CONSTITUTIONAL LAW OF INDIA

AUSTRALIA
The Law Book Company Ltd.
Sydney : Melbourne : Brisbane

CANADA AND U.S.A.
The Carswell Company Ltd.
Agincourt, Ontario

ISRAEL
Steimatzky's Agency Ltd.
Jerusalem : Tel Aviv : Haifa

MALAYSIA : SINGAPORE : BRUNEI
Malayan Law Journal (Pte) Ltd.
Singapore

NEW ZEALAND
Sweet & Maxwell (N.Z.) Ltd.
Auckland

PAKISTAN
Pakistan Law House
Karachi

CONSTITUTIONAL LAW OF INDIA

A Critical Commentary

THIRD EDITION

BY

H. M. SEERVAI

Senior Advocate, M.A., LL.B., F.B.A.

Advocate-General of Maharashtra, 1957-1974

"A thousand years scarce serve to form a State;
An hour may lay it in the dust."

BYRON

VOLUME 1

N. M. TRIPATHI PRIVATE LTD., BOMBAY

SWEET & MAXWELL LTD., LONDON

1983

FIRST EDITION 1967
REPRINTED
(With Supplement) 1968
SECOND EDITION
(Vols. 1 & 2) 1975-76
(Vol. 3) 1979
THIRD EDITION
(Vol. 1) 1983

ISBN 0 421 31660 8

Rs. 260

For Volume 1

Printed by S. V. Limaye at the India Printing Works, 9 Nagindas Master Road Extension 1, Fort, Bombay 400 023, and published by H. M. Seervai, 146, M. Karve Road, Bombay 400 020. Distributors: N. M. Tripathi Pvt. Ltd., Law Publishers, 164, Samaldas Gandhi Marg, Bombay 400 002.

This book is dedicated
to
the memory of
my father and mother
the spirit of whose teachings
animates its pages
and
to
Feroza, Meher, Shirin and Navroz
who willingly gave up
their claim to
the time which would have been theirs,
in order that this book
may be written

PREFACE TO THE THIRD EDITION

For this edition I have had to increase the size of this volume by about 325 pages, not counting the 5 Appendices. I have done this to bring the case law up to date; to greatly enlarge the Introduction; to take notice of new trends; to enlarge upon topics which have assumed greater importance since the second edition was published, and to clarify important topics, which the judgments of the Supreme Court have left in an unsatisfactory state, by providing a fresh critical analysis of the problems involved. To make it easier for the reader to find out the nature of the important changes introduced in this edition, I have indicated them with some particularity in this Preface.

As the reader might be helped by placing our Constitution in its historical background, Secs. I to V of the present Introduction are mainly historical (pp. 1-51), Sec. VI being devoted to the legal framework of our Constitution.[1] By far the largest part of the history (pp. 13-48) deals with the transfer of power in India beginning with the Cripps Mission in March 1942 and ending with the transfer of power to India and Pakistan on August 15, 1947. As these years were the most critical in Indo-British relations, and have left a permanent mark on our history and our Constitution, many books written before 1070 contain excellent accounts of that period;[2] but they were written without the full knowledge to be derived from secret official documents in Great Britain which were not expected to be published till 1999. However, in 1967 it was decided to publish official documents under the editorship of independent historians who were to be given unrestricted access to the records, and the freedom to select and edit documents for publication. Between 1970 and 1980 ten volumes of *The Transfer of Power 1942-7* were published[3] under the editorship of a distinguished historian, Prof. Mansergh. These documents reveal what was passing on the British side during the five fateful years leading to the transfer of power in India. Further, the publication in 1973 of *Wavell, The Viceroy's Journal*[4] gave a first hand account of the part which Lord Wavell played in the transfer of power and thus made a valuable contribution to our knowledge of the subject. On reading these publications it seemed to me that we can now give a fresh account of the transfer of power by weaving the old and the new materials into a coherent narrative. And this is what I have tried to do briefly in Sec. IV of the Introduction. My narrative shows that many judgments passed, opinions expressed and surmises made before the

---

[1] This Section reproduces substantially the Introduction to the earlier editions of this book.

[2] For example, Maulana Azad's autobiography, *India Wins Freedom* and Mr. K. M. Munshi's *My Pilgrimage to Freedom*; Pyarelal's *Gandhi, The Last Phase*; Brecher's *Nehru, A Political Biography* and Hector Bolitho's *Jinnah*; Mr. V. P. Menon's *Transfer of Power*; Mr. Shiva Rao's *Framing of India's Constitution — A Study*; Lumby, *The Transfer of Power in India*; Mosely's *Last Days of the British Raj* and Hodson's *The Great Divide*. It may be added that Mosely and Hodson had access to some official records, but not to all; and obviously the *Viceroy's Journal* was not available to them.

[3] After the Introduction had been printed, the 11th volume was published in 1982, bringing the official record upto July 7, 1947.

[4] Edited by Sir Penderel Moon with an Introduction, Editorial Commentary, Epilogue and Notes.

official documents and the *Viceroy's Journal* were published require to be revised, corrected or rejected; and some myths have been destroyed.[5]

After Independence, the years 1975 to 1979 were the most critical in free India, and they too left a permanent mark on our history and our Constitution. In "A New Introduction" to the 3rd volume of the *Constitutional Law of India* (2nd ed.) I gave an account of that period. The proclamation of Emergency on June 25, 1975 by the President on the sole advice of Mrs. Gandhi ushered in the most shameful period in our history. I described the large scale arrests and detention of her political opponents, the imposition of a censorship such as India had never known, the gross abuse of the powers of preventive detention, the attacks on the judiciary and the amendments to our Constitution which took it towards a dictatorship. I described how the High Courts reached their finest hour when notwithstanding threats to their judges, 9 High Courts upheld the rule of law when they refused to countenance the monstrous doctrine that during the Emergency a detenu could not secure his release from preventive detention by an application for *Habeas Corpus* even if he was detained without the authority of law, or contrary to law, or under a *mala fide* order or an order based on extraneous considerations. But what the 9 High Courts refused to do, the Supreme Court did when Ray C.J., Beg, Chandrachud and Bhagwati JJ. delivered four separate judgments in the *Habeas Corpus Case*, Khanna J. dissenting. I described how, when the Supreme Court had wrapped up the face of Justice in the folds of the Emergency, Nemesis, which personifies retributive justice, stepped in by driving Mrs. Gandhi from Parliament, office and power, and by inflicting on her party a catastrophic defeat at the hands of the Janata Party, first, in the elections to the Lok Sabha in 1977 and, later, in the elections to all but three States. I showed that the reasons given for the numerous amendments made to our Constitution by the 39th and the 42nd Amendments, were specious and untenable. I then described how the Janata Government first dismantled the apparatus of tyranny, and, later, with the help of the defeated Congress party, repealed almost all the aforesaid amendments by enacting the 43rd and the 44th Amendments, which also introduced further safeguards for freedom against future abuse of power. The "New Introduction" has been reproduced as Appendix I to this volume, because it contains a contemporary account of four critical years, and because I want to keep my criticisms of the 39th and the 42nd Amendments on record. No doubt almost all the amendments have been repealed; but "what is done once may be done again". I may add that in "An Epilogue : 1980-1983" I have given a brief account of Mrs. Gandhi's return to power in 1980 after a landslide victory in the elections to the Lok Sabha and, later, in the States and some of the constitutional problems which have arisen for our country.

I have not discussed the *Habeas Corpus Case* in Chapter XI, because in another book[6] I criticised the Case and showed that the majority judgments were untenable. I had discussed the Case in its appropriate setting by placing it between Chapter I on "The Judiciary and the Emergency" and Chapter III on "The Courts and Preventive Detention",

---

[5] See para 1.55 of the text.

[6] Seervai, *The Emergency, Future Safeguards and the Habeas Corpus Case: A Criticism* (1978).

because the three Chapters had an organic unity. They were reproduced in the 3rd volume of the Constitutional Law of India (2nd ed.). However, in discussing preventive detention in Chapter XI of this volume, I was obliged to use parts of my Chapter on the *Habeas Corpus Case* in order to explain the scheme underlying Arts. 21 and 22, as also the difference between a fundamental right and an ordinary right. Since the reader would prefer to have a full discussion of the Case in its appropriate setting, I have reproduced the three Chapters as Appendices III, IV and V[7] to the present volume. In the earlier editions of this book, Chapter V dealt with the "Relations of the Union and the States". The bulk of that Chapter has been reproduced in Appendix II.

There is one omission in this volume which I regret. In *S. P. Gupta & Ors.* v. *President of India & Ors.* A.I.R. 1982 S.C. 149 (*"The Judges' Case"*), a Bench of 7 judges of the Supreme Court[8] decided far reaching questions affecting High Court Judges and their independence. I had intended to deal briefly with that case in this volume, leaving a detailed discussion to Volume II. However, I soon realized that a brief *and* accurate account cannot be given in a legal text book, of seven judgments which between them occupy 495 pages of the All India Reporter.

In view of the importance of the subject, I have greatly enlarged Chapter II on "The Interpretation of the Constitution" to take account of recent trends in statutory interpretation. My approach has been influenced by Prof. Cross's admirable and illuminating book on *Statutory Construction*, more particularly by his careful analysis of the expression "the intention of Parliament".[9] He has rightly pointed out that this expression is meaningless unless we recognize that it is used by analogy, for only human beings can have intentions, purposes or objects. "The expression is not so much a description as a linguistic convenience."[10] This analysis is useful in discussing extrinsic aids to construction. The decisions in *Dyson's Holdings Ltd.* v. *Cox* (1976) Q.B. 503 (C.A.) and *Minister of Home Affairs* v. *Fischer* (1980) A.C. 319 (P.C.) (paras 2.5 to 2.11) emphasize the need to interpret ordinary words, as for example, "family" or "child", to accord with changing social attitudes, and to that extent the rule that a statute must be interpreted as at the date of its enactment stands modified. Again, Lord Blackburn's well known statement of the "context" rule in the *River Wear Case* (1877) 2 App. Cas. 743, 766-7 has been held by Lord Wilberforce in *Prenn* v. *Simmonds* (1971) 1 W.L.R. 1381 (H.L.) to have laid down the anti-literal rule as far back as 1877, and to justify a liberal approach to interpretation. And Lord Simon of Glaisdale and Lord Reid expressed the same view in the *Black-Clawson Case* (1975) A.C. 591 (H.L.), and Lord Reid added that it is in comparatively few cases that the words of a statutory provision are only capable of one meaning. Thus by 1980, the rule of literal con-

---

[7] Originally, Appendix V ended with the strong language in which Bhagwati J. passed judgment on Mrs. Gandhi and her party after their "crushing defeat" at the polls in 1977. When Mrs. Gandhi returned to power in 1980 after a landslide victory at the polls, Bhagwati J. wrote her a letter of congratulations which has a historical interest. The relevant paragraphs of that letter have been reproduced at the end of Appendix V as a study in contrast — the effect which the defeat and victory of the same person can produce on the mind of the same judge.

[8] Bhagwati, Gupta, Fazal Ali, Tulzapurkar, Desai, Pathak and Venkataramiah JJ.

[9] *Cross, op. cit.* pp. 34-40.

[10] ibid. p. 36.

struction stood largely modified by the "context" rule. In *R.* v. *Schildkamp* (1971) A.C. 1, 10 (H.L.) Lord Reid stressed the need to recognize the reality of the legislative process, and observed that it was not very meaningful to say that the words of an Act represented the intention of Parliament, but that punctuations, cross-headings and side notes did not. And in *Ealing L. B. C.* v. *Race Relations Board* (1972) A.C. 342 (H.L.) Lord Simon of Glaisdale said much the same thing.

The most welcome development in statutory interpretation is the increasing recognition of the need to conserve forensic time and minimize the cost of litigation. It follows that too high a price is paid for doing justice if, in interpreting statutes, judges seek "light" from whatever source it can be got — no matter how uncertain or delusive the "light" may be. First, in *Beswick* v. *Beswick* (1968) A.C. 58, 74, and then in the *Black-Clawson Case*[11] Lord Reid adverted to these considerations as the reason why, on purely practical grounds, courts severely limited the use of preparatory work (*travaux préparatoire*), and why speeches were not permitted as extrinsic aids to construction. In the *Black-Clawson Case* all the Law Lords were agreed that speeches in Parliament were not permissible aids to construction, and Lord Simon of Glaisdale further referred to the American experience as justifying this view. The law that speeches were not permissible aids to construction was not new. The Privy Council had applied it to Indian statutes in *Adm.-Gen. of Bengal* v. *Prem Lall Mullick* (1895) 22 I.A. 107, 118, In *Trav.-Cochin* v. *Bombay Co. Ltd.* (1952) S.C.R. 1112 our Supreme Court adopted that decision, and the unanswerable logic[12] underlying it, namely, "that those who did not speak may not have agreed with those who did; and those who speak might differ from each other". What is new in the recent English decisions is that although the logical ground for disallowing speeches is retained, the need to conserve forensic time and minimize costs is put in the forefront. These considerations are even more important for our Supreme Court, which has the widest jurisdiction of any final court, including the power of judicial review of legislation rightly conferred on it. However, departing from its earlier decisions, the Supreme Court frequently embarks on the futile enterprise of seeking "light" from speeches in the Constituent Assembly for interpreting the Constitution. The enterprise is futile, because after an inordinate waste of the Court's time and the litigant's money, the Court comes to the inevitable conclusion that speeches throw no decisive light on the provisions to be interpreted (paras 2.38 to 2.44).[13] Waste of time and money would be prevented, and the disposal of cases speeded up, if the Supreme Court ruled at the outset, as the Privy Council did,[14] that speeches will not be permitted as aids to construction. Again, as most Supreme Court

---

[11] Which has been discussed fully in paras 2.24 to 2.30. The case also considered the admissibility of the report of an expert committee accompanied by a draft Bill which Parliament enacted into law with two immaterial variations.

[12] No judge has given an effective answer to it.

[13] See para 2.44 of the text, where Bhagwati J. appeared to draw a conclusion from a speech of Dr. Ambedkar. However, inadvertently, he overlooked a part of the same speech which nullified that conclusion.

[14] In *Krishna Ayyangar* v. *Nallaperumal Pillai* (1920) 47 I.A. 35, an objection being raised to Counsel referring to the proceedings in the Legislature, "Viscount Finlay, after consideration by their Lordships, said that any reference to the proceedings in the Legislature would be mischievous and should not be allowed." (ibid. p. 36).

judgments do not distinguish speeches in the Constituent Assembly from other proceedings there, I have, for the first time, divided those proceedings into four categories, to show that though speeches in the Assembly are not permissible aids to construction, proceedings in the three other categories do, at times, provide an aid to construction: (paras 2.31 to 2.44).

There is another matter which is even more wasteful of time and money, and is a serious impediment to speeding up judicial proceedings. A fashion has grown up in the Supreme Court to "communicate to the law abiding community . . . the glow of life-giving principles rooted in social sciences": *Organo Chemical Industries* v. *Union* A.I.R. 1979 S.C. 1803, 1804. But fine phrases are not a substitute for good law. The functions of a judge and of an expert scientific witness cannot be combined in one person. Psychology, psychiatry, sociology and penology are social sciences; but eminent authorities in these sciences differ from one another as to the very basis of their sciences; and over a wide field no firm conclusions can be drawn in those sciences. In any event, the opinion evidence of scientific experts is permitted provided it is given by witnesses who can be cross-examined. If judges feel that they are experts in one or more of the social sciences, and the benefit of their knowledge must be placed before the Court, they must be called as witnesses. Otherwise, all scientific opinions expressed by them based on materials gathered from books must be struck out from their judgments as embodying inadmissible evidence,[15] or valueless evidence because not tested by cross-examination.[16] The lengths to which this fashion can go is shown by the dissenting judgment of Bhagwati J. in *Bachan Singh's Case*: A.I.R. 1982 S.C. 1325. The majority judgment was delivered on 6th May, 1980; his judgment was promised in the middle of July 1980; it was delivered on 16th August 1982 because the research required to support a conclusion he had reached without it, was so extensive that it took him over two years to deliver his judgment.[17] It is also fashionable to speak of the "Colonial legacy". But if that legacy saves the Court's time and the litigant's money by ruling out at the outset speeches in the Constituent Assembly, or in the Legislatures, as aids to construction, and by insisting that relevant scientific evidence should be confined to expert witnesses in the box, then no person, who values the saving of forensic time, the reduction of the litigants' costs and the speedy disposal of cases, can renounce that legacy.

In Chapter VII, I have discussed the recent developments by which the Supreme Court finally reached the position that Corporations, Government Companies, Companies incorporated under the Companies Act and Registered Societies are "the State" within the meaning of Art. 12 if they are agencies or instrumentalities of the State (paras 2.11 to 2.34). Further, in the 2nd edition of this book the question whether the Judiciary is "The State" within the meaning of Art. 12 was considered in Chapter XVI on "Judicial Remedies". That discussion has now been

---

[15] To say this is not to say that scientific theories which have been universally accepted, and have passed into the currency of thought cannot be referred to by judges.

[16] See Seervai, *Constitutional Law of India*, Vol. III (2nd ed.) at pp. 1879 and 2028-29.

[17] For a criticism of that judgment see paras 11.290 to 11.292.

transferred to Chapter VII which deals, *inter alia*, with "the State" and "Fundamental Rights" (paras 7.35 to 7.52).

Bhagwati J., who delivered the judgment in *Royappa's Case* A.I.R. 1974 S.C. 555, and in three other leading cases, claimed that the decisions in the post *Royappa* period had laid bare a new dimension of Art. 14 which had escaped judges of an earlier day, namely, that "Article 14 embodies a guarantee against arbitrariness . . . and (equality) cannot be 'cribbed, cabined and confined'" within the doctrine of classification. In Chapter IX, Sec. I (*a*) I have shown that "The New Doctrine" is untenable; that far from enlarging the fundamental right to equality it has narrowed that right to one aspect of it. For, although arbitrariness and equality may be sworn enemies, equality has many more enemies than arbitrariness, and the doctrine of classification has enabled the Courts to strike down all of them (paras 9.3 to 9.13). In Sec. I (*b*) I have dealt at length with the *Bearer Bonds Case* (paras 9.45 to 9.66), first, because in the past the Supreme Court had set its face against tax evasion and against rewarding crime and criminal activities, whereas the majority judgment in the *Bearer Bonds Case* has, for the first time, upheld a law which put a premium on tax evasion, dishonesty, fraud and crime; and, secondly, because the majority judgment is most unsatisfactory.

In Sec. II of Chapter IX, I was obliged to think out afresh the correlation of Art. 14 to Arts. 15 and 16, and of Art. 15 to Art. 16 because of the increasing importance of "reverse discrimination", and because two extremely unsatisfactory judgments of the Supreme Court[18] have thrown the law on the interpretation of Arts. 15 and 16 into confusion. The discussion of Art. 16 (4) in the two judgments has become surcharged with emotion because of compassion for the plight of Sch. Castes and Sch. Tribes. The leading judgment of Krishna Iyer J. in the *Karmachari Sangh Case* is a strange mixture of sermon, prophecy and platform rhetoric; of thinly disguised contempt for persons who hold a different view from his own; and of discourteous remarks on Counsel's arguments which ran counter to his own views (see para 9.207). Moral indignation is not a substitute for a careful analysis of Arts. 15 (4) and 16 (4) interpreted in their context as parts of a group of Articles entitled "The Right to Equality". As no such analysis has been undertaken by Krishna Iyer J., I have given a fresh analysis myself in paras 9.182 to 9.203 for *Thomas's Case*, and paras 9.204 to 9.222 for the *Karmachari Sangh Case*. If the methods followed for the last 30 years to uplift Sch. Castes and Sch. Tribes have failed as pitifully as the judgment of Krishna Iyer J. suggests, it is reasonable to suppose that wrong methods have been adopted. In a public lecture, I outlined a scheme, which would cost substantial sums of money but which, I believe, would achieve within a reasonable time, the objective of Arts. 15 (4) and 16 (4), and enable members of Sch. Castes and Sch. Tribes to compete on equal terms with other communities. A brief outline of the scheme is given in paras 9.218 and 9.219. I ought to add that the Supreme Court has heard a number of petitions and/or appeals which have again raised the question of reverse discrimination; but judgments have been reserved.

---

[18] *Thomas's Case* A.I.R. 1976 S.C. 490 and the *Karmachari Sangh Case* A.I.R. 1981 S.C. 298.

In this edition for the first time I have dealt with promissory estoppel as a topic by itself, (pp. 601-634) because of its increasing importance in Administrative Law, and because the Supreme Court decisions on promissory estoppel are conflicting. I have tried to give a coherent account of the principles which emerge from a fresh study of English decisions and the decisions of our Supreme Court. In paras 10.209 to 10.211, I have considered three important judgments of the Privy Council, and in para 10.212 an important judgment of Atkin J. in *Collom's Case*. Finally, in para 10.216 I have set out the many qualifications which must be made to the proposition that "there can be no estoppel against a statute" before it can be accepted as correct.

Chapter XI on "The Right to Freedom" in its present form and arrangement is new. It is divided into three sections. Section I (pp. 691-754) deals almost entirely with the constitutional questions raised by preventive detention, including the correlation of Arts. 19 and 21—which was central to *Gopalan's Case* 1950 S.C.R. 88. Section II (pp. 754-795) deals with each of the three sub-clauses of Art. 20. Section III deals with three topics. First, with Arts. 21 and 22 (pp. 796-864), that is, with cases of preventive detention arising under various preventive detention Acts considered with reference to Arts. 21 and 22. Secondly, with the *Fundamental Rights of Prisoners* (pp. 864-873), and thirdly, with *Arts. 14, 19, 21 and the Sentence of Death* (pp. 873-893). In Vol. I (2nd ed.) of this book the constitutional aspects of preventive detention were discussed partly in Chapter XI on "The Right to Freedom" and partly in Chapter XV on "Rights to Property".[19] This unsatisfactory mode of treatment was forced on me by the *Bank Nationalization Case* A.I.R. 1970 S.C. 564. There, a single shareholder impugned the nationalization of 14 Banks on the ground that the impugned Act violated *his* fundamental rights under Arts. 14, 19 and 31. As the case involved the acquisition of property and business it fell squarely under "Rights to Property" and had to be discussed in Chapter XV. The case had not the remotest connection with preventive detention; nevertheless, 10 judges purported to overrule *Gopalan's Case* which was the leading case on preventive detention. Now that Rights to Property have ceased to be fundamental rights, and Arts. 19(1) (*f*) and 31 which conferred them have been repealed, an opportunity offered itself to place the discussion on preventive detention in one Chapter, and I have done so by placing the discussion in Sec. I, and in part of Sec. III of Chapter XI.

I have rewritten the discussion on the constitutional aspects of preventive detention in Sec. I. However, the space devoted to the majority judgment in the *Bank Nationalization Case*, and the detailed analysis I have given of that case, is not because I consider the majority judgment valuable, but because of the great importance of determining correctly the correlation of Art. 21 to Art. 19(1). The majority judgment in the *Bank Case* is one of the most unsatisfactory judgments of the Supreme Court. First, it violates the principles of natural justice because the rights of the Banks, who were not parties to the petition, were decided without hearing them (paras 11.43 and 11.44). Secondly, the judgment violates

---

[19] In Volume III of the book (2nd ed.) there was a discussion of preventive detention in Chapter XII-B on *The Habeas Corpus Case*.

the salutory general rule that in constitutional matters a Court will not decide more than is necessary to give relief to the parties. The finding in the majority judgment that the impugned Act was void because it violated Art. 31(2), made it unnecessary to decide the challenge under Arts. 14 and 19. Thirdly, it is amazing that ten judges should purport to overrule *Gopalan* on preventive detention, when the petition could not, and did not, raise any question of preventive detention. Finally, the purported overruling of *Gopalan* is indefensible because it is founded on a fundamental error, namely, that the majority in *Gopalan* had held that Art. 22 was a complete Code on preventive detention, when even the head-note to *Gopalan* in the Supreme Court Reports would have told the 10 judges that the majority in *Gopalan* had held that Art. 22 was *not* a complete code on preventive detention.

The present position of the *Bank Case vis-a-vis Gopalan* is this: In *Maneka Gandhi's Case* A.I.R. 1978 S.C. 597 Kailasam J. demonstrated the fundamental error about *Gopalan* on which the *Bank Case* was based, and further showed that the observations in the *Bank Case* about *Gopalan* were casual observations which did not have the effect of overruling *Gopalan*. In *Bachan Singh's Case* (paras 11.72 to 11.97), in which the constitutional validity of the death sentence was in issue, Sarkaria J., for the majority, upheld the view taken by the majority in *Gopalan* on every point and rejected the contrary view taken in the *Bank Case*. Further, broadly following *Gopalan*, Sarkaria J. upheld the constitutional validity of the death sentence, thus overruling the majority judgment in *Rajendra Prasad's Case*, A.I.R. 1979 S.C. 916. The Supreme Court has not formally buried the *Bank Case vis-a-vis Gopalan*; it has preferred to cut off its essential limbs. The Supreme Court's unwillingness to admit demonstrable and demonstrated error is a grave injury to the administration of justice (para 11.58).

On the fundamental rights of prisoners, the Supreme Court has continued to develop the law in the right direction: (para 11.272). Again, in the *National Security Case* A.I.R. 1982 S.C. 710, the judgment of the Supreme Court took a step forward in emphasizing that any element of punishment must be excluded from preventive detention, and gave effect to this view by observing, among other things, "We see no reason why (the detenus) should not be permitted to wear their own clothes, eat their own food, have interviews with members of their families at least once a week, and . . . have reading and writing material according to their reasonable requirements". (para 11.241). This attitude is in refreshing contrast to the callous attitude of the Supreme Court to conditions of detention during the Emergency. The *National Security Case* raised many other important questions, and they have been discussed at length in paras 11.191 to 11.212.

My thanks are due to my friends at the Bar, Mr. A. G. Noorani and Mr. Shavax J. Vazifdar, and to my friends outside the Bar, Prof. Dara Marshall, Mr. Govind Talwalkar, Prof. Sheryar Ookerjee and Miss Hira Bhandara, for help willingly given. My friend and personal secretary, Mr. M. P. B. Nair, has given me great help in everything connected with this volume; I do not think he could have done more even if the book had been his own.

As before, I am thankful to members of my family for help willingly given. My daughter Shirin relieved me of the burden of comparing the proofs with a fair part of the manuscript, and so did my son Navroz. As he is a practising advocate, I have discussed important parts of the manuscript with him, and, on occasions, I have given effect to his criticism. He also made brief notes of recent decisions to make it easier for me to bring the case law up-to-date.

My wife has gone through several drafts of the manuscript and has corrected errors which had escaped me. She went through the proofs and was responsible for correcting serious errors. The only acknowledgment I can make of her single-minded devotion to this book is to repeat what I said in the Preface to the First Edition, that this book is as much hers as mine, because without her assistance, its publication would have been indefinitely delayed.

March 16, 1983. H. M. SEERVAI

PREFACE TO THE FIRST EDITION

In a manner of speaking, this book has got itself written. It all began fifteen years ago when I read with admiration and delight Dr. Wynes's critical commentary on the Australian Constitution. As I laid down his book I could not help expressing to myself a wish that someone would try to do for the Constitution of India what Dr. Wynes had done so well for the Constitution of Australia, and I believed then that one at least of the eminent lawyers who had helped to fashion our Constitution would undertake the task. But as the Supreme Court and the High Courts handed down judgments on important constitutional questions, the wish would keep coming back, till the decision of the Supreme Court in the *Bengal Immunity Case* in 1955 made me feel that I might have to attempt the task—"some time". In September 1960, as I sat in the Supreme Court, listening to the powerful dissent of Mr. Justice Kapur in the *Nanavati Case* I realised that the time had come, though I did not then realise that the work would engage me for over six years.

As the Constitution is an organic whole, its underlying unity can best be brought out by a narrative which deals with connected topics together. Accordingly, I have departed from the method generally adopted of commenting on each Article separately. This book has been written not only for legal practitioners but also for students of law and for general readers interested in the legal aspect of our Constitution; I have therefore tried to make the narrative as simple as I could, and it is some satisfaction to me that persons not lawyers have found large parts of the book easily intelligible.

In writing this book I have borne Indian conditions in mind. It is not usual for a legal practitioner to have a well equipped library of text books and law reports, and outside the High Courts there are no adequate law libraries to which he can resort. I have therefore set out facts of cases more fully than is usual in an English text book, and have generally indicated in the footnotes the point involved in the cases cited. In citing English and American cases I have borne in mind that the English law reports are even less easily available to a legal practitioner than the Indian law reports, and that the United States Supreme Court Reports are not available at all outside the Bar libraries of the Supreme Court and the High Courts.

I have been sparing in the citation of American, Canadian and Australian cases, because few things are more misleading than the citation of cases on Constitutions very different from our own. In the early days of our Constitution, in dealing with fundamental rights, the Supreme Court and the High Courts relied heavily on American decisions, but it did not take the courts long to realize that the differences between our two constitutions are as great as the similarities, and that American authorities must first be viewed against the background of the relevant constitutional provisions in order to ascertain whether they are really applicable. In the first case of importance before the Federal Court of India, Gwyer C.J. had struck that very note of caution against the use of Canadian, Australian and American cases in the interpretation of the Constitution Act of 1935, and he set those authorities in their true perspective by observing that

". . . where relevant they will always be listened to in this Court with attention and respect as the judgments of eminent men accustomed to expound and illumine the principles of a jurisprudence similar to our own": (1939) F.C.R. at pp. 37-8.

In India the problem of writing a critical commentary presents special problems of its own. There are excellent *critical* commentaries on the Constitutions of the United States, Canada and Australia. Besides, there are legal journals of high authority, and of great weight with the legal profession, in which competent professional opinion subjects decided cases to a critical scrutiny. Such commentaries and critical literature are of invaluable assistance to the Bench and the Bar in giving a coherent picture of the law as it emerges from decided cases, which cases might otherwise appear as a "wilderness of single instances". No such conditions exist in India. A further difficulty arises from defective law reporting in India. The United States Supreme Court Reports contain a full report of counsel's arguments as the briefs filed by counsel are set out. Again, the Commonwealth Law Reports give a full report of counsels' arguments. In India, the Law Reports, including the official Reports, even of the Supreme Court, rarely contain counsel's arguments, so that the Bench and the Bar do not know what was argued and therefore cannot fully appreciate what was decided. No doubt the judgments refer to counsel's arguments, but every judge and lawyer knows that the report of an argument by a tribunal whose duty is to weigh that argument is no substitute for a report by a lawyer whose duty is to report the argument and not to weigh it.

In writing a critical commentary my object has been essentially constructive. I have stated as accurately as I can the effect of a decision; I have then considered the relevant decisions on a subject to ascertain whether they disclosed a principle or a coherent pattern, and if they did not, I have submitted what appeared to me to be the correct principle or a coherent explanation. But I have taken care to separate the statement of the law and my submissions on it. There are however a number of topics on which I have found it necessary to question the basic presuppositions underlying the judgments of the Supreme Court, and as examples I may mention delegated legislation, the waiver of fundamental rights, the doctrine of error apparent on the face of the record in *certiorari*, and the tenure at pleasure in the Union and State services. Here also I have distinguished the statement of the law, from my submissions on it. But the submissions have had to be fuller as the presuppositions had to be displaced by thinking out the matter afresh.

I realise that some of my criticisms may be mistaken; but to refuse to criticize judgments for fear of being mistaken is to abandon criticism altogether. The cause I serve is that of a correct and coherent interpretation of our Constitution. If any of my criticisms are found to be correct, the cause is served; and if any are found to be incorrect the very process of finding out my mistakes must lead to the discovery of the right reasons, or better reasons than I have been able to give, and the cause is served just as well.

The reader will not find in this commentary any reference to the sociological or the dynamic interpretation of the law, nor will he find references to social, economic and political theories supposed to underlie our Constitution. The discussions in the Constituent Assembly show that the draft Articles were supported by people for the most diverse reasons;

and such evidence as there is of the work of various committees "behind the scenes" shows that the final solution was a compromise between conflicting points of view. In any event, a Constitution confers legislative, executive and judicial power and imposes limitations on such power either expressly or by necessary implication, and the question whether the power thus conferred has been transgressed, or whether a constitutional limitation has been violated is wholly unconnected with the various theories supposed to underlie the grant or limitation of such power.

The objection to importing political, economic and social concepts into the task of constitutional interpretation has been very well expressed by Latham C.J. in the *Communist Party Case*. He said:

"It is sometimes said that legal questions before the High Court should be determined upon sociological grounds—political, economic or social. I can understand Courts being directed (as in Russia and in Germany in recent years) to determine questions in accordance with the interests of a particular political party. There the Court is provided with at least a political standard. But such a proposition as, for example, that the recent *Banking Case* [(1948) 76 C.L.R. 1] should have been determined upon political grounds and that the Court was wrong in adopting an attitude of detachment from all political considerations appears to me merely to ask the Court to vote again upon an issue upon which Parliament has already voted or could be asked to vote, and to determine whether the nationalization of banks would be a good thing or bad thing for the community. In my opinion the Court has no concern whatever with any such question. In the present case the decision of the Court should be the same whether the members of the Court believe in communism or do not believe in communism": [83 C.L.R. at pp. 148, 149].

No doubt the inclusion of fundamental rights in our Constitution, and the reasonable restrictions to which they are subject, raises questions about "reasonableness" which cannot be separated from questions of policy. However, in the discharge of his judicial duties a judge is trained to disregard his personal likes and dislikes. Again, as Mr. Justice Holmes showed in his famous dissent in the *Lochner Case*, the correct question to ask is not "Do I consider the restriction reasonable?" but "would a reasonable man necessarily consider it unreasonable?" The test therefore is not the subjective view of the judge as to reasonableness but the objective test of the reasonable man which is applied in several branches of the law. It is not realised that if a judge's social, political and economic theories were to intrude in his decision on constitutional questions, the most far-reaching questions about the method of appointing judges to the High Courts and the Supreme Court would arise. According to the English theory, which has been followed in Australia and Canada, and which we have adopted, the politics of a judge are irrelevant to his judicial functions. But once this principle is departed from, the politics of a judge become material for his appointment, as they have become material for the appointment to the Bench of the Supreme Court of the United States. Besides, our courts are courts of general jurisdiction, and are not limited to the determination of constitutional questions; and the fair and impartial decision of cases would become impossible once it becomes known that the personal views of the judge obtrude in his judicial pronouncements. That is why by convention judges are expected to abstain from public pronouncements on political, economic and social issues which are likely to come before them in their judicial capacity.

Paradoxically, the greatest danger to the administration of justice and constitutional interpretation arises from the genuine desire of judges to do justice in *each individual case*. The consequences of this desire are so grave that in *Ramappa* v. *Bajappa* [(1963) A.SC. 1633, 1637] the Supreme Court thought it necessary to say that:

"It may be that in some cases, the High Court dealing with the second appeal is inclined to take the view that what it regards to be justice or equity of the case has not been served by the findings of fact recorded by Courts of fact; but on such occasions it is necessary to remember that what is administered in Courts is justice according to law and considerations of fair play and equity however important they may be, must yield to clear and express provisions of the law. If in reaching its decisions in second appeals the High Court contravenes the express provision of s. 100 (C.P.C.) it would inevitably introduce in such decisions an element of disconcerting unpredictability which is usually associated with gambling; and that is a reproach which judicial process must constantly and scrupulously endeavour to avoid."

As against this disconcerting unpredictability, we have the example of the Privy Council which for over a century was the highest court of appeal from the Dominions and the Colonies. When in *Att.-Gen. for Ontario* v. *Canada Temperance Federation* [(1946) A.C. 193] the Privy Council was invited to overrule *Russel* v. *R.* [(1882) 7 App. Cas. 829], Viscount Simon after observing that the Privy Council was not absolutely bound by previous decisions of the Board, observed:

"But on constitutional questions it must be seldom indeed that the Board would depart from a previous decision which it may be assumed will have beeen acted on both by governments and subjects."

If the judgments of the Privy Council command great respect it is due as much to the stability of the Privy Council as a judicial tribunal, and to the predictability of its decisions, as to the eminent judges who were, and are, its members. This stability and predictability is not less necessary for our High Courts, which are the highest courts of appeal in the States, or for the Supreme Court of India, which is the highest court of appeal for the whole of India. The Supreme Court of India was therefore right in condemning that desire for justice in individual cases which converts the judicial process into a gamble.

I had intended to devote a separate chapter to the provisions of our Constitution in their application to Jammu and Kashmir. This would have required a study of the amendments made by the Constitution (Application to Jammu and Kashmir) Order, 1954, as amended from time to time. But as the writing of such a chapter would have considerably delayed the publication of this book, I decided not to include it in the present edition.

As I hold the office of the Advocate-General of Maharashtra, it is necessary to state that the opinions expressed in this book are my personal opinions.

Parts of chapters in this book have appeared in the *Law Quarterly Review* (Chap. I), *The Cambridge Law Journal* (Chap. XXIII) and in *The International and Comparative Law Quarterly* (Chap. XVI) and I am obliged to their editors for their ready consent to the inclusion in this book of materials published in their journals.

My thanks are due to many friends, to Prof. C. J. Hamson, Professor of Comparative Law in the University of Cambridge, for the interest which he has taken in the writing of this book, and for all that it owes to his wise, candid and kindly guidance; to K. S. Shavaksha, Advocate, for going through the manuscript and suggesting many improvements; to B. P. Dalal,

Remembrancer for Legal Affairs, Government of Maharashtra, for helpful discussions on fine points of legal drafting and constitutional law; to R. J. Joshi, Advocate, for helpful discussions on many topics considered in this book; to P. N. Damry, then Secretary, Finance Department of the State of Maharashtra, for assistance on matters connected with the control of public finance provided for by our Constitution; to Atul M. Setalvad and Tehmtan R. Andhyarujina, Advocates, for long and stimulating discussions on the difficult problems considered in this book, for their unfailing help in all things connected with it, and to Atul M. Setalvad for going through the proofs and comparing them with the manuscript, and to Tehmtan R. Andhyarujina for the equally laborious task of preparing the index; to Miss Hema B. Thakore and B. R. Irani, Advocates, for the care with which they have checked the citations and the references in the book, and to B. R. Irani for also preparing the table of cases; to M. P. B. Nair for the unfailing cheerfulness with which he prepared excellent typescripts of the many drafts of each chapter and for giving up well deserved vacations in order that the publication of this book may not be delayed; to R. M. D. Chamarbaugwala for his friendly advice as to the *format* of this book, for selecting and procuring the paper, and for its safe storage. My thanks are also due to the Government of Maharashtra for readily granting me four weeks' leave in order that an important chapter in this book may be completed and to the India Printing Works for the excellence and accuracy of their printing, the care with which the proofs were scrutinized before being sent to me and for their willing co-operation.

I cannot end this preface without acknowledging all that this book owes to my wife. When I broached the subject of writing this book to her, she strongly pressed me to write it. Over the years she has carefully scrutinized the various drafts of each chapter and suggested numerous improvements. Though not a lawyer, she has put questions which have led, at times, to a more accurate statement of the law. When in 1966 she found that due to the pressure of official duties this book would make little progress if I worked unaided, she spent a year in finding out references and cross references for that part of the book which had still to be written, and also in correcting the proofs as they came in. This book is as much hers as mine, for without her assistance its publication would have been indefinitely delayed.

February 22, 1967. H. M. SEERVAI

CONTENTS OF VOLUME 1

TABLE OF CASES CITED

B

C

H

I

K

Q

R

ADDENDA

P. 337, *add in the last but one line*:

In *D. K. Nakra* v. *Union*, ('83) A.SC. 130, it was held that the classification made in the Ministry of Defence Notification whereby the increased pension was payable only to those who retired after a specified date was arbitrary and violative of Art. 14. The Court declared that all pensioners shall be entitled to the liberalized pension scheme from the specified date, irrespective of the date of retirement. An application for review made in April, 1983 was reported by the newspapers to have been summarily rejected.

P. 895, *add* para 11.311A:

11.311A In *People's Union for Democratic Rights* v. *Union* (1982) A.SC. 1473, the Supreme Court held that a person who provides service to another for less than the minimum wage fixed by the Minimum Wages Act, 1948, renders forced service, which is *begar* within the meaning of Art. 23. He can therefore approach the Court to enforce his right under Art. 23 asking the Court to direct payment of the minimum wage. Article 23 protects the individual not only against the State but also against private citizens.

CORRIGENDA

P. 39, *f.n.* 29, line 2: for "para 1.54" read "para 1.55".

P. 50, para 1.77, line 8: for "*qua*" read "*quo*".

P. 157: In the marginal note to para 5.22 and in the first line of that para, for "s. 199" read "s. 119".

P. 206, line 6: for "s. 10 C.P.C." read "s. 11 C.P.C.".

P. 274, line 16: for "numger" read "number".

P. 426, *f.n.* 62, line 2: for "(1969) 2 S.C.R. 29" read "(1967) 2 S.C.R. 29".

P. 462, *f.n.* 15: Add at the end "in Vol. II".

P. 499, In para 10.35, line 18, for "*Ram Narain*" read "*Ram Nandan*".

P. 563, para 10.139, lines 14 and 16: add "in Vol. II" where reference to Chapter XIV is given.

P. 597, para 10.174, line 6: for "*Dava*" read "*Daya*".

P. 598, 5th line from bottom: for "*Dava's Case*" read "*Daya's Case*".

P. 716, *f.ns.* 97 and 98: for "see para 12 of Appendix III" read "para 12, Appendix I, Vol. II".

P. 752, line 3: for "para 10.31" read "para 10.34".

P. 766, *f.n.* 70: for "('65) A.SC. 578" read "('65) A.SC. 87".

LIST OF ABBREVIATIONS

All the Law Reports, except the All India Reporter series, are cited in the usual manner. The A.I.R. series is, however, cited in an abbreviated form, e.g.

AIR (1977)		Allahabad	:	('77) A.A.
„	„	Andhra Pradesh	:	('77) A.A.P.
„	„	Assam	:	('77) A.Ass.
„	„	Bombay	:	('77) A.B.
„	„	Calcutta	:	('77) A.Cal.
„	„	Delhi	:	('77) A.Del.
„	„	Gujarat	:	('77) A.Guj.
„	„	Himachal Pradesh	:	('77) A.H.P.
„	„	Jammu & Kashmir	:	('77) A.J.&K.
„	„	Karnataka	:	('77) A.Knt.
„	„	Kerala	:	('77) A.Ker.
„	„	Madhya Pradesh	:	('77) A.M.P.
„	„	Madras	:	('77) A.M.
„	„	Mysore	:	('77) A.Mys.
„	„	Orissa	:	('77) A.Or.
„	„	Patna	:	('77) A.Pat.
„	„	Punjab	:	('77) A.Punj.
„	„	Punjab & Haryana	:	('77) A.P. & H.
„	„	Rajasthan	:	('77) A.Raj.
„	„	Supreme Court	:	('77) A.SC.
„	„	Tamil Nadu	:	('77) A.T.N.

The full title, etc. of certain works, which have been cited in an abbreviated form, are:

Concise Oxford Dictionary: C.O.D.

Constituent Assembly Debates: C.A.D.

Seervai, H. M., *Constitutional Law of India*: Seervai.

CHAPTER I

INTRODUCTION : Mainly Historical

"Of all the sad words of tongue or pen
The saddest are these 'It might have been'."

"... it is wrong not to lay the lessons of the past before the future." [1]

—WINSTON CHURCHILL

1.1 For India, 1947 was a year of triumph and tragedy. Of triumph, because the freedom, for which hundreds had toiled and died, was won. Of tragedy, because the dream of freedom for a united India vanished when on June 3, 1947, the Prime Minister of India, Pandit Jawaharlal Nehru, announced his acceptance of the partition of India with "no joy in my heart". This acceptance had been preceded by violent communal disorders of the utmost savagery and bestiality in Bengal and Bihar; but grave as these disorders had been, they paled into insignificance before the violence and bestiality which broke out in the Punjab after the Radcliffe Award was announced on 16th August, 1947 — an Award which started a trek of over 10 million refugees, the Hindus fleeing from Pakistan to India, and the Muslims fleeing from India to Pakistan, leaving on the way men, women and children dead, defiled and mutilated. In a Broadcast to the Nation, Jawaharlal Nehru described his anguish at the happenings in Delhi and the Punjab: "My mind is full of horror of the things that I saw and that I heard. During these last few days ... I have supped my fill of horror. That indeed is the only feast that we can have now."[2] How did India come to this pass? And what drowned the dream of a united India in rivers of blood and tears? A very brief historical account would not only enable us to lay the lessons of the past before the future, but to see the remarkable achievement of the Constitution of India against its historical background.

August 1947: triumph and tragedy

SECTION I: 1835-1884

A Fateful Decision: 7th March, 1835.

"The destinies of our Indian Empire are covered with thick darkness. . . . It may be that the public mind of India may expand under our system till it has outgrown that system; that by good government we may educate our subjects into a capacity for better government; that having become instructed in European knowledge they may, in some future age, demand European institutions. Whether such a day will ever come, I know not. But never will I attempt to avert or retard it. Whenever it comes, it will be the proudest day in English history."[3]

—MACAULAY

---

[1] *The Gathering Storm*, p. vii.
[2] Brecher, *Nehru*, p. 364.
[3] Speech delivered in the House of Commons on July 10, 1833, on the India Bill, 1833.

Jan. 26, 1950: "proudest day in English history"

1.2 The proudest day in English history of which Macaulay spoke, dawned on 26th January, 1950 when the Constitution of India came into force. And it was no mere accident that the Constitution was written in English and that its framers chose of their own free will the basic principles of British Parliamentary institutions which had gradually grown up in India. How did this come about?

Macaulay and the adoption of English as medium of instruction

1.3 It is not given to many men to assist effectively in the fulfilment of their visions and their hopes. It was given to Macaulay to do so. Some time after his great speech on the India Bill, he was appointed Law Member of the Executive Council of the Gov.-General of India, Lord William Bentick. "It (was) fortunate for India", says Macaulay's biographer[4] "that a man with the tastes, and the training, of Macaulay came to her shore as one vested with authority and that he came at the moment when he did; for that moment was the very turning point of her intellectual progress." By 1834 all educational action was at a stand, for the Committee of Public Instruction was evenly divided — one half were for the continuation of the existing system of education in Arabic, Persian and Sanskrit with stipends given to students and with subsidies given for the publication of text books. The other half were for imparting elementary education in vernacular languages and higher education in English. In June 1835, the advocates of the two systems laid their opinion before the Supreme Council and on 2nd February 1835, Macaulay, as a member of the Council produced his celebrated Minute in which he adopted and defended the views of those who supported English. In the course of a vivid and closely reasoned argument, Macaulay appealed to history and gave two striking illustrations. He wrote:

Macaulay's appeal to history: two striking illustrations

"The first instance ... is the great revival of letters among Western Nations at the close of the 15th and the beginning of the 16th Century. At that time almost everything that was worth reading was contained in the writing of the ancient Greeks and Romans. Had our ancestors acted as the Committee of Public Instruction has hitherto acted; had they neglected the language of Cicero and Tacitus; had they confined their education to the old dialects of our own Island; had they printed nothing and taught nothing at Universities but the chronicles of Anglo-Saxons and romances in Norman-French, would English have been what she is now? What Greek and Latin were to the contemporaries of More and Ascham. our tongue is to the people of India."[5]

And again,

"Within the last hundred and twenty years, a nation which had previously been in a state as barbarous as that in which our ancestors were before the Crusades, has gradually emerged from the ignorance in which it was sunk and has taken its place among civilised communities. I speak of Russia. There is now in that country a large educated class, abounding with persons fit to serve the State in the highest functions and in no way inferior to the most accomplished men who adorn the best circles of Paris and London. . . . How was this change effected? Not by flattering national prejudices, not by filling the mind of the young Moscovite with old women's stories which his rude fathers had believed. . . . But (by) teaching him those foreign languages in which the greatest mass of information had been laid up and then putting that information within his reach. The languages of Western Europe civilized Russia. I cannot doubt that they will do for the Hindoo what they have done for the Tartar."[6]

---

[4] Trevelyan, *Life and Letters of Lord Macaulay*, Vol. I, (1908) p. 290.
[5] ibid. p. 291.
[6] ibid. p. 291-292.

1.4 The cogency and force of Macaulay's Minute won the day, and on 7th March 1835 the Government of Lord William Bentick announced that "The great object of the British Government ought to be the promotion of European Literature and Science among the Natives of India." From this decision was to grow a political and intellectual unity in British India such as India had never known before. In the following Sections, a brief account will be given of how the decision taken on 7th March 1835 was to transform the face of India; how the mind of India having been instructed in European knowledge demanded English Institutions; how the dream of a free India, working those free Institutions for a *United* India came near to realization when the tragedy of Partition destroyed it; and how, notwithstanding this tragedy, the Constituent Assembly of a free India — free to choose a Constitution for India — chose a democratic Constitution with a Parliamentary Cabinet form of Government on the Westminster model as part of a Federal Constitution. English transforms the face of India

1.5 The results of the New Learning were not long in coming, for the year 1857 which saw the outbreak of the Indian Mutiny saw also the establishment of the Universities of Calcutta, Madras and Bombay, formed as examining Universities on the model of the London University. English, as a medium of instruction and of official work, not only threw wide open the windows to the West, but it also unbarred the windows to India's past. Sir Percival Spear[7] has said: Calcutta, Madras and Bombay, Universities established in 1857

"The first burst of Sanskrit Scholarship in the late eighteenth century, of which Sir William Jones was the leading figure, was followed after 1830 by the harvest of European Sanskrit and Pali studies centred round the French Savant Burnouf and the German Max Muller. Whilst Europeans in India were denigrating Indian civilization in all its aspects and counting it semi-barbarians, Western savants were discovering there fresh beauties and elegancies and plumbing fresh depths of thought."[8]

1.6 By the Government of India Act, 1858, the governance of India was taken over by the Crown from the East India Company. The Indian Councils Act, 1862 for the first time associated non-officials with legislation passed by the Governor-General's Council. We have seen that three Universities were established in 1857 and the men who graduated from them very soon felt the need for Indians to be associated with the Government of their own country. The establishment of Parliamentary institutions in Canada by the British North America Act, 1867, indicated the line of Colonial development towards self-governing institutions, and set before educated Indians the same goals as were being pursued in British Colonies like Canada. This desire of Indians to be associated with the Government of India found expression in the founding of the Indian National Congress in 1885. G.I. Act, 1858 and Indian Councils Act, 1862

---

[7] *India, Pakistan and the West* (1952) Home University Library.

[8] ibid. p. 195. The reader interested in the impact of Western knowledge on Hindu and Muslim culture and modes of life will find a fascinating account in Sir Percival Spear's book. Max Muller's work on the *Sacred Books of the East* was translated into English by several scholars, and was published by the Clarendon Press in 50 volumes.

SECTION II: 1885-1937

Indian National Congress founded in 1885. Congress objectives up to the Indian Councils Act, 1909

1.7 The Indian National Congress ("the Congress") was "first conceived in an English brain." Allan Octavian Hume saw the need for a national forum in which "the picked men, the most highly educated of the nation", could meet each year to "secure greater freedom . . . a more impartial administration (and) a larger share in the management" of their own country. The first session of the Congress opened in Bombay in 1885. But as time passed, the objectives of the Congress changed, as liberal doctrines came to the fore in England, and the failure to apply them to India, aroused discontent among Indian intellectuals. The victory of Japan in the Russo-Japanese War, convinced India of what an "Asiatic" nation could achieve against a Western power. The partition of Bengal by Lord Curzon sparked off an agitation which gave rise to revolutionary violence, and produced a sharp division between the "moderates" and the "extremists" in the Congress. At the annual Sessions of the Congress in 1906, Dadabhai Naoroji, the grand old man of India, in a conciliatory presidential address tried to heal this rift when he declared that *Swaraj* (self Rule) was the goal of the Congress. However, in the annual session of the Congress in 1907, a split occurred between the moderates on the one hand and the extremists, led by Bal Gangadhar Tilak, on the other, and the extremists were expelled from the Congress. Going back a little, in 1906 a Liberal Government had come to power in England, with Lord Morley as the Secretary of State for India; and he, along with Lord Minto, the Viceroy of India, proposed reforms which were embodied in the India Councils Act, 1909. The Morley-Minto reforms, as they came to be called, enabled the moderate leaders in the Congress to claim that their efforts to secure greater association of Indians with the Government of our country had borne fruit. However, the India Councils Act, 1909, did not secure effective participation of Indians in the legislative and executive government of India.

Separate electorates — for Muslims and minorities introduced by Act of 1909

1.8 It should be noted that the Act of 1909 introduced separate electorates for Muslims and other minorities. It has been said that separate electorates were a device of the British to "divide and rule". There was an element of truth in this; but a legislative provision may be desirable, or necessary, independently of the motive which originally led to its enactment. It will be seen, as this narrative unfolds, that a failure to bear this distinction in mind, first imperilled, and then destroyed, the unity of India.

Jinnah's entry in the Congress: 1906; Lucknow Pact: 1916

1.9 The year 1906 saw the entry into the Congress of Mohamed Ali Jinnah who was to be hailed as the ambassador of Hindu-Muslim unity, of which "the Lucknow Pact" in 1916 between the Congress and the Muslim League was his crowning achievement. In November, 1916 a Session of the Congress and also of the Muslim League was held in Lucknow. In his *Pilgrimage to Freedom*, K. M. Munshi described in striking words the result of the Sessions of the Congress and the Muslim League:

"In a sense Jinnah dominated the Congress and the League at the time. He had played the key role in preparing a draft constitution for India and getting it adopted by the sessions both of the Congress and of the League.

The historical Lucknow Pact was an integral part of this constitution. Under it, the Muslims led by the League promised to work with the Hindus to achieve freedom in return for the Congress conceding to the Muslims separate electorates with weightage far in excess of their numerical strength."[9]

Later, Jinnah was to be denounced as the destroyer of Hindu-Muslim unity and the creator of Pakistan. In 1906 all this was in the future; it is enough, at this place, to note his entry into the Congress as a *nationalist* Muslim.

Effect of 1st World War on India

1.10 The First World War broke out on 4th August, 1914, and the part which India was called upon to play, and played, in that war, quickened the political aspirations of the people, and hopes rose high that England would go far to meet those aspirations. In view of the split which had occurred in the Congress, Mrs. Annie Besant, an English woman devoted to the cause of India's freedom, felt the need for a new political organisation — "The Home Rule League." She secured the moral support of Dadabhai Naoroji, then 95 years of age. However, the Subjects Committee of the Congress resisted Mrs. Besant's proposals. On 1st August, 1916, Mrs. Besant started the All India Home Rule League which could move fast enough to take advantage of the war situation. In June 1917, Mrs. Besant and her co-workers were arrested and detained. Sir Tej Bahadur Sapru and Motilal Nehru organized a Branch of the Home Rule League in Allahabad, and the Bombay Branch was reconstituted with Jinnah as its President. This political activity in India had its effect in England, and on August 20, 1917, Mr. Montagu, the Secretary of State for India, made the historic declaration that the policy of the British Government was one of "increasing association of Indians in every branch of the administration and the gradual development of self-governing institutions with a view to the progressive realization of responsible government in India as an integral part of the British Empire."[10]

Home Rule League founded; Br. Govt.'s historic declaration in 1917

G.I. Act, 1919 introduces "dyarchy" in Provinces

1.11 This declaration greatly enhanced the prestige of the Home Rule League. Mrs. Besant and her co-workers were released in September 1917, and she was elected the President of the Congress session held in Calcutta in December 1917, at which session Home Rule was adopted as part of the Congress creed. Passing over the split between Mrs. Besant and Tilak on the issue of "Dominion Status", we come to the Montagu-Chelmsford Reforms which were implemented in the Government of India Act, 1919. That Act introduced "dyarchy" in the Provinces because the Executive was divided into two parts : certain Departments were, for the first time, put in charge of elected Ministers responsible to the Legislature; the remaining departments were in charge of Government officials, namely, Members of the Governor's Executive Council. Although these reforms were not enthusiastically welcomed, they would have been worked but for two grave errors of the British. The first was the passing of the Rowlatt Act providing for preventive detention, and the second was the brutal massacre of innocent people at the Jallianwalla Bagh on the orders of General Dyer who wanted to strike terror into the hearts of those opposed to him. The proper working of the Government of India Act, 1919, was gravely hampered, when Gandhi launched his non-violent non-co-operation movement.

---

[9] Munshi, *Pilgrimage to Freedom*, p. 7.
[10] ibid. p. 9.

Entry of Mahatma Gandhi in Indian politics

1.12 Going back a little, we must note the entry into Indian politics of Mahatma Gandhi, who was to dominate the political scene till he was assassinated by a Hindu fanatic on 30th January, 1948. No other political leader has commanded the affection and devotion of the people of India as he did. His ascetic ways of living endowed him with the halo of a saint which shone the brighter because his words appealed to Hindu religious sentiment.[11] This makes it difficult to evaluate his political achievements, great as they were, for it is not easy to determine at what times the astute politician in him submerged the saint. In 1920, Gandhi was appointed President of the Home Rule League in place of Mrs. Besant, who left the League because it had become "intertwined with Religion". Gandhi changed the object of the Home Rule League from self-government within the British Empire to complete *Swaraj* — freedom from all ties with Britain. When Jinnah protested that the meeting was not competent to alter the Constitution of the League, his objection was overruled by Gandhi. Thereafter, Jinnah with 19 other members (who included Munshi) left the Home Rule League. Munshi has recorded with insight the effect of these events:

Effect of Gandhi taking over the leadership of the Congress and the Home Rule League

> "When Gandhiji forced Jinnah and his followers out of the Home Rule League and later the Congress, we all felt, with Jinnah, that a movement of an unconstitutional nature, sponsored by Gandhiji with the tremendous influence he had acquired over the masses, would inevitably result in widespread violence, barring the progressive development of self-governing institutions based on a partnership between educated Hindus and Muslims. To generate coercive power in the masses would only provoke mass conflict between the two communities, as in fact it did. With his keen sense of realities Jinnah firmly set his face against any dialogue with Gandhiji on this point."[12]

Gandhi and the Khilafat movement

1.13 Another event of importance was the support which Gandhi gave to the agitation led by two brothers, Mohamed Ali and Shaukat Ali against the abolition of the Khalifate in Turkey after the War, for the Khalif was the spiritual head of the Muslims. The agitation was essentially religious, and Gandhi believed that by supporting it he would bring about Hindu-Muslim unity. Subsequent events showed that his belief was ill founded, and a number of writers have taken the view that his support only widened the differences between Hindus and Muslims.

Simon Commission appointed in 1927

1.14 In July 1925, Lord Birkenhead, the Secretary of State for India, threw out a challenge to Indians to frame a Constitution "which carried behind it a fair measure of agreement" instead of constantly criticizing the measures adopted by the British Parliament. In this connection it may be observed that the Government of India Act, 1919, had provided for the appointment of a Commission to report on the working of the Act, at the end of 10 years. This period was shortened, and in November, 1927 a Commission, consisting exclusively of the members of the British Parliament, was appointed, with Sir John Simon as its chairman. When announcing the appointment of the Commission, Lord Birkenhead repeated the challenge which he had thrown out in 1925. The exclusion of Indians from the Commission was opposed by almost every section of political opinion in India and the Commission worked in an atmosphere of boycott

---

[11] For example, he spoke of *Ram Rajya* to describe "good government".

[12] *Munshi, op. cit.* p. 18. The tenor of Munshi's book runs counter to the insight of this passage.

and opposition. However, the challenge thrown out by Lord Birkenhead was taken up by an All Party Conference which appointed a Committee presided over by Pandit Motilal Nehru. The Committee made a Report, known as the "Nehru Report" laying down the principles for framing a Constitution for India. The Committee considered the suggestion for an All-India Federal Constitution, and expressed its willingness to consider such a Constitution for India if the Indian States realised the full implication of a Federal India.[13] The Committee rejected separate electorates for the Muslims. However, at a meeting of the Muslim League convened to consider the Report, amendments to the Report were proposed and forwarded to the Nehru Committee. These amendments provided for separate electorates for the Muslims, for weightage in the Legislatures in excess of the Muslim population and provided for residuary powers being conferred on the Provinces and not on the Central Government. The reference to residuary powers would suggest that the Muslim League considered a Federal form of Government as the appropriate form for India, the more so as the Report of the Committee showed that the Committee was prepared to consider the Federal solution as stated earlier. At an All Party Conference at which the Report and the Muslim League Amendments were considered, Jinnah pleaded for acceptance of the Amendments if "revolution and civil war"[14] were to be avoided. However, all the Amendments were rejected, and Jinnah is recorded as having said to a friend "This is the parting of the ways."[15]

Nehru Committee Report — Muslim League amendments for separate electorates rejected

Jinnah and the "parting of the ways"

1.15 It may strike the reader as odd that the Lucknow Pact, which accepted separate electorates and weighted representation for Muslims in the Legislature, should have been hailed as a symbol of Hindu-Muslim unity, and yet the amendments for separate electorates and weightage for the representation of Muslims in the Legislatures should have been rejected by the Nehru Committee and the All Party Conference. Perhaps the explanation lies in the fact that "the war of succession"[16] to the British Raj had not begun in 1916, but had begun in 1928, because full Provincial autonomy was the obvious line of political advance in India and it could not be long deferred as the Simon Commission Report in 1930 was to show. The few opportunities for averting that war were missed by the Congress and, as we shall see, the war of succession ended with the partion of India.

Rejection of the Lucknow Pact the result of "war of succession" in 1928

1.16 Between the appointment of the Simon Commission and the submission of its Report, events were moving fast. A Labour Government had come to power in Great Britain, and on October 31, 1929. the Viceroy, Lord Irwin, announced its decision to hold a Round Table Conference in England for the solution of the Indian problem, and also announced, with the concurrence of His Majesty's Government, that Dominion Status was the goal of India's political development.[17] The effect of these events on the work of the Commission was thus described by its Chairman, Sir John Simon:

Round Table Conf. announced

---

[13] Shiva Rao, *Framing of India's Constitution, A Study*, p. 13.
[14] Hector Bolitho, *Jinnah*, p. 94. [15] ibid. p. 95.
[16] This phrase was applied by Sir Evan Jenkins to describe the communal riots in the Punjab in early 1947.
[17] Gwyer and Appadorai, *Speeches and Documents on the Indian Constitution 1921-47*, Vol. 1, p. XXXVII.

"The Government's announcement was naturally made much of by Indian politicians. They were quite shrewd enough to appreciate that, after this, any detailed recommendations made by the Commission, however carefully thought out, must lose much of their original force.[18] ... The tide of constitutional advance was mounting so fast that, in the event, it swept over and buried much of the detailed considerations we had been at such pains to set out."[19]

Results of 1st Round Table Conf.

1.17 Three Round Table Conferences were held in England. At the first Round Table Conference the Congress was not represented as it refused its co-operation. Writing of this conference, V. P. Menon said:

"Contrary to general expectation, the first Round Table Conference achieved outstanding results, the most important being the unanimous agreement of all parties, including the rulers, on the issue of federation. Up to this time, an all-India federation had been regarded as only a remote possibility. But at the very outset of the Conference Sir Tej Bahadur Sapru boldly declared himself for a federal system of government for India and invited the rulers to support his suggestion. The Maharajah of Bikaner and the Nawab of Bhopal stated on behalf of the rulers that they were prepared to come into the proposed federation provided their internal sovereignty was guaranteed. Sir Muhammad Shafi for one wing of the Muslim League and Jinnah for the other, also welcomed the proposal."[20]

At the end of the Conference, the Prime Minister of England announced the policy of his Government on India and expressed the hope that those who had refused to co-operate would join in subsequent Conferences. Taking up this cue, the Viceroy entered into conversations with Congress leaders, released them from detention, and, by the "Gandhi-Irwin Pact", paved the way for the Congress to join in the deliberations of the Second Round Table Conference. The Congress sent Gandhi as its sole representative to the Second Round Table Conference.

Gandhi sole representative at 2nd Round Table Conf.

2nd Round Table Conf.: Communal Award and the "Poona Pact"

1.18 But by the time that the Second Round Table Conference was held, the political climate had changed. The labour government had been replaced by a coalition, and although Ramsay Macdonald continued to be the Prime Minister, the government was largely a Conservative government. Besides, with Congress represented by Gandhi, the minorities demanded that their claims should be settled first, and Gandhi was unable to solve the communal problem, and he returned to India with the knowledge that the Conference had only widened the differences between the Congress and the Muslim League. The failure of Indian leaders to solve the "communal problem" threw on the British government the duty of providing its own solution, and in April, 1932, the Prime Minister announced his "Communal Award". It provided for separate electorates and reservation of seats for minorities of which the Muslims and the Depressed Classes were the largest. Gandhi announced that if the Award was not changed as to the Depressed Classes (who were Hindus) he would fast unto death. Faced with this threat, several Hindu leaders started negotiations with Dr. Ambedkar, the leader of the Depressed Classes, which resulted in the "Poona Pact" which was accepted by the British Government. Under it, there was reservation of seats for the Depressed Classes, but with joint

[18] *Retrospect: The Memoirs of the Rt. Hon. Viscount Simon*, p. 152.
[19] ibid. p. 155.
[20] *The Transfer of Power in India*, p. 43.

electorates. The Third Round Table Conference produced no real change in the atmosphere for solving India's Constitutional problem.

1.19 The three Round Table Conferences were followed by a White Paper which contained the proposals of the British Government for an Indian Constitution. After these proposals had been considered by a Joint Select Committee, a Bill based on the Joint Committee's recommendations was introduced in the British Parliament in December, 1934, and after prolonged debate, it became the Government of India Act, 1935 ("G.I. Act, 35") which came into force on April 1, 1937. The merits of the G.I. Act, 35 as a legal framework for a Constitution for India will be considered in Section VI. It is enough to say that for the first time the Act introduced a Federal form of government and it conferred full provincial autonomy on the Provinces subject to certain "safeguards". As a corrolary to a federal constitution, the Act established a Federal Court in India.

Govt. of India Act, 1935

1.20 Before considering the effect of the G.I. Act, 35 on the political parties in India, we must note that Jinnah who had been invited to the first two Round Table Conferences, was not invited to the third, and in September, 1931, he settled down in England to practise before the Privy Council. While he was in England, the G.I. Act, 35, received the Royal Assent. However, in July 1933 a meeting had taken place between him and Liaquat Ali Khan[21] as a result of which Jinnah returned to India in October 1935 and became the President of the Muslim League.

Jinnah's retirement from, and return to, Indian politics

1.21 Elections to the Provincial Legislatures under the G.I. Act, 35 were held in 1937. The Congress obtained a clear majority in Madras, United Provinces, Bihar, Central Provinces and Orissa. In Bombay, it won nearly half the seats and could count from the support of some members of other parties. In Assam and North West Frontier Province it was the largest single party. Only in Bengal, the Punjab and Sind was it in a minority. Out of a total of 485 Muslim seats, the Muslim League captured only 108. The Congress contested 58 Muslim seats and won 26. After negotiations with Government and as a result of the statement by the Governor-General, Lord Linlithgow, that the "special responsibility" of the Governor did not entitle him to intervene at random in the administration of the Provinces, the Congress decided to accept office. Congress Ministries were formed in eight Provinces, including Bombay. But this moment of opportunity brought with it the need to make a vital decision: "Should the Congress form coalition ministries to include Muslim members?" The decision against coalition ministries appeared to be logically and theoretically correct, but there is a broad concensus of well informed opinion that, in practice, the decision proved diastrous. In his *Pilgrimage to Freedom,*[22] Munshi wrote:

Provincial elections in 1937

Congress refusal to form coalition ministries disastrous in practice:

> "A serious situation arose with regard to the choice of the Muslim member, wherever Congress Ministries were formed. At that time it did not appear to be formidable; but as events were to show ten years later, it was the beginning of the end of united India. . . . The situation in the United Provinces and the Province of Bombay was particularly difficult. In the United Provinces, Congress had contested 9 seats out of 66 Muslim seats and lost all; in Bombay it had contested 2 seats out of 30 and lost both."

Munshi's view

---

[21] A vivid account of this meeting and Jinnah's return to India will be found in Bolitho, *Jinnah,* pp. 104-6.

[22] *Munshi,* ibid. p. 46.

In his *Transfer of Power in India,* Menon wrote:

Menon's view

"The Congress decided to have homogenous ministries of its own and chose Muslim ministers from among those who were members of the Congress party. This was the beginning of a serious rift between the Congress and the League and was a factor which induced neutral Muslim opinion to turn to the support of Jinnah."[23]

In his Autobiography, *India Wins Freedom*[24] Maulana Abul Kalam Azad, who was the President of the Congress from 1939 to 1946, speaking of the aftermath of the 1937 elections, wrote:

Maulana Azad's view

"If the U.P. League's offer of co-operation had been accepted, the Muslim League party would for all practical purposes have merged in the Congress. Jawaharlal's action gave the Muslim League in the U.P. a new lease of life. All students of Indian politics know that it was from the U.P. that the league was reorganised. Mr. Jinnah took full advantage of the situation and started an offensive which ultimately led to partition."

In his sympathetic and appreciative but not uncritical biography of Nehru[25] Brecher wrote:

Brecher's view

"The immediate and most far-reaching effect of the Congress victory at the polls was a widening of the breach with the Muslim League. Flushed with success the Congress adopted an imperious attitude to all other political parties, a 'Himalayan blunder', for which it was to pay dearly in the years to come. Nehru himself set the tone with his haughty remark in March 1937: 'There are only two forces in India today, British imperialism, and Indian nationalism as represented by the Congress.' Jinnah was quick to retort: 'No, there is a third party, the Mussulmans.' History was to bear him out.

"The Congress went beyond contemptuous words. During the election campaign the two parties had co-operated to some extent, notably in the United Provinces where there developed a tacit understanding that a coalition government would be formed. However, this was before the elections, when the Congress did not expect a clear majority. It was no longer necessary to make concessions. The League offer of co-operation was now treated with disdain. It was not rejected outright, but a series of incredible conditions was laid down by the Congress: ..."[26]

Shiva Rao's view

1.22 Writing in 1969, Shiva Rao referred to the 1937 Elections and said that it was significant that even after the elections, Jinnah was not thinking of a separate State of Pakistan:

"In a public statement, shortly after the elections in 1937 he declared, 'nobody will welcome an honourable settlement between the Hindus and the Muslims more than I and nobody will be more ready to help it'; and he followed it with a public appeal to Gandhi to tackle this question. The latter's response was somewhat depressing: 'I wish I could do something, but I am utterly helpless. My faith in unity is bright as ever; only I see no daylight but impenetrable darkness and in such distress I cry out to God for light'."[27]

Shiva Rao asked the question: "How then did the Indian situation alter within three years to give this movement (for Pakistan) vitality?"[28] His answer can be stated thus: Not being confident of a decisive majority in the United Provinces Legislature, the Congress "had a tacit electoral understanding with the Muslim League, which extended beyond the U.P. and was designed to facilitate a working arrangement between the two organizations during elections." Muslim leaders in the U.P. looked upon the refusal to form a coalition with the Muslims as a breach of faith. Nehru's "mass contact"

---

[23] *Menon,* ibid. p. 55.
[24] *Azad,* ibid. pp. 160-61.
[25] Brecher, *Nehru, A Political Biography* (1959).
[26] ibid. p. 231.
[27] *Shiva Rao, op. cit.* p. 22.
[28] ibid.

programme, to win over Muslims (which met with little success) added a further complication. Many Muslims, even outside U.P. felt that the League's very existence was being threatened and in reply to the Congress "mass contact" programme the League launched a vigorous counter propaganda, which was so effective that in a number of bye-elections in Muslim constituencies, the Congress candidates were defeated. "These defeats showed that Nehru and the Congress had committed a serious tactical error."[29]

1.23 But the most unfortunate consequence of the decision not to form coalition Ministries was the correspondence that took place between Gandhi and Nehru on one side and Jinnah on the other, following on Jinnah's speech at Lucknow on October 15, 1937. Gandhi described the speech as "a declaration of war" to which Jinnah replied that his speech was "purely in self-defence". But the most damaging correspondence between two great leaders, Nehru and Jinnah, was the letter which Nehru wrote to Jinnah in the name of the Congress on April 6, 1938, in the course of which he said:

Damaging effect of Nehru's correspondence with Jinnah

"... Obviously, the Muslim League is an important communal organization and we deal with it as such. But we have to deal with all organizations and individuals that come within our ken. We do not determine the measure of importance or distinction they possess. . . . Inevitably, the more important the organization, the more the attention paid to it, but this importance does not come from outside recognition but from inherent strength. And the other organizations, even though they might be younger and smaller, cannot be ignored."[30]

to which Jinnah replied:

"Your tone and language again display the same arrogance and militant spirit, as if the Congress is the sovereign power. . . . I may add that, in my opinion, as I have publicly stated so often, that unless the Congress recognizes the Muslim League on a footing of complete equality and is prepared as such to negotiate for a Hindu-Muslim settlement, we shall have to wait and depend upon our 'inherent strength' which will 'determine the measure of importance or distinction' it possesses..."[31]

As will appear hereafter the unfortunate reference to "the inherent strength" which would "determine the measure of importance" to be accorded to the associations with which Congress had to deal was to have most unfortunate consequences in 1946.

SECTION III: 1937-1942

1.24 Even as the Congress Ministries took office in July, 1937, the shadow of "war" was falling increasingly over Europe. The dismemberment of Czechoslovakia at Munich and its subsequent absorption by Germany brought a European war nearer; and when Germany invaded Poland war broke out in Europe on September 3, 1939. The Governor-General, Lord Linlithgow, without consulting the Central Legislature or political leaders, declared that India was at war with Germany. Gandhi's first reaction was to offer unconditional support

Outbreak of 2nd World War

---

29 ibid, pp. 24-25. The whole discussion of the topic will be found at pp. 21-25 in his first Chapter, "Historical Background."

30 *Bolitho, op. cit.* p. 117. A full text of the letter is given in Gwyer and Appadorai, *Speeches and Documents on the Indian Constitution 1921-47*, Vol. I, at pp. 423-429. The para quoted above is from para 13 of Nehru's letter omitting the reference to various associations. Jinnah's reply which is set out above has not been given in *Gwyer and Appadorai.*

31 *Bolitho, op. cit.* p. 117.

to Great Britain, but he was overruled by the Congress Working Committee which demanded immediate independence as a condition for the co-operation of the Congress, although prominent Congress leaders left no doubt that in a struggle between free democracies and Nazi and Fascist tyranny, they were on the side of the democracies.

Congress Ministries resign; Governor's rule under s. 93, G.I. Act, 35

Lord Linlithgow's attempts to secure co-operation from the Congress were unsuccessful, and under the direction of the Congress High Command the Congress Ministries resigned between October/November 1939. Thereupon, acting under s. 93, of the G.I. Act, 35, the administration of the Provinces was taken over by the Governors. It will be recalled that Congress Ministries assumed office on the assurance given by Lord Linlithgow about the Governor's exercise of their special responsibilities. This meant the abrogation, in substance though not in form, by the Governors of their special responsibilities to protect minorities. The "gentlemen's agreement" under which Congress Ministries were sworn in had an effective sanction behind it — a threat of the Ministry's resignation if its advice was rejected. This "gentleman's agreement" was a source of grievance to the Muslim League, and when the Congress Ministries resigned, Jinnah called on his followers to observe December 22, 1940 as a "Day of Deliverance and Thanksgiving as a mark of relief that the Congress regime has at last ceased to function".

Hitler's blitzkrieg 1940; invasion of Russia 1941

1.25 Attempts to find a solution of the political problem in India continued even after the Ministries had resigned, but they made little headway. In 1940 Gandhi adopted the policy of individual *satyagraha* as a symbolic gesture of protest. However, events were moving fast in Europe, and Norway, Denmark, Holland and Belgium were overrun in Hitler's blitzkrieg. In Great Britain, Neville Chamberlain was replaced as Prime Minister by Winston Churchill. He headed a coalition government of all parties, which declared its intention to fight Hitler, "if necessary for years, if necessary alone". With the fall of France and its capitulation on June 17, 1940, England stood alone to carry on the fight. When Hitler failed to subdue England, he turned to the East and invaded Russia on June 22, 1941; and with the Japanese attack on Pearl Harbour on 9th December 1941, the United States entered into what became a global war. The destruction of the American fleet in the Pacific enabled Japan to overrun Singapore, Malaya and Burma and her armies were at the gates of India. Under the impact of the Japanese victories and conquests, the British Government felt the need of making a fresh attempt to resolve the political deadlock in India. Sir Stafford Cripps, a Member of the British Cabinet, was sent out to India to negotiate with Indian leaders, and he made an offer on behalf of the British Government which came to be known as the "Cripps Offer". The time when the offer was made was unfortunate, for, there was a feeling in India that Great Britain was likely to lose the war.[32] Consequently, the attention of the Congress was focussed not on the pro-

Japanese attack on Pearl harbour

The Cripps Mission fails

---

[32] Munshi, *Pilgrimage to Freedom*, Vol. 1, p. 75: "Sardar Patel felt convinced that the Allies were going to lose the War. Every morning, as he read the newspaper reports of German victories, he taunted me for holding the view that the Allies would win"; Azad, *India Wins Freedom*, p. 41: "Gandhiji by now inclined more and more to the view that the Allies could not win the war. He feared that it might end in the triumph of Germany and Japan, or at the best there might be a stalemate."

mise of Dominion Status, with the right of secession at the end of the War, but on obtaining immediate power at the Centre. After negotiations which, at one time, appeared to be promising, the Cripps offer was rejected, and this rejection was soon to have far reaching consequences. After further attempts made by or on behalf of the Congress to find a solution had failed, on August 8, 1942, it passed the famous "Quit India" Resolution which was to be backed by a mass movement on the largest scale of non-violent non-co-operation. The next day all the members of the Congress Working Committee were arrested and detained and, as will appear presently, the political deadlock continued till Lord Wavell's initiative after he became the Viceroy of India.

Quit India movement launched by Congress; Working Commmittee members arrested

1.26 When the Quit India movement was launched, there was a sharp difference of opinion between Gandhi on the one hand and Azad (and Nehru) on the other. Gandhi insisted on the movement being non-violent; Azad, the Congress President, said that as long as Congress leaders were free, the movement must be non-violent, but if the leaders were arrested, (as he expected they would be) the movement must be carried on by all available means.[33] As Azad had forseen, after the Congress Working Committee and the Congress leaders were arrested on 9th August 1942, violent disturbances broke out. Gandhi attributed these to the "leonine violence" unleashed by Government, and Government justified their action on the ground of the threat which such violence posed to the Defence of India against Japan.

Azad's secret instructions if leaders arrested: people free to adopt violent or non-violent methods

SECTION IV: 1942-1947
The Transfer of Power

1.27 We have an unusually full account of the five eventful years between the Quit India movement and the partition of India, because of the decision of His Majesty's Government to publish a selection of documents from the India Office records on the transfer of power and the events leading up to it. The Editors of such publication were to be independent historians "who will be given unrestricted access to the records and the freedom to select and edit documents for publication."[34] At the time of the Cripps Offer, Lord Linlithgow

Documents on *Transfer of Power 1942-47* published in 1970-80.

[33] Azad, *India Wins Freedom*, pp. 81-82: "From 14 July to 5 August, my time was taken up in a series of meetings with Congress leaders from different parts of the country. I wanted to impress on them that if the Government accepted our demand or at least allowed us to function, the movement must develop strictly according to Gandhiji's instructions. If, however, the Government arrested Gandhiji and other Congress leaders, the people would be free to adopt any method, violent or non-violent, to oppose the violence of the Government in every possible way. . . . Naturally, these instructions were secret and never made public."

[34] Ten volumes of the *Transfer of Power* have been published beginning with the Cripps Mission January/April 1942 to May 30, 1947. One further volume is to be published, dealing with events between 3rd June 1947 and 15th August 1947 when India became independent, Pakistan having become independent a day earlier. It is a remarkable work of scholarship; each volume contains an admirable introduction describing the main topics dealt with in the correspondence and a clear and concise summary of each letter or document. The object of the publication is "to make available to scholars in a convenient form the more important British historical records relating to the transfer of power". These volumes must remain indispensable to every student of Indian constitutional history and law; and many judgements expressed in various books before the documents were published require to be revised in the light of the facts disclosed in the published documents.

was the Viceroy of India and after the Quit India movement was launched, there was no effective dialogue between him and the Congress. In February 1943, Gandhi informed the Viceroy that he would undertake a fast of three weeks for "self-purification". Government's offer to release him during the fast was rejected by Gandhi, who said that in that event there would be no fast, and the Government of India refused to release him. Three members of the Viceroy's Executive Council resigned in protest; but after Gandhi's fast was over, political relations between the Congress and the Government of India remained in the doldrums. With Congress out of office, and its leaders in detention, the field was left open for the Muslim League, which greatly improved its position. A perceptive writer has said:

Gandhi's fast in detention

The Muslim League improves its position

"Jinnah and his principal henchmen in the League pointedly refrained from any active assistance to the war effort, but, unlike Congress leaders, they did not positively obstruct; and Jinnah permitted the Muslim League and Muslim League Coalition Ministries, which now, thanks partly to the Congressmen being in goal, existed in five out of eleven Provinces, to cooperate fully in all measures required for winning the war."[35]

Lord Linlithgow's term of office came to an end in October 19, 1943, and Lord Wavell became the Viceroy of India.[36]

Lord Wavell's Viceroyalty: October 20, 1943 — March 22, 1947

Lord Wavell appointed Viceroy: his liberal and unorthodox solution for the Indian problem

1.28 On July 2, 1942 Lord Wavell accepted Winston Churchill's offer to appoint him as the Viceroy of India. Churchill appointed Lord Wavell on the assumption that he would keep the *status quo* in India, and was surprised to find in his new Viceroy a person of liberal and unorthodox views for solving the political problem in India before the war against Germany and Japan was over. It was characteristic of Wavell that on August 20, 1943, he drew up a Note[37] indicating the move he was prepared to make in India, for resolving the political deadlock, and he invited the comments of the Personal Secretary to the Viceroy-designate, Mr. (later Sir Evan) Jenkins. Wavell had ended the Note by saying that in military matters he had always been an upholder of unorthodox methods when orthodox methods had failed, and he thought that orthodox methods had failed for solving the political problem in India. His secretary expressed the view that the chances of success were five to one against, but that an attempt was worth making. Obviously with reference to this move which Wavell had proposed as the Viceroy-designate, Munshi wrote:

"Lord Linlithgow was succeeded by Lord Wavell. As an ex-Commander-in-Chief of India, his appointment was not looked upon favourably by the Congress. Unfortunately, we did not know that, before coming to India as Viceroy, he had recommended to the British Government the release of Gandhiji and Nehru and their appointment in his Executive Council. This proposal, however, had been turned down by the British Government."[38]

---

[35] Sir Penderel Moon, *Wavell: The Viceroy's Journal*, p. 27.

[36] At the time of his appointment he was the Commander-in-Chief in India, having been the Commander-in-Chief in the Middle East at the outbreak of the Second World War.

[37] For the full Note see *Moon, op. cit.* at pp. 467-70.

[38] *Munshi, op. cit.* p. 90.

The proposal to which Munshi referred has been thus described by Wavell's biographer[39]:

Gist of Wavell's proposal as Viceroy-designate; proposals rejected by Churchill

"The gist of Wavell's proposition was that he should personally invite a carefully chosen group of ten leading Indians (including Gandhi, Nehru and Jinnah) to confer with him at Viceroy's House, Delhi, under conditions of extreme secrecy. 'I believe', he intended to say to them 'that a vital decision in matters of government—and I am asking you to make a vital decision for India—can be arrived at only by a few selected men of wisdom and good faith, not by counting votes.' He would offer a definite pledge that His Majesty's Government was prepared to give self-government as soon as possible, subject only to the condition that the war must be successfully concluded and that the British would be handing over to a government as capable as their own of ruling and enforcing its decisions. 'I leave you' he intended to say, 'to devise your own procedure and methods of debating the problems of India's future and advising me on it'."[40]

But Churchill would have none of these radical and immediate measures, and the new approach which Wavell wished to make was rejected.

New light thrown on Wavell's Viceroyalty by *Viceroy's Journal* and *Transfer of Power 1942-47*

1.29 The misfortune of which Munshi wrote was real, for it was only after the *Viceroy's Journal* and Vols. IV to IX of the *Transfer of Power 1942-47* were published that it became known what efforts Wavell had made to transfer power to India under a Constitution which would be just both to the Hindus and to the Muslims. Wavell persevered in his efforts notwithstanding the opposition, first of Churchill's coalition Government and later of Attlee's Labour Government. Had he been supported by the British Government in his efforts to find a just solution, it is more than arguable that the partition of India might have been averted, or, at any rate, it would have been carried out without the holocaust which followed partition. The impression that "Wavell reigned from afar, aloof and monolithic is wholly unfounded. Nobody, except Evan Jenkins and a few others, knew how inaccurate this image was until *The Viceroy's Journal* was published in 1973: nobody thereafter could possibly be in doubt."[41]

Wavell's success in staving off famine.

1.30 After he assumed office on October 20, 1943, Wavell was confronted with the aftermath of the Bengal famine. Throughout the three and a half years that he was in office, it was his personal exertion and pressure on all the Provinces in India and on the British Government which prevented the recurrence of such a famine. In his letter of October 24, 1944 to Winston Churchill, he wrote:

"I have had during the last nine months literally to fight with all the words I could command, sometimes almost intemperate, to secure food imports; without which we should undoubtedly be in the throes of another famine, and probably of uncontrolled inflation, since without these imports I could hardly have held food prices from soaring."[42]

Wavell's move for resolving political deadlock

Wavell's first move towards resolving the political deadlock was made in his address to the Central Legislature on February 17, 1944. In it, he sought the co-operation of the Congress Party "which contained much ability and high-mindedness" but was standing aloof. He expressed his inability to release those responsible for the Quit

---

39 Ronald Lewin, *The Chief: Field Marshall Lord Wavell, Commander-in-Chief and Viceroy, 1939-1947*, (1980).

40 ibid, p. 224.

41 *Lewin, op. cit.* p. 231.

42 *Moon, op. cit.* p. 95.

India movement till he was convinced that the policy of non-co-operation and obstruction had been "withdrawn — not in sack-cloth and ashes, that helps no one — but in recognition of a mistaken and unprofitable policy." This approach of the Viceroy seemed to open a door which had been closed, and, when on grounds of health Gandhi was unconditionally released from detention on May 5, 1944, fresh attempts were made to resolve the political deadlock in India. The first attempt was made by Mr. Rajagopalachari who proposed a formula, which, if accepted by the Congress and the Muslim League, would have resulted in some sort of partition between Hindu and Muslim India. Gandhi and Jinnah held discussions which began on Sept. 9, 1944 and continued for eighteen days, but they ended in failure. However the fact that Gandhi, the undisputed leader of the Congress, should have held these discussions and offered a formula for the acceptance of Jinnah, the undisputed leader of the Muslim League, involved a tacit admission that there were only two effective parties in India, the Congress and the Muslim League, for resolving the political deadlock. For that reason, Gandhi's discussions with Jinnah were criticized by eminent Congressmen as inopportune and as enhancing Jinnah's prestige. Another initiative was taken in November 1944 by an All Party Committee headed by Sir Tej Bahadur Sapru, but Wavell expected little from the Committee's proceeding, although they had the effect of delaying consideration of the proposals which he had made. The final attempt between Indian leaders, and one which appeared the most promising at one time, was the Desai-Liaquat Ali Pact.[43] The Pact was an attempt to bring about a harmonious agreement between Hindus and Muslims for the formation of a coalition Ministry at the Centre. The heart of the scheme was that the coalition Ministry was to contain "(*a*) an equal number of persons nominated by the Congress and the League in the Central Legislature (persons nominated need not be members of the Central Legislature); (*b*) the representatives of minorities (in particular Scheduled Castes and the Sikhs); and (*c*) the Commander-in-Chief."[44] The Government was to function within the framework of the existing Government of India Act. It was agreed that if such a Ministry was formed, the first step would be to release from detention, the working committee members of the Congress. The final step was to get a withdrawal of s. 93 in the Provinces and the formation, as soon as possible, of Provincial Governments on the lines of a coalition. The formation of coalition Ministries appears to have been an attempt to remove the damage which had been done to Hindu-Muslim relations by the refusal of the Congress to form coalition Ministries in 1937 referred to earlier. With the failure of this attempt by Indian leaders to find a solution of the communal problem, there disappeared the last opportunity for healing the wound inflicted on Hindu-Muslim relations by the Congress decision against coalitions in 1937. Thereafter, only one opportunity remained, as will appear hereafter. It may however be said that a controversy has arisen about the

Gandhi-Jinnah talks end in failure

Desai-Liaquat Ali Pact: formation of coalition ministries at the Centre and in Provinces

Failure of Desai-Liaquat Ali Pact

[43] So-called because it was arrived at as the result of discussions between Bhulabhai Desai, an eminent Advocate and leader of the Congress Party in the Central Legislature and Liaquat Ali Khan, a member of the Central Legislature and the right hand man of Jinnah.

[44] Setalvad, *Bhulabhai Desai*, p. 367.

genesis, the merits and the responsibility for the failure of the Desai-Liaquat Ali Pact, but it is outside the scope of this Introduction to enter into that controversy.[45]

1.31 While these attempts were being made by Indian leaders to solve the political deadlock, the Viceroy had not been idle. On Sept. 20, 1944, he sent to the Secretary of State for India a Memorandum outlining the steps to be taken for forming a coalition government at the Centre and for framing a Constitution. He said that there were difficulties and risks in his proposal, but he was satisfied that the ultimate risks would be much greater if no action was taken by His Majesty's Government, (H.M.G.) and that H.M.G. should make a determined effort towards a political settlement. He amplified this stand in his letter of Oct. 24 to Churchill. Wavell said that he had in mind "the formation of a provisional political Government of the type suggested in the Cripps declaration, within the present constitution, coupled with an earnest but not necessarily simultaneous attempt to devise means to reach a constitutional settlement". In the same letter, Wavell wrote:

Wavell's moves for resolving political deadlock

"To be effective, any move we must make must be such as to capture the Indian imagination. If India is not to be ruled by force, it must be ruled by the heart rather than by the head. Our move must be sincere and friendly, and our outlook towards India must change accordingly. I am prepared to put up proposals for a move, which will involve risks, but which I think constitute the best chance of making progress.[46] . . . It is easy to condemn any plan for betterment of the Indian situation on the ground of risk or probable failure. If we are to make any progress, we must take risks and be prepared for failure; but a move made generously and honestly, even if it failed, would do good."[47]

Wavell's recipe for any effective move

1.32 But between Wavell's ideas and their execution there fell the shadow of the British Government. Wavell could get no reply to his proposal from the British Government which tried to put off till June 1945 his visit to England to explain his proposal. But a strong protest from Wavell on March 15, 1945, that "H.M.G. *must* face the Indian problem without further delay" brought an invitation to Wavell to be in England on March 25. After protracted discussions in the "India Committee" from March 26, to May 31, 1945 (during which twenty-six meetings of the India Committee were held), discussions which can be described as fertile in objections against making any move in India, but almost sterile in constructive suggestions, the Viceroy, who had held his own, obtained permission to make a statement on behalf of H.M.G. after his return to India. On June 14, Wavell in a broadcast announced his proposals. He said that he would invite Indian leaders to a Conference to take counsel with him for forming a new executive council more representative of organized political opinion. Except for the Viceroy, and the Com-

Wavell's statement on behalf of Brit. Govt. for a conference of political leaders

---

[45] The reader interested in this controversy will find a full discussion in Setalvad, *Bhulabhai Desai* (June 1968) at pp. 242-290. The book contains a photostat copy of two documents, namely, an Explanatory Note by Bhulabhai Desai about the Pact, with Gandhi's alterations, and a copy of the original of the Pact signed by Bhulabhai Desai and Liaquat Ali Khan. Setalvad's analysis shows that Bhulabhai had undertaken the negotiations with the consent of Gandhi and the subsequent repudiation of it by the Congress was unjust and unfair to Bhulabhai Desai, a view also taken by Azad in *India Wins Freedom* at pp. 134-37. For the opposite view, see Munshi, *Pilgrimage to Freedom*, pp. 93-94.

[46] See, *The Viceroy's Journal*, pp. 98-9. [47] **ibid. p. 99.**

mander-in-Chief, the Council would be composed entirely of Indians and it would include equal representatives of caste Hindus[48] and Muslims. The Council would function within the framework of the G.I. Act, 35, but it could consider the means by which agreement could be reached for framing a new Constitution. He announced that orders had been given for the release from detention of the President and Members of the working committee of the Congress.

The Simla Conference and its failure

1.33 The Conference was held in Simla on June 25, 1945. After a hopeful start, it foundered on Jinnah's insistence that all Muslim members of the Council should be nominated by the Muslim League. Wavell announced the failure of the Conference on July 14, 1945. Characteristically, he assumed responsibility for the failure. He said that the idea of calling the Conference was his, and had the Conference succeeded, credit would have been given to him for that success. He assumed responsibility for its failure and urged that his view should be accepted and that there should be no recrimination; and he urged the leaders to exercise the greatest possible restraint. He said that he would have to consider the next step, but he reminded the Conference that the prosecution of the War against Japan, and the administration of India must be carried on by the Government for the time being in office. Several leaders who had taken part in the Conference expressed the view that the Viceroy was not responsible for the failure.

Effect of Simla Conference: Azad's view

1.34 Although the Simla Conference failed, it opened a new chapter in the political history of India. Its effect can be summed up in the words of the Congress President Maulana Azad. He said:

> "I was impressed by the frankness and sincerity of the Viceroy as he described the proposals to me. I saw that his attitude was not that of a politician but of a soldier. He spoke frankly and directly and came to the point without any attempt at beating about the bush. It struck me that his approach was very different from that of Sir Stafford Cripps. Cripps had tried to present his proposals in as favourable a light as possible. He highlighted the strong points and tried to slur over the difficulties. Lord Wavell made no attempt at embellishment and he certainly was not trying to make an impression. He put it quite bluntly that the war was still on and that Japan was a formidable enemy. In such a situation the British Government were not prepared to take any far-reaching steps. Such developments must wait till the end of the war, but he felt that the foundation for far-reaching changes could now be laid. The Executive Council would be exclusively Indian. The top administration of the country would thus come into Indian hands. Once this happened, a completely new situation would develop and further progress after the war would be assured. My interview with Lord Wavell created a new atmosphere in Simla."[49]

The events which followed the Simla Conference did not alter Azad's opinion of Wavell.

Labour's landslide victory in Brit. elections; Labour Govt. formed

1.35 The breakdown of the Simla Conference was soon followed by a landslide victory of the Labour Party at the Elections in the United Kingdom, and Labour took office with Attlee as Prime Minister, and Lord Pethick-Lawrence was appointed the Secretary of State for India. Then came the capitulation of Japan in August, 1945, and various parties in India demanded that elections for the Central and Provincial Legislatures should be held, since the War

---

[48] When objection was taken to the expression "caste Hindus" it was explained that this was to distinguish them from Hindus belonging to the Scheduled Castes.
[49] *Azad, op. cit.* p. 107.

had come to an end. On August 21, 1945, Wavell announced that elections to the Central and Provincial Assemblies would be held in the cold weather and that he would shortly go to England for consultation with H.M.G. Accordingly, Wavell visited England, and returned to India on Sept. 16, 1945. On 19th September, in his broadcast he announced on behalf of H.M.G. its firm intention to do its utmost to promote, in conjunction with leaders of Indian opinion, the early realisation of full self-government. He added that after the elections, H.M.G. earnestly hoped that ministerial responsibility would be accepted by political leaders in the Provinces. It was also proposed to convene, as soon as possible, a Constitution making body and to hold discussions with the representatives of Indian opinion after the elections whether the proposals contained in the Cripps offer of 1942 were acceptable or whether some alternative or modified scheme was preferred. Further, he had been authorised to say that as soon as the results of the Provincial Elections were published, he would take steps for forming an Executive Council which would have the support of the main parties in India. The reaction of the Congress and the Muslim League to this announcement was not favourable, and the parties were soon engrossed in campaigning for the elections. The full results of the elections became known by February, 1946. According to Munshi, they

Results of Provincial elections in India

"proved that the Muslim League dominated the Muslims as completely as the Congress dominated the Hindus. They should have been an eye-opener to some of our leaders who would not believe that Jinnah had acquired complete hold over the Muslim masses."[50]

1.36 The election campaign was fought by the Congress on the issue of Indian unity and by the Muslim League on the issue of Pakistan and the right of the League solely to represent Muslims. The intemperate speeches made by several Congress members in the election campaign led Wavell to propose to H.M.G. the steps which should be taken to avoid any wide scale disturbances of the kind which had taken place in 1942. The object was to form an Executive Council at the Centre, to set up an agreed machinery for a constitution making body and to form Provincial Ministries, preferably as coalition ministries. In view of Wavell's appreciation of the political situation in India and the steps necessary to find a bridge between Hindus and Muslims and to get an agreed solution, the Secretary of State for India announced that a Cabinet Mission would visit India to seek agreement with Indian leaders on the principles and procedure to be followed in framing a new Constitution for an independent India. A Mission consisting of Lord Pethick-Lawrence, the Secretary of State for India; Sir Stafford Cripps, President of the Board of Trade; and Mr. A. V. Alexander, the First Lord of the Admirality, arrived in India on March 24, 1946. Since the proclaimed objectives of the Congress and the Muslim League were diametrically opposite, it may appear that the Mission was set a most difficult, if not an impossible, task. "But the Mission believed, not incorrectly as it proved, that the League might accept something less than complete independence for Pakistan; and it was in this belief that they went to work."[51] It is unnecessary to refer to the long discussions which the Mission and Wavell had with various representatives of Indian public opinion,

Wavell's appreciation of Indian situation; Cabinet Mission's visit to India announced

[50] *Munshi, op. cit.* p. 98.

[51] *Moon, op. cit.* p. 226.

Azad's statement before the Cabinet Mission designed to allay Muslim's fears

more especially those representing the Congress and the Muslim League. However, it is necessary to refer to a statement which Azad submitted to the Mission. That statement was broadly approved by the Congress and will be found in Azad's *Autobiography*.[52] Its gist was that as a Muslim he was clearly of the view that the partition of India was against the interest of the Muslims themselves. However, he realised that the fears of the Muslims were genuine and required to be allayed. He said that the formula which he proposed, and which the Congress had accepted, secured whatever merit the Pakistan scheme contained, whilst avoiding all its defects and drawbacks. The basis of the Pakistan scheme was a fear of interference by the Centre in the Muslim majority areas as the Hindus would be in a majority at the Centre. The Congress allayed this fear by granting and vesting residual powers in the Provinces and it had provided for two Lists for Central subjects, one compulsory and one optional, so that if any Province so wanted it could administer all subjects itself, except the minimum delegated to the Central Government, namely, Defence, Foreign Affairs and Communication. Azad's proposals have been referred to because the Cabinet Mission Plan announced later was on the lines which Azad had suggested, though there were important variations.

Cabinet Mission's statement of May 16, 1946

1.37 After consulting leaders of political opinion in India, the Cabinet Mission tried to bring the parties together for an agreed procedure to set up a constituent body for framing a Constitution and for reconstituting the Executive Council of the Viceroy. These attempts had failed; consequently, the Mission went to Simla to prepare its own scheme which was to be put to the parties as the "recommendations" of the Mission. Wavell was of the view that they should have been put forward as an Award by the Mission, for then it would have stood a better chance of acceptance.[53] However, on 16th May 1946, the Cabinet Mission put forward its own recommendations for solving the deadlock. The Cabinet Mission Plan, as it came to be called, is too long to set out in this Introduction.[54]

Grouping of States in Sections A, B and C

The Plan was one integral whole, and, as it turned out, its most crucial provision related to the grouping of the Provinces of British India into three sections. Section A consisted of Madras, Bombay, United Provinces, Bihar, Central Provinces and Orissa; Section B consisted of the Punjab, North West Frontier Province and Sind (where the Muslims were in a majority) and Section C consisted of Bengal and Assam (where the Muslims had a small majority). According to the Cabinet Mission, the grouping in these Sections was obligatory; the groups would meet to frame a provincial Constitution and in the case of a division of opinion, the question was to be decided by a majority of the members of the groups. After such a Constitution had been framed, and fresh elections held under it, it was open for the Provinces to opt out of the group. An assurance on these lines had been given to the Muslim League and the general opinion is that this grouping led Jinnah to accept the Plan as the

---

[52] *Azad, op. cit.* pp. 142-45.

[53] See Moon, *The Viceroy's Journal*, p. 450.

[54] It is fully set out in the *Viceroy's Journal*, pp. 471-80, and in the *Transfer of Power 1942-47*, Vol. VII at pp. 582-91.

best that he could obtain, if he was not to have a truncated or a 'moth eaten Pakistan'. A reading of the official papers and the *Viceroy's Journal* leaves no doubt that the Secretary of State and Sir Stafford Cripps did not resolutely put forward this aspect in their discussions with Gandhi and with the Congress, and had Wavell's advice been followed, the bitter disputes about the interpretation of "grouping" would have been avoided at the earliest stage. When Wavell wanted that this position should be made clear to Gandhi, the Secretary of State asked him not to press it. The Cabinet Mission issued a clarification on May 25, 1946, of some points raised by the Congress and the League. The Mission stated that the Congress interpretation of Cl.15 of the Mission Plan did not "accord with the Delegation's intentions. . . . The reasons for the grouping of the Provinces are well known and this is an essential part of the scheme. . . ." As there was also a deadlock about the Executive Council, the Mission issued a Statement on June 16, that it was proposed to set up an Executive Council of 14 members (whose names were mentioned), 6 belonging to the Congress, but not including a nationalist Muslim, but including a representative of the Scheduled Caste, 5 belonging to the League, 1 Sikh, 1 Indian Christian and 1 Parsi. It was made clear that the proposed distribution was not to be treated as a precedent for the solution of any other constitutional question. The published documents show that this attempt to side step the issue of the "Nationalist Muslim" would have been accepted by the Congress *sub silentio*, but the attempt failed because Gandhi appears to have had in mind a distinction between "right" and "duty". If it was the "right" of the Congress to nominate a nationalist Muslim it could be waived; but if it was a "duty" owed to the nationalist Muslim the matter was different. He made this distinction expressly in his interview with Wavell on Sept. 26, 1946.[55] The Mission sailed for England on June 29, 1946, believing that it had obtained an agreement to a workable solution.

led Jinnah to accept the Mission's Plan

Congress and interpretation of Mission Plan

Mission announces appointments to Executive Council: appointments rejected

1.38 The departure of the Cabinet Mission left Wavell with two unresolved problems arising from the Mission's Plan and Statements, and a third problem as to the steps which might have to be taken by the British Government if the deadlock between Hindus and Muslims persisted. The first problem related to the formation of the Executive Council; the second to the convening of the Constituent Assembly after elections to it had been completed; and the third to Wavell's "Breakdown Plan" if the political deadlock continued and the law and order situation greatly deteriorated. These problems though distinct were interconnected as the published documents clearly show. However, they are dealt with separately, to present a clear picture of each problem.

Three problems facing Wavell after departure of Cabinet Mission

1.39 As to the first problem — the formation of the Executive Council — it is not necessary to consider in detail the various negotiations, with their accompanying charges and counter-charges, which took place before the Executive Council was formed, first, without, and, later, with the Muslim League representatives. The stumbling block in the way of the League joining a coalition government in the first instance was the insistence of the Congress that a nationalist Muslim must be appointed to the Executive Coun-

Formation of the Executive Council: first without, and then including, Muslim League representatives

[55] *The Transfer of Power 1942-47*, Vol. VIII, p. 595.

cil and the insistence of Jinnah that the Muslim members of the Council should be nominated by the Muslim Leage. When it became clear that the Muslim League would not join the Executive Council, a notification was issued on 24th August 1946, stating that the King had accepted the resignations of the Members of the Viceroy's Executive Council and had appointed Pandit Jawaharlal Nehru and 11 other members to the Executive Council; two other Muslim members were to be appointed later. The interim Government composed of 14 members of the Executive Council would take office on Sept. 2, 1946. On the same day, Wavell made a broadcast in which among other things, he expressed the hope that the Muslim League would accept the offer of 5 representatives to the Executive Council, an offer which was still open. After further discussions had taken place, on 26th October 1946 the Council was reconstituted and five representatives of the Muslim League joined as members. Liaquat Ali Khan was their leader, and the Muslim League had included among the five members a representative of the Scheduled Caste, Mr. Mandal.

Azad steps down as President of Congress

1.40 This brief account of the formation of the Executive Council spans a period in which the Cabinet Mission Plan for the election and functioning of the Constituent Assembly were the subject of acremonious debate. Azad had carried on negotiations on behalf of the Congress with Wavell and the Cabinet Mission. Having been the President of the Congress from 1939-46, he took the view that since the Working Committee had approved the Cabinet Mission Plan, its acceptance by the All-India Congress Committee was merely a formality and did not justify his continuing as President to conclude the negotiations about the Mission's Plan. He decided to step down, and he recommended Jawaharlal Nehru, who had Gandhi's support, for the Presidentship of the Congress. At a Session of the All-India Congress Committee held in Bombay in July, the decision of the Working Committee was ratified by a large majority, and Nehru took over the Presidentship of the Congress. But then, wrote Azad,

Nehru takes over presidentship; his unfortunate press statement

> "There happened one of those unfortunate events which change the course of history. On 10th July, Jawaharlal held a press conference in Bombay. (Answering the press) Jawaharlal stated in reply that Congress would enter the Constituent Assembly 'completely unfettered by agreement and free to meet all situations as they arose'. Press representatives further asked if this meant that the Cabinet Mission Plan would be modified. Jawaharlal replied emphatically that the Congress had agreed only to participate in the Constituent Assembly and regarded itself free to change or modify the Cabinet Mission Plan."[56]

Congress Working Committee statement fails to undo the damage

The Working Committee of the Congress tried to undo the damage done by Nehru's statement by passing a resolution which reaffirmed the acceptance of the Cabinet Mission Plan by the Congress. But the damage could not be undone. In the words of Azad:

> "Mr. Jinnah did not however accept the position and held that Jawaharlal's statement represented the real mind of the Congress.[57] He argued that if the

---

[56] *Azad, op. cit.* pp. 154-5.

[57] *Cf.* "Jawaharlal Nehru as President of the Congress on July 10, declared that the Congress would enter the Constituent Assembly 'completely unfettered by agreements and free to meet all situations as they arose.' *He spoke what was in our hearts but gave a handle to Jinnah*": *Munshi, op. cit.* p. 104. (italics supplied) Nehru's statement at the Press Conference represented a view which he firmly held. For, in an interview on 10th June with the members of the Cabinet Mission and

Congress could change so many times while the British were still in the country and power had not come to its hands, what assurance would the minorities have that once the British left, the Congress would not again change and go back to the position taken up in Jawaharlal's statement?"[58]

Following on Nehru's statement, Jinnah called a meeting of the Council of the Muslim League. At the meeting of the Council held on 27th July, 1946, two Resolutions were passed. The first resolution was to the effect that in the events that had happened, "the Muslim League Council had felt that their interests would not be safe in the Constituent Assembly and had decided that the acceptance of the scheme contained in the Cabinet Mission's statement of 16th May should be revoked."[59] The second resolution called upon the working committee to draw up a Plan for direct action and called upon all members of the League to renounce titles conferred by Government. After the resolutions had been passed, Jinnah said:

Muslim League withdraws acceptance of Cabinet Mission Plan

" 'What we have done today is the most historic act in our history. Never have we in the whole history of the League done anything except by constitutional methods and by constitutionalism. But now we are obliged and forced into this position. This day we bid goodbye to constitutional methods.' He recalled that throughout the fateful negotiations with the Cabinet Mission the other two parties, the British and the Congress, each held a pistol in their hand, the one of authority and arms and the other of mass struggle and non-co-operation. 'Today', he said, 'we have also forged a pistol and are in a position to use it'."[60]

Muslim League abandons constitutional methods and calls for "Direct Action Day"

The Working Committee of the League followed up the Council's resolution by calling upon the Muslims throughout India to observe August 16 as "Direct Action Day." The effect of Nehru's answers at his press conference and their grave aftermath in the resolutions of the Muslim League for direct action is best summed up in the words of Azad:

"Jawaharlal's mistake in 1937[61] had been bad enough. His mistake of 1946 proved even more costly. One may perhaps say in Jawaharlal's defence, that he never expected the Muslim League to resort to direct action.[62] Mr. Jinnah had never been a believer in mass movement."[63]

1.41 The Muslim League's resolutions and the killings and disorders in Calcutta on Aug. 16, created a situation of the utmost gravity. Soon after the announcement of the interim government on Aug. 24, followed by his broadcast, Wavell went to Calcutta to obtain first hand knowledge of the terrible happenings which left about 5,000 people dead, about 15,000 injured and about 1,00,000 homeless. Ac-

The great Calcutta killings

---

the Viceroy, Nehru told them: "The Congress were going to work for a strong Centre and to break the Group system and they would succeed. They did not think that Mr. Jinnah had any real place in the country. The Muslim League and the Congress each represented entirely different outlooks on the work of the Constitution-making Body and they were bound to have strong differences in the Interim Government": *Transfer of Power 1942-47*, Vol. VII, p. 855.

[58] *Azad, op. cit.* pp. 157-58. [59] *Menon, op. cit.* pp. 286-87.

[60] ibid. p. 287.

[61] In not forming a coalition Ministry in the United Provinces. *Azad, op. cit.* p. 162.

[62] Unknown to Azad, his defence of Nehru is borne out by the letter which Nehru wrote to Sir Stafford Cripps as late as 27th January, 1946. Nehru wrote: "The Muslim League leadership is far too reactionary (they are mostly landlords) and opposed to social change *to dare to indulge in any form of direct action. They are incapable of it, having spent their lives in soft jobs.* If it is once made clear that violence on their part will not help them at all, they will subside": *The Transfer of Power, 1942-47*, Vol. VI, p. 851, 854.

[63] *Azad, op. cit.* p. 162.

cording to Menon, "what (Wavell) saw and learnt convinced him that if some sort of agreement was not brought about soon, the Calcutta happenings would be repeated with varying degrees of recklessness all over India."[64] He was impressed by a statement made to him by a prominent member of the Muslim League that "if the Congress made an unequivocal statement that Provinces could not opt out of Groups except as laid down in the Statement of May 16, or the Viceroy or H.M.G. would state plainly that they would not permit any other interpretation on grouping, the League would reconsider entering the Constituent Assembly. And if the League's quota of five members was allowed to be filled, Jinnah might come in without making difficulties about a 'Nationalist Muslim'."[65]

Wavell invites Gandhi: Gandhi and Nehru refuse to make a declaration to avoid failure of Mission Plan

Wavell invited Gandhi and Nehru to meet him on Aug. 27, and at the interview after describing the happenings in Calcutta he asked whether Congress would make a declaration which he believed would satisfy the Muslim League. The declaration ran:

> "The Congress are prepared in the interests of communal harmony to accept the intention of the Statement of May 16th that provinces cannot exercise any option affecting their membership of the sections or of the groups if formed, until the decision contemplated in paragraph 19(viii) of the Statement of 16th May is taken by the new Legislature after the new constitutional arrangements have come into operation and the first general elections have been held."[66]

And he intimated that he would not undertake the responsibility of summoning the Constituent Assembly till the point was settled. "The discussions which went on for some time and now and then became rather heated, proved inconclusive. In the end Gandhiji and Nehru agreed to take away the formula."[67] Gandhi wrote to Wavell that in their discussion he had been minatory in threatening not to summon the Constituent Assembly. And Nehru by his letter rejected the formula in the statement suggested by the Viceroy. Wavell thereupon requested Nehru to put his formula before the Congress Working Committee. This was done, and Nehru wrote back to say that the Working Committee was unable to accept the Viceroy's formula. The reply further said that the Constituent Assembly must proceed, even if some people refused to come in.

Assurances given to Muslim League about grouping and interpretation of Mission's Plan on May 16, 1946

1.42 The change in the policy of the Muslim League from the pursuit of constitutional methods to direct action was the result of a bitter controversy which arose over the Grouping provisions of the Cabinet Mission Plan. As to the Cabinet Mission Plan, the published documents leave no doubt of the Mission's intention, since it was made perfectly clear by the assurances given to the representatives of the Muslim League on 16th May, 1946, before the statement was later publicly announced. At the meeting held on 16th May between Lord Pethick-Lawrence and Sir Stafford Cripps and Nawabzada Liaquat Ali Khan, Nawab Mohammed Ismail Khan and Sardar Abdul Rabb Nishtar, the following discussion took place:[68]

---

64 *Menon, op. cit.* p. 305.

65 ibid.

66 ibid. p. 306.

67 ibid. For a dramatic account of the interview see Leonard Mosely, *The Last Days of the British Raj,* (Indian ed.) pp. 37-42.

68 *The Transfer of Power, 1942-47,* Vol. VII, pp. 577-80. It was agreed that Sardar Nishtar might see the note of the meeting and take notes from it but these would not have the status of an official record: ibid. p. 579. These assurances were not communicated to the Congress.

"Nawab Mohammed Ismail Khan asked at what stage and how the Groups would be formed. The Secretary of State and Sir Stafford Cripps explained that the sections of the Constitution-making Body would meet to decide the character of the Provincial Constitutions within the Group, and *the decision would be taken by majority vote of the representatives of the Provinces within the section* (italics supplied) . . . Sardar Rab Nishtar asked whether he correctly understood that each section of the Constitution-making Body would be entitled to frame the Constitution for the Provinces within it irrespective of whether they attended or not and also to determine whether there should be a Group and what the Group subjects should be, subject only to the right of a Province to opt out after the constitution had been framed. Sir Stafford Cripps said that this was in accordance with the document. The option would be exercisable after the whole picture including the Union Constitution had been completed[69] . . . Mohammed Ismail Khan asked who would interpret the statement. Sir Stafford Cripps said that if any question arose he presumed that the Viceroy would be the deciding authority. He would act in consultation with His Majesty's Government when necessary."[70]

In a telegram to the Secretary of State, dated Sept. 11, 1946, Wavell said that Jinnah was likely to quote from the Notes of the interview with the League on 16th May,[71] and inquired whether fairness to the Congress did not require that they should be informed of those assurances. With reference to Wavell's telegram, Mr. Turnbull, (the Private Secretary to Lord Pethick-Lawrence) made a note. He wrote:

"There is no doubt that the explanations given to the Muslim League on the three points which the Viceroy mentions were in accordance with the intentions of the Mission but I doubt if the Viceroy need disclose these points to the Congress out of any sense of fairness to them. If however, Mr. Jinnah bases his case for assurances now on these statements made by the Mission, it seems necessary to tell the Congress that these were the intentions of the Mission."[72] He added: "There is a much more awkward point than the ones mentioned by the Viceroy in the record of this meeting. This is the statement by Sir Stafford Cripps at the bottom of page 3 of the record that he presumed that if any question of interpretation arose the Viceroy would be the deciding authority in consultation with H.M.G. I believe that Sir Stafford Cripps said something in a different sense to Mr. Gandhi orally but of that we have no record. The Muslim League might well take their stand on this in refuting Nehru's position that interpretation should be by the Federal Court."[73]

Why Mission and Brit. Govt. failed to stand by their promises and their intention

1.43 Why, in face of these assurances did not the Cabinet Mission in the first instance, and the British Government later, make their intention clear as Wavell asked them to do? Why did the Mission and and the British Government countenance the idea that the intention of the Mission should be interpreted by the Federal Court, and not by the Viceroy assisted by the British Government as Cripps had told the representatives of the League? The correspondence on the point is voluminous, but it makes it reasonably clear that the Mission and the British Government were unwilling to say anything which would alienate the Congress and lead it to launch a mass civil disobedience movement. In this context it may be observed that on Dec. 12, 1945, Sir Stafford Cripps had written a letter to Nehru,[74] to which Nehru had sent a lengthy reply on Jan. 27, 1946.[75] From

---

[69] ibid. p. 577.
[70] ibid. p. 579.
[71] See *f.n.* 70 above.
[72] *The Transfer of Power, 1942-47*, Vol. VIII, p. 490.
[73] ibid.
[74] "Attempts to trace this letter have not been successful": *The Transfer of Power 1942-47*, Vol. VI, p. 851, *f.n.* 2.
[75] *Transfer of Power 1942-47*, Vol. VII, pp. 851-9.

Nehru's reply it appears that Cripps had asked Nehru "what action (Nehru) would lay down to be followed if (he) were the Viceroy of India."[76] It was in this letter that Nehru had written that the Muslim League would not dare to start Direct Action, to which reference has been made earlier.[77] Sir Stafford Cripps was the leading spirit of the Cabinet Mission, and the reluctance of the Mission to do anything which would offend the Congress and lead to a resort to direct action might have been confirmed by the Muslim League's adherence to constitutional methods, and also by Nehru's opinion that there was no likelihood of the League resorting to direct action. When Nehru's prediction proved mistaken, and the Muslim League adopted the policy of direct action, followed by the tragic killings in Calcutta, a new situation was created.

Muslim League's success in elections for Constituent Assembly: Assembly convened for Dec. 9

1.44 The delay in forming a coalition interim Government at the Centre, and the dispute about convening the Constituent Assembly also aggravated the situation. The elections to the Constituent Assembly which were completed in July 1946 showed that the Congress won all the general seats except 9, and the Muslim League won 73 seats out of 78 allotted to it. This result meant that the Congress and the Muslim League were, broadly speaking, the only two parties which mattered in Indian politics. The first meeting of the Constituent Assembly had been postponed several times, but finally the meeting of the Constituent Assembly was convened for December 9, 1946 and invitations were sent out to the members who had been elected to the Constituent Assembly. As the dispute about the interpretation of the Statement of May 16 had not been resolved, Jinnah declared that the Muslim League members would not attend the meeting of the Constituent Assembly. However, nominees of the Muslim League had been admitted into the interim Government on the understanding that the League would accept the Cabinet Mission's Plan, by rescinding the Muslim League's resolution of July 27, withdrawing its acceptance of the Plan. Since a meeting of the Muslim League to reconsider this resolution was not called, and yet the nominees of the Muslim League continued to be members of the interim Government, a question arose whether they should not resign. Attempts to induce the Muslim League to accept the Mission Plan and to attend the Session of the Constituent Assembly having failed, on 23rd November 1946, Wavell told Liaquat Ali Khan that he would not agree to the League remaining in the coalition without accepting the long term Plan. Liaquat Ali Khan replied that the League members were prepared to resign whenever the Viceroy required them to do so, but they would not accept the long term Plan unless H.M.G. declared that the Provinces must meet in sections, that the representatives in the sections would decide, by a majority if necessary, whether there would be groups, and that the sections again, by a majority if necessary, would frame the Provincial constitution and the Group constitutions. Also, H.M.G. must undertake not to implement the results unless this procedure was observed. If such an undertaking was given, the League would accept the long term Plan. Wavell's arguments failed to convince Liaquat Ali Khan to accept the Plan. Liaquat's position was that "If H.M.G. was afraid of the

League members decline acceptance of Mission Plan if Brit. Govt. failed to enforce their intention: they express readiness to resign from Executive Council

---

[76] ibid. p. 851.

[77] See *f.n.* 62, *ante*.

Congress and had not the courage or honesty to maintain their own Mission's Plan, then the Muslims had been thrown to the wolves and must accept the position and do the best they could by themselves, for it was useless to expect any mercy from the Congress."[78] Faced with this intractable problem and the growing disturbances in various parts of British India, Prime Minister Attlee invited two representatives of the Congress, two of the Muslim League and a representative of the Sikhs for discussions in England. At first Nehru refused the invitation, but on a personal appeal from Attlee he accepted it; and much the same thing happened to Jinnah. In the end, Nehru representing the Congress, Jinnah and Liaquat Ali Khan representing the League and Baldev Singh representing the Sikhs, left for England along with Wavell.

1.45 Discussions were held in London between Dec. 3 to Dec. 6. Various formulas were suggested for bringing the Congress and the League together on the interpretation of the Statement of 16th May, but without success. It may be mentioned at this place that as to the correct interpretation of the Statement of May 16, the Lord Chancellor's (Viscount Jowitt) opinion had been sought by the Secretary of State for India on November 29, 1946.[79] The Lord Chancellor concluded his opinion thus:

Nehru, Jinnah, Liaquat Ali Khan, Baldev Singh and Wavell join discussions in London

"That the recommendation involves that it is for the majority of the representatives in each section taken as a whole to decide how Provincial constitutions shall be framed and to what extent, if any, they shall be grouped. I should add that I come to the above conclusion solely on the terms of the Statement (Cmd. 6821) itself. If it were legitimate to pray in aid the doctrine of 'contemporanea expositio' it is obvious that my conclusion is reinforced."[80]

Lord Chancellor confirms Muslim League's and Mission's interpretation of Plan

This opinion supported the Muslim League's view of the Grouping Provisions, a view which the Mission had throughout maintained.

1.46 However, when the attempt to bring the Congress and the League together failed, the Prime Minister, on December 6, 1946, read out to the parties a Statement on behalf of H.M.G. As this Statement was the last effective attempt to bring the Congress and the League together in framing a Constitution *for a united India*, it is set out below:

Brit. Govt.'s statement of Dec. 6 on real intention of Mission's Plan

"The Cabinet Mission have throughout maintained the view that the decisions of the sections should, in the absence of agreement to the contrary, be taken by a simple majority vote of the representatives in the sections. This view has been accepted by the Muslim League, but the Congress have put forward a different view. They have asserted that the true meaning of the Statement read as a whole is that the provinces have a right to decide both as to grouping and as to their own constitutions.

His Majesty's Government have had legal advice,[81] which confirms that the Statement of May 16 means what the Cabinet Mission have always stated was their intention. This part of the Statement as so interpreted must therefore be considered as an essential part of the scheme of May 16 for enabling the Indian people to formulate a constitution which His Majesty's Government would be prepared to submit to Parliament. It should therefore be accepted by all parties in the Constituent Assembly

It is however clear that other questions of interpretation of the Statement of May 16 may arise, and His Majesty's Government hope that if the Council

[78] *The Transfer of Power 1942-47*, Vol. IX, p. 153.
[79] *The Transfer of Power 1942-47*, Vol. IX, pp. 220-24.
[80] ibid. pp. 238-40 at p. 240.
[81] This refers to the opinion of the Lord Chancellor set out in the text.

of the Muslim League are able to agree to participate in the Constituent Assembly they will also agree, as have the Congress, that the Federal Court should be asked to decide matters of interpretation that may be referred to them by either side, and will accept such decision, so that the procedure both in the Union Constituent Assembly and in the sections may accord with the Cabinet Mission's plan.

On the matter immediately in dispute, His Majesty's Government urge the Congress to accept the view of the Cabinet Mission, in order that the way may be open for the Muslim League to reconsider their attitude.

If, in spite of this reaffirmation of the intention of the Cabinet Mission, the Constituent Assembly desires that this fundamental point should be referred for the decision of the Federal Court, such reference should be made at a very early date. It will then be reasonable that the meetings of the sections of the Constituent Assembly should be postponed until the decision of the Federal Court is known.

There has never been any prospect of success for the Constituent Assembly except on this basis of an agreed procedure. Should a constitution come to be framed by a Constituent Assembly in which a large section of the Indian population had not been represented, His Majesty's Government could not of course contemplate — as the Congress have stated they would not contemplate — forcing such a constitution upon any unwilling parts of the country."[82]

Constituent Assembly meets on Dec. 9; Nehru moves "Objectives Resolution"

1.47 Nehru returned to India to attend the meeting of the Constituent Assembly fixed for Dec. 9, 1946. Rajendra Prasad was elected President of the Constituent Assembly. Nehru, in a moving speech, introduced the famous "Objectives Resolution". Muslim League members elected to the Constituent Assembly were absent. However, since the Constituent Assembly did not frame a Constitution for the whole of India, as envisaged by the Cabinet Mission Plan, the framing of India's Constitution by the Constituent Assembly is discussed separately in Section V below.

Wavell's Breakdown Plan — reasons for its formulation and the objects to be secured

1.48 We must now turn to Wavell's third problem: the Breakdown Plan. The reasons for framing the Plan were: the communal situation which led to the Calcutta tragedy; the running down of the Secretary of State's services; the difficulty of Governors in some Provinces to run a s. 93 administration, since a Governor's powers to protect government servants was fast becoming a dead letter in face of his Ministers' threat to resign. As the British were still constitutionally responsible, they would be "blamed for the disorders, repression and corruption which will become increasingly evident in India in the future."[83] Wavell communicated his Breakdown Plan to the Secretary of State for India on 8th Sept. 1946.[84] The object of the Breakdown Plan was: "(*a*) to regain the initiative; (*b*) to withdraw British authority with the minimum disorder and loss to H.M.G. and to India, and in such a manner as is most likely to maintain the cohesion of the Armed Forces; (*c*) by administering a severe shock, to induce the political leaders to adopt a saner outlook; (*d*) to have a period during which a last effort may be made to secure agreement; and (*e*) during such period to reduce progressively our responsibilities in India thus strengthening at each successive stage our position in the remaining territory."[85] The withdrawal of control was in the first instance to be from the Provinces of Madras, Bombay, Central Provinces and Orissa. This was to be followed by complete withdrawal from India by March 31, 1948. This plan was not designed

[82] *Transfer of Power 1942-47*, Vol. X, pp. 295-6.
[83] *The Transfer of Power 1942-47*, Vol. VIII, p. 456.
[84] ibid. pp. 454-64. [85] ibid. p. 458.

merely to meet a sudden emergency; it was to be announced and acted upon, whatever happened. It will be seen that the Plan was proposed after the Muslim League had withdrawn its acceptance of the Mission's Plan and adopted the policy of direct action. After the tragic events in Calcutta, and the continued bitterness between the Congress and the Muslim League about the framing of a Constitution for India, Wavell was of the opinion that till the basic principles on which the Constituent Assembly was to function were agreed upon, the meeting of the Constituent Assembly should not be called. The British Government raised objections to the Breakdown Plan and was of the view that the interim Government which had been formed should carry on and that the meeting of the Constituent Assembly should be convened notwithstanding the Muslim League's threatened boycott.

Brit. Govt.'s objection to Breakdown Plan

1.49 On 3rd December, before discussions began between the Indian leaders and British Ministers, Wavell saw the Prime Minister, the Secretary of State for India and A. V. Alexander, and handed over to them a statement in which he analysed the Indian situation describing, first, the short term issues, and then the long term plan.[86] After the Prime Minister had read out H.M.G.'s Statement on 6th December, Wavell remained in London and strongly pressed his Breakdown Plan on the British Government. When Wavell left England for India in December, Attlee told Wavell that he had got what he wanted about his Breakdown Plan. But after Wavell's return, the British Government went back on their decision.[87]

Wavell assured Breakdown Plan accepted by Brit. Govt. which, later, went back on its acceptance

1.50 On January 5, 1947, the All-India Congress Committee "accepted" H.M.G.'s statement of December 6, but it added the following rider:

"It must be clearly understood, however, that this must not involve any compulsion of a Province and that the rights of Sikhs in the Punjab should not be jeopardized. In the event of any attempt of such compulsion, a Province or part of Province has the right to take such action as may be deemed necessary in order to give effect to the wishes of the people concerned."

The Congress and Muslim League resolutions on statement of 6th Dec.

On 31st January, 1947, the Working Committee of the Muslim League passed a resolution that it had decided not to call the Council of the League to reconsider its decision rejecting the Cabinet Mission Plan. The resolution stated that the "so-called acceptance" by the Congress of the statement of 6th December was not an acceptance at all.

1.51 Departing from chronology, it may be observed that when Nehru pleaded during the negotiations between the Congress, the Muslim League and Lord Mountbatten that the Congress had accepted the Cabinet Mission Plan as interpreted by the statement of December 6 and that therefore it should be enforced as an award, Mountbatten said that "he did not think that the Congress would be regarded as having accepted the Mission's Plan. . . ."[88] No other view was possible in face of the rider to the resolution of January 5, 1947. The political deadlock in India was complete, and Wavell's attempts to persuade the parties to work the Cabinet Mission's Plan, as it was intended by the Mission, failed.

Mountbatten's view: Congress had not accepted Mission's Plan

---

[86] *The Transfer of Power 1942-47*, Vol. IX, pp. 240-43.
[87] Moon, *Viceroy's Journal*: Epilogue, p. 457.
[88] *Transfer of Power 1942-47*, Vol. X, p. 954.

Wavell's appointment as Viceroy terminated; Mountbatten appointed Viceroy-designate

1.52 It will be recalled that Wavell's Breakdown Plan had been rejected by the British Government. The published documents make it clear that even when Wavell was in England, Attlee had approached Lord Mountbatten on December 18, 1946 to take over as Viceroy from Lord Wavell, and Mountbatten had later accepted the offer. Attlee by his letter of Jan. 31, 1947 informed Wavell that his services were being terminated. To this letter, dismissing him at short notice, Wavell sent a dignified reply.[89] On Feb. 20, 1947, the British Government issued a statement on their Indian Policy.[90] The statement announced that the transfer of power from British to Indian hands would take place not later than June 1948. However, if a Constitution was not framed in accordance with the Cabinet Mission's Plan, by a fully representative Constituent Assembly before that date, "His Majesty's Government would have to consider to whom the power of Central Government in British India should be handed over."[91] Simultaneously with this statement it was announced that Lord Wavell would be succeeded by Lord Mountbatten as Viceroy.

Brit. Govt.'s statement of Feb. 20, 1947 announcing transfer of power not later than June 1948

Wavell's services to India: Consequence of failure of Churchill and Attlee Govt. to give him full support

1.53 In Azad's words, Lord Wavell "was the initiator of a new chapter in the history of relations, between India and England."[92] Had he been allowed to take an initiative in getting together leaders of Indian public opinion as he wanted to do when he had been appointed Viceroy-designate, or had he later received full support from His Majesty's Government in his firm determination to treat *both* the Congress and the Muslim League justly in order to bring them

[89] The letters deserve to be read as a whole. See *Transfer of Power 1942-47*, Vol. IX at pp. 582-83 (Attlee's letter) and pp. 624-25 (Wavell's reply). Attlee's letter illustrates Macaulay's favourite saying, "No man was ever written down, except by himself."

[90] ibid. pp. 773-74.

[91] ibid. p. 774. It is necessary to set out the following entry in the *Viceroy's Journal*, followed by the Editor's note, in order to remove any misconception that Wavell, having pressed on H.M.G. that a date should be announced for the transfer of power to India, later gave up that suggestion.

"*February 19, 1947*: H.M.G. telegraphed adhering to their announcement; and also sent a long telegram of self-justification and accusation of myself as inconsistent, to which I think I can make an effective reply."

"*H.M.G. accused Wavell of inconsistency because, having strongly pressed when in London that a final date should be announced for the transfer of power, he had later transmitted reports from Burrows* (the Governor of Bengal) *and Jenkins* (the Governor of Punjab) *opposing such a course and predicting calamitous consequences in Bengal and the Punjab, and had himself urged that the announcement of the date should be postponed.*

"*It does not appear that Wavell ever sent his 'effective' reply. Probably he would have pointed out that in forwarding the reports of Burrows and Jenkins he had expressed the view that they were unduly pessimistic; that he had only asked for a temporary postponement of the announcement in order to make one final effort to bring the Congress and the League together in the Constituent Assembly and that from the point of view of staving off a crisis there was no longer any immediate hurry to make the announcement, since neither party really wanted to precipitate a break; and finally that, in his view, before making the announcement, H.M.G. should have some definite plan for demitting power by the due date and that they had rejected his Breakdown Plan, but had not put forward any other.*": *Penderel Moon, op. cit.* pp. 421-22. It may be added that Wavell had prepared a draft letter which contained his "effective" reply. After that draft had been amended, it was sent to Lord Pethick-Lawrence by a letter dated Feb. 22. On its receipt in London it was circulated to the India and Burma Committee. The Note made by Sir Penderel Moon broadly corresponds to Wavell's effective reply dated Feb. 22: See *Transfer of Power 1942-47*, Vol. IX, pp. 771-2, and *f.n.* 5 at p. 772.

[92] *Azad, op. cit. p.* 179.

together, it is more than arguable that he would have succeeded in bringing the parties together in a united India. Had the Cabinet Mission's Plan been announced as an Award,[93] the chances of its being worked as it was intended to be worked could have been greatly enhanced. The obstruction from the Churchill Government was intelligible, for Churchill had a blind spot about India; but the obstruction from the Attlee Government was due to its unwillingness to take unpleasant decisions. In a Note dated December 2, 1946[94] Wavell bluntly put the position as follows:

"1. The Cabinet Mission Plan was as good as could have been framed in the circumstances, and could have been put through with firmness. But neither the Mission nor H.M.G. adhered to their original intention with sufficient directness of purpose, in particular, the Mission gave Jinnah pledges on May 16 which they have not honoured. . . . 3. The Muslims are thoroughly alarmed and many of the leaders are getting desperate. They trusted to the British to give them a fair deal and feel that owing to the unwillingness and duplicity of H.M.G. they are not getting it.

"They will not come into the Constituent Assembly unless they get a very definite pledge that it will be worked in the way they were promised and that H.M.G. will not recognize the results otherwise."[95]

The reader will have noticed that the authoritative interpretation given in the Statement of 6th December, of the grouping provisions set out in para 1.37 above, had many escape clauses. If the British Government's interpretation was not accepted, it was suggested that the matter should be referred to the Federal Court. The published documents leave no doubt that the Muslim League accepted the Cabinet Mission Plan in the first instance because of the compulsory grouping provisions.[96] Wavell pressed firmly for a clear declaration that the Plan must be worked according to the intention of the Cabinet Mission. His advice was rejected. It seems bizzare that the interpretation of a Plan designed to bring the two great communities of India together should be left to a Court, and that too, in face of assurances given to the Muslim League. But in the clash of political battle, the deep significance of Jinnah's objection to a reference to the Federal Court was lost. He said: ". . . on the very threshold parties fundamentally differ in their interpretation regarding the basic terms. *Are we going to commence the proceedings of the Constituent Assembly with litigation and law suits in the Federal Court? Is this the spirit in which the future Constitution can be framed for 400 million people of this sub-continent?*"[97] (italics supplied)

1.54 Secondly, it was Wavell who insisted that a date should be fixed for the withdrawal of the British Power and a supreme effort Wavell responsible for suggest-

[93] *Cf.* "Pandit Nehru's view was that the proposals set out in the draft announcement (proposed by Mountbatten) should now be abandoned; *that the Cabinet Mission's Plan should be imposed as a settlement*; . . .": *Transfer of Power 1942-47*, Vol. X, p. 1014. (italics supplied)

[94] Prepared for discussion with the Prime Minister and other Ministers.

[95] *Transfer of Power 1942-47*, Vol. IX, pp. 240-41.

[96] *Azad, op. cit.* p. 150: "The Muslim League Council met for three days before it could come to a decision. On the final day, Mr. Jinnah had to admit that there could be no fairer solution of the minority problem than that presented in the Cabinet Mission Plan. In any case, he could not get better terms. He told the Council that the scheme presented by the Cabinet Mission was the maximum he could secure. As such he advised the Muslim League to accept the scheme and the Council voted unanimously in its favour."

[97] *Menon, op. cit.* p. 304.

ing date for withdrawal: his dismissal as a "defeatist" and its amazing sequel

should be made to bring all parties together, before partition was adopted as inevitable. For his insistence on this point he was described by Attlee as a "defeatist" and dismissed summarily. Sir Penderel Moon has aptly described the sequel:

"What followed was a striking *reductio ad absurdum* of His Majesty's Government. They had rejected Wavell's demand for the fixing of a date and had decided to dismiss him from the post of Viceroy, only to find that his proposed successor made exactly the same demand and would not agree to take office unless it was granted. So *Attlee and his Government capitulated, and soon were quite happy to take credit for a decision that had in fact been forced upon them.*"[98] (italics supplied)

Two myths destroyed by *Viceroy's Journal* and *Transfer of Power 1942-47*

1.55 The publication of the *Viceroy's Journal* (1973) and then of Volumes IV to IX of the *Transfer of Power 1942-47* (1973 to 1980) have destroyed two myths : First, that it was a benevolent Labour Government which, out of the goodness of its heart and love of freedom, transferred power to India; secondly, that Wavell who had persisted in asking His Majesty's Government to make a declaration about the withdrawal from India by a specified date was a "defeatist" who had to be removed from office in order to secure it. There is little doubt that Wavell's task was much harder than Mountbatten's. It is relatively easy to break up a joint family and partition its assets because of squabbles between its members. It is much more difficult to keep the family intact by removing, or minimizing, the causes of friction between its members and that is what Wavell resolutely set out to do. Realising that his best efforts might fail, he put forward his Breakdown Plan as early as September 1946, so that if he failed to bring the parties together, a plan worked out in good time for an orderly withdrawal of power from India could be put into effect to avoid disastrous consequences. When it became known that Wavell was leaving India, Azad issued a statement paying a glowing tribute to Wavell's services to India.[99] If Azad could have had access to the *Viceroy's Journal* and to the documents on the Transfer of Power, he would have been gratified to find that his tribute to Wavell was more than deserved, and that Wavell had lived up to his favourite saying from Sir Walter Scott : "Without courage there cannot be truth, and without truth there can be no other virtue." Attlee's Government lacked courage,[1] and India paid the price of partition, or, at any rate, the price of 600,000 people massacred and 14 million people uprooted by mass migrations.

Heavy price paid by India for Attlee Govt.'s lack of courage

Lord Mountbatten's Viceroyalty: 23rd March 1947 — 15th August 1947.

Directive to Mountbatten for demitting power

1.56 Lord Mountbatten agreed to become the Viceroy of India on the express condition that a date must be fixed for the withdrawal of British power from India, and that he should be given large powers to carry out such withdrawal. The directive issued to

[98] Penderel Moon, *The Viceroy's Journal*, p. 457.

[99] *Azad, op. cit.* p. 179.

[1] Lord Pethick-Lawrence said in a Note prepared for Attlee: "It is only fair to the Viceroy to admit that the difficulties in which we now find ourselves result from the failure to get clear satisfaction on this point (grouping). But our judgment at the time was that to press it to a final conclusion would result in the Congress not accepting the Statement of May 16th": *Transfer of Power 1942-47*, Vol. VIII, p. 504.

Mountbatten provided, among other things, that he should work for a unitary government, and make an attempt to bring the Congress and the Muslim League to agree to the acceptance of the Cabinet Mission Plan. If he was unable to do so before 1st October 1947, he was to report to His Majesty's Government what steps should be taken to secure the transfer of power by June 30, 1948.[1a]

1.57 Between the offer of the Viceroyalty of India to Mountbatten and his arrival in India on March 22, 1947, grave events were taking place in India. The qualified acceptance of H.M.G.'s Statement of 6th December 1946 by the Congress on 5th January, 1947, and the Muslim League's contention that the so-called acceptance by the Congress of the Cabinet Mission's Plan was not an acceptance at all, produced a deadlock, and Wavell's attempts to bring the Congress and the League to work the Plan failed. But all this while the situation in the Punjab was deteriorating, since the Muslim League, which was the largest single party in the Punjab Legislative Assembly, but had been unable to form a government, had launched a non-cooperation movement against the Unionist Ministry of Sir Khizar Hayat Khan Tiwana. The League used "exactly the techniques used by the Congress in their agitations of 1920 and 1930."[2] On the top of this came H.M.G.'s announcement on Feb. 20, 1947; Khizar Hayat Khan found his position untenable, and he resigned on 2nd March; and Sir Evan Jenkins, the Governor of Punjab, took over the administration of the Punjab under s. 93, G.I. Act, 35 on 5th March. On that very day the Congress Working Committee passed resolutions on H.M.G.'s Announcement of 20th February. One of the resolutions said that the events in the Punjab had shown that the province may have to be divided as a means of putting an end to violence. The political deadlock persisted, and violence in several Provinces increased by the time Mountbatten was sworn in on 23rd March. Mountbatten had been given an enlarged staff and he brought with him Lord Ismay and Sir Eric Mieville, and retained Abell as his private secretary. V. P. Menon continued as the Reforms Commissioner. Since Menon had played a leading part in drawing up a plan for partition, which was ultimately accepted, Chapters 15 to 18 of his book[3] on *The Transfer of Power in India* have high authority. However, the reader will bear in mind that by this time he had become a close confidant of Vallabhbhai Patel, and this, to some extent, coloured his judgments of men and events. Since the final volume of the *Transfer of Power 1942-47* covering the most crucial period of Mountbatten's Viceroyalty (3rd June-15th August) has not been published, it is not possible to give an independent account of Mountbatten's Viceroyalty for that period. A brief account of what Mountbatten did is given below.

Situation in Punjab deteriorates between Dec. 1946 and March 22, 1947

Khizar Hayat Khan ministry resigns

Menon and the Mountbatten Plan

1.58 As soon as he came to India, he met Gandhi, Nehru, Jinnah, Liaquat Ali Khan, Vallabhbhai Patel, Azad and other political leaders. He pressed them to accept the Cabinet Mission Plan. But as the discussions proceeded, he realised that the Plan was dead. Having reached this conclusion, Mountbatten, with the assistance of Menon and other advisers evolved a plan for the partition of India

Mountbatten's discussions with Indian leaders: visits London with plan for partition

---

[1a] For the full text of the directive see *Transfer of Power 1942-47*, Vol. IX, pp. 972-74.

[2] *Moon, op. cit.* p. 428.

[3] *Menon, op. cit.* pp. 355-423.

which would be acceptable to the Congress and to the Muslim League. It is not necessary to go through the details of the various drafts of the Plan; it is enough to say that Mountbatten carried with him to England a draft which had been shown both to Nehru and to Jinnah. A feature of the draft Plan likely to appeal to the Conservative Party in England was that power was to be transferred to two Dominions — India and Pakistan — as an interim measure, and power would be finally transferred to them before the end of 1947. On his return to India, on 3rd June 1947, Mountbatten in a broadcast announced the decision of His Majesty's Government, (which, he said, had the support of the parties in India) to partition India by the creation of two Dominions of India and Pakistan. The Viceroy's broadcast was followed by broadcasts by Nehru, Jinnah and Baldev Singh indicating their acceptance of the Plan. The Muslim League Council met on 10th June 1947 and by its resolution accepted the principles laid down in the Plan and authorised Jinnah to accept the fundamental principles and empowered him to take all steps and decisions in that behalf. A Meeting of the All India Congress Committee was held on 14th June and a resolution was moved accepting the Plan for partition. Azad felt it to be his duty to oppose the resolution. He said that "Partition was a tragedy for India and the only thing that could be said in its favour was that we have done our best to avoid division, but we had failed."[4] The debate on the resolution continued for another day. However, the intervention of Gandhi in support of the resolution was decisive. His opposition to Pakistan was well known — he had said that Pakistan could come to India only over his dead body. But he advised that circumstances had arisen which made partition unavoidable. The resolution was passed by 29 votes to 15.

Mountbatten's broadcast on partition plan; broadcasts by Nehru, Jinnah and Baldev Singh

1.59 The British Parliament swiftly implemented the decision to partition India. A Bill (which became the Indian Independence Act, 1947) was introduced in the House of Commons on 4th July, 1947 and was passed on 15th July. The next day, it was passed by the House of Lords. There were no amendments. It received the Royal Assent on 18th July. That Act created the two independent Dominions of India and Pakistan,[5] divested His Majesty's Government in the United Kingdom of responsibility for the government of the territories which immediately before August 15, 1947, were included in British India,[6] made temporary provisions for the government of each dominion and provided that the powers of the legislature of the dominion were, for the purpose of making provision for the Constitution of the dominion, to be exercisable in the first instance by the Constituent Assembly for that dominion,[7] the references to the Constituent Assembly for the Dominion of India being construed as references to the Constituent Assembly, the first sitting whereof was held on December 9, 1946, with its membership modified by certain exclusions and inclusions.[8] To complete the narrative it may be added that as a result of the machinery[9] devised for ascertaining the wishes of the people likely to be affected by partition, between

Indian Independence Act, 1947: the two Dominions of India and Pakistan

---

4 *Azad, op. cit.* p. 197.
5 s. 1.
6 s. 7(a) read with s. 1(b).
7 s. 8(1).
8 s. 19(3).
9 For the machinery adopted, see *Menon, op. cit.* pp. 394-7.

June and July, 1947, East Bengal (including Sylhet), West Punjab, Sind, Baluchistan and the North-West Frontier Province voted for Pakistan.

1.60 The bringing forward of the date for establishing the two Dominions of India and Pakistan from June 30, 1948 to August 15, 1947 posed formidable problems with inadequate time to solve them. Problems raised by fixing date on 15th Aug. 1947

First, in accordance with the Plan of June 3, 1947, it was decided to set up two Boundary Commissions, one for the partition of Punjab and the other for the partition of Bengal as also the separation of Sylhet from Assam.[10] Sir Cyril Radcliffe, the independent Chairman, landed in India on 8th July, 1947, and was told by Mountbatten, Nehru and Jinnah that he and his two Commissions had five weeks time to make an award demarcating the boundaries of the provinces to be partitioned. However, the partition of the Punjab involved a special complication, because partition would disrupt the existence of canal systems, vital to the life of the Punjab, which were developed on the basis of a single administration. Radcliffe informed Mountbatten that he wished to put a proposition to Nehru and Jinnah, namely, that they should enter into an agreement to place the administration of the canal systems under a joint administration. He put his proposition to them, only to be rebuked and rebuffed by both. The members of the two Boundary Commissions were unable to agree on really controversial matters, and, in substance, it fell to Radcliffe to make an award, which came to be known as the "Radcliffe Award". The failure of the leaders to accept Radcliffe's wise suggestion was to lead to prolonged disputes which were only settled when India and Pakistan signed the Indus Basin Development Treaty on Sept. 19, 1960 in Karachi. The Indus Water Treaty was signed by Prime Minister Nehru and President Ayub Khan as well as on behalf of the International Bank for Reconstruction and Development and the agreement concerning the financing of the project was signed by the representatives of Australia, Canada, Germany, New Zealand, Pakistan, the United Kingdom, the United States and the Bank.[11] Very little time left for award of Boundary Commission

Secondly, on what principles were the Armed Forces to be divided since both the Congress and the Muslim League insisted on having their own Armed Forces under their control. Kripalani, the Principle for dividing Armed Forces

[10] "With the consent of both parties Sir Cyril (later Lord) Radcliffe was appointed the Chairman of both Commissions. The remaining members were all High Court Judges. Thus, the members of the Bengal Commission were Justices C. C. Biswas, B. K. Mukherjea, Abu Saleh Mahomed Akram and S. A. Rahman, while the members of the Punjab Commission were Justices Meher Chand Mahajan, Teja Singh, Din Mahomed and Muhammad Munir.": *Menon, op. cit.* p. 408. For the difficulties which faced the Boundary Commission see ibid. pp. 408-410. For the Plan of June 3, see ibid. pp. 522-27.

[11] Large grants had been made by these countries and the Bank granted large and substantial loans. For a fascinating account of how the treaty came to be made and signed, see *The Law of International Drainage Basins,* edited by Gariston, Hayton and Olmstead. The main provision of the treaty was that the western rivers. Indus, Jhelum and Chinab would be available for the exclusive use and benefit of Pakistan with limited exceptions and the entire flow of the eastern rivers, Ravi, Beas and Sutlej would be available for the exclusive use and benefit of India, with limited exceptions. This division involved large construction works and link canals which were only made possible by substantial grants from the countries mentioned earlier and by loans from the World Bank and the International Bank for Reconstruction and Development.

between India and Pakistan

Congress President, pointed out that it was a question intimately connected with that of nationality. Jinnah supported this view, adding that it would be his purpose in Pakistan to observe no communal differences and that all those who lived there regardless of creed would be full-fledged citizens. It appears that at first this view found acceptance, subject to the right of members of a minority community in each State to opt out. Ultimately however, it was decided that from 15th August, India and Pakistan would have their Armed Forces composed predominantly of non-Muslims and Muslims respectively.[12]

Separate or common Governors-General for India and Pakistan

Thirdly, a question was raised whether there should be one Governor-General for the two Dominions during the transition period and whether Mountbatten should be "re-appointed". It seems surprising that such a question should have been raised at all, and even more surprising that it should have been the subject of considerable discussion till it became a contest of wills between Mountbatten and Jinnah, with Jinnah as the victor. Menon's discussion of this topic in *The Transfer of Power in India*[13] is unsatisfactory and incorrect, as is clear from the documents now published. A lively and dramatic, but a substantially accurate, account of the episode will be found in Mosely's *Last Days of the British Raj.*[14] However, the following is a brief account of the episode based on published documents. Menon had prepared a draft of "Heads of Agreement" which, it was hoped, the Indian leaders would sign.[15] Clause 6 of the Draft provided that "The Governor-General should be common to both States. We suggest that the present Governor-General should be re-appointed." A letter from Nehru to Mountbatten dated 17th May, commenting on "Proposals for Transfer of Power during Interim Period," said, among other things, "We agree to the proposal that during the interim period, the Governor-General should be common to both States, if there are two States. For our part we shall be happy if you could continue in the office and help us with your experience."[16] The record of an interview between Mountbatten and Jinnah and Liaquat Ali Khan on 17th May shows that Mountbatten wanted Jinnah's personal views as to whether Jinnah preferred Pakistan to have its own Governor-General or to share a common Governor-General with Hindustan. Jinnah, without committing himself, said that "he felt that it would be better to have two Governors-General. Also there should in his opinion, be a Representative of the Crown responsible for the division of assets between the two States,"[17] and that Mountbatten should fill that post. After further discussion Mountbatten suggested that Jinnah should send him a letter on 19th May "giving a full description of his suggestion of a supreme arbitrator and two Governors-General."

Menon's account unsatisfactory and incorrect as disclosed by published documents

---

[12] For a fuller account, see *Menon, op. cit.* pp. 405-07.

[13] See pp. 400-402. Menon has left out important documents which are to be found in the *Transfer of Power 1942-47*, Vol. X which put a different complexion on the episode, and render Menon's account incorrect.

[14] See pp. 168-177. The narrative is supported by reference to "Government of India Records", and the documents referred to in that narrative till the return of Mountbatten on June 2, are found also in the *Transfer of Power 1942-47*, Vol. X.

[15] See *Transfer of Power 1942-47*, Vol. X, pp. 841-43 (Meeting of 16th May 1947).

[16] ibid. p. 869. [17] ibid.

"However, he (Mountbatten) wished to be quite clear that he would reserve his personal position unless it was clearly stated by Mr. Jinnah in his letter that, if his scheme was found by H. M. G. to be impracticable, he would accept, as a less desirable alternative and as an interim measure, the appointment of a common Governor-General between the two States. Mr. Jinnah at first expressed himself violently opposed to this suggestion, but eventually, after prolonged discussion, he said that he would think it over. He pointed out that if H.M.G. decided, contrary to his own opinion, that his suggestion was unworkable, there would be no reason for him not to accept an alternative."[18]

It would appear that in view of Jinnah's personal opinion, two alternative drafts, marked "A" and "B" were prepared on 17th May, containing "Proposals for Transfer of Power during the Interim Period on the basis of two Independent States." Clause 2 of draft "A" provided that "If the States desire it, there will be one common Constitutional Governor-General for the two States. He will also act as Arbitrator in matters of common concern between the two States, if the Governments of the two States agree that he should do so." Clause 2 of the draft "B" said simply that "There will be a separate Governor-General for each state."[19] In a letter dated 19th May, Nehru informed Captain Brockman, (among other things), "We prefer, therefore, draft 'A' to 'B'. But if, for any reason, one of the States wants to have a separate Governor-General for this period, we have no insuperable objection to it."[20] The published documents show that Jinnah did not forward to Mountbatten the details of his suggestion of a supreme arbitrator with two Governors-General for India and Pakistan. Nor did he agree to there being a common Governor-General. It is clear however from Nehru's comment that the Congress had no insuperable objection to two Governors-General.

1.61 Volume X of *The Transfer of Power 1942-47* ends with documents dated 30th May. From this point the brief account of what happened after Mountbatten returned to India must be gathered chiefly from Mosley's *Last Days of the British Raj*, part of which is derived from "Government of India Records". It would appear that on 8th June, Lord Ismay prepared a memorandum indicating the benefits to Hindustan and Pakistan of a common Governor-General.[21] Sir Eric Meiville's interview with Liaquat Ali Khan on 20th June failed to obtain any answer about a common Governor-General, as did the interview between Mountbatten and Jinnah on 23rd June.[22] However, at a meeting on 2nd July between Jinnah and Mountbatten, Jinnah said that he had decided to become the Governor-General of Pakistan. Mountbatten argued against this decision and suggested a compromise under which Jinnah would be Officiating Governor-General in Pakistan when Mountbatten was in Delhi. Jinnah did not accept the compromise. Thereupon, Mountbatten recorded: "I asked him 'Do you realise what this will cost you?' He said sadly 'It may cost me several crores of rupees in assets', to which I replied somewhat acidly 'It may well cost you the whole of your assets and the future of Pakistan.' I then got up and left the room."[23] On the same day "a Staff meeting was

Same topic continued

[18] ibid. p. 873.
[19] ibid. pp. 888-89.
[20] ibid. p. 892.
[21] *Mosley, op. cit.* pp. 171-72.
[22] ibid. pp. 172-74.
[23] Viceroy's Personal Report No. 11, 4th July, 1947, quoted in Hudson, *The Great Divide*, p. 331.

called at Lord Ismay's house 'to consider the consequences of Mr. Jinnah's declared wish to be Governor-General of Pakistan.' The main purpose of the meeting was 'to devise a formula whereby His Excellency the Viceroy could remain Governor General of both Dominions, *and, at the same time, satisfy Mr. Jinnah's vanity*'."[24] On 5th July, Liaquat Ali Khan confirmed in a letter to Mountbatten that Jinnah had made up his mind, and requested Mountbatten formally to recommend to the King the appointment of Jinnah as Governor-General of Pakistan. The letter expressed the hope that Mountbatten would remain as Governor-General of India.[25] This whole episode is unfortunate and should never have been allowed to arise, for it is incredible that the same person could be the constitutional Governor-General of two States. The constitutional head of a Dominion must act on the advice of his ministry. The two independent Dominions would be entitled to pursue their own policies, policies which may conflict, and a constitutional head of the two Dominions would be in an impossible position if his two ministries gave him conflicting advice. Menon's explanation that the only way of giving effect to Jinnah's suggestion of a Super-Governor-General was to provide for a common Governor-General[26] is special pleading. Mountbatten correctly understood Jinnah's proposal when he asked Jinnah to give a full description of his "suggestion of a supreme arbitrator and two Governors-General." This episode left an unfortunate legacy behind. Jinnah's refusal to agree to Mountbatten becoming the Governor-General of India and also of Pakistan inflicted a wound on Mountbatten which time did not heal, and which led him to say in public, harsh and unkind things about Jinnah.

Partition not inevitable

1.62 The question has been asked, was the partition of India inevitable? Opinions on this point have differed. After the Congress committed the grave error of refusing to form coalition ministries in 1937,[27] the first opportunity of avoiding partition was the Desai-Liaquat Ali Pact which, had it been implemented with good will, might have broken the deadlock. The repudiation of Bhulabhai Desai by the Congress put an end to the hope of repairing the damage which had been done in 1937. One more opportunity remained. It was seized by Azad when he put his ideas before the Cabinet Mission, and succeeded in persuading the Congress Working Committee to adopt his plan. The Cabinet Mission Plan remained substantially the same as Azad's;[28] it would have secured a united India, and the compulsory grouping scheme in the three sections would have given the Muslims all that they could get from Pakistan, without the penalties, perils and burdens flowing from a Pakistan separated from India. It was this idea, when propounded by Azad, that commended itself to the Cabinet Mission. This opportunity of keeping India united was lost, first, because the Congress accepted the plan with a qualification which destroyed its value for the Muslim League; secondly, because of the failure of the Mission and, later, of the

---

[24] *Mosley, op. cit.* p. 174 (Government of India Records).
[25] ibid. pp. 174-75.
[26] *Menon, op. cit.* pp. 400-401.
[27] See para 1.21 above.
[28] See *Azad, op. cit.* p. 173: "He (Wavell) repeatedly told me that even from the point of the Muslim League, no better solution was possible. Since the Cabinet Mission Plan was largely based on the scheme I had formulated in my statement of 15 April, I naturally agreed."

British Government to make their intention clear before damage had been done by allowing the Congress reservations about the Cabinet Mission Plan to remain outstanding for over five months. Patel rightly complained about this delay, and expressed ". . . regret that H.M.G. did not state their position earlier if their present statement (of 6th December 1946) represented their intention; Congress is now put in a very difficult position *vis-a-vis* Assam and the Sikhs."[29] In any rational sense, partition was not inevitable. It became inevitable because Hindu leaders, including a leader as eminent as Nehru failed to realise that by 1946 "the Muslim League dominated the Muslims as the Congress dominated the Hindus,"[30] and that the Congress and the League would have to live and work together if India was to remain united.

1.63 Secondly, would the Cabinet Mission Plan have worked satisfactorily? If the Congress and the Muslim League had joined hands, the problem of the "Native States" ruled by autocratic rulers would have posed no serious difficulties, and those States would have been absorbed in a united India as they were absorbed in a divided India. No doubt the Centre would not have been a strong Centre as it is in our Constitution, but as against that, India would have had a united Army, common communications to guard its extensive and historically vulnerable frontiers, and one foreign policy. Besides, a united India could have utilised its limited resources for the welfare of the people instead of India, Pakistan and later Bangladesh spending crores of rupees on costly armaments, each State treating the other two as potential enemies. Nor would Pakistan have been split in two by the creation of Bangladesh — a State created with Indian help, but not very much more friendly to India than Pakistan. And most important of all, democratic institutions would not have been snuffed out in any part of India and replaced by military dictatorships, as in Pakistan and Bangladesh. But the plan required mutual co-operation and goodwill, a willingness to forget the past and to work for the well-being of a free and independent India. But between 1942 and 1947 goodwill and co-operation were rare commodities in India; they were not sought for, because distinguished Congress leaders confidently believed that Pakistan would have to seek reunion with India. On 19th May, 1947, Mountbatten reported to the British Cabinet that "It had become clear that the Muslim League would resort to arms if Pakistan in some form was not conceded. In the face of this threat, the Congress leaders had modified their former attitude; indeed they were now inclined to feel that it would be to their advantage to be relieved of responsibility for the Provinces that would form Pakistan, *while at the same time they were confident that those Provinces would ultimately have to seek reunion with the remainder of India.*"[31] (italics supplied) Jinnah left India

Would Cabinet Mission Plan have worked satisfactorily?

Indian leaders believed that Pakistan would have to rejoin India

[29] In an interview with Sir John Colville, Acting Viceroy, on 10th December, 1946: See *Transfer of Power* 1942-47, Vol. IX, p. 316. See also para 1.54, *f.n.* 1.

[30] See para 1.35 above. Or, as Wavell's biographer put it, "It may be asserted that this non-political soldier (Wavell) with his one eye saw more clearly than the experts in London, than some of his own advisers, and even than the sophisticated Nehru himself. Since the time of the Cripps Mission, Jinnah and the Muslim League had extended their power-base so far and so effectively that any idea of treating with them other than on the same level as Congress was doomed. This was the reality whose truth was ratified by the final split.": Lewin, *The Chief*, p. 232.

[31] *The Transfer of Power 1942-47*, Vol. X, p. 896.

for Pakistan on 7th August, 1947, with an appeal to both Hindus and Muslims to "bury the past" and wished India success and prosperity. The next day, Patel said in Delhi "The poison had been removed from the body of India. We are now one and indivisible. You cannot divide the sea or the waters of the river. As for the Muslims they have their roots, their sacred places and their centres here. I do not know what they can possibly do in Pakistan. It will not be long before they return to us."[32] Hardly the words to promote goodwill and neighbourliness either then or in the days to come.

Menon's unconscious tribute to Cabinet Mission Plan he consciously rejected

1.64 In Chapter XX of his book Menon has described the Cabinet Mission Plan, as intended by its authors, to be "no more than a facade of unity", and he said that in any event, the three tier constitution was unwieldy and carried with it the potentiality of continued friction.[33] However, by a strange irony, in an article he wrote for *The Statesman,* on 21st October, 1947 he paid an unconscious tribute to the Plan which he consciously rejected. He wrote that public opinion in India would insist on adequate military preparations, and no responsible Government would be able to resist the demand, and this would lead to counter-preparations on the Pakistan side. He added:

> "This is a danger which must be averted. Mahatma Gandhi has been insisting that freedom would lose its significance if the lot of the common man were not improved. Similarly, the agitation for Pakistan was based upon the need for the Muslims to build up their life in their own way. Neither object can be achieved if the two States' resources are frittered away in futile military preparations. It is imperative that a way be found for building up a basis of security for both.
>
> In essential respects their interests are bound up with each other. . . . *Why then should not both recognize this, and join up formally in mutual union for the three essential subjects of defence and foreign affairs (mutually dependent) and communications upon which defence depends?* In this lies salvation. (italics supplied)
>
> Pakistan may be loath to surrender the sentimental satisfaction of a separate national State for the Muslims. But a union at the top for these three subjects would not affect the separate existence of the two States for other matters."[34]

Menon's prescription self-contradictory

But it was just because Azad and the Cabinet Mission realised the vital importance of common defence, common communications and a common foreign policy for the sub-continent of India, that the Cabinet Mission Plan allocated these subjects to the Union of India while conferring on the Provinces, grouped in the three sections, all other powers, including residuary powers. When Nehru and Patel accepted partition to secure for India a federation with a strong centre, so that India would be free to develop in such manner as she thought fit, they chose partition as a lesser evil. Menon's prescription overlooks the fact that either we had to be content with a loose federation and a weak centre in order to secure the blessings of a common policy in foreign affairs, defence and communications in a united India, or be content to break up the country into India and Pakistan, each State being free to pursue policies which it considered most beneficial to itself, regardless of how they affected the other. Or, to put the choice more simply, we could have built on

---

[32] *Mosley, op. cit.* p. 248.
[33] *Menon, op. cit.* p. 447.
[34] ibid. p. 449.

trust and co-operation and remained a united country; or we could have built on distrust and disharmony and become two countries, each pursuing its own individual good. Menon's prescription is self-contradictory for it seeks to combine two contradictory alternatives.

1.65 One other cause which led the Congress to accept partition must be noted here. It was said that the interim government did not act harmoniously and did not act as a Cabinet with Nehru as the *de facto* Prime Minister. This situation was aggravated by the fact that Patel had insisted on retaining the Home Ministry and had readily agreed that the Finance Ministry be offered to the Muslim League, only to discover that Liaquat Ali Khan as the Finance Minister controlled all ministries, including the Home Ministry. The published documents disclose many discussions as to the status of the Interim Government. The position was made clear in paras 3 and 4 of Wavell's letter to Azad of May 30, 1946:[35]

Brit. Govt.'s consistent policy as to status and functioning of Executive Council

"3. I am quite clear that I did not state to you that the Interim Government would have the same powers as a Dominion Cabinet. The whole Constitutional position is entirely different. I said that I was sure that His Majesty's Government would treat the new Interim Government with the same close consultation and consideration as a Dominion Government.

Policy set out in Wavell's letter to Azad

4. His Majesty's Government had already said that they will give to the Indian Government the greatest possible freedom in the exercise of the day to day administration of the country and I need hardly assure you that it is my intention faithfully to carry out this undertaking."[36]

The Congress's claim that the Interim Government should function as a Cabinet, with Nehru as the *de facto* Prime Minister, raised questions not only of the constitutional position of the Executive Council under the G.I. Act, 35, but also about the attitude of the Muslim League to such a claim. The Muslim League saw in that claim an attempt by Congress to seize absolute executive power by eliminating the Viceroy's veto, and then dealing with the Muslims as an all powerful Cabinet. The Muslims therefore opposed the claim; and the British Government also rejected that claim by declining to go beyond the assurances given to Azad. The British Government reiterated this view in the directive issued to Mountbatten which said, among other things,

Policy reaffirmed in directive to Mountbatten

"In your relations with the Interim Government you will be guided by the general terms of the Viceroy's letter of May 30, 1946 to the President of the Congress Party (Azad) and of the statement made by the Secretary of State for India in the House of Lords on March 13, 1947. These statements made it clear that, while the Interim Government would not have the same powers as a Dominion Government, His Majesty's Government would treat the Interim Government with the same consultation and consideration as a Dominion Government, and give it the greatest possible freedom in the day to day exercise of the administration of the country".[37]

As usual, Wavell stated the correct position in direct and straightforward language. He proposed to tell Nehru:

"3. If however it was clear that the Congress will not participate in the Interim Government except on the condition that absolute power is handed over to them and the Governor-General's special powers abrogated I propose to speak in perfectly clear terms. I would say that H.M.G. have the fullest intention of handing over power to the Indians. They wish a united

Policy accurately stated by Wavell

[35] *The Transfer of Power 1942-47*, Vol. VII, p. 738.
[36] ibid.
[37] Letter dt. 18.3.1947. See *The Transfer of Power 1942-47*, Vol. IX, pp. 972-74 at p. 973.

India. But they do not recognise Congress as representing all India and have no intention of handing over power to Congress alone. While they are prepared to consider any modifications in the working of the Interim Government which are desired by *both* main parties H.M.G. will not accept unilateral demands by Congress."[38]

The British Government agreed with Wavell that they could not go beyond the position taken in his letter to Azad dated 30th May, 1946. They approved Wavell's approach, but, predictably, they wished to omit the last sentence of para 3 "because though this must be substantially our position, the enunciation of it as a principle might result in giving Jinnah an absolute veto."[39] Although H.M.G. declined to state its position in the clear and direct language which Wavell wanted to use, H.M.G.'s position was the same as his till the end.

Was haste and hurry in fixing 15th Aug. justified?

1.66 Assuming that partition had become inevitable and was accepted by the Congress and the Muslim League, was there any justification for the haste and hurry with which the date of transfer of power was brought forward from June 1948, first to October 1947[40] and then to 15th August, 1947? The last and unpublished volume of the *Transfer of Power 1942-47* holds the key to the answer, if it is to be based on a fresh assessment of published documents. However, the question has been asked and answered by many writers since 600,000 lives were lost and 14 million people "were involved in a painful and pitiful migration". Could this catastrophe, measureless in its pain, have been avoided by fixing a later date which would have gained much needed time to prevent, or at any rate, to greatly mitigate that disaster? In justification of bringing the date forward to 15th August, it has been suggested that nobody could have foreseen the magnitude and intensity of the catastrophe which followed partition. However, Mosley's narrative, in *The Last Days of the British Raj, based on Government of India Records* makes this suggestion untenable. Sir Evan Jenkins, the Governor of Punjab, gave clear and persistent warnings to Mountbatten that the Sikhs meant to make trouble if the Governments of Pakistan and India were set up before the lines of demarcation were laid down by the award of the Boundary Commission and if that award was not to their liking. Jenkins annexed a confidential report of a conversation with Gianni Khartar Singh which ended with an appeal to Jenkins not to abandon Punjab to tears and bloodshed, for there would be tears and bloodshed if the boundary problem was not suitably solved.[41] This was on 10th July, Jenkins wrote again on 13th July repeating his warning of the dangers threatening the Punjab. He wrote that communal feeling in Punjab was unbelievably bad. He added "The Sikhs believe that they will be expropriated and massacred in West Punjab and smothered by the Hindus and Congress generally in East Punjab." He requested Mountbatten to obtain the Radcliffe Award and announce it *before* 15th August "to stop panic and the mad hurrying to and fro of populations from one Dominion to the other."[42] Mountbatten obtained a statement from the leaders of the Congress and the Muslim League appealing for a peaceful transfer of power,

Governor of Punjab's repeated warnings about "tears and bloodshed" in Punjab

---

[38] *The Transfer of Power 1942-47*, Vol. VIII, pp. 114-5.
[39] ibid. pp. 124-25.
[40] *The Transfer of Power 1942-47*, Vol. X, p. 873.
[41] *Mosley, op. cit.* pp. 233-36 (Based on Government of India Records).
[42] ibid. p. 236 (Government of India Records).

and expressing the determination of the Governments of the two Dominions to secure such peaceful transfer, as also their determination to accept the Boundary Commission Award whatever it may be. A Boundary Force of 50,000 soldiers was set up for the Punjab under General Rees. However, in the beginning of August, Master Tara Singh, the Sikh leader "came into the picture", and his appeals to the Sikhs inflamed their religious and communal feelings.[43] In a final attempt to make the Viceroy and the political leaders in Delhi nip the rebellion in the bud, Jenkins sent a C.I.D. officer with considerable documentary evidence of serious conspiracies, including a conspiracy to assassinate Jinnah. On 5th August, the evidence was produced before Mountbatten, Ismay, Nehru, Patel, Jinnah and Liaquat Ali Khan.[44] On the available evidence, there is no justification for the view that disorders in the Punjab of the gravest kind could not have been foreseen. As to Bengal, Lt.-Gen. Tucker was asked whether he would like to have a force corresponding to the Punjab Boundary Force, but he said "No", for he was confident that he could effectively meet the situation with the forces at his command. However, military force did not become necessary, for Gandhi was in Bengal with Suhrawardy (the former Prime Minister of united Bengal), and they moved about together to promote communal harmony and extinguish the flames of communal violence. It was Gandhi's finest hour. His courage, his healing touch and tireless efforts succeeded, and such violence as there was, was within manageable limits. In recognition of the achievement Mountbatten wrote to Gandhi, "In the Punjab we have 50,000 soldiers and large scale rioting on our hands. In Bengal our forces consist of one man, and we have no rioting. As a serving officer, as well as an administrator, may I be allowed to pay my tribute to the One-man Boundary Force, not forgetting his second-in-Command, Mr. Suhrawardy?"[45]

suggested justification that the hollocaust could not be foreseen contrary to evidence

Gandhi's finest hour

1.67 In the inflamed communal atmosphere, the orderly transfer of power in the Punjab and Bengal depended largely on the demarcation of the boundaries between West and East Bengal, and between West and East Punjab. Therefore, the terms of reference of the two Boundary Commissions assumed great importance, because, "The Boundary Commission (was) instructed to demarcate the boundaries of Bengal on the basis of ascertaining the contiguous majority areas of Muslims and non-Muslims. In doing so, *it will also take into account other factors*."[46] The terms of reference of the Boundary Commission for the Punjab were, *mutatis mutandis*, the same. For the Sikhs and Hindus in Western Punjab and the non-Muslim inhabitants of Lahore, the precise boundary line was important, because hoping that the Commission would take into account the ownership of land under "other factors" they had stayed on. "The award would be the signal to them to collect up whatever belongings they had and go East. In the mounting glare of communal tension, the sooner they

Need for early publication of Radcliffe award and orderly transfer of power

[43] ibid. p. 241.
[44] ibid. pp. 245-47. The fact that the Government of India Records relied upon by Mosley up to May 30, 1947 are supported by the documents in Vol. X of *The Transfer of Power 1942-47* inspires confidence in his narrative of events after May 1947, when based on the Government of India Records.
[45] ibid. p. 258.
[46] Gwyer & Appadorai, *Speeches and Documents of the Indian Constitution*, Vol. II, p. 685.

knew their fate the better."[47] The part which the Boundary Commission's award and its implementation were to play in the partition of the Punjab was thus crucial to an orderly transfer of power, or at least to a transfer of power with as little bloodshed and misery as foresight and preparation could devise. Mountbatten knew this, for when 1st Oct., 1947, was the date for the interim transfer of power,[48] he proposed telling Jinnah that "It is also possible that the Boundary Commission may not be ready with their recommendations."[49] Besides, Jenkins had informed Mountbatten of the near civil war atmosphere in the Punjab, particularly the determination of the Sikhs to create trouble, even before he returned to India on 2nd June. Therefore, a date for the interim transfer of power had to be fixed at least by reference to the Boundary Commission being able to make their award well within the date fixed for the interim transfer of power so that Mountbatten, Nehru and Jinnah could study the award and take steps to see that all those who wished to cross over to the other side of the boundary line had time to do so when one central authority remained to enforce peaceful and orderly transfer. Further, the movement of people from one side of the boundary to the other, could have been protected by fully armed convoys. But the Boundary Commissions were not appointed till 30th June; Radcliffe, their independent Chairman, did not reach Delhi till 8th July. Was there any justification for bringing the date forward from 1st October to 15th August?

Mountbatten's choice of 15th Aug.: 2nd Anniversary of Japan's surrender in 1945

1.68 Why did Mountbatten choose 15th August? A recent book reports Mountbatten as having told its authors, "I thought it had to be August or September, and I then went to 15th August. Why? Because it was the second anniversary of the Japanese surrender."[50] This statement cannot be put down, as some other statements in the book have been put down, to failing memory about events which took place over thirty years earlier. For, on 15th August, as Independence Day was being celebrated in New Delhi,

Mountbatten's broadcast to U.S.A. on 15th Aug. 47

". . . Lord Mountbatten issued (sic) a broadcast to the United States of America to celebrate the second anniversary of the Allied victory over Japan. (He) said: Two years ago today, I had just returned from the Potsdam Conference and was in the Prime Minister's room in 10 Downing Street, when the news of Japanese surrender came through. Here, as I speak to you tonight in Delhi, we are celebrating an event no less momentous for the future of the world — India's Independence Day. In the Atlantic Chaster we — The British and the Americans — dedicated ourselves to champion the self-determination of people and the independence of nations. Bitter experience has taught us that it is often easier to win a war than to achieve a war aim; so let us remember August 15th — V.J. Day — not only as the celebration of a victory, but also as the fulfilment of a pledge."[51]

That 15th August 1947 was the second anniversary of the surrender of Japan may have had a historic association for Mountbatten, as he had been the Supreme Commander for South-East Asia in the War against Japan. But that fact was extraneous and irrelevant to his task — to transfer power with the least amount of bloodshed and

---

[47] *Mosley, op. cit.* p. 262. [48] See *f.n.* 40, *ante*.

[49] *Transfer of Power 1942-47*, Vol. X, p. 814.

[50] Larry Collins & Dominique Lapierre, *Mountbatten and the Partition of India, March 22—August 15, 1947* (1982) p. 49. The book takes the form of questions put by its authors to Mountbatten and his replies. The questions and answers were tape-recorded.

[51] *Menon, op. cit.* pp. 422-3.

misery. Mountbatten realised that the date he had fixed had exposed him to criticism for haste and hurry. In para 17 of the conclusions appended to a Report which he made,[52] he summarises five reasons for selecting 15th August, *but those reasons make no reference to the 2nd anniversary of the Japanese surrender*. Four of the five reasons he gave for fixing 15th August would have applied equally if the transfer had been fixed for September. The fifth reason, namely, that the leaders unanimously accepted 15th August, a date which presumably he suggested, cannot lessen his responsibility. Nor could the leaders have known how he would deal with the Boundary Commission awards.

1.69 When were the Radcliffe Awards ready? There is some dispute as to the date,[53] but there is enough evidence to show that Mountbatten did not wish to disclose them till after the Independence Day celebrations on 15th August were over. Menon's account in *The Transfer of Power in India*[54] makes out the case that since the Radcliffe awards were sent to Mountbatten on 13th August, he was not able to disclose them till *after* 15th August. This was because Mountbatten flew to Karachi on 13th August and addressed the Pakistan Constituent Assembly on the 14th (for Pakistan celebrated its Independence Day on 14th August and India on 15th August). This case is incorrect as is clear from the following account of Menon's advice to Mountbatten:

Could the Radcliffe Awards have been announced before 15th Aug. 47? Menon's account not correct

"The Viceroy had received warning of this storm at a meeting with his staff on 12th August when he was informed that the award would broadly allot the Chittagong Hill Tracts to Pakistan. Mr. V. P. Menon said that this would have a disturbing effect on Congress leaders who have been committing themselves unequivocally on the matter. If the details of the award were given them before the 15th August, he thought they might well refuse to attend the meeting of the Constituent Assembly which the Viceroy was to address on that day, or the State banquet in the evening. Lord Mountbatten, who observed that he had never known V. P. Menon to mislead him, decided that somehow the details of the award must be kept back from the leaders until after 15th August, and must then be discussed with them before publication."[55]

It is clear that Mountbatten had the awards by the 12th or 13th of August; he could have discussed them in confidence with Nehru, Jinnah and General Rees, Commander of the Punjab Boundary Force, and taken urgent and appropriate steps *before* the two Dominions came into being, and one Central Government remained in power. We have seen that Sir Evan Jenkins had asked Mountbatten to get the award *before* 15th August. Campbell-Johnson, his press attache and admiring biographer, observes:

Campbell-Johnson on withholding Radcliffe Award till after-independence

"Various points of view about publication were put forward. On administrative grounds it was argued that the earliest possible announcement would be of help to Jenkins and would enable last-minute troop movements to be made into the affected areas in advance of the transfer of power. Alternatively, it was suggested that in so far as the award would in any case be bound to touch off trouble, the best date to release would be 14th August. Mountbatten said that if he could exercise some discretion in the matter he would prefer to postpone its appearance until after the Independence Day cele-

---

[52] Report on the Last Viceroyalty submitted to His Majesty's Government in September 1948. See *Hodson, op. cit.* pp. 548-52.

[53] *Menon, op. cit.* p. 409 gives 13th August as the date when the awards were sent to Mountbatten. *Mosley op. cit.* p. 261 states "Since 9th August he had been in possession of Sir Cyril Radcliffe's boundary award." *Brecher, op. cit.* p. 355 states "apparently the reports of the Commission were ready on 9th August".

[54] pp. 408-410, read with p. 418.

[55] *Hosdon, op. cit.* pp. 350-51.

brations, feeling that the problem of its timing was one of psychology, and that the controversy and grief it was bound to arouse on both sides should not be allowed to mar independence day itself."[56]

Again, Campbell-Johnson thus describes Mountbatten's mood in the last minutes of the British Raj:

"I have known (Mountbatten) in most moods; tonight there was an air of serenity, almost detachment. *The scale of his personal achievement was too great for elation; rather his sense of history and the fitness of things at this dramatic movement when the old and the new were reconciled in himself, called for the composure*".[57] (italics supplied)

Mountbatten's attempts to justify fixing 15 Aug. 47

That the grim tragedy following partition was stamped on Mountbatten's memory is clear from the attempts he made to justify his action. For example, "Upon his return to the U.K. in June 1948, Mountbatten claimed that the transition period had been relatively peaceful. In support of this contention he noted that only 3 per cent of the population were involved in the disturbance."[58] "But", commented Brecher, "percentages are often misleading; but translated into human terms, it meant 10 million or 1 in every 35 persons (sic) in the sub-continent. Whether or not the delay would have been more catastrophic is difficult to say, for the clock of history cannot be turned back. Suffice it to note that many Indians and Pakistanis, and Englishmen, are convinced that it could not have been worse if the transfer had been postponed."[59] It is difficult to resist the correctness of the judgment passed on Mountbatten by Mosley:

Mosley's strictures on Mountbatten justified

'A prior report would have given millions of Hindus and Sikhs and Muslims a chance to pack their bags and leave. A confidential report to Nehru, Jinnah and the Punjab Border Force Commander, General Rees, would have made it possible for dispositions and arrangements to be made to allow them to leave in some semblance of order. But Mountbatten took no one into his confidence . . . and suppressed them until after Independence Day. Independence Day was happy. But millions died or lost everything as a result."[60]

Orderly transfer of power mattered a great deal

Again, Mountbatten told Mosley: "What really did anything matter to the Indians except independence?[61] The answer should have been obvious to Mountbatten: it mattered a great deal: Nehru, Jinnah and other leaders had not fought for independence in order "to sup their fill of horror" and in order to live with its accompanying estrangement between India and Pakistan for years to come.

Fresh appraisal of Wavell and his Viceroyalty

1.70 It is outside the scope of this Introduction to give a fresh appraisal of the character and achievements of Lord Wavell and Lord Mountbatten as Viceroys of India. The publication of the *Viceroy's Journal* and of the documents in Vols. IV to IX of the *Transfer of Power 1942-47* has led to a fresh appraisal of Wavell and his work. The reader interested in such appraisal will find Sir Penderel Moon's *Epilogue* to the *Viceroy's Journal* rewarding reading, for it brings out in warm colours the Viceroy and the man whose *Journal* he has edited with skill, accuracy and a sense of balance.[62] The eighth Chap-

---

[56] Campbell-Johnson, *Mission with Mountbatten*, quoted in *Mosley, op. cit.* p. 262.

[57] *Campbell-Johnson, op. cit.*, quoted by *Mosley, op. cit.* p. 263.

[58] *Brecher, op. cit.* p. 374.

[59] ibid.

[60] *Mosley, op. cit.* p. 623.

[61] ibid.

[62] Sir Penderel Moon's account has high authority, for he was a member of the Indian Civil Service from 1929 to 1944 and he has been the assistant editor of the documents published in the *Transfer of Power 1942-47* from the time that Vol. IV was ready for the press.

ter of Ronald Lewin's biography of Wavell, *The Chief,* contains an appreciative, but not uncritical, account of Wavell and his Viceroyalty. However, it emphasizes an aspect of Wavell which is not generally known. When Wavell was appointed Viceroy-designate, says Lewin, "What happened, and happened irrevocably, was that (Wavell) . . . was reaffirming the classical humanism of his earlier youth, the sense of history, of mutual justice and social order, which, in spite of years of constricting service and war time command, had never been entirely overlaid."[63] In the ninth Chapter of his book, entitled "Post script: *Other Men's Flowers*", Lewin gives an account of a highly successful and popular Anthology of English poetry compiled by Wavell as relevant to the source of Wavell's inspiration and his sense of values.[64] That source and those values are reflected in the concluding words of Wavell's speech at a farewell dinner before he came to India as Viceroy:

Wavell's humanism, and "the real mainsprings of life"

"Finally, I think that we must have in our minds always the hope of the vision that may await us at the top, the prospect of an India at peace within herself, a partner in our great Commonwealth of Nations, mother of a prosperous people, a shield for peace in the East, a busy market for trade, and yet with sufficient leisure to develop art and poetry and thought, the real mainsprings of life to which India has already contributed much to the world, a far-distant vision and I believe and hope not unattainable, and one to which I feel we must look forward."[65]

As "the real mainsprings of life" were never far from Wavell, it is not surprising that Azad found Wavell to be "a man of innate refinement and consideration for others"; Nehru's sister found him "understanding and humane",[66] and Nehru himself told Wavell that "failures and successes were only relative and that some failures were greater than successes."[67]

1.71 A fresh appraisal of Mountbatten's character and work as Viceroy of India must await the publication of the last volume of the *Transfer of Power 1942-47*. It may however be said that television films, and tape-recorded interviews published in a book[68] are not a sure passport to future fame. For "it is an irony of human life that the verdict of History occasionally overtakes us sooner than we anticipated".

Fresh appraisal of Mountbatten's Viceroyalty must be deferred

1.72 The narrative in this Introduction has left out several incidents and episodes which engaged public attention at the time but did not determine the final result.[69] However, there is one important omission: the position of the Native States, as they were then called. Once the "paramountcy" exercised by the British Crown over Native States lapsed, and the treaties between the British Crown and the rulers of Native States stood terminated when India and Pakistan became two independent Dominions, the ultimate disappearance of

Position of "Native States" not dealt with

---

63 *Lewin, op. cit.* pp. 224-5.

64 ". . . his choice of poems for *Other Men's Flowers* illuminates his own mind: a mind which, on his own confession, drew on them for sustenance in battle, in perplexity, in times of stressful decision. Cromwell and Montgomery may have turned to God for inspiration but amid the tensions of war it is evident Wavell sought comfort among the Muses." ibid. p. 247.

65 *Transfer of Power 1942-47*, Vol. IV, p. 378. The speech was made on 6th October, at a farewell dinner, in reply to a speech made by Winston Churchill.

66 *Moon, op. cit.* p. 463.

67 *Viceroy's Journal*, entry under date March 10, pp. 426-7.

68 See *f.n.* 50 to para 1.68.

69 *e.g.* The I.N.A. Trial and the Naval Mutiny in Bombay.

the rulers of Native States was a question of time. However, thanks to the skill and statesmanship of Vallabhbhai Patel, aided by Mountbatten and Menon, the Indian States were integrated with India, their rulers preserving their personal dignity and receiving tax free "privy purses". The subject has thus lost its importance. Besides, Menon has narrated "The Story of the Integration of Indian States" in a separate volume, so that the reader interested in the subject can turn with profit to his authoritative book.

Grave disorders in Delhi following partition: Gandhi's fast

1.73 The grave disorders which followed partition ultimately reached Delhi, and they were faced by Mountbatten, Nehru and his colleagues with courage, resource and resolution. In Delhi, violence against Muslims and the conditions in which Muslim refugees lived in the *Purana Quila,* and at other places, led Gandhi to undertake a fast which was to be continued till the violence against Muslims ceased, harmony between Hindus and Muslims was restored and the damage done to Muslim shrines and mosques was repaired. He broke his fast because he was satisfied with the pledge given by the people of Delhi that they would carry out the conditions he had laid down for withdrawing the fast. This brave gesture to restore sanity, and serve the cause of Hindu-Muslim unity, was later to cost him his life at the hands of a Hindu fanatic who shot Gandhi at point-blank range as he was proceeding to his prayer meeting in Birla House on 30th January 1948. Gandhi's martyrdom provoked a strong reaction against parties believed to be responsible for his murder; Nehru and Patel joined hands and successfully put down communal violence and restored order. Jawaharlal Nehru remained as Prime Minister of India till his death on 27th May, 1964. If Parliamentary institutions survived in India, when they guttered and flickered out in almost all the countries of the East, it was due in no small measure to Jawaharlal Nehru. A man of action as well as thought, he encouraged science and scientific research and their application to life and industry for improving the well-being of our people. Azad used the right words when he said that since the attainment of Independence, Nehru became the symbol of our national unity and progress.

Gandhi's martyrdom

Nehru's contribution to survival of democracy in India

SECTION V

The Constituent Assembly: The Framing of India's Constitution

Work of Constituent Assembly: Shiva Rao's *Framing of India's Constitution*

1.74 After partition, the character of the Constituent Assembly changed. It functioned as a sovereign body unfettered by any restrictions on its powers, for it had to frame a Constitution for India alone. The framing of our Constitution took the Constituent Assembly nearly three years, and its labours are reflected in the twelve volumes of *Constituent Assembly Debates.* However, it is not necessary to describe the work of the Constituent Assembly in any detail, for that has been admirably done by Shiva Rao (himself a member of the Constituent Assembly) in his 5 volumes of *The Framing of India's Constitution.* The last volume, entitled "A Study", gives a clear and synoptic view of the subject by referring to the documents in the first four volumes together with the relevant parts from the Constituent Assembly Debates. However, a few observations would not be out of place, because the circumstances under which our Constitution came to be framed are apt to be forgotten by the passage of time.

Contemporary historical background — Nazi atrocities, the Nuremberg trials; the Universal Declaration of Human Rights

1.75 The first effective step towards the transfer of power — the Simla Conference — was taken some weeks after the Second World War ended with the surrender of Germany on 8th May 1945. This surrender brought to light the horrors and infamies of German concentration camps at Auschwitz, Belsen and Buchenwald where 6 million Jews were exterminated in gas chambers. The plight of the survivors in the camps and its effect upon the world was thus described by a broadcaster: "As the shattered wrecks of once decent men and women tottered into the arms of wives and mothers, humanity bowed its head in shame." These revelations led to fresh emphasis being laid on Human Rights. The Nuremberg Trials (1945-46) of Nazi war criminals was the first step in this direction. A learned writer[70] has said:

> "It is not without significance that in the indictment at Nuremberg were included 'war crimes' and 'crimes against humanity': namely, murder, extermination, enslavement, deportation and other inhumane acts committed against any civilian population, before or during the war . . . *'whether or not in violation of the domestic law of the country where perpetrated'*: Article 6(*c*) of Charter, restricted by the court, to crimes against humanity committed during the war".[71]

The Universal Declaration of Human Rights promulgated by the United Nations to which India was a party, proclaimed basic human rights, although it did not provide any machinery for their enforcement.[72] The emphasis on human rights was not without its impact on our Constitution. The cruelties and infamies of the Nazi regime and the extermination of millions of people in gas chambers took place in times of war. In our own country gross acts of cruelty and barbarism, gravely threatening law and order, were perpetrated by members of different communities following on the partition of India. These events in war and in peace left their mark on our Constitution.

Enactment of fundamental rights and the unity of India

1.76 The history of the struggle for political freedom in India had made a declaration of fundamental rights inevitable. In fact, the Indian delegation at the Round Table Conference had pressed for the enactment of fundamental rights in the Constitution Act which, it was expected the British Parliament would pass. But at that time the British viewed the declaration of fundamental rights with scepticism, an attitude which was to change later. Fundamental rights as enacted in our Constitution not only recognize the dignity of the individual to which the Preamble refers, but also recognize their necessity for the full development of the individual and also for preserving the unity of India. Several fundamental rights although conferred on individuals and groups also secure the unity of India by removing well known sources of discord. Before partition, the Muslim community was, and even after partition still is, the

---

[70] Wortley, *Jurisprudence* (1967). [71] ibid. p. 256.

[72] Deriving its inspiration from the Universal Declaration of Human Rights, the European Convention of Human Rights was signed at Rome in 1950. The scope of the Convention was extended by subsequent protocols. A novel feature of the Convention as a treaty between States was the right which it gave to individuals to complain of breaches of the Convention by the States who were parties to it. For a full account of the Convention and the organs set up under it see Wade & Phillips, *Constitutional and Administrative Law*, pp. 534-39, (9th ed. by A. W. Bradley).

largest minority in India. The test of a Constitution, it has been said, is the protection which it gives to minorities. Article 25 confers on any person the right to practise, profess and propagate religion, and Art. 26 confers on religious denominations the right to manage their own affairs in matters of religion. Similarly, Articles 29 and 30, protect the cultural, educational and linguistic rights of minorities. These Articles thus remove the most potent sources of discord in a multiracial society. The unity of India, in the sense that India, notwithstanding its division into several States is one country, and all its inhabitants are the inhabitants of that one country, is provided for by Art. 19(1)(*d*), (*e*), (*f*) and (*g*).[73] This unity is also emphasized by Art. 14 which provides for equality before the law and the equal protection of the laws; by Art. 15 which prohibits discrimination against citizens on the grounds of religion, race, caste, sex or place of birth, and by Art. 16 which provides for equality of opportunity to all citizens in matters of public employment. By abolishing "untouchability" (Art. 17) and throwing open Hindu religious institutions of a public character to "untouchables" (Art. 25) the Constitution has tried to remove not only the greatest blot on Indian society but also a source of bitter discord. Article 12 by defining "the State" very widely, to include many authorities other than the State strictly so-called, subjects those authorities to the discipline of fundamental rights. The provision for a common citizenship, for a common electoral roll and for the freedom of inter-State trade and commerce were all designed to promote the unity of India.

Enforcement of fundamental rights: Arts. 32 and 226

1.77 But mere declaration of rights is worth little without the will or the means to enforce them. The framers of our Constitution had the will, and therefore they adopted the means, for such enforcement. To that end, Art. 13 *expressly* declared any law violating fundamental rights to be void to the extent of the violation or the contravention. Secondly, the Supreme Court was armed under Art. 32 with the power to issue the historic writs (of proved efficacy) of *habeas corpus, mandamus*, prohibition, *certiorari* and *qua warranto* for the enforcement of fundamental rights, and Art. 32 was itself made a fundamental right. Further, the High Courts were also armed with the power to issue the same writs, not only for the enforcement of fundamental rights, but also for any other purpose.

Preventive detention an unfortunate legacy

1.78 The conditions under which the Constitution was framed left one unfortunate legacy behind. No civilized country has provided for preventive detention as an ordinary legislative power in times of peace. The G.I. Act, 35, no doubt, did so, and the leaders of the freedom movement characterised the power as arbitrary and despotic. The retention of this power in our Constitution was due to the disturbed condition of the Indian sub-continent after partition. The assurances given by eminent leaders like Jawaharlal Nehru and Vallabhbhai Patel, (who had themselves been preventively detained) that these powers would not be abused were accepted, without fully realizing that powers which may be safe in the hands of Nehru and Patel, might be gravely abused in other hands, as the Emergency proclaimed in 1975 was to show. If the internal situation demanded preventive detention for five or ten years, the power ought to have been so limited. However, although the assurances of our leaders

---

[73] Art. 19(1)(*f*) was repealed by the Const. (44th Amend.) Act, 1979.

were accepted, there was great disquiet among the members of the Constituent Assembly by the deletion of the "due process" clause in what became Art. 21. Consequently, Art. 22 was enacted to provide, first, for limited due process in Art. 22(1) and (2) and, secondly, to provide safeguards as to preventive detention.

1.79 In framing our Constitution, its leading figures wisely proceeded on the footing of a broad consensus, although if the Congress party was determined to enact a particular provision, its majority would have enabled it to do so. But this consensus was severely strained when it came to enacting the language provisions of our Constitution, provisions rightly described by Granville Austin as a "half-hearted compromise".[74] Hindi was designated as the "Official Language" of India and was given a special status. The grave consequences following from the language provisions of our Constitution will be considered in the Chapter on Official Language. The division of the States on linguistic lines has introduced divisive, or at any rate, parochial, tendencies which run counter to the whole spirit, and to the numerous provisions, of our Constitution, designed to promote unity. It is enough to say that having opposed the two-nation theory based on race, language and religion, we are in danger of accepting, in substance, a ten or twelve nation theory, based only on language. In the Bombay Presidency, later the State of Bombay, Maharashtrians (who spoke Marathi) and Gujaratis (who spoke Gujarati) had lived together for over a hundred years. However, in justifying the division of the State of Bombay into Maharashtra and Gujarat, the Chief Minister of the State of Bombay said that Maharashtrians and Gujaratis could live together as neighbours but not as partners!

Official Language: a "half-hearted compromise"

Language acting as a divisive or parochial tendency

1.80 On August 29, 1947, the Constituent Assembly of India appointed a drafting committee which presented a draft constitution in February 1948. After considerable discussion, the draft as amended and altered was adopted by the Constituent Assembly on November 26, 1949. Certain Articles of the Constitution came into force at once; the remaining Articles and the Preamble came into force on January 26, 1950.[75] When the drafting committee began its work the problem of federation with the Native States had ceased to exist, as the Native States which acceded to India merged in India, their former rulers retaining only their titular dignity and certain personal privileges.

The Constituent Assembly: the Draft Constitution; the Const. of India

Section VI

The Constitution of India : Its Legal Framework

1.81 What were the objects which the framers of the Constitution set out to achieve in their Draft Constitution? What were the models to which they turned? What were the pitfalls they tried to avoid? Dr. Ambedkar, the Chairman of the drafting committee, answered some of these questions when he moved that the Constituent Assembly should take the Draft Constitution into consideration.[76] The form

The objects which the Constitution sought to achieve

[74] Granville Austin, *The Indian Constitution — Cornerstone of a Nation*, Chapter XII, p. 265.
[75] See Art. 394.
[76] *Constituent Assembly Debates*, Vol. VII, p. 31 *et seq.*

in which the speech was cast, and the popular assembly to which it was addressed, made it difficult for him to give to his analysis that precision which he would have given were he writing on the Draft Constitution. Therefore, it is not proposed to give a summary of his views, but to deal with the topics contained in or raised by his speech, and to refer to his views where necessary.

Federalism: the U.S. Const. and the Bill of Rights

1.82 Once a federal constitution was decided upon there was no lack of models to draw upon. These models fell broadly into two categories: (i) the U.S. Constitution and (ii) the Constitution Acts enacted by the British Parliament establishing federal constitutions for Canada,[77] Australia[78] and India,[79] all of which had drawn on the American experience. In speaking of the U.S. Constitution it is necessary to bear in mind the "Bill of Rights" enacted by the first ten Amendments to the Constitution so soon after its ratification that it can almost be regarded as enacted by the Constitution.[80] The U.S. Constitution originated in a revolutionary seizure of power and exhibited certain features which found no place in the Constitution Acts of Canada, Australia and India.

Our Const. adopts the British model of an executive responsible to the legislature

1.83 The U.S. Constitution adopted the doctrine of separation of powers in the mistaken view that English precedent was being followed.[81] As a consequence the executive authority of the United States was vested in the President who was independent of the legislature and not responsible to it. The Constitution of Canada and Australia, and to a limited extent the G.I. Act, 35,[82] provided for an executive responsible to the legislature. The framers of the Indian Constitution borrowed from the United States the name, and from Great Britain the position and functions, of the Chief Executive of the Union of India. He was called the President, acting, like the Sovereign of Great Britain, on the advice of his Ministers, who were responsible to the House of the People and who wielded real executive authority. The office of Vice-President was also taken from the United States, and the Vice-President of India, like the Vice-President of the United States, was not to be a member of either House of Parliament, and was to be *ex-officio* Chairman of the Second Chamber.

but the example of the American Bill of Rights followed: fundamental rights enacted in the Constitution

1.84 But if the framers of the Indian Constitution adopted the system of parliamentary executive in preference to the Presidential system adopted in the United States, there were other features of the U.S. Constitution which they adopted which are not to be found in the Constitutions of Canada or Australia. This was the result of the course which political struggle had taken in India. Although the Indian Constitution derives its legal authority from the Indian Independence Act, 1947, which conferred on the Constituent Assembly the power to frame a Constitution, it cannot be denied that the Indian Independence Act, 1947, was the result of a protracted struggle for

---

77 The British North America Act, 1867. ("B.N.A. Act, 1867.")

78 The Commonwealth of Australia Constitution Act, 1900.

79 The Government of India Act, 1935 ("G.I Act, 35".)

80 "Several states ratified the Constitution only after Washington put forward the suggestion that the desired guarantees could be added by amendment": *Corwin*, p. 840.

81 *Wynes*, p. 2.

82 The principle was applied in a qualified form and would have been fully applied had the federation come into existence and worked for some time.

political freedom. During that struggle the Indian National Congress had declared that a Constitution for free India should provide for fundamental rights and the attainment of economic and social objectives[83] and later the idea of framing a Constitution through a Constituent Assembly was adopted.[84] It is, therefore, not surprising that though the Constituent Assembly had the legal power to *enact*, and did enact, the Constitution of India, the preamble to the Constitution, following the American example, proclaimed : "We, the people of India[85] . . . in our Constituent Assembly, this Twenty-sixth day of November, 1949, do hereby adopt, enact and give to ourselves this Constitution," and declared that the objectives of the Constitution were justice, liberty, equality and fraternity. The framers of the Constitution were not content to embody its social and economic objectives merely in the Preamble. Following the example of the Irish Free State they embodied some of these objectives in Part IV of the Constitution entitled "Directive Principles of State Policy" which were declared to be fundamental in the governance of the country but were not to be enforceable by any Court.

The Preamble: "We the people . . ."

1.85 The incorporation of a Bill of Rights[86] was a feature of the U.S. Constitution which the British Parliament consistently eschewed in the Constitution Acts it enacted for Canada, Australia and India. As was to be expected this feature of the U.S. Constitution was adopted by the framers of our Constitution; but whereas the American Bill of Rights declares rights in terms apparently absolute, leaving it to the courts to limit the rights thus declared, our Constitution declares the rights and prescribes the limitations in the Constitution itself. By enacting Art. 32 the Constitution created a new fundamental right, namely, the right to move the Supreme Court by appropriate proceedings for the enforcement of the rights conferred by Part III which is entitled "Fundamental Rights".[87]

The difference in the formulation of the Bill of Rights and our fundamental rights

1.86 To remove a common misconception it ought to be stated that the machinery of Government set up by our Constitution follows in essentials the British, and not the American, model. The doctrine of the separation of powers and the doctrine that legislatures are the delegates of the people which are basic doctrines of the U.S. Constitution do not form part of the Constitution of Great Britain or the Constitution of India. Our Constitution has rejected the Presidential form of Government, that is, of an executive independent of, and not responsible to, the legislature, and adopted the British model of government by a Cabinet, that is, of an executive responsible to, and removable by, the legislature.[88] This has now been established by the

The machinery of Government in our Constitution is based on the British and not on the American model

---

[83] *Gwyer and Appadorai, op. cit.* Vol. 1, p. 243 *et seq.*

[84] See ibid. Vol. II, pp. 475-8.

[85] For a discussion of "We the People" see paras 4.5 and 4.6 of the text.

[86] The first ten Amendments and the Fourteenth Amendment to the Constitution.

[87] Fundamental rights, and the inclusion of preventive detention in the part which deals with fundamental rights, would require separate treatment by itself.

[88] See Arts. 74 and 75 for the Union Executive and Arts. 163 and 164 for the State Executive. In Great Britain the Sovereign names the Prime Minister and he in his turn submits to the Sovereign the names of his ministry for appointment. The same procedure is followed in our Constitution, the President naming the Prime Minister and the Governor naming the Chief Minister and then appointing Ministers on the advice of the Prime Minister or the Chief Minister, as the case may be.

decision of the Supreme Court in *Shamsher Singh* v. *Punjab*[89] which held that our Constitution embodies generally the parliamentary or cabinet system of Government on the British model and that the position of the President and the Governors correspond to that of the sovereign in the U.K. who is the formal head of government and must act on the advice of the Council of Ministers. As regards the legislatures, our Constitution has conferred on the House of the People, and on the Legislative Assemblies of each State, the predominant position in legislation which the British House of Commons secured for itself by the Parliament Act, 1911.[90] The privileges of the Houses of Parliament and of the Houses of the State Legislature are in terms the privileges of the British House of Commons at the commencement of the Constitution.[91] The legislative procedure in respect of finance, the provision for a consolidated fund, the scrutiny and supervision of Union and State public accounts by an independent Comptroller and Auditor-General, all follow the British model.[92] The Civil Services of the Union and the States are based on the British model, and the "spoils system",[93] which prevails in the United States and from which only the Federal Government has gradually, but not completely, freed itself,[94] has no place in India. The position of the Judges of the Supreme Court and the High Courts, and the appointment of the subordinate judiciary, follows the English and not the American model. As in England, the independence of Judges of the Supreme Court and the High Courts is secured by prescribing that they shall hold office till a stated age and that they can be removed from office only by a process analogous to impeachment. In this respect, the position of the Judges of the Superior Courts in England and the Judges of the Supreme Court and of other Courts which may be established under Art. 3, s. 1, of the U.S. Constitution, is the same. However, in England and in India, Judges are not appointed by election as they are in a number of States in the U.S. As will appear more fully from the Chapter on the "Courts and the Constitution,"[95] a judge's function in India corresponds more closely to that in England.

British Parliamentary procedure adopted

The Civil Services based on the British model

as also the appointment of judges

It is a misconception that the enactment of fundamental rights, and of Arts. 32 and 226 makes our Constitution resemble the U.S. Constitution

1.87 A vague general impression prevails in our country that the enactment of fundamental rights in the Constitution and the conferment of writ jurisdiction by Arts. 32 and 226 somehow distinguishes the Indian Constitution from the British, Canadian and Australian Constitutions, and makes it resemble the U.S. Constitution. This impression is incorrect. No doubt Great Britain has a unitary unwritten Constitution in which Parliament is supreme and sovereign so that no law passed by Parliament can be declared *ultra*

---

[89] (1975) 1 S.C.R. 814, ('74) A.SC. 2192. It may be added that there is a very limited area in which the President and the Governors can act without, or contrary to, the advice of the Council of Ministers.

[90] See Arts. 108-110 for Parliament and Arts. 196-99 for State Legislatures. The provisions regarding money bills and the conclusiveness of the Speaker's Certificate that a bill is a money bill are based on those contained in the Parliament Act, 1911.

[91] See Arts. 105 and 194.

[92] See Arts. 112-117 (Procedure in financial matters in the Union) and Arts. 202-207 (Procedure in financial matters in the States), see Arts. 148-151 for the Comptroller and Auditor-General of India.

[93] The "practice of giving public offices to adherents of successful party": *C.O.D.*

[94] Finer, *Modern Government* (1949) at pp. 828 *et seq.*

[95] See paras 3.2 and 3.3.

vires by a court of law. In this respect, the written federal Constitutions of the United States, Canada, Australia and India all differ from the British Constitution. But the doctrine of ultra vires, though not applicable to laws enacted by the British Parliament, was applied by English Courts to subordinate bodies constituted by Statute or Charter, and by the Privy Council in considering the validity of laws passed by the Colonies.[96] The enactment of a Bill of Rights in the Constitution itself no doubt indicates that the Constitution looks upon those rights as important and as rights which cannot be abrogated by ordinary process of legislation. But, in the first place, the very terminology of a Bill of Rights bespeaks its English origin, for the English Bill of Rights, 1689, declares the basic freedoms which Englishmen claimed for themselves. The Rights so declared have been enjoyed for centuries, and only a cataclysm can sweep them away. Secondly, apart from the procedural advantage conferred by Art. 32 for the enforcement of fundamental rights, a fundamental right is not different from any other right conferred by the Constitution, nor is it necessarily more important than another right which is not so described. For example, the right to carry on any business, profession, trade or calling is a fundamental right conferred by Art. 19(1) (*g*), but it is quite impossible to say that it is more important than the right conferred by Art. 301 to carry on trade freely throughout the whole of India. Both rights are constitutional rights and their violation has precisely the same consequences, namely, that any law, or executive act, violating those rights is void. Any person whose rights are violated by such a law can obtain assistance of the Court in enforcing his rights. In *Commonwealth of Australia* v. *Bank of New South Wales*,[97] Lord Porter, in discussing the effect of s. 92 of the Commonwealth of Australia Act (which provides that trade, commerce and intercourse shall be absolutely free) said:

Except for a procedural advantage, a fundamental right is not different from other constitutional rights

Some examples

"First may be mentioned an argument strenuously maintained on this appeal that s. 92 of the Constitution does not guarantee the freedom of individuals. Yet James[98] was an individual and James vindicated his freedom in hard won fights. Clearly there is here a misconception. It is true, as has been said more than once in the High Court, that s. 92 does not create any new juristic rights, but it does give the citizen of State or Commonwealth, as the case may be, the right to ignore, and, if necessary, to call on the judicial power to help him to resist, legislative or executive action which offends against the section. And this is just what James successfully did."[99]

Thirdly, provisions corresponding to those contained in a Bill of Rights are to be found in Constitutions which do not enact such a Bill and therefore differ from such a Bill only as a matter of form.

[96] In fact, a learned American writer has said that it was familiarity with this doctrine which led the U.S. Supreme Court finally to take to itself the power of declaring a law void if it conflicted with the provisions of the U.S. Constitution. He said: "One reason for the fact that the Supreme Court (of the United States) finally took this power to itself was the colonial practice. The colonial courts and on appeal the Privy Council of England had the power to declare legislative acts void if in conflict with colonial charters. The colonists consequently acquired the habit of seeing colonial laws occasionally declared void by the courts.": Willis, *Constitutional Law*, p. 75.

[97] (1950) A.C. 235.

[98] The plaintiff in *James* v. *Commonwealth of Australia* (1936) A.C. 578 and *James* v. *Cowan* (1932) A.C. 542.

[99] (1950) A.C. at p. 305.

Thus, the 1st Amendment to the U.S. Constitution provides that: "Congress shall make no law respecting the establishment of religion or prohibiting the free exercise thereof." Articles 25 to 28 confer fundamental rights which secure the freedom of religion. The Commonwealth of Australia Act does not enact a Bill of Rights, but s. 116 of that Act secures the right to religious freedom quite as effectively by providing that "The Commonwealth shall make no law for establishing any religion or for imposing any religious observance or from prohibiting the free exercise of any religion, and no religious test shall be required as a qualification for any office of public trust for the Commonwealth." Again, the 5th Amendment to the U.S. Constitution provides that ". . . Private property shall not be taken for public use without just compensation." Article 31 of our Constitution (before its repeal) declares a similar fundamental right.[1] S. 51 of the Australian Constitution secures the same right by enacting that Parliament shall have the power to make laws for the ". . . Acquisition of property on just terms from any State or person in respect of which the Parliament has the power to make laws." It is unnecessary to multiply examples because it is clear that the nature of a right is not altered by the label affixed to it.

Some fundamental rights in our Constitution, are contained in the Australian Constitution as constitutional rights

Arts. 32 and 226 in terms incorporate the high prerogative writs of English law

1.88 The provisions of Arts. 32 and 226 have given rise to a strange impression that our Constitution is unique because it embodies judicial review in the Constitution itself. We have seen that judicial review, meaning thereby, the power of a Court to pronounce a law invalid if it violates a Constitutional provision is a concomitant of all written Federal Constitutions which follow the English doctrine of *ultra vires*. Therefore Arts. 32 and 226 introduce no new principle in India; they confer on the Supreme Court and the High Courts, the power to issue the well-known English writs of *habeas corpus*, *mandamus*, *certiorari*, prohibition and *quo warranto*.[2] There is nothing peculiar to India in the power to issue these writs, because for centuries the Court of Queen's Bench in England has exercised that jurisdiction in order to control all subordinate jurisdictions. The English Colonists carried this jurisdiction with them to the United States, and power to issue these writs has been conferred on various courts in the United States. It is submitted, therefore, that Arts. 32 and 226 introduce no new jurisdiction in India and our Constitution does not differ in this respect except as a matter of form from any other Constitution which has adopted the Common Law of England.

They do not confer a new and unknown jurisdiction

Differences between the U.S. and the Indian Constitution

1.89 Our Constitution differs from the U.S. Constitution in another important respect, namely, that it provides a Constitution both for the Federation and for the States, whereas the U.S. Constitution provides a Constitution only for the Federation though it contains a few restraints on the powers of the States all of which have independent Constitutions of their own. The 10th Amendment to the U.S. Constitution gives legal content to the statement in the preamble to the U.S. Constitution "We the people . . . do ordain and establish this Constitution . . ." and also gives support to the doctrine underlying the U.S. Constitution that the legislatures

---

[1] Before the Amendment of Art. 31 it was held that "compensation" and "just compensation" meant the same thing. However, after the Amendment of Art. 31 the adequacy of compensation is not justiciable.

[2] It may be mentioned that under their charters the High Courts of Calcutta, Madras and Bombay had the power to issue these writs.

derive their power by delegation from the people, for the 10th Amendment provides that "The powers not delegated to the United States by the Constitution nor prohibited by it to the States, are reserved to the States respectively, or to the people." There is no such provision in our Constitution and ever since *R.* v. *Burah*[3] it is settled law that the legislatures established by the British Parliament were in no sense delegates of that Parliament but, within the limits of the power conferred upon them, were as supreme and sovereign as the British Parliament itself. *R.* v. *Burah* has been repeatedly approved by the Supreme Court and it is the settled law of our Constitution that the legislatures are not the delegates of the people.[4] The doctrine of immunities of instrumentality evolved by the U.S. Supreme Court, the doctrine of police powers, the doctrine of the political question have no place in our Constitution. For our Constitution is a detailed and an elaborate document containing provisions as regards the executive and the judiciary, as also for the distribution of legislative powers in three detailed lists on principles described later in this Introduction. Judicial legislation, unlike that in the United States, has a limited scope in our Constitution as regards the distribution of legislative powers, and this is true also of the fundamental and other rights conferred by the Constitution, because whereas the U.S. Constitution is a brief document which declares rights in wide general terms, leaving it to the Courts to evolve exceptions and qualifications to those rights, our Constitution, in confering rights expressly mentions the restrictions and limitations to which they are subject. It is necessary to say this in the Introduction, because observations in the judgments of the Supreme Court, and experience of arguments in Courts, show that an impression prevails that our Constitution is based on the American and not the British model; and that by reason of the enactment of fundamental rights and by reason of Arts. 32 and 226, somehow different principles of construction apply to our Constitution than are applicable to the Australian or the Canadian Constitution. For reasons already stated, it is submitted that these impressions are wholly unfounded.

Legislatures in India not the delegates of the people

1.90 A federal constitution involves a distribution of legislative powers between the Union and the States, each being supreme and sovereign in its own sphere. This distribution is made on the principle of granting powers to the Union in matters of national concern, or in matters where uniformity of laws throughout the Union is considered desirable, and of granting powers to the States in matters which concern the States or can be described as principally of local interest. The distribution generally takes one of two forms; enumerated powers are given to the Union, residuary powers being retained by the States, as in the United States and Australia, or enumerated powers are given to the States, residuary powers being given to the Union as in Canada.

Distribution of legislative power in a federation

1.91 A federal constitution, with its distribution of powers, requires a written constitution, and it is a consequence of a written constitution, according to the concept of *ultra vires* familiar to English law, that the established courts must decide whether a law violates con-

Federal constitutions are written constitutions, and generally involve the doctrine of *ultra vires*

[3] (1878) 3 App. Cas. 889, 5 I.A. 178.

[4] For delegated legislation, see the discussion on that topic in Vol. II; see also para 7.3.

stitutional limitations and declare it void to the extent that it does.[5] It follows from this that federalism gives rise to legalism. It follows also that a federal government cannot do several things which a unitary government can do; that the powers of a federal government lack flexibility for they are limited by the terms conferring the powers and can be enlarged only by an amendment of the Constitution, or by judicial interpretation. The framers of our Constitution were aware that legalism and rigidity are the inevitable consequences of federalism, and they were also aware that in part, at least, the success of a federal constitution depends upon the extent to which these evils are minimised. Dr. Ambedkar's speech lists various ways adopted by the drafting committee to minimise the rigidity and legalism of a federal constitution[6] and the questions there raised can now be considered.

The rigidity of federalism

The reasons for this rigidity and ways of mitigating it

1.92 If rigidity is a defect inherent in federalism, it is because normally federal governments have come into existence either by a surrender by States with independent constitutions of their own, of enumerated powers to the Union, as in the United States and Australia, or by the abrogation of the existing powers of the States with a fresh grant of enumerated powers to them as in Canada. The willingness of the States to part with only some of their power, and their desire that the powers given to them under the agreed Constitution should not be changed without their consent, dictate the form which any federal constitution will take, and rigidity may be the unavoidable price of federal union. For example, it is well known that leading men in Canada like John A. Macdonald, desired legislative union between the provinces, but Macdonald himself declared that only a federal union was possible and Lower Canada would never consent to a legislative union.[7] Nevertheless the working of various federal systems shows that even within the limits imposed by a federal union the method adopted for the distribution of powers, and certain other methods, may mitigate the rigidity and legalism of a federal constitution.

Features of our Constitution listed by Dr. Ambedkar as mitigating the

1.93 Dr. Ambedkar's speech[8] lists several features of the Draft Constitution which mitigated the rigidity and legalism of federalism. We will list them first and discuss them briefly, later. For the convenience of the reader, references in the speech to the Articles of the draft

[5] This is not the necessary consequence of a written constitution, federal or unitary. In the federal constitution of Switzerland "the last word does not appear to rest with the Federal Tribunal: It may declare cantonal laws invalid, but it must accept the laws of the general legislature as valid": Wheare's *Federal Government*, 3rd ed., p. 61. As regards the unitary constitution of France "Anyone in fact who bears in mind the respect paid in France from the time of the Revolution onwards to the legislation of *de facto* governments and the traditions of the French judicature, will assume with confidence that an enactment passed through the Chambers, promulgated by the President, and published in the *Bulletin des Lois*, will be held valid by every tribunal through the Republic": Dicey's *Law of the Constitution*, 10th ed., pp. 134-5. However, the doctrine of *ultra vires* is so ingrained in the Indian law that when Art. 13 of the Constitution of India expressly invalidates existing and future laws to the extent that they are repugnant to fundamental rights, Kania C.J. expressed the opinion that the Article was unnecessary and was inserted *ex majore cautela*, because even without such declaration a law contravening the Constitution would be void: See *Gopalan's Case* (1950) S.C.R. 88 at p. 100.

[6] *C.A.D.*, Vol. VII, p. 34 *et seq.*

[7] Laskin's *Canadian Constitutional Law*, 2nd ed., p. 16.

[8] *C.A.D.*, Vol. VII, p. 34 *et seq.*

constitution have been replaced by references to the Articles as enacted in the Constitution.[9]

rigidity of a federal Constitution

(1) The distribution of legislative power between the Union and the States which gives to the Union exclusive power to legislate in respect of matters contained in List I, and a concurrent power to legislate in respect of matters contained in List III of Sch. VII (Art. 246).[10]

(i) Three legislative lists: concurrent as well as exclusive legislative power

(2) The power given to Parliament to legislate on exclusively State subjects, namely,

(ii) Power of Parliament to legislate on exclusive State matters

- (*a*) Power to legislate with respect to a matter in the State List in the national interest (Art. 249).[11]
- (*b*) Power to legislate in respect of any matter in the State List if a proclamation of emergency is in operation (Art. 250).[12]
- (*c*) Power to legislate for two or more States by consent of those States (Art. 252).[13]

(iii) Proclamation of emergency

(3) Provisions for proclamation of emergency and the effect of such proclamation (Arts. 352 and 353).[14]

(iv) Provisions which operate unless Parliament provides to the contrary

(4) Provisions included in the Constitution which are to be operative "unless provision is made to the contrary by Parliament by law" or words to the same effect.

(v) Amendment of the Constitution

(5) Provisions regarding the amendment of the Constitution.

Provisions taken over from the G.I. Act, 35, except for (2)(a) and (5)

1.94 It is not clear from Dr. Ambedkar's speech whether he considered all the provisions listed above to have been devised by the Drafting Committee,[15] or whether he assumed that the origin of most of them was well known and would be covered by the general words in which he acknowledged the debt which the Draft Constitution owed to the G.I. Act, 35.[16] As will presently appear, provisions listed above in (1), (2)(*b*) and (*c*), and (3) were taken over from the G.I. Act, 35, and the provisions listed in (4) above were also contained in the G.I. Act, 35, wherever thought necessary.

Art. 246 adopts the distribution of legislative power contained in s. 100 G.I. Act, 35

1.95 As regards the distribution of legislative powers [listed in (1) above],[17] Art. 246 adopts with immaterial alterations the scheme for the distribution of legislative power contained in s. 100 of the G.I. Act, 35, and for a proper understanding of that scheme we must consider what the scheme sought to achieve. As we have seen, the distribution of legislative power generally proceeds on the basis of allocating enumerated powers to one authority (the Union or the States), and residuary powers to the other. In the United States "The powers not delegated to the United States by the Constitution, nor prohibited

---

[9] References to the draft articles are given in the footnotes.
[10] Draft Art. 217.
[11] Draft Art. 226.
[12] Draft Art. 227.
[13] Draft Art. 229.
[14] Draft Arts. 275 and 276.
[15] About Draft Arts. 275 and 276 he said: "Such a power of converting itself into a unitary State no federation possesses"; or again: ". . . it (the Draft Constitution) has added new ways of overcoming the rigidity and legalism inherent in federalism which are special to it and which are not to be found elsewhere": *C.A.D.* Vol. VII, pp. 35 and 36, respectively.
[16] "As to the accusation that the Draft Constitution has produced a good part of the provisions of the Government of India Act, 1935, I make no apologies. There is nothing to be ashamed of in borrowing. It involves no plagiarism. Nobody holds any patent rights in the fundamental ideas of a Constitution. What I am sorry about is that the provisions taken from the Government of India Act, 1935, relate mostly to the details of administration": ibid. p. 38.
[17] See para 1.93.

by it to the States, are reserved to the States respectively, or to the people."[18] The powers were thus mutually exclusive and it was left to judicial interpretation to imply a limited field of concurrent legislative action. In Australia, which followed the U.S. in preference to the Canadian example, the residuary powers are with the States, but the enumerated powers of the Commonwealth are, except as to a few of them, not exclusive so that there is a large field of concurrent legislative action although express provision is made to secure the supremacy of the Commonwealth over State law.[19] The Canadian Constitution gave the residuary powers to the Dominion, nevertheless it contained a double enumeration of exclusive legislative powers in ss. 91 and 92. The wide general words in which s. 91 conferred on the Dominion power to legislate "for the peace, order and good government" of Canada, and the equally wide general words in which s. 92 conferred power on the provinces to legislate on "property and civil rights in the provinces," gave rise to serious legal controversies involving the very existence of the federal principle.

The three lists in s. 100 attempted an exhaustive enumeration of heads of legislation

The draftsman of the G.I. Act, 35, with a view to avoid a final allocation of residuary powers between the federation and the provinces, attempted an exhaustive enumeration of heads of legislative subjects and distributed them in three legislative lists: List I being the Federal, List II being the Provincial, and List III being the Concurrent, Legislative Lists. S. 100(1) gave the federal legislature exclusive power to legislate with respect to matters in List I; s. 100(2)

the principles underlying the three lists

gave the federal legislature and, subject to s. 100(1), also the provincial legislature power to legislate in respect of matters in List III; and s. 100(3) gave the provincial legislature, subject to s. 100(1) and (2), exclusive power to legislate in respect of matters in List II. The subjects included in List I can be described as of national importance;[20] the subjects included in List III can be described as having an important national aspect in which local variations or experiments might be desirable and were not necessarily injurious to the national interest; the subjects included in List II can be described

Art. 246 adopts the basic principle of the three lists

as matters which were considered to be principally of local and provincial interest. If Art. 246 of, and Sch. VII to, the Constitution[21] mitigate the rigidity and legalism inherent in federalism, as they do, by giving Parliament a wide field of exclusive legislation and a substantial field of concurrent legislation, s. 100 of, and Sch. VII to, the G.I. Act, 35, pointed the direction and went the whole way.

Other features which mitigate rigidity: s. 107, G.I. Act, 35

1.96 There are other features of the distribution of legislative powers in three lists which have not been listed above, though they mitigate the rigidity and legalism inherent in federalism. They relate to the innovation made by s. 107 to the G.I. Act, 35, as regards the exercise of concurrent legislative powers; to the innovation in the distribution of the powers of taxation, and, lastly, to the consequences which have flowed from an attempt exhaustively to enumerate legislative subjects.

---

[18] The Tenth Amendment to the Constitution.

[19] s. 109, Commonwealth of Australia Constitution Act, 1900.

[20] The statement has to be qualified, because certain entries in List I like "Ecclesiastical Affairs, including European cemeteries" reflect the policy of "safeguards" inserted in the Act.

[21] The three lists in Sch. VII to the Constitution are based on the same principle on which the three lists of the G.I. Act, 35, were based.

1.97 In the United States, Canada and Australia it is well settled that in any irreconcilable conflict between a valid federal law and valid State law the federal law will prevail and the State law will be void to the extent of its repugnancy to the federal law. This paramountcy of federal law was generally provided for in the G.I. Act, 35, but s. 107 of that Act introduced a useful constitutional innovation in the field of concurrent legislation. It provided for the prevalence of federal law over provincial law in the concurrent field and declared that in case of conflict the provincial law would be void to the extent of its repugnancy. But sub-s. (2) provided that if a provincial law in the concurrent field contained any provisions repugnant to an earlier federal law, or an existing Indian law, in the same field, then the provincial law would prevail in the province if it had received the assent of the Governor-General or His Majesty after being reserved for the Governor-General's consideration or the signification of His Majesty's pleasure. This was subject to the provision that the federal legislature might at any time enact further legislation with respect to the same matter. S. 107 thus secured flexibility in the exercise of concurrent legislative power, for it left considerable initiative to the provincial legislatures in the concurrent field whilst providing for the ultimate prevalence of federal law, should the need arise. Art. 254 has taken over this feature of the G.I. Act, 1935, and has further conferred on Parliament the power to repeal a State law made in exercise of concurrent legislative power.[22]

S. 107 enables the provincial law to prevail over federal law in certain circumstances

thus securing greater flexibility

Art. 254 has adopted the principle of s. 107

1.98 The innovation made for the distribution of taxing power may now be mentioned. In the United States the power of taxation is conferred on the Congress in wide general terms. But the power is not exclusive except as to the imposts or duties on import or export subject to a limited exception not here material. In Canada the power of taxation is conferred in the widest terms on the Dominion, and a power of direct taxation within the province to raise revenue for provincial purposes is conferred on the provinces. Thus the taxing powers are independent but as regards direct taxation they cover an overlapping field. In Australia "The Federal power over customs and excise duties is exclusive (s. 90), but as regards other taxation the Commonwealth and State Parliaments have separate rather than concurrent powers."[23] These overlapping powers of taxation covering the same field, for example, the power to impose an income tax, have given rise to much litigation and have raised the question whether the federal power can be so exercised as to nullify the State's power of taxation. The lists contained in the Sch. VII to the G.I. Act, 35, provided for distinct and separate fields of taxation, and it is not without significance that the concurrent legislative list contains no entry relating to taxation but provides only for "fees" in respect of matters contained in the list but not including fees taken in any court. Among the important items of federal taxation are duties of customs (entry 44), duties of excise with certain exceptions (entry 45), taxes on income other than agricultural income (entry 54), taxes on the capital value of assets (entry 55), duties in respect of succession to property (entry 56). Among the items of provincial taxation

The taxing power of the federation and the provinces was mutually exclusive in the G.I. Act, 35

[22] This power may have been expressly conferred in view of the decision of the Privy Council in *Att.-Gen. for Ontario* v. *Att.-Gen. for the Dominion* (1896) A.C. 348. For a discussion of the problem involved see para 2.50.

[23] *Wynes*, p. 168.

Conflicts from overlapping powers of taxation avoided

are land revenue (entry 39), duties of excise on goods excepted from entry 45, List I (entry 40), taxes on agricultural income (entry 41), taxes on the sale of goods and on advertisements (entry 48). It will thus be seen that List I and List II of Sch. 7 thus avoid overlapping powers of taxation and proceed on the basis of allocating adequate sources of taxation for the federation and the provinces, with the result that few problems of conflicting or competing taxing powers have arisen under the G.I. Act, 35. This scheme of the legislative lists as regards taxation has been taken over by the Constitution of India with like beneficial results.

this scheme adopted in our Constitution

The consequences of an exhaustive enumeration in the lists

1.99 Lastly, we must consider the consequences which have flowed from an exhaustive enumeration of legislative subjects in the three legislative lists of the G.I. Act, 35. Such enumeration, it was hoped, would reduce litigation arising from overlapping powers expressed in wide general terms such as are to be found in ss. 91 and 92, B.N.A. Act, 1867.[24] It is true that "It would be a supreme draftsman who could so draw these lists that no charge of overlapping could be brought against them."[25] But the lists were in fact supremely well drawn, and disputes of substance arising from apparently overlapping provisions have been few and have presented no recurring and intractable problems. Our Constitution has taken over the principle of exhaustive enumeration of legislative subjects in the three legislative lists with like beneficial results. It should, however, be noted that though such enumeration was originally undertaken in order to avoid a final allocation of residuary power to the federation or the provinces, our Constitution has adopted such enumeration even though residuary powers have been given to the Union by Art. 248. However, in practice, the scope for the application of Art. 248 has not been as limited as it was intended to be.

the lists have given rise to very little litigation

This feature adopted by our Constitution, whilst giving the residuary power to the Union

Art. 249 introduces a useful, but limited innovation

1.100 The provisions of Art. 249, listed in (2)(*a*) above[26] may now be considered. Art. 249 introduced for the first time a useful innovation for securing greater flexibility in working the federation. As we have seen, the States have exclusive power to legislate on matters contained in the State List. Art. 249 provides for a situation where the national interest requires that Parliament should legislate upon a subject in the State List, and it permits parliamentary legislation subject to certain limitations. Parliament can legislate on a subject in the State List only if "the Council of States has declared by resolution supported by not less than two-thirds of the members present and voting that it is necessary or expedient in the national interest" for Parliament so to do.[27] Such a resolution remains in force for a period not exceeding one year, but may be continued if and so often as a resolution approving the continuance is passed in the manner provided for passing the original resolution. A law passed in pursuance of such resolution which Parliament is not otherwise competent to pass ceases to have effect, to the extent of such incompetency, six months after the resolution has ceased to be in force except as to things done or omitted to be done before the expiration of six months. Art. 249 is a useful provision, but as its terms show, it is meant to deal with a temporary situation, for if a subject in the State List has permanently acquired national importance it would have to be

---

[24] See *per* Gwyer C.J. in *In re The C.P. and Berar Act*, (1939) F.C.R. 18, at p. 38.

[25] *Wheare*, p. 82.

[26] See para 1.93.

placed in the Union or the Concurrent List by an amendment of the Constitution.

1.101 The provisions contained in Art. 250 and in Arts. 352 and 353 listed in (2)(*b*) and (3) above[28] may be considered together for they relate to one topic and were in fact dealt with in a single section of the G.I. Act, 35, namely, s. 102. That section provided that on the Governor-General declaring by a proclamation that a grave emergency existed whereby the security of India was threatened, whether by war or internal disturbance, the federal legislature could make laws also for a province or any part thereof in respect of matters contained in the Provincial Legislative List. In other words, on a proclamation of emergency the matters in List II became a field of concurrent legislative power with the further difference that a law passed by the federal legislature under s. 102 whether made before or after the provincial law, prevailed over the provincial law as long as the federal law continued. The proclamation of the Governor-General was to be made in his "discretion", but the proclamation was to be communicated to the Secretary of State who was to lay it before each House of the British Parliament; and the proclamation was to cease to operate at the expiration of six months unless before that time it had been approved by resolutions of both Houses of the British Parliament. These provisions were strongly condemned by Indian public opinion. But it is clear from the provisions of our Constitution that the objection was not to the nature and scope of the power but to its exercise by the Governor-General over whom the ultimate control rested with the British Parliament which claimed responsibility *for* India but was not responsible *to* India. Arts. 250, 352 and 353 of our Constitution confer the same power to issue a proclamation of emergency which is followed by the same consequences, namely, that Parliament can pass laws for a State or any part thereof in respect of the matters contained in List II. The power however is to be exercised by the President of India and requires the approval of both Houses of the Indian Parliament. Dr. Ambedkar said that these provisions made the Indian Constitution ". . . both unitary as well as federal according to the requirements of time and circumstances. In normal times, it is framed to work as a federal system. But in times of war it is so designed as to make it work as though it was a unitary system."[29] This observation is, broadly speaking, accurate and it is true that there is no such provision in the Constitutions of the United States, Canada and Australia. However, in the United States of America, Canada and Australia much the same result was arrived at by the judicial interpretation given to the war, or defence, power. For example, Dr. Wynes has observed:

S. 102, G.I. Act, 35: proclamation of emergency: adopted in Arts. 352 and 353

the effect of such proclamation: the central government has total legislative and executive power

Even in the U.S., Canada and Australia, the Federal Governments are practically unitary in times of War

"The Commonwealth has passed through two world wars as an active belligerent. If, during the Great War, the defence power as expounded by the court was availed of to an extent which evoked the comment from the Royal Commission on the Constitution in 1929 that the Commonwealth was, during the war, for practical purposes, a unified government, the Second World War produced an extension in the subjects which were considered necessary for regulation by such a Government so wide as to embrace practically every aspect of the national life."[30]

---

[27] Except for 12 members nominated by the President, the Council of States is composed of representatives of the States to be elected by the elected representatives of the Legislative Assembly of each State. See Art. 80.

[28] See para 1.93.

[29] *C.A.D.*, Vol. VII, pp. 34 and 35.

[30] *Wynes*, p. 258.

S. 102, and Arts. 352 and 353 recognize this fact

Section 102 of the G.I. Act, 35, thus gave statutory recognition to the fact that in times of war the federal government should have power to legislate even on subjects of exclusive provincial legislation. Such an express provision prevented litigation which might otherwise have arisen on the ground of lack of legislative competence. The inclusion of internal disturbance in s. 102 was open to question on the ground that it was aimed at the freedom movement in India. However, the Second World War and its aftermath gave a new meaning and content to the expression "internal disturbance," for it became a part of hot and cold war strategy to promote internal disturbance in countries considered hostile or neutral. Articles 250, 352 and 353 have, among other things, naturally taken note of this new content of the words "internal disturbance". However, the abuse of the power to declare an emergency on the grounds of internal disturbance during the Emergency proclaimed on 26th June 1975 has led to an amendment of the Constitution putting restrictions on declaring an emergency on the ground of "internal disturbance", which is now replaced by "armed rebellion".

S. 103 G.I. Act, 35: legislation for two or more States: Art. 252 adopts this section with a variation

1.102 The provisions contained in Art. 252, listed in para 1.93(2)(c) above, which empower Parliament to legislate for two or more States by consent of those States reproduces s. 103 of the G.I. Act, 35, with this difference that a law passed under s. 103 could be amended as to any particular province by the legislature of that province, whereas a law passed by Parliament under Art. 252 cannot be amended by the legislature of a State. Section 103 and Art. 252 both secure flexibility in the working of a federal government, for they enable two or more States to legislate effectively on a topic where legislative action by individual States would be ineffective or not fully effective.[31] The provisions mentioned in para 1.93(4) above[32] do not call for special mention.

Legislative powers of the Chief Executive: ss. 42 and 88, G.I. Act, 35

1.103 Two other characteristic features of our Constitution may be noticed here, and both of them have been taken over from the G.I. Act, 35. The first relates to the legislative powers of the Chief Executive in the Union and in the States, and the second relates to the failure of the constitutional machinery. Section 42 of the G.I. Act, 35, empowered the Governor-General to promulgate ordinances during the recess of the federal legislature; and s. 88 of that Act empowered the Governor to promulgate ordinances during the recess of the State legislature. These sections were strongly assailed as involving "rule by ordinance". But their incorporation in our Constitution shows, that here again, the objection was not to the nature and scope of the power but to the authorities by whom it was to be exercised. Art. 123 which deals with the legislative powers of the President empowers the President to promulgate ordinances during the recess of the Parliament, and Art. 213 confers a similar power on the Governor to promulgate ordinances during the recess of the State legislature. These provisions have secured considerable flexibility both to the Union and to the State to enact laws to meet emergent situations, as also to meet circumstances created by laws being declared void by courts of law. Grave public inconvenience would be caused if on an Act, like the Bombay Sales Tax Act, being declared

similar power conferred by Arts. 123 and 213

---

[31] As an instance of the utility of this power, see the decision in *R. M. D. Chamarbaugwalla* v. *Union* (1957) S.C.R. 930, ('57) A.SC. 628.

[32] For similar provisions in the G.I. Act, 35, see, for example, ss. 154 and 154A.

void,[33] no machinery existed whereby a valid law could be promptly promulgated to take the place of the law declared void. In this connection it must be remembered that under our Constitution a validating Act must stand the test of Part III of the Constitution.

1.104 As regards the failure of constitutional machinery, s. 45 of the G.I. Act, 35, gave power to the Governor-General to issue a proclamation if he was satisfied that a situation had arisen in which the Government of the Federation could not be carried on in accordance with the provisions of the Act. It gave the Governor-General wide powers of executive action and powers to make laws which a federal legislature would be competent to make. The functions of the Governor-General under s. 45 were to be exercised by him in his discretion and s. 93 conferred a similar power on the Governor of each province to issue a proclamation enabling him to take executive and legislative action in case of failure of constitutional machinery. These provisions were brought into force during the Second World War and were the subject of bitter criticism; but here again Art. 356 shows that the criticism was directed not to the nature and scope of the power but to the authorities by whom it was to be exercised. Art. 356 enables the President to assume to himself all or any of the functions of the Governor of the State where the constitutional machinery has broken down, but unlike the powers conferred by the G.I. Act, 35, the President is not entitled straightaway to make laws for the State. The President can only declare by proclamation that the powers of the legislature of a State shall be exercisable by or under the authority of Parliament. On that being done, Parliament can empower the President to make laws. The full implication of this power and the necessity for inserting it in the Constitution would require separate treatment by itself. It may, however, be stated here that this power has in fact been exercised by proclamation on several occasions.[34]

Failure of constitutional machinery: s. 45, G.I. Act, 35

similar provision in Art 356

1.105 The Legislative Lists of the G.I. Act, 35, did not contain any entry relating to inter-State trade and commerce.[35] Entry 27 of the Provincial Legislative List related to trade and commerce within the province and entry 29 related to the production and manufacture of goods. However, s. 297 of the Act prohibited certain restrictions on internal trade and thus secured freedom of inter-State trade and commerce by providing that no provincial legislature or government shall have power to pass any law or take any executive action prohibiting or restricting the entry into or export from a province of any goods or class of goods, and by prohibiting discriminatory taxation on goods manufactured and produced outside a province. The G.I. Act, 35, thus furnished a model which, with necessary alterations, might have been adopted by the drafting committee to secure freedom of inter-State and intra-State trade and commerce. Unfortunately, the drafting committee turned for inspiration to s. 92 of the Australian Constitution, and couched Art. 301 in language deceptively similar to that of s. 92. *Deceptively* similar, because whereas s. 92

Inter-State trade and commerce

the Govt. of India Act furnished a model

[33] As was done by the Bombay High Court in *United Motors India Ltd.* v. *Bombay* 55 Bom.L.R. 246.

[34] Action has been taken under Art. 356 in respect of the following States: The Punjab, Pepsu, Andhra, Travancore-Cochin (now Kerala), Kerala, Orissa, West Bengal, Gujarat, Rajasthan and Karnataka.

[35] Entry 42, List I, Sch. VII.

Art. 301 and s. 92 of the Australian Constitution

purports to declare absolute freedom of trade, commerce and intercourse it is clear from Arts. 302 to 304, to which Art. 301 is subject, that the freedom declared by Art. 301 is a limited freedom. This importation from Australia is surprising, first, because in Australia itself it has been said by a distinguished authority that the first paragraph of s. 92 "reads more like a slogan than as part of a legal document",[36] and secondly, because, no section of the Australian Constitution has given rise to greater litigation than s. 92; the end of such litigation was not in sight in 1948 and is not in sight even now. As was to be expected Arts. 301 to 304 have given rise to difficult and, it would seem, intractable problems[37] which are fully considered in the Chapter on Trade, Commerce and Intercourse within the Territory of India.

Arts. 301 to 304 pose intractable problems

Amendment of the Constitution

1.106 Unlike the Commonwealth of Australia Act, 1900, but like the B.N.A. Act, 1867, the G.I. Act, 35, contained no provision for its amendment. This was because the Act did not provide for the governance of a "Dominion" so that the amendment of the Act had to be left to the British Parliament. A constitution without the power of amendment is extremely rigid, for there is no way in which lessons made manifest by experience can be incorporated in the constitution. The U.S. Constitution and the Constitutions of other federations make provision for amendment.[38] The provisions of Art. 368 for the amendment of the Constitution are considered in the Chapter on Amendment of the Constitution.

Citizenship

1.107 The Constitution Acts passed by the British Parliament for Canada, Australia and India did not raise any problem as regards citizenship because all persons in those territories were the subjects of the Sovereign of the United Kingdom and there was a common citizenship. The changed status of India as a Republic made it necessary to provide for Indian citizenship and the Constitution provides for one citizenship throughout India. The American example of dual citizenship, namely, a citizenship of the United States and a citizenship of individual States was not followed because it was not relevant, for the provinces of India were not separate States with Constitutions of their own.

Dual agencies — federal and State — not established

1.108 One other feature of the U.S. Constitution has not been followed in Canada, Australia and by the G.I. Act, 35, namely, the establishments of dual agencies for carrying out federal and State laws, such as federal courts established in each State and a federal executive operating in each State to enforce federal laws. In all these constitutions there is a power to create separate federal agencies, but in fact such agencies have not been created. Our Constitution also gives such power but in fact this power has not been exercised.

Conclusion

1.109 A review of the provisions of the Constitution of India may have impressed the reader, as it has impressed the present writer, with the strange destiny of the G.I. Act, 35. Little could the framers of that Act have dreamt that in the Constitution of a free India they would find the greatest monument to their drafting skill and constitutional insight.

---

[36] Nicholas, *The Australian Constitution* (1952 ed.), p. 250.

[37] It may be stated that it is generally agreed that the drafting of Arts. 301 to 304 leaves much to be desired.

[38] Till 1949 there was no power of amendment in the B.N.A. Act, 1867.

CHAPTER II

INTERPRETATION OF THE CONSTITUTION

"I have had on many occasions, to draft Acts of Parliament, which, although they may be easy to understand, people continually try to misunderstand, and in which therefore it is not enough to attain to a degree of precision which a person reading in good faith can understand; but it is necessary to attain if possible to a degree of precision which a person reading in bad faith cannot misunderstand. It is all the better if he cannot pretend to misunderstand it."[1]

—SIR JAMES FITZJAMES STEPHEN.

2.1 A Court of Law must gather the spirit of the Constitution from the language used, and what one may believe to be the spirit of the Constitution cannot prevail if not supported by the language, which therefore must be construed according to well-established rules of interpretation uninfluenced by an assumed spirit of the Constitution.[2] Where the Constitution has not limited, either in terms or by necessary implication, the general powers conferred upon the Legislature, the Court cannot limit them upon any notion of the spirit of the Constitution.[3]

Spirit of the Constitution to be gathered from the words used

2.2 Well established rules of interpretation require that the meaning and intention of the framers of a Constitution — be it a Parliament or a Constituent Assembly — must be ascertained from the language of that Constitution itself; with the motives of those who framed it, the Court has no concern.[4] But, as Higgins J. observed[5] — "in words that have not withered or grown sterile with years"[6] —:

Well settled principles of interpretation apply to the Constitution

"although we are to interpret the words of the Constitution on the same principles of interpretation as we apply to any ordinary law, these very principles of interpretation compel us to take into account the nature and scope of the Act we are interpreting, to remember that it is a Constitution, a mechanism under which laws are to be made, and not a mere Act which declares what the law is to be."[7]

In *In re the C.P. and Berar Act, 1938*[8] (*"The Central Provinces Case"*) after quoting the observations of Lord Wright in *James* v. *Commonwealth of Australia*[9] that a Constitution must not be construed in a narrow or pedantic manner, and "that construction most beneficial to the widest possible amplitude" of its powers, must be adopted,[10] Gwyer C.J. added that:

A large and liberal construction must be given to legislative power: *The Central Provinces Case*

---

[1] *In re Castioni,* (1891) 1 Q.B. 149, 167-8.
[2] *Keshavan Madhava Menon* v. *Bombay* (1951) S.C.R. 228, 232, ('51) A.SC. 128.
[3] *A. K. Gopalan* v. *The State* (1950) S.C.R. 88, 120, ('50) A.SC. 27, *per* Kania C.J.
[4] *In re The C.P. and Berar Act, 1938* (1939) F.C.R. 18, 36, ('39) A.FC. 1, *per* Gwyer C.J.
[5] *A.-G. for New South Wales* v. *Brewery Employees Union* (1908) 6 C.L.R. 469, 611-12.
[6] *Victoria* v. *Commonwealth* (*"The Payroll Tax Case"*) (1971) 122 C.L.R. at p. 395, *per* Windeyer J.
[7] (1908) 6 C.L.R. *supra* at pp. 611-12.
[8] (1939) F.C.R. 18, ('39) A.FC. 1.
[9] (1936) A.C. 578.
[10] *British Coal Corporation* v. *R.* (1935) A.C. 500, 518.

and a Constitution must be interpreted in a broad and liberal spirit

". . . a broad and liberal spirit should inspire those whose duty it is to interpret (the Constitution); but I do not imply by this that they are free to stretch or pervert the language of the enactment in the interests of any legal or constitutional theory, or even for the purposes of supplying omissions or of correcting supposed errors. A Federal Court will not strengthen, but only derogate from, its position; if it seeks to do anything but declare the law; but it may rightly reflect that a Constitution of government is a living and organic thing, which of all Instruments has the greatest claim to be construed *ut res magis valeat quam pereat.*[11]" [12]

Prof. Cross on "the intention of Parliament": not a description but a linguistic convenience

As the object of statutory interpretation is to ascertain "the intention of the Legislature", the manner in which, and the materials from which, that intention is to be gathered, has been the subject of an increasingly wide, deep and refined analysis in the 1970s. Prof. Cross's admirable and illuminating book on *Statutory Construction* (1976) will be found instructive by the practising lawyer, "who likes to devote his spare time to the contemplation of the law".[13] Apart from a critical appraisal of recent trends in statutory interpretation, which trends are discussed in this Chapter,[14] Prof. Cross has given a careful analysis of the expression "the intention of Parliament".[15] The whole discussion repays study, but his argument is briefly this: It is meaningless to speak of the "intention of Parliament" unless it is recognized that the expression is used by analogy, but in no way synonymously with the intention of an individual concerning the general and particular effects of a document he prepares and signs. In various Statutes it is impossible to point to specific individuals (as one can point to specific testators making their Wills) who did or did not entertain the intention in question. For example,

"It has been pointed out that in a debate on what has become the Statute of Westminster, 1932, Mr. Winston Churchill and the Solicitor-General agreed that there was no obscurity in the provisions concerning the Irish Free State, although they took diametrically opposite views concerning their effect."[16]

In the result, the expression " 'the intention of Parliament' is not so much a description as a linguistic convenience."[17] The present writer would add that Parliament is treated as though it was an individual "law-maker",[18] whose intention is to be ascertained from the language which he has used in making and promulgating the law. It is submitted that this analysis of the "intention of Parliament" is helpful in considering the nature of extrinsic aids to construction, particularly the speeches of individual members, made in a Legislature or in a Constituent Assembly.

The Constitution must be read in the light of the G.I. Act, 35

2.3 Our Constitution was not written on a clean slate, because a federal constitution had been established by the G.I. Act, 35, and

". . . though that has undergone considerable change by way of repeal, modification and addition, it still remains the framework on which the present

[11] "It is better that it should live than that it should perish".
[12] (1939) F.C.R. *supra* at p. 37.
[13] Cross, *Statutory Construction* (1976) Preface vi; See also p. 170: "It is greatly to be regretted that English academic lawyers have not performed their usual functions with regard to the general principles of statutory construction". In the opinion of the present writer, Prof. Cross has made good this deficiency by his admirably lucid and critical treatment of the subject.
[14] See paras 2.20 to 2.30.
[15] *Cross, op. cit.* pp. 34-40.
[16] Geoffrey Marshall, *Constitutional Theory,* p. 76, quoted in *Cross, op. cit.* p. 34.
[17] *Cross, op. cit.* p. 36.
[18] See *Brett* v. *Brett* (1826) 3 Add 210, 216 where Sir John Nicholl (in a passage quoted in para 2.17) spoke of "the intention of the law-maker".

Constitution is built, and . . . the provisions of the Constitution must accordingly be read in the light of the provisions of the (G. I. Act, 35)."[19]

It has been stated in the Introduction that the basic scheme for the distribution of legislative power contained in the G.I. Act, 35, was taken over by the Constitution. Consequently, the principles laid down in connection with the nature and interpretation of legislative power contained in the G.I. Act, 35, are applicable, and have in fact been applied, to our Constitution.

R. v. Burah: within their limits the powers of Ind. legislatures as plenary as those of Br. Parliament

2.4 In considering the powers of the Indian Legislature,[20] the Privy Council, in *R.* v. *Burah*[21] laid down a fundamental principle for the interpretation of a written Constitution. In a classic passage, Lord Selborne said:

"The Indian Legislature has powers expressly limited by the Act of the Imperial Parliament which created it, and it can, of course, do nothing beyond the limits which circumscribe these powers. But, when acting within those limits, it is not in any sense an agent or delegate of the Imperial Parliament, but has, and was intended to have, plenary powers of legislation, as large and of the same nature, as those of Parliament itself. The established Courts of Justice, when a question arises whether the prescribed limits have been exceeded, must of necessity determine that question; and the only way in which they can properly do so, is by looking to the terms of the instrument by which, affirmatively, the legislative powers were created, and by which, negatively, they are restricted. If what has been done is legislation, within the general scope of the affirmative words which give the power, and if it violates no express condition or restriction by which that power is limited (in which category would, of course, be included any Act of the Imperial Parliament at variance with it) it is not for any Court of Justice to inquire further, or to enlarge constructively those conditions and restrictions."[22]

No decision of the Privy Council has thrown any doubt on the soundness of *Burah's Case*: on the contrary, it has been relied upon in case after case from the Dominions.[23] In *Kesavananda* v. *Kerala*[24] the majority of judges reaffirmed the correctness of the principle laid down in *Burah's Case*.[25]

Br. Coal Corp. v. *R* strict construction appropriate to penal or taxing statutes not appropriate for a Constitution

2.5 In *British Coal Corporation* v. *R.*[26] Viscount Sankey cited with approval a passage from an earlier judgment of the Privy Council[27] which had approved and incorporated the following passage from Clements, *Canadian Constitution*, 3rd ed., p. 347:

"The Privy Council, indeed has laid down that Courts of law must treat the provisions of the British North America Act by the same methods of construction and exposition which they apply to other statutes. But there are statutes and statutes; and the strict construction deemed proper in the case,

---

[19] *Per* Venkatarama Aiyar J. in *M. P. V. Sundararamier and Co.* v. *A.P.* (1958) S.C.R. 1422, 1478, ('58) A.SC. 468.

[20] Constituted under the Indian Councils Act, 1861 (24 and 25 Vict. c. 67).

[21] (1878) 5 I.A. 178, (1878) 3 App. Cas. 889.

[22] 5 I.A. at pp. 193-4.

[23] *Per* Bose J. in *In re the Delhi Laws Act, 1912* (1951) S.C.R. 747, 1111, ('51) A.SC. 332.

[24] ('73) A.SC. 1461, (1973) Supp. S.C.R. 1.

[25] ('73) A.SC. *supra* at pp. 1613-14 (Ray J.); pp. 1811-12 (Palekar J.); p. 1838 (Khanna J.); p. 1908 (Mathew J.); pp. 1070 80 (Beg J.); pp. 2041-42 (Chandrachud J.). Dwivedi J. affirmed the principle without mentioning *Burah's Case* by name: ibid. p. 2005. The view expressed by Hegde and Mukherjea JJ. that *Burah's Case* was only an authority on delegated legislation and not on the interpretation of a written Constitution (ibid. p. 1627) is, it is submitted, untenable in view of numerous decisions to the contrary. For some of those decisions see Seervai, *The Fundamental Rights Case: At the Cross Roads* 75 Bom.L.R. (Journal) p. 47 at pp. 54-7.

[26] (1935) A.C. 500, 518 (P.C.).

[27] *Edwards* v. *A.-G. for Canada* (1930) A.C. 124, 136, (P.C.).

for example, of a penal or taxing statute or one passed to regulate the affairs of an English parish, would be often subversive of Parliament's real intent if applied to an Act passed to ensure the peace, order and good government of a British Colony".

the above principle explained

The reference to "the strict construction deemed proper in the case, for example, of a penal or taxing statute" points to an important difference in the interpretation of such statutes and a constituent or organic statute like a Constitution Act, which must now be considered. When it is said that a penal statute must be strictly construed it means that when the Legislature intends the infliction of suffering or an encroachment on natural liberty or rights, it must manifest its intention with reasonable clearness,[28] for a Court will presume that the Legislature does not intend what it has not clearly expressed. The question of construction thus raised is a question of the *exercise* of power. The rule of strict construction assumes that a Legislature has power to punish particular acts; it only raises the question: Has the Legislature *exercised* that power? But the whole basis of this reasoning disappears when the question shifts from the exercise of power to the *possession* of power. That question has to be decided having regard to two considerations. The first consideration can best be given in the words of Dixon J.:

"The purpose of the enumeration of powers in s. 51 is not to define or delimit the description of law that the Parliament may make upon any of the subjects assigned to it. Speaking generally, the legislative power so given is plenary in its quality. The purpose of the enumeration is to name a subject for the purpose of assigning it to that power. The names or descriptions employed are usually of the briefest kind. It is true that certain powers do involve a description amounting almost to a formal definition; . . . But more often they are the most general names of general topics. * * * To borrow the words of Gray J. delivering the opinion of the Supreme Court in *Juilliard* v. *Greenman*:[29] 'The Constitution . . . by apt words of designation or general description, marks the outlines of the powers granted to the National Legislature; but it does not undertake, with the precision and detail of a code of laws, to enumerate the sub-divisions of those powers, or to specify all the means by which they may be carried into execution'."[30]

These observations help us to understand why the widest meaning must be given to the words used[31] in interpreting the grant of legislative power, for to give any but the widest meaning is to define or delimit words which the Constitution has not defined or delimited. The second consideration flows from the plenary nature of legislative power, so that anyone denying a particular power, or alleging a limitation on a power, must show that the power does not exist, or must show such limitation either expressly or by necessary implication from the terms of the Constitution. A strict construction of an ordinary law is based upon the presumption raised by the Courts that the Legislature does not intend what it has not clearly expressed. No presumption of a limited grant of power can be made by a court, because to limit the grant of legislative power is a constituent and

---

[28] See Maxwell, *Interpretation of Statutes*, 11th ed., pp. 253-4.

[29] (1883) 110 U.S. 421, 439, 28 L. ed. 204.

[30] *Bank of New South Wales* v. *Commonwealth of Australia* (1948) 76 C.L.R. 1, 333. Though the words refer to the grant of legislative power by s. 51 of the Australian Constitution, they are equally applicable to the legislative Lists in the 7th Schedule to our Constitution.

[31] *Navinchandra Mafatlal* v. *C.I.T., Bombay* (1955) 1 S.C.R. 829, 836-7, ('55) A.SC. 58.

not a judicial function: as observed in *Burah's Case*,[32] "it is not for a Court to enlarge constructively" the express conditions or restrictions contained in the grant of legislative power.

2.6 But though it is not for a Court to enlarge constructively the conditions and restrictions contained in the Constitution, the nature of the Constitution may be important on a question of construction. Thus, the *Federal* Constitution of Canada was held to support the view that the words "peace, order and good government" in s. 91 of the B.N.A. Act, 1867, cannot be construed literally, as such a construction would practically destroy the autonomy of the Provinces, since there was hardly a subject enumerated in s. 92[33] upon which the Parliament of Canada could not legislate to the exclusion of the Provincial Legislature.[34] In other words, the federal nature of the Constitution dictated that an interpretation which would destroy Provincial or State autonomy must be rejected in favour of an interpretation which would preserve it. Similarly, our Supreme Court held that Art. 372 does not save the Fugitive Offenders Act, 1880, enacted by the British Parliament, because the power there given to Her Majesty by Order-in-Council to place certain territories in groups was repugnant to the concept of India as a Sovereign Democratic Republic.[35]

The nature of the Constitution cannot be ignored in interpreting it

2.7 It has been said, at times, that a statute must be construed as on the day it was enacted; but this proposition is subject to qualifications. In *Dyson Holdings Ltd.* v. *Fox*[36] the question for decision was the meaning of the word "family" in the expression "member of the family". The facts of the case were briefly these: The defendant lived with the tenant of a house as if she were his wife for 21 years until his death in 1961. They never married and had no children. After his death the defendant continued to live in the house for which she paid rent as if she was his widow until the plaintiffs, who owned the house, learned in 1973 that she was not in fact his widow. The plaintiffs refused to accept further rents and brought proceedings to eject her. The trial court having decided that the defendant was not a member of the family, reluctantly ordered delivery of possession of the house to the owners. The defendant appealed. All the three Judges,[37] held that whatever may have been the position in 1950[38] the meaning of the word "family", which was a popular word, had clearly changed. Lord Denning observed:

Dyson Holdings Ltd. v. *Cox*: interpretation as on the date of enactment: the rule explained

"The word 'family' in this Statute is not used in any technical sense: but in a popular sense. It is not used in the sense in which it would be used by a studious and unworldly lawyer, but in the sense in which it would be used by a man who is 'base, common and popular' to use Shakespeare's words in Henry V, Act IV, Scene I, quoted by Sir Raymond Evershed M.R. in this

meaning of "family" ascertained by reference to current social attitudes to marriage

[32] (1878) 5 I.A. 178, (1878) 3 App. Cas. 889.

[33] S. 92 provides that Provincial Legislatures may exclusively make laws in relation to the matters enumerated therein. S. 92 corresponds to Art. 246(3) read with List II, Sch. VII, of the Constitution and s. 100(3) read with List II, Sch. VII of the G.I. Act, 35.

[34] *Per* Lord Watson in *A.-G. for Ontario* v. *A.-G. for the Dominion* (1896) A.C. 348, 361.

[35] *Madras* v. *C. G. Menon* (1955) 1 S.C.R. 280, ('54) A.SC. 517.

[36] (1976) Q.B. 503.

[37] Lord Denning M.R., James and Bridge L.JJ.

[38] When *Gammans* v. *Ekins* (1950) 2 K.B. 328 was decided by the Court of Appeal.

context in *Langdon* v. *Horton*[39] or in modern words by the ordinary man in the street: see *Brock* v. *Wollams*[40] *per* Cohen L.J."[41]

Applying this test, all the Judges were satisfied that in 1975 the common man would have answered the question whether the defendant was a "member of the family" of the deceased in the affirmative, because social attitudes to marriage had changed. Bridge L.J. made the following important observation:

> ". . . if language can change its meaning to accord with changing social attitudes, *then a decision on the meaning of a word in a statute before such a change should not continue to bind thereafter*, at all events in a case where the courts have consistently affirmed that the word is to be understood in its ordinary meaning. (Further), where the modern meaning is plain, we should, I think, be prepared to apply it retrospectively to any date, unless plainly satisfied that at that date the modern meaning would have been unacceptable."[42] (italics supplied)

same principle applies *a fortiori* to a Constitution

Examples can be multiplied, but it is not necessary to do so. Turning from the interpretation of an ordinary statute, to the interpretation of a Constitution, Prof. Cross has rightly observed : "No one would suggest that a written Constitution should be construed for all time as if the court was sitting the day after it was enacted."[43] And he quoted in support Lord Jowitt's observations in *A.-G. for Ontario* v. *A.-G. for Canada*[44], when considering the question whether the B.N.A. Act, 1867 empowered the Canadian Parliament to abolish the right of appeal from the Canadian Courts to the Privy Council. Lord Jowitt said:

> "It is, as their Lordships think, irrelevant that the question is one which may have seemed unreal at the date of the British North America Act. To such an organic statute the flexible interpretation must be given that changing circumstances require."[45]

Minister of Home Affairs v. *Fisher*: meaning of "child" in Fundamental Rights conferred by a Constitution

2.8 In *Minister of Home Affairs* v. *Fisher*,[46] the Privy Council considered the interpretation of a written Constitution — the Bermuda Constitution[47] — which provided, inter alia, for the fundamental rights of individuals. The question turned on the meaning of the word "child" in s. 11(5) of the Bermuda Constitution. That section was a part of Chapter I, headed "Protection of Fundamental Rights and Freedoms of the Individual", which Chapter contained the undernoted sections.[48]

---

39 (1951) 1 K.B. 660, 669.
40 (1949) 2 K.B. 388, 395.
41 (1976) Q.B. *supra* at p. 508.
42 ibid. p. 513.
43 *Cross*, *op. cit.* p. 46.
44 (1947) A.C. 127 (*held*, that the Parliament of Canada had power to abolish appeals from Canadian Courts to the Privy Council).
45 ibid. p. 154, quoted in *Cross*, *op. cit.* p. 46.
46 (1980) A.C. 319 (P.C.).
47 Which was brought into existence by the Bermuda Constitution Order, 1968 (Statutory Instrument 1968 No. 182) made under the Bermuda Constitution Act, 1967 of the U.K.
48 "*Sec. 1.* Whereas every person in Bermuda is entitled to fundamental rights and freedoms of the individual, that is to say, has the right whatever his race, place of origin, political opinions, colour, creed or sex, but subject to respect for the rights and freedoms of others and for the public interest, to each and all of the following, namely:—(a) life, liberty, security of the person and the protection of the law; (b) freedom of conscience, of expression and of assembly and association; and (c) protection for the privacy of his home and other property and from deprivation of property without compensation, the subsequent provisions of this Chapter shall have effect for the purpose of affording protection to the aforesaid rights and freedoms subject to such limitations of that protection as are contained in those provisions, being limitations designed to ensure that the enjoyment of the said rights and free-

2.9 The facts of the case were briefly these: Facts of the case

A Jamican mother of four illegitimate children, all born in Jamica, married Mr. Fisher, who from the date of the marriage accepted all the four children as children of his family. At all material times, the children were under 18 years of age. In 1976 the Minister of Labour and Immigration ordered the children to leave Bermuda. Their mother and her husband, Mr. Fisher, applied to the Supreme Court to quash the order and for a Declaration that the children were to be deemed to belong to Bermuda within the meaning of s. 11(5) of the Constitution of Bermuda. The Supreme Court refused a Declaration on the ground that the children were illegitimate. In allowing the appeal, the Court of Appeal held by a majority that the children were to be deemed to belong to Bermuda by virtue of Sec. 11(5)(d) of the Constitution. The Minister of Home Affairs appealed to the Privy Council.

2.10 It was submitted for the Minister, that the Bermuda Constitution was in effect an Act of the British Parliament; that in all Acts of that Parliament the word "child" meant a "legitimate child"; consequently, in s. 11(5)(d) of the Bermuda Constitution the word "child" meant a "legitimate child". Appellant's contention

2.11 It is a remarkable feature of the case that neither in the argument of Counsel nor in the judgment of the Privy Council delivered by Lord Wilberforce is any reference made to well settled principles for interpreting written Constitutions. The observations of Higgins J. and of Lord Wright quoted in para 2.2 above, and of Viscount Sankey quoted in para 2.5 — and numerous observations to the same effect in decisions of high authority — would have simplified the Privy Council's task in holding that in s. 11(5)(d) the word "child" must be given a large and liberal construction, and therefore the word "child" included an illegitimate child. However, Lord Wilberforce reached the same conclusion by the following line of reasoning. In the first place, he characterised as too rigid the submission that in Acts of the British Parliament the word "child" meant a "legitimate child", unless by express provision, or necessary implication, an illegitimate child was included. He pointed out that the change in social conditions between the 19th and the 20th Century had narrowed the gulf between legitimate and illegitimate children; and the fact that in certain kinds of Acts, dealing with specific matters like Succession, Citizenship and Wills, there was a strong presumption that the word "child" meant a "legitimate child", did not lead to the conclusion that the nature of the Acts could be disregarded in ascertaining whether an illegitimate child was not included. In the second place, there was a more radical solution to the problem of interpretation, namely, to treat a Constitutional instrument like the Bermuda Constitution, as *sui generis*, calling for principles of interpretation of its own, suitable to its character, without necessarily accepting all the presumptions that were relevant to private laws legislation. The Bermuda Constitution had certain characteristics common to several constitutions framed in the post-Colonial period, namely, that they provided for the fundamental rights of individuals,

Surprising feature of the case

considerations for holding that "child" included an illegitimate child

---

doms by any individual does not prejudice the rights and freedoms of others or the public interest.

Sec. 11. (5) For the purpose of this section, a person shall be deemed to belong to Bermuda if that person — (a) possesses Bermudian status; . . . (c) is the wife of a person to whom either of the foregoing paragraphs of this sub-section applies not living apart from such person . . .; or (d) is under the age of 18 years and is the child, stepchild or a child adopted in a manner recognised by law of a person to whom any of the foregoing paragraphs of this sub-section applies."

Effect on interpretation of conventions and declarations on human rights

which provisions were influenced by the European Convention for the Protection of Human Rights and Fundamental Freedoms (1953) which was signed and ratified by the United Kingdom, and applied to dependent territories, including Bermuda. That Convention in its turn had been influenced by the United Nations Universal Declaration of Human Rights of 1948. These antecedents, and the form of Chapter I itself, called for a generous interpretation suitable to give to individuals the full measure of the fundamental rights and freedoms referred to in the Constitution. These considerations showed that in s. 11(5)(d), the word "child" included an illegitimate child. This decision is important, first, because it dealt with the interpretation of a section conferring fundamental rights; and secondly, because lacking the guidance of settled principles for interpreting written Constitutions, the Privy Council relied for a "generous interpretation" on the fact that post-Colonial Constitutions contained provisions for fundamental rights of individuals — provisions which had been greatly influenced by the two aforesaid Declarations.

The golden rule of construction: its limitations and modifications

2.12 The golden rule of interpretation is that words should be read in their ordinary, natural and grammatical meaning subject to the rider that in construing words in a Constitution conferring legislative power the most liberal construction should be put upon the words so that they may have effect in their widest amplitude.[49] But this rider is subject to certain exceptions. Thus, a restricted meaning may be given to words if it is necessary to prevent a conflict between two exclusive jurisdictions. For example, in the *Central Provinces Case*,[50] the Federal Court recognised that the expression "duty of excise" taken by itself, was wide enough to include a tax on the sale of goods; but as power was expressly conferred on the Provincial Legislatures to impose such a tax, it could not have been intended that such a power should be rendered nugatory by the power to levy duties of excise.[51] Such a conflict could not have been intended, and it can be resolved by giving to "duties of excise" a restricted meaning, namely, that a duty of excise is a tax on the manufacture or production of goods.[52] This restricted interpretation preserves the power of Provincial Legislatures to levy a tax on the sale of goods. A restricted meaning may have to be given by considering the language of the conflicting provisions together and, if necessary, by modifying the language of the one in the light of the other.[53] In some cases such light might be thrown by the legislative history of one, or both, the powers. Thus, in the *Central Provinces Case*, the legislative history of the word "excise" in Indian legislation showed that the only kind of excise duties which were known in India by that name were duties collected from manufacturers or producers and usually payable on the issue of the excisable articles from the place of manufacture or production. In the light of this history, it was not an unreasonable inference that the British Parliament used

---

[49] *Navinchandra Mafatlal* v. *C.I.T., Bombay* (1955) 1 S.C.R. 829, 836-7, ('55) A.SC. 58.

[50] (1939) F.C.R. 18, ('39) A.FC. 1.

[51] (1939) F.C.R. *supra* at p. 44.

[52] ibid. p. 47.

[53] ibid. p. 39, citing *Citizens Insurance Co. of Canada* v. *Parsons* (1881) 7 App. Cas. 96, 108, appr. and appl. in *Harakchand* v. *Union* (1970) 1 S.C.R. 479, ('70) A.SC. 1453, 1458.

the expression "duties of excise" in the sense in which it had been used in India, where excise duties of any other kind were unknown.[54]

Legal terms must be given their legal meaning

2.13 Again, though in construing a legislative entry the widest construction must be put on the words used, unless the context, or the other parts of the Constitution, or legislative practice, require a different construction, other considerations arise when legal terms are used in a legislative entry. In such a case, the normal rule is that legal terms having, in law, acquired a definite and precise sense, the legislature must be taken to have intended that they should be understood in that sense. So, in *Madras* v. *Gannon Dunkerley & Co. (Madras) Ltd.*[55] it was held that at the time when the G.I. Act, 35 was enacted, the words "sale of goods" had a well recognised legal meaning in the general law relating to the sale of goods, and in the legislative practice relating to that topic, and must be interpreted in Entry 48, List II, Sch. 7 of the Act as having the same meaning as in the Sale of Goods Act, 1930.[56] In *Maumsell* v. *Olins*[57] Lord Simon of Glaisdale formulated the "golden rule" and the exception required by technical words, or words of art, as follows:

recent formulations of "golden rule" and exceptions to it

"(The 'golden rule') is sometimes put, (sic) that in statutes dealing with ordinary people, in their everyday lives, the language is presumed to be used in its primary ordinary sense unless this stultifies the purpose of the statute or otherwise produces some injustice, absurdity, anomaly or contradiction in which case some secondary ordinary sense may be preferred so as to obviate the injustice, absurdity, anomaly or contradiction, or fulfil the purpose of the statute; while in statutes dealing with technical matters, words which are capable of both bearing the ordinary meaning and being terms of art in the technical matter of the legislation will presumptively bear their primary meaning as such terms of art (or, if they must necessarily be modified, some secondary meaning as terms of art.")[58]

What is ambiguity?

2.14 However, the golden rule of interpretation cannot be applied where the words of a Constitution or an enactment are ambiguous. In such a situation, extrinsic aids to construction have to be resorted to. This was recognized in *Gopalan's Case*,[59] although that case did not consider what is meant by "ambiguity". A word or phrase is ambiguous when it has more than one meaning or has shades of meaning. But, as will presently appear from a discussion of decided cases, in construing a document or a statute the Court has to ascertain the intention of "them that made it" (generally described as the "mischief rule"). Such intention is to be gathered from the words used, and, normally, if the words bear a plain ordinary meaning, that meaning gives effect to the intention of the maker of the written instrument. But the plain ordinary meaning of words may be qualified by the circumstances with reference to which the words are used, so that the intention is better effectuated by giving to the words a different meaning from that which they normally bear. Therefore, although the golden rule of interpretation is that words should be read in their ordinary, natural and grammatical meaning, this rule is subject to the qualification that if such a construction produces an inconsistency or absurdity or inconvenience so great as to convince the Court that the intention could not have been to use them in their ordinary meaning, the Court would be justified in putting on

literal construction has only a *prima facie* preference

[54] (1939) F.C.R. *supra* at pp. 54-5.
[55] (1959) S.C.R. 379, ('58) A.SC. 560.
[56] (1959) S.C.R. *supra* at p. 416.
[57] (1975) A.C. 373.
[58] ibid. p. 391.
[59] (1950) S.C.R. 88, ('50) A.SC. 27.

those words some other meaning which, though less proper is one which the Court thinks the words will bear.[60] The literal construction then,

"has, in general, but *prima facie* preference. To arrive at the real meaning, it is always necessary to get an exact conception of the aim, scope, and object of the whole Act; to consider, according to Lord Coke:[61] 1. What was the law before the Act was passed; 2. What was the mischief or defect for which the law had not provided; 3. What remedy Parliament has appointed; and 4. The reason of the remedy."[62]

Rule in *Heydon's Case* adopted by the Sup. Ct. in *Chamarbaugwala's Case* and in *Bengal Immunity Case*

It has been said that in order properly to interpret any statute it is as necessary now as it was when Lord Coke reported on *Heydon's Case* to consider the matters there stated.[63] In *R. M. D. Chamarbaugwala* v. *Union*[64] Venkatarama Aiyar J. cited with approval the passage from *Maxwell* setting out the rule in *Heydon's Case*, and he added that the principles there laid down were well settled and had been applied by our Supreme Court in *Bengal Immunity Co. Ltd.* v. *Bihar*[65]. *Chamarbaugwalla's Case*[66] may be given as an illustration of the practical application of the rules laid down in *Heydon's Case.* In *Chamarbaugwalla's Case*, the validity of the Prize Competitions Act, 1955, was impugned on the ground that the definition of 'prize competition', if literally construed, included prize competitions involving substantial skill as well as prize competitions of a gambling nature, and as the definition was one and inseverable, the whole law was void as violating Art. 19(1)(g). It was contended that the words of the section being clear and unambiguous, there was no scope for restricting their meaning by interpretation. In rejecting this argument Venkatarama Aiyar J. referred to the passage in Maxwell setting out the rule in *Heydon's Case* and, applying those principles, held that the legislative history of the impugned law showed that prize competitions involving skill had presented no problems to the Legislature, and that having regard to that history, and also to the language used in the Act, the definition must, by construction, be limited to prize competitions of a gambling nature.

Underlying principles of *Heydon's Case* explained in *River Wear Case*

2.15 The most satisfactory discussion of the subject is to be found in Lord Blackburn's judgment in the *River Wear Case*[67] ("Lord Blackburn's judgment"). The facts of that case were these:

The steamship *Natalian* was attempting under stress of weather to enter the Sunderland Docks belonging to the Appellants, and while it was still in the open sea about 40 or 50 yards from the pier it struck the ground, canted with its head south and drifted bodily ashore. The crew was rescued from the ship. The tide was low at the time; and as the tide rose, the flood and the storm drifted the ship against the pier and caused damage amounting to £2825.13s. The respondents were the owners of the ship and the question was whether they were liable to damages under the provisions of s. 74 of the Harbour, Docks and Piers Act of 1847.[68]

---

[60] *River Wear Commissioners* v. *Adamson* (1877) 2 App. Cas. 743 at pp. 764-5, *per* Lord Blackburn. See *Maxwell*, p. 6.

[61] *Heydon's Case* (1584) 3 Rep. 7b; *Marshalsea Case* (1613) 10 Rep. 73a.

[62] *Maxwell*, pp. 18-19.

[63] *Per* Lindley M.R. *In re Mayfair Property* Co. (1898) 2 Ch. 28, 35.

[64] (1957) S.C.R. 930, 936, ('57) A.SC. 628 (the reference was to *Maxwell*, 10th ed., p. 19).

[65] (1955) 2 S.C.R. 603, 633, ('55) A.SC. 661.

[66] (1957) S.C.R. *supra.*

[67] *River Wear Commissioners* v. *Adamson* (1877) 2 App. Cas. 743.

[68] ibid. p. 744, *f.n.* 1.

The trial court reluctantly held that the respondents were liable on a plain reading of s. 74. The Court of Appeal reversed this decision substantially on the ground that no person could be saddled with liability for an Act of God. The House of Lords dismissed the appeal, Lord Gordon dissenting.[69] Lord Blackburn's judgment contains a masterly exposition of the law and the judgment must be read as a whole. But his view can be stated thus : In interpreting words the object is to ascertain the intention expressed by the words used. But words may have different meanings according to the circumstances with reference to which they are used. Thus, words innocent in themselves may be shown to be libellous if circumstances are established which would justify an innuendo, that is, a secondary meaning which the words do not ordinarily bear. The same principle applies in construing written instruments. Thus the will of a testator is construed by trying to ascertain his intention with reference to his affairs, so that the same words used by another testator with reference to a different state of affairs may have a different meaning. The same principle was applied to the construction of a statute by Lord Coke in *Heydon's Case.* After referring to the history of the law before s. 74 had been enacted, Lord Blackburn said that:

Lord Blackburn's judgment: object of interpretation is to ascertain intention of writer of a document

Meaning of words depends upon context

"neither in a general nor a special Act, could the Legislature have meant (if the words were at all understood) to shift the burden of a misfortune befalling the owner of the pier, from the owner of the pier, who at Common Law would bear it, to the owner of a ship wholly free from blame, and involved, without fault of his, in a common misfortune. It may have been said but could hardly have been intended to be said."[70]

The object of s. 74 was to give the owners of harbours, docks and piers more protection than they had at Common Law; the mischief to be remedied being the expenses of litigation in fixing liability on the proper party, the remedy provided being that the owners should be liable without proof of how the accident occurred. The hardship produced, and the injustice worked, by a literal construction of s. 74 was so great as to justify the Court in putting on the words any meaning which they would bear in order to avoid it. In the *Eastman Case*[71] Lord Halsbury quoted the following passage from Lord Blackburn's judgment:

literal meaning qualified by context to avoid grave hardship or injustice

Lord Blackburn's judgment followed in the *Eastman Case*

"In all cases the object is to see what is the intention expressed by the words used. But, from the imperfections of language, it is impossible to know what that intention is without inquiring further, and seeing what the circumstances were with reference to which the words were used and what was the object appearing from those circumstances, which the person using them had in view."[72]

---

[69] Lord Cairns, whilst not concurring with the wide observations of the Court of Appeal about an Act of God, looked to the previous state of the law, the mischief to be remedied and the terms of the section and held that the clause related only to procedure and to the mode in which the right of action for damages already existing was to be asserted, and that it did not create a right of action for damages where no right of action existed before. Lord O'Hagan observed: "We must take care that a hard case shall not make a bad law, but we must also take care, that we do not attribute to Parliament the intention of injustice so very flagrant without coercive necessity" (ibid. p. 758) and he said that there was no such coercive necessity on a view of the language of the section and the object of the law.

[70] ibid. pp. 766-7.

[71] *Eastman Photographic Materials Co.* v. *Comptroller General of Patents, Designs and Trade Marks* (1898) A.C. 571.

[72] ibid. pp. 575-6. (*held,* that the object of the law was that a particular individual could not be allowed to take exclusive possession of any part of the English

Lord Halsbury used this passage to support his view that in considering the meaning of a word in a later Act, passed after a Commission had reported on the defects of the earlier Act, there was ". . . no more accurate source of information as to what was the evil or defect which the Act of Parliament now under construction was intended to remedy can be imagined than the Report of that Commission."[73]

and in *Prenn* v. *Simmonds*

2.16 Although the *Hannover Case*[74] considered in the next para marks a great advance in statutory interpretation, by rightly emphasizing the importance of construing a word in its context as widely defined in that case, it did not refer to Lord Blackburn's judgment. However, it has been frequently referred to in later decisions of the House of Lords. Thus, in *Prenn* v. *Simmonds*[75] Lord Wilberforce[76] said that:

"In order for the agreement of July 6, 1960, to be understood, it must be placed in its context. *The time has long passed when agreements, even those under seal, were isolated from the matrix of facts in which they were set and interpreted purely on internal linguistic considerations.* There is no need to appeal here to any modern, anti-literal, tendencies, for Loard Blackburn's well-known judgment in *River Wear Commissioners* v. *Adamson*[77] provides ample warrant for a liberal approach. We must, as he said, inquire beyond the language and see what the circumstances were with reference to which the words were used, and the object, appearing from those circumstances, which the person using them had in view."[78] (italics supplied)

and in *Black-Clausson Ltd.* v. *Papierwerke A. G.*

The reader will have noticed that Lord Wilberforce treated Lord Blackburn's judgment as representing an "anti-literal tendency" as far back as 1878. Again, in *Black-Clawson Ltd.* v. *Papierwerke A. G.*[79] Lord Simon of Glaisdale quoted, first, the italicized words from the above observations of Lord Wilberforce, and, secondly, he referred to the *Eastman Case* in which Lord Halsbury had quoted, and applied, the passage from Lord Blackburn's judgment set out in para 2.15. It may be added that in the *Black-Clawson Case*, Lord Reid found it unnecessary to cite authorities for the proposition that it is in comparatively few cases that the words of a statutory provision are only capable of one meaning, and for the proposition that "one must read the words, (with more than one meaning) in the context of the Act read as a whole and one is entitled to go beyond that."[80]

"ambiguity" considered in the

2.17 The question of "ambiguity" was considered at length in the *Hanover Case*[81] with reference to the Preamble of an Act as an aid

---

language. This object was in the mind of the framers of the earlier Act when they used the phrase 'fancy word' as part of the definition of what might be registered as a trade mark. That word, and the qualifications to which it was subject, gave rise to much litigation, and the Act in question was meant to alter that state of the law, and therefore cases decided under the earlier Act had no bearing on the later Act.)

[73] ibid. p. 576. These observations were quoted and applied by Lord Hodson in *Dullewe* v. *Dullewe* (1969) 2 A.C. 313 at p. 320 (P.C.); and by Lords Dilhorne and Simon of Glaisdale in the *Black-Clawson Case* (1975) A.C. 591 at p. 621 and at p. 648 respectively.

[74] *A.-G.* v. *Prince Ernest Augustus of Hanover* (1957) A.C. 436.

[75] (1971) 1 W.L.R. 1381 (H.L.).

[76] With whom Lord Reid, Lord Donovan and Lord Pearson agreed.

[77] (1877) 2 App. Cas. 743, *supra*.

[78] (1971) 1 W.L.R. *supra* at pp. 1383-84.

[79] (1975) A.C. 591.

[80] ibid. p. 613.

[81] (1957) A.C. 436.

to construction. The preamble is a part of the Act,[82] however, "it is a settled rule that the preamble cannot be made use of to control the enactments themselves where they are expressed in clear and unambiguous terms."[83] To this rule, Lord Davey added the subsidiary rule that an ambiguity must not be created or imagined in order to bring in the aid of the preamble.[84] But Lord Simonds said that words, and particularly general words, took their colour and content from their context, and context in its widest sense included other enacting provisions of the same statute, its preamble, the existing state of the law, other statutes *in pari materia*, and the mischief, which by these and other legitimate means, the court can find, that the statute was designed to remove.[85] Consequently, it would often be difficult to say that any terms were clear and unambiguous till they were studied in their context. Therefore, the rule mentioned by Lord Davey meant little, and was better expressed by saying that the context of the preamble was not to influence the meaning otherwise ascribable to the enacting part unless there were compelling reasons for it.[86] *It was not a compelling reason that the provisions of the enacting part went beyond the terms of the Preamble, and still less could a preamble affect the meaning of the enacting words when its own meaning was in doubt.*[87] According to Lord Normand, the preamble was not of the same weight as an aid to the construction of a section of the Act, as are other relevant enacting words to be found elsewhere in the Act, or even in related Acts. Further, the Act may go beyond, or it may fall short of, the indications that may be gathered from the preamble. Again, the preamble cannot be of much, or any, assistance in construing provisions which embody qualifications or exceptions from the operation of the general purposes of the Act. *It is only when the preamble conveys a clear and definite meaning in comparison with relatively obscure or indefinite enacting words that the preamble may legitimately prevail.*[88] According to Lord Somervell,

Hanover Case

Lord Simond's view

Lord Normand's view

Lord Somervell's view

"It is unreal to proceed as if the court looked first at the provision in dispute without knowing whether it was contained in a Finance Act or a Public Health Act. The title and the general scope of the Act constitute the background of the context. When a court comes to the Act itself, bearing in mind any relevant extraneous matters, there is, in my opinion, one compelling rule. The whole or any part of the Act may be referred to and relied on. It is, I hope, not disrespectful to regret that the subject was not left where Sir John Nicholl left it in 1826. 'The key to the opening of every law is the reason and spirit of the law — it is the *animus imponentis,* the intention of the law-maker, expressed in the law itself, taken as a whole. Hence, to arrive at the true meaning of any particular phrase in a statute, that particular phrase

[82] *Salkeld* v. *Johnson* (1848) 2 Exch. 256, 283; *Davies* v. *Kennedy* (1869) L.R. 3 Eq. 668, 698; *A.-G.* v. *Prince Ernest Augustus* (1957) A.C. 436 where the Act including the preamble is treated as the whole document to be construed; *Craies, op. cit.* pp. 200-201; the view of Holt J. to the contrary in *Mills* v. *Wilkins* (1704) 6 Mod. 62 is not in accord with modern authorities.

[83] Per Chitty L.J. in *Powell* v. *Kempton Park Race-Course Co.* (1897) 2 Q.B. 242, 299; approved by Lord Davy in the same case in the House of Lords (1899) A.C. 143, 185.

[84] *f.n.* 83 above.

[85] *A.-G.* v. *Prince Ernest Augustus* (1957) A.C. 436 at pp. 460-61; see *Craies,* p. 203, *f.n.* 2.

[86] (1957) A.C. at p. 463; *Halsbury* (3rd ed.) Vol. 36, p. 370 *f.n.* (b).

[87] (1957) A.C. at p. 463.

[88] ibid. p. 467, *per* Lord Normand; *Maxwell,* p. 7.

is not to be viewed, detached from its context in the statute: it is to be viewed in connection with its whole context — meaning by this as well the title and preamble as the purview or enacting part of the statute'.[89]" [90]

Similar principles laid down by the U.S. Sup. Ct.: Extrinsic aid not forbidden no matter how clear words may appear on a superficial view

2.18 Similar principles have been laid down by the U.S. Supreme Court. Indeed, resort to explanatory legislative history has been declared not to be forbidden *no matter how clear the words may first appear on superficial examination.*[91] Thus in *Harrison* v. *Northern Trust Co.*[92] the question for determination was the meaning of the words "payable out of" in s. 807 of the Revenue Act of 1932.[93] The lower Court had refused to consider the legislative history of s. 807 on the ground that the words were unambiguous. Rejecting this view, Murphy J. said:

> "But words are inexact tools at best and for that reason there is wisely no rule of the law forbidding resort to explanatory legislative history no matter how 'clear the words may appear on superficial examination'.[94] . . . So, accepting the Circuit Court's interpretation of Illinois law as to the incidence of the tax, we think it should have considered the legislative history of s. 807 to determine in just what sense Congress used the words 'payable out of'. The Committee reports on s. 807 demonstrate that it was intended as 'a legislative reversal of a decision' in *Edwards* v. *Slocum*[95] . . . and that Congress used the words 'payable out of' in the sense of 'diminished or reduced by' the payment of the tax."[96]

Rules of literal construction modified by "context"

2.19 Our discussion has shown that the rule of literal construction now stands modified by the principle that words, however clear they may appear to be, must be read in the "context" in which they appear. And if they appear in an Act, the whole Act, or the relevant parts of it dealing with the subject in hand, must be looked at. And "context" includes intrinsic and extrinsic aids to construction.

Recent trends in statutory interpretation in England

2.20 Questions relating to extrinsic aids to construction have been increasingly engaging the attention of Courts in India and in England. Therefore, it would be convenient at this place to consider the recent trends in statutory interpretation before considering their impact on the interpretation of our Constitution. The importance attached to "context" in statutory interpretation, has gone hand in

---

[89] *Brett* v. *Brett* (1826) 3 Add. 210, 216.

[90] (1957) A.C. *supra* at p. 473.

[91] *American Jurisprudence* (1st ed.), Vol. 50, p. 275, citing the case in the next footnote. In *A.-G.* v. *Prince Ernest Augustus* (1957) A.C. 436, at pp. 461 and 463, Lord Simonds made similar observations.

[92] (1942) 317 U.S. 476, 87 L. ed. 407.

[93] *S. 807*: "Sections 303(*a*)(3) and 303(b)(3) of the Revenue Act of 1926 are amended by inserting after the first sentence of each a new sentence to read as follows: 'If the tax imposed by s. 301, or any estate, succession, legacy, or inheritance taxes, are, either by the terms of the will, by the law of the jurisdiction under which the estate is administered, or by the law of the jurisdiction imposing the particular tax, payable in whole or in part out of the bequests, legacies, or devises otherwise deductible under this paragraph, then the amount deductible under this paragraph shall be the amount of such bequests, legacies, or devises reduced by the amount of such taxes."

[94] *U.S.* v. *American Trucking Association* (1930) 310 U.S. 534, 543, 544, 84 L. ed. 1345, 1350, 1351. See also *U.S.* v. *Dickerson* (1939) 310 U.S. 554, 562, 84 L. ed. 1356, 1362.

[95] (1923) 264 U.S. 61, 68 L. ed. 564.

[96] 317 U.S. at 479-80, 87 L. ed. 410-11. The reader interested in pursuing this inquiry further will find the materials collected in Crawford on *Statutory Construction* at p. 381 *et seq.* and in *American Jurisprudence*, 1st ed., Vol. 50, p. 274 *et seq.* It may be added that the American Courts permit reference to sources of information which are rejected in English Courts and have been rejected by the Supreme Court, namely, speeches by Members in Parliament, debates in Parliament and the like.

hand with an analysis of the phrase "intention of Parliament" and of the factors that go to make up the whole legislative process resulting in an Act of Parliament. Once it is realised that the "intention of Parliament" "is not a description but a linguistic convenience" (para 2.2 above) the whole legislative process assumes importance for statutory interpretation. This new approach emphasises, first, the realities of the legislative process; secondly, the close relationship between the draftsman of an Act and the court of construction; and, thirdly, the practical grounds on which English Courts limit the use of "*travaux préperatoires*" (preparatory work) as an aid to construction.

the new approach

2.21 As to the realities of the legislative process, in *R.* v. *Schildkamp*[97] Lord Reid dealt with it in considering whether, and to what extent, weight should be given to punctuation, cross headings and side notes (marginal notes) to an Act. He said:

R. v. *Schildkamp*: recognizing the realities of the legislative process

"Taking a strict view, one can say that these should be disregarded because they are not the product of anything done in Parliament. I have never heard of any attempt to move that any of them should be altered or amended and between the introduction of a Bill and the Royal Assent they can be, and often are altered by officials of Parliament acting in conjunction with the draftsman.

But *it may be more realistic to accept the Act as printed as being the product of the whole legislative process* and to give due weight to everything found in the printed Act. *I say more realistic,* because in very many cases the provision before the Court was never even mentioned in debate in either House and it may be that its wording was never scrutinised by any member of either House. In such a case it is not very meaningful to say that the words of the Act represent the intention of Parliament, but that punctuations, cross headings and side notes do not."[98] (italics supplied)

Again, in *Ealing L. B. C.* v. *Race Relations Board*,[99] Lord Simon of Glaisdale enlarged upon "the reality of the matter" when a court ascertains the intention of the legislature. And, in that context, he also dwelt upon the close relationship between the draftsman of an Act and the court of construction. In interpreting an Act of Parliament, the court sometimes asked itself what the draftsman must have intended. This was reasonable, because the draftsman would know the intention of the legislative initiator (nowadays almost always an organ of the executive); he would know what canons of construction the courts would apply; and accordingly he would express himself in such a way as to give effect to the legislative intention. No doubt Parliament, in enacting legislation, assumes responsibility for the draftsman's language. But *the reality is that only a minority of legislators will attend the debates on the legislation.* Failing special interest in the subject-matter of the legislation, what will demand their attention will be something on the face of the proposed legislation which alerts them to a questionable matter. Accordingly, such canons of construction as that words in a non-technical statute will primarily be interpreted according to their ordinary meaning, or that a statute establishing a criminal offence will be expected to use plain and unequivocal language to delimit the ambit of the offence (i.e. that such a statute will be construed restrictively) are not only useful as part of that common code of juristic communication by which the draftsman signals legislative

Also emphasized in *Ealing L. B. C.* v. *Race Relations Board*

importance of the draftsman in the legislative process

[97] (1971) A.C. 1.
[98] ibid. p. 10.
[99] (1972) A.C. 342.

intention, but are also constitutionally salutary in helping to ensure that legislators are not left in doubt as to what they are taking responsibility for.

Maumsell v. *Olins*: importance of the draftsman again emphasized

2.22 In *Maumsell* v. *Olins*[1] Lord Simon of Glaisdale, — after setting out the "golden rule", and the exceptions to it, (quoted at the end of para 2.13 above) — once again emphasized the close connection between the draftsman of an Act and the court of construction when he observed:

> "It is essential that this 'golden rule' is adhered to. An English court of construction must put itself in the place of the draftsman, and ascertain the meaning of the words used in the light of all the circumstances known by the draftsman — especially the 'mischief' which is the subject matter of the statutory remedy. . . . The canons of construction — including first and foremost, the 'golden rule' — constitute a code of communication between the draftsman and the court of construction. Observing the code on his side, the draftsman will use language in such a way that its meaning represents what Parliament means to say; and it is only by observance of the code by the court on its own side that a divergence can be avoided between its interpretation of what the words mean from what Parliament meant to say."[2]

This was said in a dissenting judgment prepared in collaboration with Lord Diplock. However, as Prof. Cross has rightly observed, that fact "in no way detracts from the authoritative nature of this statement."[3] Besides, in a concurring judgment in *Black-Clawson* v. *Papierwerke A. G.*,[4] which will be considered later, Lord Simon emphasised the reality of the Parliamentary process, the close relation between the draftsman of an Act and the Court of construction.

Beswick v. *Beswick*: use of "preparatory work" *e.g.* legislative debates rejected for practical reasons, including time and costs

2.23 As to the limited use of *travaux préperatoires* (preparatory work), Lord Reid observed in *Beswick* v. *Beswick*[5] that

> "For purely practical reasons we do not permit debates in either House to be cited; it would add greatly to the time and expense involved in preparing cases, involving the construction of a statute if Counsel were expected to read all the debates in Hansard, and it would often be impracticable for counsel to get access to at least the older reports of debates in Select Committees of the House of Commons; moreover, in a very large proportion of cases such a search, even if practicable, would throw no light on the question before the court. But I can see no objection to investigating in the present case the antecedents of s. 56 (of the Law of Property Act, 1925)."[6]

It may be added that Lord Reid's reference to time and expense would apply not only to the proceedings before the court of first instance, but also to appeals heard by the Court of Appeal and by the House of Lords. In *Ealing L. B. C.* v. *Race Relations Board*,[7] Lord Simon said that although "preparatory work" may be useful sometimes it was open to abuse and waste *because an individual legislator may support a measure under the belief that it had a particular meaning and there was no means of ascertaining whether the other members of the legislature agreed.* Further, by extending the material of judicial scrutiny the cost of litigation was inevitably increased. Finally, the legislative history of an English Statute would require a reference to successive drafts of a Bill, heads of instruction to the draftsman, departmental papers and minutes of executive committees, before the Bill becomes an Act.[8] The objection to this

considerations again emphasized by Lord Simon of Glaisdale

---

[1] (1975) A.C. 373.
[2] ibid. p. 391.
[3] *Cross*, *op. cit.* p. 43.
[4] (1975) A.C. 591.
[5] (1968) A.C. 58.
[6] ibid. p. 74.
[7] (1972) A.C. 342.
[8] ibid. p. 361.

material does not apply to an explanatory memorandum accompanying a complicated measure which is often useful both in informing the legislators of all the details for which they are assuming responsibility and in assisting the Courts in their task of interpretation.[9] As will appear later, Lord Simon again emphasised the practical reasons for the limited use of preparatory work in the *Black-Clawson Case* considered below.

2.24 The new approach to interpretation is fully exemplified in the *Black-Clawson Case*. That case turned on the true interpretation of the undernoted Sec. 8(1) and (3)[10] of the Foreign Judgments (Reciprocal Enforcement) Act, 1933 ("the 1933 Act"). The facts of the case were these: New approach fully exemplified in the *Black-Clawson Case*

The plaintiffs, an English Company, became holders in due course of two Bills of Exchange accepted by the predecessors of the defendants, a West German Company without any assets in England. The bills were drawn, negotiated and payable in England. The plaintiffs became their holders in due course shortly before action on them would have become time-barred in six years from their acceptance. In German law the period of limitation was three years. The English Company brought proceedings in the District Court of Munich and in England in the High Court. The German Court dismissed the plaintiff's suit on the ground that the limitation period of three years prescribed by German substantive law relating to bills of exchange had expired. The English company appealed to the House of Lords.

It was held by Lord Denning, in the Court of Appeal, that s. 8(1) dealt with "cause of action estoppel" and s. 8(3) with "issue estoppel", and s. 8(1) prevented Black-Clawson from suing in England.[11] In the House of Lords, Lord Dilhorne said that although after 1964 the expressions "cause of action estoppel" and "issue estoppel" were common, this division into two species of estoppel was not recognised, and those expressions were not used, in 1933. Lord Simon observed that the concepts of "cause of action" and "issue estoppel" had not been developed by 1933 and could not possibly be what Parliament and the draftsman had then in mind.[12]

2.25 By a majority of 4:1[13] the House of Lords allowed the appeal. Lord Reid held that s. 8(1) had no application, but if it did apply, he agreed, with difficulty, with Lords Dilhorne, Wilberforce and Simon that the appeal should be allowed. These three Law Lords held that s. 8(1) only operated to make foreign judgments conclusive between *Black-Clawson Case* in the House of Lords

---

[9] ibid. In India it is called "The Statement of Objects and Reasons".

[10] s. 8. "(1) . . . a judgment to which Part I of this Act applies or would have applied if a sum of money had been payable thereunder, . . . shall be recognised in any court in the United Kingdom as conclusive between the parties thereto in all proceedings founded on the same cause of action and may be relied on by way of defence or counterclaim in any such proceedings. . . . (3) Nothing in this section shall be taken to prevent any court in the United Kingdom recognizing any judgment as conclusive of any matter of law or fact decided therein, if that judgment would have been so recognized before the passing of this Act."

[11] (1975) A.C. *supra* at p. 620.

[12] Ibid. p. 644. Lord Simon said that his first reaction was that the Court of Appeal was right and s. 8(1) dealt with "cause of action estoppel and s. 8(3) with issue estoppel". But he realized his error, namely, that he was looking at s. 8 with 1974 eyes, whereas the Act had been enacted in 1933, in which year those two concepts had not been developed or used: ibid. pp. 643-4. See also p. 651 where he held that s. 8(3) did not apply and was not inserted to deal with issue estoppel as opposed to cause of action estoppel dealt with in s. 8(1). Lord Wilberforce agreed with Lord Simon that s. 8(3) had no application: see ibid. pp. 633-4.

[13] Lord Reid, Lord Dilhorne, Lord Wilberforce and Lord Simon of Glaisdale, Lord Diplock dissenting.

the parties as to the matter thereby adjudicated upon, and since the foreign judgment in the instant case was not a decision on the merits, but a decision that the plaintiff's case was barred by limitation, proceedings by the English Company in the English Courts were not barred. All the Law Lords, except Lord Diplock, held that s. 8(1) was not one of the few provisions of a statute of which it could be said that it had only one meaning. As the words of the section were ambiguous the Court was entitled to refer to intrinsic and extrinsic aids to construction. This raised the question whether, and to what extent, "legislative history" or parts of that history, can be resorted to as an aid to construction.

Legislative history of the 1933 Act

2.26 The legislative history of the 1933 Act was that a Committee, which included eminent lawyers and was presided over by Lord Justice Greer, had been appointed, and the Committee made a Report ("the Report") which contained the Committee's recommendations, together with a draft Bill and Notes on clauses. With two immaterial alterations, Parliament enacted the draft Bill into the 1933 Act. One of the questions for determination by the House of Lords was, whether the Report could be looked at, and if so, to what extent. It should be noted that the Report was linked to the 1933 Act in a very special way, namely, that the draft Bill attached to the Report was enacted by Parliament into the 1933 Act with immaterial alterations. And the difference of opinion on interpretation between Lords Reid, Wilberforce and Diplock on the one hand, and Lords Dilhorne and Simon of Glaisdale on the other, arose from the very special way in which the Report was linked to the 1933 Act.

Parliamentary debates not admissible in interpretation

2.27 All the law Lords agreed that speeches made by Ministers and/or Members of Parliament and recorded in *Hansard* could not be looked at as extrinsic aids to construction;[14] and, secondly, that the court could look at the Report for ascertaining the state of the law as it was, or was understood to be, at the time when the 1933 Act was passed[15] and also for ascertaining "the mischief", which was disclosed by the previous state of the law and for the remedy which Parliament had provided in enacting the 1933 Act.[16] But on the question whether the Court was entitled to look at the Committee's recommendations, the draft Bill and the Notes on Clauses, as extrinsic aids to construction, Lords Reid, Wilberforce and Diplock held that they could not be looked at. Lord Dilhorne held that they could be looked at; and, "as at present advised", Lord Simon was of much the same view.

2.28 The views of the five Law Lords as to the admissibility of the recommendations, the draft Bill and the Notes on Clauses are given below:

(*a*) Lord Reid's view

(a) *Lord Reid* said that the construction of the provisions of an Act was for the court, and if the court was to take evidence about the intention of Parliament, the court would have to reverse its existing practice of not allowing, as aids to statutory interpretation, references

---

[14] ibid. p. 614 (Lord Reid); p. 623 (Lord Dilhorne); p. 629 (Lord Wilberforce); p. 638 (Lord Diplock); p. 651 (Lord Simon).

[15] ibid. p. 614 (Lord Reid); p. 622 (Lord Dilhorne); p. 629 (Lord Wilberforce); p. 638 (Lord Diplock); p. 648 (Lord Simon).

[16] See *f.n.* 15 above.

to Parliamentary Debates recorded in *Hansard*. Resort to *Hansard* would create practical difficulties, because the questions before the Court were rarely those which came before Parliament, and assuming that the promulgators of the Bill could be said to reflect the intention of Parliament, they may never have thought of the question which was before the Court. Further, at best, the Court might get materials from which dubious inferences may be drawn as to the intention of Parliament: "The difficulties in assessing any references there made in Parliament to the question before the Court are such that . . . our best course is to adhere to the present practice." It would follow, *a fortiori*, that the Court should disregard expression of intention by Committees or Commissions which are reported before the Bill was introduced.

(b) *Lord Wilberforce* agreed with Lord Reid, and added that it was not proper or desirable to make use of the Report of a Committee or Commission *or for that matter, anything reported as said in Parliament*, or in official Notes on Clauses as to what the proposed enactment was to mean or what the Committee or Commission thought it meant.[17] He gave two reasons for his view : The first was a practical reason, namely, that the Court would then have to interpret two documents and not one — one the Bill, and the other the commentary on it in the Report. The second reason, according to him, was based on the important constitutional principle that after Parliament had enacted a law, the task of interpreting and applying it to individual cases was assigned to the Courts *and to no one else*, and "it would be a degradation of that process if Courts were to be a reflecting mirror of what some interpreting agency may say."[18] *(b) Lord Wilberforce's view*

(c) *Lord Diplock* said: *(c) Lord Diplock's view*

"The acceptance of the rule of law as a constitutional principle requires that a citizen, before committing himself to any course of action, should be able to know in advance what are the legal consequences that will flow from it. Where those consequences are regulated by a statute the source of that knowledge is what the statute says. In construing it the court must give effect to what the words of the statute would be reasonably understood to mean by those whose conduct it regulates. That any or all of the individual members of the two Houses of the Parliament that passed it may have thought the words bore a different meaning cannot affect the matter. Parliament, under our Constitution, is sovereign only in respect of what it expresses by the words used in the legislation it has passed."[19]

However Lord Diplock accepted the view that in case of ambiguity, the Court could look at the Report to ascertain the previous state of the law and the mischief which the Act under consideration was designed to remedy.[20] However, his dissent was primarily based on his view that the words to be construed were not ambiguous.

(d) *Lord Dilhorne* held that it was legitimate to look at the recommendations contained in the Report, to the Notes on clauses and to the draft Bill when, as in the instant case, it had been enacted into an Act with immaterial alterations. He said: *(d) Lord Dilhorne's view*

"The reason why one is entitled to consider what was the mischief at which the Act was aimed is surely that that will throw a revealing light on the object and purpose of the Act, that is to say the intention of Parliament; and,

---

[17] He said that on this point he agreed with Lord Diplock.
[18] ibid. p. 629. [19] ibid. p. 638.
[20] ibid.

applying Lord Halsbury's observations . . . what more accurate source of information both as to the law at the time and as to the evil or defect which the Act was intended to remedy can be imagined than the report of such a committee, or for that matter the reports of the Law Commission?"[21]

Lord Dilhorne said that the contrary view imposed on judges the risk of being selective in their reading of such Reports, selective between what could, and what could not, be read, and this drew an artificial line which served no useful purpose. After referring to Lord Denning's observations in *Letang* v. *Cooper*,[22] Lord Dilhorne added:

"While I . . . agree that recommendations of a committee may not help much when there is a possibility that Parliament may have decided to do something different, where there is no such possibility, as where the draft Bill has been enacted without alteration, in my opinion, it can safely be assumed that it was Parliament's intention to do what the committee recommended and to achieve the object the committee had in mind. Then, in my view the recommendations of the committee and their observations on their draft Bill may form a valuable aid to construction which the courts should not be inhibited from taking into account."[23]

"It does not follow that if one can have regard to the whole of a committee's report, one ought also to be able to refer to Hansard to see what the Minister in charge of a Bill has said it was intended to do. In the course of the passage of a Bill through both Houses there may be many statements by Ministers, and what is said by a Minister in introducing a Bill in one House is no sure guide as to the intention of the enactment, for changes of intention may occur during its passage."[24]

(*e*) Lord Simon of Glaisdale's view

(e) *Lord Simon of Glaisdale* emphasized the close relationship between the draftsman of an Act and the court of construction and the practical considerations for limiting to reasonable proportions the search for "light" from "legislative history" or other sources. As in interpreting all written material, so in interpreting an Act, what is to be ascertained is the meaning of what Parliament has said in the Act and not what Parliament meant to say.[25] This was not a self-evident juristic truth, for, it could be argued that in a Parliamentary democracy, effect should be given to what Parliament meant to say, since that would truly reflect "the desired influence of the citizens on the decision making which affects themselves." To this, Lord Simon gave three answers:

Practical reasons for rejecting preparatory work

"First, in interpretation of all written material the law in this country has set great pragmatic store on limiting the material available for forensic scrutiny; *society generally thereby enjoys the advantages of economy in forensic man-power and time.* By concentrating on the meaning of what has been said, to the exclusion of what was meant to be said, the material for scrutiny is greatly reduced. Specifically, *experience in the United States has tended to show that scrutiny of the legislative proceedings is apt to be a disappointingly misleading and wasteful guide to the legislative intention.* Secondly, interpretation cannot be concerned wholly with what the promulgator of a written

---

[21] ibid. p. 622. Lord Halsbury's observations have been set out in para 2.15 above.

[22] (1965) 1 Q.B. 222, 240 [Lord Denning said, *inter alia*, ". . . But you cannot look at what the committee recommended, or at least, if you do look at it, you should not be unduly influenced by it. It does not help you much, (because) Parliament may, and often does, decide to do something different to cure the mischief."]

[23] (1975) A.C. *supra* at p. 623.

[24] ibid. This is obviously an answer to Lord Reid's observations which have been referred to earlier in the text.

[25] ibid. p. 645. Lord Reid also said: "We are seeking not what Parliament meant, but the true meaning of what Parliament said": ibid. p. 613.

instrument meant by it: interpretation must also frequently be concerned with the reasonable expectation of those who may be affected thereby . . . in statutory construction, the court is not solely concerned with what the citizens, through their parliamentary representatives, meant to say; it is also concerned with the reasonable expectation of those citizens who are affected by the statute, and whose understanding of the meaning of what was said is therefore relevant. *The sovereignty of Parliament runs in tandem with the rule of objective law.* Thirdly, if the draftsman uses the tools of his trade correctly, the meaning of his words should actually represent what their promulgator meant to say. And the court of construction, retracing the same path in the opposite direction, should arrive, via the meaning of what was said, at what the promulgator meant to say.

There are, however, two riders . . . to this last consideration. First, draftsmen's offices . . . and courts . . . are all manned by fallible human beings; with the result that the court's exposition of the meaning of what Parliament has said is inherently liable to differ from what Parliament meant to say. The object of the parliamentary and forensic techniques should be to minimise such liability to error; so that artificial rules which stand unnecessarily in the way (i.e., which cannot be used as a code of communication) should be eliminated. Secondly, most words in the English language have a number of shades of meaning . . . The draftsman therefore needs the full co-operation of the court of construction: they must be tuned in on the same wavelength. In order to understand the meaning of the words which the draftsman has used to convey what Parliament meant to say, the court must so far retrace the path of the draftsman as actually to put itself in his position and that of Parliament. The *expositio* must be both *contemporanea* and *eodem loco*."[26] (italics supplied)

Importance of the draftsman in interpretation emphasized

Lord Simon developed further the reference to the draftsman of the Act by observing that if regard was to be had to Parliament's understanding of the law as it existed when a later Act was enacted, the following considerations must be borne in mind. A testator making a will may not know the law — he may never have heard of the rule in *Gundry* v. *Pinniger*,[27] but few draftsmen of wills could be ignorant of the rule. Similarly, many M.P.s before 1969 did not know that the legal interpretation put on the word "child" was that it meant a "legitimate child", but the draftsman of a statute would know this rule, and a court of construction will conclude that the use of the word "child" was to carry into legal effect what Parliament had intended. Lord Simon added:

The effect of the current technique of a draft bill with commentary on interpretation explained

"But the technique of a draft Bill with commentary is so common nowadays in reports to Parliament as to excuse, I hope, some expatiation on the matter. The argument against recourse to such a commentary is that if what Parliament or parliamentarians (or, indeed, any promulgators of a written instrument) think is the meaning of what is said is irrelevant, so must be the opinion of any draftsman, including the draftsman of a Bill annexed to a report to Parliament. But . . . I find this less than conclusive. In essence, *drafting, enactment and interpretation are integral parts of the process* of translating the volition of the electorate into rules which will bind themselves. If it comes about that the declared meaning of a statutory provision is not what Parliament meant, the system is at fault. Sometimes the fault is merely a reflection of human fallibility. But where the fault arises from a technical refusal to consider relevant material, such refusal requires justification. The commentary on a draft Bill in a report to Parliament is not merely an expression of opinion — even if it were only that, it would be an expression of expert opinion, and I can see no more reason for excluding it than any other relevant matter of expert opinion. But actually it is more: that experts publicly expressed the view that a certain draft would have such-and-such an effect is

[26] ibid. pp. 645-46.

[27] (1851) 12 Beav. 94, (1852) 1 De G.M. & G. 502. "Next-of-kin *ex parte materna*: Under a gift to next-of-kin *ex parte materna*, next-of-kin *ex parte paterna*, who happen to be also next-of-kin *ex parte materna*, will not be excluded, except by express words": Theobald *on Wills*, 13th ed., para 1001.

one of the facts within the shared knowledge of Parliament and the citizenry. To refuse to consider such a commentary, when Parliament has legislated on the basis and faith of it, is for the interpreter to fail to put himself in the real position of the promulgator of the instrument before essaying its interpretation. It is refusing to follow what is perhaps the most important clue to meaning. It is perversely neglecting the reality, while chasing shadows. As Aneurin Bevan said: 'Why read the crystal when you can read the book?' Here the book is already open: it is merely a matter of reading on. *Certainly, a court of construction cannot be precluded from saying that what the committee thought as to the meaning of its draft was incorrect. But that is one thing: to dismiss, out of hand and for all purposes,* an authoritative opinion in the light of which Parliament has legislated is quite another. So, *as at present advised,* I think that your Lordships would have been entitled, if necessary to consider the commentary of the Greer committee on the draft Bill."[28] (italics supplied)

Submission: the views of Lords Dilhorne and Simon re. draft Bill enacted without change are correct

2.29 The *Black-Clawson Case* has been dealt with at some length because it brings together the recent trends in statutory interpretation. It is submitted that in respect of a draft Bill which, without change, is enacted into an Act by Parliament, the views of Lords Dilhorne and Simon are cogent, and ought to be preferred to those of Lords Reid, Wilberforce and Diplock. Lord Dilhorne has effectively answered the objection of Lord Reid that if the Report of the Committee and notes on clauses are to be admitted, the practice against references to *Hansard* for statutory interpretation would have to be abrogated. Lord Dilhorne rightly pointed out the great difference between the report of an expert committee with a draft Bill attached, which Bill is bodily enacted into an Act, and the speeches made by ministers and/or members in Parliament at different stages before the Bill becomes an Act. As to the observations of Lord Wilberforce that ". . . it would be a degradation of that process if courts were to be merely a reflecting mirror of what some interpreting agency may say," has rightly provoked the following comment from Prof. Cross:

"It would indeed. But, if a judge who is *ex hypothesi* in doubt about the meaning of a statutory provision, takes note of what its author thought it meant *it is a little tendencious to describe him as a 'reflecting mirror'.* He is not obliged to act on the author's meaning and there are famous instances in which French courts have not acted on the intentions revealed in the *travaux préperatoires* which they have consulted."[29] (italics supplied)

It need hardly be added that different considerations apply to a report made by a committee of experts if an Act is enacted which departs materially from the recommendations made in that report. However, such a report could be looked at to ascertain what the law was, or was understood to be, before the subsequent Act was enacted, and also for the mischief disclosed by the law which, according to the committee, required to be remedied.

The importance of conserving judicial and forensic time and saving of time and costs emphasized

2.30 Lords Reid, Dilhorne and Wilberforce referred, in passing, to the practical grounds for limiting the use of preparatory material in statutory interpretation, although as we have seen, Lord Reid set out the practical reasons fully in *Beswick* v. *Beswick*.[30] Lord Reid's observations in *Beswick* v. *Beswick* and Lord Simon's observations in the *Black-Clawson Case* show that the administration of justice does not take place in a vacuum, but in a human society. Conservation of judicial and forensic power, as also the saving of time and

---

[28] (1975) A.C. *supra* at pp. 651-52. [29] *Cross, op. cit.* p. 139.
[30] See para 2.23.

costs are important considerations if justice is to be done. It follows that too high a price is paid for doing justice if judges seek "light" from whatever source it can be got — no matter how flickering and uncertain the "light", or how delusive it might turn out to be. Lord Reid's and Lord Simon's analysis is helpful when we consider whether, and to what extent, proceedings in the Constituent Assembly can be used as aids to interpreting the provisions of our Constitution.

2.31 The question whether speeches in the Constituent Assembly can be used to interpret the provisions of our Constitution has been increasingly raised before our Supreme Court. It is submitted that Supreme Court decisions are not satisfactory, because the Supreme Court has not asked the right question. The right question to ask was not whether speeches in the Constituent Assembly are admissible as extrinsic aids to construction, but whether, any, and if so what, part or parts of the proceedings in the Constituent Assembly are admissible as extrinsic aids to construction. This requires a fresh approach to the question different from the one adopted by the Supreme Court, and in the earlier editions of this book.

Admissibility of speeches in the Const. Assembly as aids to interpretation: a fresh approach required

2.32 The proceedings of the Constituent Assembly ("the proceedings") fall, broadly speaking, into four classes: (i) the presentation of the draft Constitutions, because several drafts were presented to the Constituent Assembly; (ii) Considerations of amendments proposed to draft Articles or sub-Articles; (iii) Reports of the various Committees appointed by the Assembly; and (iv) Speeches made in the Constituent Assembly, particularly, the speeches made by its leading figures ("speeches").

Four categories of proceedings of the Const. Assembly

2.33 It is necessary to distinguish the proceedings in the first three classes [para 2.32 (i), (ii) and (iii)] from the fourth class, namely, speeches. This distinction has not generally been borne in mind in decided cases. For reasons given in paras 2.34 to 2.36, it is submitted that in certain situations, proceedings in the first three classes are admissible as extrinsic aids to construction; but that speeches are not.

Necessary to distinguish the speeches in Const. Assembly from remaining categories of its proceedings

2.34 As to the changes made in various draft Constitutions in the process of framing the Constitution [para 2.32 (i)], they can be of value as extrinsic aids to construction. For example, in the Draft Constitution of October 1947, Part III was entitled "Fundamental Rights including Directive Principles of State Policy."[31] This title would suggest that Directive Principles were included in Fundamental Rights. Chapters II and III of Part III dealt respectively with Fundamental Rights[32] and Directive Principles of State Policy.[33] However, in the draft Constitution of 21st February 1948, Part III was entitled "Fundamental Rights" and Part IV was entitled "Directive Principles of State Policy." In considering the nature and scope of Fundamental Rights *vis-a-vis* Directive Principles of State Policy, this change would lead to a reasonable inference that the framers of our Constitution realised the difference between Fundamental Rights and Directive Principles of State Policy by excluding the Directives from Fundamental Rights and placing them in a separate Part of the Constitution.

(i) Changes in various drafts of the Constitution

---

[31] Shiva Rao, *Framing of India's Constitution*, Vol. III, p. 7 *et seq.*
[32] ibid. p. 7.
[33] ibid. p. 12.

(ii) Report of the Drafting Committee

2.35 As to the Report of the Drafting Committee [para 2.32 (ii)], it has been said to possess a higher value than speeches made in the Constituent Assembly, and can be a helpful extrinsic aid to construction.[34] Thus the Report of the Drafting Committee substituting in Draft Art. 15 (now Art. 21) the words "procedure established by law" for the words "due process of law" on the ground that the substituted words were "more specific" showed, first, that the amendment sought to remove the mischief of the vague and indefinite concept of "due process" as evolved by the U.S. Supreme Court. Secondly, that the attention of the Assembly was called to two different expressions, and, finally, that the change was deliberate and not the result of inadvertence. These considerations would negative any construction which would equate "procedure established by law" with "due process" in the U.S.A.

Amendments moved in the Const. Assembly

2.36 As to amendments moved in the Constituent Assembly, [para 2.32 (iii)] the proposal of an amendment and its rejection by the Assembly might be helpful if a question arises whether a word was inadvertently omitted in an Article and ought to be supplied by the Court as required by the context or whether the omission was deliberate. For example, Art. 304(*b*) enables the State to put "reasonable" restrictions on the freedom of trade and commerce in the public interest, whereas Art. 302 enables Parliament to put "such restrictions" on the freedom of trade and commerce as may be required in the public interest. If a question arises whether the omission in Art. 302 of the word "reasonable" before the word "restrictions" was inadvertent, or was deliberate, the fact that an amendment which inserted the word "reasonable" before the word "restrictions" was rejected, leads to the inference that the omission was deliberate, and a different standard was to be applied to the restrictions imposed by Parliament, from those imposed by the State. In the above example, the rejection of the amendment was deliberately designed to make a distinction between the power conferred on the State Legislatures by Art. 304(b) and the power conferred on Parliament by Art. 302. However, the rejection of an amendment does not always lead to the conclusion that the change proposed was negatived; it may be that the amendment was considered unnecessary.[35]

Admissibility of speeches in Const. Assembly considered

2.37 As to speeches [para 2.32 (iv)], judicial decisions on the admissibility of speeches in the Constituent Assembly as extrinsic aids to construction, a clear distinction has not been made between the first three classes of proceedings on the one hand, and speeches on the other. It has been submitted in paras 2.34 to 2.36 above that in respect of the first three classes in para 2.32, in certain situations, they may afford help in interpreting the provisions of the Constitution where extrinsic aids to construction are required or admissible. However, speeches in the Constituent Assembly are in a very different category and there are authoritative pronouncements of the Supreme Court, giving cogent reasons against admitting speeches for interpreting any Article of the Constitution. We have seen that in the *Black-Clawson Case* all the five Law Lords were agreed that

[34] (1950) S.C.R. 88 at p. 111, 274.

[35] *Fundamental Rights Case* (1973) Supp. S.C.R. at pp. 303-4; ('73) A.SC. at p. 1617.

speeches in Parliament cannot be admitted for interpreting a statute. But before considering the decisions of the Supreme Court, it is necessary to refer to two judgments of the Federal Court on the admissibility of a Report made to the British Parliament which preceded the enactment of the G.I. Act, 35. The reference by Gwyer C.J. in the *Central Provinces Case*[36] to the White Paper (The Proposals for Indian Constitutional Reform) and the Report of the Joint Select Committee thereon was taken to mean that such references were permissible aids for ascertaining the meaning of the words used in the G.I. Act, 35. But, in *Suraj Narain Anand* v. *N. W. Frontier Province*[37] Gwyer C.J. said that it was necessary to remove the misapprehension caused by his reference to the White Paper. He said that he had referred to the White Paper and the Report upon it as "historical facts" and had emphasised in the same passage that a Court was only concerned with what Parliament had in fact said. It is submitted that Gwyer C.J.'s disclaimer does less than justice to his earlier judgment. He referred to the White Paper and the Report not as mere historical facts but to negative the contention that a tax on the sale of goods was limited only to a turnover tax. The whole point of the reference was that if Parliament had meant to confer on the Provincial Legislature the limited power of levying a turnover tax, that precise tax had been brought to its notice by the White Paper, and it would not have "deliberately used words which so effectively cloaked its real intention when it was so simple a matter to make that intention clear beyond any possibility of doubt."[38] Both the original reference and the subsequent disclaimer are correct, if rightly understood. The original reference was meant to negative a suggested meaning which sought to equate two expressions essentially different. The fact that Parliament did not use the words "tax on turnover" which was suggested in the White Paper reasonably leads to the inference that a tax on the sale of goods did not mean *only* a tax on turnover. This is so, first, because ordinarily, different words mean different things, and secondly, because a violently inept expression would not be used to describe ideas capable of being expressed in apt words ordinarily used for that purpose. Words in a Statute must be taken to be used correctly and exactly, and the onus on those who assert that they are used loosely or inexactly is a heavy one.[39] The subsequent disclaimer is correct because when a suggested meaning has been rejected by reference to legislative history, the task of ascertaining the real meaning from the words themselves still remains.

The Central Prov. Case and the White Paper on Indian reforms

Suraj Narain's Case

A criticism and suggested reconciliation

2.38 As to the decisions of our Supreme Court, in *Trav.-Cochin* v. *Bombay Company Ltd.*[40] the Supreme Court ruled that speeches made by the members of the Constituent Assembly in the course of the debates on the draft Constitution could not be used as aids for interpreting any article of the Constitution. Patanjali Sastri C.J., speaking for a Constitution Bench observed:

Trav.-Cochin v. Bombay Co. Ltd.: speeches in Const. Assembly not permissible aids to construction

---

[36] (1939) F.C.R. 18 at p. 46.
[37] (1941) F.C.R. 37, 41-42, ('42) A.FC. 3.
[38] (1939) F.C.R. at p. 47.
[39] *Halsbury*, Vol. 36 (3rd ed.) p. 393; *New Plymouth Borough Council* v. *Taranaki Electric Power Board* (1933) A.C. 680, 682 (P.C.).
[40] (1952) S.C.R. 1112, ('52) A.SC. 366.

". . . the use made by the learned Judges below of the speeches made by the members of the Constituent Assembly in the course of the debates on the draft Constitution is unwarranted. That this form of extrinsic aid to the interpretation of statutes is not admissible has been generally accepted in England, and the same rule has been observed in the construction of Indian Statutes — See *Administrator-General of Bengal* v. *Prem Nath Mallick*.[41] The reason behind the rule was explained by one of us in *Gopalan's Case*[42] thus: 'A speech made in the course of the debate on a bill could at best be indicative of the intent of the speaker, but it could not reflect the inarticulate mental process lying behind the majority vote which carried the Bill. Nor is it reasonable to assume that the minds of all those legislators were in accord.' Or, as it is more tersely put in an American case — 'Those who did not speak may not have agreed with those who did; and those who spoke might differ from each other.': *United States* v. *Trans-Missouri Freight Association*.[43]" [44]

Kesavananda v. Kerala submission for Kerala

2.39 It is not necessary to refer to judgments which have relied upon speeches made in the Constituent Assembly without considering the question whether they were admissible for interpreting the Constitution. However, this question was squarely raised in *Kesavananda* v. *Kerala*[45] ("*The Fundamental Rights Case*"). The speeches in the Constituent Assembly having been extensively referred to by both the Petitioners and some of the Respondents, a question arose whether they were admissible for interpreting the provisions of our Constitution. It was submitted for the State of Kerala that in three decisions of the Supreme Court, namely, *I. C. Golak Nath* v. *Punjab*,[46] *Madhav Rao* v. *Union*[47] ("*The Privy Purse Case*") and *Union* v. *H. S. Dhillon*[48] had altered the rule laid down in the *Trav.-Cochin Case*.

Submission rejected by 4 judges: *Trav.-Cochin Case* laid down correct law

2.40 Of the 13 Judges constituting the Bench in the *Fundamental Rights Case*, 6 Judges dealt with the law as laid down in the *Trav.-Cochin Case*. Sikri C.J.,[49] Hegde and Mukherjea JJ.[50] and Chandrachud J.[51] held that the three cases relied upon on behalf of the State of Kerala had not altered the law as laid down in the *Trav.-Cochin Case*. Reddy J. dealt with the question without express reference to the *Trav.-Cochin Case* and held that the debates in the Constituent Assembly could be looked at for interpreting Articles of the Constitution. But he failed to distinguish between the three classes of proceedings referred to in para 2.33 above and speeches referred to in the fourth class, so that he failed to isolate the question whether speeches of individual members in the Constituent Assembly can furnish any aid for interpreting the Constitution.[52] Mathew J. expressly referred to the *Trav.-Cochin Case* and the three cases which were said to have altered the rule of interpretation laid down in that case. He held that the rigid rule applied by the British Courts and adopted in the *Trav.-Cochin Case* for interpreting the Constitution should not be applied in its rigour to the interpretation of the Constitution because whatever was of probative value was not to be excluded in interpreting the Constitution.[53] It is submitted that if

---

41 (1895) 22 I.A. 107, 118 (P.C.).
42 (1950) S.C.R. 88, ('50) A.SC. 27.
43 (1897) 169 U.S. 290 at p. 318.
44 (1952) S.C.R. 1112 at p. 1121, ('52) A.SC. 366.
45 (1973) Supp. S.C.R. 1, ('73) A.SC. 1461.
46 (1967) 2 S.C.R. 762, ('67) A.SC. 1643.
47 (1971) 3 S.C.R. 9, ('71) A.SC. 530.
48 (1972) 2 S.C.R. 33, ('72) A.SC. 1061.
49 ('73) A.SC. *supra* at pp. 1515-6.
50 ibid. pp. 1633-4.
51 ibid. p. 2054.
52 ibid. pp. 1727-28.
53 ibid. pp. 1917-18.

these observations refer to the first three classes of proceedings referred to in para 2.33 above, his observations would not have been disputed by the other Judges, who held that speeches in the Constituent Assembly were not admissible as aids to interpreting the Constitution. But Mathew J. did not answer, *as no judge has been able to answer*, the crucial reasons for excluding speeches, namely, that the Article or sub-Articles may have been passed by other members of the Constituent Assembly for reasons very different from those given by the Speaker. Secondly, conflicting speeches on the same article may have been made by different members in the Constituent Assembly which would be difficult to reconcile. Finally, Mathew J. overlooked the cogent reasons which Lord Reid had given in 1968, and Lord Simon of Glaisdale in 1972 for limiting the use of preparatory work on practical grounds. These reasons apply with greater force to the Supreme Court of India which has a heavy load of work and whose time is wasted by going through the speeches of members in 12 volumes of the *Constituent Assembly Debates*.

Submission: criticism of 3 cases mentioned in para 2.39

2.41 It is submitted that in so far as Sikri C.J., Hegde and Mukherjee JJ. and Chandrachud J. held that speeches were not admissible extrinsic aids to the interpretation of our Constitution, their decision is correct. However, it is submitted that in the three cases mentioned in para 2.39 above, Judges referred to opinions of individual members of the Constituent Assembly which supported their view, and this use is quite unintelligible unless it was meant to fortify the conclusion, which, without it, might lack conviction. The words of Prof. de Smith, used by him in a different context, are applicable here, namely, that it is more profitable to concentrate on what the court has done than on what it has said.[54] It is submitted that the undernoted quotation from the judgment of 7 Judges pronounced by Shah J. in *Madhav Rao's Case*[55] clearly shows that the Judges read into Art. 291 (Privy Purses) the speech made by Sardar Vallabhbhai Patel as Home Minister.[56] It is submitted that there is nothing in the language of Art. 291, read with Art. 363, about any *quid pro quo*, and in fact the language is incapable of bearing any such meaning. The reason at times given for reference to speeches is that they are referred to as a matter of history. Apart from other objections to such use, the history resorted to by the Supreme Court is seldom the whole history. If history was to be referred to for throwing light upon the question whether the "right to privy purses" was justiciable or not, the most decisive piece of history was to be found not in the speech of Sardar Vallabhbhai Patel, but in the

[54] *de Smith*, 3rd ed., p. 77. [55] (1971) 3 S.C.R. 9, ('71) A.SC. 530.

[56] ('71) A.SC. at p. 570: "(Home Minister): 'The minimum which we would offer to them as *quid pro quo* for parting with their ruling powers was to guarantee to them privy purses and certain privileges on a reasonable and defined basis. The privy purse settlements are therefore in the nature of consideration for the surrender by the Rulers of all their ruling powers and also for the dissolution of the States as separate units'. (Shah J.): The Constituent Assembly resolved to honour, without reservation, the promises made to the Princes from time to time. Clauses in the draft Constitution relating to the obligation of the Union to pay the privy purses and recognition of certain rights, privileges and dignities till then enjoyed by the Princes, were intended to incorporate a just *quid pro quo* for surrender by them of their authority and powers and dissolution of their States."

speech of Shri T. T. Krishnamachari, which was the only speech made when the adoption of draft Art. 302A (the present Art. 291), and draft Art. 302AA (the present Art. 363) was moved, and passed. In that speech he made it clear that draft Art. 302A (Art. 291) was one of the Articles which was to be non-justiciable by any court. Mitter J. has set out the speech in full in his dissenting judgment.[57] It is unnecessary to pursue this criticism further since the Supreme Court has now authoritatively declared that speeches of members of Parliament or of Constituent Assembly are not permissible aids to construction.

Mysore v. Bidap

2.42 In *Mysore* v. *R. V. Bidap*[58] the question of the admissibility of debates in the Constituent Assembly as aids to interpretation arose under the following circumstances : One Bidap had been appointed a member of the Mysore Public Service Commission by the Governor of Mysore on March 20, 1967. While his term as a member was continuing, the Governor appointed him Chairman of the Commission with effect from February 15, 1969. The State took the view that his term of office for 6 years had to be reckoned from March 20, 1967, so that he ceased to be the Chairman on March 19, 1973. Bidap contended that his term as Chairman for 6 years would end, having regard to Arts. 316(3) and 319(*d*), on February 15, 1975, that is, 6 years after his appointment as Chairman. The High Court upheld his contention, and the State appealed to the Supreme Court.

Krishna Iyer J.: no concluded view on admissibility of speeches as aids to construction

2.43 Delivering the judgment of the Court,[59] Krishna Iyer J. referred to the judgment in the *Trav.-Cochin Case* and cited the passages from it which have been quoted in para 2.38 above. He did not refer to the *Fundamental Rights Case*[60] in which 4 out of 6 judges, who considered the question had held that the Supreme Court had not departed from the law laid down in the *Trav.-Cochin Case.*[61] The question turned on the interpretation of Arts. 316(3) and 319(*d*),[62] read with Art. 316(1A) which speaks of the *office* of a Chairman. Having referred to the *Trav.-Cochin Case*, Krishna Iyer J. referred to the view taken in the United States and in certain Western countries according to which debates in the legislature could be used as aids to interpreting the Constitution. It is not necessary to refer to this view because, having considered the speeches in the Constituent Assembly, he said:

"The law of statutory construction is a strategic branch of jurisprudence which must, it may be felt, respond to the great social changes *but a conclusive pronouncement on the particular point arising here need not detain us because nothing decisive as between the alternative interpretations flows from a reli-*

---

57 ibid. p. 592.

58 (1974) 1 S.C.R. 589, ('73) A.SC. 2555.

59 For himself, Ray C.J., Palekar, Chandrachud and Bhagwati JJ.

60 (1973) Supp. S.C.R. 1, ('73) A.SC. 1461.

61 See para 2.40 above.

62 *Art. 316.* * * * (3) A person who holds office as a member of a Public Service Commission shall, on the expiration of his term of office, be ineligible for reappointment to that office. *Art. 319.* * * * (d) a member other than the Chairman of a State Public Service Commission shall be eligible for appointment as the Chairman or any other member of the Union Public Service Commission or as the Chairman of that or any other State Public Service Commission, but not for any other employment either under the Government of India or under the Government of a State.

ance on the Constituent Assembly proceedings or the broad purposes of the statutory scheme."[63] (italics supplied)

There was some further reference to the debates to ascertain the object of the Articles under consideration, but it is submitted that the whole discussion was wholly unnecessary because Krishna Iyer J. held that Arts. 316(3), 316(1A) and 319(*d*) made a clear distinction between membership of the Commission and the office which a member may hold. A member who is appointed a Chairman cannot be said to be re-appointed because re-appointment postulates the identity of the office to which a person is to be re-appointed. Since a member who is appointed a Chairman did not hold *that* office before his appointment, he could not be said to be re-appointed. It is submitted that the discussion in Court about speeches in the Constituent Assembly was so much time wasted; and waste of time not only consumes judicial power in a Court which has a heavy work load, but also adds substantially to the cost of litigation, as has been pointed out by the House of Lords in the cases discussed in paras 2.23, 2.27 and 2.30 above. These practical considerations give an additional reason for not departing from the view taken by 4 judges in the *Fundamental Rights Case* that the law laid down in the *Trav.-Cochin Case* had not been altered, namely, that speeches in the legislature or in the Constituent Assembly are not permissible aids to interpretation.

Fagu Shaw v. W.B.: reliance on Bidap's Case; open to objections to that case

2.44 Bhagwati J., in a dissenting judgment in *Fagu Shaw* v. *W.B.*[64] relied on *Bidap's Case* (which we have considered above) and all the objections which have been pointed out against that case apply equally to the judgment of Bhagwati J. and need not be repeated here. Bhagwati J. extracted the following passage from Dr. Ambedkar's speech in the Constituent Assembly to support the view that a law providing for preventive detention must fix the maximum period. ". . . Thirdly, *in every case whether it is a case which is required to be placed before the judicial board or not, Parliament shall prescribe the maximum period of detention.* . . ."[65] It is submitted that this reference is unhelpful as is shown by the following questions and answers:

Dr. Ambedkar: ". . . Those who want that a maximum sentence may be fixed will please note the provision of cl.(4) where it has been definitely stated that in making such a law Parliament will also fix the maximum period."

Pandit Kunzru: "The word is 'may'."

Dr. Ambedkar: " 'May' is 'shall'."

Pandit Kunzru: "Parliament may or may not do that."

Dr. Ambedkar: "*That is true.* But if it does, it will fix the maximum".[66] (italics supplied)

It is unnecessary to multiply judgments which have referred to speeches in the Legislature or the Constituent Assembly. It is submitted that speeches in the Constituent Assembly are not permissible aids to the interpretation of our Constitution, for reasons fully set out in paras 2.23, 2.27 and 2.30 above.

---

[63] (1974) 1 S.C.R. *supra* at p. 594, ('73) A.SC. at p. 2558.
[64] (1975) 3 S.C.R. 365, ('74) A.SC. 613.
[65] ('74) A.SC. *supra* at p. 629. [66] *C.A.D.* Vol. 9, p. 1563.

Conflict between legislative powers: the doctrine of "pith and substance"

2.45 A distribution of legislative powers between the Union and the States in mutually exclusive lists at times gives rise to the question whether a law purporting to be made under one or more legislative entries in an authorised list is in fact legislation under one or more entries in the forbidden list. When such questions arose under ss. 91 and 92 of the B.N.A. Act, 1867, the Privy Council evolved the rule of pith and substance as a rule of interpretation for their solution. When similar questions arose under s. 100 of the G.I. Act, 35, in *Subrahmanyan Chettiar* v. *Muthuswami Goundan*[67] Gwyer C.J. observed that in enacting those provisions the British Parliament had the provisions of ss. 91 and 92 of the B.N.A. Act, 1867, as interpreted by the Judicial Committee, in mind, and the B.N.A. Act presented an exact analogy to the Indian Act even to the overriding provision of s. 100(1), G.I. Act, 35. Accordingly he held that the doctrine of pith and substance evolved by the Privy Council with reference to the Canadian Constitution can be applied under the G.I. Act, 35. This view was approved by the Privy Council, in *Prafulla Kumar Mukherjee* v. *Bank of Khulna*.[68] There, it was argued that though the doctrine of pith and substance may be applicable to Canada and Australia, in India the difficulty in dividing legislative powers had been foreseen. Accordingly, three and not two Lists had been prepared in order to cover the whole field with a definite priority attributed to the Lists, so that anything contained in List I was reserved for the Federal Legislature and however incidentally it may be touched upon in an Act of the Provincial Legislature that Act was *ultra vires* in whole or part as the case may be. The Privy Council rejected this argument observing that it was not possible to make so clean a cut between the powers of the various legislatures and that they were bound to overlap. Lord Porter observed:

The doctrine applied to G.I. Act, 35

> "As Sir Maurice Gywer C.J. said in *Subramanyam Chettiar Case*:[69] 'it must inevitably happen from time to time that legislation, though purporting to deal with a subject in one list, touches also on a subject in another list, and the different provisions of the enactment may be so closely inter-twined that blind observance to a strictly verbal interpretation would result in a large number of statutes being declared invalid because the legislature enacting them may appear to have legislated in a forbidden sphere. Hence the rule which has been evolved by the Judicial Committee, whereby the impugned statute is examined to ascertain its 'pith and substance,' or its 'true nature and character,' for the purpose of determining whether it is legislation with respect to matters in this list or in that.' Their Lordships agree that this passage correctly describes the grounds on which the rule is founded, and that it applies to Indian as well as to Dominion legislation."[70]

and to our Constitution

Prafulla Kumar Mukherjee's Case has been repeatedly approved by the Supreme Court as laying down the correct rule to be applied in resolving conflicts which arise from overlapping powers in mutually exclusive Lists.[71] It may be added as a corollary of the pith and substance rule that once it is found that in pith and substance an impugned Act is a law on a permitted field any incidental encroachment on a forbidden field does not affect the competence of the

---

[67] (1940) F.C.R. 188, ('41) A.FC. 47.

[68] (1947) 74 I.A. 23, 43, ('47) A.PC. 60.

[69] (1940) F.C.R. *supra* at p. 201.

[70] 74 I.A. at p. 43.

[71] *Bombay* v. *Narothamdas Jethabhai* (1951) S.C.R. 51, 64-5; 72-3; *Bombay* v. *F. N. Balsara* (1951) S.C.R. 682, ('51) A.SC. 318.

legislature to enact that Act.[72] A discussion of decided cases on the pith and substance rule will be found in the Chapter on the Legislative Power of the Union and the States,[73] but the rule may be illustrated by reference to the issues in *Subrahmanyan Chettiar's Case.*[74] The Madras Agriculturists Relief Act, 1938, contained provisions to scale down all debts secured or unsecured due from an agriculturist whether payable under a decree or order of a civil or revenue Court or otherwise with certain exceptions which are not material. The Act contained no reference to promissory notes or any form of negotiable instruments. The Federal Legislature had exclusive power to legislate with respect to cheques, bills of exchange, promissory notes and like instruments (List I, Entry 28), and the provisions of the Madras Act were in conflict with the existing law under Entry 28, namely, the Negotiable Instruments Act, 1881. It was, therefore, contended that the Madras Act was wholly void or, at any rate, was void in so far as it affected debts evidenced or secured by promissory notes or negotiable instruments. The Federal Court held that the Madras Act was not in pith and substance a law with respect to negotiable instruments or promissory notes. The fact that many, or even most, of the debts were in practice evidenced by negotiable instruments or promissory notes was an accidental circumstance which could not affect the question.[75]

Supremacy of Union over State law: Art. 254(1)

2.46 Either by an express provision, like s. 109 of the Commonwealth of Australia Act, or by judicial decisions as in the United States and Canada,[76] it is well settled that where a federal law conflicts with a State law on the same subject, the federal law must prevail. In India although an attempt was made to make the three Lists mutually exclusive, it became necessary to provide for the contingency of a conflict between the powers of the Union and the powers of the State. Accordingly, Art. 246(1) and (2), and Art. 254(1) provide that to the extent to which a State law is in conflict with or repugnant to a Union law, which Parliament is competent to enact, the Union law shall prevail and the State law shall be void to the extent of its repugnancy. Such a provision is necessary because "an absurd situation would result if two inconsistent laws, each of equal validity, could exist side by side within the same territory."[77] This general rule is subject to the qualification contained in Art. 254(2) to be considered presently. The rule as to the prevalence of the Union over the State law in case of conflict applies not only to Parliament's exclusive power to legislate in respect of matters in List I but applies equally to its power to legislate in respect of matters in List III, subject to Art. 254(2). However, an attempt must first be made to see whether a conflict can be avoided by construction. If such a reconciliation should prove impossible ". . . then, and only then, will the *non-obstante* clause operate and the federal power prevail; for the clause ought to be regarded as a last resource, a witness to the imperfections of human expression and the fallibility of legal draftsmanship."[78]

The exception contained in Art. 254(2)

Conflict between Union and State Law avoided

[72] (1951) S.C.R. *supra* at p. 72.
[73] See Volume II.
[74] (1940) F.C.R. 188.
[75] Ibid. p. 202.
[76] See *Gibbons* v. *Ogden* (1824) Wheat. 1, 210-11, 6 L. ed. 23, 73; *Att.-Gen. for Ontario* v. *Att.-Gen. for the Dominion* (1896) A.C. 348, 366-7.
[77] *Per* Gwyer C.J. in *Subrahmanyan Chettiar* v. *Muthuswami Goundan* (1940) F.C.R. *supra* at p. 200, ('41) A.FC. 47.
[78] *The C.P. and Berar Case* (1939) F.C.R. 18, 44, ('39) A.FC. 1.

Questions raised by Art. 254: (i) repugnancy; (ii) power to repeal

2.47 Here we must consider two questions, one raised by Art. 246(1) and (2) read with Art. 254(1), and the other by Art. 254(2). The first question is, "What is repugnancy?" The second question is whether the reference contained in Art. 254(2) to the power of Parliament to repeal a law made by a State in the concurrent field means that the State Legislatures cannot repeal an existing law on a subject falling within List III, or a law made by Parliament in the exercise of its concurrent legislative power. These questions are treated separately in the following paragraphs.

(i) repugnancy

2.48 In considering whether a State law is repugnant to a law made by Parliament, two questions arise : first, is the law made by Parliament a valid law? For, if it is not, no question of its repugnancy to a State law can arise. If however, it is a valid law, the question as to what constitutes repugnancy directly arises. The Supreme Court has considered the question of repugnancy in several cases and in *Deepchand* v. *U.P.*[79] the result of the authorities was thus stated by Subba Rao J.:

The test for determining repugnancy: *Deepchand's Case*

"Nicholas in his Australian Constitution, 2nd Edition, page 303, refers to three tests of inconsistency or repugnancy:

'(1) There may be inconsistency in the actual terms of the competing statutes; (2) Though there may be no direct conflict, a State law may be inoperative because the Commonwealth law, or the award of the Commonwealth Court, is intended to be a complete exhaustive code; and (3) Even in the absence of intention, a conflict may arise when both State and Commonwealth seek to exercise their powers over the same subject-matter.'

This Court in *Ch. Tika Ramji* v. *U.P.*[80] accepted the said three rules, among others, as useful guides to test the question of repugnancy. In *Zaverbhai Amaidas* v. *Bombay*[81] this Court laid down a similar test. At page 807, it is stated:

'The principle embodied in section 107(2) and Article 254(2) is that when there is legislation covering the same ground both by the Centre and by the Province, both of them being competent to enact the same, the law of the Centre should prevail over that of the State.'

Repugnancy between two statutes may thus be ascertained on the basis of the following three principles:

(1) Whether there is direct conflict between the two provisions;

(2) Whether Parliament intended to lay down an exhaustive code in respect of the subject-matter replacing the Act of the State Legislature; and

(3) Whether the law made by Parliament and the law made by the State Legislature occupy the same field."[82]

Tika Ramji's Case

It may be mentioned that Bhagwati J. in considering the test of repugnancy in *Tika Ramji's Case*[83] extracted the following passage from *Shyamakant Lal* v. *Rambhajan Singh*:[84]

"When the question is whether a Provincial legislation is repugnant to an existing Indian law, the onus of showing its repugnancy and the extent to which it is repugnant should be on the party attacking its validity. There ought to be a presumption in favour of its validity, and every effort should be made to reconcile them and construe both so as to avoid their being repugnant to each other; and care should be taken to see whether the two do not really operate in different fields without encroachment. *Further, repugnancy*

---

[79] (1959) Supp. 2 S.C.R. 8, ('59) A.SC. 648.
[80] (1956) S.C.R. 393, ('59) A.SC. 676.
[81] (1955) 1 S.C.R. 799, ('54) A.SC. 752.
[82] (1959) Supp. 2 S.C.R. *supra* at p. 43.
[83] (1956) S.C.R. *supra*.
[84] (1939) F.C.R. 193, 212, ('39) A.FC. 74.

must exist in fact, and not depend merely on a possibility. 'Their Lordships can discover no adequate grounds for holding that there exists repugnancy between the two laws in districts of the Province of Ontario where the prohibitions of the Canadian Act are not and may never be in force': *Att.-Gen. for Ontario* v. *Att.-Gen. for the Dominion*."[85]

2.49 The reference to *Att.-Gen. for Ontario* v. *Att.-Gen. for the Dominion* requires explanation. It is not an authority for the general proposition that there must be an actual and not a possible conflict. The conflict alleged in that case was between the prohibitions contained in the Canada Temperance Act, 1886, and s. 18 of the Ontario Act, 53, Vict. c. 56, called "an Act to approve the liquor licencing Acts" as explained by the Ontario Act, 54 Vic. c. 46, an "Act respecting local option in the matter of liquor selling." The Privy Council observed that the Canada Temperance Act was permissive; it could be brought into force in a district by the requisite number of votes cast by the electors, but it was open to them to reject the provisions of the second part in which case the option to bring those provisions into force was abolished for three years. Consequently, the Ontario Act and the Canada Temperance Act could never be in force at the same time, for if the option contained under the Canada Temperance Act was not exercised, the Canadian law would not be in force in the State of Ontario and no question of a conflict could arise. The case therefore only decided that where a law was not immediately applicable to the whole of Canada, but was contingently applicable in one or more district or districts of a State, there could be no conflict between the provisions of such a law and a State law on the subject as long as the contingency had not happened to bring the Canadian law into effect.[86] The Privy Council decision is not an authority against the proposition, accepted by Bhagwati J. himself, that if the Federal Legislature evinces an intention to cover the whole field, such an intention would not be defeated because a rule or order within the competence of the Federal Legislature was not in fact made. The passage extracted by Bhagwati J., and its application, was considered in *Orissa* v. *Tulloch & Co.*[87] where the Supreme Court said that the submission based on Bhagwati J.'s observations was without force, "besides being based on a misapprehension of the true legal position." The Supreme Court did not consider the Privy Council judgment on which Bhagwati J. had based his opinion, but merely affirmed the other principles, which Bhagwati J. had himself affirmed. However, the observations in *Tulloch's Case* are correct for reasons already given in explaining the Privy Council judgment. Strictly speaking, *Tulloch's Case* raised no questions of repugnancy, but only of power. The question there was whether a State law under entry 23, List II, namely, the Orissa Mining Areas Development Fund Act, 1952, which provided for the recovery of certain fees, remained in operation after Parliament had enacted the Mines and Mineral Regulation and Development Act, 1954, under entry 54, List I. As

A.-G. for *Ontario* v. *A.-G. for the Dominion*

Tulloch's Case: repugnancy

Strictly that case raised only a question of power

[85] (1896) A.C. 348, 369-70.

[86] The above view of *A.-G. for Ontario* v. *A.-G. for the Dominion* was taken by the Supreme Court in *Municipal Council, Palai* v. *T. J. Joseph* ('63) A.SC. 1561, 1566, and the case was distinguished on that ground from the case before the court. *Joseph's Case* was fol. in *T. S. Agarwal* v. *Jt. Registrar Co-op. Societies* ('71) A.M.P. 86, 87 (1971) M.P.L.J. 110 [*held*, that s. 67(2), Co-operative Societies Act, 1960, was not void under Art. 254 on the ground of s. 30, Advocates Act, since s. 30 had not been brought into force.]

[87] ('64) A.SC. 1284 at p. 1291.

the power of the State Legislature under entry 23, List II, is made expressly subject to a law made under entry 54, List I, once the Union law evinced an intention to occupy the whole field, the State Legislature lost its power to enact such a law, so that the State lacked executive authority to collect the fees in respect of mines and minerals which were *thereafter* to be recovered under the law made by Parliament.[88] The question therefore was one of lack of legislative power, and consequently of executive authority to recover the fees. The real controversy was whether in enacting the Mines and Minerals Regulation and Development Act, 1957, Parliament had evinced an intention to cover the whole field of regulating mines and minerals; for if it had, the power of the State Legislature to legislate at all was excluded; if it had not, but had evinced an intention to regulate mines and minerals only to a limited extent, the power of the State Legislature would have continued in respect of regulation of mines and minerals not covered by the Central Law. On a plain reading of the Act, the Supreme Court rightly held that the Central Act had evinced an intention to cover the total field and therefore the State Legislature lacked legislative competence and executive authority in respect of mines and minerals or of any fees charged in respect of mining and mineral rights *from the time* the Central Act came into force.

Obiter in *Zaverbhai's Case* about power to repeal a State law under List III

2.50 The second question turns on a comparison of the terms of s. 107(2) of the G.I. Act, 35, with those of Art. 254(2) to which we have adverted above. In *Zaverbhai Amaidas* v. *Bombay*[89] Venkatarama Ayyar J. observed:

". . . in a situation similar to that under s. 107(2) of the Government of India Act, it was observed by Lord Watson in *Att.-Gen. for Ontario* v. *Att.-Gen. for the Dominion* (1896) A.C. 348, that though a law enacted by the Parliament of Canada and within its competence would override Provincial legislation covering the same field, the Dominion Parliament had no authority conferred upon it under the Constitution to enact a statute repealing directly any Provincial statute. That would appear to have been under s. 107(2) . . . with reference to the subjects mentioned in the Concurrent List. Now, by the Proviso to Art, 254(2) the Constitution has enlarged the powers of Parliament, and under that proviso, Parliament can do what the Central Legislature could not under s. 107(2) . . . and enact a law adding to, amending, varying or repealing a law of State, when it relates to a matter mentioned in the Concurrent List."

Obiter not followed in *Zoolfiqar Ali's Case* by Tarkunde J.

In *Official Trustee* v. *Zoolfiqar Ali*[91] it was urged that these observations showed that in the concurrent field State legislatures could not repeal a law made by Parliament or an existing law since, unlike Parliament, they lacked an express power to repeal. Tarkunde J. held that the observations were neither the *ratio decidendi* of the case,

---

[88] In *Tulloch's Case*, the Court cited the observations of Gajendragadkar J. in the *Hingir-Rampur Coal Co. Case* (1961) 2 S.C.R. 537, 557 ". . . if a Central Act had been passed which contains a declaration by Parliament as required by Entry 54, and if the said declaration covers the field occupied by the impugned Act the impugned Act would be *ultra vires*, not because of any repugnance between the two statutes, but because the State Legislature had no jurisdiction to pass the law. The limitation imposed by the latter part of Entry 23 is a limitation on the legislative competence of the State Legislature itself."

[89] (1955) 1 S.C.R. 799, ('54) A.SC. 752.

[90] ibid. at p. 806.

[91] *Official Trustee* v. *Zoolfiqar Ali*, reported *sub-nom.* on appeal in *Zoolfiqar Ali* v. *Official Trustee*, 69 Bom.L.R. 326, 335.

nor even considered *obiter dicta,* but were mere casual observations entitled to respect, but not binding on a court. He said that, even so, he would have given effect to them but for the reasons he gave in his judgment.[92]

2.51 On appeal, the appeal court agreed with Tarkunde J.'s view that the observations of Venkatarama Aiyar J. in *Zaverbhai's Case* were casual observations not binding on a court.[93] The appeal court upheld Tarkunde J.'s finding that the State legislature had power to repeal a law on matters in the concurrent list. After referring to s. 292 of the G.I. Act, 35, as also to the corresponding provisions of Art. 372, the court held that power to repeal was a part of legislative power and it was not necessary to confer that power separately.[94] This view was further supported by the consideration that a power to legislate includes the power to vary or amend, and every such variation or amendment is a *pro tanto* repeal of the existing provisions.[95] The court also held that the proviso to Art. 254(2)[96] did not confer a power to repeal. It was in negative terms, and assumed that Parliament possessed legislative power but stated *ex majore cautela* that nothing in Art. 254(2) was to affect that power.

Obiter not followed by the Appellate Court

2.52 Article 248 departs from the scheme of the G.I. Act, 35, and allocates residuary powers of legislation to Parliament. But as the legislative Lists run into great detail and were designed to exhaust all topics of legislation, the occasion for resorting to the "residuary" Article would be limited. However, there are not the same compelling reasons under our Constitution to treat Article 248 as the very last resort, as there were in the G.I. Act, 35[97] for under that Act if it was found that a particular matter did not fall within the three Lists of Sch. 7 no legislature in India was competent to legislate on it *until* the Governor-General issued a notification under s. 104 empowering either the Federal or the Provincial legislature to enact a law with respect to such matter.

Art. 248: residuary power of legislation conferred on Parliament

2.53 In *M. Karunanidhi* v. *Union*[98] Fazal Ali J. reviewed the authorities on "repugnancy" under Art. 254[99] and held that the following propositions emerged from decided cases:

Authorities on repugnancy reviewed

"1. That in order to decide the question of repugnancy it must be shown that the two enactments contain inconsistent and irreconcilable provisions, so that they cannot stand together or operate in the same field.

---

[92] ibid. pp. 335-342.
[93] *Zoolfiqar Ali* v. *Official Trustee,* 69 Bom.L.R. 326.
[94] ibid. p. 368. [95] ibid. p. 372.
[96] "Nothing in this clause shall prevent Parliament from enacting at any time any law with respect to the same matter including a law adding to, amending, varying or repealing the law so made by the legislature of the State."
[97] "But resort to that residual power should be the very last refuge. It is only when all the categories in the three Lists are absolutely exhausted that one can think of falling back upon a *nondescript." Per* Sulaiman J. in *Subrahmaniyan Chettiar* v. *Muthuswami Goundan* (1940) F.C.R. 188, 212, ('41) A.FC. 47.
[98] (1979) 3 S.C.R. 254, ('79) A.SC. 898.
[99] *Hume* v. *Palmer* 38 C.L.R. 441; *Ex p. McLean* 43 C.L.R. 472; *Zaverbhai Amaidas* v. *Bombay* (1955) 1 S.C.R. 799, ('54) A.SC. 752; *Tika Ramji* v. *U.P.* (1956) S.C.R. 393, ('56) A.SC. 676; *Om Prakash Gupta* v. *U.P.* (1957) S.C.R. 423, ('57) A.SC. 458; *Deep Chand* v. *U.P.* (1959) 2 Supp. S.C.R. 8, ('59) A.SC. 648; *Orissa* v. *M. A. Tulloch & Co.* (1964) 4 S.C.R. 461, ('64) A.SC. 1284; *T. S. Baliah* v. *T. S. Rangachari* (1969) 3 S.C.R. 65, ('69) A.SC. 701.

2. That there can be no repeal by implication unless the inconsistency appears on the face of the two statutes.

3. That where the two statutes occupy a particular field, but there is room or possibility of both the statutes operating in the same field without coming into collision with each other, no repugnancy results.

4. That where there is no inconsistency but a statute occupying the same field seeks to create distinct and separate offences, no question of repugnancy arises and both the statutes continue to operate in the same field."[1]

Applying these principles, Fazal Ali J. held that there was no repugnancy between the provisions of Tamil Nadu Public Men (Criminal Misconduct) Act and the Indian Penal Code or the Prevention of Corruption Act. The substituted s. 29 of the Tamil Nadu Act was decisive, for it provided that "the provisions of the Act shall be in addition to and not in derogation of, any other law for the time being in force, and nothing contained herein shall exempt any public man from any proceeding by way of investigation or otherwise which might, apart from this Act, be instituted against him."[2]

Principle of "harmonious construction"

2.54 If there is an apparent or real conflict between two provisions of the Constitution, how is that conflict to be resolved? The problem thus raised is not peculiar to the interpretation of a Constitution but is common to the interpretation of all statutes. The principles for resolving such a conflict are well known and are to be found in standard books on statutory construction, but the Supreme Court of India has compendiously described them as "the principle of harmonious construction." The name is a little unfortunate, for it might suggest that it is the function of the Court somehow to produce harmony between various provisions of a statute. But the principle underlying the rule of harmonious construction is itself correct if certain relevant considerations are borne in mind. That principle does not require a Court first to produce disharmony by construction in order to resolve it thereafter by harmonious construction. For, as the Judges said in the House of Lords in *Warburton* v. *Loveland*,[3]

conflict must be avoided, if possible, by construction

"No rule of construction can require that when the words of one part of a statute convey a clear meaning . . . it shall be necessary to introduce another part of a Statute which speaks with less perspicuity and of which the words may be capable of such construction as by possibility to diminish the efficacy of the first part."[4]

This passage was cited and applied by Barton J. in construing the provisions of ss. 89, 92 and 93 of the Australian Constitution. He said:

"Applying those expressions to these sections I should say they amount to this: Seeing that sec. 89 has an absolutely clear meaning, the rules of construction do not require us to introduce another part of the Statute which speaks with less perspicuity, and to apply that part to the construction of sec. 89. That would have the effect of diminishing the clearness of sec. 89, and appears to me to be an absolute inversion of the rule which is applicable in such a case. *Hardcastle*, in his work on the Interpretation of Statutes (3rd ed.)

---

[1] ('79) A.SC. at p. 910.

[2] In view of the substituted s. 29, it is submitted that a discussion of the authorities on "repugnancy" was hardly necessary.

[3] (1832) 2 D. & Cl. 480, 500, 5 E.R. 499.

[4] See Craies on *Statute Law*, 6th ed., p. 99; the quotation from *Warburton* v. *Loveland* given in Craies is not correct. The above passage was quoted with approval by Palekar J. in *Kesavananda* v. *Kerala* ('73) A.SC. 1461, 1811, and has been quoted with approval by Ray C.J. delivering the unanimous Opinion of seven judges in *In Re Presidential Election 1974*, (1974) 2 S.C.C. 33, 54, (1975) 1 S.C.R. 504.

p. 111, says: 'It is only when, as the Court said in *Palmer's Case* (1784) 1 Leach., 355, any part of an Act of Parliament is penned obscurely, and other passages can elucidate that obscurity, recourse ought to be had to such context for that purpose'."[5]

Secondly, the conflict between two provisions may be merely apparent as when their objects or subjects are different:

"... It is sometimes found that the conflict of two statutes is apparent only, as their objects are different and the language of each is restricted, ... to its own object or subject. When their language is so confined, they run in parallel lines, without meeting."[6] Again, "... distinct provisions of the Constitution are repugnant to each other in such a way as to be irreconcilable only when they are related to the same subject or adopted for the same purpose and cannot be enforced without material and substantial conflict."[7]

The conflict may be only apparent

2.55 If, however, the conflict is not apparent but is real, the principle of harmonious construction comes into play. That principle was clearly enunciated by Venkatarama Aiyar J. in *Sri Venkataramana Devaru* v. *Mysore*[8] and may be stated thus: When there are in an enactment two provisions which cannot be reconciled with each other, they should be so interpreted that, if possible, effect can be given to both. It follows from this that a construction which would render one provision wholly nugatory must be rejected in favour of a construction which gives effect to both provisions. Applying the principle, it was held that the right conferred by Art. 26(*b*) on every religious denomination to manage its own affairs in matters of religion did not include the right to prohibit any class or section of Hindus from entering a public temple because Art. 25(2)(*b*) expressly saved existing or future laws providing for throwing open public temples to all classes and sections of Hindus. Art. 26(*b*) had to be narrowly construed if Art. 25(2)(*b*) was not to be rendered nugatory. The important thing to note is that the principle of harmonious construction is misapplied if it leads to one of the two provisions being rendered nugatory, for that is the very result which the rule is designed to avoid. The misapplication of this principle in the minority judgment in *Sharma's Case*,[9] in the majority judgment in *K. M. Nanavati* v. *Bombay*[10] and in the majority Opinion in *President's Reference No. 1 of 1964* will be considered when dealing with those cases.[11] But the real nature of the principle of harmonious construction has been best brought out by Sarkar J. in his dissenting Opinion in the *President's Reference No. 1 of 1964*, in his analysis of the application of that principle in *M.S.M. Sharma* v. *Sri Krishna Sinha*.[12] His reasoning may be stated thus: Art. 19(1)(*a*) and Art. 194(3) do not *prima facie* conflict. But when the privileges of the British House of Commons are read into Art. 194(3), one of those privileges is the privilege of a House of the Legislature to prohibit publication of any of its proceedings. When so read, there is a conflict with Art. 19(1)(*a*) which refers to the freedom of speech and expression which includes the freedom of publication. If Art. 19(1)(*a*) were given full effect

If conflict is real, effect should be given to *both* provisions as far as possible

The principle of harmonious construction best explained by Sarkar J.

[5] *Tasmania* v. *Commonwealth of Australia* (1904) 1 C.L.R. 329 at 357.
[6] Maxwell, *Interpretation of Statutes*, 11th ed. pp. 162-3.
[7] *American Jurisprudence*, 2nd ed., Vol. 16, p. 247.
[8] (1958) S.C.R. 895 at p. 918.
[9] (1959) Supp. (1) S.C.R. 806, ('59) A.SC. 395.
[10] (1961) 1 S.C.R. 497, ('61) A.SC. 112.
[11] See Volume II.
[12] (1959) Supp. (1) S.C.R. *supra*.

the privilege of the House to prohibit publication would be completely destroyed. Therefore, Art. 19(1)(*a*) has to be so interpreted as to exclude from its ambit the privilege of a House of the Legislature to prohibit publication of its proceedings. To say, as Subba Rao J. said in his dissenting judgment in *Sharma's Case*,[13] that Art. 19(1)(*a*) prevailed over Art. 194(3) would be not to harmonise the two provisions but to wipe out that part of Art. 194(3) which conferred on the Legislature the privilege to prohibit publication of its proceedings. It is not an answer to say, as Subba Rao J. said, that if the privilege of the Legislature to prohibit publication of its proceedings was wiped out, other privileges still remained, as for example, the right to exclude strangers from the precincts of the Legislature, for there was never any conflict between freedom of speech and expression and the right to exclude strangers from the precincts of the Legislature. Sarkar J. summed up the position by saying: "We are concerned with harmonising two conflicting provisions by giving both the best effect possible and that is not done by cutting the gordian knot by removing the conflicting part out of the statute." It is clear from what has been said above, that in a large number of cases the principle of harmonious construction merely applies the rule that where there is a general provision of the law dealing with a subject, and a special provision dealing with the same subject, the special prevails over the general. The privileges of the Legislature to prohibit publication was a special provision which impinged on the general provision which guaranteed the freedom of speech and expression. The special provision therefore prevailed over the general for otherwise it would be wholly defeated. We have seen that an analogous principle was applied in the *Central Provinces Case*[14] where it was said that though the words "duties of excise" were capable of including a tax on the first or subsequent sale of goods, that meaning could not be given in view of the fact that the power to levy a tax on the sale of goods, conferred on the provincial Legislature, would have been wholly destroyed if duties of excise were given that wide meaning.

Decisions of other Courts to be used with caution

2.56 The decisions on the Canadian, Australian and the U.S. Constitutions must be used with great caution when the object is to ascertain the meaning of words used to confer federal and provincial powers,

> "for in the last analysis the decision must depend upon the words of the Constitution which the Court is interpreting and since no two Constitutions are in identical terms, it is extremely unsafe to assume that a decision on one of them can be applied without qualification to another. This may be so even where the words or expressions used are the same in both cases, for a word or phrase may take a colour from its context and bear different senses accordingly."[15]

Thus, the decisions on the meaning given to the expression "duties of excise" in the Canadian, Australian and U.S. Constitutions were not found helpful in determining its meaning in the G.I. Act, 35, because in none of those Constitutions was the power to levy duties of excise found set in opposition to an express power to levy a tax

---

[13] ibid. p. 881.
[14] (1939) F.C.R. 18, *supra*.
[15] *The Central Provinces Case* (1939) F.C.R. 18, 38, ('39) A.FC. 1.

on the sale of goods such as was found in the G.I. Act.[16] Similarly, the wide meaning given by Marshall C.J. in *Brown* v. *Maryland*[17] to the word "import" was held inapplicable to the word "import" in entry 19, List, I, Sch. VII, of the G.I. Act, 35, because in the U.S. Constitution the widest meaning could be given to the Commerce Clause as it was not necessary to reconcile that clause with any other clause conferring legislative power on the States. In Entry 19, List I, the word "import" had to be given a limited meaning in order to give effect to the very general words of Entry 31 of List II.[18]

2.57 The resemblance between ss. 91 and 92 of the B.N.A. Act, 1867 and s. 100(1) and (3) of the G.I. Act, 35, was rightly emphasised by Gwyer C.J. as we have already seen.[19] Since Art. 246 in substance reproduces s. 100 the observations of Gwyer C.J. on s. 100 apply equally to Art. 246.

Applicability of Canadian decisions

2.58 Australian decisions require to be used with great caution because the scheme for the distribution of legislative powers in the two Constitutions is very different. The Federal Government in Australia is a Government of enumerated powers, most of which are not exclusive, the residuary power remaining with the States. In our Constitution mutually exclusive powers of legislation are conferred on the Union and the States, in Legislative Lists I and II, the residuary power remaining with the Union. Australian decisions have been relied upon in interpreting Part XIII of the Constitution because of the apparent similarity of Art. 301 to s. 92 of the Australian Constitution. But this subject has been considered in detail in a later Chapter.[20]

Australian decisions: Distribution of legislative power very different in our Constitution

2.59 In the early days of the Australian Constitution, considerable reliance was placed on the U.S. decisions. In the *Engineers' Case*[21] this trend was reversed, and it was held that American authorities, however, illustrious the tribunal may be, were not a secure basis on which to build fundamentally with respect to the Australian Constitution. This is because the difference between the two Constitutions is fundamental, namely, that the Australian Constitution is based on responsible government, a government under which the executive is directly responsible to and is almost the creature of the Legislature, and the U.S. Constitution is not. Since our Constitution (like that of Australia), is based on the principle of responsible government the observations of Issacs J. in the *Engineer's Case* apply to it directly, but with the qualifications which will presently appear.

U.S. decisions not a secure basis for interpreting the Australian Constitution

2.60 Though our Constitution resembles the Australian Constitution as far as responsible government is concerned, it differs from the Australian and resembles the U.S. Constitution in two respects. First, the Australian Constitution owes its efficacy to an Act of the British Parliament. But according to the preamble to the Constitutions of the U.S. and India, they have been given by the people to themselves. This aspect of the preamble to the U.S. Constitution is given positive

nor our Constitution

---

[16] (1939) F.C.R. *supra* at p. 43.
[17] (1827) 12 Wheat. 419, 6 L. ed. 678.
[18] *Bombay* v. *F. N. Balsara* (1951) S.C.R. 682, 700, ('51) A.SC. 318.
[19] *Subrahmanyan Chettiar's Case* (1940) F.C.R. 188, *supra*. See para 2.45.
[20] See Vol. II: Trade, Commerce and Intercourse within the Territory of India.
[21] (1920) 28 C.L.R. 129, *per* Issacs J.

content by the 10th Amendment which provides that the powers not delegated to the United States by the Constitution nor reserved to the States are reserved to the people. There is no such provision in our Constitution; in fact it has been the settled law in India since *Burah's Case*[22] that the legislatures in India are in no sense delegates in the exercise of their powers.[23] It is submitted that this part of the preamble has a sentimental and not a legal effect in India. No rights are reserved to the people and the Constitution can be, and has been, amended without any reference to them. Secondly, unlike the Australian Constitution but like the U.S. Constitution our Constitution has included a Bill of Rights in the Constitution itself. This feature of our Constitution raised novel problems of interpretation, since no Constitution enacted by the British Parliament till then had contained any such Bill of Rights. Therefore it is not surprising that judges and lawyers should have turned for guidance to the U.S. Supreme Court which had faced such problems and had suggested from time to time the lines of their solution.

A critical appraisal of U.S. decisions discloses important difference between the U.S. and the Indian Constitution

2.61 But the first uncritical enthusiasm for American decisions gradually wore off as the differences, no less than the resemblances, between the United States and our Constitution became increasingly clear. The following are the most important of those differences:

(a) *Gopalan's Case*[24] established that in using the words "according to procedure established by law" in Art. 21 instead of the words "according to the due process of law" our Constitution had deliberately abstained from adopting the due process clause of the 5th and 14th amendments to the U.S. Constitution.

(b) A separation of legislative, executive and judicial powers is an essential feature of the U.S. Constitution. Our Constitution does not recognise such a separation, though these powers are separately dealt with in the Constitution.[25]

(c) The fundamental rights granted by the U.S. Constitution are expressed in wide general terms with the result that the restrictions on those rights have had to be evolved by judicial decisions. Generally speaking, the limitations, subject to which fundamental rights are given in our Constitution, are defined in the Constitution itself with the result that the nature of those restrictions must be ascertained from the words of the Constitution.[26] Art. 14 is an important exception, and American authorities have been relied upon most heavily in interpreting that Article.

American decisions most helpful on Art. 14

2.62 While the distinguishing features of our Constitution make it necessary to use American decisions with caution, they have been drawn upon freely in ascertaining the content of fundamental rights as opposed to the restrictions to which they are subject. Thus the right to the protection of equal laws (Art. 14) has been given a content by practically taking over the theory of classification developed by the U.S. Supreme Court. Similarly, in considering the scope and extent of the rights conferred by Art. 19, particularly the freedom of

---

[22] (1878), 5 I.A. 178, (1878) 3 App. Cas. 889.

[23] An implication has been drawn from the fact that the people have given the Constitution to themselves: *per* Patanjali Sastri J. in *Gopalan's Case* (1950) S.C.R. 88, 198, ('50) A.SC. 27. However, his own view in *In re The Delhi Laws Act, 1912*, (1951) S.C.R. 747, 883-84, ('51) A.SC. 332 shows that his earlier view was mistaken.

[24] (1950) S.C.R. 88, ('50) A.SC. 27.

[25] *In re The Delhi Laws Act, 1912* (1951) S.C.R. 747, 831 (*per* Fazal Ali J.); 883 (*per* Patanjali Sastri J.) 965 (*per* Mukherjea J.); 1067 (*per* Das J.).

[26] See *Gopalan's Case* (1950) S.C.R. *supra* at pp. 108-9.

speech and expression, and the freedom of association, it has been held by our Supreme Court that the U.S. decisions may furnish helpful guidance[27] but this view is open to question.[28]

The danger of importing American doctrines into our Constitution

2.63 If American decisions require to be used with caution, doctrines evolved by the U.S. Supreme Court in the context of the U.S. Constitution require to be scrutinised even more carefully before introducing them into our Constitution. As will appear hereafter, our Constitution has deliberately rejected the due process clause of the U.S. Constitution[29] with the result that it is not necessary in India to evolve a doctrine of police power in order to mitigate the rigour of the due process clause. Again, the distribution of legislative power between the Union and the States in two detailed and mutually exclusive Lists, with a detailed concurrent List, and the inclusion in the Part on fundamental rights of the limitations to which the rights are subject, leave no room for reading into our Constitution the theories evolved in the context of the U.S. Constitution. Words like "police power" and "power of eminent domain" were freely used in the earlier judgments of our Supreme Court and they have been employed even for interpreting the words of Arts. 19 and 31. Different constructions have been put on Art. 31 according as it was held to embody the power of eminent domain or to embody police power as well.[30]

"Police power", "eminent domain"

2.64 Having regard to the principles laid down by the Privy Council for construing a written Constitution, principles approved and applied by our Supreme Court, it is impermissible to inquire whether Art. 31 embodies the doctrine of police power or power of eminent domain or both, and still more impermissible to consider the content of police power or the power of eminent domain in the United States and assume that the framers of our Constitution intended to embody those doctrines in our Constitution. In the country of their origin, both the due process clause and the doctrine of police powers have been held to be vague and indeterminate concepts fluctuating with the views of individual Judges constituting the U.S. Supreme Court at any time.[31] It is submitted that Bose J. laid down the correct principle for interpreting our Constitution when he said:

Objections to their introduction into our Constitution

". . . I deprecate, . . . the use of doubtful words like 'police power', 'social control', 'eminent domain' and the like. I say doubtful, not because they are devoid of meaning but because they have different shades of meaning in different countries and because they represent powers which spring from widely differing sources. In my opinion, it is wrong to assume that these powers are inherent in the State in India and then to say how far the Constitution regulates and fits in with them. We have to interpret the plain provisions of the Constitution and it is for jurists and students of law, not for judges, to see whether our Constitution also provides for these powers and it is for them to determine whether the shape which they take in India resemble any of the varying forms which they assume in other countries."[32]

---

[27] *Express Newspapers (Private) Ltd.* v. *Union of India* (1959) S.C.R. 12, 121, ('58) A.SC. 578.

[28] See Chapter X.

[29] See Appendix III.

[30] See the conflicting views expressed by Mahajan and Das JJ. in *Dwarakadas Shrinivas* v. *Sholapur Spg. & Wvg. Co.* (1954) S.C.R. 674, ('54) A.SC. 119.

[31] An elaborate discussion of this topic will be found in *Gopalan's Case* (1950) S.C.R. 88, ('50) A.SC. 27.

[32] *Sholapur Mills Case* (1954) S.C.R. *supra* at pp. 731-2.

The decisions of the Privy Council before Jan. 26, 1950

2.65 The Privy Council was the final appellate tribunal for the British Dominions, Colonies and Protectorates, and s. 212 of the G.I. Act, 35, made the law declared by the Federal Court and by any jûdgment of the Privy Council to be binding on all Courts in British India. Since an appeal lay from the judgments of the Federal Court to the Privy Council, the law declared by the Privy Council prevailed over the law declared by the Federal Court. Appeals to the Privy Council were abolished by the Abolition of Privy Council Jurisdiction Act, 1949, and the question has arisen whether decisions of the Privy Council rendered before the Constitution came into force on January 26, 1950, are binding on the courts in India. The correct view appears to be that unless overruled, expressly or impliedly, by the Supreme Court they are binding on all courts in India, but are not binding on the Supreme Court.[33] Accordingly, the decisions of the Privy Council on the G.I. Act, 35, including those on the principles of interpretation of that Act, would apply to the interpretation of the corresponding provisions of the Constitution unless the Supreme Court takes a different view. However, broadly speaking, the Supreme Court has approved and applied those principles to our Constitution.

binding on all courts, except the Sup. Ct. unless overruled by the Sup. Ct.

Construction of express power *vis-a-vis* residuary power

2.66 In *Madras* v. *Boddu Paidanna & Sons*[34] Gwyer C.J. observed:

"It is natural enough, when considering the ambit of an express power in relation to an unspecified residuary power, to give a broad interpretation to the former at the expense of the latter; and this indeed is the principle upon which the Judicial Committee have for the most part interpreted ss. 91 and 92 of the British North America Act. The case however is different where, as in the Indian Act, there are two complementary powers, each expressed in precise and definite terms. There can be no reason in such a case for giving a broader interpretation to one power rather than to the other."[35]

In applying this principle to our Constitution, it must be remembered that though the G.I. Act, 35, did not confer the residuary power of legislation on either the Federal or the Provincial Legislature, our Constitution has conferred residuary powers of legislation on Parliament by Art. 248 and entry 97, List I.

Aswini Kumar Ghosh's Case

2.67 It is well settled that the proceedings of Indian Legislatures are not legitimate aids to the construction of Indian Statutes for the same reasons for which they are excluded from consideration in the construction of Statutes passed by the British legislatures[36] and that no statement made on the introduction of the measure or its discussion can be looked at as affording any guidance as to the meaning of the words.[37] In *Aswini Kumar Ghosh* v. *Arabinda Bose*[38] the Supreme Court took the same view and held that the Statement of

---

[33] This question has been dealt with at length in the Chapter on the Union Judiciary.

[34] (1942) F.C.R. 90, 105.

[35] ibid. Cited with approval in *Ram Krishna Ramnath Agarwal of Kamptee* v. *Secretary, Municipal Committee* (1950) S.C.R. 15, 22, ('50) A.SC. 10, foll. in *Servants of India Society* v. *Charity Commissioner* (1961) Bom. 381, ('62) A.B. 12, 15, 63 Bom. L.R. 379.

[36] *Adm.-Gen. of Bengal* v. *Prem Lal Mullick* (1895) 22 I.A. 107, 118, 22 Cal. 788.

[37] *Krishna Ayyangar* v. *Nallaperumal Pillai* (1919) 47 I.A. 33, 42, 22 Bom.L.R. 568.

[38] (1953) S.C.R. 1, (1952) A.SC. 369, foll. in *N. R. Revanna* v. *State* ('74) A.Knt. 31, 33-4.

Objects and Reasons could not be referred to for the construction of a section. The reference to "Statements of Objects and Reasons" requires clarification. A statement of objects and reasons may express the individual opinion of the person who introduces the Bill. Thus the statement of objects and reasons annexed to the Bill which became the Prize Competition Act, 1955, stated that the proposed legislation fell under Entry 34 of the State List, "Betting and Gambling". That opinion cannot be taken into account, first, because it is on a question which is for the Court to decide, secondly because it may be mistaken, and lastly because other members who voted for the Bill may not share it. But if the Statement of Objects and Reasons refers to facts which are matters of history, or common knowledge, and which are capable of independent proof, it is submitted that the statement can be looked at for the purposes of construction provided that on well settled principles of construction, the materials there stated furnish relevant extrinsic aids to construction. For example, if the mischief to be remedied is set out in the Statement of Objects and Reasons, as for example, that the reversal by the Supreme Court of its own earlier decision has rendered taxes collected pursuant to that decision illegal, and the bill proposes to validate those taxes, the statement can be referred to if the mischief to be remedied and the remedy provided become relevant for purposes of construction. This subject is considered more fully later in this Chapter. We have seen that the Statement of Objects and Reasons cannot be used for interpreting the provisions of the Act. However, in *W.B.* v. *Subodh Gopal Bose*[39] Das J.[40] held

Statement of Objects and Reasons—a clarification

Subodh Gopal Bose's Case: limited use of Statement of Objects and Reasons

[39] (1954) S.C.R. 587, 628; foll. in *M. K. Ranganathan* v. *Madras* ('55) A.SC. 604, 608; fol. in *Hakim Singh* v. *Shiv Sagar* ('73) A.A. 596, 630; *Jagdish Pandey* v. *Chancellor, Bihar University* (1968) 1 S.C.R. 231, ('68) A.SC. 353, 356 ["We are entitled to look to (the Statement of Objects and Reasons) to see what was the state of affairs when the section came to be passed." The court did so in order to ascertain whether the dates mentioned in the impugned section were selected arbitrarily, in which case they would violate Art. 14; however, in the light of the Statement of Objects and Reasons it was held that the dates were not selected arbitrarily.] The same view was expressed by Grover J. in *J.R.G. Mfg. Association* v. *Union* (1970) 2 S.C.R. 68, ('70) A.SC. 1589, 1596, without any reference to decided cases. He referred to the statement of objects and reasons for s. 12 of the Rubber Amendment Act, 1960, to show the mischief which the law was designed to prevent. Having regard to that mischief the court held that the section did not violate Art. 14 by conferring arbitrary and unbridled power on the Board which was "a high powered body" whose actions were subject to the control of government.

[40] Foll. in *A. Thangal Kunju Musaliar* v. *M. Venkitachalam Potti* (1955) 2 S.C.R. 1196, ('56) A.SC. 246, 265. In *Shyamlal* v. *Gujarat* (1965) 2 S.C.R. 457, ('65) A.SC. 1251, 1255, Shah J. referred to a speech delivered by the Lt.-Governor, not for interpreting the words used by the legislature but "to ascertain the historical setting in which the statute which is parent to s. 94(1) (of the Act) came to be enacted." The above cases were referred to and foll. in *G. S. Chooramani* v. *U.P.* ('69) A.A. 43, 48 (*held*, that the statement of objects and reasons, and the speech of the Finance Minister while introducing the Bill to abolish Thekedari Rights, could be looked at to show ". . . the historical setting of the problem and the assurances on which the Act was sought to be introduced.") *Workmen of F.T. & R. Co.* v. *Management* ('73) A.SC. 1227, 1239 (Without reference to decided cases, *held*, that the Statement of Objects and Reasons cannot be taken into account for the purpose of interpreting the plain words of the section. But it gives an indication as to what the Legislature wanted to achieve. *Held, further*, that the Statement of Objects and Reasons showed that the limitations imposed on the powers of an Industrial Tribunal by various decisions were intended to be removed); *A. C. Sharma* v. *Delhi Administration* ('73) A.SC. 913, 917; *Jamuna Prasad* v. *Kishorilal* ('73) A. Cal. 204, 209 (Supreme Court decisions on the Statement of Objects and Reasons followed).

that the Statement of Objects and Reasons could be referred to for the limited purpose of ascertaining the conditions prevailing at the time which actuated the sponsor of the Bill to introduce the same and the extent and urgency of the evil which he sought to remedy, since these were matters relevant for deciding whether the restrictions were reasonable within the meaning of Arts. 19(2) to (6). Ever since that decision, the Statement of Objects and Reasons has been referred to for the purpose indicated by Das J. But can the Statement of Objects and Reasons annexed to a Bill which ultimately becomes a Constitutional Amendment be referred to as an extrinsic aid to construction? In *Kochunni's Case*[41] Subba Rao J. delivering the judgment of the majority, extracted from the Statement of Objects and Reasons for the Constitution (4th Amendment) Act, 1955, that part which was relevant to the acquisition of estates and added:

Can Statement of Objects and Reasons etc. be used to aid construction?

Kochunni's Case: Construction of Art. 31A

"*The object was, therefore, to bring about a change in the agricultural economy but not to recognize or confer any title in the whole or part of an estate of junior members of a family.*[42] This Court has held in *Aswini Kumar Ghose* v. *Arabinda Bose*[43] that the statement of objects and reasons is not admissible as an aid to the construction of a statute. But we are referring to it only for the limited purpose of ascertaining the conditions prevailing at the time the bill was introduced, and the purpose for which the amendment was made."[44] (italics supplied)

Kochunni's Case is considered at length later in this book but the question of constitutional interpretation which arose for decision in that case was whether the definition of an "estate" or "rights" in relation to an estate contained in Art. 31A(2) was to be given its literal meaning or was to be construed as limited to a law for the acquisition of estates or for the modification or extinguishment of rights in estates if the law was a law for agrarian reform. The majority held that the meaning must be so restricted; the minority held that apart from the Statement of Objects and Reasons, Art. 31A(2) contained no restrictions on the general language there used which must therefore be given its literal meaning. The question of principle thus raised has become confused because in *P. Vajravelu Mudaliar* v. *Special Deputy Collector, Madras*[45-46] Subba Rao J. said that in *Kochunni's Case* he had not relied on the Statement of Objects and Reasons for the construction of Art. 31A(1)(*a*) and (2). It is submitted that in *Kochunni's Case* Subba Rao J. did rely on the Statement of Objects and Reasons for putting a restricted, and not a literal, meaning on the definition of an estate and rights in an estate; and if he had not done so, he could not have arrived at the conclusion to which he came. It is submitted further that this reliance was correct, and in accord with well-settled principles of construction and that its subsequent repudiation appears to be based on the mistaken view that such reliance was contrary to settled principles of construction.

Mudaliar's Case explains the use of the statement of objects etc. in *Kochunni's Case*: a criticism

---

[41] (1960) 3 S.C.R. 887, ('60) A.SC. 1080.

[42] The italicised words indicate the nature of the law impugned before the Court.

[43] (1953) S.C.R. 1, ('52) A.SC. 369.

[44] (1960) 3 S.C.R. *supra* at p. 899. It will be seen that the last sentence repeats what Das J. had said as regards the use of the Statement of Objects and Reasons.

[45-46] (1965) 1 S.C.R. 614, 620-21, ('65) A.SC. 1017.

Circumstances under which the Statement of Objects etc. can be used to aid construction

2.68 On the question of construction the real issue did not emerge clearly in *Kochunni's Case*, but the interpretation there adopted, and the criticism to which it was subjected, led Subba Rao J. in *Mudaliar's Case* to advert to a ground[47] which, had it been adverted to in *Kochunni's Case*, would have provided a consistent and logical basis for referring to the Statement of Objects and Reasons and restricting Art. 31A(1)(*a*) and (2) in the manner he did. The real issue in *Kochunni's Case* was this : Art. 31(2) provides that private property cannot be acquired except under a law providing for such acquisition for a public purpose and on payment of compensation. Art. 31A was inserted by the Constitution (1st Amendment) Act, 1951, and was subsequently amended by the Constitution (4th Amendment) Act, 1955, and, after the judgment in *Kochunni's Case*, by the Constitution (17th Amendment) Act, 1964. Each Amendment Act was introduced as a Bill with a Statement of Objects and Reasons attached to it.[48] The effect of Art. 31A(1)(*a*) and (2) was to exclude the operation of Art. 31(2), so that in respect of the acquisition of an estate or for the extinguishment or modification of rights in estates, a law could not be impugned on the ground that it subserved no public purpose and did not provide for payment of compensation. If a strictly literal interpretation was given to the word "estate" or to "rights" in an estate, especially after the Constitution (17th Amendment) Act, almost all lands in India would constitute estates, and a law providing for acquisition of land would be a law for the acquisition of an estate and need not comply with the requirements of Art 31(2) which would therefore become a dead letter as regards land. But Art. 31(2) embodies a valuable fundamental right; that Article was amended by the Constitution (4th Amendment) Act, which made it explicit that a law for the acquisition or requisition of property must satisfy two requirements : there must be a public purpose and the law must provide for payment of compensation, although the amendment made the adequacy of compensation non-justiciable. The 4th Amendment Act which amended Art. 31(2) also amended Art. 31A(2). If it was intended that Art. 31A(1)(*a*) and (2) should in substance repeal Art. 31(2), the Constitutional Amendment would have said so, instead of affirming the two requirements of Art. 31(2). The legislative history of Art. 31 and of Arts. 31A and 31B has been set out in another part of this book. The reasons for the Amendments are matters of common knowledge and within recent memory, if they have not passed into history : the amendments were designed to remedy the deficiencies of the existing law. The Statement of Objects and Reasons relating to the 1st Amendment records facts which are capable of independent verification, namely, that challenges to agrarian laws or laws relating to land reform were pending in Courts and were holding up large schemes of land legislation through dilatory and wasteful litigation. The Statement of Objects and Reasons relating to the 4th Amendment records the fact that Arts. 31A and 31B had succeeded in preventing the challenge under Arts. 14, 19 and 31 to Zamindari legislation, but that there

Statement of Objects etc. to Constitutional Amendments records matters of history, the mischief to be remedied, etc.

---

[47] The ground was that a literal interpretation would make Art. 31(2) practically a dead letter.

[48] For the Bills and the Statement of Objects and Reasons see Appendix 2 to the Constitution of India, pp. A-219 to A-229.

were other measures of land reform which were exposed to a similar challenge which it was desired to put beyond such challenge and decisions of the Supreme Court were referred to in that context. The Statement of Objects and Reasons relating to the 17th Amendment referred to the decisions of the Supreme Court which had held that *ryotwari* tenure in Kerala did not fall within the definition of an "estate" and accordingly the amendment added that tenure. Running through all these Statements is the central idea that large schemes of agrarian reform or land reform ought not to be defeated by a challenge under Arts. 14, 19 and 31. These Statements do not merely express the opinion of one person but they refer to facts which show the mischief to be remedied and the remedy provided by the amendment. If Art. 31(2) was to have any practical content in relation to land, the history of the various amendments showed that

Art. 31A confined to acquisition for agrarian reform by reference to the statement of objects and reasons to avoid Art. 31(2) becoming practically nugatory

Art. 31A(1)(*a*) and (2) did not deal with a law for the acquisition of an estate or for the extinguishment or modification of rights in estates which had nothing to do with agrarian or land reform. This conclusion is not reached by saying, as Subba Rao J. said later, that a law for the acquisition of an estate must be a law for the acquisition of a tenure which is called an estate[49-50] for most, if not all, land in India is held on some tenure or the other, and by definition most land in India would be "an estate" and a law providing for acquisition of land must therefore be a law for the acquisition of "an estate". The conclusion at which Subba Rao J. arrived in *Kochunni's Case*, namely, that such laws must have relation to agrarian reform can be derived only from considering the history of the law, the mischief to be remedied and the remedy which was supplied. As these are recorded in the Statement of Objects and Reasons and are capable of independent verification, on settled principles of construction the statement can be resorted to for giving a restricted meaning to Art. 31A(1)(*a*) and (2).

Same principle applied by the U.S. Sup. Ct. in interpreting the 13th and 14th Amendments

2.69 Questions of Constitutional limitations do not arise in England, and English authorities on statutory interpretation do not throw light on them. But they have arisen in the United States and the principles mentioned above have been applied in interpreting Constitutional Amendments. Thus the meaning to be given to the 13th and 14th Amendments to the U.S. Constitution was considered in the *Slaughter House Cases*[51] and the majority of the Supreme Court construed those amendments in the light of the known history of the times which was within their memory. The literal construction of the 13th Amendment, which was pressed on the Court, would have brought "servitudes" which were not personal servitudes like slavery, peonage and involuntary servitude by imprisonment in jail, within the 13th Amendment; but the Supreme Court rejected that interpretation on the ground that the known purpose for which the Amendment was made, namely, the abolition of negro slavery made such a construction untenable. Again, in interpreting the words "privileges and immunities of the Citizens of the United States" the majority declined to put a construction which would obliterate the privileges and immunities of citizens of various States, and for that purpose also

---

49-50 See *Mudaliar's Case*, (1965) 1 S.C.R. 614, ('65) A.SC. 1017.
51 (1872) 16 Wal 36, 21 L. ed. 395.

they referred to the history of the times and to the object which the Amendments was designed to secure. It is submitted, therefore, that though extrinsic aids to construction must be used with caution and judgment where the words have a plain meaning, they are permissible aids and might in certain circumstances be decisive. If the proclaimed object of a law results in hardship or injustice it is not for a Court to say that effect should not be given to words which clearly express that object. But where the known object is against producing hardship and injustice it is open to the Court to resort to extrinsic aids to construction, and put a construction which avoids hardship, injustice or absurdity. It is hardly necessary to add that the assistance to be derived from the Statement of Objects and Reasons will depend upon its contents. If the contents do not lead to any clear conclusion as to the object of the law, no assistance can be derived from the Statement.

Fundamental rights and other constitutional rights

2.70 It is necessary to consider the place which fundamental rights occupy in our Constitution, because misconceptions about that place are a fruitful source of error in interpreting the Constitution. It is common to find in the judgments of various Courts the use of quasi-religious terminology in describing fundamental rights. Thus, it is a "sacred" duty of the Court to safeguard fundamental rights and it would be a "sacrilege" to whittle down those rights;[52] again, fundamental rights are of a "transcendental" character.[53] It is submitted that an understanding of the nature of a Constitutional right is obscured by the use of emotional and mystical language. Every right conferred by the Constitution, whether in the Part relating to fundamental rights or in any other Part, is a Constitutional right; any person entitled to that right can enforce it through a Court of Law. Nor is the importance of a right determined by the part of the Constitution in which it is placed. For example, the right to carry on any occupation, trade or business is a fundamental right under Art. 19(1)(*g*); the freedom of trade, commerce and intercourse throughout the territory of India is not a fundamental right because it is declared in Art. 301; but for that reason it is not possible to say that the freedom conferred by Art. 19(1)(*g*) is more important than the freedom conferred by Art. 301. It is well settled that provisions of the Constitution are of equal authority unless expressly or by necessary implication subordinated to others.[54] The only difference between a fundamental right and other rights conferred by the Constitution lies in the fact that Art. 32 confers a guaranteed fundamental right on a person to move the Supreme Court for the enforcement of his fundamental rights and enables that Court to enforce them by issuing an appropriate writ, order or direction as mentioned in that Article. This difference is discussed fully in the Chapter on Judicial Remedies. We have seen that neither the presence of fundamental rights nor the provisions for judicial review make any difference to the well settled principles of interpreting a written Constitution.[55]

Violation of every constitutional right gives a cause of action

[52] See for example, the judgment of Bhagwati J. in *Basheshar Nath* v. *C.I.T., Delhi and Rajasthan* (1959) Supp. 1 S.C.R. 528, 557 and 565, ('59) A.SC. 149.

[53] See for example the judgment of Subba Rao J. in *M. S. M. Sharma* v. *Sri Krishna Sinha* (1959) Supp. 1 S.C.R. 806, 874, ('59) A.SC. 395.

[54] *Hari Vishnu Kamath* v. *Syed Ahmad Ishaque* (1955) 1 S.C.R. 1104, ('55) A.SC. 233.

[55] See paras 1.87 and 1.88.

The parts of the Constitution and headings given to Articles as aids to construction

2.71 It is a relevant consideration in interpreting two Articles of the Constitution that they are in two different parts.[56] There is ample authority that one is entitled to have regard to indicia afforded by the arrangement of sections and from other indications.[57] The arrangement of sections into parts and their headings are substantive parts of the Act and "they are gradually winning recognition as a kind of preamble to the enactments which they precede limiting or explaining their operation."[58] Kapur J. in his dissenting judgment in *Nanavati's Case* applied this principle to Arts. 142(1) and 161 observing that these Articles appear in different parts dealing with different subjects, thus showing that they operate in separate fields and are not intended to overlap so as to be restrictive of each other. In *U.P.* v. *Manbodhan Lal Srivastava*[59] Sinha C.J. considered it a relevant matter in interpreting Art. 320(*c*) to point out that it appeared in Chapter II, Part XIV, which dealt with the constitution and the duties of Public Service Commissions and not under Chapter I, Part XIV, which dealt with the Services and conferred certain rights on Government servants. In *Indu Bhushan De* v. *State*[60] it was held that marginal notes in the Constitution, unlike those in Acts of the British Parliament, are parts of the Constitution and *prima facie*, furnish some proof as to their meaning and purpose.[61]

Marginal Notes

Directive Principles of State Policy

2.72 Part IV of the Constitution (Arts. 36-51) contains Directive Principles of State Policy. The role which Part IV plays in the Constitution of India, both substantively and for interpreting other provisions of the Constitution, is considered in Chapter XVI.

The Common Law

2.73 It is not necessary in this Chapter to consider the larger question of how the Common Law came to India and the part which it played, and plays in Indian Law.[62] In the earlier editions of this book, the question whether the common law doctrine that the Crown is not bound by a Statute unless expressly or by necessary implication named therein was discussed at some length by reference to two conflicting judgments of the Supreme Court, namely, *Director of Rationing* v. *Corporation of Calcutta*[63] and *Legal Remembrancer* v. *Calcutta Corporation*.[64] It was submitted that the earlier case was rightly decided. However, the question has lost much of its importance by passage of time and the reader who is interested in the detailed discussion will find it in the second edition of this book at pp. 44 to 49.

---

[56] *Per* Kapur J. in *K. M. Nanavati* v. *Bombay* (1961) 1 S.C.R. 497, 561, ('61) A.SC. 112.

[57] ibid. citing *Dorma* v. *Newcastle-upon-Tyne Corporation* (1940) 2 K.B. 204, 217.

[58] ibid. citing Craies on *Statute Law*, 5th ed., p. 195 (6th ed., p. 210); see also *Inglis* v. *Robertson* (1898) A.C. 616, 630, *per* Lord Herschell; and *Nokes* v. *Doncaster Amalgamated Colliers* (1940) A.C. 1114, *per* Lord Simon, L.C.

[59] (1958) S.C.R. 533, ('57) A.SC. 912. [60] ('72) A.Cal. 160.

[61] ibid. p. 168, following the observations of Das C.J. in *Bengal Immunity Co. Ltd.* v. *Bihar* (1955) 2 S.C.R. 603, ('55) A.SC. 661 (*held*, that the marginal note to Art. 247 showed that the power given to Parliament to establish additional courts was limited to only "certain" additional courts.) See para 2.21 for Lord Reid's view.

[62] The reader interested in the question is referred to the *Common Law in India* by M. C. Setalvad (Hamlyn Lectures).

[63] (1961) 1 S.C.R. 158, ('60) A.SC. 1355.

[64] (1967) 2 S.C.R. 170, ('67) A.SC. 997.

2.74 The distribution of legislative power between federal and state governments in the Constitution of Canada, Australia, the G.I. Act, 35 and the Constitution of India, takes the form of giving power to make laws "in relation to"[65] or "in respect of"[66] certain topics. The expression "in respect of" and "in relation to" in the context have the same meaning. But it is submitted that there is a distinction between a law "in respect of" a subject-matter and a law "affecting" that subject-matter. In borderline cases it may be difficult to decide whether a law is "in respect of" a certain matter or merely "affects" such matter, but the fact that a distinction may be difficult to make in some cases is no reason for denying its existence. Two cases decided by the Privy Council bring out this distinction clearly, and one of them in terms accepts the above distinction. In *Att.-Gen. for Saskatchewan* v. *Att.-Gen. for Canada*[67] the Privy Council considered the validity of the Farm Security Act, 1944, of Saskatchewan, the main object of which was to lighten the contractual obligations of a mortgagor or purchaser of farm land in the event of there being in any year a "crop failure". S.6(3) of that Act provided for reducing the contractual rate of interest, a topic exclusively assigned to the Parliament of Canada. By a majority the Supreme Court of Canada held the section *ultra vires*. In upholding the majority judgment Viscount Simon L.C. said:

"In respect of", "In relation to"

"In relation to" and "affecting"

Distinction brought out by two Privy Council decisions (i) *A.G. for Saskatchewan* v. *A.G. for Canada*

"But, as Rand J. points out, there is a distinction between legislation 'in relation to' agriculture and legislation which may produce a favourable effect on the strength and stability of that industry. Consequential effects are not the same thing as legislative subject-matter. It is 'the true nature and character of the legislation' — not its ultimate economic results — that matters.[68] Here, what is sought to be statutorily modified is a contract between two parties one of which is an agriculturist but the other of which is a lender of money. However broadly the phrase 'agriculture in the Province' may be construed, and whatever advantages to the farmers the re-shaping of their mortgages or agreements for sale might confer, their Lordships are unable to take the view that this legislation can be regarded as valid on the ground that it is enacted in relation to agriculture."[69]

2.75 In *Ladore* v. *Bennett*[70] the Privy Council had to consider the validity of the City of Windsor (Amalgamation) Act, 1935, and the Amending Act of 1936, of the Ontario Provincial Legislature. By that Act four adjoining Municipalities which were in financial difficulties and unable to meet the debenture interest and maturing principal, part of which was payable outside the Province, were amalgamated as the City of Windsor. The City of Windsor (Amalgamation) Amendment Act, 1936, provided for the framing of a scheme whereby the amounts due as principal and interest could be scaled down. A scheme was framed providing for the scaling down of interest and it was contended that the law was invalid, first because it was legislation "in relation to" interest which, as we have seen, was exclusively assigned to the Parliament of Canada, and secondly, because it was legislation relating to bankruptcy which was also a subject of such exclusive legislation. Lord Atkin rejected these contentions holding

(ii) *Ladore* v. *Bennett*

[65] See ss. 91 and 92 of the B.N.A. Act, 1867.
[66] See ss. 51 and 52 of the Australian Constitution for the powers conferred on Parliament; s. 100 of the G.I. Act, 35 and Art. 246 of the Constitution of India.
[67] (1949) A.C. 110.
[68] *Russel* v. *R.* (1882) 7 App. Cas. 829, 840.
[69] (1949) A.C. 110, at p. 123.
[70] (1939) A.C. 468.

that on the evidence it was clear that the financial position of the four Municipalities was such that the proper functioning of Municipal Corporations became impossible. The law was not a law relating to insolvency, though the insolvency of the Municipalities was an occasion for amalgamating them and incorporating a new Municipality. The law thus came under s. 92(8) of the B.N.A. Act, 1867, namely, Municipal Institutions in the Province. It was not only the right but the duty of the Provincial Legislature to provide for the proper functioning of municipal institutions on which the health and well-being of the inhabitants depended. The power to create a Corporation included the power to dissolve it, and if the Corporations had been dissolved their debts and liabilities would have become unenforceable. If so, the power to create another Corporation carried with it the power to provide how much of the liabilities of the dissolved Corporations should be taken over or discharged by the new Corporation. The fact that the interest payable on debentures was also payable to some person outside the Province did not alter the nature of the legislation but was a mere incidental consequence of legislation in relation to Municipal Institutions in the Province. Every person outside a State dealing with a Corporation took the risk of losing his money if the Corporation was dissolved.

The distinction between "in relation to" and "affecting" a subject matter

2.76 It is submitted that these two cases clearly bring out the distinction between a law "in relation to" a subject-matter and a law "affecting" that subject matter. In the first case, the law "affected" agriculture but was directly "in relation to" interest on which there was existing Dominion Legislation. In the second case, interest on debentures was "affected" but that was a consequence of a law "in relation to" Municipal Institutions.

Directory and mandatory provisions

2.77 The question sometimes arises whether certain provisions of the Constitution are merely directory or whether they are mandatory, in the sense that failure to observe them renders an act null and void. Dr. Wynes has said:

> "Whether a statutory provision is mandatory or directory is often a question of some difficulty, but in general it may be said that the provisions of the Constitution should be regarded as mandatory where such construction is possible.[71] Those sections which relate to the procedure of the Houses and other political matters are generally directory only inasmuch as the Courts have no immediate power of control over such matters."[72]

Srivastava's Case

2.78 The question about the mandatory or directory nature of Constitutional provisions arose in *U.P.* v. *Manbhodan Lal Srivastava.*[73] The Supreme Court had to decide whether the respondent's dismissal was null and void because the State Government failed to consult the Public Service Commission as required by Art. 320(3)(c). The Supreme Court held that the dismissal was not void. It appears to have propounded two tests:

---

[71] *Wynes,* p. 29, citing Cooley, *Constitutional Limitations,* 154, 155; Black, *Interpretation*, pp. 21-22; Halsbury, *Laws of England,* 2nd ed., vol. 31, pp. 529, *et sqq.* See also *Dignan* v. *Australian Steamships Pty. Ltd.* (1931) 45 C.L.R. 188; *Montreal Street Rly. Co.* v. *Normandin* (1917) A.C. 170, 174, 175; *R.* v. *Brisbane Licensing Court* (1920) 28 C.L.R. 23. See also *Clydesdale* v. *Hughes* (1934-35) 51 C.L.R. 518.
[72] *Wynes*, p. 29.
[73] (1958) S.C.R. 533, ('57) A.SC. 912.

First, ". . . does the Constitution provide for the contingency as to what is to happen in the event of non-compliance with the requirements of Art. 320(3)(c)? It does not, either in express terms or by implication, provide that the result of such a non-compliance is to invalidate the proceedings ending with the final order of the Government."[74]

Two tests: (i) express or implied provision for consequences of non-compliance

Secondly, it cited with approval the test laid down by the Privy Council in *Montreal Street Railway Co.* v. *Normandin*,[75] namely,

"The question whether provisions in a statute are directory or imperative has very frequently arisen in this country, but it has been said that no general rule can be laid down, and that in every case the object of the statute must be looked at. The cases of the subject will be found collected in Maxwell on Statutes, 5th ed. p. 596[76] and following pages. When the provisions of a statute relate to the performance of a public duty and the case is such that to hold null and void acts done in neglect of this duty would work serious general inconvenience, or injustice to persons who have no control over those entrusted with the duty, and at the same time would not promote the main object of the Legislature, it has been the practice to hold such provisions to be directory only, the neglect of them, though punishable, not affecting the validity of the acts done."[77]

(ii) the test laid down by the Privy Council and followed in *Khemka's Case*

The above test had been followed by the Federal Court in *Biswanath Khemka* v. *R.*[78] and the Supreme Court approved that decision. Applying this test, and having regard to the frame of Art. 320, which used the word "shall" in every sub-clause, the Court held that Art. 320(3)(c) was merely directory. *Srivastava's Case* was followed in *Ram Gopal* v. *M.P.*[79]

2.79 In *V. R. Sutaria* v. *N. P. Bhanvadia*[80] the Supreme Court considered the question whether a deviation from the form of oath prescribed by Art. 173, read with Sch. III, was such as to vitiate the whole election. The non-compliance consisted of a wrong translation in the oath in Gujarati where the Legislative Assembly of the State of Gujarat was described as "Rajya Sabha". The court held that that mis-description did not vitiate the essence of an oath, and therefore literal compliance with the terms of Art. 173, and Sch. III, was not necessary.[81]

Form of oath: wrong translation

---

[74] (1958) S.C.R. *supra* at pp. 544-45. [75] (1917) A.C. 170, 174-5.
[76] See now Maxwell, *Interpretation*, 11th ed., pp. 362-73.
[77] (1958) S.C.R. *supra* at p. 545.
[78] (1945) F.C.R. 99, ('45) A.FC. 67, 49 C.W.N. (F.R.) 62.
[79] (1970) 1 S.C.R. 472, ('70) A.SC. 158, 160.
[80] (1969) 2 S.C.R. 627, ('70) A.SC. 765, 768.
[81] The Court cited in support: (i) *Kamraj Nadar* v. *Kunju Thevan* (1959) S.C.R. 583, ('58) A.SC. 687 (The Court declined to reject the election petition on the ground that the deposit provided for under Sec. 117, Representation of the People Act was made in favour of the Election Commission and not in favour of the Secretary of that Commission as provided in the section); (ii) *Murarka Rhadeshyam Ram Krishna* v. *Rupsingh Rathod* (1964) 3 S.C.R. 573, ('64) A.SC. 1545 [The Court rejected the contention that s. 81(3) of the Representation of the People Act had not been complied with because copy of the election petition served on the appellant was not a true copy. The court held that that only meant a copy so true that nobody could by any possibility misunderstand it]. *U.P.* v. *Manbodhan Lal Srivastava* (1958) S.C.R. 533, ('57) A.SC. 912 was also referred to for showing that the word "shall" was not always mandatory in *Punjab* v. *Satya Pal* ('69) A.SC. 903 where the Court examined the several tests to determine when the provisions of a statute might be treated as mandatory and when not. These cases showed that non-compliance with the provisions of a statute would not necessarily render a proceeding invalid if by considering its nature, its design and the consequences which followed from its non-observation one was not led to the conclusion that the Legislature or the Constitution makers intended that there should be no departure from the strict letter of the law.

Use of Dictionaries

2.80 In *R.* v. *Peters*[82] Lord Coleridge observed:

"I am quite aware that dictionaries are not to be taken as authoritative exponents of the meanings of words used in Acts of Parliament, *but it is a well-known rule of courts of law that words should be taken to be used in their ordinary sense, and we are therefore sent for instruction to these books.*"[83] (italics supplied)

Submission: current disparagement of the use of dictionaries unhelpful and unjustified

and in construing the provisions of statutes and Constitutions dictionaries have been frequently resorted to. The present writer does not share the current fashion which looks upon the reference to a dictionary as playing the lexicographer's role which is somehow below the dignity of constitutional interpretation. Glowing words like "the significance of words is not formal but vital," and that "we must think things rather than words" do not help in finding the correct meaning of words and thereby gathering the intention which lies behind them. If the draftsman of the Constitution felt any doubt about the meaning of an ordinary English word which he proposed to use, or had used, he would resolve that doubt by consulting standard dictionaries, for there is no other way of resolving that doubt, and the draftsman would assume that if those who have to interpret his words also have a doubt, they will resolve it likewise. Further, a detailed Constitution like ours is drafted as an instrument of Government designed to secure the well-being of the people. It is not designed to stimulate juristic and philosophical thought, or to stimulate historical research in interpreting the Constitution, for, any such design would mark a grave failure of precise and careful draftsmanship. The draftsman must be credited with the elementary knowledge that his words would be understood in their ordinary sense and that, as Khanna J. felicitously put it, "it has not yet been erected into a legal maxim of Constitutional construction *that words were meant to conceal thoughts.*"[84] (italics supplied). The observations of Lord Simon of Glaisdale in the *Black-Clawson Case* cited in para 2.28(*e*) of the text that "In essence, drafting, enactment and interpretation are integral parts of the process of translating the volition of the electorate into rules which will bind themselves" support the view expressed above.

---

[82] (1886) 16 Q.B.D. 636 at p. 641; see *Maxwell*, 12th ed., p. 55; *Craies*, 7th ed., p. 161.

[83] *Maxwell*, 12th ed., p. 55.

[84] *Kesavananda* v. *Kerala* (1973) Supp. S.C.R. 1, ('73) A.SC. 1461 at p. 1838.

CHAPTER III

COURTS AND THE CONSTITUTION

3.1 Once a law has been passed by the British Parliament and has received Royal Assent, no question of its validity can arise in British courts, because Parliament is supreme and sovereign. However, in Federal Constitutions, the question not infrequently arises whether the law passed by a legislature is valid having regard to the distribution of legislative powers and other Constitutional limitations. When such a question arises, the courts of the country must decide it.[1] The grave responsibility of declaring a law unconstitutional has made courts reluctant to refuse to give effect to the will of the legislature. The judiciary is a branch of the Government co-ordinate with the legislature and the executive, although it may appear to occupy a position of superiority.[2] In deciding upon the validity of laws, judges have borne in mind that the function of making laws has been entrusted to the elected representatives of the people and the function of the courts is to interpret those laws and not to act as a third or revising Chamber.[3] Accordingly, the courts are guided by the following rules in discharging their solemn duty to declare laws passed by a legislature unconstitutional:

Federal Constitutions and the power to declare a law void

Courts are not a third legislative chamber: rules observed in considering the validity of a law

(1) There is a presumption in favour of constitutionality,[4] and a law will not be declared unconstitutional unless the case is so clear as to be free from doubt; "to doubt the constitutionality of a law is to resolve it in favour of its validity."[5]

(i) presumption of constitutionality

(2) Where the validity of a statute is questioned and there are two interpretations, one of which would make the law valid and the other void, the former must be preferred and the validity of the law

(ii) preference of a construction which would make a law

---

[1] *R* v. *Burah,* (1878) 5 I.A. 178, 193, (1878) 3 App. Cas. 889, 4 Cal. 172.

[2] Contrast the observations of Taft C.J. in *Ex.p. Grossman* (1924) 267 U.S. 87 at p. 120, 69 L. ed. 527, 535: ". . . The fact is that the Judiciary, quite as much as Congress and the Executive, are dependent on the co-operation of the other two, that government may go on. Indeed, while the Constitution has made the Judiciary as independent of the other branches as is practicable, it is, as often remarked, the weakest of the three. It must look for a continuity of necessary co-operation, in the possible reluctance of either of the other branches, to the force of public opinion."

[3] *Fram N. Balsara* v. *Bombay* (1951) Bom. 17, 33, ('51) A.B. 210, 52 Bom.L.R. 799; on app., sub. nom., (1951) S.C.R. 682, ('51) A.SC. 318.

[4] *V. M. Syed Mohammad & Co.* v. *Andhra* (1954) S.C.R. 1117, ('54) A.SC. 314; *Madhubhai Amathalal Gandhi* v. *Union* (1961) 1 S.C.R. 191, 209, ('61) A.SC. 21; *Rameshwarlal* v. *Union* ('70) A.Cal. 520, 526. The presumption is in favour of the constitutionality of a statute and all circumstances which might lead to the statute being upheld must be presumed by the court and must be shown not to exist by the person challenging the validity of the Act; *Dalip Singh* v. *Rakha Ram* ('60) A. Punj. 176; *Durga Parshad* v. *Custodian, E.P.* (1960) 2 Punj. 159, ('60) A.Punj. 341 F.B.; *Manohar Lal* v. *The State* (1957) Punj. 155; *Kishori Lal* v. *The State* (1957) Punj. 1388; ('57) A.Punj. 244; *Jupiter General Insurance Co. Ltd.* v. *A. Rajagopalan* (1952) Punj. 11, ('52) A.Punj. 9; *Kadiyala Chandrayya* v. *Andhra* (1957) Andh. 44, ('57) A.A.P. 261; *Firm Soma Rajaiah* v. *S.T.O.* (1954) Hyd. 76, ('54) A.Hyd. 50.

[5] *American Jurisprudence,* Vol. 11, pp. 719-720; *Jupiter General Insurance Co. Ltd.* v. *A. Rajagopalan, supra; Firm Soma Rajaiah* v. *S.T.O.* ('54) A.Hyd. 50, 52; *Durga Parshad* v. *Custodian, E.P., supra*: ". . . then there is the general principle of the construction of statutes that a reasonable doubt must be resolved in favour of the legislative action and the Act sustained".

valid: Macleod's Case

upheld. Thus, in *Macleod* v. *Att.-Gen. for N.S.W.*,[6] the Privy Council had to consider the meaning of "wheresoever" in s. 54 of the Criminal Law Amendment Act, 1883.[7] The Privy Council held that the word "wheresoever" must be read "wheresoever in this Colony the offence is committed", because, if the word were interpreted literally the section would be *ultra vires* the Colonial legislature. The principle of *Macleod's Case* was adopted in *In re The Hindu Women's Rights to Property Act.*[8] That was a reference by the Governor-General to the Federal Court for opinion whether the Hindu Women's Rights to Property Act, 1937 and the Hindu Women's Rights to Property (Amendment) Act, 1938 (both Central Acts), were valid. Those Acts were designed to secure to Hindu women better rights in succession to the property of a deceased Hindu as also to regulate devolution, by survivorship, of property. The reference was made necessary, partly because the Central Legislature had no power to legislate in respect of agricultural land. Gwyer C.J. applied the principle of *Macleod's Case* and said that when a legislature with limited and restricted power used a word of such wide and general import as "property", the presumption must be that it was using that word with reference to that kind of property with respect to which it was competent to legislate and to no other. Unless the Act was to be regarded as wholly meaningless and ineffective, the word "property" must be read as "property other than agricultural property."[9] Where an impugned section confers uncanalised power if read literally but it can be "read down", it should be so read in order to uphold the section.[10] Similarly, the Supreme Court held that it was reasonable to interpret ss. 3 and 4 of the Punjab Cattle Fairs (Regulation) Act, 1968, as not authorizing the violation of Arts. 19 and 31.[11]

---

[6] (1891) A.C. 455 (P.C.).

[7] ibid. p. 456: *s. 54.* "Whosoever being married marries another person during the life of the former husband or wife, wheresoever such second marriage takes place, shall be liable to penal servitude for seven years."

[8] (1941) F.C.R. 12, ('42) A.FC. 72.

[9] (1941) F.C.R. *supra* at pp. 26-27; the principle that the legislature must be presumed to know the limits of its powers was adopted in *Bombay* v. *R.M.D. Chamarbaugwala* (1957) S.C.R. 874 and it was held that if the tax on prize competitions could be referred to either entry 60 or 62 of the legislative list, it must be referred to entry 62 because the tax would be valid in its entirety while if it was referred to entry 60 it would to a very large extent be void: *Kedar Nath Singh* v. *Bihar* (1962) Supp. 2 S.C.R. 769, 810-11, where the Supreme Court gave a limited meaning to the word "sedition" in s. 124A, I.P.C.; fol. in *R. L. Arora* v. *U.P.* (1964) Supp. 6 S.C.R. 784, 797, where the court put a limited construction on s. 4(1)(aa) of the Land Acquisition Act; fol. in *W.B.* v. *Ruttonjee & Co.* ('70) A.Cal. 548, 554, where the court put a limited construction on the word "control" in s. 8(1), Bengal Excise Act, 1909, as amended in 1965. The above principle was also fol. in *Jothi Timber Mart* v. *Calicut Municipality* (1970) 1 S.C.R. 629, ('70) A.SC. 264, where Shah J. held that the wide words "brought into the city", used in s. 126, Calicut City Municipal Act, must be read to mean "brought into the city for consumption, use or sale therein" in order that the legislative power conferred by entry 52, List II, Sch. 7 of the Constitution was not transgressed; *M.P.* v. *D.N.C.P. Hill Colliery Co.* ('72) A.SC. 614, 621 (*held*, that a court construing a provision of law must presume that the intention of the authority making it was not to exceed its power, but to enact a valid law). See also *L.M. Co.* v. *T.D. Board* ('72) A.Mys. 299.

[10] *Jagdish Pandey* v. *Chancellor, Bihar University* (1968) 1 S.C.R. 231, ('68) A.SC. 353, 357 [*held*, that s. 4 of the Bihar University (Amendment) Act, 1962, should be read so as to save it from conferring uncanalised power on the chancellor; and so read it did not violate Art. 14.]

[11] *Amritsar Municipality* v. *Punjab* ('69) A.SC. 1100, 1105 (*held*, that it was implicit in ss. 3 and 4 that the monopoly created in favour of the State to

(3) The court will not decide Constitutional questions if a case is capable of being decided on other grounds.[12]

(iii) constitutional issue not decided if case can be decided on other grounds

(4) The court will not decide a larger Constitutional question than is required by the case before it.[13]

(iv) a larger constitutional question not decided

(5) The court will not hear an objection as to the constitutionality of a law by a person whose rights are not affected by it.[14]

(v) nor at the instance of a party not aggrieved

(6) A Statute cannot be declared unconstitutional merely because in the opinion of the Court it violates one or more of the principles of liberty, or the spirit of the Constitution, unless such principles and that spirit are found in the terms of the Constitution. Thus, in *A. K. Gopalan* v. *State*,[15] Kania C.J. cited with approval the following observations of Gwyer C.J.:

(vi) statutes not declared void as violating "the spirit of the Constitution" which is not expressed in words

"... especially is this true of a Federal Constitution with its nice balance of jurisdictions. I conceive that a broad and liberal spirit should inspire those whose duty it is to interpret it; but I do not imply by this that they are free to stretch or pervert the language of the enactment in the interest of any legal or constitutional theory or even for the purpose of supplying omissions or of correcting supposed errors."[16]

and then continued:

"Where the fundamental law has not limited, either in terms or by necessary implication, the general powers conferred upon the Legislature we cannot declare a limitation under the notion of having discovered something in the spirit of the Constitution which is not even mentioned in the instrument. . . . But it is only in express constitutional provisions limiting legislative power and controlling the temporary will of a majority by a permanent and paramount law settled by the deliberate wisdom of the nation that one can find a safe and solid ground for the authority of the Courts of justice to declare void any legislative enactment. Any assumption of authority beyond this would be *to place in the hands of the judiciary powers too great and too indefinite either for its own security or the protection of private rights*."[17] (italics supplied).

The same view was repeated by S. R. Das J. in *Keshavan Madhava Menon* v. *Bombay*:[18]

"An argument founded on what is claimed to be the spirit of the Constitution is always attractive, for it has a powerful appeal to sentiment and emotion; but a Court of Law has to gather the spirit of the Constitution from the language of the Constitution. What one may believe or think to be the spirit of the Constitution cannot prevail if the language of the Constitution does not support

hold and manage cattle fairs required that the State should do so on its own property and not on property belonging to local authorities or private owners); *M.P.* v. *C. J. Patel* ('72) A.SC. 971, 973 (treated as settled law that where there are two interpretations of a statute possible that interpretation which would make the statute constitutional must be preferred to that which would make is unconstitutional); *Ram Sarup* v. *Samunder Singh* ('72) A.P. & H. 280.

[12] Cooley: *Constitutional Law*, 4th ed., p. 192; *American Jurisprudence*, Vol. 11, p. 723; *Basheshar Nath* v. *C.I.T. Delhi & Rajasthan* (1959) Supp. 1 S.C.R. 528, 589-90, ('59) A.SC. 149.

[13] See f.n. 12 above; also *Suraj Mull Mohta & Co.* v. *A. V. Visvanatha Sastri* (1955) 1 S.C.R. 448, 449, ('54) A.SC. 545. In *M. M. Pathak* v. *Union* (1978) 3 S.C.R. 334, ('78) A.SC. 803, in the context of alternative challenge to the impugned Act under Art. 19(1)(*f*), Bhagwati J. observed: "It is the settled practice of this Court to decide no more than what is absolutely necessary for the decision of a case" ('78) A.SC. at p. 828. Accordingly the Court having accepted the main argument, did not decide the question under Art. 19(1)(*f*).

[14] *Hans Muller Nurenburg* v. *Supdt., Presidency Jail, Calcutta* (1955) 1 S.C.R. 1284, 1295, ('55) A.SC. 367.

[15] (1950) S.C.R. 88, 120, ('50) A.SC. 27.

[16] *In re C.P. & Berar Act, 1938*, (1939) F.C.R. 18, 37, ('39) A.FC. 1.

[17] (1950) S.C.R. at pp. 120-21.

[18] (1951) S.C.R. 228, 232-33, ('51) A.SC. 128.

that view. . . . It is, therefore, quite clear that the Court should construe the language of Art. 13(1) according to the established rules of interpretation and arrive at its true meaning uninfluenced by any assumed spirit of the Constitution."

(vii) Court not concerned with the wisdom or justice of a law if the Constitution is not violated

(7) In pronouncing on the constitutional validity of a statute, the Court is not concerned with the wisdom or unwisdom, the justice or injustice of the law. If that which is passed into law is within the scope of the power conferred on a Legislature and violates no restrictions on that power, the law must be upheld whatever a Court may think of it.[19]

(8) Ordinarily, courts should not pronounce on the validity of an Act, or part of an Act, which has not been brought into force, because till then the question of validity would be merely academic. Art. 143 confers advisory jurisdiction only on the Supreme Court, which therefore can exercise that jurisdiction *as provided in Art. 143*.[20]

Illustrations of rule (7)

3.2 On the whole, rule (7) above has been adhered to by the Supreme Court as is clear from the observations of Kania C.J. and Das J. set out in (6) above. The attitude towards Judicial review reflected in the present rule is most strikingly illustrated by the following observations of Latham C.J. in the *Australian Communist Party* v. *Commonwealth*:[21]

"I am aware that it is sometimes said that legal questions before the High Court should be determined upon sociological grounds — political economic or social. I can understand Courts being directed (as in Russia and Germany in recent years) to determine questions in accordance with the interest of a particular political party. There, the Court is provided with at least a political standard. But such a proposition as, for example, that the recent *Banking Case*[22] should have been determined upon political grounds and that the Court was wrong in adopting an attitude of detachment from all political considerations appears to me merely to ask the Court to vote again upon an issue upon which Parliament had already voted or could be asked to vote and to determine whether the nationalisation of banks would be a good thing or bad thing for the community. In my opinion, the Court has no concern whatsoever with any such question. In the present case, the decision of the Court should be the same whether the members of the Court believe in communism or do not believe in communism."

The position occupied by our Supreme Court more closely resembles that of the Supreme Court of Australia than that of the U.S. Supreme Court. The U.S. Supreme Court is not the final Court of Appeal in Civil and Criminal cases throughout the United States. It has appellate jurisdiction to control inferior Courts but its principal work is as a Constitutional Court. Our Supreme Court is a final Court of Appeal in all matters from all the Courts in India and not merely on Constitutional matters. It has a limited Original Jurisdiction under Art. 32 and an exclusive original jurisdiction in disputes between the Union and the States. The Supreme Court of Australia is a final Court of Appeal in Australia in all matters Civil, Criminal and Constitutional, except *inter se* matters where an appeal lies to the

---

[19] *Fram N. Balsara* v. *Bombay* (1951) Bom. 17, ('51) A.B. 210, 52 Bom.L.R. 799, 820; on app., sub nom., (1951) S.C.R. 682, ('51) A.SC. 318. For Australian and American cases, see Wynes, p. 15.

[20] *Chandra Sekhar* v. *Orissa* ('72) A.SC. 486-8, (the High Court ought not to have pronounced on the validity of Ch. 4, Orissa Land Reforms Act, 1960, as amended in 1965. For the same reason the Supreme Court declined to consider the validity of Ch. 4.)

[21] (1950-51) 83 C.L.R. 1, 148-9.

[22] (1948) 76 C.L.R. 1; on app., *sub. nom.*, (1949) 79 C.L.R. 497, (1950) A.C. 235.

Privy Council with the certificate of the High Court.[23] The importance of adhering to the rule of interpretation now being considered can best be expressed in the words of Prof. Finer:

"But courts of justice cannot afford the charge of error or bias. For the courts of justice are not only concerned with constitutional cases but with other cases, in which states, individuals, and corporations are in conflict: where people sue one against the other, where the state sues citizens: where, in short, the whole mass of claims under admitted law is decided. The multitude does not minutely discriminate, and when it mistrusts for one thing it may mistrust for another, though the cases are poles asunder; . . ."[24]

A departure from this rule and the adoption of a rule allowing political, economic and social considerations to determine judgments would raise serious problems about the appointment of Judges to the High Courts and the Supreme Court of India. And here again, the problems can best be described in the words of Prof. Finer:

"Since what shall be the law depends upon a majority of five judges out of nine, it is clear that the appointment of each judge is of great moment. It is not surprising, therefore, to find that on the occasion of a vacancy, the organs of opinion — press, party managers, Congress, President, 'political circles' just on the fringe of official politics, the Congressional lobbies, the hotels of Washington, the seminars and common rooms of universities, passengers aboard crack railway trains and airplanes — excitedly discuss the prospect. There is almost as much ado about a Supreme Court appointment in the United States as there is in the choice of a new party leader — a possible prime minister — in parliamentary countries, with perhaps just a little less overt noise."[25]

No such thing happens in India.[26]

3.3 Dr. Wynes has said that the U.S. Supreme Court ". . . has perforce become embroiled in discussions of what are really and in truth political questions, from the necessity of assigning some meaning to the various 'Bill of Rights' provisions."[27] And Prof. Finer's observations about the appointment of judges quoted above emphasise the same point. However, the inclusion of Fundamental Rights in our Constitution has not raised the same problems in India largely because: Fundamental Rights

(1) The U.S. Constitution came into existence as a result of the desire to combine several sovereign States into a Federal Union, so that the rights not granted to the Union were reserved to the States. Thus State Rights and Federal Rights had political overtones in the United States. In India, there were no Sovereign independent States to be federated, and State Rights and Federal Rights raised no such acute political controversies, as they did, and do, raise in the United States. (2) The U.S. Constitution treats the Legislatures as the delegates of the people who cannot transgress the powers delegated to them without forfeiting their trust. In India it has been settled law since *R. v. Burah*[28] that Indian Legislatures were in no sense the delegates of the British Parliament which conferred the power, but that within the limits of their power, the Legislatures were as supreme and sovereign as the British Parliament itself. Again, in India no rights are reserved to the people. (3) The Bill of Rights in the U.S. Constitution confers rights in broad general terms leaving the restrictions to be determined by Courts of law. Our Constitution declares Fundamental Rights and defines the limitations of those Rights in the Constitution itself. Art. 14 is an exception to this general rule, but the theory of classification evolved by the U.S. Supreme Court has in substance

Factors which have prevented the Courts in India from being involved in political controversies

---

[23] The exception "does not appear to be more than a theoretical possibility": *Wynes*, p. 487.

[24] *The Theory and Practice of Modern Government*, pp. 151-2.

[25] op. cit., 149; the passage relates to the appointment of Judges to the U.S. Supreme Court.

[26] For a further discussion of the topic see the Chapter on the Union Judiciary.

[27] Wynes, 3rd ed., p. vii.

[28] (1878) 5 I.A. 178, (1878) 3 App. Cas. 889, 4 Cal. 172.

been written into Art. 14 by judicial decisions as will appear later in this book.[29] (4) The due process clause of the 5th and the 14th Amendment has been the most potent source of political and social controversies in the United States. The power wielded by the Supreme Court under that clause is wide and indefinite, it being left to the majority of the Court to decide what is due process and what is not. (5) The courts in India started with the ingrained traditions of the British administration of justice according to which judges do not get involved in political or social controversies. This attitude was clearly expressed in the classic test of "reasonableness" laid down by Patanjali Sastri C.J. which is set out in full in Chapter X. The judicial approach embodied in that test was maintained by the courts till the decision in *Golak Nath*[30] in February 1967.

In the result, the view of the judicial function mentioned in Rules (6) and (7) in para 3.1 has not been affected by the inclusion of Fundamental Rights in our Constitution.

Stare decisis and the Sup. Ct.: *The Bengal Immunity Case*

3.4 The law declared by the Supreme Court is made binding on all courts by Art. 141, but in *Bengal Immunity Co. Ltd.* v. *Bihar*[31] this Article has been interpreted to mean that it does not include the Supreme Court itself.

The review of authorities by Jagannadhadas J.

3.5 As the above case was the first case before the Supreme Court in which the question arose, the matter was fully considered by the court though, in an unsatisfactory way, as pointed out by Jagannadhadas J.[32] The decision of the Supreme Court in *Bombay* v. *United Motors (India) Ltd.*[33] decided by a majority of 4 to 1, directly covered the appeal which should have been dismissed. As Jagannadhadas J. observed, the binding nature of the earlier judgment should have been considered first, instead of which the discussion took the form of challenging the correctness of that decision straight away. All the judgments deal with the practice of superior Courts as regards the binding nature of their own judgments. It is submitted that the most satisfactory discussion of the subject will be found in the judgment of Jagannadhadas J. and the effect of it may be stated thus: In 1955, the House of Lords was the only Tribunal which held that its decisions were absolutely binding on itself: *London Street Tramways Ltd.* v. *London County Council.*[34] The Privy Council which was the highest Tribunal of Appeal from the Dominions and the Colonies, had the power to re-consider its own decisions on *Constitutional questions.* When invited to reverse its decision in *Russel's Case*[35] the Privy Council said: ". . . on constitutional questions it must be seldom indeed that the Board would depart from a previous decision which it may be assumed will have been acted on both by governments and subjects."[36] The High Court of Australia also reserved to itself the power to reconsider its own decisions, but ". . . *not*, . . . upon a mere suggestion that some or all of the members of the later Court might arrive at a different conclusion if the matter were *res integra.* Otherwise there would be great danger

---

29 See para 2.61.
30 *I. C. Golak Nath* v. *Punjab* (1967) 2 S.C.R. 762, 895, ('67) A.SC. 1643, 1660.
31 (1955) 2 S.C.R. 603, ('55) A.SC. 661.
32 ibid. p. 739.
33 (1953) S.C.R. 1069, ('53) A.SC. 252.
34 (1898) A.C. 375, 380, [for the exception to this rule see *Midland Silicones Ltd.* v. *Scuttons Ltd.* (1962) A.C. 446]. On July 26, 1966, the House of Lords announced that it would no longer consider itself absolutely bound by its own decisions. For a text of the announcement, see Salmond, *Jurisprudence*, 12th ed., p. ix.
35 (1881-82) 7 App. Cas. 829.
36 *Att.-Gen. for Ontario* v. *Canada Temperance Federation* (1946) A.C. 193, 206.

of a want of continuity in the interpretation of the law."[37] In the same case Barton J. stated that the strongest reason for overruling an earlier decision was that it was manifestly wrong *and* its maintenance was injurious to the public interest. In *Att.-Gen. for New South Wales* v. *Perpetual Trustee Co. Ltd.*[38] the High Court refused to overrule its former decision. Dixon J. would have preferred a view contrary to the earlier decision if the matter had been *res integra* but he said:

". . . there appears to me to be no ground for reconsidering the decision in *Quince's Case*[39] unless it be a sufficient ground simply that the opposite conclusion is to be preferred. It is evident that the decision was reached only after a very full examination of the question. It cannot be said that any compelling consideration or important authority was overlooked or that the decision conflicts with well established principle or fails to go with a definite stream of authority. It is a recent and well considered decision upon what is evidently a highly disputable question."[40]

The U.S. Supreme Court has freely exercised the right to reconsider its own decisions on the Constitution.

The grave consequences of a reversal of its judgment by a final court

3.6 In the *Bengal Immunity Case*,[41] Jagannadhadas J. had no difficulty in showing that the previous judgment had been given after an elaborate argument lasting for twelve working days and after eight States had intervened. The arguments addressed to the larger Bench were those urged before, *and rejected by*, the earlier Bench. He held, it is submitted rightly, that there was no justification for overruling such a judgment. This conclusion is reinforced when it is realised that out of the 7 judges constituting the larger Bench, 3 judges actually took the view that the earlier judgment was right. Experience has shown the correctness of Jagannadhadas, J.'s observation that:

Fears expressed in dissenting judgments in the *Bengal Immunity Case* realized

"The finality of the decisions of this Court, which is the Court of last resort, will be greatly weakened and much mischief done if we treat our own judgments, even though recent, as open to reconsideration."[42]

and the fears expressed by B. P. Sinha J. have come true:

"Under the Constitution and even otherwise, this Court is naturally looked upon by the country as the custodian of law and the Constitution, and if this Court were to review its previous decisions simply on the ground that another view is possible, the litigant public may be encouraged to think that it is always worthwhile taking a chance with the highest Court in the land."[43]

In *I.T.O. Tuticorin* v. *T. S. D. Nadar*[44] Hegde J. in his dissenting judgment observed that:

". . . the decisions of this Court should not be overruled excepting under compelling circumstances. It is only when this Court is fully convinced that public interest of a substantial character would be jeopardized by a previous decision of this Court, this Court should overrule that decision. *Every time this Court over-rules its previous decision, the confidence of the public in the soundness of the decision of this Court is bound to be shaken.* Reconsideration of the decisions of this Court should be confined to questions of great public importance. In law finality is of utmost importance. *Legal problems should not be treated as mere subjects for mental exercise.* This Court must overrule its previous decisions only when it comes to the conclusion that it is manifestly wrong, not upon a mere suggestion that some or all of the members of the later Court might arrive at a different conclusion if the matter was *res integra*."[45] (italics supplied)

---

[37] *The Tramways Case (No. 1)* (1914) 18 C.L.R. 54, *per* Griffith C.J. at p. 58.
[38] (1951-2) 85 C.L.R. 237.
[39] (1943) 68 C.L.R. 227.
[40] ibid. 85 C.L.R. at p. 244.
[41] (1955) 2 S.C.R. 603, ('55) A.SC. 661.
[42] (1955) 2 S.C.R. *supra* at p. 743.
[43] ibid. p. 839.
[44] ('68) A.SC. 623.
[45] ibid. p. 636. *Cf.* "Undoubtedly, reversal of a precedent may cause injustice to those who have shaped their conduct in reliance upon it; but this is an argu-

The present writer has heard Counsel in the Bombay High Court refer to a 3 to 2 judgment of the Supreme Court in some such words as these: "This is a divided judgment of the Supreme Court and my client would like to take a chance with a larger Bench." Many Counsel act on this assumption who do not openly proclaim it. It is submitted that frequent references to a larger Bench in Constitutional matters have an unsettling effect on the law, are productive of great public inconvenience[46] and derogate from the authority of a final Court as rightly pointed out by Jagannadhadas and Sinha JJ. This power should be reserved for exceptional cases where the previous decisions were rendered in ignorance of provisions of the law or in the absence of material and relevant facts or were manifestly wrong *and* productive of public mischief.[47] The knowledge that judgments of the Court can be corrected by a larger Bench, would also have the psychological effect of making an ordinary Constitutional Bench of the Supreme Court feel that there is another authority which can set it right, so that the extreme precision of language and rigour of discussion required of a final Court would lose something of their urgency.

Severability **3.7** We have seen that where two interpretations are possible, a Court will accept that interpretation which will uphold the validity of the law. If, however, this is not possible, it becomes necessary to decide whether the law is bad as a whole, or whether the bad part can be severed from the good part. The question of construction, and the question of severability are thus two distinct questions.[48]

Principles laid down in *Chamarbaugwalla's Case* **3.8** The whole question of construction and severability was exhaustively considered in *R. M. D. Chamarbaugwalla* v. *Union.*[49] There, the question to be decided was whether the definition of a prize competition in s. 2(*d*) of the Prize Competitions Act, 1955, which was wide enough to cover both competitions of skill and gambling competitions, could be limited, by construction, to gambling competitions, and the literal meaning of the words was relied upon to show that it could not be so limited. Venkatarama Aiyar J. held that the literal meaning had only a *prima facie* preference in a Court, but to arrive at the real meaning:

". . . 'it is always necessary to get an exact conception of the aim, scope and object of the whole Act; to consider, according to Lord Coke: (1) What was the law before the Act was passed; (2) What was the mischief or defect for

---

ment for extreme care in overruling precedents rather than for a complete denial of the powers. Certainly, *if a court follows no consistent policy and frequently changes from one view to another, disrespect for the law results, since a chance majority may affect the decision*": (italics supplied). Paton, *A Text-Book of Jurisprudence*, 4th ed., pp. 223-4.

[46] The Privy Council had this inconvenience in mind when it said that in Constitutional matters the Board would seldom depart from a previous decision *which it may be assumed will have been acted on both by Governments and subjects*: see para 3.5.

[47] Judged by this test the reversal in the *Bengal Immunity Case, supra*, (1955) 2 S.C.R. 603, of the *United Motors Case, supra* (1953) S.C.R. 1069, ('53) A.SC. 252, 408 was unjustified.

[48] This was pointed out by Gwyer C.J. in the *Hindu Women's Property Case* (1941) F.C.R. 12, 27, ('41) A.FC. 72: "the Court does not seek to divide the Act into two parts, viz. the part which the Legislature was competent, and the part which it was incompetent, to enact. It holds that, on the true construction of the Act and especially of the word 'property' as used in it, no part of the Act was beyond the Legislature's powers."

[49] (1957) S.C.R. 930, ('57) A.SC. 628.

which the law had not provided; (3) What remedy Parliament has appointed; and (4) The reason for the remedy.' The reference here is to *Heydon's Case*.[50] These are principles well settled, and were applied by this Court in *Bengal Immunity Company Ltd.* v. *Bihar*.[51]"[52]

Applying the above rules of construction he held that the words "prize competition" must be interpreted to mean "prize competitions of a gambling nature."

3.9 Assuming that the above view was wrong, he considered the question of severability. There are two kinds of severability: a statutory provision may contain distinct and separate words dealing with distinct and separate topics, as for example, one sub-section may provide a rule of law for the future and another sub-section may apply it retrospectively. The first sub-section may be valid and the second void. In such a case, the Court may delete the second sub-section by treating it as severable.[53]

Two kinds of severability (i) severability by striking out a provision in whole or in part

3.10 There is however a different kind of severability recognized by the Courts, namely, severability in application, or separability in enforcement. The question of severability in application or enforcement arises when an impugned provision is one indivisible whole, as for instance, the definition of a word. Here severability cannot be applied by deleting an offending provision and leaving the rest standing. It becomes necessary therefore to inquire whether the impugned definition embraces distinct classes or categories of subject-matter in respect to some of which the Legislature has no power to legislate or is otherwise subject to a Constitutional limitation. If it is found that the definition does cover distinct and separate classes or categories, the Court will restrain the enforcement of the law in respect of that class of subjects in respect of which the law is invalid. This might be done by granting a perpetual injunction restraining the enforcement of the law on the forbidden field. The judgment in *Chamarbaugwalla's Case*[54] applied this principle to the definition of prize competitions as will presently appear.

(ii) Severability in application,

3.11 The principle of severability in application was first adopted by our Supreme Court when dealing with the contention that a tax law must be declared wholly void if it was bad in part as transgressing Constitutional limitations. Sastri C.J., delivering the majority judgment, observed: "It is a sound rule to extend severability to include separability in enforcement . . . and we are of opinion that the principle should be applied in dealing with taxing statutes. . . ."[55] He referred to the decision in *Bowman* v. *Continental Oil Co.*[56] In *Chamarbaugwalla's Case*[57] it was argued that this rule was exceptional and applied only to taxing statutes. But Venkatarama Aiyar J. rejected this contention.[58] After a careful scrutiny of English, American and Indian authorities on severability, he summarised the effect of the authorities thus:

was first applied to taxing statutes by the Sup. Ct.,

but is not restricted to such statutes

[50] (1584) 3 W.Rep. 16, 76 E.R. 637.
[51] (1955) 2 S.C.R. 603, 633, ('55) A.SC. 661.
[52] (1957) S.C.R. 930, 936.
[53] See *Punjab* v. *Daulat Singh* (1946) 73 I.A. 59, (1946) F.C.R. 1, ('46) A.PC. 66. The Privy Council severed a retrospective provision by deletion of the words "either before or" from the early part of the section under consideration.
[54] (1957) S.C.R. 930, ('57) A.SC. 628.
[55] *Bombay* v. *United Motors (India) Ltd.* (1953) S.C.R. 1069, ('53) A.SC. 252.
[56] (1920) 256 U.S. 642, 65 L. ed. 1139. [57] (1957) S.C.R. 930, ('57) A.SC. 628.
[58] (1957) S.C.R. *supra* at p. 945.

Principles formulated in *Chamarbaugwalla's Case*

"1. In determining whether the valid parts of a statute are separable from the invalid parts thereof, it is the intention of the legislature that is the determining factor. The test to be applied is whether the legislature would have enacted the valid part if it had known that the rest of the statute was invalid. *Vide Corpus Juris Secundum,* Vol. 82, p. 156; Sutherland on Statutory Construction, Vol. 2, pp. 176-177.[59]

2. If the valid and invalid provisions are so inextricably mixed up that they cannot be separated from one another, then the invalidity of a portion must result in the invalidity of the Act in its entirety. On the other hand, if they are so distinct and separate that after striking out what is invalid, what remains is in itself a complete code independent of the rest, then it will be upheld notwithstanding that the rest has become unenforceable. *Vide* Cooley's Constitutional Limitations, Vol. 1, at pp. 360-361; Crawford on Statutory Construction, pp. 217-218.

3. Even when the provisions which are valid are distinct and separate from those which are invalid, if they all form part of a single scheme which is intended to be operative as a whole, then also the invalidity of a part will result in the failure of the whole. *Vide* Crawford on Statutory Construction, pp. 218-219.

4. Likewise, when the valid and invalid parts of a statute are independent and do not form part of a scheme but what is left after omitting the invalid portion is so thin and truncated as to be in substance different from what it was when it emerged out of the legislature, then also it will be rejected in its entirety.

5. The separability of the valid and invalid provisions of a statute does not depend on whether the law is enacted in the same section or different sections (*vide* Cooley's Constitutional Limitations, Vol. 1, pp. 361-362); it is not the form, but the substance of the matter that is material, and that has to be ascertained on an examination of the Act as a whole and of the setting of the relevant provisions therein.

6. If after the invalid portion is expunged from the statute what remains cannot be enforced without making alterations and modifications therein, then the whole of it must be struck down as void, as otherwise it will amount to judicial legislation. *Vide* Sutherland on Statutory Construction, Vol. 2, p. 194.

7. In determining the legislative intent on the question of separability, it will be legitimate to take into account the history of the legislation, its object, the title and the preamble to it. *Vide* Sutherland on Statutory Construction; Vol. 2, pp. 177-178."[60]

their application to the case

Applying these tests Venkatarama Aiyar J. held that competitions fell into two distinct classes, competitions of skill and competitions of a gambling nature; the difference between the two was as clearcut as the difference between commercial and wagering contracts. On the facts it might be difficult to say whether a competition fell within one class or the other,[61] but when the true character of the competition was determined, it must fall within one class or the other. If the Court were to ask itself, would the Parliament have enacted the law if it did not apply to competitions of skill, there could be no doubt having regard to the history of the legislation that the answer must be in the affirmative. The restriction of the Act to competitions of a gambling nature did not affect either the texture or colour of the Act nor did it require any of its provisions to be re-written and

---

[59] *I.T.O., Assam* v. *Lawrence Singh* ('68) A.SC. 658 (*held,* that having regard to the reasons which persuaded the legislature to grant exemption, there was no doubt that it would have granted that exemption even if it were aware that it was beyond its competence to exclude government servants from the exemption in question).

[60] ibid. pp. 950-952. The above propositions were set out and fol. in *G. S. Chooramani* v. *U.P.* ('69) A.A. 43, 55-6.

[61] This difficulty would arise even if the definition of a prize competition was *expressly* limited to gambling competitions.

accordingly they must be treated as severable in their application and the enforcement of the law to competitions of skill would be restrained by an appropriate order. It is submitted that the acceptance of severability in application is clearly right. The time has long gone by when mere technicalities were permitted to defeat the ends of justice. There is no reason why a law should be invalidated as a whole, when there are large parts of it which are valid. Nor can the citizen legitimately complain of a procedure which protects him by restraining the enforcement of the invalid portion of the law by a permanent injunction.

3.12 In *H. R. Banthia* v. *Union,*[62] Ramaswami J. quoted a passage from Coolley's *Constitutional Limitations*[63] and held that the provisions of the Gold Control Act, 1968, which the court had struck down were not inextricably bound up with the remaining provisions of the Act which therefore were valid. No reference was made to *Chamarbaugwalla's Case,*[64] considered in para 3.11 above, although Ramaswami J. applied the second proposition there laid down by Venkatarama Aiyar J.

Severability clauses

3.13 The question of severability has been discussed above without reference to "severability clauses". A statute may contain a clause to the following effect:

"Every Act shall be read and construed subject to the Constitution, and so as not to exceed the Legislative power of the Commonwealth, to the intent that where any enactment thereof would, but for this section, have been construed as being in excess of that power, it shall nevertheless be a valid enactment to the extent to which it is not in excess of that power."

In Australia, a clause in these terms has been embodied in s. 15A of the Acts Interpretation Act, and a similar provision concerning the rules, regulations and bye-laws made in pursuance of statutory authority is made in s. 46(*b*) of that Act.[65] In India this practice has not been followed.

The utility of such clauses

3.14 A severability clause is of considerable importance when the Court is faced with the question: "Would the Legislature have enacted the law if the invalid portions were deleted?" for the clause gives the answer and absolves the Court from arriving at its own decision. It has, however, been held that the clause is an aid to construction and is not a binding command. A very useful discussion of severability clauses will be found in *Wynes,*[66] but the following paragraph sums up the result of the authorities:

'In the *Banking Case,*[67] Dixon J. reviewed the position reached on this question and stated his own view at length. . . . His Honour said: 'The effect of (severability) clauses is to reverse the presumption that a statute is to operate as a whole, so that the intention of the Legislature is to be taken *prima facie* to be that the enactment should be divisible and that any parts found constitutionally unobjectionable should be carried into effect independently of those which fail. To displace the application of this new presumption to any given situation arising under the statute by reason of the invalidation of part, it must sufficiently appear that the invalid provision forms part of an inseparable context.' But, added His Honour, in applying secs. 15A and 46(*b*), the Courts had insisted that once it appeared that rejection of the invalid part

---

[62] (1970) 1 S.C.R. 479, ('70) A.SC. 1433, 1467-8.
[63] 8th ed., p. 360.
[64] (1957) S.C.R. 930, ('57) A.SC. 628.
[65] Wynes, pp. 50-51.
[66] ibid. pp. 50-54.
[67] (1948) 76 C.L.R. 1, 371 on app. *sub. nom.*, (1949) 79 C.L.R. 497, (1950) A.C. 235, (1949) 2 All E.R. 755.

would mean a different operation of the valid part or produce a different result, the whole must fail. This consideration supplied a strong logical ground for holding provisions to be inseverable, since in such a case there was a strong inference that Parliament did not intend that anything less than the whole Act should be law. At a later stage His Honour refers to the rule 'that provisions are to be considered severable and general words distributable.' "[68]

Colourable legislation

3.15 A Legislature lacking legislative power or subject to a Constitutional prohibition may frame its legislation so as to make it appear to be within its legislative power or to be free from the constitutional prohibition. Such a law is "colourable" legislation, meaning thereby that while pretending to be a law in the exercise of undoubted power, it is in fact a law on a prohibited field.

Gajapati's Case: the Sup. Ct. approves Privy Council decisions:

3.16 The question of colourable legislation was fully discussed by the Supreme Court in *K. C. Gajapati Narayan Deo* v. *Orissa*,[69] a decision which has been treated as settling the law on the subject.[70] However, before discussing that case, it would be convenient to refer to the decisions of the Privy Council in appeals from Canada and Australia, where the same question had been raised, because the Supreme Court has referred to some of those decisions with approval, and adopted the principles there laid down.

(i) *Union Colliery Case*

3.17 In *Union Colliery Co. of British Columbia* v. *Bryden*,[71] the Privy Council held that s. 4 of the impugned Act, which prohibited Chinamen of full age from employment in underground coal workings, was not a law relating to Provincial Undertakings,[72] nor a law relating to property and Civil Rights in the Province,[73] but was in pith and substance a law relating to naturalisation of aliens,[74] a subject of exclusive Dominion legislative power. Accordingly, s. 4 was *ultra vires* of the Provincial Legislature. In *Att.-Gen. for Ontario* v. *Reciprocal Insurers*,[75] the Privy Council had to consider, *inter alia*, an attempt by the Dominion of Canada to control contracts of insurance within a province. The Dominion having failed to secure that control by the Insurance Act of 1910, which was declared *ultra vires* by the Privy Council,[76] tried to achieve the same object by resorting to the Criminal Law of Canada. A Dominion Act of 1917, inserted s. 508(*c*) in the Criminal Code which made it an offence for any person to solicit or accept any insurance risk except on behalf or as agent of a Company duly licensed under the Insurance Act, 1917, of Canada. The Dominion contended that its power to legislate on Criminal Law was unfettered and that the impugned law was *intra vires*. Rejecting this contention, the Privy Council observed that this claim was a claim to legislate on every topic of exclusive Provincial legislation by resorting to the entry on Criminal Law, and that such a claim could not be allowed consistently with the principles governing the interpretation of Ss. 91 and 92 of the B.N.A. Act, 1867.

(ii) *A.G. for Ontario* v. *Reciprocal Insurers*

"It is one thing, for example, to declare corruption in municipal elections, or negligence of a given order in the management of railway trains, to be a criminal offence and punishable under the Criminal Code; it is another thing to

---

[68] Wynes, 3rd ed., pp. 51-2.
[69] (1954) S.C.R. 1, ('53) A.SC. 375.
[70] *Sonapur Tea Co.* v. *Deputy Commissioner* (1962) 1 S.C.R. 724, ('62) A.SC. 137, 140.
[71] (1899) A.C. 580.
[72] S. 92(10), B.N.A. Act, 1867.
[73] ibid. s. 92(13).
[74] ibid. s. 91(25).
[75] (1924) A.C. 328.
[76] *Att.-Gen. for Canada* v. *Att.-Gen. for Alberta* (1916) 1 A.C. 588.

make use of the machinery of the criminal law for the purpose of assuming control of municipal corporations or of Provincial railways."[77]

Accordingly, s. 508(*c*) was held void on the ground that though in form a law relating to Criminal Law, in substance it was an attempt to legislate on one or more topics of exclusive Provincial legislation.

3.18 In *Att.-Gen. for Alberta* v. *Att.-Gen. for Canada*,[78] the question of colourable legislation arose with the addition of a new feature, namely, that the colourable legislation was contained not in a single statute, but in a number of statutes taken together. A Bill passed by the Legislative Assembly of the Province of Alberta entitled "An Act respecting the Taxation of Banks" and reserved by the Lt.-Governor of Alberta for the significance of the pleasure of the Governor-General in Council imposed on every Corporation or Joint Stock Company other than the Bank of Canada incorporated for the purpose of doing Banking or the Savings Bank business in the Province, an annual tax in addition to any tax payable under any other Act, of (*a*) ½ per cent on the paid-up capital, and (*b*) 1 per cent on the reserve fund and undivided profits, the tax to be payable to the Provincial Secretary on behalf of His Majesty for use of the Province. The question for the determination of the Privy Council was whether the taxation was in order to the raising of a revenue for Provincial purposes within the meaning of s. 92(2) of the B.N.A. Act, 1867, or whether it was in substance a tax on banks and savings banks which fell within s. 91(15) and (16) respectively of that Act. It was held that the law was in no sense one relating to taxation for provincial purposes but was a law designed to prevent the functioning of banks and savings banks in the Privinces both of which subjects were exclusive subjects of Dominion legislation. The law was colourable because:

A.G. for Alberta v. *A.G. for Canada*

(1) No other body, Corporation, Institution or person was the subject of taxation under the Bill, and "it is strange to find the Province singling out, 'in order to the raising of a revenue for Provincial purposes,' banks and savings banks and no other wealthy Corporation, body or persons in the Province."[79]

Grounds for holding the law colourable

(2) "Under the guise of discriminatory taxation in the Province it would be easy not only to impair, but even to render wholly nugatory, the exclusive legislative authority of the Dominion over a number of the classes of subjects specifically mentioned in s. 91 by making them valueless. Instances could be found in bills of exchange, and promissory notes, patents, and copyrights, which could be so heavily taxed as entirely to destroy their use as well as their value in the Province. A number of other illustrations could be given arising under s. 92(10). No one would suggest . . . that Provincial legislation of this character would be valid"[80]

(3) Admitting that a test applicable to every case of overlapping powers specified in ss. 91 and 92 is more than elusive, yet it is often comparatively easy to determine that the particular piece of legislation is an encroachment on a forbidden territory.[81]

(4) In considering the effect of the Act, the Court must take into account any public general knowledge of which the Court would take Judicial notice, and may in a proper case require to be informed by evidence as to what the effect will be: "Clearly, the Acts passed by the Provincial Legislature may be considered, for it is often impossible to determine the effect of the Act under examination without taking into account any other Act operating, or intended to operate, or recently operating in the Province."[82]

[77] (1924) A.C. 328 at p. 343.
[78] (1939) A.C. 117.
[79] ibid. p. 131.
[80] ibid. pp. 128-9.
[81] ibid. p. 129.
[82] ibid. p. 130.

(5) "It is not competent either for the Dominion or the Province under the guise, or the pretence, or in the form of an exercise of its own powers, to carry out an object which is beyond its powers and a trespass on the exclusive powers of the other: *Att.-Gen. for Ontario* v. *Reciprocal Insurers*,[83] *In re The Insurance Act of Canada*.[84]"[85] The increase in tax brought about by the impugned Act was so great that the facts were sufficient to show that such a rate of taxation must be prohibitive in fact and must be known to the Alberta Legislature to be prohibitive.[86]

(6) Whilst the Court is not concerned with the question whether taxation is light or heavy, this argument cannot prevail in a case where the taxation was in a practical sense prohibitive of the business taxed.[87]

(7) The argument stated in (6) above is reinforced by a study of the various Acts of the Alberta Legislature which showed that the impugned law was part of a legislative plan to prevent the operation within the Province of banking institutions which had been called into existence and given the necessary powers to conduct their business by the only proper authority, the Parliament of Canada.[88]

(8) While the Privy Council has declined to invalidate the exercise of a taxing power on an anticipatory argument, that if the power was abused it would interfere with the exercise of exclusive Dominion power: *Bank of Toronto* v. *Lambe*;[89] the position is different where the argument is based not on a possible abuse of power but on the actual abuse of the power which has the effect of destroying an exercise of exclusive Dominion power.[90]

Moran's Case: legislative schemes

3.19 In *W. R. Moran Pty. Ltd.* v. *Dy. Commissioner of Taxation for N.S.W.*,[91] the Privy Council had to consider whether a legislative scheme adopted by the Commonwealth and the States of Australia was a colourable scheme involving discriminatory taxation forbidden by s. 51(ii) of the Australian Constitution. S. 51(ii) empowers the Commonwealth Parliament to make laws with respect to "taxation; but so as not to discriminate between States or parts of States": The power thus conferred is subject to the provisions of the Constitution which include s. 96 which provides:

"*Financial Assistance to States.* During a period of ten years after the establishment of the Commonwealth and thereafter until the Parliament otherwise provides, the Parliament may grant financial assistance to any State on such terms and conditions as the Parliament thinks fit."

There was nothing disguised about the scheme which had been evolved by the Commonwealth in consultation with the States, and the whole of it was set out in the preamble to the Wheat Industries Assistance Act, 1938. The scheme was carried out through a series of Commonwealth Acts and by certain State Acts passed by the various States. The scheme and the manner of carrying it out may be stated thus:

"In pursuance of a joint Commonwealth and State scheme to ensure to wheat growers in all the Australian States a 'payable price' for their produce, a number of Acts were passed by the Commonwealth Parliament imposing taxes on flour sold in Australia for home consumption so as to provide a fund available for the payment of moneys to wheat growers. Those Acts included the Flour Tax (Stocks) Act, No. 50 of 1938, which imposed a tax on flour in excess of 1,000 lbs. held in stock on December 5, 1938, by any person other than the manufacturer of the flour; the Flour Tax (Wheat Industry Assistance) Assessment Act, No. 48 of 1938, which provided the machinery relating to the imposition, assessment and collection of the taxes imposed by the various Acts; and the Wheat Industry Assistance Act, No. 53 of 1938, which provided for a fund into which the taxes were to be paid, and out of which

---

[83] (1924) A.C. 328, 342.
[84] (1932) A.C. 41.
[85] (1939) A.C. at pp. 130-1.
[86] ibid. p. 132.
[87] ibid. p. 133.
[88] ibid.
[89] (1887) 12 App. Cas. 575, 576.
[90] (1939) A.C. at pp. 133-5.
[91] (1940) A.C. 838 at p. 839, (1940) 3 All E.R. 269.

certain payments were to be made to the States of financial assistance for payment to wheat growers in accordance with State legislation. In the case of the State of Tasmania, however, where the quantity of wheat grown was relatively insignificant and wheat was imported, the taxes on flour were imposed by the Federal legislation at the same rate as in the other States, but it was agreed as part of the scheme, and was provided by s. 14 of the Wheat Industry Assistance Act, No. 53 of 1938, that a special grant should be made to Tasmania, not subject to any Federal statutory conditions, but intended to be applied by the Government of Tasmania in paying back to Tasmanian millers and others nearly the whole of the flour tax paid by them, and provision to give effect to that purpose was made by the Flour Tax Relief Act, No. 40 of 1938, of the State of Tasmania."[92]

grounds for holding that the scheme was not colourable

The Privy Council held that the scheme was not colourable legislation, but in arriving at this conclusion, it laid down certain propositions which are important in considering colourable legislation:

(1) The prohibition of s. 51(ii) against discrimination is not got over by enacting a taxation Act containing no discrimination followed by an Appropriation Act or a Tax Assessment Act containing such discrimination. In the opinion of the Privy Council, a Taxation Act, an Appropriation Act and a Tax Assessment Act are all laws with respect to taxation or related to taxation and must be taken together.[93]

(2) ". . . where there is admittedly a scheme of proposed legislation, it seems to be necessary when the 'pith and substance' or 'scope and effect' of any one of the Acts is under consideration, to treat them together and to see how they interact. The separate parts of a machine have little meaning if examined without reference to the function they will discharge in the machine."[94]

(3) That while s. 96 did not prohibit discrimination, the Privy Council made it clear that as then advised, the Commonwealth Parliament could not exercise its powers under s. 96 with a complete disregard of the prohibition contained in s. 51(ii) or so as altogether to nullify that Constitutional safeguard. Under the guise or pretence of assisting a State with money, the real purpose and substance of the Act might simply be to effect discrimination in regard to taxation. Such an Act might well be *ultra vires* of the Commonwealth Parliament.[95]

Gajapati's Case: Privy Council decisions applied

3.20 In *Gajapati's Case*,[96] already referred to, the challenge on the ground of colourable legislation, or fraud on the Constitution, was based on the following facts:

"The Bill relating to the Orissa Estates Abolition Act, 1952, was published in the Gazette on the 3rd January, 1950. It contained a provision that any sum payable for agricultural income-tax for the previous year should be deducted from the gross asset of an estate for the purpose of arriving at its net income on the basis on which compensation was payable to the estate owners. On the 8th January, 1950, a Bill to amend the Orissa Agricultural Income-tax Act of 1947 so as to enhance the highest rate of tax from 3 annas in the rupee to 4 annas and reduce the highest slab from Rs. 30,000 to Rs. 20,000 was published in the Gazette. This Bill was dropped by the next Chief Minister who introduced a revised Bill on the 22nd July 1950, enhancing the highest rate of 12 annas 6 pies in the rupee and reducing highest slab to Rs. 15,000 and this was passed into law in August 1950. It was contended that the Orissa Agricultural Income-tax (Amendment) Act of 1950 was a fraud on the Constitution and as such invalid as it was a colourable legislation to effect a drastic reduction in the compensation payable under the Estates Abolition Act."[97]

The appellant's contention was that the Agricultural Income-tax Act was a fraud on the Constitution and was a colourable law because its object was to reduce the compensation payable for the acquisition of

---

92 (1940) A.C. at pp. 838-9.
93 ibid. p. 854.
94 ibid. p. 849. This is an amplification of Rule 4 in para 3.18.
95 ibid. p. 858. This was said to be the language of caution.
96 (1954) S.C.R. 1, ('53) A.SC. 375.
97 (1954) S.C.R. *supra* at p. 1.

land, contrary to the requirements of the Constitution as regards the payment of compensation. The argument appears to have been that as compensation was to be calculated on the basis of capitalising income, the tax was designed only to reduce the compensation to a small fraction of what would otherwise be payable. It may be mentioned that the impugned law was covered by Art. 31(4) with the result that it could not be questioned on the ground that it was not for a public purpose or that it did not provide for compensation. Mukherjea J., observed that the doctrine of colourable legislation did not involve any question of *bona fides* or *mala fides* on the part of the legislature. The whole doctrine resolved itself into a question of the competency of a particular legislature to enact a particular law.[98] The idea conveyed by the expression 'colourable legislation' was that although apparently the Legislature, in passing a statute purported to act within the limits of its powers, yet in substance and in reality, it transgressed those powers, the transgression being veiled by what appears on a proper examination to be a mere pretence or disguise: *The Att.-Gen. for Ontario* v. *Reciprocal Insurers.*[99] He said that:

Colourable legislation raises a question of legislative power, and not of the *bona fides* of the legislature

". . . In cases like these, the enquiry must always be as to the true nature and character of the challenged legislation . . . and not the form alone that will determine as to whether or not it relates to a subject which is within the power of the legislative authority. For the purpose of this investigation the court could certainly examine the effect of the legislation and take into consideration its object, purpose or design. But these are only relevant for the purpose of ascertaining the true character and substance of the enactment and the class of subjects of legislation to which it really belongs and not for finding out the motives which induced the legislature to exercise its powers. It is said by Lefroy in his well known work on Canadian Constitution that even if the legislature avow on the face of an Act that it intends thereby to legislate in reference to a subject over which it has no jurisdiction, yet if the enacting clauses of the Act bring the legislation within its powers, the Act cannot be considered *ultra vires.*"[1]

After considering *The Union Colliery Case;*[2] *Att.-Gen. for Alberta* v. *Att.-Gen. for Canada;*[3] *and Moran's Case,*[4] Mukherjea J. said:

The basis of the doctrine of colourable legislation

"The whole doctrine of colourable legislation is based upon the maxim that you cannot do indirectly what you cannot do directly. If a legislature is competent to do a thing directly, then the mere fact that it attempted to do it in an indirect or disguised manner, cannot make the Act invalid."[5]

Since, under Entry 42, List III, Sch. VII, any principle of compensation could be adopted and since under Art. 31(4) the adequacy of compensation could not be gone into, the appellant's case for colourable legislation failed. The decision of the Supreme Court in *Bihar* v. *Maharajadhiraja Sir Kameshwar Singh,*[6] was strongly relied on, but was distinguished by the Court. As the law was covered by Art. 31(4), the decision is clearly right. But if the law were not so covered, it is submitted that a very serious question of colourable legislation would have arisen, namely, whether the taxing power of the State could be used to defeat the requirements of Art. 31(2) as regards the payment of compensation which at that time was taken to mean adequate compensation.

---

[98] (1954) S.C.R. *supra* at p. 11.
[99] (1924) A.C. 328, 337.
[1] (1954) S.C.R. 1, 12, referring to Lefroy on *Canadian Constitution,* p. 75.
[2] (1899) A.C. 580.
[3] (1939) A.C. 117, 130.
[4] (1940) A.C. 838, (1940) 3 All E.R. 269.
[5] (1954) S.C.R. 1, 19-20.
[6] (1952) S.C.R. 889, ('52) A.SC. 252.

3.21 In *Kameshwar Singh's Case*[7] the whole law relating to acquisition of estates was challenged but certain provisions of the law were challenged as colourable legislation or as a fraud on the Constitution. As to the provisions contained in ss. 4(*b*) and 23(*f*) of the Bihar Land Reforms Act, 1950, the Court held by a majority of 3 to 2 that they were colourable legislation and were void. S. 4(*b*) provided that all arrears of rent whether they had merged into a decree or not, were to vest in Government and 50 per cent of those rents were to be added to the compensation payable to the land holder. Mahajan and Chandrasekhara Aiyer JJ. held that Art. 31(4) referred only to that part of Art. 31(2) which provided for the payment of compensation and that a public purpose was inherent in the concept of acquisition of property under the then legislative entries 36 and 42. They held that while the adequacy of compensation could not be determined by the Court under Art. 31(4), the Court was not precluded from considering whether there was a public purpose, and they held that the acquisition of arrears of rent on payment of 50 per cent of their value cannot be held to be for a public purpose. Mukherjea J., who agreed in the conclusion, was prepared to assume that Art. 31(4) referred both to public purpose and to compensation; but he held that the real object of s. 4(*b*) was to deprive the proprietor of his money which was not a subject-matter for acquisition under the powers of eminent domain without giving anything in exchange and in the guise of acting under Entry 42, the Legislature had in truth and substance evaded and nullified its provision altogether and therefore s. 4(*b*) was void.

Kameshwar Singh's case

Mukherjea J.: two provisions colourable

3.22 S. 23(*f*) provided for a deduction representing 4 to 12½ per cent of the gross assets as "cost of works for the benefits of raiyats" in ascertaining the net assets on which compensation was to be based. The Court held that this provision was purely arbitrary and had no relation to facts and was merely designed to aviod paying compensation under the guise of laying down principles of compensation. Mahajan, Mukherjea and Chandrasekhara Aiyer JJ. held that Entry 42 of List III did not permit laying down principles which would deny compensation but applied to principles for determining payment of compensation. Accordingly, s. 23(*f*) was merely a colourable device.

S. 23(f) Bihar Land Reforms Act held colourable by the majority

3.23 When *Kameshwar Singh's Case*[8] was strongly pressed in *Gajapati's Case*[9] Mukherjea J. distinguished it by saying that the two provisions held colourable in the earlier case: ". . . purported to have been enacted under entry 42 of List III, Schedule VII of the Constitution, namely, principles on which compensation for property acquired is to be determined and the form and manner in which their compensation is to be given."[10] Accordingly, the majority in that case held that the item of deduction provided for in s. 23(*f*) was a fictitious item wholly unrelated to the facts. There was no definable pre-existing liability on the part of the landlord to execute works of any kind for the benefit of raiyats. What was attempted to be done was to bring within the scope of the legislation something which not being existent could have no conceivable relation to any principle of compensation. It had therefore been held to be colourable legislation, which though

Kameshwar Singh's Case distinguished in Gajapati's Case

[7] ibid.
[8] (1952) S.C.R. 889, ('52) A.SC. 252.
[9] (1954) S.C.R. 1, ('53) A.SC. 375.
[10] (1954) S.C.R. at p. 17.

purporting to have been made under Entry 42 could not factually come within its scope.[11] The same principle was applicable as to the arrears of rent which had become due to the landlord without giving him any compensation whatsoever. Taking the whole and returning the half meant nothing more or less than taking the half and this, it was held, could not be regarded as a principle of compensation in any sense of the word.[12] It is submitted that the decision of the majority in *Kameshwar Singh's Case* was correct and the distinction made by Mukherjea J. in *Gajapati's Case* correctly brings out the difference between the two cases.

Gajapati's Case followed in several Sup. Ct. decisions

3.24 *Gajapati's Case* has been repeatedly cited and followed by the Supreme Court as laying down the correct principles for determining colourable legislation. Applying those principles, it has been held (i) that Ch. IV-A, Motor Vehicles Act, was not a colourable device to transfer the business of citizens to the State or a Corporation owned or controlled by the State;[13] (ii) that s. 22(1), Vindhya Pradesh Abolition of Jagirs and Land Reforms Act, 1952, was not colourable legislation;[14] (iii) that a tax on prize competitions was not void on the ground that it was colourable;[15] (iv) that the imposition of a sales tax on cane jaggery was not colourable;[16] (v) that the Kerala Agrarian Relations Act, 1961, was not a colourable device to take away the moneys of the land owners or the persons from whom excess land was taken away for the purpose of adding to the revenue of the State;[17] (vi) that the tax levied by the U.P. Large Land Holdings Tax Act, 1957, was not confiscatory and was not colourable;[18] (vii) that a tax on lands and buildings imposed by s. 4, M.P. *Nagriya Sampati Kar Adhiniyam*, 1964, was not colourable legislation.[19] (viii) that the Excise duty levied under s. 2 of the Iron Ores Mines Labour Welfare Cess Act, 1961, was not colourable as Entry 84, List I, Sch. 7 directly covered the duty.[20] However, in *Maharana Shri Jayavantsinghji*

---

[11] ibid. p. 17. [12] ibid. p. 17.

[13] *G. Nageswara Rao* v. *A.P. State Road Transport Corpn.* (1959) Supp. 1 S.C.R. 319, ('59) A.SC. 308.

[14] *V.P.* v. *Moradhwaj Singh* (1960) 3 S.C.R. 106, 112-13, ('60) A.SC. 796 (after citing *Gajapati's Case* it was said that it was not proper for the Judicial Commissioner to ascribe motives to the Legislature as he did by saying that the provision was made for creating inconvenience to a class whom the Legislature did not like.)

[15] *R.M.D.C. (Mysore) Private Ltd.* v. *Mysore* (1962) 3 S.C.R. 230, 243-44, ('62) A.SC. 594 (the argument was that the object of the tax was not revenue, but control of betting and gambling and therefore the tax was colourable, a contention which was repelled by saying that since the tax was within the power of the Legislature, the motives for the tax were irrelevant. The decision is correct, but the assumption that a tax cannot be used for purposes other than revenue is ill-founded; a tax is a recognized instrument of social control and heavy taxes on luxuries are an example of such control.)

[16] *T. G. Venkataraman* v. *Madras*, 1969 (2) S.C.C. 299, 305 (if the Legislature has the power to impose a tax, its validity is not open to challenge on a plea of colourable exercise of power.)

[17] *Karimbil Kunhikoman* v. *Kerala* (1962) Supp. 1 S.C.R. 829, 835, ('62) A.SC. 723.

[18] *Jagannath Baksh Singh* v. *U.P.* (1963) 1 S.C.R. 220, 238-9, ('62) A.SC. 1563 [citing *K. T. Moopil Nair* v. *Kerala* (1961) 3 S.C.R. 77, ('61) A.SC. 552, as an instance where a land tax was struck down as colourable. *Moopil Nair's Case* held that the tax was confiscatory, was discriminatory and violated Arts. 14 and 19; it contains no discussion on principles governing colourable legislation.]

[19] *D. Kasturchandji* v. *State* ('67) A.M.P. 268.

[20] *Nagappa* v. *I.O.M. Cess Commissioner* ('68) A.Mys. 42, 45-6.

Ranmalsinghji v. *Gujarat*[21] S. K. Das J. (for himself and Sinha C.J.) held, applying the principle of *Gajapati's Case,* that ss. 3, 4 and 6 of the Bombay Land Tenure Abolition Laws (Amendment) Act, 1958, were colourable legislation, since under the guise of defining a permanent tenant or changing a rule of evidence, they reduced the purchase price which had become payable to tenure holders on April 1, 1959.

3.25 The principle of colourable legislation was applied to subordinate delegated legislation in *Assam Co. Ltd.* v. *Assam.*[22]

3.26 In *Mahendra Lal* v. *U.P.*[23] the Supreme Court held that the constitutionality of an Act must be judged on the basis of the Constitution as it was on the date the Act was passed subject to any retrospective amendment of the Constitution.[24] *Mahendra Lal's Case* was followed and extended to determining the constitutionality of statutory orders.[25]

---

[21] (1962) Supp. 2 S.C.R. 411, 441, ('62) A.SC. 821.

[22] ('70) A.A. & N. 40 [*held*, that under s. 334 of the Assam Municipal Act, 1957, a town committee was to be constituted when "improved arrangements are required within a specified area". In the present case, s. 4(1) of the Act was applied by the impugned notification to an area having better arrangements than those which could be provided by the town committee; the notification was therefore colourable legislation and was invalid.]

[23] (1963) Supp. 1 S.C.R. 912, ('63) A.SC. 1019.

[24] (1963) Supp. 1 S.C.R. *supra* at p. 929 [*held*, that the observation in *Bombay Dyeing & Mfg. Co. Ltd.* v. *Bombay* (1958) S.C.R. 1122 that the validity of a law must be judged as it stood at the date of the petition, could not be interprcted as controverting the proposition in the text, because otherwise, a law would be prospective or retrospective according to the date on which the petition was filed —a result which it would be impossible to accept.]

[25] *State* v. *Annam* ('69) A.Ker. 38, 54 (F.B.). (The principle was applied to determine the constitutional validity of the Kerala Rice & Paddy Procurement by Levy Order, 1966.)

CHAPTER IV

PREAMBLE

The Preamble **4.1** The Preamble to our Constitution declares: "WE, THE PEOPLE OF INDIA, having solemnly resolved to constitute India into a SOVEREIGN *SOCIALIST SECULAR* DEMOCRATIC REPUBLIC and to secure to all its citizens:

JUSTICE, social, economic and political;

LIBERTY of thought, expression, belief, faith and worship;

EQUALITY of status and of opportunity; and to promote among them all

FRATERNITY assuring the dignity of the individual and the unity *and integrity* of the Nation;

IN OUR CONSTITUENT ASSEMBLY this twenty-sixth day of November, 1949, do HEREBY ADOPT, ENACT AND GIVE TO OURSELVES THIS CONSTITUTION."[1]

Preamble amended: a criticism **4.2** The changes made in the Preamble call for a few comments. First, it would be patently false to say that the people of India, on the 26th day of November, 1949, resolved to constitute India into a "Sovereign Socialist Secular Democratic Republic." What they did was to constitute India into a Sovereign Democratic Republic. A Preamble to a Constitution indicates the objectives of the founding fathers (who claimed to speak on behalf of the people of India), and since the Preamble is a part of the Constitution as held in the *Fundamental Rights Case*,[2] the Preamble can be amended. But such a result can only be produced by setting out the original Preamble with the introductory words "WHEREAS the people of India in their Constituent Assembly enacted the following Preamble and WHEREAS Parliament in the . . . year of the Republic desires to add to the Preamble, be it enacted as follows: After the word 'sovereign' add the words 'socialist secular'." Any other way of amending the Preamble would be historically false and would involve a patent contradiction. As Gwyer C.J. observed in *Bhola Prasad's Case*,[3]

> "But we doubt very much whether a preamble retrospectively inserted in 1940 in an Act passed 25 years before can be looked at by the Court for the purpose of discovering what the true intention of the Legislature was at the earlier date. A Legislature can always enact that the law is, and shall be deemed always to have been, such and such; but that is a wholly different thing from imputing to dead and gone legislators a particular intention merely because their successors at the present day think that they might or ought to have had it."[4]

"Socialist" and "Secular" required to be defined **4.3** Whether the Preamble at all needed amendment is a question of policy. However, it may be observed that the word "socialist" would require to be defined. It is a word of many meanings, and its appropriation by the Soviet Union would seem to suggest that a

---

1 The italicized words "*SOCIALIST SECULAR*" and "*and integrity*" were added by the 42nd Amendment.

2 *Kesavananda* v. *Kerala* (1973) Supp. S.C.R. 1, ('73) A.SC. 1461.

3 (1942) F.C.R. 17.

4 ibid. p. 29.

socialist form of government can be a dictatorship, which is foreign to our Constitution. In fact, an amendment to the Preamble moved by Maulana Hasrat Mohani which spoke of "We the people of India having solemnly resolved to constitute India into a Union of Indian Socialistic Republic to be called U.I.S.R. on the lines of the U.S.S.R." was rejected as inconsistent with our Constitution.[5] Secondly, the word "secular" is not precise and would itself require to be defined. "Secular" may be opposed to "religious" in the sense that a secular State can be an anti-religious State. In this sense, the Constitution of India is not secular, because the right to the freedom of religion is a guaranteed fundamental right. The word "secular" may mean that as far as the State is concerned, it does not support any religion out of public funds, nor does it penalise the profession and practice of any religion or the right to manage religious institutions as provided in Arts. 25 and 26. The secular nature of our Constitution has to be gathered from these and other Articles of our Constitution, like the Articles relating to a common Citizenship (Part II) and Articles 15, 16 and 29(2). Good drafting would require that ambiguous words should not be put into a Preamble without a reason and as far as one can see, there is no reason for putting in the word "socialist" and the word "secular", for the content of those concepts themselves would have to be found in the enacting parts of the Constitution, and by themselves the two words have certain associations which are inconsistent with the enacting provisions of our Constitution. The words "equality, fraternity, liberty" as well as the word "justice" in the original Preamble are not precise, but they have been historically associated with the struggle for freedom. The insertion of the word "integrity" in the sentence beginning with "Fraternity" adds to the Preamble what had been added by the 16th Amendment in Art. 19 and in the Third Schedule to the Constitution.

4.4 Realising that the words "secular" and "socialist" required to be defined, the 45th Amendment Bill (which became the 44th Amendment) proposed an amendment of Art. 366 by inserting definitions of the words "secular" and "socialist".[6] However, this amendment was not accepted by the Council of States. Consequently, the words "secular" and "socialist" remain undefined, and it becomes unnecessary to consider the correctness of the suggested definition. In *Excel Wear* v. *Union*[7] the Supreme Court held that the addition of the word "Socialist" in the Preamble might enable the Court to lean more and more in favour of nationalization and State ownership of an industry. However, as long as the private ownership of industries was recognized, and governed an overwhelmingly large proportion of our economic structure, the principles of socialism and social justice could not be pushed to such an extent as to ignore completely,

but remain undefined:

Excel Wear v *Union* on effect of "Socialist"

[5] *C.A.D.*, Vol. X, pp. 435-37.

[6] The Constitution (Forty fifth) Amendment Bill, 1978: *Cl. 44. Amendment of Article 366.*—Article 366 of the Constitution shall be *renumbered* as clause (2) of that article, and before clause (2) as so renumbered, the following clause shall be *inserted*, namely:— "(1) In the Preamble to this Constitution,— (1) the expression 'REPUBLIC' as qualified by the expression 'SECULAR', means a republic in which there is equal respect for all religions; and (2) the expression 'REPUBLIC' as qualified by the expression 'SOCIALIST', means a republic in which there is freedom from all forms of exploitation, social, political and economic.

[7] (1979) 1 S.C.R. 1009, ('79) A.SC. 25.

or to a very large extent, the interest of another section of the public — the private owners of the undertakings.[8]

Legislative history: Preamble a part of the Constitution

4.5 At the second reading of the draft Constitution a member suggested that the preamble should be considered at the third reading. The President of the Constituent Assembly said that this could not be done, because the Constitution as a whole had to be passed in its second reading, and the preamble was a part of the Constitution.[9] After various amendments to the preamble had been rejected, the motion "that the preamble do stand part of the Constitution" was adopted.[10] Part XVIII of the draft Constitution (Part XXII of our Constitution) provided for a few Articles coming into force on November 26, 1949, and a member of the Constituent Assembly suggested that the preamble should also come into force on that day. This suggestion was rejected, Sir Alladi Krishnaswami Ayyar observing that the preamble would come into force when the Constitution came into force.[11] It is obvious that the preamble which declared India to be a Republic could not possibly come into force on November 26, 1949, for India continued to be a Dominion till January 26, 1950.

Above history overlooked in the *Berubari Opinion*

4.6 In *In re Berubari Union & Exchange of Enclaves*[12] the Supreme Court held that the preamble to the Constitution was, in the words of Story,

"'a key to open the mind of the makers' which may show the general purposes for which they made the several provisions in the Constitution; but nevertheless the preamble is not a part of the Constitution, and, as Willoughby has observed of the preamble to the American Constitution, 'It has never been regarded as the source of any substantive power conferred on the Government of the United States, or any of its Departments. Such powers embrace only those expressly granted in the body of the Constitution and such as may be implied from those so granted.'[13]"[14]

It is obvious that the history of the preamble had not been brought to the attention of the court; otherwise it would not have said that the preamble was not a part of our Constitution. In *Keshavananda* v. *Kerala*[15] the *Berubari Opinion* was relied upon to support the petitioner's case that the preamble was not a part of the Constitution and since Art. 368 provided for the amendment of "this Constitution", the preamble was unamendable; consequently, the amending power must be so construed as not to permit a destruction of the noble objectives declared by the preamble, because it could not have been intended that the amended Constitution should conflict with an unamendable preamble. This argument collapsed when the history of the preamble was placed before the Supreme Court, which rightly held that the preamble was a part of our Constitution, several judges observing that on this point, the *Berubari Opinion* was wrong.[16]

---

8 ('79) A.SC. *supra* at pp. 36-7.
9 *C.A.D.*, Vol. 10, p. 429.
10 ibid. p. 456.
11 ibid. pp. 415-18.
12 (1960) 3 S.C.R. 250, 281-2, ('60) A.SC. 845.
13 ibid.
14 It was stated in the first edition of this book that the statement that the preamble was not a part of the Constitution was not in accordance with modern authorities and was not correct. See para 2.17, *f.n.* 82.
15 (1973) Supp. S.C.R. 1, ('73) A.SC. 1461.
16 ('73) A.SC. at p. 1503 (Sikri C.J.); pp. 1578, 1579-80 (Shelat and Grover JJ.); pp. 1678-9 (Ray J.); p. 1815 (Palekar J.); pp. 1875-6 (Khanna J.: Preamble a provision of the Constitution within the meaning of Art. 394); pp. 1927-8 (Mathew J.); p. 1992 (Dwivedi J.); p. 2041 (Chandrachud J.).

4.7 For a full discussion of the place of the preamble in statutory interpretation, the reader is referred to standard books on the subject.[17] However, the reader will find certain well settled principles for the interpretation of the preamble in para 2.17 of the text. Place of the Preamble in interpreting the Constitution

4.8 In *Kesavananda's Case* a question arose whether the court could inquire into the correctness of the declaration "We the People" because, factually, it is well known that our Constitution was framed by the Constituent Assembly which was elected on a very narrow franchise, and the Constitution was not submitted to the people for ratification. On this point different views were expressed in *Kesavananda's Case* by Hegde J. on the one hand and by Mathew J. on the other.[18] However, it is not necessary to enter into this controversy, for the Indian Independence Act, 1947, undoubtedly gave legal authority to the Constituent Assembly (which had met for the first time in New Delhi on December 9, 1946) to frame a Constitution for India. Whether the authority of the Constitution is derived from the Indian Independence Act, 1947, which partitioned British India into the Dominions of India and Pakistan, (a partition which the leaders of an undivided India *accepted*), and which, as a consequence, altered the composition of the Constituent Assembly of India by certain exclusions and inclusions [*ibid.* s. 19(3)], or whether the authority is derived from the People, as recited in the preamble, is purely academic. The reason is that the Supreme Court owes its existence to the Constitution. Again, the Constitution provided that judges of the High Courts in any Province, holding office immediately before the commencement of the Constitution, *unless they had elected otherwise*, should become judges of the High Court in the corresponding State on the commencement of the Constitution (Art. 376), and subsequent appointments had to be made *under* the Constitution. Consequently, a challenge to the validity of the Constitution is impossible before the Supreme Court or the High Courts, for a prayer to declare the Constitution invalid, would result in a declaration that those courts are illegally constituted and therefore lack jurisdiction to decide any matter whatsoever. "We the people": effect of

4.9 As to the Constitution being made by the "People", it is submitted that almost all that can be profitably said on the subject has been said by Prof. Wheare with his usual insight and brevity: Prof. Wheare on "We the people"

"In India 'the people' enact the Constitution 'in our Constituent Assembly', but that Assembly was composed of representatives elected by a minority of the people of India and the Constitution itself was never submitted to the people directly. Is it not unreal in any case to speak of 'the people' enacting a Constitution 'in' or 'through' a constituent assembly? It is seldom indeed that the people are asked even to approve a Constitution ostensibly enacted in their name.

Moreover, once a Constitution is enacted, even when it has been submitted to the people for approval, it binds thereafter not only the institutions which it establishes, but also the people itself. They may amend the Constitution, if at all, only by the methods which the Constitution itself provides."[19]

4.10 The Preamble loomed very large in the *Fundamental Rights Case*, for it was contended that in view of the noble objectives of the Preamble and amendment of the Constitution

---

[17] Maxwell, *Interpretation of Statutes,* 11th ed., pp. 43-48; 12th ed., pp. 6-9; Craies on *Statute Law*, 7th ed., pp. 199-206; *Halsbury*, Vol. 36, 3rd ed., pp. 370-71.
[18] ('73) A.SC. at pp. 1623-4 (Hegde J.); at pp. 1921, 1927-8 (Mathew J.).
[19] Wheare, *Modern Constitutions,* (1960) pp. 89-90.

Preamble, limitations should be *implied* on the amending power (Art. 368), even if the words "amendment of this Constitution" were given the widest meaning. This topic is considered in the Chapter on the Amendment of the Constitution in Vol. II.

Preamble: its three parts

4.11 The preamble can be divided into the following parts:

(*a*) The People of India in their Constituent Assembly adopted, enacted and gave to themselves "this Constitution" (*i.e.* the Constitution of India : Art. 393).

(*b*) The People of India solemnly resolved to constitute India into a (i) Sovereign (ii) Democratic (iii) Republic.

(*c*) The People of India solemnly resolved to secure to all its citizens the four objectives mentioned in the Preamble. We have already dealt with (*a*) above in paras 4.8 and 4.9 and need not discuss it further.

"Sovereign democratic republic": content of *democratic* found in provisions of the Constitution

4.12 As to para 4.11(*b*) above, when it is said that India is a *Sovereign* Democratic Republic, it means that both externally and internally India is sovereign. Where precisely internal sovereignty resides need not be considered at this place. The word "Democratic" by itself, or even in the phrase "democratic constitution", is ambiguous, for as pointed out by Prof. Finer,

> ". . . no political terms have been so subjected to contradictory definitions as 'democracy' and 'democratic' since it has become fashionable and profitable for every and any state to style itself in this way. The Soviet Union and communist states of Eastern Europe, the Chinese People's Republic, North Korea and North Vietnam all call themselves democracies. So does Nasser's Egypt; so does General Stoessner's Paraguay; so did Sukarno's Indonesia. *Yet, if anything is clear, it is that these states do not all meet the same definition of democracy*."[20] (italics supplied)

However, though the preamble does not tell us what kind of "democratic" Republic is established in India, the enacting provisions of our Constitution show that, broadly speaking, the Constitution has set up a parliamentary democracy of the type established in the federal Constitutions of Canada and Australia. The word "Republic" presents no particular difficulty.

Justice, liberty equality and fraternity used absolutely

4.13 As to para 4.11(*c*) above, the following observations can be made:

Justice alone written into an Article: Art. 38

(*a*) The words "justice, liberty, equality and fraternity" are words of passion and power — the last three were the watchwords of the French Revolution. If they are to retain their power to move men's hearts and to stir them to action, the words must be used absolutely — as they are used in the preamble. But do they throw any light on the provisions of the Constitution? The only one of the four objectives which is directly incorporated in any Article is "Justice, social, economic and political", for Art. 38 provides:

> "The State shall strive to promote the welfare of the people by securing and protecting as effectively as it may a social order in which *justice, social, economic and political,* shall inform all the institutions of the national life." (italics supplied)

And Art. 39 amplifies the concept of justice by providing that the State shall *in particular* (that is, especially) direct its policy towards securing the objectives set out of Clauses (*a*) to (*f*) of that Article.

---

[20] Finer, *Comparative Government* (1970) pp. 62-3.

(*b*) The second objective in the Preamble is not Liberty generally, but liberty of thought, expression, belief, faith and worship. This objective in its absoluteness means different things to different men, and is not reflected in any Article of the Constitution. However, subject to public order, morality and health, this objective can be related to Art. 25, which confers on every person the freedom of conscience and the right freely to profess, practice and propagate religion, for such freedom necessarily requires liberty of thought, expression, belief, faith and worship. Further, it is possible to hold that liberty of thought and expression also covers the freedom of speech and expression conferred by Art. 19(1)(*a*), but here the liberty is even more severely curtailed than it is in Art. 25 as is clear from Art. 19(2) which provides:

Liberty in the Constitution not absolute

"Nothing in sub-clause (a) of clause (1) shall affect the operation of any existing law, or prevent the State from making any law, in so far as such law imposes reasonable restrictions on the exercise of the right conferred by the said sub-clause in the interests of the security of the State, friendly relations with foreign States, public order, decency or morality, or in relation to contempt of court, defamation or incitement to an offence."

The result, therefore, is that the enacting provisions of our Constitution fall far short of the Liberty mentioned in the Preamble. However, there is one respect in which the liberty in Art. 25 goes beyond the Preamble, for whereas the Preamble secures liberty to citizens, Art. 25, (unlike Art. 19), is not limited to citizens but extends to every person.

(*c*) (i) The third objective is not equality *generally*, but equality of status and opportunity. Equality has two aspects, negative and positive; equality may be achieved to some extent by removing inequality. Slavery was a most flagrant denial of the equality of human beings as human beings; and when slavery was abolished in the United States by the 13th Amendment, and the slave acquired the status of a citizen under the 14th Amendment, the slave secured, with other citizens, the status of a human being and a citizen. Again, for centuries a great blot on Indian society was "untouchability" — a doctrine held by our Supreme Court to be a part of Hindu religion[21] — under which millions of men, women and children were "untouchable": their presence in a temple defiled the temple, and their touch, and in some places, even their shadow, defiled or polluted other Hindus. The abolition of untouchability by Art. 17, like the abolition of slavery in the United States, secured to millions of Indian citizens equality of status as human beings. The throwing open of Hindu Temples (other than private temples) to "untouchables" secured to them equality of status in matters of religion [Art. 25(2)] and the injunction to the State not to discriminate against citizens on the grounds of race, religion or caste, secured to "untouchables" equality of status by giving them equal access to shops, restaurants, hotels and places of public entertainment, and also the equal right to the use of wells, tanks, burning ghats (for the disposal of the dead) and places of public resort which are dedicated to the public or maintained wholly or partly out of State funds [Art. 15(2)]. But though restored to the status of human beings, "untouchables" belonged to "backward classes", and Art. 15(4) enables the State to discriminate

Equality of status and opportunity: its implications

Arts. 17 and 25

Arts. 15 and 16

[21] *Sri Venkataramana Devaru* v. *Mysore* (1958) S.C.R. 895, 1005.

in their favour by taking steps to secure their advancement, and Art. 16(4) increases their opportunities of employment in the public service of the Union or the States, because posts in those services can be reserved for them. These are massive achievements.

Equality of status and not attainable opportunity absolutely

(ii) But equality of status and opportunity, used absolutely, as they are in the Preamble, are incapable of realization, because they mean more than the removal of inequality. No one believes that an Indian peasant is equal in status and opportunities with the Prime Minister of India. Again, opportunity is partly a matter of chance, partly a matter of capacity to seize the opportunity should it come. Opportunity can make or mar a man's life according as he rises to the opportunity or sinks under its weight. Besides, the opportunity may be for good as well as evil.[22]

Nor do they mean uniform mediocrity: Art. 18

(iii) Nor does equality of status involve a dead level of mediocrity. Art. 18 abolishes titles, and by abolishing hereditary titles, it abolishes the artificial inequality resulting from birth. However, Art. 18 does not seek to discourage, but to encourage distinction due to merit, for it provides that "No title, *not being a military or academic distinction,* shall be conferred by the State." (italics supplied)

Art.14 goes beyond the Preamble

(iv) Article 14 which is the general Article on equality does not in terms provide for equality of status and opportunity. It provides that the State shall not deny to any person equality before the law or the equal protection of the laws. To some extent, these provisions help to secure equality of status and opportunity, but the doctrine of classification makes large inroads on the concept of equality of status and opportunity as the reader will find from our discussion of Equality in Chapter IX. In one respect, Art. 14 goes beyond the Preamble, because Art. 14 is not limited to citizens alone. Here again, it is not the Preamble which enables us to interpret the relevant Articles; it is the relevant Articles which throw light on the Preamble which goes beyond, and falls short of, those Articles.

"Fraternity" — not reflected in any Article

(*d*) "Fraternity", the fourth objective in the Preamble, was added by the Drafting Committee because

> "the committee felt that the need for fraternal concord and goodwill in India was never greater than now and that this particular aim of the Constitution should be emphasized by special reference in the preamble."[23]

Fraternity as an object is not reflected in any Article of the Constitution — no Constitution and no law can produce brotherly feeling or concord. There are provisions of the Constitution which are designed to promote fraternity, such as a common citizenship (Art. 5) and the right of citizens of India to move freely throughout the territory of India, to reside and settle in any part of India, or to acquire, hold and dispose of property, to practise any profession, or to carry on any occupation, trade or calling in any part of India [Art. 19(1)(*d*) to (*g*)].

---

[22] *Cf.* "O, Opportunity, thy guilt is great!
'Tis thou that executest the traitor's treason;
Thou sett'st the wolf where he the lamb may get;
Whoever plots the sin, thou point'st the season;
'Tis thou that spurn'st at right, at law, at reason;
And in thy shady cell where none may spy him,
Sits Sin, to seize the souls that wander by him."
— Shakespeare.

[23] Shiva Rao, *The Framing of the Indian Constitution,* Vol. III, p. 510.

There are however, other provisions which militate against fraternity, such as the division of States on linguistic lines and the provisions relating to language. A fair and evenhanded executive administration can do more to promote fraternity than any constitutional or legal provision. The fourth objective refers to a moral and political ideal, and it can throw no light on the interpretation of the Constitution, nor does any provision of the Constitution give a clear content to fraternity.

Submission: objectives in the Preamble themselves need interpretation as they are ambiguous

(*e*) It is submitted that the result of the discussion in (*a*) to (*d*) above shows that the four objectives set out in the preamble are themselves ambiguous and they cannot throw any light on the provisions of the Constitution because they stand in need of interpretation themselves.[24] It is submitted that the fact that the judgments of the Supreme Court which have referred to the Preamble have not adverted to the fact that the objectives of the Preamble are ambiguous, does not have the effect of making ambiguous objectives clear and distinct.

Rights to property not mentioned in the Preamble

4.14 Since the Preamble played a large part in *Kesavananda's Case* which was primarily concerned with the rights of property, it may be mentioned that rights of property find no place in the Preamble. The emphasis of the Preamble is on "justice, social, economic and political," which objective is embodied and amplified in the Directive Principles of State Policy noted earlier. However, the impact of the Preamble on the amending power will be considered in Vol. II. The concept of justice, social, economic and political is more conveniently dealt with in the Chapter on the Directive Principles of State Policy.

---

[24] *Cf.* "Still less can the preamble affect the meaning of the enacting words when its own meaning is in doubt": *per* Lord Simonds in *A.-G.* v. *Prince Ernest Augustus of Hanover* (1957) A.C. at p. 463; "it is only when (a preamble) conveys a clear and definite meaning in comparison with relatively obscure or indefinite enacting words that the preamble may legitimately prevail"; *per* Lord Normand, ibid. p. 466. See para 2.17 of the text.

CHAPTER V

FEDERALISM IN INDIA

The Emergency has brought the question about the federal nature of our Constitution to the fore

5.1 In the first and second editions of this book a separate Chapter was not devoted to Federalism in India. However, the Emergency and its aftermath have brought the question of Federalism into prominence and made it necessary to devote a Chapter to it. During the Emergency, Congress Ministries abdicated their duties to the Centre — responsible State Ministries could never have advised ratification of the 39th Amendment at one or two days' notice. The existence of the Congress governments at the Centre and in a large number of States for over 25 years prevented problems of Federal Government from coming to the fore. However, when the Janata Party came to power at the Centre and in a large number of States, after the Parliamentary and State elections held in 1977, the few States in which Congress Ministries continued to function suddenly became aware that our Constitution was a federal one; that the States had rights of their own which could be enforced against the Centre. Recent decisions of the Supreme Court[1] have brought to the fore the question whether our Constitution is federal.

The current doctrine of the Sup. Ct.

5.2 Ever since the decision in *W.B.* v. *Union*[2] it has been the doctrine of our Supreme Court that the unitary features in our Constitution are so many that the Federal features almost disappear. In *Rajasthan* v. *Union* Beg C.J. said:

> "In a sense, therefore, the Indian Union is federal. But, the extent of federalism in it is largely watered down by the needs of progress and development of a country which has to be nationally integrated, politically and economically co-ordinated, and socially, intellectually, and spiritually uplifted."[3]

Submission: the current doctrine is incorrect

It is submitted that this view is based on an imperfect study of our own and other Federal constitutions. It will be shown in this Chapter that almost all the features on which the Supreme Court has relied to support its doctrine, will be found on examination to be features present in constitutions which are undisputably federal. The present writer gave reasons for this view in an Essay which he wrote for the University of Mexico on *Federalism in India* — as part of a projected volume on *Federalism in Asia.* However, the University decided to publish the Essay in a separate volume, after translating it into Spanish, under the title *La Federalismo En La India.* For reasons into which it is not necessary to enter, the Essay was not published in English. However, parts of that Essay have been used in this Chapter with the kind permission of the University of Mexico.

W.B. v. *Union*

5.3 In *W.B.* v. *Union*[4] the majority judgment of the Supreme Court held that the Union was entitled to the coal mines vested in the State of West Bengal. The discussion on Federalism and Sovereignty in the majority judgment is very unsatisfactory, and instead of con-

---

[1] *Rajasthan* v. *Union* (1978) 1 S.C.R. 1, ('77) A.SC. 1361; *Karnataka* v. *Union* (1978) 2 S.C.R. 1; ('78) A.SC. 68.
[2] (1964) 1 S.C.R. 371, ('63) A.SC. 1241.
[3] (1978) 1 S.C.R. at p. 34, ('77) A.SC. at p. 1382.
[4] *Supra.*

sidering it in detail, it would lead to a briefer and clearer discussion of Federalism if the so-called "unitary" features are considered independently and shown to be present in admittedly federal constitutions. And the same observation would apply to the views expressed by Beg. C.J. in *Rajasthan* v. *Union* set out above.

The test laid down by Prof. Wheare as supplemented by Prof. Sawer applied. A federal situation existed in India

5.4 A theoretical discussion of Federalism is not necessary. The test laid down by Prof. Wheare in his classic work[5] has been generally applied to our Constitution and, broadly speaking, that test can be accepted, subject to its being supplemented by the illuminating discussion of Prof. Sawer[6] in which he rightly said that it is necessary to inquire whether a federal situation existed in a country before it adopted a federal constitution. Writing of India, he said: "The subcontinent of India was another area which by reason of size, population, regional (including linguistic) differences and communication problems presented an obvious federal situation, if not the possibility of several distinct Nations."[7] The following historical account of how our Constitution adopted the federal solution amply supports Prof. Sawer's conclusion that a federal situation clearly existed in India.

(a) *Federalism in India: Mainly Historical*

G.I. Act, 35 adopted a federal solution; the reasons for this choice

5.5 The Montague-Chelmsford Report (1918) envisaged a federal solution for the problem of political freedom for British India as a distant prospect, observing that the conditions for a federation did not then exist because the Provinces of India were not self-governing States which could surrender certain powers to a federal government (para 120, p. 78). The Simon Commission Report quoted this para and said that it remained equally true in 1929. The Simon Commission did not recommend a federal solution, though it envisaged it as a distant goal.[8] Why then did the British Parliament provide a federal Constitution for India, disregarding the views expressed in two Reports? First, the British have never been wedded to theories of government, but have tried to establish political institutions which would work. Secondly, the demand for substantial political advance in British India had become almost irresistible, and each political advance brought the full transfer of power to Indian hands nearer. Speaking broadly, the Provinces of British India were closely linked by common communications: roads, railways, posts and telegraphs, telephone; by a common official language, which was also the medium of instruction; by a common system of administration — some of the important executive offices in the Provinces were manned by members of all-India services; by a common economic policy affecting all the Provinces of British India. Further, the political struggle against the British had produced a sense of national cohesion, and the desire to be free from foreign rule and to form a united India had taken root. No doubt there were differences of race, religion and language; but these differences would point to a federal solution as obviously the right one. Therefore, to the leaders of the political struggle in British India, a federal solution offered the best chance of an early

[5] Wheare, *Federal Government*, 4th edn. (1963).
[6] Sawer, *Modern Federalism* (1969).
[7] ibid. p. 44.
[8] Gwyer & Appadorai, *Speeches and Documents on the Indian Constitution*, Vol. 1, pp. 213-14.

realisation of their goal — political freedom for the whole of India. Thirdly, the British Crown had entered into treaties and covenants with Indian Rulers under which they acknowledged the Crown's suzerainty in return for the protection of the British power against external aggression and internal disorder. The Rulers of Indian States welcomed a federal India, as a part of the British Empire, because it offered them the best chance of retaining their autocratic powers which were protected by their treaties with the British Crown. Besides, by accepting the federal solution, the Rulers hoped to slow down the agitation for the democratization of their States which otherwise would flow irresistibly from British India. Finally, the British had vast trading interests in India, which they naturally wished to protect, and they saw in the accession of Indian States to a federal India, a conservative element, whose interests coincided with theirs, and therefore offered the best prospects of securing their vast interests in India. Thus a situation existed in which all the parties affected were interested in providing a federal solution.

Actual working of the G.I. Act, 35, favoured a federal solution for the future

5.6 But if the G.I. Act, 35 adopted a federal solution for the reasons given above, the actual working of the Act favoured a federal solution *for the future*, notwithstanding the fact that the federal provisions of the G.I. Act, 35 did not come into effect. Responsible Congress Ministries functioned under the federal distribution of powers in the States; and the Federal Court of India and the Privy Council decided questions as to the scope of the respective powers of the Provinces and the Central Government. It was realized that a federal Constitution could work satisfactorily in British India. Besides, the Second World War and its aftermath of partition strongly favoured an effective, as opposed to a loose, federation. No doubt for a while the light of hope shone on the Indian political scene when a Constituent Assembly was elected according to the Cabinet Mission Plan,[9] when, in order to avoid a partition of British India between Hindu India and Muslim India, the objectives resolution which was moved in the Constituent Assembly on 13th December 1946, envisaged a loose federation with the residuary powers of legislation given to the Provinces (States) and a legally enforceable Bill of Rights providing, among other things, for the protection of minorities. But the high hopes for a united India faded, and the leaders of political parties accepted the partition of British India into India and Pakistan. The British Parliament implemented this decision by passing the Indian Independence Act, 1947, which created the two independent Dominions of India and Pakistan.

The Indian Independence Act, 47, made an effective federal solution easier

5.7 With the passing of this Act, it was no longer necessary to provide a loose federal Constitution for India. Secondly, s. 7(1)(*b*) of the Act abrogated all treaties between the British Crown and the Indian rulers, thus leaving them to fend for themselves, for they could no longer count on British protection against external aggression and internal disorder. The "liquidation" of Native States by the merger of their territories into the Provinces of India, was a question of time, and was almost accomplished before our Constitution was finally adopted on 26th November, 1949. The elimination of Indian

[9] See para 1.37 of the text.

States and the partition of British India made an effective federal solution easier.

5.8 If the British Parliament adopted the Federal solution in the G.I. Act, 35 because a federal situation existed in British India and all the parties involved desired it, the conditions in 1947-49 were even more favourable to a federal solution. Two major obstacles to an effective, as opposed to a loose, federal Constitution were removed by the creation of Pakistan, and by the liquidation of the Indian States. No doubt, the conditions for a federal solution which existed in British India did not exist in the Indian States to the same extent. Yet, common communications, the close contacts brought about by trade, commerce and intercourse between the Indian States and British India, the control exercised over the Indian States by the Governor-General of India, and years of political agitation sponsored by the Congress in the Indian States for the participation of the people in their own governments had made the people in the States feel their identity with the people of British India. The merger of several Indian States into the Dominion of India completed the process of integration, and enabled the former subjects of Indian States to play their part in working our Constitution. In the result, it is not an objection to the federal nature of our Constitution that it was not formed by independent self-governing Provinces coming together to form a Union. Conditions existed in India which pointed to a federal solution as the right one for a sovereign democratic Republic and the solution was embodied in our Constitution.

The conditions for a federal solution more favourable in 1947-9 than in 1935

(b) *Federalism and the Constitution of India*

5.9 In framing a federal Constitution, the Constituent Assembly had many models to draw upon, but it wisely decided to take the G.I. Act, 35 as the basis on which the new Constitution was to be framed. For, once the various "safeguards" in the G.I. Act, 35 were removed, its provisions could easily be adapted to a Parliamentary system of federal government which came to be the object of political struggle in India. Leaders of political opinion in India had demanded Dominion Status such as was enjoyed by Canada and Australia, and the Constitutions of those countries, enacted by the British Parliament, embodied a Parliamentary system of federal government which had been framed on the British model subject to the necessary difference involved in a federal, as opposed to a unitary Constitution, like that of Great Britain. The decision to adopt the G.I. Act, 35 as the basis of the new Constitution had the great advantage of making the transition from British rule to the new Republic of India without any break with the past; the old laws and constitutional provisions continued without a break; and thus secured for India the advantage which an evolutionary change has over a revolutionary break with the past. As will presently appear, the G.I. Act, 35 had great merits as an instrument of federal government.

Our Constitution adopts the basic scheme of G.I. Act, 35, and its distribution of legislative power

5.10 Article 1 declares that India is a Union of States. Adopting the test of Federalism propounded by Prof. Wheare (supplemented by the view of Prof. Sawer as to a "federal situation") he rightly observes that "*any definition of federal government which failed to include*

India a Union of States. Any definition of federalism which failed

to include the U.S.A. would be unreal

the United States would be thereby condemned as unreal."[10] (italics supplied). The U.S. Constitution established an association of States where powers are divided between a general government, which in certain matters is independent of State governments, and State governments which, in certain matters are independent of the general government, so that both the general and State governments operate directly upon the people who are therefore subject to two governments. An examination of the U.S. Constitution shows that the principle of organization upon which it is based, ("the federal principle") is that the field of government is divided between a general authority and regional authorities which are not subordinate one to another.[11] In order to be called federal, it is not necessary that a Constitution should adopt the federal principle completely. It is enough if the federal principle is the predominant principle in the Constitution. Thus, till 1913, members of the Upper House of the U.S. Congress were elected by the Legislatures of the States, and to that extent the general legislature of the United States was dependent upon State Legislatures. That position has been changed by the XVIIth Amendment which provides for the election of Senators by the people of the States. But even before 1913, the U.S. Constitution, was rightly looked upon as a Federal Constitution, because the federal principle was predominant in it.[12]

The federal principle must be dominant in a federal constitution

Federal Constitution and Federal Government

5.11 But it is not enough to say that, in law, a Constitution is federal; we must inquire further and find out whether the Constitution works as a federal government. For the law of the Constitution is one thing; the practice is another.[13] The mere presence of unitary features in a Constitution, which may make a Constitution quasi-federal in law, does not prevent the Constitution from being predominantly federal in practice.[14]

Has India a federal constitution?

5.12 Judged by these tests, has India a federal Constitution and a federal government? The following paragraphs will furnish the answer which is summed up in para 5.36 below.

(c) *Distribution of Legislative Power*

Distribution of Legislative power in G.I. Act, 35 — exhaustive legislative lists to avoid allocation of residuary power

5.13 The most important feature of a federal constitution is the distribution of legislative power between the Centre and the States; and our Constitution has bodily adopted *the scheme* of the G.I. Act, 35 with small verbal changes, with substantially enlarged Legislative Lists of Schedule 7. Before the G.I. Act, 35 was enacted, the British Parliament had enacted a Federal Constitution for Canada in the British North America Act, 1867 ("the Canadian Constitution") and a Federal Constitution for Australia in the Commonwealth of Australia Constitution Act, 1900 ("the Australian Constitution"). The Canadian Constitution conferred enumerated powers on the Provinces and residuary powers on the Centre; but this was done by reference to two Legislative Lists contained in ss. 91 and 92 of the Act, a concurrent legislative list in respect of agriculture and immi-

---

[10] Wheare, *Federal Government*, 4th edn., p. 1.
[11] ibid. p. 2. [12] ibid. p. 3.
[13] ibid. p. 19.
[14] See Prof. Wheare's discussion of the Canadian Constitution in the course of which he shows that in spite of the presence of unitary features, in practice the Constitution is worked predominantly on the federal principle: ibid. pp. 17-20.

gration being provided for in s. 95. The Australian Constitution, following the American model, conferred enumerated powers on the centre (s. 51) only very few of which were exclusive (s. 52) and conferred residuary powers on the States. However, in the G.I. Act, 35, the British Parliament had to solve the problem posed by the demand of the Muslim minority that residuary power of legislation should be conferred on the Provinces, and the demand of the Hindu majority that residuary power should be conferred on the Federation. The G.I. Act, 35 solved this intractable problem, *and avoided the allocation of residuary powers either to the Provinces or to the Federation* by adopting the device of exhaustively enumerating every conceivable subject of legislative power and putting it in one or other of the three Lists of the 7th Schedule to the Act. As to matters in List I, the Federal Legislature had exclusive legislative power; as to matters in List II, the Provincial Legislatures had exclusive legislative power; and as to matters in List III, the Central and the Provincial Legislatures had concurrent legislative power. The method thus adopted left little scope for the residuary power; but to guard against human fallibility and the limitations of human foresight the G.I. Act, 35 conferred the residuary power on the Governor-General (to be exercised in his discretion) to place any subject not found in the three Lists in any of those Lists. The scheme of the three Lists has been taken over by our Constitution with the difference that the three Lists have been greatly enlarged, *and the residuary power has been conferred on Parliament.*

The scheme of G.I. Act, 35 Sch. VII adopted by our Constitution; residuary power allotted to Parliament

5.14 What model did the G.I. Act, 35 draw upon for the distribution of legislative power? Sir Maurice Gwyer C.J. answered this question when he observed: ". . . it can scarcely be doubted that (the British) Parliament had the provisions of ss. 91 and 92 of the British North America Act, 1867, in mind when it enacted the 1935 Act."[15] And he added, "As interpreted by the Judicial Committee, the British North America Act presents an exact analogy to the Indian Act, even to the overriding provisions (of the 1935 Act)."[16] It may be noted here that our Constitution followed the Canadian model in two other respects. First, the federal union in Canada was not brought about by independent States, having constitutions of their own, coming together to form a Union, because, as pointed out by Dr. Wynes,

G.I. Act, 35 followed the model of the Canadian Constitution re. distribution of legislative powers

Two other resemblances pointed out

". . . the old Provinces of Canada, Nova Scotia, and New Brunswick were formed into one Dominion under the name of Canada *which was re-divided into new Provinces.*"[17]

Our Constitution also constituted new States which had arisen from the merger of the former Native States into the Provinces of India and there were no pre-existing States with constitutions of their own. Secondly, a glance at the Canadian and the Indian Constitutions will show that both of them provide a Constitution for the federation and also for the States. This would follow from the desire of reconstituted Provinces to unite and to form a federal Union. Theoretically, it was possible for the Constituent Assembly to have adopted a unitary

Our Constitution adopts the scheme of the G.I. Act, 35 and adopts a federal solution

---

[15] *Per* Gwyer C.J. in *Subrahmanyan Chettiar* v. *Muthuswami Goundan* (1940) F.C.R. 188, 200.

[16] ibid. p. 201.

[17] Wynes, *Legislative, Executive and Judicial Powers in Australia*, 5th edn., p. 3. The new Provinces were: Ontario, Quebec, Nova Scotia and New Brunswick.

Constitution. But the actual working of provincial autonomy in the Provinces of British India, where ministries responsible to the Legislature had functioned effectively, made such a step impracticable, because the Provinces would have refused to give up the powers they had enjoyed from 1937 till the Indian Independence Act was passed in 1947.

Benefits derived from adopting the scheme of G.I. Act, 35

5.15 In adopting the scheme of the G.I Act, 35 our Constitution had the benefit of the innovations which that Act had introduced in the distribution of legislative power. Any Constitution which by its defective drafting, or by its provisions, gives rise to constant litigation to determine the scope and ambit of the respective powers of the Centre and the States, must impede the smooth working of the Constitution. The G.I. Act, 35 was the third Federal Constitution enacted by the British Parliament. Consequently, the draftsmen of the Act profited by the experience gained from the working of the Canadian and the Australian Constitutions not only on the political plane, but also as interpreted by the highest courts of those countries and by the Privy Council. As we have seen, the G.I. Act, 35 adopted the Canadian model; however, it greatly improved upon the model so as to avoid the defects disclosed by the distribution of legislative power in ss. 91 and 92 of the Canadian Constitution. The most important entries in those sections were couched in wide general terms, which demanded repeated attempts to reconcile them in each case. Thus, the power to legislate for peace, order and good government conferred on the Dominion by s. 91 had to be reconciled with the power of the Provinces to make laws on property and civil rights in the Provinces [Sec. 92(13)]; and the power of the Dominion to make laws for the raising of money by any mode or system of taxation [Sec. 91(3)] with the powers of the Provinces to make laws for "direct taxation within the Provinces in order to the raising of a revenue for provincial purposes" [Sec. 92(2)]. Our Constitution in adopting the G.I. Act, 35 had the benefit of the superbly drawn legislative Lists of that Act which contained very little overlapping. The effect of such overlapping as there was, was soon settled by the decisions of the Federal Court and the Privy Council; and there was surprisingly little litigation arising from the conflict of legislative powers allotted to the Federation and to the Provinces. Our Constitution also embodied the innovation which had been made in drafting the Lists of the 7th Schedule to the G.I. Act, 35, namely, that the subjects of legislation mentioned in each List were made mutually exclusive as far as possible. For example, entry 20, List I provides for Pilgrimages to places outside India; entry 7, List II provides for Pilgrimages other than Pilgrimages to places outside India. Again, entries relating to taxation were separated from entries relating to general subjects of legislative power. For example, entry 41, List I, provides for "Trade and Commerce with foreign countries; import and export across customs frontiers," entry 83, List I provides for "Duties of customs including export duties". Further, taxing entries were made mutually exclusive, as for example, entry 82, List I provides for "Taxes on income other than agricultural income"; entry 46, List II provides for "Taxes on agricultural income". It is significant that the Concurrent List contains no tax, but provides only for fees. *This mode of distribution of legislative power has the effect of securing to the States exclusive*

G.I. Act, 35 and our Constitution avoid overlapping entries in List I and II, Sch. VII

legislative power to raise revenues by taxes which could not ordinarily be impinged upon by the Centre. We will discuss the sources of revenue of the Centre and the States later.[18] As stated earlier, our Constitution confers the residuary power of legislation on the Centre. However, the thing to note is that this does not in any way militate against the federal nature of our Constitution. The U.S. and the Australian Constitutions, which are undisputably federal, confer the residuary power on *the States* and *not* on the United States.

(d) *Distribution of Executive Power*

5.16 Normally, executive authority is co-extensive with legislative authority.[19] This general rule would have extended the executive authority of the Union to the States as to matters in the Concurrent Legislative List; but the proviso to Art. 73(1) expressly states that the executive power of the Union shall not extend in any State to matters within the legislative competence of the State except to the extent that the Constitution, or a law made by Parliament, provides otherwise.[20] The distribution of mutually exclusive powers between the Union and the States, including the power to raise revenue by taxes operating on mutually exclusive spheres, introduces in the Constitution a most important part of the federal principle.

Executive power ordinarily co-extensive with legislative power

(e) *The War or Emergency Power*

5.17 In Federal Constitutions, like those of the United States, Australia and Canada, the defence or war power is conferred on the Federation. The power, which is limited in times of peace, expands in times of war or imminent threat of war; *and during a war, for practical purposes, these federal governments function as unitary governments*, because modern total war requires that the total resources of the whole country should be mobilised under Central control. But the extent of the war power is left to judicial interpretation; and though, in times of war the courts are disposed to concede to Legislatures very wide powers, a certain amount of doubt or uncertainty must remain as to how far the federal legislature can trench upon the powers exclusively exercisable by the States. Following s. 102 of the G.I. Act, 35, Art. 352 provided that the President may issue a proclamation if satisfied that a grave emergency exists whereby the security of the whole or any part of India is threatened by war, or external aggression or internal disturbance;' and Art. 250 provides that on such proclamation being issued, Parliament shall have the power, during the time the Proclamation is in force, to legislate on matters exclusively in the State List (List II). This provision enables India to function as a unitary State when threatened by external aggression or internal disturbance; and as the right of the Union to legislate on subjects in the exclusive State List is expressly provided for, the legislative competence of Parliament over the whole field of legislation is put beyond dispute. *This apparent departure from the federal principle however, merely provides expressly for what in fact*

War or Emergency power in federal States: in times of war federal States act as unitary States

Art. 352 enacts *de jure* what happens *de facto* in federal States

[18] See para 5.30 *et seqq.*
[19] See Arts. 73 and 162, at pp. A-25 and A-51 respectively.
[20] Sec. 8(a) read with proviso (i) of the G.I. Act, 35 had made a similar provision.

happens in federations in times of war or imminent threat of war. As Dr. Wynes has said of the Australian Constitution,

Australia functioned as a unitary State in two World Wars

"If during the Great War, the defence power as expounded by the Court was availed of to an extent which evoked the comment from the Royal Commission on the Constitution in 1929 that the Commonwealth (of Australia) was, during the war, for practical purposes, a unified government (Report p. 120), the Second World War produced an extension in the subjects which were considered necessary for regulation by such a Government so wide as to embrace practically every aspect of the national life."[21]

There is however this difference that if the proclamation of emergency continues after the state of emergency has ended, then in the absence of such continuance being proved to be *mala fide*, courts in India would not invalidate actions taken during the Proclamation of Emergency, whereas in the United States, Canada and Australia, the Courts scrutinise any infringement of State power once a war is over, or soon after it is over. But to continue a proclamation after the need for it has ceased to exist is to abuse the power conferred by Art. 352, by using the power for a purpose for which it was *not* granted. The effect of such abuse would have to be considered in relation to a federal government as opposed to a federal Constitution.

The abuse of Art. 352

(f) *Territory of the States*

Parliament's power to alter the territory of States — the difference between theory and practice

5.18 Under our Constitution, Parliament has the power to alter the boundaries of the States, or to distribute the territories of a State among other States, as happened with the State of Hyderabad. And this power can be exercised without the consent of the States concerned. As a matter of law this is a serious departure from the federal principle. But in practice it is not the Union which has re-drawn the map of India; on the contrary, the hands of a reluctant Union have been forced by extra-constitutional agitation in the States, since most of them wanted to be regrouped on a linguistic basis. There are signs of a hardening attitude on the part of the Union against dividing existing States; and the way in which the Union dealt with the agitation in Andhra Pradesh for a separate State for Telangana (which is part of Andhra Pradesh) shows that demands for breaking up existing States, by carving out new States from them, will meet much greater resistance from the Union in the future. For a time the President's Rule was imposed on Andhra Pradesh, and after months of negotiations, a "six point formula" was evolved (and generally accepted by the parties affected), which was designed to meet the grievances of the Telangana region, which remained as part of Andhra Pradesh. The 32nd Amendment was passed, and Article 371D was inserted in the Constitution to make *special provisions* for the State of Andhra Pradesh; further Art. 371E enabled Parliament by law to establish a Central University for Andhra Pradesh.

(g) *Failure of Constitutional Machinery*

Provisions re. failure of constitutional machinery, *if properly exercised*, uphold the federal principle

5.19 As the British Parliament claimed ultimate responsibility for the Government of India, and the right to determine the pace of India's political advance towards complete self-government, ss. 45 and 92 of the G.I. Act, 35 contained provisions to deal with a failure of constitutional machinery, because one of the proclaimed objects of the Congress was to enter the legislatures in order to wreck them

[21] Wynes, p. 203.

from within. On being satisfied that there was a failure of constitutional machinery in the Federation or in a Province, the Governor-General (in respect of the Federation) and a Governor (in respect of a Province) could issue a proclamation which enabled them to exercise their powers in their discretion and also enabled them to assume to themselves the powers of the Federal and a Provincial legislature respectively. These provisions were severely criticized as being directed against the freedom movement. However, the utility of such a proclamation in case of a failure of constitutional machinery in a State was realized when the Constitution came to be enacted, and Arts. 356 and 357 provide that the President may issue a proclamation in case of such a failure, and provide for the powers which he can assume on issuing such proclamation. At first blush this provision may appear to be a serious departure from the federal principle, but a consideration of other federal constitutions shows that *if properly exercised*, these powers uphold the federal principle. The Constitution of the United States and Australia — which are federal Constitutions — provide only for the Constitution of the general governments; the States have constitutions of their own which remain in full force except to the extent that they are inconsistent with the Constitutions of the United States and Australia respectively. Our Constitution, like that of Canada, provides a Constitution both for the Union (the general government) and the States. The general government in the United States, Australia and India are governments of Sovereign States which enjoy full external sovereignty. But the possession of external sovereignty by a country does not affect its federal structure. The United States has, and the States composing it do not have, external sovereignty. And yet the United States has indisputably a federal Constitution. This is because in federal States, it is the division of internal sovereignty between the general and State governments which is relevant in considering the question whether a Constitution is federal. That the Indian Legislatures are as supreme and sovereign within their own spheres as the British Parliament itself has been established as far back as 1878 by *R.* v. *Burah*[22] and has never been doubted since.

The possession of external sovereignty by the Union irrelevant to the federal principle

5.20 Is it contrary to the federal principle that the States should be prevented from working the Constitution in a manner not permitted by the Constitution? Taking the United States first, Article 4, s. 4 requires the United States to guarantee to every State in the Union a republican form of government. The Constitution thus enjoins that each State of the Union must have a republican form of government. If a State were to adopt a non-republican form of government, the United States would be under an obligation to intervene, and to restore by force, if necessary, a republican form of government to the State. And for this purpose the United States must act on its own initiative, for it is unlikely that the people who had destroyed the republican form of government would ask the United States to restore it.[23] *Article 4, s. 4 shows that it is not inconsistent with the federal principle that a State should be prevented from working its own Constitution contrary to the mandate of the U.S. Constitution.*

Article 4, s. 4 of U.S. Const. treated as a precedent for Art. 355 of our Constitution

Preventing State action contrary to the Federal Const. not inconsistent with the federal principle

[22] (1878) 3 App. Cas. 889, 5 I.A. 178. [23] Willis, *Constitutional Law*, p. 451.

The power thus conferred on the United States is very wide, for the U.S. Supreme Court has held in *Luther* v. *Borden*[24] that it is for the Congress to restore republican governments to States, and the question as to when a State government had ceased to be republican was a political question and was not justiciable.

The *Debs Case* — application by the States for federal assistance to suppress domestic violence loses its importance

5.21 Not only does Article 4, s. 4 provide a guarantee of a republican form of government but it also obliges the United States to protect each State from foreign invasion; and, *on application by the legislature or the executive of a State,* against domestic violence. It may be said that this provision respects the federal principle, because the United States cannot intervene to suppress domestic violence *without an application by the State.* But in practice this is not so. Article 4, s. 4 has lost its importance after the *Debs Case*[25] which held that domestic violence may affect the execution of powers entrusted to the United States by the Constitution. Consequently, the United States had the power and the duty to use "the entire strength of the Nation . . . to enforce in any part of the land the full and free exercise of all national powers and the security of all rights entrusted by the Constitution to its care."[26] An interesting and instructive account of how the attempts of the Southern States in the United States to defy the orders of the U.S. Supreme Court, and other Federal Courts, to desegregate schools will be found in Kelly and Harbinson, *The American Constitution* at p. 864 *et seqq.* (5th ed.). But a brief account of it is given here. Governor Orval Faubus called out the Arkansas National Guard, which acting under the Governor's proclamation alleging the necessity of maintaining law and order, effectively barred prospective Negro students from entering the white high-school building at Little Rock. A series of Court's orders were disregarded. Acting on President Eisenhower's instructions, the Att.-General obtained an injunction against the Governor, ordering him and the National Guard to cease from blocking enforcement of the federal court's orders. The Governor thereupon withdrew the National Guard. However, Negro students were prevented from entering the school by a large and unruly mob. On September 25, 1957, the President dispatched several companies of the United States Army to Little Rock, in effect putting the city under martial law. He took this action under a provision of the federal law, which authorised the President to suppress insurrection and unlawful combination that hindered execution of either State or Federal law. Mob resistance immediately disappeared, and several Negro students thereupon entered the school without further interference. (ibid. p. 866). This was not an isolated action of the President of the United States. When, after protracted litigation against the University of Mississippi, the Supreme Court directed that one James Meredith, a Negro, be admitted as a student, the Governor of the State took charge of the University, using state and local police to block the attempts of Meredith, now escorted by U.S. marshals, to register. President Kennedy issued a proclamation on September 29, 1962 addressed to the officials and people of the State of Mississippi, warning them to cease their resistance to federal

Two illustrations

[24] 7 How. 1.

[25] 158 U.S. 564.

[26] ibid. p. 582: see *The Constitution of the United States of America, Revised and Annotated* (1964) at p. 796.

authority. On the next day, University officials capitulated and agreed to allow Meredith now accompanied by several hundred United States marshals, to register. Riots approaching the proportions of an insurrection broke out. President Kennedy sent several thousand regular U.S. Army troops to the town, as well as several units of the Mississippi National Guards, to put down the insurrection and the resistance to federal law collapsed. (ibid. p. 869). In other words, "the entire strength of the Nation" was used to put down forcible resistance to the enforcement of federal law. It will be seen that as the request of the State is not necessary for the United States to enforce its own rights, the importance of observing the formalities required by Art. 4, s. 4 has declined.[27]

5.22 Section 199 of the Australian Constitution requires the Commonwealth to protect every State against invasion, and, on the application of the executive government of the State, against domestic violence. Section 119 is obviously modelled on Art. 4, s. 4 of the U.S. Constitution, and the position in Australia is the same as in the United States. In his book on the Australian Constitution,[28] Dr. Wynes quoted *Luther* v. *Borden* in support of his view that the determination by the Commonwealth that domestic violence exists as a fact is final and conclusive and cannot be investigated by any Court.[29] And he observes that the State's request is not necessary when the Commonwealth acts in respect of domestic violence for the execution of its powers or for the protection of Commonwealth property or services.[30]

S. 199 of the Australian Constitution — the law in *Debs Case* applies

5.23 The above discussion shows that even in admittedly federal Constitutions, the general government has the power to ensure that the State Constitution is worked as required by the Federal Constitution, and has also the power to suppress by force, if necessary, domestic violence in a State, so that the Federal Constitution can function as it was intended to function. If such a power did not exist, Federal government itself would be at the mercy of one or more States. *A power essential for the existence of federal government cannot be said to impair the federal principle.* If this is true of federal Constitutions which provide only a Constitution for the general government, it cannot be less true of our Constitution which, like that of Canada, provides a Constitution both for the general and the State governments. We will now consider the relevant provisions of our Constitution.

Power essential to preserve federal government cannot impair the federal principle

5.24 Article 355 imposes on the Union the duty to protect every State against external aggression and internal disturbance, and also the duty to ensure that the government of every State is carried on in accordance with the provisions of the Constitution. The resemblance of Art. 355 to Art. 4, s. 4 of the U.S. Constitution is obvious. In fact in proposing draft Art. 277A (now Art. 355) Dr. Ambedkar referred to the said Art. 4, s. 4 as a precedent.[31] It is clear that in respect of internal disturbance the request of the State is not necessary; but, for the reasons given earlier, the requirement of a request from a

Article 355 explained in the light of above discussion

[27] See Corwin, *The President: Office and Powers*, pp. 135-6 (1957).
[28] Wynes, pp. 229-30.
[29] ibid. p. 230.
[30] ibid.
[31] *C.A.D.*, Vol. 9, p. 175.

State has lost its importance even in the United States and in Australia. The same considerations apply in India, for internal disturbance in a State would prevent the Union from executing the powers entrusted to it, and interfere with its property and services in the States, so that the Union could deal with such disturbances on its own with "the entire strength of the Nation." The second duty cast upon the Union corresponds to the obligation laid upon the United States to guarantee a republican form of government to each State. The U.S. Constitution leaves the State Constitutions in full force, except to the extent that they are inconsistent with its provisions. The effect of the guarantee of a republican form of government is best described by saying that there is written into each State Constitution a requirement, *which no State Constitution can abrogate,* that the government of that State shall, in law and fact, be republican. If this provision is contravened by any State, the contravention would entail the intervention of the federal government, which can use all the force necessary to re-establish a republican form of government in that State. The duty cast on the Union of India to ensure that the government of each State is carried on in accordance with the Constitution could have been enforced by the Union by the use of the necessary force; but for dealing with the situation, the method first adopted by the G.I. Act, 35 was considered more satisfactory and was adopted in the Constitution. A proclamation of failure of constitutional machinery made it legally possible for the Union to establish a stable government in the State with a view to re-establishing a government in the State which would be conducted in accordance with the Constitution.

The abuse of powers conferred by Art. 356 considered in the discussion of *Rajasthan* v. *Union*

5.25 The powers conferred by Art. 356 have been gravely abused; and if it is desired to prevent, or minimize such abuse, constitutional amendments would have to be made. The reader interested in pursuing this subject further will find it discussed in Chapter V, Section II, pp. 102-118 of the present writer's book *The Emergency, Future Safeguards and the Habeas Corpus Case: A Criticism.* In fact the 44th Amendment has amended Art. 356, though in the submission of the present writer the amendment does not go far enough. The question whether the abuse of the power under Art. 356 is amenable to judicial review, and if so, to what extent, will be considered when the Supreme Court's decision in *Rajasthan* v. *Union*[32] is fully discussed.

(h) *Administrative Relations Between the Union and the States*

The Central concept of federalism

5.26 In considering whether a Constitution is federal or not, we must never lose sight of the central concept of federalism, namely, that every person in a State is subject to laws made by two different authorities — the Federal Legislature and the Legislature of his State. And since laws have to be enforced by the executive, either separate Federal and State agencies may be entrusted with such enforcement or, as in our Constitution, State agencies may be entrusted with the enforcement of Federal laws. A failure to bear the central concept of federalism (and its necessary corollaries) in mind has been responsible for the erroneous view that in our Constitution

[32] (1978) 1 S.C.R. 1, ('77) A.SC. 1361.

federalism is "watered down". Articles 245 to 255 having provided for the legislative relations between the Union and the States, Arts. 256 to 258A provide for the administrative relations between the Union and the States. Since Parliament has exclusive jurisdiction to pass laws with respect to matters in List I, and the State legislatures have exclusive jurisdiction to pass laws with respect to matters in List II, and both Parliament and State Legislatures have power and concurrent jurisdiction to pass laws with respect to matters in List III, a question arises, what would happen if there was a conflict between a valid Union Law and a valid State Law? In Canada, judicial decisions have held that an attempt must be made to reconcile conflicting Federal and Provincial laws, but if the two laws cannot be reconciled, then the Federal Law would prevail over the Provincial law.[33] If that were not so, "an absurd situation would result if two inconsistent laws, each of equal validity, could exist side by side."[34] Section 109 of the Australian Constitution expressly provides that a valid Federal Law shall prevail over a State Law in case of irreconcilable conflict. Article 254(1) makes the same provision in case of conflict between a Union law and a State law. However, following the innovation made by s. 107 of the G.I. Act, 35, Art. 254(2) provides that if a law passed by a State Legislature in respect of a matter in the concurrent Legislative List receives the President's assent, then, such a law, if inconsistent with the law passed by Parliament, would prevail in *that State*, subject to the power of Parliament to repeal such a law either directly, or by passing a law inconsistent with it.

A valid federal law must prevail over a valid State law in case of conflict

5.27 Having regard to this priority of a valid Union law over a valid State law where they conflict, it became necessary to provide for the exercise of executive power which is co-extensive with legislative power, except that in respect of List III, executive power of the Union does not extend to a State unless expressly so authorised by the Constitution or by a law made by Parliament. If Union laws are to be enforced in each State, the proper working of a Federal government requires that the executive power of the State governments must be so exercised as to ensure compliance with laws made by Parliament (or existing law) which apply in that State. And, logically, the executive power of the Union would extend to giving such direction to a State as may appear to the Government of India to be necessary for that purpose, and Art. 256 so provides. Article 256 does not in any way derogate from the federal principle but gives effect to it, since laws made by Parliament operate in the States. Whereas Federal and State Courts operate side by side in the United States, under our Constitution there is only one set of courts with the Supreme Court at its apex. Entry 95, List I, entry 65, List II and entry 46, List III all run as follows: "Jurisdiction and powers of all courts other than the Supreme Court in respect of matters in this list" except that entry 95, List I also refers to "admirality jurisdiction." Thus special jurisdiction in respect of matters in the three Lists can be conferred on the State judiciary.

Priority of valid exercise of Union executive power over valid exercise of State executive power: Arts. 256 and 257

[33] *Att.-Gen. for Ontario* v. *Att.-Gen. for the Dominion* (1896) A.C. 348, 366-7 (P.C.).

[34] *Per* Gwyer C.J. in *Subramanyan Chettiar* v. *Muthuswamy Goundan* (1940) F.C.R. at p. 200.

The enforcement of the Union laws is secured by the law enforcement machinery of the State. Again, Art. 257 provides for the control of the Union over the States in certain matters. Just as in the case of a conflict between a valid State law and a valid Union law, the latter law prevails, so also a question may arise as to the conflict between the valid exercise of executive power by the Union and the States and, equally logically, Art. 257 provides that the executive power of every State shall be so exercised as not to impede or prejudice the exercise of the executive power of the Union. To make this general declaration effective, Art. 257 provides that the executive power of the Union shall extend to giving of such directions to a State as may appear to the Government of India to be necessary for that purpose. Such a provision is essential to the harmonious exercise of executive power by the Union and by the States, and also to effectuate the provision of our Constitution that the executive power of the Union is co-extensive with its legislative power. Further, it is essential for securing the means of communication between the States, and for protecting Railways which run through the States, that the Union Government should have power to require the State Governments to maintain and protect such communication and such railways, and Art. 257(2) and (3) so provide. Such provisions are necessary, because the States have exclusive legislative and executive power over "land". But Article 257(4) recognizes the fact that carrying out the directions as to means of communication and railways would involve extra expense, and recognizes the Union's obligation to defray such expense, the amount of such expense being fixed by agreement, and in default of agreement, by an arbitrator appointed by the Chief Justice of India.

Art. 365—sanction to secure enforcement of valid exercise of Union's executive power

5.28 The sanction behind the power of the Union to give directions is found in Art. 365 which provides that where any State has failed to comply with, or to give effect to, any direction given in the exercise of the executive power of the Union under any of the provisions of the Constitution, it shall be lawful for the President to hold that a situation has arisen in which the Government of the State cannot be carried on in accordance with the provisions of the Constitution. This sanction is necessary if directions given by the Union are not to be flouted with impugnity by the States. As far as the present writer is aware, directions under Art. 257(2) have been issued only once to a State. However, the power conferred by Art. 365 is not absolute; it is subject to the conditions mentioned in Art. 365 and is therefore open to judicial review. For example, if the Union government purported to give directions about the exercise of executive power in any field reserved for the State executive, *which power does not collide with, or prejudice the exercise of, the Union's executive power,* such a direction would be invalid, and the imposition of the President's Rule under Art. 365 would be void for non-compliance with the condition precedent laid down by Art. 365. Further, the language of Art. 365 is suggestive. It confers *a power* by use of the words "it shall be lawful"; it does not impose *an obligation*. The objection that a constitution cannot be Federal if the Union could give directions to the State as aforesaid is based on a misconception for, as we have seen, the executive authority of the Federation extends also to the States,

Art. 365 confers a *power*; it does not impose *an obligation* and it is essential for the working of a federal Constitution that the Union executive should have power to discharge its duty by giving appropriate directions to the State executive without being obliged to set up separate Federal agencies for the enforcement of Federal laws. To utilize existing State agencies is cheaper and more effective, and also avoids conflicts of jurisdiction between Union and State agencies. This aspect is emphasized by Art. 258 which enables the President to confer power on the State Governments *with their consent* in matters to which the executive power of the Union extends. Article 258A enables the Governor of a State with the consent of the Government of India to entrust to that Government functions in respect of matters to which the executive power of the State extends. The administrative relations contained in Arts. 256 to 258A are a counterpart of the legislative divisions between the Union and the States and are designed to ensure effective exercise by the Union of its own powers, as stated in sub-section (g) above.

(i) *Federalism and the Importance of the Matters Allocated to the Union and the States*

5.29 It cannot be an objection to the Federal principle embodied in our Constitution that the States were not separate sovereign States before the Constitution. As we saw in paras 5.5 to 5.8 above, first, the British Parliament, and then our Constitution adopted a Federal solution, *because a federal situation existed in India.* In the framework of our Constitution the word "sovereign" is ambiguous and misleading. Externally, that is, in international law, India is a sovereign State, and the States are not; but this is equally true of the United States, Canada and Australia (whose constitutions are clearly federal), *so that external sovereignty vesting in the country as a whole is not inconsistent with the federal principle.* But within India, neither the Union nor the States possess internal sovereignty, because the legislative, executive and judicial powers of India are divided between the Union and the States. No doubt legislative powers in matters of national importance are assigned in federal Constitutions to the federal government, like war and peace, the armed forces, foreign relations, customs, currency, coinage, railways, etc. But India is a Union of States, and the functions assigned to the States are of high importance though of a different kind. With his usual insight, Sir Maurice Gwyer C.J. said of the allocation of powers under the G.I. Act, 35,

"Sovereignty" — internal and external. The latter not relevant to federalism

Functions assigned to the States are of high importance

> "I mention, only to dismiss, the argument that the new autonomy of the Provinces and the expenditure necessary to administer and maintain the vital services committed to their charge require that every intendment should be made in favour of the provincial taxing power. I should never *deny the high importance of the provincial functions; but the Centre has also great responsibilities though of another kind, and it is not for this Court to weigh one against the other.*"[35] (italics supplied)

And, speaking of the powers of Indian Legislatures, he observed in another case:

[35] *In re the C.P. & Berar Act, 1938,* (1939) F.C.R. 18 at p. 44.

Burah's Case: within the limits of their powers Indian legislatures as supreme and sovereign as the British Parliament

"We must again refer to the fundamental proposition enunciated in *The Queen* v. *Burah*,[36] *that Indian Legislatures within their own sphere have plenary powers of legislation as large and of the same nature as those of (the British) Parliament itself. If that was true in 1878, it cannot be less true in 1942.* Every intendment ought therefore to be made in favour of a Legislature which is exercising the powers conferred on it. Its enactments ought not to be subjected to the minute scrutiny which may be appropriate to an examination of the by-laws of a body exercising only delegated powers, nor is the generality of its power to legislate on a particular subject to be cut down by the arbitrary introduction of far-fetched and impertinent limitations."[37] (italics supplied)

If this was true in 1942 of the 1935 Act, which contained numerous "safeguards", it cannot be less true of the powers conferred by our Constitution on State Legislatures functioning under a system of cabinet government with Ministers responsible to legislative assemblies elected on a universal franchise.

Subjects of legislation allotted to the States are not of "subordinate concern"

5.30 The above observations have been made not only because the *West Bengal Case* belittles the power and position of the States, but because so eminent a writer on Federalism as Prof. Wheare has expressed the opinion that in India

"... the powers granted in the exclusive Union List and in the concurrent list cover, as in Western Germany, almost all subjects of importance, and what is left to the exclusive authority of the States tends to be of subordinate concern."[38]

If by "subordinate" is meant "not important", then, with respect, the present writer does not agree with his assessment of the exclusive State List. Public order, the police, administration of justice, local government, public health and sanitation, to mention but a few, are matters of great importance; and so are agriculture, water (subject to Union control of the waters of inter-State rivers), land, and fisheries. Again, the allocation of taxes between the Union and the States is mutually exclusive, and the taxes allocated exclusively to the States are not negligible. Thus sales tax is an expanding source of revenue in India as it becomes increasingly industrialized under the successive five year plans. In the industrialized State of Maharashtra, the yield from Sales Tax was about Rs. 1,580 million for the year 1971-72, and the estimate for the year 1972-73 was about Rs. 1,780 million. For the year ending 31st March, 1978, the yield from sales tax practically doubled, and reached Rs. 3,550 million. With the increasing urbanisation of India, property taxes, that is, taxes on lands and buildings, are also likely to be a substantial source of revenue. Again, with the development of agriculture on modern lines, with large irrigation schemes going into operation, agricultural income-tax might soon develop into a most important source of revenue. The attitude of the Central Government towards agricultural income-tax has been gradually changing, first, because to let large agricultural incomes go free of income-tax, is inequitable and unjust; secondly because the increasing needs of the States cannot be met solely out of Central grants and there is increasing pressure on the States from the Centre to introduce agricultural income-tax. The Direct Tax Enquiry Committee in its Final Report (December 1971) unanimously recommended the imposition of an agricultural

Taxing powers of the Union and the States mutually exclusive: important taxes allotted to the States

Changed attitude of the Union to the imposition of agricultural income-tax by the States

---

36 (1878) 3 App. Cas. 889, 5 I.A. 178.
37 *Bhola Prasad* v. *R.* (1942) F.C.R. 17 at p. 27.
38 Wheare, *Federal Government,* p. 27.

income-tax as a means of preventing evasion of income-tax on non-agricultural income and also to redress the injustice to urban tax payers who had been subsidising agricultural income by bearing the full burden of agricultural development schemes.[39] The Finance Act of 1973, which provides for the levy and collection of income-tax, does not directly bring agricultural income to tax, since that is an exclusive State subject; but it does so by providing that the net agricultural income of an assessee shall be added to his other income for determining the higher rate of tax payable on his non-agricultural income than he would have paid if he had no agricultural income. The reluctance of the States to impose an agricultural income-tax is understandable, for taxes do not attract votes. But the large public expenditure on irrigation and other agricultural inputs like fertilisers, combined with what has come to be called "the green revolution" has made it unacceptable that the farmer's income should be income-tax free, when much smaller non-agricultural incomes are taxed. The provisions of the Finance Act noted above show that it is the accepted policy of the Union that land, and income from land, should make their contribution to the financial resources of the States, as is done by other kinds of property, and as is done by non-agricultural income. It may be added that the Administrative Reforms Commission in a unanimous Report on Centre-State Relationships (June, 1969) observed:

"In this context, we would emphasize that the States cannot expect Central resources to be made available to them in order to compensate them for their unwillingness to tap their own resources to the required extent. Some of the State Governments are very chary of levying taxes and rates on those who are direct beneficiaries on heavy investments made by the Government on big projects, like irrigation and power projects, and on whom the levy of such taxes and rates will not become a great burden. To refrain from making such levies, under the wrong notion that they will lead to unpopularity, will only result in unequal and unjust treatment being meted out to different classes or groups of persons in the State. While the State government must, no doubt be anxious to increase the tempo of development in their States, they must be equally keen on maximising the revenues from the development projects."[40]

and followed it up with the recommendation:

"The State Governments should adequately tax the direct beneficiaries of the heavy investments in big projects like the Irrigation and Power projects."[41]

5.31 Further, the financial resources of the States are not limited by the taxes exclusively allotted to the States under entries 45 to 63, List II. The States have additional sources of revenue. First, there are duties levied by the Union, but collected *and appropriated by the States*: Art. 268. Secondly, there are taxes levied and collected by the Union under Art. 269 which are assigned to the States and must be distributed among the States in accordance with such principles of distribution as may be formulated by Parliament by law. Thirdly, under Art. 270 taxes on income, other than agricultural income, though levied and collected by the Government of India must be distributed between the Union and the States in the manner provided by Art. 270(2). Six successive Finance Commissions have increased the share of the States from 50 to 80 per cent of the income-tax collected after deducting the tax attributable to Union territories

Financial resources of the States *not* limited to taxes exclusively allotted to the States

[39] See pp. 40-42 of the Report.
[40] *Administrative Reforms Commission Report*, June, 1969, p. 19.
[41] ibid.

and Union emoluments. Though, in theory, the recommendations of the Finance Commission are not binding on the President, in practice, effect has been given to those recommendations.

Finance Commissions and increasing share of the States in income-tax collected by the Union

5.32 In 1978, the Seventh Finance Commission has made its Report, and the Union Government has accepted it. It has raised the share of the States in the net collection from income-tax (after deducting 2.19 per cent attributable to Union Territories) to 85 per cent. Further, it has recommended that the net proceeds of the additional excise duty on the generation of electricity should be paid over to each State in an amount equal to the duty collected from or attributable to that State. The Commission also recommended that the payment of the net additional excise duty on sugar and textiles (after retaining 3.271 and 2.192 per cent respectively as attributable to the Union territories) should be paid to the States according to the percentages set out in the Commission's Report.

(j) *Emergency Powers during Internal Disturbance*

Abuse of emergency powers during the Emergency

5.33 The abuse of this power during the Emergency (proclaimed in June 1975) has branded the word "Emergency" with infamy. There is no doubt that the framers of our Constitution intended those provisions to safeguard a free democratic Constitution from internal subversion by force or violence. The fact that no such emergency was proclaimed from the time when the Constitution came into force on 26th January, 1950 to 25th June, 1975 shows that the provision for proclamation of internal emergency was designed as an ultimate safeguard. It may be said that emergencies proclaimed as a result of external aggression may have made a proclamation of emergency on the ground of internal disturbance unnecessary. But the attitude adopted by the people of India in uniting to meet external aggression *irrespective of party affiliation* makes it unreasonable to hold such a view. However, the Emergency proclaimed in 1975 has shown the grave danger to the Federal principle by such a proclamation, more so, when it was accompanied by an amendment of the Constitution which prolonged the life of the Legislatures from 5 to 6 years which duration could have been indefinitely extended, since Mrs. Gandhi's party possessed the requisite majorities in the two Houses of Parliament and in the requisite number of State legislatures. Although the way in which our Constitution is working is important for determining whether the Federal principle prevails, it is equally true that a gross abuse of power is not an indication of the structure of a Constitution as it was designed to be worked and as it was in fact worked in normal times. In the undernoted work the present writer has expressed the view that Emergency powers are unnecessary in dealing with internal disorder or violence and he adheres to that view.[42] However, the 44th Amendment has restricted this power to *armed rebellion* and has provided safeguards for issuing a proclamation on that account and safeguards against its automatic continuation. That the power to put down any rebellion in a State of a Federation is not inconsistent with the Federal principle is clear from

Substitution of "armed rebellion" for "internal disturbance" in Art. 352 by the 44th Amendment

---

[42] Seervai, *Emergency, Future Safeguards and the Habeas Corpus Case: A Criticism*, pp. 96-102.

what has been said in sub-section (g) above. For, as we have seen, such a rebellion or insurgency affects the exercise of the legitimate powers of the Union and the Union can put it down by force.

(k) *Dependence of the Union on the States*

5.34 It has been customary to emphasize the dependence of the States on the Union. To redress the balance, it is necessary to point out the dependence of the Union on the States in several important respects. First and foremost, Parliament (the Central Legislature) is dependent upon the States, because one of its Houses, the Council of States, is elected by the Legislative Assemblies of the States. Where the ruling party, or group of parties, in the House of the People has a majority but not an overwhelming majority, the Council of States can have a very important voice in the passage of legislation other than financial Bills. Secondly, a Bill to amend the Constitution requires to be passed by each House of Parliament separately by an absolute majority in that House and by not less than two-thirds of those present and voting. Since the Council of States is indirectly elected by the State Legislatures, the State Legislatures have an important say in the amendment of the Constitution because of the requirement of special majorities in each House. Thirdly, the very important matters mentioned in the proviso to Art. 368 (Amendment of the Constitution) cannot be amended unless the amendments passed by Parliament are ratified by not less than half the number of Legislatures of the States. Ratification is thus required, *inter alia,* for changes in the Legislative Lists, in the Union and State Judiciary, in the election of the President and in amending the amending Article itself. Fourthly, the amendment of Art. 352 by the 44th Amendment gives the Council of States a most important voice in the declaration of Emergency, because a proclamation of emergency must be approved by *each House* separately by majorities required for an amendment of the Constitution; and the continuance of the proclamation for a further period or periods requires to be approved by each House by the same majorities. Fifthly, the executive power of the Union is vested in the President of India who is not directly elected by the people but is elected by an electoral college consisting of (a) the elected members of the Legislative Assemblies of the States and (b) the elected members of both Houses of Parliament. There is a parity of votes between members of all the Legislative Assemblies taken together, and all the members of the two Houses of Parliament taken together. Directly the State Legislatures have substantial voting power in electing the President; that power is increased indirectly through the Council of States, which is elected by the Legislative Assemblies of States. The result therefore is that they have a very substantial say in the election of the President of India. No doubt the President is the constitutional head of government, but he has a real discretion in exceptional but important cases as has been pointed out in *Samsher Singh's Case.*[43] It may be that the organisation of political parties at times may not give full play to the part which the States have in Parliament, through election of the President, but the power

Matters in which the Union is dependent on the States

[43] ('74) A.SC. at p. 2230.

is unquestionably there. That power has been clearly manifested by the Council of States in which *the ruling party* was in a substantial minority in 1977-1979.

Has India a federal government?

5.35 The question whether India worked as a *federal government* is difficult to answer, first, because the materials for forming a conclusion are not available; secondly, because the dominance of the Congress Party in the Centre and in a large number of States muted the problems of federal government; thirdly, the phenomenon of "defection" and the pastime of "toppling governments" introduced a distracting feature in State governments, which did not command a stable majority, and thus made it difficult to examine the working of a federal government. One failure of federal *government* arose from the abuse of the power to impose the President's Rule. The 44th Amendment has done something to remove this abuse; and the courts could do more if they did not shirk their responsibility of deciding the legal rights of the States against the Union by referring to the "political thicket" or "the prohibited field".

Conclusions

A summary of the discussion on Federalism which shows that the Federal principle is not "watered down" in our Constitution

5.36 The result of our discussion can be summed up thus:

(a) It is no objection to our Constitution being federal that the States were not independent States before they became parts of a Federation. A Federal situation existed, first, when the British Parliament adopted a federal solution in the G.I. Act, 35, and secondly, when the Constituent Assembly adopted a federal solution in our Constitution.

(b) Parliament's power to alter the boundaries of States without their consent is a breach of the federal principle, but in fact it is not Parliament which has, on its own, altered the boundaries of States. By extra constitutional agitation, the States have forced Parliament to alter the boundaries of States. In practice, therefore, the federal principle has not been violated.

(c) The allocation of the residuary power of legislation to Parliament (i.e. the Federation) is irrelevant for determining the federal nature of a Constitution. The U.S. and the Australian Constitutions do not confer the residuary power on the Federation but on the States, yet those Constitutions are indisputably federal.

(d) External sovereignty is not relevant to the federal nature of a Constitution, for such sovereignty must belong to the country as a whole. But the division of internal sovereignty by a distribution of legislative powers is an essential feature of federalism, and our Constitution possesses that feature. With limited exceptions, the Australian Constitution confers overlapping legislative powers on the States and the Commonwealth, whereas List II, Sch. VII of our Constitution confers exclusive powers of legislation on the States, thus emphasizing the federal nature of our Constitution.

(e) The enactment in Art. 352 of the emergency power arising from war or external aggression which threatens the security of India merely recognizes *de jure* what happens *de facto* in great federal countries like the U.S., Canada and Australia in times of war, or imminent threat of war, because in war, these federal countries act as though they were unitary. The presence in our Constitution of exclusive legislative powers conferred on the States makes it reasonable to provide that during the emergency created by war or external aggression, the Union should have power to legislate on topics exclusively assigned to the States and to take corresponding executive action. The Emergency Provisions therefore do not dilute the principle of Federalism, although the abuse of those provisions by continuing the emergency when the occasion which caused it had ceased to exist does detract from the principle of federal *government.* The Amendments introduced in Art. 352 by the 44th Amendment have, to a considerable extent, reduced the chances of such abuse. And by deleting the clauses which made the declaration and the continuance of emergency by the President conclusive, the 44th Amendment has provided opportunity for judicial review which, it is submitted, the Courts should not lightly decline when as a matter of common knowledge, the emergency has ceased to exist. This deletion of the conclusive satisfaction of the President has been prompted not only by the abuse of the proclamation of emergency arising out of war or external aggression, but, even more, by the wholly unjustified proclamation of emergency issued in 1975 to protect the personal position of the Prime Minister.

(f) The power to proclaim an emergency originally on the ground of internal disturbance, but now only on the ground of armed rebellion, does not detract from the principle of federalism because such a power, as we have seen, exists in indisputably federal constitutions. *Deb's Case* has established that internal violence would ordinarily interfere with the powers of the Federal Government to enforce its own laws and to take necessary executive action. Consequently, such interference can be put down with the total force of the United States. And the same position obtains in Australia.

(g) The provisions of Art. 355 imposing a duty on the Union to protect a State against external aggression and internal disorder are not inconsistent with the federal principle. The War Power belongs to the Union in all federal governments, and therefore the defence of a State against external aggression is essential in any federal government. As to internal disturbance, the position reached in *Deb's Case* shows that the absence of an application by the State does not materially affect the federal principle. Such application has lost its importance in the United States and in Australia.

(h) Since it is of the essence of the Federal principle that both Federal and State laws operate on the same individual, it must follow that in case of conflict of a valid Federal law and a valid State law, the Federal law must prevail and our Constitution so provides in Art. 254, with an exception noted earlier which does not affect the present discussion.

(i) It follows from what is stated in (g) above, that Federal laws must be implemented in the States and that the Federal executive must have power to take appropriate executive action under Federal laws in the State, including the enforcement of those laws. Whether this is done by setting up in each State a parallel Federal machinery of law enforcement, or by using the existing State machinery, is a matter governed by practical expediency which does not affect the Federal principle. In the United States, a defiance of Federal law can be, *and, as we have seen, has been* put down by the use of Armed Forces of the U.S. and the National Militia of the States. This is not inconsistent with the Federal principle in the United States. Our Constitution has adopted the method of empowering the Union Government to give directions to the States to give effect to the Union law and to prevent obstruction in the working of the Union law. Such a power, though different in form, is in substance the same as the power of the Federal government in the U.S. to enforce its laws, if necessary by force. Therefore, the power to give directions to the State governments does not violate the Federal principle.

(j) Article 356 (read with Art. 355) which provides for the failure of constitutional machinery was based on Art. 4, s. 4 of the U.S. Constitution and Art. 356, like Art. 4, s. 4, is not inconsistent with the Federal principle. As stated earlier, these provisions were meant to be the last resort, but have been gravely abused and can therefore be said to affect the working of the Constitution as a *Federal Government*. But the recent amendment of Art. 356 by the 44th Amendment, and the submission to be made hereafter that the doctrine of the Political Question does not apply in India, show that the Courts can now take a more active part in preventing a *mala fide* or improper exercise of the power to impose a President's Rule, unfettered by the American doctrine of the political question.

(k) The view that unimportant matters were assigned to the States cannot be sustained in face of the very important subjects assigned to the States in List II, and the same applies to taxing powers of the States, which are made mutually exclusive of the taxing powers of the Union so that ordinarily the States have independent source of revenue of their own. The legislative entries relating to taxes in List II show that the sources of revenue available to the States are substantial and would increasingly become more substantial. In addition to the exclusive taxing powers of the States, the States become entitled either to appropriate taxes collected by the Union or to a share in the taxes collected by the Union.

Principle of federalism not watered down in our Constitution

5.37 In the result, the view expressed in Supreme Court judgments that the principle of Federalism has been watered down in our Constitution is not supported by an examination of its provisions when compared with corresponding provisions in admittedly federal Constitutions. For the reasons given above, the federal principle is dominant in our Constitution.

CHAPTER VI

TERRITORIES, NEW STATES AND CITIZENSHIP

PART I

India in the British Commonwealth of Nations and in International Law

International status of India before and after the Ind. Independence Act, 1947

6.1 Although India was a member of international organizations like the League of Nations and the United Nations Organization, and although she exercised the treaty-making power in her own right, she was not regarded as a sovereign State and as a normal subject of international law as long as her internal and external relations rested ultimately on the British Government and Parliament.[1] However, under the Indian Independence Act, 1947, India became an independent State, and under our Constitution she became a Sovereign Democratic Republic. However India "declared and affirmed (her) desire to continue her full membership of the British Commonwealth of Nations, her acceptance of the King as the symbol of the free association of its independent member Nations and as such the Head of the Commonwealth." In accepting and recognising India's continued membership in terms of the above declaration, the Governments of the other Commonwealth countries affirmed that the basis of their own membership, namely, the allegiance to the Crown had not changed.[2]

India remains a member of the Br. Commonwealth of Nations

India a sovereign democratic republic

6.2 The Drafting Committee in submitting the draft Constitution stated that the Committee had altered the Preamble by substituting the words "Sovereign Democratic Republic" for the words "Sovereign Independent Republic" because the idea of independence was included in sovereignty and added nothing to it. Sovereignty has an internal as well as an external aspect but in this Chapter we are concerned with external sovereignty. It has been said that "in consequence of its external independence, a State can, unless restricted by treaty, manage its international affairs according to its discretion; in particular, it can enter into alliances and conclude other treaties, send and receive diplomatic envoys, acquire and cede territory, make war and peace."[3] Our Constitution confers on the Union of India legislative and executive power which embraces the total field of external sovereignty. Under Arts. 245 and 246 read with the following entries in List I, Sch. VII, Parliament has exclusive power to legislate on: 1. The defence of India; 9. preventive detention for reasons connected with defence and foreign affairs; 10. foreign affairs and all matters which bring the Union into relation with any foreign country; 11. diplomatic corps and trade representation; 12. United Nations Organization; 13. participation in international conferences and other bodies and implementation of decisions made thereat; 14. entering into treaties and agreements and conven-

External sovereignty

Our Constitution confers on the Union total legislative and executive powers as regards external sovereignty: express powers cover the whole field,

---

[1] Oppenheim, *International Law*, 8th ed., Vol. 1, p. 209.
[2] ibid. pp. 209-10. [3] ibid. pp. 286-87.

tions with foreign countries; 15. war and peace; 16. foreign jurisdiction; 17. citizenship, naturalisation and aliens; 18. extradition; 19. emigration and expulsion from India, passports and visas; 25. maritime shipping and navigation; 37. foreign loans; 41. trade and commerce with foreign countries, import and export across Customs frontiers, definition of Customs frontiers; 83. duties of Customs, including duties on export; 57. fishing and fisheries beyond territorial waters. It is difficult to see what aspect of external sovereignty is left out from this exhaustive enumeration of powers, but if any aspect were left out, it would be covered by Art. 248 and entry 97, List I, Sch. VII, which confer residuary powers of legislation on the Union. Consequently in India no part of external sovereignty can be outside the Constitution, since the residuary power would cover it. And Art. 73 provides that the executive power of the Union is co-extensive with its exclusive legislative power.

but in any event the residuary power would cover anything left out

Power to acquire and cede territory: the *Berubari Opinion*

6.3 It is an aspect of external sovereignty that a Sovereign State can acquire and cede territory. Does India possess that power (i) under our Constitution or (ii) outside it as an attribute of sovereignty? What has been said above clearly establishes that no aspect of external sovereignty can fall outside our Constitution; but since the Supreme Court in its advisory opinion in *In re Berubari Union and Exchange of Enclaves*[4] expressed the view that the power to acquire and cede territory was a sovereign power which existed outside the Constitution, it is necessary to consider the question further. However, as the *Berubari Opinion* not only overlooked Art. 248, and entry 97, List I, Sch. VII, but also other relevant provisions of the Constitution, it would lead to a clearer understanding of that opinion to consider first, the provisions thus left out.

In the U.S., the power to acquire and cede territory included in the treaty making, or foreign affairs power

6.4 The power to acquire and cede territory has been considered in the United States as necessarily involved either in the war and treaty-making power, or in the power relating to foreign affairs. Notwithstanding *obiter dicta* that State territory cannot be ceded under a treaty without the consent of that State,[5] the general trend of authority is that State territory may be ceded without such consent:

State territory can be ceded without the State's consent

"The better opinion would seem to be, that such a power of cession of the territory of a State without its consent does reside exclusively in the treaty-making power, under the Constitution of the United States yet sound discretion would forbid the exercise of it without the consent of the local government who are interested, except in cases of great necessity, in which the consent might be presumed."[6]

This appears to be substantially the view of Marshall and Story[7] and of commentators like Prof. Willoughby, Prof. Corwin and Dr. Schwartz.[8] Bearing in mind the well-settled principle that entries in the Legislative Lists must be widely construed, and that all powers embraced by the terms of an entry must be taken to have

---

[4] (1960) 3 S.C.R. 250, ('60) A.SC. 845.

[5] *Per* Field J. in *DeGeofroy* v. *Riggs* (1889) 133 U.S. 258, 33 L. ed. 642; *per* White J. in *Downes* v. *Bidwell* (1900) 182 U.S. 244, 45 L. ed. 1088.

[6] Kent, 1 Comm. 166-167 and Note; see *Lattimer* v. *Poteet* (1840) 14 Pet 4, 14, 10 L. ed. 328, 333.

[7] See Willoughby *on the Constitution*, 2nd ed., Vol. 1, p. 575.

[8] *Willoughby*, ibid. p. 576; *Corwin*, p. 481; Schwartz, *The Powers of Government*, Vol. II, pp. 141-2.

been conferred, it is submitted that acquisition or cession following war and declaration of peace would be covered by the power to declare war and make peace along with the treaty-making power, and the power to acquire or cede territory in times of peace would be equally covered by the power to deal with foreign affairs and to make treaties. The width of the treaty-making power is emphasized by Art. 253. Under Art. 253, in implementing a treaty, agreement or convention with another country or countries (entry 14, List I) or any decision made in any international conference, association or other body (entry 13, List I) the limitations imposed by Art. 245 and Art. 246(3) are removed and the total field of legislation is open to the Union Parliament. The importance attached to treaties and international obligations is further emphasized by Art. 51 which makes it a directive of State Policy, to foster respect for international law and treaty obligations in dealings of organized peoples with one another. It is submitted, therefore, that the power to acquire and cede territory is a legislative and executive power covered by the express provisions of List I mentioned above. In any event, the power would be included in Art. 248 and entry 97, List I, Sch. VII.

Submission: express powers in List I cover the power to acquire and cede territory; in any event, At. 248 and entry 97, List I, would do so

6.5 It may be mentioned here that Art. 253 of our Constitution appears to have been enacted in order to avoid the difficulties such as were experienced by Canada in implementing international agreements or conventions. S. 132, B.N.A. Act, 1867, confers upon the Parliament and Government of Canada, "all powers necessary or proper for performing the obligations of Canada or any Province thereof as part of the British Empire towards foreign countries arising under treaties between the Empire and such foreign countries." The Privy Council referred to this section and upheld the power of the Dominion Government to implement the Paris Convention for the International Regulation of Aviation signed and ratified by Canada *as part of the British Empire.*[9] Again, by reference to the residuary powers of legislation, the Privy Council upheld the power to implement a convention with foreign countries on Broadcasting which Canada had entered into *separately* with those countries.[10] However, the Privy Council struck down as *ultra vires* three labour Acts passed by the Dominion Parliament in 1935 which gave effect to the draft convention adopted by the International Labour Organization in accordance with the treaty of Versailles and ratified by Canada.[11] The Privy Council held that the Dominion could not merely by making promises to foreign countries clothe itself with legislative authority inconsistent with the Constitution which gave it birth,[12] and as the impugned laws related to "property and civil rights in the Province", a subject of exclusive provincial legislative power under s. 92(13), B.N.A. Act, they were void. In other words, the Privy Council held that a power to implement a treaty did not include a power to legislate on a subject of exclusive provincial legislation. To prevent such a position arising in India, Art. 253 enables Parliament to implement a treaty by law even if the subject-matter of the law is a subject of exclusive State legislation.

Art. 253 avoids the difficulties experienced by Canada in implementing treaties

[9] *In re Control of Aeronautics* (1932) A.C. 54.
[10] *In re Regulation and Control of Radio Communications* (1932) A.C. 304.
[11] *A.-G. for Canada* v. *A.-G. for Ontario* (1937) A.C. 326.
[12] ibid. p. 352.

R. Monteiro v. Goa; Art. 253, entries 13 and 14, List I and the Geneva Conventions Act, 1960

6.6 In *R. Monteiro* v. *Goa*[13] the Supreme Court considered the effect of implementing conventions under Art. 253, read with entries 13 and 14 of List I, in connection with the Geneva Conventions Act, 1960 ("the Act"). The appellant was a resident of Goa, and after its annexation by India, he chose to retain his Portuguese nationality, and he applied for, and obtained, a temporary permit to stay in India. He did not apply for the renewal of the permit when it expired, so he was ordered to leave Goa. As he disobeyed the order, he was prosecuted. His defence was that the order of deportation was *ultra vires* the Act; and that he had committed no offence as he was protected by the Act.

Effect of the Geneva Conventions Act, 1960

6.7 In rejecting the appellant's defence, the Supreme Court laid down the following propositions:

(a) the protection given by Art. 47, Sch. IV of the Act, to persons in the appellant's position, enured only during military conflict, and not after the conflict had ceased and the territory had been annexed by the occupying power. As conflict had ceased when Goa was annexed on December 20, 1961, the appellant was not protected by the Act;[14] (b) the Act by itself gave no remedy to the appellant, as the Conventions were not made enforceable against the Government;[15] (c) it cannot be doubted that the reception and residence of an alien is a matter of discretion, and every State has, by reason of its own territorial supremacy the legal right and the competence to exclude aliens from the whole or part of its territory[16] and an alien excluded from the State's territory had no right to maintain an action in the States' courts to enforce a right to stay in the said territory.[17]

The internal aspect of the treaty-making power: the effect of Constitutional limitations

6.8 The power to make treaties or enter into binding agreements with other nations, has an international as well as an internal aspect. In International Law, nations are assumed to know where the treaty-making power resides, as well as the internal limitations on that power.[18] As regards the internal aspect of a treaty or agreement, the Constitutional limitations, if any, on the treaty-making power would come into play. For example, in the United States although it is for the President to negotiate a treaty, his power is to be exercised on the advice and with the consent of the Senate. If the Senate refuses its consent, or gives it subject to conditions, then the treaty does not become a law of the United States as provided by Art. 6, cl. 2, and would have no operation in the United States, although it may involve a breach of the treaty with the foreign nation. Again, where a treaty imposes an obligation which affects the rights of the inhabitants of a State, say, India, the treaty would have to be implemented by a law, and the same would be the position if the treaty involved expenditure of public funds because these can only be appropriated in the manner provided for in the Constitution. Although the power to enter into treaties and implement them is in terms absolute, having regard to the fact that we have a written federal Constitution, a Court would imply limitations on that power as they have been implied in the United States although no treaty entered into by the United States has been held constitutionally void. A treaty, for instance, cannot make provisions which would, in effect, amend

---

13 (1970) 1 S.C.R. 87, ('70) A.SC. 329.
14 ibid. pp. 334-7.
15 ibid. p. 334.
16 ibid. p. 332.
17 ibid., where *Musgrove* v. *Chun Teeong Tay* (1891) A.C. 272 is given in support of the proposition.
18 Willoughby, *Constitution of the United States*, p. 528.

the Constitution, or give up the form of Government set up by the Constitution, for, it could not have been intended that a power conferred by the Constitution should, without an amendment of the Constitution, alter the Constitution.

6.9 The question whether the acquisition or cession of territory can be brought about by a law referable to Arts. 2 and 3 or whether it can be brought about only by an amendment of the Constitution will be considered in the second part of this Chapter dealing with the Union and its territories.

Whether territory can be acquired or ceded by a law under Arts. 2 and 3

PART II

The Territories of India

6.10 India, that is Bharat, is a Union of States [Art. 1(1)]. The Drafting Committee substituted the word "Union" for the word "Federation" because it preferred to follow the language of the Preamble to the B.N.A. Act, 1867; the Committee said that there were advantages in describing India as a "Union", although its Constitution was federal in structure. Amplifying this view in the Constituent Assembly, Dr. Ambedkar said that the unitary government of South Africa was called a Union so that it was not contrary to usage to describe India as a Union. The Committee wanted to make it clear that though India was to be a Federation, the Federation was not the result of an agreement by the States to join a Federation, and that the Federation, not being the result of an agreement no State had the right to secede from it. The Federation was a Union because it was indissoluble.[19] It is submitted that the word "Union" conveys no such meaning, and if it was intended to make the Union "indissoluble", the obvious way was to describe India as "an indissoluble Union of States"[20] However, the definition of India as a Union of States emphasizes the important part which the States have to play in our Constitution,[21] for apart from the States, India does not exist.

India a Union of States

"Union" preferred to "federation" to show that the Union was indissoluble

6.11 In federal Governments, it is customary to provide that the territory of a State shall not be altered without its consent (apart from the case of cession forced by necessity arising from war or threat of war). However, the position in India has been fully considered earlier.[22]

Parliamentary power to alter the territory of States

6.12 In our Constitution as originally enacted, India, that is Bharat, was declared to be a Union of States: Art. 1(1). The States and their territories were specified in Part A, B and C of the First Schedule

The Union and its territories on Jan. 26, 1950 — Part

---

[19] *C.A.D.*, Vol. 7, p. 43.

[20] See the Preamble to the Australian Constitution which declares that the States had agreed "to unite in one indissoluble Federal Commonwealth".

[21] "The Constitution itself says by Art. 1 that India is a Union of States and in interpreting the Constitution one must keep in view the essential structure of a federal or quasi-federal Constitution, namely, that the units of the Union have also certain powers as has the Union": *Automobile Transport Ltd.* v. *Rajasthan* ('62) A.SC. 1406, 1416.

[22] See para 5.18.

A, B and C States [Art. 1(2)],[23] and the territory of India consisted of the territory of the States, the territories specified in Part D of the First Schedule (Andaman and Nicobar Islands) and such other territories as may be acquired.[24] On the day our Constitution came into force (January 26, 1950), the Adaptation of Laws Order, 1950, was promulgated by the President of India in the exercise of the powers conferred on him by Art. 372(2), and it came into force the same day. The Adaptation Order substituted a new section 3 in the General Clauses Act, 1897, and the new s. 3(41) and (58) were as follows:

Art. 372: Adaptation of Laws Order, 1950, adapts the General Clauses Act

Definition of "Part A, B and C States"

"s. 3(41) 'Part A State' shall mean a State for the time being specified in Part A of the First Schedule to the Constitution, 'Part B State' shall mean a State for the time being specified in Part B of that Schedule and 'Part C State' shall mean a State for the time being specified in Part C of that Schedule or a territory for the time being administered by the President under the provisions of article 243 of the Constitution."

"s. 3(58) 'State' shall mean a Part A State, a Part B State or a Part C State."

Under Art. 367(1), the General Clauses Act, 1897, with the adaptations and modifications made by the President under Art. 372 is applicable to the interpretation of the Constitution with the result that India, which is a Union of States consists of Part A, Part B and Part C States, because by virtue of the above sections the territory of Andaman and Nicobar Islands and any other territory not shown in Sch. I are included in Part C States. If a question of the cession of territory under Art. 3 had arisen before the Constitution (7th Amendment) Act, it is clear that the word "State" in Art. 3 included Andaman and Nicobar Islands or any other territory of India.

Territory in Part D, Sch. I, included in the definition of Part C States

Constitution (7th Amend.) Act, Sch. I amended: Part I — States, Part II — Union Territory

6.13 Section 12 of the State Reorganization Act, 1956, amended the First Schedule of the Constitution by amending Parts A, B and C thereof.[25] However, by the Constitution (7th Amendment) Act, the Division of the States into A, B and C States and the territory mentioned in Part D of the First Schedule was altered. The First Schedule was amended and was divided into two parts: Part I described "The States", and Part II — described "The Union Territories." The Union territories, with the exception of Andaman and Nicobar Islands, consisted of five States which were formerly Part C States. The First Schedule has been amended from time to time.[26] Arts. 1(2) and 3(*b*) India consisted of the Territories of the States, the Union Territories thereof be as specified in the First Schedule, and the Territory of India consisted of the Territories of the States, the Union Territories specified in the First Schedule and any other territory which may be acquired. However, by the Adaptation of Laws (No. 1) Order, 1956, made under Art. 372A, the definition of "States" in s. 3(58) of the General Clauses Act was amended to run as follows:

Arts. 1(2) and 3(*b*) amended

Art. 372A: Adaptation of Laws (No. 1) Order, 1956

Definition of "State" amended

" 'State' — (a) as respects any period before the commencement of the Constitution (Seventh Amendment) Act, 1956, shall mean a Part A State, a Part B State, or a Part C State; and (b) as respects any period after such commencement, shall mean a State specified in the First Schedule to the Constitution and shall include a Union territory."

---

[23] The Report of the Drafting Committee observed that Part A, B and C States corresponded to "the existing Governor's Provinces, Chief Commissioner's Provinces and Indian States."

[24] For the number of A, B and C States, see pp. A-146 to A-151.

[25] See p. A-146.

[26] Changes made from time to time will be found at p. A-146 *et seq.*

6.14 In our Constitution as originally enacted, Part VIII dealt with Part C States. Under Art. 239, Part C States were to be administered by the President acting to such extent as he thought fit, through a Chief Commissioner or a Lt.-Governor. Art. 240 provided for the creation or continuance of local legislatures, or a Council of Advisers or Ministers or both with such constitution, powers and functions in each case as may be specified in the law. Such a law was not to be deemed to be an amendment of the Constitution within Art. 368 notwithstanding that the law contained any provision which amended, or had the effect of amending, the Constitution. Art. 242 continued the constitution, powers and functions of the Coorg Legislative Council as they existed immediately before the commencement of the Constitution until Parliament by law otherwise provided.

Jan. 26, 1950: Chapter VIII contained provisions for Part C States

6.15 In 1951 Parliament passed the Government of Part C States Act (Act XLIX of 1951) to provide for Legislative Assemblies, Councils of Ministers and Councils of Advisers for Part C States. S. 21(1) of the Act defined the extent of legislative power there conferred, and s. 21(2) provided that "Nothing in sub-cl. (1) was to derogate from the power conferred on Parliament by the Constitution to make laws with respect to any matter for a State or any part thereof." The result therefore was that notwithstanding the conferment of legislative power on Legislative Assemblies, Parliament retained an overriding power to make laws for Part C States. S. 22 of the Act secured supremacy of the Union law in case of conflict, whether such law was made before or after the law made by the Legislature of a Part C State.

The Government of Part C States Act, 1951

6.16 The Constitution as enacted provided in Part IX (which consisted of one Article - Art. 243) for the administration of the territories specified in Part D of the First Schedule and other territories not specified in that Schedule. Art. 243 provided that the territories were to be administered by the President acting to such extent as he thought fit through a Chief Commissioner or other authority appointed by him. Further, the President had power to make regulations for the peace and good government of any territory and any regulation so made could repeal or amend by law made by Parliament or any existing law applicable to the territory; such regulation was to have the effect of an Act of Parliament applying to such territory.

Jan. 26, 1950: Part IX contained provisions for the territories in Sch. I, Part D

6.17 The Constitution (7th Amendment) Act altered the scheme described above for the administration of Part C States and Part D States. Part IX was repealed, and the title of Part VIII was altered to that of "The Union Territories", and Sch. I was amended. Art. 239 as amended empowered the President to administer the Union Territory through an Administrator to be appointed by him and provided that notwithstanding anything contained in Part VI the President may appoint a Governor of a State as an administrator of an adjoining Union Territory, and the Governor so appointed was to exercise his function as such Administrator independently of his Council of Ministers. Art. 240 empowered the President to make regulations for the peace, order and good government of the Union Territory of the Andaman and Nicobar Islands, the Laccadive and Minicoy and Amindevi Islands. Such regulations could repeal or amend any Act

Part IX repealed and Part VIII amended by the Const. (7th Amend.) Act made by Parliament or any existing law applicable to the Union Territory and such regulations were to have the effect of an Act of Parliament applying to such territory. Art. 242 which related to Coorg was repealed.

The Const. (14th Amend.) Act

6.18 The Constitution (14th Amendment) Act, 1962, added Pondicherry as the ninth item in the First Schedule, Part II, and inserted Art. 239A enabling Parliament by law to create for the Union Territories of Himachal Pradesh, Manipur, Tripura, Goa, Daman and Diu and Pondicherry, local legislatures or Councils of Ministers or both with such constitution, powers and functions as may be specified in such law. Any such law was not to be deemed an amendment of the Constitution under Art. 368 notwithstanding that it contained any provision which amended, or had the effect of amending, the Constitution. Art. 240 was amended by adding Pondicherry in Cl. 1(*a*), and by adding a proviso that when any body was created under Art. 239A to function as the legislature in the Union Territory of Goa, Daman and Diu or Pondicherry, the President was not to make regulations for the peace, progress and good government of that Union Territory with effect from the day appointed for the first meeting of the Legislature. In 1956, Parliament enacted the Territorial Councils Act, 1956, to provide for the establishment of Territorial Councils for the Union Territories of Himachal Pradesh, Manipur and Tripura. In 1963, Parliament passed the Government of Union Territories Act, 1963, providing for the Legislative Assemblies and Councils of Ministers of certain Union Territories. S. 18 enables the legislatures so created to legislate on matters mentioned in List II and List III, Sch. 7, but the section expressly provides that such power is not to derogate from the power conferred on Parliament by the Constitution to make laws in respect of any Union Territory or part thereof. The result therefore is that though Union Territories have to some extent been approximated to the States, they are not assimilated to the States and the overriding power, legislative and executive, remains with Parliament and the Union Government respectively. The First Schedule (pp. A-142 to A-151) has been amended several times and the States of Haryana, Himachal Pradesh and Meghalaya have been created, as also the Union Territories of Mizoram and Arunachal Pradesh. The Sixth Schedule (pp. A-161 to A-176) has been amended to include the Tribal Areas of Assam, Meghalaya and the Union Territory of Mizoram.

The Berubari Opinion

6.19 We can now consider the *Berubari Opinion*[27] in which the Supreme Court considered Arts. 1, 2 and 3. That case arose out of the Indo-Pakistan Agreement ("the Agreement") for the division of the Berubari Union and for the exchange of Cooch-Behar enclaves. We will, first, state the law laid down by the Supreme Court and then submit that the law so laid down is wrong. The Supreme Court rejected the argument that the agreement merely brought about a change in the boundary prescribed by the Radcliffe Award[28] and held that the agreement involved a cession of Indian territory. Therefore, the question to be determined was whether such cession could be effected by a law made by Parliament under Art. 3, or whether

Power to cede territory a sovereign power outside the Constitution

[27] (1960) 3 S.C.R. 250, ('60) A.SC. 845.
[28] (1960) 3 S.C.R. *supra* at p. 275.

it could only be effected by amending the Constitution under Art. 368. Gajendragadkar J. said that the question had to be considered against the historical background that the Provinces of India were not independent States before they became part of a Federation, and that the Constitution "contemplated changes of the territorial limits of the constituent States and there was no guarantee about their territorial integrity."[29] He rejected the argument, based on the Preamble to the Constitution, that the territory of India could not be ceded at all, observing that the Preamble was not a source of power, and consequently not a source of limitation of power. Art. 1(3)(*c*) did not confer the power to acquire territory,[30] and Art. 3 did not expressly confer the power to cede territory. The power to acquire and cede territory was a sovereign power which existed outside the Constitution.[31] Article 2, which enabled Parliament by law to admit into the Union, or establish, new States, showed that foreign territories, which on acquisition became a part of the territory of India under Art. 1(3)(*c*), could by law be admitted into the Union.[32] The acquisition of foreign territory in the exercise of sovereignty automatically made that territory a part of India, and after such territory was factually made part of India, it could be assimilated by law made under Art. 2 or Art. 3(*a*) or (*b*). Territory acquired by India may be formed into a new State or be united to another State under Art. 3(*a*). Article 3(*c*), which empowered Parliament by law to "diminish the territory of any State", did not refer to ceding territory to another State. Article 3(*b*) to (*e*) does not refer to Union Territory:

Art. 3(*c*) refers to territory of a State, so Union Territory not covered by it

"In other words, if an increase or diminution in areas of the Union Territory is contemplated or the alteration of their boundaries or name is proposed, it cannot be effected by law relatable to Art. 3. This position is of *considerable* assistance in interpreting Art. 3(c)."[33] (italics supplied)

Accordingly, the court held that the agreement could not be implemented by a law made under Art. 3 but could only be implemented by an amendment of the Constitution. As a result of this judgment, the Constitution (9th Amendment) Act was passed to implement the agreement.

6.20 The observations of Gajendragadkar J. that the boundaries of Union Territories could not be effected by a law relatable to Art. 3,[34] since "State" in Art. 3 did not include Union Territories, were *obiter*, once the court held that the Berubari Agreement did not merely bring about a change of boundaries between India and Pakistan, but involved a cession of Indian territory. However, in *Ram Kishore* v. *Union*[35] the same learned judge stated that, in the *Berubari Opinion*, the court had overlooked the definition of "State" in the General Clauses Act, 1897, which Act, *with the adaptations made by the President under Art. 372,* applied to the interpretation of the Constitution *by virtue of Art. 367(1)*. According to s. 3(58)(*b*) of the General Clauses Act, the word "State", as respects any period after the Constitution (7th Amendment) Act, 1956, included Union Territory. Consequently, Gajendragadkar J. said that on that point the *Berubari*

Ram Kishore v. *Union*

[29] ibid. p. 285.
[30] ibid. p. 282.
[31] ibid. p. 291.
[32] ibid. p. 287.
[33] ibid. p. 290.
[34] Quoted in para 6.19 above.
[35] (1966) 1 S.C.R. 430, ('66) A.SC. 644.

Opinion was mistaken, and he added, "to that extent the *incidental* reason given in support of the main conclusion is not justified".[36] If the matter rested here, the main reason given for the *Berubari Opinion* is clearly wrong, for no power can be outside our Constitution, since Parliament possesses the residuary power of legislation. However, in *Advance Insurance Co.* v. *Gurudasmal*[37] Hidayatullah C.J. said that Gajendragadkar C.J.'s statement in *Ram Kishore's Case* that the adaptation of the General Clauses Act was made under Art. 372 was *per incuriam,* as the proper reference ought to have been to Art. 372A. It is submitted that in correcting one error, Hidayatullah C.J. has fallen into another error, because on the language of Art. 367, the General Clauses Act, 1897 applies to the interpretation of the Constitution subject to adaptations made under Art. 372. Under Art. 367, Gajendragadkar C.J. could have applied the General Clauses Act to the interpretation of the Constitution only if the adaptation had been made under Art. 372. The reference to Art. 372 was not *per incuriam,* if Art. 367 was to be invoked. What was *per incuriam* was that the adaptation of the General Clauses Act to which he referred had been made under Art. 372A, so that *prima facie,* Art. 367 did not apply. But for the Constitution (18th Amendment) Act, 1966, a difficult question of construction would have arisen as to the "incidental reason" given in support of the *Berubari Opinion.* However, it is unnecessary to consider that question here, for the 18th Amendment has put the "incidental reason" out of the way, by the insertion of two Explanations in Art. 3 which make it clear that "State" includes Union Territory in Art. 3(*a*) to 3(*e*) but not in the proviso.

Advance Ins. Co. v. *Gurudasmal*: a criticism

18th Amendment puts the construction of Art. 3 beyond doubt

Submission: *Berubari Opinion* wrong

6.21 It is clear from the above discussion that the *Berubari Opinion* is wrong. It is submitted that the Constitution (9th Amendment) Act was wholly unnecessary, and a law referable to Art. 3 would have been adequate to implement the agreement.

Maganbhai v. *Union* questions about boundary disputes directly raised

6.22 The question, whether an agreement between India and Pakistan, settling disputed questions about their boundaries, could be effective without legislation and/or without a constitutional amendment, did not arise in the *Berubari Opinion* once the court held that the Berubari Agreement did not merely effect a change in boundaries, but involved a cession of Indian territory. Nor did that question arise in *Ram Kishore's Case* in which the petitioners sought to restrain the implementation of the Constitution (9th Amendment) Act, — which incorporated the Berubari Agreement — on the ground that having regard to the real facts it was incapable of implementation.[38] However, that question directly arose in *Maganbhai* v. *Union.*[39] There, the dispute about the boundary between India and Pakistan in the Rann of Kutch, which had led to an armed conflict, was brought to an end by referring the dispute to an International Tribunal, by whose award both countries agreed to be bound. The complicated facts of the case are set out in the judgments.[40] The Tribunal's award, by a majority, upheld, *inter alia,* the claim of Pakistan

---

[36] (1966) 1 S.C.R. *supra* at p. 438.
[37] (1970) 3 S.C.R. 881, ('70) A.SC. 1126.
[38] (1966) 1 S.C.R. at p. 435, ('66) A.SC. 641.
[39] (1969) 3 S.C.R. 254, ('69) A.SC. 783.
[40] (1969) 3 S.C.R. *supra* at pp. 260-9; 289-96.

to three sectors of the Rann.[41] The Petitioners did not dispute that the Union Government could enter into a covenant to be bound by the decision of an International Tribunal, and that its award would be binding on India; they merely contended that a constitutional amendment was necessary, since the award affected the territorial limits of India.

6.23 The Petitioners alleged that the treaty violated their fundamental rights to move freely throughout the territory of India and to reside and settle in any part of the territory of India [Art. 19(1)(*d*) and (*e*)]. "The nature of the territory precludes any other claim being made."[42] The *locus standi* of the petitioners to maintain a petition under Art. 32 was doubtful, but the court heard the petitions on the merits, observing that this course "was not to be taken as establishing a precedent."[43]

The petitioner's case

6.24 Hidayatullah C.J. delivered the majority,[44] and Shah J. a concurring, judgment. Upto a point the two judgments lay down the same principles, but in the majority judgment they are obscured by irrelevant historical digressions. Hidayatullah C.J.'s survey of the treaty-making power under other Constitutions is irrelevant since those Constitutions confer the power in terms very different from those of our Constitution.[45] Nor is the evolution of the treaty-making power in the United Kingdom helpful or relevant, once the judgment gives "the settled law of modern times."[46] For a clear understanding of the two judgments, we will consider, first, the propositions affirmed by both the judgments and then refer to the points on which the two judgments differ.

The majority and the concerning judgments

6.25 Both judgments refer with approval to the observations of Sir Robert Philmore in *In re Parlement Belge*[47] that the use of the treaty-making prerogative of the Crown to confer on a civilian ship the privileges of a ship of war was unprecedented and unconstitutional.[48] Both judgments also refer with approval to *Walker* v. *Baird*,[49] where the Judicial Committee held that acts done in derogation of the plaintiff's private rights in his lobster factory, under powers conferred by a treaty between Her Majesty and the French Government, could not be defended as acts of State into which the courts could not inquire, and that such a defence was no answer to the action.[50] Both judgments held that Lord Atkin's observations in

Propositions affirmed by both judgments

[41] ibid. p. 296, where the three sectors are fully described.

[42] ibid. p. 300: "There are no local residents, no private property, and no agriculture. For four months in the year it is mostly under water, for the rest of the year it is marshy land".

[43] "The only person who can claim deprivation of fundamental rights, is Mr. Madhu Limaye, although in his case also the *connection was temporary and almost ephemeral.* . . . But we are not to be taken as establishing a precedent for this Court which declines to issue a writ of *mandamus* except at the instance of a party whose fundamental rights are *directly and substantially invaded* or are in imminent danger of being so invaded." (italics supplied): ibid. p. 270.

[44] For himself, Ramaswami, Mitter and Grover JJ.

[45] (1969) 3 S.C.R. *supra* at pp. 271-2. [46] ibid. p. 273.

[47] (1879) 4 P.D. 129, reversed on a different point in (1880) 5 P.D. 197.

[48] (1969) 3 S.C.R. *supra* at p. 298 (Shah J.) and at pp. 273-4 (Hidayatullah C.J.).

[49] (1892) A.C. 491 (J.C.).

[50] (1969) 3 S.C.R. *supra* at p. 273 (Hidayatullah C.J.); p. 298 (Shah J.).

A.-G. for Canada v. *A.-G. for Ontario*[51] were valid in the context of our Constitution.[52] Lord Atkin observed that within the British Empire there was a well-established rule that the making of a treaty was an executive act, while the performance of its obligation, if they entailed the alteration of the existing domestic law, would require legislation. The creation of the obligations undertaken in treaties, and the assent to their form and quality, were undisputably the function of the executive alone. But Parliament might refuse to perform those obligations and so leave the State in default.[53] Both judgments held that the settlement of a dispute about the alignment of an undefined boundary between India and Pakistan involved no cession of territory by either State, and such settlement did not require either a constitutional amendment or parliamentary legislation, but could be effected by the executive.[54]

Settlement of boundary dispute not a cession of territory, and can be effected by the executive

The judgment of Shah J. contains a clear statement of the law on the treatymaking power. The majority judgment unsatisfactory

6.26 However, on a true nature of the power under our Constitution to make a treaty, or to implement a treaty, agreement or convention with a foreign State, a clear statement of the law can be given from the judgment of Shah J., but not from that of Hidayatullah C.J. Shah J. held that our Constitution did not make the power to enter into a treaty, whether in *peace or in war,* conditional on passing legislation. Under Art. 73 the executive power of the Union of India was co-extensive with the legislative power of Parliament, and the power to legislate in respect of treaties was conferred on Parliament by entries 10 and 14, List I, Sch. 7.[55] The petitioner's contention that the power to make, or to implement a treaty, agreement or convention, could only be exercised under the authority of law was based on a misreading of Art. 253. The effect of Art. 253 was, that if a treaty etc. dealt with a subject within the competence of the State Legislatures, then, notwithstanding Art. 246(3), Parliament alone had power to make laws implementing such treaty etc. Further, Art. 253 dealt with legislative power, and did not circumscribe the executive power conferred by Art. 73. The executive might incur obligations by entering into treaties, etc.; but if such obligations did not restrict the rights of citizens or others, or modify the laws of the State, no legislation was necessary; but if such obligations did affect such rights or modify such laws, legislation would be necessary.[56]

Shah J. expressed no opinion on the *Berubari Opinion*

6.27 Since both judgments held that the dispute about the Rann of Kutch involved no cession of Indian territory, the question whether cession of territory could be effected only by a constitutional amendment did not arise and, very rightly, Shah J. did not express any opinion on the correctness of the *Berubari Opinion.* However, Hidayatullah C.J. said:

A criticism of the majority judgment on the *Berubari Opinion*

"The precedents of this Court are clear only on one point, namely, that no cession of Indian territory can take place without a constitutional amendment. Must a boundary dispute and its settlement by an arbitral tribunal be put on the same footing?"[57]

---

[51] (1937) A.C. 326.

[52] Shah J. said so: (1969) 3 S.C.R. *supra* at p. 299; Hidayatullah C.J. appears to say much the same thing: ibid. p. 274.

[53] (1937) A.C. *supra* at p. 347; see (1969) 3 S.C.R. *supra* at p. 299 (Shah J.); pp. 273-4 (Hidayatullah C.J.).

[54] (1969) 3 S.C.R. *supra* at pp. 288-9 (Hidayatullah C.J.); p. 299 (Shah J.).

[55] See p. A-177.

[56] (1969) 3 S.C.R. *supra* at p. 299.

[57] ibid. p. 283.

If these observations treat it as settled law that a cession of territory requires a constitutional amendment, they are *obiter*, and for the reasons already given in paras 6.20 and 6.21, they are clearly wrong.

6.28 It is difficult to state what exactly was laid down by Hidayatullah C.J. about the treaty-making power under our Constitution. The survey of the English practice, and the distinctions made in England between cession of territory in times of peace and in times of war, and between the cession of territory held in free-hold by the Crown and cession of territory not so held, is unhelpful, because our Constitution makes no such distinctions. Majority judgment and the treaty-making power

6.29 Hidayatullah C.J. referred to entries 14 and 15[58] of List. I, Sch. 7[59] and stated that they must be read with Art. 253. He added: Majority judgment: Art. 253, read with entries 14 and 15, not correctly interpreted

"In point of fact (Art. 253) adds nothing to . . . Entries 14 and 15 . . . but confers exclusive power of law-making upon Parliament."[60]

It is submitted that Shah J. has correctly stated the effect of Art. 253 and the observations of Hidayatullah C.J. do not state the law correctly. The exclusive power to legislate under entries 14 and 15 must be distinguished from the subject matter of treaties, etc., because such subject matter may fall within the exclusive legislative competence of State Legislatures under List II. Article 253 has been enacted in order to make it clear that in respect of treaties, etc., Parliament has exclusive legislative power *notwithstanding that their subject matter may relate to matters in List II.*[61]

6.30 The Chief Justice's reference to s. 113 of the Evidence Act is not easily intelligible. That section was declared *ultra vires* the provincial Legislature in *Damodar Govardhan* v. *Deoram Kanji*,[62] and therefore the statement that "in British India advantage was taken of s. 113 of the Evidence Act in cases of cession to Native States, Prince or Ruler"[63] is not correct. The majority judgment and s. 113 Evidence Act

6.31 It would be unprofitable to attempt to deduce any further principles from the judgment of the Chief Justice, and it is submitted that the concurring judgment of Shah J. accurately states the law on the treaty-making power under our Constitution, and the power to settle disputed boundaries between India and any other country. Submission: the judgment of Shah J. accurately states the law

6.32 In *S. R. Bhansali* v. *Union*[64] it was held that mere physical possession of territory by force of arms did not amount to "acquisition" within the meaning of Arts. 1(3)(*c*) and 2 till the territory was annexed; the territory conquered during the India-Pakistan War of December 1971, had not become part of the territory of India.[65] *S. R. Bhansali* v. *Union*

---

58 See p. A-177.
59 (1969) 3 S.C.R. *supra* at p. 276.
60 ibid. p. 277.
61 See para 6.5.
62 (1876) 1 A.C. 332. He referred to *Damodar Govardhan's Case* in another context: (1969) 3 S.C.R. *supra* at pp. 275, 276. His observations as to what that case decided about the treaty making power are not supported by the judgment.
63 (1969) 3 S.C.R. *supra* at p. 276.
64 ('73) A.Raj. 49.
65 ibid. pp. 50-51. (The petitioner's contention that the conquered territory could not be ceded under the Simla Agreement was met by saying that since no part of the cause of action arose within the court's jurisdiction, the court could not deal with that question. It is submitted that once the court held that Pakistan territory had not been "acquired", the question of ceding it to Pakistan did not arise).

Art. 3: reference to the Bill altering boundaries etc. to the State legislatures for ascertaining its views

6.33 So far we have considered the question of acquisition or cession, and an enlargement or diminution of the territories of States. But as stated earlier, any Bill for the purpose of making a law contemplated by Art. 3 can be introduced in either House only on the recommendation of the President, and where the law affects the area, the boundary or the name of any State, the Bill embodying the law has been referred by the President to the Legislature of the affected State for ascertaining its views thereon within the time specified or within such further time as the President may give. In *Manohar Lal* v. *Union*[66] the petitioner contended that the Punjab Reorganisation Act, 1962, was invalid because the Bill which was subsequently enacted into the impugned Act had not been referred to the State legislature as required by the proviso to Art. 3. In rejecting the contention the court held that the President had issued a proclamation under Art. 356 expressing his satisfaction that the Government of the State of Punjab could not be carried on in accordance with the Constitution, and under Art. 356(1)(*c*) had suspended the operation of the proviso to Art. 3 in so far as it referred to sending the Bill to the State legislature for its opinion and also suspended Art. 174(1) and 2(*a*). As the President had suspended the power of the Governor to summon the State Legislature, and suspended the relevant part of the proviso to Art. 3, the impugned law was validly enacted because the exercise of power under Art. 356 prevailed over the requirement of the relevant part of the proviso to Art. 3.[67]

Manohar Lal v. Union: exercise of power under Art. 356 prevails over requirement of Art. 3

Babulal Parate's Case: amendments germane to the Bill permitted

6.34 The scope of the proviso to Art. 3 was determined by the Supreme Court in *Babulal Parate* v. *Bombay*.[68] There, a Bill had been introduced in the House of the People on the report of the States Reorganisation Commission, and as recommended by the President under the proviso to Art. 3 had contained a proposal for the formation of three separate units, namely (1) Union Territory of Bombay, (2) Maharashtra, including Marathwada and Vidarbha and (3) Gujarat, including Saurashtra and Cutch. The President referred this Bill to the State Legislatures concerned and obtained their views. Subsequently, Parliament amended some of the clauses and passed the Bill which came to be known as the States Reorganisation Act, 1956. That Act by s. 8(1) constituted a composite State of Bombay instead of the three separate units as originally proposed in the Bill. The appellant contended that the Act contravened Art. 3 since the Bombay Legislature had not been given an opportunity of expressing its views on the formation of the composite State. In negativing this contention the Supreme Court held that the word "purpose" in the words of the proviso "no Bill for the purpose" obviously had reference to the power of making a law in respect of the matters mentioned in the substantive part. Further, the proviso laid down two conditions and in the second condition what the President had to refer

66 ('70) A.Del. 178.

67 ibid. p. 180 [*held*, further, that the suspension of the relevant part of the proviso to Art. 3 was an incidental and consequential provision within the meaning of Art. 356(1)(*c*).]

68 (1960) 1 S.C.R. 605, ('60) A.SC. 51.

to the State Legislature for its opinion was the proposal contained in a Bill. The proviso did not contemplate that if Parliament subsequently modified that proposal, there must be a fresh Bill or a fresh reference to the State Legislature. The Court said that where amendments to a Bill were not to be introduced without the recommendation of the President, our Constitution expressly provided for it, as for example, in Art. 117. Under Art. 122 the proceedings in Parliament could not be questioned on the ground of irregularity, and the Rules of the Legislature permitted an amendment germane to the proposition. The debates in the State Legislature showed that opinions had been expressed on all aspects of the matter.[69] Although the amendment substantially altered the character of the original proposal it was still germane to the proposal and the Bill as amended was not in reality a new Bill.

A law under Arts. 2, 3 and 4(1) is not to be deemed an amendment of the Constitution

6.35 But for the provisions of Art. 4, any law altering the boundaries of a State, or a law ceding the territory of a State would require an amendment of the Constitution and the procedure prescribed by Art. 368 would have to be followed. However, Art. 4 provides that a law under Arts. 2 and 3 shall contain the necessary provisions for the amendment of Sch. I and Sch. IV and such supplemental, incidental and consequential provisions as Parliament may consider necessary. And Art. 4(2) provides that a law referred to in Art. 2, 3 and 4(1) is not to be deemed to be an amendment of the Constitution for the purposes of Art. 368.

Part III

Citizenship

Citizenship before the Constitution: the British Nationality Act, 1948

6.36 Till India became a Sovereign Democratic Republic, the question of citizenship or nationality raised no problems, because all subjects of the British Empire and Commonwealth possessed a common British nationality. The position under the British Nationality Act, 1948, had been stated thus:

"*Citizenship.* The British Nationality Act, 1948, which came into force on 1st January 1949, is a measure on which general agreement was reached with Canada, Australia, New Zealand, the Union of South Africa, India, Pakistan, Southern Rhodesia and Ceylon, and which has been followed by citizenship laws on similar lines in most of these countries.

This legislation provides a method of giving effect to the principles that each of the self-governing countries of the Commonwealth (including Southern Rhodesia although it had not yet acquired full Dominion status) should by its own legislation determine who are its citizens, that those citizens should be declared to be British subjects, and that citizens of the other territories within the Commonwealth should be recognized as British subjects."[70]

Ind. Citizenship Act, 1955, and

Section 11 of our Citizenship Act, 1955, provides that every person who is a citizen of a Commonwealth country specified in the First

[69] It may be mentioned that the opinion of the Legislature of the State of Bombay was not expressed by a formal resolution but it was resolved to forward the debates in the Legislative Assembly and in the Legislative Council as expressing the opinion of the Legislature.

[70] *Halsbury*, 3rd ed., Vol. 1 at p. 529, paragraph 1024.

Commonwealth citizenship

Schedule[71] shall by virtue of that citizenship, have the status of Commonwealth citizen in India. Art. 367(3) provides that for the purposes of the Constitution "foreign state" means any State other than India, provided that subject to the provisions of any law made by Parliament the President may by order declare any State not to be a foreign state for such purpose as may be specified in the order. Accordingly the Constitution (Declaration as to Foreign States) Order, 1950, was promulgated,[72] whereby every country within the Commonwealth was declared not to be a foreign state for the purpose of the Constitution. The effect of this declaration is not that the citizens of all Commonwealth countries, of which Pakistan is one, become Indian citizens even for the purpose of Articles like Arts. 7 and 9 which do not contain the words "foreign state". Again, a Commonwealth citizen is not a citizen within the meaning of Art. 19. It is clear from S. 12 of the Citizenship Act, 1955,[73] that in the absence of a notification conferring the rights of a citizen of India on a Commonwealth citizen, he cannot claim such rights.[74]

Commonwealth countries not "foreign" countries for certain purposes

6.37 A detailed discussion of the terms "subject", "citizen", "nationality", "alien" and "domicile" is outside the scope of this work, but a brief description of these terms may be given here. In an article on "Citizenship and Allegiance"[75] Salmond wrote:

Citizenship and residence

"In all civilized communities the title of state-membership is twofold, and the members of the body politic are of two classes accordingly. The two titles are citizenship and residence, the former being a personal, the latter merely a territorial, bond between the state and the individual. The former is a title of permanent, the latter one of temporary, membership of the political community. The State, therefore, consists, in the first place, of all those who by virtue of this personal and permanent relationship are its citizens or subjects, and, in the second place, of all those who for the time being reside within its territory, and so possess a temporary and territorial title to state-membership. Both classes are equally members of the body politic, so long as their title lasts; for both have claims to the protection of the laws and government of the state, and to such laws and government both alike owe obedience and fidelity. They are alike subject to the dominion of the state and it is in the interests of both that the state exists and fulfils its functions. . . . The practical importance of the distinction between the two forms of state-membership lies chiefly in the superior privileges possessed by citizens or subjects. Citizenship

---

[71] The First Schedule mentions the following Commonwealth countries: A. (1) United Kingdom, (2) Canada, (3) Commonwealth of Australia, (4) New Zealand, (5) Union of South Africa, (6) Pakistan, (7) Ceylon, (8) Federation of Rhodesia and Nyasaland, (9) Ghana, (10) Federation of Malaya, (11) Singapore; B. Republic of Ireland. An explanation to the First Schedule provides that "United Kingdom" means the United Kingdom of Great Britain and Northern Ireland, and including the Channel Islands, the Isle of Man and all Colonies; "Commonwealth of Australia" includes the territory of Papua and the territory of Norfolk Islands.

[72] Gazette of India Extraordinary, p. 80n, d. January 23, 1950.

[73] "12. *Power to confer rights of Indian citizen on citizens of certain countries*: (1) The Central Government may, by order notified in the Official Gazette, make provisions on a basis of reciprocity for the conferment of all or any of the rights of a citizen of India on the citizens of any country specified in the First Schedule. (2) Any order made under sub-section (1) shall have effect notwithstanding anything inconsistent therewith contained in any law other than the Constitution of India or this Act."

[74] *Noor Mohammad* v. *State* ('56) A.M.B. 211, fol. in *Naziranbai* v. *State* ('57) A.M.B. 1.

[75] (1901) 17 *L.Q.R.* 270.

is a title to rights which are not available for aliens. Citizens are members *optimo jure*, while aliens stand on a lower level in the scale of legal right."[76]

The State has thus jurisdiction not only over its citizens but also over resident aliens. "Non-resident aliens, on the other hand, possess no title of membership and stand altogether outside the body politic".[77] The term, "alien" is the subject of statutory definition in many countries, but at common law an alien was a subject of a foreign State who was not born within the allegiance of the Crown.[78] The term "national"

The State has no jurisdiction over non-resident aliens; definitions: (i) alien

(ii) "national"

"... is frequently used as synonymous with 'citizen'. However, the former term has a broader significance than the latter, being applicable to all persons owing permanent allegiance to a state, while the latter usually signifies the possession of special rights, such as the right of suffrage not enjoyed by all nationals."[79]

According to Oppenheim[80]

"Nationality of an individual is his quality of being a subject of a certain State, and therefore its citizen. . . . In general, it matters not, as far as the Law of Nations is concerned, that Municipal Laws may distinguish between different kinds of subjects — for instance, those who enjoy full political rights, and are on that account named citizens and those who are less favoured, and are on that account not named citizens."

(iii) "Nationality"

Again, it has been said that

"Nationality represents a man's political status, by virtue of which he owes allegiance to some particular country; domicile indicates his civil status and it provides the law by which his personal rights and obligations are determined. Nationality depends, apart from naturalization, on the place of birth or on parentage; domicile, is constituted by residence in a particular country *animo manendi*. It follows that a man may be a national of one country but domiciled in another."[81]

6.38 Part II of our Constitution provides for citizenship at the commencement of the Constitution (Arts. 5 to 9) and for its continuance thereafter subject to any law that may be made by Parliament (Art. 10). Art. 11 enables Parliament to provide for citizenship after the commencement of the Constitution, and it expressly provides that nothing in Arts. 5 to 10 ". . . shall derogate from the power of Parliament to make any provision with respect to the acquisition of citizenship and of other matters relating to citizenship." Under entry 17, List I, Sch. 7, Parliament has exclusive power to make laws on "citizenship, naturalisation and aliens", the last two being clearly the "other matters relating to citizenship" mentioned in Art. 11. However, the power to legislate on citizenship is "subject to the provisions of the Constitution" (Art. 246) and Art. 11 confers on Parliament the power to override Arts. 5 to 10. Theoretically, a power to legislate on "citizenship" carries with it a power to abolish citizenship altogether[82] but in the context of our Constitution such a power does not exist because the concept of citizenship is embedded in our Constitution and is basic to it. First, certain fundamental rights are conferred on citizens which are not conferred on non-citizens (e.g. Arts. 15,

Citizenship at the commencement of the Constitution and after

Art. 11: power of Parliament to override Arts. 5 to 10

Submission: no power to abolish citizenship

[76] ibid. pp. 270-71. [77] ibid. p. 270.
[78] Jowitt: *Dictionary of English Law*, Vol. 1, p. 83 (2nd ed.).
[79] *Encyclopedia Brittanica*, Vol. 16, p. 151.
[80] *International Law*, Vol. 1, 8th ed., pp. 642 to 644.
[81] Cheshire, *Private International Law*, 6th ed., p. 194.
[82] As the power to make a law "with respect to intoxicating liquors and narcotic drugs . . ." carries with it the power to prohibit the use or manufacture of such liquor: *Bhola Prasad* v. *R.* (1942) F.C.R. 17, 25.

16, 19 and 29). Secondly, certain public offices can be held only by citizens: The President of India (Art. 58); the Attorney-General of India and the Advocate Generals of the States [Art. 76(1) read with Art. 124(3) and Art. 165 read with Art. 217(2)]; Judges of the Supreme Court [Art. 124(3)] and of the High Courts [Art. 217(2)] and the Governors of the States (Art. 157). Finally, election to the House of the People and to the Legislative Assemblies of States is on the basis of adult suffrage, that is to say, every person who is a citizen of India over 21 years of age, is entitled to be registered as a voter, subject to limited exceptions (Art. 326).

No "State" citizenship in India

6.39 Unlike the United States, the component States of India are not, and never had been, independent units, and there is no such thing as "a citizen of West Bengal". The Constitution recognizes only one form of citizenship for the whole country and there cannot be double citizenship: one for the Union and the other for a State.[83] But a common citizenship must not be confused with a common Indian domicile and it was rightly so held in *Radhabai* v. *Bombay*.[84] After stating that Provincial domicile was recognized in Canada and Australia[85] the judgment said:

Citizenship not to be confused with domicile

"... under the Constitution each State in the Indian Union has its own Legislature, which is empowered to enact laws on certain subjects. Although therefore the laws passed by the Central Legislature may apply to all the States, each State has its own system of laws. The State Legislatures are also competent to legislate on matters such as marriage, divorce, success on, testacy, or intestacy, rights in regard to which depend upon domicile. There is no unity of laws in the Union in regard to many of these matters. In the words of the Privy Council in *Att.-Gen. for Alberta* v. *Cook*,[86] the indicia of domicile, 'uniformity of law, civil institutions existing within ascertained territorial limits, and juristic authority in being there for the administration of the law under which rights attributable to domicile are claimed' are all found in the Provinces or States. The persons residing in any State, such as the State of Bombay, and having an intention to continue residence in that State for an unlimited time or to make their permanent home in that State can therefore be said to have the domicile of that State."

State domicile recognized: *Joshi's Case*

This view was also taken by the Supreme Court in *D. P. Joshi* v. *M.B.*[87] In delivering the majority judgment, Venkatarama Ayyar, J. for himself, Mukherjea C.J., Bose and Sinha JJ. (Jagannadhadas J. dissenting), said:

"It was argued that under the Constitution there can be only a single citizenship for the whole of India, and that it would run counter to that notion to hold that the State could make laws based on domicile. . . . But citizenship and domicile represent two different conceptions. Citizenship has reference to the political status of a person, and domicile to his civil rights. A classic statement of the law on this subject is that of Lord Westbury in *Udny* v. *Udny*.[88] . . . Under the Constitution, article 5, which defines citizenship, itself proceeds on the basis that it is different from domicile, because under that article, domicile is not by itself sufficient to confer on a person the status of a citizen of this country."[89]

---

[83] *Hem Chandra* v. *Speaker, Legislative Assembly* ('56) A.Cal. 378, 381-2, 60 C.W.N. 555.

[84] (1955) Bom. 1039, ('55) A.B. 439, 442, 57 Bom.L.R. 827.

[85] ('55) A.B. at p. 442.

[86] (1926) A.C. 444.

[87] (1955) 1 S.C.R. 1215, ('55) A.SC. 334; applied in *Malkiat Singh* v. *State* ('69) A.P. & H. 250, 255.

[88] (1869) L.R. 1 Sc. & Div. 441, 457.

[89] (1955) 1 S.C.R. 1215, *supra* at pp. 1221-3; see p. 1222 where the passage from Lord Westbury's judgment is set out.

In *State* v. *Narayandas Mangilal*[90] a Full Bench overruled *Radhabai's Case* holding, among other things, that ". . . in India we have one citizenship, the citizenship of India. We have one domicile—the domicile in India. . . ." Unfortunately, the decision in *Joshi's Case*[91] was not cited, and therefore on this part of the case the judgment is not good law as it is a judgment *per incuriam* contrary to the law laid down by the Supreme Court.

6.40 Article 5 provides that at the commencement of the Constitution every person who is domiciled in the territory of India and (*a*) who was born in that territory; or (*b*) either of whose parents was born in that territory, or (*c*) who has been ordinarily residing in that territory for not less than 5 years immediately before the commencement of the Constitution, shall be a citizen of India. The three conditions which have to be satisfied in addition to domicile are alternative and not cumulative.[92] It has been said that the concept of domicile can be illustrated but is difficult to define; that the simplest definition though not an absolute one, is that given by Chitty J.[93] namely, "That place is properly the domicile of a person in which his habitation is fixed without any present intention of removing therefrom."[94] Two elements are necessary under the English law for the existence of domicile: (i) a residence of a particular kind, and (ii) an intention of a particular kind. There must be both the factum and the animus. The residence need not be continuous, but it must be definite, not purely fleeting. The intention must be a present intention to reside for ever in the country where the residence has been taken up.[95] In a later decision, it has been said that 'domicile' means "residence with the intention of living and dying in the country".[96] In *Union* v. *Karam Ali*[97] the respondent's family originally resided in a district, now part of Pakistan. However, in 1922 the family came to a village in Assam and resided there as permanent inhabitants and carried on business in dry fish. On the partition of India, the family did not leave Assam, but purchased landed property in Assam. The respondent challenged the "quit India" notice on the ground that they were citizens of India. In dismissing the appeal, the court held, it is submitted rightly, that on the above facts the respondents' case fell within Art. 5, for they had established that they were domiciled in India and were ordinarily residents of India for not less than five years before the coming into force of our Constitution. Art. 6 had no application, for before the partition of India on August 15, 1947, migration could only mean coming to India from outside India, and not coming from one part of India (now Pakistan) to another part of India (now in India). In 1922 India was one undivided country.

Art. 5: conditions of citizenship at the commencement of the Constitution

"Domicile" defined

[90] (1957) Bom. 880, ('58) A.B. 68, 71, 59 Bom.L.R. 901.
[91] *Supra.*
[92] *Abdul Sattar* v. *Gujarat* ('65) A.SC. 810.
[93] *Craignish* v. *Craignish* (1892) 2 Ch. 180, 192.
[94] *Per* Mahajan C.J. in *Central Bank of India Ltd.* v. *Ram Narain* (1955) 1 S.C.R. 697, 703, ('55) A.SC. 36, fol. in *Abdul Ghani* v. *State* (1956) Madh.Bh. 216, ('56) A.M.B. 250, 252.
[95] (1955) 1 S.C.R. *supra* at p. 703.
[96] *Shanno Devi* v. *Mangal Sain,* (1961) 1 S.C.R. 576, ('61) A.SC. 58, 62.
[97] ('70) A.A. & N. 14, 16.

Acquisition of Indian domicile before the Constitution: Art. 5(*c*)

6.41 In view of Art. 5(*c*) the concept of domicile acquires importance because independently of birth or descent a person domiciled in India and ordinarily residing in India for a period of five years before the commencement of the Constitution is a citizen of India at the commencement of the Constitution. Speaking generally, birth in India or descent from parents in India is likely to be accompanied by an Indian domicile. The question however assumes importance where a person's domicile of origin is not Indian but he claims to have acquired a domicile of choice in India. It has been held that the burden of proving such domicile of choice is on the person who asserts it.[98] Normally considerable evidence would be required to prove such an intention. However, in the circumstances prevailing between 1st March, 1947, and the commencement of the Constitution, the migration by a Muslim from India to Pakistan, except for a temporary purpose, would easily lead to the inference that he intended to make Pakistan his permanent home. Again, as we have seen, nationality and domicile are two different concepts. Therefore, although the father of a person may continue to be a Goan national that person can give up his Goan domicile and acquire an Indian domicile.[99] A wife migrating to Pakistan with her husband in December 1947 acquires her husband's domicile in Pakistan and loses her Indian domicile. She can acquire an Indian domicile, but she cannot force her entry into India and reside there against its laws. If she came to India on a visa which limited her stay to 45 days, her stay after that period, as extended, became unlawful unless her case was covered by Arts. 5 to 10; but on the facts, Arts. 5, 6, 7, 8 and 10 did not apply to her case.[1] The question whether a company can be a citizen has frequently arisen under Art. 19 and is dealt with in considering that Article.

Change of domicile: evidence and burden of proof

Migration of Muslims to Pakistan

---

[98] *Kedar Pandey* v. *Narain Bikra* ('66) A.SC. 160 (affirming the judgment of the Patna High Court, it was held on the evidence that the burden of proof had been discharged; the question arose in respect of an election under the Representation of the People Act which provides that a person cannot be chosen to fill a seat in the Legislative Assembly of a State unless he is an elector for any Assembly and a person cannot be an elector unless he is a citizen of India).

[99] *Michael* v. *State* (1956) Bom. 954, ('56) A.B. 729, 58 Bom.L.R. 825 (*held* on the facts that a person born in Goa of Goan parents who came to India in his boyhood, was educated there, resided in Bombay since then and did his father's business in Bombay had established his Indian domicile; fol. in *K. S. Irani* v. *State* ('72) A.B. 357, 74 Bom.L.R. 271. [The petitioner was not only born, brought up and educated in India, but also on attaining majority he served in an Ordinance factory and started a business of his own in Sholapur, making India his permanent home. His wife also permanently resided in India. He had never left India after his birth. *Held*, that at the commencement of the Constitution the petitioner was domiciled in India. Even assuming that his domicile of origin was Iranian, as his father and mother hailed from Iran, in law, he acquired a domicile of choice in India before the commencement of the Constitution. He thus became a citizen of India under Art. 5 as he was born in India and had been ordinarily residing in India, for not less than 5 years immediately preceding the commencement of the Constitution: ('72) A.B. at pp. 363-4.] *Sultan Ahmed* v. *Dy. Commissioner of Police* ('60) A.Cal. 740 [where the petitioner who was born in East Bengal (now East Pakistan) came to Calcutta in 1943, continued to live and work in India for 17 years, had openly taken an Indian passport and there was nothing to show that he had an intention of going back to his place of birth; held, that he had established his Indian domicile and was a citizen under Art. 5].

[1] *Kharimunnisa* v. *M.P.* (1954) Nag. 798, ('55) A.N. 6 (the Court however added "We can only emphasize for the consideration of the authorities concerned that this is a hard and unfortunate case where a young and helpless woman is suffering for the act of another and deserves to be treated with that sympathy, which is characteristic of the best traditions of Indian chivalry. This country has never

6.42 Articles 6 and 7 deal with the problem created by the partition of India into the Dominions of India and Pakistan. Before the partition, the inhabitants of undivided India were British Indian subjects. The disturbances which preceded the partition by a few months and which continued thereafter led to a large-scale migration of people from one part of undivided India to another. The effect of partition on the minds of the people who were migrating from one part of the territory of undivided India to another was thus described by Mahajan C.J.:

Problems created by the partition of India: Art. 6 and 7

". . . in October or November, 1947, men's minds were in a state of flux. The partition of India and the events that followed in its wake in both Pakistan and India were unprecedented and it is difficult to cite any historical precedent for the situation that arose. Minds of people affected by this partition and who were living in those parts were completely unhinged and unbalanced and there was hardly any occasion to form intentions requisite for acquiring domicile in one place or another. People vacillated and altered their programmes from day to day as events happened. They went backward and forward; families were sent from one place to another for the sake of safety. Most of those displaced from West Pakistan had no permanent homes in India where they could go and take up abode. They overnight became refugees, living in camps in Pakistan or India. No one, as a matter of fact, at the moment thought that when he was leaving Pakistan for India or *vice versa* that he was for ever abandoning the place of his ancestors."[2]

The effect of partition described: No settled intention of migrants to acquire a new domicile

6.43 Article 6 provides that notwithstanding anything in Art. 5, a person who has migrated to India from Pakistan shall be deemed to be a citizen of India at the commencement of the Constitution, if (*a*) he or either of his parents or any of his grandparents was born in India as defined in the G.I. Act, 35, as originally enacted;[3] and (*b*)(i) where such person has so migrated before July 19, 1948,[4] he has been ordinarily resident in the territory of India since the date of his migration or (ii) where such person has so migrated on or after July 19, 1948, he has been registered as a citizen of India by an officer appointed in that behalf by the Government of the Dominion of India on an application made by him therefore to such an officer before the commencement of the Constitution in the form and manner prescribed by that Government, provided that no person shall be so registered unless he has been residing in India for at least six months immediately preceding the date of his application. In *Shanno Devi* v. *Mangal Sain*[5] the Supreme Court held that "migrated to the territory of India" meant migrated at any time before the commencement of the Constitution to a place now in the territory of India. Further, though the word 'migrate' is capable of a wide construction, namely,

Migrants to India from Pakistan to be deemed to be Ind. citizens: conditions for such citizenship

---

been known to refuse an asylum to any person who driven by circumstances, supplicated her protection. The case of a helpless widow who has young children to maintain and cannot live any independent existence without the support of her relatives in India, deserves all the greater consideration.")

[2] *Central Bank* v. *Ram Narain* (1955) 1 S.C.R. *supra* at p. 705, ('55) A.SC. 36.

[3] S. 311(i) of the G.I. Act, 35, as originally enacted defined India to mean "British India together with all territories of any Indian Ruler under the suzerainty of His Majesty, all territories under the suzerainty of such an Indian Ruler, tribal areas, and any other territories which His Majesty in Council may, from time to time, after ascertaining the views of the Federal Government and the Federal Legislature, declare to be part of India." British India was defined by the same section to mean "all territories for the time being comprised within the Governor's Provinces and the Chief Commissioners' Provinces."

[4] The Permit system was introduced on July 19, 1948.

[5] (1961) 1 S.C.R. 576, ('61) A.SC. 58; fol. in *Abdul Barik* v. *Union* ('64) A.Cal. 324.

"coming from one place to another", and also of a narrow construction, namely, "coming from one place to another with the intention of residing permanently in the latter place", in Art. 6 it is used in the narrow sense, having regard to the purpose for which the Article was enacted, a conclusion which is supported by the language of the Proviso to Art. 7.[6] *Shanno Devi's Case* was overruled in *Kulathil* v. *Kerala*[7] by a majority of 5 to 1, Hidayatullah J. dissenting. The majority held that in Arts. 6 and 7 the word "migrate" was used in the wider sense of moving from one country to another with the qualification that such movement was not for a short visit or for a special purpose.[8] The majority and the minority judgments do not refer to the effect of the proviso to Art. 7 on the construction of Arts. 6 and 7, though *Shanoo Devi's Case* had expressly relied on that proviso. The majority judgments hold that Art. 5 expressly refers to domicile, and therefore domicile is excluded by the *non obstante* clause with which Arts. 6 and 7 begin.[9] This conclusion was said to be supported by the observations of Mahajan C.J. in *Ram Narain's Case*,[10] namely, that in October/November, 1947, men's minds were in a state of flux as a result of the partition of India and in October/November, 1947, they were incapable of forming an intention requisite to change their domicile.

Shanoo Devi's Case overruled by Kulathil's Case

Submission: *Shanoo Devi's Case* wrongly overruled

6.44 It is submitted that *Kulathil's Case* wrongly overruled *Shanoo Devi's Case*. However, *Kulathil's Case* requires a fuller discussion of the effect of the partition of British India (hereafter called "partition"), on domicile than was found necessary in the first edition of this book. Such a discussion can best begin by considering the judgment of Mahajan C.J. in *Central Bank* v. *Ram Narain*[11] on which the majority judgments in *Kulathil's Case* relied. One Ram Narain had been given cash-credit facilities by the Mailasi Branch, Multan District, of the Central Bank against the security of goods which were to remain in his possession in the bank's godowns as trustee for the bank. Due to the disturbances which followed partition, there was

Ram Narain's Case

---

[6] (1961) 1 S.C.R. *supra* at p. 587 ("It is of interest to notice in this connection the proviso to Art. 7. . . . The proviso deals with some of these persons who after such migration to Pakistan have returned to India. It appears that when this return is under a permit for re-settlement or permanent return — that is, re-settlement in India or return to India with the intention to reside here permanently — the main provisions of Art. 7 will not apply and for this under Art. 6 of the Constitution such a person would be deemed to have migrated to India after the 19th July 1948. That the return to India of such migrant has to be under a permit for re-settlement or permanent return in order that he might escape the loss of citizenship is a strong reason for thinking that in Art. 6 the intention to reside in India permanently is implicit in the use of the phrase 'migrated to the territory of India'.")

[7] ('66) A.SC. 1614; fol. in *Bali Ram* v. *Mysore* ('73) A.SC. 506 (*held*, that the appellants submission that he migrated to India was repelled by his Pakistani passport, by the visa granted by the State of W.B. and the members of his family staying in Pakistan); fol. in *Mashkurul Hasan* v. *Union* ('67) A.A. 565 and in *Intaz Ali* v. *Supdt. of Police* ('71) A.A. & N. 81, 82-3.

[8] It is difficult to understand the reservation made. If the movement is not for a short visit or for a special purpose, for what is the movement meant, in the context of the impending and actual partition of India? In the context, such movement, if not for a special purpose or for a short visit, would normally be for the purpose of making that country his home.

[9] "Notwithstanding anything contained in Art. 5 . . ." and "Notwithstanding anything contained in Arts. 5 and 6. . . ."

[10] (1955) 1 S.C.R. 697, ('55) A.SC. 36. The passage is set out in para 6.42 above.

[11] (1955) 1 S.C.R. 697, *supra*.

no one to safeguard the Bank's godowns. The goods deposited by Ram Narain were stolen and he booked them for Karachi on 9th November, 1947, and realised Rs. 1,97,702 as the price of the goods. As he failed to pay that amount to the Bank when demanded, the Bank applied for, and obtained, from the Government of East Punjab, sanction to prosecute him for offences under ss. 380 and 454 I.P.C. as he was residing in Hodel, District Gurgaon, India.

Ram Narain's contentions

6.45 Ram Narain contended that the East Punjab Government had no jurisdiction to sanction his prosecution because when the alleged offences were committed he was domiciled in Pakistan since the District of Multan went to Pakistan on partition. The lower courts held that Ram Narain had not acquired Pakistani nationality merely by staying in Pakistan between August 15, 1947, and November 10, 1947, when he came to India, for during all this time he had the desire and the intention to revert to the Indian nationality, because he sent his family to India in October, 1947, wound up his business, migrated to India in November, 1947, and never returned to Pakistan. Accordingly the sanction to prosecute was competent. On appeal to the High Court, Ram Narain's appeal was allowed. On appeal by the Bank to the Supreme Court, the question to be determined was whether at the time of the alleged offence, Ram Narain had a Pakistani domicile, for if he had, he could not be prosecuted for an offence committed in Pakistan in view of s. 4, I.P.C., and s. 188, Cr.P.C. Mahajan C.J. laid down several propositions about the law of domicile as recognised by private international law without express reference to standard works on that subject, but those works fully support his propositions. He held that

Mahajan C.J.: the law of domicile in private international law

(*a*) no person can be without a domicile, and to make this rule effective, the law assigned to every person at his birth, a domicile of origin, which prevailed until a new domicile was acquired;[12]

(*b*) to acquire a domicile

"... two constituent elements that are necessary by English Law for the existence of domicile are: (1) a residence of a particular kind, and (2) an intention of a particular kind. There must be the factum and there must be the animus. The residence need not be continuous but it must be indefinite, not purely fleeting. The intention must be a present intention to reside for ever in the country where the residence has been taken up."[13]

(*c*) the domicile of origin, if one may use the expression,[14] of Ram Narain

"... was in the district of Multan and when the district of Multan fell by the partition of India in Pakistan, Ram Narain had to be assigned Pakistani domicile till the time he expressed his unequivocal intention of giving up that domicile and acquiring Indian domicile and also took up his residence in India. His domicile cannot be determined by his family coming to India and without any finding that he had established a home for himself. Even if the animus can be ascribed to him the factum of residence is wanting in his case; and in the absence of that fact, an Indian domicile cannot be ascribed to Ram Narain."[15]

---

[12] (1955) 1 S.C.R. 704. See also Dicey & Morris, *The Conflict of Laws*, 8th ed., pp. 81, 84 and 86.

[13] (1955) 1 S.C.R. 703. See also Dicey & Morris, *supra*, pp. 86-96.

[14] The reason for this doubt is that most of the inhabitants of British India had a British Indian domicile of origin, but this got converted into an Indian or a Pakistani domicile, as the case may be, on partition.

[15] (1955) 1 S.C.R. 706.

Submission: special feature of *Ram Narain's Case*

Accordingly, the Bank's appeal was dismissed. When Mahajan C.J. said that in October/November, 1947, men's minds were in a state of flux and that under the circumstances there was hardly any occasion to form intentions requisite to acquire a domicile in one place or the other, he spoke in the context of a British Indian subject resident in what became a part of Pakistan, who acquired by operation of law, a Pakistani domicile, but who had not migrated to India at the relevant time. It is submitted that this aspect of the case has been overlooked in the majority judgments in *Kulathil's Case*.

Submission:

6.46 It is submitted that the key to the problem lies in the fact that on partition, the British Indian domicile of origin got converted into an Indian or Pakistani domicile as a matter of law. Had partition been peaceful, it would have become necessary to provide for the nationality and the domicile of persons who found themselves saddled with a nationality and domicile against their will.[16] But partition was accompanied by grave violence and disorder, and what could not be done by agreement was done by Arts. 6 and 7. However, in order to interpret those Articles aright, it is necessary to have regard to the basis on which British India was partitioned, and the events which followed partition. Partition was born of the theory that the Hindus and the Muslims constituted two nations, and consequently predominantly Muslim provinces, or parts of provinces, should go to Pakistan, and predominantly Hindu provinces, or parts of provinces, should go to India, and actual partition followed these lines. The boundaries between East and West Punjab, and between East and West Bengal, were fixed by the Radcliffe Award on August 13, 1947. The basis on which partition was effected, and the nature of the disorders which broke out, led to a "painful and often pitiful" migration of twelve million people[17]—of Hindus from Pakistan into India, and of Muslims from India into Pakistan. The events which preceded and followed partition, created a situation not dissimilar to that created by war, and this was recognized by the Administration of Evacuee Property Acts passed in India and Pakistan. The migrants from Pakistan to India and from India to Pakistan, abandoned their property, and it became necessary to appoint Custodians of Evacuee Property on the lines of Custodians of Enemy Property appointed during a war. The ultimate disposal of evacuee property was to be settled by agreement between the Governments of India and Pakistan; but no such agreement has been reached so far. Again, the acquisition of evacuee property was withdrawn from the protection of Art. 31(2) by Art. 31(5)(*b*)(iii).[18] It has become necessary to set out these circumstances because, although in ordinary times a person alleging an intention to change

---

[16] Oppenheim, *International Law*, Vol. 1, 8th ed., pp. 552-4 ("The hardship of the inhabitants being handed over to a new sovereign against their will can be lessened by a provision in the treaty of cession binding the acquiring State to give the inhabitants of the ceded territory the option of retaining their old citizenship on making an express declaration").

[17] Spear, *India, Pakistan and the West* (H.U.L.) 2nd ed., p. 210.

[18] Art. 31(5): "Nothing in clause (2) shall affect . . . (b) the provisions of any law which the State may hereafter make . . . (iii) in pursuance of any agreement entered into between the Government of the Dominion of India or the Government of India and the Government of any other country, or otherwise, with respect to property declared by law to be evacuee property."

his domicile of origin has a very heavy burden of proof to discharge, a change of domicile from Pakistani to Indian domicile would present little difficulty, if in pursuance of such intention, a person migrated to India. *Ram Narain's Case* established that *it was not enough that a Hindu residing in Pakistan should entertain an intention to acquire an Indian domicile: it was necessary that he should give effect to that intention by actually coming to India and making India his home.* But the judgment clearly implied, that if Ram Narain had come to India, an intention to make India his home would not have been difficult to establish, having regard to the circumstances attending partition.

6.47 Articles 5, 6 and 7 deal with three distinct but connected topics. Art. 5 deals with the citizenship of persons who remained in the territory allotted to India. These persons became Indian citizens if they had their domicile in India by birth or descent, or if they had been domiciled in India and were ordinarily resident in the territory of India for not less than five years immediately preceding the commencement of the Constitution. Art. 6 deals with persons of British Indian domicile who happened to reside in the territory allotted to Pakistan and who therefore acquired a Pakistani domicile by law. Art. 5 would not apply to such persons, for, *ex hypothesi* their domicile was the Pakistani domicile to start with. But such persons might wish to acquire an Indian domicile, and to become citizens of India, and Art. 6 provided for that contingency. Art. 7 dealt with persons who left the territory of India after 1st March, 1947, for the territory included in Pakistan. Such persons were not to be deemed to be citizens of India notwithstanding that they had a British Indian domicile by birth, descent or residence from March, 1947, to 15th August, 1947, or who by operation of law acquired an Indian domicile by reason of residence in the territory allotted to India. Accordingly, Arts. 6 and 7 provide for persons who, having acquired a Pakistani domicile, wanted to come to India; and for persons who, having acquired an Indian domicile, wished to acquire a Pakistani domicile. The proviso to Art. 7 however recognised the fact that some of the persons who left India for Pakistan, might have done so under the stress of events, or under an apprehension of future difficulties which did not materialise, and who therefore desired to return to India. For those persons, a provision was made that if they returned to the territory of India under a permit for resettlement or permanent return, issued by or under the authority of any law, such persons were to be deemed to be citizens of India within Art. 6(*b*)(ii). It is submitted that the provisions of Arts. 6 and 7 show that the concept of domicile is implicit in the use of the word "migrate" as held in *Shanno Devi's Case* and that the *non obstante* clause with which these Articles open does not exclude that concept as mistakenly held in *Kulathil's Case*. Art. 6 and proviso to Art. 7 provide for persons who are to be "deemed to be citizens" of India because they could not be citizens of India under Art. 5. The requirement of Art. 6(*b*)(i) that the migrant to India before July 19, 1948, should be *resident* in India from the date of such migration till the commencement of the Constitution, and of Art. 6(*b*)(ii) that the migrant after that date must have been registered as an Indian citizen

Inter-relation of Arts. 5, 6 and 7

which registration could not be effected without six months' residence before the application for registration shows that the intention to make India the migrant's home is implicit in the word "migrate". The conclusion is reinforced by the proviso to Art. 7 that a migrant to Pakistan who returns to India under a permit for *re-settlement* or *permanent return* shall be deemed to be a citizen within the meaning of Art. 6(1)(*b*).

Art. 7: migrants from India to Pakistan deemed not to be citizens

6.48 Article 7 provides that notwithstanding anything in Arts. 5 and 6 a person who, after March 1, 1947, migrated from India to Pakistan shall not be deemed to be a citizen of India. It is submitted that the word 'migrate' in Art. 7 is used in the same narrow sense in which it has been used in Art. 6, namely, going from India to Pakistan, with the intention of residing permanently in Pakistan and it has been so held by the Supreme Court.[19] Further, it has been held by the Supreme Court that migration to which Art. 7 refers means migration between March 1, 1947, and January 26, 1950.[20]

Art. 7, proviso: migrants returning to India under a permit etc. deemed to have migrated to India within Art. 6(*b*)

Art. 7 *Kumar Amar Singh's Case*:

6.49 Article 7 is subject to the Proviso that it does not apply to a person who after having so migrated to Pakistan has returned to India under a permit for resettlement or permanent return issued by or under the authority of any law and every such person shall, for the purposes of Art. 6(*b*) be deemed to have migrated to India after July 19, 1948. The scope of Art. 7 was considered in *Bihar* v. *Kumar Amar Singh*.[21] Two questions arose for decision on the following facts: One Kumar Rani, who was admittedly born in the territory of India, and claimed to be the lawfully wedded wife of an Indian citizen whose domicile was Indian at all material times, left India for Pakistan in July 1948, returning to India in December 1948 on a temporary permit and went back to Pakistan in April 1949. On May 14, 1950, she came back to India under a permanent permit obtained from the High Commissioner for India in Pakistan, which was cancelled on July 12, 1950, because it was wrongly issued without the concurrence of the Government as required by the rules made under the Influx of Pakistan (Control) Act, 1949. She contended, first, that she had never ceased to be a citizen of India because she was born in India and her domicile was the domicile of her husband which was Indian and consequently she was a citizen

---

[19] *Abdul Sattar* v. *Gujarat* ('65) A.SC. 810, 813, citing *Shanno Devi* v. *Mangal Sain* (1961) 1 S.C.R. 576, ('61) A.SC. 58, for the proposition that leaving India casually for a specific purpose without intending to settle down permanently in Pakistan would not amount to migration. See also *A.P.* v. *Abdul Khader* (1962) 1 S.C.R. 737, 743, ('61) A.SC. 1467, *per* Sarkar J.: "Clearly, a short visit to Pakistan would not amount to migrating to that country." *Shanno Devi's Case* was followed in *Afzar Ali* v. *State* ('61) A.Or. 174; *Golam Rasul* v. *Supdt. of Police* ('65) A.Cal. 302 (also citing *Abdul Sattar's Case, supra*). See also *Badruzzaman* v. *State* ('51) A.A. 16 fol. in *Shabbir Husain* v. *U.P.* ('52) A.A. 257; *Hussain Abidi* v. *Hyderabad* ('55) A.Hyd. 34; and in *Abdul Ghani* v. *State* (1956) Madh.Bh. 216, ('56) A.M.B. 250, 253. The observations in *Habatullah* v. *State* ('64) A.Guj. 128, 135, that "in the case of migration, a person leaves the country of his permanent home, but that, at the back of his mind there is always the intention to return to the country of his domicile . . ." are contrary to the law as laid down by the Supreme Court and are not correct.

[20] *M.P.* v. *Peer Mohd.* ('63) A.SC. 645; fol. in *State* v. *Korban Khan* ('65) A.Or. 145; *Abdul Sattar* v. *Gujarat* ('65) A.SC. 810, 812; *Firoze Meheruddin* v. *Sub-Divisional Officer* ('61) A.M.P. 110 [the contrary view taken in *Noor Mohd.* v. *State* ('56) A.M.B. 211 is no longer good law.]

[21] (1955) 1 S.C.R. 1259, ('55) A.SC. 282.

of India. She contended, alternatively, that the Proviso to Art. 7 applied to her since she had returned to India on a permanent permit and the subsequent cancellation of the permit was illegal and irrelevant. The Supreme Court held that in upholding her first contention the High Court had overlooked Art. 7, and that even if she was an Indian citizen under Art. 5,

"Art. 7 clearly overrides Art. 5. It is peremptory in its scope and makes no exception for such a case, i.e. of the wife migrating to Pakistan leaving her husband in India. Even such a wife must be deemed not to be a citizen of India unless the particular facts bring her case within the Proviso to Art. 7."[22]

(i) Art. 7 overrides Art. 5

Her second contention failed as the Proviso did not apply to an unauthorised issue of an invalid permit which was subsequently cancelled by a reasoned order:

". . . the permit has been cancelled in a reasoned order on the ground that, on the facts of the case, the consent of the State Government concerned should have been obtained before the permit could be issued. This is a case, therefore, not of a valid permanent permit having been issued and the permit holder returning to India on the strength thereof and the same having been arbitrarily cancelled. It is the case of an unauthorised issue of an invalid permit which has been properly cancelled. Hence the proviso to Article 7 can have no possible application."[23]

(ii) Art. 7 (proviso), does not apply to invalid permit properly cancelled

In the above case, the fact that the domicile of the wife who had migrated to Pakistan continued to be that of her husband, namely, Indian domicile, was not relevant because Art. 7 (which applies to migration before January 26, 1950) overrides Art. 5.

Domicile of married women and minor children: difficulties arising from their "migration" to Pakistan

6.50 The meaning which the Supreme Court had rightly given to the word "migrate", namely, going to Pakistan with the intention of making Pakistan a permanent home creates no difficulty in the case of an adult male, for when he "migrates" to Pakistan he thereby changes his domicile of origin to that of Pakistan and conversely, if his domicile is not changed, he cannot be said to have "migrated" to Pakistan. However, under the principles of private international law, the domicile of a wife follows that of her husband, and the domicile of a minor child follows that of his father, and in certain cases, of his mother, and the wife and minor child are incapable of changing their domicile by any voluntary act. A question therefore arises whether a married woman or a minor can "migrate", since migration as defined by the Supreme Court would involve a change of domicile, and a married woman and a minor child cannot change their domicile. The answer to this difficulty is that the intention to make Pakistan a permanent home is a fact which has also certain legal consequences as regards domicile; but Art. 7 is concerned with the intention as a fact and not with its legal consequences. Therefore the case of an adult married woman migrating to Pakistan presents no difficulty. As regards a minor no difficulty arises if the minor's father migrates with the minor for it has been held that in that event, the father does not have Indian nationality under Art. 7 and the minor must also be taken to have lost the nationality unless

A suggested solution of the difficulties: Art. 7 is concerned with the *intention* to migrate *as a fact*

[22] (1955) 1 S.C.R., *supra* at p. 1264, fol. in: *Ali Ahmad* v. *E.R. Officer* ('65) A.Cal. 1. (Art. 7 is peremptory in its scope and makes no exception for a citizen migrating to Pakistan leaving his wife in India); *Abdul Gafar* v. *Gujarat* ('63) A.Guj. 48; *Naziranbai* v. *State* ('57) A.M.B. 1; *Mohammed Naseeruddin* v. *A.P.* ('60) A.A.P. 106; *Fazal Dad* v. *M.P.* ('64) A.M.P. 272. See also *Wahid Mian* v. *State* (61) A.A. 111. (Art. 7 is an explanation to both Arts. 5 and 6.)

[23] (1955) 1 S.C.R. *supra* at p. 1265.

according to the permit system rules he comes to India with a permit for re-settlement or residence;[24] and the mere fact that the maternal grandfather of the minor was a citizen of India, that the minor was staying with him all along and that the petitioner intended to reside in India permanently would not give him Indian citizenship unless he got himself registered as an Indian citizen under s. 5(4) of the Citizenship Act.[25] However, if the minor migrates to Pakistan independently of his father, who remains in India, a question arises whether a minor can form an *intention* to make Pakistan his permanent home, which is an essential requirement of "migration". As regards an infant in arms the question would answer itself, for an infant cannot have such an intention. However, the rule enacted in s. 11 of the Contract Act that a minor's contract is void (and broadly speaking a person under 18 years of age is a minor) does not indicate any general policy of the law[26] as is shown by ss. 82 and 83 I.P.C. which respectively provide that "nothing is an offence which is done by a child under seven years of age" and "nothing is an offence which is done by a child between seven and twelve years of age, who has not attained sufficient maturity of understanding to judge the nature and consequences of his conduct on that occasion." Again, s. 17(3), Guardian and Wards Act, 1890, enables the Court to consider the preference of the minor if the minor is old enough to form an intelligent preference. It is submitted that the question whether a minor has sufficient maturity of understanding to form an intention of making Pakistan his home is a question of fact to be decided on the evidence. If the question is answered in the affirmative, the fact is established which attracts Art. 7, and as it overrides Art. 5 in the case of a married woman, it equally overrides Art. 5 in the case of such a minor. It is submitted that the contrary view taken in certain cases is not correct.[27]

State v. Abdul Sattar

6.51 The meaning of the word "migration" was considered in *State* v. *Abdul Sattar*[28] under very unusual circumstances. The respondent, a constable in the Assam Police Department, opted for service in Pakistan in 1947, apprehending that his permanent home State, where he owned cultivable land, would be included in Pakistan. He was

---

[24] *State* v. *Abdul Hamid* (1957) Punj. 974, ('57) A.Punj. 86, 87 (the judgment mixes up citizenship and nationality. It was enough to have said that on the migration of the father and his minor child to Pakistan before January 26, 1950, they ceased to be Indian citizens under Art. 7); *Ali Hossain* v. *W.B.* ('61) A.Cal. 482 (if an adult person migrates to Pakistan after 1-3-1947, and voluntarily obtains a Pakistani passport, he ceases to be an Indian citizen. If he subsequently intends to become an Indian citizen, he must obtain a permit for permanent return; if the Indian Government is not willing to grant him such permit, it cannot be compelled to do so).

[25] *Mohammad Umar* v. *State* ('61) A.Or. 150, relying on *State* v. *Abdul Hamid* (1957) Punj. 974, ('57) A.Punj. 86 and *Kulsum Bibi* v. *District Magistrate, Kanpur* ('53) A.A. 178, (1953) A.L.J. 25.

[26] *State* v. *Abdul Sattar* ('63) A.Guj. 226 (a minor may not be able to contract but there was nothing in the Constitution to show that he could not migrate.)

[27] e.g. *Mukhtar Ahmad* v. *U.P.* ('65) A.A. 191 [*held* that since a minor could not change his domicile, the minor remained an Indian citizen under Art. 5. This argument was rejected by the Supreme Court in *Kumar Amarsingh's Case* (1955) 1 S.C.R. 1259, and should have been rejected in *Mukhtar Ahmad's Case* if it was found that the minor could form the requisite intention, since Art. 7 overrides Art. 5].

[28] ('78) A.Gau. 48.

released from service in India to join service in Pakistan. However, as his home State was not included in Pakistan, he never went to Pakistan at any time and remained all along in India, and took to cultivation. It was held that the ordinary meaning of the word "migration" was "change of abode, removal from one country or climate to another". Consequently, two elements were necessary to constitute migration: a mental desire to go to another country and the physical departure for that country. As the respondent had never left India, his mere desire at one time to leave India was not sufficient to constitute migration and he had not lost his Indian citizenship.

Prof. Cheshire and minor's domicile

6.52 Although the rule that the domicile of a minor child follows that of his father is stated in absolute terms it has been said by Prof. Cheshire that

> ". . . it is to be hoped that should the occasion arise it will not be pressed to its logical conclusion. Suppose, for instance, that a father deserts his son, leaves him in his domicile of origin and himself acquires a fresh domicile elsewhere. Or suppose that he is divorced for adultery and the custody of the children is given to his wife. In such cases as these it is scarcely credible that a court would affirm the inevitability of a common domicile."[29]

His view adopted in Rashid Hasan v. Union

It is submitted that in *Rashid Hasan* v. *Union*[30] the court rightly adopted this view under the following circumstances: the petitioner was born of Indian parents in India and resided in India for more than five years immediately preceding the commencement of the Constitution. He was left in India by his father who migrated to Pakistan. The petitioner continued to live in India, was enrolled as a voter and contested the election for and was elected as Chairman of his Town Area Committee. The court held that the father had deserted the petitioner[31] and in the circumstances the domicile of the petitioner continued to be Indian and he remained an Indian citizen. The undernoted cases[32] were distinguished on the ground that in all of them the minor had migrated to Pakistan.

Indians residing abroad: when deemed to be Ind. citizens

6.53 Article 8 provides that notwithstanding anything in Art. 5, any person who, or either of whose parents or any of whose grand-parents was born in India as defined in the G.I. Act, 35 (as originally enacted),[33] and who is ordinarily residing in a country outside India as so defined, shall be deemed to be a citizen of India if he has been registered as a citizen of India by the diplomatic or consular representative of India in the country where he is for the time being residing on an application made by him therefor to such representative whether before or after the commencement of the Constitution in the form and manner prescribed by the Government of the Dominion of India or the Government of India. This Article confers citizenship on Indian nationals residing abroad on their complying with its provisions.

Art. 9 effect of voluntary acquisition of foreign citizenship on Ind. citizenship

Art. 9 provides that a person shall not be a citizen of India by virtue of Art. 5 or shall not be deemed to be such citizen by virtue of Art. 6 or 8 if he has voluntarily acquired the citizenship of any foreign State. Art. 9 thus provides against dual citizenship subject

---

[29] Cheshire, *Private International Law*, 6th ed., pp. 190-1.

[30] ('67) A.A. 154, 155.

[31] This finding is implicit in the judgment.

[32] *Mst. Allah Bandi* v. *Union* ('54) A.A. 456, (1954) A.L.J. 156; *Karimunnisa* v. *M.P.* (1954) Nag. 798, ('55) A.N. 6 (see *f.n.* 1 *ante*); *State* v. *Abdul Hamid* (1957) Punj. 974, ('57) A.Punj. 86 (see *f.n.* 24 *ante*); *Mohammad Umar* v. *State* ('61) A.Or. 150 (see *f.n.* 25 *ante*).

[33] See *f.n.* 3 *ante*.

to the qualification that the Citizenship Act, 1955, recognises Commonwealth citizenship. In *M.P.* v. *Peer Mohd.*[34] Gajendragadkar J. said that

Peer Mohd.'s Case: Art. 9 applies to such acquisition *before* Jan., 1950

"... it is clear that the acquisition of the citizenship of any foreign State to which this Article refers is acquisition made prior to the commencement of the Constitution. 'Has voluntarily acquired' can have no other meaning, and ... the application of Art. 9 is confined to the case of acquisition of citizenship of foreign State prior to the commencement of the Constitution."

The use of the words "has acquired" in the present perfect tense was treated as conclusive in favour of this construction. If foreign citizenship was acquired subsequent to January 26, 1950, and before the Citizenship Act, 1955 came into force and thereafter, that was covered by the provisions of the Citizenship Act.[35] Gajendragadkar C.J.'s statement in *Abdul Sattar* v. *Gujarat*[36] that Art. 9 applied to migration which had taken place after January 26, 1950, was clearly wrong, and was later described by the Supreme Court as due to an "oversight."[37] The decision in *Peer Mohamed's Case* is correct, even though it involves the strange result that before the enactment of the Citizenship Act, 1955, the acquisition of a foreign citizenship did not involve the loss of Indian citizenship. Parliament realized this in enacting s. 9 of the Citizenship Act, which provides that "any citizen of India who ... voluntarily acquires, *or has at any time between January 26, 1950, and the commencement of this Act, voluntarily acquired* the citizenship of another country shall, upon such acquisition, *or as the case may be, such commencement,* cease to be a citizen of India." (italics supplied). S. 9 thus accepts the consequences of the manner in which Art. 9 has been framed, namely, that if foreign citizenship is acquired after the commencement of the Constitution and before the commencement of the Citizenship Act, the person acquiring such foreign citizenship ceases to be a citizen only upon the commencement of the Act. However, it has been held that where a person continued to be in India upto July, 1950, *prima facie,* by virtue of Art. 5 read with Art. 7 he was a citizen of India on the commencement of the Constitution and continued to be so upto the date of the offence committed by him in July/August 1950 unless he showed under Art. 9 that he had voluntarily acquired the citizenship of a foreign country.[38]

Submission: *Peer Mohd.'s Case* correct

S. 9, Citizenship Act, 1955 and voluntary acquisition of citizenship of another country between Jan. 26, 1950 and the commencement of the Act

Arts. 10 and 11: continuance of Ind. citizenship after Jan. 26, 1950; power of Parliament to enact citizenship laws

6.54 Article 10 provides for continuance of citizenship at the commencement of the Constitution subject to any law made by Parliament. Art. 11 enables Parliament to legislate on the acquisition and termination of citizenship after the commencement of the Constitution, and it also enables Parliament to legislate on the continuance of citizenship at the commencement of the Constitution even to the extent of overriding or modifying the provisions of Arts. 5 to 9. In the exercise of its powers Parliament enacted the Citizenship Act

---

[34] ('63) A.SC. 645 at p. 648.
[35] ibid. pp. 648-9, citing *Izhar Ahmed Khan* v. *Union* (1962) Supp. 3 S.C.R. 235, ('62) A.SC. 1052.
[36] ('65) A.SC. 810, 812.
[37] *Kulathil* v. *Kerala* ('66) A.SC. 1614, 1619 (the observations were *obiter* and were made "to correct a slip which has occurred in *Abdul Sattar's Case*.")
[38] *Mobarik Ali Ahmed* v. *Bombay* (1958) S.C.R. 328, ('57) A.SC. 857, 866-7.

which received the President's assent on December 30, 1955, and was gazetted the same day. S. 2 is the interpretation section.[39] Ss. 3, 4, 5 and 6 provide respectively for citizenship by birth, descent, registration and naturalization as follows:

The Citizenship Act, 1955:

Citizenship by birth

S. 3. (1) Except as provided in sub-section (2) of this section, every person born in India on or after the 26th January, 1950, shall be a citizen of India by birth.

(2) A person shall not be such a citizen by virtue of this section if at the time of his birth — (*a*) his father possesses such immunity from suits and legal process as is accorded to an envoy of a foreign sovereign power accredited to the President of India and is not a citizen of India; or (*b*) his father is an enemy alien and the birth occurs in a place then under occupation by the enemy.

Citizenship by descent

S. 4. (1) A person born outside India on or after the 26th January, 1950, shall be a citizen of India by descent if his father is a citizen of India at the time of his birth:

Provided that if the father of such a person was citizen of India by descent only, that person shall not be a citizen of India by virtue of the section unless — (*a*) his birth is registered at an Indian consulate within one year of its occurrence or the commencement of this Act, whichever is later, or, with the permission of the Central Government, after the expiry of the said period; or (*b*) his father is, at the time of his birth, in service under a Government in India.

(2) If the Central Government so directs, a birth shall be deemed for the purposes of this section to have been registered with its permission, notwithstanding that its permission was not obtained before the registration.

(3) For the purposes of the proviso to sub-section (1), any male person born outside undivided India who was, or was deemed to be a citizen of India at the commencement of the Constitution shall be deemed to be a citizen of India by descent only.

Citizenship by registration

S. 5. (1) Subject to the provisions of this section and such conditions and restrictions as may be prescribed, the prescribed authority may, on application made in this behalf, register as a citizen of India any person who is not already such citizen by virtue of the Constitution or by virtue of any of the other provisions of this Act and belongs to any of the following categories: (*a*) persons of Indian origin who are ordinarily resident in India and have been so resident for six months immediately before making an application for registration; (*b*) persons of Indian origin who are ordinarily resident in any country or place outside undivided India; (*c*) women who are, or have been, married to citizens of India; (*d*) minor children of persons who are citizens of India; and (*e*) persons of full age and capacity who are citizens of a country specified in the First Schedule:

Provided that in prescribing the conditions and restrictions subject to which persons of any such country may be registered as citizens of India under this clause, the Central Government shall have due regard to the conditions subject to which citizens of India may, by law or practice of that country, become citizens of that country by registration.

---

[39] The following definitions are important: S. 2(1)(*d*) . . . "minor" means a person who has not attained the age of eighteen years; S. 2(1)(*f*) "person" does not include any company or association or body of individuals, whether incorporated or not; sub-secs. S. 2(2): For the purposes of this Act, a person born aboard a registered ship or aircraft, or aboard an unregistered ship or aircraft of the Government of any country, shall be deemed to have been born in the place in which the ship or aircraft was registered or, as the case may be, in that country; S. 2(3) Any reference in this Act to the status or description of the father of a person at the time of that person's birth shall, in relation to a person born after the death of his father, be construed as a reference to the status or description of the father at the time of the father's death; and where that death occurred before, and the birth occurs after, the commencement of this Act, the status or description which would have been applicable to the father had he died after the commencement of this Act shall be deemed to be the status or description applicable to him at the time of his death; S. 2(4) For the purposes of this Act, a person shall be deemed to be of full age if he is not a minor, and of full capacity if he is not of unsound mind.

Explanation.—For the purposes of this sub-section, a person shall be deemed to be of Indian origin if he, or either of his parents, or any of his grand-parents, was born in undivided India.

(2) No person being of full age shall be registered as a citizen of India under sub-section (1) until he has taken the oath of allegiance in the form specified in the Second Schedule.

(3) No person who has renounced, or has been deprived of, his Indian citizenship, or whose Indian citizenship has terminated, under this Act shall be registered as a citizen of India under sub-section (i) except by order of the Central Government.

(4) The Central Government may, if satisfied that there are special circumstances justifying such registration, cause any minor to be registered as a citizen of India.

(5) A person registered under this section shall be a citizen of India by registration as from the date on which he is so registered; and a person registered under the provisions of clause (*b*)(ii) of Article 6 or Article 8 of the Constitution shall be deemed to be a citizen of India by registration as from the commencement of the Constitution or the date on which he was so registered, whichever may be later.

Citizenship by naturalization

S. 6. (1) Where an application is made in the prescribed manner by any person of full age and capacity who is not a citizen of a country specified in the First Schedule for the grant of a certificate of naturalisation to him, the Central Government may, if satisfied that the applicant is qualified for naturalisation under the provisions of the Third Schedule, grant to him, a certificate of naturalisation:

Provided that, if in the opinion of the Central Government, the applicant is a person who has rendered distinguished service to the cause of science, philosophy, art, literature, world peace or human progress generally, it may waive all or any of the conditions specified in the Third Schedule.

(2) The person to whom a certificate of naturalisation is granted under sub-section (i) shall, on taking the oath of allegiance in the form specified in the Second Schedule, be a citizen of India by naturalisation as from the date on which that certificate is granted.

Ss. 8 and 10 provide respectively for renunciation of citizenship and for deprivation of citizenship:

Renunciation of citizenship

S. 8. (1) If any citizen of India of full age and capacity, who is also a citizen or national of another country, makes in the prescribed manner a declaration renouncing his Indian citizenship, the declaration shall be registered by the prescribed authority; and, upon such registration, that person shall cease to be a citizen of India:

Provided that if any such declaration is made during any war in which India may be engaged, registration thereof shall be withheld until the Central Government otherwise directs.

(2) Where a male person ceases to be a citizen of India under sub-section (1), every minor child of that person shall thereupon cease to be a citizen of India:

Provided that any such child may, within one year after attaining full age, make a declaration that he wishes to resume Indian citizenship and shall thereupon again become a citizen of India.

(3) For the purposes of this section, any woman who is, or has been, married shall be deemed to be of full age.

Deprivation of citizenship

S. 10. (1) A citizen of India who is such by naturalisation or by virtue only of clause (*c*) of Article 5 of the Constitution or by registration otherwise than under clause (*b*)(ii) of Article 6 of the Constitution or clause (*a*) of sub-section (1) of section 5 of this Act shall cease to be a citizen of India, if he is deprived of that citizenship by an order of the Central Government under this section.

(2) Subject to the provisions of this section, the Central Government may, by order, deprive any such citizen of Indian citizenship, if it is satisfied that (*a*) the registration or certificate of naturalisation was obtained by means of fraud, false representation or the concealment of any material fact; or (*b*) that citizen has shown himself by act or speech to be disloyal or disaffected towards the Constitution of India as by law established; or (*c*) that citizen has, during

any war in which India may be engaged, unlawfully traded or communicated with an enemy or been engaged in, or associated with, any business that was to his knowledge carried on in such manner as to assist an enemy in that war; or (*d*) that citizen has within five years after registration or naturalization, been sentenced to imprisonment for a term of not less than two years; or (*e*) that citizen has been ordinarily resident out of India for a continuous period of seven years, and during that period, has neither been at any time a student of any educational institution in a country outside India or in the service of a Government in India or of an international organisation of which India is a member, nor registered annually in the prescribed manner at an Indian Consulate his intention to retain his citizenship of India.

(3) The Central Government shall not deprive a person of citizenship under this section unless it is satisfied that it is not conducive to the public good that that person should continue to be a citizen of India.

(4) Before making an order under this section, the Central Government shall give the person against whom the order is proposed to be made notice in writing informing him of the ground on which it is proposed to be made and, if the order is proposed to be made on any of the grounds specified in sub-section (2) other than clause (*e*) thereof, of his right, upon making application therefor in prescribed manner, to have his case referred to a committee of inquiry under this section.

(5) If the order is proposed to be made against a person on any of the grounds specified in the sub-section (2) other than clause (*e*) thereof and that person so applies in the prescribed manner, the Central Government shall, and in any other case it may, refer the case to a Committee of Inquiry consisting of a chairman (being a person who has for at least ten years held a judicial office) and two other members appointed by the Central Government in this behalf.

(6) The Committee of Inquiry shall, on such reference, hold the inquiry in such manner as may be prescribed and submit its report to the Central Government; and the Central Government shall ordinarily be guided by such report in making an order under this section.

S. 9(1) and (2) of the Citizenship Act, 1955, hereafter called s. 9(1) and s. 9(2) are as follows:

Termination of citizenship

S. 9. (1) Any citizen of India who by naturalisation, registration or otherwise voluntarily acquires, or has at any time between the 26th January 1950, and the commencement of this Act voluntarily acquired, the citizenship of another country shall, upon such acquisition or, as the case may be, such commencement, cease to be a citizen of India:

Provided that nothing in this sub-section shall apply to a citizen of India who, during any war in which India may be engaged, voluntarily acquires the citizenship of another country, until the Central Government otherwise directs.

(2) If any question arises as to whether, when or how any person has acquired the citizenship of another country, it shall be determined by such authority, in such manner, and having regard to such rules of evidence, as may be prescribed in this behalf.

Rule 30, Citizenship Rules

Rule 30 of the Citizenship Rules provides (i) that if any question arises as to whether, when or how any person has acquired the citizenship of another country, the authority to determine such question shall, for the purpose of s. 9(2), be the Central Government, and (ii) the Central Government shall, in determining any such question have due regard to the rules of evidence specified in Sch. 3. Rule 3 of Sch. 3, hereafter called Rule 3, is as follows:

Rule 3, Sch. 3: effect of obtaining a foreign passport

"The fact that a citizen of India has obtained on any date a passport from the Government of any other country shall be conclusive proof of his having voluntarily acquired the citizenship of that country before that date."

In *U.P.* v. *Shah Mahomed*[40] the Supreme Court held that s. 9(1) could not be given a prospective operation only, for its language left

[40] ('69) A.SC. 1234, 1236 [the judgment under appeal was reversed. That judgment had relied on the decision in *Abida Khatoon* v. *U.P.* ('63) A.A. 260, which had

no doubt that it would cover all cases of an Indian citizen acquiring foreign nationality between January 26, 1950 and the commencement of the Act, and also cases of acquiring such citizenship after its commencement.

Question of *acquisition* of foreign citizenship to be determined by authority under R. 30

6.55 It was held in *A.P.* v. *Abdul Khadar*[41] that once it was shown that a person was a citizen of India at the commencement of the Constitution, and the question to be decided was whether he had acquired the citizenship of another country, that question could not be decided by the Courts in the first instance as the authority to decide it was the authority mentioned in Rule 30 of the Citizenship Rules. It was further held that the fact that the Central Government had refused to extend the visa granted by Indian authorities to the respondent, who was an Indian citizen at the commencement of the Constitution, but who had come on a Pakistani passport did not warrant the inference that the Government had come to the conclusion that the respondent had acquired the citizenship of Pakistan. For, in order that there may be a decision by the Central Government whether he had acquired foreign nationality, an inquiry as laid down under Rule 30 had to be made and no such inquiry had been made. Again, the Supreme Court has held that s. 9 (2) barred the jurisdiction of Civil Courts to try the questions there mentioned since it provided that those questions were to be determined by the prescribed authority which necessarily implied that they could not be decided by anyone else. However, the bar only applied to determining the question whether a citizen of India had acquired the citizenship of another country or when or how he acquired it. Where a person's claim to be an Indian citizen was resisted on the ground that having migrated to Pakistan in 1948 he never acquired Indian citizenship, that might follow from Art. 7 and the jurisdiction of the Court to decide that question was not affected by s. 9 (2). If a Court upheld this contention, the suit must be dismissed. It was only when it was found that on January 26, 1950, the person had been an Indian citizen that a question of renunciation of that citizenship could arise. As the Court could not decide that question, the proper thing for the Court would be to stay the suit till the Central Government had decided that question, and dispose of the rest of the suit in the light of the Central Government's decision.[42] It was also held that an order of deportation passed by the State Government against a Pakistani found in the State could not be sustained if there had been no inquiry by the Central Government under s. 9 (2) about his status.[43]

Courts not precluded from determining questions not covered by R. 30

---

taken the view that s. 9(2) was not retrospective. The Supreme Court held that *Abida Khatoon's Case* was wrongly decided.]

41 ('61) A.SC. 1467, 1469; *M.P.* v. *Peer Mahomed* ('63) A.SC. 645 [whether a person had lost his Indian citizenship under s. 9(1) by acquiring a Pakistani passport was a question to be decided by the Central Government and not by the Court].

42 *Akbar Khan* v. *Union* (1962) 1 S.C.R. 779, ('62) A.SC. 70, fol. in *Union* v. *Yakub Ali Khan* ('63) A.A. 205 (since the only question raised before the Court was whether the plaintiff had migrated to Pakistan and thus lost his Indian citizenship, the question of acquisition of Pakistani citizenship did not arise and the Court had jurisdiction to decide the question raised in the suit); fol. in *State* v. *Ghoraishi* ('64) A.B. 235. (S. 9 does not exclude jurisdiction of the Court where the question is whether a person is an Indian citizen under Art. 5, or is deemed to be an Indian citizen under Art. 6).

43 *A.P.* v. *Syed Mohd. Khan* (1962) Supp. 3 S.C.R. 288, ('62) A.SC. 1778

6.56 The effect of s. 9 (2) read with Rule 3 was considered in several cases and has led to a difference of judicial opinion which has persisted even in the Supreme Court. In *Mohammad Khan* v. *A.P.*[44] it was held that a passport was not evidence of citizenship and Rule 3 was void as it went beyond the scope of s. 9 (2). In *Sharafat Ali Khan* v. *U.P.*[45] it was held that the mere acquisition of a foreign passport would normally be considered sufficient only to raise a rebuttable presumption of voluntary acquisition of foreign citizenship. Rule 3 was binding only on the Central Government but not on the Court. The fact that a person declared himself to be a Pakistani national in order to obtain a passport may be capable of explanation and was in fact explained on the facts of the present case which were these: the petitioner's father had been murdered on 8th March, 1956, and it was essential for him to return to India with the utmost speed and the only way in which he could do so was by making a false declaration and obtaining a Pakistani passport. Broome J. said:

Conflicting decisions on the effect of R. 3

> "It is idle to suggest that he should have sent an application to the Indian authorities for the grant of an Indian passport, for with the best will in the world those authorities could not possibly have sent the application through the various 'proper channels', made all necessary enquiries in Rampur and elsewhere and completed the essential formalities in less than a year or so (even assuming that they were ready and willing to treat the petitioner as an Indian national and to grant him a passport accordingly). Indeed, those who have had occasion to deal with Government departments in such matters would probably consider one year to be a gross under-estimate of the time required for the purpose.
>
> The result was that the petitioner, if he wanted to reach India in time to be of any service to his bereaved mother and younger brother and sisters, had no alternative but to apply for a Pakistani passport (which could of course be had for the asking).[46]

The acquisition of a passport under these circumstances was no evidence that the petitioner had voluntarily acquired the citizenship of another country. In *Ghaurul Hasan* v. *Rajasthan*,[47] Wanchoo C.J. dissented from the view expressed by Subba Rao C.J. in *Mahomed Khan's Case*[48] that Rule 3 was void, and in *State* v. *Sharifbhai Jamalbhai*[49] Vyas, J. also dissented from that view. Again, in *Mahomed Usman* v. *Madras*[50] Rajagopala Ayyengar J. in an elaborate judgment held that Rule 3 was not void. As Counsel appearing for the parties did not rely on the reasoning of Subba Rao C.J. in *Mohamed Khan's Case* nor of Wanchoo C.J. in *Ghaurul Hasan's Case* nor of Vyas J. in *Sharafbhai's Case*, it was found unnecessary to consider those cases.

6.57 It is not necessary to discuss these judgments in detail since the Supreme Court considered the matter at length in *Izhar Ahmed Khan* v. *Union.*[51] However, the difference of judicial opinion persisted even in the Supreme Court. Gajendragadkar J. delivering the majority judgment for himself, Wanchoo and Rajagopala Ayyan-

Conflict resolved by the Sup. Ct.: *Ishar Ahmed Khan's Case*, by a 3:2 decision, the

[44] ('57) A.A.P. 1047.
[45] ('60) A.A. 637, (1960) A.L.J. 461.
[46] ('60) A.A. at p. 640.
[47] (1958) 8 Raj. 928, ('58) A.Raj. 172.
[48] ('57) A.A.P. 1047, *supra*.
[49] (1958) Bom. 1422, ('59) A.B. 192, 60 Bom.L.R. 1186 (Sharafbhai was not represented before the Court and it is unfortunate that the Court did not appoint a Counsel *amicus curiae* to present his case to the Court).
[50] ('61) A.M. 129.
[51] (1962) Supp. 3 S.C.R. 235, ('62) A.SC. 1052.

majority holding the Rule valid

gar JJ.[52] held that Rule 3 was a rule of evidence and not a rule of substantive law, and was therefore valid. Das Gupta J. for himself and Sarkar J. held that Rule 3 was a rule of substantive law and therefore was void. It is submitted that the majority judgment is *clearly* wrong and productive of great public mischief. As the questions considered by the judgment go far beyond the validity of Rule 3, they are dealt with at some length. The conclusion that Rule 3 is valid is based on the following propositions:

Submission: majority view wrong *and* productive of public mischief

Grounds underlying the majority view:

(i) juristic views do not disclose an identity of views

(1) Though due importance must be given to juristic opinion, which takes the view that irrebuttable presumptions are matters of substantive law, the views expressed by jurists "do not disclose an identity of approach and their conclusions show different shades of opinion."[53]

(ii) no difference in principle between rebuttable and irrebuttable presumptions and between estoppel and conclusive proof

(2) Rebuttable presumptions are "rightly" conceded to be rules of evidence. When a rebuttable presumption provides that on proof of fact A, the Court shall presume that fact B is proved, unless the contrary is established, the effect of the presumption is to take away the discretion of the Court to attach such weight as it likes to the probative value of fact A. If that is so, it makes no difference that the law adds conclusive strength to the probative value of fact A in relation to the proof of fact B. Nor does it make any difference that a conclusive presumption prevents a person against whom it operates from disproving the existence of fact B. Estoppel, which is "admitted" to be a part of the law of evidence, also prevents a person against whom it operates from proving the true facts.

(iii) when irrebuttable presumptions are rules of evidence

(3) The correct rule about irrebuttable presumption is that if fact A is inherently relevant in proving the existence of fact B, then a rule prescribing either a rebuttable presumption or an irrebuttable presumption would be a rule of evidence. If,, however, fact A is inherently not relevant, in proving the existence of fact B, or has no probative value in that behalf, an irrebuttable presumption would be a rule of substantive law.

(iv) *Domingo's Case*: does not support the view that passport is not legal evidence of citizenship

(4) The contention that a passport is not legal evidence of citizenship and therefore not relevant to it is not supported by the decision in *Domingo Urtetiqui* v. *John N. D'Arcy*[54] as the Court was divided in its opinion on that point.

(v) Pakistani law relevant

(5) In dealing with the question, the requirements by the Government of Pakistan for the issue of a passport are relevant.

(vi) legislative history: conclusive presumptions a part of the law *of evidence,* and are

(6) From 1872, conclusive presumptions are part of the *law of evidence* and the legislative power to make laws on evidence and oaths (entry 12, List III, Sch. 7) must therefore include conclusive presumptions. Previous legislative practice is relevant in considering the

---

[52] It will be noticed that the case involved a consideration of the conflicting decisions of the High Courts, and these included the judgments delivered by Wanchoo and Rajagopala Ayyangar JJ. It is submitted that it would be a salutary rule for the Supreme Court to adopt that a Judge of the Supreme Court whose judgment in a High Court requires consideration should not be a member of the Supreme Court Bench charged with that duty.

[53] ('62) A.SC., *supra*, p. 1062.

[54] (1835) 9 Pet. 692, 9 L. ed. 276.

scope of legislative power: *In re The Central Provinces and Berar Act No. XIV of 1938*.[55]

therefore *rules* of evidence

"There can, therefore be no doubt that the expression '*rules of evidence*' construed in the light of the Indian legal and legislative history would include some rules of conclusive proof and . . . it would be idle to contend that the impugned rule is a part of the substantive law merely because it prescribes a conclusive presumption."[56] (italics supplied)

A criticism of the majority view: (i) legislative history against the view that procedural laws do not contain rules of substantive law

6.58 It is submitted that the majority judgment proceeds on a misapprehension of the nature of the law of evidence and the nature of presumptions, rebuttable and irrebuttable. No doubt, legislative practice shows that conclusive presumptions are part of *the law* of evidence in India, but it is a long step, *and an illegitimate step,* to describe everything contained in that law as *rules of* evidence, as opposed to rules of substantive law. It is submitted that there is no legislative practice that none of the provisions of a procedural law should contain rules of substantive law; in fact, *the practice is otherwise.* Thus, the Civil Procedure Code confers rights of appeal which are substantive rights and are not mere matters of procedure.[57] Again, the Limitation Act bars the remedy and not the right and is therefore correctly regarded as a procedural law. However, s. 28 of that Act provides for the extinguishment of right to property and is clearly a rule of substantive law which not only divests the right of the true owner, but invests the person in adverse possession with the right of ownership. Therefore legislative practice does not prevent a *law of evidence* from containing rules of substantive law such as estoppel and conclusive presumptions.

(ii) rebuttable presumptions affect only the burden of proof; irrebuttable presumptions affect the rights of parties

6.59 The majority judgment is in error in holding that the difference between a rebuttable presumption and an irrebuttable presumption is merely one of degree of the probative value of the fact from which another fact is to be presumed; it is submitted that the difference is not one of degree but of kind. A rebuttable presumption, as its very name shows, affects only the burden of proof. A party in whose favour a rebuttable presumption is raised has only to prove fact *A* if he wants the Court to hold that fact *B* is proved; but that proof does not conclude the rights of the opposite party, who is left free to disprove that fact. For example, in jurisdictions where a blood test is treated as establishing or negativing paternity, a rebutable presumption of legitimacy during the subsistence of a valid marriage could be disproved by showing that a blood test does not support legitimacy. Therefore, rebuttable presumptions do not conclude the rights of parties but shift only the burden of proof. Irrebuttable presumptions on the other hand directly affect the rights of all parties because on fact *A* being proved, fact *B* must be taken to have been proved and no evidence can be offered in disproof of it.

(iii) the concession that estoppel is a rule of evidence was mistaken

6.60 It is unfortunate that it appears to have been conceded before the Supreme Court that estoppel is a rule of evidence, and the attention of the Court was not drawn to the statement of the law in Halsbury,[58] namely, "Estoppel is often described as a rule of evidence, but

[55] (1939) F.C.R. 18 at p. 53. [56] ('62) A.SC., *supra*, at p. 1066.

[57] *Colonial Sugar Refining Co.* v. *Irving* (1905) A.C. 369; *Delhi Cloth & General Mills Co.* v. *I.T.C., Delhi* (1927) 54 I.A. 421; *Bombay* v. *Supreme General Film Exchange Ltd.* (1960) 3 S.C.R. 640, ('60) A.SC. 980. See Mulla, *Code of Civil Procedure*, 13th ed., Vol. 1, p. 418.

[58] Vol. 15, p. 168.

for estoppel is more correctly described as a rule of substantive law: Canada & Dominion Sugar Co.'s Case

the whole concept is more correctly viewed as a substantive rule of law," a proposition clearly laid down by Lord Wright in *Canada and Dominion Sugar Co. Ltd.* v. *Canadian National* (*West Indies*) *Steamships Ltd.*[59] Both estoppel and conclusive proof are part of substantive law, based on public policy. The doctrine of *estoppel by record* is embodied as the doctrine of *res judicata* in s. 10, C.P.C., and the Supreme Court has held that the doctrine is based on public policy and has actually the effect of displacing the fundamental right guaranteed by Art. 32.[60] Estoppel by conduct proceeds on the rule of substantive law and equity that where one person has led another person to believe a thing to be true to the prejudice of that person, it is not right, or just, or moral, to permit the first-mentioned person to deny the truth of that which he formerly asserted. As this rule is for the benefit of the person who has been misled it is open to that person to waive it and in this respect, estoppel as a rule of substantive law, differs from conclusive proof where on proof of fact *A* irrespective of the party against whom it is offered, fact *B* must be treated as proved.

(iv) the principle underlying conclusive presumptions: public policy requires that the real state of things should not be inquired into

6.61 The majority judgment does not inquire into the principles which form the basis of conclusive presumptions. Conclusive presumptions are enacted by the legislature, where in public interest it is desired to shut out inquiry about the real state of facts. This is done because the benefit derived by individuals from being permitted to prove the real state of things is outweighed by the disadvantage to the public at large from such inquiry. Thus, the certificate of incorporation of a company is conclusive proof that all the preliminary requirements for incorporation have been complied with. To provide otherwise would be to unsettle all commercial dealings with companies if it should turn out that some requirement of incorporation had not been complied with, with the result that all actions of the company would be without legal authority. Similarly, the conclusiveness of the declaration of public purpose under s. 6 of the Land Acquisition Act is meant to prevent land acquisition proceedings being held up in order to ascertain whether a public purpose exists or not. A conclusive presumption that children born during the subsistence of a valid marriage, *the parties to which have access to each other,* are legitimate, is meant to protect innocent parties, namely, the children, from the grave consequences of illegitimacy, and is also meant to prevent inquiry into intimate domestic relations. Conclusive presumptions protect as well as affect the rights of persons. The rights of the children are protected, as legitimacy is conclusively presumed. The rights of persons which would arise on proof of illegitimacy are directly affected, but they are so affected because of a rule of substantive law based on public policy. Thus the difference between a rebuttable and an unrebuttable presumption is not one of degree, as mistakenly held by the majority, but one of kind. The former affects only the burden of proof; leaving the rights of the parties untouched; the latter directly affects, and is

---

[59] (1947) A.C. 46 (P.C.) at p. 56. The passage in the judgment of Lord Wright is set out in Chapter VIII.

[60] *Daryao* v. *U.P.* (1962) 1 S.C.R. 574, ('61) A.SC. 1457, citing *Halsbury*, Vol. 15, para 357.

intended to affect, the rights of parties on grounds of public policy. Phipson, in his *Law of Evidence* states:

Phipson's view supported by provisions like s. 82, I.P.C.

"In many cases, so-called conclusive presumptions are rules which belong, properly speaking, to the various branches of substantive law and not to the law of evidence, such as the presumption that an infant under eight is incapable of committing a felony. . . ."[61]

In India, the truth of this proposition is exemplified by s. 82 of the Penal Code which provides that "nothing is an offence which is done by a child under seven years of age." It is submitted that except for the difference in age, there is no difference in substance or effect between s. 82, which is a provision of substantive law, and the conclusive presumption of English law that a child under eight years of age is incapable of committing an offence.

(v) the majority judgment misreads *Domingo's Case*

6.62 The majority judgment holds that the observations of Thomson J. in *Domingo Urteriqui* v. *John N. D'Arcy*,[62] namely, "Whether the passport *per se* was legal and competent evidence of the fact of citizenship, we are of the opinion that it was not," are not helpful because the Court was divided in opinion. It is submitted that this is a misreading of the judgment. The full passage is as follows:

"There is some diversity of opinion on the bench, with respect to *the admissibility in evidence* of this passport, arising, in some measure, from the circumstances under which the offer was made, and its connection with other matters which had been given in evidence. Upon the general and abstract question, whether the passport, *per se*, was legal and competent evidence of the fact of citizenship, we are of opinion that it was not."[63] (italics supplied)

The distinction made is between the question as to the admissibility in evidence of the passport having regard to the facts of the case, and the abstract question whether a passport *per se* was legal and competent evidence of the fact of citizenship. On the first question there was a division of opinion; on the second there was none.

(vi) false statement about citizenship does not establish that citizenship

6.63 It is submitted that a little reflection would show that a false statement made by an applicant for a passport that he was a citizen would not establish that fact; a man cannot make himself a citizen of another country by making a false declaration to that effect. If, for instance, a Pakistani citizen made a false declaration that he was an Indian citizen and obtained an Indian passport it would not make him an Indian citizen, for a statement in a passport that the applicant was an Indian citizen is not one of the modes of acquiring Indian citizenship under that Act, nor is it one of the modes by which a person can be said to be a citizen at the commencement of the Constitution as provided in Part II of our Constitution. The above view is supported by *Joyce* v. *Director of Public Prosecutions*.[64] That case would not have involved a point of law of exceptional importance if the false statement by Joyce that he was a British subject had the effect of making him one, for there was no doubt at all that a British subject could be punished for treason committed in a foreign country. Nor was it the case of the Crown that Joyce was debarred from alleging that he was not a British subject.[65] The judgment of the House of Lords shows that the difficult question which arose in that case was whether in obtaining a British passport, Joyce who had been a resi-

Joyce v. *Director of Public Prosecutions*

---

[61] Phipson on *Evidence*, 10th ed., p. 836.
[62] (1835) 9 L. ed. 276; 9 Pet. 692.
[63] ibid. at p. 279.
[64] (1946) A.C. 347, (H.L.).
[65] ibid. at p. 371.

dent alien, extended his allegiance to the British Crown because he secured the protection which the passport gave him as a British subject. As Lord Jowitt L.C. said: "The question is not whether he obtained British citizenship by obtaining the passport, but whether by its receipt he extended his duty of allegiance beyond the moment when he left the shores of this country."[66] It is submitted that the majority judgment was wrong in holding that a passport was evidence of citizenship and that a person who made a false statement in an application for a passport that he was a citizen of the country giving him the passport was "estopped" from contending that he was not such a citizen. There can be no estoppel against a statute, for so to hold would be to add a mode of acquisition of citizenship contrary to the law of the land. Again, the requirements of a particular country in respect of application for passports is irrelevant to an inquiry into the validity of a rule which makes the acquisition of a passport of *any* country other than India conclusive proof of acquisition of foreign citizenship; and the fact that a passport is generally granted to the nationals of a country does not prevent a State from granting a passport to the national of another country. Examples are not wanting where countries have granted passports to nationals who had been denied passports by the authorities of their own countries.

A false statement about citizenship cannot operate as an estoppel — no estoppel against a statute

Requirements of a country as regards passports irrelevant to the validity of R. 3

(vii) Even if R. 3 were a rule of evidence, it is void as defeating the requirement of s. 9(1)

6.64 Though the whole case was argued and decided on the basis that if Rule 3 was a rule of substantive law it was outside the rule-making power which authorised the making of rules of evidence only, there is another line of reasoning which leads to the conclusion that the Rule is void. S. 9 (1) makes the termination of Indian citizenship depend upon the *voluntary* acquisition of citizenship of another country. S. 9 (2) enables rules to be made for determining the question whether any person has voluntarily acquired the citizenship of another country, for though the word "voluntary" is not expressly contained in s. 9 (2), it must be read into it, if s. 9 (1) is not to be nugatory. Therefore, even if Rule 3 were a rule of evidence and not a rule of substantive law, still a rule made under an Act must carry out, and not nullify, the provisions of the Act. Thus it has been held that a rule imposing a limitation not contained in an Act[67] or a rule enlarging the provisions of an Act[68] woud be *ultra vires* and void. Under s. 9 (1) the acquisition of foreign citizenship must be *voluntary;* but the question whether a person has acted voluntarily raises a question about the state of his mind, and therefore of fact.[69] Any rule which shuts out an inquiry into that state of mind by making it de-

---

[66] ibid. p. 370.

[67] *Bombay* v. *United Motors (India) Ltd.* (1953) S.C.R. 1069, 1096, ('53) A.SC. 252. "This limitation, it was claimed, was beyond the competence of the rule-making authority. The argument is not without force, and it must be held that the Sales Tax Rules 5(2)(i) is *ultra vires* the rule-making authority and therefore void."

[68] *Parbhani Transport Ltd.* v. *G. V. Bedekar* (1960) Bom. 87, 102, ('60) A.B. 278, 61 Bom.L.R. 1572. "It would appear from (s. 64) that only one appeal is contemplated by it. . . . Therefore, the rules framed by the State Government under s. 68 had to confine themselves to the appeals contemplated by s. 64. It was clearly beyond the powers of the State Government to make a rule providing for a second appeal, when the Act itself provides for one appeal."

[69] 'A fact means and includes . . . (2) any mental condition of which any person is conscious' (S. 3 of the Evidence Act); "The state of a man's mind, as has been said, is as much a fact as the state of his digestion": *Sabhapati* v. *Huntley* ('38) A.P.C. 91, 97.

pend arbitrarily upon the acquisition of a passport is repugnant to s. 9 (1) and therefore *ultra vires* and void.

6.65 In England statutory rules are called statutory instruments and it is settled law that "Instruments and bye-laws made under statutory powers . . . must not be in excess of the statutory power authorising them, nor repugnant to that statute or to general principles of law."[70] The above line of inquiry is directly relevant to the decision of the Supreme Court in *Md. Ayub Khan* v. *Commr. of Police, Madras.*[71] There the Supreme Court was invited to reconsider its judgment in *Izhar Ahmed's Case*[72] but declined to do so, giving as an additional reason that it had been followed in *A.P.* v. *Syed Mohd. Khan.*[73] The Court however interpreted Rule 3 so as to rob a passport of its conclusiveness. The Court rejected the contention that s. 9 prescribed an objective test and had nothing to do with intention, and that the word "voluntary" was used in contra-distinction to the phrase "by operation of law".[74] The Court also rejected the view, which appears to have been accepted by Rajagopala Ayyengar J., as a Judge of the Madras High Court[75] that the question whether a passport was voluntarily obtained must be decided by the foreign country, the representative of which issued the passport, Shah J. observing that it was impossible to hold that the termination of Indian citizenship depended upon the action of the foreign country in issuing the passport. The Court however held that the mere receipt of a passport by a person did not attract the operation of Rule 3 unless it was shown that the passport was received *voluntarily*. If a plea was raised that the person was compelled to take, or was by fraud or misrepresentation induced to receive, a passport *without any intention of renouncing his Indian citizenship* it would be difficult to say that such a passport was obtained voluntarily.[76] The Supreme Court therefore recognised that the crucial question to determine was whether a person in acquiring a passport intended to renounce his Indian citizenship. However, as the Court refused to reconsider *Izhar Ahmed's Case*, it was driven to read into the word "obtained" the words "voluntarily obtained." To lawyer and layman alike, it must seem odd that a Court should strike out, in effect, the word "voluntarily" from s. 9 (1), where it exists, and should then insert it in Rule 3, where it does not exist, on the ground that only a voluntary acquisition of foreign citizenship terminates Indian citizenship. It is submitted that though the decision in *Md. Ayub Khan's Case* goes some way to mitigate the

rules repugnant to the statute are void

Md. Ayub Khan's Case

---

[70] Maxwell, *Interpretation of Statutes*, 11th ed., p. 290 and f.n. 54.

[71] ('65) A.SC. 1623.

[72] (1962) Supp. 3 S.C.R. 235, ('62) A.SC. 1052.

[73] (1962) Supp. 3 S.C.R. 288, ('62) A.SC. 1778. On this point the Court merely said: "The point raised by the Appellants in these appeals is, therefore, concluded in (the Government's) favour by (*Ahmed Khan's Case*). This position is not disputed by the respondents." It is difficult to see how this decision adds weight to the earlier one.

[74] ('65) A.SC. *supra* p. 1628. As *Mahomed Usman* v. *State* ('61) A.M. 129, 143 expressed the view that the rule invalidating a contract on the ground of mistake could not be applied to interpret the word "voluntarily", which was used in contra-distinction to "by operation of law", it is no longer good law.

[75] ('61) A.M. 129, 143.

[76] ('65) A.SC. *supra* at p. 1628.

manifest injustice of *Izhar Ahmed's Case,* it does not go far enough, and if the intention to relinquish Indian citizenship is to be read into a rule which is meant to shut out an inquiry into that intention, the simplest and most satisfactory way to give effect to the express words of s. 9 (1) is to hold that Rule 3 is *ultra vires,* both because it is not a rule of evidence and because it is repugnant to s. 9 (1). It is submitted that *Izhar Ahmed's Case* should be overruled, as it is *obviously* wrong *and* productive of the most serious injury that can be done to an Indian citizen, namely, to deprive him of his Indian citizenship.

Submission: *Izar Ahmed's Case* wrongly decided

CHAPTER VII

FUNDAMENTAL RIGHTS — GENERAL CONSIDERATIONS: "THE STATE" AND "FUNDAMENTAL RIGHTS"

Fundamental rights enacted in the Constitution itself

7.1 The historical and political developments in India made it inevitable that a Bill of Rights, or Fundamental Rights, as we call them, should be enacted in our Constitution.[1] The British Indian Delegation which attended the Round Table Conferences in England had pressed for such inclusion in the Bill which was to become the G.I. Act, 35. This demand was rejected because general declarations had not much value unless there existed the will and the means to enforce them, and the history of the decade preceding the Bill would justify a cynic in saying that "the surest way of securing the destruction of a fundamental right was to include it as such in a Constitutional instrument."[2]

Art. 32: the right to move the Sup. Ct. for the enforcement of fundamental rights is itself a fundamental right

7.2 Our Constitution followed the American precedent and enacted fundamental rights in the Constitution itself. But it met a part of the objection against fundamental rights by providing effective means for their enforcement. This was done by arming the Supreme Court, and the High Courts, with power to issue writs of *habeas corpus, mandamus,* prohibition, *certiorari* and *quo warranto* whose efficacy in securing the liberty of the subject, the performance of public duty, the due administration of justice by inferior tribunals or Courts and the holding of a public office by lawful authority had long been proved in England. The Constitution went further and by Art. 32 made the right to move the Supreme Court for an appropriate writ for the protection of fundamental rights, itself a fundamental right.

No rights are reserved to the people under our Constitution, and our Legislatures are not the "delegates" of the people

7.3 In *Gopalan's Case*[3] Sastri J. said that the people of India in delegating to the legislature, the executive and the judiciary their respective powers reserved to themselves certain fundamental rights, so called because they had been retained by the people and made paramount to the delegated powers as in the American model. Further consideration of delegated legislation and separation of powers led him to accept the British, as opposed to the American, view, that the maxim *delegata potestas non potest delegari* did not apply to our legislatures which within the limits of their powers were as supreme and sovereign as the British Parliament;[4] and that our Constitution, unlike the American, was not based on the doctrine of the separation of powers. He said:

"It is true to say that, in a sense, the people delegated to the legislative, executive and the judicial organs of the State their respective powers while reserving to themselves the fundamental rights which they made paramount by providing that the State shall not make any law which takes away or abridges the rights conferred by that Part. To this extent the Indian Constitution may be said to have been based on the American model, but this is far from making the principle of separation of powers, as interpreted by the

---

[1] See para 1.85.
[2] See *W.B.* v. *Subodh Gopal Bose* (1954) S.C.R. 587, 615-16, ('54) A.SC. 92.
[3] (1950) S.C.R. 88, 198, ('50) A.SC. 27.
[4] *Delhi Laws Case* (1951) S.C.R. 747, 863, 878, ('51) A.SC. 332.

American courts, an essential part of the Indian Constitution or making the Indian Legislatures the delegates of the people so as to attract the application of the maxim."[5]

Reasons for the above view

It is submitted that in our Constitution no rights are reserved to the people. First, we have no provision like the 10th Amendment to the U.S. Constitution which expressly reserves to the people powers not delegated under the Constitution or denied to the States. Secondly, once the theory that the legislatures are the delegates of the people is given up, as Patanjali Sastri J. rightly gave it up, the theory that in *delegating* certain powers to the legislatures the people reserved fundamental rights to themselves lacks any foundation. Thirdly, the prohibition in Art. 13(2) against making laws which violate fundamental rights, and the declaration that laws so made shall be void does not amount to the reservation of fundamental rights to the people; Art. 13(2) states explicitly and by way of abundant caution[6] what is implicit in all constitutional limitations, namely, that a law contravening such limitations is void. Thus, the legislature is equally prohibited from making a law contravening Art. 286, or Arts. 301 to 304, for a law contravening those articles would undoubtedly be held void at the instance of a party whose rights were violated by such contravention. Lastly, fundamental rights can be amended by Parliament by following the procedure prescribed by Art. 368 for the amendment of the Constitution and the procedure does not require the consent of the people who are supposed to have reserved those rights to themselves.[7]

The enactment of fundamental rights has proved its value

7.4 It is outside the scope of this book to examine the theory underlying the inclusion of fundamental rights in a written Constitution, or to consider whether fundamental rights should or should not have been included in our Constitution. The actual working of the Constitution for over thirty years, however, shows that such inclusion has been more than justified. The Law Reports bear witness to the fact that legislative and executive interference with fundamental rights has been effectively checked by the Courts. However, the Law Reports tell only a small part of the tale because for one case that goes to a Court there are hundreds in which action violating fundamental rights has been restrained by the knowledge that a cheap and effective remedy exists for their enforcement. Those whose duty it is to advise the State or Local Authorities find that their advice to do what is fair and just gains in weight by a reference to fundamental rights, which, on the whole, are based on concepts of freedom, justice and fair play. It may be mentioned that the English attitude to fundamental rights has undergone a change after our Constitution was enacted.[8] In 1960 Canada enacted a Bill of Rights with a noble preamble.[9]

The change in the English attitude to fundamental rights

Canada enacts a Bill of Rights

---

[5](1951) S.C.R. at p. 883.

[6] *Per* Kania C.J. in *Gopalan's Case* (1950) S.C.R. 88, 100, ('50) A.SC. 27.

[7] The view that fundamental rights cannot be amended under Art. 368 is considered in the Chapter on Amendment of the Constitution in Vol. II.

[8] See the able article on "Fundamental Rights in the Commonwealth" by Prof. de Smith in the *International and Comparative Law Quarterly*, vol. 10, p. 83 *et seq.* and pp. 236-37.

[9] In 1981, the Canada Act was enacted by the British Parliament to repatriate the Constitution to Canada. "This Act is to be cited as the Constitution Act, 1981, and the Constitution Acts 1867 to 1975 (No. 2) and this Act may be cited together as the Constitution Acts, 1867 to 1981." Part I, Schedule B to the Constitution Act,

7.5 Part III, which deals with Fundamental Rights, consists of 26 Articles, which are arranged under the following sub-headings: (1) *General*: Arts. 12 and 13; (2) *Right to Equality*: Arts. 14 to 18; (3) *Right to Freedom*: Arts. 19 to 22; (4) *Right against Exploitation*: Arts. 23 and 24; (5) *Right to Freedom of Religion*: Arts. 25 to 28; (6) *Cultural and Educational Rights*: Arts. 29 and 30; (7) *Right to Property*: Arts. 31 (now deleted), 31A, 31B and 31C; (8) *Right to Constitutional Remedies*: Arts. 32 to 35. These different Rights are considered in detail later. However, the fundamental rights grouped under the eight sub-titles mentioned above, do not deal with mutually exclusive subjects. Thus, Art. 19 (1) (*f*) puts the right to acquire, hold, and dispose of property under the title "Right to Freedom" but it is clear that Art. 19 (1) (*f*) also deals with the "Right to Property", the title under which Arts. 31, 31A, 31B and 31C are grouped. Similarly, Art. 17 which abolishes untouchability appears under the title "Equality"; but the throwing open of Hindu Religious Institutions to "untouchables" is secured by Art. 25 (2) (*b*) which appears under the title "Right to the freedom of Religion". The scope of each Article in Part III and the inter-relation of various Articles will be considered in detail in its appropriate place. The Scheme of Part III

7.6 The Articles in Part III make a distinction between a "citizen" and "a person". Certain fundamental rights are conferred on any person, *e.g.*, the right to equality contained in Art. 14 and the right to property contained in Art. 31; certain fundamental rights are conferred only on citizens, *e.g.* the right to freedom contained in Art. 19. In order to make the fundamental rights more effective, Art. 12 defines "the State" and Art. 13 (3) (*a*) defines "law" very widely.[10] The definition of "the State" is considered fully in this Chapter, and the definition of "law" in the next. Art. 12 provides: Part III and the distinction between "citizen" and "person" "State" and "law" defined widely

"In this Part, unless the context otherwise requires, 'the State' includes the Government and Parliament of India and the Government and the Legislature of each of the States and all local or other authorities within the territory of India or under the control of the Government of India."[11]

7.7 The State consists of three great departments, the Legislature, the Executive and the Judiciary. The definition of "the State" in Art. 12 is an inclusive definition and does not expressly mention the Judiciary, but it is submitted that the inclusive definition of the word "State" does not exclude the Judiciary. However, this aspect of the definition will be considered later.

7.8 As interpreted by the Supreme Court in *Masthan Sahib* v. *Chief Commr., Pondicherry*[12] and *K. S. Ramamurthy* v. *Chief. Commr., Pondicherry*,[13] Art. 12 would run as follows: Art. 12 as interpreted by the Sup. Ct.

1981 provides for the Canadian Charter of Rights and Freedoms (or for fundamental rights as we call them). S. 24(1) provides for the enforcement of guaranteed rights and freedoms.

[10] *Shri Ram Krishna Dalmia* v. *Shri Justice S. R. Tendolkar* (1959) S.C.R. 279, 302; ('58) A.SC. 538: "Article 14 protects all persons from discrimination by the legislative as well as by the executive organ of the State. 'State' is defined in Art. 12 as including the Government and 'law' is defined in Art. 13 as including any notification or order. It has to be conceded, therefore, that it is open to the petitioners also to question the constitutionality of the notification".

[11] Art. 7 of the Draft Constitution corresponded to Art. 12 except that the words "or under the control of the Government of India" were added in Art. 12.

[12] (1962) 1 Supp. S.C.R. 981, ('63) A.SC. 533.

[13] (1964) 1 S.C.R. 656, ('63) A.SC. 1464.

"In this Part, unless the context otherwise requires, 'the State' includes (i) the Government and Parliament of India, (ii) the Government and the legislature of each State and (iii) (*a*) all local or other authorities within the territory of India, (*b*) all local or other authorities under the control of the Government of India."[14]

The words "or under the control" govern "local or other authorities"

In *Ramamurthy's Case*, the Supreme Court repelled the contention that the words "or under the control of the Government of India" qualified the word "territory", first, because it was opposed to the grammatical construction of the Article and, secondly, because it was opposed to the scheme of the Article which dealt with three kinds of authorities which constituted the "State", namely, the legislature and the executive of the Union and the States and local or other authorities. Again, local or other authorities fall into two categories: those which are within the territory of India and those which are under the control of the Government of India, even if not within the territory of India. In the two cases decided by the Supreme Court the questions for determination were (i) whether an appeal under Art. 136 lay against an order passed by the Chief Commissioner, Pondicherry, as an Appellate Authority under the Motor Vehicles Act and (ii) whether a writ could be issued in respect of that order under Art. 32. On the Government of India answering the question put to it in *Masthan's Case*[15] that at the relevant time Pondicherry was not a part of the territory of India,[16] an appeal under Art. 136 was held incompetent,[17] a decision which governed *Ramamurthy's Case*.[18] As to Art. 32, the majority in *Masthan's Case* said that though there was no territorial limitation on the jurisdiction of the Supreme Court under Art. 32, having regard to the provisions of Arts. 12, 142 and 144, the Supreme Court could issue a writ in respect of an executive or administrative act of an authority under the control of the Government of India, since that Government would be in a position to enforce that order on such authority. However, as the impugned order was passed by a quasi-judicial authority, such authority could not be described as under the control of the Government of India and therefore the issue of the writ would be futile as obedience to it could not be secured by the Government of India. Sarkar and Das Gupta JJ. dissented.[19] In *Ramamurthy's Case*, however, the Supreme Court unanimously held that a writ could not be issued against a quasi-judicial authority because it could not be considered to be an authority under the control of the Government of India and was therefore outside the definition of "The State" in Art. 12 and the fundamental rights guaranteed by the Constitution were available against the State as defined in Art. 12. The fact that at the time when the appeal and petition were heard Pondicherry had become a part of the territory of India did not affect the question, for, if the order when passed could not be impugned, to allow it to be impugned later would be to give the Constitution a retrospective effect which it did not possess.

Masthan's Case: when a writ will not be issued under Art. 32

---

[14] ('63) A.SC. *supra* at pp. 1467-8.
[15] ('63) A.SC. *supra* at pp. 538-39.
[16] ('62) A.SC. 797, 802-3.
[17] ('63) A.SC. *supra* at p. 536.
[18] ('63) A.SC. 1464, 1466.
[19] ('63) A.SC. 533, 540 (1st hearing of *Mastan's Case* decided on 28.4.1961); 2nd hearing decided on 8.12.1961 reported earlier in ('62) A.SC. 797, 806.

7.9 The development of the law as to "other authorities" which fall within the definition of "the State" in Art. 12 must be traced through the following four cases: (i) *Electricity Board, Rajasthan* v. *Mohan Lal*[20] decided *by a bench of 5 judges;* (ii) *Sukhdev Singh* v. *Bhagatram*[21] (*"Sukhdev's Case"*) decided *by a bench of 5 judges;* (iii) *R. D. Shetty* v. *International Airport Authority*[22] (*"The Airport Case"*) decided *by a bench of 3 judges*: and (iv) *Ajay Hasia* v. *Khalid Mujib*[23] (*"Hasia's Case"*) decided *by a bench of 5 judges.*

Development of law as to "other authorities": four leading cases

7.10 There was a conflict of authority as to the meaning of "other authorities" in Art. 12.[24] One view was that the words should be construed *ejusdem generis,* and the other that the word "authority" meant "a body exercising power" and in Art. 12 that power meant a power to issue rules, by-laws, or regulations having the force of law.[25] In *The Rajasthan Electricity Board Case,*[26] the Supreme Court overruled the decisions in *University of Madras* v. *Shanta Bai*[27], *Devadas* v. *Karnataka Engineering College*[28] and *Kishan Gopal Ramchand Sharma* v. *Punjab University*[29] all of which had construed "other authorities" *ejusdem generis.* After explaining the principles underlying the *ejusdem generis* rule by reference to *Craies*[30] and *Maxwell*[31], the court held that the rule did not apply because there was no genus common to the named bodies, nor could they be placed in one single category on any rational basis.[32] The court held that the Electricity Board fell within the definition of "the State" in Art. 12.

Earlier conflict of authority now resolved

---

20 (1967) 3 S.C.R. 377, ('67) A.SC. 1857.
21 (1975) 3 S.C.R. 619, ('75) A.SC. 1331.
22 ('79) A.SC. 1628. 23 ('81) A.SC. 487.
24 *University of Madras* v. *Shanta Bai* ('54) A.M. 67, 68 (*held,* that a University was not a "State"); fol. in *Devadas* v. *Karnataka Engineering College* ('64) A.Mys. 6 (*held,* that the respondent college was not a "State"), and in *Ena Gosh* v. *W.B.* ('62) A.Cal. 420 (*held,* that the Sarojini Naidu College, which was sponsored by the Government was not a "State"; see also *Surendra Kumar* v. *Central Board of Secondary Education, Ajmer* (1957) 7 Raj. 665, ('57) A.Raj. 206, where it was held without any discussion of the subject that the fact that the Government of India had control over the Central Board of Secondary Education did not make the Board a "State" within the meaning of Art. 12. It is submitted that it would be necessary to consider the Board's powers before deciding whether it was a "State".
25 *Namboodripad* v. *C.D. Board* ('56) A.Tr.-Co. 19 (*held,* that the Cochin Dewaswom Board constituted under the Travancore-Cochin Hindu Religious Institutions Act, 1950, though not a "local authority" was clearly an "other authority" mentioned in Art. 12); see also *Kesava* v. *Mysore* ('56) A.Mys. 20 (*held,* that under the Constitution, the Public Service Commission did not possess even the power to implement its own decision without referring to the State Government and was not "a State" within the meaning of Art. 12.)
26 ('67) A.SC. 1857; fol. in *Umesh Chandra* v. *V. N. Singh* ('68) A.P. 3 (F.B.) (*held,* that a University fell within the definition of "State" in Art. 12); applied in *K. C. Verma* v. *Bokaro Steel Ltd.* ('71) A.P. 137 (*held,* that the respondent company was a separate entity from its shareholders; no governmental or quasi-governmental powers had been conferred on it and it was not a "State" within Art. 12). See also *Abdul Rehman* v. *State* ('70) A.J. & K. 133 (F.B.) (*held,* that a corporation or a Government undertaking, even if the Government owned the undertaking or corporation, was not a "State" within Art. 12 unless it was created by statute with powers which included power to give directions the disobedience of which was punishable as an offence); *R. D. Singh* v. *Secy., B.S.S.I. Corpn.* ('74) A.P. 213.
27 (1954) Mad. 426, ('54) A.M. 67. 28 ('64) A.Mys. 6.
29 (1965) 2 Punj. 480, ('66) A.Punj. 34. 30 *Statute Law,* 6th ed., p. 181.
31 *Interpretation of Statutes,* 11th ed., pp. 326-7.
32 ('67) A.SC. 1857. In *Ujjam Bai* v. *U.P.* (1963) 1 S.C.R. 778, ('62) A.SC. 1621, Rajagopala Ayyangar had expressed the same view at p. 969: "Again, Art. 12 winds up the list of authorities falling within the definition by referring to 'other authorities' within the territory of India which cannot, obviously, be read as *ejusdem*

Same topic continued

7.11 As to the meaning of the words "other authorities" there was a difference of opinion between the majority judgment delivered by Bhargava J. and the concurring judgment of Shah J. This difference does not call for a discussion in view of the subsequent development of the law. In holding that the State Electricity Board fell within the definition of "the State" in Art. 12, the majority adopted the test that a statutory auhority "would be within the meaning of 'other authorities' if it has been invested with statutory power to issue binding directions to the parties, the disobedience of which would entail penal consequences or it has the sovereign power to make rules and regulations having the force of law."[33]

Sukhdev's Case

7.12 In *Sukhdev's Case*[34] the Supreme Court considered its earlier decisions on the meaning of the word "authorities" in Art. 12. The question arose in three appeals in which dismissed employees claimed reinstatement respectively from the Oil and Natural Gas Commission, the Life Insurance Corporation and the Industrial Finance Corporation ("the three Corporations") which were incorporated under the Natural Oil & Gas Commission Act, 1959, the Life Insurance Corporation Act, 1956, and the Industrial Finance Corporation Act 1948. Three judgments were delivered. Ray C.J. delivered the majority judgment for himself and Chandrachud and Gupta JJ.; Mathew J. delivered a concurring judgment; Alagiriswamy J. delivered a dissenting judgment.

Ray C.J. and the majority view

7.13 Ray C.J. considered the relevant provisions of the three Acts. The State contended: (i) that Regulations made under a Statute affecting matters of internal management "do not have a statutory binding character".[35] Regulations provided the terms and conditions of employment and thereafter the employment of any person was contractual; (ii) that the three Corporations were not "other authorities" within the meaning of Art. 12. Ray C.J. rejected these contentions. He held that Rules and Regulations made in exercise of statutory authority were subordinate delegated legislation, which, if validly made, had the full force and effect of a law. He held that Rules and Regulations have the characteristics of law. The three Corporations had no free hand in framing the conditions and terms of service, but were bound to apply the terms and conditions as laid down in the Regulations. There was no substantial difference between Rules and Regulations because both were subordinate legislation under powers conferred by Statutes.[36] "These regulations are not only binding on the authorities but also on the public."[37] Regulations framed by a Company under the Companies Act could not be equated to Regulations framed by a corporate body created by statute. A company was not a statutory body because it was not

---

generis with either the Government and the Legislatures or local authorities. The words are of wide amplitude and capable of comprehending every authority created under a statute and functioning within the territory of India. There is no characterisation of the nature of the 'authority' in this residuary clause and consequently it must include every type of authority set up under a statute for the purpose of administering laws enacted by the Parliament or by the State including those vested with the duty to make decisions in order to implement those laws": The above passage was quoted in ('67) A.SC. *supra* at pp. 1862-3.

[33] *Per* Bhagwati J. in the *Airport Case* ('79) A.SC. 1628, 1646.

[34] ('75) A.SC. 1331.

[35] ('75) A.SC. at p. 1336.

[36] ibid. p. 1341.

[37] ibid. p. 1338.

created by Statute, but was incorporated in accordance with the provisions of a statute — the Companies Act.[38] Ray C.J. considered a number of Supreme Court decisions on "the character of regulations"[39] but the discussion of cases cannot be set out profitably, because having considered each decision he has not deduced the principle or principles underlying those decisions.

7.14 As to whether the three Corporations were "other authorities", Ray C.J. adopted, as we have seen in para 7.12 above, the test laid down by the majority in the *Rajasthan Electricity Board Case*. He stated his conclusions thus: Conclusion reached by Ray C.J.

"For the foregoing reasons, we hold that rules and regulations framed by the Oil and Natural Gas Commission, Life Insurance Corporation and the Industrial Finance Corporation have the force of law. The employees of these statutory bodies have a statutory status and they are entitled to declaration of being in employment when their dismissal or removal is in contravention of statutory provisions. By way of abundant caution we state that these employees are not servants of the Union or the State. These statutory bodies are 'authorities' within the meaning of Article 12. . . ."[40]

7.15 In a concurring judgment, Mathew J. adopted a new line of approach, which, as will appear hereafter, has been adopted unanimously by 5 judges in *Hasia's Case*.[41] The judgment of Mathew J. is closely reasoned and repays study as a whole. The following is a brief account of the reasoning by which he held that the three Corporations were "other authorities" within the meaning of Art. 12 and were "the State" as defined in that Article. Mathew J. held that the *Rajasthan Electricity Board Case*[42] laid down a test which would be satisfied by the Oil and Natural Gas Commission because of the provisions of s. 25.[43] However, he held, it is submitted rightly, that the two other Corporations would not satisfy the test. He added that the question still remained Concurring judgment of Mathew J.: A new approach

"whether despite the fact that there are no provisions for issuing binding directions to third parties the disobedience of which would entail penal consequences, the corporations set up under statutes to carry on business of public importance or which is fundamental to the life of the people can be considered as 'State' within the meaning of Art. 12."[44]

7.16 Mathew J. observed that the concept of "State" had changed radically in recent years and the State could no longer be looked upon simply as "a coercive machinery weilding the thunderbolt of authority".[45] Part IV of the Constitution (Directive Principles of State Policy) showed the extent of the services which the State was expected to undertake and render for the welfare of the people. Therefore, New approach developed

"the question for consideration is whether a public corporation set up under a special statute to carry on a business or service which Parliament thinks necessary to be carried on in the interest of the nation is an agency or instrumentality of the State and would be subject to the limitations expressed in Article 13(2) of the Constitution. A State is an abstract entity. It can only act through the instrumentality or agency of natural or juridicial persons. Therefore, there is nothing strange in the notion of the State acting through a corporation and making it an agency or instrumentality of the State."[46]

---

[38] ibid. p. 1339.
[39] ibid. pp. 1339-41.
[40] ('75) A.SC. *supra* at p. 1348.
[41] ('79) A.SC. 1628; see para 7.29.
[42] (1967) 3 S.C.R. 377, ('67) A.SC. 1857.
[43] ('75) A.SC. *supra* at p. 1349.
[44] ibid.
[45] ibid.
[46] ibid. p. 1350.

Mathew J. observed that in English Law, chartered Corporations of the 17th, 18th and 19th centuries were expanded as a device by which the political State got something done. They were far more like the bodies corporate which we call "public authorities" today.[47] Few in the 17th or 18th centuries would have disputed that such corporations were agencies of the State. In the United States, in *McCullough* v. *Maryland*[48] it was held that to charter a corporation was incidental to, or in aid of, governmental functions, and *qua* the Federal Government, such corporations were agencies of the Federal Government subject to the constitutional limitations imposed on an agency of the Federal Government. A public corporation was usually established by a statute passed by Parliament in the United Kingdom, charged with carrying out specified governmental functions in the national interest. Such functions have been confined to a comparatively restricted field. A public corporation was not a general multi-purpose authority. Its administration was in the hands of a Board appointed by the competent Minister. The employees of public corporations were not civil servants.

Condition of liability of public corporations as "the State"

7.17 Our Constitution has been framed on the basis that limitations should exist on the exercise of power by the State; but the essential problem of liberty and equality was freedom from arbitrary restrictions. The Constitution should be so interpreted that the governing power, wherever located, must be subjected to fundamental constitutional limitations. The tendency in the United States is to bring more and more activity within the reach of constitutional limitations as is evidenced by *Marsh* v. *Alabama*.[49] But how far can this expansion go? Under Art. 13(2) it is State action of a particular kind that is prohibited. Individual invasion of individual rights is not, generally speaking, covered by Art. 13(2). For, although Arts. 17, 23 and 24 show that fundamental rights can be violated by private individuals and relief against them would be available under Art. 32, still, by and large, Art. 13(2) is directed against State action. A public corporation being the creation of the State, is subject to the same constitutional limitations as the State itself. Two conditions are necessary, namely, that the Corporation must be created by the State and it must invade the constitutional rights of individuals.[50]

The proposed test

7.18 But when can a Corporation be looked upon as an agency of the State for subjecting it to constitutional limitations? No easy answer is possible. But the following considerations may be helpful in answering the question. A mere finding of State control of a Corporation, or of unusual financial help, may not be sufficient to characterize the Corporation's operations as State action. But a

---

[47] It may be noticed that the definition of "State" mentions local authorities and the Municipality and the Port Trust are local authorities as defined in the General Clauses Act.

[48] (1819) 4 Wheat 316.

[49] (1946) 326 U.S. 501, 90 L. ed. 265. (A corporation owned a "company town". Marsh offered his pamphlet and preached his doctrine on one of the town corners. He was fined 5 dollars. The U.S. Supreme Court held that the operation of a town was a public function and although the town was private property in the sense of being owned by a corporation, yet, the corporation was privately performing a public function. Consequently, it was subject to the constitutional standards regarding civil rights and equal protection of the law which applied to the State).

[50] ('75) A.SC. *supra* at p. 1351.

finding of State financial support plus an unusual degree of control over management and policies might lead to characterising the acts of the Corporation as State action. Another factor may be considered. The combination of State assistance with assigning important public functions to the Corporation might lead to the conclusion that the Corporation should be classified as a State agency.[51] A State may help a Corporation otherwise than by financial assistance, *e.g.*, by granting it the power of eminent domain, or by creating a monopoly in its favour or by granting it tax exemptions.[52]

7.19 Applying these tests, Mathew J. held that the Life Insurance Corporation and the Industrial Finance Corporation were agencies or instrumentalities of the State and were thus the State within the meaning of Art. 12. As to the Life Insurance Corporation, the Central Government had contributed the original capital of the Corporation; part of the profits went to the Central Government; the Central Government exercised control over the policy of the Corporation and the Corporation carried on business of great public importance in which it held a monopoly. Mathew J. said that he would draw similar conclusions about the Industrial Finance Corporation from the provisions of the Industrial Finance Corporation Act.[53]

The test applied

7.20 The line of reasoning developed by Mathew J. can also be supported on the additional ground that it prevents a large-scale evasion of fundamental rights by transferring work done in Government Departments to statutory Corporations, whilst retaining Government control. Company legislation in India has enacted provisions against the abuse of the corporate personality of the company, when combined with limited liability. Courts have torn the corporate veil in certain cases and the growing tendency is to look behind the legal personality to the reality behind it. Mathew J. achieved the same result, but by a different route, namely, by drawing out the implications of Art. 13 (2). And although he mentioned liberty and equality without express reference to Art. 14, he laid great stress on subjecting arbitrary action of the State to constitutional limitations. Subsequent decisions of the Supreme Court have supported his view by drawing out one of the implications of Art. 14, namely, that arbitrary and capricious action by the State violates the equal protection of the laws guaranteed by Art. 14.

Submission: Mathew J.'s reasoning can be supported on additional grounds

7.21 In the *Airport Case*[54] the doctrine of agency and State instrumentality was adopted by Bhagwati J.[55] The problem to be solved in that case was thus stated by Bhagwati J.:

The Airport Case: Bhagwati J. prefers the view of Mathew J.

"This appeal by special leave raises interesting questions of law in the area of public law. What are the constitutional obligations on the State when it

[51] ibid. p. 1354.

[52] ibid. pp. 1354-56 where several decisions of the U.S. Supreme Court are cited. But the decision in *Kerr* v. *Enoch Pratt Free Library* [(1945) 149 F.2d. 212 (4th cir.) cert. denied, 326 U.S. 721] is striking. The library system in question was established by private donation in 1882, but by 1944, 99 per cent of the system's budget was supplied by the city. Title to the library property was held by the city, employees were paid by the city, and a high degree of budget control was available to the city government. On these facts, the Court of Appeals required the trustees managing the system to abandon a discriminatory admissions policy for its library training courses.

[53] ibid. p. 1356.

[54] ('79) A.SC. 1628.

[55] For himself, Tulzapurkar and Pathak JJ.

takes action in exercise of its statutory or executive power? Is the State entitled to deal with its property in any manner it likes or award a contract to any person it chooses without any constitutional limitations upon it? What are the parameters of the statutory or executive power in the matter of awarding a contract or dealing with its property? These questions fall in the sphere of both Administrative Law and Constitutional law and they assume special significance in a modern welfare State which is committed to egalitarian values and dedicated to the rule of law. But these questions cannot be decided in the abstract. They can be determined only against the background of facts and hence we shall proceed to state the facts giving rise to the appeal."[56]

Facts of the *Airport Case*

7.22 The facts of the case, and the large amount of litigation to which they gave rise, are set out in the judgment. But the following brief facts are necessary for an appreciation of the judgment. The International Airport Authority ("the Authority") is a body corporate constituted under the International Airport Authority Act, 1971. The Director of the Authority issued a Notice inviting tenders for putting up and running a second class restaurant and two snack bars at the International Airport at Bombay. Paragraph 1 of the Notice stated that

"Sealed tenders in the prescribed form are hereby invited from Registered IInd Class Hoteliers having at least 5 years' experience, for putting up and running a IInd Class Restaurant and two Snack Bars at this Airport for a period of 3 years". Paragraph (8) of the notice made it clear that "the acceptance of the tender will rest with the Airport Director who does not bind himself to accept any tender and reserves to himself the right to reject all or any of the tenders received without assigning any reasons therefor."[57]

Six tenders were received. The 4th Respondent's tender offered the highest licence fee, the remaining five offering decreasing amounts as licence fee. The 4th Respondent's tender was complete, the tenders of the remaining five were incomplete. The 4th Respondent was not a "Registered II class Hotelier having at least 5 years' experience"; but had considerable experience in running canteens for big corporations. After correspondence between the 4th Respondent and the Director of the Authority, the Director accepted the 4th Respondent's tender. One K. C. Irani, one of the five tenderers, instituted legal proceedings to question the Director's decision. After Irani had failed in two successive suits to get an interim stay, the appellant, who had not put in a tender, filed a writ petition which was rejected by the Bombay High Court. He applied for, and obtained, special leave to appeal to the Supreme Court.

A preliminary contention rejected

7.23 It is enough for the purposes of the present discussion to state that the Supreme Court found, first, that it was a condition for the acceptance of a tender that the person tendering must be a Registered IInd Class Hotelier of at least 5 years' experience, and the 4th Respondent did not satisfy that condition and his tender could not have been accepted. However, it was contended for the Authority that as it was not bound to accept any tender, it could have rejected all the tenders and given the licence to the 4th Respondent by private negotiations. The Court rejected this contention by observing that the process of inviting tenders had not been terminated, so that a contract by negotiations could be entered into. The Authority accepted the 4th Respondent's tender, and as held earlier, the 4th Respondent's tender could not be accepted as he did not fulfil a condition of the tender Notice.

[56] ('79) A.SC. at p. 1629. [57] ibid.

7.24 The Authority and the 4th Respondent contended that the appellant had no *locus standi*, for, as he had not submitted a tender, he had suffered no injury by the impugned grant of the licence to the 4th Respondent. Bhagwati J. rejected this contention by observing that the real grievance of the Appellant was that had he known that the condition of the tenderer being a Registered II Class Hotelier with at least 5 years' experience would be disregarded, or not insisted on, he would have submitted a tender. Appellant's *locus standi*

7.25 The question whether the Director's acceptance of the 4th Respondent's tender was invalid was considered, first, as a matter of administrative law. Bhagwati J. said that it was a well settled rule of administrative law that an executive authority must be rigorously held to the standards by which it professes its actions to be judged and it must scrupulously adhere to those standards, for any violation of those standards would render the executive act invalid. This enunciation of the law by Frankfurter J.[58] was accepted and applied in India in *A. S. Ahluwalia* v. *Punjab*[59] and in *Sukhdev* v. *Bhagatram*.[60] Frankfurter J. stated the rule as part of administrative law, and did not support it by reference to the equality clause of the 14th Amendment to the U.S. Constitution. The recent trend in England was in the same direction as Prof. Wade's *Administrative Law* (4th ed.)[61] clearly showed. Bhagwati J. observed that there was no reason why we should not adopt the same view as part of the developing administrative law in India. For whatever view one may take of the concept of the rule of law, the great purpose underlying the concept is the protection of the individual against arbitrary exercise of power. Every action of the executive must be informed with reason and should be free from arbitrariness. Bhagwati J. said that in a welfare State, Question considered as a matter of administrative law

"Government was the regulator and dispenser of benefits and special services and a provider of a large number of benefits including jobs, contracts, licences, quotas, mineral rights etc. . . . The valuables dispensed by Government take many forms, but they all share one characteristic. They are steadily taking the place of traditional forms of wealth. . . . Some of these forms of wealth may be in the nature of legal rights, but the large majority of them are in the nature of privileges. But on that account can it be said that they do not enjoy any protection? . . We do not think so."[62]

Bhagwati J. held that Government did not stand in the same position as a private individual, and in the matter of dispensing this new wealth, Government could not act arbitrarily. He supported his view by referring to the Supreme Court's decision in *Erusian Equipment and Chemicals Ltd.* v. *W.B.*[63]

7.26 Bhagwati J. then considered the question whether the Authority as a Corporation was "the State". Following the line of reasoning adopted by Mathew J. to show that Corporations created by the State could be looked upon as agencies or instrumentalities of the State if they satisfied certain tests, Bhagwati J. referred to *Sukhdev* v. *Bhagatram* in which the majority followed the test laid down by Airport Authority held to be "the State"

[58] 359 U.S. 535, 3 L. ed. 2d. 1012.
[59] (1975) 3 S.C.R. 82, ('75) A.SC. 984.
[60] (1975) 3 S.C.R. 619, ('75) A.SC. 1331.
[61] pp. 540-41.
[62] ('79) A.SC. at pp. 1636-7.
[63] (1975) 2 S.C.R. 674, ('75) A.SC. 266.

the majority in the *Rajasthan Electricity Board Case* for determining when a body corporate created by a statute can be considered to be the State. Bhagwati J. added:

"Whilst accepting the test laid down in *Rajasthan Electricity Board* v. *Mohan Lal* (supra) and followed by Ray, C.J. in *Sukhdev* v. *Bhagatram* (supra), we would, for reasons already discussed, prefer to adopt the test of Governmental instrumentality or agency as one more test and perhaps a more satisfactory one for determining whether a statutory corporation, body or other authority falls within the definition of 'State'. If a statutory corporation, body or other authority is an instrumentality or agency of Government, it would be an 'authority' and therefore 'State' within the meaning of that expression in Article 12."[64]

He dealt with, and distinguished, the undernoted cases[65] as not affecting the conclusion set out in the above paragraph. Applying the result of the above discussion to the International Airport Authority of India in the light of the provisions of the Act incorporating it, Bhagwati J. said:

"These provisions clearly show that every test discussed above is satisfied in the case of the 1st respondent and they leave no doubt that the 1st respondent is an instrumentality or agency of the Central Government and falls within the definition of 'State' both on the narrow view taken by the majority in *Sukhdev* v. *Bhagatram* (supra) as also on the broader view of Mathew J., adopted by us. It is therefore obvious that both having regard to the constitutional mandate of Article 14 as also the judicially evolved rule of administrative law, the 1st respondent was not entitled to act arbitrarily in accepting the tender of the 4th respondent, but was bound to conform to the standard or norm laid down in paragraph 1 of the notice inviting tenders which required that only a person running a registered IInd Class hotel or restaurant and having at least 5 years' experience as such should be eligible to tender."[66]

Reasons for refusing relief

7.27 However, relief was refused to the Appellant because of his conduct, including delay, and also because it was doubtful whether the petition was filed *bona fide,* and because the 4th Respondent had incurred considerable expense and had in fact put up the restaurant and the snack bars. The court held that in these circumstances it would be iniquitous to set aside the contract.

The test applied by Mathew J. adopted by 5 judges in *Hasia's Case*

7.28 It is submitted that the line of reasoning adopted by Mathew J. in *Sukhdev Singh's Case* and adopted by Bhagwati J. for himself, Tulzapurkar and Pathak JJ. in the *Airport Case* marks a development, in the right direction, of administrative law and the clear emphasis put on Art. 14 as negativing arbitrary action on the part of the State. It is submitted that the broader test applied by Mathew J., and accepted by Bhagwati J., for determining whether a Corporation is to be considered as "the State" is to be preferred to the narrower test laid down by the majority in the *Rajasthan Electricity Board Case* and adopted by the majority in *Sukhdev's Case*. The above submission[67] is now supported by the unanimous decision of 5 judges in *Hasia's Case* considered in paras 7.29 to 7.34 below.

---

[64] ('79) A.SC. at pp. 1646-7.

[65] *Praga Tools Corp.* v. *C. A. Imanual* (1969) 3 S.C.R. 773; *Heavy Engineering Mazdoor Union* v. *Bihar* (1969) 3 S.C.R. 995; *S. L. Agarwal* v. *General Manager, Hindustan Steel Ltd.* (1970) 3 S.C.R. 363, and *Sabhajit Tewari* v. *Union* (1975) 1 S.C.C. 485.

[66] ('69) A.SC. at p. 1650.

[67] See Seervai, *Constitutional Law of India,* Vol. III, 2nd ed., p. 1851.

7.29 *Hasia's Case*[69] marks the culmination of the process which Mathew J. started as to the meaning of "other authorities" in Art. 12. In *Hasia's Case* the question for determination arose out of writ petitions filed under Art. 32 challenging the validity of admissions to the Regional Engineering College, Srinagar ("the College") which was one of 15 Engineering Colleges in India sponsored by the Govt. of India. The College was run by a Society ("the Society") registered under the Jammu and Kashmir Registration of Societies Act, 1893. The question was whether the Society was "the State" under Art. 12, for only if it was the State could the admissions to the College be challenged as violating Art. 14. Bhagwati J. delivering the unanimous judgment of a Constitution Bench[70] scrutinized the Memorandum of Association and the Rules of the Society[71] and held that the Society was an instrumentality or agency of the State and Central Governments and the Society was an authority under Art. 12, for reasons we have set out in paras 7.30 to 7.34 below.

Hasia's Case

7.30 Bhagwati J. started the discussion with his judgment in the *Airport Case,* and he quoted several passages from that judgment.[72] But it is unnecessary to refer to them because, as we have seen, in the *Airport Case* he preferred the views of Mathew J. in *Sukhdev's Case* to that of the majority, and we have already considered the views of Mathew J. at length.[73] In *Hasia's Case,* Bhagwati J. said that if agencies and instrumentalities of government were not held to be "other authorities" under Art. 12, then,

Consequences of not holding agencies or instrumentalities of Govt. to be "the State"

". . . it would be the easiest thing for the government to assign to a plurality of corporations almost every State business such as Post and Telegraph, TV and Radio, Rail Road and Telephones — in short every economic activity — and thereby cheat the people of India out of the Fundamental Rights guaranteed to them. That would be a mockery of the Constitution and nothing short of treachery and breach of faith with the people of India, because, though apparently the Corporation will be carrying out these functions, it will in truth and reality be the Government which will be controlling the corporation and carrying out these functions through the instrumentality or agency of the corporation. We cannot by a process of judicial construction allow the Fundamental Rights to be rendered futile and meaningless and thereby wipe out Chapter III from the Constitution. That would be contrary to the constitutional faith of the post *Maneka Gandhi* era."[74]

Conversion of Govt. Depts. into Corporations to circumvent fundamental rights

7.31 Bhagwati J. formulated the relevant tests for determining whether a corporation was an agency or instrumentality of government as follows:

Tests to determine when corporation an agency or instrumentality of Govt.

"(*a*) One thing is clear that if the entire share capital of the corporation is held by Government it would go a long way towards indicating that the corporation is an instrumentality or agency of Government; (*b*) Where the financial assistance of the State is so much as to meet almost (the) entire expenditure of the corporation, it would afford some indication of the corporation being impregnated with governmental character; (*c*) It may also be a

---

69 ('81) A.SC. 487; foll. in *A. M. Ahamed & Co.* v. *Union* ('82) A.Mad. 247, 252. [*Held,* that the National Agricultural Co-op. Federation of India Ltd. (NAFED), a co-operative society registered under the Delhi Co-operative Societies Act, in relation to its activities as a canalising agency for export of onions to Singapore and Malaysia was "the State" as it was an "authority" within Art. 12].

70 For himself, Chandrachud C.J. and Krishna Iyer, Fazal Ali and Koshal JJ.

71 See ('81) A.SC. at pp. 489-90 where the relevant clauses of the Memorandum and the relevant Rules are set out.

72 ('81) A.SC. *supra* at pp. 494-6.

73 See paras 7.15 to 7.20.

74 ('81) A.SC. at pp. 493-4.

relevant factor . . . whether the corporation enjoys monopoly status which is the (sic) State conferred or State protected; (*d*) Existence of 'deep and pervasive State control may afford an indication that the Corporation is a State agency or instrumentality'; (*e*) If the functions of the corporation are of public importance and closely related to governmental functions, it would be a relevant factor in classifying the corporation as an instrumentality or agency of Government; (*f*) 'Specifically, if a department of Govt. is transferred to a corporation, it would be a strong factor supportive of this inference' of the corporation being an instrumentality or agency of Government."[75]

If on applying these tests it is found that a corporation is an agency or instrumentality of Government, it is the State under Art. 12. Bhagwati J. held that for the purpose of determining whether a Corporation was "the State" under Art. 12 it mattered not whether it was created by, or under, a statute; or was a Government company, or a company incorporated under the Companies Act; or was a society formed under the Societies Registration Act or any other similar statute. Whatever the machinery by which the corporation was created, if it was an instrumentality or agency of Government, it was "the State" under Art. 12.[76]

Mathew J.'s view in *Sukhdev's Case* now accepted doctrine

7.32 This part of the judgment of Bhagwati J. marks a great advance over the earlier decisions of the Supreme Court. But the most important advance lies in the fact that the view of Mathew J. in *Sukhdev's Case,* which was preferred by three judges in the *Airport Case,* has now become the established doctrine laid down by a unanimous judgment of five judges. However, the definition of "the State" in Art. 12 was only for the purpose of Part III and the fact that a corporation was "the State" under Art. 12 (or under Art. 36) did not make a corporation "the State" for the purpose of Part XIV (Services under the Union and the States) or any other Part of our Constitution.[77] It would follow that servants of a corporation which is the State under Art. 12, do not thereby become persons in the employ of the Union and the States.

7.33 It is not necessary to consider the challenge to the action of the College on the merits, or to deal with the views expressed by the

---

[75] ibid. p. 496. The judgment in *Hasia's Case* was delivered on 13th Nov., 1980 by Bhagwati J. for a Constitution Bench which included Krishna Iyer J. On 13th Nov., 1980, Krishna Iyer J. for himself and Reddy J. delivered the judgment in *Som Prakash* v. *Union* ('81) A.SC. 212. In that case Krishna Iyer J. referred to *U.P. Warehousing Corpn.* v. *Vijay Narain* ('80) A.SC. 840, which had held that the U.P. Warehousing Corporation was "the State" as defined in Art. 12, and observed: "The Court reviewed many decisions, Indian and English, and upheld the employee's contention that the writ could and should issue to such a body if illegality were established. It is significant that pointed reference has been made to *Sukhdev Singh* (1975) 3 S.C.R. 619, ('75) A.SC. 1331, *Airport Authority* ('79) A.SC. 1628 and the judgment of the House of Lords in *Malloch* v. *Aberdeen Corpn.* (1971) 1 W.L.R. 1578. Sarkaria J. adverted to the observations of Lord Wilberforce that in cases where there is an element of public employment or service, or support by statute or something in the nature of public office or status, the Court would correct illegal acts": ('81) A.SC. at p. 220. Krishna Iyer J. propounded five tests for determining when an agency or instrumentality of the state can be considered to be an "authority" within the meaning of Art. 12 and, therefore, "the State". It appears likely that the judgment of Krishna Iyer J. was available to Bhagwati J. before he delivered the judgment in *Hasia's Case,* because, except for the test set out in (*b*) in para 7.31 above, the remaining five tests laid down by Krishna Iyer J. appear to have been re-arranged and bodily incorporated by Bhagwati J. except for an incorrect insertion of "the" in test (c) in para 7.31.

[76] ibid. p. 496. [77] ibid. p. 497.

court on Art. 14. These views are considered in the Chapter on Equality.

7.34 In view of the development of the law as to the interpretation of "other authorities" in Art. 12, it would be unprofitable to consider the decisions of the Supreme Court, or of the High Courts which are, or on the facts of the case may be, inconsistent with *Hasia's Case,* because they stand overruled by that Case.

Whether the Judiciary is included in "the State"

7.35 We must now consider whether the Judiciary is "the State" as defined in Art. 12, because if it is, it must conform to fundamental rights conferred by Part III of our Constitution. Article 14 (Right to Equality) provides: *"The State shall not deny* to any person equality before the law or *the equal protection of the laws within the territory of India".* In our Constitution, the italicized words have been borrowed from the 14th Amendment to the U.S. Constitution, which provides: "Nor shall any State . . . deny to any person within its jurisdiction the equal protection of the laws." As will appear hereafter,[78] Art. 14 is the one Article in which our Courts have drawn most heavily on the decisions of the U.S. Supreme Court, and the whole doctrine of "classification", evolved by the U.S Supreme Court, has very rightly been adopted by our Courts. In the United States, it is well settled that the judiciary is within the prohibition of the 14th Amendment. A standard text book[79] states the position thus:

In the U.S. the prohibitions of 14th Amendment apply to the Judiciary

"The prohibitions of the Amendment 'have reference to action of the political body denominated by a State, by whatever instruments or in whatever modes that action may be taken. A State acts by its legislative, its executive, *or its judicial authorities.* It can act in no other way. The constitutional provision, therefore, must mean that no agency of the State, or of the officers or agents by whom its powers are exerted shall deny to any person within its jurisdiction the equal protection of the laws. Whoever, by virtue of public position under a State Government . . . denies or takes away the equal protection of the laws, violates the constitutional inhibitions; and as he acts in the name and for the State and is clothed with the States' power, his act is that of the State'."[80] (italics supplied)

Observations to the same effect in *Budhan Choudhry's Case*

7.36 In *Budhan Choudhry* v. *Bihar*[81] the question whether Article 14 could be violated by the Judiciary was raised but not decided, although the observations of Das J. would suggest that the Judiciary had to conform to Art. 14. Das J. said:

". . . It is suggested that discrimination may be brought about . . . even (by) the judiciary and the inhibition of Art. 14 extends to all actions of the State denying equal protection of the laws whether it be the action of any one of the three limbs of the State. It has, however, to be remembered that, in the language of Frankfurter J. in *Snowden* v. *Hughes*[82] 'the Constitution does not assure uniformity of decisions or immunity from merely erroneous action, whether by the Courts or the executive agencies of a State.' The judicial decision must of necessity depend on the facts and circumstances of each particular case and what may superficially appear to be an unequal application of the law may not necessarily amount to a denial of equal protection of law unless there is shown to be present in it an element of intentional and purposeful discrimination. [See *per* Stone, C.J. in *Snowden* v. *Hughes* (*supra*)]. It may be mentioned at once that in the present case there is no suggestion

---

[78] The question is fully discussed in Chapter IX.

[79] *The Constitution of the United States of America,* Analysis and Interpretation, 4th ed. (Congressional Edn.) p. 1462.

[80] *Ex p. Virginia* (1880) 100 U.S. 339, 346-47.

[81] (1955) 1 S.C.R. 1045, ('55) A.SC. 191.

[82] (1944) 321 U.S. 1, 88 L. ed. 497.

whatever that there has been at any stage any intentional or purposeful discrimination as against the appellants by the Sub-Divisional Magistrate or the District Magistrate or the section 30 Magistrate who actually tried the accused."[83]

Frankfurter J.: Judiciary subject to 14th Amendment

Das J. extracted one passage from the judgment of Frankfurter J. in *Snowden* v. *Hughes,* but there is another passage which is directly relevant:

"And if the highest Court of a State should candidly deny to one litigant a rule of law which it concededly would apply to all other litigants in similar situation, could it escape condemnation as an unjust discrimination and therefore a denial of the equal protection of the laws?"[84]

Mirajkar's Case

7.37 The question whether the judiciary was "the State" as defined by Art. 12 was raised before the Supreme Court in Art. 32 Writ petitions in *Naresh Sridhar Mirajkar* v. *Maharashtra*[85] ("*Mirajkar's Case*"). The matter arose out of a sensational libel case, *K. M. D. Thackersey* v. *R. K. Karanjia* (unreported) in the Bombay High Court in which hearings had been held in public. One Goda, who had been examined earlier, was recalled for further examination, when he applied that his evidence should not be allowed to be reported, because reports of his evidence earlier had injured him in his business. Although the trial continued to be held in public, Tarkunde J. orally directed that Goda's further evidence should not be reported. The next day, the defendant's counsel submitted that the above order ought not to have been passed, and, in any event, the judge should pass a written order. The judge adhered to his order and declined to pass a written order. A writ petition to quash the judge's order was dismissed by the Bombay High Court on the ground that a writ could not issue from a bench of the High Court to another bench, or to a single judge, of the same Court. The present petitions were filed by journalists (who were affected by the judge's order), contending that it violated their rights to the freedom of speech and expression guaranteed by Art. 19(1)(*a*), and that a writ should be issued quashing the judge's order. The petitions were heard by a bench of nine judges. Five judgments were delivered: Gajendragadkar C.J. delivered a judgment for himself, Wanchoo, Mudholkar, Sikri and Ramaswamy JJ. ("the majority judgment") dismissing the petitions; Sarkar, Shah and Bachawat JJ. each delivered separate concurring judgments dismissing the petitions. Hidayatullah J. delivered a dissenting judgment, allowing the petitions. He accurately formulated the questions for determination as follows:

Order prohibiting the publication of a witness's evidence taken in open court

Order impugned as violating fundamental rights by a petition under Art. 32

Questions for the determination of the Sup. Ct.

"(i) Can a court, which is holding a public trial from which the public is not excluded, suppress the publication of the deposition of a witness, heard not *in camera* but in open court, on the request of the witness that his business will suffer; (ii) does such an order breach (the) fundamental right of freedom of speech and expression entitling persons affected to invoke Art. 32; and (iii) if so, can this court issue a writ to a High Court?"[86]

The reader will have noticed that the question whether the judiciary was "the State" squarely arose in *Mirajkar's Case,* because only if the judiciary were "the State" could any question of enforcing the

---

[83] (1955) 1 S.C.R. *supra* at p. 1054.
[84] (1944) 321 U.S. 1, 16; 88 L. ed. 497, 507, citing *A. Baques Jr. & Sons* v. *Fort Street Union Depot Co.,* 169 U.S. 567, 42 L. ed. 853, 859.
[85] (1966) 3 S.C.R. 744, ('67) A.SC. 1.
[86] ('67) A.SC. at p. 25.

violation of fundamental rights under Art. 32 against the judiciary arise: see question (ii) above. Although this question is inextricably connected with the writ jurisdiction of the Supreme Court under Art. 32, it appears to the present writer that the question whether the judiciary is "the State" is most appropriately discussed in this Chapter in which the scope of Art. 12 is being fully considered. This is all the more so because Art. 32 (which is itself a fundamental right) shows that in our Constitution rights and remedies go together. Reverting to the questions formulated by Hidayatullah J. as will appear hereafter, the first question raises the further question whether Tarkunde J.'s order enjoined a perpetual prohibition against the publication of Goda's evidence, or a prohibition limited to the duration of the trial. The second question mentioned by Hidayatullah J. raises the wider question whether the judiciary is subject to fundamental rights. Since the majority judgment and the concurring judgments, expressly limit their decision to the violation of the fundamental rights under Art. 19(1), it will be necessary to discuss the wider question independently of the judgments.

The scheme of the present discussion

7.38 It is proposed, first, to state briefly the effect of the majority, the concurring and the dissenting judgments; secondly, to consider whether the judiciary is subject to fundamental rights; thirdly, to consider the correctness of the majority judgment and the concurring judgments that Art. 19(1)(*a*) was not violated by Tarkunde J.'s order, and finally, to consider whether a writ of *certiorari* lies from the Supreme Court to a judge or judges of the High Court whose judicial action involves a violation of fundamental rights.

Submission: the dissenting judgment has placed the correct construction on the impugned order

7.39 It is difficult to understand why the majority judgment held that Tarkunde J.'s order imposed a ban on the publication of Goda's evidence *only during the trial of the suit.* It is submitted that Hidayatullah J. was right when he said that "as the intention was to save Goda's business from harm, it is reasonable to think that the prohibition was perpetual and that is how the matter appears to have been understood . . . because no report of his deposition has since appeared in any newspaper". The majority judgment considered the authorities relating to the holding of a trial *in camera* and held that a judge had inherent jurisdiction to hold a trial *in camera* if he was satisfied that in no other way could justice be done. If a judge wrongly ordered a trial *in camera* he acted not without jurisdiction, but in the mistaken exercise of jurisdiction. On this assumption the majority held that the order was passed by Tarkunde J. acting as a judge, and just as his order would be binding between the parties and could not be questioned except on appeal so also an order made by a judge in a judicial proceeding affecting third parties, and in that sense collateral, stood in the same position. Assuming that the order incidentally affected the fundamental rights of the petitioners, that did not involve a violation of a fundamental right.[87]

Majority view: impugned order was not without jurisdiction, Art. 19 not violated

[87] Reference was made to the observations of Kania C.J. in *A. K. Gopalan* v. *The State* (1950) S.C.R. 88 at p. 105, which was followed in *Ram Singh* v. *Delhi* (1951) S.C.R. 451, 456; *Express Newspapers Pr. Ltd.* v. *Union* (1959) S.C.R. 112, 129-30, and *Atiabari Tea Co. Ltd.* v. *Assam* (1961) 1 S.C.R. 809, 864.

Art. 19: majority view—*Ujjam Bai's Case* followed. Even if Art. 19 were violated, a writ would not lie to a High Ct.

7.40 The majority judgment considered the question whether Art. 14 could be violated by a judge in his judicial capacity and said that the observations of Das J. in *Budhan Chowdhury's Case* were at most *obiter* and that a contrary view had been taken, also *obiter*, in other judgments of the Supreme Court. Having held that there was no violation of a fundamental right under Art. 19 (1) (*a*) and having limited their decision to the alleged violation of that Article, the majority proceeded to decide whether under Art. 32 a writ of *certiorari* lay against the High Court and held that it did not. The majority referred to the decision in *Ujjam Bai* v. *U.P.*[88] to show that the wrong action of a judicial or quasi-judicial tribunal in the exercise of admitted jurisdiction, did not violate fundamental rights. Assuming that a fundamental right had been violated, the majority judgment considered whether a writ of *certiorari* under Art. 32 was available against the High Court. The discussion on *certiorari* is not very satisfactory and that part of the judgment will be considered more fully later. Sarkar J. agreed with the majority in holding that the court had inherent jurisdiction to hear a matter *in camera* and that an erroneous exercise of that power did not violate fundamental rights and he treated *Ujjam Bai's Case* as conclusive on that point. He held that the order of Tarkunde J. indirectly affected the fundamental right under Art. 19 (1) (*a*), but that right was subject to reasonable restrictions, and the power to prohibit publication must be treated as a reasonable restriction. He referred to *R.* v. *Chancellor of St. Edmundsbury and Ipswich Diocese Ex p. White*[89] as showing that an inferior court was conceived in English law in that context as a court of limited jurisdiction. He confessed that the question was somewhat hazy, but on the whole he also held, *obiter*, that a writ did not lie to the High Court. Shah J. took the same view as the majority, but he made two striking reservations. He said that the court was only concerned with the fundamental rights under Art. 19, which rights were subject to reasonable restrictions. However, the freedoms declared by Arts. 20, 21 and 22 were in terms absolute and were not liable to be tested on the touchstone of reasonableness,[90] and considerations relevant to those Articles would not be relevant to Art. 19. Secondly,

Sarkar J.

Shah J.: the two reservations made by him

> ". . . if this Court possesses authority to issue a writ in respect of an adjudication by a Court, the circumstance that the High Court has also power to issue a writ of *certiorari* which may be issued by this Court in enforcement of a fundamental right, whereas the Subordinate Courts have not, will not warrant the distinction sought to be made on behalf of the respondents. I am therefore unable to agree that in the matter of issue of a writ of *certiorari* against the order of any Court, a distinction may be made between the order of the District Court or the Subordinate Court and an order of the High Court."[91]

Bachawat J.

Bachawat J. took the same view as the majority, but he rightly did not deal with the question whether the Supreme Court could issue a writ against the High Court.

---

[88] (1963) 1 S.C.R. 778, ('62) A.SC. 1621.
[89] (1947) 1 K.B. 263.
[90] ('67) A.SC. 1, 38.
[91] ('67) A.SC. *supra* at p. 37.

7.41 Hidayatullah J. held that the order of Tarkunde J. enjoined a perpetual prohibition and that the order was without jurisdiction. If there was one point on which the law lords were agreed in *Scott* v. *Scott*[92] it was that there was no jurisdiction to enjoin a perpetual prohibition of the evidence given *in camera* except in cases not material to the present inquiry.[93] Secondly, even if there was jurisdiction to hold a proceeding *in camera,* the order was made when the court was not sitting *in camera* and a judge had no jurisdiction at all to prohibit the publication of evidence when the hearing was not *in camera.* The right of publication flowed from the fact that such publication merely enlarged the area of the court and communicated to all that which all had the right to know.[94] He held that the judiciary was subject to fundamental rights and he considered several other Articles in Part III in order better to understand the alleged violation of Art. 19(1). He held that as the order was without jurisdiction, the fundamental right to the freedom of speech was violated. Therefore, it became directly necessary for him to decide whether a writ lay to the High Court under Art. 32, and on a careful review of the authorities and of the language of Arts. 32 and 226, he held that such a writ lay. This part of the judgment will be considered more fully later.

Dissenting judgment of Hidayatullah J.: (i) impugned order enjoined a perpetual prohibition and was without jurisdiction

(ii) the judiciary was subject to fundamental rights, and Tarkunde J.'s order had violated Art. 19

(iii) and a writ lay to quash the order

7.42 We must now consider whether the judiciary is subject to fundamental rights, independently of the judgment in *Mirajkar's Case.* Article 12, which defines "the State" for the purposes of Part III, does not expressly exclude the judiciary, and though Art. 12 does not expressly include the judiciary, it is submitted that the judiciary, with the legislature and the executive, is included in the ordinary meaning of a "State" as one of the three great departments of a State; and further, that the ordinary meaning is not outside the inclusive definition of "the State" given in Art. 12. This conclusion is supported by Art. 13 which declares that any law, rule, regulation and the like, which violates fundamental rights, is void. The judiciary in India has rule-making powers and if it were not "the State" for the

Is the judiciary subject to fundamental rights? Art. 12: "the State" includes the Judiciary

Art. 13: rules of court violating fundamental rights are void

---

[92] (1913) A.C. 417.

[93] "My Lords, as to the injunction of perpetual secrecy, there is not a judgment of authority to justify it. The supposed analogy of trade secrets or private correspondence is no analogy at all": *per* Lord Halsbury, p. 433; "But to say that all subsequent publication can be forbidden and every one can be ordained to keep perpetual silence as to what passed at the trial is far in excess of the jurisdiction and is indeed an unwarrantable interference with the rights of the subject. It is not that a court ought to refrain from exercising its power in such a way. *It is that the court does not possess such power*": *per* Earl Loreburn, p. 448 (italics supplied); "I am of opinion that the order to hear this case in camera was beyond the power of the judge to pronounce. I am further of opinion that, even on the assumption that such an order had been within his power, it was beyond his power to impose a suppression of all reports of what passed at the trial after the trial had come to an end. . . . What has happened is a usurpation — a usurpation which could not have been allowed even as a prerogative of the Crown, and most certainly must be denied to the judges of the land. To remit the maintenance of constitutional right to the region of judicial discretion is to shift the foundations of freedom from the rock to the sand": *per* Lord Shaw, pp. 476-7. In *McPherson* v. *McPherson* (1936) A.C. 177 at 205. the Privy Council referred to *Scott* v. *Scott* and said that in the opinion of the House of Lords "the order directing the proceedings of the trial to be held in camera was so completely beyond the powers of the court that although obtained at the instance of the appellant herself, it might be disobeyed by her with impunity."

[94] *McDougall* v. *Knight* (1889) 14 App. Cas. 194.

purposes of Part III (fundamental rights), rules made by the courts could not be impugned as violating fundamental rights. But the Supreme Court has struck down a rule made by it as violating fundamental rights.[95] Again, the Chief Justice of a High Court has the power to appoint officers of the High Court and if an appointment discriminates against other applicants on the ground of race, religion, caste or sex it would be void as violating Art. 16. It may however be said that these examples only establish that the judiciary, when exercising legislative power, as in making rules, or executive power, as in making appointments to public offices, is subject to fundamental rights and those examples do not establish that a judge, *acting as a judge,* is subject to fundamental rights in the sense that he can be called to account for a violation of fundamental rights. It is submitted that the referring judgment of Venkatarama Aiyar J. in *Ujjam Bai's Case*[96] and the dissenting judgment of Rajagopala Ayyangar J. in the same case[97] show that there is intrinsic evidence in Art. 32 that the judiciary *in its judicial capacity* is subject to fundamental rights. Article 32 is by its terms limited to the enforcement of fundamental rights and the right to apply to the Supreme Court for the writs mentioned in Art. 32 is itself a fundamental right. A writ of *certiorari* undoubtedly lies to a court *stricto sensu,* though it also lies to bodies or authorities which are not courts *stricto sensu* but are under an obligation to act judicially or quasi-judicially. Therefore if a writ of *certiorari* lies under Art. 32 for the enforcement of fundamental rights, *it must follow that there are some fundamental rights which can be violated by a judge acting judicially in a court stricto sensu.* The referring judgment of Venkatarama Aiyar J. records that it was conceded[98], and it is submitted rightly, that there were certain Articles of the Constitution specifically directed to the judiciary, *e.g.,* Art. 20 and that a violation by a court of Art. 20 would attract the writ of *certiorari* under Art. 32.

Art. 16 applies to the Chief Justice of a High Court

Judicial action and fundamental rights

Inclusion in Art. 32 of writs of prohibition and *certiorari* show that judicial action can violate fundamental rights

Certain Articles in Part III are specially directed to the judiciary *e.g.* Art. 20

The judiciary wields the judicial power of the State

7.43 Again, the judiciary wields the judicial power of the State, and Art. 144 emphasises the fact that judgments would be worth little if the full authority of the State were not exerted to give effect to them.

7.44 We have seen that in the United States it is well settled that the judiciary is within the prohibition of the 14th Amendment. As Art. 14 corresponds to the 14th Amendment, there is no reason why the cogent judgments of the U.S. Supreme Court should not apply equally to the judiciary in India. This is all the more so, in view of the fact mentioned earlier that the inclusion of the writ of *certiorari* in Art. 32 (which is itself a fundamental right) clearly shows that some fundamental rights can be violated by Courts *stricto sensu.* It may be that the violation of Art. 14 by a judge may

---

[95] *Premchand Garg* v. *Excise Commr., U.P., Allahabad* (1963) Supp. (1) S.C.R. 885, ('63) A.SC. 996, dist. in *Lala Ram* v. *Supreme Court of India* (1967) 2 S.C.R. 14, ('67) A.SC. 847 [*held,* that whereas a rule requiring security for costs in a petition under Art. 32 would violate a fundamental right and was therefore void, the same could not be said of an application for review under O. 40, r. 2 of the Supreme Court Rules, 1966, for such an application was not one for the enforcement of fundamental rights. Accordingly, O. 42, r. 2(2) was valid].

[96] (1963) 1 S.C.R. 778, 818-9, ('62) A.SC. 1621.

[97] (1963) 1 S.C.R. *supra* at pp. 969-70. [98] ibid. pp. 819-20.

be difficult to prove, but the numerous decisions in the United States show that if proved "it cannot escape condemnation as an unjust discrimination". There is nothing to show that the framers of our Constitution, when they adopted the very words of the 14th Amendment "the State shall not deny to any person . . . the equal protection of the laws" intended to exempt the judiciary in India from a prohibition to which the judiciary in the United States was subject. On the contrary, in conferring on the Supreme Court the power to issue the writ of *certiorari* for the enforcement of fundamental rights, the framers emphasised the fact that judicial acts violating fundamental rights must be quashed by *certiorari* exactly as legislative and executive acts violating fundamental rights would be struck down by a declaration of invalidity accompanied by an appropriate writ issued under Art. 32.

Submission: Art. 32 emphasises the fact that the judiciary is subject to fundamental rights

7.45 It is difficult to understand why the possibility of a judge violating the prohibition of Art. 14 should be brushed aside by our Supreme Court as fanciful speculation — eminent judges in the United States have not considered the violation by the judiciary of the equality clause of the 14th Amendment to be fanciful, and have repeatedly asserted that the equality clause binds the judiciary as it binds the legislature and the executive. Violation of Art. 14 by a judge may be difficult to prove, but if proved it must be condemned under Art. 32. If, for instance, a judge denied discretionary orders of a particular kind to members of one community, whilst granting them under similar circumstances to members of another community, it is difficult to see how the Supreme Court could escape its duty of striking down such action as violative of fundamental rights. To suggest that the aggrieved person should exhaust the remedies of a first appeal, a second appeal and an appeal to the Supreme Court, is to suggest that he is to be deprived of his fundamental right under Art. 32 of having a speedy and effective remedy.

No reason for treating judicial violation of Art. 14 as fanciful speculation

The majority view involves an abdication by the Sup. Ct. of its duty to enforce fundamental rights under Art. 14

7.46 The question of the violation of the fundamental rights under Art. 19 will be considered later in connection with *Mirajkar's Case*. But it is submitted that the provisions of Art. 15 (2) (*b*) apply to a judge sitting as a judge and regulating the procedure of his court. A judge who violates Art. 17 by refusing to an "untouchable", entry to a court where he acts as a judge would be violating a fundamental right. Again, a judge who compels a person accused of an offence to answer incriminating questions, violates Art. 20 (3), and there is no reason why the accused should go through the whole trial and then resort to an appeal to secure redress, instead of invoking Art. 32. Subject to the provisions of Art. 22 (3), Art. 22 (1) confers on a person accused of an offence the right to be defended by a legal practitioner of his choice. If that right is denied to him by a judge, it is submitted that a fundamental right is violated and the accused is not obliged to go through a trial by engaging another legal practitioner and making the violation of his right a ground of appeal, instead of applying to the Supreme Court under Art. 32. It is submitted that Hidayatullah J. was right when he held that a breach by a judge of the provisions of several Articles relating to fundamental rights, could not be excluded from the writ jurisdiction of the Supreme Court, and the reservation made by Shah J. to which we have referred earlier, suggests, though it does not decide, that

Submission: Arts. 15(2) (*b*), 17, 20(3) and 22(1) can be violated by a judge acting as a judge

Hidayatullah J.'s view of Arts. 20 to 22 is correct. *Mirajkar's Case* was followed in *S. N. Koya* v. *L.M. & A. Islands*.[99]

If the construction put by the majority on the impugned order is correct, Art. 19 was not violated

7.47 We must now consider whether the majority judgment and the other concurring judgments were right in holding that the order of Tarkunde J. did not violate the fundamental rights of the petitioners under Art. 19 (1) (*a*). The answer to this question depends upon the construction of that order. If Tarkunde J. had jurisdiction to pass the order, then it would be correct to say that no matter how grievously he erred in the exercise of his jurisdiction, the order did not violate the fundamental right to the freedom of speech and expression which includes the freedom of communication and the freedom of the press. For reasons already given[1] it is submitted that Hidayatullah J. was right when he held that the order contained a perpetual prohibition against publication of the evidence and the order was beyond the jurisdiction of Tarkunde J., and using the language of the Privy Council in *McPherson* v. *McPherson*,[2] we may say that it was an order that could be disobeyed with impunity. If this is the correct view, it is submitted that Hidayatullah J. rightly held that it violated the petitioner's freedom of speech and expression guaranteed by Art. 19 (1) (*a*).[3] The reference in the majority judgment, and in the concurring judgments, to the test of direct and incidental violation is inapplicable, for whatever may be the reason why Tarkunde J. made the order, an order prohibiting publication of evidence directly violates the freedom of the press.[4]

Submission: but the construction put by the majority is not correct and the order violated Art. 19(1)(*a*) as held by Hidayatullah J.

Does a writ lie from the Sup. Ct. to the High Cts.? Majority view that it does not, is *obiter*. The *obiter* suffers from the infirmity that Arts. in Part III addressed to the judiciary were not considered

7.48 Can the Supreme Court issue a writ under Art. 32 against the High Court for violation of fundamental rights? The majority view that a writ did not lie, is clearly *obiter* because the point did not call for decision on the finding that fundamental rights were not violated. But apart from being *obiter*, these observations are unfortunate, because, the majority judgment and the concurring judgments expressly confined themselves to the violation of Art. 19 and did not consider whether it could ever have been intended that fundamental rights directed to the judiciary could be set at nought by the judiciary and the party affected by such violation should be left to the expensive procedure and hazard of successive appeals or be driven to appeal to the *discretionary* power of the Supreme Court under Art. 136. A rule of the Supreme Court demanding an excessive deposit before admitting a writ petition was struck down as fettering a fundamental right; a rule providing for even a larger security would not be vulnerable in an appeal from a suit or other proceeding. It is submitted that unless the High Courts were clearly excluded from the

---

99 ('67) A.Ker. 259.

1 See para 7.40.

2 (1936) A.C. 177.

3 Assuming that there was any doubt on the principles involved in holding a trial *in camera*, the following illustration brings out the real constitutional position: assume that the Supreme Court laid down that it was beyond the jurisdiction of any judge to enjoin a perpetual prohibition in respect of evidence taken *in camera*, and a High Court judge thereafter imposed such perpetual prohibition notwithstanding that judgment, has he, or has he not, violated the fundamental right guaranteed under Art. 19(1)(*a*)? It is submitted that there can be only one answer, and that is that he has clearly violated the fundamental right.

4 The argument that the ban on slaughter of cattle was not directed to any "business" but was meant to protect cattle was rejected by the Supreme Court which said that whatever may be the object of the law, its effect on business was direct and immediate.

writ jurisdiction of the Supreme Court, the provisions of Arts. 14, 20, 21 and 22 show that an appropriate writ would be available against the action of a judge who violated the rights contained in those Articles. We have said that the discussion in the majority and the other concurring judgments about the nature of the writ jurisdiction is not satisfactory. It is not clear whether the majority judgment purported to propound a theory of its own as regards the writ of *certiorari*, or whether it purported to follow the English authorities which it cited "incidentally", to show that a writ of *certiorari* would not lie from the court of Queen's Bench to an inferior court of civil jurisdiction. The majority judgment cited the following observations from *Halsbury*:[5]

The majority view that *certiorari* does not lie in England to an inferior court, is incorrect

"In the case of judgments of inferior courts of civil jurisdiction, it has been suggested that *certiorari* might be granted to quash them for want of jurisdiction[6] inasmuch as an error did not lie upon that ground. But there appears to be no reported case in which the judgment of an inferior court of civil jurisdiction has been quashed on *certiorari*, either for want of jurisdiction, or on any other ground." . . . The court said: "These observations would indicate that in England the judicial orders passed by civil courts of plenary jurisdiction in or in relation to matters brought before them are not held to be amenable to the jurisdiction to issue writs of *certiorari*."[7]

7.49 Unfortunately the attention of the court was not called to the Supplement to *Halsbury* (1965) which showed that the statement quoted above was not correct and that a writ to quash the decision of an inferior court did lie. In any event, the question is put beyond doubt by *R.* v. *Worthington Evans*,[8] *Kemp* v. *Balne*,[9] *Colonial Bank of Australasia* v. *William*,[10] and *R.* v. *Hurst*.[11] It is submitted that on principle, a writ of prohibition or *certiorari* must lie from a superior to an inferior court, and it could not be disputed in England that a county court is inferior to the High Court of Justice except where by statute it exercises the powers of the High Court.[12] In *P. V. Somaraju* v. *Munsiff Magistrate, Bhimavaram*[13] after referring to the English decisions cited above, but without reference to *Mirajkar's Case*, it was held that a writ of *certiorari* lies to subordinate civil courts which are inferior courts for the purpose of Art. 226.[14] Nor is it relevant to consider whether the court is a court of record or not,

as is shown by the Supplement to *Halsbury* (1965) and by decided cases

The distinction between a court of record and a court not of record is irrelevant, as is

[5] *Halsbury*, Vol. 11, pp. 129-30.

[6] *Kemp* v. *Balne* (1844) 1 Dow. & L. 885, 887.

[7] ('67) A.SC. 1, 18.

[8] (1959) 2 Q.B. 145 ("We are satisfied that in a proper case this court has power by *certiorari* to bring up and quash the order of a county court judge made without jurisdiction in that behalf").

[9] (1844) 1 Dow. & L. 885.

[10] (1874) 5 P.C. 417.

[11] (1960) 2 Q.B. 133 [The Queen's Bench issued a writ of *certiorari* to quash an order of the county court and it was issued notwithstanding the provisions of the County Courts Act, 1959, which provided only for a limited removal on matters by *certiorari* to the High Court. Lord Parker C.J. said: "I am quite satisfied that *certiorari* will lie against a county court judge if he has acted without jurisdiction, notwithstanding the provisions of the County Courts Act, 1959, to which I have referred." (ibid. p. 143). See also *de Smith*, p. 323: "'*No certiorari' clauses*. . . . It has been held that *certiorari* would issue notwithstanding the presence of words taking away the right to apply for it . . . if the inferior tribunal . . . lacked or exceeded jurisdiction . . ." citing, *inter alia*: *R.* v. *Hurst* and *R.* v. *Worthington Evans* in support.]

[12] ('67) A.SC. 1, 34.

[13] ('68) A.A.P. 22.

[14] ibid. p. 27 (The court observed that whatever may be the position in England where a writ of *certiorari* could be taken away by statute, in India, the power to issue writs conferred on the High Courts could not be so taken away, and a writ of *certiorari* lay against inferior courts.)

the distinction between superior and inferior courts for purposes other than the issue of *certiorari*

because the county courts in England are by statute constituted courts of record[15] and as has been said above, writs of *certiorari* lie to them. Again, the division of courts into superior and inferior courts for other purposes is not relevant to the issue of the writ of *certiorari* or prohibition. One of the lines dividing superior courts from inferior courts is that nothing is outside the jurisdiction of a superior court unless it is shown to be so, and nothing is within the jurisdiction of an inferior court unless it clearly so appears on the face of the proceedings. But this definition is irrelevant to the issue of a writ of prohibition[16] and, it is submitted, to a writ of *certiorari.* For, according to this definition, the eccleciastical courts in England and the Judicial Committee of the Privy Council when hearing eccleciastical appeals are superior courts, yet a writ of prohibition lies to them; and it is settled law that a writ of prohibition issues from a superior to an inferior court, that is to say, for the purpose of issuing the writ. The judgment of Goddard C.J. in *R.* v. *Chancellor of St. Edmundsbury, etc.*[17] to the effect that because a writ of prohibition lay to the eccleciastical courts it did not follow that they were inferior courts has been shown by Mr. D. M. Gordon[18] to be opposed to the total volume of authority[19] and to the judgments of Viscount Cave L.C., Lords Atkinson and Shaw in *Re Clifford and O'Sullivan*[20] approving the following definition of prohibition from *Short and Mellor*: "A judicial writ issuing out of a court of superior jurisdiction and directed to an inferior court for the purpose of preventing the inferior court from usurping jurisdiction. . . ." It is also opposed to the observations of Atkin L.J. in *R.* v. *Electricity Commissioners*:[21] "I can see no difference in principle between *certiorari* and prohibition except that the latter may be invoked at an earlier stage." Again, "apart from all authority, what possible explanation can be suggested of one court's ability to command another, than that the latter is subordinate? The wording of the writ of prohibition is 'We therefore, prohibit you. . . .' How can it be argued that this is the sort of language used between equals?"[22] It is submitted therefore that the fact that the court is a superior court for the purposes of assuming that everything is within its jurisdiction until it is shown to be otherwise, is not relevant to the question whether a writ of prohibition or *certiorari* lies.

A criticism of *R.* v. *Chancellor of St. Edmundsbury*

7.50 It is submitted that the correct question to ask is whether the High Courts are inferior courts *vis-a-vis* the Supreme Court for the purpose of issuing writs of *certiorari* and other appropriate writs under Art. 32. That the Supreme Court has the undoubted power to issue writs of *certiorari* under Art. 32 cannot be disputed, and as that power is limited to issuing writs for the purpose of enforcement of fundamental rights (which is itself a guaranteed fundamental right), the writ must lie to every court subordinate to the Supreme

15 *Halsbury*, Vol. 9, p. 346, and *f.n.* (i).

16 ibid. p. 348.

17 (1947) 1 K.B. 263, 272-3.

18 *Certiorari to an Ecclesiastical Court*, (1947) 63 L.Q.R. 208.

19 3 Bl. Comm. 112; Sellon's *King's Bench Practice*, 2nd ed., Vol. 2, p. 308; Holdsworth, *History of English Law*, Vol. 1, p. 229; Short and Mellor, *Crown Office Practice*, 2nd ed., p. 258; *Halsbury*, 2nd ed., Vol. 9, p. 30.

20 (1921) 2 A.C. 570 at 582, 585.

21 (1924) 1 K.B. 171, 201.

22 (1947) 63 L.Q.R. *supra* at p. 212.

Court whose action violates a fundamental right and is therefore capable of correction by the Supreme Court. Hidayatullah J. has correctly considered the scheme of Articles 32 and 226 and the effect of his careful review may be stated thus: the Supreme Court has been given the right to issue these writs for the protection of fundamental rights, and there is no express exclusion to the exercise of that power, it must follow therefore that whenever there is a violation of fundamental rights by a court or judicial tribunal a writ must *prima facie* lie. This conclusion is strengthened by the provision of Art. 226. If the power to issue writs were conferred on the Supreme Court alone it would be difficult for it to protect single-handed the people from the violation of their fundamental rights; consequently, power to issue writs was also given to all the High Courts in India. However, Art. 226(2) contained an express provision that nothing contained in Art. 226(1) should derogate from the power of the Supreme Court to issue writs, which must mean that the grant of this power to the High Courts did not in any way prevent the Supreme Court from issuing writs. This express exclusion supported the conclusion that the mere fact that the High Courts had power to issue writs of *certiorari* was not to affect the power of the Supreme Court to issue such writs for the purpose of enforcing fundamental rights. That the Supreme Court and the High Courts are not co-ordinate courts is clear from the fact that an appeal in all civil and criminal matters lies to the Supreme Court and even where no appeals are provided, the Supreme Court has power under Art. 136 to entertain an appeal from any determination by the High Courts *at any stage*.

The view of Hidayatullah J. on the scheme of Arts. 32 and 226: a writ lies from the Sup. Ct. to the High Cts. under Art. 32

7.51 The reference made in the majority judgment[23] to *Daryao* v. *U.P.*[24] which applied the doctrine of *res judicata* to petitions under Art. 32 is based on a misconception. *Mirajkar's Case* denies to a person the right to obtain an appropriate writ for the violation of his fundamental rights by a judge of the High Court in his judicial capacity. *Daryao's Case* does not deny the right of a person, whose fundamental rights are violated, to apply for an appropriate writ for their enforcement. It merely recognises the fact that the aggrieved person has two rights available to him: (i) a guaranteed fundamental right to apply to the Supreme Court for an appropriate writ; (ii) a right, which is not a fundamental right, to apply to a High Court also, for an appropriate writ. The choice lies with him which right he will exercise. If he exercises the right to approach the High Court, and the High Court *goes into the merits of his claim*, and dismisses it, the result is that there is a finding of the court against him that his fundamental rights have not been violated. That decision, subject to appeal, is *res judicata* between him and the other party. If thereafter he cannot apply under Art. 32, it is because by his own action he has obtained a decision which cannot be displaced till it is reversed in appeal. If the Supreme Court were to hear the same matter under Art. 32 and it arrived at a contrary view, there would be two conflicting decisions, each equally binding on the parties, which would be absurd. *Daryao's Case*

Daryao's Case has no resemblance to the denial of a fundamental right in *Mirajkar's Case*

---

[23] ('67) A.SC. 1, 17.
[24] (1962) 1 S.C.R. 574, ('61) A.SC. 1457.

merely holds that an approach to the High Court under Art. 226 has certain legal consequences which cannot be ignored by entertaining an independent petition under Art. 32 in respect of the same matter. The person whose fundamental rights have been violated can have no grievance if he himself voluntarily resorted to Art. 226 and not to Art. 32. Nor can he rationally contend that the determination of the High Court should be treated as though it was of no effect.

Submission: the dissenting judgment of Hidayatullah J. is correct

7.52 It is submitted that the dissenting judgment of Hidayatullah J. is correct on all the three questions raised in the petitions. It is to be hoped that the large number of *obiter dicta* in *Mirajkar's Case* will hereafter be treated as such by the Supreme Court and rejected, or will be "strictly confined to the facts of that case."

CHAPTER VIII

VIOLATION OF FUNDAMENTAL RIGHTS: ART. 13

"LAW" AND FUNDAMENTAL RIGHTS

8.1 Article 13 has been considered in several cases and has been the subject of conflicting decisions of our Supreme Court. The U.S. Constitution contains no express provision that a law contravening the Constitution is *pro tanto* void. But that position was established by Marshall C.J. in *Marbury* v. *Madison*.[1] He said that those who framed written constitutions contemplated them as forming the fundamental and paramount law of the nation, and the theory of every such government must be that an act of the legislature repugnant to the Constitution was void. The particular phraseology of the U.S. Constitution confirmed and strengthened the principle that a law repugnant to the Constitution was void. The principle thus established was familiar to the American colonists, for the colonial courts, and on appeal, the Privy Council in England, had the power to declare legislative acts void if in conflict with Colonial Charters. It is not surprising, therefore, that Kania C.J. said that

Art. 13 embodies the doctrine of *ultra vires*

"The inclusion of article 13(1) and (2) . . . appears to be a matter of abundant caution. Even in their absence, if any of the fundamental rights was infringed by any legislative enactment, the Court has always the power to declare the enactment, to the extent it transgresses the limits, invalid."[2]

It is submitted that this view is clearly right as to the express declaration of invalidity contained in those sub-articles.

8.2 However, before considering the conflicting decisions, it is necessary to consider the meaning of "law" and "law in force." Art. 13(3) (*a*) and (*b*) provide:

Definitions: "law", "law in force"

"13. (3) (*a*) 'law' includes any Ordinance, order, bye-law, rule, regulation, notification, custom or usage having in the territory of India the force of law; (*b*) 'laws in force' includes laws passed or made by a Legislature or other competent authority in the territory of India before the commencement of this Constitution and not previously repealed, notwithstanding that any such law or any part thereof may not be then in operation either at all or in particular areas."

Art. 13(3) (*a*) defines "law" very widely by an inclusive definition. It does not expressly include a law enacted by the legislature, for such an enactment is obviously law. The definition of law includes: (i) an Ordinance, because it is made in the exercise of the legislative powers of the *executive*; (ii) an order, bye-law, rule, regulation and notification having the force of law because *ordinarily* they fall in the category of subordinate delegated legislation and are not enacted by the legislature; (iii) custom or usage having the force of law because they are not enacted law at all. This extended definition appears to have been given to "law" in order to forestall a possible contention that law can only mean law enacted

---

[1] (1803) 1 Cranch 137, 177-79, 2 L. ed. 60.
[2] *A. K. Gopalan* v. *State* (1950) S.C.R. 88, 100, ('50) A.SC. 27.

by the legislature. In view of this, the omission of an amendment of the Constitution from Art. 13(3)(*a*) is significant.[3]

and "existing law"

8.3 The expression "law in force" is used in Art. 13(1) and in Art. 372 and is defined in identical terms by Art. 13(3)(*b*) and Art. 372, Expl. 1. Art. 366, which contains "definitions", does not define "law in force" but defines "existing law" to mean: "any law, ordinance, order, bye-law, rule or regulation passed or made before the commencement of this Constitution by any Legislature, authority or person having power to make such a law, ordinance, order, bye-law, rule or regulation": Art. 366(10). The expression "existing law" is used, for example, in Art. 19(2) to (6) and the difference in the definition of "existing law" and "law in force" has been relied upon to support the argument that "existing law" is narrower than "law in force", for, whereas by express definition "law in force" includes a law even if it is not in operation at all, or not in operation in a particular area, a law cannot be said to exist if it is not in operation. The argument was rejected in *Bombay* v. *Heman Alreja*,[4] the Court holding that notwithstanding the difference of language, the two expressions meant the same thing. In *Edward Mills Co. Ltd.* v. *Ajmer*[5] the Supreme Court held that there was no material difference between the two expressions "existing law" and "law in force". It is submitted that the conclusion is correct, and the following historical account given by Chagla C.J. in *Alreja's Case* supports that conclusion.

"law in force" and "existing law" mean the same thing

Legislative history: ss. 292 and 293, G.I. Act, 35

Sections 292 and 293 of the G.I. Act, 35 (which correspond to Art. 372), used the expression "law in force", but the marginal note to s. 292 was "existing law of India to continue in force", and s. 293 was "adaptation of existing Indian laws etc." Before the G.I. Act, 35, came into force on April 1, 1937, it was realised that the use of the expression "law in force" might create difficulties in carrying out the intention of the British Parliament. For, though "existing law" would include all law whether it was in actual operation or was capable of being brought into operation under the powers conferred by such law, "law in force" might be taken to mean only that part of the law which was actually in operation and not that part which was capable of being brought into operation, for, a law cannot be said to be *in force* when it is not brought into operation at all. Realising this difficulty, the British Parliament enacted on February 18, 1937, the India and Burma (Existing Laws) Act, 1937, being an Act "to explain and amend ss. 292 and 293 of the G.I. Act, Act, 35".[6]

amended and explained by the India and Burma (Existing Laws) Act, 1937

---

[3] See *Kesavananda* v. *Kerala* (1973) Supp. S.C.R. 1, ('73) A.SC. 1461 at p. 1800 where Palekar J. has substantially taken the view expressed above. See also p. 1997 where much the same view is expressed by Dwivedi J.

[4] ('52) A.B. 16, 53 Bom.L.R. 837.

[5] (1955) 1 S.C.R. 735, ('55) A.SC. 25.

[6] S. 1 of that Act was as follows: "1. (1) For the purpose of sections 292 and 293 of the Government of India Act, 1935, which provide for the existing laws of British India to continue in force therein after the date of the commencement of Part III of the said Act, subject to the power of His Majesty in Council to make such adaptations and modifications in any such law as appear to His Majesty to be necessary or expedient for bringing the provisions of the law into accord with the provisions of the said Act,—

(i) a law passed or made before the said date by a Legislature or other competent Authority in British India, and not previously repealed, is, for the removal of doubts, hereby declared to be a law in force immediately before that date, not-

Thus, the British Parliament was not content to leave ss. 292 and 293 to be interpreted in the light of the marginal notes which spoke of "existing law", but indicated in the body of the amending Act itself, and in its title, that those sections dealt with "existing law". In view of this history, the British Parliament did not repeat the mistake when it enacted s. 18, Indian Independence Act, 1947. That section made "provisions as to existing law" and sub-clause (3) provided: "Save as otherwise expressly provided in this Act, the law of British India and the several parts thereof *existing immediately before the appointed day shall*, so far as applicable and with the necessary adaptations continue as the law of each of the new Dominions and the several parts thereof . . ." (italics supplied). This history of English Parliamentary legislation was overlooked, and the phraseology of ss. 292 and 293, as amended in 1937, and the marginal notes thereto, were stereotyped in Art. 372 and the explanation to that Article was also used in Art. 13 (3) (*b*). It is submitted that the above legislative history clearly shows that the expression "law in force" was used in the previous Constitution Acts to mean "existing law", and is used in the same sense in our Constitution.

S. 18, Indian Independence Act, 1947, mentioned only "existing law"

Art. 372 reproduces ss. 292 and 293, G.I. Act, 35

8.4 It may be said at the outset that in *Sankari Prasad Singh Deo* v. *Union*[7] the Supreme Court unanimously held that an amendment of the Constitution under Art. 368 was not "law" within the meaning of Art. 13 (3) (*a*). The Court distinguished between a law made in the exercise of *legislative* power and a law made in the exercise of *constituent* power and held that Art. 13 (3) (*a*) applied only to a law made in the exercise of legislative power. This distinction was affirmed by a majority of 3 to 2 in *Sajjan Singh* v. *Rajasthan*,[8] Hidayatullah and Mudholkar JJ. observing that they wished to consider the matter further before accepting it. These cases were overruled in *I. C. Golak Nath* v. *Punjab*[9]; but *Golak Nath's Case* was decisively overruled in *Kesavananda* v. *Kerala*[10] and the view that "law" did not include an amendment of the Constitution was reaffirmed. However, the matter was set at rest by the Constitution (24th Amendment) Act, 1972, which inserted a new sub-Art. (4) in Art. 13 which expressly excluded an amendment of the Constitution from Art. 13.

Amendment of the Constitution is not "Law" within Art. 13(3): *Sankari Prasad's Case* and *Sajjan Singh's Case*

8.5 It has been held that in Art. 13 "law" includes custom or usage having the force of law. Accordingly, in a number of cases, customary laws of pre-emption have been held void as violating Art.

"Law" includes custom and usage

---

withstanding that it, or parts of it, may not then be in operation, either at all or in particular areas;

(ii) any such law which immediately before the said date has extra-territorial effect as well as effect in British India shall, subject to any such adaptations and modifications as aforesaid, continue to have extra-territorial effect;

(iii) the power of His Majesty in Council to make in an existing Indian law such adaptations and modifications as aforesaid shall be deemed to include power to declare any such law, or any part thereof, to be repealed, if it appears to His Majesty in Council that its continuance is unnecessary or inexpedient in view of the provisions of the said Act;

(iv) nothing in the said sections shall be construed as continuing any temporary Act in force beyond the date fixed for its expiration."

[7] (1952) S.C.R. 89, ('51) A.SC. 458.
[8] (1965) 1 S.C.R. 933, ('65) A.SC. 845.
[9] (1967) S.C.R. 762, ('67) A.SC. 1653.
[10] (1973) Supp. S.C.R. 1, ('73) A.SC. 1461.

19(1)(*f*).[11] Again, in *Dasaratha Rama Rao* v. *A.P.*[12] it was held that even if there was a custom which had been recognized by law with regard to hereditary village officers, that custom had to yield to a fundamental right. In *Baijnath* v. *Ram Nath*[13] it was held that assuming that there was a custom under which hereditary *yogis* could force their ministrations on their *yajmans*, such a custom would be void as violating Art.25.

and also a notification

8.6 Article 13(3) expressly refers to a notification. In *Madhubhai Amathalal Gandhi* v. *Union*[14] the Supreme Court held that if an Act was a self-contained one, and the notification issued under it only re-stated the provisions of the Act, the notification could not be questioned as violating fundamental rights if the validity of the Act was admitted. If, however, an Act conferred power on the State in general terms and the notification issued under the Act infringed fundamental rights, the notification could be impugned as violating fundamental rights since a notification issued under an Act was law.[15] In *Narayanappa* v. *Mysore*[16] the Supreme Court held that a scheme framed under Chapter IVA, Motor Vehicles Act, was "law" within the meaning of Art. 19(6) read with Art. 13(3)(*a*).[17] In *Edward Mills Co. Ltd.* v. *Ajmer*,[18] it was held that the "order" which was included in the definition of "law" had to be of a legislative and not of an executive character, but that the Order made by the Governor-General under s. 93(3), G. I. Act, 35, was not a mere executive order, and was "law".

"Order" in Art. 13(3)(*a*) must be of a legislative character

The nature of an absolute Ruler's Orders

8.7 The nature of orders issued by an absolute Ruler has been considered in several cases. First, in *Ameerunnissa Begum* v. *Mahaboob Begum*[19] and then in *Director of Endowments, Hyderabad* v. *Akram Ali*[20] it was held that the *firman* of the Nizam, an absolute Ruler, had the force of law; Bose J. observing in *Akram Ali's Case* that since the Nizam's word was law in Hyderabad, it did not matter whether his action in issuing the *firman* was called legislation, or executive action, or judicial determination, since there was no clear cut dividing line between the various functions of an absolute Ruler whose will was law.[21] In these two cases it does not appear to have been argued that a useful distinction could be made between the legislative action of the Nizam and his executive action in entering into an agreement or in making a grant.[22] However, in *Madhaorao Phalke* v. *M.P.*[23] Gajendragadkar J. did consider the question whether the relevant *Kalambandhis* issued by the Ruler of Gwalior amounted to existing law within the meaning of Art. 372 or whether they amounted merely to executive action. Using much the same language as Bose J. had used in describing the Nizam's *firman*,[24]

---

11 See Chap. X.
12 (1961) 2 S.C.R. 931, ('61) A.SC. 564, 570.
13 ('51) A.H.P. 32 (the finding was that there was no such custom).
14 (1961) 1 S.C.R. 191, ('61) A.SC. 21, 25.
15 (1961) 1 S.C.R. *supra* at p. 199.
16 (1960) 3 S.C.R. 742, ('60) A.SC. 1073.
17 (1960) 3 S.C.R. *supra* at pp. 752-53.
18 (1955) 1 S.C.R. 735, ('55) A.SC. 25.
19 (1953) S.C.R. 404, ('53) A.SC. 91.
20 ('56) A.SC. 60.
21 ibid.
22 *R. N. Pratap Singh Deo* v. *Orissa* (1964) 7 S.C.R. 112, 118, ('64) A.SC. 1793.
23 (1961) 1 S.C.R. 957, ('61) A.SC. 298.
24 (1961) 1 S.C.R. at p. 964.

Gajendragadkar J. referred to the two earlier decisions of the Supreme Court as justifying the view that what was true of the Nizam's *firman*, ". . . would be equally true about all effective orders issued by the Ruler of Gwalior . . . (and it was) also clear that an order issued by an absolute monarch in an Indian State which had the force of law would amount to an existing law under Art. 372. . . ."[25] Referring to the State's contention that there was a distinction between *Kanuns* (laws) which were, and *Kalambandhis* which were not, published in the gazette, and which should be treated as executive orders, Gajendragadkar J. considered the character, content and purpose of the orders and observed: "The words used in describing the several orders issued by the Ruler can afford no material assistance in determining their character. In this connection *it is necessary to recall that all orders issued by the absolute Monarch had the force of law.*"[26] (italics supplied). An examination of the *Kalambandhis* showed that it was difficult to distinguish them from laws; "in any event they must be treated as rules or regulations having the force of law."[27] Consequently, the impugned executive orders purporting to set aside the *Kalambandhis* were void.

8.8 In the above cases the court failed to distinguish between the nature of a Ruler's order, as long as he remained an absolute Ruler and the nature of his order when it became necessary to decide whether that order was law within Art. 372. However, this distinction was realised in subsequent cases; and in *Umaid Mills Ltd.* v. *Union*[28], in *R. N. Pratap Singh Deo* v. *Orissa*[29] and in *Union* v. *Gwalior Rayon Silk Mfg. (Wvg.) Co. Ltd.*[30] the Supreme Court held that the cases discussed in para 8.6 above were not intended to lay down the broad general proposition that in the case of an absolute Ruler, no distinction could be made between his legislative and executive acts. In the *Gwalior Rayon Case,* Wanchoo J. observed that though the order of an absolute Ruler was not liable to challenge by anyone in the State, as long as he remained such Ruler, and in that sense his word was law in the State,

Above cases distinguished. Ruler's Order may be law, agreement, grant, or executive action

> ". . . We cannot impute to the Constitution-makers an intention to continue each and every order of an absolute Ruler as a law whatsoever be its nature. When Art. 372 of the Constitution speaks of continuance of laws in 1950 the jurisprudential distinction between legislative, judicial and executive acts must have been present in the mind of the Constitution-makers and that distinction must always be kept in mind by courts in deciding whether a particular order of an absolute Ruler is law . . . under Art. 372."[31]

Consequently, in considering whether an order of an absolute Ruler was law within the meaning of Art. 372, or was an executive act

---

[25] ibid. p. 965. [26] ibid. p. 967.

[27] ibid. p. 969.

[28] (1963) Supp. 2 S.C.R. 515, ('63) A.SC. 953 (*held,* that an agreement entered into by a Ruler which rested on the consent of two parties must be distinguished from an executive or legislative act of the Ruler. Consequently, an agreement between a Ruler and a company to exempt it not only from State Excise duty but from Federal Excise duty and not only from State income-tax but from Federal income-tax or super-tax or surcharge was not law, for, the Ruler had no power to exempt from Federal Excise or Federal income-tax. An assurance to amend the law in future cannot be treated as present law); *Gujarat* v. *Vora Fiddali* (1964) 6 S.C.R. 461, ('64) A.SC. 1043 (for a full discussion of this case, see Vol. II.)

[29] (1964) 7 S.C.R. 112, ('64) A.SC. 1793.

[30] (1964) 7 S.C.R. 892, ('64) A.SC. 1903.

[31] (1964) 7 S.C.R. at p. 903.

resting on agreement, or on grant, it was necessary to consider such relevant factors as the nature of the order, its scope and effect, its general setting and context and the method adopted by the Ruler in promulgating legislative, as distinguished from executive, orders. Accordingly, in *Deo's Case*[32] it was held that a grant of Rs. 500 per month, for life, made by a Ruler to his brother, in pursuance of a family custom was a gift pure and simple and was not law. And in the *Gwalior Rayon Case* it was held that an order of a Ruler granting exemption from income-tax to the respondents was not law. And the same view has been taken in *M.P.* v. *Bhargavendra Singh*,[33] and in *Gujarat* v. *R. B. Chandrachud*.[34]

Rules and circulars for admission to educational institutions assumed to be law

8.9 In *D. P. Joshi* v. *M.B.*[35] it was assumed that a rule for admission to a Medical College was a law open to challenge under Arts. 14 and 15, the majority repelling the challenge and the minority upholding it and the same view was taken of the Communal G. O. in *Madras* v. *Smt. Champakam Dorairajan*[36] and also in *Bombay* v. *Bombay Education Society*,[37] where a circular issued by the State of Bombay as regards the medium of instruction was held void as it violated Art. 19 (1) and Art. 337. It may however be added that even if an order or notification issued by Government were not "law" within the meaning of Art. 13 (3) (*a*), it could still be struck down as violating fundamental rights wherever the State was prohibited from denying certain rights to "any person" or to a "citizen". In *Bidi Supply Co.* v. *Union*[38] the Supreme Court held that an omnibus order of transfer such as had been made in the case was not authorised by s. 5 (7) (*a*) of the Income-tax Act. The order was held to violate Art. 14 because "Here 'the state' which includes its Income-tax department has by an illegal order denied to the petitioner, as compared with other Bidi merchants who are similarly situate, equality before the law or the equal protection of the laws. . . ."[39] However, in *Dwarka Nath* v. *Bihar*[40] it was held that the Bihar Education Code, Art. 182, had no statutory or other authority which could give it the force of law.[41] Accordingly, it was held that the Code could not deprive the Managing Committee of its rights in the properties of the school under its management.

but even otherwise, they can be struck down if they violate a prohibition enacted against the State

Questions raised by Art. 13

8.10 We must now consider the effect of Art. 13 on existing laws and laws made by the legislatures set up under our Constitution. Decided cases show that in considering the effect of Art. 13, three related questions have to be considered or are generally considered, namely, first, whether Art. 13 (1) is retrospective, secondly, whether there is any distinction between lack of legislative competence and violation of constitutional limitations and, finally, whether fundamental rights can be waived.

---

[32] (1964) 7 S.C.R. 112, at p. 121.

[33] ('66) A.SC. 704, 706 [*held*, relying on *Deo's Case* (1964) 7 S.C.R. 112, that the grant of a monthly allowance made by the Ruler to his brother was not law.]

[34] ('71) A.SC. 846 (*held*, that an order of the Maharaja of Baroda granting a pension and premature retirement compensation to a civil servant of the State was an executive act and was not law.)

[35] (1955) 1 S.C.R. 1215, ('55) A.SC. 334.

[36] (1951) S.C.R. 525, ('51) A.SC. 226.

[37] (1955) 1 S.C.R. 568, ('54) A.SC. 561.

[38] (1956) S.C.R. 267, ('56) A.SC. 479.

[39] (1956) S.C.R. at p. 277.

[40] ('54) A.SC. 249.

[41] ibid. p. 253. This conclusion was reached in view of the statement contained in the preface to the Education Code set out at p. 253 of the judgment.

8.11 In *Keshavan Madhava Menon* v. *Bombay*[42] ("*Menon's Case*") the effect of Art. 13(1) was considered in order to decide whether a prosecution commenced [under s. 18, Indian Press (Emergency Powers) Act, 1931] before the coming into effect of the Constitution, could be continued after the Constitution came into force if the Act became void as violating Art. 19(1)(*a*) and (2). Das J. for the majority, held that the prosecution could be continued, because the provisions of the Constitution were not retrospective, unless made so expressly or by necessary intendment, and because there was nothing in the language of Art. 13(1) which indicated that it was retrospective. He rejected the view of the High Court that the effect of Art. 13(1) was that of the repeal of a Statute;[43] Art. 13(1) did not render existing laws void *ab initio* but only to the extent of their inconsistency with fundamental rights. In other words, after the commencement of the Constitution, no existing law could be allowed to stand in the way of the exercise of fundamental rights. Such inconsistent laws were not wiped off or obliterated from the statute book, for so to hold, would be to give fundamental rights a retrospective effect which the court held they had not. The statute operated in respect of all matters or events which took place before the Constitution came into force, and the statute also operated on non-citizens after the Constitution came into force. In *Pannalal Binjraj* v. *Union*[45] the court followed *Menon's Case* and held that Art. 13 had no retrospective effect. Certain observations of the Supreme Court in *Shanti Sarup* v. *Union*[46] have, at times, been relied upon to show that Art. 13 is, in substance, retrospective. In that case, after observing that the impugned order had been passed in 1952, and therefore there was no question of Art. 13 having a retrospective operation, the court said:

Keshavan Madhava Menon's Case:

the Constitution is not retrospective

Art. 31(1) not retrospective and does not render existing laws void *ab initio*

> "But even assuming that the deprivation took place earlier and at a time when the Constitution had not come into force, the order effecting the deprivation which continued from day to day must be held to have come into conflict with the fundamental rights of the petitioner as soon as the Constitution came into force and became void on and from that date under Art. 13(1) of the Constitution."[47]

However, in the undernoted decisions,[48] it has been held that these observations do not support the proposition that where the rights of a person were concluded, or extinguished, by a valid law before the commencement of the Constitution, he could re-open the question of his rights on the ground that the law under which they were concluded, or extinguished, violated fundamental rights, and had therefore become void after the Constitution came into force.

---

[42] (1951) S.C.R. 228, ('51) A.SC. 128; foll. in *Babu* v. *Municipal Board, Kheri* ('76) A.A. 328 [*held*, that as the resolution of the Notified Area Committee dated 29th March, 1948 violated Art. 19(1)(*g*), it could not be enforced after the commencement of the Constitution.]

[43] (1951) S.C.R. *supra* at p. 235.

[44] ibid.

[45] (1957) S.C.R. 233, ('57) A.SC. 397.

[46] ('55) A.SC. 624, 628.

[47] ibid. p. 628.

[48] *Guru Datta Sharma* v. *Bihar* (1962) 2 S.C.R. 292, 323, ('61) A.SC. 1684, 1698; *Sri Jagatguru* v. *Commr. H.R.C. Endowments* (1962) 3 S.C.R. 252, 262; *Rabindranath Bose* v. *Union* ('70) A.SC. 470, 476-7.

Pesikaka's Case: the effect of a declaration of invalidity

8.12 In *Behram Khurshed Pesikaka v. Bombay*[49] the effect of Art. 13 (1) was considered again under the following circumstances: In *Bombay* v. *F. N. Balsara*,[50] the Supreme Court held that certain provisions of the Bombay Prohibition Act, 1949 (a pre-Constitution Statute), in so far as they prohibited the possession, use and consumption of medicinal preparations were void as violating Art. 19 (1) (*f*). Pesikaka was prosecuted under the Act and pleaded that he had taken medicine containing alcohol. The question arose whether the burden of proving that fact was on him, and as incidental to that question, it became necessary to consider the legal effect of the declaration by the Supreme Court that s. 13 (*b*) of the Bombay Prohibition Act, 1949, in so far as it affected liquid medicinal and toilet preparations containing alcohol, was invalid as it infringed Art. 19 (1) (*f*). The appeal was first heard by a bench of three judges who by a majority of two to one dismissed it. But a review application was granted and the constitutional question was referred to a Constitution Bench.

The first hearing: a declaration of invalidity does not repeal or amend a law; different views expressed on the distinction between lack of legislative power and restrictions on legislative power

8.13 At the first hearing all the judges were agreed that a declaration by a Court that part of a section was invalid did not repeal or amend that section, or add a proviso or exception to it, because repeal or amendment was a legislative function.[51] Bhagwati J. appears to have taken the view that a statute void in whole or part for unconstitutionality was void *ab initio*. Venkatarama Aiyar J., with whom Jagannadhadas J. was inclined to agree, held that a distinction must be made between unconstitutionality arising from lack of legislative competence and that arising from a violation of constitutional limitations on legislative power. A law made without legislative competence was a nullity; a law violating a constitutional prohibition enacted for the benefit of the public generally was also a nullity,[52] but a law violating a constitutional prohibition enacted for individuals was not a nullity but was merely unenforceable. Such unconstitutionality could be waived, and in that case the law became enforceable. At the second hearing, Mahajan C.J. after referring to *Menon's Case* said:

The second hearing: the majority view: (i) a law declared invalid is "notionally obliterated" *qua* citizens

"The result . . . of this pronouncement is that the part of the section of an existing law which is unconstitutional is not law, and is null and void. For determining the rights and obligations of citizens the part declared void should be notionally taken to be obliterated from the section for all intents and purposes, though it may remain written on the statute book and be a good law when a question arises for determination of rights and obligations incurred prior to 26th January, 1950, and also for the determination of rights of persons who have not been given fundamental rights by the Constitution."[54]

A criticism of this view

It is difficult to understand what is meant by "notionally . . . obliterated" from the section. In his dissenting judgment Das J. rightly said that to hold that the invalid part was obliterated would be tantamount to saying covertly that the judicial declaration had

[49] (1955) 1 S.C.R. 613, ('55) A.SC. 123.
[50] (1951) S.C.R. 682, ('51) A.SC. 318.
[51] (1955) 1 S.C.R. *supra* at pp. 621, 628-29, 638.
[52] It is submitted that the proposition that a law violating a constitutional prohibition enacted for the benefit of the public was a nullity is not correct; the learned Judge himself omitted it from his very full discussion in *M. P. V. Sundararamier* v. *A.P.* (1958) S.C.R. 1422, ('58) A.SC. 468: See para 8.17.
[53] (1955) 1 S.C.R. *supra* at pp. 639-40. [54] ibid. pp. 651-52.

to that extent amended the section.[55] If, as held in *Menon's Case*, "void" did not mean "repealed", and if "Art. 13(1) cannot be read as obliterating the entire operation of inconsistent laws", it is submitted that there is no scope for an unconstitutional provision being "notionally . . . obliterated." The theory of eclipse, to be presently noticed, is quite inconsistent with any obliteration, actual or notional. Mahajan C.J. also rejected the distinction between a law void for lack of legislative power and a law void for violating a constitutional fetter or limitation on legislative power observing that "Both these declarations of unconstitutionality go to the root of the power itself and there is no real distinction between them. They represent but two aspects of want of legislative power."[56] Without finally deciding the matter he expressed the opinion that fundamental rights were enacted in the Constitution as a matter of constitutional policy and not for the benefit of individuals and they could not be waived.

(ii) there is no distinction between lack of legislative power and restrictions on legislative power

8.14 In *Saghir Ahmad* v. *U.P.*[57] Mukherjea J. stated that it was sound law that "A statute void for unconstitutionality is dead and cannot be vitalized by a subsequent amendment of the Constitution removing the constitutional objection but must be re-enacted." Accordingly, it was held that the U.P. Road Transport Act, 1951, was void under Art. 13(2) as it violated Art. 19(1)(*g*), and was not protected by Art. 19(6) as originally enacted.

Saghir Ahmad's Case: a law void for unconstitutionality is void *ab initio*

8.15 However, the matter was reconsidered in *Bhikaji Narain Dhakras* v. *M.P.*[58] under the following circumstances: The C.P. and Berar Motor Vehicles (Amendment) Act, 1947, amended s. 43, Motor Vehicles Act, 1939, by introducing provisions which authorized the Provincial Government to take up the entire motor transport business in the Province, and run it in competition with and even to the exclusion of motor transport operators. These provisions, though valid when enacted, became void on the coming into force of the Constitution, as they violated Art. 19(1)(*g*). However, on June 18, 1951, the Constitution was amended so as to authorise the State to carry on business "whether to the exclusion, complete or partial, of citizens or otherwise." After this amendment, Government issued a notification and its validity was challenged. Das Actg. C.J. held that the question raised by the respondents, namely, that though s. 43 was void between January 26, 1950, and June 18, 1951, the amendment of Art. 19(6) had the effect of removing the constitutional invalidity of s. 43 which from the date of the amendment became valid and operative, had not been raised and considered in *Saghir Ahmad's Case*[59] or in *Pesikaka's Case*,[60] and it was, therefore, open to the Court to consider that question which involved the construction of Art. 13. After referring to the meaning given to the word "void" in *Menon's Case*, Das Actg. C.J. said for the Court:

Bhikaji Narain Dhakras's Case

the question there raised not considered in *Pesikaka's Case* nor in *Saghir Ahmad's Case*

"The true position is that the impugned law became, as it were, eclipsed, for the time being, by the fundamental right. The effect of the Constitution (First Amendment) Act, 1951, was to remove the shadow and to make the

The doctrine of "eclipse": a law violat-

[55] ibid. pp. 667-68.
[56] ibid. p. 652.
[57] (1955) 1 S.C.R. 707, 728, ('54) A.SC. 128, citing Cooley, *Constitutional Limitations*, Vol. I, p. 384, note.
[58] (1955) 2 S.C.R. 589, ('55) A.SC. 781.
[59] (1955) 1 S.C.R. 707, ('54) A.SC. 728.
[60] (1955) 1 S.C.R. 613, ('55) A.SC. 123.

ing fundamental rights is not void *ab initio*, but remains moribund

impugned Act free from all blemish or infirmity. If that were not so, then it is not intelligible what 'existing law' could have been sought to be saved from the operation of article 19(1)(*g*) by the amended clause (6) in so far as it sanctioned the creation of State monopoly, for, *ex hypothesi*, all existing laws creating such monopoly had already become void at the date of the commencement of the Constitution in view of clause (6) as it then stood. The American authorities refer only to post-Constitution laws which were inconsistent with the provisions of the Constitution. Such laws never came to life but were still born as it were. The American authorities, therefore, cannot fully apply to pre-Constitution laws which were perfectly valid before the Constitution. But apart from this distinction between pre-Constitution and post-Constitution laws on which, however we need not rest our decision, it must be held that these American authorities can have no application to our Constitution. All laws, existing or future, which are inconsistent with the provisions of Part III of our Constitution are, by the express provision of article 13, rendered void 'to the extent of such inconsistency'. Such laws were not dead for all purposes. They existed for the purposes of pre-Constitution rights and liabilities and they remained operative, even after the Constitution, as against non-citizens. It is only as against the citizens that they remained in a dormant or moribund condition."[61]

The decision not rested on the distinction between pre- and post-Constitutional laws

It is clear that these observations are not restricted to Art. 13(1), which deals with pre-Constitution laws, but apply also to Art. 13(2), which deals with post-Constitutional laws, because the Court did not rest its decision on the distinction made in American decisions between pre-Constitution and post-Constitution laws. It is submitted that the theory of eclipse is based on the premise that a law which violates fundamental rights is not a nullity or void *ab initio*, but remains unenforceable (that is, in a moribund condition); and secondly, it implicitly recognizes the distinction between a law void for legislative competence and a law void for violating fundamental rights. This judgment in substance overrules the judgment of Mahajan C.J. in *Pesikaka's Case*, and it has been so held by Chagla C.J. in *C. R. H. Readymoney Ltd.* v. *Bombay*.[62] The distinction between lack of legislative competence and violation of constitutional limitations was again recognized by Das C.J. when he laid down the three tests which the Court must apply when the validity of a law was challenged.[63]

Sundararamier's Case

8.16 The whole question was again fully discussed by Venkatarama Aiyar J. in delivering the majority judgment in *M. P. V. Sundararamier* v. *A.P.*[64] The Sales Tax Laws of several States were adapted by the President in the exercise of his powers under Art. 372(2) by enacting a section which reproduced verbatim the explanation to Art. 286(1)(*a*). That explanation had been interpreted by the Supreme Court in *Bombay* v. *United Motors India Ltd.*[65] in which, by a majority of 4:1, it was held that though the sales falling within the Explanation would, in fact, be in the course of inter-State trade, they became, by reason of the fiction introduced by the Explanation, intra-State sales, and could be taxed by the State within which the goods were delivered for consumption. Several States claimed to tax "explanation sales", as they came to be called,

[61] (1955) 2 S.C.R. 589, *supra* at pp. 599-600.
[62] (1958) Bom. 128, 141, ('58) A.B. 181, 59 Bom.L.R. 786.
[63] *Bombay* v. *R. M. D. Chamarbaugwala* (1957) S.C.R. 874, ('57) A.SC. 699.
[64] (1958) S.C.R. 1422, ('58) A.SC. 468. Sarkar J., dissented on the construction of the impugned provisions and therefore did not consider the questions discussed by Venkatarama Aiyar J.
[65] (1953) S.C.R. 1069, ('53) A.SC. 252.

and this claim was resisted in some cases. The petitioner in the present case challenged the validity of the demand by the State on the ground that the sales were immune from tax under Art. 286(2). While the petitions were pending, the Supreme Court held in *Bengal Immunity Co. Ltd.* v. *Bihar*[66] by a majority of 4 : 3, that the *United Motors Case* was wrongly decided, and that "explanation sales" could not be taxed, having regard to Art. 286(2), till Parliament lifted the ban against such a tax. As several States had acted on the earlier Supreme Court judgment, at first a validating Ordinance, and then the Sales Tax Laws Validation Act, 1956, were passed.[67] As the present petitions had not been disposed of by the High Court, the State pleaded the Validation Act in bar, and the petitioner rejoined by challenging its constitutional validity. Several contentions were urged before the Supreme Court, but the one relevant to the present discussion was formulated thus: Notwithstanding the provisions of the Validating Act, no action to start fresh proceedings could be taken under s. 22 of the Andhra (Madras) Act, because when enacted on July 2, 1952, it was void as violating Art. 286(2). An unconstitutional law was a nullity and must be treated as *non est*, and the Validating Act could not revive a law which, when enacted, was dead or non-existent. Unless s. 22 was re-enacted retrospectively no action could be taken by reason of the Validating Act.[68] The majority judgment observed that s. 22 was only conditional legislation, conditional on Parliament lifting the ban under Art. 286(2), and therefore the question of its constitutionality did not arise; however, it was considered more satisfactory to deal with the argument on its merits.[69] The question thus raised, and decided, related to a post-Constitution law.

The petitioner's case: s. 22, Andhra (Madras) Act, enacted in 1952, was void *ab initio*, and could not be validated without re-enactment

Majority judgment: (i) s. 22 was conditional legislation

8.17 Venkatarama Aiyar J. said that a law made without legislative competence and a law violating constitutional limitations on legislative power were both unconstitutional and both had ". . . the same reckoning in a court of law; they are both of them unenforceable. But does it follow from this that both the laws are of the same quality and character, and stand on the same footing for all purposes?"[70] The answer given in the judgment may be stated thus: The preponderance of authority in the United States was in favour of the view that while a law on a topic not within the competence of a legislature was a nullity, a law on a topic within its competence but violating constitutional prohibitions was only unenforceable. An important consequence of this distinction was that a law void for lack of legislative competence being absolutely null and void, a subsequent cession of that legislative topic to the legislature would not revive the law which was still-born and the law would have to be re-enacted. A law within legislative competence but

(ii) petitioner's case rejected: the real issue stated

American authorities recognize the distinction between lack of legislative power and restrictions on legislative power

[66] (1955) 2 S.C.R. 603, ('55) A.SC. 661.

[67] The relevant section of the Act is set out in (1958) S.C.R. *supra* at p. 1439.

[68] (1958) S.C.R. *supra* at pp. 1467-68.

[69] This does not make the judgment *obiter* because the conclusion that the law was conditional legislation raises the further question: Can a legislature legislate conditionally if it lacks legislative competence? If there is no distinction between lack of legislative competence and the constitutional fetters on the power to legislate, there would be no power to legislate conditionally. See para 8.19, proposition (6).

[70] (1958) S.C.R. *supra* at p. 1469.

violative of constitutional limitations was unenforceable by reason of those limitations, but once the limitations were removed the law become effective.[71] Having considered the American authorities, the judgment then considered decisions of our Supreme Court. It held that the observations of Mahajan J. in *Pesikaka's Case*[72] that *qua* citizens that part of s. 13(*b*) of the Bombay Prohibition Act, 1949, which had been declared invalid by the Supreme Court "had to be regarded as null and void" could not in the context imply that the impugned law must be regarded as *non est* so as to be incapable of taking effect when the bar was removed. They meant only that the Act was unenforceable by reason of the bar. The observations in *A. V. Fernandez* v. *Kerala*[73] were distinguished on the ground that the point for decision in that case was the effect of the ban under Art. 286; as the ban had not been lifted, the effect on the existing law of lifting it did not fall to be considered, and the observations in that judgment could not be read as implying that s. 22 of the Madras Act must be taken to have been blotted out of the statute book. Having explained *Pesikaka's Case*[74] and distinguished *Fernandez's Case*[75] Venkatarama Aiyar J. observed that the case directly in point was *Dhakras's Case*.[76] He summed up the result of the authorities thus:

Indian authorities considered: *Pesikaka's case* explained, and *Fernandez's Case* distinguished

Dhakras's Case directly in point

Conclusion: a law unconstitutional in part not void *ab initio*

"Where an enactment is unconstitutional in part but valid as to the rest, assuming of course that the two portions are severable, it cannot be held to have been wiped out of the statute book as it admittedly must remain there for the purpose of enforcement of the valid portion thereof, and being on the statute book, even that portion which is unenforceable on the ground that it

---

[71] The authorities cited in support were: Willoughby, *Constitution of the United States*, Vol. 1, p. 11; Cooley, *Constitutional Law*, at p. 201; *Wilkerson* v. *Rahrer* (1890) 140 U.S. 545, 35 L. ed. 572. This case is instructive. The State of Kansas had enacted a law in 1889 forbidding the sale of intoxicating liquor. Prohibition of intoxicating liquor was within the police power of the State; but in so far as the law applied to sales in the course of inter-State trade it was bad as violating the Commerce Clause of the U.S. Constitution. In 1890 Congress passed an Act declaring that imported liquors or liquids shall, upon arrival in a State, fall within the category of domestic articles of a similar nature. Rahrer was prosecuted after the Act of Congress under the Kansas Law of 1889, and the question was whether the prosecution was sustainable without a re-enactment of the Kansas Law of 1889. Reversing the judgment of the Circuit Court which discharged Rahrer, the U.S. Supreme Court held that the prosecution was maintainable: "This is not the case of a law enacted in the unauthorised exercise of a power exclusively confided to Congress, but of a law which it was competent for the State to pass, but which could not operate upon articles occupying a certain situation until the passage of the Act of Congress. That Act in terms removed the obstacle, and we perceive no adequate ground for adjudging that a re-enactment of the state law was required before it could have the effect upon imported, which it had always had upon a domestic, property." The judgment of Lord Macdermott C.J. in *Ulster Transport Authority* v. *James Brown & Sons Ltd.* (1953) North Ir. Rep. 79, was also relied upon: (1958) S.C.R. 1422, at pp. 1470-71.

[72] (1955) 1 S.C.R. 613, 614, ('55) A.SC. 123.

[73] (1957) S.C.R. 837, 850-51, ('57) A.SC. 657. "In our opinion, s. 26 (of the T.-C. General Sales Tax Act) in cases falling within the categories specified under Art. 286 . . . has the effect of setting at nought and of obliterating in regard thereto the provisions contained in the Act relating to the imposition of tax on the sale or purchase of such goods. . . . So far as sales falling within the categories specified in Art. 286 . . . and the corresponding section 26 of the Act are concerned, they are, as it were, taken out of the purview of the Act. . . ."

[74] (1955) 1 S.C.R. 613, ('55) A.SC. 123. [75] (1957) S.C.R. 837, ('57) A.SC. 657.

[76] (1955) 2 S.C.R. 589, ('55) A.SC. 781.

is unconstitutional will operate *proprio vigore* when the Constitutional bar is removed, and there is no need for a fresh legislation. . . ."[77]

In the view the Court took it was found unnecessary to decide whether it would make any difference in the result if the impugned provision was unconstitutional in its entirety."[78]

8.18 The following propositions emerge from the above cases:

Propositions which emerge from the cases discussed so far

(1) There is a distinction between a law unconstitutional for lack of legislative power and a law unconstitutional because violative of provisions of the Constitution other than those which relate to the distribution of legislative power.[79]

(2) A law which is unconstitutional for lack of legislative competence is void *ab initio*: a law which is unconstitutional for violation of constitutional limitations is unenforceable as long as it continues to violate constitutional limitations.[80] Such a law, whether pre-Constitution or post-Constitution, is not wholly void if it violates fundamental rights; it is merely eclipsed by the fundamental right and remains, as it were, in a moribund condition as long as the shadow of fundamental rights falls upon it. When that shadow is removed the law begins to operate *proprio vigore* from the date of such removal unless it is retrospective.[81]

(3) A law void for lack of legislative competence is not revived if legislative power is subsequently given to the legislature which enacted it; a law partly void because of violation of constitutional limitations operates *proprio vigore* when the limitations are removed.[82]

(4) When a Court declares a law to be unconstitutional, that declaration does not repeal or amend the law,[83] for to repeal or amend a law is a legislative and not a judicial function.[84]

(5) The word "void" in Art. 13(1) and (2) does not mean "repealed",[85] nor is a law declared void under Art. 13(1) or (2) obliterated from the statute book. Such a law is not wholly void but by the express terms of the article is void only to the extent of its repugnancy to, or contravention of, the provisions of Part III relating to fundamental rights.[86]

8.19 However, the actual decision in *Sundararamier's Case* that s. 22 of the Act was conditional legislation, conditional on Parliament lifting the ban under Art. 286, justifies, it is submitted, the following proposition:

Submission: a further proposition is implied in the actual decision in *Sundararamier's Case*

(6) An important distinction between a legislature lacking legislative competence to enact a law and a legislature which has such competence subject to restrictions on its power is that in the first case the legislature cannot legislate conditionally on the power to legislate being given to it later; in the second case it can legislate conditionally on the law taking effect from the

---

[77] (1958) S.C.R. 1422, at pp. 1474-75. [78] ibid. p. 1475.

[79] *Sundararamier's Case* (1958) S.C.R. 1422, 1468-9, ('58) A.SC. 468.

[80] ibid. pp. 1474-75. The observations of Mahajan C.J. in *Pesikaka's Case*, (1955) 1 S.C.R. 613, 652, ('55) A.SC. 123, (cited above), denying the distinction between legislative competence and violation of constitutional limitations must be treated as overruled. His judgment was considered, and it was held that his words "null and void" did not mean that the law was *non est* but they only meant that the law was not enforceable.

[81] *Dhakras's Case*, (1955) 2 S.C.R. 589, 599-600, ('55) A.SC. 781, treated as directly in point and followed in *Sundararamier's Case, supra*. See para 8.17. This case clearly dealt with a post-constitutional law, for the impugned section was enacted on July 2, 1952.

[82] See f.n. 81 above.

[83] *Pesikaka's Case* (1955) 1 S.C.R. 613, ('55) A.SC. 123; *per* Bhagwati J. (1955) 1 S.C.R. at pp. 620-21, Jagannadhadas J., ibid. p. 628; Venkatarama Aiyar J., ibid. pp. 635-36.

[84] *Pesikaka's Case, supra* at pp. 636, 655, 661.

[85] *Menon's Case*, (1951) S.C.R. 228, 235, ('51) A.SC. 128. See para 8.11.

[86] See para 8.11.

time when the limitation on its power is removed. When it is said that s. 22 of the Act is conditional legislation, it means that the Madras Legislature was competent to pass a law in 1952 providing that *as and when Parliament lifted the ban under Art. 286(2),* "explanation sales" should be subject to sales tax prescribed by that Act.

Two Sup. Ct. judgments:

(i) *Basheshar Nath's Case*

8.20 Two judgments of the Supreme Court must now be considered, namely, *Basheshar Nath* v. *C.I.T.*[87] and *Deep Chand* v. *U.P.*[88] since they lay down propositions opposed to those set out above,[89] but without any reference to *Sundararamier's Case.* In *Basheshar Nath's Case*, the appellant had entered into a settlement of his income-tax liabilities under s. 8A, Taxation of Income (Investigation Commission) Act, 1947, and had made part payments of moneys due under the settlement. After the settlement was made the Supreme Court held that s. 5(1) of the Act violated Art. 14 and was void. When an attempt was made to recover the balance of the moneys from the appellant, he disputed the validity of the settlement on the ground that s. 8A of the Act was void since s. 5(1) of the Act on which it was founded was void. The respondent contended that the settlement was not void, but that even if it was, the appellant had entered into the agreement voluntarily and had therefore waived his right under Art. 14. The question of waiver will be considered in detail later.[90] However, two judges discussed the question whether there was any distinction between lack of legislative competence and violation of constitutional limitations. S. K. Das J. held that there was a clear distinction between the two,[91] while Subba Rao J. held that there was not.[92] It is submitted that the judgment of Subba Rao J. is a judgment *per incuriam* because it does not consider *Sundararamier's Case*[93] which directly decided that point and held that there was a clear distinction between lack of legislative competence and violation of constitutional limitations. That case cannot be overruled by the judgment of a single judge and ". . . in any event it is a salutary rule that a judge is not to be assumed to have intended to overrule or disapprove of an authority which has not been cited to him and which he does not even mention."[94] It may be added that *Basheshar Nath's Case* discussed the question of waiver of fundamental rights contrary to the wise and well settled rule that a Court will not pronounce on a constitutional question unless it is absolutely necessary to do so.[95] Strictly speaking, no constitutional question arose at all if it was held, as in fact it was held by S. K. Das J., that there was no waiver of fundamental right at all. The observations of Subba Rao J. are, therefore, not only *per incuriam*, but *obiter.*

Subba Rao J. denied the distinction between lack of legislative power and limitation on legislative power; submission: judgment *obiter* and *per incuriam*

---

[87] (1959) Supp. 1 S.C.R. 528, ('59) A.SC. 149.

[88] (1959) Supp. 2 S.C.R. 8, ('59) A.SC. 648.

[89] See para 8.18.

[90] See para 8.28 *et seq.*

[91] (1959) Supp. 1 S.C.R. *supra* at p. 593.

[92] ibid. p. 619.

[93] (1958) S.C.R. 1422, ('58) A.SC. 468; and *f.n.* 80 *ante.*

[94] *Per* Lord Reid in *Ridge* v. *Baldwin*, (1964) A.C. 40, 79.

[95] S. K. Das J. adverted to this rule and regretted a departure from it by his brother judges: (1959) Supp. 1 S.C.R. *supra* at p. 590; for the rule, see 11 *American Jurisprudence*, p. 72; Rottschaefer, *Constitutional Law*, 1939, pp. 26-7; Cooley, *Constitutional Law*, 4th ed., p. 191; the rule was reiterated by Gajendragadkar J. in *Bihar* v. *R.B.H.R.M. Jute Mills* (1960) 2 S.C.R. 331, 336, ('60) A.SC. 378.

8.21 In *Deep Chand's Case*,[96] the appellant impugned the constitutionality of the U.P. Transport Services (Development) Act, 1955, on the ground that it violated Art. 31. All the judges held that the Act did not violate Art. 31. Consequently, it was wholly unnecessary to consider whether there was a distinction between lack of legislative competence and violation of constitutional limitations and this was pointed out in the minority judgment of Das C.J. and Sinha J.[97] Subba Rao J. who delivered the judgment of the majority, again adverted to the distinction which he had made in *Basheshar Nath's Case* and adhered to what he had stated there. It is submitted, first, that these observations are *obiter* and also *per incuriam* because here also *Sundararamier's Case* was neither cited nor considered and that here though it was open to three judges of the Supreme Court who constituted the majority to overrule a judgment of four judges, in fact they have not done so.

(ii) *Deep Chand's Case*: Subba Rao J., adheres to his view in *Basheshar Nath's Case*

Submission: judgment *obiter* and also *per incuriam*

8.22 In *Mahendra Lal Jaini* v. *U.P.*,[98] without any reference to *Sundararamier's Case*, the Supreme Court again reviewed the authorities,[99] and held (i) that the doctrine of eclipse applied only to pre-Constitution and not to post-Constitution laws; (ii) that the words "to the extent of the inconsistency" or "to the extent of the contravention" were designed to save parts of a law which did not contravene, or were not inconsistent with, fundamental rights; (iii) that the meaning of the word "void" in Art. 13(1) and (2) was the same; (iv) however, pre-Constitution laws violating fundamental rights were valid when enacted and could therefore be revived under the doctrine of eclipse, whereas post-Constitution laws violating fundamental rights were "still-born" and *non est* and could not be revived. In dealing with the argument, based on Supreme Court decisions, that a law violating Art. 19 would be void *qua* citizens but valid *qua* non-citizens, Wanchoo J. said:

Mahendra Lal's Case

"Theoretically the laws falling under the latter category (i.e. contravening Art. 19) may be valid *qua* non-citizens; *but that is a wholly unrealistic consideration and it seems to us that such notionally partial valid existence of the said laws on the strength of hypothetical and pedantic considerations* cannot justify the application of the doctrine of eclipse to them."[1] (italics supplied)

It is submitted that the expressions "wholly unrealistic", "notionally partial valid existence" and "hypothetical and pedantic considerations" obscured the real issue from the court, namely, whether a post-Constitution law contravening Art. 19 which would be void *qua* citizens but valid *qua* non-citizens could be said to be still-born or *non-est*. It is submitted that the decision in *Mahendra Lal's Case* apart from being *per incuriam*, is clearly wrong, and has in effect been overruled by the decision in *Ambica Mills Case*[2] discussed in para 8.24 below.

Submission: judgment *per incuriam* and in substance over-ruled by *Ambica Mills Case*

8.23 In *L. Jagannath* v. *Authorised Officer*[3] the Supreme Court reviewed decisions which applied the doctrine of eclipse to laws

L. Jagannath's Case unhelpful

[96] (1959) Supp. 2 S.C.R. 8, ('59) A.SC. 648.
[97] (1959) Supp. 2 S.C.R. *supra* at p. 12.
[98] (1963) Supp. 1 S.C.R. 912, ('63) A.SC. 1019.
[99] (1963) Supp. 1 S.C.R. *supra* at pp. 929-35.
[1] ibid. p. 941.
[2] *Gujarat* v. *Shri Ambica Mills* (1974) 3 S.C.R. 760, ('74) A.SC. 1300.
[3] (1972) 1 S.C.R. 1055, ('72) A.SC. 425.

contravening Art. 13(2) as also decisions which held that laws contravening Art. 13(2) were still-born and void *ab initio*, and observed:

> "In our view, although decisions of the American Supreme Court and the comments of well-known commentators like Willoughby and Cooley have great persuasive force, we need not interpret our Constitution by too much reliance on them. Nor is it necessary to scrutinise too closely the decisions wherein views appear to have been expressed that a law which is void under Art. 13(2) is to be treated as still-born. Equally unfruitful would it be to consider the doctrine of eclipse."[4]

It is submitted that these observations are unhelpful because they leave the conflict unresolved, and give no guidance for the future. Further, the review of earlier authorities was unnecessary, once the court held that irrespective of those authorities the challenge to the impugned Act failed *on the express terms* of Art. 31B.[5] In the result, the observations quoted above are mere *obiter dicta*.

Ambica Mills Case

8.24 In the *Ambica Mills Case* the respondents were a company registered under the Companies Act, and they impugned certain provisions of a labour law and the rules made thereunder.[6] The High Court held that the impugned provisions violated Art. 19 and were void. Consequently, as the Act was still-born and *non est*, the respondents could challenge the demand made under the Act as not authorised by law. The Supreme Court allowed the appeal. As to the finding of the High Court that the impugned provisions violated Art. 14, Mathew J.[7] held that Art. 14 was not violated; and as to the High Court's finding that the impugned provisions set out earlier violated Art. 19, he observed that it was unnecessary to consider the correctness of the High Court's decision,[8] and he would proceed on the assumption that the impugned provisions were void as violating the fundamental rights of citizen-employees under Art. 19(1)(*f*); Mathew J. said that it had been "settled by the decisions of this court"[9] that a Corporation was not a citizen for the purposes of Art. 19, and added, "The real question, therefore, is, even if a law takes away or abridges the fundamental rights of citizens under Art. 19(1)(*f*), whether it would be void and therefore *non est*?"

Corporations not citizens: the real issue

The principle laid down in *Menon's Case*

8.25 Mathew J. held that *Menon's Case* clearly held

> ". . . that even though a law which is inconsistent with fundamental rights under Art. 19 would become void after the commencement of the Constitu-

---

[4] (1972) 1 S.C.R. *supra* at p. 1069-70. [5] ibid. p. 1070.

[6] Secs. 3, 6A and 7, Bombay Labour Welfare Act, 1953; s. 13, Bombay Labour Welfare Fund (Gujarat Extension and Amendment) Act, 1961 and Rules 3 and 4 of the Bombay Labour Welfare Fund Rules, 1953.

[7] For himself, Ray C.J., Khanna, Chandrachud and Alagiriswami JJ.

[8] Because it was a wise tradition with the courts not to adjudge on the constitutionality of a statute except where the legal rights of litigants were in actual controversy; and as part of this rule was the principle that a party *qua* whom the law was constitutional would not be heard to attack the law on the ground that it was unconstitutional *qua* others: "A person ordinarily is precluded from challenging the constitutionality of governmental action by invoking the rights of others and it is not sufficient that the statute or administrative regulation is unconstitutional as to other persons or classes of persons; it must affirmatively appear that the person attacking the statute comes within the class of persons affected by it.": *U.S.* v. *Raines* (1960) 362 U.S. 17, 4 L.ed. 2d. 524.

[9] ('74) A.SC. *supra*, p. 1306 referring to *Tata Eng. & Loco. Co. Ltd.* v. *Bihar* (1964) 6 S.C.R. 885, ('65) A.SC. 40; *R. C. Cooper* v. *Union* (1970) 3 S.C.R. 530, ('70) A.SC. 564; *Bennett Coleman and Co.* v. *Union* (1973) 2 S.C.R. 757, ('73) A.SC. 106.

tion, the law would still continue in force in so far as non-citizens are concerned. This decision takes the view that the word 'void' in Art. 13(1) would not have the effect of wiping out pre-Constitution laws from the statute book, that they will continue to be operative so far as non-citizens are concerned, notwithstanding the fact that they are inconsistent with the fundamental rights of citizens and therefore become void under Art. 13(1)".[10]

He then referred to, and stated the effect of, all the cases, including *Sundararamier's Case*, which have been discussed in paras 8.9 to 8.23 above. Since *Mahendra Lal's Case* declared the law after a review of earlier authorities, except *Sundararamier's Case*, Mathew J. devoted his judgment to a critical examination of *Mahendra Lal's Case* and a careful analysis of Art. 13(2). The following propositions emerge from his judgment:

Mahendra Lal's Case critically examined

Propositions emerging from *Ambica Mills Case*: a law valid *qua* non-citizens but void *qua* citizens not still-born or *non est*

(*a*) If, as held in *Mahendra Lal's Case*, the word "void" in Art. 13(1) and (2) had the same meaning, it was difficult to understand why a pre-Constitution law violating Art. 19 should remain operative against non-citizens after the commencement of the Constitution and a similar post-Constitution law should not remain operative against non-citizens. The fact that the pre-Constitution law was valid when enacted was irrelevant to its continuing to operate against non-citizens, notwithstanding the provisions of Art. 13(1), after the Constitution came into force. The real reason why the law remained operative was that only that law became void under Art. 13(1) which took away or abridged the fundamental rights under Part III, and since Art. 19(1) does not confer any fundamental rights on non-citizens, such a law remained operative *qua* non-citizens. If so, a similar post-Constitution law would also remain operative *qua* non-citizens.

(*b*) Rights do not exist in a vacuum. They must inhere in some person natural or juridical. And under Part III they inhere even in fluctuating bodies like religious denominations (e.g. Art. 26) or racial and linguistic minorities (e.g. Art. 30).

(*c*) The scheme underlying Art. 13(1) and Art. 13(2) is the same: Art. 13(1) makes a pre-Constitution law void *to the extent of its inconsistency* with fundamental rights; Art. 13(2) makes a post-Constitution law void *to the extent of its contravention* of fundamental rights. In both cases the law remains operative *qua* non-citizens, because Art. 19 does not confer any fundamental rights on non-citizens. ". . . the voidness is not *in rem*[11] but to the extent only of the inconsistency or contravention. . . . Therefore 'void' in Art. 13(2) can only mean void as against persons whose fundamental rights are taken away or abridged by law. The law might be 'still-born' so far as the persons, entities or denominations whose fundamental rights are taken away or abridged but there is no reason why the law should be void or still-born as against those who have no such rights."[12]

(*d*) The argument that the expression "to the extent of the contravention" in Art. 13(2) meant that only that part of the law which contravened fundamental rights (e.g. a section of an Act) would be void and not the whole Act, and that the said expression did not mean that the law would be void only as regards persons or entities whose fundamental rights had been taken away or abridged was not correct. First, there was no reason why the framers of the Constitution should want to provide that other sections which did not violate fundamental rights should not be void, and in any event, such an absolute statement would be wrong, because those other sections would be void if they were inseverable from the section which violated fundamental rights.[13] Secondly, the expression "any law" in the first part of Art. 13(2) and

---

[10] ('74) A.SC. *supra* at p. 1307. Mathew J. also cited passages from *Pesikaka's Case* and *Dhakras's Case* which repeated the same propositions.

[11] The words "*in rem*" are usually applied to a right which is available against the world as opposed to a right *in personam*, which is only available against certain persons. The expression "the voidness is not *in rem*" is meant to convey that Art. 13(1) and (2) does not make a law contravening Arts. 19, 26 or 30 void against the world but only void against citizens, religious denominations and religious and linguistic minorities respectively.

[12] ibid. p. 1310. [13] ibid.

in the second part of Art. 13(2) refers to the same law by using the same expression "any law". The first part says that the State shall not make "any law" which takes away or abridges fundamental rights. The second part refers to the same law when it provides "*any law* made in contravention of this clause shall be void", for, it is only such law as takes away or abridges fundamental rights which is declared to be void.

(*e*) As to the contention that the opening words of Art. 13(2) "the State shall not make any law" was a paramount constitutional mandate which showed that there was a lack of power to enact such law, Mathew J. observed that the question arose: "What was the mandate?" The mandate was not to take away or abridge fundamental rights conferred by Part III and the mandate was not disobeyed if fundamental rights were not abridged or taken away.

Basis of *Sundararamier's Case* not necessary to consider

8.26 Having come to the above conclusion on construction, Mathew J. said that it was not necessary to consider "whether that conclusion could be arrived at except on the basis of the distinction drawn by Venkatarama Aiyar J. in *Sundararamier's Case*[14] (between lack of legislative power and violation of constitutional limitations) which distinction had been rejected in *Deepchand's Case* and *Mahendra Lal's Case,* without adverting to *Sundararamier's Case*.[15]

"However, we venture to think that there is nothing strange in the notion of a legislature having no inherent legislative capacity or power to take away or abridge by a law the fundamental rights conferred on citizens and yet having legislative power to pass the same law in respect of non-citizens who have no such fundamental rights to be taken away or abridged. In other words, the legislative incapacity subjectwise with reference to Arts. 245 and 246 in this context would be the taking away or abridging by law the fundamental rights under Art. 19 of citizens."[16]

Mathew J. then observed that the doctrine, of "void *ab initio*" was gradually being eroded, but found it unnecessary to pursue the discussion further.

The law partly clarified by *Ambica Mills Case*

8.27 Does the *Ambica Mills Case* help in removing some of the contradictions involved in the Supreme Court judgments we have been considering? It is submitted that the *Ambica Mills Case* has put the following propositions on a sound logical foundation based on a plain interpretation of Arts. 13(1) and (2):

(*a*) Where fundamental rights have been conferred only on some persons, natural or juristic, a pre-Constitution or post-Constitution law contravening those rights is void *qua* those persons, but is valid *qua* other persons on whom those rights have not been conferred; (*b*) it cannot be said of the laws mentioned in (*a*) above that they are still-born or *non est*.

Submission: doctrine of eclipse must apply to pre- and post-Constitution laws

Thus the *Ambica Mills Case* has removed some of the confusion caused by previous decisions. Further, though the doctrine of eclipse was not in issue in the *Ambica Mills Case*, the propositions emerging from it lead to the conclusion that the doctrine of eclipse must apply both to pre-Constitution and post-Constitution laws. For, if the doctrine has been applied to pre-Constitution laws because it could not be said of them that they were still-born or *non est*, it must equally be applied to similar post-Constitution laws, for, equally, it cannot be said of them that they are still-born or *non est*.

---

[14] ibid. p. 1311. [15] ibid. [16] ibid.

Ambica Mills Case not helpful on distinction between lack of legislative competence and violation of constitutional limitations

8.28 Since Mathew J. did not pause to consider the distinction made by Venkatarama Aiyar J. in *Sundararamier's Case* between lack of legislative power and violation of constitutional limitations, the judgment in the *Ambica Mills Case* is not helpful on the validity of that distinction. The observations of Mathew J. quoted in paragraph 8.26 above do not help in answering that question, though, they do seem to suggest that violation of fundamental rights *qua* persons on whom they are conferred may go to lack of power. It is submitted, however, that in the context of the judgment the above passage does not deal with the question and that therefore it is necessary to discuss the correct position at this place. We have seen that when a law is impugned as violating constitutional limitations, it may be possible to save parts of the law by applying the doctrine of severability. As stated earlier in paras 3.10 and 3.11, there are two types of severability. In the first, the provision violating constitutional limitations may be distinct and severable, and the court would uphold the rest of the Act by severing such distinct provisions and declaring them void. But the impugned law may be one and inseverable, so that no specific provision of the Act could be declared to be void. In such circumstances, the doctrine of severability in application or enforcement would apply. When Mathew J. held in the *Ambica Mills Case* that on the assumption that the impugned law violated Art. 19(1), it was valid *qua* non-citizens (the Ambica Mills was a non-citizen), he applied the doctrine of severability in application, because in Art. 19 the Constitution itself makes a distinction between citizens and non-citizens. Consequently, *qua* citizens, the court would restrain the enforcement of the Act by a permanent injunction or *mandamus*. It is submitted that in such a situation a distinction must be made between lack of legislative power and violation of constitutional limitations because it would be self-contradictory to say of one indivisible law that there was and was not power to enact it. The situation is more satisfactorily described by saying that there was legislative power to enact the law, but as to some persons real or juristic, the power was exercised in disregard of constitutional limitations with the result that the law could not be enforced against such persons. This conclusion is further supported by the submission made above, that the judgment of Mathew J. leads to the conclusion that the doctrine of eclipse must apply equally to pre-Constitution and post-Constitution laws which violate rights conferred only on some persons or entities. For the main point of the doctrine of eclipse is that if a limitation put on legislative power by fundamental rights or any other constitutional limitation is removed, the law operates without re-enactment, for, the law then no longer violates fundamental rights and not having been wiped off the Statute Book (or become *non est*) it is revived without re-enactment. Thirdly, as S. K. Das J. observed in his dissenting judgment in *Basheshar Nath's Case*:[17]

Submission: *Sundararamier's Case* rightly distinguished lack of legislative competence from violation of constitutional limitations

". . . the Article itself recognizes the distinction between absence of legislative power which will make the law made by an incompetent legislature *wholly* void, and exercise of legislative power in contravention of a restriction or check on such power, which will make the law void to the extent of the

[17] (1959) Supp. 1 S.C.R. 528, 593, ('59) A.SC. 149.

inconsistency or contravention. The use of the words 'to the extent of the inconsistency' and 'to the extent of the contravention' indubitably points to such a distinction, and indeed this was pointed out in *Bhikaji Narain Dhakras* v. *M.P.*"[18]

and the same distinction is clearly made in the classic passage from the judgment of Lord Selbourne in *R.* v. *Burah*:[19]

"... the terms of the instrument by which, *affirmatively, the legislative powers were created* and by which, *negatively they are restricted.* If what has been done is *legislation, within the general scope of the affirmative words which give the power,* and if it *violates no express condition or restriction by which the power is limited* ... it is not for any court of justice to inquire further." (italics supplied)

It is submitted that both as a matter of language and as a matter of law, there is a clear distinction between lack of power and disregarding a restriction on power as regards a part of the subject matter of that power. It is submitted therefore that Venkatarama Aiyar J. was right in the distinction which he made between lack of legislative power and violation of constitutional limitations; and the most important result of this distinction is that a legislature having legislative power can legislate conditionally on the limitation on its power being removed, whereas a legislature not possessing legislative power cannot legislate at all.

Basheshar Nath's Case and waiver of fundamental rights

8.29 We have seen that in *Basheshar Nath's Case*[20] no constitutional question of waiver of fundamental rights arose until it was first established that the appellant had waived his rights. However, as the judges expressed their views on the waiver of fundamental rights, these views must now be considered.

Das C.J. and Kapur J.: right under Art. 14 cannot be waived

8.30 Limiting their decision to Art. 14, Das C.J. and Kapur J. held that the right conferred by Art. 14 could not be waived. Bhagwati J. expressed the view that the Constitution was "sacrosanct"[21] that it would be a "sacrilege" to whittle down fundamental rights,[22] that it was the "sacred" duty of the Supreme Court to safeguard fundamental rights.[23] It is not necessary to inquire in detail whether this view is correct; it is enough to say that the provisions for amendment contained in the Constitution, and the amendments in fact made in fundamental rights by constitutional amendments show that there is nothing "sacred" or "sacrosanct" about fundamental rights.[24] Bhagwati J. further held that fundamental rights could not be waived for the following reasons: The Preamble to our Constitution, the provisions of Art. 13 and the language in which fundamental rights were cast could lead to only one conclusion, namely, that the distinction drawn in the United States between fundamental rights which could be waived because enacted primarily for the benefit of an individual, and fundamental rights which could not be waived because enacted for the benefit of the public, could

Bhagwati J.: No fundamental right can be waived, and the distinction made in the U.S. to

[18] (1955) 2 S.C.R. 589, ('55) A.SC. 781.
[19] (1878) 5 I.A. 178, 193-4, (1878) 3 App. Cas. 889.
[20] (1959) Supp. 1 S.C.R. 528, ('59) A.SC. 149.
[21] ibid. p. 564. [22] ibid. p. 565.
[23] ibid. p. 557.
[24] S. K. Das J. made the same point in rejecting the argument that fundamental rights were natural rights retained by the people which could never be interfered with. After referring to Arts. 33 to 35 he said "if they were natural rights, the Constitution could not have given power to Parliament to modify them.": ibid. p. 605.

have no application in India. The Preambles to the U.S. and the Indian Constitutions showed that the two Constitutions were framed for securing very different objectives. Besides, the U.S. Constitution was a bare outline of government and nothing more; ours was a detailed Constitution in which the rights, and the restrictions to which they were subject, were mentioned in the Constitution itself. To allow the doctrine of waiver would be to import limitations into our Constitution for which there was no justification. Ours was a nascent democracy and it was the sacred duty of the Supreme Court to safeguard fundamental rights. He adopted the passage from the judgment of Das C.J. in the present case,[25] and said that Mahajan C.J. had stated the law correctly in *Pesikaka's Case*[26] when he said that all fundamental rights were embodied in the Constitution on grounds of public policy and they could not be waived. The difficulties which S. K. Das J. had pointed out if it were held that fundamental rights could not be waived, were "more imaginary than real."[27]

justify waiver do not apply to our Constitution — the two Constitutions are not in *pari materia* as shown by their preambles

8.31 Subba Rao J. whilst admitting that U.S. decisions recognized the doctrine of waiver of constitutional rights, referred to the distinction between the U.S. and the Indian Constitutions in much the same language as Bhagwati J. had used, and concluded that no limitations should be placed on fundamental rights other than those contained in the Constitution. He said that he had scrutinised for himself each Article in Part III and had come to the conclusion that no prejudice would be caused if the doctrine of waiver were not applied.[28] He added:

Subba Rao J. expressed the same view

"A large majority of our people are economically poor, educationally backward and politically not yet conscious of their rights. Individually or even collectively, they cannot be pitted against the State organizations and institutions, nor can they meet them on equal terms. In such circumstances, it is the duty of this Court to protect their rights against themselves."[29]

8.32 S. K. Das J. dissented, holding that there were no such differences between the U.S. and the Indian Constitutions as would make the doctrine of waiver applicable to the former and not to the latter. The correct test to apply to each fundamental right was to inquire whether it conferred a right on a person primarily for his benefit. If it did, that right could be waived.[30] It is submitted that the view of S. K. Das J. is correct. However, the majority view has such far-reaching constitutional implications that it becomes necessary to examine it more closely. For this purpose, it would lead to a clearer understanding of the problem to consider, first, the views of Bhagwati and Subba Rao JJ. that all fundamental rights were based on public policy and could not be waived, and then to consider the views of Das C.J. and Sinha J. that there were special reasons for holding that the equality clause on the 14th Amendment to the U.S. Constitution and the same provision made in Art. 14 could not be waived.

Dissenting judgment: there is no such difference between the two Constitutions as to make the American doctrine inapplicable

Submission: the dissenting view is correct

[25] ibid. p. 560. [26] (1955) 1 S.C.R. 613, ('55) A.SC. 123.
[27] (1959) Supp. 1 S.C.R. *supra* at pp. 563-64.
[28] ibid. p. 617. [29] ibid. p. 618.
[30] ibid. pp. 597-98.

The whole question re-examined: considerations relevant to the U.S. Constitution overlooked by Bhagwati and Subba Rao JJ.:

8.33 Bhagwati and Subba Rao JJ. were aware that the U.S. decisions, applying waiver and estoppel to constitutional rights, were so many, and so cogent, that it would be strange if they did not apply to our Constitution if the two Constitutions were in *pari materia* as regards fundamental rights. They, however, held that those decisions were inapplicable because the two Constitutions were materially different, the difference in their respective preambles[31] being treated as decisive of the matter. It is submitted that the conclusion is unjustified and has been reached (i) by failing to notice the Declaration of Independence, which preceded the U.S. Constitution, and the Bill of Rights, and other constitutional Amendments, which followed the ratification of that Constitution, and (ii) by reading the preamble to the U.S. Constitution, which was a preamble to the Constitution *without* the Bill of Rights, as throwing a light on the Constitution *which now contains* a Bill of Rights.

(i) The Declaration of Independence and its relation to U.S. Constitution

8.34 The Declaration of Independence is a basic document in relation to the U.S. Constitution. In *Butchers' Union Co.* v. *Crescent City Co.*,[32] Field J. observed that:

"... certain inherent rights lie at the foundation of all governmental action, and upon a recognition of them alone can free institutions be maintained. These inherent rights have never been more happily expressed than in the Declaration of Independence that new evangel of liberty to the people: 'We hold these truths to be self-evident', that is, so plain that their truth is recognized upon their mere statement, 'that all men are endowed,' not by edicts of Emperors or decrees of Parliament or Acts of Congress, but 'by their Creator, with certain inalienable rights' that is, rights which cannot be bartered away or given away except in punishment of crime; 'and that among these are life, liberty and the pursuit of happiness, and to secure these,' not grant them but secure them, 'governments are instituted among men, deriving their just powers from the consent of the governed.'"

And in *Gulf C. & S. F. R. Co.* v. *Ellis*,[33] Brewer, J. said that it was always safe to read the letter of the Constitution in the spirit of the Declaration of Independence. In view of these decisions it is difficult to see any material difference between the American and Indian Constitutions as regards fundamental rights; if anything the American theory recognizes certain human rights as inalienably given by God and the Indian theory does not.

(ii) The U.S. Constitution enacted without a Bill of Rights, which was enacted later by the first ten Amendments

8.35 At the end of its labours, the Constitutional Convention rejected a proposal for incorporating a Bill of Rights. This rejection furnished an argument against ratification of the Constitution, and several States ratified it only after the suggestion put forward by George Washington that the desired guarantee could be added by amendment. Shortly after the First Congress was convened, Madison introduced a series of amendments, designed "to quiet the apprehension of many that without some such declaration of rights the government would assume, and might be held to possess, the

[31] (*a*) "We the people of the United States, in Order to form a more perfect Union, establish Justice, insure domestic Tranquility, provide for the common defence, promote the general Welfare, and secure the Blessings of Liberty to ourselves and our Posterity, do ordain and establish this Constitution for the United States of America."

(b) For the Preamble to our Constitution, see p. A-1.

[32] (1883) 111 U.S. 746 at pp. 756-7, 28 L. ed. 585, 591.

[33] (1896) 165 U.S. 150, 41 L. ed. 666, 670.

power to trespass upon those rights of persons and property which by The Declaration of Independence were affirmed to be inalienable."[34] It need hardly be said that the Rights declared by the first ten amendments are looked upon as fundamental rights in America, and a large number of them would be so regarded in India. The 13th and 14th Amendments were further landmarks in the protection of fundamental rights. The 13th Amendment abolished slavery and gave Congress power to enforce the abolition by appropriate legislation.[35] The first section of the 14th Amendment is so far-reaching that it must be given in full:

The 13th and 14th Amendments

"All persons born or naturalized in the United States and subject to the jurisdiction thereof, are citizens of the United States and of the State wherein they reside. No State shall make or enforce any law which shall abridge the privileges or immunities of citizens of the United States; nor shall any State deprive any person of life, liberty, or property, without due process of law; nor deny to any person within its jurisdiction the equal protection of the laws."

Fundamental Rights in the U.S. and in the Indian Constitutions in *pari materia*

8.36 A comparison of the U.S. Bill of Rights (the first ten amendments), and Amendments 13 and 14, with the Chapter of Fundamental Rights in our Constitution shows that both in the nature and extent of the rights guaranteed and in the procedure for vindicating them, the U.S. Constitution on the whole goes further. It has become necessary to say this because it seems surprising that anyone can compare fundamental rights in the U.S. and the Indian Constitutions without realizing that these rights are as fundamental in America as they are in India, and that on the whole the American Bill of Rights goes further, and contains no reservation for preventive detention.

The Preamble to the U.S Constitution considered by Bhagwati and Subba Rao JJ. was to the Constitution without a Bill of Rights and later amendments

8.37 The U.S. Constitution was submitted for ratification to the Conventions of the States, it being provided by Article VII that ratification by the Conventions of nine States was to be sufficient for the establishment of the Constitution between the States so ratifying the same.[36] The Preamble to the Constitution therefore was to the Constitution which did not contain the Bill of Rights nor the 13th and 14th Amendments. Therefore, the Preamble to the Constitution did not refer to, and could not be expected to throw any light on, the fundamental rights which were enacted later. It is submitted that this aspect of the matter has been overlooked by Bhagwati and Subba Rao JJ. with the result that they have used the Preamble for a purpose for which it was not meant. It is submitted that the conclusion arrived at by Bhagwati and Subba Rao JJ. that the two Constitutions are materially different in their objectives so far as fundamental rights are concerned cannot be supported.

Submission: the view of Bhagwati and Subba Rao JJ. cannot be sustained

---

[34] Cited in Corwin, *Constitution of the United States of America*, at p. 840. Corwin cites in this connection, *Monongahela Navigation Co.* v. *United States* (1892) 148 U.S. 312, 324, 37 L. ed. 463. The facts stated in this paragraph are taken from Corwin.

[35] The resemblance of the 13th Amendment to Art. 17 of the Constitution of India will be apparent. Slavery was a denial of the idea that all men are created equal exactly as untouchability was a denial of equality. The 13th Amendment abolished slavery and armed the Congress with power to effectuate the abolition. Art. 17 abolished untouchability and armed Parliament with power to effectuate its abolition.

[36] New Hampshire was the ninth State to ratify. Therefore, on June 21, 1788, the Constitution became effective. See *Corwin*, p. 14.

As the two Constitutions are in *pari materia*, the doctrine of waiver must apply to our Constitution

8.38 If fundamental rights in the U.S. and the Indian Constitutions are broadly speaking similar, the question naturally arises as to why several fundamental rights can be waived in the United States and no fundamental right can be waived in India. It would be extravagant to suppose that fundamental rights were embodied in our Constitution as a matter of public policy but were not so embodied in the U.S. Constitution.[37] It would be even more extravagant to suppose that eminent American judges in the U.S. Supreme Court, and in the State Courts, were either ignorant of, or consistently overlooked, the relation of public policy to waiver of fundamental rights. If such extravagant conclusions are to be avoided, it is necessary to consider the place of "waiver" in the administration of justice, and the relation of waiver and estoppel to public policy.[38]

The nature of waiver must be considered

The Constitution assumes a country governed by law, and does not exclude considerations relevant to the administration of justice such as rules of evidence, etc.

8.39 The enforcement of fundamental rights by the Courts is part of the administration of justice. In granting fundamental rights, and in providing the means for their enforcement through Courts of law, our Constitution cannot be said to have abrogated considerations relevant to the administration of justice; in fact the securing of justice is one of the objectives of our Constitution. Rules of evidence, rules of procedure, Statutes of Limitation in civil and even in criminal cases, and the doctrine of *res judicata*, all apply to the enforcement of fundamental rights as they do to the enforcement of other rights. Part III of our Constitution says nothing about these matters because it assumes a country governed by law. The proposition that no limitation on a constitutional right can be permitted except that which is expressly contained in the Constitution is correct if rightly understood;[39] but is wholly incorrect if laws of procedure, evidence, limitation and *res judicata*, to mention only a few, are treated as importing limitations on fundamental rights.[40] In fact in *Daryao* v. *U.P.*,[41] the Supreme Court held that the rule of *res judicata* applied to the fundamental right guaranteed by Art. 32. Gajendragadkar J. said:

Daryao's Case: *res judicata* held to be based on public policy by the Sup. Ct. and held to bar the right under Art. 32

> ". . . the basis on which the said rule rests is founded on considerations of public policy. It is in the interest of the public at large that a finality should attach to the binding decisions pronounced by Courts of competent jurisdiction, and it is also in the public interest that individuals should not be vexed twice over with the same kind of litigation. If these two principles form the foundation of the general rule of *res judicata* they cannot be treated as irrelevant or inadmissible even in dealing with fundamental rights in petitions filed under Art. 32."[42]

---

[37] In fact Bhagwati J. has himself stated that the framers of our Constitution followed the American view of the Bill of Rights espoused by Jefferson: (1959) Supp. 1 S.C.R. 528, pp. 558-59. Sastri C.J. had said the same thing in *W.B.* v. *Subodh Gopal Bose* (1954) S.C.R. 587, 616, ('54) A.SC. 92.

[38] It may be stated that though waiver and estoppel are distinct concepts they are frequently used interchangeably: 56 *American Jurisprudence*, pp. 103-4. They cover an overlapping field.

[39] The passage from *R.* v. *Burah* (1878) 5 I.A. 178, (1878) 3 App. Cas. 889, quoted in para 8.28 brings out the correct sense in which the proposition is true.

[40] In conceivable circumstances, a rule of evidence, procedure or limitation may unreasonably burden a fundamental right and may then be struck down as void. But that does not affect the general argument.

[41] (1962) 1 S.C.R. 574, 583 ('61) A.SC. 1457.

[42] (1962) 1 S.C.R. *supra* at pp. 582-83.

8.40 The decision of the Supreme Court in *Tilokchand Motichand* v. *H. B. Munshi*[43] supports the view expressed in para 8.39 above. The petitioner contended that as Art. 32 confers a fundamental right, that right could not be defeated by the plea of laches or delay. In rejecting this contention, Bachawat J. held that though a writ under Art. 32 issued as a matter of course if a breach of a fundamental right was established, that did not mean that "... *in giving relief under Art. 32 the court must ignore and trample under foot all laws of procedure, evidence, limitation, res judicata and the like* ..."[44] (italics supplied). In *Rabindra Nath* v. *Union*[45] the Supreme Court was asked to reconsider the decision in *Motichand's Case* but after full consideration, declined to do so, and reaffirmed the principles of that case.[46]

Tilokchand Motichand's Case supports view in 8.39 above

8.41 Waiver and estoppel are part of the general law on grounds of public policy; *res judicata* is frequently referred to as estoppel by record.[47] We have used the expression "waiver or estoppel" because "the terms 'estoppel' and 'waiver' are often loosely used interchangeably",[48] and because waiver by conduct and estoppel by conduct are not easy to distinguish. As to estoppel, it has been said that though it may cause injustice if misapplied, if rightly applied it is founded upon reason and justice, and is a principle of good morals as well as of law, and that it often enables right and justice to triumph where nothing else known to jurisprudence can do so.[49] In *Daniels* v. *Tearney*[50] Swayne J. said:

Waiver and estoppel are also based on public policy

and are applied in the U.S. to Constitutional rights: *Daniels* v. *Tearney*

"The principle of estoppel thus applied, has its foundations in a wise and salutary policy. It is a means of repose. It promotes fair dealing ... and it often gives triumph to right and justice where nothing else known to our jurisprudence can, by its operation, secure those ends. Like the Statute of Limitations, it is a conservator, and without it society could not well go on."

In the above case the defendant avoided execution under a law which enabled him to do so on executing a bond in favour of the plaintiff. When the plaintiff sued him on the bond, the defendant contended that the law under which he had executed the bond was unconstitutional as it violated the U.S. Constitution. In rejecting the contention the Court said: "Not to apply the principle of estoppel to the bond in this case would, it seems to us, involve a mockery in judicial administration and a violation of the plainest principles of reason and justice."[51]

8.42 The view taken of estoppel in England is the same:[52]

"There was, perhaps, a time when estoppels were described as odious and as such were viewed with suspicion and reluctance. ... But in more modern times the law of estoppel and waiver has developed and has become recognized as a beneficial branch of law. That great lawyer Sir Fredrick Pollock has described the doctrine of estoppel as 'a simple and wholly untechnical con-

The same view is taken of estoppel in England: estoppel is more

---

[43] (1969) 2 S.C.R. 824, ('70) A.SC. 898.
[44] ('70) A.SC. at p. 908. For a full discussion of the case, see Vol. II.
[45] ('70) A.SC. 470, (1970) 2 S.C.R. 697.
[46] ('70) A.SC. at p. 470.
[47] *Halsbury*, (3rd ed.) Vol. 15, pp. 168-9.
[48] 56 *American Jurisprudence*, pp. 103-4.
[49] 19 *American Jurisprudence*, p. 602; see *per* Denning L.J. in *Charles Rickards Ltd.* v. *Oppenhaim* (1950) 1 K.B. 616, 623.
[50] (1880) 102 U.S. 415, 422, 26 L. ed. 187.
[51] ibid.
[52] *Canadian and Dominion Sugar Co. Ltd.* v. *Canadian National (West Indies) Steamships Ltd.* (1947) A.C. 46 (P.C.).

properly described as a substantive rule of law:

ception, perhaps the most powerful and flexible instrument to be found in any system of Court jurisprudence'. . . . Estoppel is often described as a rule of evidence, as, indeed, it may be so described. But the whole concept is more correctly viewed as a substantive rule of law."[53]

estoppel has been extended

But the law has gone further, and the injustice and unfairness which estoppel could not reach[54] have now been reached by the doctrine of quasi-estoppel:

by the doctrine of equitable estoppel

"Whether it be called waiver or forbearance on his part, or an agreed variation or substituted performance, does not matter. It is a kind of estoppel. By his conduct he evinced an intention to affect their legal relations. He made, in effect, a promise not to insist on his strict legal rights. That promise was intended to be acted on, and was in fact acted on. He cannot afterwards go back on it."[55]

Waiver of rights for the benefit of individuals is firmly established in Indian Law

8.43 The law in India is equally well-settled. In *AL. AR. Vellayan Chettiar (Decd.)* v. *Madras*[56] the Privy Council held that there was no inconsistency between the proposition that the provisions of s. 80, C.P.C. were mandatory and must be enforced by the Court and that they may be waived by the authority for whose benefit they were provided. The Privy Council decision in *Gaekwar, Baroda State Railway* v. *Hafiz Habib-Ul-Haq*[57] was distinguished on the ground that the provisions of ss. 86 and 87, C.P.C., which in effect made the consent of the Gov.-Gen.-in-Council a condition of a suit being brought against a Sovereign Prince, were enacted, not, or not merely, for the benefit of the Sovereign Prince, but to serve an important public purpose and therefore such consent could not be waived by the Sovereign Prince.

The nature of waiver

8.44 What is the nature of waiver? Waiver proceeds on the basis that a man not under legal disability is the best judge of his own interest and if, with knowledge of a right or privilege conferred on him by statute, contract or otherwise for his benefit, he intentionally gives up the right or privilege, or chooses not to exercise the right or privilege to its full extent, he has a right to do so. In order to establish waiver it is necessary to establish that the person waiving his right had full knowledge of the right or privilege, and that the right or privilege was conferred principally for his benefit and not principally for the benefit of the public, for in the latter case it would be against the policy of the law to allow him to waive it.[58] Bhagwati and Subba Rao JJ. do not dispute these propositions as regards rights under a contract or statute, and it is submitted

No rational ground for not applying waiver to fundamental rights

that there is no sound reason for refusing to apply the principles to constitutional rights, once it is realized that the doctrine of waiver and estoppel is based on public policy, namely, the plainest requirement of justice, good faith and fairness. Once it is established that Fundamental Rights in the U.S. and the Indian Constitutions are *in pari materia,* and that public policy in America does not

---

[53] ibid. at pp. 55, 56, *per* Lord Wright; see *Halsbury,* (3rd ed). Vol. 15, p. 168.

[54] Because, it was sometimes said, the doctrine of estoppel applied only to the representation of existing or past facts and not to representations about future conduct; also, the representations must have led the person to whom they were made to act to his detriment.

[55] *Charles Rickards Ltd.* v. *Oppenhaim* (1950) 1 K.B. 616, 623, *per* Denning L.J.; see also Anson, *Law of Contracts,* 23rd ed., pp. 104-111, 450-51.

[56] (1947) 74 I.A. 223, 49 Bom.L.R. 794, ('47) A.PC. 197.

[57] (1938) 65 I.A. 182, ('38) A.PC. 165.

[58] *Halsbury,* (3rd ed.) Vol. 14, pp. 637, 638.

preclude the waiver of fundamental rights, no rational grounds can be suggested why such waiver should be precluded in India. That India is a nascent democracy, and its people ignorant and illiterate, may justify a Court in scrutinizing with care a plea of waiver, and in insisting on strict proof that a person alleged to have waived his right did so voluntarily with full knowledge of his rights. But a nascent democracy begins ill if it begins by countenancing bad faith, and disregarding the pledged word given after full knowledge, and if it upholds claims which "involve a mockery in judicial administration and a violation of the plainest principle of reason and justice".[59]

The argument of "nascent democracy" involves a mockery of justice

8.45 We must now consider the views of Das C.J. and Kapur J. that the equality provisions of Art. 14 could not be waived. The reasons given for this view are: (i) Art. 14 (like the 14th Amendment to the U.S. Constitution) is an admonition to the State and it does not confer a right on any person such as is conferred by certain other articles, e.g. Art. 19. The benefit which accrues to an individual is an incidental and necessary consequence of the admonition; (ii) Art. 14 contains no such relaxation of the restrictions imposed such as are contained in certain other articles, e.g. Art. 19; (iii) no American decision is forthcoming to show that the equality clause of the 14th Amendment (which like Art. 14 is an admonition to the State) can be waived; (iv) it is not open to the State to disobey the constitutional mandate merely because a person tells the State that it may do so.[60]

The views of Das C.J. and Kapur J: the reasons underlying those views

8.46 It is submitted that the above reasons cannot be sustained:

Submission: the reasons are not sustainable (i) It is not correct that Art. 14 does not directly confer a right

(i) It is not correct that Art. 14 does not directly confer a right on any person. A right may be conferred on a person by affirmative words of grant; but it can be conferred equally by enacting a prohibition against those who, but for such prohibition, would be free to disregard such right.[61] Further, Art. 14 forms part of a group of articles which is entitled "right to equality", and it confers a right on every person to obtain equal protection of the laws by prohibiting the State from denying such equality. Again, Part III of the Constitution deals with fundamental rights, and Art. 14 deals with one such right — the right to equality. This conclusion is supported by Art. 13 (2) which enjoins the State not to make any law "which takes away or abridges the *rights* conferred by this Part," and by Art. 32 (1) which declares that the right to move the Supreme Court by an appropriate proceeding "for the enforcement of the rights conferred by this

---

[59] *Daniels* v. *Tearney, supra* (1880) 102 U.S. 415, 422.

[60] "In the face of such an unequivocal admonition administered by the Constitution, which is the supreme law of the land, is it open to the State to disobey the constitutional mandate merely because a person tells the State that it may do so? If the Constitution asks the State as to why the State did not carry out its behest, will it be any answer for the State to make that 'true, you directed me not to deny any person equality before the law, but this person said that I could do so, for he had no objection to my doing it'. I do not think the State will be in any better position than the position in which Adam found himself when God asked him as to why he had eaten the forbidden fruit and the State's above answer will be as futile as was that of Adam who pleaded that the woman had tempted him and so he ate the forbidden fruit." *Per* Das C.J. in *Basheshar Nath* v. *C.I.T.*, (1959) Supp. 1 S.C.R. 528 at pp. 552-53.

[61] *Punjab* v. *Daulat Singh* (1946) 73 I.A. 59, 73-4, ('46) A.PC. 66; *W.B.* v. *Union* (1964) S.C.R. 371, 431, ('63) A.SC. 1241.

Part" is guaranteed. There can, therefore, be no doubt that Art. 14 confers on every person a "right to equality".

(ii) even if the right under Art. 14 were absolute, it can still be waived

(ii) It is not easy to see the force of the Chief Justice's observation that Art. 14 contains no such relaxation as is contained for example, in Art. 19. If this means that the right contained in Art. 14 is absolute, then, apart from any question of public policy, an absolute right can be waived as easily as a limited right. But the suggestion that Art. 14 confers an absolute right is not correct, because the whole theory of classification has been incorporated into Art. 14 by judicial decisions. In form Art. 14 prohibits the State from denying to any person the equal protection of the laws; but in substance the Article leaves a wide discretion to the State as to the persons, places and things to which the law is to be applied, and the basis on which they are to be classified. The simple words of Art. 14 convey the impression that the right to the equal protection of the laws is something clear-cut. But the theory of classification, rightly adopted by the Courts, shows that few questions can be answered with less certainty than the question whether a particular law denies to any person the equal protection of the laws. In any given case only a final court can set the question at rest.

(iii) American decisions show that the equality clause of the U.S. Constitution can be waived: *Michael* v. *Louisiana*

(iii) No American decision may have been cited to the Court for the proposition that the equality clause of the 14th Amendment can be waived, but there *are* American decisions which establish that very proposition. Das C.J. appears to have assumed that American decisions on waiver in relation to jury trials were unconnected with the waiver of the equality clause of the 14th Amendment, but this assumption is not correct. A long line of decisions of the U.S. Supreme Court has laid down that " A systematic and arbitrary exclusion of negroes from grand and petit jury lists because of their race and colour constitutes a denial to a negro charged with crime of the equal protection of the laws guaranteed by the Fourteenth Amendment."[62] These decisions also show that where the objection to a grand and petit jury on the ground of violation of the equality clause of the 14th Amendment had been raised in the trial court, the U.S. Supreme Court, reversing the state Courts, has repeatedly upheld the objection. In this context, the question was asked, Can the denial of the equal protection Clause of the 14th Amendment involved in selecting a jury systematically excluding negroes, be waived by a negro accused? In *Michael* v. *Louisiana*[63] both the majority and the minority judgments of the U.S. Supreme Court held that it could be so waived.[64] The majority held on the facts of the case before them that the accused had sufficient opportunity to assert their constitutional right to the equality clause and the Due Process Clause of the 14th Amendment. The minority held that

---

[62] *Hale* v. *Kentucky* (1937) 303 U.S. 613, 82 L. ed. 1050-51; *Neal* v. *Delaware* (1880) 103 U.S. 370, 396, 26 L. ed. 567, 574; *Carter* v. *Texas* (1899) 177 U.S. 442, 44 L. ed. 839, 841; *Norris* v. *Alabama* (1934) 294 U.S. 587, 79 L. ed. 1074.

[63] (1955) 350 U.S. 91, 100 L. ed. 83.

[64] Delivering the opinion of the court, Clark J. said: "It is beyond question that under the Due Process Clause of the Fourteenth Amendment Louisiana may attach reasonable time limitations to the assertion of federal constitutional rights. More particularly, the State may require prompt assertion of the right to callenge discriminatory practices in the make-up of a grand jury.": ibid. 350 U.S. at p. 97, 100 L. ed. at p. 91.

they had not. The whole position is thus summed up in the dissenting judgment delivered by Mr. Justice Black:

". . . since the adoption of the Fourteenth Amendment this court has consistently held that systematic exclusion of negroes from grand-jury service violates the Federal Constitution. See *Patton* v. *Mississippi*, 332 U.S. 463, 465, 92 L. ed. 76, 78, 79 . . . and cases there cited. The Court holds, however, that these petitioners had a reasonable opportunity to challenge the composition of the grand jury indicting them but failed to do so thereby waiving their constitutional and statutory rights to have the charges against them considered by a fair and legal grand jury. Without going into the facts of each particular case, I think that the record shows that there was no such reasonable opportunity afforded to the petitioners Michael and Poret or their counsel."[65]

This case clearly establishes that the constitutional right to the equal protection of the laws can be waived and further shows that a period as short as three days was considered by the majority of the Court reasonable for the assertion of his constitutional right by an accused. It is submitted that the principle accepted both by the majority and the minority of the judges of the U.S. Supreme Court is clearly right. It would be manifestly unjust to allow an accused person who was aware of his right to challenge a jury on the ground of discrimination to lie by, take the chance of a verdict in his favour, and when the verdict goes against him, to turn round and say that the whole proceedings were invalid because he could not waive his constitutional right. The decisions of the U.S. Supreme Court dealing with juries constituted in violation of the equal protection clause of the 14th Amendment are in line with the decisions on that clause generally. Thus, it has been held that constitutional guarantees of equal rights and privileges are for the benefit of only those persons whose rights are affected and cannot be taken advantage of by another person.[66] Again, a person cannot complain of the possible unequal operation of a statute on others less favourably situated than he is,[67] and our Supreme Court has accepted this as correct.[68] American and Indian decisions on the equality clause show that the right to equality is conferred for the benefit of an individual and he alone is entitled to complain of its violation.

and a time limit can be prescribed for the assertion of a constitutional right

The guarantee of equality is for the benefit of those whose rights are affected: *Hans Muller's Case*

[65] 350 U.S. at pp. 102-3, 100 L. ed. at p. 94.
[66] 11 *American Jurisprudence*, p. 757. [67] ibid.
[68] *Hans Muller Nurenburg* v. *Superintendent, Presidency Jail, Calcutta* (1955) 1 S.C.R. 1284, 1295, ('55) A.SC. 367; *Matajog Dobey* v. *H. C. Bhari* (1955) 2 S.C.R. 925, 932, ('56) A.SC. 44 [". . . the petitioners who are complainants cannot be heard to say so (i.e. that they were discriminated against) for there is no discrimination as against any complainant".]; *Kunj Beharilal Agarwal* v. *Union* (1963) 2 S.C.R. 1, 25-6; ('63) A.SC. 518 [*held*, that the allegation that Arts. 14 and 16(1) were violated was without factual basis. In fact the petitioner's position was improved and he was given a limited seniority by the impugned order as compared to the rights which he possessed on January 26, 1950. Therefore, the order, far from adversely affecting him, really conferred upon him larger rights than he previously possessed.]; The above cases did not refer to *Hans Muller's Case*. However, it was referred to in *Malabar Tile Works* v. *Union* (1967) 2 Ker. 109, ('68) A.Ker. 143, 145, where the court observed that the same principle had been affirmed in the other two Supreme Court decisions mentioned in this note. It was accordingly held that the petitioners could not impugn s. 1(3) and (5) of the Payment of Bonus Act, 1965, on the ground of discrimination between a factory and an establishment because they were either owners or occupiers of a factory and s. 1(5) applied only to an establishment other than a factory. As the petitioners were in a more advantageous position, they were not aggrieved by the alleged different treatment and could not complain of discrimination. The same proposition was affirmed in *Gujarat* v. *Shri Ambica Mills* ('74) A.SC. at p. 1306. See para 8.24 and *f.n.* 8 above.

The waiver of a right gives no permission to the State to violate it

(iv) The passing of a law by the Legislature, or the issue of a general notification by the executive, does not require the consent of persons who are affected by such law or notification. When, therefore, a person waives his constitutional right under Art. 14 in respect of a law or notification which denies him that right, he does not thereby permit the legislature or the executive to violate the constitutional injunction. Waiver of a constitutional right assumes that the person is aware of such violation and knows that he can assert his right but considers such assertion unnecessary or undesirable for reasons satisfactory to himself.

Basheshar Nath's Case illustrates the undesirability of deciding constitutional issues which do not arise

8.47 One of the penalties which a lawyer pays for the present mode of law-reporting in India is that in most cases he does not know what was argued before the Court. This is true of *Basheshar Nath's Case.* But this case also furnishes an example of the extreme undesirability of a Court pronouncing on large constitutional questions which do not directly arise. The fundamental right alleged to have been violated in that case was the right to equality under Art. 14. The question of waiver of even that right did not directly arise, if there was no waiver in fact. The question of waiver of other fundamental rights did not arise at all, and it is submitted that the discussion of that question in the judgments shows that a careful scrutiny by the judge[69] is not a substitute for arguments at the bar on points directly involved in a case. These observations become necessary because, as we have seen, several lines of inquiry have not been considered by the judgments, nor do they consider two further lines of inquiry which are necessary for a satisfactory determination of the question of waiver of fundamental rights: First, is any person obliged by our Constitution to assert his fundamental rights if they are violated? Secondly, if he is not, is he free to assert those rights to such extent as he thinks fit? An extremely important line of cases in the United States throws valuable light on these questions. Under Art. 3, sec. 2 (3) of the U.S. Constitution, and under the *Sixth Amendment*, an accused person in all criminal prosecutions is entitled to a trial by an impartial jury of the State. A question has frequently arisen whether that right could be waived, and it led to a conflict of opinion. One view was that the right could not be waived, first, because a trial by jury went to the constitution of the court and to its jurisdiction and, secondly, because the State had an interest in the life and liberties of its citizens, and it was against public policy to allow these to be affected or taken away without a trial in the mode prescribed by the Constitution. On a construction of the relevant provisions, the U.S. Supreme Court held that a trial by jury did not go to the jurisdiction of the court but merely conferred a right upon an accused person.[70] The second ground in support of the view mentioned above was at one time adopted by the U.S. Supreme Court in *Jordan* v. *Masachusetts.*[71] But in *Patton* v. *United States*[72]

Two further lines of inquiry

the earlier and the later view about the waiver of jury trial in the U.S.

---

[69] "It is said that such an inflexible rule would, in certain cases, defeat the very object for which the fundamental rights are created. I have carefully scrutinized the Articles in Part III of the Constitution of India, and they do not, in my view, disclose any such anomaly. . . ." *Per* Subba Rao J. in *Basheshar Nath's Case* (1959) Supp. 1 S.C.R. 528 at p. 612.

[70] *Patton* v. *United States* (1929) 281 U.S. 276, 298, 74 L. ed. 854, 863.

[71] (1911) 225 U.S. 167, 170, 56 L. ed. 1038.

[72] *Supra.*

the Supreme Court "saw through the sophistry involved in the holdings that a jury trial could not be waived",[73] and held that such a right could be waived because every time a person pleaded guilty he waived a trial by jury, and it would be surprising if a man was free to waive a trial altogether but was not free to waive a particular mode of trial.[74] The public policy arguments were disposed of in a passage which is directly relevant to the waiver of fundamental rights under our Constitution:

Public policy not so inconsistent as to allow waiver of jury trial by a plea of guilty, but not the waiver of a particular mode of trial

"It is difficult to see why the fact, frequently suggested, that the accused may plead guilty and thus dispense with a trial altogether, does not effectively disclose the fallacy of the public policy contention; for if the state may interpose the claim of public interest between the accused and his desire to waive a jury trial, *a fortiori* it should be able to interpose a like claim between him and his determination to avoid any form of trial by admitting his guilt. If he be free to decide the question for himself in the latter case, notwithstanding the interest of society in the preservation of his life and liberty, why should he be denied the power to do so in the former? It is no answer to say that by pleading guilty there is nothing left for a jury to try, for that simply ignores the question, which is not what is the effect of the plea? The answer to which is fairly obvious, but, in view of the interest of the public in the life and liberty of the accused, can the plea be accepted and acted upon, or must the question of guilt be submitted to a jury at all events? Moreover, the suggestion is wholly beside the point, which is, that public policy is not so inconsistent as to permit the accused to dispense with *every* form of trial by a plea of guilty, and yet forbid him to dispense with a *particular* form of trial by consent"?[75]

8.48 It is submitted that the correct line of inquiry as regards the waiver of fundamental rights is to ask: (1) is any person under an obligation to assert his fundamental rights against their violation by the State? (2) if not, is any authority appointed by the Constitution to vindicate those rights on his behalf against his will? (3) if not, should he not be free to make the best arrangements for himself in face of such violation? It is obvious that there is no obligation laid on a person to assert his fundamental rights against their violation by the State, and equally obvious that no authority has been appointed to vindicate those rights on his behalf. If so, it is submitted, adapting the language of the U.S. Supreme Court, that public policy is not so inconsistent as to leave it open to a person not to assert his fundamental rights at all and yet prevent him from securing such mitigation of the violation as he considers satisfactory. Again, if the law can interpose public policy between a person and the waiver by him of his fundamental rights, it must have effective power to do so if he decides not to assert them at all. But we know that there is no such interposition in the last mentioned case; therefore there should be no such interposition in the case of waiver.

The line of inquiry about waiver of fundamental rights and public policy

the later view about waiver of jury trial in the U.S. directly applies

[73] Willis, *Constitutional Law*, p. 559.

[74] "It matters not whether the defendant is, in fact, guilty; the plea of guilty is just as effectual as if such was the case. Reasons other than the fact that he is guilty may induce a defendant to so plead, and thereby the state may be deprived of the services of the citizen, and yet the state never actually interferes in such case, and the right of the defendant to so plead has never been doubted. He must be permitted to judge for himself in this respect. So in the case at Bar. The defendant may have consented to be tried by eleven jurors, because his witnesses were then present, and he might not be able to get them again, or that it was best he should be tried by the jury as thus constituted. Why should he not be permitted to do so?": 281 U.S. at p. 304, 74 L. ed. at p. 866.

[75] 281 U.S. at pp. 305-6, 74 L. ed. at pp. 866-7.

Compromise of a dispute involving a violation of fundamental rights

8.49 What has been stated above leads to another aspect of the same question, namely, can a person settle a dispute between himself and the State if the dispute involves the determination of the question whether his fundamental right has been violated? If fundamental rights embody rules of public policy any such settlement must be void, and yet such settlements take place daily outside the courts, and frequently within the courts with the full approval of the judge. The discussion of the waiver of fundamental rights in the judgments of the Supreme Court overlooks the fact that most of these rights depend for their existence on the determination of complicated questions of opinion, of fact and law, of times and seasons. Thus, the question whether a law violates the equal protection of the laws guaranteed by Art. 14 raises difficult questions as to *the basis* of the classification adopted by the law, whether the classification is based on a differentia related to the object to be achieved by the law, whether a particular class against whom the law is directed is one which stands most in need of such law, and the like, and the wide differences of opinion exhibited in the judgments of our Supreme Court show that the questions are questions of doubt and uncertainty. The same is true of all the freedoms guaranteed by Art. 19(1), because they are all subject to "reasonable restrictions" specified in sub-articles (2) to (6) and reasonable restrictions raise questions of fact, opinion, times and seasons on which widely different views can honestly be held. Thus, it is not possible to say in advance as a matter of certainty that a fundamental right has been violated and the presumption of constitutionality which the law rightly raises in favour of a law imposes a burden on the person alleging unconstitutionality which it is not easy to discharge. In such a situation the parties to the dispute should be free to settle the matter by a compromise. Even if one of the parties was mistaken as to the law it has been held that that is no ground for setting aside the compromise if the parties were in difficulty and in doubt and wished to put an end to the disputes and to avoid or to terminate litigation. The real point to note in a compromise of a matter involving an alleged violation of fundamental rights is that the aggrieved party thereby does not give up or abandon his right. That which is abandoned in a compromise is not the ultimate right of the party, but his right in having the assistance of the court to the determination and, if admitted or held good to the enforcement of it.[76] It is submitted that the above considerations reinforce the conclusion arrived at in an earlier part of this Chapter,[77] that, speaking generally, fundamental rights are conferred primarily for the benefit of individuals and can, therefore, be waived, and can form the subject of a lawful compromise. Whether any particular article in Part III embodies rules of public policy and whether the right conferred by it cannot be waived are different matters. The frame of Art. 17, for example, suggests that the rights there conferred are conferred not merely for the benefit of individuals but as a matter of public policy because the enforcement of any disability arising out of untouchability forbidden by that Article is made an offence punishable in accordance with law.

The validity of such a compromise examined

---

[76] See Kerr, *Fraud and Mistake*, 7th ed., p. 147; Pollock and Mulla, *Contract and Specific Relief Acts*, 8th ed., p. 206.

[77] See para 8.44.

8.50 Statutes of limitation were at one time looked upon with disfavour[78] but it is now generally recognised that "the law is founded on public policy, its aim being to secure the quiet of the community to suppress fraud and perjury, to quicken diligence and to prevent oppression".[79] Are statutes of limitation constitutional when they prescribe period of limitation for the enforcement of constitutional rights? Statutes of limitation do not bar the right but merely bar the remedy;[80] therefore, they do not prevent the enforcement of constitutional rights but only require such rights to be asserted within a particular time, subject to the qualification that an unreasonably short period of limitation would prevent the enforcement of such rights in a practical sense and the law prescribing such period would be void. The above propositions, which are submitted on principle, are supported by American decisions. Thus, it was held in *Atchafalaya Land Co.* v. *William Cypress Co.*[81] that a statute prescribing a six years' limitation for suits to annul patents from the State or any transfer of property by a sub-division of the State was held not to deny due process of law or contract obligations when used to annul certain patents granting land. The Court said:

The law of limitation and fundamental rights

Statutes of limitation held applicable to fundamental rights in the U.S.

"... none of the invoked provisions of the Constitution ... are offended even under the construction plaintiffs in error give to the asserted grant to the Board of Commissioners and its conveyance to Wisner and Dresser. The Act of Prescription was a proper exercise of sovereignty. The state could recognize, as it did recognize, that there might be claims derived from it, asserted or to be asserted, rightfully or wrongfully, involving conflicts which should be decided and quieted in the public interest, and therefore enacted the statute. And such is the rationale of statutes of limitations. They do not necessarily lessen rights of property or impair the obligation of contracts. Their requirement is that the rights and obligations be asserted within a prescribed time. If that be adequate, the requirement is legal, and its justice and wisdom have the testimony of the practices of the world."

And earlier[82] and later[83] cases have taken the same view.

8.51 Do statutes of limitation affect the jurisdiction and powers of a Court? If jurisdiction is conferred on a Court not by the Constitution but by law, the question would be academic because the appropriate Legislature has the power to confer or exclude jurisdiction. But the question is of practical importance in respect of the jurisdiction and powers conferred on Courts by our Constitution, as for example, by Arts. 32(2), 129, 131 to 136, and 143 on the Supreme Court, and by Arts. 226 to 228 on the High Courts. What is the "jurisdiction" of a Court? Sometimes "judicial power" and "jurisdiction" are spoken of interchangeably, but this is not correct, because judicial power is at any time exercised by all the Courts, though none of the Courts possess all the jurisdiction for the exercise of judicial power. Thus our Supreme Court has jurisdiction in writ matters, but limited only to the enforcement of fundamental rights. Again, its original jurisdiction is limited by the provisions of Art. 131. Similarly, the High Courts have no jurisdiction to try suits which are

Statutes of limitation do not affect the jurisdiction of a Court

jurisdiction and judicial power distinguished

[78] See Rustomji, *Law of Limitation*, 6th ed., p. 9.
[79] Whitley Stokes: *Anglo Indian Codes*, Vol. II, p. 940. This passage was quoted by Bachawat J. in *Tilokchand Motichand's Case* ('70) A.SC. 898 at p. 909.
[80] *Bombay Dyeing & Mfg. Co. Ltd.* v. *Bombay* (1958) S.C.R. 1122 at pp. 1134-5.
[81] (1921) 258 U.S. 188 at 197; 66 L. ed. 559 at 563.
[82] *e.g. Montoya* v. *Gonzales* (1913) 232 U.S. 375, 378, 58 L.ed. 645, 650.
[83] *e.g. Mattason* v. *Department of Labour* (1934) 293 U.S. 151, 79 L. ed. 251.

exclusively triable by the Supreme Court under Art. 131. But the jurisdiction exercised by a Court involves the exercise of judicial power. Judicial power has been defined as:

". . . the power which every sovereign authority must of necessity have to decide controversies between its subjects, or between itself and its subjects, whether the rights relate to life, liberty or property. The exercise of this power does not begin until some tribunal which has power to give a binding and authoritative decision (whether subject to appeal or not) is called upon to take action."[84]

And jurisdiction has been defined to mean

". . . the authority which a court has to decide matters that are litigated before it or to take cognisance of matters presented in a formal way for its decision. The limits of this authority are imposed by the statute, charter, or commission under which the court is constituted, and may be extended or restricted by the like means."[85]

Conclusion **8.52** It is a necessary feature of judicial power, as of jurisdiction, that matters must be litigated before a court or presented to a court in a formal way for its decision. Now a Statute of Limitation does not ordinarily prevent a person from litigating a matter before a court, nor from presenting a matter for the formal determination of a court, and therefor it cannot affect the courts' jurisdiction. Nor does such a statute take away any powers of the courts — it merely regulates the time within which such powers are to be invoked. No doubt the fact that suits or proceedings are barred by limitation may result in fewer suits being filed and fewer proceedings being instituted; but the jurisdiction of a court does not depend upon the frequency or infrequency of its exercise.[86] Thus the Supreme Court had, and has, exclusive jurisdiction under the Constitution to entertain suits by a State against the Union, and the fact that the jurisdiction was not invoked for ten years made no difference to the jurisdiction.

---

[84] *Per* Griffith C.J. in *Huddart, Parker Pty. Ltd.* v. *Moorehead* (1908-09) 8 C.L.R. 330 at p. 357, approved by the Privy Council first, in *Shell Co. of Australia Ltd.* v. *Federal Commr. of Taxation* (1931) A.C. 275 (J.C.) at p. 295 and secondly in *Labour Relations Board of Saskatchewan* v. *John East Iron Works Ltd.* (1949) A.C. 134, 149.

[85] *Halsbury,* (3rd ed.) Vol. 9, pp. 350-51.

[86] See the observations of Gwyer C.J. in *United Provinces* v. *Atiqua Begum* (1940) F.C.R. 110, 137 (". . . I should have been disposed to say that the jurisdiction and powers of the Court are not affected merely because certain executive orders are not allowed to be questioned in any Court", and the observations of Rowland J. in his dissenting judgment in *R.* v. *Benoari Lal Sarma* (1943) F.C.R. 79 at pp. 152-53; see *Sankari Prasad Singh Deo* v. *Union* (1951) S.C.R. 89, 108, ('51) A.SC. 458 (where it was held that Arts. 31A and 31B did not affect the powers of the Supreme Court under Arts. 32 and 136, or of the High Courts under Art. 226, and those powers "remain just the same as they were before: only a certain class of case has been excluded from the purview of Part III and the courts could no longer interfere, not because their powers were curtailed in any manner or to any extent, but because there would be no occasion hereafter for the exercise of their power in such cases").

CHAPTER IX

RIGHT TO EQUALITY

"Four score and seven years ago our fathers brought forth on this continent a new nation conceived in liberty and dedicated to the proposition that all men are created equal.

"We are engaged in a great civil war, testing whether that nation, or any nation so conceived and so dedicated, can long endure."

— ABRAHAM LINCOLN : Gettysburg Address.

Preliminary

9.1 Liberty and equality are words of passion and power. They were the watchwords of the French Revolution; they inspired the unforgettable words of Abraham Lincoln's Gettysburg Address; and the U.S. Congress gave them practical effect in the 13th Amendment, which abolished slavery, and in the 14th Amendment, which provided that "the State shall not deny to any person within its jurisdiction . . . the equal protection of the laws." Conscious of this history, our founding fathers not only put Liberty and Equality in the Preamble to our Constitution but gave them practical effect in Art. 17 which abolished "Untouchability," and in Art. 14 which provides that "the State shall not deny to any person equality before the law and the equal protection of the laws in the territory of India." Few Articles of our Constitution were more heavily drawn upon in the early days of our Constitution than Art. 14, and it is not surprising that the decisions of the U.S. Supreme Court on "the equal protection of the laws" in the 14th Amendment were freely cited to interpret the same words in Art. 14. However, decisions of our Supreme Court, and the High Courts soon put the guarantee of equality in its proper perspective.

9.2 Under the heading "Right to Equality" are grouped Articles 14 to 18. Article 14 raised many problems but the principles for solving them were well settled by 1960.[1] Article 14 is dealt with in Section I of this Chapter. Articles 15 and 16 have increasingly engaged the attention of the Supreme Court and as Art. 17 has a vital impact on the doctrine of Equality, Arts. 15 to 17 are dealt with together in Section II. However, the discussion of Art. 14 on the one hand, and Arts. 15 to 17 on the other in two separate sections should not conceal from the reader the great importance of determining the co-relation of Arts. 14, 15 and 16 if the concept of equality embodied in these Articles is to be fully understood. Of Art. 18, it is enough to observe that it applied the theory of Equality in another direction by abolishing all titles which were not military or academic distinctions. Article 18 appears to have been framed under the mistaken belief that the U.S. precedent was being followed. Art. 1, s. 9, cl. 8 of the U.S. Constitution provides that :

Art. 18: abolition of titles

"No Title of nobility shall be granted by the United States: And no person holding any office of profit or trust under them, shall, without the consent of the Congress, accept of any present, emolument, office, or title, of any kind whatever, from any king, prince or foreign State."

---

[1] ('79) A.SC. 478, 508.

But the difference between the above Article and Art. 18 is that whereas the U.S. Constitution forbids the grant of titles of *nobility,* Art. 18 forbids the grant of any title which is not a military or academic distinction. A title of nobility is hereditary, and has no necessary connection with merit when the title descends to the subsequent holders of it. But titles can be conferred in recognition of merit, and the theory of equality does not require that merit should not be recognised. Art. 18 itself shows that titles may be conferred in recognition of "military and academic distinction"; but why such recognition should be limited to military and academic distinctions it is impossible to explain. However, there is a difference between theory and practice, and a regular "Honours List" appears once a year in India. It is difficult to believe that "Padma Shri" or "Padma Bhushan" or "Padma Vibhushan", and the like, are "academic" distinctions. However, it is important to determine accurately the correlation of Arts. 14, 15 and 16, if the concept of equality embodied in these Articles is to be fully understood. Nor must the vital impact of Art. 17 on the doctrine of equality be overlooked.

SECTION I : ARTICLE 14

"What is obvious is not always known, and what is known is not always present."[2]

DR. JOHNSON : Preface to the Dictionary.

(a) *The New Doctrine*

Claim for new doctrine: *Royappa* has "added a new dimension to Art. 14"

9.3 In 1979, Chandrachud C.J. said that as far back as 1960 "it was said by this Court in *Kangshari Haldar* that the propositions applicable to cases arising under Art. 14 have been repeated so many times that they now sound platitudinous."[3] And he added that if that was true in 1960, it would be even more true in 1979. In this he was clearly right, as the treatment of Art. 14 in the first two editions of this book clearly shows. However, a number of judgments delivered after 1974 have claimed that the Supreme Court for the first time laid bare in *Royappa's Case*[4] (decided in 1974) "a new dimension" of Art. 14, which had somehow escaped all the judges of an earlier day. In that case, the petitioner, an I.A.S. Officer, challenged an order of transfer, on several grounds, including the violation of Art. 14. Ray C.J. for himself, and Palekar J., dismissed the petition, but did not deal with Art. 14. In a concurring judgment, Bhagwati J. for himself, Chandrachud and Krishna Iyer JJ. dealt with the challenge under Art. 14 and made the claim to have laid bare a new dimension of Art. 14. That claim was repeated in *Maneka Gandhi's Case*[5], in the *Airport Case*[6], and in *Hasia's Case*[7], — cases in which execu-

Claim repeated in three Sup. Ct. decisions

---

[2] present : ready at hand.

[3] *In re Special Courts Bill, 1978,* (1979) 2 S.C.R. 476, ('79) A.SC. 478, at p. 508.

[4] *E. P. Royappa* v. *T. N.* (1974) 2 S.C.R. 348, ('74) A.SC. 555.

[5] *Maneka Gandhi* v. *Union* (1978) 2 S.C.R. 621, ('78) A.SC. 597 (refusal of a passport).

[6] *R. D. Shetty* v. *Airport Authority* (1979) 3 S.C.R. 1014, ('79) A.SC. 1628 (acceptance of a tender for running a canteen).

[7] *Ajay Hasia* v. *Khalid Mujib* ('81) A.SC. 487 (whether the admissions to an Engineering College were valid).

tive action was challenged as violating Art. 14. In *Hasia's Case*, the claim was formulated thus:

"The true scope and ambit of Article 14 has been the subject matter of numerous decisions . . . It is sufficient to state that the content and reach of Article 14 must not be confused with the doctrine of classification. Unfortunately, in the early stages of the evolution of our constitutional law, Article 14 came to be identified with the doctrine of classification because the view taken was that Article forbids discrimination and there would be no discrimination where classification making the differentia (sic) fulfils two conditions, namely, (i) that the classification is founded on an intelligible differentia which distinguishes persons or things that are grouped together from others left out of the group; and (ii) that that differentia has a rational relation to the object sought to be achieved by the impugned legislative or executive action. It was for the first time in *E. P. Royappa* v. *State of Tamil Nadu*[8] that *this Court laid bare a new dimension of Article 14* and pointed out that that Article has *highly activist magnitude* and *it embodies a guarantee against arbitrariness*. . . . We cannot countenance any attempt to truncate its all-embracing scope and meaning, for to do so would be to violate *its activist magnitude*. Equality is a dynamic concept with many aspects and dimensions and it cannot be 'cribbed, cabined and confined' within traditional and doctrinaire limits. From a *positivistic point of view*, equality is antithetic to arbitrariness. In fact, equality and arbitrariness are sworn enemies; one belongs to the rule of law in a republic while the other, to the whim and caprice of an absolute monarch. Where an act is arbitrary it is implicit in it that it is unequal both according to political logic and constitutional law and is therefore violative of Article 14, and if it affects any matter relating to public employment, it is also violative of Article 16. *Articles 14 and 16 strike at arbitrariness* in State action and ensure fairness and equality of treatment."[9] (italics supplied)

* * * *

"Now . . . (as to) the requirement of Art. 14; what is the content and reach of the great equalising principle enunciated in this article? There can be no doubt that it is a founding faith of the Constitution. It is indeed the pillar on which rests securely the foundation of our democratic republic. And therefore, it must not be subjected to a narrow, pedantic or lexicographic approach. No attempt should be made to truncate its all-embracing scope and meaning for, to do so would be to violate its *activist magnitude*. Equality is a dynamic concept with many aspects and dimensions and it cannot be imprisoned within traditional and doctrinaire limits . . . Article 14 strikes at arbitrariness in State action and ensures fairness and equality of treatment. The principle of *reasonableness*, which legally as well as philosophically, is an essential element of *equality* or *non-arbitrariness* pervades Article 14 like a brooding omnipresence. This was again reiterated by this Court in *International Airport Authority's Case*[10] . . It must therefore now be taken to be well settled that what Article 14 strikes at is arbitrariness because *an action that is arbitrary, must necessarily involve negation of equality. The doctrine of classification which is evolved by the Courts is not paraphrase of Article 14 nor is it the objective and end of that Article.* It is merely a judicial *formula for determining whether the legislative or executive action in question is arbitrary and therefore constituting denial of equality.* If the classification is not reasonable and does not satisfy the two conditions referred to above, the impugned legislative or executive action would plainly be arbitrary and the guarantee of equality under Article 14 would be breached."[11] (italics supplied)

The claim made by Bhagwati J. and his brother judges of having laid bare a "new dimension" of Art. 14 is hereafter referred to as the "new doctrine".

Positive and negative aspect of the new doctrine

9.4 The claim made in these passages is that *Royappa's Case* pointed out for the first time that *"Art. 14 embodies a guarantee against arbitrariness* . . . and (equality) cannot be 'cribbed, cabined and con-

[8] (1974) 2 S.C.R. *supra*.
[9] ('81) A.SC. *supra* at p. 498.
[10] (1979) 3 S.C.R. *supra*.
[11] ('81) A.SC. *supra* at p. 499.

fined' within traditional and doctrinaire limits" — an obvious reference to the doctrine of classification (which is hereafter referred to as "the old doctrine"). The conclusion drawn in these passages is that classification "is merely a judicial formula for determining whether the legislative or the executive action is arbitrary and therefore constitutes a denial of equality." The new doctrine has both a positive and a negative aspect. Positively it asserts that Art. 14 embodies a guarantee against arbitrariness, and negatively, that the "traditional and doctrinaire theory of classification" was not correct, for it failed to recognize that Art. 14 embodied a guarantee against arbitrariness. It will be submitted presently that the new doctrine is clearly wrong, and the old doctrine is clearly right. For, apart from the various infirmities of the new doctrine, it equates a part to the whole. No doubt arbitrary actions ordinarily violate equality; but it is simply not true that whatever violates equality must be arbitrary. The large numger of decided cases, before and after *Royappa's Case,* make it obvious that many laws and executive actions have been struck down as violating equality without their being arbitrary. Further, it will be submitted that in a liberal democratic Constitution like ours, it would be inappropriate to characterize laws as arbitrary.

New doctrine dealt with first as it is untenable

9.5 The new doctrine confronts the writer of a critical commentary on the Constitutional Law of India with the problem of presentation and exposition. Should he discuss at length the old doctrine — which is now stated to be no longer the law on the guarantee of equality — or should he start with the new doctrine, show that it is clearly wrong and the old doctrine clearly right, and thereafter discuss the old doctrine in its manifold aspects? After much reflection, the second course has been adopted as leading to the clearest understanding of the right to equality conferred by Art. 14.

Submission: The old doctrine clearly right and the new doctrine clearly wrong

9.6 The passages from *Hasia's Case* set out above, read more like a sermon on equality than a careful analysis of the scope and nature of the right to equality guaranteed to every person by Art. 14. However, stripped of rhetoric, and the use of fashionable phrases like "dynamic aspects" and "activist magnitude" (whose appropriateness we need not stop to examine), it is claimed for the new doctrine that it explains, as the "doctrinaire" theory of classification does not, the true scope of the right to equality. One of the risks which judges run by being "dynamic", or "active", is, that at times, their activity may carry them away from truth and reality, and this is precisely what has happened to Bhagwati J. and his brother judges in propounding the new doctrine. It is submitted, first, that the old doctrine is the *only* doctrine which brings out the full scope of "the equal protection of the laws" guaranteed to every person by Art. 14, and, secondly, that the new doctrine is untenable for the following reasons:

Reasons for submission that new doctrine is untenable

(*a*) *The new doctrine hangs in the air,* because it is propounded without reference to the terms in which the guaranteed right to "the equal protection of the laws" is conferred.

(*b*) The new doctrine involves the logical fallacy of the undistributed middle or the fallacy of simple conversion as explained in para 9.8 below.

(*c*) The new doctrine fails to distinguish between the violation of equality by a law and its violation by executive action.

(*d*) The new doctrine fails to analyze certain concepts like "arbitrary", "law", "executive action" or "discretionary power" and fails to recognize the necessary implication of numerous Supreme Court decisions on classification.

If any reader feels that in discussing the new doctrine the present writer states what is obvious and, even elementary, he can only say that the words of Dr. Johnson quoted at the beginning of the present Section also apply, although rarely, to the judgments of the Supreme Court, and if those judgments deny the obvious, then the obvious must be stated simply.

New doctrine hangs in the air

9.7 *The new doctrine hangs in the air,* because it propounds a theory of equality without reference to the terms in which Art. 14 confers the right to equality. Article 14 has two limbs: the State is not to deny to any person (i) "equality before the law" or (ii) "the equal protection of the laws". The expression "equality before the law", means, broadly speaking, that except in a very limited class of cases[12], a Court administering justice is not concerned with the status or position of the parties appearing before it; "the law is no respector of persons". However, what is meant by "the equal protection of the laws"? As we have seen, these words were taken from the 14th Amendment, and our founding fathers were well aware that for over 150 years, numerous decisions of the U.S. Supreme Court had evolved the doctrine of classification to explain and give a content to "the equal protection of the laws." Before judges propound a new doctrine about Art. 14, they must ask themselves the question: "What does 'the equal protection of the laws' mean?" Obviously they cannot brush aside this question as "a lexicographical exercise", because the scope and nature of a right cannot be determined independently of the words in which that right is conferred.

Doctrine of classification gives content and significance to the guarantee of "equal protection of the laws"

9.8 Since the new doctrine has been propounded by judges without asking and answering the question "What is meant by 'the equal protection of the laws'?" we must answer that question. If all men were created equal, and remained equal throughout their lives, then the same laws would apply to all men. But we *know* that men are unequal; consequently, a right conferred on persons that they shall not be denied "the equal protection of the laws" cannot mean the protection of the same laws for all. It is here that the doctrine of classification, (the old doctrine) steps in, and gives content and significance to the guarantee of the equal protection of the laws. Equal protection of the laws must mean the protection of equal laws for all persons *similarly situated.* To separate persons similarly situated from those who are not, we must *discriminate,*[13] that is, "act on the basis of a difference between" persons, or "observe distinctions carefully" between persons who are, and persons who are not, similarly situated. But as the distinction is to be made for the purpose of making a law, how must the distinction be related to the law? This is

[12] *e.g.* public servants cannot be prosecuted for certain offences without the sanction of the appropriate authorities: see s. 164, I.P.C. read with s. 197, Cr. P.C.

[13] *Cf.* "It must be presumed that (the Legislature's) *discriminations* are based on adequate grounds". (italics supplied). See para 9.32(1).

Central test for permissible classification

answered by the central test for a permissible classification: "Permissible classification must satisfy two conditions, namely, (i) it must be founded on an intelligible differentia which distinguishes persons or things that are grouped together from others left out of the group, and (ii) the differentia must have a rational relation to the object sought to be achieved by the statute in question", with the qualification that "the differentia and the object are different (so) that the object by itself cannot be the basis of the classification."[14] A law based on a permissible classification fulfils the guarantee of the equal protection of the laws and is valid; a law based on an impermissible classification violates that guarantee and is void. It is difficult to see why Bhagwati J. and his brother judges, describe the theory of classification as "doctrinaire",[15] because there is nothing unpractical about a doctrine which effectively secures the equal protection of the laws to persons by declaring laws based on impermissible classifications to be invalid, whilst leaving to the State a wide field for making laws based on permissible classifications. The theory that "what Article 14 strikes at is arbitrariness because an action that is arbitrary, must necessarily involve the negation of equality" conceals obvious fallacies, as explained in para 9.9 below. Besides, the new doctrine is based on *a priori* ideas about the "activist magnitude" and the "dynamic concept" of Art. 14—*a priori*, because divorced from the words in which the guarantee is conferred. However, the claim that the new doctrine does, and the old doctrine does not, give full effect to the guarantee of the equal protection of the laws, is examined in detail in paras 9.9 to 9.13 below.

New doctrine involves fallacy of the "undistributed middle" and/or the fallacy of "simple conversion"

9.9 The new theory involves the fallacy of the undistributed middle. A standard book on Logic[16] explains the fallacy thus:

"Consider the following standard-form categorical syllogism:

All dogs are mammals
All cats are mammals
____
Therefore all cats are dogs.

The middle term 'Mammals' is not distributed in either premiss, and this violates (Rule 2, *In a valid categorical syllogism, the middle term must be distributed in at least one premiss*). Any syllogism which violates Rule 2 is said to commit the *Fallacy of the Undistributed Middle*. It should be clear by the following considerations that any syllogism which violates this rule is invalid. The conclusion of any categorical syllogism asserts a connection between two terms. The premisses justify asserting such a connection only if they assert that each of the two terms is connected with a third term in such a way that the first two are appropriately connected with each other *through* or *by means of* the third. For the two terms of the conclusion really to be connected through the third, at least one of them must be related to the *whole* of the class designated by the third or middle term. Otherwise each may be connected with a *different part* of that class, and not necessarily connected with each other

---

[14] See para 9.32 (c) and (d).

[15] *doctrinaire*: theoretical or unpractical (*C.O.D.*).

[16] Copi, *Introduction to Logic*, 2nd ed. pp 189-90. See also *Oxford Essays in Jurisprudence* (First Series) edited by A. G. Guest. Chapter VII, "Logic in the Law" by A. G. Guest at p. 194: "In *Stuart* v. *Diplock* 43 Ch.D. 343, 352, Bowen J. restated counsel's argument in the form of a syllogism in order to show that it contained the fallacy of the undistributed middle. (The syllogism was: "All ladies outfitters sell combinations; the Defendants sell combinations, therefore the Defendants are ladies outfitters.")

at all. This is obviously what occurs in the example. Dogs are included in *part* of the class of mammals, and cats are also included in *part* of the class of mammals. But different *parts* of that class may be (and, in this case are) involved, so the middle term does not connect the syllogism's major and minor terms. For it to connect them, *all* of the class designated by it must be referred to in at least one premiss, which is to say that in a valid syllogism the middle term must be *distributed* in at least one premiss."[17]

The new doctrine is based on the following premisses:

All arbitrary actions violate equality.
Some laws violate equality.

But from these premisses no conclusion can be drawn, because the middle term "equality" is undistributed in both the major and minor premisses. If a conclusion were drawn, namely, "therefore some laws are arbitrary actions" it would be as inaccurate as the conclusion that "all cats are dogs" in the illustration given by Copi. However, it may be that judges who interpret Art. 14 without referring to its language may, inadvertently, commit the not uncommon fallacy of "simple conversion". If All A is B, it would be a fallacy of simple conversion to conclude that All B is A. For example, to conclude from the proposition "All men are mortal", that "All mortals are men" is to commit the fallacy of simple conversion, because, obviously, all living beings are mortal. Equally, it is a fallacy of simple conversion to conclude from the premiss "All arbitrary actions violate equality" that "All that violates equality are arbitrary actions".

Meaning of "arbitrary" and "discretionary"

9.10 Since the new doctrine involves logical fallacies, that would be enough to show that the doctrine is untenable. But this conclusion is fortified by analyzing certain concepts like "arbitrary", "law", "executive action" and "discretionary power". First, it is necessary to define "arbitrary". "Arbitrary" is defined in the Shorter Oxford Dictionary (3rd ed.) as follows: "2. *Law* relating to or dependent on the discretion of an arbiter, discretionary, not fixed. 3. based on mere opinion or preference *hence* capricious. 4. unrestrained in the exercise of will, absolute *hence* despotic." These definitions show, first that "arbitrary" involves the voluntary action of a person on whom the arbitrary power is conferred. But as we have seen in para 2.1 of the text, we cannot attribute will or intention to Parliament (or a Legislature) except figuratively and as a linguistic device.[18] Secondly, we do speak of harsh, oppressive, unjust, or cruel laws; because it is possible to characterize laws by reference to their content, nature and/or effect. However, under a Constitution such as ours we do not speak of "arbitrary laws". The phrase "arbitrary laws" is appropriate to describe laws made by absolute monarchs or dictators, because they can make laws in the "unrestrained exercise of their will". Thirdly, the definitions show the close connection

---

[17] ibid. pp. 189-90.

[18] *Cf.* "It may be made clear at the outset that the doctrine of colourable legislation does not involve any question of *bona fides* or *mala fides* on the part of the legislature. The whole doctrine resolves itself into the question of competency of a particular legislature to enact a particular law. If the legislature is competent to pass a particular law, the motives which impelled it to act are really irrelevant. On the other hand, if the legislature lacks competency, the question of motive does not arise at all. Whether a statute is constitutional or not is thus always a question of power: *Vide* Cooley's *Constitutional Limitations*, Vol. I, p. 379": *Per* Mukherjea J. in *K. C. Gajapati Narayan Deo* v. *Orissa* (1954) S.C.R. 1 at pp. 10-11.

between arbitrary power and discretionary power, which is dealt with later.

Law violating Art. 14 and arbitrariness

9.11 Further, when a law based on impermissible classification is struck down for violating the equal protection of the laws, that does not involve a finding that the law is "arbitrary". The question whether persons or things are classified on the basis of an intelligible differentia reasonably related to the object of the law, raises questions of fact, evaluation and law on which honest persons may differ in good faith. The reversal by an appellate court of a trial court's judgment upholding a classification, and the reversal by the Supreme Court of the appellate court's judgment, as not infrequently happens, shows that highly trained and independent judges can, and do, hold different views as to whether a particular classification is permissible or not, and no question of upholding arbitrariness arises if different views are taken. This conclusion is reinforced by the large number of dissenting judgments in our Supreme Court either upholding, by a majority, a classification which the dissenting judges would strike down, or striking down, by a majority, a classification which the dissenting judges would uphold. If judges of the highest standing can differ as to whether a classification is permissible or impermissible without raising any question of arbitrariness, those who *draft Bills* and those who pass them into Acts might well take the view that the Acts were based on a permissible classification. Besides, impermissible classification may be the result of inadvertence or negligence.

Relation between "arbitrary" and "discretionary"

9.12 Bhagwati J. and his brother judges did not consider the close relation between *arbitrary* and *discretionary* power. The conferment of wide discretionary power is, broadly speaking, a confession that it is not possible to lay down rules for the exercise of that power. Two illustrations may be given—one from criminal law and the other from industrial law. The Penal Code lays down (with rare exceptions where a particular sentence must be imposed) the maximum punishment by way of fine and/or imprisonment which can be inflicted on persons found guilty of committing specified offences. A discretion conferred on judges and magistrates which ranges from a small fine to a substantial fine together with the maximum term of imprisonment prescribed by the law can only be described as arbitrary, for no rules and no guidelines can be given for the exercise of the discretionary power. And yet the circumstances under which crimes are committed, and the matters of extenuation and aggravation to be taken into account in deciding on the punishment, are so various, that a power, in essence arbitrary, must be conferred on judges and magistrates if justice is to be done. If the conferment of arbitrary power by itself violated Art. 14, all punishments prescribed by the Penal Code would be void. However, apart from the doctrine of necessity, the doctrine of classification makes it clear that equality is violated by treating persons similarly situated differently and, except in the rarest of cases, no two persons convicted of the same offence are similarly situated. The second illustration is furnished by s. 10 of the Industrial Disputes Act which confers on the appropriate Government a discretion to refer an industrial dispute to one of several authorities set up under the Act. In upholding this discretion the Supreme Court held that the criteria for exercising the discretion were enacted in the Act itself and it was not possible to lay down further rules for the exercise of that discretion as no two cases of actual or apprehended industrial disputes were alike and in such disputes in a particular establishment or undertaking, each dispute had to be treated according to the situation prevalent in the undertaking.[19] In other words, the question of wide discretionary power violating Art. 14 cannot arise where it is to be exercised with reference to situations, no two of which are alike. These examples can be multiplied, and several examples will be found in para 9.106 below in which wide discretionary powers have been upheld because they were not capable of being governed by further rules.

Equality has many more sworn enemies than arbitrariness

9.13 In conclusion, it is submitted, first, that the new doctrine is untenable for the reasons given above; and, secondly, that instead of enlarging the fundamental right to equality it has narrowed it to one aspect of equality. The graphic words in *Hasia's Case* that "In fact equality and arbitrariness are sworn enemies" has made the Court forget that equality has many more sworn enemies than arbitrariness, and the old doctrine of classification has enabled the Courts to strike down all of them. Finally, the new doctrine obscures the clear light which the old doctrine has thrown on many aspects of equality.

Section I : Article 14

(b) *The Old Doctrine.*

Some questions raised by Art. 14

9.14 Before dealing with the decided cases we must consider some of the questions posed by Art. 14: (*a*) What light is thrown on the Article by the form in which it is cast? (*b*) Against whom is the Article directed? (*c*) What is the nature of the right which is conferred by the Article?

The form of the Article: it confers a right by enacting a prohibition

9.15 Article 14 confers a right by enacting a prohibition which in form, at least, is absolute. In this respect, Art. 14 has been said to differ from Art. 19. "It will be observed that, so far as (Art. 14) is concerned, there is no relaxation of the restriction imposed by it such as there are in some of the other Articles, e.g., Article 19, Cls. (2) to (6)."[20] But, these observations, though formally correct, overlook the fact that Art. 14 is not really absolute, since the doctrine of classification has been incorporated in it by judicial decisions.[21] Article 14, as interpreted by the courts, would run in some such words as these: The State shall not deny to any person equality before the law or equal protection of the laws provided that nothing herein contained shall prevent the State from making

Though absolute in form, the doctrine of classification has been incorporated in it

---

[19] *Niemla Textile Finishing Mills Ltd.* v. *2nd Punjab Tribunal* (1957) S.C.R. 335, ('57) A.SC. 329; *R. S. Navigation Co.* v. *Radha Nath* (1957) 9 Ass. 353, ('60) A.Ass. 39.

[20] *Per* Das C.J. in *Basheshar Nath* v. *C.I.T.* (1959) Supp. (1) S.C.R. 528, 552, ('59) A.SC. 149.

[21] *Makhan Lal Malhotra* v. *Union* (1961) 2 S.C.R. 120, 130, ('61) A.SC. 392; *Bishnu Charan* v. *Orissa* ('52) A.Or. 42; *Sakhi Chand* v. *Central Co-op. Bank* ('55) A.Pep. 129.

a law based on or involving a classification founded on an intellible differentia having a rational relation to the object sought to be achieved by the law.

Against whom is the Article directed?

9.16 The prohibition contained in Art. 14 is directed against the State, as widely defined by Art. 12, for the purposes of Part III (Fundamental Rights).[22] The prohibition of Art. 14 is thus addressed not only to the legislature but also to the executive, and not only to the Government but also to local and other authorities; but it is not directed against private individuals.[23] In *Erusian Equipment and Chemicals Ltd.* v. *W.B.*[24] the Supreme Court applied Arts. 14 and 19 to a contract. It held that

Art. 14 applied to contract

"The State can enter into contract with any person it chooses. No person has a fundamental right to insist that the Government must enter into a contract with him. A citizen has a right to earn livelihood and to pursue any trade. A citizen has right to claim equal treatment to enter into a contract which may be proper, necessary and essential to his lawful calling."[25] Further, "Blacklisting has the effect of preventing a person from the privilege and advantage of entering into lawful relationship with the Government for purposes of gain. The fact that a disability is created by the order of *blacklisting* indicates that the relevant authority is to have an objective satisfaction. *Fundamentals of fair play require that the person concerned should be given an opportunity to represent his case before he is put on the blacklist.*"[26] (italics supplied)

and to a lease: *Radhakrishna Agarwal's Case*

The question whether Art. 14 applied to a contract between a citizen and the State was also considered in *Radhakrishna Agarwal* v. *Bihar*.[27] There, the petitioner filed two writ petitions challenging the increase of royalty payable under a lease, entered into by the petitioners with the respondent, which provided for an increase of royalty every three years in consultation with the lessee, and also the cancellation of the lease. Clause 4 of the lease required the lessee to establish a factory in Bihar within a period of five years from the date of the agreement for processing of seeds and extracting oil from them, failing which the lease would be cancelled. The petitioner contended that Art. 14 had been violated, both by the increase of royalty and by the cancellation of the lease, because the lease had been entered into in exercise of the executive powers of the State, and such executive power was subject to the provision of fundamental rights. The Patna High Court rejected this contention, but granted a certificate for appeal to the Supreme Court. The Supreme Court held that the exercise of the State's power to enter into a contract in the exercise of the power conferred by Art. 298, and in the form prescribed by Art. 299, would attract the provisions of Art. 14 *at the threshold*, before the contract was entered into, as held in *Erusian Equipment and Chemicals Ltd.* v. *W.B.*[28] However, the Supreme Court held that once the contract had been entered into, the

---

[22] See para 7.6.

[23] See *P. D. Shamdasani* v. *Central Bank of India Ltd.* (1952) S.C.R. 391, 393, ('52) A.SC. 59. That was a case under Arts. 19 and 31, but the position is the same under Art. 14.

[24] (1975) 2 S.C.R. 674, ('75) A.SC. 266; foll. in *J. Vilangandan* v. *Executive Engineer* (*P.W.D.*) ('78) A.SC. 930, 932.

[25] ('75) A.SC. *supra* at p. 268. [26] ibid p. 269.

[27] (1977) 3 S.C.R. 249, ('77) A.SC. 1496.

[28] (1975) 2 S.C.R. 674, ('75) A.SC. 266.

rights of parties were governed by the contract and a breach of its terms gave rise to no question as to the violation of Art. 14. The Supreme Court said that the Patna High Court had rightly divided the types of cases in which breaches of alleged obligations by the State, or its agents, could be set up, into three categories, namely,

"(i) Where a petitioner makes a grievance of breach of promise on the part of the State in cases where on assurance of promise made by the State he has acted to his prejudice and predicament, but the agreement is short, of a contract within the meaning of Art. 299 of the Constitution; (ii) Where the contract entered into between the person aggrieved and the State is in exercise of a statutory power under certain Act or Rules, framed thereunder and the petitioner alleges a breach on the part of the State; and (iii) Where the contract entered into between the State and the person aggrieved is non-statutory and purely contractual and the rights and liabilities of the parties are governed by the terms of the contract, and the petitioner complains about breach of such contract by the State."[29]

The Supreme Court observed that the Patna High Court had rightly held that the petitioner's case fell in the third category, and Art. 14 was not attracted.

9.17 It is submitted that the proposition that Art. 14 was not attracted may be correct on the facts of the case, but is too wide, for in certain situations it would be incorrect. If a Government enters into leases of similar and equal plots of land ("the said plots") for a rent fixed under the lease, but to be increased periodically in consultation with the lessee, the increase made by Government being binding on the lessee, it is clear that government cannot increase the rent differently for each of the said plots without violating Art. 14. In *Agarwal's Case*, the Solicitor-General stated that the question of Art. 14 would arise only if increase of the petitioner's rent were being compared with the rent of other lessees. The Supreme Court expressed some doubt whether Art. 14 would be attracted but stated that there was no case made out for the application of Art. 14. It is submitted that if *a law* cannot confer arbitrary power on Government, to enter into leases and increase the rents of similar plots arbitrarily at its discretion, neither can Government discriminate by *executive action* between lessees occupying the same position, by favouring some and disfavouring other lessees. Article 14 forbids such arbitrary action.

Submission: Sup. Ct.'s proposition too wide

9.18 The form of Art. 14 may suggest that there is an opposition between the State and a "person" so that the State is not protected by Art. 14. If there was only one State in India there would be something to be said for this view. But there are several States in India and the Union of India is a State. The question therefore arises whether when State A enacts a law, it can deny to States B, C and D equality before the law, or the equal protection of the laws. This question assumes further importance because Art. 12 defines the "State" as including local and other authorities within the territory of India. Therefore it is necessary to consider whether the State is a person within the meaning of Art. 14. Different views have been expressed on this question, some of which appear to have been

Is the State a person protected by Art. 14?

[29] ('77) A.SC. at pp. 1500-1501.

coloured by the view that fundamental rights are conferred on the people and not on the State. It would lead to a clearer understanding of the problem if we consider it first on principle, and then on authority.

Natural and legal persons: a corporation is a legal person

9.19 In legal theory a person is "any being whom the law regards as capable of rights or duties"[30] and as so defined, persons are either natural or legal. A natural person is a human being. Legal persons are beings, real or imaginary, who for the purposes of legal reasoning are treated in greater or less degree in the same way as human beings.[31] A corporation, which is an entity distinct and separate from its members, is an example of a legal person. In considering whether the State is a corporation, and therefore a person, Salmond explains how in England the monarchical form of Government has made it unnecessary to treat the State as a corporation, i.e. a legal person.[32] However,

Historical reasons for the State not being treated as a corporation in England

In Australia the States are bodies corporate and politic

"The Commonwealth of Australia, for example and also the constituent Australian States are to be deemed for certain purposes bodies politic and corporate for by virtue of Australian Legislation they can now sue and be sued in their names; and possess other attributes of personality; thus, an action will now lie at the suit of the State of Victoria against the State of New South Wales . . ."[33]

Submission: the provisions of our Constitution show that the Union and the States are legal persons

It is submitted that in India the Union of India and the States are legal persons. Part III (Fundamental Rights) imposes several duties on the State, and provides for their enforcement by the Supreme Court and the High Courts: Arts. 32 and 226. Part IV (Directive Principles of State Policy) imposes on the State a duty to apply the directive principles in making laws, though those principles cannot be enforced in a court of law: Art. 37. The executive power of the Union and of each State extends to the carrying on of any trade or business and to the acquisition, holding and disposal of property and the making of contracts for any purpose: Art. 298; and the Government of India and the Government of a State may sue or be sued: Art. 300. The Union and the States have power to borrow money: Arts. 292 and 293. The property of the Union is exempt from State taxation except as Parliament may otherwise provide: Art. 285; and the property and income of the State is exempt from Union taxation except that Parliament may by law provide for imposing a tax on the income of a business carried on by a State and on the property used by such State for such business: Art. 289. Property accruing by *escheat* or lapse or *bona vacantia* vests in the Union or the States as provided by Art. 296. These provisions clearly show, that the Union of India and the States have rights and obligations which can be enforced one against the other and against private individuals and private or public bodies.[34] The existence of a monarchy in England which has prevented the State from being

and can enforce rights and obligations one agaist the other

[30] Salmond, Jurisprudence, 11th ed., p. 350 (the definition is sufficiently accurate for the purpose of this discussion).

[31] ibid. pp. 350-51.

[32] ibid. pp. 372-76.

[33] ibid p. 375; see also *Wynes*, p. 371.

[34] That the Union of India and the States can enforce rights one against the other is emphasised by Art. 131 which confers on the Supreme Court exclusive Original Jurisdiction to try any dispute between the Government of India and any State or States on the one side, and one or more other States on the other, or between two or more States.

recognized as a juristic person has, as we have seen, lost some of its force in self-governing Dominions like Australia,[35] and in India the position is clearer still, because there is no authority in India of which it can be said that it acts in the right of the Union or acts in the right of the States but is still one and indivisible, as the Crown is in Australia. It is submitted that for the reasons given above, the States in India are bodies politic and corporate and in this respect they resemble the States of the United States, where a State has been held to be a corporation.[36]

9.20 This conclusion is strengthened by the consideration that strange consequences would follow if it were held that the State was not a person within the meaning of Art. 14 and the other Articles in Part III, particularly Art. 31, (which was deleted in 1979.) It is well settled that the words in a Constitution are to be given the widest meaning and, secondly, that a construction which would lead to absurd results must be rejected in favour of a construction which would avoid them. If the State were not a person within the meaning of Part III of the Constitution, Art. 31(1) would not apply to the States, so that State A could deprive State B of its property in State A without the authority of law.[37] Again, if, for example, the States of Karnataka and Maharashtra maintain separate Government Depots in Rajasthan for the sale of the same variety of cloth, Rajasthan would be free to tax the same goods sold by the two Depots at different rates of tax on the ground that Art. 14 does not protect the States. It is submitted that it is unreasonable to suppose that the framers of the Constitution intended to produce such results,[38] and it is equally unreasonable to suppose that a Constitution which recognizes equality before the law and the equal protection of the laws as a fundamental right, enjoyed even by aliens, would deny that right to the State.

Strange consequences of the Union and the States not being persons: equality can be denied by one State to another, and property of one State in another can be confiscated

9.21 The question whether the State is a person within the meaning of Art. 14 has been considered in *Moti Lal* v. *U.P.*,[39] in *Amraoti Electric Supply Co.* v. *Dist. and Sessions Judge, Amraoti*,[40] *Kesheoprasad* v. *State*[41] and *Shiv Parshad* v. *Punjab*,[42] but none of them raised the question whether in relation to the impugned law of one State, other States affected by that law could be regarded as persons within the meaning of Art. 14. Again, these cases made a distinction between the trading activities of a State and its governmental activities, apparently holding that as regards governmental activities, a State was not a person. Therefore, these cases do not discuss comprehensively the question whether a State is a person but deal only

Decided cases do not raise the question whether the Union and the States are persons *inter se*

Conflicting judicial views as to whether the State is a person

---

[35] See *f.n.* 33 above.

[36] "Even a State may be regarded broadly as a Corporation inasmuch as it is a legal being, capable of transacting same kinds of business like a natural person, and such a being is a Corporation." 13 *American Jurisprudence*, 2d. p. 550.

[37] It has been held in *In re Allocation of Lands and Buildings in a Chief Commissioner's Province* (1943) F.C.R. 20, ('43) A.FC. 13, 47, that in lands or buildings vested in His Majesty for the purposes of a Province outside the territorial limits of the Province, the rights of the Provincial Government over them are analogous to those of a private owner.

[38] The absurd consequences of holding that fundamental rights are not available to a State were pointed out by Sinha C.J. in *W.B.* v. *Union* ('63) A.SC. 1241, 1264.

[39] (1951) 1 All. 269, ('51) A.A. 257 (F.B.)

[40] (1952) Nag. 830, ('53) A.N. 35.

[41] (1955) Nag. 459, ('55) A.N. 177.

[42] (1957) Punj. 310, ('57) A. Punj. 150.

with one aspect of that question. In *Moti Lal* v. *U.P.*[43] the judgments of the Full Bench disclose a difference of judicial opinion. It is not clear whether Malick C.J. considered the State to be a person within the meaning of Art. 14, but his observations suggest that he did not.[44] Mootham and Wanchoo JJ. did not deal with this question, but they adopted the distinction made in *P. & O. Steam Navigation Co.* v. *Secretary of State*[45] between the governmental and the trading activities of the East India Co., namely, that in respect of its trading activities the East India Co. was subject to the same liabilities as private individuals. They held that in running a motor transport service the State was engaged in a trading activity and could not secure preference to itself, and that s. 42 (3) (a) of the Motor Vehicles Act was void. Sapru and Agarwalla JJ. considered the question jurisprudentially, and held that the State was a juristic person. After citing well-known textbooks on *Jurisprudence*, Sapru J. concluded that

> ". . . the position of the State as a 'great juristic person' is not identical with that of a juristic person in all respects. At the same time, when the State engages itself in a commercial undertaking, trade or business or enters into a contract, it is acting, to use the language of Prof. Holland, 'as a quasi-private juristic person' who should have in that sphere of business no more rights than any other private citizens."[46]

Agarwala J. held that there was no doubt that the State itself was a "person". But he also distinguished the governmental from the trading activities of the State. He referred to Arts. 20, 27 and 31 as showing that the word "person" in the Constitution included corporations.

9.22 The majority judgments in *Moti Lal's Case* were relied on and followed in *Amraoti Electric Supply Co.* v. *Dist. and Sessions Judge, Amraoti*.[47] In *Kesheoprasad* v. *State*[48] the two earlier cases were considered but were held inapplicable. It was held that "the word 'State' was used in the special sense understood in Art. 12 which took it out of the category of a person". It was only when the State engaged in any activity which was outside the scope of its ordinary functions of government that the question of its being a "person" for the purposes of Art. 14, could arise. The discussion is not very satisfactory, but the decision turned principally on the view that the activity of Government there impugned was a governmental activity. In *Shiv Parshad* v. *Punjab*[49] the above cases were considered and were held to be inapplicable. The Court held, without any discussion of the jurisprudential question involved, that the State was not a person when, acting as such, the State reserved to itself certain rights which it denied to others, and consequently Art. 14 was not applicable. It is submitted that the fact that the powers, rights, duties and obligations of a State are unlike those of any other person,

---

43 ('51) A.A. at p. 272: "If the word 'person' in Art. 14 is interpreted to include the State then the provisions of Art. 14 would appear to be in conflict with the provisions of Art. 289. Reading the Constitution as a whole I am inclined to the view that it was not intended that the Government of a State should be placed on the same footing as any person carrying on a business." It is submitted that the provisions of Art. 289 cannot be in conflict with Art. 14 for, Art. 14 applies to existing law or to law to be made under the Constitution and has no application to another Article of the Constitution itself.

44 ibid.

45 (1861) 5 Bom. H.C.R. App. 1.

46 ('51) A.A. at p. 305.

47 (1952) Nag. 830, ('53) A.N. 35.

48 (1955) Nag. 459, ('55) A.N. 177.

49 (1957) Punj. 310, ('57) A.Punj. 150.

natural or legal, is not relevant to the question whether the State is a person, just as the fact that one corporation possesses extensive, and another limited, powers is not relevant to the question whether they are both corporations. If the State has rights and obligations which are unique, that only means that the State is a unique person and that for the purpose of Art. 14, in most situations, if not in all, the State will be in a class by itself.

Submission: the distinction between governmental and trading activities of a State is irrelevant to the question of the State being a person

9.23 The right which Art. 14 confers by enacting a prohibition is conferred on every person and not merely on citizens. It protects a person against a law, but not against any agreement or contract.[50] And law in Art. 14 is not confined to the law enacted by a legislature, but includes any order or notification.[51] Thus, Art. 14 protects a person not only against legislation but also against executive orders or notifications.[52] This is not surprising, for the protection given by Art. 14 would be worth little if a law enacted by the legislature could not violate it but executive action could. As Lord Atkin said in another context: "The Constitution is not to be mocked by substituting executive for legislative interference with freedom".[53] But for the fact that the contrary was argued before the Supreme Court, it would be unnecessary to say that "law" in Art. 14 would include procedural law, and the Supreme Court has so held.[54]

The protection of Art. 14 extends to executive action by the State but not to agreements or contracts

9.24 In determining whether an impugned law violates Art. 14, is it necessary that the law should be enacted "with an evil eye and an unequal hand", or that it should make "purposeful or intentional discrimination"? The answer is, "No". Thus Mukherjea J. said

An intention to violate Art. 14 not necessary

"... If it is established that the person complaining has been discriminated against as a result of legislation and denied equal privileges with others occupying the same position, I do not think that it is incumbent upon him ... to assert and to prove that in making the law, the legislature was actuated by a hostile or inimical intention against a particular person or class."[55]

And Fazal Ali J., after referring to American cases which spoke of "purposeful or intentional discrimination"[56] said:

"I suggest ... that it will be extremely unsafe to lay down that unless there was evidence that discrimination was 'purposeful or intentional' (Art. 14) would not be infringed. ... It should be noted that there is no reference to intention in Art. 14 and the gravamen of that Article is equality of treatment. In my opinion, it will be dangerous to introduce a subjective test when the Article itself lays down a clear and objective test."[57]

---

[50] *Shantabai* v. *Bombay* (1959) S.C.R. 265, ('58) A.SC. 532.

[51] See Chapter VIII.

[52] *W.B.* v. *Anwar Ali Sarkar* (1952) S.C.R. 284, 294, ('52) A.SC. 75, *per* Patanjali Sastri C.J.; *Basheshar Nath* v. *C.I.T.* (1959) Supp. 1 S.C.R. 528, 552 ("... Art. 14 protects us from both legislative and executive tyranny by way of discrimination.")

[53] *James* v. *Cowan* (1932) A.C. 542, 558, (1932) All E.R. Rep. 413. These observations of Lord Atkin were quoted with approval in *Ram Singh* v. *A.P.* ('70) A.A.P. 314, 316 [*held*, that in view of the decisions referred to in *f.n.* 52 above, the judgment in *K. Bhaskaran* v. *Kerala* ('58) A.Ker. 333, was no longer good law.]

[54] *W.B.* v. *Anwar Ali Sarkar, supra, per* Fazal Ali and Mukherjea JJ. (with whom Mahajan J. concurred) (1952) S.C.R. at p. 332; *per* Das J., ibid. p. 337; *per* Chandrasekhara Aiyar J., ibid. p. 347.

[55] ibid. p. 324.

[56] ibid. p. 310. See also para 9.25 of the text.

[57] ibid. p. 311; see also *Cracknell* v. *U.P.* (1963) 1 All. 29, ('52) A.A. 746. "The intention with which a law is made is hardly relevant for the consideration of the contentions raised by the petitioner (viz. that the impugned law violated Arts. 14, 15 and 19). We have to see whether any particular provision of the law infringes any provisions of the Constitution. If it does, then whatever may be the intention

The correct test

The decision is correct, but it is submitted that the correct test for answering the question was laid down in *Punjab* v. *Daulat Singh*,[58] namely, that the effect of the impugned Act on the personal right conferred by Art. 14 must be ascertained, and if the Act involved an infringement of such right, the object of the Act, however laudable, would not obviate the prohibition contained in Art. 14.[59] The Supreme Court approved this test in *Bombay* v. *Bombay Education Society*[60] where Das J. said that the test was implicit in *Madras* v. *Champakam Dorairajan*.[61] Art. 14 confers a personal right by enacting a prohibition; and the only question which has to be determined when a law is said to violate the right is to inquire whether the prohibition has been violated.[62] If the prohibition has been violated, the law will be void, however laudable the motives of its makers; and if the prohibition has not been violated, the utmost malignity on the part of the law-makers will not make it void.

The test of equality *qua* executive action in U.S.A.

9.25 Can the same test be applied to the executive administration of a law which does not violate equality, or are there practical considerations which modify the test? In the United States, historical considerations and the nature of the American federation, have led to a modification of the test when executive action under a State law is alleged to violate the equality provisions of the 14th Amendment. The federating States were independent States with Constitutions of their own, and a hierarchy of courts with a State Supreme Court at the apex. Under the U.S. Constitution, the federal government is a government of enumerated powers; and federal courts function in the States to determine questions of federal law and questions arising under the U.S. Constitution. It is against this background that Stone C.J. said in *Snowden* v. *Hughes*:[63]

Snowden v. *Hughes*

"The unlawful administration by state officers of a state statute fair on its face, resulting in its unequal application to those who are entitled to be treated alike, is not a denial of equal protection unless *there is shown to be present in it an element of intentional or purposeful discrimination*."[64] * * * "*A construction of the equal protection clause which would find a violation of federal right in every departure by state officers from state law is not to be favoured*."[65] (italics supplied)

And Frankfurter J. said:

"*The Constitution does not assure uniformity of decisions or immunity from merely erroneous action, whether by the courts or the executive agencies of a state*."[66] * * * "Our question is not whether a remedy is available for such

---

of the Legislature, it must be held to be void"; *Sundareswarar Devasthanam* v. *Marimuthu* (1963) Mad. 1054, ('63) A.M. 369, 376, quoting *Royster Guano Co.* v. *Virginia* (1919) 64 L.ed. 989 at p. 991: "It follows that it is arbitrary in effect; and nonetheless because it is probable that the unequal operation of the taxing system was due to inadvertence rather than design."

58 (1946) 73 I.A. 59, ('46) A.PC. 66 (In connection with s. 298, G.I. Act, 35, which prohibited discrimination on the ground of race, religion, etc.).

59 (1946) 73 I.A. *supra* at p. 74, *per* Lord Thankerton.

60 (1955) 1 S.C.R. 568, 583-4, ('54) A.SC. 561, *per* Das J.

61 (1951) S.C.R. 525, 530, ('51) A.SC. 226.

62 This is subject to the qualification laid down by the Supreme Court in *Syed Quasim Razvi* v. *Hyderabad* (1953) S.C.R. 589, ('53) A.SC. 156, which is discussed in para 9.82. It has been said that the words "equality before the law" have been taken from English law, and the words "equal protection of the laws" have been taken from the equality clauses of the U.S. Constitution.

63 321 U.S. 1, 88 L. ed. 497.

64 ibid. p. 1, 8; ibid. p. 497, 503.

65 ibid. p. 1, 11-12; ibid. p. 497, 505.

66 ibid. p. 1, 15; ibid. pp. 506-507.

an illegality, but whether it is available in the first instance in a federal court. *Such a problem of federal judicial control must be placed in the historic context of the relationship of the federal courts to the states,* with due regard for the natural sensitiveness of the states and for the appropriate responsibility of state courts to correct the action of lower state courts and state officials."[67] (italics supplied)

9.26 In *Sioux City Bridge Co.* v. *Dakota County*[68] the U.S. Supreme Court had to deal with a slightly different problem: under a state statute, property tax was to be levied on the full value of the property. A Bridge Company was taxed on the full value of its property, while other property in the county was assessed at only 55 per cent of its value. Without going into the question of alleged discrimination, the State Supreme Court held, following its earlier decisions, that when the law provided for taxing the full value of property, the correct procedure was to have the value of the property which had been assessed below its value, raised. The U.S. Supreme Court held that the State Supreme Court's decision left the appellant without any remedy whatever against discrimination, because it was utterly impossible for him, by any judicial proceeding, to secure an increase in the assessment of the great mass of under-assessed property in the taxing district. The U.S. Supreme Court held that the right of a tax payer whose property alone was assessed at 100 per cent of its true value, when other properties were assessed at 55 per cent of their true value, was to have his assessment reduced to 55 per cent. This *Sioux City Bridge Co.'s Case*

". . . conclusion is based on the principle that where it is impossible to secure both the standards of the true value, and the uniformity and equality required by law, the latter requirement is to be preferred as the just and ultimate purpose of the law. In substance and effect, the decision of the Nebraska supreme court in this case upholds the violation of the the 14th Amendment to the injury of the Bridge Company."[69]

The Court remanded the matter for a further hearing on discrimination to find whether there was intentional discrimination between the value of the Bridge Company's property and that of all other real property, adding: ". . . mere errors of judgment do not support a claim of discrimination, but that there must be something more,— something which, in effect, *amounts to an intentional violation* of the essential principle of practical uniformity."[70] (italics supplied)

9.27 Most of the considerations which weighed with the U.S. Supreme Court do not obtain in India. Before the Constitution, the Provinces of British India were not independent sovereign states with Constitutions of their own, nor was there a hierarchy of State as opposed to Federal courts. Our Constitution applies both to the Union and the States, the residuary power of legislation being with the Union. Again, although there is power to create Federal Courts Considerations relevant to the test in U.S.A. not relevant in India

[67] ibid. p. 1, 16; ibid. p. 507.

[68] 260 U.S. 441, 67 L. ed. 340.

[69] ibid. p. 441, 446-7; ibid. p. 340, 343. It is submitted that the State Supreme Court was right, and the reversal of its decision by the U.S. Supreme Court is clearly wrong. It would be surprising if the law of the State was so defective that the taxing authority could not be compelled to perform its statutory duty; and it would be even more surprising if the State Supreme Court laid down a course of action which was impossible. Apart from a bald statement that the decision under appeal left the petitioner without any remedy, the U.S. Supreme Court has given no reasons why the State Courts were powerless to compel the performance of a mandatory statutory duty.

[70] ibid. p. 441; ibid. p. 340, 343.

to administer federal laws, that power has not been exercised. The High Court is the highest court in a state, but High Courts are expressly made subject to the appellate jurisdiction of the Supreme Court and the law laid down by the Supreme Court is binding on all the High Courts and the courts subordinate to them. We must now consider the decisions of our Supreme Court.

Nevertheless *Snowden* v. *Hughes* followed by our Sup. Ct.

9.28 In *Budhan Choudhry* v. *Bihar*[71] a power to be judicially exercised by a magistrate to send a case for trial to a Sec. 30 (Cr.P.C.) Magistrate, or to commit it to Sessions was impugned as violating Art. 14. In dealing with this contention Das C.J. cited *Snowden* v. *Hughes*,[72] and added that it was not the appellant's case that there had been any *intentional or purposeful* discrimination against him. A similar view was taken in *J. & K.* v. *Ghulam Rasool*.[73] The respondent had applied to the High Court of Jammu and Kashmir under Art. 32 (2A) for the enforcement of his fundamental right. He complained that he had been arbitrarily suspended and demoted in disregard of the relevant Civil Service Rules which had the force of law and that consequently, Art. 14 had been violated. Rejecting this contention, Sarkar J. observed:

> ". . . even if the rules are a law and the respondent has not been given the benefit of them, all that can be said to have happened is that the appellant has acted in breach of the law. But that does not amount to a violation of the right to the equal protection of the laws. We are not aware of any authority in support of that proposition and none has been cited to us. Nor are we able to find any support for it in principle. It is not the respondent's case that other servants of the appellant had been given the benefit of those Rules and such benefit has been *designedly denied only to him*."[74] (italics supplied)

Again, in *Narain Dass* v. *Improvement Trust, Amritsar*[75] the Supreme Court held that hostile discrimination against the appellants by the executive, in refusing exemption under s. 53, Punjab Town Improvement Act, 1922, had not been established; consequently there was no denial of equality. In any event, ". . . merely because some other party has erroneously succeeded in getting his lands exempted ostensibly under that section, that by itself would not clothe the present appellants with a right to secure exemption for their lands. The rule of equality before the law or of equal protection of the laws under Art. 14 cannot be invoked in such a case."[76] It will be seen that the Supreme Court adopted the test of intentional and purposeful discrimination by executive action in dealing with an alleged violation of Art. 14 and this has been done without adverting to the circumstances which led the U.S. Supreme Court to do so. It is submitted

Submission: the test of executive denial of equality requires reconsideration

---

[71] (1955) 1 S.C.R. 1045, ('55) A.SC. 191.

[72] The quotation is given in para 9.25 above (see the first sentence).

[73] (1961) 3 S.C.R. 969, ('61) A.SC. 1301.

[74] ('61) A.SC. at p. 1302. In the Mysore High Court, Hegde J. took the same view in *H. J. Siddappa* v. *Mysore* ('67) A.Mys. 67, 71: ("Every wrong interpretation of a Rule or law does not amount to a *hostile discrimination*. What is of the essence is hostile discrimination — *an intentional unequal treatment of persons similarly placed*. We are unable to agree . . . that any and every contravention of a Rule brings the case within Art. 14 and the equality clause requires that if one person is wrongly selected, everyone else similarly situated is also entitled to be selected. This contention is wholly untenable. In cases of this nature, there is no hostile discrimination against anyone. In such a case there is no question of contravention of Art. 14"). (italics supplied)

[75] ('72) A.SC. 865.

[76] ibid. p. 871; fol. in *Sashi Bhushan Prasad Singh* v. *State* ('82) A.P. 55, 59.

that the question of discrimination by executive action requires further consideration, because there are situations in which Art. 14 can be invoked. But before doing so, we must refer to the following passage from *Dhanraj Mills Ltd.* v. *B. K. Kocher*[77] which has been cited with approval in other cases[78] dealing with discrimination by executive action:

Dhanraj Mills Case

". . . a clear distinction must be borne in mind between the law and the administration of the law. If the law itself permits discrimination, even though the law may appear to be fair and undiscriminatory, the Court may interfere and say (sic) 'We are more concerned with how the law actually works rather than how it appears in black and white.' . . . One may even have a case where in exercising the discretion vested in officers under the statute, the State may, as a policy of administration, require its officers to exercise the discretion unfairly and unequally . . . even in such a case the Court may interfere and say . . . the administrative orders suggest behind them a policy of the State of discrimination. But . . . the position is different when a subject comes to the Court and challenges a specific act of an individual officer as being in contravention of Art. 14. The officer in acting contrary to Art. 14 (is acting contrary) to the law and not in conformity . . . with the law. . . . In such a case the subject comes to Court not for protection under Art. 14, but for protection against the dishonest, arbitrary or capricious act of the officer. The Court is not powerless to give the subject protection against a dishonest officer, but that protection cannot be sought under Art. 14 or under Art. 226."[79]

Dhanraj Mills Case was a petition under Art. 226, and it is submitted that the judgment is clearly wrong when it holds that no relief under Art. 226 is available against "the dishonest, arbitrary or capricious" action of the officer. If the dishonest action intentionally and purposefully discriminated against the petitioner, the decisions which we have considered earlier are agreed that the petitioner's right to equality under Art. 14 would be violated, and relief under Art. 226 would be available. Again, if the officer acted contrary to the law, and in breach of it, then, in a petition under Art. 226, a writ of *mandamus* would lie to compel him to perform his statutory duty or to abstain from acting contrary to law. It is submitted that if an officer acts contrary to Art. 14 he denies to the person affected by his action equal protection of the laws, and such a person can complain that his right under Art. 14 has been violated. If a deliberate intention on the part of the executive to violate the law is actionable under Art. 14, it is difficult to see why a deliberate violation of the law in an individual case by an executive officer is not actionable under Art. 14. The above submission is supported by a judgment of the U.S. Supreme Court delivered by Brandeis J. in *Iowa-Des Moines National Bank* v. *Bennett*:[80]

Submission: judgment clearly wrong *qua* Art. 226, and *qua* intentional and purposeful discrimination

A criticism of the *Dhanraj Mills Case*

"The prohibition of the 14th Amendment, it is true, has reference exclusively to action by the State, as distinguished from action by private individuals. . . . But acts done 'by virtue of a public position under a State Government and in the name and for the State' . . . are not to be treated as if they were the acts of private individuals, although in doing them the official acted contrary to an express command of the State law. When a State official, acting under color of state authority, invades, in the course of his duties, a private right secured by the federal Constitution, that right is violated, even if the

---

[77] (1952) Bom. 335, ('51) A.B. 132, 135, 53 Bom.L.R. 393.

[78] *Nathmal* v. *Commr., Civil Supplies* (1951) 1 Raj. 674, ('52) A.Raj. 74, 76; *Dinesh Charan* v. *M.B.* (1953) Mad.Bha. 393, ('53) A.M.B. 165, 172.

[79] ('51) A.B. *supra* at p. 135.

[80] (1931) 284 U.S. 239, 76 L. ed. 265.

state officer not only exceeded his authority but disregarded special commands of the state law."[81]

Discrimination by executive action which is not intentional and purposeful

9.29 Granted that intentional and purposeful discrimination by executive action violates equality, and entitles the person discriminated against to obtain relief under Art. 32 or Art. 226, does it follow that if a person is in fact denied equality by executive officers, but not intentionally or purposely, that the person aggrieved should be denied the cheap and speedy remedy under Art. 32 and/or Art. 226? In considering some of the situations which may arise, we have seen that the main consideration which led the U.S. Supreme Court to limit the violation of equality under the 14th Amendment to intentional and purposeful discrimination was, that finding a denial of equality in the action of state officers acting under state laws, would convert what were essentially state questions to be decided by state courts, into federal questions, to be decided by Federal Courts. For reasons given in para 9.27 above, these considerations have no relevance in India.

Two situations: First situation

9.30 We will now consider the following situations:

(i) A law provides that on *any* person satisfying prescribed conditions for trading in a particular commodity a licence to trade in that commodity *shall* be granted by designated officers. Two thousand persons complying with the prescribed conditions, apply for and are granted licences. Thirty persons, complying with the prescribed conditions, apply for but are refused licences by the designated officers, but not because of any hostile and purposeful discrimination against those thirty persons. In this situation it is submitted that there is no compelling reason for applying a different test of discrimination to executive action than is applied to a law, namely, to consider the effect of the officers' action on the right of the persons aggrieved. Under Art. 226 a *mandamus* would clearly lie against the officers to compel them to perform a mandatory duty; but unless the officers' action is held to violate the applicants' right to equality, a petition to the Supreme Court under Art. 32 for a writ of *mandamus* would not lie. It is submitted that there is no reason why an obvious denial of equality should not be carried directly to the Supreme Court under Art. 32.

Submission

Second situation

(ii) A law provides that if certain prescribed conditions are *not* fulfilled, a licence to trade in a particular commodity shall *not* be granted to *any* person by designated officers. Two thousand persons who have not fulfilled the prescribed conditions apply for and are *not* granted licences by the designated officers. Thirty persons who have *not fulfilled* the prescribed conditions apply for and *are granted* licences by the designated officers as a result of inadvertance, mistake or even bribery. Can any one or more of the 2,000 persons who have been refused licences, apply to the High Court or the Supreme Court to direct the designated officers to grant them a licence? The answer must be: No, for the applicants having been rightly refused a licence,

Submission

[81] ibid. pp. 245-6. In the United States, the consideration that such a view would convert every violation of a state law contrary to the 14th Amendment into a federal question might require the test of intentional and purposeful discrimination to be applied; but, as stated in the text, such a consideration has no relevance in India.

they cannot complain that their right to obtain a licence had been violated. Article 14 requires that persons similarly situated must be treated equally; but Art. 14 does not confer on any person a right to which he is not entitled under a valid law.[82] And yet, by refusing licences to the 2,000 applicants and granting them to 30 applicants, who ought also to have been refused licences, persons similarly situated have been treated unequally. Is there no remedy against a clear violation of the right to equality? It is submitted, that a writ of *mandamus* should lie at the instance of any one of the 2,000 applicants against the designated officers, directing them to cancel the licences granted to the thirty applicants. The difficulty in this solution would be one of *locus standi*, for a writ is available to enforce a person's rights, and *ex hypothesi*, the applicant had no right to a licence. However the applicant has a right to the equal protection of the law, and a violation of that right should give him sufficient *locus standi*. If the applicant can show that the licence refused to him has been granted to a rival trader to whom it ought equally to have been refused, the applicant would have a sufficient *locus standi* even for the protection of his business interests.[83] But even if a trader who has been refused a licence cannot show such injury, he can complain of a violation of his right to equality by public officers entrusted with a public duty and courts are increasingly inclined to accord *locus standi* to persons whose rights have been violated.[84]

Locus standi

9.31 We have seen that the U.S. Supreme Court has recognized this fact and held that "equal protection of the laws" in the U.S. Constitution meant the protection of equal laws that operate alike on all persons under like circumstances.[85] The theory of classification adopted by the American Courts was a necessary consequence of the concept underlying the equality clause, namely, that a law must operate alike on all persons under like circumstances. This concept negatives class legislation[86] because to single out members of a class is to treat *some* persons who are similarly situated alike whilst treating others also similarly situated, differently. For example, a law

Equal protection of the laws: classification

[82] The above submission is supported by *T. V. Setty* v. *Bangalore Municipality* ('68) A.Mys. 251 where the court held that Art. 14 could not be understood to require the prescribed authorities to act illegally by granting a licence contrary to the provisions of the Bangalore Municipal Corporation Act, merely because they had acted illegally in other cases.

[83] *R.* v. *Thames Magistrates Court, ex. p. Greenbaum* (1957) 55 L.G.R. 129 referred to in de Smith's *Judicial Review of Administrative Action*, p. 366, for the proposition that "an unsuccessful applicant for a street trader's licence was held to have *locus standi* to apply for *certiorari* to quash the grant of a pitch to a rival although he had no *locus standi* to appear at the proceedings when the pitch was allocated."

[84] The observations in the *Bangalore Municipality Case, supra*, that the "petitioner has not impleaded the licencees in whose favour he has alleged there has been discrimination. In the absence of those licencees as parties in the present petition, and without giving them an opportunity to meet the allegation of discrimination in their favour" would suggest that the petitioner had a *locus standi*. See *de Smith, op. cit.* p. 366 "Standing has been accorded to local rate payers (in respect of) a breach of standing orders relating to the placing of contracts [*R.* v. *Hereford Corpn. ex. p. Harrower* (1970) 1 W.L.R. 1424 (*mandamus*) although they had suffered no more detriment *qua* ratepayers than other members of their class".]

[85] *Anwar Ali Sarkar's Case* (1952) S.C.R. 284, 294, ('52) A.SC. 75.

[86] *Shri Ram Krishna Dalmia* v. *Justice S. R. Tendolkar* (1959) S.C.R. 279, 296, ('58) A.SC. 538, as also the cases there referred to.

which prescribes that members of community A shall pay a tax of five per cent on their incomes whereas members of community B, similarly situated, shall pay a tax of ten per cent on their incomes, violates the principle of "classification" because though members of the two communities are similarly situated, as regards their incomes, they are treated differently. This illustration brings out the meaning of the paradoxical statement that the equality clause forbids class legislation but does not forbid classification, for though classification involves putting persons or things together in a class, the equality clause requires that the class thus formed must not leave out any person or thing which falls within the class, as the class formed for the purpose of class legislation unmistakably does.

Doctrine of classification adopted in India

9.32 Article 14 "combines the English doctrine of the rule of law with the equal protection clause of the 14th Amendment."[87] In adopting the doctrine of classification laid down by the U.S. Supreme Court, our Supreme Court has merely adopted a doctrine which makes explicit what is implicit in the very concept of the protection of equal laws.[88] But though the theory of classification is easy to state, its application is beset by many difficulties and necessitates several refinements. The true meaning and scope of Art. 14 has been explained in several decisions of the Supreme Court; they[89] were referred to and their effect summarised by Das C.J. in *Dalmia's Case*.[90] As the summary deals with a number of topics, it would be convenient to regroup the principles there stated. The following propositions are estabished by *Dalmia's Case* and the other cases to which it refers:

Scope of Art. 14 explained in *Dalmia's Case*

(a) Article 14 condemns discrimination not only by substantive law but by a law of procedure;[91]

(b) Art. 14 forbids class legislation but does not forbid classification;[92]

(c) Permissible classification must satisfy two conditions, namely, (i) it must be founded on an intelligible differentia which distinguishes persons or things that are grouped together from others left out of the group, and (ii) the dif-

---

[87] *Per* Das C.J. in *Basheshar Nath* v. *C.I.T. Delhi and Rajasthan* (1959) Supp. 1 S.C.R. 528, 551, ('59) A.SC. 149.

[88] Bose J. expressed the opinion that the theory of classification did not supply the only or the true test: *Anwar Ali Sarkar's Case* (1952) S.C.R. 284, 361, ('52) A.SC. 75. It is submitted that this opinion is not correct. The fact that questions of reasonableness are difficult to decide, *or* that the standard of the reasonable man is "mythical" [(1952) S.C.R. at p. 360] does not prevent courts from daily deciding such questions and applying the "mythical test". As an example of a perfect classification which would still not be accepted by the Courts, Bose J. mentioned a provision that all persons of sub-standard intelligence should be tried summarily as such a trial was fairer to them (ibid. p. 361). If the assumption of fairness were granted the classification would be upheld. But the assumption is unfounded, for it is not fair to remove the safeguards of an ordinary trial in the case of a person of sub-standard intelligence; if anything, the safeguards require to be increased.

[89] *Chiranjit Lal Chowdhuri* v. *Union* (1950) S.C.R. 869, ('51) A.SC. 41; *Bombay* v. *F. N. Balsara* (1951) S.C.R. 682, ('51) A.SC. 318; *Anwar Ali Sarkar's Case* (1952) S.C.R. 284, ('52) A.SC. 75; *Kathi Raning Rawat* v. *Saurashtra* (1952) A.SC. 123; *Lachmandas Kewalram Ahuja* v. *Bombay* (1952) S.C.R. 710, ('52) A.SC. 235; *Quasim Razvi's Case* (1953) S.C.R. 589, ('53) A.SC. 156; *Habeeb Mohamed* v. *Hyderabad* (1953) S.C.R. 661, ('53) A.SC. 287; *Budhan Chowdhury* v. *Bihar* (1955) 1 S.C.R. 1045, ('55) A.SC. 191.

[90] (1959) S.C.R. 279, 296-8, ('58) A.SC. 538.

[91] (1959) S.C.R. at p. 297.

[92] ibid. p. 296.

ferentia must have a rational relation to the object sought to be achieved by the statute in question;[93]

(d) The differentia and object are different elements and it follows that the object by itself cannot be the basis of the classification;[94]

(e) In permissible classification mathematical nicety and perfect equality are not required. Similarity, not identity of treatment, is enough;[95]

(f) The classification may be founded on different bases, namely, geographical or according to objects or occupations or the like;[96]

(g) If a law deals equally with members of a well-defined class, it is not obnoxious and it is not open to the charge of denial of equal protection on the ground that it has no application to other persons;[97]

(h) Even a single individual may be in a class by himself on account of some special circumstances or reasons applicable to him and not applicable to others; a law may be constitutional even though it relates to a single individual who is in a class by himself;[98]

(i) The legislature is free to recognize degrees of harm and may confine its restrictions to those cases where the need is deemed to be the clearest;[99]

(j) There is always a presumption in favour of the constitutionality of an enactment and the burden is upon him who attacks it to show that there has been a clear transgression of the constitutional principles (sic);[1]

(k) In order to sustain the presumption of constitutionality, the court may take into consideration matters of common knowledge, matters of common re-

---

[93] ibid. pp. 296-7. See *per* Das J. in *Anwar Ali Sarkar's Case*, (1952) S.C.R. at pp. 340-41; foll. in *Om Prakash* v. *J. & K.* ('81) A.SC. 1001. [*held*, that the allotment of raisin, contrary to the industrial policy, to some allottees violated Art. 14.]

[94] *Per* Das J. in *Anwar Ali Sarkar's Case, supra*, (1952) S.C.R. at p. 341; for his application of the principle to the case before him, see para 9.76; *R. Prasad Mohan Lal* v. *I.T.A. Tribunal* ('70) A.A. 620, 638-9: "If the two tests are satisfied it is not for the courts to see to the wisdom of the basis for the classification. It may be demonstrated that the scheme is not the best in the circumstances, and the choice of the legislature may be shown to be erroneous, but the classification will not be subject to judicial interference on these grounds [*vide* Shah J. speaking for the majority in *Jalan Trading Co.* v. *Mill Mazdoor Sabha* ('67) A.SC. 691, para 27.]"

[95] *Per* Fazl Ali J. in *Balsara's Case, supra*, (1951) S.C.R. 682 at pp. 709-10, citing Willis,, *Constitutional Law*. See also *per* Chandrasekhara Aiyar J. in *Anwar Ali Sarkar's Case, supra*, (1952) S.C.R. at pp. 349-50; *R. Prasad Mohan Lal* v. *I.T.A. Tribunal* ('70) A.A. 620 (F.B.) at p. 639: "A general classification cannot be justified on the basis of exceptional cases: Civil Appeal No. 1832 of 1968 decided by the Supreme Court on 12.12.1968 (S.C.) [In other words general classification cannot fail because of exceptional cases.]"

[96] *Dalmia's Case, supra*, (1959) S.C.R. 279, at p. 297. It need hardly be added that it may be founded on the difference between persons; *S.I.S. Mills Assn.* v. *Union* ('72) A.A.P. 75, 81-82 [the grouping of factories zone-wise (India being divided into 15 zones) for fixing the price of sugar was upheld.]

[97] *Bombay* v. *F.N. Balsara* (1951) S.C.R. 682, 709.

[98] (1959) S.C.R. *supra* at p. 297, proposition (*a*).

[99] ibid. p. 297, proposition (*d*); *Khyerbari Tea Co.* v. *Assam* (1964) 5 S.C.R. 975, ('64) A.SC. 925, fol. in *Naguppa* v. *I.O.M. Cess Commr.* ('68) A.Mys. 42.

[1] (1959) S.C.R. *supra* at p. 297, proposition (b). (The words "transgression of the constitutional *principles*" clearly mean transgression of the provisions of the Constitution); *U.P. Electric Co.* v. *U.P.* ('70) A.SC. 21, 24; *U.P.* v. *Kartar Singh* (1964) 6 S.C.R. 679, 687, ('64) A.SC. 1135; *G. D. Kalkar* v. *Chief Controller* (1967) 2 S.C.R. 29, 34, ('67) A.SC. 839, where Subba Rao C.J. cited three earlier decisions of the Supreme Court: *Banarsi Das* v. *U.P.* (1956) S.C.R. 357, ('56) A.SC. 520; *All India Station Masters' & Asst. Station Masters' Assn.* v. *Gen. Manager, C. Rly.* (1960) 2 S.C.R. 311, ('60) A.SC. 384; *Gen. Manager, S. Rly.* v. *Rangachari* (1962) 2 S.C.R. 586, ('62) A.SC. 36. All the above cases were referred to and fol. in *J. & K.* v. *T. N. Khosa* ('74) A.SC. 1 at p. 9; *Sultan Singh* v. *Asst. Registrar* ('72) A.A. 159, 165-6; *C. Basu* v. *Calcutta C.J.* ('72) A.Cal. 470, 480-81; *Laxmi Cotton Traders* v. *State* ('69) A.Punj. 12, 22.

port, the history of the times and may assume every state of facts which can be conceived;[2]

(l) It must be presumed that the legislature understands and correctly appreciates the need of its own people, that its laws are directed to problems made manifest by experience and that its discriminations are based on adequate grounds;[3]

(m) While good faith and knowledge of the existing conditions on the part of a legislature are to be presumed, if there is nothing on the face of the law or the surrounding circumstances brought to the notice of the court on which the classification may reasonably be regarded as based, the presumption of constitutionality cannot be carried to the extent of always holding that there must be some undisclosed and unknown reasons for subjecting certain individuals or corporations to hostile or discriminatory legislation.[4] The principle must be borne in mind in deciding whether a law violates Art. 14.

Advisory Opinion: *In re the Special Courts Bill*

9.33 In an Advisory Opinion under Art. 143[5], Chandrachud C.J. observed that as far back as 1960 it had been said that propositions applicable to cases under Art. 14 had been repeated so often that they sounded platitudinous, and if this was so in 1960, it was not less so in 1979. However, even at the cost of repetition, it was desirable to state "the propositions which emerged from the judgments of the Supreme Court"[6] because the matter was being heard by a Bench of 7 judges. The propositions which he laid down[7] suffer from two infirmities. First, as the Supreme Court was exercising advisory jurisdiction, and was not laying down the law within the meaning of Art. 141[8], the Chief Justice should have refrained from re-formulating well settled principles applicable to Art. 14. Secondly, in re-formulating the propositions which are said "to emerge from the judgments of the Supreme Court", the case, or cases from which the propositions are said to emerge are not cited. Consequently, it is not possible to check whether the propositions are correctly laid down. Further, there are serious practical objections to a court re-formulating well settled principles, namely, that it creates uncertainty in the law and encourages needless litigation, because Advocates would

---

[2] (1959) S.C.R. *supra* at p. 297, proposition (*e*); fol. in *Ramraj Singh* v. *State* ('69) A.B. 333.

[3] ibid. p. 297, proposition (*c*).

[4] ibid. pp. 297-8, proposition (*f*); *Ram Prasad Narayan Sahi* v. *Bihar* (1953) S.C.R. 1129, ('53) A.SC. 215. See *R. Prasad Mohan Lal* v. *I.T.A. Tribunal* ('70) A.A. 620 (F.B.) where Chanda J. summarized the principles of classification laid down by decided cases. He reiterated propositions (*c*), (*e*), (*f*), (*g*), (*i*) and (*l*) above; but paras 7 to 9 of the judgment at pp. 638-9 carry the principles further, and these have been noted in their appropriate places in the text.

[5] *In re the Special Courts Bill* (1979) 2 S.C.R. 476, ('79) A.SC. 478. (The nature of an advisory opinion will be discussed in the Chapter on the Union Judiciary).

[6] ('79) A.SC. at p. 508.

[7] They are set out in para 9.34 below.

[8] In *R. K. Garg* v. *Union* ('81) A.SC. 2138, ("*The Bearer Bonds Case*"), Bhagwati J. delivering the majority judgment said that the latest and most comprehensive statement of the propositions relating to Art. 14 was to be found in the judgment of Chandrachud J. in *In re the Special Courts Bill,* and that judgment was binding on the Court because it was a judgment of 7 judges. In this he was in error, for Chandrachud J. was aware that decisions of high authority, as also juristic opinion, had held that such a judgment does not lay down the law, and that an Advisory Opinion had no greater effect than the opinion of Law Officers. Consequently, Chandrachud J. had himself observed "The question may have to be considered more fully on a future occasion . . .": ('79) A.SC. at p. 519. Bhagwati J. was a party to this judgment and in overlooking the nature of an Advisory Opinion and the express reservation made by Chandrachud J. about considering the matter on a future occasion, Bhagwati J.'s remarks are *per incuriam.*

naturally fasten on the differences between the wording of the earlier propositions and their re-formulation. It is submitted that the law was carefully formulated by Das C.J. in *Dalmia's Case*[9] and as para 9.32 above shows, the propositions there laid down are capable of being briefly stated. If the Supreme Court thought fit to re-formulate the propositions there laid down, the most satisfactory way would have been to start with the propositions in *Dalmia's Case* and then to indicate whether subsequent decisions had confirmed, added to, or modified those propositions. This would have made the law certain and easy to understand and would have discouraged needless litigation. However, as the Chief Justice has re-formulated well settled principles, the present writer has set them out without further comment in the next para.

Scope of Art. 14 reformulated

9.34 "1. The first part of Article 14, which was adopted from the Irish Constitution, is a declaration of equality of the civil rights of all persons within the territories of India. It enshrines a basic principle of republicanism. The second part, which is a corollary of the first and is based on the last clause of the first section of the Fourteenth Amendment of the American Constitution, enjoins that equal protection shall be secured to all such persons in the enjoyment of their rights and liberties without discrimination or favouritism. It is a pledge of the protection of equal laws, that is, laws that operate alike on all persons under like circumstances.

2. The State, in the exercise of its governmental power, has of necessity to make laws operating differently on different groups or classes of persons within its territory to attain particular ends in giving effect to its policies, and it must possess for that purpose, large powers of distinguishing and classifying persons or things to be subjected to such laws.

3. The constitutional command to the State to afford equal protection of its laws sets a goal not attainable by the invention and application of a precise formula. Therefore, classification need not be constituted by an exact or scientific exclusion or inclusion of persons or things. The Courts should not insist on delusive exactness or apply doctrinaire tests for determining the validity of classification in any given case. Classification is justified if it is not palpably arbitrary.

4. The principle underlying the guarantee of Article 14 is not that the same rules of law should be applicable to all persons within the Indian territory or that the same remedies should be made available to them irrespective of differences of circumstances. It only means that all persons similarly circumstanced shall be treated alike, both in privileges conferred and liabilities imposed. Equal laws would have to be applied to all in the same situation, and there should be no discrimination between one person and another, if as regards the subject-matter of the legislation, their position is substantially the same.

5. By the process of classification, the State has the power of determining who should be regarded as a class for purposes of legislation and in relation to a law enacted on a particular subject. This power, no doubt, in some degree is likely to produce some inequality; but if a law deals with the liberties of a number of well-defined classes, it is not open to the charge of denial of equal protection on the ground that it has no application to other persons. Classification thus means segregation in classes which have a systematic relation, usually found in common properties and characteristics. It postulates a rational basis and does not mean herding together of certain persons and classes arbitrarily.

6. The law can make and set apart the classes according to the needs and exigencies of the society and as suggested by experience. It can recognise even degrees of evil, but the classification should never be arbitrary, artificial or evasive.

7. The classification must not be arbitrary but must be rational, that is to say, it must not only be based on some qualities or characteristics which are

---

[9] (1959) S.C.R. 279, ('58) A.SC. 538.

to be found in all the persons grouped together and not in others who are left out, but those qualities or characteristics must have a reasonable relation to the object of the legislation. In order to pass the test, two conditions must be fulfilled, namely, (i) that the classification must be founded on an intelligible differentia which distinguishes those that are grouped together from others and (ii) that that differentia must have a rational relation to the object sought to be achieved by the Act.

8. The differentia which is the basis of the classification and the object of the Act are distinct things and what is necessary is that there must be a nexus between them. In short, while Article 14 forbids class discrimination by conferring privileges or imposing liabilities upon persons arbitrarily selected out of a large number of other persons similarly situated in relation to the privileges sought to be conferred or the liabilities proposed to be imposed, it does not forbid classification for the purpose of legislation, provided such classification is not arbitrary in the sense above mentioned.

9. If the legislative policy is clear and definite and is an effective method of carrying out that policy a discretion is vested by the statute upon a body of administrators or officers to make selective application of the law to certain classes or groups of persons, the statute itself cannot be condemned as a piece of discriminatory legislation. In such cases, the power given to the executive body would import a duty on it to classify the subject-matter of legislation in accordance with the objective indicated in the statute. If the administrative body proceeds to classify persons or things on a basis which has no rational relation to the objective of the legislature, its action can be annulled as offending against the equal protection clause. On the other hand, if the statute itself does not disclose a definite policy or objective and it confers authority on another to make selection at its pleasure, the statute would be held on the face of it to be discriminatory, irrespective of the way in which it is applied.

10. Whether a law conferring discretionary powers on an administrative authority is constitutionally valid or not, should not be determined on the assumption that such authority will act in an arbitrary manner in exercising the discretion committed to it. Abuse of power given by law does occur; but the validity of the law cannot be contested because of such an apprehension. Discretionary power is not necessarily a discriminatory power.

11. Classification necessarily implies the making of a distinction or discrimination between persons classified and those who are not members of that class. It is the essence of a classification that upon the class are cast duties and burdens different from those resting upon the general public. Indeed, the very idea of classification is that of inequality, so that it goes without saying that the mere fact of inequality in no manner determines the matter of constitutionality.

12. Whether an enactment providing for special procedure for the trial of certain offences is or is not discriminatory and violative of Article 14 must be determined in each case as it arises, for no general rule applicable to all cases can safely be laid down. A practical assessment of the operation of the law in the particular circumstances is necessary.

13. A rule of procedure laid down by law comes as much within the purview of Article 14 as any rule of substantive law and it is necessary that all litigants, who are similarly situated, are able to avail themselves of the same procedural rights for relief and for defence with like protection and without discrimination."[10]

U.P. Electric Co. v. U.P.

9.35 The technical formulation of proposition (b) in para 9.32 above[11] has, at times, blurred the basic principle underlying Art. 14, namely, that the laws must operate equally on all persons *under like circumstances.* When Art. 14 is invoked, the first thing to consider is whether the persons between whom discrimination is alleged,

---

10 ('79) A.SC. at pp. 508-510.

11 Discussed more fully in para 9.31 of the text.

fall in the same class. In *U.P. Electric Co.* v. *U.P.*[12] Shah J. rightly observed:

"Art. 14 . . . ensures equality among equals. Its aim is to protect persons similarly placed, against discriminatory treatment. . . . A person setting up a grievance of denial of equal treatment by law must establish that between persons similarly circumstanced, some were treated to their prejudice."[13]

Mandawar's Case: equality not violated if the sources of two laws are different

9.36 Further, Art. 14 is not violated by two laws dealing with the same subject-matter, if the sources of the two laws are different.[14] This was laid down in *Mandawar's Case* in repelling the contention that the scale of dearness allowance laid down for State government servants was discriminatory compared with the one laid down for Union government servants for doing the same class of work. The court observed:

"Art. 14 does not authorize the striking down of a law of one State on the ground that in contrast with the law of another State on the same subject, its provisions are discriminatory. Nor does it contemplate a law of the Centre or of the State dealing with similar subjects being held to be unconstitutional by a process of comparative study of the provisions of the two enactments. The sources of authority for the two statutes being different, Art. 14 can have no application."[15]

The principle laid down above is correct, but the reference to different sources of law is likely to be misleading if it is treated as laying down a mechanical test. For example, the Criminal Procedure Code ("the Code") is a Central law; but criminal procedure is a topic of concurrent legislative power under entry 2, List III, Sch. 7. A State legislature's power to amend an existing or Central law in the concurrent field is subject to Art. 14, and the law as amended would be void if it violated Art. 14. Thus, if a State legislature amended the

---

[12] (1969) 3 S.C.R. 865, ('70) A.SC. 21.

[13] ('70) A.SC. at p. 24. (*a*) The judgment shows that this principle had not been kept in mind in the earlier decision of the Supreme Court in *U.P. Electric Co.* v. *U.P.* ('68) A.SC. 1099; (*b*) [*held*, applying this principle, that the discrimination alleged by the appellant company between itself and Hind Lamps Private Ltd., (a factory manufacturing electric equipment within the area of supply of the company), could not be sustained, because the appellant company were suppliers of electricity and the Hind Lamps Company were consumers of electricity and they did not therefore fall within the same class. As regards the alleged discrimination between consumers of electricity *inter se*, Shah J. observed that from the fact that Hind Lamps and consumers supplied by the appellant company were all consumers of electricity, it did not follow that they belonged to the same class. Besides, no consumer had made any such complaint.]

[14] *M.P.* v. *G. C. Mandawar* (1955) 1 S.C.R. 599, ('54) A.SC. 493, fol. in *Benson Transport* v. *A.P.* ('62) A.A.P. 103, where the court held that the Motor Vehicles (Taxation of Passengers and Goods) (A.P. Amendment) Act, 1959, did not violate Art. 14, because the tax levied in Madras under the law prevailing there could not be compared with the tax levied in Andhra Pradesh. *Mandawar's Case* was reaffirmed in *Lachhman Das* v. *Punjab* (1963) 2 S.C.R. 353, ('63) A.SC. 222, 233; *Mandawar's Case* was applied in *Surendra Kumar* v. *Central Board of Secondary Education* (1957) 7 Raj. 665, ('57) A.Raj. 204, (*held*, that the fixing of an age limit by two different authorities, namely, the Rajasthan University Board of High School and Intermediate Examination and the Central Board of Secondary Education, Ajmer, cannot contravene Art. 14 as the two authorities were distinct and separate.) *Mandawar's Case* was applied in *Narottamdas* v. *M.P.* ('64) A.SC. 1667 (upholding the provisions of M.P. Minimum Wages Fixation Act, 1962, which fixed minimum rates of wages only in respect of some of the employments enumerated in the schedule to the Central Minimum Wages Act which continued to apply to the remaining employments); *Mandawar's Case* and *Lachhman Das's Case, supra*, were fol. in *K. K. Collieries* v. *State* ('71) A.P. 328, 336-7.

[15] (1955) 1 S.C.R. 599 at p. 606.

Code by providing a harsher procedure for some persons, whilst leaving other persons similarly situated to be dealt with under the more lenient provisions of the Code, the amendment would be void as violating Art. 14 notwithstanding that the sources of the two laws were different. In *Nazeria Motor Service* v. *A.P.*[16] without any reference to *Mandawar's Case,* the Supreme Court held that "no question of discrimination can arise when taxes are being imposed under two different sets of laws in States or geographical areas."[17]

Decisions of the Sup. Ct. on Art. 14 fall in five classes: *per* Das C.J. in *Dalmia's Case*

9.37 In *Dalmia's Case*[18] after stating several of the above propositions, Das C.J. said that decisions of the Supreme Court affirming those principles, showed that the decisions fell in one of five classes: (i) a statute may itself indicate the persons or things to whom its provisions were intended to apply and the basis of the classification of such persons or things may appear on the face of the statute or may be gathered from the surrounding circumstances known to, or brought to the attention of the Court. If the classification satisfied the test laid down in the above propositions, the law would be upheld;[19] (ii) a statute may direct its provisions against one individual person or thing or against several individual persons or things but no reasonable basis of classification may appear on the face of it or be deducible from the surrounding circumstances or matters of common knowledge. Such a law would be declared void;[20] (iii) a statute may not make any classification of persons or things for the purpose of applying its provisions but may leave it to the discretion of the Government to select and classify persons or things to whom its provisions should apply. The mere fact that no classification was made by the statute or that discretion was left to Government would not lead to the law being struck down, but the Court woud inquire whether the statute contained any principle or policy for guiding the exercise of discretion by Government in the matter of selection or classification and if it did not, the statute would be struck down on the ground that it conferred arbitrary and uncontrolled power on Government to discriminate between persons or things similarly situated, so that the discrimination was inherent in the statute itself;[21] (iv) if however, in the case last mentioned, the statute laid down a policy or principle for the guidance of the exercise of discretion by Government in the

---

16 (1969) 2 S.C.C. 576.

17 ibid. p. 581.

18 (1959) S.C.R. 279, *supra.*

19 ibid. p. 298, citing *Chiranjit Lal Chowdhuri* v. *Union* (1950) S.C.R. 869, ('51) A.SC. 41; *Bombay* v. *F. N. Balsara* (1951) S.C.R. 682, ('51) A.SC. 318; *Kedar Nath Bajoria* v. *W.B.* (1954) S.C.R. 30, ('53) A.SC. 404; *V. M. Syed Mohammad & Co.* v. *Andhra* (1953) S.C.R. 1117, ('54) A.SC. 314; *Budhan Chowdhury* v. *Bihar* (1955) 1 S.C.R. 1045, ('55) A.SC. 191.

20 (1959) S.C.R. *supra* at p. 299, citing *Ameerunnissa Begum* v. *Mahboob Begum* (1953) S.C.R. 404, ('53) A.SC. 91; and *Ramprasad Narain Sahi* v. *Bihar* (1953) S.C.R. 1129, ('53) A.SC. 215.

21 (1959) S.C.R. at p. 299, citing *Anwar Ali Sarkar's Case* (1952) S.C.R. 284, ('52) A.SC. 75; *Dwarka Prasad Laxmi Narain* v. *U.P.* (1954) S.C.R. 803, ('54) A.SC. 224; *Dhirendra Kumar Mandal* v. *Superintendent & Remembrencer, Legal Affairs* (1955) 1 S.C.R. 224, ('54) A.SC. 424 (it is submitted that *Dwarka Prasad's Case* was not decided on the basis of a discretionary power conferred on Government; the discretionary power was conferred on the Coal Controller who could delegate that power to any person whatsoever); *J. & K.* v. *T. N. Khosa* ('74) A.SC. 1, 10 (*held,* fol. *Dalmia's Case* that reasons need not appear on the face of the rule or law which affects the classification); *Ramraj Sinh* v. *State* ('69) A.B. 333.

matter of such selection or classification, the law would be upheld;[22] (v) if in the case last mentioned, Government in making the selection or classification did not proceed on or follow such policy or principle, the executive action, but not the statute, would be condemned as unconstitutional.[23] It is submitted that one very important class of cases has been left out in the above classification, namely, where discretionary power is conferred by statute on public officials either directly, or by Government in the exercise of powers of delegation contained in the statute. This class of cases raises questions different from those raised by discretion conferred on Government.

an additional class suggested

9.38 The five classes of cases mentioned by Das C.J. fall into two broad classes. Classes (i) and (ii) deal with the theory of classification made by the statute itself. Classes (iii), (iv) and (v) deal with the conferment of discretionary power. Various kinds of classifications have been upheld in decided cases and a large number of them will be noted in this Chapter. However, classification valid for one purpose may not be valid for another. Thus, the classification made between companies employing more than fifty workmen and less than fifty workmen may be relevant and justifiable in considering the provisions of a law dealing with factory legislation but it would ordinarily be irrelevant for the purposes of income-tax. However, before dealing with the classifications upheld or struck down by the Courts we will consider cases where certain broad classifications have been dealt with, such as the classification between the State and individuals or bodies, between local or other public authorities and private persons, the theory of classification as applied to taxing statutes, or to merged territories or territories governed by various States Reorganization Acts. Thereafter, we will deal with the question of conferment of discretionary power. The doctrine of classification presents no real difficulty in principle though opinions may differ on the validity of particular classifications. However, the theory of discretionary power raises serious diffi-

The five classes fall into two classes: (i) classification made by the Statute (ii) conferment of discretionary power

Certain broad classifications considered first

[22] (1959) S.C.R. at p. 300, citing *Kathi Raning Rawat* v. *Saurashtra* (1952) S.C.R. 435, ('52) A.SC. 123; *Suraj Prakash* v. *The State* ('64) A.A.P. 356 (the discretion given to the State Government to extend the provision of the Public Gambling Act to particular areas was held valid as the long title and preamble to the Act gave sufficient guidance).

[23] ibid. p. 300. In *Jyoti Pershad* v. *Delhi* (1962) 2 S.C.R. 125, ('61) A.SC. 1602, the Supreme Court, after referring to the above summary made by Das C.J. made a summary "on slightly different lines": (1) If a statute or rule applied unequally to persons or things similarly situated, that would involve a direct violation of Art. 14, and the statute or rule would have to be struck down. (2) the statute or rule may not enact a discriminatory rule, but might confer discretionary power on an authority, without laying down any policy, or disclosing any tangible or intelligible purpose, thus clothing the authority with unguided and arbitrary powers enabling the authority to discriminate. Here, the statute or the rule would violate Art. 14 and must be struck down. (3) However, as to (2) above, it was not essential that rules for the guidance of the authority should be laid down expressly in the statute or the rule. Such guidance may be obtained (*a*) from the preamble, read in the light of surrounding circumstances which necessitated the legislation, in conjunction with facts of which the court can take judicial notice, or of which it might be apprised by affidavits; or (*b*) from the policy and purpose of the enactments, as gathered from the other operative provisions applicable to analogous or comparable situations, or generally from the object sought to be achieved by the enactment. (4) As to the circumstances under which (1) above does not apply, see ('61) A.SC. at p. 1609 [proposition (3)].

culties. In America where the doctrine is reinforced by the doctrine of separation of powers and the doctrine against delegation of legislative power, the law cannot be stated with certainty. In India, where these theories do not operate, the position is not very different, for as will appear hereafter, a part of the uncertainty is inherent in the nature of discretionary power.

Classification between the State and private individuals or bodies

9.39 The question whether the State can be treated as a class by itself has been considered in several cases and the overwhelming weight of authority shows that for most, if not for all, purposes, the State is in a class by itself. This position of the State was recognized in Indian law long before the Constitution came into force and continues to be recognized under our Constitution. At one time it was possible to distinguish between the governmental and the trading activities of government, but that distinction has lost much of its force because the State is now engaged in activities which, at one time, were not considered as the essential activities of the State but are so considered now. The main ground for distinguishing between the State and individual persons or bodies is that all activities of the State are public in the sense that they are either undertaken on behalf of the public or the loss or gain arising from them falls upon the public. It is on this ground that a special machinery has been devised for recovering public demands, and longer periods of time have been prescribed for the enforcement of demands by Government. Also, in the administration of criminal law, all prosecutions are by the State, and this is so even where a prosecution arises from a private complaint. Again, in matters of Civil Procedure, the law takes into account the fact that the constitutional requirements imposed upon Government involve delay. For when any claim is made against Government, the claim has to be considered by several departments, official sanction to resist the claim has to be obtained and these requirements necessarily take time. We will now consider the various classes of cases in which the special position of Government has been recognized.

Revenue Recovery and Public Demands Acts upheld even when used to enforce a demand of the Union: *Halai's Case*

9.40 "Revenue Recovery Acts" and "Public Demands Recovery Acts" have been on the statute book for over a century. These Acts differ from state to state and the question whether they violate Art. 14 falls into two parts. As to the law of each state, the only question which arises is whether the special coercive machinery made available to a state for the recovery of a public demand is based on a valid classification. As to a public demand of the Union of India, in addition to that question a further question arises, namely, whether Art. 14 is violated if a Union demand is enforced in the various States of India through the machinery of different local Recovery Acts. In *Purshottam Govindji Halai* v. *B. M. Desai*[24] it was contended that s. 46(2), Income-tax Act, violated Art. 14 when it required the Collector on receipt of the requisite certificate from an Income-tax Officer to proceed to recover from the assessee the amounts specified in the certificate, as if it were an arrear of land revenue. Now, the various State Acts for the recovery of arrears of land revenue prescribe different machinery for such recovery, and the provisions in some Acts are harsher than those contained in

[24] (1955) 2 S.C.R. 887, ('56) A.SC. 20.

others. It was argued that as income-tax was a subject of exclusive Union legislation, and its recovery an exclusive Union responsibility, the machinery for the recovery of income-tax ought to be uniform throughout India, since all defaulters who did not pay a Union demand were similarly situated. As s. 46(2) authorised Collectors in different states to adopt a machinery which differed from state to state, the defaulters were treated differently in the different states, and s. 46(2) was void as violating Art. 14. Applying the principles laid down in *Budhan Chowdhury's Case*[25] the Supreme Court rejected this argument. It said that the assessed amount of tax was a public demand and the Union Government found ready to hand in various states a machinery which each state in its wisdom had devised as appropriate for the recovery of its own demands.[26] As to the recovery of arrears of land revenue, defaulters of one state could not complain of the denial of the equal protection of laws because of the differences in the modes of recovery in several states, because the people of one state and the people of another state were not similarly situated; their needs, as understood by their own legislatures, were different from those of the people of other states. It was not unreasonable that the Union Government should adopt for the recovery of its own public demand, a machinery found suitable for recovery of public demands in various states. The grouping of income-tax defaulters in different states was territorial classification based on an intelligible differentia reasonably related to the object of the law. Further, the Income-tax Act classified people in various groups and taxed them differently. On the same principle, there could be no objection to the people of a backward area, which may be in need of a tax remission, being exempted from taxation either wholly or in part. If that was right when a question of imposition arose, it could not be wrong when the matter was one of recovery—". . . the two together make up the full measure of the burden and if it is permissible to vary the burden at one end it must be equally valid to vary at the other for the same or similar reasons."[27]

Manna Lal's Case: Public Demands Acts upheld on the ground that the State was in a class by itself

9.41 The question whether the state could be treated as a class by itself was not raised in *Halai's Case*, but it was raised and decided in *Manna Lal* v. *Collector, Jhalawar*.[28] There it was contended that s. 2(5), Sch. Cl. (6) Rajasthan Public Demands Recovery Act, 1952, violated Art. 14 for it enabled Government to recover a loan due to the State Bank of Jhalawar, that is, moneys due to Government in respect of its trading activities, through the coercive machinery of the Act. In rejecting this contention, the Court said: ". . . the Government, even as a banker, can be legitimately put in a separate class. The dues of the Government of a State are the dues of the entire people of the State. This being the position, a law giving

[25] (1955) 1 S.C.R. 1045, ('55) A.SC. 191.

[26] "There is a strong presumption that a legislature understands and correctly appreciates the needs of its own people, that its laws are directed to problems made manifest by experience, and that its discriminations are based upon adequate grounds": *Middleton* v. *Texas Power & Light Co.* (1918) 249 U.S. 152, 157, 63 L. ed. 527, 531.

[27] (1955) 2 S.C.R. 887 at pp. 900-901; this case was followed in *Collector of Malabar* v. *Erimal Ebrahim Hajee* (1957) S.C.R. 970, ('57) A.SC. 688.

[28] (1961) 2 S.C.R. 962, ('61) A.SC. 828.

special facility for the recovery of such dues cannot, . . . be said to offend Art. 14."[29] *Manna Lal's Case* was reaffirmed in *Lachhman Das* v. *Punjab*.[30] The Supreme Court held by a majority, Subba Rao J. dissenting, that as the funds of the Patiala State Bank belonged to the State, a law which provided for State funds being advanced to customers through a State Bank could also provide for its being recovered as revenue by the coercive process available for the collection of revenue. The same view has been taken by several High Courts.[31] Similarly, the priority given to state debts, or the preference given to state debts, has been upheld.[32] The special position accorded to the State in the recovery of public demands has at times been accorded to public demands of local authorities like Municipalities.[33] *Halai's Case*,[34] *Ibrahim's Case*,[35] and *Manna Lal's Case*[36] were regarded in *Nav Ratanmal* v. *Rajasthan*[37] as establishing the special position of Government in respect of the recovery of public demands, and those decisions were considered relevant in deciding whether the 60 year period prescribed for suits by Government by Art. 149, Limitation Act, 1908[38] violated Art. 14. The Supreme Court held that Art. 149, Limitation Act, did not violate Art. 14. After referring to the historical background against which

Lachhman Das's Case: principle applied to money lent by a State Bank

---

[29] (1961) 2 S.C.R. at p. 970, ('61) A.SC. at p. 828.

[30] (1963) 2 S.C.R. 353, ('63) A.SC. 222.

[31] *Badri Batan Lal* v. *V.P.* ('52) A.V.P. 18 (upholding a law granting special facilities to the State Bank of Datia for the realisation of its claims as arrears of land revenue); *Attelliswamy* v. *Hyderabad* ('53) A.Hyd. 109 (upholding s. 43, Hyderabad Abkari Act which provided that moneys due to Government in respect of leases granted for the tapping of toddy trees would be recovered as arrears of land revenue); foll. in *Mukundayya* v. *A.P.* (1959) Andh.Pra. 19, ('59) A.A.P. 394, *Kuppuswamy* v. *Madras* ('57) A.M. 23, (1956) 2 M.L.J. 185 (upholding s. 52, Madras Revenue Recovery Act, 1864, which provided for recovery of sums due to the Provincial Government including compensation for any loss or damage sustained by them in consequence of a breach of contract being recovered as arrears of land revenue). The last case was relied on in *Rajalingam* v. *State* ('68) A.A.P. 156.

[32] *Builders Supply Corpn.* v. *Union* (1965) 2 S.C.R. 289; ('65) A.SC. 1704 [*held*, that there was a consensus of judicial opinion that arrears of tax due to the State can claim priority over private debts; *held*, further that rules of Common Law relating to substantive rights adopted in India and enforced by judicial decisions amounted to "law in force" in India within the meaning of Art. 372(1). Consequently, the priority of Crown debts which had been recognized by Indian High Courts before 1950 continued to be in force in our country]; *Bank of India* v. *John Bowman* (1955) Bom. 654, ('55) A.B. 305, 57 Bom.L.R. 345 (upholding the priority given to State debts over private debts of the same class); *J. R. Kimtee* v. *Kishendas* (1955) Hyd. 510, ('55) A.Hyd. 194 [upholding the exclusion of public demands from the scaling down of debts of Jagirdars, (due to their impoverished position) under the Hyderabad Jagirdar's Debt Settlement Act, 1952]; *Kesheoprasad* v. *State* (1955) Nag. 459, ('55) A.N. 177 (upholding the C.P. & Berar Excise Act, 1915, authorizing recovery of licence fees as arrears of land revenue. It is difficult to see why a discussion whether the State was a person was necessary if the court held, as it did, that the discrimination was based on a differentia reasonably related to the object of the law); rel. on in *Shiv Parshad* v. *Punjab* (1959) Punj. 310, ('57) A.Punj. 150, (upholding s. 44, Prov. Insolvency Act, 1920, which provided for preferential payment of taxes due to the State).

[33] *Corporation of Trivandrum* v. *Muhammad Haneefa* (1598) Ker. 227, ('58) A. Ker. 61 [upholding s. 409, Trivandrum City Municipal Act and Rule 31(2) which provided for the recovery of Municipal dues as arrears of land revenue].

[34] *Supra*.

[35] *Supra*.

[36] *Supra*.

[37] (1962) 2 S.C.R. 324, ('61) A.SC. 1704.

[38] Now Art. 112, Limitation Act, 1963, has reduced the period to 30 years.

Art. 149 of the Act had to be considered[39], the Court said that there was first the fact that if a claim by Government became barred, the loss fell on the public, that is, on the community in general, to the benefit of a private individual who would thus gain an advantage by lapse of time: "That itself would appear to indicate a sufficient ground for differentiating between the claims of an individual and the claim of the community at large." Further, it was well known that governmental machinery did not move as quickly as non-governmental, because Government being an impersonal body there had to be departmental correspondence, consultations, obtaining of sanctions according to rules, and these necessarily took time, a fact recognized by O. 27, rr. 5 and 7, C.P.C.[40]

Special position of Government recognized in *Nav Ratanmal's Case*: longer period of limitation upheld

9.42 The special position of Government has also been recognized under s. 80, C.P.C., which provides for a statutory notice to Government or to a public officer acting in his official capacity. S. 80 was challenged as violating Art. 14 but its constitutional validity was upheld.[41] The special position occupied by Government in the administration of Criminal Law has also been recognized. Thus, the Government's right under s. 417, Cr. P.C., to appeal from an acquittal has been held not to violate Art. 14 because such a right has not been conferred on a private complainant.[42] The following are some of the other provisions in which the special position of Government has been recognized: the M.P. Government Premises (Eviction) Act, 1952;[43] the Orissa Motor Vehicles (Regulation of Stage Carriage and

The special position of Government recognized by s. 80, C.P.C.: s. 80 upheld

The special position of Govt. in criminal law recognized

[39] The Court said that Art. 149 was part of a law of limitation which was a statute of repose. However, the position filled by a plaintiff, as also the public interest had not been overlooked in the Limitation Act. A plaintiff under a legal disability to institute a suit was entitled to an extension of the period of limitation by taking into account the period of such disability. Again, s. 10 of the Act protected public interest by providing that there was to be no period of limitation for the breach of an express trust, the maxim *vigilantibus et non dormientibus jura subveniunt* (the vigilant and not the sleepy are assisted by the laws) was a rule for the subject; the maxim *nullum tempus occurit regi* (no time runs against the King) was in general applicable to the Crown: (1962) 2 S.C.R. *supra* at pp. 330-31.

[40] ibid. p. 331. For similar reasons the longer period of prescription provided for Government by s. 15, Easements Act, 1882, was upheld in *Chadami Lal* v. *General Manager, W. Rly.* (1962) 1 All. 58, ('62) A.A. 159.

[41] *Andhra* v. *Prasada Rao* (1956) Andh. Pra. 114, ('57) A.A.P. 675; see *Narain Mal* v. *Ganpat Singh* (1957) 7 Raj. 229, ('57) A.Raj. 73, where it was held, upholding s. 55, Rajasthan Court of Wards Act, 1951, that the same considerations which applied to a notice under s. 80 C.P.C. applied to a notice where the estate of a Jagirdar is managed through a Court of Wards.

[42] *Nasrullah* v. *State* ('55) A.A. 124, (1954) A.L.J. 429 (proposition affirmed without any discussion); *Abdul Ali* v. *Mt. Jannat* ('57) A.A. 552 (upholding s. 417, Cr. P.C., the Court held that the classification between the State and private individuals was justified, first, because the State was not likely to file frivolous appeals and, secondly, because the State would not be guided by feelings of revenge as a private complainant might very often be; an appeal by the State would be filed in the public interest); *In re Bokkasam Krishnayya* ('57) A.A.P. 163; rel. on in *State* v. *Shankar* (1958) 1 All. 306, ('58) A.A. 432; *Mysore* v. *Nanja* (1957) Mys. 159, ('58) A.Mys. 48.

[43] *G. Solomon* v. *Competent Authority* (1957) Madh. Pra. 613, ('58) A.M.P. 330 [the classification between Government and private landlords was supported by citing the observations of the Supreme Court in *Baburao Shantaram More* v. *Bombay Housing Board* (1954) S.C.R. 572, ('54) A.SC. 153, which upheld an exemption granted to Government or the local authority or the Housing Board from the provisions of the Rent Act. Having regard to the delays involved in the ordinary procedure for eviction of tenants, the Court held that it was not unreasonable to arm the Competent Authority with summary powers]; *Brig. Commdr., Meerut* v.

Other special provisions upheld

Public Carriers Service) Act, 1947, which conferred a monopoly on a joint stock company in which the Union and the State Government together would have a controlling interest;[44] Entry 16, Sch. 1, Bombay Court Fees Act, 1959, which required a litigant tax payer to pay Court fees on an application under s. 66(2), Income-tax Act, to the High Court, but did not require such fees to be paid by the Commissioner of Income-tax on a similar application;[45] s. 4, Bombay Rents, Hotel and Lodging Houses (Rates Control) Act, 1947, read with ss. 3-3a, Bombay Housing Board Act, 1948, (as amended in 1951), which exempted properties belonging to the Government, Local Authority or the Housing Board from the provisions of the Bombay Rent Act;[46] s. 11(2), Bihar Buildings (Lease, Rent and Eviction) Control Act, 1947, which makes special provision for the benefit of public servants.[47]

Classification based on historical and geographical considerations

9.43 The existence of different laws in the former Indian States raised the question whether on the merger of those States into larger units and on the merger of several of those units into the States of India, those laws became void as violating Art. 14. The same problem has been raised by the successive States Re-organization Acts passed by Parliament. Decided cases show that the weight of authority is in favour of the view that laws which were in force in a State, or part of a State, which had a distinct and separate existence did not become void on the merger or the re-organization of a State on the ground that in other parts of the merged, or recognized, State, similar laws were not in force. A classification based on historical reasons has been held, it is submitted rightly,

---

Ganga Prasad ('56) A.A. 507, (1956) A.L.J. 251, foll. in *Moinuddin* v *Dy. Director* (1957) 2 All. 302, ('56) A.A. 684 (in these cases it was held that the Government Premises Eviction Act of 1950 violated Art. 14 and was void. The decisions did not dispute the validity of a classification between Government and private individuals but proceeded on the ground that the provisions of the Act were not reasonably related to the object of the law); *Sucha Singh* v. *Administrative Officer,* ('63) A.A. 526 (F.B.), (1963) A.L.J. 311; [*Bir Pratap Singh* v. *U.P.* (1960) A.L.J. 52 was overruled]. The special machinery provided for recovery of private lands in unauthorised occupation, was upheld, following *Manna Lal's Case* (1961) 2 S.C.R. 962, ('61) A.SC. 828, and *Nav Rattanmal's Case* (1962) 2 S.C.R. 324, ('61) A.SC. 1704.

[44] *Lokanath Misra* v. *Orissa* ('52) A.Or. 42.

[45] *C. N. Bros.* v. *I.T.C.* ('61) A.Guj. (F.B.) 144 (*held,* that the Union and the States were vitally interested in the collection of taxes and there was nothing objectionable in the classification made by the impugned law).

[46] *Baburao Shantaram More* v. *Bombay Housing Board* (1954) S.C.R. 572, ('54) A.SC. 153 (in upholding the exemption the Court observed that Government had set up the Board to solve the accommodation problem and it was not to be expected that Government or a Local Authority or the Board would be actuated by any profit-making motive so as to unduly enhance rents or eject the tenants from their respective properties as private landlords are likely to be. This reason justified putting the tenants of Government, the Local Authorities and the Board in one class and the tenants of private individuals or bodies in another class); *Ram Pratap* v. *Union* (1953) Bom. 200, 54 Bom.L.R. 927, ('53) A.B. 170 [upholding the exemption granted to Government by s. 4(1), Bombay Rents, Hotel and Lodging Houses (Rates Control) Act, 1947]; *Nabin Chandra Gantayet* v. *Orissa* (1957) Cut. 71, ('57) A.Or. 56 (upholding the exemption given to Government under the Orissa Tenancy Relief Act, 1955, the Court observed that the Legislature was the best judge to decide whether the evil of arbitrary eviction was so great as to necessitate legislation for the protection of tenants of private landlords only or also of tenants of Government).

[47] *Santi Devi* v. *Dy. Commr., Hazaribagh* ('67) A.P. 333; fol. in *Nandalal Sinha* v. *Dist. Magistrate, Hazaribagh* ('67) A.P. 334, 336.

Merger of former Indian States, and "reorganization of States": different laws in the same State upheld

to justify the existence of such laws. Thus, in *Bhaiyalal Shukla* v. *M.P.*[48] the C.P. and Berar Sales Tax Act, 1947, as extended to Vindhya Pradesh was held not to violate Art. 14 because the sales tax law in Vindhya Pradesh was different from that in other parts of Madhya Pradesh of which it became a part. These different laws were upheld because the differentiation arose from historical and geographical classification based on historical reasons. In *Anant Prasad Lakshminivas Generiwal* v. *A.P.*[49] the above decision was applied, and the Hyderabad Endowment Regulation, 1940, and the rules framed thereunder, were upheld, though two different laws were in force in respect to religious endowments in the two areas of the State of Andhra Pradesh one of which came to that State from the State of Madras in 1953 and the other from the former State of Hyderabad in 1956.[50] For the same reasons the Bhopal State Agricultural Income-tax Act, 1957, which imposed an agricultural income-tax in Bhopal which was not imposed upon agricultural income earned for the rest of Madhya Pradesh was upheld.[51] The following laws were also upheld: the Patiala Recovery of State Dues Act, notwithstanding that after the States Reorganization Act, 1956, it applied only in the territories of the erstwhile Pepsu Union and not in other parts of the State of Punjab;[52] s. 4, Saurashtra Local Development Fund Act, 1956, imposing a levy only on the occupants of the villages of Saurashtra while occupants in other places in the State of Bombay were not liable to such imposition;[53] the Jaipur District

[48] (1962) Supp. 2 S.C.R. 257, ('62) A.SC. 981.

[49] (1963) Supp. 1 S.C.R. 844, ('63) A.SC. 853.

[50] ("We are told that steps are being taken to assimilate the laws in the two parts of the State and bring them under one common pattern. But that naturally takes time and the complete assimilation of all laws has not yet taken place. We are further told that the question of having one law for public trusts of religious or charitable nature, is under the active consideration of the State Government. In these circumstances it would not be right to strike down all laws prevailing in the two parts of the State, because of certain difference in them arising out of historical reasons": (1963) Supp. 1 S.C.R. at p. 861. It is not clear whether the Court upheld the classification because it had been informed that uniform laws were in contemplation); fol. in *Narayana Reddi* v. *A.P.* ('64) A.A.P. 373 at 377 (upholding the provisions of the Hyderabad Markets Act which confined the application of the Act to Hyderabad and Secunderabad in Andhra Pradesh. The provision was justified as based on geographical and historical considerations arising out of the re-organization of States). *Anant Prasad's Case* was fol. in *D. Cawasji & Co.* v. *State* ('69) A. Mys. 23, the court observing that the decision in *Anant Prasad's Case* was not based on any assurance given by the government that uniformity of laws would be brought about in the near future.

[51] *M.P.* v. *Bhopal Sugar Industries* ('64) A.SC. 1179; fol. in *Vishwesha Tirtha Swamiar* v. *Mysore* (1972) 1 S.C.R. 137, ('71) A.SC. 2377 [upholding the validity of the Mysore Land Revenue (Surcharge) Act, 1961, as amended in 1962. A temporary surcharge levied on the basis of existing rates while settlement and survey were being done in the re-organized State did not violate Art. 14.]

[52] *Lachman Das* v. *Punjab* (1963) 2 S.C.R. 353, ('63) A.SC. 222 (upheld by a majority); *Tilakram Rambaksh* v. *Bank of Patiala* (1959) Punj. 1384, ('59) A.Punj. 440; *Bhagwan Kaur* v. *Punjab* ('63) A.Punj. 522 (s. 32-B, Punjab Tenancy and Agricultural Lands Act, 1955, was upheld for the same reason); *Nanjundaswamy* v. *Mysore* ('63) A.Mys. 202 (upholding different salary scales payable as a result of State re-organization to civil servants who had opted to retain their existing pay scales which were higher than those in Mysore). *Lachhman Das's Case* was fol. in *Ram Parshad* v. *Punjab* ('66) A.SC. 1607.

[53] *Jadeja Habhubha* v. *State* (1959) Bom. 41, ('59) A.B. 43, 60 Bom.L.R. 1191 [the reason actually given for the decision is not very satisfactory: ". . . (the) contention in its ultimate analysis would mean that until uniform legislation is in-

Boards Act, 1947, although District Boards existed only in one part of Rajasthan;[54] s. 1, Marwar Tenancy Act, 1949, and the Marwar Land Revenue Act, 1949, which Acts were enacted for the welfare of all classes within the area which was formerly the State of Marwar;[55] the Berar Regulation of Agricultural Laws Act, 1951;[56] ss. 8 (3) (iv) 1-A, Utkal University Act, 1943, which provided that out of fourteen registered graduates elected to the Senate four must be from merged States;[57] the allocation of thirty per cent of the seats in Colleges to the students of Hyderabad and Secunderabad as against seventy per cent reserved seats for the rest of the Telengana area;[58] s. 60 (1) (ccc), C.P.C. (as amended by the Patiala Relief of Indebtedness) Act, 1999 B.K., although it applied only to the erstwhile State of Pepsu by virtue of s. 119, States Reorganization Act, 1956.[59] How-

---

troduced, all local laws would be bad. The position is so obviously untenable that it does not need to be elaborated considerably." It is submitted that the correct ground for the decision would be either that the different laws are justified on historical grounds unless such grounds are unavailing in particular cases or, alternatively, that differences in local conditions justify different local laws].

[54] *Madan Singh* v. *Collector, Sikar* (1953) Raj. 606, ('54) A.Raj. 104 at 117 [the precise grounds of this decision are not clear but it would appear that it is rested on the fact that the State of Rajasthan was constituted by merging a number of territories which were formerly under Indian Princes and in varying stages of development. Reference was also made to Jaipur being a progressive State. The citation of the following passage from *Bowman* v. *Lewis* (1880) 101 U.S. 22, 32, 25 L. ed. 989, 992-93, namely, "If a Mexican State should be acquired by treaty and added to an adjoining State or part of a State, in the United States and the two should be erected into a new State, it cannot be doubted that such new State might allow the Mexican laws and judicature to continue unchanged in the one portion, and the common law and its corresponding judicature in the other portion. Such an arrangement would not be prohibited by any fair construction of the 14th Amendment. It would not be based on any respect of persons or classes, but on municipal considerations alone, and a regard to the welfare of all classes within the particular territory or jurisdiction" would suggest that the real basis of the decision is that the classification can be justified on historical grounds].

[55] *Raja Hari Singh* v. *State* (1954) Raj. 274, ('54) A.Raj. 117 (*held*, that having regard to the progressive nature of the law it could be allowed to continue even if similar progressive laws did not exist in other parts of Rajasthan. As the Act applied to the whole of Marwar there was no discrimination between Jagir and Khalsa lands. It is submitted that the correct ground for the decision is that such laws can be upheld as based on a geographical classification arising from historical causes irrespective of the question whether the law is progressive or not).

[56] *Bhaurao Atmaram* v. *S. D. O. Chandur* ('57) A.N. 1 (F.B.) (". . . the tenancy law in the Central Provinces is different from that in the merged territories or that prevailing in the alienated and unalienated villages in Berar. The classification complained of already existed in the State. . . . The protection afforded to tenants of unalienated lands in Berar under the Berar Land Revenue Code was limited. The agricultural, social and economic conditions in the three territories are also different and require different treatment to achieve the goal of efficient agriculture. It is therefore reasonable to make different provisions for these three territories even though the object, that is, efficient agriculture is the same." ibid. p. 4).

[57] *Ajoy Kumar* v. *Siala Behari* (1957) Cut. 526, ('57) A.Or. 159 (the representation given to areas which had merged in the Province of Orissa was upheld because those areas were not as advanced in matters of education as the original Province of Orissa).

[58] *Muralidhar* v. *A.P.* (1959) Andh. Pra. 137, ('59) A.A.P. 437 (the reservation was made as a result of s. 113, States Reorganisation Act, and the various notifications issued thereunder by the concerned authorities. The reservation was upheld on the ground that the policy underlying s. 113 and the notifications was to extend equal facilities and opportunities to students belonging to areas which once formed part of the Hyderabad State but were now included in other States).

[59] *Sampat Kumar* v. *Nathu Ram* (1958) Punj. 1445, ('58) A.Punj. 326 [the reasons given for the decision are not satisfactory. *Ramjilal's Case* (1951) S.C.R. 127, ('51)

ever, in *Brijmohan* v. *Rajasthan*[60] it was held that the Prevention of Unequal Marriages Act, 1945, which applied to "the domiciled residents" of the old Jaipur State, now a part of Rajasthan, could not be upheld as being founded on a reasonable and permissible classification and was void. Historical and geographical classification is not limited to cases arising out of merger agreements or the reorganisation of States: ". . . it was settled law that in order to give effect to the policy of the Government clearly indicated in the statute in question, it is open to the executive authorities to make a geographical classification so as to apply the law to selected areas with a view ultimately to cover the whole territory for which the law was enacted."[61]

Historical and geographical classifications not limited to merger agreements, etc.

9.44 At one time the decision in *Ramjilal* v. *I.T.O. Mohindargarh*[62] was mistakenly taken to mean that as tax laws were governed by Art. 265 they were not subject to fundamental rights. This view was not correct, for all that the case decided was that Art. 31 (1) did not apply to taxation, since express provision had been made by Art. 265 for the levy of taxes. In fact, the court considered and repelled the challenge under Art. 14 *on merits*. But it is now settled that tax laws are subject to fundamental rights.[63] However, it was held in *East India Tobacco Co.* v. *A.P.*[64] that the wide latitude given by our Constitution to the legislature in classification for taxation was correctly described in the following words:

Art. 14 applies to tax laws

"A State does not have to tax everything in order to tax something. It is allowed to pick and choose districts, objects, persons, methods and even rates for taxation if it does so reasonably. . . . The (U.S.) Supreme Court has been practical and has permitted a very wide latitude in classification for taxation."[65]

The *Tobacco Case* was cited with approval in *Khyerbari Tea Co. Ltd.* v. *Assam*[66] and both decisions were applied and followed in

A.SC. 97, was relied upon as furnishing guidance. It is submitted that the analogy of pending proceedings is not applicable but the decision is correct on the ground that a geographical classification based on historical reasons is valid].

[60] (1960) 10 Raj. 12, ('60) A.Raj. 118.

[61] *Bahadur Singh* v. *Union* (unreported judgment of the Supreme Court) quoted in *Balley Singh* v. *State* ('67) A.A. 341, 344-5 (*held*, that the prohibition of the cultivation of poppy in some areas, and not in others, under the Opium Act, 1878, and the Dangerous Drugs Act, 1930, was valid).

[62] (1951) S.C.R. 127, ('51) A.SC. 97.

[63] *Purshottam Govindji Halai* v. *B. M. Desai* (1955) 2 S.C.R. 887, ('56) A.SC. 20; *K. T. Moopil Nair* v. *Kerala* (1961) 3 S.C.R. 77, ('61) A.SC. 552; *Khandige Sham Bhat* v. *Agricultural I.T.O.* ('63) A.SC. 591, (1963) 3 S.C.R. 809, (citing the above cases) *held*, further, that a larger discretion is permitted to the legislatures in classification for taxation than in other matters.

[64] (1963) 1 S.C.R. 404, 409, ('62) A.SC. 1733 (The classification between Virginia and "country" tobacco was upheld).

[65] *Willis*, p. 587. The same passage was quoted with approval in *V. V. R. Varma* v. *Union* (1969) 3 S.C.R. 827, ('69) A.SC. 1094, 1098 (*held*, that in considering a Hindu undivided family as a unit of taxation under the Expenditure Tax Act and not a non-Hindu undivided family, Parliament had not attempted "obvious inequality"); appld. in *T. G. Venkataraman* v. *Madras* (1970) 1 S.C.R. 615, ('70) A.SC. 508, 511-12; foll. in *Avinder Singh* v. *Punjab* (1979) 1 S.C.R. 845, ('79) A.SC. 321, 325 [*held*, that a levy of a tax of Re. 1 per bottle of foreign liquor did not violate Art. 14. The Court also referred to *Abdul Shakoor & Co.'s Case* (1964) 8 S.C.R. 217 at 230, ('64) A.SC. 1729 at pp. 1734-5.]

[66] (1964) 5 S.C.R. 975, 1010 (*held*, that the impugned Act did not violate Art. 14 in taxing tea and jute — which were the main produce of the State of Assam — and not other commodities).

Karnataka v. *Hansa Corpn.*[67] The first two decisions have been followed in other cases.[68] The same principles were affirmed in *Rai Ramkrishna* v. *Bihar*,[69] where the court also considered the circumstances under which tax laws would be struck down as violating Arts. 14 and 19:

"... the power of taxing the people and their property is an essential attribute of the Government and Government may legitimately exercise the said power by reference to the objects to which it is applicable to the utmost extent to which Government thinks it expedient to do so. The objects to be taxed so long as they happen to be within the legislative competence of the Legislature can be taxed . . . according to the exigencies of its needs, because there can be no doubt that the State is entitled to raise revenue by taxation. The quantum of tax levied . . . the conditions subject to which it is levied, the manner in which it is sought to be recovered, are all matters within the competence of the Legislature, and in dealing with the contention . . . that the taxing statute contravenes Art. 19, Courts would naturally be circumspect and cautious. Where for instance it appears that the taxing statute is plainly discriminatory, or provides no procedural machinery for assessment and levy of the tax, or that it is confiscatory, Courts would be justified in striking down the impugned statute as unconstitutional. In such cases, the character of the material provisions of the impugned statute is such that the Court would feel justified in taking the view that, in substance, the taxing statute is a cloak adopted by the Legislature for achieving its confiscatory purposes. This is illustrated by . . . *Kunnathat Thathunni Moopil Nair* v. *Kerala*[70] where a taxing statute was struck down because it suffered from several fatal infirmities. On the other hand, . . . (in) *Jagannath Baksh Singh* v. *U.P.*[71] . . . a challenge to the taxing statute on the ground that its provisions were unreasonable was rejected and it was observed that unless the infirmities in the impugned statute were of such a serious nature as to justify its description as a colourable exercise of legislative power, the Court would uphold a taxing statute."[72]

Decided cases show that a classification may be made not only for the imposition or recovery of a tax, but also to prevent an evasion

---

[67] ('81) A.SC. 463 [*held,* that a "population criterion would provide a reasonable basis for classification for selectively levying the tax by choosing local area and by specifying different rates so as to make the tax productive. Therefore . . . the classification . . . was (reasonable)." ibid. p. 470.

[68] *Nagappa* v. *I.O.M. Cess Commr.* ('68) A.Mys. 48 (the court repelled the contention that s. 2, Iron Ore Mines Labour Welfare Act, 1961, which levied an excise duty on iron ore, violated Art. 14, because no duty was levied on the mining of other metals); *Sushil Chander* v. *State* ('69) A.A. 317, 325, 332 (*held,* that the exclusion of agriculture from, and the exemption granted to the armed forces under, the impugned Act, which imposed a tax on professions etc., was not discriminatory); *R. Prasad Mohan Lal* v. *I.T.A. Tribunal* ('70) A.A. 620 (F.B.) at p. 639, proposition (9).

[69] ('63) A.SC. 1667, 1673 [In view of the earlier Supreme Court decisions it was conceded that taxing statutes "were not beyond the pale" of constitutional limitations imposed by Arts. 14 and 19 or the test of reasonableness laid down in Art. 304(b).]

[70] (1961) 3 S.C.R. 77, ('61) A.SC. 552, fol. in *State* v. *Kunhippokker Kutty* (1966) 2 Ker. 313, ('67) A.Ker. 114 (*held,* that the classification of buildings on the basis of floor area as adopted in the Kerala Buildings Tax Act, 1961, violated Art. 14 as it was not founded on an intelligible differentia nor had it any relation to the object of the Act).

[71] (1963) 1 S.C.R. 220, ('62) A.SC. 1563; cited and fol. in *Asst. Commr. of Urban Land Tax* v. *Buckhingham Carnatic Co. Ltd.* 1969 (2) S.C.C. 55, 69 [*held,* that the tax of 4 per cent of the value of urban land did not violate Art. 19(1)(*f*) and (*g*), even though the tax was levied retrospectively].

[72] ('63) A.SC. 1667 at p. 1673, fol. in *Sushil Chander* v. *State* ('69) A.A. 317, 332; for similar observations, see *T. G. Venkataraman* v. *Madras* (1970) 1 S.C.R. 615, ('70) A.SC. 508, 511-12.

of tax.[73] The following classifications have been upheld on the ground that they were based on a differentia reasonably related to the object of the taxing statutes: BETWEEN:—pending proceedings and fresh proceedings;[74] a person carrying on a business in partnership with other persons, men or women, and with his major children;[75] holding companies and other companies;[76] assessments commenced under a later law;[77] the State and the assessee;[78] assessees whose assessments have been set aside and re-assessment ordered and other assessees;[79] registered firms which had, and registered firms which had not, committed default attracting a penalty;[80] existing firms and firms which came into existence during the assessment year;[81] persons whose assessments had been completed (or were not pending) before a specified date, and those whose assessments had not

Income-tax

---

[73] See, for example, *f.ns.* 75 and 76 below.

[74] *Ramji Lal* v. *I.T.O., Mohindargarh* (1951) S.C.R. 127, ('51) A.SC. 97 [in rejecting the contention that the petitioner who was a resident of Nabha was assessed in Kapurthala, the Supreme Court observed, first, that the discrimination, if any, was brought about by the fact that there was no income-tax in Nabha before the impugned Act came into force, and, secondly, that a provision that pending proceedings should be concluded according to law applicable at the time when the rights or liabilities accrued and the proceedings commenced was founded on a reasonable classification of assessees; the observations about pending proceedings were applied in *Ram Kumar* v. *I.T.C.* ('63) A.A. 451 in upholding s. 3, Income-tax (Amendment) Act, 1950]; *Straw Products Ltd.* v. *I.T.O.* ('67) A.M.P. 34, 44 (applying *Ramjilal's Case*, the classification between assessees whose assessment had been completed and assessees whose assessments were not completed, was upheld); *R. Prasad Mohan Lal* v. *I.T.A. Tribunal* ('70) A.A. 620 [upholding the classification made by cls. (*a*) and (*b*) of s. 297(2) of the Income-tax Act, 1961. It was further held that the fact that a better classification could be made was no ground for holding the classification made by the Act void].

[75] *B. M. Amina Umma* v. *I.T.O.* (1955) Mad. 702, ('54) A.M. 1120, 1126 [In upholding s. 16(3)(*a*)(ii), Income-tax Act, as amended by Act 4 of 1937, the court upheld the classification as necessary to give effect to the object of the provision, namely, preventing the evasion of a just tax liability]; cited with approval in *Balaji* v. *I.T.O.* (1962) 2 S.C.R. 983, ('62) A.SC. 123 [where it was held that s. 16 (3)(*a*)(ii) did not violate Art. 14 as the classification made was related to the object of the Act which was to prevent tax evasion. A similar device would not ordinarily be resorted to by individuals by entering into partnerships with persons other than those mentioned in the sub-section, as it would involve the risk of the third party turning round and asserting his own rights]; fol. in *Umed Rai* v. *I.T.O.* ('65) A.P. 114.

[76] *C. W. Spencer* v. *I.T.O.* (1957) Mad. 251, ('57) A.M. 133, (upholding s. 23A, Income-tax Act, 1922, *held*, that the classification was related to the object of the law which was to prevent tax evasion).

[77] *Hukumchand Mills* v. *M.P.* ('64) A.SC. 1329, 1333 [upholding the Madhya Bharat Taxation on Income (Validating) Act, 1954].

[78] *R. M. Seshadri* v. *2nd Addl. I.T.O.* (1954) Mad. 1236, ('54) A.M. 806 [upholding s. 33(3), Income-tax Act, 1922].

[79] *P. Ganesh Nayak* v. *C.T.O.* ('64) A.Mys. 240 [differing from Chagla C.J. and agreeing with Desai J. in *S. C. Prashar* v. *Vasantsen Dwarkadas* (1956) Bom. 374, ('56) A.B. 530, 58 Bom.L.R. 184; also citing *C.I.T., B. & O.* v. *Lakshmi Singh* ('63) A.SC. 1394, 1398, in which the Supreme Court was evenly divided, with Sarkar J. appearing to take the view that the classification may be legitimate.]

[80] *Jain Bros.* v. *Union* (1970) 3 S.C.R. 253, ('70) A.SC. 778, 785-6 [upholding the validity of s. 271(2), Income-tax Act, 1961, which made the classification].

[81] *Firm Nagappa Chettiar* v. *I.T.C.* ('65) A.M. 424 [upholding R. 2, as amended in 1952, made under s. 59(1), Income-tax Act, which required that a partnership should be registered before the close of the preceding year but provided that in respect of a partnership coming into existence during the year, it should be registered within six months from the commencement of the partnership or before the end of the year, whichever is earlier. The classification was justified on the ground that it was designed to prevent false claims of partnership being made].

been completed (or were pending) before that date;[82] assessees whose income has escaped assessment according as such income is one lakh of rupees and more or less than one lakh of rupees;[83] a lower rate of tax on small incomes and a higher rate of tax on large incomes;[84] income from salaries and income from all other sources;[85] assessees in one State (Madhya Bharat) and in other States of India;[86] the classification made by s. 10(26)(*a*), Income-tax Act, 1961, for the purpose of exemption between the income of a member of a Scheduled Tribe accruing or arising from any source in the area, State or Union Territories specified in the said clause (26), and the income from a source outside such area, State or Union Territory;[87] agricultural income-tax on income from tea plantations and on income from rubber plantations;[88] sale of machinery to Government and to others;[89] individual agriculturists and partnership firms and companies doing agricultural business;[90] purchasers

---

[82] ('70) A.SC. *supra* at p. 784 [*held*, that s. 297(2), Income-tax Act, 1961, which came into force on 1.4.1962, was valid and the provision that assessment proceedings which were pending on 1.4.1962 were to be governed by the old Act, and assessment proceedings which were not pending were to be governed by the new Act, was based on a valid classification]; *Paramanand* v. *Addl. I.T.O.* (1958) Mys. 10, ('58) A.Mys. 70 (the classification was based on an objective test, namely, whether the assessment in question had been completed by April 1, 1952); *M. M. Isphahani* v. *I.T.C.* ('69) A.Cal. 264 [upholding the validity of s. 297(2)(*d*)(i) of the Income-tax Act, 1961]; The decision in *R. Prasad Mohan Lal* v. *I.T.A. Tribunal* ('70) A.A. 620 (F.B.) in so far as it upholds the validity of the classification made by s. 297(2)(*a*) and (*b*) is in accord with the decision of the Supreme Court in *Jain Bros.' Case*, *supra*, and is good law. But the decision on the classification made by s. 297(2)(*f*) and (*g*) is contrary to *Jain Bros.' Case* and is no longer good law.

[83] *Rashid & Sons* v. *I.T.O.* ('64) A.SC. 1190 [Upholding s. 34(1)(*a*) of the Income-tax Act].

[84] *Sukhlall* v. *I.T.O.* ('59) A.Cal. 444 (a graduated scale of income-tax, the rate of tax rising with the rise of income as provided by the Finance Act, 1957, was upheld as based on a valid classification).

[85] *Ved Vyas* v. *I.T.O.* ('65) A.A. 37 [upholding the provisions of the Finance Act, 1963, which excluded the salaried class of persons from the levy of a surcharge; salaries had been taxed since the Income-tax Act, 1922, on the basis of the Finance Act current during the year in which they were received].

[86] *Hukumchand Mills* v. *M.P.* ('59) A.M.P. 195 [upholding the Madhya Bharat Tax on Income (Validating) Act, 1954, *held*, that as the assessments made by the Madhya Bharat authorities were illegal and liable to be set aside, the Legislature chose the least harmful of the two courses, namely, validating the assessments instead of refunding the tax and going through the whole process of assessment over again. The classification was valid as Madhya Bharat assessees formed a class by themselves when a new law was introduced].

[87] *I.T.O. Shillong* v. *N. T. R. Rymbai* ('76) A.SC. 670 [*held*, that the object of the above classification was not only to benefit members of the Scheduled Tribes residing in the specified area but also to benefit such areas economically. The Court distinguished the decision in *I.T.O. Assam* v. *Lawrence Singh* ('68) A.SC. 658 as dealing with a different classification which was held invalid, namely, between members of Scheduled Tribes in Government service and those not in Government service].

[88] *Travancore Rubber and Tea Co.* v. *Kerala* ('64) A.SC. 572 [upholding s. 5, explanation (2), (Kerala) Agricultural Income-tax Act, 1950, on the ground that income derived from sale of tea grown and manufactured by a seller is partly derived from land, by agriculture and partly from business. That is not the case with the income derived from the sale of rubber].

[89] *Chittoor Transport Co.* v. *I.T.O.* ('65) A.A.P. 196 [upholding s. 10(2)(vi)(*b*), Proviso, the court said that the provision was designed to prevent abuse of the concession].

[90] *Prativa Sasmal* v. *Agricultural I.T.O.* ('58) A.Cal. 585, 61 C.W.N. 791 [upholding s. 7(1), Bengal Agricultural Income-tax Act, 1944, "It was said in an affidavit . . . and that statement was accepted by the Court that individual agriculturists

and sellers;[91] vegetable in the popular sense and a vegetable in a technical sense;[92] vegetable oils other than mustard oil and rape oil and mustard oil and rape oil;[93] traders or shop-keepers who merely sell, and persons who personally make gold ornaments, or own manufacturing establishments employing artisans for that purpose;[94] food and drink sold in hotels, boarding houses or restaurants and food and drink sold outside these places;[95] a registered and an unregistered dealer;[96] a manufacturer who purchases tobacco from a dealer and a manufacturer who purchases it from the grower;[97] sales through commission agents who account fully for all collections made and sales through commission agents who do not so account;[98] cane jaggery and palm jaggery;[99] tobacco of one quality and tobacco of another;[1] the transaction of purchase and the transaction of sale;[2]

---

were generally illiterate and kept no books of accounts, whereas partnership firms and companies kept books of accounts. There was therefore sufficient basis for treating them separately."]

91 *V.M.S. & Co.* v. *Madras* ('53) A.M. 105, (1952) 2 M.L.J. 598.

92 *Ram Bux* v. *Rajasthan* ('63) A.SC. 351 [upholding s. 4(2), Sch. 2, Item 2, Rajasthan Sales Tax Act, 1954, *held*, that the word 'vegetable' was used in its popular sense and did not include *pan* (betel leaves), and a conditional exemption of sales tax on betel leaves was based on a valid classification.]

93 *Satyanarayan Mahabir* v. *State* ('71) A.A. & N. 83 (*held*, that the classification of mustard oil and rape oil from vegetable oil did not make the classification unreasonable. The nature of the commodities in question was different and the consumers of the commodities may also be different).

94 *C. Krishna Murthy* v. *Orissa* (1964) 7 S.C.R. 185, ('64) A.SC. 1581 [upholding s. 2, Orissa Sales Tax (Validating) Act].

95 *Chandrayya* v. *Andhra* (1957) Andh. Pra. 44, ('57) A.A.P. 261 [in upholding s. 3(1)(b) Proviso, Madras General Sales Tax Act, 1939, the court upheld this classification as reasonable, dissenting from *Krishna Iyer* v. *Madras* (1956) Mad. 1368, ('56) A.M. 480, (1956) 2 M.L.J. 179, where it had been hold that the Proviso violated Art. 14].

96 *Ghanshyamdas* v. *Regional Asst. Commr. of Sales Tax* ('64) A.SC. 766, 776 [*per* Raghubir Dayal J. upholding the action of the S.T.O. under s. 11(2) and (4) C.P. & Berar Sales Tax Act]; *V. M. S. Mohamed & Co.* v. *State* (1956) Andh. Pra. 070, ('57) A.A.P. 408 (upholding ss. 5 and 6A, Madras General Sales Tax Act), fol. in. *S.A.S. & Co.* v. *C.T.O.* ('58) A.A.P. 425; *Adhi* v. *Madras* (1957) Mad. 694, ('57) A.M. 603.

97 *Tobacco Trading Co.* v. *Asst. Commercial Tax Officer* (1957) Mad. 493, ('57) A.M. 325, (1957) 1 M.L.J. 321 [upholding the Madras General Sales Tax Act, 1939, as amended by the Madras General Sales Tax Act and Madras Tobacco Sales & Registration (Amendment) Act, 1955, s. 5(vii), and (viii), it was held that there was a legitimate distinction because on purchases from a dealer there was no payment of tax whereas purchases from a grower required payment of a purchase tax which after payment could be refunded in full].

98 *Sri T.V.T. & B. Firm* v. *C.T.O., Rajahmundry* (1968) 2 S.C.R. 476, ('68) A.SC. 784, 788.

99 *T. G. Venkataraman* v. *Madras* (1970) 1 S.C.R. 615, ('70) A.SC. 508, 511 (cane jaggery is made from the juice of sugar-cane; palm jaggery by boiling "neera" from palm and other trees. The two kinds of jaggery were sold at different prices, distributed through different channels and were consumed by different sections of the community. Cane jaggery and palm jaggery were commercially different articles).

1. *Butchaia* v. *Andhra* (1958) Andh. Pra. 225, ('58) A.A.P. 294 [upholding s. 5, Item (VIII), Madras General Sales Tax Act, 1939, as amended by the Andhra Act, 1955, *held*, that the levy of a tax on virginia tobacco, when no tax was levied on 'natu' tobacco, was based on the distinction that virginia tobacco was considered a luxury which could bear the tax, whereas 'natu' tobacco was not so considered].

2 *Buchi Rajahyya* v. *Hyderabad* (1953) Hyd. 673, ('54) A.Hyd. 1 (F.B.) [upholding s. 26 and r. 5(2), Hyderabad General Sales Tax Act, the majority held that where an Act permitted both a sales and a purchase tax, a rule providing that in respect of certain commodities a tax should be paid on the transaction of purchase was not discriminatory].

goods in one area and goods in another area;[3] the State carrying on trade with the object of encouraging Cottage Industries and persons carrying on trade generally;[4] goods conveyed by Railways and goods conveyed by private motor transport;[5] purchases of hides and skins and purchases of other commodities;[6] between garments and hosiery including hosiery garments;[7] tobacco in broken leaf form and tobacco other than flue-cured and not actually used in the manufacture of cigarettes, smoking-mixture for pipes and cigarettes and bidis in the whole leaf form;[8] defaulters in payment of excise dues in Hyderabad

Excise

and others when bidding at an auction;[9] goods produced in big establishments and similar goods produced by small weavers in the mofussil;[10] employers who employ fifty or more workers and employers who employ less than fifty, or manufacturers whose manufacturing process is being carried on with the aid of power exceeding 2 H.P. and those using less than 2 H.P.;[11] mill-made dhotis made by spinning-

---

[3] *Firm Soma Raja* v. *S.T.O.* (1954) Hyd. 76, ('54) A.Hyd. 50 (since the tax was legislatively competent, a territorial classification was not open to question).

[4] *Firm Jaswant Rai* v. *S.T.O.* ('55) A.A. 585 [upholding ss. 2(*c*) and 4(1)(*b*), U.P. Sales Tax Act, 1948, *held*, that in view of the absence of a profit-making motive, the State can be treated as a class apart from dealers who carry on business for profit. Similar considerations apply to the Spinners' Association and the Gandhi Ashram, Meerut].

[5] *Rama Transport Co.* v. *U.P.* ('57) A.A. 448 [upholding s. 28 and R. 83, U.P. Sales Tax Act, 1948, as amended in 1956, the Court said that in the case of transport by Railways, there was no ground for any apprehension that a smaller quantity of goods would be shown as having been consigned whereas in the case of private motor transport, an apprehension was felt by the Legislature and was reflected in s. 28(1) which provided for the setting up of check-posts with a view to preventing evasion of sales tax]; *cf. Swaranavar Nashar* v. *Mysore* ('63) A.Mys. 49 where a classification between passengers carried by public carrier vehicles or by a stage carriage and passengers carried by a taxi was upheld.

[6] *V. M. Syed Mohammad & Co.* v. *Andhra* (1954) S.C.R. 1117, ('54) A.SC. 314 (*held*, that there is a presumption in favour of the validity of legislative classification and the appellant had not discharged the burden of proof that the classification was unreasonable, when sales tax was levied on purchases of hides and skins and not on purchases of other commodities).

[7] *Jaipur Hosiery Mills* v. *Rajasthan* ('71) A.SC. 1330 [upholding a notification under s. 4(2) Rajasthan Sales Tax Act, 1950].

[8] *Jagannath* v. *Union* (1962) 2 S.C.R. 118, ('62) A.SC. 148 [upholding the Central Excise and Salt Act, 1944, Sch. I, Entry 4(1), Items 5 and 6, *held*, that the two types of tobacco were different in their use and could be looked upon as two different commodities].

[9] *K. Ramulu* v. *Dy. Commr. of Excise* ('65) A.A.P. 20, 24 [upholding a circular issued under s. 3(1)(*a*), Andhra Pradesh (Telengana Area) Abkari Act and R. 7(1)(*b*) which placed restrictions on the entry into the auction hall of those bidders who were defaulters in paying excise revenue of recent years as based on a proper classification even though such a restriction is placed on defaulters of recent years in Hyderabad District only. Excise arrears in Hyderabad District were rupees 48 lakhs whereas in all the other districts put together they amounted to rupees 93 lakhs; hence more stringent action was taken in the case of habitual defaulters in the Hyderabad area].

[10] *Orient Weaving Mills (Pvt.) Ltd.* v. *Union* (1962) Supp. (3) S.C.R. 481, ('63) A.SC. 98 [upholding R. 8(1), Central Excise Rules, 1944, and notification granting exemption to co-operative societies, *held*, that there was a clear classification between goods produced in big establishments and by small weavers who were usually illiterate and poor and suffered from hardships to which big establishments were not subject. The fact that individual weavers had joined themselves into a Co-operative Society to increase their efficiency should not be used against them].

[11] *British India Corporation Ltd.* v. *Collector of Central Excise, Allahabad* (1963) 3 S.C.R. 642, ('63) A.SC. 104 [upholding Sch. I, item 17, Central Excise & Salt Act, 1944, *held*, that a classification dependent upon the size of an establishment or upon

cum-weaving mills and other dhotis;[12] dealers in tobacco carrying on business within the limits of Municipalities, notified areas, etc., and manufacturers and dealers carrying on business in other parts of the State;[13] toll tax imposed on vehicles and tax imposed on trains;[14] urban and rural areas.[15]

The *Bearer Bonds Case*

9.45 In the *Bearer Bonds Case* (*R. K. Garg* v. *Union*)[16] a remarkable majority judgment ("the majority judgment") was delivered by Bhagwati J., for himself, Chandrachud C.J., Fazl Ali and A. N. Sen JJ., upholding the validity of the Special Bearer Bonds (Immunity and Exemptions) Act, 1981 ("the impugned Act"), Gupta J. dissenting.[17] The majority judgment is remarkable because till it was delivered, the Supreme Court had set its face against tax evasion and against rewarding crime and criminal activities. Thus, in *Balaji* v. *I.T.O.*[18] the Supreme Court held that under Art. 14, a classification could be made to prevent evasion of tax, and it upheld a provision of the Income-tax Act which treated the income derived from a partnership by a man, his wife and minor children as his income, because such a provision prevented him from evading income-tax, or reducing its incidence. Again, in the *Prize Competition Case*,[19] the Supreme Court having held that the prize competitions were of a gambling nature, held further that gambling and other criminal or immoral activities "carried on for profit" could not be treated as "business" protected by the fundamental right to carry on business conferred by Art. 19(1)(*g*). For example, hiring goondas to assault, rob and murder, or trafficking in women, or the sale of pornographic literature was not "business" entitled to the protection of Art. 19(1)(*g*). This view was reaffirmed and applied by Krishna Iyer J. in the *Money Lenders' Case*.[20] No doubt, the Supreme Court has extended

Sup. Ct. had set its face against tax evasion, rewarding crime and criminal activities: *Balaji's Case; Prize Competition Case; Moneylenders' Case*

---

the extent of power employed is well-known, and frequently to be found, and it affords a proper basis for classification in imposing an Excise duty. It is permissible to exempt small traders from the burdens of such a duty].

[12] *Mewar Textile Mills* v. *Union* ('55) A.Raj. 114 [upholding s. 3(2), Dhotis (Additional Excise Duty) Act, 1953, *held*, that the classification was made with the object of affording protection to those employed in the small industry of hand-made dhotis; the same restriction was not considered necessary in the case of Weaving Mills as they were required to purchase yarn from the Spinning Mills and had to pay the middleman's profit and could not produce dhotis as cheaply as the mills which did both spinning and weaving].

[13] *Gopi Parshad* v. *Punjab* (1957) Punj. 184, ('57) A.Punj. 45.

[14] *Raghbir* v. *Hardwar Municipality* ('56) A.A. 324, (1955) A.L.J. 735 [upholding s. 128(i), (vii) and (xv) U.P. Municipalities Act, 1916, *held*, that the tax, though measured by the number of passengers, was really a tax on vehicles for the use of municipal roads. Trains did not enter the municipal limits nor did they use municipal roads].

[15] *D. Kasturchandji* v. *State* ('67) A.M.P. 268 (*held*, that a tax on land and building in urban areas did not violate Art. 14 notwithstanding that no such tax was imposed in rural areas since lands and buildings in the rural and urban areas constituted two distinct and defined classes of property).

[16] ('81) A.SC. 2138.

[17] On Sept. 2, 1981 an Order was passed by the majority dismissing Mr. Garg's petition and other allied petitions. The judgment of Bhagwati J. for the majority was delivered on Oct. 20, 1981 and the dissenting judgment of Gupta J. was delivered on Nov. 13, 1981.

[18] (1962) 2 S.C.R. 983, ('62) A.SC. 123.

[19] *Bombay* v. *R. M. D. Chamarbaugwala* (1957) S.C.R. 874, 920 *et sqq.*, ('57) A.SC. 699.

[20] *Fatehchand* v. *Maharashtra* (1977) 2 S.C.R. 828, 840, ('77) A.SC. 1825, 1833. See further, para 10.11 of the text.

the protection of Art. 14 to persons charged with criminal offences, by holding that Art. 14 required that persons charged with the same offences must be tried by the same, or by a substantially similar, procedure. But the Supreme Court did not thereby condone, much less reward, the alleged criminals, but merely ensured that if they were similarly situated, they should receive the equal protection of the laws. In the majority judgment, the Supreme Court has, for the first time, upheld a classification which puts a premium on tax evasion, dishonesty, fraud and crime, and which rewards the tax dodger by granting him immunities and exemptions under the Income-tax, Wealth-tax and the Gift-Tax Acts ("the three Acts"), while saddling the honest tax payer with the continued obligation to bear the heavy burden of paying the tax under all, or one or more of the three Acts.

Majority judgment for the first time puts premium on tax evasion, dishonesty, fraud and crime

9.46 A judgment which puts a premium on tax evasion, dishonesty, fraud and crime has nothing to recommend it, unless, for the most cogent reasons leading to an almost inevitable conclusion, no other judgment was possible. Far from this being the case, the majority judgment suffers from the grave infirmities set out in paras 9.52 to 9.66 below.

Submission: majority judgment clearly wrong; dissenting judgment clearly right on Art. 14

9.47 The *Bearer Bonds Case* arose out of an Art. 32 petition filed by Mr. Garg, a Senior Advocate,[21] who contended that the Bearer Bonds Ordinance, and the impugned Act which replaced it, were void as they violated Art. 14. Further, the Ordinance was void also because under Art. 123 the President of India had no power to promulgate it. The present discussion is confined to the challenge to the impugned Act under Art. 14, since the Act reproduced the Ordinance with an immaterial variation. The majority judgment dismissed the petitions because the object of the impugned Act being to canalise black money for productive purposes, the classification between those who had, and those who did not have, black money, was a valid classification. It will be submitted that for reasons appearing hereafter, the majority judgment is clearly wrong and the dissenting judgment of Gupta J. is clearly right.

Preamble and provisions of the Act set out

9.48 As the Preamble to the Act ("the Preamble") and the provisions of ss. 3 and 4 of the impugned Act are important, they are given in the undernoted foot note.[22] Gupta J. rightly emphasized the

---

[21] There were other similar petitions which were heard together with Mr. Garg's petition.

[22] *Preamble*: "Whereas for effective economic and social planning it is necessary to canalise for productive purposes black money which has become a serious threat to the national economy; And whereas with a view to such canalisation the Central Government has decided to issue at par certain bearer bonds to be known as the Special Bearer Bonds, 1991, of the face value of ten thousand rupees and redemption value, after ten years, of twelve thousand rupees; and whereas it is expedient to provide for certain immunities and exemptions to render it possible for persons in possession of black money to invest the same in the said Bonds. . . ." *S.* (3) (1) "Notwithstanding anything contained in any other law for the time being in force:— (*a*) no person who has subscribed to or has otherwise acquired Special Bearer Bonds shall be required to disclose, for any purpose whatsoever, the nature and source of acquisition of such Bonds; (*b*) no inquiry or investigation shall be commenced against any person under any such law on the ground that such person has subscribed to or has otherwise acquired Special Bearer Bonds; and (*c*) the fact that a person has subscribed to or has otherwise acquired Special Bearer Bonds shall not be taken into account and shall be inadmissible as evidence in any pro-

importance of ss. 5, 6 and 7 of the impugned Act and summed up their effect thus:

"The marginal notes against Sections 5, 6 and 7 indicate that these sections are amendments respectively of the Income-tax Act of 1961, Wealth-Tax Act of 1957 and Gift-Tax Act of 1958. Section 5 excludes Special Bearer Bonds, 1991, from the capital asset of an assessee and exempts the premium payable on the redemption of the Bonds from income-tax. Section 6 exempts the Bonds from wealth-tax. Section 7 exempts from gift-tax property in the form of these Bonds."[23]

At times it is necessary, and desirable, to pass an order whilst deferring the judgment to a later date. Such a course, however, may have the disadvantage, namely, that the impugned law may be amended in a manner which might require further consideration before delivering the judgment, for such amendment may introduce a new factor bearing on the challenge to the impugned Act. In the *Bearer Bonds Case,* the impugned Act read with the form of the Bearer Bonds, showed that on maturity, the holder of the Bond was entitled, on presentation, to the payment of Rs. 12,000 in cash.[24] After the majority of judges had passed an Order on Sept. 2, 1981, dismissing the petitions but before the majority judgment was delivered, by an amendment of the Income-tax Act, a new section 269TT was inserted (with effect from Sept. 19, 1981) in Chapter XX-B entitled

Amendment of Income-tax Act re. Bearer Bonds s. 269TT

---

ceedings relating to any offence or the imposition of any penalty under any such law. (2) Nothing in sub-section (1) shall apply in relation to prosecution for any offence punishable under Chap. IX or Chap. XVII of the Indian Penal Code, the Prevention of Corruption Act, 1947 or any offence which is punishable under any other law and which is similar to an offence punishable under either of those Chapters or under that Act or for the purpose of enforcement of any civil liability. *Explanation*:—For the purpose of this sub-section 'civil liability' does not include liability by way of tax under any law for the time being in force."

Sec. 4 "Without prejudice to the generality of the provisions of Sec. 3, the subscription to, or acquisition of Special Bearer Bonds by any person shall not be taken into account for the purpose of any proceedings under the Income-tax Act, 1961 (hereinafter referred to as the Income-tax Act), the Wealth-Tax Act, 1957 (hereinafter referred to as the Wealth-Tax Act), or the Gift Tax Act, 1958 (hereinafter referred to as the Gift-Tax Act), and, in particular, no person who has subscribed to, or has otherwise acquired, the said Bonds shall be entitled — (*a*) to claim any set-off or relief in any assessment, re-assessment, appeal, reference or other proceeding under the Income-tax Act or to reopen any assessment or re-assessment made under that Act on the ground that he has subscribed to or has otherwise acquired the said Bonds; (*b*) to claim, in relation to any period before the date of maturity of the said Bonds, that any asset which is includable in his net wealth for any assessment year under the Wealth-Tax Act has been converted into the said Bonds; or (*c*) to claim, in relation to any period before the date of maturity of the said Bonds, that any asset held by him or any sum credited in his books of account or otherwise held by him represents the consideration received by him for the transfer of the said Bonds."

[23] ('81) A.SC. *supra* at p. 2159.

[24]

"Rs. 10,000 (Rupees Ten thousand)	GOVERNMENT OF INDIA SPECIAL BEARER BONDS, 1991	Rs. 10,000 No. ....

The President of India hereby promises to pay the bearer at any office of the Reserve Bank of India or any branch of the State Bank of India and its Subsidiary Banks in India a sum of

RUPEES TWELVE THOUSAND ONLY

on the expiry of a period of ten years from the date of sale hereof.

No other interest will be payable on the Bond."

"Requirement of mode of payment in certain cases to counteract evasion of tax", namely:

S.269TT. "Notwithstanding anything contained in any other law for the time being in force, the amount payable on redemption of Special Bearer Bonds 1991 shall be paid only by account payee cheque or account payee bank draft drawn in the name of such person to whom such payment has to be made."

It will be noticed that although the immunities and exemptions from the three Acts were conferred by ss. 3 to 7 of the impugned Act, the amendment relating to the payment of the Bearer Bonds was not made in the impugned Act, where one would expect it to be made, but in the Income-tax Act. The reader will not find any reference to this amendment in the majority judgment or in the dissenting judgment in the *Bearer Bonds Case,* although if the Order had not been passed *(and become effective)* the amendment would have required consideration before the judgment was delivered.

Legal character of Bearer Bonds explained

9.49 At this place we must consider the legal character of Bearer Bonds. First, Bearer Bonds are "a species of securities for money paid or advanced (as opposed to registered Bonds), which originated in America but which may be classified as a negotiable security in English law: *Edelstein* v. *Schuler & Co.* (1902) 2 K.B. 144."[25] *Edelstein's Case* shows (See pp. 146-7) that Bearer Bonds were and are issued by companies or corporations, some of them giving an option to the purchaser either to register the Bonds with the company, or to buy the Bearer Bonds without registration. In the first case the Bonds could not be negotiated by delivery until the registration was cancelled; in the second case they could be. The impugned Act authorises the issue of Special Bearer Bonds and Sec. 3 speaks of "a person who has subscribed to or has otherwise acquired the Special Bearer Bonds" and s. 4 does likewise. The most obvious way of "otherwise acquiring" the Bearer Bonds is by purchase, and this harmonizes with the character of "Bearer Bonds", namely, that they are negotiated and pass from hand to hand by delivery. The majority judgment has interpreted the Act in such a manner as to make the Bearer Bonds *not negotiable* by delivery, thus destroying their essential character. This topic is fully dealt with in para 9.58 below. Secondly, the promise to pay the bearer Rs. 12,000 contained in the Special Bearer Bonds is a promise to pay in cash, which alone is legal tender. In India, currency notes issued by the Reserve Bank of India are legal tender for any amount.[26] As issued under the impugned Act,[27] the essential character of the Bonds, as their form shows, was that they were to pass from hand to hand by delivery and were to be paid for *in cash* at maturity. And although from Sept. 19, 1981, s. 269TT of the Income-tax Act made it obligatory to pay the amount due on the Bonds at maturity by a crossed payee's account cheque or bank draft to the person entitled to payment (that is, the holder of the Bonds) the form of the Bonds remained unchanged till the list closed on Jan. 9, 1982, with the result that the purchaser of the Bonds against delivery would not have his attention

25 *Jowitt's Dictionary of English Law,* Vol. 1, p. 200.

26 See s. 28 of the Reserve Bank of India Act, 1934.

27 Before the insertion of s. 269TT in the Income-tax Act, with effect from Sept. 19, 1981.

drawn to the fact that payment at maturity was to be made by a crossed account payee cheque or bank draft, and not in cash to the bearer.

"Black money": its meaning and implications

9.50 The words "black money" have been used in the majority judgment without ascertaining their true meaning and implication. However, Gupta J. rightly emphasized the meaning and implications of "black money". He adopted the following meaning from the Wanchoo Committee's Report[28]:

"It (black money) is, as its name suggests, 'tainted' money — money which is not clean or which has a stigma attached to it . . . Black is a colour which is generally associated with evil. While it symbolises something which violates moral, social or legal norms, it also suggests a veil of secrecy shrouding it. The term 'black money' consequently has both these implications. It not only stands for money earned by violating legal provisions — even social conscience — but also suggests that such money is kept secret and not accounted for. Today the term 'black money' is generally used to denote unaccounted money or concealed income and/or undisclosed wealth, as well as money involved in transactions wholly or partly suppressed."[29]

It is clear therefore that the holder of black money, apart from violating several other laws, has violated the provisions of all or one or other of the three Acts.

Presumpton of constitutionality. References to matters of common knowledge, etc., subject to two qualifications

9.51 The majority judgment has rightly observed that under Art. 14 there is a presumption of constitutionality and the burden lies on him who assails an Act to show that Art. 14 is violated. In order to strengthen the presumption of constitutionality, "the Court may take into consideration matters of common knowledge, matters of common report, the history of the times and may assume every state of facts which can be conceived existing at the time of legislation."[30] It is submitted that this accurate statement of the law is subject to two qualifications. First, the power to take into account matters of common knowledge, common report and the history of the times does not empower the Court to refer to those matters and that history, only partially or selectively. Secondly, the power to assume every state of facts which can be *conceived* does not empower the Court to disregard the case of the State in enacting an Act, especially when that case is supported by matters of common knowledge, the history of the times and/or by the provisions of the impugned law. The majority judgment has violated both these necessary qualifications.

Propositions emerging from judgment of Bhagwati J.

9.52 Bhagwati J. for the majority held that:

(*a*) "The problem of black money was an obstinate economic problem which had been defying the Government for quite sometime and it was in order to resolve this problem that, *other efforts having failed*, the legislature decided to enact the Act, even though the effect of its provisions might be *to confer certain undeserved advantages on tax evaders* in possession of black money."[31] (italics supplied)

(*b*) Although the impugned Act did not, *in terms*, prohibit the purchase of the Bearer Bonds with "white money", two considerations, namely, (i) the provisions of the Act rightly construed, and (ii) the fact that no person would invest white money at 2 per cent simple

---

[28] The Taxation Enquiry Committee presided over by the former Chief Justice of India, Mr. Justice Wanchoo.

[29] ('81) A.SC. *supra* at p. 2158. [30] ibid. p. 2147.

[31] ibid. p. 2156.

interest, tax-free payable on maturity after 10 years,[32] limit the purchase of the Bonds to black money.

(*c*) Just as no one would pay white money to buy the Bonds, so also no holder of the Bonds would sell them for black money because the whole object of subscribing to the Bonds was to convert black money into white "in order to avoid the risk of being found in possession of black money".[33]

(*d*) The immunity granted by ss. 3 and 4 was strictly limited. On this point the judgment is self-contradictory. At one place Bhagwati J. was at pains to point out that if, independently of the Bonds, the taxing authorities could unearth black money, then, the tax dodger would be liable for all the consequences of his failure to discharge his liabilities under the three Acts. The obvious answer to this observation is that if independently of the Bonds, black money could have been unearthed, there would have been no need to issue the Bonds. Bhagwati J. himself gave that very answer in repelling the argument that the issue of the Bonds would prevent the search and seizure of black money. Describing the argument as "highly theoretical", he said, "If it had been possible to detect and discover a substantial part of black money in circulation . . . *there would have been no need to enact the impugned Act.* It is precisely because, in spite of considerable efforts made by the tax authorities including carrying out of searches and seizures, the bulk of black money remained secreted and could not be unearthed that the impugned Act had to be enacted."[34] (italics supplied) As the later part of the judgment destroys the earlier, the emphasis thrown on the limited nature of the immunity need not detain us further.

(*e*) The impugned Act was based on an intelligible classification between those who have, and those who do not have, black money, and this classification had a nexus with the object of the law, namely, to canalise black money for productive purposes.[35]

Three Voluntary Disclosure Schemes: Court's failure to ascertain amount of disclosure of fourth scheme (1975)

9.53 The propositions in para 9.52 (*a*) to (*c*) above, involve, in part at least, matters of common knowledge, common report and the history of the times on which the Court can rely to sustain the validity of the impugned Act. The majority judgment rightly referred to three Voluntary Disclosure Schemes; the first unearthed Rs. 70.20 crores of concealed income; the second unearthed Rs. 52.11 crores and the third "had a slightly better response" as it unearthed Rs. 145 crores.[36] As to the Voluntary Disclosure Scheme of 1975, the majority judgment said that the amount of black money unearthed was not on the record. It is submitted that the Court, when exercising its power to rely on matters of common knowledge and the history of the times, must inform itself *fully* about those matters. If the amount unearthed by the 1975 scheme was not on the record, nothing was easier than to have asked the Att.-General to supply it to the Court, as it was relevant to the decision in the

---

[32] ibid. p. 2155.
[33] ibid. p. 2152.
[34] ibid. p. 2150.
[35] ibid. p. 2155.
[36] ibid. pp. 2148-49; (i) The Scheme of 1951 (The Tyagi Scheme); (ii) Sec. 68 of the Finance Act, 1965 (The 60:40 Scheme); (iii) Sec. 24 of the Finance Act (No. 2)) 1965. (For the benefit of the foreign reader: Rs. 1 crore means Rs. 10 million). "Slightly better response" is an odd way of describing an increase from Rs. 52 crores to Rs. 145 crores.

case. Besides, the information was easily available from well-known publications like the "Economic Survey 1975-76".[37] That Survey would have shown the Court that:

"Under the Voluntary Disclosure of Income and Wealth Ordinance, 1975, total amount disclosed has been provisionally placed at Rs. 1578 crores of which incomes disclosed have amounted to Rs. 744 crores and wealth Rs. 834 crores. Income-tax and wealth-tax payable respectively on these disclosed amounts are estimated to be Rs. 241 crores and Rs. 7.7 crores respectively, of which Rs. 159 crores of income-tax and Rs. 4.2 crores of wealth-tax have been already paid. Besides, Rs. 4.9 crores have been invested in specified securities."[38]

The Reserve Bank of India's Bulletin for November, 1976[39] would have shown that "Income-tax and wealth-tax payable on amounts disclosed are estimated at Rs. 241 crores and Rs. 7.7 crores respectively; and according to revised estimates, subscriptions to the 5¾ per cent Bonds 1985 related to disclosed income and wealth amounted to Rs. 40 crores."[40] And the Annual Survey of the Reserve Bank of India for 1975-76 (p. ix) would have shown that the Reserve Bank looked upon the result of the Voluntary Disclosure Scheme of 1975 as a success. Bhagwati J. could not possibly have described this attempt in 1975 to unearth "black money" as a failure. The black money unearthed by the sale of the Bearer Bonds was Rs. 963 crores when the list closed on 9th January, 1982.[41]

Important features of earlier Voluntary Disclosure Schemes

9.54 At this place we must note the following important features of the earlier Voluntary Disclosure Schemes: (*a*) The person making the disclosure revealed his identity when he made a written declaration; consequently, from the time of his disclosure, he would in the future become subject to the attention of the taxing authorities; (*b*) the immunities and the tax benefit granted were granted once for all; thereafter, the person making the disclosure would have to comply with the provisions of all or one or more of the three Acts. The scheme had an intelligible principle, namely, to get the tax dodger to confess voluntarily his wrong doing; to exempt him from penal consequences; to require him to make a substantial payment of the undisclosed income and/or wealth as tax and then bring the balance into his accounts. The Bearer Bonds depart radically from this scheme. No doubt the Bonds were open for subscription till January 9, 1982. But when that date passed, the distinction between "a subscriber" and a person "who otherwise acquired the Bonds" became meaningless since from the beginning no one could say *who* the "subscriber" was. Secondly, the tax dodger was not brought within the taxing system in respect of the black money he had accumulated from the time he purchased the Bonds. Thirdly, not only have the immunities been given to him from penalties and prosecutions[42] but tax reliefs under the three Acts have also been given to him for a period of 10 years. The provisions of the impugned Act considered in the majority and the dissenting judgments left no doubt that at the end of 10 years the Bonds were repayable in

[37] It is a priced publication published by the Govt. of India each year.
[38] *Economic Survey 1975-76* at pp. 24-25.
[39] at p. 782.
[40] ibid.
[41] *Economic Survey 1981-82* at p. 39.
[42] Except under the Prevention of Corruption Act for bribing a public officer.

cash; since the whole object of the Act in issuing Bearer Bonds was to enable the holder of the Bonds to conceal his identity. However, s. 269TT of the Income-tax Act has changed the mode of payment into payment by a crossed payee account cheque or bank draft.

Examples of conferring *"certain undeserved advantages on the tax evader"*: Italicized words an abuse of language

9.55 Bhagwati J. has described the Act as conferring "certain undeserved advantages on the tax evaders." Adapting the felicitous words of Fowler[43] "use general statements in your judgments and your reader gets a sillhouette; illustrate your statements and he has it 'in the round'." As Bhagwati J. has not illustrated this statement, we will illustrate the "certain undeserved advantages (conferred) on tax evaders" so that the reader can see the picture vividly "in the round". Let us assume that two tax payers, *A* and *B* had each an income of Rs. 5,00,000 (five lacs) a year at the time when the tax payable in excess of an income of Rs. 1 lac was 92.5 per cent, and for an income in excess of Rs. 2.5 lacs was 97.5 per cent. For three successive years, *A*, the honest tax payer, disclosed the whole income and paid each year on the income in excess of Rs. 2.5 lacs a sum of Rs. 2,43,750 as income-tax, that is, he paid income-tax aggregating to Rs. 7,31,250, *retaining for himself a sum of Rs. 18,750 out of an income of Rs. 7,50,000.* *B*, the dishonest tax payer, disclosed only half his income and concealed his income in excess of Rs. 2.5 lacs without being found out. At the end of three years, he will have amassed a fortune of Rs. 7,50,000. *A* has contributed in the three years Rs. 7,31,250 for productive purposes which are served by the 5-Year Plans to be referred to hereafter. *B* will have withheld this amount. For depriving the State of Rs. 7,31,250 to be used towards productive purposes, by dishonesty, fraud and crime, *B* is to be rewarded not only by being allowed to keep Rs. 7,50,000 intact but also by loading him with benefits of tax exemption under the three Acts. It is submitted that it would be an abuse of language to describe this situation as conferring "certain undeserved tax advantages". And, be it noted that our illustration leaves out the benefits under the Wealth and Gift-tax Acts. And although the Estate Duty Act is not amended, *B* can escape estate duty (i) if he dies within 10 years because his heirs can take possession of the Bonds; (ii) if he has gifted the Bonds before his death.

Submission: No warrant for saying all modes of unearthing black money had failed

9.56 In view of what has been set out in para 9.52 to 9.55 above, it is submitted that there is no warrant for one of the propositions on which the majority judgment is founded, namely, that all other modes of unearthing black money had failed. This proposition is directly opposed to the case of the Union of India as is clear from the dissenting judgment of Gupta J. who said:

> "I asked the Att.-General if it was his case that all attempts to unearth black money had failed, and the present scheme was the only course open. His answer was that that was not his case. The affidavits filed on behalf of the Union of India also does not make such a case. Clearly, the impugned Act puts a premium on dishonesty without even a justification of necessity — that the situation in the country left no option."[44]

---

[43] ". . . define and your reader gets a sillhouette; illustrate, and he has it 'in the round'." From the Preface to the 2nd ed., *Concise Oxford Dictionary* (6th ed.)

[44] ('81) A.SC. at p. 2162.

Finally, the elaborate Preamble to the Act does not assert, as it could not, that there was no other way of unearthing black money.

9.57 The propositions in para 9.52 (*b*) and (*c*) above, require to be dealt with together, because their combined effect is to deprive the Bearer Bonds of their essential character of negotiability by delivery. The proposition in para 9.52 (*b*) above, *viz.* that although the impugned Act does not in terms prohibit the investment of white money in the Bonds, if the provisions of the impugned Act are rightly construed, they limit the investment in Bearer Bonds to investment of black money, is correct. This is because the honest tax payer does not need the immunities conferred by s. 3 and, secondly, because he is in effect prevented from subscribing to the Bearer Bonds with white money from his disclosed wealth. This result follows from s. 4 (*b*) which prevents him from proving his purchase of the Bonds from his disclosed wealth so that if he invested Rs. 5 lacs in the Bonds from his disclosed wealth, he would still be subject to wealth-tax on Rs. 5 lacs, although the Bonds are exempt from wealth-tax! However, the proposition in para 9.52 (*c*) above, namely, that the subscriber or holder of Bearer Bonds would not negotiate them for black money because his whole object was to convert his black money into white money in order to avoid the risk of his being detected in the possession of black money is unwarranted. It has also the effect of making the Bearer Bonds not negotiable—no person would buy Bearer Bonds with white money, and no subscriber would sell them for black money! The majority judgment thus destroys the essential characteristic of the Bearer Bonds, namely, that they are negotiable by delivery. A construction which produces that result must, *prima facie*, be based on an error, and so it turns out to be. First, such a result is opposed to the express provisions of the impugned Act which confer immunities and exemptions from the provisions of the three Acts, not only on the subscriber but also on those who have acquired the Bonds "otherwise" than by subscription, and the most obvious way of otherwise acquiring them is by purchasing them against delivery. Secondly, the theory that a person holding black money would invest it in Bearer Bonds with a view to convert his black money into white money *in order to avoid the risk of detection of his possessing black money* is unfounded and was known to the majority to be unfounded. For, as we have seen, in brushing aside the argument that the issue of Bearer Bonds would prevent the search and seizure of black money, Bhagwati J. said that if search and seizure could have unearthed black money, there would have been no need to issue the Bonds. It follows from this that the risk of detection was either non-existent or negligible, and would not deter the holder of the Bonds from selling them for black money. It is clear that the assumption that the holder of Bearer Bonds would not sell it for black money for fear of detection is unfounded, and the Bearer Bonds retain the character they were intended to have—negotiability by delivery. It is submitted that the basis of the judgment is gravely shaken by a construction which deprives the Bearer Bonds of their essential character, and does so on an unjustified assumption. This grave error has its impact on the majority judgment, for it supports the submission that the scheme of issuing Bearer Bonds was inherently such that the object of

Majority judgment destroys essential feature of Bearer Bonds — negotiability

Majority view based on error

preventing accumulation of black money would be defeated, since the Bearer Bonds themselves would be a means for continuing a parallel black money economy.

Why shd. the honest tax payer be denied tax benefits under the Act?

9.58 We have seen above that the view expressed in the majority judgment that the provisions of the impugned Act rightly construed limit the investment to black money is correct. But the question naturally arises: "Why should the honest tax payer be denied the benefit of an investment in a tax-free security issued by the Government of India if he desires to make the investment openly and without concealment?" The definition of Bearer Bonds and the decision in *Edelstein's Case* referred to in para 9.49 above, show that there is nothing inconsistent with the nature of Bearer Bonds for an option to be given to the purchaser either to register or not to register Bearer Bonds. In order to avoid discrimination, there is no reason why provision should not have been made for the honest tax payers wishing to invest their white money in the Bonds, to register the Bonds with the Reserve Bank after paying for them by a crossed account payee cheque or bank draft payable to the Reserve Bank, and why honest tax payers should be precluded from proving that they had purchased the Bonds, and thus obtain tax benefits under the three Acts. This is clearly unreasonable and blatantly discriminatory. Bhagwati J. realised the force of this objection, and he met it by asserting that no one would invest white money in Bonds yielding interest at the rate of 2 per cent a year tax-free, payable at the end of 10 years when the investor could obtain 15 to 40 per cent interest in the market. Therefore, from the practical point of view, this contingency must be treated as theoretical, or so rare that it can be ignored. It is submitted that no court should make such an assertion unless the Court possessed, or was prepared to acquire in the course of the hearing, full knowledge of the money market, of investments in the market and the effect of tax-free securities on the investor in view of the high rates of taxation on income, gifts and wealth. It is submitted that for the reasons given below, the majority judgment shows no such knowledge. As to the statement that persons possessing white money would not invest in tax free securities, it is submitted that the majority judgment has overlooked a number of considerations which would have made it clear to the majority of judges that their proposition was untenable. First, confining ourselves to income-tax, at the rate of taxation mentioned earlier, namely, 97.5 per cent on income in excess of Rs. 2.5 lacs and 92.5 per cent for income in excess of Rs. 1 lac, a tax-free investment yielding 2 per cent interest is a very attractive proposition. The Government of India knew this, for it always put a limit either of Rs. 35,000 or Rs. 25,000 for a single individual, and double that amount for joint holders on tax-free securities issued by it. Although described as part of the "small savings" movement, the principal attraction of these tax free investments has been for persons in high income brackets. Thus, to an investor paying 97.5 per cent tax on income over Rs. 2.5 lacs, a tax-free income of 2.5[45] per cent even though paid at the end of 10 years is not unattractive, for he may not stand in need of present

Submission: No justification for holding that nobody would invest in 2% tax free Bonds

[45] This rate of 2.5 per cent is taken for facility of calculation.

income which would be again swallowed up in tax. In order to retain Rs. 2.50 tax free, he must have a taxable income of Rs. 100. Even if he could earn 40 per cent interest as stated by Bhagwati J., he would have to pay 97.5 per cent as tax on the interest earned, which would leave him with Re. 1 and not Rs. 2.50 per Rs. 100, as the tax-free investment would. This is altogether apart from the fact that the Court assumes rates of interest between 15 to 40 per cent in the market in spite of the well known fact (i) that large sums of money had been and were being raised by companies by issuing redeemable debentures carrying originally 9, 10 and, at present 13 per cent interest, so that investors do invest at 13 per cent interest even though income-tax is deducted at the source; (ii) fixed term deposits with banks for a period of 5 years used to yield at the relevant time 9 to 10 per cent interest, and substantial amounts in fixed deposits were made by investors. This is because investors know that the higher the rate of interest, the greater is the danger to the safety of the capital and many investors would prefer the safety of their capital to taking hazardous risks of earning 40 per cent interest. All these considerations show the attractiveness of tax-free investments to investors with large incomes, and Government, realizing this, has limited tax-free investments by putting a strict limit on individual and joint holdings *till the Bearer Bonds were issued,* and an unlimited tax-free investment permitted.

9.59 In the above calculation, the present writer has taken rates of income-tax which prevailed over a period of time; however when the case was being heard, the maximum rate of income-tax (including surcharge) was 66 per cent with an obligation to make a compulsory deposit in respect of income for a period of 5 years,[46] at 15 per cent for income over Rs. 70,000. Consequently, the benefit of 2 per cent tax-free income would be very much less than the benefit described above (say, nearly 6 per cent). But a person with a large income and large wealth, wishing to invest in 2 per cent tax-free Bearer Bonds would have to make a reasonable guess of the rates of direct taxes for a period of 10 years. At the time when the Bonds were issued all the portents indicated a rise, *inter alia,* in the rate of income-tax to meet the demands of Five-Year Plans. It is clear therefore that the benefit in respect of tax-free interest of 2 per cent would come to about 6 per cent taxable, but increasing with every increase in the maximum rate of income-tax including a surcharge. However, the accumulated interest on Bearer Bonds is paid after 10 years. And it is well known that people with large wealth and large incomes would prefer to receive accumulated interest on their capital which, being tax free, in substance becomes part of the capital. The undernoted example illustrates this preference of people with large wealth and large incomes.[47]

Income-tax benefit when case was heard

---

[46] The compulsory deposit freezes the amount of deposit for 5 years. Interest (taxable) is paid on the deposit.

[47] Some companies in the U.K. took to declaring what were called "tailored dividends", i.e. those share holders who did not need the dividend to be paid to them in the form of money would opt to have shares representing the value of the dividends payable to them; and those who needed the income were paid their dividends in the usual way. This loophole in the tax was plugged by a provision that a company should either distribute shares in lieu of dividends or pay divi-

Benefit under the Gift Tax Act

9.60 Turning to the Gift-tax Act, let us assume that *A* has a *disclosed,* and *B* has an undisclosed taxable wealth of Rs. 20 lacs. *A* desires to make a gift of Rs. 3 lacs each to his two children who have attained majority. He would have to pay a gift-tax of Rs. 1,31,500. Had he been permitted to subscribe to the Bearer Bonds with white money paid by a cheque, he could gift 30 Bonds to each of his children and save Rs. 1,31,500 as tax. Secondly, since the Bonds would have been registered and paid for by cheque (white money) his children could sell them for white money and invest the proceeds so as to secure a good income.[48] *A* is substantially relieved of his responsibility to provide for his two children, and if he survives for two years after making the gift, his estate will not have to pay estate duty on Rs. 6 lacs. The impugned Act denies these benefits to *A*, the honest tax payer. However, *B*, the tax evader who has subscribed to the Bearer Bonds can make a gift of 30 Bearer Bonds to each of his two children who have attained majority and save Rs. 1,31,500 payable as gift-tax. And the Bonds so gifted would not be exigible the estate duty if *B* dies within two years of making the gift, for no one can inquire how and when his children came to possess the Bonds. Finally, turning to the Wealth-tax Act, investment in the Bonds is exempt from wealth tax and at higher ranges of wealth the saving in tax is substantial. For example, for a person having a taxable wealth of Rs. 20 lacs, and not needing the income of the whole amount, an investment in the Bearer Bonds of Rs. 5 lacs would secure him tax relief of Rs. 23,278 each year. It is submitted that the benefits offered by the Bearer Bonds as regards income-tax, gift-tax and wealth-tax are very substantial, and investors with large wealth and/or income would readily invest white money in purchasing Bearer Bonds openly. It follows that the assumption in the majority judgment that no one would invest in tax-free investments at 2 per cent is contrary to matters of common knowledge, of common report and the history of the times or which could have been easily discovered by a Court if it had tried to make the discovery, instead of basing its decision on incomplete and imperfect material. The discrimination caused by denying to the honest tax payer the benefits of investment without limit free from income, gift and wealth tax was met only by the answer that for practical purposes no one would invest white money in Bearer Bonds. Once the answer is shown to be based on untenable assumptions, it is submitted that this discrimination against the honest tax payer becomes undisputable. On that ground alone, the impugned Act should have been held void as violating Art. 14.

Benefit under the Wealth Tax Act

Discrimination against honest tax payer undisputable

Legislative powers under which Bonds issued

9.61 But the matter does not rest here. It is submitted that the real question in the case was not raised and answered, namely, "Under what legislative power or powers did Parliament enact the impugned Act?" because, the nature of the Act is relevant to the question of classification. The impugned Act (i) authorized the issue of Special Bearer Bonds; (ii) provided for immunities and exemptions

dends in the ordinary way. But if dividends were paid to some shareholders and shares issued to other shareholders, then, the amount received by way of shares would be treated as income and taxed accordingly.

[48] The Govt. of India has issued taxable 6-year Bonds carrying interest at 12 per cent (taxable). There is no limit to the amount which can be invested in these Bonds.

under the three Acts. The legislative power to issue the Bearer Bonds, falls under entry 35, List I, Sch. 7 (Public debt of the Union); but, as the Preamble clearly shows, *the Bearer Bonds would not have taken off the ground* if the impugned Act had not provided for the immunities and exemptions granted under the provisions of the three Acts. The legislative power to enact the Income-tax, the Wealth-Tax and the Gift-Tax Acts fall respectively under entry 82, List I, entry 86 and/or entry 97, List I, and under entry 97, List I. In essence, the impugned Act is a taxing statute, for, instead of calling upon the holder of black money to pay a substantial part of his concealed income or wealth towards income-tax and wealth-tax (as was the case in several Voluntary Disclosure Schemes) the impugned Act requires him to lend money to Government at 2 per cent simple interest to be paid at the end of 10 years.[49] The immunities conferred on the holder of the Bonds from the provisions of the three Acts and the tax benefits conferred on him, flow *not from the Bonds,* that is, not from the legislative power relating to the public debt of the Union, but from ss. 3 to 7 of the impugned Act. A further consequence of ss. 3 to 7 must be noted at this place. The fact that the immunities and exemptions under the three Acts have been conferred on the subscriber or holder of the Bonds shows that but for the impugned Act, the subscriber or holder would fall within the provision of all or one or other of the three Acts. The reader will have noticed that all the Voluntary Disclosure Schemes discussed earlier used the Income-tax and/or the Wealth Tax Act to unearth black money, and the impugned Act does the same.

The impugned Act in essence a taxing statute

9.62 Once it is realized that the Act, or at any rate, the most important part of it, is in essence a taxing Act, the classification made in the majority judgment between those who have, and those who do not have, black money, is superficial, and the real classification, as Gupta J. has rightly pointed out, is between tax evaders and honest tax payers.[50] For, under the law, both the classes were and are under an obligation to pay the taxes under all or one or other of the three Acts. Ever since the early 1950s, when the first 5-Year Plan was put into effect, one of the objectives of mobilising resources by taxation and by other means like public borrowing has been to use the money so raised for the productive purposes served by the 5-Year Plans. Therefore, to raise money by taxation and to unearth black money and subject it to tax (as in the various Voluntary Disclosure Schemes) has been one of the objects of taxing statutes. Under Art. 14 a permissible classification must be based on an intelligible differentia which distinguishes those that are grouped together from others, and the differentia must be reasonably related to the object of the statute. However, the object of the statute cannot fur-

Submission: Real classification — between "tax evaders" and "honest tax payers"

Collecting tax to be used for productive purposes an *object* of tax laws: grave doubt if it can furnish a valid differentia

[49] The Bearer Bonds contain a promise to pay the bearer not Rs. 10,000 but Rs. 12,000. However, s. 5 of the impugned Act exempts the "premium" paid on the Bonds at maturity from income-tax. Although Rs. 2,000 are described as a premium, the statement in the Bond that *no other interest* will be payable on the Bond shows that Rs. 2,000 represents 2 per cent simple interest a year payable at the end of 10 years.

[50] ('81) A.SC. at p. 2159.

nish the differentia because the object and the differentia are distinct and separate.[51] Das J. held in *Anwar Ali Sarkar's Case*:

"The provision for the speedier trial of certain offences is, therefore, the object of the Act. To achieve this object, offences or cases have to be classified upon the basis of some differentia which will distinguish those offences or cases from others and which will have a reasonable relation to the recited object of the Act. The differentia and the object being, as I have said, different elements, it follows that the object by itself cannot be the basis of the classification of offences or the cases, for, in the absence of any special circumstances which may distinguish one offence or one class of offences or one class of cases from another offence, or class of offences or class of cases, speedier trial is desirable in the disposal of all offences or classes of offences or classes of cases."[52]

Differentia not reasonably related to the object of the law

The object of the impugned Act is not merely to unearth black money but to unearth it *for the purpose of canalizing it for productive purposes*. But that has been one of the objects of the three taxing Acts since the early 1950s and it is submitted that it is a matter of the gravest doubt whether the classification between tax evaders and honest tax payers is permissible since the object of the Act cannot supply a differentia, and since the differentia and object are distinct and separate. However, in any event, the differentia must be *intelligible* and must be *reasonably* related to the object of the law. The provisions of the Act discriminate between tax evaders and honest tax payers by giving tax benefits under the three Acts to tax evaders and by denying those benefits to the honest tax payers. Adapting the language of *Anwar Ali Sarkar's Case*[53], the honest tax payers can ask: "Why are we being singled out from the class liable to pay taxes under all or one or other of the three Acts, by being denied the benefits under those Acts which benefits are conferred by the impugned Act on tax evaders?" The only answer can be: "Because you were honest and paid your taxes and because tax evaders by dishonesty, fraud and crime[54] did not pay their taxes either fully or partially." This answer is a *reductio ad absurdum* of the classification made between tax evaders and honest tax payers for the purpose of protecting and also rewarding the former by tax benefits, and penalizing the latter by denying them those tax benefits.[55] No classification can be described as reasonable which leads to such absurd results, for what is absurd is, by definition, unreasonable.

Whether morality and ethics relevant to classification: view of Gupta J.

9.63 The question was raised and discussed both in the majority and minority judgments whether considerations of morality and ethics are relevant to a classification under Art. 14. Gupta J. rightly said that:

---

[51] *W.B.* v. *Anwar Ali Sarkar* (1952) S.C.R. 284 at pp. 334-5 *per* S. R. Das J.

[52] ibid. p. 341.

[53] ibid. p. 309.

[54] See the Income-tax Act, Chapter XXII (Offences and Prosecutions). Under s. 276CC, wilful failure to furnish a return is punishable with rigorous imprisonment for *not less than* 6 months but which may extend to 7 years if the tax evaded is over Rs. 1 lac, and rigorous imprisonment for *not less than* 3 months which may extend to 3 years if the tax evaded is under Rs. 1 lac. And similar punishment is provided by s. 277 for false statements in any verification under the Act (which have been accepted as true) and which the person making them knows to be false or does not believe to be true.

[55] It need hardly be said that a classification between tax evaders and honest tax payers for the purpose of preventing tax evasion, and for punishing tax evaders and, if thought fit, rewarding honest tax payers is both intelligible and reasonable.

"The concept of reasonableness does not exclude notions of morality and ethics. I do not see how it can be disputed that in the circumstances of a given case considerations of morality and ethics may have a bearing on the reasonableness of the law in question."[56]

Bhagwati J. said:

View of Bhagwati J.: "laws reeking with immorality"

". . . we are concerned here only with the constitutional validity of the Act and not with its morality. Of course, when we say this we do not wish to suggest that morality can in no case have relevance to the constitutional validity of a legislation. There may be cases where the provisions of a statute may be *so reeking with immorality* that the legislation can be readily condemned as arbitrary or irrational and hence violative of Article 14. But the test in every such case would be not whether the provisions of the statute offend against morality but whether they are arbitrary and irrational having regard to all the facts and circumstances of the case. Immorality by itself is not a ground of constitutional challenge and it obviously cannot be, because morality is essentially a subjective value, except in so far as it may be reflected in any provision of the Constitution or may have crystallised into some well-accepted norm of special behaviour."[57] (italics supplied)

Submission: Impugned Act "reeking with immorality"

Leaving morality aside to start with, the tax evader is guilty of crimes which are considered so serious that departing from the normal rule of criminal law (namely, that only the maximum sentence is prescribed for an offence,) secs. 276CC and 277 of the Income-tax Act[58] prescribe a minimum sentence of 6 and 3 months rigorous imprisonment. Further, making a false declaration of income or wealth in a tax return is punishable under s. 192 (read with s. 191) of the Penal Code for fabricating false evidence. In other words fabricating false evidence has been looked upon as a serious crime under the Criminal Law of India for over 120 years. Secondly, why does not the impugned Act "reek with immorality"? In order to secure personal gain, tax evaders cause grave injury to the nation and to national economy; they do so by dishonesty, fraud and crime; their actions put a most unfair burden on the honest tax payers, and successful tax evasion corrupts public morality. If a law which *rewards* such persons and penalizes honest tax payers does not reek with immorality, what law will? The majority judgment ought to have, but did not, ask this question. Had it done so, it is difficult to believe that it would not have struck down the impugned Act for "reeking with immorality", for to have done otherwise would have outraged the sense of justice and morality of the ordinary men and women which sustains free democracies.

S. 269TT, I.T. Act laudable object likely to be defeated by extensive evasion

9.64 Two other matters require mention here. We have seen that the newly added s. 269TT of the Income-tax Act requires that the amount payable on the Bearer Bonds at the end of 10 years is payable by a crossed order payee account cheque or bank draft. No doubt this was meant to meet the objection that at maturity the money payable on the Bonds would revert to its status as black money. The object no doubt is laudable, but the manner in which the provision was made is open to objection. Section 269TT came into force on Sept. 19, 1981. The subscription list was closed on Jan. 9, 1982, but the promise to pay Rs. 12,000 on each Bond was not amended to

---

[56] ('81) A.SC. at p. 2162. He had earlier (at p. 2161) referred to Friedmann's "Legal Theory" (5th ed., p. 80) in which it is pointed out that expressions like "a reasonable and fair price" or a "fair and equitable restitution" mean "nothing except in conjunction with the social conditions of the time."

[57] ibid. pp. 2155-6.

[58] See *f.n.* 54 *ante*.

incorporate the change which materially altered the secrecy promised to the tax evader, so that persons who might buy the Bonds could know where they stood. Secondly, once the subscription list was closed no one could say who was the subscriber who invested black money in the Bonds and who was the holder, since title to the Bonds would pass by delivery. Thirdly, if the Bonds can be purchased with black money as has been submitted in para 9.57 above, the object of unearthing black money will have substantially failed. Fourthly, it is a matter of grave doubt whether s. 269TT will succeed in its object: Bonds will be presented in *benami* or fictitious names and addresses; banks will be under an obligation to open accounts, and are not expected to have an agency for verifying the genuineness of the name of the person presenting the cheque and of his address. Finally, the experience of the demonetization of high denomination notes (Rs. 1,000 and Rs. 10,000), which demonetization was brought about with secrecy and surprise, shows that with a ten year notice to the holders of black money, the most extensive evasion will take place. Probably it was a realization of this fact which led the framers of the original scheme to promise to pay "the bearer" Rs. 12,000 per Bond in cash which would prevent the identity of the holder from being disclosed.

Majority judgment considered at length lest it form an evil precedent

9.65 The present writer has dealt with the *Bearer Bonds Case* at length because the use which the majority judgment has made of the presumption of constitutionality and of matters of common knowledge, common report and the history of the times is so unsatisfactory and so clearly wrong, that a detailed criticism was necessary. The reason for doing so is best explained by the following observations of Lopes L.J. in *Farquharson* v. *Morgan*[59]:

> "The reason why, notwithstanding such acquiescence, a prohibition is granted where the want of jurisdiction is apparent on the face of the proceedings, is explained by Lord Denman in *Bodenham* v. *Ricketts*[60] to be for the sake of the public, lest 'the case might become a precedent if allowed to stand without impeachment' . . ."

Observations in *Maneka Gandhi* and *Royappa* "so much wasted eloquence"

9.66 It was said by Bhagwati J. for the majority that in matters affecting economic activities and taxation the Court should pay particular deference to legislative judgment and exercise self-restraint. Mr. Justice Gupta replied tartly by observing:

> "To pass the test of reasonableness if it was enough that there should be a differentia which should have some connection with the object of the Act, then these observations made in *Maneka Gandhi* and *Royappa* would be so much wasted eloquence."[61]

We may add that the reader will find it odd that Bhagwati J., who spoke of the post-*Royappa* period as having enlarged the boundaries of the fundamental right to equality guaranteed by Art. 14, and who spoke of the guarantee of equality in Art. 14 as a "dynamic concept", and as having an "activist magnitude", should lapse into utter *passivity* at the mere mention of the words: economic affairs and/or taxation. In the result, the majority judgment is clearing wrong, is productive of great public mischief and is out of line with Supreme Court judgments which refused to countenance tax evasion or to

---

[59] (1894) 1 Q.B. 552 at p. 559. [60] 6 N. & M. 170.
[61] ('81) A.SC. at p. 2161.

give the protection of fundamental rights to immoral and/or criminal activities.

Entities which are in a class by themselves

9.67 Reverting to the general doctrine of classification, the following classifications have been upheld on the ground that the entity was in a class by itself: treating a religious institution, e.g. a Temple;[62] or a Durgah (Shrine of a Pir or saint);[63] or a single industrial unit like a textile mill;[64] a State Bank;[65] or an only undertaking of its kind;[66] or co-operative societies;[67] or the Prime Minister of India.[68] It has been held that summary procedure for contempt of court is in a class by itself and Art. 14 is not violated because the procedure laid down in the Cr.P.C. is different.[69] However, in *Vice-Chancellor, Osmania University* v. *Chancellor*[70] the Supreme Court held that the Vice-Chancellor (the appellant) holding office at the

---

[62] *Shri Govindlalji* v. *Rajasthan* ('63) A.SC. 1938 (upholding the Rajasthan Nath Dwara Temple Act, 1959, the Court said that the Shri Nath Dwara Shrine held a unique position amongst the Hindu shrines in the State of Rajasthan and no Temple could be regarded as comparable with it. It was open to the Legislature to pass the impugned Act if it thought that it was essential to safeguard the interests of the Temple); *Bira Kishore Deb* v. *Orissa* ('64) A.SC. 1501 [upholding Shri Jagannath Temple Act, 1955, which contained provisions in many respects different from the general Orissa Hindu Religious Endowments Act, 1952, the preceding case was relied on. The same view had been taken by the Orissa High Court in *Rama Chandra* v. *Orissa* (1958) Cut. 369, ('59) A. Or. 5, where the Court had taken judicial notice that the Temple was in a class by itself].

[63] *Syed Hussain Ali* v. *Durgah Committee* (1959) 9 Raj. 424, ('59) A.Raj. 177 [S.1, Durgah Kwaja Sahib Act, 1955, was upheld as the Durgah was in a class by itself; reversed on other points: *Durgah Committee* v. *Syed Hussain Ali* (1962) 1 S.C.R. 383, ('61) A.SC. 1402.

[64] *Chiranjit Lal Chowdhuri* v. *Union* (1950) S.C.R. 869, ('51) A.SC. 41 [upholding the Sholapur Spg. & Wvg. Co. (Emergency provisions) Ordinance, 1950, *held*, that there was nothing before the Court to show that the Sholapur Mills had been singled out from other Mills similarly situated].

[65] *Lachhman Das* v. *Punjab* (1963) 2 S.C.R. 353, ('63) A.SC. 222 (the Patiala State Bank was held to be in a class by itself); *Kurian* v. *Union* ('62) A.Ker. 267 (upholding s. 49A, Banking Companies Act, 1949, *held* that the Reserve Bank, the State Bank and Co-operative Banks functioned under separate statutes and formed classes by themselves).

[66] *In re Oriental Gas Co.* ('61) A.Cal. 267, 65 C.W.N. 545 (upholding the Oriental Gas Co. Act, 1960).

[67] *C. P. Khanna* v. *V. K. Kalaghatgi* ('70) A.B. 201, (1970) Bom. 805, 72 Bom. L.R. 295 [*held*, that there was no reason why co-operative societies should not be treated as a class by themselves: ('70) A.B. p. 203; *held* further, that ss. 91 and 96 of the Maharashtra Co-opertive Societies Act, 1961, and the rules framed thereunder, which provided for compulsory arbitration in a dispurte between a society and third persons, under certain limited circumstances did not violate Art. 14 and the special procedure prescribed was reasonably related to the object of the law: ibid. p. 204].

[68] *P. V. Shastri* v. *Union* ('74) A.Del. 1, 8 (F.B.) [*held*, that in view of the importance and the nature of the duties of her office, the Prime Minister constituted a class by herself, and the Ministry of Defence memorandum of August 17, 1968 as to the use of the I.A.F. aircraft by the Prime Minister for non-official purposes, including election purposes, did not violate Art. 14. The object of the impugned memorandum was to ensure the personal safety of the Prime Minister, and to enable her to deal with official business with promptitude so that national interests may not suffer. The business of Government cannot come to a standstill, and the Prime Minister continued to function as head of the Government during such tours, and conducted official business each day and had to be contacted for such business wherever she was: proposition (*a*) in *Dalmia's Case* followed. See proposition (*h*) in para 9.32 of the text].

[69] *Sher Singh* v. *R. P. Kapur* ('68) A.Punj. 217, 230.

[70] (1967) 2 S.C.R. 214, ('67) A.SC. 1305.

time when the Osmania University Amendment Act, 1966 (Second Amendment Act) was passed, was not in a class by himself, as opposed to Vice-Chancellors to be appointed thereafter. Consequently, s. 13 (*a*) of the Second Amendment Act was void as violating Art. 14. For, whereas all succeeding Vice-Chancellors could be removed from their office only for misbehaviour or incapacity, after due inquiry by a person who was or had been a High Court Judge, s. 13 (*a*) provided for the removal of the appellant within a period of three months from the Act coming into force. Even assuming that the existing Vice-Chancellor could be treated as a class by himself, such a classification was not founded on any intelligible differentia which distinguished him from other Vice-Chancellors, and had no rational relation to the object of the statute.

9.68 Since Art. 19 (1) (*g*) and 6 (*ii*) enables a total monopoly to be created in any trade, business, industry or service in favour of the State or a Corporation owned and controlled by the State, it would follow that Art. 19 (1) (*g*) and (6) (*ii*) itself treats the State and State Corporations differently from citizens, and therefore the creation of a monopoly in favour of a state Corporation cannot be impugned as violating Art. 14. Without referring to Art. 19 (1) (*g*) and (6) (*ii*) the Supreme Court held that the canalization of export in mica

Canalization of imports

through a State Corporation did not violate Art. 14 because ". . . there is neither any competition nor any choice in the matter of a grant of licence. *It is a total exclusion of citizens in order to enable all the country's exports* (*in mica*) *to be made by one* licencee."[71] (italics supplied)

Other classifications upheld

9.69 The following classifications have been upheld as based on a differentia reasonably related to the object of the impugned law, namely, BETWEEN: Rulers of Indian States and other persons;[72] ordinary suits and suits on negotiable instruments;[73] agriculturists

Civil procedure

and non-agriculturists;[74] an application for execution of a decree made within, and made after, a year from the date of the decree,

---

[71] *Daruka & Co.* v. *Union* ('73) A.SC. 2711, 2716.

[72] *Mohanlal Jain* v. *H. H. Maharaja Sri Sawai Man Singhji* (1962) 1 S.C.R. 702, ('62) A.SC. 73 (upholding s. 87-B, C.P.C., which made that classification. The court also referred to Art. 362 which provided that in making laws, the Legislatures should have due regard to the guarantees or assurances given under a covenant to a Native Ruler with respect to the personal rights, privileges and dignities of such Ruler); *Bashishat Chand Rai* v. *Radhika Devi* (1951) Punj. 470, ('52) A. Punj. 97 (*held*, that an exemption from personal attendance should be given under s. 133, C.P.C. to the Rana of Kothi and that such exemption did not violate Art. 14 in view of the covenants entered into with Indian Rulers and in view of the express provisions of Art. 362 of the Constitution); *Bhimaji Narasu* v. *Vijayasinvarao* (1955) Bom. 62, ('55) A.B. 195, 57 Bom. L.R. 60.

[73] *Ambalal Purusottamdas & Co.* v. *Jawarlal* ('53) A.Cal. 758, 57 C.W.N. 744 (upholding O. 37, C.P.C., *held*, that there was a reason for making a difference between the two classes of suits and that the defendants in these two classes were not similarly situated. The importance of commercial cases justified the summary procedure of O. 37 and that procedure was available to every one without discrimination); *Amarendra Nath* v. *Bikash Chandra* (1958) 1 Cal. 576, ('57) A.Cal. 534 (*held*, that the fact that O. 37, C.P.C. did not apply to the City Court did not make the City Court Act discriminatory. It is submitted that the reasons given for this conclusion are not satisfactory).

[74] *Rura Ram* v. *Gurbachaa* ('54) A.Punj. 254, [upholding s. 60(1)(c) C.P.C.].

or between a party and the legal representative of a party;[75] vexatious litigants and other litigants;[76] persons living outside the limits of original jurisdiction of the Calcutta High Court and those living within those limits;[77] rural and urban areas;[78] information received from an accused person in the custody of a police officer which leads to the discovery of a fact as the result of such information, and such information which does not lead to such discovery;[79] a person accused of an offence and an approver;[80] principal offenders and offenders who played a subordinate part;[81] public servants who discharge responsible duties and perform important functions and public servants whose duties and functions are less important;[82] warrant cases instituted on Police Report and those instituted by private complainants;[83] rule-making powers of District Magistrates

Criminal procedure

[75] *Pichayya* v. *Andhra* ('57) A.A.P. 136 (upholding O. 21, R. 22, C.P.C., *held*, that there was good reason for not insisting on a notice where the decree-holder was diligent or when the applicant was a decree-holder and that there was equally good reason for requiring a notice when the decree-holder had not been diligent and in the case of legal representatives of a deceased judgment-debtor for they may not know that a decree had been obtained against the deceased).

[76] *P. H. Mawle* v. *A.P.* ('65) A.SC. 1827 [upholding the Madras (Vexatious Litigation) (Prevention) Act, 1949].

[77] *C. Basu* v. *Calcutta C.J.* ('72) A.Cal. 470, 479; *Navinchandra v. Bachubhai* ('69) A.Guj. 124 [held, that R. 39, Ahmedabad Small Causes Court Rules read with O. 37, R. 3 C.P.C. did not violate Art. 14 — *Ambalal's Case, supra* and *Lakshmandas Devidas Kapadia* v. *Mathurdas Dwarkadas* (1956) Bom. 218, 57 Bom.L.R. 1118 rel. on].

[78] *Tej Bahadur* v. *State* ('54) A.A. 655, (1954) A.L.J. 681 (upholding the U.P. Panchayat Raj Act, 1947, which recognized the necessity for simple remedies and simple procedure in rural areas); *Natbar Jan* v. *State* ('55) A.Cal. 138, 59 C.W.N. 729 [upholding the provision that ss. 162 and 172, Cr.P.C., should not apply to the town of Calcutta].

[79] *U.P.* v. *Deoman Upadhyaya* (1961) 1 S.C.R. 14, ('60) A.SC. 1125, 1132 [the Supreme Court reversed the judgment under appeal [reported in *Deoman Upadhyaya* v. *State* ('60) A.A. 1, (1959) A.L.J. 651 (F.B.)] and held that s. 27, Evidence Act which made that classification and s. 162(2), Cr.P.C., which made that distinction were valid since the discovery of a fact was a guarantee of the truth of the statement and the sections were based on a valid classification].

[80] *T. P. Mohideen* v. *Madras* ('65) A.M. 461 (s. 337, Cr.P.C. does not fail to give protection to an approver. It only authorises abstention from prosecution of an accused for the successful prosecution of certain other persons and for getting the best evidence against them).

[81] *Sirajuddin* v. *State* (1967) 3 Mad. 659, ('68) A.M. 117 ["Under s. 494 Cr.P.C. any Public Prosecutor may with the consent of court withdraw from the prosecution of any person. Where interests of justice may require that every offender should be booked, equally interests of justice may require that where it is not possible, some at least are arraigned and the rest retained for giving evidence at the trial. The policy of not securing judicial pardon to accomplices and bringing them as approvers but retaining them at the sole discretion of the prosecution may be open to question; but that cannot by itself invalidate the arraignment of the persons actually put up for trial. If it is laid down that all participants in a crime should be put up for trial, grave consequences may ensue": ('68) A.M. at p. 125]; affirmed in *Sirajuddin* v. *State* ('71) A.SC. 520, 529, (1970) 3 S.C.R. 931.

[82] *Matajog Dobey* v. *H. C. Bhari* (1955) 2 S.C.R. 925, ('56) A.SC. 44 (upholding s. 197, Cr.P.C., *held*, that the section was meant to give protection to public servants from harassment resulting from vexatious prosecutions; and that discretionary power was not necessarily discriminatory); *Ghanairam* v. *State* (1954) Nag. 661, ('54) A.Nag. 265.

[83] *Macherla Hanumantha Rao* v. *A.P.* (1958) S.C.R. 396, ('57) A.SC. 927 (upholding ss. 207, 207-A, Cr.P.C., the court held that they were based on a relevant consideration, namely, whether or not there had been a previous investigation by a responsible public servant whose duty it was to detect crime and bring offenders

and those of Commissioners of Police;[84] public servants who are defamed and private persons who are defamed;[85] an offence of one kind and an offence of a different kind;[86] juvenile and adult offenders;[87] students who migrate to a University and students who belong to it;[88] privately managed educational institutions and those maintained by a State Government, Central Government and local bodies;[89] continuous and discontinuous previous service;[90] appointments, dismissal, removal, termination of service or reduction in rank of any teacher in a non-government college made between November 27, 1961, and March, 1962, and appointments etc. made at any other time;[91] candidates passing multi-purpose examinations and candidates passing other examinations;[92] repatriates who are more re-settled and repatriates who are less re-settled;[93] persons who have taken part in sports or extra-curricular activities for a long time and persons who have taken such part for a short time;[94] abducted

Education

---

to book. The object was to ensure the speedy disposal of warrant cases instituted on Police reports without in any way prejudicing the accused); fol. in *Veeraraghavulu* v. *State* (1958) Andh. Pra. 143, ('58) A.A.P. 301; *S. Kotiswamy* v. *Andhra* ('58) A.A.P. 90; *Provat Kumar* v. *W.B.* ('56) A.Cal. 602, 60 C.W.N. 913 (upholding s. 207-A, Cr.P.C.).

84 *Indulal* v. *State* ('63) A.Guj. 259, (1963) 4 Guj. L.R. 209 upholding s. 33(1)(*r*)(ii), Bombay Police Act, 1951. Distinction upheld as based on a valid geographical classification.

85 *M. Tyagi* v. *U.P.* ('59) A.A.21 (the classification made by ss. 198 and 198-B, Cr.P.C. was justified as reasonably related to the object that a public servant's time should not be wasted in litigation); *R. Sankar* v. *State* (1959) Ker. 195, ('59) A.Ker 100; *K. V. Ramaniah* v. *Special Public Prosecutor* ('61) A.A.P. 190 (the public interest which is absent in s. 198 is present in s. 198-B); *In re E. V. K. Sampath* ('61) A.M. 318, (1961) 1 M.L.J. 328.

86 *Bindeshwari Mandal* v. *Birju* (1958) 37 Pat. 1183, ('59) A.P. 46 (upholding ss. 260, 263 and 264, Cr.P.C., *held*, that different procedures for summary trials and ordinary trials were based on a reasonable classification); *Dal Chand* v. *State* (1953) 1 All. 856, ('53) A.A. 123 (upholding a notification under s. 269, Cr.P.C. which provided that only certain specific offences, including the offence of dacoity, should be tried by a jury); *Badri Prasad* v. *State* ('53) A.A. 494, (1953) A.L.J. 160 [upholding s. 269(1), Cr.P.C.]; fol. in *Radha Nath* v. *State* ('53) A.Cal. 602, 58 C.W.N. 243, *Dal Chand's Case supra* was relied on.

87 *In re Anthony* ('60) A.M. 308 (upholding R. 7 made under s. 44, Madras Children's Act, *held*, that the distinction made was related to the object of the Act which was eminently reasonable, namely, to secure a more informal procedure for the trial of offences committed by juveniles as also for securing more humane methods of punishing such offences).

88 *Samir Kumar* v. *Someswar* ('53) A.Cal. 783 (the above classification justified the Syndicate making special rules under s. 25, University Act, 1904, for students who migrated to it from another University).

89 *Katra Education Society* v. *U.P.* (1966) 3 S.C.R. 328, ('66) A.SC. 1307 (classification was upheld on the basis of the facts and circumstances disclosed in the affidavit of the respondent which justified such a classification).

90 *E. P. John* v. *State* ('57) A.Tr.-Co. 265 (upholding reservation of seats in pre-professional Medical Classes for candidates passing multi-purpose examinations).

91 *Jagdish Pandey* v. *Chancellor, Bihar University* (1968) 1 S.C.R. 231, ('68) A.SC. 353, (*held*, that the Statement of Objects and Reasons showed that the dates were not arbitrarily selected).

92 *Nageswara Rao* v. *Principal, Medical College* ('62) A.A.P. 212 (upholding reservation of seats in pre-professional Medical Classes for candidates passing multi-purpose examinations).

93 *Rita* v. *Union* ('73) A.SC. 1050 (this classification was adopted for reservation of seats for pre-medical and M.B.B.S. courses).

94 *K. Sudhir* v. *Principal, G. Medical College* ('70) A.A.P. 404 [upholding R. 3(*a*) and Appendix I for selection of candidates for admission to the Medical Colleges in Andhra area of Andhra Pradesh].

Muslims in some States of India and other persons in India;[95] an evacuee and an intending evacuee;[96] a rural house which is part of a holding and one which is not part of a holding but is an independent unit;[97] an evacuee and a person not an evacuee;[98] mortgagees of property of Muslim Evacuees and mortgagees of other property;[99] creditors holding decrees against evacuees and creditors holding decrees against non-evacuees;[1] the posts of village accountants which were abolished and those which were not;[2] superior and subordinate police officers;[3] candidates to be appointed to a post by direct recruitment and those already in service;[4] government servants occupying a higher rank and getting higher pay and those occupying a lower rank with lower pay;[5] matriculate tracers with a higher pay scale and non-matriculate tracers with a lower pay scale;[6] persons working in the Central Secretariat Service and persons working in the Railways;[7] Advocates practising in the Rajasthan High Court and courts subordinate thereto and those practising in the rest of India;[8] persons

Evacuee law, and abducted persons

Government Service

[95] *Punjab* v. *Ajaib Singh* (1953) S.C.R. 254, ('53) A.SC. 10 (abducted Muslims constitute a well defined class and the application of the Act to the several States of India after having obtained their consent to the passing of the Act is based on a geographical classification designed to protect similar interests of a well-defined class of persons in those States).

[96] *Mohammad Saheb Mahboob* v. *Dy. Custodian General* (1962) 2 S.C.R. 371, ('61) A.SC. 1657.

[97] *Makhan Lal Malhotra* v. *Union* (1961) 2 S.C.R. 120, ('61) A.SC. 392 [upholding R. 5 of the Rules framed under the Displaced Persons (Claims) Supplementary Act, 1954, and R. 65 of the Rules made under the Displaced Persons (Compensation and Rehabilitation) Act, 1954, which made that classification for rehabilitating displaced persons].

[98] *Asiatic Engineering Co.* v. *Achhu Ram* (1952) 2 All. 838, ('51) A.A. 746 (F.B.) [upholding ss. 2(*d*), (*f*), and 10. Administration of Evacuee Property Act, 1950, *held*, that being an evacuee could be the basis for a reasonable classification]; *M. B. Namazi* v. *Dy. Custodian of Evacuee Property, Madras,* ('51) A.M. 930, (1951) 2 M.L.J. 1 (upholding the Administration of Evacuee Property Ordinance, 1949, *held*, that persons who migrated to Pakistan after March 1, 1947, had to be treated as non-resident aliens and that the Ordinance merely provided for taking into custody the property left in India and for safeguarding the interests of evacuees who left India abandoning their properties).

[99] *S. Raghbir Singh* v. *Union* (1955) Punj. 509, ('54) A.Punj. 261 [upholding s. 9, Evacuee Interest (Separation) Act, 1951].

[1] *N. S. Gujral* v. *Custodian, Evacuee Property* (1968) 1 S.C.R. 497, ('68) A.SC. 457, 460 [upholding s. 12 of the Displaced Persons (Compensation and Rehabilitation) Act, 1954, which vested evacuee property in government with the result that a decree against an evacuee could not be executed against that property].

[2] *Honnalige Gowda* v. *Mysore* ('64) A.Mys. 84, 106 ("there is no similarity of the required degree, between posts of village accountants, which are abolished, and those that are not").

[3] *Banarsi Das* v. *U.P.* (1956) S.C.R. 357, ('56) A.SC. 520; *Banarsi Das* v. *U.P.* ('55) A.A. 33, (1954) A.L.J. 618 (before the Allahabad H.C.); *Shiva Nandan* v. *W.B.* ('54) A.Cal. 60, 58 C.W.N. 18.

[4] *Khem Chand Tejwani* v. *Rajasthan* (1958) 8 Raj. 37, ('58) A.Raj. 242 (different instructions relating to the medical fitness of government servants were upheld on the ground that the candidates who may be promoted from government service may have deserved their promotion by their meritorious service although they did not satisfy the conditions laid down for candidates for direct recruitment in respect of age or physical fitness).

[5] *Rajgopal* v. *Supdt. of Police* ('65) A.M. 103 [upholding the Madras Civil Service (Disciplinary Proceedings Tribunal) Rules, 1955].

[6] *Mysore* v. *P. Narasinga Rao* (1968) 1 S.C.R. 407, ('68) A.SC. 349.

[7] *C. A. Rajendran* v. *Union* (1968) 1 S.C.R. 721, ('68) A.SC. 507, 513.

[8] *Munni Lal* v. *State* ('70) A.Raj. 164, 167 [upholding R. 15(ii), Rajasthan Higher Judicial Service Rules, 1969].

holding Class I and Class II posts and Class III and Class IV posts;[9] senior inspecting engineers and sectional officers;[10] government servants working in one Institute (the Indian Institute of Technology, Kharagpur) and other government servants;[11] those who had lost their offices for political reasons and those who had not;[12] representative trade unions and other trade unions;[13] employers and employees;[14] industries closed down by an employer through circumstances beyond his control and industries closed down by an employer otherwise;[15] persons with incomes over four hundred rupees per month and those with smaller incomes;[16] right to appear by Counsel in Civil Courts but not Industrial Tribunals;[17-18] one land tenure and another;[19] public and private companies and companies and firms or individuals;[20] villages where consolidation of holdings was taking place and those in which it was not;[21] allottees in the States of Punjab

Industrial and labour laws

Land and tenancy legislation

---

[9] ('68) A.SC. *supra* at p. 514 [*held*, that having regard to "the requirements of efficiency in the higher echelons of service . . . the classification (*viz.* reservation of seats for Scheduled Castes and Scheduled Tribes) in Classes III & IV but not in Classes I & II . . . is reasonable"].

[10] *D. N. V. Chellam* v. *Rly. Board* ('71) A.A. 382, 385 (*held*, that there was nothing to show that their duties were the same; in fact the duties appeared to be different).

[11] *Amulya Kumar* v. *Union* (1960) 1 Punj. 781, ('60) A.Punj. 284, 286 [upholding s. 5, Indian Institute of Technology (Kharagpur) Act, 1956].

[12] *Purushotham* v. *Venkatappa* ('52) A.M. 150, (1951) 2 M.L.J. 561 [upholding the Madras Restoration of Village Officers (Validation) Act, 1938. The Act, it was said, merely did justice to those who had lost their offices for political reasons].

[13] *Raja Kulkarni* v. *Bombay* (1954) S.C.R. 384, ('54) A.SC. 73 (upholding ss. 12 and 13, Bombay Industrial Relations Act, whereby a trade union with a certain percentage of membership was allowed to represent the workers as a class to the exclusion of others, the Court observed that it was open to the appellant to secure a larger membership and claim precedence over the existing representative union); *J. C. Mills* v. *Chairman, Industrial Court* ('53) A.M.B. 231 (upholding s. 73A, Bombay Industrial Relations Act, 1947).

[14] *South India Bank* v. *Pichuthayappan* ('53) A.M. 326, (1953) 1 M.L.J. 306 (s. 41, Madras Shops and Establishments Act, 1947); on appeal ('54) A.M. 377. In both these cases the impugned Act was upheld on the ground that it was designed to protect the workmen whose bargaining power was not equal to that of their employers; *M.D. Jute Mills* v. *L.A.T.* ('54) A.A. 161 [upholding s. 14, proviso, Industrial Disputes (Appellate Tribunal) Act, 1950, and rejecting the argument that the proviso in substance gave a right of appeal only to the workmen and was therefore discriminatory].

[15] *Rajkumar Singh* v. *Authority under the Payment of Wages Act* ('60) A.M.P. 307 (upholding s. 25 FFF, Industrial Disputes Act).

[16] *Milkhi Ram* v. *Punjab* (1964) 2 Punj. 767, ('64) A.Punj. 513, 514 (upholding the provision that a part of the bonus given to persons earning more than 400 rupees should be invested in National Savings and similar Government Certificates on the ground that the Payment of Wages Act was enacted in order to protect industrial employees not getting high salaries).

[17-18] *Rangaswamy* v. *Industrial Tribunal* (1954) Mad. 800, ('54) A.M. 553 [upholding s. 36(4), Industrial Disputes (Appellate Tribunal) Act, 1950, which denied the right to appear by Counsel to a party to a proceeding before an Industrial Tribunal].

[19] *B. K. Nanjundeswara* v. *Coorg* (1955) Mys. 117, ('57) A.Mys. 93 [upholding the classification of tenures into *Jama* and *Sagu* in Coorg].

[20] *Mangalbhai* v. *Gujarat* ('64) A.Guj. 82 at 99, 100 (upholding the classification for the purpose of the Land Acquisition Act).

[21] *Attar Singh* v. *U.P.* (1959) Supp. (1) S.C.R. 928, ('59) A.SC. 564 (upholding the classification made by ss. 8, 9 and 10 read with s. 49, U.P. Consolidation of Holdings Act, 1954, as amended, the Court upheld the two different procedures having regard to the need of a more expeditious procedure to put through consolidation); *S. Gursaran Singh* v. *Punjab* (1955) Punj. 459, ('55) A.Punj. 161 [the East

and Pepsu and allottees outside those States;[22] schemes validated by an Act and schemes framed after that Act;[23] members of a family and outsiders;[24] landlord and tenant;[25] decree holders of tenants of "holdings" and other decree holders;[26] displaced and non-displaced persons;[27] private properties of Indian Rulers and other properties;[28] private lands of Rulers and lands belonging to other persons;[29] Presidency Towns and the Mofussil;[30] *Melpattomdar* and other agricultural lessees;[31] new and dislodged motor vehicle operators from the date when a nationalisation policy was introduced;[32] permit holders and non-permit holders;[33] motor operators having more and motor opera- Motor Vehicles Act, etc.

Punjab Holdings (Consolidation and Prevention of Fragmentation) Act, 1948, s. 40]; *Mukhtar Singh* v. *U.P.* ('57) A.A. 297, (1956) A.L.J. 878 (upholding the U.P. Consolidation of Holdings Act, 1953, the Court said that where an area is declared to be under consolidation proceedings it is necessary that the proceedings should terminate within a reasonable time. There may be hundreds of cases relating to title, boundaries and possession in respect of holdings or plots contained in those holdings. It is well known that the ordinary procedure takes a long time to come to an end, and if ordinary procedure was followed, consolidation proceedings may be held up for an indefinite time. A different and more expeditious procedure is therefore essential).

[22] *Jagmohan Singh* v. *Union* ('65) A.Punj. 163 (the classification appears to have been upheld as a valid geographical classification).

[23] *Sohan Lal Kirpa Ram* v. *Punjab* ('65) A.Punj. 212 [upholding s. 2, Punjab Development of Damaged Areas (Validation) Act, 1963, which does not give a right of filing objections afresh in respect of validated schemes, which right is available to other persons in respect of schemes framed after the validating Act].

[24] *Krishna Pillai* v. *Parukutty Ammal* ('52) A.M. 33, (1951) 2 M.L.J. 496 [upholding s. 4(*a*), Partition Act, which gives a preference to members of a family over others to buy the property at a valuation by the Court].

[25] *Pirthi Singh* v. *Pepsu* (1954) Pep. 433, ('53) A.Pep. 161 [upholding s. 10, Patiala and East Punjab States Union (Abolition of Biswadari) Ordinance (2006), which gave the tenants the right to buy the shares that the landlords were to get out of the holdings on partition].

[26] *Vishnu* v. *Poulo* (1952) Tr.-Co. 670, ('53) A.Tr.-Co. 327 [upholding the Trav.-Cochin Holdings (Stay of Execution Proceedings) Act, 1950, *held*, that the law gave temporary relief to all tenants of a particular class against all decree-holders who had obtained decrees against that class].

[27] *Bhagirath* v. *Punjab* ('54) A.Punj. 167, 56 P.L.R. 1 (F.B.) (upholding the Punjab Security of Land Tenures Act, 1953).

[28] *Pratap Kesari* v. *Orissa* ('61) A.Or. 131 [upholding the Orissa Private Lands of Rulers (Assessment of Rent) Act, 1958, *held*, that the lands belonging to Rulers which had been exempted from taxation could properly be looked upon as a class by itself].

[29] *Ratnaprova Devi* v. *Orissa* ('64) A.SC. 1195 [upholding s. 6, Orissa Private Lands of Rulers (Assessment of Rent) Act, 1958, *held*, in the absence of evidence to the contrary, that s. 6 provided tests which were equitable and the State could rely on the presumption of constitutionality].

[30] *Narasinhachariar* v. *E.B.S., 3rd Branch* ('55) A.M. 135 (in upholding s. 69, Transfer of Property Act, the Court said that the power of the mortgagee to sell under s. 69 came from England and got extended to India as it was absolutely necessary for promoting quick credit. It was restricted to the Presidency Towns as its extension to the mofussil was considered likely to lend itself to abuse).

[31] *Krishnan Nair* v. *Abdu* ('65) A.Ker. 39 (F.B.) [the position of *melpattomdar* is more that of a usufructuary mortgagee than of a lessee. In enacting s. 11(*a*), Kerala Agriculturists Debt Relief Act, 1958, the Legislature thought that an agriculturist who had parted with the trees of his land on a *melpattom* was in a like case with one who had parted with land on usufructuary mortgage].

[32] *Shah Transport Co.* v. *State* (1953) Nag. 110, ('52) A.N. 353; *Balwant Raj* v. *Govt. of Madras* ('63) A.M. 265 [upholding s. 68-G(2), Motor Vehicles Act, 1939].

[33] *S. N. Transport Co.* v. *S.T.A.* (1958) 1 Cal. 486, ('57) A.Cal. 638 (upholding R. 57A, Motor Vehicles Rules, *held*, that the classification was designed to prevent a monopoly).

tors having less than 20 vehicles;[34] a Co-operative Society which runs a Transport Service and a private operator running such service;[35] permit-holders and non-permit holders;[36] a legal practitioner engaged for fees on behalf of or against a Municipality and one not so engaged;[37] Class I and Class II Panchayats based on population-cum-income basis;[38] specified localities in a Municipal area and other localities in that area;[39] residential and non-residential and industrial premises;[40] tenanted buildings used for residential purposes and other tenanted buildings, existing buildings and buildings constructed after the impugned Act, buildings constructed at one period and buildings constructed at two other periods;[41] tenants of corporation premises and tenants of non-corporation premises;[42] premises subject to a Rent Control Act and premises not so subject;[43] District Boards which had committed errors, omissions or defects in form and procedure of publication and District Boards which had not committed such errors, etc.;[44] the employees about whom the State Government has formed an opinion that they are unfit to be retained in the service of a Municipal Committee and those about whom no such opinion has been formed;[45] *Zilla Parishads* and *Gaon Sabhas* and *Kshetra Samitis*;[46] members of

Municipal law

---

[34] *Bata Singh* v. *State* ('58) A.M.P. 193 (upholding R. 49-A, C.P. & Berar Motor Vehicles Rules, 1940, *held*, that the classification was based on requirements of efficiency and it must be assumed that the requirement was the result of experience).

[35] *Brahm Dutt* v. *Peoples' Co-op. Transport Society Ltd.* (1961) 1 Punj. 283, ('61) A.Punj. 24 [upholding s. 47(1), Proviso, Motor Vehicles Act].

[36] *Gopalchandra* v. *W.B.* ('62) A.Cal. 183 (upholding r. 57-A, Bengal Motor Vehicles Rules, 1940).

[37] *Bishnu Charan* v. *Orissa* ('52) A.Or. 11 [upholding s. 16(1)(ix), Orissa Municipal Act, 1950, which disqualified a legal practitioner engaged for or against the Municipality, from being elected a Councillor].

[38] *M. A. Haji* v. *M. K. Kurup* (1954) Mad. 201, ('54) A.M. 360 (upholding R. 9 of the Rules made under the Madras Village Panchayats Act, 1950, prescribing open voting for Class II and secret ballot for Class I Panchayats).

[39] *Hirabhai Ashabhai* v. *Bombay* ('55) A.B. 185, 56 Bom.L.R. 1035 (upholding the introduction of payment of water charges in specific localities under s. 169, Bombay Municipal Corporation Act, 1888).

[40] *Sethumadhavan* v. *Vishakhapatnam Municipality* ('64) A.A.P. 280 (upholding the classification for the purpose of making a charge of Rs. 4, 6 and 9 respectively for 1000 gallons of water).

[41] *V. J. Ferreira* v. *Bombay Municipality* ('72) A.SC. 845, 854-7, (1972) 2 S.C.R. 257 [the above classifications were made by the Bombay Buildings Repairs and Reconstruction Board Act, 1969, for the purpose of levying a tax on buildings under s. 27 of the Act. Section 28 which granted exemption was held not to violate Art. 14 as each group set out in s. 28 formed a distinct class by itself from tenanted residential premises: ('72) A.SC. at p. 857].

[42] *Bibi Batool* v. *City Civil Court* (1972) Bom. 917, ('72) A.B. 254, 74 Bom.L.R. 22 (upholding the validity of s. 105-B of the Bombay Municipal Corporation Act, 1888 which made the above classification).

[43] *Calcutta Corporation* v. *Padma Debi* ('57) A.Cal. 466, 61 C.W.N. 129 [*held*, that accepting the classification made by ss. 3 and 5 of the W.B. Premises Rent Control (Temporary Provisions) Act, 1950, which classification was not challenged before the Court, there was no reason why the valuation of the premises to which the Rent Control Act did not apply should not be governed by different principles from those applicable to premises where the rent was controlled]; affd. on other points: *Corporation of Calcutta* v. *Padma Debi* (1962) 3 S.C.R. 49, ('62) A.SC. 151.

[44] *Jiwan Lal* v. *Rajasthan* (1958) 8 Raj. 492, ('59) A.Raj. 86 (upholding s. 2, Rajasthan Municipal Board Validation Act, 1956).

[45] *Arjan Singh* v. *Punjab* (1960) 2 Punj. 645, ('60) A.Punj. 554.

[46] *Sarju Prasad* v. *State* ('70) A.A. 571, 582.

the *gram panchayat* and the *sarpanch* of the gram panchayat;[47] Sikh and Hindu Religious Trusts and Jain Religious Trusts;[48] Hindu, Mahommadan or Christian Endowments;[49] office-holders of a Temple and outsiders;[50] Hindus, Sikhs and Jains;[51] the Trustee of a Muth and the Trustee of a Temple;[52] old and newly constructed premises;[53] pending suits and fresh suits;[54] houses built before a certain date and houses built after;[55] between tenancies under and over a particular rent;[56] one town and another;[57] superior officers (Tahsildars) and

Religious and Charitable Endowments

Rent Control

---

[47] *Kista Reddy* v. *Collector Karimnagar* ('70) A.A.P. 180, 190-91 (F.B.) (upholding ss. 16-25 of the A.P. Gram Panchayat Act, 1964).

[48] *Mahant Moti Das* v. *S. P. Sahi* (1959) Supp. 2 S.C.R. 563, ('59) A.SC. 942 [the above decision covered also the decisions in *Mahant Ramsaroopdasji* v. *S. P. Sahi* (1959) Supp. 2 S.C.R. 583, ('59) A.SC. 951, and *Bihar* v. *Bhabapritananda Ojha* (1959) Supp. 2 S.C.R. 624, ('59) A.SC. 1073: the needs of Jains and Hindus are not the same, in the matter of the administration of their respective religious trusts, as the needs of the Sikhs].

[49] *Lakshmindra Theertha Swamiar* v. *Commr., Hindu Religious Endowments, Madras* ('52) A.M. 613, (1952) 1 M.L.J. 557 (the classification had existed for nearly a century. It was not based solely on religion as institutions included in the classification were religious as well as secular. Art. 14 did not prevent the Legislature from enacting laws in respect of one set of Institutions reserving the other types of Institutions for consideration at a future date.

[50] *Dandaiah* v. *Venkatarama* ('54) A.M. 500, (1953) 2 M.L.J. 550 (upholding s. 87, Madras Hindu Religious and Charitable Endowments Act, 1951, which enabled the Trustees of a Temple to recover Temple property by a summary procedure, instead of driving the office-holder to a Civil Court to establish his title, the object of the Act being the protection of Temple properties).

[51] *Bijayananda* v. *Bihar* (1953) 32 Pat. 1148, ('54) A.P. 266 [upholding ss. 2(*e*), 5, 7 and 8, Bihar Hindu Religious Trusts Act, 1951, *held*, that the petitioner had not discharged the burden of showing that Hindus, Sikhs and Jains were similarly situated].

[52] *G. Sitharamamma* v. *Dy. Commissioner* ('58) A.A.P. 319 (upholding ss. 45 and 52, Madras Hindu Religious and Charitable Endowments Act, 1950, *held*, that the Trustee of a Muth had rights as well as duties; the Trustee of a Temple had only duties and the impugned sections recognized this distinction).

[53] *Roshan Lal Mehra* v. *Ishwar Das* (1962) 2 S.C.R. 947, ('62) A.SC. 646; foll. in *Ram Lal Kapur & Sons (P) Ltd.* v. *Ram Nath* (1963) 2 S.C.R. 242, ('63) A.SC. 1060 (upholding the different procedures for fixing standard rent prescribed by s. 7A, Sch. 4, Delhi and Ajmer-Marwara Rent Control Act, 1947).

[54] *S. B. Trading Co. Ltd.* v. *Shyam Lal Ram Chandra* (1953) 2 Cal. 15, ('51) A.Cal. 539 [the W.B. Premises Rent Control (Temporary Provisions) Act, 1950, s. 18(5) as amended by W.B. Act 62 of 1950].

[55] *Raman Das* v. *U.P.* (1953) 1 All. 970, ('52) A.A. 703, 706 (F.B.) (s. 7, Proviso, U.P. Temporary Control of Rent and Eviction Act, 1947, made a distinction between houses built before July 1, 1946, and those built thereafter, the object being to encourage the building of new houses by exempting them from rent control); *Mohd. Shafi* v. *First Addl. Munsif* ('65) A.A. 23; *Basudev* v. *Damodar Lal* ('71) A.Raj. 115; *Dalip Singh* v. *Rakha Ram* (1959) Punj. 2189, ('60) A.Punj. 176 [upholding a notification issued under the East Punjab Rent Restriction Act, 1949, *held*, that the object was to encourage the construction of new buildings]; see also *A. S. Ruben* v. *Narayan Moreshwar* (1953) Bom. 230, ('53) A.B. 174, 54 Bom.L.R. 950, where s. 13(1)(*g*) explanation (*a*), Bombay Rents, Hotel and Lodging House Control Act was upheld as the provision there made preventing landlords, purchasing properties after January 1, 1947, from recovering possession even if they reasonably and *bona fide* required it for their own use was justified on the ground that from that date there was a sudden boom in the purchase of properties leading to a large-scale eviction of tenants but for the impugned provision; *C. Achiah* v. *P. Gopalakrishna* ('66) A.A.P. 51 [upholding s. 32(*b*) A.P. Buildings (Lease, Rent and Eviction) Act, 1960, which exempted buildings constructed on or after August 26, 1957, from the operation of the Act].

[56] *Raval & Co.* v. *Ramachandran* (1966) 2 Mad.437, ('67) A.M. 57, 70 (F.B.).

[57] *Milap Chand* v. *Dwarka Das* (1954) Raj. 958, ('54) A.Raj. 252 [upholding the Rajasthan Premises (Control of Rent and Eviction) Act, 1950, *held*, that although

Trade, Commerce and industry

inferior officers;[58] butchers who slaughter cattle and butchers who slaughter sheep or goats;[59] Associations dealing with hedge contracts for a long time (twenty years) and Associations recently formed;[60] an insurance company whose license remained wholly cancelled for less than 6 months before the appointed day;[61] active and non-active members of a Stock-exchange;[62] exporters who had exported a particular quantity of goods during a stated period and those who had not;[63] exporters of mica scrap and waste and exporters of mica powder;[64] dealers or refiners and non-dealers;[65] sugar produced by the vacuum-pan process and sugar produced by other methods;[66] food

---

there was no classification indicated in the Act, the known facts justified the application of rent control to such towns as in the opinion of government required such control].

[58] *Rawat* v. *Rajasthan* (1957) 7 Raj. 878, ('57) A.Raj. 343 [upholding ss. 4A, and 4B, Rajasthan Produce Rents Regulations (Second Amendment) Act, 1953, which provided that when a Tahsildar went to the spot to appraise crops he was not required to be assisted by assessors but when subordinate officers went to assess the crops they were to be so assisted].

[59] *Mohd. Hanif Quareshi* v. *Bihar* (1959) S.C.R. 629, ('58) A.SC. 731 (upholding the Bihar Preservation and Improvement of Animals Act, 1955, the C.P. and Berar Animal Preservation Act, 1949, *held* that the classification was based on the usefulness of various animals to society).

[60] *M. B. Cotton Assn. Ltd.* v. *Union* ('54) A.SC. 634 (upholding the exemption under cl. 4, Cotton Control Order, 1950, given to associations of long standing, *held*, that hedging in cotton trading, like insurance and banking, required experience and as it vitally affected the welfare of a large section of the people of India and India's economic stability in world markets it could not be lightly entrusted to inexperienced hands).

[61] *N. Assurance Co.* v. *Union* ('73) A.SC. 602, 607, (1973) 2 S.C.R. 940 [so held by a majority of 3:2 in upholding the validity of ss. 2(*e*) and 15(*a*) of the General Insurance (Emergency Provisions) Act, 1971 because an insurance company whose licence was wholly cancelled for six months before the appointed day was defunct, and could not be revived, whereas a company in the other class could be revived. The temporal differentia between the two classes had a rational relation to the object of the law, namely, the protection of the policy holders].

[62] *Madhubhai Amathalal Gandhi* v. *Union* (1961) 1 S.C.R. 191, ('61) A.SC. 21 [upholding a notification under s. 4, Securities Contracts (Regulation) Act, 1956, which laid down a condition that a person applying for membership of the Bombay Stock Exchange must have been an active member of the Indian Stock Exchange Ltd. for twelve months immediately preceding August 6, 1957].

[63] *P. V. Sivarajan* v. *Union* (1959) Supp. 1 S.C.R. 779, ('59) A.SC. 556 (upholding the classification of traders made by rr. 18 and 19 framed under s. 26, Coir Industry Act, 1933).

[64] *Daruka & Co.* v. *Union* ('73) A.SC. 2711, 2719, (1974) 1 S.C.R. 570 (*held*, that the exclusion of mica powder from an export canalization scheme but not mica scrap or mica waste was based on an intelligible differentia, namely, to develop mica powder industry in India).

[65] *Gem Palace* v. *Union* ('70) A.Raj. 225, 231 [upholding the validity of s. 16(7), Gold Control Act, 1968].

[66] *Lord Krishna Sugar Mills Ltd.* v. *Union* (1960) 1 S.C.R. 39, ('59) A.SC. 1124 (the classification was upheld by a majority which held that the government was the best judge as to which commodities were more likely to earn foreign exchange and the classification made was reasonably related to the object of the Act, namely, earning foreign exchange); *Andhra Sugars Ltd.* v. *A.P.* ('68) A.SC. 599, 608, (1968) 1 S.C.R. 705 (*held*, "that the differential treatment of the factories producing sugar by means of vacuum pans, *khandsari* units producing sugar by the open pan process and cane growers using cane for the manufacture of jaggery is reasonable and has a rational relation to the object of taxation. There are marked differences between the three classes of users of cane and their capacity to pay the tax. The legislature could reasonably treat the . . . users of cane differently for purposes of levy").

and drink served in restaurants and eating houses;[67] trade in country liquor and other trades;[68] between petty dealers and big dealers;[69] manufacturers and dealers;[70] licenced dealers and certified goldsmiths;[71] persons in management of companies and other persons;[72] newspapers and news agencies;[73] between universal (U) films and adult (A) films, and between films and other forms of art;[74] banking and non-banking companies;[75] banking companies and private moneylenders;[76] between conventional chits and prize chits;[77] permanent cinema owners and touring cinema owners;[78] those who trade by

---

[67] *Gyan Prakash* v. *State* ('68) A.Mys. 61, 66 (upholding s. 32 of the Mysore Rent Control Act, 1961, which provided for fixation of fair rates for articles sold in hotels and lodging houses but not for articles sold in restaurants and eating houses).

[68] *Amar Chandra* v. *Excise Collector, Tripura* (1973) 1 S.C.R. 533, ('72) A.SC. 1863 ["In view of the injurious effect of excessive consumption of liquor on health, this trade or business must be treated as a class by itself and it cannot be treated on the same basis as other trades": ('72) A.SC. at p. 1868].

[69] *A. K. A. Setty & Sons* v. *State* ('70) A.Mys. 289 (upholding the exclusion from the operation of the Licensing Orders of dealers who kept for sale, at any one time less than ten quintals of any one food grain, or less than twenty five quintals of all foodgrains taken together).

[70] *Narendra Kumar* v. *Union* (1960) 2 S.C.R. 375, ('60) A.SC. 430 (upholding cls. 3 and 4, Non-Ferrous Metal Control Order, 1958, which made that classification).

[71] *H. R. Banthia* v. *Union* (1970) 1 S.C.R. 479, ('70) A.SC. 1453, (*held*, that the classification was reasonable, and was reasonably related to the object of the law).

[72] *Raja Narayanlal Bansilal* v. *Maneck Pheroz Mistri* (1961) 1 S.C.R. 417, ('61) A.SC. 29 [the Supreme Court upheld ss. 239 and 240, Indian Companies Act, 1956, which made this classification by denying to persons in management of companies the protection afforded to witnesses under s. 132, Evidence Act and to accused persons under s. 161(1) and (2) Cr.P.C., on the ground that it was necessary to treat persons managing companies as a class by themselves and to provide for necessary safeguards and checks against a possible abuse of powers vesting in them. In the High Court, Chagla C.J. rightly referred to the history of the law and pointed out that in England the rule against self-incrimination did not apply to examinations in bankruptcy, and under the provisions of the Companies Act, both exceptions being based on the need of protecting the public interest.] [See *Narayanlal Bansilal* v. *Maneck Pheroz Mistri* (1959) Bom. 952, ('59) A.B. 320, 61 Bom. L.R. 220, 260-262.]

[73] *P.T.I.* v. *Union* ('74) A.SC. 1044, 1053, (1975) 3 S.C.R. 499, (*held*, that the classification was based on the nature of the service rendered).

[74] *K. A. Abbas* v. *Union* (1971) 2 S.C.R. 446, ('71) A.SC. 481. See ('71) A.SC. p. 489, where elaborate reasons for the above classifications are given.

[75] *Joseph Kuruvilla Vellukunnel* v. *Reserve Bank* (1962) Supp. (3) S.C.R. 632, ('62) A.SC. 1371 [upholding ss. 38(1) and (3)(b)(iii), Banking Companies Act, 1949, *held*, that the fact that the procedure under ss. 38(1) and 38(3)(b)(iii) may be involved in some cases and the procedure of the Companies Act in others did not violate Art. 14 because the different procedures were designed to suit different situations and it could not be said that the Reserve Bank would act arbitrarily from case to case].

[76] *Catholic Bank of India* v. *George Jacob* (1967) 1 Ker. 567, ('68) A.Ker. 3 (F.B.) [upholding s. 2(c)(xi) of the Kerala Agriculturists Debt Relief Act, 1958, *held*, that the special treatment given to banks was justified, as banks, unlike private money-lenders, did not charge usurious interest, and, secondly, the advance by a bank of a sum exceeding Rs. 1,500 at a time under a single transaction would be to persons who did not belong to the poorer sections of the State].

[77] *Srinivasa Enterprises* v. *Union* ('81) A.SC. 504 [*held*, that the distinction was justified and was supported by an expert committee's report].

[78] *Rasdeep Touring Talkies* v. *Dist. Magistrate, Karnal* (1966) 2 Punj. 341, ('67) A.Punj. 219 (the business of the two classes of cinema owners was regulated by separate sets of rules).

employing outside labour and those who trade with the assistance of members of their own family;[79] comparatively larger and comparatively smaller producers requiring the former to deliver a proportionately greater quantity of grain to Government;[80] consumer quota holders who deal with mills in the "first control period" and quota holders who do not so deal;[81] food carried by rail or motor vehicles and food carried by other means;[82] those who own less than ten acres of land and those who own more;[83] Presidency Towns like Madras and places outside Presidency Towns;[84] the quality and value of goods and their use;[85] certain crops grown in large quantities in the State and crops sparsely grown;[86] Military and Naval messes and canteens and other messes and canteens;[87] cargo boats and passenger boats;[88] small and

Miscellaneous

[79] *Mathrumal* v. *Chief Inspector of Shops, Kanpur* ('52) A.A. 773, (1952) A.L.J. 409 [*Chiranjit Lal's Case*, (1950) S.C.R. 869, ('51) A.SC. 41 applied: U.P. Shops and Commercial Establishments Act, 1947, s. 4].

[80] *S. M. Anzar Husnain* v. *Bihar* (1952) 31 Pat. 203, ('52) A.P. 220 (The Bihar Agricultural Levies Order, 1950).

[81] *V. Menon* v. *Development Dept., Madras* ('52) A.M. 715, (1952) 1 M.L.J. 532 (the Cotton Textile Control Order, 1948, Cl. 30: It was held that consumer quota holders who did not deal with mills in the first control period were rightly treated as newcomers).

[82] *Har Murat* v. *State* (1954) 1 All. 546, ('53) A.A. 545, 546 [the U.P. Foodgrains Movement Control Order, 1949, cl. 3(ii)].

[83] *Atulya Kumar* v. *Director of Procurement and Supply* ('53) A.Cal. 548, 57 C.W.N. 397 [West Bengal Food Grains (Intensive Procurement) Order, 1952].

[84] *Mohd. Zackeria* v. *Srinivas & Co.* ('57) A.M. 403 [the fact that under s. 9(*e*), Presidency Towns Insolvency Act, 1909, it was a sufficient cause in adjudging a person insolvent if his property remained under attachment for 21 days whereas under s. 6(*e*), Provincial Insolvencies Act, 1920, the attached property of the debtor had to be sold in execution of a decree for the payment of money before the transaction could be considered to be an act of insolvency, was not violative of Art. 14 as the entire economic structure and the tempo of life in Presidency towns and places outside such towns were different]; *Anant Reddy* v. *Hyderabad* ('54) A.Hyd. 221 [upholding the validity of separate Police Acts for the City and the Districts, namely, the Hyderabad District Police Act. The classification was justified on the ground that it existed in different parts of India. It is submitted that the more satisfactory ground for the classification is that given in *In re B. N. Ramakrishna* ('55) A.M. 100, namely, that the problems of investigation, detection and prosecution of crimes are different in big cities from what they are outside those cities and in rural areas. Accordingly, the validity of the Madras City Police Act and the Madras District Police Act was upheld. It was further held that the Madras City Police Act did not violate Art. 14 as the presumption raised by s. 65 was reasonable and necessary for investigation of crime in a big city like Madras]; *Narayana Reddi* v. *A.P.* ('64) A.A.P. 373 (upholding the application of the Hyderabad Markets Act to Hyderabad and Secunderabad and not to other places).

[85] *Sethi Marble and Stone Industries, Chittorgarh* v. *Rajasthan* (1958) 8 Raj. 311, ('58) A.Raj. 140 (the Rajasthan Minor Mineral Concession Rules, 1955, Sch. 1, which prescribed rates of royalty dependent on the quality and value of goods).

[86] *Balwantrai Bhikhabhai Parekh* v. *South Kanara Market Committee* (1958) Mys. 206, ('59) A.Mys. 29 (the Madras Agricultural Crops Markets Act, 1933, s. 5).

[87] *Bombay* v. *F. N. Balsara* (1951) S.C.R. 682, 711-12, ('51) A.SC. 318 (s. 39, Bombay Prohibition Act, 1949, empowered the Provincial Government to permit the use or consumption of foreign liquor on cargo boats, war ships and troop ships and in Military and Naval messes and canteens. The High Court had held that the Armed Forces did not constitute a separate class under our Constitution and, in any event, the classification made by s. 39 had no reasonable relation to the object of the Act. Reversing the High Court, *held*, that the Armed Forces were a class by themselves, that they had their traditions and mode of life, conditioned and regulated by rules which were the product of experience. Drinking among the Forces was properly and carefully regulated. When drinking was regulated among a class of persons by specific rules and regulations and drunkenness was made an

large taxis;[89] "first informants" who are homeless and other homeless persons;[90] goods which are or can be easily smuggled and which are not or cannot be easily smuggled;[91] Advocates who plead, those who plead and act, and those who only act;[92] the possession by Advocates of a special professional qualification coupled with practice on the Original Side of the Bombay High Court and the absence of such qualification and practice;[93] scales of pay and allowances for administrative work and for field work in an Insurance Corporation;[94] diploma holders and degree holders;[95] a person specially trained and experienced in engineering in tele-communication and a person not so trained;[96] land holders who obtained decrees against tenants before a certain date and those who did not;[97] between *bustees* (hovels) and owners of bustees;[98] a partition that took place before and after the Madras Aliyasanthana (Mysore Amendment) Act, 1962 came into

---

offence, the relaxation of the law in their case was not likely to produce the same evil results as it may produce under other circumstances).

[88] (1951) S.C.R. *supra* at p. 712. (the exemption from the prohibition law, granted to cargo boats was justified on the ground that ". . . cargo boats have to be on the sea for long periods, the number of persons affected by the exemption is comparatively small, and they are mostly sojourners who stay at the port for a short time and then go away").

[89] *Harman Singh* v. *R.T.A., Calcutta Region* (1954) S.C.R. 371, ('54) A.SC. 190 (upholding different rates of fares for large and small taxis under s. 42, Motor Vehicles Act, 1939).

[90] *Bombay* v. *Bhanji Munji* (1955) 1 S.C.R. 777, ('55) A.SC. 41, (*held*, that allotting requisitioned premises to first informants who had given information about suppressed vacancies was a reasonable test in ascertaining who amongst the vast class of the homeless which existed in Bombay were to get the benefit of available accommodation. In the High Court Chagla C.J. had held that the policy of allotting vacant premises to first informants was discriminatory and the classification could not possibly be looked upon as a reasonable classification. The Supreme Court reversed the judgment and held, in substance, that the classification was reasonable and observed that the equitable maxim that "equity helps the vigilant" also pointed in the same direction).

[91] *Babulal Amthalal Mehta* v. *Collector of Customs* (1957) S.C.R. 1110, ('57) A.SC. 877 (upholding s. 178-A, Sea Customs Act, 1878).

[92] *Pabitra Kumar* v. *W.B.* ('64) A.SC. 593, 599 (1964) 5 S.C.R. 45 (upholding the allocation of separate rooms in the High Courts to the three classes of practitioners).

[93] *Manibhai Gopalji Desai* v. *Union* ('60) A.B. 83, 61 Bom. L.R. 976 (upholding reservations of seats by the High Court for Advocates, O.S. under s. 4(3), Bar Councils Act, 1926. The validity of the section was also supported on the alternative ground that the right created by the Act was not a Common Law right or a natural right or a right flowing from the Constitution but was a franchise dependent upon the law and therefore the right could not be asserted to a larger extent than was permitted by the law creating it).

[94] *Sunil Kumar* v. *Zonal Manager, E.Z., L.I.C.* ('62) A.Cal. 75 [the Life Insurance Corporation Act, 1956, s. 11(2) and the categorization Order, December 30, 1957]; *Girija Shankar* v. *Zonal Manager, L.I.C.* ('63) A.Cal. 574, 577; *Murari Mohan* v. *L.I.C.* ('64) A.Cal. 388, 390.

[95] *J. & K.* v. *T. N. Khosa* (1974) 1 S.C.R. 771, ('74) A.SC. 1 (*held*, that the classification was valid in considering promotion of persons drawn from different sources and integrated into one service).

[96] *Ramesh Prasad* v. *Bihar* (1978) 1 S.C.R. 787, ('78) A.SC. 327 (the present case held covered by the case in *f.n.* 95 above).

[97] *Seshayya* v. *Narasimhacharyulu* (1955) Mad. 1151, ('55) A.M. 252, (1955) 1 M.L.J. 439 (the land holders who had spent much time, money and energy in obtaining decrees and fighting out their cases, deserved in law and equity, the small concession given to them).

[98] *Sambhu Nath* v. *Calcutta Municipality* (1978) 2 S.C.R. 606, ('78) A.SC. 768.

force;[99] those who were and those who were not Wards of Court;[1] creditors of a class of *Taluqdars* and creditors of other persons;[2] between claims of banks and co-operative societies and claims of private money-lenders;[3] co-operative societies and other societies;[4] Hindu and Muslim women;[5] citizen and non-citizen;[6] "trespassers" whose claim or title is *bona fide* and "trespassers" whose claim is not *bona fide*;[7] refined oil and hydrogenated oil.[8]

9.70 Classifications based on administrative convenience have been upheld in *Bombay* v. *United Motors*;[9] *Bishwambhar Singh* v. *Orissa*[10] and *Ram Chandra Palai* v. *Orissa*.[11] A classification made by the Constitution itself cannot be struck down as violating Art. 14. Accordingly, the distinction made between the State and Union Territories by s. 54 of the Union Territories Act, 1963, was valid.[12]

Classifications held invalid

9.71 The following classifications were held to be no classification at all or classification not reasonably related to the object of the impugned law. BETWEEN:—persons of "rank" and other persons;[13]

---

[99] *Ratnamala* v. *State* ('68) A.Mys. 216, 236.

[1] *Maharaja G. P. Sahi* v. *Bihar* (1951) 30 Pat. 735, ('51) A.P. 570 [upholding s. 3(2) Majority Act, 1875].

[2] *Jethalal* v. *D. S. A. Laxmanwala* ('53) A.Sau. 177 (upholding a notification which prohibited a Taluqdar whose estate was taken under agency management from entering into a contract involving him or his estate in a pecuniary liability and which provided that if the contract was made it was to be void).

[3] *Chandmal* v. *M.P.* ('67) A.M.P. 52 (upholding Reg. 4 of the M.B. Scheduled Tribes Debt Relief Regulations, 1962, *held*, that the object of Reg. 4 was to protect members of the Scheduled Tribes from being exploited by "the superior intelligence" and devices of private moneylenders).

[4] *C. P. Khanna* v. *V. K. Kalghatgi* ('70) A.B. 201, 202-3 [upholding ss. 91 and 96, Maharashtra Co-op. Societies Act, 1961, and rules framed thereunder, *held*, that co-operative societies could be treated as a class by themselves].

[5] *Abdulla Khan* v. *Chandni Bi* ('56) A.Bhop. 71 (upholding the Hindu Women's Right of Residence and Separate Maintenance Act, 1944, *held*, that non-application of the Act to Muslims did not violate Art. 14 as the Legislature must have regard to the development of a community and would be reluctant to pass legislation on matters affecting religion).

[6] *Everett Orient Line* v. *Jasjit Singh* ('62) A.Cal. 308 (upholding s. 52-A, Sea Customs Act, 1878, whereby non-citizens are prohibited from the shipping business).

[7] *Abdul Aziz* v. *U.P.* ('66) A.A. 517, (1966) A.L.J. 99 (upholding s. 122-B of the U.P. Zamindari Abolition and Land Reforms Act, 1951).

[8] *Tungabhadra Industries* v. *State* ('66) A.A.P. 85 (F.B.) (the difference between refined oil and hydrogenated oil justified the exemption of sales tax being withdrawn from refined oil but being continued for hydrogenated oil).

[9] (1953) S.C.R. 1069, 1096-7, ('53) A.SC. 252 (*held*, that the maximum taxable turnover for general and special tax fixed by ss. 5 and 10 respectively of the Bombay Sales Tax Act, 1952, was based on a classification justified by administrative convenience).

[10] (1954) S.C.R. 842, 855, ('54) A.SC. 139 (*held*, that the power conferred on the State Government by s. 3, Orissa Estates Abolition Act, 1950, to declare from time to time that the estates specified in the notification had passed to and had become vested in the State free from all encumbrances did not violate Art. 14 but was based on administrative necessity since it would have been a colossal task to take over all estates at one and the same time. Such action would have broken down the entire administrative machinery); fol. in *Thakur Amarsinghji* v. *Rajasthan* (1955) 2 S.C.R. 303, 366-7, ('55) A.SC. 504 (upholding a provision authorising the State to resume different classes of jagir lands on different dates).

[11] (1956) S.C.R. 28, 39, ('56) A.SC. 298 (provisions for carrying out schemes for State transport service depending on the administrative convenience of the State government were held not to violate Art. 14).

[12] *Moti Ram* v. *Union* ('66) A.H.P. 25.

[13] *Sher Singh* v. *Ghansi Ram* (1954) Raj. 450, ('54) A.Raj. 233 [upholding that s. 133, C.P.C. (before its Amendment in 1956) was void as the power of exemption

habitual criminals who have acquired a bad reputation and habitual criminals who have not acquired such reputation;[14] territories to which Parts (I) and (II) of the Fugitive Offenders Act, 1881, applied and other territories;[15] persons who could publish news sheets without being liable to be punished and persons who could not publish news sheets without such liability;[16] directly recruited *mamalatdars* and promotee *mamalatdars*;[17] employees who have throughout been in the Indian Railway administration and employees whose previous services were with Railway Companies;[18] the rich and the poor;[19] settlements of lands belonging to a Raj, made by the Court of Wards with one person and settlements made with other persons;[20] land acquired for housing schemes;[21] or for flood control and pre-

Civil and Criminal Procedure

Land legislation

---

related to individuals, and the word "rank" did not supply any basis for classification. S. 133 C.P.C. was amended in 1956 and conferred exemption from personal appearance in court on the following persons: (i) The President of India; (ii) the Vice-President of India; (iii) the Speaker of the House of the People; (iv) the Ministers of the Union; (v) the Judges of the Supreme Court; (vi) Governors of States and Administrators of Union Territories; (vii) Speakers of the State Legislative Assemblies; (viii) the Chairman of the State Legislative Councils; (ix) the Ministers of States; (x) the Judges of the High Courts; (xi) the persons to whom s. 87B applied].

[14] *Deodat Rai* v. *State* (1951) 2 All. 745, ('51) A.A. 718 [*held*, that s. 3(1) (*a*), (*b*) and (*c*) U.P. Prevention of Crimes (Special Powers) Temporary Act, 1949, violated Art. 14 since there was no reason why habitual criminals who had not acquired a bad reputation should be dealt with under s. 110, Cr.P.C., while those who had acquired a bad reputation should be dealt with under the Act, since the special procedure prescribed by the Act had nothing to do with the question of a bad reputation].

[15] *In re C. G. Menon* ('53) A.M. 729, (1953) 2 M.L.J. 61 (*held*, that there was no rational connection between the territorial classification made by the Act and the object of the Act, namely, the surrender of a fugitive offender; the State appealed to the Supreme Court which confirmed the judgment on the different ground that having regard to the scheme of the Act, it became inapplicable to India when she became a sovereign democratic Republic: *Madras* v. *C. G. Menon* (1955) 1 S.C.R. 280, ('54) A.SC. 517.

[16] *Rama Shankar* v *State* ('54) A.A. 562 [*held*, that ss. 15 and 18, Press (Emergency Powers) Act, 1939, violated Art. 14 as there was nothing in the Act to guide the District Magistrate in putting persons in the one class or the other].

[17] *S. M. Pandit* v. *Gujarat* ('72) A.SC. 252.

[18] *Railway Board* v. *A. Pichumani* ('72) A.SC. 508, 514, (1972) 2 S.C.R. 187 (*held*, that the part of a Note which obliged railway employees whose previous services had been with companies to retire at the age of 58 whereas employees whose services had been with the railway administration were permitted to retire at 60 violated Art. 14).

[19] *M. D. Sir Kameshwar Singh* v. *Bihar* (1951) 30 Pat. 454, ('51) A.P. 91 (S.B.) (*held*, that the provisions of the Bihar Land Reforms Act, 1950, which provided for compensation at 20 times the net income in the case of the poor man and 3 times the net income in the case of the rich man did not make a reasonable classification since the object of the law was to pay compensation, that is, the present value of the property that was being acquired; the principle of progressive taxation did not apply to compensation for land acquired).

[20] *Ram Prasad Narayan Sahey* v. *Bihar* (1953) S.C.R. 1129, ('53) A.SC. 215 (*held*, that the Sathi Land Restoration Act, 1950 was void, as it singled out a particular individual from his fellow subjects and visited him with a disability which was not imposed on others, and against which even the right to complain was taken away; *held*, also that the Act was highly discriminatory. The Act sought to nullify a settlement made by the Court of Wards which was in management of the Bethiah Raj, it would appear under political pressure, as it was found on evidence that other settlements of lands belonging to the Bethiah Raj on similar terms had not been proceeded against, or sought to be invalidated).

[21] *P. Vajravelu Mudaliar* v. *Spl. Dy. Collector, Madras* (1965) 1 S.C.R. 614, ('65) A.SC. 1017.

Municipalities

Religious trusts

Trade, Commerce, etc.

vention of erosion;[22] and land acquired for other public purposes; the State and persons;[23] the Chairman, Vice-Chairman, and Councillors of Municipal Councils and officers and servants of such Councils;[24] trustees of Temples in the Travancore area and Trustees of Temples in the Cochin area;[25] all Jains of the Swetambar sect over 21 years of age staying in Bihar and all other Jains of the same sect staying outside Bihar;[26] manufacturers who had cleared and manufacturers who had not cleared goods during the financial year;[27] licence holders who are co-operative societies and licence holders who are not;[28] the Press Trust of India and other news agencies;[29] between small scale industrial units established before 1959 and those established after 1959;[30] penalty proceedings in respect of assessment

---

[22] *Dy. Commr. Kamrup* v. *Durganath* ('68) A.SC. 394, 405, (1968) 1 S.C.R. 561.

[23] *U.P.* v. *Raj Narain* ('61) A.A. 432 [*held*, that bye-law 3(1) of the bye-laws of the Agra Municipal Board was void as it permitted the State if encroachment was allowed to have been made on its land to get the encroachment removed in a summary way, whereas for an encroachment on the land of some other person that person was required to file a suit for its removal. It is submitted that the decision is not correct, having regard to the fact that there is a substantial distinction between the State and private individuals and any encroachment on the property of the State is an encroachment upon public property for which a speedy remedy may very well be provided].

[24] *Bhupendra Kumar* v. *Orissa* (1959) Cut. 203, ('60) A.Or. 46 [*held*, that s. 5(1), Orissa Municipal Election (Validation) Ordinance, 1959, was void on the ground that s. 375, Orissa Municipal Act, 1950, made the Chairman, the Vice-Chairman, the Councillors and officers and servants of the Municipal Council liable for the loss caused on a misapplication of the money or other property of the Municipal Council on account of his illegal act, omission, neglect or misconduct, whereas by virtue of s. 5(1) of the Ordinance the Chairman, Vice-Chairman and Councillors would escape such liability while officers and servants of the Municipal Councils would continue to be liable. There was no reasonable basis for this classification which was arbitrary].

[25] *Kumaran* v. *C. D. Board* ('54) A.Tr.-Co. 515 [*held*, that s. 87(3), Trav.-Cochin Hindu Religious Institutions Act, violated Art. 14 as there was no reason for treating trustees of Temples in the Cochin and Travancore areas differently].

[26] *Labh Chandra* v. *State* ('69) A.P. 209 (*held*, that a rule made by government enabling all Swetambar Jains over 21 years of age staying in Bihar to be on an electoral roll while Swetambar Jains outside Bihar could be on the roll only if they had donated Rs. 500 within 10 years to the Trust violated Art. 14].

[27] *A. Match Industries* v. *Union* ('71) A.A.P. 69 [*held*, that an excise duty on matches was imposed on the basis of output, the imposition of a higher duty on manufacturers who had not cleared goods had no reasonable connection with the object of the law (ibid. p. 72): *Mayflower Farm Inc.* v. *Peter G. Ten Eyck* 297 U.S. 266, 80 L. ed. 675 rel. on].

[28] *Ramanlal* v. *M. S. Palinkar* ('61) A.Guj. 38 [the State in issuing executive instructions entrusting wholesale distribution of sugar to co-operative societies to the exclusion of other licence holders did not proceed on any rational classification as it was unrelated to the object of the Essential Commodities Act, 1955. The court held (it is submitted, incorrectly) that since the action impugned was executive action, intentional and purposeful discrimination had to be established. It further held that there was nothing to show that the discrimination was not intentional and purposeful].

[29] *P.T.I.* v. *Union* ('74) A.SC. 1044, 1055 (1975) 3 S.C.R. 499, (*held*, that the fact that the P.T.I. had the status of a national news agency was irrelevant to the criterion adopted by the Wage Board in fixing wages, namely, the gross revenue of newspapers and news agencies. The placing of the P.T.I. in Class II, when according to the criterion adopted it should have been placed in Class III was clearly discriminatory).

[30] *Ram Lubhaya Kapur* v. *Union* ('73) A.P. & H. 297 (*held*, that government's decision to allocate imported shoddy wool and woollen rags only to small scale industrial units established before 1959 was arbitrary, and the classification had no rational or intelligible differentia which would distinguish the units established before and after 1959).

completed before and after 1st April, 1962;[31] Hindus and non-Hindus, and Hindus of one area and Hindus of another area in the same State;[32] undivided families and other families;[33] female and male proprietors of estates;[34] disputes which have continued for a long time between rival claimants and disputes which have not so continued;[35] medical practitioners in the Vidarbha Region and the Hyderabad areas of Maharashtra and medical practitioners in the Bombay areas of Maharashtra;[36] B.Sc. (Honours) and B.Sc. (Pass) students regardless of the marks obtained by them;[37] French and Portuguese nationals and other foreign nationals;[38] the maintenance allowance of dependents of Jagirdars or State Grantees whose maintenance allowances were fixed by courts and those whose allowances were fixed by executive officers;[39] persons who apply for probate in respect of an estate valued at under Rs. one lac and persons applying for probate in respect of an estate exceeding one lac of rupees;[40] members of Scheduled

Miscellaneous

---

[31] *R. Prasad Mohan Lal* v. *I.T.A. Tribunal* ('70) A.A. 620 (F.B.).

[32] *Sheokaran Singh* v. *Doulatram* ('55) A.Raj. 201 (F.B.) (*held*, that the law of *Damdupat* involved a distinction between Hindus and non-Hindus only on the ground of religion or race and secondly that as the rule of *Damdupat* prevailed only in some parts of Rajasthan it could not be upheld as a local custom because the law of *Damdupat* was essentially a matter of Civil law and there was no reason why Hindus of some areas should be subject to it and of others not).

[33] *Mammad Keyi* v. *W.T.O.* (1961) 2 Ker. 368, ('62) A.Ker. 110 (*held*, that s. 3, Wealth Tax Act, 1957 violated Art. 14 as Hindu undivided families of wealth had been singled out from other similar joint families in the country).

[34] *Cracknell* v. *U.P.* (1953) 1 All. 29, ('52) A.A. 746 [*held*, that s. 8(1)(*b*), U.P. Court of Wards Act, 1912, violated Art. 14 as the classification between female and male proprietors was arbitrary and placed female proprietors in a disadvantageous position]; *Raj Rajeshwari Devi* v. *U.P.* ('54) A.A. 608.

[35] *Ameerunnissa Begum* v. *Mahaboob Begum* (1953) S.C.R. 404, ('53) A.SC. 91 (holding the Waliuddolla Succession Act, 1950, void, the Supreme Court said that the continuance of a dispute even for a long period of time between two sets of rival claimants to the property of a private person was not a circumstance of such unusual nature as would invest the case with special or exceptional features and make it a class by itself. The Act in singling out two groups of persons consisting of two women and their children out of those who claimed to be related to the late Nawab and preventing them from establishing their rights in Courts of Law under their personal law, violated Art. 14).

[36] *Rukmani* v. *Maharashtra* (1968) Bom. 1445, ('70) A.B. 10, 71 Bom.L.R. 71 [*held*, that ss. 18(2)(b)(ii) and s. 33 which made the classification must be struck down].

[37] *R. S. Singh* v. *Darbhanga Medical College* ('69) A.P. 11 [although B.Sc. (Honours) students formed a separate class there was no reasonable nexus between the class and admitting them automatically to a medical college irrespective of the marks obtained by B.Sc. (Pass) students].

[38] *L. C. Menzes* v. *Madras* ('52) A.M. 734, (1952) 2 M.L.J. 237 (*held*, that a classification made by a Government Order, for the purposes of issuing liquor permits, between Portuguese and French citizens of the Portuguese and French Settlements in India and foreign nationals was arbitrary since such Portuguese and French nationals were also foreign nationals).

[39] *Shiv Kalyan Singh* v. *Bhur Singh* (1954) Raj. 182 (*held*, that the Jaipur *Hitkarni* Committee Rules did not provide a better procedure for fixing the maintenance allowance as compared with the fixation by a court and the classification could not be upheld).

[40] *L. Raymond* v. *Y. B. Yakchee* ('57) A.A. 207, (1957) A.L.J. 176 (*held*, that Sch. I, Art. II, U.P. Court Fees Act, 1870, Cls. 4 to 8 contravened Art. 14. The classification was directly opposed to the object of the law which was progressively high taxation on an estate, for even on the construction contended for by the State, the first lac of rupees in an estate of over a lac of rupees escaped taxation).

Tribes in government service and those not in government service;[41] and between the children of University employees who were either poor or were rendering meritorious service to the University and other candidates for admission to a State Medical College.[42]

Discrimination arising from choice by a person

9.72 Where a statute treats every person alike and the discrimination, if any, arises from the choice made by a person, the statute does not contravene Art. 14.[43] Where, however, a taxing Act makes no attempt to adopt any rational classification the Act contravenes Art. 14 and is void.[44]

9.73 In *Moti Ram* v. *M.P.*[45] the Supreme Court had directed that the petitioner, a poor mason, should be released on bail to the satisfaction of the Chief Judicial Magistrate. The Chief Judicial Magistrate required a bail of Rs. 10,000, and refused to accept the petitioner's brother as a surety because his assets were in another district. On an application by the Petitioner to the Supreme Court, Krishna Iyer J. held that it shocked one's conscience that a poor mason should be called upon to give bail of Rs. 10,000 and the insistence by the Magistrate that the surety should be from his own district was clearly discriminatory. Krishna Iyer J. observed that an accused arrested outside his district may not know anybody with property at the place where he was arrested. He added:

---

41 *I.T.O., Assam* v. *Lawrence Singh* (1968) 2 S.C.R. 165, ('68) A.SC. 658 [*held*, that the classification made by the words "provided that such member is not in the service of Government" found in s. 4(3)(xxi) of the Income-tax Act, 1922, and by the words "who is not in service of the Government" in s. 10(26) of the Income-tax Act, 1961, had no rational nexus with granting exemption from income-tax to members of the Scheduled Tribes in Government service whilst not granting the same exemption to members of the Scheduled Tribes who were not in Government service. *Held further*, that the aforesaid words were severable and having regard to the reasons which persuaded the Legislature to grant exemption there was no doubt that it would have granted that exemption even if it was aware that it was beyond its competence to exclude Government servants from the exemption in question].

42 *Umesh Chandra* v. *V. N. Singh*, 46 Pat. 616, ('68) A.P. 3, 10 (F.B.) (*held*, that there was no reasonable nexus between the object of the law, namely, to provide for proper selection of candidates for admission to a medical course and the pecuniary difficulties or meritorious services rendered by the employees of the University).

43 *Chittoor Motor Transport Co.* v. *I.T.O.* ('66) A.SC. 570 [*held*, that s. 10(2)(vib) of the Income-tax Act, 1922, did not violate Art. 14. Rightly interpreted, that section provided that if an assessee sold to a person other than the Government at any time before the expiry of 10 years from the end of the year in which a motor vehicle was acquired, the allowance in respect of it was deemed to have been wrongly allowed for the purposes of the Act; but if the assessee sold it to the Government no such consequence followed. There was no discrimination, because every person had the right to sell the motor-car to the Government, or to any other person].

44 *Kerala* v. *Haji K. Kutty* (1969) 1 S.C.R. 645, ('69) A.SC. 378 [*held*, that s. 4 of the Kerala Building Tax Act, 1961, read with the Schedule to the Act, violated Art. 14 as they adopted merely the floor area of the building as the basis of the tax irrespective of all other considerations. "Where objects, persons or transactions essentially dissimilar are treated by the imposition of a uniform tax, discrimination may result, for, refusal to make rational classification may itself in some cases operate as a denial of equality": ibid. p. 380: *K. T. Moopil Nair* v. *Kerala* (1961) 3 S.C.R. 77, ('61) A.SC. 552 followed].

45 ('78) A.SC. 1594, (1979) 1 S.C.R. 335.

"What law prescribes sureties from outside or non-regional language applications? What law prescribes the geographical discrimination implicit in asking for sureties from the court district? This tendency takes many forms, sometimes geographic, sometimes linguistic, sometimes legalistic. Art. 14 protects all Indians *qua* Indians within the territory of India. Art. 350 sanctions representation to any authority, including a court, for redress of grievances in any language used in the Union of India. Equality before the law implies that even a vakalat or affirmation made in any State language according to the law in that State must be accepted everywhere in the territory of India save where a valid legislation to the contrary exists. Otherwise, an adivasi will be unfree in Free India, and likewise many other minorities. This divagation has become necessary to still the judicial beginnings, and to inhibit the process of making Indians aliens in their own homeland. Swaraj is made of united stuff."[46]

9.74 In *S. Garg* v. *K. M. Garg*,[47] Deshpande J. held that there was no rule of Hindu Law that the husband had an absolute right to choose the matrimonial home. It would depend, in the first instance, on an agreement before marriage; and the observations in Mulla's *Hindu Law* that such an agreement would be void, required reconsideration in the light of modern conditions. A law conferring an absolute right on the husband to choose the matrimonial home, would be void as violating Art. 14.[48]

9.75 We must now consider the question of the conferment of discretionary power in relation to Art. 14. As this branch of the law was developed by the Supreme Court in a series of cases in which two different procedures were prescribed for the trial of criminal offences, we will consider those cases first. Both before and after the Constitution, several States had enacted laws empowering the State Governments to set up Special Courts for the trial of "such offences or classes of offences, or cases or classes of cases as the State Government may by general or special order in writing direct",[49] or for the trial of "cases" allotted to the Special Judge,[50] or for the trial of "any offence or class of offences" which the Military Governor may by general or special order direct.[51] The procedure prescribed by all these laws for the trial of cases was materially different from that prescribed by the Criminal Procedure Code for the trial of offences generally, and this special procedure was challenged as violative of Art. 14 in *Anwar Ali Sarkar's Case*,[52] *Kathi Raning Rawat's Case*,[53] *Ahuja's Case*,[54] *Qasim Razvi's Case*[55]

Discretionary power: power to prescribe different procedures for criminal trials

---

[46] ('78) A.SC. *supra* at pp. 1600-1601.

[47] ('78) A.Del. 296 (A husband's application for the restitution of conjugal rights).

[48] On the facts it was held, first, that the wife was earning a much higher income and was not obliged to resign her post; secondly, that the husband's conduct showed that he wanted to obtain money from her in addition to the very large dowry which he had obtained, and that he flaunted to her, his relations with other women. The Court held that the wife was justified in not staying with her husband. The order of restitution of conjugal rights, under appeal, was set aside.

[49] S. 5(1), W.B. Special Courts Act, 1950 (impugned in *Anwar Ali Sarkar's Case, infra*); s. 11, Saurashtra State Public Safety (3rd. Amendment) Ordinance (impugned in *Kathi Raning Rawat's Case, infra*); s. 12, Bombay Public Safety Measures Act, 1947 (impugned in *Ahuja's Case, infra*).

[50] S. 4(1), W.B. Criminal Law Amendment (Special Courts) Act, 1949 (impugned in *Kedar Nath Bajoria's Case, infra*).

[51] Special Tribunal Regulation, Hyderabad (impugned in *Quasim Razvi's Case, infra*).

[52] (1952) S.C.R. 284, ('52) A.SC. 75.

[53] (1952) S.C.R. 435, ('52) A.SC. 123.

[54] (1952) S.C.R. 710, ('52) A.SC. 235.

[55] (1953) S.C.R. 589, ('53) A.SC. 156.

and *Kedar Nath Bajoria's Case*.[56] All these cases raised the question whether the special procedure prescribed by the impugned law was discriminatory, and except for the doubt expressed by Sastri C.J. in *Ahuja's Case*[57] the Judges had no difficulty in holding that the procedure was discriminatory, as it clearly was. The next question considered was whether the special procedure could be justified on the basis of permissible classification, and this question produced a remarkable divergence of opinion in each case, and from case to case.

Anwar Ali Sarkar's Case

9.76 In *Anwar Ali Sarkar's Case*,[58] the majority (Fazl Ali, Mahajan, Mukherjea, Chandrasekhara Aiyar and Bose JJ.) held that s. 5(1), West Bengal Act, 1950, was wholly void. Das J. in a concurring judgment held that s. 5(1) was void only to the extent that it referred to "cases". Sastri C.J. in his dissent held that s. 5(1) was valid. Fazl Ali, Mahajan, Mukherjea and Chandrasekhara Aiyar JJ. accepted the theory of classification, and held that s. 5(1) conferred unfettered and arbitrary power on Government to classify offences or cases at its pleasure, since the Act did not disclose or lay down any policy to guide the discretion of Government in classifying cases or offences. The reference in the Preamble to the necessity for speedier trial of offences could not control the plain meaning of s. 5(1);[59] but even if the words of the Preamble were read into, or, with the words of s. 5(1), the words "speedier trial" were too vague and uncertain to afford any basis for a rational classification.[60] Das J. held that the part of s. 5(1) which referred to "cases" was outside the Preamble,[61] which referred only to "offences" or "classes of offences". The *speedier trial* mentioned in the preamble was the object of the impugned law and the object by itself could not be the basis of the classification.[62] However, circumstances attending a crime may furnish a basis for classifying "offences" or "classes of offences" or "classes of cases"[63] as requiring speedier trial, in which event s. 5(1) by necessary implication empowered the State to make such classification in the light of the object set out in the Preamble. If the Government made an arbitrary or impermissible classification, such classification, and not the law, would be struck down.[64] Fazl Ali and Mukherjea JJ. rejected this position although in the case to be considered next they practically accepted it. Fazl Ali J. rejected the position because its acceptance would mean that even palpable discrimination made by an Act couched in general terms could not be challenged; nor could executive action under the law be challenged because the executive could plead that it was

---

[56] (1954) S.C.R. 30, ('53) A.SC. 404.
[57] (1952) S.C.R. 710, 718, ('52) A.SC. 235.
[58] (1952) S.C.R. 284, ('52) A.SC. 75.
[59] Mukherjea J. (with whom Mahajan J. concurred) (1952) S.C.R. 284 at pp. 327-28; Das J., ibid. p. 340; Chandrasekhara Aiyar J. ibid. at p. 353.
[60] Mukherjea J. (Mahajan J. agreeing), ibid. p. 328; Das J. ibid. pp. 340-41; Chadrasekhara Aiyar J., ibid. p. 343.
[61] ibid. p. 345. [62] ibid. p. 335.
[63] ibid. p. 343: ". . . crimes of murder, arson, loot and rape committed on a large scale during communal riots in particular localities . . . are they not really different from a case of stray murder, arson, loot and rape in another district which may not be affected by any communal upheaval?"
[64] ibid. p, 344.

authorized by the law.[65] Mukherjea J. rejected the position by saying that when the statute itself made a discrimination without any reasonable basis it would be invalidated for violating Art. 14 and the question as to how the law was actually worked might not be material. He held that in the case before him the statute itself made a discrimination.[66] It is submitted that the majority view is correct, and Sastri C.J.'s dissent does not answer the questions raised, and answered, by the majority.

Kathi Raning Rawat's Case

9.77 *Kathi Raning Rawat's Case*[67] was heard by the same Bench which heard *Anwar Ali Sarkar's Case*[68] and the impugned provisions of the Saurashtra Ordinance were substantially the same as those impugned in *Anwar Ali Sarkar's Case* with the following differences: the procedure prescribed was free from some of the objectionable features of the West Bengal Ordinance but even so it was sufficiently prejudicial to the accused to be discriminatory. However, the preamble was different; it referred to the need "to provide for public safety, maintenance of public order and the preservation of peace and tranquility in the State of Saurashtra." The Ordinance was a pre-Constitution Ordinance.[69] The case was heard along with *Anwar Ali Sarkar's Case*[70] "but was adjourned to enable the respondent State to file an affidavit explaining the circumstances" under which the impugned order was passed.[71] Although s. 11 of the Ordinance was in terms identical with s. 5(1) of the West Bengal Act, the majority (Sastri C.J., Fazl Ali, Mukherjea and Das JJ.) held, according to the Chief Justice, that s. 11 was valid in its entirety, and according to the rest that it was valid as to that part which referred to "offences", "classes of offences" and "classes of cases". Mahajan, Chandrasekhara Aiyar and Bose JJ. held that s. 11 violated Art. 14 and was void. Sastri C.J. adhered to his view in *Anwar Ali Sarkar's Case* and found the present case an *a fortiori*.[72] The State's affidavit furnished an additional ground for holding that there was a "two-fold classification on the lines of type and territory adopted in the impugned Ordinance read with the notification issued thereunder". Fazl Ali J. found in the preamble a decisive factor distinguishing the present case from *Anwar Ali Sarkar's Case*, for it gave guidance to Government in classifying "offences", "classes of offences" or "classes of cases" for being tried by the Special procedure.[73] Mukherjea J. arrived at the same conclusion on the basis of the preamble taken along with the circumstances disclosed in the Government's affidavit.[74] Das J. adhered to his earlier position.[75] Mahajan and Chandrasekhara Aiyar JJ.

The majority judgments

dissenting judgments

[65] "I think the fallacy of the argument lies in overlooking the fact that 'insidious discrimination complained of is incorporated in the Act itself', it being so drafted that whenever any discrimination is made such discrimination would be ultimately traceable to it." *Per* Fazl Ali J., ibid. pp. 309-10.

[66] ibid. p. 331.

[67] (1952) S.C.R. 435, ('52) A.SC. 123.

[68] (1952) S.C.R. 284, ('52) A.SC. 75.

[69] The West Bengal Act was a post-Constitution Act, but it was a verbatim reproduction of a pre-Constitution Ordinance: *Per* Fazl Ali J. (1952) S.C.R. at p. 306.

[70] (1952) S.C.R. 284, ('52) A.SC. 75.

[71] (1952) S.C.R. at p. 439.

[72] ibid. p. 441.

[73] ibid. pp. 449-50. As he could not conceal his repugnance to this type of legislation he expressed his feelings that "the legislatures should have recourse to legislation such as the present only in very special circumstances": ibid. p. 450.

[74] ibid. pp. 460-62.

[75] ibid. p. 475.

found the case covered by *Anwar Ali Sarkar's Case*. Mahajan J. said that the plain words of s. 11 could not be controlled by "the familiar and conventional phraseology" of the preamble.[76] Chandrasekhara Aiyar J. said that the need to provide for public safety, maintenance of public order, and the preservation of peace and tranquility in the State by itself indicated no classification, as the object was a general one, and every law dealing with the commission and punishment of offences was based on the need referred to in the preamble.[77] Both Mahajan J.[78] and Chandrasekhara Aiyar J.[79] said that the discrimination inherent in the Act was reflected in the notification, in which cognate offences, that is, offences presenting the same characteristic features, had been separately dealt with; some were to be tried by the Special Court, and others by the ordinary Courts. Mukherjea J. realized the force of these observations, but he did not meet them;[80] he merely said that even if the force of the observations was recognized, the accused had been charged with murder under s. 302, I.P.C. and there was no offence in the I.P.C. which could be placed on an identical footing with murder. Therefore it was not open to the accused to raise the question that the Act was discriminatory in respect of other offences.[81] Bose J. repeated his views on the equality clause, and agreed with Mahajan and Chandrasekhara Aiyar JJ.

Submission: the dissenting judgments are correct

9.78 It is submitted that the minority judgments are correct. If, as Mukherjea J. held, the appellant was not entitled to complain of discrimination because he had not been discriminated against, there was no need at all to consider the constitutional validity of the impugned Act. And if the constitutional validity of the Act was to be decided, it was irrelevant that the appellant had no *locus standi* to complain of inequality. Again, the issue as it presented itself to Fazl Ali J.[82] was not the real issue. The real issue was not, can a legislature under any circumstances lay down a special procedure for the trial of a particular class of offences; or did recourse to a simplified and less cumbrous procedure for the trial of those offences, even when abnormal conditions prevailed, amount to a violation of Art. 14?[83] The real issue was whether the legislature had classified offences, or classes of offences or classes of cases which required to be tried by a special procedure having regard to the nature of the offences or cases and the abnormal circumstances attending them, or alternatively, whether the legislature had indicated any principles on which Government were under an obligation[84] to classify offences, classes of offences or classes of cases which required to be so tried. It is submitted that Mahajan J. was right in saying that the plain unambiguous language of s. 11 could not be controlled by the preamble;[85]

---

[76] ibid. p. 453.
[77] ibid. p. 476.
[78] ibid. p. 452.
[79] ibid. p, 476.
[80] General observations that the equality clause did not require abstract symmetry cannot be said to meet objections going far beyond abstract symmetry.
[81] (1952) S.C.R. at pp. 465-66.
[82] ibid. p. 450.
[83] ibid.
[84] Fazl Ali J. speaks of the Government being *expected* to select only such offences etc.: ibid. p. 449.
[85] ibid. p. 453.

indeed, Mukherjea J. had said so in *Anwar Ali Sarkar's Case.*[86] But even if the preamble is used to throw light on s. 11, the majority judgments give no answer to the cogent objection of Chandrasekhara Aiyar J. that the "need" expressed in the preamble is at the basis of all criminal law.[87] The need to provide for public safety, maintenance of public order, and the preservation of peace and tranquility cannot furnish the differentia for classifying offences or classes of offences, first, for the reason given by Chandrasekhara Aiyar J., and secondly, because the need referred to in the preamble is the *object* of the Act, and the differentia and the object are different elements and the object by itself cannot be the differentia.[88]

9.79 The admission of an affidavit on behalf of the State to show the circumstances under which the law was passed was a confession that without the affidavit no principle of classification was to be found in the Act. If the plain unambiguous words of an Act cannot be controlled by the preamble, it would be surprising if an affidavit, made years after the Act, setting out the circumstances under which it was passed, could have the effect of controlling such plain unambiguous words, by limiting their effect to the circumstances set out in the affidavit. Such use of an affidavit is opposed to all principles of construction. Besides, to make the ambit of a law depend not upon a publicly declared policy, as by declaring it in the preamble, but upon *ex post facto* explanations given years later by a Government servant is to deprive law of its essential feature, namely, that it is publicly promulgated, so that those governed by it can shape their conduct accordingly. The danger of using such an extrinsic aid to interpretation becomes apparent when two responsible officers give different and contrary explanations *of the same policy* in two different High Courts.[89]

A criticism of admitting affidavit evidence to control the language of an Act

The danger of using such affidavits

---

[86] (1952) S.C.R. 284, ('52) A.SC. 75: "I agree . . . that the express provision of an enactment, if it is clear and unambiguous, cannot be curtailed or extended with the aid of the preamble to the Act. It is only when the object or meaning of the enactment is not clear that recourse can be had to the preamble to explain it" (1952) S.C.R. pp. 327-8.

[87] (1952) S.C.R. at p. 476.

[88] See para 9.32, proposition (*d*).

[89] In *East India Commercial Co.* v. *Customs Collector* ('57) A.Cal. 606 the question was whether the import control policy laid down in the Red Book was a notified order under s. 3(1), Imports and Exports Control Act. An affidavit was filed by the Jt. Secretary of the Govt. of India, Ministry of Commerce, stating it as true to his knowledge that the Red Book was a notified order under s. 3(1): (ibid. p. 611). If so, the policy had statutory force. In Misc. Application No. 264 of 1960, *M/s. Shams & Co.* v. *N. Swami & Anr.* (unreported), the Jt. Chief Controller of Imports and Exports swore an affidavit stating: "I say that the Import Trade Control Policy Book issued by the Govt. of India contains only the import and export policy proposed to be followed by the Government during the relevant period. I further say that the said policy is declared by the Government in exercise of its executive function and the provisions of the said policy book referred to in the petition do not confer any legal right on the members of the public including the petitioner. I further say that the said policy book is prepared for the purpose of regulating the grant of import licence and, therefore, does not confer any right to the members of the public to obtain any import licence from the Government under it, even assuming that any person has complied with the terms and provisions of the said policy book."

Ahuja's Case

9.80 *Ahuja's Case*[90] raised the question whether a power to refer cases to a special tribunal whose procedure was prejudicial to the accused as compared with the general law violated Art. 14.[91] The question would have been completely covered by *Anwar Ali Sarkar's Case*[92] if a new question had not been raised, namely, that assuming that the impugned law became void after the coming into effect of the Constitution, did such invalidity affect a trial commenced before, but concluded after, the Constitution came into force? Sastri C.J. answered the question in the negative. Das J., for himself, Mahajan, Mukherjea and Chandrasekhara Aiyar JJ. answered it in the affirmative. Sastri C.J. held, first, that the Constitution was not retrospective as held in *Menon's Case*,[93] secondly, that persons whose trials had commenced before the Constitution came into force were not similarly circumstanced, and the equality clause was not violated in treating differently those whose trial began after January 26, 1950; and lastly, that the Special Judge was competent to try the case when he began it before January 26, 1950, and the impugned Act was validly applied. The rest was merely working out the application of the Act.[94] Das J. held that *Anwar Ali Sarkar's Case* directly applied and *Menon's Case* did not, for it related to substantive rights, that is, to acts which before the Constitution amounted to an offence under the impugned Act, but which if done after the Constitution would not be an offence, and all that the case decided was that as the Constitution was not retrospective, it did not obliterate the offences completed before the Constitution came into force and therefore the offender could be proceeded against. However, the question raised by a procedural law was different. No one had a vested right in any course of procedure,[95] and it must follow as a corollary that nobody had a vested liability in matters of procedure. Again, persons whose cases were sent to the special tribunal before January 26, 1950, did not constitute a different class from those whose cases were sent after that date because such a classification had no nexus with the object of the Act[96] which was wide enough to cover both. *Keshoram Poddar's Case*[97] which was relied upon by Sastri C.J. did not apply, because it did not deal with proceedings commenced under a valid law being continued after the law had become void as violating a constitutional prohibition.[98] Das J. held that the continuation of the trial under a discriminatory procedure

The dissenting judgment

The majority judgment

---

[90] (1952) S.C.R. 710, ('52) A.SC. 235.

[91] Except for the doubt expressed by Sastri C.J. (1952) S.C.R. at p. 718, the other Judges had no difficulty in holding that the special procedure was discriminatory.

[92] (1952) S.C.R. 284, ('52) A.SC. 75.

[93] (1951) S.C.R. 228, ('51) A.SC. 128.

[94] He arrived at this conclusion after citing with approval the following passage from the judgment of the Privy Council in *Keshoram Poddar* v. *Nundo Lal Mullick* (1927) 54 I.A.152, 156, ('27) A.PC. 97: "The application of the Act is when the parties begin to move under it. This was done in the present case before March, 1924. The rest is merely the working out of the application."

[95] Citing Maxwell, *Interpretation of Statutes*, 9th ed., p. 232; now see, 11th ed., p. 216.

[96] (1952) S.C.R. 710, 733: "The avowed objects of the Act recited in the preamble are the expediency of consolidating and amending the law relating to the security of the State, maintenance of public order and maintenance of supplies and services essential to the community in the State of Bombay."

[97] *Supra.*

[98] (1952) S.C.R. at pp. 735-36.

made the trial void, and ". . . the Special Judge's jurisdiction came to an end, for he was enjoined to proceed only according to the special procedure and that procedure having become void as stated above, he could not proceed at all as a Judge of a Special Court constituted under the impugned Act."[99]

Qasim Razvi's Case

9.81 In *Syed Qasim Razvi* v. *Hyderabad*[1] the impugned law was substantially the same as in *Ahuja's Case*;[2] the Appellants' case had been individually referred to the Special Tribunal on October 6, 1949, and the trial was completed in September, 1950. The special procedure was prejudicial to the accused as compared with the procedure applicable to the trial of crimes generally. On these features being established, *Ahuja's Case* directly applied. However, Sastri C.J. for himself, Mukherjea and Chandrasekhara Aiyar JJ., held that it did not apply; Ghulam Hasan and Bose JJ. held that it did. Mukherjea and Chandrasekhara Aiyar JJ. had been parties to the majority judgment in *Ahuja's Case* which decided, first, that the decision in *Keshoram Poddar's Case* on which Sastri C.J. had relied had no application,[3] and secondly, that after the Constitution came into force the Special Judge lost his jurisdiction because he was appointed a judge to try cases by the special procedure prescribed by the Act and that procedure became void after the Constitution. Both these points were necessary for the decision of that case, for the question to be decided was: Can it be said that a trial lawfully begun cannot be continued, and a jurisdiction rightly assumed by a Judge is lost, because the law which governed the trial and conferred the jurisdiction became void after the Constitution? Therefore, it is submitted that even if it was open to three judges to overrule, in substance, the judgment of four judges on an issue which directly arose and was definitely decided,[4] they have not purported to do so.

The majority judgments

Submission: even if it is open to three judges in substance to overrule a judgment of four judges, they have not done so

9.82 The majority judgment in *Qasim Razvi's Case*[5] held that when a trial which had commenced under a special procedure became void, the correct question to ask was not whether the impugned procedure was discriminatory but whether the procedure in fact followed was discriminatory. Thus, though the law authorised a summary procedure and the recording of a memorandum of evidence in a summary manner, in fact the warrant procedure had been followed and evidence had been recorded *in extenso* in *Razvi's Case*. The conduct of proceedings in English was not discriminatory because though the ordinary court proceedings in Hyderabad were conducted in Urdu, "Urdu is certainly not the spoken language of even the majority of the people within the Hyderabad State".[6] The provisions entitling the Tribunal

The majority judgment in *Qasim Razvi's Case*

[99] ibid. p. 735.

[1] (1953) S.C.R. 589, ('53) A.SC. 156.

[2] (1952) S.C.R. 710, ('52) A.SC. 235.

[3] (1952) S.C.R. 710, 736. ('52) A.SC. 235.

[4] Mukherjea and Chandrasekhara Aiyar JJ. laid themselves open to the dry observations of Ghulam Hasan J. that "My learned brothers are certainly in a better position to interpret the decision in . . . . (*Ahuja's Case*) and to say whether their intention was not to declare the Act bad, whether or not its discriminatory provisions were applied in fact. It is impossible for me to go behind the actual words used in the decision and my conclusion is based entirely upon the language and the reasoning adopted in that case.": *Qasim Razvi* v. *Hyderabad* (1953) S.C.R. 589, 639, ('53) A.SC. 156.

[5] (1953) S.C.R. 589, ('53) A.SC. 156.

[6] (1953) S.C.R. 589, 598; see para 9.84 for the answer given by Bose J.

Dissenting judgments

to refuse to call witnesses, and the provisions disentitling the accused to a *de novo* trial were not material since the tribunal did not in fact refuse to call witnesses, and the events did not happen which could have raised the question of a *de novo* trial. Ghulam Hasan J. and Bose J. held that *Ahuja's Case* applied, for, as there held, the jurisdiction of the special Judge came to an end on the Act becoming void, as the impugned Act contained departures from the ordinary law which were prejudicial to the accused, namely, provisions which prevented the accused from applying for revision[7] and bail even after the Constitution came into force. Bose J. referred *also* to the absence of committal proceedings, the right to demand a *de novo* trial, the right to adopt a summary procedure and the elimination of Urdu as additional features prejudicial to the accused. Both the Judges held that in judging the validity of the law it is irrelevant to consider what has been done under it.

Submission: the dissenting judgments are correct

9.83 It is submitted that both on the law and on the facts the minority judgments are right. On the law, apart from the fact that the three judges did not purport to overrule four, the reasons given in *Ahuja's Case*[8] for holding that the law became void, and the Special Judge ceased to have jurisdiction, are unanswerable. It is submitted that there are further reasons for saying that the majority decision is wrong. Art. 14 is not limited to future law; it is expressly extended by Art. 13 to laws enacted before Art. 14 came into force, and such laws are declared to be void to the extent of their repugnancy with Art. 14. The majority decision amounts to saying that the Court will not pronounce on the constitutionality of pre-Constitution procedural laws in a case begun before the Constitution but will only consider whether the procedure actually followed was violative of equality. It is submitted that there is no justification for declining to discharge a duty which the Supreme Court itself has declared to be inescapable.[9] in fact there is no warrant in principle for applying one test to a case under a pre-Constitution law where the law has been set in motion before January 26, 1950, and another test to the same law where action is taken under it after the Constitution. In *Ahuja's Case,* Sastri C.J. justified such different treatment by saying that the two types of cases fell into two distinct classes, but the four judges who were parties to the majority judgment in that case rejected this classification as based

---

[7] There was evidence in the case that the order of the tribunal dated December 15, 1949, was carried in revision to the High Court, but the revision application was dismissed on February 25, 1950. "The office, it appears, noted that under s. 7, Cl.2 of the Regulation there could not be any revision but the learned Chief Justice in rejecting the revision petition merely said that he saw no reason to interfere 'at this stage'. I do not think that the order of rejection meant that the stage of interference was not appropriate and that he would have the right to interfere at a later stage, say at the time of the appeal. The learned Chief Justice could not have been unaware of the fact that no revision was competent against an order of the Tribunal under the Regulation.": (1953) S.C.R. at p. 638.

[8] (1952) S.C.R. 710, ('52) A.SC. 235.

[9] "This Court is thus constituted the protector and guarantor of fundamental rights, and it cannot, consistently with the responsibility so laid upon it, refuse to entertain applications seeking protection against infringements of such rights.": *Romesh Thappar* v. *Madras* (1950) S.C.R. 594, 597, ('50) A.SC. 124.

on no rational differentia related to the object of the Act.[10] The majority judgment in the present case does not repudiate this rejection of the classification which Sastri C.J. had made. Therefore, to hold the provisions of the West Bengal Ordinance and Act of 1950 void and to set aside the conviction of Anwar Ali Sarkar, whose case was referred to the Special Court on January 26, 1950,[11] without inquiring whether the procedure in fact followed was discriminatory and yet not to declare the Hyderabad Regulation void and not to set aside the conviction of Syed Qasim Razvi is to discriminate between two accused persons similarly situated on the basis of a classification held to be untenable by the Supreme Court.

9.84 The observations of Mukherjea J. that the use of English was not discriminatory as Urdu was not the language of even a majority of the people of Hyderabad, and therefore the provision of the Regulation that the Tribunal's proceedings shall be in English was not void, were answered with satisfying finality by Bose J.:

"In Hyderabad the court language in practice is Urdu and so great is the importance attached to it that neither judges nor counsel are permitted to function there unless they know that language. Indeed, the matter was carried to such lengths that one of the appellants was refused the services of an eminent King's Counsel from England on the ground that the latter did not know the court language Urdu. But at the same time the appellants were tried in a language which the gentleman in question did know and which was the language of the Special Tribunal. And an even greater anomaly, the President of the Tribunal himself did not know Urdu. I am unable to brush this aside as a matter of no consequence. It is to my mind material and vital and cuts at the root of this trial. I find it impossible to say that this is not discrimination continued after the Constitution. . . . There is to my mind something grotesquely fantastic in insisting on Urdu knowing counsel in a tribunal whose proceedings are to be conducted in English and at the same time rigidly excluding counsel who do not know Urdu and who do know English."[12]

It may be added that *Qasim Razvi's Case* received its judicial obituary from Das C.J.[13] who said that "the observations made in the majority judgment (in *Qasim Razvi's Case*) should not be extended but must be kept strictly confined to the special facts of that case", and from S. K. Das J. whose observations suggest that the minority judgments were right.[14]

Qasim Razvi's Case to be "strictly confined to the special facts of that case"

9.85 *Kedar Nath Bajoria* v. *W.B.*[15] marked a further retreat by the Supreme Court. The appellant was charged with having committed offences under ss. 120B and 420, I.P.C., and s. 5(2), Prevention of Corruption Act, 1947, and his case was allotted to the Special Court

Kedar Nath Bajoria's Case

[10] *Ahuja's Case, supra,* (1952) S.C.R. 710, 733, *per* Das J. Bose J. rightly cites this view of the majority and rightly concludes that "the majority considered it relevant and important to determine the post-constitutional validity of an enactment which was valid up to the date of the Constitution by the application of post-constitutional standards and tests.": *Qasim Razvi's Case,* (1953) S.C.R. 589, 619.

[11] *Anwar Ali Sarkar's Case* (1952) S.C.R. 284, 289, ('52) A.SC. 75.

[12] (1953) S.C.R. 589 at pp. 622-23. *Qasim Razvi's Case* was followed in *Habeeb Mahomed* v. *Hyderabad* (1953) S.C.R. 661, ('53) A.SC. 287.

[13] *Basheshar Nath* v. *C.I.T. Delhi & Rajasthan* (1959) Supp. (1) S.C.R. 528, 547, ('59) A.SC. 149.

[14] "The minority judgments, however, very pertinently pointed out that the discriminatory provisions were an integral part of the Regulation under which the accused person in that case was tried and in fact the discriminatory provisions were applied.": (1959) Supp. (1) S.C.R. 528, 581, ('59) A.SC. 149.

[15] (1954) S.C.R. 30, ('53) A.SC. 404.

constituted under s. 3, West Bengal Criminal Law Amendment Act. The trial commenced on January 3, 1950, and judgment was delivered on August 29, 1950, by the Special Judge convicting the appellant. The preamble to the West Bengal Criminal Law Amendment Act declared that "It is expedient to provide for the more speedy trial and more effective punishment of certain offences" which were set out in a schedule annexed to the Act. Sec. 4(1) of the Act empowered the Provincial Government to allot cases for trial to a Special Judge. The appellant contended that his case was covered by *Anwar Ali Sarkar's Case*[16] and that therefore the continuation of the trial before the Special Judge violated Art. 14 and was void. The majority held that the question whether the impugned law violated Art. 14 was to be determined in each case. After considering the earlier cases, the majority held that conferring a discretion on the State Government to refer cases to special Tribunals did not violate Art. 14 as the discretion had to be exercised in the light of the policy of the Act. Bose J. dissented, and held that the Act having made a classification of offences and the schedule having provided for the same class of persons, power could not be validly conferred on the State Government to pick out certain persons belonging to that class and send them for trial before a Special Judge. In fact, the Legislature itself could not have picked up the cases of accused *X*, *Y* and *Z* and sent them to trial before a Special Judge while leaving out the cases of other persons similarly situated. It is submitted that the dissenting judgment is correct.

Submission: dissenting judgment is correct

The principle established by the above decisions

9.86 The above cases establish that where two procedures are prescribed by law and one of the two is harsher or more onerous than the other, the harsher procedure cannot be justified unless it is based on a reasonable classification either made by the law itself or made by the executive in the exercise of its discretion in the light of the policy or object of the Act. In the following cases, different procedures prescribed by the impugned law or laws were held to be based on a reasonable classification reasonably related to the object of the law and consequently not open to challenge under Art. 14: the provisions of a law that pending proceedings should be concluded according to the law applicable at the time when the rights or liabilities accrued and the proceedings commenced;[17] the provisions of the Criminal Law Amendment Act, 1952, setting up Special Courts and providing a special procedure for dealing with offences of bribery and corruption;[18] procedure prescribed under s. 27(4) of the City of

Cases where different procedures were upheld

[16] (1952) S.C.R. 284, ('52) A.SC. 75.

[17] *Ramjilal* v. *I.T.O. Mohindargarh* (1951) S.C.R. 127, 135, ('51) A.SC. 97; *Rao Shiv Bahadur Singh* v. *V.P.* (1953) S.C.R. 1188, 1197, ('53) A.SC. 394, (pending proceedings constitute a separate class and can be dealt with separately by reason of the exigencies of the situation which such pendency itself calls for).

[18] *Asgarali Nazarali* v. *Bombay* (1957) S.C.R. 678, ('57) A.SC. 503 (the offences of bribery and corruption having become rampant and it being necessary to enact measures for eliminating all possible delay in bringing offenders to book, provisions for a speedy trial were founded on a valid classification); *Macherla Hanumantha Rao* v. *A.P.* (1958) S.C.R. 396, ('57) A.SC. 927 (ss. 207 and 207-A, Cr.P.C., which prescribe a different procedure for committing the accused to the Sessions Court, are based on the relevant consideration whether or not there had been a previous inquiry by a responsible public servant whose duty it was to discover crime and to bring criminals to speedy justice).

Bombay Police Act and the procedure under the ordinary law;[19] the provisions of s. 4, Prevention of Corruption Act, which on proof of certain facts, raised a presumption in the case of Government servants who were charged with the offences of bribery and corruption;[20] the proviso to s. 421 (1), Cr.P.C., in so far as it denied an opportunity to be heard to a convicted person in jail, before the Court dismissed his appeal summarily, while such an opportunity was given to a convicted person who presented his appeal in person or to a convicted person appearing through an Advocate.[21] It is submitted that though, as stated in the judgment, a person in jail who cannot appear in person, or through an Advocate, occupies a different position from that of a convicted person who can appear in person or through an Advocate, this difference is not rationally related to the right of the person to be heard in a judicial proceeding before the matter is decided against him, and the provision is discriminatory. The provisions of the M.B. Panchayat Act were upheld first, because the departure from ordinary procedure laid down in the Cr.P.C. was neither substantial nor real. The changes were so minor that they did not really prejudice the accused. Only minor offences were triable by the Panchayat and the punishment inflicted was also small, namely a fine of 100 rupees. These factors furnished a basis for a valid classification.[22] The different procedures prescribed by ss. 3 and 7 of the Suppression of Immoral Traffic in Women and Girls Act, 1956, which provided for the punishment of persons guilty of offences of carrying on prostitution near any place of public religious worship, educational institution, hostel, hospital, nursing home or such other public place or of being a keeper of premises allowed to be used for purpose aforesaid, and the provisions of s. 18 which provide for the attachment of premises used for the purposes of prostitution as aforesaid dealt with two distinct classes of cases.[23] Again, ss. 131 and 132 of the Income-tax Act, 1961, did not violate Art. 14 because the different procedures prescribed by them did not operate on the same field.[24] In *Batahari Jena* v. *State*[25] it was held that two sets of rules operating simultaneously relating to compulsory retirement of government servants, one of which was more stringent and harsh, were not necessarily violative of Art. 14.[26] In

---

19 *Gurbachan Singh* v. *Bombay* (1952) S.C.R. 737, ('52) A.SC. 221; fol. in *Raja Sukhnandan* v. *State* ('72) A.A. 498, 502 (upholding s. 3, U.P. Control of Goonda Act, 1971 which prescribed a different procedure for dealing with goondas from that prescribed by the Cr.P.C.)

20 *Shri C. I. Emden* v. *U.P.* (1960) 2 S.C.R. 592, ('60) A.SC. 548 (the difficulty of bringing home the charge and the need of eradicating bribery and corruption among public servants justified the classification of Government servants charged with bribery and corruption in a separate class).

21 *Pratap Singh* v. *V.P.* (1961) 2 S.C.R. 509, ('61) A.SC. 586.

22 *Khachu* v. *M.P.* ('64) A.M.P. 239.

23 *Sub-Divisional Magistrate, Delhi* v. *Ram Kali* ('68) A.SC. 1, 5, (1968) 1 S.C.R. 205 [*held*, that ss. 3 and 7 dealt with the punishment of offences whereas s. 18 provided for preventive action with the result that there was a valid classification justifying two distinct procedures. The challenge under Art. 19(1)(*d*)(*e*) and (*f*) was not pressed. The challenge under Art. 19(1)(*f*) and (*g*) had been repelled.]

24 *Chiranji Lal* v. *R. Prasad* ('67) A.Raj. 61.

25 ('68) A.Or.44.

26 ibid. p. 56 (*held*, that both sets of rules were equally applicable to all employees, without discrimination. *Held*, further, that conditions under which the two sets of rules came into play were different).

Ramtanu Co-op. Housing Society v. *Maharashtra*[27] it was held that the provisions of the Maharashtra Industrial Development Act, 1961, relating to acquisition of land did not create a procedural discrimination *vis-a-vis* the Land Acquisition Act. The Land Acquisition Act was a general Act and provided, *inter alia,* for acquisition by companies. The Maharashtra Act was a special Act for the sole purpose of development of industrial areas through the agency of a corporation. The two Acts were not similar in situations and circumstances.[28] In *In re P. Bapanaiah*[29] it was held that the impugned R. 126-P[30] was not discriminatory when compared to s. 256(2) Cr.P.C. which prescribed a maximum imprisonment of six months. Having regard to the object of the Defence of India Act which provided for a national emergency, higher punishment was necessary to effectuate its object, and the difference in punishment was based on a valid classification. However, a question of authorities being able to resort to two remedies cannot arise where the law providing a special procedure bars the jurisdiction of the civil or revenue courts to entertain a suit or proceeding in relation to the matter covered by that law.[31]

Different procedures first held invalid, but later held valid: Service cases

9.87 In the following cases, the Supreme Court first held that the different procedures prescribed by a law or by different laws were discriminatory, but later distinguished those cases holding that such provisions were not discriminatory:

(*a*) The dismissal of a Government servant under "Tribunal Rules" which did not provide for an appeal against the finding of the Tribunal, was discriminatory because an appeal was available to a Government servant against whom a disciplinary inquiry was held under "Service Rules".[32] However, first, in *Jagannath Prasad Sharma* v. *U.P.*[33] and then, in *Orissa* v. *Bidyabhushan Mohapatra,*[34] the Supreme Court held that the absence of a right of appeal from one of the two sets of service rules was not discriminatory. In *Sharma's Case,* the earlier case was distinguished on the ground that it was there conceded that the rules were discriminatory and the only question to be decided was whether at the relevant time only one set of rules was in force. It is submitted that this distinction is not correct and that the Supreme Court came to an independent conclusion that such rules were discriminatory:

> "The Tribunal Rules do contemplate an inquiry by a person not connected with the department of the public servant and the rules also provide that before passing an order to the prejudice of the public servant concerned, the Public Service Commission shall be consulted, but those compensatory safeguards do not, *in our judgment,* make the procedure prescribed by the Tribunal Rules any the less discriminatory."[35] (italics supplied)

---

[27] ('70) A.SC. 1771, (1971) 1 S.C.R. 719.
[28] ('70) A.SC. at p. 1777. [29] ('70) A.A.P. 47.
[30] Of Defence of India (Part XII-A) Gold Control Rules, 1962.
[31] *Dasaudha Singh* v. *Haryana* ('73) A.SC. 710, 714, (1973) 2 S.C.R. 1006 (*held,* that the provisions of s. 7 read with s. 11, E.P. Utilization of Lands Act, 1949, which might result in the eviction of a tenant, if he failed to deliver the property to the owner or to the person specified in the order did not violate Art. 14. The Act did not leave the authorities free to pursue two or more remedies, since s. 14-A of the Act barred the jurisdiction of civil or revenue courts).
[32] *Orissa* v. *Dhirendra Nath Das* ('61) A.SC. 1715.
[33] (1962) 1 S.C.R. 151, ('61) A.SC. 1245.
[34] (1963) 1 S.C.R. 648, ('63) A.SC. 779.
[35] *Orissa* v. *Dhirendra Nath Das, supra* ('61) A.SC. at p. 1717.

It is submitted that the earlier decision was correct because the right of appeal has always been held to be a valuable substantive right and if that right is denied under one set of rules, that set of rules is disadvantageous to the Government servant and therefore on the principles laid down in a long line of cases,[36] proceedings under those rules must be held to be discriminatory. Submission: earlier decision correct

(*b*) In *Bidi Supply Co.* v. *Union*[37] the majority judgment held that s. 5(7-A) read with s. 22(2) of the Income-tax Act did not authorise an omnibus transfer of cases, and consequently it was not necessary to consider the constitutional validity of s. 5(7-A). As the Income-tax authorities had by an illegal executive order picked out the petitioner and transferred all his cases by an order unlimited in point of time, the order was clearly discriminatory as it inflicted considerable inconvenience and harassment on the petitioner as compared with other bidi merchants who were similarly situated. Bose J. concurred in the result, but he held that ss. 5(7-A) and 64(5)(*b*) of the Income-tax Act were *ultra vires* and void as offending against Art. 14. He repeated his criticism of the theory of classification[38] and held that "power given to authorities to be exercised on their subjective satisfaction would render fundamental rights pointless".[39] However, in *Pannalal Binjraj* v. *Union*[40] it was held that the harassment and inconvenience caused to an assessee by a transfer of his case to an area in which he would not ordinarily be assessed was not conclusive. The right to be assessed in a particular locality was not an absolute right but had to yield to the exigencies of tax collection. The power to transfer cases was vested in high public authorities and though it was discretionary, discretionary power was not necessarily discriminatory. Besides, there was a presumption that public acts were properly performed.[41] Accordingly, it was held that the transfer of cases did not involve a violation of Art. 14. If the decision had been rested on the above grounds it would not be open to serious question, but Bhagwati J. went further and held that the discretion vested in public officers ". . . had to be looked at from two points of view, namely, (1) Does it admit of the possibility of any real and substantial discrimination, and (2) Does it impinge on a fundamental right guaranteed by the Constitution. Art. 14 can be invoked only if both these conditions are satisfied."[42] It is submitted that the second test overlooks the fact that Art. 14 itself confers a fundamental right and it is not necessary for a person asserting that right to prove that another fundamental right of his has been violated. Again, in dealing with the objection that the *mala fide* exercise of discretion is well-nigh impossible to prove, Bhagwati

Income-tax Cases; *Bidi Supply Co.'s Case*

Pannalal Binjraj's Case

A criticism of two points decided in the case, though the decision is correct

---

[36] See para 9.76 *et sqq.*
[37] (1956) S.C.R. 267, ('56) A.SC. 479.
[38] See para 9.32, *f.n.* 88.
[39] This view of Bose J. has not been accepted in subsequent decisions.
[40] (1957) S.C.R. 233, ('57) A.SC. 397.
[41] The principle that discretionary power is not discriminatory and abuse of power is not to be presumed was applied in *Kishan Das* v. *Delhi Development Authority* ('64) A.Punj. 384 [upholding s. 64(*a*) U.P.Town Improvement Act, 1919, as applied to Delhi]; fol. in *C. Lingam* v. *Union* ('71) A.SC. 474, 477, (1971) 2 S.C.R. 871 (the power to grant a permit was vested in high ranking officers, namely, the Dist. Collector and the Deputy Commr. of Civil Supplies).
[42] (1957) S.C.R. *supra* at p. 262.

J. observed that the proof required was a *prima facie* proof and he referred to *R.* v. *Carr-Briant*.[43] It is difficult to see the applicability of that case.[44] It is settled law that allegations of *mala fides* must be strictly proved and the practical impossibility of discharging that burden has been judicially recognized.[45] Further, the relevant data to prove that there are other persons similarly situated would be with the income-tax office, and rival traders are unlikely to confide their income-tax liabilities to a petitioner who alleges that they are more favourably treated. If the power to transfer cases is to be upheld, it must be on the ground that the discretion has to be exercised for the purposes of the Act, and it is reasonable and necessary that such a discretion should be conferred for the proper assessment and collection of income-tax.

Cases in which different procedures were held invalid:

9.88 In the following cases, it was held that the different procedures prescribed by the impugned law or laws violated Art. 14 since persons similarly situated were treated differently to the prejudice of some of them:

Income-tax cases

(*a*) S. 34, Income-tax Act, 1922, and s. 5 (4), Taxation of Income (Investigation Commission) Act, 1947, deal with all persons who have similar characteristics, namely, that they have not truly disclosed their income and have evaded payment of tax on income. As the procedure prescribed by the Taxation of Income (Investigation Commission) Act, 1947, was substantially more drastic and therefore prejudicial to the assessee, than that under the Indian Income-tax Act, s. 5 (4) and the procedure prescribed by the impugned Act, in so far as it affected the persons proceeded against under s. 5 (4) was void as violating Art. 14.[46] As a result of this decision, s. 34, Income-tax Act was amended by the Indian Income-tax (Amendment) Act, 1954, and the effect of that amendment was canvassed in cases (*b*) and (*c*) below.

(*b*) S. 34, Income-tax Act, as amended by the Indian Income-tax (Amendment) Act, 1954, operated on the same field as s. 5 (1), Taxation of Income (Investigation Commission) Act, 1947. Assuming that the provisions of s. 5 (1) were based on a rational classification, they became void and unenforceable under Art. 14 because the procedure prescribed by the Taxation of Income (Investigation Commission) Act, 1947, was more drastic, and therefore prejudicial to the assessee, than that contained in the Income-tax Act.[47]

---

[43] (1943) K.B. 607, (1943) 2 All E.R. 156.

[44] It was there held that when either by statute or common law, some matter was presumed against an accused person, "unless the contrary is proved", the jury should be directed that the burden of proof on the accused was less than that required at the hands of the prosecution in proving the case beyond a reasonable doubt and that this burden may be discharged by evidence satisfying the jury of the probability of that which the accused is called upon to establish.

[45] ". . . no doubt he (i.e. the person exercising the power) must not exercise the power in bad faith, but the field in which this kind of question arises is such that the reservation in the case of bad faith is hardly more than a formality." *Per* Lord Radcliffe in *Nakkuda Ali* v. *M.F.de S. Jayaratne* (1951) A.C.66, 67.

[46] *Suraj Mall Mohta & Co.* v. *A. V. Vishwanatha Sastri* (1955) 1 S.C.R. 448, ('54) A.SC. 545, rel. on in *Lakshmi Bags Mfg. Co.* v. *State* ('69) A.Mys. 295 [*held*, that s. 12A, Mysore Sales Tax Act, 1957 (before the amendment of s. 22 of the Act) was void as violating Art. 14].

[47] *Meenakshi Mills Ltd., Madurai* v. *A. V. Vishwanatha Sastri* (1955) 1 S.C.R. 787, ('55) A.SC. 13.

(c) S. 5(1), Taxation of Income (Investigation Commission) Act, 1947, was based on a rational classification because "substantial evaders of income-tax" formed a class by themselves. Had s. 34(1), Income-tax Act, not been amended in 1948 and in 1954, the Court would have upheld the validity of s. 5(1) following *A Thangal Kunju Musaliar* v. *M. Venkitachalam Potti.*[48] However, as a result of the two amendments, s. 5(1) and s. 34(1) applied to the same class of persons and the fact that the cases of some persons had been referred before 1st September, 1948, to the Income-tax Investigation Commission did not constitute such persons into a separate class requiring different treatment. As the procedure prescribed by the Taxation of Income (Investigation Commission) Act, 1947, was more drastic and therefore prejudicial to the assessee, as compared with the procedure under the Income-tax Act, s. 5(1) violated Art. 14 and was void.[49]

(d) Ss. 37(1) and 37(2), Income-tax Act, 1922, contained distinct and independent powers covering the same subject and answering the same purpose. As the power under s. 37(2) was much more drastic and onerous than the power under s. 37(1), s. 37(2) violated Art. 14 and was *ultra vires* and void.[50]

(e) S. 10(3) and (4) of the Rajasthan Entertainments Tax Act, 1957, provided two methods for dealing with offences mentioned in cls. (*a*) to (*e*) of s. 10, and as s. 10(4) gave no guidance for the exercise of power conferred by sub-sec. (4), and as s. 10(3) conferred unguided and absolute discretion, s. 10(3) violated Art. 14 and was void.[51]

Removal of a member of a Municipality

(f) S. 14(*e*), Punjab Municipalities Act, 1911, entirely covered s. 16(1) of that Act. S. 16(1) provided for the removal of a member of the Municipality in the public interest and s. 14(*e*) also made the provision for such removal in the public interest. However, whereas under s. 16, provision was made for hearing the member to be removed, no such provision was made by s. 14(*e*) which was therefore more drastic than s. 16(1) and as Government could resort to either section, s. 14(*e*) was clearly discriminatory.[52]

---

[48] (1955) 2 S.C.R. 1190, ('56) A.SC. 246 [it was held in that case that s. 5(1), Travancore Taxation on Income (Investigation Commission) Act, 1947, and s. 47(1), Travancore Income-tax Act 1121 (which corresponded to s. 34(1), Indian Income-tax Act as it stood before its amendment in 1948) did not cover the same field and that therefore s. 5(1), Travancore Act did not violate Art. 14].

[49] *M. Ct. Muthiah* v. *C.I.T. Madras* (1955) 2 S.C.R. 1247, ('56) A.SC. 269; In *Ranjit Singh* v. *I.T.C.* (1962) 1 S.C.R. 966, ('62) A.SC. 92, the above cases were distinguished on the ground that they dealt with the operation of a discriminatory procedure under the different provisions of the Taxation of Income (Investigation Commission) Act, 1947, after the commencement of the Constitution, whereas in the case before the Court the settlement of the petitioner's tax liability had been effected before the coming into effect of the Constitution, and as the Constitution was not retrospective, the settlement and the steps taken for its enforcement could not be set aside as violating Art. 14. The procedure prescribed for the enforcement of the settlement by s. 8(*a*)(2) of the Act was not discriminatory as it applied equally to all persons in the same class. Again, it was open to the Legislature to make a law as to how particular government dues were to be recovered and if the law applied equally to all persons similarly situated it was not open to question under Art. 14.

[50] *S. Doongarmal Agency* v. *K. E. Johnson* ('64) A.Ass. 1 (F.B.) (*per* Naidu and Dutta JJ., Mehrotra C.J. dissenting).

[51] *Galbaji* v. *C.T.O., Sirohi* ('71) A.Raj. 106, 109.

[52] *Ram Dial* v. *Punjab* (1965) 2 S.C.R. 858, ('65) A.SC. 1518.

Acquisition of property under different laws

9.89 In *P. Vajravelu Mudaliar* v. *Dy. Collector*[53] the Land Acquisition (Madras) Amendment Act, 1961 was struck down not on the ground that the compensation was inadequate, which it obviously was, but on the ground that two laws were in force in the State providing for land acquisition: that contained in s. 23, Land Acquisition Act, 1894, for acquisition of land generally and the other, the amended provisions of the Land Acquisition Act which applied only to the acquisition of land for housing purposes. The Supreme Court held that there was no reasonable classification to justify this distinction. The amended Act treated persons similarly situated differently by the mere accident that the land of some persons was required for purposes of housing and of others for other purposes. Thus, if waste land was acquired for purposes of building a network of hospitals or for buildings required by a University and the mere accident that it was wanted for one purpose rather than another was not relevant for determining the compensation for land, which was of the same quality. *Vajravelu's Case* was followed in *Balammal* v. *Madras*[54] and the Supreme Court held that the impugned law[55] violated Art. 14, since it deprived the owners of property, acquired for the Town Expansion Scheme, of the 15 per cent solatium provided in the Land Acquisition Act, 1894.[56] In *Nagpur Improvement Trust* v. *Vithal Rao*[57] the Supreme Court followed the above cases and held that the impugned law[58] violated Art. 14. Article 14 conferred an individual right, and ordinarily, Land Acquisition laws, which provided for compensation varying with the public purpose for which the land was acquired were not based on a valid classification, since such laws enabled owners of land similarly situated to be treated differently. To the owner of land the purpose for which the land was acquired was immaterial.[59] The position would be different where the owner of land himself was the recepient of benefits from an improvement scheme, and the benefit to him was taken into consideration in fixing compensation.[60] In *Gujarat* v. *Shantilal*,[61] *Vajravelu's Case* was distinguished, and it was held that ss. 53 and 67 of the Bombay Town Planning Act, 1955 did not violate Art. 14 because the method of determining compensation in respect of lands which were subject to the Town Planning Scheme was prescribed by the Act, and there was no option under that Act to acquire

---

53 (1965) 1 S.C.R. 614, ('65) A.SC. 1017.

54 (1969) 1 S.C.R. 90, ('68) A.SC. 1425.

55 Cl. 6(2) of the Schedule to the Madras City Improvement Trust Act, 1950 read with s. 73.

56 ('68) A.SC. *supra* at pp. 1428-9.

57 (1973) 3 S.C.R. 39, ('73) A.SC. 689.

58 Paras 10(2) and 10(3) of the Schedule to the Nagpur Improvement Trust Act in so far as they added a new clause 3(*a*) to s. 23 and a proviso to s. 23(2) of the Land Acquisition Act, 1894.

59 ('73) A.SC. *supra* at p. 693.

60 ibid. p. 693. The argument that the view taken in the judgment would prevent social objectives from being achieved, and that paying a smaller amount in some cases only took into account the unearned increment in increase of land value, was met by saying that if the object of the law was to tax unearned increment, then all unearned increment should be taxed and not only the unearned increment of some owners of land leaving other owners untouched: ibid. p. 694.

61 ('69) A.SC. 634, 654, (1969) 3 S.C.R. 341.

the land either under the Land Acquisition Act or under the Town Planning Act.

9.90 The question of two procedures came to a head when the results of the majority judgment in the *Northern India Caterers Ltd.* v. *Punjab*[62] (*"the Caterers' Case"*) made themselves felt and led to its being overruled in *Maganlal Chhaganlal* v. *Municipal Corpn., Greater Bombay*[63] (*"the Municipal Corpn. Case"*). We will consider, first, the majority and minority judgments in the *Caterers' Case*; secondly, the results which flowed from the majority judgment in that case; and, finally, the constitutional doctrine which emerged from the overruling of the *Caterers' Case* in the *Municipal Corpn. Case*.

Two procedures: *Caterers' Case* and its subsequent overruling

9.91 In the *Caterers' Case* the appellants were required to show cause under s. 4, Punjab Public Premises and Land (Eviction and Rent Recovery) Act, 1959, why they should not be evicted as unauthorised occupants of government premises called "Mount View Hotel", which had been leased to them. The appellants impugned s. 5 of the Act as violating Art. 14, on the ground that the procedure there prescribed was more prejudicial than the ordinary procedure of an ejectment suit, and government could arbitrarily adopt one of the two procedures. Shelat J. delivering the majority judgment[64] upheld this contention. He held that even assuming that occupants of premises belonging to Government or local authorities formed a different class from occupants of premises belonging to other landlords, decisions of the Supreme Court[65] had established ". . . that discrimination would result if there are two available procedures one more drastic or prejudicial to the party concerned than the other and which can be applied at the arbitrary will of the authority."[66]

Caterers' Case: majority judgment

9.92 In a dissenting judgment of remarkable cogency and grasp of the underlying principles of decided cases, Bachawat J. said that Art. 14 did not "require a fanatical approach to the problem of equality before the law." He held that:

Caterers' Case: Bachawat J.'s dissenting judgment

(*a*) Art. 14 permitted Government being treated differently in matters of substantive and procedural law as by providing a longer period of limitation for suits by Government,[67] conferring on Government priority in payment of its claims,[68] exempting Government from the provisions of rent control legislation as regards government buildings whilst protecting Government as a lessee of non-Government buildings;[69]

(*b*) "It is settled by our previous decisions that the Revenue Recovery Acts and other Acts creating special tribunals and procedure for the expeditious recovery of revenue and State dues are in the public interest and do not violate

[62] (1967) 3 S.C.R. 399, ('67) A.SC. 1581.

[63] (1975) 1 S.C.R. 1, ('74) A.SC. 2009, 1974 (2) S.C.C. 402; foll. in *Gujarat* v. *Patel Bava Karsan* ('80) A.SC. 1144 and *Amathabhai* v. *C. D. Patel* ('82) A.SC. 782, 783.

[64] For himself, Subba Rao C.J. and Vaidyalingam J.

[65] *W.B.* v. *Anwar Ali Sarkar* (1952) S.C.R. 284, ('52) A.SC. 75; *Suraj Mall Mohta & Co.* v. *A. V. Visvanatha Sastri* (1955) 1 S.C.R. 448, ('54) A.SC. 545; *Banarsi Das* v. *Cane Commr., U.P.* (1963) Supp. 2 S.C.R. 760, ('63) A.SC. 1417.

[66] ('67) A.SC. *supra* at p. 1587.

[67] *Nav Rattanmal* v. *Rajasthan* (1962) 2 S.C.R. 324, ('61) A.SC. 1704.

[68] *Builders Supply Corpn.* v. *Union* (1965) 2 S.C.R. 289, ('65) A.SC. 1061.

[69] *Baburao Shantaram More* v. *Bombay Housing Board* (1954) S.C.R. 572, ('54) A.SC. 153.

Art. 14[70] . . . If quick recovery of revenue is in the public interest, expeditious recovery of State property from which revenue is derived is, a *fortiori* in the public interest. The impugned Act has properly devised a special machinery for the speedy recovery of premises belonging to the Government;"[71]

(c) A classification between premises belonging to Government, District Boards, Municipal Committees, Notified Area Committees and Panchayats on the one hand and premises belonging to private persons on the other had reasonable relation to the object of the Act and a similar classification had been upheld in *Baburao Shantaram More* v. *Bombay Housing Board*;[72, 73]

(d) On the question whether Art. 14 was violated by an option given to Government to proceed under the impugned Act, the decisions of the Supreme Court on the Revenue Recovery Acts were conclusive in favour of Government that Art. 14 was not violated;[74]

(e) "Without violating Art. 14, the law may allow a litigant a free choice of remedies, proceedings and tribunals for the redress of his grievances. The plaintiff may have a choice of claiming specific relief or damages. As *dominus litis*, he has the option of suing in one of several courts having concurrent jurisdiction, and the defendant cannot insist that he must be sued at a place where he can more conveniently carry on the litigation. The plaintiff may even fix the original and appellate forums on the basis of his own arbitrary valuation. For a suit on a negotiable instrument, he may instead of choosing the ordinary procedure, adopt the summary procedure of Order XXXVII of the Code of Civil Procedure and shut out the defence altogether unless leave to defend is obtained. A landlord may evict a tenant by a suit or by a summary proceeding under Chap. VII of the Presidency Small Cause Courts Act. An aggrieved party may be free to choose one of several types of tribunals and modes of proceeding. He may obtain a rectification of the share register by a suit or by an application to the Court taking company matters or by appealing to an administrative tribunal against the refusal of the company to register the transfer of shares."[75]

(f) "The law does not violate Art. 14 because it gives an aggrieved party the free choice of remedies and proceedings for the redress of his grievances. In *Arizona Copper Co.* v. *Hammer*[76] . . . Pitney J. said, 'election of remedies is an option very frequently given by the law to a person entitled to an action — an option normally exercised to his own advantage as a matter of course'."[77]

(g) The Supreme Court of India had struck down harsh, oppressive and unjust laws giving the Government an arbitrary power of directing a summary trial of offences by a special criminal court instead of trial by the ordinary courts or laws subjecting assessees to the inquisitorial procedure of the Taxation of Income (Investigation Commission) Act, 1947. But even in such cases, the Supreme Court had observed that if there had been a provision for reviewing the conclusion of the Investigation Commission, the Act might have been sustained.[78] Even an Act giving the executive an option of sending a case for trial by a special criminal court is not necessarily violative of Art. 14.[79] "We have upheld an Act empowering an administrative tribunal trying an offence to send the case to a court for trial if the case deserves more severe punishment: *Shanti Prasad Jain* v. *Director of Enforcement* (1963) 2 S.C.R. 297, 303-4, ('62) A.SC. 1764."[80]

---

70 ('67) A.SC. *supra* at p. 1589, citing *Manna Lal* v. *Collector of Jhalawar* (1961) 2 S.C.R. 962, ('61) A.SC. 828; *Nav Rattanmal* v. *Rajasthan* (1962) 2 S.C.R. *supra* at p. 332; *Collector of Malabar* v. *Erimal Ebrahim Hajee* (1957) S.C.R. 970, ('57) A.SC. 688; *Purshottam Govindji Halai* v. *B. M. Desai* (1955) 2 S.C.R. 887, ('56) A.SC. 20; *Lachhman Das* v. *Punjab* (1963) 2 S.C.R. 353, ('63) A.SC. 222.

71 ('67) A.SC. *supra* at p. 1589.

72 (1954) S.C.R. 572, *supra*.

73 ('67) A.SC. *supra* at p. 1589.

74 ibid.

75 ibid. at pp. 1589-90.

76 (1918) 250 U.S. 400, 63 L. ed. 1058.

77 ('67) A.SC. *supra* at p. 1590.

78 *Suraj Mall Mohta & Co.* v. *A. V. Visvanatha Sastri* (1955) 1 S.C.R. *supra* at p. 466.

79 Citing *Kanshari Haldar* v. *W.B.* (1960) 2 S.C.R. 646, ('60) A.SC. 457.

80 See ('67) A.SC. *supra* at p. 1589.

(*h*) The impugned Act was not unfair or oppressive. The unauthorised occupant had the full opportunity of being heard and of producing his evidence before the collector and of obtaining a review of the Collector's order by an appeal to the commissioner, and in appropriate cases, he could apply for a writ of *certiorari* from the High Court: "If we strike down the Act, we shall be giving a free charter to unauthorized occupants and to officers squatting on public premises after they have vacated their offices to continue in occupation for an indefinite time until they are evicted by dilatory procedure of a title suit."[81]

(*i*) The argument based upon the option of the Government to file a suit was unreal because in practice Government was unlikely to file a suit in a case where it could seek relief under the Act.[82]

Submission: dissenting judgment is unanswerable

He upheld the Act as it did not suffer from any blemish. The reasons given in the dissenting judgment have been set out at length because, it is submitted, they are unanswerable, and the majority judgment made no attempt to answer them or to deal with the cases on which they were based. However, it would save repetition if the unassailable character of the reasons given by Bachawat J. and the correctness of his approach to the problem of equality, are considered after we have discussed the *Municipal Corpn. Case.*

Caterers' Case overruled by *Municipal Corpn. Case*

9.93-94 The question for decision in the *Municipal Corpn. Case* was whether the provisions of Chapter V-A of the Bombay Municipal Corporation Act, as also of the Bombay Government Premises (Eviction) Act, 1955 (before its amendment as a result of the *Caterers' Case*), which provided a special procedure for evicting an unauthorised occupant from Municipal premises, and for evicting a person from Government premises,[85] violated Art. 14 because it was open to the prescribed authorities either to resort to the special procedure for eviction or to file a suit. The appellant relied on the *Caterers' Case* as concluding the appeal in his favour. Three judgments were delivered: the leading majority judgment by Alagiriswami J. for himself, Ray C.J. and Palekar and Mathew JJ., and a concurring judgment by Bhagwati J. for himself and Krishna Iyer J. Both these judgments overruled the *Caterers' Case.*[86] Khanna J., after an elaborate discussion of the circumstances under which the Supreme Court would be justified in overruling its earlier decision, held that "no sufficient ground had been shown for overruling the view expressed by the majority in the (*Caterers' Case*)"[87] though he concurred in dismissing the appeal because the procedure prescribed by the impugned provisions was not onerous or drastic when compared with that contained in the C.P.C.

---

[81] ibid. at p. 1590. [82] ibid.

[83] *Per* Alagiriswami J. in the *Municipal Corpn. Case* 1974 (2) S.C.C. *supra* at p. 412. He referred to *Abdul Rashid* v. *Asst. Engineer (Highways)* ('70) A.M. 387; *M. Begum* v. *State* ('71) A.A.P. 382; *Meherunnisa Begum* v. *A.P.* (1970) Andh.L.T. 88; *Bhartiya Hotel* v. *Union* ('68) A.P. 476.

[84] *Per* Alagiriswami J., 1974 (2) S.C.C. *supra* at p. 412.

[85] ibid. pp. 409-10 (Alagiriswami J.) and pp. 428-31 (Bhagwati J.) where a summary of the relevant statutory provisions is given.

[86] ibid. p. 423: "We, therefore, find ourselves unable to agree with the majority in the (*Caterers' Case*)", *per* Alagiriswami J.; ibid p. 450: "We are of the view that the decision in (the *Caterers' Case*) does not present the correct law, and must be overruled", *per* Bhagwati J.

[87] ibid. pp. 427-8.

Submission: the difference in the approach to Art. 14 —Alagiriswami J.'s approach is correct

9.95 We must notice at the outset that the leading majority judgment and the concurring judgment disclose an important difference in their approach to Art. 14. Alagiriswami J. repeated the words of Bachawat J. that "Article 14 does not require a fanatical approach".[88] It is submitted that this view is clearly right, and its repudiation by Bhagwati J. in the following passage is clearly wrong. He said:

"But the point we wish to make, and we cannot over-emphasise it, that Art. 14 enunciates a vital principle which lies at the core of our republicanism and shines like a beacon light pointing towards the goal of classless egalitarian socio-economic order which we promised to build ourselves when we made a tryst with destiny on that fateful day when we adopted our Constitution. If we have to choose between fanatical devotion to this great principle of equality and feeble allegiance to it, we would unhesitatingly prefer to err on the side of the former as against the latter. We should be breaking our faith with this high and noble principle which is pregnant with hope for the common man and which is at once a goal as well as a pursuit, for history shows that it is by insidious encroachments made in the name of pragmatism and expediency that freedom and liberty are gradually but imperceptibly eroded and we should not allow the same fate to overtake equality and egalitarianism in the name of expediency and practical convenience."[89]

Submission: the approach of Bhagwati J. is clearly erroneous

9.96 That "Art. 14 . . . shines like a beacon light pointing towards the goal of *classless egalitarian socio-economic order* which *we promised to build for ourselves* when we made a tryst with destiny . . . *when we adopted our Constitution*" (italics supplied) is simply not true. The legislative history (i) of the property provisions of the Constitution; (ii) of fundamental rights and the limitations to which those rights were to be subject, and (iii) of the separation of justiciable fundamental rights from non-justiciable directive principles of state policy, shows that grave differences existed between the prominent members of the Constituent Assembly, who helped to fashion our Constitution, as to its social and economic objectives, and the compromise solutions which were finally adopted. "A classless egalitarian socio-economic order" may be the goal of a school of thought or the creed of some political parties. But the Constitution of India no more enacted that goal, or that creed, than the Constitution of the United States enacted Herbert Spencer's Social Statics. This was well brought out by Sastri C.J. in his classic formulation of the test of "reasonableness"[90] in which he reminded judges of "the sobering reflection that the Constitution is meant not only for people of their way of thinking, but for all . . ."[91] Again, the words "classless egalitarian socio-economic order" convey no precise meaning; and the word "classless" is singularly inept with reference to Art. 14, which has been consistently interpreted to mean that persons, equally with things and places, can be put into classes — on which the whole theory of classification is based. Finally, several provisions of the Constitution clearly recognize classes.[92] Again, the observations that "If we have to choose between *fanatical devotion* to this great principle of equality and *feeble allegiance* to it, we would unhesitatingly prefer to err on the side of the former as against the latter" (italics supplied) creates a false antithesis be-

---

[88] ibid. p. 424. [89] ibid. pp. 435-6.
[90] A test which has been repeatedly cited with approval: see Chap. X.
[91] *Madras* v. *V. G. Row* (1952) S.C.R. 596, 607, ('52) A.SC. 196.
[92] See, for example, Art. 15(4); (page A-7); Art. 25(2)(*b*): (page A-11); the privileges conferred on Rulers of Indian States by Arts. 291, 362-63: (see pp. A-96, A-126).

tween "fanatical" and "feeble", and asserts a proposition which could hardly have been intended. A "fanatic" is "a person exhibiting excessive enthusiasm and uncritical devotion usually towards some controversial matter (as in religion, politics or philosophy) and commonly urging his belief zealously and with unreasonable and uncompromising insistence"[93]; hence *fanatical.* Bhagwati J. could hardly have intended to convey that his devotion to the doctrine of equality was excessive and unreasonable, for, reason and judgment are the hallmark of the judicial process. When it is said that "Art. 14 does not require a fanatical approach" what is meant is not that the doctrine of equality should be held "feebly", but that it should be applied reasonably. It has become necessary to say this because the quasi-religious terminology[94] of Bhagwati J.'s passage obscures the central issue, and robs the concurring judgment of much of its value, apart from the fact that the law laid down by the Supreme Court has to be found in the leading majority judgment of Alagiriswami J.

Alagiriswami J.'s review of earlier cases

9.97 We will consider, first, the propositions which emerge from a review of the authorities undertaken by Alagiriswami J. and, secondly, whether the review has clarified the law. The following propositions emerge from the judgment:

The propositions emerging from the Judgment of Alagiriswami J.

(i) Art. 14 does not demand a fanatical approach.[95]

(ii) "It was not and could not be argued that the Acts in so far as they provided for special procedures to the State and the Municipal Corporation were invalid.[96] . . . It cannot now be contended that special provision of law applying to Government and public bodies is not based upon reasonable classification or that it offends Art. 14."[97]

(iii) "One finds it difficult to reconcile oneself to the position that the mere possibility of resort to the Civil Court should make invalid a procedure which would otherwise be valid. It can very well be argued that as long as a procedure does not by itself violate either Art. 19 or Art. 14 and is thus constitutionally valid, the fact that that procedure is more onerous and harsher than the procedure in the ordinary civil Courts, should not make that procedure void merely because the authority competent to take action can resort to that procedure in the case of some and ordinary Civil Court procedure in the case of others. That a constitutionally valid provision of law should be held to be void because there is a possibility of its being resorted to in the case of some and the ordinary Civil Court procedure in the case of others somehow makes one feel uneasy and that has been responsible for the attempts to get round the reasoning which is the basis in the decision in *Northern India Caterers' Case* (supra)."[98]

(iv) A review of Supreme Court decisions (in their chronological order)[99] can be summarized thus: "Where a statute providing for a more drastic procedure different from the ordinary procedure covers the whole field covered by the ordinary procedure, as in *Anwar Ali Sarkar's Case* and *Suraj Mal Mohta's Case* without any guidelines as to the class of cases in which either procedure is to be resorted to, the statute will be hit by Art. 14.

---

[93] Webster, *Third New International Dictionary.*

[94] The word "fanatic" is derived from *fanum,* temple.

[95] 1974 (2) S.C.C. *supra,* p. 424.

[96] ibid. pp. 410-11 [citing cases which had been cited by Bachawat J. (see para 9.91 and *f.ns.* 65 to 70) with the addition of *Asgarali Nazarali Singaporawalla* v. *Bombay* (1957) S.C.R. 678, ('57) A.SC. 503].

[97] 1974 (2) S.C.C. *supra* at p. 411. [98] ibid. pp. 412-13.

[99] *Anwar Ali Sarkar's Case, Kathi Raning Rawat's Case, Lachmandas Ahuja's Case, Suraj Mall Mohta's Case (Shree Meenakshi Mills Case* and *Muthia's Case* being on the same lines as *Suraj Mall Mohta's Case* required no separate discussion), *Thangal Kunju Musaliar's Case; Kedar Nath Bajoria's Case, Kangsari Haldar's Case, Jyoti Pershad's Case.*

Even there, as mentioned in *Suraj Mall Mohta's Case* (*supra*) a provision for appeal may cure the defect. Further, in such cases if from the preamble and surrounding circumstances, as well as the provisions of the statute themselves explained and amplified by affidavits, necessary guidelines could be inferred as in *Saurashtra Case* (*supra*) and *Jyoti Pershad's Case* (*supra*) the statute will not be hit by Art. 14. Then again where the statute itself covers only a class of cases as in *Haldar's Case* (*supra*) and *Bajoria's Case* (*supra*) the statute will not be bad. The fact that in such cases the executive will choose which cases are to be tried under the special procedure will not affect the validity of the statute. Therefore, the contention that the mere availability of two procedures will vitiate one of them, that is the special procedure, is not supported by reason or authority."[1]

(v) As to the impugned Acts (*a*) the purpose behind them, namely, the speedy recovery of Government and Municipal premises gave sufficient guidance to the authorities on whom power was conferred; (*b*) given this guidance, officers would be expected to avail themselves of the speedy procedure under the Acts and not resort to the dilatory procedure of a civil suit; (*c*) "In considering whether the officers would be discriminating between one set of persons and another one has got to take into account normal human behaviour and not behaviour which is abnormal. It is not every fancied possibility of discrimination that we must take into account. . . . Discrimination may be possible but is very improbable."

Alternative procedure not so unconscionable as to attract Art. 14

9.98 Alagiriswami J. reviewed the earlier decisions on the assumption that the impugned Acts provided a harsher procedure which would be prejudicial to the persons governed by it. But after examining the provisions of the impugned Acts, Alagiriswami J. observed:

"On the whole, considering the object with which these special procedures were enacted by the Legislature we would not be prepared to hold that the difference between the two procedures *is so unconscionable as to attract the vice of discrimination.* After all, Art. 14 does not demand a fanatical approach."[2] (italics supplied)

How does the law stand to-day?

9.99 How does the law on two procedures stand to-day? It is unfortunate that Alagiriswami J. did not state to what extent he agreed with Bachawat J. but comparison of the propositions laid down by Bachawat J. and Alagiriswami J. discloses a large measure of agreement. We wll first discuss the law with reference to the propositions emerging from the judgment of Alagiriswami J. which are set out in para 9.97 above.

Propositions common to the judgment of Alagiriswami J. and Bachawat J.:

9.100 As to proposition (i) in para 9.97 above, it adopts the words of Bachawat J. in indicating the correct approach to Art. 14. This approach has important consequences which are not expressly drawn out by Alagiriswami J. but are stated in his judgment as is clear from proposition (v) in para 9.97 above.[3] It is submitted that in laying down the correct approach to Art. 14 and the consequences which flow from it, Alagiriswami J. has given effect to two propositions laid down by Das C.J. in *Dalmia's Case*,[4] and repeatedly accepted thereafter. Thus, the proposition in *Dalmia's Case* that the burden of proving discrimination lies on the person who alleges it means that he must establish that discrimination would be *a certain, or a pro-*

The consequences of the right approach to Art. 14

---

[1] 1974 (2) S.C.C. *supra* at p. 412. [2] ibid. p. 424.

[3] These propositions are implicit in the judgment of Bachawat J. [see para 9.92 (*i*)] in which Bachawat J. brushed aside the argument about the alternative remedy of a suit as unreal and unlikely to be resorted to in practice.

[4] See propositions (*j*) and (*i*) in para 9.32 of the text.

bable, result of the impugned law[5]—it is not enough to establish that discrimination may be a *possible result*. Again, when it is said in *Dalmia's Case* that in order to sustain the constitutionality of a statute the court must have regard to matters of common knowledge, common report and must assume every state of facts which can be conceived,[6] it follows that the court must have regard to normal, and not to abnormal, human behaviour. It is submitted that the majority judgment in the *Caterers' Case* overlooked the fact that though the doctrine of classification and the exercise of discretionary power are analytically distinct, there are some considerations which apply to both the doctrines, as the propositions from *Dalmia's Case* referred to above clearly show.

9.101 As to proposition (ii) in para 9.97 above, it is self-explanatory; but its full import becomes even clearer when read with the propositions from the judgment of Bachawat J. in para 9.92 (*a*) and (*c*) above. As to proposition (iii) in para 9.97 above, it indicates the necessity for a reasonable approach to Art. 14. This is emphasized by the fact that as the majority judgment in the *Caterers' Case* did not adopt such an approach, the various High Courts tried to get over the reasoning of that judgment.

Para 9.97(ii) read with para 9.92 (*a*) and (*c*)

Need for reasonable approach to Art. 14

9.102 As to proposition (iv) in para 9.97 above, so far as it goes, it must be taken as an authoritative statement following on a review of the earlier decisions of the Supreme Court. It is however, submitted that the following observations "where a statute providing for a more drastic procedure different from the ordinary procedure covers the whole field, covered by the ordinary procedure . . . without any guidelines as to the classes of cases in which the other procedure is to be resorted to, the statute will be hit by Art. 14. Even there, as mentioned in *Suraj Mal Mohta's Case* (*supra*) a provision for appeal may cure the defect" merely state what the cases have decided, but do not state the principle on which the exception was made. It is submitted that Bachawat J. stated the principle when he said that the Supreme Court of India had struck down harsh, oppressive and unjust laws giving an arbitrary power of directing a summary trial of the offences by a special criminal court instead of trial by the ordinary courts, or laws subjecting assessees to the inquisitorial process of the Taxation of Income (Investigation Commission) Act, 1947, the Supreme Court observing that even in such cases an appeal or review may have saved it.[7] Bachawat J. also observed that the impugned Act was not unfair or oppressive for the reasons stated in proposition (*h*) in para 9.92. It is submitted that the principles deduced by Bachawat J. in the propositions referred to above is the correct basis for the exception to the rule where the two procedures cover the whole field. It is submitted that Alagiriswami J. has, in

Review of earlier decisions by Alagiriswami J. and Bachawat J.

[5] See s. 3 of the Evidence Act: "A fact is said to be proved when, after considering the matters before it, the Court either believes it to exist, or considers its existence so probable that a prudent man ought, under the circumstances of the particular case, to act upon the supposition that it exists."

[6] *Cf.* s. 114, Evidence Act: "The Court may presume the existence of any fact which it thinks likely to have happened, regard being had to the common course of natural events, human conduct and public and private business, in their relation to facts of the particular case. *Illustrations.* The Court may presume — . . . (*e*) that judicial and official acts have been regularly performed; . . ."

[7] See para 9.92 (*g*) of the text.

fact, adopted that principle when, dealing with the Acts impugned in the *Municipal Corpn. Case*, he said that the difference between the two procedures was not "so unconscionable as to attract the vice of discrimination". The principle, therefore, is that the Court will strike down harsh, oppressive or unconscionable laws prescribing a procedure other than the ordinary procedure.

The Revenue Recovery Acts: the effect of Sup. Ct. decisions upholding them

9.103 It is difficult to account for the fact that Alagiriswami J.'s elaborate review of the authorities leaves out a line of authorities relating to Revenue Recovery Acts which Bachawat J. considered conclusive on the point.[8] Those decisions upheld the summary procedure of recovering public dues although such a procedure did not exclude the ordinary procedure of a suit, or other methods indicated by the Act.[9] If an unbroken line of Supreme Court decisions upheld such an alternative procedure, Bachawat J. rightly held that if recovery of debts due to Government by a summary process did not violate Art. 14, the recovery of public premises which produced such revenue (or which were required for a public purpose)[10] would, *a fortiori*, not violate Art. 14. No doubt, in the revenue recovery cases it does not appear to have been argued that the mere existence of an alternative remedy would violate Art. 14. It may be, that realising this, Bachawat J. pointed out as an independent, supporting argument that "without violating Art. 14 the law may allow a litigant a free choice of remedies, proceedings and tribunals for the redress of his grievance,"[11] and further quoted in support the observation of Pitney J. in *Arizona Copper Co.* v. *Hammer* set out in para 9.92 above.[12] It is submitted that the law laid down by Bachawat J. is

Bachawat J.: Art. 14 not violated by allowing litigants a free choice of remedies

Arizona Copper Co's Case rightly applied by Bachawat J.

[8] See para 9.92, propositions (*b*) and (*d*) of the text.

[9] See Kanga & Palkhivala, *Income Tax*, 6th ed., Vol. I, p. 936, "Modes of Recovery".

[10] The words in parenthesis were not used by Bachawat J., but on principle they are justified.

[11] See para 9.92, proposition (*e*) of the text and *illustrations there given.*

[12] In his concurring judgment in the *Municipal Corpn. Case*, Bhagwati J. said that the observations of Bachawat J. that "without violating Art. 14, the law may allow a litigant a free choice of remedies, proceedings and tribunals for the redress of his grievances" were not borne out by the observation of Pitney J. in *Arizona Copper Co.'s Case* [which Bachawat J. had quoted: see para 9.92(f) above], if it was read in the context of the question to be decided in that case. ". . . What Mr. Justice Pitney had in mind when he made this observation was the existence of several rights to relief arising out of the same act, and not the existence of several remedies in reference to a single right to relief": 1974 (2) S.C.C. *supra*, p. 436. It is submitted, first, that on a fair reading of Pitney J.'s judgment, it is not susceptible of this interpretation. The argument before Pitney J. was that ". . . the Arizona System . . . denies (employers) equal protection because it confers upon the employee *a free choice among several remedies*" (italics supplied). It was this argument which Pitney J. repelled by saying ". . . and election of remedies is an option very frequently given by the law to a person entitled to an action — an option normally exercised to his own advantage as a matter of course." If Pitney J. merely meant that there was no question of different remedies, but only of different rights, it is difficult to believe that he would have effectively concealed his meaning by talking of remedies when he meant rights. Bhagwati J.'s observations as to what Pitney J. had in mind are based on a misconception due mainly to the ambiguity of the word "right". If *A* violates *B's* right, and the law gives *B* a remedy, the remedy has been described as a "sanctioning right" (Salmond, *Jurisprudence*, 12th ed., pp. 100-101) or as a "remedial right" (Paton, *Jurisprudence*, 4th ed., p. 487). However, a sanctioning right or a remedial right has no independent existence; it springs into existence only when a right, which the law recognizes and protects, is violated. In the *Arizona Case*, the employee had the right that injury should not

correct, and the instances which he has given of alternative remedies allowed to litigants directly support his argument: The above discussion will have shown that the propositions laid down by Bachawat J. in his dissenting judgment in the *Caterer's Case* are unanswerable and have the additional advantage of stating the law with a clarity and sharpness which would have been lost by an elaborate formal review of the authorities. The *Municipal Corpn. Case* was followed by the Supreme Court in *Pandya Nadar* v. *T.N.*[13] where the Supreme Court held that the Tamil Nadu Land Encroachments Act, 1905 and its impugned provisions did not violate Art. 14 and the case was covered by the *Municipal Corpn. Case.* These two decisions were followed in *Shrinivasa Kandasari Sugars* v. *State.*[14]

9.104 Now that the majority judgment in the *Caterers' Case* has been overruled, it is not necessary to refer to High Court decisions which followed that judgment, for those decisions are no longer good law. Nor is it necessary to refer to cases which "distinguished" the majority judgment, for, the question of two procedures must now be decided in the light of the leading majority judgment in the *Municipal Corpn. Case.* Decisions which followed or "distinguished" the *Caterers' Case*

9.105 In the following cases, it was held that the impugned law violated Art. 14, as it was not based on a valid classification: Laws held void because they were based on an invalid classification

(*a*) A notification issued under s. 269(1), Cr.P.C., withdrawing a group of cases known as the "Burdwan Test Relief Fraud Case"[15] from a jury. The notification did not disclose any classification on the face of it, but the High Court held that the case possesses ". . . the common features that a mass of evidence regarding the genuineness of thumb impressions regarding the existence or otherwise of person or persons required consideration and this was bound to take such a long time that it would be very difficult if not impossible

be caused to him in the course of his especially dangerous occupation. That right was violated, and he suffered a wrong, when injury was caused to him in the course of his employment. For the violation of his right, the laws of Arizona gave him three remedies — each with advantages and disadvantages of its own — leaving him free to choose *one* of the three remedies, and, normally, he would choose the one most advantageous to himself. When Bhagwati J. described the situation by saying that there were "several *rights* to relief arising from the same act" (italics supplied) he used words which meant the same thing as "several remedies in respect of the same act", for a *remedy* is defined as "the relief (as damages . . .) given by a court for a wrong" (Webster); but the court cannot give a party any relief unless the law gives him a right to that relief. In the case before Bhagwati J., Government's right to the possession of its property was violated by an unauthorized occupant. For the violation of this right, the law gave Government two remedies, one of which it could choose, and normally it would choose the one most advantageous to itself. In principle, the situations in the *Arizona Case* and the *Caterers' Case* were the same, and Bachawat J. rightly interpreted and applied Pitney J.'s observations in the *Arizona Case* to the case before him.

[13] (1975) 1 S.C.R. 333, ('74) A.SC. 2044.

[14] ('76) A.A.P. 93 (*held,* that the two procedures mentioned in ss. 29 and 31 of the Andhra Pradesh State Financial Corporation Act, 1951, did not violate Art. 14. From a combined reading of the Objects and Reasons and several sections of the Act, the requisite guidance could be inferred, especially when a very responsible authority was vested with the power of selecting either of the two procedures. A body like the Financial Corporation would like to act in a realistic manner, keeping in view the interests of the Corporation, industry, commerce and the general public).

[15] *Dhirendra Kumar Mandal* v. *Supdt. and Remembrancer of Legal Affairs* (1955) 1 S.C.R. 224, ('54) A.SC. 424.

for a juror to keep proper measure of the evidence".[16] The Supreme Court held that the suggested classification had no rational basis for there was no reason to believe that the assessors, who assisted the judge instead of jurors, would keep "proper measure of the evidence" more easily than the jurors.[17]

(*b*) S. 36 (1), East Punjab Public Safety Act, 1949, was based on a valid classification of territory into "dangerously disturbed areas" and other areas. However, when the State of Delhi ceased to be a dangerously disturbed area, the continuation of the summons procedure prescribed under s. 36 (1) became clearly discriminatory.[18]

(*c*) A Rule which provided that no person was eligible for appointment for a post of District Munsiff unless he possessed the following qualifications, namely: "that he must be practising as an Advocate of the High Court[19] and must be actually practising in Courts of Civil or Criminal jurisdiction in India for a period of not less than three years" violated Art. 14 and it was not founded on any rational classification related to the duties to be discharged by a District Munsiff. The rule, as framed, could not be supported on the ground that a lawyer of the High Court of Andhra would be familiar with local laws because such a lawyer was eligible for appointment even if he had been actually practising in Civil or Criminal Courts in India, that is, outside Andhra.[20]

(*d*) S. 14, Madhya Pradesh Public Security Measures Act, 1950, in so far as it empowers the State to direct the trial of any case by a special judge.[21]

Cases in which wide discretionary powers were upheld: Criminal law

9.106 In the following cases, discretion conferred in wide general terms has been held not to violate Art. 14 on the ground that the discretionary power there conferred was not capable of being regulated by further rules: wide powers to be exercised on the subjective satisfaction of Government in the discharge of its duty to maintain law and order, such powers, however, not being unguided because they could be exercised only on the State Government, or its delegate, being satisfied that such exercise was necessary for the purposes mentioned in the impugned sections;[22] the power conferred

[16] ibid. pp. 233-34. [17] *Dhirendra's Case, supra.*

[18] *Gopichand* v. *Delhi Administration* (1959) Supp. 2 S.C.R. 87, ('59) A.SC. 609.

[19] As a matter of construction this was held by the Supreme Court to refer to the High Court of Andhra Pradesh.

[20] *Panduranga Rao* v. *Andhra Public Service Commission* (1963) 1 S.C.R. 707, 712, ('63) A.SC. 268.

[21] *Jagjivanram* v. *State* (1952) Nag. 14, ('52) A.Nag. 118. See the editorial note in the A.I.R. suggesting that the case required reconsideration in the light of *Anwar Ali Sarkar's Case,* (1952) S.C.R. 284, ('52) A.SC. 75.

[22] *Virendra* v. *Punjab* (1958) S.C.R. 308, ('57) A.SC. 896 [upholding s. 2, Punjab Special Powers (Press) Act, 1956, Das C.J. said: "The Court is wholly unsuited to gauge the seriousness of the situation for it cannot be in possession of materials which are available only to the Executive Government" and that wide powers to be exercised on the subjective satisfaction of Government could not but be regarded as reasonable restrictions within the meaning of Art. 19(1)(*a*) and (*b*). Swift decision and swift effective action must be of the essence of those powers and the exercise of it must be left to the subjective satisfaction of Government charged with the duty of maintaining law and order. Further, the power was conferred on the State Government and could be delegated by the State Government alone, and if there was abuse of power the action of the executive and not the law would be struck down].

on the Commissioner of Police under s. 27(1), City Police Act;[23] the power conferred by s. 3(1)(*b*), Preventive Detention Act, 1950;[24] the discretionary power conferred on the Vice-Chancellor to impose punishment for the maintenance of discipline under s. 12(5), Allahabad University Act, 1921, and the Statutes made under it;[25] the discretion conferred on the appropriate Government under s. 10, Industrial Disputes Act, to refer an industrial dispute to the one or the other of the authorities set up under the Act. In upholding this discretion, the Supreme Court held that the criteria for exercising the discretion were enacted in the Act itself and it was not possible to lay down further rules for the exercise of that discretion as no two cases of actual or apprehended industrial disputes were alike and in such disputes in a particular establishment or undertaking, each dispute had to be treated according to the situation prevalent in the undertaking;[26] the discretion vested in Government to resort either to s. 5(1)(*a*) or s. 5(1)(*b*), Minimum Wages Act, 1948, to collect the necessary data for fixing a minimum wage;[27] the discretion vested in Government under s. 3 or 4, Orissa Estates Abolition Act, 1951, as the discretion had to be exercised in the light of the policy of the Act which was to abolish the right, title and interest in the land of intermediaries by whatever name called. It was imperative to leave a discretion to Government because it would have been a colossal task to take over all the estates at the same time; it would have broken down the machinery of administration and it would have been difficult to arrange for the requisite finance all at once;[28] the discretion conferred on the President by s. 69(*a*), U.P. Holdings Act, 1916, as it was to be exercised after examining all the circumstances of the case;[29] s. 15, U.P. Consolidation of Holdings Act, 1953, which laid down the principles for the guidance of the discretionary power there conferred, but qualified those principles by the words "as far as possible";[30] the discretionary

Education

Industrial Law

Land legislation

---

[23] *Gurbachan Singh* v. *Bombay* (1952) S.C.R. 737, ('52) A.SC. 221 (*held*, that the law was certainly an extraordinary one, but the object of the law would be wholly defeated if a right to confront or to cross-examine the witness was given to the suspect. The power to initiate proceedings was vested in a very high and responsible officer who was expected to act with caution and impartiality while discharging his duties); *C.B. Boarding & Lodging Co.* v. *Mysore* (1970) 2 S.C.R. 600, ('70) A.SC. 2042, 2048 [*held*, that the power under s. 5(1), Minimum Wages Act, 1948, was conferred not on any petty officer but on the State Government which could be trusted to exercise that power to further the purpose of the Act].

[24] *Mohd. Iqbal* v. *Supdt., Central Jail* ('69) A.Del. 45 [*held*, that s. 3(1)(*b*) applied to all foreigners and there were guiding principles governing the exercise of power by the executive. The power was accompanied by several safeguards].

[25] *Ram Chander* v. *Allahabad University* ('56) A.A. 46; *Wasim Ahmed* v. *Secretary, B.H.S. & I.E., U.P.* ('61) A.A. 290.

[26] *Niemla Textile Finishing Mills Ltd.* v. *2nd. Punjab Tribunal* (1957) S.C.R. 335, ('57) A.SC. 329; *R.S. Navigation Co.* v. *Radha Nath* (1957) 9 Ass. 353, ('60) A.Ass. 39.

[27] *C.B. Boarding & Lodging Co.* v. *Mysore* (1970) 2 S.C.R. 600, ('70) A.SC. 2042 (*held*, that it was not the law that guidance for the exercise of the power should be gathered from the provisions of the Act. Such guidance could also be gathered from the mischief to be remedied, the preamble to the Act or even from the scheme of the Act).

[28] *Biswambhar Singh* v. *Orissa* (1954) S.C.R. 842, ('54) A.SC. 139.

[29] *Seoti Prasad* v. *Raghubir Dutt* ('60) A.A. 273.

[30] *Rani* v. *Dy. Director of Consolidation* ('59) A.A. 525, (1959) A.L.J. 438 (*held*, that the qualifying words were absolutely necessary in view of the fact that the

Municipal law

power conferred on the State Government by s. 47A (3) U.P. Municipalities Act, 1916, as it was limited to considering the two courses indicated in that section and no further rules for the guidance of discretion were feasible because the reasons given by the President may be various;[31] the wide discretion conferred on the State Government under s. 35, Punjab Aid to Industries Act, 1935, where it was not possible for the Legislature to visualise every kind of contingency and where, further, the discretion referred only to a minor matter of procedure not affecting the substantial liability of any individual but merely determining whether an additional mode of recovery was to be resorted to or not;[32] the discretion to fix different freight rates under the powers contained in s. 28, Railways Act, 1890.[33]

Trade, business, etc.

Bishun Narain's Case: Govt. Service

9.107 In *Bishun Narain* v. *U.P.*[34] the Supreme Court held that a Notification which provided the date of retirement of those who had completed 55 years but not 58 years up to December 31, 1961, did not contravene Art. 14 for it treated all persons alike.[35] The Court observed that different government servants had no doubt to retire at different ages but there was no right to be continued in service after the age of superannuation—the retention of public servants after the age fixed for retirement depended upon their efficiency and the exigencies of public service. This decision was followed in *Assam* v. *Premadhar*[36] where the Supreme Court held that a notification allowing the retention of civil servants after superannuation, having regard to the service, and considerations of physical fitness and efficiency, did not violate Art. 14, for it treated all government servants alike.

Cases in which there was sufficient guidance for the exercise of discretionary power: Criminal Law

9.108 In the following cases, the discretion there conferred was held not to be arbitrary and unfettered as the impugned law contained sufficient guidance for the exercise of that discretion: s. 125 of the Army Act which enabled certain officers to decide whether a case should be tried by a Court Martial or by an ordinary Criminal Court;[37] the power conferred on the Director of Enforcement by

---

process of compulsory consolidation was a very difficult and complicated one in the peculiar conditions prevalent in the State. What could be done in one village may not be possible in another).

[31] *Abdul Wajid* v. *U.P.* ('55) A.A. 708.

[32] *Harish Chand* v. *Collector of Amritsar* (1958) Punj. 1390, ('59) A.Punj. 19, 60 P.L.R. 620 (F.B.).

[33] *Ranbir Singh* v. *Chief Commercial Superintendent* ('61) A.Punj. 268, 271, 63 P.L.R. 206 (different transport conditions, geographical location of States, the form of transport facilities available at the destination station and competition with other kinds of transport are some of the factors which require consideration for determining whether the distinctive or territorial treatment is reasonable or not. The general public interest and the effect of charges on the development of the country as a whole are also a good ground for fixing differential rates. There can be no undue preference if there is no competition between the persons favoured and the persons put in a disadvantageous position by the fixing of the impugned rates).

[34] (1965) 1 S.C.R. 693, ('65) A.SC. 1567.

[35] ('65) A.SC. *supra* at p. 1570.

[36] (1971) 1 S.C.R. 503, ('70) A.SC. 1314.

[37] *Ram Sarup* v. *Union* (1964) 5 S.C.R. 931, ('65) A.SC. 247, 251 (*held*, that although s. 125 itself did not give any guidance, there was enough in the policy of the Act to give such guidance. The Court upheld the contention of the Att.-Gen. that if any section of the Act violated Art. 14, or any other fundamental right, it must be taken that the section was a law made by Parliament under Art. 33 abridging such a right).

s. 23D, proviso, of the Foreign Exchange Regulation Act, 1947, to make a complaint to the court, instead of adjudicating the penalty himself;[38] the power to order remand under s. 344, Cr.P.C.;[39] the power conferred by s. 52, Prisons Act, 1894, on the superintendent to forward the case of an individual prisoner to the District Judge;[40] the discretion given to the University Service Commission and, ultimately, to the Chancellor of the University under s. 4, Bihar State Universities (Amendment) Act, 1964;[41] the power conferred by Cl. 3(5) read with Cls. 36 and 15, Kerala Education Bill, as the power was guided by a policy laid down in the Preamble of the Bill and by the more distinct statement of policy in Cls. 3(2)(A), (B) and (C);[42] the discretion conferred by s. 3(3)(*a*)(iv), Minimum Wages Act, 1948;[43] the discretionary power conferred by s. 5, Employee's Provident Fund Act, 1952;[44] the power conferred on the Reserve Bank by s. 38(3)(*b*)(ii), Banking Companies Act, 1949;[45] s. 85 of the Factories Act, 1948;[46] the power conferred by ss. 4 and 6, Land Acquisition Act, 1894, read with s. 3(*f*)(2) as amended by the Bombay Act VII of 1958;[47] the power conferred by s. 18,

Education

Industrial Law

Land acquisition, land laws, land reforms

---

[38] *Rayala Corpn.* v. *Director of Enforcement* (1970) 1 S.C.R. 639, ('70) A.SC. 494 [the court read s. 23(1) to mean that the Director of Enforcement must in the first instance proceed under the principal clause of s. 23D (1); if at any stage of that inquiry he came to the conclusion that the penalty which he could impose was inadequate, only then, and not before, could he file a complaint under the proviso to s. 23D(1). The criterion for making a choice between two procedures was contained in the proviso to s. 23D(1). The Court put this interpretation on the relevant sections on the principle that an interpretation which would make the law valid must be preferred to an interpretation which would make the law void].

[39] *A. Lakshmanrao* v. *Judl. Magistrate, Parvatipuram* (1971) 2 S.C.R. 822, ('71) A.SC. 186 ("the power conferred being judicial, the absence of an express precise standard for determination of the question would not render the section unconstitutional"): ('71) A.SC. *supra* at p. 191.

[40] *State* v. *Chandra Bali Singh* ('60) A.A. 124, (1959) A.L.J. 682 (the power was to be exercised only when the prisoner was guilty of frequently committing jail offences or when the Supdt. was of the opinion that he could not adequately punish the offender).

[41] *Jagdish* v. *Vice-Chancellor, Bihar University* ('65) A.P. 11 (the object of the section was to enable scrutiny to be made of certain appointments within a specified time and discretion was conferred on the authorities to enable them to consider any particular case. There being a presumption of constitutionality it was not enough for the petitioner to allege that the power given under s. 4 was so unreasonable that it violated Art. 14).

[42] *In re The Kerala Education Bill, 1957*, (1959) S.C.R. 995, ('58) A.SC. 956 [the word "may" in sub-cl. 3 meant "If the existence of the purpose is established and the conditions of the exercise of the discretion are fulfilled, the Government would be under an obligation to exercise its discretion in the furtherance of such purpose": *Julius* v. *Lord Bishop of Oxford* (1880) 5 App.Cas. 214].

[43] *Bhikusa Yamasa* v. *A.T.B. Union* (1959) Bom. 1175, ('59) A.B. 299, 61 Bom.L.R. 764 (the section left no scope for the Government to make an arbitrary discrimination between different localities).

[44] *Hindustan Electric Co.* v. *R.P.F. Commr.* ('59) A.Punj. 27 [the power was not without guidance as indicated more particularly by ss. 1(3) and (4), 16(1)(*b*), 16(2) and (6)].

[45] *Reserve Bank of India* v. *Palai Central Bank Ltd.* ('61) A.Ker. 268, 279 (the words "the continuance of the banking company is prejudicial to the interests of its depositors" are ample guidance to the Reserve Bank for the exercise of its discretion whether it should take the company into liquidation by making an application).

[46] *B. Y. Kashatriya (P) Ltd.* v. *Union* (1964) 1 S.C.R. 860, ('63) A.SC. 1591; rel. on in *Raojibhai Savjibhai & Bros.* v. *Gujarat* ('67) A.Guj. 111.

[47] *Sadrudin* v. *J. H. Patwardhan* ('65) A.B. 224 (there are sufficient criteria or safeguards indicated and abuse of discretionary power is not to be presumed).

East Punjab Holdings (Consolidation and Prevention of Fragmentation) Act, 1948, to reserve land for common purposes;[48] s. 14(2), Manipur Land Revenue and Land Reforms Act, 1960;[49] the power to pass an order of removal under s. 7, Punjab Small Towns Act, 1922;[50] the power conferred by s. 17(1) of the Land Acquisition Act;[51] the power conferred by s. 7, Bombay Tenancy and Agricultural Lands Act, 1948;[52] the power conferred on the State Government by s. 1(2), Bihar Khosi Area (Restoration of land to Ryotwari) Act, 1951, to notify certain areas;[53] the discretion conferred on the Competent Authority under s. 19, Slum Areas (Improvement and Slum Clearance) Act, 1956;[54] the provisions of the Bombay Town Planning Act, 1955;[55] the power given to the Municipal Board under s. 128(1), U.P. Municipalities Act, 1916, to impose the taxes there mentioned in any part of the Municipality;[56] the discretion conferred on the State Government by s. 59, Bombay District Municipalities Act, 1901, enabling it to restrain the levy of tax even after its imposition with the sanction of Government;[57] the power conferred on a Municipality by s. 247, U.P. Municipalities Act, 1916;[58] the power to remove encroachment conferred by s. 185, Gujarat Municipalities Act, 1964;[59] the power conferred on the S.T.A. by s. 44(5), Motor Vehicles Act, 1939 (if authorised in that behalf by rules made under s. 68) to delegate such of its powers and functions

Municipal law

Motor Vehicles Act

---

[48] *Basti Ram* v. *Punjab* ('65) A.Punj. 269 (r. 16 of the rules made under the Act provides the requisite fetter).

[49] *Ibotombi* v. *Chief Commr.* ('65) A.Mani. 35 (the power of the Administrator is restricted because he can allot lands only for the purpose of industry or public-utility and not for any other purpose).

[50] *Prithi Chand* v. *Lt.-Governor* ('62) A.H.P. 59 (the power was to be exercised in the light of the policy of the Act, namely, that the order was to be passed if a member was unfit to act or was persistently remiss in the discharge of his duties as a member, and abuse of power was not to be assumed).

[51] *R. L. Arora* v. *U.P.* (1958) 2 All. 184, ('58) A.A. 872 (the power can be exercised in the public interest when there was urgency); *Arjan Singh* v. *Punjab* (1958) Punj. 1451, ('59) A.Punj. 538 (discretionary power is not discriminatory); *Sarju Prasad* v. *U.P.* ('62) A.A. 221, (1962) A.L.J. 96; *Ram Sewak* v. *U.P.* ('63) A.A. 24; *Ishwarlal* v. *Gujarat* (1968) 2 S.C.R. 267, ('68) A.SC. 870 [*held*, affirming the judgment of the Gujarat High Court in (1967) Guj. 620 that the principle and policy for guidance of the State Government for issuing directions was laid down and the classification of land on the basis of urgency of acquisition was reasonable].

[52] *Parashram Damodhar* v. *Bombay* ('57) A.B. 252, 59 Bom.L.R. 616 (the power was to be exercised after taking into consideration the public interest, the situation and the productive capacity of land and other factors relevant to land).

[53] *Chhaya Devi* v. *Bihar* (1957) 35 Pat. 847, ('57) A.P. 44 (the power was to be exercised in the light of the preamble which referred to the areas of the Khosi river and to lands of raiyats which were sold for arrears of rent or were treated as abandoned, as also to certain districts which were chosen because they were affected by the floods).

[54] *Jyoti Pershad* v. *Administrator for Delhi* (1962) 2 S.C.R. 125, 141, ('61) A.SC. 1602 (though the Act does not lay down rules for the exercise of discretion, the preamble and the operative provisions of the Act give a sufficient guidance for the exercise of that discretion.

[55] *K. L. Gupte* v. *Corpn., Greater Bombay* (1968) 1 S.C.R. 674, ('68) A.SC. 303, 316.

[56] *Gopal Narain* v. *U.P.* (1964) 4 S.C.R. 869, ('64) A.SC. 370 (the power is controlled by the purpose underlying the Act.)

[57] *Anand Municipality* v. *State* ('56) A.B. 368, 57 Bom.L.R. 1088 (the discretion was guided by the scheme of the Act).

[58] *Smt. Mithan* v. *Municipal Board, Orai* ('58) A.A. 603, (1958) A.L.J. 398 [the power was guided by the provisions mentioned in s. 247(1)(*a*), (*b*) and (*c*)].

[59] *Parasram* v. *Kalol Municipality* ('72) A.Guj. 54 (s. 185 gave a complete guideline: ibid. p. 60).

to such authority or person and subject to such restrictions, limitations and conditions as may be prescribed by the said rules;[60] the power conferred by s. 68B, Motor Vehicles Act, 1939;[61] ss. 128, 131 and 133 of the U.P. Municipalities Act, 1916, show that the rate of tax to be levied and the persons or class of persons liable to pay the tax have a reasonable relation to the subjects liable to pay the tax under the Act. The rate to be imposed and the persons liable to pay the tax are to be ascertained by a quasi-judicial procedure subject to revision by the State Government. The sections do not confer arbitrary power on the Municipal Board;[62] R. 38 of the Medicinal and Toilet Preparations (Excise Duties) Rules, 1956;[63] the provisions of ss. 22(3), (4) and (6) of the Rajasthan Sales Tax Act, 1954;[64] the power conferred by s. 3, Income-tax Act, 1922, which enables the imposition of a tax on an association of persons or the members of an association individually;[65] although the powers conferred by s. 132(1) of the Income-tax Act, 1961, are very wide and drastic, there is sufficient guidance for their exercise;[66] the power conferred by s. 52 of the Income-tax Act, 1922;[67] the provisions of s. 3-A, U.P. Sales Tax Act, 1948;[68] s. 6, Madras Urban Land Tax Act, 1966;[69] the power given to the Cane Commissioner under s. 15, U.P. Sugarcane (Regulation, Supply and Purchase) Order, 1954;[70] the provisions of r. 218 made under s. 36(2), E. Bengal and Assam Excise Act, 1910, which gave the State Government a discretion to fix different periods of licence for settlement of country spirit shops;[71]

Tax laws: Municipal rates

Excise, Sales Tax, Income-tax, Sugarcane Cess

[60] *Dhanmull Sowcar* v. *Secretary, R.T.A.* (1957) Mad. 461, ('57) A.M. 387 (the power so conferred on the State Government is not without guidance).

[61] *M. S. Sadananda* v. *State* ('69) A.Mys. 319, 330 (*held*, that ss. 68C and 68D gave sufficient guidance for the exercise of power).

[62] *N.N.C. & P. Works, Bharatpur* v. *State* ('67) A.Raj. 42.

[64] *Nathulal Fatehpuria* v. *State* ('68) A.Raj. 151 (the exercise of the power was to be guided by the policy of collecting tax and preventing evasion. The sections also contained further safeguards).

[65] *Meyyappa* v. *I.T.O.* ('65) A.M. 60 at p. 75 (the discretion conferred by the section on officers is not unguided but a judicial discretion. The principles laid down by the Supreme Court in *Jyoti Pershad* v. *Delhi, supra*, stated and applied); *M. M. Ipoh* v. *I.T.C. Madras* (1968) 1 S.C.R. 65, ('68) A.SC. 317 [*held*, relying on *Jyoti Pershad* v. *Delhi, supra*, that although s. 3 of the Income-tax Act did not lay down any principle for guidance of the I.T.O., the policy underlying the scheme of the Act, gave such guidance. Further, the I.T.O.'s decision was not final, but was subject to appeal].

[66] *Chiranji Lal* v. *R. Prasad* ('67) A.Raj. 71 [following the decision in *Surajmal* v. *C.I.T.* ('61) A.Cal. 578 on s. 37(2), Indian Income-tax Act, 1922, which was considered to be in *pari materia* with s. 132(1)].

[67] *Baliah* v. *Rangachari* (1969) 3 S.C.R. 65, ('69) A.SC. 701 (*held*, that the institution of a complaint under s. 52 was circumscribed by sufficient safeguards).

[68] *H. L. M. Biri Works* v. *S.T.O.* ('59) A.A. 208, (1958) A.L.J. 719 (there was sufficient check on the exercise of the power conferred on the State Government, having regard to the nature of the power conferred).

[69] *Asst. Commr. of Urban Land Tax* v. *Buckingham Carnatic Co. Ltd.* 1969 (2) S.C.C. 55, 65 (the procedure for assessment for the Urban Land Tax in Chapter III of the Act showed that the opinion of the Asst. Collector was not subjective and arbitrary, but was objective; his decision was quasi-judicial and subject to appeals).

[70] *Ch. Tika Ramji* v. *U.P.* (1956) S.C.R. 393, ('56) A.SC. 676 (the power was not arbitrary and unfettered as it was well defined and was subject to an appeal to the State Government).

[71] *Gajendra Nath* v. *Padma Kanta* ('60) A.Ass. 218 (the reasons given in the judgment are not very clear but it appears that as a bottling system had been introduced in two areas, the State Government believed that a settlement for a period of

Trade, commerce and business

the power conferred on government by s. 15, Forward Contracts (Regulation) Act, 1959, to select a commodity for the prohibition or regulation of forward trading in it;[72] the power conferred on the Administrator by s. 52, read with the amended s. 27(6) of the Gold Control Act, 1968;[73] the power given to the administrator under s. 28 to permit or refuse to permit the carrying on of money lending business in the same premises where the business of a goldsmith is being carried on;[74] the power conferred on the Commissioner of Police by s. 39, Calcutta Police Act, 1886, to refuse a licence for an eating house;[75] the power conferred by s. 105, Sea Customs Act;[76] the discretion conferred upon the Marketing Committee under ss. 4(2), Proviso 5-A of the Bombay Agricultural Produce Markets Act, 1939, as extended to the Delhi Territories;[77] the provisions of the Madras Essential Articles (Control and Requisition) (Temporary Powers) Act, 1949 (as amended by the Andhra Act I of 1955);[78] the power to issue directions under s. 3(6), Bihar Rice and Paddy Procurement Order, 1970;[79] R. 39 of the Bihar Co-operative Societies Rules, 1959.[80]

Uncanalized power "read down"

9.109 Where an impugned section confers uncanalised power if read literally but is capable of being "read down", it should be so read in order to uphold the section.[81]

---

two years was necessary to give effect to the policy underlying the bottling system: ibid. p. 222).

72 *Raghubar Dayal Jai Prakash* v. *Union* (1962) 3 S.C.R. 547, ('62) A.SC. 262 (the purpose for which the power was to be used, and the machinery created for investigation afforded sufficient guidance); fol. in *Jullunder Rubber Goods Mfrs. Assn.* v. *Union* 1969 (2) S.C.C. 644 [*held*, that the amendment of s. 12 of the Rubber Act, 1947 by the Rubber (Amendment) Act, 1960, did not confer arbitrary and unfettered power on the Rubber Board which was "a high powered body" and its actions were subject to the control of government]; *Modern Hindu Hotel* v. *Mysore* (1964) Mys.L.J. (Supp.) 202 [*held*, that the power conferred on the competent authority by s. 32(1), (2) and (3) of the Mysore Rent Control Act, 1961, to fix fair rent was not unfettered as there was sufficient guidance in the purpose of the Act]; fol. in *Gyan Prakash* v. *State* ('68) A.Mys. 61, 64.

73 *Gem Palace* v. *Union* ('70) A.Raj. 225, 232 [*held*, that s. 27(6) after its amendment contained sufficient guidance for the exercise of his powers under s. 52].

74 *B.S.B.M. Assn.* v. *Union* ('71) A.P. 240, 248 [*held*, fol. the decision in *Banthia's Case* (1970) 1 S.C.R. 479, ('70) A.SC. 1453, that "s. 5(1) requires that the administrator should have regard to the policy of the Act in making his orders"].

75 *Mohd. Soleman* v. *State* ('65) A.Cal. 312 (the power is not arbitrary and unfettered as there is sufficient guidance in the preamble and the policy of the Act).

76 *Sreeram Durgaprasad* v. *D.C., Customs Department* ('65) A.A.P. 294, 300 (both by itself and along with other provisions of the Act, there is sufficient guidance to the warrant officer for taking action under s. 105); *Gopikisan* v. *Asst. Collector of Customs, Raipur* ('67) A.SC. 1298, 1301, (1967) 2 S.C.R. 340 (s. 105 of the Customs Act, 1962, contained sufficient guidance: the search had to be of goods liable to be confiscated and of documents relevant to proceedings under the Act).

77 *Ram Rachhpal* v. *Union* ('60) A.Punj. 439, 62 P.L.R. 612 (the power is not arbitrary, first, because reasons have to be given for granting or cancelling a licence, and secondly because certain conditions and requirements have to be complied with before licences can be cancelled).

78 *Secy. to Govt., P.W. & T. Dept.* v. *A.G. Factory* ('59) A.A.P. 538 (the powers are to be exercised for maintenance or increase in supply of essential commodities, or securing equitable distribution and availability at fair price, etc.).

79 *T. M. Prasad* v. *State* ('72) A.P. 250, 258 (the power had to be exercised within the ambit of the Procurement Order).

80 *H. Bhagat* v. *A.R., Co-op. Societies* ('68) A.P. 211, 216 (*held*, that if the rule were read with the preamble it did not contain unfettered power. There was also the safeguard of an appeal).

81 *Jagdish Pandey* v. *Chancellor, Bihar University* ('68) A.SC. 353, 357, (1968)

9.110 The discretionary power conferred in the following cases was held to violate Art. 14: In relation to properties of persons belonging to a royal family and properties belonging to other persons;[82] the power conferred by s. 40 (4) (c), Administration of Evacuee Property Act, 1950, to refuse to confirm any transaction;[83] the power conferred by Rule 2 (2) of the Liberalized Pension Rules to compulsorily retire a government servant;[84] the power conferred by s. 40 (4), U.P. Industrial Disputes Rules, 1947;[85] between persons whose property was acquired for rehabilitation and those whose property was acquired for other purposes;[86] between one pending litigant and another;[87] between allottees with regard to whose lands consolidation schemes were published between December 31, 1951, and January 1, 1956, and allottees in whose cases the said schemes were published after January 1, 1956;[88] the discretion conferred on the Commissioner and the Corporation of Calcutta under ss. 237 and 245 of the Calcutta Municipal Act, 1951;[89] the power conferred by para 63, second Proviso, U.P. Gaon Samaj Manual, as it conferred an absolute arbitrary and uncontrolled power on the State Government or the Collector to follow one method in respect of the transfer of one fishery right and a totally different method in respect of the transfer of another fishery right or even to follow no procedure at all and to do just what they liked;[90] inviting offers for advance purchase

Discretionary power held void: Civil Procedure

Evacuee Law

Govt. service

Industrial Law

Land laws, Land reform

Municipal Law

Trade and business

---

1 S.C.R. 231 [*held*, that s. 4 of the Bihar University (Amendment) Act, 1962, should be read down so as to save it from conferring uncanalised power on the Chancellor, and so read down it did not violate Art. 14].

[82] *Budh Singh* v. *Mohd. Yasin* (1957) 7 Raj. 495, ('57) A.Raj. 304 (*held*, that the notification of the former ruler of Tonk which exempted properties belonging to persons of the royal family of Tonk from attachment was not based on a reasonable classification and was therefore invalid).

[83] *Vittalji* v. *Dy. Custodian of Evacuee Property* (1955) Mad. 972, ('55) A.M. 75 (*held*, that the section conferred unfettered discretion to refuse to confirm any transaction. The section however was severable).

[84] *G. B. Nesrikar* v. *Union* ('72) *A.Mys.* 71 (the power was unguided as it did not prescribe the requirement of public interest for its exercise).

[85] *U.P. Shramik Maha Sangh* v. *U.P.* ('60) A.A. 45 (*held*, that the sub-rule vested the Labour Commissioner with an absolute power to approve or reject a federation and the power was unguided by any principle or criteria).

[86] *H. P. Khandelwal* v. *U.P.* ('55) A.A. 12, (1954) A.L.J. 673 [*held*, that s. 11(1), Provisos, U.P. Land Acquisition (Rehabilitation of Refugees) Act, 1948, violated Art. 14. There was no reasonable connection between acquiring property for rehabilitation and paying a smaller compensation than would be paid for acquiring the same property for any other purpose].

[87] *Balabhau Manaji* v. *Bapuji Satwaji* (1957) Bom. 728, ('57) A.B. 233, 60 Bom.L.R. 18 (F.B.) [*held*, that s. 242(3), M.P. Land Revenue Code, violated Art. 14 because, though a classification could be made on the basis of time, there was no rational ground for safeguarding the rights of some pending litigants and taking away the rights of others: it had not been shown that the date fixed as a dividing line was fixed for administrative convenience].

[88] *Punjab* v. *S. Kehar Singh* (1958) Punj. 2136, ('59) A.Punj. 8 (F.B.) [ss. 3 and 4, Punjab Consolidation of Lands Proceedings (Validation) Act, 1957, violated Art. 14, as the classification there made was arbitrary and unreasonable].

[89] *S. M. Nawab Ariff* v. *Corporation of Calcutta* ('60) A.Cal. 158 [*held*, by the majority, that the Act laid down no principle or policy for guiding the discretion of the Commissioner and the Corporation in the matter of selection or classification of defaulters in deciding whether any particular defaulter should be proceeded against by way of a suit (s. 251) or by other modes (ss. 237 and 245). It was held further that one of the procedures, namely, by distraint as provided under s. 237 was very much more onerous than the procedure of a suit prescribed under s. 251 and that s. 237 was void].

[90] *Mohammad Ismail* v. *District Magistrate* ('57) A.A. 487, (1957) A.L.J. 763.

of kendu leaves from purchasers during previous years who had carried out their obligations to the satisfaction of Government as opposed to other purchasers;[91] between one part of the State and another;[92] the discretionary power conferred by s. 71(2) of the Rajasthan Excise Act, 1950;[93] between sales of food articles within and outside hotels;[94] the discretionary power given to the officer under r. 7 made under s. 23, Cochin Abkari Act, 1077;[95] the power conferred by r. 62-A, of the Assam Drug Rules, 1945;[96] Rr. 3(1) and (2) framed under the Grants-in-Aid Code.[97]

Two further questions on discretionary power

9.111 The question of discretionary power has been considered in this Chapter and also in Chapter X in connection with Art. 19.[98] However, two questions must be considered at this place: (i) If a law authorises the State to delegate its discretionary power to whomsoever it likes, would the grant of such power of delegation make the discretionary power void? (ii) Does the mere conferment of unguided discretionary power invalidate a law?

Power to delegate discretionary power

9.112 It is believed that no case has directly held that wide discretionary powers are void because the State or any other body or authority on whom they have been conferred have power to delegate them to whomsoever they please. However, in several decisions of the Supreme Court, the high standing of the body or authority on whom wide discretionary powers have been conferred has been held relevant in upholding the grant of discretionary power. Thus, in *Gurbachan Singh* v. *Bombay*[99] Mukherjea J. upheld the power of

---

[91] *Rasbihari* v. *Orissa* (1969) 3 S.C.R. 374, ('69) A.SC. 1081 [*held*, that exclusion of all persons interested in the trade "who were not in the previous year's licensees" was *ex facie* arbitrary and had no direct relation to the object of preventing exploitation of pluckers and growers of Kendu leaves, nor had it any just or reasonable relation to securing of the full benefit from the trade to the State: ('69) A.SC. at pp. 1087-8. The challenge to the law under Art. 19 is dealt with in Chap. X].

[92] *Birdi Chand* v. *Rajasthan* (1957) 7 Raj. 906, ('58) A.Raj. 26 (in holding that Part IV of the Marwar Relief of Indebtedness Act, 1941, violated Art. 14, the Court said that there was no basis for coming to the conclusion that the part of Rajasthan to which the Act applied has something peculiar which would require the law, as compared with the other parts of the State. It is submitted that the decision is not correct because the geographical classification can be justified on historical grounds, namely, that Marwar was at one time a State by itself).

[93] *Rao Manohar Singh* v. *Rajasthan* (1954) Raj. 113 ('54) A.Raj. 85 (F.B.) [*held*, that s. 71(2) was void on the ground that neither the preamble nor the provisions of the Act showed any basis for an exemption to be granted; that exemption could be granted in the case of a single person as well. The section put uncontrolled and unbridled power in the hands of Government].

[94] *Seetharamaiah* v. *Asst. S.T.O.* (1956) Mys. 402, ('57) A.Mys. 63 [*held*, that s. 3(1)(b) Proviso 11, Mysore Sales Tax Act, 1948, violated Art. 14, as the classification could not be assumed to be rational or to have a just relation to the object of the law].

[95] *P. J. Joseph* v. *Asst. Excise Commissioner* (1952) A.Tr.-Co. 146 (the power given to the officer by r. 7 was a naked and arbitrary power and had a potency of being exercised with unjust discrimination as there were no principles or standards for guiding or regulating the exercise of the power).

[96] *Rasiklal Ghosh & Sons.* v. *Insp. of Drugs* ('60) A.Ass. 94 (*held*, R. 62-A was void on the ground that it conferred unfettered power to grant or refuse a licence. The correctness of this decision is open to question. The Drug Rules embody a policy for the control and proper dispensing of drugs and as drugs are not innocuous articles of commerce it is necessary to confer a wide discretion on competent authorities).

[97] *Sakharkherda Education Society* v. *State* ('68) A.B. 91, 69 Bom.L.R. 690 (*held*, that the rules were vague and afforded no guidance).

[98] See Chapter X.

[99] (1952) S.C.R. 737, ('52) A.SC. 221.

externment conferred on the Commissioner of Police, *inter alia*, on the ground that "... the power to initiate proceedings under the Act has been vested in a very high and responsible officer and he is expected to act with caution and impartiality while discharging his duties under the Act."[1] Similarly, in upholding the power vested in the Income-tax Commissioner and the Central Board of Revenue under the Income-tax Act, to transfer certain cases, Bhagwati J. observed: "... This power is vested not in minor officials, but in top-ranking authorities like the Commissioner of Income-tax and the Central Board of Revenue, who act on the information supplied to them by the Income-tax officers concerned."[2] Similarly, the Supreme Court held[3] that power under s. 5(1), Minimum Wages Act, 1948 was conferred not on any petty officer but on the State Government which could be trusted to exercise that power to further the purpose of the Act. On the other hand, in *Dwarka Prasad Lakshmi Narain* v. *U.P.*[4] Mukherjea J. in striking down Cl. 4(3) of the Coal Control Order said:

"... The licensing authority has been given an absolute power to grant or refuse to grant, renew or refuse to renew, suspend, revoke, cancel or modify any licence under this order. ... Not only so, the power could be exercised by *any person* to whom the State Coal Controller may choose to delegate the same and the choice can be made in favour of any and every person. It seems to us that such provision cannot be held to be reasonable."

These observations were distinguished in *Virendra* v. *Punjab*[5] by Das C.J. who said:

"... In the first place, the discretion is given in the first instance to the State Government itself and not to a very subordinate officer like the licensing officer as was done in *Dwarka Prasad's Case*. ... It is true that the State Government may delegate the power to any officer or person but the fact that the power of delegation is to be exercised by the State Government itself was some safeguard against an abuse of this power of delegation."[6]

The case was also distinguished on the ground that there was no policy underlying the Coal Control Order whereas there was a policy underlying the impugned law which would afford guidance to the authority exercising discretionary power. The result of the authorities appears to be that the vesting of discretionary power in the State or public authorities of a very high standing is treated as a guarantee that the power will be used fairly and with a sense of responsibility. The conferment of wide discretionary power on minor or subordinate officials weakens, if it does not destroy, that guarantee, and might lead the Court to hold that the conferment of such power was unreasonable.

The result of the authorities

9.113 Of few laws can it be said that they embody no policy, for as the Privy Council observed in *Province of Bombay* v. *Bombay Municipal Corporation* "every statute must be supposed to be 'for the

Conferment of unfettered discretionary power and its consequences

[1] (1952) S.C.R. *supra* at p. 744.
[2] *Pannalal Binjraj* v. *Union* (1957) S.C.R. 233, 257, ('57) A.SC. 397.
[3] *C.B. Boarding & Lodging Co.* v. *Mysore* (1970) 2 S.C.R. 600, ('70) A.SC. 2042, 2048.
[4] (1954) S.C.R. 803, 812-3, ('54) A.SC. 224.
[5] (1958) S.C.R. 308, ('57) A.SC. 896.
[6] (1958) S.C.R. at p. 321; *K. L. Gupte* v. *Corpn., Greater Bombay* ('68) A.SC. 303, 316, (1968) 1 S.C.R. 674 (wide discretionary power was conferred on the Municipal Commissioner himself or the Chief Officer of a Municipal Borough).

public good' at least in intention"[7] and, therefore, of few laws can it be said that they confer unfettered discretionary power since the policy of the law affords guidance for the exercise of discretionary power. But assuming that an unfettered discretionary power were conferred, is that enough to render that provision void irrespective of the question whether in fact the power was exercised arbitrarily or capriciously? This question has been considered in the United States in connection with the equality clause of the 14th Amendment to the U.S. Constitution, and Prof. Willis answered it as follows:

The view of Prof. Willis

"Perhaps the best view on the subject is that 'due process' and 'equality' are not violated by the mere conference of unguided power, but only by its arbitrary exercise by those upon whom conferred.[8] If this is the correct position, the only question that would then arise would be the delegation of legislative power. If a statute declares a definite policy, there is a sufficiently definite standard for the rule against the delegation of legislative power, and also for equality if the standard is reasonable. If no standard is set up to avoid the violation of equality, those exercising the power must act as though they were administering a valid standard."[9]

Submission: his view is correct

Subject to the qualification that the rule laid down by Prof. Willis should be treated as a general, and not as an absolute rule,[10] the present writer agrees with it. It is submitted that there is no reason for striking down a provision because it confers unguided power if the power has not been exercised at all or in fact the person exercising the power has acted on a reasonable standard.

Power to exempt from the operation of a law

9.114 The above proposition can best be illustrated by reference to the power of exemption conferred by most statutes on the executive. On this question, the attitude of the Supreme Court is not consistent. In enacting a general law, it is not possible to foresee every situation or to envisage every contingency and to provide specially for it by excluding the operation of the law wholly or in part in respect of such situation or such contingency. Power is therefore conferred on the executive to exempt persons or bodies from all or any of the provisions of the law. In respect of laws which disclose a policy, such a power must be exercised in the light of the policy and the mere conferment of discretionary power would not invalidate that power. But on the assumption that there are some laws which disclose no policy, the power cannot be struck down because there is nothing unreasonable in giving a power to meet unforeseen situations. The unreasonableness must be found, if at all, in the exercise of that power. If the power is exercised according to a rule, which appears to a Court to be reasonable, the Court will uphold the exercise of that power; if on the other hand the exercise of power is arbitrary or capricious, such exercise of power will be struck down. This view was clearly taken by the Supreme Cour in *F. N. Balsara* v. *Bombay*.[11] There, the High Court, after adverting to the observations of Prof. Willis, quoted above, and without pronouncing on their correctness, held that ss. 52, 53 and 139 (*c*), Bombay Prohibition Act, 1948, were invalid on

Balsara's Case rightly upholds such power

---

[7] (1946) 72 I.A. 271, 276, ('47) A.PC. 34.
[8] *Plymouth Coal Co.* v. *Pennsylvania* (1914) 232 U.S. 531, 58 L.ed. 713.
[9] Willis, *Constitutional Law*, pp. 586-87.
[10] The qualification is discussed in paras 9.116 and 9.121 of the text.
[11] (1951) S.C.R. 682, ('51) A.SC. 318.

the ground of delegation of legislative power.[12] In reversing this judgment, the Supreme Court held that

". . . Delegation of the character which these sections involve cannot in our view be held to be invalid. . . . The Legislature, while legislating cannot foresee and provide for all future contingencies, and s. 52 does no more than enable the duly authorised officer to meet the contingencies and deal with various situations as they arise. The same considerations will apply to ss. 53, and 139(c)."[13]

It is submitted that the above view accurately indicates the necessity for delegation of discretionary power and the necessity of a power to exempt from the provisions of an Act or the rules and regulations made under it. However, without adverting to these principles, the Supreme Court, by a majority, held that a power to exempt contained in s. 7, Travancore-Cochin Land Tax Act, 1955[14] gave uncanalised, unlimited and arbitrary power to Government to pick and choose in the matter of land or grant total or partial exemption from the provisions of the Act and it also suffered from the vice of discrimination.[15] It has been submitted in another part of this book[16] that the majority decision is incorrect, but on the question of Art. 14 and delegation of power, it is submitted that no pronouncement on the section was called for, because in fact, no exemption had been granted. Secondly, the impugned Act provided for a tax of Rupees 2 per acre in place of a number of taxes in the nature of land revenue and a power to remit or exempt persons from land revenue has been a normal feature of revenue laws in India. There are several contingencies in which exemption from land tax would be clearly reasonable, for example, a part of a territory may suffer from drought or pestilence or from an epidemic disease from which the rest of the territory is free. In such a case, a uniform exemption granted to the affected part depending upon the severity of the drought or pestilence or epidemic would be clearly reasonable and based on rational grounds. It is submitted that the view taken in *Balsara's Case* of the power to exempt is correct and is based on principles repeatedly affirmed by the Supreme Court in upholding the grant of discretionary power. It may be mentioned that no weight appears to have been given in *Moopil Nair's Case* to the fact that the discretionary power was conferred on the State Government which was expected to use it fairly and justly till the contrary was proved.[17] In *Ram Bachan* v. *Bihar*[18] the power of exemption conferred by s. 82(1) (*ff*) of the Bihar and Orissa Municipal Act, 1922, was impugned on the ground that it conferred an arbitrary power on Government to exempt any classes or professions,

Moopil Nair's Case

Submission: wrongly decided on this point also

[12] S. 52 empowered Government to grant licences in cases other than those specifically provided for under the Act; s. 53 empowered Government, *inter alia*, to vary, or substitute any of the conditions of the licence laid down in the Act and s. 139(c) empowered Government to exempt any person or institution from the observance of all or any of the provisions of the Act or any rule, or regulation or order made thereunder.

[13] (1951) S.C.R. *supra* at p. 747.

[14] *S. 7*: "This Act is not applicable to lands held or leased by the Government or any land or class of lands which the Government might by notification in the Gazette either wholly or partly exempt from the provisions of this Act."

[15] *K. T. Moopil Nair* v. *Kerala* (1961) 3 S.C.R. 77, 93.

[16] See Chapter X.

[17] *Pannalal Binjraj* v. *Union* (1957) S.C.R. 233, 258, ('57) A.SC. 397.

[18] (1967) 3 S.C.R. 1, ('67) A.SC. 1404, 1407.

trades or callings from a profession tax imposed by the Act without giving any guidance as to the classes to be exempted. In rejecting this contention, the Supreme Court said:

"We do not find it necessary to deal with this academic point because, first, the Government has not exercised this power and, secondly, even if we were to hold this proviso to be violative of Art. 14, it would be severable and would not give any relief to the petitioner."[19]

Exemption Sections

9.115 Decisions of the Supreme Court before and after the decision in *Moopil Nair's Case*[20] show that an exemption section is valid if there is guidance for its exercise, because the power to exempt must be used to further the policy and purpose of the Act.[21] The policy and purpose of the Act is to be gathered from the preamble and other provisions of the Act.[22] However, an order made under a valid exemption section may be held void if it is contrary to the policy or purpose of the Act.[23]

Khan Chand's Case

9.116 *Punjab* v. *Khan Chand*[24] is considered at this place because in his dissenting judgment Mathew J. cited with approval the passage from Prof. Willis set out in para 9.113 above, and held that the passage indicated the correct rule to apply when a law was impugned as violating Art. 14 on the ground that it conferred unguided discretionary power.[25] It is submitted that he was right if he treated it as a general, and not as an absolute, rule.[26] However, it raised several questions, all of which are considered below.

Khan Chand's Case: acquisition of movable

9.117 In *Khan Chand's Case* the East Punjab Movable Property (Requisitioning) Act, 1947 ("the Act") was impugned as violating Arts. 14 and 19. The relevant sections are set out in the majority

---

[19] ('67) A.SC. *supra* at p. 1407. [20] (1961) 3 S.C.R. 77, ('61) A.SC. 552.

[21] *P. J. Irani* v. *Madras* (1962) 2 S.C.R. 169, ('61) A.SC. 1731 [s. 13 of the Madras Buildings (Lease and Rent Control) Act, 1949, did not violate Art. 14 on the ground of conferring unfettered and unbridled power. The power was to be exercised in order to further the policy and purpose of the Act, namely, to prevent unreasonable eviction of tenants: *Sirdar Inder Singh* v. *Rajasthan* (1957) S.C.R. 605, 621, ('51) A.SC. 510 rel. on].

[22] *Harishankar Bagla* v. *M.P.* (1955) 1 S.C.R. 380, 381, ('54) A.SC. 465 [s. 3, Essential Supplies (Temporary Powers) Act, 1946, did not confer any unfettered discretion because the discretion was to be exercised in the light of the policy of the Act as gathered from its preamble and from the other provisions of the Act]; foll. in *Sirdar Inder Singh* v. *Rajasthan* (1957) S.C.R. 605, 621 and in *P. J. Irani* v. *Madras* (1962) 2 S.C.R. 169, 181; *Jyoti Pershad* v. *Delhi* (1962) 2 S.C.R. 125, ('61) A.SC. 1602.

[23] *Harishankar Bagla* v. *M.P.* (1955) 1 S.C.R. *supra* at pp. 387-8: "The conferment of such a discretion cannot be called invalid and if there is an abuse of the power there is ample power in the Courts to undo the mischief"; *Jyoti Pershad* v. *Delhi, supra* [s. 19, Slum Areas (Improvement and Clearance) Act, 1956, did not confer arbitrary and unfettered power and was valid; further, the impugned order passed under the Act was valid as it was in line with the policy and purpose of the Act]; *P. J. Irani* v. *Madras, supra* (*held*, by a majority of 3 to 2, that the order granting exemption was void as it was contrary to the policy and purposes of the Act). The last two cases were relied on in *Rudra Talkies* v. *Prem Sagar & Co.* ('67) A.Punj. 348 [upholding s. 10 of the Punjab Cinemas (Regulations) Act 1952, which conferred on the government a general power of exemption]. *Jyoti Pershad's Case* was quoted with approval in *K. L. Gupte* v. *Corpn., Greater Bombay* ('68) A.SC. 303, 312-4.

[24] (1974) 2 S.C.R. 768, ('74) A.SC. 543.

[25] However, he held that the impugned law contained sufficient guidance for its exercise.

[26] For a discussion of this qualification see para 9.113 of the text.

judgment of Khanna J.;[27] however, s. 2 is set out in the undernoted footnote.[28] Except for the extremely limited exception contained in the proviso to s. 2(1), every kind of movable property could be requisitioned under the Act, which was a pre-Constitution Act; and under s. 3 there was power to acquire property which had been requisitioned. The Act did not provide that the requisition was only to be for a public purpose; consequently, there was no obligation to state the public purpose for which the movable property was being requisitioned. The power of requisition could be delegated to any officer, and not merely to officers of high standing. The following questions were considered by the Court: (*a*) Could the requirement of a public purpose be read into the Act? (*b*) Would the mention of a public purpose in the Act have saved it from invalidity under Art. 14? (*c*) If the requirement of a public purpose could not be read into the Act, was it necessary to strike down the law?

property; public purpose not mentioned in the Act

9.118 Khanna J. held that public purpose could not be read into the Act,[29] for to do so would amount to judicial legislation.[30] He expressed a tentative opinion that if "public purpose", or any specified purpose, had been mentioned in the Act "it *might* have been possible to sustain s. 2".[31] (italics supplied). He held that the Act contained unfettered, unguided power and it must be struck down, adding that "it would be wrong to assume that there is an element of judicial arrogance in the act of the Courts in striking down an enactment".[32] Before considering the dissenting judgment, it may be stated that it was not argued before the Supreme Court, that even if a public purpose could be read into the Act, the Act would have to be struck down because of its procedural infirmities.

Act held void by the majority

9.119 In his dissenting judgment, Mathew J. held, first, that nothing turned

Mathew J.'s dissent: public purpose implied

"upon the presence or absence of such phrases as 'public interest', 'public good' or 'public purpose' . . . Courts and parties all assume that the legislature always wants protection of the public interest, to serve public cause and do things for public good or to exercise powers for public purpose

[27] For himself, Ray C.J. and Alagiriswami and Bhagwati JJ.: ('74) A.SC. *supra* at p. 545.

[28] *S. 2(1)* : The State Government, if it considers it necessary or expedient so to do, may by order in writing requisition any moveable property and make such further orders as may be necessary or expedient in connection with the requisitioning: Provided that no property used for the purpose of religious worship and no aircraft or anything forming part of an aircraft or connected with the operation, repair or maintenance of aircraft, shall be requisitioned. (2) When the State Government makes any order under sub-sec. (1) it may use or deal when the property in such manner as may appear to it to be expedient.

[29] *Inter alia*, because legislation in *pari materia* showed that the requirement of a public purpose was expressly provided for: ('74) A.SC. *supra* at p. 548.

[30] ('74) A.SC. at p. 548.

[31] ibid. "as was done by the Gujarat High Court in *Jayantilal Parshottamdas* v. *Gujarat* (1970) 11 Guj.L.R. 403."

[32] ibid. This was presumably a reply to the observations of Mathew J. in his dissenting judgment when he said "Our attempt must be to preserve and not destroy. Respect for a coordinate branch of the Government as well as the presumption of constitutionality demands it. Before a duly enacted law can be judicially nullified, it must be forbidden by some explicit restriction in the Constitution. Our duty of deference to those who have the responsibility for making the laws has great relevance in this context. The attitude of judicial humility which this consideration enjoins is not an abdication of the judicial function": ibid. p. 554.

and always intends that administrators act justly and reasonably whether the legislature says so in the statute or not. . . ."[33]

Secondly, that on reading the section no Court could or would say that the power conferred on the Government could be exercised for a private purpose—public purpose was implied in the section.[34] Finally, the expression "necessary and expedient" used in s. 2(1) gave adequate guidance when read in juxtaposition with the implied public purpose.[35] However, in the alternative, Mathew J. held that even if it be held that the Act conferred unfettered, unguided power, the correct view to take was that indicated by Prof. Willis (set out in para 9.113 above), and the Court should not strike down the Act, but only executive action under it, if such action showed an abuse of discretionary power.[36]

Prof. Willis's view adopted

Submission: Mathew J. rightly implied public purpose

9.120 It is submitted that on "public purpose", Mathew J. was clearly right for the reasons which he gave.[37] Further, it is submitted that reading "public purpose" into the Act would have involved no judicial legislation; it would merely have made explicit what was implicit in the Act. In any event, since public and private purposes constitute two distinct classes, the operation of the Act could have been confined to requisition for a public purpose by applying the doctrine of severability in application.[38]

Submission: Act void because of procedural infirmities: the qualification to Prof. Willis's view

9.121 However, it is submitted that neither by reading "public purpose" into the Act, nor by adopting Prof. Willis's statement of the law, could the Act have been upheld. For, underlying the theory of "guided" power, as well as Prof. Willis's statement of the law, is the assumption that it is not necessary to strike down the law because the Court can give effective relief to the aggrieved party by striking down executive action under the impugned law if such action showed an abuse of power. If this assumption does not hold, having regard to the scope and nature of a particular enactment, the underlying basis is destroyed, and it is submitted that the law itself would have to be struck down.[39] The Act in *Khan Chand's Case* enabled every kind of movable property to be requisitioned (with an insignificant exception) and, if necessary, acquired later. Movable property may be (*a*) perishable and consumable, like vegetables or fish; (*b*) consumable, like rice or cotton; and (*c*) relatively durable, like furniture. In cases (*a*) and (*b*), the requisition of property must be followed by its acquisition, and within a very short time no evidence of the character, condition, quantity and quality of the movable property would be available by the production of the property acquired,

---

[33] "See Keneth Culp Davis, *Administrative Law Treatise,* (1959) Vol. 1, p. 87."

[34] ('74) A.SC. *supra* at p. 551, quoting Hood Phillips, *Constitutional and Administrative Law,* pp. 623-4: "The purpose for which a power is given may not be specified in the enabling Act, but that does not necessarily prevent the Court from inferring the purpose and holding that the power has been abused."

[35] ibid. p. 552: ". . . 'Necessary' means 'what is indispensable, needful or essential' and 'expedient' means useful for effecting a desired result, fit or suitable for the purpose'."

[36] ibid. p. 554.

[37] His view is supported by the observations of the Privy Council quoted in para 9.113 of the text.

[38] See para 3.11 of the text where the doctrine has been explained fully.

[39] *Cessante ratione legis cessat ipsa lex* ("Reason is the soul of the law, and when the reason of any particular law ceases, so does the law itself": *Brooms Legal Maxims,* 10th ed. p. 97).

because the property would have been consumed. The Act applied to the whole State, and to almost every kind of movable property. Unless therefore a satisfactory procedure was devised to preserve independent written record of the movable property requisitioned, its character, etc., the aggrieved person would lack the necessary evidence to establish a violation of Art. 14 by an abuse of discretionary power. In a practical sense the Court would be powerless to grant relief to the aggrieved party on the ground of abuse of power, because there would be no independent evidence of the character, condition, quantity and quality of the movable property acquired on the basis of which the aggrieved party could discharge the burden of proof that lies on him to show that he had been discriminated against by an abuse of discretionary power.

9.122 In *Haryana* v. *Darshana Devi*[40] the Supreme Court refused Special Leave and confirmed the decision of the High Court holding that the provisions of O. 33 of C.P.C. (suit in *forma pauperis*) applied to proceedings before a Claims Tribunal established under the Motor Vehicles Act. The Court observed that:

"If the State itself should travesty the basic principle *in the teeth of Arts. 14* and 39(*a*), where an indigent widow is involved, a second look at its policy is overdue. The Court must give the benefit of doubt against levy of a price to enter the temple of justice until one day the whole issue of the validity of profit-making through sale of civil justice, disguised as court-fee, is fully reviewed by this Court."[41] (italics supplied)

Section II

Right to Equality: Articles 15 to 17

9.123 Since Arts. 15(4) and 16(4) enable reservations to be made for backward classes in educational institutions and in public employment respectively, these Articles have increasingly engaged the attention of our Courts, for these Articles provide for "reverse discrimination", as it has come to be called. Reverse discrimination has caused much controversy, especially as it has been in force for over 30 years. The law on the correlation of Arts. 15 and 16 has been in an untidy state, because cases decided under Art. 16 refer to principles laid down in cases decided under Art. 15 and *vice versa*. But even so, the law was reasonably certain till the judgments in *Kerala* v. *N. M. Thomas*[42] ("*Thomas's Case*") introduced considerable confusion in the law. It is proposed to consider the correlation of Arts. 14, 15 and 16 without reference to decided cases in the first instance.

Reverse discrimination

Correlation between Arts. 14, 15 and 16

9.124 The legislative history of Arts. 14 to 16 has been given in detail by Shiva Rao[43], but the reader will find the following brief account not unhelpful. Part III of the draft Constitution of 21st Feb., 1948 provided for fundamental rights. Under the caption "Rights of Equality" were placed not only Arts. 9 to 12 (which correspond to Arts 15 to 18 of our Constitution) but also Arts. 13, 14 and 15 (which correspond to Arts. 19, 20 and 21 of our Constitution) except that the

Legislative history of Arts. 14 to 16

---

40 (1979) 3 S.C.R. 184, ('79) A.SC. 855.
41 ibid. p. 856.
42 (1976) 1 S.C.R. 906, ('76) A.SC. 490.
43 Shiva Rao, *Framing of India's Constitution: A Study* pp. 179 to 201.

provision in Art. 15 "nor shall any person be denied equality before the law or the equal protection of the laws" was detached at the revision stage from Art. 15 (now Art. 21) and put in as the present Article 14. Further, in our Constitution as enacted, Arts. 14 to 18 were put under the caption "Right to Equality" and Arts. 19 to 21 under the caption "Right to Freedom". As to draft Art. 10(4) [now Art. 16(4)], the drafting Committee was of the opinion that the word "backward" should be inserted before the words "class of citizens,"[44] and the Committee inserted that word in the Draft Constitution although it was not there in Clause 10(4) as passed by the Constituent Assembly. Explaining this action of the Committee, Dr. Ambedkar said:

Dr. Ambedkar: reason for inserting "backward" in Art. 16(4): 16(4) was an exception

". . . they (the honourable Members) will find that the view of those who believe and hold that there shall be equality of opportunity, has been embodied in sub-clause (1) of Article 10. It is a generic principle. At the same time, . . . we had to reconcile this formula with the demand made by certain communities that the administration which has now — for historical reasons — been controlled by one community or a few communities, that situation should disappear and that the others also must have an opportunity of getting into the public services. Supposing, . . . we were to concede in full the demand of those communities who have not been so far employed in the public services to the fullest extent, what would really happen is, we shall be completely destroying the first proposition upon which we are all agreed, namely, that there shall be an equality of opportunity. Let me give an illustration. Supposing, . . . reservations were made for a community or a collection of communities, the total of which came to something like 70 per cent of the total posts under the State and only 30 per cent are retained as the unreserved. Could anybody say that the reservation of 30 per cent as open to general competition would be satisfactory from the point of view of giving effect to the first principle, namely, that there shall be equality of opportunity? It cannot be in my judgment. Therefore the seats to be reserved, if the reservation is to be consistent with sub-clause (1) of Article 10, must be confined to a minority of seats. It is then only that the first principle could find its place in the Constitution and effective in operation. . . . I am sure (the honourable Members) will agree that unless you use some such qualifying phrase as 'backward' the exception made in favour of reservation will ultimately eat up the rule altogether. Nothing of the rule will remain. That I think, . . . is the justification why the Drafting Committee undertook . . . the responsibility of introducing the word 'backward' which, I admit, did not originally find a place in the fundamental right in the way in which it was passed by this Assembly."[45]

Sub-cl. (4) added to Art. 15 because of a Sup. Ct. judgment

9.125 Article 15, as originally enacted, contained only three sub-clauses. Sub-clause (4) was inserted by the Constitution (1st Amendment) Act, 1951, as a result of the decision in *Madras* v. *Champakam Dorairajan*.[46] In that case, the Supreme Court struck down the "Communal G.O." as violating Art. 15 or Art. 29(2). Das J. observed:

"Seeing, however, that clause (4) was inserted in Article 16, the omission of such an express provision from article 29 cannot but be regarded as significant. It may well be that the intention of the Constitution was not to introduce at all communal considerations in matters of admission into any educational institution maintained by the State or receiving aid out of State funds."[47]

"The object of (the 1st.) Amendment was to bring Arts. 15 and 29 in line with Art. 16(4)."[48] However, Art. 16(4) refers to "backward

[44] See *f.n.* to draft Art. 10.
[45] *C.A.D.* Vol. 7, pp. 701-02.
[46] (1951) S.C.R. 525, ('51) A.SC. 226.
[47] *Per* Das J. (for himself, Kania C.J. and Sastri, Fazal Ali, Mahajan, Mukherjea and Bose JJ.) (1951) S.C.R. at p. 532.
[48] *M. R. Balaji* v. *Mysore* (1963) 1 S.C.R. 439, 455, ('63) A.SC. 649, 657.

class of citizens", whereas Art. 15(4) refers to "socially and educationally backward class of citizens or for Scheduled Castes and Scheduled Tribes." The difference between Art. 15(4) and Art. 16(4) is striking, but, as will appear hereafter, the words "backward classes" have been judicially interpreted as covering the same classes as are referred to in Art. 15(4).[49]

9.126 Judgments of our Supreme Court, including the judgments in *Thomas's Case,* state that Arts. 15 and 16 are "facets" of Art. 14 which provides that the State shall not deny to any person equality before the law or the equal protection of the laws. One need not quarrel with the word "facet" as long as it does not conceal the departure made by Arts. 15 and 16 from the general rule of equality in Art. 14. First, Art. 14 applies to *any person,* that is, to citizens and non-citizens alike; whereas Arts. 15 and 16 apply *only to citizens.* Article 15(1) provides that the State shall not discriminate against any citizen on grounds only of religion, race, sex, place of birth or any of them ("prohibited grounds"). Reading Art. 14 and Art. 15(1) together it follows that the right to equality guaranteed by Art. 14 to *any person* does not carry with it the right against discrimination on the prohibited grounds. For, if Art. 14 conferred on citizen and non-citizen alike the right against discrimination on the prohibited grounds, then Art. 15(1) could not confer that very right on *citizens alone.* However, Art. 15(1) does not mean that *in fact* non-citizens are being discriminated against on the prohibited grounds. It only means that if non-citizens were so discriminated against, they could not complain of the violation of the fundamental right of equality, because Art. 15(1) does not apply to them, and Art. 14, by itself, does not carry with it the right against discrimination on the prohibited grounds. Secondly, a classification permitted *qua* citizens by Art. 14[50] *e.g.* a classification based on sex or place of birth, is forbidden by Art. 15, so that Art. 15 prohibits a classification which Art. 14 may permit.[51] Again, although Art. 15(1) is directed to the State, Art. 15(2) is directed also to private individuals.

Are Arts. 15 and 16 "facets" of Art. 14? The concept of "facets" examined

The difference between Arts. 14 and 15

9.127 Article 16(1) provides that all citizens shall have equality of opportunity in matters relating to public employment or appointment to any post in the State (as widely defined by Art. 12). Unlike other rights to equality, after equal opportunity has been given to all citi-

Equality of opportunity in matters of public employment

---

[49] See para 9.159 *post.*

[50] *Yusuf Abdul Aziz* v. *Bombay* (1954) S.C.R. 930, 932, ('54) A.SC. 321: "Article 14 is general and must be read with the other provisions which set out the ambit of fundamental rights. Sex is a sound classification and although there can be no discrimination in general on that ground the Constitution itself provides for special provisions in the case of women . . ." *per* Bose J.

[51] It may be noted that classifications permissible under Art. 14 are forbidden not only by Art. 15, but are forbidden also by Arts. 303 and 304(*a*). For, in order to develop trade and commerce in State A, it may be desirable to discriminate between State A and other States by giving preference to trade and commerce of State A. Such a discrimination would be based on a reasonable classification reasonably related to the object of the law and would be valid under Art. 14. However, in the larger interest of India, constitutional limitations have been imposed on the legislative power of Parliament and the State Legislatures so as to prevent discrimination or preference by virtue of any entry in the Legislative Lists, relating to trade and commerce and a provision has also been made in Art. 304(*a*) to prohibit the imposition of discriminatory taxes on goods manufactured or produced in other States.

zens, the person selected becomes an employee of the State, and a part of the machinery which runs the State. Consequently, considerations different from those connected with Arts. 14 or 15 come into play, because the efficient functioning of State Services is essential for the welfare both of the people and the State, and Art. 335[52] recognizes this.

14th Amendment to U.S. Const. (Equality) does not carry with it equality of opportunity in public employment

9.128 But the statement that Arts. 15 and 16 are "facets" of the general doctrine of equality in Art. 14 is misleading if it is taken to mean that any Constitution which provides that the State shall not deny to any person the equal protection of the laws, (as the U.S. Constitution does) must carry with it the right to equality of opportunity in public employment as a specialized application of the general doctrine of equality. In the United States not only was there no equality of opportunity in matters relating to public employment but its opposite, the "spoils system", prevailed. As Prof. Finer put it,

"But the spoils system on a really grand scale began when Andrew Jackson became President in 1828. . . ."[53] The theory that to the victor belongs the spoils of victory — meaning the distribution of public offices — was enunciated by William L. Mercy, a United States Senator.[54] The Federal Government has very largely freed itself of the stain of this system by successive laws which enlarged the jurisdiction of the Civil Services Commission to hold open competitive examinations. Consequently, on June 30, 1947, employees numbering 1,698,568 out of 1,849,781 employees in the Civilian Branch of the Executive, were subject to the competitive requirements of the Civil Service.[55] However, "the largest amount of 'spoils' are in the state and the municipal services: the Federal Government has cleaned itself."[55]

The reasons for the spoils system

Far from public employment being considered as a matter of right, the spoils system was based on the theory that no one had the right to public employment. This was because Article II, Sec. 2(2) of the U.S. Constitution provides that

"He (the President) shall have power, by and with the advice and consent of the Senate, to make treaties, provided two-thirds of the Senators present concur; and he shall nominate, and, by and with the advice and consent of the Senate, shall appoint ambassadors, other public ministers and consuls, judges of the Supreme Court, and all other officers of the United States, whose appointments are not herein otherwise provided for and which shall be established by law; but the Congress may by law vest the appointment of such inferior officers, as they think proper, in the President alone, in the courts of law, or in the heads of departments."

The existence of the spoils system in the United States is relevant, because it was well known to the framers of our Constitution, and they knew that in the United States the doctrine of equality did not carry with it, as a necessary corrolary, the doctrine of equality of opportunity in matters of public employment which was governed by the law of master and servant. Consequently, the right was expressly conferred by Art. 16, since we have not adopted the spoils system.

Presidential notifications on Sch. Castes and Sch. Tribes

9.129 The reference to Sch. Castes and the Sch. Tribes in Art. 15 makes it necessary to refer to Arts. 341 and 342,[56] which authorize the President to issue a notified order in respect of each State specifying

---

[52] See p. A-113.
[53] Finer, *Theory and Practice of Modern Government* (1949) p. 292.
[54] ibid. [55] ibid. p. 829.
[56] See pp. A-115, A-117.

the castes, races or tribes which are to be regarded as Sch. Castes and Art. 342 makes *mutatis mutandis* the same provision for Sch. Tribes. Since a question has been raised in *Thomas's Case* whether Sch. Castes are castes in the ordinary sense of the word, it may be stated that the President has issued the Constitution (Scheduled Castes) Order, 1950 and the Constitution (Scheduled Castes) Union Territories Order, 1951. Clause (2) of the 1950 Order provides for *castes*, *races* or *tribes* which are to be deemed Sch. Castes in the territories of the States mentioned in Parts 1 to 30 of the Order. Para 3 of the Order provides that "notwithstanding anything contained in para (2), no person professing a religion different from the Hindu or Sikh religion shall be deemed to be a member of the Scheduled Castes" and the same provision is made in the 1951 Order. Two conclusions follow from the above Orders: First, that the classification of races, castes and tribes is based on *religion*, namely, the Hindu or Sikh religion, and discrimination on the ground of religion is forbidden by Art. 16(2), exactly as discrimination on the ground of race or caste is forbidden. Secondly, the inclusion of the word "tribes" in the Scheduled Castes Order of 1950 and 1951 shows that there are tribes who practise the Hindu or Sikh religion; otherwise their inclusion in the said Orders would be meaningless. The Scheduled Tribes Order issued by the President does not refer to the Hindu or Sikh religion, but we have seen that to belong to a tribe is not inconsistent with a person professing the Hindu or Sikh region.

Sch. Castes based on Hindu or Sikh religion

9.130 The expression "on grounds only" in Art. 15(1) and (2) and in Art. 16(2) requires explanation, which is best given by reference to s. 298(1), G.I. Act, 35, which used that very expression in prohibiting discrimination on grounds similar to those contained in Arts. 15 and 16.[57] In *Punjab* v. *Daulat Singh*[58] s. 298(1) was considered under the following circumstances: s. 13A, which was added to the Punjab Alienation of Land Act, 1900, with retrospective effect[59] was impugned as violating s. 298(1). By a majority, the Federal Court held that the Act contravened s. 298(1) in some cases, and remanded the case for ascertaining facts in the light of their directions. Beaumont J., who dissented, emphasised the words "on the ground only", observing that the true basis of the impugned Act was not discrimination only, or even principally, on one or more of the grounds specified in s. 298(1), but the true object of the Act was to avoid a method of evading the principal Act though in achieving that object some persons whose only disqualification was a lack of particular descent might be affected. In decisively rejecting this view, the Privy Council observed:

Discrimination "on grounds only" of religion, etc.

Punjab v. *Daulat Singh* and discrimination "on grounds only" of descent, etc.

"Their Lordships are unable to accept this as the correct test. In their view, it is not a question of whether the impugned Act is based only on one or more of the grounds specified in s. 298 sub-s. (1), but whether its operation may result in a prohibition only on these grounds. The proper test as to whether

---

[57] *S. 298(1)*: "No subject of His Majesty domiciled in India shall on grounds only of religion, place of birth, descent, colour or any of them be ineligible for office under the Crown in India, or be prohibited on any such grounds from acquiring, holding or disposing of property or carrying on any occupation, trade, business or profession in British India."

[58] (1946) 73 I.A. 59, (1946) F.C.R. 1, ('46) A.PC. 66, *per* Lord Thankerton.

[59] The retrospective operation was not saved by a subsequent amendment of s. 298(2).

there is a contravention of the sub-section is to ascertain the reaction of the impugned Act on the personal right conferred by the sub-section, and, while the scope and object of the Act may be of assistance in determining the effect of the operation of the Act on a proper construction of its provisions, if the effect of the Act so determined involves an infringement of such personal right, the object of the Act, however laudable, will not obviate the prohibition of sub-s. (1)."[60]

followed in *Bombay Education Society's Case*

In *Bombay* v. *Bombay Education Society*[61] S. R. Das J. cited the above passage as laying down the correct test and added:

"Whatever the object, the immediate ground and direct cause for the denial is that the mother tongue of the pupil is not English. Adapting the language of Lord Thankerton, it may be said that the laudable object of the impugned order does not obviate the prohibition of Article 29(2) because the effect of the order involves an infringement of this fundamental right, and that effect is brought about by denying admission only on the ground of language."[62]

And Das J. said that this very test was implicit in an earlier decision of the Supreme Court, namely, *Madras* v. *Smt. Champakam Dorairajan.*[63]

Arts. 15(4), 16(4): discrimination in reverse. An illustration

9.131 Since Arts. 15(4) and 16(4) permit discrimination in reverse to be practised by reserving seats in educational institutions and by reserving posts or appointments in public service, the extent of such reservation assumes great importance for the citizen, for the public generally and for the State. An instructive illustration of such appointments to unreserved and reserved posts is furnished by the facts of *Devadasan's Case.*[64] Out of 45 appointments to be made, 16 were made from unreserved seats and 29 from candidates belonging to the Sch. Castes and Tribes. The petitioner complained that although he had obtained 61 per cent marks in the competitive examination, he was not appointed, whereas the percentage of marks secured by some out of the 29 appointees belonging to the Sch. Castes and Sch. Tribes was as low as 29.[65] The petitioner who had obtained 61 per cent marks would naturally feel a deep sense of resentment and injustice at being passed over in favour of candidates who had obtained 29 per cent marks and who, rationally speaking, were not comparable to him. The injury to the public is that they have to deal with less able public servants. The injury to the State is a less efficient public service, and the blame which Government must shoulder for the shortcomings and blunders of its servants. These facts do not disappear because it is said that to redress a great historical wrong done to a section of Hindu Society (for, as we have seen, no one can be deemed to belong to the Scheduled Castes unless he professes the Hindu or the Sikh religion) the individual must put up with the feeling of resentment and injustice, and the public and the State must put up with a less efficient public service—at least for a reasonable time. But these indisputable evils make it imperative to ascertain the extent to which they must be accepted. Till *Thomas's Case,* decisions of the Supreme Court on Arts. 15(4) and

---

[60] (1946) 73 I.A. 59, 74.
[61] (1955) 1 S.C.R. 568, 583-4, ('54) A.SC. 561.
[62] (1955) 1 S.C.R. *supra* at p. 584. [63] (1951) S.C.R. 525, 530, ('51) A.SC. 226.
[64] *Devadasan* v. *Union* (1964) 4 S.C.R. 680, ('64) A.SC. 179. For appointments to a public office or post, through competitive examinations, the order of merit of the candidates is determined by the marks obtained at such examinations, with the addition, at times, of a specified percentage of marks for extra curricular activities.
[65] (1964) 4 S.C.R. at p. 683.

16 (4) had held that these Articles were exceptions and that, speaking generally, reservations should be less than fifty per cent. Against this uniform trend of authority there was one dissent in *Devadasan's Case* from Subba Rao J. There the majority[66] held that Art. 16 (4) was an exception; that reservation in public employment must be less than fifty per cent. As the effect of the impugned "carry forward rule" was to reserve 64.4 per cent of posts, the majority held that the rule was unconstitutional and partly allowed the petition. Subba Rao J. held that Art. 16 (4) was not an exception, and the rule was valid. For himself, he would have dismissed the petition. We must now examine his views.

Subba Rao J.'s dissent

9.132 Subba Rao J. said:

Subba Rao and Krishna Iyer JJ.'s theory of a "legislative device"

"The expression 'nothing in this article' is a legislative device to express its intention in a most emphatic way that the power conferred thereunder is not limited in any way by the main provision but falls outside it. It has not really carved out an exception, but has preserved a power untrammelled by the other provisions of the Article."[67]

The theory here propounded is hereafter described as the "theory of a legislative device". In *Thomas's Case*, Krishna Iyer J. cited with approval the above passage without stating that it was from a dissenting judgment.[68] However, he supported the passage by reference to authority. He said, "Art. 16 (4) need not be a saving clause but put in (sic) due to the over anxiety of the draftsman to make matters clear beyond possibility of doubt (see for instance 59 I.A. 206)."[69] Mathew J. did not cite the said passage but, without any supporting authority, he used language very similar to that used by Subba Rao J. Mathew J. said:

"If equality of opportunity guaranteed under Article 16(1) means effective material equality, then Article 16(4) is not an exception to Article 16(1). It is only an emphatic way of putting the extent to which equality of opportunity could be carried viz., even upto the point of making reservation."[70]

Pemsell's Case: specific exemptions inserted *ex majori cautela*

9.133 Before examining the theory of a legislative device propounded by Subba Rao J., and adopted by Krishna Iyer J., we must deal with the *Shaw Wallace Case* because it does not support that theory, but only deals with the interpretation and effect of provisions inserted in an Act *ex majori cautela*. The leading authority on that subject is the decision of the House of Lords in *Commissioners for Special Purposes* v. *Pemsell*,[71] which was cited by the respondents' Counsel in the *Shaw Wallace Case*.[72] In *Pemsell's Case* the question was whether the words "charitable purposes" in the Act were to be given the technical meaning they had in English law, or whether they were to be limited to the relief of poverty, since the Act applied not only to England but also to Scotland. The appellant contended, *inter alia*, that the expression "charitable purposes" did not have its technical meaning in English law[73] but must be limited

---

[66] Mudholkar J. for himself, S. K. Das Actg., C.J. and Raghubar Dayal and Ayyangar JJ. *Devdasan's Case* is considered fully in para 9.234, *post*.

[67] ('64) A.SC. at p. 190.

[68] ('76) A.SC. 490, 535-6.

[69] *I.T.C.* v. *Shaw Wallace & Co.* 59 I.A. 206.

[70] ('76) A.SC. at p. 519.

[71] (1891) A.C. 531.

[72] 59 I.A. 211.

[73] Trusts for: (i) the relief of poverty; (ii) the advancement of education; (iii) the advancement of religion and (iv) for other purposes beneficial to the community not falling under any of the heads (i) to (iii): *per* Lord Macnaghten, (1891) A.C. at p. 583.

to the relief of poverty, because the Act contained a special exemption in favour of funds dedicated to the repair of Cathedrals, Colleges, Churches and places of worship. By a majority of 4 : 2,[74] this contention was rejected. Speaking of the special exemption, Lord Herschell said:

"I think that an argument derived from the specific mention of certain subjects in the exemptions found in a taxing statute are of little weight. Such specific exemptions are often introduced *ex majori cautela* to quiet the fears of those whose interests are engaged or sympathies aroused in favour of some particular institution, and who are apprehensive that it may not be held to fall within a general exemption."[75]

The law is well settled, and is thus set out in *Halsbury*:

"In some statutes, and particularly in private statutes provisos and exceptions are to be found *which are not strictly necessary, since they except*, from the enactments to which they are attached, *matters which would not in any event be covered by those enactments*, but are inserted *ex abundanti cautela* to allay the fear of those who might think that their interests might be affected; and in such cases no implication can be derived from the proviso or exception as to the scope of the enactment."[76] (italics supplied)

Shaw Wallace Case: proviso inserted *ex majori cautela*

9.134 We must now consider the decision in the *Shaw Wallace Case*. There, the question for determination was whether the two sums of money received by Shaw Wallace & Co. from two companies as compensation for the closure of two agencies was "income" within the meaning of the Indian Income-tax Act, 1922. The appellant contended that the undernoted provision[77] showed that the word "income" had a wider meaning than would ordinarily be given to it. Rejecting this argument, the Privy Council observed:

"Their Lordships do not think that any of these sums, apart from their exemption, could be regarded in any scheme of taxation as income, and they think that the clause must be due to the over anxiety of the draftsman to make this clear beyond possibility of doubt. They cannot construe it as enlarging the word 'income' so as to include receipts of any kind which are not specially exempted. They do not think that the clause is of any assistance to the appellant."[78]

Above case has no application to Arts. 15(4), 16(4)

In other words, the proviso could not be used to enlarge the meaning of a provision in the Act, and, further, that even apart from the exemption given by cl. (v), none of the items mentioned in cl. (v) could be looked upon as income in any scheme of taxation. This means that Clause (v) was inserted *ex majori cautela*, for even if it were struck out, the items in cl. (v) were not income and could not be taxed as income. The reader will have noticed that the Privy Council applied the principles laid down in *Pemsell's Case*. It is submitted that for reasons which will appear hereafter, the decision in the *Shaw Wallace Case* can have no application to the interpreta-

---

[74] Lord Watson, Lord Herschell, Lord Macnaghten and Lord Morris; Lord Halsbury L.C. and Lord Bramwell dissenting.

[75] (1891) A.C. at p. 574.

[76] *Halsbury*, Vol. 36 (3rd ed.) at pp. 400 to 401. Footnotes (*e*) to (*l*) to this passage have been omitted.

[77] Sub-Sec. 3 said that the Act "shall not apply to the following classes of *income*" and sub-clause (*v*) provided: "Any capital sum received in commutation of the whole or a portion of a pension, or in the nature of consolidated compensation for death or injuries, or in payment of any insurance policy, or as the accumulated balance at the credit of a subscriber to any such provident fund."

[78] 59 I.A. at p. 214.

tion and effect of the words "Nothing in this article" in Art. 15(3) and (4) and in Art. 16(3) and (5).

9.135 Before examining the theory of a legislative device it is necessary to set out certain propositions which are relevant to our discussion. Fundamental rights impose constitutional limitations on the legislative and executive power of the State and any law or executive action which violates fundamental rights is, *pro tanto*, void under Art. 13(2). Secondly, it is obvious, if not elementary, that in Art. 16(1) no classification can be made which is prohibited by Art. 16(2); but the prohibition under Art. 16(2) can be relaxed by a proviso or an exception. On the construction of provisos, a leading text book states: "The effect of an excepting or qualifying proviso, according to the ordinary rules of construction, is to except out of the preceding portion of the enactment, or to qualify something enacted therein, which but for the proviso would be within it.[79]" [80] **Three basic propositions stated**

9.136 It is submitted that the theory of a legislative device is untenable because: **Reasons why the theory of legislative device is untenable**

(*a*) it ignores the scheme of Arts. 15 and 16, and, more particularly, the relation of clauses (1) and (2) of Arts. 15 and 16, to clauses (3) and (4) of Art. 15 and to clauses (3), (4) and (5) of Art. 16 respectively;

(*b*) it ignores the fact that the words "nothing in this article" appear as the opening words not only in Art. 16(4) but also in Art. 15(3) and (4) and in Art. 16(3) and (5) and in those four sub-clauses the opening words are not a legislative device;

(*c*) it ignores the fact that it is impossible to argue that clauses (3) and (4) of Art. 15 and clauses (3) and (5) of Art. 16 were inserted *ex majori cautela*;

(*d*) it ignores the legislative history of Art. 16(4) which shows that Art. 16(4) was an exception to Art. 16(1);

(*e*) it ignores decisions of high authority which show that the words "nothing in this Act" or "nothing in this Article" are apt words for introducing an exception;

(*f*) when the passage propounding the theory of a legislative device is examined it will be found that it is difficult to give the words in the passage a rational meaning, and at any rate the theory leads to absurd results.

9.137 The scheme of Arts. 15 and 16 is, broadly speaking, similar. Article 15(1) confers on every citizen a fundamental right not to be discriminated against on the grounds only of religion, race, caste, sex or place of birth ("the prohibited grounds") or any of them, and Art. 15(2) confers the right not to be subjected to any disability, liability, restriction or condition, on the prohibited grounds, with regard to specified matters. Article 16(1) confers on every citizen a fundamental right to equality of opportunity in matters **The scheme of Arts. 15, 16**

---

[79] The object of this rule is to ensure that effect is given to the true intention of the legislature and is not designed for the purpose of defeating that intention: *Leveridge* v. *Kennedy* (1960) N.Z.L.R.1.

[80] Craies on *Statute Law*, p. 218 (7th ed.).

of public employment; and Article 16 (2) gives effect and content to that right by prohibiting discrimination in matters of public employment on the prohibited grounds with the addition of "residence" as a prohibited ground. The thing to note is that Arts. 15 (1) and (2) and 16 (1) and (2) confer fundamental *rights* on every citizen. However, Clauses (3) and (4) of Art. 15 and Art. 16 do not confer any *rights* but merely confer a *discretionary power*. Article 15 (3) and (4) and Art. 16 (4) confer that power on the State; Art. 16 (3) confers that *power* not on the State but on Parliament alone. The question naturally arises: How is the discretionary *power* in Arts. 15 and 16 related to the fundamental *rights* conferred by those Articles? Article 15 (1) prohibits discrimination only on the ground of sex; therefore a discrimination in favour of women would necessarily discriminate against men only on the ground of sex, and would be void. The discretionary power in Art. 15 (3) relaxes this prohibition in favour of women by expressly authorizing such discrimination by way of an exception. Article 15 (3) is not inserted *ex majori cautela* for if it were struck out discrimination in favour of women could not be made.

In Art. 15(4) opening words not a legislative device; they introduce an exception

9.138 Turning to Art. 15 (4), we have seen that the Supreme Court's decision in *Champakam Dorairajan's Case* led to its enactment, because the Court held that in the absence of a provision in Art. 15 corresponding to Art. 16 (4), reservation for backward classes could not be made in educational institutions without violating Art. 15 or Art. 29 (2).[81] Consequently, in Art. 15 (4) "Nothing in this article" introduce a proviso or exception to Art. 15 (1) and also to Art. 29 (2), because Arts. 15 (1) and 29 (2) without the proviso were held to prevent special provision being made for backward classes. In Art. 15 (4) the words "Nothing in this article" are clearly not a legislative device. It is just because the main provision—Art. 15 (1)—without Art. 15 (4) prevented special provisions from being made, as held by the Supreme Court, that Art. 15 (4) was enacted.[82]

Opening words of Art. 16(3) not a legislative device; they introduce a limited exception

9.139 We have seen that Art. 16 (2) prohibits, *inter alia*, discrimination in public service on the ground only of *residence*, and any such discrimination would be void. Article 16 (3) contains a *limited* relaxation of this prohibition in the form of a discretionary power. The relaxation is limited, first, because although the prohibition operates *against the State*, the relaxation is only *in favour of Parliament* (and *not* in favour of the State) if it enacts a law

---

[81] See para 9.125.

[82] In the Bill [which became the Constitution (1st Amendment) Act, 1951] it was proposed to amend Art. 15(3) by adding after the word "children" the words "or for the educational, economic or social advancement of any backward class of citizens." The Statement of Objects and Reasons attached to the amending Bill states: "It is laid down in Article 46 as a directive principle of State policy that the State should promote with special care the educational and economic interests of the weaker sections of the people and protect them from social injustice. In order that any special provision that the State may make for the educational, economic or social advancement of any backward class of citizens may not be challenged on the ground of being discriminatory, it is proposed that Article 15(3) should be suitably amplified." In the Constitution (1st Amendment) Act, 1951, the power to make special provision for backward classes was put in a separate clause (4) for the very same purpose, namely, to save such provisions from the challenge on the ground of discrimination prohibited by Art. 15(1) and Art. 29(2).

prescribing any requirement as to residence within a State or Union territory for employment or appointment to an office in public service. Secondly, it is limited because the prohibition in Art. 16 (4) continues to operate against executive action by the State. In Art. 16 (3), the words "nothing in this Article" introduce a limited proviso or exception and are not "a legislative device". Further, it is unarguable that Art. 16 (3) was inserted *ex majori cautela*, for if it were struck out even a partial relaxation of discrimination on the ground of "residence" would be barred by the prohibition in Art. 16 (2).

Opening words of Art. 16(5) not a legislative device; they introduce a limited exception

9.140 We have seen that Art. 16 (2) prohibits discrimination in public service on the ground of religion, and any such discrimination would be void. Article 16 (5) *partially* relaxes this prohibition in one particular situation. There are offices in public services "in connection with the affairs of any religious or denominational[83] institution", including membership of its governing body. Article 16 (5) does not relax generally the prohibition against discrimination on the ground of religion contained in Art. 16 (2) but only in respect of the provisions of a law dealing with the particular situation described above. In Art. 16 (5), the words "nothing in this article" introduce an exception to the prohibition of discrimination on the ground of religion in respect of a specified kind of law, and is not a legislative device. It will be noticed that Art. 16 (5), unlike Art. 15 (3) and (4) and Art. 16 (3), does not *directly* confer a *power*. But as the law referred to in Art. 16 (5) is not limited to existing law, it is submitted that Art. 16 (5), by necessary implication, confers a power to enact such a law if it should become necessary to do so. Article 16 (5) is not enacted *ex majori cautela* for if it were struck out the law of the kind indicated in Art. 16 (5) would be void.

Opening words in Art. 16(4) must have same meaning as in Arts. 15(3), (4), 16(3), (5)

9.141 We have seen that the words "nothing in this article" are not "a legislative device" in Art. 15 (3) and (4) and Art. 16 (3) and (5). It would follow that the same meaning must be attached to those words in Art. 16 (4). The position of Art. 16 (4) between Art. 16 (3) and (5), both of which introduce exceptions, further strengthens that conclusion, for it harmonizes with the scheme that the first two clauses confer rights and the remaining three clauses confer, by way of exception, a power to derogate from those rights. Further, on a plain reading of Art. 16 (4) it is obvious that without the provision there made, the reservation for backward classes could not be made. This plain reading is supported by the unanimous judgment of 7 judges of the Supreme Court in *Champakam Dorairajan's Case*, when they held that the presence in Art. 16 of the provision in Art. 16 (4) enabled reservations to be made in public service, whereas the absence of a similar provision in Arts. 15 and 29 made a reservation in educational institutions for backward classes void as violating the fundamental rights guaranteed by Arts. 15 and 29 (2). In the result, the theory of a legislative device propounded by Subba Rao J. and adopted by Krishna Iyer J. is untenable.

[83] In the *Shirur Mutt Case* (1954) S.C.R. p. 1055 at p. 1022 [('54) A.SC. 282,] Mukherjea J. in considering the expression "any religious denomination" quoted the definition of "denomination" given in the Oxford Dictionary, namely, "a collection of individuals classed together under the same name; a religious sect or body having a common faith and organization and designated by a distinctive name."

Legislative history: Art. 16(4) an exception

9.142 If there was any doubt whether Art. 16(4) carved out a proviso or exception or not—and it is submitted that there is no doubt—the legislative history of Art. 16(4) set out in para 9.124 above clearly supports the view that Art. 16(4) is an exception to the rule of equality of opportunity conferred in affirmative terms by Art. 16(1) and made effective by the prohibitions enacted in Art. 16(2). The word "backward" was inserted before the words "class of citizens" by the Drafting Committee on its own responsibility in the Draft Constitution as a word of limitation, so that the exception permitting reservations in public employment to be made might not swallow up the rule of equality of opportunity in matters of public employment.

Decisions on "nothing in this Act/ Article": the words introduce an exception

9.143 The decisions of Indian and English Courts support the view that the words "Nothing in this Act and/or Section" or "nothing in this article and/or sub-article" are apt words to introduce an exception. In *Automobile Transport Ltd.* v. *Rajasthan*[84] S. K. Das J. for himself, Kapoor and Sarkar JJ. interpreted Art. 303(2) which opened with the words "Nothing in cl. (1)" as creating an exception. He said: "Art. 303(2) again carves out an exception to the restriction placed by Art. 303(1) on the powers of Parliament by providing that nothing in Art. 303(1) shall prevent Parliament from making. . ."[85] Hidayatullah J. for himself, Ayyangar and Mudholkar JJ. in their dissenting judgment also treated Art. 303(2) as an exception to Art. 303(1).[86] Again, in *Dormer* v. *Newcastle-on-Tyne Corporation*[87],

". . . section 65 in a group of sections from section 62 onwards in a private Act at the side of which was a note 'Sewers — Sanitary arrangements,' provided that 'nothing in the Act shall authorise the Corporation of Newcastle-on-Tyne to commit a nuisance,' and the Improvement Act of 1885 by section 22 authorised the corporation to erect posts, rails and fences for the protection of passengers and traffic, it was argued that this authority must be read subject to the proviso as to nuisance; but the court held that the proviso affected only the group of sections to which it was attached and was not a proviso to section 22.[88]"[89]

There is therefore high authority for the view that words like "nothing in this article" are apt words to introduce an excepting or qualifying proviso.

No rational meaning can be given to theory of legislative device. Theory untenable

9.144 Finally, no rational meaning can be given to the words in which the theory of the legislative device was propounded, and in any event, the theory leads to absurd results. Subba Rao J. said:

"The expression 'nothing in this article' is a legislative device to express its intention in a most emphatic way that the power conferred thereunder is not limited in any way by the main provision but falls outside it. It has not really carved out an exception, but has preserved a power untrammelled by other provisions of the Article."[90]

The expression "the power conferred thereunder" refers to Art. 16(4), and the expression "the main provisions" obviously refer to Art. 16(1) and (2) which confer fundamental rights. But for the express assertion that Art. 16(4) has not carved out an exception, it would have been possible to interpret the above passage as a round

[84] (1963) 1 S.C.R. 491, ('62) A.SC. 1406.
[85] ('62) A.SC. at p. 1418.
[86] ibid. p. 1454.
[87] (1940) 2 K.B. 204.
[88] ibid.
[89] Craies on *Statute Law*, 7th ed. p. 219.
[90] ('64) A.SC. at p. 190.

about way of saying that Art. 16(4) carved out an exception. For the power conferred by an exception to a right can be rationally described as "outside" the right, or as being "untrammelled" by the right to which it is an exception. But if Art. 16(4) is not an exception what intelligible meaning can be given to the power conferred by Art. 16(4) as being "outside" or as being "untrammelled" by the rights conferred by Art. 16(1) and (2)? Subba Rao J. failed to notice that the *power* conferred by Art. 16(4) was a power *to do something*, and that "something" related to the rights conferred by Art. 16(1) and (2). If there was nothing in Art. 16(1) and (2) which could prevent the exercise by the State of the power conferred by clause (4) of Art. 16, the opening words of clause (4) "nothing in this article" would be meaningless unless it was said that clause (4) was inserted *ex majori cautela*. But we have seen above that to say that a provision is inserted *ex majori cautela* is to say that even without the provision the result would be the same, so that if the provision were struck off, the Act would remain unaffected. But Art. 16(4) cannot be struck off without seriously affecting the provisions of Art. 16, because the reservations for backward class of citizens, which include Sch. Castes, would violate the prohibition of discrimination on the ground of religion and caste, because, as we have seen, nobody can be deemed to be a member of the Sch. Caste unless he professes the Hindu or the Sikh religion : para 9.129. If Clause (4) of Art. 16 is looked upon as outside of, or *unconnected* with, the fundamental rights conferred by clauses (1) and (2) of Art. 16, we would have the absurd result that in the same Article clause (1) and (2) prohibit discrimination *inter alia* on the ground of religion and/or caste and clause (4) confer an *independent* power to disregard the prohibition. It is submitted that the theory of a legislative device is untenable on an examination of the passage in which Subba Rao J. formulated it.

9.145 The discussion so far in Sec. II will enable the reader to view decided cases on Arts. 15 and 16 in their proper perspective. As Art. 15 confers a right only on citizens it must follow that it cannot be invoked by non-citizens.[91] However, in *Yusuf Abdul Aziz* v. *State*[92] Chagla C.J. held that even if a non-citizen could not invoke Art. 15 it was open to him to contend that the law under which he was prosecuted was a void law as it violated Art. 15. It is submitted that the above view proceeds on the mistaken assumption that a law violating fundamental rights conferred only on citizens is void in its entirety. As we have seen, such a law is valid and can be enforced against non-citizens on whom a fundamental right has not been conferred.[93] Chagla C.J.'s view has been dissented from in *Everett*

Art. 15 can be invoked only by citizens

[91] *M. B. Namazi* v. *Dy. Custodian of Evacuee Property, Madras* ('51) A.M. 930, (1951) 2 M.L.J. 1 (Art. 15 could not be invoked by a person who had migrated from India to Pakistan after March 1, 1947); *Everett Orient Line Inc.* v. *Jasjit Singh* ('59) A.Cal. 237, 63 C.W.N. 986.

[92] (1952) Bom. 449, ('51) A.B. 470, 53 Bom.L.R. 736.

[93] See paras 8.13 and 8.16; see also *Behram Khurshed Pesikaka* v. *Bombay* (1955) 1 S.C.R. 613 at pp. 651-52, ('55) A.SC. 123; *Bhikaji Narain Dhakras* v. *M.P.* (1955) 2 S.C.R. 589, 599, ('55) A.SC. 781 ("the law continued in force, even after the commencement of the Constitution, with respect to persons who were not citizens and could not claim the fundamental right").

Orient Line v. *Jasjit Singh.*[94] In *Arvind Mills* v. *State*[95] Bhagwati J. without discussion of the relevant authorities and relying on *Dwarkadas Shrinivas* v. *Sholapur Spg. & Wvg. Co. Ltd.*[96] held that although a corporation could not claim any fundamental rights, it could still establish that the impugned law was void as violating fundamental rights and claim that as the law was unconstitutional the corporation was entitled to relief. This decision has been followed in *Prithvi Cotton Mills* v. *Broach Municipality.*[97] It is submitted that Art. 31, which was considered in *Dwarkadas Shrinivas's Case,* was not limited to citizens and therefore that case is not an authority for the proposition that a corporation, which is not a citizen, can claim relief on the ground that the impugned law violated fundamental rights *qua* citizens. It is submitted that the decisions of the Gujarat High Court are erroneous. The whole question was considered in *Zoolfiquar Ali* v. *Official Trustee.*[98] There, relying on the observations of Chagla C.J. in *State* v. *Yusuf Abdul Aziz*[99] it was contended that though the claimants 6, 7 and 8 could not claim fundamental rights under Art. 19, they were not precluded from showing that the impugned law violated Art. 19 and was void. The court held that it was doubtful whether *Abdul Aziz's Case* was good law having regard to the language of Art. 13 itself. In any event, the court held that later decisions of the Supreme Court had taken a contrary view. Thus, in *Behram Khurshid Pesikaka* v. *Bombay*[1] the Supreme Court had held that a law void under Art. 13 (1) "should be notionally taken to be obliterated from the section for all intents and purposes though it may yet remain on the Statute Book and be a good law . . . *for the determination of rights of persons who have not been given fundamental rights by the Constitution*". (italics supplied). The same view was taken by the Supreme Court in *Bhikaji Narain Dhakras* v. *M.P.*[2] where the Supreme Court held that a law void under Art. 13 (1) "continued in force even after the commencement of the Constitution, *with respect to persons who were not citizens or could not claim fundamental rights*". (italics supplied) After referring to the Supreme Court judgments, the High Court observed:

> "Quite apart from the question whether the law is void or voidable, whether it is temporarily eclipsed or still-born, the fact remains that an essential condition to the applicability of Art. 19(1) has not been fulfilled in so far as the person who is claiming to enforce that right is not a citizen. It seems to us a mere play of words to say that although he is not a citizen he is still entitled to show that the law is void, when in effect he cannot take advantage of that law. In our opinion, therefore, these claimants are not entitled to take advantage of Art. 19 for the simple reason that they are not citizens, nor are they entitled to show that the law is void and, therefore, should not be enforced."[3]

It is submitted that this decision is clearly right. Article 13 (2) provides that a legislature shall not make any law taking away or abridging the rights contained in Part III. But a law denying to non-citizens the rights conferred by Part III on citizens alone is not hit by Art. 13 (2), since those rights are not conferred on non-citizens.

---

94 ('59) A.Cal. 237, 240, 63 C.W.N. 986.
95 (1966) Guj. 313, (1966) 7 Guj.L.R. 156, 198-9.
96 (1954) S.C.R. 674, ('54) A.SC. 119.
97 ('68) A.Guj. 124.
98 69 Bom.L.R. 326.
99 53 Bom.L.R. 736.
1 (1955) 1 S.C.R. 613, ('55) A.SC. 123.
2 (1955) 2 S.C.R. 589, ('55) A.SC. 781.
3 69 Bom.L.R. at p. 363.

A law denying those rights both to citizens and non-citizens is clearly severable; it is invalid *qua* citizen and valid *qua* non-citizen. In *Gujarat* v. *Shri Ambica Mills*[4] the Supreme Court settled this controversy when it held that as the respondents were a joint stock company, and were not citizens, they could not complain of a violation of Art. 19, nor could they claim that the law was void and *non-est,* for as against non-citizens the law was valid, since Art. 19 conferred fundamental rights *only* on citizens. It is submitted that *Abdul Aziz's Case* and the *Arvind Mills Case* are no longer good law.

Personal law and Art. 13(3)*b*)

9.146 Questions have arisen whether the personal law of the Hindus, or of any other community, is "law" within the meaning of Art. 13 (3) (*b*) and Art. 372 (3), Expl. 1, and whether an alteration of the personal law of one community, without a similar alteration in that of others, violates equality. In *State* v. *Narsu Appa Mali,*[5] Chagla C.J. and Gajendragadkar J. in considering the validity of the Bombay Prevention of Hindu Bigamous Marriages Act, 1946, said that personal law was not included in the "law" referred to in Art. 13 (3) (*a*) and was not the "law in force" saved by Art. 372 (3), and defined in Art. 13 (3) (*b*). In *Srinivasa Iyer* v. *Saraswathi Ammal,*[6] in dealing with the Madras Hindu Bigamous (Prevention and Divorce) Act, 1949, the Court found it unnecessary to consider whether personal law of the Hindus was a "law" within the meaning of Art. 13 (3) (*a*) or "law in force" within the meaning of Art. 13 (3) (*b*) and Art. 372 (3). We have seen that there is no difference between the expression "existing law" and "law in force"[7] and consequently, personal law would be "existing law" and "law in force". This conclusion is strengthened by the consideration that custom, usage and statutory law are so inextricably mixed up in personal law that it would be difficult to ascertain the residue of personal law outside them; it was, therefore, necessary to treat the whole of personal law as existing law or law in force under Art. 372 and to continue it subject to the provisions of the Constitution and subject to the legislative power of the appropriate legislature. In *Narsu Appa's Case,* both the judges said that Art. 17 indicated that personal law was not included in the expression "law" or "law in force", for otherwise, that Article would be wholly unnecessary, since untouchability would have become void (presumably as violating equality). It is submitted that the argument based on Art. 17 is not correct. First, but for Art. 17 it could have been argued that untouchability was a part of religion,[8] and the freedom to practise religion guaranteed by Art. 25 involved the enforcement of the disabilities attached to untouchability. The throwing open of public temples to "untouchables", which is expressly provided for by Art. 25, did not mean that as a part of religious practice other disabilities could not be enforced. Secondly, the object of Art. 17 was not merely to abolish untouchability, but to implement such abolition by imposing an obligation on Parliament to make the enforcement of disabilities attaching to untouchability punishable by

Narsu Appa Mali's Case: personal law not "law" under Art. 13(3)(*a*)

Submission: personal law is "law"

[4] ('74) A.SC. 1300. See paras 8.24 to 8.28 of the text where the case has been fully discussed.

[5] (1951) Bom. 775. ('52) A.B. 84, 53 Bom.L.R. 779.

[6] (1953) Mad. 78, ('52) A.M. 193. [7] See para 8.2.

[8] The Supreme Court upheld this argument in *Devaru's Case* (1958) S.C.R. 895, 911.

law. Thirdly, it is not uncommon in a Constitution to make express provision for matters to which its makers attach great importance, instead of leaving them to the dilatory and hazardous process of litigation. Finally, entry 5, List III, Sch. 7[9] clearly recognizes personal law, as law which Parliament and State legislatures can enact, alter or repeal. For all these reasons it is submitted that the personal law of a community is "law", and is "law in force" or "existing law", within the meaning of the Constitution.

The above submission supported by judicial decisions

9.147 Decisions of the Courts support the above conclusion. Thus the customary law of pre-emption has been held void in a number of cases as violating Art. 19(1) (*f*).[10] It has also been held that in enforcing the law of *damdupat* as between Hindus, or at any rate, in cases where the debtor was a Hindu, the State would be discriminating between Hindus and non-Hindus on the ground of their religion. Therefore, the rule of *damdupat* as known to Hindu law, violated Art. 15 and was void.[11] In *Arumugha* v. *Narayana*[12] it was held that a customary right obtained by members of two communities to the exclusive use of a well must be rejected, for in view of Art. 15, such custom was neither reasonable nor in accordance with enlightened modern ideas of the utility of public wells.

Arts. 14 and 15 and the reform of personal law

9.148 Measures of social reform in personal law have been held not to violate Art. 14 or Art. 15. In rejecting the argument that the Bombay Prevention of Hindu Bigamous Marriage Act, 1946, discriminated between Hindus and Muslims by enforcing monogamy on Hindus and not on Muslims, the Court said that Art. 14 was not violated as the State was free to embark on social reforms in stages. Even if personal law fell within the expression "law in force" used in Art. 13(1), the impugned law did not violate Art. 15 as it did not discriminate on the ground only of religion. The special penalties provided in the Act, which were more stringent than those provided in the Penal Code, were justified on the ground that having regard to the outlook of the Hindus it may have been considered necessary to impose severer penalties in order effectively to implement the law.[13] The same question was considered more fully in *Srinivasa Iyer* v. *Saraswathi Ammal*:[14] In holding that the Madras Hindu Bigamous (Prevention and Divorce) Act, 1949, did not violate Art. 15 or Art. 25, the Court observed that the Act did not discriminate between Hindus and Mohammedans on the ground of religion. Entries 6 and 7, List III, Sch. 7, G.I. Act, 35 (which correspond to entry 5, List III, Sch. 7 of our Constitution) under which the impugned Act was passed, conferred legislative power to enact, alter, or repeal personal laws. Though these legislative entries could not abrogate fundamental rights, they gave an indication that the Hindus had preserved a personal law peculiar to themselves and that the Muslims

Laws upheld as not violating Art. 15

[9] See p. A-185. [10] See Chapter X.

[11] *Sheokaransingh* v. *Daulatram* ('55) A.Raj. 201.

[12] ('58) A.M. 282.

[13] *State* v. *Narsu Appa Mali* (1951) Bom. 775, ('52) A.B. 84, 53 Bom.L.R. 779.

[14] (1953) Mad. 78, ('52) A.M. 193; *G. Sambireddy* v. *G. Jayamma* ('72) A.A.P. 156 (F.B.). [The court referred with approval to the case in *f.n.* 13 above and to *Saraswathi Ammal's Case* and held ss. 11 and 17 of the Hindu Marriages Act, 1956 did not violate Art. 15(1), as ss. 5(1), 11 and 17 merely introduced a social reform for the class of persons to whom the Act applied].

had done likewise, and that personal law was not based only on religion. The essence of the classification was not religion. As regards Art. 25, religious practice could be controlled in the interest of social welfare and therefore Art. 15 (1) was not violated. The Court said that to accept the argument of the petitioner would be to render the personal laws of the Hindus, the Muslims, and others, void, for those laws contained different provisions in respect of various matters. In *H. B. Singh* v. *T. N. H. Ongbi Bhani Devi*[15] it was held that the Hindu Marriage Act, 1955, which imposed monogamy on the Hindus was valid and did not violate Art. 14, 15 or 25. In *Chennamma* v. *Dyana Setty*[16] it was held that s. 23, Mysore Hindu Law Women's Rights Act, 1953, which conferred on a Hindu woman governed by the *mitakshara* school of Hindu law, a right to claim maintenance against her husband on the ground that he had kept a concubine did not violate Art. 15.[17] It is submitted that these decisions are correct and that in introducing social reform, the State is entitled to proceed by stages and to consider whether any particular community governed by the personal law is ripe enough for the reform proposed.[18]

Other laws upheld

9.149 The challenge to the Hindu Succession Act, 1956, under Art. 14 on the ground that it discriminated between the powers of alienation of males and females was rejected as devoid of force, in view of Art. 15. The Court said that women as a class were different from men as a class and the legislature had merely removed the disability attaching to women; there was no discrimination *inter se* a class.[19] In *Sangannagouda* v. *Kalkangouda*[20] it was said that *lingayats* were within the fold of Hinduism and belonged to the fourth class. The classification of *lingayats* among *sudras* did not violate Arts. 14, 15 and 17 and there was no discrimination against *lingayats*. On the contrary, an enlarged right was given to *lingayats* to adopt even a wife's sister's son. No question of untouchability arose in the case, and if it was felt that the word "sudra" had an uncomplimentary connotation, it was for the legislature to change the nomenclature. In *Bhabani Prosad* v. *Sm. Sarat Sundari*,[21] it was held that s. 14, Hindu Succession Act, 1956, did not discriminate between citizens on the ground of place of birth but applied equally to the *mitakshara* as well as the *dayabhaga* school of Hindu law.

Classification based on residence not violative of Art. 15: *D. P. Joshi's Case*

9.150 We have seen that Art. 16 (2) includes "residence" among the grounds on which discrimination cannot be made. The absence of that ground in Art. 15 has been noticed, and a classification based on residence has been upheld. In *D. P. Joshi* v. *M. B.*[22] the Supreme Court, by a majority of 4 to 1, upheld a rule which exempted all

---

[15] ('59) A.Mani. 20. [16] (1953) Mys. 41, ('53) A.Mys. 136.

[17] The Court referred to the decisions in *Srinivasa Iyer* v. *Saraswathi Ammal* (1953) Mad. 78, ('52) A.M. 193, (1951) 2 M.L.J. 649 and to *Bombay* v. *Narasu Appa Mali* (1951) Bom. 775, ('52) A.B. 84, 53 Bom.L.R. 779, in support of the view that the universal application of a law was not the test or criterion to brand a law as discriminatory. Citizens of India were governed by personal laws and when a law applied to one and all of a class alike, the law was not discriminatory.

[18] It may be mentioned that before 1865 polygamy prevailed among the Parsis. In 1865, on the demand of the community itself, polygamy was abolished and monogamy enforced.

[19] *Kaur Singh* v. *Jaggar Singh* ('61) A.Punj. 489, 63 P.L.R. 537.

[20] ('60) A.Mys. 147. [21] ('57) A.Cal. 527.

[22] (1955) 1 S.C.R. 1215, ('55) A.SC. 334.

students who were "*bona fide* residents" of Madhya Bharat from the payment of capitation fees. The definition of *bona fide* residents contained a reference to domicile in Madhya Bharat. The majority held that on a true construction of the rule, "domicile" was used in the sense of residence, that there was a distinction between domicile and citizenship, and therefore a rule giving preference on the ground of residence did not violate Art. 15(1). The rule did not contravene Art. 14 as it was based on a reasonable classification. This decision was followed in *N. Vasundara* v. *Mysore*[23], in *Jayantilal* v. *Saurashtra*[24] and in *Ramakrishna* v. *Osmania University*.[25] The same view was taken in *Rustom* v. *M.B.*[26], *P. Sagar* v. *State*[27] and in *Arun Narayan* v. *State*.[28].

The difference between Art. 14 and Arts. 15 and 16

9.151 Although the word "discriminate" is not used in Art. 14, the expression "discriminate against" is used in Arts. 15 and 16 and the expression means, according to the Oxford Dictionary, "to make an adverse distinction with regard to; to distinguish unfavourably from others." In *Kathi Raning Rawat* v. *Saurashtra*[29] after referring to the above definition, Sastri C.J. brought out the difference between Art. 14 on the one hand, and Arts. 15 and 16 on the other as regards burden of proof by observing that:

> ". . . Discrimination thus involves an element of unfavourable bias and it is in that sense that the expression has to be understood in this context. If such bias is disclosed and is based on any of the grounds mentioned in Articles 15 and 16, it may well be that the statute will, without more, incur condemnation as violating a specific constitutional prohibition unless it is saved by one or other of the provisos to those articles. But the position under Art. 14 is different. Equal protection claims under that article are examined with the presumption that the State action is reasonable and justified."[30]

It is obvious that a discrimination made by the Constitution cannot be questioned as violating Art. 14 and it was so held by Beg J. in *Union* v. *K. S. Subramanian*.[31] Several decisions under Art. 15(3) considered in para 9.155 of the text illustrate the same principle.

---

[23] (1971) Supp. S.C.R. 381, ('71) A.SC. 1439 (*held*, that R. 3 of Mysore Rules for selecting candidates for admission to pre-professional/B.Sc. Part I course leading to M.B.B.S. in Government medical colleges imposing a condition of residence for a minimum period of 10 years in the State of Mysore in addition to the condition of being domiciled in that State did not violate Art. 14).

[24] ('56) A.Sau. 54 (upholding a Huzur order of the former Limdi State allowing free education to subjects of the former Limdi State on the ground that the preference was given on the basis of residence).

[25] (1963) Andh.Pr. 198, ('62) A.A.P. 120 (upholding r. 6 of the Osmania University on the ground that it was based on residence and not on place of birth).

[26] (1954) Madh.Bh. 87, ('54) A.M.B. 119 (upholding a discrimination made in admission to educational institutions on the ground of residence).

[27] ('68) A.A.P. 165 [*held*, upholding R. 6 (Telengana) and R. 7 (Andhra) for selection for admission to Medical Colleges in Telengana and Andhra areas, that the territorial division made for purposes of admission was valid and the rules did not violate Arts. 14 to 16].

[28] ('76) A.Knt. 174 [*held*, following the two Supreme Court decisions, particularly *N. Vasundhara* v. *Mysore* that, as held in that case, the requirement of domicile and residence for 10 years in the State of Mysore (now Karnataka) as a condition of eligibility for admission to Medical Colleges did not violate Art. 14].

[29] (1952) S.C.R. 435, ('52) A.SC. 123.

[30] (1952) S.C.R. at p. 442; *Jalan Trading Co.* v. *Mill Mazdoor Sabha* (1967) 1 S.C.R. 15, ('67) A.SC. 691, 703.

[31] (1977) 1 S.C.R. 87, ('76) A.SC. 2433 (*held*, that as the provisions of Art. 311 do not apply to those who hold posts "connected with defence", the respondent could not invoke Arts. 14 and 16, against a discrimination made by the Constitution itself).

9.152 A challenge to a law or an executive act on the ground that it violated Art. 15 or any other Article must be pleaded and proved if it is to succeed. Therefore, where the petitioner alleged that he had been excluded from the *maidan* surrounding Fort William in Calcutta, the petition was dismissed because there was no pleading and no sufficient proof that the petitioner had been discriminated against by reason of race.[32] Again, a plea that a certain notification was based on a discrimination on the ground of place of birth, was a plea under Art. 15 and not under Art. 14, and where the plea under Art. 15 had neither been pleaded nor proved, the Court would not allow it to be raised at the stage of revision.[33] Finally, if a person failed to establish a right, he would necessarily fail to establish the violation of a fundamental right. Thus, where the petitioner complained that the State had violated Art. 15 in granting a concession in school fees to members of specified castes, who, or whose parents had been converted to Christianity and in not extending that concession to those whose grand-parents or remoter ancestors had been converted to Christianity, it was held that as the petitioner had no right to any concessional fee the question of a violation of Art. 15 did not arise.[34]

Conditions necessary to attract Art. 15 must be pleaded and proved

9.153 The following provisions have been held not to violate Art. 15: s. 2(1) (*a*), Abducted Persons (Recovery and Restoration) Act, 1949;[35] the limited power of alienating ancestral land in Punjab;[36] s. 19E, Punjab Security of Land Tenures Act, 1953, and s. 32KK, Pepsu Tenancy and Agricultural Land Act, 1959;[37] Punjab Land Reforms Act, 1973;[38] the Hyderabad Prevention of Agricultural Land Alienation Act (1330F);[39] the provisions of s. 60(1) (*c*), C.P.C., which

Provisions held not violative of Art. 15

---

[32] *Alfred M. Deane* v. *Commissioner of Police* ('61) A.Cal. 664, 64 C.W.N. 348 (the Court held that the *maidan* surrounding Fort William in Calcutta, except those parts of it set apart for a particular purpose, could be said to be a place of public resort maintained out of State funds within the meaning of Art. 15).

[33] *P.B.M.C.M. Union* v. *Commissioner of Police* ('61) A.Cal. 125 (S.B.), 65 C.W.N. 213.

[34] *In re M. Thomas* ('53) A.M. 21, (1952) 2 M.L.J. 450.

[35] *Ajaib Singh* v. Punjab (1952) Punj. 381, ('52) A.Punj. 309 [*held*, that the abducted person might not even be a Muslim at the time of his or her being taken into custody; on appeal in *Punjab* v. *Ajaib Singh* (1953) S.C.R. 254, ('53) A.SC. 10, the plea under Art. 15 was given up, the Court observing that the High Court had rightly rejected the plea; rel. on in *Sohan Singh* v. *State* ('55) A.Pep. 1].

[36] *Nathu* v. *Ralla* ('51) A.Punj. 445 (*held*, that whoever lived in the Punjab whether Jat, Rajaput, or anybody and whatever his race, his power of alienation over ancestral land was limited and there was no infringement of Art. 15).

[37] *Bhagat Gobind Singh* v. *Punjab* (1963) 1 Punj. 500, ('63) A.Punj. 319.

[38] *Sucha Singh* v. *State* ('74) A.P. & H. 162 (*held*, that Art. 15 was not violated by s. 5 of the Act merely because the holder or owner was allowed to select a separate permissible area in respect of each adult son but not in respect of each adult daughter. The Act was legislation in respect of the holders or owners of land as to the permissible area which they could hold and the Act made no discrimination in that respect between men and women holders or owners; and, secondly, because the discrimination was not on the ground of sex but on the ground that "a daughter has to go to another family after her marriage in due course, marriage being a normal custom which is universally practised.": ibid. p. 171.

[39] *Narasappa* v. *Shaik Hazrat* ('60) A.Mys. 59 (*held*, that the Act safeguarded the agricultural classes and not persons belonging to a particular community like the Muslims or Hindus or Christians. The basis of classification was not religion but avocation in life, namely, agriculture. The Court observed that a person who took the benefit of a statute could not challenge it).

exempted houses and buildings, etc., belonging to agriculturists from attachment;[40] s. 5, Punjab Court of Wards Act; [41] s. 10, Indian Divorce Act, which required a woman to prove not only adultery by her husband but also desertion and cruelty;[42] para 3, W. B. Food Grains (Movement and Control) Order, 1951;[43] a notification purporting to acquire land for housing accommodation for harijans ("untouchables");[44] s. 4, Money-lenders (Regulation of Transactions) Act, 1939.[45]

Provisions held violative of Art. 15

9.154 The following were held to violate Art. 15(1): any law providing for an election to local bodies on the basis of separate electorates for members of different religious communities unless such a law was protected by Art. 15(4);[46] the formation of certain constituencies for the purpose of elections to a Panchayat on the basis of caste by taking out people of certain castes from one area and putting them in another in de-limiting the Wards for the purpose of benefiting a particular community;[47] s. 15, Buschahar Alienation of Land Regulation (1986B);[48] the requisition of land under the Bombay Land Requisition Act, 1948, for the construction of a Harijan colony *before the amendment of Art. 15*;[49] the exemption granted under s. 15(5), Police Act[50], to the Harijan and Muslim inhabitants of certain villages in which an additional police force was stationed, from the levy of the cost of such force on the ground that they were

---

40 *Rura Ram* v. *Gurbachana* ('54) A.Punj. 254 (there was nothing to indicate that the privilege conferred by the section upon agriculturists proceeded upon the place of birth of the agriculturist).

41 *Harmahendra Singh* v. *Punjab* (1953) VI Punj. 279, ('53) A.Punj. 30 (*held*, that however undesirable it may be to pass the law, it was not hit by Art. 15 which prohibited discrimination on the grounds there mentioned. As regards Art. 14, the section was based on a valid classification).

42 *Dr. Dwarka Bai* v. *Prof. Nainan* ('53) A.M. 792, 800 (without expressing a final view, the Court observed that s. 10 did not violate Arts. 13 and 15 since the consequences of adultery by a man and adultery by a women were different, in that a husband committing adultery did not bear a child as a result of it nor was the wife bound to maintain any child; whereas if the wife committed adultery and bore a child as a result of such adultery, the husband would have to treat it as his legitimate child and would have to maintain that child).

43 *Indra Narayan* v. *W.B.* ('52) A.Cal. 61 (*held*, that the delimitation of the areas made by the order was not made on the ground that a person was born within a certain area. Control was imposed on the movement of foodgrains in the interest of the general public and it became necessary to forbid foodgrains from being moved out of a cordoned area except under a permit.

44 *Moosa* v. *Kerala* ('60) A.Ker. 355 (*held*, that after the amendment of Art. 15, the decision in *Jagwant Kaur* v. *Bombay* [see f.n. 49, *infra*] was no longer good law).

45 *J. P. Misser* v. *B. Das* (1952) 31 Pat. 963, ('53) A.P. 259 (*held*, that s. 4 did not violate Arts. 14 and 15 as the bar under that section applied to all money-lenders equally, whoever they were, and if they gave a loan within the limits of the State without being registered under the Money-Lenders Act).

46 *Nain Sukh Das* v. *U.P.* (1953) S.C.R. 1184, ('53) A.SC. 384.

47 *Bhopal Singh* v. *Rajasthan* (1957) 7 Raj. 1049, ('58) A.Raj. 41.

48 *Jai Lal* v. *Padam Singh* ('54) A.H.P. 23 (*held*, that s. 15 was void as it clearly discriminated in favour of one set of judgment-debtors on the ground of caste).

49 *Jagwant Kaur* v. *Bombay* (1953) Bom. 44, ('52) A.B. 461, 54 Bom.L.R. 678 [It was rightly held that the Directives of State Policy in Art. 46 did not control Art. 15(1)].

50 *Rajasthan* v. *Thakur Pratap Singh* ('60) A.SC. 1208 [*held*, that the exemption discriminated against the law-abiding members of other communities and in favour of the Muslims and Harijan communities (assuming that every one of them was peace-loving and law-abiding) on the basis only of caste or religion].

members of law-abiding communities. In *Radha Charan* v. *State*[51] it was held that R. 6(2) of the Orissa Statutory Judicial Service Rules, 1963, purporting to disqualify women from being appointed District Judges on marriage violated Art. 14 as the disqualification was on the ground of sex only. It is submitted that Rule 6(2) violated Art. 15 which prohibits discrimination on the ground of sex.

9.155 Article 15(2) is self-explanatory. It provides that no citizen shall be subjected to any disability, liability, restriction or condition with regard to access to shops, public restaurants, hotels and places of public entertainment[52] or with regard to the use of wells, tanks, bathing ghats, roads and places of public resort maintained wholly or partially out of State funds or dedicated to the use of the general public, on grounds only of religion, race, caste, sex, place of birth or any of them. In so far as such disability arises out of "untouchability", while Art. 15(2) forbids the enforcement of such disability, Art. 17 makes such enforcement punishable as an offence. Art.15(2)

9.156 Article 15(3) provides that "nothing in this Article shall prevent the State from making any special provision for women and children". This sub-Article is in the nature of an exception or proviso, but its drafting leaves much to be desired. Since Art. 15(1) does not make *age* a prohibited ground of discrimination, the reference to children in Art. 15(3) appears pointless as observed in *Anjali* v. *W.B.*[53] Again, read literally, Art. 15(3) would apply only to future laws, and that is how Mukherji J. read it in *Mahadeb Jiew* v. *B. B. Sen.*[54] However, such a construction would be irrational, for it would be absurd to permit a legislature to make special provisions for women and children for the future and yet invalidate existing laws which already made such provision. In fact, the object of Art. 15(3) is so plain that in *Yusuf Abdul Aziz* v. *Bombay*[55] Bose J. repelled the challenge under Art. 15(1) to s. 497 I.P.C. (which had been enacted in 1860), by holding that the section was protected by Art. 15(3). It is submitted that by construction Art. 15(3) must be treated as applying to both existing and future laws. And the reference to children must be treated as an independent substantive provision putting a discrimination in favour of children beyond

Art. 15(3): defective drafting

Reference to "children" inept in the context

The plain meaning of Art. 15 would lead to absurd results

---

[51] ('69) A.Or. 237, 240-41 (The court said that it was significant that Art. 217 did not preclude married women from being appointed judges of the High Courts).

[52] On the subject of places of public entertainment, see *Halsbury*, Vol. 37 (3rd ed.) pp. 1-72.

[53] ('52) A.Cal. 825, 56 C.W.N. 801.

[54] ('51) A.Cal. 563, 568, 55 C.W.N. 453 [the case decided that O. 25, r. 1(3), C.P.C., did not violate Art. 15(1) as it did not discriminate against men only on the ground of sex. It is submitted that the decision is more securely rested on the ground that O. 25, r. 1(3), C.P.C. is covered by Art. 15(3)]. In *Dattatraya Motiram* v. *Bombay* (1953) Bom. 842, ('53) A.B. 311, 55 Bom.L.R. 323, Chagla C.J. held that Art. 15(3) applied to both existing laws and laws which the State may make in the future. It is submitted that the decision is correct but the difficulty created by the language of Art. 15(3) is not met by saying as the judgment says, that Art. 372 preserves all existing law and that before an existing law is shown to be invalid, it must be established that it violates a fundamental right, and that as Art. 15(3) enables a special provision to be made, the impugned law is not void. But this begs the question which is whether the special provision could be made only prospectively, that is, after January 26, 1950, or also covers provisions already made.

[55] (1954) S.C.R. 930, ('54) A.SC. 321.

challenge on the ground of discrimination. In *Abdul Aziz's Case*, one Yusuf Abdul Aziz was charged with an offence under s. 497, I.P.C. (adultery). The case was removed under Art. 228 to the High Court for the determination of the question raised by the accused that s. 497 was void as violating Arts. 14 and 15. The challenge under Art. 14 was repelled by saying that the sub-section created an offence limited to adultery committed by a man and did not extend the offence to adultery committed by a woman. The law created no inequality because it operated equally on all. The challenge under Art. 15(1) was based on the last part of s. 497 which provided that the wife was not to be punished as an abettor. As the accused was not a citizen he was not entitled to invoke Art. 15(1) but as we have seen, Chagla C.J. mistakenly held that he was entitled to show that he was being prosecuted under a void law. Chagla C.J. repelled the challenge under Art. 15(1) by observing that the difference of treatment was not based on the ground of sex, but on the ground of the social position of women in India.[56] Strictly speaking, the question of justifying the law on the merits under Art. 15(1) did not arise if Art. 15(3) covered the law.[57] On appeal,[58] Bose J. held that the challenge under Art. 15(1) was effectively met by referring to Art. 15(3). In dismissing the appeal, he said:

Does Art. 15(3) refer to discrimination in favour of women?

"It was argued that clause (3) should be confined to provisions which are beneficial to women and cannot be used to give them a licence to commit and abet crimes. We are unable to read any such restriction into the clause; nor are we able to agree that a provision which prohibits punishment is tantamount to a licence to commit the offence of which punishment has been prohibited. Art. 14 is general and must be read with the other provisions which set out the ambit of fundamental rights. Sex is a sound classification and although there can be no discrimination in general on that ground, the Constitution itself provides for special provisions in the case of women and children. The two articles read together validate the impugned clause in section 497 of the Indian Penal Code."[59]

---

[56] The authors of the I.P.C. said: ". . . We cannot but feel that there are some peculiarities in the state of society in this country which may well lead a humane man to pause before he determines to punish the infidelity of wives. The condition of the women of this country is . . . (that) they are married while still children; they are often neglected for other wives while still young. They share the attentions of a husband with several rivals. To make laws for punishing the inconstancy of the wife, while the law admits the privilege of the husband to fill his zenana with women, is a course which we are most reluctant to adopt. We are not so visionary as to think of attacking, by law, an evil so deeply rooted in the manners of the people of this country as polygamy. We leave it to the slow, but we trust the certain, operation of education and of time. But while it exists, while it continues to produce its never failing effects on the happiness and respectability of women, we are not inclined to throw into a scale, already too much depressed, the additional weight of the penal law" (quoted in Ratanlal and Dhiralal, *Law of Crimes*, 20th ed., pp. 1269-70).

[57] In the concluding part of his judgment Chagla C.J. said: "In this connection we would like to add that it is possible to take the view that the alleged discrimination in favour of women is saved by . . . Art. 15(3)"; See also *Girdhar Gopal* v. *State* ('53) A.M.B. 147, where it was held that s. 354, I.P.C. which made an assault or use of criminal force whether by a man or woman with intent to outrage the modesty of a woman punishable was based on a valid classification under Art. 14, and did not violate Art. 15(1) as it did not discriminate on grounds only of sex but also on considerations of propriety, public morals, decency, decorum and rectitude. It is submitted that the decision is correct but should be rested on the ground that the section was covered by Art. 15(3).

[58] (1954) S.C.R. 930, ('54) A.SC. 321.

[59] (1954) S.C.R. *supra* at pp. 931-2.

9.157 The above observations might suggest that the special provision contemplated by Art. 15 (3) is not limited to provisions which discriminate *in favour* of women. It is submitted that this question in a general form did not arise and was not considered by the Supreme Court. It has however been raised and considered by the High Courts. In *Mahadeb Jiew* v. *B. B. Sen*[60] Mukherji J. in a well-considered judgment observed that the word "discriminate against" involved a comparison, and that one could not "discriminate *against*" a person, without discriminating "*in favour of*" someone else. The special provision for women mentioned in Art. 15 (3) could not be interpreted to authorise a discrimination against women, first, because Art. 15 (3) did not use the expression "discriminate against" but used the different expression "special provisions for". Secondly, the word "for" in the context meant "in favour of".[61] The intention clearly was to protect the interests of women and children, which according to the framers of the Constitution required protection. This interpretation gave a clear and coherent interpretation to Art. 15 (1) and (3) because a provision discriminating in favour of women would necessarily discriminate against men and would therefore constitute an exception to the prohibition of discrimination on the ground of sex contained in Art. 15 (1). This decision was followed by Bose J. in *Anjali* v. *State of W.B.*[62] On appeal[63], Chakravarti Acg. C.J. admitted the possibility that the word "for" might mean "concerning", on which construction Art. 15 (3) might justify a discrimination against women; but he held that in the context of the whole Article, the words "special provisions for women" meant "special provisions in favour of women". In *Dattatraya Motiram* v. *Bombay*[64] Chagla C.J. held that as a result of the joint operation of Art. 15 (1) and Art. 15 (3) the State could discriminate in favour of women against men, but it could not discriminate in favour of men against women. Accordingly, a reservation of seats for women in an election to a Municipality was upheld as covered by Art. 15 (3), as also a reservation of 30 per cent of seats for women candidates for admission to Medical Colleges.[65] However, in *Savitri* v. *K. K. Bose*[66] it was held that the word "provision" in Art. 15 (3) was used in the sense of a legislative enactment, a rule, a regulation and a general order. The word "provision" could not be read as including a decision given

The better view is that it does

---

[60] ('51) A.Cal. 563, 55 C.W.N. 453.

[61] *Cf. The C.O.D.* p. 474: "for": "in defence or support or *favour of*" (italics supplied).

[62] ('52) A.Cal. 825.

[63] *Anjali* v. *W.B.* ('52) A.Cal. 825, 56 C.W.N. 801 [*held*, that the impugned order of the Director of Public Instruction not to admit women students in certain colleges was intended to promote the development of a new college for women and ultimately to make it a well-established and self-sufficient organization and was a special provision under Art. 15(3), made in the interest of and for the benefit of the women students of our country].

[64] (1953) Bom. 842, ('53) A.B. 311, 55 Bom.L.R. 323.

[65] *P. Sagar* v. *State* ('68) A.A.P. 165, 174 [fol. an earlier judgment in *Sukhdev* v. *A.P.* reported in (1966) 1 Andh.W.R. 294].

[66] ('72) A.A. 305 [*held*, that since no special provision had been made in respect of granting liquor licences to women, preference given to women applicants in granting liquor licence on the ground that they were women was given on an irrelevant ground and also violated Art. 15(1)].

Submission: Art. 15(3) permits discrimination in favour of, and not against, women

in a particular case or matter. In *Mt. Choki* v. *State*[67] the Court upheld the provision of s. 497(1), Cr.P.C. which enabled women and children to be released on bail in circumstances under which men could not be released, by observing that under Art. 15(3) special provisions could be made *in favour of* women and children but not against them. It is submitted that this view is correct and that it effectuates both the general policy underlying Art. 15(1) and the necessity of making an exception in favour of women and children, whose position requires special protection. Consequently, it has been rightly held that s. 8(1)(*d*)[68] and s. 8(1)(*b*)[69] of the U.P. Court of Wards Act, 1912, made a classification prejudicial to women on the ground of sex and was void under Art. 15.

Art. 15(4): special provision for backward classes

9.158 As the number of candidates seeking admission to colleges far exceeds the number of seats available, the validity of orders passed by government reserving seats for Scheduled Castes, Scheduled Tribes and Backward classes in engineering, medical and other colleges providing technical education has been considered in a number of cases after clause (4) had been inserted in Art. 15 under circumstances noted earlier. The Supreme Court considered Art. 15(4) in *M. R. Balaji* v. *Mysore*[70], *Heggade Janardhan Subbarye* v. *Mysore*[71] and *R. Chitralekha* v. *Mysore*,[72] which must be read together as the second case "clarified" the first, and the third "explained" a part of it. In *Balaji's Case*, the Order of the Mysore Government reserving seats was the fifth Order impugned in Court.[73] The questions thus raised were of extreme importance, for they involved the two fundamental rights guaranteed to citizens by Art. 15(1) and Art. 29(2) on the one hand, and the promotion of the educational and economic interests of the weaker sections of the people mentioned in Art. 46 on the other. There was also the national interest which must suffer if qualified and competent students were unreasonably excluded from higher university education. It was against this background that the Supreme Court considered Art. 15(4). That Article, and Arts. 29(2), 46, and 340 to 342 form a group of Articles making special provision for the advancement of any socially and educationally backward classes of citizens in matters of admission to educational institutions.[74] It was not disputed that these Articles justified a reservation of seats for the Scheduled Castes and Scheduled Tribes and for Backward classes; the dispute was about the extent of such special provision, and the tests to be applied for determining backward classes. The impugned Order was based on the report of the Nagan Gowda Committee, and the judgment in *Balaji's Case* considered that report, and other reports, dealing with backward classes and the reservation to be made for them in educational institutions. However, the Court first

Balaji's Case: reservation of seats in educational institutions

---

67 ('57) A.Raj. 10.
68 *Cracknell* v. *U.P.* (1953) 1 All. 29, ('52) A.A. 746.
69 *Raj Rajeshwari Devi* v. *U.P.* ('54) A.A. 608.
70 (1963) Supp. 1 S.C.R. 439, ('63) A.SC. 649.
71 (1963) Supp. 1 S.C.R. 475, ('63) A.SC. 702.
72 (1964) 6 S.C.R. 368, ('64) A.SC. 1823.
73 See (1963) Supp. 1 S.C.R. *supra* at pp. 445-48, where the various orders are set out.
74 ('64) A.SC. *supra* at p. 1833, *per* Subba Rao J.

dealt with certain preliminary contentions and held that: (1) the appointment of a Commission under Art. 340(1) and the laying of a copy of its report before each House of Parliament was not a necessary condition before taking action under Art. 15(4);[75] (ii) the language of Art. 340(1) showed that it was the Union or the State Government which had to take action and not the President;[76] (iii) provision under Art. 15(4) could be made by an executive order and legislation was not necessary for that purpose.[77]

9.159 On the main issues, the Supreme Court held that (*i*) the bracketing of socially and educationally backward classes with the Scheduled Castes and Tribes in Art. 15(4), and the provision in Art. 338(3) that the references to Scheduled Castes and Tribes were to be construed as including such backward classes as the President may by order specify on receipt of the report of the Commission appointed under Art. 340(1), showed that in the matter of their backwardness they were comparable to Scheduled Castes and Tribes;[78] (*ii*) the concept of backward classes was not relative in the sense that any class which was backward in relation to the most advanced class in the community must be included in it;[79] (*iii*) the backwardness must be *both* social *and* educational and not *either* social *or* educational;[80] (*iv*) Art. 15(4) referred to backward classes and not to backward castes; indeed the test of caste would break down as regards backward communities which had no caste;[81] (*v*) caste was *a* relevant factor in determining social backwardness. As regards Hindus, caste

The meaning of "backward classes"

the test of backwardness: caste may be *a* relevant factor

". . . may be a relevant factor to consider in determining . . . social backwardness . . . (but) it cannot be made the sole or the dominant test. . . . Social backwardness is on the ultimate analysis the result of poverty, to a very large extent . . . social backwardness which results from poverty is likely to be aggravated by considerations of caste to which the poor citizens may belong, but that only shows the relevance of both caste and poverty in determining the backwardness of citizens."[82]

(*vi*) the occupations followed by certain classes (which are looked upon as inferior) may contribute to social backwardness;[83] and so may the habitation of people, for, in a sense, the problem of social backwardness is the problem of rural India;[84] (*vii*) that the impugned order made a classification based only on caste without regard to other relevant factors and such a classification was not permissible under Art. 15(4);[85] (*viii*) the division of backward classes into backward and more backward classes was in substance a division of the population into the most advanced and *the rest*, *the rest* being divided into backward and more backward classes and this was not warranted by Art. 15(4);[86] (*ix*) the propriety of the literacy test

Classification in the impugned circular invalid on several grounds

[75] (1963) Supp. 1 S.C.R. *supra* at p. 456.
[76] ibid. p. 457.
[77] ibid. [fol. in *P. Sagar* v. *State* ('68) A.A.P. 165, 173].
[78] ibid. p. 458.
[79] ibid. p. 459.
[80] ibid.
[81] ibid.
[82] ibid. pp. 460-61 (this test was subsequently explained in *Chitralekha's Case*).
[83] ibid. p. 461.
[84] ibid.
[85] ibid. pp. 462-63.
[86] ibid. pp. 465-66. The impugned order treated 90 per cent of the population as backward.

adopted in the impugned order was doubtful;[87] but even if it were correct, to classify any class as backward, the average of that class must be "well below 6.9 per thousand;[88] the impugned order was void as it classified communities which were just below 6.9 per 1,000 as backward.[89] In *B. C. Swain* v. *W. & T. Dept.*,[90] it was held that although Harijans do not fall within Scheduled Castes and Scheduled Tribes, the court could take judicial notice of the fact that Harijans were socially and educationally backward.

The extent of reservation: Art. 15(4) an exception to Art. 15(1)

9.160 As regards the extent of the reservation permitted by Art. 15 (4) it was held that that sub-Article was a special provision for Scheduled Castes and Tribes and Backward Classes and it would be unreasonable to construe that provision *as justifying even a total reservation of seats for such classes, as contended for by the State.*[91] Art. 15 (4) was a special provision in derogation of the fundamental rights of citizens under Art. 15 (1) and Art. 29 (2), to both of which Art. 15 (4) was a proviso. Again, the national interest could not be ignored, and that interest would suffer if students with superior qualifications and merit were unreasonably excluded from admission into Colleges.[92] The Supreme Court held that speaking generally, the reservation must be less than 50 per cent[93] without laying down any hard and fast rule *as to how much less.* In a later case the Supreme Court upheld a reservation of 48 per cent for Scheduled Castes, Scheduled Tribes and Backward classes.[94] As the impugned order reserved 68 per cent seats for Sch. Castes and Tribes and Backward Classes, it was void on that ground also. This judgment was "clarified" in *Janardhan's Case*[95] by saying that it had not in any way invalidated the reservation for Scheduled Castes and Scheduled Tribes of 15 and 3 per cent respectively, which had remained constant in all the impugned orders. It is submitted that the disadvantage of the clarification is that it concealed from the Court the difference between Art. 16 (4), which speaks for reservations in favour of any "backward class of citizens", and Art. 15 (4) which speaks of any provision for the advancement of any socially and educationally backward classes of citizens *or* for the Scheduled Castes and Sche-

must ordinarily be less than fifty per cent

The above decision "clarified" in *Janardhan's Case*

---

[87] ibid. p. 463. The Nagan Gowda Committees' Report found that the average for the whole State of students in the three highest classes in the High Schools was 6.9 per 1000. Any caste or community which had an average below 6.9 per 1000 was classified as backward and any caste or community whose average was 50 per cent of 6.9 per 1000 was classed as more backward.

[88] ibid. p. 464. The Court did not define "well below" but indicated that an average of 5 per 1000 for the Muslim community was not well below the State average of 6.9 per 1000.

[89] ibid. p. 464.

[90] ('74) A.Or. 115 [*held*, that the impugned Govt. order suggesting the leasing out of certain roadside lands on an annual basis to landless Harijans, preference being given to Fisheries Co-operative Society of landless Harijans was not discriminatory as it fell within Art. 15(4)].

[91] (1963) Supp. 1 S.C.R. *supra* at p. 467. Although the judgment does not refer to the well-settled principle of construction that a proviso should not be held to nullify the section to which it is a proviso [*Kottaya* v. *R.* 48 Bom.L.R. 508, 514 (P.C.)], in fact, the judgment applies that principle.

[92] ibid. pp. 467-69.

[93] ibid. p. 470. Applied in *Ramesh Chander* v. *Punjab* ('66) A.Punj. 476.

[94] *D. N. Chanchala* v. *Mysore* (1971) Supp. S.C.R. 608, ('71) A.SC. 1762, 1771 [the Court referred to *A. Periakaruppan* v. *T.N.* (1970) 2 S.C.R. 430, ('71) A.SC. 2303, 2309 where a reservation of 41 per cent for the same classes had been upheld.

[95] (1963) Supp. 1 S.C.R. 475, ('63) A.SC. 702.

duled Tribes. *Janardhan's Case* clarified that in *Balaji's Case* no challenge had been made to the reservation of 15% and 3% in favour of Scheduled Castes and Scheduled Tribes respectively ("the said reservation"). Therefore, although the Court in *Balaji's Case* quashed the whole order, it was not to be taken as having quashed the said reservation. If the Court had inquired why no challenge had been made to the said reservation, it would have discovered that under Art. 15(4), special provision could be made for two separate categories (i) socially and educationally backward classes of citizens, *or* (ii) for Sch. Castes and Sch. Tribes. As to (i) above, the question whether caste can be the *sole* criterion is relevant, and the decision in *Balaji's Case* that it cannot be, is correct. But as to (ii) above, Sch. Castes and Sch. Tribes are the subject of a distinct and separate power introduced by the disjunctive word *or*. The question whether in the case of Sch. Castes and Sch. Tribes, caste can be the sole criterion, or whether they are socially and educationally backward becomes irrelevant under Art. 15(4). Once reasonable reservations are made for members of Sch. Castes and Sch. Tribes, no further question survives, because the condition for the exercise of the State's power under Art. 15(4) are satisfied. This is not to say that the Court cannot take judicial notice that Sch. Castes and Sch. Tribes are socially and educationally backward. It only means that such backwardness is irrelevant.

Sch. Castes and Sch. Tribes the subject of a separate power

9.161 *Chitralekha's Case* "explained" *Balaji's Case* by saying that though caste was a relevant test for determining the social backwardness of citizens, it was not obligatory to apply that test and a determination of social backwardness was not void merely because it ignored caste if such determination was based on other relevant criteria.[96] *Chitralekha's Case* was followed by the Supreme Court in *K. S. Jayasree* v. *Kerala*.[97] There, the State of Kerala had appointed a Commission to inquire into the social and educational conditions of the people, and to report as to what sections of the people in Kerala should be treated as socially and educationally backward classes. Following on the recommendations in the Commission's Report[98] Government directed that members of backward classes with an annual income of Rs. 10,000 would not be eligible for seats reserved for backward classes in Medical Colleges. The Supreme Court held that neither caste by itself nor poverty by itself constituted backwardness. But though poverty by itself was not the determining factor, poverty was a relevant factor in determining social backwardness. Confining the benefit of reservation of seats to members of backward classes who were poor gave a benefit, where it was necessary, to uplift the backward classes. Accordingly, the Government's direction was held to be valid.[99]. In

and "explained" in *Chitralekha's Case*

[96] ('64) A.SC. 1823, 1833; *R. Chitralekha* v. *Mysore* (1964) 6 S.C.R. 368, 369, ('64) A.SC. 1823. In *Skaria Francis* v. *State* ('67) A.Ker. 128, *Balaji's Case* and *Chitralekha's Case* were relied on, and it was held that where a means-cum-caste or community test was adopted to determine the backwardness of a class, the mere fact that the income of a person was less than the limit of income fixed by the test would not entitle him to claim that he belonged to a backward class.

[97] ('76) A.SC. 2381, (1977) 1 S.C.R. 194.

[98] ('76) A.SC. pp. 2384-5 where a summary of the Report is given.

[99] In *R. Shrinivasa* v. *Chairman, Selection Board*, ('81) A.Knt. 86, the petitioner who belonged to a backward class family with an income of over Rs. 10,000 a year

Chamaraja v. *Mysore*[99a] the discretion conferred on the State under Art. 15(4) was very wide and was not regulated by any other provision of the Constitution. Merely because Art. 336 had reserved certain posts for a particular community in addition to what they might get under Art. 29(2), it did not follow that the same was true of Art. 15(4).

P. Rajendran v. Madras: districtwise reservation violates Art. 14

9.162 In *P. Rajendran* v. *Madras*[99b] the Supreme Court held that though the list of backward classes prepared by the Madras Government described them by reference to caste, and though the reservation of seats based on caste alone would be invalid, considerations of caste were not irrelevant to the question of backwardness[99c] as held in *M. R. Balaji* v. *Mysore*.[99d] The court was satisfied by the explanation given by the Madras Government in its affidavit, that the castes mentioned in the list were socially and educationally backward.[99e] But, the court held that the reservation made districtwise violated Art. 14, because there was no reasonable nexus between a districtwise classification and the admitted object of the law, to secure the best candidates for admission to the Medical College.[99f]

Chitra Ghosh v. Union

9.163 In *Chitra Ghosh* v. *Union*[99g] under the rules made by the Central Government admission to the Maulana Azad Medical College

---

got himself adopted into another backward class family with an income of less than Rs. 10,000 a year. Rule 5(3) of the Karnataka Selection Rules was similar to the Rule considered in *Jayasree's Case*. The petitioner claimed the right to be admitted to a reserved seat as the income of his adoptive father was less than Rs. 10,000. Rejecting the claim, the Court held that reading the relevant rules, "there was no room for doubt that the intention of the State Government was only to make reservations in favour of persons who belonged to a backward class in the family of their birth and not in favour of persons who chose to get themselves adopted to a family of a lower income or shortly before applying for the M.B.B.S. Course": ibid. p. 88.

[99a] ('67) A.Mys. 21 (upholding the validity of an order reserving 30 per cent of seats in professional and technical colleges for socially and educationally backward classes but making the reservation available only to the extent that they did not get adequate representation in the merit pool).

[99b] ('68) A.SC. 1012, (1968) 2 S.C.R. 786.

[99c] ('68) A.SC. at p. 1015.

[99d] (1963) Supp. 1 S.C.R. 439, 459-60; ('63) A.SC. 649 at p. 659. *Balaji's Case, Chitralekha's Case* and *Rajendran's Case* were fol. in *A.P.* v. *Sagar* (1968) 3 S.C.R. 595, ('68) A.SC. 1379 and reservation of seats for backward classes in medical institutions based *ex facie* on castes without taking into account considerations relevant for determining backward classes and without putting materials before the court to justify it could not be sustained under Art. 15(4). The above cases were fol. in *A.P.* v. *U.S.V. Balaram* (1972) 3 S.C.R. 247, ('72) A.SC. 1375 [*held*, that since Art. 15(4) is a proviso or exception to Arts. 15(1) and 29(2), the conditions which justify a departure from Art. 15(1) must be strictly established; *held further*, that once a common test had been prescribed for admission to the M.B.B.S. course, namely, Higher Secondary Course (multi-purpose) and pre-University candidates, there could be no valid classification between the two. Even assuming that such a classification was valid, it had no reasonable relation to the object sought to be achieved, namely, selecting the best candidates for admission to the Medical Colleges. Consequently, the reservation of 40 per cent for H.S.C. candidates violated Art. 14].

[99e] The Court accepted the explanation as it had not been traversed by any affidavit in rejoinder: ('68) A.SC. at p. 1015.

[99f] The court made no consequential order because candidates who had already been selected on the basis of districtwise classification had not been joined as parties, and the appellant agreed that the selection of candidates should not be disturbed especially as it was too late for the rejected candidates to be admitted to College for the ensuing examination: ibid. pp. 1014, 1017.

("the College") was confined to the undernoted categories of students.[99h] One hundred twenty-five students were admitted annually to the College; 15 per cent and 5 per cent seats were reserved, respectively, for Sch. Caste and Sch. Tribe students; 25 per cent of the seats (excluding seats reserved for Government of India nominees) were reserved for girl students who were taken on the basis of merit. Twenty-three seats were reserved for categories (c) to (*h*) mentioned in f.n. 99h. The provisions for reserving seats were challenged as violating Arts. 14, 15 and 29(2). In repelling the challenge, the Supreme Court held that Art. 15 did not apply, as the classification was not based on grounds prohibited by that Article; in fact, Art. 15(4) expressly authorised special provisions for the advancement of socially and educationally backward class of citizens. Art. 29(2) did not apply, as the classification was not based on the grounds prohibited by that Article. Art. 14 was not violated because the classification was reasonable.[99i] In upholding the validity of the categories of students who were entitled to admission, the Supreme Court said that the main purpose of admission to a medical college was to impart education in the theory and practice of medicine, and *the sources from which students were to be drawn was primarily to be determined by the authority which maintained the institution* which, in the case before the court, was the Central Government. Though,

"the object of selection for admission is to secure the best possible material, (this) can surely be achieved by making proper rules in the matter of selection but there can be no doubt that such selection has to be confined to the sources that are intended to supply the material. If the sources have been classified in the manner done in the present case it is difficult to see how that classification has no rational nexus with the object of imparting medical education and also of selection for the purpose."[99j]

It is submitted that, in substance, this decision has over-ruled the decision in *P. Rajendran's Case*, in so far as it held that the *sole* object of medical education was to secure the best available candidates. For, the present decision holds that the best available candidates are not to be determined absolutely, but are to be the best candidates available from the various categories of students entitled to admission to a college.

[99g] (1970) 1 S.C.R. 413, ('70) A.SC. 35; foll. in *Y. Shanta* v. *Govt. Medical College* ('78) A.Knt. 66 [*held*, after construing the relevant rules of the Karnataka Medical College (Examination to Post-graduate Course) Rules, 1977, for selecting candidates, that where a candidate was denied admission in a subject of her choice because she had been selected in another subject, Art. 14 was violated].

[99h] (a) Residents of Delhi . . .; (b) Sons/daughters of Central Government servants posted in Delhi at the time of the admission; (ii) Candidate whose father is dead and who is wholly dependent on brother/sister who is a Central Government servant posted in Delhi at the time of the admission; (c) Sons/daughters of residents of Union Territories specified below including displaced persons registered therein and sponsored by their respective Administration (Sic) of Territory; (i) Himachal Pradesh; (ii) Tripura; (iii) Manipur; (iv) Naga Hills; (v) N.E.F.A.; (vi) Andaman; (d) Sons/daughters of Central Government servants posted in Indian Missions abroad; (e) Cultural Scholars; (f) Colombo Plan Scholars; (g) Thailand Scholars; (h) Jammu & Kashmir State Scholars.

[99i] For a detailed consideration of each category, see ('70) A.SC. *supra* pp. 38-9.

[99j] ('70) A.SC. at p. 39; *N. Kanakadurga* v. *K. Medical College* ('72) A.A.P. 82, 92-93 (*held*, that Art. 14 did not apply to a private Medical College because it was not the "State" within the meaning of Art. 12; *held further*, that even if Art. 14 did apply. *Chitra Ghosh's Case* justified the conclusion that the reservation of 140 seats for candidates from the Telengana region did not violate Art. 14).

A. Periakaruppan v. T.N.

9.164 However, in *A. Periakaruppan* v. *T. N.*[1], without reference to *Chitra Ghosh's Case*, the Supreme Court held that a unit-wise classification adopted by the State for admission to medical colleges, violated Arts. 14 and 15 as it did not secure the object of selecting the best candidates available. The fact that students were free to apply to any unit did not take the scheme outside the mischief of Arts. 14 and 15, for the students had been advised as far as possible to apply to the unit nearest to their place of residence.[2] Since the minimum number of marks required for being selected in some units was less than that required for selection in others, the scheme was *prima facie* discriminatory,[3] and the court was not satisfied with the explanation offered by Government in support of the discrimination.[4] Following *Balaji's Case*, *Chitralekha's Case* and *Rajendran's Case*, the Court upheld the classification of backward classes with reference to caste.[5] But the court rightly observed that the object of the reservation would be defeated if on the inclusion of a class in a list of backward classes, that class was treated as backward for all times. For the object of the reservation was to give special facilities to backward classes in order that in course of time they may cease to be backward. Consequently, Government should keep under review the question of the reservation of seats for backward classes;[6] and the fact that the backward classes had secured about 50 per cent of the seats in the general pool showed that the need for a *de novo* examination of the whole question of reserved seats.[7] The Court held that a reservation of 41 per cent of seats was not excessive.[8] However, *P. Rajendran's Case* and *Periakaruppan's Case* were distinguished by the Supreme Court in *D. N. Chanchala* v. *Mysore*[9] where it was held that where the State established three universities, and different Government medical colleges were affiliated to these universities.

> "there is nothing undesirable in ensuring that those attached to such universities have their ambitions to have specialised training . . . in medicine, satisfied through colleges affiliated to their own universities. *Such a basis for selection has not the disadvantage of districtwise or unitwise selection as any student from any part of the state can pass the qualifying examination in any of the three universities irrespective of the place of his birth or residence.*"[10] (italics supplied)

Kerala v. T. P. Roshana: University-wise student strength violated Art. 14

In considering the extent of the reservation, 15 seats reserved for candidates who took up family planning programmes must be excluded, for such a reservation was not a reservation "as understood by Art. 15".[11] *Chanchala's Case* was followed in *Kerala* v. *T. P. Roshana*.[12] Krishna Iyer J. held that the scheme adopted by the

---

[1] (1970) 2 S.C.R. 430, ('71) A.SC. 2303.
[2] ('71) A.SC. at p. 2306.
[3] ibid.
[4] ibid. where the explanation offered and rejected is discussed.
[5] ibid. pp. 2309-11.
[6] ibid. p. 2311.
[7] ibid.
[8] ibid. p. 2309.
[9] (1971) Supp. S.C.R. 608, ('71) A.SC. 1762.
[10] ('71) A.SC. at p. 1769 (Further, the rules conferred a discretion on the selection committee to admit outsiders who had passed the qualifying examination or its equivalent upto 20 per cent of the seats available).
[11] ibid. p. 1770; rel. on in *Subash Chandra* v. *State* ('73) A.A. 295, 298 and extended to reservation for nominees of the Central Government.
[12] (1979) 2 S.C.R. 974, ('79) A.SC. 765.

Kerala Government for admission of students to Medical Colleges[13] violated Art. 14, because:

"... the injection of the University-wise student-strength is drawing the red-herring across the trail — an irrelevance that invalidates the scheme. We cannot see the nexus between the registered student-strength and the seats to be allotted. The fewer the colleges the fewer the pre-degree or degree students. And so, the linkage of the division of seats with the registered student-strength would make an irrational inroad into the University-wise allocation. Such a formula would be a punishment for backwardness, not a promotion of their advancement. We cannot uphold the discriminatory paring down based on unreason."[14]

Treating the reilef to be given on the petition as a matter of emergency, Krishna Iyer J. claimed that the Supreme Court had wide powers under Art. 136, to do justice. Since the orders were passed, if not with consent, with the acquiescence of parties, and bearing in mind that the order was limited to a year, in which time no real injury would be done to the standards of medical education in Kerala, it is unnecessary to consider whether the powers claimed by Krishna Iyer J. actually belong to the Supreme Court under Art. 136. It is enough to say that the claim appears to be extremely dubious. In *State* v. *Rafia Rahim*[15] it was held that a scheme of selection for admission of students to Medical Colleges on assessment of merit of students drawn from different Universities with no uniformity of standards violated Art. 14. The consequences of this decision would have been that students who had already been selected would have to be removed in the midst of their studies and those who had not been selected could not profitably carry on their studies in the time left, especially as time would elapse before the right machinery was set up, and fresh students admitted. The Court held that under the circumstances it was a proper exercise of discretion to dismiss the petition since no practicable relief could be granted. However, the Court granted a declaration that the impugned scheme violated Art. 14. The Court opined that the best scheme for selection of students to Medical Colleges would be to select candidates by holding a uniform entrance examination to secure uniformity of standards.

U.P. v. *Pradip Tandon*: reservation for candidates from rural areas violated Art. 15

9.165 In *U.P.* v. *Pradip Tandon*[16] reservation of seats in medical colleges for candidates from rural, the Hill and Uttarkhand areas in Uttar Pradesh was justified on the ground that the areas were socially and educationally backward areas. The reservation was also justified on geographical or territorial basis. Ray C.J. for himself, Mathew and Untwalia JJ. said that Art. 15 (4) speaks of a socially and educationally backward class of citizens; and Art. 15 (4) did not enable the State to bring socially and educationally backward *areas* within the protection of Art. 15 (4).[17] After setting out the test of backwardness,[18] Ray C.J. held that the Hill and Uttarkhand areas in U.P. were instances of a socially and educationally backward class of citizens because they satisfied the test of social and educational backwardness which is set out in some detail.[19] As to rural areas,

---

[13] The scheme is set out in ('79) A.SC. at p. 767.
[14] ibid p. 774.
[15] ('78) A.Ker. 176 (F.B.).
[16] (1975) 2 S.C.R. 761, ('75) A.SC. 563.
[17] ('75) A.SC. at p. 566.
[18] ibid. p. 567.
[19] ibid., where the tests are set out at some length.

Ray C.J. observed that the 1971 census showed that 80.1 per cent of the population lived in rural areas and 19.9 per cent in cities and towns and he observed:

"It is incomprehensible as to how 80.1 per cent of the people in rural areas or 7 crores in rural parts of U.P. can be suggested to be socially backward because of poverty. Further, it is also not possible to predicate poverty as the common trait of rural people. This Court (in an earlier case)[20] said that if poverty is the exclusive test a large population in our country would be socially and educationally backward class of citizens."[21] Further, "80 per cent of the population (in U.P.) in rural areas cannot be said to be a homogenous class by itself. They are not of the same kind. Their occupation is different. Their standards are different. Their lives are different. Population cannot be a class by itself. Rural element does not make it a class. To suggest that the rural areas are socially and educationally backward is to have reservation for the majority of the State."[22]

Ray C.J. said that "No reservation can be made on the basis of place of birth, as this would offend Art. 15."[23] He distinguished *D. P. Joshi's Case*[24] (see para 9.149) on the ground that the Court there distinguished between place of birth and residence. But the classification made in the present case could not be upheld as there was no classification based on residence between students coming from within the State and others coming from outside. "The object of providing medical education to students in U.P. is to secure the best possible students for admission to these colleges."[25] So, the Court held that the reservation for rural areas aggregating to 131 seats was unconstitutional, but the reservation for Hills and Uttarkhand area was valid. The above case was referred to in *Arti* v. *J. & K.*[26] where for admission to medical colleges, more than 95 per cent of villages were classified as socially and educationally backward calling for a reserved quota in order to rectify the imbalance in different parts of the State. The Supreme Court held that there was no intelligible data for sustaining that classification, and the classification made was arbitrary and therefore invalid.

Reservation of seats in educational institutions

9.166 An order of the Kerala Government reserving seats in the Medical Colleges of Kerala (*a*) for Ezhavas, Muslims and Latin Catholics (including Anglo-Catholics) on the ground that they belonged to socially and educationally backward classes; (*b*) in favour of the children of registered medical practitioners; (*c*) for outstanding sportsmen, came up for consideration in *Kerala* v. *R. Jacob.*[27] The Court struck down the reservation in favour of the children of medical practitioners on the ground that it was based on a classification which had no rational relation to the object to be secured. It upheld the reservation for outstanding sportsmen on the ground that it was based on a valid classification. It upheld the

[20] *Parimoo* v. *J. & K.* (1973) 3 S.C.R. 236, ('73) A.SC. 930.
[21] ('75) A.SC. at p. 568. [22] ibid. p. 568.
[23] This was clear from the certificate to be submitted by a candidate for reserved seats from rural areas that "he was born in the rural area and had a permanent home there": ibid. p. 569.
[24] (1955) 1 S.C.R. 1215, ('55) A.SC. 334.
[25] ('75) A.SC. at p. 570. [26] ('81) A.SC. 1009.
[27] (1964) 2 Ker. 53, ('64) A.Ker. 316; foll. in *State* v. *Rafia Rahim* ('78) A.Ker. 176 (F.B.) (*held*, following the above case, and for the reasons there given, that the reservation of seats from the geographic area of Malabar, a socially and educationally backward area, was valid as a legitimate geographical classification). *Rafia Rahim's Case* was followed and applied in *Susan Thomas* v. *State* ('78) A.Ker. 199.

reservations for Ezhavas etc. on the ground that the reservation was covered by Art. 15 (4) and the respondent had failed to discharge the burden of proof that the Ezhavas etc. did not belong to the backward classes. It is submitted that the burden of proof was wrongly placed and the Court overlooked the difference between Art. 14 and Art. 15, namely, that a person who alleges a violation of equality (Art. 14) has to prove it because he must overcome the presumption of constitutionality; but a person who alleges the violation of Art. 15 (1) has to show that a discrimination has been made only on the ground of religion, caste, etc. and the law would be struck down as prohibited by Art. 15 unless it was justified as falling within Art. 15 (3) and (4).[28] But as Art. 15 (3) and (4) are exceptions to Art. 15 (1) the burden of proving that the discrimination fell within the exception would be on the person alleging it.

9.167 Provisions reserving a maximum number of seats for backward classes have been considered in a number of cases. In *V. Raghuramulu* v. *A.P.*[29] it was held that the provision in a circular issued by the State of Andhra that a maximum of 15 per cent of the total number of seats in any faculty may be reserved for backward communities proceeded on the assumption that in no event could a larger percentage be secured by those classes in open competition. Where such assumption was belied, the reservation, far from conferring a right, abridged a fundamental right. However, the Court did not declare the whole order void, but directed that it should be applied where the underlying assumption was found to exist and not where that assumption was belied. Again, in *P. Sundarsan* v. *A.P.*[30] it was held that a rule reserving seats for backward classes ought not to be so worded as to prevent members of backward classes from getting larger numbers of seats on their merits because in that event, it would contravene their fundamental rights under Art. 29 (2). Nor could the rule be worked so as to divide the matter in two compartments, namely, that some students belonging to backward classes were to be allowed to compete for the general pool and some for the reserved seats, as that would cause great hardship to students belonging to other communities. All the seats should be pooled guaranteeing a minimum number of seats for backward classes. Where a list of backward classes for educational purposes was notified by government, and a community included in the list was eliminated from the prospectus of certain educational institutions for selection of a course of study, it was held that the elimination was not justified since government had not altered the aforesaid notified list.[31]

Reservation of seats must be for a minimum and not for a maximum number of seats

9.168 These decisions establish that a rule reserving a maximum number of seats for backward classes would be void whenever students of the backward classes became eligible on merit for a

The result of cases already considered

---

[28] See para 9.3.

[29] (1957) Andh.Pr. 772, ('58) A.A.P. 129.

[30] ('58) A.A.P. 569. See also *V. V. Giri* v. *Dippala Suri Dora* (1960) 1 S.C.R. 426, ('59) A.SC. 1318, where it was held as regards Art. 330 that the reservation of seats as therein specified was intended to guarantee a *minimum* number of seats to the Scheduled Castes and Tribes; therefore if members of those castes and tribes secured additional seats by election to general unreserved seats, there would be no repugnancy at all.

[31] *P. Susila* v. *State* ('70) A.M. 399, 400.

larger number of seats than those reserved for them; but the Court will not strike down such reservation but will prevent its operating to the disadvantage of students of backward classes.

Reservation of seats on grounds not forbidden by Art. 15(1)

9.169 However, reservation of seats not based on the ground of religion, race, caste, sex, place of birth or any of them, is not violative of Art. 15. Thus it was held that where a certain percentage of the total number of seats to a pre-professional course in Medicine was reserved for students who had passed a "multi-purpose" examination, the reservation did not attract Art. 14.[32]

Subhashini v. *State*: reservations falling outside Art. 15(4)

9.170 In *Subhashini* v. *State*[33] Hegde J. explained that any reservation made under Art. 15 (4) could only be for the benefit of socially and educationally backward classes of citizens or for Scheduled Castes and Tribes. However, there was nothing unconstitutional or illegal in reservations made for students coming from other States, cultural scholars of Indian origin domiciled abroad, Colombo Plan scholars, students of Indian origin migrating from Burma, students from Asian and African countries and Union Territories and it was not for the Courts to consider whether those reservations were politically wise, though it may be said that they appeared to be in the right direction. Classification based on lawful State policy was not violative of Art. 14. Reservations made in favour of Armed Services and Ex-servicemen including those who were in the Armed Services in the second World War could not be challenged as being discriminative in character.[34] The same question was raised in *H. J. Siddappa* v. *Mysore*,[35] but not decided as it had not been raised in the pleading and as the parties affected were not before the Court. *Subhashini's Case* was followed in *P. Sagar* v. *State*[36]. However, in *Vinod Sagar Sood* v. *State*[37] it was held that "Rules for admission in Medical Colleges, Dental Colleges, 1966" were merely administrative instructions and the reservation of seats in medical and dental colleges for the sons and daughters of political suffers, contained therein, did not justify the issue of a writ of *certiorari* for cancelling the admission of a student or for compelling the authority to admit a student who was refused admission. It was further held that Art. 14 was not violated. The court however deprecated the practice of reserving seats for the sons and daughters of political sufferers. It is submitted that even an administrative order or direction cannot discriminate between persons, and unless the court came to the conclusion that such reservation was based on a reasonable classification reasonably related to the object of the "Rules", such reservation clearly violated Art. 14. A writ of *certiorari* did not lie in respect of an administrative act, but a writ of *mandamus* was clearly available.

Guntur Medical College v. *Mohan Rao*: Christian

9.171 In *Guntur Medical College* v. *Mohan Rao*[38] the Supreme Court considered the question whether M.R., who was born to Christian converts from Hinduism (who originally belonged to a Scheduled

---

[32] *Nageswara Rao* v. *Principal, Medical College* ('62) A.A.P. 213.
[33] ('66) A.Mys. 40.
[34] ibid. pp. 45-6.
[35] ('67) A.Mys. 67.
[36] ('68) A.A.P. 165, 173-4 (upholding reservation of seats for nominees of the Government of India).
[37] ('67) A.M.P. 182.
[38] (1976) 3 S.C.R. 1046, ('76) A.SC. 1904.

Caste) could claim the benefit of reservation of seats in a Medical College for Scheduled Castes, after embracing Hinduism. That question arose from the following facts:

convert from Sch. Caste embracing Hinduism

The parents of M.R. originally professed the Hindu religion, and belonged to the Madiga caste which was admittedly a caste deemed to be a Scheduled Caste in the State of Andhra Pradesh. They were both converted to Christianity and the case proceeded on the footing that when M.R. was born they were Christians. M.R. applied for admission to the Gandhi Medical College in 1973 as a member of a backward class. As he did not get admission, he got converted to Hinduism and applied for admission as a member of the Madiga caste. He was admitted to College but later, the admission was cancelled by the Principal on the interpretation of the relevant rules. M.R. filed a writ petition which was allowed by a single Judge and affirmed by the Appellate Bench. Leave to appeal to the Supreme Court was refused, but the Supreme Court granted Special Leave on condition that the admission of M.R. was not to be disturbed and that the appellants would bear the costs of the appeal in any event.

Bhagwati J. observed that when special leave was granted, the Supreme Court had not considered the question in any case. But before the matter was heard, Bhagwati J. had held in *C. M. Arumugam* v. *S. Rajagopal*[39] that the view taken in India since 1886 was that on re-conversion to Hinduism, a person again became a member of the caste in which he was born, and to which he belonged before conversion to another religion, *provided that the members of the caste accepted him as a member*. Neither principle nor authority compelled the Court to disregard this view which had prevailed for almost a century. Bhagwati J. held that the principle of *Arumugam's Case* directly applied to the question whether M.R. could be said to belong to a Scheduled Caste. This would have involved an inquiry whether M.R. had been accepted by the caste as a member; but as the State had given an undertaking that M.R.'s admission would not be disturbed, the Court found it unnecessary to decide that question.

9.172 In *Raju V. B.* v. *State*[40] it was held that concession granted to members of Scheduled Castes and Scheduled Tribes in respect of deposits for purposes of standing as a candidate for elections was not discriminatory as it was a special provision for the benefit of members of the Sch. Castes and Tribes who were economically backward and financially incapable of contesting elections, and is not discriminatory and is covered by Art. 15(4). [The judgment does not mention Art. 15(4).]

Raju V. B. v. *State*: concessions to Sch. Castes and Tribes

9.173 In *Mahendra Nath* v. *Assam*[41] it was held that in making a settlement of Mahals of forest produce, Government could give preference under Art. 15(4) to a member of a Scheduled Tribe. But where such a person does not produce a requisite certificate in support of his claim that he was a member of a Sch. Tribe, nor was there any other evidence to show that he was a member of a Sch. Tribe, giving him preference would be arbitrary and capricious and would be struck down.[42]

Mahendra Nath v. *Assam*: preference under Art. 15(4) given to member of Sch. Tribe

---

[39] (1976) 3 S.C.R. 82, ('76) A.SC. 939.
[40] ('76) A.Guj. 66. [41] ('70) A.A. & N. 32.
[42] ibid. p. 34 (*held*, that the preference given by the impugned order was arbitrary and capricious; that it must be set aside as it violated the petitioner's fundamental right to equality. The original settlement of the *Mahal* made with the petitioner was to stand).

Art. 16(1): discrimination in public employment forbidden *qua* citizens

9.174 We have seen that the "spoils" system does not prevail in India and that our civil service is based on the English model.[43] In fact the principle of recruitment by open competition was first applied in India and then applied in England. Article 16 confers on every citizen a right to equality of opportunity "in matters relating to employment or appointment to any office under the State", and further provides that he shall not be ineligible for, or be discriminated against in respect of, any employment or office under the State, on the ground only of religion, race, caste, descent, place of birth, residence or any of them.

Service under the State

9.175 Article 16, read with Art. 12, shows that service or employment under the State means service or appointment under the Government and Parliament of India, under the Government and legislatures of the States and under local or other authorities within the territory of India or under the control of the Government of India. Lord Wright has said:

> "The word 'office' is of indefinite content. Its various meanings cover four columns of the New English Dictionary, but I take as the most relevant for purposes of this case the following: 'A position or place to which certain duties are attached, especially one of a more or less public character.' This, I think, roughly corresponds with such approaches to a definition as have been attempted in the authorities. . . ."[44]

Motiram's Case: the word "under" indicates subordination

This definition, speaking broadly, covers the "office" referred to in Art. 16. However, the office has to be *under* the State. The effect of the word *under* was considered by Chagla C.J.[45] where he said that employment or appointment to any office under the State showed that the word "appointment" must be read *ejusdem generis* with the word employment and such appointment or employment indicated that the person so appointed or employed held a position of subordination to the State and the same position obtained as regards the word "office" in Art. 16(2). Consequently, it was held that a Councillor elected under the Bombay Municipal Boroughs Act was a part of the Municipality and therefore far from being a person who held office under the Local Authority, he was a part of the Local Authority itself, and Art. 16(1) did not apply to election to a Local Authority.

The right conferred by Art. 16(1) and (2) is an individual right: the limitations of the right

9.176 We must now consider the nature and extent of this right and the limitations to which it is subject. Article 16(1) and (2) confers a right on each individual citizen,[46] a fact which is important in considering the effect of Art. 16(4). Article 16(1) does not confer a right to *obtain* public employment but it does confer a right to an equality of opportunity for being considered for such employment. Article 16 does not exclude selective tests, nor does it preclude the laying down of qualifications for office, not only of mental excellence but also of physical fitness, sense of discipline, moral integrity, loyalty to the State, etc. Where the appointment requires technical know-

---

[43] See para 9.128.
[44] *McMillan* v. *Guest* (1942) A.C. 561, 566.
[45] *Dattatreya Motiram* v. *Bombay* (1953) Bom. 842, ('53) A.B. 311.
[46] See *Devadasan* v. *Union* (1964) 4 S.C.R. 680, ('64) A.SC. 179, 187.

ledge, evidence of such knowledge may be required.[47] Further, Government is entitled to have regard to the character and antecedents of candidates for appointment to public office.[48] Again since the equality of opportunity "is in respect of any employment", Art. 16 cannot be confined to the initial matters prior to the act of employment, but includes other matters relating to employment such as provisions about the salary and periodical increments therein, terms as to leave, gratuity and pension and as to the age of superannuation. It also includes promotion to selection posts.[49] But seniority by itself cannot confer an absolute right to promotion re-

The content of the equality guaranteed by Art. 16

Seniority and equality of opportunity

---

[47] *Sukhnandan* v. *Bihar* (1956) 35 Pat. 1, ('57) A.P. 617; *Banarsi Das* v. *U.P.* (1956) S.C.R. 357, ('56) A.SC. 520 (Government could prescribe rules for the selection of candidates. Selection for appointment in government service had to be on a competitive basis and those whose past services were free from blemish were better qualified than those who were not); fol. in *Sampath* v. *Madras* ('62) A.M. 485 (the granting of exemption to some government servants and not to others was not by itself violative of Art. 16); *Gen. Manager, S.Rly.* v. *Rangachari* (1962) 2 S.C.R. 586, ('62) A.SC. 36; *V. K. Namboodri* v. *Union* ('65) A.Ker. 185 [although under Art. 259(2) the Armed Forces of Part B States became a part of the Armed Forces of the Union of India, that Article did not *ipso facto* entitle members of the State force to hold the same rank in the Armed Forces of the Union. They had to be accepted as conforming to the Indian Army standards. Arts. 14 and 16 were not violated because officers of the Travancore-Cochin State force were screened by the Indian Army Selection Board and officers of the Armed Forces of the Union were not]; *N. Rudraradhaya* v. *Mysore* ('61) A.Mys. 247 (the State was entitled to prescribe qualifications and lay down standards in order to secure the best service and to ensure that the State was well served); *Gurbachan Singh* v. *Pepsu* (1955) Pep. 703, ('56) A.Pep. 26 [Art. 16(1) was not violated where candidates were selected on merit and where they were all subjected to the same rules and tests. The discrimination between persons who were accepted and persons who were rejected was inevitable in every selection for employment or appointment]; *Mohd. Hussain* v. *Hyderabad* (1953) Hyd. 498, ('53) A.Hyd. 298; *Sardul Singh* v. *I.-G. of Police* ('70) A.P. & H. 481 (F.B.) (*held*, that Art. 16 does not confer a right to promotion but a right to be considered for promotion; *held further*, that a process of grading, screening and progressive selection for promotion can be prescribed without violating Art. 16).

[48] *Sugatha Prasad* v. *Kerala* ('65) A.Ker. 19 [where the petitioners were given provisional appointments pending investigation into their character and antecedents and they were not given a permanent appointment because the appointing authority was not satisfied about their character and antecedents, Art. 16(1) and (2) was not violated]; *K. George* v. *Kerala* ('64) A.Ker. 238 [the petitioner was recommended by the Public Service Commission for appointment as Munsiff but Government did not appoint him because on verification of his character and antecedents he was found to be a communist and not suitable for the office; *held*, that there was no lack of *bona fides* on the part of Government nor was its decision based on irrelevant considerations. Government had a large discretion in prescribing the qualifications for a post and Art. 16(1) had not been violated]; *Sadanandan* v. *Kerala* (1962) 1 Ker. 59 (Government were entitled to take the character and antecedents of the petitioner into account; and where the same uniform principle was applied to the petitioner and all other persons whose names had been recommended by the Public Service Commission, Art. 16 was not violated); *Madhusudanan* v. *Kerala* ('61) A.Ker. 203 [Art. 16(1) covers the whole period during which a public servant is employed and thereby prevents such servants being treated arbitrarily].

[49] *General Manager, S.Rly.* v. *Rangachari* (1962) 2 S.C.R. 586, ('62) A.SC. 36, approving the view taken in *Pandurang Kashinath More* v. *Union* (1958) Bom. 1266, ('59) A.B. 134, 60 Bom.L.R. 342, and in *Sukhnandan* v. *Bihar* (1956) 35 Pat. 1, ('57) A.P. 617, and disapproving the contrary view taken in *Moinuddin* v. *U.P.* (1950) 2 All. 33, ('60) A.A. 484. In view of the decision in *Rangachari's Case, supra*, the decision in *Sudhir Kumar* v. *W.B.* ('62) A.Cal. 587, that promotions do not fall under Art. 16 is no longer good law; *Mohan Lal* v. *State* (1965) 15 Raj. 707, ('66) A.Raj. 1 (Art. 16 was violated when an employee who was on deputation was not considered for promotion); foll. in *S. S. Sharma* v. *Union* ('81) A.SC. 588, 594 [Art. 16(4) extends to reservation in selection posts].

gardless of other considerations, for Art. 16(1) does not prohibit the prescription of reasonable rules of selection.[50] In *Jaisinghani* v. *Union*[51] the Supreme Court held that Rule 1(*f*) (iii) of the Rules of Seniority which provided for the weightage of three years for seniority for I.T.Os promoted to Class I, Grade II from the Department over officers in the same grade who were directly recruited by a competitive examination was based on a reasonable classification and did not violate Arts 14 and 16. Rule 1(*f*) (*iv*) [which was closely connected with Rule 1(*f*) (*iii*)] was also based on a valid classification and did not violate Arts. 14 and 16. However, an order of Government promoting a junior in supersession of a senior, without considering the claim of a senior for promotion when it was due to him, was quashed as violating Art. 16, even though the promotion was a temporary one.[52] Again, equality of opportunity in matters of public employment is denied where in making a temporary appointment to the post of lecturer, the case of one of two clinical tutors in Pediatrics was not considered at all.[53] Where from 200 officers most of whom were junior to the respondent, he alone was reverted from his officiating post to his substantive post, Arts. 14 and 16 were violated in the circumstances of the case.[54] In *Punjab* v. *Hira Lal*[55], respondent No. 1 impugned the promotion of respondent No. 3 (who belonged to a Sch. Caste) ignoring the claim of respondent No. 1 who was senior to respondent No. 3. The High Court allowed the petition, but the Supreme Court held that this had been done on hypothetical grounds. Reversing the judgment, Hegde J. observed:

> "But the equality contemplated by [Art. 16(1)] is not an embodied equality. It is subject to several exceptions and one of the exceptions is that provided in Art. 16(4). . . ."[56] And he observed later, "The exception provided under Art. 16(4) should not make the rule embodied in Art. 16(1) meaningless."[57]

But where two petitioners were appointed to two out of three temporary posts, their period of appointment came to an end as soon as the two posts were abolished, and their services could be legally terminated by the State. The petitioners could not claim any legal right to the third post on the ground of seniority, and if either of them

---

[50] *M. A. Moqeem* v. *Mysore* ('63) A.Mys. 219.

[51] (1967) 2 S.C.R. 703, ('67) A.SC. 1427, 1432-3. *Jagannath* v. *U.P.* (1962) 1 S.C.R. 151, ('61) A.SC. 1245 and *Jaisinghani's Case* were foll. in *Dwarka Dhish* v. *State* ('78) A.M.P. 119 (F.B.) (appointment to posts as to 50 per cent by direct recruitment and 50 per cent by promotion held not to violate Art. 16).

[52] *A. N. Nagnoor* v. *Mysore* ('64) A.Mys. 229; rel. on in *Anand Swarup* v. *State* (1965) 15 Raj. 1013, ('66) A.Raj. 8 (Art. 16 was violated when a junior officer was promoted and a senior officer was overlooked); *Sheo Dayal Sinha* v. *Bihar & Ors.* ('81) A.SC. 1543 (The appellants and respondents were members of the Bihar Agricultural Service Class I. The respondents though junior were promoted on an *ad hoc* basis pending report of the Public Service Commission. Since only the respondents' cases were referred to the Commission, the appellants impugned the orders of promotion. *Held*, that as the appellants' cases had not been considered for promotion, the impugned orders violated Arts. 14 and 16 and the orders were quashed except for the order of a promotee who had retired).

[53] *Swayambar Prasad* v. *State* ('72) A.Raj. 69.

[54] *U.P.* v. *Sughar Singh* (1974) 2 S.C.R. 335, ('74) A.SC. 423 [*held*, that as the reversion was admitted to be on the basis of an adverse entry in the respondent's character roll, it was a reduction in rank and the order was void for non-compliance with Art. 311(2)].

[55] ('71) A.SC. 1777, (1971) 3 S.C.R. 267.

[56] ('71) A.SC. at p. 1779. [57] ibid. p. 1780.

was not appointed to the third post, there was no discrimination against them within the meaning of Arts. 14 and 16.[58]

Art. 16 not applicable to a contract to sell goods

9.177 Article 16 has no application to a contract for the sale of goods to the State. Thus Art. 16 has been held not to apply to a contractor who supplied milk to a Government Hospital, because both in its terms and in the collocation of the words Art. 16(1) indicated that it was confined to "employment" by the State and had reference to employment in service rather than as contractors. ". . . there may be cases in which the contract may include within itself an element of service" but no such question arose in the case before the Court.[59] Again, Art. 16 can have no application to a case where certain students were refused admission to a certain College.[60]

Art. 16(1) and (2) and the judicial service: *Roy's Case*

9.178 In *High Court, Calcutta* v. *Amar Kumar Roy*[61] the respondent was a munsiff in the W.B. Civil Service (Judicial) and, as such, had issued an injunction in his own favour in a case where he was the plaintiff. His case was considered by the High Court for inclusion of names in the panel of officers to officiate as subordinate judges, but his name was excluded, and on his representation, the Registrar intimated that the High Court had decided to consider his case next year. So, the respondent, who was the senior-most munsiff, lost eight places in the cadre of subordinate judges, and he filed a suit in the City Court contending that the withholding of promotion was in substance a penalty. The trial Court decreed the suit. In allowing the appeal, which had been filed by special leave, the Supreme Court held that there was no cause of action for the suit, and held further that under Art. 235, the High Court was the sole authority to decide the fitness of a munsiff to be appointed as a subordinate judge and the exercise of its power was not justiciable. It is submitted that both these conclusions are clearly incorrect. Since the Supreme Court dealt with the respondent's case under Art. 16(1), he had obviously a cause of action if he substantiated his allegation that he had been denied equality of opportunity. In fact, the judgment held, *on the merits*, that he had been afforded equality of opportunity because his case had been carefully considered and his promotion was held over for a year because of his action in granting an injunction in his own favour as a munsiff. Again, although the fitness for promotion may be within the jurisdiction of the High Court, it is not correct to say that the exercise of the power is not justiciable. If it could be shown on evidence that the power was exercised arbitrarily or for a collateral purpose, as for instance, for favouring a relative of one of the appointing judges, or considerations extraneous to his fitness were taken into account, the question of fitness to be appointed would be clearly justiciable.

A criticism of the above case

---

[58] *Brajanandan Prasad* v. *Bihar* ('55) A.P. 353.
[59] *C. K. Achuthan* v. *Kerala* (1959) Supp. 1 S.C.R. 787, 791, ('59) A.SC. 490.
[60] *Om Prakash Dhri* v. *Punjab* (1951) Punj. 344, ('51) A.Punj. 93 [the argument for the application of Art. 16 was an unusual one, namely, that unless students were admitted into a College, they would not be eligible for Government service. The Court held that Art. 15(1) would apply if a person were kept out from or admitted into any College or educational institution on the ground solely of religion, sex, etc. But as no such ground had been made out, the petition failed].
[61] (1963) 1 S.C.R. 437, ('62) A.SC. 1704.

Equality between equals

9.179 However, equality of opportunity in matters of employment can be predicted only as between persons who are either seeking the same employment or have obtained it. Thus in *All India S.M. and A.S.M.'s Assn.* v. *Gen. Manager, Central Rly.*[62] it was held that assuming that the determination of matters relating to employment were within Art. 16 (1), such equality of opportunity in matters of promotion must mean equality as between members of the same class of employees and not equality between members of separate independent classes. As Road-side Station Masters and Guards were recruited and trained separately and had separate avenues of promotion, they formed two distinct and separate classes between whom there was no scope for predicating equality or inequality of opportunity in matters of promotion. Whether a classification is reasonable depends upon the facts of each case and the circumstances obtaining at the time the recruitment is made. Unless the classification between two sources of recruitment is unjust on the face of it, the burden of proving that the classification violates Art. 16 is upon the person who alleges such violation.[63]

Art. 16 does not forbid the creation of different grades in Government service

9.180 Again, the abstract doctrine of equal pay for equal work has nothing to do with Art. 14, and incremental scales of pay can be validly fixed dependent upon the duration of an officer's service. Accordingly, it was held that Art. 14 was not violated where the pay scales of I.T.Os., Class I and II, were different though they did

[62] (1960) 2 S.C.R. 311, ('60) A.SC. 384; fol. in *Govind Dattatray* v. *Ch. Controller of Imports & Exports* (1969) 2 S.C.R. 29, ('67) A.SC. 839 (*held*, that where a statute made a classification between two sources of recruitment, then, unless the classification was unjust on the face of it, the onus lay upon the party attacking the classification to show that it was unreasonable and violated Art. 16. *Held further*, that unless the ratio fixed for recruitment to posts from different sources was so unreasonable as to amount to discrimination, the court could not strike down or suggest a different ratio); *U. S. Menon* v. *Rajasthan* (1967) 3 S.C.R. 430, ('68) A.SC. 81, 84 [*held*, that Arts. 14 and 16 were not violated because under the Rajasthan Civil Service (Rationalisation of Pay Scales) Rules & Schedules, 1956, special pay was admissible to the members of the Rajasthan Administrative Service but not to the members of the Rajasthan Secretariat Service]; and rel. on in *Sham Sunder* v. *Union* (1969) 1 S.C.R. 312, ('69) A.SC. 212, 215 and in *Unikat Sankunni* v. *State* ('67) A.Raj. 128, 132-3; see also *Mysore* v. *P. Narasinga Rao* (1968) 1 S.C.R. 407, ('68) A.SC. 349 (*held*, that the classification of tracers into matriculate tracers with higher pay scales and non-matriculate tracers with lower pay scales did not violate Art. 14 and 16. Ramaswami J. met the argument that general education had no relevance to the technical branches of the public service by quoting with approval the following passage from Macaulay: "Men who have been engaged, upto one and two and twenty, in studies which have no immediate connection with the business of any profession, and the effect of which is merely to open, to invigorate, and enrich the mind, will generally be found, in the business of every profession, superior to men who have at eighteen or nineteen devoted themselves to the special studies of their calling. Indeed early superiority in literature and science generally indicates the existence of some qualities which are securities against vice — industry, self-denial, a taste for pleasure not sensual, a laudable desire of honourable distinction, a still more laudable desire to obtain the approbation of friends and relations. We therefore, think that the intellectual test about to be established will be found in practice to be also the best moral test that can be devised.": ibid. p. 352. The above case was distinguished in *S. M. Pandit* v. *Gujarat* ('72) A.SC. 252 and it was held that where directly recruited *Mamlatdars* had the same designation, same pay scale and same functions, and their posts were inter-changeable, they formed one class, and government could not discriminate between them for promotion to the posts of Deputy Collectors.

[63] *Govind Dattatray* v. *Chief Controller of Imports & Exports* (1967) 2 S.C.R. 29, ('67) A.SC. 839, 842.

the same kind of work. Although Art. 16(1) applied to promotion, that Article was not violated where the rules made an I.T.O., Class I, eligible for appointment as Asst. Commissioner, whilst making an I.T.O., Class II, eligible for appointment as I.T.O., Class I, but not for appointment as Asst. Commissioner. This was because Art. 16 did not forbid the creation of different grades in Government service, and there was no inequality of opportunity between persons holding posts in the same grade.[64] In *Punjab* v. *Joginder Singh*[65] the majority decision went still further, and held that although by the order dated September 27, 1957, teachers in the erstwhile Board Schools became employees of Government and were given the same scales and grades of pay as were applicable to their counterparts in the State cadre, except for this equality of grade and pay there was no integration of the two cadres. Therefore, it was not the Punjab Educational Service (Provincialised cadre) Class III Rules that created the two distinct cadres but they existed independently of the rules. As they were two distinct services, there was no question of *inter se* seniority between members of the two services nor of any comparison between the two in matters of promotion for founding an argument based on Art. 14 or Art. 16(1). They started, and continued, dissimilarly, and any dissimilarity in their treatment would not be a denial of equal opportunity. Equality of opportunity in matters of public employment is not violated by a scheme which relates pay scales to educational qualifications having reasonable nexus with the nature of the service.[66] Where recruitment to a cadre was from two sources, namely, direct recruits and promotees, and a rotational system was in force, there was no violation of Art. 16(1) by following the rotational system of fixing seniority.[67] However, the rotational system could not apply when there was only one source of recruitment, and fixation of seniority by rotation in such a case violated Art. 16(1).[68] In *C. A. Rajendran*

---

[64] *Kishori* v. *Union* ('62) A.SC. 1139. This case and *Joginder Singh's Case* (see f.n. 65 below) were rel. on in *B.H.P.S.T. Assn.* v. *B.S. Project* ('69) A.M.P. 43 (*held*, that as the qualifications, method of recruitment and avenues of promotion were different for Hindi and English School teachers, they formed two distinct and separate classes and hence disparity in chances of promotion between members of the two classes did not violate Art. 16).

[65] (1963) Supp. 2 S.C.R. 169, ('63) A.SC. 913.

[66] *B. C. K. Murthy* v. *State* ('72) A.Mys. 88 [*Mysore* v. *Narasingha P. Rao* (1968) 1 S.C.R. 407, ('68) A.SC. 349, rel. on].

[67] *Mervyn Coutinho* v. *Collector* (1966) 3 S.C.R. 600, ('67) A.SC. 52.

[68] (1966) 3 S.C.R. *supra* at p. 606; fol. in *Roshan Lal* v. *Union* (1968) 1 S.C.R. 185, ('67) A.SC. 1889 (*held*, that once there was absorption of direct recruits and promotees in one cadre no discrimination could be made between them for future promotion and such discrimination violated Arts. 14 and 16). The above cases were fol. in *Satya Kumar* v. *State* ('71) A.A.P. 320, 329-30 (*held*, that once a provisional seniority list of employees was framed, the whole State must be treated as one unit and promotion must be made strictly according to that list. Promotions made on the basis of regional lists would be violative of Art. 16); and in *Gen. Manager, S.C.Rly.* v. *A.V.R. Siddhanti* ('72) A.A.P. 252 (F.B.) (*held*, that since the absorption of direct recruits and others was from an integrated Grain Shop Department, no discrimination could be shown on the ground of the differences that existed between various sources prior to the recruitment to the Grain Shop Department for the purpose of fixing seniority); *Roshan Lal's Case* was rel. on in *Kamal Mukharji* v. *Union* ('70) A.Cal. 250 [*held*, that where the posts of Upper Division Assistant and Junior Stenographer having the same pay were in practice classed together for further promotion, non-statutory rules subsequently framed which retrospectively

v. *Union*[69] the Supreme Court observed that it was well established that there could be a reasonable classification of employment for the purpose of appointment by promotion and that a classification as between direct recruits and promotees was reasonable.[70]

Art. 16 and promotion in service

9.181 The question of equality of opportunity for promotion was considered in *Ram Sharan* v. *Dy. I.G. of Police, Ajmer,*[71] where the Supreme Court upheld the "three-tier" system evolved for the Police force in the State of Rajasthan on the ground of efficiency of the force, even though as a result of that system employee *A* in one range, who may be junior to employee *B* in another range, may get a promotion, and *B* may not. The Court held that knowledge of local conditions was necessary for the efficient working of the first and second tiers, and it was only in the third tier that it was not insisted upon. Balancing the claims of equality of opportunity in public employment against the necessity of an efficient Police force, the three-tier system did not violate Art. 16(1). However, in *Manendra Prasad* v. *Ranchi Regn. Dev. Authority*[72] the petitioner was promoted as accountant on condition that if he did not pass the Local Body Accounts examination he would be reverted. As he did not pass the examination, he was reverted. Respondent No. 3 was also appointed as accountant but the same condition was not imposed on him, on the ground that he was the member of a Sch. Tribe. The Court held that in the absence of reservation of posts for members of Sch. Tribes this was a discrimination between equals and violated Art. 16, and the order of reversion was quashed. The question of equality of opportunity in matters of public employment was again considered in *C. C. Padmanabhan* v. *Director of Public Instruction*[73] on the following facts. Each appellant was an Assistant Educational Officer ("A.E.O.") for more than 6 years continuously, when in implementation of instructions issued by Government that every A.E.O. after 6 years of service should be transferred back as High School Assistant ("H.S.A."), the appellants were reverted as H.S.As. The Supreme Court held that the post of A.E.O. was a promotion post *vis-a-vis* the post of H.S.A. and consequently the two posts could not be treated as inter-changeable. The reversion of the appellants therefore violated Art. 16. In any event, even if the post of an A.E.O. was not higher than that of an H.S.A., the direction that A.E.Os. after 6 years of service should be transferred back as H.S.As. was not based on any principle and was wholly arbitrary and therefore violated Art. 14. The order of reversion was set aside.

Thomas v. *Kerala*: exemption from necessary

9.182 *Thomas* v. *Kerala*[74] is important, not because of what the High Court decided according to well settled law, but because of the reversal of the High Court's judgment by the Supreme Court

differentiated the two posts for purposes of promotion, and applied the rules to employees appointed before the rules were promulgated, would contravene Arts. 14 and 16(1)].

[69] (1968) 1 S.C.R. 721, ('68) A.SC. 507.

[70] ('68) A.SC. at p. 513, citing *Mervyn Coutinho* v. *Collector* (1966) 3 S.C.R. 600, ('67) A.SC. 52.

[71] (1964) 7 S.C.R. 228, ('64) A.SC. 1559.

[72] ('81) A.P. 208.

[73] ('81) A.SC. 64.

[74] (1974) Ker. 549.

which will be considered later. The facts of the case were briefly these: The petitioner was a Lower Division Clerk in the Registration Department. For promotion to the Upper Division on the basis of seniority, Lower Division Clerks had to pass a test in three prescribed subjects. The petitioner complained that although he had passed all the tests by Nov. 2, 1971, he had not been promoted to the Upper Division, because of the concession given to Lower Division Clerks who were members of the Sch. Castes and Sch. Tribes, and who were promoted even though they had not passed the tests. The concession was given as the result of the undernoted representation.[75] The petitioner contended that Rule 13AA[76] and the orders passed thereunder (hereafter compendiously described as "Rule 13AA") were *ultra vires* and void for violating Art. 16.

qualification for promotion for Sch. Castes and Tribes

9.183 In the High Court, the State defended Rule 13AA, first, as protected by Art. 16(4) and, secondly, as protected by Art. 15(4) in any event. Dealing with the defence of Rule 13AA under Art. 16(4), Govindan Nair C.J. said that it was well settled by *Rangachari's Case* that Art. 16(1) and (2) embodied guarantees in respect of matters other than provisions for reservation of posts for the backward class of citizens under Art. 16(4).[77] Again, the Chief Justice cited the passage from the judgment of Sastri C.J. in *Kathi Raning Rawat's Case* (set out in para 9.151 of the text) for the proposition that there was no presumption that any action taken under Art. 16 was reasonable as there was in any action taken under Art. 14. Applying these principles to Rule 13AA, he said that as the Rule was intended to apply only to Sch. Castes and Tribes, it was clearly hit by Art. 16(2) and was not protected by Art. 16(4) because

Such exemption not protected by Art. 16(4) or 15(4),

"What has been done is not to reserve appointments or posts in favour of any backward class of citizens or for Sch. Castes and Tribes. *As a matter of fact reservations had already been made in the matter of appointments or posts.* What has been attempted by (Rule 13AA) is to exempt persons from possessing the necessary qualifications. . . . The action therefore cannot be supported under Art. 16(4)."[78] (italics supplied)

Further, Art. 335 showed that the claims of members of Sch. Castes and Tribes must be consistent with the efficiency of public service. To grant for long periods of time wholesale exemptions from the qualifications considered necessary for the satisfactory discharge of the duties of a particular post, thus enabling unqualified persons to occupy posts, when qualified persons were available to fill those posts cannot be conducive to the efficiency of administration. In the case before the Court "the choosing of the unfit was so heavy", namely, 34 out of 51 persons, that it was clearly arbitrary and unreasonable and directly violated Art. 335. As to the defence of

and was not conducive to efficiency of public service — Art. 335

75 The representation has been set out in ('76) A.SC. at p. 503: The President, Kerala Harijan Samskarika Kshema Samithy, Trivandrum had brought to the notice of the Government that a large number of Harijan employees were facing immediate reversion from their posts for want of test qualification and had therefore requested that all Sch. Caste and Sch. Tribe employees may be granted temporary exemption from passing the obligatory Departmental test for a period of two years with immediate effect.

76 Rule 13AA was introduced on Jan. 13, 1972 in the Kerala State and Subordinate Service Rules, 1958. The Rule is set out in ('76) A.SC. at p. 494.

77 *Rangachari's Case* ('62) A.SC. 36 at p. 42.

78 (1974) Ker. at pp. 556-7.

Rule 13AA under Art. 15(4), the history of cl. (4) showed that it was inserted in Art. 15 as the result of a judgment which held that reservations for backward classes in educational institutions could not be made under Art. 15 in the absence of a special provision like Art. 16(4). If reservation of posts and appointments could be made under Art. 15(4), then Art. 16(4) would be rendered redundant. Therefore, Rule 13AA was not protected by Art. 15(4). But even if Art. 15(4) were applied, Rule 13AA could not be defended, for Art. 15(4) was an exception to Art. 15(1) and could never be used for obliterating the rule.[79] Rule 13AA was held void as violating Art. 16(2). It is submitted that the judgment is clearly right. It is further submitted that if Rule 13AA was not supported by the State as making a valid classification under Art. 16(1), it must have been realized that a glance at Art. 16(2) would have put an end to that defence. In view of what happened in the Supreme Court, it should be noted that the judges of the Kerala High Court did not allow the hardship of the members of the Sch. Castes and Tribes who were before them to deflect their judgment in laying down the law, for it is well known that hard cases tend to make bad law. On a certificate granted by the High Court, the State appealed to the Supreme Court. This brings us to *Kerala* v. *N. M. Thomas*[80] ("*Thomas's Case*") which is considered below. It may however be added that apart from the reasons given by the High Court for holding that Art. 15(4) did not apply, it is clear that for reservations in public employment a *special provision* in favour of backward classes, which include Sch. Castes and Tribes, *already existed*. Therefore, sound principles of interpretation require that the reservations which can be made for socially and educationally backward classes, or for Sch. Castes and Tribes, must relate to matters other than those relating to employment in public service. This is all the more so because Art. 15(4) was inserted in Art. 15 by a Constitutional Amendment, as there was no provision corresponding to Art. 16(4) in Art. 15.

Submission: judgment is clearly right

Kerala v. *N. M. Thomas* ("*Thomas's Case*")

9.184 It is not easy to say why the appeal was heard by a Bench of 7 Judges.[81] It is submitted that having regard to the total volume of Supreme Court decisions[82] which had held that Art. 15(4) and 16(4) were exceptions (except for a lone dissent by Subba Rao J.),

[79] ibid. p. 558, citing *Devadasan's Case* ('64) A.SC. 179 at p. 187.

[80] (1976) 1 S.C.R. 906, ('76) A.SC. 490.

[81] Ray C.J., Khanna, Mathew, Beg, Krishna Iyer, Gupta and Fazal Ali JJ.

[82] *Champakam Dorairajan's Case* (1951) S.C.R. 525 (7 Judges) [*held*, that in the absence of a special provision in Art. 15 like that contained in Art. 16(4) (which enabled reservations to be made in public employment) no reservations could be made in educational institutions contrary to Art. 15(1). This judgment led to the insertion of Art. 15(4) in Art. 15]; *Rangachari's Case* (5 Judges) ["Art. 16(4) in substance provides for an exception to the fundamental rights guaranteed by Art. 16(1) and (2) . . ." *per* Gajendragadkar J. ('62) A.SC. 36 at p. 42. See also p. 45 *per* Wanchoo J. and p. 48 *per* Ayyangar J.]; *Balaji's Case* ('63) A.SC. 649, 662 (5 Judges) [Art. 15(4) is "a provision in the nature of an exception . . ."]; *C. A. Rajendran* v. *Union* ('68) A.SC. 507, 512 (5 Judges) [*held*, in rejecting the contention that Art. 16(4) was not an exception that, "it is well settled that cl. (4) of Art. 16 is an exception . . ."]. The above judgments were unanimous judgments of Constitution Benches. In *Devadasan's Case*, as we have seen, 4 out of 5 Judges held that Art. 16(4) was an exception. In *Punjab* v. *Hira Lal* ('71) A.SC. 1777, 1780, it was said that "the exception provided in Art. 16(4) should not make the rule embodied in Art. 16(1) meaningless." (per Hegde J.).

judicial discipline required that those decisions should be followed. If, however, the Bench felt that those decisions were clearly wrong and productive of public mischief and required to be reconsidered, it is submitted that this conclusion should have been stated in the judgment and steps taken to give a hearing to parties likely to be affected.[83] Finally, it is submitted that the reversal of a long line of authorities on Arts. 15 (4) and 16 (4) required reconsideration of Arts. 14, 15 and 16, on the lines indicated below. For, as long as it was held that Arts. 15 (4) and 16 (4) were exceptions, it became unnecessary to consider in detail: (*A*) the co-relation of Arts. 14, 15 and 16; (*B*) the scheme of Arts. 15 and 16 and the light which it throws on Arts. 15 (4) and 16 (4); (*C*) the terms of the Constitution (Scheduled Castes) Orders 1950 and 1951, and particularly Cl. 3 thereof. Such reconsideration was essential if a clear and coherent doctrine was to be authoritatively laid down as to the nature and extent of the fundamental rights conferred by Arts. 15 and 16. It is submitted that no such reconsideration has been undertaken in *Thomas's Case;* in fact the judgments are very unsatisfactory, and no coherent pattern emerges from them. It was in order to make the infirmities of the majority judgment clear to the reader that the present writer found it necessary to undertake such reconsideration in paras 9.123 to 9.144 above, and in paras 9.188 to 9.190 below.

Submissions: *Thomas's Case* very unsatisfactory; earlier decisions not reconsidered

9.185 Although 5 of the 7 Judges concurred in the Order, the concurring judgment of Beg J., rejects the central propositions of 4 out of the 5 judges, namely, Ray C.J., Mathew, Krishna Iyer and Fazal Ali JJ. ("four majority Judges"). Beg J. held, first, that Lower Division Clerks formed only one class and the fact that some of its members were socially and economically backward was not material or even relevant, because their entry into the class of Lower Division Clerks "must be deemed to indicate that they no longer suffer from the handicaps of a backward class."[84] Secondly, he was quite clear that Art. 16 (1) and (2) had to be read together and that "If Scheduled Castes do not come within the ambit of Art. 16 (2) but, as a backward class of citizens, escape direct prohibition, it is because the provision of Art. 16 (4) makes such an escape possible."[85] He was equally clear that the backward classes could escape the mandate of Art. 16 (1) "if they came within *the only exception* contained in Art. 16 (4) . . ."[86] (italics supplied). It is clear therefore that although he agreed with the final Order dismissing the appeal on the question of law involved, his judgment is opposed to that of the four majority judges. On the legal issue therefore, the majority consists of four Judges as Beg J. repudiated the basis of their judgments, and agreed with the dissenting Judges.

Beg J. rejects the central propositions in the four other majority judgments

9.186 The following questions were considered and decided by the four majority judges:

Questions considered and decided by four majority judges

(*a*) Was Rule 13AA supported by a valid classification under Art. 16(1)?

(*b*) Was the word "caste" in the expression "Scheduled Castes" used in the ordinary sense?

---

[83] In such a case it is the invariable practice to issue notices to the Att.-Gen., to the Advs.-Gen. and to give an opportunity to parties interested to intervene.
[84] ('76) A.SC. at pp. 521-22. [85] ibid. p. 521.
[86] ibid.

(c) Was Art. 16(4) an exception to Art. 16(2)?

(d) Were Arts. 15 and 16 "facets" of Art. 14 which conferred the right to equality on any person?

(e) Did the decisions of the U.S. Supreme Court on the equality clause of the 14th Amendment assist in the interpretation of Art. 16?

(f) What is the nature of the *equality* of opportunity guaranteed by Art. 16?

(g) What weight should be given to the maintenance of efficiency in public service in making reservations for Sch. Castes and Tribes?

Submission: doctrine of classification misapplied

9.187 With reference to para 9.186 (*a*) above, the four majority Judges cited many decisions which showed that the doctrine of classification applied to Art. 16 (1), and that doctrine required that the equality of opportunity under Art. 16 (1) was, as we have seen in para 9.179 above, equality between equals. But this exercise undertaken by the four majority judges was unnecessary, and the doctrine of equality between equals was misapplied because the four Judges asked the wrong question and, not surprisingly, gave the wrong answers. The right question to ask was not, "Can Rule 13AA be defended as a valid classification under Art. 16 (1) ?", but "Can any classification be made under Art. 16 (1) on grounds prohibited by Art. 16 (2) ?" The question answers itself: It is elementary and obvious that no classification based on grounds which the Constitution prohibits, as Art. 16 (2) does, can be made under Art. 16 (1), although Art. 16 (1) clearly permits classification. This is because the fundamental right to equality of opportunity in matters of public employment ("equality of opportunity") conferred in positive terms is effectively enforced by Art. 16 (2), which in a negative form prohibits discrimination in matters of public employment on the "grounds only of religion, race, caste, sex, descent, place of birth and residence or any of them" ("the prohibited grounds"). For, if discrimination on the prohibited grounds was not forbidden, the equality of opportunity in matters of public employment guaranteed by Art. 16 (1) woud be illusory. Therefore the equality of opportunity guaranteed by Art. 16 is to be found in Art. 16 (1) and (2) *read together*. If authority were wanted for the above proposition which follows on a plain reading of Art. 16 (1) and (2), it is furnished by the Supreme Court decision in *Rangachari's Case* given as far back as 1961. Speaking of Art. 16 (2), Gajendragadkar J. said:

Classification forbidden by Art. 16(2) cannot be made under Art. 16(1)

Rangachari's Case: Art. 16(1) and (2) must be read together

". . . this sub-Art. emphatically brings out in a negative form what is guaranteed affirmatively by Art. 16(1). Discrimination is a double-edged weapon; it would operate in favour of some persons and not against others; and Art. 16(2) prohibits discrimination and *thus assures the effective enforcement of the fundamental right to equality of opportunity guaranteed by Art. 16(1).*"[87] (italics supplied)

Since no classification can be made which is forbidden by Art. 16 (2), the only other questions which survived were: Since Rule 13AA makes a discrimination in favour of Sch. Castes and Tribes, is the discrimination based on religion and/or caste and/or race and/or descent prohibited by Art. 16 (2)? If yes, is Rule 13AA protected by any other clause of Art. 16?

Submission: implication of definition

9.188 As to para 9.186 (*b*) above, it is a surprising feature of *Thomas's Case* that although there was some discussion by the Judges as to

[87] ('62) A.SC. 36, 42.

whether Sch. Castes were castes in the ordinary sense[88], none of the judgments refer to the implication of the definition of Sch. Castes in Art. 366(24).[89] Why are Sch. *Castes* defined to mean castes, races or tribes, whom the President may by public notification specify under Art. 341? If castes, races and tribes had nothing to do with caste, why were they included in the definition of Sch. Castes? The answer is that the concepts of race, tribe and caste run into each other as pointed out in the next paragraph. Nor does any judgment in *Thomas's Case* refer to the Sch. Castes Orders of 1950 and 1951 promulgated by the President for the States and the Union Territories respectively, which we have discussed in para 9.129 of the text. Had the Judges done so, they would have found Cl. 3 of the said Orders determinative of the question before them. For, as we have seen, Cl. 3 provides that no person shall be deemed to be a member of a Sch. Caste who "professes a religion different from the Hindu or the Sikh religion" or, to put it bluntly, unless he professes the Hindu or the Sikh religion.[90] To be a member of a Sch. Caste it is not enough that he belongs to the caste, race, or tribe specified by the President in the Order; these will avail him nothing if he embraces Buddhism, Islam, Christianity or any other religion. By definition Sch. Castes are based on caste and race, two grounds of discrimination prohibited by Art. 16(2), and under Cl. 3 of the President's Order, *religion* is one of the *determinative* factors in a person being a member of a Sch. Caste, and religion is also a ground of discrimination prohibited by Art. 16(2). It is true that Art. 16(2) does not mention "tribe" as observed by Mathew J. in *Thomas's Case*,[91] but this observation though formally correct will be shown below to be incorrect as a matter of substance.

of Sch. Castes not realized

Sch. Castes Orders of 1950, and particularly cl. 3 thereof not referred to

No one not professing the Hindu or the Sikh religion can be a member of a Sch. Caste; classification based on religion

9.189 We have seen that the definition of Sch. Castes and the President's Orders speak of castes, races or tribes which are deemed to be Sch. Castes, and a reference to a standard Dictionary will show that the concepts of race, tribe and caste run into each other, and also involve the concept of descent. The Shorter Oxford Dictionary defines race, tribe and caste as follows:

Definitions of race, tribe and caste

RACE: "1. A group of persons, animals, or plants, connected by a common descent or origin. 2. A limited group of persons descended from a common ancestor; b. a tribe, nation or people regarded as common stock; c. a group of several tribes of peoples forming a distinct ethenic stock."

TRIBE: "1. A group of persons forming a community and claiming descent from a common anscestor; specially each of the 12 divisions of the people of Israel claiming descent from the 12 sons of Jacob; b. a particular race of recognized ancestry; 3. A race of people; now applied especially to a primary aggregate of people in a primitive or barbarous condition, under a head man or chief."

CASTE: "[Adapted from Spanish or Portuguese *casta*, race, lineage; origin pure (stock or breed)]. 1. A race, stock, breed; 2. specially one of the hereditary classes into which society in India has long been divided 'the members of each caste are socially equal, have the same religious rites and generally

[88] Ray C.J., and Mathew, Krishna Iyer and Fazal Ali JJ. held that Sch. Castes were not castes in the ordinary sense: See ('76) A.SC. at p. 501 (Ray C.J.); at p. 519 (Mathew J.); at p. 535 (Krishna Iyer J.) at p. 549 (Fazal Ali J.).

[89] See p. A-129.

[90] The rare case of a Sch. Caste member being an atheist or an agnostic may technically justify the oblique language of Cl. 3 of the Order.

[91] ('76) A.SC. at p. 519.

follow some occupation or profession; they have no social intercourse with those of another caste'. The original castes were: '1st. *Brahmins* or priestly caste; 2nd the *Kshatriyas* or military caste; 3rd *Vaisya* or merchants, 4th the *Sudras* or artisans and labourers'. Now almost every variety has its occupation as its caste."

Submission: Sch. Castes are castes in the ordinary sense

9.190 It will be seen that race and tribe are based on common descent — a ground of discrimination forbidden by Art. 16(2). And it is well known that tribes may break up into castes. As pointed out by Mr. Enthowen, "Tribe and caste, therefore, are different ways of looking at the same social groups, the tribe being the forerunner of the caste."[92] It is submitted that the answer given by Gupta J. to the suggestion that Sch. Castes are not castes in the ordinary sense is decisive and is borne out by a scrutiny of the castes notified in the Presidential Order. He said:

"It is claimed that the expression 'Scheduled Castes' does not refer to any caste of the Hindu Society but connotes a backward class of citizens. A look at article 341 will show that the expression means a number of existing social castes listed in a schedule; castes do not cease to be castes being put in a schedule though backwardness has come to be associated with them."[93]

Part IV in the Schedule to the Constitution (Scheduled Castes) Order 1950 refers to Gujarat, which was a part of the Province of Bombay till 1960. Item 2 mentions *Bakad* as a Scheduled Caste. It also mentions under Item 3, *inter alia, Chambhar*. An authoritative work on the *Tribes and Castes of Bombay* by R. E. Enthowen, I.C.S., Supdt. of Ethnography, Bombay Presidency, has given an account of these castes. He states of the Bakad *caste* that "Bakads are Hindus. They worship village gods and goddesses and the ancestral dieties."[94] "*Chambhar*: Thus, *Chambhar* has been applied to other castes and tribes of this Presidency, such as the *Kathi* etc."[95] He further mentions "the caste follows the Hindu law of inheritance and professes Hinduism".[96] It is needless to labour the point. For, the answer given by Gupta J. is further borne out by reference to a standard work on Castes and Tribes. Further, our discussion has shown that although the observation that Art. 16(2) does not mention tribes is formally correct, it is incorrrect as a matter of substance. The Scheduled Tribes Order does not make it obligatory for the member of a tribe to profess the Hindu or the Sikh religion, presumably because, although as we have seen, several tribes follow the Hindu religion and have been included in the Sch. Castes, some tribes follow an animistic form of religion and they require protection as aboriginal tribes.[97] It is clear therefore that the Sch. Castes are based on religion, on race, on caste and on descent; and Sch. Tribes are based on race and descent. Therefore, the discrimination in favour of Sch. Castes and Tribes made by Rule 13AA falls

Submission: Sch. Castes are based on religion, race, caste and descent; appeal should have been dismissed

---

[92] Enthowen, *The Tribes and Castes of Bombay*, Vol. I, p. vi (1920). See also "The Ahirs and Gujars, immigrant *tribes* of great importance, are now broken into many caste sections such as those found in Shimpis, Sonars, Sutars, Chambhars, etc.": ibid. p. vi. (italics supplied)

[93] ('76) A.SC. at p. 542.

[94] *Enthowen*, p. 55.

[95] ibid. p. 260.

[96] ibid. p. 267.

[97] See *per* Mukherjea J. in *A. K. Gopalan* v. *The State* (1950) S.C.R. 88 at p. 259: "The scheduled tribes, as is well known, are a backward and unsophisticated class of people who are liable to be imposed upon by shrewd and designing persons. Hence there are various provisions disabling them from alienating even their own properties except under special conditions."

squarely within Art. 16(2). As Rule 13AA was not, and could not have been, defended under Art. 16(4), the State's appeal should have been dismissed.

9.191 As to para 9.186(*c*) above, the view expressed by the four majority judges that Art. 16(4) is not an exception[98] has been fully discussed in paras 9.132 to 9.144 above and has been shown to be untenable. The view is also opposed to the legislative history of Art. 16(4) (see para 9.142 above) and, we may add, to the legislative history of Art. 15(4).

Submission: view of four majority judges that Art. 16(4) is not an exception is erroneous

9.192 As to para 9.186(*d*) above, we have already explained in paras 9.126 to 9.129 the misconceptions which may arise from the use of the expression "Arts. 15 and 16 are facets of Art. 14." It only remains to add that Arts. 15 and 16 which deny to non-citizens the fundamental rights against discrimination conferred by Art. 15(1) and (2) and the fundamental rights to equality of opportunity in matters of public employment conferred by Art. 16(1) and (2) cannot, with propriety, be described as a "facet" of the fundamental right to equality conferred by Art. 14 on citizens and *non-citizens alike*.

Misconception arising from Arts. 15 and 16 being "facets" of Art. 14

9.193 As to para 9.186(*e*) above, the decisions of the U.S. Supreme Court on the equality clause of the 14th Amendment freely cited by Mathew and Krishna Iyer JJ. cannot throw any light on Art. 16. First, because there is no provision corresponding to Art. 16 in the U.S. Constitution; and, secondly, because in the United States the equality clause of the 14th Amendment does not carry with it *as a necessary corollary* a right to equality of opportunity in matters of public employment. On the contrary, as we have seen in para 9.128 above, the "spoils system" which is the opposite of equality of opportunity in matters of public employment, prevailed, and still prevails in the United States.

Submission: decisions of U.S. Supreme Court unhelpful

9.194 As to para 9.186(*f*) and (*g*) above, the majority judgments are one further illustration that hard cases make bad law. Khanna J. said as much when he observed: "Out of our concern for the facts of one individual case, we must not adopt a construction the effect of which might be to open the door for making all kinds of inroads into a great ideal and desideratum like that of equality of opportunity."[99] What the case called for was not moral indignation at a historical wrong done to whole communities, legitimate though it may be in its proper place, nor eloquence and rhetoric, nor moral and political philosophising. The concept of "equality of opportunity" called for a careful analysis of the concept, *not in the abstract*, but in the context of public employment and the object or purpose which public employment is meant to subserve. Article 335 is a reminder of this. The earlier Supreme Court decisions, which held that Art. 16(4) was an exception, limited the admitted evil following from reservation in public service to reservation which is less than 50 per cent. But following on *Thomas's Case* the State of Karnataka has reserved 68 per cent of seats in educational institu-

Further infirmities of the majority judgments pointed out

---

[98] See ('76) A.SC. at p. 499 (Ray C.J.); at p. 519 (Mathew J.); at pp. 535-6 (Krishna Iyer J.) and at pp. 552-3 (Fazal Ali J.).

[99] ('76) A.SC. at p. 510.

tions and 68 per cent of posts in public services, a reservation which has been upheld by the High Court.[1] So, contrary to the intention of the founders, a reservation which was to be an exception and was to be confined to a minority of seats[2] is now allowed to destroy the rule of equality of opportunity. A result so contrary to the intention of the founders, contrary to the plain language of Arts. 15 and 16, and contrary to public interest in sound educational institutions and in an efficient public service, can be accepted only for reasons so cogent that they lead only to one conclusion and no other. Far from this being so, the conclusion of the four majority judges suffers not only from the grave infirmities we have pointed out earlier but is based on inapplicable and inept analogies, and on a moral and political philosophy misapplied to the problems raised by Art. 16(4).

"Real equality": the analogy of handicap horse racing given by Subba Rao J.

9.195 In his dissenting judgment in *Devadasan's Case* Subba Rao J. dealt with the "real nature" of equality. He gave the following instance of the true concept of equality. He said :

"Two horses are set down to run a race — one is a first class race horse and the other an ordinary one. Both are made to run from the same starting point. Though theoretically they are given equal opportunity to run the race, in practice the ordinary horse is not given an equal opportunity to compete with the race horse. Indeed, that is denied to it. So, a handicap may be given either in the nature of extra weight or a start from a longer distance. By doing so, what would otherwise have been a farce of a competition would be made a real one."[3]

He said that the makers of the Constitution had introduced Art. 16(4) in view of centuries of calculated oppression of a considerable section of our people. In the light of this he propounded the theory of a legislative device in the passage set out in para 9.132 above. It is a little unfortunate that Subba Rao J. should have selected his example from *handicap* horse racing, for, had he glanced at a book, or even an article, on horse racing and breeding, like the article in the *Encyclopedia Britannica* on the subject, he would have realised how inept his illustration was in the context of public service. First, in actual races, a first class race horse is *not* made to run a race with an ordinary horse. Secondly, horse racing is concerned with two things: first, providing opportunities for *excellence* and for improving the breed of horses, and, secondly, to encourage gambling. The *Encyclopedia* article states that:

"As a touchstone for excellence in competition, and hence for selecting animals to improve the breed five English classic races, all exclusively for 3 year olds became the central concern of British racing . . ."[4] and "Handicaps are open to horses of specified age and sex. . . . Weights are assigned by an official handicapper, whose task, *in theory is to equalize the chances of all the potential runners;* in practice this is not possible, of course, but *horses of lesser ability* do have an improved *chance* of finishing ahead of their betters. The uncertainties resulting from difference in weights carried have caused the amount of wagering on the principal handicaps to be among the largest totals of a season. Classic winners and other top flight horses normally avoid encounters

[1] At the time of writing, an appeal has been pending before the Supreme Court.

[2] See para 9.124 of the text. Dr. Ambedkar asked: "Could anybody say that the reservation of 30 per cent as open to general competition would be consistent with giving effect to the first principle, namely, that there shall be equality of opportunity? It cannot be in my judgment."

[3] ('64) A.SC. at p. 189.

[4] *Encyclopedia Britannica*, Vol. 11, Horse Racing and Breeding, p. 717. (1970).

under handicap conditions, when the risk of defeat is not balanced by the prestige to be gained by winning over second class competition".[5] (italics supplied)

9.196 Superficially, the analogy of handicap racing is attractive, but a little reflection will show how inappropriate the analogy is. Further, we are concerned not with the concept of "equality of opportunity" in the abstract, but with the very different concept of "equality of opportunity *in matters of public employment*". First, the object of classic races (that is, without any handicap) is to promote excellence,[6] and having found out excellence to improve the breed. Reservation of seats for backward classes is *ex hypothesi not* designed to find out excellence: to prefer a third class candidate (with 29 per cent marks) to a first class candidate (with 61 per cent marks), as in *Devadasan's Case*, is not to promote excellence but to disregard excellence as irrelevant or superfluous. Secondly, handicap races are run between second class horses, and experience has shown that the task of equalizing unequal horses is so uncertain that it adds to the gambling nature of a horse race and thus promotes gambling on the largest scale. It is odd to compare recruitment to public service to gambling; but it is odder still to overlook the method of recruitment to public employment or service, and the object or purpose which a public service is designed to subserve. What is the method by which candidates are to be recruited to public service? Article 320 (1) gives the answer: "It shall be the duty of the Union and the State Public Service Commissions to conduct examinations for appointments to the services of the Union and the services of the States respectively". The framers of our Constitution were familiar with the method of recruiting members of public services, and they entrusted the conduct of examinations to independent Commissions in the belief that, if fairly conducted, candidates would be selected on merit, uninfluenced by nepotism, corruption, or by communal and caste bias. This method had produced a first class civil service, and in spite of repeated criticisms of examinations as a test of merit, they found no other method of selecting candidates which would produce even the same, much less, better, results.

Submission: analogy of horse racing inappropriate

9.197 The judgment of Mathew J. on the real nature of equality is based partly on observations of eminent writers and partly on his inferences from those observations. He quoted the following passage from Prof. Harold Laski:

Mathew J. on "real equality"

"Equality means, in the second place, that adequate opportunities are laid open to all. By adequate opportunities we cannot imply equal opportunities in a sense that implies identity of original chance. The native endowments of men are by no means equal. Children who are brought up in an atmosphere where things of the mind are accounted highly are bound to start the race of life with advantages no legislation can secure. Parental character will inevitably affect profoundly the equality of the children whom it touches. So long, therefore, as the family endures — and there seems little reason to anticipate or to desire its disappearance — the varying environments it will create make the notion of equal opportunities a fantastic one."[7]

Prof. Laski: equality and the family

---

[5] ibid. The article on the same subject in the 1951 edition made much the same point about handicap racing.

[6] Classic races designed to promote excellence do offer an analogy, for it is the object of such races to put horses in an order of merit, according to their performance. The object of competitive examinations is to put candidates in an order of merit according to their performance.

[7] ('76) A.SC. at p. 514.

No exception can be taken to this passage and the idea there expressed has been more precisely stated by another distinguished writer.[8] However, does the conclusion which Mathew J. drew from Laski's observations and the manner in which he applied it in the following passages really follow?

Mathew J.'s views on "equality of opportunity"

"Though complete identity of equality of opportunity is impossible in this world, measures compensatory in character and which are calculated to mitigate surmountable obstacles to ensure equality of opportunity can never incur the wrath of Article 16(1)."[9]

"The notion of equality of opportunity is a notion that a limited good shall in fact be allocated on the grounds which do not *a priori* exclude any section of those that desire it.[10] All sections of people desire and claim representation in the public service of the country, but the available number of posts are limited and therefore, even though all sections of people might desire to get posts, it is practically impossible to satisfy the desire. The question therefore is: On what basis can any citizen or class of citizens be excluded from his or their fair share of representation? Article 335 postulates that members of Scheduled Castes and Scheduled Tribes have a claim to representation in the public service both of the Union and the States and that the claim has to be taken into consideration consistently with the maintenance of efficiency of administration in the making of appointments to services of the Union and the States. As I said, the notion of equality of opportunity has meaning only when a limited good or, in the present context, a limited number of posts, should be allocated on grounds which do not *a priori* exclude any section of citizens of those that desire it."[11]

A criticism of his views

9.198 It is submitted that Mathew J. has lost sight of the fact that under our Constitution recruitment to public service was to be, and in fact is, by open competitive examinations, and that he had to fit in his theory of equality of opportunity in public employment into that frame work. Further, the provisions of our Constitution give no countenance to his theory that "The notion of equality of opportunity is a notion that a limited good shall in fact be allocated on grounds which do not *a priori* exclude any section of those that desire it", if by that is meant that communities or sections of communities have a *right* to be "represented" in public service, or a claim to be so represented. Leaving aside Sch. Castes and Sch. Tribes, and leaving aside Art. 16(4) for the present, Art. 16(1) read with Art. 16(2) negatives any such claim. Unreserved seats are to be filled by open competition, and the question whether a community is over represented or under represented is irrelevant to a selection based on merit as disclosed by the examination results. Article 16(2) prevents exclusion of candidates on *a priori* grounds, *e.g.* the rejection of candidates on the ground that they are "untouchables", or on the ground that they do not belong to a "martial race or tribe" or because they belong to "criminal tribes",

---

[8] Allen, *Aspects of Justice*, p. 31: "For example, we hear much today of 'social justice'. I am not sure that those who use the term most glibly know very clearly what they mean by it. Some mean distribution, or 'redistribution,' of wealth; some interpret it as *'equality of opportunity' — a misleading term, since opportunity can never be equal among human beings who have unequal capacities to grasp it;* many, I suspect, mean simply that it is unjust that anybody should be more fortunate than themselves; and the more intelligent mean that it is just — I would rather say benevolent — that every effort should be made at least to mitigate the asperities of natural human inequality and that no obstacles should be offered, but rather help offered to practicable opportunities of self-improvement." (italics supplied)

[9] ('76) A.SC. at p. 514.

[10] See Williams on "The Idea of Equality" in *Justice and Equality*, ed. Hugh A. Badan, p. 116.

[11] ('76) A.SC. at p. 514.

and the like. Article 335[12] refers *only* to Sch. Castes and Tribes; it says that their claims shall be considered *consistently with the maintenance of efficiency of administration.* The italicised words, though frequently repeated in the four majority judgments are not given any practical content. However, those words bring out the cardinal fact that public services exist to supply an efficient administration for the benefit of the people of the States or the Union, and not for providing "jobs", or limited "goods", to any section of people. That the efficiency of administration is the deciding factor is clear from the unanimous judgment of 5 Judges of the Supreme Court in *C. A. Rajendran* v. *Union,*[13] which is considered in greater detail in para 9.236 below. There, it was contended that Art. 16(4) created a fundamental right in favour of backward classes and was not an exception. This contention was rejected, the Court holding that Art. 16(4) conferred no right but only a discretionary power, and that Art. 16(4) was an exception to Art. 16(1). But the important thing to note in this Case is that when Government found that quota reservations were harmful from the point of efficiency of Railway Service, the reservations were withdrawn and the Supreme Court upheld the withdrawal.

Art. 16(4) and Art. 335 create no rights, unlike Arts. 330 and 332, in favour of Sch. Castes and Tribes

9.199 That Art. 16(4) creates no rights but confers a discretionary power, and Art. 335 does likewise, is clear if the language of these Articles is contrasted with that of Arts. 330 and 332 which provide that seats *shall* be reserved for Sch. Castes and Tribes in the House of the People and in the Legislative Assemblies of every State. The only qualification for being a candidate at an election to the House of the People, or to a Legislative Assembly, is that the candidate must be a citizen of India, and must not be less than 25 years of age and has not incurred one or more of a limited number of disqualifications. Consequently, a mandatory reservation of seats for Sch. Castes and Tribes, on historical grounds, in a representative body is intelligible, for *excellence in the representative is not a requirement* for being a candidate at an election. Even so, under Art. 334 the reservation ran counter to the policy of the Congress and it was originally intended to last for 10 years. But the reservation has become a political issue, and by successive Constitutional amendments it now stands extended from 10 to 40 years.

Further infirmities of the "handicap" theory pointed out

9.200 As we have seen, Subba Rao J. spoke of giving backward class persons a handicap to secure an equality of opportunity. However, what he overlooked was that if a candidate is given a "handicap" he can get into public service; but once there, a third class candidate will, ordinarily, remain third class; and a first class candidate will, ordinarily, remain first class. Public service cannot be efficiently run by "handicapped" persons. Mathew J. gave another illustration. He quoted Benard I. O. Williams[14] for the proposition that where recruitment to the army was limited to warrior class and the objection to

---

[12] *Art. 335 : Claims of Scheduled Castes and Scheduled Tribes to services and posts.* — The claims of the members of the Scheduled Castes and the Scheduled Tribes shall be taken into consideration, consistently with the maintenance of efficiency of administration, in the making of appointments to services and posts in connection with the affairs of the Union or of a State.

[13] (1968) 1 S.C.R. 721, ('68) A.SC. 507.

[14] ('76) A.SC. at pp. 514-5.

that had been met by saying, "we are not excluding anyone for being poor; we exclude people for being weak, and it is unfortunate that those who are poor are also weak." Mathew J. held that it was not a satisfactory answer, because the connection between the poor and the undernourished was well known. But the example which he gives is the clearest refutation of his theory, because he could not have intended to suggest that in order to produce real equality, the weak and the undernourished should be recruited to the army, in which physical fitness is vital.

Submission: Mathew J.'s contrast between language of Art. 14 and Art. 16(1) is not correct

9.201 Some other observations of Mathew J. must be noted here. He contrasted the language of Art. 14 which, according to him, emphasised "the negative character of the duty of the State, while the emphasis of Art. 16(1) is on the mandatory aspect, namely, that there should be equality of opportunity for all citizens. . ."[15] It is submitted that the alleged contrast is based on several misconceptions. As to Art. 14 Mathew J. looked to the form and not to the substance, for as we have seen, though negative in form it is positive in effect: it confers a right to equality on every person by prohibiting the State from denying it.[16] The right would be no different if it were put in an affirmative form: "Every person shall be accorded equality before the law and the protection of equal laws". This right would *necessarily* restrain the State from denying it to any person. Secondly, the reference to Art. 16(1) as though it were the sole repository of the right to equality of opportunity in matters of public employment is clearly wrong. As pointed out by Gajendragadkar J.[17] the right to equality of opportunity is conferred positively by Art. 16(1) and its enforcement is made effective by Art. 16(2) which though negative in form is positive in effect: "No citizen shall . . . be discriminated against . . ." This injunction is necessarily addressed to the State, although the State is not mentioned, because it is only the State which can discriminate against a citizen on the prohibited grounds in respect of any employment or office *under the State.* Therefore Art. 16(1) and (2) is as much an injunction against the State as is Art. 14. In fact, Art. 13(2) makes every fundamental right an injunction against the State not to violate it.

Submission: Mathew J.'s reference to Arts. 29(1) and 30(1) irrelevant and unhelpful

9.202 Again, it is submitted that the reference by Mathew J. to the rights conferred on minorities by Arts. 29(1) and 30(1) is irrelevant and unhelpful in interpreting Art. 16(1) and (2). First, these Articles do not deal with equality. Secondly, these Articles confer fundamental rights on minorities, which will remain minorities. Article 16(4) and Art. 335 do not confer *rights* on backward classes; those Articles as we have seen merely confer discretionary power. Further, the whole object of Arts. 16(4) and 335 was to uplift the backward classes; they were meant to be a help and not a permanent crutch. Consequently, the exercise of discretionary power was expected to fade away. Articles 29(1) and 30(1) conferred fundamental rights which were designed to endure. Thirdly, as to his reference to the judgment which he delivered for himself and Chandrachud J. in *St. Xavier's College* v. *Gujarat*,[18] it is enough to say at present, what will be discussed fully in Chapter XII, that the reference is unhelp-

---

15 ('76) A.SC. at p. 516.

16 See para 8.46(*i*).

17 See para 9.187 of the text.

18 (1975) 1 S.C.R. 173, ('74) A.SC. 1389.

ful, because no two judgments in that case were agreed as to "the real reason for the protection of minorities in a democratic State". Even otherwise Arts. 29 (1) and 30 (1) must be interpreted according to their terms, and not by the different philosophies supposed to underlie those Articles. But the most decisive objection against reference to minority rights is that Art. 16 (1) and (2) does not protect the rights of minorities by conferring on them a right, *as minorities,* to obtain reservation of seats in public service. There are many minorities which do not belong to backward classes of citizens, and Art. 16 confers no special rights on such minorities in order to promote "real equality", but leaves them to face open competition for unreserved seats.

9.203 Our discussion has shown that the four majority judgments are untenable; consequently, it would be unprofitable to analyse each judgment in order to show that the four judgments do not disclose any coherent pattern or a common *ratio.* It may be added that in *Akhil Bharatiya Soshit Karmachari Sangh* v. *Union*[19] (*the "Karmachari Sangh Case"*), which is discussed in paras 9.204 to 9.218 below, Krishna Iyer J. (with whom Reddy J. concurred) has held, *contrary to his view* in *Thomas's Case,* that Art. 16 (4) is an exception and that it saves reservations for SCs *assuming* SCs are castes. This change of view lends support to the present writer's submission that the four majority judgments are clearly wrong, productive of great public mischief and ought to be overruled.

Submission: *Thomas's Case* wrongly decided

9.204 The *Karmachari Sangh Case* is important, first, because it enlarged the *locus standi* of petitioners in public interest litigation; secondly, because the question of reservation of quotas for members of the Scheduled Castes and Scheduled Tribes[20] was directly raised and the correct interpretation of Art. 16 (4) was directly put in issue. Finally, the change in the position of Krishna Iyer J. referred to in para 9.203 above on two crucial issues in *Thomas's Case* has deprived that case of its authority by destroying its foundation, although Krishna Iyer and Reddy JJ., followed the majority view in *Thomas's Case.* Our present discussion is confined to the issues raised under Art. 16.

The *Karmachari Sangh Case*: the interpretation of Art. 16(4) was directly raised

9.205 The *Karmachari Sangh Case* came before the Supreme Court on writ petitions which impugned ten circulars issued by the Railway Board fixing reservation quotas for members of SCs and STs in promotion posts, including circulars for the "carry forward rules". The reader will find the gist of the impugned circulars in the leading judgment of Krishna Iyer J. Three judgments were delivered, dismissing the petitions and upholding the validity of the ten circulars. However, as to the circulars laying down the *carry forward rule,* Krishna Iyer J. added the rider that the rule *"shall not result,* in any given year, in the selection of SC and ST candidates considerably in excess of 50% . . ."[21] This rider, like the rest of his judgment, is lacking in precision and will lead to further litigation. For, what does "considerably" in excess of 50% mean? Since "considerable" means "much",[22] the rider means "not much in excess of 50%". This

Petitions dismissed, with a rider added to the "carry forward rule"

---

[19] (1981) 2 S.C.R. 185, ('81) A.SC. 298.

[20] As the judgments use the abbreviation SCs and STs for Sch. Castes and Sch. Tribes, those abbreviations are used in the discussion of this case.

[21] ('81) A.SC. at p. 321. [22] *C.O.D.*

leaves Counsel free to argue, and Judges free to decide, that 55, 60, 65 or even a larger percentage, is not "much in excess" of 50%. It may be added that in reaching their decision, all the Judges followed *Thomas's Case.* Although Reddy J. agreed with "the reasoning and conclusions" of Krishna Iyer J.[23], he made ". . . certain general observations because I expect the same questions to be raised repeatedly in different situations . . . and it is just as well that I project my prosaic and pedestrian point of view, without going into the detail or depth already explored by (Krishna Iyer J.)"[24].

Reddy J. agrees with Krishna Iyer J.

Judgment of Pathak J., a dissenting judgment in substance though not in form

9.206 Pathak J.'s judgment is, in substance, though not in form, a dissenting judgment. He said that his brother Judges had "held against the petitioners on the several contentions raised in the case. *With respect, I find myself unable to agree with all that they have said.* I intend to confine myself here to certain aspects of the case which appear to possess a fundamental importance."[25] (italics supplied) He concentrated his attention on the "carry forward rules" and he referred to Gajendragadkar J.'s judgment in *Balaji's Case* which laid down that broadly speaking, a special provision for reservation should be less than 50 per cent. Pathak J. observed that *Balaji's Case* pointed out the need for striking a balance between several relevant considerations in making reservations. He then referred to *Devadasan's Case,* in which a carry forward rule which would result in a quota reservation of 68% was struck down by a majority of 4 : 1, and it was further held that every year must be treated as a separate year for recruitment. Pathak J. then expressed his own view as follows:

The view of Pathak J.: a maximum of 50% for reserved quota was fair and reasonable

"It seems to me that apart from the impact that an excessive reservation in a particular year is bound to have on the general community of citizens, there is the further far-reaching significance this assumes in the context of Article 335. The maintenance of efficiency of administration is bound to be adversely affected if general candidates of high merit are correspondingly excluded from recruitment because the large bulk of the vacancies, numbering anything over 50%, is allotted to the reserved quota. In view of a maximum age-limit invariably prescribed, some of such meritorious candidates may be lost to the service altogether. Viewed in that light, a maximum of 50% for reserved quotas in their totality is a rule which appears fair and reasonable, just and equitable, and violation of which would contravene Article 335".[26]

However, he said that there was an apparent conflict between *Devadasan's Case* and *Thomas's Case* and in view of the last mentioned case, since his brother Judges had upheld the carry forward rule he went along with them after having expressed his own view. It is not clear whether Pathak J. had the judgment of Krishna Iyer J. before him when he wrote his judgment. However, the change in the view of Krishna Iyer J. (Reddy J. agreeing with him) pointed out in para 9.210 below, has deprived *Thomas's Case* of its authority by destroying its foundation. Pathak J. was therefore entitled to follow *Devadasan's Case* and his view that the total maximum reservations should not exceed 50% becomes unanswerable, because, a rule must have a larger operation than the exception to it, if the exception is not to become the rule.

---

23 ('81) A.SC. at p. 340.
24 ibid. pp. 333-4.
25 ibid. p. 331.
26 ibid. p. 333.

9.207 The leading judgment of Krishna Iyer J. poses a serious problem of exposition for a commentator. The judgment is a strange mixture of sermon, prophecy and platform rhetoric; of thinly disguised contempt for those who take a different view from his own,[27] of discourteous remarks on Counsel's arguments which ran counter to his own views,[28] accompanied by the recurrent theme song of strong moral indignation at the unjust and inhuman treatment to which the depressed classes were subjected for centuries and at their sad plight even to-day. After much reflection, the present writer has decided that he cannot, with propriety, deal with the judgment as it might be dealt with outside a textbook. Therefore, the reader must decide for himself what he thinks of the tone, the temper, the approach and the reasoning of Krishna Iyer J's judgment. In this task the reader may be helped by the observation of Mr. Justice Frankfurter[29] that "if Judges want to be preachers, they should dedicate themselves to the pulpit; if Judges want to be primary shapers of policy, the Legislature is their place. Self-willed Judges are the least defensible offenders of government under law."[30] We will confine the discussion of the judgment of Krishna Iyer J. to examining some of the arguments by which he reached his conclusions.

The leading judgment of Krishna Iyer J. poses a serious problem of exposition

9.208 As we have seen, the question whether Arts. 15(4) and 16(4) were an exception or not had presented no difficulty except for the judgment of Subba Rao J. (adopted by Krishna Iyer J. in *Thomas's Case*) that Art. 16(4) was not an exception. Now that Krishna Iyer J. has held that Art. 16(4) is an exception,[31] the question of extrinsic aids to construction does not arise. However, Krishna Iyer J. quoted a passage (set out in the undernoted Law Reports)[32] from the final address of Dr. Ambedkar to the Constituent Assembly,[33] "not to interpret but to illumine the scheme of the equality code"[34] ("the equality code"). But this passage gives an incorrect impression of Dr. Ambedkar's final address. He was not thinking of the SCs and STs or of the equality code as the following passage clearly shows:

Krishna Iyer J. now holds Art. 16(4) to be an exception

and quotes Dr. Ambedkar "not to interpret but to illumine"

"I remember the days when politically minded Indians resented the expression 'the people of India'. They preferred the expression 'the Indian nation'. I am of opinion that in believing that we are a nation we are *cherishing a great delusion*. How can people *divided into several thousands of castes* be a nation? The sooner we realise that we are not as yet a nation in the social

A passage from Dr. Ambedkar's final address left out

[27] When the Report of the Railway Accidents Enquiry Committee, 1968 was relied upon, Krishna Iyer J. observed: "*It is true that the Report has a slant against the SC and ST promotion policy* . . ." ('81) A.SC. at p. 317 (italics supplied)

[28] *E.g.* "Social realists will read these pessimistic figures of the last ten years which prove the myth and negate the *neurotic rhetoric* about the SCs and STs . . .": ('81) A.SC. at p. 318 (italics supplied); "A mere formula of reservation is not the factum of recruitment. That is *morbid fancy*": ibid. p. 319 (italics supplied); "I divagate and make these observations *to debunk the exaggerated argument* about *harijans* and *girijans* being sub-standard": ibid. p. 329 (italics supplied).

[29] He is one of the persons whom Krishna Iyer J. has quoted in his judgment. Quotations from other eminent men include Tolstoy, Vivekananda, Jawaharlal Nehru, Cardozo, Prof. Griffiths, Landis and Dr. Ambedkar.

[30] *Government Under Law*, p. 31.

[31] See para 9.210 of the text.

[32] (1981) 2 S.C.R. at pp. 199-200 (the quotation ends with the italicised words at p. 200); ('81) A.SC. at p. 304. The quotation ends with the words (emphasis supplied).

[33] From Keer, *Ambedkar: Life and Mission*, p. 412.

[34] ('81) A.SC. at p. 304.

and psychological sense of the word, the better for us. For, then only we shall realise the necessity of becoming a nation and seriously think of ways and means of realising the goal. The realisation of this goal is going to be very difficult — far more difficult than it has been in the United States. The United States has no caste problem. In India there are castes. The castes are anti-national. In the first place because they bring about separation in social life. They are anti-national also because they generate jealousy and antipathy between caste and caste. But we must overcome all these difficulties if we wish to become a nation in reality. For, fraternity can be a fact only when there is a nation. Without fraternity, equality and liberty will be no deeper than coats of paint."[35] (italics supplied)

Theme of Dr. Ambedkar's final address not concerned with Art. 16(4) or "the equality code"

Dr. Ambedkar appealed to the poeple who had given themselves a new Constitution, but who were nevertheless divided into thousands of castes and sub-castes, even among the higher castes, for a change of heart in their personal and social dealings with one another; he was not thinking in terms of constitutional arrangements for SCs and STs. The theme of his final address was that no constitutional arrangements for equality and for the backward classes could break down the barriers which separated thousands of castes in their social and personal intercourse without a resolute effort by the people to break down those barriers.

Three odd features in Krishna Iyer J.'s search for "illumination"

9.209 It seems odd that in search of illumination on the equality code Krishna Iyer J. should turn to a biography of Dr. Ambedkar for a quotation from his final address to the Constituent Assembly, instead of turning to that address as a whole in the Constituent Assembly Debates, Vol. 12. It is odder still to refer to an address in which Dr. Ambedkar did not deal with the equality code but expressed his hopes and fears as to the working of the Constitution, in the framing of which, as Chairman of the Drafting Committee, he had played an important part. But the oddest thing a Judge can do in seeking illumination on the equality code is to leave out the only speech which Dr. Ambedkar made directly on Art. 16(4) to justify the insertion of the word "backward" in Draft Art. 10 [now 16(4)],—a speech which made the scheme of Art. 16 luminously clear.[36] No doubt that speech, (the relevant parts of which have been set out in para 9.124 above) ran counter to the doctrine propounded on Art. 16 by Krishna Iyer J. in the *Karmachari Sangh Case*.[37] But a Judge who seeks *illumination* in such odd ways leaves himself open to the criticism that such a judge "drops the mantle of a judge and assumes the robes of an Advocate, and the change does not become him well."[38]

Dr. Ambedkar's speech directly on Art. 16(4) left out

---

[35] *C.A.D.* Vol. 12 at p. 980.

[36] It was not as though his speech lay buried in the volumes of the Constituent Assembly Debates. In criticising *Thomas's Case*, Dr. Ambedkar's speech on Art. 16(4) was referred to and the reference to the Constituent Assembly Debates given, in Seervai, *Constitutional Law of India*, (2nd ed.) Vol. III (1979) at p. 1865.

[37] ('81) A.SC. at p. 304. The reader will have noticed further that Dr. Ambedkar, (whom Krishna Iyer J. described as "a *mahar* by birth and a fighter to his last breath against the Himalayan injustice to the *Harijan* fellow millions stigmatized by their genetic handicap": ('81) A.SC. at p. 303) in spite of the personal indignities inflicted upon him in his childhood by reason of his "genetic handicap", preserved a balanced outlook in his speech defending the insertion of the word "backward" in Art. 16(4): see para 9.124 above. Krishna Iyer J., who suffered from no such genetic handicap, was unable as a Judge to preserve a similar outlook because of his indignation at the treatment of persons with "genetic handicaps".

[38] *Jones* v. *National Coal Board* (1957) 2 Q.B. 55 at p. 64. These words were applied by Denning L.J. to a judge whose excessive interventions during a trial had made a fair trial impossible. A new trial was ordered.

9.210 We must now refer, first, to the passages of the judgment of Krishna Iyer J. in which he was prepared to proceed on the footing that SCs were castes, and secondly, to the passages of the judgment in which he clearly said that Art. 16(4) was an exception to Art. 16(1) and (2). There are three passages the first of which covers both the points:

Krishna Iyer J., accepts that Art. 16(4) is an exception and is prepared to assume Sch. Castes are Castes: illustrative passages

(*A*) "Since a contrary view is possible and has been taken by some Judges, *a verdict need not be rested on the view that SCs are not castes.* Even assuming they are, classification if permitted will validate the differential rules for promotion. *Moreover, Art. 16(4) is an exception to Art. 16(2).*"[39] (italics supplied)

(*B*) "The success of State action under Art. 16(4) consists in the speed with which result oriented reservation withers away as no longer a need, not in the ever widening and everlasting operation of *an exception* [Art. 16(4)] as if it were a super-fundamental right to continue backward all the time."[40] (italics supplied)

(*C*) "The first sub-Article speaks of equality and the second sub-Article amplifies its content by expressly interdicting 'caste' as a ground of discrimination.[41] Article 16(4) imparts to the seemingly static equality embedded in Article 16(1) a dynamic quality by importing equalisation strategies geared to the eventual achievement of equality as permissible State action, viewed as an amplification of Art. 16(1) *or as an exception to it.* The same observations will hold good for the sub-articles of Article 15."[42] (italics supplied)

When in the passage in (*C*) above Krishna Iyer J. spoke of Art. 16(4) being an amplification of Art. 16(1), these words can only mean that Art. 16(4) was an exception, since he rightly said that Art. 16(2) expressly interdicted caste as a ground of discrimination.

9.211 Having regard to Krishna Iyer J.'s change of view on the two grounds which were basic to *Thomas's Case*, could he, with reason, assert that "even though we would, we could not, and even if we could, we would not" depart *inter alia*, from *Thomas's Case*?[43] It is submitted that since *Thomas's Case* did not directly involve reservation of posts under Art. 16(4), the Judges were not bound by observations in that case on Art. 16(4). In any event, the Judges were not bound after Krishna Iyer J. (with whose reasoning and conclusion Reddy J. agreed), had changed his view on the two principal reasons on which *Thomas's Case* was based. No doubt that decision was also rested on the ground that Art. 16(1) permitted classification. But, as we have seen, no classification can be made which is forbidden by Art. 16(2)—hence the view that SCs were not castes. However, once Krishna Iyer J. decided not to rest his decision on that ground but assumed that SCs were castes, and once he rightly said that Art. 16(2) interdicted discrimination on the ground of caste, and that reservations would be saved by Art. 16(4) (which was an exception), the total reasoning of *Thomas's Case* was destroyed. It is submitted that in the *Karmachari Sangh Case* it should

The change in Krishna Iyer's view destroys the basis of the majority decision in *Thomas's Case*

---

[39] ('81) A.SC. at p. 322. Our discussion has shown that SCs are castes and any discrimination in their favour would be based on religion, caste, race or descent which are prohibited grounds of discrimination under Art. 16(2) unless they are saved by Art. 16(4).

[40] ibid. p. 306.

[41] ibid. p. 310. This has obvious reference to Art. 16(2) although the passage does not expressly refer to that Article.

[42] ibid. [43] ibid. p. 308.

have been held that *Thomas's Case* was wrongly decided,[44] and that case could no longer be followed.

Krishna Iyer J. a party to *Thomas's Case* and also to the *Karmachari Sangh Case*

9.212 The reader will have noticed the coincidence by which discrimination in favour of SCs and STs was upheld in *Thomas's Case* and in the *Karmachari Sangh Case* (to both of which Krishna Iyer J. was a party) on directly conflicting grounds. In *Thomas's Case*, the discrimination in favour of SCs and STs could not have been upheld if SCs were castes, unless Art. 16(4) was an exception, and applied to the facts of that case, which it did not. The majority of the Court held that SCs were *not castes* and Art. 16(4) was *not* an *exception.* In the *Karmachari Sangh Case* discrimination in favour of SCs by reservation quotas could not have been upheld unless Art. 16(4), (which is a special provisions providing for reservation of posts in public service) was an exception to both Art. 16(1) and 16(2). Krishna Iyer J. held that Art. 16(4) *was* an exception—giving up Subba Rao's J.'s theory of a legislative device; nor did he affirm that SCs were not castes: he assumed that they were. It is submitted that the grounds on which the *Karmachari Sangh Case* was decided support our submission—made after a detailed analysis of Arts. 15 and 16 and of the President's Orders notifying SCs—that *Thomas's Case* was wrongly decided, and that a hard case had made bad law.

The *extent* of reservations in favour of SCs and STs directly arose

9.213 But once it was held, contrary to the decision in *Thomas's Case* that Art. 16(4) was an exception, the question of the extent of the reservation directly arose. And with *Thomas's Case* out of the way, and Subba Rao J.'s theory of a legislative device given up, the matter was concluded by an overwhelming weight of authority that the reservation under Art. 16 should, broadly not exceed 50%. The reasons for this conclusion have been fully set out earlier and need not be repeated here. Two further observations fall to be made. First, that Pathak J. has accurately stated the law in the passage set out in para 9.206 above. Had he considered the impact of the judgments of this two brother Judges on *Thomas's Case*, he would not have felt constrained by the authority of that case. Secondly, Krishna Iyer J. rightly observed in the passage set out in para 9.210 (*C*) above that what applied to Art. 16(4) applied to Art. 15(4). This is important, for the largest use made of Art. 15(4) has been to reserve seats for backward classes and SCs and STs in educational institutions, with the result that students of high merit would be prevented from pursuing studies for which they are qualified, to the detriment of the public and of standards of education in Colleges which provide training in Arts, Science and for professional examinations. These questions require further discussion, and this is best done by referring to a passage from the judgment of Krishna Iyer J. which, in the submission of the present writer, shows the power of truth to assert itself. He said:

---

44 The elaborate discussion of Krishna Iyer J. of cases which have held that classification can be made under Art. 16(1) [see ('81) A.SC. pp. 320-22] is unnecessary once he proceeded on the footing that SCs are castes.

"This is not mere harmonious statutory construction of Art. 16(1) and (4) but insightful perception of our constitutional culture, reflecting the current of resurgent India bent on making, out of a sick and stratified society of inequality and poverty, a brave new Bharat. If freedom, justice and equal opportunity to unfold one's own personality belong alike to *bhangi* and *brahmin*, prince and pauper, if the *panchama* proletariate is to *feel* the social transformation Art. 16(4) promises, the State must apply equalising techniques which will enlarge their opportunities and thereby progressively diminish the need for props. The success of State action under Art. 16(4) consists in the speed with which result-oriented reservation withers away as no longer a need, not in the everwidening and everlasting operation of an exception [Art. 16(4)] as if it were a super-fundamental right to continue backward all the time. To lend immorality to the reservation policy is to defeat its *raison d'etre;* to politicise this provision for communal support and Party ends is to subvert the solemn undertaking of Art. 16(1), to casteify 'reservation' even beyond the dismal groups of backward-most people, euphemistically described as SC & ST, is to run a grave constitutional risk. Caste, *ipso facto,* is not class in a secular State."[45]

Krishna Iyer J.'s view: Art. 16(4) does not confer a fundamental right to be backward for all time

The observations in this passage are opposed to the tenor of his judgment, although they may have been prompted by matters of common knowledge of which a Court will take notice.[46] But this passage raises the second important question, which fell for determination in the *Karmachari Sangh Case*, namely, "what is the extent of reservations under Art. 16(4), and how far is that extent controlled by the efficiency of administration required by Art. 335?" On the record before the Court, it was held that the carry forward rule did not *in fact* lead to a reservation for SCs and STs exceeding 50%; on the contrary it fell far below 50%. It is not necessary for us to consider whether the finding of fact is correct,[47] because Krishna Iyer J. has not limited his decision to the facts of the case. He has laid down as a general rule how far reservations under a carry forward rule can be carried, namely, that the rule must not result in reservations considerably in excess of 50%. However, Krishna Iyer J.'s discussion of efficiency and merit is very unsatisfactory, coloured as it is by his own ideas of efficiency and merit. But the question of efficiency or merit has to be decided within the framework of our Constitution as it is, and not as Krishna Iyer J. would have it be. As we have seen, recruitment to services is by an open competitive examination conducted by the Union and State Public Service Commissions whose members have been made independent of the executive. The underlying postulates of this system are that such examinations, if fairly conducted, eliminate favouritism, nepotism and corruption which would prevent the best candidates from being recruited to the public services; and, secondly, that candidates who pass the examination in the first class will, *normally*, make more efficient public servants than those who pass the examinations in the second class, and candidates who pass in the second class will, normally, make more efficient public servants than those who pass in the third class. Even in reserving posts or appointments under Art. 16(4) the order of merit among SC and ST candidates is adhered to. If the results of examinations could be ignored, it would be farcical to hold examinations.

The extent of reservations and efficiency of administration

Submission: Krishna Iyer J.'s discussion of merit and efficiency very unsatisfactory

The underlying postulates of open competitive examination

[45] ('81) A.SC. at p. 306.

[46] Since some time, statements have been made by men in power that "the question of reservations is not negotiable".

[47] That would require a study of the record which is not available to the present writer.

Krishna Iyer J.'s dislike of examinations and of emphasis on efficiency

9.214 It is clear from his judgment that Krishna Iyer J. does not like examinations for which Art. 320 (1) provides nor does he like the emphasis on efficiency of administration placed by Art. 335 when the claims of SCs and STs to employment in the services of the Union and the States are to be considered. This is clear from what he states in his judgment. He said:

Krishna Iyer J. on "merit" and "suitability"

> "A democracy of talent is an inarticulate major premise of *our culture*. (italics supplied).[48] The fundamental question arises as to what is 'merit' and 'suitability'. Elitists whose sympathies with the masses have dried up are, from the standards of the Indian people, least suitable to run Government and least meritorious to handle state business, if we envision a Service State in which the millions are the consumers. A sensitized heart and a vibrant head, tuned to the tears of the people, will speedily quicken the developmental needs of the country, including its rural stretches and slum squalour. Sincere dedication and intellectual integrity — these are some of the major components of 'merit' and 'suitability' — not degrees from Oxford or Cambridge, Harvard or Stanford or Simian, though Indian, institutions. Unfortunately, the very orientation of our selection process is distorted and those like the candidates from the SC & ST who, from their birth, have had a traumatic understanding of the conditions of agrestic India have, in one sense, more capability than those who have lived under affluent circumstances and are callous to the human lot of the sorrowing masses. Moreover, our examination system makes memory the master of 'merit' and banishes creativity into exile. We need not enter these areas where a fundamental transformation and a radical reorientation even in the assessment of the qualities needed by the personnel in the Administration and the socialist values to be possessed by the echelons in office is a consummation devoutly to be wished. This may have to be subjected to a national debate. The colonial hangover still clings to our selection processes with superstitious tenacity and narrower concepts of efficiency and merit are readily evolved to push out Gandhis and J.Ps, Ambedkars and Nehrus, to mention but a few who knew the heart-beats of the people. I divagate and make these observations only to debunk the exaggerated argument about harijans and girijans being sub-standard."[49]

Submission: his tests for ascertaining "merit" and "suitability" impracticable

It is submitted that new theories are not always right and old theories are not always wrong. A little reflection would show how impracticable is the test proposed by Krishna Iyer J. for ascertaining merit or suitability. Thousands of candidates appear for the Indian Administrative Examinations each year, (to take only one examination). How does one determine "a sensitised heart and a vibrant head" and how are candidates to be put in an order of merit for possessing a sensitised heart and vibrant head since only a relatively small number of candidates are to be selected? And the same questions would have to be asked about "sincere dedication and intellectual integrity". Further, these qualities are manifested over a period of time, and attempts to determine them would have to last for years and not for days. It would be unprofitable to pursue this subject further.

Submissions: (i) Krishna Iyer J.'s rider to carry forward rule clearly wrong

9.215 It is submitted, that Krishna Iyer J. has failed to realize the necessary implication of his finding that Art. 16 (4) is an exception. Consequently, the rider that he added to the carry forward rule, namely, that the rule must not result in reservations *considerably* in excess of 50% is clearly wrong, both on principle and on the

---

[48] This is a strange thing to say for a judge who repeatedly used strong words to denounce the inhuman treatment meted out for centuries to SCs and STs (who constitute a fifth of the population). A culture which produces this result cannot have "excellence" as its premise — inarticulate or articulate.

[49] ('81) A.SC. p. 329. But Gandhi, Nehru and Ambedkar had foreign degrees/qualifications!

overwhelming weight of authority. Again, it is submitted that his whole approach to the problem is distorted by excessive preoccupation with the sad plight of SCs and STs and the historical wrong done to them. For, he has overlooked the fact that there were five parties before the Court, and if Courts are to do justice, it must be justice to all the parties and not only to one of them. The five parties were: First, the State, to whose service candidates are to be recruited. Secondly, the public, as the very phrase "public servant" shows. Thirdly, the petitioners, who were discriminated against by the reservations in favour of members of SCs and STs. Fourthly, members of SCs and STs in whose favour discrimination was made by fixing reservation quotas. And, fifthly, the services, that is, each service considered as a whole. A service which lacks an *esprit de corps*, that is, consciousness of and pride in belonging to a particular service, lacks an element essential to an efficient and harmonious administration. To balance the claims of these parties, in considering reservation quotas, requires critical analysis and calm deliberation; anger at the treatment meted out to classes to which one of the parties belongs does not help, for anger has been rightly likened "to a hasty servant who runs away before he has heard half the message". Further,

(ii) Krishna Iyer J. overlooked that there were 5 parties before the court

"It is necessary to remember that in litigation there are more parties than one, that it is wrong to gratify the plaintiff to the detriment of the defendant, and that, while sympathy is a most commendable quality, it never appears in a less attractive guise than when it is practised at the expense of somebody else."[50]

Sympathy in an unattractive guise

If past injustice done to members of SCs and STs because of the accident of their birth calls for condemnation, so does injustice done to members of "advanced classes" because of the accident of their birth. It may be that members of "advanced classes" may have to bear for a time, as best as they can, the injustice done to them by reverse discrimination, if a long standing historical wrong has to be righted. But 32 years have gone by since our Constitution came into force; and every year that passes increases the individual's sense of injustice and injury. It is submitted that Judges who have to balance the claims of all the parties affected by any action under Art. 16(4) ought to reflect that if the injustices of the past are to be strongly denounced now, then the future will denounce quite as strongly the injustices suffered by members of "advanced classes" since 1950.

Injustices of the past and injustices since 1950: a need for balance

9.216 The most important quesiton before the Court in the *Karmachari Sangh Case* was, "since Art. 16(4) permits discrimination in favour of backward classes including SCs and STs, how far can relaxation of standards in favour of SCs and STs go, consistently with the efficiency of administration required by Art. 335 and demanded by the public interest?" In answering this question lessons to be learnt from earlier judgments of the Supreme Court ought not to be ignored. It is possible to brush aside the Report of a Railway Enquiry Committee as "slanted"[51] or as based on a "hunch"[52] and to proclaim that "Courts are not credulity in robes!"[53]

The relaxation of standards in favour of SCs and STs and efficiency

[50] Lord Hewart, *Not Without Prejudice*, at p. 228.
[51] ('81) A.SC. at p. 317. [52] ibid. p. 317.
[53] ibid. p. 316.

Lessons learnt from earlier Sup. Ct. decisions

It is not possible to brush aside facts and opinions recorded in Supreme Court decisions. Thus in *C. A. Rajendran* v. *Union*[54] when the Railway Board found that quota reservations were harmful from the point of view of the efficiency of Railway Service, the reservations were withdrawn, the challenge to the withdrawal failed.[55] Again, there is an instructive passage in *A. Periakaruppan* v. *T. N.*,[56] and although it refers to reservations under Art. 15(4) the same principles apply to reservations under Art. 16(4). Hegde J. said:

". . . all the same the Government should not proceed on the basis that once a class is considered as a backward class, it should continue to be backward class for all times. Such an approach would defeat the very purpose of the reservation because once a class reaches a stage of progress which some modern writers call as take off stage then competition is necessary for their future progress. The Government should always keep under review the question of reservation of seats and only the classes which are really socially and educationally backward should be allowed to have the benefit of reservation. Reservation of seats should not be allowed to become a vested interest. The fact that candidates of backward classes have secured about 50% of the seats in the general pool does show that the time has come for a *de novo* comprehensive examination of the question. It must be remembered that the Government's decision in this regard is open to judicial review."[57]

It follows from the above judgments that it is not true that if reservations are made once, they cannot be revoked if experience shows that the efficiency of the public service has suffered as a consequence. Again, the very fact that backward classes do well in unreserved seats requires that Government should keep the list of backward classes under regular review, and remove those backward classes from the list who no longer need the help which Art. 16(4) was designed to provide, if the object of Art. 16(4) was not to be defeated. A failure to do this would be subject to judicial review. It is a matter of common knowledge that reservation of places for the backward classes has become a vote-catching or vote-losing issue. Krishna Iyer J. was aware of this when he said ". . . to politicise this provision for communal support is to subvert the solemn undertaking of Art. 16(4) . . ."[58] In this situation, the role of a federal court as the interpreter and guardian of the Constitution comes into play, and the exercise by the Court of its power would be welcomed by most politicians as taking a load off their backs. If the list of backward classes and the failure to revise it, where such revision is necessary, is subject to judicial review, so also the relaxation of standards and the degree of such relaxation becomes the subject of judicial review, for circumstances may show that the relaxation goes so far that efficiency must suffer.

Krishna Iyer J. on use of Art. 16(4) for "political support"

The role of a federal court: judicial review of relaxation of standards

Open competition and relaxation of standards

9.217 In considering relaxation of standards, where examinations are the determining factor, it is obvious that a line must be drawn somewhere between the first, the second and the third class. Therefore, on the border line of each class, there is a field in which some relaxation for a reasonable time in favour of SCs and STs would not appear unreasonable and unjust. For example, if 60% marks

[54] (1968) 1 S.C.R. 721, ('68) A.SC. 507.

[55] *C. A. Rajendran's Case* is referred to by Krishna Iyer J. in ('81) A.SC. at p. 327, but not on this point.

[56] (1970) 2 S.C.R. 430, ('71) A.SC. 2303.

[57] ('71) A.SC. at p. 2311. Reddy J. has referred to the judgment of Hegde J., but not on this point: see ('81) A.SC. at p. 338.

[58] ('81) A.SC. at p. 306.

is the bare minimum for obtaining a first class, it is difficult to say that a candidate who has obtained 59% marks and is placed in the second class, would be "appreciably less efficient" than a first class candidate. And the same may be said of a very high second class. It is not possible to lay down precisely the area dividing the second class from the first in which it can be said that the second class candidate, especially belonging to SC and ST with their social handicaps, would be appreciably less efficient in public service. But it is one thing to say that a second class candidate who has got 55% marks is not "substantially less efficient" than a candidate who has got a bare first class. It is another thing to prefer a high second class candidate to a high first class candidate, who has obtained 70% marks. A study of Government resolutions on reservation quotas in public services shows a progressive abandonment of standards, and in several cases separate examinations are held for SCs and STs on the ground that notwithstanding great relaxation of the standards, SC and ST candidates do not easily qualify for selection in open competitive examinations. It is submitted that to hold separate examinations is, first, to destroy the basis of comparison of merit between SC and ST candidates and other candidates. Secondly, if a class is *ex hypothesi* unable to compete on its own in an open competitive examination, the standard of separate examinations held for them must necessarily be low. There is one aspect of this question which is likely to be overlooked, or brushed aside, but which nevertheless is essential for a well organised and efficient public service. We have already spoken of an *esprit de corps* as an essential element for an efficient and harmonious public service. It is not possible to maintain an *esprit de corps* for any appreciable period of time if the pride in the service is destroyed, first by division in the services based on caste, and, even more, where reservations are made in promotion posts in favour of members of SCs and STs who are not rationally comparable in merit to the persons left out. A person who, but for the reservation, would have walked into the higher post on his merit, must be more than human if he is not deeply resentful of the injustice done to him, and of his having to serve under a person vastly his inferior in merit. Here it may be observed that at one place in his judgment, Krishna Iyer J. in dealing with a circular says that the minimum qualifications were not relaxed. But every Judge ought to know that normally minimum qualifications mean nothing at all, in deciding questions of merit and efficiency. The minimum qualification for being a Judge of the High Court is, *inter alia*, 10 years standing (not practice) as an Advocate of a High Court. Thousands of persons on the rolls of advocates qualify for a High Court judgeship because they possess the minimum qualifications. But to appoint a person who has 10 years standing at the Bar but has never practised, or has little or no practice, would be rightly condemned as a most improper exercise of power. Similarly, where a graduate degree is the minimum qualification, it only means that those who are not graduates do not qualify at all for being selected. It does not mean that a candidate who has secured the minimum percentage of marks for a third class is to be appointed in preference to a first class or a high second class

"Minimum qualifications" mean nothing in judging merit

candidate. It is submitted that where relaxation of standards in favour of members of SCs and STs is such that the efficiency of service must suffer, the relaxation must be struck down both in the interest of the public and of the service itself.

Present writer's suggested scheme to achieve the objective of Art. 16(4)

9.218 But does our criticism of *Thomas's Case* and the *Karmachari Sangh's Case* and of the approach of a number of judges to the problem mean that the operation of Art. 16(4) should be made ineffective? The answer is, "No". To submit that an exception should be narrowly construed, and that more than lip service should be paid to efficiency of public administration, is in no way to disparage the end, or the proper means by which that end can be achieved within the framework of our Constitution. The judgments of Mathew J. in *Thomas's Case* and of Krishna Iyer J. in the *Karmachari Sangh Case* range so widely over the issues involved in discrimination in the reverse, that the present writer would like to place before the reader some ideas which he expressed in a public lecture on reverse discrimination. It seems to him that if attempts made to recruit members of SCs and STs to public services for 31 years have failed as pitifully as the judgment of Krishna Iyer J. suggests and as the progressive abandonment of standards shows, it is reasonable to suppose that mistaken methods have been adopted so far. Philosophical discussions about real equality are not helpful, and the analogy of a handicap in horse racing is delusive for reasons fully set out in paras 9.195 and 9.196 above. In *Thomas's Case*, Mathew J. relied upon the observations of Harold Laski[59] and said that to produce complete equality, we would have to begin with the family. But he added that since that was not possible, we must adopt compensatory measures. The idea of compensatory measures is sound, but Mathew J.'s application of it is not. The method which the present writer will suggest cannot be adopted by merely professing sympathy for members of SCs and STs, which costs nothing, nor by showing sympathy by fixing reservation quotas for SCs and STs which also, broadly speaking, costs nothing. The method suggested by the present writer would involve a substantial expenditure of money, but it is believed that within a reasonable period of time, the expenditure would more than repay itself, apart from adding greatly to human happiness, national wellbeing and national unity. The phrase "genetic handicap" used by Krishna Iyer J. is unfortunate, as it might suggest that SC and ST children suffer from hereditary defects. What was intended to be conveyed was that such children are handicapped by the conditions in which their families live, and by their lack of means. The present writer shares the general view that, by and large, intellectual capacity and general ability are more or less evenly divided among peoples. A successful attempt to remove the handicap of SC and ST children must therefore begin with the school, since it is not practicable to begin with the family.

The present methods have failed

The scheme in broad outline: to uplift SCs and STs we must begin from the

9.219 The central idea of the scheme, whose details would have to be worked out, is to adopt measures which would put SC and ST children as near to children more favourably placed as circumstances permit. One of the most serious handicaps of SC and ST children is

[59]See para 9.197 above.

that their parents find it necessary to increase the family income by making even very small children earn a small income by part time work, as for example, by selling newspapers. The time so taken up is withdrawn from studies and other activities of the school; a handicap from which children more fortunately placed are free. The compensatory measures to remove this handicap are: free education, free supply of text books and other school requisites; free supply of uniforms where prescribed. But to remove the temptation of SC and ST parents to make their children earn by part time work, it is necessary to provide a daily stipend or grant[60] for each SC and ST child which would leave him free to do school work and participate in other activities which are a part of education in schools. We must begin with the primary school, for the object of the scheme is not only to put SC and ST children on a level with others but to give them an opportunity of showing their talents and abilities. Before the SC and ST child's primary education is completed, a number of such children will have shown promise as students. Special attention should be paid to them in the secondary school, and in addition to a daily stipend, merit scholarships, reserved for SC and ST students should be awarded on their results as a recognition of their work and also to encourage them to further effort in their studies. And these proposals should be applied to high school education and to education in Colleges, with the difference that the amount of the grant or stipend and the merit scholarships would have to be increased.[61] It is believed that if this scheme is followed, then within a reasonable time we would have SC and ST candidates for public service who can compete successfully against other candidates. It does seem odd that instead of starting from the school, Government circulars provide that if substandard SC and ST candidates are promoted they should be given training for six months to bring them upto the required standard and if they fail to come up to the standard they should be reverted. It is more reasonable and also more practical to start encouraging and helping SC and ST children to develop their capacities and abilities during their formative years in schools and colleges so that by the time the ablest among them come to compete for public service they can do so on equal terms with other candidates. If there is a better or a different scheme from the one suggested here, it should be adopted, so long as it starts with SC and ST children when they are at school.

primary school

The necessary compensatory measures

9.220 It is not necessary to deal separately with the judgment of Reddy J. since he agreed with the reasoning and conclusions of Krishna Iyer J. However, there is one part of the judgment of Reddy J. which calls for special mention, because the increasing tendency of some Supreme Court judges to refer to learned treatises propounding new theories poses a grave threat to the proper, efficient, speedy and relatively inexpensive administration of justice. Reddy J. said:

Reddy J. and Rawls' "A Theory of Justice"

---

[60] In several countries substantial grants are made to every student even in colleges.

[61] Whether the free facilities and the daily stipend made available to SC and ST children should be continued beyond the secondary school for children who show no aptitude for, or satisfactory progress in, their school studies, would require serious consideration, partly because the financial resources of the State are not unlimited.

"John Rawls in *A Theory of Justice*[62] demands the priority of equality in a distributive sense and the setting up of a social system 'so that no one gains or loses from his arbitrary place in the distribution of natural assets or his own initial position in society without giving or receiving compensatory advantages in return.' His basic principle of social justice is: "All social primary goods — liberty and opportunity, income and wealth and the bases of self respect — are to be distributed equally unless an unequal distribution of any or all these goods is to the advantage of the least favoured'. One of the essential elements of his conception of social justice is what he calls the principle of redress: 'This is the principle that undeserved inequalities call for redress; and since inequalities of birth and talent are somehow to be compensated for'. Society must, therefore, treat more favourably those with fewer native assets and those born into less favourable social positions. If the statement that the 'Equality of Opportunity must yield to Equality of Results', and if the fulfilment of Art. 16(1) in Art. 16(4) ever needed a philosophical foundation, it is furnished by Rawls' Theory of Justice and the Redress Principle."[63]

Rawl's theory disputed by competent critics

Reddy J. does not appear to be aware that the theory which he put forward as though it was an axiom of universal acceptance has been seriously disputed by competent critics. Prof. Barry, in his critical examination of the principal doctrines of Rawls' *Theory of Justice* has said that "Rawls' 'Theory of Justice' does not work and that many of his individual arguments are unsound."[64] A Critical Notice of Rawls' *Theory of Justice* in the leading philosophical Journal, *Mind*,[65] by D. D. Raphael, Imperial College, University of London, concludes with the words: "Needless to say, there are many other features of this large and complex book that invite comment, but I have confined myself to two main theses because of their originality. Each of them, it seems to me, founders completely. Why then do I say that the book is an important one? Just because these two theses are novel and hold out the promise of new light on old problems. It is sad that the problem fades so soon."[66] For the reasons given below it is submitted that Reddy J. should have abstained from incorporating in his judgment Rawls' main principles of social justice especially because he expected the same questions to arise repeatedly in the future.

Reasons why Reddy J. should have abstained from reference to Rawls' "A Theory of Justice"

9.221 The following submissions are made on Reddy J.'s excursion into the moral and political philosophy and propounded in Rawls' *A Theory of Justice*:

(*a*) It is opposed to well settled principles of interpretation.[67]

(*b*) Assuming that Art. 16(1) and (4) have "an underlying philosophy", it must be a philosophy known to, and generally accepted by, the framers of our Constitution before the Article was finally enacted in November, 1949. A new philosophical theory propounded in 1972 cannot underlie a provision enacted in 1949 !

(*c*) Would Reddy J. have given up, or materially altered, his interpretation of Art. 16(1) and (4) if Rawls' theory of social justice was shown to be untenable, or so disputable that it would be unsafe to act upon it? If the answer is "No", as would appear from his judgment[68]

---

[62] Oxford University Press (1972), pp. 587, Index 589-600.
[63] ('81) A.SC. at p. 336.
[64] Barry, *A Liberal Theory of Justice*, Clarendon Press, Oxford, pp. 168. (1973; revised and reprinted 1975). Prof. Barry was Professor of Government at the University of Essex before becoming a Fellow of Nuffield College, Oxford, in 1972.
[65] *Mind*, Vol. 74 at pp. 118 to 127.
[66] ibid. p. 127.
[67] See Chapter II of this book.
[68] Because he supports his judgment by referring to the earlier decisions of the Supreme Court.

then the reference to Rawls' theory is not only superfluous but irrelevant because even if the theory were rejected, Reddy J.'s interpretation of Art. 16(1) and (4) would remain the same. Consequently, any discussion of Rawls' theory, when the judgment of Reddy J. is relied upon before another Bench of the Supreme Court, would be wasteful of judicial and forensic time, and would put the parties to needless costs. If, however, the answer is "Yes", the position is even more disturbing, for the learned Judge has not considered the problems which his judgment would pose if other judges had to consider his judgment. We will assume that the Judges hearing the matter. and Counsel arguing before them, are familiar with moral and political philosophy. Even so, a reading of Rawls' book is not the work of a few days, but of weeks. Surely, it would be absurd to ask the Supreme Court to decide the correctness of Rawls' theory for interpreting Art. 16(1) and (2) when competent critics have rejected the theory after a careful analysis. Further, Reddy J.'s references to Rawls' put Counsel in an embarassing position. Not many Counsel would brush aside his reference to Rawls' as irrelevant and as reflecting the personal views of Reddy J., for such a course would appear to be disrespectful to a Supreme Court Judge. Since the part which Rawls' Theory would play in the argument before the Court would not be known till the hearing begins before the Supreme Court, what must Counsel do who consider, as the present writer does, that Rawls' Theory is untenable, and the interpretation put by Reddy J. on Art. 16(1) and (4) is incorrect? What would be Counsel's answer if asked by the Court, "Have you read Rawl's *Theory of Justice?* And what have you to say about the correctness of the principles which Reddy J. draws from Rawls' Theory?" A variety of answers suggest themselves, depending on the training, temper and attitude of Counsel to the Court. But it is unnecessary to consider the possible answers, because the present writer believes that had Reddy J. reflected on the problems which his reference to Rawls' Theory would pose for his brother Judges, for Counsel and for parties (who would have to pay for the time consumed in the study and discussion in Court of difficult moral and philosophical problems), Reddy J. would not have referred to Rawls' Theory, or would have qualified his reference in some such words as these: "For myself, I find Rawls' Theory, and the principle I have extracted, satisfactory and helpful in understanding what I believe to be the philosophy of Art. 16(1) and (4). But I do not rest my judgment on that philosophy. The interpretation I have put on Art. 16(1) and (4) is supported by the judgments of this Court, including the judgment in *Thomas's Case.*"[69]

U.S. decisions on reverse discrimination not discussed

9.222 In view of our detailed criticism of the majority judgment in *Thomas's Case* and of the judgment of Krishna Iyer J. (with whom Reddy J. concurred) in the *Karmachari Sangh Case,* it is not necessary to deal with decisions which have followed *Thomas's Case* or the *Karmachari Sangh Case,* because the same criticism would apply to those decisions. Again, the present writer considers it unnecessary to deal with the decision of the U.S. Supreme Court in *University of California Regents* v. *Bakke*[70] in which the U.S. Supreme Court struck down reverse discrimination which raised the constitutional question

[69] ('76) A.SC. 490.

[70] (1978) 57 L.ed. 2d. 750.

because U.S. Constitution has no provision like Arts. 15(4) and 16(4)

of violation of the equality clause of the 14th Amendment, or to discuss subsequent decisions which did not raise a constitutional question but raised the question of reverse discrimination under a Federal Law. These decisions are not discussed because the U.S. Constitution contains no provisions corresponding to Arts. 15(4) and 16(4) which expressly authorise reverse discrimination to the extent therein mentioned.

Discrimination arising from re-organization of States

9.223 A discrimination not created by Government, but arising out of the provisions of the State Re-organization Act and the options given therein, resulting in different pay scales does not violate Art. 14 as there is a valid classification, and it does not amount to denying equality of opportunity guaranteed by Art. 16.[71]

Art. 16 and termination of service

9.224 Where a person who had been appointed on a temporary basis was discharged from service after notice, it was held that Art. 16(1) was inapplicable because he had not been denied any opportunity of employment or of appointment. He had been treated just like any other person to whom an offer of temporary employment was made. There can be no grievance against an offer of temporary employment on special terms as opposed to permanent employment.[72] Again, it was said that assuming that Art. 16(1) may be violated by an arbitrary and discriminatory termination of service, such termination must first be established. The fact that the services of an employee were terminated while employees junior to him were retained in service did not by itself prove unequal treatment.[73] However, in *Govt. Branch Press* v. *T. B. Belliappa*[74] it was held that where the services of the respondent, a temporary servant, were terminated without assigning any reason, and his juniors in service, who were also temporary, were retained, and the respondent had specifically averred discrimination against himself, which averment had not been controverted by the appellant, the requirements of Art. 14 and Art. 16 were violated. The contention that the relationship between the appellant and the respondent was that of master and servant was rejected as inapplicable to a Government servant. It was observed, *obiter,* that even outside government service the rigid law of master and servant had been eroded by judicial decisions.[75]

Art. 16 and compulsory retirement

9.225 A question has arisen whether a rule providing for compulsory premature retirement from Government service violates Art. 16(1). In *Shivcharana* v. *Mysore*[76] the Supreme Court held, first, that the law in relation to the validity of rules permitting compulsory premature retirement from Government service had been well settled by the prior decisions of the Supreme Court which did not require to be reconsidered.[77] Secondly, it held that Note (1) to r. 285, Mysore

---

[71] *Nanjundaswamy* v. *Mysore* ('63) A.Mys. 202.

[72] *Satish Chandra Anand* v. *Union* (1953) S.C.R. 655, ('53) A.SC. 250; referred to and foll. in *V. Singh* v. *Addl. Director, Agriculture* ('60) A.A. 647.

[73] *Union* v. *P. K. More* ('62) A.SC. 630.

[74] (1979) 2 S.C.R. 458, ('79) A.SC. 429.

[75] The contention urged before the Supreme Court that the respondent's service had been terminated because of a show cause notice, which had not been proceeded with, was rejected on the ground that consistently the appellant had maintained that the respondent's service had been terminated under a power to terminate without assigning any reasons.

[76] ('65) A.SC. 280.

Civil Service Rules, 1958, applied to all Government servants and as such was not open to challenge under Art. 14 or Art. 16 (1).[78] The same view has been taken of r. 465, Civil Service Regulation (as adopted in U.P.), which provided for compulsory retirement.[79] In *Nanak Singh* v. *Union*[80] it was held that since Senior Inspectors of Station Accounts and Senior Accountants were not similarly situated, prescribing different ages of retirement for the two classes of officers did not violate Art. 16 (1).[81]

9.226 The following orders etc. were held to violate Art. 16 (1): the last part of rule 9 (2) of Mysore Recruitment of Gazetted Probationers Rules, 1958;[82] an order imposing an arbitrary ban against a person whose services under Government were terminated from ever being employed in Government service;[83] a notification whereby bifurcation was effected, affecting prevalent practice and promotion according to seniority and promotion of juniors over seniors in the same class;[84] where an order by the State Government picked out a certain person for preferential treatment;[85] an order appointing an Assessment and Estate Officer of a Municipality when the post had not been advertised and persons with the requisite qualifications had not been given an opportunity to apply for it;[86] an order accepting the recommendations of the Pay Commission with reference to the research staff of the Forest Research Institute and Colleges, Dehra Dun, but giving prospective effect to those recommendations whereas in the case of all other government servants, government accepted those recommendations and gave them retrospective effect from July 1, 1959;[87] provisions requiring permission before marriage and

Orders etc. held violative of Art. 16(1)

[77] This subject is discussed fully in the Chapter on Services under the Union and the States in Vol. II.

[78] ('65) A.SC. *supra* at p. 282.

[79] *Abdul Ahad* v. *I.G. of Police* ('65) A.A. 142.

[80] ('70) A.Del. 71.

[81] ibid. p. 76.

[82] *Mysore* v. *S. R. Jayaram* (1968) 1 S.C.R. 349, ('68) A.SC. 346, 348 [". . . recruitment by open competition aims at ensuring equality of opportunity in the matter of employment and obtaining the services of the most meritorious candidates. Rules 1 to 8, 9(1) and the first part of Rule 9(2) seek to achieve this aim. The last part of Rule 9(2) subverts and destroys the basic objectives of the preceding rules. It vests in the Government an arbitrary power of patronage. Though R. 9(1) requires the appointment of successful candidates to Class I posts in the order of merit and thereafter to Class II posts in the order of merit, Rule 9(1) is subject to Rule 9(2), and under the cover of Rule 9(2), Government can even arrogate to itself the power of assigning a Class I post to a less meritorious and a Class II post to a more meritorious candidate"].

[83] *Krishan Chander Nayar* v. *Chairman, Central Tractor Organization* (1962) 3 S.C.R. 187, ('62) A.SC. 602 (*held*, that though an employee whose services were once terminated might or might not stand on an equal footing with other candidates not under such a ban, his case must be considered on its merits).

[84] *Brijlal* v. *Punjab* ('65) A.Punj. 401 (it was also held that the notification violated R. 16, Punjab Services Integration Rules, 1957).

[85] *Baij Nath* v. *U.P.* ('65) A.A. 151 (*held*, that the order was discriminatory as regards the petitioner and the other candidates who had applied for the posts. Rule 4, U.P. Primary Education Rules did not contemplate any such discrimination).

[86] *Dandekar* v. *R. C. Rathi* ('63) A.M.P. 17 (it was held that the Municipality was "State" as defined in Art. 12, and its Estate Officer held an office under the State).

[87] *Purshottam Lal* v. *Union* ('73) A.SC. 1088 at 1091. (The court rejected the contention of the Union that the case of the Research Staff had not been referred to the Pay Commission).

the denial to married women of the right of employment in public services.[88]

Art. 16: Miscellaneous

9.227 A division of two classes of the members of the same services belonging to the same cadre for the purpose of creating differences in opportunity for promotion violated Arts. 14 and 16.[89] Where the Maharashtra State Electricity Board issued an advertisement for filling up posts without mentioning that a relaxation in conditions as to qualifications and experience from the prescribed requirements would be made in appropriate cases, equal opportunity of employment was not given to departmental and non-departmental candidates and Art. 16 was voilated.[90] Retrenchment from Government service of a person higher on the list whilst retaining persons lower on the list—no reason being given why such a course was followed—violates Art. 16.[91] Equality of opportunity in matters of public employment cannot be denied to a citizen on an *ex parte* finding that he was dishonest.[92] Failure to consider the claim of a government employee otherwise qualified for consideration for promotion violates Arts. 14 and 16.[93] Where selection for promotion was made by an authority not empowered to make the selection, Art. 16 was violated.[94]

Equality of opportunity—making vacancies known

9.228 How is equality of opportunity in public employment to be secured? It is submitted that where there is direct recruitment to a service, equality of opportunity would require that the posts be advertised. However, it is well known that after initial recruitment, appointments to higher posts in the service are, at times, made partly by promotion and partly directly, or at times wholly by promotion. Where the appointment is partly by promotion and partly by direct employment, it would be necessary to advertise the posts. Where, however, the appointment is by promotion among those already employed, equality of opportunity does not necessarily require that the appointment should be advertised but it does require that the case of each person eligible for promotion should be fairly considered. However, in *Paramatma Sharan* v. *Chief Justice*,[95] it was held with reference to the post of Asst. Registrar and Secretary to the Chief Justice that the equality of opportunity contemplated by Art. 16 did not mean that in every case of appointment or recruitment to service or promotion, the State should invite applications for such appointment or promotion, "the emphasis is that as between *A* and *B* there should be no discrimination in the matter of appoint-

---

[88] *C. B. Muthamma* v. *Union* ('79) A.SC. 1868 [*held*, that *prima facie* R. 8(1) of the Indian Foreign Service (Conduct and Discipline) Rules, 1951 and R. 18(4) of the Indian Foreign Service (Recruitment of Cadre and Promotion) Rules, 1961 were violative of Art. 16(2) as they discriminate against women on the ground of sex. As R. 18(4) was repealed during the pendency of the petition and repeal of R. 8(2) was being gazetted, no order was passed on the petition, because pending the petition, the petitioner had been promoted to be the Ambassador of India to the Hague. Government also agreed that the respondent would consider the question of the petitioner's seniority].

[89] *Mysore* v. *Krishna Murthy* (1973) 2 S.C.R. 575, ('73) A.SC. 1146.

[90] *M.S.E.B. Engineer's Assn.* v. *M.S.E. Board* ('68) A.B. 65.

[91] *Viney Kumar* v. *State* ('68) A.Raj. 227, 233.

[92] *M. K. Mathulla* v. *N. N. Wanchoo* ('70) A.Del. 195, 201-202.

[93] *A. C. Mitra* v. *State* ('70) A.Or. 19, 21.

[94] *Sachidananda* v. *Union* ('71) A.Or. 6.

[95] ('64) A.Raj. 13.

ment." As the relevant facts do not appear clearly from the judgment, it is submitted that the decision would be correct if appointment to the post were limited to promotion from among persons in a particular service or services. If, however, the post was also open for direct recruitment, it is submitted that the equality of opportunity conferred by Art. 16 would be denied if the fact of vacancy in the post was not advertised.

Hereditary Officers Acts violate Art. 16(1)

9.229 As "descent" is a forbidden ground of classification it follows that various Hereditary Officers Acts became void after the commencement of the Constitution. Thus, in *Gazula Dasaratha Rama Rao* v. *A.P.*,[96] the Supreme Court held, first, that the office of a village munsiff under the Madras Hereditary Village Officers Act, 1895, was an "office under the State", within Art. 16(1) and (2); and, secondly, that as s. 6(1) of the Act provided that in choosing persons to fill new offices, the Collector should select the persons whom he considered the best qualified from among the last holders of the offices which had been abolished, s. 6(1) discriminated on the ground of descent only and was void as contravening Art. 16(2). And a similar view has been taken of hereditary offices in other cases.[97] However, where an applicant with hereditary qualifications was the only candidate for the post of a village headman and he was appointed, it could not be said that he was chosen on the overriding consideration of heredity.[98] But, a discrimination made, not on the ground of the unsuitability of women for a particular kind of public employment does not violate Art. 16(2).[99] An order removing a temporary government servant on the only ground that he was a non-Andhra violates Art. 16(2) and is void, for Art. 16(2) does not make any distinction between a temporary and a permanent post, but applies with equal rigour to both temporary and permanent

Discrimination on the ground of place of birth

[96] (1961) 2 S.C.R. 931, ('61) A.SC. 564, 572.

[97] *Balakrishna Hegde* v. *Shankara Hegde* ('62) A.Mys. 233 [the offices held by village officers fell within the meaning of "offices under the State" in Art. 16(1) and (2) and the application of the principle of hereditary succession violated Art. 16(1) and (2). The appointing authority must consider the claims of the candidates disregarding principles of hereditary succession, and as the impugned orders had applied the principles of hereditary succession, they were set aside]; *Bhaskar* v. *Arjun* (1962) Cut. 203, ('62) A.Or. 167 [the office of a village artisan under the Madras Hereditary Village Officers Act, 1895, was an office under the State as contemplated by Art. 16. S. 12 of the Act which recognized the customary law of succession to the office of a village artisan like that of village blacksmith solely on the ground of descent violated Art. 16(2) and was void]; *Bhimo* v. *Mohan* ('71) A.Or. 118 [*held*, that s. 12 of the Madras Hereditary Field Officers Act, 1895 violated Art. 16(2). *Held further*, that *Bhaskar* v. *Arjun*, *supra* was correctly decided and that *Sattamma* v. *Satyanarayana* (see *f.n.* 98 below) was wrongly decided].

[98] *Rishikesavan* v. *Srinivasa* ('65) A.M. 178 [*Rama Rao's Case* (1961) 2 S.C.R. 93, *supra* was distinguished on the ground mentioned in the text, and the Court added that a person who had not applied for the post could not challenge the appointment of another]. See also *Sattemma* v. *Satyanarayana* ('63) A.A.P. 375 (where also *Rama Rao's Case*, *supra*, was distinguished with reference to the language of certain provisions of the Madras Hereditary Village Officers Act, 1895).

[99] *Raghubans* v. *State* ('72) A.P. & H. 117 [*held*, that a pre-Constitution order of the Governor making women ineligible to hold posts in men's jails other than clerks or matrons did not violate Art. 16(2) as it was passed primarily on considerations of suitability and efficiency. A woman acting as a warder, or other official, in a jail for men would have to be in contact with "hardened and ribald criminals guilty of heinous crimes of violence and sex." To maintain discipline among them would put a woman into an awkward and even hazardous position — more hazardous than that of male officials. Efficiency of service would also suffer].

posts under the State; and it is not permissible to engraft limitations upon fundamental rights.[1]

Art. 16(3) is an exception to Art. 16(2)

9.230 Article 16(3) is an exception to Art. 16(2), which forbids discrimination on the ground of residence, for Art. 16(3) enables Parliament to make a law prescribing in regard to a class or classes of employment or appointment to an office under the Government of all or any local or other authority within a State or Union Territory, any requirement as to residence within that State or Union Territory prior to such employment or appointment. The language of Art. 16(3) shows that it does not apply to employment under the Union Government not connected with a Union Territory, obviously because the Union Government operates throughout India. Article 16(3) is designed to prevent parochialism in public employment by the Government of a State or by any local or other authority within a State or Union Territory. In the exercise of powers conferred by Art. 16(3), Parliament has enacted the Public Employment (Requirement as to Residence) Act, 1957, which was brought into force on March 21, 1959. By s. 2 it repealed existing laws prescribing requirements as to residence which were in force in any State or Union Territory by virtue of Art. 35(b). S. 3 enables the Central Government to make rules in respect of certain classes of public employment in certain areas prescribing requirements as regards residence,[2] and s. 4 provides that rules so made must be laid before each House of Parliament and are subject to such modifications as Parliament may make. S. 5 provides that s. 3 and all rules made thereunder are to cease to have effect on the expiration of five years from the commencement of the Act, but such cesser is not to affect the validity of appointments made previously, pursuant to the Act. By the Public Employment (Requirement as to Residence) Amendment Act, 1964, s. 4 of the principal Act relating to Parliamentary scrutiny of rules was amended. S. 5 was amended by substituting a period of ten years for the original period of five years, and appointments made under the existing rules after the period of five years and before the commencement of the amending Act, were validated.

Parliamentary legislation in 1957 under Art. 16(3)

and in 1964

A. V. S. N. Rao's Case: No power to prescribe residence in part of a State *e.g.* in Telengana

9.231 In *A. V. S. N. Rao* v. *A.P.*[3] the Supreme Court held that Art. 16(3) was an exception to the rules laid down in Art. 16(1) and (2) and must be narrowly construed,[4] and, therefore, Parliament had no power to prescribe residence in part of a State (Telengana) as a qualification for employment by the State in Andhra Pradesh as was provided in s. 3(2)(*b*) of the Public Employment (Requirement as to Residence) Act, 1957. Accordingly, the Court held that s. 3 *in so far as it related to* Telengana, and Rule 3 of the Rules made under the Act, were *ultra vires*.[5] The Court expressed no opinion on the question whether the *mulki rules* existing in the

---

[1] *Jaikiraman* v. *A.P.* ('59) A.A.P. 185.

[2] The rule-making power extends to prescribing requirements as regards residence in respect of any subordinate service or post under the State Government of Andhra Pradesh or under the control of the Administrator of Himachal Pradesh, Manipur or Tripura and any service or post under a local authority (other than a Cantonment Board) within the Telengana area of Andhra Pradesh or within the Union Territory of Himachal Pradesh, Manipur or Tripura.

[3] (1970) 1 S.C.R. 115, ('70) A.SC. 422.

[4] ('70) A.SC. *supra* at p. 425.

[5] ibid. pp. 425-6.

former Hyderabad State continued to operate by virtue of Art. 35 (*b*) since that question had not been raised in the petition.[6] But that very question was decided in *P. L. Rao* v. *A.P.*[7] The case raised two questions: (i) Did s. 2 of the Public Employment (Requirement as to Residence) Act, 1957, survive once s. 3 had been declared invalid so far as Telengana was concerned? (ii) If s. 2 did not survive, were the *mulki* rules operative? On the first question a full bench held that s. 2 did not survive. It was common ground that ss. 4 and 5 were inextricably connected with s. 3 and they became void along with it. The remaining s. 2 was a repealing section, and Parliament would not have enacted it had it known that ss. 3 to to 5 were invalid.[8] No doubt s. 2 was a general provision and was not limited to Telengana, but then so was s. 3. The Supreme Court had applied the doctrine of severability in application[9] in *A. V. S. N. Rao's Case* and held s. 3 invalid in so far as it related to Telengana; applying the same principle the High Court held that s. 2 was invalid to the same extent.[10] On the second question the full bench held that the *mulki* rules continued in operation once s. 2, which repealed them, was void. Kumarayya C.J. and Ekbote, J. two of the judges constituting the full bench, held that the rules had not to satisfy the requirement of Art. 16 (3), or strictly conform to it, if in pith and substance it was a law relating to the matter prescribing residential qualifications. The rules were continued by Art. 35 (*b*), and their validity could not be challenged on the ground that they were contrary to any Article in the Constitution.[11] In any event, all the three members of the full bench held that even if it was assumed that the law in force had to satisfy the test of Art. 16 (3) in regard to the residential qualification of the entire State, and not of a part of the State, the *mulki* rules satisfied the test when the Constitution came into force in the Hyderabad State. They continued to be in force until altered or repealed or amended by Parliament as provided in Art. 35 (*b*), and they had not become invalid on the reorganisation of the States. Parliament did repeal those rules, but as the repeal was ineffective, they continued to be in force. The full bench decision in *P. L. Rao's Case* was overruled by another full bench in *V. V. Reddy* v. *A.P.*[12] which held that the *mulki* rules were not valid and operative after the formation of the State of Andhra Pradesh. In any event, they did not survive, and could not be deemed to be valid and operative in view of the Supreme Court decision in *A. V. S. N. Rao's Case*.[13] This decision was reversed by the Supreme Court on appeal in *A.P.* v. *V. V. Reddy*.[14] That judgment was to have unexpected and far-reaching consequences, for, as a consequence of it, grave disorder broke out in the State of Andhra Pradesh accompanied by a demand for a separate State of Telengana. A "President's Rule" was imposed on the State, and partition of the State was averted by the Constitution (32nd

---

[6] ibid. p. 426. [7] ('71) A.A.P. 118 (F.B.).
[8] ibid. p. 123.
[9] *R M. D. Chamarbaugwala* v. *Union* (1957) S.C.R. 930, ('57) A.SC. 628.
[10] ('71) A.A.P. *supra* at p. 124.
[11] *Per* Kumarayya C.J. and Ekbote, J.: ibid. pp. 129-30.
[12] (1973) 1 Andh.L.T. 1 (F.B.). [13] ('70) A.SC. *supra*.
[14] ('73) A.SC. 827.

Amendment) Act, 1973. Since the Supreme Court decision was based on a true construction of Art. 35, read with Art. 372, the whole case is considered under Art. 35.[15]

Raghunanda Rao's Case

9.232 In *Raghunanda Rao* v. *Orissa*[16] it was held that r. 5 of the Orissa Administrative Service and the Orissa Subordinate Administrative Service Rules, 1950, prescribed only a test of language and this was not forbidden by Art. 15 or 16. Secondly that till Parliament made a law relating to the recruitment as to residence for public service, the effect of Art. 16(3) read with Art 35(*a*) was that till Parliament made a law prescribing residence as a requirement, the existing laws continued under Art. 372.

Art. 16(4): the nature and extent of reservation for backward classes

9.233 The question of the nature and extent of the reservation which can be made in public employment has been considered by the Supreme Court in several cases. In *Venkataramana* v. *Madras*[17] a Communal G.O. of the Madras Government which reserved posts not only for Harijans and backward classes, but also for other communities, namely, Muslims, Christians, non-Brahmins (Hindus), and Brahmins was held to violate Art. 16. In *Gen. Manager, S. Rly.* v. *Rangachari*[18] it was held by a majority that it would be unreasonable to treat "posts" as a term of art and equate it with "ex-cadre" posts. The "posts" were "inside" the service and not outside. The condition precedent for the exercise of the power conferred by Art. 16(4) was that any backward class of citizens was not adequately represented in the service. This may refer either to numerical inadequacy of representation or even to the qualitative inadequacy of representation. Socially and educationally backward classes required not only that they should have adequate representation in the lowest rung but that they should aspire to secure representation in selection posts as well. This construction would effectuate the intention of the Constitution-makers. *Rangachari's Case* has been followed or relied on in the undernoted cases.[19] After the above case was decided, the question of the nature and extent of the reservation of seats in educational institutions was considered by the Supreme Court in *M. R. Balaji* v. *Mysore*.[20] That

Rangachari's Case: inadequate representation may be quantitative or qualitative

---

[15] See the Chapter on Right to Judicial Remedies.

[16] (1955) Cut. 510, ('55) A.Or. 113.

[17] ('51) A.SC. 229. As however the selections had been made by the Public Service Commission and persons selected had taken their posts, the court did not order the Public Service Commission to cancel the selections already made, since all the posts had not been filled up and there was no difficulty in considering the application of the petitioners without reference to the Communal G.O.

[18] (1962) 2 S.C.R. 586, ('62) A.SC. 36.

[19] Fol. in *Bhabendra Chandra* v. *P.M.G., Assam Circle* ('68) A.A. & N. 9; rel. on in *C. S. Devasahayam* v. *State* ('69) A.M. 118 (*held*, that where in the civil service in the State of Madras the age of superannuation was raised to 58 only in some of the services, the criterion applied being the dearth of experienced officers and the need for obtaining qualified officers, and applying that test the age of superannuation was not raised in the commercial tax department, there was no violation of Arts. 15 and 16); rel. on in *R. N. Pramanick* v. *Union* ('69) A.Cal. 576, 577 [*held*, that Art. 16(4) must be read with Art. 335, so that no reservation or special provision in favour of members of the Sch. Castes can be carried to the length of impairing the "efficiency of the administration." The respondents had not violated the Constitution in providing that merit was to be the only consideration for promotion to the higher grade even though there was reservation for Sch. Castes for recruitment to the lower post.]

[20] (1963) Supp. 1 S.C.R. 439, ('63) A.SC. 649.

case has been considered in detail earlier;[21] but as will appear from the case to be considered presently, *Balaji's Case* referred to Art. 15(4) and the Court said:

Observations on Art. 16(4) in *Balaji's Case*

"Therefore, what is true in regard to Art. 15(4) is equally true in regard to Art. 16(4) . . . that the Constitution-makers assumed, . . . that while making adequate reservation under Art. 16(4), care would be taken not to provide for unreasonable, excessive or extravagant reservation, for that would, by eliminating general competition in a large field and by creating wide-spread dissatisfaction amongst the employees, materially affect efficiency. Therefore, like the special provision improperly made under Art. 15(4), reservation made under Art. 16(4) beyond the permissible and legitimate limits would be liable to be challenged as a fraud on the Constitution."[22]

Devadasan's Case: "carry forward" rule and Art. 16(4)

9.234 The scope of Art. 16(4) was considered in *Devadasan* v. *Union*[23] under the following circumstances. By a Government of India Resolution dated September 13, 1950, as "modified by" supplementary instructions dated January 28, 1952, and Office Memorandum dated May 7, 1955, the Government reserved a certain percentage of vacancies for Sch. Castes and Sch. Tribes, adopting the principle of "carry forward" in the second and third year. The actual effect of the carry forward rule for the year in question was that a little over 64 per cent of vacancies were reserved for Sch. Castes and Sch. Tribes.[24] By a majority of 4 to 1, the Supreme Court held that Art. 16 conferred a right on each individual citizen seeking employment or appointment to an office under the State, and that in order to effectuate that right each year of recruitment must be considered by itself, and the reservation for backward communities each year should not be so excessive as to create a monopoly or to interfere unduly with the legitimate claims of other communities. Art. 16(4) was a proviso or an explanation to Art. 16(1), and the opening words of Art. 16(4) "Nothing in this Article shall prevent etc. . . ." could not be so construed as to nullify the express guarantees contained in Art. 16(1) and (2). "A proviso or an exception cannot be so interpreted as to nullify or destroy the main provision. To hold that unlimited reservation of appointments could be made under Cl. (4) would in effect efface the guarantee contained in Cl. (1) or at best make it illusory."[25] After citing the observations in *Balaji's Case* on Art. 16(4), quoted earlier,[26] the Court said that what was there laid down about reservation of seats in educational institutions applied equally to reservation of posts under Art. 16(4), namely, that generally speaking, the reservation ought to be less than 50 per cent. As the reservation in the present case was as high as 64 per cent the "carry forward" rule "as modified" in 1955 was unconstitutional.[27] It is submitted that the majority view is clearly right. The dissenting judgment of Subba Rao J. has already been discussed and shown to be untenable. *Balaji's Case* and *Devadasan's Case* were relied on in *M. Natarajan* v. *D.G.P. & T.*,

Observations in *Balaji's Case* applied

---

[21] See para 9.158 *et seq.*
[22] (1963) Supp. 1 S.C.R. *supra* at p. 474.
[23] (1964) 4 S.C.R. 680, ('64) A.SC. 179. [24] ('64) A.SC. at p. 187.
[25] ibid. p. 187. See also para 9.160, *f.n.* 81.
[26] See para 9.233.
[27] See (1963) Supp. 1 S.C.R. *supra* at p. 471: "Therefore, we are satisfied that the reservation of 68 per cent directed by the impugned order is plainly inconsistent with Art. 15(4)."

New Delhi[28] and it was held that as the Railway Mail Service and the Post Office were two distinct and independent branches of the Postal Department, the clubbing together of the two departments for the sole purpose of selecting Sch. Caste candidates violated Art. 16(4) and was illegal.[29]

Tewari's Case: Order in *Devadasan's Case* explained

9.235 The actual order passed in the above case, namely, "In the result, the petition succeeds partially and the carry forward rule, as modified in 1955 is declared invalid" led to the case of *B. N. Tewari* v. *Union*[30] in which it was contended that the effect of the Supreme Court's declaration was to revive the earlier rule which had been *modified* and on the basis of that rule, the petitioner was entitled to claim to be appointed to the post of Section Officer (Asst. Superintendent). Without expressly admitting that the phraseology of the order was incorrect, the Court held that the order of 1952 had not been modified but had in fact been cancelled by Government, with the result that the order of 1952 was non-existent.[31] As the Supreme Court applied *Balaji's Case* to Art. 16(4), the decision in *Kesava* v. *Mysore*[32] upholding the order of the Mysore Government which had classified all candidates other than Brahmins as backward communities cannot be supported since it proceeds on the classification of the "most advanced" and "the rest", which was held to be void in *Balaji's Case*.

C. A. Rajendran v. Union:

9.236 In *C. A. Rajendran* v. *Union*[33] questions not raised and considered in *Rangachari's Case* or in *Devadasan's Case* were raised and decided by a unanimous decision of a Constitution Bench of the Supreme Court.[34] The petitioner was a permanent assistant in Grade IV, (Class III, non-gazetted ministerial) of the Railway Board Secretariat Service. The next post to which the petitioner claimed promotion was that of section officer which was classified as Class II, Grade III. It was stated on behalf of Government that after *Rangachari's Case* the whole policy of reservation of posts was reviewed by the Union Government. As a result of the review, it was found that "quotas of promotion were harmful from the point of view of efficiency of Railway Service"[35] and the earlier circulars fixing such quotas were withdrawn. It was contended for the petitioner (i) that Art. 16(4) was not an exception engrafted on Art. 16, and (ii) that Art. 16(4) guaranteed a fundamental right to Sch. Castes and Sch. Tribes and backward classes and as such it was untrammelled by any other provision of the Constitution.[36] Ramaswami J. said that the relevant law on the subject was settled. He referred to *Rangachari's Case* and *Balaji's Case* which had held that Art. 16(4) and Art. 15(4) were in the nature of exceptions and

Petitioner's contentions: (i) Art. 16(4) not an exception (ii) Art. 16(4) conferred a fundamental right on

---

28 ('70) A.M. 458.

29 ibid. 459 (the court observed that 2 out of 3 posts of Inspectors in the Rly. Mail Service were reserved for Sch. Castes, that is, 66.66 per cent. of seats were reserved, whereas the Supreme Court had held that the reservation should not exceed fifty per cent).

30 ('65) A.SC. 1430.

31 On facts, the Supreme Court held that even if the rule of 1952 was treated as revived, the petitioner was not entitled to claim the appointment.

32 ('54) A.Mys. 20.

33 (1968) 1 S.C.R. 721, ('68) A.SC. 507.

34 Wanchoo C.J., Ramaswami, Bachawat, Mitter and Hegde JJ.

35 ('68) A.SC. at p. 513.

36 ibid. p. 510.

had to be strictly construed, and that in making reservations regard must be had to the efficiency of public service referred to in Art. 335, the Supreme Court considered the submission that Art. 16 (4) itself conferred a fundamental right and it was not open to the Government to withdraw the benefits conferred on Sch. Castes and Sch. Tribes by its earlier orders. In support of this contention, reliance had been placed on the dissenting judgment of Subba Rao J. in *Devadasan's Case* that Art. 16 (4) was not really an exception, but merely preserved a power untramelled by the other provisions of the Article. After observing that the majority judgment in *Devadasan's Case* had held that Art. 16 (4) was an exception, and that it could not render nugatory or illusory the guarantee conferred by Art. 16 (1) and (2), Ramaswami J. said: Sch. Castes etc.

"Our conclusion therefore is that Article 16(4) does not confer any right on the petitioner and there is no constitutional duty imposed on the Government to make a reservation for Scheduled Castes and Scheduled Tribes either at the initial stage of recruitment or at the stage of promotion. In other words Article 16(4) is an enabling provision and confers a discretionary power on the State to make a reservation of appointments in favour of backward class of citizens which, in its opinion, is not adequately represented in the Services of the State. We are accordingly of the opinion that the petitioner is unable to make good his submission on this aspect of the case."[37]

Court unanimously held Art. 16(4) is an exception, and confers no fundamental right

In the result, the Constitution Bench negatived the contention that Art. 16 (4) was not an exception to Art. 16 (1) and (2) and further negatived the contention that Art. 16 (4) conferred a fundamental right. On the contrary the Court held that Art. 16 (4) merely conferred a discretionary power.

9.237 *Balaji's Case* and *Rajendran's Case*[38] were followed and the principles there laid down were re-affirmed in *Janki Prasad* v. *J. & K.*[39] After a careful analysis of the J. & K. Sch. Castes and Backward Classes Reservation Rules of 1970, the Supreme Court held that they violated Art. 16 as the principles governing the reservation of posts in the employment of the State had not been correctly applied. Again, in *Triloki Nath* v. *J. & K.*[40] it was held that a direction to secretaries to select candidates "keeping in view the policy of adequate representation of such elements as were not adequately represented in the service" was not a provision reserving appointments or posts in favour of backward classes, and the direction violated Art. 16 (1) and (2) and was void.[41] In *Sudhakar* v. *State*[42] it was said that the reservation of seats for Sch. Castes and Tribes in public services and posts mentioned in Art. 335 was subject

---

[37] ('68) A.SC. at p. 513. [38] See para 9.158 *et seq.*

[39] (1973) 3 S.C.R. 236, ('73) A.SC. 930 [*held*, that mere educational backwardness or social backwardness did not by itself make a class of citizens backward. It was well settled that the expression "socially and educationally backward class of citizens" under Art. 15(4) and the expression "any backward class of citizens" in Art. 16(4) meant the same thing. In order to qualify for being called "a backward class of citizen" he must be a member of a socially and educationally backward class. Applying this test it was held that the J. & K. Sch. Castes and Backward Classes Reservation Rules of 1970 were unconstitutional. For a detailed discussion of the rules directly in issue, and held unconstitutional, see ('73) A.SC. at pp. 939-44].

[40] (1969) 1 S.C.R. 103, ('69) A.SC. 1, 4.

[41] See *Makhan Lal* v. *J. & K.* (1971) 3 S.C.R. 832, ('71) A.SC. 2206, where an attempt was made to circumvent the law declared in *Triloki Nath's Case*. The Supreme Court held that the attempt failed.

[42] ('70) A.Or. 224.

to the paramount consideration that such persons were fit for the appointment, having regard to the maintenance of efficiency of the administration. Consequently, candidates of Sch. Castes or Tribes found unfit could not claim to be appointed to public services despite the reservations made for such castes or tribes. When a member of the Sch. Caste was recommended for a Class B post because he belonged to the Sch. Caste, he could not claim to be appointed to a Class A post on the ground that seats in that class had been reserved for Sch. Castes and Tribes.

Art. 16(4) cannot be used to demote a person lawfully promoted

9.238 However, Art. 16 (4) cannot be utilised to demote a person lawfully appointed. It was so held in *Sudama Prashad* v. *Divisional Supdt., W. Rly.*[43] under the following circumstances: On a panel approved for promotion, *A*'s name appeared above *B*'s and he was entitled to preferential treatment for promotion to a higher post not reserved for the Sch. Caste. Both *A* and *B* were promoted in an officiating capacity to the post of a Chief Clerk. While *A* was retained in that post, *B* was reverted to the post of Head Clerk. On *B* obtaining a certificate, for the first time, that he belonged to a Sch. Caste, and filing a representation to the authorities to revert *A* in order to give him (*B*) an opportunity to be promoted, *A* was reverted by a speaking order which gave as the only reason for reverting him that it was being done to make room for *B*, who belonged to the Sch. Caste. The order reverting *A* was held to violate Art. 16 and was set aside.

9.239 Article 16 (4) applies only if two conditions are satisfied: (i) the class of citizens in backward socially and educationally and (ii) that class is not adequately represented in the service under the State. Art. 16 (4) cannot be invoked merely because a class of citizens is not adequately represented in such service.[44]

Art. 16(5)

9.240 Art. 16 (5) is self-explanatory and is an exception to Art. 16 (1) to the extent that it forbids discrimination in public employment on the ground of religion. Article 16 (5) excludes offices in connection with the affairs of any religious or denominational[45] institution, or the membership of a governing body thereof from the operation of Art. 16 (1). This exclusion is a logical consequence of the right to the freedom of religion guaranteed by Arts. 26 and 27.

Art. 17: "untouchability" abolished

9.241 It would be outside the scope of this work to give a historical account of the origin and practice of "untouchability", or of the various attempts made by social reformers and political leaders to put an end to the practice of "untouchability", which, like slavery, was a denial of human equality in an acute form. Since references are to be found in decided cases, and in statutes, to the word "Harijan" it may be observed that the word is a euphemism

---

[43] ('65) A.Raj. 108.

[44] *Triloki Nath* v. *J. & K.* ('67) A.SC. 1283, 1286, (1967) 2 S.C.R. 265 [If the contention was accepted that inadequacy of representation was the sole condition for invoking Art. 16(4), "it would really exclude the backward classes from the benefit of Art. 16(4) and confer the benefit only on a class of citizens who, though rich and cultured, have taken to other avocation of life." The case was remanded to the High Court for ascertaining whether the Mahommedans in the entire State of Jammu & Kashmir and the Hindus of the Jammu Province were backward].

[45] That is, an institution run according to the principles of a church or religious sect. (*C.O.D.*).

for "untouchables", and it means "the children of God" and conveys indirectly that they have been abandoned by men. The removal of untouchability was for long an item in the programme of the Indian National Congress, and, as was to be expected, the Constitution by Art. 17 abolished "untouchability" and made the enforcement of disabilities attaching to it an offence punishable by law to be enacted by Parliament.

Arts. 17 and 35: the Untouchability (Offences) Act, 1955

9.242 Article 17 which makes the practice of untouchability an offence must be read with Art. 35(*a*) (ii) which confers upon Parliament the *exclusive power* to make laws prescribing punishment for those acts which are declared to be offences under Part III. Article 35(*b*) continues existing laws which provide punishment for any act which is made an offence under Part III, subject to adaptation or modification under Art. 372. In the exercise of the powers conferred by Art. 35, Parliament has enacted the Untouchability (Offences) Act, 1955. The Act defines: a "hotel" to include a refreshment room, a boarding house, a building, a tent and a vessel; a "place of public entertainment" to include any place to which the public are admitted and in which entertainment is provided or held, and "entertainment" to include any exhibition, performance, game, sport and any other form of amusement; a "shop" to mean any premises where goods are sold and to include a laundry, a hair-cutting saloon and any other place where services are rendered to customers; a "place of public worship" is defined as follows:

". . . a place, by whatever name known, which is used as a place of public religious worship or which is dedicated generally to, or is used generally by, persons professing any religion or belonging to any religious denomination or any section thereof, for the performance of any religious service, or for offering prayers therein; and includes all lands and subsidiary shrines appurtenant or attached to any such place."

The meaning of "untouchability" in Art. 17 and in the above Act

9.243 Both Art. 17 and the Act place the word "untouchability" in inverted commas. Accordingly, it has been held that the subject-matter of Art. 17 is not untouchability in its literal or grammatical sense, but the practice as it developed historically in India and that the word "untouchability" is used in that sense in the Act. A literal construction of the term would include persons who are treated as untouchables either temporarily or otherwise for various reasons such as their suffering from an epidemic or contageous disease or on account of social boycott resulting from caste or other disputes. Where the acts and conduct complained of may at the most amount to an instigation to social boycott between Jains, such conduct does not come within the mischief of the Act.[46] That "untouchability" refers to the practice among Hindus is further emphasized by Art. 25(2)(*b*) which excludes from Art. 25(1) any existing or future law providing for the throwing open of Hindu Religious Institutions of a public character to all classes and sections of Hindus.

The Untouchability (Offences) Act, 1955

9.244 The Act prescribes punishment which may extend to imprisonment for six months or a fine which may extend to five hundred rupees or both, for anyone enforcing, on the ground of "untouch-

[46] *Devarajaiah* v. *Padmanna* ('58) A.Mys. 84 (see para 2.69 for the case in which the U.S. Supreme Court also placed a limited construction on the word "slavery" in the 13th Amendment).

ability", religious disabilities (s. 3), social disabilities (s. 4), or for refusal to admit persons to hospitals, etc. (s. 5), for refusing to sell goods or render services (s. 6) and for "other offences" arising from untouchability (s. 7), the object of s. 7 being to ensure that persons are not deterred from exercising any right accruing to them by reason of the abolition of "untouchability" by Art. 17. S. 8 empowers a Court convicting a person under s. 6 for refusing to sell goods or for refusing to render services to cancel a licence held by him for the purpose of such sale or business or to suspend it for such period as the Court deems fit. S. 9 provides for suspension or resumption of grants made by Government to the Manager or Trustee of a place of public worship, who is convicted of an offence under the Act. The penalty for the abetment of offences is the same as that provided for the offence (s. 10) and for subsequent convictions the punishment has to be *both* imprisonment *and* fine (s. 11). S. 12 provides that where an act constituting an offence under the Act is committed in relation to a member of a Sch. Caste as defined in Art. 366 (24), then the court shall presume, unless the contrary is proved, that such an act was committed on the ground of "untouchability". S. 13 bars the jurisdiction of Civil Courts in any suit or proceeding or execution of a decree which involves a claim contrary to the provisions of the Act, and Courts are directed not to recognize any custom or usage imposing any disability on any person on the ground of "untouchability". S. 14 provides for offences by Companies. S. 15 makes offences under the Act cognisable and, "with the permission of the Court", compoundable. S. 16 gives the Act an overriding effect over other laws except as otherwise expressly provided in the Act. S. 17 repeals a large number of State Acts designed to remove social and religious disabilities arising from "untouchability". However, as regards existing law, which is not repealed by Parliament, we have seen that it continues in force, subject to adaptation under Art. 372. Accordingly, it has been held that the Madras Temple Entry Authorising Act, 1947, as amended by the Madras Act 13 of 1949, did not violate any provision of the Constitution, because, to prevent certain classes of Hindus who were once called "depressed classes" from entering a public temple was certainly to practise "untouchability" and the Act prohibited "untouchability" in pursuance of a policy which found expression in Art. 17. As the Act was covered by Art. 35 (*a*) (ii), it continued in force till repealed.[47] In *State* v. *Gulab Singh*,[48] without any reference to Art. 35 (*b*) (ii), the Court held that the U.P. Removal of Social Disabilities Act, 1947, continued till repeal by Parliament. That Act has now been repealed by the Untouchability Offences Act, 1955.

Arts. 15, 35 and the power of State Legislatures

9.245 As the power of State Legislatures to make laws prescribing punishment for acts declared to be offences under Art. 17, is taken away by Art. 35 in respect of post-Constitution laws, the Madhya Bharat Harijan Disabilities Removal (Amendment) Act, 1950, which was enacted after the Constitution came into force, and dealt with the question of sentences so as to amend the law which was in force

[47] *P. S. Charya* v. *Madras* ('56) A.M. 541.
[48] ('53) A.A. 483.

at the commencement of the Constitution, was *ultra vires*, as the Madhya Bharat Legislature lacked legislative competence to enact it.[49]

9.246 In *Sangannagouda* v. *Kalkangouda*[50] it was held that the classification of *Lingayats* among *sudras* did not contravene Arts. 14, 15 and 17. In fact, the Act gave them larger powers of adoption than they otherwise had. In *Pavadai Gounder* v. *State*[51] it was held that the acquisition of land for constructing a colony for Harijans did not violate Art. 17.[52]

Lingayats

Acquisition for Harijans

---

[49] *State* v. *Kishan* ('55) A.M.B. 207.
[50] ('60) A.Mys. 147.
[51] ('73) A.M. 458.
[52] ibid. p. 459 [*held*, further that Art. 17 prohibited singling out Harijans for hostile treatment as a socially backward community; and, that to uphold the contention that such a scheme would amount to practising untouchability resulting in segregation would defeat the very purpose of Arts. 15(4), 16(4) and Articles dealing with Directive Principles of State Policy].

CHAPTER X

RIGHT TO FREEDOM

ARTICLE 19

[NOTE: As originally enacted, Art. 19(1)(*a*) to (*g*) conferred on every citizen seven fundamental rights. The discussion of Art. 19 in this Chapter therefore deals with all the seven rights. However, the reader will bear in mind that Art. 19(1)(*f*) has been repealed, (as also Art. 31) by the Constitution (44th Amendment) Act, 1979, with effect from June 20, 1979.]

Scheme of this Chapter

10.1 In this Chapter we will consider, first, the general questions raised by Art. 19, and, secondly, each individual right conferred by Art. 19 and the restrictions to which it is subject. In the next Chapter we will consider the relation of Art. 19 to Arts. 20, 21 and 22, all of which have been placed under the title "Right to Freedom".

Rights have presented no serious difficulties: controversy has centred on "restriction"

10.2 The content of the rights embodied in Art. 19(1) (*a*) to (*g*) has not presented any serious, or intractable difficulties, and such questions as have arisen have been solved without difficulty. The questions which have most engaged the attention of the Courts have centred round the restrictions to which these rights are subject. For a time, different views were expressed on the question whether the word "restrictions" in Arts. 19(2) to (6) included "prohibition", till the Supreme Court answered it in the affirmative in *Narendra Kumar* v. *Union.*[1] In that case, Das Gupta J. reviewed the earlier decisions of the Supreme Court with the following result: the observations of Kania C. J. and Das J. in *A. K. Gopalan* v. *State*[2] that "restriction" did not mean "deprivation" were made in the context of a conflict between Art. 19(1) (*d*) and Art. 21 and could not have been intended for general application. In *Saghir Ahmad* v. *U.P.*[3] and in *Bombay* v. *R. M. D. Chamarbaugwalla*[4] the question whether restrictions included prohibition was raised but was left open. However, in *Chintaman Rao* v. *M.P.*[5], in *Cooverjee B. Bharucha* v. *Excise Commr. and the Chief Commr., Ajmer*[6] and in *M. B. Cotton Association Ltd.* v. *Union*[7] the Court held that the law would be valid or invalid according as the interference with fundamental rights was reasonable or not in the interest of the general public. In all these cases "prohibition" was treated as only a kind of "restriction". After the above review Das Gupta J. added that any other view would defeat the intention of the Constitution. This conclusion was supported by the language of Art. 13 (which prohibits the making of laws "inconsistent" with, or "taking away the rights" conferred by, Part III of the Constitution):

after some conflict, "restriction" held to include "prohibition"

"It is reasonable to think that the makers of the Constitution considered the word 'restriction' to be sufficiently wide to save laws 'inconsistent' with Art. 19(1), or 'taking away the rights' conferred by the Article, provided this inconsistency or taking away was reasonable in the interests of the different matters mentioned in the clause. There can be no doubt therefore that they

---

[1] (1960) 2 S.C.R. 375, ('60) A.SC. 430.
[2] (1950) S.C.R. 88, 106, 301, ('50) A.SC. 27.
[3] (1955) 1 S.C.R. 707, ('54) A.SC. 728. [4] (1957) S.C.R. 874, ('57) A.SC. 699.
[5] (1950) S.C.R. 759, ('51) A.SC. 118. [6] (1954) S.C.R. 873, ('54) A.SC. 220.
[7] ('54) A.SC. 634.

intended the word 'restriction' to include cases of 'prohibition' also. The contention that a law prohibiting the exercise of a fundamental right is in no case saved, cannot therefore be accepted."[8]

In the result, cases which decided that a law was void because reasonable restrictions in Art. 19 (5) and (6) did not include prohibition, are no longer good law on that point and require to be reconsidered.[9] Contrary view no longer good law

10.3 A question connected with the one just discussed was decided in *Bombay* v. *R. M. D. Chamarbaugwalla*.[10] That case raised the question whether the Bombay Prize Competition Act, which regulated prize competitions of a gambling nature, violated Art. 19 (1) (*g*), and it became necessary to decide whether there could be "trade" or "business" in gambling. The respondent contended that even a criminal or immoral activity, if it yielded a profit or income, must be looked upon as trade or business and was therefore protected by Art. 19 (1) (*g*). The Court rightly negatived this contention, holding that crime was not "business" as had been pointed out in *F. A. Lindsay, A. E. Woodward and W. Hiscox* v. *The Commissioners, Inland Revenue*[11] and in *Southern* (*Inspector of Taxes*) v. *A. B.*[12] In the last mentioned case, Finlay J. said that

Activities not entitled to the protection of Art. 19: *Chamarbaugwalla's Case*

there can be no "business" in gambling

". . . assuming . . . that a burglar and his occupation do not come within Sch. D of the Income-tax Act, 1918, the reason is that what he does is not an earning of profit by a 'trade' within Case I of the Schedule and not that, while carrying on a 'trade' within Case I, he is taken out of the operation of the Case by some consideration of illegality".[13]

The references made by Das C.J.[14] in *Chamarbaugwalla's Case* to the Rig Veda, to the Mahabharata, to Manu, Yajnavalkya, Kautilya (who advocated State control of gambling) and to the Hedaya have met with some criticism. These references were made to repel the contention that the condemnation of gambling was not universal. If the decisions of the U.S. Supreme Court, the Supreme Courts of Australia or Canada, or the decisions of the Privy Council can be referred to for showing the evils of gambling, there is no reason why references should not be made to Hindu Law and to Hindu religious books, or to Mahomedan Law, to show that gambling had been condemned in India from ancient times. In a later case, upholding ss. 6 and 8, United States of Gwalior and Indore-Malwa (Madhya Bharat) Gambling Act, the Supreme Court held that since the Act was not challenged for lack of legislative competence, once it was conceded that gambling was an evil, that gambling-houses flourished and that the detection of gambling was extremely difficult, a law to root out gambling was in the public interest, and

Other cases on gambling

---

[8] *Narendra Kumar's Case,* (1960) 2 S.C.R. *supra* at p. 387.

[9] For example, in *Ramunni Kurup* v. *Panchayat Board, Badagara* (1954) Mad. 513, ('54) A.M. 754, s. 81(1), Madras Village Panchayat Act, 1950, and the notification issued thereunder, closing down private markets, were held void solely on the ground that Art. 19(5) contemplated the regulation, and not the total prohibition, of the exercise of that right. It is submitted that the question whether on the facts of the case a closing down of the market was a reasonable restriction under Art. 19(5) would have to be considered on its merits.

[10] (1957) S.C.R. 874, ('57) A.SC. 699.

[11] (1932) 18 T.C. 43, *per* Lord President Clyde.

[12] (1933) 1 K.B. 713, *per* Lord Sands.

[13] (1933) 1 K.B. 713, 719.

[14] (1957) S.C.R. *supra* at pp. 921-3.

the Act was constitutionally valid.[15] In *Mahesh Chandra Gupta* v. *State*[16] it was held that prize-competitions kindled a gambling outlook in the public and induced them to submit entries far in excess of their means, and consequently, restrictions on the prizes offered and the number of entries permitted were reasonable. It is submitted that if the Court found that the competitions were of a gambling nature, they were covered by *Chamarbaugwalla's Case*[17] and the question of reasonableness of restrictions did not arise since Art. 19(1)(*g*) could not be invoked. Though prize-competitions of a gambling nature are not "business" protected by Art. 19(1)(*g*), different considerations apply to prize-competitions involving substantial skill. This was held in *R. M. D. Chamarbaugwalla* v. *Union*.[18] There, the validity of the Prize Competitions Act, 1955, enacted by Parliament, was impugned on the ground that the definition of prize-competitions in s. 2(*d*) included prize-competitions of a gambling nature as well as prize-competitions involving substantial skill, and the restrictions imposed by the Act were unreasonable as to prize-competitions involving substantial skill and as the definition was inseverable, the whole Act was void. In a careful judgment, which is a leading authority on severability, Venkatarama Aiyar J. held that the definition must be confined only to prize-competitions of a gambling nature by construction but that in any event, the doctrine of severability in enforcement applied, and the Court could restrain enforcement of the Act as regards prize-competitions involving substantial skill. In this context, Venkatarama Aiyar J. made observations which show that had it become necessary to do so, he would have held that the provisions of the Act were void as regards prize-competitions involving substantial skill. He said:

Distinction between gambling, prize-competitions and those involving substantial skill

"As regards competitions which involve substantial skill, however, different considerations arise. They are business activities, the protection of which is guaranteed by Art. 19(1)(*g*), and the question would have to be determined with reference to those competitions whether ss. 4 and 5 and rr. 11 and 12 are reasonable restrictions enacted in public interest. But (Counsel) has fairly conceded before us that on the materials on record in these proceedings, he could not maintain that the restrictions contained in those provisions are saved by Art. 19(6) as being reasonable and in the public interest."[19]

Prohibition of practising prostitution upheld

10.4 In *Malerkotla* v. *Mohd. Mushtaq*[20] the Court considered s. 152, Punjab Municipal Act, 1911, which enabled a Municipal Committee by public notice to prohibit in any specified part of the Municipality the keeping of a brothel, and the residence of any person who practised prostitution. A number of persons were prosecuted for practising prostitution and others for being wilful parties to such practice. The Magistrate, as also the Sessions Judge, who tried the

---

[15] *Kishan Chander* v. *M.P.* (1964) 1 S.C.R. 765, ('65) A.SC. 307. The precise argument for the appellants is not clear from the judgment but it would appear that the argument was not that gambling was entitled to the protection of Art. 19(1)(*g*), — for *Chamarbaugwalla's Case* had held that it was not, — but that the provisions of the Act, including those relating to the burden of proof, imposed unreasonable restrictions on the possession of innocent articles like playing-cards and dice. The court negatived this contention observing that the Act provided safeguards against victimisation of innocent persons.

[16] ('64) A.A. 572.

[17] (1957) S.C.R. 874, ('57) A.SC. 699.

[18] (1957) S.C.R. 930. ('57) A.SC. 628.

[19] (1957) S.C.R. 930, 935.

[20] ('60) A.Punj. 18 [see *Mithan* v. *Municipal Board* ('58) A.A. 603, where an order passed by a Magistrate against the petitioner directing her to stop the use of her house for habitual prostitution was upheld as a reasonable restriction].

case found the facts established. The Sessions Judge however held, in substance, that s. 152 violated the rights of the accused to practise their profession in a certain locality; and that the Municipality had uprooted those people without providing accommodation for them. Reversing the Sessions Court, the High Court held that the Order of the former Ruler was not immutable and that the legislature could by enacting subsequent laws, revoke or amend such an order.[21] Although the High Court did not expressly say so, it held, in substance, that prostitution and the running of a brothel were not "occupation", "trade" or "business" entitled to the protection of Art. 19 and therefore it was competent for the Municipal Committee to prohibit the practice of prostitution or the keeping of a brothel. The Municipality was under no obligation to provide alternative accommodation as it was not the function of a public body like the Municipal Committee to offer facilities to prostitutes to practise prostitution.

10.5 Following *Chamarbaugwalla's Case* it was held in *T. K. Abraham* v. *Trav.-Cochin*[22] that tobacco was as deleterious as liquor and there was no fundamental right to carry on trade in it. Again, it has been held that s. 178-A, Sea Customs Act, does not violate Art. 19 (1) (*f*) and (*g*) because no one can claim fundamental rights in smuggled goods.[23] In *U.P.* v. *Kartar Singh*[24] the Supreme Court held that no person had a fundamental right under Art. 19 (1) (*g*) to trade in adulterated foodstuffs.[25] It was held in *In re N. V. Natarajan*[26] that s. 5, Madras Prevention of Insults to National Honour Act, 1957, did not violate Art. 19 (1) (*f*) as the wilful burning of a copy of the Constitution is not included in the fundamental right to acquire, hold and dispose of property. In *In re Sant Ram*[27] the Supreme Court appears to have held that the "occupation" of a tout is not business or occupation protected by Art. 19 (1) (*g*) since that occupation has a corrupting influence on the administration of justice. In *Bahadur Singh* v. *Union*[28] the

No fundamental right to trade (i) in deleterious articles or (ii) in smuggled goods or (iii) in adulterated foodstuffs

No fundamental right to insult national honour

Occupation of a 'tout' not protected by Art. 19(1)(*g*)

[21] The Court invoked the maxim "It is an everlasting law, that no positive and human law shall be perpetual, and a clause which excludes abrogation is not good from its commencement." It might have equally involked the following observations from *Douglas* v. *Kentucky* (1897) 168 U.S. 488, 42 L.ed. 553, 555, which were cited with approval by our Supreme Court in *Bombay* v. *R. M. D. Chamarbaugwalla* (1957) S.C.R. 874, 924: "Can the Legislature of a State contract away its power to establish such regulations as are reasonably necessary from time to time to protect the public morals against the evils of lotteries?"

[22] (1958) Ker. 148 (F.B.), ('58) A.Ker. 129 (*Cooverjee Bharucha's Case* was also referred to).

[23] *Boota Singh* v. *State* ('61) A.Punj. 21, 62 P.L.R. 772, foll. *Balbir Singh* v. *Collector of C.E. & L.C.* ('60) A.Punj. 488, and *Punjab* v. *Krishan Lal* ('60) A.Punj. 664.

[24] (1964) 6 S.C.R. 679, 687, ('64) A.SC. 1135.

[25] See *A.P.G. & S.M. Assocn.* v. *Union* ('71) A.SC. 2346, 2347, where, presumably, in view of the above judgment it was conceded that there was no fundamental right to carry on business in adulterated or misbranded foodstuffs.

[26] (1964) 2 Mad. 889, ('65) A.M. 11, 14.

[27] (1960) 3 S.C.R. 499, ('60) A.SC. 932, 935; see *Secretary, Advocates Association* v. *Phool Din* (1953) 1 All. 930, ('52) A.A. 491, where it was held that it was permissible under Art. 19(6) to prohibit a profession if it was in the public interest to do so and that permitting a tout to function was not in the public interest.

[28] Unreported judgment quoted and fol. in *Balley Singh* v. *State* ('67) A.A. 341 [*held*, that the provisions of the Opium Act, 1857, and the Dangerous Drugs Act, 1930, prohibiting the cultivation of poppy did not violate Art. 19(1)(*g*)].

Supreme Court referred to *Cooverji Bharucha's Case* and held that the cultivation of poppy could be prohibited where there was evidence that the cultivators conveyed opium and its derivatives beyond the frontiers of the country.

Consequences of a business not being protected by Art. 19(1)(*g*)

10.6 One of the corollaries of a "profession", "trade", "business" or "occupation" not being entitled to the protection of Art. 19 (1) (*g*), or being such as can be prohibited under Art. 19 (6) was pointed out in *Sheoshankar* v. *State.*[29] There, the Court held that the C.P. and Berar Prohibition Act, 1938, did not violate Art. 19 (1) (*f*) because the legislature having come to the conclusion that the consumption of intoxicating liquor was not in the public interest, intoxicating liquor must be regarded as a noxious object and it ceased to be a legitimate object of "property" or of "commerce", for, what had been rendered contraband could not be the object of property. The Court cited American decisions which fully established this proposition. Thus, in *Mugler* v. *Kansas*[30], in *Clarke* v. *Haberle Crystal Springs Brewing Co.*[31] and in *Ziffrin* v. *Reeves*,[32] the U.S. Supreme Court held respectively (i) that prohibition upon the use of property for purposes that were declared by valid legislation to be injurious to the health, morals and safety of the community was within the power of the State which could declare that any place kept and maintained for the illegal manufacture and sale of intoxicating liquors shall be deemed a common nuisance and could be abated; (ii) that when a business was extinguished as noxious under the Constitution, the owners could not demand compensation from the Government; (iii) that property (whisky) removed from prohibited channels of transportation and distribution which was subject to seizure under the police power could not be regarded as a proper article of commerce. This doctrine was not limited to liquor laws. In *Miller* v. *Schoene*[33] it was held that ornamental cedar trees may be declared a nuisance to prevent the infecting of apple orchards in the vicinity with cedar rust,[34] and in *Clason* v. *Indiana*[35] the right of the State not to recognize dead horses as legitimate articles of inter-State commerce was upheld as a sanitary and health measure. However, the observations in *Rajindra Singh* v. *Union*[36] that ". . . nothing can be the subject of property which is not recognized by law to be such and similarly when the law withdraws such recognition a thing from which recognition is withdrawn ceases to be property," are too wide. Under our Constitution, which protects the rights of property, and provides for compensation for acquisition of property, the State cannot divest well-recognized and innocuous kinds of property of their character. It is one thing to divest infected food or deleterious drinks of their character as property. It is an altogether different thing to divest ordinary food and drink of such character. The first is permissible; the second is not.

Effect on property used in such "business": property divested of its character

Submission: innocuous kinds of property cannot be divested of their character without justification

---

[29] (1951) Nag. 646, ('51) A.Nag. 58 at p. 84.
[30] (1887) 123 U.S. 623, 31 L.ed. 205.
[31] (1929) 280 U.S. 384, 74 L.ed. 498.
[32] (1939) 308 U.S. 132, 84 L.ed. 128.
[33] (1927) 276 U.S. 272, 72 L.ed. 568.
[34] The Court found it unnecessary to weigh the nicety whether such trees were a common law nuisance or could be declared a nuisance by statute.
[35] (1938) 306 U.S. 439, 83 L.ed. 858.
[36] ('63) A.Punj. 461.

10.7 In *Krishnan Kumar v. J. & K.*[37] Subba Rao C.J. in rejecting the contention that there could be no "business" in liquor, observed that the morality or otherwise of a deal did not affect its character as a business and that therefore dealing in liquor was business.[38] The observations of Das C.J., in *Bombay* v. *R. M. D. Chamarbaugwalla*[39] that gambling could not be regarded as trade or business within the meaning of Art. 19(1) (*f*) and (*g*) and Art. 301[40] were distinguished as being limited to gambling. It is submitted that the observations that the quality of a deal does not affect the quality of an activity as business proceeds on a total misconception of the decision in *Chamarbaugwalla's Case.* In that case it was contended that crime or inherently vicious activities must be treated as business or trade within the meaning of Arts. 19(1) (*f*) and (*g*) and Art. 301 and then restricted or prohibited according to its heinousness.[41] The definition of "business" there suggested was "all activities carried on with a view to earning profit."[42] Das C.J. rightly rejected this approach, and his judgment, far from leading to "incoherence in thought and expression" with which Subba Rao C. J. apparently characterised it,[43] focussed attention on the real issue. Subba Rao C.J. asked: if dealing in *ghee*[44] is business, why not dealing in liquor? He would have got the correct answer if he had asked: if dealing in *ghee* is business, why not dealing in slaves or trafficking in women or dealing in counterfeit coins or currency notes? The question has only to be asked to realise, as the English judgments which Das C. J. quoted showed, that the ordinary English word "business" or "trade" does not include crime:

Krishan Kumar's Case — submission: wrongly decided

"That crime is not a business is also recognised in *F. A. Lindsay, A. E. Woodward and W. Hiscox* v. *The Commissioners of Inland Revenue*[45] (*per* Lord President Clyde and *per* Lord Sands) and in *Southern, (H.M. Inspector of Taxes)* v. *A.B.*[46] The fact that regulatory provisions have been enacted to control gambling by issuing licences and by imposing taxes does not in any way alter the nature of gambling which is inherently vicious and pernicious."[47]

It is submitted that Das C.J. was right in holding that activities which are criminal, as also dealing in articles or goods which are *res extra commercium*, could not have been intended to be permitted in the first instance by Art. 19(1) (*f*) and (*g*) relating to fundamental rights to property, trade or business, or by Art. 301 relating to the freedom of trade and commerce, with permission to the State to restrict or prohibit them. The question whether liquor is inherently vicious or not, may admit of a difference of opinion. But in our Constitution, liquor is looked upon as inherently vicious, because the directive principles of State policy, which are fundamental in the governance of the country (Art. 37) require that the State should endeavour to bring about the prohibition of consumption of liquor (Art. 47). This topic is more fully discussed in the Chapter on Directive Principles of State Policy. But apart from Art. 47, the fact that liquor can be totally prohibited, and such

Submission: *Chamarbaugwalla's Case* rightly decided

---

[37] ('67) A.SC. 1368, (1967) 3 S.C.R. 50.
[38] ('67) A.SC. p. 1371.
[39] (1957) S.C.R. 874, ('57) A.SC. 699.
[40] (1957) S.C.R. *supra* at p. 925.
[41] ibid. p. 920.
[42] ibid.
[43] ('67) A.SC. *supra* at p. 1371.
[44] Clarified butter at one time generally used for frying.
[45] 18 T.C. 43.
[46] (1933) 1 K.B. 713.
[47] (1957) S.C.R. *supra* at p. 926.

prohibition upheld, not only in India but in the United States and Canada, shows that it is regarded as inherently vicious and the State may treat the possession or consumption of alcohol as a crime and thus divest liquor of its character as property which can be the subject of trade or business. We have seen in para 10.6 above, that Hidayatullah J. so held in *Sheoshankar's Case*. It has now been held by the Supreme Court in *Southern Pharmaceuticals & Chemicals* v. *Kerala*[48] that no citizen has any fundamental right under Art. 19(1)(*g*) to carry on trade in noxious and dangerous goods such as intoxicants. Apart altogether from the submission that the theoretical basis of *Chamarbaugwalla's Case* is correct, the practical consequence of holding that liquor is not *res extra commercium* is not different, for it has been held that a law introducing total prohibition of alcoholic liquor does not violate Art. 19(1)(*f*) and (*g*) and *a fortiori* would not violate Art. 301.

Fatechand's Case: whether money lending could claim the freedom of trade

10.8 The question whether money-lending was a business which could claim the freedom of trade and commerce guaranteed under Art. 301 was raised and decided in *Fatehchand* v. *Maharashtra*[49] by Krishna Iyer J. who delivered the unanimous judgment of the Supreme Court.[50] The appeals arose out of writ petitions filed in Bombay High Court in 1976 when a proclamation of emergency was in force, so that the protection of Art. 19(1)(*f*) and (*g*) was not available to challenge the provisions of the Maharashtra Debt Relief Act, 1976. That Act did not prohibit the business of money-lending, but it wiped out all debts due to money-lenders upto a certain date and obliged them to return to the debtors the securities obtained from the debtors as a security for their debts.

Krishna Iyer J's admonition of counsel

10.9 The Emergency was not an ideal time to argue "constitutional issues of great moment"; but Counsel for different Appellants discharged their duty to their clients as best as they could. The exercise by Counsel of their right to address the Court annoyed the Court, as is clear from the following observations of Krishna Iyer J.: "We dismiss these appeals and writ petitions, leaving the parties to bear their costs, *although we had at least on one occasion sufficient provocation to make a different direction*."[51] (Italics supplied). The Court however, took the unusual course of admonishing Counsel by saying:

"A bunch of counsel, led by Shri Nariman and seconded by Shri B. Sen, have lashed out against the vires of the Maharashtra Debt Relief Act, 1976 (for short, the Debt Act). The former has focussed on the fatal flaw in the Act based on Article 301 of the Constitution and the latter has concentrated his fire on the incompetency of the State Legislature to enact the Debt Act. A plurality of submissions by a procession of lawyers has followed, although the principal points have been comprehensively covered by Shri Nariman and Shri B. Sen. To encore is not to augment, and yet, some counsel, who had not much to supplement, claimed the right to be heard and exercised it *ad libitum*, essaying what had already been forcefully urged and forgetting that a fine,

---

48 ('81) A.SC. 1863, 1872. [So held in repelling a challenge to ss. 12A, 12B, 14(*e*) and (*f*) and 68A of the Kerala Abkari Act and Rr. 13 and 16 of the Kerala Rectified Spirit Rule, 1972. However, the Court held further that as to provisions relating to medicinal and toilet preparations capable of being used as alcoholic beverages (ibid p. 1872) or as substitutes for alcoholic beverages (ibid p. 1878), those provisions imposed reasonable restrictions on the citizen's rights under Art. 19(1)(*g*)].

49 (1977) 2 S.C.R. 828, ('77) A.SC. 1825.

50 For himself, Ray C.J. and Beg, Bhagwati and Fazal Ali JJ.

51 (1977) 2 S.C.R. at p. 861, ('77) A.SC. at p. 1848.

fresh presentation of a case is apt to be staled by a second version of it and pejorated by a third repetition. While in constitutional issues of great moment this Court is reluctant to ration oral submission it is important, by comity of the Bench and the Bar, to conserve judicial time in the name of public justice so that internal allocation, avoiding overlapping may be organised among many counsel who may appear in several appeals, substantially dealing with the same points. A happy husbandry of advocacy is helpful for judge and lawyer alike and to streamline forensic business is the joint responsibility of both the limbs of the institution of justice."[52]

10.10 Two comments must be made on this admonition. First, it is much fairer to counsel discharging a difficult duty in arguing "constitutional issues of great moment" to stop them on the ground of unjustified repetition, than to attack them in a judgment to which they cannot reply. Secondly, if the conservation of judicial time in the name of public justice is desirable, and is said to be the joint responsibility of the Bench and the Bar, Judges must also make their contribution by writing judgments which will not waste judicial time by the difficulty of trying to find out what the judgment says or means. *Adapting* the words of Fowler, "before a judge allows himself to be tempted by the more showy qualities of good writing, he must be direct, simple, brief, vigorous and lucid".[53] Anyone who has read the judgments of Krishna Iyer J. will have been struck by his extensive knowledge, his judicial courage and independence, his willingness to think out things afresh, and his passionate desire to do justice. But his judgments are robbed of much of their value because they cannot be read without several dictionaries by one's side, and, even when so read, the judgments leave the Bench and the Bar guessing as to what *precisely* he meant to say.[54]

Two criticisms of the admonition

10.11 The present writer has felt obliged to refer to the language of the judgment in *Fatehchand's Case*—and his observations apply

Difficulty of stating

[52] (1977) 2 S.C.R. at p. 832, ('77) A.SC. at pp. 1827-8.

[53] Sir Earnest Gower, *The Complete Plain Words*, 1st edn. p. 79, quoting Fowler.

[54] For example, we all know that to call a man a "Shylock" is to call him a hard-hearted and grasping money-lender. But, who is an "*asuric*" Shylock? [(1977) 2 S.C.R. at p. 849, ('77) A.SC. at p. 1840]. The *C.O.D.* (6th edn.) does not record "*asuric*". Justice Holmes's famous epigram "The life of the law is not logic but experience" is well known. Are we helped by being told: "The life of the law is not neat noesis but actual experience." (ibid. p. 848; p. 1839). What is "noesis"? The C.O.D. (6th edn. 1976) does not record the word "noesis"; it tells us that "noetic" means: "of the intellect, purely intellectual or abstract; (in singular or plural) science of the intellect." Again, repetition of an argument by different Counsel in different ways is nothing new, but why send the Bench and the Bar in search of "allomorphic" (ibid. p. 837; p. 1831) combinations? The C.O.D. defines "allomorph" (noun) to mean "one of two or more forms of a morpheme; hence allomorphic (adjective)." And a morpheme means "morphological element considered in functional relations to a linguistic system; smallest meaningful unit of a language." And "morphology" in the context means "study of the form of words; system of forms in a language, hence morphological (adjective)." Even with this patient tracking down of the meaning of "allomorphic", the reader will be no wiser at the end than when he began his search. Leaving single words aside, what *precise* meaning is conveyed by "rural cum-slum economics"? (ibid. p. 832; p. 1827), "poverty jurisprudence" (ibid. p. 848; p. 1839), or "development jurisprudence" (ibid.), or the "taboo of traumatic trade"? (ibid. p. 840; p. 1833). And surely the epigramatic saying "to encore is not to augment" (ibid. p. 832; p. 1828) says exactly the opposite of what the learned judge wished to say, for, an "encore" is given in response to the demand of the audience that the *same performer* should perform the same piece over again, or perform a different piece — so charmed is the audience by his first performance!

Krishna Iyer J's reasoning

to other judgments of Krishna Iyer J.—partly in response to the learned judge's appeal to the Bench and the Bar to save judicial time in the interest of justice, and partly to explain the difficulty of unearthing the reasoning of *Fatehchand's Case* from the rhetoric in which it is buried. However, it is believed that the reasoning runs something like this: One type of money-lending is business and is connected with business, for most businesses run on moneys borrowed from banks, institutions of credit and other public agencies. This type of money-lending presents no problem and is clearly trade or business. However, the impugned Act dealt with a different kind of money-lending (hereafter referred to as merely as "money-lending") namely, rural and allied money-lending to agriculturists and urban workmen by money-lenders. In support of the Act, the State contended, first, that such money-lending was so pernicious that it could be treated by the law as not a trade or business at all.[55] Alternatively, if such money-lending was trade or business, the restrictions imposed on it by the Act were reasonable, within the meaning of Art. 304(*b*). The Court held that money-lending was not a trade or business, but, if it was, the Act imposed reasonable restrictions on the business of money-lending within the meaning of Art. 304(*b*). The evil of money-lending was not confined to isolated cases, but was widespread, as it affected a very large number of agricultural and urban debtors. Considerable evidence was produced before the trial Court and the Supreme Court.[56] This evidence showed that money-lending could be looked upon as a pernicious activity. In the past, "Many Conferences, Commissions and resultant enactments before and after Independence provided but marginal protection for the rural debtor. Even licensing was evaded by the money-lender successfully and conciliation machinery proved a mirage. Statutes made of sterner stuff became the desideratum."[57] In other words, previous legislative attempts to grant relief to the debtors had failed, either because resolute attempts were not made to enforce the law or because of the illiteracy, ignorance and above all, the need of the borrower, or because of the dishonesty or trickery of the money-lender or by a combination of all these factors. The question before the Court therefore was a "simple" one, namely, in view of all this evidence, and the failure of earlier laws to relieve the borrower, could a legislature, without violating any constitutional limitations, wipe out all debts and restore the security given for the debts to the borrowers? There can be no doubt that the legislature was competent to enact the Act, for the power to legislate in respect of money-lending and money-lenders would, in appropriate cases, enable the Legislature to wipe

Two types of money lending: the first is "business", the second is not

The evils of money lending

Money lending not "business": observations of Das C.J. quoted with approval

---

[55] ". . . whether rural and allied money-lending is so abominable as to be 'bastardized by the law' ": *per* Krishna Iyer J., (1977) 2 S.C.R. at p. 840; ('77) A.SC. at p. 1834.

[56] The Supreme Court judgment referred to: (a) Current Trends in Rural Indebtedness by M. Gopalan and V. Kulandaiswamy — *Eastern Economist*, April 23, 1976; *Rural Savings in India* by Prof. P. G. Panikar; (b) *Social Security Measures in India* by Dr. Bhattacharya; (c) *Concise History of the Indian Economy* by Dhiresh Bhattacharya; (d) *Indian Economy* by A. N. Agarwal; (e) *Agricultural Problems of India* by Dr. C. B. Mamoria and (f) the *Report* of a High Power Committee appointed by the Government of Maharashtra to make recommendations for the relief of rural and urban indebtedness.

[57] (1977) 2 S.C.R. at p. 846, ('77) A.SC. at p. 1838.

out debts. The Supreme Court upheld the State's contention that money-lending was not a trade or business. After quoting a passage from the judgment of Das C.J. in *Chamarbaugwala's Case*, Krishna Iyer J. said :

"We have no hesitation, in our hearts and our heads, to hold that every systematic, profit-oriented activity, however sinister, suppressive or socially diabolic, cannot *ipso facto*, exalt itself into a trade. Incorporation of Directive Principles of State Policy casting the high duty upon the State to strive to promote the welfare of the people by securing and protecting as effectively as it may a social order in which justice — social, economic, and political — shall inform all the institutions of the national life, is not idle print but command to action. We can never forget, except at our peril, that the Constitution obligates the State to ensure an adequate means of livelihood to its citizens and to see that the health and strength of workers, men and women are not abused, that exploitation, moral and material, shall be extradited. . . . At this point, the legal culture and the public morals of a nation may merge, economic justice and taboo of traumatic trade may meet and jurisprudence may frown upon dark and deadly dealings."[58]

In view of the evidence which had been produced before the Supreme Court of this type of money-lending, a reasonable person could take the view that such money-lending was not "trade or business" within the meaning of Art. 301. In any event, if the legislature took that view, a Court could not hold that it was wrong. It may be added that the judgment does not put the case as we have set it out above, but that appears to be the underlying reasoning of the judgment, stripped of its highly emotional rhetoric.

Sup. Ct. aware of another view of money lending

10.12 The Supreme Court was aware that the State Legislature's view of money-lending was not the only one which could be taken of money-lending, because the cases before the Court had another side. One of the authorities quoted in the judgment had said that institutional agencies provided only 50 per cent of the total rural credit needs.[59] Therefore, if the economic conditions of agriculturists and urban labourers obliged them to borrow money, where was that money to come from, to satisfy the remaining 50 per cent of the needs of the borrowers? Once the need to borrow was admitted, the necessity of fulfilling the need would be inescapable, so that even if the Act wiped out existing debts, the money-lender may still come into his own, and might even try to make up the money he had lost as a result of the Act. This other side of the picture does not appear clearly from the judgment. But the Supreme Court was aware of it, for, having painted the money-lender in the blackest colours, the Supreme Court found it necessary to add:

"A concluding caveat"

"A concluding caveat. The poignant purpose of ending exploitative rural-urban lending to the weaker members of society is the validating virtue of this legislation, viewed from the constitutional angle. But, as (Counsel) at some stage mentioned — and the learned Attorney-General also concurred — mere farewell to existing debts is prone to prove a teasing illusion or promise of unreality unless the administration fills the credit gap by an easy, accessible and need-based network of humane credit agencies, coupled with employment opportunities for the small man. The experience of the past has not inspired adequate confidence."[60]

In plain English, the Court said: "We have held that the law is valid. We know that there is not enough money to enable agriculturists and

[58] (1977) 2 S.C.R. at p. 840, ('77) A.SC. at p. 1833.
[59] (1977) 2 S.C.R. at p. 842, ('77) A.SC. at p. 1835.
[60] (1977) 2 S.C.R. at p. 860, ('77) A.SC. at p. 1848.

urban labourers to borrow all the money they need from institutional agencies. We know also that agriculturists and urban labourers must borrow the extra money. We hope that *somehow* the money will be found. The experience of the past does not inspire 'adequate confidence'. Therefore, we give the State good advice, and hope for the best." However that may be, if the reasoning underlying the judgment is as we have stated it to be, the judgment is correct. For, if, as the Supreme Court held, the Maharashtra Legislature could reasonably take the view of money-lending which it did, a court could not say that the Legislature was wrong; it is not for a court to consider whether the object of the law could have been better achieved by different methods.[61]

Submission: the judgment is correct

Phatumma v. *Kerala* Submission: Case covered by *Fatehchand's Case*; discussion of money lending unnecessary

10.13 In *Phathumma* v. *Kerala*[62] the validity of s. 20 of the Kerala Agriculturists' Debt Relief Act, 1970 was challenged, first, for lack of legislative competence; secondly, as violative of Art. 19 and, thirdly, as violative of Art. 14. Two judgments were delivered.[63] The section is too long to quote but it has been set out in full in the concurring judgment.[64] After the view of money-lending taken in *Fatehchand's Case,* which Fazal Ali J. referred to with approval, it is difficult to understand why Fazal Ali J. thought it necessary to discuss money-lending and the need for relief of agricultural indebtedness at length. If, as held in *Fatehchand's Case,* money-lending is not trade or business and is not entitled to the protection of fundamental rights under Art. 19 (1) (*g*), the challenge under Art. 19 did not survive. In any event, if the total wiping out of the debts in the Maharashtra Act was upheld, including the return of security given in respect of the debt, the provisions for restoration of property of agriculturists sold in execution of the decree on repayment of purchase price, in the manner specified by s. 20, must be upheld. In any event, the restrictions imposed by the Act must be held to be reasonable. Therefore, it is not necessary to refer to the passages quoted by Fazal Ali J. on the test to be applied for determining the reasonableness of a law.

S. 20 makes a valid classification

10.14 As to Art. 14, s. 20 of the Act made a distinction between the decree holder, who had become the purchaser of the property which was sold in execution of a mortgage decree, and a stranger who had purchased such property at a Court sale. Both the judgments rightly held that such a classification was a valid classification. The decree holder was familiar with the conditions of the judgment-debtor, whereas a stranger purchaser was not. Again, s. 20 distinguished between a sale by the agriculturists and treated the pur-

---

[61] In the 3rd. volume of the 2nd edition of this book at pp. 1874-80 and at pp. 2026-8, the present writer had criticised the style in which Krishna Iyer J. wrote his judgments. His retirement from office makes it unnecessary to reproduce that criticism.

[62] (1978) 2 S.C.R. 537, ('78) A.SC. 771. It may be mentioned that 1,02,867 suits were filed in various courts in the State in which suits no relief could be granted to the debtor because the date originally fixed for relief had expired. The date was therefore extended by an Amendment. The above facts are relevant as showing the extent of the indebtedness and the loss by agriculturists of their property and they need for relief granted by the Act.

[63] One by Fazal Ali J. for himself and for Beg C.J., Krishna Iyer and Jaswant Singh JJ. and a concurring judgment by Shinghal J. for himself, Bhagwati and Tulzapurkar JJ.

[64] ('78) A.SC. at pp. 789-90.

chaser differently from the purchaser at a Court sale. Here again, the Court rightly held, that there was a valid classification.

10.15 Although the main judgment raised the question of legislative competence, it does not deal with it. The concurring judgment held that the law was clearly covered by entry 30, List II, namely, "Money-lending and money-lenders; relief of agricultural indebtedness." It was argued that the section gave relief when by sale of property the debt had ceased to exist. The Court held that there was no reason why relief from indebtedness should be limited to subsisting indebtedness and could not cover the necessity of providing relief to agriculturists who had lost their immovable property by Court sales in execution of decrees against them and who had been rendered destitute. The decision of the Supreme Court in *Navinchandra Mafatlal* v. *C.I.T., Bombay*[65] was cited to show that in construing words of a legislative entry, the most liberal construction should be put upon the words, so that they may have effect in their widest amplitude, and laws may not have to be declared void on a mere technicality.[66]

The relation of "restrictions" to "rights"

10.16 Two further questions of a general nature arise in connection with the "restrictions" permitted by Art. 19 (2) to (6). First, what is the relation of the restrictions to the right which they restrict? It has been said that "it is the *rights* which are fundamental, not the limitations".[67] Such observations, it is submitted, are misleading, for they overlook the fact that what is granted is not an absolute right but a right subject to permissible restrictions. That the rights conferred by Art. 19 (1) are not absolute is obvious from the nature of those rights. In England, where several of them have been enjoyed for centuries, they have been subject to well-recognized limitations. Thus freedom of speech does not mean the freedom to say whatever one likes, but freedom of speech subject to the laws of libel, sedition, blasphemy and the like. Again, the right of assembly is subject to the assembly being peaceful and not causing a breach of the public peace. In the United States where the English colonists carried these rights with them, they were embodied in the Bill of Rights, and for a long time the U.S. Supreme Court treated them as subject to the limitations recognized in England, although, as we shall see, the form in which the First Amendment embodied the right to the freedom of speech led to a departure from English law. In India, the well-recognized limitations on the rights embodied in Art. 19 (1) (*a*) to (*g*) are expressly incorporated in Art. 19 (2) to (6). The rights represent the claims of the individual, the limitations protect the claims of other individuals and the claims of society or the State; to say that the rights are fundamental and the limitations are not is to destroy the balance which Art. 19 was designed to achieve. To say this is not to belittle those rights but only to say that the rights are not absolute and can be enjoyed only in an orderly society.

"restrictions" in Art. 19 fall into four groups

10.17 The restrictions which can be imposed on the seven fundamental rights contained in Art. 19 (1) fall into four groups which are not mutually exclusive but overlap in parts. The restrictions which Art. 19 (2) enables the State to put on the freedom of speech and

---

65 (1955) 1 S.C.R. 829, ('55) A.SC. 58.
66 ('78) A.SC. *supra* at p. 780.
67 See, *e.g. Ram Singh* v. *Delhi* (1951) S.C.R. 451, 467, ('51) A.SC. 270, *per* Bose J.

expression include, among others, restrictions in the interest of (*i*) the sovereignty and integrity of India; (*ii*) public order; and (*iii*) morality; but these are the only restrictions which, under Art. 19 (4), the State can put on the freedom to form associations or unions, and the first two are the only restrictions which under Art. 19 (3) the State can place on the right to assemble peaceably and without arms. Art. 19 (5) enables the State to put restriction on three fundamental rights, namely, the right to move freely throughout the territory of India, the right to settle in any part of the territory of India and to acquire, hold and dispose of property, (*i*) in the interest of the general public and (*ii*) for the protection of the interest of the Sch. Tribes. As will be more fully explained hereafter, the wording of the three rights and the identity of the grounds on which they can be restricted, led the majority of Judges in *Gopalan's Case*[68] to hold that the three rights were different facets of one central idea, namely, that though India is divided into States, for her citizens India is one country and they can move freely anywhere in India, settle in any part of India and acquire, hold and dispose of property, which, in the context of the preceding rights, must mean "anywhere in India". That restrictions can be put on these rights not only in the public interest, but for the protection of the interests of the Sch. Tribes has been taken to indicate that the right to move freely does not refer to freedom of movement but to freedom to move *throughout the territory of India.* As Mukherjea J. said in *Gopalan's Case*:

"... The scheduled tribes, as is well known, are a backward and unsophisticated class of people who are liable to be imposed upon by shrewd and designing persons. Hence there are various provisions disabling them from alienating even their own properties except under special conditions. In their interest and for their benefit, laws may be made restricting the ordinary right of citizens to go or settle in particular areas or acquire property in them. The reference to the interest of scheduled tribes makes it quite clear that the free movement spoken of in the clause relates not to general rights of locomotion but to the particular right of shifting or moving from one part of the Indian territory to another, without any sort of discriminatory barriers."[69]

The test of "reasonableness"

10.18 Secondly, what is the test for determining whether a restriction is reasonable within the meaning of Art. 19? This question must be decided in the context of a federal Constitution where the Courts have the power to declare a law invalid if it violates a constitutional limitation. We have seen that a Court is not a second or revising Chamber from the decision of the Legislature and that it is only in the clearest case that a Court will declare a law invalid.[70] The test of reasonableness laid down by Sastri C.J. in *Madras* v. *V. G. Row*[71] has generally been accepted as correct. He said:

***Row's Case* lays down the generally accepted test**

"It is important ... to bear in mind that the test of reasonableness, wherever prescribed, should be applied to each individual statute impugned, and no abstract standard, or general pattern of reasonableness can be laid down as applicable to all cases. The nature of the right alleged to have been infringed, the underlying purpose of the restrictions imposed, the extent and urgency of the evil sought to be remedied thereby, the disproportion of the imposition, the prevailing conditions at the time, should all enter into the judicial verdict. In evaluating such elusive factors and forming their own conception of what is reasonable, in all the circumstances of a given case, it is inevitable that

[68] (1950) S.C.R. 88, ('50) A.SC. 27.
[69] ibid. p. 259. See also *Chandmal* v. *M.P.* ('67) A.M.P. 52, 55.
[70] See para 3.1.
[71] (1952) S.C.R. 597, 607, ('52) A.SC. 196.

the social philosophy and the scale of values of the judges participating in the decision should play an important part, and the limit to their interference with legislative judgment in such cases can only be dictated by their sense of responsibility and self-restraint and the sobering reflection that the Constitution is meant not only for people of their way of thinking but for all, and that the majority of the elected representatives of the people have, in authorizing the imposition of the restrictions, considered them to be reasonable."[72]

10.19 In *Chintaman Rao* v. *M. P.*, Mahajan J. said that "reasonable restriction" means that the

the "*bidi*" *case* amplifies the dictates of reason

". . . limitation imposed on a person in enjoyment of the right should not be arbitrary or of an excessive nature, beyond what is required in the interests of the public. The word 'reasonable' implies intelligent care and deliberation, that is, the choice of a course which reason dictates. Legislation which arbitrarily or excessively invades the right cannot be said to contain the quality of reasonableness and unless it strikes a proper balance between the freedom guaranteed in article 19(1)(g) and the social control permitted by article 19(6) it must be held to be wanting in that quality."[73]

This passage does not refer to the nature of the business sought to be restrained, but in *Cooverjee Bharucha's Case*[74] Mahajan C.J. said:

the nature of the business is important in judging the reasonableness of restrictions

". . . in order to determine the reasonableness of the restriction regard must be had to the nature of the business. . . . It can also not be denied that the State has the power to prohibit trades which are illegal or immoral or injurious to the health and welfare of the public. Laws prohibiting trades in noxious or dangerous goods or trafficking in women cannot be held to be illegal as enacting a prohibition and not a mere regulation. The nature of the business is, therefore, an important element in deciding the reasonableness of the restrictions. The right of every citizen to pursue any lawful trade or business is obviously subject to such reasonable conditions as may be deemed by the governing authority . . . essential to the safety, health, peace, order and morals of the community. Some occupations by the noise made in their pursuit, some by the odours they engender, and some by the dangers accompanying them, require regulations as to the locality in which they may be conducted. Some, by the dangerous character of the articles used, manufactured or sold, require also special qualifications in the parties permitted to use, manufacture or sell them."[75]

The above tests may be supplemented by the following observations of Holmes J. in his classic dissent in *Lochner* v. *New York*:[76]

Lochner v. *New York*: would a

[72] This passage has been repeatedly cited with approval: *Phathumma* v. *Kerala* (1978) 2 S.C.R. 537, ('78) A.SC. 771 at p. 777; *Maharashtra* v. *H. N. Rao* (1969) 2 S.C.R. 392, ('70) A.SC. 1157, 1163; *H. R. Banthia* v. *Union* (1970) 1 S.C.R. 479, ('70) A.SC. 1453, (1969) 2 S.C.C. 167, 181; *U.P.* v. *Kaushaila* (1964) 4 S.C.R. 1002, 1012-13, ('64) A.SC. 416; *Virendra* v. *Punjab* (1958) S.C.R. 308, 318, ('57) A.SC. 896, 900; *Mohd. Hanif Quareshi* v. *Bihar* (1959) S.C.R. 629, 660-61, ('58) A.SC. 731, 744; *Abdul Hakim Quareishi* v. *Bihar* (1961) 2 S.C.R. 610, 620, ('61) A.SC. 448; *Lord Krishna Sugar Mills* v. *Union* (1960) 1 S.C.R. 39, ('59) A.SC. 1124, 1132; *Mineral Development Ltd.* v. *Bihar* (1960) 2 S.C.R. 609, ('60) A.SC. 468, 470; *Ranojirao* v. *M.P.* ('65) A.M.P. 77, 84; *Kannan* v. *Kerala* (1966) 1 Ker. 199, ('66) A.Ker. 143 (F.B.); *Gem Palace* v. *Union* ('70) A.Raj. 225, 227; *Syed Habib* v. *Kamal Chand* ('69) A.Raj. 31, 36.

[73] *Chintaman Rao* v. *M.P.* (1950) S.C.R. 759, 763, ('51) A.SC. 118; cited with approval in *Phathumma* v. *Kerala*, ('78) A.SC. 771; and in ('64) A.SC. *supra* at p. 422; fol. in: *Ranojirao* v. *M.P., supra; Anumathi Sadhukhan* v. *A. K. Chatterjee* ('57) A.Cal. 90, 92; *Partap R. & T. Factory* v. *State* (1965) 2 Punj. 32, ('66) A.Punj. 16, 24 (where the above test was applied without expressly referring to the passage); *Syed Habib* v. *Kamal Chand, supra; Maharashtra* v. *H. N. Rao, supra.*

[74] (1954) S.C.R. 873, ('54) A.SC. 220; *Govinda Pillai* v. *Padmanabha Pillai* ('65) A.Ker. 123 (F.B.) which held that a complete prohibition of trade in *kesari dal*, which is poisonous to human beings though, it would appear, harmless as fodder, would be justified as a reasonable restriction on the right to carry on trade assuming that trade in poisonous food grains like *kesari dal* was not regarded as *res extra commercium*: ibid. p. 128.

[75] ibid. p. 879. It will be seen that Mahajan C.J. *assumed*, what has subsequently been *decided*, that restrictions in Art. 19 include prohibition.

[76] (1904) 198 U.S. 45, 49 L.ed. 937.

reasonable man consider the restrictions reasonable?

"This case is decided upon an economic theory which a large part of the country does not entertain. If it were a question whether I agreed with that theory, I should desire to study it further and long before making up my mind. But I do not conceive that to be my duty, *because I strongly believe that my agreement or disagreement has nothing to do with the right of a majority to embody their opinions in law.* It is settled by various decisions of this court that state constitutions and state laws may regulate life in many ways which we as legislators might think as injudicious, or if you like as tyrannical, as this, and which, equally with this, interfere with the liberty to contract. . . . Some of these laws (upheld by the court) embody convictions or prejudices which judges are likely to share. Some may not. . . . I think that the word 'liberty,' in the 14th Amendment, is perverted when it is held to prevent the natural outcome of a dominant opinion, unless it can be said that a rational and fair man necessarily would admit that the statute proposed would infringe fundamental principles as they have been understood by the traditions of our people and our law. . . . A reasonable man might think (the impugned statute) a proper measure on the score of health. Men whom I certainly could not pronounce unreasonable would uphold it as a first instalment of a general regulation of the hours of work."[77] (italics supplied)

The judge's personal opinions are irrelevant

Thus, the test to be applied is not whether a judge personally considers particular restrictions unreasonable, but whether a reasonable man would necessarily consider them unreasonable. This caution is necessary if the judicial restraint of which Sastri C.J. spoke is to be maintained.[78] As a learned American writer has said, "the Court's power has been maintained by a wise refusal to employ it in unequal combat".[79]

Reasonableness to be judged with reference to the right which is restricted

10.20 Although restrictions may be put on the different rights contained in Art. 19(1) on a common ground, e.g. "in the interest of public order" on the rights contained in Art. 19(1) (*a*), (*b*) and (*c*), or on the ground of the "interest of the general public" as on the rights contained in Art. 19(1) (*d*) to (*g*), the reasonableness of the restriction has to be judged not with reference to the ground on which it can be imposed, but with reference to the fundamental right which is restricted. Consequently,

". . . a decision dealing with the validity of restrictions imposed on one of the rights conferred by Art. 19(1) cannot have much value as a precedent for adjudging the validity of the restrictions imposed on another right, even when the constitutional criterion is the same, namely, reasonableness, as the conclusion must depend on the cumulative effect of the varying facts and circumstances of each case."[80]

Reasonableness and Art. 14

10.21 A cognate question has arisen whether Art. 14 involves the concept of reasonableness and whether reasonableness in Art. 14 is the same as reasonableness under Art. 19. In *Surajmal* v. *I.T.C.*[81] P. B. Mukharji J. said that on a plain comparison of the language of Arts. 14 and 19, no question of reasonableness arose on the language of Art. 14 as distinguished from the specific words

---

[77] ibid. p. 949.

[78] The breakdown of this restraint in the U.S. Supreme Court led to a serious conflict between President Roosevelt and the Supreme Court in which the President called upon the Congress to pass a law reforming the Supreme Court. The Supreme Court saved itself by reversing its previous decisions. For an interesting account of this conflict, see "Struggle for Judicial Supremacy" by Robert H. Jackson, who was the Att.-General in President Roosevelt's administration, and later became a Judge of the U.S. Supreme Court.

[79] Roche, "Judicial Self-Restraint", *49 American Political Science Review,* 722 (1955), quoted in Forkosch, *Constitutional Law,* p. 59.

[80] *Madras* v. *V. G. Row* (1952) S.C.R. 597, 611, ('52) A.SC. 196.

[81] ('61) A.Cal. 578.

"reasonable restrictions" appearing in Art. 19(2) to (6). The only way in which reasonableness entered into Art. 14 was that the law required a reasonable classification having a reasonable nexus to the object of the law. In considering reasonable restrictions under Art. 19, the Court has not to consider the reasonableness of the law but only the reasonableness of the restrictions and to that extent only is legislative policy under review in a Court of law. A legislation may pass the test of reasonable restriction within the meaning of Art. 19. To read into Arts. 14 and 19 an equal standard of reasonableness would be to introduce in India the concept of "due process" of the American Law, and our Supreme Court has repeatedly held that "due process" does not apply to our Constitution.

Factors to be taken into account in judging reasonableness

10.22 Certain general considerations have been laid down in amplifying the tests of reasonableness stated above. Thus in considering whether restrictions are reasonable it is relevant to consider whether the law imposing them is temporary or permanent.[82] Again, where the State has to take swift decisions to meet emergent circumstances of apprehended danger, restrictions may be considered reasonable which would not be considered reasonable otherwise.[83] The reasonableness of both the substantive and the procedural provisions of the law must be considered,[84] and it is necessary to inquire whether the impugned law provides reasonable safeguards, as for example, by conferring a right of appeal or review, or a right to have the matter judicially determined.[85]

Reasonableness and Art. 19(1)(f) and (g)

10.23 Certain special questions about the reasonableness of restrictions have arisen in connection with Art. 19(1) (*f*) and (*g*) and they have had to be considered in the context of a planned economy. The decisions of the Supreme Court in connection with the import and export of goods show that the judgment of Government that particular restrictions are necessary is for practical purposes conclusive as to their reasonableness.[86] Again, though the Supreme Court has said more than once that tax laws are subject to Art. 19(1) (*f*) and (*g*), it is submitted that Art. 19(1) (*f*) and (*g*) has a very limited application to tax laws. The cases in which tax laws were held to be subject to Art. 19 were really cases where it could be said that under the guise of imposing a tax, the law confiscated property. It is submitted that the reasonableness of a

Reasonableness and tax laws

[82] *Dr. N. B. Khare* v. *Delhi* (1950) S.C.R. 519, 526, ('50) A.SC. 211; *Madras* v. *V. G. Row* (1952) S.C.R. 597, ('52) A.SC. 196 ["what may be regarded as a reasonable restriction imposed under such a statute (i.e. a temporary statute) will not necessarily be considered reasonable under the impugned Act, as the latter is a permanent measure, and any declaration made thereunder would continue in operation for an indefinite period until the Government should think fit to cancel it": ibid. pp. 609-10; *Gyan Prakash* v. *State* ('68) A.Mys. 61, 67 (upholding Part VI of the Mysore Rent Control Act, 1962, which was a temporary Act).

[83] See *Row's Case*, (1952) S.C.R. *supra* at p. 609.

[84] (1950) S.C.R. *supra* at pp. 524, 532; affirmed in *Row's Case* (1952) S.C.R. *supra* at pp. 606-7; *Nabin Chandra* v. *Orissa* ('57) A.Or. 56.

[85] ibid. at pp. 607-8; in *Jagdish Vastralaya* v. *Bihar* ('64) A.P. 180, it was held that s. 26(3), Bihar Shops & Establishments Act, 1954, as amended in 1959 did not impose unreasonable restrictions because it did not provide for a right of appeal. The authority under the amended s. 26 was an officer who had held judicial office or had judicial experience.

[86] See para 10.171.

taxing statute would be wholly beyond the competence of a Court for it involves an evaluation of factors which the Court is neither entitled, nor competent, to evaluate. The objects to be taxed, the persons to be taxed, the amount of the tax to be levied, the political, social and economic policies which a tax is designed to subserve, are all matters of political and legislative judgment, and they have been entrusted to the legislature and not to the Courts. As long as a tax retains its avowed character and does not confiscate property to the State under the guise of a tax, the reasonableness of a tax cannot be questioned.

Is a corporation a "citizen"?

10.24 In Part III of our Constitution, certain fundamental rights are conferred on "any person" or "all persons", *e.g.* by Arts. 14 and 25 (1) respectively, while other fundamental rights are conferred on "citizens" as in the present Art. 19 and in Arts. 15 and 16. As Art. 19 confers fundamental rights only on citizens, obviously aliens or foreigners cannot claim those rights. But can Corporations claim those rights? This question has assumed great importance, because increasingly, public and private business and trade is extensively carried on by companies, corporations, or registered societies. For example, newspapers are largely owned and published by public or private companies; trade unions are, at times, treated as bodies corporate; and property is owned by companies and corporations for their business. Valuable fundamental rights conferred by Art. 19 would be denied to companies and corporations if they were not citizens. The difficulty in treating a corporation as a "citizen" arose from the House of Lords' decision in *Salomon* v. *Salomon & Co.*[87] which held that a "one man company" was nevertheless a legal entity distinct and separate from its shareholders. *Salomon's Case* decisively rejected the theory that the company was the agent of its members or shareholders. Ever since *Salomon's Case* was decided, the principle that a company was a distinct legal entity separate from its members became a part of the law of India, and was applied to bodies corporate which were not companies. In the second edition of this book the question whether corporations were citizens was discussed at some length.[88] However, subsequent developments of the law have made a detailed discussion unnecessary for reasons which will presently appear.

Salomon v. *Saloman*: a corporation a separate entity from its members

10.25 Is a Corporation a citizen? This question was discussed at length in paras 15.59 to 15.68 in the second edition of this book with reference to conflicting decisions of the Supreme Court. However, that discussion is not reproduced here because of the submission made below that the whole subject requires to be considered afresh in view of the recent trend of Supreme Court decisions. The following is a brief account of important decisions of the Supreme Court. In *State Trading Corporation of India Ltd.* v. *C.T.O.*[89] a Bench of 9 Supreme Court judges held, by a majority of 7:2, that the State Trading Corporation (a corporation registered under the Companies Act) was not a citizen within the meaning of Art. 19, and therefore could not invoke Art. 19. In this case the

Cases holding that a corporation is not a citizen

[87] (1897) A.C. 22.
[88] See *Seervai*, Vol. I (2nd ed.) pp. 677-686.
[89] (1964) 4 S.C.R. 99, ('63) A.SC. 1811.

Supreme Court was not invited to "tear the corporate veil" but it was invited to do so in the *Telco Case*.[90] The Court declined to do so, observing that after the *State Trading Corporation Case* it was not possible to tear the corporate veil, for to do so would be to do indirectly what could not be done directly. Further, although the corporate veil had at times been torn in a limited number of cases in company law, the Court was not prepared to extend those cases further. The Court added that if it was desired to treat companies or corporations as citizens, that could be done by an amendment of the Citizenship Act. It may be observed that the question whether a company can claim to be a citizen has been linked with the question whether the totality, or the majority, of its shareholders were Indian citizens or foreigners. In *Indo-China Steam Navigation Co.* v. *Jasjit Singh*[91] the Supreme Court held that Art. 19(1) (*f*) was not available to a company, and more so to a "foreign" company. Secondly, that under Art. 31(1) a person could be deprived of property by authority of law and could challenge such deprivation only if Art. 19(1) were available. In the *Bank Nationalization Case*[92] the Supreme Court in effect decided the rights of the fourteen nationalized Banks under Art. 19(1) (*f*) on the petition of one shareholder, who claimed to be also a director of the Central Bank of India Ltd., without purporting to overrule earlier Supreme Court decisions. In the *Bennet Coleman Case*[93] Ray J. after referring to the *State Trading Corporation Case*, the *Telco Case*[94] and the *Express Newspapers* and the *Sakal Case*[95] observed that the *Bank Nationalization Case* had established that fundamental rights of shareholders as citizens were not lost when they associated together to form a company; and if their fundamental rights as shareholders were impaired by State action, their rights as shareholders would be protected. Ray J. developed the theory of agency holding that the shareholders acted through their company as its agents. After the *Bennet Coleman Case*, Mathew J. delivering the judgment of the Supreme Court in the *Ambica Mills Case*[96] referred to the *Bank Nationalization Case*, but he said that it was settled law that a corporation was not a citizen and could not claim fundamental rights under Art. 19.

The Ct declined to tear the corporate veil: the *Telco Case*

Cases holding that fundamental rights of shareholders not taken away by their membership of a corporation

10.26 It is submitted that the present state of the law is unsatisfactory, and the time is ripe for the whole question to be considered afresh in view of the tendency of the Courts to afford relief to shareholders of corporations and in view of the increasing tendency, even in Company Law, to tear the corporate veil. Further, the Supreme Court has now finally decided that (i) a State Corporation; (ii) a Government Company; (iii) a Company incorporated under the Companies Act; and (iv) a registered society are "the State" within the meaning of Art. 12 if in substance they are an agency or instrumentality of the State, notwithstanding that, in law, a body corporate is a separate legal entity from the

Submission: time ripe for a reconsideration of the whole question

---

[90] *The Tata Engineering & Locomotive Co. Ltd.* v. *Bihar* (1964) 6 S.C.R. 885, ('65) A.SC. 40.
[91] (1964) 6 S.C.R. 594, ('64) A.SC. 1140.
[92] *R. C. Cooper* v. *Union* (1970) S.C.R. 530, ('70) A.SC. 564.
[93] (1973) 2 S.C.R. 757, ('73) A.SC. 106.
[94] ('73) A.SC. at p. 112.
[95] ibid. pp. 112-3.
[96] *Gujarat* v. *Shri Ambica Mills* (1974) 3 S.C.R. 760, ('74) A.SC. 1300, 1306.

Corporate veil torn to determine whether a corporation is "the State"

members composing it.[97] If the corporate veil can be torn so that *the employees* of corporate bodies might not be deprived of their fundamental rights, there is no rational ground for not tearing the corporate veil so that *the shareholders or members* of a corporation who have ultimate control of the corporation may not be denied their fundamental rights. But before a question can arise whether a corporation is a citizen, two conditions must be satisfied. First, all or a majority of its shareholders must be Indian citizens; and, secondly, its management and control must be in the hands of Indian citizens. If both these conditions are satisfied, then the correct ground for holding that such a corporation is a citizen is that a Court will look behind the corporate veil to the persons, who in substance, though not in legal theory, control the management and run the company. This would also get rid of the absurd anamoly that although a partnership firm carrying on a small business can enforce its fundamental rights under Art. 19, companies, State corporations, Government companies and corporations created by statute carrying on business on the most extensive scale cannot claim those rights. It is submitted that although Gajendragadkar J. may have been right in holding in 1964 that the corporate veil could not be torn, and the tearing of the corporate veil must be limited to very narrow grounds, the passage of time has eroded that doctrine. Consequently, instead of treating the company as an agent of its shareholders, which it clearly is not, it would be more accurate to say that the Court will look behind the separate entity of the company to the shareholders who carry on the business, if the valuable fundamental rights conferred by Art. 19 are not to be defeated. This is not an ideal solution,[98] but it is the best that is to be had, since Parliament has not amended the Citizenship Act, as suggested by Gajendragadkar C.J. This suggestion itself shows that there is nothing incongruous in a Corporation being a citizen.

Submission: corporate veil should be torn if two conditions are satisfied

---

[97] See paras 7.13 to 7.32 of the text.

[98] With large companies, corporations or registered societies, this solution is unlikely to present practical difficulties. However, with Private Limited Companies established with a small capital, difficulties have arisen principally when the Court grants an interim stay of the operation of the impugned law or order. The grant of a stay is, no doubt, discretionary, and in granting it the Court would protect the interests of both parties as by requiring the deposit of the whole, or part, of the amount at stake, or by requiring a bank guarantee. But the case of a small private limited company presents a special problem. For example, a Private Limited Company with a capital of Rs. 5,000 held by two Indian citizens ran a prize competition of a gambling nature with a turnover of lacs of rupees. The company applied for, and obtained, a stay of the tax levied on each entry for the prize competition. The fact that the two shareholders were Indian citizens, enabled the company to claim the rights conferred by Art. 19(1). However, on the petitions being dismissed with costs by the Supreme Court, the heavy tax liability became incapable of being realized, as the Private Limited Company had no assets to meet it. If in a similar situation, a Private Limited Company invites the Court to tear the corporate veil to protect the fundamental rights of the shareholders, that is, for the benefit of the shareholders, justice requires that if the challenge to the impugned law or order fails and the company is unable to meet its liability, that the shareholders for whose benefit the corporate veil had been torn should bear the burden. In such a situation the judge has one of two options — he can refuse the stay or he can grant it on condition that the shareholders, who must be joined as parties, agree that in the event of the Company being unable to meet its liability, the shareholders would personally do so.

Freedom of Speech and Expression

10.27 Article 19 (1) (*a*) provides that "all citizens shall have the right to freedom of speech and expression." Article 19 (2) as originally enacted provided that

Art. 19(2) before and after amendment

"Nothing in sub-clause (*a*) of Cl. (1) shall affect the operation of any existing law in so far as it relates to, or prevents the State from making any law relating to, libel, slander, defamation, contempt of Court or any matter which offends against decency or morality or which *undermines the security* of, or *tends to overthrow*, the State."

This sub-Article was retrospectively amended by the Constitution (1st Amendment) Act, 1951, which provides

"(2) Nothing in sub-clause (*a*) of clause (1) shall affect the operation of any existing law, or prevent the State from making any law, in so far as such law imposes reasonable restrictions on the exercise of the right conferred by the said sub-clause in the interests of the security of the State, friendly relations with foreign States, public order, decency or morality, or in relation to contempt of Court, defamation or incitement to an offence."

As the First Amendment to the U.S. Constitution has been referred to by our Supreme Court in considering Art. 19 (1) (*a*) the relevant part of that Amendment is given below:

"Congress shall make no law . . . abridging the freedom of speech, or of the press."

Although Art. 19 (1) (*a*) does not mention the freedom of the press it was early settled by judicial decisions that freedom of speech and expression includes freedom of the press and circulation.[99] But,

Freedom of speech and expression includes freedom of the press: the extent of that freedom

". . . being only a right flowing from the freedom of speech and expression, the liberty of the Press in India stands on no higher footing than the freedom of speech and expression of a citizen and that no privilege attaches to the Press as such, that is to say, as distinct from the freedom of the citizen. In short, as regards citizens running a newspaper the position under our Constitution is the same as it was when the Judicial Committee decided . . . in *Arnold* v. *R*.[1] and as regards non-citizens the position may even be worse."[2]

---

[99] *Romesh Thappar* v. *Madras* (1950) S.C.R. 594, 597, ('50) A.SC. 124. ". . . there can be no doubt that freedom of speech and expression includes freedom of propagation of ideas, and that freedom is ensured by the freedom of circulation. 'Liberty of circulation is as essential to that freedom as the liberty of publication. Indeed, without circulation, the publication would be of little value': *Ex. p. Jackson* (1877) 96 U.S. 727, 736; 24 L. ed. 877; see also *Lovell* v. *City of Griffin* (1937) 303 U.S. 444, 82 L. ed. 949"; *Brij Bhushan* v. *Delhi* (1950) S.C.R. 605, 608, ('50) A.SC. 129: "There can be little doubt that the imposition of pre-censorship on a journal is a restriction on the liberty of the press which is an essential part of the right to freedom of speech and expression declared by Art. 19(1)(*a*)"; *Srinivasa* v. *Madras* ('51) A.M. 70, (1951) 1 M.L.J. 115. *Romesh Thappar's Case* was cited with approval in *Express Newspapers (Private) Ltd.* v. *Union* (1959) S.C.R. 12 at p. 120 (see also the discussion on freedom of the press at pp. 118-128); the *Express Newspapers Case*, and also the *Sakal Case* (1962) 3 S.C.R. 842, ('62) A.SC. 305 were cited with approval in *Bennett Coleman & Co. Ltd.* v. *Union* (1967) 2 S.C.R. 757, ('67) A.SC. 106 at pp. 117-8. The proposition in the text is too well settled to need the citation of other authorities.

[1] (1914) 41 I.A. 149, 169: "Their Lordships regret to find that there appeared on the one side in this case the time-worn fallacy that some kind of privilege attaches to the profession of the Press as distinguished from the members of the public. The freedom of the journalist is an ordinary part of the freedom of the subject, and to whatever lengths the subject in general may go, so also may the journalist, but, apart from statute law, his privilege is no other and no higher. The responsibilities which attach to his power in the dissemination of printed matter may, and in the case of a conscientious journalist do, make him more careful; but the range of his assertions, his criticisms, or his comments, is as wide as, and no wider than, that of any other subject. No privilege attaches to his position."

[2] *M. S. M. Sharma* v. *Shri Sri Krishna Sinha* (1959) Supp. 1 S.C.R. 806 at 838;

In *Express Newspapers (Private) Ltd.* v. *Union*[3] Bhagwati J. said that there was a paucity of authority in India on the nature, scope and extent of the fundamental right to the freedom of speech and expression and he added:

The Express Newspapers Case: Art. 19(1)(*a*) based on the 1st Amendment to U.S. Constitution

"... .the fundamental right to the freedom of speech and expression enshrined in ... our Constitution is based on (the provisions in) Amendment I of the Constitution of the United States ... and it would be therefore legitimate and proper to refer to those decisions of the Supreme Court of the United States of America in order to appreciate the true nature, scope and extent of this right in spite of the warning administered by this Court against use of American and other cases."[4]

Submission: the provisions of the two Constitutions are essentially different

It is submitted that the provisions of the two Constitutions as to freedom of speech and expression are essentially different, the difference being accentuated by provisions in our Constitution for preventive detention which have no counterpart in the U.S. Constitution. The First Amendment to the U.S. Constitution enacts an absolute prohibition, so that a heavy burden lies on anyone transgressing it to justify such transgression. Again, since the Amendment contains no exceptions, it is not surprising that exceptions have had to be evolved by judicial decisions which have limited the scope of such exceptions with increasing stringency. The position in India is different. The right to the freedom of speech and expression, and the limitations on that right, are contained in Art. 19(1) (*a*) read with sub-Art. (2). Laws which fall under sub-Art. (2) are expressly permitted by our Constitution and the problem in India is to determine whether an impugned law falls within Art. 19(2), and that is essentially a problem of construction. No doubt Art. 19(2) authorises the imposition of "reasonable restrictions", and in the end, the question of reasonableness is a question for a Court to decide. However, a law made in respect of the matters referred to in Art. 19(2) must *prima facie* be presumed to be constitutionally valid and due weight must be given to the legislative judgment on the question of reasonableness, though that judgment is subject to judicial review. It is difficult, if not impossible, to read into the words "reasonable restrictions" the test of "clear and present danger" evolved by the U.S. Supreme Court in dealing with the freedom of speech and the press. The diffference between the First Amendment and Art. 19(1) (*a*) was noted by Douglas J. in *Kingsley Corporation* v. *Regents of the University of New York*.[5] In holding that all pre-censorship of cinema films was constitutionally void, he said:

difference noticed by the U.S. Supreme Court

Kingsley Corporation Case

"If we had a provision in our Constitution for 'reasonable' regulation of the press such as India has included in hers[6] there would be room for argument that censorship in the interest of morality would be permissible."

---

fol. in *Ramnarayan* v. *State* ('70) A.M.P. 102, 105. In *Sewak Ram* v. *R. K. Karanjia* ('82) A.SC. 6, the passage from the judgment of the Privy Council set out in *f.n.* 1 above was quoted with approval.

[3] (1959) S.C.R. 12, 121-2; ('58) A.SC. 578.

[4] The warning was given in *Trav.-Cochin* v. *Bombay Co. Ltd.* (1952) S.C.R. 1112, 1120, ('52) A.SC. 366; *Bombay* v. *R. M. D. Chamarbaugwalla* (1957) S.C.R. 874, 918, ('57) A.SC. 699.

[5] 360 U.S. 684, 698, 3 L. ed. 2d. 1512, 1522.

[6] "Art. 19(2) of the Indian Constitution permits 'reasonable restrictions' on the exercise of the right of freedom of speech and expression, in the interest *inter alia*, of decency or morality, defamation or incitement to an offence. This limitation is strictly construed: any restriction amounting to an imposition which will 'operate

10.28 The above submission is reinforced by the fact that preventive detention for reasons connected with the security of a State, the maintenance of public order and the maintenance of supplies and services essential to the community is a subject of concurrent legislative power under Entry 3, List III, Sch. VII, and Art. 22 (3) to (7) provides safeguards of a very limited nature in respect of such detention. Safeguards for preventive detention are unusual visitors in the realm of fundamental rights, but their presence in the Part containing Fundamental Rights emphasizes the fact that though the freedoms conferred by our Constitution are valuable and highly prized human freedoms, even they must yield to the interest which society has in public order. Thus, in *Ram Singh* v. *Delhi*[7] the Supreme Court held that even though a law restricting freedom of speech and expression is not solely directed against undermining the security of the State or its overthrow, but is made generally in the interest of public order, it may not be protected by the unamended Art. 19 (2) and may therefore be void; an order of preventive detention cannot be held to be invalid merely because the detention was made with a view to prevent the making of speeches prejudicial to the maintenance of public order. It has become necessary to point out the radical difference between the provisions as to freedom of speech in the U.S. Constitution and our own, because the observations in the *Express Newspapers Case*[8] would otherwise lead to the application of tests in India which are wholly inconsistent with Art. 19 (1) (*a*) and (2). It is submitted that in *Santokh Singh* v. *Delhi Administration*[9] the Supreme Court has, in substance, overruled the observations of Bhagwati J. set out above, when it observed:

No provision for preventive detention in U.S. Constitution

Ram Singh's Case: order for preventive detention not bad because made to prevent the making of speeches

"In our opinion, it is hardly fruitful to refer to the American decisions particularly when this Court has more than once clearly enunciated the scope and effect of Art. 19(1)(*a*) and 19(2). . . . Our Constitution provides reasonably precise, general guidance in this matter. *It would thus be misleading to construe it in the light of American decisions given in a different context.*"[10] (italics supplied)

10.29 It has been rightly observed that to say that a thing is constitutional, is not to say that it is desirable.[11] Therefore, to say that restraints on the freedom of speech and expression are permissible under our Constitution is not to say that any particular restraint is desirable or ought to be imposed. The freedom of thought and expression, and the freedom of the press, are not only valuable freedoms in themselves, but are basic to a democratic form of Government which proceeds on the theory that problems of Government can be solved by the free exchange of thought and by public discussion. In the earlier editions of this book, it was said that a plea for freedom of thought, speech and expression is not necessary, nor is it necessary to refer to classic pleas for the liberty of thought to show that restraint on the freedom of thought "hinders

The great value attached to free speech in our Constitution

harshly' on speech or the press will be held invalid. . . . See *R. M. Seshadri* v. *District Magistrate, Tanjore* (1955) 1 S.C.R. 686, 690, ('54) A.SC. 747."

[7] (1951) S.C.R. 451, ('51) A.SC. 270. [8] (1959) S.C.R. 12, ('58) A.SC. 578.

[9] (1973) 3 S.C.R. 533, ('73) A.SC. 1091, 1095.

[10] ('73) A.SC. at p. 1095.

[11] *Dennis* v. *U.S.* (1950) 341 U.S. 494, 552-3, 95 L. ed. 1137, 1175 (*per* Frankfurter J.).

and retards the importation of our richest Merchandise, Truth." The high value attached to this freedom in our Constitution can therefore be taken as the basis of any discussion on the subject. However, the censorship imposed in 1975 (under the guise of an Emergency) on freedom of speech and expression, including the freedom of the press, the like of which India had never known, has made it necessary to say that no opportunity should be missed to emphasize the vital importance of freedom of speech and expression, which includes freedom to dissent, to a free democracy like ours. And any encroachment on such freedom should be resisted by every legal means made available to citizens by our Constitution. For, an injury to one citizen, or to one newspaper, is an injury to all citizens and to all newspapers. But the "invocation of constitutional liberties as part of the strategy for overthrowing them presents a dilemma to a free people",[12] a dilemma which has produced a sharp conflict of judicial opinion in the United States, as will presently appear. Our Constitution has resolved this dilemma by providing that even freedom of speech must yield to public order, for in the words of Jackson J. "the choice is not between order and liberty, but between liberty with order and anarchy without either"[13] and that doctrinaire logic must be tempered with a little practical wisdom, if a Bill of Rights is not to be converted into a "suicide pact".

But even free speech must yield to the requirements of public order

Changing attitudes in the U.S.: Blackstone's view adopted in 1897

10.30 The changing attitudes in the United States to the freedom of speech and press may briefly be stated as follows: The First Amendment was framed in the background of Blackstone's classic statement that the liberty of the press

> "consists in laying no previous restraints upon publications, and not in freedom from censure for criminal matter when published. Every free man has an undoubted right in law to air what sentiment he pleases before the public; to forbid this, is to destroy the freedom of the press: but if he publishes what is improper, mischievous, or illegal, he must take the consequences of his own temerity. To subject the press to the restrictive power of a licenser, . . . is to subject all freedom of sentiment to the prejudices of one man, and make him the arbitrary and infallible judge of all controverted points in learning, religion and Government. But to punish . . . any dangerous or offensive writings, which, when published, shall on a fair and impartial trial be adjudged of pernicious tendency, is necessary for the preservation of peace and good order, of Government and religion, the only solid foundations of civil liberty. Thus, the will of individuals is still left free; the abuse only of that free will is the object of legal punishment."[14]

The framers of the First Amendment had apparently no intention to change the law as stated by Blackstone, for as late as 1897 the U.S. Supreme Court declared:

> ". . . the first ten Amendments . . . commonly known as the Bill of Rights, were not intended to lay down any novel principles of government, but simply to embody certain guarantees and immunities which we had inherited from our English ancestors, and which had from time immemorial been subject to certain well recognized exceptions arising from the necessities of the case. In incorporating these principles into the fundamental law there was no intention of disregarding the exceptions, which continued to be recognised as if they had been formally expressed."[15]

---

12 *Per* Jackson J. dissenting in *Terminiello* v. *Chicago* (1948) 337 U.S. 1, 36, 93 L. ed. 1131, 1150.

13 93 L. ed. *supra* at p. 1151.

14 *Corwin*, p. 769.

15 *Robertson* v. *Baldwin* (1897) 165 U.S. 275, 281, 41 L. ed. 715.

Holmes J. speaking for the Court in 1907, said:

Same view affirmed by Holmes J. in 1907

"... the main purpose of such constitutional provisions is 'to prevent all such *previous restraints* upon publications as had been practised by other governments', and they generally do not prevent the subsequent punishment of such as may be deemed contrary to the public welfare. . . . The preliminary freedom extends as well to the false as to the true; the subsequent punishment may extend as well to the true as to the false."[16]

This was an uncompromising affirmation of Blackstone's view, but a change began to appear later, and the test of "clear and present danger" was formulated by Holmes J. in *Schenck* v. *U.S.*[17]

Change of view in 1918: the test of "clear and present danger" propounded by Holmes J.

"We admit that in many places and in ordinary times the defendants, in saying all that was said in the circular, would have been within their constitutional rights. But the character of every act depends upon the circumstances in which it is done . . . . The law's stringent protection of free speech would not protect a man in falsely shouting 'fire' in a theatre, and causing panic. It does not even protect a man from an injunction against uttering words that may have all the effect of force. . . . *The question in every case is whether the words used are used in such circumstances and are of such a nature as to create a clear and present danger that they will bring about the substantive evils that Congress has a right to prevent. It is a question of proximity and degree.*" (italics supplied)

Developing this theory in a famous passage he said:

"Persecution for the expression of opinions seems to me perfectly logical. If you have no doubt of your premises or your power and want a certain result with all your heart you naturally express your wishes in law and sweep away all opposition. To allow opposition by speech seems to indicate that you think the speech impotent, as when a man says that he has squared the circle, or that you do not care wholeheartedly for the result, or that you doubt either your power or your premises. But when men have realized that time has upset many fighting faiths, they may come to believe even more than they believe the very foundations of their own conduct that the ultimate good desired is better reached by free trade in ideas, — that the best test of truth is the power of the thought to get itself accepted in the competition of the market; and that truth is the only ground upon which their wishes safely can be carried out. That, at any rate, is the theory of our Constitution. It is an experiment, as all life is an experiment."[18]

Subsequent decisions of the U.S. Supreme Court show the difficult problems posed by the subversive activities of organized totalitarian parties—communist or fascist—working in secret through highly trained men committed to the subversion of the State and to a denial of the freedoms embodied in the U.S. Constitution. The time and method of overthrowing or subverting the State are decided by the party, which would naturally choose the moment when Government is embarrassed or in difficulties. Must the "clear and present danger" test be applied to the subversive activities of such a party? In two very powerful dissents Jackson J. said, it is submitted rightly, that Holmes's test had no application to the problems thus raised. In *Terminiello* v. *Chicago*[19] he said:

Controversies in the U.S. over the test of "clear and present danger"

"Invocation of constitutional liberties as part of the strategy for over-throwing them presents a dilemma to a free people which may not be soluble by constitutional logic alone. . . . This Court has gone far toward accepting the doctrine that civil liberty means the removal of all restraints from these crowds and that all local attempts to maintain order are impairments of the liberty of the citizen. The choice is not between order and liberty. It is between liberty

Jackson J.'s dissent in *Terminiello's Case*

---

[16] *Patterson* v. *Colorado* (1906) 205 U.S. 454, 462, 51 L. ed. 879, 881.
[17] (1918) 249 U.S. 47, 52, 63 L. ed. 470, 473-4.
[18] *Abrams* v. *U.S.* (1919) 250 U.S. 616, 629; 62 L. ed. 1173, 1180.
[19] (1948) 337 U.S. 1, 36-7; 93 L. ed. 1131, 1150-51.

with order and anarchy without either. There is danger that, if the Court does not temper its doctrinaire logic with a little practical wisdom, it will convert the constitutional Bill of Rights into a suicide pact."

repeated in *Dennis* v. *United States*

Again, in *Dennis* v. *United States*[20] after observing that he would save the "clear and present danger" test as a rule of reason in the kind of cases for which it was devised, he continued:

"Unless we are to hold our Government captive in a judge-made verbal trap, we must approach the problem of a well-organized, nation-wide conspiracy, such as I have described, as realistically as our predecessors faced the trivialities that were being prosecuted until they were checked with a rule of reason. I think reason is lacking for applying that test to this case."[21]

In order to apply that test to the kind of case before the Court, it would have to appraise imponderables,

"including international and national phenomena which baffle the best informed foreign offices and our most experienced politicians. We would have to foresee and predict the effectiveness of Communist propaganda, opportunities for infiltration, whether and when, a time will come that they consider propitious for action, and whether and how fast our existing government will deteriorate. And we would have to speculate as to whether an approaching Communist coup would not be anticipated by a nationalistic fascist movement. No doctrine can be sound whose application requires us to make a prophecy of that sort in the guise of a legal decision. The judicial process simply is not adequate to a trial of such far-flung issues."[22]

The test of "clear and present danger" rejected by our Supreme Court

The test of "clear and present danger" has been rejected by our Supreme Court because the framework of our Constitution differed from that of the U.S. Constitution.[23] It is submitted that the framers of our Constitution appear to have taken the view which Lord Sumner expressed in a passage as famous as that of Holmes J.:

Lord Sumner's approach in *Bowman* v. *Secular Society* adopted by our Courts

"The words, as well as the acts, which tend to endanger society differ from time to time in proportion as society is stable or insecure in fact, or is believed by its reasonable members to be open to assault. In the present day meetings or processions are held lawful which a hundred and fifty years ago would have been deemed seditious, and this is not because the law is weaker or has changed, but because, the times having changed, society is stronger than before. In the present day reasonable men do not apprehend the dissolution or downfall of society because religion is publicly assailed by methods not scandalous. Whether it is possible that in the future irreligious attacks, designed to undermine fundamental institutions of our society, may come to be criminal in themselves, as constituting a public danger, is a matter that does not arise. The fact that opinion grounded on experience has moved one way does not in law preclude the possibility of its moving on fresh experiences in the other; nor does it bind succeeding generations, when conditions have again changed. After all, the question whether a given opinion is a danger to society is a question of the times and is a question of fact. I desire to say nothing that would limit the right of society to protect itself by process of law from the dangers of the movement, whatever that right may be, but only to say that, experience having proved dangers once thought real to be now negligible, and dangers once very possibly imminent to have now passed away, there is nothing in the general rules as to blasphemy and irreligion

---

[20] (1950) 341 U.S. 494, 95 L. ed. 1137. [21] 95 L. ed. *supra* at pp. 1183, 1184.

[22] ibid. p. 1184. Vinson C.J. with the concurrence of Reed, Burton and Minton JJ. held that the case satisfied the test of "clear and present danger". Frankfurter J. concurred in the result but said of the "clear and present danger test": ". . . It were far better that the phrase be abandoned than that it be sounded once more to hide from the believers in an absolute right of free speech the plain fact that the interest in speech, profoundly important as it is, is no more conclusive in judicial review than other attributes of democracy or than a determination of the people's representatives that a measure is necessary to assure the safety of government itself." (ibid. p. 1171).

[23] *Babulal Parate* v. *Maharashtra* (1961) 3 S.C.R. 423, ('61) A.SC. 884.

. . . which prevents us from varying their application to the particular circumstances of our time in accordance with that experience."[24]

and judgments of the Indian Courts show that the approach indicated by Lord Sumner is best adapted for determining the reasonableness of restrictions.

A literal reading of Art. 19(2) should not be adopted

10.31 Before considering Supreme Court decisions on Art. 19 (2), we must consider at the outset whether the requirement of reasonable restrictions apply to a law relating to defamation, contempt of court or incitement to an offence. In *State* v. *Editor, Matrubhumi*[25] the Court said:

". . . whether the qualification of reasonable restrictions applies also to law relating to defamation or contempt of court admits of doubt, for removing words not material Art. 19(2) would read . . . 'Nothing in sub-cl. (*a*) of cl. (1) shall affect the operation of any existing law or prevent the State from making any law in so far as such law imposes reasonable restrictions in the exercise of the right conferred by the said sub-clause . . . in relation to contempt of court, defamation or incitement to an offence.' Read in this way, cl. (2) . . . does not sound to be good English and conveys no meaning. Therefore, one way of reading clause (2) is that the words in so far as such law imposes reasonable restrictions on the exercise of the right conferred by the said sub-clause do not relate to any existing law or do not prevent the State from making any law in relation to contempt of Court, defamation or incitement to an offence. It is, however, unnecessary for the purpose of the present case to decide this point."

There is considerable force in the doubt expressed. However, it is submitted that a literal reading ought not to be allowed to prevail because it would then be open to a legislature to make a law of defamation providing that the truth of a statement shall be no defence to defamation in a civil action, and no defence in a criminal prosecution for defamation, even if it is made for the public good. To uphold unrestricted legislative power to make true statements for the public good, a crime, would be to reduce to a mockery the fundamental right to freedom of speech and expression. As the main object of the Article is clear, it cannot be reduced to a nullity by the draftsman's unskilfulness, and the Court would be entitled, and indeed bound, to interpret the Article so as to avoid such a result.[26] By a simple transposition of the words used in the material part of the Article, it would read:

"Nothing in sub-clause (*a*) of clause (1) shall affect the operation of any existing law or prevent the State from making any law . . . *in relation to contempt of Court, defamation or incitement to an offence* in so far as such law imposes reasonable restrictions on the exercise of the right conferred by the said sub-clause (1)(*a*)." (The italicised words are those which have been transposed.)

and it is submitted that the Article should be so read.

The unamended Art. 19(2)

10.32 We must now consider the decisions of the Supreme Court in *Romesh Thappar* v. *Madras*[27] and *Brij Bhushan* v. *Delhi*,[28] both of which were decided on the unamended Art. 19 (2). These cases appear to have been heard together[29] and the majority decision in

[24] *Bowman* v. *Secular Society Ltd.* (1917) A.C. 406, 466-7.
[25] ('55) A.Or. 36, 39.
[26] *Salmon* v. *Duncombe* (1886) 11 App. Cas. 627; see *Maxwell*, p. 221.
[27] (1950) S.C.R. 594, ('50) A.SC. 124.
[28] (1950) S.C.R. 605, ('50) A.SC. 129.
[29] In *Romesh Thappar's Case*, Fazl Ali J. refers to the reasons given by him in *Brij Bhushan's Case* as deciding the issue.

Romesh Thappar's Case: majority view

those cases led to a retrospective amendment of Art. 19(2). In *Romesh Thappar's Case* the majority held that s. 9(1-A), of the Madras Maintenance of Public Order Act, 1949, authorised the imposition of restrictions for the purposes of securing public safety and for the maintenance of public order and that these purposes were wider than those relating to the security, or to the overthrow, of the State. As the restrictions imposed were wide enough to cover permissible as well as impermissible restrictions, the law must be struck down as a whole, since the restraint put on the freedom of speech was not justified by Art. 19(2). The omission of the word 'sedition' from Art. 19(2), although it had been included in the draft Article,[30] was taken as indicating that criticism of Government exciting disaffection or bad feeling was not to be regarded as justifying restrictions on the freedom of speech and expression unless it was such as to undermine the security of the State or tended to its overthrow.

Dissent of Fazl Ali J.

Fazl Ali J. dissented. He held that though literally construed the Act may justify restrictions even in cases of trivial offences, in the context of the Act, it could only relate to serious offences affecting public order. He explained the omission of the word 'sedition' by saying that it had given rise to a conflict of judicial opinion between the Federal Court and the Privy Council, and the framers of the Constitution avoided the word by using words wide enough to include sedition as an offence affecting public order.

Brij Bhushan's Case

In *Brij Bhushan's Case*, an order issued under s. 7(1) (*c*), East Punjab Public Safety Act, 1949, imposed pre-censorship on an English Weekly on the ground that it was necessary to maintain public safety and public order. The majority judgment quoted a passage from *Blackstone's Commentaries*[31] to show that pre-censorship was a restraint on freedom of speech. For the rest, the decision was concluded by the majority decision in *Romesh Thappar's Case*.

Fazl Ali J. adheres to his dissent

Fazl Ali J. adhered to his dissent in *Romesh Thappar's Case*. Though the matter is now academic in view of the subsequent amendment, it is submitted that the dissenting judgment is correct. For, if two interpretations were possible, it was the duty of the Court to give a narrower interpretation to the words used in the Act in order to save its validity.

Retrospective amendment of Art. 19(2)

However, as stated earlier, Art. 19(2) was amended with retrospective effect and the view taken by Fazl Ali J. appears to have been accepted by the insertion in the Article of the words "public order". The effect of the retrospective Amendment was considered in *Bihar* v. *Shailabala Devi*[32] where s. 4(1) (*a*), Indian Press (Emergency Powers) Act, 1931, was impugned as violating Art. 19(1) (*a*).

Shailabala Devi's Case, Romesh Thapar's Case, and Brij Bhushan's Case inapplicable after amendment

Mahajan J. held that *Romesh Thappar's Case* and *Brij Bhushan's Case*[33] had no application and that those decisions had been misunderstood and misapplied in the lower Court. In any event, he held that they had no application after the amendment which introduced the words "public order" in Art. 19(2).

Jumuna Prasad's Case:

10.33 Several statutory provisions have been impugned on the ground that they violated Art. 19(1) (*a*) and were not saved by Art. 19(2). Before dealing with decided cases, a few general observations may be made. First, Art. 19(1) (*a*) has no application to

[30] Draft Article 13(2).
[31] A fuller quotation of the passage is set out in para 10.30.
[32] (1952) S.C.R. 654, ('52) A.SC. 329. [33] *Supra*.

a law which confers certain statutory rights subject to certain statutory restrictions, including restrictions on the freedom of speech. Thus, in *Jumuna Prasad* v. *Lachhi Ram*[34] the Supreme Court held that ss. 123(5) and 124(5), Representation of the people Act, 1951, did not interfere with a citizen's fundamental right to the freedom of speech; they merely prescribed conditions to be observed if he wanted to enter Parliament. The right to contest an election was not a common law right, but a right created by a statute to be exercised on the conditions there laid down. If a person wished to exercise his right to freedom of speech, the impugned sections did not prevent his doing so; he could exercise that right and not stand as a candidate for Parliament. Similarly, in *Sakhawat Ali* v. *Orissa*[35] the Supreme Court held that s. 16(1) (ix), Orissa Municipal Act, 1950, by which a paid legal practitioner on behalf of or against the Municipality was disqualified for election to a seat in such Municipality did not violate the legal practitioner's right under Art. 19(1) (*g*). The right to stand as a candidate for an election was not a fundamental right and it was open to the petitioner to practise as a legal practitioner and not stand as a candidate for an election. Secondly, as observed by the Supreme Court in *Ramji Lal Modi* v. *U.P.*[36] the ambit of the amended Art. 19(2) is very wide, for the words "in the interests of" are much wider than the words "for the maintenance of". In that case, s. 295A, I.P.C., was impugned as violating Art. 19(1) (*a*). It was contended that insults to the religion or religious belief of a class of citizens of India may not lead to public disorder in some cases and therefore a law, making such insults punishable could not be described to be in the interest of public order. In rejecting this argument, the court said that Art. 19(2)

restrictions on speeh imposed by the Representation of the People Act upheld

Right to stand as a candidate for an election not a fundamental right: *Sakhawat Ali* v. *Orissa*

the words "in the interests of" much wider than the words "for the maintenance of": *Ramji Lal Modi's Case*

". . . protects a law imposing reasonable restrictions on the exercise of the right to freedom of speech and expression 'in the interest of public order', which is much wider than 'for maintenance of' public order. If, therefore, certain activities have a tendency to cause public disorder, a law penalising such activities as an offence cannot but be held to be a law imposing reason-

---

[34] (1955) 1 S.C.R. 608, ('54) A.SC. 686; fol. in *H. A. K. Rao* v. *Institute of Chartered Accountants* ('65) A.Mys. 112 (upholding provisions which prohibited canvassing of votes by visiting places of business or residences of voters or in any other manner. The right to canvass etc. was incidental to a statutory right and such incidental rights could be regulated by statute. The restrictions were reasonable); also fol. in *Bhauri Lal* v. *S.D.O., Jamatra* ('73) A.P. 1 (F.B.) at pp. 14-5 [*held*, that the right to acquire title by adverse possession was a statutory right under the Limitation Act and not a common law right; hence ss. 42 and 69, Santal Parganas Tenancy (Supplementary Provisions) Act, 1949, did not attract Art. 19(1)(*f*). S. 20(5), 3rd. proviso of the same Act did not violate Art. 19(1)(*f*) because it did away with the right to hold and dispose of property in respect of which a person had acquired title by adverse possession]; *Harbans Lal* v. *State* ('71) A.P. & H. 379, 380 (*held*, without reference to authorities, that the right to vote was not a fundamental right but a statutory right, and the right must be exercised according to validly made rules).

[35] (1955) 1 S.C.R. 1004, ('55) A.SC. 166 [*Jumuna Prasad's Case* was not cited or referred to. The Court further added that if disqualification were treated as a restriction, it was a reasonable restriction for preserving the purity of public life. In *Bishnu Charan* v. *Orissa* ('52) A.Or. 11, the same view had been taken of s. 16(1)(*ix*)].

[36] (1957) S.C.R. 860, ('57) A.SC. 620; fol. in *Public Prosecutor* v. *Ramaswami* ('64) A.M. 258.

able restrictions 'in the interests of public order' although in some cases those activities may not actually lead to a breach of public order."[37]

Jang Bahadur's Case: rights under Art. 19(1) must not violate the rights of others.

Lastly, in *Jang Bahadur* v. *Principal, Mohindra College*,[38] Teja Singh C.J. said that apart from the qualifications contained in Cls. (2) to (6) of Art. 19, there was the further qualification that the rights conferred by Art. 19 (1) must not violate the rights of others. In that case, the petitioner had written a highly defamatory circular defaming, among others, the respondent, who was the Principal of the College in which the petitioner was studying. The respondent rusticated the petitioner, who contended that such rustication violated the freedom of speech guaranteed to him under Art. 19 (1) (*a*). In repelling the contention, the court said that the rights conferred by Art. 19 (1) were subject to the qualification that they did not violate the rights of others; thus the right to move freely throughout the territory of India did not confer the right to walk over other people's property. In any event, Art. 19 (1) (*a*) did not entitle the petitioner to defame the respondent and the action taken by the respondent was in the interest of discipline and did not violate Art. 19 (1) (*a*).

"Sedition": s. 124A I.P.C.: conflicting views about its validity

10.34 We have seen that the draft Article which corresponded to Art. 19 (2) contained the word 'sedition'. The omission of this word in Art. 19 (2) gave rise to a comment in *Romesh Thappar's Case* and was explained by Fazal Ali J. in *Brij Bhushan's Case*. However, the constitutional validity of s. 124A, I.P.C.[39] which defined the offence of 'sedition', was directly raised in several cases and a brief statement of the state of the law relating to sedition is necessary for an understanding of the constitutional issue involved. A full historical account of s. 124A, I.P.C. will be found in *Kedar Nath Singh* v. *Bihar*[40] to be presently noticed, but the position may be briefly stated thus: there is considerable authority in English law for the view that "public disorder", or incitement to, or reasonable likelihood of, public disorder, is the gist of the offence of sedition and that the acts or words complained of must either incite to disorder or must be such as to satisfy reasonable men that that is their intention or tendency. In *Niharendu Dutt Majumdar* v. *R.*[41] Gwyer C.J. expressed this view in a brilliant and masterly exposition of the law of sedition. On the other hand, in his charge to the jury, in *R.* v. *Bal Gangadhar Tilak*[42] Strachey J. had said:

Two views of the nature of sedition: Gwyer C.J.'s view in *Majumdar's Case*

". . . the express words (of s. 124A, I.P.C. itself) . . . make exciting or attempting to excite certain feelings, and not the inducing or attempting to induce

---

[37] ('57) A.SC. *supra* at p. 622. The distinction emphasised above was repeated in *Virendra* v. *Punjab* (1958) S.C.R. 308, 317-8, ('57) A.SC. 896. The above decisions were followed in *Mohamad Khan* v. *Kerala* ('64) A.Ker. 104 where s. 31, T.C. Public Safety Measures Act was upheld on the ground that rightly interpreted it punished only the publication of a false rumour or report or information. Even otherwise the restrictions imposed by it were reasonable.

[38] ('51) A.Pep. 59.

[39] S. 124A. *Sedition.*—"Whoever by words, either spoken or written, or by signs, or by visible representation, or otherwise, brings or attempts to bring into hatred or contempt, or excites or attempts to excite disaffection towards, the Government established by law in India, shall be punished. . . ."

[40] (1962) Supp. (2) S.C.R. 769, ('62) A.SC. 955; *G. V. Godse* v. *Union* ('71) A.B. 56, 72 [*held*, that for the reasons given in *Kedar Nath Singh's Case* in upholding s. 124A, I.P.C., and in *Ramjilal Mody's Case* (*f.n.* 36 above) in upholding s. 295A, I.P.C., the impugned s. 153A, I.P.C. did not violate Art. 19(1)(*a*) since the acts made punishable by s. 153A were clearly those calculated to disturb public order].

[41] (1942) F.C.R. 38, ('42) A.FC. 22. [42] (1898) 22 Bom. 112.

to any course of action such as rebellion or forcible resistance, the test of guilt. . . ."[43]

In *R.* v. *Sadashiv Narayan Bhalerao*[44] the Privy Council approved the charge of Strachey J., and disapproved the judgment of Gwyer C.J. by saying that the English authorities on sedition were not relevant in considering the offence defined in s. 124A, I.P.C. The Privy Council said that the word 'sedition' was not mentioned in the section but only in the marginal note to indicate the offence, and the nature of the offence must be found from the terms of the section itself. Thus at the commencement of the Constitution two views had been taken of 'sedition': that of Gwyer C.J. based on English authorities and that of the Privy Council based on the language of s. 124A, I.P.C. This difference of view produced conflicting decisions in the High Courts when s. 124A was impugned as violating Art. 19 (1) (*a*).

The Privy Council view in *Bhalerao's Case*

10.35 In *Tara Singh Gopichand* v. *State*[45] it was held that s. 124A, I.P.C., was void as violating Art. 19 (1) (*a*). For, under s. 124A, sedition consisted in exciting or attempting to excite in others certain bad feelings towards the Government, and in some instances at least, the unsuccessful attempt to excite such feelings would not undermine or tend to overthrow the State, and the whole section was invalidated, relying on *Romesh Thappar's Case*.[46] *Gopichand's Case* was distinguished in *D. Soren* v. *State*[47] by saying that the position had been altered by the amendment of Art. 19 (2) and that the reasoning in *Romesh Thappar's Case* no longer applied to the amended Art. 19 (2). Das J. referred to the two views of sedition mentioned above and held that the Court must, if possible, accept that view which would validate the law and reject that view which would invalidate it. He said that the view taken by Gwyer C.J. was correct and that the Privy Council had taken an unduly literal view. However, even if that view were adopted, Lord Sumner's observations in *Bowman* v. *Secular Society Ltd.*[48] would justify the Court in giving a liberal interpretation to the section in order to avoid constitutional invalidity. But in *Ram Narain* v. *State*[49] it was held that in view of *Majumdar's Case*, s. 124A, I.P.C., was invalid. This conflict was resolved by the Supreme Court in *Kedar Nath Singh* v. *Bihar*[50] by holding that, *rightly interpreted*, s. 124A did not violate Art. 19 (1) (*a*). After setting out the history of s. 124A, and the different views expressed by the Federal Court and the Privy Council, the Supreme Court said that it was well settled that if two views of a constitutional provision were possible, that view ought to be adopted which would validate the provision, in preference to the view which would invalidate it. After referring to the distinction which had been made by the Supreme Court in *Ramji Lal Modi* v. *U.P.*[51] between the words "in the interest of" and

s. 124A I.P.C. held valid by some Courts and void by others

Supreme Court resolves the conflict in *Kedar Nath's Case*

[43] 22 Bom. *supra* at p. 135.
[44] (1947) 74 I.A. 89, 49 Bom.L.R. 526, ('47) A.PC. 82.
[45] (1951) Punj. 193, ('51) A.Punj. 27.
[46] (1950) S.C.R. 594, ('50) A.SC. 124.
[47] (1953) Pat. 1104, ('54) A.P. 254.
[48] Quoted in para 10.30.
[49] (1958) 2 All. 84, (F.B.), ('59) A.A. 101.
[50] (1962) Supp. (2) S.C.R. 769, ('62) A.SC. 955; fol. in *Wajieh Uddnin* v. *State* ('63) A.A. 335, (1963) A.L.J. 21, and s. 153-A I.P.C. was held not violative of Art. 19(1)(*a*).
[51] (1954) S.C.R. 608, ('54) A.SC. 686.

the words "for the maintenance of" which distinction had also been adverted to in *Soren's Case*[52], the Court said:

"... the expression 'the Government established by law' ... is the visible symbol of the State. The very existence of the State will be in jeopardy if the Government established by law is subverted. Hence the continued existence of a Government established by law is an essential condition of the stability of the State. That is why 'sedition' as the offence in s. 124A has been characterised, comes under Chapter VI relating to offences against the State. Hence any acts within the meaning of s. 124A which have the effect of subverting the Government by bringing that Government into contempt or hatred or creating disaffection against it, would be within the penal statute because the feeling of disloyalty to the Government established by law or enmity to it imports the idea of tendency to public disorder by the use of actual violence or incitement to violence. In other words, any written or spoken words, etc., which have implicit in them the idea of subverting Government by violent means, which are compendiously included in the term 'revolution', have been made penal by the section in question. But the section has taken care to indicate clearly that strong words used to express disapprobation of the measures of Government with a view to their improvement or alteration by lawful means would not come within the section. Similarly, comments, however strongly worded, expressing disapprobation of actions of the Government, without exciting those feelings which generate the inclination to cause public disorder by acts of violence, would not be penal. In other words, disloyalty to Government established by law is not the same thing as commenting in strong terms upon the measures or acts of Government, or its agencies, so as to ameliorate the condition of the people or to secure the cancellation or alteration of those acts or measures by lawful means, that is to say, without exciting those feelings of enmity and disloyalty which imply incitement to public disorder or the use of violence."[53]

S. 124A, I.P.C. valid on a true construction: Gwyer C.J.'s view adopted

The Supreme Court held that s. 124A[54] was constitutionally valid once its application was limited to acts involving an intention or a tendency to create disorder or disturbance of law and order or incitement to violence. In view of this judgment it is submitted that the decision in *Balroop Sharma* v. *U.P.*[55] is no longer good law. There, it was held that s. 108, Cr.P.C., which provided that a person could be proceeded against for disseminating any seditious matter did not violate Art. 19 (1) (*a*) even if a law providing for sedition (s. 124A, I.P.C.) was void, because no one had the fundamental right to disseminate seditious matter. It is submitted that if the matter disseminated did not fall within the definition of 'sedition' as laid down by the Supreme Court, the matter could not be looked upon as seditious and there would be a clear right to disseminate that matter.

S. 144 Cr.P.C. held valid

10.36 In *V. G. Deshpandey* v. *City Magistrate*[56] the question whether s. 144, Cr.P.C., violated Art. 19 (1) (*a*) was raised but not decided.

---

[52] *Supra*.

[53] (1962) Supp. (2) S.C.R. 769, 805-6, ('62) A.SC. 955; *Indramani Singh* v. *Manipur* ('56) A.Mani. 9 (upholding s. 124A, I.P.C.). In *State* v. *Ramanand Tiwari* ('56) A.P. 188, it was held that s. 5, Bihar Essential Services Maintenance Act, did not go beyond the constitutionally permissible limit if its provisions were subject to the three explanations mentioned in s. 124-A, I.P.C. Read in the context of s. 3, s. 5 of the Bihar Act was easily intelligible.

[54] Also s. 505, I.P.C.

[55] ('56) A.A. 270, (1956) A.L.J. 148. In so far as it was held in *State* v. *Hariprasad Jethalal* ('52) A.Sau. 25 that s. 4(1)(*d*) of the Press (Emergency Powers) Act, 1931, violated Art. 19(1)(*a*) because every news sheet which brings Government into contempt does not necessarily undermine the security of the State, the case would require reconsideration in view of the Supreme Court decision in *Kedar Nath's Case*. The decision, however was rendered on the unamended Article 19(2).

[56] ('53) A.A. 577, (1953) A.L.J. 419 [*held*, that if a magistrate apprehended a breach of the peace he had a right to pass an order under s. 144 Cr.P.C. and without

However, in *Raj Narain* v. *Dist. Magistrate*[57] it was held that s. 144, Cr.P.C. imposed reasonable restrictions on the right conferred by Art. 19(1)(*a*) and (*b*). The same view was taken by the Supreme Court in *Babulal Parate* v. *Maharashtra*.[58] In that case it was contended that the section violated Art. 19(1)(*a*) and (*b*), and the test of clear and present danger laid down in *Schenck's Case*[59] was invoked in support. The Supreme Court rejected the test by saying that the framework of our Constitution was different from that of the United States, and there was nothing in the U.S. Constitution corresponding to Art. 19(2) to (6).[60] S. 144, Cr.P.C., did not impose unreasonable restrictions on the rights conferred by Art. 19(1)(*a*) and (*b*) because (i) the power there conferred was to be exercised by a Magistrate in an emergency and was conditioned by the objects for which it was to be exercised; (ii) even where there was an *ex parte* order, there was an opportunity to be heard and the order could be cancelled or modified; (iii) the order was subject to judicial review; (iv) no one had a right to cause obstruction, annoyance, injury, etc. to another; (v) the order was of a limited duration.[61] This decision was followed in *Ram Manohar Lohia* v. *State*.[62]

Babulal Parate's Case: the "clear and present danger test" rejected by our Supreme Court

10.37 In *Santokh Singh* v. *Delhi Administration*,[63] s. 9, Punjab Security of the State Act, 1953[64] was impugned as violating Art. 19(1)(*a*). The Supreme Court rejected this contention and held that reading s. 9 and Art. 19(2) it was obvious that the only matter specifically contained in s. 9—in addition to those stated in Art. 19(2)—related to the offending speech, words or other publication, which "tends to overthrow the State". This additional matter clearly fell within the expression "incitement to an offence prejudicial to the security of the State" contained in s. 9, and within the words in Art. 19(2) "reasonable restrictions . . . in the interest of . . .

Santokh Singh's Case and Art. 19(2)

violating Art. 19(1)(*a*), direct a person not to make a speech which might cause a breach of the peace. The question whether there was such an apprehension must be left to the magistrate and unless his order was on the face of it absurd or *mala fide*, the Court would not interfere].

[57] ('56) A.A. 481, (1956) A.L.J. 671.

[58] (1961) 3 S.C.R. 423, ('61) A.SC. 884. In view of this decision *Kamla Kant* v. *Bihar* (1962) 41 Pat. 871, ('62) A.P. 292 which held that s. 144 Cr.P.C. violated Art. 19(1)(*b*), (*c*) and (*d*), is not good law. The decision in *Babulal Parate's Case* was fol. in *Ram Manohar Lohia* v. *State* ('68) A.A. 110, (1967) A.L.J. 573; *Madhu Limaye* v. *S.D.M., Monghyr* (1971) 2 S.C.R. 711, ('71) A.SC. 2486 ["All these matters were considered by this court in *Babulal Parate's Case*. . . . We have reconsidered all these matters and are satisfied that there are sufficient safeguards available to the person affected by the order and the restrictions therefore are reasonable. We are of the opinion that s. 144 (Cr.P.C.) is not unconstitutional if properly applied and the fact that it may be abused is no ground for striking it down": ('71) A.SC. at p. 2497]. It is not clear whether the whole section has been held "not unconstitutional" or whether this pronouncement is subject to the observation at p. 2496 "But the second portion of sub-s. 5 (of s. 144) was declared violative of Art. 19 in (*Bihar* v. *K. K. Misra*) 1969 (3) S.C.C. 337", ('71) A.SC. 1643.

[59] (1918) 249 U.S. 47, 52, 63 L. ed. 470, 473-4.

[60] ('61) A.SC. *supra* at pp. 890-91.

[61] *State* v. *Deadley Misra* ('54) A.A. 738, (1954) A.L.J. 440 [after the amendment of Art. 19(2) there can be no doubt that s. 144, Cr.P.C. was never in conflict with Art. 19(1)(*a*)].

[62] ('68) A.A. 100, 104, (1967) A.L.J. 573.

[63] (1973) 3 S.C.R. 533, ('73) A.SC. 1091.

[64] ('73) A.SC. p. 1093 where the section is set out.

security of the State", since "anything tending to overthrow the State must necessarily be prejudicial to the security of the State."[65]

K. Narayanan's Case: content of freedom of speech and expression

10.38 In *K. Narayanan* v. *State*[66] it was held that the freedom of speech and expression guaranteed by Art. 19(1)(*a*) included the freedom to acquire knowledge, to read books and periodicals and read any type of literature, subject only to reasonable restrictions being placed on such right. It was further held, that the detention of a person under a law, such as the Maintenance of Internal Security Act, 1971, had the necessary consequences of excluding the exercise by him of the freedoms guaranteed by Art. 19(1)(*b*), (*c*), (*d*), (*e*) and (*g*), but it did not exclude the right under Art. 19(1)(*a*) though such freedom can be subject to reasonable restrictions on the grounds mentioned in Art. 19(2). Consequently, cl. 19(1)(*b*) of the Kerala Security Prisoners' Order, 1971,[67] which empowered government to direct that security prisoners may not receive books etc. considered impermissible by government, did not violate Art. 19(2), for the power conferred by the order, read in the light of the preamble and the object of the Act under which the order was made, fell within reasonable restrictions which could be placed on the right conferred by Art. 19(1)(*a*). However, an order providing that "Mao literature" should not be made available to security prisoners was very vague; and having regard to the fact that books made available to the petitioner[68] contained passages inciting to violence and endangering the security of the State, whereas the books of Mao denied to the petitioner, contained no such passages, the court felt constrained to set aside the impugned order, it being expressly provided that the government could pass further orders after considering what was stated in the judgment.

Riotous behaviour not protected by Art 19(1) (*a*) and (*b*)

10.39 In *Linghanna* v. *Mysore*[69] it was held that the rights to freedom of speech and expression and freedom to assemble peaceably, were not an answer to a charge against the accused that he behaved riotously at a private or even at a public meeting or that he behaved in a violent, indecorous or disorderly manner by insisting on the meeting being conducted in a particular language or in a particular way. The right of the accused to freedom of speech gave him no right to insist that the proceedings should be conducted in *Kannada* because the conveners of the meeting had a right to conduct it in any language they thought fit.

Restrictions imposed by the Dramatic Performance Act:

10.40 In *State* v. *Baboo Lal*[70] the court had to consider whether ss. 3 and 4, Dramatic Performance Act, 1876, in whole or in part, violated Art. 19(1)(*a*) and whether a prohibitory order issued under s. 3 was void. It was held that the substantive provisions of the sections were

---

[65] *Ram Manohar Lohia's Case* (1960) 2 S.C.R. 821, ('60) A.SC. 633 was distinguished on the ground that the law there impugned was in very different terms. The Supreme Court refused to read down s. 9 on the analogy of *Kedar Nath Singh* v. *Bihar* (1962) Supp. (2) S.C.R. 769, ('62) A.SC. 955, observing that "in view of the comprehensive sweep of Art. 19(2) we are unable to restrict s. 9 of the Act only to those speeches and expressions which incite or tend to incite violence": ('73) A.SC. at pp. 1094-5.

[66] ('73) A.Ker. 97 (F.B.).

[67] ibid. p. 99 where it is set out.

[68] *The State and Revolution* by Lenin; Lenin on *War and Peace; National Liberation War in Viet Nam* by Gen. Giap.

[69] (1953) Mys. 388, ('54) A.Mys. 12.

[70] (1957) 1 All. 399, ('56) A.A. 571.

reasonable having regard to the distinction between the written and the spoken word, namely, that the written word could be confiscated before it did any harm, whereas the spoken word could do great harm as soon as it was uttered. Therefore, it was necessary in the interest of public order and the security of the State that the State should have power to deal in an emergent manner with the spoken word. The power to prohibit the performance of plays which contained scandalous or defamatory matter or which were likely to deprave or corrupt an audience, imposed a reasonable restriction. However, s. 3(*b*) which enabled a play to be prohibited if the proposed performance "was likely to excite feelings of disaffection to the Government established by law in British India" had become void when the Constitution was enacted. To forbid a play because it represented an ideology different from that of the ruling party cannot possibly be regarded as a reasonable restriction on the freedom of speech. It is submitted that the finding that s. 3(*b*) had become void cannot be sustained after *Kedar Nath's Case*[71] since disaffection against Government established by law can be punished, though such disaffection is something different from a mere criticism of the actions and policies of the Government in power. However, in *Babulal's Case* the Court rightly held that the procedural provisions of the Dramatic Performance Act imposed unreasonable restrictions on the right guaranteed by Art. 19(1) (*a*) as they left the decision of the question to the subjective satisfaction of the District Magistrate and made no provision for a hearing before any order was passed nor for a review or appeal from such order.[72] Similarly, ss. 3, 4, 6 and 8, Dramatic Performance Ordinance, 1949, were held to impose unreasonable restrictions since no rules had been prescribed under s. 11 providing for a notice to be given to the person affected and providing for the constitution of the tribunal.[73]

substantive provisions reasonable

procedural provisions unreasonable

10.41 In *Gopal Das v. Assam*[74] it was held that s. 11, Press (Objectionable Matter) Act, 1951, could not be held void as imposing an unreasonable restriction on the fundamental rights of freedom of speech and expression [Art. 19(1) (*a*)] or the pursuit of any lawful avocation [Art. 19(1) (*g*)] merely because the law did not provide that before passing an order under that section, Government should give any notice to the person affected thereby, to show cause against the action proposed to be taken. It was of the essence of the action to be taken under s. 11 that it should be taken promptly. However, the Act provided ample safeguards. The Governor could not take any action under s. 11 unless the principal Law Officer or the Adv.-Gen. of the State as the case may be, or the Att.-Gen. of India, certified that the offending pamphlet or booklet contained objectionable matter. Again, the aggrieved person could move the High Court against Government's order within sixty days. Since these safeguards were real, the restrictions imposed on the fundamental rights were reasonable.

S. 11, Press (Objectionable Matter) Act upheld: swift action of the essence of the section

and there were ample safeguards

---

[71] (1962) Supp. (2) S.C.R. 769, ('62) A.SC. 955.

[72] ('56) A.A. 571, *supra;* fol. in *Harnam Singh* v. *Punjab* ('58) A.Punj. 243; *Chanan Singh* v. *Union* ('61) A.Punj. 272.

[73] *Madan Lal Kapur* v. *Rajasthan* (1952) Raj. 993, ('53) A.Raj. 162.

[74] *Gopal Das* v. *State* (1954) 6 Ass. 399, ('54) A.Ass. 193; see also *Shantilal Vadilal* v. *Bombay* (1954) Bom. 1245, ('54) A.B. 508, 56 Bom.L.R. 709.

Restrictions on the use of loud-speakers

10.42 In *Rajni Kant* v. *State*[75] it was held that the use of mechanical instruments like loudspeakers and amplifiers was not covered by the guarantee of freedom of speech and expression, and consequently, a Municipal bye-law which required a permit of the Executive Officer for using a loudspeaker did not infringe Art. 19 (1) (*a*). It is submitted that the correct position is that since there is a fundamental right to freedom of speech and expression, that right extends to mechanical devices which amplify speech, but in so far as these devices are likely to cause noise, or disturbance, or nuisance, reasonable restrictions could be placed on the use of such devices as regards the time, place and manner of using them, and a Municipal bye-law providing for such reasonable restrictions is valid. This view has been taken in *Indulal* v. *State.*[76]

The right of free speech extends to the use of mechanical devices: *Indulal's Case*

Other cases on free speech

10.43 The right to the freedom of speech and expression is not violated by a law[77] which requires that the name of the printer and publisher and the place of printing and publication should be printed legibly on every book or paper.[78] Nor is such right violated by s. 3 (2), M.P. Official Languages Act, 1950, because Art. 19 (1) (*a*) is not intended to cover the question of official languages, which is separately provided for in Part XVII of the Constitution.[79]

Freedom of speech and commercial advertisements: *Hamdarad Dawakhana Case*

10.44 In *Hamdarad Dawakhana* (*Wakf*) *Lal Kuan* v. *Union*[80] a question arose whether an advertisement designed to promote the sale of certain medicines was protected by Art. 19 (1) (*a*). The matter arose out of the provisions of the Drug and Magic Remedies (Objectionable Advertisements) Act, 1954. As stated in its preamble, the Act was passed "to control the advertisements of drugs in certain cases, to prohibit the advertisement for certain purposes of remedies alleged to possess magic qualities and to provide for matters connected thereto". The Court said that when a provision was challenged as violating a fundamental right, it was necessary to ascertain its true nature and character, that is, its subject-matter, the area in which it was intended to operate, its purport and intent. In order to do this, it was legitimate to consider the history of the legislation, the mischief intended to be suppressed, the remedy proposed by the Legislature, the true reason for that remedy and the surrounding circumstances and conditions. There was a presumption in favour of the constitutionality of an enactment. An examination of the legislative history and the surrounding circumstances showed that the object of the Act was to prevent self-medication and self-treatment by prohibiting instruments which may be used to advocate them or which tended to spread the evil, and not merely to stop all advertisements offending against morality

---

[75] ('58) A.A. 360, (1958) A.L.J. 56. [76] ('63) A.Guj. 259.

[77] *E.g.*, s. 3 of the Press and Registration of Books Act, 1867.

[78] *In re G. Alavandar* ('57) A.M. 427, (1957) M.L.J. 136 (such a provision is designed to inform the public as to who is responsible for the printing and publication. Such requirement is a reasonable restriction on freedom of the press which is not higher than the freedom of speech and expression enjoyed by individuals. The provision does not restrict the freedom of speech but prevents it from degenerating into a licence without remedy both for the State and individual citizens as regards defamatory, seditious, blasphemous and obscene matters or contempts of Court).

[79] *L. M. Wakhare* v. *State* ('59) A.M.P. 208.

[80] (1960) 2 S.C.R. 671, ('60) A.SC. 554.

and decency. Although an advertisement was a form of speech, its true character was reflected by the object for the promotion of which it was employed. It was only when an advertisement was concerned with the expression or propagation of ideas that it could be said to relate to the freedom of speech. The right to publish and distribute a commercial advertisement advertising an individual's personal business was not a part of the freedom of speech guaranteed by our Constitution. The provisions of the Act which prohibited advertisements commending the efficacy, value and importance of certain drugs in the treatment of particular diseases, did not fall under Art. 19(1)(*a*). The scope and object of the Act, its true nature and character was not interference with the freedom of speech but was the imposition of restrictions on trade and business. The wide definition of the word "advertisement" was necessary if the object of the law was not to be defeated. The provisions of the Act, except s. 8, did not violate the petitioner's fundamental rights. S. 8, which empowered seizure and detention of documents, articles or things which the prescribed authority had reason to believe contravened the provisions of the Act, imposed unreasonable restrictions on the right of the petitioners and was void. S. 3(*d*), which empowered Government to add to the diseases within the mischief of s. 3, was an impermissible delegation of legislative power and was therefore void.[81] But ss. 3(*a*) and (8) were severable, and the validity of the remaining provisions of the Act was therefore not affected.

Commercial advertisements do not fall under Art. 19(1)(*a*)

Contempt proceedings in *In re Sham Lal* and *In re Mulgaokar* as offshoots of *Habeas Corpus Case*

10.45 In the earlier editions of this book the difference between the American and Indian law as to contempt of court *vis-a-vis* freedom of speech was discussed with reference to decided cases,[82] but it was not felt necessary to deal with the law of contempt as such. The judgments of the Supreme Court in *In re Sham Lal*[83] and *In re S. Mulgaokar*[84] make it necessary to do so, more especially because of the use which Beg C.J. made of the contempt proceedings in *Sham Lal's Case* and *Mulgaokar's Case*, and because of Krishna Iyer J.'s inconclusive essay in "contempt jurisprudence" in *Mulgaokar's Case*. We will consider contempt of court in three interconnected aspects: (*a*) *vis-a-vis* the freedom of speech and expression; (*b*) whether a law of contempt can be said to be reasonable, no matter what it contains; and (*c*) whether the existing law of contempt is reasonable. Thereafter, we will consider the judgments of the Supreme Court in *In re Sham Lal* and *In re S. Mulgaokar*. It may however be stated that it is difficult to set out fully the facts of these two cases because the words said to constitute contempt (the "offending words") are not set out in the judgments although it is usual to do so as the reader will find from the cases discussed in paras 10.46 to 10.51 below, except where contempt is admitted.

---

[81] This aspect is considered further in the Chapter on Delegated Legislation in Vol. II.
[82] See *Seervai*, Vol. 1, 2nd ed., pp. 560-63.
[83] (1978) 2 S.C.R. 581, ('78) A.SC. 489.
[84] (1978) 3 S.C.R. 162, ('78) A.SC. 727.

Contempt of Court and Art. 19(1)(*a*) and (2)

10.46 Article 19 (1) (*a*) confers on every citizen the right to the freedom of speech and expression which includes the freedom of the press. Article 19 (2), so far as it is relevant, saves existing laws and permits the enactment of future laws which impose *reasonable restrictions* on the right of free speech, *inter alia,* in relation to contempt of court, (and also defamation). No doubt the law relating to contempt of court was well known to the framers of the Constitution—but so were various other laws. But the framers allowed such laws, present and future, to operate only if the restrictions imposed by the laws of the kind mentioned in Art. 19 (2) were reasonable. Consequently, the restrictions which could be imposed, *inter alia,* on the freedom of speech in relation to the contempt of court (or defamation) must be reasonable. Thus, a law relating to defamation, which provided that truth, spoken or written, for the public good shall not be a defence in a libel action would impose restrictions which would be unreasonable. Would the position be any different if a law were to enact that truth should not be a defence to a charge of contempt of court, if it consists of scandalizing a judge? If a Minister takes bribes, or shows favour to his relations in the discharge of his public duties, an article in a newspaper making specific charges would be a libel. However, an action for libel would fail if it were shown that the specific charges were true. In a criminal prosecution for libel, the prosecution would fail if it were shown that specific charges were true and it was for the public good that they should be made. But is there one law for a corrupt Minister and another for a corrupt judge? When a senior judge of the U.S. Court of Appeals was prosecuted for corruption and bribery (due to a public-spirited attorney, Thomas E. Dewey) and was sentenced to two years' imprisonment and a fine of ten thousand dollars, the convicted judge in his appeal to the U.S. Supreme Court urged that "From a broad viewpoint, it serves no public policy for a high judicial officer *to be convicted of a judicial crime. It tends to destroy the confidence of the people in the courts."* As one would expect, the Supreme Court rejected the plea (as it rejected his other pleas). Would any court in India take a different view? If, as the present writer believes, no court would, by what process of reasoning would the same court punish for contempt the writer of an article who, in sober language, sets out specific acts of bribery and is able successfully to prove them? These and other connected questions make it necessary to set out the law of contempt which falls under the category of scandalising a judge.

Any aspect of the law of contempt of court must stand the test of "reasonableness"

The Bahamas Case

10.47 The first important decision is *In the Matter of a Special Reference from Bahamas Islands*[85] (the "*Bahamas Case*"). It was a special reference on a case by the Secretary of State for the Colonies and was heard by a strong Board.[86] The offending words are set out at pp. 139-141 of the Report and have been admirably summed up in the first sentence of the passage quoted below. In

---

[85] (1893) A.C. 138 (P.C.).

[86] The Lord Chancellor, The Lord Chief Justice, Lord Watson, Lord Hobhouse, Lord Ashbourne, The Master of the Rolls, Lord Macnaughten, Lord Hannen, Lord Shaw, Sir Richard Couch and Lord Justice Bowen.

that case, the Chief Justice of a Colony had written letters to a newspaper and in reply,

"a man had, in a letter published in a newspaper, held up the Chief Justice . . . to public ridicule in the grossest manner, representing him as an utterly incompetent judge, and a shirker of his work, and suggesting that it would be a providential thing if he were to die. The Board, consisting of eleven members of the Judicial Committee, did not give a formal judgment — it is not the practice in such cases to do so — but reported that the letter complained of, though it might have been made the subject of proceedings for libel, was not, in the circumstances, calculated to obstruct or interfere with the course of justice or the due administration of the law, and therefore did not constitute a contempt of court."[87]

Distinction between libel on a judge and contempt by scandalising a judge

In other words, when a Chief Justice was foolish enough to enter into a newspaper controversy, he exposed himself to a reply sufficient to blast the career of any judge and yet an exceptionally strong Board of 11 judges held that there was no contempt. The theory that the judge has an integrated personality, and any attack on a judge which reduces the people's confidence in him as a judge is contempt, becomes untenable; the Colonial Chief Justice was brought into contempt and ridicule, but this was held not to amount to contempt of court. This decision is important when considering the judgment of Beg C.J. in *In re S. Mulgaokar* because Beg C.J.'s letter to the Chief Justice of the High Courts had nothing to do with his judicial work, or even his administrative work (if that were relevant).

Extra-judicial pronouncements

10.48 The second decision of the Privy Council, in *McLeod* v. *St. Aubyn*,[88] is also important. The head-note accurately states the effect of the judgment:

***McLeod* v. *St. Aubyn* — the judge made to pay the costs of appeal to the Privy Council**

"Contempt of Court may be committed by publication of scandalous matter respecting the Court after adjudication as well as pending a case before it. In England committals for such contempts have become obsolete: in small colonies consisting principally of coloured populations they may still be necessary in proper cases:—

But *held*, that where the appellant was neither printer nor publisher nor writer of such scandalous matter, but had innocently lent the paper containing it to a friend without knowledge of its contents, he was neither constructively nor necessarily guilty of contempt of Court, and that the judge who committed him must pay the costs of appeal to Her Majesty in Council."[89]

The observations that committals for such contempt had become obsolete were too wide. Again, notwithstanding the reference to "small Colonies principally of coloured people" the Privy Council found that the appellant had committed no contempt and made the judge pay the costs.

10.49 Having found the appellant guilty of circulating a libel which the respondent held to be contempt of court, he adjourned the case to give the appellant an opportunity to tender an apology. The terms of the apology are important, because the Appellant refused to apologize for a crime which he had not committed, for to apologize in those terms would have been to state an untruth. The Privy Council held that the Appellant had committed no contempt. They held that:

Apology offered was sufficient for the judge to have stayed his hand.

"It would be extraordinary if every person who innocently handed over a newspaper or lent one to a friend, with no knowledge of its containing anything

[87] *R.* v. *Nicholls* 12 C.L.R. 280 at p. 285.
[88] (1899) A.C. 549.
[89] ibid.

objectionable, could be thereby constructively but necessarily guilty of a contempt of a Court because the said newspaper happened to contain scandalous matter reflecting on the Court. . . Their Lordships are also of opinion the apology offered by the appellant before his committal contains sufficient to have called on the respondent to stay his hand. *It is an unconditional expression of regret for the act for which he was arraigned.*[90] (italics supplied)

An apology genuinely offered always mitigates the punishment for contempt. But a person cannot truthfully apologize if he charges a judge with having taken bribes if he has in his possession evidence which leaves no doubt about the correctness of the charge.

Ambard v. Att.-Gen. of Trinidad and Tobago

10.50 The third decision, *Ambard* v. *Att.-Gen. of Trinidad and Tobago*[91] contains Lord Atkin's classic statement of the law of contempt. The matter arose out of an article written in a newspaper, entitled "The Human element". The article pointed out the different sentences awarded in two cases which appeared to the writer to be similar, in one of which he considered that the sentence was too light and in the other that the sentence was not heavy enough. He was held guilty of contempt. Special leave was given to appeal to the Privy Council.[92] After observing that the Privy Council found no evidence to justify the finding that the article was written with the intention of lowering the dignity of the Court, or had that effect, Lord Atkin said:

Lord Atkin's classic statement of the law—"justice is not a cloistered virtue"

"But whether the authority and position of an individual judge, or the due administration of justice, is concerned, no wrong is committed by any member of the public who exercises the ordinary right of criticizing, in good faith, in private or public, the public act done in the seat of justice. The path of criticism is a public way: the wrong headed are permitted to err therein: provided that members of the public abstain from imputing improper motives to those taking part in the administration of justice, and are genuinely exercising a right of criticism, and not acting in malice or attempting to impair the administration of justice, they are immune. Justice is not a cloistered virtue: she must be allowed to suffer the scrutiny and respectful, even though outspoken, comments of ordinary men.[93] If to say that the human element enters into the awarding of punishment be contempt of Court it is to be feared that few in or out of the profession would escape.[94] . . . *If criticism of decisions could only safely be made by persons who accurately knew the relevant law, who would be protected? There is no suggestion that the law was intentionally mis-stated.*"[95] (italics supplied)

Contempt and freedom of the press

Lord Atkin said that the case had been discussed at some length because it concerned ". . . the liberty of the Press, which is no more than the liberty of any member of the public, to criticize temperately and fairly, but freely, any episode in the administration of justice."[96]

R. v. Commr. of Police Ex p. Blackburn: the importance of the freedom of the press emphasised

10.51 In *R.* v. *Commr. of Police Ex p. Blackburn* (*No. 2*),[97] Mr. Quintin Hogg, Q.C. wrote an article in "Punch", in which, among other things, he said: "The recent judgment of the Court of Appeal is a strange example of a blindness which sometimes descends on the best of judges . . . it is to be hoped that the Courts will remember the golden rule of judges in the matter of obiter dicta. Silence is always an option."[98] It was admitted at the hearing of the contempt proceedings that the reference to the Court of Appeal was a mis-

---

[90] ibid. p. 562.
[91] (1936) A.C. 322 (P.C.).
[92] The Privy Council held that it had jurisdiction to hear the matter: (1936) A.C. at pp. 328-9. The offending article is set out at pp. 330-333.
[93] (1936) A.C. at p. 335.
[94] ibid. p. 336.
[95] ibid. p. 337.
[96] ibid.
[97] (1968) 2 Q.B. 150.
[98] ibid. p. 154.

take, and the reference should have been to the Divisional Court. Notwithstanding this, in three separate but concurring judgments, the Court held that there was no contempt. In this case, even greater emphasis was laid on the freedom of speech than had been laid by Lord Atkin. Lord Denning said:

Lord Denning M.R.

"Let me say at once that we will never use this jurisdiction as a means to uphold our own dignity. That must rest on surer foundations. Nor will we use it to suppress those who speak against us. We do not fear criticism, nor do we resent it. *For there is something far more important at stake. It is no less than freedom of speech itself.* It is the right of every man, in Parliament or out of it, in the Press or over the broadcast, to make fair comment, even outspoken comment, on matters of public interest. . . . Mr. Quintin Hogg has criticised the court, but in so doing he is exercising his undoubted right. The article contains an error, no doubt, but errors do not make it a contempt of court. *We must uphold his right to the uttermost.*"[99] (italics supplied)

Salmon L.J. said:

Salmon L.J.

"It is the inalienable right of everyone to comment fairly upon any matter of public importance. This right is one of the pillars of individual liberty — freedom of speech, which our courts have always unfailingly upheld. . . . The criticism here complained of, however rumbustious, however wide of the mark, whether expressed in good taste or in bad taste, seems to me to be well within (the limits of reasonable courtesy and good faith").[1]

Edmund Davies L.J. said:

Edmund Davies L.J.

"The right to fair criticism is part of the birth-right of all subjects of Her Majesty. Though it has its boundaries, that right covers a wide expanse, and its curtailment must be jealously guarded against. It applies to the judgments of the courts as to all other topics of public importance."[2]

It will be seen that progressively there is increasing emphasis on freedom of speech. In India, the position must be even stronger than it is in England, because freedom of speech, which includes the freedom of the press, is a fundamental right although subject, *inter alia*, to reasonable restrictions imposed by the law governing contempt of court. The current tendency has not been to restrict freedom of speech by resorting to the power to commit for contempt of court.

R. v. Nicholls: imputation of want of impartiality in a judge and the public interest

10.52 *R.* v. *Nicholls*[3] decided by the High Court of Australia is a most instructive case. There, the contempt complained of arose from an article written by Nicholls in a newspaper, entitled "A Modest Judge". That article arose from the undernoted exchange between Counsel and Higgins J. presiding over the Commonwealth Court of Conciliation and Arbitration.[4] Griffiths C.J. after referring to the Privy Council Report in the *Bahamas Case* in the passage set out in para 10.47 above, observed:

---

[99] ibid. p. 155.
[1] ibid. pp. 155-6.
[2] ibid. p. 156.
[3] 12 C.L.R. 280.
[4] "*Mr. Starke.*—Of all the labour organizations I have ever heard of Broken Hill (in?) that field seem to be the strongest and about the most tyrannous I have ever heard of. They not only do not do their work but they break their agreements with impunity and they are encouraged by their Unions and by the Government of this country.

Higgins J.—I will not allow you to speak in that way of the Government of this country. You have no right to speak in that way, and you will understand I will not listen to it.

Mr. Starke.—I am entitled to put forward any view I like for my clients.

Higgins J.—You are not entitled to speak disrespectfully of those above us.

Mr. Starke.—I am not speaking disrespectfully.

Higgins J.—If that is not disrespectful I do not know what is.

Griffiths C.J.: Want of impartiality in a judge, subject of fair comment and not necessarily contempt

"It is said by Mr. Weigall that they suggest a want of impartiality, but we do not find that in them, *and I am not prepared to accede to the proposition that an imputation of want of impartiality to a Judge is necessarily a contempt of Court.* On the contrary, I think that, if any Judge of this Court or of any other Court were to make a public utterance of such character as to be likely to impair the confidence of the public, or of suitors or any class of suitors in the impartiality of the Court in any matter likely to be brought before it, any public comment on such an utterance, if it were a fair comment would, *so far from being a contempt of Court, be for the public benefit,* and would be entitled to similar protection to that which comment upon matters of public interest is entitled under the law of libel."[5] (italics supplied)

Submission: the above view is clearly right

It is submitted that Griffiths C.J.'s statement of the law is clearly right. Proceedings for contempt of Court are meant to prevent obstruction to, or interference with, the administration of justice. Scurrilous or abusive attacks on a judge would shake the public confidence, and would interfere with the administration of justice. But a judge who makes public pronouncements which throw a grave doubt on his impartiality, himself becomes an offender against the administration of justice. And since there is no way of setting such a judge right except by impeachment, a cumbrous procedure seldom resorted to, the interest of justice itself requires that there should be public criticism of the impropriety of making such public pronouncements. In *R.* v. *Commr. of Police Ex P. Blackburn* (*No.* 2) referred to earlier, Lord Denning said:

"All we would ask is that those who criticise us will remember that, from the nature of our office, we cannot reply to their criticisms. We cannot enter into public controversy. Still less into political controversy."[6]

A judge who makes extra judicial public pronouncements which show that he lacks impartiality, departs from the line of conduct dictated by his office.

Reddy's Case: Sup. Ct. adopts distinction between libel and contempt made in the *Bahamas Case*

10.53 The distinction made by the Privy Council in the *Bahamas Case* between a libel of a judge and contempt of court was adopted by our Supreme Court. In *Bathina Ramakrishna Reddy* v. *Madras*[7] Mukherjea J.[8] dealt with contempt of court in a newspaper article. He observed that it was clear from the observations of the Privy Council in the *Bahamas Case* that ". . . a libel attacking the integrity of a judge may not in the circumstances of a particular case amount to contempt at all, although it may be the subject matter of libel proceedings."[9] He continued:

Allegations of corruption against a judge, if true, require to be brought to light in the public interest

"The article in question is a scurrilous attack on the integrity and honesty of a judicial officer. Specific instances have been given where the officer is alleged to have taken bribes or behaved with impropriety to litigants who did not satisfy his dishonest demands. *If the allegations were true, obviously it would be to the benefit of the public to bring these matters into light.* But if they were false, they cannot but undermine the confidence of the public in the administration of justice and bring the judiciary into disrepute."[10] (italics supplied)

Mr. Starke.—I spoke of the tyranny of these Unions at Broken Hill.

Higgins J.—I will not allow you to speak in that form of a Government of the country and those above us. If you do not comply with my rules, you will leave the Court.": 12 C.L.R. at p. 282.

[5] ibid. p. 286.

[6] (1968) 2 Q.B. at p. 155.

[7] (1952) S.C.R. 425.

[8] For himself, Sastri C.J., Meher Chand Mahajan, Das and Chandrasekhara Aiyar JJ.

[9] ibid. p. 434.

[10] ibid.

Since a later judgment of the Supreme Court purports to interpret *Reddy's Case*, it may be noted that the High Court considered that it was open to the appellant to substantiate the allegations which he had made. However, "As the appellant was not prepared to substantiate the allegations which he made and which he admitted to be based on hearsay"[11] he was found guilty of contempt. So, two issues arose: Were the allegations true? If not, was it any defence to say that Reddy *in good faith* believed them to be true? Mukherjea J. rightly held that if the allegations were true it would be to the benefit of the public to bring them to light. But since Reddy had not attempted to substantiate his allegations the question still remained, was it a defence to say that he believed in good faith that the allegations were true? It was in this context that Mukherjea J. said:

If such allegations are not true, whether making them in good faith would be a defence

"The appellant, though he took sole responsibility regarding the publication of the article, was not in a position to substantiate by evidence any of the allegations made therein. He admitted that the statement was based on hearsay. Rumours may have reached him from various sources, but before he published the article it was incumbent upon him as a reasonable man to attempt to verify the informations he received and ascertain, as far as he could, whether the facts were true or mere concocted lies. He does not appear to have made any endeavour in this direction. As the appellant did not act with reasonable care and caution, he cannot be said to have acted *bona fide, even if good faith can be held to be a defence at all in a proceeding for contempt.*"[12] (italics supplied)

10.54 In *Brahma Prakash Sharma* v. *U.P.*,[13] the Executive Committee of the District Bar Association received several complaints against the way in which the judicial magistrates and revenue officers of the district disposed of cases and behaved towards litigants and lawyers and the Association passed a resolution which stated:

Sharma's Case: Representation by a Bar Association to persons in authority over the judicial officers against whom representation made

"It was their considered opinion that the two officers are thoroughly incompetent in law, do not inspire confidence in their judicial work, are given to state wrong facts when passing orders and are overbearing and discourteous to the litigant public and lawyers alike."[14]

and gave a list of complaints against the officers. This resolution was passed in camera, typed by the President of the Association himself and was forwarded confidentially to the District Magistrate, the Commissioner of the Division, the Chief Secretary and the Premier of the State. On being found guilty of contempt of court by the High Court, the appellants appealed to the Supreme Court. Mukherjea J. (for himself, Patanjali Sastri C.J., S. R. Das, Gulam Hassan and Bhagwati JJ.) referred to the undernoted English authorities[15] and also to his earlier decision in *Reddy* v. *Madras*. He observed that very little publicity had been given to the resolution, that representations were made to four specified persons who were the official superiors of the officers concerned. The Association had acted in good faith, with no intention to interfere with the administration of justice. After referring to some of the allegations,

[11] ibid. p. 427.
[12] ibid. pp. 434-35.
[13] (1953) S.C.R. 1169, ('54) A.SC. 10.
[14] (1953) S.C.R. at p. 1170.
[15] Namely, *MacLeod* v. *St. Aubyn* (1899) A.C. 549; *R.* v. *Gray* (1900) 2 Q.B. 36; *Ambard* v. *Att.-Gen. for Trinidad and Tobago* (1936) A.C. 322, 335; *The Bahamas Case* (1893) A.C. 138 and *R.* v. *Nicholls* 12 C.L.R. 280.

Mukherjea J. observed:

Patent illegality of procedure by judicial officers — must be brought to the notice of Dist. Magistrate.

"It is undoubtedly a grave charge that the Revenue Officer hears two cases simultaneously and allows the Court Reader to do the work for him. If true, it is a patent illegality and is precisely a matter which should be brought to the notice of the District Magistrate who is the administrative head of these officers."[16]

Sweeping remarks made in good faith

As to the observation that the officers were thoroughly incompetent in law and their judicial work did not inspire confidence, Mukherjea J. observed: "These remarks are certainly of a sweeping nature and can scarcely be justified. Assuming, however, that this portion of the resolution is defamatory, the question arises whether it can be held to amount to contempt of court."[17] After observing that "It may be that pleas of justification or privilege are not strictly speaking available to the defendant in contempt proceedings,"[18] he held that in considering whether a defamatory statement amounted to contempt, the Court had to consider all the surrounding circumstances and materials before the Court, particularly the limited publication of the libel. The Court held that the contempt, *if any*, was of a technical character and that after the affidavits filed in the High Court, the proceedings against the appellants should have been dropped. The judgment of the High Court was reversed.

Perspective Publications v. Maharashtra

10.55 We must now refer to *Perspective Publications* v. *Maharashtra.*[19] The matter arose out of an article which the High Court held contained a clear imputation of dishonesty to a judge trying a libel action. No attempt had been made to justify the allegation and in fact it had been established that some of the material allegations were wrong and incorrect. After a review of the authorities, Grover J. extracted five propositions[20] and then observed:

The question whether "truth" is a defence *"merely of academic interest"* as the material statements were in fact false

"As regards the third contention no attempt was made before the High Court to substantiate that the facts stated in the article were true or were founded on correct data. It may be that truthfulness or factual correctness is a good defence in an action for libel, but in the law of contempt there are hardly any English or Indian cases in which such defence has been recognized. It is true that in the case of *Bathina Ramakrishna Reddy*[21] there was some discussion about the *bona fides* of the person responsible for the publication but that was apparently done to dispose of the contention which had been raised on the point. It is quite clear that the submission made was considered on the assumption that good faith can be held to be a defence in a proceeding for contempt. The words '*even if good faith can be held to be a defence at all in a proceeding for contempt*' show that this Court did not lay down affirmatively that good faith can be set up as a defence in contempt proceedings. *At any rate, this point is merely of academic interest* because no attempt was made before the High Court to establish the truthfulness of the facts stated in the article. On the other hand, it was established that some of the material allegations were altogether wrong and incorrect."[22] (italics supplied)

Submission: Mukherjea J.'s statement in *Reddy's Case* that truth was a defence

It is submitted, first, that a final court ought not to lay down the law if it is "merely of academic interest". Secondly, the law so laid down overlooks the judgment of Griffiths C.J. in *R.* v. *Nicholls.* Thirdly, Grover J. overlooked the material part of *Reddy's Case*, for, as we have seen, Mukherjea J. held that if the allegations were true

[16] (1953) S.C.R. at pp. 1181-82. [17] ibid. p. 1182.
[18] ibid. pp. 1182-83.
[19] (1969) 2 S.C.R. 779, ('71) A.SC. 222. This case has been relied on in *C. K. Daphtary* v. *O. P. Gupta* discussed in para 10.56.
[20] (1969) 2 S.C.R. at pp. 791-2, ('71) A.SC. at p. 230.
[21] (1952) S.C.R. 425 *supra.*
[22] (1969) 2 S.C.R. at p. 792, ('71) A.SC. at p. 230.

it was in the public interest that they should be brought to light. This judgment of 5 judges was clearly binding on Grover J. It was with reference to Reddy's defence that he had published the article in good faith believing the allegations to be true that Mukherjea J. used the expression "if good faith can be held to be a defence at all". It is obvious that the plea that the allegations are true is very different from the plea that the allegations were believed in good faith to be true. It is submitted that on the question whether truth is a complete defence, the judgment of Grover J. is a judgment *per incuriam* and is clearly wrong.

overlooked as also *R.* v. *Nicholls*

10.56 The decision of the Supreme Court in *C. K. Daphtary* v. *O. P. Gupta*[23] is an unsatisfactory decision. The matters from which the contempt proceedings arose were as follows: Gupta was in the judicial service and on a complaint by the District Judge of Gupta's improper conduct with a woman, whose case was before Gupta—*a complaint which the District Judge later withdrew for reasons stated*—a disciplinary inquiry was held, and Gupta was dismissed from service. His suit for wrongful dismissal was dismissed by the District Court. The High Court, after a careful scrutiny of the evidence, allowed Gupta's appeal. On appeal to the Supreme Court, after certain interlocutory proceedings, the judgment of the High Court was reversed. The conduct of one of the judges in the interlocutory proceedings, and at the hearing of the appeal, was made the subject of an attempt to initiate proceedings for his impeachment. In that connection, Gupta appears to have assisted in preparing a booklet setting out the case for the impeachment.[24] It may be added that it was shown that Gupta not only had the booklet circulated to members of Parliament but also to several other persons and it was also offered for sale. The present writer had occasion to read and study the said booklet.[25] This case was not dealt with in the text of the second edition since in the present writer's opinion, a fair discussion of the merits of the case was not possible unless the booklet was read as a whole, and all the points which Gupta purported to make in his favour were considered. Further, having regard to the wide publicity which Gupta gave to the booklet, and the further abuse which he heaped upon the judge who had been scandalized in the booklet, the judgment could have been rested on the facts of the case. Further, his defence that there could not be contempt of a retired judge could also have been disposed of on the facts of the case. For, it was in evidence that proceedings for contempt for scandalizing the judge was started when the judge was on the Bench and that Gupta avoided the execution of an arrest warrant till the judge had retired. On these facts it was clear that a person cannot commit contempt by scandalizing a sitting judge, avoid execution of an arrest warrant and then contend that there was no contempt. A man cannot take advantage of his own wrong to convert contempt of a sitting judge into contempt of a retired judge.

C. K. Daphtary v. *O. P. Gupta*: Submission: not a satisfactory decision, although it could be justified on the facts of the case

---

23 (1971) Supp. S.C.R. 76, ('71) A.SC. 1132.

24 No impeachment proceedings were in fact adopted as the Speaker did not accept the impeachment notice.

25 As it was put to him in his capacity as Advocate-General of Maharashtra whether he did not think that the Bombay Bar should take some action in respect of the said booklet.

Three general propositions of law in *Gupta's Case* are considered below

10.57 However, the Supreme Court did not rest the decision on the special facts of the case but proceeded to lay down general propositions of law. The present discussion is limited to three questions of law, namely,

(a) Is the law relating to contempt of court unreasonable in whole or in part?

(b) Is the truth of an allegation made about a judge a defence to a charge of contempt if it is expressed in sober language?

(c) Can scandalous allegations relating to a judge who has retired be looked upon as contempt of court?

Freedom of speech and contempt of Court: Submission — right questions not asked

10.58 As to para 10.57 (a) above, it is submitted that Sikri C.J. failed to ask the right questions and therefore gave the wrong answers. The contemnor contended that existing law as to contempt of court imposed unreasonable restrictions on the freedom of speech and therefore the law was void as it was not saved by Art. 19 (2). The first petitioner contended that the existing law of contempt was not a law within the meaning of law given by Art. 13 (3). In this connection it was said that the Supreme Court derived its power to punish for contempt of itself from Art. 129. Secondly, that the existing law of contempt was not a law governed by Art. 19 (2), and finally that the existing law imposed reasonable restrictions within the meaning of Art. 19 (2).

Submission: The whole discussion whether existing law of contempt was "law" was misconceived

10.59 Sikri C.J. said that it was not necessary to decide whether the existing law of contempt was a law within the meaning of Art. 13 (3) (*a*) since the Court came to the conclusion that the existing law imposed reasonable restrictions within the meaning of Art. 19 (2). He then said:

> "Apart from this, the Constitution makes this Court the guardian of fundamental rights conferred by the Constitution and it would not desire to enforce any law which imposes unreasonable restrictions on the precious right of freedom of speech and expression guaranteed by the Constitution."[26]

It is submitted, first, that the total discussion about "law" was misconceived. The existing law of contempt is continued by Art. 372,[27] but "subject to the provisions of the Constitution", and Art. 19 (2) is a provision of the Constitution. Secondly, the undernoted entry 77, List I,[28] expressly makes the contempt of the Supreme Court a subject of legislative power. Thirdly, the definition of "law" in Art. 13 (3) is inclusive and is not helpful. Nor is it necessary to resort to Art. 13 (3) because Art. 19 (2) treats existing law relating to contempt *as a law* within the meaning of Art. 19 (2). Omitting unnecessary words, Art. 19 (2) reads: "Nothing in sub-clause (*a*) of clause (1) shall affect the operation of any *existing law* or prevent the State from making any law in so far as such law imposes reasonable restrictions on the right conferred by sub-clause (*a*) in relation to contempt of Court." Article 19 (1) (*a*) is not excluded by the operation of the existing law relating to contempt of Court; it is excluded only to the extent that the existing law imposes *reasonable restrictions* on the freedom of speech. Article 129, which confers on the Supreme

Art. 19(2) clearly treats existing law of contempt as "law"

---

26 ('71) A.SC. at p. 1141. 27 See pp. A-139-140.

28 List I, Entry 77: "Constitution, organisation, jurisdiction and powers of the Supreme Court (including contempt of such Court), and the fees taken therein; persons entitled to practise before the Supreme Court."

Court the power to punish for contempt of itself, necessarily refers to the existing law of contempt of court, subject to the legislative power of Parliament. Thus, the Contempt of Courts Act, 1971, in terms deals, *inter alia,* with contempt of the Supreme Court, and makes certain modifications in the general law of contempt. The question therefore was not whether in a general sense the existing law of contempt was reasonable, but whether any particular aspect of the law of contempt was reasonable or unreasonable. No general proposition can be laid down without examining each aspect of the law, and ascertaining whether that aspect imposes reasonable restrictions. Thus, if it was a part of the law, that a person committed contempt if he truthfully published the fact that a judge had received a bribe for giving a judgment in a party's favour, then it is submitted that the law would be void as imposing unreasonable restrictions on the freedom of speech and expression. First, because the judge who took that bribe was false to his oath, to do justice without fear or favour. Secondly, Art. 124(4) provides for the impeachment of a judge for proved misbehaviour, and the judge who accepted the bribe was guilty not only of gross misbehaviour but also of a crime.[29] It would be absurd to say that although Art. 124(4) provides for the removal of a judge for proved misbehaviour, no one can offer proof of such misbehaviour except on the pain of being sent to jail for contempt of court. Finally, a judge who takes a bribe is not acting as a judge but using his position as a judge to secure illicit personal gain. As Mukherjea J. rightly held, the interest of justice requires that the judge's misbehaviour should be brought to light.

Submission: each aspect of existing law of contempt must stand the test of reasonableness *e.g.* if true allegations that a judge received bribes constitute contempt, the law violates Art. 19(1)(*a*) and is void

10.60 As to para 10.57 (*b*) above, in addition to what has been said already, it may be observed that the fact that the Supreme Court is constituted the guardian of fundamental rights and would not uphold any law which is unreasonable, is a *petitio principi* for it assumes the very thing to be proved. If, without a scrutiny of an impugned part of the law of contempt, the Supreme Court holds it reasonable, the fact that the Supreme Court is a guardian of fundamental rights would not make the law reasonable. It is submitted that in that event, the Supreme Court would have inadvertently failed to be a *vigilant* guardian, and its finding would be clearly erroneous.

Submission: That the Sup. Ct. is constituted guardian of fundamental rights is irrelevant to the reasonableness of a law

10.61 The general proposition that truth cannot be a defence, after the court has found that the statements made by Gupta were untrue, is incorrect. It ignores the decision of the Supreme Court itself in *Reddy's Case*; it ignores the decision of the High Court of Australia in *R.* v. *Nicholls.* If two views are possible of a particular provision of the law, that interpretation which would make the law valid must be preferred to that which would make it void.[30] The view taken by Mukherjea J. in *Reddy's Case* that truth would be a defence to a charge of contempt would make the law valid; the view expressed by Grover J. and by Sikri C.J. would, it is submitted, make the law void. Therefore, the first view must be preferred to the second. A

Submission: on truth not being a defence *Gupta's Case* is incorrect

The view of Mukherjea J. must be preferred to that of Sikri C.J.

---

[29] Under s. 161 of the Indian Penal Code read with s. 21. Section 161 provides that a public servant who takes gratification other than legal remuneration in respect of an official act shall be punished with imprisonment for a term which may extend to three years or with fine or with both. And under s. 21 a judge is a public servant.

[30] *Kedarnath Singh* v. *Bihar* (1962) Supp. 2 S.C.R. 769, ('62) A.SC. 955.

to save the validity of the law of contempt

similar situation arose with reference to the word "sedition". The subject is fully discussed in the text,[31] but it can be briefly stated thus: Section 124 of the Indian Penal Code, which dealt with the offence of "sedition", was impugned as violating Art. 19(1) (*a*). The Bombay High Court had taken one view of s. 127; Gwyer C.J. delivering a judgment of the Federal Court disapproved that view and propounded a different view. The Privy Council approved the Bombay view and overruled the view taken by Gwyer C.J. The Supreme Court held that if the Privy Council's view of "sedition" were adopted, s. 124 would be void as violating Art. 19(1) (*a*). However, if Gwyer C.J.'s view of s. 124 were adopted, s. 124 would be valid. Consequently, adopting Gwyer C.J.'s view, the Supreme Court held s. 124 valid. It is submitted that the same line of reasoning applies to a law relating to contempt of Court.

Contempt by scandalizing a retired judge — law laid down in *Gupta's Case* too wide

10.62 As to para 10.57 (*c*) above, the proposition that there could be contempt of court of a retired judge could be supported on the special facts of *Gupta's Case*. But the general proposition that there can be contempt of court by scandalizing a retired judge because it would shake the confidence of the people in the administration of justice is too wide. Scurrilous or abusive language falsely attributing dishonesty, bias or corruption to a sitting judge shakes the confidence of the public, because no one would feel safe in appearing before him. And punishing the contemnor is a mode of establishing to the public that the allegations made are false and/or insulting. None of these considerations apply to a retired judge, because he has ceased to be a part of the administration of justice. Further, the retired judge is not without a remedy. A civil action, or a criminal prosecution, for libel is available to him.

Criticism of retired judge's misconduct in biographies and in history

10.63 Biographies of eminent lawyers and judges contain comments on judicial misbehaviour of judges or shocking bias of judges in the discharge of their judicial duties; and history has branded a number of judges as infamous. But no one has thought of hauling up those authors for contempt. That some judges will be biased at times, that some judges may be corrupt or may misbehave does not shake the confidence of the public in respect of judges generally. The provision in our Constitution for the removal of a judge for proved misbehaviour shows that the framers were aware that in a few cases judges will not be free from human infirmity.

Statements made by parties about judicial misconduct to secure redress from a higher Court

10.64 It may be mentioned that Sikri C.J. has made no distinction between a contempt alleged to have been committed by a party to a legal proceeding, which was the case before him, and contempt alleged to have been committed in respect of the same proceedings by a member of the public. An application for the transfer of a case because of the judge's misconduct, or an application for a new trial on the ground that the judge's conduct of the case made a fair trial impossible involve a serious reflection on the judge, but the aggrieved party can protect his interest only by bringing the judge's misconduct to the attention of a higher court entitled to grant him relief. And Advocates who after careful verification of the facts sign the relevant application or memorandum of appeal are obviously dis-

[31] See paras 10.34 and 10.35.

charging their duty. Two examples from reported decisions ordering a new trial will suffice. No one could have read the report of *Hobbs* v. *Tinling*[32] without realising that Lord Hewart L.C.J. showed a marked and pronounced bias against the plaintiff and the trial was so unfair that a fresh trial was ordered. Nor can anyone read the report of *Jones* v. *National Coal Board*[33] without realising that Mr. Justice Hallet's conduct of the trial rendered a fair trial impossible. Notice of appeal on behalf of the plaintiffs stated:

Applications for new trial on the ground that the party did not get a fair trial: *Hobbs* v. *Tinling; Jones* v. *National Coal Board*

"That the nature and extent of the judge's interruptions during the hearing of the evidence called on behalf of the defendants made it virtually impossible for counsel for the plaintiff to put the plaintiff's case properly or adequately or to cross-examine witnesses called on behalf of the defendants adequately or effectively."[34]

At the hearing Counsel for the defendants asked for, and obtained, permission to raise *mutatis mutandis* the same ground on behalf of the defendants. All the judicial courtesy shown to the trial judge by emphasising that he acted from the best of motives cannot disguise the unfairness of the trial. For a judge must have done much to drive the Court of Appeal to discuss the role of a judge in a trial.[35] After doing so, Lord Denning observed:

"If he goes beyond this, *he drops the mantle of a judge and assumes the robe of an advocate; and the change does not become him well.* Lord Chancellor Bacon spoke right[36] when he said that: 'Patience and gravity of hearing is an essential part of justice, and an over-speaking judge is no well-tuned cymbal'."[37] (italics supplied)

A fresh trial was ordered. Such observations on the conduct of a trial judge far from shaking confidence in the administration of justice, establish such confidence, because people know that when the judge has misconducted himself there is a remedy. But it is not always possible for a party to appeal, because the cost may be prohibitive. In that event, it is submitted that there is no reason why a newspaper should not, after carefully veryfying the facts, make the same observations which the Court of Appeal had made including a reference to the purity of the judge's motives.

10.65 In *Baradakanta* v. *Registra, Orissa H.C.*[38] Art. 235 was considered in the context of a criminal contempt of Court as defined in s. 2(c), Contempt of Courts Act.[39] Palekar J. (for himself, Ray C.J. and Chandrachud J.) observed that no comprehensive definition of the "administration of justice" had been brought to the attention of the Court. Palekar J. said that administration of justice did not consist merely in the adjudication of disputes between parties. Article 235 entrusted to the High Court (and not to individual judges) disciplinary control over the subordinate judiciary, and the exercise of disciplinary jurisdiction by the High Court was essential for the administration of justice. Consequently, vilificatory criticism of a judge functioning as a judge even in an administrative or non-adjudicatory matter amounted to criminal contempt.[40] Further, a

Baradakanta's Case: Art. 235 and contempt of court in respect of administrative work of the High Court in holding a departmental inquiry. The majority view

---

[32] (1929) 2 K.B. 1. [33] (1957) 2 K.B. 55.
[34] ibid. p. 61. [35] ibid. p. 64.
[36] Essays of Counsels Civil and Moral, Of Judicature.
[37] (1957) 2 K.B. *supra* at p. 64. [38] (1974) 2 S.C.R. 282, ('74) A.SC. 710.
[39] See para 10.74 and *f.n.* 72 in which the definition is set out.
[40] ('74) A.SC. at pp. 724-5.

right of appeal did not give a right to commit contempt of court.[41] The administrative inquiry in the appellant's conduct as a judge was so clearly connected with the administration of justice, and the contempt was so gross that on the facts the decision is right. The judgment did not purport to lay down the whole law of contempt, and it did not consider the importance to be given to the right to freedom of speech and expression. But in his concurring judgment Krishna Iyer J. (for himself and Bhagwati J.) rightly referred to *R.* v. *Commr. of Police of the Metropolis Ex p. Blackburn* (*No. 2*)[42] in which all the three Lord Justices emphasised the fact that the power of committing for contempt could not be used to stifle freedom of speech. Lord Denning M. R. said:

Important aspects emphasized in the concurring judgment of Krishna Iyer J.

> "Nor will we use (the contempt jurisdiction) to suppress those who speak against us. We do not fear criticism, nor do we resent it. For there is something far more important at stake. *It is no less than freedom of speech itself* . . . Mr. Quintin Hogg has criticised the court, but in so doing, he is exercising his undoubted right. The article contains an error, no doubt, but errors do not make it a contempt of court. *We must uphold his right to the uttermost.*"[43] (italics supplied)

Again, the majority judgment in *Baradakanta's Case* does not deal with the "vilification" of a judge, if such vilification takes the form of complaint made in good faith to persons in authority to prevent abuses in the administration of justice. To say of a judge that he takes bribes and decides in favour of those who bribe him would be to "vilify" the judge if it was untrue or stated without belief in its truth. But to report a judge who takes bribes to persons in authority for action or for further investigation cannot be contempt, for otherwise the disciplinary jurisdiction of the High Court can never be invoked without risking committal for contempt of court.[44] And the same is true of judges of superior courts. It would be surprising if Lord Chancellor Bacon could be impeached for taking bribes and deprived of his office in the 1620s, but a judge of a superior court in the 1970s could not be dealt with likewise on complaints made in good faith to persons in authority. The judgment of the Allahabad High Court, which Krishna Iyer J. cited, said as much.[45] It is submitted that the approach of Krishna Iyer J. to contempt of court is to be preferred to that of the majority, subject to this that the American approach to freedom of speech in general, and to contempt of court in particular, is not applicable in India.[46]

Submission: Krishna Iyer J.'s approach to contempt of court ought to be preferred to the approach of the majority

---

[41] ibid. p. 720. [42] (1968) 2 Q.B. 150.

[43] ibid. p. 155. Salmon L.J. and Edmund Davies L.J. expressed similar views.

[44] This is recognized in s. 6 of the Contempt of Courts Act, 1971: "A person shall not be guilty of contempt of court in respect of any statement made by him in good faith concerning the presiding officer of a subordinate court to (*a*) any other subordinate court (*b*) the High Court to which it is subordinate. *Explanation.*—In this section, 'subordinate court' means subordinate to a High Court."

[45] ('74) A.SC. supra at pp. 733-4. He quoted the following passage: "It would indeed be extraordinary if the law should provide a remedy — the conduct of even a member of the highest Judicial Tribunal in the exercise of his judicial office may be the subject of enquiry with a view to see whether he is fit to continue to hold that office—and yet no one should be able to initiate proceedings for an enquiry by a complaint to the appropriate authority by reason of a fear of being punished for contempt, and I can find no justification for this view": *R.* v. *B. S. Nayyar* ('50) A.A. 549, 554.

[46] See paras 10.27, 10.28, 10.72 and 10.73 of the text.

10.66 Reverting to *Sham Lal's Case* and *Mulgaokar's Case* it must be observed that s. 14 of the Contempt of Courts Act, 1971, deals with contempt of the Supreme Court *ex facie* the Court, and expressly provides that the judges in whose presence contempt of court has been committed shall not hear the contempt matter if the contemnor desired that the matter be heard by a different judge. In view of the fact that contempt *ex facie* the court is the most serious and requires to be repressed with a strong hand, and in view of the principle underlying s. 14 it is submitted that Beg C.J. should not have allowed the contempt notices to be placed before a Bench of which he was a member. In *Sham Lal's Case* he was one of the majority judges in the *Habeas Corpus Case* whose judgments had been assailed; and, as his dissenting judgment against dropping the contempt proceedings shows, a fair trial of the contempt proceedings was not possible before a judge who was convinced that he was right and had followed the only course open to any judge. If the matter had been placed before him and his brother judges, he ought to have inquired at the outset whether Counsel appearing for the contemnor desired that the matter be placed before a Bench of which he was not a member. Similarly, in *Mulgaokar's Case,* his confidential letter to the Chief Justices of the High Courts was the subject of attack and the same principles apply here as they apply to *Sham Lal's Case.*

Sham Lal's Case and *Mulgaokar's Case*: Submission

Beg C.J. should have had the matter placed before a Bench of which he was not a member

10.67 Taking up *Mulgaokar's Case* first, the facts were briefly these: Beg C.J. addressed a confidential letter to the Chief Justices of the High Courts in India suggesting that a code of conduct laying down rules for the guidance of judges should be drawn up by the Chief Justices in a conference. According to him, he made certain suggestions which were merely illustrative, which were to have been the subject of discussion in conference, so that such rules as the Chief Justices considered proper could be framed. The words complained of contained *inter alia,* the following: "So adverse has been the criticism, that the Supreme Court Judges, some of whom had prepared the draft Code, have disowned it." According to Beg C.J. these words came near contempt, first, because according to him, judges of the Supreme Court were not even aware of the contents of the letter, and, secondly, because the words would suggest that the judges lacked moral courage to stand by what they have done by disowning it. In *Mulgaokar's Case* the whole court decided to drop the proceedings "for reasons to be recorded later."[47] In his judgment Beg C.J. referred *inter alia,* to the judgments of Krishna Iyer J. and Kailasam J. In "A Concluding Note" Krishna Iyer J. described his own judgment as "a long and inconclusive essay in contempt jurisprudence bearing on scandalising the judges *qua* judges," aware that not high falutin rhetoric but hard-headed realism, illumined by constitutional values, must set the limits and interpret the statute."[48] In "An Afterword", Krishna Iyer J. said:

Facts of *Mulgaokar's Case*

Court decided to drop the proceedings

Krishna Iyer J.'s "inconclusive essay in contempt jurisprudence"

---

[47] ('78) A.SC. at p. 747. The accuracy of Beg C.J.'s account of the confidential letter was disputed by Mr. Mulgaokar in an article entitled "The Judiciary and the Claims of Public Interest" in the *Indian Express* dated March 1, 1978 at p. 6. He rightly pointed out that although Beg C.J. purported to agree with Kailasam J. that observations on the merits would be improper once the proceedings were dropped, the observations actually made "are bound to be widely interpreted as applying to the editorial conduct of the *Indian Express.* We therefore owe it to ourselves to enter our defence."

[48] ('78) A.SC. at p. 746.

"An afterword has become necessitous (sic) because the learned Chief Justice has, in his reasons, made some critical observations on men and matters based on his rich experience, high responsibility and urge to right wrongs. *While respecting his feeling of hurt* and attempt to set the record straight regarding his prior judgment and letters on canons of judicial ethics, I desist from comments on the author or the article, including its correctness and propriety, for fear that an indelible word, writ incautiously, *may fester into an incurable wound*."[49] (italics supplied)

In a brief judgment, Kailasam J. rightly said that the judgment of Krishna Iyer J. need not be dealt with as it was admittedly *obiter*, As to the judgment of Beg C.J., once the court had decided to drop the contempt proceedings *without calling upon Counsel to deal with the case*, "it is not right and proper to make any comments about the facts of the case . . . I refrain from referring to the publication in the 'The Indian Express' or about the article in the newspaper by Shri A. G. Noorani."[50] It is submitted that Krishna Iyer J. was in error in launching on "an inconclusive essay in contempt jurisprudence". A brief judgment, such as was delivered by Untwalia and Kailasam JJ. in *Sham Lal's Case*, would have upheld the dignity of the Court much better. A judgment delivered after the Court had decided to drop the proceedings, and had not heard Counsel for the parties, has little value, if indeed it is not void for violating the principles of natural justice.

Mulgaokar's Case: offending words did not relate to any judicial act of Beg C.J.

10.68 It may be observed that no action of the Chief Justice in his judicial capacity was assailed. Neither the Constitution nor any law imposes on the Chief Justice a duty of formulating codes of conduct for the High Court and/or the Supreme Court judges. Consequently, the letter was a voluntary exercise in law reform. Secondly, the secrecy accompanying the proposals was out of place, for, a code of judicial ethics is not a matter merely for the Chief Justices but for the whole judiciary, the Bar and the public. Thirdly, the Chief Justices' conference has no legal status: it is an informal gathering of Chief Justices to exchange views on problems affecting the administration of justice. Its proceedings are not public, so that the discussions in the conference are not subjected to public and professional criticism. It is believed that when the Conference was originally started, resolutions were not passed unless all the Chief Justices present agreed. Later, that practice has been departed from and resolutions have been passed by majorities; and resolutions passed unanimously at one time find the Chief Justices divided on the same subject at another time. Finally, the Chief Justices's idea that a code of judicial ethics was wanted on the lines of the Code of Judicial Ethics for Judges in the United States, necessarily implied that the conduct of judges of the superior courts had fallen from the high level of which the High Courts and the Supreme Court had been proud. This implication, if true, coming from the Chief Justice of India, would reflect adversely on the superior judiciary in India. Since Beg C.J. has referred in his judgment to the Code of Judicial Ethics in the United States, the following quotation from the well known book on *Tipping the Scales* appears to the present writer to give a complete answer:

Code of Judicial Ethics suggested by Beg C.J.

Mr. Cecil's comment on the Code of Judicial Ethics in the U.S.A. a complete answer to Beg C.J.

[49] ibid.

[50] ibid. p. 747.

"In 1962 the American Judicature Society published a *Handbook of Judges*. It was full of . . . wise sayings, delivered from ancient times to the present day. Judges were also recommended in the Handbook to read nineteen other books and further publications of the Society 'too numerous to list'. *But the trouble is that telling judges how to behave is ineffective.* Reputable American judges do not require these home-tutors, while the disreputable presumably do not read them. *What is required is a tradition of integrity in the judicial system and that has not yet been established in the U.S.A.*"[51] (italics supplied)

The same topic continued

10.69 Any article which criticised the proposals made secretly by the Chief Justice of India on a matter of such public importance as a code of judicial ethics can hardly be treated as contempt in the sense of lowering the position, dignity and authority of the judge in the administration of justice. In this connection, it may be mentioned that the Chief Justice of India had no supervisory jurisdiction over the Chief Justices or of the judges of the High Courts, and if the reactions of the Chief Justices of the High Courts were adverse, it is not surprising, having regard to what was proposed to be done. And since the code of ethics was to be enforced by disciplinary sanctions, the resentment of the judiciary becomes more intelligible. Beyond the above observations, no further comment is called for, except to say that the judgment of Krishna Iyer J. refers to a large number of decided cases on contempt, but it is unnecessary to deal with his judgment, because he himself describes his discussion as inconclusive.

Facts of *Sham Lal's Case*

10.70 Coming to *Sham Lal's Case,* the facts were briefly these: An amended notice was issued to *The Times of India* on 11th January 1978 to show cause why proceedings for contempt should not be initiated against it in respect of *a news item on the Supreme Court's judgment in the Habeas Corpus Case.* The Notice was heard by Beg C.J., Untwalia and Kailasam JJ. In a brief order, Untwalia, and Kailasam JJ. said that they had considered the pros and cons of the matter, and were of the view that it was not a fit case in which formal proceedings for contempt should be started; and they ordered that the proceeding should be dropped. Beg C.J. dissented, and delivered a judgment in which he sought to defend the majority decision in the *Habeas Corpus Case* against what he considered to be improperly motivated attacks on that judgment. He said, "Nevertheless, certain interested persons with motives which are to be presumed to be ulterior and unhealthy, have continued to misrepresent to the public that what the majority of judges of this Court held was that rights to life and liberty themselves were suspended."[52]

Proceedings dropped by the majority

Beg C.J.'s dissent

Beg C.J.'s defence of the majority judgments in the *Habeas Corpus Case* in his dissenting judgment

10.71 It is most unfortunate that Beg C.J. should have thought fit to defend his own judgment against public criticism. It is submitted that the wiser course for Beg C.J. would have been to follow the rule laid down by Lord Atkin for himself, namely, not to discuss publicly any judgment of his once it had been delivered.[53] The question raised by the issue of the "Notice" to the *Times of India* was first, whether formal proceedings for contempt should be initiated in respect of the statements made by the *Times of India* about the Supreme Court judgments in the *Habeas Corpus Case,* and secondly, if such proceedings were initiated, whether the offending words constituted contempt of court. The question whether the majority judgments in

---

[51] Cecil, *Tipping the Scales*, pp. 13-14. [52] ('78) A.SC. at p. 481.
[53] See Heuston, *Liversidge* v. *Anderson in Retrospect*, 86 L.Q.R. 33 at p. 56.

the *Habeas Corpus Case* ("the majority judgments") were right or wrong, did not directly arise, because judgments may be completely wrong, and yet the offending words about them may amount to contempt of court. However, once it was decided by a majority to drop the proceedings, it is submitted that a judgment dissenting from that course could not, with propriety, go into the question whether the majority judgments were right or wrong, much less whether they were the only judgments which could have been delivered. His defence of his judgment in the *Habeas Corpus Case* will be considered separately in a full discussion of that case.

Freedom of speech and contempt of Court: difference between Indian and American Law

10.72 Reverting to freedom of speech, it has been submitted above that Art. 19(1) (*a*) read with sub-Art. (2) is very different from the First Amendment to the U.S. Constitution and that the test of "clear and present danger" is inapplicable to the freedom of speech and expression guaranteed by our Constitution. Nowhere is the difference more marked than in cases of contempt of court decided in the United States and in India. We have seen that the First Amendment to the U.S. Constitution contains an absolute prohibition; however, Art. 19(2) expressly saves restrictions in relation to contempt of court. The power to commit for contempt has been held to be inherent in every Court of Record, and the High Courts in India have exercised that power according to well-recognized principles governing its exercise in England.[54] In the United States the guarantee of the freedom of speech and press has been construed to mean that the test of "clear and present danger" applies also to proceedings for contempt of court and a latitude is permitted in the United States both as regards insulting observations about a judge and as regards pending matters which would not be permitted in India or in England. Thus, in *Pennekamp* v. *Florida*[55] the Supreme Court reversed the concurrent judgments of the State Court which had held that the publications complained of were an attempt to abase the Court and were therefore contempt. The effect of the Supreme Court judgment has been stated thus:

The test of "clear and present danger" applied to contempt of court in the United States

"Newspaper editorials intimating bias on the part of the courts towards those who are charged with crime, with specific reference to cases where indictments have been held insufficient and to the dismissal of 'padlock' suits to close alleged gambling places, and a cartoon which pictured a robed compliant figure as a judge on the bench tossing aside formal charges to hand a document marked 'Defendant dismissed' to a powerful figure close at his left arm and of an intentionally drawn criminal type while at the right a futile individual labeled 'public interest' vainly protests, did not create such a clear and present danger to the administration of justice as to be punishable as contempt consistently with the constitutional right of free speech."[56]

It is needless to multiply cases. The whole position has been summed up thus:

---

[54] "It is a contempt of any Court of Justice to disturb and obstruct the Court by insulting it in its presence and at a time when it is actually sitting"; and "any act done or any writing published which is calculated to bring the Court or a Judge into contempt or to lower his authority or to interfere with the due course of justice or lawful process of the Court is a contempt of Court"; "Speeches or writings misrepresenting the proceeding of the Court or prejudicing the public or against a party are contempts.": *Halsbury*, 3rd ed., Vol. 8, p. 5 and p. 7 respectively.

[55] (1945) 328 U.S. 331, 90 L. ed. 1295. [56] ibid.

"Punishment for contempt is in violation of the constitutional guarantee of free speech and press, in absence of a showing that the utterances created a 'clear and present danger' to the administration of justice according to the facts and circumstances involved in the particular case. Under the clear and present danger rule, comment by the press on administration of justice, to be punishable as contempt without violating the right of free speech, must have evil consequences extremely serious and the degree of imminence must be extremely high.

The possibility of engendering disrespect for the judiciary as a result of the published criticism of a judge is not such a substantive evil as will justify impairment of the constitutional right of freedom of speech and press. And the mere fact that misstatements and misrepresentations are contained in articles criticizing judicial action is not decisive. And this is so even though the misrepresentation is deliberate.

There are some intimations that under the right of free speech the right to criticize judicial action has a greater scope where the judiciary is elective.

Beyond these general principles, no definition can give an answer to the question as to what is meant by clear and present danger to a fair administration of justice."[57]

Indian law different *Namboodripad's Case*: communist view of the judiciary

10.73 The view taken in India is different. In *E. M. S. Namboodripad* v. *T. N. Nambiar*,[58] the Supreme Court held that while Art. 19 (1) (*a*) guaranteed the freedom of speech and expression, Art. 19 (2) showed that it was also intended that contempt of court should not be committed in exercising that right. The case arose out of a press conference held by the appellant, the chief minister of Kerala, in which he said that the judiciary was "an instrument of oppression" and that the judges "were guided and dominated by class hatred, class interests and class prejudices, instinctively favouring the rich against the poor". Hidayatullah C.J. held that this was a clear case of contempt.[59] It is submitted that the judgment is correct in the result, but is unsatisfactory when it attempts to summarize

Submission: discussion of the true communist doctrine irrelevant

". . . into a very small compass, many thousands of words in which these doctrines have been debated from Plekhanov to Lenin through the thoughts of Kautsky, Kerensky, Lesalle, Belinsky and others who attempted a middle line between the revisionism of Bernstein and the Bolshevik views of Lenin".[60] "We have done so because Mr. V. K. Krishna Menon[61] sneered that many people learn about communism through Middleton Murray."[62]

It is submitted that the sneer of counsel ought not to have launched the court on an inquiry as to the true communist creed about the judiciary in a capitalist society, for such an inquiry would require months of study in several languages before a correct conclusion could be reached—if at all! Further, such an inquiry was wholly irrelevant, for the real issue before the court was not whether the appellant had rightly stated the communist creed, as he contended, or had been mistaken about it, as held by the court. The real issue was whether his words were likely "to raise in the minds of the people a general dissatisfaction with and distrust of all judicial decisions",[63] and the Supreme Court rightly answered the issue in the affirmative. It is submitted that the appellant's words would have constituted contempt of court even if it was demonstrated

---

[57] See annotation 2, *Terminiello* v. *Chicago* (1948) 93 L. ed. 1131 at pp. 1151 *et seq.*

[58] (1971) 1 S.C.R. 697, ('70) A.SC. 2015.

[59] Surprisingly enough the Supreme Court reduced the fine of Rs. 1000 imposed upon the appellant to a nominal fine of Rs. 50: ('70) A.SC. pp. 2016, 2024-5.

[60] ibid. p. 2023.

[61] Counsel for the appellant.

[62] ('70) A.SC. *supra* at p. 2023.

[63] ibid. p. 2024.

that he had correctly stated the communist creed, for having regard to the forum which he had selected, namely, a press conference, and the audience he hoped to reach,—the newspaper reading public —it was clear that he was not discussing theoretically a political doctrine, but was asserting that his words were true of the Indian judiciary. He showed his consciousness of what he was doing when he said at the press conference, "The High Court and the Supreme Court can haul me up if they want".[64] In *Leo Roy Frey* v. *R. Prasad*[65] it was held that the power of courts to punish for publication calculated to obstruct the due course of justice and law was not restricted by constitutional guarantees of the liberty of the press and that the liberty of the press was subordinate to the independence of the judiciary and the proper administration of justice. In *State* v. *Ram Chander*[66] the Court said:

Leo Roy Frey v. R. Prasad

State v. Ram Chander

"Freedom of press, liberty of speech and action, so far as they do not contravene the law of contempt are to prevail without let or hindrance. But at the same time the maintenance of dignity of the Courts is one of the cardinal principles of rule of law in a free democratic country and when the criticism which may otherwise be couched in language that appears to be mere criticism results in undermining the dignity of Courts and course of justice in the land it must be held repugnant and punished. No court can look with equanimity on a publication which may have tendency to interfere with the administration of justice."[67]

Rao Harnarain Singh's Case

Again in *Rao Harnarain Singh* v. *Gumani Ram Arya*[68] it was said that no notion of the liberty of the Press can stand in the way of the inherent power of the Court to punish for contempt, and Art. 19(2) applied. However, it has been said[69] that where a pending case in respect of which contempt is alleged to have been committed is a case of defamation and the person defamed is a politician (or a public man) an important question arises. In view of the guarantee of freedom of speech there ought to be freedom to criticize the activities of public men, and though a preliminary trial by the press should be put down, where there is no intention to prejudice the trial, but the contempt is alleged to consist in the tendency to prejudice such trial, the Court would have to take several matters into account. Where a newspaper asserts that what it has said is true and is prepared to prove it in a criminal court, it would be straining the law of contempt to use it to put down such criticism in the public interest. *In re Hiren Bose*[70] it was held that though the press is free to criticize the judicial system under Art. 19(1)(*a*), and though justice is not a cloistered virtue intolerant of criticism, the press cannot commit contempt of court in the garb of criticism.

In re Hiren Bose

---

[64] ibid. p. 2017.

[65] (1958) Punj. 1723, ('58) A.Punj. 377.

[66] ('59) A.Punj. 41.

[67] ibid. p. 42. See also *State* v. *Vikar Ahmed* (1954) Hyd. 270, ('54) A.Hyd. 175.

[68] (1958) Punj. 1272, ('58) A.Punj. 273; see also *Bijoyananda* v. *Balakrushna* ('53) A.Or. 249. The above cases were relied on in *Sher Singh* v. *R. P. Kapur* ('68) A.Punj. 217, 230 (*held*, that "contempt of court" was in a class by itself and the summary procedure provided for it was a reasonable restriction in the public interest).

[69] *State* v. *Editors, Matrubhumi* ('54) A.Or. 149.

[70] ('69) A.Cal. 1 (S.B.) (*held*, that the article in question was not a mere libel on the judges, but used language which was likely to undermine the dignity of, and impair the respect for, the High Court, and the editor was guilty of contempt of court).

10.74 Contempt of court has not been defined either in the General Clauses Act or in the Constitution although contempt of court is mentioned in Arts. 19(2) and 129, and in entry 77, List I, Sch. 7. In *Legal Remembrancer* v. *B. B. Das Gupta*[71] the court rightly observed that the framers of the Constitution thought it unnecessary to define contempt of court, since judicial decisions in England and in India had given a well-recognized meaning to the words.[72] In *Lakhan Singh* v. *Balbir Singh*[73] it was held that the law of contempt as laid down by British and Indian Courts imposed nothing but reasonable restrictions on the exercise of the right of freedom of speech and expression. The test of clear and present danger laid down in *Schenck's Case*[74] was rejected, because even in the United States there was a division of opinion on its suitability and because under our Constitution all that the court had to decide was whether the restriction was reasonable.

The "clear and present danger test" rejected

10.75 In *Virendra* v. *Punjab*[75] the Supreme Court had to consider the validity of ss. 2 and 3 of the Punjab Special Powers (Press) Act, 1956,[76] which authorised the imposition of drastic restrictions on the freedom of the press. The facts giving rise to the petition were these: A "Save Hindi Agitation" was started by the Hindi Raksha Samiti and was joined by the Arya Samaj:

***Virendra's Case*: restraints on freedom of the press**

> "the agitation apparently followed the usual course and pattern of political agitation of this kind with its attendant demonstrations, slogans and satyagraha by the volunteers and lathi charge by the police, and it culminated in the Save Hindi agitation volunteers' forcible entry into the Secretariat of the Punjab Government at Chandigarh."[77]

---

[71] (1953) Pat. 1069, ('54) A.P. 203; rel. on in *K. P. Noordeen* v. *A. K. Gopalan* ('68) A.Ker. 301, 309 (*held*, that a law which prohibited speech with reference to a case which was pending or imminent in such manner as to interfere with the course of justice, and which provided for the punishment of such interference after due trial, imposed only reasonable restrictions, substantive and procedural, on the freedom of speech). The observations in *R. K. Garg* v. *S. A. Azad* ('57) A.A. 37 that contempt of court was not defined because it was intended to keep it flexible in the light of Art. 19(2) are, it is, submitted, not correct.

[72] However, the Contempt of Courts Act, 1971, has defined "Contempt of Court" as follows (unless the context otherwise requires): (*a*) "contempt of court" means civil contempt or criminal contempt; (*b*) "civil contempt" means wilful disobedience to any judgment, decree, direction, order, writ or other process of a court or wilful breach of an undertaking given to a court; (*c*) "criminal contempt" means the publication (whether by words, spoken or written, or by signs, or by visible representations or otherwise) of any matter or the doing of any other act whatsoever which — (*i*) scandalises or tends to scandalise, or lowers or tends to lower the authority of, any court; or (*ii*) prejudices, or interferes or tends to interfere with, or obstructs or tends to obstruct, the administration of justice in any other manner. It will be seen that the definition enacts in a statutory form the well-recognized meaning which the words "contempt of court" had acquired in England and in India. In view of this definition, the argument seriously pressed in *E. T. Sen* v. *E. Narayanan* ('69) A.Del. 201 (F.B.) and rejected after an elaborate discussion of Supreme Court decisions no longer survives. It is submitted that independently of the definition, the argument was untenable as the Full Bench judgment clearly shows.

[73] (1953) 1 All. 796, ('53) A.A. 342.

[74] (1918) 249 U.S. 47, 53 L. ed. 470, 473-4. In *Babulal Parate's Case* (1961) 3 S.C.R. 423, ('61) A.SC. 884, our Supreme Court rejected the test of clear and present danger laid down in *Schenck's Case*: see para 10.36 of the text.

[75] (1958) S.C.R. 308, ('57) A.SC. 896.

[76] See (1958) S.C.R. *supra* at pp. 312-3 for the material provisions of ss. 2 and 3.

[77] (1958) S.C.R. *supra* at p. 314.

Under these circumstances, an order was issued against the petitioner under s. 2 (1) (*a*) of the Act prohibiting him from publishing any article, report, news item, etc. relating to the activities of the "Save Hindi Agitation" for a period of two months. An order was also passed under s. 3 prohibiting him from bringing into Punjab the newspaper printed and published at Delhi. Das C.J. cited with approval the test of reasonableness laid down in *Row's Case*[78] and applying that test he said that the abuse by the press of its great power, the powerful influence of newspapers for good or evil on their readers, the large circulation and the easy facilities for such circulation must all enter into the judicial verdict in considering the reasonableness of an impugned restriction upon the press. Normal social interest demanded freedom of the press, but society's interest in public order might require reasonable subordination of the social interest in free speech to the needs of social interest in public order. The agitation might have taken a violent turn disturbing public tranquility and public order in the State which was on the border of a foreign State where tranquility was essential for the safety of the State. If power for speedy action had to be given, wide powers to be exercised on the subjective satisfaction of Government had to be conferred on the authorities.[79] The power was not unfettered as the purposes for which it was to be exercised were specified, and abuse of discretionary power was not to be presumed. As the order under s. 2 (1) (*a*) was of a limited duration and there was a right of representation against it, Das C.J. held that s. 2 (1) (*a*) was valid. He held, however that s. 3 was void as the order made under it need not be limited in point of time and there was no provision for a representation being made against it by the person aggrieved. This decision shows that restrictions more stringent than pre-censorship could be imposed in the interest of public order and the publication of certain matters could be totally prohibited for a limited period of time.

Restraints imposed on the subjective satisfaction of Government upheld

10.76 *Ramji Lal Modi's Case*[80] and *Virendra's Case*[81] were followed (i) in *N. Veerabhrahmam* v. *State*[82] and it was held that s. 99A, Cr.P.C., did not violate Art. 19 (1) (*a*) as it was covered by Art. 19 (2). It left a person free to write books without offending deliberately the religious sentiments of other citizens and (ii) in *Indulal K. Yagnik* v. *State*[83] where it was held that s. 3 of the Police (Incitement to Disaffection) Act, 1922, did not violate Art. 19 (1) (*a*) as it was protected by Art. 19 (2). In view of the explanation to s. 3 and in view of s. 4, it could not be held that the restriction imposed by s. 3 was unlimited, or that it included in its purview even innocent expressions of disapprobation against Government or its measures, or conditions of service of the constabulary.

---

[78] See para 10.18.

[79] "Quick decision and swift and effective action must be of the essence of those powers and the exercise of it must, therefore, be left to the subjective satisfaction of the Government charged with the duty of maintaining law and order. To make the exercise of these powers justiciable and subject to the judicial scrutiny will defeat the very purpose of the enactment": (1958) S.C.R. *supra* at pp. 320-1.

[80] (1957) S.C.R. 860, ('57) A.SC. 620. [81] (1958) S.C.R. 308, ('57) A.SC. 896.

[82] ('59) A.A.P. 572.

[83] (1960) Bom. 305, ('60) A.B. 399, 62 Bom.L.R. 206.

10.77 We have seen that in *Ramji Lal Modi's Case*[84] and again in *Virendra's Case*[85] the Supreme Court emphasized the distinction between the words "for the maintenance of" occurring in the unamended Art. 19 (2) and the words "in the interests of" occurring in the amended Article. One of the conclusions to be drawn from these cases is that if an activity has a tendency to cause public disorder it can be penalised even though in some cases that activity may not result in a breach of public order. It is now necessary to consider the decision of the Allahabad High Court in *Ram Manohar Lohia* v. *Supdt., Central Prison*[86] which was delivered before the two Supreme Court cases mentioned above. There, the petitioner applied for a writ of *habeas corpus* contending that s. 3, U.P. Special Powers Act, 1932, under which he was detained was void as violating Art. 19 (1) (*a*). The application was heard by Desai and Chaturvedi JJ., but as they differed, the points of difference were referred to Agarwala J. who agreed with Desai J. in allowing the petition. As stated in the preamble, the U.P. Special Powers Act was enacted in 1932 in order "to make provisions against and to take powers to deal with instigation to the illegal refusal of the payment of certain liabilities". The Act was to remain in force for one year, but the period was extended, and in 1940, the Act was made permanent. The Act was to come into force in those Districts to which it was extended by a Notification in the State Gazette. Between April and June, 1954, the Act was extended to 33 Districts including Farrukhabad District. S. 3 of the Act, and the definition of liability occurring therein in s. 2 are as follows:

Virendra's Case followed

Ram Manohar Lohia's Case: the High Court decision

Difference between Desai and Chaturvedi JJ. referred to Agarwala J.

"Whoever by words either spoken or written or by signs or by visible representations or otherwise instigates expressly or by implication, any person or class of persons not to pay or to defer payment of any liability, shall be punishable with imprisonment which may extend to six months, or with fine, extending to Rs. 250/- or with both.

The word 'liability' is defined in s. 2 to mean: (1) land revenue, (2) any sum recoverable as arrears of land revenue, (3) any tax, rate, cess or other due or amount, (4) as above, payable to any local authority, (5) rent of agricultural land, (6) anything recoverable as arrears of, or (7) along with rent of agricultural land."

Desai J. quoted extensively from American decisions on the First Amendment to the U.S. Constitution and held that the impugned restrictions were not in the interest of public order, because "the words 'in the interest of public order' mean 'for the maintenance of public order'," a conclusion which cannot be sustained in view of the clear distinction made between the two expressions in the Supreme Court judgments considered above.[87] Chaturvedi J., it is submitted rightly, distinguished the American authorities, and the test of "present and clear danger" there laid down, by saying that the provisions of our Constitution relating to freedom of speech were very different from those contained in the U.S. Constitution. He said that an exhortation to the members of the public not to obey the laws in general, or any particular law, was likely to disturb the state of tranquility prevailing among the members of the public, and the preaching of disobedience of valid laws was

The views of Desai J.

Chaturvedi J.

---

[84] (1957) S.C.R. *supra*.
[85] (1958) S.C.R. *supra*.
[86] (1955) 1 All. 355, ('55) A.A. 193; affd. (1960) 2 S.C.R. 821, ('60) A.SC. 633.
[87] See para 10.33 and *f.n.* 37 thereto.

meant to disturb the public tranquility. Criticism of a law was one thing, exhortation to disobey duly promulgated and valid laws was another, and such exhortation had a tendency to disturb the state of tranquility which, according to the Supreme Court in *Romesh Thappar's Case*[88] was comprised in the concept of public order. The law had remained inoperative from 1940 till April 1954, and only when the State Government decided to apply its provisions to a particular area did those provisions become operative. This feature showed that the law was in the nature of emergency legislation and was to be brought into force when in the opinion of the Government an emergency existed. That was an additional reason for holding that the restrictions imposed by the Act were reasonable. He expressed a doubt whether rent of agricultural land payable by private persons, which was included in the definition of 'liability', could be upheld as valid, but that question did not arise in the case, and the provision was severable. Agarwala J. agreed with Desai J. He drew heavily on the American cases, and his view was coloured by the fact that great men had been at times obliged to disobey the law as a matter of conscience, as for example, Socrates and Mahatma Gandhi.[89] Agarwala J. appears to have thought that unless action led to violence or breach of the peace it would not be prohibited in the interest of public order. The actual decision however is rested on the ground that though a large-scale action for non-payment of taxes or violation of laws may in extreme case lead to a disturbance of public order unless such cases could be separated, the impugned provisions could not be sustained. In view of *Ramji Lal Modi's Case*[90] and *Virendra* v. *Punjab*[91] it is submitted that the decision of Chaturvedi J. is correct.

Ram Manohar Lohia's Case: the Supreme Court decision

10.78 However, the Supreme Court affirmed the majority decision in *Lohia's Case.*[92] After referring to the history of the law as originating in the no-tax campaign started in 1932 against British Rule by the Indian National Congress[93] and after referring to the Preamble and to the provisions of the impugned Act, Subba Rao J. analysed s. 3, read with s. 2, into several concrete instances and concluded:

"In its wide amplitude the section takes in the innocent and the guilty persons, *bona fide* and *mala fide* advice, individuals and class, abstention from payment and deferment of payment, expressed or implied instigation, indirect or direct instigation, liability due not only to Government but to any authority or landholder. In short, no person, whether legal adviser or a friend or a well-wisher of a person instigated can escape the tentacles of this section, though in fact the rent due has been collected through coercive process or otherwise."[94]

It is difficult to state precisely what Subba Rao J. meant to say in an elaborate analysis of the amended Art. 19(2); he certainly did not

---

[88] (1950) S.C.R. 594, ('50) A.SC. 124.

[89] It is submitted that the learned Judge overlooked the fact that although Socrates and Mahatma Gandhi proclaimed the right to disobey a law, neither of them disputed that the State was entitled to visit such disobedience with punishment. In fact, Socrates submitted to the extreme penalty of the law rather than run away from Athens, maintaining that a punishment prescribed by law must be suffered.

[90] (1957) S.C.R. *supra*.

[91] (1958) S.C.R. *supra*.

[92] *Supdt. Central Prison, Fategarh* v. *Ram Manohar Lohia* (1960) 2 S.C.R. 821, ('60) A.SC. 633.

[93] It is difficult to assess the weight which that factor had in the judicial verdict.

[94] (1960) 2 S.C.R. *supra* pp. 827-8.

dispute the distinction made by the Supreme Court between the expressions "for the maintenance of public order" and "in the interest of public order". But it is submitted, that contrary to the terms of those decisions, he held that the distinction was only this, that whereas the expression "for the maintenance of public order" meant that the restrictions directly referred to such maintenance, "in the interest of public order" meant that it was merely implied. The Supreme Court held that the same result would follow by considering the question from the point of view of reasonable restrictions. There must be direct and proximate cause between public order and the restriction and not a very remote or fanciful cause. It is submitted that this part of the judgment is also incorrect. Whether restrictions are reasonable or unreasonable depends upon the content of the permissible restrictions and the judgments of the Supreme Court which led to the Constitutional Amendment show that restrictions which may be "reasonable restrictions in the interest of public order" would not be reasonable restrictions in the interest of public safety. It is submitted that the decision of the Supreme Court in *Lohia's Case* is incorrect as it overlooks the following considerations. If the definition contained in an Act falls into distinct and separate parts, or if there are indications in an Act that though not expressly divided into several parts, it is capable of being so divided, then, the whole definition will not be struck down as void but only the offending part.[95] Secondly, if the literal construction of the words used in an enactment leads to an absurd result and would involve constitutional invalidity, the Court must, if possible, put an interpretation which avoids such absurdity and unconstitutionality. For this purpose, the preamble to the Act and the mischief which the Act was designed to remedy are relevant.[96] Therefore, if the definition of liability in s. 2 of the Act, read with s. 3, and construed literally, converts an innocent act into an offence, it is not only permissible, but necessary, for the Court to read the sections so as to avoid such absurdity and unconstitutionality. The preamble to the Act shows that it was designed to make provision against and to deal with instigation to the *illegal refusal of the payment* of certain liabilities (italics supplied). Therefore, friendly advice not to pay the liabilities because they are disputed or not due, cannot fall within the terms of the section read in the light of the preamble, for the advice or opinion which is forbidden by the Act must be limited to those which can be described as incitement to an illegal refusal to pay liabilities. The Supreme Court should have read the sections in the light of the preamble and thus saved them from invalidity, unless as regards a clearly severable part it found the part void, as Chaturvedi J. found a small part void. And lastly, the fact that an Act is not immediately operative but is to be brought into operation when, in the opinion of the Executive Government,

A criticism of the Supreme Court decision

Submission: Sup. Ct.'s decision is incorrect: relevant considerations overlooked

[95] In *Bombay* v. *F. N. Balsara* (1951) S.C.R. 682, ('51) A.SC. 318, the Supreme Court found in the Bombay Prohibition Act an indication that the words "all liquids consisting of, or containing alcohol" occurring in the definition of liquor in that Act were capable of being separated into, and had in fact been separated into several items in the Act, including liquid, toilet and medicinal preparations containing alcohol. Accordingly, it held that the definition was valid except to the extent of liquid, toilet and medicinal preparations containing alcohol: (1951) S.C.R. at p. 719.

[96] See *Maxwell*, p. 43 *et seq;* Craies p. 201 *et seq.*

circumstances justify its being brought into operation shows that the Legislature left it to the judgment of the executive to decide whether the circumstances justified the application of the law. Accordingly, when the law is brought into force it is an expression of the opinion of the executive Government that circumstances have arisen which require the provisions of the Act to be applied, and *prima facie* that judgment is entitled to respect unless it is affirmatively shown that the judgment is wrong. That, in effect, was the view of Chaturvedi J. and it is submitted that that view is correct. It is submitted that the earlier Supreme Court decisions were right and the correct question to ask was: Have the prohibited activities a tendency to create a breach of public order? And it is immaterial that in some cases, there is no breach of public order. To say that an exortation to disobey the law by refusing to pay taxes or other Government dues would not have a tendency to affect public order, would be to run counter to the facts of history not in one, but in a number of countries. It is submitted that the judgment is contrary to well-settled principles laid down by the Supreme Court itself, and ought to be overruled as being clearly wrong and productive of public mischief.

Submission: *Ram Manohar Lohia's Case* ought to be overruled

Restrictions on freedom of speech in the interest of decency or morality

10.79 The freedom of speech guaranteed by Art. 19 (1) (*a*) is subject to reasonable restrictions in the interest of decency or morality. Indecent exposure and indecent publications are misdemeanours at common law.[97] S. 292, I.P.C. makes it an offence to possess obscene publications for purposes of sale or to sell such publications. This section was introduced by the Obscene Publications Act, 1925, to give effect to Art. 1 of the International Convention for the Suppression of Traffic in Obscene Publications signed by India in 1923 at Geneva. A discussion of the law of obscenity is outside the scope of this book. Courts in India had applied the test of obscenity laid down by Cockburn C.J. in *Hicklin's Case*:[98]

Obscenity: the test in *Hicklin's Case* adopted

> ". . . whether the tendency of the matter charged as obscenity is to deprave and corrupt those whose minds are open to such immoral influences, and into whose hands a publication of this sort may fall . . . it is quite certain that it would suggest to the minds of the young of either sex, or even persons of more advanced years, thoughts of a most impure and libidinous character."

This test was approved by the Supreme Court in *Ranjit D. Udeshi* v. *Maharashtra.*[99] The appellant was convicted under s. 292 I.P.C. for being in possession, for purposes of sale, of "Lady Chatterley's Lover" (unexpurgated edition) and for selling a copy of it. In rejecting the appellant's contention[1] that s. 292 violated Art. 19 (1) (*a*), the Court approved the test laid down in *Hicklin's Case* and held that s. 292 was valid as it did not go beyond "obscenity" which fell directly within the words "public decency or morality" mentioned in Art. 19 (2). On the same ground, s. 3 (6) Press (Objectionable Matter) Act, 1951, in so far as it includes words which may be grossly indecent, scurrilous or obscene, and ss. 4 and 6 were upheld as falling under Art. 19 (2).[2] Similarly, in *Shanker & Co.* v. *Madras,*[3] s. 1, Press (Objectionable Matter) Act, 1951, was held not to violate Art.

---

97 *Halsbury,* Vol. 10 (3rd ed.) p. 666.
98 (1863) 3 Q.B. 360, 371.
99 (1965) 1 S.C.R. 65, ('65) A.SC. 881.
1 ibid.
2 *Krishna Sharma* v. *State* ('54) A.Sau. 28.
3 ('55) A.M. 498, (1955) 2 M.L.J. 319.

19 (1) (*a*) and (*g*), the court adopting the test of obscenity laid down in *Hicklin's Case*.

10.80 In *K. A. Abbas* v. *Union*[4] a Constitution Bench of the Supreme Court considered important questions relating to pre-censorship of cinematograph films in relation to the fundamental right of freedom of speech and expression: Art. 19 (1) (*a*). The petitioner challenged the action of the Board of Film Censors in refusing a "U" certificate for his film "*A Tale of Four Cities*",[5] which action was varied by the Central Government which offered to give a "U" certificate provided certain cuts were made in the film. Before the hearing, judges and counsel saw the film, and when at the hearing, the Solicitor-General, who had not seen the film, appeared, the court desired the Att.-General to appear at the hearing as he had seen the film. The Att.-General accordingly appeared, but intimated to the Court that the Central Government had decided to grant a "U" certificate to the film.[6] On this, the petition did not survive, for, the petitioner's grievance was completely redressed. He, however, applied for an amendment enabling him to raise the question of pre-censorship in general, in order that persons who invested money in making films may have guidance on this important constitutional question. The permission was granted, and the questions raised by the amendment were considered in the judgment.

Abbas's Case and pre-censorship of cinematograph films

10.81 It is submitted that the procedure adopted was unfortunate, because the court did not decide any actual controversy arising between the parties, but decided a controversy which might arise in the future. In the present case this was particularly unfortunate, for the petitioner had, in a paper entitled "Creative Expression" declared himself in favour of pre-censorship[7] and it would be difficult for him to press before the Supreme Court the minority view taken in several U.S. cases that all pre-censorship was unconstitutional, as violating the freedom of speech. It is submitted that the precedent thus created of delivering what, in substance, was an advisory opinion, is unfortunate, and ought not to be followed. Of the four issues raised by the petitioner, two did not survive, when the Solicitor-General stated that Government would set on foot legislation to secure that there would be a reasonable time limit fixed for the decision of the authorities censoring films and that an appeal should lie to a court or a tribunal and not to the Central Government.[8] The two issues which survived therefore, were

Submission: procedure followed unsatisfactory

The two issues decided in *Abbas's Case*

"(*a*) that pre-censorship itself cannot be tolerated under the freedom of speech and expression; (*b*) that even if it were a legitimate restraint on the freedom, it must be exercised on very definite principles which leave no room for arbitrary action."[9]

10.82 After observing that it was not necessary to trace the history of film censorship in India, as that had been admirably done by the Khosla Committee in its Report, Hidayatullah C.J. observed that the Cinematograph Act, 1952 (as amended in 1959) established a Board of Film Censors and provided for advisory panels at regional

A historical account of film censorship

[4] (1971) 2 S.C.R. 446, ('71) A.SC. 481.
[5] The nature of the film is described at pp. 483-4, ('71) A.SC. *supra*.
[6] ibid. p. 485.
[7] ibid. p. 489.
[8] ibid. p. 485.
[9] ibid.

centres. The Board, after examining the film or having it examined, could

(*a*) sanction the film for unrestricted public exhibition; (*b*) sanction the film for public exhibition restricted to adults; (*c*) direct such excisions and modifications in the film before sanctioning the film to any unrestricted public exhibition or for public exhibition restricted to adults; and (*d*) refuse to sanction the film for public exhibition.[10]

Ss. 5B and 5C of the Act laid down principles for guidance and for appeals.[11] S. 5B enabled the Government to lay down principles to guide the censoring authority by issuing directions and, in the exercise of that power, Government had issued such directions.[12] Hidayatullah C.J. observed that pre-censorship was only an aspect of censorship, and censorship of cinematograph films was "universal"; in fact, the petitioner had himself "pronounced strongly in favour of (censorship)".[13] The Court observed that it had been almost universally recognised that motion pictures must be treated differently from other forms of art and expression, because of a motion picture's instant appeal both to the sight and to hearing, and because a motion picture had become more true to life than even the theatre or any other form of artistic representation. Its effect, particularly on children and immature adolescents, was great. Accordingly a classification of pictures as "A" (for adults only) and "U" (for universal exhibition) was a valid classification. The U.S. decisions were considered by the Court in detail,[14] and their effect was briefly stated.[15]

Pre-censorship part of censorship of films, which was universal

Classification of films into "A" and "U" valid

Pre-censorship and classification of films into "U" and "A" not violative of Art. 19(1)(*a*)

10.83 The review of American law on censorship was followed by a review of the English law and it was stated that the rules there followed were those laid down by Mr. T. P. O'Cornor in 1918. The necessity for censorship was admitted, and restrictions as regards audiences to which the film could be shown were also provided for. The relevance of the T. P. O'Cornor's Rules in India was that, broadly speaking, censorship proceeded on the line of those rules.[16] Considering the limitations which could be put on the freedom of speech under Art. 19(2), Hidayatullah C.J. affirmed the view expressed by him in *Ranjit D. Udeshi* v. *Maharashtra*[17] that the right to the freedom of speech could not be claimed for obscenity, and that s. 292 I.P.C. embodied reasonable restrictions on that right because the law against obscenity, rightly understood and applied, did no more than secure public decency and morality. In view of the

---

[10] ibid. p. 487; before action under clause (*b*) to (*d*) was taken, the producer was allowed to present his views.
[11] The sections are set out at p. 487, ibid.
[12] The principles are set out or described at pp. 487-9, ibid.
[13] In a paper entitled "Creative Expression" written by him: ibid. p. 489.
[14] The cases considered were: *Mutual Film Corpn.* v. *Industrial Commission of Ohio* (1915) 236 U.S. 230, 59 L. ed. 552; *Schenck* v. *United States* (1919) 249 U.S. 47, 63 L. ed. 470; *Whitney* v. *California* (1927) 274 U.S. 357, 71 L. ed. 1095 (the last two cases propound the theory of "clear and present danger"); *Near* v. *Minnesota* (1931) 283 U.S. 697, 75 L. ed. 1357; *Chaplinsky* v. *New Hampshire* (1941) 315 U.S. 567, 85 L. ed. 1031; *Burstyn* v. *Wilson* (1951) 343 U.S. 495, 96 L. ed. 1098; *Kingsley International Pictures Corp.* v. *Regents* (1959) 360 U.S. 684, 3 L. ed. 2d 1512; *Freedman* v. *Maryland* (1965) 380 U.S. 51, 13 L. ed. 2d 649; *Teitel Film Corp.* v. *Cusack* (1966) 390 U.S. 139, 19 L. ed. 2d 66; *Times Film Corpn.* v. *Chicago* (1961) 365 U.S. 43, 5 L. ed. 2d 403.
[15] ('71) A.SC. *supra* at p. 492.
[16] ibid. p. 493.
[17] (1965) 1 S.C.R. 65, 70, ('65) A.SC. 881.

express provisions of our Constitution, the American and British precedents could not be decisive. The language of the 1st Amendment to the U.S. Constitution was absolute in terms, and the difference between that Amendment and the Indian law had been recognized by Mr. Justice Douglas himself, who consistently held that pre-censorship was unconstitutional.[18] Accordingly, the Court held that pre-censorship of films, their classification according to age groups and suitability for unrestricted exhibition with or without excisions was a valid exercise of the state's power in the interest of public morality and decency. The Court held that s. 5B (2) could not be challenged as imposing unreasonable restrictions.

Rules for guidance of film censors approved with a direction that regard should be had to preserving and promoting art

10.84 The Court upheld the general principles which had been laid down for the guidance of censors and said that the test of obscenity and the principles laid down in *Udeshi's Case* applied *mutatis mutandis* to an obscene cinematograph film.[19] The Supreme Court however, observed that the principles followed had one real flaw, namely, ". . . a total absence of any direction which would tend to preserve art and promote it. This artistic appeal or presentation of an episode robs it of its vulgarity and harm and this appears to be completely forgotten."[20] The reservation for artistic representation is correct, but is unlikely to offer any practical guidance to the censor who must form his own opinion about the artistic ability of the members of the audience who are likely to see the film.[21] The Court affirmed the *Hicklin test* of obscenity and stated that the evidence of experts on the question of obscenity was not relevant for in the end the question would have to be decided by the judges.[22]

Submission

10.85 In *V. K. Javali* v. *Mysore*,[23] the Supreme Court held that the speech made by the appellant, an Inspector of Education in the service of the State of Bombay, to the effect that Kannada, as the mother-tongue, as a medium of instruction, should be ahead of Hindi, fell outside Art. 19 (2). The speech was made with the permission of the Director of Education and was delivered at a prize-giving function arranged by the Hindi Prachar Sabha, Dharwar, and it could not rationally be said to lead to a disturbance of public order as envisaged by Art. 19 (2), even if the widest meaning were given to "public order".

Javali's Case: advocacy of Kannada as a medium of instruction outside Art. 19(2)

10.86 Again, the freedom of speech is subject to reasonable restrictions imposed on such freedom by a law relating to defamation. In view of this express provision contained in Art. 19 (2) it is not surprising that s. 499, I.P.C. (defamation), has been held not to

Freedom of speech subject to reasonable restrictions imposed by a law

[18] See quotation at the end of para 10.27 of the text.

[19] The Supreme Court adopted as its own summary those principles given by the Khosla Committee: see ('71) A.SC. 497, 498.

[20] ibid. p. 497. (Illustrations of artistic presentation of subjects otherwise objectionable are given at pp. 498-9 ibid.)

[21] *Cf.* "Now, who shall arbitrate?
Ten men love what I hate,
Shun what I follow, slight what I receive;
Ten who in ears and eyes
Match me: we all surmise,
They this thing and I that: whom shall my soul believe?"
—Browning.

[22] ('71) A.SC. *supra* at p. 497.

[23] ('66) A.SC. 1387.

relating to defamation

violate Art. 19(1)(*a*).[24] It has also been held that the freedom of the press, which is no higher than that of a citizen, cannot be used to infringe the law relating to defamation.[25]

Freedom to assemble peaceably and without arms

Prohibition of meetings for a limited time upheld

10.87 Article 19(1)(*b*) guarantees the right of assembly, limited to assembling peaceably and without arms, and the right is subject to reasonable restrictions in the interest of public order. In *In re Annadurai*[26] it was held that s. 41, Madras City Police Act, 1888, did not violate Art. 19(1)(*a*) and (*b*), for the section laid down certain conditions to be observed by the Commissioner before passing an order prohibiting public meetings, and one such condition was that he considered such prohibition necessary for the preservation of public peace or public safety. Although no time limit was fixed for such order, having regard to a convention for over 3 years such orders had been limited to 14 days at a time. The Court however observed that an order exceeding 14 days would be held invalid. Again, though the section did not contain an express provision enabling persons affected to approach Government against the Commissioner's orders, ". . . everybody including the accused knew that the Government, under whom the Commissioner was directly working, could be approached for rescinding or modifying such orders, though what orders the Government would pass would depend on the merits of the case".[27] Further, there is no right to hold meetings on private property belonging to others, and accordingly it has been held that instructions issued by the Railway Authorities forbidding the holding of meetings at the actual place of work such as workshops, stores and office-compounds without permission did not contravene Art. 19(1)(*b*). The case of absolute restrictions in residential areas belonging to the Railway was left to be decided when it arose.[28]

No right to hold meetings on other people's property

The nature of the right to take out a procession

10.88 What is the nature of the right to take out a procession, and is it a fundamental right? It is submitted that in taking out a procession, two fundamental rights are being exercised, namely, to assemble peaceably and without arms and to move freely throughout the territory of India, and the rights are subject to the restrictions under Art. 19(3) and Art. 19(5) respectively. If the procession carries placards or shouts slogans, or halts from time to time and speeches are made, the right to freedom of speech and expression is also being exercised and is subject to restrictions under Art. 19(2). Thus, it has been held that s. 126, Representation of the People Act, 1951, which prohibits the holding or attending of any public meeting within any constituency on the date or dates on which polling is taking place for an election was a law relating to the holding of public meetings passed in the interest of public order.[29] In *Gopal*

Restrictions on procession

---

[24] *K. V. Ramanaiah* v. *Special Public Prosecutor* ('61) A.A.P. 190.

[25] *M. B. Kanwar* v. *State* ('63) A.Punj. 201; *K. P. Narayanan* v. *Mahendrasingh* (1956) Nag. 439, ('57) A.N. 19.

[26] (1958) Mad. 865, ('59) A.M. 63.

[27] (1958) Mad. *supra* at p. 871.

[28] *Railway Board* v. *Niranjan Singh* ('63) A.Punj. 336.

[29] *Rameshwar* v. *State* (1955) 34 Pat. 855, ('57) A.P. 252.

Charan v. *Daitary Nandy*[30] it has been held that the right to lead a procession is neither an easement nor a customary right, but a fundamental right. In *M. Manjooran* v. *State*[31] in upholding s. 26, Travancore Police Act, 1952, it was said that restrictions can amount to a total prohibition of the exercise of the right even when the prohibition is strictly circumscribed in time and operative area to suit the exigencies of definite threats to public order. Prohibition under s. 26 of this type of processions in public, threatening public order, is covered by Art. 19 (3). In *State* v. *Mangala*[32] it was held that s. 14, U.P. Opium Smoking Act, 1934, which prohibited an assembly for purposes of smoking opium did not violate Art. 19 (3). The case does not contain any discussion on the nature of the restriction permitted by Art. 19 (3) namely, "in the interest of public order", but it is submitted that if it were necessary to consider the matter, it can be held that having regard to the deleterious nature of opium and the fact that it is an article which no one has a *right* to possess, the right of assembly for smoking opium is not a right covered by Art. 19 (1) (*b*).

may include total prohibition

10.89 Important questions as to meetings and processions on highways arose in *Himatlal* v. *Police Commr., Ahmedabad.*[33] The petitioner, who was the secretary of the All-India Students' Federation, applied to the Commissioner of Police for permission to hold a public meeting near Panch Kuva Darwaja, Ahmedabad, on September 5, 1969, in connection with the All-India Students' strike sponsored by the Federation. Permission to hold the meeting was refused ". . . inasmuch as a meeting was held on August 7, 1969 under similar permission whereafter certain elements had indulged in rioting and caused mischief to private and public properties, regarding which a crime also was registered . . . in view of the present position, it is not possible to grant such permission in order to maintain law and order."[34]

Himatlal's Case: meetings and processions on highways

10.90 The petitioner filed a writ petition in the Gujarat High Court (i) to quash the order refusing permission; (ii) to declare s. 33 (1) (*o*) read with s. 33 (7) of the Bombay Police Act, 1951, void; (iii) to declare Rules 7-11, 14 and 15 of the Rules for processions and public meetings void;[35] (iv) to declare that the petitioner was entitled to hold the meeting without the permission of the respondent.[36] Section 33 (1) (*o*) was impugned as conferring excessive delegation of legislative power and as violating Art. 14 as it conferred uncontrolled, naked and arbitrary power on the Commissioner of Police to grant or refuse permission. Section 33 (1) and the Rules made thereunder were also impugned as violating his right to the freedom of speech and the right to assemble peaceably guaranteed by Art. 19 (1) (*a*) and (*b*).

Provisions enabling meetings on highways impugned as violating Art. 19(1)(*a*) and (*b*)

10.91 When the petition reached hearing it had become infructuous as the day for holding the meeting had passed. However, as the petitioner would have had occasion to apply for similar permission in

Petition dismissed by the High Court

---

30 ('61) A.Or. 167.
31 (1953) Tr.-Co. 930, ('54) A.Tr.-Co. 47.
32 ('57) A.A. 753, (1957) A.L.J. 595.
33 (1973) 2 S.C.R. 266, ('73) A.SC. 87, on appeal from the Gujarat High Court: see (1971) 12 Guj.L.R. 13.
34 ('73) A.SC. *supra* at p. 90.
35 ibid. pp. 90-91 (where the relevant section and the Rules are set out).
36 ibid. p. 90.

the future, the Gujarat High Court, in a careful judgment dealt with the petitioner's contention on the merits. It held, first, that the power to regulate did not include total prohibition, but restrictions would include partial prohibition, as where a procession is asked to take one route and not another; and, secondly, that the Act and the Rules did not confer an arbitrary unbridled power because a perusal of the Act and the Rules showed that there was a clear policy which would guide the exercise of the discretionary power conferred upon the Commissioner of Police. Accordingly, the petition was dismissed.

Appeal allowed by Sup. Court: propositions emerging from leading majority judgment

10.92 On appeal, the Supreme Court unanimously held[37] that r. 7 was void but rejected all the other contentions of the appellant. Sikri C.J. delivered the leading judgment for himself, Ray and Reddy JJ., separate concurring judgments being delivered by Mathew and Beg JJ. Since the law declared by the Supreme Court must be found in the judgment of the majority of judges, the propositions which emerge from the judgment of Sikri C.J. are set out below:

(*a*) on the facts, Art. 19(1)(*a*) was not attracted.[38]

(*b*) In India, a citizen had, before the Constitution, a right to hold meetings on public streets subject to the control of the appropriate authority regarding the time and place of meeting, and subject to considerations of public order. This conclusion was said to follow from the decision of the Privy Council in *Manzur Hasan* v. *Muhammad Zaman*[39] which was followed by the Supreme Court in *Sheikh Paru Bux* v. *Kalandi Pati*.[40] Although these decisions related to processions, Indian Statutes, notably the Police Acts, deal with assemblies and processions on the same basis, for as pointed out by Benson J. a procession is but an assembly in motion.[41] Consequently, rules made under the Bombay Police Act, 1951 which required prior permission for holding meetings were not *ultra vires* s. 33(1) of the Act.[42]

(*c*) Since the right to hold public meetings flows from Art. 19(1)(*b*) and (*d*), the State cannot impose unreasonable restrictions upon it.[43] Article 19(*b*) read with Art. 13 protects the citizen from State action, and these articles have nothing to do with the right to assemble on private streets or property without the consent of the owners or occupiers of private property.[44]

(*d*) Section 33(1)(*o*) of the Act enables the Commissioner to make rules to regulate assemblies and processions; without such rules, in crowded public streets it would be impossible for citizens to exercise their rights. Not only was s. 33(1)(*o*) not *ultra vires* but it can be said to be enacted in aid of the rights under Art. 19(1)(*b*) and (*d*).

(*e*) Rule 7,[45] framed under s. 33(1)(*o*) was void as it did not give any guidance to the officer authorised by the Commissioner of Police as to the circumstances in which he could refuse permission to hold a public meeting. The

---

37 *Himatlal* v. *Police Commr., Ahmedabad* ('73) A.SC. 87.

38 ibid. p. 95.

39 52 I.A. 61, ('25) A.PC. 36.

40 ('70) A.SC. 1885, (1969) 2 S.C.R. 563.

41 26 Mad. 554 at p. 587.

42 ('73) A.SC. *supra* at p. 95; see also pp. 90-91, where the relevant parts of the section are set out.

43 ibid. p. 95.

44 ibid. This proposition was meant to distinguish the observations in *Railway Board* v. *N. Singh* (see para 10.123 *post*).

45 *Rule 7*: "No public meeting with or without loudspeaker, shall be held on the public street within the jurisdiction of the Commissionarate of Police, Ahmedabad City unless the necessary permission in writing has been obtained from the officer authorised by the Commissioner of Police."

marginal note[46] or the scheme of the Act did not give any guidance to the concerned officer, for, it was "too much to expect him to look at the scheme of the Act and decide that his discretion is limited."[47]

Sikri C.J. held that Rule 7 was void as it infringed Art. 19(1)(*b*).

Submission: law laid down by the majority not correct

10.93 It is submitted that the law laid down by the majority judgment is not correct, because,

(*i*) the judgment did not consider the right which persons in India have over public highways; as a consequence it wrongly equated the right to hold public meetings on highways with the right to take out processions along highways;

(*ii*) the judgment of the Privy Council in *Manzur Hasan* v. *Muhammed Zaman*[48] which was approved and applied in *Sheikh Paru Bux* v. *Kalandi Pati*[49] lends no support for equating the right to hold public meetings on highways with the right to take out processions.

(*iii*) The proposition that the right to hold public meetings on highways does not involve freedom of speech and expression is untenable; consequently, the Court failed to consider the kinds of restrictions which could be imposed upon that right under Art. 19(2).

(*iv*) Proposition (*e*) in para 10.92 above is contrary to numerous decisions of the Supreme Court.

Submission: the right to take out processions *prima facie* lawful, and meetings on highways *prima facie* unlawful

10.94 As to para 10.93(i) above, the right to take out processions or to hold public meetings on highways necessarily depends upon the rights which persons in India have over highways. In *Saghir Ahmed* v. *U.P.*[50] the Supreme Court held that the English law of highways had been applied all along in India;[51] and both in English and Indian law, the ordinary user of a highway is for persons to pass and re-pass. A highway could also be used for vehicles to pass and re-pass. Since every person has a right to move over the highway, movement is the characteristic feature of the right of persons over the highway. Since a public meeting is a static assembly of people, it is clear that members of a meeting are not exercising their right as individuals over the highway. Prof. de Smith has brought out the distinction between the two rights as follows:

"Stationary gatherings on highways are generally regarded as trespass at common law against the person or body in whom the highway is vested, unless sanction of the owner (usually a local authority) is obtained. This is because the primary purpose to which a highway is dedicated is passage and re-passage.[52] And since a public procession involves people marching down a highway, *participation is prima facie lawful* except perhaps while the procession is assembling. But a procession may well constitute an unlawful obstruction of the highway or a public nuisance.

"The general rule that meetings on highways are trespasses is derived from private law. *It gives no weight to public interest in freedom of expression*, and it seems ripe for reconsideration by the courts. In any event, the principle of dedication to passage and re-passage is subject to exceptions indeterminate in scope — ancillary activities such as holding private conversations and shopping are not trespasses nor are brief stoppages by motor cars,[53] but what

---

[46] "Power to make rules for regulation of traffic and for preservation of order in public place, etc."

[47] ('73) A.SC. *supra* at p. 96.

[48] 52 I.A. 61, *supra*.

[49] ('70) A.SC. *supra*.

[50] (1955) 1 S.C.R. 707, ('54) A.SC. 728.

[51] (1955) 1 S.C.R. at p. 715.

[52] See *e.g. Ex p. Lewis* (1886) 21 Q.B.D. at 197; *Harrison* v. *Duke of Rutland* (1893) 1 Q.B. 142; *Hickman* v. *Masy* (1900) 1 Q.B. 752. . . . See, however *Burden* v. *Rigley* (1911) 1 K.B. 337 where it was held that a meeting held on a highway was not necessarily unlawful.

[53] See *Iveagh* v. *Martin* (1961) 1 Q.B. 232; *Randell* v. *Tarrant* (1955) 1 W.L.R. 255. For picketing as obstruction, see *Hume* v. *Broome* (1973) 2 W.L.R. 773.

of distributing leaflets or soliciting answers from passers-by to questionnaires?[54] — and it would be sensible to replace the prevailing concept by one which equates trespass with unreasonable user. Seldom would a large meeting in a public thoroughfare be a reasonable use."[55] (italics supplied)

Submission: *Manzur Hasan's Case* (P.C.) and *Sheikh Paru Bux's Case* do not justify equating meetings on highways with processions

10.95 As to para 10.93 (ii) above, the right to take out religious processions is not decisive on the nature of the right to take out processions generally. Under our Constitution, the right to take out a religious procession *simpliciter* would also fall under Art. 25 (1) as involving the right freely to profess, practise and propagate religion. In *Manzur Hasan* v. *Muhammad Zaman*[56] on which Sikri C.J. relied, the whole dispute arose because the appellants, who were Shias, contended that they had a right to take out processions with proper religious observances during the period of *Muharram*; that while passing by a Sunni Mosque they were entitled to perform *matam* (wailing) from time to time, and they objected to the *modus vivendi* which had been found by the Magistrate, namely, that the procession should stop wailing some distance before approaching the mosque and resume wailing after they had passed some distance from the Mosque. The Privy Council held, approving the decisions of the Madras High Court, that there was a right to conduct a religious procession with its appropriate observance along a highway, and that a suit to declare that right was competent. The Privy Council confirmed the declaration granted by the District Judge, with the addition of certain words, and explained why the declaration had been granted instead of the appeal being dismissed. The declaration, with the italicised words added by the Privy Council, together with the said explanation, are set out below:

Declaration: "It is declared that, subject to the orders of the local authorities regulating the traffic, *to the Magistrate's directions and the rights of the people,* the plaintiffs have got the right to make short stays on the road at the back of the Juma Masjid at Aurangabad for the performance of the 'matam'. The defendants, specially those named in the plaint, are hereby prohibited from making interference in the performance of 'matam'." ". . . if their Lordships were simply to dismiss the appeal the effect would be misunderstood in India. Every different sect or religion, whose places of worship are upon the routes where the processions of those with whom they do not agree pass, would appeal to the judgment as settling that the functions of the procession should cease as it passed them. But if the declaration as made by the District Judge is granted the magistrate will still be able to make any arrangement they choose, and if they choose, to repeat the order that forbade doing 'matam" within a certain distance of the mosque. That order would be an order passed in respect of special circumstances, not a general pronouncement as to rights."[57]

The declaration granted, and the explanation given, by the Privy Council show that the right of the processionists to march on a highway is subject to the right of passage of other persons; that a procession is subject to traffic regulations meant to ensure the enjoyment of the right of passage by the public; that even the right to perform a religious observance may be restricted by a magistrate on the facts of a particular case. In *Sheikh Paru Bux* v. *Kalandi*

[54] Brownlie, *The Law Relating to Public Order*, pp. 140-45.
[55] S.A. de Smith, *Constitutional and Administrative Law*, 2nd ed., pp. 500-501.
[56] 52 I.A. supra. [57] ibid. p. 68.

Pati[58] the Supreme Court gave a declaration in the form adopted by the Privy Council. But these decisions lend no support to the conclusion that there is a right to hold public meetings on highways, for in those cases no question arose about public meetings. No doubt a procession is an assembly in motion, and consequently each member of the procession is merely exercising his right of passage over the road. A public meeting is a static assembly, and its members are not making use of the road for passage over it. If Police Acts deal both with processions and public meetings, it is because processions on highways, and public meetings on highways, involve problems of regulating the use of highways as well as problems of law and order. Further, the right of freedom of speech and expression is an important ingredient of a public meeting, and a law regulating that aspect of public meetings can impose restrictions permitted by Art. 19(2), *in addition to restrictions* permitted by Art. 19(3) and (5).

By definition a public meeting involves freedom of speech and expression

10.96 As to para 10.93(iii) above, a public meeting may be defined as "a meeting held for the purpose of discussing or expressing views on matters of public interest, and which the public or any section thereof is invited to attend".[59] It is obvious that a public meeting necessarily involves the freedom of speech and expression: the petitioner rightly pleaded that the Commissioner's order violated Art. 19(1) (*a*); and it is difficult to understand the bald statement in the judgment of Sikri C.J. that "We do not think that Art. 19(1) (*a*) is attracted on the facts of this case".[60] Nothing turned on the facts of the case, because in fact no meeting was held. The case was decided by the High Court and the Supreme Court by considering whether the impugned order could be upheld in face of the constitutional objections raised by the petitioner. It is submitted that the right to the freedom of speech was obviously involved when the holding of the meeting was not permitted; consequently the law laid down by the majority suffers from the grave infirmity that the majority failed to consider whether the Act and/or the rules could be sustained under Art. 19(2).

Submission: majority judgment erred in holding that Art. 19(1)(*a*) not attracted

10.97 As to para 10.93(iv) above, it is submitted that once the leading majority judgment found that there was a policy underlying the Act, which would guide the exercise of discretionary power, numerous judgments of the Supreme Court[61] require the Court to hold that the Act and the Rules did not confer unfettered arbitrary power. The statement that "it is too much to expect (the Commr. of Police) to look at the scheme of the Act and decide that his discretion is limited" could have been said in every case where discretion was given to public officers to be exercised in the light of the policy of the Act and the purpose for which the rules were to be made. It is submitted that on this part of the case the judgment is contrary to a large volume of authority and is clearly erroneous.

Submission: once there was policy underlying the exercise of discretionary power, rule 7 could not be struck down

---

[58] ('70) A.SC. 1885. It was also held that an agreement arrived at between important members of the Hindu and the Muslim communities as to taking out processions on public roads before Mosques accompanied with music filed in proceedings under s. 107, Cr.P.C. was not binding on the communities as the agreement was not arrived at in a civil suit filed in a representative capacity.

[59] Hood Phillips, *Constitutional and Administrative Law*, 5th ed., p. 431.

[60] ('73) A.SC. *supra* at p. 95.

[61] See paras 9.108 and 10.173 of the text.

The judgment of Mathew J.: a criticism

10.98 As regards the concurring judgment of Mathew J. it is submitted that it fails to distinguish between the right to take out processions on highways, which is *prima facie* lawful, and the right to hold public meetings on highways, which is *prima facie* unlawful, though not necessarily illegal. As to the statement that "public meetings in open spaces and public streets forms part of the tradition of our national life . . . and people have come to regard it as a part of their privileges and immunities" it is a mere assertion unsupported by any historical evidence, or by decisions of the Indian Courts or of the Privy Council. As Beg J. has rightly pointed out,

> "Whatever may be the law in America, we have not been shown any authority for the proposition that there is an unconditional right of holding a public meeting at every public place, much less on a public thoroughfare or street in this country, as a necessary incident of the fundamental rights of either free speech or of assembly."[62]

As to Rule 7, Mathew J. proceeded on the assumption that there was a fundamental right to hold public meetings on highways and held that on that assumption the rule was clearly arbitrary. It is submitted that there is no right to hold public meetings on highways such as there is to take out processions on highways, and the assumption is not tenable for reasons set out in para 10.95 above. Once it is found, as the High Court of Gujarat found, and the leading majority judgment also found, that there is a policy underlying the Act which should guide the discretion of the Commissioner, the power conferred on him cannot be looked upon as arbitrary or unfettered. In dealing with this point it is not irrelevant to observe that in the case before the Supreme Court reasons had been given by the Commissioner of Police, and the question of the arbitrary exercise of power did not call for decision once the challenge to the Act on the ground of Art. 14 and Art. 19(1)(*b*) and (*d*) had been repelled. The same observations apply to the finding of Beg J. that Rule 7 conferred arbitrary power and it would be open to the Commissioner to give permission to influential people and refuse it to others. It is submitted that it has been settled by numerous decisions of the Supreme Court, first, that abuse of power is not to be assumed;[63] secondly, that there is a presumption that power will be exercised for the purpose for which it is conferred, and, thirdly, that if the abuse of power is established, the executive act would be struck down, but not the power itself. It is submitted that the majority judgment is clearly wrong and productive of public mischief and should be overruled.

Judgment of Beg J.: a criticism

Submission: majority judgment clearly wrong

Conflict between fundamental rights claimed by different classes of persons

10.99 What would happen if the fundamental rights of citizens came in collision? The question arose when s. 7, Criminal Law Amendment Act, 1932, was challenged on the ground that it violated freedom of speech in so far as it put restrictions on peaceful picketing. It was held that where two fundamental rights collided, namely, the right of one group of persons to freedom of speech to dissuade people from trading with others came into conflict with the right of the

[62] ('73) A.SC. *supra* at p. 105. Beg J. rightly distinguished the right to take out processions on highways from using highways for holding public meetings: ibid. pp. 104-105.

[63] See para 9.87, *f.n.* 41 of the text.

citizen to trade, a Court would not hold such restrictions on the freedom of speech to be unreasonable and would not declare s. 7 void as contravening Art. 19 (1) (*a*).[64]

Freedom to form associations and unions

Row's Case: restrictions on association held unreasonable

10.100 We have seen that *Madras* v. *V. G. Row*[65] is the leading case on the test of reasonableness to be applied to a restriction on a fundamental right; but it is also a leading case on the right to form an association. The question there decided arose out of a notification issued on March 10, 1950, under s. 15 (2) (*b*), Indian Criminal Law Amendment Act, 1908 (as amended in 1950), declaring the "People's Education Society" an unlawful association. No notice was required to be given, and none was given, to the respondent (who was the Secretary of the society), or to any office-bearer, that the society had been declared an unlawful association, but the impugned notification was published in the official Gazette as required by the Act. The respondent contended that s. 15 (2) (*b*) and the notification was void as they violated his right to form an association under Art. 19 (1) (*c*). The objects of the society can broadly be described as the advancement of knowledge; but an affidavit on behalf of Government stated that the ostensible objects were a mere camouflage, and that the society was using its funds in actively helping the Communist party in Madras, which had been declared unlawful in August 1949. As a matter of construction, the Supreme Court held that under s. 15 (2) (*b*) as amended, as under the old s. 16, the factual existence or otherwise of the grounds for declaring an association unlawful was to be determined on the subjective satisfaction of Government and was not justiciable.[66] No doubt s. 15 (2) (*b*) imposed restrictions in the interest of public order, but the question remained whether they were reasonable. After setting out the test of reasonableness mentioned earlier,[67] the Court said that not only the duration and extent, but also the circumstances under which the restrictions were imposed, must be considered, because both substantive and procedural provisions of a law must satisfy the test of reasonableness. As the curtailment of the right to form associations and unions would have serious reactions in the religious, political and economic fields, a law empowering the executive government to impose restrictions on such a right, without allowing the factual and legal grounds of such imposition to be tested by a judicial inquiry, must ordinarily be considered unreasonable:

Restrictions on association imposed on the subjective satisfaction of Govt., ordinarily unreasonable

"The formula of subjective satisfaction of the Government or of its officers, with an Advisory Board thrown in to review the materials on which the Government seeks to override a basic freedom guaranteed to the citizen, may be viewed as reasonable only in very exceptional circumstances and within the narrowest limits, and cannot receive judicial approval as a general pattern of reasonable restrictions on fundamental rights."[68]

---

[64] *In re Vengan* (1952) Mad. 553, ('52) A.M. 95; *Damodar Ganesh* v. *State* ('51) A.B. 459, 53 Bom.L.R. 739.

[65] (1952) S.C.R. 597, ('52) A.SC. 196; fol. in *Krishna Warrier* v. *State* ('53) A.Tr.-Co. 174 (s. 23, Trav.-Cochin Public Safety Measures Act, 1950, held void as there was no provision for judicial review of the declaration nor any reference to an Advisory Board).

[66] (1952) S.C.R. 597, 604.

[67] See para 10.18.

[68] (1952) S.C.R. *supra* at p. 608.

Gopalan's Case[69] was distinguished because preventive detention, and the machinery of an Advisory Committee, were sanctioned by the Constitution itself and no question of the reasonableness of a law of preventive detention could arise in view of the language of Art. 21.[70] *Dr. Khare's Case*[71] was distinguished because externment, like preventive detention, was a precautionary measure and both involved an element of emergency. That factor was absent in the present case because the grounds for declaring an association unlawful under s. 15 (1) (*b*) were factual and it was unreasonable to shut out judicial inquiry in respect of such factual grounds. Again the Act considered in *Dr. Khare's Case* was a temporary Act, whereas the impugned Act was a permanent Act. Finally, the absence of an obligation to serve the notice on the office-bearers of the society made the restrictions unreasonable as it exposed them to penal consequences without notice to them that the association had been declared unlawful. Accordingly, s. 15 (2) (*b*) was held void.

Associations and Industrial Law: *Raja Kulkarni's Case*

10.101 The violation of the right to form associations has been alleged in cases arising under laws relating to industrial disputes, to trade or business and to the conduct of government servants. In *Raja Kulkarni* v. *Bombay*,[72] s. 27, Industrial Disputes (Appellate Tribunal) Act, 1950, was impugned as violating Art. 19 (1) (*a*) (Freedom of Speech) and (*c*) (Freedom of Association). The Supreme Court held that the provision that a trade union with a certain percentage of membership would be allowed to the exclusion of others to represent the workers as a class before the Appellate Tribunal, did not in any way impinge upon the freedom of speech of textile workers or their right to form an association. Further, there was nothing to prevent workers from forming an association representing a larger percentage of workers than the one already in existence and thus acquiring the right to represent the workers before the Appellate Tribunal to the exclusion of other unions. In *K. R. W. Union* v. *Registrar*[73] it was held that an order under s. 8, Trade Union Act, 1926, registering a new trade union without reference to the existing union was not violative of Art. 19 (1) (*c*). The right to be recognised by Government or the right to represent workmen was not absolute. Art. 19 (1) (*c*) did not confer on any individual or association the right to carry on trade union activities free of competition from rivals; therefore, State action which introduced new competitors could not be challenged as contravening Art. 19 (1) (*c*). Since an order of the registrar under s. 8 granting recognition to a rival union did not place any restrictions on the fundamental rights of the existing union, that union had no *locus standi* to file a writ petition under Art. 226. Again, it has been held that s. 36AB (1) (*a*) and (*b*), Banking Laws (Amendment) Act, 1968, did not violate the right to freedom of speech, expression and peaceable assembly guaranteed by Art. 19 (1) (*a*) and (*b*) as they

---

69 (1950) S.C.R. 88, ('50) A.SC. 27.
70 (1952) S.C.R. *supra* at p. 608.
71 (1950) S.C.R. 519, ('50) A.SC. 211.
72 (1954) S.C.R. 384, ('54) A.SC. 73.
73 ('67) A.Cal. 507.

fell within the exceptions mentioned in Art. 19(2);[74] s. 36AB(1)(c) of the Act did not violate the right to freedom of speech.[75]

10.102 Does the right to form an association imply a right (i) not to form it, (ii) not to be compelled to form or join it? There is authority for the proposition that the positive right implies the negative *as part of one right.* In *West Virginia State Board of Education* v. *Barnette*[76] the U.S. Supreme Court had to consider whether the freedom of speech and religion guaranteed by the First Amendment was violated by a compulsory flag salutation ceremony accompanied by a pledge to be taken by the pupil saluting the flag. The question raised was important because an affirmative answer involved the overruling of an 8 to 1 decision of the U.S. Supreme Court itself in *Minersville School District* v. *Gobitis.*[77] Both the *Gobitis Case* and the *West Virginia Case* concerned Jehovah's Witnesses, a sect of Christians whose religious beliefs included a literal version of Exodus Ch. 20, vv. 4 and 5: "Thou shalt not make unto thee any graven image, or any likeness of anything that is in heaven above, or that is in the earth beneath, or that is in the water under the earth; thou shalt not bow down thyself to them, nor serve them." They considered the flag as an image within the Commandment and therefore they refused to salute it. In the *Gobitis Case* they succeeded in obtaining an injunction from the lower Courts, but the Supreme Court allowed the appeal holding that freedom of speech and religion must yield to national unity and security and if the legislatures of States considered that the flag-salutation ceremony promoted national unity and security it was not for the Court to say that they were wrong. Stone J. dissented. In the *West Virginia Case* the Supreme Court overruled the *Gobitis Case* by a 6 to 3 majority, Black and Douglas JJ. declaring that reflection had convinced them that though the principle they laid down in the *Gobitis Case* was correct, the application of it to the facts was wrong, and they concurred in overruling it.

Does the right include the right to form or join an association?

American cases: a positive fundamental right implies the negative as a fundamental right

Gobitis Case overruled in the *West Virginia Case*

10.103 Having regard to the religious beliefs of Jehovah's Witnesses, Jackson J., who delivered the majority judgment, could have rested it on the narrow ground that the flag-salutation and the pledge required by the Board of Education violated that part of the First Amendment which protected the free exercise of religion. However, the majority judgment overruled the *Gobitis Case* on the wider ground that the compulsory flag-salutation ceremony and the accompanying pledge invaded "the sphere of the intellect and spirit" which the First Amendment protected[78] and that to sustain the compulsory flag-salute would require the absurd conclusion that a Bill of Rights which guaranteed the individual's right to speak his own mind, left it open to public authorities to compel him to utter what was not in his mind.[79] No official, high or low, could prescribe

[74] *M. Ramu* v. *Govt. of India* ('70) A.M. 331 (*held,* that the fundamental right did not include the right to obstruct persons entering the place of business or to prevent entry of persons into the bank premises).

[75] ibid. p. 333 (*held,* that the section only prohibited acts for which there was no reasonable excuse and which were calculated to undermine the depositor's confidence in the bank).

[76] (1942) 319 U.S. 624, 87 L. ed. 1628.

[77] (1939) 310 U.S. 586, 84 L. ed. 1375.

[78] (1942) 319 U.S. 624; 87 L. ed. 1628.

[79] ibid. pp. 634; 1635.

Freedom of speech violated by a law compelling a person to speak

what shall be orthodox in politics, nationalism or other matters of opinion, or force citizens to confess by word or act their faith therein.[80] Thus, freedom of speech and worship was violated by a law which compelled a person to act or speak contrary to his will or belief. Murphy J. concurred and said that the right to the freedom of thought and of religion included both the right to speak freely and the right to refrain from speaking at all, except where an essential function of government may require it for the preservation of an orderly society, as in the compulsion to give evidence in a Court.[81]

Art. 19(1)(g) held to involve the right not to carry on a business etc.

10.104 In *Indian Metal and Metallurgical Corpn.* v. *Industrial Tribunal, Madras*[82] the Madras High Court took a similar view of the right to carry on trade or business, guaranteed by Art. 19(1) (*g*):

"If a citizen has got a right to carry on business we think it follows that, he must be at liberty not to carry it on if he so chooses. A person can no more be compelled to carry on a business than a person can be compelled to acquire or hold property . . . (Counsel) was really unable to convince us how anyone can be compelled to carry on a business against his will and yet be said to enjoy a right to carry on a business. . . ."

Tika Ramji's Case

The questions considered above arose in *Tika Ramji* v. *U.P.*[83] where the provisions of the U.P. Sugarcane (Regulation of Supply and Purchase) Act, 1953, and two Notifications issued by the U.P. Government were impugned, *inter alia,* as violating Art. 19(1) (*c*). The petitioner contended that the provision relating to the supply of sugarcane by a Co-operative Society to factories manufacturing sugar would, in substance, compel him to join such a society, thus violating his fundamental right under Art. 19(1) (*c*) not to form, or join, an association. Bhagwati J. said:

Bhagwati J.'s view: the right not to form an association not a fundamental right

". . . assuming that the right to form an association implies a right not to form an association, it does not follow that the negative right must also be regarded as a fundamental right. The citizens of India have many rights which have not been given the sanctity of fundamental rights and there is nothing absurd or uncommon if the positive right alone is made a fundamental right. The whole fallacy in the argument urged on behalf of the petitioners lies in this that it ignores that there is no compulsion at all on any cane grower to become a member of the Canegrowers' Co-operative Society."[84]

It is submitted that the above passage mixes up several distinct concepts, fails to consider the real problem presented to the Court for solution, and offers a solution which is no solution at all. When the petitioner urged that the right to form an association implied the right not to form it, his contention was that both rights were one integral right guaranteed by Art. 19(1) (*c*) and it begs the question to say that the negative right is not a fundamental right. Nor is it an answer to say that the fallacy in the argument was that there was no compulsion on any cane-grower to become a member of the society, because the argument was not a simple but a composite argument, namely, that if business could be done only through a canegrowers' society, then, in substance, there was a compulsion to become a member of the society. That contention could be rejected by saying that he was not compelled, without deciding the question whether the negative implied in a fundamental right was a part of that fundamental right. The con-

80 ibid. pp. 642; 1639.
81 ibid. pp. 645; 1641.
82 ('53) A.M. 98, 101, (1952) 1 M.L.J. 481.
83 (1956) S.C.R. 393, ('56) A.SC. 676.
84 (1956) S.C.R. *supra* at p. 443.

stitutional question can arise for decision only on the assumption that even if the petitioner were compelled to become a member of an association, he could not complain of the violation of any fundamental right. It is submitted that the right to form an association carries with it the right not to form it, or the right not to be compelled to form or join an association. The observations of Bhagwati J. that the negative right was not a fundamental right are not correct, and are, in fact, inconsistent with the view expressed by him in a later case,[85] that "freedom" involved absence of restraint or control from outside. However, the actual decision in *Tika Ramji's Case* is correct. In *Sitharamachary* v. *Sr. Dy. Inspector of Schools*[86] it was held, it is submitted rightly, that the right to form an association necessarily implied a right not to be a member of an association. Accordingly, it was held that rules which made it obligatory for all teachers in elementary schools to become members of an association were void as violating Art. 19 (1) (*c*).

Sitharamachary's Case

10.105 In *Excel Wear* v. *Union*[87] the Supreme Court considered the question whether the right to carry on a business carried with it the right not to carry it on in the sense of closing it down. The questions arose in three Writ Petitions, one of them having been filed by a partnership, and the other two by limited companies, challenging the validity of s. 25-O and s. 25-R of the Industrial Disputes Act[88] ("the Act"). Briefly put, s. 25-O prevented a person from closing down his business even if the reasons given by him were cogent and justified such closure, provided that government was of the opinion that it was not in the public interest, that is, in the interest of labour. The petitioners urged several infirmities in s. 25-O which have been set out in the judgment.[89] The important points were that there was no obligation on Government to give any reasons; that even if there was justification for the closure it was left to government to refuse to give permission; that there was no provision for appeal or review; and that the orders which were in fact passed were brief and cryptic and the reason given for refusing permission would apply to the case of every closure. Section 25-R provided that the persons contravening s. 25-O were liable to be imprisoned and fined.

Excel Wear v. Union

The validity of a law preventing closure of a business challenged

10.106 The Supreme Court held that a person who was carrying on a business and had exercised his right to carry it on as a part of his fundamental right, had the right of discontinuing his business. But although the two rights were integrally connected, the right to discontinue the business could not be equated with deciding in the first instance not to carry on the business. In the latter case, no question of imposing reasonable restrictions on the right could arise, because in fact no business was being carried on. But once a person decided to carry on a business that right was subject to reasonable restrictions in the public interest and equally the connected negative right of discontinuing the business might also be subject to reasonable restrictions in the public interest.

Sup. Ct's view: right to carry on, or not to carry on business both subject to reasonable restrictions

---

[85] *Express Newspapers (P.) Ltd.* v. *Union* (1959) S.C.R. 12, 119, ('58) A.SC. 578.
[86] ('58) A.A.P. 78.
[87] (1979) 1 S.C.R. 1009, ('79) A.SC. 25.
[88] ('79) A.SC. at pp. 32-3 where the sections have been set out.
[89] ibid. p. 35.

Reasonable and unreasonable restrictions on the right to close down a business

10.107 After a careful examination of the various infirmities of the impugned provisions, the Supreme Court held that although prohibiting the frivolous or capricious closing down of a business might be upheld as a reasonable restriction, to say that in the interest of labour or to prevent unemployment, a closure necessitated by bad industrial relations, or by threats of personal violence or by fear of violence or by heavy and successive losses incurred by the company was unreasonable. And although restrictions in certain circumstances may extend to extinction, there was all the greater reason to scrutinize the reasonableness of the law. The Court rejected the argument based on the presence in the Preamble to our Constitution of the word "Socialist". Because, apart from the fact that the word "Socialist" had many meanings in different countries and at different times, and even assuming that the word "Socialist" in the Preamble might lead a Court to look favourably on legislation for nationalisation of business, still, as long as private business existed, the word "Socialist" could not be carried to the extent of eliminating all interests other than those of workmen. A further argument based on Art. 31C, as amended by the 42nd Amendment was rejected, the Court holding that the Amendment was not retrospective and that laws enacted during the Emergency had not the effect of depriving people of their rights once the Emergency was over. The Court also rejected the argument that s. 25-O did not compel a person to carry on a business, but merely affected property belonging to the business.

A criticism of the above decision

10.108 It is submitted that s. 25-O and s. 25-R were rightly struck down as they placed unreasonable restrictions on the right to carry on business. But in so far as the decision suggests that a law to compel a person to carry on a business if circumstances justifying its closure were not reasonable is open to grave doubt. First, the phrase "not carrying on the business" is ambiguous. A citizen carrying on a business may decide not to carry it on either temporarily, as in the case of a lock-out, or permanently. The temporary closure of a business, as by a lock-out, would be subject to reasonable restrictions imposed by industrial law—lock-outs may be legal or illegal. But a citizen's decision to close down the business by exercising his right not to carry it on raises very different questions. It would not be profitable to discuss the question in the absence of concrete cases. But the following considerations may be helpful in answering the question when it arises. Confining ourselves to business carried on by an individual citizen or by a body of citizens, as in a partnership, the liability of individual citizens for the debts and obligations of the business is unlimited. All business involves taking risks and the risk of loss. But as business is carried on with a view to profit,[90] the risk is undertaken under the belief that if it materializes, and the business suffers a loss, the business can be closed down. Would any prudent businessman carry on a business till he has suffered "repeated and heavy losses"? The right to carry on a business is a part of the right to freedom, and it is not conferred subject to the condition that it must be exercised only if there are reasonable

[90] Partnership is the relation between persons who have agreed to share the profits of a business carried on by all or any of them acting for all: s. 4 of the Partnership Act, 1932.

grounds for believing that the business will be continued indefinitely or during the life of the citizen. If there is no such fetter for starting a business, would there be any justification for imposing that fetter on the integrally connected right of not carrying it on? Again, what is meant by frivolous and capricious closing down of a business in the sense of deciding to close it down for good? A doctor, a lawyer or an engineer can stop his practice for a variety of reasons or just to please himself. Why cannot the owner of a business do likewise, and with greater reason? For whereas professional men are called upon to exercise their personal skill, the owner of a business must not only exercise personal skill, but must find the finance and must face conditions in our own country, and the world, over which he has no control. This is not to say that if in running a business he employs workmen to whom the industrial law applies, that he cannot be required to make reasonable compensation to the workmen for losing their employment. But to say that he must carry on the business if there are no reasonable grounds to close it down, is to force him to work against his will which is a characteristic of slavery or forced labour and not of freedom.

Damyanti v. Union: the right to form associations

10.109 In *Damyanti* v. *Union*[91] the Supreme Court decided important questions as to the right to form associations. The facts of the case were briefly these: The Hindi Sahitya Sammelan was a society registered under the Societies Registration Act, 1860, with the principal object of developing and promoting the propagation of Hindi. The Sammelan's bye-laws provided for three classes of members, and for constituting a governing body, a working committee and several other committees. The Sammelan owned lands and buildings at various places. The U.P. Legislature passed the U.P. Hindi Sahitya Sammelan Act, 1956, under which a statutory body was created called the "Hindi Sahitya Sammelan". The High Court declared the Act void on the ground that it terminated the existence of the original Sammelan, and thus violated the right of members of the original Sammelan to form associations guaranteed by Art. 19(1)(c). Thereupon, Parliament, purporting to act under entry 63, List I, Sch. 7,[92] enacted the Hindi Sahitya Sammelan Act, 1962, which declared the original Sammelan to be an institution of national importance, and vested its property in a new Sammelan which was constituted a body corporate. All the existing members of the original Sammelan were made members of the new Sammelan; but many outsiders were also made members by the Act. The rules framed under the Act prescribed qualifications for enrolling new members, who could be admitted without the voluntary consent of the original members of the Sammelan. The court held that the guaranteed right to form associations was not limited merely to the initial stage of forming an association, for then that right could be rendered nugatory by a law, passed after the association had been formed, which violated that right. The right to form an association carried with it the right to continue to be members of that association, and the further right of not being compelled to have members forced upon the associations without the volition of its members and

---

[91] (1971) 3 S.C.R. 840, ('71) A.SC. 966. [92] See p. A-179.

the right not to be associated with persons with whom the members of the association did not want to be associated. "(Any) law altering the composition of the Association compulsorily will be a breach of the right to form the association."[93] On a careful examination of the provisions of the Act and the rules, the Supreme Court held that the Act was void as it violated this composite right.[94] *Damyanti's Case* lends support to the submissions made in para 10.104 above, that the right to form associations involves the right not to form them.

The real question not raised in *Tika Ramji's Case*

10.110 Because of the manner in which Bhagwati J. dealt with the challenge under Art. 19(1)(*c*), the real question in *Tika Ramji's Case* was not raised and decided. The petitioner's contention squarely raised the question of the relation of Art. 19(1)(*c*) to Art. 19(1)(*g*). For, accepting the contention that the right to form an association included the right not to be compelled to join an association, did it follow that canalising the trade in sugarcane through a canegrowers' society was not a reasonable restriction on the right to carry on trade or business? And if it was, then was it any objection to such restriction that it required the petitioner to join a co-operative society if he wanted to carry on that business?

but raised and decided in *All India Bank Employees' Case*

All India Bank Employees' Association v. *National Industrial Tribunal*[95] raised this very question, namely, the relation of the rights conferred by Art. 19(1)(*c*) to the rights conferred by Art. 19(1)(*g*). The petitioners impugned s. 34A, Banking Companies Act,[96] as violating Art. 19(1)(*c*). The effect of s. 34A was that no tribunal could compel the production and inspection of any books of account or other documents or require a Bank to furnish or disclose any statement or information if the Banking Company claimed such document or statement or information to be of a confidential nature relating to secret reserves and to provision for bad and doubtful debts. If a dispute was pending and a question was raised whether any amount from the reserves or other provisions should be taken into account by a tribunal, the tribunal could refer the matter to the Reserve Bank of India whose certificate as to the amount which could be taken into account, was made final and conclusive. In challenging the validity of s. 34A it was admitted that the section did not prevent the workmen from forming unions, or put any impediment to their doing so; but it was said that Art. 19(1)(*c*) should not be read literally and that the right to form unions carried

---

[93] ('71) A.SC. *supra* at p. 972.

[94] The Supreme Court referred to two judgments as indirectly supporting its view: *O. K. Ghosh* v. *E. X. Joseph* (1963) Supp. 1 S.C.R. 789, ('63) A.SC. 812 and *Madras* v. *V. G. Row* (1952) S.C.R. 597, ('52) A.SC. 196. As to *Ghosh's Case,* the Supreme Court referred to the judgment of the High Court which had held that "the word 'form' . . . must refer not only to the initial commencement of the association but also to the continuance of the association as such."

[95] (1962) 3 S.C.R. 269, ('62) A.SC. 171.

[96] The circumstances leading to the enactment of s. 34A are set out in ('62) A.SC. 171, 174-177. The immediate cause for enacting the section was that although the Banking Companies Act did not require the disclosure of bad and doubtful debts, and other usual and proper provisions, the appellants in an industrial dispute asked for such disclosure, presumably because of observations made earlier by the Jeejibhoy Tribunal that such disclosure was necessary for ascertaining a Bank's capacity to pay.

with it a guarantee of their effective functioning[97] and unions could not function effectively in respect of industrial disputes if relevant and necessary materials were shut out under the provisions of the Act. In other words, the freedom to form unions carried with it the concomittant right that such unions should be able to achiëve the objects for which they were formed. The Supreme Court negatived this contention. It said that unions were not restricted to workmen, that employers' unions may be formed in order to earn a profit, and that a guarantee for the effective functioning of unions would lead to the conclusion that restrictions on their right to earn profits could be put only in the interests of public order and morality. Such a construction ran basically counter to the scheme of Art. 19, and to the provisions of Art. 19 (1) (*g*) and (6). The restrictions which could be imposed upon the right to form an association were limited to restrictions in the interest of public order and morality. The restrictions which could be imposed on the right to carry on any trade, business, profession or calling were reasonable restrictions in the public interest, and if the guarantee for the effective functioning of an association was a part of the right, then restrictions could not be imposed in the public interest on the business of an association. Again, an association of workmen may claim the right of collective bargaining and the right to strike, yet the right to strike could not by implication be treated as part of the right to form associations, for if it were so treated it would not be possible to put restrictions on the right in the public interest (as is done by the Industrial Disputes Act), which restrictions would be permissible under Art. 19 (6), but not under Art. 19 (4). The correct position was that the right to form unions did not carry with it a fundamental right for the union so formed to achieve every objective for which it was formed. Rights relating to business had to be decided by the criteria laid down in Art. 19 (6) relating to business.

right to form unions does not carry a guarantee of their effective functioning

The business of an association must be governed by considerations relevant to Art. 19(1)(*g*) and (6)

10.111 The above decision was applied in *Raghubar Dayal* v. *Union*.[98] There ss. 5, 6 and 10, Forward Contracts (Regulation) Act, 1952, were impugned as violating Art. 19 (1) (*c*). Originally, *gur* was outside the ambit of the Forward Contract (Regulation) Act, but as a result of experience gained in working the Act, *gur* was brought within its ambit. The application of s. 15 of the Act necessitated the fixing of rates under s. 16 at which all forward contracts outstanding on that date would be closed. No association had been granted recognition before the impugned notification dated February 11, 1959, but existing associations in certain places were accorded recognition after an inquiry as to whether they conformed to the requirements of the Act. Associations subsequently formed were similarly recognised. The petitioners belonged to the associations which were not recognised till June 1959. They contended that if the object of an association was lawful, no restrictions could be placed upon it except in the interest of public order and morality; that freedom to form an association carried with it the right to determine its internal arrangements as regards its manage-

The above case applied in *Dayal's Case*: restrictions on associations doing business in forward contracts upheld

[97] This contention was upheld in *U.P. Shramik Maha Sangh* v. *U.P.* ('60) A.A. 45.

[98] (1962) 3 S.C.R. 547, ('62) A.SC. 263.

ment, the framing of its bye-laws, regulations and the like. In rejecting the argument, the Court held, first, that s. 6 did not impose any restriction on the formation of an association, but imposed restrictions only for the purposes of "recognition". Since it was not disputed that forward trading might have undesirable consequences and might, under certain circumstances, resemble gambling, and that reasonable restrictions could be imposed in the public interest on such trading, the Court held that it was a matter for the legislative judgment what instrument should be chosen for the purpose of dealing in forward contracts.[99]

10.112 In *D. A. V. College, Jullundur* v. *Punjab*[1] the petitioners (an Association of Arya Samajis) contended that their compulsory affiliation to the Guru Nanak University affected the aims and objects of the Association, and therefore the freedom to form associations guaranteed by Art. 19(1)(c) was violated. The Supreme Court said that the fallacy of the argument had been repelled by the *All-India Bank Employees' Case* and *Raghubar Dayal's Case*, considered in paras 10.110 and 10.111 above.[2]

No fundamental right to strike

10.113 In *Radhey Shyam* v. *P. M. G., Nagpur*[3] the *All India Bank Employees' Association Case*[4] was referred to as establishing that under Art. 19(1) there was no fundamental right to strike, and it was held that ss. 3, 4 and 5, Essential Services Maintenance Ordinance, 1960, did not violate Art. 19(1)(*a*) and (*b*); they merely dealt with illegal strikes, and did not in any way restrict freedom of speech and expression nor restrict anyone from assembling peaceably and without arms. The fact that action in furtherance of the strike took the form of speeches or demonstrations would make no difference.

Balakotaiah's Case: no violation of right to form associations

10.114 *P. Balakotiaiah* v. *Union*[5] raised the question whether rules 3 and 7, Railway Service (Safeguarding of National Security) Rules, 1949, violated Art. 19(1)(*c*). The appellants contended that their services were terminated, because they were communists and trade unionists and consequently the orders terminating their services under r. 3 amounted in substance to a denial to them of the freedom to form associations. In negativing this contention, the Court said:

---

[99] (1962) 3 S.C.R. at p. 564; in view of the above decisions, the observations in *U.P. Shramik Maha Sangh* v. *U.P.* ('60) A.A. p. 45, 49, that the "purpose of an association is an integral part of the right, and if the purpose is restricted, the right is inevitably restricted. The right to form an association is not a right to be exercised in a vacuum or an empty or a paper right. The enjoyment and fulfilment of the right begins with the fulfilment of the purpose for which the association is formed" is no longer good law.

[1] (1971) Supp. S.C.R. 688, ('71) A.SC. 1737.

[2] ('71) A.SC. at pp. 1746-7. [*Damayanti's Case* (see para 10.109 above) was distinguished on the ground that in that case the Act interfered with the composition of the society in constituting the Sammelan and so violated the rights of the original members of the Society to form an association guaranteed under Art. 19(1)(c). No such thing was intended, or effected, by s. 5, Punjab University Act].

[3] (1964) 7 S.C.R. 403, ('65) A.SC. 311; in *S. Vasudevan* v. *S. D. Mital* (1961) 63 Bom.L.R. 774 in upholding s. 3(1) and 7, Essential Services Maintenance Ordinance, 1960, the Court observed that the right not to work did not include the right to receive pay without working.

[4] (1962) 3 S.C.R. 269, 292, ('62) A.SC. 171.

[5] (1958) S.C.R. 1052, ('58) A.SC. 232.

"The orders do not prevent them from continuing to be Communists or trade unionists. Their rights in that behalf remain after the impugned orders precisely what they were before. The real complaint of the appellants is that their services have been terminated; but that involves, apart from Art. 311, no infringement of any of their Constitutional rights. The appellants have no doubt a fundamental right to be continued in employment by the State, and when their services are terminated by the State they cannot complain of the infringement of any of their Constitutional rights, when no question of violation of Art. 311 arises."[6]

10.115 In *Kameshwar Prasad* v. *Bihar*,[7] *Balakotaiah's Case* was distinguished on the ground that the validity of the Service Rule was not disputed in that case. *Kameshwar Prasad's Case* raised the question of the validity or r. 4-A, Bihar Government Servants' Conduct Rules (1956), which ran: "No Government servant shall participate in any demonstration or resort to any form of strike in connection with any matter pertaining to his condition of service." The Supreme Court held that a person did not lose his fundamental rights by joining government service, a conclusion which was said to receive support from Art. 33 which provides that the fundamental rights of members of the armed forces, or forces charged with the maintenance of public order, can be abridged or abrogated by law, thus implying that the fundamental rights of other government servants cannot be abrogated or abridged. The Court held that although Rule 4-A was valid in so far as it referred to strikes, it was void in so far as it referred to demonstrations, because it violated the freedom of speech and assembly guaranteed by Art. 19(1) (*a*) and (*b*). The vice of the rule was that it was not confined to those forms of demonstration which might lead to a breach of public tranquility, but applied even to demonstrations which were incapable of causing such breach. The Court however added that although the membership of a public service did not deprive a government servant of his fundamental rights, restrictions may be put on his right to freedom of speech and expression in matters arising from his official position, as for example, restrictions against disclosure of information obtained in the course of his official duties. It is submitted that the implication drawn from Art. 33 is a *non sequitur*. Art. 19 confers fundamental rights which are not absolute, but are subject to *reasonable restrictions*. Art 33 enables Parliament by law to restrict or abrogate fundamental rights, which can only mean that *greater restrictions* can be put on the fundamental rights than are permitted by Art. 19. But from this it does not follow that the interests of discipline are irrelevant in considering the *lesser restrictions* permitted under Art. 19. The reasonableness of any restriction has to be judged by reference to the fundamental right which is restricted,

Kameshwar Prasad's Case: service rule against demonstrations and strikes

Rule valid as regards strikes, but void as regards demonstrations

---

[6] (1958) S.C.R. *supra* at p. 1064. The case is also an authority for the important proposition that when an authority passes an order within its competence, the order cannot fail because it purports to be made under a wrong provision; fol. in *Afzal Ullah* v. *U.P.* (1964) 4 S.C.R. 991, 1000, ('64) A.SC. 264; both these cases fol. in *J.K. Steel Ltd.* v. *Union* (1969) 2 S.C.R. 481, ('70) A.SC. 1173; 1188.

[7] (1962) 3 Supp. S.C.R. 369, ('62) A.SC. 1166; fol. in *K. G. Pillai* v. *Comptroller and Auditor-General* ('63) A.Punj. 390; *M. L. Kandhari* v. *Union* ('64) A.Punj. 143; *Madan Lal* v. *Dy. Inspector General of Police* ('63) A.Raj. 136 [*held*, that Rr. 23 and 23A, Rajasthan Government Servants' and Pensioners' Conduct Rules which prohibited government servants from becoming members of associations not recognized by government, such recognition being left to the arbitrary discretion of government, violated Art. 19(1)(*c*). *Kameshwar Prasad's Case, supra*, was referred to.]

and restrictions on government servants in the interest of discipline would be germane to the right conferred by Art. 19(1)(g). The Supreme Court has itself held that the fundamental right conferred by Art. 16, to equality of opportunity in public employment, does not exclude selective tests to determine, among other things, a sense of discipline. Thus, in *Banarasi Das* v. *U.P.*[8] Sinha J. said that Art. 16 was not violated when Government exercised its right to exclude those persons who had betrayed a lack of proper sense of discipline.[9] He added

> "In our opinion, it is open to the appointing authority . . . to lay down such pre-requisite conditions of appointment as would be conducive to the maintenance of proper discipline amongst Government servants. If persons already under Government employment on part-time basis had shown themselves not to be amenable to proper discipline in Government offices, it was open to Government not to appoint such persons . . . because such persons could not be said to be as efficient as those who . . . had shown greater sense of responsibility to their employers."[10]

It is submitted that it would be surprising if a sense of discipline were relevant in selecting candidates for public employment but became irrelevant once the employment had been secured. The above discussion furnishes an additional reason for saying that *Kameshwar Prasad's Case* was wrongly decided.

Kameshwar's Case applied in Ghosh's Case

10.116 *Kameshwar Prasad's Case* was applied in *O. K. Ghosh* v. *E. X. Joseph*[11] and r. 4-A, Central Civil Service (Conduct) Rules, 1955, which was in the same terms as Rule 4-A, Bihar Rules, was held void in so far as it referred to demonstrations. Rule 4-B of the Central Rules provided that a government servant was not to join an association which had not within 6 months of its formation obtained recognition of Government under the rules prescribed for such recognition or where recognition had been refused or withdrawn. The Supreme Court said that r. 4-B raised the question of the meaning of the words "public order" in Art. 19(2) and (4), which must have the same meaning in the two sub-Articles. But restriction in the interest of public order did not mean that a restriction was justified however remote may be its connection with public order. The correct view was that taken in *Lohia's Case*[12] namely, "The connection contemplated between restriction and public order must . . . be real and proximate and not far-fetched or problematical."[13] Accordingly, r. 4-B was invalid, because recognition may be refused or withdrawn on grounds wholly unconnected with public order, and the right under Art. 19(1)(c) was thus made subject to a greater restriction than was permitted by Art. 19(4). However, the question of reasonable restrictions can arise only if

Rules prohibiting membership of associations not recognized by Govt. violates Art. 19(1)(*c*) and is void

---

[8] (1956) S.C.R. 357, ('56) A.SC. 520. [9] (1956) S.C.R. at p. 360.
[10] ibid. p. 361.
[11] (1963) Supp. 1 S.C.R. 789, ('63) A.SC. 812; see *Ramakrishnaiah* v. *President, Dist. Board* (1952) Mad. 57, ('52) A.M. 253, where it was held that the Rules contained in a Government circular forbidding the existence of, and dissolving any teachers' union not conforming to certain rules and compelling teachers in Local Board or Municipal Schools to obtain the permission of the Board or Council concerned before forming unions, and prohibiting teachers in recognized elementary schools, from becoming members of teachers' unions or other teachers' organizations not constituted in accordance with the orders of Government, were void as violating Art. 19(1)(c).
[12] (1960) 2 S.C.R. 821, ('60) A.SC. 633.
[13] Quoting Sastri J. in *R.* v. *Basudev* (1949) F.C.R. 657, 661.

they are imposed by a valid "law" as defined in Art. 13. Accordingly, it was held that as rules 70 and 72 of the Government Servants' Conduct Rules, 1950 (Travancore-Cochin), were not framed under Art. 309, they were not law and hence could not impose restrictions on fundamental rights, and the prosecution of a government servant for violating the rules which provided that government servants shall not take part in politics and elections was void under Art. 19.[14] Again, the dismissal of a government servant on account of his alleged membership, or his alleged participation in the activities, of a political party, without a hearing, violated Art. 19 (1) (*c*).[15]

10.117 In view of the decision in *Kameshwar Prasad's Case*, the decision in *Bhagelu* v. *Civil Surgeon*[16] upholding the validity of r. 5-B of the Government Servants' Conduct Rules, which is substantially in the same terms as r. 4-B of the Central Government Rules, is no longer good law. Similarly, it is submitted that the decision in *V. C. Chacko* v. *State*[17] is no longer good law. That case raised the question whether rr. 63, 64 and 65 of the Government Servants' Conduct Rules, 1950, violated Art. 19 (1) (*a*), (*b*) or (*c*). R. 63 prohibited a Government servant from uttering, writing or otherwise criticizing in public or in any meeting or association or body, any policy pursued or action taken by Government and from participating in such discussion or criticism. If the only restrictions which could be put on the right of freedom of speech and association were those contained in Art. 19 (2) and (3), r. 63 could not be upheld as valid. The real justification for such a rule is that the conduct thereby prohibited would be subversive of discipline, subversive of the detachment and impartiality which a government servant is expected to show in the discharge of his duty and subversive of the confidence which must exist between superior and subordinate in the service hierarchy. However, in *Kameshwar Prasad's Case*,[18] the Supreme Court decisively rejected considerations of discipline by referring to the implication to be drawn from Art. 33. The decision in *Hazi Mohammad* v. *Dist. S. Board*[19] that restrictions placed on teachers of primary schools getting mixed up with political institutions were reasonable restrictions, is no longer good law.

10.118 The service rules which have been considered so far, prohibited government servants from becoming members of associations unless they were recognized or approved. A different question arises where there is no such prohibition against joining an association but conditions are prescribed for an association desiring to obtain recognition from Government or to speak on behalf of the members of the services. In *Bhagelu* v. *Civil Surgeon*[20] it was held that para 97, Manual of Government Orders constituted a reasonable restriction within the meaning of Art. 19 (1) (*g*). As regards Art. 19 (1) (c) it was held that there was no restriction placed by that

No right to "recognition" of unions

---

[14] *Gopinathan* v. *Kerala* ('64) A.Ker. 227.

[15] *Director of Edn.* v. *R. P. Pandey* ('71) A.A. 371 (Ordinarily, a restriction on the right of association will not be reasonable if the right is abridged without a hearing).

[16] (1959) 1 All. 787, ('60) A.A. 353.

[17] (1957) Ker. 1020, ('57) A.Ker. 7.

[18] *Supra.*

[19] ('58) A.Cal. 401.

[20] (1959) 1 All. 787, ('60) A.A. 353.

paragraph on the right to form associations. It is submitted that the decision is correct.

Position emerging from Supreme Court decisions unsatisfactory

10.119 The position which emerges from the Supreme Court judgments cannot be considered satisfactory. A law which upholds the right of a government servant to take part in political controversies, and which upholds his right to comment in public on the incompetence or incapacity of his departmental or political head has nothing to commend it. Such a law must destroy the high standards required of a civil service, as well as its unity and cohesion which are so essential to the smooth and efficient working of executive government. It is submitted that this aspect of the problem has not received sufficient attention from the Supreme Court and that had it done so, one of two possible solutions would have been adopted. What is the object which the impugned rules are designed to subserve and what is the mischief which they are designed to avoid? The underlying object of these rules is to secure certain standards of conduct which are necessary for the proper working of the public service. It has been said of the standards expected in the British Civil Service that:

Object of impugned service rules: efficient working of public service

> ". . . there are spheres of activity legitimately open to the ordinary citizens in which the civil servant can play no part or only a limited part. He is not to indulge in political or party controversy lest by so doing he should appear no longer the disinterested adviser of Ministers or able impartially to execute their policy. He is bound to maintain a proper reticence in discussing public affairs and more particularly those with which his own Department is concerned. And lastly, his position clearly imposes upon him restrictions in matters of commerce and business from which the ordinary citizen is free."[21]

The whole basis of the Civil Service is that the civil servant must carry out the policies of the Government of the day, whatever its political complexion may be. It is his duty to give detached, objective advice on matters within the scope of his duty, and this detachment and objectivity would be destroyed were he actively engaged in political controversy. Again, in his dealings with members of the public, in considering their complaints and grievances, the same detachment and impartiality is expected of him and these would also be impaired, if not destroyed, were it known that he was a political partisan. The first solution which presents itself is that which has been already adopted by the Supreme Court in *Balakotaiah's Case*[22] and in *Jumuna Prasad's Case*.[23] The first case shows that such rules do not fetter the citizen's freedom of speech and expression or his right to form associations; he is free to exercise his right to the freedom of speech and association. If, however, he decides to exercise those rights, such exercise may bring about the determination of his service with the State. As he has no fundamental right to remain in the service of the State, the rules do not deprive him of any fundamental right. The only question which can arise is a question under Art. 311. It is submitted that there is nothing surprising in this result, because every citizen who decides to assert his rights under Art. 19 must take the consequences of such assertion. A Cabinet Minister has the right to freedom of speech

Suggested solution (i) *Balakotaiah's Case* and *Jumuna Prasad's Case* should be applied

---

[21] Finer, *The Theory and Practice of Modern Government*, 2nd edn., p. 870 (quoting from the Report of a Board of Enquiry on the standards of conduct expected in the British Civil Services, ibid. p. 869).

[22] See para 10.114.

[23] See para 10.33.

and expression. But if he chooses to exercise it by open attacks on the Cabinet, he can do so only on the basis of his resignation or dismissal.[24] The same view of the law was taken in a different context in *Jumuna Prasad's Case*. There, the petitioner complained of restrictions on his freedom of speech contained in the Representation of the People Act. His complaint was rejected on the ground that it was only if he wished to be elected to a Legislature, that the Act restricted his right to freedom of speech, but it was open to him to assert that right and not stand as a candidate for the Legislature. He had no fundamental right to stand as a candidate for the Legislature. It was a right conferred by statute subject to restrictions there provided and it was for him to decide whether he wished to assert his fundamental right under Art. 19 (1) (*a*) or whether he preferred to have the rights conferred by the statute.

10.120 The second solution of the problem can be found in recognising the fact that a civil servant is following a profession or occupation within the meaning of Art. 19 (1) (*g*). Whereas his right to freedom of speech and expression, or the right to form an association can be subject only to reasonable restrictions in the interest of public order or morality, his right to carry on his profession or calling can be made subject to reasonable restrictions in the public interest. If the true scope and object of an impugned rule is not to deal with freedom of speech or freedom of association but to secure standards of conduct necessary for the efficient and proper discharge of a profession or calling, in the public interest, then such restrictions can be justified under Art. 19 (6), although they cannot be justified under Art. 19 (2) and (3). This solution of the problem is supported by the principle underlying the judgments of the Supreme Court considered earlier,[25] namely, that in considering the validity of a law imposing reasonable restrictions on the right to practise any business, trade, profession or occupation, the criteria relevant to reasonable restrictions on business must be adopted and it is no objection to such reasonable restrictions in the public interest, that they affect some other right which the person carrying on the trade or business independently possesses, such as the right to form associations.

(ii) the rights of a civil servant can be restricted under Art. 19(1)(g) as civil service is a profession or occupation

10.121 The discussion in paras 10.115, 10.119 and 10.120 shows that *Kameshwar Prasad's Case* was wrongly decided and is productive of public mischief and ought to be overruled.

Kameshwar Prasad's Case wrongly decided

---

[24] In *Divakaran Nair* v. *Tra.-Cochin* ('58) A.Ker. 283, the Court said: "As Holmes J. observed in *McAuliffe* v. *New Bedford* (1892) 155 Mass. 216, where a service rule against soliciting moneys for any political purposes was challenged by a policeman, 'The petitioner may have a constitutional right to talk politics, but he has no constitutional right to be a policeman. There are few employments for hire in which the servant does not agree to suspend his constitutional right of free speech, as well as of idleness, by the implied terms of his contract. The servant cannot complain, as he takes the employment on the terms which are offered to him'."; see the annotation to *United Public Workers* v. *Mitchell* (1949) 330 U.S. 75, 91 L. ed. 754, 791-2. See also *Adler* v. *Board of Education* (1951) 342 U.S. 485, 96 L. ed. 517. In *Divakaran Nair's Case, supra,* it was held that rr. 80(*a*), 81 and 82, Government Servants' (Conduct) Rules, prohibiting non-government servants' membership of government servants' associations, impose reasonable restrictions.

[25] See paras 10.110, 10.111.

No right to recognition

10.122 It has been held that although there is no fundamental right to obtain recognition of an association from Government, recognition by Government may attain constitutional importance where, without such recognition, a fundamental right to form an association under Art. 19 (1) (*c*) would be illusory. No restriction on the right to form associations could be permitted unless it was reasonable.[26] It is submitted that this decision is contrary to the decision in the *All India Bank Employees' Case*[27] where the Supreme Court held that the observations of Das C.J. in the *Kerala Education Bill Case*[28]—that without the recognition of educational institutions the right granted by Art. 30 (1) would be rendered nugatory—were made in the context of Art. 30 (1) and that they did not purport to lay down any general principle for the construction of Art. 19. Again, in *Dayal's Case* the Supreme Court held that the right guaranteed by Art. 19 (1) (*c*) to form associations does not involve a guaranteed right to recognition.[29]

Art. 19(1) (*a*), (*b*), (*c*) and private property

10.123 In *Railway Board, New Delhi* v. *N. Singh*[30] the Supreme Court held that the freedoms guaranteed under Art. 19 (1) (*a*) (*b*) and (*c*) did not include the right to exercise them in properties belonging to others.[31]

The right to move freely throughout the territory of India

and

The right to reside and settle in any part of India

Nature of right conferred by Art. 19(1)(*d*)

10.124 In *Gopalan's Case*[32] it was held by the majority that preventive or punitive detention did not violate the right under Art. 19 (1) (*d*) which was not a right *simpliciter* to move about freely, but a right to move about freely throughout India. *Gopalan's Case* is discussed fully in Chapter XI. However, questions of violation of Art. 19 (1) (*d*) and (*e*) have arisen in connection with externment orders. In *Dr. N. B. Khare* v. *Delhi,*[33] s. 4 (1) (*c*), (3), (6),[34] East Punjab Public Safety Act, 1949, was impugned as violating Art. 19 (1) (*d*) and (*e*). By a majority of 3 to 2 the Supreme Court upheld its validity. The Court said that both the substantive and the procedural provisions must be considered in judging the reasonable-

Dr. Khare's Case: validity of externment orders upheld

---

[26] *Eastern Railway Employees' Congress* v. *Gen. Manager, E. Rly.* ('65) A.Cal. 389 [*O. K. Ghosh* v. *E. X. Joseph* ('63) A.SC. 812 rel. on and also *In re the Kerala Education Bill, 1957,* (1959) S.C.R. 995, ('58) A.SC. 956: "scholars of unrecognised schools are not permitted to avail themselves of the opportunities for higher education in the University and are not eligible for entering the public service and without recognition the rights under Art. 30(1) cannot be effectively exercised."]

[27] (1962) 3 S.C.R. 269, ('62) A.SC. 171.

[28] (1959) S.C.R. *supra*.

[29] (1962) 3 S.C.R. 547, 564, ('62) A.SC. 263, "Could it be contended that there is a right in the association guaranteed by the Constitution to obtain recognition?"

[30] (1969) 3 S.C.R. 548, ('69) A.SC. 966.

[31] ('69) A.SC. at p. 970 (*held*, that the instructions issued by the General Manager prohibiting railway employees from holding meetings within railway premises, including open grounds forming part of those premises, did not violate Art. 19).

[32] (1950) S.C.R. 88, ('50) A.SC. 27. [33] (1950) S.C.R. 519, ('50) A.SC. 211.

[34] That section (i) empowered government, or a Dist. Magistrate, to extern persons on the satisfaction of the externing authority, which satisfaction was made final, (ii) authorised externment for an indefinite period, and (iii) provided that the authority may communicate the grounds of externment.

ness of the restrictions. Normally, an externment order was not to remain in force for more than three months, and though Government had power to extend the order indefinitely the whole Act was in force only up to August 14, 1951, and therefore an order passed under it would expire on that date. A three month period could not be considered unreasonable when Art. 22(4) to (7), which provided for the much severer restrictions of preventive detention, permitted such detention for a period of 3 months without any remedy. As regards the provisions that Government "may" communicate their reasons to the externee, in the context, the word "may" meant "must". The actual particulars given to the petitioner were not vague but specific, namely, that his activities were of a communal nature tending to arouse feelings of hostility between the majority and minority communities and were prejudicial to the maintenance of law and order. Although Mukherjea J. dissented, he nevertheless held that to vest authority in particular officers to take prompt action under emergent circumstances entirely on their own responsibility or personal satisfaction was not necessarily unreasonable.[35] In *Gurbachan Singh* v. *Bombay*[36] the petitioner challenged an externment order, made under s. 27(1), City of Bombay Police Act, 1902, directing him to remove himself outside Greater Bombay, on the ground that the section authorising the making of the order violated Art. 19(1)(*d*) and (*e*). In upholding s. 27(1), the Court held that the section imposed reasonable restrictions in the public interest both in its substantive and procedural requirements. The substantive requirements were reasonable because the order could not remain in force for more than two years and could be cancelled earlier in a proper case by the Commissioner. The procedural requirements were reasonable because the proposed externee was to be told the material allegations against him and had an opportunity of meeting them, with a right to appear by a lawyer and with the right to lead evidence as to character. The denial of the right to cross-examine police informants arose from the fact that the law dealt with exceptional cases, where fear of harm to their persons and properties made persons afraid to depose in public against bad characters. The whole object of the law would be defeated if such cross-examination were allowed. The power to pass an externment order was vested in a very high officer who was expected to exercise it with caution and impartiality. Similarly, in *Hari Khemu Gawali* v. *Dy. Commr. of Police, Bombay*,[37] the validity of s. 57, Bombay Police Act, 1951, was upheld. After stating that s. 57 was an instance of preventive action and that its substantive and procedural provisions must be examined to see whether it imposed reasonable restrictions, the Court found that *Gurbachan Singh's Case* was very near the present one; in fact s. 57 provided a surer foundation for the proposed internment order by requiring that the person must have been convicted for an offence. The objection that a person might be asked to remove himself from the State was met by saying that having regard to the scheme of the Act, such a case would not ordinarily arise. The further objection that the Act did not provide for an advisory board such as is provided for in cases of

Externment orders under Police Acts upheld: (*g*) *Gurbachan Singh's Case*

Above case followed: (i) *Khemu Gawali's Case*

[35] (1950) S.C.R. *supra* at p. 533.
[36] (1952) S.C.R. 737, ('52) A.SC. 221.
[37] (1956) S.C.R. 506, ('56) A.SC. 559.

preventive detention was met by saying that it was not a universal rule that in the absence of an advisory board a law to prevent the commission of offences must be held unconstitutional. Since externment, like preventive detention, was largely precautionary and based on suspicion, the procedure did not violate the rules of natural justice. Further, the externment order could be passed only by the Commissioner of Police or by a Dist. Magistrate or a specially-empowered sub-Div. Magistrate. The right of appeal to Government was real and not illusory, and though its order on appeal was final, the Act expressly provided that the order could be challenged in a court on three specified grounds. In *Bhagubhai Dullabhabhai Bhandari* v. *Dist. Magistrate, Thana,*[38] s. 56, Bombay Police Act, 1951, was upheld since *Gurbachan Singh's Case* concluded the constitutional challenge under Art. 19 (1) (*d*) against the petitioner.

(ii) *Bhandari's Case*

Order under Goondas Act held void for lack of necessary safeguards

10.125 However, in *M.P.* v. *Baldeo Prasad*[39] the above cases on externment were held not to apply to an order under ss. 4 and 4-A, C.P. & Berar Goondas Act, 1946, as amended in 1950. It was held that when a law authorised preventive action against citizens, it must provide expressly that the specified authorities should satisfy themselves that the condition laid down by the statute existed before they acted under it. Though it was a condition precedent to any action under the Act that the person sought to be proceeded against was a goonda, the Act failed to provide that the District Magistrate should first find that the person to be proceeded against *was* a goonda. Nor did the Act provide any guidance whatsoever in that regard. The definition of a goonda was an inclusive definition and did not indicate the test for deciding whether a person fell within the first part of the definition or not. Nor did the Act afford an opportunity to the person proceeded against to show that he was not a goonda. However laudable the object of the Act, it was void as it failed to provide the necessary safeguards.[40] Again, in *M.P.* v. *Bharat Singh*[41] it was held that s. 3 (1) (*b*) of the M.P. Public Security Act, 1959, which enabled restrictions to be imposed upon a person requiring him to reside in such place as may be specified in the order, violated Art. 19 (1) (*d*) and (*e*) and was void. The sub-section did not provide that he should be supplied with residence, maintenance or means of livelihood, although the place may be one in which he may have no residential accommodation and no way of honestly securing the means of subsistence.[42] In *W.B.* v. *Ashok Dey*[43] it was held that *assuming that Art. 19 (1) (d) was attracted* to the case of preventive detention, restrictions imposed

Bharat Singh's Case

Ashok Dey's Case: preventive detention and Art. 19(1)(*d*)

---

[38] (1956) S.C.R. 533, ('56) A.SC. 585. [39] (1961) 1 S.C.R. 970, ('61) A.SC. 293.

[40] *Baldeo's Case* was rel. on in *Sarbananda* v. *State* ('69) A.Cal. 474, 476 [*held*, that para 5(*c*) with its proviso to the W.B. Rice and Paddy Control Order, 1966 was vague and it imposed unreasonable restrictions upon the freedom guaranteed by Arts. 19(1)(*f*) and (*g*).]

[41] (1967) 2 S.C.R. 454, ('67) A.SC. 1170.

[42] ('67) A.SC. at p. 1172 [*held*, that the reasonable restrictions which could be put under the sub-section on the fundamental rights of a person, were inseverable from the unreasonable restrictions which could be put on such rights, and the subsection must be struck down as a whole. In taking this view the Court appears to have been influenced by the consideration that an order imposing reasonable restrictions on the movement of a person and maintaining supervision over him could appropriately be made under s. 3(1)(*c*) and (*d*) of the Act.]

[43] ('72) A.SC. 1660, 1665, (1972) 2 S.C.R. 434.

by the W.B. (Prevention of Violent Activities) Act, 1970, on the right to move freely throughout the territory of India with a view to prevent him from acting in any manner prejudicial to the security of West Bengal or maintenance of public order, were clearly in the interest of the general public.

Deportation of prostitutes upheld

10.126 In upholding the validity of s. 20, Suppression of Immoral Traffic in Women and Girls Act, 1956, against a challenge under Art. 19(1) (*d*) and (*e*) the Supreme Court said: "Once it is held that the activities of a prostitute in a particular area having regard to the conditions obtaining therein, are so subversive of public morals and so destructive of public health that it is necessary in public interest to deport her from that place, the restriction should be held to be reasonable."[44]

Restrictions on the right of residence upheld

Restrictions on movement of habitual offenders upheld

Restrictions in the interest of the Sch. Tribes upheld

10.127 Just as deportation laws have been upheld, laws restricting the right of residence have also been upheld. Thus, in *P. Arumugham* v. *Madras*[45] ss. 5, 6 and 16(1), Madras Restrictions of Habitual Offenders, Act, 1948, were upheld as imposing reasonable restrictions on the right of free movement of habitual offenders; and in *Anant Reddy* v. *Hyderabad*,[46] s. 26, Hyderabad City Police Act (1348F), which contained provisions for making a person reside in a particular place, was upheld as imposing reasonable restrictions on the right of free movement and the right to reside anywhere. In *Shiva Nandan* v. *W.B.*,[47] in upholding s. 7, Police Act, 1861, the provisions of s. 7(*b*) which prescribed confinement in quarters for a period not exceeding fifteen days, the court said that the restrictions were reasonable. In *Dhan Bahadur Ghorti* v. *State*,[48] the long-standing custom in the Garo Hills in the interest of the people there that no Nepali or foreigner should be allowed in the Garo village without the permission of the Dy. Commissioner (which permission was refused to the petitioner after due inquiry), was upheld under Art. 19(5) as a reasonable restriction in the interests of the protection of the Sch. Tribes. In *Chandmal* v. *M.P.*[49] Regs. 5 and 7 to 20 of the M.B. Sch. Tribes Debt Relief Regulations, 1962, were upheld as imposing reasonable restrictions for the protection of the Sch. Tribes.

Deportation of a citizen for breach of permit regulations held void

10.128 *Ebrahim Vazir Mavat* v. *Bombay*,[50] raised the question whether a law authorizing the deportation of an Indian citizen for committing a breach of permit, or passport regulations was valid, having regard to Art. 19(1) (*d*) and (*e*). The matter arose out of orders passed under s. 7, Influx from Pakistan (Control) Act, 1949, which provided:

---

[44] *U.P.* v. *Kaushailiya* ('64) A.SC. 416, 418; *Kamla China* v. *State* ('63) A.Punj. 36; *Seetharamamma* v. *Sambasiva Rao* ('64) A.A.P. 400; *Shama Bai* v. *U.P.* ('59) A.A. 57 [Suppression of Immoral Traffic in Women and Girls Act, 1956, imposes reasonable restrictions. Even if the Act violated the fundamental right under Art. 19(1)(*g*), the prohibition contained in Art. 23 (traffic in human beings) must prevail.]

[45] (1953) Mad. 937, ('53) A.M. 664.

[46] ('54) A.Hyd. 221.

[47] ('54) A.Cal. 60 [this seems to be an alternative ground. The Court rightly said that Art. 19(1)(*d*) had to be read with Art. 21].

[48] (1952) 4 Ass. 320, ('53) A.Ass. 61.

[49] ('67) A.M.P. 52, 55.

[50] (1954) S.C.R. 933, ('54) A.SC. 229.

". . . Without prejudice to the provisions contained in s. 5, the Central Government may, by general or special order, direct the removal from India of any person who has committed, or against whom a reasonable suspicion exists that he has committed an offence under this Act, and thereupon any officer of Government shall have all reasonable powers necessary to enforce such direction."

In the judgment under appeal the Bombay High Court had upheld the the validity of s. 7. The Allahabad High Court had however held[51] that s. 7 was void as violating Art. 19 (1) (*d*) and (*e*). The Supreme Court held that s. 7 was void as regards citizens, as it violated Art. 19 (1) (*e*).[52] A law which virtually denied citizenship to a citizen upon a mere breach of permit regulations could not be justified as imposing a reasonable restriction, for the punishment was utterly disproportionate to the gravity of the offence.[53]

Demand for security for lack of means void under Art. 19(1)(*d*) and (*e*)

10.129 It has been held that the fact that a person had no means of livelihood or residence in a town where he was hauled up under s. 109, Cr.P.C., could not be accepted as a ground for directing him to furnish security under s. 109 as it would be a denial of his fundamental rights under Art. 19 (1) (*d*) and (*e*).[54] In *Nanhu Lal* v. *Gaya L. H. Committee*[55] it was held that where railway authorities, in the interest of the general public, and especially of pilgrims visiting a place during a particular period, regulated entry into a railway platform by imposing restrictions on the sale of platform-tickets during that particular period, such restrictions did not violate Art. 19 (1) (*d*). A railway platform, though a public place, was not public property. It was the property of the Railway and, in the case before the court, the property of the Union of India. The authorities had a right to restrict the issue of platform-tickets and regulate entry to the station platform.

Restrictions on entry into public places like railway platforms

Arts. 19(1)(*e*) and 21 do not affect the Court's jurisdiction as to the custody of minors

10.130 In *Marggarate* v. *Chacko*[56] it was held that if the Court, as *parens partriae,* came to the conclusion that in the paramount interest of the minor it was necessary to entrust the minor to the care and custody of one of its parents who was residing outside India, the Court had full power to pass orders permitting the child to be removed out of India. There was nothing in Art. 19 (1) (*e*) or Art. 21 which abrogated to any extent the Court's jurisdiction in that respect. It was further held, that the custody of the children should be given to the mother and she should be permitted to remove them to Germany on the conditions mentioned in the judgment.[57]

Miscellaneous cases involving a challenge under Art. 19(1)(*c*) and one or

10.131 Certain miscellaneous cases may be mentioned here, in which provisions were challenged as violating Art. 19 (1) (*c*) and one or more of the other fundamental rights guaranteed under Art. 19 (1). In *Narayan Prosad* v. *Indian Iron and Steel Co.*,[58] the Iron and Steel Amalgamation Ordinance 8 of 1952 and 79 of 1952 were impugned as

---

[51] *Shabbir Husain* v. *U.P.* (1952) 1 All. 513, ('52) A.A. 257.
[52] Very rightly it was not contended that it was void as regards non-citizens.
[53] *Ebrahim Vazir's Case*, (1954) S.C.R. *supra* at p. 938.
[54] *Ganga Ram* v. *State* ('56) A.Him.Pra. 43.
[55] ('64) A.P. 98.
[56] ('70) A.Ker. 1, 10 (F.B.).
[57] ibid. p. 13. After a contest in the German courts, those courts had given the custody of the children to the mother. The Kerala High Court held that (subject to changed circumstances, if any) the court should respect the orders of the German Courts; and the High Court was confident that though the conditions on which the High Court had passed the order could not be enforced in Germany, German Courts would enforce them out of respect for Indian Courts.
[58] ('53) A.Cal. 695.

violating Art. 19 (1) (*c*). This contention was repelled, the court saying that the Ordinances did not interfere with the right of shareholders to form associations, for they could, after the amalgamation, sell their shares if they did not want to continue as members. Again, the Ordinance did not affect the shareholders' rights under Art. 19 (1) (*f*) and (*g*), but even if they did, they were saved by Art. 19 (5) and (6). In *Jatindra Nath* v. *Jadavpur University*[59] it was held that s. 2 (3) and (4), Jadavpur University Act, 1955, did not violate the applicant's right under Art. 19 (1) (*c*) as there was explicit and implicit recognition in the Act that the nucleus was the National Council of Education of which the applicant was a member. Since under the Rules of that Council a life-member had no right of property in the assets held by the association, the petitioner could not complain of the violation of Art. 19 (1) (*f*) either. In *In re Sockalingam*[60] it was held that the surrender under the Indian Extradition Act of a person who had committed an offence to which the Act applied did not violate Art. 19 (1) (*c*) and (*d*). The imprisonment of a criminal, or a person arrested and detained according to law for an alleged crime, did not cover any fundamental right, since extradition was a specific subject of legislative power. It followed that the rendition of the offender for an extraditable offence was not in derogation of fundamental rights. In *Punjab* v. *Ajaib Singh*[61] the Supreme Court held that the Abducted Persons (Recovery and Restoration) Act, 1949, did not violate Art. 19 (1) (*d*) and (*e*) and Art. 21 and that the matter was concluded by the judgment in *Gopalan's Case.*[62] The Supreme Court decision was followed in *Ram Singh* v. *Union.*[63] In *Bimla Devi* v. *Chaturvedi*[64] the Allahabad High Court held that the effect of the Abducted Persons (Recovery and Restoration) Act, 1949, was not to deport a citizen but to restore an abducted person. In *Sanghar Umar* v. *State*[65] the Court struck down the extraordinary provisions of the Nawanagar Fauz Hazri Dara Act (2003) as violative of Art. 19 (1) (*d*) and (*e*) as imposing unreasonable restrictions on perfectly innocent persons.[66]

more other clauses of Art. 19(1)

10.132 An extraordinary judgment was delivered in *A. V. Chandel* v. *Delhi University.*[67] The relevant facts were briefly these:

Chandel v. *Delhi University*

A student C was admitted to the Delhi University on 9th August 1977. It would appear that the first List of admissions to the M.A., Philosophy Class, was issued on 21st July 1977. As some seats remained vacant, a second list was notified to applicants in order of merit. (The judgment does not mention the date of the notification). Thereafter, a third List was issued on 9th August, 1977 for admission, and the candidates were asked to apply between 9th and 11th August, 1977. *C* applied on the 10th August. He wanted to contest the election to the office of the Vice-President of the Student's Union. The last day and the latest time for receiving nomination papers was 10th August, 1977 at or before 2 p.m. As *C*'s Nomination paper was presented after 2 p.m. it was rejected.

---

[59] ('60) A.Cal. 120, 63 C.W.N. 914.
[60] (1960) Mad. 829, ('60) A.M. 548.
[61] (1953) S.C.R. 254, 271, ('53) A.SC. 10.
[62] (1950) S.C.R. 88, ('50) A.SC. 27. In fact Counsel did not maintain the contrary view expressed by the dissenting judge in the High Court.
[63] ('54) A.Punj. 145.
[64] (1953) 2 All. 735, ('53) A.A. 613.
[65] ('52) A.Sau. 124.
[66] The extraordinary nature of the provisions clearly appear from the judgment.
[67] ('78) A.Del. 308.

Unsatisfactory nature of the writ petition

10.133 A writ petition was filed "in a hurry"; consequently, the case was allowed to be argued "on admitted facts" because the petition raised "pure questions of law". It is submitted that this is unsatisfactory, because the case with which the petitioner came to the Court remains unknown, nor does the reader know what facts were admitted and whether they were all the facts relevant for deciding the issue. Allegedly important constitutional questions ought not to be decided without proper pleadings. The Court held that the rejection of the nomination paper violated the petitioner's fundamental right to education.

Reasons for not dealing with the judgment at length

10.134 It is not proposed to deal with the judgment at any length, first, because being a High Court judgment it does not lay down the law for the whole of India; secondly, because the major premise of the judgment that education is a fundamental right is so obviously wrong that the elaborate and learned discussion by which it is supported does not call for detailed examination, and, finally, because a good deal of reasoning in the judgment will be found untenable by most readers.

Correct question not asked

10.135 The judgment states that the University Students' Union ("the Union") is not mentioned in the Delhi University Act, 1924. *Prima facie* therefore it is not one of the authorities of the University. That the Executive Council of the University approved the Constitution of the Union does not answer the question: was the Union an autonomous body? The composition of the Students' Council, the objects of the Union and the activities which the Union was to undertake, all support the view that the Union was an autonomous body and was not a body obliged to act under the orders or direction of the University. The Court has not asked this question and, naturally, has not recorded any finding on it. But unless the Court recorded a finding, for reasons stated, that the Union was not an autonomous body but was controlled by, and was obliged to follow the orders and directions of, the University, there would be no justification for holding that the rejection of *C*'s nomination paper was an act of the University and therefore of the State as defined by Art. 12. No such finding has been recorded.

Reasons for holding that "education" was a "fundamental right"

10.136 The Court held that education was a fundamental right under our Constitution because: (*a*) education is a natural right; (*b*) because the Declaration of Human Rights looks upon education as a fundamental right; (*c*) Art. 41 (Directives of State Policy) talks of "right to education"; (*d*) originally right to education was put in the Draft Constitution in the Chapter on Fundamental Rights, but later transferred to the Chapter on directives, because the former "were more easily enforceable than the latter."[68]

Submission: the reasons are untenable

10.137 It is submitted that these reasons show a complete confusion about the nature of fundamental rights. The fact that education is a natural right; that the Declaration of Human Rights treats it as a fundamental right, that Art. 41 speaks of "the right to education" is completely irrelevant. Article 13(2) makes it clear that fundamental rights under our Constitution are "rights conferred by this Part" (i.e. Part III). A right to education is not a right conferred

[68] ibid. p. 311.

by any Article in Part III. And the fact noted by the Court that in the Draft Constitution the right to education was put in the Chapter on Fundamental Rights but was later transferred to Part IV (Directive Principles) shows conclusively that the right to education was deliberately not conferred as a fundamental right. The statement in the judgment that this was because fundamental rights are more easily enforceable would suggest that Directive Principles are enforceable but with difficulty, but this is contrary to Art. 37 which states that the Directive Principles are not enforceable. Further, the following observations betray the same confusion: "However, once the State takes action by legislation or otherwise to make the right to education available to every eligible person the statutory right or statutory facility should stand in practice (if not in theory) on the footing of a fundamental right."[69] A right recognized or conferred by the University Act is *not* a right conferred by Part III of the Constitution, and is therefore not a fundamental right.

10.138 It is submitted that the suggestion that in the alternative the right to education could be inferred from Art. 19(1)(*a*) to (*c*) hardly needs serious consideration. It stands refuted by the fact that the right to education was transferred from the Chapter on Fundamental Rights (which are legally enforceable) to the Chapter on Directive Principles (which are not legally enforceable). As the result of a deliberate act of choice, the framers of our Constitution did not make the right to education a fundamental right; in face of this it would be absurd to suggest that they left it to judges to spell out the right to education as a fundamental right from Art. 19(1)(*a*) to (*c*).

The above submission applies to the "alternative" argument

Right to acquire, hold and dispose of property

10.139 The Constitution (44th Amendment) Act, 1979 deleted Art. 19(1)(*f*) (the right to acquire, hold and dispose of property) and Art. 31 (the acquisition or requisitioning of property) and inserted a new Article 300A. The reasons given for the Amendment give no assistance in solving the difficult problems to which the Amendments will give rise. As the repeal is not retrospective but comes into effect from June 20, 1979 the discussion of Art. 19(1)(*f*) is retained, first, because Art. 19(1)(*f*) will apply to all laws enacted before June 20, 1979, and executive action taken under them: and secondly because the right to acquire, hold and dispose of property is inextricably mixed up with several fundamental rights in Art. 19(1) and with other fundamental rights. However, it is the repeal of Art. 31 which raises the most difficult problems, and they have been dealt with in Chapter XIV. Since the history of these Amendments is relevant both to Art. 19(1)(*f*) and Art. 31, it is most conveniently dealt with in Chapter XIV which deals with the Right to Property. It is therefore suggested that the reader should, at this place, turn to paras 14.1 to 14.7 before proceeding with the discussion of Art. 19(1)(*f*) which follows.

The 44th Amendment and the prospective repeal of Arts. 19(1)(*f*) and 31 w.e.f. 20-6-1979

10.140 Before a person can complain that a law violates his right to acquire, hold and dispose of property, he must establish that the right which he claims is a right to property. "Property" is not defined in Indian law. S. 3(26), General Clauses Act, defines "immovable pro-

"Property" within the meaning of Art. 19(1)(*f*)

[69] ibid.

perty" as including "land, benefits to arise out of land and things attached to the earth or permanently fastened to anything attached to the earth"; and s. 3(36) defines moveable property as property of every description except immovable property. S. 3, Transfer of Property Act, defines "attached to the earth" occurring in s. 3(26) of the General Clauses Act. Property consists of a bundle of rights, some of which the law treats as themselves capable of separate acquisition and possession or enjoyment. Thus the owner of land can lease it, or mortgage it, and unless forbidden by law, leases and mortgages can be transferred. In *W.B.* v. *Subodh Gopal Bose*[70] Jagannadhadas J. said that in the context of Art. 19(1) (*f*) and Art. 31(2) only that can be called "property" which can be the subject-matter of acquisition or taking possession. Consequently, it excluded, for instance, a bare individual right, out of the bundle of rights which go to make up property, as being itself property within Art. 31(2), unless such individual right was itself recognised as property, e.g. an easement, a *profits-a-prendre,* and the like. But a right to annual undertenures cannot itself be treated as property for it is not capable of independent acquisition or possession. The depravation of such right is a restriction on the exercise of the main rights as regards the main property itself and must fall under Art. 19(1) (*f*) and (5). And the same view was expressed in *Rajindra Singh* v. *Union.*[71] However, the above propositions must be qualified when dealing with the rights of hereditary trustees of temples, or other religious institutions. In a series of decisions it has been held that the right to manage such institutions as hereditary trustees is a right to property.[72] In *N. S. Gujral* v. *Custodian, Evacuee Property,*[73] it was held that s. 12 of the Displaced Persons (Compensation and Rehabilitation) Act, 1954, did not in any manner affect a money decree held by an Indian citizen against a person who, subsequent to the passing of the decree, had become an evacuee, for the decree-holder had at no time any right in the property which vested in the Central Government on issue of a notification under s. 12 of the Act. Nor did s. 12 provide for the acquisition of the decree-holder's right to acquire, hold and dispose of property, namely, the decree, against a person who had subsequently become an evacuee. Art. 19(1) (*f*) therefore had no application.

Rights held not to be rights of "property"

10.141 The following rights have been held not to be rights to property within Art. 19(1) (*f*): the right of a quasi-permanent allottee under the provisions of the Administration of Evacuee Property Act, read with the notification issued thereunder;[74] the right of a *Mutavali;*[75] the right of the Tilkayat of the Nathdwara Temple to the possession and management of the temple property;[76] the right

---

[70] (1954) S.C.R. 587, 673, ('54) A.SC. 92. [71] ('63) A.Punj. 461.

[72] *Narayanan Nambudripad* v. *Madras* ('54) A.M. 385, (1953) 2 M.L.J. 699; fol. in *Kumaran Nambudiri* v. *Cochin Dewaswom Board* ('54) A.Tr.-Co. 515 (F.B.); *Namboodripad* v. *C.D. Board* (1956) Tr.-Co. 741, ('56) A.Tr.-Co. 19 (F.B.); *Chathu Madia* v. *Commr., H.R. & C.E.* (1958) Ker. 451, ('58) A.Ker. 57.

[73] (1968) 1 S.C.R. 497, ('68) A.SC. 457.

[74] *Amar Singh* v. *Custodian, Evacuee Property* (1957) S.C.R. 801, ('57) A.SC. 599.

[75] *Hafiz Mohammad* v. *U.P.S.C. Board of Waqfs* ('65) A.A. 333.

[76] *Mahant Sri Jagannath* v. *Orissa* (1954) S.C.R. 1046, ('54) A.SC. 400.

of a landlord to eject his tenants;[77] the right of recognition as a Ruler under Art. 366 (22), and the rights that accrue by virtue of that recognition;[78] the village offices abolished by the Mysore Village Offices Abolition Act, 1961.[79] Again, where the petitioner acquired a colliery in transgression of the rules validly made under the Mineral Concession Rules, it was held that he did not have sufficient interest in the property to raise questions about the constitutional validity of r. 39, Coal Mines (Conservation and Safety) Rules, 1954.[80] But though a right may not itself be a right of property, and therefore incapable of acquisition and requisition under Art. 31 (2) and (2A), a restriction or a prohibition on the exercise of that right would raise a question under Art. 19 (1) (*f*) and (5) if the right were a part of the bundle of rights constituting property. Again, a person alleging a violation of his right to hold property must be able to establish his title to that property. Thus in *Bokaro & Ramgur Ltd.* v. *Bihar*[81] it was held that if the petitioner's title to property was in dispute and was subject to adjudication in proceedings legally constituted, *e.g.* an inquiry under s. 4 (*h*), Bihar Land Reforms Act, 1950, he could not complain of the violation of his fundamental right till his title was established as a result of the inquiry. Similarly where the alleged fundamental right of a petitioner was dependent on whether the property transferred to her was evacuee property, and where the decision of the authority having jurisdiction to determine that question had become final, she not having questioned it, and where such decision was not a nullity or could not be otherwise got rid of, she could not complain of the violation of her rights under Art. 19 (1) (*f*) or Art. 31.[82] Again, if the right to property was lost before the coming into effect of the Constitution, Art. 19 (1) (*f*) could not be invoked. Thus, in *Narayana* v. *Andhra*[83] it was held that whatever rights a *mahant* might have had under a *sanad* or a scheme framed by the Court, they had been extinguished by s. 2, Madras Act of 1933, and Art. 19 did not apply as the alleged right had ceased to exist long before the Constitution came into force.

Pre-emption on the ground of vicinage: conflicting views

10.142 The question whether a customary or a statutory right of pre-emption on the ground of vicinage violated Art. 14 or Art. 19 (1) (*f*) gave rise to a conflict of judicial opinion. One view was that a law of pre-emption violated Art. 19 (1) (*f*) and was void;[84]

---

[77] *Per* Jagannadhadas J. in *W.B.* v. *Subodh Gopal Bose* (1954) S.C.R. 587, ('54) A.SC. 92.

[78] *Rajindra Singh* v. *Union* ('63) A.Punj. 461 (the rights granted by the Constitution to the United States of Rajasthan are political rights and are not justiciable).

[79] *Honnalige Gowda* v. *Mysore* ('64) A.Mys. 84, 106.

[80] *Biswanath Prasad* v. *Union* ('65) A.SC. 821, 825, (1965) 1 S.C.R. 49.

[81] (1962) Supp. (3) S.C.R. 831, ('63) A.SC. 516.

[82] *Aniyoth Kunhamina Umma* v. *Ministry of Rehabilitation* (1961) 1 S.C.R. 505, ('62) A.SC. 1616.

[83] (1959) Andh.Pra. 254, ('59) A.A.P. 471.

[84] *Abdul Hakim* v. *Jan Mohammad* (1952) 1 All. 149, ('51) A.A. 247 (*held*, that the Agra Pre-emption Act, 1922 was invalid); *Rulia Ram* v. *Sadh Ram* ('52) A.Pep. 190 (F.B.) (the Patiala Alienation of Land Act and Pepsu Pre-emption Act held invalid); *Panch Gujar Gaur Brahmans* v. *Amar Singh* (1954) Raj. 84, ('54) A.Raj. 100; *Siremal* v. *Kanti Lal* (1954) Raj. 853, ('54) A.Raj. 195; *Moti Bai* v. *Kand Kari Channaya* (1954) Hyd. 85, ('54) A.Hyd. 161 (F.B.) (customary law of pre-emption in Hyderabad held void); *Rangnath* v. *Babu Rao* ('56) A.Hyd. 120; *Babulal* v. *Gowardhandas* ('56) A.M.B. 1 (F.B.) [s. 12(1)(5) and (6), Gwalior Pre-emption Act held in-

Conflict resolved: *Bhau Ram's Case*

the other that it did not violate Art. 19(1) (*f*) and was valid.[85] The conflict was resolved by the Supreme Court in *Bhau Ram* v. *Brij Nath*[86] though the question produced sharp differences of opinion in the Supreme Court itself, the majority, Wanchoo J. (for himself, Gajendragadkar and Rajagopala Ayyangar JJ.) holding that pre-emption on the ground of vicinage was void, and Sarkar J. (for himself and Das Gupta J.) holding that it was valid. Wanchoo J. said that even if the liability under a law of pre-emption attached to the property, it would still amount to a restriction on the right to acquire, hold and dispose of property, and the question must arise whether such a restriction was reasonable. That reasonableness must be judged not by considerations relevant to pre-Constitution laws but in the light of fundamental rights. The right of preemption conferred by the Rewa State Pre-emption Act, 1946, did not have any effect on the prices of the property, but it gave rise to litigation and the disadvantages of the law outweighed its advantages. Such a right affected the purchaser of property who would have to face litigation in order to hold the property, if at all. Art. 15 prohibited discrimination on the grounds of religion, race, caste, sect, place of birth or any of them, and though the ostensible reason for the law was vicinage, the real reason was to prevent a stranger from acquiring property in any area which had been populated by a class of people. In effect, therefore, the law of pre-emption based on vicinage was really meant to prevent people belonging to a different religion, race, or caste from acquiring property. These considerations had no force after the Constitution and a law which imposed restrictions on those grounds must be held unreasonable. Further there was no question of consolidation of holdings in urban areas[87] and as there was no way of severing the provisions of the Rewa Act from its application to urban or house property, the entire provision based on vicinage must be struck down, even if something could be said in its favour with reference to agricultural holdings. The same conclusion applied to the right of pre-emption conferred by the Punjab Pre-emption Act, 1913. In a powerful dissenting judgment, Sarkar J. held that the right of pre-emption did not impose unreasonable restrictions on the right to acquire, hold and dispose of property. The Supreme Court itself had upheld the customary right of pre-emption, from which it must follow that the custom was

Majority view: pre-emption on the ground of vicinage void

Dissent by Sarkar J.

valid]; *Kishori* v. *Board of Revenue* (1957) 7 Raj. 588, ('57) A.Raj. 182 (the law of pre-emption on the ground of vicinage held void); *Girdhari* v. *Jawala* ('57) A.Raj. 203 (ss. 6 and 15, Alwar Pre-emption Act, 1946, held void); *Dhani Ram* v. *Bhairon Prasad* (1959) 9 Raj. 156, ('59) A.Raj. 78; *Yakub Mohd.* v. *Karim* ('60) A.M.P. 191 [s. 11(6), Bhopal Pre-emption Act, 1934, conferring a right of pre-emption by vicinage held void]; *Yusuf Ali* v. *Lakshmi Narayan* ('61) A.M.P. 311.

[85] *Uttam Singh* v. *Kartar Singh* ('54) A.Punj. 55 (F.B.) 55 P.L.R. 500 (upholding ss. 15 and 16 Punjab Pre-emption Act); *Kesar Devi* v. *Nanak Singh* ('58) A.Punj. 44, 60 P.L.R. 151; *Sardha Ram* v. *Haji Abdul* ('60) A.Punj. 196 (F.B.), 62 P.L.R. 201; *Ramchandra* v. *Janardan* (1955) Nag. 378 ('55) A.Nag. 225 (F.B.); *Sant Ram* v. *Labh Singh* ('62) A.A. 199.

[86] (1962) 3 Supp. S.C.R. 724, ('62) A.SC. 1476, fol. in *Motilal* v. *Basantlal* ('63) A.P. 145; *Saliman Bibi* v. *Hafiz Mohammad* ('64) A.A. 372.

[87] This assumption is questionable. It is obvious that small urban property in ill-ventilated alleys and by-lanes may with advantage be improved by consolidation, and not infrequently slum clearance involves consolidation of holdings.

considered reasonable, otherwise it would not have been upheld. If the various Courts had held the custom reasonable before the Constitution, there had not been any such vast change in the social and economic structure of the country which would justify the view that a restriction reasonable before 1950 had since then become unreasonable. A careful consideration of the advantages and disadvantages both to the vendor and vendee showed that the advantages predominated over the disadvantages. As to the vendor he was prevented from selling the land at an excessive price, and had to be content with its fair market value, but such a restriction was not unreasonable. The vendor's right to sell his property to anyone he liked was of sentimental and not of practical value. As against this, there was the advantage that as to agricultural lands the law of pre-emption enabled holdings to be consolidated, and as to urban land it enabled the owner of land to acquire property in the vicinity. Therefore, the right must be held to be reasonable. It is submitted that the dissenting judgment is correct. There were no materials before the Court from which it could have said that the real ground of the law was different from the ostensible ground. Such a conclusion can be based only on a careful analysis of factual data, and none such were put before the Court.

Submission: Dissenting judgment is correct

10.143 As to the right of pre-emption given to a co-sharer the whole Court held that the restriction imposed was reasonable, as the introduction of a stranger would cause difficulties of management which would be greater if it was an urban residential house; and the same reasoning applied to the right of pre-emption where the sale was of property which had a street-entrance or a staircase in common with other properties. As to the right of pre-emption created by the Berar Land Revenue Code, 1929, the right was of a limited nature, being confined to occupants in a survey number, who were co-sharers or akin to co-sharers. Accordingly, the right to pre-emption was really in respect of co-sharers and resulted in consolidation of holdings generally upto about 30 acres. In this respect, and because the right related to agricultural land, the restriction was reasonable.[88]

Right of pre-emption of co-sharers upheld

10.144 In *Ram Sarup* v. *Munshi*[89] the Supreme Court referred to *Bhau Ram's Case*[90] and said that the question to consider was, whether judged by the present-day circumstances and needs of the community, the restrictions imposed by a pre-emption law were reasonable. S. 15, Punjab Pre-emption Act, before its amendment, provided that the right to pre-emption in agricultural land and village immovable property should vest, where the sale was by a sole owner,

S. 15, Punjab Pre-emption Act

---

[88] *Bhau Ram* v. *Brij Nath* (1962) 3 Supp. S.C.R. 724, ('62) A.SC. 1476, 1483; fol. in *Mahboob Hasan* v. *Ram Bharosey* ('66) A.A. 271; (1965) A.L.J. 1178 [*held*, that the custom of pre-emption in Mohammedan law was not void as regards pre-emption by a *Shafi-i-Sharik* (a co-sharer in the property). The custom of pre-emption was void as regards a *Shafi-i-jar* (owner of property adjoining the property sought to be pre-empted). As regards pre-emption by a *Shafi-i-Khalit* (a participator in immunities and appendages, such as a right of way or a right to discharge water), its validity would depend upon the nature of the claim]; *Sewalal* v. *Param Lalanju* ('56) A.V.P. 9 (this was subsequently the view taken of the Rewa State Pre-emption Act, 1946, by the Court).

[89] (1963) 3 S.C.R. 858, ('63) A.SC. 553.

[90] (1962) 3 Supp. S.C.R. *supra.*

in the son or daughter or son's son or daughter's son of the vendor. The Full Bench judgment in *Uttam Singh* v. *Kartar Singh*[91] had said that the objects of ss. 15 and 16 of the Act were: (i) to preserve the integrity of the village and the village community; (ii) to avoid fragmentation of holdings; (iii) to implement the agnatic theory of the law of succession; (iv) to reduce the chances of litigation and friction and to promote public order and domestic comfort; and (v) to promote private and public decency and convenience. According to the Supreme Court the reference to public or domestic comfort and to private and public decency and convenience obviously had relevance to urban immovable property dealt with under s. 16.[92] The avoidance of chances of litigation and of fragmentation of holdings could not sustain the law because a pre-emption law in its turn gave rise to litigation, and fragmentation of holdings was not avoided by giving a right of pre-emption to the heirs of a sole owner. However, the objective of preserving the integrity of the village and the village community and the implementation of the agnatic rule of succession was sufficient to sustain the constitutionality of the law. After the amendment of s. 15, the right was extended to the brother or brother's son of the vendor and to the father's brother or father's brother's son of the vendor, but the heirs mentioned in the amended s. 15, though not presently entitled to the property, would have reasonable expectation of succeeding to the property, an expectation founded on and promoted by the consciousness of the community,

Act upheld in view of strong sentimental value attached to keeping property in the family

"If the social consciousness did engender such feelings, and taking into account the very strong sentimental value that is attached to the continued possession of family property in the Punjab, it could not be said that the restriction on the right of free alienation imposed by s. 15(1)(*a*) . . ." was unreasonable.[93]

The provisions of s. 15, which gave a right of pre-emption to landowners who jointly and severally held lands in respect of a particular survey number under s. 61 of the Punjab Land Revenue Act, were valid as they were covered by the decision in *Bhau Ram's Case* upholding the validity of similar provisions in the Berar Land Revenue Code. *Bhau Ram's Case*[94] was followed in *Sant Ram* v. *Labh Singh*.[95] The only additional point decided was that custom was "law" within Art. 13 (3) (*a*), and Art. 13 (3) (*b*) did not in any way cut down the definition in Art. 13 (3) (*a*). The definition in Art. 13 (3) (*b*) was inclusive, and it merely extended the definition in Art. 13 (3) (*a*) by providing that a law on the Statute book which was not in operation was also included in the definition of "law" in Art. 13 (3) (*a*).[96]

---

[91] ('54) A.Punj. 55 (F.B.), 55 P.L.R. 500.

[92] It is submitted that this assumption is questionable. It could hardly have been intended to suggest that 'public order and domestic comfort' were irrelevant to a village community or that public decency and convenience were irrelevant either.

[93] (1963) 3 S.C.R. 858, 875, ('63) A.SC. 553.

[94] (1962) 3 Supp. S.C.R. *supra*.

[95] (1964) 7 S.C.R. 756, ('65) A.SC. 314.

[96] ('65) A.SC. *supra* at p. 316. In view of the Supreme Court judgment, the decisions in *Mohammad Umar* v. *Amir Mohammad* ('58) A.M.P. 423; *Bhimrao* v. *Patilbua Ramkishan* ('60) A.B. 552, 62 Bom.L.R. 574; *Sheo Kumar* v. *Sudama Devi* ('62) A.P. 125 (F.B.) and *Nathuni Ram* v. *Gopinath* ('62) A.P. 226 are no longer good law.

10.145 Before a person can complain that a restriction on a fundamental right is unreasonable, he must show that he has a fundamental right.[97] Thus, where an order of allotment of a house made before the Constitution came into force was challenged as violating Art. 19 (1) (*f*) on the ground that dispossession of the landlord took place after the Constitution came into force, the Court held that as the petitioner's right to retain possession of the house came to an end as a result of the order of requisition before the Constitution came into force, he had no fundamental right which he could assert under the Constitution. Similarly, when the property rights of the appellant, a Matadhipathi, had been taken away before the coming into effect of the Constitution by a scheme framed under the Madras Hindu Religious Endowments Act, 1927, he could not claim to enforce fundamental rights under Art. 19 (1) (*f*) merely because the implementation of the scheme had been delayed till after the Constitution due to protracted litigation and obstruction by them.[98] It has been held that the right to get elected as a Managing Director or appointed as a Chief Executive Officer of a banking company was a statutory and not a common law right.[99] Sales tax collected by the seller, which tax was declared *ultra vires*, belonged to the purchasers and the seller had no property in it.[1]

Violation of fundamental rights: the right must be established first

10.146 Laws made for the control of rents of agricultural lands and holdings or to prevent the eviction of tenants or both have been upheld. Again, various Rent Acts or Rent and Eviction Acts have been upheld having regard to the acute scarcity of housing accommodation which arose during the second world war and has persisted thereafter. Thus, the Rajasthan (Protection of Tenants) Ordinance, 1949, was upheld on the ground that it did not restrict the right of the owner himself to cultivate his lands but only prevented him when he had induced a tenant on the land from getting rid of him without sufficient cause. A law which required an owner, not himself a tiller of the soil, to assure the tiller some fixity of tenure cannot, on that ground alone, be said to be unreasonable. The temporary character of the Ordinance was also a factor to be taken into account in adjudging its reasonableness.[2] So also, the Trav.-Cochin Holdings (Stay of Execution) Proceedings Act, 1950, was held not to violate Art. 19 (1) (*f*) as it was a temporary Act designed to afford relief to a large section of the public.[3] The fol-

Laws for control of rents and eviction of tenants upheld

---

[97] *D. K. Nabhirajiah* v. *Mysore* (1952) S.C.R. 744, ('52) A.SC. 339.

[98] *Rajendraswami* v. *Commissioner, H.R. & C.E.* (1964) 8 S.C.R. 252, ('65) A.SC. 502.

[99] *E. Ambooken* v. *Reserve Bank of India* ('66) A.Ker. 6, 8. The Court cited the following decisions to show that it was doubtful whether the right to be a Managing Director was a fundamental right: *Digambar Aruk* v. *Nanda Aruk* (1957) Cut. 485, ('57) A.Or. 281 [the Court relied on *Mulchand* v. *Mukund* ('52) A.B. 296 and *Rangaswamy* v. *Industrial Tribunal* ('54) A.M. 553 in which it was held that the right of lawyers to practise was not absolute but was subject to the restrictions imposed by statutes governing them]; *Aruk's Case, supra*, was relied on in *B. Naik* v. *Co-operative Societies, Cuttack* (1958) ('58) A.Or. 217. In *Lachhman Dass* v. *Punjab* (1963) 2 S.C.R. 353, ('63) A.SC. 222, the question was not finally decided, but the Court observed that the contention that Art. 19 had no application to a law which was attracted by reason of a contract deserved consideration.

[1] *I.C. Corporation* v. *Bihar* (1966) 45 Pat. 631, ('66) A.P. 54.

[2] *Inder Singh* v. *Rajasthan* (1957) S.C.R. 605, ('57) A.SC. 510.

[3] *Vishnu* v. *Poulo* ('53) A.Tr.-Co. 327.

lowing provisions have been upheld: S. 3, Madras Estates Land (Reduction of Rent) Act, 1949;[4] s. 4(1), Madras Cultivating Tenants Act, 1955;[5] s. 27, U.P. Tenancy (Amendment) Act, 1947;[6] s. 27, Santhal Parganas Settlement Regulations, 1872;[7] s. 46(1), proviso (*c*) of the Chota Nagpur Tenancy Act, 1908, as amended by the Bihar Act 25 of 1947;[8] Rajasthan Produce Rents Regulating Act, 1951;[9] s. 1, Marwar Tenancy Act, 1949, and s. 1 Marwar Land Revenue Act, 1959;[10] s. 3, Orissa Tenants Relief Act, 1955;[11] s. 17(4), proviso, as amended, of the W. B. Premises Tenancy Act, 1956;[12] s. 3, Mysore Tenants Temporary (Protection from Eviction) Act, 1961, was upheld on the ground that it preserved the *status quo* and prevented the eviction of tenants who might under the new law be able to retain possession of lands from which their eviction was ordered. It was a temporary measure till a permanent law was enacted and it did not impose unreasonable restrictions.[13] Similarly, s. 3(3)(*a*), Mysore Rent and Accommodation Act, 1951, was upheld. That section applied when the owner did not want the house for his own use, in which case it could make no reasonable difference to him if a private individual, instead of the Government or its servant were chosen as the tenant. There were ample safeguards against an unsuitable person being foisted on the owner as his tenant, namely, an appeal to the District Judge and the right to move the High Court in revision against the tenant actually chosen.[14] A provision empowering Government to issue directions for the allotment of premises in favour of any public servant was valid as it imposed reasonable restrictions on the normal right of a landlord to select his own tenant.[15] The following provisions, namely, ss. 11, 16, 18 and 18B, Bihar Buildings (Lease, Rent and Eviction) Control

---

[4] *State* v. *Kannapalli Chinna Venkata Chalamayya Sastri* (1963) 1 S.C.R. 155, ('62) A.SC. 1687 (the reduction of the prevailing rents to the *ryotwari* levels was a reasonable restriction on the landholder of an estate to hold his property; accordingly, the notification fixing the reduction of rents approximately to the level of assessment levied on lands on *ryotwari* areas in the neighbourhood was upheld).

[5] *N. Sundararaja* v. *Sub-Collector, Dindigul* ('57) A.M. 333, (1957) 1 M.L.J. 307.

[6] *Khairunnisa* v. *Ganga Prasad* ('61) A.A. 191 [reinstatement of ejected tenants under that section is not acquisition; the section does not violate the right of the new tenant as under Art. 31(1) that right has been taken away].

[7] *Basini Goalin* v. *Amrit Gon* ('61) A.P. 276 (the restrictions regarding the transfer of holdings laid down in a. 27 were in the interest of the ryots in the District with a view to maintain their social status, to preserve their culture and to prevent the extinction of the village community).

[8] *Sasti Pado* v. *Anandi Chaudhari* ('67) A.P. 25 (the restrictions placed on the transfer of holdings were designed to prevent absentee landlordism of agricultural land and also to prevent occupancy raiyats from being converted into landless labourers).

[9] *Shersingh* v. *Rajasthan* ('54) A.Raj. 65 (tenancy laws aiming at the welfare of the tenancy, which form a large part of the population, have always been a feature of ameliorating legislation in our country).

[10] *Raja Hari Singh* v. *State* (1954) 4 Raj. 274, ('54) A.Raj. 117 [a law laying down principles of fixing rents and determining the rights of tenants and landlords with respect to the nature of the tenure and ejectment are a feature of progressive statutes and do not violate Art. 19(1)(*f*)].

[11] *Nabin Chandra* v. *Orissa* ('57) A.Or. 56.

[12] *Sanjib Kumar* v. *Nathmal* ('72) A.Cal. 524 (the section gave extra protection to the tenant to avoid forfeiture for non-payment of rent).

[13] *Sangappa* v. *Mohammadhanif Saheb* ('64) A.Mys. 43.

[14] *S. P. Jinadathappa* v. *R. P. Sharma* (1962) 2 S.C.R. 22, ('61) A.SC. 1523.

[15] *Maimunnisa Begum* v. *Dy. Commissioner, Bangalore* ('67) A.Mys. 107.

Act;[16] the Madras Buildings (Lease and Rent Control) Act, 1946;[17] ss. 32(1), (2) and (3) of the Mysore Rent Control Act, 1961;[18] the W. B. Premises Rent Control (Temporary Provisions) Act, 1950;[19] the U.P. (Temporary) Control of Rent and Eviction Act, 1947;[20] U.P. Rent Control and Eviction Act, 1951;[21] were upheld as necessary to meet the scarcity of housing accommodation. In *Bajrapani Naidu* v. *N. T. C. Talkies*,[22] the Supreme Court upheld the validity of s. 9, Madras City Tenants' Protection Act, 1922, which enabled tenants to purchase the property leased to them on determination of the lease. The law applied to a limited class of landlords who, in breach of the mutual understanding that as long as the rent was paid the land would not be resumed sought to obtain possession of the land in order to secure an unearned increment as a result of conditions produced by the first World War; and it was manifestly in the public interest to effectuate the understanding between landlord and tenant and to conserve building material by maintaining existing buildings for which the leases were granted.

10.147 The shortage of accommodation and the difficulty and delay involved in the ordinary process of law in evicting an unauthorised occupant of Government premises led to the passing of the Government Premises (Eviction) Act, 1950. The necessity of allowing Government to adopt summary methods for the eviction of persons in wrongful occupation of Government residential premises was not disputed. However, ss. 2(*a*), 3, 4, 5 and 6 of the Act were held void on the ground of unreasonableness because the powers of the Competent Authority under the Act were very wide and capable of abuse, and the protection provided by the Act to the occupant was wholly inadequate. The only right given to any person affected by the order of the Competent Authority under s. 5 was by way of appeal to the Central Government, which meant an officer appointed by the Central Government, and the protection thus afforded was almost illusory. The section gave no right to the person affected to be heard by the Appellate authority. Again, ss. 3 and 4 contained no provision for giving a show cause notice to the person affected and the jurisdiction of the Court had been expressly barred. Further, the title to the property of a person was to be decided according to the subjective satisfaction of a person who may have

Government Premises Eviction Acts before amendment in 1958

Held void as procedural provisions were un reasonable

[16] *Ram Nath* v. *Sukumari* ('54) A.P. 211; *Santi Devi* v. *Dy. Commissioner* ('67) A.P. 333, 334 [*held*, that s. 11(2) of the Act did not impose unreasonable restrictions on the right to hold property]; fol. in *Nandalal Sinha* v. *Dist. Magistrate, Hazaribagh* ('67) A.P. 334.

[17] *Vencatachellum* v. *Kabalamurthy* ('55) A.M. 350.

[18] *Gyan Prakash* v. *State* ('68) A.Mys. 61.

[19] *S.B. Trading Co.* v. *Shyamlal* ('51) A.Cal. 539; *Iswari Prosad* v. *N. R. Sen* ('52) A.Cal. 273 (F.B.).

[20] *Ram Krishna* v. *Radhamal* (1953) 2 All. 849; *Prem Shankar* v. *U.P. Provincial Co.-op. Bank* ('53) A.A. 51; *Sarojini Devi* v. *Rent (C. & E.) Officer* ('56) A.A. 110, (1955) A.L.J. 657 [it would appear that it was held that there was no violation of Art. 19(1)(*f*) because the impugned section was not discretionary].

[21] *Raman Das* v. *U.P.* (1953) 1 All. 970, ('52) A.A. 703 (F.B.); *Ram Katori* v. *Rent Control & Eviction Officer* ('53) A.A. 543, (1953) A.L.J. 237.

[22] (1964) 6 S.C.R. 1015, ('64) A.SC. 1440 (the law was upheld by the majority, *viz.* Shah J. for himself, Gajendragadkar C.J., and Sikri J., Wanchoo and Rajagopala Ayyangar JJ. expressing no opinion on this point); see also *Sundareswarar Devasthanam* v. *Marimuthu* ('63) A.M. 369 (where s. 9, Madras City Tenants Protection Act, 1922, re-enacted by the Madras Act 13 of 1960, was upheld).

no qualification for deciding questions of title, and a person may even lose his own property while being precluded from even complaining about it to any Civil Court.[23]

Nature of right to property in occupation of tenants: *Kishan Singh's Case*

10.148 What is the nature of a fundamental right which a citizen has to hold and enjoy property which is cultivated by a tenant? In *Kishan Singh* v. *Rajasthan*[24] the Supreme Court held that the fundamental right of a citizen to hold and enjoy property imports only a right to recover reasonable rent when the lands are cultivated by a tenant. Therefore a legislation whose object is to fix a fair and equitable rent cannot be said to invade that right. If the rent fixed was reasonable with reference to a period subsequent to the settlement it must be reasonable for the period prior to it as well, and if the settlement was not an encroachment on the right of a holder as regards the future, it cannot be an encroachment as regards the past. The decision might be correct on the facts,[25] but it is submitted that the statement that the only right of an owner of property occupied by a tenant is the right to receive a reasonable rent is incorrect. The right of the owner of land is to get as much return, or enjoyment, out of it as he can get. It might carry with it the right to eject the tenant. These rights may be made subject to reasonable restrictions—eviction of tenants may be regulated or forbidden, and rents may be fixed, by law; but such laws must pass the test of reasonable restrictions. Therefore the impugned law can be upheld not on the ground that the fundamental right is limited to recovering a reasonable rent but because fixing a reasonable rent might, under certain circumstances, be a reasonable restriction on the right to hold property.

a criticism

Right to hold a fair, a right to property, protected by Art. 19(1)(*f*)

10.149 In *Ganpatisinghji* v. *Ajmer*[26] it was held by a majority[27] that a right to hold a fair on one's own land was a fundamental right under Art. 19 (1) (*f*) which could only be restricted in the manner permitted by Art. 19 (5). The holding of an annual fair was also an occupation or business within the meaning of Art. 19 (1) (*g*). Therefore a citizen had also a fundamental right to engage in the occupation on his land provided that it did not infringe any law imposing "reasonable restrictions" on that right in the interest of the general public.

Cattle slaughter cases

10.150 *Mohd. Hanif Quareshi* v. *Bihar*[28] is a case of very great importance, both because of the constitutional questions raised and because of the strong feelings which are roused by the slaughter of cattle, particularly cows. The petitioners were Muslims of the Quareshi community, whose members were engaged in the trade of butchers and its subsidiary undertakings such as sale of hides, glue, etc. Some of the petitioners slaughtered cattle and not sheep or goats. It

---

[23] *Brig. Commdr., Meerut* v. *Ganga Prasad* ('56) A.A. 507, (1956) 54 A.L.J. 251; *Satish Chander* v. *Delhi Improvement Trust* (1958) Punj. 195, ('58) A.Punj. 1 [the above two cases were relied on in *Mahendralal* v. *Tripura* ('59) A.Trip. 21 in declaring the unamended Act, void].

[24] (1955) 2 S.C.R. 531, ('55) A.SC. 795.

[25] Assuming that the circumstances justified such a restriction.

[26] ('54) A.Ajm. 17.

[27] The minority declined to express any opinion on the Constitutional question because the appeal was capable of being disposed of on the ground that the rules under which action was taken were *ultra vires* of the statute and were therefore void.

[28] (1959) S.C.R. 629, ('58) A.SC. 731.

was alleged that there were 500 butchers in Patna and 2 lakhs in Bihar. Some of the petitioners owned tanning factories or were gut merchants or were butchers or cattle dealers. The petitioners challenged the laws of different States aimed at preventing the slaughter of cattle. Das C.J. summarised the impugned laws thus:

"... under the Bihar Act there is in the State of Bihar a total ban on slaughter of all categories of animals of the species of bovine cattle. In Uttar Pradesh there is, under the U.P. Act, a total ban on the slaughter of cows and her progeny which include bulls, bullocks, heifer or calves. The buffaloes (male or female adults or calves) are completely outside the protection of the Act. In the present Madhya Pradesh and the districts which formerly formed part of Madhya Pradesh but have since been transferred to the State of Bombay and where the Madhya Pradesh law including the Madhya Pradesh Act still applies, there is a total ban on the slaughter of cow, male or female calves of a cow, bulls, bullocks, or heifers and the slaughter of buffaloes (male or female adults or calves) are controlled in that their slaughter is permitted under certificate granted by the proper authorities mentioned in the Act. No exception has been made in any of these three Acts permitting slaughter of cattle even for *bona fide* religious purposes such as has been made, say, in the Bombay Animal Preservation Act, 1948."[29]

Laws totally prohibiting slaughter of cattle directly affect rights under Art. 19(1)(*f*) and (*g*)

The questions raised under Arts. 14 and 25(1) are not relevant to this discussion[30] which is confined to the questions raised under Art. 19(1)(*g*). The respondents contended that Art. 19(1)(*g*) was violated only by a law which directly violated its provisions; that the impugned Acts were designed to secure the preservation, protection and improvement of stock and their real aim was not to take away or abridge anybody's rights under Art. 19(1)(*g*). In rejecting this contention the Supreme Court said:

"There can be no mistake about the directness of these legislations *vis-a-vis* the petitioners and other butchers and the effect of these legislations on their rights is direct and instantaneous as soon as they are brought into force."[31]

After referring to the test of reasonableness laid down in the undernoted cases,[32] and after giving a brief historical account on the question of slaughter of cattle, Das C.J. said:

Importance of cattle in Indian agriculture

"... after the recent partition of the country this agitation against the slaughter of cows has been further intensified. While ... the constitutional question before us cannot be decided on grounds of mere sentiment, however passionate it may be, we, nevertheless, think that it has to be taken into consideration, though only as one of many elements, in arriving at a judicial verdict as to the reasonableness of the restrictions."[33]

After giving the figures of the cattle wealth of India,[34] of the yield of milk,[35] and of the shortage of milk,[36] Das C.J. quoted the observations of the Report on the Marketing of Cattle in India that "The cow and the working bullock have on their patient back the whole structure

---

[29] (1959) S.C.R. *supra* at p. 646.

[30] The challenge under Art. 14 was met by saying that there was a valid classification between those who slaughtered bovine cattle and those who slaughtered sheep and goats; and the challenge under Art. 25(1) was met by saying that it had not been established on the evidence that the slaughter of cows on certain days was a part of the Mohammedan religion.

[31] (1959) S.C.R. *supra* at p. 655.

[32] *Madras* v. *V. G. Row* (1952) S.C.R. 597, 607, ('52) A.SC. 196; *W.B.* v. *Subodh Gopal Bose* (1954) S.C.R. 587, 627, ('54) A.SC. 92; *Ebrahim Vazir Mavat* v. *Bombay* (1954) S.C.R. 933, 949-50, ('54) A.SC. 229; and *Bihar* v. *Maharajadhiraj Sir Kameshwar Singh* (1952) S.C.R. 889, 941, ('52) A.SC. 252.

[33] (1959) S.C.R. *supra* at p. 664.

[34] ibid. p. 665.

[35] ibid. p. 666.

[36] ibid. p. 667.

Adverse effects of maintaining unfit and decrepit cattle

of Indian agriculture." Turning to the other side of the picture, Das C.J. said:

"First, there was a loss of business, and consequently of livelihood, to a very large number of people who, on an average, earned from the business about Rs. 150 to Rs. 200 per month.[37] Secondly, the total ban on slaughter of cattle would deprive large numbers of people of cheap cattle-beef which was a staple item in their diet and thus accentuate the existing malnutrition.[38] Thirdly, such a total ban would aggravate the evils of surplus, useless and inefficient cattle, namely, that without proper feeding, the breed of cattle cannot be improved, and the feeding of useless and inefficient cattle prevents proper feeding of fit cattle.[39] Fourthly, old and inefficient cattle, being left to fend for themselves, would roam about for food and run wild and be a source of danger to the community and to crop production; their presence in the midst of fit cattle adversely affecting the breed of cattle.[40] *Gosadans* did not meet this menace of useless cattle. Without taking the cost of fodder into account, the cost of maintaining one useless animal was Rs. 19 or Rs. 18 per year, compared with the national *per capita* expenditure of Rs. 4.9 on education."

Das C.J. continued:

"When the conscience of the individual or the community did not prevent the Hindu owner from selling his dry cow to the butcher for a paltry sum of Rs. 30 to Rs. 40 per head, when the Hindu sentiment for the divinity and sanctity attributed to the cow has to be propped up by legislative compulsion, when . . . the Dharmada and Brit collected by the Hindu businessmen on each commercial transaction ostensibly for the benefit of the cow is not made available in full and finally when Goshalas have had to be closed down for want of funds and public support, when the country cannot spend more than Rs. 5 *per capita* per annum on the education of the people, it seems to be . . . illogical and extravagant, bordering on incongruity . . . preserving useless cattle at a cost of Rs. 19 or Rs. 18 per head per annum and which will, for its success, admittedly have to depend on the same elusive and illusory public support or 75 per cent subsidy from the Central Government."[41]

The grim fate of useless cattle: they are left to slow death; ban on cow-slaughter upheld as an exception

After having drawn the grimmest picture of the attempt to preserve useless cattle by saying that the "Preservation of these useless animals by sending them to concentration camps to fend for themselves is to leave them to a process of slow death and does no good to them",[42] the Court justified the total ban on cow-slaughter in these words:

". . . the she-buffalo and the breeding bulls and working bullocks (both cattle and buffaloes) for their value, present and future, do not run the same amount of danger as a dry cow does. Regulation of slaughter of animals above a specified age may not be quite adequate protection for the cow but may be quite sufficient for the breeding bulls and working bullocks and the she-buffaloes. These considerations induce us to make an exception even in favour of the old and decrepit cows. *The Counsel for the petitioners, be it said to their credit, did not contend otherwise.*"[43] (italics supplied)

Court's justification of the exception

The sentence in italics above is misleading, for it suggests that Counsel did not wish to offend religious sentiment, and the total exemption against slaughtering of cows was a mere rationalization. This led the present writer in the earlier editions of this book to say that it was difficult to understand why it was creditable for Counsel not to argue a point which arose necessarily from the reasons relevant to the slaughter of unfit cattle, and from the grim picture presented to, and accepted by, the Court, of the fate of old and decrepit

---

[37] This consideration was held relevant on a question of reasonableness in *Saghir Ahmad* v. *U.P.* (1955) 1 S.C.R. 707, 724, ('54) A.SC. 728.
[38] (1959) S.C.R. *supra* at pp. 672-3.
[39] ibid. pp. 673-6.
[40] ibid. p. 676.
[41] ibid. p. 680.
[42] ibid. p. 685.
[43] ibid. pp. 687-8.

cows. However, there was a factual justification for the reasoning of the above quoted passage to be found in the earlier part of the judgment. After having pointed out the very low yield of milk per cow in India, in contrast to the very high yield in other countries, Das C.J. said that judged purely from the economic point of view, it would be necessary to eliminate cattle which yielded 2 lbs. or less of milk per day. However, such drastic action would mean the elimination of more than 90 per cent of the cows in India. But that would involve a loss of about 70,00,000 tons out of 97,00,000 tons of annual gross production of milk from cows, apart from a number of bullocks produced by the cows.[44] In a country where there was an acute shortage of milk, and the milk *per capita* was grossly inadequate, such a loss would be catastrophic. This factual basis can support the exception made in favour of the cow. The Court's conclusions were:

A summary of the Court's conclusions

"... (i) that a total ban on the slaughter of cows of all ages and calves of cows and calves of she-buffaloes, male and female, is quite reasonable and valid and is in consonance with the directive principles laid down in Art. 48; (ii) that a total ban on slaughter of she-buffaloes or breeding bulls or working bullocks (cattle as well as buffaloes) as long as they are useful as milch or draught cattle is also reasonable and valid and (iii) that a total ban on the slaughter of she-buffaloes, bulls and bullocks (cattle or buffalo) after they cease to be capable of yielding milk or of breeding or working as draught animals cannot be supported as reasonable in the interest of the general public."[45]

Accordingly, the provisions of the three Acts which imposed a total ban on the third category were held to be unconstitutional and void.

Legislative amendments, designed to prevent slaughter of

10.151 This decision had a strange sequel. It was followed by legislative amendments[46] designed to prevent the slaughter of cattle after they ceased to be capable of yielding milk or of breeding or of work-

[44] ibid. p. 666.

[45] ibid. p. 688. *Mohd. Hanif Qureshi's Case* was fol. in *Abdul Ameed* v. *Chitradurga Municipality* ('65) A.Mys. 281 and it was held that though the right to trade in beef was a fundamental right under Art. 19(1)(*g*) and could be subjected to reasonable restrictions, no restrictions could be considered reasonable which conferred on the licensing authority an arbitrary power to cancel a licence, for such arbitrary power in respect of a trade would make the content of the fundamental right under Art. 19(1)(*g*) illusory: ibid. p. 283. It is submitted that in *Maina Bai* v. *M.P.* ('65) A.M.P. 247 this aspect has not been considered. A power to grant a permit for opening a new rice mill depending upon the subjective satisfaction of the authority granting the permit would render the fundamental right under Art. 19(1)(*g*) illusory and cannot be upheld as a reasonable restriction on the right to carry on trade or business. In *N.K.K. Samaj* v. *Nagpur Corporation* ('59) A.B. 112 it was held that the prohibition by the Nagpur Corporation of the sale of meat in weekly markets violated Art. 19(1)(*g*), and was invalid.

[46] S. 3, Bihar Preservation and Improvement of Animals (Amendment) Act, 1955, prohibited the slaughter of a bull, bullock or she-buffalo except when it was over 25 years of age and had become useless. R. 3, Bihar Preservation and Improvement of Animal Rules, 1960, prescribed that a certificate for slaughtering animals may be granted only with the concurrence of the Veterinary Officer and the Chairman or Chief Officer of a District Board, and if the two differed, then according to the decision of the sub-divisional Animal Husbandry Officer. S. 3, U.P. Prevention of Cow Slaughter (Amendment) Act, 1959, permitted the slaughter of a bull or bullock only if it was over 20 years of age and was permanently unfit. It however provided that the animal should not be slaughtered within 20 days of the grant of a certificate that it was fit to be slaughtered, and gave a right of appeal to any person aggrieved by the order granting the certificate. S. 4(1)(*b*), M.P. Agricultural Cattle Preservation Act, 1959, provided that no bull or bullock or buffalo could be slaughtered except upon a certificate issued by the Competent Authority and s. 4(2)(*a*) provided that no certificate should be issued unless the animal was over 20 years of age and was unfit for work or breeding. S. 4(3) gave the right of appeal to any person aggrieved by the Order of the Competent Authority. S. 5 provided that no

cattle held void

ing as draught animals. In *Abdul Hakim Quraishi* v. *Bihar*,[47] these amendments were again challenged as violating Art. 19 (1) (*g*). In addition to urging some of the grounds which had been held to justify the slaughter of old and unfit cattle, the petitioners contended that as a result of the raising of the age-limit there would be no bullocks or buffaloes or she-buffaloes available for slaughter as few of the animals survived in India up to the age of 15 years and that millions of members of the minority community would be deprived of cattle-beef which was a staple item of their diet. Affidavits on behalf of the States tried to justify the raising of the limit from 15 to 20 years or 25 years. On a careful consideration of the evidence, the Court held that:

"... the almost unanimous opinion of experts is that after the age of 15, bulls, bullocks and buffaloes are no longer useful for breeding, draught and other purposes and whatever little use they may have then is greatly offset by the economic disadvantages of feeding and maintaining unserviceable cattle — disadvantages to which we had referred in much greater detail in *Mohd. Hanif Qureshi's Case* (1959) S.C.R. 629."[48]

Accordingly, the Court held that s. 3 of the Bihar Act, in so far as it raised the age-limit to 25 years, was void as an unreasonable restriction. R. 3 was void because it prescribed a cumbrous and expensive procedure which would involve so much expenditure of time and money that it would practically prohibit the slaughter of cattle. S. 3 of the U.P. Act was void because, apart from prescribing the unduly high age of 20 years, before a certificate for slaughter was given, the animal must fulfil two conditions as to (i) age and (ii) permanent unfitness, and the Court said:

"We consider this to be a demonstrably unreasonable restriction. In *Mohd. Hanif Qureshi's Case* (1959) S.C.R. 629, this Court has said that a total ban on the slaughter of bulls and bullocks after they had ceased to be capable of breeding or working as draught animals was not in the interests of the general public. Yet this is exactly what the impugned provision does by imposing a double restriction. It lays down that even if the animal is permanently unserviceable, no certificate can be given unless it is more than 20 years in age. The restriction will in effect put an end to the trade of the petitioners."[49]

The provision against slaughter within 20 years, and the right to appeal given to anyone from such an order was also unreasonable as it would practically put an end to the slaughter of unfit cattle. S. 4 of the M.P. Act was void for the same reasons which applied to s. 3 of the U.P. Act, and s. 5 which imposed restrictions as to the time when the cattle could be slaughtered was also open to the same objection. Accordingly, the impugned provisions were declared void.

Attempt to circumvent *Mohd. Quareshi's Case*: notification declared void

The notification impugned in *Md. Faruk* v. *M.P.*[50] was described by the Supreme Court as "apparently another attempt though on a restricted scale, to circumvent the judgment of this Court in *Mohd. Hanif Quareshi's Case* ..."[51] The effect of the impugned notification was to prohibit the slaughter of bulls and bullocks within the Munici-

animal should be slaughtered within 10 days of the issue of the certificate and where an appeal was preferred against the grant of a certificate, till the time such appeal was disposed of.

47 (1961) 2 S.C.R. 610, ('61) A.SC. 448.
48 (1961) 2 S.C.R. *supra* at p. 622.
49 ibid. p. 626.
50 (1970) 1 S.C.R. 156, ('70) A.SC. 93.
51 ('70) A.SC. *supra* at p. 95.

pality of Jabalpur, and the notification imposed a direct restriction upon the petitioners' rights under Art. 19(1) (*g*). In allowing the petition, Shah J. speaking for a Bench of five judges, said:

"The sentiments of a section of the people may be hurt by permitting slaughter of bulls and bullocks in premises maintained by a local authority. But a prohibition imposed on the exercise of a fundamental right to carry on an occupation, trade or business will not be regarded as reasonable, if it is imposed not in the interest of the general public, but merely to respect the susceptibilities and sentiments of a section of the people whose way of life, belief or thought is not the same as that of the claimant."[52]

H. N. Rao's Case: provisions for disposal of animal carcasses held valid

10.152 In *Maharashtra* v. *H. N. Rao*[53] the Supreme Court allowed the appeal and upheld the validity of s. 385, Bombay Municipal Corporation Act, 1888.[54] That section imposed upon the owner of an animal or the occupier of the premises in or upon which the animal died, or the person having charge of the animal, the duty to remove the carcass at his own expense with the permission of the Commissioner, or to have it removed by the Corporation and pay the prescribed fee. In 1962 the Corporation resolved to grant a contract authorizing removal of carcasses under s. 385 in respect of certain "Wards" to a society, and declared that no other person or agency was authorized under s. 385 to remove or dispose of carcasses. The Court held that carcasses of dead animals were property, but they constituted a nuisance, and for the promotion of public health and for the prevention of danger to the community, it was necessary that the carcasses should be removed expeditiously and disposed of in a manner which would cause the least nuisance. A law making such provision was *prima facie* in the public interest; but to attract the protection of Art. 19(5) the restrictions imposed by such law must be reasonable, that is, they should not be arbitrary or excessive;[55] but the restrictions imposed by s. 385 were not arbitrary or excessive. The High Court had held that s. 385 imposed unreasonable restrictions for it made no difference whether the carcass was disposed of by a purchaser from the owner or by a contractor who purchased it from the Corporation. But the Supreme Court said that these observations ignored the uncontroverted evidence on record[56] that meat and fat from the carcasses were used by unscrupulous persons for adulterating food of the community. This could not be effectively prevented unless the person authorized to dispose of carcasses was under the strict control and supervision of the Corporation. The possibility that a better scheme might have been, but had not been, designed to secure the same result, would not make the restriction imposed by the impugned scheme unreasonable.[57]

Carcasses of dead animals constitute a nuisance, and the impugned provisions were reasonable

Religious & Charitable Endowments

10.153 Provisions in Religious or Charitable Endowments Acts for carrying out the objects of any trust and for the better administra-

---

[52] ibid. pp. 96-7.
[53] (1969) 2 S.C.R. 392, ('70) A.SC. 1157.
[54] ('70) A.SC. at pp. 1160-61 where the section is set out.
[55] ibid. p. 1161. [56] ibid.
[57] ibid. pp. 1162-3. A similar view had been expressed in *Bombay* v. *Bhanji Munji* (1955) 1 S.C.R. 777, 785: "A wide discretion must be left to Government to carry out the policy of the Act. . . . So long as this is done . . . reasonably, the Courts cannot interfere simply because other methods are also possible, even if the Courts think they are better, for in the end Government must be left to determine which of many possible schemes is the best."

—Provisions for proper working of endowments upheld

tion, protection and preservation of properties,[58] or for the better and more convenient discharge of the trustees' duty[59] or for keeping accounts of gifts made to the head of a *math* and for the utilisation of the same according to the customs and usages of an Institution[60] are valid as they impose reasonable restrictions in the public interest on trustees whose duty it is to carry out their trust. However, in considering the reasonableness of restrictions imposed on religious trusts the impact of Arts. 25 and 26 must not be overlooked.[61]

Religious Trusts

---

[58] *Moti Das* v. *S. P. Sahi* (1959) Supp. (2) S.C.R. 563, ('59) A.SC. 942. This decision also covers the decision in *Bihar* v. *Bhabapritananda Ojha* (1959) Supp. (2) S.C.R. 624, ('59) A.SC. 1073, upholding the validity of ss. 28 and 32, Bihar Hindu Religious Trusts Act, 1959; *Namboodripad* v. *C.D. Board* (1956) Tr.-Co. 74 (F.B.), ('56) A.Tr.-Co. 19 [where the plaintiff was the hereditary trustee of a temple his right as *Uralan* constituted property within the meaning of Art. 19(1)(*f*). Provisions for safeguarding religious institutions of a particular faith and for avoiding friction and mis-management must be considered reasonable restrictions in the interest of the general public]; *P.B.N.C. Committee* v. *A.P.* ('58) A.A.P. 773 (the appointment of a Treasurer and the vesting of the properties in him for the purposes specified in the Charitable Endowments Act would not offend the fundamental rights of the members of the Society, either under Art. 19 or Art. 31); *Pubbiri* v. *S. Govinda* ('58) A.M. 147, (1957) 2 M.L.J. 617 (s. 87, Madras Hindu Religious and Charitable Endowments Act, 1951, was upheld on the ground that it was designed to recover properties from trustees who had been dismissed by committees appointed under the Act when they neglected or refused to hand over trust properties); *Raja of Kozhikode* v. *Commr. H.R. & C.E.* ('61) A.Ker. 87 (upholding s. 45, Madras Hindu Religious and Charitable Endowments Act, 1951, as it provided for the removal of trustees on five grounds which showed that the power was to be exercised only when danger to the endowment was reasonably apprehended); *Rama Nayar* v. *Dy. Commr. H.R. & C.E.* ('63) A.M. 205 (the rule which directs trustees to lease out lands by public auction is eminently a reasonable restriction in the public interest).

[59] *Anant Prasad* v. *A.P.* (1963) Supp. (1) S.C.R. 844, ('63) A.SC. 853 (upholding ss. 3 to 11, Hyderabad Endowment Regulations, 1940 [except s. 4(*b*) on wihch it was not necessary to pronounce].

[60] *S. T. Swamiar* v. *Commr. Hindu Religious Endowments* ('63) A.SC. 966 [upholding ss. 52(1)(*g*) and 55, Madras Hindu Religious Endowments Act, 1951, as in force in the Madras area of the State of Mysore]; *Durgah Committee* v. *Hussain Ali* ('61) A.SC. 1402, (1962) 1 S.C.R. 383 [*held*, reversing the judgment under appeal in *Hussain Syed Hussain Ali* v. *Durgah Committee* (1959) Raj. 424, ('59) A.Raj. 177 that s. 11(*f*) and (*h*), Durgah Kwaja Saheb Act, 1955, merely regulated the discharge of duties by *Khadims* and by *Sajjadanashins*. Ss. 2(*d*), (v) and 14 of the Act did not affect the offerings which were made to *Khadims* and therefore did not violate Art. 19(1)(*f*) and (*g*)]. In *Bashiruddin Ashraf* v. *Bihar* (1957) S.C.R. 1032, ('57) A.SC. 645, the provisions of s. 58(1) and the penal provisions of s. 65, Bihar Waqfs Act, 1948, were held not to violate Art. 19(1)(*g*). S. 58(1) required a *mutavalli* of every Waqf to prepare a budget and send it to the Majlis, and s. 58(2) to (6) conferred certain powers on the Majlis, which the Court held did not in any way interfere with the Waqf, and in any event were severable. S. 65 provided punishment for failure to prepare and furnish the budget to the Majlis. The petitioner who was convicted under s. 65 impugned the validity of s. 58 but the court held that the provisions as regards the preparation of a budget were necessary to ensure that a Waqf was properly administered and that the income of the Waqf was duly appropriated for the purposes for which the Waqf had been founded. Nothing in s. 58 amounted to unreasonable restrictions on the duties of the *mutavalli* as a person administering the Waqf: *Hafiz Mohammad* v. *U.P.S.C. Board of Waqfs* ('65) A.A. 333 [*held*, that the right of a *mutavalli* is not equivalent to that of a Mahant, it is a right to the management of the property and not a proprietary right. His duties are purely of a secular character, he is not the head of a spiritual fraternity differing in all these respects from a Mahant. A *mutavalli* is nothing more than a servant of the founder of the Waqf].

[61] This aspect is considered more fully in Chapter XII.

Art. 19 (1) (*f*) applies both to concrete and abstract rights of property, and the word "property" in that Article should be given a liberal and wide meaning, and so interpreted, should be extended to those well-recognized types of interest which have an insignia or characteristic of proprietary right. In the case of a Mahant the ingredients both of office and property, of duties and personal interest are blended together and the Mahant has the right to enjoy the property or beneficial interest so long as he is entitled to hold office. To take away this beneficial interest and leave him merely to discharge his duties would be to destroy his character as a Mahant and the restrictions imposed on his right to enjoy property must be held unreasonable.[62] Section 46, A.P. Charitable and Hindu Religious Institutions and Endowments Act, 1966, which mentioned the grounds on which a *Mathadhipati* or a trustee could be removed, and conferred a power to suspend them pending an inquiry for such removal, imposed reasonable restrictions within the meaning of Art. 19 (1) (*f*) and (5) on the rights of the *Mathadhipati*.[63] But, the settling of a scheme under ss. 38, 39 and the Proviso to s. 46, Orissa Hindu Religious Endowments Act, 1939, in regard to a religious institution by an Executive Officer without the intervention of any judicial tribunal amounted to imposing an unreasonable restriction upon the right of property of the superior of a religious institution which right is blended with his office. The Proviso to s. 46, contained an unreasonable restriction on the discretion of the trustees in regard to the spending of surplus income for such purposes as were mentioned in s. 46.[64] However, in *G. Sitharamamma* v. *Dy. Commr* [65] it was said that assuming that a trustee was the owner of property, still, unlike the trustee of a *math* the trustee of a temple had no beneficial interest in property and the restrictions imposed by ss. 45-52, Madras Hindu Religious and Charitable Endowments Act, 1951, were reasonable. However, the *Tilkayat* was merely a custodian, manager and trustee of the temple and no more; his position was not similar to that of a Mahant or Shebait, and his right to possession and management of the property could not be regarded as a right to property under Art. 19 (1) (*f*), and, for the same reason, under Art. 31 (2). Even if in theory the *Tilkayat* could be regarded as a Mahant or Shebait, the absolute and strict supervision which the Udaipur Durbar could exercise had the result that the right could not be equated with the totality of the powers generally possessed by a Mahant and even by a Shebait; consequently, the right of management could not be considered to be a right to property under Arts. 19 (1) (*f*) and 31 (2). Even if the right were a right to property, the restrictions imposed by the relevant provisions of the Rajasthan Nathdwara Temple Act, 1959, were reasonable restrictions designed to provide for the regulation and the proper administration of the properties of the temple.[66] The above case was relied on in *Bira Kishore Deb* v. *Orissa*[67] and it was

Ingredients of property and office blend in the case of a Mahant

What amounts to unreasonable restrictions on the Mahant's right to property

The position of a custodian, manager and trustee of a temple, different from the Mahant's

---

[62] *Commissioner, H.R.E., Madras* v. *Sri Lakshmindra Thirtha Swamiar* (1954) S.C.R. 1005, ('54) A.SC. 282.
[63] *Digyadarsan R. R. Varu* v. *A.P.* ('70) A.SC. 181, 187; s. 46 is set out at p. 184.
[64] *Mahant Sri Jagannath* v. *Orissa* (1954) S.C.R. 1046, ('54) A.SC. 400.
[65] ('58) A.A.P. 319.
[66] *Tilkayat Shri Govindlalji* v. *Rajasthan* (1964) 1 S.C.R. 561, ('63) A.SC. 1638.
[67] (1964) 7 S.C.R. 32, ('64) A.SC. 1501.

held that s. 6, Shri Jagannath Temple Act, 1954, which took away the sole management of the temple vested in the Raja of Puri and his ancestors, was not unconstitutional, first, because the right was not property in the present case, as it carried no beneficial enjoyment of any property with it and, secondly, because that right had not been acquired by the State. The Act extinguished the sole right of the Raja to manage the property and in its place it created a body for administering the temple. Thus the office of one functionary was brought to an end, and that of another created, and this could not be called acquisition of the extinguished office, or the vesting of it in the new body holding it. The restrictions put on the Raja's sole right to manage the property were reasonable. The Act had not taken away his right as *Adya Sevak* and could not be attacked as depriving him of his rights to property, for s. 8 preserved those rights.[68] In *K. A. Samajam* v. *Commr. H.R. & C.E., Hyderabad,*[69] relying on *Tilkayat Case* and *Bira Kishore Deb's Case,* the Supreme Court held that the office of a hereditary trustee[70] was not "property" within the meaning of Art. 19(1) (*f*). The position of a bare trustee of a religious endowment could not be equated with that of a *Mahant,* a *Shibait* or a *Mathadhipati.* For, in these cases, the ingredients of both office and property, of duties and personal interest are blended together. The Supreme Court held that the observations to the contrary in *Sambhuda Murthi Mudaliar* v. *Madras*[71] were *obiter* and did not lay down the correct law.

Tax laws and fundamental rights

10.154 Tax laws are subject to fundamental rights[72] under Art. 19. The most frequent challenge to tax laws is under Art. 19(1) (*f*) and (*g*) though a tax law can be challenged under the other heads of Art. 19(1). Thus in the *Express Newspapers* (*Private*) *Ltd.* v. *Union*[73] there was an unsuccessful challenge to the decision of a Wage Board on the ground that the wages fixed by it interfered with the freedom of the press which was included in the freedom of speech. However, the Court referred with approval to *Grosjean* v. *American Press Co.*[74] for the proposition that a statute imposing a tax on the business of publishing advertisements would be void if it was found to be a deliberate and calculated device in the guise of a tax to limit the circulation of information to which the public was entitled in virtue of the constitutional guarantees.[75]

A right must be established before complaining of its violation

10.155 A person cannot challenge a tax as violating his fundamental right under Art. 19(1) (*f*) or 19(1) (*g*) if he had no right to obtain a tax concession at the time when he challenged the law. Thus, in *Dalmia Dadri Cement Co.* v. *C.I.T.*[76] it was held that the imposition of a tax on the petitioners could not be challenged as violating their right of property, because, the income-tax concession granted to them had come to an end before our Constitution came into force.

---

[68] ('64) A.SC. at p. 1508.
[69] (1971) 2 S.C.R. 878, ('71) A.SC. 891, 897.
[70] Where such trustee was a bare trustee and claimed no interest in the trust property.
[71] (1970) 2 S.C.R. 424.
[72] See para 10.23.
[73] (1959) S.C.R. 12, ('58) A.SC. 578.
[74] (1935) 297 U.S. 233, 249, 80 L. ed. 660, 668.
[75] *Express Newspapers' Case, supra.*
[76] (1959) S.C.R. 729, ('58) A.SC. 816.

10.156 A tax law cannot be challenged merely on the ground that the rate of tax is very high[77] unless the tax is a colourable device to confiscate property.[78] In *Moopil Nair's Case*[79] a tax on land was declared void as violating Arts. 14 and 19(1) (*f*). The principle that a tax which is discriminatory is void as violating Art. 14 is indisputable, and it is equally indisputable that a tax which is a colourable device for acquiring property violates Art. 19(1) (*f*). For example, a law imposing an income-tax of 100 paise in the rupee would be void because it does not tax income but confiscates it. Therefore, though the principle is not in dispute, its application in the majority judgment in *Moopil Nair's Case* is open to very serious question as is clear from the convincing dissent of Sarkar J. The case arose out of the imposition of a tax of Rs. 2 per acre of land under the Trav.-Cochin Land Tax Act, 1955, as amended in 1957. The tax also applied to forest land which was governed by the Madras Preservation of Private Forests Act, 1949. The Land Tax Act was challenged on a number of grounds, of which the following are material to the present discussion. Pending a survey of the land, the Act provided for a provisional assessment of land, and for making adjustments in such provisional assessment; there was, however, no obligation to complete the survey within a stated time. The Act did not require that the person to be taxed should make a return nor did it provide for giving him a hearing. As regards the forest land to which the tax applied, some petitioners contended that as a result of the operation of the Madras Preservation of Private Forests Act, the tax payable was 15 to 20 times the income derived from the forest. Government could exempt lands from the operation of the Act there being no guidance for the exercise of the power. On these facts, the majority held that the law violated Arts. 14 and 19(1) (*f*), that the procedural provisions as regards the imposition of tax were unreasonable restrictions on the right to hold property, that the tax was confiscatory and that the power to grant exemption conferred arbitrary and unguided power, and therefore the Act was void. On the dis-

Tax law cannot be challenged because rate of tax is high, unless the rate is confiscatory

A discriminatory tax is void: *Moopil Nair's Case*

Majority view: Land Tax Act held void as violating Arts. 14, 19(1)(*f*) and 31

[77] *Jagannath* v. *Union* (1962) 2 S.C.R. 118, ('62) A.SC. 148 ("it is obvious that a challenge to a tax law on the mere ground that the tariff imposed by the tax law is heavy cannot be entertained"); *Jagannath Baksh Singh* v. *U.P.* (1963) 1 S.C.R. 220, 240, ('62) A.SC. 1563 [There is no doubt that the decision in the case of *K. T. Moopil Nair (infra)* is not an authority for the proposition that in testing the validity of a taxing statute, the Court can embark upon an inquiry whether the tax imposed by the statute is unreasonably high and whether it should have been fixed at a lower level." On the facts it was held that the tax was not confiscatory]; *Calcutta Corporation* v. *Liberty Cinema* (1965) 2 S.C.R. 477, ('65) A.SC. 1107 (an increase of licence fee on a Cinema House from Rs. 400 in 1948 to Rs. 6,000 in 1958 did not amount to expropriation as the Cinema House could collect Rs. 1,000 per show); *Ayodhya Naidu* v. *Madras* ('65) A.M. 349 [the quantum of tax was a matter within the competence of the legislature. There was no indication that the purpose of the Madras Motor Vehicle Taxation (Amendment) Act, 1962, was confiscatory. It was in the nature of a compensatory tax].

[78] *K. T. Moopil Nair* v. *Kerala* (1961) 3 S.C.R. 77, ('61) A.SC. 552; *Pithapuram T.T.C. & S.M. Union* v. *State* ('58) A.A.P. 558 [*prima facie* taxation cannot be said to be an abridgment of the fundamental rights under Art. 19(1)(*g*). If however, the pith and substance of the legislation is to impose taxes which are prohibitive or amount to unreasonable restrictions, they must be justified under Art. 19(6)]. *Moopil Nair's Case* was rel. on in *N. Kunhali Haji* v. *Kerala* ('66) A.Ker. 14, 17 and it was held that a tax on lands and buildings based on floor area violated Art. 14 as it failed to make a proper classification.

[79] *Supra*.

criminatory nature of the tax the majority held that this was a case where equality of treatment really resulted in inequality, since all lands were taxed equally without any reference to their yield. The confiscatory nature of the tax was spelt out by taking the case of the tax imposed on forest land.[80]

Sarkar J.'s dissent

10.157 It is submitted that, except possibly in the case of forest land, there appears to have been no evidence at all that the tax was confiscatory. As regards discrimination, as rightly pointed out by Sarkar J. the tax on land did not violate Art. 14 as it was based on an intelligible differentia reasonably related to the object of the law. The differentia adopted was the area of the land owned by a person. The object of the law was to provide a low and uniform rate of basic tax to replace all other dues payable to Government in respect of the ownership of land. Accordingly, there was nothing unreasonable in fixing the basic tax with reference to the area of the land owned by a person. To say that this classification was bad because it imposed an unequal burden of tax on the owners of land, and that owners of less productive land would have a larger burden put on them, was to assume that a tax on land could be imposed only according to its productivity, for which assumption there was no warrant. It would lead to the conclusion that unproductive land cannot be taxed at all, which would mean that the State's power to tax land would be inoperative in respect of unproductive land. Sarkar J. rightly said that if the argument were accepted in the present case, it would apply to all taxing laws which would then have to be correlated to the income or profit which would be made and this would have very far-reaching consequences.[81] Further, the fact that some owners of land may be able to pay the tax from the income and others may have to find it from other sources may be a matter of some hardship but that was not a ground for assuming that the tax was unconstitutional.

Submission: dissenting judgment is correct except, possibly, as regards forest lands

10.158 However, the validity of the tax on forest lands requires to be considered separately. The facts stated by Sarkar J. show that the relevant evidence was not before the Court:

> "Taking by way of illustration Petition No. 13, it is pointed out that the income from the forest with which that petition is concerned was Rs. 8,477 for the year 1956-57 while the tax payable under the Act for more or less the same period was Rs. 1,51,000. I am unable to hold that because of this the Act offends Art. 19(1)(*f*) and (*g*). It is not stated that the land is not capable of producing any income other than the income from the forest standing on it. There is nothing to show that in all times to come the income from the land including the income from the forest, will be less than the tax imposed on it by the Act. The area of the land concerned in Petition No. 13 is enormous being about 75,500 acres."[82]

The above facts required further investigation, for, the petitioners' case led to the incredible conclusion that the income from the forest was about one-tenth of a rupee per annum per acre! However,

---

[80] In *Ratan Chand* v. *Panchayat Samiti, Sojat* ('67) A.Raj. 142, Rr. 12, 13 and 14 of the Rajasthan Panchayat Samitis Taxation Rules, 1960, which imposed a tax on the basis of income, were held void as violating Art. 19(1)(*f*) as they provided for an assessment to tax without giving the assessee a hearing.

[81] For example, would a sales tax at 10 paise per rupee be discriminatory if some articles on which it is imposed involve less profit than others?

[82] (1961) 3 S.C.R. *supra* at pp. 104-5.

accepting the facts as correct, the small income was due to the operation of the Madras Act, and it is possible to take the view, contrary to that taken by Sarkar J., that in respect of forest land governed by the Madras Act, the tax would be confiscatory in effect, though not in intent, and to that extent was void as long as the Madras Act, and the executive action taken under it, remained unaltered. It is settled law that the principle of severability in enforcement applies to taxing, and indeed to any Statute,[83] and an injunction could be issued restraining the State from recovering tax from forest lands. That lands subject to a special law like the Forest Act can be treated differently from other lands is obvious.

Submission: Sarkar J.'s judgment is correct as regards procedural requirements

10.159 As regards the procedural requirement of the law, it is submitted that the dissenting judgment of Sarkar J. is correct. The difference between surveyed and unsurveyed lands justified the imposition of a provisional assessment. Nor was any elaborate procedure necessary when the tax to be levied was at a uniform rate of Rs. 2 per acre. If the Act did not provide for a hearing or an opportunity then the Court would be justified in implying such a requirement in order to save the validity of the Act. If these requirements were violated in any particular case, the executive act of assessment, and not the law, would be struck down. As regards power to grant an exemption the subject has been discussed in an earlier part of this book.[84] In fact no exemption had been granted, but in any event, the section was severable and the Act could be applied without it. It is submitted therefore that though the abstract principles laid down in the case are correct, in their application to the facts of the case, the majority decision is wrong except possibly as regards the forest lands, provided the facts stated by the petitioners were found on a careful scrutiny of the evidence to be correct.

***Twyford's Case*: uniform tax per acre held valid**

10.160 The grave consequences of *Moopil Nair's Case* were realized in *Twyford Tea Co.* v. *Kerala*[85] where, by a majority of 3 : 2 the Supreme Court held the impugned taxing Act valid.[86] The Act imposed a uniform tax of Rs. 50 per acre on lands used for seven kinds of plantations. Schedule 2 to the Act gave a formula which, by reference to the number of trees or plants grown, tried to equalize the area of different plantations, on which area the uniform tax was levied. Holding that the Act was valid, Hidayatullah C.J. said:

"The uniform tax falls more heavily on some plantations than on others because the profits are widely discrepant. But does that involve a discrimination? If the answer be in the affirmative, *hardly any tax direct or indirect would escape the same censure for taxes touch purses of different lengths and the very uniformity of the tax and its equal treatment would become its undoing. The rich and the poor pay the same taxes irrespective of their incomes in many instances such as the sales-tax and the profession tax etc.*"[87] (italics supplied)

---

[83] *Bombay* v. *United Motors (India) Ltd.* (1953) S.C.R. 1069, 1098-9, ('53) A.SC. 252, approved and held not limited to taxing statutes in *R. M. D. Chamarbaugwalla* v. *Union* (1957) S.C.R. 930, 945, ('57) A.SC. 628.

[84] See para 9.114.

[85] (1970) 3 S.C.R. 383, ('70) A.SC. 1133.

[86] The Kerala Plantation (Additional Tax) Act, 1960, as amended by the Kerala Plantation (Additional Tax) Amendment Act, 1967.

[87] ('70) A.SC. *supra* at p. 1136.

After quoting the passage from Willis which was approved in the *East India Tobacco Co.* v. *A.P.*[88] Hidayatullah C.J. observed that if production must always be taken into account, there would have to be a settlement of land for every year, and the tax would become a kind of income-tax. As to the burden of proving inequality, Hidayatullah C.J. said:

"The burden is proving not possible 'inequality' but hostile 'unequal' treatment. *This is more so when uniform taxes are levied.* It is not proved to us how the different plantations can be said to be 'hostilely or unequally' treated. A uniform wheel tax on cars does not take into account the value of the car, the mileage it runs or in the case of taxis the profits it makes and the miles per gallon it delivers. An Ambassador taxi and a Fiat taxi give different out-turn in terms of money and mileage. Cinemas pay the same show fee. We do not take a doctrinnaire view of equality".[89] (italics supplied)

Submission: *Moopil Nair's Case* wrongly decided

It is submitted that this is a circuitious way of saying that *Moopil Nair's* Case was wrongly decided. If absurd consequences would have flowed from holding the tax invalid, as Hidayatullah C.J. pointed out, it is because *Moopil Nair's Case* converted the legislative entry "tax on land" to read "tax on productivity or income from land" contrary to the settled rule that a Court cannot re-write a legislative entry which is plain and unambiguous. It is submitted that the grounds given by Hidayatullah C.J. for holding the Act valid show that the dissenting judgment of Sarkar J. in *Moopil Nair's Case* was correct, and that the majority judgment required to be overruled.

Pattabhiraman's Case: unguided power

10.161 In *V. Pattabhiraman* v. *Asst. Commr., Urban Land Tax,*[90] it was held that s. 6, Madras Urban Land Tax Act, 1966, conferred an unguided power on the Asst. Commissioner to fix the market value of urban land and that the test laid down for determining the market value was

". . . *per se* quite an arbitrary estimate, . . . the words 'if sold in the open market' will be quite meaningless in many cases as there is no open market in built-up areas and such market is not even conceivable."[91]

But the levy of a tax lawfully imposed under a statute within the competence of the Legislature, cannot be deemed to infringe the fundamental rights guaranteed by Art. 19(1) (*f*) and (*g*).[92]

Retrospective validation of tax upheld: *Rai Ramkrishna's Case*

10.162 Normally a retrospective validation of a tax law does not amount to imposing unreasonable restrictions on the rights conferred by Art. 19(1) (*f*) and (*g*). Thus, in *Rai Ramkrishna* v. *Bihar*[93] it was held that the power to make a law carried with it the power to give it retrospective operation and included the subsidiary power of validating laws which had been declared invalid. Under the Bihar Finance Act, 1950, a tax was levied on passengers and goods carried by public service motor-vehicles in Bihar. Suits challenging the validity of the tax were dismissed by the High Court on May 8, 1952, and appeals therefrom were pending in the Supreme Court till 1960,

[88] (1963) 1 S.C.R. 404, 410, ('62) A.SC. 1733. The passage from *Willis* is set out in para 9.44 of the text.

[89] ('70) A.SC. *supra* at p. 1138.

[90] ('71) A.M. 61 (F.B.).

[91] ibid. p. 71 (*per* Anantanarayanan C.J.)

[92] *Bhopal Sugar Industries* v. *S.T.O., Bhopal* (1964) 1 S.C.R. 488, ('67) A.SC. 549, 552 (the question whether the tax has been properly levied is not one for the determination by the High Court under Art. 226 but for the taxing authority).

[93] (1964) 1 S.C.R. 897, ('63) A.SC. 1667; *Chhotabhai Patel & Co.* v. *Union* ('52) A.N. 139 [upholding s. 7(2), Finance Act, 1951, which imposed a tax retrospectively].

and were allowed on December 12, 1960. The Bihar Taxation on Passengers and Goods (Carriage by Public Service Motor Vehicles) Act, 1961, was passed on September 23, 1961, with retrospective effect from April 1, 1950. It was contended that the Act was unreasonable because it was practically impossible to pass on the tax to the passengers from whom it was expected to be collected. The Supreme Court held that the character of a tax was not altered because it was given retrospective operation, and that the mere length of period during which retrospective operation was given to a taxing statute was not by itself enough to invalidate it. The Supreme Court referred to the facts of the present case, mentioned above, to show that ten years had elapsed between the filing of the suits by the plaintiffs and the conclusion of the proceedings in their favour in the Supreme Court. The above decision has been followed in *C. Krishna Moorthy* v. *Orissa*,[94] *in Narottamdas* v. *M.P.*[95] and *Jawharmal* v. *Rajasthan*.[96] In *Krishnamurthy & Co.* v. *Madras*[97] it was held that ss. 2 and 4, Madras General Sales Tax (3rd Amendment) Act, 1967, which gave retrospective operation to the provisions of ss. 2 and 4, did not violate Art. 19(1)(*g*). The sections had been passed to rectify and remove the difficulty created by the limited interpretation given to "mineral oils" by the High Court, and to validate past levy and collection of tax on all kinds of non-lubricating mineral oils. The fact that a dealer was not in a position to pass on the sales tax to others did not affect the competence of the legislature to enact a law imposing sales tax retrospectively.[98]

Provisions against evasion of tax upheld

10.163 Provisions in taxing statutes designed to prevent evasion of tax do not amount to unreasonable restrictions within the meaning of Art. 19(1)(*f*) and (*g*). Thus, ss. 16(3)(*a*)(*i*) and (*ii*) of the Income-tax Act, which imposed on a person a tax in respect of the income earned by his wife and minor child in partnership business, was not unreasonable as it was designed to prevent evasion of tax by carrying on business nominally in the name of a wife or minor child.[99] Similarly, the provision of the Wealth Tax Act, 1957, refusing to recognize a transfer in favour of a wife and minor children living with the assessee where such transfer was not for adequate consi-

---

[94] (1964) 7 S.C.R. 185, ('64) A.SC. 1581 [*held*, that s. 2, Orissa Sales Tax (Validation) Act, 1961 was not *ultra vires* because it withdrew an exemption in respect of gold ornaments retrospectively, for though the fact that a provision was retrospective was relevant on reasonableness, the retrospective effect was for a short time and, in any event, under the circumstances, it was not an unreasonable restriction in the public interest].

[95] ('64) A.SC. 1667 (upholding the validity of ss. 3 and 4, M.P. Minimum Wages Fixation Act, 1962, notwithstanding that they had retrospective operation).

[96] ('66) A.SC. 764 at pp. 770 and 773; fol. in *V. Pattabhiraman* v. *Asst. Commr., Urban Land Tax* ('71) A.M. 61 (F.B.) at p. 96 (the power to levy urban land tax retrospectively under the Madras Urban Land Tax Act, 1966, was upheld).

[97] (1973) 2 S.C.R. 54, ('72) A.SC. 2455.

[98] The Court referred to an article in 73 *Harvard Law Review* p. 692 at p. 705 where it was observed, *inter alia*, that "the individual who claims that a vested right has arisen from the defect (in legislation) is seeking a windfall since had the legislature's or administrator's action had the effect it was intended to and could have had, no such right would have arisen."

[99] *Balaji* v. *I.T.O.* (1962) 2 S.C.R. 983, ('63) A.SC. 123; fol. in *Umedray* v. *I.T.C.* ('65) A.P. 114, 116 and in *S. Srinivasan* v. *I.T.C., Madras* ('67) A.SC. 517, (1967) 1 S.C.R. 727; *Srinivasan* v. *I.T.C.* ('63) A.M. 348 (point conceded in view of *Balaji's Case, supra*); *Chandrasekhara* v. *I.T.C.* ('51) A.M. 897.

deration was upheld as designed to prevent large-scale evasion of tax; the transfers were recognized as valid for all other purposes.[1] For the same reason, ss. 2 (6A) and 12 (1B) (as introduced by the Finance Act, XV of 1955), by which a loan made to a shareholder by a private controlled company was taxable as dividend, were held not to violate Art. 19 (1) (*f*) and (*g*) as they were designed to prevent evasion of income-tax.[2] Again, provisions made in a taxing law to prevent fraud and to secure payment of tax which had become due could not be regarded as unreasonable even if those provisions resulted in the prohibition or extinction of a business. Thus, in *M. A. Rahman* v. *A.P.*,[3] the provisions of s. 4 (6), Madras Sales on Motor Spirit Tax (Andhra Pradesh Amendment Act, 1958) and r. 14 for cancellation of the registration of dealers for failure to pay the tax or for fraudulently evading the payment of it, were held to be reasonable as they were designed to secure the speedy payment of a liability admittedly due to the State. They were all the more reasonable because a sales tax on motor spirit is recovered from the purchaser in the price charged to him for the petrol.

Provisions to prevent fraud and secure payment of tax upheld

Search and seizure do not violate Art. 19 (1)(*f*)

10.164 Although Art. 19 (1) (*f*), unlike the 4th Amendment to the U.S. Constitution does not protect the citizen from "unreasonable searches and seizures," in *M. P. Sharma* v. *Satish Chandra*[4] s. 96 (5), Cr.P.C. which authorized search and seizure, was impugned as violating Art. 19 (1) (*f*) and (5). The Supreme Court held that search by itself was not a restriction on the right to hold property and though seizure was a restriction, it was only temporary and limited for the purpose of investigation. A law providing for search and seizure could not *per se* be regarded as unreasonable.

Restrictions on the right to hold property held reasonable: licensing provisions for arms and explosives

10.165 The following provisions have been upheld as imposing reasonable restrictions on the right guaranteed under Art. 19 (1) (*f*): the licensing provisions of ss. 14 and 16, Arms Act, 1878;[5] the provisions of the Explosives Act, 1884;[6] restrictions imposed by a notification in respect of chloral hydrate which is a narcotic;[7] s. 11 (*d*), M.P. Opium Act, 1878, which provides for a compulsory confiscation

---

1 *Narayanamurthy* v. *Commr. of Wealth Tax* ('64) A.Or. 128.

2 *Navnit Lal* v. *I.T.A.A.C.* (1965) 1 S.C.R. 909, ('65) A.SC. 1375; *Kannan* v. *Kerala* (1966) 1 Ker. 199, ('66) A.Ker. 143 [s. 17(2A), T.C. Sales Tax Act (11 of 1125) imposed reasonable restrictions having regard to the ". . . ever increasing tendency for the evasion of payment of taxes of all kinds including sales tax . . ." Accordingly, Art. 19(1)(*f*) and (*g*) were not violated].

3 (1962) 1 S.C.R. 694, ('61) A.SC. 1471.

4 (1954) S.C.R. 1077, ('54) A.SC. 300.

5 *Mahendra Bahadur* v. *M.P.* ('53) A.M.B. 236 (the restrictions were necessary to the preservation of peace and for the prevention of danger to life and property); *Narasimha* v. *District Magistrate* ('53) A.M. 476 (the requirement of a licence prescribed by R. 33, Arms Act Rules were reasonable; the discretion to grant or refuse a licence was not arbitrary but was to be exercised judicially); rel. on in *Kishore Singh* v. *Rajasthan* ('54) A.Raj. 264, as establishing that the Arms Act must be treated as restricting the right to acquire, hold and dispose of fire-arms and not as conferring a privilege on the person to whom the licence under the Act was granted.

6 *In re Sundara* ('53) A.M. 142 (the restrictions imposed on the acquisition, holding and disposal of explosives and explosive substances were reasonable).

7 *Indian C. & P. Works* v. *A.P.* ('64) A.A.P. 430.

of property used in transporting opium;[8] the Punjab Opium (Restrictions on Oral Consumption) Rules, 1957;[9] the scheme of regulation introduced in the Bombay Prohibition Act, 1949, by the amending Act 26 of 1952, in so far as it relates to medicinal and toilet preparations fit for use as intoxicating liquor;[10] the provisions of the Delhi Intoxicating Spirituous Preparations (Import, Export, Transport, Possession & Sale Rules), 1952, (as amended upto December, 13, 1961);[11] s. 126, Cantonments Act, 1924, which requires the owner and in default, the occupier, to repair ruinous structures;[12] s. 5A, Punjab Irrigation and Drainage Works Act, 1848;[13] Patiala Recovery of State Dues Act;[14] s. 65, Kerala Revenue Recovery Act, 1968;[15] s. 52, Madras Revenue Recovery Act, 1864;[16] ss. 13, 15, 17 and 25, Punjab Court of Wards Act, 1903;[17] ss. 132 and 132-A of the Income-tax Act, 1961, and R. 112 and 112-A of the Rules;[18] s. 3, Andhra Inams

restrictions on dangerous drugs, abuse of medicinal and toilet preparations

to prevent danger to life or property

for the protection and recovery of revenue

---

[8] *Mehtab Singh & Sons* v. *M.P.* ('65) A.M.P. 37 (the provision for confiscating the vehicles even of innocent persons was upheld as necessary to control opium and prevent smuggling of opium); *Jamnadas* v. *C. L. Nangia* ('65) A.Guj. 215 [the provisions of r. 9(2), Central Excise Rules, 1944, which provided for confiscating goods without providing a machinery and procedure was not unreasonable as the right to hold the goods was affected only when demand was made under r. 9(2) and the right to object had been provided under s. 33, Central Excise and Salt Act, 1944].

[9] *Arjan Das* v. *Punjab* ('58) A.Punj. 400, (*held*, that where regulation of a commodity included its total prohibition, the question depended upon the nature of the commodity. The rules in effect introduced rationing leading to complete prohibition; the directive contained in Art. 47 also applied and the rules were not unreasonable).

[10] *C.R.H. Readymoney Ltd.* v. *State* ('56) A.B. 304 [upholding ss. 12(*c*) and (*d*) and 13(*b*) of the Act as amended].

[11] *Pritpal Singh* v. *Chief Commr. of Delhi* (1966) 1 Punj. 775, ('66) A.Punj. 4, 14 (the provisions were meant to prevent misuse of or abuse of medicinal preparations and were not unreasonable).

[12] *Ram Narayan* v. *Dinapore Cannt. Board* ('58) A.P. 71 (there is no constitutional right to keep one's property in such a state as to be dangerous to human beings).

[13] *Sashibhusan* v. *Bihar* ('56) A.P. 493 (the section applied only in cases of emergency and it was not unreasonable in an emergency where there was danger to life and property, that the State Government should proceed to direct execution of the irrigation and private work without giving notice and without hearing objections preferred by parties).

[14] *Tilakram Rambaksh* v. *Bank of Patiala* ('59) A.Punj. 440 (the Act had no direct connection with the taking away of any property or hindering any person from practising any trade or business. It did not set up an abitrary or unreasonable machinery for the determination of liability).

[15] *C. P. Joseph* v. *State* (1973) 1 Ker. 178, ('73) A.Ker. 89, 93 (*held*, that as the section provided for the arrest and detention under the Act for deliberate and wilful withholding of payment by a defaulter, who was is a position to pay, the provision for detention was a reasonable restriction in the public interest).

[16] *Rajalingam* v. *State* ('68) A.A.P. 156, 160.

[17] *Harmahendra Singh* v. *Punjab* ('53) A.Punj. 30 (if for the purposes of protecting the revenues of the State and for ensuring that there was no discontent among tenants, laws of the kind such as the Punjab Court of Wards Act were passed by Government, it could not be said that they were an unreasonable interference with the fundamental rights of persons).

[18] *Pooran Mal* v. *Director of Inspection etc.* ('74) A.SC. 348 (*held*, that the provisions were directed against persons who were believed on good grounds to have illegally evaded payment of tax on their income and property. Drastic measures to get at such income and property, with a view to recover government dues, were justified in themselves. In the interest of the community it was right that fiscal authorities, should have sufficient powers to prevent large scale tax evasion; the powers were vested in the highest officers and there were sufficient safeguards for the exercise of the powers).

preservation of forests; regulation of mines, etc.

Land reform and Town Planning

Miscellaneous cases

(Assessment) Act, 1955, which levied full assessment on Inam lands;[19] s. 3(2) Madras Preservation of Private Forests Act, 1947;[20] Rr. 4 and 6, Orissa Timber and Forest Produce Transit Rules, 1958;[21] s. 5, Mines and Minerals (Development and Regulation) Act, 1948;[22] ss. 6(6) and 17(3), Bihar Mica Act, 1947;[23] ss. 3 and 4, Bombay Land Tenures Abolition and Recovery of Records Act, 1953;[24] s. 9(4) (*a*) (i), Madras Estates Abolition and Conversion into Ryotwari (A. P. Amendment) Act, 1957[25] s. 24, W. B. Non-Agricultural Tenancy Act, 1949;[26] the Punjab Development of Damaged Areas Act, 1951;[27] s. 354[28] and ss. 354-R and 354-RA, Bombay Municipal Corporation Act, 1888;[29] s. 376A, Bombay Provincial Municipal Corporation Act, 1949, empowering the Commissioner to compel owners and occupiers of property to abate acts of civic nuisance and/or danger to the public health;[30] bye-law (4) made under s. 458 of the above Act, prohibiting the keeping of milch cattle in the city walled area for trade in milk;[31] R. 13(*a*) of Assam Rules for settlement of fisheries;[32] levy of cess on residential buildings under s. 27, Bom-

---

[19] *V. Sesha Sarma* v. *A.P.* ('60) A.A.P. 461 (s. 3 expressly excluded cases where the grant was of land revenue only).

[20] *V. K. Balarama Chetty* v. *Madras* ('58) A.A.P. 93 (the Act was a temporary measure designed to prevent the indiscriminate destruction of private forests without affecting the customary rights of landholders. The restrictions were reasonable both in their substantive and procedural aspects. Quasi-judicial power was conferred on the Collector subject to a right of appeal to the State Government).

[21] *Kasi Prasad* v. *Orissa* ('63) A.Or. 24 [the rules were merely regulatory and did not violate Art. 19(1)(*f*) and (*g*)].

[22] *Mineral Development Ltd.* v. *Union* ('54) A.P. 340.

[23] *Srikant Lal* v. *Bihar* ('58) A.P. 496 (although the Act did not provide for the controller hearing the parties before removing the mines from the licensee, such hearing was implicit in the section. The power though wide, was subject to sufficient safeguards).

[24] *Rinarbai* v. *Bombay* ('62) A.Guj. 18 (the object of the legislation was to preserve the records. There was no disturbance of the right to property in the records and the provisions were regulatory in their nature).

[25] *Bhanojirao* v. *A.P.* ('62) A.A.P. 157 (the impugned clause merely vested in Government the right to appeal with retrospective effect with the consequence that the finality attached to the decision of Settlement Officer was nullified. A citizen had no fundamental right that any adjudication in his favour should have an attribute of finality).

[26] *Shibsankar* v. *Prabartak Sangha* (1967) 2 S.C.R. 558, ('67) A.SC. 940.

[27] *Bachan Singh* v. *Punjab* (1971) 3 S.C.R. 762, ('71) A.SC. 2164, 2169-70 (*held*, that the provisions of the Act clearly indicated that they were reasonable and were designed to serve the interest of the general public, namely, the execution of schemes in a planned manner for the improvement of the damaged areas of the City of Amritsar. The fact that some buildings in those areas were newly built, or that some buildings were not damaged did not justify an impediment being placed in the way of a scheme which was designed to achieve a social purpose, and was for the public good).

[28] *Diwanchand* v. *N. M. Shah* ('72) A.B. 316, 322.

[29] *Bombay Municipal Corpn.* v. *Pancham* (1965) 1 S.C.R. 542, ('65) A.SC. 1008 [*held*, that the defendant's interest in demised premises was property within Art. 19(1)(*f*), but that the restrictions imposed on his rights under ss. 354-R and 354-RA were reasonable].

[30] *Valjibhai* v. *Ahmedabad Municipality* ('73) A.Guj. 211, 212.

[31] ibid. pp. 214-5.

[32] *Surendranath* v. *State* ('73) A.Gau. 6 [*held*, that the reservation of 60 per cent of fisheries for co-operative fishery societies consisting solely of the members of the Sch. Castes did not violate Art. 19(1)(*f*) and (*g*) as it was made to promote the economic interests of the Sch. Castes in furtherance of Art. 46. Having regard to the decisions of the Supreme Court under Arts. 15 and 16 which held that the special provisions for Sch. Castes and Tribes and Backward Classes should not exceed 50

bay Buildings Repairs and Reconstruction Board Act, 1969[33] s. 31(1), Companies Act;[34] ss. 3 and 4, High Denomination Bank Notes (Demonetization) Ordinance, 1946;[35] Sch. I of M.P. Sch. Tribes Debt Relief Regulations, 1962, and of M.P. *Anusuchit Jan Jati Rini Sahayata Adhiniyam,* 1967;[36] s. 40,[37] and s. 43 of the Administration of Evacuee Property Act, 1950;[38] an order for the sale of composite property comprising a sugar mill in order to realize the money value of the shareholdings of evacuees in that mill;[39] s. 28(2), Provincial Insolvency Act, 1920, which vests the insolvent's properties in the Court or the Receiver;[40] s. 13(2) Hyderabad Atyat Enquiries Act, 1952;[41] s. 52, Madras Revenue Recovery Act, 1864;[42] s. 18, Illustration (*b*) of the Easements Act, 1882;[43] s. 99A, Cr.P.C.;[44] s. 51 of the

---

per cent, the present decision seems to be doubtful; it is more than arguable that such reservation was an unreasonable restriction and was not in the public interest].

[33] *V. J. Ferreira* v. *Bombay Municipality* (1972) 2 S.C.R. 257, ('72) A.SC. 845, 75 Bom.L.R. 1 (*held*, upholding s. 27 that the purpose of a tax could not be regarded as private merely because some persons might receive more benefits from the use of its proceeds than others, or because the tax was imposed for a purpose other than revenue. The principle that funds raised by taxation could not be expended for private use did not prevent the legislature from looking at *the ultimate* rather than *the immediate* result of the expenditure. The test was not as to who received the money, but the character of the purpose for which it was to be expended. *Held further*, that the imposition of the cess on residential buildings even though they were in sound and good condition, and even though they would not require structural repairs for the entire period of the Act, did not amount to an unreasonable restriction).

[34] *Bank of Hindustan* v. *Suryanarayana Rao* ('57) A.M. 702 [the absolute discretion given to the company to accept or reject an application for registration of the transfer of shares under the Articles of Association, and which was recognised by s. 34(1) was reasonable in the interest of the company and was the basis of the contract between the shareholders].

[35] *Ram Lal* v. *State* ('54) A.A. 758.

[36] *Vallabhdas* v. *Sikanya* ('73) A.M.P. 116, 119 (*held*, that the impugned provisions did not prohibit the business of money-lending as such but only limited the rate of interest when money was lent to a member of the tribal community).

[37] *Mohd. Habibbuddin* v. *Hyderabad* ('53) A.Hyd. 157 (the section is based on the necessity for ascertaining the genuineness and legality of transfers by evacuees).

[38] *Mohd. Hamid* v. *Asst. Custodian of Evacuee Property* ('63) A.A. 101 (the restrictions imposed upon the heirs of evacuees were reasonable).

[39] *Azimunnissa* v. *Dy. Custodian of Evacuee Property* (1961) 2 S.C.R. 91, ('61) A.SC. 365 (it was found as a fact that the value of the shares of non-evacuees represented a large sum of money. They had not claimed it from the Custodian of Evacuee Property. Equally, the non-evacuees were not prepared to pay to the Custodian the money value of the shares of the evacuees. Under the circumstances, the sale of the property and the division of the sale-proceeds was the only mode of separation available and the order of the Competent Officer for sale could not be termed unreasonable).

[40] *Kripa Nath* v. *Ganga Prasad* ('62) A.A. 256, 260-61 [such vesting was a reasonable restriction; even if it constituted total prohibition, it would be covered by *Narendra Kumar's Case,* (1960) 2 S.C.R. 375, ('60) A.SC. 430.

[41] *Sikander Jehan Begum* v. *A.P.* (1962) Supp. (2) S.C.R. 226, ('62) A.SC. 996 [having regard to the special character of the property dealt with by the section, it could not be impugned as violating Art. 19(1)(*f*)].

[42] *Rajalingam* v. *State* ('68) A.A.P. 156, 160 (*held*, the restrictions were clearly reasonable).

[43] *Syed Habib* v. *Kamal Chand* ('69) A.Raj. 31, 36 [*held*, that the illustration was designed to secure a customary easement of privacy and s. 18, Ill. (*b*) in its application to Jaipur City did not violate Art. 19(1)(*f*)].

[44] *G. V. Godse* v. *Union* ('71) A.B. 56 (S.B.) [*held*, that the fact that the order of forfeiture operated throughout India, or the fact that there was no provision for hearing before the order was passed, or the fact that government had power to

Electricity Act, 1910 read with s. 10, Telegraph Act;[45] s. 9 (2) of the Laccadive, Minicoy and Amindevi Islands (Debts Conciliation and Grant of Loans) Regulations, 1964, as amended in 1970;[46] R. 39 of the Ahmedabad Small Causes Court Rules, read with O. 37, R. 3, C.P.C.[47]

Unreasonable restrictions: Art. 19(1)(*f*)

10.166 The following have been held to impose unreasonable restrictions on the right to hold property guaranteed by Art. 19 (1) (*f*): The imposition of a wage structure on a news agency (the P.T.I.) which was far in excess of what the employees themselves demanded and which was also beyond the financial capacity of the establishment;[48] s. 63, Kerala University Act, 1969;[49] cl. 13 (3) (vi), proviso, C.P. and Berar Letting of Houses and Rent Control Order, 1949.[50]

Social and industrial welfare legislation

10.167 The Directives of State Policy that the State shall endeavour to secure to all workers, agricultural, industrial, or otherwise, work, a living wage, conditions of work ensuring a decent standard of life and full enjoyment of leisure and social and cultural opportunities (Art. 43); that the State shall promote with special care the educational and economic interests of the weaker sections of the people (Art. 46), and that it shall regard the raising of the level of nutrition and the standard of living of its people and the improvement of public health as among its primary duties (Art. 47) would justify a large body of legislation broadly described as social and industrial welfare legislation. Such legislation, as was to be expected, has been upheld against challenge under Art. 19 (1) (*f*) or 19 (1) (*g*) or both. Thus, in *Manohar Lal* v. *Punjab*,[51] s. 7 (1), Punjab Trade Employees Act, 1940, which required every shop or commercial establishment to remain closed on a "closed day" in the week, was upheld as a law made in the exercise of social control. It was con-

upheld from challenge under Art. 19(1)(*f*) and (*g*): Shop Establishment Acts

---

pass the order of forfeiture on its subjective satisfaction, did not involve a violation of Art. 19(1)(*a*), (*f*) and (*g*); *held further*, that the fact that s. 99A did not provide for withdrawal of the order of forfeiture or for the copies of the books seized did not involve a violation of Art. 19(1)(*a*) and (*f*)].

[45] *B.P. & T. Products* v. *K.S.E. Board* ('72) A.Ker. 47 (F.B.) (the section allowed the laying of electric supply lines on private property with as little damage as possible).

[46] *P.A.S.M. Koya* v. *Union* ('72) A.Ker. 85 [*held*, that as the section provided for recovery of the principal amount together with a reasonable rate of interest, it was protected by Art. 19(5)].

[47] *Navinchandra* v. *Bachubhai* (1968) Guj. 191, ('69) A.Guj. 124 (*held*, that the restrictions put on the manner in which the defendant could defend the cause where the C.P.C. applied was in the public interest. *Held further*, that there was no fundamental right to defend a suit and the law could restrict that right). It is submitted that the second finding is not correct, for the right to property cannot be taken away by putting unreasonable restrictions on the right to defend a suit involving a claim to property. The correct position is that the summary procedure prescribes reasonable restrictions on the right to defend, which are in the public interest.

[48] *P.T.I.* v. *Union* (1975) 3 S.C.R. 499, ('74) A.SC. 1044, 1058.

[49] *Kerala* v. *Mother Provincial* (1971) 1 S.C.R. 734, ('70) A.SC. 2079, 2086 [*held*, that as s. 63 violated Art. 19(1)(*f*) as to minority educational institutions and as s. 63 applied to minority and majority institutions alike, the section was wholly void].

[50] *Ramcharan* v. *R. Dy. Collector* ('71) A.B. 203 [*held*, that the impugned provision, as interpreted by the Full Bench in *Eknath* v. *Shankarrao* ('71) A.B.1 denied to the landlord the right to use his own house even if he genuinely needed it, because his own house or a part thereof in which he was living; was either unsuitable or inadequate for his needs. The fact that such restriction was not imposed on the landlords in the rest of India, showed that the restriction was unreasonable: ibid. pp. 209-212].

[51] (1961) 2 S.C.R. 343, ('61) A.SC. 418.

tended in that case that the establishment which was kept open on a closed day did not engage any workmen, but was run by members of the family of the owner of the establishment and therefore the restrictions imposed by the law were unreasonable restrictions on the right to carry on trade or business. The Supreme Court held that the Act regulated business in the interest of the health and welfare not merely of those employed in the trade, but of all those engaged in it. It was also designed to protect the owner and the members of his family and their health and welfare from themselves. Further, the impugned provisions could also be sustained on the ground that they prevented the evasion of the provisions specially designed for the protection of workmen employed. Acts innocent in themselves may be prohibited, and the restrictions in that regard would be reasonable if they were necessary to secure an efficient enforcement of valid provisions, and the inclusion of a reasonable margin to ensure effective enforcement would not stamp a law, otherwise valid, with unconstitutionality. Accordingly, the provisions were justified also on the ground of administrative convenience and the proper enforcement of the law without evasion.[52] Following this decision, the Supreme Court upheld ss. 7 and 9, Punjab Shops and Establishments Act, 1958, which regulated the hours of work in shops and establishments, observing that judged by the test of reasonableness, a forty-eight hour week, with one weekly holiday, could not be said to have gone beyond what, by modern standards, were necessary conditions for ensuring the health and efficiency of the employees.[53] Again, in *Basti Sugar Mills* v. *Ram Ujagar*[54] the Supreme Court upheld s. 2(1)(iv), U.P. Industrial Disputes Act, 1952, on the ground that it was designed to prevent owners of industry from evading the provisions of the Act through the device of engaging a contractor for doing the work which was ordinarily done as part of such industry. In upholding s. 26, Bihar Shops and Establishments Act, 1957,[55] the Patna High Court observed that the object of the Act was to carry out the Directives of State Policy contained in Arts. 41, 43 and 46. For similar reasons, the provisions of the Employees' Provident Fund Act, 1952[56] and of the Employees' State Insurance Act, 1948[57] were upheld. For the same

Industrial Disputes Act

[52] The Court relied on *Manohar Lal* v. *State* (1951) S.C.R. 671, 675, ('51) A.SC. 315, where similar observations were made when the identical provision was challenged on other grounds.

[53] *Ramdhandas* v. *Punjab* (1962) 1 S.C.R. 852, ('61) A.SC. 1559; *Mathrumal* v. *Chief Inspector of Shops* ('52) A.A. 773 (upholding the U.P. Shops and Establishments Act, 1947); *Sadasivan* v. *Madras* ('57) A.M. 144 (upholding ss. 6 and 11, Madras Shops and Establishments Act, 1947); *Mir Zahiruddin* v. *Mysore* ('57) A.Mys. 64 (upholding s. 11, Mysore Shops and Establishments Act, 1947); *G. Mangaraju* v. *Asst. Labour Inspector* ('59) A.A.P. 604; *Ram Chander* v. *State* ('63) A.Punj. 148 (upholding the Punjab Shops and Commercial Establishments Act, 1958).

[54] (1964) 2 S.C.R. 838, ('64) A.SC. 355.

[55] *Jugal Kishore* v. *Labour Commissioner* ('58) A.P. 442.

[56] *Hindustan Electric Co.* v. *R.P.F. Commr.* ('59) A.Punj. 27 (upholding s. 5 of the Act which enabled the Central Government to frame the scheme for the establishment of Provident Funds); *R.P.F., Commr.* v. *Lakshmi Ratten Engineering Works* ('62) A.Punj. 507; *R.P.F. Commr.* v. *F.I. Industries* ('64) A.Punj. 85 (upholding s. 5 of the Act which required employers to make contributions towards an Employees' Prov. Fund).

[57] *K. C. Sarma* v. *Regional Director, E.S.I. Corporation* ('62) A.Ass. 120 (the whole object of the Act was to provide for benefits to employees in case of sickness,

reasons, the challenge to the provisions of the Industrial Disputes Act, 1947, has been repelled. Upholding s. 15, Industrial Disputes Act, the Court said that it carried out the Directives of State Policy contained in Art. 43[58] and that s. 15 did not put unreasonable restrictions on the right to carry on trade or business.

Provisions of Industrial Disputes Act upheld

10.168 Other sections of the Industrial Disputes Act upheld are: s. 3, which dealt with orders to be made in relation to strikes, lockouts, terms and conditions of employment and the like did not interfere with the right to hold and dispose of property;[59] s. 10, which confers a discretion on Government to refer an industrial dispute to an industrial tribunal of which the Court said that the discretion was not unfettered but had to be exercised in the light of the policy of the Act;[60] s. 25FFF, which imposes upon an employer, who closes down his business, an obligation to make compensation to workmen rendered unemployed.[61] In *G. C. Bez Barua* v. *Assam*[62] the validity of the Industrial Disputes Act was upheld on the ground that it was legislation designed to secure social justice. Again, an award made by a tribunal appointed under s. 10, Industrial Disputes Act, ordering the reinstatement of a workman wrongly dismissed, was upheld, the Court observing that it was not satisfied that the award placed any restriction on the right guaranteed by Art. 19(1)(*g*), but that even if it did, the restriction was reasonable.[63] This case was cited with approval in *Shreekrishnanarayana* v. *Republic of India*[64] where the Court upheld the award by a tribunal directing payment to be made to a workman wrongfully dismissed.

Minimum Wage legislation upheld: *Bijay Mills Case*

10.169 The provisions of ss. 3, 4 and 25, Minimum Wages Act, 1948, were challenged as violating Art. 19(1)(*g*) in *Bijay Cotton Mills Ltd.* v. *Ajmer*[65] under unusual circumstances. An industrial dispute was pending between the petitioner company and its workmen. In

---

maternity and employment injury and to make provision for certain other matters in relation to health, and an obligation to contribute to a fund for these purposes could not be described as imposing unreasonable restrictions).

58 *C. P. Sarathy* v. *Madras* ('51) A.M. 191.

59 *Basti Sugar Mills* v. *U.P.* ('54) A.A. 538 (F.B.) [it held further that an order for the payment of bonus did not violate Art. 19(1)(*f*)].

60 *Neimala Textile Furnishing Mills Ltd.* v. *2nd Punjab Tribunal* (1957) S.C.R. 335 fol. in *R.S. Navigation Co.* v. *Radhanath* ('60) A.Ass. 39.

61 *Rajkumarsingh* v. *Authority, P.W. Act,* ('60) A.M.P. 307.

62 ('54) A.Ass. 161.

63 *East India Industries (Madras) Ltd.* v. *Industrial Tribunal* ('55) A.M. 242.

64 ('58) A.Ker. 136.

65 (1955) 1 S.C.R. 752, ('55) A.SC. 33; fol. in *Gulamahamed* v. *Bombay* ('62) A.B. 97; *U. Unichoyi* v. *Kerala* (1962) 1 S.C.R. 947, ('62) A.SC. 12 (in view of the decisions of the Supreme Court, the validity of the Minimum Wages Act could no longer be questioned); *D. M. S. Rao* v. *Kerala* ('63) A.Ker. 115; *Narottamdas* v. *M.P.* ('64) A.M.P. 45 (upholding s. 3, M.P. Minimum Wages Fixation Act, 1962); rel. on in *N.B. Coal Co.* v. *Jt. Director of Mines* ('73) A.Cal. 17 [*held,* that regulation 191(1) and (2) Coal Mines Regulations, 1957, were meant to meet a social need and afford protection to workmen against physical injuries while in employment in mines. The fact that the industry as a whole was not capable of meeting the financial burden could not afford any constitutional sanction to carry on such trade and Art. 19(1)(*f*) and (*g*) were not violated: ibid. p. 22. *Sivrajan* v. *Union* (1959) Supp. 1 S.C.R. 779, ('59) A.SC. 556, and *Huthesing Mfg. Co.* v. *Union* (1960) 3 S.C.R. 528, ('60) A.SC. 923 were also rel. on. Oddly enough, the Court observed that the Central Govt. should adjudge whether the petitioners' claim that the industry was not in a position to bear the burden of the additional expense resulting from the impugned regulation

November 1951, the tribunal made an award holding that the earning capacity of the mill precluded the award of higher rates of wages and higher dearness allowance. While the employees' appeal to the Appellate Tribunal was pending, steps were taken to fix minimum wages of labourers in the textile industry and the wages were fixed at Rs. 56. Thereafter, the Appellate Tribunal heard the appeal and remanded the matter to an industrial tribunal which rejected the basis upon which the minimum wages had been fixed at Rs. 56 and fixed the minimum wages including dearness allowance at Rs. 35. The company closed down in April 1953. There were about 1,500 workmen and several hundreds of them approached the management with a request to open the mills, offering to work at the wages fixed by the industrial tribunal. In view however of the fixation of minimum wages, the mill could not be opened. Accordingly, petitions were presented under Art. 32, by the petitioning company and, by a large number of workmen. It was contended, first, that the Minimum Wages Act put unreasonable restrictions both on the rights of the employers and the employees and gave unfettered power to the appropriate Government to fix wages; secondly, that the restrictions imposed by the Act were unreasonable and oppressive with regard to one class of employers, namely, those who, for purely economic reasons, were not able to pay the minimum wage but had no intention to exploit labour at all. The Court held that the securing of living wages to labourers, which ensures not only their physical subsistence but also the maintenance of health and decency, was conducive to the general interest of the public, and was in fact a directive principle of State Policy embodied in Art. 43. The fixation of minimum wages was necessary to prevent exploitation of labour by employers, and the interest of the general public required these restrictions. The inability of the employers to pay the amount required and their good intentions were irrelevant. Accordingly, the impugned provisions were held not to violate Art. 19(1)(*g*). It is submitted that this case is illustrative of the unwillingness to criticize current dogmas in employer-employee relations. That workers require to be protected from their employers, and that employers with a capacity to pay should not be able to beat down workmen by their

A criticism of the *Bijay Mills Case*

was correct in which event Government, as the bulk purchaser of coal should revise the price paid by it.] See also *Crown Aluminium Works* v. *Their Workmen* (1958) S.C.R. 651, ('58) A.SC. 30 ("There is however one principle which admits of no exception. No industry has a right to exist unless it is able to pay its workmen at least a bare minimum wage"); fol. in *W.C.E. Federation* v. *State* (1967) 2 Ker. 182, ('68) A.Ker. 18, 19 (*held*, that Government should be directed to hold a fresh inquiry as the Committee for fixation of minimum wage had taken into account the capacity to pay in the following passage of its report, "No doubt the principle of 'capacity to pay' is a relevant factor to be considered in the fixation of minimum wages, especially in India where the industry has not developed very much and where the burden on the land is too heavy even now. It will be unwise to compel some industries to close down on account of their inability to pay the minimum wages prescribed when the country is faced with the problem of great unemployment and it is straining every nerve to develop industries and put herself in the industrial map of the world. If some industries cease to operate not only will the country's industrial development be retarded but many workers will also be thrown out of employment": ibid. pp. 20-21. It is submitted that the Committee's report showed an awareness that the theoretical dogma, laid down by the Courts, would have serious consequences, namely, unemployment which the State is unable to remedy, and it supports the criticism of the dogma in the text).

superior bargaining power is not in dispute. But the Supreme Court had before it the decision of an independent body—the industrial tribunal—that the company was unable to pay the minimum monthly wage of Rs. 56, and that the monthly wage should be Rs. 35. If the whole object of the law is to prevent exploitation and provide decent wages, it is difficult to see how that object is achieved by forcing an industrial enterprise to close down. To the knowledge of the present writer no court has undertaken to answer the question, "If a labourer cannot live except on Rs. 56 per month (as is assumed by the fixation under the Minimum Wages Act) how is it proposed to make him subsist on no wage at all, if as a consequence of the inability of a company to pay, it closes down?"

Regulation of property and business: licences and permits

10.170 Licences or permits are well recognized modes of regulating the use of property, or the conduct of a trade or business, and difficult and complicated questions have arisen under Art. 19(1) (*f*) and (*g*) from the grant or refusal of licences or permits. The first and most important question is: Can the exercise or enjoyment of fundamental rights be made dependent upon the exercise of discretion conferred on a named authority? This question has given rise to a wider diversity of judicial opinion. In *Bidi Supply Co.* v. *Union*[66] Bose J. in his dissenting judgment said that no power resting on the subjective satisfaction of an executive authority, or a quasi-judicial body, or even Parliament itself, could ever be conferred if the Chapter on Fundamental Rights was not to lose its point. On the other hand, in *Virendra Singh's Case*[67] Das C.J. said that quick decision and swift and effective action was the essence of the power to maintain public order, and the exercise of it must therefore be left to the subjective satisfaction of Government charged with the duty of maintaining law and order; to make the power subject to judicial scrutiny would be to defeat the very purpose for which it was conferred. It would lead to a clearer understanding of the problem to consider, first, the law about discretionary power before the Constitution came into force, and then to ascertain what light that law throws on the provisions of the Constitution and to what extent that law requires to be modified in the light of the Constitution. As observed in *Govindji Vithaldas & Co.* v. *Municipal Corporation, Ahmedabad*[68] the law as regards the exercise of discretionary power has long been well settled:

Can fundamental rights be restricted on the subjective satisfaction of the executive: different views

Law governing discretionary power before the Constitution

"Where, as in a multitude of Acts, something is left to be done according to the discretion of the authority on whom the power of doing it is conferred, the discretion must be exercised honestly and in the spirit of the statute, otherwise the act done would not fall within the statute. 'According to his discretion' means, it has been said, according to the rules of reason and justice, not private opinion; according to law and not humour; it is to be, not arbitrary, vague and fanciful, but legal and regular; to be exercised, not capriciously, but on judicial grounds and for substantial reasons. And it must be exercised within the limits to which an honest man competent to the discharge of his office ought to confine himself, that is, within the limits and for the objects intended by the legislature."[69]

---

[66] (1956) S.C.R. 267, ('56) A.SC. 479.
[67] (1958) S.C.R. 308 at p. 320, ('57) A.SC. 896.
[68] (1957) Bom. 147, ('59) A.B. 26, 59 Bom.L.R. 129, citing *Maxwell*, 10th ed., p. 123; *K. Koteswararao* v. *State* ('68) A.A.P. 129, 134.
[69] *Maxwell*, pp. 117-8.

It is submitted that on this view of discretionary power few statutes could be held to confer absolute, arbitrary and unfettered power, for there are few statutes of which it can be said that they have no policy underlying them. However, in the absence of constitutional limitations, such as those contained in the Chapter on Fundamental Rights, it would be open to a legislature to confer absolute and unfettered power on any authority, which the Courts would then be obliged to uphold. But under our Constitution, the conferment of such power would have to satnd the test of constitutional limitations. There is an element of truth in the observations of Bose J., mentioned earlier, that to make fundamental rights depend upon the subjective satisfaction of an authority is to deprive them of their value; but the problems of a complex society do not admit of the clear-cut and easy solution suggested by him. The only thing which can be said with some confidence is that where discretionary power without safeguard and without appeal is conferred, it must be justified as necessary or reasonable under the circumstances. In what follows, we will consider the classes of cases which have arisen, and the solutions which have been found in respect of them.

Under our Constitution, conferment of unfettered discretionary power requires to be justified

10.171 Apart from the basic objection to the conferment of arbitrary discretionary power mentioned by Bose J., the objection to such power has been forcibly stated by Mukherjea J. in *Dwaraka Prasad Laxmi Narain* v. *U.P.*[70] ("the *Coal Control Case*"). There, Cl. 4(3), U.P. Coal Control Order, 1953, was impugned as giving the licensing authority an absolute power to grant or refuse to grant, renew or refuse to renew, suspend, revoke, cancel or modify any licence under that order, the only obilgation on the licensing authority being to record the reasons for the action taken. No appeal or revision was provided for and the power could be exercised not only by the State Coal Controller but by *any person whatsoever* to whom he may delegate his power. Mukherjea J. said that some amount of discretion would have to be conferred on the Authority, but

Objection to the conferment of unfettered power: the *Coal Control Case*

"... A law or order, which confers arbitrary and uncontrolled power upon the executive in the matter of regulating trade or business in normally available commodities cannot but be held to be unreasonable.... The Order commits to the unrestrained will of a single individual the power to grant, withhold or cancel licences in any way he chooses and there is nothing in the Order which could ensure the proper exercise of the power or operate as a check upon injustice that might result from its improper execution. ... It was pointed out and with perfect propriety by Mr. Justice Mathews[71] that the action or non-action of officers placed in such position may proceed from enmity or prejudice, from partisan zeal or animosity, from favouritism and other improper influences and motives which are easy of concealment and difficult to be detected and exposed, and consequently the injustice capable of being wrought under cover of such unrestricted power becomes apparent to every man, without the necessity of detailed investigation."[72]

Subject to the exceptions to be noted hereafter, the principles there laid down are correct, though their application in the case appears doubtful. First, it could have been held that the grant or refusal of a licence was a quasi-judicial function and the recording of reasons for the action taken, further strengthens that view. The

The *Coal Control Case* overlooked the guidance given by the policy of the Act

[70] (1954) S.C.R. 803, ('54) A.SC. 224.
[71] *Yick Wo* v. *Hopkins* 118 U.S. 356 at p. 373.
[72] (1954) S.C.R. at pp. 811-3.

fact that no appeal was provided for, from such quasi-judicial decision, would still leave such decision open to the supervisory jurisdiction of the Court by *certiorari* and by appeal under Art. 136. Secondly, it does not appear to have been argued before the Court that the impugned order was passed under s. 3(2), Essential Supplies Act, 1946, and that the discretion of the Controller was to be guided by the policy underlying that Act, a view later expressed by the Supreme Court itself in *Rajasthan* v. *Nath Mal.*[73] However, this aspect of the matter has been emphasised in later cases. It would have been simpler to say that the *Coal Control Case* overlooked the guidance to be derived from the policy underlying s. 3 of the Act, and to that extent the case was wrongly decided. But without saying so, the Courts have purported to distinguish the case on grounds which, it is submitted, are insubstantial. In *Harishankar Bagla* v. *M.P.*,[74] a case repeatedly followed or relied on,[75] the Supreme Court upheld Cl. 3, Cotton Textiles (Control of Movement) Order, observing that the discretion there conferred had to be exercised in the light of the policy underlying the Order. Referring to this case, Chagla C.J. observed that the discretion conferred by Cl. 3 upon the Textile Commissioner

Guidance given by the policy of the Act emphasized in later cases

Harishankar Bagla's Case

"... seems to be as absolute and as uncontrolled as the discretion conferred upon the licensing authority in *Dwaraka Prasad's Case*. The order itself does not seem to lay down any directions as to how this discretion had to be exercised by the Textile Commissioner. No right of appeal was provided against this decision and it does not even seem that he had to record his reasons for refusing a permit to a person who applied for it. . . . Therefore, it is clear . . . that if the Court can discover a policy underlying the law and if a discretion is conferred under that law, then the Court must hold that the discretion is to be exercised not in an arbitrary manner, not in a capricious manner, not in an uncontrolled manner, but in a manner so as to effectuate the policy of the law. Again, as pointed out by the Supreme Court, if the discretion is not exercised in this manner, then there is no exercise of the power at all, there is an abuse of the power, and the Court has ample jurisdiction to rectify that abuse of power."[76]

Control of essential commodities upheld

10.172 Restrictions imposed on the rights of property as regards essential commodities have been generally upheld. Thus, the Bihar Agriculturists Levy Order, 1950;[77] the W. B. Food Grains (Intensive Procurement) Order, 1952;[78] Cl. 13(*f*), Fruits Products Order, 1955,

---

[73] (1954) S.C.R. 982, 985, ('54) A.SC. 307.

[74] (1955) 1 S.C.R. 380, ('54) A.SC. 465; *Hiralal* v. *State* ('53) A.N. 58 [upholding Cl. 3, Cotton Textiles (Control of Movement) Order, 1948 because the requirement of a permit was not an unreasonable restriction on a citizen's right under Art. 19(1)(*f*) and (*g*)].

[75] *e.g. State* v. *Haidarali* ('57) A.M.P. 179 (F.B.) (upholding ss. 3 and 4, Essential Supplies Act); *Thanmal* v. *Union* ('59) A.Raj. 206 [upholding Cl. 21(3)(*c*), and 5(*h*), Essential Commodities Act]; *State* v. *Dhanraj Mills* ('60) A.B. 453 [upholding Cl. 21(3)(*c*), Cotton Textile (Control) Order, 1948]; *V. L. Patel & Co.* v. *M.P.* ('65) A.M.P. 211 (upholding rr. 3 and 4 made under s. 41, Forests Act, 1929, requiring a permit for transit of timber because the grant or refusal of a permit under the rules was governed by the policy enunciated in the Act); *K. Ganeshilal* v. *State* ('67) A.Raj. 90, 96 (*held*, that the Export Prohibition Order, 1965, did not confer unfettered power as the power was to be exercised to effectuate the policy of the order. Art. 14 was therefore not violated); *Chuni Singh* v. *Union* ('68) A.Del. 196, 200 [upholding cl. 3, Delhi Coarse Grain (Export Control) Order, 1966].

[76] *Govindji Vithaldas & Co.* v. *Municipal Corprn., Ahmedabad* (1957) Bom. 147, ('59) A.B. 26, 28-29, 59 Bom.L.R. 129.

[77] *Mohd. Anzar Husain* v. *Bihar* ('52) A.P. 220.

[78] *Atulya Kumar* v. *Director of Procurement and Supply* ('53) A.Cal. 548, fol in *Ghrita Mohan* v. *Addl. Dist. Magistrate* ('54) A.Cal. 97.

issued under s. 3 (1) Essential Commodities Act;[79] Cl. 4 of the M.P. Paddy Procurement (Levy) Order, 1955;[80] Cl. 5 of the M.P. Wheat Stock Requisitioning Order, 1958;[81] were upheld. In *Rajasthan* v. *Nath Mal*[82] the Supreme Court held that the first portion of Cl. 25, Rajasthan Food Grains Control Order, 1949, relating to the freezing of stocks of food grains did not violate Art. 19 (1) (*f*) because such freezing was reasonably related to the object which the Act was intended to achieve, namely, to secure the equitable distribution and availability at fair prices and to regulate transport, distribution, disposal and acquisition of an essential commodity such as food grains. However, it was held that the last portion of Cl. 25, which enabled the acquiring authority to acquire the stock at such prices as it thought fit, was void both under Art. 19 (1) (*g*) and Art. 31 (2), (i) because it placed unreasonable restrictions on carrying on trade or business in that it enabled Government to acquire stocks from traders at half the market rate, or even less, and thus destroy their business, and (ii) because the clause vested the power in the authority to acquire the stocks at any price without fixing the amount of compensation or the principles of compensation, and thus violated Art. 31 (2). It has also been held that not only the law, but also orders made under it, must be reasonable, when the freedom of trade is restricted.[83]

acquisition of essential commodities at any price held void

10.173 However, though the general rule is clear, where the grant or refusal of a license or permit depends upon a large number of imponderable factors such as questions of State policy and foreign relations, it is clear that the grant of discretionary power is in substance, though not in form, absolute. This has been recognised by the Supreme Court in cases dealing with import and export, and in other cases where similar considerations apply.

Discretionary power: imponderable factors

10.174 As has been said earlier, the judgment of the Government that it was necessary to impose certain restrictions on the import and export of goods was, for practical purposes, conclusive and incapable of being displaced. This is the result of the decision of the Supreme Court in *Glass Chatons Importers and Users' Assn.* v. *Union*[84] which was adopted and carried further in *Dava* v. *Jt. Chief Controller of Imports and Exports.*[85] In the first case, some of the petitioners were importers, and some were actual users, of glass chatons which formed an important part of the raw material for the manufacture of glass bangles and other similar articles. Since 1955, the matter was regulated by the Imports (Control) Order, 1955 (made under ss. 3 and 4A, Import and Export Control Act, 1947), which prohibited imports, *inter alia*, of glass chatons except under a licence. From January 1957 to the end of March 1958, the import

Judgment of Govt. on import and export of goods practically conclusive: the *Glass Chatons* Case

---

[79] *Hamdarad Dawakhana* v. *Union* (1965) 2 S.C.R. 192, ('65) A.SC. 1167 (as the restrictions imposed by the clause were reasonable the fact that they incidentally tended to affect the appellant's trade mark did not render the impugned order invalid).

[80] *Baijnath Prasad* v. *State* ('68) A.M.P. 26, 28.

[81] *Baldoo* v. *M.P.* ('66) A.M.P. 273, 278.

[82] (1954) S.C.R. 982, ('54) A.SC. 307.

[83] *Oudh Sugar Mills Ltd.* v. *Union* ('70) A.SC. 1070 [held, that the refusal to extend the time for the disposal of free sugar was unreasonable on the facts of the case].

[84] (1962) 1 S.C.R. 862, ('61) A.SC. 1514.

[85] (1963) 2 S.C.R. 73, ('62) A.SC. 1796.

was permitted only under an Export Promotion Scheme. Licences were however issued in favour of the State Trading Corporation for the import of glass chatons, under para 6(*h*) of the Order which provided that licences may be refused if the licensing authority decided to canalise import. Para 6(*h*) was impugned as violating Art. 19(1)(*g*). In rejecting this contention, the Court said that an import policy was an integral part of the general economic policy of a country. Consequently, an import policy must have regard not only to its impact on internal and international trade, but also on monetary policy, on agriculture and industry and on political policies involving friendship, neutrality and hostility with other countries. A Court would not have adequate materials to say whether a particular policy was in the interest of the general public; but even if it had such materials, in many cases more than one view could be taken of a particular policy. Consequently, a very heavy burden lay on a person to establish that a particular import policy was not in the interest of the general public for the Court would proceed on the assumption that it was. But though the decision of Government that import should be canalised, may be difficult to challenge, the selection of a particular agency may be open to challenge on the ground that it violated Art. 14 or any fundamental

Dava's Case

right.[86] In *Dava's Case*[87] the appellants had acquired leases of certain manganese mines in Madhya Pradesh in 1952 and 1955. There was a very small internal demand for manganese in India and most of the manganese mined was exported. Export of manganese was subjected to progressively increasing restrictions under s. 3, Imports and Exports Control Act, 1947, and Cl. 6(*h*), Exports Control Order, such exports being confined to established exporters and to the State Trading Corporation. The appellant was not an established exporter, having regard to the time when he acquired the mining leases, and he impugned s. 3 of the Act and Cl. 6(*h*) of the Order as violating Art. 19(1)(*g*). In view of the decision in the *Glass Chatons Case*, the validity of Cl. 6(*h*) was not disputed. By a majority (Subba Rao J. dissenting), the Court held that the exclusion of persons who were not established exporters was a reasonable restriction on the appellant's right to carry on business. It is submitted that since the State Trading Corporation was not made a party, the majority view may be justified; but the facts mentioned in the dissenting judgment raised a serious question of the reasonableness of the restrictions, and it might have been more satisfactory to have brought the State Trading Corporation on record as a party whose presence was necessary for the proper determination of the matters in issue. *Dava's Case* and the *Glass Chatons Case* were followed in *Daruka & Co.* v. *Union.*[88]

Import and export: arbitrary power cannot

10.175 Though the judgment of Government that it is necessary to impose certain restrictions on the import and export of goods, is for practical purposes conclusive and incapable of being displaced,[89]

---

[86] (1962) 1 S.C.R. *supra* at p. 866. [87] (1963) 2 S.C.R. *supra*.

[88] (1974) 1 S.C.R. 570, ('73) A.SC. 2711 [the dominant purpose of the impugned scheme was canalization of export through the Trading Corporation, and the scheme did not violate Art. 19(1)(*g*). The impugned scheme was framed pursuant to s. 3(1)(*a*), Imports & Exports Control Act, 1947, and cl. 6(1) Export Control Order, 1968].

[89] See para 10.174 of the text.

it does not follow that Government can exercise arbitrary power in imposing restrictions on the import and export of goods, as rightly held by the Supreme Court in the cases considered below. In *Ramchand Jagdish Chand* v. *Union*[90] the petitioner contended that under the Export Promotion Scheme he had become entitled to an import licence for 66.2/3 per cent of the export value of certain goods exported and of 100 per cent in the case of other goods exported and that an import licence for the full value had been wrongly refused, a licence for a much smaller value having been given to him. He contended (*i*) that this action of the licensing authority violated his fundamental right under Art. 19(1) (*g*); and (*ii*) that the licensing authorities had discriminated between him and other merchants similarly situated, thus violating Art. 14. In rejecting these contentions, Shah J. held that the fundamental right under Art. 19(1) (*g*) was subject to reasonable restrictions in the interest of the general public, and the right of the State to impose controls on imports in the larger interests of the State had not been denied. Power to grant licences had been conferred upon high officers of the State and the power was not uncanalised or arbitrary. Secondly, under the relevant regulation, the petitioner had no right to obtain an import licence to the extent of 66.2/3 per cent and 100 per cent respectively, because the policy provided for the grant of an import licence *upto these percentages.* Shah J. said:

be claimed: *Ramchand's Case*

Ramchand Jagdish Chand v. *Union*: export promotion scheme

"The power is plainly discretionary. It is true that the discretion has to be exercised reasonably and not arbitrarily. The licensing authority would normally issue an import licence for 100 per cent of the value of the goods exported, *but having regard to special considerations such as difficult foreign exchange position or other matters which have a bearing on the general interest of the State, import licences for a smaller percentage may be granted to the exporters.* But by the use of the expression 'upto the following percentage of the rupee equivalent' power to fix arbitrarily a percentage of the value of the goods exported for awarding an import licence is not granted."[91] (italics supplied)

In that case, malpractices in respect of export having been brought to the notice of Government, a Committee was appointed to consider the question. The Committee considered the petitioner's case, along with eleven other cases, giving him an opportunity to present his case, and as a result of the Committee's recommendations the import licence was granted for a lesser value. Such action could not be said to violate Art. 19(1) (*g*). As to Art. 14, Shah J. held that no case for discrimination had been made out.

10.176 In *Probhudas* v. *Union*[92] the Supreme Court considered a special export promotion scheme for engineering goods. There also, the petitioner contended that he had not received an import licence for the full value under that scheme. Without reference to *Ramchand's Case*[93] *on this point,* the Supreme Court observed:

Probhudas v. *Union*: export promotion scheme

"The Licensing Authority would normally issue an import licence upto the monetary extent prescribed but, having regard to the special considerations such as difficult foreign exchange position or other matters which have a bearing on the general interest of the State, import licences for a smaller percentage may be granted to the exporters. It may be assumed that by the use of the expression 'upto the monetary extent mentioned in Annexure V' in Cl. 5.4,

[90] (1962) 3 S.C.R. 72, ('63) A.SC. 563.
[91] (1962) 3 S.C.R. *supra* at p. 80.
[92] ('66) A.SC. 1044.
[93] (1962) 3 S.C.R. *supra.*

the authorities are not clothed with the arbitrary power to fix the percentage of the value of the goods exported for awarding an import licence."[94]

The Supreme Court held that the value of the import entitlement had not been arbitrarily reduced. As to the violation of Art. 14, the Supreme Court referred to *Ramchand's Case* and observed that the petitioner had not established that he had been unjustifiably given discriminatory treatment.

Amin Chand's Case: import quotas

10.177 In *Controller* v. *Amin Chand,*[95] the Supreme Court had to consider the effect of administrative instructions in respect of import quotas. The Central Government issued the Import (Control) Order in exercise of the powers conferred by s. 3 of the Imports & Exports (Control) Act, 1947. The order provided for a system of licensing and R. 3 thereof provided that no person could import goods specified in the schedule except under a licence granted by the proper authority. In order to guide the licensing authorities, the Central Government issued administrative instructions providing for granting licences to "established importers" for a specified period called the "basic period". The instructions also provided for the division of quota rights of a firm amongst its partners when the firm was dissolved, namely, that on dissolution, the partners would get their quota rights according to the agreement between them. Quotas were fixed for the purpose of informing the licensing authorities that a particular person had been recognized as an established importer and it was for the licensing authorities to issue a licence to the quota-holder, in accordance with the licensing policy for the relevant period. The respondent was a partner of a firm which had been dissolved in January 1957, and on March 4, 1957, he applied to the Chief Controller of Imports on behalf of the dissolved firm for a division of the quota between the partners. As the application for a licence for the January/June period had to be made by 31st March, the respondent applied for the grant of a licence for that period on 25th March 1957 without mentioning his quota as required by the instructions, because the Chief Controller had not approved the division of quota rights. In September 1957 the Chief Controller informed the respondent that instructions had been issued to the Jt. Chief Controller of Imports & Exports, who was the licensing authority. That officer informed the respondent that a licence could not be issued since the transfer of quota rights in the respondent's favour were recognised by the Chief Controller after the expiry of the licensing period. After an unsuccessful appeal to the authorities, the respondent moved the High Court for an appropriate writ which was granted. By a majority of 4 to 1,[96] the Supreme Court held, on a construction of the relevant provisions, that the instructions conferred a right on members of a dissolved firm to obtain quota rights as provided in the agreement to divide the quota, and that the licensing authority could not refuse to grant a licence on the ground that the division of the quota had not been approved till after the expiry of the licensing period. The approval, when given, related back to the date of the agreement, and as no order made by Government prohibiting the import of goods

[94] ('66) A.SC. *supra* at p. 1046.
[95] (1966) 1 S.C.R. 262, ('66) A.SC. 478.
[96] Mudholkar J. dissenting.

had been produced, it was open to the licensing authority to issue a licence for the period January/June 1957, even if there was a change of policy thereafter.

Promissory Estoppel : The High Trees Case[97]

10.178 Decisions of our Supreme Court on promissory estoppel are in an unsatisfactory state, largely due to the Court's failure in some cases to realize that very different considerations arise when promissory estoppel is pleaded against Government or public authorities from those which arise where promissory estoppel is pleaded against private parties. The most satisfactory way of presenting a clear picture to the reader of the doctrine of promissory estoppel against Government or public authorities in India is to give a brief account of that doctrine in England and then consider Supreme Court decisions which purport to apply that doctrine in India.

Sup. Ct. decisions on promissory estoppel in an unsatisfactory state

10.179 It all began when one of the most distinguished Judges of our day—Lord Denning—brought his formidable legal equipment to bear on an apparently simple case which came before him as a Judge of the first instance: the *High Trees Case*. Before he decided that case two propositions had been firmly established in the common law. First, the House of Lords had held in *Jorden* v. *Money*[98] that no estoppel can be founded except upon a representation as to an existing fact. As Denning J. put it, ". . . as was said in *Jorden* v. *Money* a representation as to the future must be embodied in a contract or be nothing".[99] Again, the House of Lords had reluctantly held in *Foakes* v. *Beer*[1] that a promise, even if accepted, to pay a smaller sum in discharge of a liability to pay a larger sum was without consideration and could not be enforced. In view of these decisions, the *High Trees Case*[2] appeared to be concluded against the defendants, first, because the representation there made was not about an existing fact but as to what was to be done in the future; and, secondly, because a promise to pay a smaller sum in satisfaction of a liability to pay a larger sum lacked consideration and could not be enforced.

The *High Trees Case*

Jorden v. *Money*, and

Foakes v. *Beer* appeared to be against the defendants

10.180 Denning J. held on the facts that had the plaintiffs claimed to recover arrears of rent upto 1945 they would have been precluded from doing so by promissory estoppel. However, as the plaintiffs claimed to recover at the rate of £2,500 from September 1945, they were entitled to do so on a true interpretation of the scope of the arrangement between the parties. He said:

Denning J. appeals to principles of equity laid down in two Cases

"The law has not been standing still since *Jorden* v. *Money*. There has been a series of decisions over the last 50 years which although they are said to be cases of estoppel are not really such. They are cases in which a promise was made, which was intended to create legal relations, and which, to the knowledge

[97] *Central London Property Trust Ltd.* v. *High Trees House Ltd.* (1947) K.B. 130.
[98] (1854) 5 H.L.C. 185.
[99] (1947) K.B. *supra* at p. 134.
[1] (1884) 9 App. Cas. 605.
[2] "The facts were quite simple. During the war, many people left London owing to the bombing. Flats were empty. In one block, where the flats were let on 99 year leases at £2500 a year, (by the plaintiff to the defendant) the landlord (the plaintiff) had agreed to reduce it by half and to accept £1250 a year. When the bombing was over, and the tenants came back, the landlord sought to recover the full £2500 a year": Lord Denning, *The Discipline of the Law*, p. 203.

of the person making the promise, was going to be acted on by the person to whom it was made, and which was in fact acted on. In such cases the Courts have said that the promise must be honoured . . . The Courts have not gone so far as to give a cause of action in damages for the breach of such promise, but they have refused to allow the party making it to act inconsistently with it. It is in that sense, and that sense only, that such a promise gives rise to an estoppel. The decisions are the natural result of the fusion of law and equity: For the cases of *Hughes* v. *Metropolitan Rail Co.*[3] and *Birmingham District Land Co.* v. *London and N.W. Rly Co.*[4] . . . afford a sufficient basis for saying that a party would not be allowed in equity to go back on such a promise."[5]

Principle of equity applied by House of Lords in *Hughes* v. *Metropolitan Rail Co.*

In *Hughes* v. *Metropolitan Rail Co.* the House of Lords dealt with a claim to forfeit a lease for failure to comply with a six months' notice to repair. The defence was that negotiations had taken place between the parties after the notice, and this precluded the lessor from contending that the notice became effective on the expiry of six months. In upholding the lessee's claim, Lord Cairns L.C. said:

". . . it is the first principle upon which all Courts of Equity proceed, that if parties who have entered into definite and distinct terms involving certain legal results — certain penalties or legal forfeiture — afterwards by their own act or with their own consent enter upon a course of negotiations which has the effect of leaving one of the parties to suppose that the strict rights arising under the contract will not be enforced, or will be kept in suspense or held in abeyance, the person who otherwise might have enforced those rights will not be allowed to enforce them, where it would be inequitable having regard to the dealings which have thus taken place between the parties."[6]

Principle not limited to forfeiture cases

But was this principle limited to the forfeiture of a lease? In *Birmingham and District Land Co.* v. *London and N. W. Rly Co.*[7] a strong Court of Appeal[8] held that this principle was not so limited. Bowen L.J. said:

Bowen L.J. states the general principle of equity

"It is a principle which lies outside forfeiture, and everything connected with forfeiture, as will be seen in a moment by reflection. It was applied in *Hughes* v. *Metropolitan Rail Co.*[9] in a case in which equity could not relieve against forfeiture upon the mere ground that it was forfeiture, but could interfere only because there had been something in the nature of acquiescence, or negotiations between the parties, which made it inequitable to allow the forfeiture to be enforced. . . . It seems to me to amount to this, that if persons who have contractual rights against others induce by their conduct those against whom they have such rights to believe that such rights will either not be enforced or will be kept in suspense or abeyance for some particular time, those persons will not be allowed by a Court of Equity to enforce the rights until such time has elapsed, without at all events placing the parties in the same position as they were before."[10]

High Trees principle extended to a public authority; *Robertson's Case*

10.181 The *High Trees Case* is now the leading case on promissory estoppel. But that case was between private persons. In *Robertson* v. *Minister of Pensions*[11] ("*Robertson's Case*") Denning J. applied the *High Trees* principle, although one of the parties was the Minister of Pensions. In view of the House of Lords decision in the *Falmouth Case* referred to in the next para, the facts of *Robertson's* Case require to be set out more fully than are set out in the head note to the Report.[12] It is also necessary to set out the legal framework in which Robertson's appeal had to be decided. Robertson, who

[3] (1877) 2 App. Cas. 439 (H.L.).
[4] (1888) 40 Ch.D. 268.
[5] (1947) K.B. *supra* at pp. 134-5.
[6] (1877) 2 App. Cas. at p. 448.
[7] (1889) 40 Ch.D 268.
[8] Cotton, Lindley and Bowen L.JJ.
[9] (1877) 2 App. Cas. *supra*.
[10] (1889) 40 Ch.D. at p. 286,
[11] (1949) 1 K.B. 227.
[12] ibid.

was a Colonel, suffered the injury in question in December, 1939. In March, 1941 he wrote to the Director of Personal Services at the War Office requesting that the question of the attributability of the disability arising from his injury to war service should be considered. In his reply of April 8, 1941, the Director wrote, *inter alia*, that "your case has been duly considered and your disability has been accepted as attributable to military service". Relying on this letter, Robertson took no steps to obtain a medical opinion. Further, X-ray plates (showing the nature of his injury) which were then available were thereafter lost. The Minister of Pensions later decided that Robertson's disability was not attributable to military service and the pensions appeal tribunal affirmed that decision. Robertson appealed on the ground that the Minister of Pensions was bound by the War Office letter of April 8, 1941. The legal framework within which the appeal had to be decided was this: By a Royal Warrant of Sept. 15, 1939 the entire establishment of disablement claims in respect of service after Sept. 2, 1939 was transferred from the War Office to the Minister of Pensions. The Royal Warrant of June, 1940, which was in force when the letter of April 8, 1941 was written, dealt with all claims in respect of war injuries, that is, pensions, retired disability pay, allowances and medical expenses. Article 5 of the Warrant laid down the conditions under which a disability shall or shall not be accepted as attributable to military service. The thing to note is that Robertson's claim in respect of the injury suffered in Dec. 1939 was governed by the Royal Warrants which had transferred the determination of that question from the War Office to the Minister of Pensions so that the War Office had no legal authority over the subject matter of Robertson's claim and, *a fortiori*, no legal authority to admit the claim as was done by the letter of April 8, 1941. The Minister of Pensions contended that the War Office letter of April 8, 1941 did not bind him and did not bind the Crown. The facts and the legal framework in which *Robertson's Case* had to be decided have been set out at some length because the impact of the House of Lords rejection in the *Falmouth Case* of the principle which Denning J. applied in *Robertson's Case* is considered more fully in paras 10.204 to 10.207 below. Denning J. formulated the *High Trees* principle thus: ". . . If a man gives a promise or assurance which he intends to be binding on him and to be acted on by the person to whom it is given, then, once it is acted upon, he is bound by it."[13]

Extension of High Trees principle in Robertson's Case and in the Falmouth Case

10.182 But in *Robertson's Case*, Denning J. laid down another principle, (obviously to supplement and give effect to the *High Trees* principle) which is best formulated in his own words in *Falmouth Boat Construction Co. Ltd.* v. *Howell*,[14] ("the *Falmouth Case*"). There, the plaintiffs, who were ship repairers, claimed from the defendant a sum of money for alterations done to a ship at the order of the defendant. The defendant resisted the claim *inter alia* on the ground that work done in contravention of the provisions of a statute could not be made the subject of an action.[15] Denning L.J. said that the "essence of the argument for the defendant is that a written licence (from the licensing officer) was necessary and no oral

[13] ibid. at p. 231.
[14] (1950) 2 K.B. 16.
[15] *Bostel Bros. Ltd.* v. *Hurlock* (1949) 1 K.B. 74, 79.

permission could take its place; nor could any of its terms or conditions be waived by any oral dispensation."[16] Denning L.J. said that assuming that the original order postulated a licence in writing, nevertheless it could be varied without any publicity or formality. But assuming that he was wrong about this, he would apply the principle he had applied in *Robertson's Case*:

"The principle is this: whenever government officers, in their dealings with a subject, take on themselves to assume authority in a matter with which he is concerned, the subject is entitled to rely on their having the authority which they assume and he ought not to suffer if they exceed it.[17]

Overruled by House of Lords in the *Falmouth Case*: Lord Simonds

On appeal to the House or Lords[18] Lord Simonds quoted the above passage and said:

"My Lords, I know of no such principle in our law nor was any authority for it cited. The illegality of an act is the same whether or not the actor has been misled by an assumption of authority on the part of a government officer however high or low in the hierarchy. I do not doubt that in criminal proceedings it would be a material factor that the actor had been thus misled if knowledge was a necessary element of the offence, and in any case it would have a bearing on the sentence. . . . But that is not the question. The question is whether the character of an act done in face of a statutory prohibition is affected by the fact that it has been induced by a misleading assumption of authority. In my opinion the answer is clearly No. Such an answer may make more difficult the task of the citizen who is anxious to walk in the narrow way, but that does not justify a different answer being given."[19]

Two further questions about promissory estoppel considered

10.183 It is outside the scope of this book to give a detailed account of promissory estoppel; the reader will find Chapter XIV (Promissory Estoppel) of Spencer Bower and Turner's classic book on *Estoppel by Representation* (3rd ed.) instructive and rewarding reading. Lord Denning's *Discipline of the Law*[20] contains an entrancing account of how he started the doctrine of promissory estoppel in the *High Trees Case* and how he developed it. He can justly claim that the doctrine "caused at the time some eyebrows to be raised in high quarters. But they have been lowered since. The solution was so obviously just that no one could gainsay it".[21] But before parting with the doctrine of promissory estoppel two questions remain to be answered. First, must a promissory estoppel, falling short of a contract,[22] "be closely analogous in many respects to a promise having contractual effect"?[23] Secondly, is the Crown amenable to the law of estoppel by representation? On the first question, the position is summed up in *Spencer Bower and Turner*, as follows:

"Both principle and authority, however, afford some support for a statement of the principle which, while insisting upon a sufficient legal relationship already existing between the parties before the estoppel can be founded, yet does not too strictly require that the parties shall have been *contractually*

---

16 (1950) 2 K.B. at p. 23.

17 ibid. p. 26.

18 *Howell* v. *Falmouth Boat Construction Co. Ltd.* (1951) A.C. 837.

19 ibid. p. 845. Lord Normand said: "But . . . neither a minister nor any subordinate officer of the Crown can by any conduct or representation bar the Crown from enforcing a statutory prohibition or entitle the subject to maintain that there has been no breach of it." (ibid. p. 849). The appeal was however dismissed for the reasons given by Lord Normand, and concurred in by the other Law Lords.

20 pp. 197-223.

21 ibid. p. 222.

22 For, if there were a contract there would be no need to resort to promissory estoppel.

23 *Spencer Bower and Turner*, op. cit. p. 176.

bound *inter se* by a legal contract. Some other relationship, similar to a contractual relationship, may perhaps suffice — but there must be a similar relationship."[24]

As to the second question, the statement that the Crown is amenable to an estoppel by representation requires qualifications due to the complexities of modern government. The question whether a representation made by one department of Govermnent is binding upon another department depends upon whether the department making the representation had been entrusted by the legislature with the subject matter to which the representation relates. Secondly, the question whether the representation made by an officer of one department, acting within the scope of his authority, is binding on another department, also depends on whether the first mentioned department was entrusted with statutory authority over the subject matter,[25] to which the representation relates. Further, there can be no estoppel contrary to a statutory prohibition, nor can the Crown be estopped from exercising an unfettered statutory discretion entrusted to it for the public good.

Indo-Afghan Case: promissory estoppel

10.183-A In the three cases considered in paras 10.175 to 10.177 no question of promissory estoppel appears to have been raised. These cases establish that the authorities charged with the administration of an import policy, cannot act arbitrarily or capriciously and can be directed by the Court to discharge their duty in granting licences, if the facts of a case justify such direction. The whole question was more elaborately considered in *Union* v. *Indo-Afghan Agencies*.[26] That case again involved the consideration of an export promotion scheme under which on exporting goods to Afghanistan of the f.o.b. value of Rs. 5,03,471.73 p. the respondents became entitled to get an import entitlement certificate *equal* to 100 per cent of the f.o.b. value of their export, unless the appropriate authority reduced the quota on the ground that the value of the goods had been over-invoiced. No opportunity had been given to the respondents to meet the allegation that the goods had been over-invoiced. Without deciding the question whether the import policy was legislative or executive in character, the Court held that even if it were executive in character, the Courts had the power, in appropriate cases, to compel the performance of the obligation imposed by the scheme upon the authorities, citing in support the three judgments of the Supreme Court considered earlier. The argument of the Union is not easy to understand; but relying on *Rederiaktiebolaget Amphitrite* v. *R*.[27] it was contended that it was open to the Textile Commissioner to reduce the import entitlement below the f.o.b. value to the goods exported and that the exercise of the power conferred upon him was not limited by the terms of the scheme and was not open to judicial review as long as it was exercised in good faith. The Supreme Court held that the observations in the case relied upon were very wide, and cited with approval the following observations of Denning J. in *Robertson's Case*, namely,

---

[24] ibid. p. 380. The careful discussion of the subject in para 349 (pp. 378-384) supports the statement of principle in the above passage.

[25] ibid. pp. 121-22.

[26] (1968) 2 S.C.R. 366, ('68) A.SC. 718.

[27] (1921) 3 K.B. 500.

"The Crown cannot escape by saying that estoppels do not bind the Crown, for that doctrine has long been exploded. Nor can the Crown escape by praying in aid the doctrine of executive necessity, that is, the doctrine that the Crown cannot bind itself so as to fetter its future executive action."[28]

and Shah J. held that this doctrine applied in India. He rejected the Union's contention and held that under our Constitution no person could be deprived of his right or liberty except under the authority of law, and that the Courts were competent and bound to protect the rights of an aggrieved citizen. The Union "somewhat faintly urged" that to enforce on it the policy announced by Government would amount to enforcing contractual rights even though the contract did not comply with Art. 299. The Court rejected the argument, holding that the respondents did not seek to enforce a contractual right, but an equity arising in their favour after they had carried out their part under the policy announced by the Government. The Court observed that the Supreme Court had laid down that licensing authorities were not entitled *at their whim* to ignore the promises made by Government: to concede such a power would be to strike at the very root of the rule of law. As to the contention that the entitlement certificate had been refused because of under-invoicing, the Court held that no opportunity had been given to the respondents to meet any such case, and the decision to reduce the quota without giving an opportunity to the respondents to present their case was violative of natural justice and could not be upheld. The Supreme Court contrasted the failure to give an opportunity to the respondents to meet the case against them with the full opportunity given to the petitioner in *Ramchand's Case.*[29]

Discussion of promissory estoppel not necessary

10.184 It is not clear whether the discussion of promissory estoppel was really necessary. It is probable that the respondents did not invoke Art. 19 because it was suspended during the Proclamation of Emergency. But Art. 14 was available to challenge the exercise of power under the Import and Export Control Order passed in the exercise of powers conferred by the Imports and Exports Control Act, 1947. The power claimed by the Union was a naked, arbitrary power to do what it liked, and any action based on such a claim must violate Art. 14.

Submission: discussion of promissory estoppel misleading

10.185 It is submitted that the decision is correct, but the discussion of promissory estoppel is likely to be misleading unless the judgment is properly understood. The authorities considered by the Supreme Court, and the conclusions drawn from them, by Shah J. in the present case, merely affirm the proposition that the Government could not go back upon promises made in the exercise of discretionary power as embodied in a scheme, *merely on a whim.* The judgment of Shah J. in the present case, and the judgments in the earlier cases considered by him, do not suggest that even if the foreign exchange position had radically changed against India, the promises made for the exercise of discretionary power would still be binding on the Union and would be enforced by the Courts. If Shah J.'s judgment did lay down such a proposition, it is submitted that it would be clearly wrong. First, a promissory estoppel cannot stand on a higher footing than a contract entered into between a

---

[28] (1949) 1 K.B. 227 at p. 231. [29] (1962) 3 S.C.R. *supra.*

citizen or subject and a public authority, and it is settled by numerous decisions that no public authority entrusted with discretionary power to be exercised for the public good can bind itself by a contract not to exercise that discretion when the public good demands its exercise. In *Commrs. of Crown Lands* v. *Page*[30] Devlin L. J. accurately set out the effect of decided cases thus:

Devlin L.J. accurately states the law

"When the Crown, or any other person, is entrusted, whether by virtue of the prerogative or by statute, with discretionary powers to be exercised for the public good, it does not, when making a private contract in general terms, undertake (and it may be that it could not even with the use of specific language validly undertake)[31] to fetter itself in the use of those powers, and in the exercise of its discretion. This principle has been accepted in a number of authorities: it is sufficient to mention *Ayr Harbour Trustees* v. *Oswald*;[32] *Rederiaktiebolaget Amphitrite* v. *R.*;[33] *Board of Trade* v. *Temperley Steam Shipping Co. Ltd.*[34] and *William Cory & Sons Ltd.* v. *City of London Corporation.*[35]" [36]

In the same case, Lord Evershed M.R. said:

Lord Evershed M.R. on effect of House of Lords' decision in *Falmouth Case*

". . . upon the question of the implied covenant for quiet enjoyment we were referred to the view expressed by Denning J. in *Robertson* v. *Minister of Pensions*[37] to the effect that in the present day and age no distinction should be drawn as to *the legal effect of its or their actions between the Crown and ordinary subjects, so that the effect of a representation made by the Crown could no longer be qualified so as to be subject to the future exercise by the Crown of its executive authority.* The case was, however, upon its facts, very different from the present; and the judge's general proposition was disapproved by Viscount Simonds and Lord Normand in the later case of *Howell* v. *Falmouth Boat Construction Co. Ltd.*[38] I do not, therefore, think that Mr. Dunn's contention upon this point can be sustained by reference to *Robertson's Case.*[39]"[40]

These observations are relevant, because the observations of Denning J. in *Robertson's Case*, which we have italicised in the above passage, were rightly held by Lord Evershed M.R. to have been disapproved by Lord Simonds and Lord Normand. Secondly, Devlin L.J. rightly pointed out that the Crown cannot fetter itself in the exercise of discretionary power entrusted to it for the public good. To complete this discussion it may be added that in *Wells* v. *Minister of Housing*[41] Lord Denning M.R. himself observed: "Now I know that a public authority cannot be estopped from doing its public duty; but I do think that it can be estopped from relying on technicalities and this is a technicality."[42] In the result, the above discussion makes it clear that the standards applicable for enforcing promissory estoppel between private parties cannot be applied without large qualifications to enforcing promissory estoppel

Wells v. *Minister of Housing*

---

[30] (1960) 2 Q.B. 274, 291.

[31] See *York Corporation* v. *Henry Leetham & Sons Ltd.* (1924) 1 Ch. 557. There, the plaintiffs who were invested with statutory powers of charging such tolls, within limits, as they may deem necessary for carrying on their undertakings in which the public were interested, had bound themselves for a period, the duration of which depended upon the volition of the defendants not to exercise their powers against him. Russell J. held that the agreements on the dates of their execution were *ultra vires*, and that an *ultra vires* agreement could not become *intra vires* by reason of estoppel, lapse of time, ratification, acquiescence or delay.

[32] (1883) 8 App.Cas. 623 (H.L.).

[33] (1921) 3 K.B. 500.

[34] (1926) 26 Ll.L.R. 76; affd. (1927) 27 Ll.L.R. 230, C.A.

[35] (1951) 2 K.B. 476, C.A.

[36] (1960) 2 Q.B. *supra* at p. 291.

[37] (1949) 1 K.B. 227.

[38] (1951) A.C. 837.

[39] (1949) 1 K.B. 227, *supra*.

[40] (1960) 2 Q.B. *supra* at pp. 287-8.

[41] (1967) 1 W.L.R. 1000.

[42] ibid. p. 1044.

against Government or public authorities. In referring to the observations of Denning J. in *Robertson's Case*, (para 10.183 above) Shah J. overlooked the considerations set out above, and further overlooked the fact that to have accepted that principle would have enabled executive authorities, who lacked statutory powers, to acquire those powers by representing that they possessed them: a principle destructive of the whole doctrine of *ultra vires*. In this connection, the decision in *Southend-on-Sea Corporation* v. *Hodson (Wickford) Ltd.*[43] is very important, because Lord Parker L.C.J. held that a representation made by the Corporation, assuming it to be a pure representation of fact, on which representation the respondents had acted, could not operate to bind or prevent the exercise by the Local Planning Authority of their statutory discretion under Sec. 23, Town and Country Planning Act, 1947, in deciding whether to serve an enforcement notice, since this discretion was intended to be exercised for the benefit of the public or a section thereof. Further, there was no logical distinction *quoad* estoppel, between the prevention or hindrance of a positive statutory duty and the prevention or hindrance of the exercise of a statutory discretion. It is clear that if an express or implied term in a contract binding an authority not to exercise a discretion vested in it for the public good is *ultra vires*, a representation to the same effect, but not amounting to a contract, cannot validly furnish the ground for an equitable estoppel if it is shown that public good requires the exercise of the power contrary to the representation.

Considerations overlooked by Shah J.

The *Century Mills Case*

10.186 In the *Century Spg. & Mfg. Co. Ltd.* v. *Ulhasnagar Municipality*[44] ("the *Century Mills Case*") in remanding the petition to the High Court, which had dismissed it *in limine*, Shah J. said that in the *Indo-Afghan Case* the Supreme Court had approved of the passage from Lord Denning's judgment in *Robertson's Case* (set out in para 10.183 above) and had said that it applied to India. Shah J. observed that in the present case the Court was not concerned with the extension of that principle which was disapproved by Lord Simonds in the *Falmouth Case*, and he added:

> "If our nascent democracy is to thrive different standards of conduct for the people and the public bodies cannot ordinarily be permitted. A public body is, in our judgment, not exempt from liability to carry out its obligations arising out of representations made by it relying upon which a citizen has altered his position."[45]

The reference to the observations of Denning J. adopted by Shah J. in the *Indo-Afghan Case* is open to all the objections which we have set out in criticising the *Indo-Afghan Case*. Further, the reference to standards of conduct in a nascent democracy overlooks the fact that public authorities are, and private parties are not, charged with protecting the public interest; and the protection of the public interest must, to that extent, require different standards to be applied to private persons and to public authorities.

Turner Morrison's Case: estoppel

10.187 The Supreme Court's decision in *Turner Morrison* v. *Hungerford*[46] raised a question of promissory estoppel between private parties and would not have required consideration here, but

[43] See para 10.2.
[44] (1970) 3 S.C.R. 854, ('70) A.SC. 1021.
[45] (1970) 3 S.C.R. at p. 860.
[46] (1972) 3 S.C.R. 711, ('72) A.SC. 1311.

for the fact that Hegde J. referred not only to the *High Trees Case*, but also to the *Indo-Afghan Case*[47] and to the acceptance by the Supreme Court of the principles enunciated by Denning J. in *Robertson's Case*. Hegde J. added that "the rule laid down in these decisions undoubtedly advance the cause of justice and hence we have no hesitation in accepting it."[48] Since Hegde J. was dealing with the case of promissory estoppel between private parties, he was not called upon to decide, and he did not decide, whether the same considerations applied to a plea of estoppel against public authorities. However, if his references to the *Indo-Afghan Case* and *Robertson's Case* are taken to mean that the same considerations apply to a plea of estoppel against public authorities as apply to private parties, then such a view is clearly wrong for the reasons set out earlier in this discussion. between private parties

10.188 We must now consider three decisions of the Supreme Court which *seemed* to hold that there can be no estoppel against public authorities. In *M. R. Pillai* v. *Kerala*[49] (*"Pillai's Case"*) the plea of estoppel arose under the following circumstances: *Pillai's Case*

By an order dated Nov. 2, 1968, the Government of Kerala ("the Government") directed that the Vigilance Commissioner would hold office for five years or till he attained the age of 60 years whichever was earlier. The post of the Vigilance Commissioner was a temporary post, and by an order dated Nov. 15, 1968 sanction was accorded to the continuance of that post till Feb. 28, 1970. In an agreement dated Dec. 20, 1968 between Pillai and the Government it was agreed that Pillai's appointment was to be for a period of 5 years from Oct. 3, 1968 or till he attained the age of 60 years whichever was earlier. It was further provided that Pillai was not to be removed or suspended from office except in the manner provided for the removal or suspension of the Chairman or Member of the State Public Service Commission. By an order dated Feb. 24, 1970, the Government ordered that the post of the Vigilance Commissioner should be abolished from Feb. 28, 1970, as Government considered that there was no need to have a Vigilance Commissioner. Circumstances said to give rise to a promissory estoppel

Pillai challenged the abolition of the post, on three grounds: first, that it amounted to his removal from service within the meaning of Art. 311 of the Constitution, and Art. 311 had not been complied with; secondly, that the abolition of the post was *mala fide*; and, thirdly, that he had entered into an agreement with Government, and by accepting its offer he had changed his position and the State was estopped from altering the terms of the agreement on the principle of estoppel.[50] The High Court rejected all these contentions, and dismissed Pillai's petition, and the Supreme Court, agreeing with the High Court, dismissed his appeal. In the present discussion we are only concerned with Pillai's plea of estoppel.

10.189 Dealing with the plea of estoppel, Ray C.J. said: Ray C.J. on principles governing estoppel against the State: *American Jurisprudence* quoted

"The High Court was correct in holding that no estoppel could arise against the State in regard to abolition of post. The appellant Ramanathan Pillai knew that the post was temporary. In American Jurisprudence 2d at page 783 paragraph 123 it is stated 'Generally, a state is not subject to an estoppel to the same extent as in (sic) an individual or a private corporation. Otherwise it might be rendered helpless to assert its powers in government. Therefore as a general rule the doctrine of estoppel will not be applied against the state in its governmental, public or sovereign capacity. *An exception however arises in the application of estoppel to the State where it is necessary to prevent*

[47] (1972) 3 S.C.R. at pp. 725-6. [48] ibid. p. 726.
[49] (1974) 1 S.C.R. 515, ('73) A.SC. 2641.
[50] (1974) 1 S.C.R. at p. 518.

fraud or manifest injustice'. The estoppel alleged by the appellant Ramanathan Pillai was on the ground that he entered into an agreement and thereby changed his position to his detriment. The High Court rightly held that the courts exclude the operation of the doctrine of estoppel, *when it is found that the authority against whom estoppel is pleaded has owed a duty to the public against whom the estoppel cannot fairly operate.*"[51] (italics supplied)

Apart from American Jurisprudence there is overwhelming English authority that public officers cannot be prevented by estoppel from doing a public duty

10.190 The citation from *American Jurisprudence* in the above passage cannot be read as meaning that in no case can the doctrine of estoppel apply to the State. The words we have italicised in the above passage show that the general rule recognizes the fact that different considerations arise in applying promissory estoppel to the State from those which arise when applying it to private parties. The decision of Ray C.J. is correct for, quite apart from *American Jurisprudence,* we have seen that there is overwhelming authority of the English Courts, including that of Denning L.J. himself (see para 10.185) that a public authority cannot be estopped from doing its duty. In *Pillai's Case,* if Government *bona fide*[52] came to the conclusion that it was no longer necessary to have a Vigilance Commissioner, then public interest required that the post should be abolished. However, the emphasis thrown on the fact that Pillai knew that the post was temporary was unnecessary for the decision and was unjustified as it overlooked important facts. Before Pillai's appointment as Vigilance Commissioner, the following facts were known *both* to Pillai and to the Government, namely, that the post was temporary, and that by an order dated Nov. 15, 1968 the post had been continued upto Feb. 28, 1970. If with knowledge of these facts *both the Government and Pillai* entered into an agreement on Dec. 20, 1968 (in respect of a post which would come to an end in 1 year, 2 months and 11 days from the date of the agreement) whereby the Government appointed Pillai Vigilance Commissioner for 5 *years,* implicit in this appointment was a representation that Government would exercise its powers to extend, from time to time, the duration of the temporary post at least to cover the period of 5 years. On any other assumption it would have been meaningless to have appointed Pillai for 5 years. It is submitted that Pillai was justified in believing that Government would not have offered to appoint him for a period of 5 years from Oct. 3, 1968,[53] unless it was prepared to extend the duration of the temporary post. In accepting the post Pillai did act on Government's offer to his prejudice, and a question of promissory estoppel clearly arose. If Pillai's plea of promissory estoppel failed, it is because it would have failed even if the Government had *expressly* provided in the agreement to extend the duration of the temporary post to cover the period of 5 years, for no government could bind itself not to exercise its power to abolish a post if public interest required it. It is therefore not correct to say, as Bhagwati J. said in a later case considered in para 10.198 below, that the facts did not justify a plea of promissory estoppel or that the decision on that plea was *obiter.* The facts rightly understood raised

Emphasis on Pillai's knowledge that the post was temporary unnecessary and unjustified

Pillai's plea of equitable estoppel would have failed even if there was express agreement to continue the post for 5 years

---

[51] ibid. p. 526.

[52] Ray C.J. rejected Pillai's contention that the abolition of the post was *mala fide*: (1974) 1 S.C.R. at p. 527.

[53] Before the agreement was entered into, Pillai had been appointed Vigilance Commissioner on the death of the previous incumbent of the office.

the plea of promissory estoppel; it was necessary to decide the question and the decision of a Constitution Bench was binding on Bhagwati and Tulzapurkar JJ., quite apart from the fact that the decision was correct.

Agarwala's Case

10.191 In *Asst. Custodian, E.P.* v. *B. K. Agarwala*[54] ("*Agarwala's Case*") the question of promissory estoppel arose in this way: *N*, the wife of a police officer of the United Provinces, was in Teheran along with her husband in 1942. She had purchased a property in Lucknow. She migrated to Pakistan from Teheran in 1948. On June 24, 1949, the United Provinces Administration of Evacuee Property Ordinance, 1949, came into force. Under that Ordinance evacuee property meant any property in which an evacuee has any right or interest. Under s. 2(c) (ii) of the Ordinance, *N* was an evacuee because she was a resident of Pakistan after partition and therefore she was unable to occupy, supervise or manage her property in Uttar Pradesh. As she was an evacuee on the *coming into force of the Ordinance*, her property at Lucknow became evacuee property, and under s. 5 of the Ordinance the property automatically vested in the Custodian of Evacuee Property.[55] *N* came to India in 1962 and sold her property in Lucknow to the 1st respondent and one Mrs. Jain. From what has been said earlier, the property in Lucknow was evacuee property vesting in the Custodian long before the sale of that property. However, before purchasing the property, the 1st respondent inquired of the 1st Appellant, the Asst. Custodian of Evacuee Property, whether the Lucknow property was an evacuee property, and received the reply that it was not evacuee property. On March 25, 1963, the 1st Appellant passed an order declaring the property evacuee property. On March 7, 1964, a notification was issued under the Displaced Persons (Compensation and Rehabilitation) Act, 1954, acquiring the Lucknow property. Failing to get redress, the 1st respondent filed the petition out of which the appeal to the Supreme Court arose. A Division Bench of the High Court held that *N* was not an evacuee under s. 2(c) (*i*) of the Ordinance and the Bench refused to consider whether *N* was an evacuee under s. 2(c) (*ii*). Reversing the High Court, the Supreme Court held that *N* was an evacuee under s. 2(c) (*ii*).[56] Therefore, relying on the principle laid down by Denning J. in *Robertson's Case* (para 10.182 above) it was contended for the Respondents that the reply given by the 1st Appellant (the Assistant Custodian) to the 1st respondent's inquiry stating that the property was not evacuee property operated as an equitable estoppel since the respondent had purchased the Lucknow property relying on the reply of the 1st respondent. It is clear that if the broad principle which Denning J. laid down in *Robertson's Case* was the law, a case of promissory estoppel clearly arose. For, the Asst. Custodian had assumed authority to answer the 1st respondent's inquiry and had informed him that the property was not evacuee property. The 1st respondent was entitled to act, and had acted on it to his detriment, and the Asst.

Circumstances giving rise to a plea of promissory estoppel

If *Robertson's Case* accurately laid down the law, a plea of equitable estoppel arose

[54] (1975) 2 S.C.R. 359, ('74) A.SC. 2325.
[55] ('74) A.SC. at p. 2326; the Court said: "It should be noticed that an evacuee property automatically vests in the Custodian, and the notification under s. 6 of the Ordinance is not a necessary condition for such vesting": ibid.
[56] ibid. pp. 2326-7.

Alagiriswami J. rejected the Robertson principle, as the House of Lords had laid down the correct law

Custodian was estopped from contending that the property was evacuee property. Alagiriswami J. repelled the respondent's plea of estoppel by saying that the reliance placed on *Robertson's Case* did not help the respondents because the observations of Lord Denning had been disapproved by the House of Lords in the *Falmouth Case* by Lord Simonds and Lord Normand[57] and Alagiriswami J. added: "We are of the opinion that the view taken by the House of Lords is the correct one and not the one taken by Lord Denning."[58] It is clear that the observations on estoppel were not *obiter dicta,* because the plea of estoppel required to be decided before the appeal could be allowed. Secondly, Alagiriswami J. and Mathew J. laid down the law within the meaning of Art. 141 when they held that the view taken by the House of Lords, disapproving the principle laid down by Denning J., was correct. The reader will recall that in the *Century Mills Case,* Shah J. expressly said that the Court was not concerned with the extension of the principle in *Robertson's Case* which was disapproved by Lord Simonds in the *Falmouth Case* (para 10.186 above). The question left open by Shah J. was decided when Alagiriswami and Mathew JJ. held that the decision of the House of Lords in the *Falmouth Case* was correct.

Agarwala's Case concluded the question left open in the Century Mills Case

Ram Kumar's Case

10.192 In *Excise Commr.* v. *Ram Kumar*[59] (*"Ram Kumar's Case"*), the facts of the case were briefly these:

> In the State of Uttar Pradesh auction sales used to be held during February and March for licences to be granted for the sale of country liquor or spirit (hereafter referred to as "liquor"). Before holding the auctions, rates of excise duty and prices of different varieties of liquor as also the conditions of licences for sale of liquor were announced. No announcement was, however, made as to whether the exemption from sales tax in respect of liquor granted by Notification dated April 6, 1959 was or was not likely to be withdrawn[60] but in reply to the query made by (the respondents in six out of 127 appeals) at the time of the auction they were told by the authorities that there was no sales tax on the sale of liquor.[61] The respondents, who participated in the auctions and were the highest bidders, were granted licences for retail sale of liquor for the period April 1, 1969 to March 31, 1970.[62] It was one of the conditions of the licences granted to the respondents that "they would lift the fixed minimum quantity of liquor and sell the same at their allotted shops and in case of failure or default to do so they would be liable to pay compensation equal to the amount of the excise duty leviable on the unlifted quantity. . . ."[63] All the respondents failed to lift the minimum quantity of liquor and they were required by the excise authorities to pay, by way of compensation, the amount of excise duty on the shortfalls.

The two questions raised in Ram Kumar's Case

10.193 The respondents challenged this demand as unconstitutional and void in 127 Writ petitions filed in the High Court. Six of those respondents also challenged the notification imposing a sales tax on the ground that the Government did not announce at the time of the auction that the earlier notification was likely to be withdrawn, and, in fact, the appellants informed the respondents at the time of the auction that there was no sales tax on liquor and therefore they were estopped from making a demand to recover sales tax from them. The High Court decided the point common to all the petitions against the appellant, and also upheld the plea of estoppel raised by the six res-

High Ct. decided both against the appellant

---

57 ibid. p. 2327 where the relevant passages from the judgments of Denning J., Lord Simonds and Lord Normand are set out.

58 ibid.

59 (1976) Supp. S.C.R. 532, ('76) A.SC. 2237.

60 (1976) Supp. S.C.R. at p. 535.

61 ibid. p. 537.

62 ibid. p. 535.

63 ibid. p. 537.

pondents. The appellant appealed to the Supreme Court by special leave. The Supreme Court held that the demand made by the appellant though disguised as a claim for compensation was in reality a claim for excise duty on the unlifted quantity of liquor, and the demand was void and unenforceable as it was not authorized by any provision of the U.P. Excise Act, 1910. In fact, the question for the Court's determination had been settled by the *ratio* of the Supreme Court's decision in *B. C. Bannerjee* v. *M.P.*[64] The appeal on this point was dismissed.

Second question: plea of estoppel upheld by High Ct. Reversal by Sup. Ct. not *obiter dicta*

10.194 As the High Court had upheld the claim of six respondents that the Appellant was estopped from demanding and recovering sales tax from them, it became *necessary* for the Supreme Court to decide the appeal whether the claim of estoppel which the High Court had upheld was valid. The law laid down on estoppel was therefore not *obiter dicta.* And the observations in a later case that "in this case there was factually no foundation for invoking the doctrine of promissory estoppel" (see para 10.198 below) are completely irrelevant once the High Court had upheld the plea, and the Supreme Court had to decide, as a matter of law, whether the High Court was right. Before considering the Supreme Court's decision on the plea of estoppel, it appears to the present writer that certain features of the case have not received their due importance. First, why were the rates of excise duty announced before holding the auction? Obviously because the bid which a person would make for obtaining the retail licence would depend upon the taxes payable, for although the excise duty can be passed on to the consumer, the question would still remain whether the sum which would be paid by the individual consumer would leave a sufficient margin of profit to the bidder. Secondly, the exemption of liquor from sales tax from 1959 to the time of holding the auctions in 1969 might not unreasonably lead the bidders to think that in deciding on what amount to bid, the additional burden of sales tax need not be taken into account in determining the amount of the bid. In any event, the six respondents who actually made an inquiry before the auction clearly thought so, and the answer from the authorities that there was no sales tax on liquor, would mean, *in the context of announcing the rates of excise duty, before the auction,* that the bidders need not take the burden of sales tax into account in determining the amount of the bid they wished to make. The answer that "there was no sales tax on the sales of country liquor" cannot be equated with "there is *at present* no sales tax on country liquor" or "no sales tax has been announced till today", for these modes of answering the question would have put bidders on notice that in making their bids they must be prepared for the imposition of sales tax and adjust their bids accordingly. Since the judgment of the Allahabad High Court under appeal is not reported, it is not possible to say whether the Court treated the answer to the query as a representation that there would be no sales tax on the sale of liquor, a representation on which the six respondents acted to their detriment. But the present writer would not be surprised if the High Court took that view, and, in any event, it seems to him that such a view is a reasonable one to take for the reasons set

Submission: Certain features of the Case have not received due importance

[64] (1971) 1 S.C.R. 844 at 850.

out above. This view is also implicit in the judgment of the Supreme Court, for Jaswant Singh J. did not allow the appellant's appeal on the ground that the six respondents had failed to establish a factual basis for a promissory estoppel. They treated the answer given to the six respondents' questions as a representation on which they acted to their detriment, but held that as a matter of law such an estoppel would not prevent the State from imposing a sales tax in the exercise of its statutory powers. On the law laid down by the Supreme Court, even if there had been an express representation that no sales tax would be imposed during the period April 1, 1969 to March 31, 1970, such a representation would not have operated as a promissory estoppel, if no question of *mala fides* arose.

Submission: Was the notification imposing sales tax issued by the Govt. *mala fide*?

10.195 Before setting out briefly the law on promissory estoppel laid down in *Ram Kumar's Case,* it may be observed that the tax was not imposed by the legislature, but by the executive, namely, the State Government, which imposed the tax by issuing the Notification of 1969. Therefore, the question whether the State Government acted *mala fide* would arise although Counsel and the Supreme Court do not appear to have looked at the facts and circumstances from this point of view. It is easy to say, as the Supreme Court said, that the State required to raise revenue for its manifold needs; but the needs existed from 1959 to 1969. Further, auctioning licenses for the sale of country liquor is a mode of raising revenue and the Government was trying to raise *the maximum amount of revenue,* since normally licences would be granted, as in fact they were granted in the present case, to the highest bidders. To the amount offered as a bid, that is, to the revenue so raised, the taxes imposed on the sale of country liquor was most material; therefore the rates of excise duty on country liquor were announced *before* the auction. Now, till the auctions were held, was there no need to raise further revenue by imposing a sales tax? How did the need suddenly arise *a day after* the one year period of the license? It is submitted that the Government appears to have been emboldened in imposing this burden *a day after* the license because having secured the maximum bid (that is, revenue) without the bidder taking sales tax into account, it had made sure of securing excise duty under the guise of compensation if the minimum quantity was not lifted and sold. It is not clear whether the 127 respondents were unable to lift the minimum quantity because of a 10 per cent sales tax imposed a day after their licence periods had begun, but *prima facie* this might well have been so. When the Supreme Court struck down the condition which would have enabled Government to recover excise duty under the guise of compensation, the Government lost that excise revenue.

Submissions: facts must be scrutinized and public interest proved to the satisfaction of the Ct. before rejecting a plea of promissory estoppel

It is submitted that when promissory estoppel is pleaded against the executive or a public authority the facts must be carefully scrutinized, and if they disclose fraudulent conduct, as they appear to do in the present case, the authority should be estopped as Ray C.J. held (para 10.189 above) in order to prevent fraud. Secondly, where public purpose is urged, then it must be proved to the satisfaction of the Court, as Bhagwati J. rightly held in the case considered in para 10.198 *et seq.*

The law laid down in Ram Kumar's Case

10.196 As to promissory estoppel, Jaswant Singh J. held that "It is now well settled by a catena of decisions that there can be no question of estoppel against the Government in the exercise of its legislative, sovereign or executive powers."[65] He then referred to the judgment of Ray C.J. in *Pillai's Case*[66] and to *Kerala v. G.R. Silk Mfg. (Wvg.)* Co.[67] (The *"Gwalior Rayon Case"*) in which Palekar J. delivering the majority judgment observed:

"We do not see how an agreement of the Government can preclude legislation on the subject. The High Court has rightly pointed out that the surrender by Government of its legislative powers to be used for public good cannot avail the company or operate against the Government as equitable estoppel."[68]

Jaswant Singh J. then referred to *Agarwala's Case* in which the Supreme Court had stated that in the *Falmouth Case* the House of Lords had laid down the correct law when it disapproved the observations of Denning J. in *Robertson's Case.* He then referred to *Malhotra and Sons* v. *Union*[69] where he said it was rightly held that:

"The courts will only bind the Government by its promise to prevent manifest injustice or fraud and will not make the Government a slave of its policy for all times to come when the Government acts in its Governmental, public or sovereign capacity."[70]

He thereafter referred to the decision of the U.S. Supreme Court in *Federal Crop Insurance Corporation* v. *Marrill*[71] and quoted from it the following passage:

"It is too late in the day to urge that the Government is just another private litigant, for purposes of charging it with liability, whenever it takes over a business theretofore conducted by private enterprise or engages in competition with private ventures . . . Whatever the form in which the Government functions, anyone entering into an arrangement with the Government takes the risk of having accurately ascertained that he who purports to act for the Government stays within the bounds of his authority. . . . And this is so even though, as here, the agent himself may have been unaware of the limitations upon his authority . . . 'Men must turn square corners when they deal with the Government', does not reflect a callous outlook. It merely expresses the duty of all courts to observe the conditions defined by Congress for charging the public treasury."[72]

A criticism of Ram Kumar's Case

He held that the High Court was wrong in sustaining a plea of estoppel. It is submitted that the law on promissory estoppel has been correctly laid down by Jaswant Singh J. except that his statement that "there can be no question of estoppel against the Government in the exercise of its legislative, sovereign or executive powers" is not correct as the decisions of the courts amply show.

The Sugar Mills Case and Jit Ram's Case

10.197 We must now consider two important Supreme Court judgments: the first delivered by Bhagwati J. for himself and Tulzapurkar J. in *M.P. Sugar Mills* v. *U.P.*[73] (The *"Sugar Mills Case"*) and the second delivered by Kailasam J. for himself and Fazal Ali J. in *M/s. Jit Ram Shiv Kumar* v. *Haryana*[74], (*"Jit Ram's Case"*) which contains a detailed criticism of the judgment in the

---

65 ibid. p. 538.
66 (1974) 1 S.C.R. 515, ('73) A.SC. 2641.
67 ('73) A.SC. 2734.
68 (1976) Supp. S.C.R. at p. 539.
69 ('76) A. J. & K. 41.
70 (1976) Supp. S.C.R. at pp. 539-40.
71 (1947) 332 U.S. 380, 92 L.ed. 10.
72 (1976) Supp. S.C.R. at p. 540.
73 (1979) 2 S.C.R. 641, ('79) A.SC. 621.
74 ('80) A.SC. 1285.

Sugar Mills Case. It was that criticism which decided the present writer to treat promissory estoppel against the State and public authorities at some length as a topic by itself.

The facts of the *Sugar Mills Case*

10.198 The facts of the *Sugar Mills Case* were briefly these: The U.P. Government announced that anyone setting up industries in the State would get a three-year "tax holiday" from sales tax from the date when the industry commenced operations. The M.P. Sugar Mills (the Petitioners) wrote to the Chief Secretary of the U.P. Government asking him to confirm whether in the event of their setting up a factory in U.P. they would get three years' concession from sales tax, and the Chief Secretary confirmed that they would get such concession. The correspondence between the parties[75] showed that the Chief Secretary,[76] on behalf of Government, clearly represented to the Petitioners that on the Mills being erected, the "tax holiday" would be given to them for three years. Later, the Government changed its mind, and issued a Notification stating that a partial tax concession would be given. Even this concession was later withdrawn. But before such withdrawal, the Petitioners had stated in a letter to Government that they would be able to pay tax only at the concessional rate. As government repudiated its obligation, the Petitioners filed a writ petition in the High Court. Originally, the petition did not raise the plea of equitable estoppel, but by an amendment that plea was raised. The government urged, first, that by accepting the liability to pay tax at concessional rates the Petitioners had waived their right to claim exemption from tax.[77] Secondly, that the Chief Secretary had no authority to bind the Government, and thirdly, that the doctrine of equitable estoppel did not apply to Government. The High Court dismissed the petition primarily on the ground of waiver.

Non-Compliance with Art. 299

10.199 But for the fact that Art. 299 required that a contract entered into by a State must be expressed to be made by the Governor and must be executed on his behalf by such person and in such manner as he may direct, there would have been no need to resort to equitable estoppel. For, the facts set out earlier clearly establish a contract.

Reasons for not summarizing Bhagwati J.'s review of authorities on promissory estoppel

10.200 In his judgment, Bhagwati J. reviewed at length the law of promissory estoppel in England and the United States. It is not proposed to give a summary of that review for three reasons. First, because the review requires to be read as a whole; secondly, because we have already set out briefly the English law on promissory estoppel against the Crown and public authorities in paras 10.179 to 10.183 above; and finally, because the reader will find a full discussion of the subject in the undernoted books.[78] However, Bhagwati J.'s

---

[75] ('79) A.SC. at pp. 625-27, where the correspondence is referred to.

[76] He also happened to be an adviser to the Governor, as Uttar Pradesh was under the President's Rule.

[77] Bhagwati J. rejected the plea of waiver, first, because it had not been pleaded, and waiver must be pleaded and proved. Secondly, two conditions were necessary for waiver to operate: a full knowledge of the right and a giving up of that right with full knowledge. And these conditions were not established on the facts of the case. Further, the doctrine of equitable estoppel could not be treated as so firmly established that, relying on it, the petitioners gave up their right to full exemption from tax, and contented themselves with a partial concession. In fact, the plea of equitable estoppel had not been raised in the petition in the first instance. There was no presumption that every one knew all the law: *Martindale* v. *Falkner* (1846) 2 C.B. 706; *Evans* v. *Bartlam* (1937) A.C. 473. As Lord Atkin put it, "There is not and never has been a presumption that everyone knows the law. There is the rule that the ignorance of the law does not excuse, a maxim of a very different scope and application": (1937) A.C. 479, *supra*.

[78] Spencer Bower and Turner, *Estoppel by Representation*, (3rd ed.) Chapter XIV, Promissory Estoppel; Lord Denning, *Discipline of the Law* (1979) at pp. 197-223.

review of Supreme Court decisions on promissory estoppel is unsatisfactory. First, his discussion of the three earlier Supreme Court decisions (which we have discussed in paras 10.189 to 10.197 above) is not correct, partly because he failed to realise that private parties and public authorities do not stand on the same footing when it comes to enforcing a promissory estoppel; and, secondly, because the accurate propositions which he laid down on the law of promissory estoppel against the State and public authorities are accompanied by observations inconsistent with the law so laid down. Again, it is unfortunate that the attention of the Court was not called to s. 63, *Illustration* (b) of the Contract Act[79] which deliberately departed from the English law.[80] *Illustration* (b) clearly shows that in India the payment of a smaller sum of money, *e.g.* Rs. 2,000, if accepted in full satisfaction of a larger sum of money, *e.g.* Rs. 5,000, discharges the whole debt of Rs. 5,000. Section 63 and *Illustration* (b) would have made it unnecessary for Bhagwati J. to consider the criticism levelled in England and, even in India, against the doctrine of consideration. *The High Trees Case* would not have arisen at all if acceptance of a promise to pay a rent of £1250 per annum in satisfaction of a liability of £2500 per annum had amounted in England to a discharge of the liability to pay £2500. The only question which would have survived would have been the true scope of the agreement, namely, whether the agreement was limited in point of time, as Denning J. held that it was. Further, s. 10 of the Contract Act makes "consideration" an essential part of a contract and as long as the law remains unaltered, no amount of criticism by authorities, however eminent, can displace that requirement.

Submission: Bhagwati J.'s review of Sup. Ct. authorities unsatisfactory

Attention of the Court not called to s. 63, ill. (*b*) of the Contract Act

10.201 Before discussing the judgment of Bhagwati J. further, the reader will recall that in the *Indo-Afghan Case*, Shah J. did not refer to the House of Lords' decision in the *Falmouth Case* or the extended principle which Denning J. had laid down in *Robertson's Case*. And although in the *Century Mills Case* Shah J. did refer to the overruling by the House of Lords of Denning J.'s extension of the principle in *Robertson's Case*, Shah J. said that the Court was not concerned with the extended principle, so that the impact of the House of Lords decision on the principles of *Robertson's Case* was not considered and remained open for future consideration by the Supreme Court. The question thus left open by Shah J. was, as we said earlier, concluded by Alagiriswami and Mathew JJ. when they held in *Agarwala's Case* that the view taken by the House of Lords in the *Falmouth Case* was correct and not the view taken by Lord Denning. The law so laid down was quoted with approval by Jaswant Singh and Fazal Ali JJ. in *Ram Kumar's Case* (para 10.196).

Question left open in the *Century Mills Case* concluded by *Agarwala's Case*

---

[79] *Sec. 63. Promisee may dispense with or remit performance of promise.* — Every promisee may dispense with or remit, wholly or in part, the performance of the promise made to him, or may extend the time for such performance, or may accept instead of it any satisfaction which he thinks fit. *Illustration* (b): "*A* owes *B* 5,000 rupees. *A* pays to *B* and *B* accepts, in satisfaction of the whole debt, 2,000 rupees paid at the time and place at which the 5,000 rupees were payable. The whole debt is discharged."

[80] See Pollock & Mulla, *Indian Contract and Specific Relief Acts*, 9th ed. p. 450.

A closer look at *Robertson's Case* and the impact of the *Falmouth Case* on it is necessary

10.202 What propositions of law about promissory estoppel emerge from the elaborate review of authorities by Bhagwati J. in the *Sugar Mills Case* and the equally elaborate review by Kailasam J. in *Jit Ram's Case*?[81] If this discussion is to be kept within reasonable limits, we must look more closely at *Robertson's Case*, because Bhagwati J. has laid great stress on the fact that the principles laid down by Denning J. in *Robertson's Case* were accepted by Shah J. in the *Indo-Afghan Case* (para 10.183 above) and again in the *Turner Morrison Case* (para 10.187 above). Secondly, we must consider the impact of the House of Lords' decision in the *Falmouth Case* on the principles laid down by Denning J. in *Robertson's Case*, including in such impact subsequent decisions of the English Courts. Finally, we must inquire what qualifications to the *Robertson* principles are accepted by Bhagwati J., and whether some parts of his judgment are inconsistent with such acceptance, as Kailasam J. is at pains to point out.

Bhagwati J. accepted the *ratio* of Lord Normand's judgment in *Falmouth Case*,

10.203 Bhagwati J. accepted the rejection by Lord Simonds and Lord Normand of the extended principle enunciated by Lord Denning in *Robertson's Case* as laying down the correct law. But Bhagwati J. rightly observed that this rejection did not mean that there could be no estoppel against the Crown or public authorities. Further, Bhagwati J. accepted the following *ratio* of Lord Normand's judgment, ("the said *ratio*") namely: ". . . neither a minister nor any subordinate officer of the Crown can by any conduct or representation bar the Crown from enforcing a statutory prohibition or entitle a subject to say that there has been no breach of it",[82] as correctly laying down the law on estoppel. However, he failed to realize that the consequences of accepting the said *ratio* as correct had to be worked out by reference to *Robertson's Case* itself, for it was the principle of that case which Denning J. had applied in the *Falmouth Case*, and which the House of Lords overruled.

but failed to realize the consequence of such acceptance

An analysis of propositions emerging from *Robertson's Case*

10.204 The facts and the legal framework in which *Robertson's Case* had to be decided have been fully set out in para 10.181 above and need not be repeated here. We will first analyse the propositions which emerge from the judgment in *Robertson's Case*, and then consider the consequences of applying the said *ratio* to that case. In *Robertson's Case*, Denning J. affirmed the *High Trees* principle which laid down the doctrine of promissory estoppel between subjects. He then applied that principle to the assurance given by an official of the War Office. This second principle was an intermediate step, or a connecting bridge, linking the *High Trees* principle to the third principle by which Denning J. made the Minister of Pensions and, through him, the Crown, responsible for the assurance of the War Office, even though the War Office had no legal authority to deal with Robertson's claim. The three principles which Denning J. laid down in *Robertson's Case* are given below for convenience of reference, although two of them have been set out earlier. They will be referred to as the first, the second and the third principle.

---

[81] The review is designed to show that the conclusions drawn by Bhagwati J. are partly incorrect.

[82] ('79) A.SC. at p. 647.

The three principles

(i) *The first or the High Trees Principle*: "If a man gives a promise or assurance which he intends to be binding on him and to be acted on by the person to whom it is given, then once it is acted upon, he is bound by it": (para 10.181 above).

(ii) *The Second or the Connecting Principle*: ". . . in the present day and age no distinction should be drawn as to the legal effect of its or their action between the Crown and ordinary subjects, so that the effect of a representation made by the Crown could no longer be qualified so as to be subject to the future exercise by the Crown of its executive authority."[83]

(iii) *The Third or the Extended Principle*: "The principle is this: Whenever government officers, in their dealings with a subject, take on themselves to assume authority in a matter with which he is concerned, the subject is entitled to rely on their having the authority which they assume. He does not know the limits of their authority, and he ought not to suffer if they exceed it. That was the principle which I applied in (*Robertson's Case*)"[84] (para 10.182 above).

The formulation of the second principle

10.205 The formulation of the second principle is taken from Lord Evershed's judgment (see para 10.185 above) and it accurately describes the principle which Denning J. laid down in *Robertson's Case*. For, in that Case, Denning J. said: "What then is the result in law? If this was a question between subjects a person who gave such an assurance as that contained in the War Office letter would be held bound by it. . . . (Robertson) did, therefore on faith of the War Office letter forbear from getting (a medical opinion). That is sufficient to make the letter binding. The case falls within (the *High Trees* principle)".[85] It will be seen that if Robertson was to succeed, the question which Denning J. had to decide was not whether the War Office was bound by the letter of April 8, 1941, but whether the Crown was bound by it. Denning J. equated the War Office letter to a letter written by one subject to another, as a first step towards holding the Crown bound by the *High Trees* principle, supplemented by the third or the extended principle.

The consequence of applying Lord Normand's *ratio* to *Robertson's Case*

10.206 Did the *ratio* of Lord Normand's judgment apply to *Robertson's Case*, and, if so, how would that case have been decided? As the said *ratio* resulted in the House of Lords rejecting the third or extended principle in *Robertson's Case*, it obviously applied to that case; and it applied in this way. In the said *ratio* Lord Normand spoke of "a statutory prohibition". In *Robertson's Case*, the War Office was necessarily prohibited by the Royal Warrants from dealing with Robertson's claim because the Warrants transferred that power from the War Office to the Minister of Pensions. If the War Office had no legal authority to deal with Robertson's claim, then, *a fortiori*, they could give no assurances in relation to it which could operate as an estoppel. Therefore, the Minister of Pensions was not barred by the representation of the War Office official from enforcing a statutory prohibition against the War Office. In the result, Robertson's appeal would have failed because the only ground on which it was

Robertson's appeal would have

[83] (1960) 2 Q.B. at pp. 287-8.
[84] *Falmouth Boat Construction Co. Ltd.* v. *Howell* (1950) 2 K.B. 16 at p. 18.
[85] (1949) 1 K.B. 227 at pp. 230-31.

failed; the *ratio* also destroyed the second principle laid down by Denning J.

allowed was rejected by the House of Lords. Further, the said *ratio* also destroyed the second, or the connecting principle, laid down by Lord Denning, who had equated representations made by public officials to representations by subjects. For it is clear that the representation made by the officer of a department which had no legal authority to deal with the subject matter to which the representation related, cannot bind even the department, because a body with limited powers cannot exercise a power not entrusted to it, either expressly or by necessary implication. In other words, representations by public officials serving in various departments of the State cannot be equated to representations by subjects, because such representations raise the further question whether the representations relate to a subject matter over which their departments have legal authority. No such question ordinarily arises between subjects; consequently, the same standard cannot be applied to representations by public officials as is applied to subjects. As will appear hereafter, Bhagwati J. had not realized the effect of Lord Normand's judgment on the second or connecting principle in *Robertson's Case*. In the result, the only one of the three principles enunciated by Denning J. which survives the judgment of the House of Lords is the *High Trees* principle. It may be added that it is not without significance that in the very full discussion of the *High Trees* principle and its development in his *Discipline of the Law*,[86] Lord Denning has made no reference either to *Robertson's Case* or to the *Falmouth Case* which in terms rejected the third principle he had laid down in *Robertson's Case*. This omission is unfortunate; but it appears to be a recognition of the fact that the very wide principle he laid down in *Robertson's Case* to prevent grave injustice being done to Robertson, could not be sustained.[87] As we have seen, Lord Denning in *Wells* v. *Minister of Housing*[88] (para 10.185 above) rightly observed that he was aware that a public authority could not be estopped from doing its public duty.

The omission of *Robertson's Case* and the *Falmouth Case* in Lord Denning's book

House of Lords dismissed the appeal in *Falmouth Case*

10.207 In the *Falmouth Case*, Denning J. got over the difficulty posed by the requirement of an Order passed in 1940 under the authority of the Emergency Powers (Defence) Act, 1939, on its true construction (which construction might have required that permission to repair ships should be by a written licence), by applying the third principle in *Robertson's Case* thus giving effect to the oral permission which had been given to repair the ship. However, as we have seen, Lord Simonds and Lord Normand rejected this "short way to a decision which avoids the necessity of construing the Order of 1940. . . ". Nevertheless, the appeal was dismissed because it was held on a true construction of the relevant provision that although a licence had to be in writing, such a licence operated retrospectively to cover work done previously under oral permission, because repair had to be done under official supervision in emergency conditions created by the war. Therefore, the work

[86] Pages 197 to 293.

[87] This case further illustrates the well known saying that "hard cases make bad law". The Minister of Pension's repudiation of the assurance to Robertson contained in the War Office letter appears so unfair and unjust, that judges would struggle hard to prevent such unfairness and injustice.

[88] (1967) 1 W.L.R. 1000 at p. 1044.

covered by the licence was done legally, and the plaintiff was entitled to recover the amount claimed by him. However, Lord Normand's observations about a part of the paintiff's claim are of great importance on a matter of principle. He said:

An important principle laid down by Lord Normand

"There is more difficulty about the cocktail bar, which I shall assume was not within the terms of the application, and, therefore, not within the terms of the written licence. I think, however, that when the officer authorized to grant licences with retrospective effect comes forward to depone that all the work done in fact had his authority, any defect in the licence which he had power to cure and which ought to have been cured should be disregarded. In such a case, too, I would decline to apply the rule that money cannot be recovered for services given or materials supplied in breach of a statutory prohibition. To do so would be to stretch the precedents beyond reason and to pass from reality into formalism and make believe."[89]

This passage is important, because it shows that the rule that "what is done in contravention of the provisions of an Act of Parliament cannot be the subject of an action"—a rule which applies equally to a Rule or Order lawfully made under the authority of that Act —is a matter of substance and not of form or technicality. The work on the cocktail bar was not covered, even retrospectively, by the written licence. But it had been done pursuant to the oral directions of an official who had the power to cover, and who ought to have covered, that work by a written licence. Under these circumstances to say that repairs to the cocktail bar were effected in contravention of an Order lawfully made, would be to permit the form or a technicality to prevail over the reason and substance of the rule. In *Wells* v. *Minister of Housing*[90] Lord Denning referred to the above passage from Lord Normand's judgment in support of his proposition that although a public authority cannot be estopped from doing its public duty, it can be stopped from relying on technicalities. He said that in the *Falmouth Case* "a defect in the licence (about the cocktail bar) was disregarded by the House of Lords".[91]

later applied by Lord Denning

10.208 The result of our discussion is that observations of Shah J. which suggest that the same considerations apply to public authorities as apply to private parties in relation to promissory estoppel, and the acceptance and amplification of those observations by Bhagwati J. in the *Sugar Mills Case*[92] are not correct and cannot be accepted. However, the following observations of Denning J. in *Robertson's Case* require further consideration:

The result of our discussion on the judgments of Shah J. and Bhagwati J.

"The Crown cannot escape by saying that estoppels do not bind the Crown, for that doctrine has long been exploded. Nor can the Crown escape by praying in aid the doctrine of executive necessity, that is, the doctrine that the Crown cannot bind itself so as to fetter its future executive action" (para 10.183 above).

Our discussion has shown that these two propositions in their broad generality cannot survive the House of Lords' decision in the *Falmouth Case,* or Lord Denning's own judgment in *Wells* v. *Minister of Housing.* However, the question still remains, "how far is the Crown amenable to estoppel, and how far can the Crown fetter its discretionary power?" In England the matter is complicated by the Sovereign's prerogative; in India there is no such

[89] (1951) A.C. 837 at p. 848.
[90] (1967) 1 W.L.R. 1000, 1007.
[91] ibid.
[92] See ('79) A.SC. at pp. 638-9.

complication. In the following discussion we will therefore refer to an estoppel against the State so that the discussion may not get entangled in fine points of the Sovereign's prerogative.

Is the State amenable to estoppel?

10.209 The question whether the State is amenable to estoppel has several aspects which require to be distinguished. The Government of India and the Government of a State can sue and be sued as provided in Art. 300. Consequently, matters become *"res judicata"* (which is described as "estoppel by record") between the State and the party by whom or against whom a suit has been filed or a proceeding brought. Secondly, the State can acquire, hold and dispose of property and can carry on any trade or business. If State A grants a lease for 30 years to *X*, a private citizen, the State is ordinarily in the same position as a private landlord, and is amenable to estoppel by representation or conduct. It has been so held in numerous decisions. The facts of *Att.-Gen. of Victoria* v. *Ettershank*[93] and the decision of the Privy Council in that case are instructive. The facts material for this discussion were briefly these:

Ettershank's Case: Lease granted under the provisions of a statute

In June 1865. Strong, after the payment of a year's rent was put in possession of an allotment of land according to the Land Act of 1862 (as amended in 1865) "subject to the usual covenant for payment of rent, and a condition for re-entry on non-payment thereof". He failed to cultivate, build or enclose within a year as required by s. 36 of the Act. In April 1869 the allotment was declared to be forfeited for non-payment of rent, non-compliance with the provisions and non-performance of covenants incident to tenure under the Act. In 1872 Ettershank entered into a treaty for the purchase of the allotment from Strong. But before concluding an agreement, he had an interview with *Grant*, the President of the Board of Lands and Works, in April 1872, and told *Grant* of his wish to purchase, if he could do so with safety, and asked if the Government could take the back rent and issue the lease. *Grant* took time to make inquiries, and on a second interview told Ettershank that he found on inquiry that the land had been gazetted as forfeited some years ago, but there was nothing to prevent *Grant* taking the back rent and issuing the lease and that he would do so. Ettershank, on that assurance said that he would purchase, and *Grant* gave instructions for the lease. In July 1872 a lease was executed by the Governor back dated to 29th June 1865, and Ettershank was registered as the proprietor of the lease. Ettershank had been in possession of the allotment since then. After the lease had been issued, *Grant* ceased to be President and was succeeded by Casey, who refused to receive the back rent when tendered by Ettershank and disputed his title to the allotment and to the grant of the fee simple.[94]

Ettershank filed a suit under a petition of right claiming, *inter alia*, to be entitled to the grant in fee simple of the lease as the registered proprietor of the lease. It was contended for the Appellant that the grant of a lease after the forfeiture of the lease was not a waiver of forfeiture. The lease was granted under a legislative enactment and therefore it was a lease, *the terms of which were in the public interest. Equity did not grant relief against a statute or against those provisions of a lease which had been introduced by the express direction of the legislature.* The respondent got what he bargained for, namely, a void lease. The representation made by *Grant* to the respondent, if *Grant* had been the lessor and Strong the lessee would have been of serious import; but the lease rested upon legislation *and Grant had no power to alter that legislation by his representations.* The reader will have noticed that the stand taken was that there could be no estoppel against a statute or statutory leases

---

[93] (1875) L.R. 6 P.C. 354.

[94] ibid. pp. 364-5.

the terms of which were conceived in the public interest. The Privy Council rejected all these contentions. It held that the grant of a lease in 1872 amounted to a waiver of all previous forfeitures under the circumstances of the present case. When the Governor executed the lease it must be presumed that it was intended to waive any forfeitures and affirm an existing tenancy. The argument that Ettershank got what he bargained for, namely, a void lease, had no foundation for it was not denied that Ettershank on applying for the lease was led to believe by *Grant* that it would be issued for an existing interest which he might safely purchase. Further, none of the terms required to be inserted in leases by the Act rendered the lease void, but only voidable at the option of the lessor, and if so, forfeiture for breaches of covenants could be waived. The respondent contended that even if there had been no waiver, equity would relieve against forfeiture for non-payment of rent; but the appellant tried to meet this contention by submitting that these interests being Crown lands, and governed by statutory regulations, the ordinary relief afforded by the Court could not be granted, because in giving relief the Court proceeded on the presumption that the condition of forfeiture was intended merely as security for the payment of the rent, and this presumption could not be made in the case of conditions imposed by a statute. Rejecting this contention the Privy Council observed:

The Privy Council rejects the Crown's contentions about waiver

"This would be so, where a statute, either expressly or by necessary implication, annexes a condition to an estate, making it determinable on non-payment of rent, without more. But that is not the present case. . . . When, therefore, the statute authorizes a lease with these usual and well understood-provisions it is reasonable to suppose that the Legislature intended that it should operate as a contract of like nature made between private persons. The statute does not . . . (make) the lease void on non-payment; and there is nothing to indicate that it meant the condition of re-entry to have a more stringent effect, or to be regarded otherwise than the like condition in ordinary leases."[95]

Equitable relief available where the Act puts the Crown in the position of an ordinary lessor

The reader will have noticed that *Grant*, as President of the Board of Lands and Works had authority to deal with the grant of leases and to waive forfeitures. The assurance which *Grant* gave was not of an existing fact but of his intention to receive rent and grant a lease in the future. Therefore on the construction rightly put on the Land Acts by the Privy Council, a case of promissory estoppel clearly arose. Counsel for Ettershank did not have the doctrine of promissory estoppel to rely on. But if his argument had to be urged after the *High Trees Case* he would have made out all the requirements of a promissory estoppel. He said:

"Even if there had been no waiver, still Ettershank in 1872 went to the head of the Government Department and received from him the assurance that he could and would receive the back rent and issue the lease. Ettershank purchased on the faith of such assurance, and the Government cannot now be heard to contend that it granted a void lease, after its own representation that it would issue a lease for an existing interest which it might safely purchase."[96]

The Privy Council held in favour of the respondent by applying the doctrine of waiver,[97] and, as we have seen, waiver and estoppel have frequently been used interchangeably (para 8.41).

---

[95] ibid. p. 370.
[96] ibid. at p. 358.
[97] The Privy Council held in the alternative that if there was no waiver, a

The importance of *Ettershank's Case*

10.210 *Ettershank's Case* is of great importance for it shows that there are statutes and statutes; and if the Court finds on a true construction of a statute that it puts Government and private persons in the same position, then the bald statement that there could be no estoppel against a statute would require to be qualified. However, this topic, and the related topic of "executive necessity" is more conveniently dealt with later (see paras 10.215 and 10.216).

Devenport v. *The Queen*, also a case of a lease governed by the provisions of statutes

10.211 In *Devenport* v. *The Queen*[98] a lease of Crown Lands[99] was granted to the respondent. The lessee failed to perform his covenant to cultivate one-sixth of the said lands within a year from the allotment thereof. However, rent for the whole term of years was subsequently received by the Government with full knowledge of the above breach but a notification in the Gazettes of 1869, 1870 and 1871 announced that it was received conditionally and without prejudice to the rights of Government. An action of ejectment was brought in the name of Her Majesty against the appellant as the tenant in possession. The questions for determination were: whether the lease was forfeited, and, if so, whether the forfeiture could be, and was, waived by the Crown. The Privy Council decided the appeal on the assumption that a forfeiture had accrued, and addressed itself to the question whether it had been waived by the receipt of rent. It was contended for the Crown that the proviso to s. 8 of the 1863 Act, made the lease absolutely void, and not voidable only. The Supreme Court of Queensland took this view, and further decided that the Legislature having imposed this condition, the Crown could not dispense with it. The Privy Council observed that s. 5 of the Leasing Act left the form of the lease to the discretion of the Governor, showing thereby that a lease by way of contract was contemplated, although based on the provisions of the statute. The lease actually granted was made subject to the terms, conditions, penalties and forfeitures contained in the Act. But the Privy Council said that there was nothing in the form of the lease inconsistent with the Acts. The covenants of the lease afforded the means of conveniently enforcing the obligations of the lessee. Section 8 of the Reserves Act provided that "if any person selecting lands in an agricultural reserve shall fail to occupy and improve the same, as required by s. 7 of this Act, then the right and interest of such selector to the land shall cease and determine. . . ." On this provision, the Privy Council observed:

Privy Council held that the statutes did not make the lease absolutely void, but only voidable at the option of the lessor in case of breach by the lessee

"Does then the proviso of forfeiture in s. 8 of the *Reserves Act* when read into such a lease as the present, make the term *ipso facto* void or voidable only upon a breach of the condition? In a long series of decisions the Courts have construed clauses of forfeiture in leases declaring in terms, however clear and strong, that they shall be void on breach of conditions by the lessees, to mean that they are voidable only at the option of the lessors. The same rule of construction has been applied to other contracts where a party bound

---

lessee in possession was entitled both under the Act and the terms of the lease to relief in equity against forfeiture for non-payment of rent, and to a decree for specific performance on proper terms.

[98] (1877-8) 3 App.Cas. 115.

[99] Granted under the Agricultural Reserves Act, 1863 and the Leasing Act, 1866.

by a condition has sought to take advantage of his own breach of it to annul the contract."[1]

The argument of the Crown that this rule of construction was inapplicable when a legislature had imposed a condition was met by saying that even where a statute provided that if the purchaser at an auction refused to pay the auction duty, his bidding "should be null and void to all intents and purposes", it was held in *Malins* v. *Freeman*[2] that the bidding was void only at the option of the seller, though the object of the Act was to protect the revenue. Coltman J. said: "It is so contrary to justice that a party should avoid his own contract by his own wrong that, unless constrained, we should not adopt a construction favourable to such a view."[3] No doubt a legislature may express clearly an intention to the contrary, but the Privy Council found no such clear intention in the present case. The Legislature may well have meant to leave to the Crown acting by its responsible ministers the option which other lessors in case of similar conditions were entitled to exercise.[4]

The Crown had waived the forfeiture

Having found waiver established as a fact, the Privy Council held that where rent was received as rent but under protest after knowledge of the breach of the condition, the waiver of forfeiture was complete and the protest was inoperative: *Croft* v. *Lumley*.[5] In a later case, *R.* v. *Paulson*,[6] the Privy Council again reaffirmed the principle that a lessor who accepts rent knowing that there was a breach of a covenant in the lease thereby irrevocably elects to treat the lease as subsisting and is precluded from claiming a forfeiture. The Privy Council held that the presence in a lease or contract of a provision requiring a waiver to be expressed in writing did not render the above principle inapplicable.[7] A number of cases were cited in support of these propositions including *Croft* v. *Lumley* (*supra*), the Privy Council adding that "The case of *Devenport* v. *The Queen* resembles the present case in many respects."

The above principle reaffirmed by the Privy Council in *R.* v. *Paulson*

10.212 Finally, in *Att.-Gen. to His Royal Highness the Prince of Wales* v. *Collom*[8] the question whether the Crown was bound by an estoppel *in pais* (that is, estoppel by representation) was considered and decided. The facts of the case are complicated and too long to set out here,[9] but those facts raised the question whether a case for an estoppel by representation had been made out against the Crown. The judgment of Atkin J. on this point is accurately set out in the 3rd finding in the head-note to the report:

Collom's Case: Crown bound by estoppel by representation

---

[1] (1887-8) 3 App.Cas. *supra* at pp. 128-9, citing *Doe* v. *Bancks* 4 B.&A. 401; *Roberts* v. *Davey* 2 B. & Ad. 664 (the words were that licence "should cease, determine, and be utterly void and of no effect to all intents and purposes") and other cases cited in the notes to *Devenport's Case* 1 Sm.L.C. 41.

[2] 4 Bing. N.C. 395.

[3] (1887-8) 3 App.Cas. *supra* at p. 129.

[4] ibid. pp. 129-30.

[5] 6 H.L.C. 672 (H.L.). The Privy Council referred, *inter alia*, to the opinion given to the House of Lords by a "very learned Judge Mr. Justice Williams": see 3 App.Cas. *supra* at p. 131.

[6] (1921) 1 A.C. 271 (P.C.).

[7] ibid. p. 283. At p. 286 the Privy Council observed. "It may well be that many cases may occur to which the clause as to waiver would be applicable; their Lordships think that it is not applicable in the present case under all its circumstances."

[8] (1916) 2 K.B. 193.

[9] ibid. pp. 194-199 where they are fully set out.

"*Held*: (3) Following the principle laid down in *Ramsden* v. *Dyson* (1866) L.R. 1 H.L. 129, 140, that in regard to the Duchy's claim to the house at W.Z. the defendant had established a good equitable defence based on estoppel, the expenditure on the house having been made to the knowledge of the agent to the Dutchy and on the property which the defendant reasonably believed to be her own and that such equitable defence was good against the Crown. *Held*, therefore, that in the result the defendant had established her title, and the information must be dismissed."[10]

Jit Ram's Case: right to levy *octroi* duty renounced for ever as a condition for sale of land

10.213 Before considering the doctrine that there can be no estoppel against a statute, and the connected doctrine that public authorities cannot be estopped from doing their public duties, it would be convenient to consider the judgment of Kailasam J. in *Jit Ram's Case*.[11] In that case, the question of estoppel arose under these circumstances:

The Municipal Committee of Bahadurgarh ("the Committee") established Mandi Fateh ("the Mandi") to improve trade in those areas. The Committee decided that purchasers of plots for sale in the Mandi would not be required to pay octroi duty on goods imported within the Mandi, and by resolutions in 1916 and 1917 the Committee decided that the Mandi should remain *immune from octroi duty for ever*. The Commissioner first objected to this proposal, but later withdrew his objection on the representation by the Committee that if the octroi duty was to be levied, there would be no purchaser for plots and the whole scheme would fail. Plots were sold on the basis that the Mandi would remain immune from octroi duty for ever. After certain intermediate steps the Committee on 21.7.1965 requested Government to cancel the Committee's resolution of 2.3.1954 which provided that the Mandi would remain free from octroi duty according to the terms of the proclamation of sale relating to the sale of the plots. The State of Haryana, which had come into existence in 1964, by its memo dated 30.10.1967 approved the said resolution of 1965 and cancelled the Committee's resolution of 2.3.1954. Thereupon, the Committee began charging octroi duty on goods imported into the Mandi.

Challenge to the levy of octroi in breach of condition

The petitioners contended that the Committee's resolution of 1965 and the approval accorded to it by the State of Haryana were illegal, *ultra vires* and without jurisdiction.

Petition dismissed by the H. Ct.

10.214 The High Court dismissed the petition holding that under s. 62-A of the Punjab Municipal Act, 48/1953, Government was entitled to direct the Committee to impose octroi duty, and even if the Committee was found to have erred in imposing the octroi duty, the powers of the State under the law could not be questioned. Secondly, it was not within the competence of the Committee to grant any exemption from octroi duty and this act *ultra vires* of its powers could not be enforced.[12] The Supreme Court agreed with the High Court on both these grounds for dismissing the petition.[13] However, the Supreme Court went into the question whether the Committee and its successors were bound by a promissory estoppel. After an elaborate review of authorities on promissory estoppel including the *Sugar Mills Case*, Kailasam J. held that the Municipality was not estopped as the representation made by it was beyond the scope of its authority. The levy of tax being for a public purpose i.e. the revenues of the State as laid down in *Ram Kumar's Case*, the plea of estoppel was not available. As will appear hereafter, the decision is clearly right, and in conformity with the law laid down as far back as 1883. It may be added that in countries where corruption is rampant it is essential to maintain the doctrine of *ultra vires*, however

The Sup. Ct. discussed the plea of equitable estoppel and held against the appellant

[10] ibid. p. 194.
[11] ('80) A.SC. 1248.
[12] ibid. p. 1288.
[13] ibid. p. 1289.

immoral the result may appear to be in individual cases. Lord Denning overlooked this aspect of promissory estoppel in *Robertson's Case*. For, although the assurances given to Robertson were honestly and fairly given, where stakes are high, assurances might be procured by bribes, especially as bribery is difficult to prove.

10.215 However, the importance of *Jit Ram's Case* lies in the following five propositions which Kailasam J. laid down about the scope of the doctrine of promissory estoppel as a result of his review of the authorities:

Jit Ram's Case: five propositions laid down on promissory estoppel

"(1) The plea of promissory estoppel is not available against the exercise of the legislative functions of the State.

(2) The doctrine cannot be invoked for preventing the Government from discharging its functions under the law.

(3) When the officer of the Government acts outside the scope of his authority, the plea of promissory estoppel is not available. The doctrine of *ultra vires* will come into operation and the Government cannot be held bound by the unauthorised acts of its officers.

(4) When the officer acts within the scope of his authority under a scheme and enters into an agreement and makes a representation and a person acting on that representation puts himself in a disadvantageous position, the Court is entitled to require the officer to act according to the scheme and the agreement or representation. The Officer cannot arbitrarily act on his mere whim and ignore his promise on some undefined and undisclosed grounds of necessity or change the conditions to the prejudice of the person who had acted upon such representation and put himself in a disadvantageous position.

(5) The officer would be justified in changing the terms of the agreement to the prejudice of the other party on special considerations such as difficult foreign exchange position or other matters which have a bearing on general interest of the State."[14]

Kailasam J. rightly pointed out that in the *Sugar Mills Case*, Bhagwati J. laid down propositions which correspond to propositions 1 to 3 set out above.

10.215A Having regard to the increasing importance of promissory estoppel in constitutional law, the above propositions must be critically examined. Proposition (1) above which speaks of "the exercise of the legislative functions of the State" is better expressed by the form in which it is usually put, namely, "that a party cannot set up an estoppel in the face of a statute."[15] For the phrase "legislative functions" may refer to the *procedure* for enacting laws with which, broadly speaking, the Courts are not concerned; or it may refer to the Statute which emerges after the procedure for enacting it has been followed with which Courts are very much concerned. Propositions (2) and (3) are closely connected with, and follow from, proposition (1). Propositions (4) and (5) deal with the conferment of discretionary power, and indicate the circumstances under which a plea of estoppel can or cannot be raised against the exercise of discretionary power. However, these propositions require a number of qualifications to be made, and they are explained and set out below.

These propositions require critical examination

10.216 The proposition "that a party cannot set up an estoppel in the face of a statute" takes us to acts done under the statute; and that, in its turn, makes it necessary to examine the provisions of a statute to see whether they preclude a plea of estoppel in respect of action

Examination of the doctrine that there can be no estoppel against a statute

[14] ibid. p. 1302.
[15] *Kok Hoong* v. *Leong Cheong Kweng Mines Ltd.* (1964) A.C. 996, 1015 (P.C.).

taken under the statute. Such an examination leads to the following results:

The rule stated, subject to qualification in (b) below

(*a*) If an Act imposes on Government, or on a public authority a statutory duty to carry out certain acts in the interest of the public, then the Government or a public authority cannot preclude itself by estoppel *in pais* (that is, by representation) from performing its duty and asserting legal rights accordingly.[16] We have seen that this proposition was clearly laid down by Lord Simonds and Lord Normand in the *Falmouth Case,* and that Bhagwati J. accepted the *ratio* of Lord Normand's judgment as correct.

(*b*) However, the above proposition requires to be qualified by saying that public interest is a matter of substance and not of form or technicality for reasons fully set out in para 10.207 above.

Two classes of statutes which make certain transactions void

(c) A statute may enact a provision directing that a particular transaction shall be void or unenforceable. But such statutes fall into two classes:

(i) Statutes which make a transaction void on the general ground of social policy. Thus s. 10 read with s. 11 of the Indian Contract Act makes a minor's "contract" void. In *Sadik Ali Khan* v. *Jai Kishore,*[17] the Privy Council held that a deed executed by a minor was a nullity and incapable of founding an estoppel.

(ii) ". . . there are statutes which though declaring transactions to be unenforceable or void are nevertheless not essentially prohibitory and so do not preclude estoppel.[18]

Halsbury on "*Estoppel against statute*"

(*d*) In *Halsbury*, under the title *Estoppel against statute* it is said that "the doctrine of estoppel cannot be invoked to render valid a transaction which the legislature has, on grounds of general policy, enacted to be invalid" Footnote 1 to this proposition says, "As to whether this is the right test, see *Kok Hoong* v. *Leong Cheong Kweng Mines Ltd.* 1964 A.C. 993, 1016 . . ."[19] In that case, Lord Radcliffe said:

The test in *Kok Hoong's Case*

> "It has been said that the question whether an estoppel is to be allowed or not depends on whether the enactment or rule of law relied upon is imposed 'in the public interest' or 'on grounds of general public policy.'[20] But a principle as widely stated as this might prove to be rather an elusive guide, since there is no statute, at least public general statute, for which this claim might not be made. In their Lordships' opinion, a more direct test to apply in any case such as at present, where the laws of moneylending or monetory security are involved, is to ask whether the law that confronts the estoppel can be seen to represent a social policy to which the court must give effect in the interests of the public generally or some section of the public, despite any rules of evidence as between themselves that the parties may have created by their conduct or otherwise. Thus the laws of gaming or usury[21] override an estoppel: so do the provisions of the Rent Restriction Acts with regard to orders for possession of controlled tenancies."[22]

---

[16] ibid. p. 1015 *per* Lord Radcliffe.

[17] (1928) A.PC. 152, 30 Bom.L.R. 1346.

[18] (1964) A.C. *supra* at p. 1015. Lord Radcliffe gives examples of such statutes at pp. 1015-6.

[19] *Halsbury,* Vol. 16 (4th ed.) para 1515, *f.n.* 1.

[20] [See *In re A Bankruptcy Notice* (1924) 2 Ch. 76, 97, *per* Atkin L.J.].

[21] *Carter* v. *James* (1844) 13 M.&W. 138.

[22] *Welch* v. *Nagy* (1950) 1 K.B. 455.

And Lord Radcliffe added:

"In all such cases there is no room for the application of another general and familiar principle of the law that a man may, if he wishes, disclaim a statutory provision enacted for his benefit, for what is for his benefit and what is for his protection are not synonymous terms. Nor is it open to the Court to give sanction to departures from any law that reflects such a policy, even though the party concerned has himself behaved in such a way as would otherwise tie his hands. See In re Stapleford Colliery (1880) 14 Ch.D. 432, 441 C.A."[23]

Distinction between provisions of the law which can and cannot be waived

(*e*) Two decisions of the Privy Council on s. 80 of the C.P.C. on the one hand, and ss. 86 and 87 of the C.P.C. on the other, bring out the distinction between a mandatory provision of the law for the benefit of a party, which benefit the party can waive, and mandatory provisions of the law for the protection of a party which protection cannot be waived as explained in para 8.48 above.

Public policy may place the state in the same position as private parties in commercial and business transactions

(*f*) But public policy may itself require that in laws governing business or commercial transactions, or dealings with property, Government and private persons should be put on the same footing subject to limited exceptions,[24] with the result that representations or conduct which would raise an estoppel between private parties to a contract would equally raise an estoppel where Government is one of the parties (see para 10.212). And this is so even where the contract or lease contains provisions required to be inserted therein by a statute as in *Ettershank's Case* (paras 10.209 and 10.210) or in *Davenport* v. *The Queen* (para 10.211).

Subject to the qualification in (g) herein

(*g*) However, although the proposition in (*f*) above is correct in a large number of situations, and the Government cannot "escape from any contract which it finds disadvantageous by saying that it never promised to act otherwise than for the public good"[25] — because fulfilment of contracts by government, as by private persons, is for the public good — yet in certain situations it may become necessary to take action, in the public interest in exercise of governmental powers *de hors* the contract and the public purpose which the contract subserves. The case of *Commrs. of Crown Lands* v. *Page*[26] illustrates this distinction. In a lease granted by the Crown for 25 years there was an implied covenant for quiet enjoyment. In 1945 the Minister of Works requisitioned the premises in the exercise of powers under Defence (General) Regulations, 1939. The premises were derequisitioned in 1955. The lessee contended that she had been "evicted" by the lessor (the Crown) and no rent was payable. Rejecting this contention Devlin J. held, it is submitted rightly, that even if there had been an express covenant regarding quiet enjoyment it must by necessary implication be read to exclude those measures affecting the nation as a whole which the Crown took for the public good.[27]

Commrs. of Crown Lands v. Page

---

[23] (1964) A.C. *supra* at p. 1116-7.

[24] For example, contracts entered into by the Union or State Governments must comply with the requirements of Art. 299. In *Jit Ram's Case,* Kailasam J. has referred to Supreme Court decisions which have held that estoppel and waiver are not available against the non-observance of those requirements: ('80) A.SC. 1285, 1290.

[25] *Commrs. of Crown Lands* v. *Page* (1960) 2 Q.B. 274, at p. 293.

[26] ibid.

[27] ibid. at p. 292. "No one can imagine, for example, that when the Crown makes a contract which could not be fulfilled in time of war, it is pledging itself not to declare war for so long as the contract lasts": ibid. (*per* Devlin L.J.).

Two questions raised by conferment of discretionary power

(*h*) Where a statute confers on Government or a public officer discretionary power, two questions arise. First, can he fetter the future exercise of his discretionary power? Secondly, can he contend that discretionary power enables him to act in the public interest, and as long as he acts in good faith his actions are unreviewable by a Court?

The two lines of cases according as public law or private law considerations are appropriate

(*i*) The question whether a public authority can fetter the future exercise of his power requires a scrutiny of the statute, rule or regulation which confers the discretionary power. The decided cases fall into two broad categories according as the law conferring the power involves considerations appropriate to public law or to private law. As to laws conferring discretionary power where public law considerations are appropriate, Lord Birkenhead said in *Stockport Corpn.* v. *Birkdale Electricity Co. Ltd.*[28] that the well-established principle of law was

"... that if a person or public body is entrusted by the Legislature with certain powers and duties expressly or impliedly for public purposes, those persons or bodies cannot divest themselves of those powers or duties. They cannot enter into any contract or take any action incompatible with the due exercise of their powers or the discharge of their duties."[29]

Discretionary power governed by public law consideration: Lord Blackburn's classic formulation of the principle

The classic statement of this principle is to be found in the judgment of Lord Blackburn in *Ayr Harbour Trustees* v. *Oswald*[30]

"I think that where the legislature confer powers on any body to take lands compulsorily for a particular purpose, it is on the ground that the using of that land for that purpose will be for the public good. Whether that body be one which is seeking to make a profit for shareholders, or, as in the present case, a body of trustees acting solely for the public good, I think in either case the powers conferred on the body empowered to take the land compulsorily are intrusted to them, and their successors, to be used for the furtherance of that object which the legislature has thought sufficiently for the public good to justify it in entrusting them with such powers; and, consequently, that a contract purporting to bind them and their successors not to use those powers is void."[31]

The reader will have noticed that the judgment of Kailasam J. in *Jit Ram's Case* fell squarely within this principle when he held that the Municipal Committee could not by a contract give up its power to levy octroi duty. (see para 10.213). In the graphic words of Lord Sumner, the Municipal Committee had "renounced a part of their statutory birthright".[32]

Exercise of discretionary power where private law considerations are appropriate: the *Bournemouth Corpn. Case*:

(*j*) However, the two decisions discussed below, illustrate the line of cases in which, the future exercise of discretionary power conferred by or under a statute is governed by considerations appropriate to private law. *Stourcliffe Estates Co. Ltd.* v. *Corpn. of Bournemouth*[33] is instructive. There, the Bournemouth Corporation which had power under s. 164 of the Public Health Act, 1875 to purchase land for the purpose of being used as public parks or pleasure grounds; and under s. 85 of the Bournemouth Improvement Act, 1892, the Corporation had power, *inter alia,* to construct a urinal or urinals. By agreement, the Corporation purchased land from the plaintiff company and covenanted with the company that the Corporation would

[28] (1926) A.C. 355.
[29] ibid. p. 364.
[30] (1883) 8 App.Cas. 623.
[31] ibid. p. 634.
[32] (1926) A.C. *supra* at p. 371.
[33] (1910) 2 Ch. 12.

"preserve and keep the land to be devoted to pleasure ground purposes as an open space for the enjoyment of the public in such manner and form as the corporation shall think best in the interest of the public subject to no building or erections of any kind being put thereupon except such structures as summer houses a band stand or shelters not more than 12 feet in height for the accommodation and convenience of the public."[34]

Covenant in purchase of land by agreement given by the Corpn.

The Corporation proposed to construct urinals on the pleasure ground; and the Plaintiff brought an action to restrain the corporation from doing so. The Corporation contended, first, that the urinal fell within the covenant which permitted the erection of a shelter, a contention which was rejected by the Trial Court and the Court of Appeal. The main contention urged by the Corporation was that by the said covenant the Corporation had fettered the future exercise of its statutory powers, and the covenant was *ultra vires* the Corporation and void, on the principle of *Ayr Harbour Case* [which has been set out in (i) above]. This contention was rejected by both the Courts which held that the line of cases of which the *Ayr Harbour Case* was the leading case, had no application. Buckley L.J. brought out most clearly the legal issue involved. But before stating his reasoning, it may be observed that it is obvious that to confer on a public authority the power to enter into contracts necessarily means that as long as the contract subsists, the powers of the public authority are limited by the terms of that contract. Consequently, if a public authority cannot in any case fetter the future exercise of its statutory discretion, it would be unable to enter into a contract, and it would be absurd to confer on it the power to enter into a contract. Buckley L.J. said that both on principle and on authority, the agreement with the plaintiff company was not *ultra vires* the Corporation. He observed that s. 164 of the Public Health Act conferred on the Corporation the power to purchase land by agreement, and s. 176 of that Act also conferred on the Corporation the power to acquire land compulsorily. These two modes of acquiring land, the first by agreement and the second by compulsory acquisition were different. To acquire land compulsorily, the purpose for which it was being acquired by the Corporation had to be indicated. The adjoining owners may, on a local inquiry, object to the land being acquired for the purpose. A Local Government Board might authorize the Corporation to acquire land either absolutely or subject to conditions and modifications and the Corporation would be limited as regards the way in which they were to use the land for the purpose for which it was acquired. Reasonable conditions on the user of the land to be acquired for a public park may be imposed, as for example, that the park should be closed at certain stated hours and the like. The case before the Court was not one of compulsory acquisition. However, the Corporation's power to purchase land also involved a definite purpose, in respect of which they were entitled to acquire land by agreement. The Corporation could say "We offer to buy your land and we will bind ourselves not to put a urinal there".[35] It was said that in doing so the Corporation would be divesting itself of its powers under s. 85 which conferred on the Corporation the power to erect urinals. Buckley L.J. rightly observed that s. 85 only meant that it was not an improper

Lord Blackburn's principle not applicable. Buckley L.J. brings out the issues involved

[34] ibid. pp. 12-13.

[35] ibid. p. 22.

expenditure for the Corporation to erect urinals in proper places but it was not necessary that with every piece of land which the Corporation should buy, the Corporation should acquire the right to put up urinals. On authority, Buckley L.J. said that the *Ayr Harbour Case* had no application:

"I fail to see how (that Case) has any application to this case. There you find particular lands which the particular authority is authorized to take upon the footing that they want them for their undertaking, and for the purposes of their undertaking the statute has said they shall have certain powers. The House (of Lords) only decided that as regards land thus acquired the authority cannot release the powers which the Act of Parliament has attached to those lands. In the present case I think it clear that the corporation were entitled to acquire this land subject to the limitation expressed in the covenant to this deed."[36]

The *Southport Corpn. Case*: supply of electricity in the exercise of statutory powers

The above case related to the purchase of land under a contract. The decision of the House of Lords in *Birkdale Dist. Electricity Supply Co.* v. *Southport Corpn.*[37] is the leading authority on the question whether in a commercial contract a public authority could bind itself to exercise its powers in the future in a specified way. In the *Southport Case*, Orders passed under the authority of the Electric Lighting Act of 1882, the Birkdale Urban Dist. Council ("the Council") were empowered to supply and distribute electricity for all public and private purposes within the Urban District of Birkdale as then constituted. The power of the Council was transferred to the appellant company with the approval of the Board of Trade, and the contractual rights and obligations of the Council were transferred to the respondent Corporation. The Council had power to charge up to a certain maximum price for the supply of electricity. But the Council had the authority to make special agreements with particular consumers as to price. The Company agreed with the Council not to charge higher price than those charged in the adjoining borough of Southport. The company having begun to charge higher prices than those charged by the Corporation, the Corporation brought an action to restrain the company's breach of the aforesaid agreement. The company contended that the agreement was *ultra vires, inter alia,* under the general law applicable to statutory undertakings. For the company, reliance was placed on the well-settled principle which Lord Birkenhead enunciated, which has been set out in para 10.215 (*i*) above. The House of Lords held that the principle of those cases had no application to the present case. It seems to have been argued that in entering into an agreement the Council fettered its power because the Southport Corporation may charge a very small price, relying upon their power to raise revenue by increasing the rates and if this happened the company would suffer serious losses and be unable to discharge its functions under the Act properly. Dealing with this argument, Lord Sumner said:

An agreement fixing the price to be charged in the future not *ultra vires* and does not attract Lord Blackburn's principle

Observations of Lord Sumner

"My Lords, this hypothesis is conceivable, though neither from the evidence nor the argument have I gathered why these machinations should be attributed to the respondents or be tolerated by their outraged ratepayers. Municipal finance is capable of much curious development, but I think that among ordinary ratepayers a passion to supply current below cost price to private consumers is purely academic. If it exists at Southport, I think it should be proved by testimony."[38]

---

[36] ibid. p. 23.
[37] (1926) A.C. 355.
[38] ibid. pp. 372-3.

Lord Sumner observed that there was no true analogy between cases like *Ayr Harbour Case* and the present one. He said:

Lord Sumner distinguished the *Ayr Harbour Case*

"On examining the facts in the *Ayr Harbour Case* it is plain that, in effect, the trustees did not merely propose to covenant in a manner that committed the business of the harbour to restricted lines in the future; they were to forbear, once and for all, to acquire all that the statute intended them to acquire, for, though technically they acquired the whole of the land, they were to sterilize part of their acquisition, so far as the statutory purpose of their undertaking was concerned. . . . If the Ayr trustees had reduced the acquisition price by covenanting with the respondent for a perpetual right to moor his barges, free of tolls, at any wharf they might construct on the water front of the land acquired, the decision might, and I think would, have been different."[39]

It may be added that as to the argument that the agreement was *ultra vires* and void as it might result in the company suffering serious losses, thereby disabling itself from performing its duties under the Act, the judgments in the Court of Appeal and the House of Lords show that the question whether the company made a profit or suffered a loss, or the question whether the agreement was commercially prudent or imprudent was irrelevant to the powers conferred by the Act. In this context, Sargent L.J. observed:

Sargent L.J. on "extra-ordinary" extension of the doctrine of *ultra vires*

". . . That is one of the risks which has to be run by a concern carried on for the purpose of profit. In my judgment it would be an extraordinary extension of this doctrine of *ultra vires* or repugnancy to say that in such a case as this, a commercial undertaking was deprived of its ordinary discretion as to fixing the price at which the services rendered or commodity supplied should be rendered or supplied"[40]

The decision of the House of Lords shows that a corporation or company charged with the duty of supplying a public service under the provisions of an Act, or Orders made thereunder, with power to enter into contracts does not fetter the future exercise of its powers if it enters into a commercial contract on commercial considerations. And this is not the less so because what was considered to be a prudent contract turns out to be imprudent. Such risks are incidental to carrying on business.

Discussion has covered the first three propositions in *Jit Ram's Case*

10.217 Our discussion in para 10.216 above has covered the first three propositions laid down by Kailasam J. in *Jit Ram's Case* set out in para 10.215 above. These propositions are correct as far as they go, but they require to be explained, qualified and modified in the manner explained in para 10.216 above.

A criticism of the 4th and 5th proposition in *Jit Ram's Case*

10.218 Proposition (4) in para 20.215 above can hardly be said to lay down a proposition about promissory estoppel, because it envisages an officer acting within the scope of his authority (i) under a scheme *and* (ii) entering into an agreement and (iii) making a representation to a person who acts on it to his disadvantage. But the situation thus described has not arisen in the cases which have come before the Supreme Court. The export promotion schemes which have come before the Supreme Court have differed in their provisions, and different considerations apply to different schemes. Secondly, in such schemes, officers who administer them do not enter into "agreements". Their task has been to allot import or export quotas. It would be unprofitable to pursue this discussion further, for the proposition postulates that there is a "scheme" and no single

[39] ibid. p. 371.

[40] (1925) 1 Ch. *supra* at p. 824.

proposition can be affirmed about different schemes. Thus, in *Ramchand's Case* an export promotion scheme for artsilk sarees, fabrics, garments, hosiery, etc., was announced. Government having come to learn of malpractices by importers of artsilk yarns[41] suspended the scheme, but directed that pending applications with the port licensing authorities would be scrutinized by a Committee appointed by the Government of India. As stated earlier,[42–99] on a scrutiny by the Committee the petitioner's claim for 100 per cent quota under the scheme was reduced, and the reduction was upheld as imposing a reasonable restriction in the public interest on the right to carry on business. Proposition (5) is consequential on proposition (4) and for the same reasons it need not be discussed further.

The great merit of Bhagwati J.'s judgment in the *Sugar Mills Case*

10.219 In the result some of the wide propositions in the judgment of Bhagwati J. in the *Sugar Mills Case* cannot be sustained in the light of our discussion on promissory estoppel. However, the great merit of his judgment lies in his reaffirming the proposition that the Crown in England and the State in India is amenable to promissory estoppel in certain situations. And although there can be no promissory estoppel against public authorities discharging public duties in the "public interest", the phrase "public interest" is not a magical incantation which bars judicial review. On the contrary, an alleged public interest which is said to justify a departure from a representation on which a person has acted to his detriment must be proved to the satisfaction of the Court. The present writer would like to add that keeping faith with persons by honouring representations solemnly made by the state or by public officials acting within the scope of their authority, and entrusted with authority over the subject matter of the representation, is itself a public interest of high value. For, few greater injuries can be done to a State than that its people should cease to believe the pledged word of the State or of public officials discharging public duties.

Right to acquire, hold and dispose of property

Narendra Kumar's Case

10.220 *Narendra Kumar's Case*[1] has been considered earlier[2] as an authority for the proposition that "restrictions" in Art. 19(2) to (6) include prohibition; it must now be considered in connection with the circumstances under which "prohibition" may be upheld as involving "reasonable restrictions". In that case the petitioners challenged Cls. 3 and 4, Non-ferrous Metal Control Order, 1958, made under s. 3, Essential Commodities Act, 1955. The effect of the order was that trade in copper could only be carried on according to a permit issued in accordance with such principles as the Central Government may specify. No principles were specified in a communication to the Chief Industrial Adviser. The petitioners who had applied for, but were refused, permits, impugned Cls. 3 and 4 of the Order, read with the principles communicated by Government to the Chief Adviser, as violating their rights under Art. 19 and

restrictions amounting to prohibition upheld: control of import of copper

---

[41] See ('63) A.SC. at pp. 565-8 where some of the malpractices have been described.

[42–99] See para 10.175.

[1] (1960) 2 S.C.R. 375, ('60) A.SC. 430.

[2] See para 10.2.

as violating their rights under Art. 14 since the principles discriminated between manufacturers and dealers. Before dealing with these contentions, the Court observed:

Test of reasonableness

"In applying the test of reasonableness, the court has to consider the question in the background of the facts and circumstances under which the order was made, taking into account *the nature of the evil sought to be remedied by such law, the ratio of the harm caused to individual citizens by the proposed remedy, to the beneficial effect reasonably expected to result to the general public.* It will also be necessary to consider . . . whether the restraint caused by the law is more than was necessary in the interest of the general public."[3] (italics supplied)

The Court held that Cls. 3 and 4 imposed reasonable restrictions having regard to the following considerations: very little copper was produced in India although copper was very largely required by industries in India. For this reason copper was kept on an open general licence, but as the foreign exchange position worsened, a licensing system was introduced, both for established importers and actual consumers. Later licences were granted only to established importers. The results were disastrous, as established importers exploited their monopoly position and prices shot up from Rs. 2,221 a ton to Rs. 3,477 a ton. It was not disputed that public interest was seriously affected. It was to meet this situation that the impugned orders were passed. Under the circumstances a permit system with price control must be regarded as reasonable. The elimination of the middleman, which would result from the commission being fixed at three and a half per cent was also, under the circumstances, justifiable. Consequently Cls. 3 and 4 did not violate Art. 19(1)(*g*).[4]

Premier Automobiles Case

10.221 In *Premier Automobiles Ltd.* v. *Union*[5] the petitioners challenged the price of three cars, manufactured by them, which had been fixed under the undernoted provisions.[6] For reasons which do not appear from the judgment, the Court recommended to the Government of India to appoint a Commission for the purpose of suggesting a fair price for the three cars, and a Commission was appointed.[7] After it had made its report, and the prices had been fixed accordingly, for reasons which must have appeared adequate to the parties, including the Union of India,

The agreement between the parties

"Counsel of all the parties and the learned Att.-General are agreed that irrespective of the technical or legal points that may be involved, we should base our judgment on examination of correct and rational principles and should direct deviations from the report of the Commission which was an expert body presided over by a former Judge of a High Court only when it is shown that there has been a departure from established principles or the conclusions of the Commission are shown to be demonstrably wrong or erroneous."[8]

---

[3] (1960) 2 S.C.R. *supra* at pp. 387-8.

[4] *Bhatnagars & Co. Ltd.* v. *Union* (1957) S.C.R. 701, ('57) A.SC. 478; raised similar questions. There, the import policy was impugned as violative of Art. 19(1)(*g*) on the ground, among others, that canalising the import trade in soda ash through two big companies, namely, Imperial Chemical Industries (India) Ltd., and Tata Oil Mills Co. Ltd., created a monopoly and in any event, violated the petitioner's right to carry on business guaranteed by Art. 19(1)(*g*). After setting out considerations relevant in considering an import policy, the Court found that the canalisation of trade in soda ash was necessary to prevent fluctuations in the market and accordingly the restrictions imposed by the policy did not violate Art. 19(1)(*g*).

[5] (1972) 2 S.C.R. 524, ('72) A.SC. 1690.

[6] The Motor Car Distribution and Sale Control (Amendment) Order, 1969, passed under s. 18G of the Industries (Development and Regulation) Act, 1951.

[7] ibid. pp. 531-2. [8] ibid. p. 535.

The Court's judgment was delivered according to this agreement. In the course of its judgment, the Supreme Court said:

"The concept of fair price fixed under s. 18G takes in all the elements to make it fair for the consumer leaving a reasonable margin of profit to the manufacturer without which no one will engage in any manufacturing activity."[9]

After an elaborate discussion, the Court gave certain directions, and further directed that the prices should be revised every six months bearing in mind the relevant principles. In other words, in substance, the Court provided an escalator clause for fixing the prices of cars. It is unnecessary to discuss this judgment further in view of the observations made on it in *Shree Meenakshi Mills* v. *Union.*[10] The Supreme Court said:

The limitations of the *Premier Automobiles Case*

"*The Premier Automobiles* . . . decision does not consider that the concept of fair prices varies with circumstances in which and the purposes for which the price control is sought to be imposed. This decision *because of the special agreement there* does not consider that the fixation of fair price with a view to holding the price line may be stultified by allowing periodic increase in price."[11] (italics supplied)

Meenakshi Mills Case

10.222 In *Shree Meenakshi Mills Case,*[12] the notifications fixing the price of cotton yarn and directing the producer to deliver yarn only to five channels of distribution mentioned therein were impugned on various grounds of which the contentions relating to the present discussion were, that if contrary to the petitioner's submission, the provisions of the Cotton Textile Control Order were interpreted as conferring arbitrary power on the Textile Commissioner to fix prices for yarn unrelated to the cost of production and reasonable profits to the producer, those provisions were void as violating, *inter alia,* Arts. 19(*f*) and (*g*); that as the impugned notification had fixed the price of cotton yarn arbitrarily, and without referring to relevant factors such as cost of production and reasonable return, such notification was wholly arbitrary and based on irrelevant considerations and was therefore void, as violating the petitioner's fundamental rights.[13] The provisions for canalization were also impugned; but the Supreme Court repelled this challenge, it is submitted rightly, by reference to the *Glass Chatons Case, Dava's Case* and *Daruka's Case* considered above.[14] The Supreme Court set out in great detail the history of Government's attempts since 1960 to provide for fair prices for cotton textiles, including the reports of Tariff Commissions and the report of the Commodity Control Committee. This history dealt with the technical problems involved in fixing the fair price of textiles (which include yarn) and is too long to set out here.[15] After setting out the history, the Court observed:

History of price fixation of textiles

Considerations relevant to fixing a fair price with a view to hold the price line

"In a largely free economy when controls have to be introduced to ensure availability of consumer goods like foodstuff, cloth and the like at a fair price it is an impracticable proposition to require the Government to go through the exercise like that of a Commission to fix the prices. The Tariff Board and the Tariff Commission *did not deal with the question of fixing prices with a view only to holding price line* and in the circumstances that justify giving pre-eminent preference to the interest of the consumer or general public over that of the producers of the commodity and the dealers. *Even these Commis-*

---

[9] ibid. pp. 549-50.
[10] (1974) 2 S.C.R. 398, ('74) A.SC. 366.
[11] ('74) A.SC. at p. 380.
[12] *Supra.*
[13] ('74) A.SC. at pp. 374-5.
[14] See para 10.174 of the text.
[15] ('74) A.SC. at pp. 373-8.

sions cannot always make a correct estimate of a price which is fair to all because there are intricacies of the trade of all profit making enterprises which a Commission may not be able to probe. As an illustration, *the Tariff Commission Report points out that many textile mills use cotton mixes with a view to reducing cost and the result of such mixes* is difficult to discern.

When available stocks go underground and the Government has to step in to control distribution and availability in public interest fixing of price can, therefore, be only empirical. Market prices at a time when the goods did not go underground and were freely available, *the capacity of the consumer specially in case of consumer goods like foodstuff, cloth etc. the amount of loss which the industry is able to absorb after having made huge profits in prosperous years,* all these enter into the calculation of a fair price in an exigency created by artificial shortages."[16] (italics supplied)

It adopted the test of reasonableness laid down in *Narendra Kumar's Case* (set out in para 10.220 above) and observed that in that case in order to make copper available at a reasonable price, the elimination of middlemen was justified. The Court then referred to *Union* v. *Bhanamal Gulzarimal*[17] where, in upholding the fixation of maximum price of iron and steel,[18] Gajendragadkar J. observed that in considering the validity of the impugned notification it was not enough to show that a particular registered stock holder suffered loss, but if

The test of reasonableness: *Narendra Kumar's Case*

Bhanamal Gulzarimal's Case

". . . it is shown that in a large majority of cases, if not all, the impugned notification would adversely affect the fundamental right of the dealers guaranteed under Arts. 19(1)(*f*) and (*g*) that may constitute a serious infirmity in the validity of the notification."[19]

The Court referred to the unreported decision of the Supreme Court in *Sri Krishna Rice Mills* v. *Jt. Director (Food), Vijayawada*[20] where it was held that s. 3 of the Essential Commodities Act sufficiently specified the principles on the basis of which prices should be fixed. In that case, in respect of rice procured by government under the impugned notification, the maximum price fixed was lower than the price which the Mills had paid for it. It was held that unless the fixation of the price was unfair the impugned notification would not be invalid.

Sri Krishna Rice Mills' Case

"The Court found that the prices fixed were fair, because the reason for the reduction of prices of December, 1957 was that new crop came into the market from November, 1957 and the market prices of rice fell. When prices fall, traders who had made purchases at higher prices have to sell at the reduced rates and therefore, they cannot complain against rise and fall of prices due to economic factors in an open market. Just as the industry cannot complain of rise and fall of prices due to economic factors in an open market they cannot similarly complain of increase or reduction of prices as a result of notification under s. 3(1) of the Essential Commodities Act, 1955 because that increase or reduction is also based on economic factors."[21]

Rajasthan v. *Nathmal*[22] was distinguished. Two cases, which had been relied upon for the petitioners, namely, *Panipat Co-op. Sugar*

Cases distinguished

---

[16] ibid. p. 381.

[17] (1960) 2 S.C.R. 627, ('60) A.SC. 475.

[18] Under the Iron and Steel (Control of Production and Distribution) Order, 1941 issued pursuant to s. 3 of the Essential Commodities Act.

[19] ('60) A.SC. *supra* at p. 482.

[20] ('74) A.SC. *supra* at p. 378: C.A. Nos. 1026-31 of 1963; Judgment delivered on 27.1.1965 (S.C.).

[21] ibid. p. 378.

[22] (1954) S.C.R. 982, ('54) A.SC. 307; it had also been distinguished in *Union* v. *Bhanamal Gulzarimal, supra.* It is submitted that the distinction made in *Bhanamal's Case* is correct.

Mills v. *Union*[23] and *Anakapalle Co-op. Agricultural & Industrial Society Ltd.* v. *Union*[24] were also distinguished as arising under s. 3(3C) of the Essential Commodities Act and as not relevant to the discussion before the Court. In summarising the conclusion, the Court observed that in determining the reasonableness of a restriction in the field of industry, trade or commerce the mere fact that some of those who were engaged in them alleged that they suffered a loss after the imposition of the law would not render the law unreasonable. By its very nature, industry, trade or commerce went through periods of prosperity and adversity on account of economic and sometimes social and political factors. In fixing the fair price of consumer goods, the machinery of a Tariff Commission and the like may not be practicable since a correct estimate could not be made of certain factors.[25] The petition was dismissed.

Conclusion: trade and business involve loss as well as gain

The importance of *Meenakshi Mills Case*

10.223 *Shree Meenakshi Mills Case* is important because it emphasises, for the first time, that if the object of the law is to hold the price line, so as to make certain essential commodities available to the public or to the trade, at a fair price, it must be borne in mind that trade and business is not always carried on at a profit; that losses may also have to be suffered, and that therefore an automatic revision of prices to secure a "fair return" would, under certain circumstances, nullify the very object of the law. The implications of this judgment would have to be worked out in several cases, dealing with different situations, before a reasonably clear principle can be laid down. But *Meenakshi Mills Case* marks a departure from the fixed belief that trade and business must automatically yield a "reasonable return".

Restrictions to prevent evasion of import and export control upheld: S. 178-A, Sea Customs Act and gold smuggling

10.224 Just as the executive judgment that a particular export or import policy is necessary has been upheld, so also has the legislative judgment been upheld that certain policies are necessary to prevent the evasion of import and export control through smuggling. This can best be illustrated by reference to a number of cases under s. 178-A, Sea Customs Act, which applies to gold, gold manufactures, diamonds, etc., and other goods which may be notified by the Central Government in that behalf, and it provides that where goods to which that section applies are seized under the Act in the reasonable belief that they were smuggled goods, the burden of proving that they were not smuggled goods is on the person from whose possession the goods were seized. Confining this discussion to the smuggling of gold, from 1939 gold could be imported into India only with the permission of the Reserve Bank of India. These restrictions on the import of gold led to a great disparity between the internal and the international price of gold, and furnished a great incentive to smuggling, which besides depriving the State of its revenue, also posed a grave threat to national economy. The Taxation Inquiry Commission recommended that smuggling should be made a criminal offence and that the onus of proof in respect of smuggling should be shifted to the accused. S. 178-A carried out the latter recommendation. S. 178-A was impugned as

---

[23] (1973) 2 S.C.R. 860, ('73) A.SC. 537.
[24] (1973) 2 S.C.R. 882, ('73) A.SC. 734.
[25] ('74) A.SC. *supra* at p. 381.

violating Art. 14 in *Babulal Amthalal Mehta* v. *Collector of Customs, Calcutta*[26] but the Supreme Court repelled the challenge. That case did not decide any challenge to s. 178-A under Art. 19(1) (*f*) or (*g*).[27] But that challenge was made in *M. G. Abrol* v. *Amichand*[28] and was upheld by K. T. Desai J. on the ground that the burden of proof was incapable of being discharged. The Madras High Court adopted the same view in *N. S. Chetty* v. *Collector of Customs.*[29] The Nagpur Bench of the Bombay High Court in *Pukhraj Jain* v. *D. R. Kohli*[30] dissented from the Bombay and Madras judgments and held the section valid, apparently because of certain administrative directions issued by the Central Board of Revenue in relation to s. 178-A.[31] In *Collector of Customs* v. *Sampathu Chetty*[32] the Supreme Court upheld the validity of s. 178-A. Although several issues were raised in the appeal, the principal argument in support of the unreasonableness of s. 178-A was that it was impossible for a person to discharge the burden of proof that the gold, or the gold articles, in his possession had entered India with the permission of the Reserve Bank of India. Gold had no earmark, was capable of infinite manipulation by fusion and fission, and large quantities of gold had been imported into India before the requirement of a permit from the Reserve Bank was imposed. The position as regards the import of gold and the quantity of gold in India as stated by K. T. Desai J. in the Bombay case was accepted by all the parties as correct.[33] The Supreme Court said that s. 106, Evidence Act, had not been challenged as unconstitutional, and therefore there was nothing unconstitutional in throwing the burden of proof on a person when the relevant facts were within his special knowledge, and *prima facie* the person in possession of gold was best qualified to account for his possession. Where gold was seized from persons charged with being concerned in the act of illicit transportation, it was not disputed that the burden of proof could be laid upon them. Nor was it disputed that a person in possession of gold could be asked to explain his possession. The Supreme Court held that the above classes of cases would constitute most of the cases in which suspicion or information of the type which led to seizure and the ensuing proceedings would occur. But s. 178-A also applied to a person who was able to account for his possession though the person or persons from whom he purchased the gold may be unable to account for their possession. After referring to the test of reasonableness laid down in *Row's Case*[34] the Supreme Court said that though gold was not a noxious or dangerous commodity in itself, gold-smuggling had assumed proportions which threatened the national economy and the effective fulfilment of the objectives of foreign trade control. Apart from its effect on revenue and deleterious effect on legitimate trade, it required an expensive machinery for law enforcement because of the extensive coast-line and large land frontiers of India. The Taxation Inquiry Commission

Conflicting decisions on the validity of s. 178-A

S. 178-A upheld by the Supreme Court

[26] (1957) S.C.R. 1110, ('57) A.SC. 877.
[27] See ('62) A.SC. 316, at pp. 324-5.
[28] 62 Bom.L.R. 1043.
[29] ('59) A.M. 142.
[30] (1959) Bom. 1771; 61 Bom.L.R. 1230.
[31] In *Collector of Customs* v. *Sampathu Chetty* (1962) 3 S.C.R. 786, ('62) A.SC. 316 at pp. 322-3, it was rightly held that administrative directions would not make a law valid if it was otherwise void.
[32] (1962) 3 S.C.R. *supra*.
[33] See ('62) A.SC. 316 at p. 326 where the statement is set out in full.
[34] See para 10.18.

S. 178-A held reasonable even though oppressive in marginal cases

had said that it was necessary "... that stringent measures both legal and administrative should be adopted with a view to minimising the scope of this evil." Since the objective to be attained was within legislative power, and since without a provision of the type enacted in s. 178-A, that objective could not be effectively attained, the Supreme Court said that s. 178-A must be held to impose reasonable restrictions even though in marginal cases it operated harshly or oppressively. It cited its earlier decision in *Manhori Lal* v. *Punjab*[35] and *Ramdhandas* v. *Punjab*[36] to show that acts innocent in themselves may be prohibited, and that restrictions in that regard may be held reasonable, if they were necessary to secure the efficient enforcement of a valid law.[37] In *Harakchand* (*H. R. Banthia*) v. *Union*[38] ("*Banthia's Case*") without reference to its earlier decisions[39] the Supreme Court held that in considering the reasonableness of gold control, the evil effects of smuggling of gold on the national economy must be borne in mind.[40] The Court struck down ss. 27 (2) (*d*),[41] 27 (6), 32, 46, 88 and 100 of the Gold (Control) Act, 1968, as imposing unreasonable restrictions under Art. 19. The Court further held that if ss. 27 (2) (*d*) and 27 (6) were invalid, the final scheme contemplated by the rest of s. 27 was unworkable, and Parliament would have to enact fresh legislation or, in the alternative, to make necessary rules under s. 114 of the Act. Following the decision in *Banthia's Case*, it was held in *Gem Palace* v. *Union*[42] that s. 6 (1) of the Gold (Control) Act which enabled the Administrator to demand a "return" from any person in respect of the transactions there mentioned, *inter alia*, imposed unreasonable restrictions and was invalid. However, the provisions of s. 16 (5),[43] s. 27 (8),[44] and s. 52 read with the amended s. 27 (6), were held not to impose unreasonable restrictions. In *B. Narasimhalu* v. *Central Govt.*[46] it was held that Rule 3 (ee) of the Gold Control (Licensing of Dealers) Rules, 1969, made under s. 114 of the Gold Control Act, 1968,[47] was *ultra vires* the rule making power as it did not carry out the purposes of the Act, and was unconstitutional as it put unreasonable restrictions on the fundamental right of gold dealers to carry on their business. Rule 3 (ee) also violated Art. 14 as it laid down no guidelines for determining when turnover was

---

35 (1961) 2 S.C.R. 343, ('61) A.SC. 418. 36 (1962) 1 S.C.R. 852, ('61) A.SC. 1559.

37 Fol. and appl. in *Gem Palace* v. *Union* ('70) A.Raj. 225, 227 (*held*, that in considering the reasonableness of the restrictions imposed by the Gold Control Act, 1968, the grave injury caused to the economy of India by the smuggling of gold must be borne in mind).

38 (1970) 1 S.C.R. 479, ('70) A.SC. 1453.

39 *Collector of Customs* v. *Sampathu Chetty* ('62) A.SC. 316, 322-3, where the Court pointed out the evil effects on the economy of the country by the smuggling of gold.

40 The Court referred to and applied the test of reasonableness given by Sastri C.J. in *Madras* v. *V. G. Row* (1952) S.C.R. 597, 607 (see para 10.18 of the text).

41 Set out in ('70) A.SC. *supra* at pp. 1456-7.

42 ('70) A.Raj. 225. 43 ibid. p. 230.

44 ibid. pp. 231-2. 45 ibid. p. 233.

46 ('76) A.M. 224.

47 *R. 3(ee)*: That the turnover of the applicant in the twelve months immediately preceding the date of application for renewal of the licence was too low. *Explanation*: For the purpose of this clause, low turnover means a turnover which is on the average, not more than 50 grammes per month except where the applicant satisfies the Administrator that there are sufficient reasons for an average monthly turnover of lower than 50 grammes.

"too low", and the Explanation to the Rule conferred arbitrary power on the licensing authorities to treat a low turnover as not a low turnover in granting a renewal of licence. After the above decision was given, R. 3(ee) was amended to remove the defects which had been pointed out by the Madras High Court. Accordingly, in *Sohan Lal* v. *Union*[48] it was held that R. 3(ee) as amended in 1976 did not violate Art. 19(1)(*g*) and Art. 14.

10.225 In *Badri Prasad* v. *Collector, C.E.*[49] several provisions of the Gold Control Act, 1968 were again challenged. The Court held that s. 16(1) of the Act which required a pawn broker to make monthly declarations in a prescribed form did not impose unreasonable restrictions on his rights under Art. 19(1)(*f*) and (*g*). Again, s. 68 which provided for confiscation proceedings but did not provide for giving a notice to the pawn broker prior to confiscation proceedings caused him no prejudice since under s. 99 a pawn broker was presumed to be the owner of gold and he could appear and show cause for not taking any penal action against him. However, the Court held that s. 71 which provided for confiscation of gold on the failure of the pawn broker to submit monthly returns imposed unreasonable restrictions on a person's right to acquire, hold and dispose of gold and gold ornaments and was void as violating Art. 19(1)(*f*) and (*g*). In *Kashi Nath* v. *Collector, C.E.*,[50] the Court held that though they were bound by the law laid down by the Supreme Court, the *ratio* of the decision should not be extended to points which did not arise for adjudication in that case. The Court held that although ss. 71 and 73 of the Act were held unconstitutional by the Supreme Court in *Badri Prasad's Case,* those sections had been amended and the unreasonableness of confiscating the property of the real owner in the hands of a pawn broker merely for his omission to make a declaration under s. 16 had been mitigated by suitable amendment. Sections 71 and 73 as amended were therefore *intra vires*. Consequently, ss. 74 and 75 which were dependent on ss. 71 and 72 were also *intra vires*.

10.226 That a Court would not be in a position to pronounce on the reasonableness of an import-export policy because it involved the weighing of several imponderable factors which involve political judgment, and would have to conform to the policies which command the support of the legislatures, is true also of tax laws, as is clear from the cases considered earlier[51] and is true of all laws where the policy content is very large. Thus, in ***Joseph Vellukunnel*** v. ***Reserve Bank of India***[52] the Court upheld by a majority of 3 to 2 the constitutional validity of s. 38(1) and (3)(*b*)(iii), Banking Companies Act, on the ground that there may be occasions and situations in which the legislature may with reason think that the determination of an issue may be left to an expert executive like the Reserve Bank rather than to Courts, without incurring the penalty of having the law

Power of the Reserve Bank to apply for winding up a bank; upheld by a majority

[48] ('79) A.A. 93.
[49] (1971) Supp. S.C.R. 254, ('71) A.SC. 1170.
[50] ('76) A.A. 35.
[51] See para 9.44.
[52] (1962) Supp. (3) S.C.R. 632, ('62) A.SC. 137; *E. Ambooken* v. *Reserve Bank of India* ('66) A.Ker. 6, 11 (s. 35-B of the Banking Companies Act was valid as action under it was governed by the object and purposes of the Act. The refusal to approve the appointment of the petitioner as Managing Director was upheld on the assumption that the right to act as a Managing Director was a fundamental right, although the Court considered such an assumption doubtful).

declared void, as violating Art. 19(1)(*f*) and (*g*). In view of the history of the establishment of the Reserve Bank as the Central Bank for India, its position as a bankers' bank, its control over banking companies and banking in India, its position as an issuing bank, its power to license banks and cancel their licences, and numerous other powers, it was unanswerable that as between the Court and the Reserve Bank, the momentous decision to wind up a tottering or unsafe banking company in the interest of depositors may reasonably be left to the Reserve Bank. No doubt the Court could also, given the time, perform this task. But where swift action was necessary, the Reserve Bank had, and the Court had not, the relevant material within its knowledge, so that if immediate action were demanded it would be impossible for the Court to reach a conclusion unguided by the Reserve Bank. In a dissenting judgment Kapur J. held that any law which enabled the company to be wound up on the subjective satisfaction of the Reserve Bank, was unconstitutional. If there was urgency, and a proper case was made out, the Court would act with promptitude and make such interim orders as the facts of the case may require, for example, the appointment of a provisional liquidator. It is submitted that the majority judgment is correct, and that Kapur J. did not attach sufficient importance to the fact that the Reserve Bank had, and the Court did not have, materials on which to form a judgment. Actual experience of the winding up of banking companies shows that an investigation into the affairs of banks to ascertain their real financial position would be a work of months, if not years.

Kapur J.'s dissent

Submission: majority judgment is correct

Cases in which arbitrary discretionary power held justified

10.227 Though the conferment of arbitrary discretionary power may expose a statute to challenge, there are certain exceptions, namely, (i) where it is difficult or impracticable to lay down a definite or comprehensive rule; (ii) where a licence is to be granted having regard to the personal fitness of the applicant; (iii) matters involving the exercise of discretion as to details in enforcing valid statutes.[53] In *Ram Gopal* v. *M.P.*[54] it was held that the impugned r. 12[55] did not violate Arts. 14 and 16. The contention that r. 12 conferred arbitrary and unguided discretion was devoid of merit, because the services of a temporary Government servant would have to be terminated whenever Government thought it necessary or expedient to do so for administrative reasons. As it was impossible to define beforehand all the circumstances in which the discretion could be exercised, such discretion had necessarily to be left to Government. But it must be added that where swift action and speedy decision are wanted for the maintenance of law and order or for the prevention of danger or injury to the public, a power exercisable on the subjective satisfaction of an authority must be upheld.[56]

Discretionary power to grant licences for places of public entertainment

10.228 Various Municipal Acts and Police Acts confer discretionary power on named authorities to grant licences and the question has often arisen whether the conferment of discretion to grant such licence violates fundamental rights. The requirement of a licence for a place of public entertainment was considered by the Supreme Court

[53] *Lumsden Club* v. *Punjab* (1957) Punj. 166, ('57) A.Punj. 20.
[54] (1970) 1 S.C.R. 472, ('70) A.SC. 158.
[55] M.P. Government Servants (Temporary and quasi-temporary Service) Rules, 1960.
[56] See, for example, *Virendra's Case* (1958) S.C.R. 308, 320, ('57) A.SC. 896.

in *Kishen Chand Arora* v. *Commr. of Police, Calcutta.*[57] It was contended that s. 39, Calcutta Police Act, 1866, gave naked and uncanalised power to the Commissioner to grant or refuse a licence, and no criteria had been laid down in the Act to guide his discretion, and no provision made for a hearing before the grant or refusal of a licence. By a majority of 3 to 2 Wanchoo J. for himself, Kapur and Gajendragadkar JJ. held that the discretion conferred by s. 39 was not absolute and unfettered and did not violate Art. 19 (1) (*g*) and added:

Power upheld by the majority in *Kishen Chand Arora's Case*

"We see no unfairness or unreasonableness in reading the section to mean that the Commissioner shall satisfy himself (i) that the person applying for a licence is the keeper of an eating house, meaning thereby that he has a place where he can carry on the business or trade and that he actually and effectively has control and possession of that place, (ii) that the keeper is a person of good behaviour so that the eating house may not become a resort of criminals and persons of ill-repute, and (iii) that the keeper is in a position to prevent drunkenness and disorder among those who come to the eating house. This section appears in the Police Act, the purpose of which is to maintain law and order and that is why we find that the two objects to be secured when granting licences are the good behaviour of the keeper himself and the prevention of drunkenness and disorder among those who frequent the eating house."[58]

If the conditions mentioned above were satisfied, it was not open to the Commissioner to refuse to grant a licence. The mere fact that there were no provisions for giving a hearing to the person applying for a licence did not necessarily constitute an unreasonable restriction on fundamental rights, and no case has been cited to that effect. Wanchoo J. relied on *Nakkuda Ali's Case*[59] for holding that it was quite possible to act reasonably without acting judicially. Subba Rao J. for himself and Sinha C.J. held that arbitrariness was writ large in s. 39; that as a matter of construction the absolute discretion of the Commissioner was not cut down by the conditions referred to in that section, and that even if the two conditions could be read into the first part of s. 39, even so, without deciding the question whether the discretion was judicial or executive,[60] the absence of an obligation to give a hearing and the absence of any provision for an appeal led to the conclusion that the restriction on the right to carry on trade or business was an unreasonable restriction. The majority judgment falls into two parts: that dealing with the nature of the discretion exercised by the Commissioner and that dealing with the omission in the Act to provide for a hearing. On the first part, it is submitted that the majority judgment is correct when it finds the principles for guidance in the Act itself; though its observations would suggest that this was being done particularly because the Act was a pre-Constitution Act. On the second part it is submitted that the decision is incorrect and the reference to *Nakkuda Ali's Case* was unfortunate. That case decided that when the Controller cancelled a licence he was withdrawing a privilege, but in India a licence is not a privilege but a matter of right and, secondly, as will appear

Dissenting judgment

A criticism of the decision

[57] (1961) 3 S.C.R. 135, ('61) A.SC. 705, fol. in *Commissioner of Police* v. *Lakshmi Chand* ('62) A.Cal. 556.

[58] (1961) 3 S.C.R. at pp. 144-5.

[59] (1951) A.C. 66.

[60] It is difficult to understand this reservation, for if the discretion is judicial it is amenable to *certiorari* or to an appeal to the Supreme Court under Art. 136 and the main objection to the reasonableness of conferring a discretion on the Commissioner would disappear.

hereafter,[61] the judgment in *Nakkuda Ali's Case* has been disapproved by the House of Lords in *Ridge* v. *Baldwin*.[62] It is submitted that now that it has been established that it is not necessary for an Act to contain a super-added obligation to act judicially, the grant or refusal of a licence on which the right of the person to acquire, hold and dispose of property or to carry on any trade, business or profession depends must be considered to impose an obligation to act quasi-judicially even if there is no express provision in the Act for such a hearing. As will be shown later in this book, such a duty has been implied in a number of statutes.[63] The majority view on the first part of the case has been taken by several High Courts. Thus, in *S. D. Shetty* v. *K. D. Billimoria*[64] it was held that the impugned rule provided for the grant of a licence to suitable persons for the purposes of keeping a place of public entertainment and the power to grant licences was not arbitrary and unfettered. Again, in *Govindji Vithaldas & Co.* v. *Municipal Corporation, Ahmedabad*[65] it was held that s. 376(5), Bombay Provincial Municipal Corporation Act, 1949, did not confer arbitrary and unbridled discretion on the Commissioner to refuse a licence and that it could be withheld only for a good cause. The Commissioner's discretion had to be guided by the policy underlying the Act. The Court also adverted to the provisions of the Act which showed that the exercise of the Commissioner's powers was subject to supervision and control. The same view was taken in *P. J. George* v. *Municipal Commr.*,[66] in *Municipal H.O., Ongole* v. *Ranganayakulu*,[67] in *K. Md. Khassim* v. *Municipal Council, Ootacamund*[68] and in *Mohamed Amanullah* v. *Quilon Municipality*.[69] Again, in *Sankaran Mooss* v. *Kerala*[70] the power given to Government by ss. 4 and 5, Electricity Act, 1910, was upheld as it was not an arbitrary power to revoke a licence but was hedged in with safeguards. Again, in *Allhanoor* v. *District Magistrate*,[71] the power given to the District Magistrate by s. 5, Explosives Act, 1884 to recommend the refusal of a licence to a particular person because he was undesirable was upheld both on the ground that it was very difficult to frame laws or rules to cover all cases and also on the ground that the legislative policy was clear and the power had to be exercised in the light of it. The power conferred by s. 13, Bombay Town Planning Act on the Commissioner to refuse the commencement certificate was not uncontrolled and uncanalised power if the provisions of the Act were borne in mind and the rules framed thereunder complied with. The fact that no appeal was provided was not material as the authority

The majority view taken in a number of cases

[61] See Vol. II.
[62] (1964) A.C. 40.
[63] See Vol. II.
[64] ('59) A.B. 346; 60 Bom.L.R. 1314.
[65] (1957) Bom. 147, ('59) A.B. 26; 59 Bom.L.R. 129.
[66] ('57) Tr.-Co. 249 [upholding ss. 255(3), 296(4) and 329(1) and (2) Cochin Municipalities Act, (1113)].
[67] ('62) A.A.P. 379 [upholding s. 249(3), Madras District Municipalities Act, 1920, dissenting, it is submitted rightly, from the decisions on that very section].
[68] ('56) A.M. 181, (1955) 2 M.L.J. 684.
[69] ('62) A.Ker. 30 [upholding s. 267(7) Travancore District Municipalities Act].
[70] ('65) A.Ker. 253.
[71] (1956) 6 Raj. 592, ('56) A.Raj. 153; see also *Narasimha Reddy* v. *Dist. Magistrate, Cudappah* ('53) A.M. 476, (1953) 1 M.L.J. 418, rel. on in *G. Raja Reddy* v. *Collector, Nizamabad* ('60) A.A.P. 384 (the licensing system for the sale or keeping for sale of fire-arms was reasonable only if reasons were recorded for grant or refusal of a licence).

on whom power was conferred was no less a person than the Municipal Commissioner himself.[72]

10.229 The decisions in respect of the control of drugs have not been uniform. In *Rasiklal Ghose & Sons* v. *Inspector of Drugs*[73] it was held that the discretion given to the authority under r. 62-A, Assam Drug Rules 1945, to grant or refuse to grant a licence was uncontrolled and was discriminatory and was an unreasonable restriction on the right to carry on business, and the same view was taken in *Shambu Nath & Sons* v. *Punjab*[74] with reference to rr. 27 and 30, Punjab Manufacture of Drug Rules, 1932. This decision was however reversed on appeal. In *Punjab* v. *Shambu Nath & Sons*[75] the Appeal Court observed that rr. 27 and 30 (1) dealt with dangerous drugs, that the Dangerous Drugs Act, 1930, was passed as a result of the Geneva Convention relating to dangerous drugs, and the Act was designed to suppress contraband traffic in, and the abuse of, dangerous drugs, especially those derived from opium, Indian hemp, etc. The provision in the Act enabling an authority to grant or refuse a licence without disclosing his reasons could not be held invalid, first, because the drugs in respect of which the power was exercised were dangerous; secondly, because the personal suitability of the licensee was important, and lastly because it could not be assumed that the officer would exercise his powers improperly and without applying his mind to all the relevant considerations. The Court referred to the decisions in *Cooverjee B. Bharucha* v. *Excise Commissioner*,[76] *Harishankar Bagla* v. *M.P.*[77] and *Niemala Textile Finishing Mills Ltd.* v. *2nd Punjab Industrial Tribunal*[78] to show that having regard to the nature of the business and the circumstances of the case the grant of an absolute discretion had been upheld in those cases. The reference to the last two cases would suggest, though the judgment does not say so, that the exercise of the discretion would have to be governed by the policy underlying the statute. This aspect was, however, emphasised in *Natwarlal Ambalal* v. *Bombay*.[79] There the Court held that the nature of the business was relevant in considering discretionary powers, that drugs were not ordinary articles which could be sold at will in the market, that the Act and the rules disclosed a policy underlying the Act and that the discretion in granting or refusing a licence would have to be exercised in the light of that policy. It is submitted that the view taken by the Bombay High Court is correct. The discretionary power to grant or refuse a licence or permit has been upheld not only on the ground that it must be exercised in the light of the policy underlying the law which confers such power, but also on the ground that the discretionary power is accompanied by safeguards and is not unfettered.

Control of drugs: conflicting views

---

[72] *K. L. Gupte* v. *Corporation, Greater Bombay* (1968) 1 S.C.R. 274, at p. 297, ('68) A.SC. 303, 316; fol. in *C. Lingam* v. *Union* ('71) A.SC. 474, 476-7 (". . . it has been pointed out in more than one decision of this Court that when the power had to be exercised by one of the highest officers the fact that no appeal has been provided for is a matter of no moment").

[73] ('60) A.Ass. 94.

[74] (1958) Punj. 1709, ('59) A.Punj. 526.

[75] ('59) A.Punj. 606.

[76] (1954) S.C.R. 873, ('54) A.SC. 220.

[77] (1955) 1 S.C.R. 380, *supra*.

[78] (1957) S.C.R. 335, ('57) A.SC. 329.

[79] 58 Bom.L.R. 221.

10.230 In *A.P.G. & S.M. Asscn.* v. *Union*[80] the Supreme Court upheld the validity of s. 16 of the Prevention of Food Adulteration Act, 1954. Section 16 created an offence of absolute liability for storing, selling, distributing, importing into India or manufacturing for sale adulterated or misbranded foodstuffs, and provided a minimum sentence of six months' imprisonment for the commission of the offence. The Supreme Court held that:

"The nature of the trade in foodstuffs, the channels of supply and the movement of goods from trader to trader and the fertile sources of adulteration and misbranding make it extremely difficult in a large majority of cases to establish affirmatively that storage or sale of adulterated or misbranded foodstuffs was with a guilty mind. Provisions in the statute book creating absolute liability for sale of adulterated food are fairly common."[81]

Consequently, s. 16 imposed reasonable restrictions in the public interest, for it was designed to protect the public by ensuring the purity of food supplied to the people.[82] Further, the severity of the penalties prescribed were not disproportionate to the gravity of the offence.[83]

Requirement of a licence or permit can be imposed only under a valid law

10.231 Although the requirement of a licence or permit can be justified as a reasonable restriction on the right to acquire, hold and dispose of property or to carry on a trade or business, such a requirement can be imposed only by a valid law, which expression includes a rule, regulation and notification, having the force of law. If such a requirement is imposed by an invalid law, the restrictions must be held violative of the fundamental right.[84] Licensing cases illustrate the general proposition that any restriction imposed on the rights conferred by Art. 19(1) (*f*) and (*g*) is void if imposed by an invalid law, or without the authority of, or contrary to the provisions of, a valid law. Thus where a District Magistrate cancelled a declaration made under s. 5, Press and Registration of Books Act, 1867 on the ground that the newspaper bore the same title as that of an existing newspaper without giving the petitioner an opportunity of being heard as required by s. 8B of the Act, it was held that the Magistrate's action was illegal and infringed the petitioner's fundamental rights to carry on the occupation of the editor and publisher of a newspaper.[85]

10.232 Municipal Bye-laws, and purported action under them, have been impugned as violating Art. 19(1) (*g*). Thus, in *Rashid Ahmed* v. *Municipal Board, Kairana*[86] the petitioner impugned the action

---

[80] (1971) 1 S.C.R. 166, ('71) A.SC. 2346.

[81] ('71) A.SC. at p. 2349. The Court observed that s. 3 of the English Food & Drugs Act, 1938, imposed an absolute liability: *Lindley* v. *George W. Horner & Co. Ltd.* (1950) 1 All E.R. 234; *Lamb* v. *Sunderland & District Creamary Ltd.* (1951) 1 All E.R. 923. The provisions of s. 3 were re-enacted in s. 2 of the Food & Drugs Act, 1955. In *Quality Dairies (York) Ltd.* v. *Pedley* (1952) 1 K.B. 275 it was held that Reg. 26 of the Milk & Dairies Regulations, 1949, created an offence of absolute liability.

[82] ibid. pp. 2348-49. [83] ibid. p. 2350.

[84] *Mohammad Yasin* v. *Town Area Committee* (1952) S.C.R. 572, ('52) A.SC. 115; *Bengal Immunity Co. Ltd.* v. *Bihar* (1955) 2 S.C.R. 603, ('55) A.SC. 661; *Mahabirprasad* v. *B. S. Gupta* ('57) A.M.P. 109.

[85] *G. D. Sharma* v. *Dist. Magistrate, Jammu* ('73) A.SC. 213, 215, (1973) 2 S.C.R. 969.

[86] (1950) S.C.R. 566, ('50) A.SC. 163; fol. in *Haji Ismail* v. *Malerkotla Municipality* ('62) A.Punj. 364; *Malerkotla Municipality* v. *Haji Ismail* ('67) A.Punj. 32 [*held*, that the Municipal bye-law created a monopoly of selling vegetables in favour of

taken by the Board as violating Art. 19(1)(*g*). In anticipation of certain bye-laws coming into force, the Board sold by auction to *X* the monopoly right to carry on the trade of selling vegetables wholesale for three years. Bye-law 2 of the Bye-laws made by the Board provided that:

"No person shall establish any new market or place for wholesale transaction without obtaining the previous permission of the Board and no person shall sell or expose for sale any vegetable, fruit, etc. at any place other than that fixed by the Board for the purpose."[87]

The petitioner applied for permission to sell vegetables wholesale but it was refused without assigning reasons, the actual reason being that the Board had sold the monopoly right to one *X*. When the petitioner carried on his business as a wholesale dealer in vegetables notwithstanding the refusal to grant permission, he was prosecuted for a breach of bye-law 2. The Supreme Court held that the bye-law contemplated that permission to set up a market or place for wholesale dealings may be given but this had been refused to the petitioner. If a licence was required it could be refused under s. 241(2)(*a*), U.P. Municipal Act, 1916, only on the ground that the market or place failed to comply with the conditions prescribed by or under the Act, but none had been prescribed. The action of the Board in refusing the licence, and in prosecuting the petitioner, violated Art. 19(1)(*g*), and the Board was directed to withdraw the prosecution and was restrained from interfering with his business except under bye-laws made according to law.[88]

refusal of licence held void

10.233 *Mohammad Yasin* v. *Town Area Committee, Jallalabad*[89] raised a similar question and also the further question whether a licence fee imposed under an *ultra vires* bye-law was void as infringing Art. 19(1)(*g*). Unlike the bye-law in *Rashid Ahmed's Case*[90] the impugned bye-law did not in terms prohibit anyone from dealing in fruits and vegetables, and accordingly, *Rashid Ahmed's Case* was held not to govern the present case. However, the Court found great force in the argument that the bye-laws in substance, and in a business sense, prohibited all wholesale dealings in fruits or vegetables except by the person to whom the Municipality had sold the right to sell vegetables and collect the commissions which wholesale dealers used to get from the sellers. The Court did not definitely pronounce the bye-laws void as imposing unreasonable restrictions (though its observations suggest that it would have done so if it were necessary) because it held that the licence fee imposed by the Committee was imposed under *ultra vires* bye-laws and therefore

***Mohammad Yasin's Case*: a licence fee imposed under an *ultra vires* bye law violates Art. 19(1)(g)**

". . . the bye-laws cannot be said to constitute a valid law which alone may, under Art. 19(6) . . . impose a restriction on the right conferred by Art. 19(1)(*g*). In the absence of any valid law authorising it, such illegal imposition must undoubtedly operate as an illegal restraint and must infringe the unfettered

---

four persons who were the highest bidders and imposed unreasonable restrictions on the right to carry on business: *Rashid Ahmed* v. *Municipal Board* ('50) A.SC. 163 rel. on].

87 (1950) S.C.R. at p. 570.

88 ibid. p. 572, for the actual terms of the order.

89 (1952) S.C.R. 572, ('52) A.SC. 115.

90 (1950) S.C.R. 566, ('50) A.SC. 163.

right of the wholesale dealer to carry on his occupation, trade or business which is guaranteed to him by Art. 19(1)(*g*) . . ."[91]

Regulations by licences and permits must comply with Art. 19(5) and (6)

10.234 Licences or permits are a well-recognized form of regulating the use of property or the conduct of a trade or business. Such regulation, however, must conform to Art. 19 (1) (*f*) and (*g*) and it will be upheld only if it imposes reasonable restrictions in the interest of the general public. Thus, in *Harishankar Bagla* v. *M.P.*[92] it was held that Cl. 3, Cotton Textiles (Control of Movement) Order, 1945, did not deprive a citizen of his right to dispose of or transfer cotton textiles purchased by him but only required him to take a permit from the Textile Commissioner to enable him to transport them. As cotton textiles were an essential commodity, the requirement of a permit to transport such commodities by road or rail or by other means of transport contained in a temporary Act could not be regarded as an unreasonable restriction on the citizen's right under Art. 19 (1) (*f*) and (*g*).[93] Similarly, in *P. V. Sivarajan* v. *Union*[94] it was held that since the regulation of the coir industry was in the public interest, it was obviously for the rule-making authority to decide whether in granting permits or licences the qualitative or quantitative test should be applied; granting licences or permits for import or export on a quantitative basis was not unknown. Accordingly, the impugned rr. 18, 19, 20 (1) (*a*), 21 and 22 (*a*) made under s. 26, Coir Industry Act, 1953, did not violate Art. 19 (1) (*g*). However, in *Corporation of Calcutta* v. *Calcutta Tramways Co. Ltd.*,[95] the Supreme Court held that the provisions of the parenthetical clause in s. 437 (1) (*b*), Calcutta Municipal Act, 1951, which made the opinion of the Municipality as to the necessity of a licence conclusive and precluded a challenge to it in any court, imposed unreasonable restrictions on the right to carry on trade guaranteed by Art. 19 (1) (*g*). The conferment of such power was an unreasonable restriction as it put the carrying on of trade within the limits of the Municipal Corporation entirely at its mercy if it chose to exercise that power capriciously, arbitrarily or unreasonably, though not *mala fide*. However, the provision was severable[96] and the whole section was not invalid as held by the Calcutta High Court.

Requirement of a licence, of the necessity of which the Municipality was the conclusive judge, struck down

---

[91] (1950) S.C.R. *supra* at p. 581; appl. in *S. K. Srivastava* v. *V.K. & Co.* ('70) A.Cal. 527, 534 [*held*, that the right conferred by Art. 19(1)(*g*) was violated where the imposition, or collection, of duty was *ultra vires*]; *Pusparaj & Co.* v. *Collector of Balasore* ('73) A.Or. 6 [*held*, that when the Collector exercised control over the petitioners in the matter of equitable distribution of tubes and tyres without the authority of law, Art. 19(1)(*g*) was violated; although his order might be reasonable, since it was made to give effect to an arrangement between the interested parties, it was without the authority of law].

[92] (1955) 1 S.C.R. 380, ('54) A.SC. 465.

[93] Applying the above decision, it was held in *Union* v. *Bhanamal Gulzarimal Ltd.* (1960) 2 S.C.R. 627, ('60) A.SC. 475, that Cl. II-B of the Iron & Steel (Control of Production and Distribution) Order, 1941, was valid.

[94] (1959) Supp. (1) S.C.R. 779, ('59) A.SC. 556. *Sivarajan's Case* and *Hari Shankar Bagla's Case* were rel. on in *Union* v. *B. & A.P. Exchange* ('73) A.A. 205; *Diwan Sugar & General Mills* v. *Union* (1959) Supp. (2) S.C.R. 123, ('59) A.SC. 626.

[95] (1964) 5 S.C.R. 25, ('64) A.SC. 1279.

[96] The tests of severability were laid down in *Chamarbaugwalla's Case* (1957) S.C.R. 930, ('57) A.SC. 628.

10.235 If the requirement of the grant of a licence or permit is valid, on the ground that such requirement imposes reasonable restrictions in the public interest, it must follow that reasonable provisions for the cancellation of such a licence or permit must also be valid. Thus, in *Fedco (P) Ltd.* v. *S. N. Bilgrami*[97] the cancellation of a licence obtained by fraud or misrepresentation was held not to violate the rights under Art. 19(1) (*f*) and (*g*). Having regard to the fact that the entire scheme of control and regulation of imports by licence was based on the assumption that the licence was granted on a correct statement of relevant facts, the basis of the grant disappeared if it had been obtained by fraud or misrepresentation and consequently the cancellation of such a licence must be considered reasonable. Similarly, in *Mineral Development Ltd.* v. *Bihar*,[98] the validity of s. 25, Bihar Mica Act, 1948, which empowered Government to cancel a licence was upheld, first, because the power was entrusted to the highest executive authority which ordinarily could be trusted to exercise it honestly, impartially and in the public interest, and secondly because s. 25 provided clearly ascertainable objective standards for the State Government to apply to the facts of each case. Again, the discretion of Government under s. 25(1) (*c*) was fettered by two restrictions. There must be *repeated* failure to comply with the Act and rules, and a reasonable opportunity to show cause must be given to the licensee. Cancellation of a licence did not debar a person from applying for a fresh licence; only the application could not be granted without the previous sanction of Government. The restrictions imposed by s. 25(1) (*c*) were not unreasonable.

Provisions for cancellation of a licence or permit upheld

the *Fedco Case*

the *Mineral Development Case*

10.236 In considering the reasonableness of a law under Art. 19, is the Court limited to considering the impugned law, or can it have regard to other laws in existence dealing with the same subject as part of a scheme? In *Lord Krishna Sugar Mills Ltd.* v. *Union*[99] the Supreme Court held by a majority, Sarkar J. dissenting, that in judging the reasonableness of a law the Court would look not only at surrounding circumstances, but at all contemporaneous legislation passed as part of a single scheme. The reasonableness of the restrictions, and not the law, had to be ascertained, and if a restriction in one law was offset by a countervailing advantage conferred by another law as part of the same legislative plan, the Court must take that law into account.[1] Accordingly, the majority held that the promotion of export in respect of sugar under the Sugar Promotion Act, 1958, did not amount to an unreasonable restriction upon the right conferred by Art. 19(1) (*f*) and (*g*), because arrangements had been made to save owners of factories from the loss sustained by the export of sugar, which loss was borne by consumers in India and not by producers. There was a real possibility of the loss being recouped by sales in the country, and the loss itself was so small that it did not amount to an unreasonable restriction. Sarkar J. dissented, holding that a laudable object cannot make a restriction reasonable which otherwise was unreasonable, and that a restriction which imposed a loss on the manufacturers was not reasonable.

In judging reasonableness of restrictions, the Court can look at other laws if they are part of a scheme: *Krishna Sugar Mills Case*

[97] (1960) 2 S.C.R. 408, ('60) A.SC. 415. [98] (1960) 2 S.C.R. 609, ('60) A.SC. 468.
[99] (1960) 1 S.C.R. 39, ('59) A.SC. 1124.
[1] *Pillai* v. *Mudanayake* (1953) A.C. 514.

Marketing legislation upheld: Nadar's Case

10.237 *Arunachala Nadar* v. *Madras*[2] raised important questions about the validity of marketing legislation in India. The Madras Commercial Crops Markets Act, 1933, was impugned as violating Art. 19 (1) (*g*). In a carefully considered judgment the Madras High Court[3] upheld the validity of the Act. However, s. 5 (4) (*a*) which conferred on the Collector an unlimited and uncontrolled discretion to grant or refuse a licence was held void on the ground that a provision which made the exercise of a fundamental right dependent on the absolute discretion of administrative authorities was unconstitutional. This however, did not invalidate the whole licensing system but only meant that all applicants were entitled to obtain a licence on the payment of a prescribed fee. In dismissing the appeals from this decision the Supreme Court held that the impugned Act was the result of a long exploratory investigation by experts and was enacted to regulate the buying and selling of commercial crops by providing suitable and regulated markets, by eliminating middlemen and bringing face to face the producer and the buyer so that they might meet on equal terms, thereby eradicating, or at any rate reducing, the scope for exploitation in dealings. Such an Act could not be said to impose unreasonable restrictions on the right to carry on business unless it was clearly established that its provisions were too drastic, unnecessarily harsh and overreached the scope of the object to achieve which it was enacted. The Act, Rules and Bye-laws framed thereunder had the long-term target of providing a network of markets in which correct weighment would be secured, storage facilities provided and equal powers of bargaining ensured so that the growers may bring their commercial crops to market and sell them at reasonable prices. Having regard to the scheme of the Act, the impugned provisions of the Act constituted reasonable restrictions on a citizen's right to carry on business and were valid.[4] Although the judgment of the Supreme Court declares all the impugned provisions valid, it contains no reasons for holding s. 5 (4) (*a*) valid contrary to the judgment of the Madras High Court; in fact s. 5 (4) (*a*) is nowhere discussed and appears to have been overlooked. In view of this decision the Supreme Court held in *Mohammad Hussain* v. *Bombay*[5] that ss. 4, 4A, 5, 5A and 5AA, Bombay Agricultural Produce Markets Act, 1939, did not violate Art. 19 (1) (*g*) and were valid. And in *Muhammadbhai* v. *Gujarat*[6]

The above case followed in other cases

---

[2] (1959) Supp. (1) S.C.R. 92, ('59) A.SC. 300; rel. on in *Hrudananda Sahu* v. *Orissa* ('61) A.Or. 81 (upholding ss. 4 and 14 Orissa Agricultural Produce Markets Act, 1957; the imposition of market fees and licence fees was held not to be the imposition of a tax); rel. on in *Mukhtiar Chand* v. *Marketing Committee* ('65) A.Punj. 33 [upholding r. 26, Punjab Agricultural Produce Markets (General) Rules, 1962. If experience had shown that weighing by hand-scales had led to malpractices, corruption, wastage of time and inconvenience, the prescribing of the use of only beam-scales could not be considered unreasonable as it was likely to reduce the chances of exploitation by middlemen and profiteers].

[3] *Kutti Keya* v. *State* ('54) A.M. 621, (1954) 1 M.L.J. 117.

[4] (1959) Supp. (1) S.C.R. 92 *supra* at p. 104; see also *B. B. Parekh* v. *S.K.M. Committee* ('59) A.Mys. 29 (the object of the Madras Agricultural Produce Markets Act, 1937, was to secure the growers an adequate price from the buyers); fol. in *K. U. V. Mandal* v. *M.P.* ('65) A.M.P. 6, 10 [upholding s. 3 M.P. Agricultural Produce Markets (Validation) Act, 1962, as imposing restrictions which were not unreasonable].

[5] (1962) 2 S.C.R. 659, ('62) A.SC. 97.

[6] (1962) 3 Supp. S.C.R. 875, ('62) A.SC. 1517.

it was held that there was no radical departure from the scheme of the Act made by the amendments introduced by the Bombay Ordinance 1 of 1961, and therefore the reason which led the Court to uphold the validity of the Bombay Agricultural Markets Act, 1939, and the Rules and Bye-laws made under it, still held good. Following *Nadar's Case*[7] and *Hussain's Case*[8] the regulatory provisions of the Hyderabad Markets Act were upheld as imposing reasonable restrictions in the interest of the growers of agricultural produce to the community at large.[9]

The Right to practise a profession and to carry on trade, business or occupation

10.238 Article 19 (1) (*g*) confers on a citizen the right to practise a profession or carry on any trade, business or occupation, subject to the restrictions contained in Art. 19 (6) which, as will appear later, was amended by the Constitution (1st Amendment) Act, 1951. Questions connected with Art. 19 (1) (*g*) have been referred to in different contexts earlier; it would however be convenient to state the result of the earlier discussion briefly at this place. Art. 19 (1) (*g*) confers a right and not an obligation. Therefore, it carries within it the right not to carry on a trade or business.[10] Secondly, the Supreme Court has held that there cannot be "trade" or "business" in immoral or criminal activities, and in any event, such activities can be totally prohibited.[11] Thirdly, where another fundamental right, *e.g.* the right to form an association collides with the right to carry on a business, the restrictions which can be imposed on that right are not limited to Art. 19 (3) but extend to Art. 19 (6). **Result of earlier discussion**

10.239 If a right is claimed under Art. 19, the question whether the person claiming that right is a citizen is outside Art. 19, and it is only when he establishes his citizenship that a question of the **The question whether a person is a citizen, is outside Art. 19**

---

[7] *Supra.* [8] *Supra.*

[9] *Narayana Reddy* v. *A.P.* ('64) A.A.P. 373; *Thakur Prasad* v. *Bihar* ('65) A.P. 267 (upholding ss. 4 and 15, Bihar Agricultural Produce Markets Act, 1960, which were similar in material respects to those upheld in *Nadar's Case* and *Hussain's Case, supra*).

[10] *Indian Metal and Metallurgical Corpn.* v. *Industrial Tribunal, Madras* ('53) A.M. 98, 101, (1952) 1 M.L.J. 481 (for the relevant portion of the judgment see para 10.104 *ante*; it was also held that an award under the Industrial Disputes Act compelling the continuance of business was void); *K. N. Joglekar* v. *Barsi Light Rly. Co. Ltd.* ('55) A.B. 294, 298 ["It may be . . . that the right to carry on a business must imply the right to carry on a business as the owner . . . likes, including the right to close it down when he chooses, and if the Legislature were to put a restriction upon the right of a businessman to close his business, it may be that the case may fall within the ambit of Art. 19(1)(*g*)." The Court however held that s. 25F, Industrial Disputes Act, did not have that effect]. *Joglekar's Case* was reversed in appeal on another point by the Supreme Court in *Sub-nom. Hari Prasad* v. *Authority, Payment of Wages Act* ('57) A.SC. 121, but the Court did not decide the question under Art. 19(1)(*g*); relying on the cases mentioned in the *f.n.* it was held in *Rajkumarsingh* v. *Authority, Payment of Wages Act* ('60) A.M.P. 307, that the running of any business being a right and not an obligation, an industrial concern had the liberty to carry it on or to close it down particularly when it did not yield any profit; *J.K. Hosiery Factory* v. *L.A.T.* ('56) A.A. 498, 500 (*held*, that the word "discharged" in s. 22, Industrial Disputes Act did not include discharge arising from closure of business. It was a fundamental right of an employer to close down his business).

[11] See para 10.3.

To invoke Art. 19, a right, and a fundamental right, must be established

violation of his right can arise.[12] Secondly, it must be shown that the law violates the right to practise a profession, etc., if the challenge under Art. 19 (1) (*g*) is not to fail. For example, it has been held that study in a University is not an "occupation" within the meaning of Art. 19 (1) (*g*). Since a student cannot be said to be following an occupation in the generally accepted sense of the term, the regulations of the Calcutta University regarding migration of students did not violate any right under Art. 19 (1) (*g*).[13] Thirdly, before a person can complain of the violation of a fundamental right, it must be established that the right claimed is, first, a legal right and secondly, that it is a fundamental right. Accordingly, it has been held that a petition writer had no legal right, let alone a fundamental right, to carry on his profession or business in the Collectorate compound. He may have a grievance against the withdrawal of the permission, but no legal remedy, unless it was in breach of contract.[14] It has also been held that the right to collect tolls in a Municipal Market under a licence was a statutory and not a fundamental right,[15] and likewise, that a citizen has no fundamental right to carry on the business of stevedoring at docks owned and controlled by the Port Commissioners, for a statute or bye-law may create a statutory right, but not a fundamental right.[16] Similarly, the right to challenge an election is not a fundamental right.[17] Again, no person has a right to a certificate in the nature of a testimonial. Accordingly, where there was no provision of law requiring a person to hold a certificate for exercising the profession of a guide it was held that the cancellation of the certificate by the Police did not attract Art. 19 (1) (*g*).[18] Finally, fundamental rights in Art. 19 are guaranteed against the State and have nothing to do with the rights of citizens *inter se*. Consequently, when it was argued that Art. 19 abrogated the law of torts it was held in *Datta Mal Chiranji Lal* v. *L. L. Prasad*[19] that it did not, and that a suit for an injunction preventing the defendant from running a flour mill on the ground that it constituted a nuisance did not attract Art. 19. Again, Government, like a private individual, is free not to enter into a contract with a person, and accordingly, the refusal of Government to deal with a black-listed contractor did not violate the contractor's fundamental right to carry on business.[20] And the same view was taken in *Ram Krishna* v. *Union*[21]

---

[12] *Mahomed Usman* v. *Madras* ('61) A.M. 129.

[13] *Samir Kumar* v. *Someswar* ('53) A.Cal. 783 (the decision is correct, because the word 'occupation' takes its colour from employment, business and calling, with which it is bracketed).

[14] *Mohd. Yasin* v. *District Magistrate* ('54) A.A. 317 (the order actually passed did invade the petitioner's fundamental right when it provided that "no application or papers written by him should be entertained in any Court", but the Court held that this order was beyond the power of the officer making it, and was void).

[15] *Mahboob Khan* v. *Dy. Commissioner* ('53) A.Ass. 145.

[16] *Commissioners, Calcutta Port* v. *Asit Ranjan* ('62) A.Cal. 530.

[17] *Bhuvanesh Bhushan* v. *Election Tribunal* ('58) A.A. 587.

[18] *Jagdamba Prasad* v. *Senior Supdt. of Police* ('59) A.A. 573.

[19] ('60) A.A. 632.

[20] *K. Bhaskaran* v. *Kerala* ('58) A.Ker. 333.

[21] ('69) A.Cal. 18. The case made a distinction between the non-statutory sphere unaffected by any statutory control order, and the statutory sphere and the freedom of Government to enter into contracts with such persons as they liked was affirmed with reference to the non-statutory sphere.

relying on the observations of the Supreme Court in *Achutan* v. *Kerala*.[22] Where the Government of Saurashtra issued a notification declaring that a "Bhayat" grant had lapsed on the petitioner becoming a ruler, it was held that as the grant was not absolute, the petitioner could not found his claim on any violation of his fundamental right, namely, deprivation of property by State action.[23]

10.240 We must now consider the *Sakal Newspapers (P) Ltd.* v. *Union*[24] and *Bennett Coleman & Co.* v. *Union*[25] both of which dealt with restrictions on newspapers and squarely raised the question of the inter-relation of Art. 19 (1) (*a*) and 19 (1) (*g*). But the unanimous judgment in the *Sakal Case* considered that question perfunctorily, and the majority judgment in the *Bennett Coleman Case* did no better. To avoid repetition it would be convenient to consider the decision of the *Sakal Case* without any comment and then consider the far-reaching issues raised by the *Bennett Coleman Case*, in which the *Sakal Case* was considered. The *Sakal* and the *Bennett Coleman Cases*: relation of Art. 19(1)(*a*) and 19(1)(*g*) not considered

10.241 In the *Sakal Case* the undernoted provisions were impugned as violating Art. 19 (1) (*f*).[26] The Supreme Court upheld the challenge. In dealing with the argument that the publication of a newspaper involved not merely the freedom of speech and expression but also the carrying on of business, so that reasonable restrictions could be put on the business activities of a newspaper, the Supreme Court observed: *The Sakal Case*

". . . the right of freedom of speech cannot be taken away with the object of placing restrictions on the business activities of a citizen. Freedom of speech can be *restricted only in the interests of the security of the State, friendly relations with foreign States, public order, decency or morality or in relation to contempt of court, defamation or incitement to an offence*. It cannot, like the freedom to carry on business, be curtailed in the interest of the general public. If a law directly affecting it is challenged it is no answer that the restrictions enacted by it are justifiable under cls. (3) to (6). . . . Viewing the question from this angle it would be seen that the reference to the Press being a business and to the restriction imposed by the impugned Act being referable or justified as a proper restriction on the right to carry on the business of publishing a newspaper *would be wholly irrelevant* for considering whether the impugned Act infringes or does not infringe the freedom guaranteed by Art. 19(1)(*a*)."[27] (italics supplied)

10.242 In the *Bennett Coleman Case* the newsprint policy passed by the Government under ss. 3 and 4A of the Imports Control Act, 1947, was impugned as violating Art. 19 (1) (*a*) and 14. Three judgements were delivered. The majority judgment by Ray J. for himself, Sikri C.J. and Reddy J. held that the impugned policy violated Arts. 14 and 19 (1) (*a*); in a separate judgment Beg J. concurred in the result; and a dissenting judgment by Mathew J. held that the impugned policy was valid. The Bennett *Coleman Case*

---

[22] (1959) Supp. (1) S.C.R. 787, ('59) A.SC. 490.
[23] *S.V.V.S.V. Vadia* v. *Saurashtra* (1960) 3 S.C.R. 521, ('67) A.SC. 346.
[24] (1962) 3 S.C.R. 842, ('62) A.SC. 305.
[25] (1973) 2 S.C.R. 757, ('73) A.SC. 106.
[26] The Newspaper (Price Page) Act, 1956, which empowered the Central Government to regulate the prices of newspapers in relation to their pages and sizes and to regulate the allocation of the space for advertising matter; and the Daily Newspapers (Price and Page) Order, 1960, made under the Act fixed the minimum number of pages that might be published by a newspaper according to the prices charged and prescribed the number of supplements that could be issued.
[27] (1962) 3 S.C.R. *supra* at pp. 863-4.

Facts of the case

10.243 The facts of the *Bennett Coleman Case* are complicated, and the details of the newsprint policy of 1962 and the newsprint policy of 1971-72 are too long to be set out here.[28] Briefly stated the facts material for the decision of the case were these: Newsprint is the raw material for newspapers and periodicals. Till 1957 newsprint was wholly imported, but thereafter one paper mill set up in India was the only source of indigenous supply. The distribution of newsprint has been controlled since 1939,[29] and newsprint is an essential commodity under s. 2(*a*) (vii), Essential Commodities Act, 1955. The newsprint policy was laid down by the Newsprint Control Order, 1962 till it was replaced by the impugned policy of 1972-73.[30] In 1971-72 due to the suspension of U.S. aid there was a reduction of 11,000 tonnes in the import of newsprint, and the newsprint available for distribution was less than what it was in 1971-72, and the imported and domestic newsprint had to be rationed. "Before 1972-73, the newsprint allocation policy was based on the page level of 1957 coupled with circulation figures of 1961-62, and all allotments were calculated with allowable increases and adjustments, from year to year on that basis."[31] Fixation of page level for calculating the entitlement of quota for a newspaper was not a new feature introduced by the impugned policy.[32]

Rival contentions

10.244 The petitioners impugned the new newsprint policy on the following grounds:

"(*a*) No evening paper or new edition could be started by a common ownership unit, (i.e. a newspaper establishment or concern owning two or more news interest newspapers including at least one daily) even within the authorised quota of newsprint; (*b*) there was a limitation on the maximum number of pages to 10, no adjusting being permitted between circulation and the pages so as to increase the pages; (*c*) no interchangeability was permitted between the different papers of common ownership unit or different editions of the same paper; (*d*) allowance of 20 per cent increase in page level upto maximum of 10 had been given to newspapers with less than 10 pages; (*e*) a big newspaper was prohibited and prevented from increasing the number of pages, page area and periodicity by reducing circulation to meet its requirement even within its admissible quota; (*f*) there was distinction in entitlement between newspapers with an average of more than 10 pages as compared with newspapers of 10 or less than 10 pages."[33]

The Union of India contended that

(i) the newsprint policy did not directly and immediately deal with the right of freedom of speech and expression conferred by Art. 19(1)(*a*), and the right under Art. 19(1)(*a*) was not violated though the freedom of speech and expression was incidentally or consequentially abridged;[34] (ii) the subject matter of the policy was rationing of imported commodity and its equitable distribution; (iii) one method of controlling import was to regulate the use and disposition of goods after they were bought.[35]

---

[28] ibid. pp. 765-67 where the details have been set out.

[29] ibid. p. 799. Further, Art. 369 vests the control of production, supply and distribution of newsprint within the exclusive jurisdiction of Parliament for 5 years from the commencement of the Constitution.

[30] ibid. pp. 800-801 where cl. 3 and Sch. I to the Order are set out, as also a new cl. 3A introduced on December 29, 1962.

[31] ibid. p. 807.

[32] ibid. p. 808.

[33] ibid. pp. 757-8 where the head note sets out the grounds of challenge.

[34] ibid. p. 778.

[35] ibid. p. 779.

10.245 It may be stated that in addition to the challenge under Arts. 14 and 19 there was a challenge to the *vires* of the policy on the ground that it was not warranted by the Import Control Act and the Import Control Order, and a further contention that the policy was without the authority of law. Beg J. concurred in the result, and held that the policy was without the authority of law. The majority judgment *appears* to have held that the policy was *ultra vires* the Act and the Order.[36] If this were so, a decision on the challenge under Arts. 14 and 19 was unnecessary. It is not necessary to deal with the *vires* of the policy beyond saying that the present writer is in agreement with the decision of Mathew J. on this point.[37] The present discussion is confined to the challenge under Arts. 14 and 19. In that context it may be observed that both the majority and the dissenting judgments agreed that the right of government to import newsprint and to control its distribution fairly and equitably could not be denied.[38] But apart from this agreement the conflict between the majority and the dissenting judgments is so extensive and so fundamental, and the issues really involved in the case are of such far-reaching constitutional importance, that it becomes necessary, first, to formulate the questions which called for decision, and then to consider the manner in which those questions were dealt with in the majority and the dissenting judgments.

Challenges to the policy other than those under Arts. 14 and 19

Present discussion limited to Arts. 14 and 19

Radical differences between majority and dissenting judgments

(*a*) What test must be applied to determine the validity or invalidity of a law which is impugned as violating one of the rights conferred by Art. 19(1) if the exercise of that right involves the exercise of one or more other rights conferred by Art. 19(1)?

(*b*) What is the scope and ambit of the freedom of speech, which includes the freedom of the press? If in a factual situation two views can be taken of that freedom, is the legislature, or the executive authorized by law, free to adopt one of the two views? Does the presumption of constitutionality apply in such a case?

(*c*) Is there any warrant for the assumption that any law, or executive action authorized by law, which increases the price of a newspaper or which diminishes the revenue from advertisement must necessarily violate Art. 19(1)(*a*)?

(*d*) Does the doctrine of equality require that existing inequalities should be perpetuated? If such inequality has been brought about partly or wholly by legislative or executive action can such inequality be removed by legislative or executive action?[39]

The questions that called for decision

10.246 As to question (a) in para 10.245, above, the majority judgment adopted the two tests laid down in *Bank Nationalization Case*,[40] namely,

The test of validity of a law

"First it is not the object of the authority making the law impairing the right of the citizen nor the form of action that determines the invasion of the right. Secondly, it is the effect of the law and the action upon the right which attracts the jurisdiction of the court to grant relief. The direct operation of the Act upon the rights forms the real test."[41]

impugned as violating Art. 19(1)(*a*): the majority judgment;

---

[36] ibid. p. 758 (vi) and pp. 780-81. [37] ibid. pp. 823-6.

[38] ibid. p. 778 (Ray J.); p. 802 (Mathew J.).

[39] The judgment dealt with two other questions: (i) Whether the petitioner being a joint stock company were entitled to invoke Art. 19; (ii) whether the impugned policy in so far as it restricted actual user of newsprint had the authority of law. Question (i) above has been considered in paras 10.24 to 10.26 *ante*, but question (ii) is outside the scope of the discussion of the constitutional questions considered in the text.

[40] (1970) 3 S.C.R. 530, ('70) A.SC. 564.

[41] (1973) 2 S.C.R. *supra* at p. 781.

Mathew J. said that in the area of free speech the following test had been firmly established in the *Express Newspapers Case*:

and the dissenting judgment

"The impugned Act, judged by its provisions, was not such a law but was a beneficient legislation intended to regulate the conditions of service of the working journalists and the consequences aforesaid could not be the direct and inevitable result of it. Although there could be no doubt that it directly affected the press and fell outside the categories of protection mentioned in Art. 19(2), it had not the effect of taking away or abridging the freedom of speech and expression of the petitioner and did not, therefore, infringe Art. 19(1)(*a*) of the Constitution."[42]

and the same test had been applied in *Naresh Shridhar Mirajkar* v. *Maharashtra*.[43] Mathew J. added that

"The pith and substance test, although not strictly appropriate, might serve a useful purpose in the process of deciding whether the provisions in question which work some interference with the freedom of speech are essentially regulatory in character (see the observation of Lord Porter in *Commonwealth of Australia* v. *Bank of New South Wales*).[44]" [45]

Submission: the test applied by Mathew J. correct in substance

10.247 It is submitted (i) that the test which Mathew J. treated as established by the *Express Newspapers Case* is correct, in substance, but it has a much stronger foundation than the one on which he rested it; and (ii) that the test laid down in the *Bank Nationalization Case* is not correct in its application to Art. 19. First, in that case the question of considering Art. 19 did not arise, once the Court held that the impugned Act violated Art. 31, so that the observations on Art. 19 were not necessary for deciding the case.[46] Secondly, in the *Bank Nationalization Case* the Court considered the co-relation of Art. 19(1)(*f*) to Art. 31, and was not called upon to consider, and did not consider, the co-relation between the rights conferred by Art. 19(1)(*a*) to (*g*), read with Art. 19(2) to (6). However, such co-relation was considered by the Supreme Court in the *Bank Employees' Case* and in *Raghubar Dayal's Case*,[47] and it is unfortunate that although they were directly relevant, they were overlooked in the *Sakal Case* and in the *Bennett Coleman Case*. Before stating the effect of the decisions which were overlooked, it may be observed that the freedom of speech includes the freedom of the press, though it is not expressly mentioned in Art. 19(1)(*a*).[48] Consequently, a person carrying on the business of publishing a newspaper has not only the right to the freedom of speech and expression [Art. 19(1)(*a*)]; but has also the right to carry on business [Art. 19(1)(*g*)], the right to acquire, hold and dispose of property for the purpose of his business [Art. 19(1)(*f*)], and for the same purpose, the right to move freely throughout the territory

Infirmities of the test applied by the majority

Bank Nationalization Case did not consider co-relation of Art. 19(1)(*a*) to 19(1)(*g*)

Two decisions which considered such co-relation overlooked in the *Bennett Coleman Case*

---

[42] ibid. pp. 805-6.

[43] ibid. p. 805. [(1966) 3 S.C.R. 744, 764, where an order prohibiting the evidence of a witness made by Tarkunde J. was impugned as violating Art. 19(1)(*a*). See paras 7.37 and 7.39 *ante*].

[44] (1950) A.C. 235, 312-3.

[45] (1973) 2 S.C.R. *supra* at p. 807.

[46] See Appendix III.

[47] See paras 10.110 and 10.111 of the text. These cases were treated by the Supreme Court as settling the law: see *D.A.V. College, Jullundur* v. *Punjab* (1971) Supp. S.C.R. 688, ('71) A.SC. 1737 (and para 10.112 of the text).

[48] See para 10.27 of the text. Discussions in the Constituent Assembly show that the question of the freedom of the press was specifically raised by Prof. K. T. Shah, and Dr. Ambedkar said that freedom of expression covered the freedom of the press; though it is not easy to see why the freedom of the press was not expressly mentioned. See *C.A.D.* Vol. 7, pp. 715, 780.

of India [Art. 19 (1) (*d*)]; to reside and settle in any part of India [Art. 19 (1) (*e*)]; and, if he is so minded, the right to form associations by doing his business in partnership with other persons [Art. 19 (1) (*c*)].

10.248 But if the publisher of a newspaper claims several fundamental rights under Art. 19 (1) in respect of his business, it would be absurd for him to claim exemption from the restrictions to which those rights are subject. And, in the *Bank Employees' Case*, the Supreme Court pointed out the absurd consequences of accepting such a claim.[49] In that case the Supreme Court held that though the right to form a trade union (an association) was subject only to the reasonable restrictions mentioned in Art. 19 (3), the business activities of the trade union were subject to the reasonable restrictions mentioned in Art. 19 (6). This conclusion was based on the scheme of Art. 19 and the light thrown on the fundamental rights conferred by Art. 19 (1) (*a*) to (*f*) by the restrictions to which those rights were subject. This decision was followed in *Raghubar Dayal's Case* where the Supreme Court held that an association formed to do business in forward contracts was subject to the restrictions which could be imposed on that business under Art. 19 (6).

Bank Employees' Case

Raghubar Dayal's Case

10.249 It is submitted that those decisions establish that when more than one fundamental right conferred by Art. 19 (1) inheres in a person, (or a number of persons), the legislature has power to put on each fundamental right the restrictions to which that right is subject. Since the publisher of a newspaper has the right to the freedom of the press, a law can put only those restrictions on his right which are permitted by Art. 19 (2); but since he has the right to carry on his business of publishing a newspaper, a law can put reasonable restrictions on that right in the interest of the general public. But such restrictions may *affect* the freedom of the press. Here, the exercise by the legislature of its undoubted power under Art. 19 (6) *appears* to conflict with the right conferred by Art. 19 (1) (*a*) and the restrictions which can be put on that right under Art. 19 (2). How is that conflict to be resolved? That was the central issue in the *Bennett Coleman Case*. The majority judgment did not raise that issue, and the dissenting judgment raised it partially. It is submitted that the doctrine of pith and substance furnishes a solution of the apparent conflict, and the majority judgment was in error in holding that

Apparent conflict between restrictions on business and the freedom of the press

Submission: pith and substance test wrongly rejected

"the test of pith and substance of the subject matter and of direct and of incidental effect of legislation are relevant to the question of legislative competence but they are irrelevant to the question of infringement of fundamental rights."[51]

And even Mathew J. said that the pith and substance test *although not strictly appropriate* may serve a useful purpose. It is submitted that relevant authorities were not brought to the attention of the

Relevant authorities not cited

---

[49] (1962) 3 S.C.R. at pp. 288-9. These decisions were taken by the Supreme Court as settling the law in *D.A.V. College, Jullundur* v. *Punjab* ('71) A.SC. 1737 which is discussed in para 10.112 of the text.

[50] The head note makes this statement explicit. "The pith and substance doctrine is used in ascertaining whether an Act falls under one Entry while incidentally encroaching upon another Entry. Such a question does not arise here": (1973) 2 S.C.R. *supra* at p. 759.

[51] ibid. p. 780.

Supreme Court, and they show that the doctrine of pith and substance is not limited to resolving conflicts between legislative powers conferred on Federal and State Legislatures with reference to Legislative Lists.

Gallager v. Lynn

10.250 In *Gallager* v. *Lynn*[52] the Milk and Milk Products Act (Northern Ireland) 1934 was impugned as violating s. 4 of the Government of Ireland Act, 1920. It is clear that the challenge was to a law made under a unitary Constitution which placed a limitation on the legislative power of the Parliament of Northern Ireland by prohibiting it from enacting a law in respect of "trade with any place out of the part of Ireland within their jurisdiction. . . ."[53] In rejecting that challenge Lord Atkin said:[54]

". . . the short answer . . . is that this Milk Act is not a law 'in respect of' trade; but is a law for the peace, order and good government of Northern Ireland 'in respect of' precautions taken to secure the health of the inhabitants of Northern Ireland by protecting them from the dangers of an unregulated supply of milk. These questions affecting *limitation on the legislative powers of subordinate parliaments or the distribution of powers between parliaments in a federal system are now familiar.* . . . It is well established that you are to look at the 'true nature and character of the legislation',[55] 'the pith and substance of the legislation.' *If*, on the view of the statute as a whole, . . . *the substance of the legislation is within the express powers, then it is not invalidated if incidentally it affects matters which are outside the authorized field.* The legislation must not under the guise of dealing with one matter in fact encroach upon the forbidden field. Nor are you to look only at the object of the legislator. An Act may have a perfectly lawful object, *e.g.*, to promote the health of the inhabitants, but may seek to achieve that object by invalid methods, *e.g.*, a direct prohibition of any trade within a foreign country. In other words, you may certainly consider the clauses of an Act to see whether they are passed 'in respect of' the forbidden subject."[56] (italics supplied)

Subramanyan Chettiar's Case

In *Subramanyan Chettiar's Case*[57] Varadachariar J., in his concurring judgment, referred with approval to *Gallager* v. *Lynn*. He said:

"It will be clear from the decisions that the rules of interpretation were evolved only as a matter of reasonableness and common sense and out of the necessity of satisfactorily solving conflicts from the inevitable overlapping of subjects in any distribution of legislative powers. That they need not be limited to any special system of federal constitution is made clear by the fact that in *Gallager* v. *Lynn*, Lord Atkin applied the 'pith and substance' rule when dealing with a question arising under the Government of Ireland Act — which did not embody a federal system at all — . . ."[58]

Submission: pith and substance doctrine applicable to resolving conflicts between restrictions permitted by Art. 19(2) to (6)

10.251 It is submitted that the very same question arises when a law passed by a competent legislature is impugned as violating fundamental rights conferred by Art. 19 (1), and considerations of "reasonableness and common sense" dictate the same solution. The seven fundamental rights conferred by Art. 19 (1) impose limitations on the legislative powers of Parliament and the State Legislatures. But the limitations are not absolute: in respect of *each* fundamental right, the power of the legislatures to put restrictions to which that right is subject is expressly preserved. Therefore, the Constitution confers on the appropriate legislature, *inter alia*, the power to make laws

---

52 (1937) A.C. 863 (H.L.).
53 ibid. p. 869 where the relevant provisions are set out.
54 Lords Tankerton, Macmillan, Wright and Maugham stated that they agreed with Lord Atkin's judgment.
55 *Russell* v. *R.* (1882) 7 App.Cas. 829.
56 (1937) A.C. *supra* at pp. 869-70.
57 (1940) F.C.R. 188.
58 ibid. pp. 236-7.

which place reasonable restrictions in the public interest on the right to carry on a business. If the true nature and character of the law made in the exercise of that power, or the pith and substance of that law, is that it imposes reasonable restrictions on the right to carry on a business, then, "it is not invalidated if incidentally it affects matters which are outside the authorised field."[59] Any other construction would lead to absurd results and would nullify the express powers conferred by the Constitution on the legislatures. For the publisher of a newspaper to claim six fundamental rights in respect of his business, and yet contend that five of those rights are exempted from the restrictions to which they are subject would be absurd, because the rights are conferred subject to the permitted restrictions. Two illustrations will bring out this absurdity.

Absurd consequences of rejecting the doctrine: two illustrations

(*a*) Entry 92, List I, Sch. 7 confers on Parliament the power to make laws imposing a tax on the sale or purchase of newspapers and on advertisements published therein. It may be noticed that the restrictions which can be put on fundamental rights under Art. 19 (2) to (6) do not refer to a tax at all. But a tax has been held to be a restriction and, ordinarily, a reasonable restriction, *inter alia,* on business. A tax on the sale of newspapers might diminish the circulation of newspapers by increasing the cost to the purchasers. Again, a tax on advertisements published in newspapers might diminish the revenue from advertisements by making them more costly. Consequently, the tax may affect the freedom of the press. But, unless an express legislative power in respect of newspapers is to be rendered nugatory, it must be held that a law imposing a tax on the sale of newspapers, or on advertisements published therein, is not a law *in respect of* the freedom of the press, but is in pith and substance a revenue law which imposes reasonable restrictions on the *business* of publishing newspapers.[60] However, though the incidental effect of such a law on the freedom of the press does not invalidate that law, the extent to which the tax impinges on the freedom of speech would be relevant. If the rate of tax were so high, that it would put a large number of newspapers out of circulation, the tax would be struck down as imposing an unreasonable restriction on the business of publishing newspapers, having regard to the intimate connection of that business with the freedom of the press.[61] It may also be relevant if the factual situation justified the conclusion that under the guise of a revenue law imposing restrictions on business, in fact

(*a*) Entry 92, List I: sales tax on newspapers and advertisements

Incidental effect on freedom of the press cannot nullify entry 92

[59] See *Gallager* v. *Lynn*: para 10.250 above.

[60] The framers of our Constitution did not take the same view of a tax on the sale of newspapers as has been taken in the United States, where such a tax was looked upon as a hated tax imposed by the British to suppress the freedom of the press. In *Grosjean* v. *American Press Co.* 297 U.S. 233, 80 L.ed. 661, the U.S. Supreme Court referred to this history in striking down a tax of two per cent on newspapers whose circulation exceeded 20,000 copies a week. The Court said: "(in) view of the persistent search for new subjects of taxation, it is not without significance that, with the single exception of the Louisiana statute, so far as we can discover, no State during the 150 years of our national existence has undertaken to impose a tax like that now in question.": ibid. pp. 250-51; p. 669. In view of entry 92, List I, *Grosjean's Case* can have no application in India.

[61] For the test of reasonableness see paras 10.18 and 10.100 of the text. The nature of the right infringed and the impact of such infringement on the religious, political and economic fields would be relevant in deciding whether the restriction was reasonable.

the very high rate of tax impinged not incidentally but directly on the freedom of the press.

(b) Express Newspapers Case: Law for the welfare of labour upheld by Sup. Ct. inspite of indirect effect on freedom of the press

(*b*) The *Express Newspapers Case* furnishes another illustration. The Working Journalists Act there impugned was a law in respect of the "welfare of labour including conditions of work....": entry 24, List III, Sch. 7. The Supreme Court repelled the challenge to it under Art. 19(1) (*a*) by observing that the direct effect of the Act was not to abridge the freedom of the press. The principles of wage fixation which the Supreme Court approved[62] involved the consequence that the weakest units in the newspaper industry might have to close down[63] with the consequence that the freedom of the press might be affected; nevertheless the challenge under Art. 19(1) (*a*) was repelled. No doubt the Supreme Court upheld the Act by applying to it the test of direct and indirect effect on the fundamental right conferred by Art. 19(1) (*a*), but this test is only a less satisfactory way of saying that in pith and substance the impugned law was *in respect of* the welfare of labour and not *in respect of* the freedom of the press.

Submission: *Bennett Coleman's Case* applied a wrong test

It is submitted that the above discussion shows that the test adopted by the majority judgment in *Bennett Coleman's Case* for determining the validity of a law impugned as violating the fundamental right conferred by Art. 19(1) (*a*) to (*g*) has been formulated without considering the situation where several fundamental rights inhere in a person in respect of the business of publishing newspapers; that the test is incorrect, and it would be unprofitable to speculate whether the majority would have reached the same conclusion on Art. 19 if the correct test had been adopted. It is submitted that in substance, though not in form, Mathew J. adopted the correct test and the conclusions which he reached are correct. This submission is reinforced by the discussion in paras 10.252 and 10.253 below.

Freedom of the press and monopoly in the newspaper industry

10.252 As to question (*b*) in para 10.245 above, this question partly overlaps question (*a*) considered above, and it would be convenient to deal with this overlapping aspect first. In several countries monopolies, or monopolistic practices, in trade or business have been treated as evils calling for appropriate remedy. In the United States, the Sherman Anti-Trust Law was designed to prevent monopolies and monopolistic tendencies in industry, and the application of that Act to news agencies was upheld by the U.S. Supreme Court in *Associated Press* v. *U.S.*[64] and to newspapers in *Citizen Publishing Co.* v. *U.S.*[65] In the *Associated Press Case*, Black J. observed

Anti-Trust Laws against monopolistic tendencies applied to news agencies by U.S. Sup. Ct.

"It would be strange indeed . . . if the grave concern for freedom of the press which prompted the adoption of the First Amendment *should be read as a command that the government was without power to protect that freedom* . . . That Amendment rests on the assumption that the widest possible dissemination of information from diverse and antagonistic sources is essential to the welfare of the public, that a free press is the condition of a free society. *Surely a command that the Government itself shall not impede the free flow of ideas does not afford non-governmental combinations a refuge if they impose restraints upon that constitutionally guaranteed freedom.* Freedom to

---

[62] (1959) S.C.R. at pp. 92-3.

[63] ibid. p. 135: ". . . those who are marginally situated may not be able to bear the strain and may in conceivable cases have to disappear after closing down their establishments."

[64] 326 U.S. 1; 89 L.ed. 2013.

[65] 394 U.S. 131, 139-40; 22 L.ed. 2d. 148, 156-7.

publish is guaranteed by the Constitution, *but freedom to combine is not.* Freedom of the press from Governmental interference under the First Amendment does not sanction repression of that freedom by private interests. *The First Amendment affords not the slightest support for the contention that a combination to trade in news and views has any constitutional validity.*"[66] (italics supplied)

and this passage was quoted with approval, and applied, by Roberts J., in the second case mentioned above. It has been said earlier[67] that the decisions of the U.S. Supreme Court on the freedom of speech and of the press do not apply to our Constitution. In the United States the First Amendment is absolute in its terms: "Congress shall make no law . . . abridging the freedom of speech, or of the press. . . . "Therefore, before a Court can engraft an exception to this absolute prohibition the necessity for such exception must be established. But in India, the right is expressly made subject to a large number of specified restrictions. However, this only means that in the United States the area of the freedom of speech and the press is much larger than it is in India. If, in spite of this, the U.S. Supreme Court has upheld the validity of laws against monopolies, *a fortiori,* such laws must be upheld in India where the area of freedom is smaller than in the United States. But a law against monopoly can be justified only as a reasonable restriction on business imposed under Art. 19(6).

and to newspapers

Submission

***a fortiori* similar restrictions must be valid in India**

10.253 Nor are the evils of monopolies peculiar to the United States. In *Kesavananda* v. *Kerala,*[68] Mathew J., after observing that in his dissenting judgment in the *Bennett Coleman Case* he had referred to certain aspects of the modern press, added: "(Counsel) has rightly emphasized its commercial character and how that aspect though connected with freedom of speech might require control."[69] He referred to some observations of Lord Bryce on "The Press".[70] But the following observations of Lord Bryce are pertinent here:

Evils of monopoly not peculiar to U.S.A.

". . . the best remedy against whatever dangers the dominance of the press involves is to be found in the free and full competition of independent newspapers. It is the predominance in one particular area or among the members of one particular class, of a single paper, or of several controlled by the same person or group and working for the same ends, that threatens the formation of a fair and enlightened public opinion. *The tyranny of monopoly is even worse in opinion than in commerce.* . . . How could the dictatorship of such a syndicated press be resisted? The remedy proposed for industrial monopolies is nationalization, but here nationalization would aggravate the evil, making the State itself the tyrant. *Recourse might be needed to drastic legislation of a kind not yet tried.*"[71] (italics supplied)

Lord Bryce on monopoly in the press and the danger to the freedom of the press

---

[66] 326 U.S. *supra* at p. 20. This case was distinguished in the majority judgment by saying that it merely showed that there was power in the United States to regulate the newspaper industry: (1973) 2 S.C.R. at p. 784. However, "to regulate" is to subject to guidance or restrictions (*S.O.D.*), and under our Constitution, Art. 19(1)(*g*) read with Art. 19(6) in terms confers power on the legislatures to put reasonable restrictions on business which, as we have seen, must include the business of publishing a newspaper. For a discussion of the power of Indian legislatures to legislate on monopolies see para 10.253 of the text. It is submitted that the distinction made in the majority judgment is based on a misconception, and is untenable.

[67] See paras 10.27 and 10.28 of the text.

[68] ('73) A.SC. at pp. 1963-4.

[69] ibid. p. 1964.

[70] ibid. p. 1964: Bryce, *Modern Democracies,* Vol. 1, pp. 101-124.

[71] *Bryce, op. cit.* pp. 121-22.

U.K. legislation re. merger and monopolies applicable to newspapers

This was in 1920. In 1965 the British Parliament enacted the Monopolies and Merger Act, 1965, which applied to Newspaper Mergers.[72] Section 8 (3) of the Act provided that

"In deciding whether or not the transfer may be expected to operate against the public interest the Commission must take into account all matters which appear in the particular circumstances to be relevant and having regard (amongst other things) *to the need for accurate presentation of news and free expression of opinion.*"[73]

Power to legislate on industrial and commercial monopolies under our Constitution

In India, "Commercial and industrial monopolies, combines and trusts" is a head of concurrent legislative power,[74] which shows that the framers of our Constitution were aware of the evils which *may* flow from monopolies etc. Mathew J. referred to the Reports of the Mahalanobis Committee and the Press Commission[75] to point out the danger to the freedom of the press from newspapers which hold a monopolistic position.[76] It is submitted that the above considerations establish that whatever may be the ambit of the freedom of speech and expression, the business activity of the press which has the effect of curtailing that freedom by a monopolistic combination is antagonistic to the freedom which is conferred by Art. 19 (1) (*a*) and a law which removes such monopoly or monopolistic combinations, far from diminishing freedom actually increases it.

Scope of freedom of the press *vis-a-vis* rationing of newsprint

10.254 This leads us to the second part of question (*b*) in para 10.245 above. Mathew J. has reached the right conclusion on the nature of the freedom of speech and of the press and as to the reasons why such freedom is highly regarded as a necessary condition of the working of a free democracy, and his careful and learned discussion will repay study. His conclusions are based on juristic considerations and on theories some of which may admit of dispute. However, it is submitted that his decision can be rested on a simpler ground. First, it has been held that commercial advertisements in newspapers do not fall within the protection of Art. 19 (1) (*a*).[77] Secondly, where newsprint is a scarce commodity and has to be rationed, to deny extra newsprint to newspapers with fewer pages in order to grant newsprint to newspapers so that they could increase the number of their pages, would be a denial of freedom of speech and expression to the former. Thirdly, it is submitted that it is impossible to say *a priori* whether freedom of speech and of the press is increased by allowing newspapers to reduce their circulation and increase their pages, instead of requiring such newspapers to maintain or increase their circulation whilst diminishing the number of pages. It is equally impossible to say, *a priori*, that allowing newspapers which have fewer pages to increase the number of pages, which might also increase their circulation, would not promote freedom instead of restricting it. The

Submission

---

[72] See *Halsbury,* 1974 Supplement, Vol. II, Vol. 38, para 120B. A discussion of the provisions of that Act is outside the scope of this work.

[73] ibid., *note* 11.

[74] Entry 21, List III, Sch. 7.

[75] (1973) 2 S.C.R. at pp. 812-3.

[76] ibid. These references show that there was evidence before the Court of monopolistic tendencies in the Indian press, a conclusion supported by the fact that there were chains of newspapers under a common ownership. The bald statement in the majority judgment that "The Press is not exposed to any mischief of monopolistic combination" (ibid. p. 797) overlooks this evidence apart from ignoring the experience in other countries.

[77] *Hamdarad Dawakhana (Wakf) Lal Kuan* v. *Union* (1960) 2 S.C.R. 671, ('60) A.SC. 554.

factual situation therefore is that two views can be reasonably taken of freedom of speech and expression and it is submitted that in such a situation, the choice of one such view as a basis of policy is a matter of legislative judgment and not of judicial determination. Further, the presumption of constitutionality would apply, and cannot be displaced since, as shown above, two views can be reasonably taken.

Increase of cost and freedom of the press: Submission: implied assumption in the majority judgment not correct

10.255 As to question (*c*) in para 10.245 above, it is submitted that it is an underlying assumption of the majority judgment in the *Benett Coleman Case* that anything which increased the price of newspapers, or which diminished the revenue from advertisements, must violate Art. 19(1)(*a*). But, as we have seen, laws for the welfare of labour, laws restraining monopoly and monopolistic combination and laws imposing a tax on the sale or purchase of newspapers or on advertisements published therein might, and probably would, increase the price and might diminish the revenue from advertisements. For reasons given earlier, these laws cannot be declared void merely because they would, to some extent, abridge the freedom of speech and the press. Further, it may be observed that the majority judgment in the *Bennett Coleman Case*, and the theory prevailing at the time was that all price fixation must ensure a reasonable return and if such fixation put a business undertaking to loss, must necessarily be invalid. The decision in the *Meenakshi Mills Case*[78] has reversed that trend.

Challenge under Art. 14

10.256 As to question (*d*) in para 10.245 above, the majority judgment appears to assume that the doctrine of equality requires the existing inequalities to be perpetuated. The majority judgment applied the doctrine that inequality resulted if unequals were treated equally. We have considered this doctrine earlier, and pointed out that the majority judgment of the Supreme Court in *Twyford Tea Co.'s Case* has rightly described the absurd consequences which would follow if the above doctrine were applied in all cases.[79] The whole trend of modern legislation is in favour of removing inequalities which can be removed, and this trend is in consonance with the concept of equality. It would be strange indeed if a Constitution, whose proclaimed object is to secure equality of status and opportunity to its citizens, should, in its enacting part (Art. 14), require that equality of status and opportunity should be denied to citizens, and that the *status quo* should be maintained. If, as an accident of earlier policies, well-established newspapers were given a larger quota of newsprint related to their circulation, and permitted to have a larger number of pages, with the result that newspapers which come into existence at a later date were deprived of necessary newsprint to increase their pages, it is difficult to see which doctrine of equality required this inequality be perpetuated. It is submitted that Mathew J. rightly upheld the policy on this ground, though he also supported his conclusion by reference to the active concept of equality developed in *Griffin* v. *Illinois*[80] and *Douglas* v. *California*.[81]

Submission: dissenting judgment of Mathew J. is correct

---

[78] See para 10.222 *et seq.* where the case has been fully discussed.

[79] See paras 10.157 and 10.160 of the text.

[80] 351 U.S. 12, 100 L.ed. 891. (Denial of an appeal to an indigent appellant unable to pay the charges for a short hand transcript).

[81] 372 U.S. 353, 9 L.ed. 2d. 811 (Denial of counsel before an Appellate Court).

Those cases involved a challenge both under the equality and due process clauses of the 14th Amendment, and it is not clear how far considerations relevant to due process influenced the decision on the equality clause. Secondly, the impressive dissents of four judges in the first case, and of three judges in the second, make it unsafe to rest the conclusion on the active concept of equality, more especially when the due process clause was expressly eliminated by the framers of our Constitution from Art. 21.

Conclusion

10.257 The above discussion shows that Mathew J. applied the correct test and reached the correct conclusions on the challenge to the impugned policy under Art. 14; and that he applied substantially the correct test and reached the correct conclusions as to the challenge under Art 19.[82] These conclusions are, it is submitted, strengthened by several considerations referred to in the above discussion, especially those relating to the inter-relation of Art. 19(1) (*a*) read with Art. 19(2) and of Art. 19(1) (*g*) read with Art. 19(6).

"Monopoly": Art. 19(6)

10.258 Would the creation of a monopoly fall within the meaning of "reasonable restrictions" on trade, business, etc.? This question arose for consideration under Art. 19(6) as originally enacted in our Constitution, and it involved an interpretation of Art. 19(6). As the construction of the amended Art. 19(6) was considered at length by the Supreme Court in a case which will be considered later,[83] the correct construction will be considered in connection with that judgment. However, the amended Art. 19(6) provides for what may compendiously be described as a monopoly, the original and the amended Articles are set out below:

before and after the 4th Amendment

Art. 19(6): "Nothing in sub-clause (*g*) of the said clause shall affect the operation of any existing law in so far as it imposes, or prevent the State from making any law imposing, in the interests of the general public, reasonable restrictions on the exercise of the right conferred by the said sub-clause, and, in particular, nothing in the said sub-clause shall affect the operation of any existing law in so far as it prescribes or empowers any authority to prescribe, or prevent the State from making any law prescribing or empowering any authority to prescribe, the professional or technical qualifications necessary for practising any profession or carrying on any occupation, trade or business."

Art. 19(6) (amended): "Nothing in sub-clause (*g*) of the said clause shall affect the operation of any existing law in so far as it imposes, or prevent the State from making any law imposing, in the interests of the general public, reasonable restrictions on the exercise of the right conferred by the said sub-clause, and, in particular, nothing in the said sub-clause, shall affect the operation of any existing law in so far as it relates to, or prevent the State from making any law relating to (i) the professional or technical qualifications necessary for practising any profession or carrying on any occupation, trade or business, or (ii) the carrying on by the State or by a corporation owned or controlled by the State, of any trade, business, industry or service, whether to the exclusion, complete or partial, of citizens or otherwise."

---

[82] The above discussion also shows that it is not possible to sustain the wide general observations in the *Sakal Case* (see para 10.241 above), namely, that the only restrictions which can be put on the freedom of speech and expression are those permitted by Art. 19(2), and that restrictions which can be put on business under Art. 19(6) are irrelevant in considering an alleged infringement of freedom of speech and expression.

[83] See para 10.259 *et seq.*

It will be noticed that the frame of Art. 19(6) remains the same after its amendment as it was before; the original Art. 19(6) fell into two parts; these are retained as they were, the second part being enlarged by the addition of Art. 19(6)(ii). As it is relevant to a Supreme Court decision to be considered later, it may be mentioned that the words "in particular" appear both in the original and in the amended Art. 19(6). The question whether a monopoly violated the rights conferred by Art. 19(1)(*g*) was considered in *Saghir Ahmad* v. *U.P.*[84] with reference to the unamended Art. 19(6). The monopoly there impugned was in road transport and the court left open the question whether the words "reasonable restrictions" included prohibition;[85] if they did not, then a monopoly must be judged on the touch-stone of "reasonable restrictions". In considering whether a monopoly imposed reasonable restrictions regard must be had to the directive of State policy contained in Art. 39(*a*) that the State shall secure to all citizens, men and women equally, the right to an adequate means of livelihood. Accordingly, the loss of livelihood to a large number of people, resulting from the creation of a monopoly was relevant in judging its reasonableness. Further, the nature of the business must also be considered. As there was nothing noxious about the business of road transport, before a monopoly in road transport could be upheld as reasonable, materials must be placed before the Court for that purpose. As no material had been placed before the Court to justify the monopoly, the Court held that the monopoly imposed unreasonable restrictions and was void.[86] As the amendment of Art. 19(6) was not retrospective, Mukherjea J. held that the case before the Court had to be decided on the unamended Article; however, he added that if a case had to be decided after the amendment of Art. 19(6), the monopoly could not be impugned as violating Art. 19(1)(*g*):

Saghir Ahmad's Case: reasonableness of a monopoly must be justified

Monopoly in motor transport held void

"... the amendment does not make the establishment of such monopoly a reasonable restriction within the meaning of the first clause of Art. 19(6). The result of the amendment is that the State would not have to justify such action as reasonable at all in a Court of law and no objection is to be taken to it on the ground that it is an infringement of the right guaranteed under Art. 19(1)(*g*) ..."[87]

The effect of the 4th Amendment: reasonableness not to be justified

---

[84] (1955) 1 S.C.R. 707, ('54) A.SC. 728; *Gopal Rao* v. *Shiv Ramiah* (1952) Hyd. 481, ('53) A.Hyd. 1 [*held*, that a suit for a declaration of the plaintiff's exclusive right to perform "Purohitgiri" did not lie as it would violate Art. 19(1)(*g*) since the right claimed would exclude others from carrying on the same profession in the village]; rel. on in *Maniram* v. *Pannalal* ('62) A.M.P. 275, [*held*, that a custom giving exclusive right to some *chamars* to remove carcasses of animals dying in a village was void as violating Art. 19(1)(*f*) and (*g*)]

[85] It has now been decided that they include prohibition. See para 10.2 of the text.

[86] In *Rajasthan* v. *Mohan Lal* ('71) A.SC. 2068 (without any reference to this statement of the law in *Saghir Ahmed's Case*) the Supreme Court observed that "The Constitution forbids grant by the State to a citizen of monopoly right to carry on the business of plying buses undertaken in the agreements. The manner in which the agreements were to be performed became illegal as a result of the Constitution." It is submitted that this proposition is too wide, and the correct law on the subject was laid down by Mukherjea J., namely, "before a monopoly can be upheld as reasonable, materials must be placed before the Court for that purpose."

[87] (1955) 1 S.C.R. *supra* at p. 727, fol. in *Jain T. & G. Trading Co.* v. *U.P.* ('57) A.A. 320.

Akadasi's Case

10.259 In *Akadasi* v. *Orissa*[88] questions arising from the creation of monopoly were fully considered under the amended Art. 19(6), in connection with the provisions of the Orissa Kendu Leaves (Control of Trade) Act, 1961. The petitioner owned about eighty acres of land on which he grew kendu leaves which are used in the manufacture of *bidis.* Since the Act came into force, the State acquired a monopoly in the trade of kendu leaves and the petitioner challenged the Act as contravening Art. 19(1) (*f*) and (*g*). Three questions were considered by the Supreme Court: (1) What is the effect of the amendment made in Art. 19(6) by inserting sub-Article (ii)? (2) What is the nature of the law which is covered by Art. 19(6) (ii)? (3) Does Art. 19(6) (ii) authorise the State to employ agents other than the Departments of the State or members of the Service of the States?

Observations of Mukherjea J. in *Sagir Ahmad's Case* not accepted

(1) In *Akadasi's Case* the observations of Mukherjea J. on the effect of the amended Art. 19(6) were not accepted on the ground, first, that in that case the question did not arise and, secondly, because the impact of Art. 19(6) on Art. 19(1) (*f*) had not been considered.[89] Mukherjea J.'s observations were rejected for the following reasons: the legislative history of the amendment of Art. 19(6) showed that laws passed by the State[90] creating a monopoly, as for example, in State Transport, had been struck down as violating Art. 19(1) (*g*).[91] It was thus realised that the legislative power to create a monopoly did not preclude a challenge under Art. 19(1) (*g*) and, accordingly, Art. 19(6) was amended by adding Art. 19(6) (ii) which provided in effect that the creation of a complete or partial monopoly was not to be affected because it contravened Art. 19(1) (*g*). The question was, what was the scope and effect of the amendment on the interpretation of Art. 19(6)?

The scope of the amended Art. 19(6) considered: approach to the construction of Art. 19(6) indicated

"In attempting to construe Art. 19(6), . . . a literal construction may not be quite appropriate. The task of construing important Constitutional provisions like Art. 19(6) cannot always be accomplished by treating the said problem as a mere exercise in grammar. In interpreting such a provision, it is essential to bear in mind the political or the economic philosophy underlying the provisions in question, and that would necessarily involve the adoption of a liberal and not a literal and mechanical approach to the problem."[92]

After considering the philosophy of socialism and State ownership, and the various theories underlying nationalisation, and after holding that the approach to nationalisation could be either doctrinaire or pragmatic, the Court said:

"The amendment made by the Legislature in Art. 19(6) shows that according to the Legislature, a law relating to the creation of State monopoly should be presumed to be in the interests of the general public."[93]

and proceeded to say that the theory underlying the amendment appeared to be doctrinaire and not pragmatic and for that reason the argument on behalf of the petitioner, that a State monopoly must be justified by showing that it imposed reasonable restrictions

---

88 (1963) Supp. (2) S.C.R. 691, ('63) A.SC. 1047; rel. on in *Vrajlal Manilal & Co.* v. *State* ('66) A.M.P. 301, 306 [*held*, that the M.P. Tendu Patta (Vyapar Viniyaman) Adhiniyam, 1964, was protected by Art. 19(6)].

89 The validity of the second ground is discussed in para 10.266.

90 In the exercise of their legislative power under Entry 21, List III. Sch. VII (Commercial and Industrial Monopoly, Combines and Trusts).

91 As for example, in *Moti Lal* v. *U.P.* (1951) 1 All. 269, ('51) A.A. 257 (F.B.).

92 (1963) Supp. (2) S.C.R. *supra* at p. 704.

93 ibid. p. 704.

in the interests of the general public, had to be rejected. The framers of the Constitution had assumed that a monopoly would be covered by Art. 19 (6) but when their assumption was invalidated by judicial decisions, it was thought necessary to "clarify the intention of the Constitution" by making the amendment. It was because the amendment was made for the purposes of clarification "that it begins with the words 'in particular'." The Court concluded:

"These words indicate that restrictions imposed on the fundamental rights guaranteed by Art. 19(1)(*g*) which are reasonable and which are in the interests of the general public, are saved by Art. 19(6) as it originally stood; the subject-matter covered by the said provision being justiciable, and the amendment adds that the State monopolies or nationalisation Schemes which may be introduced by legislation, are an illustration of reasonable restrictions imposed in the interests of the general public and must be treated as such. That is why the question about the validity of the laws covered by the amendment is no longer left to be tried in Courts. This brings out the doctrinaire approach adopted by the amendment in respect of a State monopoly as such."[94]

A criticism: approach contrary to settled principles of construction

It is submitted that the whole approach to the interpretation of Art. 19 (6) before and after its amendment is contrary to well-settled principles of constitutional interpretation, and the interpretation actually put is clearly wrong. We have seen[95] that the cardinal rule of interpretation of the Constitution is to give to the words their plain grammatical meaning, and if such meaning is clear and results in no absurdity or grave inconvenience, no further question of interpretation arises. If however, the plain meaning of the words leads to absurdity or grave inconvenience, or there is an ambiguity, resort can be had to well-known extrinsic aids to interpretation. But the philosophical, social or economic theories supposed to underlie a particular provision is clearly not one of such extrinsic aids to construction.[96] Again, the discussion about the "doctrinaire" or "pragmatic" theory of a monopoly may be relevant, if at all, to a law creating a monopoly, but is wholly irrelevant to Art. 19 (6) (ii). That Article does not confer legislative power or compel the making of a law. It saves a law creating a monopoly from a particular constitutional challenge, whether such a law is based on the doctrinaire theory, or the pragmatic theory, or on no theory at all. The danger of first propounding theories, and then interpreting provisions to give effect to those theories is demonstrated by the remark of the Supreme Court that "it is because the amendment was thus made for the purposes of clarification that it begins with the words 'in particular' ".[97] The remark overlooks the unamended Art. 19 (6), in which the words "in particular" occur in the same place and for the same purpose as they do in the amended Article, and there was nothing "to clarify" in the unamended Article. Therefore, the real question to ask was: what is the interpretation of the unamended Article, and does the amended Article affect such interpretation in any manner? It is submitted that the unamended Article fell into two separate parts, namely,

Irrelevance of theories of monopoly: Art. 19(6) not a source of legislative power

[94] ibid. p. 706.
[95] See paras 2.12, 2.14 *et seq.*
[96] See para 2.2 and the references there given to the judgment of Gwyer C.J. in the *Central Provinces Case*, (1939) F.C.R. 18, 37, ('39) A.FC. 1.
[97] (1963) Supp. (2) S.C.R. *supra* at p. 706.

The frame of the unamended Art. 19(6)

Part I: "Nothing in sub-clause (*g*) of the said clause [19(1)] shall affect the operation of any exisiting law in so far as it imposes or prevents the State from making any law imposing, in the interests of the general public, reasonable restrictions on the exercise of the right coferred by the said clause";

Part II: "and, in particular, nothing in the said sub-clause shall affect the operation of any existing law in so far as it prescribes or empowers any authority to prescribe, or prevent the State from making any law prescribing or empowering any authority to prescribe, the professional or technical qualifications necessary for practising any profession or carrying on any occupation, trade or business."

remains the same after amendment

The expression "in particular" means: "in distinction from others; particularly, especially"[98] and it emphasises the fact that a provision is especially made for the class of laws mentioned in the second part. That the two parts are separate is also clear from the repetition of the words "nothing in sub-clause (*g*) shall affect" in the first part, and "nothing in the said sub-clause [i.e. sub-cl. (*g*)] shall affect" occurring in the second part. The words "reasonable restrictions" find a place in the first part but not in the second. Therefore, when the opening words of the second part say that nothing contained in Art. 19(1)(*g*) is to affect the laws described in the second part, no requirement of reasonableness is prescribed for those laws. The amendment not only does not weaken, but strengthens the above conclusion. The view which the Courts had taken was that a monopoly had to be justified as imposing reasonable restrictions under the first part of Art. 19(6), such reasonableness being justiciable. If the amendment was designed to nullify this view, and a monopoly was not to be judged on the touchstone of "reasonable restrictions" which were justiciable, that result was best achieved by putting a monopoly in the second part where no question of reasonableness and, therefore, of justiciability, arose; and that is what the amendment has done. To say as the Supreme Court said, that the words "in particular" show that what follows them in the second part is an illustration of what is contained in the first part, is first, to ignore the meaning of the phrase "in particular"; and secondly, to misunderstand the nature of the first part, and the nature of an illustration of the first part. The first part refers to existing and future laws imposing reasonable restrictions, and decisions of the Supreme Court show that the reasonableness of restrictions is justiciable. If that is the general characteristic of a law under the first part, an illustration of that law must exhibit the same general characteristic, namely, that it must be an instance of a law imposing reasonable restrictions which are justiciable, but that is exactly what the Supreme Court says a law creating a monopoly is not. The result therefore is that on a correct interpretation of Art. 19(6) the requirement of reasonableness applies to the first part but does not apply to sub-clauses (i) and (ii) of the second part. It is submitted therefore that the interpretation placed by the Supreme Court in *Akadasi's Case* on Art. 19(6) after its amendment is incorrect, is contrary to the language of the sub-Article and is opposed to well-settled principles of constitutional interpretation. The interpretation placed by Mukherjea J. is correct and is in conformity with the plain language of the Article.

The requirement of reasonableness does not apply to Art. 19(6)(*i*) and (*ii*)

Submission: Mukherjea J.'s view is correct

[98] *Shorter Oxford Dictionary,* (1959) 3rd. ed. p. 1439.

(2) The Supreme Court then considered the nature of a law covered by Art. 19 (6) (ii): what is meant by "laws in relation to" a monopoly? It was held that it must mean those parts of the law which were absolutely essential for the creation of a monopoly, and that other provisions in such a law must satisfy the test of the first part of Art. 19 (6). The conclusion is correct, though "monopoly" is a compendious expression for the words actually used in the Article, namely, "the carrying on by the State of any trade, business, industry or service, *whether to the exclusion complete or partial*, of citizens or otherwise" (italics supplied). The decision can be rested on the language of the Article itself, from which it follows that it is that part of the law which relates to the carrying on of trade *to the exclusion of others*, which is protected, and therefore if a law providing for the carrying on of trade to the exclusion of others contains provisions which can be said not to relate to such exclusion, it is not protected by Art. 19 (6) (ii). Provisions of a law creating a monopoly which are not an integral part of it, but are subsidiary, incidental or helpful to the operation of monopoly, did not fall under Art. 19 (6) (ii), but had to be justified under the first part of Art. 19 (6). This part of the decision was followed in *Vrajlal M. & Co.* v. *M.P.*[99] where the Supreme Court upheld the validity of s. 5, M.P. Tendu Patta Vyapar Viniyaman Adhiniyam, 1964, and R. 9 of the rules made thereunder, by putting a restricted interpretation on them.[1] In *Amritsar Municipality* v. *Punjab*[2] the Supreme Court followed the principle laid down in the *Akadasi Case* and held that the exclusion of citizens from holding cattle fairs was "basically and essentially" necessary for creating a state monopoly, and the monopoly was protected by Art. 19 (6). The restrictions on the rights of citizens under Art. 19 (1) (*b*), (*d*) and (*f*) must be regarded as reasonable within the meaning of Art. 19 (3) and (5) as those restrictions were necessary to make the monopoly effective, and their reasonableness must be judged in the light of Art. 19 (6).[3]

What law is covered by Art. 19(6)(*ii*)? only those parts of a law essential to the creation of a monopoly

Submission: all ancillary and subsidiary provisions covered

(3) As to the question whether the trade, etc., protected by Art. 19 (6) (ii) could be carried on through agents, the Court held that the State could only act through human agency and could carry on trade or business through a government department or through officers who were members of a public service. But there may be cases where these modes of carrying on trade or business were not suitable, as for example, where the trade was seasonal, as in the case before the Court, and in such cases Government could engage agents working for and on behalf of Government for a remuneration and not on their own account or in their own interest. Agency in this strict sense was permissible and was within the scope of Art.

Trade protected by Art. 19(6)(*ii*) can be carried on through agents working for Govt. and *not* on their own account

[99] (1970) 1 S.C.R. 400, ('70) A.SC. 129.

[1] ('70) A.SC. at pp. 136-7 [*held*, that the section and the rules required that a manufacturer must have a permit to move the leaves purchased from the unit or units where he had purchased them to his warehouse outside and from there to his branches and also when he transported them to his "sattedars". But it was not intended that permission would be necessary when the leaves were distributed for the manufacture of bidis by the *sattedar* to the *mazdoors* whom he employed. This restricted interpretation carried out the object of the law and avoided constitutional invalidity under Art. 19(1)(*g*)].

[2] (1969) 3 S.C.R. 447, ('69) A.SC. 1100.

[3] ('69) A.SC. at pp. 1104-1105.

19(6) (ii). If, however, such an agent could be shown to work for his own interest or benefit, such agency was outside Art. 19(6) (ii). Although therefore the Court upheld the validity of the section which provided for the appointment of agents, it held that having regard to the actual contracts entered into with the agents it could not be said that they were working solely for and on behalf of Government for a remuneration and therefore the actual appointment of agents was not protected by Art. 19(6) (ii) and was not authorised by the provisions of the Act. In *T. Mishra* v. *Orissa*[4] the Supreme Court applied the principles laid down in *Akadasi's Case* relating to working a monopoly through agents, and held that ss. 3(2) (*a*), 8(1) (as amended in 1969), Orissa Kendu Leaves (Control of Trade) Act, 1961 and Rules 5-B(6), (7), (8), (9) and (16); 6(3) and 7(1) made under the Act did not violate Art. 19(1) (*g*).

agents employed working also on their own: actual appointment of agents not protected

Impact of Art. 19(6) on the right in Art. 19(1)(*f*)

10.260 The impact of the amendment in Art. 19(6), on the right conferred in Art. 19(1) (*f*), was also considered in the *Akadasi Case*. Adopting the test laid down by Kania C.J. in *Gopalan's Case*[5] and approved in *Ram Singh's Case*[6] and in the *Express Newspapers Case*[7] the Supreme Court held that

"... in dealing with the attack against the validity of a law creating state monopoly on the ground that its provisions impinge upon the other fundamental rights guaranteed by Art. 19(1), it would be necessary to decide what is the purpose of the Act and its direct effect. If the direct effect of the Act is to impinge upon any other right guaranteed by Art. 19(1), its validity will have to be tested in the light of the corresponding clauses in Art. 19; if the effect on the said right is indirect or remote, then its validity cannot be successfully challenged."[8]

Submission: impact of Art. 19(1)(*g*) on 19(1)(*f*) irrelevant to the meaning to be given to 19(6)(*ii*)

This view is clearly right, but it is difficult to see what the impact of Art. 19(6) on the right conferred by Art. 19(1) (*f*) has to do with the meaning to be given to Art. 19(6), and why Mukherjea J.'s interpretation of Art. 19(6) (ii) is to be rejected because he did not consider that impact. Whether a law protected under Art. 19(6) (ii) directly violates a right conferred by Arts. 19(1) (*a*) to (*f*) and must therefore conform to the requirements of Art. 19(2) to (5) can have no bearing on the meaning of Art. 19(6).

The *Ennadu Case*

10.261 Important questions relating to Art. 19(1) (*a*), and Art. 14 were decided in *Ushodaya Publications (P) Ltd.* v. *A.P.*[9] ("the *Ennadu Case*"). The 1st petitioner, Ushodaya Publications (Private) Ltd., ("the company") owned a leading Telugu daily *Ennadu*[10], the 2nd petitioner being the Chairman of the Board of Directors of the company, and also the printer and publisher of *Ennadu*. *Ennadu* had been started in 1974 and it was claimed by the company that within a period of 5 years it had reached a daily circulation of over

---

[4] ('71) A.SC. 733. The above principle was followed in *Lakshmi Chand* v. *Shankar Lal* ('76) A.H.P. 69. [*held*, that ss. 7 and 8 of the Himachal Pradesh Urban Rent Control Act, 1978 were reasonably capable of the construction that they operated prospectively and therefore Art. 20(1) was not attracted].

[5] (1950) S.C.R. 88, 100-101, ('50) A.SC. 27.

[6] (1951) S.C.R. 451, 457, ('51) A.SC. 270.

[7] (1959) S.C.R. 12, 129-135, ('58) A.SC. 578.

[8] *Akadasi's Case*, (1963) Supp. (2) S.C.R. *supra* at p. 709.

[9] ('81) A.A.P. 109 (F.B.).

[10] Which was published from Hyderabad, Vishakapatanam and Vijayawada.

two lacs, which was said to be the highest circulation for a newspaper in the State. In a writ petition, the petitioners prayed that the Government Order ("the G.O.") dated 10-8-1979 should be quashed. Under the G.O., all advertisements of government departments/ public sector undertakings/government companies were to be released only by the Director of Information and Public Relations ("the Director") to various newspapers, keeping in view the subject matter of the advertisement. When the petition was filed, guidelines had not been laid down for the distribution of advertisements under the G.O., but such guidelines were laid down before the petition was heard.[11] The petitioners contended that the G.O. with guidelines were violative of Art. 19 (1) (*a*) because they imposed restrictions on the freedom of speech and expression, which included the freedom of the press, beyond the limits permitted by Art. 19 (2), and also because the restrictions were vague and imprecise and lacked distinctness in respect of the factors disqualifying a newspaper from receiving Government advertisements; further, the G.O. violated Art. 14 because it conferred unfettered and unregulated discretion in respect of a fundamental right. The criteria adopted for the release of advertisements were irrational and not germane to the object of issuing advertisements which was to ensure the widest possible coverage; that the G.O. had been implemented in a discriminatory manner and particulars of the discrimination were given; finally it was contended that the G.O. had been issued *mala fide* and with the object of punishing *Ennadu* for its strong criticism of the Government and its ministers. The Court rejected the last two contentions as not justified by the materials placed before it.[12]

Govt.'s Order relating to advertisements challenged as violating Art. 19(1)(*a*)

and as violating Art. 14

10.262 Kuppuswami Acg. C.J. treated it as settled that the freedom of speech and expression conferred by Art. 19 (1) (*a*) included the freedom of the press, which was an aspect of freedom of speech and expression and was an integral part of free speech, as held in the undernoted decisions.[13] Further, freedom of circulation of newspapers was necessarily involved in freedom of speech and expression, and was a part of it, and therefore enjoyed the protection of Art. 19 (1) (*a*) as held in *Romesh Thapar's Case*.[14] The G.O. was impugned on the ground that it directly affected the circulation of the petitioner's newspaper and infringed the right of the freedom of the press guaranteed under Art. 19 (1) (*a*). The Acg. Chief Justice considered the decisions in the *Sakal Case* and the *Bennett Coleman Case* and held that they did not assist the petitioners. In those cases restrictions had been placed on the right to advertise in the newspapers; but in the present case, the Company had no right to obtain advertisements, and the G.O. did not place any restriction on the freedom of the press or on circulation. This fact distinguished the present case from the *Sakal Case* and *Bennett Coleman Case*. Further, the facts in *In re Kerala Education Bill*[15] bore no resem-

Challenge under Art. 19(1) (*a*) rejected

[11] ibid. pp. 112-13 where the guidelines are set out.
[12] ibid. pp. 121-22.
[13] *Express Newspapers Case* (1959) S.C.R. 12, ('58) A.SC. 578; *Sakal Papers (P) Ltd.* v. *Union* (1962) 3 S.C.R. 842, ('62) A.SC. 305; *Bennett Coleman & Co. Ltd.* v. *Union* (1973) 2 S.C.R. 757, ('73) A.SC. 106 and *Maneka Gandhi* v. *Union* (1978) 2 S.C.R. 621, ('78) A.SC. 597.
[14] (1950) S.C.R. 594, ('50) A.SC. 124.
[15] (1959) S.C.R. 995, ('58) A.SC. 956.

blance to the facts in the present case.[16] Besides, as held in the *Hamdarad Dawakhana Case*,[17] commercial advertisements do not fall within the freedom of speech referred to in Art. 19 (1) (*a*).[18]

The importance of the *Ennadu Case*: application of the enlarged scope of Art.14 in the *Airport Case*

10.263 The importance of the *Ennadu Case* lies in the manner in which the court dealt with the challenge to the G.O., and the guidelines, under Art. 14. Having held that the petitioner had no right to obtain advertisements from Government Departments, etc., the Court used the enlarged scope of Art. 14 to give the petitioners, in substance, a right ot challenge the G.O. and the guidelines. The petitioners relied on the *Airport Case*[19] and on *E.E. & C. Ltd.* v *W.B.*,[20] and

"In view of these decisions, the learned Adv.-General fairly conceded that it is open to the petitioners to attack the G.O. on the ground of discrimination and violation of Art. 14 . . ."[21]

The Court observed that Government raised crores of rupees as revenue, and as Government was the guardian of the State's finances it was its duty to use the revenue for the benefit of all concerned. Government spent a considerable portion of its funds on advertisements, and

"It should not use the power over such large funds in its hands to muzzle the press or as a weapon to punish newspapers which criticise its policies and actions. It has to use the funds in a reasonable manner consistently with the object of the advertisement viz. to educate and inform the public about the activities of the Government."[22]

After holding that circulation of a newspaper could not be the only criterion—for then smaller newspapers would be denied all Government advertisements—the Court said that the main attack had been on paragraph 2 of the G.O. (read with the guidelines) which provided that Government advertisements should not be given to newspapers adopting "any of the following tones", namely, "(i) Anti-national; (ii) Communal; (iii) Rabid, abusive; (iv) provoking tensions between different sections of the society; (v) Distorting news for mischievous purpose; (vi) Character assassination, blackmailing and attacks on individuals or mud-slinging without proper and truthful evidence and intimidation; (vii) Fomenting group rivalries and quarrels and thereby indulging in mischievous gossip-mongering and sensationalism; (viii) Abusive and slanderous attacks on Government or its functionaries".[23] The Court held that conditions (i), (ii), (iv) and (vi) were valid. However, conditions (iii), (v) and (vii) had to be struck down. Condition (iii) had to be struck down because "rabid" meant "raging, fanatical", and it was difficult to decide whether any view expressed by a newspaper was fanatical or abusive. A newspaper may be fanatical about what it considered a right cause, and may be abusive against what it considered to be injurious to society or to the community. The same was true of condition (v) because it was difficult to decide whether a newspaper distorted news and if so whether it was for a mischievous purpose. Again, as to condition (vii) it was difficult to say

---

[16] ('81) A.A.P. at p. 117.
[17] See para 10.44 where the case is fully discussed.
[18] ('81) A.A.P. at p. 115.
[19] *R. D. Shetty* v. *International Airport Authority of India* ('79) A.SC. 1628.
[20] ('75) A.SC. 266, 268.
[21] ('81) A.A.P. at p. 118.
[22] ibid.
[23] ibid. pp. 119-20.

whether a newspaper took side with a particular group for fomenting group rivalries, and views might differ whether a news item amounts to gossip mongering and sensationalism.[24] In the result the writ petition was allowed to the extent that conditions (iii), (v) and (vii) of the guidelines were struck down as violative of Art. 14. Further, the direction given to the Visakhapatanam Municipality not to issue advertisements was contrary to the G.O., and the Court granted a declaration that "the G.O. will not apply to municipalities and local bodies which do not come within the definition of 'Public Sector' undertakings and Government Companies'."[25]

Relief granted to the petitioners

10.264 In *Combined Traders* v. *State*[26] it was held that where Government which was the absolute owner of a reserved forest, sold the produce of the forest by public auction, and bluegum wood was sold subject to the condition, that it should not be transported outside the district, the auction purchaser would take the wood subject to that condition. For, the whole matter rested in contract and the purchaser could not complain of a violation of his rights under Art. 19 (1) (*f*) and (*g*) or under Art. 301. No citizen could claim that he had a fundamental right to purchase property owned by Government.

Combined Traders* v. *State

10.265 Can Government's dealings with the assets and properties vested in it ("government property") give rise to a claim that such dealings violate the fundamental rights guaranteed by Part III of our Constitution? Again, can government be restrained from dealing with government property contrary to its duty, because contrary to the purpose for which such property is vested in government? Put plainly, can the Union or any State government say "We know that this Government property is worth Rs. 5 crores but we will sell it for Rs. 1 crore — a Government, like a private individual, can do what it likes with its 'own' property"?

Government's dealings with property and assets vested in it

10.266 It is clear from Art. 294[27] that assets and properties are vested in the Union or the State governments for the purpose of the Union or the States, and entry 32, List I, and entry 35, List II, Sch. VII[28] confer express legislative power in respect of the property of the Union, and in respect of works, lands and buildings vested in a State, which legislative power is subject to the provisions of our Constitution (Arts. 245, 246), and, therefore, to fundamental rights and other constitutional limitations. No law and no executive action under the said entries can violate fundamental rights.[29] Again, our Constitution provides for the levying, collection and expenditure of revenue of the Union and the States. Such revenues are to be expended for the purposes of the Union or the States; and Art. 282[30] shows that an express provision was considered necessary to enable the Union and the States to make grants out of their revenue for purposes which were not the purposes of the Union or the States,[31] provided the grant was for *a public purpose*. The above provisions show that the

Property vested for purposes of the Union or of the States: Constitutional provisions and limitations

[24] ibid. p. 120.
[25] ibid. p. 123.
[26] ('76) A.M. 169.
[27] See p. A-97.
[28] See pp. A-178, A-183.
[29] See para 9.17 of the text.
[30] *Art. 282: Expenditure defrayable by the Union or a* State out of its revenues. — The Union or a State may make any grants for any public purpose, *notwithstanding that the purpose is not one with respect to which Parliament or the Legislature of the State, as the case may be, may make laws.* (italics supplied)
[31] See the words italicised in *f.n.* 30 above.

Union and the States hold their assets and properties impressed with an obligation to use them for their respective purposes which are public purposes; that legislative and executive action in relation to government property is subject to constitutional limitations. Property belonging to private persons or bodies is not subject to constitutional limitations;[32] within the law, a private person can do what he likes with his property; he may squander it, or give it away; in dealings with his property he may prefer one community to another, and so on.

Art. 14 and the special position of Govt. — its underlying principle

10.267 The above conclusion is strengthened by decisions under Art. 14. We have seen[33] that for most purposes Government is in a class by itself, so that special procedures for the speedy recovery of government dues or government *premises* can be provided without violating equality, and likewise a longer period of limitation can be prescribed for government than for private persons. The principle underlying these, and other similar provisions, has been well expressed by the Supreme Court when it said that *"the dues of Government* of a State (even as a Banker) *are the dues of the entire people* of the State. . ."[34] (italics supplied), and again, ". . . if a claim by Government became barred, the loss fell on the public, that is, *on the community in general,* to the benefit of a private individual. . ."[35] (italics supplied). It is submitted that if Government is given special rights, remedies and privileges in order to preserve, protect and recover government property, it is because such property belongs to the entire people of the State in the sense that government holds property for their benefit. Consequently, it is submitted that no government can claim the right to do what it likes with its "own" property, as for example, deliberately dispose of it either at an undervalue, or to serve a private, as opposed to a public, purpose.

Submission

The position in U.S.A. is the same

10.268 The position in the United States is the same. In *Van Brocklin* v. *Anderson*[36] the U.S. Supreme Court said that:

> "The United States does not and cannot hold property, as a monarch may, for private or personal purposes. All the property and revenues of the United States must be held and applied, as all taxes, duties, imposts and excises must be laid and collected, to pay the debts and provide for the common defence and general welfare of the United States."

In *U.S.* v. *Insley,*[37] after quoting this passage, the Supreme Court said: "In the present case, the United States holds the title to the property in question as it holds all other property, for public purposes and not for private purposes."

Rasbihari v. *Orissa*

10.269 We will now consider decided cases on Art. 14 and 19. In *Rasbihari* v. *Orissa*[38] the Supreme Court dealt with the Orissa Kendu Leaves (Control of Trade) Act, 1961 ("the Act"), under which the State had assumed a monopoly to trade in Kendu leaves.[39] The challenge in *Rasbihari's Case* was to the scheme adopted by Government

---

[32] Except for limited exceptions provided in Art. 15(2) and 17.
[33] Paras 9.40 to 9.42 of the text.
[34] See the quotation in para 9.41 at pp. 301-2 *ante.*
[35] See p. 303, *ante.*
[36] (1884-85) 117 U.S. 151, 158, 29 L.ed. 845, 847.
[37] (1887-88) 130 U.S. 263, 265, 32 L.ed. 968, 969.
[38] (1969) 3 S.C.R. 374, ('69) A.SC. 1081.
[39] This Act had been challenged earlier in *Akadasi's Case* which has been fully discussed in para 10.259 above.

under s. 10 of the Act,[40] namely, that government invited offers for advance purchases only from persons who had purchased Kendu leaves from individual units during 1967. The petitioners challenged the scheme as a colourable device to make it appear constitutional under Art. 19(1) (*g*) and 6(ii), whereas it was intended for the benefit of the supporters of the party in power and to increase party funds to the detriment of the public.[41] The Government after purporting to make a defence on facts,[42] contended that the exercise of the discretion under s. 10 "was not amenable to the writ jurisdiction of the High Court."[43] The following propositions emerge from the Supreme Court's judgment:

Propositions emerging from *Rasbihari's Case*

(*a*) As held in *Akadasi's Case,* (i) the expression "law relating to monopoly" covered only provisions integrally and essentially connected with the creation of a monopoly and provisions which were incidental or subsidiary to the creation of the monopoly must stand the test of Art. 19(1); (ii) the Act "cannot be used by the State for the private benefit of agents; it must only be administered for the benefit of the general public and any arrangement in which under the guise of a monopoly the State permitted a set of persons to make profit for themselves by carrying on business in Kendu leaves on their own behalf is invalid."[44]

(*b*) "S. 10 of the Act is a counterpart of s. 3 and authorises the Government to sell or otherwise dispose of Kendu leaves in such manner as the Government may direct. If the monopoly of purchasing Kendu leaves by s. 3 is valid, *in so far as it is intended to be administered only for the benefit of the State, the sale or disposal of Kendu leaves by the Government must also be in the public interest and not to serve the private interests of any person or class of persons.*"[45] (italics supplied)

(*c*) "If the scheme . . . creates a class of middlemen who would purchase from the Government Kendu leaves at concessional rates and would earn large profits disproportionate to the nature of the service rendered or duty performed by them, it cannot claim the protection of Art. 19(6)(*ii*)."[46]

(*d*) "S. 10 leaves the method of sale or disposal of Kendu leaves to the Government as they think fit. The action of the Government if conceived and executed in the interest of the general public is not open to judicial scrutiny. But it is not given to the Government thereby to create a monopoly in favour of third parties from their own monopoly."[47]

(*e*) The impugned scheme was not integrally and essentially connected with the creation of a monopoly by the Act and the scheme must stand the test of Art. 19(6). As no attempt was made by government to support the scheme as imposing reasonable restrictions under Art. 19(6), it violated Arts. 14 and 19(1)(*g*) and was void.[48]

Duty to act in the interest of the general public stressed

On the facts, the Supreme Court held that the State had given no explanation why an offer made by a well-known manufacturer of bidis to purchase the entire crop of Kendu leaves for Rs. 3 crores had been turned down. If the interests of the State alone were to be considered, the State stood to gain Rs. 1 crore. As the period for which the Kendu leaves had been sold had expired and the parties who had entered into contracts were not before the court, the

---

[40] *S. 10*: "Kendu leaves purchases by Government or by their officers or agents under this Act shall be sold or otherwise disposed of in such manner as Government may direct."

[41] For the full details of the challenge see ('69) A.SC. *supra* at p. 1085. In the view which the court took of the legal position, the court found it unnecessary to consider whether government acted in the interest of their party men and to increase party funds in devising this scheme.

[42] ibid.

[43] ibid.

[44] ibid. p. 1086.

[45] ibid. p. 1087.

[46] ibid.

[47] ibid.

[48] ibid. p. 1088.

Supreme Court could not declare such contracts void. However, it directed that Government should invite tenders for the purchase of Kendu leaves for the next season from all persons interested in the trade, and added: "We trust that in accepting tenders, the State Government will act in the interest of the general public and not of any class of traders so that in the next season the State may get the entire benefit of the monopoly in trade in Kendu leaves."[49]

Cooverjee Bharucha's Case: characteristics of the liquor trade

10.270 In *Cooverjee Bharucha's Case*[50] the petitioner impugned the provisions of Excise Regulation, 1915, and the auction rules made thereunder as violating Art. 19(1)(*g*) as they purported to create a monopoly of trade in intoxicating liquor in favour of a few persons, and because "the provisions of the Regulation regarding the levy of licence fees with the avowed object of raising a big source of revenue also seriously affected the fundamental rights of the petitioner under Art. 19(1)(*g*). . . .[51] In rejecting these contentions, Mahajan C.J. laid down the test of reasonableness set out in para 10.19 above, and held

(*a*) that no citizen had an inherent right to sell intoxicating liquor, and the State could prohibit trade in liquor altogether."[52]

(b) "Elimination and exclusion from business is inherent in the nature of liquor business *and it will hardly be proper to apply to such a business principles applicable to trades which all could carry (on)*. The provisions of the regulation cannot be attacked merely on the ground that they create a monopoly. Properly speaking, there can be a monopoly only when a trade which could be carried on by all persons is entrusted by law to one or more persons to the exclusion of the general public. Such, however, is not the case with the business of liquor."[53] (italics supplied)

(c) That the contention that the charge of fee by public auction was excessive and not in the nature of a fee but a tax ignored the fact "that the licence fee as a licence fee is more in the nature of a tax than a licence fee. One of the purposes of the regulation is to raise revenue."[54]

Having regard to the clear decision that considerations relating to ordinary trades are inapplicable to trade in intoxicating liquors, a discussion of any Supreme Court decision relating to trade in intoxicating liquors would appear to be irrelevant to a discussion on property belonging to government. However, it becomes necessary to do so, since some observations of the Supreme Court in *Orissa* v. *Harinarayan*[55] (to be considered next)—a case dealing with the auction of liquor shops—have been mistakenly interpreted as applying to Government property in general. We must now consider that case.

Harinarayan's Case: auction for the sale of liquor

10.271 In *Harinarayan's Case*[56] the first respondent, who carried on the business of selling country liquor, bid at an auction for the exclusive privilege of selling by retail, country liquor in eight specified shops. His bid was the highest, but Government rejected it on the ground that it was too low as a result of collusions among bidders. Government ordered the Excise Commissioner to invite tenders. Government accepted the tender in respect of one shop, but rejected other tenders as the price offered was inadequate. "Thereafter it sold

---

[49] ibid. pp. 1088-9.
[50] (1954) S.C.R. 873.
[51] ibid. pp. 875-76.
[52] ibid. pp. 880-81.
[53] ibid. p. 881.
[54] ibid. p. 882.
[55] (1972) 3 S.C.R. 784, ('72) A.SC. 1816.
[56] ibid.

the seven shops by negotiating with some of the tenderers. *The price realized was substantially more than that offered either at the auction or as per tenders*"[57] (italics supplied). The respondents did not challenge the validity of any of the provisions in the Act before the Supreme Court.[58] Their contention was that the power which government retained "to accept or reject any bid without assigning any reason therefor" in cl. (6) of the government order under s. 29 (2) of the Act was an arbitrary power and therefore violative of Arts. 14 and 19. The High Court upheld this contention. In allowing the appeal Hegde J. observed that though business in liquor must be treated as business within the meaning of Art. 19 (1) (*g*),[59] this was subject to the test of reasonableness of restrictions laid down in *Cooverji Bharucha's Case*[60] and he adopted the propositions from that case which are set out in para 10.270 (*a*) and (*c*) above, and he also accepted the radical difference between trade in liquor and in ordinary commodities, pointed out by Mahajan J.: para 10.270 (*b*).[61] In addition, Hegde J. held:

(i) that the power which Government had reserved under cl. (6) was no more than the power conferred on government by ss. 22 and 29 of the Act; *it was not possible to challenge the validity of the power without challenging the validity of s. 29 itself, which the petitioners had not done.*

(ii) that even apart from the power conferred by ss. 22 and 29, cl. (6) could not be considered to be unconstitutional. . . . The High Court "was wholly wrong in thinking that the purpose of ss. 22 and 29 was not to raise revenue."[62]

(iii) that the "Government is *the guardian of the finances of the State* and it is expected to protect the financial interests of the State. Hence quite naturally the legislature had empowered the Government to see that there was no leakage of its revenue. . . . *Public auctions are held to get the best possible price.* Once these aspects are recognized there appears to be no basis for contending that the owner of the privileges in question who had offered to sell them cannot decline to accept the highest bid if he thinks that the price offered is inadequate."[63] (italics supplied)

Govt. as guardian of State finances: duty to get the best price for conferring the right to sell liquor

(iv) "If the government is the exclusive owner of these privileges, reliance on Art. 19(1)(*g*) or Art. 14 becomes irrelevant. Citizens cannot have any fundamental right to trade or carry on business in the properties or rights belonging to the Government. Nor can there be any infringement of Art. 14 if the Government tries to get the best price. . . . *The sale in question was only a mode of raising revenues.* Assuming that the question of arbitrary or unguided power could arise, the power to accept or reject the highest bid was given to the highest authority in the State, namely, Government, which was

---

[57] ('72) A.SC. at p. 1818.

[58] ibid. p. 1821. The court said that ". . . this was possibly in their own interest. They are not interested in raising any contention which might vitiate the auctions held." The relevant provisions of the Bihar and Orissa Excise Act, 1915, and the Order issued under s. 29 of the Act are set out at pp. 1819-21, ibid. S. 29 is as follows: "(1) Instead of or in addition to, any duty leviable under this Act, the State Government may accept payment of a sum in consideration of the grant of any exclusive privilege under s. 22. (2) The sum payable under sub-s. (1) shall be determined as follows: (a) by calling tenders or by auction or otherwise as the State Government may, by general or special order direct; and (b) by such authority and subject to such control as may be specified in such order." "Excise revenue" was defined as including "any payment to be made to the State Government under s. 29": s. 2(9).

[59] As held in *Krishna Kumar Narula* v. *J.&K.* (1967) 3 S.C.R. 50, ('67) A.SC. 1368.

[60] Set out in para 10.19 of the text.

[61] "The decision in *Lala Harichand Sarda* v. *Mizo Dist. Council* (1967) 1 S.C.R. 1012, ('67) A.SC. 829, relied on by the writ petitioner does not bear on the point under consideration. It deals with power to grant licence to trade in some ordinary commodity under Lushai Hill Dist. Regulation": ('72) A.SC. *supra* at p. 1822.

[62] ('72) A.SC. *supra* at p. 1822. [63] ibid.

expected to safeguard the fianances of the State. Such power cannot be considered as an arbitrary power. *If that power is exercised for any collateral purpose, the exercise of the power will be struck down.*"[64] (italics supplied)

Proposition (iv) in para 10.271 explained

10.272 Some of the expressions used in the first two sentences in proposition (iv) above are unfortunate and if not carefully considered in their context are liable to be misunderstood and misapplied.[65] The statement that "Government is the owner of these privileges" is not accurate: the exclusive privilege of selling liquor belongs not to Government, but to the party who pays the licence fee for that privilege. Government has the *right* under the Excise Act to *sell* the exclusive privilege, but this *right* to raise revenue by charging a licence fee cannot be called a privilege. Nor can the right be accurately called the property of Government: Government has the *power* to raise revenue by auctioning or otherwise disposing of liquor shops. Hegde J. appears to have been aware of this, for in the second sentence in proposition (iv) he speaks of Government's property or *right*. Further, these observations were made in the context of trade in liquor to which no citizen has a right and which can be prohibited altogether, and which Hegde J. distinguished from trade in ordinary commodities to which very different considerations applied. And finally those observations were made in a case dealing with the raising of revenue, and Hegde J. repeatedly emphasised the *Government's duty to secure the highest revenue for the State.* In this context Hegde J. was right in saying that no question of violation of Art. 14 arises if out of several modes of raising revenue, that which would raise the highest revenue is preferred. Again, no question of the violation of Art. 19(1) (*g*) arises because as Mahajan J. said in *Cooverjee Bharucha's Case* exclusion and elimination is in the nature of the liquor business, and since the licence fee for the sale of the sole privilege of selling liquor is a mode of raising revenue, no one can legitimately complain of violation of Art. 19(1) (*g*) if that privilege is conferred on the party who pays the highest fee. It is submitted that *Harinarayan's Case* is misapplied if it is held to justify the disposal of Government property at less than its full value, except where such disposal secures other benefits which make up for the disposal at a lesser value: Hegde J. said that if Government exercised its power for a collateral purpose, the exercise of that power would be struck down. *Harinarayan's Case* was followed in *Hari Shankar* v. *Dy. E. & T. Commr.*[66] in which Chandrachud J. stated that the true position governing dealings in intoxicants was as stated in the undernoted cases.[67] Both these cases were followed in *S. T. Thimappa & Sons* v. *State.*[68]

---

[64] ibid.

[65] As they were in *State* v. *Rajendra Singh* ('73) A.A. 337.

[66] (1975) 3 S.C.R. 254, ('75) A.SC. 1121.

[67] *Balsara's Case* (1951) S.C.R. 682, ('51) A.SC. 318; *Cooverjee's Case* (1954) S.C.R. 873, ('54) A.SC. 220; *Kidwai's Case* (1957) S.C.R. 295, ('57) A.SC. 414; *Nagendra Nath's Case* (1958) S.C.R. 1240, ('58) A.SC. 398; *Amar Chakraborty's Case* (1973) 1 S.C.R. 533, ('72) A.SC. 1863; *R.M.D.C. Case* (1957) S.C.R. 874, ('57) A.SC. 699 as interpreted in *Harinarayan Jaiswal's Case* (1972) 3 S.C.R. 784, ('72) A.SC. 1816. Chandrachud J. held that there was no fundamental right to do trade or business in intoxicants: ('75) A.SC. at p. 1132.

[68] ('78) A.Knt. 17, 20-21.

Rajendra Singh's Case in the trial Court

10.273 In *Rajendra Singh* v. *State*[69] (which was reversed on appeal)[70] the petition related to the auction of Borang trees growing in a reserved forest, which was government property. At the impugned auction of Borang trees Government had directed that they should be auctioned only to those who were pencil or slate manufacturers. The petitioner challenged this auction as violative of Arts. 14 and 19. The trial judge observed that if "the auction had been kept open for all . . . normally the auction would have fetched a higher price." Government justified its omission to hold an open auction on the ground that the limited auction was held to protect the pencil and slate industry in the State which needed Borang wood, a commodity in short supply. The hearing of the petition was adjourned to enable the State Counsel to find out whether the agreements entered into with the purchasers at the impugned auction contained any restrictive clauses prohibiting the sale of Borang wood by the pencil or slate manufacturers, and whether the agreements contained any clause as to the maximum price which these persons would charge when effecting the sale. *The State Counsel made a statement that there were no restrictive clauses*; that the purchaser could sell the wood of Borang trees to any person and at any price agreed between seller and purchaser; and that there was no restrictive clause in the agreement to prevent the export of the wood outside the State of U.P.[71] It is implicit in the judgment of the trial judge that if the Government had made good its justification, he would have upheld the impugned auction; but the statement made by the State Counsel made that justification untenable.[72] The trial judge quoted passages from the judgments of the U.S. Supreme Court set out in para 10.268 above, and also referred to *Rasbihari's Case*, discussed in para 10.269 above.[73] Applying the principles of these cases, he held that Government was under an obligation to secure the highest price for Borang trees and the classification made by Government was untenable. He distinguished the decision in *Harinarayan's Case* by saying that the observations there made were to be read in the context of the law granting exclusive licences in respect of intoxicants and he observed that the Supreme Court had emphasized the fact that public auctions were held for the grant of the exclusive right to sell intoxicants and to secure the best price.

Rajendra Singh's Case: decision of the appellate court is clearly wrong

10.274 The above judgment was reversed in appeal.[74] The appellate judgment is not satisfactory, for it is not clear whether the court held that Government could do what it liked with its property, purporting to rely on *Harinarayan's Case*, or whether it accepted Government's justification that the limited auction was held in order to secure to the State the benefits arising from the pencil and slate industry which had grown up in the State. It is submitted that the appellate judgment is clearly wrong. It makes no reference to the

---

[69] ('73) A.A. 37.
[70] In *State* v. *Rajendra Singh* ('73) A.A. 337.
[71] ('73) A.A. *supra* at p. 40.
[72] It is not so stated in express words but that is the necessary implication of adjourning the hearing for the purpose set out above.
[73] ibid. pp. 39-40.
[74] *State* v. *Rajendra Singh* ('73) A.A. 337.

statement made by Government Counsel, which rendered Government's justification untenable. Further, the Appellate Court wrongly interpreted and misapplied the Supreme Court's judgment in *Harinarayan's Case*, for the reasons given in para 10.271 above.

Disposal of Govt. property at an undervalue is, *prima facie* a public wrong

10.275 The above discussion has shown that a disposal of Government property at an undervalue is, *prima facie* a public wrong because it is a breach of Government's duty to deal with government property for the benefit of the State and not for the benefit of private parties at the expense of the State. Though judicial remedies are considered in Volume II, the present discussion would be incomplete if the appropriate judicial remedy were not considered at this place. A writ of *mandamus* compelling Government to do its duty, and/or restraining it from committing a breach of its duty, would clearly lie. The only question is, at whose instance? It is unlikely, though not impossible, that a State Government would openly claim that even if it disposed of Government property at a gross undervalue, no one had *locus standi* to bring it to book by moving the court for a writ of *mandamus*. If such a plea were taken, it is submitted that it would fail for the following reasons: Even in England the technicalities of *locus standi* are yielding to the need to ensure that the injury done to the public should be redressed by the enforcement of the law. As to *locus standi*, Prof. de Smith referred to the view that in applications for *mandamus*, as in applications for *certiorari*, *locus standi* was not restricted by any rule of common law, and that the courts could grant an application made by any member of the public.[75] After observing that the courts had, on occasions, shown the utmost liberality in granting applications made by persons whose interest in the performance of duty was tenuous, and after giving examples of such liberal approach, he summed up the position thus: "Normally the applicant's interest must be more substantial than the general interests of other members of the community or interest group to which he belongs, *but it is impossible to say that this is at all a firm rule*"[76] (*italics supplied*).

Mandamus and *locus standi* in respect of such public wrong

English decisions on *locus standi*

Relator actions and *locus standi* in England

10.276 In connection with *locus standi* it must be borne in mind that in England the Att.-General represents the public interest, and can bring an action to vindicate public rights in the country, which rights are not confined to cases of public nuisance. And he can grant leave to a relator, who may have no personal interest of his own, to file such action. In England a stricter view can be taken of *locus standi* because relator actions furnish a recognized remedy to vindicate public rights. But in a recent case of great importance, *Att.-Gen.* v. *I.B.A.*[77] which raised the question of the *locus standi* of a private person to move the court for an injunction, without obtaining the Att.-General's leave as a relator, against the Independent Broadcasting Authority to restrain it from exhibiting an indecent film. The Court after granting an interim injunction, held, at the hearing, that he could have applied for the Att.-General's

Att.-Gen. v. *I.B.A.*

---

[75] S.A. de Smith, *Judicial Review of Administrative Action*, 3rd. ed. p. 492 referring to D.C.M. Yardley, "*Prohibition* and *Mandamus* and the Problem of *Locus Standi*" 73 L.Q.R. 534, 539.

[76] ibid. p. 493.

[77] (1973) 1 Q.B. 629.

leave. However, in his judgment Lord Denning M. R. made important observations on *locus standi*. He said that the Court had been right in granting interim injunction on the uncontroverted facts before it. And though after full hearing the Court raised the injunction, the Att.-General having granted his leave to the applicant as a relator, Lord Denning added that as a last resort, if the Att.-General refused leave in a proper case, or improperly or unreasonably delayed giving leave, or his machinery worked too slowly, then a member of the public who had a sufficient interest could apply for a declaration and, in appropriate cases, an injunction. Lord Denning said that he "would not restrict the circumstances in which an individual may be held to have sufficient interest".[78] Lord Denning referred to recent cases[79] in which Mr. Blackburn applied to the Court for *mandamus* on the ground that the Commissioner of Police was not doing his duty in regard to gaming and pornography, and added, "Mr. Blackburn had sufficient interest, even though it is shared with thousands".[80] Lord Denning concluded:

Lord Denning on *locus standi*

"Person interested" not given a restricted meaning. Mr. Blackburn's enforcement of public duties

". . . I regard it as a matter of high constitutional principle that if there is good ground for supposing that a government department or a public authority is transgressing the law, or is about to transgress it in a way which offends or injures thousands of Her Majesty's subjects, then, in the last resort, any of those offended or injured can draw it to the attention of the courts of law and seek to have the law enforced. But this, I would emphasize, is only in the last resort when there is no other remedy reasonably available to secure that the law is obeyed."[81]

10.277 It is submitted that if this is the law of *locus standi* in England, where relator actions are available to a member of the public to vindicate public rights, *a fortiori*, a member of the public in India must have *locus standi* to vindicate public rights where relator actions are not available except in the case of public nuisance (s. 91, C.P.C.).[82] No doubt a disposal of Government property at an undervalue which benefits private persons would ordinarily attract Art. 14, as in *Rasbihari's Case*, and any one of the prospective purchasers would have *locus standi* as persons interested to apply for a *mandamus*. But where the value of the property is very great, the number of prospective purchasers would be small, and it may be that members of that class may not apply for a *mandamus* because of fear of offending Government by legal action or because of hope of getting benefits for themselves. In such circumstances the English authorities discussed above show that any member of the public has *locus standi* to apply for a *mandamus* to prevent a public wrong. As the grant of *mandamus* is discretionary, the discretion of the judge is a safeguard against abuse. But where a member of the public makes a *prima facie* case for breach of public duty, our courts call for a return from the Government or any public authority, and there can be no abuse of legal process where,

Submissions about *locus standi* in India

[78] ibid. p. 649.

[79] *R.* v. *Commr. of Police of the Metropolis, Ex. p. Blackburn* (1968) 2 Q.B. 118, 137, 139 (gaming); *R.* v. *Commr. of Police of the Metropolis Ex. p. Blackburn (No. 3)* (1973) 1 Q.B. 241 (pornography).

[80] (1973) 1 Q.B. 629 at p. 649.

[81] ibid.

[82] For unlike the Att.-General in England, who represents the public interest generally, in India, the Att.-General of India and the Advocates-General of the States represent the public interest in a limited number of matters.

instead of justifying its action on the merits, a Government takes the stand that a member of the public has no *locus standi* to question its action however correct his complaint may be. Such a claim to be above the law has been rightly rejected by the English and Indian courts. The question is more fully discussed in Volume II.

Art. 19(6)(*ii*) held to exclude challenge on the ground that a monopoly was created: illustrative cases

10.278 The amendment of Art. 19 (6) has been considered in several cases and it has been held, for example, to exclude all argument that the ousting of private stage-carriage services created a virtual monopoly in favour of the State or a Corporation owned and controlled by the State.[83] Again, it has been held that the right of the State to carry on trade or business was recognised by Art. 298 and the authority to exclude competitors in the field of such trade or business was derived from Entry 21, List III, Sch. 7, and the exercise of that power was protected from challenge under Art. 19 (1) (*g*) by Art. 19 (6) (ii). It was therefore not necessary that a law excluding others from business should itself confer an authority on the State to carry on trade or business.[84] The Punjab Cattle Fairs (Regulation) Act, 1968, which gave the State a monopoly of holding and managing cattle fairs was protected by Art. 19 (1) (*g*) read with Art. 19 (6), and the restrictions imposed on the rights of citizens under Art. 19 (1) (*b*), (*d*) and (*f*) must be held to be reasonable as they were necessary to make the monopoly effective.[85] In any event, since "law" under Art. 13 (3) (*a*) included any Ordinance, Order, Bye-law, Rule, Regulation, Notification, Custom, etc. the scheme framed under s. 68 (*c*) of the Motor Vehicles Act may properly be looked upon as a law authorising Government to exclude others from competition in road transport. Although Art. 19 (6) protected a monopoly from challenge under Art. 19 (1) (*g*) its terms indicated that the State may carry on any business either as a monopoly, complete or partial, or in competition with any citizen and such competition would not have the effect of infringing any fundamental right of a citizen. As the plying of buses as stage carriages was a commercial enterprise, it was open to Government to apply for a permit under s. 42 (3) (*a*) read with s. 42 (1) of the Motor Vehicles Act, 1939, as amended in 1956, and Government was not obliged to proceed only under the provisions of Chapter IV-A which conferred on Governmnet certain special rights to run its buses.[86] In *Veerappa Pillai* v. *Raman and Raman Ltd.*[87] there are

---

[83] *Ram Chandra* v. *Orissa* (1956) S.C.R. 28, ('56) A.SC. 298, 304; fol. in *Bhiman Singh* v. *Assam* ('57) A.Ass. 139.

[84] *Narayanappa* v. *Mysore* (1960) 3 S.C.R. 742, ('60) A.SC. 1073, 1077-9; *Dosa Satyanarayanamurty* v. *A.P. State Road Transport Corpn.* (1961) 1 S.C.R. 642, ('61) A.SC. 82. It was held that Art. 19(6)(ii) protected a law for carrying on business or service to the exclusion, complete or partial, of all citizens; it may exclude some citizens only; it may provide for business in the entire State or in a part of the State. Consequently, s. 68(*c*) of the Motor Vehicles Act does not violate Art. 19.

[85] *Amritsar Municipality* v. *Punjab* (1969) 3 S.C.R. 447, ('69) A.SC. 1100, 1105-6.

[86] *Parbhani Transport Co-op. Society Ltd.* v. *R.T.A. Aurangabad* (1960) 3 S.C.R. 177, ('60) A.SC. 801; *Parbhani Transport Co.* v. *G. V. Bedekar* ('60) A.B. 278 [*held*, that in view of the amended Art. 19(6), Ch. IV-A, Motor Vehicles Act, must be upheld. *Held further*, that the provisions of that chapter were in addition to, and not in substitution of the other provisions of the Act under which the State could apply for a permit]; rel. on in *Narendra Kumar* v. *State* ('72) A.A. 55, 60 [*held*, that the restrictions placed by Ch. IV-A in furtherance of the policy of nationalization were saved by Art. 19(6)].

[87] (1952) S.C.R. 583, 595-6, ('52) A.SC. 192.

observations which would suggest that a person has no fundamental right to ply motor vehicles on public pathways, and that the grant of a licence or permit is a mere privilege, to be granted at the discretion of the authorities. These observations are not good law and it has been held that a citizen has a fundamental right to ply motor vehicles on the public pathways under Art. 19 (1) (*g*) and any infringement of that right by the State could be justified only if it fell under Art. 19 (6).[88]

10.279 *Mannalal Jain* v. *Assam*[89] raised the question whether Cl. 5 (*e*), Assam Food Grains (Licensing and Control) Order, 1961[90] provided for a monopoly, and if it did not, whether the grant of licences only to co-operative societies, violated the petitioner's rights under Arts. 14 and 19. The Supreme Court held that Cl. 5 (*e*) did not provide for a monopoly, but only enabled the licensing authority to prefer a co-operative society in certain circumstances, since there may be cases or localities where the consideration set out in sub-cl. (*e*) may override other considerations. As to interpreted, it could not be said that the sub-clause was unrelated to the object mentioned in s. 3 of the Act. But beyond this point a difference of opinion arose in the court. The majority consisting of Sinha C.J., S. K. Das and Rajagopala Ayyangar JJ. held that the repeated applications of the petitioner for a licence were turned down by the licensing authority solely for the purpose of granting a monopoly to co-operatives. And though Cl. 5 (*e*) did not violate Art. 14, as it was based on a reasonable classification reasonably related to the object of the Act, the discrimination made against the petitioner by the licensing authority was discrimination in the administration of the law based on the executive instructions of Government. It was the duty of the licensing authority to consider the application for a licence ignoring those instructions, which were not in consonance with the provisions of Cl. 5 (*e*). Accordingly, the majority held that the order refusing a licence violated the petitioner's rights under Arts. 14 and 19. Although the judgment does not in terms say so, the finding appears to be based on the proposition that as the different treatment meted out to the petitioner and to co-operative societies, was not justified by any law, it violated Art. 14; and as he was denied the rights guaranteed by Art. 19 (1) (*f*) and (*g*) also by an order without the authority of law, the order violated Art. 19 (1) (*f*) and (*g*). Sarkar and Mudholkar JJ. dissented. Sarkar J. treated *Narendra Kumar* v. *Union*[91] and the *Glass Chatons Importers and Users' Association* v. *Union*[92] as determinative of the

Mannalal Jain's Case

majority view

minority view

[88] *Raman & Raman Ltd.* v. *Madras* (1959) Supp. (2) S.C.R. 227, ('59) A.SC. 694, 697 [citing *C.S.S. Motor Service, Tenkasi* v. *Madras* (1953) Mad. 304, 330, 334 ('53) A.M. 279, 288, 289], *Saghir Ahmad* v. *U.P.* (1955) 1 S.C.R. 707, 719, ('54) A.SC. 728.

[89] (1962) 3 S.C.R. 936, ('62) A.SC. 386; *Dist. Collector, Hyderabad* v. *Ibrahim & Co.* ('66) A.A.P. 310 (striking down a Government Order which created a monopoly in favour of a co-operative society). *Mannalal Jain's Case* was fol. in *C. P. Khanna* v. *V. K. Kalaghatgi* (1970) Bom. 805, ('70) A.B. 201, 72 Bom.L.R. 295 (*held*, that an exception could be made in favour of co-operative societies by providing compulsory arbitration in disputes between a society and third parties in certain limited circumstances and such a provision did not violate Arts. 14 or 19).

[90] Made in the exercise of the powers conferred by s. 3 of the Essential Commodities Act, 1955, read with the notification by which the said powers were delegated by the Central Government to the Govt. of Assam.

[91] (1960) 2 S.C.R. 375, ('60) A.SC. 430. [92] (1962) 1 S.C.R. 862, ('61) A.SC. 1514.

case before him. It is submitted that those cases dealt with the policy governing the export and import of goods, and considerations which led the Court to uphold the restrictions imposed in those cases as reasonable restrictions would be mostly inapplicable to domestic trade in an essential commodity. It is submitted that the view of Sarkar J. that no monopoly was created because licences were granted to several co-operative societies and not to one society alone,[93] is not correct for a monopoly can be created in favour of a number of persons.[94]

Submission: majority view is correct

Hrudananda v. Rev. Div. Commr., Cuttack: creation of a monopoly an administrative action

10.280 In *Hrudananda* v. *Rev. Divnl. Commr., Cuttack*[95] the question of the creation of a monopoly by administrative action was considered on the following facts:

A and B were the highest bidders in a public auction for the lease of two quarries. The auction notice did not contain any statement that the quarries would be settled with co-operative societies if they agreed to pay the amount offered by the highest bidders. The authorities recommended the settling of the quarries with A and B. The Tashildar reported that the previous lessee, the co-operative society C, had defaulted and misconducted itself in several ways. Nevertheless, the respondent directed that the quarries be settled with C. On a writ petition being filed, he defended his action by reference to instructions contained in a letter which he said he was obliged to act upon and therefore settled the quarries with C.

The Court held that a monopoly can only be created under the authority of law and not by an administrative order. It was open to the State to prefer co-operative societies if the State was of the opinion that granting the lease to a co-operative society would facilitate the object of any law in force. The Court held that a settlement which sought to exclude A and B from carying on trade with government violated Art. 19(1)(*g*) read with Art. 14. The settlement had created a monopoly at the threshold to the exclusion of the highest bidders thus denying equality of opportunity to trade with Government.[96] The matter was remitted to Government to consider the bids of A and B afresh.

---

93 See (1962) 3 S.C.R. *supra* at p. 965.

94 "Monopoly. 2. An exclusive privilege (conferred by the Sovereign or the State) of selling some commodity or trading with a particular place or country: (illustration) 2. The monopoly of the right to print the Bible in England is still possessed by the Universities of Oxford and Cambridge, and Her Majesty's printer for England.": *Shorter Oxford Dictionary* (1959), p. 1276. In *Lal Chand* v. *D.F.&C.S. Controller* ('65) A.Punj. 410, *Mannalal Jain's Case* was relied upon and it was held that the retail and wholesale distribution of sugar entrusted to co-operative societies to the exclusion of other licensed dealers violated Art. 14 and was void. It is submitted that in that event it would also be void under Art. 19(1)(*g*); *Partap R. & T. Factory* v. *State* (1965) 2 Punj. 32, ('66) A.Punj. 16 [*Mannalal Jain's Case* and *Lalchand's Case* were apparently referred to with approval and it was held that a monopoly in resin created by an executive order imposed unreasonable restrictions on the right guaranteed by Art. 19(1)(*g*). The facts of the case disclosed a shocking abuse of power, and the creation of a monopoly was also held to be *mala fide*]; *N. V. Subba Rao* v. *State* ('68) A.A.P. 98, 100 ("It is always open to the Municipal Commissioner to keep in view the existing circumstances and after hearing the petitioners' or other persons' objections, if they are raised before him, decide independently whether the licence should be granted to the 3rd respondent or not. He need not be influenced by any direction given by the Government or any observation made by this Court even in this order. He is the licensing authority, and it is for him to keep the relevant matters (in mind) and keep out all irrelevant considerations and decide the matter in accordance with law.")

95 ('79) A.Or. 13.

96 ('77) A.SC. 1498 and ('75) A.SC. 286 were relied on.

Ramnarain Prasad v. Dist. Magistrate

10.281 In *Ramnarain Prasad* v. *Dist. Magistrate*,[97] Condition 10 of the wholesale foodgrains dealers licence issued under the Bihar Food Grains Dealers (Licensing) Order, 1967, was impugned as violative of Art. 19, because it enabled Government to give directions to the dealer, *inter alia*, to purchase foodgrains. It was held that the direction given to the petitioner to buy 500 quintals of grain was not by itself unreasonable, because in times of scarcity, it would be reasonable in the public interest for government to ensure that a buffer stock was built up. As to the contention that a particular order directing the petitioner to buy 500 quintals of grain *by a particular day* was unreasonable, it was held that as the petitioner had not availed himself of the right of appeal, and as his averment in the petition was denied in the respondent's affidavit, which denial was not controverted by the petitioner, the Court would not go into the question of the reasonableness of the Order.[98]

"The Bidi Case": restriction on manufacture of *bidis* held unreasonable

10.282 In *Chintaman Rao* v. *M.P.*[99] s. 4, C.P. & Berar Regulation of Manufacture of Bidis (Agricultural Purposes) Act, 1948, and an order issued under it were impugned as violating the petitioner's rights under Art. 19(1)(*g*). After laying down the test of reasonableness set out earlier[1] the Court held that the restrictions placed on the right to carry on business were arbitrary and unreasonable and in excess of what was required to be achieved by the object of the Act. The manufacturers of *bidis* were not only prohibited from employing agricultural labourers in the area but were prohibited from engaging any person whether from within the area or from the neighbouring areas or from any other part in India. Again, the prohibition affected not only agricultural labourers in the area but those who did no agricultural work, as well as old, aged and infirm persons who would not be expected to do agricultural work but might engage in the occupation of making *bidis*. As the absolute prohibition covered both permissible and impermissible restrictions it could not be upheld even as regards permissible restrictions.[2]

Conditions in Cinematograph Licences: (*i*) unreasonable

10.283 *R. M. Seshadri* v. *Dist. Magistrate, Tanjore*[3] raised the question of the validity of condition 4(*a*) and special condition 3 imposed in a cinematograph licence in exercise of the powers contained in s. 8, Cinematograph Act, 1898. The Supreme Court held that condition 4(*a*) enabled Government to compel a licensee to exhibit a film of any length without reference to the time occupied. Again, there were no guiding principles for the exercise of that discretion. The special Condition 3 enabled Government to compel the exhibition of a film of *not less* than 2,000 feet without specifying the maximum length of the film. Condition 4(*a*) and special condition 3 thus imposed unreasonable restrictions and were void as infringing Art. 19(1)(*g*). The above case was distinguished in *M. A. Baig* v. *State*[4] and it was held that conditions 3(*a*) and (*b*) in the licence granted

(*ii*) reasonable

---

[97] ('78) A.Pat. 245.
[98] The petition was however allowed because, the licence was cancelled without giving the petitioner an opportunity to show cause against such cancellation.
[99] (1950) S.C.R. 759, ('51) A.SC. 118. [1] See para 10.19.
[2] In so far as this case dealt with severability, it has been discussed in *R.M.D. Chamarbaugwalla* v. *Union* (1957) S.C.R. 930, 949-50; ('57) A.SC. 628.
[3] (1955) 1 S.C.R. 686, ('54) A.SC. 747. [4] ('61) A.A.P. 126.

under the Hyderabad Cinema Rules requiring Cinema Houses to exhibit films of length *not exceeding* 2,000 feet approved and certified by the Central Government and the Film Advisory Board, depicting educational, cultural and current events and also documentary films, imposed reasonable restrictions.

Unfettered power to refuse admission to the Bar upheld

10.284 In *Babul Chandra* v. *Chief Justice and Judges of the Patna High Court*[5] the petitioner impugned s. 9(1), Indian Bar Councils Act, 1926, which expressly provided that the rules ". . . shall not limit or in any way affect the power of the High Court to refuse admission to any person at its discretion" on the ground that it imposed unreasonable restrictions on his right to practise the profession of the law. The Supreme Court held that such unfettered discretion had to be given to some authority and there could not be a more appropriate authority than the High Court. It is submitted that the reasoning is not correct. The assumption that an unfettered discretion to prevent a person from being admitted to a profession must reside somewhere appears to be unfounded, and, in any event, even if a wide discretion has to be conferred, there is no reason why permissible safeguards such as the giving of reasons and an opportunity of questioning those reasons, should not be provided.

A criticism

Restrictions on the right to practise a profession

10.285 Under Art. 19(6) reasonable restrictions can be imposed on the exercise of a right to practise a profession, and technical and professional qualifications may be prescribed for exercising such profession. In *Taracharan Mukherjee* v. *B. C. Das Gupta*[6] it was held that the W. B. Clinical Establishment Act, and the rules made thereunder, imposed reasonable restrictions in the interest of the general public. It was open to Government to prescribe the qualifications for running a physical therapy establishment. Physiotherapeutics was a branch of medical science requiring specialised knowledge, technical training and proper equipment. The State could not allow unqualified or inexperienced men to play with the life and limbs of citizens. It must discourage quacks from practising medicine or unqualified men from practising law.

Restrictions held reasonable

10.286 The following provisions have been held to impose reasonable restrictions on the right to carry on trade, business, etc., contained in Art. 19(1)(*g*): S. 153-B, Companies Act, under which a company can make an offer to acquire the shares of another company;[7] s. 22, Banking Companies Act, under which no company can carry on the business of banking without a licence from the Reserve Bank;[8] s. 49-A, Banking Companies Act, 1949, which prohibits private banks from receiving deposits or allowing withdrawals by

Company Law

---

[5] ('54) A.SC. 524. [6] ('54) A.Cal. 138.

[7] *S. Viswanathan* v. *E.I.D. & S. Factories Ltd.* ('57) A.M. 341 (the observations about reasonableness are *obiter*; it was also held that the rights and obligations of shareholders were created by statute and were subject to limitations contained in that statute).

[8] *Sajjan Bank* v. *Reserve Bank of India* ('61) A.M. 8 (the power to grant a licence is given to the Reserve Bank which is a statutory body entrusted with regulating the credit of the country and there is sufficient guidance for the exercise of the power).

cheque;[9] the provisions of s. 10, Madras Money Lenders Act, 1957;[10] or the provisions of rr. 15, 18, 21, 22, 23, 34 and 36, Central Excise Rules;[11] provisions designed to prevent the abuse of denatured spirituous preparations such as French polish and varnish;[12] s. 27(2) of the Payment of Bonus Act, 1965;[13] Condition No. 9 in licence form B under Mysore (Wholesale Dealers Licensing) Order, 1964, which prohibited a wholesale dealer selling without a permit to another wholesale dealer in the State;[14] Conditions 3, 4 and 10 of wholesale as well as retail licences issued under Licensing Orders of the State of Mysore;[15] Cl. 11(*b*) of the Licensing Orders of the State of Mysore which conferred on the Enforcement Officer the power to carry out a search when he had reason to believe that there had been a contravention of the Orders or of the conditions of the licence;[16] s. 3(*c*), W.B. Hindu Social Disabilities Removal Act, 1948, which required that no Hindu shall merely on the ground that he belonged to a particular class or caste be denied any service whatsoever whether in connection with civic, social or religious practices or rights by a Hindu who habitually rendered such services in the course of his profession;[17] the upgrading of electricity tariffs by government under s. 3, Madras Essential Articles Control and Requisitioning (Temporary Powers) Act, 1949, as amended by the Andhra Act 1, 1955;[18] the control imposed by paragraph 15, W.B. Rice Mills Control Order, 1949;[19] provisions for regulating business,

restrictions to prevent abuse

Miscellaneous cases

---

[9] *Kurian* v. *Union* ('62) A.Ker. 267. [10] *Nichani* v. *Madras* ('64) A.M. 30.

[11] *T. R. Raju* v. *Union* ('60) A.A.P. 498 (the provisions were designed to prevent the evasion of excise duties on tobacco.

[12] *Chandulal* v. *Gujarat* ('64) A.Guj. 59 [upholding rr. 22 (except Proviso), 32(9), (10) and 37, Gujarat Denatured Spirituous Preparation Rules, as such provisions effectuated the policy of prohibition which was a Directive of State Policy under Art. 47].

[13] *Malabar Tile Works* v. *Union* ('68) A.Ker. 143, 146 [*held*, that apart from the fact that Art. 19 was not available to the petitioner in view of the Proclamation of Emergency by the President, the restrictions imposed by s. 27(2)(*b*) or (*c*) were reasonable. Those provisions had been made for the purpose of ascertaining whether any of the provisions of the Act had been complied with, and they did not in any manner interfere with the fundamental right under Art. 19(1)(*g*). The possibility of a person being accused of any offence did not give immunity to him from being examined for a lawful purpose. The examination contemplated under cl. (*c*) was not for the purposes of establishing any offence against the person examined, but only for the purpose of ascertaining whether any of the provisions of the Act had been complied with].

[14] *A. K. A. Setty & Sons* v. *State* ('70) A.Mys. 289, 293 (*held*, that the restrictions were reasonable having regard to the necessity for preventing hoarding and cornering of food-grains).

[15] ibid. pp. 293-4 (Conditions 3, 4 and 10, respectively, required the dealer: to maintain a register of daily account containing the specified particulars; to submit a true return, in the prescribed form to the licensing authority; and to issue a true receipt or invoice).

[16] ibid. p. 296.

[17] *Banamali Das* v. *Pakhu Bhandari* ('51) A.Cal. 167 (the case arose out of a prosecution of the accused, Bhandari, a barber, who had refused his services to the complainant because of his low caste).

[18] *Secy., G.P.W. & T. Dept.* v. *A.G. Factory* ('59) A.A.P. 538 (the Court held that there was a fundamental right to enter into a contract but there was no fundamental right not to have the terms of the contract regulated by law, and s. 3 did not affect the right or impose any restrictions, but even if it did, the restrictions were reasonable).

[19] *Anumati Sadhukhan* v. *Asst. Regional Controller* ('53) A.Cal. 187 (the fact that the order rendered the running of the complainant's rice-mill uneconomical, did not make the impugned restrictions unreasonable).

e.g., a pawn-broker's business, through the machinery of a licence;[20] s. 9, Evacuees Interest (Separation) Act, 1951, which restricted excessive rates of interest;[21] or the business of plying rickshaws by human labour;[22] s. 43-A, Motor Vehicles Act, read with s. 43 (1) (*b*) (iii) enabling government to issue directions regarding the grant of permits to persons whose existing permits were cancelled or modified under s. 68F;[23] a provision requiring the R.T.A. to have regard to the grant of permits on existing services;[24] Rule 216 (2) and (3) (i) made under s. 70, Motor Vehicles Act, 1939;[25] an order under s. 33, Bombay Police Act, 1951 (as extended to Delhi) restricting the plying and parking of trucks on a particular road for a fixed period of the day;[26] s. 19 (*a*) (iii), Drugs Act, 1940, as amended in 1955, which required that the true formula or lists of ingredients of the drugs concerned, should be displayed on the cartons or labels of the patent or proprietary medicines, because a buyer was entitled to know the ingredients contained in the article he purchased so that he might not be cheated, imposed on or deceived;[27] rules imposing vicarious liability on a licensee;[28] the power to demand security for the payment of sales tax from a dealer;[29] s. 57, Specific Relief Act, 1877,

---

[20] *M. Kevalchand* v. *Madras* ('57) A.M. 514 (upholding ss. 3, 4 and various other sections of the Madras Pawn Brokers Act, 1943).

[21] *Sampuran Singh* v. *Competent Officer* ('55) A.Pep. 148; rel. on in *Ram Kripal* v. *A.C.G., Evacuee Property, Lucknow* ('72) A.P. 38 [upholding s. 9(2) of the Evacuee Interest (Separation) Act, 1951].

[22] *S. Iqubal Singh* v. *Municipal Board* ('59) A.A. 186 [upholding s. 298(2), List I, Part H-(c), U.P. Municipalities Act, 1916. The provisions for the licensing of rickshaws were made with a view gradually to limit human labour for transporting human beings and to avoid congestion]; *Satya Ranjan* v. *Commr. of Police, Calcutta* ('55) A.Cal. 417 (restrictions put on the number of rickshaws under the Calcutta Hackney Carriage Act, 1919, and rules, were reasonable. The Judge expressed the view that the right to exploit human beings as beasts of burden could hardly claim the dignity of a fundamental right though he decided the case on the basis of such a right).

[23] *Tulsi Ram* v. *Road Transport Co.* ('62) A.P. 57 (though the provision was valid, an order passed under it may be open to question on other grounds).

[24] *Malik Ram* v. *R.T.A.* ('56) A.Raj. 142 (F.B.) [upholding s. 47(1)(*c*), Motor Vehicles Act, 1939, the Court observed that excessive competition may bring down the standard of services or may lead to existing services being discontinued to the detriment of the public].

[25] *Mysore* v. *K. G. Jagannath* (1973) 3 S.C.R. 770, ('73) A.SC. 2165, 2168-9 ("Stage carriage operators exclusively in cities and towns form a class by themselves and the exemption in their case has a direct relation to the objective sought to be achieved. . . . The rule is one of general application which can be justified as being in the interest of the general travelling public.")

[26] *Sukhdev Sahai* v. *Dist. Magistrate* ('71) A.Del. 237, 239 [*held*, that as the order was passed to secure the safety and convenience of the public and to abate what amounted to a nuisance, the order imposed reasonable restrictions on the petitioner's rights under Art. 19(1)(*g*)].

[27] *K. L. Chaturvedi* v. *M.P.* ('60) A.M.P. 389.

[28] *V. Rice & Oil Mills* v. *Collector, C.E.* ('61) A.A.P. 350 (upholding R. 225, Central Excise Rules which imposed such liability, the court observing that it was the licensee's liability to observe the conditions of his licence); see also *Shivdev Singh* v. *Bihar* ('63) A.P. 201 where on the application of a similar principle, it was held that s. 48, Bihar Town Planning and Improvement Trust Act, 1951, did not violate Art. 19(1)(*f*) and (*g*). That Act did not provide for service of notice on premises sought to be acquired, whether such occupiers were entered in the Municipal assessment list or not. The court held, that it was the duty of the occupier to get his name entered as such in the Municipal assessment list.

[29] *Durga Prosad* v. *C.T.O.* ('56) A.Cal. 596 [in upholding s. 7, 4(*a*) Bengal Finance (Sales Tax) Act, it was held that the section did not confer arbitrary discretion but that it had to be exercised subject to two limitations: (i) it is to be

which empowers a court to enforce a negative covenant;[30] provisions designed to remove a nuisance or to control things injurious to public health and well-being;[31] the penalties, including imprisonment, imposed by s. 92 (read with s. 101) of the Factories Act, 1948;[32] and s. 4(1)(*r*), Cr.P.C., requiring a person not a lawyer, to obtain the permission of the Court before he could appear for an accused.[33]

Restrictions held unreasonable

10.287 The following provisions have been held to impose unreasonable restrictions on the right to carry on trade, business, etc., contained in Art. 19(1)(*g*): A notification issued under the Motor Vehicles Act and the Madras Traffic Rules, prohibiting the passage of hand-carts on certain main roads during the day time;[34] Cls. 4(3), (5), 5(1) and (2) of the Bihar Cotton Cloth and Yarn Control Order which conferred upon the Cloth Controller an unfettered and uncontrolled discretion to refuse to renew a licence, or to cancel a licence;[35] Rr. 3(1) and (2) of the Grants-in-aid Code;[36] R. 3(iv) of the Punjab Cinemas (Regulations) Rules, 1952 (as amended in 1955), under which a licence to a touring cinema could not be granted if there was a permanent cinema in that place;[37] s. 15 of the Punjab

---

demanded "for good or sufficient reasons" and (ii) the security must be "reasonable security"].

[30] *Sunilchand* v. *Aryodaya Spg. & Wvg. Mills* ('64) A.Guj. 115 [the court followed *Godavari Sugar Mills Ltd.* v. *K.T.S. Kamgar Sabha* (1961) 3 S.C.R. 342, ('61) A.SC. 1016, in so far as it laid down that judicial decisions could not impose unreasonable restrictions on fundamental rights. It is submitted that the correct ground on which the decision should be rested is that if a person *sui juris*, and not under a disability, enters into a contract not to do a thing, there is nothing unreasonable in compelling him to perform his agreement by an injunction].

[31] *Maharashtra* v. *H. N. Rao* (1969) 2 S.C.R. 392, ('70) A.SC. 1157, 1162-4 (*held*, that a law compelling the owner of a carcass to remove it at his own expense, or by paying a fee for such removal, to a designated place, thereby preventing him from selling the carcass, imposes reasonable restrictions in the public interest, as the law is designed to protect public health and to abate a grave nuisance); *Cherry Hosiery Mills* v. *S. K. Ghose* ('59) A.Cal. 397 (upholding the Bengal Smoke Nuisance Act, 1905); *Jibaneswar* v. *A. B. Mukherjee* ('64) A.Cal. 45 (upholding the W.B. Closing of Canals Act, 1958. The Act was justified by considerations of the health and growth of the city of Calcutta, and the restrictions on the right of the petitioner to ply boats, assuming that they had such a right, were reasonable); *Narasimharao* v. *A.P.* ('64) A.A.P. 501 (upholding s. 10, Prevention of Food Adulteration Act, 1954, the court held that there were various safeguards in the Act including one contained in s. 10-A).

[32] *Ramanlal Chimanlal* v. *State* ('67) A.Guj. 148.

[33] *D. A. S. Swami* v. *Kubendran* ('67) A.M. 276, 277-8, (1967) 1 M.L.J. 27.

[34] *State* v. *Murray & Co.* ('65) A.M. 301 [the Court followed *Chintaman Rao* v. *M.P.* (1950) S.C.R. 759, ('51) A.SC. 118. The Court added that its orders were without prejudice to the right of the Commr. of Police to regulate the time during which such carts, or other slow-moving vehicles, would be allowed to pass, and also to regulate the weight and capacity of such carts].

[35] *Banwarilal* v. *Cloth Controller* ('54) A.P. 325 (it was held that the clauses were unreasonable from the procedural point of view).

[36] *Sakharkherda Education Society* v. *State* ('68) A.B. 91, 69, Bom. L.R. 690 (the rules provided no guidance for non-recognition of schools. They did not provide for hearing the party affected and they had the effect of preventing the petitioners from carrying on the business of running their school).

[37] *Rasdeep Touring Talkies* v. *Dist. Magistrate, Karnal* (1966) 2 Punj. 341, ('67) A.Punj. 219, 224 (*held*, on the facts, including previous history, that the refusal of a licence to a touring cinema to exhibit films during the Kurukshetra fair which lakhs of people were likely to visit, was unreasonable, for the one permanent cinema with a sitting accommodation of 470 persons could not possibly meet the requirement of the large number of visitors. The rule thwarted, rather than advanced, the purpose of the Act under which it was made).

Cattle Fairs (Regulation) Act, 1968;[38] and s. 9 of the Capital of Punjab (Development and Regulation) Act, 1952.[39]

Acquisition of land not for a public purpose: Arts. 14 and 19 violated

10.288 Acquisition of lands belonging to one industrialist, on the ground that the lands acquired were far in excess of his requirements, in order to develop the lands and allot them to other industrialists was not an acquisition for a public purpose since the conclusion that the lands acquired were far in excess of the industrialist's requirements was reached without any material justifying it and was such as no reasonable person could have arrived at. Government's action violated Arts. 14 and 19.[40]

---

[38] *Amritsar Municipality* v. *Punjab* (1969) 3 S.C.R. 447, ('69) A.SC. 1100, 1106 (s. 15 authorized the State to call upon a panchayat samiti or a municipal committee to make a prescribed deposit in the Cattle Fair Fund, and compelled those authorities to abide by the directions given by the State).

[39] *Jagdish Chand* v. *Punjab* (1973) 2 S.C.R. 97, ('72) A.SC. 2587 [The Act provided for forfeiture of any part of the money paid at an auction sale and for resumption of the land without providing any relief against forfeiture. The Act therefore allowed two procedures without any guidance as to the circumstances under which one of the two procedures was to be followed. The section violated Arts. 14 and 19]. It will be noticed that the provision for the forfeiture of the money paid and for resumption of the land without any relief against forfeiture was an instance of what Bachawat J. called (in the *Caterers' Case*) "harsh and oppressive laws" which the Supreme Court had struck down: see para 9.92 of the text.

[40] *Godrej & Boyce Mfg. Co.* v. *State* ('69) A.M. 305 (*held*, that government's action was a *bona fide* misuse of power).

CHAPTER XI

RIGHT TO FREEDOM

SECTION I

Articles 20, 21 and 22

The correlation of Art. 19 to Arts. 20, 21 and 22 and Sup. Ct. decisions on such correlation

11.1 The correlation of Art. 21 to Art. 19 on the one hand and Arts. 20 and 22 on the other presents difficult problems of exposition, because several decisions of the Supreme Court have left the subject in some confusion. The correlation of Art. 21 to Art. 19 was one of the central issues in *A. K. Gopalan* v. *The State*[1] ("*Gopalan's Case*") where it was contended that "personal liberty" in Art. 21 included all the freedoms conferred by Art. 19(1)(*a*) to (*g*), and that, in any event, it included the right to free movement conferred by Art. 19(1)(*d*). As preventive detention in times of peace is repugnant to civilized societies — a repugnance which the Judges shared — all the Judges considered the matter in great detail and with great care. The correctness of the law laid down in *Gopalan's Case* was never seriously doubted by any judgment of the Supreme Court till in *R. C. Cooper* v. *Union*[2] ("*The Bank Nationalization Case*"), a Bench of 11 Judges, by a majority of 10 : 1, "reconsidered" *Gopalan's Case* and held that it was wrongly decided because, according to the Court, its main premiss, namely, that Art. 22 was a complete code was wrong, and also because the majority in *Gopalan's Case* treated the fundamental rights conferred by various Articles as mutually exclusive. It may be added that three majority Judges in *Gopalan's Case* held that Art. 22 was *not* a complete code; and they did *not* hold that fundamental rights conferred by different Articles were mutually exclusive, as will appear hereafter.[3] The reason given for such "reconsideration" was that in two Supreme Court decisions a different view had been taken from that taken in *Gopalan's Case* and in several Supreme Court decisions which had followed *Gopalan's Case*. Reliance was placed on the observations of Subba Rao J. in *Kavalappara Koltarathil Kochuni* v. *Madras*[4] where he observed that "the decision of this Court in *Bhanji Munji's Case*[5] no longer holds the field after the Constitution (4th Amendment) Act, 1955."[6] These observations were unnecessarily wide, and they were soon corrected in *Sitabati Devi* v. *W.B.*[7] The second decision was the decision in *M.P.* v *Ranoji Rao*[8] but that was a judgment *per incuriam* because the relevant Supreme Court judgments were not considered. *The Bank Nationalization Case*, in so far as it dealt with *Gopalan's Case* was followed in *S. N. Sarkar* v. *W.B.*[9] and in *Khudiram* v. *W.B.*[10] both of which repeated the

Gopalan's Case and after

The *Bank Nationalization Case* and after

---

[1] (1950) S.C.R. 88, ('50) A.SC. 27.
[2] (1970) 3 S.C.R. 530, ('70) A.SC. 564.
[3] See para 11.14 below.
[4] (1960) 3 S.C.R. 887, ('60) A.SC. 1080.
[5] (1955) 1 S.C.R. 777, ('55) A.SC. 41.
[6] (1960) 3 S.C.R. *supra* at p. 916.
[7] (1967) 2 S.C.R. 949 (decided on December 1, 1961).
[8] (1968) 3 S.C.R. 481, ('68) A.SC. 1053.
[9] (1974) 1 S.C.R. 1, ('73) A.SC. 1425.
[10] (1975) 2 S.C.R. 832, ('75) A.SC. 550.

observations in the *Bank Nationalization Case* that the majority of Judges in *Gopalan's Case* held that Art. 22 was a complete code. These cases were also relied on in *A. D. M. Jabalpur* v. *Shivkant Shukla*[11] ("*The Habeas Corpus Case*"). However, in the *Habeas Corpus Case*, the correlation of Art. 19 to Art. 21 was considered at a time when there was a Proclamation of Emergency on the ground of internal disturbance, and the right to move the Court, *inter alia*, for the enforcement of the fundamental right conferred by Art. 21 was suspended, a fact which added a new dimension to the co-relation of Arts. 19 and 22. All these cases were referred to in *Maneka Gandhi* v. *Union*[12] and they will be considered in their appropriate place.

The three questions raised by Art. 21

11.2 Article 21 raises the following important questions:

(i) What is the meaning of the expression "personal liberty" used in Art. 21?

(ii) Does "personal liberty" include all or any of the freedoms conferred on citizens by Art. 19 (1) (*a*) to (*e*) and (*g*)?

(iii) How is a fundamental right related to an ordinary legal right?

The legislative history of Art. 21 throws light on it

11.3 In the light of the various Supreme Court decisions mentioned earlier, the most satisfactory way of dealing with Art. 21 is first to set out its legislative history because it has not been fully set out in any decision, and that history throws valuable light on the nature, scope and effect of Arts. 19, 21 and 22.

The legislative history of Art. 21

11.4 The legislative history of Art. 21 is this: Draft Art. 15, as originally passed by the Constituent Assembly, provided that "No person shall be deprived of his life or liberty without due process of law. . . ." The Drafting Committee suggested two changes in this Article: (i) the addition of the word "personal" before the word "liberty" and (ii) the substitution of the expression "except according to procedure established by law" for the words "without due process of law". The reason given for the first change was that "otherwise (liberty) might be construed very widely so as to include even the freedoms already dealt with in Art. 13" (now Art. 19). The reason given for the second change was that "the (substituted) expression was more specific (Cf. Art. XXXI of the Japanese Constitution 1946)."[13] The reason given for the first change was clearly right, for Draft Art. 13 (now Art. 19) conferred certain freedoms *only on citizens*, whereas Art. 15 (now Art. 21) applied to citizens and non-citizens alike, and it was wise to foreclose the argument that the word "liberty" included the freedoms which had been denied to non-citizens by Draft Art. 13. The reason given for the second change may be literally correct but was not candid. Both substantive and procedural "due process" were well established in the United States, and though the concept of "due process" was vague and flexible (or imprecise) it was used to enforce certain standards to which according to the majority of Judges of the U.S. Supreme Court substantive and procedural laws had to conform. However,

The reason for adding "personal" before "liberty"

The reason for substituting "procedure established by law" for "due process of law"

---

[11] (1976) Supp. S.C.R. 172, ('76) A.SC. 1207.

[12] (1978) 2 S.C.R. 621, ('78) A.SC. 597.

[13] Note of the Drafting Committee in the Draft Constitution forwarded by Dr. Ambedkar to the President of the Constituent Assembly on 21st February, 1948.

the abuse of *substantive* due process by the U.S. Supreme Court produced second thoughts, and "due process" was replaced by "procedure established by law". This change was the result of a discussion which the Constitutional Adviser, Sir B. N. Rau had with Mr. Justice Frankfurter of the U.S. Supreme Court. By substituting for the words "due process of law" the expression "except according to procedure established by law" the Drafting Committee did not make the American concept of "due process" more precise as a matter of drafting — *the Committee gave up that concept altogether.*

Legislative history of Art. 22 — Arts. (1) and (2) introduced to give the substance of "due process"

11.5 Although the Draft Constitution contained Art. 15, it did not, in the first instance, contain any Article corresponding to Art. 22 of the Constitution. When the proposal to delete "due process" suggested by the Drafting Committee was debated in the Constituent Assembly on 6th December, 1948,[14] and then on 13th December, 1948,[15] there was strong opposition to the proposal; nevertheless the Drafting Committee's suggestion was accepted by the Constituent Assembly.[16] However, the Assembly's vote did not finally settle the matter, for dissatisfaction with the deletion of "due process" continued inside and outside the Assembly. On September 15, 1949, Dr. Ambedkar moved that a new Article 15A (which, as amended, corresponds to Art. 22 of our Constitution) be adopted. Speaking on the motion, he said:

"We are therefore now, by introducing Article 15A, making, if I may say so, compensation for what was done then in passing article 15. *In other words, we are providing for the substance of the law of 'due process' by the introduction of article 15A.* Article 15A merely lifts from the provisions of the Criminal Procedure Code two of the most fundamental principles which every civilized country follows as principles of international justice. It is quite true that these two provisions contained in clause (1) and clause (2) are already to be found in the Criminal Procedure Code and therefore probably it might be said that we are really not making any very fundamental change. But we are, as I contend, making a fundamental change because what we are doing by the introduction of article 15A is to put a limitation upon the authority both of Parliament as well as of the Provincial Legislature not to abrogate these two provisions, because they are now introduced in our Constitution it self. It is quite true that the enthusiasts for personal liberty are probably not content with the provisions of clause (1) and (2). They probably want something more by way of further safeguards against the inroads of the executive and the legislatures upon the personal liberty of the citizen. I personally think that while I sympathise with them that probably this article might have been expanded to include some further safeguards, I am quite satisfied that the provisions contained are sufficient *against illegal or arbitrary arrests.*"[17] (italics supplied)

Article 15A, with certain amendments, was passed as it now stands in Art. 22 of our Constitution. For the sake of convenience, Draft Articles 15 and 15A will hereafter be referred to by their present counterparts, Arts. 21 and 22. In *Gopalan's Case* the attention of the Supreme Court was drawn to the legislative history of Art. 21 which showed why the expression "due process of law" was replaced by the expression "procedure established by law". However, it is unfortunate that the legislative history of Art. 22, and particularly of Clauses (1) and (2), whereby the substance of "due process" was reintroduced, was not brought to the attention of the Supreme

Unfortunately the legislative history of Art. 22 was

[14] C.A.D., Vol. VII, pp. 842-857. [15] ibid. pp. 999-1001.
[16] See Shiva Rao, *The Framing of India's Constitution, A Study*, pp. 235-8.
[17] *C.A.D.* Vol. IX, p. 1497.

not brought to the attention of the Sup. Ct. in *Gopalan's Case*

Court. Had this legislative history been brought to the Court's attention, a number of problems which caused the Judges grave concern in *Gopalan's Case* would have been simplified. The Court could then have dealt with two aspects of Art. 21, namely, the *procedural due process* available to every person (not preventively detained) before he was deprived of his life or personal liberty, and the attenuated procedural safeguards available to a person preventively detained, because Art. 22(1) and (2) were expressly excluded in the case of preventive detention. The legislative history would also have led to simpler answers being given to the contentions urged on behalf of Gopalan. However, the full impact of Art. 22(1) and (2) on Art. 21, and on the contentions raised on behalf of Gopalan will be considered later in their appropriate place.

Defective drafting of Arts. 21 and 22 — a suggested re-drafting

11.6 It is also unfortunate that Arts. 21 and 22 were not taken up together in the Constituent Assembly and Art. 21 re-drafted in the light of Art. 22. If Clauses (1) and (2) of Art. 22 were meant to reintroduce the substance of "due process", then, those Clauses ought to have been put in Art 21 from which "due process" had been removed. There would have been several advantages in re-numbering Art. 21 as Art. 21(1), and transferring to it, as sub-Articles (2) and (3), sub-Articles (1) and (2) of Art. 22, and re-numbering the sub-Articles of Art. 22 accordingly, and by inserting a new marginal note. For one thing, the Supreme Court would have seen at a glance that procedural due process was a part of Art. 21 itself. Articles 21 and 22 would then have been re-drafted as follows:

Art. 21. Protection of life and personal liberty—(1) No person shall be deprived of his life or personal liberty except according to procedure established by law.

(2) No person who is arrested shall be detained in custody without being informed, as soon as may be, of the grounds for such arrest nor shall he be denied the right to consult, and to be defended by, a legal practitioner of his choice.

(3) Every person who is arrested and detained in custody shall be produced before the nearest magistrate within a period of twenty-four hours of such arrest excluding the time necessary for the journey from the place of arrest to the court of the magistrate and no such person shall be detained in custody beyond the said period without the authority of a magistrate.

Art. 22. Art. 21(2) and (3) not to apply to enemy aliens and persons preventively detained; preventive detention.—(1) Nothing in Art. 21(2) and (3) shall apply—

(*a*) to any person who for the time being is an enemy alien; or

(*b*) to any person who is arrested or detained under any law providing for preventive detention.

(2) No law providing for preventive detention shall authorise the detention of a person for a longer period than three months unless—

(*a*) an Advisory Board consisting of persons who are, or have been, or are qualified to be appointed as, Judges of a High Court has reported before the expiration of the said period of three months that there is in its opinion sufficient cause for such detention;

Provided that nothing in this sub-clause shall authorize the detention of any person beyond the maximum period prescribed by any law made by Parliament under sub-clause (*b*) of clause (5); or

(*b*) such person is detained in accordance with the provisions of any law made by Parliament under sub-clauses (*a*) and (*b*) of clause (5).

(3) When any person is detained in pursuance of an order made under any law providing for preventive detention, the authority making the order shall,

as soon as may be, communicate to such person the grounds on which the order has been made and shall afford him the earliest opportunity of making a representation against the order.

(4) Nothing in clause (3) shall require the authority making any such order as is referred to in that clause to disclose facts which such authority considers to be against the public interest to disclose.

(5) Parliament may by law prescribe—

(*a*) the circumstances under which, and the class or classes of cases in which, a person may be detained for a period longer than three months under any law providing for preventive detention without obtaining the opinion of an Advisory Board in accordance with the provisions of sub-clause (*a*) of clause (2);

(*b*) the maximum period for which any person may in any class or classes of cases be detained under any law providing for preventive detention; and

(*c*) the procedure to be followed by an Advisory Board in an inquiry under sub-clause (*a*) of Clause (2).

The advantages of the suggested re-drafting

11.7 The advantages of re-drafting the two Articles would have been: (i) more precise draftsmanship, because the appropriate place for the two sub-Articles which "gave the substance of due process" was in Art. 21 from which "due process" had been removed; (ii) as Art. 21 stands and as "law" was interpreted in *Gopalan's Case*, Art. 21, taken by itself, *appears at first blush* open to the objection that it does not confer a fundamental right. For, if "law" in Art. 21 means a law enacted by a Legislature, as rightly held in *Gopalan's Case*, then Art. 21, as it stands, appears to confer no fundamental right, for fundamental rights are limitations on legislative power, and Art. 21 contains no such limitation since it only requires the authority of "law". The inclusion of sub-Arts. (2) and (3) would have removed this objection, because the law referred to in Art. 21(1) must, at least, conform to the requirements of sub-Arts. (2) and (3), which clearly impose limitations on legislative power; (iii) such re-drafting would have made it easy to interpret the expression "personal liberty", because Clauses (2) and (3) were "already to be found in the Criminal Procedure Code . . ." as Dr. Ambedkar rightly pointed out in his speech.

The correlation of Art. 19 to Arts. 21 and 22 best considered by referring to *Gopalan's Case*

11.8 Against the background of this legislative history, the discussion of Art. 21 and its relation to Arts. 19 and 22 can most conveniently begin by considering *Gopalan's Case*. The present discussion does not deal with the Supreme Court's interpretation of the Preventive Detention Act, 1950 ("the Detention Act"), which will be discussed separately under Art. 22. In *Gopalan's Case*, Gopalan, who was a citizen, challenged the validity of his detention on the wide ground that the Detention Act, under which he was detained, was void as violating Arts. 19 and 21, and also on the narrow ground that the Act did not comply with the requirements of Art. 22. The present discussion is confined to the wider challenge under Arts. 19 and 21.

Contentions urged in *Gopalan's Case*

11.9 Counsel for Gopalan contended that the Detention Act contravened Art. 21.[18] and was void because:

(*a*) *Personal liberty* included the freedoms conferred by Art. 19(1)(*a*) to (*e*) and (*g*) and the impugned law did not satisfy the test of Art. 19(2) to (6).[19]

---

[18] Which provides that no person shall be deprived of life or personal liberty save by procedure established by law.

[19] (1950) S.C.R. *supra* at p. 100.

(*b*) In the alternative, the impugned law directly violated Gopalan's right to move freely throughout the territory of India [Art. 19(1)(*d*)] because the freedom of movement is of the essence of *personal liberty* and the impugned Act did not satisfy the test of Art. 19(5).[20]

(*c*) Article 19(1) and Art. 21 should be read together because *Art. 19(1) dealt with substantive rights and Art. 21 dealt with procedural rights.*[21]

(*d*) The reference in Art. 21 to "procedure established by law" meant "due process of law", and the impugned Act did not satisfy the requirement of "due process".[22]

(*e*) In any event, the word "law" in Art. 21 meant not State enacted law, but *jus naturale* or the principles of natural justice. The impugned Act did not comply with the requirements of natural justice.[23]

The basis of *Gopalan's* contention that Art. 21 applied to preventive detention was countered by saying that Art. 22 was a complete code

It will be seen that the proposition that Art. 21 applied to a law of preventive detention was the foundation of *all* the reasons (*a*) to (*e*) which were urged for submitting that the Detention Act was void. The Att.-General tried to strike at the root of these reasons by contending that Art. 21 did not apply to preventive detention, *because Art. 22 was a complete code relating to preventive detention.* If the Att.-General's argument had been accepted, then reasons (*a*) to (*e*) would have required no consideration, since the validity of the impugned Act would have to be tested only by Art. 22.

Six judgments delivered in *Gopalan's Case* in view of the important questions raised

11.10 As the questions raised were of great constitutional importance, all the six judges delivered separate judgments in which the arguments of both sides were considered at length.[24] Kania C.J., Sastri, Mahajan, Mukherjea and Das JJ. (Fazl Ali J. dissenting) held that Art. 19 did not apply to a law of preventive detention, although as a result of an order of detention, the rights referred to in Art. 19(1) (*a*) to (*e*) and (*g*) in general, and the right referred to in Art. 19(1) (*d*) in particular, may be restricted or abridged. Consequently, the constitutional validity of such a law could not be judged in the light of the tests prescribed in Art. 19(5). Mahajan J. held that whatever may be the precise scope of Art. 19(1) (*d*) and Art. 19(5), the provisions of Art. 19(5) did not apply to a law of preventive detention because there was a special self-contained provision in Art. 22 regulating it. Das J. held that Art. 19(1) postulated a legal capacity to exercise the rights guaranteed by it and if a citizen lost the freedom of his person because he was lawfully detained on a conviction for an offence, or otherwise, he could not claim the rights under Art. 19(1) (*a*) to (*e*) and (*g*).[25–27] Likewise, if a citizen's property was compulsorily acquired under Art. 31 he could not claim the right under sub-cl. (*f*) of Art. 19(1) with respect to that property. In short, the rights under sub-cls. (*a*) to (*e*) and (*g*) ended where lawful detention began, and therefore the validity of the Detention Act could not be judged by Art. 19(5). Fazl Ali J. in his dissent held that preventive detention was a direct infringement of the right guaranteed by Art. 19(1) (*d*) even if that Article was narrowly construed, and a law of preventive detention was therefore subject to such limited judicial review as was permitted by Art. 19(5).

---

[20] ibid. p. 101.
[21] ibid. p. 103.
[22] ibid. p. 107 *et seq.*
[23] ibid. p. 204.
[24] The judgments occupy 250 pages of the Supreme Court Reports.
[25–27] Sastri J. took the same view; (1950) S.C.R. *supra* at pp. 191-2.

11.11 With reference to para 11.9 (*a*) above, the majority of judges in *Gopalan's Case* did *not* hold that Art. 22 was a complete code. Kania C.J., Sastri and Das JJ. held that Art. 22 was *not* a complete code on preventive detention; Mukherjea J. held that it was unnecessary to decide that question; Mahajan J. alone of all the judges, held that Art. 22 was a complete Code. This will be clear from the following quotations:

The majority in *Gopalan* held that Art. 22 was not a complete code

Kania C.J.: "The learned Att.-Gen. contended that the subject of preventive detention does not fall under Art. 21 at all and is covered wholly by Art. 22. *According to him, Art. 22 is a complete code. I am unable to accept that contention.*"[28] (italics supplied)

Sastri J.: "The learned Att.-Gen. contended that Art. 21 did not apply to preventive detention at all *as Art. 22(4) to (7) formed a complete code* of constitutional safeguards in respect of preventive detention. . . . *I am unable to agree with this view.*"[29] (italics supplied)

Das J.: "The learned Att.-Gen. on the other hand, has at one stage of his argument, urged that Art. 21 has nothing to do with preventive detention at all and that preventive detention is wholly covered by *Art. 22(4) to (7) which by themselves constitute a complete Code. I am unable to accede to this extreme point also.*"[30] (italics supplied)

Mukherjea J.: "It is also unnecessary to enter into a discussion *on the question raised by the learned Att.-Gen.* as to whether *Art. 22 by itself is a self-contained Code* with regard to the law of Preventive Detention and whether or not the procedure it lays down is exhaustive. Even if the procedure is not exhaustive, it is not permissible to supplement it by application of the rules of natural justice."[31] (italics supplied)

Mahajan J.: "I now proceed to consider the first question that was canvassed before us by the learned Att.-Gen., i.e. that Article 22 of the Constitution read with the entries in the 7th Schedule *was a complete Code on the subject of preventive detention*, and that being so, the other articles of Part III could not be invoked in the consideration of the validity of the impugned statute . . . I am satisfied on a review of the whole scheme of the Constitution that the intention was to make Article 22 self-contained in respect of the laws on the subject of preventive detention."[32] (italics supplied)

11.12 The argument that preventive detention infringed the rights specified in Art. 19 (1) (*a*) to (*e*) and (*g*) was met by Kania C.J. by saying that if it were accepted in the case of preventive detention it must equally be accepted in the case of punitive detention for offences under the Penal Code, in which case punitive detention would be illegal in respect of several offences. Such a conclusion must be avoided if possible, and it was clearly not the outcome of our Constitution. He said:

Kania C.J. pointed out the absurd consequences of applying Art. 19 to preventive detention

"The article has to be read without any pre-conceived notions. So read, it clearly means that the legislation to be examined must be directly in respect of one of the rights mentioned in the sub-clauses. If there is a legislation directly attempting to control a citizen's freedom of speech or expression, or his right to assemble peaceably and without arms, etc., the question whether that legislation is saved by the relevant saving clause of Article 19 will arise. If, however, the legislation is not directly in respect of any of these subjects, but as a result of the operation of other legislation, for instance, for punitive or preventive detention, his right under any of these sub-clauses is abridged, the question of the application of Article 19 does not arise. The true approach is only to consider the directness of the legislation and not what will be the result of the detention *otherwise valid*, on the mode of the detenue's life."[33] (italics supplied)

---

[28] (1950) S.C.R. *supra* at pp. 115-6.
[29] ibid. p. 207.
[30] ibid. p. 324.
[31] ibid. p. 279.
[32] ibid. pp. 225, 226.
[33] ibid. pp. 100-1. [The above passage was cited with approval by Sastri J. in

Fazl Ali J.: Art. 19 does not apply to punitive detention

In his dissenting judgment Fazl Ali J. after saying that "no calamitous or untoward result would follow even if the provisions of the Penal Code became justiciable",[34] added:

> "The Indian Penal Code does not primarily or necessarily impose restrictions on the freedom of movement and it is not correct to say that it is a law imposing restrictions on the right to move freely. Its primary object is to punish crime and not to restrict movement. . . . But if it (the punishment) consists in imprisonment there is a restriction on movement. This restraint is imposed not under a law imposing restrictions on movement but under a law defining crime and making it punishable. The punishment is correlated directly with the violation of some other person's right and not with the right of movement (of) the offender himself . . . the (I.P.C.) does not come within the ambit of the words 'law imposing restrictions on the right to move freely'."[35]

Submission: the same considerations apply to preventive detention

It will be seen that Fazl Ali J. applied to punitive detention *the same test* as was applied by Kania C.J. in the passage cited earlier. It is submitted that Fazl Ali J. overlooked the "primary object" of a law of preventive detention, which is put beyond doubt by the language of the undernoted legislative entry.[36] Adapting the language which Fazl Ali J. applied to punitive detention under the Penal Code, it can be said that a law of preventive detention is not a law primarily or necessarily imposing restrictions on the right to move freely, but is correlated directly with the apprehended violation by the detenu of the rights of others by disturbing public safety or public order or by disrupting supplies and services essential to the community. It is submitted that the distinction made by Fazl Ali J. between punitive and preventive detention is not correct. He was reconciled to punitive detention because it was imposed after a trial and was subject to appeals which may be taken right up to the Supreme Court. But that is because a crime has to be proved by evidence, and Courts are best qualified to judge whether a conviction is proper. Preventive detention does not admit of such a trial, because the whole case for such detention rests upon apprehended, and not actual danger. As Lord Finlay L.C. said:

> ". . . no tribunal for investigating the question whether circumstances of suspicion exist warranting some restraint can be imagined less appropriate than a Court of Law. No crime is charged. The question is whether there is ground for suspicion whether a particular person may be disposed to help the enemy."[37]

Art. 21 and Art. 19(1)(*d*): an alternative argument—Art. 19(1)(*d*) was said to affect

11.13 *Gopalan's Case* shows that when the contention that personal liberty in Art. 21 attracted Art. 19 (1) (*a*) to (*e*) and (*g*) was urged before the Court, it was soon realized that it would render imprisonment under "the Penal Code, *e.g.* for theft, cheating, forgery and even ordinary assault . . . illegal";[38] as it would not be protected

Ram Singh v. *Delhi* (1951) S.C.R. 451, 457, ('51) A.SC. 270, where he added, "similar conclusions expressed by the other learned Judges will be found at (1950) S.C.R. pp. 194, 229, 256 and 305."] Although Mahajan and Bose JJ. dissented on the merits there was no dissent on this point. Kania C.J.'s view was also adopted in the *Express Newspapers Case* (1959) S.C.R. 12, 129-135, ('58) A.SC. 578.

34 (1950) S.C.R. *supra* at p. 145. 35 ibid. pp. 145-46.

36 Entry 3, List III, Sch. VII: "Preventive detention for reasons connected with the security of the State, the maintenance of public order or the maintenance of supplies and services essential to the community. . . ."

37 *R.* v. *Halliday* (1917) A.C. 260, 269.

38 (1950) S.C.R. *supra* at p. 100 *per* Kania C.J.; pp. 192-3 *per* Sastri J.

by sub-Art. (2).[39] If such an absurd result was to be avoided some other construction must be adopted. In urging the alternative ground [para 11.9 (*b*)], counsel for Gopalan personal liberty *directly*

"... drew a distinction between the right conferred by sub-clause (*d*) [of Art. 19(1)] and those conferred by other sub-clauses. He urged, referring to *Blackstone's Commentaries*, that personal liberty consisted 'in moving one's person to whatever place one's inclination might direct', and that any law which deprived such power of locomotion was a *direct invasion* of the right mentioned in sub-clause (*d*), whereas it interfered only indirectly and consequentially with the rights mentioned in the other sub-clauses."[40] (italics supplied)

Therefore, the test whether a law directly affected the rights conferred by Art. 19 (1) (as set out by Kania C.J. and by Fazl Ali J.) or indirectly affected them was put in issue by Counsel for Gopalan in order to avoid a construction which would lead to absurd results. This distinction was accepted, but its application to Art. 19 (1) (*d*) was rejected for the reasons set out in the next paragraph.

Art. 19(1)(*d*) did not confer a right of free movement *simpliciter*, but a right to move freely throughout India

11.14 With reference to para 11.9 (*b*) above, Kania C.J., Sastri, Mukherjea and Das JJ. (Fazl Ali J. dissenting) held that in Art. 19 (1) (*d*) the concept of the right "to move freely throughout the territory of India" was entirely different from the concept of the "right to personal liberty" in Art. 21, and Art. 19 should not therefore be read as controlled by Art. 21. Kania C.J. said that in the right "to move freely throughout the territory of India", the emphasis was not on "free movement" *simpliciter*, but on the right to move freely *throughout the territory of India* and that Art. 19 (1) (*d*) read with sub-Art. (5), meant that if restrictions were put on the movement of a citizen from State to State or even within a State, such restrictions must satisfy the requirements of Art. 19 (5), and that Art. 19 (1) (*d*) had nothing to do with detention, preventive or punitive. This position was made clear by Art. 19 (5) which permitted "reasonable restrictions" to be imposed on the right in the interest of the general public or the protection of the interest of any Scheduled Tribe. Kania C.J. said:

Kania C.J.

"It is difficult to conceive of a reasonable restriction necessary in the interest of the *general* public for confining a person in a cell. Such restriction may be appropriate to prevent a person from going from one Province to another or one area to another, having regard to local conditions prevailing in particular areas. The point however is made abundantly clear by the alternative, namely, for the protection of the interests of any Scheduled Tribe. What protection of the interests of a Scheduled Tribe requires the confinement of a man in a cell? On the other hand, preventing the movement of a person from one part of the territory of India to another and the question of reasonable restriction imposed to protect the interest of a Scheduled Tribe is clearly intelligible and often noticed in the course of the administration of the country."[41]

---

[39] ibid. p. 303 "To say that every crime undermines the security of the State and therefore every section of the Indian Penal Code, irrespective of whether it has any reference to speech or expression, is a law within the meaning of this clause is wholly unconvincing and betrays only a vain and forlorn attempt to find an explanation for meeting the argument that any conviction by a Court of law must necessarily infringe Article 19(1)(*a*). There can be no getting away from the fact that a detention as a result of a conviction impairs the freedom of speech far beyond what is permissible under clause (2) of Article 19": *per* Das J.

[40] ibid. p. 193 *per* Sastri J.

[41] ibid. pp. 102-3.

Sastri J. Mukherjea J. Das J.

Sastri J. said that Art. 19 (1) (*d*) emphasized the factual unity of India which a narrow-minded provincialism would deny.[42] Mukherjea J. also held that Art. 19 (1) (*d*) was designed to secure the unity of India in spite of its being divided into a number of States. He supported this conclusion by observing that Art. 19 (1) (*d*) (*e*) and (*f*) had to be read together with Art. 19 (5) which applied to all the three sub-clauses.[43] Das J. expressed the same view as was expressed by Sastri J.[44] This conclusion was not based on any theory that Art. 19 (1) and Art. 21 were mutually exclusive, but on an *interpretation* of the language of Art. 19 (1) (*d*) read with Art. 19 (5), namely, that Art. 19 (1) (*d*) did not deal with a person's freedom of movement *simpliciter* but with his freedom of movement *throughout the territory of India.* The whole discussion *on the merits* would have been unnecessary if Art. 19 (1) and Art. 21 had been held to be mutually exclusive. Assuming that the right to move freely was of the essence of personal liberty, the majority held that it did not fall under Art. 19 (1) (*d*) which conferred a different right, namely, "the right to move freely *throughout the territory of India*".

Some judges referred to the report of Drafting Committee and the reason for adding the word "personal" before liberty

11.15 In further support of the above conclusion, some of the Judges referred to the Drafting Committee's Report on Draft Art. 15 (now Art. 21) which inserted the word "personal" before the word "liberty". The Report stated that "the word 'liberty' should be qualified by the word 'personal' before it, for otherwise it might be construed very widely *so as to include even the freedoms already dealt with in Art. 13* (now Art. 19)". (italics supplied) Sastri J. said that the "acceptance of this suggestion shows that whatever may be the generally accepted connotation of the expression 'personal liberty' it was used in Art. 21 in a sense which excludes the freedom dealt with in Art. 19. . . ."[45] Mukherjea J. said: "If the views of the Drafting Committee were accepted by the Constituent

---

[42] "Sub-cl. (*d*) of Cl. (1) does not refer to the freedom of movement *simpliciter* but guarantees the right to move freely 'throughout the territory of India'. Sub. cl. (*e*) similarly guarantees the right to reside and settle in any part of the territory of India and Cl. (5) authorises the imposition of 'reasonable restrictions' on these rights in the interests of the general public or for the protection of the interests of any Scheduled Tribe. Reading these provisions together, it is reasonably clear that they were designed primarily to emphasize the factual unity of the territory of India and to secure the right of a free citizen to move from one place in India to another and to reside and settle in any part of India unhampered by any barriers which narrow-minded provincialism may seek to interpose": ibid. p. 191.

[43] ibid. pp. 258-9. He added that a comparison of the provisions in Art. 19(1)(*d*) to (*f*) with similar provisions in other constitutions supported this conclusion. The rights embodied in Art. 19(1)(*d*) to (*f*) are embodied in Art. 75 in the Constitution of the Free City of Danzig, in identical language, but they are differentiated from the "liberty of the person" which is "described as inviolable except by virtue of law" by Art. 74. The same distinction is made by Arts. 111 and 114 of the Constitution of the German Reich. Mukherjea J. said that the right to move freely throughout the territory of India had nothing to do with the rights of emigration; and he referred to the Danzig and the German Constitutions, which confer a right to move freely throughout the territory, to show that separate Articles, namely, Arts. 76 and 112 respectively, guarantee the rights of emigration (ibid. pp. 260-1); for a similar reference by Das J. to the Danzig and German Constitutions, see ibid. p. 322.

[44] ". . . in sub-cl. (*d*) the real emphasis is on the words 'throughout the territory of India'. The purpose of Art. 19(1)(*d*) is to guarantee that there shall be no State barrier. It gives protection against provincialism. It has nothing to do with the freedom of the person as such.": ibid. p. 302.

[45] ibid. pp. 194-5.

Assembly, the intention obviously was to exclude the contents of Art. 19 from the concept of 'personal liberty' as used in Art. 21."[46] Das J. did not base his judgment on the Report, nor did he pronounce on its admissibility, but observed that "if it were permissible to refer to the Drafting Committee Report, it would be another answer to the contentions of learned Counsel for the petitioner that personal liberty as a substantive right was protected by Art. 19."[47]

Reasons for rejecting the contention that Art. 21 dealt with *procedural*, and Art. 19 with *substantive* rights

11.16 Counsel's submission in para 11.9(*c*) above that Art. 19(1) conferred substantive rights and Art. 21 conferred procedural rights raised a question of far-reaching importance, namely, the nature of the rights conferred by Arts. 19(1) and 21. This question was carefully considered by the Judges who constituted the majority in *Gopalan's Case* (other than Mahajan J. who held Art. 22 to be a complete code). In rejecting the submission in para 11.9(*c*), some of the Judges pointed out that Arts. 19(1) and 21 did not operate on the same field, because, whereas Art. 19(1) conferred rights only on citizens, Art. 21 conferred rights on all persons.[48] Again, if Art. 21 conferred only procedural rights, then the most fundamental right of all, the right to life, was nowhere provided for in our Constitution, and, in any event, if there was no substantive right what would the procedural right protect? Similarly, if non-citizens had no substantive right to personal liberty, what would the procedure protect?[49] The majority held that Art. 21 conferred also substantive rights to life and personal liberty.[50] Mukherjea J. observed:

The majority view: Art. 21 deals with both substantive and procedural rights

"It is not correct to say . . . that Art. 21 is confined to matters of procedure only. There must be a substantive law, under which the State is empowered to deprive a man of his life and personal liberty and such a law must be a valid law which the legislature is competent to enact within the limits of the powers assigned to it and which does not transgress any of the fundamental rights that the Constitution lays down. Thus a person cannot be convicted or punished under an *ex post facto* law, or a law which compels the accused to incriminate himself in a criminal trial or punishes him for the same offence more than once."[51]

It may be observed that far from holding that the fundamental rights conferred by different Articles were mutually exclusive, Mukherjea J. held that a substantive law authorizing the deprivation of life must conform to the requirements of other fundamental rights, *e.g.* those contained in Art. 20(1) to (3). It is submitted that the majority rightly rejected the contention that Art. 21 conferred only procedural rights. But why was this contention urged at all? No definite answer can be given in the absence of a report of counsel's argument. But the reason for the contention that Art. 21 dealt with

---

[46] ibid. pp. 262-3. Mukherjea J. said that debates in the Constituent Assembly were not admissible as aids to construction; but as to the report of the Drafting Committee, on which both the sides had relied, there were decided cases in which a higher value has been attached to them than to the debates on the floor of the House: ibid. p. 274.

[47] ibid. p 297.

[48] ibid. p. 195 (Sastri J.); p. 257 (Mukherjea J.); p. 297 (Das J.).

[49] ibid. pp. 195, 257, 297.

[50] ibid. p. 195. [Sastri J. observed that "the right to life is the most difficult to define and its protection generally takes the form of a declaration that no person shall be deprived of it save by due process of law or by authority of law"; p. 257 (Mukherjea J.); pp. 295-7 (Das J.)].

[51] ibid. p. 255.

procedural rights may have been that to urge that Art. 21 also conferred substantive rights would have destroyed the central argument that Art. 19(1) and Art. 21 should be read together. Because, apart from the fact that the right to life is not mentioned in Art. 19(1), if "personal liberty" in Art. 21 conferred both substantive and procedural rights, it could easily be *demonstrated* that Art. 19(1) and 21 could not be read together. For, if the substantive rights conferred by Art. 21 were to include the substantive rights conferred by Art. 19(1), it would mean that the very rights denied to non-citizens by Art. 19(1) were conferred on them by Art. 21, which would be absurd.

Majority view: "law" meant a law enacted by legislatures, and not "natural justice"

11.17 With reference to the contention in para 11.9(*d*) and (*e*) above, Kania C.J., Mukherjea and Das JJ. (Fazl Ali J. dissenting) held that in Art. 21 the word "law" had been used in the sense of "State-made law" and not in the sense of law embodying the principles of natural justice; and "procedure established by law" meant "a law made by the Union Parliament or by Legislatures of the States", and it was not proper to consider this expression in the light of the expression "due process of law" as interpreted by the U.S. Supreme Court. Sastri J. held that "law" in Art. 21 did not mean *jus naturale* but meant positive or State-made law. "Procedure established by law" did not however mean any procedure which may be prescribed by a competent legislature, but the ordinary well-established criminal procedure, that is, those settled usages and normal modes of procedure sanctioned by the Criminal Procedure Code which is the general law of criminal procedure in our country. Fazl Ali J. held that whatever "procedure established by law" may mean, it must include (i) notice, (ii) opportunity to be heard, (iii) impartial tribunal, and (iv) orderly course of procedure.

Submission: the majority rightly held that "procedure established by law" did not mean "due process of law"

11.18 It is submitted that the majority judgments rightly held that "procedure established by law" did not mean "due process of law" as understood in the United States. In the first place, the Report of the Drafting Committee showed that the words "except according to procedure established by law" were substituted for the words "without due process of law" because the substituted expression was more specific. That Report could be resorted to in case of ambiguity, and also to show that the precise phrase "due process of law" had been brought to the attention of the Constituent Assembly which rejected it in favour of the expression "procedure established by law" and that therefore, *prima facie*, the two expressions did not mean the same thing.[52] Secondly, it is submitted, that the words "due process of law" have been given an interpretation by the U.S. Supreme Court which those words do not *necessarily* bear as a matter of English. In England, where they originated, they have been traced to the famous words of Magna Carta:

The origin of the words "due process" in England

> "No free man shall be arrested or detained in prison or deprived of his freedom or outlawed or banished or in any way molested and we will not set forth against him, nor send against him, unless by the lawful judgment of his Peers, and by the law of the land."

[52] See para 2.37.

However, the actual expression "due process of the law" was used in the following Clause of the Statute 28, Edw. III, c. 3 (1354) "That no man of what estate or condition shall be put out of land or tenement nor taken, nor imprisoned nor disinherited nor put to death without being brought in answer by due process of the law."[53] In the Petition of Right the violation of this Statute was urged by averring that contrary to the Statute, people had been arrested and detained without any cause shown other than the order of the King.[54] It is clear that "due process of the law" in England conveyed the idea of arrest or imprisonment *according to the law of the land*, as opposed to the arbitrary order of the King or his Council, and the procedural safeguards considered necessary in the United States were not a necessary part of the concept in England. Thirdly, quite apart from the meaning given to those words in England, the whole basis of interpreting the due process clause as it has been interpreted in the United States is to be found in the word "due".[55] This word does not occur in Art. 21 and in fact was deleted from it. Lastly, the interpretation put on the due process clause by the U.S. Supreme Court has been characterised by the utmost vagueness and "due process" means what the five Judges of that Court say it means. If the object of the Drafting Committee was to substitute a more precise expression, that object would be completely defeated by reading into the precise words of our Constitution a concept as vague and indefinite as "the due process" of the United States. Several judgments in *Gopalan's Case* have pointed out that the interpretation given to the "due process" clause in the United States had to be supplemented by developing the theory of Police powers of the States; and Das J. said:

Due process in the United States

". . . it will be incongrous to import the doctrine of due process of law without its palliative, the doctrine of police powers. It is impossible to read the last mentioned doctrine into Article 21."[56]

The words "procedure established by law" are clear and unambiguous and do not require any construction.[57] The reason why the judges in *Gopalan's Case* gave such anxious thought to the meaning of the phrase "procedure established by law" was that if these words meant what they said, legislatures in India would have an unfettered power to prescribe such procedure as they thought fit.[58] However,

[53] "That expression had its roots in the expression *'per legem terrae'* (law of the land) used in Magna Carta . . . however, the words 'due process of law' were used in a statute . . . 28, Edw. III, Ch. 3": *Per* Fazl Ali J. (1950) S.C.R. *supra* at p. 159; Mukherjea J. at p. 266.

[54] Cls. IV and V of the Petition of Right.

[55] " 'The Judges of Aragon began by setting aside laws and ended by making them.' And all this sweeping development could only be possible because of the presence of one little word 'due' which, in its content, knows no bound and is not subject to any fixed definition. Whenever a substantive law or some procedure laid down in any law did not find favour with the majority of the learned Judges of the Supreme Court it was not reasonable and, therefore, it was not 'due'.": *Per* Das J. (1950) S.C.R. *supra* at p. 312.

[56] (1950) S.C.R. *supra* at p. 317.

[57] "No extrinsic aid is needed to interpret the words of Art. 21, which, in my opinion, are not ambiguous": *per* Kania C.J. (1950) S.C.R. *supra* at p. 111.

[58] As will appear later, a full appreciation of Art. 22(1) and (2) would have shown that to a large extent these fears were groundless, and that Art. 22(1) and (2) contained valuable safeguards against arbitrary and unfair procedure.

the majority rightly held that "procedure established by law" meant "procedure prescribed by a legislature".

The compromise solution of Sastri J. Submission: it is untenable, and unnecessary

11.19 The compromise solution suggested by Sastri J. is, it is submitted, untenable, because in substance it reads into the words "procedure established by law" the words "existing procedure under the Criminal Procedure Code". But the legislature has the power to amend or abrogate the Code. Sastri J. realised this, and said that though an *ad hoc* procedure could not be devised by a special law, the fundamental principles underlying the Code could be abrogated altogether for the trial of all offences.[59] It is submitted that there is nothing in the language of Art. 21 to support a conclusion which is self-contradictory and is opposed to well-settled principles of construction. However, if, as we suggested above, Art. 21 had been redrafted by transferring to it Clauses (*a*) and (*b*) of Art. 22, it is submitted that Sastri J. would have found it unnecessary to propound this compromise solution, for two of the most important safeguards of life and personal liberty contained in the Criminal Procedure Code would have been enacted in Art. 21 which undoubtedly confers a fundamental right.

Does Art. 22(1) and (2) give the substance of "due process"?

11.20 Although, as a matter of construction, the words "procedure established by law" do not mean "due process of law" as understood in the United States, where it includes both substantive and procedural due process, the question still remains whether Art. 22(1) and (2) does not give the substance of "due process" as claimed by Dr. Ambedkar (see para 11.5 above). Since the Supreme Court in *Gopalan's Case* dealt with preventive detention [Art. 22(4) to (7)], the impact of Art. 22(1) and (2) appears not to have been fully realized since the application of Article 22(1) and (2) is expressly excluded by Art. 22(3), *inter alia,* in the case of preventive detention. However, this question is tied up with the meaning to be given to the expression "personal liberty" in Art. 21, and is best considered in that context.

Gopalan's Case and "personal liberty"

11.21 In *Gopalan's Case* a large number of questions were considered by the Judges, including the meaning of the expression "personal liberty" in Art. 21. However, as different views were expressed by different Judges, no common pattern emerges from the judgments which can be said to fix authoritatively the correlation of Art. 19 to Arts. 20, 21 and 22, or the meaning of the expression "personal liberty". As the object of this book is to give a correct and coherent interpretation of our Constitution, we will consider the correlation of Art. 19 to Arts. 20, 21 and 22, as also the meaning of "personal liberty" in Art. 21, independently of decided cases. This course has been followed because the decisions which purport to "reconsider" *Gopalan's Case* suffer from such grave infirmities that an attempt to state the law by reference to those decisions would present a confused and distorted picture of the scheme underlying Arts. 19 to 22 which appear under the common heading "Right to Freedom". Having given our own interpretation first, we will then consider in detail the relevant decisions of the Supreme Court. *However, the reader should note at this place that the law laid down by the*

Author's submission on "personal liberty" independently of decided cases

---

[59] (1950) S.C.R. *supra* at p. 206.

Supreme Court on "personal liberty" and the correlation of Arts. 19 and 21 is set out in para 11.53 and 11.57, as modified and qualified by the majority judgment of the Supreme Court in Bachan Singh's Case considered in para 11.72 et seq. below, and the views expressed in the present discussion are the views of the present writer as to the underlying scheme of Arts. 19 to 21.

Kharak Singh v. U.P.

11.22 Before attempting to give a coherent explanation of the underlying scheme of Arts. 19 to 22, we must consider *Kharak Singh* v. *U.P.*[60] There, the question for decision was whether the U.P. Police Regulation 236 violated Art. 19(1)(*d*) or Art. 21. The Regulation was not passed under the authority of any law, and the Supreme Court rightly held that if it violated a fundamental right under Art. 19, the reasonableness of the Regulation was irrelevant, for reasonable restrictions could be put on such a right only by a law; and if it violated Art. 21 it must be held void, for the right contained in Art. 21 could not be taken away without the authority of law. On the question whether any provision of the Regulation violated fundamental rights, there was a difference of opinion. By a majority, the Court held that the only provision which was void was Reg. 236(*b*), which authorized domiciliary visits at night, which the Court interpreted as conferring on the police authorities the right to knock at night at the door of the person under surveillance, to awake him if he was asleep, to oblige him to open the door and to let the police in to satisfy themselves about him. The actual decision of the majority is correct, but it is submitted that the reasoning of the majority and the minority judgments is very unsatisfactory. The majority judgment cited a large number of American authorities on the due process clause, namely, "that the State shall not deprive any person of life, liberty or property without due process of law". *The majority expressly declined to give a final opinion on the relation between Art. 19 and Art. 21*, or the content of the expression "procedure established by law",[61] because:

A criticism of *Kharak Singh's Case*

"In view of the very limited nature of the question before us it is unnecessary to pause to consider either the precise relationship between the 'liberties' in Art. 19(1)(*a*) and (*d*) on the one hand and that in Art. 21 on the other, or the content and significance of the words 'procedure established by law' in the latter article, both of which were the subject of elaborate consideration by this Court in *A. K. Gopalan* v. *Madras*."[62]

And yet, the majority judgment adopted the view of "personal liberty" taken by Das J. in *Gopalan's Case* without realizing that the majority of judges had taken a different view in that case. Nor does the judgment consider the impact of Arts. 20 and 22, which also appear under the common heading "Right to Freedom". Further, the majority judgment puts on the words "right to move freely throughout the territory of India" a meaning directly contrary to the meaning given to those words by the majority of Judges in *Gopalan's Case*, (including Das J.) for the majority judgment in the present case says:

---

[60] (1964) 1 S.C.R. 332, ('63) A.SC. 1295.
[61] (1964) 1 S.C.R. *supra* at p. 345, ('63) A.SC. *supra* at p. 1301.
[62] (1950) S.C.R. *supra*.

"Taking first Art. 19(1)(*d*) the 'freedom' here guaranteed is a right 'to move freely' throughout the territory of India. *Omitting as immaterial for the present purpose the last words defining the geographical area of the guaranteed movement*, we agree that the right to 'move' denotes nothing more than a right of locomotion, and that in the context the adverb 'freely' would only connote that the freedom to move is without restriction and is absolute, i.e. to move wherever one likes, whenever one likes and however one likes subject to any valid law enacted or made under Cl. 5"[63] (italics supplied)

This passage states as the law the opinion in the dissenting judgment of Fazl Ali J., forgetting that the majority in *Gopalan's Case* had held that the concluding words of Art. 19 (1) (*d*) were *not only not immaterial but were determinative of the right there conferred*, and that the right was not one of free locomotion but a distinct and independent right of free movement *throughout the territory of India*. It is unnecessary to consider the minority judgment which goes further, but is open to the same objections as the majority judgment. It may be added that the construction put by the majority on Reg. 236 required no elaborate discussion of the meaning of Art. 19 (1) (*d*) and Art. 21, for domiciliary visits which knock up a person from sleep, compel him to open the door and to allow persons to enter his house unquestionably impose restraints on his person. It is submitted that in *Kharak Singh's Case*, the majority declined to lay down the relationship between Art. 19 and Art. 21; and the construction which the majority put on Art. 19 (1) (*d*) and Art. 21 is contrary to the decision in *Gopalan's Case*, and is, besides, incorrect.

An attempt to give a coherent account of the correlation of Art. 19 to Arts. 20, 21 and 22

11.23 In what follows, an attempt is made to give a coherent explanation of the scheme underlying the correlation of Arts. 19 to 21 and 22, in the light of (i) the legislative history of Arts. 21 and 22 including the conclusions which can be drawn from Art. 22 (1) and (2); (ii) the suggestions contained in the judgments in *Gopalan's Case* particularly in the judgment of Mukherjea J. who said:

Mukherjea J.'s explanation

"Art. 19 . . . gives a list of individual liberties and prescribes in the various clauses the restraints that may be placed upon them by law, so that they may not conflict with public welfare or general morality. On the other hand, Arts. 20, 21 and 22 are primarily concerned with penal enactments or other law under which personal safety or liberty of persons would be taken away in the interests of the Society and they set down the limits within which State control should be exercised. Art. 19 uses the expression 'freedom' and mentions the several forms and aspects of it which are secured to individuals, together with the limitations that could be placed upon them in the general interest of the society. Arts. 20, 21 and 22 . . . do not make use of the expression 'freedom' and they lay down the restrictions that are to be placed on State control where an individual is sought to be deprived of his life or personal liberty. The right to the safety of one's life and limbs and to enjoyment of *personal liberty*, in the sense of freedom from physical restraint and coercion of any sort, are the inherent birth rights of a man. The essence of these rights consists in restraining others from interfering with them and hence they cannot be described in terms of 'freedom' to do particular things . . ."[64]

Arts. 19 to 22 fall into two parts: Art. 19 and Arts. 20 to 22

First, Art. 19 confers the freedoms there mentioned on citizens alone[65] whereas the rights conferred by Arts. 20 to 22 are not limited to citizens but apply to all persons. Secondly, Art. 19 does not deal with the right to life which is dealt with in Art. 21. Articles 19

---

[63] (1964) 1 S.C.R. *supra* at p. 344. [64] (1950) S.C.R. *supra* at p. 254.
[65] Corporations and non-citizens are not entitled to these freedoms.

to 22, which appear under the heading, "Right to Freedom", fall into two parts — Art. 19 on the one hand and Arts. 20 to 22 on the other. Article 19 mentions the word "freedom" and provides for the freedom which a citizen has *to do things*; Arts. 20 to 22 do not mention the word "freedom" but they secure the freedom of a person by providing that certain things *shall not be done to him*. Although Arts. 20 to 22 are negative in form, they are positive in effect, because by preventing restraint on the person, except under certain circumstances, they secure the freedom of the person in all other cases. We are assisted in ascertaining the meaning of "personal liberty", first, by the position which Art. 21 occupies, namely, between Art. 20 on the one hand and Art. 22(1) and (2) on the other. Secondly, by the context in which the words "personal liberty" appear in Art. 21. Article 20(1) secures freedom of the person by prohibiting *ex post facto* laws, that is, laws making an act or omission an offence which was lawful when done or omitted to be done, so that a person cannot be imprisoned under an *ex post facto* law.[66] Article 20(2) secures the freedom of the person by providing that a person who has been prosecuted and punished for an offence shall not be again prosecuted and punished for the same offence. In other words, he cannot be imprisoned a second time for the same offence. Article 20(3) secures the freedom of the person, for it provides that a person shall not be compelled to give evidence which would amount to an admission or confession of a crime, for on that admission or confession his person may be put under restraint by his being imprisoned. Article 21 which provides that no person is to be deprived of life or personal liberty "except according to procedure established by law", is clearly designed to protect a person from physical constraint. Deprivation of life is physical constraint on a person in its most extreme form, for on such constraint being applied the person ceases to exist. The words "personal liberty" take their colour from the words "deprived of his life", and mean freedom of the person from external constraint.

Arts. 20 to 22(1) and (2) secure freedom by preventing restraint on the person

The Scheme of Art. 20(1), (2) and (3) explained

11.24 The above conclusion is reinforced by Art. 22(1) and (2). Article 22 falls into two parts, namely, Art. 22(1) and (2) and Art. 22(3) to (7). Article 22(1) and (2) contains valuable safeguards against an unfair procedure for depriving a person of life and personal liberty. Article 21 having provided against arbitrary arrest, that is, without the authority of law, Art. 22(1) and (2) deals with a matter closely allied to the freedom from arbitrary arrest, namely, freedom from oppression while under arrest. Article 22(1) provides that a person who is arrested cannot be detained without being informed as soon as may be of the grounds of such arrest, nor can he be denied the right to consult, and to be defended by, a legal practitioner of his choice. Article 22(2) provides that every person who is arrested and detained in custody must be produced before the nearest Magistrate within twenty-four hours of his arrest, and no such person shall be detained in custody beyond that period

Art. 22(1) and (2) read with Art. 21 provide valuable safeguards against unfair procedure

[66] The present writer has not overlooked the fact that a law may impose only a fine; but since a law referred to in Art. 20(1) to (3) may also impose a sentence of imprisonment, the argument in the text is not affected by the fact that the provisions of Art. 20 also protect a person from the deprivation of his property by a fine, as a punishment for an offence.

Art. 22(1) and (2) puts fetters on legislative powers and secures a fair procedure for arrest and trial

without the authority of a Magistrate. Thus, the assistance of a legal practitioner and the authority of a Magistrate are interposed between the arrested person and those arresting him. *Article 22(1) and (2) imposes fetters on legislative power because no procedure can be validly prescribed contrary to the requirements of Art. 22(1) and (2).* When these requirements are examined closely, they will be found to contain valuable safeguards for a fair procedure. They confer on the accused the right (*a*) to be informed of the grounds of arrest; (*b*) to consult and to be defended by a legal practitioner of the arrested person's choice; (*c*) to be produced before a Magistrate within 24 hours, and (*d*) the right not to be kept in detention beyond 24 hours except by an order of the Magistrate.[67] The implications of the right to be informed of the grounds of arrest and to consult and to be defended by a legal practitioner were not considered in *Gopalan's Case* because in cases of preventive detention, those rights are expressly excluded by Art. 22(3). However, the right of an arrested person to be defended by Counsel carries with it the right to have the charge against him formulated and the right to defend himself against that charge. Formulation of a charge and a defence against it necessarily involves a trial of some kind, and carries with it the right of testing the evidence in support of the charge by cross-examination and also of destroying it by affirmative evidence. Consequently, any procedure prescribed must be a judicial procedure, if the constitutional right of an arrested person to defend himself is not to become ineffective. Such a judicial procedure ensures for the accused a right to approach the High Court under Art. 226 and the Supreme Court under Arts. 32 and 136 even if no appeals are provided. It will have been noticed that the subject matter of Arts. 20, 21 and 22 falls squarely under criminal or penal law.

Meaning of "personal liberty" given above in harmony with English Constitutional Law: *Halsbury* on right to personal liberty

11.25 The meaning we have given to the expression "personal liberty" is in harmony with the meaning given to it in English Constitutional Law. In Halsbury's *Laws of England* the law has been stated thus:

> "*Right to personal liberty*: The right to personal liberty and immunity from wrongful detention is enshrined in Magna Carta and is enforceable by the Writ of *habeas corpus* and actions for false imprisonment. A person may be arrested by warrant issued by a justice or, in certain circumstances, without a warrant. If a person is arrested without a warrant, he must be informed of the reason for his arrest and, if retained in custody, he must be brought before a magistrates' court as soon as is practicable. Closely connected with the right to personal liberty is the right to be protected against unfair or oppressive police methods in the interrogation of suspects."[68]

Dicey on "personal liberty"

The same view has been taken by leading authorities on English Constitutional Law. According to *Dicey*,

> "The right to personal liberty as understood in England means in substance a person's right not to be subjected to imprisonment, arrest, or other physical coercion in any manner that does not admit of legal justification."[69]

---

[67] The observations of Das J. in *Gopalan's Case* (1950) S.C.R. *supra* p. 325, ". . . these four procedural requirements are very . . . similar to the requirements of the procedural 'due process of law' as enumerated by Willis" gain greater force once the implications of Art. 22(1) and (2) are fully realized.

[68] *Halsbury*, Vol. 8 (4th ed.) para 832. (Footnotes have been omitted).

[69] Dicey, *The Law of the Constitution*, 10th ed., pp. 207-208.

In *Wade and Phillips*[70] under the caption "Personal freedom" it is said:

Wade & Phillips on "personal liberty"

"There are two main aspects of the law relating to individual liberty: first the grounds on which an individual may be deprived of his physical liberty; second, the remedies which an individual has if he wishes to contest the legality of such detention."[71]

Prof. de Smith summed up the position perceptively when he wrote:

Prof. de Smith on traditional approach to civil liberties in Britain

"The traditional legal approach to civil liberties in Britain can be summed up in three propositions. First, freedoms are not to be guaranteed by statements of general principles. Secondly, *they are residual.* Freedom of public assembly, for example, means the liberty to gather wherever one chooses, except in so far as others are legally entitled to prevent the assembly from being held or in so far as the holding or the conduct of an assembly is a civil wrong or a criminal offence. *To define the content of liberty one has to subtract from its totality the sum of the legal restraints to which it is subject.*[72] Thirdly, for every wrongful encroachment upon one's liberty there is a remedy awarded by an independent court of justice. *Ubi jus, ibi remedium.*"[73] (There is no wrong without a remedy). (italics supplied)

Before the Constitution the position in India was the same

11.26 Before our Constitution came into force on January 26, 1950, the position in India was the same as in England. Indian law, like English law, in dealing with the freedoms of the individual, has relied ". . . 'on the principle that what is not prohibited is permitted and . . . therefore on keeping within acceptable limits, and providing precise definitions of, the restrictions imposed by the civil and criminal law' on the individual's freedom".[74] A person enjoyed the freedom to do everything except the doing of things for which he could be deprived of his physical liberty. In an appeal from Nigeria, Lord Atkin said in an oft quoted passage:

Lord Atkin on interference with liberty or property of a subject

"In accordance with British jurisprudence no member of the executive can interfere with the liberty or property of a British subject except on the condition that he can support the legality of his action before a court of justice."[75]

And in *Liversidge* v. *Anderson*[76] Lord Atkin spoke of "a principle which again is one of the pillars of liberty in that in English law

---

[70] *Constitutional and Administrative Law,* 9th ed. by A. W. Bradley, Professor of Constitutional Law in the University of Edinburgh (1977).

[71] ibid. p. 442 (Footnotes have been omitted). The following ten grounds of *detention* have been set out at pp. 442-3: (*a*) Arrest and detention pending trial on a criminal charge; (*b*) Sentence of imprisonment or detention (for example, in a Borstal institution) imposed after conviction by a court on a criminal charge; (*c*) Imprisonment for civil debt; (*d*) Imprisonment for contempt of court and for contempt of Parliament; (*e*) Detention of mental patients; (*f*) Detention of a child in need of care or control under the Children and Young Persons Acts 1933 to 1969; (*g*) The exercise of parental authority over an infant; (*h*) Detention of persons under the Extradition Act 1870, the Fugitive Offenders Act 1967 and the Immigration Act 1971 (for example, pending a decision by the Home Secretary on whether an individual is to be deported or extradited); (*i*) Detention of persons subject to military law by the service authorities and detention under the Visiting Forces Act 1952; (*j*) Detention of persons and restrictions on movement imposed under anti-terrorist legislation.

[72] *Cf.* "Free speech does not mean free speech: it means speech hedged in by all the laws against defamation, blasphemey, sedition and so forth": *Per* Lord Wright in *James* v. *Commonwealth of Australia* (1936) A.C. 578, 627 (P.C.).

[73] Prof. de Smith, *Constitutional and Administrative Law,* (2nd ed.) p. 452.

[74] *Wade and Phillips, op. cit.* pp. 465-6 citing the Report of the Committee on Privacy: Cmnd 5012, 1972, p. 10.

[75] *Eshugbayi Eleko* v. *Govt. of Nigeria* (1931) A.C. 662, 670. Quoted with approval by Sastri J. in *Gopalan's Case* (1950) S.C.R. at p. 204; also by Das C.J. in *Basheshar Nath's Case* (1959) 1 Supp. S.C.R. 528, 552.

[76] (1942) A.C. 206.

every imprisonment is prima facie unlawful and it is for a person directing imprisonment to justify his act".[77]

The principles though common, operated differently in England and in India

11.27 But these principles operated differently in England and in India, and, in the early days of the Indian National Congress, the nationalist complaint was that Indian subjects of Her Majesty were being denied the freedoms and the rights enjoyed by her subjects in England, accompanied by a demand for the same freedoms and rights as were enjoyed by subjects in England. Besides, if the extent of human freedom depended on the restrictions laid upon it by law, the ambit of such freedom could be narrowed, and was in fact narrowed, in India, by numerous laws. It is against this background that a demand arose for the enactment of fundamental rights in the Constitution itself, so that cherished human freedoms would not be at the mercy of chance majorities in elected legislatures. Although the freedoms conferred by Art. 19 are, and have been, enjoyed in England for generations, and appear, if anything, more secure there than they are in India, a demand has been increasingly made in England for an entrenched and/or unentrenched Bill of Rights. However, the method of securing human freedoms conferred by Art. 19 in India remains the same, but with one important difference *qua* citizens. Citizens of India enjoy many more freedoms than are conferred by Art. 19(1); all that Art. 19(1) (*a*) to (*g*) has done is to select seven freedoms whose high value has long been recognized in free civilized societies. Article 19, like other Articles conferring fundamental rights, acts as a limitation on legislative power. Further, Art. 19 does not secure the rights conferred by it by a *mere declaration*; Art. 13 makes all laws abridging or abrogating fundamental rights *pro tanto* void, and Arts. 32 and 226 arm the Supreme Court and the High Courts with power to issue appropriate writs against laws and executive acts violating fundamental rights. Although, therefore the framers of our Constitution have departed from Prof. de Smith's first proposition, namely, "First, freedoms are not to be guaranteed by statements of general principles", the framers did so by meeting the underlying objection to such "statements of general principles". Prof. de Smith described the underlying objection thus:

(Margin notes: The demand for the enactment in the Constitution of fundamental rights — Art. 19(1) provides for freedoms long recognized in free civilized countries — The underlying objection to affirmation of fundamental human rights: our Constitution meets that objection)

"There is something peculiarly exasperating about a broad affirmation of fundamental human rights unaccompanied by any machinery of giving them legal effect. This is what Dicey had in mind: 'The Habeas Corpus Acts declare no principle and define no rights, but are for practical purposes worth a hundred constitutional articles guaranteeing individual liberty.' Had he been alive in 1948, he might have added 'or a thousand Universal Declarations of Human Rights'."[78]

Prof. de Smith's propositions support the submission that "personal

11.28 But although the fundamental freedoms conferred by Art. 19 confer legally enforceable human rights, they conform to the second and third proposition stated by Prof. de Smith. A discussion of these two propositions will support our submission that "personal liberty"

[77] ibid. p. 245.

[78] *Prof. de Smith, op. cit.* at p. 452. "As stated by most of the Governments which voted for its adoption, the Declaration (of Human Rights) is not an instrument which is legally binding either directly or indirectly. . . . This absence of binding obligation probably explains the willingness of Governments to subscribe to the wide terms of the Declaration." Oppenheim, *International Law*, Vol. 1 (8th ed. edited by H. Lauterpacht).

in Art. 21 does not include the freedoms conferred by Art. 19, and will also enable us to answer the question put in para 11.2 "How is a fundamental right related to an ordinary right?" liberty" does not include the freedoms in Art. 19(1)

11.29 A glance at Art. 19 shows that the freedoms conferred on citizens by Art. 19(1)(*a*) to (*g*) *are residual*. For example, Art. 19(1)(*a*) confers on every citizen the freedom of speech. By itself this tells us nothing about the nature and extent of that freedom. However, Art. 19(2) helps us to understand the nature and extent of that freedom for it provides:

The freedoms in Art. 19(1) are "residual"

What is "freedom of speech"? That which remains after restrictions permitted by Art. 19(2) are put on that right by valid laws

> *Art. 19(2)*: Nothing in sub-clause (*a*) of clause (1) shall affect the operation of any existing law, or prevent the State from making any law, *in so far as such law imposes reasonable restrictions* on the exercise of the right conferred by the said sub-clause *in the interests of the sovereignty and integrity of India, the security of the State, friendly relations with foreign States, public order, decency or morality, or in relation to contempt of court, defamation or incitement to an offence.* (italics supplied)

Article 19(2) shows that there are existing laws which deal with freedom of speech and expression, and such laws can be made in the future. The right to freedom of speech is what remains after reasonable restrictions on the exercise of that right have been put by existing or future laws, in respect of, or in relation to the topics we have italicized in sub-cl. (2), it being understood that "restrictions" can in appropriate cases, or in certain circumstances, include "prohibition" or "deprivation".[79] And the same is true of the rights conferred by Art. 19(1)(*b*) to (*g*). This means that the citizen's right to the freedoms conferred on him by Art. 19(1)(*a*) to (*g*) is to be found in what remains after restrictions of the kind mentioned in Art. 19(2) to (6) have been placed on each right. So, under Art. 19(1)(*a*) read with Art. 19(2), free speech does not mean free speech. It means speech "hedged in" by the laws relating to decency and morality, contempt of court, defamation and other laws referred to in Art. 19(2). In a democracy, the freedoms conferred by Art. 19(1)(*a*) to (*g*) can be enlarged by legislatures by refraining from putting even reasonable restrictions on these freedoms unless such restrictions are necessary; and by repealing or amending laws which put unnecessary restrictions on those freedoms. In view of certain observations of the Supreme Court as to the Court's duty to enlarge fundamental rights, which will be considered later, it may be observed that the power of the Courts to "enlarge" the freedoms conferred by Art. 19(1)(*a*) to (*g*) is limited. Creative legal interpretation, based on sound legal principles, can, and has, brought those freedoms to classes of citizens who had been deprived of them earlier. The creative legal reasoning by which Mathew J. brought Corporations within the meaning of "other authorities" and therefore within the meaning of "the State" as defined by Art. 12, and the subsequent development based on his reasoning is a case in point.[80] This development subjected Corporations to the discipline of fundamental rights, and enabled the employees of such Corporations to claim the fundamental rights available to them

How legislatures can "enlarge" the freedoms conferred by Art. 19(1)

The court's powers to enlarge those freedoms limited: the modes of such enlargement indicated

---

[79] *Narendra Kumar* v. *Union* (1960) 2 S.C.R. 375, 387; ('60) A.SC. 430.

[80] This creative development has been fully discussed in paras 7.14 to 7.32 of the text.

against "the State" as defined in Art. 12.[81] Further, Courts can enlarge the freedoms conferred by Art. 19(1) (*a*) to (*g*) by a vigilant scrutiny of the restrictions put upon those freedoms. Since restrictions on fundamental rights can be placed only by a *valid* law the Court's duty is threefold. First, to see that the law is within the legislative competence of the Legislature which enacted the law. Secondly, that the law does not violate any fundamental right, or other constitutional limitation. And, thirdly, to scrutinize with care whether the restrictions are reasonable, a scrutiny to which the question whether the restrictions are necessary is relevant. But this threefold duty is negative: freedoms are enlarged by preventing invalid laws and unreasonable restrictions from curtailing those freedoms.

Freedoms under Art. 19(1) can be enjoyed if lawful restrictions on them are not transgressed

11.30 We have seen that the freedoms conferred by Art. 19(1) (*a*) to (*g*) are residual. As long as a citizen does not transgress *reasonable restrictions imposed on his right to those freedoms by a valid law* (for the sake of brevity the italicized words are referred to simply as "reasonable restrictions") he is free to exercise his rights to the freedoms conferred by Art. 19(1).[82]

Transgression of lawful restrictions on the freedoms conferred by Art. 19(1), bring Arts. 20 to 22(1) and (2) into play

11.31 However, if he transgresses such reasonable restrictions he will move from the world of free men, freely exercising their rights to the freedoms conferred by their rights under Art. 19(1) (*a*) to (*g*) to a world where his person is subject to physical restraint which may rob him of his freedoms *altogether,* as by a sentence of death, or *substantially* as by a sentence of imprisonment. For example, *A*, a citizen has a right to form associations under Art. 19(1) (*c*). This right is subject, *inter alia,* to reasonable restrictions in the interest of public order under Art. 19(4). If *A* forms an association for waging war against the Government of India, and joins members of the association in waging such war, he thereby commits an offence under s. 121 of the I.P.C.[83] which is punishable with death or imprisonment for life. But has *A* no fundamental rights if he transgresses reasonable restrictions on the freedoms conferred on him by Art. 19(1) (*a*) to (*g*)? He certainly has, and he shares those rights with non-citizens. In order of time, Art. 22(1) and (2) comes into play first and confers on him valuable fundamental rights. *A* must be told of the reasons for his arrest; he must be produced before a magistrate within 24 hours excluding the time it takes to take him to a magistrate; he is also entitled to consult and be defended by a lawyer of his choice. Next, Art. 21 confers on him the fundamental right not to be deprived of his life or personal liberty except according to procedure established by law. Such a law is found in the Criminal Procedure Code, and that Code takes us to the substantive

Art. 22(1) and (2) provide valuable safeguards against arrest, detention and trial

---

[81] Creative legal interpretation does not cease to be creative because its effect may be to curtail fundamental rights in the interest of the administration of justice. See the discussion of *Tilokchand Motichand* v. *H. B. Munshi* (1969) 2 S.C.R. 824, ('70) A.SC. 898, and *Rabindra Nath* v. *Union* (1969) 2 S.C.R. 193, ('70) A.SC. 470 in the Chapter on The Right to Judicial Remedies in Vol. II of this book.

[82] As he is free to enjoy several other freedoms as long as he does not transgress the prohibitions of valid laws.

[83] *S. 121*: "Whoever wages war against the Government of India or attempts to wage such war, or abets the waging of such war, shall be punished with death or imprisonment for life and shall also be liable to a fine."

law of crimes, the Indian Penal Code, which creates, defines, and prescribes the punishment for an offence which is then to be tried under the Cr. P. Code. But the fundamental rights for his protection at the trial are found in Art. 20 (3) which provides that "no person accused of an offence shall be compelled to be a witness against himself", or, to put it more simply, he cannot be forced to incriminate himself. In the example we have taken of *A* waging war against the Government of India, there is no scope for the application of two valuable safeguards provided by Art. 20 (1) and (2), but if a citizen is tried for transgressing a different provision of the law imposing reasonable restrictions on his right to the freedoms conferred by Art. 19 (1), the fundamental rights conferred by Art. 20 (1) and (2) are valuable rights.

The safeguard provided by Art. 20(3) against self incrimination

and by Art. 20(1) and (2) against *ex post facto* laws and double jeopardy

11.32-33 It follows from what we have said above, that Art. 19 on the one hand and Arts. 20, 21 and 22 (1) and (2) on the other operate in two distinct fields: Art. 19 operates in the field where a citizen who is not under physical restraint[84] can exercise his right to the freedoms conferred by Art. 19 (1) subject to reasonable restrictions. Articles 20, 21 and 22 (1) and (2) operate in the field where a person is under physical restraint under the provisions of valid laws. Again, the freedoms conferred by Art. 19 as fundamental rights are conferred only on citizens; freedoms have not been conferred on non-ciitzens *as fundamental rights*, because if need should arise, laws can be passed, or existing laws altered, in their application to non-citizens which would not stand the test of Art. 19. However, as a civilised country valuing the dignity of the individual, the founding fathers decided that when it came to depriving a person of his life or putting his person under restraint by imprisonment, justice required that the safeguards provided by Arts, 20, 21 and 22 (1) and (2) should be available to citizen and non-citizen alike before anyone is held guilty of committing a crime, and before he is sentenced to death or imprisonment.

Art. 19 and Arts. 20 to 22 operate in two distinct fields

11.34 This leads us to consider the distinction between a *fundamental* right and an *ordinary* right. This distinction is best brought out by considering fundamental rights conferred on citizens alone. Article 19 (1) (*f*) conferred on citizens the right to acquire, hold and dispose of property ("property rights")[85] and that right is necessarily implied in the right to carry on any profession, trade or business conferred by Art. 19 (1) (*g*). Does it mean that foreigners (non-citizens) in India have no property rights? It is a matter of common knowledge, which a glance at the Statute book would confirm, that foreigners have property rights in India. This is because, broadly speaking, *various statutes confer property rights without reference to the citizenship of the person* acquiring, holding and disposing of property, as for example, the Transfer of Property Act, the Contract Act, the Sale of Goods Act and the Succession Act. If the question were asked: "Where are the property rights of citizens and non-citizens to be found?" the answer must be: in the relevant

The distinction between a *fundamental* and an *ordinary* right best discussed by reference to Art. 19(1)(*f*)

The right to acquire, hold and dispose of

[84] The case of persons who, as a result of physical infirmities, cannot enjoy the freedoms conferred by Art. 19(1) is not relevant to the present discussion.

[85] This right has been repealed with effect from June 20, 1979 by the 44th Constitutional amendment.

property under Art. 19(1)(*f*) is to be found in the relevant statutes like the Transfer of Property Act, etc.

statutes, some of which have been mentioned above. This is because Art. 19 (1) (*f*) tells us nothing about the content of property rights. Article 19 (5) reminds us that there are existing laws, and laws can be made in the future in relation to property rights. So for discovering the content of property rights we must turn to relevant statutes which govern the acquisition, holding and disposal of property. For property cannot be acquired, held and disposed of unless the requirements of the relevant laws are complied with. But, it may be asked, if the right of citizen and non-citizen alike to acquire, hold and dispose of property is to be found in the relevant statutory law, why was it necessary to confer on citizens a *fundamental* right to acquire, hold and dispose of property? *The answer to this question brings out the difference between a fundamental right and an ordinary right* to property. If Art. 19 (1) (*f*) had not been enacted, Parliament and State Legislatures in the exercise of their plenary legislative power to make laws for the acquisition, holding and disposal of property could deprive persons of their property rights, or put unreasonable restrictions on the exercise of those rights.

Fundamental rights, by limiting plenary legislative power, give the citizen a higher right under Art. 19(1)(*f*)

Fundamental rights limit or restrict the exercise of plenary legislative power. If a fundamental right is conferred on *any person*, that is, on citizens and non-citizens alike, the fundamental right is a limitation on the entire legislative power in respect of that right; if it is conferred on citizens alone, it is a partial limitation on legislative power, because the limitation does not extend to non-citizens. The distinction we have made above, is very well brought out by Bose J.[86]:

> "But what article 19(1)(f) means is that whereas a law can be passed to prevent persons who are not citizens of India from acquiring and holding property in this country no such restrictions can be placed on citizens. *But in the absence of such a law* non-citizens can also acquire property in India and if they do then they cannot be deprived of it any more than citizens, save by authority of law."[87] (italics supplied)

In other words, the citizen under Art. 19 gets a higher protection in respect of statutory rights to acquire, hold and dispose of property. It will be submitted later[88] that ordinary rights of a citizen are not merged in the fundamental right to acquire, hold and dispose of property.

A summing up

11.35 To sum up: the correlation of Art. 19 to Arts. 20, 21 and 22 (1) and (2) submitted above, not only gives a clear and coherent account of the group of Articles put under the caption "Right to Freedom" based on well settled principles of construction, but the meaning we have given to the word "personal liberty" carries out the intention of the framers of our Constitution and is in conformity with the meaning which the phrase "personal liberty" bears in constitutional law. It carries out the intention of the framers of our Constitution, because it will be recalled that the Drafting Committee added the word "personal" before the word "liberty", because "otherwise (liberty) might be construed very widely so as to include the freedom already dealt with in Art. 13 (now Art. 19)". The word "per-

---

[86] *Dwarkadas Shrinivas* v. *Sholapur Spg. & Wvg. Co. Ltd.* (1954) S.C.R. 674.
[87] ibid. p. 732.
[88] In discussing the *Habeas Corpus Case.*

sonal" was meant to exclude the freedoms conferred by Art. 19; and although the Drafting Committee did not say so, such limitation had to be inserted in Art. 21 if that Article was not to lead to the absurd result that the freedoms denied to non-citizens by Art. 19 were conferred on them by Art. 21.

11.36 We must now turn to Supreme Court decisions and the interpretation put by them on Art. 21. After *Gopalan's Case* was decided, the Supreme Court in *Bombay* v. *Bhanji Munji*[89] held that Art. 19 (1) (*f*) and Art. 31 (2) were mutually exclusive. Bose J. observed:

Bhanji Munji's Case: Art. 19(1)(*f*) and Art. 31(2) mutually exclusive

". . . article 19(1)(*f*) read with clause (5) postulates the existence of property which can be enjoyed and over which rights can be exercised because otherwise the reasonable restrictions contemplated by clause (5) could not be brought into play. If there is no property which can be acquired, held or disposed of, no restriction can be placed on the exercise of the right to acquire, hold and dispose of it, and as clause (5) contemplates the placing of reasonable restrictions on the exercise of those rights it must follow that the article postulates the existence of property over which these rights can be exercised. In our opinion, this was decided in principle in *A. K. Gopalan* v. *The State of Madras*[90] where it was held that the freedoms relating to the person of a citizen guaranteed by article 19 assumes the existence of a free citizen and can no longer be enjoyed if a citizen is deprived of his liberty by the law of preventive detention. In the same way, when there is a substantially total deprivation of property which is already held and enjoyed, one must turn to article 31 to see how far that is justified."[91]

This decision had been rendered before Art. 31 had been amended by the Constitution (4th Amendment) Act, 1955 and was consistently followed.

11.37 However, after the Amendment, in *Kavalappara Kottarathil Kochuni* v. *Madras*,[92] Subba Rao J. said: "The decision of this Court in *Bhanji Munji's Case*[93] no longer holds the field after the Constitution (4th Amendment) Act, 1955." *Kochuni's Case* did not involve any question of acquisition or requisition of property, but related to deprivation of property under Art. 31 (1) which by the express provision of Art. 31 (2A) was *not* to be deemed to be acquisition or requisition of property. Thus, Subba Rao J.'s observations were unnecessarily wide. Consequently, when the petitioner in *Sitabati Devi* v. *W.B.*[94] relied on them to invalidate the W.B. Land (Requisition and Acquisition) Act, 1948, the contention was rejected by Sarkar J. who said:

Kochuni's Case: "Bhanji Munji no longer holds the field"

Sitabati's Case: observations in *Kochuni's Case* do not apply to acquisition and requisition of property

". . . *Kochuni's Case* held that after the amendment, cl. (2) of Art. 31 alone dealt with acquisition and requisition of property by the State and cl. (1) dealt with deprivation of property in other ways. This case did not deal with a law of acquisition or requisition of property by the State but was concerned with a law by which deprivation of property was brought about in other ways, which law, it held, had to satisfy Art. 19 and the principle in *Bhanji Munji's Case* which could have saved that law before the amendment could not save it after the amendment. The observation in . . . *Kochuni's Case* that *Bhanji Munji's Case* 'no longer holds the field' *has therefore, to be*

---

[89] (1955) 1 S.C.R. 777, ('55) A.SC. 41. [90] (1950) S.C.R. *supra*.
[91] (1955) 1 S.C.R. *supra* at p. 780.
[92] (1960) 3 S.C.R. 887, ('60) A.SC. 1080. (Decided on 4.5.1960).
[93] (1955) 1 S.C.R. *supra*.
[94] (1967) 2 S.C.R. 949 (decided on December 1, 1961). See also *Kamla Bala* v. *W.B.* ('60) A.Cal. 289, where the same view had been taken. *Sitabati's Case* was rel. on in *Mangalbhai* v. *Gujarat* ('64) A.Guj. 82, 90 and it was held that the observations in *Kochuni's Case* were confined only to cases falling under Art. 31(1).

understood as meaning that it no longer governs a case of deprivation of property by means other than requisition and acquisition by the State . . . Kochuni's Case was not concerned with a law of requisition or acquisition of property governed by Art. 31(2), as it now stands, and did not decide that question."[95] (italics supplied)

In other words, the proposition that "*Bhanji Munji's Case* no longer holds the field" was held not to apply to acquisition or requisition of property.

Ranojirao's Case: Art. 19(1)(*f*) and 31(2) must be read harmoniously

11.38 But in *M.P.* v. *Ranojirao*,[96] Hegde J. referred to *Kochuni's Case*, though *not* to *Sitabati Devi's Case*, in considering the constitutional validity of the M.P. Abolition of Cash Grants Act, 1963. He also relied on the majority judgment in *Kameshwar Singh's Case*[97] and on the *Bombay Dyeing Case*,[98] and held that cash grants were money or choses in action which could not be the subject matter of acquisition. Consequently, he held that the impugned law was void because, according to him, it violated Art. 19(1)(*f*) which must be construed harmoniously with Art. 31. It is submitted, first, that the judgment is self-contradictory, for if money and choses in action could not be the subject of acquisition, Art. 31(2) would have no application, and the question of its correlation to Art. 19(1)(*f*) could not arise, for the case would fall under Art. 19(1)(*f*). In the *Bombay Dyeing Case*, Venkatarama Aiyar J. put his decision in the alternative because *he did not finally decide* whether money and choses in action could not be acquired. He held that if choses in action could be acquired, then the impugned law was void as violating Art. 31(2); if choses in action could not be acquired, the impugned law was void as violating Art. 19(1)(*f*). Secondly, the Supreme Court decisions on the correlation of Art. 19(1)(*f*) to Art. 31(2) were apparently not cited to, and were clearly not considered by, Hegde J., so that his judgment is a judgment *per incuriam*. Further, he referred to the wide observations in *Kochuni's Case*, but not to *Sitabati's Case* which had restricted the wide observations in *Kochuni's Case* by observing that they did not apply to acquisition or requisition. In other words, he relied on a decision which a Constitution Bench had unanimously held to be inapplicable to acquisition or requisition of property. In the result, once Hegde J. held that money or choses in action could not be acquired, it followed that the Act fell outside Art. 31(2) and *Ranojirao's Case* could have no relevance to Art. 31(2) or its correlation to Art. 19(1)(*f*).

A criticism of *Ranojirao's Case*

Shantilal Mangaldas's Case treated *Sitabati Devi's Case* as having settled the law

In *Shantilal Mangaldas's Case* — decided after *Ranojirao's Case* — Shah J. stated that it had been settled by *Sitabati's Case* that a law for the acquisition or requisition of property cannot be tested on the criterion of Art. 19(1)(*f*) read with Art. 19(5).[99] *Kochuni's Case* and *Ranojirao's Case* have been considered above, because, sur-

[95] (1967) 2 S.C.R. *supra* at pp. 951-2.
[96] (1968) 3 S.C.R. 489, ('68) A.SC. 1053.
[97] See para 12 of Appendix III where the majority view is set out.
[98] See *f.n.* 27 to para 12 of Appendix III where the Case is discussed and Hegde J.'s error in interpreting it has been pointed out. *The Bombay Dyeing Case* held that if money or choses in action could not be acquired, the law violated Art. 31(2) as no compensation was provided; but if money or choses in action could not be acquired the law violated Art. 19(1)(*f*) as the restriction on the right conferred by that Article was not reasonable.
[99] ('69) A.SC. 634, 653.

prisingly enough, in the *Bank Nationalization Case*, they were supposed to constitute a different line of approach to the correlation of Arts. 19 and 31 from that adopted in *Gopalan's Case* and in the several decisions which had followed that case.

11.39 We must now consider the *Bank Nationalization Case* in which the Supreme Court went out of its way to consider the correlation of Art. 19 (1) (*f*) to Art. 31 (2), and overruled a long line of decisions which had settled the law. We said "went out of its way" because once the majority held that the impugned Act violated Art. 31 (2) by not laying down relevant principles, the Act was void, and a decision on Art. 19 (1) (*f*), or its correlation with Art. 31 (2), was not necessary to give relief to the petitioner. Secondly, there is nothing in the judgment to indicate that a Bench of 11 Judges was constituted to reconsider the earlier decisions, including *Gopalan's Case* ("*Gopalan*") which dealt, not with Arts. 19 and 31, but with Arts. 19 to 22. But as the majority judgment went into the question, we must consider it here.

Bank Nationalization Case "reconsiders" the correlation of Arts. 19(1)(*f*) and 31(2)

11.40 It is submitted that there was no justification for reconsidering the settled law on the correlation of Art. 19 (1) (*f*) to Art. 31 (2). The second of the so-called two divergent lines of authority consisted of *Kochuni's Case* and *Ranojirao's Case*, the first of which dealt with deprivation of property otherwise than by acquisition, and the second of which did likewise because it dealt with money or choses in action which the Court held could not be acquired. Since these cases clearly fell outside Art. 31 (2) (after the 4th Amendment), the question of the correlation of Art. 31 (2) to Art. 19 (1) (*f*) did not arise, except that in *Kochuni's Case* the correlation established before the 4th Amendment was rightly negatived after the 4th Amendment in respect of a law which fell under Art. 31 (1). It is submitted that one decision of the Supreme Court, whose wide language was soon corrected by limiting it to the kind of law with which the Court was concerned in that case, and another decision, which on the Court's finding that money or choses in action could not be acquired, fell outside Art. 31 (2), could not with propriety be described as two divergent lines of authority[1] on the correlation of Art. 31 (2) to Art. 19 (1) (*f*), and could not justify reconsidering a consistent line of authority which had become part of the constitutional law of India.

Submission: there was no justification for reconsidering the correlation of Arts. 19(1)(*f*) and 31(2)

11.41 If there was no justification for reconsidering the correlation between Art. 19 (1) (*f*) and Art. 31 (2) there was still less justification for purporting to overrule *Gopalan*. The questions for consideration in the *Bank Nationalization Case* related to the acquisition of business and property, that is, to the civil rights of parties, to which the correlation between Art. 19 (1) (*f*) and Art. 31 (2) was relevant. The questions decided in *Gopalan* did not relate to civil rights or property; they related to preventive detention, and involved a consideration of the correlation of Art. 19 (1), or, in the alternative, of Art. 19 (1) (*d*), to Arts. 20, 21 and 22, which three Articles deal with criminal law and procedure (leaving aside for the present the question of personal liberty). No doubt, as we have seen, (para 11.36),

Submission: there was no justification for "reconsidering" *Gopalan's Case*

Gopalan's Case dealt with preventive detention not with civil rights

[1] ('70) A.SC. *supra* at p. 596.

in *Bhanji Munji's Case*, Bose J. treated the correlation between Art. 19(1) (*f*) and Art. 31(2) as decided in principle by *Gopalan*; in other words, he extended the principle of *Gopalan* to the civil rights of parties affecting property. But the principle laid down with reference to the correlation of Art. 19(1) or Art. 19(1) (*d*) to Art. 20, 21 and 22 might be correct for the reasons given by the majority in *Gopalan*, whereas the extension of that principle to the correlation between Art. 19(1) (*f*) and 31(2) might be open to question. In the *Bank Nationalization Case* it was open to the Supreme Court, if it thought fit to decide more than was necessary, to disapprove the extension of the principle in *Gopalan* to the correlation between Arts. 19(1) (*f*) and Art. 31(2). But to purport to overrule *Gopalan* on Art. 19(1), or Art. 19(1) (*d*), *vis-a-vis* Arts. 20, 21 and 22 would have involved the grotesque procedure of inviting a full argument, *pro* and *contra*, on the correctness of *Gopalan* from Counsel whose clients had not the slightest interest in preventive or punitive detention! But assuming that the Court had decided to "reconsider" the correctness of *Gopalan*, then for such reconsideration to have any value, or to be of any help, it was the imperative duty of the Court, first, to invite a full argument, *pro* and *contra* about the correctness of the majority decision in *Gopalan*, and then to give in its judgment a careful analysis of the issues raised in *Gopalan*, the manner in which they were presented and argued before the Court and the way in which the Court dealt with them. No such thing appears to have been done, or even attempted, by the judges who formed the majority in the *Bank Nationalization Case*. And it is no disrespect to them to say that their discussion of *Gopalan* does not show a fraction of the care, legal knowledge and judicial skill which the judges in *Gopalan* brought to bear on every issue and every argument presented for the Court's consideration. This is not surprising, for in the *Bank Nationalization Case* a "reconsideration" of *Gopalan* was a side show; in *Gopalan*, the questions raised occupied the centre of the stage and commanded the attention of the Court all the time. The danger of deciding questions which do not arise for decision, and overruling carefully considered judgments which occupy about 250 pages of the Supreme Court Reports is clear from the following passage from the leading majority judgment of Shah J. in the *Bank Nationalization Case*. ("the judgment of Shah J.") He said:

In the *Bank Nationalization Case* it was not strictly necessary once Art. 31(2) was violated by the impugned law to consider Art. 19(1)(*f*) and Art. 31(2)

A "reconsideration" of *Gopalan* would have involved a grotesque procedure

The *Bank Nationalization Case* did not consider the correctness of *Gopalan* afresh

A fundamental error in the *Bank Nationalization Case* about *Gopalan*

"The majority of the Court (Kania C.J., and Patanjali Sastri, Mahajan, Mukherjea and Das J.J.) held that Art. 22 being a complete code relating to preventive detention, the validity of an order of detention must be determined strictly according to the terms and 'within the four corners of that Article'."[2]

To the reader who has read the judgments in *Gopalan*, or the quotations from the judges who constituted the majority set out in para 11.11, this statement made for 10 judges must seem incredible. Mahajan J. was the only judge who held that Art. 22 was a complete code; Mukherjea J. found it unnecessary to decide whether Art. 22 was a complete code; and Kania C.J., Patanjali Sastri and Das JJ., held that Art. 22 was *not* a complete code. Three errors,

[2] ibid. p. 593 *per* Shah J. for himself, Sikri, Shelat, Bhargava, Mitter, Vaidialingam, Hegde, Reddy and Dua JJ.

packed in one sentence, the third of which attributed to the majority in *Gopalan* a view precisely the opposite of that which they had expressed was to be a fertile source of error in later decisions, which, unlike the decision in the *Bank Nationalization Case*, dealt with preventive detention. It appears to the present writer that the most satisfactory way of considering the purported overruling of *Gopalan* by the *Bank Nationalization Case* is, first, to set out briefly, the facts of that case, the questions that arose for decision in that case, the majority decision, and then to set out the propositions which emerge from the majority decision. Secondly, to set out the cases which followed the *Bank Nationalization Case* in its inaccurate account of the majority decision in *Gopalan*. Thirdly, to recall the reader's attention to our discussion in paras 11.2 to 11.20 above, in which the present writer has tried to do, what the Supreme Court ought to have done in the *Bank Nationalization Case* but did not, namely, to state the issues raised in *Gopalan's Case*, the manner in which they were presented to the Court, and the manner in which the Court dealt with them. And finally, to point out the serious errors in the majority judgment in the *Bank Nationalization Case*, and the cases which followed it, in overruling *Gopalan* for doing which the foundation has been laid in paras 11.2 to 11.20 above, and by the present writer's submissions about the correlation of Art. 19 to Arts. 20, 21 and 22(1) and (2) in paras 11.21 to 11.35 above. Although we will consider the *Bank Nationalization Case* at length, the present writer would repeat his submission[3] that the majority judgment in that Case is void for violating principles of natural justice for the reasons given in para 11.44, a submission to which no answer has been, or, it is believed, can be given, so clear is the violation of natural justice.

The proposed method of dealing with the *Bank Nationalization Case*

11.42 The facts of the *Bank Nationalization Case* and the constitutional challenge to the impugned law were briefly these: First, by an Ordinance promulgated on July 19, 1969, and then by an Act ("the Act"), which was given retrospective effect from July 19, 1969,[4] 14 Indian Scheduled Banks, with deposits exceeding Rs. 50 crores, were nationalized. The Act laid down principles for determining compensation to be paid for the acquisition of the Banks. The case came before the Supreme Court under the following circumstances:

The Bank Nationalization Case

Dr. R. C. Cooper, the petitioner, held shares in the Central Bank of India Ltd., and was also its director. He was a shareholder of three other nationalized banks and he had current and fixed deposit accounts with all the four banks. He presented a petition under Art. 32 to the Supreme Court challenging the Act mainly on the following grounds: (i) that the Act was void for lack of legislative competence, since in any event a part of the Act fell within the exclusive competence of State legislatures; (ii) that the Act deprived him of his office of Director of the Central Bank of India; (iii) that the Act made a hostile discrimination between banks as a result of which the value of his interest in shares had been substantially reduced and his right to receive dividends had ceased and he had suffered financial loss; (iv) that the Act was not passed for a public purpose and thus contravened Art. 31(2); (v) that the Act violated Art. 31(2) because it did not lay down principles for deter-

The law for nationalization of banks impugned as violating the fundamental rights of a single shareholder and not as violating the fundamental rights of the Banks

[3] The submission was made in the second edition of this book (Vol. II) in para 15.50 read with para 15.49 at pp. 669-670.

[4] The Banking Companies (Acquisition and Transfer of Undertakings) Ordinance, 1969; The Banking Companies (Acquisition and Transfer of Undertakings) Act, 1969.

mining compensation; (vi) that the petitioner did not challenge the Act on the ground that it violated the fundamental rights of the Banks, but on the ground that it violated his own fundamental rights guaranteed by Arts. 14, 19 and 31. The Union of India was the only party to the petition, and seven States intervened, presumably because the question of legislative competence had been raised.

Petition not a representative petition — the Banks not joined as parties

The petition was by a single shareholder and was not a representative petition on behalf of all, or of a majority of the shareholders of the four banks. No shareholders' meeting had been called in any of the Banks, to authorize them to support the petitioner, or to file an independent petition. No Bank was a party to the petition, and none had complained that its fundamental rights had been violated.

Findings of the majority: the fundamental rights of the Banks under Arts. 14, 19 and 31 were violated by the impugned Act

11.43 For reasons which do not appear from the judgment of Shah J., the case was heard by a Bench of 11 judges.[5] Two judgments were delivered; the leading majority judgment by Shah J.[6] declaring the impugned Act void, and a dissenting judgment by Ray J. holding the Act valid. At the end of his judgment, Shah J. said:

"Accordingly we hold that (*a*) the Act is within the legislative competence of the Parliament; but (*b*) makes hostile discrimination against the named banks from carrying on banking business, whereas other banks — Indian and Foreign — are permitted to carry on banking business, and even new banks may be formed which may engage in banking business; (*c*) it in reality restricts the named banks from carrying on business other than banking as defined in Section 5(*b*) of the Banking Regulation Act, 1949; and (*d*) that the Act violates the guarantee of compensation under Art. 31(2) in that it provides for giving certain amounts determined according to principles which are not relevant in the determination of compensation of the undertaking of the named banks and by the method prescribed amounts so declared cannot be regarded as compensation."[7]

Finding (*b*) is a finding that the Bank's right to equality under Art. 14 was violated. Finding (*c*) read with the discussion in the judgment under Aat. 19 is a finding that the Bank's rights under Art. 19 were violated. Finding (*d*), read with the discussion in the judgment on Art. 31 (2) is a finding that the compensation payable to the Banks for the acquisition of their undertakings violated rights conferred on the Banks by Art. 31 (2).

---

[5] It is submitted that such a Bench should never be constituted unless a smaller Bench hearing the petition is of the opinion that any earlier decision or decisions of the Supreme Court require reconsideration, and indicates the points on which such reconsideration is required. This would enable parties affected by such reference to intervene to protect their interests. The decision in the *Bank Nationalization Case* has disclosed another important reason why such large benches should not be constituted. The earlier decisions of the Supreme Court show that when a law was challenged as violating Arts. 14, 19 and 31, the Court acted with judicial self-restraint by refusing to decide the challenge under Arts. 14 and 19 once it upheld the challenge under Art. 31: See *Dwarkadas Shrinivas's Case* (1954) S.C.R. at p. 716. The *Bank Nationalization Case* shows that such judicial self-restraint cannot be counted upon at all times, and extremely important questions of law may be decided as to the interpretation of various Articles conferring fundamental rights, when such interpretation is not necessary for giving relief to the party moving the Court. Thus judgments may be overruled without the parties being under a necessity to bestow on them a fraction of the time which was bestowed on the arguments and decision of the cases overruled.

[6] For himself, Sikri, Shelat, Bhargava, Mitter, Vaidialingam, Hegde, Grover, Reddy and Dua JJ.

[7] ('70) A.SC. *supra* at p. 615.

11.44 It is clear that the rights of the banks were decided in their absence and without their being heard. The petitioner came to Court expressly stating that he did not challenge the Act as violating the Bank's fundamental rights but as violating his own, and the Court ended up by deciding that the Act violated the Bank's fundamental rights under Arts. 14, 19 and 31. If the petitioner wanted to base the violation of his own fundamental rights on the violation of the Bank's fundamental rights, he would have had to join the Banks as respondents to the petition. But his petition showed that that was not his case and he advisedly did not join the Banks as parties to the petition. It is submitted that the majority judgment was rendered in violation of the principles of natural justice. As the present writer said in a lecture:

The rights of the Banks decided without the Banks being parties, and without hearing them

"The Banks might or might not have supported the petitioner; the Banks might or might not have satisfied the Court that the compensation given was adequate; the Banks might or might not have told the Court that incorrect principles may give a larger compensation than correct principles might give; and that the Court ought to uphold the law; the Banks might or might not have told the Court that they could not assert that they wanted to carry on new banking business or non-banking business without calling a meeting of the shareholders and ascertaining the view of the majority of shareholders. However, it was necessary to hear the Banks before a final decision, affecting their rights, was arrived at, and the banks were not heard."[8]

Submission: majority judgment is a nullity having been rendered in violation of the principles of natural justice

It is submitted that the majority judgment is null and void because the Supreme Court has repeatedly held that any judgment affecting the rights of parties rendered in violation of the principles of natural justice is void.[9]

---

[8] These words have been taken from a lecture which the present writer delivered on the *Bank Nationalization Case* at the University of Bombay on April 2, 1970, which has been published. Some of the material there used has been incorporated in the present discussion. With reference to the submission made in the lecture that the majority judgment was rendered in violation of natural justice, the present writer was asked and answered a question which is thus recorded in *f.n.* 2, p. 3 of the printed lecture: "At the end of the lecture a question was put to me whether, apart from theory, the principles of natural justice could be invoked unless the party invoking them was prejudiced; and the Bank Nationalization Act subsequently passed showed that the Banks were not prejudiced. I replied that the question whether a person was prejudiced or not could only be determined after he had been heard; secondly, that when the Supreme Court struck down the Bank Nationalization Act, it did not, and could not know, whether another Act would award a larger or a smaller compensation; and finally that it was not at all clear that the arbitration provisions of the Act struck down by the Supreme Court would not have secured a larger compensation than has been provided for in the later Act. I stated that when the shares of the Tata Industrial Bank Ltd. were taken over by the Central Bank of India Ltd., it was on the basis that one share of the Tata Industrial Bank was worth Rs. 15. Those shareholders who resorted to arbitration proceedings got anything between Rs. 18 to Rs. 22.50 for each share of the Tata Industrial Bank Ltd." The arbitration provisions referred to above was a reference to the determination by the Tribunal of the compensation payable according to the principles laid down in Sch. II.

[9] See for example *Orissa* v. *Dr.* (*Miss*) *Binapani Dei* ('67) A.SC. 1269, at p. 1271: "If there is power to decide to the prejudice of a person, duty to act judicially is implicit in the exercise of such power. If the essentials of justice are ignored and an order to the prejudice of a person is made, *the order is a nullity*" (italics supplied). It need hardly be added that the right to be heard before a decision affecting a person's rights is rendered is an essential of justice. The Supreme Court has taken the view of the majority in *Ridge* v. *Baldwin* (1964) A.C. 40 that a decision given in violation of the principles of natural justice is void and not voidable.

Propositions emerging from the *Bank Nationalization Case*

11.45 The following propositions emerge from the *Bank Nationalization Case*:

(*a*) "The majority of the court (Kania C.J. and Sastri, Mahajan, Mukherjea and Das JJ.) held that Art. 22 *being a complete code* relating to preventive detention, the validity of an order of detention must be determined strictly according to the terms and 'within the four corners of that Article'."[10] (italics supplied)

(*b*) "(The) majority (in *Gopalan's Case*) held that a person detained may not claim that the freedom guaranteed by Art. 19(1)(*d*) was infringed by his detention, and that the validity of the law providing for making orders of detention will not be tested in the light of the reasonableness of the restrictions imposed thereby on the freedom of movement, nor on the ground that his right to personal liberty is infringed otherwise than according to the procedure established by law."[11]

(*c*) "(*Gopalan's*) *Case* has formed the nucleus of the theory that the protection of the guarantee of a fundamental freedom must be adjudged in the light of the object of State action in relation to the individual's right and not upon its influence upon the guarantee of the fundamental freedom, and as a corollary thereto, that the freedoms under Arts. 19, 21, 22 and 31 are exclusive — each article enacting a code relating to protection of distinct rights."[12]

(*d*) "Kania C.J., proceeded on the theory that different articles guarantee distinct rights. He observed at p. 100 '. . . it (Art. 19) * * * means that the legislation to be examined must be directly in respect of one of the rights mentioned in the sub-clauses. If there is a legislation directly attempting to control a citizen's freedom of speech or expression, or his right to assemble peaceably and without arms, etc., the question whether that legislation is saved by the relevant saving clause of Art. 19 will arise. If, however, the legislation is not directly in respect of any of these subjects, but as a result of the operation of other legislation, * * * the question of the application of Art. 19 does not arise. The true approach is only to consider the directness of the legislation and not what will be the result of the detention otherwise valid, on the mode of the detenu's life'."[13]

(*e*) "The principle underlying the judgment of the majority was extended to the protection of the freedom in respect of property and it was held that Art. 19(1)(*f*) and Art. 31 were mutually exclusive . . ."[14]

(*f*) The "weighty pronouncements of the eminent judges who gave shape to the concept that the extent of the protection of important guarantees such as *the liberty of person*, and right to property, depends on the form and object of State action and not upon its direct operation upon the individual's freedom"[15] did not correctly lay down the law.[16] (italics supplied)

(*g*) "But it is not the object of the authority making the law impairing the right of a citizen, nor the form of action that determines the protection he can claim: the extent of the protection against an impairment of a fundamental right is determined not by the object of the Legislature nor by the form of the action but by the direct operation upon the individual's rights."[17]

(*h*) ". . . each freedom has different dimensions. . . . The true character of the limitation under the two provisions is not different. Clause (5) of Art. 19 and clause (1) and (2) of Art. 31 are parts of a single pattern. Art. 19(1)(*f*) enunciates the basic right to property of the citizens and Art. 19(5) and clauses (1) and (2) of Art. 31 deal with limitation which may be placed by law subject to which the right may be exercised."[18]

---

[10] ibid. p. 593.
[11] ibid.
[12] ibid.
[13] ibid. pp. 593-4.
[14] ibid. p. 595 citing the observations of (i) Das J. in *Gopalan's Case* (1950) S.C.R. 88; (ii) *Chiranjit Lal Chowdhuri's Case* (1950) S.C.R. 809, at p. 919; (iii) *Subodh Gopal Bose's Case* (1954) S.C.R. 587: "The principle so stated was given a more concrete shape"; and (iv) of Bose J. in *Bhanji Munji's Case* (1955) 1 S.C.R. 777.
[15] ibid. p. 596.
[16] ibid.
[17] ibid.
[18] ibid.

(*i*) "If the acquisition is for a public purpose, *substantive reasonableness of the restriction which includes deprivation may unless otherwise established, be presumed*, but enquiry into reasonableness of the procedural provisions will not be excluded. For instance if a tribunal is authorised by an Act to determine compensation for property compulsorily acquired, *without hearing the owner of the property*, the Act would be liable to be struck down under Art. 19(1)(*f*)."[19] (italics supplied)

(*j*) ". . . the validity of 'law' which authorizes deprivation of property and 'a law' which authorizes compulsory acquisition for a public purpose must be adjudged by the same test."[20]

Sarkar's Case: the interpretation of Art. 22(7)(*a*). The interpretation in *Gopalan* on this point overruled

11.46 We must now consider other decisions of the Supreme Court which have referred to, or considered the impact of, the *Bank Nationalization Case* on *Gopalan's Case*. In *S. N. Sarkar* v. *W.B.*[21] the question for determination was the meaning to be placed on Art. 22 (7) (*a*).[22] The majority of judges in *Gopalan*, namely, Kania C.J., Patanjali Sastri, Mukherjea and Das JJ. (Fazl Ali and Mahajan JJ. dissenting) held that Art. 22 (7) (*a*) meant that Parliament might prescribe *either* the circumstances under which *or* the class or classes of cases in which, a person can be detained for a longer period than three months without obtaining the opinion of an Advisory Board in accordance with the provisions of Clause (4) (*a*). In other words, the majority interpreted the word "and", which is usually conjunctive, as "or", which is usually disjunctive. Accordingly, they held s. 12 of the Preventive Detention Act, 1950 valid. Fazl Ali and Mahajan JJ. held that Art. 22 (7) (*a*) meant that it was necessary for Parliament to prescribe *both* the circumstances *and* the class or classes of cases, (different expressions with different meanings), and the prescription of one without the other was not enough. In other words the dissenting judges treated "and" as conjunctive, which is the meaning which it usually bears. The reader will have noted that this part of *Gopalan* raised a question as to the interpretation of Art. 22 (4) (*a*) and (*b*) and (7) (*a*) which was distinct and separate from the majority decision on the correlation of Art. 19 (1), or 19 (1) (*d*) to Arts. 21 and 22. In *Sarkar's Case*, the petitioner, who was preventively detained under the provisions of the Maintenance of Internal Security Act, 1971 ("the Act"), challenged the validity of his detention on the ground that s. 17A of the Act (which corresponded to s. 12 of the Preventive Detention Act, 1950), did not comply with the requirements of Art 22 (7) (*a*) which, on its true construction meant that it was necessary for Parliament to prescribe

---

[19] ibid. pp. 596-7. [20] ibid. p. 597.
[21] (1974) 1 S.C.R. 1, ('73) A.SC. 1425.
[22] *Art. 22, Clause* (4): "No law providing for preventive detention shall authorise the detention of a person for a longer period than three months unless — (*a*) an Advisory Board consisting of persons who are, or have been, or are qualified to be appointed as, Judges of a High Court has reported before the expiration of the said period of three months that there is in its opinion sufficient cause for such detention: Provided that nothing in this sub-clause shall authorise the detention of any person beyond the maximum period prescribed by any law made by Parliament under sub-clause (*b*) of Clause (7), or (*b*) such person is detained in accordance with the provisions of any law made by Parliament under sub-clauses (*a*) and (*b*) of Clause (7)."

Clause (7): Parliament may by law prescribe — (*a*) the circumstances under which, and the class or classes of cases in which, a person may be detained for a period longer than three months under any law providing for preventive detention without obtaining the opinion of an Advisory Board in accordance with the provisions of sub-clause (*a*) of clause (4); . . ."

both the circumstances under which, and the class or classes of cases in which, a person may be detained for a longer period than three months without obtaining the opinion of an Advisory Board. In other words, the Constitution Bench, which heard the matter in the first instance, was invited to reconsider the interpretation put on Art. 22 (7) (*a*) in *Gopalan* and adopt the minority view in that case. Accordingly, a larger Bench of seven judges heard the matter.

In *Sarkar's Case*, Shelat A.C.J. repeated the 3 errors in the *Bank Nationalization Case* about *Gopalan* and added another error of his own

11.47 After setting out the principles on which the Supreme Court would reconsider an earlier decision, Shelat A.C.J. added:

"Further, the major premise of the majority decision that Art. 22 was a self-contained code and the provisions of the law would not have to be considered in the light of the provisions of Art. 19 was disapproved in (the *Bank Nationalization Case*). Nevertheless, we have to bear in mind the accepted rule that earlier decisions are not to be upset except upon a clear compulsion, especially when the legislature has acted upon, as perhaps Parliament did in enacting s. 17A."[23]

Sarkar's Case will be considered more fully later. However, for the purpose of our present discussion it is enough to say that the Court overruled the interpretation put by the majority in *Gopalan* on Art. 22 (7) (*a*), and accepted the minority view. Accordingly, the Court held s. 17A invalid on the ground that it did not comply with the requirements of Art. 22 (7) (*a*).[24]

In *Sarkar's Case* a "reconsideration" of *Gopalan* on Arts. 19 and 21 was not necessary and was not undertaken

11.48 It was open to a Bench of seven judges to reconsider *Gopalan* also on the correlation of Art. 19 (1) or 19 (1) (*d*) to Arts. 21 and 22, for the case before the Court did not deal with rights of property but dealt *directly* with preventive detention. An argument for the petitioner assailing several provisions of the Act under Art. 14 gave such an opportunity; and had the Court considered the challenge under Art. 14, the first question on reconsideration would have been whether the majority in *Gopalan* had expressed the view which the judgment of Shah J., had incorrectly attributed to them. However, as we shall see later, the Bench did not do so. Shelat A.C.J. said:

The errors of the *Bank Nationalization Case* repeated with one additional error

"In *Gopalan* . . . the majority court had held that Art. 22 was a self-contained Code and therefore a law of preventive detention did not have to satisfy the requirements of Arts. 19, 14 and 21. . . . the aforesaid premise of the majority in *Gopalan* . . . was disapproved and therefore it no longer holds the field. Though (the *Bank Nationalization Case*) . . . dealt with the inter-relationship of Art. 19 and Art. 31, the basic approach to construing the fundamental rights guaranteed in the different provisions of the Constitution adopted in this case held the major premise of the majority in *Gopalan* . . . to be incorrect."[25]

No question of "Art. 14" arose in *Gopalan*, and Art. 14 was not dealt with

It will be seen that in the above passage, Shelat A.C.J. not only repeated the three errors in the judgment of Shah J., but added a fourth error of his own when he referred to "Art. 14". In *Gopalan* there was no challenge to the impugned Act under Art. 14. Therefore, the majority and the minority in *Gopalan* did not deal with Art. 14, much less hold that it did not apply. Shelat A.C.J. described the statement attributed by Shah J. to the majority in *Gopalan* as the major premiss of *Gopalan*; and as it was disapproved in the *Bank Nationalization Case*. Shelat A.C.J. said that *Gopalan* no longer held the field. He realized that the *Bank Nationalization Case* dealt with the inter-relationship of Arts. 19

---

23 ('73) A.SC. *supra* at p. 1435. 24 ibid. p. 1441.
25 ibid.

and 31, but he added "the basic approach to construing fundamental rights guaranteed under different provisions of the Constitution in this case held the major premiss of the majority in *Gopalan* . . . to be incorrect". The learned judge added that "in view of this constructional position" Counsel assailed certain provisions of the Act as violating Art. 14 and others as imposing unreasonable restrictions. Before dealing with the challenge under Art. 14, it is clear that Shelat A.C.J. did not consider the majority decision in *Gopalan* for himself but rested his decision on the judgment of Shah J. Secondly, Shelat A.C.J. said that as the Supreme Court had disapproved of the *major premiss* of *Gopalan* it no longer held the field. It is obvious that if Shah J. stated the "major premiss" of *Gopalan* erroneously by attributing to the majority in *Gopalan* a view which was the opposite of what the majority held, his own argument based on an erroneous premiss cannot be sustained. That Shelat A.C.J. based his judgment on what Shah J. had said, and not on a fresh reading of Gopalan is clear from the fact that even without going to the passages from the judgments of Kania C.J., Patanjali Sastri, Mahajan, Mukherjea and Das JJ. quoted in para 11.11 above, a glance at the head note in the Supreme Court Reports would have disclosed the true position. The head note reads: "*Per* Kania C.J., Patanjali Sastri and Das J. (Mahajan J. *dissenting*)—Article 22 does not form a complete Code of constitutional safeguards relating to preventive detention. . . ."[26]

Sarkar's challenge to the impugned law under Arts. 14 and 19 not considered because not necessary

Submission: Shelat A. C.J.'s observations about *Gopalan* cannot be sustained because of the fundamental error in the *Bank Nationalization Case*

11.49 What is said above about the judgment of Shelat A.C.J. is not surprising, for the refusal of the Court, to entertain the challenge under Arts. 14 and 19, made a reconsideration, or fresh appraisal, of Gopalan unnecessary. The reason for such refusal was stated thus:

Submission: Shelat A. C. J. did not reconsider *Gopalan* afresh on Arts. 19 and 21

"However, in the view we have taken of s. 17A of the Act we need not go into them as in accordance with the practice followed by this Court we need not decide more than what is necessary. We, therefore, do not express any views on the aforesaid contentions raised by counsel. It is, therefore, enough for us to declare S. 17A as not having satisfied the requirements laid down in cl. (7)(*a*) of Article 22 and therefore bad."[27]

It is submitted, first, that the practice followed by Shelat A.C.J. is correct; and the disregard of that practice in the judgment of Shah J. was clearly wrong, and has led the Court into grave and demonstrable errors. Secondly, *Sarkar's Case* carries the *Bank Nationalization Case* no further, for in *Sarkar's Case*, Shelat A.C.J. merely relied on the judgment of Shah J. and rightly declined to undertake a reconsideration of *Gopalan* which a consideration of the challenge under Arts. 14 and 19 would have involved.

11.50 The decision in *Fagu Shaw* v. *W.B.*[28] is important. There, the petitioners, who were preventively detained, challenged the validity of their detention on the ground that s. 13 of the Maintenance of Internal Security Act, 1971 (as amended) did not fix a maximum period of detention, as it was obligatory on Parliament to do under Art. 22(7) (*b*). Mathew J. for himself, Ray C.J. and Chandrachud J. held, first, that it was not obligatory under Art. 22(7)(*b*) for Parlia-

Fagu Shaw's Case: interpretation of Art. 22 (7)(*b*)

[26] (1950) S.C.R. 88 at p. 90.
[27] ('73) A.SC. at p. 1442.
[28] (1974) 2 S.C.R. 832, ('74) A.SC. 613.

ment to fix the maximum period of detention, and, secondly, that in fact the impugned law had fixed the maximum period of detention. Alagiriswami J. dissented on the first point, and held that under Art. 22(7)(*b*) it was obligatory on Parliament to fix a maximum period of detention; but he agreed with Mathew J. that the Act had fixed the maximum period. He also agreed with the order that the constitutional questions having been decided against the petitioners, their petitions should be listed for hearing before the appropriate Bench. Bhagwati J. dissented on both points and would have allowed the petitions and directed that the petitioners be set at liberty. This case will be discussed fully later, but for the purpose of the present discussion the judgment of Alagiriswami J. is important. He observed that the legislative power of preventive detention arose under entry 9, List I and entry 3, List III. Article 22, being an Article in Part III (Fundamental Rights) read with Art. 13(2), is a restriction on legislative powers of Parliament and State Legislatures. He then said:

Per Alagiriswami J.:— Kania C.J., Patanjali Sastri and Das JJ. held Art. 22 was *not* a complete code

"Of the learned Judges who dealt with *Gopalan's Case . . . Kania C.J., Patanjali Sastri and Das JJ.* took the view *that Art. 22 does not form a complete code of constitutional safeguards relating to preventive detention.*[29] Mahajan J. thought that it contained a self-contained Code . . ."[30] (italics supplied)

Nevertheless, in 2 subsequent judgments Bhagwati J. repeats the fundamental errors

The judgment of Bhagwati J. shows that he had read the judgment of Alagiriswami J.[31] and it would appear to the reader impossible that Bhagwati J., or any other judge should repeat the erroneous statement from the judgment of Shah J. after Alagiriswami J. had accurately pointed out that Kania C.J., Patanjali Sastri and Das JJ. had held that Art. 22 was *not* a complete code of constitutional safeguards in relation to preventive detention. However, in law, as in life, it is unsafe to confuse the impossible with the unlikely, and in two judgments which are considered later, Bhagwati J. was to repeat the errors in the judgment of Shah J. and Shelat A.C.J.

Saha's Case: impugned law of preventive detention challenged under Art. 14, 19, 21 and 22

11.51 In *H. Saha* v. *W.B.*[32] the petitioner, who was preventively detained under the Maintenance of Internal Security Act, 1971, challenged his detention on the ground that the provisions of the Act under which he was detained violated Arts. 14, 19, 21 and 22. The challenge under Art. 19 was obviously based on the *Bank Nationalization Case* and its disapproval of what it believed to be the majority judgments in *Gopalan*. Ray C.J., who delivered the judgment for himself, Reddy, Mathew, Beg and Alagiriswami JJ. observed that it was not open to a person punitively detained

Ray C.J. on Arts. 19 and 22

"to say that the imprisonment should be tested with reference to Art. 19 for its reasonableness. A law which attracts Art. 19 therefore must be such as is capable of being tested to be reasonable under clauses (2) to (5) of Art 19."[33]

---

[29] The italicised words reproduce the head note in (1950) S.C.R. at p. 90, the accuracy of which is borne out by the quotations in para 11.11 above.

[30] ('74) A.SC. *supra* at p. 623.

[31] ('74) A.SC. *supra* at p. 633 where Bhagwati J. said: ". . . if we look at the judgment of Dua J., and particularly the portion extracted in the judgment of brother Alagiriswami J. . . ."

[32] (1975) 1 S.C.R. 778, ('74) A.SC. 2154.

[33] ('74) A.SC. at pp. 2157-8.

Having expressed a view which coincided with that of Kania C.J., Patanjali Sastri, Mukherjea and Das JJ. that Art. 19 did not apply where a person was preventively detained, Ray C.J. said: "This Court in (*Gopalan's Case*) held that Art. 22 was a complete code and Art. 19 is not invoked in those cases (i.e. cases of preventive detention)."[34] The first part of the statement is clearly wrong and was probably taken from the judgment of Shah J., which had been relied upon for the petitioners, but the second part about Art. 19 is clearly right. When it was urged that *Gopalan* no longer held the field after the *Bank Nationalization Case*, Ray C.J. gave the following answer which shows that the Court did not accept the correlation between Art. 19 (1) (*f*) and Art. 31 (2) laid down in that case, but "explained" the decision by reference to Art. 19 (1) (*g*). Ray C.J. said:

Ray C.J. "explains" the *Bank Nationalization Case* on Art. 19(1)(*f*) and Art. 31(2),

> "Article 19(1)(*f*) deals with the right to acquire, hold and dispose of property. It is apparent that after a person's property has been acquired by the State he cannot acquire, hold or dispose of the same property. In the *Bank Nationalization Case* (*supra*) it is said that the acquisition which left the Banks free to do business other than banking was rendered unreasonable by reason of the Banks being deprived of the wherewithal to carry on the business. The right guaranteed under Article 19(1)(*g*) to carry on any occupation, trade or business were therefore held to be directly invaded by the nationalization of Banks. It is in this context, that the *Bank Nationalization Case* (*supra*) held that in spite of Article 31(2) the acquisition of property directly impinged on the right of the Banks to carry on business other than Banking guaranteed under Art. 19(1)(*g*) and Art. 31(2) was not a protection against infringement of that guaranteed right."[35]

That the Court did not accept the *Bank Nationalization Case* as correctly laying down the law on Art. 19 is clear from the observation of Ray C.J. that "*We may proceed on the assumption* that the Act which is for preventive detention may be tested with regard to its reasonableness with reference to Art. 19."[36] (italics supplied) No Court proceeds on an assumption on a matter which is directly covered by the judgment of ten judges of the Supreme Court. It may be observed that the view expressed by Ray C.J. about the correlation of Art. 19 (1) (*f*) to Art. 31 (2) was expressed by Hegde J. in the *Fundamental Rights Case*[37] in upholding the validity of the amendment of Art. 31 by the insertion of a new sub-clause (2B) which provided that "Nothing in sub-cl. (*f*) of cl. (1) of Art. 19 shall affect any such law as is referred to in cl. (2)." Hegde J. said:

and proceeds on the *assumption* that Art. 19 applied to preventive detention

> "[Art. 31(2B)] has no real impact on the right conferred by Art. 31(2). Article 31(2) empowers the State to compulsorily acquire or requisition property for public purpose. Where property is acquired or requisitioned for a public purpose, the right of the owner of the property to hold or dispose it of is necessarily lost."[38]

Hegde J.: Art. 19(1)(*f*) and Art. 31(2) mutually exclusive

It may be added that the consideration by Ray C.J. of the challenge under Art. 14 does not show that he impliedly held *Gopalan* to be wrongly decided, for as we have seen, there was no challenge in *Gopalan's Case* under Art. 14, and the Court obviously could not, and did not hold that Art. 22 excluded the application of Art. 14. In the result, *Saha's Case* did not accept the *Bank Nationalization Case*

Submission: *Bank Nationalization Case* not accepted but "explained"

---

[34] ibid. p. 2158. [35] ibid.
[36] ibid.
[37] *Kesavananda* v. *Kerala* (1973) Supp. S.C.R. 1, ('73) A.SC. 1461. Hegde J. was a party to the judgment of Shah J. in the *Bank Nationalization Case*.
[38] ('73) A.SC. at p. 1640. This means that Hegde J. had come round to the view taken by Bose J. in *Bhanji Munji's Case*.

but "explained" it; it did not independently reconsider *Gopalan* on the accuracy of the doctrine attributed to it in the judgment of Shah J.[39]

The judgment of Shah J. receives no additional support from subsequent judgments

11.52 In the result the judgment of Shah J. in the *Bank Nationalization Case* in so far as it "disapproved" the "major premiss" in *Gopalan's Case* can derive no strength from *Sarkar's Case* in which Shelat A.C.J. merely repeated the errors of Shah J., nor does it derive independent strength from *Saha's Case* for the reasons given above. On the contrary, the judgment of Alagiriswami J. in *Fagu Shaw's Case* has, in effect, deprived the judgment of Shah J. of its authority by showing that it is founded on demonstrable errors.

11.53 We must now consider two judgments of Bhagwati J. In *Khudiram* v. *W.B.*[40] the petitioner, who had been preventively detained under the Maintenance of Internal Security Act, 1971, challenged an order for his detention under s. 3(2) of the Act on several grounds, but for the purpose of this discussion we are concerned only with the view taken by the majority in *Gopalan* as to Art. 22 Bhagwati J. observed:

> "The view taken by the majority in (*Gopalan's Case*) was that Art. 22 is a self-contained Code, and therefore, a law of preventive detention does not have to satisfy the requirements of Arts. 14, 19 and 21."[41]

The reader will have noticed that the above observations repeat what Shelat A.C.J. had said in *Sarkar's Case*; and our criticism of that case applies equally to the observations of Bhagwati J. Having made those observations, Bhagwati J. referred to the *Bank Nationalization Case*, to *Sarkar's Case* and *Saha's Case*, for support. It is unnecessary to repeat what we have said about those cases beyond saying that error is not converted into truth by being repeated a number of times. Bhagwati J. concluded his discussion by the emphatic declaration that:

> "This question, thus, stands concluded and a final seal is put on this controversy and in view of these decisions, *it is not open to anyone now to contend that a law of preventive detention, which falls within Art. 22 does not have to meet the requirement of Art. 14 or Art. 19.*"[42]

The extraordinary claim made in the words we have italicised above[43] calls for four observations. First, his omission to refer to the judgment of Alagiriswami J. in *Fagu Shaw's Case* robs his survey of decided cases of any value, for Bhagwati J. made no attempt to show that Alagiriswami J. was in error when he said that Kania C.J., Patanjali Sastri and Das JJ. held that Art. 22 was *not* a complete code. Secondly, the "controversy" about Art. 14 is unreal; it was not created by the majority judgment in *Gopalan, which did not deal with Art. 14 at all*, nor by the judgment of Shah J. in the *Bank Nationalization Case*; it was an error in the judgment of Shelat

---

[39] This is not surprising, for Alagiriswamy J. who was a party to *Fagu Shaw's Case* had pointed out correctly what the majority in *Gopalan* had held.

[40] (1975) 2 S.C.R. 832, ('75) A.SC. 550.

[41] ('75) A.SC. at p. 558.

[42] ibid. p. 559.

[43] The reader familiar with the history of science will be reminded by these words of how the Papacy believed that the seal was put on the controversy whether the sun went round the earth, when the Inquisition forced Galileo to recant his support for Copernicus that the earth went round the sun. Yet, for the 200 years that his book was proscribed by the Papacy the earth went round the sun each day.

A.C.J. in *Sarkar's Case,* which Bhagwati J. repeated. Thirdly, our discussion of *Sarkar's Case* and *Saha's Case* will satisfy the reader that Bhagwati J.'s discussion of those cases is incorrect. Finally, the statement that "it is not open to anyone now to contend" may be intended to prevent Counsel from arguing the matter, but it could not prevent a judge (or judges) in a later case from not only "contending" to the contrary, but from demonstrating that the earlier judgments were based on a fundamental error.

The facts of *Maneka Gandhi's Case*

11.54 In a second judgment Bhagwati J. again returned to the subject in *Maneka Gandhi* v. *Union*[44] (*"Maneka Gandhi's Case"*). Maneka Gandhi's petition was heard by a Bench of seven judges, and the facts giving rise to the petition were these:

The petitioner's passport was impounded "in public interest" by an order of July 2, 1977. The Government of India declined "in the interest of the general public" to furnish the petitioner with reasons for the order. The petitioner challenged s. 10(3) of the Passports Act, 1967, as violative of Art. 14 and also of 19(1)(*a*) and (*g*) and Art. 21: of Art. 19(1)(*a*) and (*g*) as it permitted restrictions to be imposed which cannot be imposed under Art. 19(2) and (6); and of Art. 21 as it did not prescribe a "procedure" within the meaning of Art. 21. Finally, s. 10(3)(c) was void as conferring an arbitrary power as it did not provide for giving a hearing to the holder of the passport before it was impounded. Before the matter was heard, the reason for impounding the passport was disclosed in the affidavit of the Government of India. The reason was that the petitioner's passport was impounded because her presence was likely to be required in connection with the proceedings before a Commission of Inquiry. Before the hearing was concluded, the following statement was filed on behalf of the Government:

Statement filed by Government

"(1) The Government is agreeable to considering any representation that may be made by the petitioner in respect of the impounding of her passport and giving her an opportunity in the matter. The opportunity will be given within two weeks of the receipt of the representation. It is clarified that in the present case, the grounds for impounding the passport are those mentioned in the affidavit in reply dated 18th August, 1977 of Shri Ghosh except those mentioned in para 2(xi). (2) The representation of the petitioner will be dealt with expeditiously in accordance with law. (3) In the event of the decision of impounding the passport having (being?) confirmed, it is clarified that the duration of the impounding will not exceed a period of six months from the date of the decision that may be taken on the petitioner's representation. (4) Pending the consideration of the petitioner's representation and until the decision of the Government of India thereon, the petitioner's passport shall remain in custody of this Hon'ble Court. (5) This will be without prejudice to the power of the Government of India to take such action as it may be advised in accordance with the provisions of the Passport Act in respect of the petitioner's passport."[45]

Five judgments delivered: Beg C.J. would have allowed the petition with costs; the other judges passed no "formal order" in view of Government's statement

11.55 Five separate judgments were delivered, namely, by Beg C.J.; by Chandrachud J; by Bhagwati J., for himself and Untwalia and Fazal Ali JJ.; by Krishna Iyer J.; and by Kailasam J. Beg C.J. said that in view of the Att.-General's statement

". . . it seems that no further action by this Court is necessary. In view, however, of what is practically an admission that the order actually passed on 7th July, 1977, is neither fair nor the procedure proper, I would, speaking for myself quash this order and direct the return of the impounded passport to the petitioner. I also think that the petitioner is entitled to her costs."[46]

However, the order passed by the Court was:

"Having regard to the majority view, and, in view of the statement made by the learned Attorney-General to which reference has already been made in

---

[44] (1978) 2 S.C.R. 621, ('78) A.SC. 597. [45] ('78) A.SC. at p. 699.
[46] ibid. p. 612.

the judgments we do not think it necessary to formally interfere with the impugned order. We, accordingly dispose of the Writ Petition without passing any formal order. The passport will remain in the custody of the Registrar of this Court until further orders. There will be no order as to costs."[47]

A criticism of the court's order

It is submitted that the order proposed by Beg C.J. was clearly right and it had the merit of disposing of the petition by a final order. The order of the Court is unsatisfactory. It says, "We, accordingly dispose of the petition without passing any formal order." First, a petition can only be disposed of by being allowed, or dismissed (in whole or in part) or by allowing it to be withdrawn. Secondly, if the petition is disposed of, how can the passport remain in the custody of the Court *till further orders*, for in that case something remains to be done before the petition is disposed of. Thirdly, in substance, though not in form, the majority passed an "informal" order in terms of the Att.-General's statement.

Maneka Gandhi's Case raised no question of preventive detention; yet Chandrachud and Bhagwati JJ. repeat the errors of the *Bank Nationalization Case*

11.56 The case dealt with a large number of important questions, including questions connected with the grant, impounding or refusal of a passport. However, the present discussion is limited to the correlation of Art. 21 to Art. 19. The reader will have seen from the narrative of facts that the case raised no question of preventive detention which would require a reconsideration of *Gopalan's Case* on the correlation of Art. 19 to 21 *in the context of preventive detention.* Bhagwati J. and Chandrachud J. repeated the erroneous statements of Shah J. in the *Bank Nationalization Case* and *Sarkar's Case.* But in *Maneka Gandhi's Case* this repetition of error was in spite of the judgment of Kailasam J. which made the following important points on the correlation of Art. 19 to Art. 21:

Kailasam J. on the *Bank Nationalization Case*: he corrects its errors and states the correct position

(*a*) "The decision of the *Bank Nationalization Case* in so far as it relates to Arts. 19(1) and Art. 21 is in the nature of *obiter dicta.* Though it is a decision of a Court of 11 judges and is entitled to the highest regard, as the Court had not applied its mind or decided the specific question and as (it) is in the nature of a general casual observation on a point not calling for decision and *not obviously argued before it*[48] the case cannot be taken as an authority on the proposition in question. The Court cannot be said to have declared the law on the subject when no occasion arose for it to consider and decide the question."[49]

(*b*) Since the Court ruled that the impugned Act violated Art. 31(2), the interrelationship of Art. 19(1)(*f*) to Art. 31(2) was not strictly necessary for the purpose of giving relief to the petitioner.[50]

(*c*) The Court was not concerned with the question whether the decision of the *Bank Nationalization Case* on the interrelation of Art. 19(1)(*f*) and Art. 31(2) were "in the nature of *obiter dicta*", nevertheless "it is necessary to state that the decision proceeded on some erroneous assumptions . . . (In *Gopalan's Case*) it was assumed that 'the majority of the Court (Kania C.J., and Patanjali Sastri, Mahajan, Mukherjea and Das JJ.) held that Art. 22 being a complete code relating to preventive detention the validity of an order of detention must be determined strictly according to the terms and within the four corners of that article.' *This statement is not borne out from* the text of the judgments in *Gopalan's Case.*"[51] (italics supplied)

(*d*) Having set out the relevant passages from the judgments in *Gopalan's Case* (which have been set out in para 11.11 above, which show that the majority of three judges had held that Art. 22 was not a complete code) Kailasam J. said: "It is thus seen that the assumption in the *Bank Nationali-*

---

[47] ibid. p. 694.
[48] See para 11.40 above where the same point has been made.
[49] ('78) A.SC. *supra* at pp. 681-82.
[50] ibid. p. 682 (see also para 11.39 above).
[51] ibid.

zation Case that the majority of the Court (in *Gopalan*) held that Art. 22 is a complete code is erroneous and the basis of the decision stands shaken. If the *obiter dicta* on the wrong assumption is to be taken as the correct position in law it would lead to strange results."[52]

(*e*) "For the reasons stated above [which included 'the strange results' referred to in (*d*) above] (the) *obiter dicta* in the *Bank Nationalization Case* that a legislation under Art. 21 should also satisfy the requirements of Art. 19(1)(*f*) cannot be taken as correct law. The Court has not considered the reasoning in *Gopalan's Case* and overruled it."[53]

11.57 It is submitted that the propositions which emerge from the judgment of Kailasam J. about the purported overruling of *Gopalan* in the *Bank Nationalization Case*, and the erroneous assumption made in that case about *Gopalan* are unanswerable, and the other judges have made no attempt to answer them presumably because of their view of the Court's function *vis-a-vis* fundamental rights. This is clear from the following observations of Bhagwati J. which lay down the law on the meaning of "personal liberty" in Art. 21. Bhagwati J. said:

Submission: propositions (*a*) to (*e*) above are unanswerable

"It is indeed difficult to see on what principle we can refuse to give its plain natural meaning to the expression 'personal liberty' as used in Art. 21 and read it in a narrow and restricted sense so as to exclude those attributes of personal liberty which are specifically dealt with in Article 19. We do not think that this would be a correct way of interpreting the provisions of the Constitution conferring fundamental rights. *The attempt of the court should be to expand the reach and ambit of fundamental rights rather than attenuate their meaning and content by a process of judicial construction.*"[54] (italics supplied)

11.58 We will deal with these observations presently, but the persistence of the Court in perpetuating the error of the *Bank Nationalization Case* about *Gopalan's Case* (hereafter referred to as "fundamental error") raises a question which is crucial to the proper discharge of the judicial function. Kailasam J. demonstrated the fundamental error by quoting the words used by Kania C.J., Patanjali Sastri and Das JJ. The accuracy of the quotations cannot be, and has not been, questioned by Bhagwati J. and his brother judges. Faced with this demonstration of a fundamental error, what is the duty of the judges of the Supreme Court? It is submitted that the judges in *Maneka Gandhi's Case* who repeated the fundamental error of the *Bank Nationalization Case*, after the error had been pointed out by Kailasam J., have, unwittingly, done a grave injury to the judicial process. For it means that Supreme Court judges do not mind resting their judgments on a fundamental error so long as it subserves a desirable end. But it is submitted, *that this substitutes the rule of judges for the rule of law.* Secondly, it would shock the ordinary man's idea of a Court of Justice to be told that judgments can be rested on a fundamental error, if the judges consider that the error serves a desirable end. But there is no general agreement about ends—what may appear a desirable end to one judge, may appear undesirable to another. To make the interpretation of the Constitution and the law dependent upon the individual views of a shifting majority of judges is subversive of law and justice. It is submitted that

Submission: persistence in demonstrated fundamental error does a grave injury to the judicial process

[52] ibid. The "strange results" are set out at pp. 682-83.
[53] ibid. p. 683.
[54] ibid. pp. 621-22.

Aristotle went to the root of the matter when he said: "Plato is dear to me, but dearer still is truth".[55] Adapting his words, a judge should say to himself: "Fundamental rights are dear to me, but dearer still is truth, and justice founded on truth, and they must prevail in a Court of Justice." This is altogether apart from what every judge knows, namely, that the sanction of truth is that it holds together, and the sanction *against* falsehood is that it falls apart.

The interpretation of "personal liberty" by Bhagwati J. in *Maneka Gandhi's Case*

11.59 In considering the interpretation given to the words "personal liberty" in Art. 21 *vis-a-vis* Art. 19 it is enough to confine our attention to the leading judgment of Bhagwati J. for himself, Untwalia and Fazal Ali JJ., since Beg C.J. expressed his general agreement with that judgment,[56] and Chandrachud J. expressed his entire agreement with it in so far as it dealt with Arts. 19 and 21. It is not proposed to deal with the judgment of Krishna Iyer J. because it is not the judgment of the Court, nor a judgment of the majority. All the faults of style and exposition, which have been criticized in paras 10.10 and 10.11 above in considering his judgment in *Fatehchand's Case*—faults which increased as the years went by—are to be found in the present judgment, and, in the submission of the present writer, a detailed criticism is not called for and would not be profitable.[57]

That interpretation must stand or fall by the correctness of the propositions which emerge from the *Bank Nationalization Case*

11.60 The interpretation put by Bhagwati J. on "personal liberty" in Art. 21 is based on what was said in the *Bank Nationalization Case* and the cases which followed it. Consequently, his interpretation must stand or fall by the correctness of the *Bank Nationalization Case* in so far as it purported to overrule *Gopalan.* And that takes us to the propositions which emerge from the *Bank Nationalization Case* which have been set out in para 11.45 above. But before considering those propositions, a few observations are necessary. The question of deprivation of "personal liberty" under Art. 21 arose in the *Habeas Corpus Case*,[58] which will be considered by itself later. Beg C.J., who believes that in that Case the majority gave the only answer possible[59] notwithstanding that he admitted that the actual order passed by the majority was wrong,[60] referred to the *Habeas Corpus Case* at a number of places in *Maneka Gandhi's Case*. Chandrachud J. and Bhagwati J., who were parties to the majority judgments, and who both took the narrowest view of the right against being deprived of life and personal liberty "except according to procedure established by law" make no reference to that case. Consequently, the *Habeas Corpus Case* plays no part in

The *Habeas Corpus Case*

[55] The *Oxford Dictionary of Quotations*, 2nd ed. p. 14.

[56] ('78) A.SC. *supra* at p. 614.

[57] How unprofitable such a criticism would be, will become apparent to the reader from the following passage in his judgment: "Thus humble pride of patriotic heritage would have been pre-empted had the ancient kings and medieval rulers banished foreign travel as our imperial masters nearly did. And to look at the little letters of the text of part III *de hors* the Discovery of India and the Destiny of Bharat or the divinity of the soul and the dignity of the person highlighted in the Preamble unduly obsessed with individual aberrations of yesteryears or vague hunches leading to current fears, is a persilanimous (sic) exercise in constitutional perception": ('78) A.SC. at p. 655.

[58] *A. D. M. Jabalpur* v. *Shivkant Shukla* (1976) Supp. S.C.R. 172, ('76) A.SC. 1207.

[59] ('78) A.SC. 489 at p. 495.

[60] ibid. at p. 494.

the discussion on Art. 19 and 21 in *Maneka Gandhi's Case*. Secondly, *Maneka Gandhi's Case*, like the *Bank Nationalization Case*, raised no question about preventive detention, which was the central issue in *Gopalan's Case*. Thirdly, the judges who decided the *Bank Nationalization Case* did not apply their minds independently to *Gopalan's Case* and their observations on *Gopalan's Case* are not considered *obiter dicta*, but are *unconsidered* casual observations. Unconsidered, because a look at the head note to *Gopalan's Case* in the Supreme Court Reports would have shown their observations to be untenable. Kailasam J. was right in saying that the *Bank Nationalization Case* laid down no law within the meaning of Art. 141 on the correlation of Arts. 19 and 22, but only made casual observations about *Gopalan*. Fourthly, in a final Court which lays down the law binding on all Courts in India, (Art. 141), a desire to enlarge the scope of fundamental rights does not absolve the Court from giving effect to the intention of the framers of the Constitution as expressed in the Drafting Committee's Report, to which intention, effect was given by the Constituent Assembly. Nor does it absolve the Court from applying well settled principles of construction which require, *inter alia*, that constitutional provisions should not be interpreted in isolation, but in their context as Bhagwati J. himself rightly pointed out.[61] Nor again does it absolve the Supreme Court from a careful examination and close analysis of well reasoned judgments of an earlier Bench, and all the more so when that decision had become a part of the constitutional law of India on the correlation of Art. 19 to Arts. 21 and 22. We must now deal with the propositions which emerge from the *Bank Nationalization Case* which have been set out in para 11.45 above.

plays no part in this discussion

11.61 As to proposition (*a*) in para 11.45, the statement that in *Gopalan* the majority held that Art. 22 was a complete Code has been demonstrated to be a gross error for the proposition states the opposite of what the majority in fact held. A well known legal maxim reminds us that "Reason is the soul of the law, and when the reason of any particular law ceases, so does the law itself".[62] Adapting this maxim, and applying it to the reason given in a judgment on a crucial point, we can say: "Reason is the soul of a judgment, and if that reason ceases (because untenable) the judgment ceases to apply." As the reader will see from the following discussion, a fundamental error is an unstable foundation even for unconsidered casual statements about *Gopalan's Case*.

A criticism of proposition (*a*) in para 11.45

11.62 As to proposition (*b*) in para 11.45, the statement that the majority held that the validity of the detention could not be tested

Submission: proposition

[61] Bhagwati J. himself laid down impeccable principles for interpreting an Article of the Constitution. In *Union* v. *Sankalchand* (1978) 1 S.C.R. 423, ('77) A.SC. 2328, he said: "The words used in a statute cannot be read in isolation: Their colour and content are derived from their context and, therefore, every word in a statute must be examined in its context. And when I use the word 'context', I mean it in its widest sense 'as including not only other enacting provisions of the same statute, but its preamble, the existing state of the law, other statutes in pari materia and the mischief which — the statute was intended to remedy.' The context is of the greatest importance in the interpretation of the words used in a statute.": ('77) A.SC. at p. 2358.

[62] "*Cessante Ratione Legis Cessat Ipsa Lex*" (Co. Littleton 70b) *Broom's Legal Maxims*, 10th ed. p. 97.

(*b*) in para 11.45 not easy to understand

"on the ground that his right to personal liberty is infringed otherwise than according to procedure established by law" is not easy to understand, and appears to be the result partly of the fundamental error about *Gopalan* and partly of a failure to realize that Art. 21 applies both to punitive and preventive detention, and the procedure established by law varies accordingly. The procedure prescribed by law for arrest, detention, trial and conviction resulting in a sentence of imprisonment must conform to Art. 22 (1) and (2), to Art. 20, to Art. 14 and any other relevant Article like Art. 17. However, to preventive detention Art. 20 has no application, and Art. 22 (1) and (2) is expressly excluded. It is this exclusion which led the judges in *Gopalan's Case* to give the most anxious consideration to every argument urged on behalf of Gopalan. However, this exclusion had the unfortunate consequence that the Court was not called upon to consider the scope and effect of the valuable safeguard provided by Art. 22 (1) and (2) and their impact on Art. 21.

Proposition (*c*) in para 11.45 falls into two parts: the main proposition and its "corollary" Submission: the main proposition is not tenable

11.63 As to proposition (*c*) in para 11.45, it falls into two parts, the main proposition and the "corollary" said to follow from it. The main proposition is dealt with in this para. The "corollary" is more conveniently dealt with in para 11.65 below. The main proposition overlooks the context in which the Court in *Gopalan's Case* considered the test to be applied for determining whether a law violated fundamental rights. Secondly, the alternative submission made for Gopalan that preventive detention *directly* interfered with the right to move freely, which is the essence of "personal liberty" guaranteed by Art. 19 (1) (*d*) and therefore must stand the test of reasonableness under Art. 19 (5) put the *direct* violation of Art. 19 (1) (*d*) in issue before the Court. The problem thus raised is best explained by referring to the dissenting judgment of Fazl Ali J. in which he accepted this contention urged on behalf of *Gopalan*. However, he was confronted with the question, does the test of reasonable restrictions under Art. 19 (5) apply to punitive detention for a crime under the Indian Penal Code? In the passage set out in para 11.12 above, Fazl Ali J. replied that it did not. He said that the I.P.C. could not be described as a law primarily or necessarily imposing restrictions on the right to move freely; the restriction was imposed on free movement under a law defining crime and making it punishable. "The punishment is correlated directly to the violation of some other person's right and not with the right of movement possessed by the offender himself." To lawyer and layman alike it would seem absurd that the Constitution conferred on a prisoner lawfully sentenced to imprisonment, the right "to move freely *throughout the territory of India*" when, ordinarily, he cannot move out of a jail! Therefore, the object or purpose of the law on the right of free movement became relevant. Again, imprisonment under the I.P.C. could not be subjected to the test of reasonable restrictions permitted by Art. 19 (2) because, as we have seen, it would render imprisonment for theft, cheating, forgery and even ordinary assault illegal as it would not be protected by Art. 19 (2): (see para 11.13). The test propounded by Kania C.J. was propounded to avoid absurd results, and Fazl Ali J. did likewise in the case of punitive detention. But, whereas Kania C.J. rightly observed that no valid distinction can be made between punitive and preventive detention, Fazl Ali J. erroneously made that distinction. (See para 11.12.) It is submitted that the main proposition is not tenable.

11.64 As to proposition (*d*) in para 11.45 above, it sets out the passage which Shah J. extracted in the *Bank Nationalization Case* from the judgment of Kania C.J. But Shah J. overlooked the importance of the following sentence: "the true approach is only to consider the directness of the legislation and not what effect will the result of the detention *otherwise valid* on the mode of the detenu's life." (italics supplied) First, the test was propounded in the context of Art. 19(1) and Arts. 21 and 22. Secondly, the words "otherwise valid" which qualify the word "detention" go to the heart of the problem, and can be best explained in layman's language as follows: "If a person is validly detained in prison under a valid law for preventive or punitive detention, surely, the necessary consequence of the detention must be to affect his life. The freedoms he enjoyed when he was free are no longer available to him, or are available to him to a very limited extent." The same test can be put in a different way on the lines of our earlier discussion.[63] The freedoms conferred by Art. 19(1)(*a*) to (*g*) are circumscribed and restrained by the reasonable restrictions imposed on them by valid laws to the extent permitted by Art. 19(2) to (6). For disregarding such restrictions laws not infrequently provide a sanction in the form of imprisonment. If a citizen claims to exercise the seven freedoms disregarding the lawful restrictions on them, he puts himself outside Art. 19, and cannot claim its protection. If he is imprisoned for such transgression, he has, by his own action, given up the protection of Art. 19, and he loses his power, and, in effect, his right to those freedoms except in a most attenuated form. For example, Art. 19(1)(*f*) conferred on every citizen a right to acquire, hold and dispose of property; but the Article conferred no right to acquire property by committing crimes like theft, receiving stolen property knowing it to be stolen, forgery and the like. In fact, as the reader will recall, Das C.J. held in *Chamarbauqwalla's Case* that crime and criminal activities cannot claim the protection of Art. 19, and his views had the approval of a later Bench of the Supreme Court in *Fatehchand's Case* (see para 10.11). In the result, Kania C.J. did not hold that Art. 21 and Art. 19 were mutually exclusive on any theory that Articles conferring fundamental rights are mutually exclusive. As imprisonment brings about deprivation of "personal liberty" (Art. 21), Kania C.J. rightly observed that the nature of the fundamental freedoms conferred by Art. 19(1) as a whole, or even by Art. 19(1)(*d*), was such that they could not be enjoyed in their entirety, or at any rate, substantially, by a person who has been imprisoned after complying with Art. 21 and other relevant Articles. But mutual exclusiveness between two Articles of the Constitution conferring fundamental rights is not limited to punishment for transgressing the restrictions on those rights. The content of two fundamental rights may be such that they cannot both be enjoyed together. Thus Art. 19(1)(*f*) conferred on a citizen the right to acquire, hold and dispose of property subject to reasonable

Proposition (*d*) in para 11.45 discussed, and shown to be untenable

---

[63] See para 11.31.

restrictions. Article 31 conferred on the State the power to acquire property for a public purpose and conferred on the owner of the property a fundamental right to insist that it could only be acquired for a public purpose and on payment of compensation. In *Bhanji Munji's Case* it was rightly held that if property was lawfully acquired, the question of reasonableness of the restriction which can be imposed on the right to acquire, hold and dispose of property could not arise. This settled law was departed from by Hegde J. in *Ranojirao's Case* (see para 11.38), and by the majority judgment in the *Bank Nationalization Case* to which Hegde J. was a party. However, Hegde J. changed his view in the *Fundamental Rights Case* and made observations which showed that *Bhanji Munji's Case* was rightly decided (para 11.51). It is submitted that proposition (d) in para 11.45 is untenable.

The "corollary" in proposition (*c*) in para 11.45 examined

Submission: the "corollary" did not follow from *Gopalan's Case*, but follows from the fundamental error in the *Bank Nationalization Case*

11.65 It is now convenient to deal with the "corollary" said to follow from the main proposition in para 11.45 (c). The "corollary" runs: "that the freedoms under Arts. 19, 21, 22 and 31 are exclusive, each Article enacting a code relating to the protection of distinct rights." It is submitted that there is no foundation for the assertion that this "corollary" follows from *Gopalan's Case*, or the cases which followed it. The "corollary" of which Shah J. spoke, follows from the fundamental error in his judgment, and also from not applying his mind to what *Gopalan's Case* decided, and from running counter to several decisions of the Supreme Court *after Gopalan's Case* and *before* the decision in the *Bank Nationalization Case*. Shah J. has not referred to Art. 14 in the "corollary", but as Shelat A.C.J. and Bhagwati J. have done so, purporting to state the effect of the judgment of Shah J., we will consider the "corollary" as if it referred to Art. 14 as well.

The "corollary" examined with reference to: Art. 14

11.66 In discussing the "corollary" we start with the obvious proposition that punitive detention and preventive detention deprive a person of his "personal liberty" to which Art. 21 refers. We will now deal with Arts. 14, 19, 21, 22 and 31.

(i) Article 14 was not considered in *Gopalan's Case* because there was no challenge to the impugned law under Art. 14; nor was Art. 31 considered, although Das J. referred to it by way of illustration (see para 11.10 above). *Gopalan's Case* did not hold that Art. 14 enacted a complete code of freedom which was exclusive of other Articles in Part III (Fundamental Rights). Nor did *Gopalan's Case* give rise to any such theory. In the series of cases beginning with *Anwar Ali Sarkar's Case* and ending with *Kedarnath Bajoria's Case*, which we have considered in paras 9.76 to 9.85 of the text, the conviction and imprisonment of the accused were challenged under Art. 14. The challenge succeeded in *Anwar Ali Sarkar's Case*, the majority (Fazl Ali, Mahajan, Mukherjea, Chandrasekhara Aiyar and Bose J. holding the impugned law wholly void. Das J. concurred, but held the impugned law partially void). (See para 9.76). Patanjali Sastri C.J. dissented. It will be recalled that Sastri C.J., Fazl Ali, Mahajan, Mukherjea and Das JJ. were parties to the judgments in *Gopalan's Case*, but the idea never occurred to them that Arts. 14 and 21 being complete codes, Art. 14 could not apply to deprivation of personal liberty by procedure established by law. It was obvious to the judges that the law had to be a valid law, and if it violated Art. 14 it would be void. In the cases which we considered in paras 9.77 to 9.85, the challenge to conviction by special courts under Art. 14 was considered on the merits in each case.

(ii) We have already seen that in *Gopalan's Case* exclusiveness of Art. 19(1) and Art. 21 was not based on the theory that these Articles and Art. 22 were a complete code (see para 11.64).

(iii) Article 21 is obviously not a complete Code, for, in punitive detention after arrest and trial other Articles in Part III are attracted. We have seen that Art. 14 is attracted, and the judges who tried *Gopalan's Case* knew that Art. 20 and 22(1) and (2) were attracted. As to Art. 20 Das J. said:

"I come to article 20 which is concerned with providing protection against what are well known as *ex post facto* laws, double jeopardy and self-incrimination. This article constitutes a limitation on the absolute legislative power which would, but for this article, be exercisable by Parliament or the State Legislatures under article 246 read with the legislative lists. If the Legislature disobeys this limitation the Court will certainly prevent it. Article 20 has no bearing on preventive detention laws and I pass on."[64]

As to Art. 20, Mukherjea J. said in the passage set out in para 11.16 that a person cannot be convicted and punished under an *ex post facto* law, or a law which compelled the accused to incriminate himself or which punished him for the same offence more than once.[65] Mukherjea J. added "Again a law providing for arrest and detention must conform to the limitations prescribed by Art. 22(1) and (2). These provisions indeed have been withdrawn expressly in case of preventive detention. . . ."[66] Again, Art. 17, was not in issue in *Gopalan's Case*, but there can be no doubt, that a law or executive action which enforced against an "untouchable" who is preventively or punitively detained, disabilities arising from untouchability, would be struck down as violating Art. 17 read with Art. 35(*b*).

(iv) As to Art. 31, we have seen that Art. 19(1)(*f*) and Art. 31(2) were held to be mutually exclusive not on any theory that each Article was a self-contained code in respect of the right conferred by that Article, but because the nature of the rights was such that both could not be enjoyed together: *Bhanji Munji's Case*. That case was decided at a time when it had been held that Art. 31(1) and (2) dealt with the same topic—acquisition and requisition. However, after Art. 31 had been amended by the 4th Amendment by the insertion of sub-Article (2B) the link between Art. 31(1) and Art. 31(2) was severed, and deprivation of property otherwise than by acquisition or requisition was taken out of Art. 31(2) and fell within Art. 31(1). As Art. 31(1) applied both to non-citizens and citizens, if a non-citizen was deprived of property by a valid law, which imposed unreasonable restrictions on his right to hold property, he had no remedy, for he could not invoke the help of Art. 19(1)(*f*) which applied only to citizens. However, a citizen can challenge the same law on the ground that by imposing unreasonable restrictions on that right, the law violates his right to hold property under Art. 19(1)(*f*). And if he established the unreasonableness

Art.31

Bhanji Munji's Case

[64] (1950) S.C.R. 88 at p. 306. [65] ibid. p. 255.
[66] ibid.

of the law, the Court would strike it down. This is what the Supreme Court did in the *Bombay Dyeing Case*.[67] Venkatarama Aiyar J. struck down the impugned Act on one of two alternative grounds without deciding which of the two grounds was the right one. He said that if money and choses in action could be acquired, the impugned law was void as it did not provide for compensation as required by Art. 31 (2). If, however, money and choses in action could not be acquired, the law was void because it deprived the owner of its right under Art. 19 (1) (*f*) to hold its property by imposing unreasonable restrictions on that right. This decision clearly proves that the mutual exclusiveness of Art. 19 (1) (*f*) and Art. 31 (2) was based on the ground that once property had been acquired by a valid law, the person could not rationally claim to hold it, much less to hold it subject to reasonable restrictions. But once deprivation of property *simpliciter* was taken out of acquisition and requisition of property provided for by Art. 31 (2), the reason for the mutual exclusiveness of Art. 19 (1) (*f*) and Art. 31 (2) disappeared, and Art. 31 (1) and Art. 19 (1) (*f*), both became available to citizens deprived of their property. In fact, the power to make a law depriving a citizen of his property under Art. 31 (1) is subject to the limitation put on that power by Art. 19 (1) (*f*). Nor are Arts. 19 (1) (*f*), 20, 21, 22 (1) and (2) and 31 (2) mutually exclusive. A citizen who has been imprisoned for committing a crime, after complying with Art. 22 (1) and (2), Art. 21 and Art. 20, could not have been deprived of his property except for a public purpose and on payment of compensation as required by Art. 31 (2). In the result, the "corollary" in proposition (c) in para 11.45 above is untenable.

The Bombay Dyeing Case

Submission: the "corollary" is untenable

Propositon (*e*) in para 11.45

(v) As to proposition (e), it is true that Art. 19 (1) (*f*) and Art. 31 (2) were held to be mutually exclusive. However, this was not for the reason given by Shah J. in proposition (e) but for the reasons fully set out in para 11.66 (iv) above.

Propositions (*f*) and (*g*) propound one single test

11.67 As to propositions (f) and (g) in para 11.45 above, they have been set out separately to bring out the two aspects of one single test propounded by Shah J. Proposition (*f*) states that the judges who decided *Gopalan's Case* laid down the wrong test, whereas proposition (*g*) purports to lay down the correct test to be applied in determining whether an impugned law has violated a fundamental right. Secondly, setting out proposition (*f*) separately will enable the reader to see more clearly that it is incorrect, because it negatives an important qualification laid down, first, by the Privy Council and then adopted by our Supreme Court in 1955 as will appear presently. Before dealing with propositions (*f*) and (*g*) it may be observed that for the purpose of applying the test in proposition (*g*) Shah J. made no distinction between the challenge to an Act because it violated one fundamental right, and the challenge to an Act because it violated more than one fundamental right — whether such fundamental rights were inter-related or not. We will first deal with the situation in which an Act is challenged because it violated only one fundamental right. We have seen in para 9.130 that the question first arose under s. 298 of the G.I. Act, 35,[68] which, like Arts. 15 (2), 16 (2), 29 (2) prohibited

---

[67] See para 11.38 of the text.
[68] See *f.n.* 57 at p. 391 *ante*, where it is set out.

discrimination on "the ground only" of religion, place of birth, descent, etc. In this context, Lord Thankerton laid down the following test for determining whether an impugned Act violated the personal right conferred by s. 298. He said:

The test laid down by the Privy Council under s. 298 G.I. Act

"Their Lordships are unable to accept this as the correct test. In their view, it is not a question of whether the impugned Act is based only on one or more of the grounds specified in s. 298 sub-s. (1), but whether its operation may result in a prohibition only on these grounds. The proper test as to whether there is a contravention of the sub-section is to ascertain the reaction of the impugned Act on the personal right conferred by the sub-section, and, *while the scope and object of the Act may be of assistance in determining the effect of the operation of the Act on a proper construction of its provisions*, if the effect of the Act so determined involves an infringement of such personal right, the object of the Act, however laudable, will not obviate the prohibition of sub-s. (1)."[69] (italics supplied)

This test was laid down by the Privy Council with the precision which characterized its judgments, as the qualification introduced by the italicised words in the above passage clearly show. It was this test which Das J.[70] adopted and applied in *Bombay* v. *Bombay Education Society* when he held that the impugned circular denied to all pupils whose mother tongue was not English, admission in certain schools "on the ground only" of language, thereby contravening Art. 29(2). And Das J. added that the same principle was implicit in *Champakam Dorairajan's Case*.[71] Therefore, the test of the direct impact of a law on the fundamental right to ascertain whether that right had been infringed is not new, as proposition (*g*) seems to suggest. However, the test which Lord Thankerton laid down contained a very important qualification which Shah J. disregarded, and in fact, would have looked upon as incorrect. It will be submitted that the test laid down in propositions (*f*) and (*g*) as one test, is incorrect, because of what is stated in proposition (*f*). Consequently, the "eminent judges" who decided *Gopalan's Case* and the two other cases in 1951 and 1955 referred to earlier, laid down no such theory as has been attributed to them by Shah J. They laid down the correct test, whereas Shah J. laid down a test which is incorrect for the reason given above. Therefore, the claim of Shah J., and his nine companion judges, to have laid down a new and correct test is unfounded, and can only be attributed to the fact that the earlier decisions to which we have referred were not brought to the attention of the majority judges or were not present to their minds, when they decided the *Bank Nationalization Case*.

The above test accepted by the Sup. Ct.: expressly in one case and impliedly in another

The above cases not considered

Submission: the Privy Council and the Sup. Ct. laid down the correct test; the test laid down by Shah J. is incorrect

11.68 But the Privy Council and the Supreme Court laid down the above test in the following context: the fundamental right alleged to have been violated (i) was absolute in its terms; (ii) affected the civil rights of the injured party; (iii) and did not relate to two or more inter-related fundamental rights. However, the words in which the test was formulated ". . . must (as every word of every judgment) be read *secundum subjectum materiam*.[72] They were appropriate to their context and must be read in their context."[73] So read, the test

The context in which the Privy Council and the Sup. Ct. laid down the test

[69] See para 9.130 of the text.
[70] For himself, Mahajan C.J. and Hasan, Bhagwati and Jagannadhadas JJ.
[71] See para 9.130 of the text. [72] According to the subject matter.
[73] *Commonwealth of Australia* v. *Bank of New South Wales* (1950) A.C. 235 at p. 308 (P.C.) *per* Lord Porter for himself, and Lords Simonds, Normand, Morton and MacDermott.

Situations not dealt with by the Privy Council and the Sup. Ct.

laid down by Lord Thankerton is correct. But it is a salutary practice of final tribunals, like the Privy Council and the Supreme Court, not to decide more than is necessary in constitutional cases. So, the Privy Council and the Supreme Court in the decisions we have referred to, did not deal with the following different situations, namely, where the law was impugned as violating (*a*) a fundamental right not absolute in its terms but one subject to permitted restrictions; (*b*) a number of inter-related fundamental rights conferred by the same Article [as in Art. 19 (1) or by different Articles; (*c*) a fundamental right to "personal liberty" (Art. 21) *vis-a-vis* punitive or preventive detention under the Indian Penal Code or under a Preventive Detention Act, so that the complaint of the injured party was not limited to civil rights. But in the *Bank Nationalization Case,* Shah J. disregarded this salutary practice and decided constitutional questions which were not necessary for giving relief to the injured party. For, once the majority held that the impugned law violated the fundamental right conferred by Art. 31 (2) in absolute terms, the law was void, it was unnecessary to consider the challenge under Art. 19 (1) (*f*) and (*g*) (which conferred fundamental rights subject to reasonable restrictions), or the correlation of Art. 19 (1) (*f*) to Art. 31 (2). And it was wholly inappropriate to purport to overrule *Gopalan's Case* in which the principal constitutional question was the effect of the deprivation of "personal liberty" by punitive and preventive detention, after complying with Art. 21, which confers a fundamental right. However, having decided on an excursion into the unnecessary, and, *qua Gopalan's Case,* into the unexplored,[74] Shah J. failed to consider whether a test appropriate to the alleged violation of a single fundamental right conferred in absolute terms[75] and affecting only the civil rights of parties, was appropriate to the three situations (*a*), (*b*) and (*c*) set out earlier in this para. In paras 11.63 to 11.65 we have dealt with these situations, and have shown that the principal proposition and the "corollary", said to follow from it, in proposition (*c*) in para 11.45 and proposition (*d*) in the same para were untenable. The reasoning in paras 11.63 to 11.65 applies equally to propositions (*f*) and (*g*) in para 11.45. It is submitted that propositions (*f*) and (*g*) are untenable.

The failure of Shah J. to consider tests applicable to different situations

Propositions (*h*) to (*i*) in para 11.45 examined

11.69 As to propositions (*h*) to (*i*) in para 11.45 above our discussion in para 11.65 (iv) has shown the real reason for the mutual exclusiveness of Art. 19 (1) (*f*) and Art. 31 (1) and (2), as long as they were interpreted as dealing with acquisition and requisition, and the mutual exclusiveness of Art. 19 (1) (*f*) and Art. 31 (2) after Art. 31 (2A) had severed the link between sub-cls. (1) and (2) of Art. 31. Further, we have seen that *qua* citizens Art. 19 (1) (*f*) and 31 (1) ceased to be mutually exclusive after the insertion of sub-cl. (2A) in Art. 31. The express exclusion of Art. 19 (1) (*f*) from Art. 31 (2) by the insertion of sub-cl. (2B) in Art. 31 was designed to nullify the decision in the *Bank Nationalization Case* and to restore the law treated as well settled by *Sitabati's Case,* namely, that Art. 19 (1) (*f*) and Art. 31 (2) were mutually exclusive (see para 11.38 above).

---

[74] A reading of the judgment of Shah J. leaves little doubt that the correctness or otherwise of the majority in *Gopalan's Case* was not even remotely canvassed or discussed in the *Bank Nationalization Case.*

[75] As was the right conferred by s. 298, G.I. Act, 35 and Art. 29(2).

11.70 The above analysis of the *Bank Nationalization Case* may have filled the reader, as it has filled the present writer, with surprise that in purporting to overrule *Gopalan's Case* ten judges of the Supreme Court should have attributed their own errors to the eminent judges who decided *Gopalan's Case.* And surprise turns to amazement when in *Sarkar's Case,* in *Khudiram's Case* and in *Maneka Gandhi's Case,* those errors should have been repeated, notwithstanding that in *Maneka Gandhi's Case,* a clear-sighted judge — Kailasam J. — demonstrated the fundamental error in the *Bank Nationalization Case* and gave cogent reasons for holding that the observations of Shah J. in the *Bank Nationalization Case* on the interrelation of Arts. 19 to 21 were casual observations which did not have the effect of overruling *Gopalan's Case.* However, the dissent of Kailasam J., which remained unanswered in the majority judgments, set the stage, should an opportunity present itself, for reconsidering the *Bank Nationalization Case vis-a-vis Gopalan's Case.*

The effect of the above analysis of the *Bank Nationalization Case*

The dissent of Kailasam J. in *Maneka Gandhi's Case* sets the stage for a reconsideration of earlier decisions

11.71 That opportunity came in *Bachan Singh* v. *Punjab*[76] ("*Bachan Singh's Case*") under the following circumstances: In *Rajendra Prasad* v. *U.P.*[77] ("*Rajendra Prasad's Case*"), the majority judgment of Krishna Iyer and Desai JJ., (Sen J. dissenting), took a view of the "special reasons" for imposing the death sentence, which, according to Kailasam J. in *Bachan Singh's Case* when it was first heard by a Bench of two judges was contrary to the decision of a Constitution Bench in *Jagmohan Singh* v. *U.P.*[78] After pointing out the reasons for this view, Kailasam J. without expressing his own view on the questions involved, in agreement with Sarkaria, J., directed that the papers be placed before the Chief Justice to constitute a larger Bench to resolve this conflict. Thereafter several persons convicted of murder and sentenced to death presented writ petitions under Art. 32 challenging the constitutional validity of the death penalty. Accordingly, *Bachan Singh's Case,* and the other petitions, were placed before a Bench consisting of Chandrachud C. J. and Bhagwati, Sarkaria, Gupta and Untwalia JJ.

Bachan Singh's Case

11.72 As *Bachan Singh's Case* was heard by a Bench of five judges, an application was made that in view of the judgment in *Maneka Gandhi's Case* its impact on Arts. 21, 19 and 14 and their interrelationship should be considered by a larger Bench. The Solicitor-General objected to this course as involving avoidable delay, but he said that ". . . he would have no objection on the ground of *stare decisis* to a fresh consideration of the whole problem by this very Bench." Acting on this concession, the Bench heard the matter and the majority judgment contains an elaborate discussion of *Gopalan's Case.* Sarkaria J. delivered the judgment for himself, Chandrachud C.J., Gupta and Untwalia JJ. on May 5, 1980 upholding the constitutional validity of the death sentence.[79] Bhagwati J. merely passed an order holding s. 302 (murder) unconstitutional in so far as it provided for the death penalty. He added "I shall give my reasons for this view on the day on which the Court reopens after the summer vacation".[80] However, instead of delivering the judgment in the third week of July 1980 when the Court reopened, he delivered a

Heard by a Bench of 5 judges

The concession of the Sol. General: *stare decisis* not invoked

Sarkaria J. delivers majority judgment

Bhagwati J. delivered a dissenting judgment 2 years later

---

[76] ('80) A.SC. 898.
[77] (1979) 3 S.C.R. 646, ('79) A.SC. 916.
[78] (1973) 2 S.C.R. 541, ('73) A.SC. 947.
[79] ('80) A.SC. 898.
[80] ibid. p. 945.

judgment on 16th August 1982 (reported in the October number of 1982 A.I.R. S.C.). In concluding his judgment he said: "I must express my profound regret at the long delay in delivering this judgment but the reason is that there was a considerable mass of material which had to be collected from various sources and then examined and analysed and this took a large amount of time."[81]

Only part of the majority judgment considered for the purpose of the present discussion

11.73 In so far as *Bachan Singh's Case* deals with the constitutional validity of the death sentence, it will be considered under the topic "Articles 14, 19, 21 and the sentence of death" later in this book. But it was not possible to consider the impact of *Bachan Singh's Case* on the *Bank Nationalization Case* and *Gopalan's Case* till the dissenting judgment of Bhagwati J. became available in October 1982 and could be studied. This was all the more so because Bachan Singh and the other petitioners relied on Bhagwati J.'s leading judgment in *Maneka Gandhi's Case* for a reconsideration of the inter-relation of Arts. 14, 19 and 21. However, the delay of over two years caused by the delivery of the dissenting judgment in August, 1982, has not prevented a coherent exposition of the subject. For, if, as we have submitted earlier, Bhagwati J.'s judgment in *Maneka Gandhi's Case* had to stand or fall by the correctness of the majority judgment in the *Bank Nationalization Case*, then *Bachan Singh's Case* is best considered at this place because it had to reconsider *Gopalan's Case*, the *Bank Nationalization Case* and *Maneka Gandhi's Case*.

The Bench hearing *Bachan Singh's Case* free to reconsider decisions of larger Benches

11.74 The fact that the majority judgment in the *Bank Nationalization Case* was delivered by ten judges, and the fact that *Maneka Gandhi's Case* was decided by seven judges did not stand in the way of the Supreme Court overruling, modifying or qualifying those decisions on the inter-relation of Art. 19 and Art. 21, because, as stated earlier, the Solicitor-General conceded that he did not invoke the doctrine of *stare decisis* and that this very Bench could consider the problems involved afresh, left the Court free to overrule, qualify or modify earlier judgments on the constitutional points raised by *Bachan Singh's Case*.

Sarkaria J. did not seize the opportunity for a full reconsideration of earlier decisions

11.75 However, although an opportunity presented itself to resolve the confusion caused by the *Bank Nationalization Case*, and the cases which followed it, Sarkaria J. for the majority did not seize it, as Lord Reid seized it in *Ridge* v. *Baldwin*[82] with conspicuous success. If the Supreme Court lacked its Lord Reid, it is because of the inexplicable reluctance of the Supreme Court to say plainly that earlier judges can commit mistakes, even when flagrant mistakes are pointed out. Judgments are "clarified", "explained", "confined to the facts of the case", "are not to be extended beyond the particular law" — anything but a plain clear statement that "the earlier judgments are clearly erroneous, and must be overruled". It has become necessary to say this for two reasons. First, the method followed in *Bachan Singh's Case* must encourage further litigation, because it is difficult to say what survives of the *Bank Nationalization Case*, and the cases which followed it, after the judgment in *Bachan Singh's Case* has been delivered. Secondly, the dissent of Kailasam J., which strikes at the root of the *Bank Nationalization Case* is not referred to at all,

---

[81] ('82) A.SC. 1325. 1392.

[82] (1964) A.C. p. 40.

and remains unanswered, and, in the submission of the present writer, unanswerable.[83]

11.76 We will presently deal with the advance made towards a correct statement of the law by Sarkaria J. But it may be observed that his exposition is unsatisfactory for a Court re-considering the earlier decisions in order to find out the correct test to determine whether there was one test to determine the violation of a fundamental right by an impugned law or whether there was more than one test. Secondly, Sarkaria J. failed to inquire whether the inter-relation of certain Articles in Part III had any effect on the test to be applied. Finally, bearing in mind that *Bachan Singh's Case* dealt with punitive detention as an alternative to the total deprivation of personal liberty by a sentence of death, a reconsideration of the earlier decisions made it necessary for the Court to ask: Unsatisfactory features of Sarkaria J.'s judgment

(i) Was it the "major premiss" of the majority judgments in *Gopalan's Case* that Art. 22 was a complete Code of constitutional safeguards relating to preventive detention as held in the *Bank Nationalization Case* and the cases which followed that decision?

(ii) If the answer is "No", as the quotations from the judgments of Kania C.J., Patanjali Sastri and Das JJ. accurately summed up in the head note to *Gopalan's Case* in the Supreme Court Reports clearly shows, what survives of the elaborate superstructure raised by the *Bank Nationalization Case* on the foundation of a grave and fundamental error?

(iii) Are the observations in the *Bank Nationalization Case* on *Gopalan's Case* in reference to the inter-relation of Art. 19(1) and Art. 21 unconsidered casual observations not binding on any court, much less the Supreme Court?

(iv) What was the test applied in earlier decisions of the Supreme Court to determine whether an impugned law violated a fundamental right affecting only the civil rights of parties?

A failure to raise and answer these questions has robbed the reconsideration of the earlier decision of the much greater value which it would have had. However, the judgment goes a fair way towards a more accurate statement of the law as will presently appear. The judgment makes an advance towards a more accurate statement of the law

11.77 Sarkaria J. said that two principal questions fell for consideration in the case: Questions raised by *Bachan Singh's Case*

"(i) Whether death penalty provided for the offence of murder in S. 302, Penal Code is unconstitutional.

(ii) If the answer to the foregoing question be in the negative, whether the sentencing procedure provided in Sec. 354(3) of the Code of Criminal Procedure, 1973 (Act 2 of 1974) is unconstitutional on the ground that it invests the Court with unguided and untrammelled discretion and allows death sentence to be arbitrarily or freakishly imposed on a person found guilty of murder or any other capital offence punishable under the Indian Penal Code with death or, in the alternative, with imprisonment for life."[84]

11.78 After setting out the legislative history of the death penalty[85] and after setting out the grounds on which Counsel urged that the death penalty must be regarded as an "unreasonable restriction" on the six freedoms granted by Art. 19(1), Sarkaria J. examined Art. 19(1)(*a*) to (*e*) and (*g*). The following propositions emerge from his examination: Propositions emerging from Sarkaria J.'s judgment on Art. 19(1)(*a*) to (*e*) and (*g*)

[83] It is not as though Sarkaria J. ignored dissenting judgments. He referred to the dissenting judgment of Mathew J. in the *Bennett Coleman Case*. See ('80) A.SC. 898 at p. 914.

[84] ('80) A.SC. *supra* at p. 905.

[85] ibid. pp. 905-906.

(A) An analysis of Art. 19(1)(*a*) to (*e*) and (*g*) shows that the rights there mentioned are not absolute; they have to be exercised so as not to injure the rights of others. Secondly, they are subject to the power of the State to make laws imposing reasonable restrictions, which may even extend to prohibition, on the exercise of those rights — a power which if properly exercised, is the best guarantee of those freedoms.

(B) "The argument that the provisions of the Penal Code prescribing death as an alternative penalty for murder have to be tested on the ground of Art. 19(1) appears to proceed on the fallacy that the freedoms guaranteed by Art. 19(1) are absolute freedoms and they cannot be curtailed by law imposing reasonable restrictions which may amount to total prohibition."

(C) Such an argument was urged before, and rejected by Das C.J. in *Chamarbaugwala's Case*. Das C.J. held that crime and criminal activities were not protected by Art 19. "This approach to the problem still holds the field" as the passage from the judgment of Das C.J. quoted by Sarkaria J.[86] had been cited with approval by Krishna Iyer J. in *Fatehchand's Case*.[87]

(D) "In *Gopalan's Case* all the six judges held that punitive detention or imprisonment awarded as punishment after conviction for an offence under the Indian Penal Code was outside the scope of Art. 19 although this conclusion was reached by them by adopting different approaches."

(E) The argument for Gopalan that imprisonment in a cell as a result of preventive detention affected his rights under Art. 19(1)(*a*) to (*e*) and (*g*) was rejected on two grounds:

(i) that it would render several sections of the Penal Code, for theft, cheating, forgery and even ordinary assault illegal, and such a result was not the outcome of the Constitution.[88]

(ii) that the correct test was laid down in the passage[89] from his judgment which we have extracted in para 11.13. The test is to consider the direct impact of the impugned law on the fundamental right and not what would be the result of the detention otherwise valid on the mode of the detenu's life.

(iii) The contents and subject matter of Arts. 19 and 21 are thus not the same.[90]

After setting out the approach of Patanjali Sastri J.[91] Mahajan J.,[92] Mukherjea J.,[93] Das J.[94] and after pointing out that Fazal Ali J. applied to punitive detention the same test as Kania C.J. had applied to punitive and preventive detention, Sarkaria J. summed up the result which is set out in the next para.

The result of the examination stated by Sarkaria J.

11.79 "We have copiously extracted from the judgments in *Gopalan's Case*, to show that all the propositions propounded, arguments and reasons employed or approaches adopted by the learned Judges in that case, in reaching the conclusion that the Indian Penal Code, particularly those of its provisions which do not have a direct impact on the rights conferred by Art. 19 (1), is not a law imposing restrictions on those rights, have not been overruled or rendered bad by the subsequent pronouncements of this Court in *Bank Nationalization Case* or in *Maneka Gandhi's Case*. For instance, the proposition laid down by Kania C.J., Fazal Ali, Patanjali Sastri and S. R. Das, JJ. that the Indian Penal Code particularly those of its provisions which cannot be justified on the ground of reasonableness with reference to any of

---

[86] ibid. p. 908. [87] ibid.
[88] ibid. at p. 908 at which the passage from the judgment of Kania C.J. is set out.
[89] ibid., where Sarkaria J. has set out the passage.
[90] ibid. [91] ibid. at p. 909.
[92] ibid.
[93] ibid. (Sarkaria J. set out the passage from his judgment which we have set out in para 11.23 of the text).
[94] ibid. pp. 909-910.

the specified heads, such as "public order" in Clauses (2), (3) and (4), is not a law imposing restrictions on any of the rights conferred by Article 19 (1), still holds the field. *Indeed, the reasoning, explicit or implicit, in the judgments of Kania, C.J., Patanjali Sastri and S. R. Das JJ. that such a construction which treats every section of the Indian Penal Code as a law imposing 'restriction' on the rights in Article 19(1), will lead to absurdity is unassailable.* There are several offences under the Penal Code, such as theft, cheating, ordinary assault, which do not violate or affect 'public order', but only 'law and order'. These offences injure only specific individuals as distinguished from the public at large. It is by now settled that 'public order' means 'even tempo of the life of the community'. That being so, even all murders do not disturb or affect 'public order'. Some murders may be of purely private significance and the injury or harm resulting therefrom affects only specific individuals, and, consequently, such murders may not be covered by "public order" within the contemplation of Clauses (2), (3) and (4) of Article 19. Such murders do not lead to public disorder but to disorder *simpliciter*. Yet, no rational being can say that punishment of such murders is not in the general public interest. It may be noted that general public interest is not specified as a head in Clauses (2) to (4) on which restriction on the rights mentioned in Clause (1) of the Article may be justified."[95] (italics supplied)

11.80 Applying the above reasoning to murder, Sarkaria J. said: "A murder committed in given circumstances may cause only a slight tremor, the wave-length of which does not extend beyond the parameters of law and order. Another murder committed in different context and circumstances may unleash a tidal wave of such intensity, gravity and magnitude, that its impact throws out of gear the even flow of life. Nonetheless, the fact remains that for such murders which do not affect 'public order', even the provision for life imprisonment in Sec. 302, Indian Penal Code, as an alternative punishment, would not be justifiable under Cls. (2), (3) and (4) as a reasonable restriction in the interest of 'public order'. Such a construction must, therefore, be avoided. *Thus construed, Article 19 will be attracted only to such laws, the provisions of which are capable of being tested under Cls. (2) to (5) of Art. 19.*"[96] (italics supplied)

The effect of the above reasoning on punishment for murder

The test for the application of Art. 19

11.81 As to the test which we have underlined in the above quoted passage, Sarkaria J. cited a passage from the judgment of Ray C.J. in *Saha's Case* (see para 11.51 of the text) and italicized its last sentence "*A law which attracts Art. 19 therefore must be such as is capable of being tested to be reasonable under Cls. (2) to (5) of Art.19*".[97] Sarkaria J. observed that this sentence

Saha's Case implicitly approves the test applied by the majority in *Gopalan's Case*

"appears to lend implicit approval to the rule of construction adopted by the majority of . . . judges in *Gopalan's Case* whereby they excluded from the purview of Art. 19 certain provisions of the Penal Code providing for certain offences which could not be tested on the specific grounds embodied in Cls. (2) to (5) of that Article. This proposition enunciated in *Gopalan's Case* is only a product of the application of the basic cannon that a construction which would lead to absurdity should be eschewed."[98]

[95] ibid. pp. 910-911. [96] ibid. p. 911.
[97] ibid. at p. 911. (The reader will find the sentence set out in para 11.51 of the text).
[98] ibid.

The *Bank Nationalization Case* and *Maneka Gandhi's Case*

11.82 After setting out the test laid down in the *Bank Nationalization Case* which we have set out as proposition (*g*) in para 11.45 above, and certain observations of Chandrachud J. and Bhagwati J. in *Maneka Gandhi's Case,* Sarkaria J. posed the question whether the *Bank Nationalization Case* and *Maneka Gandhi's Case* had

had not given a complete go-by to the test of "direct and indirect effect", "form and object test" or "pith and substance test"

"given a complete go-by to the 'test of direct and indirect effect', sometimes described as 'form and object test' or 'pith and substance rule', which was adopted by Kania C.J. and Fazal Ali J. in *Gopalan's Case.* In our opinion, the answer to this question cannot be in the affirmative. In the first place, there is nothing much in the name. As Varadachariar J. put it in *Subrahmanyan Chettiar's Case* (1940) F.C.R. 188, such rules of interpretation were evolved only as a matter of reasonableness and common sense and out of the necessity of satisfactorily solving conflicts from the inevitable overlapping of subjects in any distribution of powers. By the same yardstick of common sense, the 'pith and substance rule' was applied to resolve the question of the constitutionality of a law assailed on the ground of its being violative of a fundamental right."[99]

Sarkaria J.'s survey of decisions since *Gopalan's Case*

11.83 Sarkaria J. added that a survey of Supreme Court decisions since *Gopalan's Case* showed that the criterion of directness which was the essence of the test of direct and indirect effect had never been totally abandoned.

"Only the mode of its application has been modified and its scope amplified by judicial activism to maintain its efficiency for solving new constitutional problems in tune with evolving concepts of rights and obligations in strident democracy."[1]

Ram Singh v. *Delhi*

The *Express Newspapers Case*

The test of direct and indirect effect ("the test") adopted in *Gopalan's Case* was approved by a full court in *Ram Singh* v. *Delhi*,[2] and although Mahajan and Bose JJ. differed on the merits, there was no dissent on this point among all the Judges. Another decision which while purporting to follow the enunciation of the test in *Gopalan's Case* "imperceptibly added another dimension to the test of directness" was the *Express Newspapers Case.*[3] N. H. Bhagwati J., delivering a unanimous judgment of a Constitution Bench observed that it could hardly be urged that the possible effect of the impact (of the impugned laws) in conceivable cases would vitiate the legislation as such. On the facts he held that effect of the measure, namely, the tendency to curtail circulation, "*would be remote which would depend upon various factors which may or may not come into play.* Unless these were the *direct or inevitable consequences* of the measures enacted in the impugned Act, it would not be possible to strike down the legislation."[4] (italics supplied). Bhagwati J. added that the impugned Act could be legitimately characterized as a measure which affected the press, but its "intention or the proximate effect and operation" was not such as to violate Art. 19(1), and therefore, it could not be held invalid. Sarkaria J. observed that a test adopted by Bhagwati J. was not very different from the test adopted by Fazal Ali J. in relation to a law providing for punitive detention. Sarkaria J. observed that the test laid down by Bhagwati J. did not discard the test adopted by Kania C.J. in *Gopalan's Case* but merely extended the application of the criterion of directness to the operation and effect of the impugned legislation.

---

[99] ibid. p. 912.
[1] ibid. p. 912.
[2] (1951) S.C.R. 451.
[3] (1959) S.C.R. 12.
[4] ('80) A.SC. *supra* at p. 913.

11.84 Again, in the *Sakal Case*[5] it was held that the "direct and immediate" effect of the impugned Order was to violate Art. 19 (1) (*a*) and the Order was invalid. Sarkaria J. observed that in this case "the emphasis had shifted from the object and subject-matter of the impugned State action to its direct and immediate effect".[6] The reader will have noticed that whereas the *Express Newspapers Case* dealt with labour legislation affecting newspapers, the impugned Order as its title "Daily Newspaper (Price and Page) Order" directly dealt with newspapers whose freedom is included in the freedom of speech and expression. Sarkaria J. referred to *Mirajkar's Case*[7] and to the observations of Gajendragadkar C.J.[8] which included *inter alia* the following observations:

The *Sakal* Case

Mirajkar's Case

"It is well settled that in examining the validity of legislation, it is legitimate to consider whether the impugned legislation is a legislation directly in respect of the subject covered by any particular article of the Constitution, or touches the said article only incidentally or indirectly. If the test of direct effect and object which is sometimes described as the pith and substance test, is thus applied in considering the validity of legislation, it would not be inappropriate to apply the same test to judicial decisions like the one with which we are concerned in the present proceedings."[9]

Sarkaria J. also referred to the observations of Mathew J. in the *Bennett Coleman Case* which has been set out in para 10.249 of the text.

11.85 The result of the survey of earlier Supreme Court decisions led Sarkaria J. to state the result thus:

The result of the survey of the earlier decision stated by Sarkaria J.

"From the above conspectus, it is clear that the test of direct and indirect effect was not scrapped. Indeed, there is no dispute that the test of 'pith and substance' of the subject-matter and of direct and of incidental effect of legislation is a very useful test to determine the question of legislative competence, i.e. in ascertaining whether an Act falls under one Entry while incidentally encroaching upon another Entry. Even for determining the validity of a legislation on the ground of infringement of fundamental rights, the subject-matter and the object of the legislation are not altogether irrelevant. For instance, if the subject-matter of the legislation directly covers any of the fundamental freedoms mentioned in Article 19(1), it must pass the test of reasonableness under the relevant head in clauses (2) to (6) of that Article. If the legislation does not directly deal with any of the rights in Article 19(1) that may not conclude the enquiry. It will have to be ascertained further whether by its direct and immediate operation, the impugned legislation abridges any of the rights enumerated in Art. 19(1)."[10]

11.86 "From a survey of the cases noticed above, a comprehensive test which can be formulated, may be restated as under:

A "comprehensive" test formulated

'Does the impugned law, in its pith and substance, whatever may be its form and object, deal with any of the fundamental rights conferred by Art. 19(1)? If it does, does it abridge or abrogate any of those rights? And even if it does not, in its pith and substance, deal with any of the fundamental rights conferred by Art. 19(1) is the direct and inevitable effect of the impugned law such as to abridge or abrogate any of those rights'?

The mere fact that impugned law incidentally, remotely or collaterally has the effect of abridging or abrogating those rights, will not satisfy the test. If the answer to the above queries be in the

[5] (1962) 3 S.C.R. 842.
[6] ('80) A.SC. *supra* at pp. 913-14.
[7] (1966) 3 S.C.R. 744.
[8] For himself, Wanchoo, Mudholkar, Sikri and Ramaswami JJ.
[9] ('80) A.SC. *supra* at p. 914.
[10] ibid.

affirmative, the impugned law in order to be valid, must pass the test of reasonableness under Article 19. But if the impact of the law on any of the rights under cl. (1) of Art. 19 is merely incidental, indirect, remote or collateral and is dependent upon factors which may or may not come into play, the anvil of Article 19 will not be available for judging its validity."[11]

The result of applying the "comprehensive" test to s. 302 I.P.C.:—s. 302 does not have to stand the test of Art. 19(1)

11.87 Applying this test to s. 299 (culpable homicide) s. 300 (murder) and s. 302 which prescribe death or imprisonment as a penalty for murder, Sarkaria J. said:

"It cannot reasonably or rationally, be contended that any of the rights mentioned in Article 19(1) of the Constitution confers the freedom to commit murder or, for the matter of that, the freedom to commit any offence whatsoever. Therefore, penal laws, that is to say, laws which define offences and prescribe punishment for the commission of offences do not attract the application of Art. 19(1). . . . But the point of the matter is that, in pith and substance, penal laws do not deal with the subject matter of rights enshrined in Article 19(1) . . . we are of the opinion that the deprivation of freedom consequent upon an order of conviction and sentence is not a direct and inevitable consequence of the penal law but is merely incidental to the order of conviction and sentence which may or may not come into play, that is to say, which may or may not be passed. Considering therefore the test formulated by us in its dual aspect, we are of the opinion that Section 302 of the Penal Code does not have to stand the test of Article 19(1) of the Constitution."[12]

Application of the "comprehensive test to s. 302 I.P.C.

11.88 In the above passage, we have set out parts of a paragraph in which Sarkaria J. applied the "comprehensive test" to the validity of the sentence of death under s. 302 I.P.C.[13] because those parts deal with one connected topic. However, these parts are interspersed with parts which have been omitted because they are not easy to understand. Before setting out and dealing with the passages which have been omitted, it is necessary to make a few observations.

Remarkable feature of Sarkaria J.'s judgment

The judgment of Sarkaria J. makes a few references to the *Bank Nationalization Case*, but it is a remarkable feature of that judgment that it has undertaken no critical examination of that case in order to ascertain its standing as an authority on the question before the Court, namely, whether punitive detention for murder and the death penalty as an alternative to it was constitutionally invalid for violating Art. 19(1). *Gopalan's Case* dealt with the question whether preventive detention must stand the test of Art. 19; but the majority of judges felt obliged to consider whether punitive detention must stand the test of Art. 19, for they saw no difference between the effect of the two kinds of detention on the rights conferred on citizens by Art. 19(1). Therefore, Sarkaria J. critically examined the views of the judges who decided *Gopalan's Case,* as a step towards answering the question before the Court. The *Bank Nationalization Case,* as we have seen, raised questions about the civil rights of parties, but raised no question about preventive or punitive detention. Consequently, as explained by Kailasam J., the casual observations in the *Bank Nationalization Case* that legislation under Art. 21 should also satisfy the requirements of Art. 19(1) (*f*) cannot be said to be

---

[11] ibid. p. 915.

[12] ibid. at p. 915. The dots in the above passage indicate parts of the paragraph in the judgment which have been left out.

[13] The reader will have noticed that the "comprehensive test" is limited to a law alleged to violate the fundamental rights conferred by Art. 19(1).

correct law (see para 11.51). Since the test supposed to have been applied in *Gopalan's Case* was the excuse for reconsidering that and other decisions which followed it, let us see how the *Bank Nationalization Case* stands after the judgment of Sarkaria J.

The *Bank Nationalization Case* after Sarkaria J.'s judgment: (*a*) *Gopalan's Case* not overruled by the *Bank Nat. Case qua* punitive detention under I.P.C. (*b*) Kania C.J.'s avoidance of absurd result unassailable (*c*) *Chamarbaugwalla's Case* holds the field (*d*) punishment for certain murders would be void. This construction must be avoided. (*e*) Test for laws attracting Art. 19(2) to (5) Test (*e*) directly contrary to test in *Bank Nat. Case*

11.89 Sarkaria J. held that:

(*a*) The *Bank Nationalization Case* and *Maneka Gandhi's Case* had not overruled or "rendered bad" the conclusion of the judges in *Gopalan's Case* "that the Indian Penal Code particularly those of its provisions which do not have a direct impact on the rights conferred by Art. 19(1), is not a law imposing restrictions on those rights."

(*b*) The reasoning, explicit and implicit, of Kania C.J., Patanjali Sastri and Das JJ. that a construction which treated every section of the Indian Penal Code as a law imposing "restriction" on the rights conferred by Art. 19(1) would lead to absurdity is unassailable and must be avoided.

(*c*) The approach of Das C.J. in *Chamarbaugwalla's Case* that crime or criminal activities were not protected by Art. 19(1) "still holds the field" as it has been approved in *Fatehchand's Case.*

(*d*) For murders which do not affect "public order" even the alternative penalty of life imprisonment provided in s. 302 would not be justifiable under Art. 19(2), (3) and (4) as a reasonable restriction in the interest of "public order". Such a construction must be avoided.

(*e*) Properly construed, "Art. 19 would be attracted to only such laws, the provisions of which are capable of being tested under Cls. (2) to (5) of Art. 19."

It will be noted that the above test is bodily taken from the judgment of Ray C.J. in *Saha's Case* which we have discussed in para 11.51 in which Ray C.J. said further: "Art. 19(1) (*f*) deals with the right to acquire, hold and dispose of property. It is apparent that after a person's property has been acquired by the State he cannot acquire, hold or dispose of that property." In other words, Ray C.J. adopted a test directly contrary to that of the majority in the *Bank Nationalization Case.*

Submission: *Bachan Singh's Case* has discredited, if not destroyed the tests in *Bank Nat. Case* and *Maneka Gandhi's Case*

11.90 It is clear from the findings of Sarkaria J. above that the view taken by the majority in *Gopalan's Case* has been upheld on every point and the contrary view taken in the *Bank Nationalization Case* has been rejected. By adopting the test of Ray C.J., a test is adopted which destroys the theory of the *Bank Nationalization Case* that a law for the acquisition of property must satisfy the test of reasonableness prescribed by Art. 19(5), and it is submitted that on the subject of our present discussion after the majority judgment in *Bachan Singh's Case* has discredited if not struck dead the tests propounded by Shah J. in the *Bank Nationalization Case* and followed in *Maneka Gandhi's Case.*

The "two fold" test adopted in *Bank Nat. Case*

11.90A Further, referring to the test laid down by the majority in the *Bank Nationalization Case,* Sarkaria J. observed:

". . . the majority adopted the twofold test for determining as to when a law violated fundamental rights, namely: '(1) It is not the object of the authority making the law impairing the right of a citizen, nor the form of action that determines the protection he can claim. (2) It is the effect of the law and of the action upon the right which attract the jurisdiction of the Court to grant relief. The direct operation of the act upon the rights forms the real test'."[14]

Submission: only one test adopted in *Bank Nat. Case*

It is submitted that the observation that the majority judgment in the *Bank Nationalization Case* applied "a twofold test" is not correct. Tests (1) and (2) quoted by Sarkaria J. are followed by these observations:

[14] ibid. p. 912.

"We are of the view that the theory that the object and form of the State action determine the extent of the protection which the aggrieved party may claim is not consistent with the constitutional scheme."[15]

In other words, Shah J. held that there is only one test, that set out in (2), the test set out in (1) not being the correct test. Secondly, the test laid down by the Privy Council and applied by the Supreme Court (see para 11.67) has not been brought to the attention of the Court in *Bachan Singh's Case* nor has it been present to its mind. The Privy Council pointed out that the *scope* and *object* of an Act may be of assistance in determining the effect of the operation of the Act.

Test laid down by the Privy Council and the Sup. Ct. earlier not brought to court's attention

Two passages in the application of the "comprehensive test"

11.90B We must now consider the two passages which have been left out from the judgment of Sarkaria J. in applying the "comprehensive" test to s. 302, I.P.C.

Passage No. 1: "We cannot, of course, say that the object of penal laws is generally such as not to involve any violation of the rights conferred by Art. 19(1) because after the decision of this Court in the *Bank Nationalization Case* the theory, that the object and form of the State action alone determine the extent of protection that may be claimed by an individual and that the effect of the State action on the fundamental right of the individual is irrelevant, stands discredited."[16]

Passage No. 2: "That again is not enough for the purpose of deciding upon the applicability of Article 19 because as the test formulated by us above shows, even if a law does not, in its pith and substance, deal with any of the fundamental rights conferred by Art. 19(1), if the direct and inevitable effect of the law is such as to abridge or abrogate any of those rights, Art. 19(1) shall have been attracted. It would then become necessary to test the validity of even a penal law on the touchstone of that Article."[17]

Passage No. 1 criticised and critically examined

11.91 As to Passage No. 1, the reference to the test laid down by the *Bank Nationalization Case* is unintelligible because to say that test stands *discredited by the Bank Nationalization Case*, is odd, when, after *Bachan Singh's Case*, the tests propounded by the *Bank Nationalization Case* on punitive detention themselves stand discredited. This is all the more so in view of the observations of Sarkaria J. that (i) the test of "direct and indirect effect" was not scrapped; (ii) that the test of "pith and substance of the subject-matter" and of direct and incidental effect of legislation was useful even for the validity of infringement of fundamental rights (because) the subject-matter and object of the legislation are not altogether irrelevant. Part of the confusion is caused by Sarkaria J.'s reference to the judgment of Varadachariar J. in *Subrahmanyan Chettiar's Case* in an imperfect way. We have set out the correct position in para 10.249 in discussing the *Bennett Coleman Case* where we pointed out that Mathew J. was in error in observing that the doctrine of "pith and substance" was not strictly appropriate where the violation of a fundamental right is alleged. Sarkaria J. did not mention the decision of the Privy Council in *Gallager* v. *Lynn* in which Lord Atkin rejected the contention that the doctrine of pith and substance applied only to resolving a conflict between the legislative powers of Federal and State Legislatures and did not apply to the unitary Constitution of Northern Ireland. However, Varadachariar J. had no hesitation in referring to *Gallager* v. *Lynn*, for it enabled him to say that the rule of pith and substance which had been evolved "as

Subrahmanyan Chettiar's Case

Gallager v. Lynn

---

[15] ('70) A.SC. 564 at p. 596. [16] ('80) A.SC. *supra* at p. 915.
[17] ibid.

a matter of reasonableness" for resolving conflicts of competing legislative powers in a federal Constitution had been applied to a unitary Constitution. But a reference to Lord Atkin's judgment would have enabled Sarkaria J. to explain, as his judgment does not, the underlying principle which would have helped him in formulating one or more tests for determining when an impugned law can be said to violate Art. 19 (1). The principle underlying the pith and substance rule is that since legislative power is conferred on competing legislatures "in respect of" specified matters, as Lord Atkin observed "(the) Legislature must not under the guise of dealing with one matter in fact encroach upon the forbidden field". The Northern Ireland legislature had power to make laws for "the peace, order and good government of Northern Ireland" but the Legislature was prohibited from enacting laws in respect of "trade with any part of Ireland not within its jurisdiction". The challenge to the Milk Act was repelled by saying that it was "not a law 'in respect of trade'; but is a law 'in respect of' precautions taken to secure the health of the inhabitants of Northern Ireland by securing them from the dangers of an unregulated supply of milk." If this was the nature of the law in "pith and substance", its incidental effect on trade outside Northern Ireland did not matter. Further, Lord Atkin said: "Nor are you to look only at the object of the legislator. An Act may have a perfectly lawful object, *e.g.*, to promote the health of its inhabitants but may seek to achieve that object by invalid methods, *e.g.*, a direct prohibition on any trade with a foreign country".[18]

Lord Atkin on "pith and substance" and the prohibited field in a unitary Constitution: The underlying principle

11.92 In discussing the *Bennett Coleman Case* we have considered in detail the application of this principle at length in paras 10.249 to 10.257 of the text, and that discussion need not be repeated here, but the reader will turn to it as relevant at this place also. But the result of that discussion may be briefly set out primarily with reference to the effect of punitive detention for offences under the Indian Penal Code.

The relevance of paras 10.249 to 10.257 at this place

11.93 The first question to ask about any law is: "*In respect of* what subject-matter or matters has the law been enacted?" If the question were asked about the Indian Penal Code,[19] the answer would be, in respect of "Criminal Law, including all matters in the Indian Penal Code . . ." under entry 1, List III, Sch. VII of the Constitution. The object of a general law of crimes is normally to define crimes and provide for their punishment. Therefore, its pith and substance is the definition and punishment of crimes. Punitive detention after conviction has the consequential effect of affecting the freedoms conferred on citizens by Art. 19 (1) because they cannot be enjoyed once he is in prison. Unless one was prepared to accept the absurd conclusion that punishment for forgery, assault and even murder in cases where it does not affect "public order" is unlawful, it must be held that the scope and/or object and/or purpose of a general law of crimes is not to deny or violate the freedoms conferred by Art. 19 (1). And the majority in *Bachan Singh's Case* rightly so held. But though the I.P.C. considered as a whole is not directed to the seven

"Pith and substance" *qua* the I.P.C.

In its general scope the I.P.C. does not violate Art. 19(1)

[18] See para 10.251 where the relevant passage from the judgment of Lord Atkin is set out.

[19] The Indian Penal Code was the general law of Crimes in India and was continued as existing law under Art. 372.

S. 124-A, I.P.C. directly deals with freedom of speech: *Kedar Nath's Case*

fundamental freedoms, particular provisions of the I.P.C. may deal with one fundamental right. Thus s. 124A of the I.P.C. (sedition) directly punished certain kinds of speech and expression. We have seen in para 10.31 of the text that the Supreme Court in *Kedar Nath's Case* interpreted s. 124A to refer only to that kind of speech and expression which affected "public order", that is, which produce grave disorder or incite to it. Criticism of Government however strong which did not have that effect was not sedition, and if s. 124A was interpreted to include such criticism, s. 124A would be void as it would be considered as placing unreasonable restrictions on the freedom of speech in the interest of "public order". In this connection, it may be observed that the hypothetical illustration given by the Solicitor-General, namely, of a law making any criticism of Government an offence and punishing the offence by imprisonment for 5 years the law would be void under *Kedar Nath's Case*. For like Art. 124A which directly affects the freedom of speech and expression, the hypthetical law would do likewise, and it could not be justified as placing reasonable restrictions on that freedom in the interest of "public order".

Passage No. 2 examined. Formulation of the law not satisfactory

11.94 The above discussion carries us to Passage No. 2 in para 11.90 above. In so far as imprisonment for a crime affects all the freedoms under Art. 19(1), it cannot be said that the Indian Penal Code is not, in pith and substance, a law of crimes. Consequently, Sarkaria J. was right in observing that penal laws do not deal with the subject-matter of rights enshrined in Art. 19(1). Passage No. 2, opens with words which indicate that an exception is being made to the general proposition. However, the formulation of the law in Passage No. 2 though intelligible is not satisfactory. For every section of an Act is a separate enactment,[20] and numerous sections of the Code create offences which deal with the subject-matter of one of the rights conferred. Chapter VI deals with offences against the State (ss. 121-130) and they are connected —some of them are designed to prevent and punish breach of "public order" as interpreted by our Supreme Court. Chapter XVII of the Indian Penal Code deals with offences against property (ss. 378-462). These sections directly deal with the right conferred by Art. 19(1) (*f*) (which was repealed only in 1979). Chapter XXI (s. 499-502) deals with Defamation and directly falls under Art. 19(1) (*a*) read with Art. 19(2). Therefore, the pith and substance of each section cannot be described without reference to the subject-matter of the section creating a crime. However, the use of the words "pith and substance" in connection with sections of the Penal Code is best illustrated by referring again to s. 124A of that Code. Section 124A is in pith and substance a provision for defining and punishing a certain crime, under entry 1, List III. But in so far as the crime is defined in respect of speech and expression, Art. 19(1) (*a*) read with Art. 19(2) contains, in the words of Lord Atkin, a prohibited field, because by virtue of Art. 13(1) and (2) read with Art. 19(1) (*a*) and (2), and Art. 246, the legislature is prohibited from putting restrictions in the interest of "public order" on freedom of

Every section of I.P.C. a separate enactment; several sections deal with one right in Art. 19(1)

The relevance of "pith and substance" to a section of the I.P.C. *vis-a-vis* one right in Art. 19(1): the prohibited field

[20] "Every section of an Act shall have effect as a substantive enactment without introductory words": s. 8, Interpretation Act, 1889. The General Clauses Act provides that " 'enactment' shall include . . . any provision in any Act. . . ."

speech and expression which does not breach "public order" as interpreted by our Supreme Court; or, to put it in less technical language, on that kind of speech and expression which does not lead to grave disorder. The Supreme Court in *Kedar Nath's Case* saved s. 124A by removing from its ambit the prohibited field. But the important thing to note is that once s. 124A as interpreted by the Supreme Court was held to be valid, a citizen duly sentenced to imprisonment under s. 124A will find that as *a consequence* of a valid law he cannot enjoy the freedoms conferred by Art. 19(1), as Kania C.J. held in *Gopalan's Case*.

Kedar Nath's Case

11.95 The above line of reasoning can be illustrated by reference to the view adopted by the Supreme Court that crime and criminal activities cannot claim the protection of Art. 19(1). However, an action which can be treated by law as a crime must be by a valid law, which involves, *inter alia*, that the law does not violate fundamental rights. In *Chamarbaugwalla's Case*, gambling was found, after an elaborate discussion, to be a *malum in se* universally condemned which could therefore be prohibited or punished as a crime —s. 294A punishes the offence of keeping a lottery office. Article 19(2) expressly refers to a law of defamation. We have seen that s. 499 of the Indian Penal Code defines the offence of defamation. It contains several exceptions which fully protect the freedom of speech and expression. The first and most important exception takes out of the offence of defamation "imputation of truth which public good requires to be made for the public good". If Ministers, public officers, people in public life, resenting a truthful exposure of their wrong doing which public interest demands, succeed in persuading Parliament or a State Legislature to delete this exception, by an amendment, such an amendment would be void. For, s. 499 deals directly with speech and expression, and under Art. 19(2) such a law punishing defamation can put reasonable restrictions on that right. It is submitted that if s. 499 was amended by deleting the first exception, the amendment would be void for entering the prohibited field of unreasonable restrictions.[21] The law in pith and substance would not be a law of defamation, but would under the guise of that law seek to achieve a prohibited object, namely, silencing public criticism when such criticism is of the essence of the freedom of speech and expression.

Defamation: s. 499 I.P.C. and Art. 19(1)(*a*) and (2)

11.96 A better illustration of the proposition in Passage No. 2 is furnished by a law imposing a tax on the sale of newspapers and a tax on advertisements therein (entry 92, List I, Sch. VII). Such a law would be regarded as in pith and substance a law imposing a permitted tax, and not as a law relating to the freedom of speech and expression. However, if Parliament resentful of the freedom of the press imposed a rate of tax which would drive most, if not all, newspapers out of existence, the law would be void because the direct impact of the law would be to violate Art. 19(1) (*a*) although in pith and substance it is a tax law. But the underlying reason for holding the law void is the same—under the guise of achieving a permitted object, raising revenue by taxation, it has entered the prohibited field of impermissible restrictions on the freedom of the

A tax on sale of newspapers and a tax on advertisements therein and Art. 19(1)(*a*)

[21] See para 10.31 of the text.

press which is included in the freedom of speech and expression guaranteed by Art. 19(1)(*a*).

A brief and critical appraisal of Sarkaria J.'s judgment

11.97 In the result, it is submitted that the majority judgment in *Bachan Singh's Case* marks an advance, for it has upheld the tests which the majority in *Gopalan's Case* applied to punitive detention, thereby destroying the *raison d'être* for the theories propounded in the *Bank Nationalization Case*. If judicial courtesy has restrained Sarkaria J. from holding that the *Bank Nationalization Case* was based on a demonstrable and demonstrated error[22] it was not because Sarkaria J. was unaware of it, for in his review of the judgment of Patanjali Sastri J. in *Gopalan's Case*, Sarkaria J. said:

> "Rejecting the argument of the Attorney-General, the learned Judge held that Clauses (4) to (7) of Article 22 do not form a complete Code and that 'the language of Article 21 is perfectly general and covers deprivation of personal liberty or incarceration, both for punitive and preventive reasons.' [(1950) S.C.R. page 207]."[23-99]

It may be kindness to the judgment of 10 judges not to pronounce that judgment dead, while cutting off its essential limbs. But it is submitted that it is a disservice to the administration of justice and to litigants to leave a judgment outstanding when little of it survives, as our discussion has clearly shown. Further, the "comprehensive test" formulated by Sarkaria J. deals with a limited number of situations. It is submitted that for determining when an impugned law violates one or more fundamental rights, different tests are required by different situations. The reader will find the subject discussed in detail in paras 10.240 to 10.256 with reference to the judgment in the *Bennett Coleman Case* and he will find the several tests to be applied discussed at length in the present chapter. The dissenting judgment of Bhagwati J. in *Bachan Singh's Case* makes no contribution to the present discussion. It concentrates on considerations which, in his opinion, make the death sentence void under Art. 14 and Art. 19. His judgment will be discussed later, but it may be mentioned at this place that he has carried his new theory of Art. 14 to its logical *reducio ad absurdum*, for if wide discretion without guide lines makes death penalty violative of Art. 14, the wide discretion, without guidelines, in imposing sentences for other offences must make them equally void under Art. 14. In other words, the provisions of the Indian Penal Code become a dead letter.

SECTION II

Article 20

Art. 20: "person", "offence" defined

11.98 We have already considered the correlation of Art. 19 to Arts. 20, 21 and 22. We must now consider the three sub-clauses of Art. 20 which deal with three distinct, but connected, topics. Reading Art. 367 with s. 3(42) and 3(47) of the General Clauses Act, the word "person" in Art. 20 includes companies and unincorporated

---

[22] That the majority in *Gopalan* (Kania C.J., Patanjali Sastri and Das JJ.) held that Art. 22 was a complete Code when the majority held that it was *not* a complete Code.

[23-99] ('80) A.SC. at p. 909. Shah J. in the *Bank Nationalization Case* said that Patanjali Sastri J. had held Art. 22 to be a complete Code.

bodies[1] and the word "offence" means any act or omission made punishable by any law for the time being in force.[2] Art. 20 (1) deals with *ex post facto* laws, though that expression has not been used. It has been said by Coke, *Nova constitutio futuris formam imponere debet, non praeteritis* (a new law ought to impose form on what is to follow, not on the past).[3] The characteristic of a law is that it prescribes a rule of conduct by which persons are to govern themselves in respect of their civil rights, and are warned in advance of the penalties they may incur under the criminal law. However, a sovereign legislature has power to legislate retrospectively, though philosophical writers have denied that any legislature ought to have such a power.[4] As retrospective laws would ordinarily work great injustice, English judges have leaned against a construction which would make the law an *ex post facto* law. But retrospective and *ex post facto* laws are within the legislative competence of the British Parliament, and effect would be given to them if the intention expressed in the statutes was clear. However, Art. I, s. 9, cl. 3 and s. 10 of the U.S. Constitution provide respectively that "No bill of attainder or *ex post facto* law shall be passed" and "No state shall . . . pass any bill of attainder, *ex post facto* law. . . ." At the time when that Constitution was adopted, many persons understood the term *ex post facto* law to "embrace all retrospective laws, or laws governing or controlling past transactions, whether . . . of a civil or criminal nature."[5] However, in *Calder* v. *Bull*,[6] Chase J. said:

Art. 20(1): *ex post facto* laws

forbidden by the U.S. Constitution

Calder v. *Bull*: all retrospective laws are not *ex post facto* laws

"Every *ex post facto* law must necessarily be retrospective; but every retrospective law is not an *ex post facto* law. The former only are prohibited. Every law that takes away or impairs rights vested agreeably to existing laws is retrospective and is generally unjust, and may be oppressive; it is a good general rule that a law should have no retrospect; but there are cases in which the laws may justly, and for the benefit of the community, and also of individuals, relate to a time antecedent to their commencement; as statutes of oblivion or of pardon. They are certainly retrospective, and literally both concerning and after the facts committed. But I do not consider any law *ex post facto* within the prohibition (of Art. I, s. 9, cl. 3), that mollifies the rigour of the criminal law, but only those that create or aggravate the crime or increase the punishment or change the rules of evidence for the purpose of conviction . . . There is a great and apparent difference between making an unlawful act lawful and the making an innocent action criminal and punishing it as a crime."[7]

Our Supreme Court appears to have adopted the language of *Calder* v. *Bull* in *Rattan Lal* v. *Punjab*[8] when it said:

The principle of the above case adopted by our Sup. Ct.

"Every law that takes away or impairs a vested right is retrospective. Every *ex post facto* law is necessarily retrospective . . . But an *ex post facto* law

[1] *Maharashtra* v. *Nagpur Electric Light and Power Co. Ltd.* (1961) Bom. 508, ('61) A.B. 242, 63 Bom.L.R. 559 [referring to Art. 20(3)].

[2] *Maqbool Hussain* v. *Bombay* (1953) S.C.R. 730, ('53) A.S.C. 325.

[3] 2 Institutes 292.

[4] See Sedgwick, *Statutory and Constitutional Law*, p. 160, cited in Craies, p. 389. It is also stated in Craies that "the French Code contains a positive provision that laws are not to have any retrospective operation. '*La loi ne dispose que pour l'avenir, elle n'a point d'effect retroactiff*'."

[5] Story, *Commentaries on the Constitution II*, Sec. 1345, cited in Corwin, p. 316.

[6] (1798) 3 Dall. 386, 391, 1 L.ed. 648, 650.

[7] Cited and approved in *Phillips* v. *Eyre* (1870) L.R. 6 Q.B. 1, 26, *per* Willes J.

[8] (1964) 7 S.C.R. 676, ('65) A.SC. 444.

which only mollifies the rigour of a criminal law does not fall within the said prohibition (of Art. 20)."[9]

Art. 20(1) materially different from Art. I, s. 9, cl. 3 of the U.S. Constitution

11.99 Although Art. 20(1) embodies the underlying objection to *ex post facto* laws, and is designed to prevent a person being punished for an act or omission which was considered neutral or innocent when done or omitted, the language of Art. 20(1) is materially different from that of Art. I, s. 9, cl. 3 of the U.S. Constitution, and naturally our Article must be interpreted according to its terms. Art. 20(1) provides

"No person shall be convicted of any offence except for violation of a law in force at the time of the commission of the act charged as an offence, nor be subjected to a penalty greater than that which might have been inflicted under the law in force at the time of the commission of the offence."

Art. 20(1) applicable to acts done before the Constitution

11.100 In *Rao Shiv Bahadur Singh* v. *V.P.*[10] it was contended that the fundamental right conferred by Art. 20(1) was not available for acts committed before the Constitution came into force as the Constitution was not retrospective. In repelling this contention the Supreme Court said that the language of Art. 20(1) was wider than that of Art I, s. 9, cl. 3 and s. 10 of the U.S. Constitution, and what was prohibited was the conviction of a person or his being subjected to a penalty under *ex post facto laws*. Our Supreme Court said:

"The prohibition under the article is not confined to the passing or the validity of the law, but extends to the conviction or the sentence . . . The fullest effect must therefore be given to the actual words used in the article."[11]

This construction did not give a retrospective operation to the fundamental right thereby recognised because

". . . All that it amounts to is that the future operation of the fundamental right . . . may also in certain cases result from acts and situations which had their commencement in the pre-Constitution period. In *R.* v. *St. Mary Whitechapel*[12] Lord Denman C.J. pointed out that a statute which in its direct operation is prospective cannot properly be called a retrospective statute because *a part* of the requisites for its action is drawn from a time antecedent to its passing. The general principle therefore that the fundamental rights have no restrospective operation is not in any way affected by giving the fullest effect to the wording of Article 20. This Article must accordingly be taken to prohibit all convictions or subjections to penalty after the Constitution in respect of *ex post facto* laws whether the same was a post-Constitution law or a pre-Constitution law."[13]

This conclusion was further supported by the language of Arts. 20(2) and 20(3), for it could not be contended that the prohibition against double jeopardy applied only when both the occasions arose after the Constitution, or that a person accused of an offence before the Constitution came into force, could be compelled to be a witness against himself, if his case was heard after the Constitution.

---

[9] (1964) 7 S.C.R. *supra* at p. 681, *per* Subba Rao J.

[10] (1953) S.C.R. 1188, ('53) A.SC. 394; referred to and applied in *G. P. Nayyar* v. *State* (1979) 2 S.C.R. 816, ('79) A.SC. 602 [*held,* that s. 2, Anti-corruption Laws (Amendment) Act, 1967, merely revised the procedure which was in force when the offence was committed, under s. 5(3) of the Prevention of Corruption Act, 1947. Consequently, the amending section did not violate Art. 20.]

[11] (1953) S.C.R. at p. 1199.

[12] 116 E.R. 811, 814.

[13] (1953) S.C.R. 1188, *supra* at pp. 1199-1200.

11.101 What is meant by *"law in force" at the time of the commission of the act charged as an offence?* Art. 372 (3), Expl. 1, shows that "a law in force" means an enacted law even if it, or parts of it, are not in operation either at all or in particular areas. It is clear that such a law is not a law in force within the meaning of Art. 20, for, if the law is not in operation it cannot constitute any act a crime during the time it is not in force. In *Shiv Bahadur Singh's Case,*[14] it was held that "a law in force" must be taken to relate not to a law "deemed to be in force" and thus brought into force, but the law factually in operation at the time or, what may be called the then existing law.[15] These observations, taken by themselves, may be interpreted to mean that wherever a law is "deemed to be in force" it is not actually in force. But such a reading of the judgment would be incorrect, for it said later,

Art. 20(1): the meaning of "law in force etc."

Shiv Bahadur Singh's Case

Art. 20(1) does not apply to a law deemed to be in force

> ". . . the phrase 'law in force' as used in Art. 20 must be understood in its natural sense as being the law in fact in existence and in operation at the time of the commission of the offence as distinct from the law 'deemed' to have become operative *by virtue of the power of (the) legislature to pass retrospective laws.*"[16] (italics supplied).

the above proposition clarified

This is clearly right, for to allow retrospective laws to be treated as laws in force *at the time the offence was committed* would be to nullify Art. 20 (1). However, all deeming provisions are not retrospective because s. 24 of the General Clauses Act[17] provides that

> "Where any Central Act or regulation is after the commencement of this Act repealed and re-enacted with or without modification, then, unless it is otherwise expressly provided, . . . any rule, form or bye-law issued under the repealed Act or regulation, shall, so far as it is not inconsistent with the provisions re-enacted, continue in force and be deemed to have been made or issued under the provisions so re-enacted unless and until it is superseded by any . . . rule formed or bye-law made or issued under the provisions so re-enacted."

Such rules are actually in force, and the deeming provision is designed to prevent their ceasing to be in force by reason of the repeal of the law under which they were made. Thus, in several cases it has been held that the Metaliferous Mines Regulations, 1926, were laws in force within the meaning of Art. 20 (1), since they were kept alive after the repeal of the Mines Act, 1923, by s. 24 of the General Clauses Act.[18] The contrary view expressed in *In re Lingareddy*[19] is based upon a misreading of *Shiv Bahadur Singh's Case.*[20] The decision in *Thapar's*

---

[14] *Supra.*

[15] ibid. p. 1201; *Pareed Lubba* v. *Neelambaran* (1966) 1 Ker. 110, ('67) A.Ker. 155 [*held,* following *Shiv Bahadur Singh's Case,* that as the omission to pay the amount due on a bid at an auction was not an offence when the bid was made, prosecution of the petitioner under s. 74, Kerala Panchayats Act, 1960, violated Art. 20(1) and must be set aside].

[16] ibid. p. 1201; *W.R.E.D. Co. Ltd.* v. *Madras* (1963) 2 S.C.R. 747, ('62) A.SC. 1753 [". . . 'law in force' in Art. 20(1) postulates the actual factual existence of the law at the relevant time and it excludes the retrospective application of any subsequent law"].

[17] Or similar provisions of the General Clauses Acts enacted by the States.

[18] *Mysore* v. *P. C. Sarangapani Mudaliar* ('60) A.Mys. 245; *Rajasthan* v. *Pannalal* (1958) 8 Raj. 59, *Karam Chand Thapar* v. *Bihar* (1958) 37 Pat. 726, ('58) A.P. 378; affd. on this point in *Chief Inspector of Mines* v. *Karam Chand Thapar* ('61) A.SC. 838, (1962) 1 S.C.R. 9; *Ram Rattan* v. *State* (1959) Punj. 19, ('59) A.Punj. 69; *Orissa* v. *Iswar Das* (1960) Cut. 162, ('60) A.Or. 180.

[19] (1955) Andh.Pra. 497, ('56) A.A.P. 24.

[20] (1953) S.C.R. 1188, *supra.*

Case[21] was applied to notifications issued under s. 33 (1), Electricity Act, 1910, and it was held that they were actually and factually in force after the amendment of s. 33 (1) by virtue of s. 24 of the General Clauses Act.[22]

S. 5(3), Prevention of Corruption Act does not create a new offence

11.102 The Supreme Court has held that s. 5 (3), Prevention of Corruption Act, 1947, did not create a new offence. It merely prescribed a rule of evidence for proving an offence of criminal misconduct as defined in s. 5 (1) for which an accused person was already under trial. It was only when a trial had commenced for criminal misconduct by doing one or more of the acts mentioned in s. 5 (1) (*a*), (*b*), (*c*) and (*d*) that s. 5 (3) came into operation. Where there was such a trial, which necessarily must be in respect of acts committed after the Prevention of Corruption Act came into force, the application of s. 5 (3) in respect of pecuniary resources of property acquired before the Prevention of Corruption Act did not violate Art. 20 (1).[23] The language of Art. 20 (1) justified this construction, although in the United States the prohibition against *ex post facto* laws has been held to include the introduction of new rules of evidence in order to procure a conviction as is shown by the passage cited earlier.[24]

A construction involving a violation of Art. 20(1) should be avoided

11.103 If a retrospective construction of a law would violate Art. 20 (1), then, if possible, such construction should be given to it, as would avoid invalidity. In *Narottamdas* v. *M.P.*[25] the Supreme Court held that on a true construction of ss. 3 and 4, M.P. Minimum Wages Fixation Act, 1962, the new rates of wages for the past period became payable not on January 1, 1959, but on June 21, 1962, and the attack on ss. 3 and 4 based on Art. 20 (1) failed. Again, in *Kanaiyalal* v. *Indumati*[26] the Supreme Court held that s. 24, Bombay Rents, Hotels and Lodging House Rates Control Act, 1947, on its proper construction, did not attract Art. 20 (1). The section could not be construed to mean that the essential service or supply should have been enjoyed at some time in the remote past. The section spoke of the tenant having been in enjoyment of the essential supply or service and that it was cut off or withheld by the landlord; this imported recent enjoyment until the supply was cut off. Similarly it has been held that ss. 2 and 4, M.P. Motor Vehicles (Taxation on Passengers) Amendment and Validating Act did not violate Art. 20 (1) because they nowhere provided a retrospective punishment or penalty. If a prosecution were launched which had that effect, Art. 20 (1) would nullify the prosecution, but not the section[27] and the same view has been taken of s. 1, Rajasthan Municipal Boards Validating Act, 1956.[28]

---

[21] ('61) A.SC. 838, *supra*.

[22] *Poona Electricity Supply Co.* v. *State* (1966) Bom. 154, ('67) A.B. 27, 67 Bom. L.R. 534.

[23] *Sajjan Singh* v. *Punjab* (1964) 4 S.C.R. 630, ('64) A.SC. 464 [the Court referred to its former decisions in *C. S. D. Swamy* v. *State* (1960) 1 S.C.R. 461, ('60) A.SC. 7 and in *Surajpal Singh* v. *U.P.* (1961) 2 S.C.R. 971, ('61) A.SC. 583, for the proposition that s. 5(3) did not create a new offence, but merely shifted the burden of proof].

[24] See para 11.98.

[25] (1964) 7 S.C.R. 820, ('64) A.SC. 1667.

[26] (1958) S.C.R. 1394, ('58) A.SC. 444.

[27] *M.P. Transport Co.* v. *M.P.* ('63) A.M.P. 339, 343.

[28] *Milakhraj* v. *Jagdish Chandra* (1957) 7 Raj. 742, ('57) A.Raj. 293 [the protection of Art. 20(1) would be available if someone took it into his head to use the validating Act as a retrospective Act. The Act itself was not hit by Art. 20(1) as it nowhere provided for retrospective creation of offences].

11.104 As will appear more fully from a discussion of Art. 20(2) and (3), the use of the words "convicted of any offence", "the commission of the act charged as an offence" in Art. 20(1), of the words "prosecuted and punished" in Art. 20(2) and "accused of any offence" in Art. 20(3) has been held to indicate that the Article deals with criminal offences and not with civil liabilities; and a failure to discharge a civil liability is not an offence, unless a statute expressly so provides. Thus, in *Hutisingh Mfg. Co.* v. *Union*[29] the Supreme Court held that s. 25FFF(1), Industrial Disputes Act, imposed neither a prohibition nor a command. For a failure to discharge the liability to pay compensation a person may be imprisoned, under the statute providing for the recovery of the amount, e.g. the Bombay Land Revenue Code. But failure to discharge a civil liability was not, unless the statute expressly so provided, an offence. The protection of Art. 20(1) was available only against punishment for an act which was treated as an offence which, when done, was not an offence. Similarly, in *Public Prosecutor* v. *Ayyappan Pillai*[30] it was held that the new provision in s. 15(b), Madras General Sales Tax Act, did not violate Art. 20(1) for it only amounted to an alternative procedure which did not make an innocent act an offence nor did it impose a greater penalty than before. The recovery of a tax as if it were a fine did not impose a greater penalty than the two modes of recovery as arrears of land revenue, or by a suit on a debt.

The language of the clauses in Art. 20 shows that the Art. deals with criminal offences

11.105 Again, the penalty referred to in Art. 20(1) must be a penalty for an offence. Thus, in *Jawala Ram* v. *Pepsu*,[31] it was held that the unauthorised use of canal water was not an offence, and the imposition of enhanced water charge under rr. 32 and 33, Pepsu Sirhind Canal Rules, was not a penalty "for an offence". Similarly, in *W.B.* v. *S. K. Ghosh*[32] it was held that s. 13(3), Criminal Law Amendment Ordinance, 1944, which provided for forfeiture in case of an offence involving embezzlement, etc. of Government money or property, merely provided a speedier remedy than that of a suit, and it did not impose any punishment or penalty within the meaning of Art. 20(1).

"Penalty" in Art. 20(1) must be a penalty for an offence

11.106 A difference of opinion exists between the Allahabad and Hyderabad High Courts on the question, whether a person staying in India after the period for which he had been granted a permit to stay had expired, was punishable under a law enacted after the period of the permit had expired. The Allahabad High Court has held that if a permit had expired and a person had overstayed in India, he could not be punished for overstaying under a rule or law enacted after he had overstayed.[33] The Hyderbad High Court has taken a contrary view.[34] It is submitted that the view taken by the Allahabad High Court is correct. When the permit was granted, it was not an offence to overstay on the expiry of the permit, and the

Overstaying in India after the expiry of a permit

[29] (1960) 3 S.C.R. 528, ('60) A.SC. 923.

[30] ('53) A.M. 337, (1953) 1 M.L.J. 157.

[31] (1962) 2 S.C.R. 503, ('62) A.SC. 1246; *Mukandi Ram* v. *Executive Engineer* ('56) A.Pep. 40 [the levy of an enhanced rate for unauthorised use of water was not a penalty within the meaning of Art. 20(3). It only created a civil liability and a criminal prosecution for such unauthorised use, was not barred by Art. 20(1)].

[32] (1963) 2 S.C.R. 111, ('63) A.SC. 255.

[33] *Mohammad Shafi* v. *State* (1953) 2 All. 859, ('52) A.A. 921; *M. Shafique* v. *State* ('56) A.A. 108.

[34] *State* v. *Hyder Ali* (1955) Hyd. 214, ('55) A.Hyd. 128 (F.B.).

overstaying was complete as soon as the permit expired. If it was not punishable at that time, it could not, without violating Art. 20(1), be made punishable by a law or a rule subsequently enacted.

Miscellaneous cases under Art. 20(1)

11.107 In *Rameshchandra* v. *State*[35] it was said that assuming that an order of externment under s. 57, Bombay Police Act, 1951, could be regarded as a penalty within the meaning of Art. 20(1), it was imposed on the externee directly, or substantially for the tendency which he exhibited on the day of the notice under s. 59. It was not a result of previous convictions and the order did not attract Art. 20(1). In *M. P. Indra & Co.* v. *Union*[36] it was held that ss. 28 and 271 of the Income-tax Act, 1961, made it clear that the overall burden of penalty was not increased retrospectively in respect of defaults committed prior to the commencement of the new Act so as to infringe Art. 20(1). The maximum limit of the penalty was not enhanced by the new Act, and under it the I.T.O. had a discretion not to inflict any penalty under the circumstances of a particular case. If a penalty were inflicted, a question might arise under Art. 20(1). In *Om Prakash* v. *State*[37] it was held that where the alleged offence of offering a bribe had been committed in 1948, the accused could not be convicted under s. 165A, I.P.C., which was introduced for the first time by s. 3, Criminal Law Amendment Act, 1952, which came into force on July 28, 1952. In *Ganendra Kumar* v. *Narayan Chandra*[38] it was held that once a person had been prosecuted under the Calcutta Municipal Act, 1923, a greater penalty under the new Calcutta Municipal Act was not justified having regard to Art. 20(1).

Art. 20(2): *Maqbool Hussain's Case*

11.108 When can a person be said to be "prosecuted" and "punished" for an "offence" within the meaning of Art. 20(2)? That was the only question which directly arose in *Maqbool Hussain* v. *Bombay*[39] but Bhagwati J. considered it in the light of Art. 20(1) and (3), and his decision has been repeatedly referred to, and relied on, by the Supreme Court and the High Courts. The facts of that case were these: on his arrival at the airport in Bombay the appellant was found in possession of 107.2 *tolas* of gold in contravention of a notification of the Government of India dated August 25, 1948. The customs authorities took action under s. 167(8), Sea Customs Act, 1878, and confiscated the gold, giving to the owner of the gold an option to pay a fine of Rs. 12,000. Nobody claimed the ownership of the gold. On March 22, 1950, a complaint was filed before the Chief Presidency Magistrate, Bombay, against the appellant, charging him under s. 8, Foreign Exchange Regulation Act, 1947, read with the aforesaid notification. The appellant filed a writ petition in the Bombay High Court and challenged the prosecution as violating Art. 20(2). It is not necessary to refer to the history of the proceedings in the High Court as it is not relevant to the present discussion. The question considered by the Supreme Court was whether the appellant's prosecution was barred by Art. 20(2) having regard to the penalty of confiscation of gold, with an option to pay a fine of Rs. 12,000, inflicted on him. We have seen[40] that in our Constitution an offence means "any act or omission made punishable by any law

---

[35] (1955) Bom. 781, ('55) A.B. 346, 57 Bom.L.R. 560.
[36] ('65) A.Raj. 104.
[37] ('57) A.A. 388, (1958) A.L.J. 764.
[38] ('53) A.Cal. 562.
[39] (1953) S.C.R. 730, ('53) A.SC. 325.
[40] See para 11.98.

for the time being in force" and as s. 167 (8), Sea Customs Act, and s. 23, Foreign Exchange Regulation Act, made the act of the appellant punishable, the act constituted an offence. But in order to attract Art. 20 (2), the appellant must have been prosecuted and punished for the same offence when proceedings were taken by the customs authorities. Bhagwati J. said that Art. 20 (2) enunciated the principle of *autrefois convict* or double jeopardy, both of which were rooted in the principles and the maxims of the English law, namely,

". . . that where a person has been convicted of an offence by a Court of competent jurisdiction the conviction is a bar to all further criminal proceedings for the same offence."[41]

and in the ancient maxim "*Nemo bis debet punire pro uno delicito*", (that no one ought to be twice punished for one offence). The principle of *autrefois convict* or of *autrefois acquit* was also recognized in s. 403 (1), Cr.P.C., and in the Fifth Amendment to the U.S. Constitution.[42] These materials formed the background of the fundamental right under Art. 20 (2). It incorporated within its scope the plea of *autrefois convict*.

The words "before a court of law or judicial tribunal" are implied in Art. 20(2) from the words used in cls. 1 to 3 of Art. 20

11.109 Although the words "before a Court of Law or Judicial Tribunal" were not to be found in Art. 20 (2), the wording of the whole Article showed that there must have been a prosecution and a punishment in respect of the same offence before a court of law or a tribunal required by law to decide the matter in controversy judicially on evidence on oath, which it must be authorised by law to administer, and not before a tribunal which entertained a departmental or administrative enquiry, even though set up by statute, but not required to proceed on legal evidence given on oath. The presence in Art. 20 (1) of the words "convicted", "commission of the act charged as an offence", "be subjected to a penalty", "commission of the offence" and in Art. 20 (2) of the words "prosecuted and punished" and in Art. 20 (3) of the words "accused of any offence" indicated that the proceedings contemplated by Art. 20 (2) were of the nature of criminal proceedings before a court of law, or a judicial tribunal, and prosecution in that context meant an initiation or starting of a proceeding of a criminal nature before a court of law or judicial tribunal in accordance with the procedure prescribed in the statute which created an offence and regulated the procedure. The provisions of the Sea Customs Act, particularly of Ch. 16 relating to offences and penalties mentioned in s. 167, and the provisions of Ch. 17 which prescribe the procedure relating to offences, appeals and the like, showed that the powers of search, arrest and detention were given to the customs authorities for the levy of customs duties, and provision was made at the same time for reference to a magistrate in all cases where search-warrants were needed and detention of the arrested persons was required. Certain offences of a serious nature were to be tried only by magistrates, who alone could inflict punishment by way of imprisonment.

". . . Even though the customs officers are invested with the power of adjudging confiscation, increased rates of duty or penalty, the highest penalty which can be inflicted is Rs. 1,000. Confiscation is no doubt one of the penalties which

---

[41] *Per* Charles J. in *R.* v. *Miles* (1890) 24 Q.B.D. 423.

[42] ". . . nor shall any person be subject for the same offence to be put in jeopardy of life or limb."

the Customs Authorities can impose but that is more in the nature of proceedings *in rem* than proceedings *in personam*, the object being to confiscate the offending goods which have been dealt with contrary to the provisions of the law and in respect of the confiscation also an option is given to the owner of the goods to pay in lieu of confiscation such fine as the officer thinks fit. All this is for the enforcement of the levy of and safeguarding the recovery of the sea customs duties. . . . We are of the opinion that the Sea Customs authorities are not a judicial tribunal and the adjudging of confiscation, increased rate of duty or penalty under the provisions of the Sea Customs Act do not constitute a judgment or order of a court or judicial tribunal necessary for the purpose of supporting a plea of double jeopardy."[43]

A criticism of some observations in *Maqbool Hussain's Case*

11.110 It is submitted that in the result, the decision is correct, but two references in the judgment were unfortunate. First, the reference to the distinction between a judicial and an administrative act was wholly unnecessary, and the conclusion that in adjudging confiscation, the customs authorities were discharging administrative and not judicial functions was clearly wrong; in later cases the Supreme Court rightly held that the customs authorities were administrative bodies discharging *judicial functions*.[44] Secondly, the reference to Rs. 1,000 as the maximum penalty which could be inflicted was also clearly wrong. This reference was apparently made in order to show that whereas powers of confiscation were powers *in rem*, the penalty inflicted *in personam* was of a small amount indicating summary powers for protecting the revenue and not powers to deal with crimes where the penalty can be unlimited. The repetition of the same statement in subsequent judgments of the Supreme Court led various High Courts to hold that the maximum penalty which could be inflicted was a thousand rupees, a view decisively rejected by the Supreme Court in *Ranchhoddas* v. *Union*.[45] It is true, as Sarkar J. observed, in that case, that even if the maximum penalty were much larger, it would not convert an administrative into a judicial act; but it is difficult to resist the conclusion that the smallness of the personal penalty was emphasized in order to show that it was more for the protection of revenue than for the punishment of the offender.

Venkataraman's Case

11.111 *Maqbool Hussain's Case* was referred to in *S. A. Venkataraman* v. *Union*.[46] That case decided that an inquiry under the Public Servants (Inquiries) Act, 1850, was a fact-finding inquiry and the fact that the Commissioner appointed under the Act had some of the trappings of a judicial tribunal did not convert a fact-finding into a judicial tribunal. It was accordingly held that the dismissal by the President of the petitioner following on a report by the Commissioner did not prevent a criminal prosecution being launched against him in respect of the acts, for some of which he had been dismissed. Mukherjea J. gave as an example the case of a member of the Bar whose name may be struck off the rolls for professional misconduct in the exercise of disciplinary jurisdiction, though the professional

---

[43] (1953) S.C.R. 730, *supra* at pp. 742-3, ('53) A.SC. 325.

[44] See *F. N. Roy* v. *Collector of Customs, Calcutta* (1957) S.C.R. 1151, 1158, ('57) A.SC. 648 ["The imposition of the fine (under s. 167, item 8, Sea Customs Act) is really a quasi-judicial act . . ."]; fol. in *Leo Roy Frey* v. *Supdt., Dist. Jail, Amritsar* (1958) S.C.R. 822, 826-7, ('58) A.SC. 119 (". . . In imposing confiscation and a penalty under the Sea Customs Act, the Collector acts judicially"). The above decisions were treated as settling the law in *Shewpujanrai I. Ltd.* v. *Collector of Customs* (1959) S.C.R. 821, ('58) A.SC. 845.

[45] (1961) 3 S.C.R. 718, ('61) A.SC. 935.

[46] (1954) S.C.R. 1150, ('54) A.SC. 375.

misconduct might also involve a criminal offence. He said that if the petitioner's contention were correct, the lawyer could not be prosecuted for the offence, even though the authority inflicting the penalty of removal was not a competent court to investigate any criminal charge. In *Leo Roy Frey* v. *Supdt., Dist. Jail, Amritsar*,[47] it became unnecessary to consider *Maqbool Hussain's Case* because the court held that the offences under s. 120B I.P.C. read with ss. 23 and 23B, Foreign Exchange Regulation Act, 1947, and s. 167 (81), Sea Customs Act, as also under other sections with which the appellants were charged before a magistrate, were distinct and separate, for conspiracy was an offence under the Penal Code, but not under the Sea Customs Act. As the offences were distinct and separate, Art. 20 (2) was not attracted.

Leo Roy Frey's Case

11.112 In *Thomas Dana* v. *Punjab*[48] the petitioners were prosecuted while attempting to smuggle a huge amount of Indian and foreign currency and other contraband goods out of India. A Collector passed orders confiscating the seized goods and imposing heavy personal penalties on the petitioners under s. 167 (8), Sea Customs Act. On a subsequent complaint by the customs authorities on the same facts, the petitioners were convicted and sentenced by a magistrate to various terms of imprisonment under ss. 23 and 23B of the Foreign Exchange Regulation Act, s. 167 (81), Sea Customs Act and s. 120B I.P.C. This conviction was impugned as violating Art. 20 (2). By a majority of 4 to 1, (Subba Rao J. dissenting), it was held that in order to claim the protection of Art. 20 (2) it was necessary to show (i) that there was a previous prosecution, (ii) as a result of which the accused was punished and that (iii) the punishment was for the same offence; and unless all the three conditions were fulfilled, the Article was not attracted. The court said that it was necessary to understand the meaning of the word "prosecute", and cited the definition given in Webster's Dictionary,[49] and in Wharton's Law Lexicon;[50] and proceeded to cite the following passage from *Maqbool Hussain's Case*:

Thomas Dana's Case: the three requirements of Art. 20(2) stated

". . . and the prosecution in this context would mean an initiation or starting of proceedings of a criminal nature before a court of law or a judicial tribunal in accordance with the procedure prescribed in the statute which creates the offence and regulates the procedure.[51]

It is not clear from the judgment whether the Court accepted the definition given in Wharton's Law Lexicon, though the citation from *Corpus Juris Secundum* that

The meaning of the word "prosecution";

"The doctrine applies to criminal prosecution only and generally to misdemeanours as well as felonies. A former conviction or acquittal does not

---

[47] (1958) S.C.R. 822, ('58) A.SC. 119.

[48] (1959) Supp. (1) S.C.R. 274, ('59) A.SC. 375, fol. in. (i) *Bombay* v. *L. R. Malwani* (1969) 2 S.C.R. 438; ('70) A.SC. 962 (*Maqbool Hussain's Case* was also followed); (ii) *In re Bapanniah* ('70) A.A.P. 47, 55 [*held*, that the petitioner had not been prosecuted within the meaning of Art. 20(2) because the Dy. Collector, Central Excise, imposed upon him a penalty of Rs. 5,000]; (iii) *B. Prasad Mohan Lal* v. *I.T.A. Tribunal* ('70) A.A. 620, 624, 635 [*held*, that s. 297(2)(*g*) did not attract the provisions of Art. 20(2) as penalties imposed by Income-tax authorities did not amount to prosecution and punishment].

[49] (1959) Supp. (1) S.C.R. *supra* at p. 284.

[50] ibid. p. 285: " 'Prosecution' means 'a proceeding either by way of indictment or information, in the criminal courts, in order to put an offender upon his trial. In all criminal prosecutions, the King is nominally the prosecutor'." (Wharton)

[51] ibid. p. 285.

ordinarily preclude subsequent *in rem* proceedings, civil actions to recover statutory penalties or exemplary damages, or proceedings to abate a nuisance."[52]

would seem to suggest that the Court accepted the distinction between criminal proceedings ordinarily so called, and proceedings taken under laws designed for the protection of revenue, or other laws which provide for remedies *in rem* and statutory penalties exigible *in personam.* It is submitted that the decision is correct, but should be rested on the ground that a prosecution means "a proceeding by way either of indictment or of information in the criminal courts, in order to put an offender on his trial; the exhibition of a criminal charge against a person before a court of justice."[53] Under the British system of jurisprudence, adopted in India, a prosecution involves a prosecutor, and a judge cannot be a prosecutor and judge at the same time. The makers of the Constitution were familiar with the concept of "a prosecution" and "a prosecutor", and also with the basic principle that a judge cannot be a prosecutor and a judge at the same time. It is therefore reasonable to assume that in Art. 20 (2), the words "prosecuted and punished" mean "prosecuted before a criminal court or tribunal on a criminal charge by a prosecutor between whom and the accused the court or tribunal has to decide." The customs authorities are constituted investigators, prosecutors and judges with an obligation to act judicially, but this does not convert them into courts or tribunals such as are known to the English and Indian law. It may be added that in *Narayanlal Bansilal* v. *M. P. Mistry*,[54] Gajendragadkar J. said that according to the majority judgment in *Dana's Case*, "prosecution" in Art. 20 (2) meant a proceeding either by way of indictment or information in a criminal court, in order to put an offender on his trial.[55]

a proceeding by way of indictment or information before a criminal court

Dana's Case so interpreted in *Bansilal's Case*

Maqbool Hussain's Case followed in several cases

11.113 The view taken in *Maqbool Hussain's Case* has been taken in several cases. Thus, it has been held that the Sea Customs authorities confiscating goods under s. 187, Sea Customs Act, are not a court or judicial tribunal necessary to support a plea of double jeopardy.[56] Again, an order under s. 15B, Madras General Sales Tax Act, 1939, sentencing the accused to pay a fine and in default to suffer imprisonment, and the further order directing that the arrears of sales tax be recovered as a fine, is not violative of Art. 20 (2) as the liability of the dealer's property to be attached and sold for the recovery of arrears of tax cannot be regarded as amounting to a prosecution of the accused.[57] Similarly, it has been held that the

---

52 ibid. p. 292.

53 *Shorter Oxford Dictionary*, 3rd ed. 1959, p. 1603. The above definition mentioned by the Supreme Court in *Thomas Dana's Case* was followed in *Bachcha Lal* v. *Lalji* ('76) A.A. 393, 394 [*held*, that the indictment must be before a criminal Court. Proceedings started for disobedience of injunction under O. 39, r. 2A, C.P.C. were not criminal proceedings, and to such proceedings the bar of Art. 20(2) did not apply.]

54 (1961) 1 S.C.R. 191, ('61) A.SC. 29.

55 Having regard to the decision in *Maqbool Hussain's Case* and in *Dana's Case*, it is submitted that the decisions in *Pritish Dey* v. *State* ('52) A.Cal. 319, 55 C.W.N. 140 and in *State* v. *Chandra Bali Singh* ('60) A.A. 124, (1959) A.L.J. 682, are not correct. Punishment inflicted by jail authorities in respect of a jail offence does not make such authorities criminal courts or tribunals so as to bar a prosecution in respect of those acts.

56 *Boota Singh* v. *State* ('61) A.Punj. 21.

57 *In re Ramadoss* ('58) A.A.P. 707.

levy of penalty under the A.P. Sales Tax Act, 1957, for a default in payment of sales tax is not a "prosecution" under Art. 20 (2).[58] It has also been held that Art. 20 contemplated proceedings of the nature of criminal proceedings, and prosecution in that context meant an initiation of proceedings of a criminal nature. The first part of Art. 20 (1) prohibited a conviction, while the second part dealt with any penalty that might be inflicted by way of punishment. Penalties imposed under s. 297 (2) (*g*), Income-tax Act, 1961, could not be regarded as a punishment awarded for an offence. Such penalty proceedings were for the protection of revenue, and Art. 20 did not apply to them.[59] It has been said in *Mohinder Pratap* v. *H. S. Director*[60] that Art. 20 (2) was not applicable to departmental proceedings, where after a departmental inquiry, Government called for the records of the case and finding the punishment imposed inadequate, imposed adequate punishment; and in *D. A. Kelshikar* v. *Bombay*[61] that proceedings in connection with the prosecution and punishment of a person must be criminal proceedings before a court of law or judicial tribunal and not departmental or administrative inquiries, even though set up by statutes, if such inquiries were not required by law to be conducted judicially and on legal evidence. It is submitted that the decision is correct, but the reference to judicial trial and legal evidence would not convert a departmental inquiry into a "prosecution". It has been held that Art. 20 (2) is inapplicable to preventive detention, for such detention is not a prosecution.[62] It has also been held that the restrictions placed by the Madras Restrictions on Habitual Offenders Act, 1949, do not amount to prosecution and punishment under Art. 20 (2).[63]

Art. 20(2) not applicable to preventive detention and other preventive measures

11.114 The requirement of Art. 20 (2) that the person must have been prosecuted and punished is conjunctive and not disjunctive.[64] Article 20 (2) therefore does not apply, where for lack of sanction the prosecution was a nullity and the accused was discharged, for where an accused was discharged for want of sanction there was no punishment, and where a man was punished departmentally, there was no prosecution.[65] Similarly, a second complaint filed after the dismissal of the first, for the complaint's absence, does not contravene Art. 20 (2).[66] And where the petitioner was imprisoned for his failure to give security, a subsequent trial for the same acts for which security proceedings were started was not barred by Art. 20.[67] Article 20 (2) prohibits the prosecution and punishment of a person

Art. 20(2): the requirement of prosecution and punishment is conjunctive, not disjunctive

---

[58] *M. Seetharamaswamy & Co.* v. *C.T.O.* ('60) A.A.P. 451, rel. on in *Natwarlal* v. *Gujarat* ('64) A.Guj. 239.

[59] *R. Prasad Mohan Lal* v. *I.T.A. Tribunal* ('70) A.A. 620 (F.B.). The judgment stated that the Income-tax Act made separate provision for prosecution and conviction before a magistrate in respect of certain offences mentioned in the Act.

[60] (1956) Punj. 94, ('56) A.Punj. 81; *Ratilal Bhogilal* v. *Gujarat* (1965) Guj. 571, ('66) A.Guj. 244 (disciplinary proceedings are not a "prosecution").

[61] ('60) A.B. 225, 61 Bom.L.R. 1625.

[62] *Ramanlal* v. *Commr. of Police* (1953) 1 Cal. 89, ('52) A.Cal. 26.

[63] *P. Arumugham* v. *Madras* (1953) Mad. 937, ('53) A.M. 664.

[64] *In re C. Devanugraham* ('52) A.M. 725, (1952) 1 M.L.J. 550; *Gopalakrishna Naidu* v. *M.P.* ('52) A.N. 170.

[65] *In re C. Devanugraham, supra*, fol. in *In re Subramania Achari* ('55) A.M. 129; *Dattu Pant* v. *Advya Chari* (1956) Hyd. 355, ('56) A.Hyd. 127.

[66] *Sri Ram Ghei* v. *Sri Ram Kishan Das* (1952) 1 All. 244, ('52) A.A. 642.

[67] *Mathai Manjuran* v. *State* ('52) A.Tr.-Co. 556.

more than once for the same offence. It does not prohibit a second prosecution and punishment for an offence for which he was previously prosecuted and acquitted.[68]

The second prosecution must be for the same offence

11.115 The language of Art. 20(2) shows that the second prosecution and punishment which are barred must be for the same offence, and in *Bombay* v. *S. L. Apte*[69] this was explained to mean an offence whose ingredients are the same. As the ingredients of the offence under s. 105, Insurance Act, and under s. 409, I.P.C. were not the same, it was held that the accused were not punished for the same offence twice but for two distinct offences constituted or made up of different ingredients, and Art. 20(2) did not apply.[70] Offences may be different even though some ingredients of the two offences are common.[71] Thus it was held that where a person was prosecuted for trying to export illegally Indian currency out of India, his prosecution under s. 167(3), 8 and (37), Sea Customs Act, did not violate Art. 20. It could not be said that he was prosecuted for the same offence three times over, for the ingredients of the three different offences in those clauses were different.[72] Again, Art. 20(2) has no application where the law provides two punishments for the same offence. Thus, s. 7, Influx from Pakistan (Control) Act, 1949, which provides for physical removal from India in addition to the punishment imposed under s. 5, does not violate Art. 20(2).[73] Nor does it apply to an alternative punishment. Thus, it was held in *Loomchand* v. *Official Liquidator*,[74] that on a correct reading of s. 282-A, Companies Act, it did not provide for double punishment but only for an alternative punishment when default was committed, and consequently Art. 20(2) was not violated. It has been held that the W. B. Food Grains (Movement Control) Order does not contravene Art. 20(2) because it does not contain any provision that a person contravening the order may be prosecuted and punished more than once for the same offence.[75]

Offences may be different even though some ingredients are common

Art. 20(2) does not apply to continuing offences

11.116 Again, Art. 20(2) does not apply to a continuing offence.[76] However, it has been held that where a default in payment of an instalment of a licence fee constitutes an offence, the failure to pay such instalments in subsequent months does not constitute different offences, for the failure to pay an instalment is complete the moment the accused fails to pay on the due date. Consequently, successive

---

[68] *M. Dev.* v. *Tripura* ('59) A.Tri. 51.

[69] (1961) 3 S.C.R. 107, ('61) A.SC. 578.

[70] (1961) 3 S.C.R. at p. 118; this decision was relied on in *Manipur* v. *Thockchom, Bira Singh,* (1964) 7 S.C.R. 123, ('65) A.SC. 578, and followed in *Ranendra Nath* v. *Union* ('65) A.Cal. 434; *Ishodanand* v. *State* ('55) A.P. 396 (possession of fire-arms without a licence, and dacoity are two distinct offences).

[71] *M. M. Gandhi* v. *Mysore* ('60) A.Mys. 111 (*held,* that the offence under s. 161 I.P.C. and the offence of criminal misconduct under s. 5, Prevention of Corruption Act, were different). *U.P.* v. *Prabhat Kumar* ('66) A.A. 349 [*held,* that an offence under s. 25 of the Arms Act and the offence punishable under s. 411, I.P.C., were different. *Held,* further, following *Keshavan Madhava Menon* v. *Bombay* (1951) S.C.R. 228, 232, ('51) A.SC. 128, that recourse could not be had to the spirit of the Constitution in interpreting constitutional provisions].

[72] *A. T. Corporation* v. *Asst. Collector of Customs* ('64) A.Cal. 347, 354.

[73] *Ebrahim Vazir* v. *Bombay* (1954) S.C.R. 933, ('54) A.SC. 229.

[74] ('53) A.M. 595, (1953) 1 M.L.J. 514.

[75] *Indra Narayan* v. *W.B.* ('52) A.Cal. 61.

[76] *Saharanpur Municipality* v. *Kripa Ram* ('65) A.A. 160.

prosecutions for the failure to pay that instalment are barred by Art. 20(2). However, it has been held that an offence under bye-law No. 2 of the Municipal Board of Saharanpur read with s. 299, U.P. Municipalities Act, is a continuing offence, and if a person is prosecuted for having committed an offence during a particular period, there is no bar to prosecuting him again for committing a similar offence on some other date and Art. 20(2) and s. 403(1) Cr. P.C. are not attracted.[77]

11.117 In *Maqbool Hussain's Case* it was said that the pleas of *autrefois acquit* and *autrefois convict* which were rooted in the principles of "English Law" were recognized in India in s. 403, Cr. P.C.[78] The terms of s. 403 show that it affords larger protection than is afforded by Art. 20(3), for whereas Art. 20(3) applies only to a person who had been prosecuted and punished for an offence, s. 403 applies *also* to a person who had been prosecuted for an offence and acquitted. The doctrines of *autrefois acquit* and *autrefois convict* have been extended to cover the doctrine of "issue estoppel", and it is not surprising that the doctrine should have been first applied in India when s. 403 was invoked.

S. 403, Cr.P.C. affords a larger protection than Art. 20(3)

S. 403 and "issue estoppel"

11.118 In India the starting point of "issue estoppel" was the Privy Council decision in *Sambasivam* v. *Public Prosecutor, Federation of Malaya.*[79] In dealing with the facts of the appeal,[80] Lord MacDermott said:

Sambasivam's Case, and "issue estoppel"

"The effect of a verdict of acquittal pronounced by a competent court on a lawful charge and after a lawful trial is not completey stated by saying that the person acquitted cannot be tried again for the same offence. To that it must be added that the verdict is binding and conclusive in all subsequent proceedings between the parties to the adjudication. The maxim "*Res judicata pro veritate accipitur*" is no less applicable to criminal than to civil proceedings. Here, the applicant having been acquitted at the first trial on the charge of having ammunition in his possession, the prosecution was bound to accept the correctness of that verdict and was precluded from taking steps to challenge it at the second trial. And the appellant was no less entitled to rely on his acquittal in so far as it might be relevant in his defence. That it was not conclusive of his innocence on the firearm charge is plain, but it undoubtedly reduced in some degree the weight of the case against him, for at the first trial the facts proved in support of one charge were clearly relevant to the other having regard to the circumstances in which the ammunition and revolver were found and the fact that they fitted each other."[81]

---

[77] ibid.

[78] *S. 403*: "A person who has been tried by a court of competent jurisdiction for an offence and convicted or acquitted of such offence shall, while such conviction or acquittal remains in force, not be liable to be tried again for the same offence, nor on the same facts for any other offence for which a different charge from the one made against him might have been made under section 236, or for which he might have been convicted under section 237."

[79] (1950) A.C. 458.

[80] The appellant was charged with two offences: (i) carrying a firearm and (ii) being in possession of ammunition. He was acquitted of the second charge. At the second trial a statement alleged to have been made by the appellant, (which he denied having made) *inter alia*, to the effect that he was in possession of ammunition was admitted. On the principle laid down by Lord MacDermott (which is set out in the text), the Privy Council was of the opinion that the statement was inseverable, and was inadmissible as a whole. However, as it was admitted without objection, it was the duty of the judge to have told the assessors that the appellant had been acquitted on the second charge at the first trial, and as this had not been done, the conviction must be quashed.

[81] (1950) A.C. *supra* at p. 479.

Sambasivam's Case fol. by the Sup. Ct.

This passage was quoted with approval by our Supreme Court in *Pritam Singh* v. *Punjab*[82] which was referred to and followed in *K. B. Gosh* v. *W. B.*[83]—both cases under s. 403.

Issue estoppel accepted in Australia

11.119 Between 1950 and 1960 the doctrine of issue estoppel was accepted and applied in Australia. *Sambasivam's Case*, as well as the Australian decisions, were considered in *R.* v. *Connelly*[84] where the plea of *autrefois acquit* and issue estoppel were raised under the following circumstances:

Connelly, along with three others was charged with murder and robbery committed in a bank. Following the rule of practice[85] the charges could not have been contained in one indictment, nor could the two indictments, one for murder and one for robbery, have been tried together. The defence of Connelly was (i) that he was not there at all, and (ii) that if he was there, he was in no way responsible for the killing that took place. Connelly was acquitted of the charge of murder. At his subsequent trial he pleaded *inter alia, autrefois acquit*; in the alternative, issue estoppel. Both these pleas were rejected by the Court of Criminal Appeal.[86]

Connelly's Case: House of Lords and issue-estoppel

11.120 The judgments of the House will repay study as they contain a masterly discussion of the pleas of *autrefois acquit* and *autrefois convict*, as also of "issue-estoppel". Lord Morris of Borth-y-Gest referred to Lord MacDermott's observations in *Sambasivam's Case* and said that they were "in tune with important judgments in Australia":

Lord Morris of Borth-y-Gest

"Thus in *Marz* v. *R.*[87] it was stated . . . that the principle of issue estoppel is 'to treat an issue of fact or law as settled once for all between the parties if it is distinctly raised and if the judgment pronounced implies its determination, necessarily as a matter of law'. So too in *Brown* v. *Robinson*[88] it was said in reference to issue estoppel that it depends upon an issue or issues having been distinctly raised and found in a former proceeding: 'Once this is done, then, so long as the finding stands if there be any subsequent litigation between the same parties no allegations legally inconsistent with the finding may be made, by one of them against the other'."[89]

Lord Morris observed that though the provisions of *res judicata* applied to criminal cases where a verdict of guilt was given by the jury it was often not possible to deduce whether it involved a particular determination; it was not possible in the present case.[90] On issue-estoppel there was a difference of approach between Lord Morris and Lord Devlin. Lord Morris treated it as an application of the doctrine of *res judicata*; Lord Devlin found difficulty in that

Lord Devlin

---

[82] ('56) A.SC. 415, 420, 422 (*held*, that as regards the accused P.S.L., his acquittal on a former trial was tantamount to a finding that the prosecution had failed to prove the possession of the revolver, Ex. P-56, by him, and in view of Lord MacDermott's observations, the possesssion of the said revolver by P.S.L. could not be proved against him in any further proceeding).

[83] (1960) 2 S.C.R. 58, ('60) A.SC. 239. The lengthy and complicated facts of the case are set out in the majority judgment.

[84] (1964) A.C. 1254.

[85] Laid down in *R.* v. *Jones* (1918) 1 K.B. 416 C.C.A.

[86] The Court of Criminal Appeal certified that "a point of law of general public importance was involved in the decision which ought to be considered by the House of Lords. . . ." Connelly appealed to the House of Lords: (1964) A.C. 1254, *supra*.

[87] (1956) 96 C.L.R. 297; for a fuller quotation from the judgment of Dixon C.J. see *Piara Singh* v. *Punjab* ('69) A.SC. 961, 964. At the same page a quotation from an earlier decision of Dixon J. on issue estoppel in *King* v. *Wilkes* 77 C.L.R. 511, 518-19 is also given.

[88] (1960) 60 S.R. (N.S.W.) 297, 301.

[89] (1964) A.C. *supra* at p. 1321.

[90] ibid. pp. 1321-2.

concept and preferred to treat *Sambasivam's Case* as an extension or aspect of the principle of *autrefois convict.* As to the plea of *res judicata*, he said that in civil cases the plea was available to both parties, but no one had suggested that in a criminal trial the plea should be available to the prosecutor. Secondly, in a criminal trial, the accused had only to establish reasonable doubt about his guilt; was that doubt to be converted into a certainty by the application of the doctrine of *res judicata*?[91] This difference of approach has also been reflected in the decisions of our Supreme Court to be considered later.

11.121 In *Manipur Administration* v. *Bira Singh*[92] the Supreme Court was invited to reconsider *Pritam Singh's Case* on the ground that Lord MacDermott's observations had been dissented from by the Court of Criminal Appeal in England,[93] and secondly, that the common law principle underlying Lord MacDermott's observations did not apply to s. 403. The Supreme Court rejected these contentions,[94] and held that the provisions of s. 403 did not exclude issue estoppel.[95] When the judgment was delivered it would appear that the decision of the House of Lords in *R.* v. *Connelly* was not available, but the court expressed the doubt, which Lord Devlin had expressed in that case, namely, whether the doctrine of *res judicata* would apply to the prosecutor. The doctrine of issue estoppel was also applied in *Piara Singh* v. *Punjab*.[96] In stating the doctrine of issue estoppel the Supreme Court relied on the cases which we have already considered[97] and stated that the principle of issue estoppel was different from the principle of double jeopardy or *autrefois convict* embodied in s. 403, Cr.P.C. and that it was based on the principle of *res judicata.* Ramaswamy J. stated the principle thus:

Supreme Court decisions on issue estoppel after 1960

Principle of issue estoppel: *res judicata, per* Ramaswamy J.

"The principle of issue-estoppel is a different principle, viz. where an issue of fact has been tried by a competent Court on a former occasion and a finding has been reached in favour of an accused, such a finding would constitute an estoppel or *res judicata* against the prosecution not as a bar to the trial and conviction of the accused for a different or distinct offence but as precluding the reception of evidence to disturb that finding of fact when the accused is tried subsequently even for a different offence which might be permitted by the terms of s. 403(2), Cr.P.C."[98] . . . "for issue-estoppel to arise, there must have been distinctly raised and inevitably decided the same issue in the earlier proceedings between the same parties."[99]

He held that the principle did not apply to the present case as the parties were different.

11.122 Lord MacDermott's observations,[1] *Pritam Singh's Case* and *Gosh's Case* were referred to and followed by Hegde J. in *Asstt. Customs Collector, Bombay* v. *L. R. Melwani.*[2] However, he observed

Principle of issue estoppel: a facet of *autrefois*

[91] He did not pursue the question further and held that on the facts the doctrine of issue-estoppel did not apply.

[92] (1964) 7 S.C.R. 123, ('65) A.SC. 87. The case arose under s. 403, Cr.P.C.

[93] *R.* v. *Connelly* (1964) A.C. 1254 where the judgment is reported.

[94] The Court observed that in *R.* v. *Connelly* the Court had not dissented from the observations of Lord MacDermott.

[95] The Court cited the observations of Wright J. in *R.* v. *Ollis*, as also the observations of Dixon J. in *King* v. *Wilkes* and *Marz* v. *R.* referred to earlier. See para 11.120 of the text.

[96] (1969) 3 S.C.R. 548, ('69) A.SC. 961 (a case under s. 403, Cr.P.C.).

[97] See *f.ns.* 82 and 83 above.

[98] ('69) A.SC. *supra* at p. 964.

[99] ibid. p. 965.

[1] See para 11.118 of the text.

[2] (1969) 2 S.C.R. 438, ('70) A.SC. 962.

acquit, per Hegde J. that the issue estoppel rule was but a facet of the doctrine of *autrefois acquit.*[3] He held that equitable estoppel could not be invoked by the respondents because the proceedings before the Collector were not criminal proceedings. And the same view of issue estoppel was taken in *A.P.* v. *Kokkili Gada.*[4]

Art. 20(3): *Sharma's Case*

11.123 Although the question which directly arose in *M. P. Sharma* v. *Satish Chandra*[5] was whether a search and seizure of documents from a person against whom a first information report had been lodged with the Police, amounted to compelling him to be a witness against himself within the meaning of Art. 20(3), the Supreme Court considered the whole doctrine against self-incrimination and how far it was embodied in Art. 20(3). As American authorities were relied on, and considered by the Court, the Fourth Amendment, and the relevant part of the Fifth Amendment, to the U.S. Constitution are given below:

The doctrine against self-incrimination examined

The 4th and 5th Amendments to the U.S. Constitution

"IV. The right of the people to be secure in their persons, houses, papers, and effects against unreasonable searches and seizures, shall not be violated; and no warrants shall issue, but upon probable cause, supported by oath or affirmation, and particularly describing the place to be searched, and the persons or things to be seized. V. No person shall be . . . compelled, in any criminal case, to be a witness against himself. . . ."

The contention that search and seizure violated Art. 19(1)(*f*) was rejected, the court holding that search by itself did not affect any right of property, and though seizure affected it, the effect was only temporary, and was a reasonable restriction on the exercise of the right.

An historical account of the doctrine against self-incrimination (i) in England

11.124 It was next contended that though search and seizure were not mentioned in Art. 20(3) they should be held to fall within it by a liberal construction. In order to ascertain the intention of the makers of the Constitution, and the scope of the Article, the Court gave a brief historical account of the doctrine against self-incrimination, the effect of which may be stated thus: in England the doctrine had a historical origin; it arose from a feeling of revulsion against the inquisitorial methods adopted, and the barbarous sentences imposed, by the Court of Star Chamber in the exercise of its criminal jurisdiction. This came to a head in the case of John Lilburn,[6] and brought about the abolition of the Star Chamber, and the firm recognition of the principle that the accused should not be put on oath and that no evidence should be taken from him. In course of time this principle was extended as a privilege to witnesses against self-incrimination in giving oral testimony or in producing documents. The Criminal Evidence Act, 1898, made an accused a competent witness, on his own behalf if he applied for it and thus introduced a change, but as to oral testimony of

---

[3] ('70) A.SC. at p. 965, thus taking the view which Lord Devlin had taken in *R.* v. *Connelly, supra.*

[4] (1969) 2 S.C.R. 1004, ('70) A.SC. 771. Shah J. referred to all the decisions on issue estoppel which we have considered in the text. He found the true basis of the rule in the judgment of Dixon J. in *King* v. *Wilkes* 77 C.L.R. 511, 518, 519 and he quoted with approval Lord Morris's statement in *Connelly's Case* (1964) A.C. 1254, 1325 ". . . there is no rule or principle to the effect that evidence which has first been used in support of a charge which is not proved may not be used to support a subsequent and different charge." In allowing the State's appeal, Shah J. held that issue estoppel did not arise on the facts of the case.

[5] (1954) S.C.R. 1077, ('54) A.SC. 300.

[6] 3 State Trials, 1315.

witnesses and the production of documents, the protection against self-incrimination continued as before.[7] These principles, before their statutory alteration in England, were carried to America and became part of its common law;[8] but the language of the Fifth Amendment was considered by American Courts to be wide enough to cover all aspects of self-incrimination as administered under the English common law, including oral testimony of witnesses and production of documents. The doctrine was further extended, and it was held that unreasonable searches and seizures of documents fell equally within the mischief of the Fourth and Fifth Amendments[9] and the documents and evidence so obtained were held inadmissible in evidence.[10]

11.125 In India, s. 3 of Act 15 of 1852 recognized that the accused in a criminal proceeding was not a competent or compellable witness for or against himself. This provision was repealed by the Evidence Act, 1872. In the meanwhile, ss. 203 and 204, Cr.P.C., 1861, provided respectively, that no oath was to be administered to the accused and it was in the discretion of the magistrate to examine him. S. 250, Cr.P.C., 1872, made compulsory a general questioning of the accused after witnesses for the prosecution had been examined; and s. 345 provided that no oath or affirmation was to be administered to the accused. These provisions were continued in the later Codes of Criminal Procedure and were incorporated into s. 342, Cr.P.C. 1898. The only later statutory change so far, in this behalf, appears to be that brought about by s. 7, Prevention of Corruption Act, 1947, which made the accused a competent witness on his own application in respect of offences under that Act. So far as witnesses were concerned, s. 3 of Act 15 of 1852 also declared the protection of witnesses against compulsion to answer incriminating questions. Thus, *when the judgment was delivered*,[11] the Indian law as regards self-incrimination continued to be the same as the English common law as regards the accused and the production of documents, but was modified as regards witnesses by compelling them to answer incriminating questions and giving them immunity from prosecution based on their answers. **(ii) in India**

11.126 Having given a brief historical account, Jagannadhadas J. observed that after the doctine against self-incrimination was established in English law, and was followed in other systems of law, its **The utility of the doctrine examined**

---

[7] *Phipson on Evidence*, 9th ed. pp. 215 and 274.

[8] *Wigmore on Evidence*, Vol. 8, pp. 301-3.

[9] *Boyd* v. *U.S.*, 116 U.S. 616.

[10] *Weeks* v. *United States* (1913) 232 U.S. 383, 58 L.ed. 652.

[11] In 1955, however, s. 61, Code of Criminal Procedure (Amendment) Act, 1955, introduced a new section, s. 342-A, which ran as follows:

"342A. Any person accused of an offence before a Criminal Court shall be a competent witness for the defence and may give evidence on oath in disproof of the charges made against him or any person charged together with him at the same trial: Provided that (*a*) he shall not be called as a witness except on his own request in writing; or (*b*) his failure to give evidence shall not be made the subject of any comment by any of the parties or the court or give rise to any presumption against himself or any person charged together with him at the same trial."

utility had been questioned and the view had been expressed that it had a tendency to defeat justice.[12] He added:

"In view of the above background, *there is no inherent reason to construe the ambit of this fundamental right as comprising a very wide range.* Nor would it be legitimate to confine it to the purely literal meaning of the words used, since it is a recognized doctrine that when appropriate a constitutional provision has to be liberally construed, so as to advance the intendment thereof and to prevent its circumvention."[13] (italics supplied)

Full effect must be given to Art. 20(3), but it is not necessary to enlarge the range of Art. 20(3)

Though apparently paradoxical, these observations mean that the area within which the doctrine against self-incrimination operates should not be enlarged, but within its limited area it should be given full effect, and not be drained of its content by any narrow interpretation or by countenancing any evasion. The effect of these observations becomes apparent from the area within which the Supreme Court confined this doctrine. The Supreme Court rejected the narrow interpretation that the doctrine applied only to the oral evidence of a person standing his trial for an offence when called to the witness stand, by saying that there was no reason to confine the content of a constitutional guarantee to this barely literal import, for, so to limit it would be to rob it of its purpose and to mistake the substance for the sound. Art. 20 (3) used the phrase "to be a witness", and a person could "be a witness" not merely by giving oral evidence, but also by producing documents or by making intelligible gestures in the case of dumb witnesses (s. 119, Evidence Act) or the like. After observing that s. 139, Evidence Act, was not a guide to the meaning of the word "witness",[14] which must be understood in its natural sense as referring to a person who furnishes evidence, the Court said:

The meaning of the words "to be a witness"

"every positive volitional act which furnishes evidence is testimony"

". . . every positive volitional act which furnishes evidence is testimony, and every testimonial compulsion connotes coercion which procures the positive volitional evidentiary acts of the person, as opposed to the negative attitude of silence or submission on his part. Nor is . . . the protection in respect of the evidence so procured . . . confined to what transpires at the trial in the court room. The phrase used in article 20(3) is 'to be a witness' and not to 'appear as a witness': It follows that the protection afforded to an accused in so far as it is related to the phrase 'to be a witness' is not merely in respect of testimonial compulsion in the court room but may well extend to compelled testimony previously obtained from him. It is available therefore to a person against whom a formal accusation relating to the commission of an offence has

---

[12] The judgment refers to *Wigmore on Evidence*, Vol. 8, pp. 314-5; Stephens, *History of the Criminal Law of England*, Vol. 1, pp. 441 and 442. The observations of *Wigmore*, to which reference is made in the judgment, are as follows: "Indirectly and ultimately it works for good — for the good of the innocent accused and of the community at large. But directly and concretely it works for ill, — for the protection of the guilty and the consequent derangement of civic order. There ought to be an end to judicial *cant* towards crime. We have already too much of what a wit has called 'justice tampered with mercy'. The privilege therefore should be kept within the limits the strictest possible." See Sarkar, *Law of Evidence*, 11th ed. p. 1192.

[13] (1954) S.C.R. *supra* at p. 1086.

[14] **These observations were held not to be well founded in the majority judgment in *Bombay* v. *Kathi Kalu Oghad* (1962) 3 S.C.R. 10, 27, ('61) A.SC. 1808.**

been levelled which in the normal course may result in prosecution. Whether it is available to other persons in other situations does not call for decision in this case."[15]

Consequently, the guarantee under Art. 20(3) was available to the petitioner against whom a first information report had been recorded as an accused therein, and it would extend to any compulsory process for production of evidentiary documents reasonably likely to support the prosecution against him.[16] The question was whether search warrants for the seizure of such documents from his custody were unconstitutional. The American authorities were distinguished, first, because the Fourth Amendment expressly provided against unreasonable searches and seizures, and, secondly, because to make a distinction between legal and illegal searches and seizures, such as was made in the American cases, would be to import into our Constitution the provisions of the Fourth Amendment. Assuming that s. 94, Cr.P.C. applied to the accused,[17] the Court held that the petitioner's theory would lead to the conclusion that some of the cases provided for in s. 96 Cr.P.C. would fall outside Art. 20(3)—an anomalous distinction for which there was no justification. In Indian law, there was no basis for the assumption that the search or seizure of a thing or document was in itself to be treated as a compelled production of it. A search warrant was addressed to an officer, and not to the person whose premises or property were to be searched; it was not an act of the accused, but of a third person.[18] In any system, a power of search and seizure was an overriding power of the State for the protection of social security, and when the Constitution-makers did not subject such power to constitutional limitations on the lines of the Fourth Amendment, there would be no justification to import that amendment into a totally different fundamental right by a process of strained construction. Further, searches of the kind dealt with by the Court involved the interposition of a magistrate, and the issue of a search warrant was normally a judicial function. For all these reasons it was held that search and seizure did not involve a violation of Art. 20(3). In view of this decision it is submitted that the finding that a notice to an accused person to show cause why his premises

The doctrine applies to compulsory production of documents

Search and seizure authorized by law, do not violate Art. 20(3)

[15] (1954) S.C.R. *supra* at p. 1088. The proposition in the last two sentences of the above quotation was adopted by the Supreme Court in *Raja Narayanlal Bansilal* v. *Maneck Pheroz Mistry* (1961) 1 S.C.R. 417, 436, ('61) A.SC. 29. In *Rameshchandra* v. *W.B.* (1969) 2 S.C.R. 461, ('70) A.SC. 940, 946, Shah J. held that the said proposition adopted in two Supreme Court decisions gave the correct meaning to the expression "accused of an offence". He held that the decision of the Supreme Court in *Bombay* v. *Kathi Kalu Oghad* (1962) 3 S.C.R. 10, ('61) A.SC. 1808 did not prescribe any different test when it said that "the person accused must have stood in the character of an accused person". These decisions were referred to and followed in *Veera Ibrahim* v. *Maharashtra* (1976) 3 S.C.R. 672, ('76) A.SC. 1167 in which *Rameshchandra* v. *W.B.* was followed. Applying the meaning given to the word "accused of an offence" by Shah J., it was held that when the Appellant's statement was recorded by the Customs Officer, the appellant was not a person accused of any offence under the Customs Act, 1962.

[16] *Swarnalingam* v. *Asst. Inspector of Labour* ('55) A.M. 716, (1955) 2 M.L.J. 268; *Swarnalingam* v. *A. L. Inspector* ('56) A.M. 165, (1955) 2 M.L.J. 267.

[17] In *Gujarat* v. *Shyamlal* (1965) 2 S.C.R. 457, ('65) A.SC. 1251, it has been held that s. 94 Cr.P.C. does not apply to an accused.

[18] The Court observed that even in America there was a strong current of dissenting judgments making the same distinction, and Justice McKenna's dissent in *Hale* v. *Henkel* (1905) 201 U.S. 43, 50 L.ed. 652 was cited as an example.

should not be searched, amounted to compelling him to produce the document[19] is not correct. *Sharma's Case* in terms held that things could be seized from the accused, or from his premises, though he could not be compelled to produce them, and that compulsory search did not violate Art. 20(3).

The effect of *Sharma's Case*: conflict of decisions as regards the admissibility of finger-prints, hand-writing, etc.

11.127 If it was hoped to settle the scope of Art. 20(3), the judgment failed of its purpose. The contrast there drawn between seizing a thing from an accused and asking him voluntarily to produce it, and the statement that every positive volitional act which furnished evidence was testimony, and that testimonial compulsion meant coercion which produced the positive volitional evidentiary acts of the person, as opposed to the negative attitude of submission and silence, led to the most unexpected results, and to a sharp difference of judicial opinion. On the one hand it was held that to compel a person to give specimen hand-writing was to compel him to be a witness against himself contrary to Art. 20(3),[20] so that s. 73, Evidence Act, which enabled the court to give directions to any person to write words, or figures, for purposes of comparison, was void in relation to an accused person.[21] And the same view was taken of finger-prints obtained from the accused, under a direction of the Court under s. 73, Evidence Act[22] or in spite of the accused's protest.[23] On the other hand, it was held that the taking of specimen handwriting, or of thumb impressions under the direction of the Court did not violate Art. 20(3).[24] In *Subayya Gounder* v. *Bhoopala*[25] it was held that although an accused could not be compelled to produce evidence against himself, such evidence could be taken or seized from him provided such taking or seizure were legally permissible. The permissibility of identification by palm, finger and footprints; the taking of the accused's pictures after arrest; blood and urine tests, the use of emetic stomach pump, or similar device, for extracting ornaments swallowed, etc.; requiring the suspect or the accused to wear or try on particular apparel, or exhibit himself, or to perform physical acts during trial, and in

---

[19] *Swarnalingam* v. *Asst. Inspector of Labour, supra.* See however *In re Sornalingam* ('55) A.M. 685, (1955) 2 M.L.J. 269, where it was held that though the accused could not be compelled to produce any document or thing, the power of a magistrate to issue a search-warrant and of the Police to search the person or the premises of the accused, was not affected.

[20] *State* v. *Ramkumar* ('57) A.M.P. 73; *Farid Ahmed* v. *State* ('60) A.Cal. 32, 63 C.W.N. 901; *Tarini Kumar* v. *State* ('60) A.Cal. 318; *Damodaran* v. *State* (1959) Ker. 749, ('60) A.Ker. 29; *Kerala* v. *Sankaran Nair* (1960) Ker. 760, ('60) A.Ker. 392 (F.B.) [*held*, that specimen handwriting taken by non-voluntary positive act from the accused, is hit by Art. 20(3)].

[21] *Farid Ahmed's Case, supra.*

[22] *Doraiswami* v. *Palaniandi* ('56) A.M. 632, (1955) 2 M.L.J. 468; *Bhaluka Behera* v. *State* (1957) Cut. 200, ('57) A.Or. 172; *Brij Bhushan* v. *State* (1957) Madh. Pra. 263, ('57) A.M.P. 106.

[23] *Balraj Bhalla* v. *Ramesh Chandra* ('60) A.A. 157, (1959) A.L.J. 812; *Nazirsingh* v. *State* ('59) A.M.P. 411 [finger-prints taken from an accused while he remained passive, were not hit by Art. 20(3), but those taken under duress, were so hit].

[24] *In re Sheik Mohd. Hussain* ('57) A.M. 47, (1956) 2 M.L.J. 427; *Bhupendra Nath* v. *Union* ('59) A.H.P. 29; *Badri Lal* v. *State* (1958) 8 Raj. 356, ('60) A.Raj. 184 [the direction to give handwriting not hit by Art. 20(3); but on refusal, no action permissible to compel]; *Mahal Chand* v. *State* ('61) A.Cal. 123 [Art. 20(3) does not cover the taking of thumb impressions or footprints].

[25] ('59) A.M. 396; the same view had been taken in *In re Palani Goundan* (1957) Mad. 66, ('57) A.M. 546.

the presence of jury, were not hit by Art. 20 (3). And the same view was taken in *Pakhar Singh* v. *State*.[26] It is not necessary to discuss these cases because the conflict thus disclosed was resolved by the Supreme Court in *Bombay* v. *Kathi Kalu Oghad*.[27]

The conflict resolved by the Sup. Ct. in *Oghad's Case*

11.128 In a number of cases[28] a question arose whether a direction under s. 94, Cr.P.C. to the accused, to produce a document, attracted Art. 20 (3). It is not necessary to consider those cases because, in *Gujarat* v. *Shyamlal*[29] the Supreme Court held by a majority of 4 to 1 that s. 94 (1), Cr.P.C. did not apply to an accused.

S. 94(1), Cr. P.C. and Art. 20(3): s. 94(1) does not apply to an accused person

11.129 Again, questions arose whether s. 27, Evidence Act, ("s. 27") violated Art. 20 (3); whether the statements made admissible by s. 27 were hit by Art. 20 (3) if they were compelled; whether the facts discovered as a result of such compelled statements were inadmissible in evidence or were hit by Art. 20 (3). In order to appreciate the constitutional issues involved the relevant provisions of the Evidence Act must be briefly stated:

S. 27 Evidence Act, and Art. 20(3)

S. 24 makes a confession by the accused irrelevant if caused by an inducement, threat or promise, proceeding from a person in authority. S. 25 provides that no confession made by a person to a police officer shall be proved against the accused. S. 26 provides that no confession made by the accused while in the custody of a police officer, unless made in the immediate presence of a magistrate, shall be proved against such person. S. 27 runs: "Provided that, when any fact is deposed to as discovered in consequence of information received from a person accused of any offence, in the custody of a police officer, so much of such information, whether it amounts to a confession or not, as relates distinctly to the fact thereby discovered, may be proved."

The Allahabad High Court expressed the view that if the statements admissible under s. 27 were compelled statements, a doubt was cast on the genuineness of the fact deposed to as discovered in consequence of such statements, and the support which the statements received from the discovery of the facts was destroyed or put in doubt.[30] As the Court found third-degree methods in one case, and brutal ill-treatment in the other, the facts discovered as a result of the compelled statement became worthless, and the constitutional question under Art. 20 (3) did not survive. However, the Court observed *obiter* that the compelled statements *and the discoveries made as a result thereof*, were hit by Art. 20 (3).[31] In *Amrut* v.

High Court decisions

---

[26] (1958) Punj. 1747, ('58) A.Punj. 294 [*held*, that compelling a person to exhibit his body for identification marks on it or to procure finger-prints by force to establish identity, was not testimonial compulsion, and that the Identification of Prisoners Act, and ss. 5 and 73 of the Evidence Act did not violate Art. 20(3)]. See also *Peare Lal* v. *State* ('61) A.Cal. 531 where it was held that a test identification parade did not violate Art. 20(3).

[27] (1962) 3 S.C.R. 10, ('61) A.SC. 1808. See para 11.128 *et. seq.*

[28] *Md. Hussain* v. *P. F. Inspector* ('57) A.M.B. 68 [*held*, that s. 94 did not violate Art. 20(3)]; *Raman Kunhappu* v. *Ali Ahamud* ('57) A.Ker. 80 [*held*, that a magistrate commits a grave violation of Art. 20(3) in issuing notice to the accused to produce in court the document impugned as forgery]; *R. C. Gupta* v. *State* (1959) 2 All. 132, ('59) A.A. 219 [s. 94, Cr.P.C. violates Art. 20(3)]; *R. K. Ashere* v. *Tempton Jahangir* ('61) A.Guj. 137 [*held*, that the question whether s. 94, Cr.P.C. violated Art. 20(3) would depend upon whether the document conveyed the personal knowledge of the accused relating to the charge against him].

[29] (1965) 2 S.C.R. 457, ('65) A.SC. 1251.

[30] *Dhoom Singh* v. *State* ('57) A.A. 197, (1957) A.L.J. 330; *Amin* v. *State* (1957) 2 All. 110, ('58) A.A. 293. The above cases were followed in *Ghazi* v. *U.P.* ('66) A.A. 142 [the statement of the accused obtained by third degree methods contravenes Art. 20(3)].

[31] ('57) A.A. *supra* at p. 203; ('58) A.A. *supra* at p. 303.

Bombay[32] it was held that statements made by the accused, which were admissible under s. 27, would be hit by Art. 20(3) if they were made to the police as a result of harassment and after continuous interrogation for several hours, and accordingly the statements so secured were excluded.[33] In *Orissa* v. *Basanta Bag*,[34] the Allahabad High Court's view was referred to, and it was said that evidence admissible under s. 27 may be inadmissible by reason of Art. 20(3) if compulsion was established.[35] And similar views were expressed in *In re Mudugula Jermiah*[36] and in *Radha Kishan* v. *State*.[37] In *Jethiya* v. *State*[38] it was held that s. 27 did not violate Art. 20(3) and that it was not permissible to presume that the information given by the accused which was admissible under s. 27 was compelled testimony. But in the last four cases the observations were *obiter*, since it was held that the statements were voluntary. The result of these cases may be stated thus: they all held (i) that s. 27 did not contravene Art. 20(3); (ii) that voluntary statements were admissible in evidence; (iii) that compelled statements were hit by Art. 20(3). The Allahabad decisions further held that the things discovered as a result of such compelled statements were also hit by Art. 20(3). As will appear from *Oghad's Case* considered below, the majority judgment laid down as the law, the three propositions set out above, the minority finding it unnecessary to pronounce an opinion on the effect of compulsion in obtaining statements as the statements before the Court were voluntary. Since the Supreme Court did not deal with the effect of compulsion on things discovered as a result of the compelled statement, that question will be considered after considering *Oghad's Case*.

their effect stated

Oghad's Case and s. 27, Evidence Act

Oghad's Case: special bench constituted to re-examine some of the propositions in Sharma's Case

11.130 In *Bombay* v. *Kathi Kalu Oghad*[39] a Bench of eleven judges was constituted to hear three appeals which involved substantial questions of law as to Art. 20(3), in order to re-examine some of the propositions laid down in *Sharma's Case*,[40] which appeared to a Bench of five judges hearing one of the three appeals, to have been too widely stated and therefore required to be stated with more particularity.[41] The questions arising in the three appeals are set out in the majority judgment,[42] but the relevant questions were these: (1) whether a direction given by a Court to an accused present in Court to give his specimen hand-writing and signature for the purpose of comparison under the provisions of s. 73, Evidence Act, violates Art. 20(3); (2) whether by the production of the specimen handwriting of the accused, he could be said to have been "a witness against himself" within the meaning of Art. 20(3); (3)

The questions considered in Oghad's Case

---

[32] (1960) Bom. 664, ('60) A.B. 488.
[33] There is no discussion about Art. 20(3).
[34] ('59) A.Or. 33.
[35] ibid. p. 37.
[36] (1956) Andh.Pra. 173, ('57) A.A.P. 611.
[37] ('60) A.Punj. 294, 61 P.L.R. 912.
[38] ('55) A.Raj. 147.
[39] (1962) 3 S.C.R. 10, ('61) A.SC. 1808; fol. in *U.P.* v. *Boota Singh* (1979) 1 S.C.R. 527, ('78) A.SC. 1770, 1788 [*held*, following *Oghad's Case*, that taking of specimen handwriting does not violate Art. 20(3) nor does it amount to giving a statement "so as to be hit by s. 162 Cr.P.C."].
[40] (1954) S.C.R. 1077, ('54) A.SC. 300.
[41] (1962) 3 S.C.R. 10, ('61) A.SC. 1808.
[42] ('61) A.SC. *supra* at pp. 1810, 1811, 1813.

whether the mere fact that the accused was in police custody when specimen handwriting had been given, could by itself amount to compulsion, apart from any other circumstances which could be urged as vitiating the consent of the accused in giving specimen handwriting; (4) whether the impressions of the appellant's palms and fingers taken from him after his arrest, which were compared with the impressions on the glass panes and phials, were not admissible evidence in view of Art. 20(3); (5) whether ss. 5 and 6, Identification of Prisoners Act, 1920, violated Art. 20(3).

The whole Court agreed on two points

but was divided 8 : 3 on other points

The reasoning underlying the majority judgment: Art. 20(3) applies only to the compelled production of one class of documents

11.131 The whole Court was agreed (i) that the expression "to be a witness" could not be limited to the evidence given in the court-room but extended to compelled testimony previously obtained from an accused; and (ii) that the protection of Art. 20(3) extended to the compelled production from the accused of documentary evidence. But the Court was divided 8 to 3 about the nature of the documentary evidence the production of which could not be compelled, as also about other issues in the case. The majority judgment was delivered by Sinha C.J.[43] and the minority judgment by Das Gupta J.[44] The reasoning underlying the majority view does not clearly emerge from the judgment; but it is believed that the following statement brings out that reasoning: leaving aside opinion evidence, "to be a witness" in relation to oral evidence means, "imparting knowledge in respect of relevant facts by a person who has personal knowledge of the facts to be communicated to a Court"[45] and, subject to the rule against hearsay evidence, to relevant facts which he has heard; and "to be a witness" is to give such evidence. If an accused cannot be compelled to give oral evidence of this kind if it incriminates him, is there any reason why that protection should be denied to him if that very evidence has been reduced to writing, or is contained in a document? The inherent logic of the doctrine led the Courts to extend the protection of Art. 20(3) to that kind of documentary evidence, which, if it were oral evidence, would be protected. But is there any reason to extend the protection to a document in the possession of the accused which incriminates him, but which does not contain evidence of the kind we have mentioned above? The majority judgment answered the question in the negative, the minority in the affirmative. The majority judgment observed that s. 139 of the Evidence Act recognized the distinction between producing a document and being a witness, for it provided: "A person summoned to produce a document does not become a witness by the mere fact that he produces it and cannot be cross-examined unless and until he is called as a witness." This distinction was well known to the framers of the Constitution, and the majority rightly held that the observation in *Sharma's Case* that s. 139 was not a guide to the meaning of the word "evidence", was not correct. In support of the majority judgment, it may be added that just as Jagannathadas J. considered it relevant to point out that the words used in Art. 20(3) were "to be a witness", and not

---

[43] For himself, Imam, Gajendragadkar, Subba Rao, Wanchoo, Raghubar Dayal, Rajagopala Ayyangar and Mudholkar JJ.

[44] For himself, S. K. Das and Sarkar JJ.

[45] (61) A.SC. 1808, *supra* at p. 1817.

"to appear as a witness", it is relevant to point out that the words used are "to be a witness", and not "to produce or give incriminatory evidence". On this part of the case it is submitted that the majority judgment is correct. The minority judgment observed that literature was replete with illustrations which showed that "to be a witness" was merely to furnish evidence and in support it cited the following lines:

The minority judgment: "to be a witness" means to furnish evidence

> "Season your admiration for a while,
> With an attent ear, till I may deliver,
> Upon the witness of these gentlemen,
> This marvel to you"
>
> (*Hamlet*, Act I, Scene 2)

The context shows that Horatio, who utters these words, refers to the two gentlemen there present who saw the ghost of Hamlet's father on two occasions, and who saw it on the third occasion *with* Horatio. Therefore, if they were witnesses, it was because they were communicating facts within their personal knowledge. Again, one of the meanings of the word "witness" is, "one who is called on, selected, or appointed to be present at a transaction, so as to be able to testify to its having taken place".[46] It is submitted that "witness" in the sense of furnishing evidence means communicating matters of personal knowledge on matters relevant to the subject under inquiry.

Submission: the majority view is correct

The majority judgment and the admissibility of finger-prints, etc.

11.132 The majority judgment said that though "to be a witness" meant furnishing evidence, and included production of documents of the kind we have mentioned above, it did not include other kinds of documents, or the giving of impressions of the thumb, palm, foot or finger, or the giving of specimen writing, or the exposing of a part of the body by an accused for the purpose of identification. The framers of the Constitution intended to protect the accused from self-incrimination on the lines of the English doctrine, but they could not have intended to put obstacles in the way of efficient and effective investigation into crime. Further, they were aware of the existing law, e.g. s. 73, Evidence Act, and ss. 5 and 6, Identification of Prisoners Act, and they could not have intended that all this existing law should be rendered void. The reason underlying the doctrine against self-incrimination also supported this conclusion. That doctrine was designed to save the accused from being compelled by hope or fear to admit facts, or to deny them, contrary to the truth, and this could be done equally in respect of documentary evidence which embodied or contained the personal knowledge of the accused. But things like finger-prints, footprints, prints of the palm, or handwriting or measurements of the body could not, in the ordinary course, be altered, and they appeared even through disguises. Therefore, there was an additional reason for holding that "to be a witness" does not refer to evidence of a kind where a false statement incriminating the accused cannot be obtained from him through hope or fear. The minority judgment took the view that the evidence of finger-prints or handwriting or the measurements of the body did involve being a witness in the sense of furnishing evidence, but it was not hit by

[46] *Shorter Oxford Dictionary*, 3rd ed. 1959, p. 2441.

Art. 20(3) because the accused did not give evidence *against* himself, since such evidence was by itself neutral. It was only when such handwriting or mark or condition was compared with admitted or proved handwriting, mark or measurements of the body that an inference for or against the accused could be made. It is submitted that on the whole, the majority view is correct.

11.133 As to statements admissible under s. 27 of the Evidence Act, the Court held that they "are not within the prohibition [of Art. 20(3)] *unless compulsion has been used in obtaining the information*"[47] (italics supplied) Secondly, the mere fact that the accused was in custody at the time he made the statement did not make it a compelled statement, though that fact, coupled with others, might establish that the statement was compelled.

S. 27, Evidence Act and Art. 20(3)

11.134 The majority judgment formulated its conclusions in the following propositions: (1) "To be a witness" in its ordinary grammatical sense means giving oral testimony in Court. Decided cases have gone beyond this strict literal interpretation, and the expression now bears the wider meaning of "bearing testimony, orally or in writing, in court or out of court, by a person accused of an offence." (2) "To be a witness" means "imparting knowledge in respect of relevant facts by oral statement or a statement in writing made or given in Court or otherwise." (3) "To be a witness" is not equivalent to "furnishing evidence" in its wider sense, that is to say, as including not merely the making of oral or written statements by an accused but also the production of documents or giving materials which may be relevant at a trial to determine the guilt or innocence of the accused. (4) Giving the impression of foot, palm or fingers, or giving specimen handwriting, or showing parts of the body by way of identification are not included in the expression "to be a witness". (5) The fact that the accused was in police custody at the time when the statement in question was made, would not, by itself, as a proposition in law, lead to the inference that the accused was compelled to make the statement, though the fact of such custody in conjunction with other circumstances, disclosed in evidence in a particular case would be a relevant consideration to determine whether the accused had been compelled to make the impugned statement.[48] (6) The mere questioning of an accused person by a police officer resulting in a voluntary statement which may ultimately turn out to be incriminatory, is not compulsion. (7) To bring the incriminatory statement within the prohibition of Art. 20(3), a person accused must have stood in the character of an accused at the time he made the statement. It is not enough that he should become an accused at any time after the statement has been made.[49] *Oghad's Case* has been treated as settling the law that unless a statement was obtained or was used under compulsion, Art. 20(3) does not come into play.[50] Where the

Conclusions formulated by the majority judgment

Oghad's Case treated as settling the law

---

[47] ('61) A.SC. *supra* at p. 1816. The majority did not hold s. 27 to be unconstitutional, but held that it was inoperative where compulsion had been used.

[48] (1962) 3 S.C.R. 10, ('61) A.SC. 1808, 1816.

[49] ('61) A.SC. *supra* at pp. 1816-7 (the propositions as given in the judgment have been re-arranged in order to bring out their logical connection and have been slightly abridged).

[50] *B. Panda* v. *Union* ('63) A.Punj. 198; also *Ahmedmiyan* v. *State* ('63) A.Guj. 159 [where it was held that a statement made voluntarily under s. 27 does not attract Art. 20(3) and the mere questioning by a police officer cannot be compulsion

appellant's conversation with Dr. M. was tape-recorded by the police with Dr. M.'s permission, and the appellant's conversation was not extracted by compulsion or duress, but was voluntary, Article 20 (3) was not violated. At the time of the conversation there was no case against the appellant. Again, Art. 21 was not violated because there was nothing unlawful or illegal in tape-recording the conversation.[51]

Nandini Satpathy's Case: scope of Art. 20(3) *vis-a-vis* s. 161(2), Cr.P.C. and s. 179, I.P.C.

11.135 In *Nandini Satpathy* v. *P. L. Dani*[52] the Supreme Court considered the scope of Art. 20 (3) *vis-a-vis* s. 161 (2) Cr.P.C. and s. 179 of the I.P.C.[53] The Appellant was a former Chief Minister of Orissa and in the course of certain inquiries which were being made against her, she was called upon to answer certain written questions. Contrary to the express provision of s. 160 (1), proviso, of the Cr.P.C., namely, "that no woman shall be required to attend at any place other than the place in which the woman resides", the Appellant was called upon to attend at a Police Station, an action which the Supreme Court condemned as a clear breach of the law. That fact was also mentioned as relevant to the mental condition of the Appellant when called upon to answer questions. The Appellant refused to answer any question claiming the protection of Art. 20 (3). On her refusal to do so, she was charged before a Magistrate for offences under s. 179, I.P.C. for refusing to answer questions put by a person in lawful authority. Her defence that she was not obliged to answer questions as they were incriminatory was rejected by the High Court and the matter came before the Supreme Court in appeal. The judgment of the Court was delivered by Krishna Iyer J. for himself, Jaswant Singh and Tulzapurkar JJ.

Points of controversy formulated

11.136 The points in controversy were formulated by the Court as follows:

"1. Is a person *likely* to be accused of crimes i.e. a suspect accused, entitled to the sanctuary of silence as one 'accused of any offence'? Is it sufficient that he is a potential — of course, not distant — candidate for accusation by the police?

---

within the meaning of Art. 20(3)]; *R. K. Dalmia* v. *Delhi Administration* (1963) 1 S.C.R. 253, 381, ('62) A.SC. 1821, 1870; *Kalawati* v. *H.P.* (1953) S.C.R. 546, ('53) A.SC. 131; *Gujarat* v. *Shyamlal* ('63) A.Guj. 178; *Kamala-Shankar* v. *Gujarat* ('63) A.Guj. 312 [a statement made in an inquiry under s. 43(1) Bombay Co-operative Societies Act, 1925, is not covered by Art. 20(3) as the Act does not contemplate any accuser or accused person. *Narayanlal Bansilal* v. *M. P. Mistry* ('61) A.SC. 29 was rel. on; *Maqbool Hussain* v. *Bombay* (1953) S.C.R. 730, ('53) A.SC. 325 and *S. A. Venkataraman* v. *Union* (1954) S.C.R. 1150, ('54) A.SC. 375 were referred to]; *Collector of Customs* v. *Kotumal* (1967) 1 Mad. 665, ('67) A.M. 263 (F.B.).

[51] *R. M. Malkani* v. *Maharashtra* (1973) 2 S.C.R. 417, ('73) A.SC. 157, 163-4 (*held*, that there had been no violation of s. 25, Telegraph Act, 1885, as erroneously held by the High Court: ibid. p. 161).

[52] (1978) 3 S.C.R. 608, ('78) A.SC. 1025.

[53] *Art. 20(3)*: "No person accused of any offence shall be compelled to be a witness against himself."

S. 161(2), Cr.P.C.: "Such person shall be bound to answer truly all questions relating to such case put to him by such officer, other than questions the answers to which would have a tendency to expose him to a criminal charge or to a penalty or forfeiture."

S. 179, I.P.C.: "Whoever, being legally bound to state the truth on any subject to any public servant refuses to answer any question demanded of him touching that subject by such public servant in the exercise of the legal powers of such public servant, shall be punished with simple imprisonment for a term which may extend to six months, or with fine which may extend to one thousand rupees, or with both."

2. Does the bar against self-incrimination operate not merely with reference to a particular accusation in regard to which the police investigator interrogates, or does it extend also to other pending or potential accusations outside the specific investigation which has led to the questioning? That is to say, can an accused person, who is being questioned by a police officer in a certain case, refuse to answer questions plainly non-criminatory so far as that case is concerned but probably exposes him to the perils of inculpation in other cases *in posse* or *in esse* elsewhere?

3. Does the constitutional shield of silence swing into action only in Court or can it barricade the 'accused' against incriminating interrogation at the stages of police investigation?

4. What is the ambit of the cryptic expression 'compelled to be a witness against himself' occurring in Article 20(3) of the Constitution? Does 'compulsion' involve physical or like pressure or duress of an unlawful texture or does it cover also the crypto-compulsion or psychic coercion, given a tense situation or officer in authority interrogating an accused person, armed with power to insist on an answer?

5. Does being 'a witness against oneself' include testimonial tendency to incriminate or probative probability of guilt flowing from the answer?

6. What are the parameters of Section 161(2) of the Cr.Procedure Code? Does tendency to expose a person to a criminal charge embrace answers which have an inculpatory impact in other criminal cases actually or about to be investigated or tried?

7. Does 'any person' in Section 161, Cr. Procedure Code include an accused person or only a witness?

8. When does an answer self-incriminate or tend to expose one to a charge? What distinguishing features mark off nocent and innocent, permissible and impermissible interrogations and answers? Is the setting relevant or should the answer, *in vacuo,* bear a guilty badge on its bosom?

9. Does *mens rea* form a necessary component of section 179 I.P.C., and, if so, what is its precise nature? Can a mere apprehension that any answer has a guilty potential salvage the accused or bring into play the exclusionary rule?

10. Where do we demarcate the boundaries of benefit of doubt in the setting of section 161(2) Cr.P.Code and Section 179 I.P.C.?"[54]

11.137 The judgment is not easy to summarise accurately, for it is overloaded with quotations from decided cases and from writings on the psychological techniques of interrogating persons suspected of having committed a crime. Certain questions considered by Krishna Iyer J. were concluded by the earlier judgments of the Supreme Court, and those questions could have been simply answered. However, Krishna Iyer J. refers to the earlier judgments and holds them binding on the Court, after a long discussion of the questions involved.

Judgment not easy to summarise accurately

11.137A The judgment falls into two parts. First, the interpretation of Art. 20(3) in the context of s. 161(2) Cr.P.C. and s. 179, I.P.C. The second part is meant to give "concretising guidelines" to "the average Police Head Constable in the Indian countryside" who would have to work "the rules of jurisprudence in a branch like this". The guide lines occupy about 4 pages of the Supreme Court Reports. They include two quotations, one from the judgment of the Supreme Court of India and the other from the Supreme Court of the United States. The guide lines also include a digression on the absence of a public defence system in India and its consequent effect on an accused person under interrogation. He indicated a "pilot project" but observed that

[54] (1978) 3 S.C.R. at pp. 619-20.

"we do not mandate but strongly suggest the adoption of such a project". It is submitted that it must be a remarkable head constable in the Indian countryside who would be able to understand, much less follow, the guide lines thus given. If the guide lines were to be given, they have to be brief, stated in plain simple language, telling the head constable the things he should do and the things he should not do when interrogating a witness in the exercise of powers conferred on him by s. 160(1) Cr.P.C. It is not proposed therefore to deal further with the guide lines beyond saying that the whole judgment shows that the question whether testimony is compelled in the sense of being obtained under duress has to be determined on the facts and circumstances of each case. Consequently, it is difficult to give guide lines which would help a head constable, because, *ex hypothesi,* he has to evaluate certain factors in relation to the person whom he is interrogating, and these factors cannot be reduced to rule, because the weight to be given to any factor must differ from individual to individual and from case to case.

The "guide lines" — a criticism

The approach to the problem

11.138 The Court rightly observed that the problem to be solved was to balance the claims of the person interrogated not to be compelled or coerced into incriminating himself and the claims of the State that investigation into crime should not be defeated by the suspected criminal sheltering himself behind the alleged iron curtain of Art. 20(3), and s. 161(2), Cr.P.C.

Submission: discussion on historical background not necessary

11.139 It is not necessary to deal with the discussion on the "Constitution and the Criminal",[55] nor is it necessary to deal at length with the discussion which purports to put Art. 20(3) and s. 161(2) into perspective except to say that as to s. 161(2) the Court held that it was substantially the same as Art. 20(3).[56] It is submitted that the long discussion on the historical background of Art. 20(3) was not necessary, because the judgment itself rightly cites the judgment of Jagannadhadas J. in *M. P. Sharma* v. *Satish Chandra*[57] which traced the historical circumstances leading to the adoption of the doctrine against self-incrimination, and the criticism to which it has been subjected in recent times. Krishna Iyer J. quoted, *inter alia,* the following passage from that judgment:

"In view of the above background, there is no inherent reason to construe the ambit of this fundamental right as comprising a very wide range. Nor would it be legitimate to confine it to the barely literal meaning of the words used, since it is a recognised doctrine that when appropriate a constitutional provision has to be liberally construed, so as to advance the intendment thereof and to prevent its circumvention . . ."[58]

The content of "any person" in s. 161 Cr.P.C.

11.140 Krishna Iyer J. held that "any person" in s. 161, Cr.P.C. included "persons then or ultimately accused". This conclusion followed from the judgment of the Privy Council in *Pakala Narayana Swamy* v. *R.*[59] which was approved by the Supreme Court in *Mahabir Mandal* v. *Bihar.*[60] Krishna Iyer J. said that he gave the answer

---

[55] ibid. pp. 621-23.
[56] ibid. p. 623.
[57] (1954) S.C.R. 1077, ('54) A.SC. 300.
[58] (1978) 3 S.C.R. at p. 632. See paras 11.124 to 11.126 for the historical background of Art. 20(3) and for the conclusion drawn by Jagannadhadas J. in the above quoted passage.
[59] ('39) A.PC. 47.
[60] (1972) 3 S.C.R. 639 at p. 657.

he did because "the decisions of our Court which set the tone and temper of the 'silence' clause and bind us willy nilly".[61]

11.141 As to the meaning to be given to the words "accused of an offence" in Art. 20 (3), after a general discussion of the undernoted Supreme Court decisions,[62] Krishna Iyer J. accepted the view there expressed, namey, that normally a person stood in the character of an accused when a first information report was lodged against him in respect of an offence before an officer competent to investigate it, or when a complaint was made relating to the commission of an offence before a Magistrate competent to try or send to another Magistrate for trial of the offence. Again, following earlier decisions, Krishna Iyer J. held that the operation of Art. 20 (3) was not confined to evidence in the Court room but was available to a person against whom a formal accusation relating to the commission of an offence has been levelled, which, in the normal course may result in prosecution,[63] and which extends to any compulsory process for production of evidentiary documents which are reasonably likely to support a prosecution against them. As to the question what is "compelled testimony", Krishna Iyer J. rightly referred to the following passage from *Kathi Kalu Oghad's Case*:

The meaning of "accused of an offence"

"Compelled testimony"

"In order that a testimony by an accused person may be said to have been self-incriminatory, the compulsion of which comes within the prohibition of the constitutional provisions, *it must be of such a character that by itself it should have the tendency of incriminating the accused,* if not also of actually doing so. In other words, it should be *a statement, which makes the case against the accused person at least probable,* considered by itself."[64]

After setting out this passage, the Court proceeded to observe:

"The problem that confronts us is amenable to reasonable solution. Relevancy is a tendency to make a fact probable. Crimination is a tendency to make guilt probable. Confession is a potency to make crime conclusive. The taint of tendency, under Art. 20(3) and section 161(1), is more or less the same. It is not a remote, recondite, freak or fanciful inference but a reasonable, real, material or probable deduction. This governing test holds good, it is pragmatic, for you *feel* the effect, its guilty portent, fairly clearly."[65]

Finally, as to the compelled testimony, Krishna Iyer J. quoted the following passage from *Oghad's Case*:

"In order to bring the evidence within the inhibition of cl. (3) of Art. 20 it must be shown not only that the person making the statement was an accused at the time he made it and that it had a material bearing on the criminality of the maker of the statement, but also that he was compelled to make that statement. 'Compulsion' in the context, must mean what in law is called 'duress'."[66]

Krishna Iyer J. gave the definition of "duress" from Jowitt's *Dictionary of English Law* and said that the question must be considered carefully against the background of circumstances disclosed in each case. It may be added that the most important part of the judgment is that which emphasizes the fact that compelled testimony is not limited to physical torture or coercion, but extends also to tech-

[61] (1978) 3 S.C.R. at p. 632.

[62] *Raja Narayanlal Bansilal* v. *Maneck Phiroz Mistry* (1961) 1 S.C.R. 417; *Bombay* v. *Kathi Kalu Oghad* (1962) 3 S.C.R. 10; *Ramesh Chandra Mehta* v. *W.B.* (1969) 2 S.C.R. 461, and *Bhagwandas Goenka* v. *Union* Cr.A.Nos. 131-132/61 dt. 20.9.1963 (Unreported).

[63] (1978) 3 S.C.R. at p. 638.

[64] ibid. p. 641.

[65] ibid.

[66] ibid. p. 642.

niques of psychological interrogation which can cause mental torture or mental compulsion in a person subjected to such interrogation.

A.P.G. & S.M. Assn. v. Union

11.142 In *A.P.G. & S.M. Assn.* v. *Union*[67] the Supreme Court held that ss. 13 (3) and 19 (1) of the Prevention of Food Adulteration Act did not contravene Art. 20 (3). S. 19 (1) provided that a plea by a vendor, prosecuted for selling adulterated or misbranded articles of food, that he was ignorant of its nature, substance, or quality, shall not be a defence. S. 19 (1) did not violate Art. 20 (3), for the vendor when charged with an offence was not thereby compelled to be a witness against himself.[68] S. 13 (3) made the report of the Director of Central Food Laboratory conclusive evidence of the facts stated therein. "It is difficult to appreciate how [s. 13 (3)] compels the vendor charged with an offence under the Act to be a witness against himself."[69]

Art. 20(3) and evidence illegally obtained

11.143 Can evidence illegally obtained be admitted in evidence? Can such evidence be objected to as contravening Art. 20 (3) or Art. 21? Now, before a person can invoke Art. 20 (3), he must establish that he is accused of an offence, that is, that a formal accusation of an offence had been made against him,[70] at the time when he was compelled to be a witness, that is, to give oral or written testimony conveying his personal knowledge about relevant facts which would incriminate him. Again, if he invokes Art. 20 (3) against "illegally obtained" evidence, he must prove that it was illegally obtained. It is necessary to say this, because in the Supreme Court decisions where "illegally" obtained evidence was objected to as contravening Art. 20 (3), the circumstances necessary for invoking Art. 20 (3) were absent.

Art. 20(3) could not be invoked in the following cases:

Yusuf Ali v. Maharashtra

(*a*) In *Yusuf Ali* v. *Maharashtra*,[71] a conversation between the appellant (the accused) and one Shaikh, who had complained that a bribe had been offered to him by the accused, was tape-recorded in an adjoining room. The police were not present in the room where the conversation took place, but they were in the adjoining room, where, unknown to the appellant, the conversation was being tape-recorded. Bachawat J. held that though the conversation was tape recorded by deception, the appellant's conversation was not compelled, for he was free to speak or not to speak. Article 20(3) did not apply because the testimony was not compelled.[72] Bachawat J. added: "The fact that the tape recording was done without his knowledge *is not of itself* an objection to its admissibility in evidence."[73] (italics supplied)

Magraj Patodia's Case

(*b*) *Magraj Patodia* v. *R. K. Birla*[74] related to an election petition. In connection with a file produced before the court by a witness, Hegde J. observed: "He seems to be a hired witness. But the fact that the document was procured by improper or even illegal means would not be a bar to its admissibility if it is relevant and its genuineness proved."[75] It is clear that Art. 20(3) was not invoked, because there was no accusation and no accused to invoke it.

---

[67] (1971) 1 S.C.R. 166, ('71) A.SC. 2346.

[68] ('71) A.SC. at p. 2351.

[69] ibid. pp. 2351-2.

[70] In *Ramesh Chandra* v. *W.B.* ('70) A.SC. 940, 948, (1969) 2 S.C.R. 461, Shah J. said that this test had been adopted in *Sharma's Case* (1954) S.C.R. 1077, ('54) A.SC. 300 and in *Bansilal's Case* (1961) 1 S.C.R. 417, ('61) A.SC. 29, and that the words used in *Oghad's Case* "the person accused must have stood in the character of an accused person" did not prescribe any different test. Shah J. added: "Normally a person stands in the character of an accused when a First Information Report is lodged against him in respect of an offence, before an offence can be investigated against him, or when a complaint is made relating to the commission of an offence before a Magistrate competent to try or send to another Magistrate for trial of the offence."

[71] (1967) 3 S.C.R. 720, ('68) A.SC. 147.

[72] ('68) A.SC. *supra* at p. 150.

[73] ibid.

[74] (1971) 2 S.C.R. 118, ('71) A.SC. 1295.

[75] ('71) A.SC. *supra* at p. 1303.

R.M. Malkani's Case

(c) In *R. M. Malkani* v. *Maharashtra*[76] a telephone conversation between the appellant and Dr. M. was tape-recorded by a police officer by attaching the tape recording instrument to the telephone instrument with Dr. M.'s authority. The admission of the tape recording in evidence was objected to on the ground that recording was illegal, since it was in contravention of s. 25 of the Telegraph Act, and also because such admission violated Art. 20(3). Rejecting these contentions, the Supreme Court held that the tape recording was not illegal;[77] that when the recording was made "there was no case against the appellant." "He was not compelled to speak or confess."[78] There was, therefore, no scope for invoking Art. 20(3). No doubt as to the contention that the evidence secured by the tape recording was illegally obtained, Ray J. observed that there was warrant for the proposition that even if the evidence were illegally obtained it was admissible. He referred to the cases we have considered above in this para and to the undernoted cases.[79] However, it is clear that the contentions as to illegality and violation of Art. 20(3) did not survive.

Pooran Mal's Case

(d) In *Pooran Mal* v. *Director of Inspection*,[80] the petitioner contended, *inter alia*, that evidence obtained by a search which was alleged to be illegal, because it was said to contravene s. 132 of the Income-tax Act, was inadmissible in evidence. The petitioner *did not impugn the validity of any section of the Evidence Act*, and the petitioner's counsel "conceded that there was no specific Article of the Constitution prohibiting the admission of evidence obtained by illegal search and seizure." He appealed to the "spirit of the Constitution as rendering such evidence inadmissible"[81] and to certain American cases. It will be seen that Art. 20(3) was not invoked obviously because Pooran Mal had not been accused of any offence. However, Palekar J. said as the Evidence Act made relevancy the only test of admissibility and did not exclude relevant evidence on the ground of illegal search, it could not be rejected because of the supposed spirit of our Constitution nor by straining the language of Art. 20(3) of our Constitution in view of the decision in *Sharma's Case*. Palekar J. said that the Indian law of Evidence was based on the English law, and cited decisions to show that evidence illegally obtained was admissible in evidence if it was relevant.[82]

Therefore, in none of the cases considered above, did the conditions for invoking Art. 20 (3) or Art. 21 exist.

Sharma's Case: legal and illegal search distinguished

11.144 All that *Sharma's Case* decided was that a search and seizure carried out according to law did not violate Art. 20 (3), and in arriving at this conclusion the Court emphasized the fact that ordinarily search and seizure had to be authorized by a judicial officer. Nor did *Sharma's Case* deal with the question whether documents illegally seized could be admitted in evidence. On the contrary, Jagannathadas J. distinguished *Boyd* v. *U.S.*[83] by saying:

"The case, therefore, does not lend support for any general doctrine that a search and seizure in all circumstances is tantamount to a compelled production in violation of the Fifth Amendment. That decision itself expressly recognizes the legality of various kinds of searches and indeed the Fourth Amendment itself shows it. Thus what that decision really established was that the obtaining of incriminating evidence by illegal search and seizure is tantamount to the violation of the Fifth Amendment. It was in this light that subsequent cases have also understood this decision. [See *Felix Gouled* v. *U.S.*[84]]."[85]

---

[76] (1973) 2 S.C.R. 417, ('73) A.SC. 157.
[77] ('73) A.SC. *supra* at p. 161. [78] ibid. p. 164.
[79] ibid. p. 162: [*Jones* v. *Owen* (1870) 34 J.P. 759; *Kuruma* v. *R.* (1955) A.C. 197 (P.C.)]; ibid. p. 163: [*R.* v. *Maqsud Ali* (1965) 2 All E.R. 464].
[80] (1974) 2 S.C.R. 704, ('74) A.SC. 348.
[81] ('74) A.SC. *supra* at p. 360. This argument was rejected by quoting the observations of Kania C.J. in *Gopalan's Case* set out in para 3.1(6) of the text.
[82] ibid. pp. 361-3. [83] 116 U.S. 616; 29 L.ed. 746.
[84] 255 U.S. 285; 65 L.ed. 647 at 651 and 653.
[85] (1954) S.C.R. *supra* at p. 1091.

Oghad's Case and s. 27, Evidence Act

11.145 It is submitted that *Oghad's Case* saved the validity of s. 27 by holding that evidence rendered admissible under that section would be hit by Art. 20(3) and rendered inadmissible only if the oral statement (i) was made by a person who stood in the position of an accused when he made the statement; (ii) that it imparted his personal knowledge in respect of relevant facts to be communicated to the Court and (iii) if he was compelled to make the statement whether before or at the trial. And statements of the kind in (ii) above which, if made orally, would be protected under Art. 20(3), would also be protected if contained in a document. Such a document would not be admissible if he was compelled out of court to hand it over, and it cannot be admitted under s. 27 as a thing discovered in consequence of the accused's statement. Nor can a court compel the accused in course of his trial to put such a document in evidence. *Sharma's Case* did not decide that a document whose production a trial court could not compel, could be seized under the order of a magistrate and *be given in evidence.* If a document obtained by a legal search and seizure cannot be admitted in evidence, *a fortiori* the same document obtained by an illegal search cannot be admitted in evidence. It is little to the point to say that the Evidence Act makes relevance the test of admissibility, for as we have seen, Art. 20(3) overrides the Evidence Act to the extent mentioned above. So far the matter is clear.

Three situations *vis-a-vis* incriminating *real* evidence

11.146 But what is the position in the following situations?

(*a*) *X* is found in possession of large number of counterfeit currency notes and is charged with counterfeiting currency notes and in the alternative with using counterfeit currency notes knowing them to be counterfeit. All attempts at discovering the counterfeiting machine having failed, the accused under torture by the Police makes the following statement: "I counterfeited currency notes and the counterfeiting machinery is concealed within the basement of the house where I live". The counterfeiting machine is found at the place indicated.

(*b*) The facts are the same as in (*a*) above, but instead of obtaining information by torture the Police illegally broke into one of several houses occupied by the accused where they found the counterfeiting machine.

(*c*) The facts are the same as in case (*b*) above, but instead of breaking into the house, the Police obtained a warrant to search it from a duly authorized Magistrate, and the machine was found, and seized under the warrant which authorised such seizure.

Submissions: Evidence in situation (*c*) admissible; in situations (*a*) and (*b*) should be rejected

11.147 As to the questions posed in para 11.146 above, (i) The situation in para 11.146 (*c*) presents no difficulty. *Sharma's Case* shows that a legal search and seizure does not contravene Art. 20(3), although the production of a thing in court, like a counterfeiting machine, may be an incriminating fact against the accused. Further, *Oghad's Case* shows that when the machine is admitted in evidence the accused has not been compelled to be a witness against himself.

(ii) Situations (*a*) and (*b*) in para 11.146 above raise serious difficulties. As to situation (*a*), there can be no doubt that the statements made under torture, which led to the discovery of the counterfeiting machine, are hit by Art. 20(3) and must be excluded from evidence because of the protection conferred on the accused by Art. 20 (3). However, can the counterfeiting machine be admitted in evidence? We have seen that Art. 20 confers a fundamental right which secures the freedom of a person by providing what *shall not be done to him.* Article 20 (3) by its terms protects a person charged with committing crime; and protects him from being compelled to give evidence, or produce documents, which may incriminate him[86] and secure his conviction. This protection is strengthened by Art. 21 which provides that no person shall be deprived of life or liberty except according to procedure established by law. Is the protection given by Art. 20 (3) to the accused by excluding evidence of statements extracted by torture[87] to be nullified by admitting the incriminating real evidence obtained as a result of evidence hit by Art. 20 (3)? It is submitted that the answer must be in the negative. First, to admit real evidence incriminating the accused, which evidence was obtained by the criminal conduct of the Police[88] would not only nullify the protection of Art. 20 (3) but would concede to crime and unlawful conduct what the Constitution denies to law and law courts, namely, to compel the accused to give incriminating testimony. Secondly, in such a situation, evidence of the counterfeiting machine is brought before the Court *contrary to the procedure established by law.* For, the procedure involved in a criminal trial does not consist merely of the Evidence Act, which relates to the relevance and admissibility of evidence. The Criminal Procedure Code contains elaborate provisions for compelling the production of things, including the power to seize things which can then be produced and exhibited at the trial. None of these provisions authorize the use of criminal methods to obtain the production of things; in fact such methods must be treated as forbidden, for they are made punishable by law. Thirdly, to allow the law enforcement agencies to become law-breakers would breed disrespect for the law, as was forcibly pointed out by the U.S. Supreme Court in the case mentioned at the end of the next paragraph. (iii) As to situation (*b*) in para 11.146 above, the first reason for rejecting such evidence given in (ii) above does not apply. But the second and third reasons given there directly apply, and, it is submitted that they are sufficient to secure the rejection of the real evidence obtained by house-breaking which is a crime.

Submissions in 11.147 (ii) and (iii) supported by decisions of U.S. Sup. Ct.

11.148 The submissions made in para 11.147 (ii) and (iii) above and the reasons underlying the submission are supported by the following history of the decisions of the U.S. Supreme Court relating to illegal search and seizure. It is outside the scope of this book to go into the details of the controversy in the United States on the question whether evidence obtained as a result of search and seizure which violate the 4th Amendment could be admitted against the accused. But the following brief account may be given: in *Adams* v. *New York*[89] it was held that the use of private papers obtained by unlawful search and seizure did not violate the guarantee under

A brief account of the U.S. decisions

[86] As explained in *Oghad's Case*.
[87] Compelled testimony would obviously include torture.
[88] Torture would expose the police who inflicted it to charges under several sections of the Penal Code.
[89] (1903) 192 U.S. 585, 48 L.ed. 575.

the 4th Amendment. This was virtually reversed in *Weeks* v. *U.S.*[90] where it was held that evidence obtained in violation of the 4th Amendment was inadmissible against the accused in Federal Courts. In *Wolf* v. *Colorado*[91] it was held that the exclusion of such evidence was not a command of the 4th Amendment, but a rule of evidence which the court had evolved in the absence of legislation by the Congress, and if the States did not adopt the *Weeks* doctrine, and by law made such evidence admissible, they were free to do so. However, in *Mapp* v. *Ohio*,[92] *Wolf's Case* was overruled by a majority of 7 to 3, and the court held that the exclusion of such evidence was a command of the 4th Amendment binding on the Federal as well as the State courts. The majority observed that to allow state officers to violate the 4th Amendment and use the evidence obtained by such violation would be to destroy the protection which that amendment was designed to give. The requirements of the 4th Amendment were enforced not to shield lawbreakers, but because "if the Government becomes a law-breaker, it breeds contempt for law; it invites every man to become a law unto himself; it invites anarchy."[93] The majority judgment said:

> "Our decision, founded on reason and truth, gives to the individual no more than that which the Constitution guarantees him, to the police officer no less than that to which honest law enforcement is entitled, and, to the courts, that judicial integrity so necessary in the true administration of justice."[94]

and that is the present position in the United States.[95]

Art. 20 must be interpreted as a whole

11.149 The assistance derived in *Maqbool Hussain's Case* from sub-Articles (1) and (3) in fixing the meaning of Art. 20(2), has also had the effect of fixing the meaning of Art. 20(3). Accordingly, in *Sharma's Case* it was held that the guarantee against testimonial compulsion was available to a person "against whom a formal accusation relating to the commission of an offence has been levelled, which in the normal course may result in a prosecution", and "prosecution", as we have seen means

> "a proceeding by way either of indictment or of information in the criminal courts in order to put an offender on his trial; exhibition of a criminal charge against the person before a Court of Justice."

The effect of these propositions has been clearly brought out in a number of cases in which the provisions of the Companies Act have been impugned as violating Art. 20(3).

Art. 20(3). and examination under the Companies Act: *Bansilal's Case*

11.150 In *Bansilal's Case*[96] the petitioner impugned s. 240 of the Companies Act as violating Art. 20(3). The Registrar of Companies, having made a report that the affairs of the Sugar Mills of which the petitioner was the Managing Agent, disclosed an unsatisfactory state of affairs, and were carried on in fraud of the contributories, Government appointed the respondent as an inspector to investigate

---

90 (1913) 232 U.S. 383, 58 L.ed. 652.
91 (1948) 338 U.S. 25, 93 L.ed. 1782.
92 (1961) 367 U.S. 643, 6 L.ed. 2d. 1081.
93 ibid. p. 1092, quoting Brandeis J.
94 ibid. p. 1093.
95 *Massiah* v. *U.S.* (1964) 377 U.S. 201, 12 L.ed. 2d. 246 (evidence illegally seized is excluded to secure enforcement of the 4th Amendment).
96 *Raja Narayanlal Bansilal* v. *Maneck Phiroze Mistry* (1961) 1 S.C.R. 417, ('61) A.SC. 29.

the affairs of the company. The inspector intimated to the petitioner that he would be examined on oath in relation to the business of the company, and called upon him to produce all books and papers relating to the company. The petitioner impugned these orders as violating Art. 20(3). The trial court and the appellate court repelled these contentions,[97] and the Supreme Court did likewise. It was contended before the Supreme Court that Art. 20(3) should be given a wide and liberal meaning, and American authorities were relied on, particularly *Boyd* v. *U.S.*[98] where Bradley J. said

Art. 20(3) does not apply to such examination

"any compulsory discovery by extorting the party's oath, or compelling production of his private books and papers, to convict him of crime or forfeit his property is contrary to the principles of free Government" and "is abhorrent to the instincts of an American. It may suit the purpose of despotic power but it cannot abide the pure atmosphere of political liberty and personal freedom."

Doctrine against self-incrimination not applied in England to Company and Bankruptcy law

Two replies were given to this eloquent plea. First, that under the English law, protection against self-incrimination had not been given in Company and Insolvency law. Thus, under s. 15 of the English Bankruptcy Act, it had been held[99] that in a public examination of a debtor, he could be compelled to answer all questions which the court may put, or allow to be put, to him, and that the answers given could be used against him in evidence; and the position under s. 270 of the English Companies Act was the same.[1] The second answer was that the Article had been interpreted by the Supreme Court in *Maqbool Hussain's Case*,[2] *Venkataraman's Case*,[3] *Sharma's Case*,[4] and *Dana's Case*,[5] and it must be interpreted in the light of those decisions, which showed that Art. 20 must be considered as a whole, and the effect of the words used in each sub-Article on those used in the other sub-Articles must be appreciated. Those decisions also showed that the character of the proceedings, as well as the character of the forum before which the proceedings were initiated, or conducted, was treated as decisive in the matter. Applying these principles, the Supreme Court held that the investigation by an inspector appointed under the Act was no more than the work of a fact-finding commission. No doubt, as a result of the inspector's report, the Central Government may sanction a criminal prosecution, but that did not change the complexion of the inspector's investigation. Further, throughout that investigation there was no accused, no accuser and no accusation against anyone that he had committed an offence. The Court said that the same view had been taken of the corresponding provisions of the English Companies Act:[6]

Art. 20(3) must be interpreted in the light of the previous decisions of the Sup. Ct.

In a proceeding under the Companies Act, there is no accused, no accuser and no accusation against any person

---

[97] *Narayanlal* v. *M. P. Mistry* (1959) Bom. 952, ('59) A.B. 320, 61 Bom.L.R. 220.

[98] (1885) 116 U.S. 616, 29 L.ed. 746.

[99] *In re Atherton* (1912) 2 K.B. 251. The Court of Appeal had cited in addition *In re Paget*, (1927) 2 Ch. 85.

[1] The Court of Appeal had cited *Buckley on the Companies Act*, p. 566, for the proposition that a person examined under s. 270 cannot refuse to answer relevant questions on the ground that by doing so he may incriminate himself.

[2] (1953) S.C.R. 730, ('53) A.SC. 325.

[3] (1954) S.C.R. 1150, ('54) A.SC. 375.

[4] (1954) S.C.R. 1077, ('54) A.SC. 300.

[5] (1959) Supp. (1) S.C.R. 274, ('59) A.SC. 375.

[6] *In Hearts of Oak Assurance Co.* v. *Att.-General* (1932) A.C. 392 (H.L.).

"It appears to me", said Lord Thankerton, ". . . that the object of the examination is merely to recover information as to the company's affairs and that it is in no sense a judicial proceeding for the purpose of trial of an offence; it is enough to point out that there are no parties before the inspector, that he alone conducts the inquiry, and that the power to examine on oath is confined to the officers, members, agents and servants of the Company."

Bansilal's Case followed

Even if the words "accused of an offence" were given a wider meaning than that given in *Sharma's Case*, it would make no difference to the result, for the appellant was at no stage accused of an offence. This decision was followed in *Joseph* v. *Narayanan*[7] and it was held that the provisions of s. 45-G, Banking Companies Act, 1949, for the public examination of certain persons, did not violate Art. 20(3). For, though a person publicly examined under that section may in some cases be compelled to be a witness against himself, he was not a person accused of an offence. It has also been held that s. 185, Companies Act did not violate Art. 20(3) because there was neither an accusation of an offence nor was the respondent compelled to be a witness against himself.[8] Following *Bansilal's Case* it was held in *United Oil Mills* v. *Collector of Customs*,[9] that when a demand was made on the day of search, and a show-cause notice was issued to the person in connection with rr. 9 and 52A, Central Excise Rules, Art. 20(3) was not attracted. In *Bhagwandas* v. *Union*[10] it was held that directions of the Reserve Bank, and answers thereto, under s. 19, Foreign Exchange Regulation Act, were not hit by Art. 20(3) as the person was not in the position of an accused when he furnished the replies. For the same reasons it has been held that Art. 20(3) did not apply to departmental inquiries into allegations against a servant, as there was no accusation and no offence within the meaning of Art. 20(3),[11] nor to proceedings taken by customs authorities other than those taken against a person before a magistrate. Thus, it has been held that a person examined under s. 171-A, Sea Customs Act, did not stand in the character of an accused; the fact that subsequent to the making of the statement he became an accused was not sufficient to attract Art. 20(3).[12] Article 20(3) did not apply to s. 27(2)(c), Payment of Bonus Act, 1965, as the examination contemplated by that section was not for the purpose of establishing any offence against the person examined, but only for the purpose of ascertaining whether any of the provisions of the Act had been complied with.[13] In view of the deci-

---

[7] (1964) 7 S.C.R. 137, ('64) A.SC. 1552, fol. in *Popular Bank (In Liquidation)* v. *Madhava Naik* ('65) A.SC. 655; See also *Suryanarayana* v. *Vijaya Commercial Bank* ('56) A.A.P. 756; *In re Central Calcutta Bank Ltd.* ('57) A.Cal. 520, 61 C.W.N. 709.

[8] *Peoples Insurance Co.* v. *Sardul Singh* ('62) A.Punj. 101, 109 (the judgment contains an elaborate discussion of the doctrine against self-incrimination, but the decision on s. 185 of the Companies Act appears to be based on *Bansilal's Case* which is expressly referred to). In *Sushil Kumar* v. *R. R. Kini* (1965) 2 Punj. 339, ('67) A.Punj. 45, the court seems to have assumed mistakenly that Art. 20(3) would apply to an examination under s. 240(5), Companies Act, if a specific question were objected to.

[9] ('63) A.Ker. 241.

[10] ('61) A.M. 47.

[11] *Srikant Upadhya* v. *Union* ('63) A.P. 38.

[12] *Laxman Padma* v. *State* ('65) A.B. 195, 67 Bom.L.R. 317; *Rainbow Trading Co.* v. *Asst. Collector of Customs* ('63) A.M. 434 (in proceedings under s. 171-A there is no prosecution before a criminal court); *Collector of Customs* v. *Kotumal* (1967) 1 Mad. 665, ('67) A.M. 263 (F.B.).

[13] *Malabar Tile Works* v. *Union* ('68) A.Ker. 143, 146.

sions of the Supreme Court, it is submitted that in so far as *Basunti Kumar* v. *Collector of Land Customs*[14] and *Shankerlal* v. *Collector of Central Excise*[15] hold that a person appearing in answer to a notice under s. 171-A, Sea Customs Act, is entitled to the protection of Art. 20(3), are not good law. In view of the Supreme Court decisions, it is submitted that the decision in *Allen Berry & Co.* v. *Vivian Bose*[16] that as s. 6, Commissions of Inquiry Act, did not confer an immunity co-extensive with one under Art. 20(3) and that therefore that Article could be invoked in proceedings before a Commission, is no longer good law.[17]

11.151 In *Mohamed Dastagir* v. *Madras*[18] the Supreme Court held that before Art. 20(3) came into play, two facts had to be established: (i) that the individual concerned was accused of an offence, (ii) that he was compelled to be a witness against himself. We have already considered cases in which the claim to the protection of Art. 20(3) failed because the first of the above facts was not established. We must now consider cases in which the claim to the protection of Art. 20(3) failed because the second of those facts had not been established, and the most obvious case is where a person voluntarily makes oral statements, or voluntarily produces documentary evidence. In *Mohamed Dastagir's Case*[19] the facts were that the appellant went to the bungalow of the Deputy Superintendent of Police to offer him a bribe in a closed envelope with a request that he might drop an action registered against him. The police officer threw the envelope at the appellant who took it up. Later, while the appellant was still in the bungalow, he was asked to produce the envelope which he had taken up. He took out of his pocket some currency notes and placed them on the table, without the envelope. The Supreme Court held that at the time the notes were produced, there was no case against him relating to an offence; even if it was assumed that there was, the circumstances did not establish that he was compelled to produce the money. No doubt he was asked to do so, but it was in his power to refuse. Consequently, Art. 20(3) did not apply.

Mohamed Dastagir's Case: two requirements of Art. 20(3)

Cases in which the accused was not "compelled": voluntary statements

11.152 A person appeared before a sub-divisional magistrate and surrendered before him, stating that he was wanted by the police in connection with his wife's murder. The magistrate on finding his *dhoti* and upper cloth blood-stained, directed his clerk and peon to seize them, and they were seized in his presence. It was held that the seizure of the blood-stained cloth from a person like the accused who wanted to surrender would be very material and relevant, and the magistrate was bound to take possession of them, as well as of the blood-stained weapon, from the accused. Consequently, it could

Seizure of incriminating material from a person voluntarily surrendering to a magistrate

[14] ('61) A.Cal. 86, 91; the earlier decision in *Calcutta M. & C. Co.* v. *Collector of Customs* ('56) A.Cal. 253, 60 C.W.N. 67, that Art. 20(3) applies to proceedings under s. 171-A, Sea Customs Act, is not correct for the same reason.

[15] (1960) Mad. 267, ('60) A.M. 225 (in fact, the judgment itself held that the person served with a notice under s. 171-A was not an accused person).

[16] ('60) A.Punj. 87.

[17] In *Ram Krishna Dalmia* v. *S. R. Tendolkar* (1959) S.C.R. 279, 293, ('58) A.SC. 538, the Supreme Court held that a Commission of Inquiry is not a judicial but a fact-finding body.

[18] (1960) 3 S.C.R. 116, ('60) A.SC. 756 [19] *Supra.*

not be said that there had been any compulsion exercised upon the accused to produce the articles and to be a witness against himself in the murder case against him.[20]

Art. 20(3), and s. 124, Bombay City Police Act, 1951

11.153 In *State* v. *Fundan Lakhanmal*[21] it was said that s. 124, Bombay Police Act, 1951, did not violate Art. 20 (3) because far from the accused person incriminating himself, he was called upon to explain his possession of property which there was reason to believe was stolen property. In *P. Rajangam* v. *Madras*[22] it was held that it was doubtful (i) whether Art. 20 (3) applied to a fact-finding inquiry contemplated by s. 176 Cr.P.C., and (ii) whether there was any accused in those proceedings as there could be no reasonable suspicion of the commission of an offence at that stage. However, persons against whom the inquiry was directed could not rely on Art. 20 (3) when they were warned that they were not compelled to give evidence and they had not, in fact, given any evidence.

and s. 176, Cr. P.C.

Art. 20(3), and s. 4, Cr.Law Amendment Ordinance

11.154 Notice under s. 4, Criminal Law Amendment Ordinance, to show cause why an interim order for attachment of property should not be made absolute, did not attract Art. 20 (3) for it did not compel a person to be a witness against himself. If in order to secure release of the property from attachment, a person revealed incidentally the whole or part of what the answer to the charge against him would be, Art. 20 (3) was not contravened.[23]

Art. 20(3) and s. 13A, Bom.Money Lenders' Act

11.155 In *State* v. *Devsi Dosa*[24] it was said that notice to produce documents under s. 13A, Bombay Money Lenders' Act, did not entitle a person to claim protection under Art. 20 (3). For, that would enlarge the scope of the Article so as to make it applicable to civil or administrative proceedings. The protection of Art. 20 (3) could not be claimed merely because the evidence might disclose some crime.

Art. 20(3) and s. 342, Cr.P.C.

11.156 A question has arisen whether s. 342 Cr.P.C. violates Art. 20 (3). Under that section, at the close of a case a judge is under an obligation to ask questions to the accused on the evidence led against him, but the accused cannot be punished for refusal to answer, or for giving false answers, though if he refuses to answer, the Court or the jury may draw such inference from the refusal as it thinks fit. In *In re B. N. Ramakrishna*[25] it was held that the answers given by the accused under s. 342 (2) Cr.P.C. did not violate Art. 20(3), first, because the answers were optional, were not on oath and were not evidence; and, secondly, because the presumption which the judge or jury could draw from the refusal to answer did not amount virtually to compulsion.[26] It is submitted that if an accused voluntarily answers the questions put to him, no question of the violation of Art. 20 (3) arises. But if his answers are not voluntary,

Ramakrishna's Case

A criticism of the case

---

[20] *In re Palani Moopan* ('55) A.M. 495, 497.

[21] (1958) Bom. 883, ('60) A.B. 377, 60 Bom.L.R. 403.

[22] (1959) Mad. 12, ('59) A.M. 294.

[23] *G. L. Salwan* v. *Union* (1960) Punj. 687, ('60) A.Punj. 351, 354.

[24] ('60) A.B. 443, 62, Bom.L.R. 316.

[25] ('55) A.M. 100.

[26] *Banwarilal* v. *State* ('56) A.A. 341, and also ('56) A.A. 385 (s. 342 did not convert the accused into a witness and did not compel him to be a witness against himself); *In re Govinda Reddy* (1957) Mys. 177, ('58) A.Mys. 150 [*held* that s. 342 Cr.P.C. does not violate Art. 20(3)].

Ramakrishna's Case raises the question, is the word "witness" used in Art. 20(3) in the technical sense of a person giving evidence on oath? It is submitted that it is not. We have seen that "to be a witness" is to furnish evidence in court or out of court, and therefore the protection given by Art. 20(3) cannot be defeated by saying that statements made by an accused are not evidence, and he is not a witness. Those statements can be considered for or against him, and statements which lead the tribunal to pronounce on the guilt or innocence of the accused are clearly evidence within the meaning of Art. 20(3). The second question raised by the judgment is whether s. 342(2) Cr.P.C. is valid. It is submitted that if an accused person is privileged from answering certain questions, no inference can be drawn against him from his refusal to answer questions, without violating the privilege conferred on him. On the corresponding provision in the Fifth Amendment to the U.S. Constitution, it is settled law that

(i) the word "witness" not used in a technical sense

(ii) drawing an adverse inference against an accused for refusal to answer questions violates Art. 20(3)

> "It is a violation of the defendant's privilege against self-incrimination to improperly, such as by unwarranted comment of the Court, prosecution, or jury, place him in the position where he must testify in order to avoid any adverse inference that may arise from his failure to do so. Thus, the trial judge may not call attention to the fact that the defendant is entitled to testify, nor may the prosecution comment during closing on the fact that the defendant claimed his privilege while on the stand."[27]

The U.S. Supreme Court has held that a provision in a State Constitution allowing the Court and counsel to comment on the accused's failure to testify, violated the federal Constitution. It has, moreover, been held that a defendant is entitled on request, to have the court instruct the jury that it is to draw no inference from his failure to take the stand and testify in his own behalf.[28] This principle is recognized by s. 342A.[29] The principle underlying the American view, and underlying s. 342A, has been recognized by our Supreme Court in respect of "Crown Privilege", in *Punjab* v. *Sodhi Sukhdev Singh*.[30] It is submitted that in so far as s. 342(2) allows a tribunal to draw an adverse inference, it is void as violating Art. 20(3), and if it should appear that the answers given by the accused, though apparently voluntary, were given under the direct or indirect suggestion of the Court, the prosecutor or the jury, that otherwise an adverse inference would be drawn against him, the answers are inadmissible under Art. 20(3).

The U.S. decisions support the above view

11.157 Since 1955, in a criminal trial the accused is a competent witness to testifying on his own behalf under s. 342A, Cr.P.C.[31] and there will be other witnesses against him. Under s. 132, Evidence Act, a witness may be compelled to give evidence which may incriminate him, but any answer which he may be *compelled* to give cannot be proved against him in any civil or criminal proceeding. It will be seen that s. 342A completely protects an accused if he does not wish to give evidence because s. 342A, proviso (*b*) prevents any

Accused a competent witness since 1955

---

[27] *American Jurisprudence* 2d. Vol. 21, p. 383.
[28] ibid.
[29] See para 11.125, *f.n.* 11 where the section is set out. Sec. 315(1) of the Code of Criminal Procedure, 1974, reproduces s. 342A without any change.
[30] (1961) 2 S.C.R. 371, 388, ('61) A.SC. 493.
[31] See *f.n.* 29 above.

adverse inference being drawn, or any adverse comments being made, against him for not giving evidence. S. 342A enables an accused to give evidence *if he desires to do so.* In the United States it is well settled that the accused by taking the stand waives the privilege conferred on him by the Fifth Amendment in respect of the matters which are the subject-matters of the charge against him, though in respect of other unconnected matters he, as a witness, cannot be compelled to incriminate himself.[32] In *Basheshar Nath's Case*,[33] Subba Rao J., who carried out a scrutiny on his own of all the fundamental rights contained in Part III, (though the only fundamental right alleged to be violated in the case related to Art. 14), said:

> "Some comment is made in regard to the right covered by Art. 20(3) and it is asked that if a person has no liberty to waive the protection under that clause, he could not give evidence even if he wanted to give it in his own interest. This argument ignores the content of the right under Art. 20(3). The fundamental right of a person is only that he should not be compelled to be a witness against himself. It would not prevent him from giving evidence voluntarily."[34]

Submission: by electing to give evidence, an accused waives Art. 20(3)

It is submitted that these observations overlook the real issue involved, namely, can an accused person decide to give evidence in his favour and then object to answer questions in cross-examination which would incriminate him? This raises the further question, whether having applied to give evidence he has waived his privilege. It is submitted that the clearest proof that the right conferred by Art. 20(3) is a privilege which can be waived, is afforded by the fact that unless he can take the stand and waive his right, the whole object of his going into the box to prove his innocence would be defeated.[35]

Dushyant Somal v. Sushma Somal

11.158 In *Dushyant Somal* v. *Sushma Somal*,[36] Art. 20(3) was invoked under unusual circumstances. The facts of the Criminal Appeal and Special Leave Petition were these:

> The appellant married the respondent in May, 1973. A daughter, Sweta, and a son, Sandeep were born in May, 1974 and April 1975 respectively. The appellant and the respondent lived separately from 1976 as a result of estrangement between them. The children lived with their mother. On an allegation that Sandeep was removed from her custody by her husband, in Sept. 1977, the wife applied under the Guardian and Wards Act for the custody

---

32 *American Jurisprudence* 2d. Vol. 21, p. 385.

33 (1959) Supp. (1) S.C.R. 528, 614, ('59) A.SC. 149.

34 ibid.

35 In *T. G. Gaokar* v. *R. N. Shukla* (1968) 3 S.C.R. 422, ('68) A.SC. 1050, Bachawat J. held that though the appellant was a person accused of an offence within the meaning of Art. 20(3), he had not been compelled to give evidence: "The necessity to enter the witness box for substantiating his defence is not such a compulsion as would attract the protection of Art. 20(3). . . . It may be very necessary for the accused person to enter the witness-box for substantiating his defence. But this is no reason for saying that the criminal trial compels him to be a witness against himself and is in violation of Art. 20(3). Compulsion in the context of Art. 20(3) must proceed from another person or authority. (He) is not compelled to be a witness if he voluntarily gives evidence in his defence": ('68) A.SC. at p. 1053. The Court expressed no opinion on the question whether Art. 20(3) would be attracted if the Customs authorities summoned the Appellant as a witness and whether in the event of his being compelled to answer the questions put to him he could claim the protection of s. 132, Evidence Act, against the use of those answers in the criminal proceedings.

36 ('81) A.SC. 1026.

of Sandeep, who was a minor. Under an *ex parte* order, and with the assistance of the police, she recovered the custody of Sandeep. According to the respondent, on Oct. 27, 1980, at 7 O'clock in the morning her son Sandeep escorted by his grandmother was waiting at a bus stop, when the appellant, accompanied by three or four persons, forcibly took away Sandeep. On the respondent's complaint, the Police registered a case under s. 363, I.P.C. (kidnapping from lawful guardianship). The respondent's search for her son having proved unavailing, she applied to the High Court under Art. 226 for a writ of *habeas corpus* directing her husband to produce her son. In answer to the *rule nisi* issued by the High Court, he denied ever having kidnapped the son. The High Court decided to examine witnesses. The respondent examined herself and her mother. The appellant chose not to cross-examine them, nor did he examine himself, or anyone else, as a witness. The High Court was satisfied on the evidence that Sandeep had been "unauthorisedly taken away" by his father from the lawful custody of his mother, and was being illegally detained by the father. A writ was issued directing the appellant to produce the child before the Court on Dec. 17, 1980 so that the custody of the child could be given to the mother. As the appellant did not do so, the High Court found him guilty of contempt of Court and directed that he be detained in civil prison until he produced the child in Court. The appeal was directed against the order committing him to prison for contempt, and the Special Leave Petition was directed against the Order of the High Court in the petition under Art. 226.

Contempt of Court and *habeas corpus* application under Art. 32

11.159 The Court held that the High Court was right in coming to the conclusion on the unchallenged testimony of the mother and the grandmother that the appellant had snatched away Sandeep when he was waiting at the bus stop in the company of his grandmother. Consequently, the writ of *habeas corpus* was rightly issued. It was submitted for the appellant that he did not give evidence or examine any witnesses on his behalf, nor did he cross-examine the mother and the grandmother because "he would be disclosing his defence in the criminal case in the criminal matter". He could not be compelled to disclose his defence as that would be contrary to Art. 20(3). The Court rejected this contention as misconceived, and made the following important observations.

"Protection against testimonial compulsion did not convert the position of a person accused of an offence into a position of privilege, with immunity from any other action contemplated by law. A criminal prosecution was not a fortress against all other actions in law. To accept the position that the pendency of a prosecution was a valid answer to a rule for *Habeas Corpus* would be to subvert the judicial process and to mock at the Criminal Justice system. All that Art. 20(3) guaranteed was that a person accused of an offence shall not be compelled to be a witness against himself, nothing less and, certainly, nothing more. Immunity against testimonial compulsion did not extend to refusal to examine and cross-examine witnesses and it was not open to a party proceeding (sic) (proceeded against) to refuse to examine himself or anyone else as a witness on his side and to cross-examine the witnesses for the opposite party on the ground of testimonial compulsion and then to contend that no relief should be given to the opposite party on the basis of the evidence adduced by the other party. We are unable to see how Art. 20(3) comes into the picture at all."[37]

However, the Supreme Court varied the High Court's Order committing the appellant to prison by substituting a sentence of three months' simple imprisonment and a fine of Rs. 500. The sentence of imprisonment or such part of it as may not have been served was to stand remitted on the appellant producing Sandeep before the High Court.

---

[37] ibid. at p. 1029.

S. 132, Evidence Act, and Art. 20(3)

Submission: an accused in not a witness within the meaning of s. 132

11.160 Does s. 132, Evidence Act apply to an accused in respect of matters connected with the offence with which he is charged? It is submitted that the accused is not a witness within the meaning of s. 132, first, because when the section was enacted, an accused person could not be a witness on his own behalf, and the section referred to witnesses who were not being tried for an offence, and, secondly, because it would be absurd for an accused person to offer to give evidence, to answer incriminating questions, and then to claim that those answers should not be used in proof of the charges for which he is being tried. He has the privilege of remaining silent. It is conferred on him by s. 342, Cr.P.C., and even more completely by Art. 20 (3). But to give evidence to prove his innocence and then to suggest that his guilt should not be proved from his own answers, would be a situation "which would delight the heart of a Gilbert and Sullivan opera audience but can hardly reflect credit on the administration of justice."[38] It is submitted, therefore, that Art. 20 (3) confers a privilege on an accused which he can waive by giving evidence. But if he is asked incriminating questions about matters with which he is not charged, or with which on the evidence before the Court he cannot be charged at the trial, in respect of those matters he is like any other witness and can claim the protection given by s. 132.

Section III

Articles 21-22

Three leading cases on Arts. 21 and 22

Gopalan's Case and preventive detention: Art. 22(3) not directly in issue; that Art. was considered in *Atma Ram's Case*

Art. 22(1) and (2) considered in *Ajaib Singh's Case*

11.161 The relation of Art. 19 to Art. 21 has been considered in detail in Section II of this Chapter. In considering the scope of Arts. 21 and 22, three decisions of the Supreme Court occupy an important position, namely, *A. K. Gopalan* v. *State*,[39] *Bombay* v. *Atma Ram Sridhar Vaidya*,[40] and *Punjab* v. *Ajaib Singh*.[41] *Gopalan's Case* is also a leading case on the constitutional scheme for preventive detention contained in Art. 22, more particularly the inter-relation of Art. 22 (3) to (7). As there was no complaint in *Gopalan's Case* that the requirements of Art. 22(5) had not been complied with, it did not become necessary to consider in detail the scope of the right under Art. 22 (5), though some important points relating to Art. 22 (5) were laid down when all the judges held that s. 14, Preventive Detention Act, 1950, was void. But the scope of Art. 22 (5) was considered in detail in *Atma Ram's Case*. As *Gopalan's Case* and *Atma Ram's Case* were cases of preventive detention, the effect of Art. 22 (1) and (2) did not fall to be considered in detail. The effect of Art. 22 (1) and (2) was considered in *Ajaib Singh's Case*.

Gopalan's Case: the majority rejected the view that Art. 22

11.162 *Gopalan's Case* was decided in the context of the Preventive Detention Act, 1950,[42] for apart from the challenge to the Act under Arts. 19 and 21 which failed, the petitioner also challenged various provisions of the Act as violative of Art. 22 itself, and it became

---

[38] *Per* Bose J. in *U.P.* v. *Mohammed Nooh* (1958) S.C.R. 595, ('58) A.SC. 86, in the context of an inquiry officer being both a witness and a judge.

[39] (1950) S.C.R. 88, ('50) A.SC. 27.

[40] (1951) S.C.R. 167, ('51) A.SC. 157.

[41] (1953) S.C.R. 254, ('53) A.SC. 10.

[42] The relevant provisions of the Act are set out in *Gopalan's Case* (1950) S.C.R. *supra* at pp. 93-4.

necessary to consider those requirements in detail. Great care was bestowed on the petitioner's case because the Court rightly looked upon preventive detention as a serious invasion of personal liberty and the judges expressed their dislike of such detention, even when they upheld it.[43] Kania C.J., Patanjali Sastri and Das JJ. rejected the contention that Art. 22 formed a complete code of constitutional safeguards relating to preventive detention. Mahajan J. dissented and held that Art. 22 was a self-contained code of constitutional safeguards relating to preventive detention and could not be examined or controlled by the provisions of Art. 21. However, the principle underlying Art. 21 had been kept in view in Art. 22, and there was no conflict between those Articles. It is submitted that the majority view is correct and Kania C.J. gave the most satisfactory exposition of it when he said:

was a complete code on preventive detention

Submission: the majority view is correct: Art. 22 must be read with Art. 21

"... in respect of arrest and detention Art. 22(1) and (2) provide safeguards. These safeguards are excluded in the case of preventive detention by Art. 22(3), but safeguards in connection with such detention are provided by Cls. (4) to (7). ... It is therefore clear that Art. 21 has to be read as supplemented by Art. 22 ... to the extent the procedure is prescribed by Art. 22 the same is to be observed; otherwise Art. 21 will apply. But if certain procedural safeguards are expressly stated as not required, or specific rules on certain points of procedure are prescribed, it seems improper to interpret these points as not covered by Art. 22 and left open for consideration under Art. 21. To the extent the points were dealt with, and included or excluded, Art. 22 is a complete code. On the points of procedure which expressly or by necessary implication are not dealt with by Art. 22, the operation of Art. 21 will remain unaffected."[44]

Kania C.J. said that neither the United States nor the Japanese Constitution provided for preventive detention in normal times, that is, without a declaration of emergency; but in our country preventive detention in normal times was recognized as a normal topic of legislation by entry 9, List I, and entry 3, List III of Sch. 7, and even the chapter on fundamental rights envisaged preventive detention in normal times in Art. 22. Under the legislative entries in Lists I and III Parliament could have made a law of preventive detention without any safeguard or without laying down any procedure for preventive detention. This "autocratic supremacy of the legislature" was curtailed by Part III and particularly by Arts. 21 and 22.

Arts. 21 and 22 are a fetter on legislative power in respect of preventive detention

11.163 In *Gopalan's Case*, Kania C.J. explained the scheme of Art. 22(3) to (7) as follows: Article 22(3) expressly provides that the safeguards contained in Art. 22(1) and (2) are not to apply to preventive detention. Article 22(4) provides that a law of preventive detention for a period longer than three months must contain a provision for the establishment of an advisory Board consisting of persons who were, or had been, or are qualified to be, judges of a High Court[45] and which Board is to report before the expiration of three months whether in its opinion, there are sufficient causes

The scheme of Art. 22

---

[43] *Per* Kania C.J. ibid. p. 117, *per* Patanjali Sastri J. ibid. p. 211, *per* Mahajan J. ibid. p. 220, *per* Mukherjea J. ibid. p. 250, per Das J. ibid. p. 288.

[44] ibid. p. 116.

[45] See *Baishnab Patnaik* v. *State* ('52) A.Or. 60 where it was held that the qualifications for appointment as a judge of a High Court as contemplated in Art. 22(4)(*a*) [and Art. 165(1)] referred only to those qualifications described in Art. 217(2), and did not refer to the age limit fixed by Art. 217(1).

for such detention. But the proviso to Art. 22 (4) further provides that even if the Board were of opinion that there was sufficient cause for detention beyond the period of three months, such detention was not permitted beyond the maximum period, if any, prescribed by Parliament under Art. 22 (7) (*b*). However, Art. 22 (4) (*a*) "is made inoperative by Art. 22 (4) (*b*) in respect of an Act for preventive detention passed by Parliament under clause (7) (*a*) and (*b*)".[46] As the impugned Act was made by Parliament, Art. 22 (4) had no application to the case. Article 22 (5) confers certain rights on a person detained and Art. 22 (6) enables Government to withhold disclosure of facts against the public interest. But reading Art. 22 (5) and (6) together, it is clear that though non-disclosure of facts is permitted, non-disclosure of "grounds" is not permitted. In so far as Art. 22 (4) and (7) permit the non-establishment of an advisory Board expressly in a law of preventive detention made by Parliament, such non-establishment is not violative of a fundamental right. Article 22 (7) (*a*), which is contained in the part on fundamental rights, permits in respect of an Act on preventive detention passed by Parliament, detention beyond the period of three months without the necessity of consulting an advisory Board, if the Act complies with the opening words of sub-Art. (7) (*a*). Sub-Article (7) (*b*) was permissive, it not being obligatory on Parliament to prescribe a maximum period. If this construction resulted in a Parliamentary law enabling the detention of a person for an indefinite period without trial, that unfortunate consequence was the result of the words of sub-Art. (7) itself and the Court could do nothing about it. Sub-Article (7) (*c*) permitted Parliament to lay down the procedure to be followed by the advisory Board in an inquiry under sub-Art. (4) (*a*). Kania C.J. and Sastri, Mukherjea and Das JJ. took the view, Fazl Ali and Mahajan JJ. dissenting, that under Art. 22 (7) Parliament must prescribe either the circumstances under which *or* the class or classes of cases in which a person may be detained for a longer period than three months without reference to an Advisory Board; it was not necessary to prescribe both. Applying this test, the matters referred to in ss. 12 (*a*) and (*b*) of the impugned Act constituted a sufficient description of such circumstances or classes of cases and s. 12 did not violate Art. 22 (7).[47] However, the subject is dealt with more fully in paras 11.179 to 11.181 in view of a later Supreme Court decision.

The majority view of Art. 22(7)

S. 14, Preventive Detention Act, 1950 held void

11.164 Section 14 of the Act[48] was impugned as violating both Art. 22 (5) and Art. 32. All the judges held that s. 14 was *ultra vires* of the Constitution. Kania C.J. held that Cls. (5) and (6) of Art. 22 showed that though Government were permitted not to disclose facts in the public interest, they were not permitted to withhold the grounds for the detention. Article 22 (5) provided that the detaining

---

[46] (1950) S.C.R. *supra* at p. 117.

[47] Das J. further held that in fact and in substance, Parliament had prescribed both in s. 12(*a*) and (*b*).

[48] The section made it an offence punishable with imprisonment or fine, or both, for any person, (which would include the person detained), to disclose the communication made under s. 7 of the grounds on which the detention order was made against any person or the representation made by him, and further barred the jurisdiction of any Court to require any officer to produce such communication or representation or to disclose the substance of either of them.

authority should communicate to the person detained the grounds "*on which the order has been made*". It was therefore essential that the grounds must be communicated with the order of preventive detention, and if they were not so communicated the requirements of Art. 22(5) were not complied with and the detention order was invalid. It was open to a detained person to contend that the grounds on which the order had been made had no connection with the order, or with the circumstances of the class or classes of cases under which the preventive detention order could be supported under s. 12 or that the grounds were vague. He must therefore be free to indicate to the Court the grounds given for his alleged detention and the representation made by him. To prevent him from disclosing those grounds and that representation to the Court would prevent him from asserting his fundamental right under Art. 22(5).[49] Patanjali Sastri,[50] Mahajan,[51] Mukherjea[52] and Das JJ.[53] agreed with this view and held *further* that the detained person's right under Art. 32 was also violated, for he could not move the Supreme Court for the assertion of his right if he was precluded from establishing that his fundamental right under Art. 22(5) had been violated. The decision of the majority of the judges that s. 14 violated Art. 32, is important as dispelling a misconception about *Gopalan's Case*. *Gopalan's Case* decided that a law of preventive or punitive detention could not be judged by the requirements of Art. 19(2) to (6), but that was because on a true construction of Art. 19 and Art. 21 it was held that the enjoyment of the rights conferred by Art. 19(1)(*a*) to (*e*) and (*g*) postulated a free person capable of enjoying those rights, and where a person lost his freedom by a valid order of punitive or preventive detention, those rights were no longer available to him. But the case did not decide that other constitutional limitations had not to be satisfied by a law of preventive detention or a law depriving a person of life of personal liberty. In fact, as we have seen, a majority of the judges held that s. 14 violated Art. 32 and was void on that ground also. The same principle was also emphasized in *Kathi Raning Rawat* v. *Saurashtra*[54] where Patanjali Sastri C.J. said:

as violating Art.22(5).

and also Art. 32

Gopalan's Case: constitutional limitations other than those in Art. 19 apply to preventive detention

"It is, . . . not correct to say that Art. 14 provides no further constitutional protection to personal liberty than what is afforded by Art. 21. Notwithstanding that its wide general language is greatly qualified in its practical application by a due recognition of the State's necessarily wide powers of legislative classification, Art. 14 remains an important bulwark against discriminatory procedural laws."[55]

Therefore, there can be no doubt that though Art. 19(1)(*a*) to (*e*) and (*g*) does not apply to a law of preventive or punitive detention, such a law is subject to the constitutional limitations of Part III.

11.165 It is outside the scope of this work to consider cases of preventive detention which turn on the interpretation of the Preventive Detention Act or on the question whether on the facts, the provisions of that Act had been complied with. Such provisions will be considered only if they raise constitutional questions.

---

[49] ibid. p. 131.
[50] ibid. p. 218.
[51] ibid. p. 244.
[52] ibid. pp. 283-5.
[53] ibid. p. 333.
[54] (1952) S.C.R. 435, ('52) A.SC. 123.
[55] (1952) S.C.R. *supra* at p. 443.

Art. 22(3) to (7) do not confer legislative power but limit that power

11.166 In *Gopalan's Case* it was said that Art. 22(3) to (7) does not confer legislative power to enact a law of preventive detention—that power is derived from entry 9, List I, and entry 3, List III of Sch. 7 read with Art. 246. Article 22(3) to (7) imposes limitations on legislative power, which the legislature cannot transgress. But the legislature is under no obligation to exercise its power to the full extent permitted by Art. 22(4), (6) and (7). Thus, Art. 22(4)(*a*) would suggest that for detention under three months it was not necessary to refer a case for opinion to an advisory Board.[56] Nor does Art. 22(4)(*a*) provide that if the Board expressed the opinion that a person's detention was not justified, he was to be released. Article 22(5) requires that the grounds on which a detention order was made against a person should be communicated to him "as soon as may be", and decided cases under the Preventive Detention Act of 1950, before its amendment in 1951, show that periods ranging from fourteen days to several months have been held not to be unreasonable, because the expression "as soon as may be" meant "as soon as circumstances permit the authority to furnish the ground".[57] However, the amendments made in the Act in 1951 show that Parliament did not exercise its powers to the full extent permitted by Art. 22(4) to (7) and in fact restricted its own powers. Thus s. 7 provides that the ground of the order of detention should be communicated to the person detained "as soon as may be but *not later than five days from the date of detention*". Section 9 provides that *every order of detention* must be referred to an advisory Board within thirty days from the date of detention. Again, s. 11(2) provides that if the advisory Board expresses an opinion that there is not sufficient cause for the detention of the person concerned, the appropriate Government shall revoke the detention order and release the person forthwith. These amendments show the difference between the possession of power and its exercise. Our Constitution confers powers adequate to meet all situations which may arise; however the exercise of power in a democratic State must depend upon the circumstances of the times.

Amendments in the Preventive Detention Act in 1951

S. 11 of the Act and Art. 22(4)

11.167 In *S. Krishnan* v. *Madras*[58] after the amendment of the Preventive Detention Act in 1951, s. 11 of the Act was impugned as violating Art. 22(4) on the ground that s. 11 did not fix any maximum period of detention but on the contrary empowered the Government in express terms to order that a detention was to continue for such period as it thought fit. Kania C.J., Sastri, Mahajan and Das JJ. held that s. 11 was not invalid on the ground that it did not fix a maximum period of detention, because the Act itself was to be in force only for one year and no detention under the

Majority view: S. 14 not violative of Art. 22(4)

---

[56] See *per* Kania C.J., (1950) S.C.R. 88, p. 117, *per* Das J., ibid. p. 326.

[57] *Raj Bahadur* v. *Hyderabad* ('53) A.Hyd. 277 (a delay of three weeks was held not to be unreasonable); *Tarapada De* v. *W.B.* (1951) S.C.R. 212, ('51) A.SC. 174 (a delay of fourteen days was held not to be unreasonable having regard to the fact that the State Government had suddenly to deal with a large number of cases on one day); *In re Pandurang* (1951) Bom. 190 (F.B.), ('51) A.B. 30 (a delay of two and a half months was held not to be unreasonable); fol. in *Santhamma* v. *Hyderabad* (1951) Hyd. 654, ('51) A.Hyd. 128 (F.B.). However, in *Sayeed Hasan* v. *Mohd. Sultanuddin Khan* (1951) Hyd. 448, ('51) A.Hyd. 79, a delay in furnishing the grounds for five months was held unreasonable.

[58] (1951) S.C.R. 621, ('51) A.SC. 301.

Act could be continued after the expiry of the Act.[59] Mahajan J. treated the point as concluded by *Gopalan's Case* where Kania C.J. had observed that it was not obligatory on Parliament to prescribe any maximum period.[60] In a strong and, it is submitted, a convincing dissent, Bose J. held that though Parliament was not obliged to fix a maximum period of detention under Art. 22(7)(*b*), if it wanted to detain a person for a longer period than three months,[61] it could only do so by providing in the Act a maximum period, and he gave cogent reasons for rejecting the view that by enacting a law for one year the maximum period had been fixed.[62] The judgment will repay study, but in view of a subsequent legislative amendment it is not necessary to set out its arguments in detail. He said that the majority judgment amounted to the Constitution telling all persons resident in the land:

Submission: the dissent of Bose J. is correct

"Here is the full extent of your liberty so far as the length of detention is concerned. We guarantee that you will not be detained beyond three months unless Parliament otherwise directs, either generally or in your particular class of case; but we empower Parliament to smash the guarantee absolutely if it so chooses without let or hindrance, without restriction. Though we authorise Parliament to prescribe a maximum limit of detention if it so chooses, we place no compulsion on it to do so and we authorise it to pass legislation which will empower any person or authority Parliament chooses to name, right down to a police constable, to arrest you and detain you as long as he pleases, for the duration of your life if he wants, so that you may linger and rot in jail till you die, as did men in the Bastille."[63]

Though he failed to convince his brother judges on legal interpretation, he appears to have convinced Parliament of the enormity of such a result, for in 1952, Parliament inserted s. 11A prescribing twelve months from the date of detention as the maximum period of detention under s. 11.

S. 11A inserted in the Act: it fixed the maximum period of detention

11.168 The words "any person" in Art. 22(7)(*b*) do not contemplate that individual attention should be paid to each case; the words used in Art. 22(7)(*b*) empower Parliament to prescribe a maximum for a class taken as a whole as had been done by s. 3, Preventive Detention (Amendment) Act, 1952. Consequently, s. 3 did not contravene Art. 22(4) and (7). The Power of Parliament to fix a maximum period does not exhaust itself once it has been exercised but can be exercised again in respect of the same detention. Section 3 was not repugnant to the Constitution on the ground that it did not fix a time-limit, for it specified the exact period of detention, namely, until the expiry of the Act, nor on the ground that a person may be indefinitely detained by periodical amendments, for Parliament had that power[64] and that very power had been upheld in *S. Krishnan* v. *Madras*.[65]

S. 3 of the Act does not violate Art. 22(4) to (7)

---

[59] See *Ram Prasad* v. *W.B.* ('55) A.Cal. 374, where this majority view was referred to but it was said that when fresh life was added to the temporary Act by a subsequent legislation, the original order of detention on the score that it was for a period beyond the life of the temporary Act under which it was made, could not be challenged, for then, the order as well as the subsequent detention must be deemed to have been made under the original Act.

[60] (1951) S.C.R. *supra* at p. 639.

[61] ibid. p. 642 *et seq.*

[62] ibid. pp. 650-2.

[63] ibid. p. 652.

[64] *Shamrao V. Parulekar* v. *District Magistrate, Thana* (1952) S.C.R. 683, ('52) A.SC. 324.

[65] (1951) S.C.R. 621, *supra*.

The meaning of "such detention" in Art. 22(4)

Lakhanpal's Case

the majority view

the dissent of Sarkar J. Submission: the dissent is correct

11.169 Although observations were made by some of the judges in *Gopalan's Case* on Art. 22(4) (*a*), the precise meaning of the words "such detention" in Art. 22(4) (*a*) was not directly laid down. That question was considered by the Supreme Court in *Puranlal Lakhanpal* v. *Union.*[66] There, s. 11(1) of the Preventive Detention Act was impugned on the ground that it contravened Art. 22(4) (*a*). S. K. Das J. for himself, Bhagwati, Imam and Kapur JJ. held that on a true construction of Art. 22(4) (*a*), s. 11 did not contravene that Article. Sarkar J. dissented and held that the section was *ultra vires* as contravening Art. 22(4) (*a*). Das J. observed that no decision directly deciding the point at issue had been brought to the notice of the Court. The observations of Kania C.J. and Fazl Ali J. in *Gopalan's Case* showed that they considered that the words "such detention" meant "detention for a period longer than three months", but Patanjali Sastri J. had taken a different view. It therefore became necessary to consider the scheme of Art. 22(3) to (7) and Das J. held that the expression "such detention" in Art. 22(4) (*a*) referred to preventive detention and not to how long a person was to be detained. It is submitted that this conclusion begs the very question to be proved, namely, the meaning to be given to the words "*such* detention". It is submitted that Sarkar J. gave cogent reasons to show, first, that the words "such detention" could have only one meaning, namely, detention of a person for a longer period than three months,[67] and secondly, that if two constructions were possible, there was no reason to prefer the construction which would make the words refer to preventive detention *simpliciter*. He rightly held that the decisions on which the majority had relied, namely, those in *Makhan Singh Tarsikka* v. *Punjab*[68] and *Dattatreya Moreshwar Pangarkar* v. *Bombay*[69] were concerned with the scheme, or the effect, of statutory provisions, and did not raise the question whether a section of the Act was invalid because it violated the requirements of a fundamental right. He rightly observed that preventive detention for a period longer than three months was a serious matter, and that the Act itself distinguished between detention for less than three months and more than three months and there was no reason why the safeguard provided in Art. 22(4) (*a*) should not extend to pronouncing on the necessity for detention for a period exceeding three months. It is submitted that if two constructions are possible, as appears to have been argued by the Solicitor-General for the Union of India, and as is clear from the observations in *Gopalan's Case* by Kania C.J.[70] and Fazl Ali J.[71] on the one hand and Sastri J. on the other,[72] a construction favourable to the subject ought to be adopted.

---

[66] (1958) S.C.R. 460, ('58) A.SC. 163.

[67] See Fowler's *Modern English Usage*, 2nd ed. p. 602: "5. the defining *such*. A useful device in drafting legal documents, where precision is all-important, is to use *such* in the sense of as defined above, so as to avoid ambiguity without having to repeat the defining words, as in *The particulars required by this section may be furnished by or on behalf of any person who is a party to the agreement . . . and where such particulars are duly furnished by or on behalf of any such person the provision of this section shall be deemed to be duly complied with on the part of all such persons.*"

[68] (1952) S.C.R. 368, ('52) A.SC. 27.

[69] (1952) S.C.R. 612, ('52) A.SC. 181.

[70] (1950) S.C.R. 88 at p. 117.

[71] ibid. at pp. 170-1.

[72] ibid. at p. 210.

11.170 But a change in preventive detention laws again raised the question which had led Bose J. to dissent in *Krishnan's Case.* In *W. B.* v. *Ashok Dey*[73] the Supreme Court followed the majority judgment in *Krishnan's Case.*[74] In *Fagu Shaw* v. *W. B.*[75] the petitioner impugned the validity of s. 13 of the Maintenance of Internal Security Act, 1971 as amended by s. 6 (*d*), Defence of India Act, 1971,[76] on the ground that it did not fix the maximum period of detention as required by Art. 22 (7) (*b*). It was contended for the respondent that (i) Art. 22 (7) did not make it obligatory to fix a maximum period, and (ii) that in any event, s. 13 *had* prescribed the maximum period. Mathew J., for himself, Ray C.J. and Chandrachud J. upheld both these contentions. Alagiriswami J. dissented as to contention (i), but agreed with the majority as to contention (ii); Bhagwati J. dissented from the majority as to both the contentions. In substance, though not in form, all the three judgments reconsidered *Krishnan's Case.* It is submitted that since the four judges held that s. 13 had fixed a maximum period, the question whether Art. 22 (7) (*b*) made it obligatory to fix a maximum period was purely academic, and a reconsideration of *Krishnan's Case* was not called for, since such reconsideration would only have the status of considered *obiter dicta.* However, the following propositions emerge from the majority judgment:

Majority view in *Krishnan's Case* re-affirmed in *Fagu Shaw's Case*

(i) The dissenting judgment of Bose J. was based on analogies which were misleading and his reasoning from them was not convincing.[77]

Propositions emerging from majority judgment in *Fagu Shaw's Case*

(ii) Under entry 3, List III, Sch. 7, Parliament and State Legislatures have plenary power to pass laws for preventive detention in respect of the subjects mentioned therein. And as ancillary to this power, or as inseparable from it, is the power to fix the period of detention. The purpose of Art. 22(4)(*a*) is to put a curb on that power as therein provided.[78]

(iii) ". . . the proviso to Art. 22(4)(*a*) means . . . that even if an advisory board reports before the expiration of 3 months that there is sufficient cause for detention, . . . the period of detention beyond three months shall not exceed the maximum period that might be fixed by any law made by Parliament under Art. 22(7)(*b*). The proviso cannot mean that even if Parliament does not pass such a law the State legislatures . . . cannot pass a law which provides for the detention of a person beyond three months."[79]

(iv) In the absence of a law under sub-cl. 7(*b*), Parliament and State legislatures could provide for detention for a period exceeding 3 months.

(v) The proviso says in effect that if Parliament fixed the maximum period under Art. 22(7)(*b*), the power of Parliament and State Legislatures to fix the period of detention under a law passed under the entry would be curtailed to that extent.[80]

(vi) "The problem here is one of cold dispassionate interpretation of the Article in question and we cannot import an obligation that Parliament 'shall'

---

[73] ('72) A.SC. 1660 (heard by a Bench of 4 Judges).

[74] *Held*, that ss. 10 to 13 of the W.B. (Prevention of Violent Activities) Act, 1970, which provided for the detention of a person for a period longer than three months, although Parliament had not fixed the maximum period under Art. 22(7)(*b*), were valid. As the sections were impugned also under Art. 19 the Supreme Court said that "assuming that Art. 19(1)(*d*) . . . is attracted to the case of preventive detention . . ." the restrictions imposed by the Act were reasonable restrictions in the interest of the general public: ibid. p. 1665.

[75] (1974) 2 S.C.R. 832, ('74) A.SC. 613.

[76] ('74) A.SC. at p. 615 where the material parts of s. 13 before amendment and as amended, are set out.

[77] ibid. pp. 617-8.

[78] ibid. p. 617.

[79] ibid.

[80] ibid.

by law prescribe the maximum period of detention. Such an obligation could only arise from an invisible radiation proceeding from a vague and speculative concept of personal liberty."[81]

(vii) "*The question whether, when Parliament passes a law under Art. 22(7)(b) fixing the maximum period of detention in a class of cases, it is exercising an independent power of fixing the maximum period of detention derived from cl. (7) of Art. 22 or a power transferred to the entries on the subject of preventive detention does not arise for consideration here. If the exercise of the power under Art. 22(7) is independent of the power conferred by the entries relating to preventive detention, the question whether a law passed by virtue of any of the entries fixing the period in excess of the maximum period fixed by a law passed under Art. 22(7)(b) would sub silentio repeal the provision in regard to the maximum period in the law passed under Art. 22(7) and make that period 'the maximum period' for the purpose of Art. 22(7)(b) does not also strictly arise for consideration.*"[82] (italics supplied)

(viii) The period of detention mentioned in the amended s. 12, namely, a period of one year from the date of detention, or termination of the emergency proclaimed by the President, whichever is later, did fix the maximum period of detention having regard to the meaning of the words "maximum period".[83] A maximum period may be measured in terms of years, months or days, as well as in terms of an occurrence of an event or the continuance of a state of affairs.[84]

As it is the majority judgment which lays down the law on the subject it is not proposed to consider the judgments of Alagiriswami J. and Bhagwati J. at this place. It will be submitted that Bhagwati J. in the present case, and Bose J. in *Krishnan's Case* reached the right conclusion though not for the reasons which they gave.

Submission: correct approach to the interpretation of Art. 22(4) to (7)

11.171 However, before pursuing the line of thought suggested by the judgment of Mathew J. [in para 11.170 (vii) above] we must refer briefly to the approach to the interpretation of Art. 22(4) to (7). First, in our country preventive detention is not limited to times of war or emergency, but is recognized as a normal topic of legislation by Sch. 7, List I entry 9 and List II, entry 3,[85] ("entry 9" and "entry 3"). Therefore, considerations relevant to interpreting preventive detention provisions in times of war or emergency are not relevant to interpreting the preventive detention provisions of our Constitution. In fact, on a proclamation of emergency, the right to move the courts for the enforcement of fundamental rights contained in Art. 22 can be suspended by a Presidential Order under Art. 359 if it were found necessary to do so. There is, therefore, no need to construe Art. 22 as though it provided only for an emergency. Secondly, Art. 22 confers fundamental rights. Article 22(1) and (2) provides safeguards for personal liberty. These safeguards are withdrawn in the case of preventive detention, and replaced

---

[81] ibid. This is in answer to the passage of Bose J. with its reference to "men rotting in jail as in the Bastille" (para 11.167 above).

[82] ibid.

[83] "Maximum" means "the highest attainable magnitude or quantity of something; a superior limit": *S.O.D.*, p. 1221 (1953) 3rd ed. The meaning of the word "period" is "course or extent of time"; "time of duration": *S.O.D.* ibid. p. 1474.

[84] Mathew J. referred to *Juggilal Kamalapat* v. *Collector of Bombay* ('46) A.B. 280 to show that detention fixed with reference to the duration of the emergency was not vague or uncertain. *Fagu Shaw's Case* was fol. in *Mohd Alam* v. *W.B.* ('74) A.SC. 917, 920 as to the meaning and effect of the expression "maximum period" in Art. 22(7)(b).

[85] See para 11.162 of the text.

by safeguards provided by Art. 22(4) to (7), which are a pale shadow of the safeguards which they replaced. Since Art. 22(4) to (7) confers fundamental rights in relation to preventive detention—and preventive detention makes grave inroads on personal liberty—Art. 22(4) to (7) must, in case of doubt, be construed in favour of the persons to be detained. The framers of our Constitution accepted preventive detention as a necessary evil; but that evil should not be aggravated by an interpretation which would drain Art. 22(4) to (7) of its contents if a reasonable alternative construction was possible which would avoid that result. Thirdly, as Bhagwati J. rightly observed in answer to Mathew J., if the Constitution has prescribed a certain requirement as a safeguard of personal liberty, it is not for a Court to question the utility of that safeguard.[86] Finally, the legislative history of preventive detention explains why the drafting of preventive detention provisions leaves much to be desired, and why an elaborate analysis is required to give a coherent account of preventive detention and the safeguards against its abuse.

Legislative history of preventive detention

11.172 In the G.I. Act, 35, preventive detention was *not* a subject matter of concurrent legislative power.[87] Preventive detention under entry 1, List I was in respect of matters over which the Federal Legislature had exclusive legislative power, and preventive detention under entry 1, List II was in respect of matters over which provincial legislatures had exclusive legislative power. In framing the legislative Lists, the framers of our Constitution departed from the scheme of the G.I. Act, 35, and entry 9 conferred exclusive legislative power on Parliament in respect of 3 heads of preventive detention, and entry 3 conferred concurrent legislative power of preventive detention in respect of three other heads of preventive detention.[88] When the Lists were first adopted, draft Article 15 (Art 21 of our Constitution) contained the "due process" clause which would have secured safeguards against improper exercise of legislative and executive powers of preventive detention. However, although the due process clause was later deleted, the legislative entries remained unchanged. This provoked strong criticism both inside and outside the Constituent Assembly, as a result of which Dr. Ambedkar moved a draft Art. 15A. He said that "by introducing Art. 15A (we are) making . . . compensation for what was done then in passing Art. 15. In other words we are providing

Legislative entries in G.I. Act, 35 and in our Constitution

Draft Art. 15A and further amendments

[86] ('74) A.SC. *supra* at pp. 631-2. Mathew J. asked: "What then is the great guarantee of personal liberty in the fixation of the maximum period of detention by Parliament if that fixation can fluctuate with the mood of Parliament?": ibid. p. 610. It is submitted that Bhagwati J. was equally right in pointing out that though in theory Parliament could fix any period at its sweet will, in practice a highly responsible representative body like Parliament was unlikely to do so. That, it may be added, is the underlying assumption of representative government.

[87] Sch. VII: *Entry 1, List I*: "Preventive detention in British India for reasons of State connected with defence, external affairs or discharge of the functions of the Crown in its relation with Indian States." *Entry 1, List II*: "Public order . . preventive detention for reasons connected with the maintenance of public order; persons subject to such detention."

[88] Sch. VII: *Entry 9, List I*: "Preventive detention for reasons connected with Defence, Foreign Affairs, or the security of India; persons subjected to such detention;" *Entry 3, List III*: "Preventive detention for reasons connected with the security of a State, the maintenance of public order, or the maintenance of supplies and services essential to the community; persons subjected to such detention."

for the substance of 'due process' by the introduction of Art. 15A".[89] As a result of prolonged discussions and criticism in the Constituent Assembly, Dr. Ambedkar accepted the undernoted amendments[90] which were adopted and the Article as amended was passed. As a result of objections raised to these Articles by the Home Ministry under Sardar Vallabhbhai Patel, Shri T. T. Krishnamachari moved certain amendments to Art. 15A,[91] providing for preventive detention for longer than three months without consulting the Advisory Board, and these amendments were adopted. His speech in support of the amendments showed no awareness of the complications which would be caused by the fact that, in part, preventive detention was a subject of concurrent legislative power.[92] However, Shri Ajit Prasad Jain expressly referred to the concurrent legislative power of the States in relation to preventive detention and suggested amendments which would avoid the complications created by that fact.[93] In his general reply, Dr. Ambedkar dealt with the amendments moved by Shri Krishnamachari, but he did not deal with the point of concurrent legislative power which had been raised by Shri Jain. This is not surprising, because the members of the Constituent Assembly felt obliged to proceed with the draft Constitution within rigid time limits[94] which did not leave much time for precise legal draftsman-

---

[89] "15A. (1) No person who is arrested shall be detained in custody without being informed, as soon as may be, of the grounds for such arrest nor shall he be denied the right to consult a legal practitioner of his choice. (2) Every person who is arrested and detained in custody shall be produced before the nearest magistrate within a period of twenty-four hours of such arrest excluding the time necessary for the journey from the place of arrest to the court of the magistrate and no such person shall be detained in custody beyond the said period without the authority of a magistrate. (3) Nothing in this article shall apply — (*a*) to any person who for the time being is an enemy alien; or (*b*) to any person who is arrested under any law providing for preventive detention: Provided that nothing in sub-clause (*b*) of clause (3) of this article shall permit the detention of a person for a longer period than three months unless — (*a*) an Advisory Board consisting of persons who are or have been or are qualified to be appointed as judges of a High Court has reported before the expiration of the said period of three months that there is in its opinion sufficient cause for such detention, or (*b*) such person is detained in accordance with the provisions of any law made by Parliament under clause (4) of this article. (4) Parliament may by law prescribe the circumstances under which and the class or classes of cases in which a person who is arrested under any law providing for preventive detention may be detained for a period longer than three months and also the maximum period for which any such person may be so detained.": *C.A.D.* Vol. 9, pp. 1496-7.

[90] "That in clause (1) of article 15A, after the word 'consult' the words, 'and be defended by' be inserted. That in clause (3) . . . for the words 'nothing in this article' the words, brackets and figures 'Nothing in clauses (1) and (2) of the article' be substituted. That after clause (3) . . . the following clauses be inserted: '(3*a*) Where an order is made in respect of any person under sub-clause (*b*) of clause (3) of this article the authority making an order shall as soon as may be communicate to him the grounds on which the order has been made and afford him the earliest opportunity of making a representation against the order. (3*b*) Nothing in clause (3*a*) of this article shall require the authority making any order under sub-clause (*b*) of clause (3) of this article to disclose the facts which such authority considers to be against the public interest to disclose.' That at the end of clause (4) . . . the following be added: 'and Parliament may also prescribe by law the procedure to be followed by an Advisory Board in any enquiry under clause (*a*) of the proviso to clause (3) of this article'.": ibid. p. 1570.

[91] C.A.D. Vol. 10, p. 531.

[92] ibid. p. 532.

[93] ibid. p. 534.

[94] See *f.n.* 95 below.

ship before the various Articles were finally adopted.[95] In the following discussion no reliance will be placed on speeches made in the Constituent Assembly, first, because they are not a permissible aid to construction[96] and, secondly, because no reliance can be placed on the passage extracted by Bhagwati J. from Dr. Ambedkar's speech in the Constituent Assembly,[97] because when Art. 15A was first discussed in the Constituent Assembly he admitted that the word in cl. (4) [now clause 7(*a*) and (*b*)] was "may" and that Parliament might or might not make a law as is clear from the following:

Dr. Ambedkar: ". . . Those who want that a maximum sentence may be fixed will please note the provision of cl. (4) where it has been definitely stated that in making such a law Parliament will also fix the maximum period." *Pandit Kunzru*: "The word is 'may'. *Dr. Ambedkar*: " 'May' is 'shall'." *Pandit Kunzru*: "Parliament may or may not do that." *Dr. Ambedkar*: "*That is true.* But if it does, it will fix the maximum."[98] (italics supplied)

It is clear that no conclusion can be drawn from the speeches of Dr. Ambedkar, for the above exchange cancels out the passage of Dr. Ambedkar's speech extracted by Bhagwati J.

11.173 It is submitted that an inquiry into the line of thought suggested by the judgment of Mathew J. shows that the assumption made by him, and in several Supreme Court judgments, that the legislative power of preventive detention under entries 9 and 3 is plenary, except for the restrictions contained in Art. 22(4) to (7), cannot be sustained. The following analysis shows that the legislative power is not plenary:

Submission: assumption that legislative power of preventive detention is plenary is not correct:

(i) Plenary power means a power which, *taken by itself*, is an absolute power to make any law of preventive detention and for all anciliary matters. Plenary concurrent legislative power in respect of preventive detention (entry 3) must mean that, apart from any question of conflict between a preventive detention law made by Parliament and such a law made by a State Legislature,[99] a State Legislature, acting under entry 3, can make the same kind of law of preventive detention for the State as Parliament, acting under entry 3, can make for the whole of India.

A new analysis of Art. 22(4) and (7)

(ii) The opening words of Art. 22(4) govern both sub-cl. (*a*) and sub-cl. (*b*). Though the opening words are negative in form, the negative is a negative pregnant, that is, it implies the positive, namely, that if the conditions mentioned in sub-cls. (*a*) and (*b*) are complied with, a law can authorize the detention of a person for a period longer than three months.

(iii) Article 22(4) and (7) deals with one main topic, namely, detention for a period longer than three months. The main topic is divided into two sub-topics: detention for a longer period

[95] See Austin, *The Indian Constitution*, p. 109: "The pressure brought by the Assembly on its leaders produced results in August and September, *those hectic months when final decisions had to be made on other tangled issues* such as federalism, compensation for property and language. On 15th September Ambedkar submitted . . . a new Art. 15A." (italics supplied); and *C.A.D.* Vol. 9, pp. 1538-9; 1564.

[96] See paras 2.38 to 2.44 of the text.

[97] ('74) A.SC. at p. 629; see *C.A.D.* Vol. 10, pp. 575-6.

[98] *C.A.D.* Vol. 9, p. 1563.

[99] Art. 254 provides for resolving such conflict.

than three months *with the intervention* of the Advisory Board and *without such intervention.* Clauses (4) and (7) are interconnected and cannot operate independently of each other. The language of Art. 22(4) compels us to read into it the provisions of sub-cls. (*a*) and (*b*) of cl. (7); and likewise the language of cl. (7) (*c*) compels us to read it into the proviso to Art. 22(4) (*a*). So read, Art. 22(4) would run in some such way as this:

Art. 22(4): No law providing for preventive detention shall authorize the detention of a person for a longer period than three months unless (except on the condition that)[1]—

(*a*) an Advisory Board consisting of persons who are, or have been, or are qualified to be appointed as, Judges of a High Court (who, acting according to the procedure to be followed by the Advisory Board in an inquiry under this sub-clause which Parliament may by law prescribe)[2] have reported before the expiration of the said period of three months that there is in its opinion sufficient cause for such detention:

Provided that nothing in this sub-clause shall authorize the detention of any person beyond the maximum period (which Parliament may by law prescribe for which any person may in any class or classes of cases be detained under any law of preventive detention),[3] or

(*b*) Such person is detained for a period longer than three months in accordance with the provisions of any law made by Parliament (which law Parliament has power to make)[4] [prescribing (1) the circumstances under which, and the class or classes of cases in which, a person may be detained for a period longer than three months under any law providing for preventive detention without obtaining the opinion of an Advisory Board in accordance with the provisions of sub-clause (*a*) of clause (4)][5] and (2) [Parliament has by law prescribed (as it has power to do) the maximum period for which any person may in any class or class of cases be detained under any law of preventive detention].[5]

(iv) Taking Art. 22(7) by itself, its opening words: "Parliament may by law prescribe" are words conferring legislative power in respect of the matters contained in sub-cls. (*a*) to (*c*). As this legislative power is conferred on Parliament alone, it cannot be a concurrent legislative power which, *by definition,* must belong both to Parliament and the State Legislatures. The power conferred on Parliament by Art. 22(7) extends not only to the three heads of preventive detention mentioned in entry 9 on which Parliament alone has power to make laws; but it also extends to three *other* heads of preventive detention mentioned in entry 3 on which Parliament has a *concurrent* legislative power, along with State Legislatures. In other words, Art. 22(4) and (7) makes no distinction between the exclusive and the concurrent legislative powers of Parliament. The only way to resolve the conflict arising out of the concurrent power conferred by entry 3 on Parliament and the State Legislatures with the exclusive power conferred on Parliament by cl. (7) is to recognize that the legislative power conferred on Parliament by Art. 22(7) (*a*) to (*c*) is not included in the concurrent legislative entry 3. It must

---

[1] Webster, *Third New International Dictionary,* p. 2503.

[2] The words in brackets read cl. (7)(*c*) into cl. (4)(*a*) to which cl. (7)(*c*) expressly refers.

[3] The words in brackets read cl. (7)(*b*) into the Proviso which expressly refers to cl. (7)(*b*).

[4] The words in brackets state the effect of the opening words of cl. (7) "Parliament may by law prescribe".

[5] The words in brackets read into Art. 22(4)(*b*) sub-clauses (*a*) and (*b*) of cl. (7) to which Art. 22(4)(*b*) expressly refers.

also be recognized that the said legislative power is not included in entry 9, first, because Art. 22 (4) and (7) makes no distinction between the exclusive and the concurrent legislative power of Parliament, and, secondly, because it would be absurd to confer on Parliament a power it already possessed. *And this reasoning applies wherever Art. 22 (4) and (7) confer an exclusive power on Parliament.*

(v) Reading Art. 22 (4) (*b*) with Art. 22 (7) (*a*) and (*b*), as we must, it is clear that Art. 22 (4) (*b*) confers on Parliament the exclusive power to make a law authorizing the detention of a person for a longer period than three months *without the intervention* of an Advisory Board.[6] Consequently, the State legislatures have no power to enact such a law under entry 3, and equally Parliament has no such power under entry 9.

(vi) The legislative power conferred on Parliament by Art. 22 (4) (*b*) read with Art. 22(7)(*a*) *and* (*b*) includes the power to prescribe the maximum period of detention if the detention is for a longer period than three months *and* such detention is *without the intervention of the Advisory Board.* It is indisputable that if Parliament decides to make a law in the exercise of its powers under Art. 22(7)(*a*) it *must* prescribe the maximum period of detention under Art. 22 (7) (*b*) as required by Art. 22 (4) (*b*) if detention under such law is to be constitutionally valid. But a law prescribing the maximum period of detention under Art. 22 (7) (*b*) not only fixes the maximum period of detention for a period longer than three months *without the intervention of an Advisory Board*, but also where the detention is for a period longer than three months *with the intervention of the Board* as the proviso to Art. 22(4)(*a*) clearly shows. Therefore, the exclusive power conferred on Parliament is one composite power which, when exercised fixes the maximum period both for detention *without the intervention of the Advisory Board* and for *detention with the intervention of the Board.* It must follow that the power to prescribe the maximum period of detention for a period longer than three months is not included in entry 3 and equally not in entry 9. The result therefore is that a State Legislature cannot validly make a law authorizing detention for a longer period than three months with the intervention of an Advisory Board if Parliament does not fix the maximum period of such detention, and neither can Parliament acting only under entries 3 and 9.

11.174 The above analysis shows that the reasoning of Mathew J. that a law of preventive detention for more than three months need not fix the maximum period of detention because, but for the restrictions imposed by Art. 22 (4) to (7), the powers under entry 3 and entry 9 are plenary, fails, because power under the said entries is not plenary. But the above analysis is not merely negative in character, it discloses a positive and coherent scheme of legislative power relating to preventive detention which is set out in paras 11.175 and 11.176 below.

Submission: assumption of majority judgment not correct

---

[6] See the re-written Art. 22(4)(*b*) in (iii) above.

Submission: A coherent scheme of legislative power relating to preventive detention

11.175 (i) The legislative power under entry 3 and entry 9, defines the heads in respect of which Parliament under entry 9, and Parliament and State Legislatures under entry 3, can pass laws for preventive detention. Article 22(4) to (7) does not refer to these heads of preventive detention, but proceeds on the basis that preventive detention laws relate to those heads.

(ii) Our Constitution divides preventive detention into two main categories: preventive detention for a period of three months or less, and preventive detention for a period longer than three months.

(iii) As to preventive detention for a period of three months or less, legislative power under entries 9 and 3 is plenary, subject only to the limitation on that power imposed by Art. 22(5) as qualified by Art. 22(6). Though *in form* the restrictions under Art. 22(5) are imposed on the executive which passes orders of detention, *in effect* they are also restrictions on legislative power under entries 9 and 3, because any law empowering the executive to disregard the limitations imposed by cl. (5) read with cl. (6) would be void.

(iv) As to preventive detention for a period longer than three months, the restrictions on the exercise of that power imposed by cl. (5) also apply to such detention. But for the rest, Art. 22(4) and (7) itself provides for preventive detention for a period longer than three months and itself authorizes such detention subject to the conditions laid down in those sub-Articles. We have seen[7] that the opening words of Art. 22(4) govern both the sub-clauses (*a*) and (*b*) and that though couched in the negative they imply a positive authorizing a law of preventive detention for a longer period than three months if the conditions laid down in sub-cls. (*a*) and (*b*) are fulfilled. This result is achieved in two ways mentioned in (v) and (vi) below:

(v) By laying down in Art. 22(4)(*a*) conditions precedent to the exercise of power under sub-cl. (*a*) which would ordinarily be a subject matter of legislative power under legislative entries. Thus, under entry 3 taken by itself, a State legislature would be free to make, (or not to make) a law providing for an Advisory Board and would be equally free to fix the composition of the Board, the time within which the Board is to make a report and the procedure to be followed by the Board. This power Parliament and the State legislatures have under entry 3, and Parliament has under entry 9 *if the detention is for a period of three months or less.* But for detention for a period longer than three months, Art. 22(4)(*a*) requires the appointment of an Advisory Board constituted in the manner prescribed in cl. (4)(*a*) which also prescribes the time within which the report of the Board is to be made. There is no scope for a different exercise of legislative power for the conditions of such exercise are fixed by Art. 22(4)(*a*) itself.

(vi) The second method by which preventive detention for a period longer than three months is taken out of the legislative entries 3 and 9 is by expressly conferring a power on Parliament alone to make laws in respect of the matters set out in Art. 22(7)(*a*), (*b*) and (*c*) read with Art. 22(4)(*a*) and (*b*). Thus, whereas legislative power

---

[7] See para 11.173 (iii) above.

under entry 3 to appoint an Advisory Board would ordinarily have carried with it a power to prescribe the procedure which the Board must follow, Art. 22 (7) (*a*) confers that power on Parliament alone. Again, whereas legislative power under entry 3 would have ordinarily carried with it the power to prescribe the maximum duration of the detention, Art. 22 (7) (*b*) confers that power on Parliament alone.

(vii) The underlying scheme of Art. 22 (4) and (7) seems to be that detention for a period of three months or less can be left to Parliament and the State Legislatures, for though preventive detention is a serious matter, the relatively short duration of three months makes it unnecessary to fetter the legislative power under entries 3 and 9 except as provided in Art. 22 (5) read with Art. 22 (6). However, detention for a longer period than three months was considered a very serious matter, and in respect of it, Art. 22 (4) (*a*) imposed the requirement of a Board constituted as provided therein, which must make a report within the time there prescribed and following the procedure prescribed by Parliament. For, though it is not obligatory on Parliament to prescribe the procedure under cl. (7) (*c*), it was realised that if Parliament considered detention for a period longer than three months necessary, Parliament would prescribe the procedure, for, without such procedure the functioning of a Board would be gravely impaired. However, the opening words of cl. (7) confer a power — they do not impose an obligation, so that if Parliament considered preventive detention for a longer period than three months unjustified, Parliament could give effect to its views by not making a law under cl. (7).

(viii) Finally, detention for a period longer than three months without the intervention of the Board was considered most serious, and Art. 22 (4) (*b*), read with Art. 22 (7) (*a*) and (*b*) conferred on Parliament the exclusive power to make a law authorizing such detention even in respect of the 3 heads of detention contained in the concurrent legislative entry 3.

(ix) The reason for conferring exclusive power on Parliament and thereby taking that power out of the legislative Lists in respect of detention for a period longer than three months appears to be that it was considered unsafe to vest that power also in the State Legislatures under the concurrent legislative list, because such powers were liable to grave abuse since State legislatures might be influenced by regional or local considerations. Conferment of power on Parliament greatly reduced the risk of abuse, first, because it is the highest legislature in the whole of India, the members of the Lok Sabha being elected by universal adult franchise and therefore representative of the whole country; and secondly, because the composition of the Rajya Sabha ensures that the interest of the States would not be neglected and that the passing gusts of political opinion would not be immediately reflected in the Rajya Sabha whose members retire as to a third every two years.

11.176 It is submitted that the above scheme of preventive detention which is disclosed as a result of "cold dispassionate analysis" (to use the words of Mathew J.) given in para 11.173 above has the effect of freeing the law of preventive detention under our Constitution from the reproach of authorizing detention without trial for the rest of a

Submission: the scheme submitted above frees preventive detention from the

monstrous result of indefinite detention

person's life. The reference made by Bose J. in his dissenting judgment in *Krishnan's Case* to men rotting in the Bastille for the rest of their lives was fully justified as pointing out the monstrous consequences of a construction of Art. 22(7) which ought to be avoided if any other construction were reasonably possible. In any event, if the construction submitted above, as disclosed by an analysis of Art. 22(4) to (7) and entry 9 and entry 3, is a reasonably possible one, then on well settled principles of interpretation, it ought to be preferred to a construction for which judges have expressed great dislike even when they have felt constrained to adopt it. Mathew J. rightly said that "malignant diseases call for drastic remedies". But the safeguards — feeble as they are — which our Constitution provided in relation to preventive detention were meant to secure that the malignancy of the disease from which the persons to be detained were alleged to suffer, was not made a cloak for the malignity of those who had it in their power to detain such persons.

Submission: the view taken in the dissenting judgment of Bose J., and Bhagwati J., is correct

11.177 It is submitted that the view taken by Bose J. in *Krishnan's Case* and by Bhagwati J. in *Fagu Shaw's Case* is correct, namely, that the power of detention for a period longer than three months is subject to the fulfilment of conditions precedent which include Parliament fixing the maximum time. If such maximum time is not fixed, the condition precedent becomes incapable of performance and the power cannot be exercised. In view of the analysis of Art. 22(4) and (7) which the present writer has adopted, it would not be profitable to discuss the dissenting judgments of Alagiriswami and Bhagwati JJ. on Art. 22(4) and (7). It may however be observed that the view expressed by Alagiriswami J. that the word "may" in the opening sentence of Art. 22(7) means "shall" is not correct. For, though in special circumstances the word "may" may be treated as "shall", ordinarily, it means "may". Secondly, the most serious objection to treating "may" as "shall" is that Parliament would be under an obligation to enact a law providing for longer detention than three months with or without the intervention of an Advisory Board, and there is no justification for holding that Parliament cannot take the view that detention for a period longer than three months is unjustified and that a law providing for such preventive detention was not required.

Submission: the finding that s. 13 fixed the maximum period is not correct

11.178 As to the finding of Mathew J. that Parliament prescribed "the maximum period" in the impugned s. 13, it is submitted that the finding is not correct. A maximum period can be fixed not merely by mentioning a period of time, as for example, one year or one year and six months, but also by reference to a contingency which must happen, as for example, the termination of the emergency proclaimed by the President. But the impugned s. 13 after amendment does not prescribe *the* maximum period which, having regard to the definite article "the" can be only one period. Section 13 prescribes two periods: one a period of one year from the date of the detention order and the other a period measured by the termination of the emergency, whichever of the two is later. If the question were asked "What is the maximum period fixed by section 13 for the detention of X?" the answer must be "no one knows", because the maximum period instead of being one fixed period is left completely fluid. It is submitted that s. 13 did not comply with the requirement of Art. 22(7)(*b*) and was therefore void as rightly held by Bhagwati J.

S. N. Sarkar's Case: majority view in Gopalan's Case of the co-relation of Arts. 22(4) and (7), and their interpretation overruled

11.179 In *S. N. Sarkar* v. *W.B.*[8] a Bench of seven judges reconsidered that part of *Gopalan's Case* which dealt with the relation of sub-cl. (4)(*a*) and (*b*) to sub-cl. (7)(*a*) and (*b*) of Art. 22. The petitioner challenged the order of detention passed under the Maintenance of Internal Security Act, 1971 (popularly called MISA) on several grounds before the High Court.[9] In appeal, he obtained leave to amend the petition challenging the validity of ss. 3, 5, 8, 11, 12 and 13 of the Act on the ground that they violated Arts. 14, 19, 21 and 22.[10] At the hearing before a Constitution Bench, the petitioner further contended that s. 17A of the Act[11] was invalid, and the Constitution Bench directed that the matter should be considered by a larger Bench because the decision in *Gopalan's Case* required reconsideration. The present discussion is confined to the challenge to s. 17A on the ground that it did not comply with the requirements of Art. 22(7).

The contentions in Sarkar's Case

11.180 The Supreme Court said that the petitioner's contentions gave rise to three questions:

(1) Whether cl. (7) is an exception to the rule laid down in cl. (4); (2) whether Parliament's power to enact a detention law is limited by the requirements laid down in cl. (7); and (3) whether setting out verbatim the heads or subjects or some of them upon which Parliament can enact such a law would mean compliance with the requirements of cl. (7).

These very questions had been considered in one form or another in *Gopalan's Case*.[12] Shelat Acg. C.J., who delivered the judgment of the Court, observed that although in that case Mukherjea J. agreed with the majority, he expressed the view that to mention the heads of preventive detention under legislative entries did not carry out the constitutional purpose of Art. 22(7)(*a*), but he was not prepared to hold the law invalid on that account.[13] Das J. also expressed the view that it would have been better if the Act had prescribed specific circumstances or a more rigid and definite specification of classes of cases, but he added, "that is crying for the ideal".[14] Fazl Ali and Mahajan JJ. dissented from the majority.

The law laid down in Sarkar's Case

11.181 It is clear from the judgment in *Sarkar's Case* that Shelat Acg. C.J. approved the dissenting judgments of Fazl Ali and Mahajan JJ. in *Gopalan's Case*. As the judgments expressly overruled the majority view in *Gopalan's Case* on the points on which the two judges dissented, it would save repetition if the position as it emerges from the judgment of Shelat Acg. C.J., and the judgments of Fazl Ali and Mahajan JJ. is given below:

---

8 (1974) 1 S.C.R. 1, ('73) A.SC. 1425.
9 (('73) A.SC. at p. 1427 where the six grounds are set out.
10 ibid. where the reasons for the challenge are fully set out.
11 Which provided for a period of detention of 21 months without consulting an Advisory Board.
12 Where the validity of s. 12 of the Preventive Detention Act, 1950 was impugned.
13 ('73) A.SC. at pp. 1433-4 where the passage is set out in full.
14 ibid. p. 1433.

(*a*) Article 22 (4) (*a*) lays down a rule to which Art. 22 (4) (*b*) read with cl. (7) (*a*) is an exception.[15]

(*b*) In Art. 22 (7) (*a*),

" 'Circumstances' would ordinarily mean situations or events extraneous to the activities of a concerned person or a group of persons, such as riots, disorders, tensions, religious, racial, regional or linguistic or such commotion which might by their pre-existence accentuate the impact of such activities affecting the security of the country or a part of it or public order. Class or classes of cases on the other hand, relate to group or groups of individuals, who by the nature of their activities fall under one particular group or groups by their common or similar objective or objectives."[16]

(*c*) "As Mahajan J. pointed out in *Gopalan* the language of cls. (4) and (7) shows that they deal with three distinct situations: (1) where the activities of the persons likely to perpetrate them though connected with the subjects in the entries, are of such a nature and consequence that three months' detention would meet the situation; (2) where the activities of the persons likely to perpetrate them are of such a nature and consequence that they need a longer period of detention, but with the intercession of an Advisory Board, and (3) where the activities and the persons likely to resort to them are of such a nature and consequence that the situations they create are such as require not only a longer period of detention, but also the dispensation of intercession by an Advisory (Board). . . . Such situations may arise not merely in cases involving the security of the nation or part or parts of it but may arise in connection with the rest of the subjects in the entries. Sabotage of essential supplies and services would in given circumstances be as dangerous as activities involving danger to the security of the State and/or public order."[17]

(*d*) There are two objections to equating the six heads contained in the legislative entries in respect of preventive detention with the circumstances and the class or classes of cases mentioned in cl. (7) (*a*):

(i) ". . . though activities of persons thought necessary for detention may vary in degrees of their impact in that depending upon the situation existing at the time, all of them, irrespective of their degree and intensity and impact, would be clubbed together so as to treat them equally in a law under cl. (7)(*a*). In such a case if the activities, which would not justify the dispensation of the safeguard of an advisory board as against those which need such dispensation, would be treated equally, with the result that in respect of all activities and all situations, Parliament would be enabled to dispense with the safeguards of the intervention of an Advisory Board."[18]

(ii) "Such a construction would amount to the Constitution saying in one breath that a law of preventive detention cannot provide for detention for a longer period than three months without reference to an Advisory Board and at the same breath and moment that Parliament, if it so chooses, can do so in respect of all or any of the subjects mentioned in the legislative field . . ."[19]

Such a construction would nullify the safeguard provided by Art. 22 (4) (*a*).

(*e*) The word "and" in cl. (7) (*a*) is conjunctive and must be read as "and" and not as "or"[20] as held by the majority in *Gopalan's Case* which the larger Bench overruled on this point. Consequently, in

---

[15] ('73) A.SC. 1441; (1950) S.C.R. p. 173 (Fazl Ali J.), ibid. p. 234 [Mahajan J.: Clause (7) "was incorporated to meet abnormal and exceptional cases"].

[16] ('73) A.SC. 1439; (1950) S.C.R. at pp. 180-81 (Fazal Ali J.); p. 236 (Mahajan J.).

[17] ('73) A.SC. at p. 1439.

[18] ('73) A.SC. pp. 1438-9; the same view was forcefully expressed by Fazl Ali J. in (1950) S.C.R. at pp. 180-81 where he labelled the three categories of preventive detention as "dangerous", "more dangerous" and "most dangerous" and said that the Constitution treated them differently. A similar view was expressed by Mahajan J. at p. 238.

[19] (1950) S.C.R. at p. 237 (Mahajan J.); referred to in ('73) A.SC. at p. 1434.

[20] ('73) A.SC. at p. 1441; (1950) S.C.R. at pp. 175-6 (Fazl Ali J.), and p. 235 "I share this view with (Fazl Ali J.)" (Mahajan J.).

order to comply with cl. (4) (*b*) read with cl. (7) (*a*), a law must prescribe *both* the circumstances under which, and the class or classes of cases in which, the advisory body can be dispensed with.[21]

(*f*) Shelat Acg. C.J. referred to the difficulty felt by Sastri J. in *Gopalan's Case* that it would be impossible for Parliament to exhaustively set out the circumstances or the class or classes of cases in a law made under cl. (7) (*a*). But Shelat Acg. C.J. said that Fazl Ali J. had met that difficulty by referring to Regulation 18B of the British Defence of the Realm Regulations 1939,[22] and Mahajan J. had met the difficulty by referring to the classification of prejudicial activities set out in R. 34 (6) of the Defence of India Rules, 1939.[23] Shelat Acg. C.J. added that such a classification was also made by R. 36 (6) of the Defence of India Rules, 1971, and by s. 3 (2) of the W.B. (Prevention of Violent Activities) Act, 1970.[24]

(*g*) Fazl Ali J. said that his reasoning proceeded on the basis that an extreme type of law such as could be made under cl. (7) (*a*) must be limited to special classes of cases and circumstances,[25] and Mahajan J. said that the view he had taken of law of preventive detention was in accord with the scheme of the law of punitive detention where offences are classified according to their gravity, as for example, simple hurt, grievous hurt, grievous hurt with dangerous weapons etc. The framers of the Constitution must have contemplated the classification of classes of cases on the same lines.[26]

In the result, Shelat Acg. C.J. held s. 17A *ultra vires* and void. In view of this decision, he found it unnecessary to consider the challenge to the other sections based largely on the decision in the *Bank Nationalization Case*.

11.182 However, in *H. Saha* v. *W.B.*[27] the Constitutional validity of the Maintenance of Internal Security Act, 1971, was challenged on the ground that the Act violated Arts. 19, 21, 22 and 14. Here again, the challenge was based on the *Bank Nationalization Case* which had held that Art. 19 (1) (*f*) and Art. 31 (2) were not mutually exclusive, disapproving of the principle said to have been adopted by the majority in *Gopalan's Case*. Ray C.J.[28] said that the petitioners contended:

H. Saha's Case: Maintenance of Internal Security Act, 1971, held valid

"First, . . . that the law of preventive detention is unreasonable, and, therefore, it violates Art. 19. Second, . . . that the Act violates Art. 21 because the guarantee of a right to be heard is infringed. Third, . . . that the Act does not lay down the just procedure for giving effect to Art. 22(5). Fourth, . . . that the Act violates Art. 14 because it permits discrimination."[29]

It is clear that the Court was of the opinion that Arts. 19 and 22 are mutually exclusive.[30] However, in view of the comments made on

---

21 ('73) A.SC. at p. 1441.
22 (1950) S.C.R. at p. 168.
23 ibid. p. 241.
24 ('73) A.SC. at p. 1441.
25 (1950) S.C.R. at p. 176.
26 ibid. p. 239.
27 ('74) A.SC. 2154.
28 For himself, Reddy, Mathew, Beg and Alagiriswami JJ.
29 ibid. p. 2155. The judgment sets out the provisions of ss. 3, 7, 8 and 10 to 15 of the Act at pp. 2155-6.
30 "Constitution has conferred rights under Art. 19 and also adopted preventive detention to prevent the greater evil of elements imperilling the security, the safety of a State and the welfare of the Nation. It is not possible to think that a person who is detained will yet be free to move or assemble or form associations or unions or have the right to reside in any part of India or have the freedom of speech or expression. Suppose a person is prosecuted for an offence of cheating

Gopalan's Case in the *Bank Nationalization Case,* Ray C.J. observed: "We may proceed on the assumption that the Act which is for preventive detention may be tested with regard to its reasonableness with reference to Art. 19."[31] This repeated "assumption" in several judgments of the Supreme Court shows that the Benches deciding those cases had grave doubts about the correctness of the *Bank Nationalization Case,* and for reasons given in Appendix III where the *Bank Nationalization Case* is considered, it is submitted that it is necessary to reconsider that case and overrule it. The following propositions emerge from the judgment of Ray C.J. upholding the Act:

Propositions emerging from *Saha's Case*

(*a*) Supreme Court decisions have laid down that a detenu has a right to be apprised of the materials on which the detention order was based or approved. Except as provided in Art. 22(6), in which case it was not necessary to disclose facts whose disclosures was considered to be against the public interest.[32]

(*b*) There was an obligation on the State to consider the detenu's representation; the advisory board had adequate power to examine all the materials and to call for additional material and also to call the detenu at his request. The constitution of the board showed that it was to consist of judges, or persons qualified to be judges, of the High Court. "The constitution of the board observes fundamentals of fair play and principles of natural justice.[33] An oral hearing was not a requirement of natural justice. Sec. 8 of the Act, which casts an obligation on the State to consider the detenu's representation afforded him all the rights guaranteed by Art. 22(5).[34]

(*c*) "The representation is to be considered by the Advisory Board by following the substance of natural justice as far as it is consistent with the nature of the impugned Act, the nature of the relative jurisdiction of the Government and of the Advisory Board. Procedural reasonableness for natural justice flows from Art. 19. Article 22(5) speaks of liberty and making of representation. The combined result of clauses (4), (5) and (6) of Art. 22 is that a procedure which permits representation will give all the facts before the Board. Article 22(5) shows that law as to detention is necessary. The requirements of that law are to be found in Art. 22. Article 22 gives the mandate as to what will happen in such circumstances."[35]

(*d*) There was no failure of justice because the order was not a speaking order. All that was necessary was that there should be a real and proper consideration of the detenu's representation by government and the advisory board.[36]

(*e*) The power conferred by s. 14 to revoke the detention order at any time showed that the authorities could consider new factors or changed circumstances. In *Fagu Shaw* v. *W.B.*[37] the Supreme Court had held that Parliament had fixed the maximum period of detention under Art. 22(7)(*b*). The further requirement of six-monthly review, as contended for by the petitioners, suggested a new provision which went not to reasonableness but to the policy of legislature and due process of law.[38]

(*f*) Sec. 8 of the Act followed the provisions of Art. 22(5) and as long as there was an obligation on the advisory board to consider the detenu's representation, the procedure was not unreasonable because the duty to consider the representation did not mean a personal hearing or a disclosure of the Board's reasons. Procedural reasonableness should not be judged by any abstract standards.[39] "The nature of the right infringed, the underlying purpose of the

---

and convicted after trial, it is not open to him to say that the imprisonment should be tested with reference to Art. 19 for its reasonableness. A law which attracts Art. 19 therefore must be such as is capable of being tested to be reasonable under cls. (2) to (5) of Art. 19": ibid. pp. 2157-8.

31 ibid. p. 2158.

32 ibid.

33 ibid.

34 ibid.

35 ibid. pp. 2158-9.

36 ibid. p. 2159.

37 ('74) A.SC. 613.

38 ('74) A.SC. 2159.

39 ibid.

restrictions imposed, the extent and urgency of the evil sought to be remedied thereby, the disproportion of the imposition to the prevailing conditions at the time, all provide the basis for considering the reasonableness of a particular provision."[40]

(*g*) "Principles of natural justice are an element in considering the reasonableness of a restriction where Art. 19 is applicable. At the stage of consideration of representation by the State Government, (its) obligation . . . is such as Art. 22(5) implies", and s. 8 of the Act followed the provisions of Art. 22(5).[41]

(*h*) "If the statutory provisions exclude (natural?) justice then the Court does not completely ignore the mandate of the legislature. The Court notices the distinction between the duty to act fairly and the duty to act judicially in accordance with natural justice. . . . The duty to act fairly is discharged even if there is not an oral hearing. Fairness denotes abstention from abuse of discretion."[42]

(*i*) Article 22 provided substantive limitations as well as procedural safeguards. "The principles of natural justice in so far as they are compatible with detention laws find a place in Art. 22 itself and also in the Act." The content of the reasonableness required is not increased even if the law is judged by the requirement of Art. 19.[43]

(*j*) "Article 14 is inapplicable because preventive detention and prosecution are not synonymous. The purposes are different. The authorities are different. The nature of proceedings are different. In a prosecution an accused is sought to be punished for a past act. In preventive detention, the past act is merely the material for inference about the future course of probable conduct on the part of the detenu."[44]

Preventive and punitive detention qualitatively different

11.183 Ray C.J. said that the power of preventive detention was qualitatively different from the power of punitive detention. The power of preventive detention was a precautionary power exercised in reasonable anticipation. It might or might not relate to an offence. It does not overlap with prosecution even if it relies on certain facts for which a prosecution may be, or may have been launched. An order of preventive detention was also not a bar to prosecution.[45] In this context, Ray C.J. said that, broadly speaking, the following propositions emerge from decided cases[46]:

---

[40] ibid.
[41] ibid.
[42] ibid.
[43] ibid. pp. 2159-60.
[44] ibid. p. 2160.
[45] ibid.
[46] ibid. The decisions referred to were: *Borjahan* v. *W.B.* ('72) A.SC. 2256 [*held*, that the mere fact that a detenu was liable to be tried in a criminal court for the commission of a criminal offence or to be proceeded against under Ch. VIII of the Cr.P.C. would not by itself debar the government from taking action for preventive detention under MISA. Cases under the Cr.P.C. whether punitive or preventive depend on the proof of objective facts which had already taken place, whereas a case under the Act providing for preventive detention depends on the subjective satisfaction of the authorities concerned that the person to be detained is likely to act in future in a manner similar to the one in which he acted in the past]; *Ashwin Kumar Ray* v. *W.B.* ('72) A.SC. 2561 (*held*, that the arrest of the petitioner in order to prosecute him under the Cr.P.C. and his enlargement on bail was no bar to the Dist.Magistrate issuing a detention order under MISA. This proposition was treated as well settled without reference to specific authorities); fol. in *Abdul Aziz* v. *Dist. Magistrate, Burdwan* ('73) A.SC. 770 (*held*, that a detention order passed during the pendency of a prosecution was invalid). Ray C.J. held that the above cases correctly laid down the principles to be followed as to whether a detention order was valid or not, and he added "The decision in *Biramchand* v. *U.P.* ('74) A.SC. 1161, a Division Bench decision of two learned judges was contrary to the cases laying down the correct principle which had been decided by three judges."

"First, merely because a detenu is liable to be tried in a criminal court for the commission of a criminal offence or to be proceeded against for preventing him from committing offences dealt with in Chapter VIII of the Cr.P.C.[47] would not by itself debar the government from taking action for his detention under (MISA); Second, the fact that the police arrests a person and later on enlarges him on bail and initiates steps to prosecute him under the Cr.P.C. and even lodges a first information report may be no bar against the Dist. Magistrate issuing the order under preventive detention; Third, where the concerned person is actually in jail custody at the time an order of detention is passed against him and is not likely to be released for a fair length of time, it may be possible to contend that there could be no satisfaction on the part of the detaining authority as to the likelihood of such a person indulging in activities which would jeopardise the security of the State or the public order; Fourth, the mere circumstance that a detention order is possible during the pendency of the prosecution will not violate the order; Fifth, the order of detention is a precautionary measure. It is based on a reasonable prognosis of the future behaviour of a person based on his past conduct in the light of surrounding circumstances."[48]

In addition to the decided cases to which Ray C.J. referred, the undernoted cases also laid down the principles to be followed as to whether a detention order was valid or not.[49] A similar view was expressed in *M. S. Khan* v. *C. C. Bose*.[50] In *Bhut Nath* v. *W.B.*[51] Krishna Iyer J. referred to *Subrati's Case* and to *Khan's Case*[52] and said that a host of decisions had made the legal position unchallengeable. He however added that "if extraneous motives adulterate the exercise of power, the Court must nullify it." He said that the following observations in *Rameshwarlal* v. *Bihar*[53] served as a warning:

"The appellant was tried for the offence and acquitted as far back as February 1967. This ground discloses carelessness which is extremely disturbing. That the detaining authority does not know that the appellant was tried and acquitted months before, and considers the pendency of the case against him as one of the grounds of detention shows that due care and attention is not being paid to such serious matters as detention without trial. If the appellant was tried and acquitted, Government was required to study the judgment of acquittal to discover whether all these allegations had any basis in fact or not. One can understand the use of the case if the acquittal was technical, but not, when the case was held to be false."[54]

Krishna Iyer J. observed that ". . . to detain a person after a Court had held the charge false was to expose oneself to the criticism of absence of due care and of rational material for subjective satisfaction." On the merits the petition was allowed, as the information injurious to the detenu on which the Dist. Magistrate acted had not been communicated to the detenu. The note of caution sounded by

---

47 "Security for keeping the peace and for good behaviour."

48 ('74) A.SC. *supra* at p. 2160.

49 *Subrati* v. *W.B.* (1973) 2 S.C.R. 990, ('73) A.SC. 207 [The judgment expressed the same view as was expressed in *Borjahan's Case* (see *f.n.* 46 above) and observed: "Even unsuccessful trial or proceedings would, therefore, not operate as a bar to a detention order or render it *mala fide*.": ('73) A.SC. at p. 210.

50 ('72) A.SC. 1670. The principle of *Hanif's Case* ('74) A.SC. 679 (see para 11.229 below) was affirmed in *Keshab Chandra* v. *W.B.* ('74) A.SC. 1739, but was held inapplicable to the impugned detention order, the validity of which was upheld.

51 (1974) 3 S.C.R. 315, ('74) A.SC. 806. Similar views had been expressed in *Kalyanmal* v. *Dist.Magistrate* ('70) A.Cal. 12, 14 (*held*, that merely because the detenu had been discharged from the criminal case, the order of detention was not *mala fide*. The criminal case was for what the detenu was alleged to have done. The detention order was passed with a view to prevent him from acting in a similar manner).

52 See *f.ns.* 49 and 50 above.

53 (1968) 2 S.C.R. 505 at p. 511, ('68) A.SC. 1303.

54 ('74) A.SC. *supra* at p. 813.

Krishna Iyer J. is clearly right, subject only to the reservation that if fresh evidence is discovered which would have secured a conviction had such evidence been available at the trial, a detention order would be justified.

11.184 The Preventive Detention Act, 1950, does not provide for the circumstances under which and the class or classes of cases in which a person may be detained for a period longer than three months without reference to an Advisory Board. However, it has been held that the omission of such a provision cannot make s. 11 (1) or s. 11A, Preventive Detention Act, *ultra vires* Art. 22 (7) (*a*). The failure of the legislature to define the circumstances and classes of cases mentioned in Art. 22 (7) (*a*) only meant that at present no Government could detain a person for more than three months without obtaining the opinion of an Advisory Board. If such an opinion had been obtained and the final order of detention passed within three months from the date of the original order of detention, the question of the invalidity of such order or the question of s. 11 (1) or 11-A, Preventive Detention Act, being *ultra vires* Art. 22 (7) could not arise.[55] s. 11(1) and s. 11A do not contravene Art. 22(7)

11.185 The gravest abuse of power during the Emergency was in preventively detaining persons—in utter disregard of the law. The Maintenance of Internal Security Act ("MISA") under which people were preventively detained, was put beyond the reach of fundamental rights by being included in Sch. 9 by the 39th Amendment. The 44th Amendment made the following changes in Art. 22 (4) to (7) by s. 3 of the amending Act ("S. 3"): The 44th Amendment and important changes made in Art. 22(4) to (7)

(*a*) Article 22 (4) was amended so as to reduce the period upto which a person could be preventively detained without consulting an Advisory Board from 3 to 2 months.

(*b*) The composition of the Advisory Board [Art. 22 (4) (*a*)] was altered to make it really independent of the executive government. Article 22 (4) (*a*) as originally enacted, provided that the Board must consist of persons who were, or had been, or were qualified to be appointed, judges of the High Courts. Since under Art. 217 (*b*) an Advocate of 10 years' standing is qualified to be a judge of a High Court, this provision would enable government to pack the Board with its own henchmen. The 44th Amendment requires that the Board must be appointed *in accordance with the recommendation of the Chief Justice of the appropriate High Court*; and the Board must consist of a Chairman and not less than two members. The Chairman must be a serving judge of the appropriate High Court, and the remaining members may be either serving or retired judges of any High Court. In the submission of the present writer, it would have been desirable not to permit retired judges of the High Court to be appointed to the Board. Presumably the difficulty of withdrawing sitting judges from the High Courts may have led to the provision for the appointment of retired judges; the further provision that such appointment must be made on the recommendation of the Chief Justice being considered a sufficient guarantee that the retired judge who was appointed would be really independent.

---

[55] *Madan Shaw* v. *State* ('72) A.Cal. 119.

(c) Article 22 (7) (a) which permitted persons to be detained for a longer period than 3 months without obtaining the opinion of the Advisory Board if the prescribed conditions of that Article were fulfilled was deleted. This deletion removed from the Constitution the greatest blot on preventive detention in India. That provision, which was a part of a fundamental right, denied to a citizen of India *in times of peace* what was not denied to a subject, or even an alien, in England in times of two World Wars, namely, a right of the detained person to have his case considered by an independent Board. Consistently with the scope of this book, the present writer has not discussed the more fundamental question whether preventive detention in times of peace has any justification at all, since great federal democracies like those of the United States, Canada and Australia are able to get on without it in times of peace. However, that question has been discussed in a separate publication[56] and the conclusion there reached is that preventive detention in times of peace is unjustified.

All amendments brought into force except the amendment of Art. 22(4) to (7)

11.186 Most of the amendments were brought into force with effect from June 20, 1979, by a Notification issued a day earlier. The rest of the amendments, *except* that made in Art. 22 (4) to (7) by s. 3 were brought into force with effect from August 1, 1979. For reasons difficult to understand, and which reflect no credit on the Janata Government—which sponsored the Amending Act—s. 3 was not brought into force. And the Congress (I) Government which succeeded the Janata Government in 1980, did nothing to repair this omission.

This omission challenged in the *National Security Case*

11.187 In *A. K. Roy* v. *Union*[57] ("the *National Security Case*") this omission was challenged before a Constitution Bench of the Supreme Court[58] under the following circumstances:

> The National Security Ordinance, 1980 ("the Ordinance") was promulgated by the President in order "to provide for preventive detention in certain cases and for matters connected therewith". It applied to the whole of India, except Jammu & Kashmir, and it came into force on Sept. 23, 1980. The Ordinance by Cl. 9 for the constitution of Advisory Boards strictly in accordance with the provisions of s. 3 of the 44th Amendment Act, in spite of the fact that the aforesaid section was not brought into force. The National Security Act was passed on December 27, 1980 replacing the Ordinance retrospectively. Section 9 of the Act makes a significant departure from Cl. 9 of the Ordinance by providing for the constitution of Advisory Boards in accordance with Art. 22(4) in its original form and not in accordance with the amendment made to that Article by s. 3 of the 44th Amendment Act.[59]

Three separate judgments delivered

11.188 The challenge to the Ordinance, and to the Act which replaced it retrospectively was dealt with in three separate judgments. The majority judgment was delivered by Chandrachud C.J. for himself, Bhagwati and Desai JJ. Gupta J. delivered a dissenting judgment. Tulzapurkar J. in a brief judgment agreed with the majority judgment that an Ordinance was "law" and agreed with the dissent

---

56 Seervai, *Emergency, Future Safeguards and the Habeas Corpus Case: A Criticism*, pp. 84-95.

57 ('82) A.SC. 710.

58 Chandrachud C.J., Bhagwati, Gupta, Tulzapurkar and Desai JJ.

59 ('82) A.SC. *supra* at p. 728.

of Gupta J. on the question of bringing into force s. 3 read with s. 1(2) of the 44th Amendment Act.[60]

Is an Ordinance "law"?

11.189 The Ordinance was challenged on 9 grounds,[61] but "this many pronged attack", said Chandrachud C.J., "on the Ordinance-making power has one central theme: 'Ordinance is not law'."[62] In the earlier editions of this book the present writer devoted one paragraph of the Introduction to the Ordinance-making power[63] and that paragraph has been reproduced as paragraph 1.103 of the present Introduction.[64] This was because it did not occur to him that anyone could seriously maintain that the exercise of the legislative powers of the Chief Executive—the President and the Governor—did not result in a law. However, since that submission was made for the petitioner in the *National Security Case*, it would be convenient to deal with it at this place.

The reasons which led the majority to hold that an Ordinance was "law"

11.190 The reasons which led the majority to hold that an Ordinance was a law can be summarized as follows:

(*a*) The power conferred by Arts. 123 and 213 had a historical origin.[65]

(*b*) Article 123 which confers power on the President appears in Chapter III of Part V of the Constitution which is entitled "Legislative powers of the President", and Art. 213, which confers similar power on the Governor of a State, appears in Part VI, Chapter IV, which is entitled "Legislative Power of the Governor".[66]

(*c*) Apart from the heading of Chapter III of Part V, Art. 123(2) provides that an ordinance promulgated under Art. 123, "shall have the same force and effect as an Act of Parliament."[67]

(*d*) Article 13(2) provides that the State shall not make any law which takes away or abridges the (fundamental) rights conferred by Part III; and Art. 13(3) provides that in that Article "law" includes, *inter alia*, an Ordinance unless the context otherwise provide.[68]

(*e*) "In view of the fact that the context does not otherwise so require, it must follow from the combined operation of Cls. (2) and (3) of Art. 13 that an Ordinance issued by the President under Art. 123, which is equated by Cl. (2) of that Article with an Act of Parliament is subject to the same constraints and limitations as an Act of Parliament."[69]

(*f*) This exact equivalence for practical purposes between Acts or laws made by Parliament and an Ordinance issued by the President is emphasized by Art. 367 which provides for the "Interpretation" of the Constitution.

Art. 367(2): "Any reference in this Constitution to Acts or laws of, or made by, Parliament, or to Acts or laws of, or made by, the Legislature of a State, shall be construed as including a reference to an Ordinance made by the President or, to an Ordinance made by a Governor, as the case may be."[70]

(*g*) The scheme adopted by our Constitution shows that "it envisages the exercise of legislative powers by the executive in stated circumstance" *e.g.* Arts. 356 and 357 — Art. 357 speaks of "the exercise of legislative powers" under the proclamation issued under Art. 356.[71]

(*h*) "The Constituent Assembly indubitably thought, despite the strong and adverse impact which the Governor-General's ordinance-making power had

---

[60] ibid. p. 756.
[61] ibid. pp. 717-8 where grounds (*a*) to (*i*) are set out.
[62] ibid. p. 718.
[63] 1st ed. pp. 18-19; 2nd ed. Vol. 1, p. 16.
[64] at pp. 64-5.
[65] ibid. at p. 719 where s. 42 of the G.I. Act, 35 has been set out. See para 1.103 of this book for a brief account of the history of Arts. 123 and 213.
[66] ibid. at pp. 719-720.
[67] ibid. p. 720.
[68] ibid.
[69] ibid.
[70] ibid.
[71] ibid. pp. 720-721.

produced on the Indian community in the pre-independence era, that it was necessary to equip the President with legislative powers in urgent situations. After all, the Constitution makers had to take into account life's realities."[72]

(*i*) " 'Grave public inconvenience would be caused if on an Act, like the Bombay Sales Tax Act, being declared void, no machinery existed whereby a valid law could be promptly promulgated to take the place of the law declared void'."[73]

(*j*) In face of the above provisions of the Constitution it was not possible to accept Counsel's submission that an Ordinance issued by the President is not law. Such Ordinance "is as much law as an Act passed by Parliament and is, fortunately and unquestionably, subject to the same inhibitions."[74]

(*k*) "The debates of the Constituent Assembly (Vol. 8, Part V, Chapter III, pp. 201 to 217) would show that the power to issue ordinances was regarded as a necessary evil. That power was to be used to meet extraordinary situations and not perverted to serve political ends. The Constituent Assembly held forth, as it were, an assurance to the people that an extraordinary power shall not be used in order to perpetuate a fraud on the Constitution which is conceived with so much faith and vision. That assurance must in all events be made good and the balance struck by the founding fathers between the powers of the government and the liberties of the people not disturbed or destroyed."[75]

The reasons which led the majority to hold that an Ordinance was "law" within the meaning of Art. 21

11.191 It was also argued that "law" in Art. 21 did not include an Ordinance having regard to the context. This argument was considered by Chandrachud C.J. and rejected for the following reasons:

(*a*) "The contention that the word 'law' in Article 21 must be construed to mean a law made by the legislature only and cannot include an ordinance, contradicts directly the express provisions of Articles 123(2) and 367(2) of the Constitution. Besides, if an ordinance is not law within the meaning of Article 21, it will stand released from the wholesome and salutary restraint imposed upon the legislative power by Article 13(2) of the Constitution."[76]

(*b*) The contention that an Ordinance could not be equated with the procedure *established* by law was unsound. "The word 'established' is used in Article 21 in order to denote and ensure that the procedure prescribed by law must be defined with certainty in order that those who are deprived of their fundamental right to life or liberty must know the precise extent of such deprivation."[77]

(*c*) The undernoted decisions of the Supreme Court[78] "illustrate that enduring rights and obligations can be created by ordinances. The fact that any particular law has a temporary duration is immaterial for the purposes of Article 21 so long as the procedure prescribed by it is definite and reasonably ascertainable. In fact, the Preventive Detention laws were in their inception of a temporary character since they had a limited duration. They were only extended from time to time."[79]

(*d*) The argument that fundamental rights conferred by Art. 21 could not be taken away by an Ordinance involved adding a proviso to Art. 123 namely, "Provided that such Ordinance shall not deprive any person of his right to life or personal liberty conferred by Art. 21 . . ."[80] But an amendment substantially to that effect was moved by Mr. Pocker when Draft Art. 102 (which corresponds to Art. 123), was discussed in the Constituent Assembly.[81] Opposing the amendment, Dr. Ambedkar said that any law made under Draft Art. 102 "would also be automatically subject to the provisions relating to fundamental rights of citizens and any such law therefore will not be able

---

[72] ibid. p. 721.

[73] ibid., [quoting from Seervai, *Constitutional Law of India* (2nd ed.) p. 16, now part of para 1.103 at pp. 64-65].

[74] ibid.

[75] ibid.

[76] ibid. p. 722.

[77] ibid.

[78] *Orissa* v. *Bhupendra Kumar Bose* (1962) Supp. (2) S.C.R. 380 at pp. 398-400, ('62) A.SC. 945, 953-4; and *Muhamadbhai Khudabux Chippa* v. *Gujarat* (1962) Supp. (3) S.C.R. 875, ('62) A.SC. 1517.

[79] ('82) A.SC. *supra* at p. 722.

[80] ibid.

[81] *C.A.D.* Vol. 8 at p. 203.

to override these provisions and there is no need for any provision as was suggested by my friend Mr. Pocker in his amendment No. 1796."[82]

(e) Again, what Art. 21 emphasizes is that the deprivation of the right to life and personal liberty must be brought about by a State-made law and not by the rules of natural law: *Gopalan's Case*.[83]

(f) Reference in this connection could usefully be made to a few undernoted representative decisions which illustrate that Art. 21 takes in laws other than those enacted by the legislature.[84]

(g) "There is no substance in the argument that the ordinance-making power, if extended to cover matters mentioned in Article 21, will destroy the basic structure of the separation of powers as envisaged by the Constitution. In the first place, Article 123(1) is a part of the Constitution as originally enacted; and secondly, our Constitution does not follow the American pattern of a strict separation of powers."[85]

Gupta J.'s dissent

11.192 Gupta J. dissented from the judgment of the Chief Justice on two of the points which arose for decision: that relating to the failure of the Central Government to bring s. 3 into force and that relating to the question whether an Ordinance was "law" within the meaning of Art. 21. It is most important to note that Gupta J. did not differ from the Chief Justice when he held that an Ordinance was law, for Gupta J. concluded his judgment by saying that on all points other than the two mentioned above, he agreed with the conclusions reached by the Chief Justice.[86] It is submitted that the reasons given by Chandrachud C.J. for holding that an Ordinance was "law" within the meaning of Art. 21 are clearly right. It is submitted, for reasons which will appear later that the view of Gupta J. that an Ordinance is not "law" cannot be sustained once it is not disputed that an Ordinance is "law". However, before examining his judgment on this point, it is helpful to call attention to certain provisions of our Constitution, besides those referred to by Chandrachud C.J., which show that an Ordinance is assimilated to legislative power, which includes the power to amend or repeal.

Additional reasons in support of the view that an Ordinance is "law"

11.193 Chandrachud C.J. referred to the inclusion of the word "Ordinance" in the definition of "law" in Cl. (3) (*a*) of Art. 13. However, the scheme of Cl. (3) (*a*) is instructive and relevant.[87] It will be noticed that Cl. (3) (*a*) found it unnecessary to include in the definition of "law" an Act of Parliament or the State Legislatures

---

[82] ibid. p. 204.

[83] (1950) S.C.R. 88 at pp. 111, 169, 199, 229, 236 and 308-309; [('50) A.SC. 27, at pp. 39, 60, 61].

[84] "*In Re Sant Ram* (1960) 3 S.C.R. 499, 506, ('60) A.SC. 932, the Rules made by the Supreme Court; in *Nagaland* v. *Ratan Singh* (1966) 3 S.C.R. 830, 851-2, ('67) A.SC. 212, the Rules made for the governance of Nagaland Hills District; in *Govind* v. *M.P.* (1975) 3 S.C.R. 946, 955-6, the Regulations made under the Police Act, in *Ratilal Bhanji Mithani* v. *Asst. Collector of Customs* (1967) 3 S.C.R. 926, 928-31, ('67) A.SC. 1639, the Rules made by the High Court under Article 225 of the Constitution; and in *Pandit M. S. M. Sharma* v. *Shri Sri Krishna Sinha* (1959) Supp. 1 S.C.R. 806, 860-61, ('59) A.SC. 395, the Rules made by a House of Legislature under Article 208, were all regarded as laying down procedure established by 'law' for the purposes of Article 21.": ('82) A.SC. *supra* at p. 723.

[85] ('82) A.SC. *supra* at p. 723.

[86] ibid. p. 756.

[87] *Cl. (3)(a)*: "law" includes any Ordinance, order, bye-law, rule, regulation, notification, custom or usage having in the territory of India the force of law. (*b*) "*laws in force*" includes laws passed or made by a Legislature or *other competent authority* in the territory of India before the commencement of this Constitution and not previously repealed, notwithstanding that any such law or any part thereof may not be then in operation either at all or in particular areas.

The scheme of Art. 13(3)(*a*)

because the primary function of Parliament and the State Legislatures is to enact laws; and what a legislature enacts is obviously law. However, to foreclose the argument that only the legislature and not the executive can exercise legislative power, cl. (3) (*a*) includes an Ordinance (which is promulgated in exercise of the legislative power of the executive) in the definition of "law". For the same reason, an order, bye-law, rule and regulation, are included because ordinarily they are examples of, and are the result of the power to enact subordinate delegated legislation. Finally, custom or usage having the force of law included all unenacted law. Therefore, nothing which can be called "law" even if not enacted by the appropriate legislature, or even if not "enacted" at all, was excluded from law in Art. 13 because it was intended that no "law" should violate fundamental rights without being *pro tanto* invalid. The words we have italicised in Cl. (3) (*b*) of Art. 13, namely, "laws in force" includes "laws passed by a Legislature or *other competent authority* . . . before the commencement of the Constitution" (italics supplied) clearly cover the legislative powers of the Governor-General and the Governor under ss. 42 and 88 of the G.I. Act, 35.

Legislative powers of the President and the Governor assimilated to those of the legislature

11.194 That the legislative powers of the President and the Governor are assimilated to those of the Legislature is clear from the provisions of Arts. 123 and 213. Broadly speaking, the legislative powers of Parliament and State Legislatures are to be found in Lists I, II and III of Sch. VII of our Constitution read with Art. 246. In the absence of a proclamation of emergency, Parliament has exclusive legislative power to make laws with respect to matters in List I and a concurrent legislative power with respect to matters in List III. Subject to the above, State Legislatures have exclusive legislative power in respect of matters in List II and a concurrent legislative power. Under Art. 254(1) in case of conflict between a valid law enacted by Parliament and a valid law enacted by a State legislature, the former would prevail; however a law passed by a State legislature in respect of matters in the Concurrent List would prevail in that State over a law made by Parliament if, being reserved for the President's consideration, it receives his assent. Ordinarily Parliament is not competent to enact a law in respect of matters in List II nor is it competent to pass a law in disregard of fundamental rights. And the same is true of State Legislatures substituting List I for List II and subject to Art. 254. If we now turn to Arts. 123 and 213 these limitations on the legislative power of Parliament and State Legislatures are expressly placed on the legislative powers of the President and the Governor. Article 123(3) provides that "If and so far as an Ordinance under this article makes any provision which Parliament would not under this Constitution be competent to enact it shall be void". The following provisos to Art. 213(1) and (3) show how the Governor's legislative powers are assimilated to that of the State Legislature:

Art. 123(3) and Art. 213 (1) and (3)

Art. 213(1): . . . Provided that the Governor shall not, without instructions from the President, promulgate any such Ordinance if — (*a*) a Bill containing the same provisions would under this Constitution have required the previous sanction of the President for the introduction thereof into the Legislature; or (*b*) he would have deemed it necessary to reserve a Bill containing the same provisions for the consideration of the President; or (*c*) an Act of the Legislature of the State containing the same provisions would under this Constitution have been invalid unless, having been reserved for the consideration of the President, it had received the assent of the President.

Art. 213(3): If and so far as an Ordinance under this article makes any provision which would not be valid if enacted in an Act of the Legislature of the State assented to by the Governor, it shall be void: Provided that, for the purposes of the provisions of this Constitution relating to the effect of an Act of the Legislature of a State which is repugnant to an Act of Parliament or an existing law with respect to a matter enumerated in the Concurrent List, an Ordinance promulgated under this article in pursuance of instructions from the President shall be deemed to be an Act of the Legislature of the State which has been reserved for the consideration of the President and assented to by him.

Except as to duration, nothing is excluded from the scope of an Ordinance which is not excluded from the scope of an Act

11.195 If, then, the legislative powers of the President and the Governors are assimilated to the powers of Parliament and the State Legislature, and an Ordinance passed by them is declared to have the same force and effect as an Act of Parliament or the Legislature of the State, it must follow that except as to the limit put on the duration of an Ordinance by Arts. 123 and 213, there is no other limitation on the legislative power of the President and the Governor if the condition precedent for the enactment of an Ordinance is fulfilled. Legislative power within its field is plenary unless limitations on it are placed by the Constitution. Those limitations apply to Acts of Parliament and State Legislatures, and they apply equally to Ordinances by the provisions of Arts. 123 and 213. Or, to put it differently, except for its duration nothing is excluded from the scope of an Ordinance which is not excluded from the scope of an Act of Parliament or of a State Legislature.

The relevance of the above submission to the dissenting judgment of Gupta J.

11.196 This last submission is directly relevant to the dissenting opinion of Gupta J. He quoted the observations of Patanjali Sastri J. in *Gopalan's Case* that the word *established* "implies some degree of firmness, permanence and general acceptance . . .". First, this was the view of one judge contrary to the view taken by the majority of four other judges who held that the expression "procedure established by law" meant "the procedure established by a legislature" (see para 11.10 at pp. 703-4 *ante*). The words of Patanjali Sastri J. quoted by Gupta J. led to the compromise solution propounded by Patanjali Sastri J. alone in *Gopalan's Case*, and in para 11.19 we have shown that this compromise solution is untenable; and in cases other than cases of preventive detention, the solution is unnecessary (para 11.19). This is because a person can be deprived of personal liberty otherwise than by preventive detention.

Acts of a legislature can be of a limited duration

11.197 Further, legislative power within the limits set for its exercise is plenary, unless that exercise is subject to limitations imposed by the Constitution either expressly or by necessary implication. Parliament and State Legislatures are competent to pass temporary Acts to meet situations which are expected to be of a limited duration. If it is no objection to a person being deprived of his personal liberty as punishment for violating the provisions of a temporary Act passed by Parliament or a State Legislature[88] there can be no

---

[88] For example, an Act declaring area X as a quarantine area for one month, and preventing entry into and exit from that area except under a special permit and providing for fine and/or simple imprisonment for violation of the provisions of the Act.

objection to a similar law being promulgated by an Ordinance which under Arts. 123 and 213 has a limited duration.

Submission: dissenting judgment of Gupta J. on "law" and Art. 21 is not correct

11.198 The natural dislike of judges, bred in the traditions of the rule of law, for preventive detention in times of peace, led Gupta J. to observe:

"There is another aspect of the matter. Article 21 not only speaks of a person's liberty but also of his life. It is difficult to think of a situation in normal times which left no time for the President to summon Parliament and required him to promulgate ordinances to take away the life or liberty of persons, unless one considered life and liberty as matters of no great importance. However, in view of the opinion of the majority upholding the validity of the Ordinance, it is unnecessary to dilate on this aspect."[89]

It is submitted that these observations are based on a misconception. Life can be "taken away" only by a valid substantive law which prescribes the death sentence as a penalty for a crime. Such a law will attract all the safeguards of Art. 22(1) and (2), of Art. 20, and of Art. 14. These safeguards show that life is not looked upon by our Constitution as of "no great consequence". It is submitted that the dissenting judgment on the interpretation of "law" in Art. 21 is incorrect.

Differences between an Act and an Ordinance pointed out

11.199 However, there are important differences between an Ordinance and an Act of Parliament or of a State Legislature. Except in rare cases[90] there is no condition precedent to the enactment of an Act. The fulfilment of a condition precedent is ordinarily a justiciable issue. The power to promulgate an Ordinance under Art. 123 is subject to two conditions precedent: (i) both the Houses of Parliament must not be in session, and (ii) the President must be satisfied that circumstances exist which render it necessary for him to take immediate action. The first condition precedent is easily verified; the second condition precedent has been discussed in the *National Security Case* and will be considered presently. No doubt the President holds a high office, but the dignity of his office is irrelevant to his being "satisfied" because it has been settled by Supreme Court decisions that the President's satisfaction, except in rare marginal cases, is the satisfaction of his Council of Ministers whose advice the President is under an obligation to follow: Art. 74. So the decision to promulgate an Ordinance is the decision of the Council of Ministers in the Union who are normally party politicians. It is reasonably settled that actual or legal *mala fides* cannot be attributed to Parliament in relation to a law passed by it. However, the Council of Ministers are not the legislature but the executive, and any action taken by the executive is open to the challenge on the ground of *mala fides*. No doubt *mala fides* is difficult to prove, but if proved it must invalidate the executive action. If the evidence given before, and the findings recorded by the Shah Commission are correct, and the material findings of fact have not been controverted by evidence to the contrary,[91] the

---

[89] ('82) A.SC. supra at p. 756.

[90] See for example Art. 249, Art. 252 and entries 52, 53 and 54 List I, Sch. VII of the Constitution.

[91] The Report has been withdrawn from circulation, but the findings of fact in para 5.34 *et seqq.*, para 5.60 and paras 5.64 to 5.68 of the Shah Commission Report which are based on official documents have not been controverted by producing other documents.

advice given to the President to issue a proclamation of Emergency in 1975 was in law *mala fide* and the proclamation was void and inoperative in law. However, these differences do not affect the nature of an Ordinance as law if the Ordinance has been *validly* promulgated.

A validly promulgated Ordinance is "law"

11.200 On the question whether the President's satisfaction is subject to judicial review, Chandrachud C.J.'s judgment is in a muted key, although his observations seem to indicate that he was of the view that the President's satisfaction is justiciable. He said that the *Rajasthan Case*[92] was often cited as an authority for the proposition that the Courts ought not to enter the "political thicket". But in that case cl. (5) of Art. 356 made the satisfaction of the President conclusive and not open to be questioned in any Court. "Clause (5) has been deleted by the 44th Amendment and, therefore, any observations made in the *Rajasthan Case* on the basis of that Clause cannot any longer hold good".[93] Earlier, the Chief Justice discussed the doctrine of "the political question" in terms which would suggest that the doctrine of the political question having been discredited in the United States, where it originated, and having become "a little more than a play on words"[94] is unlikely to be applied to India. However, Chandrachud C.J. declined to decide the question on two grounds, the second of which was enough for the purpose in hand. The second ground was that

President's "satisfaction" and judicial review: majority judgment unsatisfactory and wrong

Chandrachud C.J.'s reasons for not deciding the question

"as the petitioners had not laid any acceptable foundation for us to hold that no circumstances existed or could have existed which rendered it necessary for the President to take immediate action by promulgating the Ordinance, we are unable to entertain the contention that the pre-conditions to the exercise of the power conferred by Art. 123 are not fulfilled".[95]

This finding was enough to dispose of the question on this point. However, Chandrachud C.J. gave another ground as the first reason, namely, that the Ordinance had been replaced by an Act. He realized the force of the objection that if the justiciability of the President's satisfaction cannot be decided when it is replaced by an Act, as it almost invariably is, the question of justiciability can never be decided at all. "All the same," said the Chief Justice:

"the position is firmly established in the field of constitutional adjudication that the court will decide no more than needs to be decided in any particular case. Abstract questions present interesting challenges, but it is for scholars and textbook writers to unravel their mystique. It is not for the courts to decide questions which are but of academic importance."[96]

The "firmly established" position

First, although the principle is generally a sound one, it is not correct that the "position is firmly established" if by that it is meant to convey that it is an invariable rule. Examples are not wanting when Supreme Court judges have violated this rule to the extent of reconsidering in fact, or, in substance, earlier decisions notwithstanding this "firmly established" position. We have seen that in the *Bank Nationalization Case*, the finding that the impugned law violated Art. 31 (2) was enough to dispose of the case, and it was wholly unnecessary to consider the challenge under Arts. 14 and 19, still less to reconsider *Gopalan's Case* which dealt with pre-

A criticism: examples of the violation of the "firmly established" position

---

[92] (1978) 1 S.C.R. 1, ('77) A.SC. 1361.
[93] ('82) A.SC. *supra* at p. 724.
[94] ibid.
[95] ibid. p. 725.
[96] ibid. p. 724.

ventive detention. The 10 judges who decided the *Bank Nationalization Case* did so in disregard of the salutary precedent laid down in an identical situation, namely, in the *Sholapur Mills Case*.[97] There the impugned law was challenged as violating Art. 14, 19 and 31(1) and (2). Mahajan J. having held the impugned law void for violating Art. 31(2) observed that it was unnecessary to consider whether the law was also void as violating Arts. 14 and 19; and all the other judges limited their decision to holding the law void for violating Art. 31(2).[98] Again, we have seen in para 11.170 that in *Fagu Shaw's Case* once four out of five judges held that s. 13 of the impugned Act had fixed a maximum period, it was wholly unnecessary to decide whether Art. 22(7)(*b*) made it obligatory to fix a maximum period, and for that purpose to reconsider, in substance though not in form, *Krishnan's Case*. And several other examples can be given where judges have disregarded the "firmly established" position for no other reason than that they chose to do so. But there is a more fundamental objection to the application of the firmly established position to the situation before the Court. The Constitution puts limitations on the President's powers under Art. 123 and if the powers are transgressed, as for example, by the promulgation of an Ordinance *mala fide*, the rights of the people are affected illegally, that is, without the authority of a valid law, and it would be an abdication of judicial power to give to the Council of Ministers, in substance, immunity from illegality if it takes the form of an Ordinance. But a rule of general application is misapplied to a situation where a Court can perform its duty of upholding rights and restraining the breach of law by illegal executive action only by disregarding an otherwise salutary rule. To apply the rule, as Chandrachud C.J. applied it to the situation before him is, in the words of Lord Normand, to stretch the rule *"beyond reason and to pass from reality into formalism and make believe"*.[99] (italics supplied) Precedents for deciding an important question which cannot be decided without departing from the general rule are not wanting. Under the Bombay Land Requisition Act, 1948, the question frequently arose on whom lay the burden of proof for establishing that the requisitioned premises were "let" or "intended to be let". In *Bhanji Munji's Case*[1] Bose J., speaking for a Constitution Bench, said:

A general rule misapplied to the present case

Bhanji Munji's Case and questions of frequent occurrence which require a departure from the general rule

"The learned trial Judge threw the burden of proof on the State Government and told its learned counsel that he should proceed to prove this fact if he so desired. He replied that he did not intend to lead any evidence. It was explained to us that Government took up this attitude as it wanted a decision about where the burden lay as the question arises continually and cannot be decided when both parties adduce evidence. The learned Attorney-General gave an assurance that the possession of the petitioners in this case would not be disturbed; all he wanted was a decision on the point. In the absence of any counter evidence the learned trial Judge accepted the facts proved by the petitioners' affidavit and decided the matter in their favour. . . . In our opinion, the burden was wrongly placed."[2]

---

[97] (1954) S.C.R. 674, ('54) A.SC. 119. [98] (1954) S.C.R. *supra* at p. 716.
[99] *Howell* v. *Falmouth Boat Construction Co. Ltd.* (1951) A.C. at p. 848.
[1] (1955) 1 S.C.R. 777, ('55) A.SC. 41. [2] (1955) 1 S.C.R. at p. 786.

Petitions challenging the grant of Government contracts for 1 year, and the grant of licences and permits for one year or less are not dismissed as infructuous if they are heard after the period of one year. If important questions of law or principle are involved, those questions are decided even if no relief can be granted to the petitioner.[3] This is all the more so in public interest litigation. As a standard text book puts it:

"But in exceptional circumstances, the Courts taking a large view of public interest, have ordered the performance of a public duty when the time for performance had expired. In such cases, they have either treated the statutory time-limit as a merely directory provision,[4] or regarded the application for *mandamus* as an appropriate occasion for making a public declaration of legal rights.[5]"[6]

Chandrachud C.J. observed that the Union Government had promulgated about 200 Ordinances between 1960 and 1980 of which 19 had been passed in 1980. Having regard to the frequent use by the executive of a power to make a law of limited duration, it is submitted that for a court to allow a large section of our people's rights to be affected by what may turn out to be illegal executive action without redress can only be described as an unjustified abdication of judicial power, and all the more so because the Ordinance before the Court affected the liberty of the subject under a law of preventive detention.

Submission: an unjustified abdication of judicial power

11.201 On the question whether a *mandamus* should issue to the Central Government it is submitted that the majority judgment is very unsatisfactory and is clearly wrong and the minority judgments are clearly right. In the first place, there is a fundamental error in the observation of Chandrachud C.J. that "the power to amend the Constitution under Art. 368 ('the amending power') and the power to legislate are conferred on the same organ of the State, namely, Parliament." A glance at the provisos (*a*) to (*e*) to Art. 368 (2)[7] shows that although the power to *initiate* an amendment to the Constitution is conferred on Parliament, Parliament has no power, *by itself*, to amend some of the most important parts of the Constitution. That power belongs to each House of Parliament *acting separately* together with not less than half the number of States whose ratification to the proposed amendments is required if they relate to the

Submission: majority judgment wrong on the question of *mandamus*

A fundamental error: legislative and constituent power not conferred on the same organ of the State

[3] See for example, *Ghaio Mal & Sons* v. *Delhi* (1959) S.C.R. 1424, ('59) A.SC. 65; *Sudhir Kumar* v. *S.T.A.* ('63) A.Ass. 1; *Rashbihari* v. *Orissa* ('69) A.SC. 1081.

[4] *R.* v. *Norwich* (*Mayor*) (1830) 1 B. & Ad. 310; *Rochester* (*Mayor*) v. *R.* (1858) E.B. & E. 1024; *R.* v. *Hanley Revising Barrister* (1912) 3 K.B. 518; *R.* v. *Woodbury Licencing JJ. Ex p. Rouse* (1960) 1 W.L.R. 461 (*Mandamus* to convene licensing meeting refused after expiry of a statutory date; justices had refused licence after inadvertently fixing the date for holding the meeting too late).

[5] *Vic Restaurant Inc.* v. *Montreal* [1959] S.C.R. 58.

[6] See de Smith, *Judicial Review of Administrative Action,* 4th ed. p. 560.

[7] *Art. 368 (2), proviso*: "Provided that if such amendment seeks to make any change in — (*a*) Article 54, Article 55, Article 73, Article 162 or Article 241, or (*b*) Chapter IV of Part V, Chapter V of Part VI, or Chapter I of Part XI, or (*c*) any of the Lists in the Seventh Schedule, or (*d*) the representation of States in Parliament, or (*e*) the provisions of this article, the amendment shall also require to be ratified by the Legislatures of not less than one-half of the States by resolutions to that effect passed by those Legislatures before the Bill making provision for such amendment is presented to the President for assent."

very important matters mentioned in Art. 368 (2) proviso (*a*) to (*e*).[8] Therefore, the power to amend the Constitution does not belong to the same organ of the State, namely, Parliament, but to a constituent body. This is as it should be in a federal constitution, because States are vitally concerned with the federal features of the Constitution. And if the amending power is one of the most important powers in our Constitution, Parliament lacks that power by virtue of Art. 368 (2) proviso (*e*).

Parliament enacting laws and initiating an amendment of the Constitution are two distinct bodies or authorities just as the Constituent Assembly of India filled two distinct and radically different positions

11.202 In the second place, apart from the requirements of the provisos to Art. 368, Parliament enacting laws under the Constitution and Parliament amending the Constitution are two distinct bodies, except in name. It will be recalled that the Constituent Assembly which framed our Constitution discharged two distinct and separate functions in radically different capacities. It was a sovereign body for framing the Constitution; as a legislative body it was, in the language of constitutional law, a subordinate law-making body acting under the provisions of the G.I. Act, 35 which was an Act of the British Parliament. When our Parliament acts as a legislative body the two Houses do not have equality of status in the most important function of Parliament — the control of the public purse. First, a Money Bill can be introduced only in the House of the People: Art. 109 (1); and when a Money Bill is sent to the Council of States it can make its "recommendations" but the House of the People may accept or reject them. In respect of other Bills, if the House of the People passes it and the Council of States rejects it, or *vice versa*, then under Art. 108 (1) the President can call the two Houses in joint sessions and under Art. 108 (4) if the Bill is passed by a simple majority of members of both Houses present and voting, it "shall be deemed for the purpose of this Constitution to have been passed by both Houses" subject to provisos which are not material. These provisions show, first, that the two Houses are unequal in status and power, making the House of the People the dominant House for passing ordinary laws under the Constitution. This is because there is difference in kind between legislative and constituent power. Legislation enacted under the Constitution and subject to its provisions is "law". [Constituent power is not "law" as defined in Art. 13 (3)]. For that purpose, primacy is accorded to the House of the People which is directly elected on the basis of adult universal suffrage. The Council of States consists of representatives of each State who are elected by the elected members of the Legislative Assembly of the State. They cannot claim to represent the people of India in the same sense in which the members of the House of the People can. However, in a federal constitution it is desirable, if not necessary, that the States should be represented in the Union Legislature for the protection of State interests and the Council of States

---

[8] Articles 54 and 55 provide for the election and manner of election of the President; Arts. 73 and 162 provide for the extent of the Executive power of the Union and a State respectively, and Art. 241 provides for High Courts for Union Territories. Again, Chapter IV of Part V and Chapter V of Part VI provide, respectively, for the Union and the State Judiciary. Further, Chapter I of Part XI provides for the distribution of legislative powers which is broadly speaking by reference to the Legislative Lists of Sch. VII and any change in which requires ratification. Nor can Parliament by itself amend the representation of States in Parliament nor can Art. 368 be amended by Parliament alone.

performs that function, in theory at any rate. The thing to note is that Parliament and all Legislatures work under the Constitution and the principle of passing legislation by a simple majority,[9] while assigning a dominant position to the House of the People and Legislative Assemblies of States, accords with the generally accepted democratic principle.

11.203 However, when it comes to amending the Constitution, the scene changes. The Constitution is the Supreme Law of the land; any change in the Constitution not only affects the people of India, but it affects India — which by definition is a Union of States: Art. 1(1). Therefore, an amendment of the Constitution involves not only the people of India but equally the States. This position is recognized by Art. 368, and is recognized most decisively by denying to Parliament alone the power to amend the Constitution. It is recognized equally strongly by putting the Council of States and the House of the People in a position of equality and what is more, by giving to the Council of States a power effectively to defeat an amendment passed by the requisite majority in the House of the People. This is done by providing that an amendment of the Constitution may be initiated only by an introduction of a Bill for the purpose in either House of Parliament, thus reversing the dominance of the House of the People in respect of Money Bills which can be introduced only in that House. Secondly, the voting in each House is distinct and separate. The majority required is not a simple majority of the members present, but a two-fold requirement is imposed for each House. First, it must be a majority of the *total membership* of each House separately, and secondly, there must be a majority of not less than two-thirds of the members of that House present and voting. In practice any amendment which is controversial would require a two-thirds majority of the House, because experience shows that members have been brought to the Houses of Parliament even on stretchers to vote on a controversial amendment. In other words, the democratic principle of passing legislation by a simple majority in each House, or by a simple majority of the two Houses in joint session has been rightly abandoned for the simple reason that the amendment of the Constitution validly made becomes part of the Constitution. This marks the difference between the exercise of legislative power and constituent power. This difference is based on important considerations. First, it is designed to secure that an amendment to the Constitution is made after due deliberation and only if it commands wide support among the members of each House and among the Legislatures of the States. Secondly, a law which is passed by a simple majority by Parliament can be repealed by a simple majority if the experience of its working dictates a repeal. A constitutional amendment once made may be difficult to repeal, because the requisite majorities in each House of Parliament and ratification by the requisite numbers of States may not be forthcoming, as the Janata Government discovered in respect of a very few amendments it had proposed in the Amendment Bill, because the Janata Government had not the requisite majority in the Council of States. The difference between the ability of Parliament to repeal a law, and the inability of Parliament

The same topic continued

The difference between legislative and constituent power — the underlying reasons

Difficulty of repealing a Constitutional Amendment

[9] With a few exceptions.

by itself to repeal a provision of an Amending Act has not been given due weight in the majority judgment when Chandrachud C.J. said:

Due weight not given to that difficulty by Chandrachud C.J.

"The Parliament does not irretrievably lose its power to bring the Amendment into force by reason of the empowered in favour of the Central Government to bring it into force. If the Central Government fails to do what, according to the Parliament, it ought to have done, it would be open to the Parliament to delete Section 1(2) of the 44th Amendment Act by following the due procedure and to bring into force that Act or any of its provisions."[10]

It is not surprising that Chandrachud C.J. shrank from suggesting directly the initiation of a Constitutional Amendment which it is not within the power of Parliament by itself to pass, but wrapped up his suggestion in the circumlocutory words "by following the due procedure". Constituent power means either the power to frame a Constitution, or to amend an existing Constitution according to the provisions for its amendment. As to the Constitution as originally framed, it cannot be said that any of its provisions is invalid or void because the Constitution is the touchstone of the validity of laws passed under it, and there is no standard outside the Constitution by which the validity of its provisions can be judged. Constituent power in the sense of amending the Constitution is on a lower plane, because a Constitution can be amended only by complying with the requirements of the amending provision, as interpreted by the Supreme Court, and a purported amendment which does not comply with Art. 368 would be void. However, a validly enacted amendment becomes a part of the Constitution and thereafter its provisions are in the same position as the provisions originally enacted in the Constitution.

Questions to be raised and answered *qua* issue of a *mandamus*

11.204 The question whether a *mandamus* should or should not be issued to the Central Government to bring s. 3 into force, raised the following questions: 1. Why was power conferred on the Central Government to fix the same date, or different dates for bringing the provisions of the amending Act into force? 2. What body or authority is the source of the Central Government's power? What is the nature of this power? 3. Was it left to the Central Government to nullify the will of the constituent body by refusing to bring all or any of the provisions of the amending Act into force? 4. Or, to put it more bluntly, was the Central Government in substance made the amending authority once the constituent body had, *pro tempore* ceased to exist?

The reasons for leaving it to an outside authority to bring a Constitution or constitutional amendments into force

11.205 As to the first question, where a new Constitution supercedes and alters the scheme of the existing Constitution as the G.I. Act, 35 did when it repealed the G.I. Act 1915 (except the Preamble) the laws of India had to be adapted under the power conferred by s. 293 for that purpose. It was a formidable task and as was the case with British legislation, the adaptation was done after inviting and considering objections to the proposed adaptations from the Legal Department of every State in British India.[11] Therefore, although the Act was passed in 1935, it was brought into force on 1st April, 1937 on which date an extremely elaborate Adaptation of Laws Order was pub-

---

[10] ('82) A.SC. *supra* at p. 731.

[11] This was communicated to the present writer by Mr. Dhurandhar who was in the Legal Department of the State of Bombay.

lished, so that the new Constitution and the existing law as adapted under it came into effect on the same day. Similarly, where extensive amendments were made as by the 44th Amendment, time may be required to make the necessary arrangements. The 44th Amendment in substance undid most of the injury done to our Constitution by the 42nd Amendment. It was therefore felt that time might be needed for making suitable arrangements to implement its numerous provisions. As to s. 3 of the amending Act, Advisory Boards were to be reconstituted. They involved seconding a sitting Judge to an Advisory Board and securing the services of retired Judges whose appointment has to be approved by the Chief Justice of that High Court. These provisions might require arrangements to be made for increasing the strength of the High Court judiciary and to make arrangements for the sittings of the Board and the necessary staff required for that purpose.

Power to bring amendments into force *not* conferred by Parliament but by a constituent body

11.206 As to the second question we have seen that the power to bring the provisions of the Amendment Act was *not* conferred by Parliament but by a constituent body exercising constituent power as explained in para 11.201 to 11.203 above. The assumption in the majority judgment that it was permissible for Parliament to vest in an outside agency — in the present case the Central Government which was responsible to Parliament — the power to bring the Amendments into force is untenable. The States which ratified the Amending Act, agreed to the power being conferred on the Central Executive, although that executive is in no sense responsible to the State Legislatures.

S. 1(2) of the Amendment Act imposed a duty on the Govt.

11.207 As to questions (3) and (4) in para 11.204 above, Chandrachud C.J. gave an impeccable answer, when he said:

"We have said at the very outset of the discussion of this point that our decision on the question as to whether a *mandamus* should be issued as prayed for by the petitioners, should not be construed as any approval on our part of the *long and unexplained failure* on the part of the Central Government to bring Section 3 of the 44th Amendment Act into force. We have no doubt that in leaving it to the judgment of the Central Government to decide as to when the various provisions of the 44th Amendment should be brought into force, the Parliament could not have intended that the Central Government may exercise a kind of veto over its constituent will by not ever bringing the Amendment or some of its provisions into force. The Parliament having seen the necessity of introducing into the Constitution a provision like Section 3 of the 44th Amendment, it is not open to the Central Government to sit in judgment over the wisdom of the policy of that section."[12]

Submission: having laid down the duty, *mandamus* was refused for the most amazing reason, accompanied by a hope

He rightly held that s. 1(2) imposed upon the Central Government a *duty*, and not a discretion, to bring the provisions of the Amendment Act into force. The discretion was limited to the time or times within which the provisions were to be brought into force. Having laid down correctly the duty of the Central Government when it came to the remedy, the majority gave the most amazing answer for not issuing a *mandamus* to enforce it, namely, that Parliament had laid down no objective standard for the Central Government to exercise its discretion.[13] That a Supreme Court should proclaim itself helpless to enforce a duty is distressing; it is even more distressing because the duty related to bringing into

[12] ('82) A.SC. *supra* at p. 733.

[13] ibid.

that s. 3 would be brought into force without delay

force s. 3 which, said the Chief Justice, "affords to the detenu an assurance that his case will be considered fairly and objectively by an impartial tribunal". So having declared its helplessness on an untenable ground, as will presently appear, the majority said "We hope that the Central Government will *without further delay* bring s. 3 . . . into force." (italics supplied.) A year has gone by since the judgment was delivered on Dec. 28, 1981 and the hope remains a hope.

Baron Martin's warning that courts should not be astute to discover reasons for not issuing a *mandamus* unheeded

11.208 It is unfortunate that the majority should not have hearkened to the wise words of a great judge pronounced in 1858. Baron Martin said:

"Instead of being astute to discover reasons for not applying the great remedy for *error and misgovernment* we think it our duty to be vigilant to apply it in every case to which by any reasonable construction, it can be made applicable."[14] (italics supplied)

If this was true in 1858, it cannot be less true in 1981, and even more so for judges who not only practise "judicial activism" but proclaim it in their judgments. That the majority were astute to discover reasons for not issuing a *mandamus* is clear from the unpractical remedies suggested by them. If, said Chandrachud C.J., Parliament thought that the Central Government was not doing its duty, Parliament could censure that Government since it is responsible to Parliament. But members of a party are not known for their zeal in censuring their leaders who constitute the Government; consequently the so-called remedy is purely theoretical. Again, said Chandrachud C.J. "Parliament" in conferring the power on the Central Government does not irretrievably part with its power but can repeal s. 1(2) of the Amending Act. The untenability of this suggestion has been shown in para 11.203 above.

Submission: *Mandamus* was the obvious remedy. If no time was fixed by S. 1(2) the law implied a reasonable time: Stroud's Judicial Dictionary

11.209 However, a reference to standard text books would have shown that a *mandamus* issued to the Central Government was the obvious and appropriate remedy. It is settled law that where an act is to be done or a duty is to be discharged and no time is specified for it, the law implies that the act must be done or the duty discharged within a reasonable time having regard to the facts and circumstances of each case. Under the entry "Reasonable Time", *Stroud's Judicial Dictionary*[15] states:

"Where a contract has to be performed[16] or a duty discharged[17] within a reasonable time (or within no specified time) which connotes a reasonable time,[18] such time will have to be determined according to the circumstances of the case, and with particular reference to the means and ability of the person by whom the contract is to be performed, or the duty discharged."[19]

---

14 *Rochester Corporation* v. *R.* (1858) E.B. & E. 1024, 1033.

15 Vol. IV, 4th ed. p. 2271.

16 *Attwood* v. *Emery*, 26 L.J.C.P. 73; *Briddon* v. *Great Northern Railway*, 28 L.J. Ex. 51; *Hales* v. *London & North Western Railway*, 32 L.J.Q.B. 292; *Taylor* v. *Great Northern Railway*, L.R. 1 C.P. 385.

17 *Goodwyn* v. *Cheveley*, 28 L.J. Ex. 298.

18 *Nosotti* v. *Averbach*, 79 L.T. 414.

19 *Postlethwaite* v. *Freeland*, 5 App. Cas. 599; *Hick* v. *Raymond* (1893) A.C. 22 (see on this last case *per* Lord Herschell); *Carlton S. S. Co.* v. *Castle Co.* (1898) A.C. 490-492; CUSTOMARY; *Toms* v. *Wilson*, 32 L.J.Q.B. 33; *Brighty* v. *Norton*, 32 L.J.Q.B. 38.

This principle is embedded in our law. For example, s. 36 (2) of the Sale of Goods Act provides: "Where under the contract of sale the seller is bound to send the goods to the buyer, but no time for sending them is fixed, the seller is bound to send them within a reasonable time"; and s. 63 provides "Where in this Act any reference is made to reasonable time, the question what is a reasonable time is a question of fact".[20] The underlying principle is that where parties have incurred obligations and undertaken to discharge duties, that dominant purpose cannot be allowed to fail because the time within which the duties were to be discharged is not fixed. The law effectuates the intention of parties by assuming that they must have intended to discharge the duties within a reasonable time. When the constituent body imposed upon the Central Government a duty to bring the provisions of the 44th Amendment Act into force but left it to the discretion of the Central Government to determine the time within which the duty was to be discharged without specifying any time limit, principle and authority require that it must be discharged within a reasonable time if the deliberate intention of the constituent body was not to be defeated. When under s. 36 of the Sale of Goods Act or s. 46 of the Contract Act, the Court determines on the evidence what is reasonable time, the Court does not substitute its own judgment for that of the parties, nor does it talk of "objective criteria". It gives effect to the intention of the parties by deciding on evidence what is reasonable time on the facts of each case. So the intention of the constituent body being clear and the discretion being limited to effectuate that intention without specifying the time within which the Central Government was to do so, the Court on the evidence must effectuate that intention by deciding whether the Central Government had failed to discharge its duty within a reasonable time.

This principle is embedded in our law: the underlying principle

The Central Govt. cannot defeat the intention of the constituent body which passed the 44th Amendment

11.210 We have referred to the duties imposed by a contract, or a contract of sale, but the source of the duty does not affect the principle stated above. As a standard text book puts it, "To be enforceable by *mandamus* the duty does not necessarily have to be imposed by statute. It may be sufficient for the duty to have been imposed by charter, common law, custom or even contract".[21] The same text book states "In an Israeli case, the courts directed Ministers to perform their duty to make regulations on a topic; there had been unreasonable delay in making the regulations but no outright refusal".[22] It is submitted that the decision in the above case is clearly right.

Principle governing issue of *mandamus*: an Israeli case

11.211 On the question of unreasonable delay, the facts of the case leave no doubt that the delay was both unexplained and unreasonable. First, the amendments contained in 43 out of 44 sections of the Amendment Act had been brought into force by August 1979, with the exception of the amendments contained in s. 3. The fact that Cl. 9 of the Ordinance provided for the constitution of an Advisory Board in conformity with Art. 22 of the Constitution as amended by s. 3 of the Amendment Act showed that there were

On facts there was unreasonable and unexplained delay

[20] Section 46 of the Indian Contract Act makes the same provision for "the performance of promise where no time is specified".
[21] S. A. de Smith, *Judicial Review of Administrative Action*, 4th ed. at p. 540.
[22] ibid. p. 557, f.n. 15.

no practical difficulties in bringing s. 3 of the Amendment Act into force. Again, the observations in the majority judgment showed that the failure of the Central Government to bring s. 3 into force was "without any acceptable reason" and it should be noted that in fact no reasons were given. That an authority on whom a duty is imposed, and a limited discretion conferred in relation to that duty, cannot escape judicial scrutiny by the Court has been laid down in *Padfield* v. *Minister of Agriculture, Fisheries and Food*[23] as is clear from the following observations of the Law Lords in that case:

Judicial scrutiny cannot be evaded by giving no reasons! *Padfield's Case*

Lord Reid: "I do not agree that a decision cannot be questioned if no reasons are given. If it is the Minister's duty not to act so as to frustrate the policy and objects of the Act, and if it were to appear from all the circumstances of the case that that has been the effect of the Minister's refusal, then it appears to me that the Court must be entitled to act."[24]

Lord Hodson: "True it is that the Minister is not bound to give his reasons for refusing to exercise his discretion in a particular manner, but when, as here, the circumstances indicate a genuine complaint for which the appropriate remedy is provided if the Minister in the case in question so directs, he would not escape from the possibility of control by *mandamus* through adopting a negative attitude without explanation. As the guardian of the public interest he has a duty to protect the interest of those who claim to have been treated contrary to the public interest."[25]

Lord Pearce: "I do not regard the Minister's failure or refusal to give any reasons as a sufficient exclusion of the Court's surveillance. If all the *prima facie* reasons seem to point in favour of his taking a certain course to carry out the intentions of Parliament in respect of a power it gave him in that regard, and he gives no reason whatever for taking a contrary course, the Court may infer that he has no good reason and he is not using the power given by Parliament to carry out its intentions."[26]

Lord Upjohn: "(the Minister) is a public officer charged by Parliament with the discharge of a public discretion affecting Her Majesty's subjects; if he does not give any reason for his decision, it may be, if circumstances warrant it, that a Court may be at liberty to come to the conclusion that he had no good reason for reaching that conclusion and order a prerogative writ to issue accordingly."[27]

The observations of 4 Law Lords are directly applicable to the present case

The reader will have noticed that the views expressed in these passages are directly applicable to the failure of the Central Government to bring s. 3 into force and its failure to give any reasons to justify that failure. The observations of Chandrachud C.J. that "it is difficult to appreciate what practical difficulty can possibly prevent the Government from bringing into force the provisions of s. 3 after the passage of two-and-a-half years" show clearly that the Court found no reason, based on practical difficulties, which would justify not bringing s. 3 into force. The Central Government was charged with a public duty affecting a section of the people for whom the constituent body had provided further safeguards before they could be preventively detained. In the absence of cogent reasons for not bringing s. 3 into force, the Court was entitled, and it is submitted, was bound, to draw the conclusion that the Central Government had no reasons to give which would justify its failure to bring s. 3 into force.

Padfield's Case quoted with approval by our Sup. Ct.

11.212 *Padfield's Case* has been quoted with approval, and described as of "considerable importance" by Hegde J. in *Rohtas Industries Ltd.* v. *S. P. Agarwal*.[28] He quoted the passage from the judgment of Lord Pearce, a part of which has been set out in para 11.211 above.

---

23 (1968) A.C. 997.
24 ibid. pp. 1032-3.
25 ibid. p. 1049.
26 ibid. pp. 1053-4.
27 ibid. pp. 1061-2.
28 (1969) 3 S.C.R. 108, ('69) A.SC. 707.

Hegde J. held that no responsible authority, much less an expert body like the Central Government, could have reasonably made the impugned order on the material before it. Bachawat J. in a concurring judgment observed: "I am, therefore constrained to hold that it formed the opinion without applying the material before it." The observations of the House of Lords, and the decision of our Supreme Court show that where there is a clear duty imposed upon the public authority with a limited discretion in the exercise of that duty, in the absence of clear reasons for not discharging the duty, the Court will either quash the order, if the duty is judicial or quasi-judicial, or issue a writ of *mandamus* to enforce the duty as was done in *Padfield's Case*. That there had been gross delay on the part of the Central Government to bring s. 3 of the Amendment Act into force (without any justifying reasons for such delay) is clear from the judgment of Chandrachud C.J. in which he expressed the hope that the Central Government would "without further delay" bring s. 3 into force, an observation which necessarily implied that the Government had been guilty of gross delay. The contention that a *mandamus* should issue, because the Central Government had not brought s. 3 into force *mala fide*, was rejected because the materials before the Court did not justify a finding of *mala fides*, "although delay in implementing the will of Parliament may justifiably raise many an eyebrow."[28a] It is submitted that there was enough material before the Court to sustain a finding of *mala fides*, not in the sense of malice or dishonesty but in the sense of acting unreasonably and using the power to achieve an object other than that for which the authority believed the power had been conferred, even if the intention may be to promote another public interest[28b] Once the Court rightly held that it was not for the Central Government to sit in judgment on the wisdom of the constituent body in enacting s. 3, the fact that all other amendments were brought into force, the fact that cl. 9 of the Ordinance was in conformity with s. 3 of the Amending Act, the fact that over two years had gone by and no rational ground could be, or was, suggested for not bringing s. 3 into force, led only to one conclusion that the power was being used *mala fide*, that is, unreasonably and for a purpose for which it was not conferred. It is common learning that those who act *mala fide* do not proclaim that fact and that *mala fides* is a matter of inference from the conduct of the party. There is high authority for the proposition that when it is said that the repository of a power must not act in bad faith, this implication of the law is wide enough to cover both honesty and reasonableness.[28c] In the result, it is submitted that on the question whether a *mandamus* ought to have been issued to the Central Government, the judgment of the majority is contrary to reason, principle and authority; it is clearly wrong and productive of grave

Submission: there was enough material to support a finding of *mala fides*

Submission: a *mandamus* ought to have been issued

[28a] ('82) A.SC. *supra* at p. 734. [28b] *S. A. de Smith, op. cit.* p. 335.

[28c] *Roberts* v. *Hopwood* (1925) A.C. 578 at 604, *per* Lord Sumner. Prof. Wade points out that Lord Macnaghten had said the same thing: see *Administrative Law*, 4th ed. at p. 340. Lord Macnaghten said that a public authority vested with discretionary power "must act in good faith. And it must act reasonably. The last proposition is involved in the second, if not in the first": *Westminster Corpn.* v. *L. & N.W. Rly.* (1905) A.C. 426 at p. 430.

against the Central Govt. public mischief and ought to be overruled at the earliest opportunity. Such opportunity may present itself to the Supreme Court either on a review application[29] or on a fresh petition presented by a person preventively detained under the impugned Act, because the delay in bringing s. 3 into force even after more than a year has gone by since the judgment was delivered in December 1981, has created a fresh situation, and no Court can allow the will of a constituent body to be defeated by obstinate and unreasonable refusal of a Government to do its duty.

Mondal's Case: Art. 22(4) confirmation after 3 months illegal

11.213 In *Ujjal Mondal* v. *W.B.*[30] it was contended that the petitioner's continued detention under the W.B. (Prevention of Violent Activities) Act, 1970 was illegal since the detention order was confirmed by Government 3 months after the date of detention. On a consideration of Art. 22 (4) and the relevant provisions of the Act,[31] Mathew J. held that the detention was illegal. Article 22 (4) specified the maximum period of initial detention, and detention for a longer period than three months could only be made on the basis of the report of the Board

> ". . . the State Government has power under the Act to detain a person without trial beyond a period of 3 months but limited to a period of one year. That power the State Government may exercise on the receipt of the opinion of the Board that there is sufficient cause for the detention. When the State Government receives that opinion, it has still the option to exercise the power and to continue the detention beyond the period of 3 months or not. Confirmation is the exercise of the power to continue the detention after the expiry of the three months. Unless that power is exercised within the period of 3 months from the date of detention, the detention after the expiry of that period would be without the authority of the law."[32]

Mathew J. said that the same view had been taken by the Supreme Court in *Deb Sadhen Roy* v. *W.B.*[33] and added: "We see no reason to doubt the correctness of this decision and we follow it."[34]

Atma Ram's Case: the scheme of Art. 22(5) and (6) and s. 3 of the Act

11.214 In *Bombay* v. *Atma Ram Sridhar Vaidya*[35] Kania C.J. explained the scheme of Art. 22 (5) and (6) in the context of s. 3, Preventive Detention Act, 1950, and the effect of his judgment may be stated thus: Government may have information against a person which may fall far short of legal proof of any specific offences although it may indicate a strong probability of the impending commission of a prejudicial act. Before Government can pass an order under s. 3, it must be satisfied with respect to the individual person that his activities were directed against one or other of the three

---

[29] If the Supreme Court treated Government's refusal to respond to the Court's hope that Government would bring into force s. 3 "without further delay" as justifying a review.

[30] (1972) 3 S.C.R. 165, ('72) A.SC. 1446; foll. in *Nirmal Kumar* v. *Union* (1978) 3 S.C.R. 817, ('78) A.SC. 1155 (The Court refused to reconsider *Mondal's Case* and three other Supreme Court decisions which had taken the same view, observing that there was no material difference on the relevant point between COFEPOSA and MISA).

[31] ('72) A.SC. at p. 1448 where they are set out.

[32] ibid. p. 1449; Mathew J. referred with approval to *Aswini Kumar Banerjee* v. *State* 75 C.W.N. 866; *Kaur Singh* v. *State* ('52) A.Pep. 134; *Sangappa Mallappa* v. *Mysore* ('59) A.Mys. 7 and *Bhupati Goswami* v. *C. R. Krishnamurti* ('69) A.Ass. 14.

[33] Unreported; ('72) A.SC. *supra* at p. 1450.

[34] ibid. The same view was expressed in *Micki Khan* v. *W.B.* ('72) A.SC. 2262 and in *S. Mukherjee* v. *W.B.* ('72) A.SC. 1356.

[35] (1951) S.C.R. 167, ('51) A.SC. 157; fol. in *Md. Allabux* v. *State* ('66) A.Guj. 126.

objects mentioned in s. 3 and that it was necessary to prevent him from so acting. The wording of s. 3 clearly showed that it was the subjective satisfaction of the Central and the State Governments which had to be established, and an objective test in a court of law could not be substituted for it. But the satisfaction of Government must be based on some grounds, for there could be no satisfaction if there were no grounds for it. Opinions may differ whether certain grounds were sufficient, but if the grounds on which it was stated that the Central, or the State Government was satisfied

S. 3 requires the subjective satisfaction of the Govt.

but it must be based on some grounds

"... are such as a rational human being can consider connected in some manner with the objects which were to be prevented from being attained, the question of satisfaction except on the ground of *mala fides* cannot be challenged in a Court."[36]

However, if the grounds were such as to have no connection with the objects to be prevented, the grounds would be irrelevant and the order of detention would be invalid for not complying with Art. 22(5).[37] So far the whole court was agreed.

which must not be irrelevant

11.215 An order of preventive detention having been permitted by law to be made, certain rights were conferred on the person against whom such an order was passed. Article 22(5) conferred on him a right to be told "as soon as may be" the grounds for making the order. This was considered an elementary right in a free democratic State, for otherwise, the detenu might remain in custody without knowing why his liberty had been taken away. But as there would be no point in his knowing the ground of arrest unless he could take action to secure redress, Art. 22(5) further provided that the detained person should have the earliest opportunity of making a representation against the order of detention. However, in conveying the information to the detained person, it may be that certain facts could not be disclosed in the public interest; Art. 22(6) enabled the authority making the order not to disclose them. If the grounds supplied were not sufficient to enable the detenu to make a representation, he might if he liked ask for particulars to enable him to do so.[38]

Rights of the detenu: (i) to be informed "as soon as may be" of the grounds for the order of detention

(ii) to be afforded the earliest opportunity of making a representation

The detenu may ask for particulars

11.216 In *Khairul Haque* v. *W.B.*[39] the Supreme Court held that Art. 22(5) imposed on Government a dual obligation and conferred on the detenu a corresponding dual right, namely, (i) to have his representation independently considered by the Government, and (ii) to have that representation, on the facts and circumstances of the case,[40] considered by the Advisory Board; and Art. 22(5) required government to afford the detenu the earliest opportunity to make a representation. This implied that such representation, when made, must be considered and disposed of as expeditiously as possi-

Khairul Haque v. *W.B.* : the rights of the detenue and the obligations of Govt. under Art. 22(5)

---

[36] (1951) S.C.R. at p. 176. [37] (1950) S.C.R. 88, 130-1.

[38] (1951) S.C.R. 167, 184; see also *Safatulla Khan* v. *Chief Secretary, W.B.* ('51) A.Cal. 194; *Devi Singh* v. *Rajasthan* (1952) Raj. 569, ('52) A.Raj. 171; *Sangappa* v. *Mysore* (1957) Mys. 374, ('59) A.Mys. 7 [where privilege is claimed under Art. 22(6) the satisfaction of the authority that the disclosure was against the public interest must be proved].

[39] Unreported; rel. on in *Jayanarayan Sukul* v. *W.B.* (1970) 3 S.C.R. 225, ('70) A.SC. 675 (unexplained delay of over a month fatal to the detention order); *Sukul's Case* was fol. in *K. I. Singh* v. *Manipur* ('72) A.SC. 438 and in *Niranjan Singh* v. *M.P.* ('72) A.SC. 2215 (representation not expeditiously disposed of).

[40] The same view was expressed in *Pankaj Kumar* v. *W.B.* ('70) A.SC. 97, 100-101.

ble, for, otherwise, "an obligation to furnish the earliest opportunity to make a representation loses both its purpose and meaning." Unexplained delay in considering the detenu's application rendered the order of detention invalid.[41] This strict view was taken because preventive detention was a serious invasion of personal liberty. The question of delay is a question of fact; and if delay is satisfactorily explained the order of detention will be upheld as was done in *Nagendra Nath* v. *W.B.*[42] and *S. C. Bose* v. *Dist. Magistrate, Burdwan.*[43]

Vague and indefinite grounds: *Atma Ram's Case*: three questions considered

11.217 In a number of cases, orders of detention had been challenged on the allegation that the grounds furnished to the detained person were vague and indefinite. Thus in the judgment under appeal in *Atma Ram's Case* grounds had been supplied to the detenu, which he challenged as vague. But before his petition was heard, further particulars were furnished to him. Chagla C.J. held that if such particulars had been furnished in the first instance, they would have been sufficient to enable the detenu to make an effective representation. But the detaining authority could not justify the detention by "amplifying and improving the grounds originally furnished", and as the grounds originally furnished were not sufficient to enable the detenu to make a representation, the order of detention violated Art. 22(5) and was void. Having regard to the important questions thus raised, Kania C.J. considered three connected questions: first, the object of furnishing the detained person with grounds and the circumstances under which such grounds could be said to be vague; secondly, the meaning of the word "grounds"; and finally, whether Art. 22 forbade the furnishing of further particulars in respect of the grounds already furnished. He said that the right which Art. 22(5) conferred on the detenu enabled the Court to answer these questions. The first right was to be furnished with the grounds on which the order had been made "as soon as may be", and the second was, to be afforded the earliest opportunity of making a representation against the order. Since the grounds furnished to the detenu were the grounds on which the detaining authority was satisfied that it was necessary to make the order, *the grounds must be in existence when the order was made*. However, "the grounds" must be distinguished from the facts on which the satisfaction of Government was based. "Grounds" were conclusions drawn from the facts, and not a complete recital of the facts, and the grounds would show in which of the three categories of prejudical acts the suspected activities of the detained person were considered to fall. Therefore, no part of the grounds could be kept back from the detenu; nor could a new ground be supplied later, for, such new ground either did not

Grounds must exist when the detention order was made; "grounds" must be distinguished from the facts on which the satisfaction of Govt. was based

[41] In the following cases the unexplained delay mentioned after each case was held fatal to the detention order: *Baidya Nath Chunakar* v. *W.B.* ('72) A.SC. 1198 (29 days); *Ranjit Dam* v. *W.B.* ('72) A.SC. 1753 (19 days). Cases in *f.n.* 39 and the above cases in this f.n. were referred to in *Kanti Lal* v. *W.B.* ('72) A.SC. 1623 (28 days) which was fol. in *Sambhu Kar* v. *W.B.* ('73) A.SC. 959 (35 days); *Abdus Sukkur* v. *W.B.* ('72) A.SC. 1915 (27 days), rel. on in *Atiar Rahman* v. *W.B.* ('72) A.SC. 2529 (24 days' delay; explanation for delay held unjustified); fol. in *B. C. Dutta* v. *W.B.* ('72) A.SC. 2605; *Binode Hembram* v. *W.B.* ('72) A.SC. 2378 (40 days); *D. P. Ghosh* v. *W.B.* ('72) A.SC. 2420 (38 days); fol. in *Sudhir Dey* v. W.B. ('72) A.SC. 2623 (43 days); and in *D. N. Goswami* v. *W.B.* ('73) A.SC. 757 (25 days; explanation for delay not satisfactory); *Satyabrata* v. *W.B.* ('73) A.SC. 756 (delay of over a month, explanation for delay held unjustified); *Sk. Rashid* v. *W.B.* ('73) A.SC. 824 (35 days).

[42] ('72) A.SC. 665.

[43] ('72) A.SC. 2481.

lead to the satisfaction of Government in the first instance, in which case the detention was void, or the new ground had not been given "as soon as may be", and Art. 22(5) had been violated. The second right of being afforded the "earliest opportunity of making a representation against the order" implied that the detenu must have knowledge of the grounds on which the authorities were satisfied about the necessity of detaining him,

". . . if the representation has to be intelligible to meet the charges contained in the grounds, the information conveyed to the detained person must be sufficient to attain that object. . . . Without getting information sufficient to make a representation against the order of detention it is not possible for the man to make the representation. Indeed, the right will be only illusory but not a real right at all."[44]

The meaning of a "vague ground"

The contention that a ground was vague was best understood by reference to the opposite of vague, namely, "definite". If the ground which was supplied was incapable of being understood or defined with sufficient certainty, it was vague and the test for determining whether a ground was vague was:

The test of "vagueness"

"If on reading the ground furnished it is capable of being intelligently understood and is sufficiently definite to furnish materials to enable the detained person to make a representation against the order of detention it cannot be called vague."[45]

"Supplementary grounds": additional facts can be given but not additional grounds

The view that "supplementary grounds" could not be given, required clarification. If by supplementary grounds was meant *new conclusions* from facts, such supplementary grounds could not be given, because all the grounds on which the satisfaction of the detaining authority was based had to be given in the first instance. But if by supplementary grounds was meant not new conclusions from facts, but *additional facts* in support of the old conclusions, which were not available or were not given in the first instance, then there was nothing in the Article to forbid such grounds being furnished. On the contrary, Art. 22(5) contemplated two distinct points of time and the duration of each was left vague. The grounds were to be given "as soon as may be" and the period thus indicated must depend on the facts of each case. Again, the detained person was to be afforded the earliest opportunity of making a representation. Until he received the grounds he could make no representation, so that the making of the representation was the second stage and the words "the earliest opportunity" also depended on the facts of each case. Kania C.J. held that though fresh grounds could not be given, additional particulars in support of existing grounds could be given and on the facts of the case before the Court, what had been supplied to the respondent were not additional grounds, but further particulars of grounds already supplied. Except on the point on which the whole Court agreed as stated earlier,[46] the judgment of Kania C.J. was a majority judgment for himself, Fazl Ali, Mukherjea and Chandrasekhara Aiyar JJ., Patanjali Sastri and Das JJ. dissenting. While the criticisms in the dissenting judgments are not without force, it is submitted that on the whole, the majority judgment is correct.

[44] (1951) S.C.R. 167 at pp. 178-9.
[45] ibid. p. 185; rel. on in *Fulchand* v. *Dist. Magistrate* ('68) A.Or. 109.
[46] See para 11.214.

Tarapada De's Case: the use of the words "supplementary grounds" is not conclusive

11.218 A judgment delivered by the same Bench on the same day in *Tarapada De* v. *W.B.*[47] amplified two points which had been made in *Atma Ram's Case.* Kania C.J. explained that the words "supplementary grounds" were not conclusive. The Court had to look beyond the label to ascertain the real facts and in the case before him he held that though called "supplementary grounds", they were additional particulars in support of the existing grounds and Art. 22 did not forbid additional particulars.[48] Again, in *Atma Ram's Case*, Kania C.J. had pointed out the difference between vague grounds on the one hand and irrelevant grounds,[49] and for the reasons there given, he said in *Tarapada De's Case* that the Court could not accept the contention that if the grounds were vague and no representation was possible, there could be no satisfaction of the authority as required under s. 3 of the Preventive Detention Act. The sufficiency of the grounds which gave rise to the satisfaction of Government was not a matter for examination by the Court. The sufficiency of the grounds which would give the detained person the earliest opportunity to make a representation could be examined by the Court, but only from that point of view. The quality and characteristic of the grounds need not be the same for both tests. One person may, but another may not, be satisfied on the same ground. That question, however, was not for the determination of the Court. The second part of the inquiry was clearly open to the Court under Art. 22. Even if the grounds were not sufficient or adequate for making a representation, they might well be sufficient for the subjective satisfaction of the authorities.[50]

The difference between vague and irrelevant grounds

Other questions arising under Art. 22(5)

11.219 Where a person was ordered to be detained by a district magistrate but his period of detention was extended by an order of the State Government, he was entitled to claim that fresh grounds of detention should be supplied to him. Article 22 (5) made no distinction between one authority and another, or between an original order and an order made at a later date.[51] Though Art. 22 (5) conferred a right on a person to be told why he had been detained, it made no provision for determining the matter or method of disposing of his representation or objections against the order of detention. S. 10, Preventive Detention Act, enabled the Advisory Board to call for such information as it deemed necessary from the appropriate Government, or from any person called for the purpose through the appropriate Government, or from the detenu himself. However, Art. 22 (5) was not infringed if the Board refused to accede to the detenu's request to call for the records, for such refusal meant that the Board did not consider it necessary or essential to do so.[52]

Ram Singh's Case: difference between the majority and the minority in applying the test of vagueness

11.220 In *Ram Singh* v. *Delhi*,[53] both the majority and the minority judgments accepted the position that preventive detention was not to be judged by the requirements of Art. 19 and they adopted the test of "vagueness" laid down by Kania C.J. in *Atma Ram's Case*. However, in the application of that test, there was a difference of opinion. Kania C.J., Patanjali Sastri and S. R. Das JJ. held that as the time

---

47 (1951) S.C.R. 212, ('51) A.SC. 174.
48 (1951) S.C.R. *supra* at p. 217.
49 (1951) S.C.R. 167 at pp. 182-3.
50 (1951) S.C.R. 212 at pp. 218-9.
51 *Madan Lal* v. *Dist. Magistrate* ('51) A.Punj. 119.
52 *Srinibash Naidu* v. *W.B.* ('62) A.Cal. 162.
53 (1951) S.C.R. 451, ('51) A.SC. 270.

and place on which speeches were alleged to have been made, and their general nature and effect, namely, that they were such as to excite disaffection between Hindus and Muslims were also stated in the grounds communicated, the grounds were not too vague or indefinite to enable petitioners to make an effective representation and the detention did not violate Art. 22 (5). Mahajan J. said that a bare denial of the fact that the speeches had been made, or the bald denial that no words were used which could possibly excite disaffection between Hindus and Muslims would be an idle formality in a representation, for mere denials without cogent argument to support them would convince nobody. He held that without the knowledge of the offending words or passages or their substance, it was not possible to make a representation which would convince a detaining authority. Bose J. agreed with Mahajan J., and made the important point that it was not enough to say that the detenu, who made the speech must know what he had said, for the question was not what he had said, but what the detaining authority *thought* he had said. There may be *bona fide mistakes* in reporting. One speaker at the meeting may be confused with another speaker at the same meeting. The words used may not have been the words of the speaker, but may have been a quotation from persons to whom no criminal intent could be attributed. Bose J. said that the construction he placed on the Article placed no great, or impossible strain on the machinery of Government:

The majority view: Mahajan J.

Bose J.

"All that is required is that the authorities should bestow on the cases of these detenus a very small fraction of the thought, time and energy which the law compels in the case of even the meanest criminal who is arraigned before the Courts of this country. The fact that there is absent in the case of these persons all the usual safeguards, the glare of publicity, the right to know with precision the charge against him, the right to speak in his own defence is all the more reason why Government be thoughtful, considerate and kind and should give them the maximum help. In any case, that, in my opinion, is what the Constitution requires and I am not prepared to abate one jot or tittle of its rigours."[54]

It is submitted that the reasons given in the minority judgments are clearly right.

Submission: the minority view is correct

11.221 In *Ram Krishan Bhardwaj* v. *Delhi*[55] the Supreme Court again emphasised that preventive detention was a serious invasion of personal liberty and such meagre safeguards as the Constitution had provided against the improper exercise of the power must be jealously watched and enforced by the Courts. A layman not experienced in interpreting documents could not be expected without legal aid, which was denied to him under Art. 22 (3), to interpret the grounds in their proper sense. Therefore, the detaining authority must make its meaning clear beyond doubt and not leave the person detained to his own resources for interpreting it. Otherwise, Art. 22 (5) would be violated, for such "grounds" would be regarded as vague because it would be difficult, if not impossible, for the petitioner to make a proper representation. Again, in *Harikisan* v. *Maharashtra*,[56] after referring to *Atma Ram's Case*, the Supreme Court said that the words "communicate the grounds" meant that the knowledge of the grounds must be brought home to the detenu. Consequently, if he did not

Ram Krishan Bhardwaj v. *Delhi*: safeguards against the abuse of the power of preventive detention must be strictly enforced

The meaning and effect of the obligation to communicate the grounds

---

[54] (1951) S.C.R. *supra* at p. 472.
[55] (1953) S.C.R. 708, ('53) A.SC. 318.
[56] (1962) Supp. (2) S.C.R. 918, ('62) A.SC. 911.

of preventive detention to the detenu

know enough English to understand the grounds upon which he was detained, the grounds should be served on him in a language which he could understand. As the detenu did not know enough English, it was held that Art. 22 (5) had not been complied with. And the same view has been taken in *Chaju Ram* v. *J. & K.*[57] without any reference to *Harikisan's Case.* However, *Chaju Ram's Case* does not warrant an argument that even if a detenu knew English, it was necessary to explain the order to him in vernacular.[58] In *Hadibandhu Das* v. *Dist. Magistrate*[59] the Supreme Court held that where grounds in support of the order of detention in the English language were served on the detenu ran into 14 typed pages and referred to his activities over 13 years, besides referring to a large number of court proceedings against him and his associates, mere oral explanation by the authorities of such complicated orders without supplying him with a translation in the script and language which he understood amounted to a denial of the right of being furnished with the grounds and of being accorded an opportunity of making representations against the order of detention. In *Lallubhai Jogibhai* v. *Union*[60] Sarkaria J. observed that Art. 22 (5) required that grounds of detention must be "communicated" to the detenu, and he added:[61]

The implications of the word "communicate"

> " 'Communicate' is a strong word. It means that sufficient knowledge of the basic facts constituting the 'grounds' should be imparted effectively and fully to the detenu in writing in a language which he understands. The whole purpose of communicating the 'ground' to the detenu is to enable him to make a purposeful and effective representation. If the 'grounds' are only verbally explained to the detenu and nothing in writing is left with him, in a language which he understands, then that purpose is not served, and the constitutional mandate in Art. 22(5) is infringed. If any authority is needed on this point, which is so obvious from Art. 22(5), reference may be made to the decisions of this Court in *Harikisan* v. *Maharashtra*[62] and *Hadibandhu Das* v. *Dist. Magistrate.*[63]"[64]

The test of vagueness laid down by Kania C.J. in *Atma Ram's Case* has been followed in a large number of cases.[65] Having regard to the above test it has been held that where the detenu has made a detailed representation, he cannot contend that the grounds supplied to him were vague;[66] nor would the grounds necessarily be vague if the

---

[57] (1970) 3 S.C.R. 872, ('71) A.SC. 263, 265-6 [*held,* that Art. 22(5) was not complied with as the detenu did not understand English, in which language the detention order was served and the terms of the order were not explained to him].

[58] *Abdul Rehman* v. *J. & K.* ('71) A.SC. 266, 267.

[59] ('69) A.SC. 43, 46-7; fol. in *Lallubhai Jogibhai* v. *Union* ('81) A.SC. 728.

[60] ('81) A.SC. 728.

[61] ibid. p. 733.

[62] (1962) Supp. 2 S.C.R. 918, ('62) A.SC. 911.

[63] (1969) 1 S.C.R. 227, ('69) A.SC. 43.

[64] ('81) A.SC. *supra* at p. 733.

[65] *Naresh Chandra Ganguli* v. *W.B.* (1960) 1 S.C.R. 411, ('59) A.SC. 1335; *Puranlal Lakhanpal* v. *Union* (1958) S.C.R. 460, ('58) A.SC. 163 (the rights conferred on the detenu were analysed and the court held that it was open to the detenu to apply for further particulars in case he had any grievance); *Shibban Lal Saksena* v. *U.P.* (1954) S.C.R. 418, ('54) A.SC. 179; *Dharamdas* v. *Dist. Magistrate* ('60) A.Guj. 43; *Moolsingh* v. *State* (1958) 8 Raj. 386, ('58) A.Raj. 158 [the ground should be formulated in a precise and concise manner and should be as full and adequate as circumstances permit. A departure from this would amount to a violation of Art. 22(5)]; *Raj Bahadur* v. *Hyderabad* ('53) A.Hyd. 277; *In re Maganlal Jivabhai Patel* (1951) Bom. 546, ('51) A.B. 33, 53 Bom.L.R. 127 [furnishing grounds of detention did not mean that the grounds mentioned in s. 3(1) (*a*) and (*b*) of the Preventive Detention Act were to be mechanically copied]. *Lakhanpal's Case, supra,* was rel. on in *Fulchand* v. *Dist. Magistrate* ('68) A.Or. 109.

[66] *Ramanadhan* v. *Hyderabad* (1952) Hyd. 770, ('52) A.Hyd. 186.

only answer of the detenu to the grounds stated was to deny them.[67] However, the grounds in *Panna Ram* v. *State*[68] and in *Sushila* v. *Commr. of Police, Greater Bombay*[69] were held to be vague, and the orders of detention invalid.

Icchu Devi v. Union: copies of documents etc. relied upon in the grounds for detention must be supplied to the detenu

11.222 In *Icchu Devi* v. *Union*,[70] Bhagwati J. held that when Art. 22(5) provided that the grounds of detention must be communicated to the detenu, it meant that the entire grounds should be communicated to him. If there were any documents, statements or other material relied upon in the grounds they must also be supplied to the detenu, because being incorporated in the grounds, the grounds cannot be said to be complete without them. Copies of documents, statements and other materials, must, subject to Art. 22(6), be supplied to the detenu if Art. 22(5) was not to be violated.[71] *Icchu Devi's Case* was referred to and followed in *Lallubhai Jogibhai* v. *Union*.[72] *Icchu Devi's Case*, which was "endorsed" in *Shalini Soni* v. *Union*[73] was followed also in *Kamla* v. *Maharashtra*.[74] In *M. M. Patel* v. *Maharashtra*[75] the above cases were referred to and it was said that their rationale was

The rationale of the above obligation

"the right to be supplied with copies of the documents, statements and other materials relied upon in the grounds of detention without any undue delay flows directly as a necessary corollary from the right conferred on the detenu to be afforded the earliest opportunity of making a representation against the detention, because unless the former right is available the latter cannot be meaningfully exercised."[76]

Abdul Karim's Case: Govt. not considering representations but forwarding it to the Advisory Board — detention order invalid

11.223 In *Abdul Karim* v. *W.B.*[77] the petitioner had been detained under the Preventive Detention Act. On receiving the grounds for his detention he sent his representation to Government. In his writ petition he alleged that Government had failed to consider the representation, as it was its duty to do, and had merely forwarded the representation to the Advisory Board.[78] The Supreme Court held that though Art. 22(5) did not expressly provide that Government should consider the representation, it was implicit in Art. 22(5) that Government should do so, if the right conferred by the Article on the detenu was not to be illusory. First, if the respondent's contention were accepted, it would lead to absurd consequences. For example, the representation might disclose that the detenu was being detained as a result of mistaken identity by reason of similarity of names; and it would be absurd to suggest that even if this were true, the detenu must be

---

[67] *Shri Krishna Sharma* v. *W.B.* ('54) A.Cal. 591, 58 C.W.N. 659.

[68] ('54) A.Punj. 133: that "your places are meeting places of all murderers and 'badmashes' not only from this State, but also from Pepsu and Rajasthan. It is widely known that the members of your party and that of Mukh Ram are big schemers and do no cultivation themselves."

[69] (1951) Bom. 92, ('51) A.B. 252, 52 Bom.L.R. 794 "You, along with your associates have been collecting and are likely to collect arms and ammunition for illegal purposes and illegal activities."

[70] ('80) A.SC. 1983.

[71] ibid. p. 1989.

[72] ('81) A.SC. 728, 732.

[73] ('81) A.SC. 431.

[74] ('81) A.SC. 814.

[75] ('81) A.SC. 510.

[76] ibid. p. 513.

[77] (1969) 3 S.C.R. 479, ('69) A.SC. 1028.

[78] The respondents argued the petition on the basis that Government had not considered, and were not bound to consider, the representation, and were justified in merely forwarding it to the Advisory Board.

kept in detention till the Advisory Board made its report. Secondly, Art. 22 (4) enabled Parliament to make a law providing for preventive detention for a period less than three months without the case of detention being investigated by the Advisory Board. Article 22 (4) thus made it clear that the right conferred by Art. 22 (5) did not depend upon the duration of the period of detention, and the detenu had the right to make a representation even if the detention was for less than three months. Again, Art. 22 (7) enabled Parliament to make a law providing for preventive detention for a longer period than three months without obtaining the opinion of the Advisory Board. If such a law were passed, it could not be contended that Government was under no obligation to consider the representation of the detenu. As Art. 22 (5) had not been complied with, the petitioner was ordered to be released. *Abdul Karim's Case* was followed in *Pankaj Kumar* v. *W.B.*[79] and in *Jayanarayan* v. *W.B.*[80] in both of which the detenus were directed to be released because government had not considered their respective representations. In *Narendra* v. *B. B. Gujral*[81] the duty of Government to consider the representation made by the detenu without waiting for the opinion of the Advisory Board was emphatically reaffirmed. The Supreme Court held that this obligation arose independently of the provisions of any law for preventive detention, for it was imposed by Art. 22 (5). The Court observed that preventive detention was an anachronism in a democratic society like ours, and the repeal of MISA and the retention of preventive detention in the Conservation of Foreign Exchange and Prevention of Smuggling Activities Act did not lead to the conclusion that preventive detention could be used without any power of judicial review and without any "checks and balances".[82] The following two paras represent the Supreme Court's reaction to the gross abuse of MISA during the Emergency:

"The Constitution is all pervasive. All laws made by a State must, therefore, yield to constitutional limitations and restrictions. The citizen's right to personal liberty is guaranteed by Art. 22 irrespective of his political beliefs, class, creed or religion. This Court has forged certain procedural safeguards in the case of preventive detention of citizens. These safeguards might be designated as a regulative 'Postulate of Respect', that is, respect for the intrinsic dignity of the human person.

"In pursuit of the idealistic considerations as to the inherent worth and dignity of man, the Parliament, in the light of the experience gained recently, repealed the Maintenance of Internal Security Act. The repeal of that Act is necessitated to promote the citizen's right to personal liberty, which is a fundamental and pervasive theme of the Constitution, to guard against the preventive detention of a person for political beliefs."[83]

Detention order must be furnished on request

11.224 It has been held that a refusal to supply the detenu with the detention order on request would make the detention void. For the detenu has a right not only to challenge the grounds of the detention order but also its validity.[84]

---

79 (1970) 1 S.C.R. 543, ('70) A.SC. 97, 101.
80 (1970) 3 S.C.R. 225, ('70) A.SC. 675.
81 (1979) 2 S.C.R. 315, ('79) A.SC. 420.
82 ('79) A.SC. at p. 424.
83 ibid. p. 424 (paras 20, 21).
84 *Thiruvadinatha* v. *Dist. Magistrate* ('51) A.Tr.-Co. 130.

Right to further particulars is subject to Art. 22(6)

11.225 If the grounds furnished are not vague but the detenu thinks that he is not able to make a representation he can apply for further particulars.[85] But the Supreme Court has held that this right was subject to the limitation contained in Art. 22(6), and that under Art. 22(5) and (6) there was no obligation to communicate to the detenu the decision not to disclose the facts as well as the ambit of the non-disclosure, at the time when the grounds were furnished. However, such an obligation would arise if the detenu, feeling that the grounds were vague, asked for particulars. The obligation to communicate the decision not to disclose facts considered prejudicial in the public interest might well be implied in such a situation, but in the absence of any such request by the detenu the non-communication of the decision could not be held to have hampered his constitutional right of representation, and an obligation to communicate could not be implied in those circumstances. The fact that the detenu did not apply for particulars might well be taken into consideration in deciding whether the grounds were vague.[86] In *Bhawarlal* v. *T.N.*[87] it was held, without any reference to decided cases, that if the Appellant's complaint was not that the grounds of preventive detention supplied to him were vague, but that certain particulars were not given to him, it was open to him to apply for those particulars. If he did not do so, he could not complain that he was prevented from making an effective representation under Art. 22.

Sup. Ct. decisions in cases where some grounds are vague and/or irrelevant

11.226 We have seen that an order based on irrelevant grounds does not comply with Art. 22(5) and is invalid.[88] Again, if the grounds communicated to the detenu are vague he is denied the opportunity of making an effective representation, in violation of his right under Art. 22(5) and the order for detention must be set aside. But what happens if one or more of a number of grounds is (i) vague or (ii) irrelevant? In *Ram Krishan Bhardwaj* v. *Delhi*[89] and in *Shibban Lal Saksena* v. *U.P.*[90] the Supreme Court answered the questions by saying that even if one of the grounds for detention was vague or irrelevant the order of detention must be held void as violating Art. 22(5). The grounds furnished, and the objections raised, and upheld, in these two cases are set out in the judgment of the Supreme Court in *Dwarka Dass Bhatia* v. *J. & K.*[91] and need not be repeated here. The principle underlying these decisions was thus stated by Jagannadhadas J.:

Bhatia's Case: the underlying principle of those decisions stated

> "Where power is vested in a statutory authority to deprive the liberty of a subject on its subjective satisfaction with reference to specified matters, if that satisfaction is stated to be based on a number of grounds or for a variety of reasons, all taken together, and if some out of them are found to be non-existent or irrelevant, the very exercise of that power is bad . . . because the

---

[85] See para 11.215.

[86] *Lawrence Joachim Joseph D'Souza* v. *Bombay* (1956) S.C.R. 382, ('56) A.SC. 531 (the court also held that where an order of detention was challenged as *mala fide* what had to be established was not the want of *bona fides* on the part of the police, but want of *bona fides* on the part of the detaining authority, and none such had been established).

[87] (1979) 2 S.C.R. 633, ('79) A.SC. 541. [88] (1950) S.C.R. 88, 131.

[89] (1953) S.C.R. 708, ('53) A.SC. 318 (one ground was vague).

[90] (1954) S.C.R. 418, ('54) A.SC. 179 (two grounds were irrelevant); fol. in *P. Mukherji* v. *W.B.* (1969) 2 S.C.R. 635, ('70) A.SC. 852, (*held* that even on the assumption that two out of the four grounds were relevant, the order of detention must be set aside because of the other two irrelevant grounds.)

[91] (1956) S.C.R. 948, 952-5, ('57) A.SC. 164.

matter being one for subjective satisfaction, it must be properly based on all the reasons on which it purports to be based. If some out of them are found to be non-existent or irrelevant, the Court cannot predicate what the subjective satisfaction of the said authority would have been on the exclusion of those grounds or reasons. To uphold the validity of such an order in spite of the invalidity of some of the reasons or grounds would be to substitute the objective standards of the Court for the subjective satisfaction of the statutory authority."[92]

a qualification added to the above principle

But he added the qualification that

". . . the Court must be satisfied that the vague or irrelevant grounds are such as, if excluded, might reasonably have affected the subjective satisfaction of the appropriate authority. It is not merely because some ground or reason of a comparatively unessential nature is defective that such an order based on subjective satisfaction can be held to be invalid. The Court while anxious to safeguard the personal liberty of the individual will not lightly interfere with such orders."[93]

Applying these principles Jagannadhadas J. held that as the grounds supplied to the appellant mentioned that he was smuggling a particular type of cloth and *zari*, it being said later that he smuggled mercury, and it was found that the first two were not essential commodities and there was no evidence that the smuggling in them was inconsequential, the order of detention was void. These principles have been followed and applied by the Supreme Court in several cases, *and the impugned orders set aside.*[94]

Effect of Sup. Ct. decisions on Art. 22(5): *Prem Nath's Case*

11.227 In *Prem Nath* v. *Union*[95] the Punjab High Court said that the decisions of the Supreme Court showed

"(1) that whether the grounds given are sufficient or not is not within the ambit of the decision of the Court and it is the subjective decision of the Government which is implied;[96] (2) there must be a rational connection between the grounds stated by the Government and the objects which are to be pre-

---

[92] (1956) S.C.R. at p. 995. [93] ibid.

[94] *Rameswar Lal* v. *Bihar* (1968) 2 S.C.R. 505, ('68) A.SC. 1303 (*held*, that the grounds of detention were either non-existent or vague or otherwise deficient); *Motilal Jain* v. *Bihar* (1968) 3 S.C.R. 587, 593, ('68) A.SC. 1509 [*held*, that ground in cl. (*a*) was vague and irrelevant and in cl. (b) was non-existent. These defects were sufficient to vitiate the order of detention as it was not possible to hold that those grounds could not have influenced the decision of the detaining authority]; *Sushanta* v. *W.B.* (1969) 3 S.C.R. 138, ('69) A.SC. 1004 (*held*, that some of the grounds of detention were irrelevant to public order); *Mishrilal Jain* v. *Dist. Magistrate, Kamrup* 1971 (3) S.C.C. 693 (*held*, that it was settled law that if the grounds were vague the order must be set aside; *held further* that the grounds for detention were vague); *Biram Chand* v. *U.P.* (1974) 3 S.C.R. 813, ('74) A.SC. 1161 [one irrelevant ground sufficient to vitiate the order of detention. The case was overruled on another point in *H. Saha* v. *W.B.* ('74) A.SC. 2154, 2160. See para 11.182 of the text]; *Krishna Lal Dutta* v. *W.B.* (1974) 3 S.C.R. 449, ('74) A.SC. 955 (sole ground of detention was vague); *Prabhu Dayal* v. *Dist. Magistrate, Kamrup* (1974) 2 S.C.R. 12, ('74) A.SC. 183 (*held*, by the majority, that the order must be set aside as one of the grounds was vague for want of particulars; *held further*, that the pendency of the reference to the Advisory Board did not affect the jurisdiction of the Court to set aside the order under Art. 32); *Bhupal Chandra* v. *Arif Ali* (1974) 2 S.C.R. 277, ('74) A.SC. 255 (five out of 16 grounds of detention had no rational connection with public order); *Kuso Sah* v. *Bihar* (1974) 2 S.C.R. 195, ('74) A.SC. 156, 158 (two out of three grounds were irrelevant); *Gaya Singh* v. *State* ('68) A.P. 193, 195-6 (*held*, that the order was vitiated because some of the grounds did not exist, and some of the other grounds were vague); *Mohd. Iqbal* v. *Supdt. Central Jail* ('69) A.Del. 45, 54-6 [*held*, that though the grounds originally supplied were vague, the detenu was given further clarification. As to other facts than those supplied, privilege was claimed under Art. 22(6). The court upheld the detention order].

[95] (1956) Punj. 374, ('57) A.Punj. 235.

[96] This was amplified by reference to *Bhagat Singh* v. *R.* (1931) 58 I.A. 169, ('31) A.PC. 111, 33 Bom.L.R. 950.

vented under the statute; (3) that the grounds must not be vague and this applies to each one of the grounds communicated to the detained person, but this is subject to the claim of privilege under cl. (6) of Art. 22 of the Constitution; (4) that even if one of the grounds is vague and the others are not, the detention is not in accordance with the procedure established by law and is therefore illegal; and (5) that a detenu can challenge his detention in a Court of law on the ground of *mala fides*."[97]

11.228 Relying on the test in *Atma Ram's Case* it has been held that where the grounds on which the detention of the petitioner had been ordered had no probative value and were extraneous to the scope or purpose of the object in view as laid down by the law, the order of detention must be set aside.[98] Similarly, where admittedly most important material was placed before the detaining authority, but it turned out to be material which did not exist, it could not be said that the detaining authority had applied its mind to all the relevant and proper circumstances before an order contemplated by the Preventive Detention Act could be made.[99] Again, where good grounds for detention had been mixed up with vague, indefinite and bad grounds, the detention was not in accordance with procedure established by law and was void.[1]

Grounds having no probative value

11.229 *Shaikh Hanif* v. *W.B.*[2] decided that where material particulars of the grounds necessary for making an effective representation had not been communicated to detenus, the orders of detention must be held invalid and set aside.[3] *Hanif's Case* was followed in *Alek Mohd.* v. *W.B.*[4] and in *Debu Mahto* v. *W.B.*[5] And the same view was taken in *Mohd. Alam* v. *W.B.*[6] in *Bhut Nath* v. *W.B.*,[7] in *G. H. Mondal*

Shaikh Hanif's Case: if grounds not such as to enable effective representation, order

---

[97] ('57) A.Punj. *supra* at p. 237; *Priyatosh Mazumdar* v. *W.B.* ('63) A.Cal. 589.

[98] *Thakur Bhim Singh* v. *State* (1956) 6 Raj. 720, ('57) A.Raj. 5; *Devi Singh* v. *Rajasthan* (1952) 2 Raj. 569, ('52) A.Raj. 171; *Asha Ram* v. *State* ('50) A.A. 709.

[99] *Bal Keshav Thakrey* v. *Commissioner of Police* (1956) Bom. 792, ('56) A.B. 100, 58 Bom.L.R. 173.

[1] *Prem Dutta* v. *Supdt., Central Prison* ('54) A.A. 315, (1954) A.L.J. 6; *Bhakhtawar Singh* v. *State* (1953) Pep. 423, ('53) A.Pep. 207 [even if one of the grounds supplied to the petitioner was not clear and specific, Art. 22(5) was violated and the order of detention would be illegal]; *Sitaram Kishore* v. *Bihar* ('56) A.P. 1 (the grounds given were vague and most of them were irrelevant).

[2] (1974) 3 S.C.R. 258, ('74) A.SC. 679.

[3] ('74) A.SC. at p. 684. The court added that nothing in the judgment would preclude government from issuing fresh orders of detention against the petitioners after "full and meticulous compliance with the procedure prescribed by law."

[4] ('74) A.SC. 889 (*held*, that as important and injurious information on which the Dist. Magistrate acted had not been communicated to the petitioner, and could not have been the subject of effective representation, the *ratio* of *Hanif's Case* was attracted).

[5] ('74) A.SC. 816 (*held*, that a single act of wagon breaking could not lead any reasonable person to be subjectively satisfied about the necessity for detention and was therefore no satisfaction at all or was in any event, colourable. *Held further*, that the real ground on which the Dist. Magistrate had acted had not been communicated to the detenu so that *Hanif's Case* was attracted).

[6] (1974) 3 S.C.R. 379, ('74) A.SC. 917 (as the Dist. Magistrate had acted on other important materials apart from the grounds which had been communicated to the detenu, the detention order was invalid).

[7] (1974) 3 S.C.R. 315, ('74) A.SC. 806 (*held*, that important material which influenced the judgment of the Dist. Magistrate was not communicated to the detenu. It was also contended that the order could not be sustained as there was no justification for the continuance of the proclamation of emergency. Krishna Iyer J. held that the validity of the continuance of the emergency was not justiciable).

of detention invalid

v. *W.B.*[8] and in *Dharman Raj* v. *W.B.*[9] In *Anil Dey* v. *W.B.*[10] Krishna Iyer J. affirmed the principle of *Hanif's Case* but distinguished *Hanif's Case* on the facts before him. He said that though ordinarily one swallow did not make a summer, the grounds given to the detenu was "neither too distant nor too trifling". The action complained of showed that sophisticated signalling equipment could not be removed by a layman but that it required a certain measure of "technical skill and electrical expertise". "The technical talent, functional perversity and conveyor-belt system of collaborating instrumentalities were all implied in the episode of removal of extremely complicated parts referred to in the grounds set out."[11]

Procedure laid down in *Shaikh Hanif's Case*

11.230 The following procedure was laid down in *Shaikh Hanif* v. *W.B.*[12]: Where a detention order under s. 3 of the Maintenance of Internal Security Act is challenged by the detenu by an Art. 32 petition, the State must satisfy the Court that the detention was legal and in conformity with the provisions of the Act and of Art. 22(5). In response to the *rule nisi* issued by a Court, the Dist. Magistrate, or the authority who passed the order on his subjective satisfaction must swear the affidavit. If it is shown to the satisfaction of the Court that the affidavit of the person who passed the order cannot be furnished, the affidavit should be sworn by some responsible officer who personally dealt with, or processed, the case, and submitted it to the Minister or other officer "duly authorized under the rules of business to pass orders on behalf of Government in such matters."[13] The failure to follow this procedure is an impropriety which ordinarily will not vitiate a detention order, though it is a circumstance which would be taken into account in considering a challenge to a detention order. However, failure to follow the above procedure in cases where *mala fides* or extraneous considerations are attributed to the magistrate or the detaining authority, it may, in conjunction with other circumstances "assume the shape of a serious infirmity, leading the Court to declare the detention illegal."[14]

Effect of Presidential Order suspending right to move the Ct. under Art. 22

11.231 The Supreme Court held in *Mohd. Yaqub* v. *J. & K.*[15] that where the President made an order under Art. 359, suspending the right to move a Court for the enforcement of fundamental rights guaranteed by Art. 22(5),[16] the requirements of that Article could not apply and there was no question of furnishing any grounds under

---

8 ('74) A.SC. 895.

9 ('74) A.SC. 897.

10 ('74) A.SC. 832. The following ground was furnished to the petitioner: "That on 1.8.1972 at about 12.30 hrs. you and your associates committed theft in respect of signal materials from SPH type location box No. 513 which is situated in between UP main and UP CCR line at Dum Dum Junction North Yard (near S.S.P.) and 2 Nos. feed and transformer from the junction box near Signal No. 35 on the said place. The value of the stolen property is valued at Rs. 600/-. Your action caused disruption of train service for a considerable time affecting supplies and services.": ibid. p. 833.

11 ibid. p. 833.

12 ('74) A.SC. 679.

13 ibid. p. 682.

14 ibid. Fol. in *Mohd. Alam* v. *W.B.* (1974) 3 S.C.R. 379, ('74) A.SC. 917 (as the affidavit was not sworn by the person who had issued the order on his personal satisfaction, and as *mala fides* were alleged the affidavit was considered unsatisfactory) also fol. in *Bhut Nath* v. *W.B.* (1974) 3 S.C.R. 315, ('74) A.SC. 806, 814.

15 ('68) A.SC. 765, (1968) 2 S.C.R. 277.

16 The observations in the judgment [('68) A.SC. p. 770] that the President's Order "suspended Art. 22" is not correct having regard to the language of Art. 359.

that Article to the detenu if his detention was under the Defence of India Act or Rules.

Fresh order for detention during the pendency of a *habeas corpus* petition

11.232 If an order of detention is challenged in Court by a petition and the Government passes a fresh order of detention pending the hearing of the petition, is the fresh detention order *mala fide* and void? As the question was raised, and would normally arise on a petition for *habeas corpus*, the Supreme Court said that it was settled law that on a *habeas corpus* petition, the Court must have regard to the legality or illegality of the detention at the time of the return and not with reference to the date of the institution of the proceedings. Consequently, it was difficult to hold, in the absence of proof of *mala fides*, that the detaining authority could not supersede an earlier order of detention challenged as illegal and make a fresh order wherever possible, which complied with the requirements of the law in that behalf. The mere making of the second order did not establish that it was *mala fide*, though, if such a contention were raised, it would have to be considered on its merits in each case.[17]

Mala fides as a ground of challenge to detention orders

11.233 We have seen that detention orders can be challenged if they are *mala fide*. But detention orders are not *mala fide* simply because a district magistrate passed them shortly after the previous detention orders were set aside by the High Court, nor on the ground that only the past activities of the detenu were relied upon.[18] As a rule, the antecedents, conduct and past activities of a person or body of persons or organization would furnish reasonable ground for finding out the present attitude of that person or body. If the present conduct revealed the activities of the past, there was no reason why those activities could not be considered at all and it was a mistake to hold that the past acts or conduct either of the detenu or his associates could not be taken into account. The distance of time was immaterial unless there was no connection between the past and present activities. This was not negatived by cases where the past conduct was referred to as the sole basis for satisfaction and no fresh prejudicial act was committed by the detenu.[19]

Detention orders held illegal or void

11.234 It has been held that where a person was already detained in jail awaiting his trial for certain offences alleged to have been committed by him, a warrant under s. 3, Preventive Detention Act, would be illegal.[20] Again, if the main ground of detention be investigation of a crime, the detention of the person under the Preventive Detention Act would be colourable and improper and would amount to a circumvention of important provisions of the Constitution and as such could not be allowed.[21]

The *National Security Case*

11.235 Several questions connected with preventive detention were decided in the *National Security Case*[22] by reference to the various provisions of the National Security Act and it would be convenient to deal with them at this place. It was contended that s. 3 (1) should

---

[17] *Naranjan Singh Nathawan* v. *Punjab* (1952) S.C.R. 395, ('52) A.SC. 106; *Ram Narayan Singh* v. *Delhi* (1953) S.C.R. 652, ('53) A.SC. 277, rel. on in *Vimal Kishore* v. *U.P.* ('56) A.A. 56.

[18] *Shri Krishna Sharma* v. *W.B.* ('54) A.Cal. 591.

[19] *Salehuddin* v. *A.P.* ('59) A.A.P. 73.

[20] *Mohd. Abdur Rahman* v. *Hyderabad* ('50) A.Hyd. 66.

[21] *Narayanamma* v. *Hyderabad* ('50) A.Hyd. 66.

[22] *A. K. Roy* v. *Union* ('82) A.SC. 710.

"defence of India", "relation of India with foreign powers", "security of India" and "security of the State" in S. 3 of impugned Act not struck down for vagueness,

be struck down because the expressions "defence of India", "relation of India with foreign powers", "security of India" and "security of the State" occurring in s. 3(1) (*a*) and s. 3(2) were so vague, general and elastic that even conduct which was otherwise lawful could easily be comprehended within those expressions depending upon the whim and caprice of the detaining authority.[23] After a discussion of the authorities cited, Chandrachud C.J. held that those expressions were "in the very nature of things, difficult to define". Section 3 of the Act could not be struck down for vagueness. However,

but they must be narrowly construed by courts

"We must . . . utter a word of caution that since the concepts are not defined, undoubtedly because they are not capable of a precise definition, Courts must strive to give to those concepts a narrower construction than what the literal words suggest. While construing laws of preventive detention . . . care must be taken to restrict their application to as few situations as possible. *Indeed, that can well be the unstated premise for upholding the constitutionality of clauses like those in Section 3,* which are fraught with grave consequences to personal liberty, if construed liberally."[24] (italics supplied)

Direction given *qua* the ground of "acting in any manner prejudicial to maintenance of supplies and services essential to the community"

11.236 However, what had been said about the expressions considered earlier, did not apply to the expression "acting in any manner prejudicial to the maintenance of supplies and services essential to the community" in s. 3(2) of the Act. Chandrachud C.J. observed that the Court would not strike down s. 3(2) but would direct

". . . that no person can be detained with a view to preventing him from acting in any manner prejudicial to the maintenance of supplies and services essential to the community unless, by a law, order or notification made or published fairly in advance, the supplies and services, the maintenance of which is regarded as essential to the community and in respect of which the order of detention is proposed to be passed, are made known appropriately, to the public."[25]

Constitutional validity of the National Security Act upheld

11.237 The challenge to the validity of the National Security Act was briefly disposed of, because the validity of the Maintenance of Internal Security Act was upheld in *H. Saha's Case*[26] which held that the Act did not violate Arts. 14, 19, 21 and 22. And that Act was in *pari materia* the National Security Act. In this connection the Chief Justice observed:

The alleged "controversy" raised by Kailasam J. Sup. Ct.'s persistence in demonstrable and demonstrated error

"We need not enter into the controversy which is reflected in the dissenting judgment of Kailasam J. in *Maneka Gandhi*[27] as to whether the major premise of *Gopalan's Case*[28] really was that Art. 22 is a complete code, in itself and whether because of that premise, the decision in that case that Art. 21 excluded the personal freedom conferred by Art. 19(1) is incorrect."[29]

We have fully discussed the persistence of the Supreme Court in a demonstrable and demonstrated error.[30] It is enough to observe that a "controversy" cannot arise if the question is whether a judgment has stated "*A* is not *B*" or "*A* is *B*". The majority in *Gopalan's Case* held that Art. 22 was not a complete Code. The *Bank Nationalization Case*, and the cases which followed it, held that the majority in *Gopalan* had held that Art. 22 was a complete Code. As stated earlier, a glance at the head note in the Supreme Court Reports would

---

23 ibid. p. 735.
24 ibid. p. 737.
25 ibid. p. 738.
26 (1975) 1 S.C.R. 778, ('74) A.SC. 2154.
27 ('78) A.SC. 597.
28 (1950) S.C.R. 88, ('50) A.SC. 27.
29 ('82) A.SC. *supra* at p. 739.
30 See paras 11.48 and 11.49 of the text.

have shown to the Judges who decided the *Bank Nationalization Case*, and the Judges who without question followed it, that their assertion was factually untrue.

11.238 With reference to s. 5 of the impugned Act, which authorized detention in "such place and under such conditions as the appropriate Government may by general or special order specify", Chandrachud C.J. observed:

Directions given as to the place of detention for detenus

"Laws of preventive detention cannot, by the backdoor, introduce procedural measures of a punitive kind. Detention without trial is an evil to be suffered, but to no greater extent and in no greater measure than is minimally necessary in the interest of the country and the community. It is neither fair nor just that a detenu should have to suffer detention in 'such place' as the Government may specify. The normal rule has to be that the detenu will be kept in detention in a place which is within the environs of his or her ordinary place of residence. If a person ordinarily resides in Delhi, to keep him in detention in a far off place like Madras or Calcutta is a punitive measure by itself which, in matters of preventive detention at any rate, is not to be encouraged. Besides, keeping a person in detention in a place other than the one where he habitually resides makes it impossible for his friends and relatives to meet him or for the detenu to claim the advantages of facilities like having his own food. The requirements of administrative convenience, safety and security may justify in a given case the transfer of a detenu to a place other than that where he ordinarily resides, but that can only be by way of an exception and not as a matter of general rule. Even when a detenu is required to be kept in or transferred to a place which is other than his usual place of residence, he ought not to be sent to any far off place which, by the very reason of its distance, is likely to deprive him of the facilities to which he is entitled. Whatever smacks of punishment must be scrupulously avoided in matters of preventive detention."[31]

It is submitted that these observations are clearly right.

11.239 It was contended that the detenu must have the right to legal representation, the right of cross-examination and the right to present his evidence. Having regard to the fact that the operation of Art. 22(1) and (2) was expressly excluded in the case of preventive detention by Art. 22(3), the Court regretfully came to the conclusion that the detenu had no right to appear by a legal practitioner in the proceeding before the Advisory Board. This was however subject to qualifications: First, if a legal practitioner appeared before the Board to represent the Government's Case, the detenu must be accorded the same facility. However, as the Court was informed that several Government officers in the concerned Departments appeared before the Board to justify the detention, the Court said that:

Observations of the court on the right of detenus to legal representation after holding that they had no such right

"the Boards should not permit the authorities to do indirectly what they cannot do directly; and no one should be enabled to take shelter behind the excuse that such officers are not 'legal practitioners' or legal advisers. Regard must be had to the substance and not the form."[32]

The qualification was that the detenu should be permitted to take the aid of a friend and that when demanded, the Advisory Boards must grant that facility.[33]

Detenus entitled to assistance from friends

11.240 After an elaborate discussion of the principles of natural justice,[34] Chandrachud C.J. said:

Detenus had no right to

[31] ('82) A.SC. *supra* at p. 740.
[32] ibid. p. 747.
[33] ibid. p. 748.
[34] ibid. pp. 748-751.

cross-examine

"We are therefore of the opinion that, in the proceedings before the Advisory Board, the detenu has no right to cross-examine either the persons on the basis of whose statement the order of detention is made or the detaining authority."[35]

Detenus to be segregated from convicts

11.241 In the same connection, the Court felt obliged to give the following specific direction, namely:

"that persons who are detained under the National Security Act must be segregated from the convicts and kept in a separate part of the place of detention. It is hardly fair that those who are suspected of being engaged in prejudicial conduct should be lodged in the same ward or cell where the convicts whose crimes are established are lodged. . . . As observed by Krishna Iyer J. in *Sunil Batra*[36] the most important right of the person who is imprisoned is to the integrity of his physical person and mental personality. . . . We see no reason why (the detenus) should not be permitted to wear their own clothes, eat their own food, have interviews with members of their families at least once a week, and . . . have reading and writing material according to their reasonable requirements. Books are the best friends of man whether inside or outside the jail."[37]

Submission: direction is correct, but does not go far enough

It is submitted that the direction given above is correct. But it does not go far enough. The present writer would repeat the submission he made in another book[38]:

Submission: Detenus should be kept in civil jails

"To keep a detenu in jail and subject him to the ordinary discipline of a criminal jail is clearly to punish him, which is opposed to the concept of preventive detention. No restraint should be imposed on a person preventively detained except to the extent necessary to prevent him from committing the kind of offence which it is suspected he would commit. Therefore, the right course would be to keep detenus in a separate place of detention. If that should be impracticable, the person detained should be kept in civil jails and be treated as civil prisoners with all the facilities available to civil prisoners, subject to the requirements of security. If this appears idealistic and impracticable, we may recall what the Rowlatt Committee, which felt itself obliged to recommend preventive detention, said in this connection:

Rowlatt Committee Report recommended "non penal custody" 60 years ago

' "No interference with liberty must be penal in character. Nothing in the nature of conviction can be admitted without trial in strict legal form. If in the *supra interests of the community* the liberty of individuals is taken away, an asylum must be provided of a different order from a jail." The Committee characterised it as a power *"to continue in non-penal custody"*.'[39] (italics supplied)

This was said nearly 60 years ago. The consequences of disregarding this sound advice were seen in the evidence before the Shah Commission on November 4, 1977. The harrowing experiences narrated by eight officials who had been preventively detained, and the evidence of their wives, constrained Mr. Justice J. C. Shah to observe: 'Man's inhumanity to man seems to know no limits at all — of the officials it is still worse'[40]."[41]

Art. 22(1) and (2): *Ajaib Singh's Case*

11.242 Article 22(1) and (2) was considered by the Supreme Court in *Punjab* v. *Ajaib Singh*[42] but in view of some of the observations there made we must see what the case actually decided. The question for determination was whether the taking of a person into custody by the police and his being sent to the officer-in-charge of

---

[35] ibid. p. 751.
[36] ('80) A.SC. 1579.
[37] ('82) A.SC. *supra* p. 752.
[38] Seervai, *Emergency, Future Safeguards and the Habeas Corpus Case: A Criticism.*
[39] A. G. Noorani, "Prisons and Political Prisoners", *The Indian Express,* November 10, 1977.
[40] *The Indian Express,* November 5, 1977.
[41] Seervai, *Emergency, Future Safeguards and the Habeas Corpus Case: A Criticism,* pp. 94-95.
[42] (1953) S.C.R. 254, ('53) A.SC. 10; fol. in *Ram Singh* v. *Union* ('54) A.Punj. 145.

the nearest camp under s. 4, Abducted Persons (Recovery and Restoration) Act, 1949, was arrest and detention, and S. R. Das J. held that it was not. He said:

"*It is not, however, our purpose, nor do we consider it desirable, to attempt a precise and meticulous enunciation of the scope and ambit of this fundamental right or to enumerate exhaustively the cases that come within its protection.* Whatever else may come within the purview of Art. 22(1) and (2), suffice it to say for the purposes of this case, that we are satisfied that the physical restraint put upon an abducted person in the process of recovering and taking that person into custody without any allegation or accusation of any actual or suspected or apprehended commission by that person of any offence of a criminal or quasi-criminal nature or of any act prejudicial to the State or the public interest, and delivery of that person to the custody of the officer in charge of the nearest camp under section 4 of the impugned Act cannot be regarded as arrest and detention within the meaning of Art. 22(1) and (2)."[43] (italics supplied)

It is submitted that this conclusion is correct having regard to the setting of the Article, and to the language used in Art. 22(2) which requires the production of a person detained before a magistrate. This conclusion is further strengthened by the consideration mentioned in the judgment that otherwise, existing laws providing for arrest in civil cases would be void, and that where two constructions were possible, the one which would avoid such a result ought to be preferred.[43a] However, in his judgment, Das J. observed that there

---

[43] (1953) S.C.R. *supra* at p. 269. See also *Collector of Malabar* v. *Erimal Ebrahim Hajoo* (1957) S.C.R. 970, ('57) A.SC. 688, where the latter part of the above passage was treated as the actual decision in the case; fol. in *Krishnaiah* v. *Sub-Collector, Gudur* ('68) A.A.P. 83, 85 (F.B.) (*held*, that where arrests were made under the Madras Revenue Malversation Regulation only to recover government dues, Arts. 21 and 22 were not attracted); and in *C. P. Joseph* v. *State* ('73) A.Ker. 89 (*held*, that arrest and detention of a person under the Kerala Revenue Recovery Act, 1968, was not a punishment but a mode of recovering the amount due, and Art. 22 was not attracted). *Ajaib Singh's Case* was *apparently* followed in *Anwar* v. *J. & K.* (1971) 1 S.C.R. 637, ('71) A.SC. 337. The petitioner, a Pakistani, who had illegally and clandestinely entered India, was served with a preventive detention order with a view to expelling him from India under the Foreigners' Act, 1948. By a *habeas corpus* petition he challenged the detention order as violating Arts. 19, 21 and 22. During the pendency of the petition, the order was withdrawn, and the permission of the Supreme Court obtained to take suitable steps to deport him. Thereupon, the question arose whether "the petitioner was deprived of his personal liberty either illegally or without procedure established by law so as to require this Court to order his immediate release." The Court held that the petitioner was "clearly not entitled to any right guaranteed by Art. 19" as he was not a citizen. Article 20 was not attracted, and Art. 21 merely provided that no person shall be deprived of his Court referred to *Ajaib Singh's Case* and *apparently* following it, held that the life or personal liberty except by procedure established by law. As to Art. 22, the restraint on the petitioner's personal liberty for the purpose of taking him to the border in order to expel him from India, as provided by law, could not be considered to be an illegal custody. In arriving at this conclusion the Court took judicial notice of "the historical fact of Pakistan's extremely hostile attitude towards the State of Jammu & Kashmir", and the fact that the presence in India of Pakistani infiltrators from across the cease-fire line on the Jammu & Kashmir border demanded the strict enforcement of regulations governing the entry into, and departure from, India. The Court observed that under such circumstances ". . . the claim to personal liberty made by unlawful infiltrators from Pakistan cannot be placed above the security of the country and the maintenance of law and order.": ibid. pp. 341-2. The Court upheld the detention.

[43a] (1953) S.C.R. *supra* at pp. 268-9.

Obiter in *Ajaib Singh's Case*: Art. 22(1) and (2) available only against arrest and detention by an executive or non-judicial authority

were indications in the language of the Article to show that the protection given by that Article was available against arrest and detention by executive and non-judicial authority, the reasons given for this conclusion being that the language of Art. 21(2) was substantially the same as the language of ss. 60 and 61, Cr.P.C. Further, protection was needed more against executive action and was not required to the same extent against judicial action where the judicial mind had been applied and a warrant issued by a magistrate. Again, in the case of a warrant issued by a magistrate, the Cr.P.C. required that the nature of the offence charged should be stated in the warrant and there would be no point in informing the person arrested of the ground of his arrest as the warrant would be shown to him before arrest. It is submitted that these observations of Das J. are *obiter dicta,* in view of his express statement quoted earlier that the Court was not determining the scope and ambit of Art. 22(1) and (2.)

Various kinds of detention

11.243 For a proper understanding of *Ajaib Singh's Case* we must distinguish between various types of detention which may deprive a person of his liberty. (1) A person may be arrested and detained in order to bring him to trial for having committed an offence. Such arrest and detention may be (*a*) on a warrant issued by a magistrate or (*b*) by the police without a warrant; (2) after trial a person found guilty may be detained in prison under a sentence of the Court; (3) a person may be arrested and detained by an executive order under a law of preventive detention without any judicial inquiry or trial; (4) a person may be detained under the preventive provisions of Chapter VIII, Cr.P.C.; (5) a person may be arrested and detained under an order of a civil court in aid of civil process, or (6) under various statutes where there is no accusation of a crime or criminal conduct. *Ajaib Singh's Case* decided that the arrest and detention mentioned in (6) above did not fall under Art. 22(1) and (2), and the same reasoning would directly apply to the arrest and detention mentioned in (5) above. The *observations* in *Ajaib Singh's Case* indicate that Art. 22(1) and (2) applies to (1) (*b*) above but not to (1) (*a*) above. It will be submitted that to the extent that the observations would exclude the arrest and detention of a person on a warrant issued by a magistrate, they are not correct. However, we may complete the discussion by saying that the detention following conviction mentioned in (2) above is clearly outside Art. 22(1) and (2), while Art. 22(3) expressly excludes the operation of Art. 22(1) and (2) in the case of preventive detention mentioned in (3) above. Finally, decided cases show that Art. 22(1) and (2) does not apply to the detention mentioned in (4) above.[44]

Submission: *obiter* not correct as regards arrest and detention under a magistrate's warrant

The rights conferred by Art. 22(1) and (2)

11.244 We must now consider, first, the rights conferred by Art. 22(1) and then the rights conferred by Art. 22(2). The rights conferred by Art. 22(1) may be stated thus:

> No person who is arrested shall be detained in custody (*a*) without being informed, as soon as may be, of the grounds of his arrest, (*b*) nor shall he be denied the right to consult a legal practitioner of his choice and (*c*) to be defended by a legal practitioner of his choice.

---

[44] See para 11.250.

The right to be defended by Counsel does not appear to have been stressed, and was clearly not considered in any detail, in *Ajaib Singh's Case*. But the right of a person accused of an offence, or against whom any proceedings were taken under the Cr.P.C. is a valuable right which was recognized by s. 340, Cr.P.C.[45] Article 22 (1), on its language, makes that right a constitutional right, and unless there are compelling reasons, Art. 22 (1) ought not to be cut down by judicial construction. And yet that would be the consequence if the observations that the right conferred by Art. 22 (1) and (2) is available against executive and not against judicial orders for detention on a criminal or quasi-criminal charge were accepted as laying down the correct law. It is submitted that Art. 22 (1) makes the statutory right under s. 340 Cr.P.C. a constitutional right in respect of criminal or quasi-criminal proceedings and since the observations of Das J. do not deal with the question of the right to be defended by Counsel, they ought not to be treated as excluding such a right. Again, the words of Art. 22 (1) are "the right to be defended by a legal practitioner of his choice" and the question arises "defended against what?" They must include, in the context, "defended against the charge levelled" and not merely "defended against the legality of the arrest and detention", for, even if the arrest and detention may be justified, the charge may not be. To limit the right of an accused person to be defended by a legal practitioner of his choice to cases where he is arrested and detained by an executive authority and to deny it in cases where he is arrested under a warrant issued by a magistrate has nothing to commend it, for there is no rational ground for saying that the right to be defended by counsel is necessary where the person is arrested and detained by the police, and is not necessary where he is arrested and detained by an order of a magistrate or a judicial officer. It is submitted that the view taken in some cases decided after *Ajaib Singh's Case* that Art. 22 (1) confers a right to be defended by Counsel in proceedings of a criminal or quasi-criminal nature is correct.

The right to be defended by counsel: s. 340, Cr.P.C.

Art. 22(1) makes that right a constitutional right, but the *obiter* would deny such right

11.245 Again, the right conferred by Art. 22 (2) on the person arrested, to be produced before a magistrate within twenty-four hours, ought not to be limited to an arrest without a warrant. For the fact that a judicial mind has been applied is not crucial where it has been applied *ex parte* and without hearing the person arrested. Where a person arrested without a warrant is brought before a magistrate, the order made by the magistrate is *after hearing him*; and there is no reason why a person arrested on a warrant should be denied a right to be heard before an order for detention is made. It is submitted that it is not a safe basis for construing constitutional provisions to assume the continued existence of existing law like the Criminal Procedure Code, for such a law can be repealed or amended, and the rights conferred by it withdrawn. It is submitted that to the extent that the observations in *Ajaib Singh's Case* are based on this assumption, they are not well founded.

Submission: *obiter* in *Ajaib Singh's Case* is not correct

[45] *S. 340(1)*: "Any person accused of an offence before a Criminal Court, or against whom proceedings are instituted under this Code in any such Court, may of right be defended by a pleader." (now s. 303, Cr.P.C., 1974).

Decided cases: right under s. 340, Cr.P.C. is now a constitutional right under Art. 22(1)

11.246 In the light of the above discussion, we may now refer to decided cases. As regards the right of an accused person to be defended by a legal practitioner of his choice it has been held that the right which was conferred by s. 340 Cr.P.C.[46] had now been made a constitutional right and it was not necessary to derive that right from any statutory enactment. Thus, in *Venkayya* v. *Chinapunnaiah*[47], it was said that Art. 22 (1) and (2) did not deal with punitive detention following a conviction by a Court but laid down the minimum requirement which Parliamentary or State legislation sanctioning the arrest and detention of a person, not convicted of a crime, should conform to. The safeguards provided in Art. 22 (1) and (2) were to a large extent covered by existing provisions of the Criminal Procedure Code but their incorporation in Art. 22 had the effect of making them inviolable by ordinary legislation. And the same view was expressed in *Moti Bai* v. *State*[48] by saying that the right of an accused person under s. 340 Cr.P.C. to consult his legal adviser and to be defended by him had been put on the highest footing ever since our Constitution came into force, by Art. 22 (1) and it was really not necessary to derive that right from other enactments. Again, it was said that there was no statutory or constitutional requirement to *provide* legal assistance to an accused person, for the choice of a lawyer was "always the lookout of the accused person and that right had been guaranteed under Art. 22 (1)" and that s. 340 Cr.P.C. also enabled him to engage a lawyer of his choice.[49] The only condition necessary for a person to have a right of defence by a legal practitioner was that he must have been arrested. It was not necessary that he should be detained after arrest. If, after arrest, he was released on security, his right of defence by a legal practitioner, which accrued at the moment of his

---

[46] Although that section did not expressly refer to a pleader "chosen by the accused", such choice was implicit in it.

[47] ('54) A.A.P. 90.

[48] ('54) A.Raj. 241 (*held*, further that certain propositions seemed to follow almost axiomatically from that right, that after his arrest the accused had the right to consult a legal adviser of his choice and to be defended by him. In order that such consultation might be effective, interviews must be allowed to the Counsel when asked for, out of the hearing of the police though within their presence. Such a right must not be abused and may be granted subject to reasonable restrictions as to time and the convenience of the police authorities no less than that of the party seeking the interview. The police ought not to obstruct such interview on arbitrary and fanciful grounds with a view to deprive the accused of his fundamental right).

[49] *In re Govinda Reddy* ('58) A.Mys. 150 (the Court added that in capital cases the circular orders of the High Court showed that a Counsel should be appointed to defend the accused if he said that he had no means to engage one); rel. on in *State* v. *Dukhi Dei* ('63) A.Or. 144 (it was said that a Court of Appeal or Revision was not powerless to interfere if it found that the accused was so handicapped for want of legal aid that the proceedings against him amounted to a negation of a fair trial, but it was held on the facts that the accused had not been so handicapped). See *Digambar Aruk* v. *Nanda Aruk* ('57) A.Or. 281 [the court referred to the observations in *Ajaib Singh's Case* that Art. 22(1) and (2) was designed to give protection against the act of the executive or other non-judicial authority. Accordingly, Art. 22(1) and (2) did not apply to an order of the *Adalati Panchayat* for arrest and detention. These observations appear wholly unnecessary in view of the Court's finding that the *Adalati Panchayat* had no power to order arrest or to keep a person in custody before or during trial. The Court rightly observed that detention of the accused after conviction by a Court was outside the scope of Art. 22].

arrest, would continue because the right was a continuing right.[50] It has been held[51] that a conviction for an offence triable as a summons case by a mobile Court on a plea of guilty could not be set aside on the ground that the trial took place outside Court premises and Court hours, thereby disabling the accused from securing the assistance of Counsel when the plea of guilty was voluntary and when no plea was raised at the trial that the accused was being deprived of the assistance of Counsel.

Cases in which Art. 22(2) was held to have been violated

11.247 The right under Art. 22(2) was held to have been violated under the following circumstances: on February 17, 1954, the petitioners were arrested by a magistrate acting under s. 64 Cr.P.C.[52] for having obstructed the entry of Harijans into the temple of Sri Vishwanathji of Banaras through the main gate and thereby committing an offence punishable under the U.P. Removal of Social Disabilities Act, 1947. On the same day, the magistrate remanded the petitioners into jail custody. It was held that the magistrate, in directing the arrest of the petitioners did not act as a magistrate as contemplated under s. 167, Cr.P.C. nor had he an opportunity of applying his judicial mind to the facts of the case. After referring to *Ajaib Singh's Case*, the Court said that the arrest was made without a warrant and in the circumstances, there was no proper production of the petitioners before a competent magistrate within twenty-four hours of their arrest and, therefore, further detention in jail was illegal and unconstitutional.[53] In *Hansraj* v. *State*,[54] the accused who were licensed porters were arrested for offences alleged to have been committed under ss. 120 and 121 of the Railways Act and were put into prison. Two sets of persons were tried within the jail precincts on March 30, 1955, and two other sets were tried on March 31, 1955. No information had been given to the accused about the date of the trial, nor were they told that under Art. 22 and s. 340, Cr.P.C. they had a right to consult a legal practitioner and to be defended by him. The Court held that the right given by Art. 22, and by s. 340, Cr.P.C., had been denied to the accused and the trial conducted in such hot haste was vitiated. Similarly, where the accused were produced before a magistrate from police custody and they had no opportunity to contact any lawyer or to secure legal assistance for their defence, their plea of guilt could not be regarded as voluntary. The trial which was alleged to have begun at 7 p.m. and ended at about 8.30 p.m. must be held to have deprived the accused of legal assistance in their

---

[50] *Deodat Rai* v. *State* ('51) A.A. 718 [in order to show that the right to be defended by Counsel conferred by Art. 22(1) had been infringed, it was not necessary to show that a person arrested under an Act was actually denied the right of defence; it was sufficient that the impugned Act itself denied that right to him]; fol. in *M. Hussain* v. *Hassan Ganduvar* ('68) A.Ker. 34. The sentence on the accused was set aside because s. 18, Laccadive Islands and Minicoy Regulation, 1912, required the permission of the Collector before the accused could be represented by Counsel, thus violating his right to be defended by Counsel.

[51] *Hadu Sahu* v. *State* ('67) A.Or. 37.

[52] Which authorised a magistrate to arrest, or direct the arrest of, persons committing a crime in his presence.

[53] *Hariharanand* v. *Jailor, Dist. Jail, Banaras* ('54) A.A. 601.

[54] ('56) A.A. 641.

trial and thus resulted in a failure of justice.[55] The arrest of a person by merely informing him of the sections of certain penal provisions for the violation of which he was arrested contravened Art. 22 (1).[56] That the right to be defended by Counsel extends not only to questioning the legality of the arrest but extends also to the trial of the charge was affirmed in *Vimal Kishore Mehrotra* v. *U.P.*[57] There, it was held that the object underlying Art. 22 (1), (that the ground of arrest should be communicated to the person arrested), appeared to be that on learning about the ground of arrest the arrested person would be in a position to approach the Court of Appeal or move the High Court for a writ of *habeas corpus. The information would also enable him to prepare in time, his defence for the purpose of his trial.* The information however should be sufficient to enable the arrested person to understand why he had been arrested; the ground of arrest should be similar to the charge framed by the Court for the trial of the case. Consequently, where the charge against the petitioner was that on a certain morning he threatened a certain worker of a mill in order to dissuade him from going to work, whereas all that he was told was that he had been arrested under s. 7, Criminal Law Amendment Act, 1932, the grounds were not sufficient and Art. 22 (1) was contravened.

Art. 22(3) must be strictly construed

11.248 As Art. 22 (3) is an exception to Art. 22 (1) and (2) it must be construed strictly. Accordingly, it was held that externment or banishment was something akin to preventive detention but was not detention. S. 5 (2), U.P. Goondas Act, 1932, which made the representation by a person a matter of discretion with the advising judges must be held to infringe Art. 22 (1) and as not saved by Art. 22 (3).[58]

Art. 22(1) not violated if request to be defended by counsel was not made

11.249 But where the only complaint of the petitioner was that relatives who sought an interview with him after arrest were refused permission, which refusal resulted in a denial of opportunity to defend himself by engaging a civil lawyer through their help, but where he had made no request to the Court Martial for being defended by a lawyer and no such request had been turned down, it was held that there was no violation of Art. 22 (1).[59]

Art. 22 does not apply to detention following on a trial

11.250 It has been held that the detention to which Art. 22 refers means detention by executive authority and not detention by an order passed by a judicial tribunal *after a full trial.* Article 22 has no application to an order made under ss. 110, 118 and 123, Cr.P.C., which provide, respectively, for security for good behaviour from habitual offenders, for an order to give security where it is necessary for keeping the peace or maintaining

---

[55] *Afjal Hussain* v. *State* (1962) 12 Raj. 595, ('62) A.Raj. 216 [the Court held in substance that Art. 22(1) had been violated. It observed further that there was no justification for holding the trial late in the night on the ground that the magistrate had been pre-occupied with his executive duties].

[56] *Madhu Limaye* v. *State* ('59) A.Punj. 506 [merely telling the arrested person that he was being arrested under s. 7, Cr. Law Amendment Act and s. 143, I.P.C., could not provide him with information as to which of the many unlawful acts mentioned in those sections he was alleged to have committed. The arrest violated Art. 22(1)].

[57] (1956) 2 All. 527, ('56) A.A 56.

[58] *Inderjit Singh* v. *Delhi* ('53) A.Punj. 52.

[59] *Ram Sarup* v. *Union* (1964) 5 S.C.R. 931, ('65) A.SC. 247.

good behaviour and for an order of imprisonment if the person makes default in giving security ordered under s. 106 or s. 118, Cr.P.C. The main distinction between preventive detention referred to in Art. 22 and detention as a result of an order under s. 123, Cr.P.C., is that the detention under s. 123 is *after a full judicial inquiry.*[60]

11.251 Section 340, Cr.P.C., confers the right on a person accused of an offence or in respect of any proceedings under the Cr.P.C. the right to be defended by Counsel and it has been submitted that Art. 22(1) confers the same right in respect of a criminal charge or conduct involving suspicion of crime or criminal activity. We have seen that any procedure established by law is subject to constitutional limitations other than those contained in Art. 19(1)(*a*) to (*e*) and (*g*) and that any law which denies to a person arrested and detained for commission of an offence the right to defend himself would be void as contravening Art. 22(1). Can this right be defeated by a conclusive evidence clause? It is submitted that such a clause would be void, for, on proof of certain facts, it would prevent the accused from defending himself by leading relevant evidence. A conclusive evidence clause must be distinguished from a clause raising a rebuttable presumption, which leaves it open to the accused to rebut the evidence if he can. It is submitted that the view expressed above is supported by the decision in *Dharam Deo* v. *State*[61] where s. 25, Drugs Act, was impugned as violating the right of an accused person to defend himself. The Court held that the basic right of an accused person to defend himself was protected and s. 25 was *intra vires* the Constitution, because on a reading of the section it was clear that the report of the Government analyst was to be held conclusive only if it was not challenged according to procedure there prescribed.

Submission: the right under Art. 22(1) cannot be defeated by a conclusive evidence clause

11.252 An order of remand can only be passed by a magistrate sitting as a Court. It is immaterial where such magistrate was sitting at the time of passing the order.[62] Neither Art. 22 nor s. 167, Cr.P.C., require the production of an accused person before a magistrate on the occasion of a subsequent remand.[63] Where the petitioner was arrested without a warrant by a station officer on his

Order of remand and Art. 22

[60] *Jit Bahadur Singh* v. *State* ('53) A.A. 753, (1953) A.L.J. 438; fol. in *In re Seetharaman* ('56) A.M. 292, (1956) 1 M.L.J. 232; *Venkayya* v. *Chinna Punnaiah* ('57) A.A.P. 90 [the primary purpose of proceedings under Ch. 7 was to take security for keeping the peace or good behaviour after a judicial inquiry whereas the primary object of preventive detention laws made in conformity with Art. 22(4) and (7) was to imprison a person by executive action without judicial inquiry]; *In re Shaik Kalesha* ('57) A.A.P. 268.

[61] ('58) A.A. 865. See also *Mohanlal* v. *Vipanchandra* ('62) A.Guj. 44 [there the proviso to s. 5 of the Prevention of Food Adulteration Act which contained a conclusive evidence clause was impugned as violating Art. 19(1) and the principles of natural justice, and the Court repelled those contentions. Surprisingly, no question was raised under Art. 22(1), but here again, the Court was at pains to show that all that the proviso provided was that certain facts found by the chemical analyser could not be challenged, but a number of defences were open to the accused to show that the food was not adulterated. The object of the proviso was to ensure the finality of the test and the analysis, so as to prevent a long lapse of time between the trial and the analysis].

[62] *Prabhat Malla* v. *D. C. Kamrup* (1952) Ass. 18, ('52) A.Ass. 167; rel. on in *Prabhakar Nath* v. *Dist. Magistrate* ('60) A.A. 467, (1960) A.L.J. 206.

[63] (1952) Ass. *supra*.

own authority and where within a few minutes of the arrest the city magistrate went to the spot in his executive capacity and the petitioner was produced before such magistrate who was competent to authorize his detention in custody and the petitioner was put in jail custody on the order of such magistrate, it was held that the arrest and detention having been made by the station officer under the direction or supervision of the magistrate, it was not necessary for him to produce the accused before any magistrate and Art. 22(2) was complied with.[64] The actual time of arrest is material in order to judge whether the police authorities did produce him before a magistrate within the time specified in Art. 22(2).[65]

Arrest and detention under Revenue Recovery Acts do not violate Arts. 21 and 22: *Erimal Hajee's Case*

11.253 Arrest and detention under Revenue Recovery Acts for the enforcement of public demands have been held not to violate Arts. 21 and 22, and the Supreme Court reversed the decision in *Erimal Ebrahim Hajee* v. *Collector of Malabar*,[66] which had held to the contrary. There, s. 46(2), Indian Income-tax Act, and s. 48, Madras Revenue Recovery Act, read with s. 5 were impugned as violating Arts. 14, 21 and 22. Mack J. held that s. 48 was *ultra vires* as it violated Art. 22 and as a consequence it violated Art. 21. He further held that s. 46(2), violated Art. 14 and was void. Krishnaswamy Naidu J. held that s. 48 violated Art. 14 and violated Art. 21 to the extent that it denied the arrested person the right conferred by Art 22(2). As regards Art. 21, he held that in view of *Gopalan's Case* the existence of the law would be sufficient to support the legality of the Collector's action. After this case was decided, s. 46(2), Indian Income-tax Act, read with s. 13, Bombay City Land Revenue Act, 1877, was impugned as violating Arts. 14, 21 and 22 in *Purshottam Govindji Halai* v. *B. M. Desai*[67] where the challenge under Art. 14 was repelled after careful consideration.[68] In view of the decision in *Punjab* v. *Ajaib Singh*,[69] the challenge under Art. 22(2) was not pressed, and the challenge under Art. 21 was met by a reference to *Gopalan's Case* by saying that these provisions constituted a procedure established by law. The Court added that it was a fallacy to regard the arrest and detention of a defaulter who failed to pay income-tax as a punishment or a penalty for an offence. It was a coercive process for the recovery of tax by putting pressure on the defaulter who could get relief by paying up his dues. Later, when the Supreme Court decided the appeal from the judgment of the Madras High Court in *Collector of Malabar* v. *Erimal Ebrahim Hajee*,[70] it followed *Purshotham Halai's Case* and held that *Ajaib Singh's Case* furnished an effective reply to a challenge under Art. 22(2):

> "In the present case, the arrest was not in connection with any allegation or accusation of any actual or suspected or apprehended commission of any offence of a criminal or quasi-criminal nature. It was really an arrest for a civil debt in the process or the mode prescribed by law for recovery of arrears of land revenue."[71]

---

64 *Ram Manohar Lohia* v. *Supdt. Central Prison* (1955) 1 All. 355, ('55) A.A. 193.
65 *Shravan Kumar* v. *Supdt. Dist. Jail* ('57) A.A. 189, (1957) A.L.J. 152.
66 (1955) Mad. 999, ('54) A.M. 1091.
67 (1955) 2 S.C.R. 887, ('56) A.SC. 20.
68 See para 9.40.
69 (1953) S.C.R. 254, ('53) A.SC. 10.
70 (1957) S.C.R. 970, ('57) A.SC. 688.
71 (1957) S.C.R. *supra* at p. 977.

A similar view had been taken in other cases.[72]

11.254 The above discussion has made it clear that according to *Gopalan's Case*,[73] "procedure established by law" means procedure established by a law enacted by a competent legislature or other authority.[74] But "procedure established by law" does not mean that every detailed step of the procedure must be mentioned. Where, therefore, s. 3, Preventive Detention Act, empowered the authorities to make an order of detention on being satisfied that the conditions laid down in s. 3 existed, it was not necessary that the legislature should also prescribe the process by which the satisfaction had to be arrived at.[75] It may however be added that the violation of the right to personal liberty by a private individual is not within the purview of Art. 21 and a person whose right to personal liberty has been infringed must seek his remedy under the ordinary law and not under Art. 32.[76] Were it not that the Supreme Court was invited to hold that "life" in Art. 21 included "livelihood" it would have been unnecessary to say that it does not and the Supreme Court has so held.[77] It follows from what has been said above that where a person is deprived of life or personal liberty by a law prescribing a procedure therefor, Art. 21 is not violated. Consequently, the following provisions have been held not to violate Art. 21, namely: s. 537, Cr.P.C.;[78] the confinement of an under-trial prisoner or the arrest and detention of a person by the police under ss. 54 to 57 and s. 151, Cr.P.C.;[79] the United States of Gwalior, Indore and Malwa (M.B.) Gambling Act, 1948;[80] the procedure for the collection of a person's blood under s. 129-A, Bombay Prohibition Act, 1949;[81] ss. 4 (2) and 53, Madras Prohibition Act, 1937.[82] It equally follows from the above proposition in *Gopalan's Case* that Art. 21

"Procedure established by law" does not require every step in the procedure to be prescribed

Art. 21 not available against private individuals

Provisions held not violative of Art. 21

---

[72] *In re P. K. Velayudhan* (1955) Tra.-Co. 559, ('55) A.Tr.-Co. 220 (F.B.); *Hiralal* v. *Sub-Divisional Officer* ('56) A.A. 428.

[73] (1950) S.C.R. 88, ('50) A.SC. 27.

[74] *Ram Chandra Prasad* v. *Bihar* (1962) 2 S.C.R. 50, ('61) A.SC. 1620; *M. D. Jute Mills* v. *L.A.T.* ('54) A.A. 161 (it is not for the court to question the wisdom and policy of the Constitution by adopting the phrase 'procedure established by law' in preference to 'due process of law'); *Raj Bahadur* v. *Legal Remembrencer* ('53) A.Cal. 522, 57 C.W.N. 507; *Jagjivanram* v. *State* (1952) Nag. 14, ('52) A.N. 118; *Abdul Munim Khan* v. *Hyderabad* ('53) A.Hyd. 145 [the trial of an accused by Special Tribunal under the Hyderabad Special Tribunal Regulations (1358F) does not violate Art. 21 as the Regulation satisfied the requirement of procedure established by law]; *Abdul Khader* v. *Mysore* (1951) Mys. 284, ('51) A.Mys. 72 (F.B.).

[75] *Mohd. Athar Rizvi* v. *State* ('51) A.A. 456, (1950) A.L.J. 526.

[76] *Smt. Vidya Verma* v. *Shiv Narain Verma* (1955) 2 S.C.R. 983, ('56) A.SC. 108 [*P. D. Shamdasani* v. *Central Bank* (1952) S.C.R. 391, ('52) A.SC. 59 was followed].

[77] *In re Sant Ram* (1960) 3 S.C.R. 499, ('60) A.SC. 932 (the question was raised by a "tout" in a court of law and the court held that even on the assumption that "life" included "livelihood", the prohibition of touting did not violate Art. 14 or 19, nor was the person deprived of his livelihood, except by procedure established by law).

[78] *Chari* v. *State* ('59) A.A. 149; *Ram Kishan* v. *State* ('56) A.A. 462, (1956) A.L.J. 748.

[79] *Venkayya* v. *Chinna Punnaiah*, ('57) A.A.P. 90.

[80] *Krishnachandra* v. *M.P.* (1964) 1 S.C.R. 765, ('65) A.SC. 307 (as the Act was not beyond the legislative competence and did not violate Art. 19, the curtailment of the liberty of any person would be according to procedure established by law).

[81] *State* v. *Sheshappa* ('64) A.B. 253 at p. 257, 66 Bom.L.R. 230.

[82] *In re A. S. Krishna* (1955) Mad. 887, ('54) A.M. 993 (even if the sections prescribed a procedure slightly different from that laid down in the Cr.P.C., Art. 21 was not violated).

Art. 21 not violated

is violated where a person is sought to be deprived of his life or liberty without the authority of law. Accordingly, the following have been held to violate Art. 21: Reg. 236, cl. (*b*), U.P. Police Regulations which authorized domiciliary visits when there was no law on which such a regulation could be justified;[83] an order for compulsory medical examination, when there was no provision in the Hindu Marriages Act enabling the Court to order such examination;[84] a D.O. letter from the Ministry of States, New Delhi, to the Chief Commissioner, Manipur, which was inconsistent with the provisions of the Criminal Law Amendment Act, 1952, as it could not confer jurisdiction on the extra-Assistant Commissioner to try a case under s. 165-A, I.P.C.;[85] the detention of a person under an extradition treaty between the former Dholepur State and the British Government, which not having been incorporated into the law of that State by a legislative enactment, could not be regarded as part of the Municipal Law of Dholepur State.[86]

Fundamental Rights of Prisoners

Development of the law relating to the fundamental rights of prisoners

11.255 Of late there has been a great development in the law relating to the fundamental rights of prisoners. The disclosures in the Shah Commission Reports, and the Reports of other Commissions, as to the treatment of prisoners in preventive detention has quickened the awareness of the rights of prisoners. Newspaper articles by a person with first-hand knowledge of prison conditions has led the Supreme Court actively to intervene to prevent people being kept in jail for years without being brought to trial. All these factors have contributed to a proper administration of criminal law and to a recognition of the fundamental rights of prisoners. We will now consider the gradual development of this law by reference to decided cases.

Mukherjea J. in *Gopalan's Case*

11.256 That a person detained in prison under the sentence of a Court, or under a valid law of preventive detention did not lose all his rights was pointed out by Mukherjea J. in *Gopalan's Case*.[87] He said:

> "It may not . . . be quite accurate to state that the operation of Art. 19 . . . is limited to free citizens only and that the rights have been described in that Article on the pre-supposition that the citizens are at liberty. . . . Deprivation of personal liberty may entail as a consequence the loss or abridgement of many of their rights described in Art. 19, but that is because the nature of these rights is such that free exercise of them is not possible in the absence of personal liberty. On the other hand, the right to hold, and dispose of property which is in sub-clause (*f*) of Art. 19(1) and which is not dependent on full possession of personal liberty by the owner may not be affected if the owner is imprisoned or detained."[88]

In *Gopalan's Case* the question was discussed in the context of preventive detention, in which the safeguards provided by Art. 22(1) and (2) were withdrawn. But in detention for an alleged crime, the accused is entitled to be told of the offence with which he is charged, is entitled to consult counsel and be defended by a counsel of his choice. On conviction, where there is a right of appeal, these rights

---

83 *Kharak Singh* v. *U.P.* (1964) 1 S.C.R. 332, ('63) A.SC. 1295 (so held by the whole court.

84 *Bipinchandra* v. *Madhuriben* ('63) A.Guj. 250, 4 Guj.L.R. 890.

85 *Ukakhasia* v. *Manipur* ('56) A.Mani. 9.

86 *Birma* v. *State* ('51) A.Raj. 127.

87 (1950) S.C.R. 88, ('50) A.SC. 27.

88 (1950) S.C.R. at pp. 263-64.

are not lost. In Art. 21, the word "procedure" does not exclude substantive law, for as Mukherjea J. said in *Gopalan's Case*, "There must be a substantive law under which the State is empowered to deprive a man of his life and liberty and such a law must be a valid law which the legislature is competent to enact . . . and which does not transgress any of the fundamental rights."[89]

Maharashtra v. Prabhakar Pandurang

11.257 In *Maharashtra* v. *Prabhakar Pandurang*[90] the respondent had been preventively detained by the Government of Maharashtra under Rule 30 (1) (*b*) of the Defence of India Rules in order to prevent him from acting in a manner prejudicial to the defence of India, public safety and the maintenance of public order. With the permission of Government, the Respondent had written a book in Marathi on "Inside the Atom". The Respondent applied for permission to send the book outside the jail for publication, but his request was refused. The High Court found that the book was purely of scientific interest, and could not prejudice the defence of India, public safety and the maintenance of public order, and directed the Government to allow the detenu to send the manuscript of the book to his wife, so that it could be published. The State contended before the Supreme Court that when a person was detained he lost his freedom and was no longer a free man, and therefore he could exercise only such privileges as were conferred on him by the order of detention. At that time the proclamation of Emergency was in force, and the President's Order had provided, *inter alia,* that the right to move the Court for the enforcement of fundamental rights conferred by Art. 21 was suspended. However, Subba Rao J. observed that it was only a conditional order, that is, conditional on the right claimed by a person arising out of a violation of the Defence of India Rules. But if the right was claimed independently of the Defence of India Rules, the approach to the Court under Arts. 32 and 226 was not barred. The stand taken by the State was not that the Respondent's book was prejudicial to the safety of India etc., the stand was that as the Rules did not provide for a detenu writing a book, or sending it for publication, he could not claim a right to do so. Subba Rao J. held that the State's contention was wrong, for if it were accepted, and the rule did not provide for the supply of food to the detenu he would be starved to death. Such a construction ought not to be put on the fundamental rights of prisoners. He held that there was no law authorising government to prevent the manuscript from being sent out of jail, and therefore, in the absence of any contention that the book was prejudicial to public safety etc., the detenu had the right to have the book sent out for publication.

No law authorising Govt. to prevent a manuscript of the detenu being sent out of Jail for publication

Patnaik's Case **and the rights of prisoners**

11.258 In *D. B. M. Patnaik* v. *A.P.*[91] the petitioner had been sentenced to imprisonment and was also an undertrial prisoner in respect of a Naxalite conspiracy case. In dealing with the rights of convicts, Chandrachud J. observed:

"Convicts are not, by mere reason of the conviction, denuded of all the fundamental rights which they otherwise possess. A compulsion under the authority of law, following upon a conviction, to live in a prison-house entails by its own force the deprivation of fundamental freedoms like the right to move

[89] ibid. p. 256.
[90] (1966) 1 S.C.R. 702, ('66) A.SC. 424.
[91] (1975) 2 S.C.R. 24, ('74) A.SC. 2092.

freely throughout the territory of India or the right to 'practise' a profession. A man of profession would thus stand stripped of his right to hold consultations while serving out his sentence. But the Constitution guarantees other freedoms like the right to acquire, hold and dispose of property for the exercise of which incarceration can be no impediment. Likewise, even a convict is entitled to the precious right guaranteed by Article 21 of the Constitution that he shall not be deprived of his life or personal liberty except according to procedure established by law."[92]

Chandrachud J. referred to *Prabhakar Pandurang's Case,* and having laid down the above principles, he dealt with the petitioner's complaints (*a*) that Police officers resided in the jail areas and (*b*) that there were live electric wires placed on the top of a wall 13 feet high to prevent escape, and the petitioner contended that these violated his fundamental rights. Chandrachud J. observed that the intrusion of the Police into the jail would be against the "very essence of a scheme of ordered liberty". However, although police officers stayed in a part of the land belonging to the jail, they had no access to the jail and were not in any way concerned with it. Such residence gave no cause for complaint. It was contended that there was segregation of the prisoner with 146 Naxalite prisoners as though it was a "fascist concentration camp". The Court affirmed the principle that no person — not even a prisoner — could be deprived of his life or personal liberty except according to procedure established by law and in that context "life" meant "something more than mere animal existence" as observed by Field J. in *Munn* v. *Illinois*[93] — observations which had been approved by our Supreme Court in *Kharak Singh* v. *U.P.*[94] Chandrachud J. held that there was no satisfactory proof of the petitioners' contention that the treatment meted out to them was in violation of their right to life and personal liberty; but he added that the provisions of Art. 42 might be benevolently extended to living conditions in a jail. However, the installation of live electric wires did not in any way endanger any prisoner's life, unless the prisoner tried to escape by scaling the wall. Chandrachud J. said that whatever may be the nature and extent of the fundamental right of prisoners to life and personal liberty, they had no fundamental freedom to escape from lawful custody. Consequently, live electric wires did not deprive the prisoners of their life unless they unlawfully attempted to escape from prison.

Giasuddin's Case

11.259 In *Mohamed Giasuddin* v. *A.P.*[95] Krishna Iyer J. propounded his theory of punishment. That case is referred to because Krishna Iyer J. referred to it in his judgment in *Sunil Batra's Case,* considered below.[96] In *Giasuddin's Case* the appellant had obtained Rs. 1,200 each from four unemployed persons by promising that he would secure them jobs because of his connection with influential people. He was found guilty and convicted and sentenced to three years' imprisonment for cheating. The appeal was limited to the question of the sentence. It is practically impossible to summarise the judgment which, it is submitted, consists of a large number of pseudo-psychological and sociological statements. That justice should be tempered with mercy, and that in sentencing an accused, the reformative aspect of punishment should be borne in mind, is

92 ('74) A.SC. at p. 2094.
93 (1877) 94 U.S. 113, 24 L.ed. 77.
94 (1964) 1 S.C.R. 332, 347, ('63) A.SC. 1295, 1302.
95 (1978) 1 S.C.R. 153, ('77) A.SC. 1926.
96 See paras 11.258 *et seqq.*

nothing new. However, prescriptions of, or suggestions to prescribe psychological treatment, transcendental meditation, yoga exercises and the like are wholly outside a judge's function. All these prescriptions require organisational changes which only the State can make if they are considered appropriate. The ground on which Krishna Iyer J. reduced the sentence was that the Appellant was an educated person, his parents were old and had limited means and they, as well as the Appellant's sister and younger brother (who was unemployed), were dependent on him. The prayer that the appellant should be released on probation under s. 360 of the Cr.P.C. because he had no blemishes by way of any previous crime, was rejected as over-ambitious. The sentence was reduced to 18 months with various directions given as to how he should be treated in jail and what facilities should be given to him. As Counsel appearing for the State agreed that those directions would be carried out, it is unnecessary to deal with them further. The following passage must, however, be set out, illustrating the learned judge's conception of the judicial function, a conception which is clearly mistaken as stated earlier. Krishna Iyer J. said:

> "The affidavit on behalf of the State indicates that a tendency to turn a new page is discernible in the appellant and this has to be strengthened imaginatively by the Jail Superintendent, if need be, by affording him opportunity for initiation into Transcendental Meditation courses or like exercises provided the appellant shows an appetite in that direction and facilities are available in Hyderabad City."[97]

11.260 *Sunil Batra* v. *Delhi Administration*[98] is a case of cardinal importance on the fundamental rights of prisoners. Desai J. delivered the leading judgment[99] and Krishna Iyer J., a concurring judgment. It is not proposed to discuss the judgment of Krishna Iyer J. at any length. His concern for the forgotten men behind the bars, and his desire that they should be treated humanely are clearly right; but his distress at the injustices and inhumanities of prison life has led him to overload his judgment with excessive quotations for propositions which need no such support. He seems to be aware of this, for under the heading "The Conclusion" he said: "Now that this *dilutory* discussion overlapping at times has come to an end, I may concretise the conclusions in both the cases, *lest diffusion should leave the decision vague* or with ragged edges."[1] (italics supplied). However, two points emphasized by Krishna Iyer J. deserve to be noted,[2] because they must be taken into account in deciding the questions which were before the Court. First, that remedies and safeguards provided for prisoners, however desirable they may be, must not be over emphasized because they may not be readily available to the prisoner who finds himself for the time being in the absolute power

Sunil Batra's Case

Two points emphasized by Krishna Iyer J.

---

[97] ('77) A.SC. at p. 1935.

[98] (1979) 1 S.C.R. 392, ('78) A.SC. 1675. This case dealt with two petitions: one filed by Sunil Batra and the other by Charles Sobhraj. The judgment was delivered on August 30, 1978, and was reported in the December issue of the A.I.R. for 1978. Another petition filed by Charles Sobhraj was heard by a Bench consisting of Krishna Iyer, Desai and Reddy JJ. and judgment was delivered on 30th of August 1978, the case being reported in the October issue of A.I.R. of 1978. The judgment in the second petition must be read together with the judgment in *Sunil Batra's Case* and is dealt with immediately after the discussion of *Batra's Case*.

[99] For himself, Chandrachud C.J. and Fazal Ali and Shinghal JJ.

[1] ('78) A.SC. at p. 1722. [2] ibid.

of a minor warder or official. Secondly, under the heading "Access and the Law" Krishna Iyer J. pointed out that the Punjab Jail Manual — a collection of the bare text of certain statutes, rules and instructions running into 469 pages — used to be sold for Rs. 20/-, but in 1975 it was suddenly priced at Rs. 260.20. This increase showed the State's desire to deprive people of the knowledge of their rights under the Manual. It is not surprising that Krishna Iyer J. found such conduct shocking.

Batra's Case and Sobhraj's Case

11.261B *Batra's Case* dealt with two petitions under Art. 32: one filed by Batra, who had been sentenced to death by the District and Sessions Judge. Batra's sentence was subject to confirmation by the High Court and to a possible appeal to the Supreme Court. If everything failed, he could apply for clemency to the President. Batra complained that from the time that he was sentenced to death on 6th July, 1976 he was kept in solitary confinement till the Supreme Court intervened by an interim Order on 24th February, 1978. The second petition was filed by one Charles Sobhraj, a foreigner, who was arrested on 6th July, 1976 and detained under s. 3 of MISA. He complained that ever since he was lodged in Tihar Jail he was put in bar fetters and the fetters were retained continuously for 24 hours of the day. It was not disputed that from his detention in July 1976 till the Supreme Court made an order on 24th February, 1978 recording an assurance from Tihar Jail authorities that the fetters would be removed for 14 days, he remained in bar fetters. It may be added that the bar fetters almost completely immobilised Sobhraj. Further, notwithstanding the recommendation of the resident medical officer that the bar fetters be removed, they had not been removed.

The incredible facts disclosed by the two cases

11.262 Sunil Batra and Charles Sobhraj were unfortunate in having been cruelly treated in jail. But it was fortunate for prisoners generally that the petitions which came before the Supreme Court exhibited calculated cruelty and brutality. The facts disclosed in the two petitions would appear incredible but for the fact that they were admitted to be true.

Batra's Case and solitary confinement

11.263 Taking up *Batra's Case* first, solitary confinement was justified by the respondents under s. 30 of the Prisons Act. Batra's contention was, first, that s. 30 (2) of the Act did not justify keeping a prisoner under sentence of death in solitary confinement on the alleged ground of security. Secondly, if s. 30 (2) was construed as authorising solitary confinement, the section would be void under Arts. 14, 19 and 21. Before dealing with the contentions thus raised, Desai J. laid down certain broad principles.[3] First, that it was not open to debate that prisoners were not wholly deprived of their fundamental rights and no iron curtain could be drawn between the prisoner and the Constitution. Prisoners were entitled to all constitutional rights unless they had been constitutionally curtailed.[4] Secondly, the prisoner's liberty was in the very nature of things, circumscribed by the very fact of his confinement. Thirdly, conviction for a crime did not reduce the prisoner into a non-person whose rights were subject to the whim of the supervising administration. And the imposing of any measure within the prison system was conditional upon the

Broad principles laid down by Desai J.

---

3 ('78) A.SC. at p. 1757.
4 *Procunier* v. *Martinez* (1974) 40 L.ed. 2d 224 at p. 248.

observance of procedural safeguards.[5] Lawful imprisonment brought about necessary withdrawal or limitation of some of the prisoner's fundamental rights. This followed from considerations underlying the penal system. Finally, the question of the prisoner's fundamental rights must be viewed against the background of modern reformist theories of punishment. The Court would not take a "hands off" attitude, all the more so because a convict was in prison under an order and direction of the Court. The Court had therefore to strike a just balance between de-humanizing prison atmosphere and the preservation of internal order and discipline and maintenance of institutional security and the rehabilitation of the prisoners.[6]

11.264 For the purpose of the present discussion, it is not necessary to go into a detailed interpretation of s. 30 (2) of the Prisons Act. On a true interpretation it was held that s. 30 (2) did not justify keeping a person under sentence of death in solitary confinement. The Court interpreted the crucial words in s. 30 (2), namely, "under sentence of death" to mean that a prisoner was not under sentence of death till all steps open to the prisoner to appeal against the sentence or to appeal for mercy had been completed and an order for his execution was passed. Till that time he was not a person under the sentence of death. It was implicit in the warrant for execution of the prisoner that he was neither awarded simple nor rigorous imprisonment; the purpose behind enacting s. 366 (2) of the Cr.P.C. was to make him available for execution. After the sentence becomes executable, the prisoner may be kept in confinement apart from other prisoners with a day and night watch. But even here, unless there were special considerations, he must be within the sight of other prisoners and able to take food in their company. The Court held that if solitary confinement was inflicted on a prisoner, it was a substantive punishment in addition to the punishment awarded by the Court and that would violate Art. 20 (2). However, on the interpretation put on s. 30 (2) by the Court there was no question of the section being void for violating Art. 20 (2). Again, "Personal liberty" as used in Art. 21 has been held to include within itself all varieties of rights which go to make personal liberties of men other than those dealt with in clause (*d*) of Art. 19 (1). The burden of justifying curtailment of those liberties must rest on the State. The challenge under Art. 21 failed, because the Court read down s. 30 (2). Any law curtailing the liberty of a prisoner other than that involved in his incarceration could only be justified by a law, but procedure prescribed by law, which had been interpreted in *Maneka Gandhi's Case*[7] to mean a law which must be just and fair and not arbitrary or fanciful, for, in that event, the procedure would violate Art. 14. The Court rejected the contention that a prisoner under sentence of death could not be made the subject of a valid classification and held that on the Court's interpretation, s. 30 (2) did not violate Art. 14.

S. 30(2) of the Prisons Act did not justify solitary confinement of a person under sentence of death

11.265 Turning to the petition of Charles Sobhraj, the State contended that s. 56 of the Prisons Act, justified putting Sobhraj in fetters. The petitioner challenged the validity of s. 56 on the ground

***Sobhraj's Case* and putting prisoners in bar fetters**

---

[5] *Charles Wolff* v. *McDonnel* (1974) 41 L.ed. 2d 935, 973. A like view was taken by Chandrachud J. in *D. B. M. Patnaik* v. *A.P.* ('74) A.SC. 2092 at p. 2094, (1975) 2 S.C.R. 34.

[6] ('78) A.SC. at p. 1729.

[7] ('78) A.SC. 597, (1978) (2) S.C.R. 621.

that it conferred unguided and arbitrary power on the Superintendent to confine a prisoner in irons, and the law violated Arts. 14 and 21—the challenge under Art. 19(1) was not open to him because he was a foreigner. The Court observed that if, along with the bar fetters, the person were handcuffed, "his life, to put it mildly, would be intolerable." The bar fetters are kept day and night even when the prisoner is kept in cellular confinement. The State contended that the prisoner had no fundamental freedom to escape from lawful custody and therefore he could not complain against precautionary measures taken to prevent his escape; cl. 399(3) of the Jail Manual was relied on to furnish the sanction of law for putting a prisoner in bar fetters, but this argument was later given up. The Court carefully considered whether there were guidelines in s. 56, and whether the Court could not so interpret the section that on being read down, it did not become invalid. The substance of this discussion in the judgment was that a mere routine order would not do, that there must be reasons for putting the prisoner in fetters and his case must be reviewed periodically and the Superintendent would have himself to review the case of the prisoner at regular and frequent intervals. In this connection, the Court said: "But we cannot be oblivious to the fact that the treatment of a human being which offends human dignity, imposes avoidable torture and reduces the man to the level of a beast would certainly be arbitrary under Art. 14. Now putting bar fetters for an unusually long period without due regard to the safety of the prisoner would not certainly be justified under s. 56". However, having read down the section, and pointed out guidelines for the exercise of power under s. 56, Desai J. held that s. 56 did not violate Art. 14 or Art. 21. Accordingly, both petitions were dismissed.

Section 56, of the Prisons Act, read down

Sobhraj's Case on points other than the fundamental rights of prisoners

11.266 *Charles Sobhraj* v. *Supdt., Central Jail, Tihar*[8] must be read together with the discussion about a prisoner's fundamental rights in *Sunil Batra's Case* discussed above. Krishna Iyer J. delivered the judgment of the Court (for himself, Desai and Reddy JJ.). The facts as set out by him are these:

"The petitioner Charles Sobhraj is no longer an under-trial (prisoner) having to serve two sentences of long imprisonment. He is given all the amenities of a 'B' class prisoner. He goes on hunger strike but medical men take care of him. Ward I, where he is lodged, gives him the facilities of wards XIII and XIV where he wants to be moved. He has a record of one escape and one attempt at suicide and Interpol reports of many crimes abroad. There are several cases pending in India against him. Even so, the barbarity of bar fetters inflicted on him by a qualmless jail staff was abandoned under orders of this Court. Now, he seeks the other extreme of coddling as if a jail were a country club or good hotel. Give me finer foreigners as companions, he demands. Don't keep convict cooks and warders as jailmates in my cell he rails. Remove me from a high security ward like Ward I to a more relaxed ward like Ward 14 or 13, he solicits. These delicate and genteel requests from a prisoner with his record and potential were turned down by the Superintendent and the reasons for such rejection, based on security, rules and allergy of other inmates to be his risky fellow-inmates have been stated on oath."[9]

Krishna Iyer J. on the fundamental rights of prisoners

11.267 The judgment substantially repeats what was said in *Batra's Case*. Krishna Iyer J. summed up the position thus:

"Whenever fundamental rights are flouted or legislative protection ignored, to any prisoner's prejudice, this Court's writ will run, breaking through stone

[8] (1979) 1 S.C.R. 512, ('78) A.SC. 1514.

[9] (1979) 1 S.C.R. at pp. 518-19, ('78) A.SC. at pp. 1517-18.

walls and iron bars, to right the wrong and restore the rule of law. Then the parrot-cry of discipline will not deter, of security will not scare, of discretion will not dissuade, the judicial process. For if courts 'cave in' when great rights are gouged (out) within the sound-proof, sight-proof precincts of prison houses, where, often, dissenters and minorities are caged, Bastilles will be re-enacted. . . . Therefore we affirm that imprisonment does not spell farewell to fundamental rights although, by a realistic re-appraisal, courts will refuse to recognise the full panoply of Part III enjoyed by a free citizen."[10]

Having said this, Krishna Iyer J. pointed out countervailing considerations in determining the fundamental rights of prisoners. He held that the classification made between dangerous prisoners and ordinary prisoners, and between under-trial prisoners and convicts was reasonable — and the petitioner was a convict. "In fact, lazy relaxation on security is a professional risk inside a prison".[11] Krishna Iyer J. said that

Reasonable classification between prisoners

"The court must not rush in where the jailor fears to tread. While the country may not make the prison boss the sole sadistic arbiter of incarcerated humans, the community may be in no mood to hand over central prisons to be run by courts. Each instrumentality must function within its province."[12]

11.268 In *Hussainara Khatoon* v. *Bihar* (*No. 1*)[13] the Supreme Court dealt, *inter alia,* with the rights of undertrial prisoners on *habeas corpus* petitions which disclosed the undernoted state of affairs,[14] which the Supreme Court rightly described as shocking. Bhagwati J. observed that although our Constitution had no provision corresponding to the 6th Amendment to the U.S. Constitution, namely, "In all criminal cases, the accused shall enjoy the right to a speedy and public trial", it was implicit in Art. 21, as interpreted in *Maneka Gandhi's Case,* namely, that no person should be deprived of his life or personal liberty except by a procedure which was "reasonable, fair or just." Bhagwati J. for himself and Koshal J. held that the right to a reasonably speedy trial was a part of the fundamental right conferred by Art. 21. As to the consequences of the violation of that right, Bhagwati J. reserved orders till the Bihar Government had supplied the requisite particulars relating to undertrial prisoners, including the period of their detention without trial.

Hussainara Khatoon's Case

Orders reserved pending further information

11.269 After the Government had supplied the required particulars and proposed how it was intended to speed up investigations pending in the cases of undertrial prisoners, Bhagwati J. (for himself and Sen J.) passed, *inter alia,* the following order:

Order passed in the above case

---

[10] (1979) 1 S.C.R. at pp. 514-15, ('78) A.SC. at pp. 1515-16.
[11] (1979) 1 S.C.R. at p. 519, ('78) A.SC. at p. 1518.
[12] (1979) 1 S.C.R. at p. 519, ('78) A.SC. at p. 1518.
[13] ('79) A.SC. 1360, (1979) 3 S.C.R. 169. As there are three judgments in the same matter, the words in brackets (No. 1), (No. 2) and (No. 3) have been added in the title by the present writer to distinguish the three judgments and to avoid confusion.
[14] "This petition for a writ of *habeas corpus* discloses a shocking state of affairs in regard to administration of justice in the State of Bihar. An alarmingly large number of men and women, children including, are behind prison bars for years awaiting trial in courts of law. The offences with which some of them are charged are trivial, which, even if proved, would not warrant punishment for more than a few months, perhaps for a year or two, and yet these unfortunate forgotten specimens of humanity are in jail, deprived of their freedom, for periods ranging from three to ten years without even as much as their trial having commenced. It is a crying shame on the judicial system which permits incarceration of men and women for such long periods of time without trial.": ('79) A.SC. at p. 1361.

"We, therefore, direct the Government of Bihar to scrutinise the cases of undertrial prisoners charged with offences which are punishable with fine only or punishable with imprisonment for a term not exceeding one year or punishable with imprisonment for a term exceeding one year but not exceeding three years and release such of them who are not liable to be proceeded against by reason of the period of limitation having expired. This direction shall be carried out by the Government of Bihar within a period of six weeks from today and compliance reports containing particulars shall be submitted to this Court, first at the end of four weeks and then at the end of the next two weeks."[15]

Hussainara Khatoon (No. 2)

11.270 *Hussainara Khatoon* v. *Bihar (No. 2)*[16] came up for hearing before Bhagwati and Desai JJ., when the Supreme Court again emphasised the right of an accused to a speedy trial and gave further directions to Government.

Hussainara Khatton (No. 3)

11.271 *Hussainara Khatoon* v. *Bihar (No. 3)*[17] came again before the Supreme Court, and the judgment of Bhagwati J. (for himself, Reddy and Sen JJ.) greatly extended the rights of undertrial prisoners. Having held earlier that the right to a reasonably speedy trial was part of the fundamental right conferred by Art. 21, Bhagwati J. held, it is submitted rightly, that where undertrial prisoners were kept in jail without a trial for periods longer than the maximum terms for which they could have been sentenced, if convicted, their detention in jail was unjustified and illegal as violating Art. 21 and they must be released forthwith. Bhagwati J. held further that since a procedure for depriving a person of life or personal liberty must be "reasonable, fair and just", a procedure which did not make available legal services to an accused person who was too poor to engage a lawyer and who would have to go through the trial without the assistance of a lawyer cannot be described as reasonable, fair and just, and it was the duty of the State to provide legal assistance to an accused too poor to engage a lawyer. Bhagwati J. referred to the directive in the newly added Art. 39A which referred, *inter alia,* to free legal advice. It is submitted that Art. 22(1) furnishes a surer foundation for the proposition laid down by Bhagwati J. For, that Article provides that an arrested person shall not be denied "the right to consult, and be defended by, a legal practitioner *of his choice*". The italicised words were presumably inserted to prevent the accused being denied the choice of Counsel as happens in Communist countries. But the right to consult and be defended by Counsel is conferred as a fundamental right by Art. 22(1) and that, coupled with the reasonable procedure required by Art. 21, would put the State under an obligation to make legal assistance available to a needy accused person detained in custody.

Kishor Singh v Rajasthan — Sunil Batra's Case reaffirmed

11.272 *Kishor Singh* v. *Rajasthan*[18] disclosed a tale of brutality in jail by keeping prisoners in solitary confinement and cross-bar fetters on flimsy grounds. The Supreme Court reaffirmed what it had said in *Sunil Batra's Case* (see paras 11.263 and 11.264 above) and gave the following important direction:

Directions given as to rules and circulars under the Prisons Act

"We find that the old rules and circulars and instructions issued under the Prisons Act are read incongruously with the Constitution, especially Art. 21 and interpretation put upon it by this Court. We, therefore, direct the State Government of Rajasthan — and indeed, all the other State Governments in the country — to convert the rulings of this Court bearing on Prison

---

[15] ibid. p. 1369.
[16] ibid.
[17] ibid. p. 1377.
[18] ('81) A.SC. 625.

Administration into rules and instructions forthwith so that violation of the prisoners' freedoms can be avoided and habeas corpus litigation may not proliferate. After all, human rights are as much cherished by the State as by the citizen."[19]

There was a further feature in this case. When under the orders of the Supreme Court, one prisoner, Surjeet Singh, was being brought to the Supreme Court, he was "manhandled severely". Krishna Iyer J. spoke of

"the more disturbing episode brought to our painful notice was the violence allegedly used by the escort police on the person of one prisoner, Surjeet Singh, while in transit and testified to by the visible wounds counsel found. Shri Parekh shocked us into shame by seeking to show us the physical injuries inflicted. If the writ of this court brings a person from the Jaipur prison to judicial presence can it be that a little set of constables in custody during transit violate, with brazen brutality, and criminal immunity the person of their charges and the hands of the law hang limp in the face of such lawlessness? 'Justice without power is inefficient; power without justice is tyranny . . . justice and power must therefore be brought together, so that whatever is just may be powerful, and whatever is powerful may be just.' (Blaise Pascal)."[20-39] Assault on a prisoner on his way to the Sup. Ct.

Articles 14, 19, 21 and the Sentence of Death

11.273 In *Rajendra Prasad* v. *U.P.*[40] a Bench consisting of Krishna Iyer J., Desai J. and Sen J. considered the question as to the circumstances under which the sentence of death can be inflicted for murder. The question arose out of three Special Leave Appeals, in which the leave was limited to the question of sentence. Krishna Iyer J. delivered the majority judgment, purporting to lay down guide lines and circumstances under which alone, capital punishment could be inflicted, if the law permitting capital punishment was not to violate Arts. 14, 19 and 21. A Bench of 5 Judges of the Supreme Court had held in *Jagmohan Singh* v. *U.P.*[41] that capital punishment did not violate Arts. 14, 19 and 21 and was constitutionally valid. Krishna Iyer J. observed that after that decision, the constitutional validity of capital punishment was not open to doubt. However, the expression "special reasons" in s. 354(3), Cr.P.C. seem to have furnished him with an opportunity for stating his own views on capital punishment, namely, that the only consideration for inflicting capital punishment was not the nature of the crime, but the concern for the criminal and unless it was shown that he was a risk to the survival of society, capital punishment would not be justified. Sen J. delivered a dissenting judgment. *Rajendra Prasad* v. *U.P.*: "guidelines" for inflicting capital punishment. The majority view

11.274 It is not proposed to deal at any length with the judgment of Krishna Iyer J., although it is the majority judgment, for the reasons given in paras 11.275 to 11.278 below: Reasons for not dealing with the judgment of Krishna Iyer J.

11.275 The style in which it is written makes it difficult to give a brief and accurate summary of his judgment. In fact, his style created the appearance of a difficult problem of interpretation in the present case, where no such problem existed. Special leave, limited to the question of sentence, had been granted, and the question for decision was: "What are the circumstances under which an accused should be sentenced to death for murder?". Section 302 of the Indian His style created problems where none existed. Section 302, I.P.C.

---

[19] ibid. p. 631.
[20-39] ibid. p. 627.
[40] (1979) 3 S.C.R. 78, ('79) A.SC. 916.
[41] (1973) 2 S.C.R. 541, ('73) A.SC. 947.

Penal Code provides: "Whoever commits murder shall be punished with death or imprisonment for life . . ." The substantive law of crimes having provided two alternative punishments, the procedural law of crimes, the Criminal Procedure Code, told the judge how his discretion should be exercised. Put briefly, s. 367 (5) Cr.P.C.[42] told the judge: "If you don't sentence an accused to death for an offence punishable with death, give your reasons". The Cr.P.C. of 1955 omitted s. 367 (5) and left the matter to the judge's discretion. Section 354 (3) of the Cr.P.C. of 1973[43] told the Judge: "Don't sentence an accused to death for an offence punishable with death unless there are 'special reasons'." Section 302 I.P.C. required no interpretation —it prescribed two alternative punishments for murder. From 1898 to 1955 the Cr.P.C. showed that the sentence of death was the rule and reasons had to be recorded for not awarding it. From 1955 to 1973 sub-s. (5) of s. 367 was deleted, so that the discretion of the Judge was at large. From 1973, s. 354 (3) Cr.P.C. made imprisonment for life the rule and the sentence of death the exception to be awarded for special reasons. The only question of construction was the meaning to be given to the expression "special reasons". Therefore, the law relating to the sentence of death can be correctly stated thus:

Section 367(5) and s. 354(3) Cr.P.C.

These sections raised no problems of interpretation

A correct and simple statement of the law

"In order to decide whether to sentence an accused to death or imprisonment for life for the offence of murder, the judge must be guided by the provisions of the Criminal Procedure Code, bearing in mind that from the sentence of death being the rule between 1898 to 1955 it has become the exception from 1973."

But these are plain words, and, it would appear, beneath the dignity of a judgment. So Krishna Iyer J. wrote:

Krishna Iyer J.'s involved formulation

"The sister Codes — the Indian Penal Code and the Criminal Procedure Code — are interwoven into the texture of sentencing. So much so, the various changes in s. 367 of the Procedure Code, 1898 and its reincarnation in Section 354 of the Code of 1973 impact on the interpretation of s. 302 of the Penal Code. The art of statutory construction seeks aid from connective tissues as it were, of complementary enactments. This mode offers a penological synthesis Parliament legislatively intended. From this angle, we may examine the history of the amendments to the Procedure Code insofar as they mould the sentencing discretion vested by s. 302, I.P.C."[44]

It is submitted that the expressions "interwoven into the texture of sentencing", "reincarnation in Sec. 354", "connective tissues, as it were" and "penological synthesis" are verbiage which obscure the simple proposition that a judge must turn to the Cr.P.C. to decide whether to sentence an accused to death or imprisonment for life for the offence of murder.

No part of the judicial function for a judge to read his

11.276 It is not a part of the judicial function for a judge to read his theories on capital punishment into the Constitution. No doubt, there is a limited sense in which in interpreting the law the Judge

---

[42] *S. 367. Language of judgment, Contents of Judgment.* — * * *(5). If the accused is convicted of an offence punishable with death and the court sentences him to any punishment other than death, the Court shall in its judgment, state the reason why the sentence of death is not passed.

[43] *S. 354. Language and Contents of Judgment.* — * * * (3). When the conviction is for an offence punishable with death or, in the alternative, with imprisonment for life or imprisonment for a term of years, the judgment shall state the reasons for the sentence awarded, and, in the case of sentence of death, the special reasons for such sentence.

[44] ('79) A.SC. at p. 926, para 26.

may make law in the sense of adopting one of two or more alternatives, if such alternatives are open, or evolving a new principle to meet a new or unusual situation. But it is not given to him to write his own theories, likes and dislikes into the Constitution and the law. And if there is one lesson which Mr. Justice Holmes (whom Krishna Iyer J. quotes) taught, it is that the personal views of a judge are irrelevant in considering the reasonableness or unreasonableness of a law. The opening words of his classic dissent in *Lockner* v. *New York*[45] give his settled views of the judicial function:

personal views into the Constitution

"This case is decided upon an economic theory which a large part of the country does not entertain. If it were a question whether I agreed with that theory, I should desire to study it further and long before making up my mind. But I do not conceive that to be my duty, because I strongly believe that my agreement or disagreement has nothing to do with the right of a majority to embody their opinion in law . . . Men whom I certainly could not pronounce unreasonable would uphold it as a first instalment of a general regulation of the hours of work."[46]

Another aspect of the same matter has been put forcibly by Mr. Justice Frankfurter. Speaking on *Government Under Law*, he said: "If judges want to be preachers, they should dedicate themselves to the pulpit; if judges want to be primarily shapers of policy, the legislature is their place. Self-willed judges are the least defensible offenders of government under law."[47]

Frankfurter J. on "self willed" judges

11.277 A Judge may decide a matter on his pet theories by a judicial *ipse dixit* (or "judicial say-so" as President Roosevelt called it), in which case later judgments will brush aside the *ipse dixit*. But there are cases in which the Judge may state in his judgment theories based on the opinions of writers whom he quotes. This is what Krishna Iyer J. has done in the present case.[48] Theories of psychology, psychiatry, cultural anthropology, penology, have been stated in his judgment and have determined his conclusions. It is submitted that a Judge must distinguish sharply between two distinct and inconsistent functions, namely, that of a Judge and that of an expert witness. No scientific theory propounded in a book can form the basis of a judgment, for, it is opinion evidence. Such evidence is permitted, *inter alia*, in matters of science, but on condition that the scientific witness goes into the box and is cross-examined. And this is all the more so where there are conflicting theories propounded by men of high standing as is the case in psychology, psychiatry and penology. It is submitted that if a judge bases his judgment on the opinion of experts, those opinions must be struck out from the judgment, as based on no evidence or at its highest, on untested evidence which no court would accept. Almost the whole theoretical basis of the judgment of Krishna Iyer J. would have to be struck out as based on inadmissible opinion evidence because the opinions were not proved before the Court by calling expert witnesses.

A judge cannot combine the function of a judge with that of an expert witness, as Krishna Iyer J. has done

Submission: the whole theoretical basis of Krishna Iyer J.'s judgment must be struck out

---

45 (1904) 198 U.S. 45, 49 L.ed. 937. 46 ibid.

47 *Government Under Law*, a Seminar organized to celebrate the second centenary of the birth of Chief Justice Marshall, p. 31.

48 *Rajendra Prasad* v. *U.P.* ('79) A.SC. 916.

Art. 14 gives no authority for laying down "guidelines" for an essentially discretionary power

11.278 The fact that Art. 14 condemns arbitrariness gives no jurisdiction to a judge to lay down rules for the exercise of discretionary power conferred on judges by law. If a matter were capable of being governed by rules, it would not be left to the discretion of judges. The rules for the exercise of discretion laid down by Krishna Iyer J. contain intrinsic evidence that he was propounding his own theories and not interpreting the law. He held that a death sentence would be justified in "white collar offences" or economic offences. But no law in India carries the death penalty for such offences.

Submission: the dissenting judgment of Sen J. is correct

11.279 In the submission of the present writer, the dissenting judgment of Sen J. is correct and contains an effective refutation of the majority judgment. In his judgment, Sen J. gave the following reasons for his dissent:

Sen J.'s criticism of the majority judgment: it virtually abolishes the death sentence

"I had the advantage of reading the judgment as originally prepared by my learned brother Krishna Iyer J., which, by defining the class of cases in which a death sentence may be passed upon conviction of a person for having committed an offence of murder punishable under s. 302 of the Indian Penal Code, 1860, and by putting a restrictive construction on the words 'special reasons' appearing in s. 354, sub-sec. (3) of the Code of Criminal Procedure, 1973, does, in my opinion, virtually abolish the death sentence. I was, therefore, constrained to write this dissenting opinion, as it is difficult to share the views of my learned brother Krishna Iyer J. He has now completely revised his draft judgment in which he has endeavoured to meet my point of view, and I have had the advantage of reading it. But I see no particular reason to change my views on the subject or to rewrite or revise my dissenting opinion as the matter essentially involves a question of principle."[48a]

Having given reasons for his dissenting judgment, Sen J. succinctly summed up the stand taken by Krishna Iyer J.:

Sen J.'s succinct summary of Krishna Iyer J.'s judgment

"My learned brother Krishna Iyer J. pleads for abolition of the death penalty, in accordance with the Stockholm Declaration of the Amnesty International. He believes that the death penalty is not only physically but psychologically 'brutal', referring to the lengthy period between sentencing and execution as a 'lingering death'. He recalls the names of many patriots who faced the firing squad or died by the hangman's noose, in the cause of the country's freedoom, and pleads that it is the duty of the State to protect the life of all persons without exception. He asserts that by its application, the death penalty contradicts the very sanctity of life which all human society claims to hold among the highest values. He tells us that almost all civilised countries have abolished it as a symbol of their respect for human life, and expresses deep anguish that we, in our country, still cling to it with little regard to the basic rights of the man."[49]

Sen J. said that he did not agree with Krishna Iyer J. when he tried to equate a patriot with an ordinary criminal. "The humanistic approach should not obscure our sense of realities. When a man commits a crime against the society by committing a diabolical, cold-blooded, pre-planned murder of an innocent person the brutality of which shocks the conscience of the Court, he must face the consequences of his act."[50]

Submission: grave problems raised by the commission of murder, and mass murders for patriotic reasons

11.280 It is submitted that the problem of securing the freedom of one's country by resorting to murder, and even mass murders, as by blowing up trains or ships or aircraft, has confronted our society with one of the most difficult problems in preventing crime, in protecting innocent people and in punishing the criminals when found. To give an example from our own history, there was a time when,

---

48a ('79) A.SC. at p. 945.

49 ibid. pp. 945-6.

50 ibid. p. 946.

if an English officer, or policeman, was murdered as part of our fight for freedom, the Indian National Congress passed a resolution praising the motive but condemning the action. But when Swami Shraddhanand, the leader of a Hindu revivalist movement and a political leader, was murdered by a Muslim fanatic, Congress realized that the distinction between the motive and the action could not safely be made. A Muslim may misguidedly believe it to be his religious duty to eliminate a religious leader of the Hindus, especially if he is a political leader as well. Therefore, the resolution passed by the Congress was changed, and the murder was condemned without making any distinction between motives and action. Pope John Paul II, speaking in September 1979 to the Irish people about the I.R.A. murders said that murder was murder, whatever the motive. International air piracy is committed by people who claim to be acting from patriotic political motives. But air piracy is piracy by whatever name called, and several countries are banding together to prevent air piracy as they once banded together to wipe out piracy at sea, and succeeded. Piracy was an offence recognized by the law of Nations and the pirate was an enemy of mankind.

A historical example from India

Pope John Paul II on murders by the I.R.A.

11.281 Sen J. gave a careful analysis of the issues involved, and the different views taken of punishment in general, and capital punishment in particular. The discussion must be read as a whole and repays study. The following is a brief account of his dissenting judgment: After the judgment in *Jagmohan Singh's Case*[51] it was not open to the Court to say that except for the cases mentioned by Krishna Iyer J., infliction of capital punishment would violate Arts. 14, 19 and 21. That question stood concluded by the decision of 5 Judges. If this were so, then the opinion expressed by Krishna Iyer J. must be treated as his personal opinion, and judges were "not concerned with the morals or ethics of punishment". It is their duty to administer the law as it is, and not to say what the law should be. The question whether the scope of the death sentence should be curtailed or not was one for Parliament and not for the Court. Sen J. held that it was constitutionally and legally impermissible while hearing a Special Leave Petition on a question of sentence to restructure the Indian Penal Code and the Criminal Procedure Code so as to limit the scope of the sentence of death provided by s. 302 I.P.C. for the offence of murder. Nor was it possible to construe the expression "special reasons" occurring in s. 354(3), Cr.P.C. by a process of judicial interpretation so as virtually to abolish the death sentence.

Sen J.'s analysis of the issues involved in considering capital punishment: the validity of the death sentence concluded by *Jagmohan Singh's Case*

The opinion expressed by Krishna Iyer J. merely reflect his personal view

11.282 Sen J. set out the views of Immanuel Kant (Philosophy of Law), Montesquieu (*L'Esprit des Lois*), John Stuart Mill (in a speech in the House of Commons advocating the death penalty), Sir Henry Maine and Sir James Stephen, in support of capital punishment. Sir James Stephen pointed out the obvious fact that the deterrent effect of the death penalty was shown by the fact that every person sentenced to death would willingly secure its commutation into life imprisonment. Sen J. observed that "By reserving the death penalty for murder, the Criminal law stigmatises the gravest crime by the gravest punishment, so that the element of retribution

Views of eminent writers on the deterrent effect of the death sentence

[51] (1973) 2 S.C.R. 541, ('73) A.SC. 947.

merges into that of deterrence".[52] He observed: "It would be generally agreed that, though reform of the criminal law ought sometimes to give a lead to public opinion, it is dangerous to move too far in advance of it.[53] He traced the history of the position of capital punishment from the doctrine of Bonesena Baccaria (An Essay on Crimes and Punishment),[54] which found favour with Rousseau, Voltaire and Montesquieu. Baccaria asserted that all capital punishment was wrong in itself and unjust. He maintained that since man was not his own creator, he did not have the right to destroy human life, either individually or collectively. However, he held that two circumstances justified capital punishment. First, if the execution would prevent a revolution against a popularly established government and secondly, if the execution was the only way to deter others from committing a crime.[55] The policy of retribution is justified and sustained by ethical philosophy from Plato to Thomas Acquinas and from Kant to T. H. Green and his disciples. The deterrent effect of punishment and its general acceptance was due to the work of Bentham, Paley, John Stuart Mill and Herbert Spencer, which makes the welfare of society—"the greatest good of the greatest number"—the aim of all moral activity. Recently, in all countries this motive has been supplemented, but never supplanted, by an unquestioning faith in the deterrent effect on potential offenders, of drastic punishment. After reference to the work of Sir Samuel Romilly in removing capital punishment for a large number of offences which existed in the Statute Book, Sen J. said that Sir Samuel Romilly had observed that all punishment implied a moral accountability. It is related to injury and not only to damage or danger however great. Capital punishment does so in an eminent degree. To reduce punishment for murder to the same level as punishment for other offences would be to weaken the law. If the appeal of capital punishment were merely to fear of death, it would be a very inefficient protector of society. Punishment only protects life effectively if it produces, in possible murderers, not only fear of the consequences of committing murder, but a horrified recoil from the thing itself. The Royal Commission on Capital punishment put this briefly by saying "by building up in the community, over a long period of time a deep feeling of peculiar abhorrence for the crime of murder".[56]

The views of eminent writers who took the opposite view

Retribution and ethical philosophy

All punishment implied moral responsibility

The history of capital punishment in England

11.283 Sen J. traced the history of capital punishment in England from the Victorian days till now, including first, the temporary abolition of capital punishment for 5 years, which was later made permanent. He observes that the increase in crime, particularly political murders, has created a genuine public demand for a reassessment of the penal policy of the British Government. Two recent decisions of the Privy Council, first in *Eaton Baker* v. *R.*[57] and then *Michael de Freitas* v. *George Ramouter Benny*[58] were destructive of the theory that (i) the death penalty was an unusual punishment and (ii) any delay in carrying it out makes it so. Sen J. then discussed the judgment of the U.S. Supreme Court in

Decisions of the Privy council

[52] ('79) A.SC. *supra* at p. 948.
[53] ibid.
[54] Voltaire is said to have written a Preface to the book anonymously.
[55] ('79) A.SC. at p. 948.
[56] ibid. p. 950.
[57] (1975) A.C. 774.
[58] (1976) A.C. 239.

Furman v. *Georgia*,[59] on which Krishna Iyer J. strongly relied. A careful analysis of the judgment showed that the Supreme Court did not hold that capital punishment was, *per se*, "cruel and unusual" but only showed that the way in which capital punishment was awarded arbitrarily and capriciously, made it unusual. He held that *Furman's Case* no longer held the field in the United States itself.

The U.S. Sup. Ct.'s decision in *Furman's Case* analysed

11.284 After the *Furman* decision, the legislatures of 35 States in the United States tightened up the laws under which the death penalty was to be imposed. Two different lines were followed: some States established new procedures for capital cases designed to meet the objection of the *Furman Case.* There was a bifurcated trial with pre-sentencing hearing. The Courts of Appeal were given broader authority to decide whether the sentence of death was fair in the light of sentences for similar offences. The other line taken by certain States, including North Carolina, Louisiana and Oklahoma, was to eliminate all discretion in awarding the sentence of death. Anyone found guilty of the specified offences was to be sentenced to death. This avoided the unpredictable and fortuitous use of the death penalty which the Supreme Court condemned in the *Furman Case.*

Legislation following *Furman's Case* in 35 States of the U.S.

11.285 On July 2, 1976, the U.S. Supreme Court heard the undernoted five Appeals.[60] Three of them related to the exercise of discretionary power in sentencing an accused to death, and two of them to a mandatory death sentence. In the three cases of discretionary sentencing (*Gregg, Proffitt* and *Jurek Cases*) the Supreme Court held that the punishment of death did not invariably violate the Constitution. The reasons in *Gregg* for holding that the sentence of death did not *per se* violate the 8th and 14th Amendments were as follows:

U.S. Sup. Ct.'s decision in *Gregg, Proffitt* and *Jurek Cases* held that death penalty was not inherently cruel and unusual punishment

"First, history and precedent do not support the conclusion that the death sentence is a *per se* violation. Second, the evolving standards of decency argument has been substantially undercut in the last four years because a large segment of the enlightened population regards the death penalty as appropriate and necessary, as seen in the new legislation passed in response to Furman."[61]

The reasons given by the U.S. Supreme Court for holding that the death penalty was not inherently cruel and unusual was that

Reasons for the above view

"It served two principal social purposes, retribution and deterrence, and held that the death sentence for the crime of murder was (1) not without justification, (2) not unconstitutionally severe, and (3) not invariably disproportionate to the crime."[62]

Sen J. referred to the 35th Report of the Law Commission which held that having regard to all the circumstances, the country could not risk the abolition of capital punishment.[63] Speaking of the policy underlying the Indian Penal Code, Sen J. said:

The 35th Report of the Indian Law Commission

---

[59] (1972) 408 U.S. 238.

[60] *Gregg* v. *Georgia* (1976) 428 U.S. 153, 49 L.ed. 2d 859; *Proffitt* v. *Florida* (1976) 428 U.S. 242, 49 L.ed. 2d 913; *Jurek* v. *Texas* (1976) 428 U.S. 262, 49 L.ed. 2d 929; *Woodson* v. *North Carolina* (1976) 428 U.S. 280, 49 L.ed. 2d 944 and *Roberts* v. *Louisiana* (1976) 426 U.S. 325, 49 L.ed. 2d 974.

[61] ('79) A.SC. at p. 957.

[62] ibid.

[63] ibid. pp. 957-58.

The policy underlying the Indian Penal Code

"The basic principle of the nineteenth century Indian Penal Code, said Lord Macaulay who drafted it, is 'the principle of suppressing crime with the smallest possible amount of suffering.'[64] He lays this down as an unassailable axiom rather than as a contention for debate."[65]

Submission: the judgment of Sen J. is clearly right

It is submitted that the judgment of Sen J. is cogent and convincing. Coming to the appeals before the Court, he held that in all the three appeals, the sentence of death had been properly imposed. He further held that the guide lines given by Krishna Iyer J. would render the death penalty practically a dead letter.

A few observations on the judgment of Krishna Iyer J.

11.286 A few observations may be made on the judgment of Krishna Iyer J. Referring to a pending amendment of s. 302, I.P.C. he said that it half-fulfilled both "the humanist quintessence of the Constitution and, may be, the creed of the Father of the Nation. Gandhiji long ago wrote in the *Harijan*:

> 'God Alone Can Take Life
> Because He Alone Gives it'."[66]

The reference to half-fulfilled objective was to the fact that the amended Bill preserved the sentence of death for offences of particular brutality—the kind of cases which were before the Supreme Court! If the quotation from Mahatma Gandhi's writing is meant to emphasize the sanctity of life, it was unnecessary, but harmless. But if it was meant to answer the question before the Court in the three appeals, it obviously did not. For, it was not God, but the murderer, who took a life he could not give. And the question remained, "what is to be done to a man who breaks not only the laws of men but the law of God?" Secondly, it is not for a judge to recommend modes of reforming prisoners as by administering anti-aphrodisiac drugs or by voluntary castration. Again, a striking example given by Krishna Iyer J. ought to have demonstrated to him that if the law does not punish cruel and brutal murder with death, private vengeance may take over. He said:

> "To exemplify, supposing a boy of fifteen incited by his elder brothers, chases with them a murderer of their father and after hours of search confronts the villain and vivisect him in blood-thirsty bestiality. Do you hang the boy, blind to his dignity and tenderness intertwined?"[67]

This example shows, first, that an outrage committed on a loved father, might so infuriate persons who have seen him being killed that no retribution appears too cruel to the injured family. Further, there can be little doubt that imprisonment for life would be awarded by any Court, because the brutality of the murder would be extenuated by the fact that it was done under grave, if not sudden, provocation, and by the fact that sons who see their father killed would be deprived of self-control by their affection for their father.

Krishna Iyer J. and the *Kunju Kunju Case*

Krishna Iyer J. speaks of the "usual sex triangle"

11.287 Krishna Iyer J. commuted the sentence of death in the *Kunju Kunju Case*, and his action calls for comment. The accused who had a wife aged 28 and two children, had illicit intimacy with a young woman. She tried to dissuade him from pursuing his suit lest it should break up his home. He wrote to her that he had decided to kill his wife and children so that he and she could live

[64] Trevelyen, *Life and Letters of Lord Macaulay*, Vol. 1, p. 459.
[65] ('79) A.SC. at p. 958.
[66] ibid. p. 927.
[67] ibid. p. 931.

happily thereafter. It was a cold-blooded murder of three people but this was brushed aside by Krishna Iyer J. as "the usual sex triangle", a phrase which explains nothing about the enormity of the crime. Sen J. rightly observed:

Sen J.'s criticism

"I fail to understand what is meant by the 'eternal triangle' as a mitigating circumstance. The accused, who acted as a monster, did not even spare his two innocent minor children in order to get rid of his wife and issues through her. If the death sentence was not to be awarded in a case like this I do not see the type of offence which calls for a death sentence."[68]

The extra-ordinary reasoning of Krishna Iyer J.

11.288 Finally, the reasoning by which Krishna Iyer J. justified the commutation of the death sentence is so extraordinary that the whole paragraph is set out below:

Submission: he has over stepped the limits of the judicial function

"The crucial question is that the crime and its horrendous character except to the extent it reveals irreparable depravity and chronic propensity. (*sic*) The innocent three will not be happy because one guilty companion is also added to their number. Is Janardanan a social security risk, altogether beyond salvage by therapeutic life sentence? If he is, the pall must fall on his cadaver. If not, life must burn on. So viewed, no material, save juridical wrath and grief, is discernible to invoke social justice and revoke his fundamental right to life. A course of anti-aphrodisiac treatment or willing castration is a better recipe for this hypersexed human than outright death sentence. We have not even information on whether he was a desparate hedonist or randy rapist with 'Y' chromosomes in excess, who sipped every flower and changed every hour, so as to be a sex menace to the locality. Sentencing is a delicate process, not a blind man's buff. We commute the death sentence to life imprisonment."[69]

Krishna Iyer J.'s judgment overruled in *Bachan Singh's Case*

It is submitted that having regard to the taste and temper of the language used about "the randy rapist", and the reasoning employed to justify commutation of the death sentence, the reader will have no difficulty in concluding that Krishna Iyer J. has stepped far outside the judicial sphere. It was submitted in the second edition of this book[70] that the majority judgment was not only clearly wrong and productive of public mischief, but was subversive of the judicial function and that the judgment should be overruled. The Supreme Court, in *Bachan Singh's Case* to be considered presently, overruled the majority judgment.

Bachan Singh's Case: s. 302 I.P.C. not to stand test of Art. 19(1)

11.289 We have seen how *Bachan Singh's Case*[71] came to be heard by a Bench of 5 judges of the Supreme Court (para 11.71 above) and we noted the two principal questions which the Court had to decide (para 11.77 above where the questions are set out). We have discussed at length the question whether s. 302 I.P.C. had to stand the test of Art. 19(1), and noted the conclusion of the majority "that s. 302 . . . does not have to stand the test of Art. 19(1) . . . "[72] Before considering the other questions discussed in the majority judgment it would be convenient to refer briefly to the judgment of Bhagwati J.

Bhagwati J.'s dissenting judgment delivered after 2 years' research

11.290 Although Bhagwati J. reserved his judgment till the reopening of the Court (that is, July 1980) the judgment was not delivered till August 16, 1982. For this delay, he gave an extraordinary reason which is best set out in his own words:

"I must express my profound regret at the long delay in delivering this judgment but the reason is that *there was a considerable mass of material which had to be collected from various sources and then examined and analysed* and this took a large amount of time."[73] (italics supplied)

---

[68] ibid. pp. 962-63.
[69] ibid. p. 943.
[70] Vol. III, p. 1916.
[71] ('80) A.SC. 898.
[72] ibid. p. 915. See para 11.87 of the text.
[73] ('82) A.SC. at p. 1391.

In plain language, the judge said: "When I held s. 302 I.P.C. *ultra vires* Arts. 14 and 21 in so far as it provided for the death penalty, I did not have the material to support my conclusion. So, the material had to be collected, and it was so extensive that it took over two years to gather it and state its effect to support a conclusion which I had reached without the materials." The reader familiar with *Alice in Wonderland* will not have failed to notice the resemblance of this course of action to that ordered by the Queen in the trial of the Knave of Hearts:

Decision first, supporting materials 2 years later

"Let the jury consider its verdict", said the King.
"No, no" said the Queen. "Sentence first, verdict afterwards."

But however engaging such a course may be in an enchanting tale, that course is wholly impermissible in a judgment. This is because a judgment must be based on the pleadings, the materials brought on the record or brought to the attention of the Court, the cases cited, and the arguments urged by Advocates for the parties and the questions put from the Bench and answered from the Bar. Judicial research *after* the trial has concluded and *before* the judgment is delivered is most unusual. But if it takes place, and questions of fact or law arise which the Court thinks require further consideration, the matter must be set down for further hearing. However, judicial research, extending over two years, after the majority judgments have been delivered, is wholly impermissible because material on which the judgment is based has not been the subject of scrutiny by the Bench and the Bar. This defect renders a judgment valueless. This is because, first, the judge's qualification for carrying on the research may be open to doubt. Secondly, he may have left out relevant material or misinterpreted the material collected; his reasoning may be faulty or self-contradictory—none of these things can be pointed out to him by Advocates at the Bar, or by his colleagues on the Bench. If authority were wanted for our submission, it is not lacking.

This course impermissible in a judgment

Bhagwati J.'s judgment rendered valueless because not subjected to the scrutiny of the Bar and the Bench — Authorities for this submission

London Hospital v. *I.R.C. per* Brightman J.

In *London Hospital* v. *I.R.C.*[74] Brightman J. said:

"In conclusion I think it is desirable that I should make a brief reference to *Baldry* v. *Feintuck*.[75] Counsel for the Medical College sought to rely on that case for the proposition that a Students' Union is *prima facie* charitable. It is true that the motion proceeded on the footing that the Students' Union in that case was a charity. *The contrary, however, was never argued.* The point went by concession. I accepted the concession because I thought it correct. *But a case which proceeds on the basis of a proposition which is not tested by argument is not of much value as an authority for the validity of that proposition.* *Baldry* v. *Feintuck* has not, therefore, assisted me in reaching my conclusion in the present case."[76] (italics supplied)

Cordell v. *Second Clanfield Properties per* Megarry J.

An even more striking and apt authority is to be found in *Cordell* v. *Second Clanfield Properties*[77] where Megarry J. pointed out the difference between a text book and a judgment delivered after argument:

"I would add one comment, in amplification of certain observations that I made when during the argument Counsel cited a passage from the third edition of *Megarry and Wade's Real Property.* It seems to me that words in a book written or subscribed to by an author who is or becomes a judge have the same value as those written by any other reputable author, neither more, nor less. *The process of authorship is entirely different from that of judicial deci-*

[74] (1976) 1 W.L.R. 613.
[75] (1972) 1 W.L.R. 552.
[76] (1976) 1 W.L.R. at p. 624.
[77] (1969) 2 Ch. 10.

sion. The author, no doubt, has the benefit of a broad and comprehensive survey of his chosen subject as a whole, together with a lengthy period of gestation and intermittent opportunities for reconsideration. But he is exposed to the peril of yielding to pre-conceptions and he lacks the advantage of that impact and sharpening of purpose which the detailed facts of a particular case bring to a judge. Above all, *he has to form his ideas without the aid of the purifying ordeal of skilled argument on the specific facts of a contested case.* Argued law is tough law. . . . I would therefore, give credit to the words of any reputable author in a book or article as expressing tenable and arguable ideas, as fertilisers to them and as a convenient expression of fruits of research in print, often in apt and persuasive language. *But I would do no more than that, and in particular, I would expose those views to the testing and refined process of argument.* To-day, as of old, by good disputing shall the law be well known."[78] (italics supplied)

11.291 In his *Discipline of the Law,* Lord Denning referred to *Rahimtoola* v. *Nizam of Hyderabad*[79] in which he delivered a dissenting judgment in which he said: "My Lords, I acknowledge that in the course of this opinion I have considered some questions and authorities which were not mentioned by counsel". In his book he said that his reward was

"Discipline of the Law" by Lord Denning

"this rebuke by Lord Simonds with which all the others[80] wholeheartedly agreed:

'My Lords, . . . I must not be taken as assenting to (Lord Denning's) views upon a number of questions and authorities in regard to which the House has not had the benefit of arguments of counsel or of the judgment of the courts below.'

Thus rebuked, I may as well make a confession. On many occasions I have done my own researches and given opinion on matters on which the Court had not had the benefit of the arguments of counsel or of the judgment of the Court below. I have done this because counsel vary much in their ability and I do not think that their clients should suffer by any oversight or mistake of counsel. *If it is a new point or new matter which could alter the outcome of the case, then the right course is to inform counsel and put the case in list for further hearing.*[81] But if it is just the elaboration of existing points or matters there is no such need. . . ." (italics supplied)

The research embodied by Lord Denning in his judgment on *questions of law* was rightly disapproved by four Law Lords, although the result of the research was available to the Law Lords *before* the judgments were delivered. But researches of a judge for two years on the *pros* and *cons* of capital punishment, and research in "penology" embodied in a dissenting judgment delivered two years after must stand condemned as depriving the judgment of its essential character as a judgment. The present writer is not competent to judge the qualifications of Bhagwati J. to carry on penological

Submission: Over 2 years' research after the case is concluded deprives the judgment of its essential character

[78] ibid. pp. 16-17.

[79] (1958) A.C. 379. See *Discipline of the Law* at pp. 288-89.

[80] (1958) A.C. p. 404 (Lord Reid); p. 410 (Lord Cohen) and (Lord Somervell).

[81] See the following passage in *Seervai*, Vol. II, 2nd ed. at p. 1406: "In *Miliangos* v. *George Frank (Textiles) Ltd.* (1975) 2 W.L.R. 555 Lord Denning M.R. observed that 'A case is not decided *per incuriam* because Counsel have not cited all the relevant authorities or referred to this or that rule of Court, or statutory provision. The court does its own researches itself and consults authorities; and these may never receive mention in the judgment.' (ibid. p. 565) Notwithstanding the great authority of Lord Denning, it is submitted that this proposition is too wide, and is not correct. For the researches of the court may merely support decisions cited on either side, or cited by one side if the opposite side was unrepresented, in which case the research does no harm, and the judgment is not *per incuriam.* If however, the research discloses a case not cited by the parties which would displace the case of one of the parties, natural justice requires that the matter be set down for further argument, in which case, the question of '*per incuriam*' does not arise."

research, or the value of that research embodied in the judgment, which, in reality, is a research paper on the *pros* and *cons* of capital punishment. But as pointed out by Megarry J. in *Cordell's Case*, a research paper is misplaced on the Bench, and more so after the arguments are concluded. It is submitted that the judgment lacks the value and authority which would otherwise belong to a dissenting judgment, since the research has not been subjected to "the purifying ordeal of skilled argument."

Second objection to dissenting judgment — the judge should have disqualified himself

11.292 There is another and not less fundamental objection to the judgment which is based on what Bhagwati J. said in its opening paragraph. After quoting from Bernard Shaw's *Caesar and Cleopatra*, he said:

> "I share this sentiment because *I regard men as an embodiment of divinity and I am therefore morally against death penalty.* But my dissent is based not upon any ground of morality or ethics but is founded on constitutional issues, for as I shall presently show, death penalty does not serve any social purpose or advance any constitutional value and is totally arbitrary and unreasonable so as to be violative of Arts. 14, 19, 21 of the Constitution."[82] (italics supplied)

the more so because of his views on "judicial craftsmanship"

It is submitted that a judge who holds the view that man is an embodiment of divinity and that it is morally wrong to take the life of a man even by way of punishment, or, in other words, who holds the death penalty unholy and immoral cannot dispassionately decide the question of that penalty's validity. It is submitted that he ought to have disqualified himself from sitting on the Bench which heard the matter. This is all the more so because of his declared views on "judicial craftsmanship",[83] (views which the present writer does not share). In *Union* v. *Sankalchand*[84] Bhagwati J. observed:

> ". . . some judges may, on account of threat of transfer be induced albeit, not consciously or deliberately to do that which pleases the executive to avert such injury and *if they are competent and skilled in judicial craftsmanship it would not be difficult for them to find arguments to justify their action in falling in line with the wishes of the executive because reason is a ready-enough advocate for the decision one consciously or unconsciously desires to reach.*"[85] (italics supplied)

Bhagwati J.'s research deprived of any value because of his strong moral objection to the death penalty

The words we have italicised directly apply to a judge who believes that the death sentence is both unholy and immoral. It is submitted further that even the research of Bhagwati J. is robbed of whatever value it may have possessed because of the firm moral conviction with which he approached the subject, the more so because it is his theory that "reason is a ready-enough advocate for the decision one consciously or unconsciously desires to reach". In the result, except for his views on Art. 14, it is not proposed to discuss the dissenting judgment of Bhagwati J. any further, either because it is not a "judgment" as that word is understood in our country, or because in any event what is stated therein has no value as a judgment since it is based on research which has not been submitted to the searching scrutiny of the Bar and the Bench.

Sarkaria J. *assumption arguendo*

11.293 For some unexplained reason, although Sarkaria J. for the majority held decisively that s. 302 did not have to stand the test of

---

[82] ('82) A.SC. at p. 1330.
[83] *Union* v. *Sankalchand* ('77) A.SC. 2328 at p. 2360.
[84] ibid.
[85] ibid.

Art. 19 (1), nevertheless, he proceeded to consider the position "assuming *arguendo* that the provisions of the Penal Code, particularly those providing death penalty as an alternative punishment for murder" had to stand the test of Art. 19 (1).[86] It is submitted that the Supreme Court as the final Court ought not to detract from its authoritative statement of the law by *assuming* something to be true for the sake of argument after holding that very thing to be untrue. However, we must take the judgment as we find it, and a brief account must be given of the result of *assuming* for the sake of argument that s. 302 I.P.C. had to stand the test of Art. 19 (1). Sarkaria J. considered, first, the question of the burden of proof. He said that "no hard and fast rule of universal application in all cases can be deduced from the decisions".[87] Even if the burden was on the State to show that the restrictions were reasonable and in the public interest, then the State had discharged that burden by producing the Report of the Law Commission, 1967, and the judgment of the Supreme Court in *Jagmohan Singh's Case*.

that Art. 19(1) applies to s. 302 I.P.C.

The burden of proof

11.294 Having decided the question of burden of proof, Sarkaria J. referred to two opposite schools of thought, namely, those who favoured the abolition of capital punishment ("Abolitionists") and those who favoured retaining capital punishment ("Retentionists".) Sarkaria J. set out the arguments of the Abolitionists which had substantially been adopted by the petitioners, namely,

Arguments of Abolitionists set out

"(*a*) The death penalty is irreversible. Decided upon according to fallible processes of law by fallible human beings it can be — and actually has been — inflicted upon people innocent of any crime;

(*b*) There is no convincing evidence to show that death penalty serves any penological purpose: (i) its deterrent effect remains unproven. It has not been shown that incidence of murder has increased in countries where death penalty has been abolished after its abolition; (ii) retribution in the sense of vengeance is no longer an acceptable end of punishment; (iii) on the contrary, reformation of the criminal and his rehabilitation is the primary purpose of punishment. Imposition of death penalty nullifies that purpose;

(*c*) Execution by whatever means and for whatever offences is a cruel inhuman and degrading punishment."[88]

Leaving (a) above to be dealt with in considering the procedural aspect of the problem, Sarkaria J. dealt with question (b) above which is dealt with in the next paragraph.

11.295 Does the death penalty serve any penological purpose? To answer this question, Sarkaria J. referred to the decisions of Courts where the deterrent value of the death penalty had been recognized.[89] The decisions were *Paras Ram* v. *Punjab* (unreported), *Jagmohan's Case*[90], *Ediga Anamma* v. *A.P.*[91], *Shiv Mohan Singh* v. *State* (*Delhi Administration*)[92] and *Charles Sobhraj* v. *Supdt., Central Jail.*[93] It should be noted that except for *Jagmohan's Case,* to which Krishna Iyer J. was not a party, the judgments in all the other cases were delivered by Krishna Iyer J. However, before considering this aspect

Does the death penalty serve any penological purpose?

Decisions of Courts which stressed the deterrent effect of death penalty referred to

[86] ('80) A.SC. at p. 916.
[87] See ('80) A.SC. at pp. 916-17 where the decisions are referred to.
[88] ('80) A.SC. *supra* at p. 918. [89] ibid. pp. 918-19.
[90] (1973) 2 S.C.R. 541, ('73) A.SC. 947.
[91] (1974) 3 S.C.R. 329, ('74) A.SC. 799.
[92] (1977) 3 S.C.R. 172, ('77) A.SC. 949.
[93] (1979) 1 S.C.R. 512, ('78) A.SC. 1514.

we may complete Sarkaria J.'s reference to cases of the U.S. Supreme Court namely, *Trop* v. *Dulles*,[94] the judgment of Stewart J. in *Furman* v. *Georgia* and the judgment of Stewart J. speaking for the majority in *Gregg* v. *Georgia*.[95]

Necessary to contrast Krishna Iyer J.'s judgment in *Paras Ram's Case* with his judgment in *Kunju Kunju Case*

11.296 The reference to Supreme Court decisions is skilful because in four of these Krishna Iyer J. delivered the judgment. It is necessary to quote the language of Krishna Iyer J. in the unreported decision in *Paras Ram's Case* and contrast it with his language in the *Kunju Kunju Case* which Krishna Iyer J. would have described as representing Sacred and Profane love. The facts of the case were these: Paras Ram, who was a fanatical devotee of the Devi used to hold *Satsangs* (spiritual meetings) at which *bhajans* (sacred songs) were sung in praise of the goddess. Paras Ram ceremoniously beheaded his four year old boy at the crescendo of the morning *bhajan*. He was tried, convicted and sentenced to death for murder. The sentence was confirmed by the High Court. In a special leave petition it was contended for Paras Ram that the very monstrosity of his crime provided proof of his insanity sufficient to bring it within s. 84, I.P.C. Krishna Iyer J. summarily dismissed the petition with these words:

Murder by a father of his 4 year old boy to propitiate a goddess: Krishna Iyer J.'s view: condign punishment of death necessary

"The poignantly pathological grip of macabre superstitions on some crude Indian minds in the shape of desire to do human and animal sacrifice, in defiance of the scientific ethos of our cultural heritage and the scientific impact of our technological century, shows up in *crimes of primitive horror* such as the one we are dealing with now, where a *blood-curdling butchery* of one's own beloved son was perpetrated, aided by other 'pious' criminals, to propitiate some blood-thirsty deity. Secular India, speaking through the Court, must administer shock therapy to such anti-social 'piety', *when the manifestation is in terms of inhuman and criminal violence. When the disease is social, deterrence through court sentence must, perforce, operate* through the individual culprit coming up before court. Social justice has many facets and Judges have a sensitive, secular and civilising role in suppressing grievous injustice to humanist values by inflicting condign punishment on dangerous deviants. (emphasis added)."[96]

The accused in *Kunju Kunju Case* kills his wife, and 2 children to marry his mistress

Contrast this language with that which he used in the *Kunju Kunju Case*. The facts of the case are set out in para 11.287 but are repeated here for convenience of the reader. The accused who had a young wife aged 28 and two children had illicit intimacy with a young woman. She tried to dissuade him from pursuing his suit lest it should break up his home. He wrote to her that he had decided to kill his wife and children and live happily with her. In the secrecy of the night he cut to death his innocent wife and his innocent children. If the killing of a boy of 4 years at the height of devotional song to a goddess deserved, as it did, the description of *crime of primitive horror* where a blood-curdling *butchery of one's own beloved* son was perpetrated . . . to propitiate a blood-thirsty deity, called forth condemnation in the strongest language from Krishna Iyer J. and led him to uphold the "condign punishment" of death by dismissing the Special Leave Petition summarily, what language was called for from Krishna Iyer J. and what "condign punishment" (of death) was to be upheld when a father killed not *one child* of his in a fit of religious frenzy, but killed his wife and his *two children* in cold blood after careful preparation in order to

[94] (1958) 356 U.S. 86; 2 L.ed. 2d. 630.
[95] (1976) 428 U.S. 153; 49 L.ed. 2d. 859.
[96] ('80) A.SC. at pp. 918-19.

bring his affair with his mistress to a successful end? Surely not the reference to "the eternal triangle" nor the amazing reasoning of "the randy rapist" passage set out in para 11.288 above. His judgment in the *Kunju Kunju Case* shows what happens to a judge when he allows his personal views on the death penalty to obscure his vision and his duty as a judge. Sen J. said the true word when he described the opinion of Krishna Iyer J. that the "imposition of a death sentence outside the categories indicated would be constitutionally invalid" as "merely *an expression of his personal view*".[97] And he said equally truly that he failed to understand what was meant by "the eternal triangle" as a mitigating circumstance, adding "The accused who acted as a monster, did not spare his innocent minor children in order to get rid of his wife and issues through her. If the death sentence is not to be awarded in a case like this I do not see the type of offence which calls for a death sentence".[98]

A criticism of Krishna Iyer J.'s judgment in the *Kunju Kunju Case*

11.297 Sarkaria J. then referred to the views of some jurists and scholars of note, namely, Sir James Fitzjames Stephen[99] who emphasized the deterrent effect of death penalty; to Baccaria, who was against the death penalty except to prevent revolution and if an execution was the only way to deter others from committing crimes;[1] to Therston Sellin, the penologist[2] who said that in the last analysis, the only utilitarian argument that has to be given attention to is the one that defends capital punishment as being a uniquely powerful means of protecting the community; to Sheldon L. Messinger and Egon Bittner, who pointed out the shortcomings of Sellin's thesis.[3] Sarkaria J. said that these scholars stressed another purpose of capital punishment, namely, the incapacitation of the offender, which, in fact, was another aspect of its deterrent effect.[4] After referring to the studies relating to rehabilitation of prisoners from the Encyclopaedia Britannica Year Book 1978, pp. 593-94, and after referring to other eminent writers on capital punishment, Sarkaria J. set out the grounds given by the Law Commission Report for holding that the death sentence had a deterrent effect as a punishment.[5] After referring to the British Royal Commission Report (1949-53), Sarkaria J. observed: "We may add that whether or not death penalty in actual practice acts as a deterrent, cannot be statistically proved either way." Further, Sarkaria J. added that retribution in the sense of reprobation for the worst of crimes, namely, murder, had not been altogether outmoded and distinguished sociologists, jurists and judges had supported it. After referring to the observations of Lord Denning, Sarkaria J. referred to the view expressed by Stewart J. in *Furman's Case*. Stewart J. said, *inter alia*, that "When people begin to believe that organized society is unwilling or unable to impose upon criminal offenders the punishment they 'deserve', then there are sown the seeds of anarchy, of self-help, vigilante justice and lynch law".[6] The present writer would like to give a recent example of "self-help" of which Stewart J. spoke. In West Germany, a girl 4 or 5 years old

Sarkaria J.'s reference to the views of jurists and scholars on the deterrent effect of the death penalty

The Report of the Law Commission of India on such deterrent effect

The views of Stewart J. in *Furman's Case*

A recent example from West Germany of "self-help"

[97] *Rajendra Prasad's Case* ('79) A.SC. at p. 946.
[98] ibid. at pp. 962-63.
[99] ('80) A.SC. pp. 919-20.
[1] ibid. p. 920.
[2] ibid.
[3] ibid. pp. 920-21.
[4] ibid. p. 921.
[5] ibid. pp. 922-23.
[6] ibid. p. 923.

was brutally raped and murdered by the accused. At his trial, the girl's mother came to court and shot him dead. It was reported that a large volume of opinion supported her action. Sarkaria J. added that retribution and deterrence were not two divergent ends of capital punishment, but were convergent goals which ultimately merged into one, as was described by the Law Commission of India in its Report.[7] After referring to some other eminent writers, Sarkaria J. referred to the cruel double murder in San Francisco in which the jury of 7 men and 5 women rejected the charge of first degree murder. Public protest against the decision spontaneously manifested itself "in a burst of flame and fury". After further discussion on the same lines, Sarkaria J. referred to what happened after the *Furman Case* as Sen J. had done in *Rajendra Prasad's Case.*[8] After a long survey of varying opinion, Sarkaria J. summed up the position by saying that the question whether or not death penalty served any penological purpose was a difficult, complex and intractable issue. It had evoked strong, divergent views. For testing the constitutionality of the provision as to death penalty in s. 302, on the ground of reasonableness in the light of Arts. 19 and 21, it was not necessary to express any categorical opinion, one way or the other. The very fact that persons of reason, learning and light were deeply divided in their opinion on this issue was a ground, among others, for rejecting the argument that the retention of death penalty was totally devoid of reason and purpose.

An example from San Francisco

Sarkaria J.'s summing up: That persons of reason, learning and light were deeply divided, a ground for rejecting the argument against the retention of the death penalty

S. 302 I.P.C. does not violate Art. 19

11.298 Sarkaria J. concluded this part of the case by saying:

". . . it is not possible to hold that the provision of death penalty as an alternative punishment for murder, in s. 302, is unreasonable and not in the public interest. We would therefore, conclude that the impugned provision in s. 302 violates neither the letter nor the ethos of Art. 19."[9]

Art. 21 as expanded by *Maneka Gandhi's Case* applied

11.299 Turning to the question whether the death penalty violated Art. 21, Sarkaria J. said that Art. 21 expanded in accordance with *Maneka Gandhi's Case* would read:

"No person shall be deprived of his life or personal liberty except according to a fair, just and reasonable procedure established by a valid law." Or put positively, "A person may be deprived of his life or personal liberty in accordance with a fair, just and reasonable procedure established by law."

There are indications in our Constitution that its makers were fully aware of the existence of the death penalty for murder and other offences under the Indian Penal Code. Thus entries 1 and 2, List III, Sch. VII, specifically refer to the Indian Penal Code and the Code of Criminal Procedure; under Art. 72(1) (*c*) the President's power of pardon, etc., extends to "all cases where the sentence is a sentence of death", and under Art. 161 the Governor has the like power; Art. 134 gives a right of appeal to a person sentenced to death by the High Court after his acquittal by the trial court.[10] Sarkaria J. added:

The death penalty does not violate Art. 21 or the basic structure

"Under the successive Criminal Procedure Codes which have been in force for about 100 years, a sentence of death is to be carried out by hanging. In view of the aforesaid constitutional postulates, by no stretch of imagination can it be said that death penalty under s. 302, Penal Code, either *per se* or because of the execution by hanging, constitutes an unreasonable, cruel or unusual punishment. By reason of the same constitutional postulates, it cannot

---

7 ibid. pp. 923-4.
8 See para 11.284 above.
9 ibid. p. 929.
10 ibid. p. 930.

be said that the framers of the Constitution considered death sentence for murder or the prescribed traditional mode of its execution as a degrading punishment which would defile 'the dignity of the individual' within the contemplation of the Preamble to the Constitution. On parity of reasoning, it cannot be said that death penalty for the offence of murder violates the basic structure of the Constitution."[11]

of our Constitution

11.300 Sarkaria J. then considered the contention based on the European Convention of Human Rights and the International Covenant on Civil and Political Rights which provide, *inter alia*, as follows:

Conventions on Human Rights considered

"*Art. 6* (1) Every human being has the inherent right to life. This right shall be protected by law. No one shall be arbitrarily deprived of his life.

(2) In countries which have not abolished the death penalty, sentence of death may be imposed only for the most serious crimes in accordance with the law in force at the time of the commission of the crime . . ." Sarkaria J. added: "It will be seen that [Art. 6 (1) and (2)] do not abolish or prohibit the imposition of death penalty. . . . All that they require is that, firstly, death penalty shall not be arbitrarily inflicted; secondly, it shall be imposed only for most serious crimes in accordance with a law, which shall not be an *ex post facto* legislation. Thus the requirements of these clauses are substantially the same as the guarantees or prohibitions contained in Arts. 20 and 21 . . . India's commitment therefore does not go beyond what is provided in the Constitution and the I.P.C. and the Cr.P.C. The Penal Code prescribes death penalty as an alternative punishment only for heinous crimes which are not more than seven in number.[12] Section 354(3) of the Cr.P.C. . . . has further restricted the area of death penalty. India's penal laws, including the impugned provisions and their application, are thus entirely in accord with its international commitment."[13]

Those Conventions not violated by our Penal Laws

Sarkaria J. said "For all the foregoing reasons, we would answer the first main question in the negative".[13]

11.301 Sarkaria J. turned to Question No. II, namely, "Are the provisions of s. 354(3) Cr.P.C. unconstitutional". Those provisions had been challenged on the following grounds:

Challenge to the provisions of s. 354(3) Cr.P.C. considered

"(i) (*a*) Section 354(3) of the Cr.P.C. delegates to the Court the duty to legislate in the field of 'special reasons' for choosing between life and death, and (*b*) permits imposition of death penalty in an arbitrary and whimsical manner inasmuch as it does not lay down any rational principles or criteria for invoking this extreme sanction. [Reliance had been placed on *Furman* v. *Georgia* (Ibid.)]

(ii) If Section 354(3) is to be saved from the vice of unconstitutionality, the Court should so interpret it and define its scope that the imposition of death penalty comes to be restricted *only* to those types of grave murders and capital offences which imperil the very existence and security of the State. (Reliance for this argument has been placed on *Rajendra Prasad's Case*: *ibid.*")[14]

Sarkaria J. narrated the history of the changes in the Cr.P.C. as a result of which from the death sentence being the rule and imprisonment for life being the exception, imprisonment for life became the rule, and death sentence the exception to be awarded for "special reasons" (see para 11.275 above). Sarkaria J. further called attention to s. 235(2) Cr.P.C. of 1973,[15] to ss. 432 and 433 Cr.P.C. of 1973,[16] to the newly added s. 433-A Cr.P.C. whereby, with effect from Dec. 18, 1978 the power of commutation of a sentence for life imprisonment for an offence for which death was a punishment, could

Various sections of the Cr.P.C. referred to and considered

[11] ibid.
[12] See ibid. p. 906 where the seven offences are set out.
[13] ibid. p. 931. [14] ibid.
[15] ibid. p. 933 where the section is set out.
[16] ibid. p. 933 where the provisions of the sections are summarized.

not be exercised in order to release a person unless he had served at least 14 years of imprisonment. Sarkaria J. then referred to a group of sections[17] in which the legislature had provided valuable safeguards for the life and liberty of the subject in cases of capital sentences. These sentences had to be scrutinized with utmost caution and care by superior courts. Sarkaria J. then proceeded to consider the effect which the legislative changes had on the authority and efficacy of the propositions laid down in *Jagmohan's Case* and he summed up the propositions there laid down.[18] Put briefly, the policy of the I.P.C. and the Cr.P.C. was to define an offence with precision, prescribe only the maximum penalty and allow judges a wide discretion in fixing the degree of punishment. Secondly, no exhaustive enumeration of mitigating circumstances which would go to determine the sentence was possible because of the infinite variety of the facts of different cases. Thirdly, the impossibility of laying down standards was at the very heart of the criminal law as administered in India, which invested judges with wide discretionary power in awarding punishment. Fourthly, the view of the U.S. Supreme Court in the *Furman Case* could not be adopted in our country where the conditions were very different. Lastly, the discretion of the judge was liable to be corrected by the Court of Appeal. In view of the above, it was not possible to say that s. 302 I.P.C. violated Art. 14 because that section conferred on judges an unguided and uncontrolled discretion in awarding capital punishment or imprisonment for life. The accused could produce relevant evidence in mitigation and what remained for the judge was to decide on guilt and punishment as provided by s. 306(2) and 309(2) Cr.P.C. These sections were part of the procedure established by law and no reasons had been urged to show that those provisions were invalid. After pointing out that some of the propositions in *Jagmohan's Case* required alteration as a result of legislative changes, Sarkaria J. observed that death sentence was to be awarded only if the Court found murder of exceptionally depraved and heinous character. The legislative changes reinforced the reasons given in *Jagmohan's Case* that the impugned provisions of the Penal Code and Cr.P.C. do not offend against Arts. 14 and 21.

The changes made in the Cr.P.C. reinforce the conclusions of Jagmohan's Case

The impugned provisions of the I.P.C. and Cr. P.C. do not offend against Arts. 14 and 19

The laying down of guidelines well nigh impossible

11.302 Sarkaria J. then considered whether guide lines could be laid down for awarding the sentence of death for murder and observed that as pointed out in *Jagmohan's Case*, standardisation in the sense of laying down standards was well nigh impossible. Standardisation of the sentencing process which left little room for judicial discretion to take into account of variations of culpability within a "single-offence category" ceased to be judicial. It tended to sacrifice justice at the altar of blind uniformity. Besides, the conferring of discretion in matters of sentence was a matter for the legislature and the court could not do what Parliament in its wisdom did not do. After a lengthy discussion of *Gregg* v. *Georgia* and the companion cases which followed the decision in *Furman's Case*, Sarkaria J. observed:

The effect of Gregg v. Georgia

[17] Sections 366 to 370 of the present Cr.P.C. (corresponding to ss. 374 to 376 of the repealed Code).

[18] The summary is too long to quote in the text. However, it will be found in ('80) A.SC. at pp. 934-35 where the propositions are set out.

"Critically examined, it is clear that the decisions in *Gregg* v. *Georgia* and its companion cases demonstrate the truth of what we have said earlier, that it is neither practicable nor desirable to imprison the sentencing discretion of a judge or jury in the straight-jacket of exhaustive and rigid standards. Nevertheless, these decisions do show that it is not impossible to lay down broad guidelines as distinguished from ironcased standards, which will minimise the risk of arbitrary imposition of death penalty for murder and some other offences under the Penal Code."[19]

is that broad guidelines, not iron clad standards can be laid down

As the majority decision in *Rajendra Prasad's Case* was the occasion for constituting a larger Bench to consider the matter in the present case, Sarkaria J. observed:

"In *Rajendra Prasad*, the majority said: 'It is constitutionally permissible to swing a criminal out of corporal existence only if the security of State and society, public order and the interests of the general public compel that course as provided in Article 19(2) to (6).' Our objection is only to the word 'only'. While it may be conceded that a murder which directly threatens, or has an extreme potentiality to harm or endanger the security of State and society, public order and the interests of the general public, may provide 'special reasons' to justify the imposition of the extreme penalty on the person convicted of such a heinous murder, it is not possible to agree that imposition of death penalty on murderers who do not fall within this narrow category is constitutionally impermissible. We have discussed and held above that the impugned provisions in Section 302, Penal Code, being reasonable and in the general public interest, do not offend Article 19, or its 'ethos'; nor do they in any manner violate Articles 21 and 14. All the reasons given by us for upholding the validity of Sec. 302, Penal Code, fully apply to the case of Section 354(3), Code of Criminal Procedure, also. The same criticism applies to the view taken in *Bishnu Deo Shaw* v. *W.B.* (1979) 3 S.C.C. 714, which follows the dictum in *Rajendra Prasad* (ibid.)."[20]

Rajendra Prasad's Case: the majority view overruled

11.303 In the result, the Court rejected the contention that the provisions in s. 302 I.P.C. and s. 354(3) Cr.P.C. were unconstitutional. It is submitted that the majority decision in *Bachan Singh's Case* is clearly right.

11.303A As to the dissenting judgment of Bhagwati J., it is submitted that his finding that s. 302 I.P.C. in so far as it provides for the death penalty violated Art. 14 is a *reductio ad absurdum* of his theory of Art. 14 (Equality). It is true that the death penalty is in a class by itself; but so is the crime of murder. It is equally true that once the death sentence is carried out it cannot be reversed; but the result of murder is equally irreversible. It is therefore not surprising that for a crime which is in a class by itself, a punishment which is in a class by itself should be prescribed by s. 302 I.P.C., not to be awarded in all cases but where there are special reasons for awarding that punishment. If the fact that judges may differ in the exercise of their discretion leads to a violation of equality, then contrary to the learned judge's intention, the objection can be met by making the death penalty mandatory, thus eliminating judicial discretion. This was the unforseen, or at any rate, the unintended, consequence of *Furman's Case*. For, as Sen J. pointed out (as did Sarkaria J.), following on *Furman's Case* certain States, including North Carolina, Louisiana and Oklahoma, eliminated all discretion by making the death penalty mandatory for specified offences and the U.S. Supreme Court upheld such mandatory death sentence in *Woodson* v. *North Carolina* and *Roberts* v. *Louisiana* [see para 11.286 above and ('79) A.SC. at p. 957]. But there is a more fundamental objection to Bhagwati J.'s application of Art. 14 when

Bhagwati J.'s dissenting judgment and Art. 14—a *reductio ad absurdum* of his theory of equality

A mandatory death sentence would meet Bhagwati J.'s objection under Art. 14

---

[19] ibid. p. 942.

[20] ibid. pp. 943-44.

Bhagwati J.'s judgment would invalidate all punishments under I.P.C., and would require the winding up of all courts since they enjoy wide discretionary power

he invalidated s. 302 for violating Art. 14. If different judges exercise discretion differently in awarding punishment for the same or similar offence, then all the punishments prescribed by the Penal Code must be void as we pointed out in para 11.9 above. When that para was written, Bhagwati J.'s dissenting judgment had not been delivered. His judgment now furnishes an actual *reductio ad absurdum* of his theory of equality. But it goes further; his theory must involve the winding up of all courts, for wide discretionary powers are given to judges who, *ex hypothesi,* exercise discretion differently in the same or similar matters. Such absurd conclusions must lead any judge to retrace his steps, and reflect that the fault is not with the total volume of our laws but with his own theory of equality.

The significance of the right of self defence overlooked in the discussion of capital punishment

11.304 There is one aspect of the death sentence which requires further consideration. It has been said by Krishna Iyer J., quoting Mahatma Gandhi, that "God Alone Can Take Life, Because He Alone Gives It" (see para 11.286 above), the implication being that a judge should not be a party to taking life by inflicting the sentence of death. First, the premiss will not support the conclusion, because in cases of murder it is not God but man who has taken a life which he cannot give. Secondly, a very important provision of civil and criminal law, founded in the nature of man and his instinct of self-preservation, is being overlooked—the right of self-defence. This right in civil and criminal law has been fully discussed in paras 31 to 35 of Appendix IV and need not be repeated here. It is enough to say that our laws and the laws of several civilized countries, recognize this right. Normally, it is the duty of the State to protect the life of its people. But where a criminal suddenly threatens to kill a person, the law recognizes his right to kill his assailant in self-defence. So, the law does not look upon the taking of life in self-defence either as unnatural or morally wrong. A successful murder takes place because it is committed against a person who has no opportunity to defend himself, or is too weak to do so. It is difficult to appreciate either the logic or the morality of allowing a man to take the life of his assailant in self-defence while denying to a judge the power under stringent conditions to punish the successful assailant—who brutally or sadistically kills his helpless victim —by awarding the death penalty.

Art. 21 and contempt of court

11.305 Contempt of court cases have raised the question whether they violate Art. 21 and whether the existing practice and procedure of the High Courts can be treated as procedure established by law. In *Sheoraj* v. *A.P. Batra*[21] it was held that r. 12, Ch. 9, Rules of Court, 1951, which allowed contempt to be proved by affidavit was based on the practice in India, in England and in America, and that it was a procedure established by law; and in holding a person guilty of contempt on the basis of an affidavit, Art. 21 was not violated. In *Bombay* v. *Mr. P.*[22] it was held that the procedure followed by the High Court in contempt of court cases fell within the expression "procedure established by law" and even if such proceedings were required to be by an enacted law, cl. 38 of the Letters Patent of the Bombay High Court enabled those proceedings to be

[21] ('55) A.A. 638.

[22] ('59) A.B. 182, 60 Bom.L.R. 873.

taken and the Letters Patent were law. This decision was followed in *In the matter of Basanta Chandra Ghosh.*[23]

Action under *ultra vires* law violates Art. 21

11.306 Any action would be without the authority of law if the law was *ultra vires* on the ground of lack of legislative competence or violation of constitutional limitations. Thus, in *Hamdard Dawakhana (Wakf) Lal Kuan* v. *Union*[24] the Supreme Court held that s. 3 (*d*) and s. 8, Drugs and Magic Remedies (Objectionable Advertisements) Act, 1954, imposed unreasonable restrictions on the petitioners' fundamental rights and were therefore void. Consequently, any action taken under them was without the authority of law and contravened Art. 21. Again, on its being held that ss. 2 (1) (*a*), 3, 4, 4A and 15, Madras Maintenance of Public Order Act, 1949, contravened Arts. 21 and 22, it followed that the sections were *ultra vires* and the detention of the persons after January 26, 1950, was invalid.[25]

Acts and orders held void under Art. 21 as the procedure prescribed by law was not followed

11.307 Authority of law would be lacking where the procedure prescribed by law has not been followed or conditions laid down for the exercise of power have been exceeded, and courts have emphasized the necessity of strictly following the procedure established by law before a person could be deprived of his personal liberty.[26] Accordingly, the following acts or orders have been held to be without the authority of law and void: the recovery of an amount under s. 42, (4A) Co-operative Societies Act, 1912 (as inserted by the U.P. Act III of 1919), which did not fall within the two classes of dues payable to the society and which therefore lacked foundation, the executing authority having no power to recover the amounts as arrears of land revenue;[27] a warrant of arrest issued against a displaced person before the amendment in 1955 of the Displaced Persons (Compensation and Rehabilitation) Act, for the amount due on account of land revenue, when the record showed that it consisted of various items including *taccavi* loans for which no warrant of arrest could be issued under s. 30 of that Act;[28] where a magistrate was not justified in ordering the detention of the prisoner;[29] where the safeguards provided against improper exercise of the power of preventive detention were not observed;[30] where a bail order releasing a prisoner was passed and though the arrested person had furnished the required sureties or was permitted to sign the bail bond, he was not released pursuant to certain departmental

[23] ('60) A.P. 430 (F.B.). [24] (1960) 2 S.C.R. 671, ('60) A.SC. 554.

[25] *Venkataraman* v. *Commr. of Police, Madras* ('51) A.M. 1015 (see the editorial note that the preventive detention order which purported to validate the detention had already been repealed by s. 16 of the Preventive Detention Act, 1950).

[26] *Umraomal* v. *Rajasthan* (1954) Raj. 51, ('55) A.Raj. 6.

[27] *Mohd. Husain Ansari* v. *D.S.C.W. Co-op. Union* ('59) A.A. 733.

[28] *Prithi Singh* v. *Punjab* ('60) A.Punj. 155.

[29] *Lalmani Devi* v. *State* ('57) A.P. 689 (the court said that if people were likely to commit a breach of peace arising from the alleged kidnapping of the petitioner, proceedings should have been taken against them under s. 107, Cr.P.C. instead of detaining the prisoner in jail custody.

[30] *Dr. Ram Krishan Bhardwaj* v. *Delhi* (1953) S.C.R. 708, ('53) A.SC. 318 (the Supreme Court observed that "preventive detention is a serious invasion of personal liberty and such meagre safeguards as the Constitution has provided against the improper exercise of the power must be jealously watched and enforced by the Court").

instructions;[31] where a prosecution before a magistrate was not in accordance with procedure established by law;[32] where the procedure adopted by the District Magistrate was a clear violation of the relevant statute;[33] where the time-limits fixed under ss. 9 (1) and 10 (1), Preventive Detention Act, 1950, as amended in 1951, had not been followed.[34]

11.308 In this section we have not discussed the *Habeas Corpus Case*. In Chapter XII-B of Volume III (2nd ed.) of this book that case was discussed at length. It was preceded by Chapter XII-A entitled "THE JUDICIARY AND THE EMERGENCY" and was followed by Chapter XII-C entitled "THE COURTS AND PREVENTIVE DETENTION". The three Chapters formed an integral whole. Parts of the Chapter on the *Habeas Corpus Case* had to be incorporated in our discussion of preventive detention generally. However, for the convenience of the reader and having regard to the great importance of the *Habeas Corpus Case* in its appropriate setting, the three connected Chapters have been reproduced in Appendices III, IV and V. The reader will find Appendix IV helpful in understanding the nature of preventive detention during a proclamation of emergency when the right to move the court for the enforcement of the rights conferred by Art. 21 had been suspended as it was during the Emergency proclaimed on 25th June, 1975.

SECTION IV

Articles 23-24

Right against exploitation: Arts. 23-24

11.309 Articles 23 and 24 have been put together under the caption "Right against Exploitation". Exploitation, which means the utilization of persons for one's own ends, is opposed to the dignity of the individual, to which the preamble to our Constitution refers. It is opposed to the directives of State Policy, as for example, Art. 39 (*e*) and (*f*), which provide respectively that the State shall secure that the health and strength of workers, men and women and the tender age of children are not abused and that citizens are not forced by economic necessity to enter avocations unsuited to their age or strength; that childhood and youth are protected against exploitation and against moral and material abandonment.[35]

Art. 23(1): traffic in human beings, *begar* etc. prohibited

11.310 Article 23 (1) prohibits traffic in human beings and *begar* and other similar forms of forced labour, and provides that any contravention of Art. 23 (1) shall be an offence punishable in accordance with law. It is believed that no law has been passed under Art. 35 making such contravention punishable by law.

---

[31] *Kulandaivelan* v. *Ayinan* ('56) A.M. 639, (1956) 1 M.L.J. 469 (in substance the court found that the departmental instructions violated Art. 21).

[32] *Maqbool Hussain* v. *Bombay* (1953) S.C.R. 730, ('53) A.SC. 325 (petitions Nos. 171 and 172 of 1951 were accepted and the orders quashed).

[33] *S. P. Jaiswal* v. *State* ('53) A.Punj. 149, 155.

[34] *Parsuram Das* v. *State* (1951) Or. 529, ('52) A.Or. 208; *Umedsingh Narubha* v. *State* ('53) A.Sau. 51 [the person concerned cannot be detained for a day longer than three months unless upon the report of the Advisory Board, which means, unless action is taken on such report before the three month period allowed under Art. 22(4), for otherwise, the detention beyond the period of three months would be illegal].

[35] See also Arts. 42 and 46.

11.311 The word *begar* has not been defined in the Constitution, but it has been defined by Molseworth as "labour or service exacted by a Government or a person in power without giving remuneration for it", and in Wilson's *Glossary* as "forced labour, one pressed to carry burden for individuals or public; under old system when pressed for public service no pay was given".[36] Accordingly, it has been held that the Central Services Maintenance Ordinance, 1960, did not contravene Art. 23(1), because what Art. 23(1) prohibited was "forcing a person to work against his will without payment". Assuming that the effect of the Ordinance was to make persons work against their will, it was not work without payment and Art. 23 was not violated.[37] Again, the U.P. Removal of Social Disabilities Act was held not to contravene Art. 23, because when a person was prohibited from refusing to render service merely on the ground that the person asking for it belonged to a scheduled class, he was not thereby subjected to forced labour similar in form to *begar*.[38] Where the petitioners, who were licensed porters at a railway station, agreed to do two hours' extra work for the railway administration by entering into a contract under which they were to be paid some remuneration for extra labour, and where further they got the benefit of reduced licence fee and were allowed the privilege of free use of the railway premises for earning their livelihood, it was held that they could not be said to be doing *begar* or forced labour. The very idea of a voluntary agreement to do extra work repelled the idea of their doing forced labour.[39] Rule 3.26(*d*), Punjab Civil Service Rules, did not violate Art. 23. It simply provided that the service which the government servant took up voluntarily and on such conditions as may be laid down by the relevant rules would continue even though the government servant had attained the age of superannuation. Such continuation under the said rule was in no sense service which could be equated with *begar* or forced labour under Art. 23, for the government servant was not forced to do any work as he remained under suspension.[40]

begar: definitions

decided cases on *begar*

11.312 In holding the Chamba Force Paid Labour Act void, as violating Art. 23, the court said that conscription for the defence of the country or for the civil service were possible instances of imposition of compulsory service for public purposes under Art. 23. There could not be said to be any imposition of compulsory service for "the purpose of carrying load of Government property" by the Tahsildar or any government servant in normal times.[41] Relying on the above decision, it was held that the words "other similar form of forced labour" should be construed *ejusdem generis* and that the kind of forced labour that was contemplated by Art. 23

Art. 23(2): "compulsory service for public purposes": the scope of the expression

---

[36] These definitions are given in *S. Vasudevan* v. *S. D. Mittal* ('62) A.B. 53, 63 Bom.L.R. 773.

[37] ('62) A.B. at p. 67.

[38] *State* v. *Banwari* ('51) A.A. 615, 617, (1951) A.L.J. 282.

[39] *Dubar Goala* v. *Union* ('52) A.Cal. 496.

[40] *Per* Raghubar Dayal and Mudholkar JJ. in *Pratap Singh* v. *Punjab* ('64) A.SC. 72, 100 [the further observations that even if it were assumed that the retention in service under the rule came within the expression "forced labour", the rule would not be void in view of Art. 23(2) are really unnecessary because under the rule, no labour was exacted at all].

[41] *State* v. *Jorawar* ('53) A.H.P. 18.

had to be something in the nature of either traffic in human beings or *begar*. The conscription for police service or military service under s. 17, Police Act, did not fall under either. In any event, such conscription would fall under Art. 23 (2) as a kind of compulsory service for a public purpose. Accordingly, ss. 17 and 19, Police Act, 1861, were held not to violate Art. 23.[42]

Traffic in women: Art. 23(1)

11.313 As regards traffic in women, it was said in *Shama Bai* v. *U.P.*[43] that a mere perusal of ss. 3 to 10 and 18, Suppression of Immoral Traffic in Women and Girls Act, showed that the acts made punishable under those sections were acts which resulted in traffic in human beings. Therefore quite apart from any question of reasonable restrictions under Art. 19 (1) (*g*), those sections had been validly enacted by Parliament under Art. 23 read with Art. 35. If there was a conflict between a fundamental right guaranteed under Art. 19 and what was prohibited under Art. 23, the prohibition must prevail over the fundamental right guaranteed by Art. 19.[44]

Art. 24: prohibition of child labour in mines etc.

11.314 Article 24 provides that no child below the age of 14 years shall be employed to work in any factory or mine or engaged in any other hazardous employment. This prohibition is in line with the policies embodied in the Directives of State Policy which have been referred to earlier. It may be noted that under Art. 45, the State must endeavour to provide, within the period of 10 years from the commencement of the Constitution, free and compulsory education for all children until they complete the age of 14 years.

---

[42] *Dulal Samanta* v. *Dist. Magistrate, Howrah* ('58) A.Cal. 365, 372.
[43] ('59) A.A. 57, 62.
[44] It is submitted that the judgment could well have gone further and have held that traffic in human beings is not entitled to the protection of Art. 19 at all. See para 10.4.

CHAPTER XII

RIGHT TO FREEDOM OF RELIGION: ARTS. 25 TO 28

12.1 India is a secular but not an anti-religious State, for it guarantees the freedom of conscience and religion. Arts. 27 and 28 emphasize the secular nature of the State, for they secure to every person freedom from the payment of taxes for the promotion of any religion, and freedom from attendance at religious instruction or religious worship in certain educational institutions. Art. 25 guarantees to every person the freedom of conscience and the free profession, practice and propagation of religion; and likewise, Art. 26 guarantees to every religious denomination, or a section of it, a right to manage its own affairs in matters of religion and the right to establish and maintain institutions for religious purposes. The freedom of religion is subject to limitations which will be considered in this chapter.

India is a secular but not an anti-religious State

12.2 As the United States and Australian decisions have been referred to in connection with the freedom of religion, the relevant constitutional provisions are set out here. The First Amendment to the U.S. Constitution provides: "Congress shall make no law respecting an establishment of religion, or prohibiting the free exercise thereof; . . ." And s. 116 of the Commonwealth of Australia Act provides:

Freedom of religion in the U.S. and in Australia

"The Commonwealth shall not make any law for establishing any religion, or for imposing any religious observance, or for prohibiting the free exercise of any religion, and no religious test shall be required as a qualification for any office or public trust under the Commonwealth."

12.3 The decisions of the U.S. Supreme Court were relied on in *Narayanan Nambudripad* v. *Madras*,[1] where s. 76, Madras Hindu Religious and Charitable Endowments Act, 1951, was impugned as violating Arts. 25 and 26 on the ground that under our Constitution there was a wall of separation erected between the Church and the State as there was in the United States. In a careful judgment, which repays study, Venkatarama Aiyer J. repelled that contention and the effect of his judgment may be briefly stated thus: the First Amendment to the U.S. Constitution falls into two parts: the first prohibits the establishment of any religion, and the second guarantees freedom of religion to all persons. In the United States there has been a sharp difference of opinion about the meaning of "establishment". Grammatically, "establishment" might mean either the act of establishing, in which case the meaning of the First Amendment would be that the State should not establish any religion by law; or it may mean religious institutions which had been established, so that the prohibition of the First Amendment would extend to any legislation in respect of a religious institution. According to one view, when Madison and Jefferson said that the U.S. Constitution had erected a wall of separation between the Church and the State, they used the word "establishment" in the first, and not in the second sense. Decided cases show that in the United States it was possible to take the view that since both prohibitions were enacted in one amendment, it could not be that religion was a private purpose under the second part of the amendment and was a public purpose under the first. Our

Decisions on the 1st Amendment to the U.S. Constitution: the meaning of "establishment"

Conflict of judicial opinion in the U.S.

[1] (1955) Mad. 356, ('54) A.M. 385.

Constitution does not contain anything corresponding to the first part of the First Amendment of the U.S. Constitution. It was in the first sense of the word "establishment" that the framers of the Australian Constitution enacted s. 116, which provides in terms that the Commonwealth shall not make any laws "for establishing any religion or for imposing any religious observance."

The position under our Constitution: no wall of separation between Church and State

12.4 The argument that though our Constitution had not expressly forbidden the establishment of a religion, it had done so impliedly, was inconsistent with several express provisions of our Constitution. For though Arts. 27 and 28 contained some specific prohibitions, there are provisions in our Constitution

". . . which are inconsistent with the theory that there should be a wall of separation between Church and State. Art. 16(5) recognizes the validity of laws relating to management of religious and denominational institutions. Art. 28(2) contemplates the State itself managing educational institutions wherein religious instruction is to be imparted. And among the subjects over which both the Union and the State have legislative competence and are set out in List No. III of the 7th Schedule to the Constitution, entry No. 28 is as follows: 'Charities and charitable institutions, charitable and religious endowments and religious institutions.'"[2]

Distinction made between two aspects of religion

Art. 27 prohibits the compulsory raising of taxes in support of a religion but a distinction must be made between religion in its doctrinal and ritual aspects, which is a private purpose, and the administration of property dedicated to the public for religious purposes which is a public purpose. Thus, in *Amulya Chandra* v. *Corporation of Calcutta*[3] the Privy Council held that the acquisition of certain properties by the Corporation of Calcutta for building a *dharmsala* for accommodating pilgrims resorting to a Hindu temple, was for a public purpose.

The position before the Constitution remains enchanged

"The position in law before the Constitution thus was that while the State did not interfere in matters of religion in its doctrinal and ritual aspects treating it as a private purpose, it did exercise control over the administration of properties endowed for religious institutions treating it as a public purpose, if the institutions were themselves dedicated to the public."[4]

And the law as it stood before the Constitution has not undergone a change.

Shirur Mutt Case: Arts. 25-26

12.5 The scope and extent of the rights conferred by Arts. 25 and 26 was considered in the *Shirur Mutt Case*[5] which is the leading case on the subject and has been repeatedly followed. That case arose out of a scheme in connection with the Shirur Mutt of which the petitioner was the head or superior. The Endowment Board called upon him to show cause why a scheme should not be framed for the proper administration of the trust whereupon he challenged the validity of the Madras Religious Endowments Act, 1927, under which the scheme was framed. While the petitions were pending, the Madras Religious and Charitable Endowments Act, 1951, was passed, and the petitions were amended challenging the validity of the new Act as well. The main contention in the appeal was that having regard to the fundamental rights guaranteed by our Constitution in matters of religion and religious institutions belonging to a particular religious denomination, the law regulating the framing of a scheme was *ultra vires*

---

2 (1955) Mad. *supra* at p. 370. 3 ('22) A.P.C. 333.
4 (1955) Mad. *supra* at p. 382.
5 *Commr. Hindu Religious Endowments, Madras* v. *Sri Lakshmindra Thirtha Swamiar of Sri Shirur Mutt* (1954) S.C.R. 1005, ('54) A.SC. 282.

and void. The Supreme Court held that as in the case of a *mahant* and a *shebait*, the superior of a *Mutt* had not only duties to discharge in connection with the endowment but had a personal interest of a beneficial character which was sanctioned by custom, an interest which was much larger than that of a *shebait*. Consequently, in these three offices both the element of office and property, of duties and personal interest, were blended together and neither could be detached from the other.[6] Art. 25 secured to every person not only the freedom of religion, belief and conscience, but also the right to express his belief in such outward acts as he thought proper and to propagate or disseminate his ideas for the edification of others.[7] Although the question whether the word "persons" in Art. 25 included a corporation did not arise—for a *mathadhipati* was not a body corporate—the court said that institutions or corporations could not practise or propagate religion; that could be done only by individual persons and it was immaterial whether they propagated their personal views or the tenets for which the institution stood. It was the propagation of the belief that was protected whether it took place in a church or monastery, in a temple or a parlour.[8]

In the offices of a *mahant*, *shebait* and *mathadhipati* the elements of duties and personal interest are inextricably blended

"persons" in Art. 25 do not include institutions or corporations

12.6 As regards Art. 26, the Supreme Court quoted the definition of "denomination" given in the Oxford Dictionary, namely, "a collection of individuals classed together under the same name: a religious sect or body having a common faith and organisation and designated by a distinctive name", and said that each one of the sects and sub-sects of Hindus could certainly be called a religious denomination.[9] Since Art. 26 referred not only to denominations but also to sections thereof, a *Mutt* or spiritual fraternity represented by it was a religious denomination under Art. 26.

The meaning of "denomination" in Art. 26

12.7 The words "the right . . . to manage its own affairs in matters of religion" in Art. 26 (*b*) suggested that there were other affairs of a denomination which were not matters of religion and the question was, where was a line to be drawn? Contrasting Art. 26 (*b*) with Art. 26 (*c*) and (*d*) the Supreme Court said that the contrast showed that no legislature could take away the right of a denomination to manage its own affairs in matters of religion, whereas the right to acquire, own and administer property were not matters of religion and could be regulated by valid laws. "Religion" was not defined in our Constitution and it was not susceptible of any rigid definition.[10] The definition suggested in *Davis* v. *Benson*[11] was

Affairs of a "denomination" which are, and are not "matters of religion"

Religion is not necessarily

[6] ibid. pp. 1018-19. In *Bijayananda* v. *State* (1953) Pat. 1148, ('54) A.P. 266, which was followed in *Ramkrishna Das* v. *Bihar* ('54) A.P. 279, the position of a *mahant* or a *shebait* as also the scope of Art. 25 was discussed, but both these questions have been settled by the decision of Mukherjea J. set out in the text.

[7] ibid. p. 1021.

[8] ibid.

[9] ibid. p. 1022.

[10] In *Narayanan Nambudripad* v. *Madras* (1955) Mad. 356 at p. 377, ('54) A.M. 385, Venkatarama Aiyar J. quoted the following observations of Latham C.J. in *Adelaide Co. of Jehovah's Witnesses Inc.* v. *Commonwealth* (1943) 67 C.L.R. 116, 123, made with reference to s. 116 of the Australian Constitution: "It would be difficult, if not impossible, to devise a definition of religion which would satisfy the adherents of all the many and various religions which exist, or have existed, in the world. There are those who regard religion as consisting principally in a system of beliefs or statement of doctrine. So viewed religion may be either true or false. Others are more inclined to regard religion as prescribing a code of conduct. So viewed a religion may be good or bad. There are others who pay greater attention to religion as involving some prescribed form of ritual or religious observance. Many religious

theistic as was assumed in *Davis* v. *Benson*

neither precise nor adequate. Religion was certainly a matter of faith but it was not necessarily theistic; Buddhism and Jainism, for example, do not involve a belief in any God, or in any Intelligent First Cause. Art. 25 protected not only the freedom of religious opinion but also acts done in pursuance of religious belief as was clear from the expression "practice of religion", used in Art. 25. The Supreme Court adopted the following observations of Latham C.J.[12] as fully applicable to the protection of religion under our Constitution:

Latham C.J.'s observations applicable to the protection of religion under our Constitution

"It is sometimes suggested in discussions of the subject of freedom of religion that, though the civil Government should not interfere with religious *opinions*, it nevertheless may deal as it pleases with any *acts* which are done in pursuance of religious belief without infringing the principle of freedom of religion. It appears to me to be difficult to maintain this distinction as relevant to the interpretation of section 116. The section refers in express terms to the exercise of religion, and therefore it is intended to protect from the operation of any Commonwealth laws acts which are done in the exercise of religion. Thus the section goes far beyond protecting liberty of opinion. It protects also acts done in pursuance of religious belief as part of religion."[13]

Restrictions permitted by Arts. 25-26

12.8 The free exercise of religion under Arts. 25 and 26 is subject to restrictions imposed by the State on grounds of public order, morality and health. Art. 25 (2) (*a*) reserved the right of the State to regulate or restrict any economic, financial, political and other secular activities which may be associated with religious practice and under Art. 25 (2) (*b*) the State could legislate for social welfare and reform even though by so doing it might interfere with religious practices. The "essential part" of a religion was primarily to be ascertained with reference to the doctrine of that religion itself.

The "essential part" of religious doctrines and religious practices

"If the tenets of any religious sect of the Hindus prescribe that offerings of food should be given to the idol at particular hours of the day, that periodical ceremonies should be performed in a certain way at certain periods of the year or that there should be daily recital of sacred texts or oblations to the sacred fire, all these would be regarded as parts of religion and the mere fact that they involve expenditure of money or employment of priests and servants or the use of marketable commodities would not make them secular activities partaking of a commercial or economic character; all of them are religious practices and should be regarded as matters of religion within the meaning of article 26(*b*). What article 25(2)(*a*) contemplates is not regulation by the State of religious practices as such, the freedom of which is guaranteed by the Constitution except when they run counter to public order, health and morality, but regulation of activities which are economic, commercial or political in their character though they are associated with religious practices."[14]

---

conflicts have been concerned with matters of ritual and observance. Section 116 must be regarded as operating in relation to all these aspects of religion, irrespective of varying opinions in the community as to the truth of particular religious doctrines, as to the goodness of conduct prescribed by a particular religion, or as to the property of any particular religious observance."

[11] (1889) 133 U.S. 333, 342, 33 L.ed. 637: ". . . the term 'religion' has reference to one's views of his relation to his Creator and to the obligation they impose of reverence for His Being and character and of obedience to His will. It is often confounded with *cultus* of form or worship of a particular sect, but is distinguishable from the latter."

[12] *Adelaide Co. of Jehovah's Witnesses Inc.* v. *Commonwealth* (1943) 67 C.L.R. 116, 124.

[13] (1954) S.C.R. *supra* at p. 1024.

[14] ibid. p. 1025; fol. in *S. A. P. Srinivasamurthy* v. *Commr., C. & H.R.I. & E.* ('73) A.A.P. 325, 332 (after referring also to other Supreme Court decisions on the subject, *held*, that s. 23, A.P. Charitable and Hindu Religious Institutions and Endowments Act, 1966, did not violate Arts. 25 and 26).

After referring to the difficulties experienced in the United States and in Australia in distinguishing between religious beliefs and practices on the one hand and economic, commercial or political activities associated with religion on the other,[15] the Supreme Court said that whereas in the United States and Australia, the freedom of religion was declared in absolute terms and the courts had to evolve exceptions to that freedom, Arts. 25 and 26 embodied the limits of that freedom in the Constitution itself. Under Art. 26(b), a religious denomination or organisation enjoyed complete autonomy in deciding what rites and ceremonies were essential according to the tenets of the religion and "no outside authority had any jurisdiction to interfere with their decision in such matters".[16] The scale of expenses incurred in connection with religious observance would be a matter of administration of the denomination's property and could be controlled by secular authorities in accordance with a valid law, for it could not be the injunction of any religion to destroy the institution and its endowments by incurring wasteful expenditure on rites and ceremonies. But under Art. 26(*d*),

Essential rites and ceremonies to be determined by the denomination itself: but wasteful expenditure can be controlled

"... it is the fundamental right of a religious denomination or its representative to administer its properties in accordance with law; and law, therefore, must leave the right of administration to the religious denomination itself subject to such restrictions and regulations as it might choose to impose. A law which takes away the right of administration from the hands of a religious denomination altogether and vests it in any other authority would amount to a violation of the right guaranteed under clause (b) of Article 26."[17]

12.9 The court then dealt with the impugned provisions of the Act and refused to strike down some of them merely because they conferred powers which were capable of abuse.[18] However, s. 20(1) was held invalid as it violated Arts. 25 and 26 in so far as it empowered the Commissioner and his subordinate officers to enter any religious institution or place of worship for the purpose of exercising any power conferred or any duty imposed by or under the Act. S. 55 was held invalid as it placed unwarranted restrictions on the *mahant's* power over personal gifts. S. 56 was held invalid as it gave the Commissioner power to require a trustee to appoint a manager for administration of the secular affairs of the institution, and in case of default, to make the appointment himself. As no rigid demarcation could be made between the spiritual duties of the *mahant* and his personal interest in the trust property, the effect of the section was that the Commissioner was at liberty, at his will, to deprive the *mahant* of his right to administer the trust property even if there were no negligence or mal-administration on his part. This crippled the authority of the *mahant* and reduced his position to that of an ordinary priest or a paid servant. The above decision on Arts. 26 and 27 governed the decision in *Mahant Sri Jagannath Ramanuj Das* v. *Orissa*[19] and ss. 38 and 39 of the Orissa Hindu Religious Endowments Act, 1939, were held invalid on the ground that the settling of a scheme of a religious institution by an executive officer without the intervention of a court was an unreasonable restriction upon the right of property of a superior

The provisions of the Madras Religious and Charitable Endowments Act, 1951, which were held invalid

[15] (1954) S.C.R. *supra* at pp. 1025-8.
[16] ibid. pp. 1028-29.
[17] ibid. p. 1029.
[18] *e.g.* s. 20.
[19] (1954) S.C.R. 1046, ('54) A.SC. 400.

of the religious institution, which blended with his office. In *Digyadarsan R. R. Varu* v. *A.P.*[20] the Supreme Court held that there was nothing in ss. 46 and 47 of the A.P. Charitable and Hindu Religious Institutions and Endowments Act, 1966[21] which violated Art. 26. Section 46 stated the grounds for the removal of a *mathadhipati* or a trustee, and provided for their suspension pending an inquiry for such removal. The grounds for removal and the provision for suspension pending an inquiry were reasonable. The petitioner, a *mathadhipati*, was not prohibited or debarred by those sections from professing, practising and propagating his religion, and those sections did not contravene Art. 25(1). As regards s. 47, it differed materially from s. 56 of the repealed Act, (before its amendment), which was struck down by the Supreme Court in the *Shirur Mutt Case*.[22] Section 47 dealt only with the situation where there was a temporary vacancy in the office of the *mathadhipati*, e.g., where he had been suspended pending an inquiry under s. 46. Section 47 did not violate Art. 26(*b*) and (*d*), for it did not empower the Commissioner to interfere with the autonomy of the religious denomination to decide what rites and ceremonies were essential according to the tenets of the religion which the denomination professed or practised.[23] In *Sri K.A.S. Committee* v. *Commr., H.R. & C. Endowments*[24] it was held, following the *Shirur Mutt Case* that the Sri Kanyakaparameswari Anna Satram, founded and managed exclusively by members of Arya Vyasa Community having a special cult, peculiar tenets held, following the *Shirur Mutt Case* that the Sri Kanyakaparameswari, and whose members had made voluntary contributions enabling the association to acquire properties dedicated to the said deity, and vested in the Governing Body of the association, was a religious denominational institution within the meaning of Art. 26. It was held further that ss. 26 and 27 of the A.P. Charitable and Hindu Religious Institutions and Endowments Act, 1966 should be read down to allow the religious denomination to exercise its constitutional rights.[25]

Ratilal's Case: Davar J.'s observations indicate the protection given by Art. 26(*b*)

12.10 In *Ratilal Panachand Gandhi* v. *Bombay*,[26] certain provisions of the Bombay Public Trusts Act, 1950, were challenged as violating Arts. 25 and 26. The case dealt with two connected appeals: in the first, the appellant was a *vahivtdar* or manager of a Jain public temple or *derasar*; in the second, the appellants were the trustees of the Parsi Panchayat. The discussion of Arts. 25 and 26 was on

---

[20] (1970) 1 S.C.R. 103, ('70) A.SC. 181; *Manavedan* v. *State* ('73) A.Ker. 106 (F.B.) [*Varu's Case* and several earlier Supreme Court decisions on Art. 26 were referred to, and applying the principles there laid down, the court held that ss. 10(*a*)(*b*)(*g*) and 27(2)(*b*) did not violate Art. 26(*b*) and (*d*).]

[21] ('70) A.SC. at pp. 184-5 where the sections are set out.

[22] (1954) S.C.R. 1005; ('54) A.SC. 282.

[23] For the administration of the *Math* pending suspension s. 47(2) provided that "The Commissioner shall have due regard to the claims, if any, of the disciples of the *Math*": ('70) A.SC. *supra* at p. 185.

[24] ('79) A.A.P. 121.

[25] *Varu's Case* and earlier decisions of the Supreme Court were relied on, and the Court set aside the impugned order because it amounted to a total extinction of the institution's right to manage its own affairs and properties, and was void. However, another order appointing the Executive Officer, for the better management of the institution, which officer had to carry out all lawful directions issued by the trustees was held not to violate the right of the denomination under Art. 26.

[26] (1954) S.C.R. 1055, ('54) A.SC. 388.

the same lines as in the *Shirur Mutt Case*,[27] but as regards the tenets of the Zoroastrian religion, the Supreme Court cited with approval the observations of Davar J. in *Jamshedji* v. *Soonabai*:[28]

"If this is the belief of the community — and it is proved undoubtedly to be the belief of the Zoroastrian community — a secular Judge is bound to accept that belief — it is not for him to sit in judgment on that belief — he has no right to interfere with the conscience of a donor who makes a gift in favour of what he believes to be the advancement of his religion and for the welfare of his community or of mankind. . . ."[29]

The Supreme Court added that those observations afforded an indication of the measure of protection given by Art. 26(*b*).

Provisions of the Bombay Public Trusts Act, 1950, which were held invalid

12.11 In *Ratilal's Case*, ss. 55 and 56, which embodied the *cy pres* doctrine, were impugned as violative of fundamental rights. It is unfortunate that the Supreme Court's attention was not drawn to the Bombay decisions on *cy pres* which would have shown that those sections did not extend the *cy pres* doctrine. Nor was it pressed upon the court that the very use of the word *cy pres*, both in the marginal note and in the body of s. 56, showed that there had been no departure from the law of *cy pres* as understood in Bombay, which law, it was held, represented the law as laid down in England.[30] But on the assumption that the *cy pres* doctrine had been enlarged, the court held that ss. 55 and 56 were void as regards a religious sect or denomination, observing that a religious sect was a denomination and had the undoubted right to manage its own affairs in matters of religion; and this included the right to spend the trust property or its income for the religious purposes and objects indicated by the founder of the trust or established by usage obtaining in a particular institution. To divert the trust poverty or funds for purposes which the Charity Commissioner or the court considered expedient or proper, although the original objects of the founder could well be carried out, was an unwarranted encroachment on the freedom of religious institutions in regard to the management of their religious affairs. But apart from the tenets of the Jain religion, such encroachment was a violation of freedom of religion and of the right of a religious denomination to manage its own affairs, in matters of religion. To divert the trust money for purposes other than those for which the trust was created, the State could step in only when the trust failed or was incapable of being carried out either in whole or in part.[31]

---

[27] (1954) S.C.R. 1005, *supra*.

[28] (1909) 33 Bom. 122 [Davar J. upheld the bequest of property by a Parsi for the perpetual performance of ceremonies like *Muktad, baj, yejushni*, etc., which had been held void in *Limji Nowroji Banaji* v. *Bapuji Ruttonji Limbuwalla* (1887) 11 Bom. 441].

[29] (1954) S.C.R. *supra* at p. 1066.

[30] For a discussion of those cases, see the present writer's article "Supreme Court restores the *cy pres* Doctrine" 67 Bom.L.R. (Journal), 49.

[31] (1954) S.C.R. *supra* at pp. 1071-2. The above decision was distinguished in *Dwarikadasji* v. *Bihar* 33 Pat. 682, ('57) A.P. 615, in upholding ss. 30 and 49, Bihar Hindu Religious Trusts Act, 1951, which enacted in a statutory form the doctrine of *cy pres* as those sections contained no provision empowering the Board of Religious Trusts to divert the funds of the institution to any other purpose, if the Board took the view that the objects of the founder were "not expedient, practicable, desirable or necessary." It was also held that s. 28(2)(*j*) had no bearing on the *cy pres* doctrine and merely enacted in a statutory form the rule of the English Chancery Court that a trustee may, without the sanction of the court, convert any property of the

Fees levied by the impugned Act in *Shirur Mutt Case* do not contravene Art. 27

12.12 In the *Shirur Mutt Case* and in the *Orissa Case* it was contended that the fees levied under the Acts were in reality a tax, and such a tax (i) was beyond the legislative competence of State legislatures and (ii) violated Art. 27. The challenge based on lack of legislative competence was upheld in the first but not in the second case,[32] but the challenge under Art. 27 was rejected, the court observing:

"What is forbidden by the article is the specific appropriation of the proceeds of any tax in payment of expenses for the promotion or maintenance of any particular religion or religious denomination. The reason underlying this provision is obvious. Ours being a secular State and there being freedom of religion guaranteed by the Constitution, both to individuals and to groups, it is against the policy of the Constitution to pay out of public funds any money for the promotion or maintenance of any particular religion or religious denomination. But the object of the contribution under section 76 of the Madras Act is not fostering or preservation of the Hindu religion or any denomination within it. The purpose is to see that religious trusts and institutions, wherever they exist, are properly administered. It is a secular administration of the religious institutions that the legislature seeks to control and the object, as enunciated in the Act, is to ensure that the endowments attached to the religious institutions are properly administered and their income is duly appropriated for the purposes for which they were founded or exist. There is no question of favouring any particular religion or religious denomination in such cases."[33]

Ragunath v. State: alleged contravention of Art. 27 considered

12.13 In *Raghunath* v. *State*[34] the petitioner impugned the undernoted order[35] of the Kerala government. The petitioner prayed for a *mandamus* directing the State of Kerala and the Dist. Collector, Cannanore to forbear from spending any amount from the public funds of the Kerala State to reconstruct the places of worship destroyed during the disturbances in the State, because, according to the petitioner, such expenditure contravened Art. 27. The court quoted with approval the observations of Mukherjea J. set out in para 12.12 above,[36] and held:

(*a*) the undernoted observations of a single judge in *Varkey Devassy* v. *Kerala*[37] were not warranted, especially in view of the observations of Mukherjea J.

(*b*) Under Art. 204 "appropriations out of the Consolidated Fund are provided for; and the appropriation contemplated by Art. 27 when it says 'specifically appropriated' is only such appropriation as is contemplated by this Article. Therefore for the reason that there is no specific appropriation in the Act

---

trust into another property if such conversion was for the benefit of the trust and Arts. 19, 25 and 26 were not violated.

32 This aspect of the case is considered in Vol. II.

33 (1954) S.C.R. *supra* at p. 1045; see to the same effect (1954) S.C.R. *supra* at 1054. In *Ratilal Ghandi's Case*, there was no challenge under Art. 27.

34 ('74) A.Ker. 48.

35 "Government order that the cost of repairs or reconstruction for the restoration to the condition existing prior to the incidents of religious and educational institutions and the houses of serving defence personnel damaged will be met by Government."

36 "(which) was approved in . . . *Sri Jagannath Ramanuj Das* v. *Orissa* ('54) A.SC. 400" and in "*Moti Das* v. *S. P. Sahi* ('59) A.SC. 942, (which) again approved the earlier decisions": ibid. p. 50.

37 ('74) A.Ker. at p. 50: "This restriction on the working of the Article only applies to compulsion to pay any taxes, the proceeds of which are specifically appropriated in payment of expenses for the promotion or maintenance of any particular religion or religious denomination. This Article of the Constitution does not preclude the application of the general revenues of the State in payment of expenses for the promotion or maintenance of any particular religion. In fact, it appears to me that the Article implies that the general revenues may be utilised for such purposes": (1968) Ker.L.T. 805.

imposing a tax, it cannot be that the impost is not unconstitutional if made by a separate appropriation Act under Art. 204."[38]

(c) On the facts,[39] the "Distress Relief Fund is not a fund constituted out of taxes collected by the Government, no question of 'specific appropriation' can . . . arise as contemplated by Art. 204"[40]

(d) Even if the Distress Relief Fund were constituted out of taxes collected by Government, the resolution did not promote or maintain a particular religion or religious denomination. First, because houses, schools and places of worship belonging to both Hindus and Muslims had been damaged during the incidents and in restoring them to their original condition there was no question of promoting or maintaining any particular religion or religious denomination. The buildings were restored not because they belonged to a particular religion but because they were damaged in the incidents. And secondly because "even if places of worship belonging to one religious denomination alone were damaged and they alone are to be reconstructed even then there is no question of promotion or maintenance of that particular religion or religious denomination. If a mad and fanatic mob attacked only the places of worship of a particular religious denomination, then the restoration or reconstruction has necessarily to be of the places of worship of that particular religious denomination: still (and this is evident) there is no question of promotion or maintenance of that particular religion or religious denomination."[41]

12.14 In *Mohd. Hanif Quareshi* v. *Bihar*[42] a question was raised whether the prohibition of cow slaughter affected the religious rights of Mahomedans. It was contended that the sacrifice of a cow on the *Bakar-Id* Day was enjoined by the Quoran and/or was a part of religion. The Supreme Court held that the evidence was very unsatisfactory and the petitioners had not made out their case.[43] On the evidence, the conclusion arrived at by the court is probably correct; the only observation it is necessary to add is that a religious practice need not be universal, and a religious practice is not negatived because it is shown to be limited to certain religious denominations.

Mohd. Hanif Quareshi's Case

12.15 In *Durgah Committee, Ajmer* v. *Syed Hussain Ali*,[44] the Supreme Court held that Art. 26(c) and (d) did not create rights in any denomination or section of it; it merely safeguarded and

Durgah Committee's Case: Art. 26(c) and

[38] ('74) A.Ker. at p. 50.
[39] ibid. where they are fully set out.
[40] ibid.
[41] ibid. p. 51.
[42] (1959) S.C.R. 629, ('58) A.SC. 731.
[43] ibid. pp. 650-1.
[44] (1962) 1 S.C.R. 383, ('61) A.SC. 1402. The *Durgah Case* was followed in *Rajasthan* v. *Sajjanlal* ('75) A.SC. 706 [*held*, as the management of the temple of Rikhabdevji, with its properties had validly vested in the Ruler of Udaipur and thereafter in the successor State before the Constitution came into force on January 26, 1950, any rights as denominations, which the Swetambar or Digambar Jains, or both, had in the temple or its management had vested in the State and could not be revived, and Art. 26(*d*) did not apply; *held further*, that s. 53(5)(*a*) of the Rajasthan Public Trusts Act, 1959 does not empower the appointment of persons who do not belong to a denomination to be appointed to a public trust of that denomination. Section 52(1)(*e*), read with s. 53(5)(*a*), cannot be impugned on the ground that it does not lay down proper safeguards for leaving the administration of the properties in the hands of a denomination.] The above cases were followed in *T. Krishnan* v. *G.D.M. Committee* ('78) A.Ker. 68, 90 (F.B.) and it was held on the facts that it could not be said that the denomination had either surrendered or lost its rights in relation to the administration of the Guruvayoor Temple and its properties by any process known to the law before the commencement of the Constitution. The Court held, after a careful examination of the provisions of the Kerala Guruvayoor Devaswom Act, 1971, ("the Act") that ss. 3, 4, 11, 12, 14 to 18, 19(6), 20, 21, 24(1), (2) and (3)(*f*), 29 and 32 of the Act violated Art. 26 and were void. As these provisions were inseverable from the rest of the Act, the Court declared the whole Act void.

(*d*) does not create rights

guaranteed the continuance of rights that such denomination or section had. If the right to administer properties never vested in the denomination, or had been validly surrendered by it, or had otherwise been effectively and irretrievably lost to it, Art. 26 could not be invoked. The endowments of Durgah Khwaja Saheb had always been made on such terms as did not confer on the denomination represented by the *Khadims* the right to manage the properties endowed, which right was in the hands of officers appointed by the State. Hence the *vires* of s. 5, Durgah Khwaja Saheb Act, 1955, could not be challenged under Art. 26(*c*) and (*d*). Although it was wholly unnecessary to do so, Gajendragadkar J. said:

Obiter observations in the above case

"... it may not be out of place incidentally to strike a note of caution and observe that in order that the practices in question should be treated as a part of religion they must be regarded by the said religion as its essential and integral part; otherwise even purely secular practices which are not an essential or an integral part of religion are apt to be clothed with a religious form and may make a claim for being treated as religious practices within the meaning of Art. 26. Similarly even practices though religious may have sprung from merely superstitious beliefs and may in that sense be extraneous and unessential accretions to religion itself. Unless such practices are found to constitute an essential and integral part of a religion their claim for the protection under Art. 26 may have to be carefuly scrutinised; in other words, the protection must be confined to such religious practices as are an essential and an integral part of it and no other."[45]

A criticism of the *obiter*

It is submitted that the above *obiter* runs directly counter to the judgment of Mukherjea J. in the *Shirur Mutt Case* and substitutes the view of the court for the view of the denomination on what is essentially a matter of religion. The reference to superstitious practices is singularly unfortunate, for what is "superstition" to one section of the public may be a matter of fundamental religious belief to another. Thus, bequests for masses for the soul of a testator were held void as being for superstitious uses, till that view was overruled in *Bourne* v. *Keane*.[46] It is submitted that in dealing with the practice of religion protected by provisions like those contained in s. 116, Commonwealth of Australia Act or in Art. 26(*b*) of our Constitution, it is necessary to bear in mind the observations of Latham C.J. quoted earlier, namely, that those provisions must be regarded as operating in relation to all aspects of religion, irrespective of varying opinions in the community as to the truth of a particular religious doctrine or the goodness of conduct prescribed by a particular religion or as to the propriety of any particular religious observance. The *obiter* of Gajendragadkar J. in the *Durgah Committee Case* is also inconsistent with the observations of Mukherjea J. in *Ratilal Gandhi's Case*, that the decision in *Jamshedji* v. *Soonabai*[47] afforded an indication of the measure of protection given by Art. 26(*b*).[48]

The *obiter* is inconsistent with the previous decisions

---

[45] (1962) 1 S.C.R. *supra* at 411-12.

[46] (1919) A.C. 815. At p. 861 Lord Birkenhead L.C. concluded his judgment thus: "I am content that my decision should not involve your Lordships in the absurdity that a Roman Catholic citizen of this country may legally endow an altar for the Roman Catholic community, but may not provide funds for the administration of that sacrament which is fundamental in the belief of Roman Catholics, and without which the Church and the Altar would alike be useless." See also Jowitt, *Dictionary of English Law*, p. 1705, "Superstitious users and Trusts".

[47] 33 Bom. 122; see para 12.10. [48] See para 12.10.

12.16 The interpretation of Arts. 25 and 26 was carried a stage further by the Supreme Court in *Sardar Syedna Taher Saifuddin Saheb* v. *Bombay*.[49] The facts were briefly these: in *Hasanali* v. *Mansoorali*,[50] the Privy Council held that the petitioner, who was the *Dai-ul-Mutlak* as the head of the Dawoodi Bohra community, had the right to excommunicate any member of the community after following the procedure indicated by the Privy Council. Speaking of the effect of excommunication, the Privy Council said: "excommunication . . . necessarily involves exclusion from the exercise of religious rights in places under the trusteeship of the head of the community in which religious exercises are performed". Shortly after the Privy Council decision, the Bombay legislature passed the impugned Act to prevent the practice of excommunication "which results in the deprivation of legitimate rights and privileges of members of certain religious communities". The definition of excommunication included excommunication on purely religious grounds. The petitioner impugned the Act as violating Arts. 25 and 26. Das Gupta J. for himself, Sarkar and Mudholkar JJ. held that the Act violated Arts. 25 and 26 and was void and Ayyangar J. agreed in a separate concurring judgment. Sinha C.J. held that the Act was valid. The majority judgment delivered by Das Gupta J. established the following points: (i) after the Privy Council decision in *Hasanali's Case*, it was no longer open to dispute that the petitioner, who was a party to that case, had the right to excommunicate any member of the community with the consequences indicated by the Privy Council;[51] (ii) the decisions of the Supreme Court had placed the main principles underlying Arts. 25 and 26 beyond controversy. The first principle was that the protection of Arts. 25 and 26 was not limited to matters of doctrine or belief, but extended also to acts done in pursuance of religion; the Articles therefore contained a guarantee for rituals and observances, ceremonies and modes of worship which were integral parts of religion. The second principle was that what constituted an essential part of religion or religious practice had to be decided by the courts with reference to the doctrine of the particular religion and included practices which were regarded by the community as a part of its religion;[52] (iii) Where excommunication was itself based on religious grounds, such as lapse from the orthodox religious creed or doctrine (similar to what is considered heresy, apostasy or schism under the Canon Law), or breach of some practice considered as an essential part of the religion by the Dawoodi Bohras in general, excommunication must be held to be for the purpose of maintaining the strength of that religion. It necessarily followed that the exercise of this power on religious grounds formed part of the management by the community, through its religious head, "of its own affairs in matters of religion" guaranteed under Art. 26(*b*). As the impugned Act made even such

Sardar Syedna Taher Saifuddin Saheb's Case

The Bombay Prevention of Excommunication Act, 1949, held void by the Sup. Ct.: the majority judgment

Excommunication on religious grounds protected by Art. 26(*b*)

---

[49] (1962) Supp. 2 S.C.R. 496, ('62) A.SC. 853.
[50] (1947) 75 I.A. 1, ('48) A.PC. 66. [51] (1962) Supp. 2 S.C.R. *supra* at p. 529.
[52] ibid. p. 532; fol. in *E. R. J. Swami* v. *T.N.* ('72) A.SC. 1586, 1593 [*held*, that the *archaka* was a servant of the temple and therefore his appointment by the trustee was essentially secular, and s. 55(2) of the T.N. Hindu Religious & Charitable Endowments Act, 59 (as amended in 1971) which authorized the trustees to disregard the hereditary principle in the appointment of an *archaka* did not violate Arts. 25 and 26].

excommunication invalid and took away the power of the *Dai* as the head of the community to excommunicate even on religious grounds, the Act clearly interfered with the right of the Dawoodi Bohra community under Art. 26(*b*);[53] (iv) the excommunication of a member may affect his social rights, as the Dawoodi Bohra community was possessed of properties, and as the necessary consequence of excommunication, the excommunicated member lost his right to the enjoyment of property. The right given under Art. 26(*b*) had not however been made subject to the preservation of civil rights. Hence, the fact that civil rights were affected by the exercise of the fundamental rights under Art. 26(*b*) was of no consequence. Nor was it possible to say that excommunication was prejudicial to public order, morality and health to which the right was made subject;[54] (v) Art. 26(*b*) was subject to Art. 25(2). The Act was not covered by Art. 25(2) as it could not be regarded as a law relating to or restricting any economic, financial, political or other secular activity. The mere fact that certain civil rights might be lost by the members of the Dawoodi Bohra community as a result of excommunication even though made on religious grounds and that the Act prevented such loss did not make it a law "providing for social welfare and reform" within Art. 25(2). As the Act invalidated excommunication on any ground whatsoever, including religious grounds, it must be held to be a clear violation of Art. 26(*b*).[55] Das Gupta J. held that the view taken by the Bombay High Court in *Taher Saifuddin* v. *Tyebbhai Moosaji*[56] upholding the validity of the Act was not correct.[57]

Concurring judgment of Ayyangar J.: religion not to be "reformed" out of existence

12.17 Ayyangar J. held that if the appellant did not exclude an apostate from religious institutions he would be guilty of a grave dereliction of duty, as it was a breach of trust for a trustee of a religious institution to permit a person to be on that institution contrary to its religious tenets.[58] The Act, by depriving the head of the community of the power and the right to excommunicate and by penalising the exercise of that power, struck at the very life of the community by rendering it impotent to protect itself against dissidents and schismatics.[59] The Act violated the right to practise religion guaranteed by Art. 25(1), and it also violated Art. 26 because it interfered with the rights of the *Dai*, as the trustee of the property of the denomination, to administer that property so as to exclude

---

[53] ibid. p. 535.
[54] ibid. pp. 535-6.
[55] ibid. p. 537.
[56] ('53) A.B. 183, 55 Bom.L.R. 1.
[57] In that case Chagla C.J. followed his own judgment in *Bombay* v. *Narasu Appa Mali* (1951) Bom. 775, ('52) A.B. 84, 53 Bom.L.R. 779. He adopted as a correct definition of religion the definition in *Davis* v. *Benson* (1889) 113 U.S. 333, 33 L.ed. 637, and drew a sharp distinction between religious faith and belief, and religious practices. In *Ratilal Panachand Gandhi* v. *Bombay* (1953) Bom. 1187, ('53) A.B. 242, 55 Bom.L.R. 86, Chagla C.J. had to deal with the religion of the Jains who did not believe in a Creator. Chagla C.J. modified his definition by saying that even so, every religion must believe in a conscience and it must believe in ethics and moral precepts and he appears to have adhered to his distinction between religious belief and faith, and practices. In *Masud Alam* v. *Commissioner of Police* ('56) A.Cal. 9, 59, C.W.N. 293, the court made a sharp distinction between religious faith and belief relying upon the two Bombay decisions considered in this *f.n.* It is submitted that on this point all these cases are no longer good law in view of the judgments considered in the text.
[58] (1962) Supp. 2 S.C.R. *supra* at pp. 547-8.
[59] ibid. p. 549.

dissidents from the beneficial use of it. In the context in which the words "a measure providing for social welfare and reform" were used in Art. 25 (2) (*b*), it was intended to save the validity of only those laws which did not invade the basic and essential practices of religion guaranteed by Art. 25 (1), for, to read the Article as covering even the basic essentials would render the guarantee nugatory; and secondly, if there were a social welfare measure or reform which had that effect, there would be no need for the special provision as to throwing open all Hindu religious institutions to all classes or sections of Hindus, since the legislation contemplated by that provision would be *par excellence* one of social reform. A law providing for social welfare and reform was not intended "to 'reform' a religion out of existence or identity".[60] Just as the activities referred to in Art. 25 (2) (*a*) were obviously not of the essence of religion, similarly, the saving in Art. 25 (2) (*b*) was not intended to cover the basic essence of the creed.[61] It is submitted that the majority judgments are clearly right.

The *Tilkayat* Case

12.18 In *Tilkayat Shri Govindlalji* v. *Rajasthan*[62] Gajendragadkar J. again adverted to the rights under Arts. 25 (1) and 26 (*b*) and stated that if a matter was obviously secular and not religious, a court would be justified in rejecting its claim to be a religious practice, as based on irrational considerations. It is submitted that the real question is whether the religious denomination looks upon it as an essential part of its religion, and however irrational it may appear to persons who do not share that religious belief, the view of the denomination must prevail, for, it is not open to a court to describe as irrational that which is a part of a denomination's religion. The actual decision in the case, that the right to manage the property was a secular matter, is correct, but that is because, as pointed out by Mukherjea J., Art. 26 (*b*) when contrasted with Art. 26 (*c*) and (*d*) shows that matters of religious belief and practices are distinct and separate from the management of property of a religious denomination. The distinction between religious belief and practices which cannot be controlled, and the management of the property of a religious denomination which can be controlled to a limited extent, is recognized by the Article itself and must be enforced. But this distinction is not relevant to the question whether a religious practice is itself irrational or secular.

A criticism of the case

Sri Jagannath Temple Case

12.19 In *Raja Bira Kishore Deb* v. *Orissa*,[63] the Supreme Court held that in the absence of any indication as to which was the denomination concerned with the Sri Jagannath Temple for which the Sri Jagannath Temple Act, 1954, had been enacted and whose rights to administer the temple had been taken away, and in the absence of any claim on behalf of any denomination, the Act was not open to challenge under Art. 26 (*d*).

The effect of the *Shirur Mutt Case*

12.20 In *Jagannath Ramanuja* v. *B. K. Patra*[64] having regard to the judgment of the Supreme Court in *Sadashib Prakash* v. *Orissa*,[65] the

[60] ibid. pp. 552-3. [61] ibid. p. 553.
[62] (1964) 1 S.C.R. 561, ('63) A.SC. 1638, 1661.
[63] (1964) 7 S.C.R. 32, ('64) A.SC. 1501. [64] (1958) Cut. 666, ('59) A.Or. 117.
[65] (1956) S.C.R. 43, ('56) A.SC. 432 (*held*, that though by virtue of s. 79-A introduced by the amending Act of 1954, a scheme framed under the Orissa Hindu Religious Endowment Act, 1939, was to be deemed a scheme framed under the new

on schemes for the management of *Mutts*

court directed the Endowment Commissioner to modify the scheme in the light of the judgment in order to remove certain defects pointed out in the judgment. In doing so, the court observed that the Supreme Court decisions in the *Shirur Mutt Case* and in *Ratilal Gandhi's Case* showed that any scheme for the administration of a *Mutt* must conform to the following requirements:

(i) as the *mahant* of the *Mutt* had property rights in the endowment of the *Mutt*, unreasonable restrictions should not be placed on his enjoyment of those rights; (ii) restrictions imposed by a scheme would be unreasonable if they rendered the *mahant* unfit to discharge his duties and reduced him to the level of a servant; (iii) as the main purpose of a *Mutt* was to encourage and foster spiritual training and to strengthen the denominations of the particular school to which the *Mutt* belonged, any scheme in the administration of a *Mutt* should not hinder but should assist the *mahant* to achieve that purpose; (iv) under Art. 26(b) the *mahant* should have complete freedom to decide what rites and ceremonies were essential according to the tenets of the sect to which the *Mutt* belonged and no outside authority had any jurisdiction to interfere in such matters; (v) the scale of expenditure on such rites however could be regulated by secular authorities for the reasons given in the *Shirur Mutt Case*; (vi) though a law may regulate the administration of a *Mutt*, it must leave the administration to the religious denomination to which the *Mutt* belonged, for a law which took away the right of administration from the hands of the religious denomination and vested it in any other body would be void; (vii) the *mahant* had unfettered power to dispose of surplus income of a *Mutt* except in respect of the expenses for personal use connected with the dignity of his office. This power of disposal could not be taken away or restricted either directly or indirectly; (viii) in fixing the standard scale of expenditure for the various rites and ceremonies of the *Mutt*, if the law or a scheme required the approval of the Endowment Commissioner, such provision would not amount to an unreasonable restriction on the *mahant's* right. Personal gifts to the *mahant* by his disciples or by his admirers and worshippers were his absolute property and no law or scheme could restrict his power of disposal over the same, though if he died without disposing of those gifts, they may become part of the assets of the *Mutt*.

Principles laid down by the Sup. Ct. applied

12.21 The principles thus deduced from the Supreme Court decision or some of them have been applied in a number of cases. Thus where a religious denomination exercises its power to control management and supervision over certain institutions through its representatives elected for that purpose and where as a result of the Madras Act of 1951 the trustees could no longer be elected by the denomination but were appointed by the Commission or the Area Committee as the case may be, the denomination ceased altogether to have any control of the management of the institution in question. Accordingly, it was held that ss. 39, 41, 42 and 44 of the Madras Act were *ultra vires* as violating Art. 26.[66] Similarly, it was held[67] that even after the amendment of the Madras Hindu Religious and Charitable Endowments Act, 1951, which had been amended in 1954 as a result of the *Shirur Mutt Case*, ss. 21, 30 (2), 31 (1) and r. 10 of the rules framed under the Act were void as violating Arts. 19, 25 and 26 as they imposed unreasonable restrictions on the *mathadhipati's* right. Similarly, it has been held that r. 58 of the rules framed under the Hyderabad Endowment Regulations violated Art. 26 and was void as it gave to the State a power to scrutinise the character of the successor of a *mutavalli* which power had no

Act, it was open to an aggrieved party to attack the scheme on the ground available under the present law).

66 *Mukundaraya* v. *Mysore* ('60) A.Mys. 18.

67 ('56) A.M. 491, (1956) 1 M.L.J. 532.

reasonable relation to the object of supervising the trust. The entire elimination of persons entitled to control the dedicated property under the trust violated Art. 26 and the impugned order was void.[68] In K. *Eranna* v. *Commr. H.R. & C.E.*[69] it was held that ss. 39 and 41 of the Madras Hindu Religious and Charitable Endowments Act, 51, violated Art. 26 because government had reserved to itself absolute powers to administer the properties of religious institutions, and the religious denomination was left without any power. The provisions of ss. 9 and 22—that the officers and trustees of the religious institutions must be persons professing the Hindu religion—did not affect the absolute powers vested in Government, and "did not save the right of the religious denomination to administer the property of the temple". However, in *Rajendra* v. *Andhra*[70] it was held that s. 52, Madras Hindu Religious and Charitable Endowments Act, 1951, when interpreted in the context of the rights guaranteed to the *mathadhipati* under the judgment of the Supreme Court was not unreasonable and unconstitutional. Again, in *S.G.P. Committee* v. *Governor of Punjab*[71] it was held that ss. 148 (B) and 52 of the Punjab Sikh Gurdwaras Act, 1925, as amended in 1959, did not violate Art. 26, for the election of 35 new members of the interim Board under s. 148-B did not amount to interference in Sikh religious affairs by non-Sikhs as none of the electors and none of the members of the Board could ever be non-Sikhs. The introduction of the Governor's nominee in the interim Board did not offend against the right of Sikhs to manage their own religious affairs. Again, in *Narayan Doss* v. *T. Neeladari Rao*,[72] it was held that s. 5 (*b*) of the Commission of Enquiry Act, 1952, did not violate Arts. 25 and 26 nor was it likely to wound religious sentiments. That section gave only a limited power to the authorised officer to enter any building or place; the search and seizure of books of accounts or documents that may be found in the building or place could be effected only after observing the formalities prescribed by ss. 102 and 103, Cr.P.C. The power of seizure and search was thus hedged in by several restrictions and safeguards. Moreover, there was little danger of the search interfering with the worship in a religious institution or violating the sanctity of the institution, for it could hardly ever happen that books of accounts and documents relating to the management of a religious institution would be kept in the *sanctum sanctorum*. In *Saligram* v. *Raghavacharya*[73] it was held that Art. 26 was no bar to the appointment under O. 40, r. 1, C.P.C. of a receiver of the properties of a temple merely because a person not belonging to the religious denomination served by the temple *may* be appointed. It would be open to the parties affected to object to the appointment of a receiver who *does not belong* to the particular religious denomination.

---

[68] *Narayan Prashad* v. *Hyderabad* (1955) Hyd. 337, ('55) A.Hyd. 82. (For the impugned order and the facts which led to the passing of it see pp. 83-84).

[69] ('70) A.Mys. 191 [*held*, that Hindus, in the larger sense, including all sections of Hindus constituted a religious denomination: ibid. p. 193, relying on *Ram Chandra Deb* v. *Orissa* ('59) A.Or. 5].

[70] ('57) A.A.P. 283.

[71] (1959) Punj. 1373, ('59) A.Punj. 623.

[72] (1959) Andh.Pra. 67, ('59) A.A.P. 148.

[73] ('69) A.P. 118, 124.

Ramchandra v. State

12.22 In *Ramchandra* v. *State*[74] it was held that ss. 3 and 4 of the Ganga Sagar Mela Ordinance did not violate Art. 25. The Ordinance was designed to provide measures to safeguard the health, safety and welfare of pilgrims attending the *mela*, and that object was within the scope of permissible restrictions on the right conferred by Art. 25. The Ordinance was in aid of the freedom guaranteed by Art. 25, as it enabled pilgrims to exercise their right to the freedom of religion under more satisfactory conditions.

Art. 25(1): Orissa Freedom of Religion Act beyond legislative competence and violative of Art. 25(1)

12.23 In *Yulitha Hyde* v. *State*[75] the provisions of the Orissa Freedom of Religion Act, 1968 were impugned,[76] as beyond the legislative competence of the State legislature and as violating Art. 25(1). In upholding these contentions the court held that:

"(1) Art. 25(1) guarantees propagation of religion, and conversion is a part of the Christian religion. (2) Prohibition of conversion by 'force' or 'fraud' as defined by the Act would be covered by the limitations subject to which the right is guaranteed under Art. 25(1). (3) The definition of the term 'inducement' is vague and many proselytizing activities may be covered by the definition and the restriction in Art. 25(1) cannot be said to cover the wide definition. (4) The State Legislature has no power to enact the impugned legislation which in pith and substance is a law relating to religion. Entry No. 1 of either List II or List III does not authorize the impugned legislation."[77]

Rev. Stainislaus v. M.P.

12.24 In *Rev. Stainislaus* v. *M.P.*[78] the Supreme Court decided important questions of interpretation of Art. 25 in general, and the right to propagate religion in particular. The questions arose out of the provisions of the Madhya Pradesh Dharma Swatantra Adhiniyam, 1968 (Freedom of Religion Act) and the Orissa Freedom of Religion Act, 1968. It is a remarkable fact that notwithstanding the importance of the questions raised, the impugned provisions are not set out in the judgment[79] but the reader is left with the following summary of the provisions given by Ray C.J.:

impugned provisions not set out: Summary of the provisions

"The Madhya Pradesh Act provides for the prohibition of conversion from one religion to another by use of force or allurement, or by fraudulent means, and matters incidental thereto. The expressions 'allurement' and 'fraud' have been defined by the Act. Section 3 of the Act prohibits conversion by use of force or by allurement or by fraudulent means and Section 4 penalises such forcible conversion. Similarly, Section 3 of the Orissa Act prohibits forcible

---

[74] ('76) A.Cal. 164. [75] ('73) A.Or. 116.

[76] *Sec. 2*: "*Definitions*: In this Act unless the context otherwise requires — (*a*) 'conversion' means renouncing one religion and adopting another; (*b*) 'force' shall include a show of force or a threat of injury of any kind including threat of divine displeasure or social excommunication; (*c*) 'fraud' shall include, misrepresentation or any other fraudulent contrivance; (*d*) 'inducement' shall include the offer of a gift or gratification either in cash or in kind, and shall also include the grant of any benefit, either pecuniary or otherwise;" *Sec. 3*: *Prohibition of forcible conversion*: "No person shall convert or attempt to convert, either directly or otherwise, any person from one religious faith to another by the use of force or by inducement or by any fraudulent means nor shall any person abet any such conversion." *Sec. 4* prescribed punishment for contravention of the provisions of s. 3.

[77] The four criminal cases against the four applicants were quashed, and a *mandamus* was issued against the State government directing it not to give effect to the Act.

[78] (1977) 2 S.C.R. 611, ('77) A.SC. 908.

[79] Acts passed by various States are easily available in the law libraries of those States, but are not available in the law libraries of several other States. However, if the reader turns to *Rev. Stainislaus* v. *M.P.* ('75) A.M.P. 163, 165 and to *Yulitha Hyde* v. *State* ('73) A.Or. 116, 120, he will find the definitions and the relevant sections set out.

conversion by the use of force or by inducement or by any fraudulent means, and Section 4 penalises such forcible conversion."[80]

It is not clear whether any Statement of Objects and Reasons was attached to the Bills which were enacted into the aforesaid Acts. It is submitted that the judgment is very unsatisfactory. Forcible conversion or conversion by fraudulent means presents no difficulty in interpreting the scope of Art. 25; but what is meant by "inducement" and what is "allurement"? Because, although the judgment states that "allurement" was defined in the Madhya Pradesh Act, the definition is not given in the judgment.

12.25 Ray C.J. considered the meaning of the word "propagate" and, after negativing the biological sense, he quoted the following definitions:

Definition of the word "propagate" considered by Ray C.J.

Propagate: "to spread from person to person, or from place to place, to disseminate, diffuse (a statement, belief, practise, etc.)": *Shorter Oxford Dictionary*.

Propagate: "To transmit or spread from person to person or from place to place; carry forward or onward; diffuse; extend; as to propagate a report; to propagate the Christian religion": *Century Dictionary*, Vol. VI.[81]

It may be added that the meaning given from the *Shorter Oxford Dictionary* carries the following illustration: "to propagate the Gospel in foreign parts". The following definition of the word "propagate" from *Webster's Third International Dictionary* (1969) is important: "foster growing knowledge of, familiarity with and acceptance of". Having given the definitions of the word "propagate", Ray C.J. said:

"We have no doubt that it is in this sense that the word 'propagate' has been used in Article 25(1), for what the Article grants is not the right to convert another person to one's own religion but to transmit or spread one's religion by an exposition of its tenets. It has to be remembered that Article 25(1) guarantees 'freedom of conscience' to every citizen, and not merely to the followers of one particular religion, and that, in turn, postulates that there is no fundamental right to convert another person to one's own religion because if a person purposely undertakes the conversion of another person to his religion, as distinguished from his effort to transmit or spread the tenets of his religion, that would impinge on the 'freedom of conscience' guaranteed to all the citizens of the country alike."[82]

It is submitted that the above passage fails to analyze the several concepts embodied in Art. 25, with the result that the conclusion reached is untenable. This submission is developed in para 12.27 below.

12.26 It is unfortunate that the legislative history of Art. 25 was not brought to the attention of the Supreme Court. In Shiva Rao, *The Framing of India's Constitution—A Study*, it is observed:

Legislative history of Art. 25 overlooked

"The Minorities Sub-Committee considered this clause on April 19, 1947. The sub-committee accepted the suggestion made by M. Ruthnaswamy that certain religions like Christianity and Islam were proselytizing religions and that they should be permitted to propagate their faith. The sub-committee accordingly recommended a redraft of clause 16 which not only restored the right to free practice of religion but also secured an additional right to propagate religion."[83]

---

[80] (1977) 2 S.C.R. at p. 616, ('77) A.SC. at p. 911.
[81] ('77) A.SC. at p. 911. [82] ibid.
[83] Shiva Rao, *The Framing of India's Constitution — A Study*, p. 261.

When the matter was debated in the Constituent Assembly, there was considerable discussion on the word "propagate". In the course of the debate, Mr. T. T. Krishnamachari pointed out, what is clear from the language of Art. 25 itself, namely, that it was "perfectly open to the Hindus and the Arya Samajists to carry on their *suddhi* propaganda as it is open to the Christians, the Muslims, the Jains and the Buddhists and to every other religionist so long as it is subject to public order, morality and the other conditions that have to be observed in any civilized society". But the speech of Mr. K. M. Munshi gave the historical background of Art. 25 (1) in the paragraph set out below in which he pointed out that the insertion of the word "propagate" was the result of a compromise to reassure the minority communities, particularly the Indian Christian community. He said:

> "Moreover, I was a party from the very beginning to the compromise with the minorities, which ultimately led to many of these clauses being inserted in the Constitution and I know it was on this word that the Indian Christian community laid the greatest emphasis, not because they wanted to convert people aggressively, but because *the word 'propagate' was a fundamental part of their tenet*. Even if the word were not there, I am sure, under the freedom of speech which the Constitution guarantees it will be open to any religious community to persuade other people to join their faith. *So long as religion is religion, conversion by free exercise of the conscience has to be recognised*. The word 'propagate' in this clause is nothing very much out of the way as some people think, nor is it fraught with dangerous consequences."[84] (italics supplied)

Conclusion of Ray C.J. contrary to legislative history

12.27 We can now consider the conclusion reached by Ray C.J. in the passage set out at the end of para 12.25 above. It is clear that his conclusion runs counter to the legislative history; but that does not conclusively establish that the conclusion is clearly wrong. It is submitted that Ray C.J. did not ask the central question which was involved in the appeals before him, namely, whether conversion was a part of the Christian religion. This omission is remarkable, because the judgment of the Orissa High Court delivered on 24th October, 1972 was under appeal to the Supreme Court. That judgment was reported in *Yulitha Hyde* v. *State*[85] ("*Yulitha Hyde's Case*") and that judgment had squarely raised the central question whether conversion was a part of the Christian religion. As it will be submitted that the judgment of the Orissa High Court is clearly right, and can be supported from the language used in Art. 25 (1), it will be convenient at this place to give a brief account of that judgment.

Yulitha Hyde's Case: Conversion part of the Christian religion

12.28 In *Yulitha Hyde's Case*, the petitioners expressly averred that conversion was a part of the Christian religion. No affidavits were filed in reply by Government, and although opportunity was given to do so, the Court was informed that it was not proposed to file any affidavit in reply. Ordinarily, the Court would have accepted the untraversed allegation of the petitioners as correct, but having regard to the important issues involved, the Court considered it appropriate to examine in brief the correctness of the allegation that

---

[84] *C.A.D.* Vol. 7, p. 837.

[85] ('73) A.Or. 116. The reader reading the Supreme Court judgment will not find this case mentioned nor the fact that it was reported. The concluding portion of the judgment which refers to the judgment of the Orissa High Court dated 24th October, 1972 is the only information the reader will have that a judgment on the question was delivered by the Orissa High Court.

the propagation by adopting methods which had been made an offence under the Act, were a part of the Christian religion. After examining the evidence produced before it, the Court held:

"Counsel for the several petitioners have freely quoted from several Christian Scriptures of undoubted authority to show that propagating religion with a view to its spreading is a part of religious duty for every Christian and, therefore, must be considered as a part of the religion. *Learned Government Advocate does not dispute this assertion of fact.* We, therefore, proceed on the basis that it is the religious duty of every Christian to propagate his religion."[86] (italics supplied)

It is clear therefore, first, that it was established by evidence that conversion was a part of the Christian religion, and, secondly, that this proposition was not controverted by Counsel appearing on behalf of the State. The Orissa High Court recorded the finding that "(1) Art. 25(1) guarantees propagation of religion and conversion as a part of the Christian religion".[87] The Supreme Court, which reversed the judgment of the Orissa High Court, has made no attempt to show that the question raised and decided was either irrelevant, or was wrongly decided.

Definitions of "convert", "conversion" and "conscience"

12.29 Since Ray C.J. has raised the question whether conversion was a part of the right guaranteed by Art. 25(1), and since he has laid emphasis on the "freedom of conscience" (referred to in Art. 25), the following definitions are relevant:

Convert: "to cause to turn to a religion, belief or opinion, specially to bring to Christianity."[88]

Conversion: "the action of converting, or the fact of being converted to a religion, belief or opinion, specially to Christianity."[88]

Conscience: "freedom or liberty of conscience; system allowing all citizens free choice of religion."[89]

It is submitted that the crucial question to have asked was whether conversion was a part of the Christian religion and, if so, whether there were any considerations of public health, morality or public order, which required that the right to convert should be restricted. It is clear that conversion by force or fraud can be prevented on the ground of morality and also on the ground of public order. Further, if A converts B by force or fraud, B is deprived of his freedom of religion and freedom of conscience. The discussion that follows is confined to conversion by persuasion.

Basic misconception in the judgment of Ray C.J. as to the nature of religion pointed out

12.30 This brings us to the basic misconception in the judgment of Ray C.J. as to the nature of the freedom of religion. Dropping freedom of religion, he turned to the phrase "freedom of conscience" to suggest that if freedom of religion included the right to convert even by persuasion, it would interfere with the "freedom of conscience" of the person who was converted. The meaning of the phrase "freedom of conscience", given above, puts an end to that argument. First, Art. 25(1) confers freedom of religion—a freedom *not limited to the religion in which a person is born.* Freedom of conscience harmonizes with this, for its presence in Art. 25(1) shows that our Constitution has adopted "a system which allows free choice of religion". The right to propagate religion gives a meaning to freedom of choice, for choice involves not only knowledge but an act of

[86] ('73) A.Or. at p. 119.
[87] ibid. p. 123.
[88] The *Shorter Oxford Dictionary.*
[89] The *Concise Oxford Dictionary.*

will. A person cannot choose if he does not know what choices are open to him. To propagate religion is not to impart knowledge and to spread it more widely, but to produce intellectual and moral conviction leading to action, namely, the adoption of that religion. *Successful* propagation of religion would result in conversion.[90] Ray C.J. mistakenly believed that if A deliberately set out to convert B by propagating A's religion, that would impinge on B's "freedom of conscience". But, as we have seen, the precise opposite is true: A's propagation of his religion with a view to its being accepted by B, gives an opportunity to B to exercise his free choice of a religion.

Summing up:

12.31 To sum up: the word "religion" in the expression "the right freely to profess, practise and propagate religion" means *any* religion. Freedom of conscience gives a person freedom to choose or not to choose any one of the many religions which are being propagated. On his deciding to choose a particular religion which is being propagated with a view to its acceptance, and on his being prepared to comply with the requirements necessary to be a member of that religion, he has the freedom to be converted to that religion. Therefore, conversion does not in any way interfere with the freedom of conscience but is a fulfilment of it and gives meaning to it. It is submitted that the above view harmonizes with the legislative history of Art. 25(1) and the inclusion of the word "propagate" in it. It harmonizes with a matter of common knowledge that several religions are proselytizing religions as a matter of religious duty, and it harmonizes with the meaning of the words "propagate", "convert" and "conversion", "freedom of conscience" and with the right freely to profess and practise *religion*. It is submitted that the judgment of the Orissa High Court in *Yulitha Hyde's Case*, about conversion is clearly right for the reasons there given and also for the additional reasons given in our discussion of the Supreme Court's judgment. It is also submitted that the Supreme Court's judgment is clearly wrong, is productive of the greatest public mischief and ought to be overruled.

Submission: H. Ct. judgment in *Yulitha Hyde's Case* was correct

Legislative competence

12.32 The Supreme Court decision also dealt with the legislative competence of the Madhya Pradesh and Orissa Legislatures to enact the respective Freedom of Religion Acts. That topic is more conveniently dealt with in the Chapter on Legislative Powers of the Union and the States in Vol. II.

Art. 25 and the right to carry *kirpans*

12.33 The possession of lethal weapons like swords or daggers is controlled by law and such possession can be forbidden altogether. However, *Explanation (1)* to Art. 25 provides that the wearing and carrying of *kirpans* shall be deemed to be included in the profession of the Sikh religion. Consequently, any law which prohibited Sikhs from wearing or carrying *kirpans* would be void unless such law was justified as necessary to public order. Though not defined in

---

[90] This is true of the propagation of any doctrine, which calls for action. To give an example which is not charged with emotion, Cobden, Bright and other leaders of the free trade doctrine propagated that doctrine for the economic salvation of a protectionist United Kingdom. They preached that doctrine in Parliament and out of Parliament; they organized meetings, formed associations, engaged in public discussion and the like. Their propagation of the free trade doctrine was successful, for a great political party was converted to it and gave effect to it by repealing protectionist laws, and bringing in free trade.

the Constitution, *kirpan* means a sword and its size or shape has not been prescribed by the Sikh religion; it may therefore be a sword of any size or shape.[91] In *Explanation (1)* to Art. 25, the word *'kirpans'* has been used in the plural in relation to Sikhs and emblems. It could never have been intended that in the name of religion a Sikh could carry any number of *kirpans* or swords as a religious emblem when one of the Sikh Gurus had ordained that the *kirpan* should be worn only as one of five named emblems; nor could it have been intended that a Sikh should possess without a licence any number of arms, for the possession of which others had to take a licence. Hence, a person, as a Sikh, was entitled to possess only one sword or *kirpan*. He could not possess an extra sword without a licence.[92]

Deliberate insults to religion are not protected by Art. 25: *Ramji Lal Modi's Case*

12.34 Though a broad and liberal interpretation has been given to the right to practise and propagate religion, no countenance has been given to the plea that such a right includes the right deliberately to insult the religion of others. Thus in *Ramji Lal Modi* v. *U.P.*[93] it was held that s. 295A, I.P.C., was protected by Art. 19(2). It would be absurd to suggest that an insult to the religion of an individual could have no bearing on public order so as to attract Art. 19(2), having regard to the provisions of Arts. 25 and 26, which, while guaranteeing the freedom of religion, expressly made it subject to public order. S. 295A did not penalise every act of insult or attempt to insult the religion or religious belief of a class of citizens, but only those acts or insults or attempt to insult which were perpetrated with the deliberate and malicious intention of outraging the religious feelings of that class. Thus s. 295A penalised only the aggravated forms of insult to religion, etc. The calculated tendency of such aggravated forms of insult was clearly to disturb public order. In *S. Veerabhadran Chettiar* v. *E. V. Ramaswamy Naicker*[94] the Supreme Court held that the words "any object held sacred by any class of persons" in s. 295, I.P.C., were of general import and could not be limited to idols in temples or idols carried on the occasion of festivals, but included sacred books and any other objects which were regarded as sacred by any class of persons, whether such objects were actually worshipped or not. Courts must be circumspect in such matters and pay due regard to the religious susceptibility of different classes of persons with different beliefs, whether they shared those beliefs or not or whether those beliefs in the opinion of the court were rational or not. This decision was followed in *Public Prosecutor* v. *Ramaswami*.[95]

S. 295A, I.P.C. held valid

Morality and health: Arts. 25-26

12.35 The rights guaranteed by Arts. 25 and 26 are subject not only to public order but to morality and health. Therefore though restrictions on the freedom of religion on the grounds of morality and

---

[91] ('24) A.Lahore 600.

[92] *R.* v. *Dhyan Singh* ('52) A.A. 53: ('24) A.Lahore 600 was relied on.

[93] (1957) S.C.R. 860, 867, ('57) A.SC. 650; fol. in *Sant Das* v. *Babu Ram* ('69) A.A. 436.

[94] (1959) S.C.R. 1211, ('58) A.SC. 1032.

[95] ('64) A.M. 258. After upholding the validity of s. 295A, I.P.C., the Court allowed the appeal and convicted the accused, holding that the two articles written by him deliberately and maliciously outraged the religious feelings of the Muslim community, as the articles contained insulting and abusive language about the Koran and about Allah (God).

health would be closely scrutinized, they would be upheld if they passed such scrutiny.

Devaru's Case: the throwing open of temples — denominational temples

12.36 Article 25 (2) (*b*) which provides for the throwing open of Hindu religious institutions of a public character to all classes of Hindus and for social welfare and reform has been the subject of several decisions. In *Sri Venkataramana Devaru* v. *Mysore*[96] the trustees of the Temple of Sri Venkataramana at Mulki challenged the Madras Temple Entry Authorization Act, 1947, which had for its object the removal of the disability of Harijans from entering into Hindu public temples, after Government had turned down their application for exemption from its provisions. The appellants contended that the temple was a private temple, a contention upheld in the trial court. The High Court rejected this contention, but granted a limited decree in favour of the appellants reserving to them the right to exclude the general public during certain ceremonies in which the members of the denomination alone were entitled to participate. The question for decision of the Supreme Court was whether the right of a religious denomination to manage its own affairs in matters of religion under Art. 26 (*b*) could be subjected to, and controlled by, a law protected by Art. 25 (2) (*b*). Venkatarama Aiyar J. held that the expression "religious institutions of a public character" occurring in Art. 25 (2) (*b*) contemplated not merely a temple dedicated to the public as a whole, but also temples endowed for the benefit of sections of the public and included denominational temples as well. The court found as a fact that Sri Venkataramana Temple at Mulki was a denominational temple. After citing the meaning given to the expression "matters of religion" in the *Shirur Mutt Case*[97] according to which matters of religion in Art. 26 (*b*) included even practices which were regarded by the community as part of its religion, Venkatarama Aiyar J. said:

> ". . . under the ceremonial law pertaining to temples, who are entitled to enter into them for worship and where they are entitled to stand and worship and how the worship is to be conducted are all matters of religion. The conclusion is also implicit in Art. 25 which after declaring that all persons are entitled freely to profess, practice and propagate religion, enacts that this should not affect the operation of any law throwing open Hindu religious institutions of a public character to all classes and sections of Hindus."[98]

The right under Art. 26(*b*) is subject to the provisions of Art. 25(2)(*b*)

Under Art. 26 (*b*) the appellant would be entitled to exclude all persons other than "*Gowda Saraswath Brahmins*" from entering the temple for worship. Under Art. 25 (2) (*b*) a law throwing open public temples to all classes of Hindus was valid. The word

---

[96] (1958) S.C.R. 895, ('58) A.SC. 255. [97] (1954) S.C.R. 1005 *supra*.

[98] (1958) S.C.R. *supra* at p. 911. In *E. R. J. Swami* v. *T.N.* ('72) A.SC. 1586, 1591-2, *Devaru's Case* was referred to and relied on for the authority of *Agamas* which that case described as treatises of ceremonial law dealing with such matters as the construction of temples, installation of idols therein and conduct of the worship of the deity. According to the *Agamas*, an image (the idol) becomes defiled if there is any departure or violation of any of the rules relating to worship. In fact purificatory rites have to be performed for restoring the sanctity of the shrine; rel. on and appl. in *Kalyan Dass* v. *State* ('73) A.M. 264 [*held*, that "if in the Hindu religion a place of worship is also prescribed, then the entire temple precincts from any part of which a devotee can usefully worship has always to be held sacrosanct" (ibid. p. 226) and ". . . no non-Hindu can for pleasure and social evaluation seek entry into such temples.": (ibid. p. 269)].

"public" in its ordinary acceptation included any section of the public and the said temple would be a public institution within Art. 25 (2) (*b*) and s. 3 of the Madras Act would be within its protection. There was thus an *apparent* conflict between the two Articles. The appellants contended that the conflict could be resolved by limiting the expression "religious institutions of a public character" as meaning institutions didicated to the Hindu community in general but not denominational institutions founded for the benefit of a section of Hindus, and supported the contention by the history of the legislation.[99] In rejecting the contention, Venkatarama Aiyar J. said that the language of the Article being plain and unambiguous, it was not open to the court to read into it limitations which were not there, based on *a priori* reasoning as to the probable intention of the legislature. The intention must be gathered from the words used, and "in a court of law what is unexpressed has the same value as what is unintended". Accordingly, a denominational institution fell within Art. 25 (2) (*b*). He said that in resolving the apparent conflict, the rule of harmonious construction must be adopted.[1] Applying that rule, he held that Art. 26 (*b*) must be read as subject to Art. 25 (2) (*b*). If full effect were given to Art. 26 (*b*), it would render the provisions of Art. 25 (2) (*e*) as regards the throwing open of public Hindu temples to all Hindus nugatory. To read Art. 26 (*b*) as subject to Art. 25 (2) (*b*) would give as much effect to both provisions as was possible.

Denominational temples and the claim of a limited right to exclude the public from certain religious services

12.37 But though the right of a denomination to wholly exclude members of the public from worship in a temple must yield to the overriding right conferred by Art. 25 (2) (*b*) on the public to enter into a temple for worship, where the right claimed was not one of general and total exclusion of the public from worship at all times, but an exclusion from certain religious services which were limited by the rules of the foundation to the members of the denomination, then the question was not whether Art. 25 (2) (*b*) overrode the right so as to extinguish it, but whether it was possible so to regulate the rights of the persons protected by Art. 25 (2) (*b*) as to give effect to both the rights.

"If the denominational rights are such that to give effect to them would substantially reduce the right conferred by Art. 25(2)(b), then of course, on our conclusion that Art. 25(2)(b) prevails as against Art. 26(b), the denominational rights must vanish. But where that is not the position, and after giving effect to the rights of the denomination what is left to the public of the right of worship is something substantial and not merely the husk of it, there is no reason why we should not so construe Art. 25(2)(b) as to give effect to Art. 26(b) and recognise the rights of the denomination in respect of matters which are strictly denominational, leaving the rights of the public in other respects unaffected."[2]

In *Yagnapurushdasji* v. *Muldas*,[3] without any reference to the above judgment it was held that s. 3 of the Bombay Hindu Places of Public Worship (Entry Authorisation) Act, 1956, did not violate Art. 26 (*b*) as it did not invade the traditional and conventional manner in which the act of actual worship of the deity was allowed to be performed only by the authorised *pujaris* of the temple and by no

---

[99] For the arguments in support, see ibid. pp. 912-6.
[1] For a discussion of the principle of harmonious construction, see para 2.54.
[2] (1958) S.C.R. *supra* at p. 920. [3] ('66) A.SC. 1119.

other devotee entering the temple for *darshan*.[4] The court also held that the Swaminarayan Sampradaya Sect was not a distinct and separate sect from the Hindus and s. 3 of the Act applied to the sect.

Tejraj's Case: no right in the public to install their own deities in a denominational temple

12.38 *Tejraj* v. *M.B.*[5] raised important questions relating to denominational temples. The case arose out of the respondents' action in installing a *Shivling* in a Jain temple and prohibiting Jains from worshipping there. The court held that where the fact of a very old temple *being* a public Jain temple was admitted, and supported by documents, and there was no record of the temple having been dedicated to the Hindu public, the mere presence of a *Shivling* in the temple and the use of the temple by the Hindu community did not support the claim that the temple was also a Hindu temple. Where the temple was exclusively a public Jain temple dedicated to and for the benefit of the Jain community, and members of that community had clearly a fundamental right under Art. 25 (1) to enter and worship there according to the principles and forms of their religion. The right under Art. 25 (1) was not merely a matter of faith and belief but also of practice, of rituals and ceremonies as held by the Supreme Court in the *Shirur Mutt Case*. The presence of a *Shivling*, and the worship of it by the Hindu community was repugnant to the principles of Jainism and the Jain worship of *Tirthankaras*, and to the sentiments of the Jains who worshipped in the temple.[6] The State had no right to do what it did, namely, to introduce a *Shivling* into the temple, and to prohibit the members of the Jain community from entering the temple and from worshipping, except on the condition of Hindus being allowed to worship the *Shivling*; and the State's action violated the fundamental rights of Jains under Arts. 25 (1) and 26 (*b*) and could not be defended on the ground of its having been taken on considerations of public order, morality and health to which the right was made subject. A public Jain temple was *res extra commercium*, and its character as such temple could not be taken away by any assertion on the part of the State of a right of ownership, and the public temple could not be made a museum for an exhibition of deities and idols of all religions. In a public Jain temple, only images of deities of the Jain religion could be kept, even if the State was the owner of the temple. The argument that an order of the court would be ineffective was dismissed as incomprehensible,[7] and the respondents were directed to remove forthwith the *Shivling* they had placed in the

---

[4] ibid. p. 1127.

[5] (1957) Mad.Pra. 658, ('58) A.M.P. 115.

[6] See *Sanjib Kumar* v. *Principal, St. Paul's College* ('57) A.Cal. 524, 61 C.W.N. 717, where it was held that though an educational institution conducted by a Christian Missionary Society could not compel anyone to profess or practise the Christian religion, it could lay down that all religious practices which were carried out inside its premises should be in conformity with Christian principles. Accordingly, the refusal of the Principal, St. Paul's College, Calcutta, to allow Saraswati Pooja to be performed in the College premises, was upheld as not violating the fundamental rights of the petitioner.

[7] The court added: "Any suggestion that for certain reasons it may be difficult and even impossible for the opposition to carry out the orders of this Court can only be viewed with dismay and cannot but impel us to say that it would be the end of the Rule of Law when the State and its authorities find themselves in a position where they cannot enforce the orders of this Court and secure obedience to them."

temple and were restrained from interfering with the Jains in worshipping at the temple.[8]

12.39 The Supreme Court's decision in *Devaru's Case* and the Madhya Pradesh High Court's in *Tejraj's Case* may appear conflicting, but the conflict is merely apparent. *Devaru's Case* held that Hindu religious institutions of a public character included not only Hindu temples open to all Hindus generally, but also included denominational Hindu temples, that is to say, a law providing for the throwing open of all Hindu temples to all classes and sections of Hindus would apply also to denominational temples. This however only meant that any Hindu who wished to worship at such denominational temples was free to do so, subject to the limited exception indicated by Venkatarama Aiyar J. in *Devaru's Case*. It did not mean that any section of the Hindu community was entitled to install into a denominational temple different idols of the faith which it professed. If the section wished to worship at the temple it had to worship such Gods as were installed there. This was rightly stressed in *Tejraj's Case*.

No real conflict between *Devaru's Case* and *Tejraj's Case*

12.40 It has been held that the Madras Temple Entry Authorization Act, 1947, did not violate any provision of Part III of the Constitution. The Act applied only to religious institutions of a public character and the Act had done what Art. 25 (2) (*b*) expressly permitted.[9] In *P. S. Charya* v. *Madras*[10] it was held that Shri Krishna Devaru Temple at Shivalli in Udipi was a public temple and not a *mutt*. The Madras Temple Entry Authorization Act, 1947, as amended by the Madras Act 13 of 1953, did not violate Arts. 25 and 26. It had carried out the principles embodied in Arts. 17, 25, 26 and 35.

The Madras Temple Entry Authorization Act, 1947, upheld

12.41 Again, the violation of the right to enter a denominational temple has to be judged in the context of the law under which the right was claimed. Accordingly, it was held in *State* v. *Puranchand*[11] that where a temple in question was a purely denominational temple confined to Jains, and non-Jain caste Hindus could not enter the temple as of right, an untouchable who was a Hindu but not a Jain could not insist upon entering the temple. S. 3 of the Untouchability Offences Act, 1955, preserved

Denominational temples and the Untouchability Act, 1955

> ". . . the distinction between the places of public worship not only belonging to different religions but even between such places as belonging (sic) to different denominations or sections included in one religion."[12]

12.42 Measures of social reform have been upheld in various cases. Thus, in *Bombay* v. *Narasu Appa Mali*[13] it was held that the Bombay Prevention of Hindu Bigamous Marriage Act, 1944, did not violate Art. 25. The decision was rested on two grounds: first, that a sharp distinction must be made, between religious faith and belief, and religious practices. That ground is no longer good law. Secondly, that it was a measure of social reform covered by Art. 25 (2) (*b*) and that part of the decision is good law. Similarly, in *Srinivasa Aiyar*

Laws for enforcing monogamy on the Hindus upheld as measures of social reform

---

[8] This case is an illustration of the view expressed in the Introduction, that the enactment of fundamental rights in the Constitution itself had justified itself. The Court effectively restrained the high-handed and unwarranted action deeply injurious to the religious feelings of Jain worshippers.

[9] *V. S. R. Aiyar* v. *Narayana Pillai* (1956) Mad. 960, ('56) A.M. 528.

[10] ('56) A.M. 541, (1956) 1 M.L.J. 125.

[11] ('58) A.M.P. 352.

[12] ibid. p. 354.

[13] (1951) Bom. 775, ('52) A.B. 84, 53 Bom.L.R. 779.

v. *Saraswathi Ammal*,[14] the Madras Hindu (Bigamy, Prevention and Divorce) Act, 1949, was held to be covered by Art. 25 (2) (*b*). In *Ram Prasad* v. *U.P.*[15] it was held that r. 27, U.P. Government Servants Conduct Rules, which provided that a government servant may not marry a second wife during the existence of the first wife, without the permission of the State Government did not infringe Art. 25, because the act of performing a second marriage during the existence of the first wife could not be regarded as an integral part of Hindu religion nor could it be regarded as practising or professing or propagating Hindu religion. Even if bigamy were regarded as an integral part of the Hindu religion, the impugned rule was protected under Art. 25 (2) (*b*). Further, ss. 5, 9, 10 and 13 and the other provisions of the Hindu Marriage Act were similarly protected.

Propositions laid down by, or deducible from, Sup. Ct. decisions on Arts. 25 and 26

12.43 It would be convenient to collect at this place certain propositions laid down in, or which are supported by the reasoning of, the various Supreme Court decisions we have considered so far if we are to solve the problem of confiscatory legislation in relation to the "Right to Freedom of Religion" guaranteed by our Constitution:

(*a*) The position before our Constitution came into force was that the State did not interfere in matters of religion in its doctrinal and ritualistic aspect treating it as a private purpose; but it did exercise control over the administration of properties endowed for religious institutions (dedicated to the public) treating it as a public purpose. And this position has not changed after the Constitution.[16]

(*b*) Art. 25 secured religious freedom to all persons, that is, to all individuals.[17]

(*c*) Art. 26 conferred rights to religious freedom on every "denomination", that is, "a collection of individuals classed together under the same name: a religious sect or body having a common faith and organization and designated by a distinctive name."[18]

(*d*) Restrictions on the free exercise of the rights granted by Arts. 25 and 26 are permitted on grounds of public order, morality and health.[19]

(*e*) Art. 25 protects not only freedom of religious opinion but also acts done in pursuance of religious belief. Thus rituals, ceremonies and religious practices according to the religious tenets of a denomination are "matters of religion within the meaning of Art. 26(*b*)."[20]

(*f*) The broad general contention that under Art. 25(2)(*a*) "all secular activities which may be associated with religion but do not constitute an essential part of it are amenable to State regulation" cannot be supported. First, because what constitutes the essential part of a religion is primarily to be determined with reference to the doctrines of that religion itself. Secondly, because the fact that religious rites and ceremonies require the expenditure of money, or the purchase and use of marketable commodities would not convert the rites and ceremonies into economic or secular activities. They remain matters of religion within the meaning of Art. 26(*b*).[21]

(*g*) The language of Art. 26(*b*), which confers on every denomination the right to manage its own affairs in matters of religion would suggest that there are affairs which are not matters of religion. But though there is a distinction between affairs which are matters of religion and affairs which are not matters of religion — e.g. administration of the property of the denomination according to law — the two overlap and do not constitute two mutually exclusive classes. "Thus if the tenets of the Jain or the Parsi religion lay down that certain rites and ceremonies are to be performed at certain times and in a particular manner, . . . (no) outside authority has any right to say that these are not essential parts of religion and it is not open to the secular authority

[14] (1953) Mad. 78, ('52) A.M. 193.
[15] ('61) A.A. 334, (1961) A.L.J. 383.
[16] See para 12.3.
[17] See para 12.5.
[18] See Para 12.6.
[19] See para 12.8.
[20] ibid.
[21] (1954) S.C.R. at p. 1025.

of the State to restrict or prohibit them in any manner they like under the guise of administering the trust estate."[22]

(*h*) But the scale of expenditure can be controlled by a valid law under Art. 26(*d*) as relating to the administration of the property of the religious denomination. For it cannot be the injunction of any religion to destroy the religious institution or its endowments by wasteful expenditure on rites and ceremonies.[23]

(*i*) Reading propositions (*g*) and (*h*) together it would follow that a valid law can control the mal-administration of the trust even though it relates to religious rites and ceremonies; but a law cannot control the proper administration of the trust by providing that certain rites and ceremonies were unnecessary and ought not to be performed, or that the money expended on them can be better employed in achieving more desirable social objectives.[24]

(*j*) "The distinction between matters of religion and those of secular administration may, at times appear to be a thin one. But in cases of doubt, as Chief Justice Latham pointed out . . . [25] the Court should take a common sense view and be actuated by considerations of practical necessity."[26]

(*k*) Restrictions imposed on non-religious trusts may be valid, when the same restrictions imposed on religious trusts would be void.[27] But the Supreme Court struck down the sections impugned in *Ratilal Gandhi's Case* as constituting an unwarranted encroachment on the freedom of religious institutions. Mukherjea J. said: "A religious sect or denomination has the undoubted right . . . to manage its own affairs in matters of religion and this includes the right to spend the trust property or its income for the religious purposes and objects indicated by the founder of the trust or established by usage (of the) institution. To divert the trust property or funds for purposes which the Charity Commissioner or the Court considers expedient or proper, although the original objects of the founder can still be carried out, is to our minds an unwarrantable encroachment on the freedom of religious institutions in regard to the management of their religious affairs. . . . apart from the tenets of the Jain religion,[28] we consider it to be a violation of the freedom of religion and of the right which a religious denomination has . . . to manage its own affairs in matters of religion, to allow any secular authority to divert the trust money for purposes other than those for which the trust was created."[29]

(*l*) "Though Art. 25(1) deals with rights of individuals, *Art. 25(2) is much wider in its contents and has reference to communities, and controls both* Art. 25(1) and Art. 26(b)."[30] (italics supplied)

(*m*) The provisions of Art. 17 abolishing untouchability and of Art. 25(2)(*b*) throwing open public Hindu Religious Institutions to all Hindus were clear and specific, and effect had to be given to them however basic or essential the practice of excluding "untouchables" and other sections of Hindus, might

---

[22] *Ratilal Panachand Gandhi* v. *Bombay* (1954) S.C.R. 1055, 1065.

[23] See para 12.8.

[24] In *Basheer Ahmed* v. *State* ('76) A.Cal. 142, it was held that the Bengal Wakf Act, 1934, as amended in 1973 did not violate Arts. 25 and 26. The Act did not interfere with the right of freedom of religion and its provisions were essentially provisions for the preservation, protection and improvement of Wakf properties and these did not destroy the right of management of Wakf properties.

[25] In *Adelaide Co.* v. *Commonwealth* 67 C.L.R. 116, 129.

[26] (1954) S.C.R. *Supra* at p. 1066.

[27] ibid. p. 1071, in *Ratilal Gandhi's Case*, the Supreme Court was prepared to assume that the extended *cy pres* doctrine (see para 12.11) embodied in s. 55 and part of s. 56(1) of the Bombay Public Trusts Act, 1950, might be valid as regards non-religious charitable trusts.

[28] That religious property cannot be diverted to non-religious purposes.

[29] *Ratilal Gandhi's Case*, (1954) S.C.R. *supra* at pp. 1071-2.

[30] *Per* Venkatarama Ayyar J. in *Devaru's Case* discussed in para 12.36. Though the conflict to be resolved in that case was between Art. 25(2)(*b*) and Art. 26(*b*), the judgment had to consider the scheme of Arts. 25 and 26. In *Sardar Sayedena's Case* (see paras 12.16 and 12.17) the leading majority judgment said that in *Devaru's Case* the Supreme Court had held "that the right under Art. 26(*b*) is subject further to cl. (2) of Art. 25 . . .": (1962) Supp. 2 S.C.R. 496, 536. And the same view is implicit in the *Shirur Mutt Case*.

be to the tenets or creed of any Hindu denomination. The express provisions cut across and effaced the distinction between basic religious belief and essential religious practices on the one hand, and religious beliefs and practices which did not constitute the core of that religion on the other.[31]

(*n*) In the case of all religious denominations "limitations imposed on religious practices on the ground of public order, morality and health have already been saved by the opening words of Art. 25(1), and the saving would cover beliefs and practices even though considered essential or vital by those professing the religion."[32]

(*o*) The phrase "laws providing for social welfare and reform" were not intended to "'reform' a religion out of existence or identity". Just as Art. 25(2)(*a*) provided for "economic, financial, political or secular activity" which may be *associated* with religious practices, so also Art. 25(2)(*b*) dealt with other activities which must also be associated with religion "Just as the activities referred to in Art. 25(2)(*a*) are obviously not of the essence of the religion, similarly the saving in Art. 25(2)(*b*) is not intended to cover the basic essentials of the creed of a religion which is protected by Art. 25(1)."[33]

(*p*) The propositions considered so far show that when a right conferred on a religious denomination is made subject to law, the nature of that law and its impact on the right of a religious denomination to manage its own affairs in matters of religion must be borne in mind. For the guarantee contained in Art. 26(*b*) would be illusory if *any* law can be passed nullifying, in substance, what Art. 26(*b*) seeks to protect.

Acquisition or requisition of property belonging to a religious denomination

12.44 Questions have arisen whether the acquisition of property belonging to a religious denomination or dedicated to religious purposes violates Arts. 25 and 26. In *Bihar* v. *Kameshwar Singh*[34] certain religious institutions contended that property already dedicated to a public purpose could not be acquired for another public purpose. This argument was rejected, the court holding that property belonging to a religious institution would only change its form from immoveable property into money.[35] Following this decision, it was held in *Prankrishna* v. *Junior Assessor*[36] that W.B. Food Grains (Intensive Procurement) Order, 1952, did not violate Arts. 25 and 26, for, if the State could acquire property dedicated for religious purposes, it could equally acquire the usufruct thereof. Since adequate compensation must be paid, the religious trust would function as if the usufruct has been changed into money. Since that was the way trusts normally functioned, there could be no prejudice caused to the trust. Besides, both Arts. 25 and 26 were subject to public order and the acquisition of rice and paddy under the Food Grains Order was due to a grave public emergency, as mal-distribution of essential commodities in such times may easily result in public order being disturbed. Similarly, it was held that the acquisition of a *Devadayan inam* under s. 3, Orissa Estates Abolition Act, did not interfere with the fundamental rights guaranteed under Art. 26. There was only

---

[31] (1962) Supp. 2 S.C.R. pp. 551-2, *per* Ayyangar J.

[32] ibid. p. 552 *per* Ayyangar J. The savings would protect such laws as the abolition of *sati* (the immolation of widows on the funeral pyres of their deceased husbands) or the abolition of the institution of *devadasis* ("a dancing girl and courtesan of a temple": *Webster*) or the prevention of child marriages by raising the age of consent for marriage.

[33] ibid. p. 553; see also para 12.17.

[34] (1952) S.C.R. 889, ('52) A.SC. 252.

[35] ('52) A.SC. *supra* at p. 316; *K. W. Estates* v. *Madras* ('71) A.SC. 161, 165 [*held*, without any reference to decided cases that Art. 26(*c*) and (*d*) do not take away the right of the State to acquire property. As regards religious and charitable institutions the impugned Acts did not provide for payment of compensation in a lump sum but provided for payment of compensation to them every year as *Tasdik*. "That mode was evidently adopted in the interest of the concerned institutions."]

[36] ('54) A.Cal. 241, 88 C.W.N. 73.

a change in the form of the property, namely, from immoveable property into money.[37]

12.45 The above cases raised no difficult questions about the right to religious freedom, because the acquisition of property was on payment of adequate compensation, and the Supreme Court rightly observed that the property of the religious denomination only changed its form, and the denomination suffered no real prejudice. But confiscatory, or near confiscatory legislation, has raised difficult questions of interpretation of Arts. 25 and 26, as is clear from the Bombay and the Kerala decisions considered below. In *Laxminarayan Temple* v. *L. M. Chandore*[38] the petitioners were a religious trust, and ss. 32 to 32R of the Bombay Tenancy and Agricultural Lands Act, 1947, as amended in 1956 and 1961, applied to them. The Act extinguished the interest of landlords in agricultural land, and provided for compensation which was grossly inadequate, *but religious trusts were exempted by the Act provided certain conditions were fulfilled.* However, the respondent became the owner of the petitioners' land under the provisions of the Act before those conditions could be fulfilled, and consequently the exemption granted by the Act was not available to the petitioners. They therefore contended that ss. 32 to 32E violated Art. 26(c) and were void. The impugned sections were protected by Art. 31A, which did not preclude a challenge on the ground that the law violated Arts. 25 and 26. The following propositions emerge from the judgment of Tarkunde J.:

Arts. 25 and 26 and confiscatory legislation

Laxminarayan Temple Case: the law laid down by the Chief Justice and Mathew J. — Art. 26 re-written

(*a*) Ownership of property could not be regulated under Art. 25(2)(*a*), for such ownership could not be regarded as an activity, secular or otherwise; at any rate, it could not be regarded as an activity associated with religious practice.[39]

(*b*) There was no conflict between Art. 25(2)(*a*) and Art. 26(*c*) — such as there was between Art. 25(2)(*b*) and Art. 26(*b*)[40] — and consequently the question of Art. 26(*c*) being subordinate to Art. 25(2)(*a*) did not arise.[41]

(*c*) "Every religious denomination in the country or any section thereof would be composed mostly, if not wholly, of citizens of India. The right of a religious denomination to acquire, hold and dispose of property is, therefore, guaranteed by Art. 19(1)(*f*) . . ."[42]

(*d*) "The right to own and acquire movable and immovable property guaranteed by Art. 26(*c*) is a different right, being a part of the freedom to manage religious affairs which is guaranteed under Art. 26. . . . Art. 26(*c*) ensures that the State shall not deny to any religious denomination or any section thereof, the right which is available to other individuals or groups of individuals to own and acquire property, except where that right is required to be restricted for safeguarding or promoting public order, morality or health."[43]

(*e*) If the above interpretation of Art. 26(*c*) were not adopted, several anomalies would arise. "If we were to hold that Art. 26(*c*) guarantees to religious denominations, independently of Art. 19(1)(*f*), the right to own and acquire property, and that the said right can only be restricted in the interests of public order, morality and health, it would follow that the right of a religious denomination to own and acquire property cannot be subjected to those restrictions in the interest of the general public which do not fall within the ambit of morality and health."[44] For, ". . . every restriction which is in the interests of public order, morality or health is in the interest of the general public. But every restriction which is in the interests of the general public is not necessarily in the interests of public order, morality or health."[45]

[37] *Chintamoni Pratihari* v. *Orissa* (1957) Cut. 328, ('58) A.Or. 18.
[38] (1970) Bom. 1289, ('70) A.B. 23, 71 Bom.L.R. 197.
[39] ('70) A.B. at p. 27.
[40] ibid. (See para 12.36 where the conflict and its solution are fully discussed).
[41] ibid. p. 28.
[42] ibid.
[43] ibid.
[44] ibid.
[45] ibid.

(f) Several instances could be given of the absurd consequences which would follow if the interpretation put on Art. 26(c) by the court [in proposition (d) above] was not adopted.[46] "It could not have been the intention of the makers of the Constitution that the right of religious denominations to own and acquire property should not be subjected to . . . reasonable restrictions in the interests of the general public."[47]

(g) The legislative history of Art. 26 also supported the interpretation put on Art. 26 by the court. Draft Art. 20 (now Art. 26) did not contain any reference to the rights being subject to public order, morality and health. This limitation was added by the Constituent Assembly.

Accordingly, Tarkunde J. held that ss. 32 to 32R did not violate Art. 26 (c) because they imposed reasonable restrictions on the right of every owner of agricultural land.

Narayanan Nair's Case: the law laid down by the Chief Justice and Mathew J.—Art. 26 re-written

12.46 In *Narayanan Nair* v. *Kerala*[48] several provisions of the Kerala Land Reforms Act, 1964, which were either confiscatory, or near confiscatory, were impugned by religious denominations entitled to the protection of Art. 26.[49] These provisions were protected by Art. 31A, but that Article did not preclude a challenge under Art. 26. The majority judgment, delivered by the Chief Justice, held that the right conferred by Art. 26 (c) was not subject only to public order, morality and health, for so to hold would lead to the absurd consequence which had been pointed out in the *Laxminarayan Temple Case*.[50] Purporting to follow the decision in the *Shirur Mutt Case* and *Ratilal Gandhi's Case*,[51] the Chief Justice held that Art. 26 fell into two parts: clauses (a) and (b) dealing with what might be called the "religious" aspect of the guaranteed right, and clauses (c) to (d) with what might be called the "secular" aspect. He held that all the clauses were governed by the opening words "Subject to public order, morality and health"; and though the words, "in accordance with law", could not be read into Art. 26 (a) and (b) by construction, yet, in order to avoid the absurd consequences referred to earlier, principles of construction justified the court in reading clause (c) as governed by the words "in accordance with law" appearing in clause (d), disregarding the punctuation in the Article.[52] He observed that this construction received support from the legislative history of Art. 26.[53] As regards the contention that such a construction would render the right conferred by Art. 26 (b) illusory, the Chief Justice observed that the right was not illusory, because property could not be taken away by executive action but only by authority of law. Mathew J. who delivered a dissenting judgment on certain matters, concurred on the interpretation of Art. 26; but he referred to the history of that Article in greater detail by reference to Shiva Rao's *Framing of India's Constitution*.[54] He held that there was great force in the contention that in the light of legislative history, the omission of the words, "in accordance with

[46] The judgment gives the following examples of laws which would not apply to religious denominations: a law putting restrictions on the ownership of gold for stabilizing the currency of the country, or requiring that immoveable property exceeding a certain value shall be acquired only by a registered instrument, or requiring the owner of dilapidated property to repair or pull it down, or requiring that land should not be kept fallow for a number of years.

[47] ('70) A.B. *supra* at p. 29.

[48] ('71) A.Ker. 98 (F.B.).

[49] ibid. p. 109.

[50] ibid. pp. 109-110.

[51] See para 12.11.

[52] ('71) A.Ker. *supra* at pp. 109-110.

[53] ibid. p. 110 where the history is set out.

[54] ibid. pp. 135-6.

law" in Art. 26(*c*) was a defect of drafting. Both the judgments held that if the rights conferred by Art. 26(*a*) and (*b*) were impaired or destroyed by a law acquiring the property of a religious denomination without compensation, that was only an indirect effect of the law. And in considering the validity of a law on the ground of the violation of a fundamental right, only the direct effect of the law on the fundamental right could be taken into account.

Submission: The view taken by the Bombay and Kerala High Courts that their construction is supported by legislative history is not correct. The full history set out

12.47 It is submitted that the conclusion of the Bombay and the Kerala High Courts that the construction adopted by them was supported by the legislative history of Art. 26 is not correct. That history shows that as a result of the discussions in the Drafting Committees on fundamental rights, and on minorities,[55] the following clause was agreed upon, namely:

> "Every religious denomination shall have the right to manage its own affairs in matters of religion and subject to the general law, to own, acquire and administer property and to establish and maintain institutions for religious and charitable purposes."[56]

On May 1, 1947, the clause was adopted by the Constituent Assembly, with the addition of the words, "or any section thereof" after "denomination", and the deletion of the word, "general" from "subject to general law".[57] Except for mere drafting changes[58] this clause was embodied in the Draft Constitution of India (October 1947) prepared by the Constitutional Advisor for the consideration of the Drafting Committee.[59] At its meeting held on November 1, 1947, the Drafting Committee decided that no change was to be made in the clause;[60] but on November 8, 1947, at the suggestion of Shri N. Gopalaswami Ayyangar, the clause was revised as it now stands in Art. 26, except that the opening words "Subject to public order, morality and health" were absent.[61] This revised clause appeared in the Draft Constitution of February 1948 as Art. 20, but as a result of suggestions made by Shri Pattabhi Sitaramayya and others,[62] the Drafting Committee decided to sponsor an amendment "That in the beginning of Art. 20, the words 'subject to public order, morality and health' be added."[63] On December 7, 1948, Dr. Ambedkar moved that Art. 20 be adopted by the Constituent Assembly with the above amendment. He said:

> "Sir, it was just an omission. Honourable Members will see that these words also govern article 19; as a matter of fact they should also have governed article 20 because it is not the purpose to give absolute rights in these matters relating to religion. The State may reserve to itself the right to regulate all these institutions and their affairs whenever public order, morality or health require it."[64]

The amendment was accepted, and the amended draft Art. 20, without any change, became Art. 26.

Submission: Art. 26 cannot be re-written so as to

12.48 Article 26 runs as follows:

> "*Freedom to manage religious affairs.*—Subject to public order, morality and health, every religious denomination or any section thereof shall have the

[55] Shiva Rao, *The Framing of India's Constitution*, Vol. II, pp. 269, 270, 298.
[56] ibid. pp. 270, 298. [57] *C.A.D.* Vol. 3, pp. 286-8.
[58] *Viz.*, "subject *to the provisions of law*" in place of "subject to law", and "*moveable* and *immoveable* property" in place of "property".
[59] Shiva Rao, *The Framing of India's Constitution*, Vol. III, p. 10.
[60] ibid. p. 330. [61] ibid. pp. 350-51.
[62] Shiva Rao, *The Framing of India's Constitution*, Vol. IV, p. 42.
[63] *C.A.D.*, Vol. 7, p. 859. [64] ibid.

destroy a fundamental right

right (*a*) to establish and maintain institutions for religious and charitable purposes; (*b*) to manage its own affairs in matters of religion; (*c*) to own and acquire moveable and immoveable property, and (*d*) to administer such property in accordance with law."

We have seen that the clause as first passed by the Constituent Assembly in May 1947, (*the sub-clauses of which have been numbered by the author for convenience of reference*), ran as follows:

Every religious denomination or a section thereof shall have the right (1) to manage its own affairs in matters of religion and subject to law (2) to own, acquire and administer property and (3) to establish and maintain religious and charitable institutions.

It will be seen that the clause as revised according to Shri Ayyangar's suggestion radically altered the above clause. Clause (3) was transposed to cl. (*a*), and clause (1) to cl. (*b*), of Art. 26, Clause (2) was split up into two: "to own and acquire property" being transposed to cl. (*c*) of Art. 26, (with the addition of the word 'and') and "to administer property" was transposed to cl. (*d*). Further, in the original clause, the right "to manage its own affairs in matters of religion" (cl. 1) was *not* subject to the qualificatory clause "subject to law", which clause however qualified the rights conferred by cls. (2) and (3). In the revised clause, the qualificatory clause performs a very different function; it qualifies a part of the original cl. (2) only, namely, "to . . . administer (such) property". Since no reasons were given for the change suggested by Shri Ayyangar,—and none can be found from the published papers,—it is not possible to say that these radical changes were not intended, and that there was a mere error of drafting. Again, the original clause as revised was further changed by the amendment adopted by the Constituent Assembly that the words "Subject to public order, morality and health" be inserted at the beginning of the Article. It is submitted that Art. 26(*c*) may raise problems of legal interpretation, but they must be solved by applying well-settled principles of construction independently of the legislative history of Art. 26. Those principles *may* justify the addition of the words "in accordance with law" at the end of Art. 26(*c*) in order to avoid absurd consequences. But those principles *do not* justify the addition of words, if such addition leads to an even more absurd result—the destruction of a guaranteed fundamental right. If absurd consequences either way are to be avoided, the whole subject of the right to freedom of religion requires a closer analysis than it has received in the *Bombay* and *Kerala Cases* considered above. We will consider, first, the relevant Articles of our Constitution, and the scheme which they embody; secondly, whether the two judgments can be supported; and finally how the apparent conflict between Art. 26(*c*) and Art. 31 can be resolved.

A fuller analysis of freedom of religion required

Articles relevant to freedom of religion

12.49 The guarantee of religious freedom is not confined only to Arts. 25 to 28 which appear under the heading "Right to Freedom of Religion". The Preamble to our Constitution proclaims that the Constitution is designed to secure to *every citizen* liberty of thought, expression, belief, faith and worship. The Constitution goes further, and confers religious freedom on *every person* and on every *religious denomination*. Art. 16, which deals with equality of opportunity in matters of public employment, saves laws which provide that the incumbent of an office in a denominational institution, or a member of its governing body, shall be a person professing a particular religion or belonging to a particular denomination: Art. 16 (5). And although Arts. 29 and 30 appear under the heading "Cultural and Educational Rights", they are connected, *inter alia*, with religion and religious institutions as is clear from their terms, and as will appear more fully in the course of this discussion.

The unity of the personal and institutional aspect of religion recognized by our Constitution

12.50 It is obvious that religion has both a personal and an institutional side. No doubt, men can pray in their homes, "and hit heaven with their prayers"; but throughout the ages men have worshipped in temples, churches, mosques and the like. In practice, the personal right is inseparable from the institutional; and a person would justly complain that he had been denied the freedom of religion if the right of private worship was conceded, but the right of public worship was denied, to him. Arts. 25 to 28 recognise this two-fold aspect of religion. Subject to public order, morality and health, Art. 25 (1) confers on every person the right freely to profess, practise and propagate religion. But Art. 25 (2) expressly refers to the throwing open of Hindu religious *institutions* of a public character to all classes and sections of Hindus, thus recognising the unity of personal and institutional aspects of religious freedom. This aspect is further emphasised by Art. 26, which confers freedom of religion on *every religious denomination*; and the scheme of that Article must now be considered. The right of a religious denomination to manage its own affairs in matters of religion [Art. 26 (*b*)] would be meaningless if such denomination could not *establish* and *maintain* religious institutions: [Art. 26 (*a*)]. In India, as in England, the advancement of religion is a recognized head of charity; therefore a religious institution (of a public character) would also be a charitable institution. But works of charity are a part of many religions; a "Brother or Sister of Charity" is "a member of a religious organization devoted to charity".[65] In India, as in England, the advancement of education is also a recognized head of charity; therefore, educational institutions would be covered by the words, "charitable institutions", in Art. 26 (*a*). But denominational education is education according to the principles of a church or sect, and Art. 28 recognizes the fact that religious instruction may be imparted in educational institutions not wholly maintained by the State. However, Art. 28 (3) provides that no one shall be required to take part in any religious instruction, or religious worship, at any educational institution recognized or receiving aid from the State, except with his, or his guardian's consent.

12.51 Article 26 (*a*) and Art. 30 (1) partially overlap. We have seen that under Art. 26 (*a*), all religious denominations, whether they constitute minorities or not, are entitled to establish religious and charitable institutions; and this would include educational institutions where religious worship takes place and where religious instruction is imparted. In the case of minorities, Art. 30 (1) expressly provides that all minorities, whether based on religion or language, shall have the right to establish and administer educational institutions of their choice. Art. 29 (2) is a corollary to Art. 28 (3); for, just as an educational institution recognized by the State, or receiving aid from the

[65] *S.O.D.*

State, cannot *compel* a citizen to take part in religious instruction or worship, so also educational institutions, receiving aid from the State cannot refuse admission to a citizen on the grounds of religion, race, caste, language or any of them. Consequently, neither majority nor minority educational institutions, receiving aid from the State, can use the lever of compulsory religious worship and instruction to keep out citizens belonging to other religious denominations. It will be seen that the rights conferred by Arts. 25 to 28 are connected with those conferred by Arts. 29 and 30 and no interpretation can be put on Art. 26 without considering its effect on Arts. 29 and 30.

Submission: the right conferred expressly by Art. 26(*c*), would have been implied in Art. 26(*a*) in the absence of Art. 26(*c*)

12.52 The discussions in the Drafting Committee show that the members of the Committee knew that to confer upon *all citizens* the right to hold, acquire and dispose of property did not mean that such a right was conferred on a religious denomination[66] and it would be open to the State to deny that right to religious denominations. But they also knew that freedom of religion would have no meaning unless the religious denomination had a right to own and acquire property.[67] The decision of the Drafting Committee to confer on each denomination the right to establish and maintain religious and charitable institutions necessarily carried with it the right to own and acquire property, movable and immovable. It is submitted that even if Art. 26(c) had not expressly conferred the right to own and acquire property, the courts would have treated such right as necessarily implied by acting on the maxim that "when the law gives anything to anyone, it also gives all those things without which the thing itself would be unavailable".[68] This position becomes clear if we consider Arts. 29 and 30, particularly Art. 30(1) which provides that "all minorities whether based on religion or language, shall have the right to establish and administer educational institutions of their choice". Arts. 29 and 30 do not expressly confer the right on a religious or linguistic minority[69] to own and acquire property; but the courts would treat such a right as necessarily implied in the right conferred by Art. 30(1) on minorities, for it requires no argument to show that educational institutions cannot be *established* and *administered* unless the minorities have the right to own and acquire property. The second proviso to Art. 31(2), inserted by the 25th Amendment, recognizes the obvious fact that educational institutions own property.

Submission: *Laxminarayan*

12.53 It is submitted that the *Laxminarayan Temple Case* was wrongly decided. First, because its main assumption that the right

66 Shiva Rao, *Framing of India's Constitution,* Vol. II, pp. 269-70; *K. M. Munshi*: "The point is this. We have said that a citizen can hold property. We have not stated that a religious group can hold property. It would be competent to the Legislature to prohibit this." . . . *K. M. Panikkar*: "In various countries, laws have been passed against religious corporations holding property. For example, in France it has been held that religious corporations and religious bodies shall not hold property, and shall not have educational institutions. The French Government itself had to modify after 15 years of experience."

67 ibid. p. 270. *K. M. Munshi*: "Religious freedom is meaningless if this clause is deleted. Fundamental freedom of religion *necessarily carries with it the right for a religious denomination to retain property*." (italics supplied)

68 [5 Co. 47 *"quando lex aliquid alicui concedit, concedere videtur id sine quo res ipsa esse non protest."*]

69 Which like a religious denomination is a fluctuating body.

of a religious denomination to own and acquire property is derived from Art. 19 (1) (*f*) is obviously incorrect, because that right is conferred on *citizens* only, and as held in *Narendra Prasadji* v. *Gujarat* "a religious denomination or a section thereof is not a citizen".[70] Tarkunde J.'s statement that most of the members of a religious denomination would be Indian citizens, is unwarranted in respect of several small denominations of foreigners; but, in any event, it is irrelevant, because the right of the denomination is not the right of its individual members, but is a distinct and separate right which belongs to the denomination *as a body*. Secondly, whereas Art. 19 (1) (*f*) confers a right to "acquire, hold and dispose of property", Art. 26 (*c*) confers a right to "own and acquire movable and immovable property". The omission of the words "dispose of" is not due to inadvertence. A private individual can dispose of *his own* property at will. A religious denomination holds property on trust, and the framers of our Constitution knew that trustees of a religious, or any, charity, cannot dispose of property without the sanction of the court or any other competent authority. The difference in language between the two sub-clauses marks the difference between private property and property impressed with a trust for a section of the public.[71] It will be noticed that every religious denomination, or a section thereof, has the right to maintain *religious and charitable* institutions, that is, institutions which serve the public, or a section of it. Thirdly, the judgment is internally inconsistent, for, on the one hand it states that the rights of a religious denomination are those of citizens under Art. 19 (1) (*f*), and consequently subject to reasonable restrictions in the public interest, and on the other hand it states that in the case of religious denominations, those rights can be restrained only on grounds of public order, morality and health: See proposition (*d*) in para 12.43 above. Finally, the anomalies which Tarkunde J. pointed out, (if his construction was not adopted,) would have disappeared had he considered the relevant law on fundamental rights couched in absolute terms.

Temple Case wrongly decided

12.54 It is also submitted that *Narayanan Nair's Case* was wrongly decided. That judgment treats Art. 26 (*a*) and (*b*) on the one hand, and Art. 26 (*c*) and (*d*) on the other, as creating *two mutually exclusive classes*; the former dealing with matters of religion and the latter with secular matters. The *Shirur Mutt Case*, which is said to justify this division, makes no such division.[72] On the contrary, in that case Mukherjea J. emphasized the close connection between the secular and the religious aspect, and said that at times the line between the two is thin, so that in case of doubt the matter must be resolved by taking a commonsense view having regard to the practical necessities of the case: proposition (*j*), para 12.43. Secondly, it is not correct to say that to take away the property of a religious institution which *may have the effect* of destroying that institution is only an indirect effect; the effect is direct and imme-

Submission: *Narayanan Nair's Case* wrongly decided

[70] ('74) A.SC. 2098, 2103 (The case is considered in para 12.55 of the text).

[71] It is submitted that the above explanation gives an answer to the observation made in *Narendra Prasadji's Case, supra*: "We are not required to consider in this case why the same language is not used in the said two clauses [that is, Art. 19(1)(*f*) and 26(*c*)]."

[72] As is clear from proposition (*f*) to (*j*) in para 12.43 above.

diate, however laudable the object of the law.[73] Again, in *Narayanan Nair's Case* the court held that the words "in accordance with law" could *not* be read into Art. 26 (*a*), but failed to notice that the right to own and acquire property was implicit in Art. 26 (*a*) and that without such property, religious and charitable institutions could not be *established or maintained*; and if Art. 26 (*a*) cannot be qualified by the words "in accordance with law", neither could Art. 26 (*c*) be so qualified. On the contrary, the very fact that the right to own property is implicit in Art. 26 (*a*), which sub-Article cannot be qualified by the words "in accordance with law" might reasonably account for the absence of that qualification from Art. 26 (*c*), in which case the suggested qualification cannot be added by construction. Finally, the court made no attempt to reconcile the conflict between the exercise of power under Art. 31, read with entry 42, List III, and Art. 26 (*a*), (*b*) and (*c*).

Khajamian Wakf Case

12.55 But before considering "the anomalies" referred to in the Bombay and Kerala decisions, and how a conflict between the rights conferred on religious denominations under Art. 26 and the right conferred on the State by Art. 31, read with entry 42, List III, Sch. 7 can be resolved, hereafter referred to as "the conflict of rights", we must consider two Supreme Court cases in which that question arose. In *Khajamian Wakf* v. *Madras*[74] the undernoted Acts[75] were impugned as violating Arts. 14, 19 and 31, and Art. 26. Hegde J. said that it was unnecessary to go into the provisions of those Acts, as they were completely protected by Art. 31A which excluded any challenge under Arts. 14, 19 and 31. Hegde J. then said:

> "It was next urged that by acquiring the properties belonging to religious denominations the legislature violated Art. 26(*c*) and (*d*) which provide that religious denominations shall have the right to own and acquire movable and immovable property and administer such property in accordance with law. These provisions do not take away the right of the State to acquire property belonging to religious denominations. Those denominations can own, acquire properties and administer them in accordance with law. That does not mean that the property owned by them cannot be acquired. As a result of acquisition they cease to own that property. Thereafter their right to administer that property ceases because it is no longer their property. Art. 26 does not interfere with the right of the State to acquire property."[76]

In the absence of a report of counsel's argument it is not possible to say what argument was presented under Art. 26; but the summary manner in which the contention was brushed aside would suggest that no serious question of the destruction of the rights conferred by Art. 26 by confiscatory legislation either arose, or was raised.

followed in Narendra Prasadji's Case

However, in *Narendra Prasadji* v. *Gujarat*[77] the Supreme Court showed its awareness of the real problem though, oddly enough, it quoted and followed the observations of Hegde J. set out above. The appellant, who was the trustee of a denominational temple which owned *devasthanam* lands, challenged the constitutional validity of the Gujarat Devasthanam Inams (Abolition) Act, 1969, under which the right of the trust to 729 *bhigas* of land[78] was extinguished for grossly inadequate compensation. Goswami J., after analysing the

---

[73] See para 13.7 and *f.n.* 17.
[74] (1971) 2 S.C.R. 790, ('71) A.SC. 161.
[75] Madras Inam Estates (Abolition and Conversion into Ryotwari) Act, 1963; Madras Leaseholds (Abolition and Conversion into Ryotwari) Act, 1973; and Madras Minor Inams (Abolition and Conversion into Ryotwari) Act, 1963.
[76] (1971) 2 S.C.R. at p. 797.
[77] ('74) A.SC. 2098.
[78] About 18 acres.

provisions of Arts. 25 and 26,[79] relied on the observations of Hegde J. and repelled the challenge under Art. 26. He however observed:

"If, on the other hand, acquisition of property of a religious denomination by the State can be proved to be such as *to destroy or completely negative its right* to own and acquire movable and immovable property for even the survival of a religious institution the question may have to be examined in a different light. *That kind of factual position, however, is not taken in these appeals before us.*"[80] (italics supplied)

Sup. Ct. shows awareness of the impact of confiscatory legislation on rights conferred by Art. 26

These observations show that for the first time the Supreme Court has shown awareness that *in certain situations* a conflict of rights might arise and would have to be resolved.

Anomalies pointed out in *Laxminarayan Case* due to overlooking Sup. Ct. decisions

12.56 The anomalies which Tarkunde J. pointed out in the *Laxminarayan Case*,—which impressed the judges in *Narayanan Nair's Case*—arose because of Tarkunde J.'s mistaken assumption that if the right to acquire and own property was subject only to the restrictions on the ground of public order, morality and health, any regulatory law, not covered by "public order, morality and health" would not apply to that right. It is submitted that this assumption is contrary to several Supreme Court decisions which have held that even where rights are conferred in absolute terms, those rights are subject to regulatory laws. For example, it has been held that though the rights under Art. 30(1) are in terms absolute, regulatory laws can be made in respect of those rights because such laws do not impair or destroy the substance of the right but enable it to be enjoyed more effectively.[81] Again, fundamental rights, and all other rights, conferred by the Constitution are to be enjoyed in an orderly society. The Constitution does not make these rights subject to the laws of civil procedure, evidence, limitation, registration, municipal bye-laws and the like, because it is known that these rights are to be enjoyed in a society governed by law. Bachawat J. affirmed this view when he said that though a writ under Art. 32 (which confers a fundamental right) would issue as a matter of course if a breach of a fundamental right was established, that did not mean that "in giving relief under Art. 32 the Court must *ignore and trample under foot all kinds of laws of procedure, evidence, limitation, res judicata and the like*".[82] (italics supplied) Still again, in the *Automobile Transport (Rajasthan) Ltd.* v. *Rajasthan*;[83] Das J. for the majority, observed:

"As the language employed in Art. 301 runs unqualified, the Court, bearing in mind the fact that the provision has to be applied to the working of an orderly society has necessarily to add certain qualifications subject to which alone that freedom may be exercised.[84] . . . Regulatory measures or measures

---

[79] On this point, the judgment is unsatisfactory and is a judgment *per incuriam*, because it overlooks the careful analysis of Arts. 25 and 26 made by Venkatarama Aiyar J. in *Devaru's Case* discussed in para 12.26 above. Further, the analysis made by Goswami J. is opposed to the plain language of Arts. 25 and 26.

[80] ('74) A.SC. *supra* at p. 2103. In contrasting the rights conferred by Art. 19(1) with the rights conferred by Art. 26, Goswami J. rightly observed that Art. 19(1) conferred the various rights specified therein on citizens and that "A religious denomination or a section thereof as such, is not a citizen. In that sense the fields of the two articles may be to some extent different.": ibid. Applied in *Mahant Ram Kishan Dass* v. *Punjab* ('81) A.SC. 1576 [*held*, that as the acquisition of land belonging to and contiguous with a *samadhi* was on payment of compensation and as such acquisition did not affect the survival of the *samadhi* or substantial annihilation of the religious denomination or institution, Art. 26(c) was not violated.]

[81] See paras 13.7 and 13.12 of the text.

[82] See para 8.40 of the text.

[83] (1963) 1 S.C.R. 491.

[84] ibid. p. 521.

imposing compensatory taxes for the use of trading facilities do not come within the purview of the restrictions contemplated by Art. 301 and such measures need not comply with the requirement of the Proviso to Art. 304(*b*) . . ."[85]

It is submitted that the anomalies pointed out by Tarkunde J.[86] would have vanished if Tarkunde J. had borne the principles of the above decisions in mind.

A suggested solution of the conflict of confiscatory legislation and the rights conferred by Art. 26

12.57 We must now consider how the conflict of rights can be resolved. If a law for acquisition of property exempts property belonging to a religious denomination, or provides adequate compensation for the acquisition of such property, there is no conflict to resolve. However, if such a law does not make the aforesaid provisions, it may become necessary to resolve the conflict of rights. The rights conferred by the Constitution (as long as they remain unaltered) are meant to be real and effective rights, and it could not have been intended that they should be taken away by the simple expedient of taking away property.[87] It is submitted that there are two possible solutions for resolving the conflict of rights. First, that the courts should hold that a law which takes away the property of a religious denomination without compensation or on payment of grossly inadequate compensation would be void against all religious denominations for violating Art. 26. It is submitted that this solution is open to the objection that it does not take note of a matter of common knowledge—of which courts would take judicial notice—that churches, temples and the like possess considerable wealth in the form of movable and immovable property and if a part of that property was acquired without compensation in order to give effect, for example, to agrarian reform, the right of the religious denomination would remain substantially unimpaired. It appears to the present writer that it is because of this knowledge that the Constitution (25th Amendment) Act did not make the proviso to Art. 31 (2)[88] applicable also to religious and charitable institutions established by a religious denomination. In enacting that proviso Parliament seems to have taken note of the fact of which courts have taken judicial notice,[89] that educational institutions cannot be maintained without considerable financial assistance from the State, and that even those institutions which can be maintained out of their own resources would have to close down if school buildings, lands and property were acquired without adequate compensation. It is submitted that it does not follow from the newly enacted proviso to Art. 31 (2) that Parliament did not wish to protect the rights conferred by Art. 26 (*a*) to (*c*) on religious denominations. It would appear that having regard to the very wide disparities between the wealthiest religious endowments and the poorest, Parliament left the matter, first, to the good sense of State legislatures; and, if that failed, to the established courts of justice to see that in any case brought before them the guaranteed fundamental right was not

[85] ibid. p. 539. [86] See para 12.45(*f*), *f.n.* 46.

[87] Arts. 31A and 31C exclude a challenge under Arts. 14, 19 and 31, but *not* under Art. 26.

[88] "Provided that in making any law providing for the compulsory acquisition of any property of an educational institution established and administered by a minority, referred to in clause (1) of article 30, the State shall ensure that the amount fixed by or determined under such law for the acquisition of such property is such as would not restrict or abrogate the right guaranteed under that clause."

[89] See para 13.7 of the text.

defeated. This leads us to the second solution for resolving the conflict of rights when it arises. When any complaint is made before a court that an impugned law for the acquisition of property deprives a religious denomination of its fundamental rights under Art. 26 (*a*) to (*c*), or gravely abridges that right, the courts could restrain the enforcement of the law against the particular denomination whose rights under Art. 26 are so affected. If, for example, a place of religious worship belonging to a religious denomination is acquired for purposes of agrarian reform for an illusory, or inadequate, compensation, so that the place of worship would have to close down, the religious denomination having no money to put up another place of worship, the courts would reconcile the conflicting rights by holding that in such a situation the law should not be enforced against that religious denomination. This solution harmonizes the right of the State and the right of the denomination by giving as much effect as possible to the rights of both. If this solution is adopted the State's right to acquire property under Art. 31, 31A and 31C, read with entry 42, List III, can be freely exercised wherever it does not take away or seriously abridge the rights under Art. 26 (*a*) to (*c*). But if this solution were not adopted, the exercise of the State's right would completely destroy the rights of individual religious denominations. This is the very situation which the principle of harmonious construction is designed to remedy. And the doctrine of severability in enforcement[90] enables the courts to enforce the law in respect of the class of religious denominations whose rights under Art. 26 (*a*) to (*c*) are not taken away or substantially abridged whilst restraining its enforcement in respect of the class of religious denominations whose rights under Art. 26 (*a*) to (*c*) are taken away or substantially abridged. No doubt, as Venkatarama Aiyar J. said,[91] on the facts, it may be difficult to say in which class a religious denomination will fall; but once the facts in any case are ascertained, the religious denomination must fall in one class or the other.

Mohd. Ali Khan v. Lucknow Municipality unsatisfactory judgment

12.58 In *Mohd. Ali Khan* v. *Lucknow Municipality*[92] it was held that acquisition under the Land Acquisition Act did not violate the rights of religious freedom conferred by Arts. 25 and 26 of the Constitution. If full compensation was paid, the matter would be governed by the decision of the Supreme Court in *Bihar* v. *Kameshwar Singh*.[93] The wide ranging discussion whether a Mosque was an institution or whether a graveyard was a religious institution was unnecessary, for even if they were, if full compensation was paid, the property merely was converted from immovable to movable property. As held by the Supreme Court, the power to acquire property is not taken away. It is only if inadequate compensation is paid that the question would arise whether, first, the Mosque and/or graveyard were religious institutions. The observation that it is not necessary for a Muslim to pray in a Mosque overlooks the fact that the question is not one of necessity. The question is what is being usually done, and it is well known that religion has an institutional aspect and that prayers are offered in Mosques and that there is a sermon delivered by the preacher. As to a graveyard, the question is whether religious

---

90 See paras 3.9 to 3.11 of the text.
91 See para 3.11 of the text.
92 ('78) A.A. 280.
93 (1952) S.C.R. 889, ('52) A.SC. 252.

services are performed in a graveyard and whether that is a part of religious ordinance. It is submitted that the wide general observations do not appear *prima facie* to be justified and would require much greater evidence to support them than appears to have been led before the Court. It may be pointed out that the right of a religious denomination to maintain religious institutions is not an abstract right, because the religious Denomination maintains such institutions for the benefit of the members. An individual Muslim has the right to profess his religion. He may do so by offering prayers in his home or any public place. But he has equally a right to offer prayers in a Mosque and to listen to the sermon which may be delivered. Therefore, the individual right and the right of the denomination are not mutually exclusive and in most cases the right of the denomination is for the benefit of its individual members.

12.59 The right to take out religious processions has been fully discussed in paras 10.89 to 10.98 of the text.[94]

Miscellaneous cases

12.60 Some miscellaneous cases relating to Arts. 25 and 26 may be considered here. In connection with r. 27A of the Representation of the People (Preparation of Electoral Rolls) Rules, 1956, the court held that there was nothing either in the Hindu or the Muslim religion which could be deemed to prohibit the taking of women's photographs, though it was fairly established that among the Muslims "there was an absolute injunction against any picture or representation of the Prophet" of which the court must take judicial notice. Accordingly, r. 27A, which required a photograph being taken did not contravene Art. 25.[95] Again, it has been held that the definition of 'Hindu' was extended by *Explanation* II to Art. 25 (2) so as to include a Buddhist for the purposes of Art. 25 (2) (*b*). Hence it could not be urged that the word 'Hindu' as used in the Constitution (Sch. Castes) Order, 1950, was comprehensive enough to include Buddhists for the purposes of that order. From the fact that a special mention was made of the Sikhs, in Cl. III of the order, it would follow that the word 'Hindu' was used in the narrower sense of the orthodox Hindu religion which recognised castes and contained injunctions based on caste distinction.[96] Under Art. 26, a Roman Catholic Mission, like any religious body, had the right to establish and maintain institutions for religious and charitable purposes and to manage their affairs. The term 'administer' in Art. 30 was wide enough to cover any enforcement of discipline in regard to dress and other matters by an educational institution. Thus, the direction that *A*, an expelled nun, should not wear the 'religious habit' of a nun could not be questioned, when indisputably, nuns had a distinctive dress known as 'the religious habit', which only nuns could wear. It was not possible to countenance the argument that an expelled nun could wear the religious habit of a nun. There was nothing in Part III of the Constitution which conferred such a right either expressly or impliedly.[97]

---

[94] See also *Mohd. Siddiqui* v. *U.P.* ('54) A.A. 756, (1954) A.L.J. 645.

[95] *Nirmal Kumar* v. *Chief Electoral Officer* (1961) A.Cal. 289.

[96] *Punjabrao* v. *D. P. Mehram* ('65) A.SC. 1179.

[97] *Chinnamma* v. *Regional Director of Public Instruction, Guntur* ('64) A.A.P. 277 (as the Mission was a private body, a petition under Art. 226 complaining of an infringement of a fundamental right did not lie).

CHAPTER XIII

CULTURAL AND EDUCATIONAL RIGHTS: ARTS. 29 AND 30

"So long as the Constitution stands as it is and is not altered, it is, we conceive, the duty of this Court to uphold the fundamental rights and thereby honour our sacred obligation to the minority communities who are of our own. Throughout the ages endless inundations of men of diverse creeds, cultures and races — Aryans and non-Aryans, Dravidians and Chinese, Scythians, Huns, Pathans and Mughals — have come to this ancient land from distant regions and climes. India has welcomed them all. They have met and gathered, given and taken and got mingled, merged and lost in one body. India's tradition has thus been epitomised in the following noble lines:

'None shall be turned away
From the shore of this vast sea of humanity
That is India.'[1]

Indeed India has sent out to the world her message of goodwill enshrined and proclaimed in our National Anthem:

'Day and night, thy voice goes out from land to land,
Calling Hindus, Buddhists, Sikhs and Jains round thy throne
and Parsees, Mussalmans and Christians.
Offerings are brought to thy shrine by the East and the West
to be woven in a garland of love.
Thou bringest the hearts of all peoples into the harmony of one life,
Thou Dispenser of India's destiny,
Victory, Victory, Victory to thee.' "[2]

13.1 These words show the spirit in which the Supreme Court has enforced cultural and educational rights embodied in Arts 29 and 30— with the lone exception of the *Aligarh Muslim University Case*.[3] And the repeated enactment by legislatures of the kind of laws struck down by the Supreme Court drew from Reddy J. the following observations: Introductory

"In spite of the consistent and categorical decisions which have held invalid certain provisions of the University Acts of some of the States as interfering with the fundamental rights of management of minority institutions inherent in the right to establish educational institutions of their choice under Art. 30(1), the State of Gujarat has incorporated similar analogous provisions to those that have been declared invalid by this Court. No doubt education is a State subject, but in the exercise of that right any transgression of the fundamental right guaranteed to the minorities will have its impact beyond the borders of that State and the minorities in the rest of the country will feel apprehensive of their rights being invaded in a similar manner by other States. A kind of instability in the body politic will be created by action of a State which will be construed as a deliberate attempt to transgress the rights of the minorities where similar earlier attempts were successfully challenged and the offending provisions held invalid."[4]

By an amendment of the Constitution, Art. 15(4) made an express provision in favour of socially and educationally backward classes of citizens and for the Sch. Castes and Tribes notwithstanding Art. 29(2). The impact of Art. 15(4) on Art. 29(2) has been considered in Chapter 10 and need not be considered here.

---

[1] Poems by Rabindranath Tagore.

[2] *Per* Das C.J. in *In re The Kerala Education Bill,* (1959) S.C.R. 995, ('58) A.SC. 956.

[3] *Azeez Basha* v. *Union* (1968) 1 S.C.R. 833, ('68) A.SC. 662. See paras 13.16 to 13.23 where the case is discussed at length.

[4] *St. Xavier's College* v. *Gujarat* ('74) A.SC. 1389, 1406; 1974 (1) S.C.C. 717.

Art. 337 and Arts. 29 and 30

13.2 Article 337 must, however, be considered in connection with Arts. 29 and 30, since it makes special provisions for grants to educational institutions established by the Anglo-Indian community before March 31, 1948. In *Bombay* v. *Bombay Education Society*,[5] the Supreme Court considered Arts. 29, 30 (1) and 337 under the following circumstances: the State of Bombay issued an order in January, 1954, headed "Admissions to Schools teaching through the medium of English". The operative part of that order enjoined that from the day of the order, no primary or secondary school should admit to a school where English was used as a medium of instruction, any pupil other than a pupil belonging to a section of citizens, the language of which was English, namely, Anglo-Indians and citizens of non-Asiatic descent. Writ petitions were presented by one *P.*, a citizen of India and a member of the Indian Christian community, alleging English to be the mother-tongue of his daughter, and by one *M.*, a citizen of India and a member of the Gujarati Hindu community, alleging Gujarati to be the mother-tongue of his son, as the said daughter and son had been refused admission to a recognized Anglo-Indian school called the Barnes High School run by the Bombay Education Society. The Society and its directors also filed a petition impugning the government order. These petitions were consolidated and the High Court of Bombay issued a *mandamus* as prayed for. On appeal to the Supreme Court, two questions arose for determination: (i) the right of students who were neither Anglo-Indians nor of non-Asiatic descent to be admitted to the Barnes High School, and (ii) the right of the Barnes High School to admit such students. The court rejected the State's contention that the word "namely" in the circular was merely illustrative and that schools were free to admit not only Anglo-Indians and citizens of non-Asiatic descent, but were free to admit pupils belonging to any other section of citizens, whose language was English. But even on the assumption that the circular had that meaning, Art. 29 (2) *ex facie* put no limitation or qualification on the expression "citizen" and therefore the order violated Art. 29 (2). Nor could Art. 29 (2) be read as conferring a right only on citizens belonging to minority communities, for there were no cogent reasons for so limiting Art. 29 (2). The heading under which Arts. 29 and 30 were grouped together was quite general and did not admit any such differentiation. In fact, in *Madras* v. *Srimathi Champakam Dorairajan*[6] the Supreme Court had already held that Art. 29 (1) protected the language, script and culture of *a section of* the citizens, while Art. 29 (2) guaranteed the fundamental right of *individual citizens*. The right under Art. 29 (2) belonged to an individual as a citizen, and not as a member of any community. The argument that Art. 29 (2) prohibited admission *only* on the grounds mentioned therein, while the circular did not prohibit admission only on those grounds, was rejected, on the principle laid down by the Privy Council in *Punjab* v. *Daulat Singh*,[7] for whatever the object of the circular, the immediate ground and direct cause for the denial of the right was that the mother-tongue of the applicant was not English. Therefore, the laudable object of the impugned order did not obviate the prohibition of Art. 29 (2). The right of

Bombay Education Society's Case: circular prohibiting admission of students other than those of non-Asiatic descent and Anglo-Indians to "English medium" schools

The circular violated Art. 29(2), even if it permitted the admission of students whose language was English

Art. 29(2) confers a right on an individual citizen, independently of his membership of a community

[5] (1955) 1 S.C.R. 568, ('54) A.SC. 561.
[6] (1951) S.C.R. 525, 530, ('51) A.SC. 226.
[7] (1946) 73 I.A. 59 (see para 9.130 where the relevant passage from Lord Thankerton's judgment is set out).

minorities to establish and administer educational institutions of their choice, may be subject to the regulatory power of the State but such power did not include the right to prescribe a particular language as a medium of instruction, for,

"Where, . . . a minority like the Anglo-Indian Community, which is based, *inter alia*, on religion and language, has the fundamental right to conserve its language, script and culture . . . and has the right to establish and administer educational institutions of their choice . . . there must be implicit in such fundamental right the right to impart instruction in their own institution to the children of their own Community in their own language. To hold otherwise will be to deprive Arts. 29(1) and 30(1) of the greater part of their contents. Such being the fundamental right, the police power of the State to determine the medium of instruction must yield to this fundamental right to the extent it is necessary to give effect to it and cannot be permitted to run counter to it."[8]

The circular was void as violating Art. 337

Further, under the second proviso to Art. 337 it was a condition of the right to the additional grant there mentioned, that at least 40 per cent of the admissions to Anglo-Indian educational institutions must be made available to members of communities other than the Anglo-Indian community. Therefore, the circular was void as violating not only Art. 30(1) but also Art. 337.

Art. 29 and 30: *In re Kerala Education Bill, 1957*

13.3 Questions of great importance under Arts. 29 and 30 were raised in the President's Reference under Art. 143(1) in *In re the Kerala Education Bill, 1957*.[9] In this discussion, we are not concerned with the scope and ambit of Art. 143(1), which was considered in the opinion, nor with the challenge under Art. 14. The Reference was made because grave doubts had arisen about the validity of several provisions contained in the Bill having regard to Arts. 29 and 30. Das C.J., who delivered the majority opinion of the court (Venkatarama Aiyar J. dissenting on one of the issues involved) said that the solution of the problem required an appreciation of certain provisions of the Constitution. The "inspiring and nobly expressed preamble to our Constitution" showed that one of the cherished objects of our Constitution was to assure to all its citizens the liberty of thought, expression, belief, faith and worship. Nothing provoked and stimulated thought and expression in people more than education, which clarified our belief and faith and helped to strengthen our spirit of worship. To implement and fortify these purposes, Part III had provided certain fundamental rights. Art. 14 guaranteed equality; Art. 16 guaranteed equality of opportunity in all matters of public employment; Art. 19(1) guaranteed, among other rights, the freedom of speech and expression and the right to practise any profession or to carry on any occupation, trade or business, subject to reasonable restrictions. Art. 25 guaranteed the freedom of conscience and the right freely to profess and propagate religion, subject to limited exceptions, and Art. 26 guaranteed the right of every religious denomination, or a section thereof, to establish and maintain institutions for religious and charitable purposes; to manage its affairs in matters of religion; to acquire property and to administer it in accordance with law. Since the ideal was to constitute India into a secular State, Art. 28(1) provided that no religious instruction was to be given in educational institutions wholly maintained out of State funds and no person attending any educational institution recognized by, or receiving aid from, State funds was to be required to attend any religious worship

The importance of appreciating the scheme underlying the following constitutional provisions: the preamble to our Constitution and Arts. 14, 16, 19(1), 25, 26, 28(1), 29, 30, 41, 45, 330, 331, 334, 336 and 337

[8] (1955) 1 S.C.R. *supra* at p. 586. [9] (1959) S.C.R. 995, ('58) A.SC. 956.

that may be conducted in such institution. Arts. 29 and 30 conferred certain educational and cultural rights as fundamental rights. The Directives of State Policy were not enforceable in courts and could not override fundamental rights, but they represented the principles of State policy and Arts. 41 and 45 were referred to. Certain special rights were conferred by Arts. 330, 331, 334 and 336 on Sch. Castes and Tribes, and on the Anglo-Indian community as regards representation in the legislatures. Art. 337 made special provision for grants to Anglo-Indian educational institutions established before March 31, 1948, and that Article had a direct bearing on the question referred to the Supreme Court.

The right under Art. 30(1) is a necessary concomitant of the right conferred by Art. 29(1)

13.4 After summarising the relevant provisions of the Bill,[10] the court observed as regards Arts. 29 and 30, that as indicated by the marginal notes, their purpose was to confer fundamental rights on certain sections of the community constituting a minority community. Art. 29 (1) which conferred on any section of the citizens a right to conserve its own language, script or culture, made it obvious that a minority could effectively conserve its language, script and culture by and through educational institutions and therefore the right to establish institutions of its choice "was a necessary concomitant to the right to conserve its distinctive language, script or culture" and that right was conferred on all minorities by Art. 30 (1). That right however was subject to the right conferred by Art. 29 (2). After considering the rival contentions as to the meaning of the word "minority"[11] the Supreme Court said that it was not necessary to express a final opinion because

The meaning of "minority" not finally determined

". . . the Bill before us extends to the whole of the State of Kerala and consequently the minority must be determined by reference to the entire population of that State. By this test Christians, Muslims and Anglo-Indians will certainly be minorities in the State of Kerala."[12]

Art. 30(1) not limited to institutions established after the Constitution

13.5 Rejecting the contention that Art. 30 (1) applied only to institutions established after the date of the Constitution,[13] the court said that Art. 30 (1) gave the minorities *two* rights; (*a*) to establish, and (*b*) to administer, educational institutions of their choice. The second right clearly covered the right to administer pre-Constitution religious institutions. Rejecting the contention that the right of admission under Art. 29 (2) was limited to members of the community for whose benefit the schools were established the court observed:

The right under Art. 29(2) not limited to the community for which a school is established

"Nor is it reasonable to assume that the purpose of Art. 29(2) was to deprive minority educational institutions of the aid they receive from the State. To say that an institution which receives aid on account of its being a minority educational institution must not refuse to admit any member of any other community only on the grounds therein mentioned and then to say that as soon as such institution admits such an outsider it will cease to be a minority institution is tantamount to saying that minority institutions will not, as minority institutions, be entitled to any aid. The real import of Arts. 29(2) and Art. 30(1) seems to us to be that they clearly contemplate a minority institution with a sprinkling of outsiders admitted into it. By admitting a non-member into it the minority institution does not shed its character and cease to be a minority institution. Indeed the object of conservation of the distinct language, script and culture of a minority may be better served by propagating the same amongst non-members of the particular minority community. In our opinion, it is not possible to read this condition into Art. 30(1). . . ."[14]

---

[10] ibid. pp. 1022-30.
[11] ibid. pp. 1047-9.
[12] ibid. p. 1050.
[13] fol. in *S. K. Patro* v. *Bihar* (1970) 1 S.C.R. 172, ('70) A.SC. 259, 261.
[14] ibid. p. 1052.

13.6 Art. 30 (1) conferred certain rights not only on religious but on linguistic minorities as well. One such right was to establish educational institutions of their own choice; but that right was not limited to teaching their religion alone or their language alone. No limitation had been placed on the subjects to be taught in such educational institutions. Minorities would ordinarily desire to establish such institutions as would serve both purposes, namely, the purpose of conserving their religion, language or culture and also the purpose of giving a good general education to their children. The key to Art. 30 (1) lay in the words *"of their own choice"*. Educational institutions so established fell into three classes: (i) those which did not seek either aid or recognition from the State; (ii) those which wanted such aid; and (iii) those which wanted recognition but not aid. The Bill did not apply to the first class which required no further consideration. The second class had to be sub-divided into two classes: (*a*) those eligible for receiving grants under the Constitution and (*b*) those not so entitled but nevertheless seeking to get aid. Anglo-Indian educational institutions came within the sub-class (*a*). Art. 366 (2), which defined an "Anglo-Indian", showed that the Anglo-Indian community was a well-known minority community in India based on religion as well as language and it had been recognized as such by the Supreme Court.[15] The State's contention that such schools were only entitled to a grant under Art. 337 was negatived, for though the word "grant" was used in Art. 337, and the word "aid" in Arts. 29 (2) and 30 (2), the word "aid" covered the grant referred to in Art. 337. The conditions of grant under the Bill would infringe the rights of the educational institution not only under Art. 337 but also under Art. 30 (2). As to grants under Art. 337, clauses 3 (5), 8 (3) and 9 to 13 of the Bill[16] had, in substance and effect, infringed the fundamental rights under Art. 30 (1), and were to that extent void.

Art. 30(1) confers rights on religious as well as linguistic minorities; it puts no limitation on the subjects to be taught

The words "of their own choice" furnish a key to Art. 30(1): the three categories of schools

Provisions of the Bill which were held to violate the rights of Anglo-Indians under Arts. 30(2) and 337

13.7 In determining the constitutional validity of a measure or a provision, regard must be had to its real effect and impact on the fundamental right as repeatedly held by the Supreme Court.[17] Although there was no constitutional provision for grant-in-aid to educational institutions established by the Anglo-Indian community after 1948, or those established by other minorities at any time, it was well known that for modern educational institutions to be properly and effectively run, considerable expense was necessary which could not be met fully by fees collected from the schools, private endowments and the like, and therefore educational institutions could not be maintained efficiently without substantial aid from the State. Arts. 28 (3), 29 (2) and 30 (2) postulated that educational institutions would receive aid from State funds. The impugned Bill also contemplated making grants-in-aid. The court rejected the State's contention that any conditions could be imposed for the grant, since the schools could forego the grant and exercise their

Grant-in-aid or recognition cannot be offered on terms which involve a surrender of the right under Art. 30(1)

[15] In *Bombay* v. *Bombay Education Society* (1955) 1 S.C.R. 568, 583, ('54) A.SC. 561.

[16] Which were the subject matter of the second question referred to the court.

[17] *Rashid Ahmed* v. *Municipal Board, Kairana* (1950) S.C.R. 566, 571, ('50) A.SC. 163; *Mohammad Yasin* v. *Town Area Committee, Jalalabad* (1952) S.C.R. 572, 577, ('52) A.SC. 115, and *Bombay* v. *Bombay Education Society* (1955) 1 S.C.R. *supra* p. 583.

Art. 45 cannot override Art. 30: but reasonable restrictions can be imposed as conditions of aid or recognition

rights under Art. 30(1), and also rejected the schools' contention that no conditions at all could be imposed upon those rights. Making grants-in-aid was a governmental function which must be discharged in a reasonable manner. A Government may not make any grants or be unable to do so; but if grants *were* made, conditions must not be attached to those grants which would destroy the fundamental right. Art. 30 guaranteed a fundamental right; Art. 45 laid down Directives of State Policy making primary and secondary education free and compulsory. The right under Art. 30 was a right to establish and to *administer* educational institutions of their choice and *the right to administer effectively did not include a right to mal-administer.* The Government therefore could impose reasonable regulations to secure proper administration as a condition for giving aid or recognition. But it could not say: "I have money and I shall distribute aid but I shall not give you any aid unless you surrender to me your right of administration."[18] Legislative powers under Arts. 245 and 246 were subject to the other provisions of the Constitution including fundamental rights. The court upheld several clauses of the Bill as imposing permissible regulations, but found it impossible to support clauses 14 and 15 of the Bill,[19] as they were totally destructive of the rights guaranteed under Art. 30(1).

The same topic continued with reference to recognition of schools

13.8 As regards schools which sought recognition and not aid, the court observed that the distinct language, script or culture was not the only object of choice of minority communities, but they also desired that scholars of their educational institutions should go out into the world fully equipped with the qualifications necessary for a useful career in life. But according to the Education Code in operation, the scholars of unrecognised schools were not permitted to avail themselves of education in the University and were not eligible for entering public service. Without recognition, therefore, the educational institutions established or to be established by the minority communities could not fulfil the real objects of their choice and the right under Art. 30(1) could not be effectively exercised. Though the right to recognition was not a fundamental right, it could not be granted on condition that no fees should be taken from students attending primary and secondary classes, as that would, in effect, make it impossible for an educational institution established by a minority community to be carried on. Art. 45 required the State to provide for free and compulsory education for all children, but there was nothing to prevent the State from discharging that obligation through Government and aided schools, and Art. 45 did not require that obligation to be discharged at the expense of minority communities. The argument that minorities should not be pampered in maintaining their selfish and sectional interests, was met by the words quoted at the beginning of this chapter.

Provisions prohibiting the charging of fees in primary and secondary classes were void as violating Art. 30(1)

The above provisions were held to be valid by Venkatarama Aiyar J. in his dissenting opinion: *Barret's Case* cited in support

13.9 Venkatarama Aiyar J. held that apart from the right to a grant contained in Art. 337, there was no right to a grant under the Constitution nor any right to recognition. The minority communities could exercise their constitutional rights, for so long as they did not seek a grant or recognition, the Bill did not apply to them. Art. 45 justified the provision of the Bill that no fees should be charged in

---

18 (1959) S.C.R. *supra* at p. 1063.

19 They are summarised in (1959) S.C.R. *supra* at pp. 1027-8.

primary and secondary classes. He cited *City of Winnipeg* v. *Barret*: *City of Winnipeg* v. *Logan*[20] as an authority supporting his view. It is unfortunate that the attention of the learned judge was not drawn to the relevant constitutional provisions in Canada nor to the subsequent decisions of the Privy Council. It is outside the scope of this work to discuss in detail a difficult branch of Canadian law; but the following brief account is given in view of the dissenting judgment of Venkatarama Aiyar J. *Barret's Case* and *Logan's Case* raised the question of the interpretation of s. 22 (1) of the Constitution Act of Manitoba, 1870. But s. 22 had other sub-sections and it has been decided by later cases that s. 22 contained provisions which for the present purposes were identical with s. 93 (1), (3) and (4) of the B.N.A. Act, 1867.[21] In *Barret's Case* and in *Logan's Case* the Privy Council held, on an interpretation of s. 22 (1), and on the evidence in the case, that the Public Schools Act, 1890, did not prejudicially affect any right or privilege which the Roman Catholics enjoyed by law or practice *at the Union*. After this judgment, the Roman Catholic minority of Manitoba appealed to the Governor-General in Council under s. 22 (2) of the Manitoba Act, and he referred the question for the opinion of the Supreme Court as to whether an appeal lay, and whether it was competent to grant the reliefs prayed for. By a majority of 3 to 2 the Supreme Court held that no appeal lay. On appeal, the Privy Council observed that there was a close parallel between s. 22 of the Manitoba Act and s. 93 (1), (3) and of the B. N. A. Act, 1867, and held that an appeal lay notwithstanding the decision in *Barret's Case* and *Logan's Case*. It was further held that s. 22 (2) dealt with the rights of Protestant and Catholic *minorities*, and was not limited to rights *at the Union*. The law impugned in *Barret's Case* had seriously affected the rights of the Roman Catholics within the meaning of s. 22 (2) because the law deprived the Roman Catholics of their previously existing proportionate share of the money contributed for school purposes out of taxes, while for the new non-sectarian schools they were both taxed and assessed to rates. Accordingly, it was within the competence of the Governor-General in Council, on appeal, to grant relief; such relief did not involve the repeal of the impugned Act but could be given by an amendment removing the objections of the Catholic minority.[22]

Relevant provisions of the Canadian law not brought to the attention of the court: *Barret's Case*

Brophy's Case — a sequal to *Barret's Case* — explained and distinguished *Barret's Case*

13.10 *Brophy's Case* was followed in *Roman Catholic Separate School Trustees* v. *R.*[23] where Lord Haldane explained that whereas

Brophy's Case followed

[20] (1892) A.C. 445.

[21] *Roman Catholic Separate School Trustees* v. *R.* (1928) A.C. 363, 372.

[22] *Brophy* v. *Att.-Gen. Manitoba* (1895) A.C. 202. The present writer is indebted to a learned friend Mr. William R. Noble of Montreal, Canada, for the following account of the strange sequel to *Brophy's Case*: Immediately after the judgment, the Federal Government passed an Order-in-Council calling on the Government of Manitoba to restore to the Roman Catholic minority the rights which unconstitutionally had been taken away from them. The Government of Manitoba refused. Riots broke out, not only in Manitoba. The Federal Government introduced remedial legislation in 1896 which, after violent controversy, was withdrawn. In the next election, the "school question" was the prime issue and the cause of the Federal Government's defeat. The question is still a live source of resentment among French Canadian nationalists.

It is not surprising that the framers of our Constitution inserted safeguards for the cultural and educational rights of minorities in the Constitution itself and did not leave the protection of those rights to the executive.

[23] (1928) A.C. 363.

in *Roman Catholic Separate School Trustees* v. *R.*

a challenge under s. 22 (1) of the Manitoba Act and s. 93 (1) B.N.A. Act, was a challenge on the ground of *ultra vires* and legality, an appeal under s. 22 (2) and (3) and s. 93 (3) and (4) provided relief not on the ground of *mere* legality but on the ground of administrative propriety. The view that the rights of the appellants were not necessarily confined under sub-section (1)

Submission: *Barret's Case* was rightly not applied by the majority, and the majority opinion is correct

"... has an important bearing on the construction of that sub-section, inasmuch as it no longer takes away all remedy in cases to which the principle of *ultra vires* does not apply. It may even be that the power conferred on the Governor-General in Council enables him to take into account the considerations arising out of what had been done in the course of *de facto* administration which James L.J. excluded in delivering the judgment of the Judicial Committee in 1874, in *Maher* v. *Town of Portland*. . . ."[24]

Thus the law interpreted by the Privy Council in *Barret's Case* was not *in pari materia* with Art. 30 (1), for the scheme for the protection of minority rights in Canada was entirely different from that contained in Arts. 29 and 30. The majority judgment rightly did not refer to or rely on *Barret's Case,* and equally rightly held that the rights conferred by Art. 30 (1), which were real rights, would be destroyed if the power were conceded, to withhold grants or recognition unless those rights were surrendered.

Order directing a reservation of 80 per cent of seats for Govt. nominees in a Christian Training College held void as violating Art. 30(1)

13.11 The questions considered by the Supreme Court in the *Kerala Education Bill Case* by way of opinion were again considered by the Supreme Court in *Sidhrajbhai* v. *Gujarat.*[25] The case dealt with a number of questions but in the present discussion we are concerned with the challenge under Art. 30. The petitioners, who were Christians belonging to the United Church of Northern India, were members of the Gujarat and Kathiawar Presbyterian Joint Board referred to in the judgment as the "Society". The Society had been running several educational institutions including a Training College for teachers. On the ground that it was necessary to have a large number of trained teachers in District School Boards and authorized Municipalities, the Government issued an order directing that 80 per cent of seats in the Training College should be reserved for Government nominees and threatened that if the order was disobeyed, grant and recognition would be withdrawn from the Training College. The petitioners impugned the validity of r. 5 (2) of the rules made by the Government of Bombay for Primary Training Colleges and rr. 11-14 for recognition of private training institutions, in so far as they related to reservation of seats thereunder under orders of the Government, and the order issued pursuant thereto, as violating Art. 30 (1). The court held that Art. 26 (*a*) conferred on religious denominations a right to establish religious and charitable institutions and "in a larger sense, an educational institution may be regarded as charit-

---

[24] ibid. p. 370.

[25] (1963) 3 S.C.R. 837, ('63) A.SC. 540; fol. in *Muslim Anjuman-e-Taleem* v. *Bihar University* ('67) A.P. 148 (*held,* that if the governing body, as required by the Bihar Act 16 of 1965, were imposed on the educational institution run by Muslims, its character as an institution for modern education to Muslims would disappear. Further, its character as an institution administered by a minority community could be destroyed. Accordingly, it was held that the amending Act, and the statutes thereunder, did not apply to the institution in question, and an appropriate injunction was issued).

able".[26] But in the view which the court took of Art. 30 (1), it found it unnecessary to consider the case further under Art. 26.

Rights under Art. 30 are in terms absolute, though regulations in the interest of efficiency of instruction, etc. can be imposed

13.12 The court said that the order passed by the Government made serious inroads on the rights vested in the Society to administer the Training College. Art. 30 (1) provided that all minorities had the right to establish and administer educational institutions of their choice. Art. 30 (2), which was couched in negative terms, did not derogate from Art. 30 (1) and could not support the inference that the State was otherwise competent to discriminate so as to impose restrictions upon the substance of the right to establish and administer educational institutions by religious or linguistic minorities. For, unlike the rights contained in Art. 19, which were subject to reasonable restrictions, Art. 30 was in terms absolute, though that was not to say that reasonable restrictions in the interest of the efficiency of instruction, discipline, health, sanitation and the like may not be imposed. Such regulations were not restrictions on the substance of the right which was guaranteed, for they secured the proper functioning of the institution in educational matters. Nor did the petitioners contend that the absolute terms of Art. 30 (1) deprived the State, which paid a grant and afforded recognition to an educational institution, of the right to impose reasonable regulations. Their contention was that those regulations could only be in the interest of the institutions, such as regulations to make it an effective educational institution so as to secure excellence of training, but that regulations could not be made in the interest of outsiders. The court held that the restrictions imposed by the rules and the directions issued thereunder were manifestly not conceived in the interest of the Society. With reference to the Opinion of the Supreme Court in the *Kerala Education Bill Case* upholding certain restrictions contained in the Bill, the Supreme Court said that the Kerala Opinion had held that notwithstanding the absolute terms of Art. 30 (1), it was open to the State by legislation or by executive direction to impose reasonable regulations. No test of reasonableness was laid down nor had the Opinion held that regulation would be deemed unreasonable only if it was totally destructive of the right of the minority to administer educational institutions.[27] The court summed up the position under Art. 30 thus:

"The right established by Art. 30(1) is a fundamental right declared in terms absolute. Unlike the fundamental freedoms guaranteed by Art. 19, it is not subject to reasonable restrictions. It is intended to be a real right for the protection of the minorities in the matter of setting up of educational institutions of their own choice. The right is intended to be effective and is not to be whittled down by so-called regulative measures conceived in the interest not of the minority educational institution, but of the public or the nation as a whole. If every order which while maintaining the formal character of a minority institution destroys the power of administration is held justifiable because it is in the public or national interest, though not in its interest as an educational institution, the right guaranteed by Art. 30(1) will be but a 'teasing illusion', a promise of unreality. Regulations which may lawfully be imposed either by legislative or executive action as a condition of receiving grant or of recognition must be directed to making the institution while retaining its character as a minority institution effective as an educational institu-

[26] (1963) 3 S.C.R. *supra* at p. 848. It is submitted that an educational institution not run for private profit is clearly charitable since the advancement of education is a recognized head of charity.

[27] ibid. pp. 855-6.

tion. Such regulation must satisfy a dual test — the test of reasonableness and the test that it is regulative of the educational character of the institution and is conducive to making the institution an effective vehicle of education for the minority community or other persons who resort to it."[28]

Accordingly, to the extent that the rules authorised the reservation of seats and the direction given thereunder and to the extent of the threat of withdrawal of grant and recognition, they were held to be violative of Art. 30 (1).

Sup. Ct. decisions applied in *Patroni's Case*

13.13 The *Kerala Opinion* and *Sidhrajbhai's Case* were applied by the Full Bench of the Kerala High Court in *A. M. Patroni* v. *Kesavan*.[29] There, a Roman Catholic High School managed by Jesuit Fathers of the Calicut Mission appointed a junior member of the staff, who was a member of the Society of Jesuits as the Head-Master of the school in preference to another teacher, who was senior to him in the service of the school. The Director of Public Institution, holding that there was no justification for departing from the rule of seniority contained in r. 44, Kerala Education Rules, directed the senior teacher to be appointed. This direction was impugned as violating Art. 30 (1). The court held that as the word 'minority' had not been defined in the Constitution, it must be held that any community, religious or linguistic, which was numerically less than 50 per cent of the population of the State was entitled to the protection of Art. 30 and found as a fact that the Roman Catholics were a minority in Kerala. It was further held that the right to choose the headmaster was perhaps the most important facet of the right to administer a school and the imposition of any trammels thereon except to the extent of prescribing the requisite qualifications and experience, could not but be considered as violating Art. 30 (1) and accordingly the order was declared to be void. The court summarised the effect of the *Kerala Opinion* and the decision in *Sidharajbhai's Case* in the following propositions: 1. A school established by a minority—whether before or after the Constitution—is within the ambit of Art. 30 (1), even though it imparts general education and its students are drawn not merely from the minority community but from other communities as well; 2. the right guaranteed by Art. 30 (1) is a right that is absolute, and any law or executive direction which infringes the substance of that right is void to the extent of the infringement; 3. the absolute character of the right does not preclude regulations in the true interests of efficiency of instruction, discipline, health, sanitation, morality, public order and the like, as such regulations are not restrictions on the substance of the right guaranteed by the Constitution; 4. the fundamental right enshrined in Art. 30 (1) is intended to be effective and should not be whittled down by any regulative measure conceived in the interest, not of the minority educational institution, but of the public or the nation as a whole.[30] *Sidhrajbhai's Case* was followed in *Director of S.E., T.N.* v. *G. Arogiasamy*[31] where

The meaning of "minority" in Art. 30(1)

The impugned order held void as violating Art. 30(1) — the effect of Sup. Ct. decisions summarised

Arogiasamy's Case

---

[28] ibid. pp. 856-7.
[29] (1964) 2 Ker. 478 (F.B.), ('65) A.Ker. 75.
[30] (1964) 2 Ker. *supra* at pp. 484-5.
[31] ('71) A.M. 440. *Arogiasamy's Case* was referred to with approval in *A. Thomas* v. *Dy. Inspector of Schools* ('76) A.M. 214, 215 and it was held that it would be an unreasonable interference to tell a minority educational institution that it could not employ a more highly qualified teacher in the interest of better educational standards in the schools because it would not assist the scheme of the Government to find employment for higher grade teachers. The impugned order violated Art. 30(1) and the order was set aside.

it was held that the right of a minority community to establish and administer educational institutions of its choice [Art. 30(1)] included the right to admit students of its choice. That right could be regulated in the interest of the institution, but not of outsiders. The impugned Government regulation violated Art. 30(1) because it reduced the chances of students belonging to a minority community from getting admission to an educational institution, established and maintained for that minority, by throwing such students into competition with students of all other communities.[32] In *K. O. Varkey* v. *State*[33] it was held, following the meaning given to the word "minority" in *Patroni's Case* that Christians in Kerala were a religious minority in Kerala. As Rr. 6, 7 and 8 in Chapter XXV[34] of the Kerala Education Rules imposed unreasonable restrictions on the fundamental rights of the petitioners under Art. 30, a *mandamus* was issued restraining the respondent from enforcing them against the schools in question.[35]

K. O. Varkey's Case

13.14 The Supreme Court Opinion and its decisions have been followed in a number of cases. Thus, in *Dipendra Nath* v. *Bihar*[36] it was held that the Brahmo Samaj was a minority based on religion,[37] and a school managed and administered by the Brahmo Samaj was entitled to the protection of Art. 30(1) even though the majority of students were not of the Brahmo Samaj faith and no instruction in that faith was given. Accordingly, a Government order interfering with the management of the school was held *ultra vires* and void.[38]

The Brahmo Samaj, a religious minority entitled to the protection of Art. 30

13.15 We have seen that in the *Bombay Education Society's Case* an attempt to prohibit the use of English as a medium of instruction for persons whose mother-tongue was not English, failed. In *Shri Krishna* v. *Gujarat University*[39] the court had to consider the validity of s. 4(27) and s. 38-A of the Gujarat University Act and statutes 207 to 209 framed thereunder, which prohibited the use of English as a medium of instruction. The St. Xavier's College had been established for the promotion of the religious and cultural interests of Roman Catholics, who were a minority in Gujarat. In holding the sections and the statutes void as violating Arts. 29(1) and 30(1), the court said that the words "of their own choice" in Art. 30(1), read with

The prohibition of English as a medium of instruction held void as violating Arts. 29(1) and 30(1): the *Gujarat University Case*

[32] ibid. p. 442. The minority before the court — Roman Catholics — represented less than 10 per cent of the total population.

[33] ('69) A.Ker. 191.

[34] ibid. p. 192 where the Rules are set out. A glance at the Rules shows that they gravely interfere with the rights guaranteed by Art. 30.

[35] An unreported judgment of the same High Court had held that the rules were invalid as violating Art. 30, but the judge did not strike them down "as he was of the opinion that the rules can be enforced against minority schools in certain circumstances.": ibid. p. 193. After expressing his agreement that the rules were bad, Mathew J. added "But, when the rules are couched in language wide enough to cover restrictions upon a fundamental right both permissible and impermissible, the rules must be adjudged void to the extent they contravene the fundamental right.": ibid.

[36] 40 Pat. 783, ('62) A.P. 101 (F.B.).

[37] Following the decision in *Arya Pratinidhi Sabha* v. *Bihar* 37 Pat. 207, ('58) A.P. 359.

[38] See also *Dipendra Nath* v. *Bihar* 40 Pat. 527, ('63) A.P. 54, where the Brahmo Samaj was held to be a minority entitled to the protection of Art. 30(1) and the resolutions of the Government interfering with the management by the Bankipore Brahmo Samaj of the Bankipore Balika Vidyalaya infringed the right of the Samaj and were void as violating Art. 30(1).

[39] ('62) A.Guj. 88 (F.B.).

Art. 29 (1) meant that the minority had not only the right to conserve its language and culture but also to establish educational institutions of its choice and to administer them as members thereof. The real effect and purpose of the impugned provisions was that at least one minority, the Anglo-Indians, whose mother-tongue was English, was prohibited from establishing educational institutions of its choice and from administering them, and therefore Arts. 29 (1) and 30 (1) were violated.[40] The Gujarat University appealed to the Supreme Court,[41] which dismissed the appeal on the ground that the state lacked legislative competence to affect the medium of instruction, without discussing the question of violation of fundamental rights.

Aligarh Muslim University Case: the basis of the Sup. Ct. judgment

13.16 *Azeez Basha* v. *Union*[42] is a very important decision on the right conferred by Art. 30 (1) on linguistic and religious minorities to establish and administer educational institutions. The petitioner impugned the validity of the Aligarh Muslim University (Amendment) Act, 1965, which amended the Aligarh Muslim University Act, 1920, ("the Act of 1920"), on the ground that the amendment deprived the Muslim minority community of its right to manage the University established by the community. Before the impugned Act, an amending Act of 1951 had deleted the proviso to s. 23 (1) of the Act of 1920 according to which members of the "Court" *had* to be Muslims. That amendment had not been challenged because *in fact the set-up of the University had continued unchanged.* The effect of the two amendments was that the "Court" ceased to be the supreme governing body of the University and it was not necessary that it should consist exclusively of Muslims. The Supreme Court held that

(i) the expression "establish and administer" used in Art. 30(1) was to be read conjunctively, that is to say, two requirements had to be fulfilled under Art. 30(1), namely, that the institution was "established" by the community *and* that its administration was vested in the community. (ii) the expression "educational institutions" in Art. 30(1) was wide enough to include a University. (iii) *St. David's College, Lampeter* v. *Ministry of Education,*[43] established that the feature which distinguished a University from a body which was not a University was the power to confer its own degrees. However, before the enactment of s. 22 of the University Grants Commission Act, 1956,[44] it was open to any person or body of persons to establish a University. (iv) notwithstanding the history of facts and events which led to the establishment of the University[45] it could not be said that the University was established by the Muslim community because: (*a*) the provision of s. 6 of the Act of 1920, that the degrees conferred by the University would be recognised by the government showed that ". . . the Aligarh University when it came to be established in 1920 was not established by the Muslim minority, for the minority *could not insist* on the recognition by Government of the degrees conferred by any University established by it".[46] (italics supplied); and (*b*) the word "establish" was not a term of art and the definitions given in various dictionaries[47] showed that though one of its meanings was "to found", it was not the only meaning

---

[40] The Court added that the impugned enactments were also repugnant to the spirit of liberal toleration embodied in Art. 350-A.

[41] *Gujarat University* v. *Krishna Ragunath Mudholkar* (1963) Supp. 1 S.C.R. 112, ('63) A.SC. 703.

[42] ('68) A.SC. 662.

[43] (1951) 1 All E.R. 559.

[44] S. 22(1): "The right of conferring or granting degrees shall be exercised only by a University established or incorporated by or under a Central Act, a Provincial Act or a State Act or an institution deemed to be a University under Section 3 or an institution specially empowered by an Act of Parliament to confer or grant degrees."

[45] ('68) A.SC. *supra* at p. 665, where the history is set out. That history is not complete. The relevant history is set out in paras 13.18 and 13.19 *post.*

[46] ('68) A.SC. *supra* at p. 671.

[47] ibid. p. 672.

and in the context it meant "to bring into existence". (v) notwithstanding that under s. 23 of the Act of 1920, the "Court" was constituted the supreme governing body of the University and that the "Court" was to consist exclusively of Muslims, the other provisions of the Act of 1920, particularly those relating to the Rector and the Visitor showed that the management of the University was not vested in the Muslim community.

Consequently, the impugned Act did not contravene Art. 30(1). It is submitted that propositions (i) and (ii) above are clearly right. However, the other propositions are clearly wrong and we will consider each of them separately.

13.17 The judgment of Vaisey J. in *St. David's Case*, on which the Supreme Court relied, negatives the proposition that the *only* essential feature of a University is the power to confer its own degrees and that anybody could establish a University. Vaisey J. said:

Submission: the essential feature of a University not correctly stated

"Counsel for the plaintiffs has enumerated what he regards as *the essential qualities* which justify an institution being described as a University, and I do not think that there is much doubt that essentially, with exceptions which I will mention, St. David's possesses, those qualifications. He said, in the first place, *that it must be incorporated by the highest authority, i.e. by the sovereign power, succeeding, no doubt, to the Papal privilege which was exercised in Christendom in the middle ages by the proper, and, indeed, only, body which could incorporate and give authority to a great teaching institution.* There is no doubt that St. David's College was incorporated and that its incorporation was confirmed and strengthened by acts of the sovereign power, that is to say, by royal charter".[48] (italics supplied)

The statement of the law in *Halsbury*[49] is that "The essential feature of a University seems to be that it was incorporated as such by the sovereign power." No doubt several requisites are necessary to constitute a University, and if Vaisey J. regarded the power to confer degrees generally, as opposed to a limited power, as crucial in the case of St. David's College, it was because that college possessed the other essential qualities of a University. It is submitted that the University Grants Commission Act, to which the Supreme Court referred, merely declared existing law, which is as stated above. If this submission is correct, the whole basis of the Supreme Court judgment disappears, for the only manner in which a community could establish a University was by invoking the exercise of the sovereign power which might either take the form of a charter or an Act of the legislature, and this the Muslim community did.

13.18 As regards the history of the foundation of the University, it is submitted that all the relevant history is not to be found in the judgment. Nor is the effect of so much of the history as has been set out properly appreciated. As the case is of great importance, the history as given by the Supreme Court is set out in full:

Submission: the history of the foundation of the Aligarh University not correctly stated

"It is necessary to refer to the history previous to the establishment of the Aligarh University in order to understand the contentions raised on either side. It appears that as far back as 1870 Sir Syed Ahmad Khan thought that the backwardness of the Muslim community was due to their neglect of modern education. He therefore conceived the idea of imparting liberal education to Muslims in literature and science while at the same time instruction was to be given in Muslim religion and traditions also. With this object in mind, he organised a Committee to devise ways and means for educational re-generation of Muslims and in May 1872 a society called the Muhammadan Anglo-Oriental College Fund Committee was started for collecting subscriptions to realise the goal that Sir Syed Ahmad Khan had conceived. In consequence of the

[48] (1951) 1 All E.R. *supra* at p. 560. [49] Vol. 13, 3rd ed. p. 707.

activities of the Committee a school was opened in May, 1873. In 1876, the school became a High School and in 1877 Lord Lytton, then Viceroy of India, laid the foundation stone for the establishment of a college. The Muhammadan Anglo-Oriental College, Aligarh (hereinafter referred to as the M.A.O. College), was established thereafter and was, it is said, a flourishing institution by the time Sir Syed Ahmad Khan died in 1898. It is said that thereafter the idea of establishing a Muslim University gathered strength from year to year at the turn of the century and by 1911 some funds were collected *and a Muslim University Association was established for the purpose of establishing a teaching University at Aligarh.* Long negotiations took place between the Association and the Government of India, which eventually resulted in the establishment of the Aligarh University in 1920 by a 1920 Act. It may be mentioned that before that a large sum of money was collected by the Association for the University as the Government of India had made it a condition that rupees thirty lakhs must be collected for the university before it could be established. Further, it seems that the existing M.A.O. College was made the basis of the University and was made over to the authorities established by the 1920 Act for the administration of the university along with the properties and funds attached to the college the major part of which had been contributed by Muslims though some contributions were made by other communities as well."[50] (italics supplied)

The Preamble to the Act of 1920, refers to two societies registered under the Societies Registration Act, 1860, namely, the Muhammadan Anglo-Oriental College, Aligarh, and the Muslim University Association, and it refers to another body, the Muslim University Foundation Committee. S. 4 of the Act of 1920 provides for the dissolution of the Muhammadan Anglo-Oriental College, Aligarh, and the Muslim University Association[51] and for the transfer of all property belonging to them and all property belonging to the Muslim University Foundation Committee, to the University and such property was to be applied to the objects and purposes for which the University was incorporated.[52]

Relevant history leads only to one conclusion:

13.19 It is relevant to the history of the Aligarh Muslim University to state that five years earlier the Benaras Hindu University Act, 1915, had been enacted. At that time, the idea of establishing a Muslim University was being canvassed but had not fructified. The important thing to note is that the Bills for the creation of the Hindu University and the Muslim University were prepared as a result of long negotiations between the representatives of those communities and the Government, and the statement of objects and reasons attached to those Bills so recites. The representatives of the communities are referred to as "the promoters" of the Bills, and before the Bills were introduced their terms were settled between the representatives of the communities on the one hand and the government on the other. The two Universities represented a departure from the Universities which had been established till then, because they were established with the avowed object of imparting religious instruction to members of the community for whom they were founded. Nevertheless,

---

[50] ('68) A.SC. *supra* at p. 665.

[51] ibid. (which the Supreme Court itself described as "established for the purpose of *establishing* a teaching University at Aligarh").

[52] S. 4, sub-sec. (iv) provided: "Any will, deed or other document, *whether made or executed before or after the commencement of this Act,* which contains any bequest, gift or trust in favour either of the said Societies or of the said Committee shall, on the commencement of this Act, be construed as if the University was therein named instead of such Society or Committee". (italics supplied.) It will be seen that benefactions designed for the two Muslim Societies and for a Muslim Committee formed for the foundation of a Muslim University, were to go to the University.

Government made a grant of one lakh of rupees to each University. S. 9 of the Banaras Hindu University Act provided that the "Court" was to be the supreme governing body of the University and except for the first "Court" it was to consist *exclusively of Hindus*, a provision similar to that contained in s. 6 of the Act of 1920 that the "Court" was to be the supreme governing body of the University and was to consist *exclusively of Muslims*. It is clear therefore that the two communities asked for, and obtained, a supreme governing body in the Universities which was to consist exclusively of Hindus or Muslims respectively. In both cases, the property and assets of the existing educational institutions run by the societies formed for the benefit of the communities were vested in the University. As a condition precedent to the establishment of the Hindu and the Muslim Universities, Government required that sums of Rs. 50 lakhs and Rs. 30 lakhs should be collected by the communities and both communities collected their respective sums. S. 14 of the Hindu University Act and s. 7 of the Act of 1920 provided that those sums were to constitute a permanent endowment to meet the recurring charges of the Universities with exceptions not material to this discussion. Among the powers conferred by s. 4(2) in the Hindu University Act was the power of the "Court" to make statutes, making instruction in Hindu religion compulsory for Hindu students. Again, statute 23 of the first statutes of the Hindu University (Sch. I of the Act) provided for the creation of faculties, and further provided that members assigned to the faculty of theology had to be Hindus. On the same lines, S. 9 of the Act of 1920 conferred power on the "Court" to make statutes providing that instruction in Muslim religion be compulsory for Muslim students. S. 5 conferred on the Muslim University the power to promote Oriental and Islamic studies and give instruction in Muslim theology and religion. It is submitted that the above history leads only to one conclusion, namely, that the Hindu University was established by Hindus for Hindus, though it was open to non-Hindus to join the University. Similarly, the Muslim University was established by Muslims, for Muslims, though non-Muslims could be admitted. The fact that non-Hindus and non-Muslims could be admitted does not derogate from this conclusion because, where grants are made from public funds, public policy requires that members of other communities should not be totally excluded. In fact, in the *Kerala Opinion*[53] Das C.J. observed that an institution established and managed by a community did not lose its character as a minority institution because a sprinkling of members of the other communities were admitted to it.[54]

the Aligarh Muslim Univ. was established by Muslims for Muslims

[53] (1959) S.C.R. 995, ('58) A.SC. 956.

[54] (1959) S.C.R. *supra* at p. 1052 ["The real import of Art. 29(2) and Art. 30(1) seems to us to be that they clearly contemplate a minority institution with a sprinkling of outsiders admitted into it. By admitting a non-member into it the minority institution does not shed its character and cease to be a minority institution. Indeed the object of conservation of the distinct language, script and culture of a minority may be better served by propagating the same amongst non-members of the particular minority community."]

Submission: meaning given to "established" not correct

13.20 As regards the meaning given by the Court to the word "establish",[55] it is submitted that the meaning is not correct. It was not disputed that "to found" is one of the meanings of the verb "to establish", and it is submitted that in the context, it is the correct meaning as is clear from the definition of the verb "to found" namely, "set up or establish (*esp. with endowments*)" (italics supplied).[56] The Muslim community established the University and provided it with its total endowments. Even if the definition given by the Court were correct, namely, "to bring the University into existence", it is submitted that the Muslim community brought the University into existence in the only manner in which a University could be brought into existence, namely, by invoking the exercise by the sovereign authority of its legislative power. The Muslim community provided lands, buildings, colleges and endowments for the University, and without these the University as a body corporate would be an unreal abstraction.

The Muslims asked that the degrees of their University should be recognised and Govt. agreed

13.21 The Court repeated more than once[57] that the Muslim community could not have "insisted" on Government recognising the degrees and diplomas awarded by the Muslim University and therefore it could not be said that the Muslim community established the University. It is submitted that the word "insist" is misleading, and confuses the real issue. A community may not be able to "insist" on a thing as against Government if the parties were at arm's length, but nothing prevents a community from asking, and Government from agreeing, that the degrees of the University would be recognised by Government. That the Muslim community and the Government were not at arm's length on this question is clear from official documents[58] which show that from the earliest days, the British Government actually supported the establishment of a Muhammadan College and promised grants-in-aid although it was maintained only for a particular community.[59] Lt. Governors and Governors-General gave active support and encouragement, and Sir William Muir encouraged the scheme by giving 74 acres of land free of cost for the building of the proposed Aligarh Muslim College. It is unnecessary to dilate on this history, but it may be stated that at the meeting of the Gov.-General's Legislative Council in which the Bill was finally passed into the Aligarh Muslim University Act, 1920, the Governor-General said:

> ". . . I should like to add my congratulations to the Muslim community on the passage of this bill. *I have come here specially this morning to preside in order that I might add my good wishes and congratulations* to those which have already been uttered in this Council."[60] (italics supplied)

Submission: purpose in establishing the University would be defeated if degrees not recognized

13.22 Secondly, the Court overlooked the fact that the very object of establishing a University for a community would be defeated if its degrees were not recognized by Government. What Das C.J. said in the *Kerala Opinion*[61] in reference to schools established and managed by religious minorities directly applies to Universities so established and managed:

---

[55] See para 13.16 (iv)(b) above. The meaning given by the Court to the word "established" was applied in *Hari Manderji* v. *Magadh University* ('77) A.Pat. 12, 17.

[56] *Concise Oxford Dictionary*.

[57] ('68) A.SC. *supra* p. 671.

[58] See Jain, *The Aligarh Movement*, (1955), Chapter 10.

[59] ibid. p. 159.

[60] *Gazette of India*, September 25, 1920, Part VI, p. 1190.

[61] (1959) S.C.R. 995, 1053.

"There is no limitation placed on the subjects to be taught in such educational institutions. As such minorities will ordinarily desire that their children should be brought up properly and efficiently and be eligible for higher university education and go out in the world *fully equipped with such intellectual attainments as will make them fit for entering the public services*, educational institutions of their choice will necessarily include institutions imparting general secular education also."[62] (italics supplied)

As to the view of the Supreme Court that notwithstanding that the "Court" of the University was the supreme governing body and that it was to consist entirely of Muslims, the management of the University was not vested in the Muslim community because of the other provisions of the Act, it is submitted that the Supreme Court failed to distinguish between the management of an institution and powers of supervision and control designed to secure that the management was properly carried out. In the *Kerala Opinion* Das C.J. rightly observed that the power to manage an educational institution did not involve the power to mismanage it, and that therefore a large measure of control designed to secure proper management must be allowed to Government. The various provisions referred to in the Court's judgment merely enable the Rector and the Visitor to see that the supreme governing body of the University did not misgovern the University. The Court did not consider the fact that power to manage a University involves the power to admit students to it and in the exercise of that power the admission of students not Muslims could be regulated. If the Banaras Hindu University and the Aligarh Muslim University were not established by and for Hindus and Muslims respectively, they would not have been called the "Banaras *Hindu* University", the "Aligarh *Muslim* University". It is submitted that this aspect of the matter has been overlooked by the court.

13.23 It is submitted that this is the first case in which the Supreme Court has departed from the broad spirit in which it had decided cases on cultural and educational rights of minorities, which was reflected in the words of Das C.J. quoted at the beginning of this Chapter. In the present case, the Supreme Court has on narrow, technical grounds, which are erroneous, held that a minority community which had striven for, and obtained, the establishment of a Muslim University and endowed it with considerable property and money, had not established that University, and that provisions of the Act of 1920 vesting the supreme government of the University exclusively in Muslims did not vest the administration in Muslims. On the Supreme Court judgment there is nothing to prevent Parliament from converting the Muslim University into a University for foreign students or for backward classes. It is submitted that the decision is clearly wrong and productive of grave public mischief and should be overruled.

Submission: decision clearly wrong and should be overruled

13.24 Arts. 29 and 30 were again considered in *W. Proost* v. *Bihar*,[63] where, in an Art. 32 petition, the Principal and the Rector of St. Xavier's College, challenged s. 48-A, Bihar State University Act, 1960, as amended in 1961, as *ultra vires* Arts. 29 and 30. Whilst the petitions were pending, the Governor promulgated an Ordinance introducing s. 48-B in the Act which exempted colleges established and administered by a minority community from the provisions of

Proost's Case

[62] ibid. p. 1053.

[63] (1969) 2 S.C.R. 73, ('69) A.SC. 465.

s. 48-A, (6) to (11). Thereupon, the petitioners claimed exemption under s. 48-B and offered to withdraw the petition. The Supreme Court found that s. 48-A completely took away the autonomy of the governing body of the college, and virtually vested the control of the college in the University Service Commission.[64] On this finding, s. 48-A would have been *ultra vires* Art. 29 with regard to colleges established by minorities based on language or religion. While conceding that Roman Catholics were a minority, the respondents contended that the St. Xavier's College could not claim exemption under s. 48-B because the college admitted members of other communities and, therefore, it could not be said to be established for a minority community. In rejecting this contention, the court held that the wide language of Art. 30(1) could not be cut down by introducing into it considerations on which Art. 29(1) was based. Art. 29(1) gave general protection to minorities to conserve their language, script or culture. Art. 30(1) gave a special right to minorities to establish educational institutions of their choice. That choice was not limited to institutions designed to conserve the language, script or culture of the minority nor was that choice taken away because the minority community, having established the institution, admitted members of other communities.[65]

Mother Provincial's Case

13.25 Article 30 was again considered in *Kerala* v. *Mother Provincial*.[66] The respondent, and other parties, challenged in the Kerala High Court several provisions of the Kerala University Act, 1969, as violating *inter alia,* Art. 30(1), and the High Court partly upheld this challenge. Without express reference to the earlier decisions of the Supreme Court, Hidayatullah C.J. held that Art. 30(1) conferred two distinct rights, namely,

(i) the initial right to establish institutions of the minorities' choice. "Establishment" meant, the bringing into being of an institution by a minority community, but "it does not matter if a single philanthropic individual with his own means founds the institution or the community at large contributes the funds. The position in law is the same and the intention in either case must be to found an institution for the benefit of a minority community by a member of that community."[67] Further, it was irrelevant to this right that in addition to the minority community, "others from other communities or even from the majority community can take advantage of these institutions. Such other communities bring in income and they do not have to be turned away to enjoy the protection."[68]

(ii) The second part of the right conferred by Art. 30(1) referred to the "administration" of such institutions, that is, "the 'management of the affairs' of the institution. This management must be free of control so that the founders or their nominees can mould the institution as they think fit, and in accordance with their ideas of how the interests of the community in general and the institution in particular will be best served. No part of this management can be taken away and vested in another body without an encroachment upon the guaranteed right."[69]

Hidayatullah C.J. added that the earlier decisions of the Supreme Court[70] had established an exception, namely, that the maintenance

---

[64] ('69) A.SC. *supra* at p. 467. [65] ibid. pp. 468-9.

[66] ('70) A.SC. 2079.

[67] ibid. p. 2082. It is clear from the passage that the founding of the institution could be by a *member* or *members* of the community.

[68] ibid. p. 2082. [69] ibid.

[70] *Bombay* v. *Bombay Education Society* (1955) 1 S.C.R. 568, ('54) A.SC. 561; *Madras* v. *Champakam Dorairajan* (1951) S.C.R. 525, ('51) A.SC. 226; *In re the Kerala Education Bill, 1957* (1959) S.C.R. 995, ('58) A.SC. 956; *Sidhrajbhai* v. *Gujarat* (1963)

of standards of education was not a part of the management as such. It is submitted that this is only another way, and a less satisfactory way, of saying, what Das C.J. said in the *Kerala Opinion*, namely, that the right to manage an educational institution did not carry with it—the right to mismanage it,[71] or what Shah J. said in *Sidhrajbhai's Case*, namely, that although the right under Art. 30 was in terms absolute, that did not mean that reasonable restrictions in the interest of efficiency of instruction, discipline, health, sanitation and the like could not be imposed. Such regulations were not restrictions on the substance of the right which was guaranteed, for they secured a proper functioning of the institution in educational matters.[72]

Certain provisions impugned in *Mother Provincials' Case* held void

13.26 The Supreme Court considered the impugned provisions,[73] and applying the principles set out above, held that sub-ss. (2), (4) and (6) of ss. 48 and 49, sub-ss. (1) (i), (2), (3) and (9) of s. 53, sub-ss. (2) and (4) of s. 56, s. 58 (in so far as it removed the disqualification which the founders might not like to agree to) and s. 63 were *ultra vires* Art. 30 (1) in respect of minority institutions on the ground that they affected the administration of such institutions, and robbed the founders of that right which the Constitution desired should be theirs.[74]

Patro's Case

13.27 In *S. K. Patro* v. *Bihar*,[75] the main question for determination was whether a primary school started in 1854 at Bhagalpur, and later converted into a Higher Secondary School, was entitled to the protection of Art. 30. The appellant impugned an order passed by the Education Department setting aside the election of the President and the Secretary of the school, and directing the school to constitute a managing committee in accordance with the order. In allowing the appeal, Shah J. held that the High Court had not correctly appreciated important documentary evidence which showed that in 1854 the school was set up by local Christians in buildings erected from funds collected by them. Although substantial assistance was obtained from the Church Missionary Society of London, it could not be said on that account that the school was not established by the local Christians, with their own efforts, and was not an educational institution established by a minority.[76] In 1854 there was no settled concept of Indian citizenship, and it could not be said that the Christian Missionaries who had settled in India, and the local Christian residents of Bhagalpur did not form a minority community. No doubt Art. 30 (1) did not confer upon non-resident foreigners the right to set up educational institutions of their own choice in India

---

3 S.C.R. 837, ('63) A.SC. 540; *Gujarat University* v. *Krishna Raghunath Mudholkar* (1963) Supp. (1) S.C.R. 112, ('63) A.SC. 703; *W. Proost* v. *Bihar* (1969) 2 S.C.R. 73, ('69) A.SC. 465. Reference was also made to *Katra Education Society* v. *U.P.* (1966) 3 S.C.R. 328, ('66) A.SC. 1307, but in that case the challenge was under Art. 14, 19 and 31 and no discussion is to be found on Art. 29 or 30.

[71] See para 13.7 above. [72] See para 13.12 above.

[73] ('70) A.SC. *supra* at pp. 2082-5.

[74] ibid. pp. 2085-6. The provisions have been referred to at pp. 2083-5 of the judgment. It was stated on behalf of the respondents that if the said provisions could not be enforced against minority institutions, they would not be enforced against majority institutions. In view of this statement, the court said that it was not called upon to decide whether Art. 14 was violated as regards majority institutions.

[75] (1970) 1 S.C.R. 172, ('70) A.SC. 259. [76] ('70) A.SC. *supra* at p. 263.

—persons setting up such institutions must be resident in India and form a well-defined religious or linguistic minority. However, Art. 30 did not postulate that it could be availed of only in respect of an institution established before the Constitution by persons born and resident in British India.[77] Contrasting the language of Art. 29 with that of Art. 30, Shah J. observed that whereas the rights under Art. 29 could be claimed only by Indian citizens, Art. 30 guaranteed the right of minorities to establish and administer Educational Institutions; but Art. 30 did not expressly refer to citizenship as a qualification for the members of the minority. He said that *Proost's Case*[78] had established that Art. 30 could not be cut down by introducing in it considerations on which Art. 29 (1) was based. The fact that funds had been contributed from the United Kingdom towards setting up and developing the school, or the fact that the management of the Institution was carried on by some persons who may not have been born in India, was not a ground for denying the protection of Art. 30 (1) to the school. Further, Art. 30 (1) did not require it to be proved that all those who established the school in 1854 were Indian citizens, for in 1854 there was no Indian citizenship independently of the citizenship of the British Empire.[79]

D.A.V. College, Jullundur v. Punjab

13.28 Important questions relating to Arts. 29 and 30 were again considered by the Supreme Court in *D.A.V. College, Jullundur* v. *Punjab*.[80] The Dayanand Anglo-Vedic College, Jullundur ("the college") was run by members of the Hindu community professing the Arya Samaj faith ("the Arya Samajists"). It was originally affiliated to the Punjab University but after 1970, was compulsorily affiliated to the Guru Nanak University ("the University") under the Guru Nanak University Amritsar Act 1961 ("the Act"). The college challenged s. 4 (2) and (3) of the Act, and cls. 2 (1) (*a*) and 17 and 18 of the University Statutes on the ground that they contravened Arts. 29 and 30. The college contended that the main purpose of the University, and of the University Act, was to propagate the Sikh religion and promote the Punjabi language in the Gurumukhi script; and since the college belonged to a minority community based on religion and language—the community being adherents of the Arya Samaj Sect and denomination—the compulsory affiliation of the college to the University violated Arts. 29 (1) and 30 (1).[81]

Principles laid down

13.29 After giving the history of the Arya Samaj,[82] the Supreme Court held that though the Hindu community was a majority community in the whole of India, it was a minority community in the Punjab and the Arya Samajists though members of the Hindu community were a religious minority in the Punjab where the impugned Act operated; and the college was entitled to claim the rights under Art. 29 (1) and 30 (1) since it was established and administered by a religious minority with a script of its own. In view of this, it was unnecessary to decide whether Arya Samajists were a linguistic minority in the Punjab or whether they constituted a religious

---

[77] ibid.

[78] ('69) A.SC. 465, discussed in para 13.24 of the text.

[79] ('70) A.SC. *supra* at p. 264. [80] ('71) A.SC. 1737.

[81] There was a question raised under the States Reorganization Act, which is not relevant to the present discussion.

[82] ibid. p. 1743.

denomination within the meaning of Art. 26.[83] Dealing with the challenge under Arts. 29(1) and 30(1), the Supreme Court referred with approval to the observations in *Proost's Case* that Art. 30(1) could not be cut down by introducing in it considerations on which Art. 29(1) was based and held that

(*a*) Section 4(3) of the Act did not violate Art. 29(1), because in view of the formation of linguistic states, which had come to stay, the University had a right to provide for the education of the majority in the Punjab in the regional medium, subject to the restrictions imposed by Arts. 25 to 30. On its true construction, s. 4(3) did not require that the medium of instruction of affiliated colleges had to be Punjabi. Sec. 4(3) merely provided for the promotion of Punjabi studies, and research in, and the development of, the Punjabi language, literature and culture.[84]

(*b*) Section 4(2) of the Act did not contravene Art. 29(1) and 30(1) because that section did not compel colleges affiliated to the University either to study the religious teachings of Guru Nanak or to adopt the culture of the Sikhs. To provide for an academic study of the life and teachings—or the philosophy and culture—of any great saint of India and their relation to, and impact on, the Indian and world civilization could not be said to make a provision for religious instruction.[85]

(*c*) However, Cls. 2(1)(*a*) and 17 of Chapter V of the Statutes[86] interfered with the rights of management of the college, and those provisions could not be made a condition of affiliation. They were accordingly void as violating Art. 30(1).[87]

13.30 Clause 18 did not suffer from the same vice, as it empowered the University to prescribe by regulations the conditions governing the service and conduct of teachers, which provision was enacted in the larger interests of educational institutions to ensure their efficiency and excellence. Whether any particular regulation made in the exercise of the power violated Art. 31(1) or not would have to be decided when the regulation was made.[88]

13.31 In *D.A.V. College, Bhatinda* v. *Punjab*[89] the petitioners impugned ss. 4(2) and 5 of the Punjab University Act, 1971 ("the Act") and certain circulars and notifications as unconstitutional and void. The effect of the circulars and notifications, as well as the petitioners' contentions relating to them, have been set out in the judgment.[90] But the petitioners' main contentions were (*a*) that s. 4(2) of the Act did not empower the University to prescribe Punjabi as the sole medium of instruction; (*b*) it was not within the legislative competence of the State legislature to make Punjabi the sole medium of instruction as that power belonged only to *D.A.V. College, Bhatinda*

---

[83] ibid. p. 1744. [84] ibid. p. 1746.
[85] ibid.
[86] Briefly put, cl. 2(1)(*a*) required all affiliated colleges to have a governing body of not more than 20 persons approved by the Senate, including two representatives of the University and the Principal of the college *ex officio*. Cl. 17 required the approval of the Vice-Chancellor for the staff initially appointed and for any changes subsequently made.
[87] ('71) A.SC. 1478-9; following *In re the Kerala Education Bill* (1959) S.C.R. 995, 1053, ('58) A.SC. 956, and *Sidhrajbhai* v. *Gujarat* (1963) 3 S.C.R. 837, ('63) A.SC. 540.
[88] ('71) A.SC. *supra* at p. 1749. [89] ('71) A.SC. 1731.
[90] ibid. pp. 1732-3.

Parliament; (c) in so far as Punjabi in the Gurumukhi script was sought to be imposed on educational institutions established by Arya Samajists, which was a religious denomination, they violated Arts. 26(1), 29(1) and 30(1). The impugned notifications were, therefore, *ultra vires* and void.

Principles laid down

13.32 The following propositions emerge from the judgment:

(a) Arya Samajists who were a part of the Hindu community in the Punjab were a religious minority with a distinct script of their own and were entitled to claim the protection of Arts. 29(1) and 30(1): *D.A.V. College, Jullundur* v. *Punjab*.[91]

(b) A minority community based, *inter alia*, on religion and language had the right to preserve its language, script and culture [Art. 29(1)], and to establish and administer educational institutions of its choice [Art. 30(1)]. There was implicit in such fundamental right the right to impart instruction to the children of such community in their own language, if Arts. 29(1) and 30(1) were not to be deprived of the greater part of their content: *Bombay* v. *Bombay Education Society*.[92]

(c) The State must harmonize its power to prescribe a medium of instruction with the rights of religious and linguistic minorities, or any section of citizens, to have the medium of instruction and script of their own choice by either providing for instruction in such language or script, or by allowing affiliation with other Universities in other States where instruction is given in such medium and script. "No inconvenience or difficulties, administrative or financial, can justify the infringement of the guaranteed rights."[93]

(d) The imposition of a language as an *exclusive* medium of instruction in a University was beyond the legislative competence of State Legislatures: *Gujarat University* v. *Krishna Raghunath Mudholkar*.[94]

(e) Section 4(3) of the Act did not empower the University to prescribe Punjabi in the Gurumukhi script as an exclusive medium of instruction:

> "The University Act having compulsorily affiliated these colleges must of necessity cater to their needs and allow them to administer their institutions in their own way and impart instructions in the medium and write examinations in their own script."[95]

The impugned circulars were quashed.

A.S.E. Trust v. Director of Education: A criticism

13.33 In *A.S.E. Trust* v. *Director of Education, Delhi Administration*[96] it was held that religious minorities do not include a section of a recognized religion, as for example, different sects among Hindus. Consequently, it was held that the Arya Samaj was a reformed sect of Hinduism; it was a part of Hinduism and not a separate religion for the purposes of Art. 30(1). It was however held that Jains and Sikhs were minorities based on religion within Art. 30 since those religions were separate from Hinduism. It is submitted that the decision is clearly wrong. It has been influenced by the feeling to which Safeer J. gave expression in his concurring judgment, namely,

---

[91] ibid. pp. 1733-4 refering to ('71) A.SC. 1737, 1742-4.
[92] ibid. p. 1725.
[93] ibid. p. 1735.
[94] ibid. p. 1736.
[95] ibid. p. 1737.
[96] ('76) A.Del. 207.

"The nation has to guard against all kinds of disruptions. There is a prevailing tendency in spiritual ambition which leading to diverse expositions is causing the coming into being of various religious denominations. Such denominations ought not to be allowed to prevail as religions and should not be confounded as separate religions."[97]

It is submitted that such considerations are totally foreign to the interpretation of a fundamental right conferred on religious and linguistic minorities to establish and administer educational institutions of their choice.

D.A.V. College, Jullundur v. *Punjab* and the test to be applied

13.34 In *D.A.V. College, Jullundur* v. *Punjab*,[98] Reddy J. quoted a passage from the *Encyclopaedia Britannica*, which said of the Arya Samaj, *inter alia*, that it was a religion "completely opposed to idolatry, is sternly monotheistic and denies the efficacy of priestly intervention. Its organization and services are strongly reminiscent of Protestantism. . . ."[99] Reddy J. also quoted the following passage from the *Encyclopaedia of Religion and Ethics*:

"As Luther the German Monk was a child of the European Renaissance, so Dayanand the Gujarati monk was a child of the Indian Renaissance . . . Luther attacked indulgences, while Dayanand attacked idolatry. Luther appealed from the Roman church and the authority of tradition to the scriptures of the Old and New Testaments. Swami Dayanand appealed from the Brahmanical Church and the authority of Smriti to the earliest and most sacred of Indian Scriptures. The watchword of Luther was 'Back to the Bible'; the watchword of Dayanand was 'back to the Vedas' . . . but be it noted to the Vedas as interpreted, not by the traditional scholarship of Indian orthodoxy or by the critical scholarship of the West, but by the scholarship of the Arya Samaj alone. . . . The scripture basis of the Arya Samaj then, while formally the Vedas, is in reality a certain interpretation of the Vedas, which is not recognised as legitimate by a single Sanskrit scholar, either Indian or European, outside of the Arya Samaj".[1]

To describe the Arya Samaj as a sect of Hinduism, as the *Encyclopaedia Britannica* does, is merely to say that the Arya Samaj is a body of persons agreed upon religious doctrines different from those of an established or orthodox church (religion) from which they have separated and having distinctive common worship.[2] This is because there is nothing common between a religion based on the worship of idols and the efficacy of priestly intervention and a religion which is strictly monotheistic, is opposed to the worship of idols and to the efficacy of priestly intervention. The religious instruction which the Arya Samajists have the right to give to their children is not the Hindu religion in general, but a monotheistic religion which is opposed to idol worship and which does not believe in the efficacy of priestly intervention as Hinduism in general does. And since the Arya Samajists are a minority among the Hindus they are a minority based on religion.

Submission: the *A.S.E. Trust Case* wrongly decided

13.35 The elaborate reasoning by which Deshpande J. reached the conclusion which he did, does not call for any detailed examination in the light of what has been said above. It is enough to say that his judgment overlooks the fact that he was not called upon to interpret the word "religion" by itself, but the phrase "minorities based on religion". The conclusion which he reached flies in the face of well known facts of history, ancient and modern. Roman

[97] ibid. p. 219.
[98] ('71) A.SC. 1737.
[99] ibid. p. 1743.
[1] ibid.
[2] See *C.O.D.*, 6th ed.

Catholics and Protestants profess the Christian religion, but it is indisputable that Roman Catholics constitute a minority based on religion in Ulster where the Protestants constitute the majority; and conversely, the Protestants are a minority based on religion in Eire (Ireland) where Roman Catholics are in the majority. Similarly, Shias and Sunnis profess the Islamic religion, but in Iran for example, Sunnis are a minority based on religion. The provisions relating to the freedom of religion and protection of cultural and educational rights of religious minorities are designed to prevent persecution, or discrimination, on the ground that the minorities profess a religion which is not that of the majority. It is submitted that an elaborate analysis of the concept of religion and religious minorities which flies in the face of ancient and modern history must be rejected. It is not for a Court to cut down fundamental rights because the Court thinks that national interests require that the Hindu religion should not include minorities based on religion.

The Jain Swetamber Sect a religious minority in W.B.

13.36 In *Sree Jain Swetamber Terapanthi Vidyalaya* v. *State*[3] it was held that:

"... members of Jain Sect ... do form a minority in comparison to the total population of India as well as of West Bengal and according to the decision of the Supreme Court in *In re Kerala Education Bill, 1957* ('58) A.SC. 956 at p. 977, para 21 that the minority is to be determined by reference to the entire population of that State. The Jain Swetamber Sect is therefore a religious minority in the State of West Bengal and as such it is entitled to the benefit conferred by Arts 29 and 30. . . ."[4]

The Vidyalaya established by the said Sect.

13.37 The Court then considered the question whether the Jain Swetambar Terapanthi Vidyalaya ("the Vidyalaya") was established by members of the minority community belonging to the said sect, that is, by petitioner No. 1, the registered society. After considering the evidence the Court held that the Vidyalaya:

"was established by Petitioner No. 1 solely with the funds contributed by the members of that religious minority community viz. Jain Swetamber Terapanthi Sect primarily for the purpose of promoting their culture and religious tenets and imparting the same to the pupils belonging to their community. Therefore this institution is entitled to the benefit of Art. 30(1). . . ."[5]

The impugned orders quashed because they violated Art. 30(1)

13.38 Petitioner No. 1, and Petitioner No. 2 its Asst. Secretary, had filed a petition,

"challenging the validity of the orders passed by the West Bengal Board of Secondary Education dated 19th March 1977 and 25th July, 1977 respectively holding that the Election of members of the Managing Committee from the Guardians' Constituency was not valid and directing the appointment of an *ad hoc* Committee or an Administrator to run the administration of this School as well as to complete re-constitution of the Managing Committee in accordance with the Rules and also by the later order rejecting the prayer for Special Constitution as regards the reconstitution of the Managing Committee of this school."[6]

The Court having held that Petitioner No. 1 was entitled to the benefit of Art. 30(1), the court relying upon *Lily Kurian* v. *Sr. Levina*[7] held further that

"the impugned order rejecting the prayer for Special Constitution as 'regards the constitution and/or reconstitution of the Managing Committee of this school' is therefore wholly illegal and bad. I also hold that R. 8 of the Rules framed for Management of Recognised Non-government Institutions (Aided or

[3] ('82) A.Cal. 101.
[4] ibid. p. 111.
[5] ibid. p. 112.
[6] ibid. p. 103.
[7] ('79) A.SC. 52.

Unaided), 1969 is not applicable to this institution inasmuch as it purports to interfere with the fundamental freedom guaranteed to the religious minority, i.e. the Jain Swetamber Terapanthi Sect to administer their educational institutions according to their choice."[8]

Accordingly, the impugned orders were quashed.

13.39 We must now consider *St. Xavier's College* v. *Gujarat.*[9] It is unfortunate that the judgments do not disclose the circumstances under which a bench of 9 judges came to be constituted to hear the case, for those circumstances enable the reader to see why an elaborate discussion of the "real reason for the protection of minorities in a democratic State"[10] is to be found in some of the judgments. When the case first came before a Constitution Bench, counsel for the Teachers' Association, (Interveners), invited the court's attention to the opinion expressed by a former Chief Justice of India, Dr. P. B. Gajendragadkar,[11] to the effect that the Supreme Court decisions on Arts. 29 and 30 required re-consideration.[12] Thereupon, the court passed the undernoted order.[13] The case was later placed before a bench of 9 judges. It may be added that Dr. Gajendragadkar reverted to the subject[14] and he said:

St. Xavier's College Case: reason for constituting a bench of 9 judges to reconsider Sup. Ct. decisions on Arts. 25 and 26

"*I am, however, anxious that the problem should not be politicalised*, but should be considered in the context of academic considerations without introducing political overtones. May I earnestly suggest that the University Grants Commission and the Union and State Education Ministers should, with the co-operation of the Vice-Chancellors and the I.U.B., evolve a healthy consensus after a frank and full discussion of the pros and cons of the problem; failing that, the said authorities may consider whether it would be appropriate and advisable to move the Supreme Court to reconsider its decisions *or to move the Parliament for a suitable amendment of Art. 30(1)* which may save the

[8] ('82) A.Cal. *supra* at p. 112.

[9] ('74) A.SC. 1389 rel. on in *Hari Manderji* v. *Magadh University* ('77) A.Pat. 12, 17 (*held*, applying the meaning given in *Azeez Basha's Case* to the word "established", namely, "bring into existence", that the Shree Guru Govind College, Patna was a denominational institution established by the Sikh community.)

[10] ibid. p. 1403 (*per* Mathew J.).

[11] Tagore Law Lectures on the *Indian Parliament and Fundamental Rights*, at pp. 54-7.

[12] ibid. p. 57: "If this view is not reconsidered and colleges started all over the country by societies consisting of members belonging to religious or linguistic minorities in different regions begin to claim the protection of Art. 30(1), it would introduce confusion and chaos in the administration of University life. Indeed, when the Supreme Court considered this matter, it does not appear that all the consequences, which would flow from the view which the Supreme Court was taking in those cases, were properly brought to the notice of the Court; otherwise, I have no doubt that the Supreme Court would have issued notices to different States and through them (to) all the Universities in India to appear and assist the Court in dealing with issues of such vital importance to the University life as a whole."

[13] "Upon being mentioned by Mr. M. K. Ramamurthy and upon hearing counsel for all parties, the Court referred these writ petitions to a larger bench. The Court directed that notice of these matters be issued to the Advocate-General of all the States, the Att.-Gen. of India as well as the Union of India. The Court further directed that public notice be also issued to the Minority Institutions to enter appearance, if so advised and that the said notice will be by advertisement by the Registrar of this Court in all the English editions of the *Statesman*, the *Times of India* and the *Hindu* as well as the *Mail* (Madras Edition) at the expense of the State. Applications for amendment of the writ petitions filed in Court to-day granted. The All India University Teachers' Association will also be heard if they enter appearance in these matters."

[14] Jawaharlal Nehru Memorial Lecture (November 27-28, 1972) on *The Philosophy of National Integration*, Chap. 6, "The Role of Universities in National Integration", pp. 52-7.

present supervisory and regulatory jurisdiction of all the Universities in respect of the colleges affiliated to them?"[15] (italics supplied)

It does seem odd to suggest an amendment of the Constitution for abrogating, in substance, minority rights—which is essentially a political question—and in the same breath to express anxiety "that the problem should not be politicalised". It appears to the present writer that the philosophical and theoretical discussion about the basis of minority rights, which appears *for the first time* in Supreme Court judgments dealing with Arts. 29 and 30, is a response of the court to the suggestion for the abrogation of minority rights, made in the name of uniformity and national integration, and constitutes a reasoned rejection of the philosophy underlying that suggestion.

Provisions of the Gujarat University (Amendment) Act, 1972 impugned as violating Art. 30

13.40 The St. Xavier's College Society and the St. Xavier's College ("the College") impugned the validity of the following sections of the Gujarat University (Amendment) Act, 1972, ("the Act") principally on the ground that they violated Art. 30: Section 33A (1) (*a*), which provided for the constitution of the Governing Body and Selection Committee; ss. 40 and 41, which converted affiliated colleges into constituent colleges; and ss. 51A and 52A, which provided for the dismissal, removal and termination of the services of members of the staff of colleges, and the reference of disputes to arbitration. Although the petitioners did not impugn the validity of s. 33A (1) (*b*) (which provided for the recruitment of the Principal and the teaching staff of colleges), some of the interveners impugned the validity of that section also. A bench of 9 judges heard all the parties affected, who appeared in response to individual and public notices issued by the Supreme Court. In fact the court departed from its settled practice that an intervener was not to raise contentions which were not raised by the petitioners in view of

Decision given after hearing all interested parties

". . . the fact that notices were given to minority institutions to appear and those institutions have appeared and made their submissions a special consideration arises here for expressing the views on s. 33-A(1)(*b*) of the Act."[16]

Questions for determination by the bench of 9 judges

13.41 The larger bench was called upon to determine the following questions.

(*a*) Whether the rights conferred on religious and linguistic minorities by Art. 30 (1) were confined to the purposes set out in Art. 29 (1), namely, the preservation of the language, script or culture of the said minorities, or whether those rights extended also to establishing educational institutions imparting general "secular" education?

(*b*) Whether the grant, recognition or affiliation of an educational institution to which Art. 30 (1) applied, could be made dependent on the religious and linguistic minorities accepting conditions which would involve the surrender by such minorities of the rights conferred on them by Art. 30 (1).

(*c*) Whether the right to establish and administer educational institutions carried with it a right to grant-in-aid, and/or recognition and/or affiliation.

---

[15] ibid. p. 57.

[16] ('74) A.SC. p. 1400. (The Petitioners had not impugned the validity of this section).

The questions thus raised were not new; they had been the subject of an unbroken line of Supreme Court decisions as Reddy J. rightly pointed out.[17]

The questions not new

13.42 The discussion of the three questions set out above, falls into three parts:

The underlying scheme of the judgments in the *St. Xavier's College Case*

(*a*) An analysis of the terms of Arts. 29 and 30 as bearing on each of these questions, and a consideration of earlier decisions which had interpreted those articles;

(*b*) A discussion of the "philosophy" or "real reason" underlying the protection to minorities given by Art. 30 (1) as supporting the conclusions reached under (*a*);

(*c*) An application of the conclusions reached under (*a*) to the impugned sections to ascertain their validity.

13.43 As to para 13.42 (*a*) above, it is submitted that as a result of the analysis of Arts 29 and 30 made in the judgments, all the nine judges held that Art. 30 (1) was not limited by Art. 29 (1); that the right of religious and linguistic minorities was not limited to establish and administer educational institutions designed solely or mainly to preserve the language, script and culture of such minorities, but the right extended to establishing educational institutions imparting general "secular" education.[18] The analysis does not

Unanimous decision: Art 30(1) not limited by Art. 29: earlier decisions affirmed

[17] "*The contentions raised before us on the scope and ambit of Articles 29(1) and 30(1) are not new* but have been earlier urged before and decided by this Court. The attempt on behalf of the State of Gujarat has been to once again raise the same crucial issues which go to the root of the rights conferred on the minorities to establish educational institutions of their choice and whether the State could treat the majority and minority educational institutions equally, an issue upon which this Court has pronounced in no uncertain terms on earlier occasions. We agree with the judgment of Hon'ble the Chief Justice just pronounced . . . We would not ordinarily have found it necessary to write a separate opinion when the same thing has to be said as has been said so tersely by him, but in trying to re-state what has already been said, the *impression is sometimes created that something new is being stated or some departure from the principles already adumbrated is being made. In order to avoid giving scope to any such contention being raised,* we would merely refer to some earlier provisions already held to violate the fundamental rights of minorities guaranteed under Art. 30(1) which are analogous to the impugned provisions which, in the view this Court has already taken, can be held to be violative in their application to the minority educational institutions.": ibid. p. 1401. (italics supplied)

[18] ('74) A.SC. *supra* at pp. 1394-5 (Ray C.J.); p. 1401 (Reddy J.); pp. 1424-5 (Khanna J.); p. 1432 (Mathew J.); p. 1447 (Beg J.); pp. 1459-60 (Dwivedi J.); Dr. Gajendragadkar's view that "the right to establish and administer educational institutions which is guaranteed by Art. 30(1) is in substance, a right to safeguard the language, script and culture of the minority concerned. It is *conceivable* that a linguistic or religious minority *may start* educational institutions of its own choice *solely or mainly* with the object of preserving its own language, script and culture": *op. cit. Tagore Law Lectures,* at p. 55 (italics supplied) was rejected, it is submitted rightly, by all the judges. It is unnecessary to consider Dr. Gajendragadkar's views in detail, beyond saying, first, that they do not proceed on an analysis of the terms of Arts. 29 and 30, but on what he believed to be the intention of the framers of our Constitution which he then read into Arts. 29 and 30, a procedure which is contrary to settled principles of construction. Secondly, the fundamental right which he concedes to minorities is devoid of practical content. His language shows awareness of this: It is "conceivable" that a minority "may start" the educational institutions he describes; but in the India of 1947-50 no one would have formulated fundamental rights to protect the right to establish educational institutions resembling antiquated museum pieces. The existence of a large number of schools and colleges run by religious minorities which imparted general "secular" education,

break any new ground on the interpretation of Arts. 29 and 30 except for the point made by Ray C.J. and Palekar J. that:

"If rights under Arts. 29(1) and 30(1) are the same then the consequence will be that any section of citizens, not necessarily linguistic or religious minorities, will have the right to establish and administer educational institutions of their choice. The scope of Art. 30 rests on linguistic or religious minorities and no other section of citizens of India has such a right"[19]

and the point made by Mathew and Chandrachud JJ. that there were religious minorities who had no language, script and culture of their own on whom Art. 29 (1) conferred no rights but who were nevertheless entitled to the rights conferred by Art. 30 (1).[20] Therefore Art. 30 (1) is not limited by Art. 29 (1). The analysis was also supported by reference to one or more of the following cases: *Bombay* v. *Bombay Education Society*;[21] *In re the Kerala Education Bill, 1957*;[22] *Sidhrajbhai Sabhai* v. *Bombay*;[23] *W. Proost* v. *Bihar*;[24] *S. K. Patro* v. *State*;[25] *D.A.V. College, Jullundur* v. *Punjab*.[26] As these cases have been fully discussed in the text it is unnecessary to repeat that discussion here.

Affiliation and recognition: (i) unanimous decision — they cannot be granted on condition that rights under Art. 30(1) should be surrendered

13.44 As to affiliation or recognition, the two questions which arise are: (i) can recognition or affiliation be granted on terms involving a surrender of the rights conferred by Art. 30 (1)? (ii) Do the rights conferred by Art. 30 (1) include the right to recognition or affiliation, and what are the consequences involved in applying for and obtaining affiliation? On (i) above, all the 9 judges were agreed that recognition or affiliation cannot be offered on terms which would involve a surrender of the rights conferred by Art. 30 (1).[27] In arriving at this conclusion the larger bench did not go beyond the reasons given by Das C.J. in the *Kerala Opinion* which are set out

---

with or without compulsory "scripture" classes, was well known to the framers of our Constitution; as also the fact that those schools received recognition and grants from the State and those colleges were affiliated to Universities. The provisions of Art. 28(3) against requiring a person attending any educational institution "*recognized* by the State or *receiving aid* from State funds to take part in any *religious instruction* or *religious worship*" without his or his guardian's consent; the provision of Art. 29(2) that no citizen shall be denied admission to educational institutions *maintained* or *aided* by the State on the ground of religion, race, caste, language or any of them; the special provision made by Art. 337 for grants to Anglo-Indian educational institutions (which are minority institutions) on condition that *not less than forty percent of the annual admissions* were made available to members of *communities other than the Anglo-Indian community*, conclusively show that it is the rights of these and similar minority institutions which the framers protected and not the minority institutions which, according to Dr. Gajendragadkar, may "conceivably" be established. And finally, where special rights are conferred on minorities alone, it is obvious that minorities and majorities are treated differently, and a plea for total uniformity between the minorities and the majority contradicts the very concept of special minority rights.

[19] ibid. p. 1394. [20] ibid. p. 1432.

[21] ibid. p. 1460 (Dwivedi J.). See para 13.2 above.

[22] ibid. pp. 1394-5 (Ray C.J.); p. 1407 (Reddy J.); p. 1424 (Khanna J.); p. 1431 (Mathew J.); p. 1447 (Beg J. who agreed with Ray C.J.); p. 1460 (Dwivedi J.). See paras 13.5 and 13.6 above.

[23] ibid. p. 1407 (Reddy J.); p. 1431 (Mathew J.). See paras 13.11 and 13.12 above.

[24] ibid. p. 1395 (Ray C.J.); pp. 1424-5 (Khanna J.); p. 1431 (Mathew J.); p. 1460 (Dwivedi J.). See para 13.24 above.

[25] ibid. p. 1431 (Mathew J.). See para 13.27 above.

[26] ibid. p. 1407 (Reddy J.); p. 1431 (Mathew J.); p. 1460 (Dwivedi J.). See paras 13.28 and 13.29 above.

[27] ibid. p. 1395 (Ray C.J.); p. 1407 (Reddy J.); p. 1425 (Khanna J.); p. 1433 (Mathew J.); p. 1448 (Beg J.); p. 1461 (Dwivedi J.).

in para 13.7 above, which reasons were also repeated in subsequent decisions. However, as to (ii) above there was a difference of opinion though by 7:2 the law laid down in the earlier decisions was affirmed. Beg J. and Dwivedi J. who dissented, differed from each other, and their judgments will be considered later. However, before we consider the difference about affiliation it is necessary to refer briefly to the discussion in the judgments about the theoretical basis of the minority rights conferred by Arts. 29 (1) and 30 (1).

(ii) "right" to affiliation etc. and the scope of regulations on the "right" — earlier decisions affirmed by 7 : 2

13.45 As stated earlier, apparently as a response to the suggestion that Art. 30 (1) should be amended, the discussion serves a useful purpose as showing that the conclusions reached by the judges on a plain interpretation of the relevant provisions of the Constitution can also be supported by various considerations of political and social philosophy. Such discussion constitutes a reasoned rejection of the philosophy underlying the suggestion for abrogating, in substance, the fundamental educational rights of minorities. On the purely legal plane it produced one important result: Since an amendment of Art. 30 (1) was said to be required by the need for uniformity of control in University education and as part of national integration, several judgments dealt with the concept of equality under our Constitution in relation to minorities. Since a number of judgments refer to the Advisory Opinion of the Permanent Court of International Justice on Minority Schools in Albania[28] it may be stated that the facts and the law involved in that case are set out most fully by Khanna J.[29] Briefly, the facts were these: After the admission of Albania into the League of Nations, Albania signed a declaration about the position of minorities. Art. 4 assured to all nationals equality before the law and the enjoyment of the same civil and political rights without distinction of race, language or religion. Art. 5 provided that

Discussion in judgments on the theoretical basis of minority rights

On the legal plane, doctrine of equality *vis-a-vis* minority rights explained

Albanian Schools Case: Judgment of International Court (8 : 3) equality in fact may require unequal treatment

"Albanian nationals who belong to racial, religious or linguistic minorities will enjoy the same treatment and security in law and in fact as other Albanian nationals. In particular they shall have an equal right to maintain, manage and control at their own expense or to establish in the future, charitable, religious and social institutions, schools and other educational establishments, with the right to use their own language and to exercise their religion freely therein."[30]

In 1933 the Albania National Assembly modified Arts. 206 and 207 of the Albanian Constitution which permitted the setting up of private schools. Henceforth those articles provided as follows:

"The instruction and education of Albanian subjects are reserved to the State and will be given in State schools. Primary education is compulsory for all Albanian nationals and will be given free of charge. Private schools of all categories at present in operation will be closed."[31]

On a complaint being made to the League of Nations, the League referred the following question for the Advisory Opinion of the Permanent Court of International Justice:

"Whether, regard being had to the above-mentioned Declaration of October 2, 1921, as a whole, the Albanian Government is justified in its plea that, as the abolition of private schools in Albania constitutes a general measure applicable to the majority as well as to the minority, it is in conformity with the letter and the spirit of the stipulation."[32]

---

[28] Publications of the Court, Series A/B No. 64.
[29] ('74) A.SC. *supra* at pp. 1415-16.
[30] ibid. p. 1415.
[31] ibid.
[32] ibid.

By 8:3 the court held that the plea of the Albanian Government was not justified. In the course of its judgment, the court said:

"Whereas equality in fact may involve the necessity of differential treatment in order to attain a result which establishes an equilibrium between different situations. . . . It is easy to imagine cases in which equality of treatment of the majority and of the minority whose situation and requirements are different, would result in inequality. . . . The equality between members of the majority and of the minority must be effective, genuine equality. . . .[33]

It is submitted that Reddy J.,[34] Khanna J.[35] and Mathew J.[36] rightly referred to this judgment as laying down the correct approach to equality and minority rights. No doubt Dwivedi J. rightly said that the judgment of the International Court could throw no light on the *construction* of Art. 30(1). But that judgment does provide an answer to the view which Beg J. expressed in interpreting Art. 30(1):

"[Art. 30(1)] meant to serve as a shield of minority educational institutions against the invasion of certain rights protected by it and declared fundamental so that they are not discriminated against, cannot be converted by them into a weapon to exact unjustifiable, preferential or discriminatory treatment for minority institutions so as to obtain the benefits but to reject the obligations of statutory rights."[37]

Submission: Art. 30(1) not an exception to, but an application of, Art. 14

For, as pointed out by the International Court, preferential treatment is inherent in guaranteed minority rights if real, and not merely nominal equality is to be secured. The judgment of the International Court also enables us to see that Art. 30(1) is not an exception to the rule of equality laid down by Art. 14 but is an application of that rule to the minority rights protected by Art. 30(1).

Submission: theoretical discussion not helpful on the *interpretation* of Art. 30(1)—different theories suggested in different judgments as the basis of minority rights conferred by Art. 30(1)

13.46 Whilst admitting the value of the theoretical discussion to the extent mentioned in para 13.45 above, it is submitted that *as a matter of interpretation* it is unsatisfactory to rest the decision on what is believed to be the underlying theory of guaranteed minority rights, as is apparent from the fact that no two judgments are agreed on the theoretical basis. According to Ray C.J.:

"The real reason embodied in Art. 30(1) is the conscience of the nation that the minorities . . . are not prohibited from establishing and administering educational institutions of their choice for the purpose of giving their children the best general education, to make them complete men and women of the country. . . . This is in the true spirit of liberty, equality and fraternity through the medium of education."[38]

Khanna J. has a different and a more elaborate explanation[39] which, *inter alia,* includes the speech of Sardar Vallabhbhai Patel in which he said that it was up to the Constituent Assembly to show the hollowness of the claim made by the British that they were there to protect the interests of the minorities, and that the Assembly should prove that nobody could be more interested than the Assembly in protecting minorities in India. "Our mission is to satisfy every interest and safeguard the interest of all minorities to their satisfaction."[40] Mathew J. found the real ground in the right of parents to determine the education of their children.[41] The strangest philo-

---

[33] ibid. p. 1416. [34] ibid. p. 1406. [35] ibid. p. 1415-16.
[36] ibid. p. 1433. [37] ibid. p. 1451. [38] ibid. p. 1395.
[39] ibid. pp. 1413-16. [40] ibid. p. 1414.
[41] ibid. p. 1433. In the *Kerala Opinion* the argument for the Anglo-Indian Schools that a child was not the creature of the State and that parents had the right to get their children educated in educational institutions of their choice was rejected, Das C.J. observing that the American decisions relied upon by the schools proceeded on the "due process" clause of the 5th and the 14th Amendments, and had no application to situations arising under our Constitution: [(1959) S.C.R. at p. 1066].

sophical explanation is that given by Beg J. in dealing with a passage from the *Kerala Opinion* which described the function of education.[42] Beg J. said:

"A person of secular outlook may consider good works or performance of one's moral obligations and duties as the best form of worship. People may differ in their opinions about what is worthy of worship. But, there is little room for difference of opinion when it is asserted that the spirit which the State is bound to foster is that of pursuit and worship of the ideals set out in the Preamble to our Constitution."[43]

To those for whom religion is a living reality, it would seem strange to find the God of their worship in the Preamble to the Constitution of India. It is submitted that however relevant on the political plane such discussions may be, they are not relevant to the interpretation which the Supreme Court repeatedly gave to Arts. 29 and 30 based on its plain language. Whether minority rights were conferred as an act of generosity on the part of the majority, or whether they were conferred because of the fear of consequences of having large and discontended minorities within India, or to prevent a further fragmentation of our country, or in order to prevent claims for special weightage in the electoral system, are matters to which no definite answer can be given. Several conflicting motives may have led different members of the Constituent Assembly to join in enacting Arts. 29 and 30 in their final form.

Theoretical discussion excluded by the right approach to constitutional interpretation

13.47 On the question of affiliation and minority rights, Mathew and Chandrachud JJ. rightly expressed the view that as judges they were neither Jew nor Gentile, neither Catholic nor agnostic, and that they would not be justified in writing their private opinions (into the Constitution?) no matter how deeply they might cherish them.[44] It is submitted that effect is best given to this view if judges do not propound theories of education, of minority rights, and of unconstitutional conditions, (valuable and stimulating as those theories are) because those theories can be, and have been, disputed, and the conclusions reached by Mathew and Chandrachud JJ. would be correct even if their theories could be refuted, or substantially qualified. It is submitted that the conclusions reached by 7 out of 9 judges on affiliation are correct on the plain interpretation of the terms of the relevant Articles read in the context of fundamental rights.

Kerala Opinion explained: situations in which right to recognition, affiliation and aid implied in Art. 30(1). Four situations considered

13.48 In the *Kerala Opinion*, Das C.J. said that the right to aid or recognition was not a fundamental right, but that aid or recognition cannot be offered on conditions which would involve a surrender of those rights. These observations have been emphatically reasserted by all the 9 judges in the *St. Xavier's College Case*. But the implications of the observations have not been drawn out, except by Reddy J. in the present case It is submitted that the said observations involve the following propositions:

(*a*) Fundamental rights conferred by our Constitution are meant to be real and effective rights. This proposition is the basis of an unbroken line of Supreme Court decisions, and is not open to dispute: any law which violates or abridges a fundamental right is declared void, or *pro tanto* void, by the express terms of Art. 13 (2).

---

[42] ibid. p. 1453: "It is education that clarifies our belief and faith and helps to strengthen our spirit of worship."

[43] ibid. p. 1453.

[44] ibid. p. 1433.

(*b*) Therefore the maxim applies that "when the law gives anything to anyone, it also gives all those things without which the thing itself would be unavailable."[45]

(*c*) But the right under Art. 30 (1) cannot be enjoyed in a vaccum, because the nature and extent of the right depends upon the situation in which the right is asserted. The following situations may exist, and have in fact existed:

1st situation *1st situation*: The State may give aid and recognition to schools and may direct that scholars of unrecognized schools shall not be permitted to avail themselves of the opportunity for higher education, and shall not be eligible for entering public service.[46] The observations of Das C.J. were made in a case where this situation existed.

2nd situation *2nd situation*: A university may be an affiliating university so that an unaffiliated college would be unable to send up its students for university examinations and university degrees. Further, government may grant aid only to affiliated colleges. In principle, this situation is the same as the 1st situation, and the observations of Das C.J. directly apply.

3rd situation *3rd situation*: Government may not give grant or may be unable to do so.[47] Government may not require recognition as a condition for sending up students from schools for higher education or for eligibility for government service.

4th situation *4th situation*: The University may be a teaching university of which colleges are an integral part and the university provides teaching in each of the colleges.

Submission: *Kerala Opinion* shows that in some situations right to recognition etc. is implied in Art. 30(1) and

13.49 When Das C.J. said that there was no fundamental right to aid or recognition, he was considering the effect of Art. 30 (1) not only in the situation before him but the effect of Art. 30 (1) in other situations as well. His observations will be better understood if we inquire in respect of each situation, whether minority institutions have a right under Art. 30 (1) to aid and/or recognition and/or affiliation ("aid etc."), in the sense that without aid etc. the rights conferred by Art. 30 (1) would not be real and effective rights. It is submitted that in the 1st and 2nd situations the right to aid etc. is necessarily implied because in those situations there is no meaning in saying that though the right to aid etc. is not a fundamental right, nevertheless, aid etc. cannot be offered on terms which involve a surrender of the rights under Art. 30 (1). The *Kerala Opinion* shows that in the 1st and 2nd situations, aid etc. *cannot be refused* which means that there is a right to aid etc.[48] What is the scope of that right has to be considered separately.

Situations in which the right is not implied.

Situations raising complicated questions and a solution

13.50 In the 3rd situation the right to aid etc. is *not* necessarily implied, since the rights conferred by Art. 30 (1) can be effectively exercised without aid etc. The 4th situation is more complicated. If the Universities in a State are teaching, and not affiliating, Universities, then the law of that state must not prevent a minority college from seeking affiliation with a University outside the State as was held by the Supreme Court with reference to an affiliating univer-

---

[45] See *f.n.* 50, para 12.52 of the text. [46] (1959) S.C.R. 995, 1067.
[47] ibid.
[48] ('74) A.SC. *supra* at p. 1407 where Reddy J. has expressed the same view.

sity.[49] However, if such affiliation is impossible or inconvenient to secure, what is the fundamental right guaranteed by Art. 30 (1)? It is submitted that in a creative judgment, which breaks new ground, Reddy J. has given the correct answer: suggested by Reddy J.

"The only purpose that the fundamental right under Art. 30(1) would serve would in that case be that minorities may establish their institutions, lay down their own syllabi, provide instructions in the subjects of their choice, conduct examinations and award degrees or diplomas. Such institutions have the right to seek recognition to their degrees and diplomas and ask for aid where aid is given to other educational institutions giving a like education on the basis of the excellence achieved by them. The State is bound to give recognition to their qualifications and to the institutions and they cannot be discriminated except on the ground of want of excellence in their educational standards so far as recognition of degrees or educational qualifications is concerned and want of efficient management so far as aid is concerned."[50]

The answer given by Reddy J. is further supported by the consideration that otherwise as regards university education, Art. 30 (1) can be rendered a dead letter by the simple expedient of converting affiliating universities into teaching universities. In the *St. Xavier's College Case* 8 out of 9 judges held that this cannot be done.

13.51 On the right to affiliation, the position adopted by Dwivedi J. is apparently self-contradictory. He held, with the majority, that in the case of an affiliating university, "since the State cannot directly take away or abridge a right conferred (by) Art. 30 (1), the State cannot also indirectly take away or abridge that right by subjecting the grant of affiliation to conditions which would entail the forbidden result."[51] However, he also held that affiliation was not a fundamental right but a "statutory concept and may be obtained on the fulfilment of the conditions prescribed therefor by statute"; that there was no express grant of the right of affiliation and the right was not necessarily implied in Art. 30 (1). It is submitted that this apparent contradiction can be resolved only by analysing the situations in which there is a right to affiliation[52] and situations in which there is no such right. It is further submitted that this failure to resolve the apparent contradiction is responsible for Dwivedi J.'s dissent from the majority on provisions which converted affiliated colleges into constituent colleges, and it is submitted that this dissenting judgment is not correct. It may be added that his judgment was also coloured by the view that "affiliation of an institution *imparting religious education* or teaching only the theology of a particular religious minority may not comport with the secular character of the State."[53] (italics supplied). But he overlooked Art. 28 (2) which shows that even in an institution administered by the State, religious instruction can be given under the circumstances described in Art. 28 (2), and he also overlooked Art. 28 (3) which also shows that religious instruction might be given in educational institutions *"recognized by the State* or *receiving aid out*

Dwivedi J. on affiliation etc.

Submission: his dissent is not correct

[49] *D.A.V. College, Bhatinda* v. *Punjab* ('71) A.SC. 1733, 1735.
[50] ('74) A.SC. at p. 1407.
[51] ibid. p. 1641 [referring to the *Kerala Opinion* (1959) S.C.R. at pp. 1063-4].
[52] If the right was purely a statutory right, there would be no point in saying that it cannot be granted on terms which would involve the surrender of rights conferred by Art. 30(1). It is because in some situations the right to affiliation is implied in Art. 30(1) that the conditions of affiliation must not involve the surrender of the rights conferred by Art. 30(1).
[53] ('74) A.SC. *supra* at p. 1460.

of State funds . . ." (italics supplied) so that imparting religious instruction in minority institutions is not inconsistent with the "secular character of the State".

Beg J. on affiliation etc.

13.52 It is not easy to give an account of the position adopted by Beg J. on points on which he differed from the majority. He held that minorities had a right to establish educational institutions imparting general "secular" education. But if they exercised their right in favour of general "secular" education by applying for affiliation they were under an obligation to accept the kind of secular education which the State chose to give because "rights and duties are co-relative".[54] Article 30 (1) protected the rights of minorities but it did not entitle them to claim unjustifiable preferential or discriminatory treatment for themselves.[55] But he also held that "the price of affiliation cannot be a total abandonment of the right to establish and administer a minority institution conferred by Art. 30 (1)."[56] It is submitted that his dissent is not correct because

Reasons for the submission that Beg J.'s dissent is not correct

(*a*) Beg J. failed to ask the question whether there are situations in which it is implicit in Art. 30 (1) that minorities have a right to affiliation, if the proposition that affiliation cannot be granted on terms which involve a surrender of the right conferred by Art. 30 (1) is to have any meaning.

(*b*) His view that if the minorities exercise their right, and opt for general "secular" education, they are under an obligation to adhere to the general pattern of education is based on a misapplication of the proposition that "rights and duties are correlative." In rights not arising out of a contract—and rights conferred by Art. 30 (1) are not contractual rights—the proposition that *A* has a right involves the proposition that other persons owe *A* a correlative duty and not that *by reason of his right A* owes a duty to other persons.[57] The *right conferred* by Art. 30 (1) *on minorities* imposes *a duty on the legislature and the executive* to abstain from making any law or taking any executive action which would take away or abridge that right.

(*c*) Beg J. overlooked the fact that preferential treatment is inherent in conferring special rights on minorities, because the minorities have rights which majorities do not have. Thus Beg J. himself held that a minority institution cannot be prevented by law from seeking affiliation with a university outside the university area in which the institution is located. Again, a language, not the language of minorities, cannot be imposed as a *compulsory* medium of instruction on mino-

---

[54] ibid. p. 1447.

[55] See the quotation set out in para 13.45 of the text.

[56] ('74) A.SC. *supra* at p. 1448.

[57] Salmond, *Jurisprudence*, 12th ed. p. 221: "Every legal right has the five following characteristics:— (1) It is vested in a *person* who may be distinguished as the *owner* of the right, the *subject* of it, the person *entitled*, or the *person of inherence*. (2) It avails against a *person*, upon whom lies the correlative duty. He may be distinguished as the person *bound*, or as the *subject* of the duty, or as the *person of incidence*. (3) It obliges the person bound to an *act* or *omission* in favour of the person entitled. This may be termed the *content* of the right. (4) The act or omission relates to some *thing* (in the widest sense of that word), which may be termed the *object* or *subject-matter* of the right. (5) Every legal right has a title, that is to say, certain facts or events by reason of which the right has become vested in its owner."

rity educational institutions even if an affiliating university adopts that medium for majority institutions.[58]

(*d*) Beg J. *appears* to divide educational institutions into two classes: secular and not secular (religious?). But Art. 28 shows that there is at least a third class in which religious instruction can be given in minority institutions which *also* impart general "secular" education.

(*e*) Finally, Art. 30 (1) confers rights not only on *religious* minorities but on *linguistic* minorities as well, and read with Art. 29 (1) a linguistic minority has a fundamental right to conserve its script and language by establishing educational institutions imparting general education in every branch of knowledge through the medium of its language. The question of choosing between secular and non-secular education does not arise if the right is claimed by a linguistic minority and not as a religious minority.

Permissible regulations on the right conferred by Art. 30(1).

13.53 But what is the nature of the right to claim affiliation? In the *Kerala Opinion,* Das C.J. rejected the extreme argument of two Anglo-Indian schools and Muslim Institutions[59] that the right conferred by Art. 30 (1) was absolute and no restrictions of any kind could be placed upon that right as a condition of giving aid or recognition[60] for "the right to administer cannot obviously include the right to maladminister".[61] He held that reasonable regulations could be imposed on the exercise of the right conferred by Art. 30 (1) as a condition for granting aid or recognition. Although an Advisory Opinion is not the law declared by the Supreme Court within the meaning of Art. 141, and is not binding on all courts in India, the Opinion delivered by Das C.J. "with the utmost clarity, great (perspicacity?) and wisdom has been the text from which this Court has drawn sustenance in its subsequent decisions."[62] Judgments of the Supreme Court have added little to the Opinion delivered by Das C.J.; however, subsequent judgments have invalidated regulations of the kind which Das C.J. upheld "as at present advised" although they made "serious inroads on the right of administration and appear perilously near violating that right."[63] In *Sidhrajbhai's Case,* Shah J. observed that the right conferred by Art. 30 (1) was in terms absolute, unlike the rights conferred by Art. 19 (1) which were subject to reasonable restrictions in the public interest though that was not to say that restrictions in the interest of the efficiency of instruction, discipline, health, sanitation and the like could not be imposed.[64] The reference to the absolute terms of Art. 30 (1) was not meant to negative all regulation of the right, but to indicate the nature of the regulations which were permissible. Our discussion of Art. 19 has shown that restrictions which can be imposed in the public interest on the rights conferred by Art. 19 (1) may not only restrict the enjoyment of those rights

Sidhrajbhai's Case: the effect of the absolute terms of Art 30(1) on the nature of the regulations which are permissible

---

[58] See the observations of Das C.J. quoted in para 13.2 of the text, which were affirmed in *D.A.V. College, Jullundur* v. *Punjab*: see para 13.32(*b*) of the text.

[59] (1959) S.C.R. p. 1065.

[60] ibid. pp. 1065-6. See also pp. 1007-8 and p. 1008 for the arguments of counsel that the rights were absolute.

[61] ibid. p. 1062.

[62] ('74) A.SC. *supra* at p. 1402 *per* Reddy J.

[63] ibid., where Reddy J. has quoted the relevant passage; ibid. p. 1428 where Khanna J. described the observations of Das C.J. in upholding the regulations as "hesitant and tentative and not a final opinion."

[64] See para 13.14 of the text.

but may totally prohibit the exercise of those rights. The absolute language of Art. 30 (1) precludes restrictions of such a character being imposed on the right conferred by Art. 30 (1). But, as stated earlier,[65] rights conferred even in absolute terms have to be exercised in an organized society governed by law, and this involves regulation of rights which do not hinder, but help, the effective exercise of those rights.[66] It follows from this, that Shah J. was right when he held that regulations which can be imposed on minority institutions must be conceived in the interest of those institutions and not in the interest of the public or the nation as a whole. It is not possible to say in advance what kind of regulation of minority rights is impermissible; and the majority judgments in the *St. Xavier's College Case* content themselves with referring to earlier decisions for the kind of regulations which are impermissible because they violate Art. 30 (1).[67] As those decisions have been fully discussed earlier, it is unnecessary to repeat them here. Applying the principles laid down in the *St. Xavier's College Case*, in the light of earlier decisions, Ray C.J., Reddy J., Khanna J., Mathew J. and Beg J. (that is, 8 out of 9 judges) held that s. 40 and 41 which converted affiliated colleges into constituent colleges violated Art. 30 (1) and those sections could not have any compulsory application to colleges established and administered by religious and linguistic minorities.[68]

Ss. 40 and 41 of the Act cannot be applied to minority institutions

S. 33-A(1)(*a*) cannot be applied to minority institutions

13.54 Section 33-A (1) (*a*) provided that every college was to be under the management of a governing body which must include a representative of the University, and representatives of teachers, non-teaching staff and students of the college. These provisions were similar to those contained in ss. 48 and 49 of the Kerala University Act, 1969, and statute 2 (1) (*a*) of the Guru Nanak University Statutes[69]—provisions which the Supreme Court had held violative of Art. 30 (1).[70] Eight out of 9 judges held that s. 33-A (1) (*a*) violated Art. 30 (1) and could not be applied to minority institutions, approving and applying one or more of the following decisions: (*a*) *The Mother Provincial's*

---

[65] See para 12.56 of the text.

[66] For examples of such laws see para 12.56 of the text.

[67] ('74) A.SC. *supra* at pp. 1396-7 (Ray C.J.); pp. 1402-5 (Reddy J.); p. 1426 (Khanna J.); pp. 1444-5 (Mathew J.).

[68] ibid. p. 1398 (Ray C.J.: "A constituent college does not retain its former individual character any longer. The minority character of the college is lost. Minority institutions become part and parcel of the university"); p. 1401 (Reddy J., agreed with Ray C.J.); p. 1428 (Khanna J.: "A provision which makes it imperative that teaching in undergraduate courses can be conducted only by the University and can be imparted only by the teachers of the University plainly violates the rights of minorities . . ."); p. 1445 (Mathew J.: "On a plain reading of s. 40 it is clear that the governing body of the religious minority will be deprived of the most vital function which appertains to its right to administer the college, the teaching, training and instruction in the courses of studies in respect of which the university is competent to hold examinations"). Beg J. held s. 41(1) invalid as "(it) would have the compelling effect of making (the petitioning College) automatically a constituent unit of the University, and must, therefore, be held to be inoperative against the petitioning College. . . . S. 40 and the remaining provisions of s. 41 are all parts of the same compulsive scheme . . . which is struck by Art. 30(1).": p. 1449.

[69] ibid. pp. 1404-5 where the provisions are set out.

[70] *In re Mother Provincial's Case*, ('70) A.SC. 2079, 2084, 2086 and in *D.A.V. College Case* ('71) A.SC. 1737, 1747-8, respectively.

Case; (*b*) *Patro's Case;* (*c*) *Proost's Case* and (*d*) *D. A. V. College Case.*[71] Beg J. dissented.[72]

13.55 Section 51-A (1) (*a*) and (2) (*a*) provided that no member of the teaching, other academic and non-teaching staff was to be dismissed, removed or reduced in rank except after an inquiry in which he had been informed of the charges against him and he had been given a reasonable opportunity of being heard and making a representation on the penalty proposed to be inflicted. Again, no termination of service not amounting to dismissal or removal was to be valid unless such member had been given a reasonable opportunity of showing cause against the proposed termination. It would appear that no objection was taken to these provisions,[73] but Khanna J. considered them reasonable[74] and Mathew J. also appears to have considered them reasonable when he expressly upheld them.[75] However, s. 51-A (1) (*b*) and (2) (*b*) were impugned as violating Art. 30 (1). The provisions thus impugned corresponded to cls. 11 (1) and 12 (1), (2), (3) and (5) of the Kerala Education Bill, to ss. 53 (1), (2) and (9) and 56 (2) and (4) of the Kerala University Act, 1969 and to Statute 17 of the Guru Nanak University Statutes.[76] And though the above mentioned clauses of the Kerala Education Bill had been upheld in the *Kerala Opinion,* the other provisions set out above were held invalid in the *Mother Provincial's Case* and in the *D. A. V. College Case* respectively.[77] Section 51-A (1) (*b*) required the approval of the Vice-

S. 51-A(1)(*a*) and (2)(*a*) applicable and s. 51-A (1)(*b*) and (2)(*b*) not applicable to minority institutions

[71] ('74) A.SC. *supra* at pp. 1399-1400 [Ray C.J. applied case (*a*) above]; pp. 1402-5 [Reddy J. applied cases (*a*) and (*d*) above]; pp. 1426-7 [Khanna J. applied cases (*a*) to (*d*) above]; Dwivedi J. agreed with the majority that the section "was obnoxious to Art. 30(1)."

[72] Beg J. surveyed earlier decisions of the Supreme Court which laid down "that a provision for subjecting the managerial functions of the governing body of the college to the supervision of a statutory University Service Commission was unconstitutional." But he observed that "This, however, was not a decision in the context of a provision such as s. 38-B . . . which offers the right to the petitioning college to become quite independent and free from the administrative control of the university altogether": ibid. p. 1454. It is submitted that his observations show that he did not find the earlier decisions incorrect, but he held that if control over managerial function of minority institutions was accompanied by a provision leaving a minority college free to become autonomous, such a college cannot complain that its rights under Art. 30(1) were violated: ibid. p. 1454. And Beg J. referred to s. 38-B in more than one context to save laws otherwise invalid (s. 38-B is set out at pp. 1456-7, ibid.). It is submitted that it does not appear from the judgments in the case that any serious argument was urged on the nature, scope and validity of s. 38-A. A number of questions would arise in connection with that section itself, including the question of its validity. Thus, when s. 38-B(2) provides that if "standards of education in an affiliated college . . . are so developed that it would be in the interest of education to allow the college, institution or Department to enjoy autonomy in the specified matters", what is meant by "so developed?" Are different standards and higher standards demanded of an autonomous college than are demanded of a constituent college? And would standards of constituent colleges be the same? If not, would there be any justification in demanding a higher standard from an autonomous college than is demanded from a college whose standards are the lowest among the various constituent colleges? It is submitted that the validity of a provision for an autonomous college would have to be judged by reference to the actual language used in providing for such autonomy.

[73] ibid. p. 1400 where Ray C.J. sets out the objection.

[74] ibid. p. 1427.

[75] ibid. p. 1446, 1447.

[76] ibid. p. 1402; the provisions are set out at pp. 1403-4.

[77] ibid: "Needless to say, in so far as these decisions lay down a principle slightly different from or even contrary to the opinion on the Kerala Education Bill, they are the law laid down by this Court.": *per* Reddy J.

Chancellor, or other officer authorized by him, for the penalty to be inflicted under sub-s. 1 (*a*), and s. 51-A (2) (*b*) required similar approval for the termination of service under sub-s. (2) (*a*). Seven out of 9 judges approving and applying the earlier decision held that s. 51-A (1) (*b*) and (2) (*b*) violated Art. 30 (1) and could not be applied to minority institutions.[78] Section 52-A provided that any dispute between the governing body and any member of the teaching, other academic and non-teaching staff of an affiliated college, connected with the terms of service of such member, must be referred to a Tribunal of Arbitration consisting of one member each appointed by the governing body and by the member of the staff and an umpire appointed by the Vice-Chancellor. Seven out of 9 judges held that s. 52-A violated Art. 30 (1) and could not be applied to minority institutions. Ray C.J. said:

S. 52-A not applicable to minority institutions

> "These references to arbitration will introduce an area of litigious controversy inside the educational institution. The atmosphere of the institution will be vitiated by such proceedings. The governing body has its domestic jurisdiction. This jurisdiction will be displaced. A new jurisdiction will be created in administration."[79]

And Khanna J.[80] and Mathew J. [81] expressed similar views.

Mark Netto v. Kerala

13.56 In *Mark Netto* v. *Kerala*[82] the Supreme Court decided important questions as to Art. 30 (1). The Appellant had filed a writ petition in the Kerala High Court for quashing the order dated June 5, 1973 of the Regional Deputy Director of Public Instruction, Trivandrum and the Order dated May 2, 1974 of the District Education Officer, issued pursuant to the aforesaid order. The constitutional question for decision in the appeal was whether Rule 12 (iii) of Chapter VI of the Kerala Education Rules, 1959 ("the Rules") was void for violating Art. 30 (1).[83] It is a remarkable fact that the judgment of the Kerala High Court does not mention the fact, set out in the Supreme Court judgment, that objection to the Appellant admitting girls to the school was raised by a Girls' school in the vicinity (run by Muslims, who were also a minority community). Leave to appeal having been refused, the Supreme Court granted special leave to appeal.

---

[78] ibid. p. 1400 (Ray C.J.); pp. 1402-1404 (Reddy J.); p. 1427 (Khanna J.); pp. 1446-7 (Mathew J.). In *St. Joseph's High School* v. *Ravi Shanker* ('76) A.A. 390, 392 (F.B.) a Full Bench followed the view expressed by the aforesaid 7 out of 9 judges in the *St. Xavier's College Case* when they held that the provisions relating to the approval of the Vice-Chancellor in disciplinary matters were violative of Art. 30(1). Applying that principle to s. 16-G (3)(*a*) of the U.P. Intermediate Education Act, 1921, the Full Bench held that the said section conferred on an Inspector uncanalised and unguided power in the sense that no facts had been mentioned on the basis of which alone the Inspector might exercise his power. In the absence of any guide lines it could not be held that the power of approval conferred on the Inspector was solely a check on mal-administration of the institution. A power directly to interfere with disciplinary control of the managing body over the teachers violated Art. 30(1). Consequently, s. 16-G(3)(*a*) was not applicable to an educational institution established by a religious or linguistic minority.

[79] ibid. p. 1400. Reddy J. agreed with Ray C.J. ibid. p. 1401.

[80] ibid. p. 1428.

[81] ibid. p. 1447.

[82] ('79) A.SC. 83, (1979) 1 S.C.R. 609.

[83] It is not necessary to deal with the question whether permission given to establish the School in 1947, which was not limited in any manner covered a school for both boys and girls. The Kerala High Court held that having regard to the fact that for 25 years only boys had been admitted to the school led to the conclusion that it was a Boy's School and therefore permission under Rule 12(iii) was required. The Supreme Court differed, it is submitted rightly, from this view.

13.57 The Supreme Court, after setting out the effect of its earlier decisions on Art. 30(1), stated that the main ground for the High Court's conclusion was that as there was a Girls' School in the vicinity, it was desirable that girls should not be admitted into a Boys' School. It is submitted that although the High Court did say this, it upheld the rule on the ground that it was merely a regulatory measure for "discipline and morality", words which the High Court took from Supreme Court decisions as to the permissible regulation of an apparently absolute right. The Supreme Court pointed out that the rule itself permitted girls to be admitted into Boys' Schools if there was no Girls' School in the vicinity provided arrangements for necessary conveniences were made.[84] It is submitted that the argument that the rule was a regulatory measure in the interests of discipline and morality had to be stated to be rejected, first, because the rule itself refuted any such argument, and secondly, because reputable and long established Colleges in Kerala are co-educational, and it would be unreasonable to believe that "discipline and morality" were not maintained in those institutions. The Supreme Court held that if the rule was widely interpreted to include all schools, it would be void as violating the right of the Christian community to have schools of their own choice for teaching girls belonging to their own community. The Supreme Court held that it was not necessary to strike down the rule, but merely to say that it was inapplicable to minority communities.

Order directing Boys' Schools not to admit girls not applicable to minority communities.

13.58 It is submitted that the judgment reversing the Kerala High Court is clearly right. However, it is submitted that the crucial question was whether a Denomination's right to establish an "educational institution" of its choice did not necessarily carry with it the right to decide whether the institution should be co-educational or not, subject to reasonable conveniences being provided if girls were to be admitted to a mixed school. It is submitted that the right to establish an educational institution must include the right to decide whether it should be co-educational, subject to provisions being made for necessary conveniences for girls. In view of the judgment in *Netto's Case,* the decision of the Madras High Court in *Charles Robson* v. *State*[85] is no longer good law, for it followed the Kerala High Court's reasoning and decision in *Netto's Case,* and held that the impugned rule was a "regulation" in the interest of "discipline and morality".

Submission: right to establish a school carries with it the right to establish a co-educational school

13.59 *Lily Kurien* v. *Sr. Levina*[86] raised the question whether in view of Art. 30(1), an educational institution established and managed by a religious or linguistic minority was bound by the provisions of Ordinance 32(4) of the Ordinances framed under the Kerala University Act, 1957. The Appellant had been appointed as Principal of St. Joseph's Training College for Women, Ernakulam, in 1957. The College had been established by a religious society of Nuns belonging to the Roman Catholic Church, and was administered by a Managing Board. As a result of certain incidents, a disciplinary inquiry was held against the Appellant and she was dismissed. It is unnecessary to refer to the various proceedings which took place; it is enough to say that from the order dismissing

Lily Kurien v. *Sr. Lavina*

[84] The School had put up a separate building for admission of girls.
[85] ('78) A.M. 390. [86] ('79) A.SC. 52.

her, she appealed to the Vice-Chancellor under Ordinance 32(4), and the Vice-Chancellor held that the dismissal was unjustified and ordered that the Appellant be reinstated. When the matter reached the Kerala High Court, it held that the Vice-Chancellor had no power to reinstate the Appellant. In appeal, the Supreme Court held that a power of appeal carried with it the power to make appropriate orders and included the power to reinstate. However, after referring to its earlier decisions,[87] the Supreme Court held that the finding of 7 out of 9 judges in the *St. Xavier's College Case*[88] squarely applied to the facts of the present case. For, Ordinance 32(4) conferred wide unfettered power on the Vice-Chancellor to interfere in disciplinary matters which directly affected the administration of the institution. Consequently, Ordinance 32(4) violated Art. 30(1) and was not applicable to minority educational institutions.

on a reconsideration of those decisions

13.60 The *St. Xavier's College Case* has been considered at length because the bench of 9 judges was constituted to reconsider the earlier Supreme Court decisions after notice to, and after hearing, all the parties affected by the questions to be decided.[89] After a full hearing, the court held unanimously that the right conferred by Art. 30(1) was not limited to the purposes mentioned in Art. 29(1), and that aid, recognition and affiliation could not be granted on terms which would involve a surrender of the rights conferred by Art. 30(1), and that the earlier decisions which had so held were correct. Again, the decisions in the *St. Xavier's College Case* by majorities of 8 : 1, and 7 : 2 on the right to affiliation, and on the regulations which could be imposed on the right conferred by Art. 30(1) also held that earlier decisions were correct. It is submitted that the unanimous and majority decisions in the *St. Xavier's College Case* are clearly right, and they emphasize the rare consistency with which the Supreme Court has interpreted Arts. 29(1) and 30(1).

S. 123(3), Representation of the People Act interpreted so as not to violate Art. 29(1)

13.61 A question under Art. 29 was raised before the Supreme Court in connection with an amendment made in 1961 to the Representation of the People Act by the insertion of cl. (3) in s. 123.[90] The Supreme Court held that s. 123(3) must be interpreted in the light of the right conferred by Art. 29(1), which right, unlike the rights conferred by Art. 19(1), was absolute. Accordingly, the Supreme Court construed s. 123(3) as follows:

"It is the appeal to the electorate on a ground personal to the candidate relating to his language which attracts the ban of s. 100 read with s. 123(3) of the Representation of the People Act. Therefore, it is only when the electors are asked to vote or not to vote because of the principal language of the candidate that a corrupt practice may be deemed to be committed. Where, however, for conservation of the language of the electorate appeals are made to the electorate and promises are given that steps would be taken to conserve that language, it will not amount to a corrupt practice."[91]

---

[87] All of which have been considered in the text.

[88] See para 13.55.

[89] Notice had been given to the Central Government but ". . . probably realising the sensitive nature of the issue (the Central Government) did not put forward any contentions contrary to those already considered and decided by this Court . . ." ibid. p. 1406 (Reddy J.).

[90] "The appeal by a candidate . . . to vote or refrain from voting for any person on the ground of his . . . language, . . . for the furtherance of the prospect of the election of that candidate or for prejudicially affecting the election of any candidate."

[91] *Jagdev Singh* v. *Pratap Singh* (1964) 6 S.C.R. 750, ('65) A.SC. 183, 189.

13.62 In *All Saints High School* v. *A.P.*[92] several sections of the Andhra Pradesh recognized Private Educational Control Act, 1975 ("the Act") were impugned as violating Art. 30(1). The sections there impugned are too long to set out, but they will be found set out in the judgment of Fazal Ali J. Chandrachud C.J., Fazal Ali and Kailasam JJ. delivered three separate judgments. Chandrachud C.J. observed, it is submitted rightly, that he regarded "the matter arising before us as well settled especially after the 9 Judge Bench decision in the (*St. Xavier's College Case*) and the recent judgment in *Lily Kurian.* All that we have to do is to apply the law laid down in this decision.[93]

All Saints High School v. A.P.

13.63 It is not necessary to go through the review of cases considered by Fazal Ali J. and Kailasam J. in their judgments and to ascertain whether the conclusions drawn by them from those decisions are correct. It is enough to say that in the submission of the present writer, in his anxiety to uphold the validity of the Act, Kailasam J. has tried to read down the provisions; however, for the reason given by Chandrachud C.J., to be noticed presently, it is not possible to read down those provisions.

A general comment on the judgments of Fazal Ali and Kailasam JJ.

13.64 The Chief Justice and Fazal Ali J. held that s. 3(1) and s. 3(2)[94] violated Art. 30(1) and were invalid in their application to minority educational institutions. The reason for this conclusion, and the reason why those provisions could not be read down, is best stated in the words of Chandrachud C.J.:

S 3(1) and 3(2) held by the majority to be invalid *qua* minority educational institutions

"The form in which Sec. 3(2) is couched is apt to mislead by creating an impression that its real object is to cast an obligation on the competent authority to approve a proposal under certain conditions. Though the section provides that the competent authority 'shall' approve the proposed order if it is satisfied that it is based on adequate and reasonable grounds, its plain and necessary implication is that it shall not approve the proposal unless it is so satisfied. The conferment of such a power on an outside authority, the exercise of which is made to depend on purely subjective considerations arising out of the twin formula of adequacy and reasonableness, cannot but constitute an infringement of the right guaranteed by Article 30(1).

Reasons for the above finding

"I find it difficult to save Ss. 3(1) and 3(2) by reading them down in the light of the objects and reasons of the impugned Act. The object of the Act and the reasons that led to its passing are laudable but the Act, in its application to minority institutions, has to take care that it does not violate the fundamental right of the minorities under Article 30(1). Sections 3(1) and 3(2) are in my opinion unconstitutional in so far as they are made applicable to minority institutions since, in practice, these provisions are bound to interfere substantially with their right to administer institutions of their choice. Similar provisions were held to be void in . . . *Rev. Mother Provincial, D.A.V. College* and *Lily Kurian.* There is no distinction in principle between those provisions and the ones contained in Sections 3(1) and 3(2)."[95]

The reason why s. 3(1) and (2) cannot be read down

13.65 All the three judges were agreed that s. 4 of the Act[96] which provided for an appeal, and s. 5 which was consequential on s. 4 were invalid as violative of Art. 30(1). Chandrachud C.J. said that the provision was "too broadly worded to be sustained on the touchstone" of Art. 30(1) because:

Sections 4 and 5 of the Act held invalid by all the judges

---

[92] ('80) A.SC. 1042. [93] ibid. at p. 1046.
[94] See ibid. p. 1063 where the sections are set out.
[95] ('80) A.SC. at p. 1050.
[96] See ('80) A.SC. at p. 1070 where it is set out.

(*a*) The section conferred on the Government the power to provide by rules that an appeal may lie to such authority or officer as it designated regardless of the standing or status of that authority or officer; (*b*) The appeal was provided on all questions of fact and law "thereby throwing open the order passed by the management to the unguided scrutiny and unlimited review of the appellate authority" so that "in the exercise of the appellate power, the prescribed authority or officer can substitute his own view for that of the management, even in cases in which two views are reasonably possible;" (*c*) Whereas an appeal to the aggrieved teacher was provided against an order passed by the management, no corresponding right was conferred on the management against the order passed by the competent authority under s. 3(2) of the Act, thereby placing the management at a great disadvantage *vis-a-vis* the teacher.

Sections upheld by the majority

Fazl Ali J. agreed broadly with the above three grounds. Kailasam J. however, held s. 4, and the consequential s. 5, invalid on the limited ground that the right of appeal from the decision of the competent authority had not been conferred on the management. On the other impugned sections, namely, Ss. 3 (3) (*a*), 3 (3) (*b*), 6 and 7, Chandrachud C.J. and Kailasam J. upheld them on the ground that they were regulatory, differing in this respect from Fazl Ali. J. who held s. 3 (3) (*a*) and 3 (3) (*b*) as also Ss. 6, 8, 9, 13 and 17 were violative of Art. 30 (1). Although the considerations urged by Fazl Ali J. are not without force, on the whole, it is submitted that the view taken by Chandrachud C.J. and by Kailasam J. is the better view.

END OF VOLUME 1

NOTE

Originally, Chapter XIV entitled "THE 44TH AMENDMENT—RIGHT TO PROPERTY NO LONGER A FUNDAMENTAL RIGHT (ART. 300A)" with an accompanying Appendix No. III entitled "RIGHTS TO PROPERTY: ART. 31, 31A TO 31C" were to have been included in this Volume. However, it was found desirable to include them in Volume II as Chapter XIV and accompanying Appendix No. 1. The few references in this Volume to Chapter XIV and its accompanying Appendix No. III should be read as references to Chapter XIV and Appendix No. 1 in Volume II.

APPENDIX I

A NEW INTRODUCTION

SECTION I — THE EMERGENCY

1. I have explained in the Preface to Vol. III (2nd ed.) of this book, how the first two volumes had been overtaken by events and why it has become necessary to fill the gaps left in the book by the events of four eventful years, which followed the Proclamation of Emergency on 26th June, 1975 ("the Emergency"). In writing this New Introduction I have benefitted by the suggestion made by Prof. Bradley[1] and by Prof. Colin Turpin[2] in their appreciative reviews of the second edition of the *Constitutional Law of India*.

2. The Shah Commission Reports must, for a long time, remain our main source of information about the Emergency, and as to what happened during the Emergency. Those Reports contain a careful analysis of the extensive evidence led before the Commission. They are written in a style which is lucid and admirable in its tone and temper. If, on occasions, the Commission uses the language of indignation, it is because those occasions called for nothing less. In this New Introduction I have drawn on the Shah Commission Reports and have indicated the paragraphs of the Reports in brackets. The reader who has not secured copies of the Reports may have difficulty in obtaining copies, since the Congress (I) Government have withdrawn them from circulation. The correctness of the findings of fact based on documentary and other evidence has not been denied by producing evidence to show that the findings were incorrect.

3. Before 1975, India had passed through three periods of emergency proclaimed as a result of external aggression — the Chinese "aggression" in 1962, the Pakistani "incident" in 1965 and the Pakistani War in 1971. These Proclamations had been criticized by civil liberty groups, and were generally criticized for being continued long after the need for those proclamations had passed. In fact the Proclamation of Emergency of 1971 was in force when the Emergency was proclaimed in 1975. But, speaking broadly, the Constitution functioned as it was intended to function "by them that made it". A free press, a free Parliament and an independent judiciary ensured the working of our liberal democratic Constitution as it was intended to be worked. Parliamentary proceedings were protected under the Parliamentary Proceedings (Protection of Publication) Act, 1956. Judicial proceedings and judgments of Courts were equally freely reported, because, under the general law, the publication of judgments and a fair report of judicial proceedings, are protected. Judgments were delivered fearlessly — no judge was demoted, or transferred without his consent, because his judgment was damaging to the Government. Indeed, in the Constituent Assembly Jawaharlal Nehru had said that judges must be ". . . of the highest integrity, if necessary, people who can stand up against the executive government and whoever come in their way." And of civil liberties, he had written: "In countries with a democratic background the greatest value is therefore attached to civil liberties and people of the most diverse and mutually hostile opinions joined together in a common demand to protect this

---

[1] "For British lawyers coming fresh to the Indian Constitution, a summary of the main recent political events in India having special constitutional significance would have made the book easier to use. But this is not so much a criticism of the second edition, more a suggestion which the author may care to consider in preparing future editions.": (1978) 94 *L.Q.R.* at p. 159.

[2] "In any event the author is a lawyer first and last, and rigorously eschews any discussion on background political events. From one point of view this deliberate self-denial may be regretted, and the non-Indian reader, in particular, would have benefitted from an account which placed recent constitutional developments in their political setting.": (1977) 36 *C.L.J.* at p. 380.

foundation of all liberty and activity. . . . In India, the necessity for such joint effort embracing all groups and individuals, who believe in civil liberties is obviously even more necessary than elsewhere." This was an expanded version of Voltaire's great saying: "I disapprove of what you say, but I will defend to the death your right to say it." Up to May, 1975, India was, and was recognized to be, a great democracy. It is a strange irony of history that it should have been left to Jawaharlal Nehru's daughter to attempt to destroy his work, and to deny all that he stood for.

4. The Emergency was to spring from a fearless judicial decision. On 12th June, 1975 Sinha J. of the Allahabad High Court held that Mrs. Gandhi had been guilty of corrupt electoral practices; and he disqualified her from holding public office for six years, as the law *obliged* him to do. He stayed the operation of his order for 20 days. In her application to the Supreme Court for a stay of the order, Mrs. Gandhi unwisely prayed for an absolute stay presumably on the grounds which her eminent Counsel, Mr. N. A. Palkhivala, pressed upon Krishna Iyer J., namely, "that the Nation was solidly behind (her) as Prime Minister" and that "there were momentous consequences disastrous to the country if anything less than the total suspension of the order under Appeal were made." This prayer was unwise, for if the court gave a conditional stay, public demand that she should step down as Prime Minister would grow, as in fact it did. Undeterred by Mrs. Gandhi's position as the Prime Minister of India, or by the sombre warning of her Counsel, Krishna Iyer J. granted a conditional stay. Mrs. Gandhi was prevented from participating in the proceedings of the Lok Sabha *in her capacity as a Member* or from receiving remuneration *as a member* and was prevented from voting. However, in her capacity as Prime Minister, she was entitled to take part in the proceedings of both Houses of Parliament *but was prevented from voting.*

5. We must go back to the 12th June, 1975. The judgment against Mrs. Gandhi was followed by a spurt of political activity. To support her claim that the people of India were behind her, rallies were stage-managed in Delhi and people were brought to them in public vehicles in contravention of the requirements of the law for the use of public vehicles. Government organizations were obliged to take part in these rallies. (paras 5.4 to 5.20). The law was applied *in favour* of the Congress Party *and against* other political parties. The prohibition of meetings under Sec. 144, Cr. P.C. — which had become a normal feature around the Prime Minister's House — was relaxed to allow demonstrations and rallies staged by the Congress Party in support of Mrs. Gandhi (para 5.26).

6. Before the Emergency was actually proclaimed, Mrs. Gandhi took some Chief Ministers and some officials into her confidence and informed them of her intention to advise the President to proclaim an emergency. The Cabinet was not informed till after the Emergency had been proclaimed (para 5.34 *et seqq.*). Under the Rules of Business, work relating to the Emergency Provisions of our Constitution was allocated to the Home Ministry. Consequently, a proposal for the Proclamation of Emergency should normally come from that Ministry. The Cabinet Secretariat did not receive any proposals from the Home Ministry as to the need to proclaim an Emergency. Further, the facts alleged by Mrs. Gandhi in support of the Emergency are not borne out by official records: There was nothing alarming on the economic front; periodical reports as to law and order showed that the stituation was in complete control all over the country; the Home Ministry received no reports from State Governments indicating any deterioration in the law and order situation in the period immediately preceding the proclamation of Emergency; the Home Ministry had prepared no plans before June 25, 1975, for the imposition of internal emergency; the Intelligence Bureau had not submitted any report suggesting that the internal situation in the country warranted the imposition of internal emergency; the Home Ministry did not submit any report to the Prime Minister expressing anxiety about the internal situation in the country (para 5.60). Contrary to the Rules of Business, which required that the question of imposition of an Emergency should be brought before the Cabinet, and notwithstanding the fact that even during the Indo-Pakistani War in 1971 the proclamation of emergency was considered by the Cabinet

which was urgently summoned, Mrs. Gandhi, purporting to act under one of the Rules, advised the President to proclaim an Emergency on her sole responsibility and informed the Cabinet of the Proclamation the next day (paras 5.64 to 5.68).

7. On the above facts as found by the Shah Commission, it is clear that Mrs. Gandhi advised the proclamation of an Emergency to secure her own position as Prime Minister, and in order to forestall a public demand that after the Supreme Court had refused an absolute stay, she should step down as Prime Minister till the Supreme Court decided the appeal and the court exonerated her. This conclusion is reinforced by Mrs. Gandhi's attempts to secure her position as Prime Minister by legislative and constitutional changes. The Election Laws (Amendment) Act, 1975, provided, among other things, "that every case of disqualification under Sec. 8A shall be referred to the President, who could condone it in consultation with the Election Commission". The Constitution (39th Amendment) Act, 1975 was passed and came into force on 11th August, 1975, the very day that Mrs. Gandhi's appeal was to have been heard by the Supreme Court. A Bill to amend the Constitution by inserting, among other things, Article 329A was introduced in the House of the People on the 7th August, and passed on the same day; on 8th August it was passed by the Council of States; on 9th August the requisite number of State Legislatures ratified the Bill. The President gave his assent on August 10, 1975 on which day the Act was gazetted, and had become law on 11th August, when Mrs. Gandhi's appeal was to have been heard. Article 329A(4), in substance directed the Supreme Court to allow Mrs. Gandhi's appeal and dismiss Mr. Raj Narain's cross-appeal. The judgment of the Supreme Court declaring Art. 329A(4) invalid, has been fully discussed in Vol. II (2nd ed.) at pp. 1521-32.

8. What is the overwhelming impression left on the mind of the reader of the Shah Commission Reports? First and foremost, the collapse of character and courage in men and women holding high offices in the Union and the States. Not one Minister in Mrs. Gandhi's Cabinet resigned, although the proclamation of an emergency should have been considered by the Cabinet, and Mrs. Gandhi had procured the promulgation of the Emergency "secretly, and therefore dishonestly", in order to confront the Cabinet with an accomplished fact. After the Emergency was over, a leading Cabinet Minister said "We were told of the proclamation the next day. What could we do?" In the felicitous language of a great judge of the Bombay High Court, Sir Joseph Arnauld, this question can only be described as "the offensive language of hardened hypocricy", because the question is easily answered: the Cabinet should have threatened to resign as a body, since the Cabinet is jointly responsible to the House of the People. The conduct of the Union Cabinet, and State Cabinets, justifies the saying of a great writer, "Without courage there can be no truth, and without truth there can be no other virtue". It is clear that the motto of our country, "*Satyameva Jayate*" (Truth prevails), had lost its hold on the men and women in power.

9. The Emergency subverted the Constitution in a number of ways. There was an attack on a free press by imposing on it a censorship the like of which had not been known in India even in times of war. Court and Parliamentary proceedings were subject to censorship (para 6.17); not only were the publication of Court judgments censored but directions were given as to how judgments should be published (para 6.23). The actual working of censorship from day to day went beyond the scope of the guidelines. Orders passed by the censors were arbitrary and capricious, usually given orally, without any relation to the provisions of the law (para 6.29). During the Emergency, legislation was enacted to make censorship a part of the ordinary law of the land. Thus the Prevention of Publication of Objectionable Matters Act was passed, the Press Council of India was abolished by an Ordinance and a Bill repealing the Parliamentary Proceedings (Protection of Publication) Act, 1956 was passed (para 6.45).

10. But censorship of the press was made effective by the most infamous law in India, the Maintenance of Internal Security Act, 1971, popularly called "MISA", which provided for preventive detention. The lawless administration of that law is described in some of the most distressing pages of the Shah Commission Report.

Orders were signed in blank, people arrested and the grounds for detention got up later. India seemed to have gone back to the days of the Star Chamber which issued general warrants to arrest unspecified persons and search property. In England, general warrants were once and for all declared illegal in the 1760s. As a standard text book puts it:

"In the 1760s the general warrant cases arose out of the attempts of George III's Government to stifle the political activities of John Wilkes and others, and publications such as the *North Briton*. Three cases decided once and for all the illegality of general warrants: *Leach* v. *Money*, that a general warrant to arrest unnamed persons (the printers and publishers of the *North Briton*) against whom no charge had been formulated was illegal; *Wilkes* v. *Wood*, that the papers of an unnamed person could not be seized on such a warrant; and *Entick* v. *Carrington*, that there was no inherent power in the Secretary of State to order an arrest except for treason, and that a general search warrant purporting to give authority to the King's Messengers to take all Entick's books and papers was illegal. The sequel to these cases was a successful action against Lord Halifax as the Secretary of State who had issued the warrants. These decisions established the fundamental principle that state necessity does not justify a wrongful act. General warrants are similarly unlawful by the law of Scotland."[3]

Again, orders of detention signed in blank, to be filled in later, were not far removed from the *lettre de cachets* for imprisonment in the Bastille — a blank order signed by the King of France, which any noble or King's favourite could obtain to secure the imprisonment of his opponent or enemy. Our founding fathers believed that the Star Chamber and the Bastille belonged to an age which had passed away. Article 22(1) and (2) had secured safeguards against arbitrary arrest and detention; and Art. 22(4) to (7), while excluding Art. 22(1) and (2) in cases of preventive detention had provided limited safeguards even for preventive detention.

11. But arbitrary censorship and illegal preventive detention had to surmount one formidable obstacle — the power of the High Courts to grant relief to the aggrieved party in appropriate cases. And the High Courts stood firm. Nine High Courts held that although a detained person could not enforce his fundamental right under Art. 21 in view of the President's Order under Art. 359, he was entitled to show that the order of detention was not under or in compliance with the law or was *mala fide*. Consequently, steps were taken to "soften up" the judiciary. Although as far back as 1962, the Law Minister, himself an eminent lawyer, had told Parliament that the Government accepted the principle that a High Court judge should not be transferred without his consent, a list of 56 judges was prepared in 1976 for transfer of judges *without their consent* because their judgments were not to the liking of Government; and to overawe judges who were not on the list there was a calculated leak of the names on the list. Orders for the transfer of 16 judges without their consent were passed in May, 1976. If further transfers were not made, it was due, in part, to the courageous action of Mr. Justice Sheth of the Gujarat High Court who filed a Writ Petition challenging the validity of the order transferring him to the Andhra Pradesh High Court. A Full Bench of the Gujarat High Court held the order of transfer invalid on 4th November, 1976. Censorship blacked out any report of the judgment, as it had blacked out the names of the 16 judges who had been transferred. But the assault on the High Court Judiciary went further. Mr. Justice Rangarajan and Mr. Justice Agarwal had delivered a judgment severely critical of government in a petition for *habeas corpus* filed by a well-known journalist, Mr. Kuldip Nayar, against his illegal detention. Not only was Mr. Justice Rangarajan transferred from the Delhi to the Assam High Court, but Mr. Justice Agarwal was reverted to his post of a Sessions Judge, although the Chief Justice of the Delhi High Court had recommended his appointment as a permanent judge in a vacancy which had occurred, observing that Mr. Justice Agarwal "would be an asset to the High Court" (para 7.1). On the evidence before it, the Shah Com-

---

[3] Wade & Phillips, *Constitutional and Administrative Law*, 9th edn. by A. W. Bradley, pp. 444-5. (foot notes to the passage have been omitted).

mission held that Mrs. Gandhi's refusal to approve the appointment of Mr. Justice Agarwal to be a permanent judge of the Delhi High Court "was a misuse of authority and abuse of power" on the part of Mrs. Gandhi (para 7.14).

12. Mr. Justice Lalit, an additional Judge of the Bombay High Court, was recommended for extension of his tenure of office by the Chief Justice of that Court, a recommendation accepted by the Chief Minister, by the Governor of Maharashtra, by the Chief Justice of India and by the Minister for Law and Justice (para 7.15). There were no adverse reports against Mr. Justice Lalit. Mrs. Gandhi made a Note on the papers "I do *not* approve of giving him another term" (para 7.17). On the evidence before the Commission, which included the evidence on oath of the former Law Minister, the Commission held that the "refusal to extend the term of Mr. Justice Lalit as a judge of the High Court amounted to subversion of well established conventions and practices and amounted to abuse of authority and misuse of power by Mrs. Gandhi" (para 7.23).

13. Whilst attempts to undermine the independence of the High Court judiciary were going on, attempts were also made to "soften up" the judges of the Supreme Court of India. A party committee, called the Swaran Singh Committee,[4] had been appointed to suggest amendments to the Constitution and there were calculated leaks of proposed amendments to the Constitution: one such amendment was designed to create a body superior to the Supreme Court. Alternatively, another proposed amendment sought to curtail the power of judicial review of the Supreme Court and the High Courts.

14. While attempts to undermine the High Courts and the Supreme Court judiciary were going on, the Supreme Court delivered five separate judgments in the *Habeas Corpus Case* on 28th April, 1976. By a majority of 4 : 1 (Ray C.J., Beg, Chandrachud and Bhagwati JJ., Khanna J. dissenting), the Supreme Court brushed aside the unanimous view of 9 High Courts, whose judgments were under appeal, and passed the following Order:

"In view of the Presidential Order dated 27th June, 1975, no person has any *locus standi* to move any writ petition under Art. 226 before a High Court for *habeas corpus* or any other writ or order or direction to challenge the legality of an order of detention on the ground that the order is not under or in compliance with the Act (MISA) or is illegal or is vitiated by *mala fides* factual or legal or is based on extraneous considerations."[5]

I have dealt with the *Habeas Corpus Case* (see Appendix IV in the present volume) and put it in the setting of "The Judiciary and the Emergency" and "Courts and Preventive Detention" (Appendix III and V respectively). I will only add that my criticism in para 7 of Appendix IV that the final order of the Court in the *Habeas Corpus Case* is in conflict with at least three of the majority judgments, is borne out by the following frank admission made by Beg C.J. in *In re Sham Lal*:[6]

"It is true that this Court held that preventive detention was practically removed from judicial supervision during an Emergency. The common statement of a conclusion at the end of the judgments in the *Habeas Corpus Cases* based on the majority view but signed by all the Judges, including Khanna J., was perhaps misleading as it gave the impression that no petition at all would lie under either Article 226 or 32 to assert the right of personal liberty because the *locus standi* of the citizen was suspended. *Had a review petition been filed before us I would have certainly made it clear that the Statement of a conclusion reached by the majority did not accurately set out atleast my conclusion which is found at the end of my judgment.* It seems to me that the majority conclusion is rather loosely and vaguely expressed at the end of our judgments. A legitimate criticism could, therefore, be

---

[4] As pointed out in para 16 below, the Committee had no particular credentials to undertake such a task.

[5] (1976) Supp. S.C.R. at p. 477, ('76) A.SC. at p. 1392.

[6] (1978) 2 S.C.R. 581, ('78) A.SC. 489.

that this Court should draft and state its majority conclusions better."[7] (italics supplied)

It may be added that after condoning delay, Beg C.J. did issue a Rule on an application for the review of the *Habeas Corpus Case*. Under what circumstances that review application was dismissed remains a mystery, for, neither the newspapers nor the law reports referred to the order of dismissal or enlighten the public as to why a judgment containing an order admitted to be clearly wrong was not publicly set right.

15. My criticism of the *Habeas Corpus Case* was couched in language appropriate to a legal discussion. When the judgments were delivered, the Indian press had been muzzled — in fact the dissenting judgment was blacked out by the censor. But the press of the free world was outspoken in its condemnation. The *New York Times* used words which were prophetic. Referring to them in a separate Epilogue to his autobiography, Mr. M. C. Chagla wrote:

"The *New York Times* in a leading Article asked the people of India to raise a monument to Justice Khanna and opined that the four other judges would be remembered in infamy.[8] I presided over a dinner which the Bombay Bar gave to Justice Khanna and I observed that we had not raised a statue or a bust to him, but he can carry with him the satisfaction that there will always be a monument for him in the hearts of the people and that was a much greater tribute than something made of marble."[9]

These words reflect the almost universal reaction to the majority judgments. Mr. Justice Khanna's fearless dissent cost him the high office of the Chief Justice of India, and he resigned as a judge of the Supreme Court, when he was superseded by a judge junior to himself.

16. I have referred to the Swaran Singh Committee, appointed to consider amendments to our Constitution — a committee with no particular credentials to undertake such a task. That the Committee undertook the task when their leading political opponents were in preventive detention, when the press was muzzled and the fundamental right to freedom of speech and expression could not be enforced, and even debates in Parliament could not be reported, shows that the Committee was ignorant of, or insensitive to, the constitutional outrage of amending our Constitution extensively during the Emergency. In the language of the day the amendments were designed to "institutionalize the emergency", and no stronger proof of this can be given than the amendment which increased the life of Parliament and State Legislatures from 5 to 6 years. However, I will have occasion to refer to the 42nd Amendment later.

17. Such was the grim scene when Mrs. Gandhi decided to hold general elections to Parliament in March 1977. Conflicting explanations have been given for her decision, but the explanation generally given runs as follows: Mrs. Gandhi lacked legitimacy for her dictatorial rule; she believed that the people were behind her, a belief probably strengthened by the current slogan "India is Indira, and Indira is India". Intelligence reports led her to believe that the time chosen by her for the elections was the most appropriate, for at a later date economic difficulties would come to the surface, and the underground movement would grow stronger. The result of the elections is now a matter of history. She was swept out of Parliament, office and power, and her party suffered a catastrophic defeat.

---

[7] (1978) 2 S.C.R. at p. 588.

[8] *Cf.* President Roosevelt's message to the Congress: "Yesterday, December 7, 1941, — a day which will live in infamy — the United States of America was suddenly and deliberately attacked by the naval and air forces of the Empire of Japan."

[9] M. C. Chagla, *Roses in December, Epilogue: Emasculation of the Judiciary in Emergency* (1978), p. 15. Bharatiya Vidya Bhavan, Bombay. After these words were written, a portrait of Mr. Justice Khanna has been put up in the Second Court Room of the Supreme Court, and Chief Justice Chandrachud unveiled the portrait.

18. But the Emergency raised grave problems of constitutional law. How was it that the safeguards provided by our Constitution against abuse of power, and against arbitrary power, were swept away almost overnight? For not only had power been broadly divided between the three great departments of the State — the Legislature, the Executive and the Judiciary — but power had also been divided territorially between the Union and the States by the federal scheme of our Constitution with its distribution of legislative and executive power between the Union and the States. How came it that State governments vied with each other in doing Mrs. Gandhi's bidding notwithstanding that they were governments of separate States? No easy answers are possible. But no more imperative task awaits the citizen, the politician, the lawyer and the legislator than to find those answers if the ghost of the Emergency is to be laid for ever.

19. The Emergency and its aftermath have made it necessary to discuss the question whether our Constitution is Federal. This is now done in Chapter V.

SECTION II

THE EMERGENCY AND AMENDMENTS TO THE CONSTITUTION. "THE PATH OF DEVIATION"

20. When our Constitution was enacted, people were justly proud of it, and the judgments of the Supreme Court reflected that pride. In *Virendra Singh* v. *U.P.*[10], Bose J. for the court spoke of the Preamble to our Constitution as a "magnificent prelude" to its provisions, and in the concluding part of his judgment he said:

"But we do not found on the will of the Government. We are no longer concerned with principalities and powers. We have upon us the whole armour of the Constitution and walk from henceforth in its enlightened ways, wearing the breastplate of its protecting provisions and flashing the flaming sword of its inspiration."[11]

Sir Ernest Barker, in his *Principles of Social and Political Theory*, said:

"I ought to explain, as I end, why the preamble to the Constitution of India is printed after the table of contents. It seemed to me, when I read it, to state in a brief and pithy form the argument of much of the book; and it may accordingly serve as a key-note. I am the more moved to quote it because I am proud that the people of Indian should begin their independent life by subscribing to the principles of a political tradition which we in the West call Western, but which is now something more than Western."

In the past, when amendments were made to the Constitution, it was customary to speak of "amending the Constitution", for people had not become ashamed to call the Constitution by its proper name. During the Emergency, for those who wanted to lay rough hands on our Constitution by subversive amendments, it became fashionable to refer to the Constitution as "the Statute", obviously to create the impression that the Constitution was like any other statute. It is a matter of regret that the words "the Statute" persist in current discussions long after the attempts to subvert the Constitution by the 39th and 42nd Amendments have failed. If the *Constitution* has to be amended, that fact must be brought home to the people and not disguised under the misleading expression "The Statute".

21. The framers of our Constitution recognized the importance of securing free and fair elections to the Union and State Legislatures; consequently, they provided for the setting up of an Election Commission headed by the Chief Election Commissioner, whose independence and conditions of service were secured in the same way as they were secured for Supreme Court Judges. The Election Commission was entrusted with the superintendence, direction and control of elections, including the appointment of tribunals to try election petitions. The working of election Tribunals led the Commission to recommend that election petitions should be tried by the

---

[10] (1955) 1 S.C.R. 415, ('54) A.SC. 447. [11] (1955) 1 S.C.R. p. 438.

High Courts; and Art. 324, (as amended by the 19th Amendment), empowered the High Courts to try election petitions. Thus it was that the election petition against Mrs. Gandhi came to be tried by Sinha J. who decided it against her. This decision also showed that judges could act without fear or favour, a fact further emphasized by the refusal of Krishna Iyer J. to grant Mrs. Gandhi the absolute stay she had prayed for. Thus, Mrs. Gandhi had personal experience of judicial independence, and she did not like it. So, she set about amending the Constitution by using her position as the leader of a party which commanded the requisite majorities in the two Houses of Parliament and in the requisite number of States. The first such attempt was made in the 39th Amendment. As we have seen, Mrs. Gandhi's appeal was fixed for hearing before the Supreme Court on 10th August 1975 and between the 7th August and 11th August, the 39th Amendment was passed by the House of the People and the Council of States, was ratified by the requisite number of States and was assented to by the President. The terms of the newly added Art. 329A clearly show that the object of rushing through the 39th Amendment was to put her election to the House of the People beyond any challenge.

(a) *The 39th Amendment*

22. The 39th Amendment although mainly designed to put Mrs. Gandhi's election to Parliament beyond challenge, fell into three parts: The first part amended Art. 71 by substituting for the original Art. 71(1), namely, "All doubts and disputes arising out of or in connection with the election of a President or Vice-President shall be inquired into and decided by the Supreme Court whose decision shall be final", the following sub-Article (2): "All doubts and disputes arising out of or in connection with the election of a President or Vice-President shall be inquired into and decided by such authority or body and in such manner as may be provided for by or under any law passed by Parliament under sub-clause (1)". This Amendment substituted for the decision of the Supreme Court, the decision of a body whose composition or nature was not stated. But the arguments advanced on Mrs. Gandhi's behalf in *Indira Nehru Gandhi* v. *Raj Narain*[12] ("the *Election Case*"), which will be referred to hereafter, show that it would not have been surprising if such a law had authorised the House of the People to decide such disputes. This Amendment was calculated to obtain control for the majority party over the disputed election of the President and the Vice-President by eliminating the safeguard of an independent judicial determination of that question by the highest Court in India.

23. The Statement of Objects and Reasons for the 39th Amendment gave the following reasons for amending Art. 71:

"The President, the Vice-President, the Prime Minister and the Speaker are holders of high office. The President is not answerable to a Court of law for anything done, while in office, for the exercise of his powers. *A fortiori* matters relating to his election should not be brought before a Court of law but should be entrusted to a forum other than a Court. The same reasoning applies equally to the incumbent of the office of Vice-President, Prime Minister and Speaker."

The Law Minister, who signed his name to the Statement of Objects and Reasons, must have known that the reasons he gave were untenable. Under Art. 361, the President is not answerable to any Court for the exercise and performance of the powers and duties of his office or for any act done by him in the exercise and performance of those powers and duties. This is because acts done in the President's name are, in reality, the actions of his Council of Ministers, and, therefore, in respect of his official actions, legal remedy can be obtained not against the President but against the Government (see Art. 300).[13] But an election petition against the President impugns his actions, not as a Persident but as a private citizen. Therefore, it is absurd to equate the acts of a private citizen with the official acts of the President of India. Secondly, the reason given for the amendment of Art. 71 is refuted by

---

[12] (1976) 2 S.C.R. 347, ('75) A.SC. 2299.
[13] See *Seervai*, Vol. 2, (2nd ed.) p. 1060 (d).

Art. 361 itself, because Art. 361(4) provides that in respect of any act done or purporting to be done by the President *in his personal capacity,* a civil proceeding can be instituted against him provided that two months' notice, containing the particulars specified in sub-Art. (4), is given. If the personal acts of the President while he is President are actionable in a court of law after giving the prescribed notice, *a fortiori* his action as a private citizen in securing his election by corrupt practices must be open to challenge before the Supreme Court as the highest Court in India. And the original Art. 71(1) had rightly so provided.

24. The second part of the 39th Amendment was the following newly added Article 329A:

"329A. *Special provision as to elections to Parliament in the case of Prime Minister and Speaker:*— (1) Subject to the provisions of Chapter II of Part V [except sub-clause (*e*) of clause (1) of Article 102], no election—

(*a*) to either House of Parliament of a person who holds the office of Prime Minister at the time of such election or is appointed as Prime Minister after such election;

(*b*) to the House of the People of a person who holds the office of Speaker of that House at the time of such election or who is chosen as the Speaker of that House after such election;

shall be called in question, except before such authority [not being any such authority as is referred to in clause (*b*) of Article 329] or body and in such manner as may be provided for by or under any law made by Parliament and any such law may provide for all other matters relating to doubts and disputes in relation to such election including the grounds on which such election may be questioned.

(2) The validity of any such law as is referred to in clause (1) and the decision of any authority or body under such law shall not be called in question in any court.

(3) Where any person is appointed as Prime Minister or, as the case may be, chosen to the office of the Speaker of the House of the People, while an election petition referred to in clause (*b*) of Article 329 in respect of his election to either House of Parliament or, as the case may be, to the House of the People is pending, such election petition shall abate upon such person being appointed as Prime Minister or, as the case may be, being chosen to the office of the Speaker of the House of the People, but such election may be called in question under any such law as is referred to in clause (1).

(4) No law made by Parliament before the commencement of the Constitution (Thirty-ninth Amendment) Act, 1975, in so far as it relates to election petitions and matters connected therewith, shall apply or shall be deemed ever to have applied to or in relation to the election of any such person as is referred to in clause (1) to either House of Parliament and such election shall not be deemed to be void or ever to have become void on any ground on which such election could be declared to be void or has, before such commencement, been declared to be void under any such law and notwithstanding any order made by any court, before such commencement, declaring such election to be void, such election shall continue to be valid in all respects and any such order and any finding on which such order is based shall be and shall be deemed always to have been void and of no effect.

(5) Any appeal or cross appeal against any such order of any court as is referred to in clause (4) pending immediately before the commencement of the Constitution (Thirty-ninth Amendment) Act, 1975, before the Supreme Court shall be disposed of in conformity with the provisions of clause (4).

(6) The provisions of this article shall have effect notwithstanding anything contained in this Constitution."

25. The hearing of the *Election Case* was adjourned because by an amendment, the validity of Art. 329A was challenged by the Respondent. The Court also issued a notice to the Att.-General. At the adjourned hearing, Counsel for Mrs. Gandhi, the Att.General and also the Solicitor-General (for the Union of India), asked for the dismissal of the petition in terms of Art. 329A(4). The *Election Case* has been

discussed fully in Vol. II, Chapter XXX (2nd ed.). It is enough to say that the Supreme Court held Art. 329A(4) and (5) invalid. Mathew J. held that constituent power, that is, the power to amend a Constitution, though distinct from legislative power was still a law making power, and he held that Art. 329A(4) was not an exercise of the amending power but was the rendering of a legislative judgment, and Art. 329A(4) must therefore be held to be void.

26. The further objection to Art. 329A(4), which is relevant to the present discussion, was put by Mathew J. in the following striking passage which brings out the importance of a judicial determination of an election dispute for determining the *real representative* of the People. He said:

". . . it was an essential feature of democracy as established by the Constitution, namely, (that there should be) the resolution of an election dispute by an authority by the exercise of judicial power by ascertaining the adjudicative facts[14] and applying the relevant law for *determining the real representative of the people*."[15] (italics supplied)

As stated earlier, in view of the arguments urged on behalf of Mrs. Gandhi it would not have been surprising if power to decide election petitions had been conferred by law on the House of the People on the excuse that in the past the British House of Commons used to decide election petitions. As to this excuse, it is enough to say, first, that the trial of election petitions by the House of Commons was found so unsatisfactory because of the inevitable political bias, that in 1868 the decision of disputed elections was transferred to the courts. Secondly, the earlier practice of the House of Commons was known to the framers of the Constitution, and they marked their disapproval of that practice by providing for independent election tribunals (appointed by an independent Election Commission), to hear election petitions.

27. The third part of the 39th Amendment was the insertion of 38 Acts in the 9th Schedule so that they could not be challenged on the ground that they violated fundamental rights. It should be noted that the very first entry added to Schedule 9 was the Representation of the People Act, 1951, the Representation of the People (Amendment) Act, 1974 and the Election Laws (Amendment) Act, 1975. From one point of view, this part of the 39th Amendment was the most objectionable, because the inclusion of an Act in the 9th Schedule requires careful scrutiny, and, in the past, Select Committees, to which such Amendments were referred, have scrutinized each Act with care. For example, the Constitution 17th Amendment Bill was referred to a Select Committee, and clause 3(*a*) of that Bill proposed the inclusion of 122 Acts (numbered 21 to 142) in the 9th Schedule. Out of these, the Select Committee chose only 36 Acts for such inclusion, and included 8 other Acts which were not in the original List. The inclusion in the 39th Amendment of 38 Acts, several of them of a complicated nature, showed that no member of either House of Parliament or of the State Legislatures, even if well versed in the law, could possibly apply his mind to the question whether any of the said Acts was to be included in the 9th Schedule, and if so whether in whole or in part. The inclusion of 38 Acts under the above circumstances can only be described as an abuse of constituent power, and this will make it necessary for the Supreme Court to reconsider its decisions on the validity of the Acts included in Schedule 9.

(b) *The 42nd Amendment*

Towards Dictatorship

28. Mrs. Gandhi's attempt in Art. 329A to put her election beyond legal challenge having failed, moves were set on foot to amend the Constitution, and as stated earlier, the Swaran Singh Committee was entrusted with the task of suggesting the amendments. No one has been able to explain the need for making extensive amendments to the Constitution during an Emergency in which almost all the safeguards

---

[14] (1976) 2 S.C.R. at p. 504 *f.n.*, ('75) A.SC. at p. 2372, *f.n.* where the definition of adjudicative facts is given.

[15] (1976) 2 S.C.R. at p. 521; ('75) A.SC. at p. 2383.

of democratic freedom were suspended. The Committee made a pretence of inviting public opinion in the form of memorandums. But the amending bill was not referred to the scrutiny of a Select Committee, although in the past, all important constitutional amendments like the 1st, the 4th, the 17th and Mr. Nath Pai's Bill (which later became the 24th Amendment) had been referred to a Select Committee, and, as we have seen, the Select Committee scrutinized the proposed amendments with care. That procedure was not followed although the Amendments were large in number and far reaching in effect.

29. The 42nd Amendment amended the Preamble to the Constitution, 40 Articles and several entries in the 7th Schedule; it also introduced 14 new Articles in the Constitution. In this Introduction, I will deal only with those amendments which had the effect of damaging or destroying those features of our Constitution which were designed to secure the satisfactory working of our free democratic Constitution. The remaining Amendments will be dealt with in their appropriate places.

30. The substitution of an authority other than the Courts by the amended Art. 71 was carried a step further by the 42nd Amendment when it amended Arts. 103 and 192. Those Articles provided that the question whether any member of Parliament or of State Legislatures had incurred disqualifications mentioned in Arts. 102 and 191 respectively, should be referred to the President or the Governor as the case may be, and their decision was to be final; but that they, in their turn, were to refer the matter to the Election Commission and act according to its opinion. Therefore, in substance, the Election Commission decided the matter. In place of the Election Commission deciding the matter, the amended Art. 103 required the President to *consult* the Election Commission before deciding the matter. In Article 192, the President was substituted for the Governor, and he was to decide the dispute as to disqualifications after *consulting* the Election Commission. It is well settled that the obligation to consult a body imposes no obligation to follow its advice.[16] Consequently, in place of an independent Commission, the determination was left to the President which meant, in effect, by the Government of India. There can be no doubt that these provisions were anti-democratic and were calculated to replace a judicial determination by a political determination.

(c) *The 42nd Amendment — The Judiciary Under Attack*

31. The Delegation from British India to the Round Table Conferences held in England in the 1930s pressed for the inclusion of fundamental rights in the Bill which was to become the Government of India Act, 1935. The Joint Select Committee rejected this demand, observing that general declarations had not much value unless there existed the will and the means to enforce them. The Committee added that the history of the decade preceding the Bill would justify a cynic in saying that "the surest way of securing the destruction of a fundamental right was to include it as such in a Constitutional Instrument."[17]

32. Realizing the force of these observations, the framers of our Constitution showed their *will* to enforce fundamental rights by expressly declaring in Art. 13(1) and (2) that laws abridging or abrogating fundamental rights were *pro tanto* void. The framers also provided the *means* for the enforcement of fundamental rights by arming the Supreme Court and the High Courts with the power to issue the historic writs of *habeas corpus, mandamus, certiorari,* prohibition and *quo warranto.* These writs had proved their effectiveness in England for securing freedom from illegal arrest or detention, for the enforcement of public duties, for the control of subordinate courts, tribunals and authorities, and for ensuring that a person holding a public office could show a legal right to hold it. Further, these writs provided a speedy, effective and relatively cheap remedy when compared with the remedy by way of a suit. So great was the importance which the framers attached to these

[16] *Seervai,* Vol. 2, (2nd ed.) p. 1427, para 26.9.
[17] See para 7.1.

well tried remedies that the right to move the Supreme Court for the issue of appropriate writs for the enforcement of fundamental rights was guaranteed by Art. 32(1); that is to say, Art. 32 itself conferred a fundamental right. Again, although Art. 32 limited the power of the Supreme Court to issue writs for the enforcement of fundamental rights only, the power of the High Courts was not so limited under Art. 226 but extended also to issuing these writs *for other purposes.* The actual working of our Constitution showed that the writ jurisdiction had more than justified itself. Even during emergencies, courts had discharged their duty fearlessly. Therefore, the 42nd Amendment sought to curtail the powers of the courts, to make it difficult for the people to obtain speedy legal redress, and to make it difficult for courts to strike down invalid laws. We must now consider these amendments, but it may be added that almost all of them have been repealed by the 43rd Amendment which came into force on April 13, 1978. If they are discussed below, it is to show what happened during the Emergency, and what the permanent legacy of the Emergency would have been if Mrs. Gandhi had not been swept out of power in favour of a party pledged to restore the Constitution to its former position — a pledge which has been very largely kept.

33. In a large number of cases, an invalid Central or State Law would violate one or more fundamental rights. In such a situation, the aggrieved party had one of two options. He could approach the Supreme Court under Art. 32 for appropriate relief, in which case the matter would be finally decided. Or he could approach the High Court under Art. 226 for appropriate relief. Article 226 as originally enacted was interpreted by a majority judgment of the Supreme Court[18] as precluding the High Courts (other than the High Court having jurisdiction over New Delhi) from issuing a writ against the Union of India because it was located in New Delhi, and because the concept of a cause of action was foreign to Art. 226. Subba Rao J. dissented. He said that the framers of our Constitution could not have intended that an inhabitant of Kanya Kumari in the extreme South of India should have to go all the way to New Delhi to enforce his fundamental rights. Parliament recognized the hardship pointed out by Subba Rao J. and in 1963 the 15th Amendment inserted a new sub-Art. (1A) in Art. 226 conferring on the High Courts jurisdiction to entertain a petition under Art. 226 if the cause of action wholly or in part arose within its jurisdiction. After this amendment, a party aggrieved by the executive acts of the Union of India could apply to the High Court of his own State for a writ against the Union of India, on the ground that the executive action violated his fundamental rights as it was taken under the authority of an invalid Central Law. This history of Art. 226 shows that even in 1963 Parliament and the State Legislatures considered the speedy and effective remedy provided by Art. 226 so important that Parliament amended Art. 226 and the requisite number of States ratified it. The Amendments introduced by the 42nd Amendment were regressive, for they ran counter, first, to the clearly affirmed purpose of the framers of the Constitution to provide a speedy, effective and cheap remedy to the people to enforce their fundamental rights, and, secondly, to the re-affirmation of that purpose by Parliament and the State Legislatures by amending Art. 226 as stated above.

34. We will now consider the amendments affecting the powers of the Supreme Court and the High Courts. Article 32 was in effect amended by a newly added Art. 32A which provided that in the exercise of its powers under Art. 32 the Supreme Court would have no jurisdiction to decide the validity of a State law. Since Art. 32(1) confers a guaranteed fundamental right to approach the Supreme Court for the enforcement of fundamental rights, and since a State law may violate fundamental rights, this amendment was wholly indefensible, for it curtailed the fundamental right conferred by Art. 32(1) to which the framers attached the highest importance. As we have seen, the Law Minister in the Statement of Objects and Reasons has given many specious and untenable reasons for certain amendments. But he is entitled to the credit that he merely summarized the provisions of Art. 32A and made no attempt to defend the indefensible. No rational ground

---

[18] *Lt. Col. Khajoor Singh* v. *Union* (1961) 2 S.C.R. 828, ('61) A.SC. 532.

could be given for excluding the validity of a state Law from the scrutiny of the Supreme Court; and it is difficult to resist the conclusion that Art. 32A in effect served a notice on the Supreme Court that if its judgments were not to the liking of the Government, Parliament could easily take away its powers of judicial review altogether.

35. Articles 131A, 144A, 226A and 228A and the amendment of Art. 226 seriously curtailed the powers of the Supreme Court and the High Courts, but in view of their subsequent repeal, I will deal with them briefly. The powers of the High Courts under Art. 226 to issue writs for "other purposes" was taken away and was restricted to a narrowly defined field. Further, the power to grant interim relief was severely curtailed and in some cases taken away. No rational ground was given for depriving the High Courts of the wide powers deliberately conferred on them by the framers. Further, Art. 226A (which is the counterpart of Art. 32A) deprived the High Courts of their jurisdiction under Art. 226 to decide the validity of a Central Law. Bearing in mind that Parliament expressly amended Art. 226 by inserting a new sub-Article (1A), so that people may not be forced to go to Delhi for the enforcement of their fundamental rights if violated by executive action of the Union under an invalid Central Law, the newly amended Art. 226A was indefensible. As in the case of Art. 32A, it is difficult to resist the conclusion that Art. 226A was intended to serve a notice on the High Courts that if their judgments were not to the liking of Government, the High Courts' powers of judicial review could be taken away.

36. Article 131A carried further the idea underlying Art. 32A by conferring exclusive jurisdiction on the Supreme Court to determine the validity of a Central Law. The marginal note of Art. 131A, as well as its badly drafted provisions, show that the jurisdiction so conferred was not original jurisdiction. Article 131A contemplated that proceedings impugning the validity of a Central Law would be filed in the High Courts, and that such proceeding should be stayed by the High Courts and the question of the validity of the Central Law should be referred to the Supreme Court for its decision, and the matter disposed of in the light of the Supreme Court's decision. Since Art. 131A has been repealed it is not necessary to refer to a judgment of the Bombay High Court which interpreted it in the context of the amended Art. 226.[19] As a corollary to Art. 131A, the newly added Art. 228A precluded the High Courts from determining the validity of a Central Law.

37. But the 42nd Amendment put further impediments in the way of the people to have laws declared invalid, and further curtailed the power of the Courts to grant effective relief against action taken under invalid laws. Articles 144A and 228A(2) provided respectively that the minimum number of judges of the Supreme Court sitting for determining the validity of a Central Law should be 7, and the minimum number of the judges of a High Court sitting for determining the validity of a State Law should be 5. And in both these cases, the law was not to be held invalid except by a majority of *not less* than two-thirds of the judges hearing the matter. These provisions were designed to protect invalid Union and State Laws from effective challenge by making it more difficult and more expensive for people to approach the courts for the protection of their rights. For larger Benches involve longer and more expensive trials, and greater delay in securing trials because, in view of the existing number of judges, Chief Justices found it extremely difficult to withdraw judges from their normal work in order to constitute Benches of 7 or 5 judges. A provision requiring that a Central or State Law should not be declared invalid except by not less than two-thirds of the judges could only have been enacted without realising its absurd consequences. The Supreme Court had rightly held that "precedents which enunciate rules of law form the foundation of the administration of justice under our system",[20] and Art. 141 puts the theory of Precedents on a constitutional basis by providing that the law declared by the

---

[19] *Shantilal* v. *M. A. Rangaswamy* 79 Bom.L.R. 633.

[20] *Seervai*, Vol. II (2nd ed.) p. 1400, para 25.45; ibid. pp. 1400-1402 where the theory of precedents is discussed.

Supreme Court shall be binding on all courts in India. Superficially, it may appear strange that an important law should be struck down by a majority of 1; but it would not be strange but absurd if the validity of an important law were to be affirmed by a minority of judges. For example, if 7 out of a Bench of 11 judges of the Supreme Court held a Central Law invalid by a unanimous judgment and the remaining 4 judges held it valid by a unanimous judgment, the judgment of 4 judges would prevail over the judgment of 7 judges — because 7 judges constitute *less than* a two-thirds majority in a Bench of 11 judges. Such an absurd result would also make nonsense of Art. 141, because under it, the law declared by the Supreme Court must be found in the majority, and not in the minority judgments. Adapting the words used in another context by Mr. Justice Bose in *U.P.* v. *Mohd. Nooh*,[21] these amendments "would doubtless delight the hearts of a Gilbert and Sullivan comic opera audience", but would destroy the confidence of ordinary men and women in the law and the administration of justice if a judgment of 4 judges can prevail over a judgment of 7 judges.

38. Article 227 of our Constitution gave the widest powers of judicial and administrative supervision to High Courts over all Courts and Tribunals (except Courts Martial), within its jurisdiction. This Article had a long history. Section 107 of the Government of India Act, 1915, conferred on the High Courts supervisory jurisdiction over all Courts subject to its appellate jurisdiction, and s. 106(3) excluded matters concerning the revenue from the Original Jurisdiction of the High Courts. Section 107 had been interpreted to mean that the supervisory jurisdiction included judicial as well as administrative supervision.[22] Section 224 of the 1935 Act conferred the same supervisory jurisdiction on the High Courts as had been conferred by s. 107 except that s. 224(2) excluded judicial supervision.[23] And s. 225(1) excluded matters concerning the revenue from the original jurisdiction of High Courts, unless an Act of the appropriate legislature otherwise provided. This history was known to the framers of our Constitution, but consistently with their view of the position which the High Courts were intended to fill in our Constitution, Article 227 not only removed the restrictions imposed upon the High Courts' supervisory jurisdiction by Sec. 224(2) and 225(1) of the G.I. Act, 35 but extended the supervisory jurisdiction to "tribunals" within their jurisdiction other than Courts Martial. The 42nd Amendment attempted to restrict the supervisory jurisdiction under Art. 227 to what the High Courts possessed under the G.I. Act, 35 and if the 43rd Amendment had not restored the original Art. 227, it would have been necessary to refer at some length to a judgment of the Bombay High Court which showed that the amendment of Art. 227 had not wholly succeeded in curtailing the supervisory jurisdiction of the High Courts over such tribunals as were "Courts" and had not succeeded in excluding judicial supervision from the amended Art. 227.[24]

39. Article 77(4), which has been added by the 42nd Amendment provided: "No court or other authority shall be entitled to require the production of any rules made under clause (3) for the more convenient transaction of the business of the Government of India", and Art. 166(4), made *mutatis mutandis* the same provision as to the business of State Governments. The reason given for the change was:

"Articles 77(3) and 166(3), as originally enacted, provided for the framing of rules for the convenient transaction of Government business which rules are treated by the Government as confidential. However, courts had been found to summon these rules for production. It was considered that this should be prevented. A new clause has, therefore, been added to these Articles to provide that no court or authority shall compel production of these rules".

First, there is no reason why the rules of business should be confidential, and there are strong reasons why they should not be. Under Arts. 77(3) and 166(3) rules of

---

[21] (1958) S.C.R. 595, 616; ('58) A.SC. 86.
[22] *In re Adiraju* (1938) 1 F.L.J. 81. [23] ibid.
[24] *Shrimant Shripatrao Dajisaheb Ghatge* v. *Maharashtra* 79 Bom.L.R. p. 259 (F.B.).

business allocate business among Ministers. If a Minister *A*, in charge of a department *X*, makes a *mala fide* order against Y, either out of enemity to Y or in order to favour *Z*, and the order is impugned in court as *mala fide*, it is essential to know which Minister had been allocated department *X* under the rules of business, because the *mala fides* of the order must be brought home to the Minister who passed it. And that Minister alone could make an affidavit denying the allegation against him, if he was able to. The whole object of our founding fathers in enacting Arts. 32 and 226 was to provide a speedy and effective remedy against abuse of power, and Arts. 77(4) and 166(4) are designed to protect abuse of power by making it difficult, if not impossible, to bring home wrong-doing to the appropriate Minister or Ministers. In a democratic government responsible to the representatives of the people, the allocation of business to Ministers by the President and the Governors in the exercise of their constitutional powers cannot, and ought not to be, a secret; the more so when it delays or defeats the rights of citizens to seek redress as provided by our Constitution. Therefore, Art. 77(4) and 166(4) required to be repealed,[25] and the 44th Amendment rightly repealed them.

40. Apart from the direct attacks on the powers of the Supreme Court and the High Courts, there were indirect attacks on that power by protecting invalid laws by putting them in the 9th Schedule to our Constitution. The most infamous law in India, the Maintenance of Internal Security Act, 1971 (MISA) was included in the 9th Schedule by the 39th Amendment. The Election Manifesto of the Janata Party pledged it to repeal MISA. However, when a landside victory brought the party into power in Parliament, the Union Government showed strange hesitation in repealing MISA. In fact, with limited safeguards, a Bill sought to make preventive detention a part of the Criminal Procedure Code. However, protests within the Janata Party and in the country were so strong that the Bill was withdrawn and, at long last, MISA was repealed, and the 44th Amendment deleted it from the 9th Schedule by omitting entry 92.

41. We have seen that 14 judges of the High Court were transferred, against their will; that one of them was reverted to the post of a District Judge and one other judge's tenure of office was not extended because their judgments were not to the liking of Mrs. Gandhi. (See paras 11 and 12 above). This was an attack on the judiciary by executive action. We have also considered attacks on the judiciary by Constitutional amendments. It is equally necessary to notice attacks on the fair name and high reputation of the judiciary by responsible politicians inside and outside Parliament. In an inaugural address[26] of remarkable courage, cogency and power, Mr. Justice Tulzapurkar, the Acting Chief Justice of Bombay, dealt with these attacks because, as he said, ". . . every one of us — citizen, lawyer, legislator and Judge — is concerned to maintain the high position which Courts of Justice occupy in our country."[27] Just as a flash of lightning in a dark night lights up the scene for the beholder, so the following passage from his speech lights up the sombre judicial scene in the Emergency:

"On October 28, 1976 the Union Law Minister Shri H. R. Gokhale while replying to the three-day general discussion of the Constitution (44th Amendment) Bill indulged in the following three types of remarks:

(*a*) He recalled that some years ago a certain member of the Rajya Sabha had made the observation that the law was one generation behind, the lawyers two generations behind and Judges three generations behind (society). He added amidst laughter that 'the developments since the Rajya Sabha member made the observation, proved that the Judges are not merely three generations behind but many more.' (*b*) Referring to the judgments delivered by the Supreme Court he stated that some of the judgments were very long, running into more than 100 and 200 pages and he added: 'One does not know whether all the Judges are saying the same thing or different thing. Sometimes we do not know whether they are saying anything at all.' (*c*) Emphasising the fact that Art. 368 was being further amended to

---

[25] This paragraph reproduces para 7.35 of Seervai, *Emergency &c.* at pp. 165-6.
[26] On "Our Judicial System".
[27] 79 Bom.L.R. (Journal) p. 6 at p. 13.

ensure against a recurrence of any confrontation between Judiciary and Parliament, he hoped that the Supreme Court Judges would do a bit of 'introspection', realise that the Supreme Court was not after all that supreme and resist temptation to intrude into the fields which did not legitimately belong to them but further went on to observe without mincing words that if a confrontation recurred 'it will be a bad day for the Judiciary of this country.' (Samachar News Agency: *The Hindu* dated October 29, 1976).

"In all humility I would like to point out that in making the first remark he could be said to have spoken derisively of the judiciary; in making the second remark he could be said to have spoken contemptuously of the judiciary; and in making the third remark he could be said to have indulged in giving a threat to the judiciary and the Judges manning the same."[28]

SECTION III

THE 44TH AMENDMENT

"REVISIONISM REVISED": TOWARDS RESTORING DEMOCRACY

42. The 43rd and the 44th Amendments should be considered together. The 43rd Amendment was passed earlier, as it was essential to restore to the Supreme Court and to the Hight Courts the full powers they enjoyed before the Emergency — powers which had been seriously curtailed by the 42nd Amendment. It may be added that the 43rd and 44th Amendments were the result of a broad agreement between the ruling party in the House of the People and the Council of States and Congress opposition which was in a minority in the House of the People but held a majority in the Council of States. Reeling under the shock of electoral defeat in the Parliamentary elections held in 1977 and in the State elections which followed, the Congress party agreed to the repeal of a large part of the amendments it had introduced by the 42nd Amendment — presumably because it wished to disassociate itself with regressive amendments subverting the liberties of the people, and also from the excesses committed during the Emergency under the protection of those amendments.

43. The 44th Amendment falls broadly into three parts: First, it repealed several Articles or sub-Articles introduced by the 42nd Amendment; secondly, it provided additional safeguards against the kind of abuse which had taken place during the Emergency, and thirdly, it made amendments which were unoonnected with the 39th and 42nd Amendments introduced during the Emergency, namely, amendments converting rights of property from a "fundamental" to a "legal" right. It also amended Article 368 in a manner which will be considered at length with reference to the Chapter on the Amendment of the Constitution in Vol. II. It is unfortunate that just as the 43rd Amendment was introduced as a separate measure from the 44th, the 44th Amendment itself was not divided into two separate amending Bills, the Bill for the 44th Amendment providing for the first two parts mentioned above being introduced first, as such amendments were a matter of urgency. It was necessary to introduce a separate Amending Bill for the 45th Amendment providing for the property amendments and the amendment of Art. 368. In respect of the 44th Amendment, limited as suggested earlier, it was right to have undone the injury done to the Constitution by the near consent of all parties, including the party which had caused the injury. However, it is unfortunate that the bad precedent set by Mrs. Gandhi of not referring the 39th and 42nd Amendments to a Select Committee was followed by the Janata Party, and the normal democratic process of having the proposed amendment debated in Parliament, scrutinized by a Select Committee and considered by Parliament in the light of the Committee's Report was not followed. Chapter XIV, Vol. II (3rd ed.) will show how heavy is the price which must be paid in not submitting such amendments to the critical scrutiny of a Select Committee, with power to take evidence, examine and cross-examine

---

[28] ibid. p. 12.

witnesses. Had that procedure been followed, witnesses familiar with the Constitution would have pointed out the serious difficulties which would arise from the property amendments, as also the Amendment of Art. 368. Since those who framed and passed the new property amendments have given no guidance as to the mischief which they wanted to remedy and the result they wanted to produce, the courts will be confronted with problems far graver than those which have arisen in connection with Art. 31 or with Art. 368. Some of these difficulties, and the way in which they can be overcome have been discussed in Chapter XIV, Vol. II.

44. We have seen the attempts made by the 39th Amendment to undermine the judiciary and to interfere with electoral disputes arising from the election of the President and the Vice-President (paras 23 and 24 above) as also the attempts to subvert other provisions of the Constitution by enacting the 42nd Amendment. Broadly speaking, the 43rd and the 44th Amendments have nullified the amendments made to our Constitution by the 39th and 42nd Amendments. Further, profiting by the lessons taught by the Emergency, the 44th Amendment has introduced safeguards in our Constitution to prevent a recurrence of the abuse of power which took place during the Emergency. The changes made by the 43rd and the 44th Amendments are noted in their appropriate places in this volume. However, the following is a brief outline of the nullification by the 43rd and the 44th Amendments of several amendments made by the 39th and 42nd Amendments:

(*a*) The amendment introduced by the 39th Amendment in Art. 71 (see para 24 above), which dealt with matters relating to or connected with the election of a President or Vice-President, and substituted for the decision of electoral disputes by the Supreme Court the decision of a body whose constitution was not specified has been deleted, and the original Article 71 restored.

(*b*) The 42nd Amendment extended the duration of the House of the People (Art. 83), of State Legislatures (Art. 172) and of the Legislative Assembly of the State of Sikkim (Art. 371F) with certain transitional provisions for the last mentioned State. The 44th Amendment restored the duration of the House of the People to 5 years and made the amendment retrospective, restored the duration of the State Legislative Assemblies to the original duration of 5 years, making certain transitional provisions in certain cases, and reduced the duration of the Legislative Assembly of Sikkim from 6 to 5 years altering the transitional provisions of Art. 371F by substituting "four years" at the two places where the period of 5 years occurred in Art. 371F(c).

(*c*) Articles 103 and 192 which, as originally enacted, provided that questions as to the disqualification of members (i) of either House of Parliament or (ii) of a House of the State Legislature should be decided by the President and the Governors respectively by acting according to the opinion of the Election Commission were restored by deleting the amendment introduced by the 42nd Amendment which in substance deprived the Election Commission of its power to decide such disputes.

(*d*) The newly inserted Art. 329A(4) and (5) which was designed to secure that Mrs. Gandhi's appeal to the Supreme Court should be allowed (see para 26 above) had been declared void by the Supreme Court and therefore ceased to have any effect. However, the special provisions as to the elections to Parliament in the case of the Prime Minister and the Speaker which were contained in Art. 329A(1) and (2), which provisions were further protected by Art. 329A(6) which opened with the words "Notwithstanding anything contained in this Constitution" were omitted by the 44th Amendment, so that matters relating to the election of the Prime Minister and Speaker will be dealt with under our Constitution as originally enacted.

(*e*) The curtailment of the powers of the Supreme Court and the High Courts brought about by the 42nd Amendment have been referred to in paras 35 to 40 above. As it was a matter of urgency that the powers originally conferred on the Supreme Court and the High Courts by our Constitution should be restored, the 43rd Amendment did so by omitting Arts. 32A, 131A, 144A, 226A and 228A, which had been introduced by the 42nd Amendment, and by amending Arts. 145 and 226. These changes are noted in their appropriate places in this volume.

(*f*) The 42nd Amendment made numerous amendments in the Emergency Provisions of the Constitution. The abuse of those provisions during the Emergency brought them under close public scrutiny. The 44th Amendment has made substantial changes in the Emergency Provisions in order to provide safeguards against the abuse of those provisions which occurred during the Emergency. These provisions will be discussed in Vol. II.

(*g*) During the Emergency, the power of Preventive Detention was one of the principal means of suppressing freedom of speech and expression and of silencing all dissent. The 44th Amendment made substantial amendments in Art. 22 which provides safeguards in the case of preventive detention. The effect of these amendments has been increased by amending Art. 359(1), which now provides that the President shall *not* have power during an emergency to declare that the right to move any court for the enforcement of the fundamental rights conferred by Art. 20 and 21 shall be suspended.

45. One Amendment of cardinal importance must be noted at this place. As we have seen, during the Emergency, the protection given to the publication of Parliamentary Proceedings was withdrawn by repealing the Parliamentary Proceedings (Protection of Publication) Act, 1956 (see para 9). To prevent such gross abuse of power, the 44th Amendment added a new Art. 361A, which writes into the Constitution the protection originally given by the Parliamentary Proceedings (Protection of Publication) Act, 1956. Obviously, the protection does not apply to proceedings of Parliament or a State Legislature in secret sessions. The protection given to newspapers is also extended to reports of news broadcast by broadcasting stations, and newspapers were defined to include news agency reports for publication in newspapers.

APPENDIX II

THE RELATIONS OF THE UNION AND THE STATES *INTER SE*

[*NOTE*: This Appendix contains a large part of Chapter V as it appeared in the 1st and 2nd editions of this book. That Chapter included several paragraphs relating to (i) the Interpretation of our Constitution; (ii) the Character of the Indian Federation; (iii) Emergency Powers of our Constitution; and (iv) India in the British Commonwealth of Nations, Territories and New States. The discussion referred to in (i) above has been transferred to Chapter II which deals with the Interpretation of the Constitution; the discussion referred to in (ii) has been used in a new Chapter on *Federalism in India*; the discussion referred to in (iii) above has been deleted because the Emergency proclaimed on 25th June, 1975 has made it necessary to devote a whole Chapter to the Emergency Provisions of our Constitution, as was done in the 3rd Volume of the 2nd edition of this book which appeared in December, 1979; and the discussion referred to in (iv) above has been transferred to Chapter VI which now deals with Territories, New States and Citizenship. However, as the interconnection of widely dispersed Articles in our Constitution showing the relation of the Union and the States, Legislative, Executive and Financial, might be of interest to students and to some practitioners, it has been set out in this Appendix.]

1. The subject of this Appendix is dealt with in different parts of our Constitution, but an examination of those parts discloses the following broad pattern:

(1) *Legislative relations*:

(a) *normal*: Arts. 245, 246, 248, 253 and 254 (general) and Arts. 285 to 289 (finance).

(b) *exceptional*: Arts. 247, 249, 251 and 252.

(c) *emergency*:

(i) Created by war, external aggression or internal disorder: Arts. 352 to 354, 358, 359 read with Arts. 250 and 251;

(ii) Arising from a failure of Constitutional machinery in the States: Arts. 356 and 357;

(iii) Financial Emergency: Art. 360.

(2) *Administrative Relations*:

(a) *normal*: Arts. 256 to 261; 262 read with Arts. 73 and 1.

(b) *emergency*:

(i) Created by war, external aggression or internal disorder: Art. 353;

(ii) Arising from a breakdown of constitutional machinery in the States: Arts. 356 and 357.

(3) *Financial Relations*:

(a) *normal*: Arts. 268 to 274, 276 (taxes and duties) and Arts. 273-75 (grants).

(b) *emergency*:

(i) Created by war, external aggression or internal disorder: Art. 354;

(ii) Arising from a financial emergency: Art. 360.

The classification of the relations between the Union and the States into "Legislative Relations" and "Administrative Relations" is made in the Constitution itself, and into Financial relations is necessarily implied by it.

(1) LEGISLATIVE RELATIONS: (a) NORMAL

2. In this Appendix, legislative power is considered from a limited point of view, namely, of the legislative *relations* between the Union and the States *inter se*. The content of the legislative power of the Union and the States, and the Legislative

Lists is dealt with in Vol. II. Consequently, questions about extra-territorial legislation, retrospective legislation, validating legislation, legislative power to override contracts and the like will be dealt with in that Volume.

3. Parliament has power to legislate for the whole or part of India, and the Legislatures of States have the power to legislate for the whole or part of a State: Art. 245(1). Since India is a Sovereign State, no law made by Parliament can be held invalid because it would have extra-territorial operation, for whatever may be the position of extra-territorial legislation in international law, Courts in India must give effect to the express provision of Art. 245(2). A distribution of legislative power between the Union and the States is a normal feature of federal Government, and in India that distribution is made with reference to the three Legislative Lists of Sch. 7 to our Constitution. List I, called the "Union List", contains matters in respect of which Parliament has exclusive power to make laws. List III, called the "Concurrent List", contains matters in respect of which Parliament, and subject to the exclusive power of Parliament in respect of the Union List, the Legislatures of States have also power to make laws. Subject to the provisions mentioned above, State Legislatures have exclusive power to legislate with respect to matters in List II called the "State List". For territories of India which are not States, Parliament has power to make laws with respect to any matter notwithstanding that it is enumerated in the State List.

4. Legislative relations between the Union and the States *inter se* with reference to the entries in the three Lists in Sch. 7 cannot be understood fully without examining the general features disclosed by the entries contained in those Lists. Such an examination shows, first, that a distinction is made between general subjects of legislation and taxation, a distinction maintained by Art. 248 which confers the residuary power of legislation on Parliament; and secondly, that the main subject of legislation is dealt with in one group of entries and taxation in respect of any of those matters is dealt with in a separate group of entries.[1] Further, the entries relating to taxation in Lists I and II show that the taxing powers of the Union and of the States are mutually exclusive, a feature emphasised by the fact that the Concurrent List contains no entry relating to a tax. In List I, entries 1 to 81 deal with general matters of legislation; entries 82 to 92A deal with taxes; entry 96 deals with fees in respect of matters in the List other than Court-fees. In List II, entries 1 to 44 deal with general matters of legislation; entries 45 to 63 deal with taxes; entry 66 deals with fees in respect of matters in the List other than Court fees. That the main subject of legislation is dealt with separately from a tax in relation to that subject is clear from a comparison of entry 22, List I (Railways), with entry 89 (terminal taxes on goods or passengers carried by rail, sea or air, taxes on railway fares and freight), or again from a comparison of entry 41 (import and export across Customs frontiers; definition of Customs frontiers) with entry 83 (duties of Customs including export duties). In List II, entry 18 provides for land and for transfer and alienation of agricultural land; entries 45 to 48 provide respectively for land revenue, for taxes on agricultural income, for duties in respect of succession to agricultural land and for estate duty in respect of agricultural land. That the taxing powers of the Union and of the States are mutually exclusive is illustrated by comparing entries 82, 87 and 88, List I, which provide respectively for taxes on income other than agricultural income, for estate duty in respect of property other than agricultural property and for duties in respect of succession to property other than agricultural land, with entries 46, 47 and 48, List II, which provide respectively for taxes on agricultural income, for duties in respect of succession to agricultural land and for estate duty in respect of agricultural land. This mutual exclusiveness is also shown by the fact that List III, the concurrent legislative list, contains no entry relating to a tax, but only contains an entry for fees.[2] Thus, in our Con-

[1] *M. P. V. Sundararamier & Co.* v. *A.P.* (1958) S.C.R. 1422, 1481, ('52) A.SC. 468.

[2] Entry 35 of the Concurrent List is not an exception, because it refers to *the principles* on which taxes on mechanically propelled vehicles suitable for use on roads are the subject matter of entry 57 of the State List, subject to entry 35 of the Concurrent List.

stitution, a conflict between the taxing powers of the Union and of the States cannot arise.

5. With respect to matters other than taxation, an examination of the Lists discloses the following features:

(*a*) Certain legislative powers of Parliament with regard to matters in List I are unqualified exclusive powers, *e.g.*: Defence (entry 1), Naval, Military and Air Force (entry 2). Similarly, certain legislative powers of State Legislatures with regard to matters in List II are unqualified exclusive powers, *e.g.*, gas and gas works (entry 25), money-lending and money-lenders (entry 30).

(*b*) Certain subjects of legislation which in the first instance belong *exclusively* to the States, become the subject of exclusive Parliamentary legislation if a declaration is made as provided in the relevant entries of List I. Thus, entry 23, List II, provides for the regulation of mines and mineral development subject to the provision of List I with respect to regulation and development under the control of the Union. Entry 54 of List I provides for the regulation of mines and mineral development *to the extent to which such regulation and development under the control of the Union is declared by Parliament by law* to be expedient in the public interest. Again, entry 24, List II, provides for industries, subject to the provisions of entries 7 and 52 of List I. Entry 7, List I, provides for industries *declared by Parliament by law to be necessary for the purpose* of defence or for the prosecution of war, and entry 52 provides for industries the control of which by the Union is *declared by Parliament by law to be expedient in the public interest.* To the extent to which a declaration is made by law by Parliament the power of the State Legislatures to legislate in respect of matters in entries 23 and 24 is excluded.[3]

(*c*) There are certain legislative powers which belong exclusively to Parliament under List I, but the legislative entry deals only with a part of a subject, the remaining part falling within the exclusive legislative powers of the States by *express provision.* For example, entries 63 to 65, List I, deal with certain educational institutions and entry 66 deals with certain aspects of higher education; entry 11, List II, provides for education,[4] including Universities, but *expressly* makes this power subject to the provisions of entries 63 to 66, List I (and to the concurrent power under entry 25, List III).

(*d*) Certain powers of the State Legislatures in List II are made subject to the concurrent legislative power of the Union. Thus, entries 26 and 27, List II, provide for trade and commerce within the State and for the production, supply and distribution of goods subject to the provisions of entry 33 in List III which provides for trade and commerce in, and the production, supply and distribution of, the items mentioned in (*a*) to (*e*) of that entry.

(*e*) Parliament has exclusive power to legislate over *such part of a subject* as is mentioned in List I, the States having exclusive legislative power over *another part of the same subject.* Thus entry 43, List I, provides for the incorporation, regulation and winding up of trading corporations including banking, insurance and financial corporations, but not including co-operative societies, and entry 44 provides for the incorporation, regulation and winding up of corporations whether trading or not with objects not confined to one state but not including Universities. Entry 32, List II, provides for the incorporation, regulation and winding up of corporations other than those specified in the Union List, and Universities, unincorporated trading, literary, scientific, religious and other societies and associations; co-operative societies.

---

[3] *Hingir Rampur Coal Co.* v. *Orissa* (1961) 2 S.C.R. 537, 558-9, ('61) A.SC. 459, cited with approval in *Orissa* v. *Tulloch & Co.* ('64) A.SC. 1284 at p. 1290.

[4] The 42nd Amendment repealed entry 11, List II and inserted the following entry 25 in List III: "Education, including technical education, medical education and Universities subject to the provisions of entries 63, 64, 65 and 66, List I; vocational and technical training of labour."

(*f*) Powers *apparently exclusive* may have to be treated as concurrent *in part* having regard to the other entries. Thus land, and particularly agricultural land, is a subject of exclusive State legislation under entry 18, List II. However, entry 42, List III, provides for acquisition and requisition of property. Therefore, on sound principles of construction, though land generally is a subject of exclusive State legislative power, acquisition and requisition of land become subjects of concurrent legislative power.

6. When a conflict is alleged between a law made in the exercise of an exclusive legislative power of Parliament, and a law made in the exercise of an exclusive legislative power of State Legislatures, it is necessary to examine the nature of the executive power, since the content of that power is not the same in respect of all the matters in the Lists. Such examination is necessary to determine whether the conflict raises a question of lack of power or of repugnancy.

7. Although the legislative powers of Parliament and of the Legislatures of States are to be found by reference to the three Legislative Lists, legislative powers are also conferred by some of the Articles of the Constitution. Examples of such Articles are given in the undernoted footnote.[5]

8. We have seen[6] that the basic scheme for the distribution of legislative power contained in our Constitution has been taken over from the G.I. Act, 35, and that Arts. 245 and 246 correspond to ss. 99 and 100 of that Act. Similarly, the distribution of legislative power with reference to the three Lists has also been taken over from the G.I. Act, 35, in which the three Lists disclose almost all the features we have noted above.[7-10] The result therefore is that the principles laid down with reference to the distribution of legislative powers in the G.I. Act, 35, become applicable to the distribution of legislative power under our Constitution, as fully explained in para 2.45 of this book.

9. Article 254 retains in our Constitution the innovation introduced by the G.I. Act, 35, in respect of concurrent powers of legislation. Having regard to the varying stages of development of the various States and territories of India, it may be that in the concurrent field State Legislatures may wish to enact laws different from existing laws on the matters contained in the Concurrent List, or from laws made by Parliament under the Concurrent List. Accordingly, Article 254(2) provides that if a law made by a State Legislature in respect of matters in the Concurrent List is reserved for the consideration of the President and receives his assent, then, the State law shall prevail in that State over an existing law or a law made by Parliament, notwithstanding its repugnancy. However, s. 107(2) of the G.I. Act provided that a law made by the Provincial Legislature with the assent of the Governor-General would not preclude the Federal Legislature from time to time enacting further legislation with respect to the same subject matter. Article 254(2) provides that a law made by the State with the assent of the President shall not prevent Parliament from enacting at any time any law with respect to the same matter including a law adding to, amending, varying or repealing the law so made by a State Legislature.

10. The Supreme Court has held that Art. 248 referred to distribution of legislative powers between the Centre and the States mentioned in Parts A and B under the three Lists in Sch. VII and had no application to Part C States for which the governing provision was Art. 246(4).[11]

11. Article 253 is in aid of the legislative power contained in List I, entry 14, and will be considered in detail when dealing with the treaty making power. Article 255[12] as is clear from the marginal note, treats the requirements of previous recom-

---

[5] Arts. 2 to 4, 119, 209. [6] See para 1.95.

[7-10] The Act did not allocate the residuary power either to the Federation or to the Provinces. S. 104 enabled the Governor-General to allocate any matter not enumerated in the Lists either to the Federation or to the Provinces.

[11] *Mithan Lal* v. *Delhi* (1959) S.C.R. 445, 452, ('58) A.SC. 682.

[12] See p. A-85.

mendation or sanction as merely procedural. In *Venkatarao* v. *Bombay*[13] it was contended that the Hyderabad Tenancy and Agricultural Lands Act, 1950, not having received the assent of the President, was void, though it was conceded that the 1950 Act had been amended in 1954 and in 1958, with the assent of the President. The Supreme Court held that if the assent of the President had been given to the Amending Acts, it would be difficult to hold that the President had never assented to the parent Act of 1950. "Even if such assent had not been accorded earlier, it must be taken to have been granted when the amending Act III of 1954 was assented to."[14]

12. Article 285 provides for the exemption of the property of the Union from State taxation, *save in so far as Parliament may by law otherwise provide*, but it saves the levy of any tax on any property of the Union which property was immediately before the commencement of the Constitution liable or *treated as liable* to tax so long as that tax continues to be levied in that State. The word "property" is used in its ordinary sense as including every kind of property,[15] and the words "treated as liable" are designed to cover cases where it may be a matter of doubt whether the property was in fact or law liable to such tax.[16] Article 287 exempts from tax on electricity, electricity consumed or sold for consumption to the Government of India or for the purposes mentioned in that Article, save in so far as Parliament may by law otherwise provide. Article 288 similarly exempts the Union from tax by States in respect of water or electricity in certain cases. Article 289 exempts the property and income of a State from Union taxation except that Parliament may by law authorize the imposition of a tax in respect of a trade or business of any kind carried on by the Government of a State or any property used in connection therewith unless the trade or business has been declared by Parliament by law to be incidental to the ordinary functions of Government. It will be seen that whereas the exemption of Union property from State taxation is absolute, the immunity of the States from Union taxation is limited.

(1) Legislative Relations: (b) Exceptional

13. In the United States, Federal Courts have been constituted to administer Federal Laws,[17] and that precedent has been followed in Australia.[18] In Canada the same Courts administer both Provincial and Federal laws, although s. 101, B.N.A. Act, 1867, enables the Federal Parliament to establish Federal Courts for the better administration of federal laws.[19] The system followed in India under the G.I. Act, 35, and thereafter under our Constitution, is that the same Courts administer both Union and State laws. However, Art. 247 enables Parliament to set up Federal Courts for the better administration of Union laws made with respect to matters in List I. No such Courts have been created till now.

14. Article 249 introduces an innovation in our Constitution,[20] namely, that if a subject matter of State legislation acquires national importance for a time, then, if the Council of States declares by a resolution, supported by not less than two-thirds of the members present, that it is necessary or expedient in the national interest that Parliament should make laws with respect to any matter enumerated in the State List specified in the resolution, Parliament can make a law on such a subject. The resolution remains in force for a period of six months but can be re-

---

[13] (1970) 1 S.C.R. 317, ('70) A.SC. 126.

[14] ('70) A.SC. at p. 129. These observations were made after the Supreme Court had held that the impugned Act was protected from challenge under Art. 31B.

[15] *Corporation of Calcutta* v. *Governors of St. Thomas' School* (1949) F.C.R. 368, 376.

[16] *Governor-General of India* v. *Corporation of Calcutta* (1947) 52 C.W.N. 173, 175.

[17] See Willis, *Constitutional Law*, p. 928 *et seq.*

[18] For Federal Courts see *Wynes*, p. 456 *et seq.*, and ss. 71, 72, 75, 76 and 77, Commonwealth of Australia Act.

[19] See Laskin, *Canadian Constitutional Law*, 2nd ed. p. 801 *et seq.*

[20] See para 1.100.

newed as often as a subsequent resolution for such renewal is passed in the manner required for passing the original resolution. The power to pass a resolution mentioned in Art. 249 has been conferred on the Council of States for the obvious reason that the members of the Council (except for 12 nominated members) are elected by the State Legislatures and can therefore be expected not to override State rights unless the national interest clearly required such action. Article 251 provides that the power conferred by Art. 249 on Parliament shall not restrict the power of the Legislature of a State to make any law which it has power to make, but if such a law is repugnant to a law made under the provisions of Art. 249, then, the State law shall be void to the extent of its repugnancy to a law made by Parliament as long as such law remains in operation. Thus Art. 249, read with Art. 251, makes the subject mentioned in the resolution a subject of concurrent legislative power. Article 252 confers on Parliament the power to legislate on matters with respect to which it has no power to make laws for the States (except under Arts. 249 and 250) provided that two or more States by resolutions passed by the House of the Legislatures of those States declare that it is desirable that Parliament should legislate in respect of the matter specified in such a resolution. Article 252 corresponds to s. 103, G.I. Act, 35, but whereas s. 103 enabled the Provincial Legislatures to amend or repeal a law so made by the Federal Legislature, Art. 252(2) prevents State Legislatures from amending or repealing a law passed by Parliament. It is difficult to understand the reason for this departure, for the Article loses its utility if the power of the State Legislature is permanently taken away. Circumstances which necessitated the resolutions of State Legislatures may change, *e.g.* by the reversal of the judgment of a State High Court by the Supreme Court — as actually happened in the Prize Competition Case.[21] In any event, it has been held that surrender by two or more Legislatures of their power to legislate on a particular subject, *e.g.* betting and gambling, does not involve a surrender of a right to levy a tax in respect of it, since the power to tax is a distinct and separate power.[22]

(1) Legislative Relations: (c) Emergency

(i) *Arising from War (including War Power) or internal disturbance, and (ii) arising from a failure of Constitutional Machinery in the States.*

15. In para 1 above, we have referred to the Legislative Relations between the Union and the States under the heading (1) (c) "emergency", dividing emergency into three sub-classes: (i) created by war, external aggression or internal disorder (Arts. 352 to 354, 358, 359 read with Arts. 250 and 251); (ii) arising from a failure of Constitutional machinery in the States (Arts. 356 and 357); and (iii) Financial Emergency (Art. 360). In the first two editions of this book, topics under sub-classes (i) and (ii) were discussed at this place. However, the Emergency proclaimed on June 25, 1975 and its aftermath made it necessary to devote a whole Chapter to the subject in the 3rd Volume of the 2nd edition. Accordingly, the discussion relating to sub-classes (i) and (ii) will be found in Volume II of this book. Financial Emergency stands in a different class and is discussed in paras 16 and 17 below.

(1) Legislative Relations: (c) Emergency

(iii) *Financial Emergency.*

16. Article 360 provides that if the President is satisfied that a situation has arisen by which the financial stability or credit of the whole or part of India is threatened, he may by Proclamation make a declaration to that effect. The provisions contained in Art. 352(2) as regards the revocation of a Proclamation issued under cl. (1) thereof as also the provisions for laying the Proclamation before the Houses and the period during which the Proclamation is to operate unless supported by resolu-

---

[21] In *Bombay* v. *R. M. D. Chamarbaugwala* (1957) S.C.R. 874, ('57) A.SC. 699, the Supreme Court reversed the judgment of the Bombay High Court on every relevant point, so that neither Art. 19 nor Arts. 301-4 would have stood in the way of the validity of the Bombay Prize Competition Act there impugned.

[22] *R.M.D.C. (Mysore) Private Ltd.* v. *Mysore* (1962) 3 S.C.R. 230, ('62) A.SC. 594.

tions of the two Houses are made applicable to a Proclamation under Art. 360. The issue of such a Proclamation does not directly affect the Legislative relations between the Union and the States but it would be convenient to mention the effect of such a Proclamation at this place. During the period that such Proclamation is in operation, the executive authority of the Union extends to giving of directions to any State to observe such cannons of financial propriety as may be specified in the directions and to the giving of such other directions as the President may deem necessary and adequate for the purpose. Article 360(4) provides that "Notwithstanding anything in this Constitution—

(a) any such direction may include—

(i) a provision requiring the reduction of salaries and allowances of all or any class of persons serving in connection with the affairs of a State;

(ii) a provision requiring all Money Bills or other Bills to which the provisions of article 207 apply to be reserved for the consideration of the President after they are passed by the Legislature of the State;

(b) it shall be competent for the President during the period any Proclamation issued under this article is in operation to issue directions for the reduction of salaries and allowances of all or any class of persons serving in connection with the affairs of the Union including the Judges of the Supreme Court and the High Courts."[23]

17. The language of the opening words of sub-cl. (*a*) "any such direction may include" show that the directions are not limited to the two items there mentioned. Article 360(*b*) relates not to the State but to the Union, for, a financial emergency in one or more States may have the effect of precipitating and creating an emergency in the Union and express power is conferred to reduce the salary and allowance of all or any of the persons serving in connection with the affairs of the Union, including Judges of the Supreme Court and the High Courts. Having regard to the purpose of Art. 360, it is submitted that the directions given by the President have overriding effect. Thus, if the implementation of the laws passed by the State Legislatures or the executive policy pursued thereunder, have the effect of undermining the financial stability of credit of the State, it is submitted that the President's directions under Art. 360(3) and (4) have the effect of overriding those laws and those policies as long as the proclamation is in force. To hold otherwise would be to defeat the purpose of Art. 360 by saying that if the financial stability of the State is threatened due to the implementation of its laws, the financial emergency thus created is beyond remedy.

(2) Administrative Relations: (a) Normal

18. Article 73 provides that subject to the provisions of the Constitution, the executive power of the Union extends to matters with respect to which Parliament has power to make laws, and to the exercise of rights, authority and jurisdiction exercisable by the Government of India by virtue of any treaty or agreement. But this power is subject to the proviso that save as expressly provided in the Constitution, or in any law made by Parliament, the executive authority shall not extend in any State to matters with respect to which the Legislature of the State has *also* power to make laws.[24] The result therefore is that the executive authority of the Union is absolute in respect of matters contained in List I but is qualified as regards matters in List III. It has been held that the proviso to Art. 73(1)(*a*) is attracted only to the executive power referred to in Art. 73(1)(*a*) and not to the executive power referred to under any other provision of the Constitution, *e.g.*, Art. 298.[25] Subject

[23] This provision is meant to avoid the acute controversy which arose in England when the salaries of judges of the superior courts were reduced in 1931 by an Order in Council under the National Economy Act, 1931. See Prof. Holdsworth's article in (1931) 46 *L.Q.R.* 25.

[24] See *T.D. Corporation Ltd.* v. *Assam* ('61) A.Ass. 133, 138.

[25] ibid.

to the provisions of the Constitution, the executive power of the State extends to all matters with respect to which the Legislature of the State has power to make laws with the proviso that where the power to make laws is concurrent, the executive power of the State is subject to, and limited by, the executive power expressly conferred by the Constitution or by any law made by Parliament upon the Union or authorities thereof: Art. 162. The executive power of every State must be so exercised as to ensure compliance with the laws made by Parliament and with existing laws which apply in that State, and the executive power of the Union extends to giving such directions to a State as may appear to the Government of India to be necessary for that purpose: Art. 256. Similarly, the executive power of every State must be so exercised as not to impede or prejudice exercise of the executive power of the Union, and the executive power of the Union extends to the giving of such directions to a State as may appear to the Government of India to be necessary for that purpose. It extends also to the giving of directions to the States as to the construction and maintenance of means of communication declared in the direction to be of naval or military importance, and also as to measures to be taken for the protection of the railways within the State, the Union being under an obligation to pay to the States any *extra* costs incurred by the State in carrying out such directions: Art. 257. The sanction for enforcing directions given to any State in the exercise of the executive power of the Union under any of the provisions of the Constitution is that if any State fails to carry out such directions, it would be lawful for the President to hold that a situation has arisen in which the government of the State cannot be carried out in accordance with the provisions of the Constitution: Art. 365. The President may, with the consent of the Governor of a State entrust either conditionally or unconditionally to the Government of that State or to its officers functions in relation to matters to which the executive power of the Union extends. A law made by Parliament which applies in any State and is on a matter on which the Legislature of a State cannot make laws may confer powers and impose duties or authorize the conferring of power and the imposing of duties upon the State, its officers and authorities: Art. 258. Article 258(3) provides for payment to the State of a sum either by agreement or arbitration for the exercise of powers and the discharge of duties, referred to in Art. 258(1) and (2). Article 258A enables the Governor of a State with the consent of the Government of India to entrust to that Government or to its officers, functions in relation to any matter to which the executive power of the State extends. In *N. B. Singh* v. *Duryodhan Pradhan*[26] it was held "The relationship arising by virtue of Art. 258A cannot be said to pertain to the law of agency but is only a constitutional statutory entrustment in relation to the exercise of the executive power which is a sovereign power. . . ." The combined effect of Arts. 256, 258 and 353, is that the Central Government is competent to issue directions to a State Government calling upon it to withdraw or cancel orders of detention passed under the Defence of India Rules by the various authorities under the State's control.[27]

The Full Faith and Credit Clause

19. Article 261 provides that full faith and credit shall be given throughout the territories of India to the public Acts, records and judicial proceedings of the Union and of every State and that the manner in which and the conditions under which the Acts, records and proceedings referred to above are to be proved and the effect thereof determined shall be such as are provided by law made by Parliament. Article 261(1) and (2) corresponds to Art. 4, s. 1, of the U.S. Constitution[28] and to

[26] (1958) Cut. 440, ('59) A.Or. 58, 65.

[27] *Anant Baburao* v. *State* (1966) Bom. 803, ('67) A.B. 109, 68 Bom.L.R. 187.

[28] "Full Faith and Credit shall be given in each State to the public acts, records and judicial proceedings of every other State. . . . And the Congress may by general laws prescribe the Manner in which such acts, records and proceedings shall be proved, and the Effect thereof."

s. 118 and s. 51 (xxiv) and (xxv) of the Commonwealth of Australia Act.[29] However, Art. 261 makes a departure from the U.S. Constitution by providing that "final judgments or orders delivered or passed by Civil Courts in any part of the territory of India shall be capable of execution anywhere within that territory according to law." The "full faith and credit" clause in the American and Australian Constitutions makes no reference to the Federal Government, because, as regards the laws and public Acts and records of the Federal Government there are no State boundaries. However, our Constitution has made express references to the Union to avoid any controversy on the subject.

20. The object of the "full faith and credit" clause is obviously to prevent the States of a Federation from treating each other as foreign States by virtue of their independence in their own respective spheres. In the United States and in Australia, the Federal Government is a Government of enumerated powers, the States having independent Constitutions of their own. In India, the position is different. The States of British India never had independent Constitutions of their own, and our Constitution is a Constitution both for the Union and the States. However, within the limits of their powers, in the exclusive and in the concurrent field, the States *inter se* have plenary powers, and the "full faith and credit" clause has the effect of preventing the States from treating one another as foreign States. Whereas the "full faith and credit clause" of our Constitution provides for the execution in the territory of India of final judgments or orders passed by Civil Courts, s. 118 of the Australian Constitution read with s. 51 (xxiv) and (xxv) enables a law to be made providing for the execution of both Civil and Criminal judgments and orders. Difficult and complicated questions have arisen in the United States in connection with the "full faith and credit" clause, and the reader interested in judicial dialectics and polemics will find fascinating material in the judgments of the U.S. Supreme Court, which have been critically reviewed by Prof. Corwin[30]. He states the problems which arise in the United States as follows: "Article IV, Section 1, has had its principal operation in relation to judgments. The cases fall into two groups: First, those in which the judgment involved was offered as a basis of proceedings for its own enforcement outside the State where rendered, as for example, when an action for debt is brought in the courts of State B on a judgment for money damages rendered in State A; secondly, those in which the judgment involved was offered, in conformance with the principle of *res judicata*, in defense in a new or 'collateral' proceeding growing out of the same facts as the original suit, as for example, when a decree of divorce granted in State A is offered as barring a suit for divorce by the other party to the marriage in the courts of State B."[31]

21. In India, the first group of cases need not arise since under Art. 261(3) a final judgment obtained in a civil matter in an Indian Court can be executed throughout the territory of India, and a suit is not necessary to enforce such a judgment. It is well settled that under s. 38, read with s. 47 C.P.C., the Court executing a decree cannot examine the validity of that decree as between the parties to the decree.[32] The importance of this provision is that if a suit has to be filed on the judgment of a foreign Court it is open to challenge on well-recognized grounds which are embodied in s. 13 C.P.C. Thus, if the Court which passed the decree had no jurisdiction, the decree will not be enforced by a foreign Court. It is well settled on principles of international law that a decree passed by the Court of a State in a *personal action* against a non-resident foreigner neither domiciled in, nor owing

---

[29] *S. 118*: "Full faith and credit shall be given, throughout the Commonwealth, to the laws, the public Acts, and records, and the judicial proceedings of every State."
S. 51: "Parliament shall have power to make laws with respect to (xxiv) Service and execution throughout the Commonwealth of the Civil and Criminal process and the judgments of the Courts of the States; (xxv) The recognition throughout the Commonwealth of the laws, the public Acts, and records, and the judicial proceedings of the States."

[30] *Corwin*, pp. 739-75.

[31] ibid. p. 741.

[32] Mulla, *Code of Civil Procedure*, 14th ed., Vol. 1, p. 289 *f.n.* (*d*); and p. 327.

allegiance to, that State, is a nullity,[33] and it makes no difference that the legislature of the State authorizes its Courts to pass a decree against such a foreigner, if the whole or part of the cause of action arises in that State. No doubt the Courts of that State must give effect to the law, but the decree remains a nullity outside the State.[34] It may be added that in relation to British India, the Native States of India were foreign States and their judgments were judgments of foreign courts which had to be enforced in India either by a suit or under s. 44 C.P.C. if that section was applicable.

22. As to cases in the second group, the differences between the States of the United States, and the States of India make it unlikely that in India in the judgment of a Court "chaos can find a masterpiece". First, in the United States, the States are governments of residuary powers with independent Constitutions of their own, possessing all the powers not delegated to the Congress or not denied to the States. Secondly, there is no authority to co-ordinate the laws of different States based on different legislative policies. Consequently, questions have arisen as to how far the Courts of State A are obliged to give effect to the judgment of a Court in State B if the policy underlying the law on the same subject in State A is different. But in India, matters of all-India concern are in the Union List and other important matters having all-India aspect are in the Concurrent List.[35] If, for example, the Workmen's Compensation Acts, or laws relating to marriage and divorce, or the local amendments to Union laws on the subjects in the Concurrent List produce such conflicts as have arisen in the United States, it is reasonable to believe that Parliament would put an end to such conflict by appropriate all-India legislation. It may be added that a question arose under Art. 261 whether a decree passed by the Court of a Native State before the coming into force of the Constitution can be executed in India. The passage of time has deprived the question of practical importance, and it need not be considered here.[36]

23. As to what constitutes "public acts" and "records" of the Union and of every State, the reader is referred to any standard commentary on ss. 74 and 78 of the Evidence Act. Section 74 defines public documents and s. 78 provides for proof of certain official documents. No law has been made under Art. 261(2), but that Article in substance confers an exclusive legislative power on Parliament so that entry 12 of List III which, among other things, provides for the recognition of laws, public acts and records and judicial proceedings is to that extent overridden by Art. 261(2), if Parliament enacts a law under that Article.

River Water Disputes

24. Article 262 provides for adjudication of disputes relating to water. However, before considering that Article, it would be helpful to refer to the corresponding provisions of the G.I. Act, 35. Entry 19, List II, Sch. 7 of the Act provided for "Water, that is to say, water supplies, irrigation and canals, drainage and embankments, water storage and water power." This was because land and water were treated as essentially a matter of provincial or local concern. However, waters of Inter-State rivers were matters of concern to more than one Province, and s. 130 of the Act[37] provided for complaints as to interference with water supplies from

---

[33] *Gurdyal* v. *Raja of Faridkote* (1894) 21 I.A. 171, 22 Cal. 222.

[34] *Hussain Khan* v. *Raphael* (1901) 28 Cal. 641; *Vishwanadha Reddi* v. *Keymer* (1916) 39 Mad. 95, 100, affirmed in 44 I.A. 6.

[35] *E.g.* criminal law and procedure, marriage, divorce and family relations, the law of property, contracts and actionable wrongs, the law of bankruptcy, the law of trusts, civil procedure, evidence and workmen's compensation are some of the subjects of concurrent legislative power.

[36] The question has been fully considered and the relevant provisions of the C.P.C. and the various changes made in them, have been fully set out in *Moloji Narsing Rao* v. *Shankar Saran* ('62) A.SC. 1737, affirming ('58) A.A. 775.

[37] *Interference with Water Supplies.* "130. *Complaints as to interference with water supplies.* — If it appears to the Government of any Governor's Province or to the Ruler of any Federated State that the interests of that Province or State, or

any natural source of supply in a Governor's Province or in a Federated State. Section 131 provided. that the Governor-General might refer any such complaint to a Commission (unless he was of opinion that the issues involved were not of sufficient importance); s. 131 also provided for the Commissioner's report to be implemented, subject to an appeal to His Majesty in Council. And ss. 132 and 133 made similar provisions for resolving water disputes for the Chief Commissioners' Provinces. S. 134 barred the jurisdiction of all courts "notwithstanding anything in this Act" in respect of water disputes covered by ss. 131 to 133. In other words, provisions for resolving water disputes and barring the jurisdiction of courts, were written into the G.I. Act, 35 itself.

25. Article 262 must be read with entry 56, List I, Sch. 7, and entry 17, List II: *Art. 262. "Adjudication of disputes relating to waters of inter-State rivers and river valleys.*—(1) Parliament may by law provide for the adjudication of any dispute or complaint with respect to the use, distribution or control of the waters of, or in, any inter-State river or river valley. (2) Notwithstanding anything in this Constitution, Parliament may by law provide that neither the Supreme Court nor any other court shall exercise jurisdiction in respect of any such dispute or complaint as is referred to in clause (1)."

List I: "56. Regulation and development of inter-State rivers and river valleys to the extent to which such regulation and development under the control of the Union is declared by Parliament by law to be expedient in the public interest."
List II: "17. Water, that is to say, water supplies, irrigation and canals, drainage and embankments, water storage and water power subject to the provisions of entry 56 of List I."

The Constitution has made several departures from the provisions of the G.I. Act, 35. First, the State's legislative power over water is made subject to Parliament's power under entry 56, List I. Secondly, the machinery for resolving water disputes is not written into the Constitution itself, but is to be provided for by law by Parliament. Thirdly, the jurisdiction of all courts including the Supreme Court is not excluded by the Constitution, but Art. 262(2) empowers Parliament to provide for such exclusion by law.

26. When the first edition of this book was written, though many disputes as to the waters of inter-State rivers had arisen, none had been referred to any Tribunal; consequently, the subject attracted little attention. The picture has now changed, and after referring to the two Acts passed by Parliament, we will consider the matter more fully than was done in the first edition.

27. Parliament has enacted two laws, the River Boards Act, 1956, relating to inter-State rivers and river valleys. Section 2 of the River Boards Act declares that it is expedient in the public interest that the Central Government should take under its control the regulation and development of inter-State rivers and river valleys *to the extent hereinafter provided.* The Act has been rendered a dead letter by not appointing River Boards, although 26 years have elapsed since the Act was enacted. Consequently, the value of the declaration in s. 2 is extremely doubtful, because it could not have been intended that the State's legislative power should be *pro tanto* affected by the Act which, for practical purposes, is dead. This conclusion is supported by the words of s. 2 italicised above. It is submitted that it is more than arguable that the declaration is ineffective and inoperative as long as the Act remains inoperative. The Inter-State Water Disputes Act, 1956, by s. 4(1) bars the jurisdiction of the Supreme Court and other courts notwithstanding anything contained in any other law. The Act provides for complaints as to water disputes

---

of any of the inhabitants thereof, in the water from any natural source of supply in any Governor's or Chief Commissioner's Province or Federated State, have been, or are likely to be affected prejudicially by — (*a*) any executive action or legislation taken or passed, or proposed to be taken or passed; or (*b*) the failure of any authority to exercise any of their powers, with respect to the use, distribution or control of water from that source, the Government or Ruler may complain to the Governor-General."

made by State Governments to the Central Government, and it further provides that:

"When any request under s. 3 is received from any State Government in respect of any water dispute and the Central Government is of opinion that the water dispute cannot be settled by negotiations, the Central Government shall . . . constitute a Water Disputes Tribunal for the adjudication of the water dispute."[38]

Water dispute is defined in s. 2(c):

"(c) 'water dispute' means any dispute or difference between two or more State Governments with respect to—(i) the use, distribution or control of the waters of, or in, any inter-State river or river valley; or (ii) the interpretation of the terms of any agreement relating to the use, distribution or control of such waters or the implementation of such agreement; or (iii) the levy of any water-rate in contravention of the prohibition contained in section 7."

28. Thus the right to have a water dispute referred to a Tribunal is not absolute, but is dependent on the opinion of the Central Government that the matter cannot be settled by negotiation. It is submitted that the provisions of s. 131 of the G.I. Act, 35, were more satisfactory, for they required the Governor-General to refer a water dispute to a Commission unless he was of the opinion that the matter was not of sufficient importance. First, the advantage of writing a machinery for resolving inter-State river water disputes into the Constitution and also barring the jurisdiction of all courts is that it is not left to the Legislature to provide a machinery. In fact over 5 years elapsed before the Inter-State Water Disputes Act, 1956 ("the Act") was passed. Article 262 confers a power to make a law; it cannot impose a duty, for no court can issue a *mandamus* to a legislature to make a law. Secondly, no provision of the Constitution can be *ultra vires*, but any law, or part of a law, made under Art. 262, can be *ultra vires*. For example, s. 4(1) of the Act would have to be held *ultra vires* if the court upheld the Central Government's claim that it gave Government an absolute arbitrary power not to refer a dispute to a tribunal because in its opinion "the dispute could be settled by negotiations", even if the parties make it clear that the dispute cannot be so settled. For, the power conferred by Art. 262(2) is a power to make a law to provide for the *adjudication* of disputes and not a power to *prevent adjudication* in a practical sense by indefinite delay. However, a court is unlikely to uphold such a construction of s. 4, which would be construed to mean that the Government's opinion must be based on reasonable grounds, and once it is clear that the dispute cannot be settled by negotiations the Central Government is under a duty to refer the matter to a Tribunal; and a mandatory order could be issued directing the Government to do so. The grave injury caused to States by inordinate delay in referring a dispute to a Tribunal appears not to have been realized, and could not have been demonstrated, till the Tribunal appointed to decide the dispute relating to the waters of the River Krishna ("the Krishna Tribunal") heard the dispute, and pronounced its decision. However, this topic is considered in para 38 below.

29. To those unfamiliar with the complex issues raised by an inter-State river water dispute under a federal or quasi-federal Constitution, it seems attractive to say that such a dispute should be settled across the table in a friendly spirit, and in the national interest (described hereafter as a "political settlement"). And proposals have been canvassed that all rivers should be put under the control of the Union. It is submitted, first, that such proposals run counter to the basic scheme for the distribution of legislative power between the Union and the States, and would destroy the most valuable features of our Constitution; secondly, that a political settlement can be even more time-consuming and would not be as satisfactory as an adjudication by a Tribunal, assuming that such a settlement can be brought about at all.

---

[38] The complaint can be made in respect of "any . . . legislation passed or proposed . . . to be passed by the other State": s. 3(*a*).

30. The scheme for the distribution of legislative power between the Union and the States can be broadly described by saying that matters of national interest are put in List I which confers exclusive legislative power on Parliament: Art. 246; and matters of State or local concern are put in List II, which confers exclusive legislative power on State Legislatures: Art. 246. Secondly, taxation is regarded as a distinct matter and is separately set out in Legislative Lists I & II. Apart from entry 56, List I, and entry 17, List II,[39] the following entries are relevant:

Sch. 7, List I: Entries 82, 87 and 88 deal respectively with taxes on income other than agricultural income; estate duty in respect of property other than agricultural land; duty in respect of succession of property other than agricultural land. *List II*: Entries 14, 18, 19, 45, 46, 47, 48, 49 deal respectively with agriculture, land, forests, land revenue, taxes on agricultural income, duties in respect of succession to agricultural land, estate duty in respect of agricultural land, and taxes on lands and buildings.

Leaving aside the question of waters of inter-State rivers, it will be seen that land and water are essentially "local", that is, they are located in the territory of a State. That land is essentially "local" was held by the Privy Council in respect of entry 21, Sch. 7, List II, G.I. Act, 35 (corresponding to entry 18, List II of our Constitution):[40]

"The key to item 21 is to be found in the opening word, 'land'. That word is sufficient in itself to include every form of land, whether agricultural or not. *Land, indeed, is primarily a matter of provincial concern.* The land in each province may have its special characteristics in view of which it is necessary to legislate. . . . *It would be strange if land in provinces were to be broken up into separate portions* some outside the legislative powers of the province. Such a conflict of jurisdiction is not to be expected."[41] (italics supplied)

What Lord Wright said about land is equally true of water exclusively located within the territory of a State. Therefore, things connected with land and water, such as agriculture and irrigation, are essentially "local", and are allocated to the States. Further, land revenue, taxes on agricultural income, succession and estate duty in respect of agricultural land, taxes on lands and buildings are subjects of exclusive State legislation whereas taxes on income other than agricultural income, estate duty, and succession duty in respect of property other than agricultural land, are subjects of exclusive parliamentary legislation. These mutually exclusive powers of taxation secure to the States independent powers of taxation, several of which would be seriously impaired if all rivers were put under Union control.

31. The fact that entry 56, List I, enables the Union to exercise control over inter-State rivers does not involve a departure from the principle underlying the distribution of legislative power. For though the waters of an inter-State river pass through the territories of all the States taken together, such waters are not located in any one State; they are in a state of flow, and on well settled principles of International and Federal Law relating to the waters of an inter-State river, no State can claim exclusive ownership of such waters so as to deprive the other States of their equitable share. Secondly, as regards water located entirely within a State, legislative power for its beneficial use is vested exclusively in State Legislatures. In respect of the waters of an inter-State river, no State can effectively legislate for the beneficial use of such waters, first, because its legislative power does not extend beyond the territories of the State; secondly, because the quantum of water available to each of the States is dependent upon the equitable share of the other States; and, thirdly, a dispute about the waters of an inter-State river can arise from any actual or proposed legislation of a State, as s. 130, G.I. Act 35, and s. 2(c), Inter-State Water Disputes Act, 1956, clearly show.[42] It is for these reasons that inter-State rivers and river valleys are mentioned in entry 56, List I, Sch. 7, and the determination of disputes relating to them is provided for in Art. 262. It is

---

[39] Set out in para 25 above.
[40] *Megh Raj* v. *Allah Rakhia* 74 I.A. 12 (*per* Lord Wright).
[41] ibid. p. 20.
[42] See *f.ns.* 37 and 38 above.

submitted that the facile notion that inter-State rivers should be treated as "national assets" overlooks the fact that water flowing through the territories of States, is a valuable asset for each of the States, and, like the land in its territory, is a matter of vital concern to each State. The beneficial use of land for agriculture and the improvement of agriculture by irrigation must enure for the benefit of the whole of India; but for that reason it has never been suggested that land, agriculture, irrigation and the like are matters of national concern and should be included in the Union List. If such a result had been intended by the framers of our Constitution, they would have adopted a unitary, and not a federal, form of government. As Prof. Wheare has observed:

"It may be true that economic life is one but in federal countries this fact is not recognized, so far as the allocation of governmental powers is concerned. The legal and political pluralism of the federations is imposed upon the alleged unity of economic affairs."[43]

Further, it is necessary to observe that control by Parliament over flowing water is very different from control over static things, like mines and minerals, because the benefit derived from the exploitation of mines and minerals mostly goes to the State in which they are located. Thus, opportunities of employment, taxes on the sale of goods, octroi and similar indirect advantages all enure for the benefit of the State. The product of the mines may be made available throughout India, but the cost of obtaining or making the product, and, up to a point, of distributing it, secures substantial direct and indirect benefits to the particular State. This is not true of the waters of an inter-State river, for once the State is deprived of its fair share of such waters, which then flows to another State, not only the water, but all the direct and indirect benefits which arise from the use of such water are lost to the State.

32. So far we have considered the matter from the legal and constitutional aspect. But the belief that river water disputes are time-consuming and protracted, and therefore a political settlement is to be preferred is ill-founded, as can be demonstrated from the following narrative of facts relating to the Krishna River Water dispute:

In 1951, without the scrutiny of relevant data and without any attempt to obtain such data, an "agreement" at the political level was reached between the States of Madras, Mysore, Hyderabad and Bombay, allocating the waters of the river Krishna between those States. Mysore did not sign the "agreement", and atttempts to obtain its signature failed. Thereafter there were various States Re-organisation Acts which required the "agreement" to be re-adjusted, but attempts to secure a settlement failed. At a conference called by the Government of India on September 26 and 27, 1960, to settle the issue, no settlement was reached. On the contrary, a dispute about the allocation of water under the 1951 "agreement" was raised by the concerned States. On May 1, 1961 the Gulati Commission was appointed to determine the dependable flow of the Krishna and the feasibility of a diversion of water from the Godavari into the Krishna. In January, 1962, the Mysore government applied to the Central Government to refer the dispute to a Tribunal. On August 25, 1962, the Gulati Commission presented its report expressing its inability to determine the dependable flow for lack of data, while expressing an informed opinion that the recorded flow was less by 10 per cent, and reporting that the Godavari diversion was feasible on a study of topo sheets, but the feasibility could be finally determined only by actual field survey. On March 23, 1963, the Union Minister for Irrigation and Power laid a statement before Parliament and in his speech he said that according to legal opinion at the highest level, the "agreement" of 1951 had become void, if it was not void *ab initio*. Pending determination of the dependable flow of the river Krishna, he made what he called an "interim allocation" of 400, 600 and 800 thousand million cubic feet (T.M.C.) of the waters of the Krishna to Maharashtra, Mysore and Andhra Pradesh respectively leaving margins of safety. In the discussions which followed the Minister's statement it was admitted that the interim allo-

[43] *Federal Government*, 3rd ed. p. 134.

cation had been made on the assumption that 300 T.M.C. of water would be available as a result of the Godavari diversion, and another 300 T.M.C. of water was likely to be available from regeneration,[44] which would enure substantially for the benefit of Maharashtra and Mysore. However, it was submitted that if these assumptions were incorrect, then there was no water in the Krishna for further allocation. On June 11, 1963, the State of Maharashtra applied to the Central Government to refer the dispute to a Tribunal. On July 2, 1963, the Government of India directed Andhra Pradesh to reconstruct the recorded flow data on the basis of 3-D (three-dimensional) model experiments performed in the Hyderabad Research Station. On April 27, 1964, Andhra Pradesh sent the reconstructed flow data to the Government of India and correspondence passed between the Government of India and the State of Andhra Pradesh for nearly 3 years as to the accuracy of the experiments with inconclusive results. Meanwhile, in June 1966, the Central Water and Power Commission directed the Poona Research Station to conduct 3-D model experiments on the Vijayawada anicut model.[45] The model was completed in October 1967, and experiments were carried out between October 1967 and May 1968. Reconstructed data was supplied to the States in June 1968. Even before the 3-D model experiments were completed, Andhra Pradesh raised certain doubts about the construction of the model and its suitability for yielding accurate results. At long last, on 10th April 1969, the matter was referred to the Krishna Tribunal.

Thus, well over 8 years were spent in trying to secure a "political settlement" without securing any agreement at all. In the light of what happened before the Krishna Tribunal, the time spent on 3-D model experiments was time wasted.

33. Before the Krishna Tribunal, considerable time was taken in determining the validity of the 1951 "agreement". Although the Government of India had proceeded on the footing that the "agreement" was no longer operative, and had allocated waters on that assumption, it was powerless to enforce its view on Andhra Pradesh. The Tribunal, after elaborate arguments, held that the agreement was void as Mysore had never signed it.

34. Since 3-D model experiments had been performed for ascertaining the dependable flow of the Krishna, the States of Maharashtra and Andhra Pradesh examined expert witnesses whose evidence involved citation of text books and papers on model experiments and on hydraulics. Once evidence had been led, it became apparent that the materials supplied by Andhra Pradesh, and the materials which it said in the first instance it did not possess but which it produced after the experiments had been performed, showed that the results of the experiments could not be relied upon. Accordingly, Maharashtra and Mysore intimated to the Tribunal that they would not rely on the result of 3-D model experiments but would rest their case on the recorded flow at Vijayawada from 1901 to 1950 after making the necessary corrections which the evidence had disclosed were necessary. This involved the scrutiny of 50 years' record, and on the Tribunal being satisfied that the record required correction the best method of correcting indisputable error had to be determined. As a result of argument, and concessions made, and the massive assistance given by the Tribunal, the central issue was settled, it being agreed by the parties for the purpose of the dispute that the reconstructed recorded data disclosed a dependable flow of 2,060 T.M.C. Having ascertained the dependable flow, the Tribunal had to determine the equitable share of each State and for that purpose to study 127 project reports.[46] It is a measure of the high capacity, tireless industry

---

[44] "Regeneration or return flow: Water, having been diverted from a stream or other body of water for irrigation purposes, passes downwards to the sub-soil water table and ultimately reaches a surface stream or other body of water": Multi-lingual Technical Dictionary on Irrigation and Drainage, p. 71.

[45] The anicut had breached in September 1952, and therefore the original of the model was not available for verifying the correctness of the model.

[46] Reports ordinarily describing the objects which the project was designed to accommoplish, the estimated cost of construction and detailed technical data about the construction of the project.

and complete grasp of the difficult problems involved that the Tribunal gave its decision on December 24, 1973, that is, within four and a half years from the time it was appointed, a decision which would have been given earlier but for the inevitable interruptions which a long inquiry involves.[47]

35. It will be seen that the popular belief that the political settlement of a river water dispute would be more satisfactorily reached is demonstrably incorrect because as opposed to inconclusive discussions and investigation extending for over eight and a half years, the Tribunal, going through an enormous record and after taking elaborate oral evidence of a highly technical and scientific character gave its decision within four and a half years.

36. Further, it is extremely difficult to secure a political settlement because of its repurcussions on State Governments. Few governments would wish to take the responsibility of arriving at a settlement — which involves give and take — for fear of being charged with selling out the rights of their States. It is not without significance that the word "rival" is derived from *rivus*, a stream. Before a judicial tribunal assisted by lawyers and engineers, settlement is much easier. For, once the evidence has been produced, sifted, and its value ascertained, the gap between the parties gets narrowed down, and with the assistance of judges accustomed to bridge gaps between contesting parties settlements are reached. Thus, before the Krishna Tribunal a large number of matters were settled by agreement, including "protected users", and most important of all, the dependable flow of the Krishna.[48]

37. Apart from the illustration furnished by the Krishna River Water Dispute, the history of the Narmada River Water Dispute is instructive on this point. The dispute was relatively simple: what should be the height of the Navagam Dam which the State of Gujarat proposed to put up? If the height was 530 feet, as proposed by Gujarat, a very large tract of land in Madhya Pradesh and Maharashtra would be submerged, to which those States strongly objected. If however, the height was reduced to 210 feet, submergence would be tolerable. Secondly, after providing for Maharashtra, it was necessary to determine what was the equitable share of Gujarat and Madhya Pradesh. The dispute was referred to a Tribunal in October 1969, and after the Tribunal had done some preliminary work, the States of Gujarat, Madhya Pradesh and Maharashtra referred the dispute to arbitration of the Prime Minister of India, Smt. Indira Gandhi, on July 22, 1972. It may be added that various Ministries in Gujarat were in difficulties, and ultimately, as a result of grave disorder in the State, the State Legislative Assembly was dissolved and the State put under the President's Rule. After the matter had been pending before the Prime Minister for nearly two years, it was referred back to the Tribunal for its decision on July 12, 1974. The above facts show that serious river water disputes do not admit of a "political settlement", because water is a scarce, and for practical purposes, an irreplaceable commodity, and the States are vitally concerned in its beneficial use.

38. We may note briefly the irreparable injury which may be caused to States by an inordinate delay in referring a dispute to a Tribunal. We have seen that interim allocations were made to Andhra Pradesh (800 T.M.C.), Mysore (600 T.M.C.) and Maharashtra (400 T.M.C.) on the assumption that the Godavari diversion and regeneration would add 600 T.M.C. of water to Krishna which would redress the balance in favour of Mysore and Maharashtra. The assumption about the Godavari

---

[47] A 5-month break was caused because two Advocates General who were appearing before the Tribunal had to appear before the Supreme Court in the *Fundamental Rights Case* which began on October 31, 1972 and ended on March 22, 1973. Adjournments were necessitated by the illness of an expert witness, by the necessity of giving time to Counsel to prepare for the examination of expert witnesses and finally for analysing and putting before the Tribunal the result of an enormous volume of oral and documentary evidence.

[48] The facts about the Krishna River Dispute are personally known to the present writer who appeared for the State of Maharashtra and they have been verified with the seniormost engineers who also represented Maharashtra.

diversion failed because Andhra Pradesh refused to agree to any diversion at all, and the parties agreed that the Tribunal could not compel the diversion. As to regeneration, the Tribunal's decision allotted 7.5 cent regeneration to each State which works out at less than a third of the 300 T.M.C. assumed for the interim allocation. Since the interim allocation created "protected users" the injury done to Mysore and Maharashtra was permanent and irreversible.

39. Since the jurisdiction of courts is barred in respect of water disputes, judicial decisions are not available on the question: who can raise an inter-State river water dispute? The basis of an inter-State river water dispute is the injury caused to the rights of a State by use made of the waters of the inter-State river by another State. The States through which the river runs can obviously raise a dispute if they bring their case within the definition of river water dispute in s. 2(c) of the Inter-State Water Disputes Act, 1956 (see para 29 above). But can a State through whose territory the inter-State river does not run (hereafter called "State X") raise a dispute? It is submitted that apart from questions of shipping and navigation on national waterways (entry 24, List I), State X can raise a dispute in the following situations and in no other. First, State X may by agreement or by custom have a right to share in the waters of the inter-State river and X can complain if that right is infringed or injuriously affected. Secondly, State X may complain if the waters of the inter-State river are discharged on its territory causing flooding or any other nuisance, as for example, by the discharge of polluted water. But apart from these cases X cannot raise a river water dispute, because X has no right in or to the river, injury to which can furnish a ground for raising a dispute. Thus, the State of West Bengal can raise no dispute as to the waters of the river Krishna, for the situations described above do not exist in the case of West Bengal; and the States of Maharashtra, Mysore (now Karnataka) and Andhra Pradesh can raise no dispute about the river Ganges, for the same reason.

Co-ordination between States

40. Article 263 provides for co-ordination between States, but it is clear from its terms[49] that the Councils established under it have no sanction behind them as their functions are merely advisory and their powers extend to inquiry, investigation, discussion and making of recommendations. Thus, the Councils can inquire into and advise upon disputes which have arisen between States or investigate and discuss subjects of common interest to one or more States, or to the Union and one or more States, or they may make recommendations upon subjects of common interest and for the better co-ordination of policy with respect to that subject.

(2) ADMINISTRATIVE RELATIONS: (b) EMERGENCY

(i) *Created by War, external aggression or internal disorder.*

41. Article 353 provides that during the proclamation of emergency, the executive power of the Union extends to the giving of directions to any State as to the manner in which the executive power of that State is to be exercised; further the power of Parliament to make laws includes the power to make laws conferring powers and duties upon the Union, its officers and authorities in respect of any matter notwithstanding that it is not contained in List I, Sch. VII.

(ii) *Arising from a breakdown of Constitutional machinery.*

42. Article 356 enables the President to assume all or any of the functions of the Government of a State and all or any of the powers of the Governor or any other body or authority in the State other than the Legislature. In other words, the executive authority of the State can be taken over and exercised by the President.

---

[49] See p. A-87.

(3) FINANCIAL RELATIONS: (a) NORMAL

43. Part 12 of the Constitution deals with finance, property, contract and suits and some of these provisions may be noted here as they relate to the distribution of revenue between the Union and the States. After providing for the Consolidated Funds and public accounts of India and of the States, the Articles provide (i) for duties levied by the Union but collected and appropriated by the States: Art. 268; (ii) for taxes levied and collected by the Union but assigned to the States: Art. 269; and (iii) for taxes levied and collected by the Union and distributed between the Union and the States: Art. 270. The duties levied by the Union and collected and appropriated by the States are stamp duties (entry 91, List I), and duties of excise on medicinal and toilet preparations, alcohol or opium, Indian hemp and certain other narcotic drugs and narcotics (entry 84, List I). The proceeds in any financial year of any duty leviable within any State are not to form part of the Consolidated Fund of India but are to be assigned to that State. Duties and taxes levied and collected by the Union but assigned to the States, refer to entries 87 to 90, 92 and 92A, List I, which provide respectively for estate duty in respect of property other than agricultural land, for duties in respect of succession to property other than agricultural land, for terminal taxes on goods or passengers carried by railway, sea or air; for taxes on railway fares and freight; for taxes other than stamp duties on transactions in Stock Exchanges and Futures market; for taxes on the sale or purchase of newspapers and on advertisements published therein, for taxes on the sale or purchase of goods other than newspapers where such sale or purchase takes place in the course of inter-State trade or commerce. The net proceeds of such duties or taxes except in so far as those proceeds represent the proceeds attributable to Union Territories are not to form part of the Consolidated Fund of India but are to be assigned to the States within which that duty was leviable in that year and is to be distributed among those States in accordance with such principles of distribution as may be formulated by Parliament by law. Taxes levied and collected by the Union and distributed between the Union and the States are taxes on income other than agricultural income (entry 82, List 1) and such percentage as may be prescribed of the net proceeds in any financial year of any such tax, other than the proceeds attributable to Union Territories or to taxes payable in respect of Union emoluments is not to form part of the Consolidated Fund, but must be assigned to the States within which that tax was leviable during the year to be distributed among those States in the prescribed manner. "Prescribed" means prescribed by the President before the constitution of a Finance Commission, and thereafter prescribed by him after considering the recommendations of the Finance Commission. Article 271 provides that Parliament may at any time increase any of the duties or taxes referred to in the above Article by a surcharge for the purposes of the Union and the whole proceeds of the surcharge is to form part of the Consolidated Fund of India. Article 272 is a permissive Article which provides that Union duties of Excise other than duties of Excise on Medicinal and Toilet Preparations referred to earlier are to be levied and collected by the Government of India, but if Parliament by law so provides, payment out of the Consolidated Fund is to be made to the States to which the law imposing the duty extends of sums equivalent to the whole or any part of the net proceeds of the duty and those sums are to be distributed among the States in accordance with the principles formulated by such law. It is a misreading of Art. 272 that the duties of excise must be collected by the Government of India and not through any agency.[50] Any tax collected by the Government may be collected by their agents and need not be collected by their servants alone.[51] Article 273 relates to the levies of duties on jute and jute products as regards the State of Assam, Bihar, Orissa and West Bengal. Article 274 contains a special provision providing for the prior recommendation of the President for Bills which affect taxation in which States are interested or which varies the mean-

---

[50] *Aluminium Corporation of India* v. *Coal Board* ('59) A.Cal. 222, 231.
[51] ibid.

ing of the expression "agricultural income" as defined for the purpose of enactments relating to the Indian Income-tax Act or which affects the principles on which under the provisions of this Chapter moneys are or may be distributed to the States or which imposes any surcharge for the purpose of the Union. Article 277 contains a saving clause saving taxes, duties, cesses or fees lawfully levied by any Government or any Municipality or Local Authority before the commencement of the Constitution until provision to the contrary is made by Parliament by law. Article 275 provides for grants from the Union to certain States.

(3) Financial Relations: (b) Emergency

(i) *Created by war, external aggression or internal disorder*

44. Article 354 enables the President during a Proclamation of emergency to direct by an order that the provisions of Arts. 268 to 279 shall have effect subject to such exceptions or modifications as he thinks fit. The order so made, must be laid before each House of Parliament as soon as may be, and the directions contained in the order operate for such period not extending in any case beyond the expiration of the financial year in which the proclamation ceases to operate.

(ii) *Arising from a financial emergency*

45. This subject has already been discussed in paragraphs 16 and 17 above.

APPENDIX III

THE JUDICIARY AND THE EMERGENCY

"The Calicut Regional Engineering College student Mr. P. Rajan, 'died while in unlawful police custody at Kakayam Police Camp on March 2, 1976, as a result of continuous police torture with iron and wooden rollers'. This was admitted in the returns filed in the form of affidavits by respondents, including the former Chief Minister, Mr. K. Karunakaran before the Division Bench of the Kerala High Court. . . ."

The Times of India, 24-5-1977.

"Counsel after counsel expressed the fear that during the emergency, the executive may whip and strip and starve the detenu and if this be our judgment, even shoot him down. *Such misdeeds have not tarnished the record of Free India* and I have a diamond-bright, diamond-hard hope that such things will never come to pass."[1] (italics supplied)

per Chandrachud J.

"Furthermore, we understand *that the care and concern bestowed by the State authorities upon the welfare of detenus who are well housed well fed and well treated*, is almost maternal."[2] (italics supplied)

per Beg J.

1. Even before Justices Chandrachud and Beg had awarded good conduct certificates to the Union and State Governments, a grim tragedy had been enacted in the Kakayam Police Camp. P. Rajan, an engineering student was arrested on 29th February, 1976, and was murdered by "continuous police torture with iron and wooden rollers". The attempts of Rajan's father, Prof. Warrier, to find his son proved fruitless. On 28th April, 1976, Chief Justice Ray, and Justices Beg, Chandrachud and Bhagwati delivered four separate but concurring judgments in the *Habeas Corpus Case*, and by a majority of 4 to 1 (Mr. Justice Khanna dissenting) passed the following Order:

"In view of the Presidential Order dated 27 June, 1975, no person has *locus standi* to move any writ petition under Art. 226 before a High Court for *habeas corpus* or any other writ or order or direction to challenge the legality of an order of detention on the ground that the order is not under or in compliance with the Act[3] or is illegal or is vitiated by *mala fides* factual or legal or is based on extraneous considerations."[4]

2. In effect, if not in intent, the four judges held that in India all law was abrogated in relation to life and personal liberty. In the face of this order, there was little which Rajan's anguished father could do to find his son. But when freedom came back to India and the two "emergencies" had ended, Rajan's father resumed his search for his son by filing a *habeas corpus* petition in the Kerala High Court. The respondents, including the Chief Minister, in their first return, denied that Rajan had been arrested; and stated that the respondents did not hold Rajan in custody. After evidence had established that Rajan had been arrested and taken away by the Police, the Court directed the respondents to file a report showing the steps taken to trace Rajan. Nothing daunted, the respondents appealed to the

---

[1] *A.D.M. Jabalpur* v. *Shivkant Shukla* (1976) Supp. S.C.R. 172 at p. 414, ('76) A.SC. 1207 at p. 1349.

[2] (1976) Supp. S.C.R. at p. 370-71, ('76) A.SC. at p. 1319. The italicised words appear to have been taken from a letter written by Mr. B. K. Nehru, the then Indian High Commissioner in the United Kingdom, to the "Times": See Kuldip Nayar, *The Judgment*, pp. 84-5.

[3] The Maintenance of Internal Security Act, 1971 ("MISA").

[4] (1976) Supp. S.C.R. at p. 477, ('76) A.SC. at p. 1392.

Supreme Court, alleging that the High Court had no jurisdiction to pass the order since the appellants did not have Rajan in their custody. The appeal was dismissed. So great was the feeling of horror and outrage at the disappearance of Rajan, and the strictures which the High Court had passed on the respondents, that the Chief Minister, Mr. Karunakaran, resigned. In further affidavits filed pursuant to the Court's order, the crime of murder by torture was admitted. Before the untimely grave of Rajan, and the desolate home of his father, the words of Justices Chandrachud and Beg, quoted earlier, seem a cruel mockery. How many Rajans have perished in detention? How many have come out maimed in mind and body? How many men and women who were not detained died at the Turkman Gate in Delhi or in other places? The Shah Commission Reports have now told the grim tale. But one thing is clear. *A.D.M. Jabalpur* v. *Shivkant Shukla* (popularly called the "*Habeas Corpus Case*") and *Rajan's Case* will find a place not only in law books but will be a part of Indian history, just as the trial of the seven Bishops is a part of English history, the trial of Dred Scott is a part of American history, and the trial of Drefus is a part of French history.

3. However, Mr. Justice Khanna delivered a remarkable dissenting judgment which he concluded with the moving words of Chief Justice Hughes: "A dissent in a court of last resort . . . is an appeal to the brooding spirit of the law, to the intelligence of a future day, when a later decision may possibly correct the error into which the dissenting Judge believes the court to have been betrayed."[5] Writing in May 1976 I said, "It may be that the future to which (Mr. Justice Khanna) appealed will prefer his dissent to the majority judgments, as the future has preferred the dissent of Lord Atkin to the majority judgments of the House of Lords in the *Liversidge Case* (1942) A.C. 206."[6] I did not know then that my words would come true so soon.

4. The four judgments were delivered in the darkest hour of India's history after Independence, and they made that darkness complete. Fortunately for the four judges, censorship in India protected their judgments from professional criticism, from criticism in the press and in public, and from "the respectful but outspoken comments of ordinary men". Ordinary men and women could understand Satan saying, "Evil be thou my good", but they were bewildered and perplexed to be told by four learned judges of the Supreme Court that, in substance, the founding fathers had written into the Emergency Provisions of our Constitution, "Lawlessness be thou our law".

5. More than three years have gone by since the four judgments were delivered, and the political scene has been transformed by the ordinary men and women of India whose resolute and courageous action at the polls sent their oppressors flying in disorder and disarray. The emergency and its aftermath will, I believe, find historians to describe in memorable language how Indians by their own exertions took their country from tyranny to freedom. In that history, the judiciary will find a place. And though prophecy is hazardous, I believe that the historian will say that, speaking broadly, the High Courts reached their finest hour during the emergency; that brave and courageous judgments were delivered, and that 16 judges paid the price for such judgments by enforced transfers; that a threat of enforced transfers was kept hanging over 40 other judges but failed to deflect them from their duty; that a Bench of 3 judges of the Gujarat High Court, regardless of consequences to themselves, unanimously struck down an Order transferring a judge of the Gujarat High Court without his consent to the Andhra Pradesh High Court, that by judicial interpretation of the inconsistencies and contradictions of the four judgments in the *Habeas Corpus Case*, the High Courts kept their doors ajar which those judgments appeared to have barred and bolted.

6. As the historian turns from the High Courts to the Supreme Court his task will be harder, for the history of the Supreme Court during the emergency is a

[5] (1976) Supp. S.C.R. at p. 304, ('76) A.SC. at p. 1277. The judgment was banned by the censors: See White Paper on Misuse of Mass Media During the Internal Emergency (August 1977) Appendix 13; September: Serial No. 11.

[6] Seervai, *Constitutional Law of India*, 2nd edn., Vol. II, Addenda p. 750.

history of two different periods: the first began a day before the Emergency and ended with Prime Minister Indira Gandhi's Appeal in the *Election Case*; the second began with the *Habeas Corpus Case* and ended with the revocation of the Emergency by a defeated Mrs. Gandhi, unwilling to put into the hands of her opponents a weapon she had forged and used against them. Of the first period, the historian will say that the Supreme Court moved towards its finest hour, a day before the proclamation of Emergency, when, on 24th June, 1975, Krishna Iyer J., following judicial precedents, rejected an application made by Mrs. Gandhi that the Allahabad High Court's Order, finding her guilty of corrupt election practices and disqualifying her for 6 years, should be totally suspended. In the best traditions of the judiciary, Krishna Iyer J. granted a conditional stay of the Order under appeal, although he had been reminded by her eminent counsel, Mr. N. A. Palkhiwala, "that the nation was solidly behind (her) as Prime Minister"[7] and that "there were momentous consequences, disastrous to the country, if anything less than the total suspension of the Order under appeal were made".[7] The historian will record that the Supreme Court reached its finest hour when it struck down the newly added Art. 329A(4) which, in substance, directed the Supreme Court to allow Mrs. Gandhi's appeal and dismiss Raj Narain's cross appeal. Judges are no respectors of persons, and in declaring Art. 329A(4) invalid, judges used language in which the authentic note of the Supreme Court was heard — as when Mr. Justice Mathew said that to accept one of the arguments of the Solicitor-General "would toll the death knell of the democratic structure of the Constitution"[8] or when Mr. Justice Chandrachud said that "It is the common man's sense of justice which sustains democracies and there is a fear that [Art. 329A(4)] may outrage that sense of justice".[9] As the historian surveys the Supreme Court from this height and descends into the dark valley below — where dwell the *Habeas Corpus Case* and its numerous progeny — he will no longer hear the authentic note of the Supreme Court. "The common man's sense of justice which sustains democracies"[10] fades away, and is replaced by the dry statement that "a frank and unreserved acceptance of the proclamation of emergency, even in the teeth of one's own pre-disposition, is conducive to a more realistic appraisal of the emergency provisions".[11] Adapting John Bright's saying "that the trouble with great thinkers is that they usually think wrong", the historian will say that "the trouble with realistic appraisal is that it usually lacks reality".

7. As the historian surveys the Supreme Court during the emergency, he will conclude that he must tell the tale of two Supreme Courts, inviting his readers to "look at this picture and that". But in drawing those pictures, and in heightening the contrasts between them, one thing will attract his attention. The four judgments make no reference to the total abrogation of safeguards against absolute arbitrary power, and the abrogation of every principle of representative government. The press was muzzled, and so were the legislatures, for the Acts granting immunity to fair reports of legislative proceedings were repealed, and those proceedings could not be reported. Judicial proceedings could not be reported; public meetings could not be held without the permission of the police which was given to "the cringing and the craven"[12] and refused to sober and responsible men; a servile radio and television worked under government orders. Again, public opinion, which is the safeguard of freedom, was strangled at birth, for all means of forming and expressing public opinion were suppressed. Except in a limited class of cases, grounds of detention were not to be communicated to the detenu and his case was not to be referred to an advisory Board, the legislatures were not to be

[7] *Indira Gandhi* v. *Raj Narain* ('75) A.SC. 1590, 1593.

[8] *Smt. Indira Nehru Gandhi* v. *Raj Narain* (1976) 2 S.C.R. 347 at p. 515, ('75) A.SC. 2295 at p. 2379.

[9] (1976) 2 S.C.R. at p. 665, ('75) A.SC. at p. 2469.

[10] ibid.

[11] (1976) Supp. S.C.R. at p. 380, ('76) A.SC. at p. 1325 (*per* Chandrachud J.).

[12] *N. P. Nathwani* v. *Commr. of Police* 78 Bom.L.R. 1 at p. 74 (*per* Tulzapurkar J.).

informed about the precise number of people arrested and released, or their whereabouts.

8. With every safeguard except the Courts gone, Counsel for the detenus in the *Habeas Corpus Case* reminded the Supreme Court of the most shameful episode in human history — the extermination of 6 million people in the gas chambers of Nazi concentration camps, and pointed out that if courts abdicated their duty to see that the law was obeyed, the infamies of Hitler could take place in India. In saying this, Counsel were not alone. In one of his judgments, Chief Justice Asthana of the Allahabad High Court had observed that if he accepted the arguments of Government "the ghost of Hitler would stalk over India". How did the Supreme Court react to the infamies of Hitler? Khanna J. realized the force of Counsel's argument; he knew that it had provoked Chief Justice Ray to insult Counsel in the language of abuse. But without mentioning the Chief Justice by name, Khanna J. administered a rebuke to the Chief Justice, not the less effective because, in words of studied moderation, he reminded the Chief Justice that:

"As observed by Friedmann (*Law in a Changing Society*, 2nd edn. p. 500), *in a purely formal sense . . . even the mass murders of the Nazi regime qualify as law. This argument cannot, however, disguise the reality of the matter that hundreds of innocent lives have been taken because of the absence of rule of law.* A state of negation of rule of law would not cease to be such a state because of the fact that such a state of negation of rule of law has been brought about by statute."[13] (italics supplied)

Ray C.J. reacted violently to the reference to gas chambers:

"Some instances from different countries were referred to by some counsel for the respondents as to what happened there *when people were murdered in gas chambers* or people were otherwise murdered. Such instances are intended to produce a kind of terror and horror and are hortative in character. *People who have faith in themselves and in their country will not paint pictures of diabolic distortion and mendacious malignment* of the governance of the country. Quite often arguments are heard that extreme examples are given to test the power. If there is power, extreme examples will neither add to the power nor rob the same. Extreme examples tend only to obfuscate reason and reality."[14] (italics supplied)

Pondering over these passages, the historian will contrast the sensitivity to human suffering and the sober dignity of Mr. Justice Khanna, with the intemperate language in which Chief Justice Ray thought fit to insult Counsel by questioning their faith in themselves and in India, and by characterizing their arguments as "diabolic distortion and mendacious malignment" about the governance of their country. And what did the Chief Justice mean when he said "If there is power extreme examples will neither add to the power nor *rob the same*?"[15] (italics supplied). Did he wish to convey that even if he were satisfied that his construction would lead to the massacre of millions of his countrymen, he would still adopt that construction? If so, the lessons of the Nuremberg trials and of the punishment of men guilty of crimes against humanity were lost on him.

9. But when the historians have given their accounts of the Emergency, and described in broad outline the part played by the judiciary, they will leave it to lawyers and those versed in Constitutional law, to answer one inescapable question: Was the *Habeas Corpus Case* rightly decided, no matter how shocking it may have been in its results? I have answered that question in Appendix IV and I believe I have established that the majority judgments are clearly wrong, productive of great public mischief and have in fact produced grave public mischief and should therefore be overruled.

---

[13] (1976) Supp. S.C.R. at p. 277, ('76) A.SC. at p. 1260.
[14] (1976) Supp. S.C.R. at pp. 222-3, ('76) A.SC. 1223.
[15] (1976) Supp. S.C.R. at p. 223, ('76) A.SC. 1223.

APPENDIX IV

THE HABEAS CORPUS CASE[1]

1. The appeals decided by the Supreme Court in the *Habeas Corpus Case* arose out of *habeas corpus* applications filed by several detenus who prayed for their release from illegal preventive detention. A preliminary objection was raised by the Union and/or the State ("the State") that in view of the President's Order under Art. 359 suspending the right of any person (including a foreigner) to move any court for the enforcement of his fundamental rights under Arts. 14, 19, 21 and 22, the petitioners had no *locus standi* to maintain the petition, because, in substance, the detenus were seeking to enforce their fundamental right under Art. 21, namely, that they should not be deprived of their personal liberty except by procedure established by law. The High Courts of Allahabad, Andhra Pradesh, Bombay, Delhi, Karnataka, Madras, Madhya Pradesh, Punjab and Haryana and Rajasthan, rejected this contention and held that though the petitioners could not move the Court to enforce their fundamental right under Art. 21, they were entitled to show that the order of detention was not under or in compliance with the law or was *mala fide*. The *consensus of judicial opinion was against* the view of the four judges of the Supreme Court in the *Habeas Corpus Case*. But that consensus was brushed aside. Chandrachud J. found that the trouble with the High Court judges was that they lacked judicial detachment. He did not put it as bluntly as that; he administered his rebuke in sweet, soothing syrup:

"But at the back of one's mind is the facile distrust of executive declarations which recite threat to the security of the country, particularly by internal disturbance. *The mind then weaves cobwebs of suspicion and the Judge without the means to knowledge of full facts, covertly weighs the pros and cons of the political situation and substitutes his personal opinion for the assessment of the Executive. . . .* A frank and unreserved acceptance of the proclamation of emergency, *even in the teeth of one's own pre-disposition*, is conducive to a more realistic appraisal of the emergency provisions."[2] (italics supplied)

In other words, judges in the nine High Courts did not show the judicial detachment required from judges. Their minds were enmeshed in *cobwebs of suspicion and they substituted their personal opinions for the assessment of the executive.* By reversing their judgments Chandrachud J. reminded them of their judicial duty in a judgment which enforced that duty by precept and example.

2. And yet, as will presently appear, the High Court judges and petitioners' advocates in the Supreme Court, had a stronger hold on law and reality, and a firmer hold on human nature, than the Supreme Court, for they knew that without the restraints of law, men can be worse than beasts. The High Courts could not express "diamond-bright and diamond-hard" hopes about the Government when responsible counsel appearing before them for the Union and the States claimed that if a detenu was threatened that he would be shot or starved to death, there was no remedy till the emergency was over[3] — in other words, wives could be made widows and children fatherless without their being able to prevent murder; when a woman freedom fighter, a member of the legislature and a social worker was detained in a cell with a leper on one side and a howling female lunatic, in a condition of indescribable filth, on the other; when a young Hindu boy was not permitted to attend the funeral of his father and take part in obsequial ceremonies till an order of a High Court, from which an urgent appeal for stay had been *twice refused* by Goswami J. of the Supreme Court, enabled him to participate in the less important

---

[1] *A.D.M. Jabalpur* v. *Shivkant Shukla* (The "*Habeas Corpus Case*") (1976) Supp. S.C.R. 172, ('76) A.SC. 1207.

[2] (1976) Supp. S.C.R. at p. 380, ('76) A.SC. at p. 1325.

[3] *Bhanudas Krishna* v. *Paranjpe* 77 Bom.L.R. 599, 602-603.

ceremonies on the 13th day after his father's death. Nor could the High Court judges assert that "such misdeeds have not tarnished the record of free India", for no judge knew what was happening to the detenus once they were behind the bars, and the few cases which came before them gave them no grounds for looking at the executive with the roseate spectacles of Mr. Justice Chandrachud. Subsequent events were to show that the High Courts were right; not merely "such misdeeds", but murder by torture of an illegally detained person had taken place. And as to a "diamond-bright and diamond-hard hope", it had been ground to dust even before it had been expressed.

3. Anyone who reads and re-reads the four judgments — for they occupy 306 pages of the Supreme Court Reports — will be filled with amazement that the four judges should not have asked the central question raised by the *Habeas Corpus Case* and, even more, that they should have failed to realize the implications of the first question which the Attorney-General formulated, and the concession which he made in answering that question. We will therefore consider the question raised by the *Habeas Corpus Case* independently of the discussion in the four judgments, and will refer to those judgments in the light of our independent discussion.

4. Ask the right question, and you are on the way to a right answer; but ask the question in clear and direct language, so that the consequences of an answer, "Yes" or "No" become obvious in their stark nakedness. The right question in the *Habeas Corpus Case* was this: "Is all law in relation to life and personal liberty abrogated in India during a proclamation of emergency if a Presidential Order under Art. 359(1) provides that the right to move any court for the enforcement of a person's fundamental right under Art. 21[4] shall remain suspended?" The Att.-General *and* the four judges who constituted the majority shrank from formulating this question and giving an affirmative answer. The Att.-General did not contend that "the suspension of the right to move any court for the enforcement of the fundamental right under Art. 21" (hereinafter for the sake of brevity referred to as "suspension of Art. 21") abrogated all law. He did not contend that without passing any law, or without any existing law, government, or its officers, could pick up any person in India and hang him or keep him in preventive detention. Equally, the States in their reply to the *habeas corpus* petitions did not say, "As the right of the detenus to move any court for the enforcement of the fundamental right conferred by Art. 21 is suspended, neither the detenu nor the court can inquire under what law the detenus were detained or whether they were detained under any law".

5. The Att-General formulated two questions, the first of which was:

"Whether in view of the Presidential Order dated June 27, 1975, under cl. 1 of Art. 359, any writ petition is maintainable under Art. 226 before the High Court for *habeas corpus* to enforce the right to personal liberty of a person detained under the Maintenance of Internal Security Act on the ground that the order of detention or the continued detention, is, for any reason, not under or in compliance with the Maintenance of Internal Security Act?"[5]

The Att.-General's answer to the question was:

"Article 21 is the sole repository of the right to life and personal liberty and if the right to move any court for the enforcement of that right is suspended by the Presidential Order issued under Art. 359(1), the detenus have no *locus standi* to file the writ petition and therefore their petitions must be dismissed without any further inquiry into the relevance of the material on which the grounds of detention are based or the relevance of those grounds or the *bona fides* of the detaining authority. If the MISA permits the non-disclosure of those grounds and indeed prevents their disclosure, there is no question of inquiring into the reasons or grounds of detention and Courts must accept at its face value the subjective satisfaction of the detaining authority as recorded in the order of detention. 'There is no half-way

---

[4] "No person shall be deprived of his life or personal liberty except according to procedure established by law."

[5] (1976) Supp. S.C.R. at p. 305, ('76) A.SC. at p. 1278.

house' asserted the Attorney-General. But, *not inconsistently with the basic submission* that the detenus have no *locus standi* to file the petitions for *habeas corpus, he conceded that the court may grant relief if the detention order is on the face of it bad*, as for example, if it is passed by a person not authorised to pass it, or if it is passed for a purpose outside those mentioned in s. 3(1) of the MISA or if it does not bear any signature at all."[6] (italics supplied)

6. In a case involving the liberty of the subject, it would be strange if the Supreme Court disregarded the concession made by the Att.-General for the Union of India.[7] The Supreme Court did not do so. On the contrary, Justices Chandrachud, Beg and Bhagwati accepted the concession as rightly made. Chandrachud J. expressly said that the concession of the Attorney-General was *not inconsistent* with his basic submission as to the effect of the Presidential Order under Art. 359(1) suspending the right of any person to move any Court to enforce his rights under Art. 21. Beg J. said:

"A *prima facie* valid detention order, that is to say, one duly authenticated and passed by an officer authorised to make it, recording a purported satisfaction to detain the petitioner under the Maintenance of Internal Security Act, which is operative either before or after its confirmation by the Government, is a complete answer to a petition for a writ of *Habeas Corpus*. Once such an order is shewn to exist in response to a notice for a writ of *Habeas Corpus*, the High Court cannot inquire into its validity or vires on the ground of either *mala fides* of any kind or of non-compliance with any provision of the Maintenance of Internal Security Act in *Habeas Corpus* proceedings. The preliminary objection of the State must be accepted in such a case."[8]

Bhagwati J. said:

"Of course, this does not mean that whenever a petition for a writ of *habeas corpus* comes before the court, it must be rejected straightway without even looking at the averments made in it. The Court would have to consider whether the bar of the Presidential Order is attracted and for that purpose, the Court would have to see whether the order of detention is one made by an authority empowered to pass such an order under the Act; if it is not, it would not be State action and the petition would not be one for the enforcement of the right conferred by Art. 21. On this view in regard to the interpretation of the constitutional provision, it is unnecessary to go into the question of construction and validity of Section 18 of the Act."[9]

In this discussion we will disregard the judgment of Ray C.J., first, because it is not easy to say what propositions the Chief Justice intended to lay down — his judgment consists of a number of propositions which are not woven into a coherent whole; and, secondly, because what 3 out of 4 judges lay down is the law.

7. We therefore start with the proposition (accepted by 3 out of the 4 judges who constituted the majority) that in spite of the Presidential Order, a detenu can successfully maintain a *habeas corpus* petition if the order of preventive detention is *ex facie* ("on the face of it") bad, that is, invalid and void. An order is *ex facie* invalid and void if one looks at the order and at the provisions of the Act under which it is passed, and it becomes obvious that the order violates the requirements of the Act. Thus the Act requires an order of preventive detention to be (i) signed

---

[6] (1976) Supp. S.C.R. at pp. 376-77, ('76) A.SC. at p. 1323, *per* Chandrachud J.

[7] Especially when "On behalf of the appellants the appeals were argued by the Att.-General and the learned Addl. Solicitor-General. The learned Advocates-General of various States argued in support of their contentions" except the Advocate-General of Gujarat who generally supported the respondents: (1976) Supp. S.C.R. at p. 376, ('76) A.SC. at p. 1323.

[8] (1976) Supp. S.C.R. at pp. 371-72, ('76) A.SC. at p. 1320; see also (1976) Supp. S.C.R. at p. 339 [('76) A.SC. p. 1300] where Beg J. observed that a patently gross and illegal order of detention falling outside the Act would be amenable to *habeas corpus*; and also (1976) Supp. S.C.R. at p. 358 [('76) A.SC. p. 1311] where he observed that if the detention was patently illegal without going into the facts, a *habeas corpus* petition was maintainable.

[9] (1976) Supp. S.C.R. at pp. 463-64, ('76) A.SC. p. 1383.

(ii) by a person authorized to do so and (iii) to be based on one or more of the grounds specified in s. 3(1). An order which is not signed, or is signed by an unauthorized person, or is based on an unauthorized ground is *ex facie* invalid and void, because it is not *in compliance with the Act*. Therefore, the final order passed by the judges, namely,

"In view of the Presidential Order dated 27 June, 1975 no person has *locus standi* to move any writ petition under Art. 226 before a High Court for *habeas corpus* or any other writ or order or direction to challenge the legality of an order of detention on the ground that the order is not under or in compliance with the Act or is illegal or is vitiated by *mala fides* factual or legal or is based on extraneous considerations."

is clearly wrong and in conflict with the position accepted by three of them. *That Order* says that a petition for *habeas corpus* is *not maintainable* on the ground that an order of detention is not under or in compliance with the Act; *the judgments of three judges* say that a *habeas corpus* petition *is maintainable* if the order of detention is not in compliance with the three requirements of the Act. This contradiction between the judgments and the final order is enough to invalidate the majority judgments. That the final Order was misleading and incorrect has been subsequently admitted by Beg C.J.: see Appendix I, para 14.

8. But apart from this contradiction, there is a more fundamental reason why the three judgments are untenable — the three judges did not stop to consider the necessary consequences of the accepted position that an order of detention which is *ex facie* invalid and void can be successfully challenged an a writ of *habeas corpus* even if Art. 21 is suspended. The consequences are far reaching, and may be stated thus:

(*a*) An order of preventive detention can only be passed under the authority of a law of preventive detention. The Presidential Order need not specify any particular law for there may be a number of laws authorizing preventive detention.[10] Further, the question whether an order of preventive detention is *ex facie* invalid and void can only arise if an order is passed *under* an Act authorizing preventive detention. If this were not so, it would not be necessary to pass any Act, or different Acts, authorising preventive detention. Any person can preventively detain any other person without any law at all, which would be a *reductio ad absurdum* of the State's argument. Besides, why pass any law if compliance with its requirements were unnecessary?

(*b*) It follows that the suspension of Art. 21 does not mean that a person can be deprived of his life or personal liberty without any law at all. If a person cannot be deprived of his personal liberty by an unsigned order of detention or by an order signed by an unauthorized person or by an order issued on an unauthorized ground, it would be absurd to say that he could be deprived of his personal liberty without the authority of any law at all.

(*c*) It follows from (*a*) and (*b*) above that any executive interference with life or personal liberty must be supported by the authority of law. An arrest under an order for preventive detention would be illegal and void if the order is signed by a person not authorized to sign it. The proclamation of emergency does not abrogate the basic principle of our jurisprudence that no one can interfere with the liberty of any person unless he can point to the authority of a law justifying such interference.

(*d*) It also follows that the right of a person to move any court to enforce the fundamental right conferred by Art. 21 is a distinct and separate right from his right to move a court to order his release on the ground that the law authorizing his detention has not been complied with. For on no other ground can a detention order *ex facie* invalid and void be set aside and the detenu released on a *habeas corpus* petition during the suspension of Art. 21. It is not an explanation or, rather,

---

[10] *E.g.* Maintenance of Internal Security Act, 1971; The Defence of India Act, 1971; The Conservation of Foreign Exchange and Prevention of Smuggling Activities Act, 1974.

it is a superficial explanation to say, as Bhagwati J. said, that an order of detention signed by an unauthorized person is an act of a private person and fundamental rights are available only against the State. Apart from the fact that it is not correct that fundamental rights are available only against the State,[11] it is a superficial explanation, because the action of a public officer can be treated as that of a private person only if compliance with the requirements of a law authorizing preventive detention was necessary for a valid detention order independently of any question about fundamental rights. And, if notwithstanding the suspension of Article 21, a *habeas corpus* petition can be successfully maintained, it is only because the obligation of a public official to comply with the requirements of the law and the corresponding right of a person that action to his prejudice should not be taken without the authority of law, but only in compliance with its requirements, is distinct and separate from the person's right to enforce his fundamental rights.

9. The conclusions drawn in para 8 above are supported by the provisions of Art. 358 and Art. 359 (as amended), and it is unfortunate that the majority judgments failed to notice that the whole emphasis of Arts. 358 and 359 is on *law*. The marginal note to Art. 358, "Suspension of provisions of Art. 19" is misleading and inaccurate. Article 358 does not suspend Art. 19 *without any action on the part of the State*. Article 19 is suspended in the sense that, to use the words of Art. 358, ". . . nothing in Art. 19 shall restrict the power of the State to make any law, or take any executive action which the State would, but for the provisions contained in Part III be competent to make or take". Article 358 shows that when there is no emergency, the provisions of Art. 19, read with Art. 13(2), limit legislative, and, consequently, executive power — since broadly speaking, executive power is co-extensive with legislative power; Articles 73 and 162. Therefore, unless *a law is made after* a proclamation of emergency comes into force, any action taken under a pre-emergency law must stand the test of Art. 19. If such a law violated Art. 19 it would be void, and any executive action taken under it *even during an emergency* would also be void, although if such a law had been enacted during an emergency the law, as well as the executive action, would have been valid. It was so held in *M.P.* v. *Bharat Singh*.[12] In that case, counsel argued that although the section under which the order was passed was void for violating Art. 19(1)(*d*), and the section was not revived on the proclamation of the emergency, Art. 358 enabled executive action to be taken contrary to the provisions of Art. 19, and as the impugned executive action was taken during the emergency it was valid under Art. 358. In rejecting this argument Shah J. observed:

"All executive action which operates to the prejudice of any person must have the authority of law to support it, and the terms of Art. 358 expressly authorises the State to take legislative or executive action provided such action was competent for the State to make or take, but for the provisions contained in Part III of the Constitution. Article 358 does not purport to invest the State with arbitrary authority to take action to the prejudice of citizens and others: it merely provides that so long as the proclamation of emergency subsists laws may be enacted and executive action may be taken in pursuance of lawful authority, which if the provisions of Art. 19 were operative would have been invalid."[13]

In the *Habeas Corpus Case*, Beg J. referred to *Bharat Singh's Case* and rightly observed:

"The ground of the decision was that, although, the empowering provision could not have been challenged if it was contained in an enactment made during the emergency, yet, as the provision was made by an Act passed at a time when Article 19 was operative, the invalidity of the provision could be demonstrated despite the existence of the emergency. I do not think that there is any such case before us. It seems to me to be possible to distinguish the case on the ground that it was a case of patent voidness of the order passed so that the principle of legality, which is not suspended, could be affirmed even apart from enforcement of a specified

---

[11] See Arts. 15(2), 17, 24, 28(3), 30.
[12] ('67) A.SC. 1170.
[13] ibid. p. 1173.

fundamental right. I think it was placed on such a footing by Shah J., speaking for this Court."[14]

In other words, even during a proclamation of emergency, executive action taken without the authority of a valid law can be successfully challenged "apart from enforcement of a fundamental right". Again, the amended Art. 359(2) enacts the same provision as was enacted in Art. 358 with a difference which is immaterial — that whereas under Art. 358 on the proclamation of emergency the State can make any law in derogation of fundamental rights contained in Art. 19, under Art. 359(2) a law in derogation of any fundamental right can be made only if the Presidential Order specifies any particular Article (or Articles) conferring such fundamental right.

10. The failure to ask the right question, the failure to draw the correct conclusions from the accepted position that an order *ex facie* invalid or void can be set aside and the detenu released on an *habeas corpus* petition notwithstanding the suspension of Art. 21, and the failure to notice and give effect to the emphasis laid by Arts. 358 and 359 on the necessity of making a law if fundamental rights were to be overridden during an emergency have all contributed to the three judges reaching the totally erroneous conclusion embodied in the Order of the majority set out in para 7 above. Further, such failure has prevented the judges from analyzing three connected topics (i) the nature of fundamental rights, (ii) the relation of fundamental rights to ordinary rights, and (iii) the relation of executive power to ordinary and fundamental rights. We must give such an analysis now.

11. Our Constitution confers certain fundamental rights on *citizens alone*: *e.g.* Arts. 15, 16, 19, 29; certain other fundamental rights on *any person*: *e.g.* Arts. 14, 20, 21, 22, 25; and, again, certain other fundamental rights on *groups of persons*: *e.g.* Arts. 26 and 30. The nature of a fundamental right and its relation to an ordinary right is best brought out by considering fundamental rights conferred *on citizens alone*, which therefore are not available to aliens or foreigners. Article 19 confers well recognized fundamental rights on citizens alone. Thus every citizen has a *fundamental right* to "acquire, hold and dispose of property" ("property rights"). Does it mean that foreigners in India have no property rights? It is a matter of common knowledge, which a glance at the Statute book would confirm, that foreigners have property rights in India. This is because, broadly speaking, various statutes *confer property rights without reference to the citizenship of the person acquiring, holding and disposing of property*, as for example, the Transfer of Property Act, the Contract Act, the Sale of Goods Act and the Succession Act. If the question were asked: "Where are the property rights of citizens and non-citizens to be found?" the answer must be: in the relevant statutes, some of which have been mentioned above. The fundamental right to acquire, hold and dispose of property specified in Art. 19(1)(*f*) tells us nothing about the content of that right; for discovering that content we must turn to the relevant statutes which govern the acquisition, holding and disposal of property. For, property cannot be acquired, held or disposed of unless the requirements of the relevant laws are complied with. But, it may be asked, if the right of citizen and non-citizen alike to acquire, hold and dispose of property is to be found in the relevant statutory law, why was it necessary to confer on citizens a *fundamental* right to acquire, hold and dispose of property? *The answer to this question brings out the difference between a fundamental right, and an ordinary right to property.* If Art. 19(1)(*f*) had not been enacted, Parliament and State Legislatures in the exercise of their plenary legislative power to make laws for the acquisition, holding and disposal of property could deprive persons of their property rights, or put unreasonable restrictions on the exercise of those rights. Part III of our Constitution (Fundamental Rights) limits or restricts the exercise of plenary legislative power. If a fundamental right is conferred on *any person*, that is, on citizens and non-citizens alike, the fundamental right is a limitation on the entire legislative power in respect of that right; if it is conferred on citizens alone, it is a partial limitation on legislative power, because the limita-

[14] (1976) Supp. S.C.R. at p. 358, ('76) A.SC. at p. 1312.

tion does not extend to non-citizens. The distinction we have made above, is very well brought out by Bose J. in *Dwarkadas Shrinivas* v. *Sholapur Spg. & Wvg. Co. Ltd.*[15]:

"But what article 19(1)(*f*) means is that whereas a law can be passed to prevent persons who are not citizens of India from acquiring and holding property in this country no such restrictions can be placed on citizens. *But in the absence of such a law* non-citizens can also acquire property in India and if they do then they cannot be deprived of it any more than citizens, save by authority of law."[16] (italics supplied)

12. But unlike the American Bill of Rights, our Constitution does not confer the fundamental rights specified in Art. 19(1)(*a*) to (*g*) in absolute terms. The rights are conferred subject to the restrictions which can be imposed on those rights under Art. 19(2) to (6). The frame of Art. 19 supports our conclusion that the rights specified in Art. 19(1) do not tell us what is the content of that right — that content is to be found in the relevant laws on the subject matter of that right. For example, Art. 19(1)(*a*) provides that every citizen shall have the right to freedom of speech and expression. By itself it tells us nothing about the nature and extent of that freedom. However, Clause (2) of Art. 19 helps us to understand the nature and extent of the freedom of speech, for it provides that:

"(2) Nothing in sub-clause (*a*) of clause (1) shall affect the operation of any existing law, *in so far as such law imposes reasonable restrictions* on the exercise of the right conferred by the said sub-clause *in the interests of the sovereignty and integrity of India, the security of the State, friendly relations with foreign States, public order, decency or morality, of in relation to contempt of court, defamation or incitement to an offence.*" (italics supplied)

Article 19(2) shows that there are existing laws which deal with freedom of speech and expression and such laws can be enacted in the future. Freedom of speech is that which remains after reasonable restrictions on the exercise of that freedom have been put by existing law, or which can be put by future law in respect of, or in relation to, the topics which we have italicized in sub-cl. (2), it being understood that "restrictions" can, in appropriate cases, or in certain circumstances, include "prohibition" or "deprivation".[17] Before Part III conferred fundamental rights, as for example, the rights mentioned in Art. 19, those rights were governed by various laws. Such laws could take away or restrict the exercise of those rights unreasonably, and some laws did so. But *the rights conferred by law were protected by law, and could be enforced in courts* if those rights were violated. Fundamental rights confer on ordinary rights an additional protection by limiting plenary legislative power by specifying the kinds of restriction which alone can be placed on the exercise of those rights. Thus the right to the freedom of speech of citizen and non-citizen is to be found in various laws which apply to both. But Art. 19(1)(*a*) read with Art. 19(2) and Art. 13(1) and (2) further protects the citizen's right to the freedom of speech to the extent that unreasonable restrictions cannot be imposed on its exercise, nor can reasonable restrictions be imposed on the exercise of that right in respect of or in relation to a topic of legislation *not specified* in Art. 19(2). This protection conferred on a citizen's right to the freedom of speech against the exercise of legislative power cannot be taken away as long as Art. 19 remains in force. It is this additional protection which the non-citizen lacks, though in fact he may enjoy the same freedom of speech in India as is enjoyed by its citizens, if laws on the topic referred to in Art. 19(2) impose reasonable restrictions on the freedom of speech of citizen and non-citizen alike, as, broadly speaking, they do. And the same reasoning applies to the restrictions on the fundamental rights conferred by Art. 19(1)(*b*) to (*g*) subject to the restrictions specified in clauses (3) to (6) in respect of or in relation to topics mentioned in those sub-clauses.

13. The result of the above discussion is that the rights conferred by Art. 19(1)(*a*) to (*g*) to the freedom of speech, of association, of assembly, of movement through-

---

[15] (1954) S.C.R. 674. [16] ibid. p. 732.
[17] *Narendra Kumar* v. *Union* (1960) 2 S.C.R. 375, 387; ('60) A.SC. 430.

out the territory of India, the right to acquire, hold and dispose of property, and the right to carry on any trade, business, vocation or calling are to be found in the relevant laws on the subject, and consist of what remains after those laws had imposed permitted restrictions on the exercise of those rights. As we have seen, these statutory rights belong to citizens and non-citizens alike. If the provisions of Art. 19 had not been enacted, those rights would have been ordinary rights available to those governed by the law and enforceable as long as the law was not altered. *By making ordinary rights fundamental, those rights are not abrogated. They are given an additional protection from legislative power which ordinary rights lack.* Therefore, the fundamental rights of citizens under Art. 19 are governed by law exactly as the rights of non-citizens are governed by law, but with the difference that citizens have, and non-citizens have not, the additional protection from the exercise of plenary legislative power. It is this additional protection given to citizens that the emergency provisions of Arts. 358 and 359 remove in the sense that if the State desires to make a law in derogation of those rights *even for citizens*, it can do so, without such a law being void. But Arts. 358 and 359 confer *a power* to make a law in derogation of fundamental rights; those Articles *do not impose an obligation* to do so. And if such a law is not made, or if a law in comformity with fundamental rights is made, it is obligatory on every one bound by the law, to comply with its terms. Articles 358 and 359 by enabling Parliament and State Legislatures to make laws in derogation of the fundamental rights conferred on citizens alone, enable the State to withdraw the protection conferred by the fundamental right on citizens and thus put citizens and non-citizens on the same level during an emergency.

14. The conclusion reached in para 13 above is strengthened by the following considerations. The Proclamation of Emergency has the effect of suspending Art. 19, in the sense explained in para 9 above. But a Presidential Order under Art. 359 providing that during an emergency no person shall move the court for the enforcement of rights conferred by Art. 19 would not prevent a non-citizen from enforcing his right to acquire, hold and dispose of property which he has under the Transfer of Property Act, because Art. 19 does not apply to non-citizens. It would be absurd to say that a non-citizen can enforce his rights under the Transfer of Property Act, but a citizen cannot enforce the same rights merely because he is given an *additional* protection that those rights cannot be taken away or abridged by a law imposing unreasonable restrictions on those rights. The "suspension" of Art. 19 and the Presidential Order under Art. 359 enable the State to deprive the citizen of that additional protection, but as long as the statutory rights of the citizen remain unaltered, he can enforce them before a court of law. The absurdity of holding that a citizen deprived of his right to move the court for the enforcement of his fundamental right under Art. 19(1)*(f)* is thereby precluded from enforcing his statutory right arises only because of the belief that an ordinary statutory right merges in a fundamental right. Once the real nature of a fundamental right is realised, the doctrine of merger will be seen to be untenable. In this connection, Art. 13(1) is important, for it directly negatives the theory of merger, and it is unfortunate that this Article has not been referred to in any of the judgments in the *Habeas Corpus Case*:

Art. 13 *Laws inconsistent with or in derogation of the fundamental rights.*—(1) All laws in force in the territory of India immediately before the commencement of this Constitution, in so far as they are inconsistent with the provisions of this Part, shall, to the extent of such inconsistency, be void.

Read with the definition of "law" given in Art. 13(3), namely, " 'law' includes any Ordinance, order, by-law, rule, regulation, notification, custom or usage having in the territory of India the force of law", it is clear that all laws in force in India before the commencement of the Constitution continue as provided by Art. 372, and as is necessarily implied in Art. 13(1), except to the extent that such laws are inconsistent with the fundamental rights conferred by Part III, in which case such laws become *pro tanto* void. In the result, fundamental rights do not abrogate existing law. Existing law continues except to the extent that it is inconsistent with the provisions of Part III. Article 13(1) shows that ordinary rights, if not inconsistent with fundamental rights, stand side by side with fundamental rights.

15. However, in connection with the doctrine of merger, we must consider the decision of the Supreme Court in *Dhirubha Devisingh Gohil* v. *Bombay*[18] which was strongly relied upon for the State and which was equally strongly relied upon in the majority judgments in the *Habeas Corpus Case*. *Gohil's Case* was supposed to justify the conclusion that an ordinary statutory right became merged in a corresponding fundamental right. In paras 16 to 20 it will be shown that *Gohil's Case* justifies no such conclusion.

16. In *Gohil's Case*, the appellants had challenged the validity of the Bombay Talukdari Tenure Abolition Act, 1949 ("the Act") under Art. 226. The High Court dismissed the petition, but gave leave to appeal under Art. 133(1)(c). The appellant raised a number of contentions, but the one with which we are concerned was that in view of s. 299 of the G.I. Act, 35 ("s. 299") the legislature lacked legislative power to enact the Act. Consequently, the inclusion of the Act in Sch. IX (as item 4) did not protect the Act from challenge, because Art. 31-B and Sch. IX only protected the laws included in that Schedule from a challenge based on the violation of fundamental rights and not from a challenge on the ground of legislative competence. Before considering the judgment of the Supreme Court it is necessary to set out s. 299 and Art. 31-B:

S. 299. (1) No person shall be deprived of his property in British India save by authority of law. (2) Neither the Federal nor a Provincial Legislature *shall have power to make any law* authorising the compulsory acquisition for public purposes of any land, or any commercial or industrial undertaking, unless the law provides for the payment of compensation for the property acquired and either fixes the amount of the compensation or specifies the principles on which and the manner in which, it is to be determined. (italics supplied)

Art. 31-B. Validation of certain Acts and Regulations.—Without prejudice to the generality of the provisions contained in Article 31-A, none of the Acts and Regulations specified in the Ninth Schedule nor any of the provisions thereof shall be deemed to be void, or ever to have become void, on the ground that such Act, Regulation or provision is inconsistent with, or takes away or abridges any of the rights conferred by, any provisions of this Part, and notwithstanding any judgment, decree or order of any court or tribunal to the contrary, each of the said Acts and Regulations shall, subject to the power of any competent Legislature to repeal or amend it, continue in force.

17. In *Gohil's Case* the Supreme Court was not called upon to decide any question about the merger of an ordinary right if it was also made a fundamental right. Section 299 was a part of the G.I. Act, 35, which provided a Constitution for the governance of India — it was not an ordinary law enacted by a competent legislature. In *Gohil's Case*, it was argued for the appellant that a challenge on the ground of lack of legislative competence was a distinct and separate challenge from the challenge on the ground of the violation of fundamental rights, and Art. 31(6) was relied upon in support of this contention. Article 31(6) provides:

Art. 31. (6) Any law of the State enacted not more than eighteen months before the commencement of this Constitution may within three months from such commencement be submitted to the President for his certification; and thereupon, if the President by public notification so certifies, it shall not be called in question in any court on the ground that it contravenes the provisions of clause (2) of this article or *has contravened the provisions of sub-section (2) of Section 299 of the Government of India Act, 1935.* (italics supplied)

Jagannadhadas J. rejected this argument. In view of the importance which was attached to *Gohil's Case* in the *Habeas Corpus Case*, we will set out at length *all* the reasons for such rejection. After referring to the argument based on Art. 31(6), Jagannadhadas J. observed:

---

[18] (1955) 1 S.C.R. 691.

"It appears to us that takes too narrow a view of article 31-B. What article 31-B protects is not a mere 'contravention of the provisions' of Part III of the Constitution but an attack on the grounds that the impugned Act is 'inconsistent with or takes away or abridges *any of the rights* conferred by any provisions of this Part'. One of the rights secured to a person by Part III of the Constitution is a right that his property shall be acquired only for public purposes and under a law authorising such acquisition and providing for compensation which is either fixed by the law itself or regulated by principles specified by the law. That is also the very right which was previously secured to the person under section 299. The challenge now made to the validity of the impugned Act is based on the alleged violation of that right. Nor does this challenge cease to be in substance anything other than a challenge in respect of the violation of the said right notwithstanding that under section 299 of the Government of India Act the right is secured in terms which restricts the power of the Legislature and operates as a restraint on its competency. What under the Government of India Act was a provision relating to the competency of the Legislature, was also clearly in the nature of a fundamental right of the person affected. This appears from the Report of the Joint Parliamentary Committee on Indian Constitutional Reform, Vol. I, Part I, paragraphs 366 and 369. But it is urged, that even so, article 31-B protects only the violation of the fundamental right in so far as 'it was *conferred* by Part III of the Constitution' and that this right cannot be said to have been 'conferred' by the Constitution. We cannot agree with this contention. This is clearly a case where the concerned right which was secured under s. 299 in the form of a fetter on the competency of the Legislature and which in substance was a fundamental right, was lifted into the formal category of a fundamental right along with other fundamental rights recognised in the present Constitution. There is therefore nothing inappropriate in referring to this right which was pre-existing, *along with* the other fundamental rights for the first time secured by this Constitution, when grouping them together, as fundamental rights 'conferred' by the Constitution. What is important to notice in the phraseology of article 31-B is that the protection is not merely against the contravention of certain provisions but an attack on the ground of unconstitutional abridgement *of certain rights*. It will be illogical to construe article 31-B as affording protection only so far as these rights are taken away by an Act in violation of the provisions of the new Constitution but not when they are taken away by an Act in violation of section 299 of the Government of India Act which has been repealed. The intention of the Constitution to protect each and every one of the Acts specified in the Ninth Schedule from any challenge on the ground of violation of any of the fundamental rights secured under Part III of the Constitution, irrespective of whether they are pre-existing or new rights, is placed beyond any doubt or question by the very emphatic language of article 31-B which declares that none of the provisions of the specified Acts shall be deemed to be void or *ever to have become void* on the ground of the alleged violation of the rights indicated *and* 'notwithstanding any judgment, decree or order of any court or tribunal'. That intention is also emphasised by the positive declaration that 'each of the said Acts or Regulations shall, subject to the power of any competent Legislature to repeal or amend it, *continue in force*'."[19]

18. The following propositions emerge from the above passage:

(i) *Gohil's Case* laid down no principle of general application. It "turned on the express provisions of Act. 31-B of the Constitution".[20]

(ii) An exclusion of a challenge to laws on the ground that they violated Art. 31(2) does not automatically exclude a challenge that they violated s. 299. An express exclusion of a challenge under s. 299 is necessary, as is clear from Art. 31(6) which excludes a challenge not only under Art. 31 but also expressly excludes a challenge under s. 299.

---

[19] (1955) 1 S.C.R. at pp. 695-7.

[20] *Jeejeebhoy* v. *Asst. Collector, Thana* ('65) A.SC. 1096 at p. 1102 *per* Subba Rao J. for himself and Wanchoo, Hidayatullah, Raghubar Dayal and Sikri JJ.

(iii) For the interpretation of Art. 31-B the legislative history of s. 299 is relevant. The Report of the Joint Select Committee on Indian Constitutional Reform showed that the provision relating to the competency of the Legislature was also clearly in the nature of a fundamental right. These observations are clearly right and are supported by the history not only of s. 299, but also the history of ss. 275, 297 and 298.[21]

(iv) In the light of this history, *it was not inappropriate* to refer to the right under s. 299 which was pre-existing *along with* other fundamental rights for the first time secured by the Constitution when grouping them together as "fundamental rights conferred by the Constitution". The various expressions used in Article 31-B to which Jagannadhadas J. referred support the conclusion that Art. 31-B did not leave a challenge under s. 299 outstanding.

It is therefore clear that *Gohil's Case* turned merely on the construction of Art. 31-B, as Subba Rao J. had rightly observed, and that it did not lay down the proposition that if rights conferred by the Government of India Act, 1935, were lifted into the category of fundamental rights by the Constitution, the former rights merged in the fundamental rights. The provisions of Art. 31(6) are a standing refutation of any such theory, and Jagannadhadas J.'s elaborate analysis of the language of Art. 31-B, in the light of the legislative history of s. 299, also refutes any such theory.

19. The above conclusion is supported by the Supreme Court decision, delivered by Subba Rao J. in *Jeejeebhoy's Case*, to which a reference has been made earlier. In that case the impugned pre-Constitution law was challenged on the ground that it was void for lack of legislative competence as it contravened s. 299 since the law did not provide for compensation in the sense of a "just equivalent". The impugned law was not included in Sch. IX. It was however argued in *Jeejeebhoy's Case* that "S. 299 of the Government of India Act, 1935, declared a fundamental right of a citizen, that it was bodily lifted and introduced by the Constitution in Article 31(2) thereof and that if Art. 31-A saved an attack against the Amending Act on the ground that it infringed Art. 31(2) thereof, it would equally save the attack based on the infringement of s. 299(2) of the Government of India Act, 1935."[22] Subba Rao J. rejected that argument as far fetched. Further, in support of the validity of the impugned law, reliance was placed on *Gohil's Case* and after setting out a part of the passage from that judgment which we have set out in full, Subba Rao J. said:

"*The said decisions turned upon the express provisions of Art. 31-B of the Constitution.* Though the observations therein appear to be wide, they have no bearing on the question whether the Act was void before the Constitution came into force. *The question whether a particular Act was void before the Constitution came into force would not arise if the Constitution itself included the said Act in the Ninth Schedule and declared that the said Act should not be deemed to be void or ever to have become void.* It was possible to construe the expression 'any rights conferred by any provisions of this Part' so as to include similar pre-existing rights under the Government of India Act, 1935, *but such a construction would be quite out of place in the context* of the question whether the Legislature had the legislative competency to make the law before the Constitution came into force."[23] (italics supplied)

20. In the result, *Gohil's Case* is only an authority for the proposition that the rights conferred by the Government of India Act, and later raised formally to the level of a fundamental right, may be treated alike in a provision which, *by apt language,* shows that challenge to a law or laws was meant to be excluded not only under a fundamental right but also under a similar constitutional right conferred by the G.I. Act, 35.

21. Our discussion of the freedoms conferred by Art. 19 on citizens alone in paras 11 to 14 has brought out the distinction between a fundamental right and an

---

[21] See Shiva Rao, *The Framing of India's Constitution, A Study*, p. 174.
[22] ('65) A.SC. 1101, 1102. [23] ibid. p. 1102

ordinary right. And our subsequent discussion has shown that ordinary rights do not merge in fundamental rights. What light does our discussion throw on Article 21, since that was the principal Article considered in the *Habeas Corpus Case*? We will consider (i) the legislative history of Article 21; (ii) the effect of the interpretation put upon Article 21 by the Supreme Court in *Gopalan's Case*; and (iii) the correct interpretation of Article 21 in order to test the assumption made in the *Habeas Corpus Case* that Art. 21 is the sole repository to the right to life and personal liberty, and if the right to move the Court for the enforcement of the rights conferred by Art. 21 is suspended, life and personal liberty are without the protection of the law during an emergency.

22. The legislative history of Article 21 is well known. Draft Article 15, as originally introduced and passed by the Constituent Assembly, provided that "No person shall be deprived of his life or liberty without due process of law. . . ." The Drafting Committee suggested two changes in draft Article 15: (i) the addition of the word "personal" before the word "liberty" and (ii) the substitution of the expression "except according to procedure established by law" for the words "without due process of law". The reason for the first change was that "otherwise (liberty) might be construed very widely so as to include even the freedoms already dealt with in Art. 13" (now Art. 19 of the Constitution). The reason for the second change was that "the (substituted) expression was more specific (Cf. Art. XXXI of the Japanese Constitution 1946)".[24] The reason given for the first change was clearly right, for Art. 13 (now Art. 19) conferred certain freedoms *only on citizens*, whereas Art. 15 applied to citizens and non-citizens alike, and it would have been unwise to leave open an interpretation which would include in the word "liberty" the freedoms which had been denied to non-citizens by Art. 13. The reason given for the second change may be literally correct but was not candid. Both substantive and procedural "due process" were well established in the United States, and though the concept of "due process" was vague and flexible (or imprecise) it was used to enforce certain standards to which according to the majority of judges of the United States Supreme Court substantive and procedural laws had to conform. By substituting for the words "due process of law" the expression "except according to procedure established by law" the Drafting Committee did not make the American concept of "due process" more precise as a matter of drafting — *the Committee gave up that concept altogether.*

23. Although the Draft Constitution contained Art. 15, it did not, in the first instance, contain any article corresponding to Art. 22 of the Constitution. When the proposal to delete "due process" suggested by the Drafting Committee was debated in the Constituent Assembly on 6th December 1948,[25] and then on 13th December 1948,[26] there was strong opposition to the proposal; nevertheless the Drafting Committee's suggestion was accepted by the Constituent Assembly.[27] However, the Assembly's vote did not finally settle the matter, for dissatisfaction with the deletion of "due process" continued inside and outside the Assembly. On September 15, 1949, Dr. Ambedkar moved that a new Article 15A (which, as amended corresponds to Art. 22 of our Constitution) be adopted. Speaking on the motion, he said:

"We are therefore now, by introducing article 15A, making, if I may say so, compensation for what was done then in passing article 15. *In other words, we are providing for the substance of the law of 'due process' by the introduction of article 15A.* Article 15A merely lifts from the provisions of the Criminal Procedure Code two of the most fundamental principles which every civilised country follows as principles of international justice. It is quite true that these two provisions contained in clause (1) and clause (2) are already to be found in the Criminal Procedure Code and therefore probably it might be said that we are really not making any very fundamental change. But we are, as I contend, making a funda-

---

[24] Note of the Drafting Committee in the Draft Constitution forwarded by Dr. Ambedkar to the President of the Constituent Assembly on 21st February, 1948.
[25] *C.A.D.*, Vol. VII, pp. 842-857. [26] ibid. pp. 999-1001.
[27] See Shiva Rao, *The Framing of India's Constitution, A Study*, pp. 235-8.

mental change because what we are doing by the introduction of article 15A is to put a limitation upon the authority both of Parliament as well as of the Provincial Legislature not to abrogate these two provisions, because they are now introduced in our Constitution itself. It is quite true that the enthusiasts for personal liberty are probably not content with the provisions of clauses (1) and (2). They probably want something more by way of further safeguards against the inroads of the executive and the legislatures upon the personal liberty of the citizen. I personally think that while I sympathise with them that probably this article might have been explained to include some further safeguards, I am quite satisfied that the provisions contained are sufficient against illegal or arbitrary arrests."[28] (italics supplied)

Article 15A, with certain amendments was passed as it now stands in Art. 22 of our Constitution.

24. It is unfortunate that draft Articles 15 and 15A were not taken up together and re-drafted in the light of the new Article 15A. If the new Article 15A was meant to introduce the substance of "due process", then, clauses (1) and (2) of Art. 15A ought to have been put in Article 15 from which "due process" had been deleted. Since Articles 15 and 15A as finally adopted correspond to Articles 21 and 22 of the Constitution as enacted, for convenience we will hereafter refer to Arts. 21 and 22 of our Constitution. There would have been several advantages in re-numbering Article 21 as Art. 21(1) and transferring to it, as sub-Articles (2) and (3), sub-Articles (1) and (2) of Art. 22, and re-numbering the sub-Articles of Art. 22 accordingly, and by inserting a new marginal note. Article 21 and Art. 22 would then have been re-drafted as shown in para 11.6.

25. The advantages of re-drafting the two Articles would have been: (i) more precise draftsmanship, because the appropriate place for the two sub-Articles which "gave the substance of due process" was in Article 21 from which "due process" had been removed. (ii) As Art. 21 stands and as "law" was interpreted in *A. K. Gopalan* v. *State*[29] ("*Gopalan's Case*"), Art. 21, taken by itself, appears *at first blush* open to the objection that it does not confer a fundamental right. For, if "law" in Art. 21 means a law enacted by a legislature, as rightly held in *Gopalan's Case*, then Art. 21 appears to confer no fundamental right, for fundamental rights are limitations on legislative power and Art. 21 contains no such limitation since it only requires the authority of "law". The inclusion of sub-Articles (2) and (3) would have removed this objection, because the law referred to in Art. 21(1) must *at least* conform to the requirements of sub-Articles (2) and (3), which clearly impose limitations on legislative power. (iii) Such redrafting would have made it easy to interpret the expression "personal liberty". In *Gopalan's Case* the Supreme Court considered at great length the correct interpretation of Arts. 21 and 22 in relation to Art. 19, with reference to the provisions of the Preventive Detention Act, 1950, which were challenged on the ground that they violated Art. 19, and preventive detention must stand the test of reasonableness laid down by Art. 19(2) to (6). The great care and attention bestowed by all the judges on the questions raised by *Gopalan* is easily intelligible, having regard to the repugnance felt by the judges to preventive detention as a peace-time legislative power. This care will have become apparent to the reader from our full discussion of *Gopalan's Case* in Chapter XI of this Volume. For the present purpose it is sufficient to note that ever since *Gopalan's Case*, "law" in Art. 21 has been held to mean a "law enacted by a competent authority". Secondly, in *Gopalan's Case*, no question arose as to the impact of the emergency provisions of Arts. 352, 358 and 359 on the interpretation of Art. 21. Therefore the court was not called upon to bring out the distinction between a fundamental right and an ordinary right for the purposes of putting a correct interpretation on Art. 21. We will refer to some aspects of *Gopalan's Case* later.

26. The correct interpretation of Art. 21 raises difficult questions which have not been considered in their interrelation by the Courts so far. However, the startling

[28] *C.A.D.* Vol. IX, p. 1497. [29] (1950) S.C.R. 88, ('50) A.SC. 27.

conclusion reached in the *Habeas Corpus Case* that the effect of the President's proclamation under Art. 359 was, in substance, that no redress was available against violation of the law or against *mala fide* actions, compels an inquiry about the nature and extent of the fundamental right conferred by Art. 21.

27. The most important thing to note is that Art. 21 does not *confer* a right to life or personal liberty. Therefore, Art. 21 is not "the sole repository of the right to life and personal liberty" as the Attorney-General wrongly contended. Article 21 is one of several Articles which protects a person from being deprived of his life or personal liberty for, as will appear hereafter (para 29), Articles 14, 20 and 22(1) and (2) also protect a person from being deprived of his life and personal liberty contrary to the rights conferred by those Articles. Article 21 assumes or recognizes the fact that those rights exist and protects them from deprivation by the State. In *Gopalan's Case*, without using the technical language of Jurisprudence, Mukherjea J. said:

"The right to the safety of one's life and limbs and to enjoyment of personal liberty, in the sense of freedom from physical restraint and coercion of any sort, are the inherent birthrights of a man. The essence of these rights consists in restraining others from interfering with them and *hence they cannot be described in terms of 'freedom' to do particular things*."[30-31] (italics supplied)

In his well known work on *Jurisprudence*, Prof. Holland described six *antecedent rights in rem*, the first of which was "the right to personal safety and freedom."[32] Under the Common Law of England and under our law, primarily, and in the first instance all rights belong to living human beings. In this sense, the right to personal safety and freedom is an antecedent right, and it is *a right in rem* because it is available against everybody or, as it is generally put, "against the world at large" (*in rem*). Both the English Common Law and our law not only recognize the right to life but, it would appear, *the duty to go on living*, because both systems look upon an attempt to commit suicide as a crime, and require that a person detained in prison should be kept alive, and if necessary, be forcibly fed if he goes on a hunger strike.[33]

28. We have seen that Article 21 (draft Art. 15) as originally drafted, used the expression "save by due process of law". "Due process" was firmly established in the constitutional law of the United States and as Mukherjea J. rightly observed in *Gopalan's Case*,

". . . If the 'due process' clause which appeared in the original draft was finally retained by the Constituent Assembly, it could be safely presumed that the framers of the Indian Constitution wanted that expression to bear the same sense as it does in America. But when that form was abandoned, and another was deliberately substituted in its place, it is not possible to say that in spite of the difference in the language and expression, they should mean the same thing and convey the same idea."[34]

It is difficult to resist the conclusion that when the framers of the Constitution gave up "due process" on the ground that the expression "procedure established by law" was more precise, they lost their moorings. They did not stop to inquire what the word "procedure" would mean in the context (*a*) of deprivation of life and personal liberty mentioned in Art. 21; (*b*) of the word "law" and (*c*) of Articles 352, 358 and 359. Nor did they inquire what "personal liberty" meant beyond saying that the words "personal liberty" showed that they did not include the freedoms referred to in Art. 19.

[30-31] (1950) S.C.R. 88, at p. 254.
[32] Holland, *Jurisprudence*, p. 170 quoted in Wortley, *Jurisprudence*, p. 267 (1967).
[33] Wortley, *Jurisprudence* (1967) Ch. 13, Human Rights, 241 at p. 252: "To sum up, the English common law recognizes that once a man exists, no matter how he comes into existence, he has the right, and possibly the duty, to go on living, irrespective of his nationality, race, shape or colour." See also pp. 245-246.
[34] (1950) S.C.R. 88 at pp. 274-275.

29. The questions raised by the language of Art. 21 are these: First, ". . . 'procedure' denotes the mode of proceeding by which a legal right is enforced, as distinguished from the law which gives or defines the right."[35] But in the context of deprivation of life, this meaning cannot be given to the word "procedure" because "There must be a substantive law, under which the State is empowered to deprive a man of his life and liberty and such a law must be a valid law which the legislature is competent to enact . . . and which does not transgress any of the fundamental rights."[36]

Thus the Indian Penal Code, which is the substantive law of crimes in India, defines murder and prescribes the sentence of death or imprisonment as punishments for murder: see ss. 299 to 302, I.P.C. The Criminal Procedure Code provides, among other things, for the trial of an accused on the charge of murder, and the Evidence Act provides for rules of evidence according to which the guilt or innocence of the accused has to be established. The word "procedure" in Art. 21 therefore cannot refer merely to procedural laws. Secondly, as Mukherjea J. observed, the word "law" must mean a valid law. Thus, a law which provided that persons belonging to community X who commit murder shall be hanged, but persons belonging to community Y who commit murder of the same kind should be transported for life would be void as violating Art. 14. Similarly, a law *retrospectively* providing the punishment of death for the commission of an offence which, when committed, was not punishable with death would be void as violating Art. 20(1) which prohibits the enactment of such *ex post facto* laws. Therefore the expression "procedure established by law" cannot refer merely to procedural laws. Valid substantive laws providing for the deprivation of life and personal liberty are necessary before procedural laws can come into play. Thirdly, the word "personal" in the expression "personal liberty" requires explanation. In their anxiety to give Art. 21 as wide a content as possible, several judgments of the Supreme Court have adopted the view expressed by S. R. Das J. in *Gopalan's Case*[37]:

"(that) article 19 protects some of the important attributes of personal liberty as independent rights and the expression 'personal liberty' has been used in article 21 as a compendious term including within its meaning all the varieties of rights which go to make up the personal liberties of men."[38]

Those judgments have treated Art. 21 as protecting personal liberty other than that protected by Art. 19. Since no question of the suspension of fundamental rights under Art. 359 as originally enacted, and as subsequently amended, arose in *Gopalan's Case*, the impact of those Articles, and the consequences of such a wide view were naturally not considered by S. R. Das J. However, the view of Das J. cannot be sustained. First, it is not correct that Art. 21 contains the residue of every kind of personal liberty (as understood by Das J.) which is not to be found in Art. 19. The Preamble to our Constitution refers to "LIBERTY of thought, expression, belief, faith and worship" and the only Article which embodies this liberty, *and confers it on every person*, is Art. 25. To some extent the freedom of speech and expression mentioned in Art. 19(1)(*a*) is also covered by the liberty referred to in the Preamble, but the liberty of thought and expression in Art. 19(1)(*a*) *is limited to citizens only*. Similarly, Art. 28(3) confers freedom as to attendance at religious instruction or religious worship in certain educational institutions, and Art. 29 confers cultural and educational rights on every member of a minority community, rights which are part of the "liberty", (as Das J. understood "liberty") of every person belonging to such minority. Secondly, Das J. has not taken into account the setting of Art. 21. Articles 19 to 22 appear under the general subject heading, "Right to Freedom". Freedom has two aspects, (i) positive and (ii) negative. In the positive aspect, there is freedom *to do* things, and Art. 19(1)(*a*) to (*g*) reflects that aspect, because citizens are free to do the things mentioned in clauses (*a*) to (*g*) subject to the restrictions permitted by Art. 19(2) to (6). Therefore, Art. 19 uses the word "freedom". Articles 20, 21 and 22, which reflect the negative

[35] *Per* Lush L.J. in *Poyser* v. *Minors* (1881) 7 Q.B.D. 329, 333.
[36] *Per* Mukherjea J. in (1950) S.C.R. at p. 256.
[37] (1950) S.C.R. 88 at p. 299.
[38] ibid.

aspect of freedom do not use the word "freedom". This is because these Articles secure freedom by providing that certain things *shall not be done to a person* which would put his personal freedom and safety in jeopardy. The freedom of each person is secured by *preventing restraint or coercion on his person in certain cases.* Article 20(1) protects the person of every individual in respect of conviction for offences, by prohibiting the infliction of punishment under *ex post facto* laws. Under Article 20(2) no one can be prosecuted and punished for the same offence more than once. Under Art. 20(3) no person accused of any offence can be compelled to be a witness against himself. These provisions protect an individual's person from coercion or restraint involved in punishment for crimes. Article 22(1) and (2), as we have seen, should really have been incorporated in Art. 21. But, in any event, Articles of the Constitution, which deal with the same topic, have to be read together. So read, the arrest of a person is controlled and limited by the requirements of Art. 22(1) and (2), and thus they help to secure the person of an individual from external coercion or restraint and secure his personal liberty. The present writer considers it most unfortunate that the very careful analysis which Mukherjea J. made of Arts. 19, 20, 21 and 22 in *Gopalan's Case* should not have received the recognition and acceptance it deserved in the subsequent judgments of the Supreme Court. As Mukherjea J. observed:

"In ordinary language 'personal liberty' means liberty relating to or concerning the person or body of the individual; and 'personal liberty' in this sense is the antithesis of *physical restraint* or *coercion.* According to Dicey, who is an acknowledged authority on the subject 'personal liberty' means a personal right not to be subjected to imprisonment, arrest or other physical coercion in any manner that does not admit of legal justification (*Vide* Dicey on *Constitutional Law,* 9th edn. pp. 207-208)."[39]

In the opinion of the present writer, the meaning given by Mukherjea J. to "personal liberty", following on his analysis of Arts. 19 to 22, is correct for the reasons more fully given in para 11.23. It may be added that the clubbing together of "deprivation of life" and "personal liberty" further supports Mukherjea J.'s view, because deprivation of life is the most extreme form of coercion of the person — "the cessation of all activity which the vulgar call death".

30. The result of our discussion so far may be stated thus: Art. 21 does not *confer* a right to life or personal liberty: Art. 21 assumes or recognizes the fact that those rights exist and affords protection against the deprivation of those rights to the extent there provided. The expression "procedure established by law" does not mean merely a procedural law but must also include a substantive law. The word "law" must mean a valid law, that is, a law within the legislative competence of the legislature enacting it, which law does not violate the limitations imposed on legislative power by fundamental rights. "Personal liberty" means the liberty of the person from external restraint or coercion. Thus Art. 21 protects life and personal liberty by putting restrictions on legislative power, which under Arts. 245 and 246 is subject to the provisions of "this Constitution", and therefore subject to fundamental rights. The precise nature of this protection is difficult to state, first because among other things, such protection is dependent on reading Art. 21 along with other Articles conferring fundamental rights, such as Arts. 14, 20 and 22(1) and (2); and, secondly, because fundamental rights from their very nature refer to ordinary laws which deal with the subject matter of those rights.

31. The right to life and personal liberty which inheres in the body of a living person is recognized and protected not merely by Art. 21 but by the civil and criminal laws of India, and it is unfortunate that in the *Habeas Corpus Case* this aspect of the matter did not receive the attention which it deserved. Neither the Constitution nor any law *confers* the right to life. That right arises from the existence of a living human body. The most famous remedy for securing personal liberty, the writ of *habeas corpus,* requires the production before the court of *the*

---

[39] (1950) S.C.R. 88 at p. 262.

body of the person alleged to be illegally detained.[40-41] The Constitution gives protection against the deprivation of life and personal liberty; so do the civil and criminal laws in force in India. A standard book on Jurisprudence states that "the distinction between crimes and civil wrongs is roughly that crimes are public wrongs and civil wrongs are private wrongs".[42] But the same book rightly states that "English law, however, has certain features which prevent us drawing a clear line between these two kinds of wrong".[43] However, the most important thing to note is that the law of civil wrongs (tort) and the law of crimes meet on common ground — the right of self help, or "self redress and self protection"[44] or the right of self defence, or the right of private defence (hereafter compendiously referred to as "the right of private defence") in the case of "trespass to the person" which is thus described by a leading text book:

"*Kinds of trespass.* The security of a man's person, which is the most elementary of civil rights, may be directly attacked by actual violence inflicted or menaced, or by a deprivation of liberty. There are accordingly three kinds of trespass to the person — battery, assault and false imprisonment."[45]

As will presently appear, battery, assault and false imprisonment are also criminal offences. One remedy for the civil wrong of trespass to the person is damages[46] just as one remedy in criminal law for battery, assault and false imprisonment is a prosecution and conviction of the offender. But these remedies do not bring out the most important fact that both civil and criminal law recognize the right of a person to defend his life and personal liberty against unauthorized interference with them. The nature and extent of the right of private defence against the civil wrong of trespass to the person is set out in para 32 below, and the right of private defence recognized by the Indian Penal Code, is set out in para 33.

32. A standard book on Torts describes the Right of Self Help and the Defence of the person and property as follows:

"*Right of self-help*: There are certain classes of injuries in respect of which the party injured is not necessarily bound to resort to the courts for his remedy, but is entitled to take the law into his own hands and redress the wrong himself. Such is the right in case of trespasses to the person or property."

"*Defence of the person*: It is lawful for one man to use force towards another in the defence of his own person, but this force must not transgress the reasonable limits of the occasion, what is reasonable force being a question of fact in each case. . . . Where, however, an assault actually takes place the assailed person is not bound to stand on a passive defence, for it is a reasonable means of repelling an attack to attack in return. Nor does the law require that a man when labouring under a natural feeling of resentment consequent on gross provocation should very nicely measure the weight of his blows. A mere assault may justify a battery, but there must be some proportion between the aggression and the defence. Ordinarily violence must be repelled by ordinary means, *and a deadly weapon should not be used except against a deadly attack.* 'A man cannot justify a maim for every assault; as if A strike B, B cannot justify the drawing his sword and cutting off his hand; but it must be such an assault whereby probably his life may be in danger'. So too, in the case of unlawful arrest, 'the person arrested may use force to avoid being arrested, but he must not use more force than necessary.' "[47] (italics supplied)

33. Sections 96 to 102 of the I.P.C. are as follows:

S. 96. *Things done in private defence.*—Nothing is an offence which is done in the exercise of the right of private defence.

[40-41] Wortley, *Jurisprudence* (1967) pp. 241-2.
[42] Salmond, *Jurisprudence*, 12th edn. p. 91.
[43] ibid. p. 92.
[44] Clerk & Lindsell *on Torts*, 13th edn., Chapter 8.
[45] ibid. para 671. [46] ibid. para 748.
[47] ibid. paras 551 and 552.

S. 97. *Right of private defence of the body and of property.*—Every person has a right, subject to the restrictions contained in Section 99, to defend—

First.—His own body, and the body of any other person, against any offence affecting the human body.

Secondly.—The property, whether movable or immovable, of himself or of any other person, against any act which is an offence falling under the definition of theft, robbery, mischief or criminal trespass, or which is an attempt to commit theft, robbery or criminal trespass.

S. 99. *Acts against which there is no right of private defence.*—There is no right of private defence against an act which does not reasonably cause the apprehension of death or of grievous hurt, if done, or attempted to be done by a public servant *acting in good faith* under colour of his office, though that act may not be strictly justifiable by law. . . .

Extent to which the right may be exercised.—The right of a private defence in no case extends to the inflicting of more harm than it is necessary to inflict for the purpose of defence.

Explanation 1.—A person is not deprived of the right of private defence against an act done, or attempted to be done, by the direction of a public servant, as such, unless he knows or has reason to believe, that the person doing the act is such public servant.

Explanation 2.—A person is not deprived of the right of private defence against an act done, or attempted to be done by the direction of a public servant, unless he knows, or has reason to believe, that the person doing the act is acting by such direction, or unless such person states the authority under which he acts, or if he has authority in writing, unless he produces such authority, if demanded.

S. 100. *When the right of private defence of the body extends to causing death.*—The right of private defence of the body extends, under the restrictions mentioned in the last preceding section, to the voluntary causing of death or of any other harm to the assailant, if the offence which occasions the exercise of the right be of any of the descriptions hereinafter enumerated, namely:—

First.—Such an assault as may reasonably cause the apprehension that death will otherwise be the consequence of such assault;

Secondly.—Such an assault as may reasonably cause the apprehension that grievous hurt will otherwise be the consequence of such assault;

Thirdly.—An assault with the intention of committing rape;

Fourthly.—An assault with the intention of gratifying unnatural lust;

Fifthly.—An assault with the intention of kidnapping or abducting;

Sixthly.—An assault with the intention of wrongfully confining a person, under circumstances which may reasonably cause him to apprehend that he will be unable to have recourse to the public authorities for his release.

S. 101. *When such right extends to causing any harm other than death.*— If the offence be not of any of the descriptions enumerated in the last preceding section, the right of private defence of the body does not extend to the voluntary causing of death to the assailant, but does extend, under the restrictions mentioned in section 99, to the voluntary causing to the assailant of any harm other than death.

S. 102. *Commencement and continuance of the right of private defence of the body.*—The right of private defence of the body commences as soon as a reasonable apprehension of danger to the body arises from an attempt or threat to commit the offence though the offence may not have been committed; and it continues as long as such apprehension of danger to the body continues.

34. Neither the Law of Torts in India nor ss. 96 to 102, I.P.C. were altered during the Emergency. These laws recognize the right of private defence which extends to illegal arrest. Therefore if a public officer tried to execute an illegal warrant of preventive detention, that is, a warrant not authorized by the law under which it was issued, the person to be arrested can forcibly resist the arrest and can use such force as is necessary to prevent it. As is clear from the passage set out in para 32 above, the Law of Torts justifies him in doing so. The position under ss. 96 to 102 I.P.C. is even clearer. Section 100 shows that against the six kinds of assault there mentioned, the right to private defence of the body extends to causing death or grievous hurt to the assailant. The restriction on this is that there is no right of private defence if there is time to have recourse to public authorities. This only means that if threats are held out to commit assault at a later day, the authorities should be approached to prevent the assault. If they refuse to assist, the right of private defence remains unaffected. Again, there is no right of private defence against the action of a public officer acting *in good faith* under colour of his office if it does not cause the apprehension of death or grievous hurt even if the act is not strictly justifiable by law. In view of the Supreme Court's reference to *mala fides* not being a ground on which a *habeas corpus* petition can lie[48] it is important to note that the right of private defence extends to the actions of a public officer *if he does not act in good faith*, that is, with due care and caution (s. 52, I.P.C.) and no one who acts *mala fide* can be said to act with due care and caution. Secondly, if in effecting an arrest in execution of an illegal order of preventive detention a public officer threatens to use force and acts in a manner which causes a reasonable apprehension of death or grievous hurt, the right of private defence would extend to voluntarily causing the death of the officer or causing him grievous hurt. No doubt irregular action of a public officer not strictly justifiable by law is protected, but decided cases on the right show that illegal action, or action which is *ultra vires* or without jurisdiction is not protected, and in the exercise of the right of private defence the person threatened with arrest can repel the threat of force by force.

35. The discussion of the right of self defence has become necessary, first, to establish that Art. 21 is not the only provision which protects a person from being deprived of his life or liberty without the authority of law, since the law of civil wrongs, as well as the law of crimes, enables every person to protect himself from being deprived of his life or personal liberty by exercising his right of private defence. Secondly, the discussion has become necessary because of an argument advanced before the Supreme Court in the *Habeas Corpus Case*, namely, that if a detenu was threatened that he would be shot or illegally confined during detention, there was no legal redress because of the suspension of Art. 21, an argument which found favour with some of the judges. Thus Bhagwati J. observed:

"If the executive detains a person contrary to law or shoots him dead without justifying circumstances, it would clearly be an offence of wrongful confinement in one case and murder in the other, punishable under the relevant provisions of the Indian Penal Code, unless the case falls within the protective mantle of Section 76 or 79 and the officer who is responsible for the offence would be liable to be prosecuted, if there is no procedural bar built by the Code of Criminal Procedure against the initiation of such prosecution. The Presidential Order suspending the enforcement of Article 21 would not bar such a prosecution and the remedy under the Indian Penal Code would be very much available. *The offence of wrongful confinement or murder is an offence against the society* and any one can set the criminal law in motion for punishment of the offender. When a person takes proceedings under the Code of Criminal Procedure in connection with the offence of wrongful confinement or murder or launches a prosecution for such offence, he cannot be said to be enforcing the fundamental right of the detenu or the murdered man under Article 21 so as to attract the inhibition of the Presidential Order."[49] (italics supplied)

The italicised words invoke the broad distinction generally made between the civil wrong of trespass to the person and the criminal law, namely, that a civil wrong does an injury to the individual whereas a crime is an offence against the public (see para 31 above). Our discussion has shown that this broad distinction

---

[48] See paras 7 and 37 of this Appendix.
[49] (1976) Supp. S.C.R. at p. 461, ('76) A.SC. at pp. 1381-82.

does not bring out the central fact that, in the first instance, both civil and criminal law are concerned to protect every member of the public from being deprived unlawfully of his life or personal liberty. In other words, if the intended wrong whether civil or criminal, against the life, liberty and property of a person, can be prevented by that person himself, the purpose of the law is satisfied. It is only when a person is unable to exercise his right of private defence, or attempts to exercise the right but fails, that the question of remedy under civil and criminal law arises. Secondly, to say that a crime is a public wrong is true; but is not the whole truth. Punishment is not an end in itself; if certain acts are declared to be crimes, and if punishments for crimes are graded according to the gravity of the injury which the criminal act has the tendency to cause, it is because protection of the life, liberty and property of each member of the public requires that every member of society should abstain from acts injurious to every other member. If actions injurious to every member of the public were not prohibited and punished, then, the freedom of every member of the public would be gravely imperilled. Mukherjea J. brought out this point clearly when he said:

"No man's liberty would be worth its name if it can be violated with impunity by any wrong-doer and if his property or possessions could be preyed upon by a thief or a marauder. The society, therefore, has got to exercise certain powers *for the protection of these liberties* and to arrest, search, imprison and punish those who break the law. If these powers are properly exercised, *they themselves are the safeguards of freedom*, but they can certainly be abused. The police may arrest any man and throw him into prison without assigning any reasons; they may search his belongings on the slightest pretext; he may be subjected to a sham trial and even punished for crimes unknown to law. What the Constitution, therefore, attempts to do in declaring the rights of the people is to strike a balance between individual liberty and social control."[50] (italics supplied)

And Das J. made the same point when he said:

"Therefore, putting restraint on the freedom of wrong doing of one person *is really securing the liberty of the intended victims*. To curb the freedom of the saboteur of surreptitiously removing the fish plates from the railway lines is to ensure the safety and liberty of movement of the numerous innocent and unsuspecting passengers."[51] (italics supplied)

It is therefore clear that the view expressed by Bhagwati J. in the passage quoted above cannot be sustained for the simple reason that before an officer can shoot or unlawfully confine a detenu, the detenu can strike him dead, and can resist the unlawful confinement and if force is threatened or used to secure such unlawful confinement, the aggrieved person can use sufficient force to repel force. It would be surprising if a person could secure his life and personal liberty by taking the law in his own hands and meeting force with force, *as the law enables him to do*, and yet he should not be able to approach a court to obtain redress in due course of law from unlawful or illegal detention. No court ought to adopt a view which leads to such bizarre results unless there are compelling reasons. Our whole discussion has shown that not only were there no compelling reasons in the *Habeas Corpus Case* but that on a true interpretation of the provisions of the Constitution, there were compelling reasons for holding that a *habeas corpus* petition was clearly maintainable in respect of an illegal detention.

36. It may be said that our discussion has only shown that the final order in the *Habeas Corpus Case* is in conflict with the judgments; but this defect can be set right by bringing the order into conformity with the three judgments by adding a proviso. The corrected final order of the Court would then run thus:

"In view of the Presidential Order dated 27th June, 1975 no person has *locus standi* to move any writ petition under Art. 226 before a High Court for *habeas corpus* or any other writ or order or direction to challenge the legality of an order of detention on the ground that the order is not under or in compliance with the Act

---

[50] (1950) S.C.R. 88 at pp. 253-4. [51] ibid. p. 292.

or is illegal or is vitiated by *mala fides* factual or legal or is based on extraneous considerations.

Provided that every person has *locus standi* to maintain a *habeas corpus* petition if the order of preventive detention is unsigned, or is signed by a person not authorised to do so, or states a ground for preventive detention not authorized by the Act."

But the proviso cannot save the Court's Order because it is inconsistent with and destroys the proposition laid down in that Order. If there is *locus standi* to maintain a *habeas corpus* petition in the three cases mentioned in the proviso, it is because the order of detention is *not* in compliance with the Act and is therefore illegal as being contrary to the law. But this exception destroys the rule laid down by the court that there is *no locus standi* to maintain a *habeas corpus* petition on the ground that the detention order is "not under or in compliance with the Act or is illegal". Secondly, once it is admitted that non-compliance with the law in respect of the aforesaid three specified requirements furnishes a ground for setting aside the order of detention, and releasing the detenu on a petition for *habeas corpus*, there is no justification for limiting illegality to these three grounds. For, there is no principle on which the court can say in respect of an illegal order "thus far and no further". King Canute is said to have bid the waves of the sea "to go thus far and no further", and he failed. A Court must equally fail if it says to illegality "thus far and no further".

37. The most disturbing part of the majority judgment in the *Habeas Corpus Case* is that which held that even a *mala fide* order cannot be set aside. It is remarkable that in the leading English case of *Liversidge* v. *Anderson*[52] it was expressly stated that a preventive detention order must not be *mala fide*. This reservation in respect of a *mala fide* order was made during a world war of the utmost severity, and although the Law Lords were fully aware that an allegation of *mala fides* was difficult to prove. The Supreme Court has affirmed in numerous judgments that even where there is a conclusive declaration clause and even where the jurisdiction of the court is expressly excluded, the courts retain the jurisdiction to set aside a *mala fide* order because it is not an order authorized by law at all. As will appear later, Gajendragadkar J. made an express reservation for *mala fides* as a ground for challenging a detention order *even during an emergency proclaimed during the Chinese "aggression"*. A *mala fide* detention order may be prompted by personal malice or illwill, and if a person were detained to satisfy the malice or illwill of the detaining authority *and not for the purpose of the Act*, then, such an order is not an order under the Act and the detention would be illegal. Secondly, if the order of detention was *mala fide* in the sense that the order was passed for collateral or irrelevant purposes, as for example, to eliminate a trader from carrying on his trade because he was competing with the son of the Minister passing the order, it is clearly an act not authorized by law and is illegal.[53] The majority of the Supreme Court gave an amazing reason for holding that a *mala fide* order was not open to challenge on a *habeas corpus* petition if Art. 21 was suspended. The court said that *mala fides* was difficult to prove, and even more so when the provisions of the Maintenance of Internal Security Act prevented the court from looking into the record of the case. It is submitted that this ground is untenable and should have shocked the conscience of any court. The difficulty of proof has never been a ground for refusing relief if that difficulty is overcome and the proof furnished. In fact, matters of which a court can take judicial notice may be sufficient to prove *mala fides*. For example, if X is in jail serving a sentence for forgery, and three years of the sentence remain to be served out, an order for X's preventive detention would be clearly *mala fide*, for, no purpose would be served by preventively detaining a person who was under punitive detention with three years to go. Secondly, matters may be brought before a court on an affidavit which show *mala fides*. Thus, when the action of the censor in causing indefinite delay

---

[52] (1942) A.C. 206.
[53] *Cf. G. Sadanandan* v. *Kerala* ('66) A.SC. 1925.

in passing materials for publication in the "Indian Express" was brought before the court, an affidavit sworn by Mr. Goenka put it on record that Shri Shukla, Minister for Information & Broadcasting, had conveyed a threat to him that unless he gave up his control over the Express Group of Newspapers, he, his wife and his daughter would be preventively detained. *After putting in a formal denial, the censorship order was withdrawn.* But there can be no doubt that if the three persons had been preventively detained, and the allegation was made good on a petition for *habeas corpus* the detention order must be set aside. Finally, no clearer proof of *mala fides* of continued detention of prominent leaders could be furnished than was furnished by the public statement of the then Prime Minister that she strongly resented foreign criticism and that several leaders would have been released much earlier but for the fact that their release was asked for by foreign critics. If an order of detention could be set aside because it was unsigned, or because it was passed on a ground not permissible under the Act, *a fortiori*, a *mala fide* order must be set aside, for it is not an order under the law at all.

38. In the *Habeas Corpus Case*, the detenus strongly relied on *Makhan Singh* v. *Punjab*,[54] as concluding the matter, as indeed it did. However, that case was distinguished by the majority judges and was held not to be applicable. It therefore becomes necessary to give a careful analysis of *Makhan Singh's Case*, since no such analysis has been attempted in the majority judgments in the *Habeas Corpus Case*. In *Makhan Singh's Case*, the matter came before the Supreme Court under the following circumstances: several detenus had filed petitions in the Bombay and the Punjab High Courts under s. 491(1)(*b*) of the Cr.P.C. ["s. 491(1)(*b*)"] alleging that they had been improperly and illegally detained. The petitions were dismissed. Similar petitions before the Allahabad High Court under s. 491(1)(*b*) were allowed and the detenus directed to be released. The majority judgment shows that the petitioners had raised a number of contentions to show that their detention was illegal. However, two questions of great importance, which were common to all the petitions, were referred to a Special Bench of 7 judges of the Supreme Court. These questions arose out of one of the contentions raised by all the detenus that s. 3(2)(15)(i) and 40 of the Defence of India Act, 1962, ("the Act") and Rule 30(1)(*b*) made under the Act were invalid because they violated Articles 14, 21 and 22(4), (5) and (6) of the Constitution, and therefore they were entitled to their release. This contention raised the following two questions which were referred to a Special Bench of 7 judges:

Qn. 1. What is the true scope and effect of the Presidential Order which has been issued under Art. 359(1)? [(The court observed that) the answer to this question would depend upon a fair and reasonable construction of Art. 359(1) itself].

Qn. 2. Does the bar created by the Presidential Order issued under Art. 359(1) operate in respect of applications made by detenus under s. 491(1)(*b*) of the Code? [(The court observed that) the answer to this question would depend upon the determination of the true character of the proceedings which the detenus had taken under s. 491(1)(*b*), considered in the light of the effect of the Presidential Order issued under Art. 359(1)].

39. In addition to the two questions which were common to all the petitions, *the petitions also raised other contentions.* One such contention, namely, excessive delegation of legislative power, which did not relate to the enforcement of fundamental rights, was in fact argued on the merits before the Special Bench and unanimously decided against the detenus. Again, another contention, that the law under which the petitioners were detained was a colourable piece of legislation, was also argued and unanimously decided against the detenus by the Special Bench. There were other grounds for challenging the order of detention which are not mentioned in the report of *Makhan Singh's Case*. It has become necessary to refer to the various grounds taken by the petitioners, other than those involving a violation of fundamental rights, because in determining the scope and ambit of Article

[54] (1964) 4 S.C.R. 797, ('64) A.SC. 381.

359, it became necessary for the Bench to decide what pleas of the detenus going to the validity of their detention were barred by a Presidential Order and what pleas were not barred and therefore could be considered by the Court. The very fact that the Special Bench went into and decided on the merits the question of delegation of legislative power and of colourable legislation shows that in the cases before them, those pleas were open to the detenus; and had they been made good, they would have succeeded in obtaining their release. It is clear therefore that the decision of the Supreme Court on what pleas were barred by the Presidential Order and what pleas were not barred was not *obiter dicta* as some observations in the *Habeas Corpus Case* suggest, but was necessary for the determination of the questions raised by the petitions.

40. The President's Order under Art. 359 as it came before the Supreme Court in *Makhan Singh's Case* is as follows:

"In exercise of the powers conferred by clause (1) of Art. 359 of the Constitution, the President hereby declares that the right of any person to move any court for the enforcement of the rights conferred by Art. 14, Art. 21 and Art. 22 of the Constitution shall remain suspended for the period during which the Proclamation of Emergency issued under clause (1) of article 352 thereof on the 26th October, 1962 is in force, if such person has been deprived of any such rights under the Defence of India Act 1962 (4 of 1962) or any rule or order made thereunder."

This Order has been described as a conditional order by Subba Rao J. in *Makhan Singh's Case* and has been so described in subsequent cases. This is because the Proclamation did not bar the right of a person to enforce his rights under Arts. 14, 21 and 22 generally, but only in relation to his detention under the provisions of the Defence of India Act and Rules.

41. Two judgments were delivered in *Makhan Singh's Case*. Gajendragadkar J. (for himself, Sarkar, Wanchoo, Hidayatullah, Das Gupta and Shah JJ.) delivered the majority judgment. Subba Rao J. delivered a separate judgment concurring in part, but dissenting on one aspect of the case.[55] Gajendragadkar J. held that though the right to claim relief under s. 491(1)(*b*) was *a distinct and separate right* from that conferred by Arts. 32 and 226, in considering whether relief under s. 491(1)(*b*) was available in view of the Proclamation under Art. 359, the court had to look at the substance of the matter. If the challenge to the detention order involved invoking a fundamental right conferred by an Article specified in a proclamation, then, the effect of the Presidential Order, read with Art. 359, was to bar *any* court from granting that relief. He held that before the Constitution came into force an applicant under s. 491(1)(*a*) could challenge the legality of his detention on the ground that (i) the impugned law was passed by a legislature without legislative competence; (ii) that the impugned provisions were void for impermissible delegation of legislative power; (iii) that in detaining him the mandatory provisions of the Act had not been complied with.[56] However, after the coming into effect of the Constitution the detenu applying under s. 491(1)(*b*) could also challenge the legality of his detention on the ground that the law under which he was detained was void for violating fundamental rights. If he could not raise that plea under Arts. 32 and 226, because such a plea would involve his seeking to enforce his fundamental rights, neither could he do so under s. 491(1)(*b*). This is because although

". . . there are two remedies open to a party whose right of personal freedom has been infringed: he may move the Court for a writ under Art. 226(1) or Art. 32(1) of the Constitution, or he may take a proceeding under s. 491(1)(*b*) of the Code. But it seems to us that despite the fact that either of the two remedies can be adopted by a citizen who has been detained improperly or illegally, the right which he claims is the same if the remedy sought for is based on the ground that there has been a breach of his fundamental rights, and that is a right guaranteed to the

[55] He agreed with the majority as regards the applicability of Art. 359 to a right to move a court under Arts. 32 and 226, but not as to the exercise by the High Court of its power under s. 491(1)(b) Cr.P.C.: ('64) A.SC. at p. 405.

[56] ibid. p. 397.

citizen by the Constitution, and so, whatever is the form of the remedy adopted by the detenu, the right which he is seeking to enforce is the same."[57]

The fact that under s. 491(1)(*b*) the court could issue a writ *of habeas corpus suo motu* made no difference. For if an aggrieved party could not move the court, the court could not grant him that very same relief contrary to the provisions of Art. 359 and the President's Order. The obvious and necessary implication of Art. 359 and the President's Order was to "suspend the jurisdiction of the Court *pro tanto* . . ."[58]

42. But though the President's Order under Art. 359 barred a challenge to the law under which the detenus were detained on the ground that they were void for violating fundamental rights, the following challenges were not barred because they did not involve a plea of violation of fundamental rights by the Defence of India Act and Rules: (i) the law authorizing detention was colourable or was passed by a legislature which had no legislative competence; (ii) the detention was in violation of the mandatory provisions of the law authorising detention; (iii) the detention was in excess of the powers conferred by the Act and Rules; (iv) the detention was not under the Defence of India Act and Rules but under another law which violated fundamental rights; (v) the order of detention was passed *mala fide.* Although Gajendragadkar J. knew the difficulty of proving *mala fides,* he made a reservation for *mala fides* in the following words:

"It is true that a mere allegation that the detention is *mala fide* would not be enough; the detenu will have to prove the *mala fides.* But if the *mala fides* are alleged, the detenu cannot be precluded from substantiating his plea on the ground of the bar created by Art. 359(1) and the Presidential Order. That is another kind of plea which is outside the purview of Art. 359(1)."[59]

Gajendragadkar J. did not hold that the right under s. 491(1)(*b*) was merged in the right conferred by Art. 32 (or Art. 226). The rights under Art. 32 (or 226) and s. 491(1)(*b*) were remedial rights, and Gajendragadkar J. held that they were *two distinct rights.* But the fundamental rights conferred by Arts. 14, 21 and 22 are substantive rights which are unaffected by the different remedies for their enforcement. Consequently, if in order to exercise the two remedial rights successfully it was necessary to plead the violation of the detenu's substantive rights under Arts. 14, 21 and 22, such a plea was barred whether the detenu sought his remedy under Art. 32 (or 226) or under s. 491(1)(*b*)

43. Subba Rao J. while agreeing that no application could be made under Art. 32 and 226, which in terms referred to issuing writs for the enforcement of fundamental rights, held that s. 491(1)(*b*) conferred no right on any body nor did it provide for any one moving the court for the enforcement of fundamental rights. It conferred a power on the High Court, and if the High Court *suo motu* set aside an illegal detention order on the ground that the law under which it was passed was void for violating fundamental rights the High Court could do so. It is submitted that the view taken by Subba Rao J. of s. 491 cannot be sustained. Whenever a power is conferred on a court for the benefit of an aggrieved party, the Court is under a duty to exercise that power if circumstances exist which call for its exercise, and the aggrieved party has the right to move the court to exercise the power though he may not be able to claim the relief as of right if the remedy is discretionary. In the sense in which s. 491(1)(*b*) is said to give no right to anybody, Art. 226 equally does not give a right to anybody but merely confers a power on the High Courts to issue writs for the enforcement of fundamental rights *and for any other purpose.* However, as Ganjendragadkar J. rightly observed, though the power conferred by Art. 226 is discretionary, the discretion must be exercised judicially and a court could not capriciously or arbitrarily refuse to exercise the power on an application made to it for its exercise on the sole ground that it was discretionary.[60] The same is true of the power conferred by s. 491(1)(*b*). Besides, since s. 491 replaced the writ of *habeas corpus,* and provided for directions in the nature of *habeas corpus* it

---

[57] ibid. p. 396.
[58] ibid. p. 397.
[59] ibid. p. 400.
[60] ibid. pp. 394-5.

would be a travesty of the most famous remedy for securing personal liberty to say that a person illegally detained had no right to apply to the High Court for his release under s. 491(1)(*b*).

44. But though his view of s. 491(1)(*b*) cannot be supported, Subba Rao J. raised a point of great importance on which the majority judgment is not very satisfactory, and which point Subba Rao J. himself did not work out fully. On the proclamation of emergency under Art. 352, the consequences provided in Art. 358 and 359 follow. But in 1965 there was a striking difference in the provisions of Art. 358 and 359. We have seen that under Art. 358, Art. 19 is suspended in the sense that the State acquires the power to make laws violative of the fundamental rights conferred by Art. 19; Article 359 (as it then stood) conferred no such power. Some judgments of the Supreme Court had held that "whether the Constitution affirmatively confers powers on the legislature to make laws subjectwise or negatively prohibits it from infringing any fundamental right they represent only two aspects of want of legislative power".[61] Consequently, there is lack of legislative competence when a legislature legislates on a topic not assigned to it, and also when it legislates in violation of fundamental rights. If that is so, the following question arose in *Makhan Singh's Case*: "If the detenu can plead that he was detained under a law by a legislature which lacked legislative competence and was therefore void, why can he not plead that the law was passed by a legislature which lacked legislative competence because it had disregarded the limitation imposed on legislative power by fundamental rights?" The fact that Art. 358 authorized the making of laws contrary to the fundamental rights conferred by Art. 19, and Art. 359 did not, gave considerable support for answering the question by saying that such a plea could be raised. The answer given by Gajendragadkar J. to the above question is not very satisfactory[62] because it does not consider the effect of the striking difference between Art. 358 and Art. 359 pointed out by Subba Rao J. However, it is not necessary to discuss this difficult question further in view of the amendment of Art. 359 beyond saying that there was much to be said on both sides. In amending Art. 359, Parliament appears to have accepted the view of Subba Rao J. that Art. 359 conferred no power to make laws violative of the fundamental rights specified in the Presidential Order under Art. 359 and therefore such laws were void. The amendment of Art. 359 expressly confers the power and brings Art. 359 in line with Art. 358. The important point raised by Subba Rao J. cannot therefore arise after the amendment of Art. 359 and a discussion of that point would be academic.

45. The 1962 Order considered in *Makhan Singh's Case* has been set out in para 40 above. The 1975 Order as it was considered in the *Habeas Corpus Case* is given below:

"In exercise of the powers conferred by clause (1) of Article 359 of the Constitution, the President hereby declares that the right of any person (including a foreigner) to move any court for the enforcement of the rights conferred by Article 14, Article 21 and Article 22 of the Constitution and all proceedings pending in any court for the enforcement of the above-mentioned rights shall remain suspended for the period during which the Proclamation of Emergency made under clause (1) of Article 352 of the Constitution on the 3rd December, 1971 and on the 25th June, 1975 are both in force."[63]

The above Order was later amended to include Art. 19.

46. The detenus in the *Habeas Corpus Case* had urged that *Makhan Singh's Case* concluded the case in their favour, as indeed it did, and as the High Courts had in fact held. How did the Supreme Court get over *Makhan Singh's Case*? Before answering this question, we must set out a passage from the judgment of Subba Rao J. in *Makhan Singh's Case*, because a misunderstanding of that passage, or an uncritical application of it, has led the majority in the *Habeas Corpus Case* to hold

[61] *Deepchand* v. *U.P.* ('59) A.SC. 648, 664 quoted by Subba Rao J. in *Makhan Singh's Case* ('64) A.SC. at p. 406.
[62] ('64) A.SC. p. 403, para 44.
[63] (1976) Supp. S.C.R. at pp. 250-51, ('76) A.SC. at p. 1244.

erroneously that *Makhan Singh's Case* did not apply to the petitions before them. Subba Rao J. had said:

"But the order made by the President still leaves the door open for deciding some questions even under Art. 32 or Art. 226 of the Constitution. The order is a conditional one. In effect it says that the right remains suspended if such person has been deprived of any such right under the Defence of India Ordinance, 1962, or under any rule or order made thereunder. The condition is that the person should have been deprived of a right under the Defence of India Ordinance or under any rule or order made thereunder. If a person was deprived of such a right not under the Ordinance or a rule or order made thereunder, his right would not be suspended. If the order was made in excess of the power conferred upon the Government by the said Ordinance, it would not be covered by that order. If the detention was made *mala fide*, it would equally be not an order made under the Ordinance."[64]

He spoke of a conditional Order, but he did not stop to analyze the concept of a conditional Order, presumably because he considered it unnecessary in the case before him. He argeed with the majority in respect of the pleas open to a detenu notwithstanding the 1962 Order, and the majority judgment showed that the only plea which the detenu could not raise was that the Defence of India Act and Rules ("the said Act and Rules") was void on the ground that it violated the fundamental rights conferred on them by Arts. 14, 21 and 22. All other pleas going to the invalidity of the detention, which we have set out in para 42 above, were open to the detenu. Reading the judgments together, it is clear that the 1962 Order was conditional *in two senses* and *not one*. It was conditional, first, because the bar to the enforcement of fundamental rights conferred by Arts. 14, 21 and 22 by moving any Court (hereafter compendiously called "the bar") obviously did not apply if a person complained of a violation of such rights by a law other than the said Act and Rules. The consequence of specifying one or more laws in the Presidential Order is that it does not bar a challenge to a law not specified in the Order *even on the ground that such other law violates fundamental rights conferred by Arts. 14, 21 and 22.* Secondly, even with regard to the said Act and Rules, the bar imposed by the 1962 Order was conditional in a second sense, namely, that it did not bar all challenge to the said Act and Rules *on any ground whatsoever*. It only barred a challenge that the said Act and Rules violated fundamental rights. The effect of the 1962 Order was that *if* a detenu wanted to contend that his detention was illegal because the said Act and Rules violated his fundamental rights, *then* the 1962 Order was a bar to the detenu raising that contention. A plain reading of Art. 359 shows that no power is conferred on the President to issue an Order providing that the right of *any person* to move *any* court for *any purpose* is barred. If such a power had been conferred, and exercised, then the Presidential Order would have been absolute and not conditional. But as Art. 359 stands, the power conferred on the President is limited by the condition that the bar imposed by him must relate only to the enforcement of the fundamental rights specified in his Order and nothing else. *Makhan Singh's Case* may not have given the above analysis of Art. 359, but the conditional nature of the President's power was the basis on which the judgments held that all pleas other than the plea of the violation of fundamental rights, were open notwithstanding the 1962 Order.

47. It is obvious that the 1962 Order and the 1975 Order differed in one important respect: the 1962 Order mentioned the violation of fundamental rights by a specified law — the said Act and Rules. The 1975 Order did not specify any particular law at all. However, fundamental rights cannot be violated in the abstract or in a vacuum. They can be violated by one or more laws. In issuing an Order under Art. 359, the President may limit the bar imposed by him to the violation of the fundamental rights specified by him (*a*) by one specified law, or (*b*) by a number of specified laws. Or (*c*) he may not limit the bar at all but extend it to the violation by any law in force in India of the fundamental rights specified by him. If he chooses to limit the bar imposed by him as in (*a*) and (*b*) above, he must specify one or more laws in his Order. His Order will then be conditional in the first

[64] ('64) A.SC. at pp. 415-416.

sense we have described in para 46 above and it will not bar the plea of the aggrieved person that his fundamental rights are not violated by the laws specified in the Order but by another law and therefore he can raise every plea, including the violation of fundamental rights. For convenience, we shall call that plea a "special plea", to distinguish it from the pleas open to the aggrieved person even in respect of the law or laws specified in the Presidential Order. If however the President does not wish to limit his bar as in (c) above, his Order would apply to each and every law in India. The 1975 Order was such an Order. If the bar is not limited to one or more specified laws, it must necessarily apply to the violation of the specified fundamental rights by *any law* in force in India. If this were not so, violation of the specified fundamental rights by any law in force in India would fall outside the bar imposed by the Order, which would be absurd. But in any event, even if such an absurd construction were put on the 1975 Order that would enable the aggrieved person (the detenu) to challenge the validity of his detention *even on the ground that the law under which he was detained was void for violating the fundamental rights conferred by Arts. 14, 21 and 22.* However, the 1975 Order was *not* conditional in the first sense, since it did not limit the bar to any specified law or laws but applied the bar to *any* law. But the only consequence of the 1975 Order not being conditional in the first sense is that the special plea open in the case of conditional Orders is not open to an aggrieved party, for he can point to no law violating his fundamental rights which can fall outside the 1975 Order. However, the 1975 Order, like *any Order* that can be passed by the President under Art. 359, was a conditional Order in the second sense mentioned in para 46 above. It is only *if* a person complained that his fundamental rights under Arts. 14, 21 and 22 are violated by a law in force that the bar imposed by the 1975 Order operates.

48. The result of our discussion in paras 46 and 47 may be stated thus: the fact that the 1962 Order mentioned the said Act and Rules and was "conditional" and the 1975 Order specified no particular law or laws and was "unconditional" was immaterial. But the 1975 Order necessarily implied and covered *any law* which violated the fundamental rights conferred by Arts. 14, 21 and 22. Under the 1962 Order, all pleas were open to a detenu, other than the violation of fundamental rights by a specified law — the said Act and Rules. Under the 1975 Order, the very same pleas were open to a detenu for it makes no difference whether a *specified* law violates fundamental rights or any law (unspecified law) violates fundamental rights. This is subject to the exception explained earlier, that the "special plea" open to a detenu under the 1962 Order was not open to the detenu under the 1975 Order. Secondly, looking at the 1962 Order and the 1975 Order in the light of the power conferred by Art. 359 on the President to issue such Orders, *both orders are conditional,* for the reasons given earlier. The reader will have noticed that the above analysis explains why Beg, Chandrachud and Bhagwati JJ. accepted it as the correct position that notwithstanding the bar created by the 1975 Order, three pleas which did not relate to the violation of fundamental rights were open to a detenu, namely, that the order of detention was unsigned, or was signed by an unauthorised person, or was passed for an unauthorised purpose. In the result, *Makhan Singh's Case* directly applied to the 1975 Order.

49. We are now in a position to answer the question: How did the Supreme Court get over *Makhan Singh's Case* in the *Habeas Corpus Case*? Two grounds were given for holding that *Makhan Singh's Case* did not apply to the 1975 Order:

(*a*) that in so far as *Makhan Singh's Case* referred to the various pleas open to the detenu, notwithstanding the 1962 Order, the observations in that Case were *obiter dicta.* Bhagwati J. put it thus:

"In the first place, the question as to what were the other pleas available to a detenu in challenging the legality or propriety of his detention, despite the Presidential Order dated 3rd November, 1962, was not in issue before the Court and did not fall to be decided and the aforesaid observations made by the Court on this question were, therefore, clearly obiter."[65]

[65] (1976) Supp. S.C.R. at p. 455, ('76) A.SC. at pp. 1377-8.

(b) that the 1975 Order, unlike the 1962 Order, was unconditional and therefore the reasoning with reference to a conditional Order could not be made applicable to an unconditional Order.

50. Our discussion has shown that both the grounds, (*a*) and (*b*), are untenable. We have seen in para 39 that the observations were not *obiter dicta.* It only remains to add that as the Special Bench was constituted to decide the scope of Art. 359 and the scope of the 1962 Order, the Supreme Court had necessarily to decide to what extent the President could bar the right of any aggrieved person to move any Court for redress. On a plain reading of Art. 359, the bar which the President could impose was only with respect to the enforcement by the aggrieved person of *such of his fundamental rights* as the President may specify. The Supreme Court was entitled to say so, and did say so. The necessary consequence of this construction of Art. 359 is that all other pleas were open, and as we have seen, the Supreme Court actually considered two such pleas, namely, excessive delegation of legislative power and the plea of colourable legislation. As to the ground (*b*) above, our discussion in paras 45 to 48 has shown that the "conditional" nature of the Order made no difference to the applicability of *Makhan Singh's Case,* except that the additional special plea which was available under the 1962 Order was not available under the 1975 Order. On a correct interpretation of Art. 359 and the 1962 Order, *Makhan Singh's Case* was rightly decided and the Supreme Court was in error in rejecting that decision in the *Habeas Corpus Case.*

51. There is one aspect of the *Habeas Corpus* judgment with which we have not dealt so far. The challenge to the executive acts in the petitions before the Court related to illegal detention under a preventive detention law the like of which had not been found necessary in the previous emergencies proclaimed in India as a result of external aggression; and had not been found necessary in England even during the Second World War. The approach adopted by the Supreme Court to personal liberty raised important questions about preventive detention sufficiently important to be considered separately in Appendix V.

52. It is not possible for laymen and lawyers alike to speak of the judgments in the *Habeas Corpus Case* without strong emotion. The majority judgments gave a free charter to every petty government servant to do his will against helpless people stripped by the Supreme Court of the protection of law. A rigid censorship concealed the extent of the injury inflicted by the judgment from the public gaze. But the evidence which has come to light since then, particularly before the Shah Commission, shows how little justification there was for any judge to speak of "motherly care" shown to detenus, or to express "diamond bright and diamond hard hopes" that the kind of misdeeds which counsel for the detenus feared, if the protection of the law was withdrawn from the detenus, had not tarnished the fair record of free India, and would not do so. It is not surprising that an officer giving evidence before the Shah Commission should have found it necessary to "(bring) to the notice of the Commission, the view taken by the Supreme Court on the plea of the Att.-General that in the emergency the absolute right to life and liberty did not exist. Police officers used to discuss the attitudes of courts to find out the legal limitations on them". However, though the present writer shares the strong feelings aroused by the majority judgments, an attempt has been made in this Appendix to meet the reasoning of the majority judgments on legal grounds by a critical examination of the legal concepts involved in the decision. It may be that the politically surcharged atmosphere in which the case was argued made an argument, in part political, and in part legal, inevitable. In her broadcast announcing the Emergency, the then Prime Minister had referred to the bomb thrown at the Chief Justice. The propriety of his presiding over the Bench was doubtful, and his presence on the Bench under the circumstances must have been a source of embarrassment to counsel for the detenus. In any event, he had the shining example of the Lord Chancellor, Lord Simon, on a question of propriety in relation to the order of preventive detention in *Liversidge's Case.* "Normally", said Prof. Heuston,

"the Lord Chancellor would sit on such an important appeal, but Simon had entrusted the task to Lord Maugham, an ex-Lord Chancellor. Simon took the very proper view that it would be wrong for him to preside in the *Liversidge appeal.*

When he had been Home Secretary in the First World War he had not only signed the order for internment in the *Zadig Case* — the only place in the law reports where Simon's name appears otherwise than as counsel or judge — but he had also been the author of Regulation 14 (the equivalent of Regulation 18B): Viscount Simon, *Retrospect* (1952), p. 104."[66]

Or it may be that at that time a strictly legal argument would not have carried the weight which it would have carried under ordinary circumstances. However, the lapse of time has made a dispassionate legal examination of the *Habeas Corpus Case* possible and necessary, for, the majority judgments may have to be reconsidered sooner or later.

53. If in this Appendix the dissenting judgment of Khanna J. has not been considered in detail, it is not for lack of admiration for the judgment, or the courage which he showed in delivering it regardless of the cost and consequences to himself. It cost him the Chief Justiceship of India, but it gained for him universal esteem not only for his courage but also for his inflexible judicial independence. If his judgment is not considered in detail it is because under the theory of precedents which we have adopted, a dissenting judgment, however valuable, does not lay down the law and the object of a critical examination of the majority judgments in this Appendix was to show that those judgments are untenable in law, productive of grave public mischief and ought to be overruled at the earliest opportunity. The conclusion which Justice Khanna has reached on the effect of the suspension of Art. 21 is correct. His reminder that the rule of law did not merely mean giving effect to an enacted law was timely, and was reinforced by his reference to the mass murders of millions of Jews in Nazi concentration camps under an enacted law. However, the legal analysis in this Chapter confirms his conclusion though on different grounds from those which he has taken.

54. In Volume 1 (2nd ed.) of this book[67] the present writer observed:

"Charles Evans Hughes, in his classical history of *The Supreme Court of the United States* wrote that '. . . it remains true that in three notable instances the (Supreme) Court has suffered severely from self-inflicted wounds' and he referred to the *Dred Scott Case*, the *Legal Tender Case* and the *Income-tax Cases*. The present writer believes, that if the Supreme Court of India finds its historian, he will use the same language about *Golak Nath*, the *Bank Nationalization Case* and the *Privy Purse Case*."[67]

The judgment in the *Habeas Corpus Case* came too late for inclusion in that book. Therefore it remains to add that the *Habeas Corpus Case* is the most glaring instance in which the Supreme Court of India has suffered most severely from a self-inflicted wound.

---

[66] R. F. V. Heuston, *Liversidge* v. *Anderson in Retrospect*, 86 L.Q.R. at p. 43.
[67] *Seervai*, Vol. 1, (2nd ed.) at p. 668.

APPENDIX V

THE COURTS AND PREVENTIVE DETENTION

I. Preventive Detention

"Preventive detention laws are repugnant to democratic Constitutions and they cannot be found to exist in any of the democratic countries of the world."[1]: *per* Mahajan J.

"(Preventive Detention) is unknown in America. It was resorted to in England only during war time but no country in the world that I am aware of has made this an integral part of their Constitution as has been done in India. This is undoubtedly unfortunate . . ."[2] *per* Mukherjea J.

1. In *Gopalan's Case,* Mukherjea J. gave the following succinct and accurate account of "preventive detention", its nature and history:

"There is no authoritative definition of the term 'Preventive Detention' in Indian law, though as description of a topic of legislation it occurred in the Legislative Lists of the Government of India Act, 1935, and has been used in Item 9 of List I and Item 3 of List III in the Seventh Schedule to the Constitution. The expression has its origin in the language used by Judges or the Law Lords in England while explaining the nature of detention under Regulation 14(B) of the Defence of Realm Consolidation Act, 1914, passed on the outbreak of the First World War; and the same language was repeated in connection with the emergency regulations made during the last World War. The word 'preventive' is used in contradistinction to the word 'punitive'. To quote the words of Lord Finlay in *Rex* v. *Halliday,* 'it is not a punitive but a precautionary measure'. The object is not to punish a man for having done something but to intercept him before he does it and to prevent him from doing it. No offence is proved, nor any charge formulated; and the justification of such detention is suspicion or reasonable probability and not criminal conviction which can only be warranted by legal evidence: *Vide* Lord Macmillan in *Liversidge* v. *Anderson* (1942) A.C. 206 at p. 254."[3]

Thus, in India preventive detention is a part of the legislative power of Parliament under entry 9, List I, Sch. 7 and a part of concurrent legislative power of Parliament and the States under entry 3, List III. As legislative powers are plenary unless limited by any provision of the Constitution, Art. 22(4) to (7) provided certain safeguards. Preventive detention was discussed in the Constituent Assembly against the background of the violence which had erupted on the partition of India, and of a revolutionary movement in Telengana. Therefore, in spite of grave misgivings, the provisions relating to preventive detention were passed, all the more so because leaders of the stature of Jawaharlal Nehru and Sardar Patel thought them necessary. At that time it seemed reasonable to believe that freedom fighters who had suffered from preventive detention themselves were not likely to abuse the powers entrusted to them after freedom had been won. However, preventive detention during the latest Emergency has raised the gravest doubts as to whether preventive detention should form part of a liberal democratic Constitution like ours which is based on the Rule of Law and the "dignity of the individual". That question falls outside the present discussion. However, as some of the judgments in the *Habeas Corpus Case* refer to the two leading cases of the House of Lords on preventive detention, we must consider them first, as they throw valuable light on preventive detention.

---

[1] *A. K. Gopalan* v. *The State* (1950) S.C.R. 88, 230.
[2] ibid. p. 250.
[3] ibid. pp. 249-250.

II. THE HOUSE OF LORDS AND PREVENTIVE DETENTION

The English Experience

"Entrusting great powers, says Lord Finlay, L.C., in (*R.* v. *Halliday*)[4] Parliament can feel 'certain that such powers will be reasonably exercised'. In *Liversidge* v. *Anderson*[5] the majority of the Lords felt the same confidence in the wisdom and moderation of executive officials; *there is, apparently, something in the tranquil atmosphere of the House of Lords which stimulates faith in human nature.* The fact, is, however, that nobody on earth can be trusted with power without restraint. It is 'of an encroaching nature', and its encroachments, more often than not, are for the sake of what are sincerely believed to be good, and indeed necessary, objects."[6] (italics supplied)

"I am not going to use the argument usually put forward as a matter of courtesy that we do not believe the present Minister would be wicked but that we are afraid his successors might be. I think that any Minister is capable of being wicked when he has a body of regulations like this to administer."[7]

"But what is not forgotten, and perhaps cannot be forgotten while the common law retains its historic characteristics, is Lord Atkin's speech in *Liversidge* v. *Anderson.* It was that speech which stirred a nation in the midst of war to a new appreciation of its values, and it was that speech which has moulded and directed the minds of lawyers throughout the common law world ever since. The Atkin judgment illustrates the importance of the dissenting judgment as an institution of the common law, at least in an appellate tribunal."[8]

2. *Halliday's Case* was decided during the First World War, and *Liversidge* v. *Anderson*[9] was decided during the Second World War when England stood alone after the fall of France. The extreme gravity of the emergency was brought home to every person. Besides, the Lords were dealing with an emergency power. As Lord Atkin rightly observed, *Halliday's Case* raised a question of *ultra vires*[10] on a petition for *habeas corpus.* It was contended for the detenu that the power conferred by s. 1(1) of the Defence of the Realm Consolidation Act, 1914 "to issue regulations for the safety or the defence of the realm" did not authorize the making of Reg. 14B of the Defence of the Realm (Consolidation) Regulations, 1914, which empowered the Secretary of State to order the internment of any person "of hostile origin or association" when on the recommendation of a competent Naval or Military authority it appeared to the Secretary of State expedient for securing the public safety or the Defence of the Realm. The contention was that the general words of s. 1(1) could not authorise the detention of a person without a trial; it was necessary for Parliament expressly to so provide if such detention was considered necessary. Lord Shaw, in a powerful dissenting judgment, upheld the contention; but the majority of the House rejected it.

3. The Lord Chancellor, Lord Finlay, who delivered the leading judgment pointed out that under Regulation 14B ("the Regulation") an internment order could only be made on the recommendation of a competent Naval or Military authority. Further, the Regulation made it obligatory to state in the order of internment in respect of a person not an enemy subject that the internee could make a representation against the order of internment for the consideration of an advisory committee presided over by a person who holds or has held high judicial office. *"The regulation, therefore, provides means for ascertaining whether any complaint against the justice or necessity of the order is well founded."*[11] (italics supplied). Later in his judgment he said:

---

[4] (1917) A.C. at p. 268. [5] (1942) A.C. 206.
[6] Allen, *Law and Orders*, 3rd ed., p. 297.
[7] Herbert Morrison on Defence Regulations, *Hansard*, Vol. 352, col. 1846 — quoted in *Allen, supra* at pp. 364-65.
[8] R. F. V. Heuston, *Liversidge* v. *Anderson in Retrospect 86 L.Q.R.* at p. 66.
[9] (1942) A.C. 206. [10] ibid. at p. 238.
[11] (1917) A.C. at p. 267.

"The statute was passed at a time of supreme national danger, *which still exists.* The danger of espionage and of damage by secret agents to ships, railways, munition works, bridges, &c., had to be guarded against. The restraint imposed may be a necessary measure of precaution, and in the interests of the whole nation it may be regarded as expedient that such an order should be made in suitable cases. *This appears to me to be the meaning of the statute. Every reasonable precaution to obviate hardship which is consistent with the object of the regulation appears to have been taken.*"[12] (italics supplied)

Having emphasised the supreme national danger and the safeguards provided, Lord Finlay made observations as to the nature of preventive detention which must be set out in full as they have been repeatedly cited in English cases and have been cited with approval by our own courts. He said:

"One of the most obvious means of taking precautions against dangers such as are enumerated is to impose some restriction on the freedom of movement of persons whom there may be any reason to suspect of being disposed to help the enemy. It is to this that reg. 14B is directed. *The measure is not punitive but precautionary.*"[13] (italics supplied)

4. Lord Atkinson observed that "It is not contended in this case that the personal liberty of the subject can be invaded arbitrarily at the mere whim of the Executive."[14] And like Lord Finlay, Lord Atkinson also said that "the *precautions already referred to effectually guard* against all injustice or abuse in the administration of the regulation."[15] Lord Wrenbury in agreeing with the majority on the nature of preventive detention, made the following important observations:

"The appellant is interned under an order made under that regulation. He says the result is that the *Habeas Corpus* Act is in substance suspended when it has not been suspended in fact. This is a complete misapprehension. If his case were that he had neither hostile origin nor associations he could have his writ of *habeas corpus* on the ground that that was so, and if he established the fact he would be discharged. The application before your Lordships is for a writ of *habeas corpus,* and the ground advanced is that reg. 14B is *ultra vires.* If that were established he would be discharged."[16]

In other words, a condition precedent to the exercise of the power of detention was open to judicial review on a *habeas corpus* petition.

5. *Liversidge's Case* was decided during a war of survival such as England had never faced before. Section 2(2) of the Emergency Powers (Defence) Act, 1939 expressly authorized the making of regulations providing for preventive detention, thus removing the objection raised in *Halliday's Case* that Regulation 14B was *ultra vires* because the Act under which it was made did not expressly authorize preventive detention. Regulation 18B made under the said s. 2(2) provided for preventive detention. The material words of the Regulation were:

"If the Secretary of State *has reasonable cause* to believe any person to have been or to be of hostile origin or associations or to have been recently concerned in acts prejudicial to the public safety or the defence of the realm or in preparation or instigation of such acts and that by reason thereof it is necessary to exercise control over him he may make an order directing that he be detained." (italics supplied)

The words we have italicized were substituted for the words "is satisfied" as a result of criticism in the House of Commons, and after a "round table" discussion between members of different parties. The whole question in *Liversidge's Case* turned on the meaning of the words "has reasonable cause to believe". The majority of the House of Lords held that though the *prima facie* meaning of the words "if A.B. has reasonable cause to believe a certain circumstance" was "if there is in fact reasonable cause to believe", yet in a special context "the words might well mean if A.B.

---

[12] ibid. p. 270.
[13] ibid. p. 269.
[14] ibid. p. 271.
[15] ibid. p. 276.
[16] ibid. p. 308.

acting on what he thinks is reasonable cause (and *of course acting in good faith*) believes the thing in question".[17] (italics supplied) Lord Maugham and the Law Lords, who agreed with him, set out in their judgments what they thought were the special circumstances justifying that meaning.

6. Lord Atkin dissented. In a judgment of remarkable cogency and power, he demonstrated that the words "has reasonable cause to believe" had always meant, if there was in fact a reasonable cause whether the words were used at common law or in statutes, and that the different words used in Regulation 18B themselves supported this meaning. The distinction between the "objective" interpretation of Lord Atkin and the "subjective" interpretation of the other Law Lords is graphically brought out as the distinction between A's statement "I have a broken bone" and A's statement "I think I have a broken bone". If the judgment had rested here it would have been an "impressive contribution to the Law Reports". But, as Prof. Hueston rightly points out, "what seized the imagination of lawyer and layman alike was the passionate, almost wild rhetoric of the three concluding paragraphs":

"I view with apprehension the attitude of judges who on a mere question of construction when face to face with claims involving the liberty of the subject show themselves more executive minded than the executive. Their function is to give words their natural meaning, not perhaps in war time leaning towards liberty, but following the dictum of Pollock C.B. in *Bowditch* v. *Balchin* [(1850) 5 Ex. 378], cited with approval by Lord Wright in *Barnard* v. *Gorman* [(1941) A.C. 378, 393], 'in a case in which the liberty of the subject is concerned, we cannot go beyond the natural construction of the statute'. *In this country, amidst the clash of arms, the laws are not silent.* They may be changed, but they speak the same language in war as in peace. It has always been one of the pillars of freedom, one of the principles of liberty for which on recent authority we are now fighting, *that the judges are no respecters of persons and stand between the subject and any attempted encroachments on his liberty by the executive, alert to see that any coercive action is justified in law.* In this case I have listend to arguments which might have been addressed acceptably to the Court of King's Bench in the time of Charles I. (italics supplied)

"I protest, even if I do it alone, against a strained construction put on words with the effect of giving an uncontrolled power of imprisonment to the minister. To recapitulate: The words have only one meaning. They are used with that meaning in statements of the common law and in statutes. They have never been used in the sense now imputed to them. They are used in the Defence Regulations in the natural meaning, and when it is intended to express the meaning now imputed to them, different and apt words are used in the regulations generally and in this regulation in particular. Even if it were relevant, which it is not, there is no absurdity or no such degree of public mischief as would lead to a non-natural construction.

"I know of only one authority which might justify the suggested method of construction. 'When I use a word', Humpty Dumpty said in rather scornful tone, 'it means just what I choose it to mean, neither more nor less'. 'The question is', said Alice, 'whether you can make words mean different things'. 'The question is', said Humpty Dumpty, 'which is to be master — that is all'. (*Through the Looking Glass*, c.vi.) After all this long discussion the question is whether the words 'If a man has' can mean 'If a man thinks he has'. I am of opinion that they cannot, and that the case should be decided accordingly."[18]

7. Not till Prof. Heuston wrote his able and delightful article on *Liversidge* v. *Anderson in Retrospect* was it possible to view the judgment in its proper perspective. All lawyers know that Lord Radcliffe delivered a *coup de grace* to the subjective interpretation of expressions like "has reasonable cause to believe" when in delivering the judgment of the Privy Council he said "However read (has reasonable

---

[17] *Per* Lord Maugham (1942) A.C. at pp. 219-220.
[18] *Heuston, op. cit.* pp. 36-37.

cause to believe) must be intended in some sense as *a condition limiting the exercise of an otherwise arbitrary power*."[19] But few lawyers could have known that as Sir Cyril Radcliffe K. C. (then the Director General of the Ministry of Information) he wrote to Lord Atkin:

"I only wanted to say how entirely I agreed with every line of your judgment and what a very valuable thing it was that you were there to deliver it. I know how widely the general public responded to the view you took, and I do privately hope that it is the one that will somehow prevail before things go much further."[20]

Again, the full import of the judges being "more executive minded than the executive" was made clear by Lord Atkin in a letter to the Lord Chief Justice who had been hurt by those remarks. The words meant that:

". . . the executive charged with maintaining the defence of the country had deliberately chosen words which in their natural and only meaning gave a safeguard to the subject (i.e., the objective cause), while those of the judges whose judgments were under review, and in particular my colleagues, were impressed with the idea that the interests of the country required that the safeguard should not be there and *therefore* adopted the non-natural construction (subjective cause). That is what I called and call being more executive-minded than the executive."[21]

8. We have referred to Prof. Heuston's article to show that when the Supreme Court decided the *Habeas Corpus Case* a considerable literature had grown up round *Liversidge* v. *Anderson* and the dissent of Lord Atkin had gained general acceptance. Prof. C. K. Allen said bluntly: "This case has never had many champions among the legal profession and as against Lord Atkin's shattering dissent, it had generally been regarded as the House of Lords 'contribution to the war effort'."[22] Prof. Wade put it more suavely when, after describing Lord Atkin's judgment as "one of the *tours de force* of legal literature" he said of *Liversidge's Case* that ". . . in retrospect it stands as an isolated example to show how strongly, in exceptional circumstances, the ordinary train of legal reasoning may be deflected."[23] Lord Reid in his classic judgment in *Ridge* v. *Baldwin*[24] said:

"In many regulations there was set out an alternative safeguard more practicable in war time — the objective test that the officer must have reasonable cause to believe whatever was the crucial matter. [I leave out the very peculiar decision of this House in *Liversidge* v. *Anderson* (1942) A.C. 206]."[25]

Delivering a lecture in the Bombay University on January 10, 1979, Lord Scarman said: "The House of Lords has put the *Liversidge Case* where it belongs — in a War Museum."

It is only right to say that Prof. Heuston in the article already referred to, observed "that as a matter of law, on the construction of the relevant Regulations, the decision of the majority of the Law Lords is preferable to that of Lord Atkin."[26] He put it on the ground that Lord Atkin's judgment involved "the heresy" that the construction of words in a statute was a matter of law and not of fact. The true view supported by overwhelming weight of authority was that each statute must be interpreted in its own context.[27] There are two answers to the "true view". The first is best given in the words of Prof. C. K. Allen:

"In all the other speeches, there is not a single instance to disprove Lord Atkin's general proposition, not a single exception from the rule on which he relies. *Liversidge* v. *Anderson*, therefore, places an entirely new interpretation *on a very familiar term of art*, and, by admission, opens up what Lord Atkin calls 'the era of "subjective" cause'."[28] (italics supplied)

---

[19] *Nakkuda Ali* v. *Jayaratne* (1951) A.C. 66, 76-7.

[20] *Heuston, op. cit* p. 52. His judgment did what he hoped would be done, namely that Lord Atkin's view would prevail "before things go much further".

[21] ibid. p. 50.

[22] Allen, *Law & Orders*, 3rd edn. p. 256.

[23] H. W. R. Wade, *Administrative Law*, 3rd edn. p. 88.

[24] (1964) A.C. 40.

[25] ibid. p. 73.

[26] *Heuston, op. cit*. p. 65.

[27] ibid. p. 64.

[28] Allen, *Law & Orders*, 1st edn. p. 333 [Reprinted from (1942) *L.Q.R.* (April)].

Secondly, "the true view" misses the main point of Lord Atkin's judgment. If the words "has reasonable cause to believe" had always had one meaning whether at common law or in statutes, it is reasonable to suppose that they were used in that sense in Regulation 18B. It is unreasonable to suppose that Parliament deliberately disguised its intention by using words which had never till then conveyed any other meaning; and all the more so when after objection and debate the word "satisfied" was changed to the words "has reasonable cause to believe". In another part of his article, after referring to the extra judicial opinion of Lord Wright, that "the strength of the government's case lay largely in the provisions of the Regulation for an Advisory Committee which was established under the presidency of so powerful a judge as Mr. Justice Birkett",[29] Prof. Heuston observed:

"Indeed, the establishment of the advisory committee makes sense only on the assumption that no appeal to the courts was being granted. For no internee would trouble to query the Home Secretary's decision before the advisory committee if the Home Secretary could instead be required to justify that decision to the satisfaction of a High Court Judge, who would, if not satisfied, have the power not only to order the release of the internee, but also to require the Home Secretary to pay damages for his wrongful detention."[30]

With respect, the present writer does not agree. First, a representation to the committee would be inexpensive. The resort to a court of law, *at a time when there was no free legal aid*, would be an expensive luxury which few detenus could afford. For, as *Liversidge's Case* and the case of *Greene* v. *Secretary of State*[31] show, a *habeas corpus* petition would have to travel its way from the Divisional Court to the Court of Appeal and then to the House of Lords, and the unsuccessful party may have to pay the State's costs. In fact, Lord Maugham *dismissed the appeal with costs*. Lord Atkin told Mr. Holmes for the State that as the matter was of general importance, the majority of the House were of opinion that there should be no order as to costs. On Mr. Holmes suggesting that probably Lord Maugham's order for costs might have escaped Lord Atkin's attention, Lord Atkin said that it had not. Mr. Holmes replied that having regard to the majority view, "he would not dream of asking for costs". With the knowledge which Prof. Heuston himself has brought to light, namely, that in 95 per cent of cases the advice given by the advisory committee was followed,[32] there would be all the greater reason why internees would apply to the advisory committee instead of resorting to the courts *in the first instance*.

9. We must set out certain features of the law of preventive detention in England on which the majority of the House of Lords relied for their interpretation of the words "has reasonable cause to believe":

(*a*) The order of detention coud not be passed by any minor official but by a Secretary of State who was answerable for his actions to Parliament.[33]

(*b*) In many cases the Home Secretary would act on information which would be confidential.[34]

(*c*) "Those who are responsible for national security must be the sole judges of national security. It would be obviously undesirable that such matters should be made the subject of evidence in a court of law or otherwise discussed in public: *The Zamora* (1916) 2 A.C. 77, 107."[35]

---

[29] In (1944) 32 *Proceedings of the British Academy* 307. It is not quite correct to describe Birkett as a High Court Judge at the time of the events in question in *Liversidge*. In June 1941 he was created a Knight for his 18 months of unpaid service as Chairman, and made a judge in November of the same year: *Heuston, op. cit.* p. 64.

[30] *Heuston, op. cit.* p. 65.

[31] (1942) A.C. 284.

[32] *Heuston, op. cit.* p. 42.

[33] (1942) A.C. p. 222; see also p. 281: "For the person who is to have reasonable cause to believe is not some minor official holding a subordinate position. He is the Secretary of State."

[34] ibid. p. 221.

[35] ibid. p. 253 (Lord Macmillan).

(*d*) The Secretary of State was provided with one or more advisory Committees and that he had to report once a month to Parliament on what action he had taken and the orders he had made and the number of cases in which he declined to follow the advice of the advisory committee.[36]

(*e*) "Were the person detained left without any safeguard, this might be an argument against holding that an absolute discretion has been conferred on the Secretary of State, but the argument is the other way when it is found, as it is in this regulation, that elaborate provision is made for the safeguarding of the detained person's interests. I refer to the constitution of advisory committees to which any person aggrieved by a detention order may make representations. The duty is imposed on the chairman to inform the objector of the grounds on which the detention order has been made and to furnish him with such particulars as are in the chairman's opinion sufficient to enable him to state his case."[37]

(*f*) A challenge to the order would be open if it was not made in good faith, (the burden of proving absence of good faith lying on the detainee)[38] or in a case of mistaken identity.[39]

This is clearly right.

(*g*) "But, if the sense of the country was outraged by the system or practice of making detention orders, or indeed, by any particular order, it could make itself sufficiently felt in the Press and in Parliament to put an end to any abuse and Parliament can always amend the regulation."[40]

These observations are correct, and are very important when we consider the conditions during the recent Emergency in India.

10. We will now consider (*a*) to (*e*) above. As to (*a*) above, Lord Atkin rightly brushed aside the reference to the high status of the Secretary of State by the terse remark that "the judges are no respector of persons". As to (*b*) above, the objection that the Secretary of State would have to rely on confidential information, Lord Atkin said that the objection was answered by the very terms of the regulation which conferred on the detainee a right to make a representation against the order to an advisory committee, whose chairman was under a duty "to inform the objector of the ground on which the order has been made against him and to furnish him with such particulars as are in the opinion of the Chairman sufficient to present his case". Secondly, referring to *Green's Case*, Lord Atkin said, "It is obvious that no important reasons of State prevented the Home Secretary from disclosing the cause of his belief".[41] To these reasons we may add another "The Home Secretary repeatedly assured the House of Commons that all available evidence including *secret dossiers* was before the Committee".[42] If all the information including secret dossiers could be disclosed to a committee (sitting no doubt in secret), it is difficult to say that the grounds of detention with sufficient particulars could not be disclosed to His Majesty's Judges, if necessary, *in camera*, and, if necessary, with a claim for privilege on matters affecting public safety or security. One objection mentioned by Viscount Simon in *Duncan* v. *Cammell Laird & Co.* to a claim for privilege, namely, that judges cannot look at documents without showing them to the parties,[43] is expressly overruled by the decision of the House of Lords in *Conway* v. *Rimmer*[44] which held that on a plea of privilege, the documents should be produced for the inspection of the House of Lords (that is, the Court) and if it was found that disclosure would not be prejudicial to the public interest or that any possibility of such interest was insufficient to justify its being withheld, disclosure should be ordered. If the disclosure of secret documents can be made to an advisory committee presided over by a King's Counsel, documents can surely be inspected by His Majesty's Judges to decide the claim of

---

[36] ibid. p. 222.
[37] ibid. p. 254-5 (Lord Macmillan); see also p. 267 (Lord Wright).
[38] ibid. p. 220 (Lord Maugham); p. 259 (Lord Wright); p. 278 (Lord Romer).
[39] ibid. p. 261 (Lord Wright).
[40] ibid. p. 270 (Lord Wright).
[41] ibid. p. 241.
[42] Allen, *Law & Orders*, 3rd ed. p. 368.
[43] (1942) A.C. 624, 640-41.
[44] (1968) A.C. 910, 953 (Lord Reid).

privilege. As to (*c*) above, the observation in *The Zamora* that those who are responsible for national security must be the *sole* judges of that security cited by Viscount Simon in *Duncan* v. *Cammell Laird & Co.*[45] does not survive the overruling of that decision in *Conway* v. *Rimmer*. As to (*d*) and (*e*) above, we have already submitted that the existence of an Advisory Committee does not support the conclusion that the question whether the Secretary of State has reasonable cause to believe something, cannot be determined by the Courts. In *Greene's Case* Lord Atkin agreed with the other Law Lords in dismissing the appeal because the affidavit of the Home Secretary showed that there was reasonable cause.

11. The reader, whether layman or lawyer, will be struck by the safeguards provided for the detainee both during the First World War and the Second World War. They are listed here so that they can be contrasted later with the total absence of all safeguards during the Emergency:

(i) If the exercise of the power of preventive detention, or even a particular order, outraged the sense of the community, *"it could make itself sufficiently felt in the Press and in Parliament to put an end to any abuse* and Parliament can always amend the regulation" [9(*g*) above].

(ii) Reports of debates in Parliament (other than in Secret Sessions) were published by the press and broadcast by the B.B.C. Nobody dreamt of prohibiting the publication of judgments. Lord Atkin's dissenting judgment in *Liversidge's Case* received wide publicity; it formed the subject of leading articles and of opinion columns — to say nothing of learned articles in legal journals.

(iii) Criticism of the executive or the Prime Minister did not land the critic in preventive detention. During the First World War, Prime Minister Asquith was replaced by David Lloyd George as a result of criticism in the Press and in public. During the Second World War, Chamberlain was replaced by Winston Churchill. In spite of Churchill's unique position in England, a no-confidence motion (in the central direction of the war) was moved on July 1, 1942 in the House of Commons, and the opening paragraph of Churchill's reply indicate the freedom of the press and the radio "at a time of mortal peril":

"This long Debate has now reached its final stage. What a remarkable example it has been of the unbridled freedom of our Parliamentary institutions in time of war! Everything that could be thought-of or raked-up has been used to weaken confidence in the Government, has been used to prove that Ministers are incompetent and to weaken their confidence in themselves, to make the Army distrust the backing it is getting from the civil power, to make the workmen lose confidence in the weapons they are striving so hard to make, to represent the Government as a set of non-entities over whom the Prime Minister towers, and then to undermine him in his own heart and, if possible, before the eyes of the nation. All this poured out by cable and radio to all parts of the world, to the distress of all our friends and to the delight of all our foes. I am in favour of this freedom, which no other country would use, or dare to use, in times of mortal peril such as those through which we are passing. But the story must not end there, and I make now my appeal to the House of Commons to make sure that it does not end there."[46]

And he concluded with the words:

"If those who have assailed us are reduced to contemptible proportions and their Vote of Censure on the National Government is converted to a vote of censure upon its authors, make no mistake, a cheer will go up from every friend of Britain and every faithful servant of our cause, and the knell of disappointment will ring in the ears of the tyrants we are striving to overthrow."[47]

Thus after a two day debate, the "no confidence" motion was defeated by 475 votes to 25.

---

[45] (1942) A.C. at p. 641.

[46] *The End of the Beginning*, the Third Volume of Winston Churchill's War Speeches: Cassels, 2nd edn. Dec. 1943, p. 129.

[47] ibid. p. 149.

(iv) The power to pass an order of detention was conferred on one person — the Home Secretary — and both Sir John Anderson and Mr. Herbert Morrison, who succeeded him as Home Secretary, assured the House of Commons that they personally considered each case before issuing a detention order. It need hardly be added that the Home Secretary is answerable to the House of Commons. The Home Secretary was also under an obligation to lay before the House of Commons *at least once a month* "action taken under the Regulation" including the number of persons detained and the number of cases in which he had not followed the recommendation of the Advisory Committee: Regulation 18B(6).

(v) The detainee had the right to make a representation against the order of detention to an advisory committee. During the 18 months of the Second World War the Committee was "constituted of persons of unquestionable reputation under the chairmanship of Mr. Norman Birkett, K. C. (later Lord Birkett) and its impartiality was above suspicion . . ."[48] It is a tribute to the weight and impartiality of the Committee that in 95 per cent of cases its recommendations were accepted.

(vi) Relief from an order of detention passed *mala fide* was available on a petition for *habeas corpus* and so also in cases of mistaken identity.

III. The Supreme Court of India and Preventive Detention

The Indian Experience

". . . we wish to add that when we come across orders of this kind by which citizens are deprived of their fundamental right of liberty without a trial on the ground that the emergency proclaimed by the President in 1962 still continues and the powers conferred on the appropriate authorities by the Defence of India Rules justify the deprivation of such liberty, we feel rudely disturbed by the thought that continuous exercise of the very wide powers conferred by the Rules on the several authorities is likely to make the conscience of the said authorities insensitive if not blunt, to the paramount requirement of the Constitution that *even during Emergency, the freedom of Indian citizens cannot be taken away without the existence of the justifying necessity specified by the Rules themselves.* The tendency to treat these matters in a somewhat casual and cavalier manner which may conceivably result from *the continuous use of such unfettered powers, may ultimately pose a serious threat to the basic values on which the democratic way of life in this country is founded.* It is true that cases of this kind are rare, but even the presence of such rare cases constitutes a warning to which we think it is our duty to invite the attention of the appropriate authorities."[49] (italics supplied)

per Gajendragadkar C.J.

12. Since preventive detention orders were passed even when there was no emergency, we will first state briefly the Supreme Court's attitude to preventive detention generally. The Supreme Court held that the safeguards provided by Art. 22(4) to (7) were feeble compared to the safeguards provided by Art. 22(1) and (2) which were expressly excluded in the case of persons preventively detained. Therefore, those safeguards must be strictly enforced. Equally, the requirements of the law authorizing preventive detention must be strictly complied with. *Mala fide* detention orders were struck down and so also orders based on irrelevant considerations. Again, if the grounds supplied to the detenu included relevant as well as irrelevant grounds the whole order was ordinarily struck down. In short, the Supreme Court affirmed the duty of every Court to see that a law depriving a person of his liberty without the safeguards available even to a person charged with crime was strictly complied with.

13. The attitude of the Supreme Court to preventive detention during a proclamation of emergency arising out of external aggression (the Chinese incident) was substantially the same. No doubt if a Presidential Order barred the right of a person to enforce specified fundamental rights, the Supreme Court held that a detenu

---

[48] Allen, *Law & Orders*, 3rd edn. p. 367.
[49] *G. Sadanandan* v. *Kerala* ('66) A.SC. 1925 at p. 1930.

could not rely on those rights in support of his plea that his detention was illegal. But every other plea, including the plea of *mala fides* against the order was available to the detenu as we have explained when discussing *Makhan Singh's Case* in para 41 and 42 of Appendix IV. Nor was the reservation in favour of a plea of *mala fides* an empty formality. In *G. Sadanandan* v. *Kerala*,[50] a case decided during an emergency, Gajendragadkar C.J. (for himself and Wanchoo, Hidayatullah, Shah and Sikri JJ.) struck down an order for the preventive detention of the petitioner on the ground "that the impugned order of detention . . . and the petitioner's continued detention . . . must be characterised as clearly and plainly *mala fide*."[51] He stated the attitude of the Court to preventive detention even during an emergency in a passage which has been set out at the beginning of this Section. He affirmed the rule of law which required that even during an emergency the freedom of Indian citizens could not be taken away without the existence of justifying necessity specified by the Rules; that the continued use of unfettered powers would pose a most serious threat to the basic values on which the democratic way of life in this country was based. It is unfortunate that the wisdom and insight shown by the judges in *Sadanandan's Case* should have been forgotten in the majority judgments in the *Habeas Corpus Case*.

14. Till we come to the *Habeas Corpus Case*, the attitude of the Supreme Court to preventive detention, even during an emergency, was almost impeccable. One would have thought that if the Supreme Court adopted that attitude during emergencies created by war or external aggression, the Supreme Court would more readily adhere to that attitude during an emergency created by "internal disturbance". However, in comparing two different periods of the Supreme Court's history, it is only fair to the Supreme Court to say that between 1964-66 and 1975-77 the climate had changed. What effect the change of climate produced on the *Habeas Corpus Case*, and its aftermath, it is difficult to say. That task must be left to the historian of the Supreme Court in the hope that relevant materials for forming a judgment will be available to him, sooner or later. But the change was brought about by the following factors.

(i) From 26th January, 1950, when the Supreme Court began to function, till 25th April, 1973, by an unbroken practice the seniormost judge of the Supreme Court was appointed its Chief Justice, no matter how short his tenure as Chief Justice might be — Mr. Justice J. C. Shah had a tenure of five weeks.[52] The judgments in the *Fundamental Rights Case* [*Kesavananda* v. *Kerala* (1973) Supp. S.C.R. 1, ('73) A.SC. 1461] were delivered on April 24 and 25, 1973. On the evening of the 25th the All India Radio announced the appointment of Mr. Justice Ray as the new Chief Justice, who was junior to three of the senior-most judges. This supersession raised a country wide controversy, and the general view was that the supersession of judges would undermine the independence of the judiciary. A former Att.-General of India, Mr. C. K. Daphtary, expressed the general view thus:

"Everyone who wants to get on, to get on to the next step in the ladder, will have to conform. A line will be drawn for him and he must toe the line. I have no doubt that presently a handbook will be issued — 'Morals and Manners for Judges'. It will tell them as far as possible what is the concept, the Government's concept, of social justice, of the welfare state, of the methods to be adopted. But he is going to find himself in a fix, because there is no hard-and-fast line; it is not a line that can be chalked straight. Much will be left for him to worry about for himself as to whether what he is going to do will advance social justice or will retard it. And he will take the safe line, the safe line which he believes must be to decide in favour of the Government or the governmental institution, unless of course, and it is not an impossibility, he has been told ahead what to do."[53]

---

[50] ibid.

[51] ibid. p. 1950.

[52] Mr. Justice Imam, the seniormost judge, had not been appointed Chief Justice in 1964 because he was suffering from a physical disability following a very grave illness.

[53] *A Judiciary Made to Measure*, ed. by N. A. Palkhivala (June 1973). The views of the present writer were expressed in the *Constitutional Law of India*, 2nd edn. (1976) Vol. II, at pp. 1415 to 1420: A Note on the supersession of Judges.

(ii) The judgment of the Allahabad High Court finding Prime Minister Indira Gandhi, guilty of corrupt electoral practices, and the judgment of the Supreme Court striking down Art. 329A(4) of our Constitution, which in substance directed the Supreme Court to allow Mrs. Gandhi's appeal from the Allahabad judgment and to dismiss her opponent's cross appeal did not endear judicial independence to Mrs. Indira Gandhi's government. There were calculated leaks of proposed amendments to the Constitution: one such amendment was designed to create a body superior to the Supreme Court; alternatively another proposed amendment sought to curtail the power of judicial review of the Supreme Court and the High Courts. These leaks were intended to shake judicial nerves.

(iii) Censorship deprived the Supreme Court of the most valuable protection of judicial independence, namely, a vigilant and vocal public opinion such as had sparked off the controversy on the supersession of the three Supreme Court judges. For the first time in the history of India, judgments of the Courts could not be reported in the newspapers and were subject to censorship.

(iv) An atmosphere of terror and fear was created by mass arrests and the way in which people were treated in preventive detention. After the emergency was lifted, the Att.-General of India, Mr. Niren De, in a public interview stated that throughout the emergency he lived in an atmosphere of terror.

15. However, in the *Habeas Corpus Case*, two factors have contributed to the Supreme Court's retreat from the impeccable standards it had laid down in earlier preventive detention cases. The first factor is best stated in the words of Bhagwati J.:

". . . it is necessary to remind ourselves that the emergency provisions in Part XVIII of the Constitution make no distinction whether the emergency is on account of threat to the security of India by war or external aggression or on account of threat to the security of India by internal disturbance. The same provisions are applicable alike in both situations of emergency, irrespective of the reason for which emergency has been declared. The legal consequences are the same and, therefore, whatever interpretation we place on Article 359, clause (1) in the present case which relates to declaration of emergency on account of internal disturbance would apply equally where the emergency is declared on account of war or external aggression by a hostile power."[54]

This view cannot be sustained, because the framers of our Constitution would have assumed that the radically different character of a war and "internal disturbance" would be known to every person, including a judge, and the fact that the two kinds of emergencies were clubbed together in Art. 352 would not mislead any person into believing that the same considerations apply to both, and all the more so because of the nebulous character of the expression "internal disturbance". The expression may cover "essentially ephimeral, spasmodic or unorganized civil disorder", or "the conduct of an organized war between contending factions within a State", or it may cover "insurgency, which is a half-way house" between the two.[55] It is not necessary to show at length that the conditions created, and the necessities imposed, by war, are very different from the conditions created, and the necessities imposed, by internal disturbance. So, a brief narrative will suffice. First, a war, its continuation and termination cannot be kept secret — locked up in the bosom of the Prime Minister and a few of his colleagues. The progress of war, more especially a modern war, is made known to the world by the press, the radio and television; armies march and cities burn, or are destroyed; a blackout reminds citizens for nights on end that a war is on. Thus a war is brought home to every citizen and to every judge in the realm. It is not surprising therefore that s. 57(11) of the Evidence Act provides that the "Court shall take judicial notice of the commencement, continuation and termination of hostilities between the Government of India and other State or body of persons". It is not a mere accident that no such provision is made with reference to internal disturbance. Secondly, in a war, the danger of espionage and of damage by secret enemy agents to ships, railways,

[54] (1976) Supp. S.C.R. at p. 424, ('76) A.SC. at p. 1355.

[55] McNair and Watts, *The Legal Effects of War*, 4th edn. p. 30.

ammunition works, bridges, etc. has to be guarded against as Lord Finlay observed in *Halliday's Case* (para 3 above). Thus, a war not only involves fighting the enemy but it involves fighting the agents of the enemy, spies and saboteurs whom the enemy may have planted or may plant in the country. Thirdly, war involves the mobilisation of the man and woman power of the State, the equipment of the army, navy, air force, the recruitment and training of personnel for the armed forces, and of home guards for civil defence. It is in these conditions that preventive detention is tolerated in a free country like England, notwithstanding its departure from the ordinary criminal law. If during a war credible information is obtained about the activities of foreign agents or spies who plan to blow up bridges, power stations, ammunition dumps, and railway lines or guide aircraft by light signals during a black out, the necessity of the case requires that such agents or spies be put out of action. Civil disturbance poses none of these problems. There is no external enemy to fight; therefore all the resources of the State — the army, the navy and the air force, the armed police, the ordinary police, and railway police are at the disposal of the government to meet force with force. The clearest proof of the difference between a war, such as we had with China and later with Pakistan and the emergency created by internal disturbance is that no attempt was made to conceal the happenings in, and the progress of, the war. Parliament, the Press and the Radio gave daily, and at times hourly, reports of what was happening. In the emergency, no information was supplied to India or to the world as to how the internal disturbance was being dealt with. In fact foreign correspondents were expelled unless they subscribed to "guidelines", that is, unless they agreed to report only what the government wanted them to report. Further, it was clear from the statements made from time to time, of which the Supreme Court could not have been unaware, (since in its judgment the court spoke of what they were given to understand) that the emergency was said to be necessary "to enforce discipline", which meant (i) locking up political opponents and even party men who criticized the emergency; (ii) the prohibition of strikes and lock-outs, the freezing of wages, dearness allowance, dividends and the like; (iii) and the disciplining of the press which was never to be permitted the freedom it had enjoyed since Independence — purposes wholly foreign to the exercise of the emergency power. To take notice of these facts was not to "weave cobwebs of suspicion" about facts known to the executive and not known to the world at large, of which Mr. Justice Chandrachud spoke; it was to do what s. 114 of the Evidence Act permits a Court to do, namely, to presume the existence of any fact which it thinks is likely to have happened, regard being had to the common course of natural events, human conduct and public and private business. It is also to take notice of facts of which the Court can take judicial notice under the Evidence Act.

16. The considerations referred to at the end of para 15 lead us to the second factor which in the *Habeas Corpus Case* set the Supreme Court on the path of deviation. It is a remarkable feature of the majority judgments that they cited *Halliday's Case* and *Liversidge's Case* to derive support for their view, by pointing out that even in a country whose Constitution is based on the rule of law and which prizes and effectively protects personal liberty, preventive detention ordered on subjective satisfaction has been upheld. Our analysis of those two judgments will have shown the reader that those cases give no support for the view taken by the majority in the *Habeas Corpus Case* having regard to the circumstances and conditions which were before them. And it is a remarkable feature of the majority judgment in that case that they are totally silent about the various safeguards pointed out in those cases which led the House of Lords to uphold preventive detention at a time of mortal peril. The total absence of those safeguards in India ought to have struck any judge:

(i) In *Liversidge's Case* Lord Wright justly pointed out that if powers of preventive detention were generally abused or were abused even in a single case, a free press, and Parliament would be effective to make the sense of the community prevail and the relevant regulation would be amended. Gajendragadkar J. said much the same thing in *Makhan Singh's Case*: ". . . it may be permissible to observe that in a democratic State, the effective safeguards against the abuse of executive power whether in peace or in emergency is ultimately to be found in the existence of an *enlightened, vigilant and vocal public opinion.*"[56] (italics supplied) The Supreme Court could have taken judicial notice of the fact from various judgments of the High Courts, and in the guidelines laid down by the censors and the orders issued by Commissioners of Police, that in the Emergency with which the Court was concerned, enlightened, vigilant and vocal public opinion was effectively destroyed by censorship; and the voice of the people's representatives in Parliament did not reach the people, because the speeches made by those opposed to the government could not be reported. It is enough to give one example to be found in the Law Reports to show that no one was permitted to criticize the Emergency in public. In *N. P. Nathwani* v. *Commr. of Police*,[57] the Joint Secretary to Government submitted in his affidavit that:

"I say that the said Emergency was declared due to internal disturbance and criticising the Emergency would be tantamount to supporting internal disturbance." And again, "I submit that discussion of Emergency at a public meeting *per se* in a given case as in the present case can affect the maintenance of internal security and public order."[58]

Dealing with this submission, Tulzapurkar J. observed:

"If that be so, it would stand to reason that permission if asked for would normally be granted for public meetings where the Emergency in question would be supported or applauded, certainly not where it will be criticised, which in the words of Justice Black (in the case of *Wieman* v. *Updegraff* [(1952) 97 L. ed. 216 at p. 223] means that the State Government is preserving the freedoms (of speech and discussion) not for all but only for "the cringing and the craven'. That such a state of affairs was far from the mind of Pandit Jawaharlal Nehru will be clear from the following passage which may be extracted from his 'Selected Works', vol. 7 at pp. 410-411 which is very eloquent: 'In countries with a democratic background the greatest value is therefore attached to civil liberty and people of the most diverse and mutually hostile opinions join together in a common attempt to protect this foundation of all liberty and activity. They consider it their duty to resist even the suppression of any opinion or activity to which they are personally opposed for once the principle of such suppression is admitted it can be, and frequently has been, extended to all manner of other activities. In America, England and France powerful civil liberties unions, of a purely non-party character, have been established to resist all such encroachments and their activities have borne substantial fruit. In India the necessity for such a joint effort embracing all groups and individuals, who believe in civil liberties, is obviously even more necessary than elsewhere'."[59]

(ii) The power to order preventive detention in England was vested in one person, the Home Secretary, who was accountable to Parliament. During the Second World War, the Home Secretary assured the Commons that every case of preventive detention was personally considered by him; further, the Regulation obliged him to inform the House of the detention orders referred to the advisory committee and the number of cases in which he had not followed the committee's advice. In India, in addition to the Central Government or the State Governments, which could pass orders of preventive detention, detention orders could be passed by (a) a district magistrate; (b) an additional district magistrate empowered in this behalf by the State government, and (c) Commissioners of Police wherever they have been appointed. In short, the orders could be passed by hundreds of officers not accountable to Parliament or the State Legislatures.

(iii) Except for persons detained under preventive detention orders passed before 25th July, 1975, the detenu was not to be supplied the grounds of his detention and had no right to make any representation to an *independent advisory board.* We have seen that the majority in *Liversidge's Case* emphasized the safeguard provided by the detainee's right to make representation to an independent tribunal which

---

[56] ('64) A.SC. at pp. 403-4.
[57] 78 Bom.L.R. 1. (Decided on December 15/16, 1975).
[58] ibid. p. 70. [59] ibid. pp. 74-75.

could consider the justice or the necessity of passing the detention order or of continued detention.

(iv) The majority in *Liversidge's Case* made it clear that a *mala fide* order or an arrest as the result of mistaken identity could be successfully brought before the courts. The High Courts had said the same thing in India.

(v) It ought to have surprised any Court in India that powers not considered necessary in times of war [the Chinese aggression (1961) and the Indo-Pakistani wars of 1965 and 1971] should have been assumed in an emergency caused by "internal disturbance".

All these were facts of which judicial notice could be taken, and if they have been set out above, it is because decided cases show that if any other view was possible, a court would not uphold unfettered power entrusted to hundreds of persons without the safeguard of the detainee knowing the grounds of his detention with a *right* to make a representation against the order to an *independent* and *impartial* body. That another view was possible is clear from the dissenting judgment of Mr. Justice Khanna. That such other view was the right view has been shown in Appendix IV of this book. In the result, as to preventive detention, the *Habeas Corpus* judgment is clearly wrong and is out of line with the judgments of the Supreme Court on preventive detention even during an emergency.

Epilogue

17. The tale of the Supreme Court and preventive detention in the *Habeas Corpus Case* was to have a strange sequel. The courage, resolution and good sense of the ordinary men and women of India not only swept Mrs. Gandhi's government out of office and power, but also brought home to the Supreme Court *the reality of the emergency power and preventive detention* — very different from the "realistic appraisal of the emergency provisions" of which Mr. Justice Chandrachud had spoken in the *Habeas Corpus Case*. For, how else are we to explain the following words of Mr. Justice Bhagwati in *Rajasthan* v. *Union*?[60] He said:

"This is not a case where just an ordinary defeat has been suffered by the ruling party in a State at the elections to the Lok Sabha. There, has been a total rout of candidates belonging to the ruling party. In some of the Plaintiff-States, the ruling party has not been able to secure a single seat. Never in the history of this country has such a clear and unequivocal verdict been given by the people, never a more massive vote of no-confidence in the ruling party. When there is such crushing defeat suffered by the ruling party and the people have expressed themselves categorically against its policies, *it is symptomatic of complete alienation between the Government and the people. It is axiomatic that no Government can function efficiently and effectively in accordance with the Constitution in a democratic set up unless it enjoys the good will and support of the people. Where there is a wall of estrangement which divides the Government from the people, and there is resentment and antipathy in the hearts of the people against the Government,* it is not at all unlikely that it may lead to instability and even the administration may be paralysed."[61] (italics supplied)

18. In the events that have happened subsequently, which are well-known, the reader will have noticed the strong language in which Mr. Justice Bhagwati passed judgment on Mrs. Gandhi and her government. That she herself was defeated showed that the question of the love and affection of the people for her did not arise. Notice the words he used: "not just an ordinary defeat"; "a crushing defeat"; "a total rout"; "never a more massive vote of no confidence in the ruling party"; "complete alienation between the Government and the people"; "a wall of estrangement which divides the Government and the people"; "resentment and antipathy in the hearts of the people against the Government".

---

[60] (1978) 1 S.C.R. 1, ('77) A.SC. 1361.
[61] (1978) 1 S.C.R. at p. 85, ('77) A.SC. at p. 1416.

This Picture and That

19. In the elections for the Lok Sabha held in 1980, Mrs. Gandhi and her party won a landslide victory, and Mrs. Gandhi became the Prime Minister. Forgetting the judgment he had passed against her and her Government, Mr. Justice Bhagwati sent his congratulations to her in a letter which was later published by a newspaper. In that letter he set out his reactions to her victory, exactly as he had set out in his judgment his reactions to her and her party's defeat. The three opening paragraphs and the concluding paragraph of that letter are set out below, for the letter made judicial history, whether for good or evil it is not necessary to inquire:

"May I offer you my heartiest congratulations on your resounding victory in the elections and your triumphant return as the Prime Minister of India. It is a most remarkable achievement of which you, your friends and well-wishers can be justly proud. It is a great honour to be the Prime Minister of a country like India, but it is equally a heavy responsibility particularly since you have to build a new order out of the wreckage of the old. You have fortunately the greatest asset which any politician can ever possess, namely, the love and affection of the people.

"Your party has been voted to power with an amazing outburst, amounting almost to an avalanche, of affection and enthusiasm and now the people are looking forward to an era where there will be for everyone freedom from want and destitution. You have become the symbol of the hopes and aspirations of the poor, hungry millions of India who had so far nothing to hope for and nothing to live for and who are now looking up to you for lifting them from dirt and squalor, freeing them from poverty and ignorance.

"It is a very difficult task which lies ahead of you, but I am sure that with your iron will and firm determination, uncanny insight and dynamic vision, grand administrative capacity and vast experience, overwhelming love and affection of the people and, above all, a heart which is identified with the misery of the poor and the weak, you will be able to steer the ship of the nation safely to its cherished goal and the glorious vision of the founding fathers of the Constitution will become a living reality.

* * *

"Today the reddish glow of the rising sun is holding out the promise of a bright sunshine. May that sunshine fill our hearts with joy and bring comfort and cheer to the poor half-naked, hungry millions of our countrymen. That is my prayer to God on this occasion."

AN EPILOGUE : 1980-1983

Mrs. Gandhi's return to power

1. In 1980, Mrs. Gandhi returned to power as Prime Minister after a landslide victory for herself and her Congress (I) party in the elections to the Lok Sabha. On Feb. 17, 1980, a Proclamation under Art. 356 was issued dissolving the Legislative Assemblies of Bihar, Gujarat, Madhya Pradesh, Maharashtra, Orissa, Punjab, Rajasthan and Tamil Nadu ("the nine States"). In the elections which followed, the Congress (I) came to power in all these States except Tamil Nadu. This electoral success was largely attributed to the Prime Minister's son, Sanjay, who was looked upon as the heir apparent to the Prime Ministership. He was also responsible for bringing several "Sanjay men" into Parliament and the State Legislatures, and was credited with having a share in the appointment of Chief Ministers and Ministers in several States. However, his untimely death on June 23, 1980, when the plane he was piloting crashed, left the Sanjay men without a leader, and without the support of the second most powerful person in India. This leaderless following has created political problems which are outside the scope of this book. In this Epilogue, I will deal with the problem of Centre-State relations, which has emerged after Mrs. Gandhi's return to power.

2. This problem falls into three parts:

(*a*) What is the relation of the Union Government to (i) State Ministries which belong to the same party as the party in power in the Union, and (ii) to State Ministries which belong to a different party or parties?

(*b*) What is the position of the Governor of a State under the Constitution and his position *vis-a-vis* the President, (that is, the Union Government) at whose pleasure he holds his office?

(*c*) A Cabinet form of Government in the Union and in the States requires certain norms of conduct from Ministers. What happens if those norms are broken?

3. In our federal Constitution, the well being of the people of India as a whole does not necessarily coincide with the well being of the people of the States, for if it did coincide, we would have had a unitary, and not a federal Constitution. There are matters of national interest affecting the well being of all the people of India, like defence or foreign affairs, and in respect of these matters exclusive legislative and executive power has been assigned to Parliament and the Union Government. But there are matters of special and local interest in each State, and these matters are assigned exclusively to State Legislatures and the State Governments. Since our Parliamentary Cabinet form of Government is worked by different parties, or combinations of parties, it is obvious that the party in power in the Union is entitled to follow its own policies and priorities in matters assigned to Parliament and the Union Government so long as those policies conform to the Constitution and the law; and the same is true, *mutatis mutandis,* of parties in power in the States. The Constitution of India does not permit national policies to be pursued contrary to the special interests and well being of the people of the States in matters exclusively assigned to the States, if the State Ministries do their duty under the Constitution. The oath of the President and the oath of a Governor highlight this obvious truth. The President swears, among other things, that he will devote himself to the service and well being of the people of India, and the Governor swears to devote himself to the service and well being of the people of the State of which he is a Governor. To use the party machinery to make State Ministries toe the line of the Union Government regardless of the special interests of the people of the State is not only to violate the Constitution, but to subvert the federal principle by extra constitutional means.

4. This problem came to the fore when fresh elections were ordered in the nine States in 1980. Was this action of the Union Government justified, or was it against the federal principle embodied in our Constitution? For, under our parliamentary form of government, a duly elected ministry is entitled to continue to hold office for the full term as long as it commands the confidence of the Legislative Assembly and functions according to the Constitution and the laws. The mere fact that another party has come to power at the Centre as the result of an election is not by itself a ground for denying to State Ministries the right to serve for the full term. It may be said that Mrs. Gandhi's government was only following the "precedent" set by the Janata Government. But before a "precedent" can be relied upon it must be relevant to the situation to which it is to be applied. However, the "precedent" was not relevant, because the state of the Constitution, the state of the Nation, and the situation in the country facing Mrs. Gandhi on her return to power, bore no resemblance to the situation facing the Janata Government when it came to power. In Parliament, and in most of the State Legislatures, Mrs. Gandhi's party commanded large majorities, but by Constitutional Amendments the duration of Parliament and State Legislatures was extended by one year, securing to the party one extra year of power if it was decided not to call fresh elections. The Constitution was subverted by using the forms of law. The situation in October 1975 was described by Mr. M. C. Chagla in a speech delivered on Oct. 12, 1975 when inaugurating the All India Civil Liberties Conference.[1] His qualifications to speak on the subject were of the highest. Jawaharlal Nehru said in a letter to a critic of Chagla that "(Chagla) is the kind of person who brings credit wherever he may be placed".[2] He had been a distinguished Judge and Chief Justice of the Bombay High Court, Ambassador to the United States, High Commissioner to the United Kingdom, Minister for Foreign Affairs, and twice Minister of Education in the Union Government. In a brave speech, made during the Emergency, in which he never sacrificed light to heat, though he spoke with a passion for freedom, he said, as we now know, that there was no justification for proclaiming the Emergency. He continued:

"What is the position today? Freedom of the Press has two aspects. First, to get information and the second to purvey that information. Today, both these channels are completely blocked. No paper or no news from outside can come into this country which contains any reference to India hostile to the Prime Minister or to the Government." In Bombay, "nobody knows that Kuldip Nayar (a leading journalist) was ever arrested, nobody knows the trial took place, nobody knows that he was released and nobody knows what judgment was delivered. If you want to read the judgment you will have to go to 'London Times' which published extracts from Kuldip Nayar's Case. Therefore, even with regard to the parliamentary proceedings which are privileged under the Constitution, even with regard to Court proceedings, after all it is a public trial, and the public has a right to know what happens in a Court of Law, the censorship will not permit a trial to be reported, arguments to be reported or the speeches in Parliament reported. This is censorship.[3] . . . The question I ask myself is: Do I want to live in a police State? Or, do I want to live in a democratic State? Because, this is a police State, when a man cannot write what he wants and have it published, when newspapers cannot publish any comments, when people can be sent behind bars without any reasons being assigned, there is not much difference between a police State as existing elsewhere and what is existing here today. . . . Do I as an Indian who looks upto Mahatma Gandhi as his leader, as his preceptor want to walk with my head up, a free man saying what I like, writing what I like, expressing my comments, my dissent, my criticism or am I going to be controlled, restricted and put down by an omnipotent Government? . . . For, civil liberties mean those essential features of the society which make it a free society. Absence of civil liberties makes a society a captive society, a society which is governed not by laws but my men, a society which can be trampled upon by Government. And remember this, there is no worse form of dictatorship than what is known as constitutional dictatorship. If behind the facade

---

[1] The speech is reproduced in the Epilogue to his Autobiography, *Roses in December*, (published in 1978), at pp. 33-43.

[2] Chagla, *Roses in December*, p. 502.

[3] Chagla, *Roses in December — Epilogue*, pp. 38-39.

of the Constitution, technically observing the rules that the Constitution lays down and violating the spirit you build up a dictatorship, then you have a constitutional dictatorship. . . . 'when the night is darkest, the dawn is not far'. I see the night very dark. I am an old man and have not got long to live. But, you younger people will see the dawn. . . . For thousands of years we have survived invasions. We have survived all sorts of troubles and I think that we will survive both Indira Gandhi and her dictatorship."[4]

If the night was dark in Oct. 1975, it was to grow darker yet when in the *Habeas Corpus Case* the Supreme Court decided, in effect, that life and personal liberty in India were without the protection of law during the Emergency.

5. It was this situation which the Janata Government inherited when the people rejected Mrs. Gandhi and her party in the Lok Sabha elections in 1977. The elections were not fought on local issues of special interest to each State: they were fought on one single issue — "Democracy *v.* Dictatorship". People in the States voted unmistakably for democracy. In *Rajasthan* v. *Union*[5] Fazal Ali J. analysed the results of the Lok Sabha elections: in Uttar Pradesh, Bihar, Punjab, Haryana and Himachal Pradesh out of 85, 54, 13, 10 and 4 constituencies respectively, the Congress party did not secure a single seat; in Madhya Pradesh and Rajasthan out of 40 and 25 seats respectively the Congress secured only 1 seat each; in West Bengal out of 42 seats the Congress secured only 3 seats and in Orissa out of 21 seats the Congress secured only 4. Fazal Ali J. continued:

"It would thus appear that in the nine States . . . the Congress party was practically routed. It is also clear that the voters who voted for the candidates standing for the Lok Sabha in the States were more or less the same who had voted the Congress party in the State Assemblies during the previous elections."[6]

Fazal Ali J. summed up the result as follows:

"Thus, summarising the position in short, it is clear —

(1) that grave emergency was clamped on the whole country;
(2) that civil liberties were withdrawn to a great extent;
(3) that important fundamental rights of the people were suspended;
(4) that strict censorship on the press was placed; and
(5) that the judicial powers were crippled to a large extent.

In the new elections the Congress party suffered a major reverse in the nine States and the people displayed complete lack of confidence in the Congress party. The cumulative effect of the circumstances mentioned above may lead to a reasonable inference that the people had given a massive verdict not only against the Congress candidates who fought the elections to the Lok Sabha but also to the policies and ideologies followed by the Congress Governments as a whole whether at the Centre or in the States during the twenty months preceding the elections."[7]

This sober judicial summary was made in May, 1977. The three Shah Commission[8] Reports which appeared between March and August 1978 with their grim tale of terror and gross abuse of legislative, constituent and executive power gave content to the summary which Fazal Ali J. made from facts of common knowledge and matters of judicial notice.

6. In the 1977 elections to the Lok Sabha, the Janata Party had pledged itself to restore democratic freedoms and to put the Constitution back on the rails. The total rejection of Mrs. Gandhi and her Congress party in five out of the nine States,

---

[4] ibid. pp. 42-43.
[5] ('77) A.SC. 1361.
[6] ibid. p. 1438.
[7] ibid.
[8] Called after its Chairman, Mr. J. C. Shah, a former Supreme Court Judge, and Chief Justice of India. The Reports must remain our principal source of information about the happenings during the Emergency. The Reports have been withdrawn by the Union Government after Mrs. Gandhi came back to power. The finding of the Commission were based on official documents, supplemented by the evidence on oath of numerous witnesses. No attempt has been made to show that the findings were not correct.

and the near total rejection in the remaining four States was a massive mandate to the Janata Party to redeem its pledges. But the end for which the people of the nine States had voted could not be achieved by Parliament and the Union Government alone since democratic freedoms had been destroyed not merely by oppressive laws and executive action but also by amendments to the Constitution, which amendments Parliament could not repeal by itself. For, although constitutional amendments can be initiated only in either House of Parliament, nevertheless in the very important matters specified in Art. 368(2), provisos (*a*) to (*e*), ratification of not less than half the number of States is necessary. And this put in issue the conduct during the Emergency of Congress Ministries in the nine States, as well as the actions of Congress members in the legislatures of those States. Congress Ministers vied with one another to do Mrs. Gandhi's bidding, no matter how unlawful, oppressive or violative of the Constitution and the law. After all, did not the Congress President, Mr. Barooah, say "India is Indira and Indira is India". The State Ministries, with the support of their Legislatures, not only violated the Constitution and the Laws by executive action, but were willing participators in enacting the 39th and the 42nd Amendments into law by ratifying them at the bidding of Mrs. Gandhi.

7. The Janata Government was thus confronted with two important considerations. To allow the Congress Ministries in the nine States, after the massive vote of no confidence in them and their ways, would be looked upon by the people who had put the Janata Government into power as a great betrayal, for how could the oppressors of the preceding 20 months be allowed to remain in power after their actions and policies had been rejected? Again, what justice was to be expected from the petty tyrants of yesterday if they remained in power and authority? Secondly, to set the Constitution back on the rails it was necessary for the people of the nine States to express their will again at State elections if their mandate to free the Constitution from subversive amendments was to become effective. Both these considerations made fresh elections in the nine States necessary and inevitable. The results showed that the people were of the same mind as they had been when they had voted Mrs. Gandhi and her party out of power in the Union. They had willed the end in the Lok Sabha elections; they also willed the means in the State elections by putting the Janata Party in power in their States. As we have seen, the Janata Government dismantled the apparatus of tyranny, and restored the Constitution to its original position, by enacting the 43rd and the 44th Amendments. Mrs. Gandhi and her party had used the forms of the law in the unfree atmosphere of the Emergency to destroy some of the most valuable features of our free democratic Constitution. The Janata Government and the Janata State Ministries restored and strengthened our free democratic Constitution not merely by using the forms of law but by giving effect to the twice expressed will of the people. This was a massive achievement which cannot be forgotten because the Janata Government came to an end as a result of internal dissensions.

8. In the 1980 Lok Sabha elections the situation which faced Mrs. Gandhi was very different. She worked under a free Constitution, with the freedom of the press, the independence and the powers of the Judiciary, the rule of law and provisions for fair and free elections restored. Her landslide victory in the Lok Sabha elections in 1980 represented the swing of the electoral pendulum; it marked the dissatisfaction of the people with the Janata Government's failure to implement firmly its policies because of internal differences. The unsatisfactory working of a State Government, without violating the Constitution and the laws, is not a ground for imposing the President's rule on the States as will presently appear. In the result, the ordering of fresh elections in the States was violative of the federal principle of our Constitution; it is a precedent which ought not to be followed.

9. This leads us to consider the relations between the Union and the State Executive when both belong to the same party. Under our federal Constitution, the Prime Minister is appointed by the President, and, normally, he calls upon the leader of the party or group of parties which commands a majority in the Lok

Sabha; and the Governor appoints the Chief Minister for the State on the same lines. The Prime Minister submits the names of his ministers to the President, and the Chief Minister submits such names to the Governor of the State. If the same party is in power in the Centre and the States, how is the Chief Minister to be selected? Mrs. Gandhi, as the leader of the Congress (I) party in India, has treated the Chief Ministers, as the Mogul Emperors treated the Governors of various *subas* or provinces, namely, as deriving their authority from him on their appointment, and therefore removable by him at pleasure. If the party agreed on a Chief Minister who had her approval, he was appointed Chief Minister, and the Council of Ministers were appointed with her concurrence. If there was no agreement, the party in the State legislatures went through the ritual of leaving the selection to Mrs. Gandhi, and her nominee was appointed. She appointed Chief Ministers and removed them, as she appointed Governors and transferred them. However, a new factor came into play. The "dissidents" made their appearance. They belonged to the Congress (I) party in the State Legislature, but felt free to attack the Chief Minister or launch a campaign for his removal — a strange distortion of the parliamentary Cabinet system of Government. I will take Maharashtra as the clearest and the best example of the evils which flowed from the Prime Minister appointing Chief Ministers in Congress (I) Ministries and the reactions it produced at long last in the States.

10. After the 1980 State elections, Mrs. Gandhi appointed Mr. A. R. Antulay as Chief Minister. In August, 1981, Mr. Arun Shourie, a distinguished journalist, published an article in the *Indian Express*, entitled "Indira Gandhi as Commerce".[9] The article charged Mr. Antulay with abuse of power in allotting cement, which was an essential commodity in short supply, to big builders as *quid pro quo* for donations made to the trusts which he had created, contrary to the guidelines laid down for the equitable distribution of cement, and particulars of certain payments were given. A petition was filed by P. B. Samant and others against the State of Maharashtra, Mr. Antulay and the Union of India, in respect of arbitrary and *mala fide* distribution of cement by Mr. Antulay contrary to law, and as a *quid pro quo* for donations made to the trusts created by Mr. Antulay. The petition was admitted by Justice Pratap and on January 12, 1982, it was allowed by Justice Lentin. He rejected the version of the State and Mr. Antulay that no allocations of cement were made by Mr. Antulay; he held that the petitioners' charge of arbitrariness against Mr. Antulay in making allocations of cement was justified; he further held that nexus and *quid pro quo* between allotments made by Mr. Antulay in favour of certain builders and donations made by them directly or indirectly was established, and that once nexus and *quid pro quo* were manifest, *mala fides* on the part of Mr. Antulay was a natural sequiter. On the day the judgment was delivered, Mr. Antulay resigned, it would appear under the directions of Mrs. Gandhi. In view of recent events to be noted later, it is necessary to observe that the State and Mr. Antulay appealed from Justice Lentin's judgment. On 10th June, 1982, Justices S. K. Desai and B. L. Rele (who delivered the leading judgment) dismissed the appeal and upheld the aforesaid findings of Justice Lentin. After the appeal Court delivered its judgment, the Governor of Maharashtra, acting on his own discretion as directed by the Court in another proceeding, after giving a full hearing to Mr. Antulay, gave his sanction to the applicants, by a reasoned speaking order, to prosecute Mr. Antulay for offences under the Prevention of Corruption Act. The thing to note is that after his resignation his public position had not improved but had greatly worsened. Two Courts found his statement on oath that he had not allotted cement to be untrue by reference to documentary evidence. The Appeal Court confirmed the findings of Justice Lentin against him. The Governor gave his

---

[9] The title had reference to a trust created by Mr. Antulay not as Chief Minister but as an individual. The trust was registered with the Charity Commissioner as "Indira Gandhi Pratibha Pratishthan obviously to trade on her name. Mrs. Gandhi said that permission to use her name had not been obtained and her name was dropped from the name of the trust.

sanction to prosecute him under the Prevention of Corruption Act. Can such a person without winning the appeal to the Supreme Court from the High Court's judgment, and being found not guilty in criminal prosecution hold office as Minister or as Chief Minister? This question is considered and answered in para 12 below.

11. On the resignation of Mr. Antulay, Mrs. Gandhi chose Mr. Babasaheb Bhosale to be the Chief Minister of Maharashtra. Almost from the start a dissident group attacked Mr. Bhosale day in and day out; signature campaigns were started against and for Mr. Bhosale, and later, a campaign "Bhosale must go" was mounted. For almost a year the normal functioning of the Council of Ministers was semi-paralysed. The Chief Minister and ministers shuttled to and from Bombay to Delhi: at times they "camped" in Delhi. At last the campaign succeeded and Mr. Bhosale resigned. But before his successor could be appointed, far reaching events had taken place. Even in the 1977 Lok Sabha elections, Andhra Pradesh and Karnataka had stood by Mrs. Gandhi. In the State elections held in Andhra Pradesh and Karnataka the results announced on Jan. 5, 1983 showed that the Congress (I) had been routed in Andhra Pradesh, and had suffered a substantial defeat in Karnataka. It is reasonable to believe that these States and their people resented being treated as the obedient servants of the Union Government. The impact of these defeats on electing the successor to Mr. Bhosale was immediate. Mrs. Gandhi announced that if there were differences in the Congress (I) party in the State Legislature about appointing a leader, she would not nominate a leader, even if asked to do so. Observers from the Congress (I) party were sent from Delhi to secure a concensus, but a contest could not be avoided, for Mr. Antulay announced his decision to contest the election. Members of the Congress party in the Legislature conveyed in confidence their preference to the Congress observers sent from Delhi, and Mr. Vasantdada Patil was declared to be the leader of the Congress Party and the Chief Minister of Maharashtra. Mr. Antulay called the "election" a "fraud".

12. For the proper functioning of the Cabinet form of Government which we have adopted, the most disturbing feature of the "election" is the candidature of Mr. Antulay for leadership and for the Chief Ministership. Chief Ministers and Ministers occupy high offices of public trust, and the standard of conduct and character demanded of them is best described in their oath of office: ". . . I will faithfully and conscientiously discharge my duties as a Minister for the State (of Maharashtra) and that I will do right to all manner of people in accordance with the Constitution and the law without fear or favour, affection or ill will". It follows from the findings of two Courts that Mr. Antulay had acted directly contrary to the terms of his oath. Does our constitutional scheme permit such a person to become a Minister or Chief Minister without destroying public faith in a government of which he is a member? It is clear that our founding fathers would have looked upon such a situation as an outrage. In the Life Assurance Corporation Inquiry held by Chief Justice Chagla, he found that the deal by which the L.I.C. purchased shares from Mundhra was suspicious, that proper formalities had not been observed, that the directive for the investment was given by the Finance Secretary, but the responsibility for it must be assumed by the Finance Minister (Mr. T. T. Krishnamachari) and that the real purpose of the deal seemed to be to help Mundhra rather than to advance the interests of the Corporation.[10] Mr. Krishnamachari was a close friend of Jawaharlal Nehru whose loyalty to his friends was well known. Says Chagla:

"When it came to the question of T. T. K.'s resignation I know that he (Nehru) had set his face firmly against it; and I also know first hand that it was entirely due to Maulana Azad's intervention that the Prime Minister was compelled to call for the resignation of his Finance Minister. Azad is reported to have told Nehru that *it would cause a national scandal* if after the disclosures of my report he continued to retain T. T. K. in the Cabinet."[11] (italics supplied)

---

[10] Chagla, *Roses in December*, p. 207. [11] ibid. p. 211.

These are the standards which have ensured respect for, and the survival of, the Cabinet form of government in Great Britain, as also in Canada, Australia and New Zealand which adopted the British model, as our founding fathers did in our Constitution.

The reader will have noticed that Mr. Krishnamachari's responsibility for the wrong doing of the officers of his department was constitutional, not personal. The finding of the two Courts fixes personal responsibility on Mr. Antulay. He was found to have allotted a scarce and controlled commodity not equitably as required by the law; but arbitrarily and *mala fide* as a *quid pro quo* for donations to his trusts. If the retention of Mr. Krishnamachari in the Cabinet would cause a national scandal, notwithstanding that his responsibility was constitutional and not personal, how does one describe the scandal, national and international, which would be caused by making a person Chief Minister after two Courts have held him guilty of abuse of power and grave personal wrong doing? What respect would a ministry led by him in Maharashtra command in India, and among countries of the Commonwealth who have adopted the Westminster model as we have done? Again, the reputation of an All India Party is also directly involved. Can such a party allow such a person, belonging to the party, to stand as a candidate for Chief Ministership without injury to the Party, the State and the Country? If such a person stands as a candidate, the most obvious course for the party is to expel him from the party for proposing to follow a line of conduct which must bring the party into disrepute. If for any reason this obvious course is not adopted, the only other alternative is for the Congress Party to officially repudiate his candidature as injurious to the party, to the State, and to the country. No doubt the problem did not call for an immediate solution since Mr. Antulay was defeated. But a solution of it must be found and announced soon if the respect for our democratic institutions inside and outside our country is not to be lost. Caesar's wife, the saying goes, must be above *suspicion;* she certainly could not survive *proof* of her guilt.

13. The events leading up to the resignation of Mr. Antulay and the subsequent events including the sanction given by the Governor to prosecute Mr. Antulay have raised important questions about the position of the Governor. The present position is very unsatisfactory: however, it will be fully discussed in the Chapter on the Union and the State Executive in Vol. II of this book. It is enough to say that the tenure of the Governor's office at the pleasure of the President, which means, in effect, the Union Government, is most unsatisfactory and is liable to grave abuse. The Governor has certain powers under the Constitution. He is not the servant or agent of the President as the Governor's oath of office clearly shows. The exercise of the power to remove or transfer a Governor must cause grave disquiet in the public mind. For example, during the hearing of the petition against Mr. Antulay, culminating in the judgment of Mr. Justice Lentin, Air Chief Marshal Mehra was the Governor of Maharashtra. Under the Constitution, a report by the Governor on the working of the State Ministry is contemplated: Art. 356. Sometime after Mr. Antulay resigned, Mr. Mehra was transferred from the office of Governor of Maharashtra to the office of the Governor of Rajasthan, without any reason being assigned, and he was succeeded by Air Chief Marshal Latif, who, after the appeal Court judgment, gave sanction to prosecute Mr. Antulay as stated earlier. Public confidence in the position and authority of the Governor would be gravely impaired by happenings of this kind. It will be suggested in a full discussion on the Governor's position that his tenure of office must be fixed for a period of 5 years. However, as there is no provision in our Constitution for removing a Governor by a process of impeachment, such as there is for the removal of the President, such a provision should be introduced in the Constitution.

14. As this Epilogue was going to the Press, Mrs. Gandhi announced in Parliament on March 24, 1983 the appointment of a Commission to be presided over by a former Supreme Court judge, Justice Sarkaria, to review Centre-State relations and to recommend such changes as may be appropriate within the constitutional framework. The appointment of the Commission is clearly a step in the right direction.

15. The recent happenings in Assam, and the holding of elections in a situation where it became necessary to call out para military forces in the first instance and the army in the second, have raised acute political controversies especially as the elections left a trail of blood and arson and left about 5,000 people dead. A discussion of that controversy is outside the scope of this book. But there is one clear question of constitutional law which emerges about "foreigners" who "infiltrated" into India from what was East Pakistan, now Bangla Desh. If it is admitted, or proved, that people came from East Pakistan to India after January 26, 1950, they are not citizens of India and cannot be on the electoral roll for the elections to State or Union Legislatures, because under Art. 326 only citizens are entitled to be registered as voters. Article 6 of the Constitution provided for Indian citizenship of persons who, or either of whose parents or grand-parents were born in India, *and* who had migrated from Pakistan (i.e. East and West Pakistan) before 19th July, 1948 and after 19th July 1948 but before the commencement of the Constitution on January 26, 1950. After the commencement of the Constitution the only way in which such migrants can become Indian citizens is by registration or naturalization under ss. 5 and 6 of the Citizenship Act respectively.

THE CONSTITUTION OF INDIA

AUTHOR'S NOTE

As indicated in the Preamble, the Constitution of India was enacted on November 26, 1949, and Arts. 5, 6, 7, 8, 9, 60, 324, 366, 367, 379, 380, 388, 391, 392, 393 and 394 came into force on that day. The rest of the Constitution came into force on January 26, 1950: (Art. 394).

The Constitution has been amended on forty-four occasions by the following amending Acts:

1. The Constitution (1st Amendment) Act, 1951, which came into force on 18th June, 1951, but certain provisions were made retrospective.
2. The Constitution (2nd Amendment) Act, 1952, which came into force on 1st May, 1953.
3. The Constitution (3rd Amendment) Act, 1954, which came into force on 22nd February, 1955.
4. The Constitution (4th Amendment) Act, 1955, which came into force on 27th April, 1955, but certain provisions were made retrospective.
5. The Constitution (5th Amendment) Act, 1955, which came into force on 24th December, 1955.
6. The Constitution (6th Amendment) Act, 1955, which came into force on 11th September, 1956.
7. The Constitution (7th Amendment) Act, 1956, which came into force on 1st November, 1956.
8. The Constitution (8th Amendment) Act, 1959, which came into force on 5th January, 1960.
9. The Constitution (9th Amendment) Act, 1960, which came into force on the appointed day, the appointed day being 17th January, 1961.
10. The Constitution (10th Amendment) Act, 1961, which came into force on 16th August, 1961.
11. The Constitution (11th Amendment) Act, 1961, which came into force on 19th December, 1961.
12. The Constitution (12th Amendment) Act, 1962, which was deemed to have come into force on 20th December, 1961.
13. The Constitution (13th Amendment) Act, 1962, which came into force on 1st December, 1963.
14. The Constitution (14th Amendment) Act, 1962, which came into force on 28th December, 1962, but certain provisions of which were brought into force as from 16th August, 1962.
15. The Constitution (15th Amendment) Act, 1963, which came into force on 5th October, 1963.
16. The Constitution (16th Amendment) Act, 1963, which came into force on 5th October, 1963.
17. The Constitution (17th Amendment) Act, 1964, which came into force on 20th June, 1964, but certain provisions of which were made retrospective.
18. The Constitution (18th Amendment) Act, 1966, which came into force on 27th August, 1966.
19. The Constitution (19th Amendment) Act, 1966, which came into force on 11th December, 1966.
20. The Constitution (20th Amendment) Act, 1966, which came into force on 22nd December, 1966.
21. The Constitution (21st Amendment) Act, 1967, which came into force on 10th April, 1967.
22. The Constitution (22nd Amendment) Act, 1969, which came into force on 25th September, 1969.
23. The Constitution (23rd Amendment) Act, 1969, which came into force on 23rd January, 1970.

24. The Constitution (24th Amendment) Act, 1971, which came into force on 5th November, 1971.
25. The Constitution (25th Amendment) Act, 1971, which came into force on 20th April, 1972.
26. The Constitution (26th Amendment) Act, 1971, which came into force on 28th December, 1971.
27. The Constitution (27th Amendment) Act, 1971 parts whereof came into force on 30th December, 1971 and the other parts came into force on 28th February, 1972.
28. The Constitution (28th Amendment) Act, 1972, which came into force from 29th August, 1972.
29. The Constitution (29th Amendment) Act, 1972, which came into force on 9th June, 1972.
30. The Constitution (30th Amendment) Act, 1972, which came into force from 27th February, 1973.
31. The Constitution (31st Amendment) Act, 1973 which came into force from 17th October, 1973.
32. The Constitution (32nd Amendment) Act, 1973 which came into force from 3rd May, 1974.
33. The Constitution (33rd Amendment) Act, 1974 which came into force from 10th May, 1974.
34. The Constitution (34th Amendment) Act, 1974 which came into force from 7th September, 1974.
35. The Constitution (35th Amendment) Act, 1974 which came into force from 22nd February, 1975.
36. The Constitution (36th Amendment) Act, 1975 which came into force from 16th May, 1975.
37. The Constitution (37th Amendment) Act, 1975 which came into force from 3rd May, 1975.
38. The Constitution (38th Amendment) Act, 1975 which came into force from 1st August, 1975.
39. The Constitution (39th Amendment) Act, 1975 which came into force from 10th August, 1975.
40. The Constitution (40th Amendment) Act, 1976 which came into force from 27th May, 1976.
41. The Constitution (41st Amendment) Act, 1976 which came into force from 7th November, 1976.
42. The Constitution (42nd Amendment) Act, 1976 which came into force from 18th December, 1976.
43. The Constitution (43rd Amendment) Act, 1977 which came into force from 13th April, 1978.
44. The Constitution (44th Amendment) Act, 1978 parts whereof came into force from 10th June 1979, and certain other parts came into force from 20th June 1979 and 1st August 1979 respectively.

The provisions of all the various amendments referred to above have been incorporated in the text of the Constitution printed in this work. For convenience of reference the various amended or repealed provisions have been given in foot notes in appropriate places so that the state of the law at any given time can be ascertained with minimum inconvenience. As the effect of the various amending Acts and Orders has been fully indicated in the text, those Acts and Orders have not been re-printed.

References to corresponding provisions in the Government of India Act, 1935, are indicated at the bottom of each Article for convenience of reference.

References to statutory provisions have been given under Entries in the 7th Schedule, where the Union Legislature has made the requisite declaration, and asserted the power of Parliament to legislate with respect to specified industries, highways, etc.

The Constitution applies to the State of Jammu and Kashmir with certain exceptions and modifications as provided in article 370 and the Constitution (Application to Jammu and Kashmir) Order, 1954, which has been included as an Appendix to the text of the Constitution. The exceptions and modifications specified in this Order are with reference to the text of the Constitution on the 20th day of June, 1964 as amended by the subsequent amendments to the Constitution which have been made applicable to the State (vide clause 2 of the Order). As some of the amendments made in the Constitution during the period from the 20th day of June, 1964 to the 10th day of August, 1975 [the date of assent of the Constitution (Thirty-ninth Amendment) Act, 1975] and all the amendments made thereafter have not yet been applied to the State of Jammu and Kashmir, a re-statement of the exceptions and modifications has been included in the said Appendix.

THE CONSTITUTION OF INDIA

PREAMBLE

WE, THE PEOPLE OF INDIA, having solemnly resolved to constitute India into a [1][SOVEREIGN SOCIALIST SECULAR DEMOCRATIC REPUBLIC] and to secure to all its citizens:

JUSTICE, social, economic and political;

LIBERTY of thought, expression, belief, faith and worship;

EQUALITY of status and of opportunity;

and to promote among them all

FRATERNITY assuring the dignity of the individual and the [2][unity and integrity of the Nation];

IN OUR CONSTITUENT ASSEMBLY this twenty-sixth day of November, 1949, do HEREBY ADOPT, ENACT AND GIVE TO OURSELVES THIS CONSTITUTION.

PART I

THE UNION AND ITS TERRITORY

1. *Name and territory of the Union.*—(1) India, that is Bharat, shall be a Union of States.

[3][(2) The States and the territories thereof shall be as specified in the First Schedule.]

(3) The territory of India shall comprise—

(*a*) the territories of the States;

[4][(*b*) the Union territories specified in the First Schedule; and]

(*c*) such other territories as may be acquired.

2. *Admission or establishment of new States.*—Parliament may by law admit into the Union, or establish, new States on such terms and conditions as it thinks fit.

[s. 290, G.I. Act]

[5]**2A.** [*Sikkim to be associated with the Union.*] *Rep. by the Constitution (Thirty-sixth Amendment) Act,* 1975, s. 5 (*w.e.f.* 26-4-1975).

3. *Formation of new States and alteration of areas, boundaries or names of existing States.*—Parliament may by law—

(*a*) form a new State by separation of territory from any State or by uniting two or more States or parts of States or by uniting any territory to a part of any State;

(*b*) increase the area of any State;

(*c*) diminish the area of any State;

(*d*) alter the boundaries of any State;

(*e*) alter the name of any State:

---

[1] Subs. by the Const. (42nd Am.) Act, 1976, s. 2, for "SOVEREIGN DEMOCRATIC REPUBLIC" (w.e.f. 3-1-1977).

[2] Subs. by s. 2, *ibid.*, for "unity of the Nation" (w.e.f. 3-1-1977).

[3] Subs. by the Const. (7th Am.) Act, 1956, s. 2, w.e.f. 1.11.1956 for:

(2) The States and the territories thereof shall be the States and their territories specified in Parts A, B and C of the First Schedule.

[4] Subs. by s. 2, *ibid.*, for:

(*b*) the territories specified in Part D of the First Schedule.

[5] Ins. by the Const. (35th Am.) Act, 1974, s. 2 (w.e.f. 1.3.1975). The repealed Article read as follows:

2A. *Sikkim to be associated with the Union.*—Sikkim, which comprises the territories specified in the Tenth Schedule, shall be associated with the Union on the terms and conditions set out in that Schedule.

[6][Provided that no Bill for the purpose shall be introduced in either House of Parliament except on the recommendation of the President and unless, where the proposal contained in the Bill affects the area, boundaries or name of any of the States[7] * * *, the Bill has been referred by the President to the Legislature of that State for expressing its views thereon within such period as may be specified in the reference or within such further period as the President may allow and the period so specified or allowed has expired.] [s. 290, G.I. Act]

[8][*Explanation I.*—In this article, in clauses (*a*) to (*e*), "State" includes a Union territory, but in the proviso, "State" does not include a Union territory.

Explanation II.—The power conferred on Parliament by clause (*a*) includes the power to form a new State or Union territory by uniting a part of any State or Union territory to any other State or Union territory.]

4. *Laws made under articles 2 and 3 to provide for the amendment of the First and the Fourth Schedules and supplemental, incidental and consequential matters.*—(1) Any law referred to in article 2 or article 3 shall contain such provisions for the amendment of the First Schedule and the Fourth Schedule as may be necessary to give effect to the provisions of the law and may also contain such supplemental, incidental and consequential provisions (including provisions as to representation in Parliament and in the Legislature or Legislatures of the State or States affected by such law) as Parliament may deem necessary.

(2) No such law as aforesaid shall be deemed to be an amendment of this Constitution for the purposes of article 368.

PART II

CITIZENSHIP

5. *Citizenship at the commencement of the Constitution.*—At the commencement of this Constitution, every person who has his domicile in the territory of India and—

(*a*) who was born in the territory of India; or

(*b*) either of whose parents was born in the territory of India; or

(*c*) who has been ordinarily resident in the territory of India for not less than five years immediately preceding such commencement,

shall be a citizen of India.

6. *Rights of citizenship of certain persons who have migrated to India from Pakistan.*—Notwithstanding anything in article 5, a person who has migrated to the territory of India from the territory now included in Pakistan shall be deemed to be a citizen of India at the commencement of this Constitution if—

(*a*) he or either of his parents or any of his grand-parents was born in India as defined in the Government of India Act, 1935 (as originally enacted); and

(*b*) (*i*) in the case where such person has so migrated before the nineteenth day of July, 1948, he has been ordinarily resident in the territory of India since the date of his migration, or

(*ii*) in the case where such person has so migrated on or after the nineteenth day of July, 1948, he has been registered as a citizen of India by an officer appointed in that behalf by the Government of the Dominion of

---

[6] Subs. by the Const. (5th Am.) Act, 1955, s. 2, w.e.f. 11.9.1956 for:

Provided that no Bill for the purpose shall be introduced in either House of Parliament except on the recommendation of the President and unless, where the proposal contained in the Bill affects the boundaries of any State or States specified in Part A or Part B of the First Schedule or the name or names of any such State or States, the views of the Legislature of the State or, as the case may be, of each of the States both with respect to the proposal to introduce the Bill and with respect to the provisions thereof have been ascertained by the President.

[7] The words and letters "specified in Part A or Part B of the First Schedule" omitted by the Cons. (7th Am.) Act, 1956, s. 29 and Sch. w.e.f. 1.11.1956.

[8] Ins. by the Const. (18th Am.) Act, 1966, s. 2, w.e.f. 27.8.1966.

India on an application made by him therefor to such officer before the commencement of this Constitution in the form and manner prescribed by that Government:

Provided that no person shall be so registered unless he has been resident in the territory of India for at least six months immediately preceding the date of his application.

7. *Rights of citizenship of certain migrants to Pakistan.*—Notwithstanding anything in articles 5 and 6, a person who has after the first day of March, 1947, migrated from the territory of India to the territory now included in Pakistan shall not be deemed to be a citizen of India:

Provided that nothing in this article shall apply to a person who, after having so migrated to the territory now included in Pakistan, has returned to the territory of India under a permit for resettlement or permanent return issued by or under the authority of any law and every such person shall for the purposes of clause (*b*) of article 6 be deemed to have migrated to the territory of India after the nineteenth day of July, 1948.

8. *Rights of citizenship of certain persons of Indian origin residing outside India.*—Notwithstanding anything in article 5, any person who or either of whose parents or any of whose grand-parents was born in India as defined in the Government of India Act, 1935 (as originally enacted), and who is ordinarily residing in any country outside India as so defined shall be deemed to be a citizen of India if he has been registered as a citizen of India by the diplomatic or consular representative of India in the country where he is for the time being residing on an application made by him therefor to such diplomatic or consular representative, whether before or after the commencement of this Constitution, in the form and manner prescribed by the Government of the Dominion of India or the Government of India.

9. *Persons voluntarily acquiring citizenship of a foreign State not to be citizens.*—No person shall be a citizen of India by virtue of article 5, or be deemed to be a citizen of India by virtue of article 6 or article 8, if he has voluntarily acquired the citizenship of any foreign State.

10. *Continuance of the rights of citizenship.*—Every person who is or is deemed to be a citizen of India under any of the foregoing provisions of this Part shall, subject to the provisions of any law that may be made by Parliament, continue to be such citizen.

11. *Parliament to regulate the right of citizenship by law.*—Nothing in the foregoing provisions of this Part shall derogate from the power of Parliament to make any provision with respect to the acquisition and termination of citizenship and all other matters relating to citizenship.[9]

PART III

FUNDAMENTAL RIGHTS

General

12. *Definition.*—In this Part, unless the context otherwise requires, "the State" includes the Government and Parliament of India and the Government and the Legislature of each of the States and all local or other authorities within the territory of India or under the control of the Government of India.

13. *Laws inconsistent with or in derogation of the fundamental rights.*—(1) All laws in force in the territory of India immediately before the commencement of this Constitution, in so far as they are inconsistent with the provisions of this Part, shall, to the extent of such inconsistency, be void.

---

[9] Parliament has enacted the Citizenship Act, 1955, regulating rights of citizenship.

(2) The State shall not make any law which takes away or abridges the rights conferred by this Part and any law made in contravention of this clause shall, to the extent of the contravention, be void.

(3) In this article, unless the context otherwise requires,—

(a) "law" includes any Ordinance, order, bye-law, rule, regulation, notification, custom or usage having in the territory of India the force of law;

(b) "laws in force" includes laws passed or made by a Legislature or other competent authority in the territory of India before the commencement of this Constitution and not previously repealed, notwithstanding that any such law or any part thereof may not be then in operation either at all or in particular areas.

[10][(4) Nothing in this article shall apply to any amendment of this Constitution made under article 368.]

Right to Equality

14. *Equality before law.*—The State shall not deny to any person equality before the law or the equal protection of the laws within the territory of India.

15. *Prohibition of discrimination on grounds of religion, race, caste, sex or place of birth.*—(1) The State shall not discriminate against any citizen on grounds only of religion, race, caste, sex, place of birth or any of them.

(2) No citizen shall, on grounds only of religion, race, caste, sex, place of birth or any of them, be subject to any disability, liability, restriction or condition with regard to—

(a) access to shops, public restaurants, hotels and places of public entertainment; or

(b) the use of wells, tanks, bathing ghats, roads and places of public resort maintained wholly or partly out of State funds or dedicated to the use of the general public.

(3) Nothing in this article shall prevent the State from making any special provision for women and children.

[11][(4) Nothing in this article or in clause (2) of article 29 shall prevent the State from making any special provision for the advancement of any socially and educationally backward classes of citizens or for the Scheduled Castes and the Scheduled Tribes.] [s. 298, G.I. Act]

16. *Equality of opportunity in matters of public employment.*—(1) There shall be equality of opportunity for all citizens in matters relating to employment or appointment to any office under the State.

(2) No citizen shall, on grounds only of religion, race, caste, sex, descent, place of birth, residence or any of them, be ineligible for, or discriminated against in respect of, any employment or office under the State.

(3) Nothing in this article shall prevent Parliament from making any law prescribing, in regard to a class or classes of employment or appointment to an office [12][under the Government of, or any local or other authority within, a State or Union territory, any requirement as to residence within that State or Union territory] prior to such employment or appointment.

(4) Nothing in this article shall prevent the State from making any provision for the reservation of appointments or posts in favour of any backward class of citizens which, in the opinion of the State is not adequately represented in the services under the State.

---

[10] Ins. by the Const. (24th Am.) Act, 1971, s. 2, w.e.f. 5.11.1971.

[11] Added by the Const. (1st Am.) Act, 1951, s. 2, w.e.f. 18.6.1951.

[12] Subs. by the Constitution (Seventh Amendment) Act, 1956, s. 29 and Sch., for "under any State specified in the First Schedule or any local or other authority within its territory, any requirement as to residence within that State", w.e.f. 1.11.1956.

(5) Nothing in this article shall affect the operation of any law which provides that the incumbent of an office in connection with the affairs of any religious or denominational institution or any member of the governing body thereof shall be a person professing a particular religion or belonging to a particular denomination.

[s. 275, 298, G.I. Act]

17. *Abolition of Untouchability.*—"Untouchability" is abolished and its practice in any form is forbidden. The enforcement of any disability arising out of "Untouchability" shall be an offence punishable in accordance with law.

18. *Abolition of titles.*—(1) No title, not being a military or academic distinction, shall be conferred by the State.

(2) No citizen of India shall accept any title from any foreign State.

(3) No person who is not a citizen of India shall, while he holds any office of profit or trust under the State, accept without the consent of the President any title from any foreign State.

(4) No person holding any office of profit or trust under the State shall, without the consent of the President, accept any present, emolument, or office of any kind from or under any foreign State.

Right to Freedom

19. *Protection of certain rights regarding freedom of speech, etc.*—(1) All citizens shall have the right—

(*a*) to freedom of speech and expression;

(*b*) to assemble peaceably and without arms;

(*c*) to form associations or unions;

(*d*) to move freely throughout the territory of India;

(*e*) to reside and settle in any part of the territory of India;[13] [and]

[14]* * * *

(*g*) to practise any profession, or to carry on any occupation, trade or business.

[15][(2) Nothing in sub-clause (*a*) of clause (1) shall affect the operation of any existing law, or prevent the State from making any law, in so far as such law imposes reasonable restrictions on the exercise of the right conferred by the said sub-clause in the interests of [16][the sovereignty and integrity of India,] the security of the State, friendly relations with foreign States, public order, decency or morality, or in relation to contempt of court, defamation or incitement to an offence.]

(3) Nothing in sub-clause (*b*) of the said clause shall affect the operation of any existing law in so far as it imposes, or prevent the State from making any law imposing, in the interests of [16][the sovereignty and integrity of India or] public

---

[13] Ins. by the Const. (44th Am.) Act, 1978, s. 2 (w.e.f. 20.6.1979).

[14] Sub-cl. (*f*) omitted by s. 2, *ibid*, w.e.f. 20.6.1979. The original sub-Article was as follows: "(f) to acquire, hold and dispose of property; and"

[15] Subs. by the Const. (1st Am.) Act, 1951, s. 3, for cl. (2) (with retrospective effect), on 18.6.1951, for:

(2) Nothing in sub-clause (*a*) of clause (1) shall affect the operation of any existing law in so far as it relates to, or prevent the State from making any law relating to libel, slander, defamation, contempt of Court or any matter which offends against decency or morality or which undermines the security of, or tends to overthrow, the State.

Sec. 3(2) of the Am. Act also provides:

No law in force in the territory of India, immediately before the commencement of the Constitution which is consistent with the provisions of article 19 of the Constitution as amended by sub-section (1) of this section shall be deemed to be void, or ever to have become void, on the ground only that, being a law which takes away or abridges the right conferred by sub-clause (*a*) of clause (1) of the said article, its operation was not saved by clause (2) of that article as originally enacted.

Explanation.—In this sub-section, the expression "law in force" has the same meaning as in clause (1) of article 13 of the Constitution.

[16] Ins. by the Const. (16th Am.) Act, 1963, s. 2.

order, reasonable restrictions on the exercise of the right conferred by the said sub-clause.

(4) Nothing in sub-clause (*c*) of the said clause shall affect the operation of any existing law in so far as it imposes, or prevent the State from making any law imposing, in the interests of [16][the sovereignty and integrity of India or] public order or morality, reasonable restrictions on the exercise of the right conferred by the said sub-clause.

(5) Nothing in [17][sub-clauses (*d*) and (*e*)] of the said clause shall affect the operation of any existing law in so far as it imposes, or prevent the State from making any law imposing, reasonable restrictions on the exercise of any of the rights conferred by the said sub-clauses either in the interests of the general public or for the protection of the interests of any Scheduled Tribe.

(6) Nothing in sub-clause (*g*) of the said clause shall affect the operation of any existing law in so far as it imposes, or prevent the State from making any law imposing, in the interests of the general public, reasonable restrictions on the exercise of the right conferred by the said sub-clause, and, in particular, [18][nothing in the said sub-clause shall affect the operation of any existing law in so far as it relates to, or prevent the State from making any law relating to,—

(*i*) the professional or technical qualifications necessary for practising any profession or carrying on any occupation, trade or business, or

(*ii*) the carrying on by the State, or by a corporation owned or controlled by the State, of any trade, business, industry or service, whether to the exclusion, complete or partial, of citizens or otherwise].

20. *Protection in respect of conviction for offences.*—(1) No person shall be convicted of any offence except for violation of a law in force at the time of the commission of the act charged as an offence, nor be subjected to a penalty greater than that which might have been inflicted under the law in force at the time of the commission of the offence.

(2) No person shall be prosecuted and punished for the same offence more than once.

(3) No person accused of any offence shall be compelled to be a witness against himself.

21. *Protection of life and personal liberty.*—No person shall be deprived of his life or personal liberty except according to procedure established by law.

[19]**22.** *Protection against arrest and detention in certain cases.*—(1) No person who is arrested shall be detained in custody without being informed, as soon as may be, of the grounds for such arrest nor shall he be denied the right to consult, and to be defended by, a legal practitioner of his choice.

---

[17] Subs. by the Const. (44th Am.) Act, 1978, s. 2, for "sub-clauses (*d*), (*e*) and (*f*)" (w.e.f. 20-6-1979).

[18] Subs. by the Const. (1st Am.) Act, 1951, w.e.f. 18.6.1951 for:

nothing in the said sub-clause shall affect the operation of any existing law in so far as it prescribes or empowers any authority to prescribe, the professional or technical qualifications necessary for practising any profession or carrying on any occupation, trade or business.

[19] On the enforcement of s. 3 of the Const. (44th Am.) Act, 1978, Art. 22 shall stand amended as directed in s. 3 of that Act. The text of s. 3 of that Act is as follows:

[3. *Amendment of article* 22.—In article 22 of the Constitution,—

(*a*) for clause (4), the following clause shall be substituted, namely:—

'(4) No law providing for preventive detention shall authorise the detention of a person for a longer period than two months unless an Advisory Board constituted in accordance with the recommendations of the Chief Justice of the appropriate High Court has reported before the expiration of the said period of two months that there is in its opinion sufficient cause for such detention:

Provided that an Advisory Board shall consist of a Chairman and not less than two other members, and the Chairman shall be

(2) Every person who is arrested and detained in custody shall be produced before the nearest magistrate within a period of twenty-four hours of such arrest excluding the time necessary for the journey from the place of arrest to the court of the magistrate and no such person shall be detained in custody beyond the said period without the authority of a magistrate.

(3) Nothing in clauses (1) and (2) shall apply—

(*a*) to any person who for the time being is an enemy alien; or

(*b*) to any person who is arrested or detained under any law providing for preventive detention.

(4) No law providing for preventive detention shall authorise the detention of a person for a longer period than three months unless—

(*a*) an Advisory Board consisting of persons who are, or have been, or are qualified to be appointed as, Judges of a High Court has reported before the expiration of the said period of three months that there is in its opinion sufficient cause for such detention:

Provided that nothing in this sub-clause shall authorise the detention of any person beyond the maximum period prescribed by any law made by Parliament under sub-clause (*b*) of clause (7); or

(*b*) such person is detained in accordance with the provisions of any law made by Parliament under sub-clauses (*a*) and (*b*) of clause (7).

(5) When any person is detained in pursuance of an order made under any law providing for preventive detention, the authority making the order shall, as soon as may be, communicate to such person the grounds on which the order has been made and shall afford him the earliest opportunity of making a representation against the order.

(6) Nothing in clause (5) shall require the authority making any such order as is referred to in that clause to disclose facts which such authority considers to be against the public interest to disclose.

(7) Parliament may by law prescribe—

(*a*) the circumstances under which, and the class or classes of cases in which, a person may be detained for a period longer than three months

---

a serving Judge of the appropriate High Court and the other members shall be serving or retired Judges of any High Court:

Provided further that nothing in this clause shall authorise the detention of any person beyond the maximum period prescribed by any law made by Parliament under sub-clause (*a*) of clause (7).

Explanation.—In this clause, "appropriate High Court" means,—

(*i*) in the case of the detention of a person in pursuance of an order of detention made by the Government of India or an officer or authority subordinate to that Government, the High Court for the Union territory of Delhi;

(*ii*) in the case of the detention of a person in pursuance of an order of detention made by the Government of any State (other than a Union territory), the High Court for that State; and

(*iii*) in the case of the detention of a person in pursuance of an order of detention made by the administrator of a Union territory or an officer or authority subordinate to such administrator, such High Court as may be specified by or under any law made by Parliament in this behalf.';

(*b*) in clause (7),—

(*i*) sub-clause (*a*) shall be omitted;

(*ii*) sub-clause (*b*) shall be re-lettered as sub-clause (*a*); and

(*iii*) sub-clause (*c*) shall be re-lettered as sub-clause (*b*) and in the sub-clause as so re-lettered, for the words, brackets, letter and figure "sub-clause (*a*) of clause (4)", the word, brackets and figure "clause (4)" shall be substituted.]

Note: This amendment had not been brought into force till this text of the Constitution was in the press.

under any law providing for preventive detention without obtaining the opinion of an Advisory Board in accordance with the provisions of sub-clause (*a*) of clause (4);

(*b*) the maximum period for which any person may in any class or classes of cases be detained under any law providing for preventive detention; and

(*c*) the procedure to be followed by an Advisory Board in an inquiry under sub-clause (*a*) of clause (4).

Right against Exploitation

23. *Prohibition of traffic in human beings and forced labour.*—(1) Traffic in human beings and *begar* and other similar forms of forced labour are prohibited and any contravention of this provision shall be an offence punishable in accordance with law.

(2) Nothing in this article shall prevent the State from imposing compulsory service for public purposes, and in imposing such service the State shall not make any discrimination on grounds only of religion, race, caste or class or any of them.

24. *Prohibition of employment of children in factories, etc.*—No child below the age of fourteen years shall be employed to work in any factory or mine or engaged in any other hazardous employment.

Right to Freedom of Religion

25. *Freedom of conscience and free profession, practice and propagation of religion.*—(1) Subject to public order, morality and health and to the other provisions of this Part, all persons are equally entitled to freedom of conscience and the right freely to profess, practise and propagate religion.

(2) Nothing in this article shall affect the operation of any existing law or prevent the State from making any law—

(*a*) regulating or restricting any economic, financial, political or other secular activity which may be associated with religious practice;

(*b*) providing for social welfare and reform or the throwing open of Hindu religious institutions of a public character to all classes and sections of Hindus.

Explanation I.—The wearing and carrying of *kirpans* shall be deemed to be included in the profession of the Sikh religion.

Explanation II.—In sub-clause (*b*) of clause (2), the reference to Hindus shall be construed as including a reference to persons professing the Sikh, Jaina or Buddhist religion, and the reference to Hindu religious institutions shall be construed accordingly.

26. *Freedom to manage religious affairs.*—Subject to public order, morality and health, every religious denomination or any section thereof shall have the right—

(*a*) to establish and maintain institutions for religious and charitable purposes;

(*b*) to manage its own affairs in matters of religion;

(*c*) to own and acquire movable and immovable property; and

(*d*) to administer such property in accordance with law.

27. *Freedom as to payment of taxes for promotion of any particular religion.*—No person shall be compelled to pay any taxes, the proceeds of which are specifically appropriated in payment of expenses for the promotion or maintenance of any particular religion or religious denomination.

28. *Freedom as to attendance at religious instruction or religious worship in certain educational institutions.*—(1) No religious instruction shall be provided in any educational institution wholly maintained out of State funds.

(2) Nothing in clause (1) shall apply to an educational institution which is administered by the State but has been established under any endowment or trust which requires that religious instruction shall be imparted in such institution.

(3) No person attending any educational institution recognised by the State or receiving aid out of State funds shall be required to take part in any religious instruction that may be imparted in such institution or to attend any religious worship that may be conducted in such institution or in any premises attached thereto unless such person or, if such person is a minor, his guardian has given his consent thereto.

Cultural and Educational Rights

29. *Protection of interests of minorities.*—(1) Any section of the citizens residing in the territory of India or any part thereof having a distinct language, script or culture of its own shall have the right to conserve the same.

(2) No citizen shall be denied admission into any educational institution maintained by the State or receiving aid out of State funds on grounds only of religion, race, caste, language or any of them.

30. *Right of minorities to establish and administer educational institutions.*—(1) All minorities, whether based on religion or language, shall have the right to establish and administer educational institutions of their choice.

[20][(1A) In making any law providing for the compulsory acquisition of any property of an educational institution established and administered by a minority, referred to in clause (1), the State shall ensure that the amount fixed by or determined under such law for the acquisition of such property is such as would not restrict or abrogate the right guaranteed under that clause.]

(2) The State shall not, in granting aid to educational institutions, discriminate against any educational institution on the ground that it is under the management of a minority, whether based on religion or language.

[21]* * *

31. [*Compulsory acquisition of property.*] *Rep. by the Constitution (Forty-fourth Amendment) Act,* 1978, *s.* 6 (*w.e.f.* 20-6-1979).

[Article 31, which appeared under the sub-title "Right to Property", before its repeal by the Const. (44th Am.) Act, 1978, stood as follows]:

"**31.** *Compulsory acquisition of property.*—(1) No person shall be deprived of his property save by authority of law.

[22][(2) No property shall be compulsorily acquired or requisitioned save for a public purpose and save by authority of a law which provides for acquisition or requisitioning of the property for an amount which may be fixed by such law or which may be determined in accordance with such principles and given in such manner as may be specified in such law; and no such law shall be called in question in any

---

[20] Ins. by the Const. (44th Am.) Act, 1978, s. 4, w.e.f. 20.6.1979.

[21] The sub-heading *"Right to Property"* omitted by s. 5 ibid. w.e.f. 20.6.1979.

[22] Subs. by the Const. (25th Am.) Act, 1971, w.e.f. 20.4.1972 for:

(2) No property shall be compulsorily acquired or requisitioned save for a public purpose and save by authority of a law which provides for compensation for the property so acquired or requisitioned and either fixes the amount of the compensation or specifies the principles on which, and the manner in which, the compensation is to be determined and given; and no such law shall be called in question in any court on the ground that the compensation provided by that law is not adequate.

Prior to 27.4.1955, when the Const. (4th Am.) Act, 1955, came into force, sub-Art. (2) was as follows:—

(2) No property, movable or immovable, including any interest in, or in any company owning, any commercial or industrial undertaking, shall be taken possession of or acquired for public purposes under any law authorising the taking of such possession or such acquisition, unless the law provides for compensation for the property taken possession of or acquired and either fixes the amount of the compensation, or specifies the principles on which, and the manner in which, the compensation is to be determined and given.

court on the ground that the amount so fixed or determined is not adequate or that the whole or any part of such amount is to be given otherwise than in cash;

Provided that in making any law providing for the compulsory acquisition of any property of an educational institution established and administered by a minority, referred to in clause (1) of article 30, the State shall ensure that the amount fixed or determined under such law for the acquisition of such property is such as would not restrict or abrogate the right guaranteed under that clause.]

[23][(2A) Where a law does not provide for the transfer of the ownership or right to possession of any property to the State or to a corporation owned or controlled by the State, it shall not be deemed to provide for the compulsory acquisition or requisitioning of property, notwithstanding that it deprives any person of his property.]

[24][(2B) Nothing in sub-clause (*f*) of clause (1) of article 19 shall affect any such law as is referred to in clause (2).]

(3) No such law as is referred to in clause (2) made by the Legislature of a State shall have effect unless such law, having been reserved for the consideration of the President, has received his assent.

(4) If any Bill pending at the commencement of this Constitution in the Legislature of a State has, after it has been passed by such Legislature, been reserved for the consideration of the President and has received his assent, then, notwithstanding anything in this Constitution, the law so assented to shall not be called in question in any court on the ground that it contravenes the provisions of clause (2).

(5) Nothing in clause (2) shall affect—

(*a*) the provisions of any existing law other than a law to which the provisions of clause (6) apply, or

(*b*) the provisions of any law which the State may hereafter make—

(*i*) for the purpose of imposing or levying any tax or penalty, or

(*ii*) for the promotion of public health or the prevention of danger to life or property, or

(*iii*) in pursuance of any agreement entered into between the Government of the Dominion of India or the Government of India and the Government of any other country, or otherwise, with respect to property declared by law to be evacuee property.

(6) Any law of the State enacted not more than eighteen months before the commencement of this Constitution may within three months from such commencement be submitted to the President for his certification; and thereupon, if the President by public notification so certifies, it shall not be called in question in any court on the ground that it contravenes the provisions of clause (2) of this article or has contravened the provisions of sub-section (2) of section 299 of the Government of India Act, 1935." [s. 299, G.I. Act]

[25][*Saving of Certain Laws*]

[26][**31A.** *Saving of laws providing for acquisition of estates, etc.*—[27][(1) Notwithstanding anything contained in article 13, no law providing for—

(*a*) the acquisition by the State of any estate or of any rights therein or the extinguishment or modification of any such rights, or

---

[23] Inserted by the Const. (4th Am.) Act, 1955, w.e.f. 27.4.1955.
[24] Inserted by the Const. (25th Am.) Act, 1971, w.e.f. 20.4.1972.
[25] Ins. by the Const. (42nd Am.) Act, 1976, s. 3 w.e.f. 3.1.1977.
[26] Ins. by the Const. (1st Am.) Act, 1951, s. 4, with retrospective effect.
[27] Subs. by the Const. (4th Am.) Act, 1955, s. 3, for clause (1), with retrospective effect. The original clause (1) as inserted in 1951 was:

"(1) Notwithstanding anything in the foregoing provisions of this Part, no law providing for the acquisition by the State of any estate or of any rights therein or for the extinguishment or modification of any such rights shall

(*b*) the taking over of the management of any property by the State for a limited period either in the public interest or in order to secure the proper management of the property, or

(*c*) the amalgamation of two or more corporations either in the public interest or in order to secure the proper management of any of the corporations, or

(*d*) the extinguishment or modification of any rights of managing agents, secretaries and treasurers, managing directors, directors or managers of corporations, or of any voting rights of shareholders thereof, or

(*e*) the extinguishment or modification of any rights accruing by virtue of any agreement, lease or licence for the purpose of searching for, or winning, any mineral or mineral oil, or the premature termination or cancellation of any such agreement, lease or licence,

shall be deemed to be void on the ground that it is inconsistent with, or takes away or abridges any of the rights conferred by [28][article 14 or article 19]:

Provided that where such law is a law made by the Legislature of a State, the provisions of this article shall not apply thereto unless such law, having been reserved for the consideration of the President, has received his assent:

[29][Provided further that where any law makes any provision for the acquisition by the State of any estate and where any land comprised therein is held by a person under his personal cultivation, it shall not be lawful for the State to acquire any portion of such land as is within the ceiling limit applicable to him under any law for the time being in force or any building or structure standing thereon or appurtenant thereto, unless the law relating to the acquisition of such land, building or structure, provides for payment of compensation at a rate which shall not be less than the market value thereof.]

(2) In this article,—

[30][(*a*) the expression "estate" shall, in relation to any local area, have the same meaning as that expression or its local equivalent has in the existing law relating to land tenures in force in that area and shall also include—

(*i*) any *Jagir, inam* or *muafi* or other similar grant and in the States of [31][Tamil Nadu] and [32][Kerala,] any *janmam* right;

(*ii*) any land held under ryotwari settlement;

(*iii*) any land held or let for purposes of agriculture or for purposes ancillary thereto, including waste land, forest land, land for pas-

---

be deemed to be void on the ground that it is inconsistent with, or takes away or abridges any of the rights conferred by, any provisions of this Part:

Provided that where such law is a law made by the Legislature of a State, the provisions of this article shall not apply thereto unless such law, having been reserved for the consideration of the President, has received his assent."

[28] Subs. by the Const. (44th Am.) Act, 1978, s. 7, for "article 14, article 19 or article 31" (w.e.f. 20.6.1979).

[29] Ins. by the Const. (17th Am.) Act, 1964, s. 2, w.e.f. 20.6.1964.

[30] Subs. by the Const. (17th Am.) Act, 1964, s. 2, for sub-clause (*a*), on 20.6.1964 (with retrospective effect from 26.1.1950). As originally enacted by the Const. (1st Am.) Act, 1951, on 18.6.1951 w.e.f. 26.1.1950, sub-clause (*a*) was as follows:

(*a*) the expression "estate" shall, in relation to any local area, have the same meaning as that expression or its local equivalent has in the existing law relating to land tenures in force in that area, and shall also include any *jagir, inam* or *muafi* or other similar grant;

The Const. (4th Am.) Act, 1955, inserted on 27.4.1955, w.e.f. 26.1.1950, the following words at the end of the sub-clause:

"and in the States of Madras and Travancore-Cochin, any *janmam* right,"

[31] Subs. by the Madras State (Alteration of Name) Act, 1968 (53 of 1968), s. 4, for "Madras", w.e.f. 14.1.1969.

[32] Subs. by the Const. (7th Am.) Act, 1956, for "Travancore-Cochin" w.e.f. 1.11.1956.

ture or sites of buildings and other structures occupied by cultivators of land, agricultural labourers and village artisans;]

(b) the expression "rights", in relation to an estate, shall include any rights vesting in a proprietor, sub-proprietor, under-proprietor, tenure-holder, [33][*raiyat, under-raiyat*] or other intermediary and any rights or privileges in respect of land revenue.]

[34][**31B.** *Validation of certain Acts and Regulations.*—Without prejudice to the generality of the provisions contained in article 31A, none of the Acts and Regulations specified in the Ninth Schedule nor any of the provisions thereof shall be deemed to be void, or ever to have become void, on the ground that such Act, Regulation or provision is inconsistent with, or takes away or abridges any of the rights conferred by, any provisions of this Part, and notwithstanding any judgment, decree or order of any court or tribunal to the contrary, each of the said Acts and Regulations shall, subject to the power of any competent Legislature to repeal or amend it, continue in force.]

[35][**31C.** *Saving of laws giving effect to certain directive principles.*—Notwithstanding anything contained in article 13, no law giving effect to the policy of the State towards securing [36][all or any of the principles laid down in Part IV] shall be deemed to be void on the ground that it is inconsistent with, or takes away or abridges any of the rights conferred by [37][article 14 or article 19]; [38]*and no law containing a declaration that it is for giving effect to such policy shall be called in question in any court on the ground that it does not give effect to such policy:*

Provided that where such law is made by the Legislature of a State, the provisions of this article shall not apply thereto unless such law, having been reserved for the consideration of the President, has received his assent.]

[39]**31D.** [*Saving of laws in respect of anti-national activities.*] *Rep. by the Constitution* (*Forty-third Amendment*) *Act*, 1977, *s.* 2 (*w.e.f.* 13-4-1978).

---

[33] Ins. by the Const. (4th Am.) Act, 1955, s. 3, on 27.4.1955 w.e.f. 26.1.1950.

[34] Ins. by the Const. (1st Am.) Act, 1951, s. 5, w.e.f. 18.6.1951.

[35] Ins. by the Const. (25th Am.) Act, 1971, s. 3, w.e.f. 20.4.1972.

[36] Subs. by the Const. (42nd Am.) Act, 1976, s. 4, for "the principles specified in clause (b) or clause (c) of article 39" w.e.f. 3.1.1977.

[37] Subs. by the Const. (44th Am.) Act, 1978, s. 8, for "article 14, article 19 or article 31" w.e.f. 20.6.1979.

[38] In *Kesavananda Bharati* vs. *The State of Kerala* (1973) Supp. S.C.R. 1, the Supreme Court held the provision in italics to be invalid.

[39] Ins. by the Const. (42nd Am.) Act, 1976, s. 5 w.e.f. 3.1.1977. The repealed clause ran as follows:

"5. *Insertion of new article 31D.*—After article 31C of the Constitution and before the sub-heading *'Right to Constitutional Remedies'*, the following article shall be inserted, namely:—

'31D. *Saving of laws in respect of anti-national activities.*—(1) Notwithstanding anything contained in article 13, no law providing for—(*a*) the prevention of prohibition of anti-national activities; or (*b*) the prevention of formation of, or the prohibition of, anti-national associations,

shall be deemed to be void on the ground that it is inconsistent with, or takes away or abridges any of the rights conferred by, article 14, article 19 or article 31.

(2) Notwithstanding anything in this Constitution, Parliament shall have, and the legislature of a State shall not have, power to make laws with respect to any of the matters referred to in sub-clause (*a*) or sub-clause (*b*) of clause (1).

(3) Any law with respect to any matter referred to in sub-clause (*a*) or sub-clause (*b*) of clause (1) which is in force immediately before the commencement of section 5 of the Const. (42nd Am.) Act, 1976, shall continue in force until altered or repealed or amended by Parliament.

(4) In this article,—

(*a*) "association" means an association of persons;

(*b*) "anti-national activity" in relation to an individual or association, means any action taken by such individual or association—

(*i*) which is intended, or which supports any claim, to bring about, on any ground whatsoever, the cession of a part of the terri-

Right to Constitutional Remedies

32. *Remedies for enforcement of rights conferred by this Part.*—(1) The right to move the Supreme Court by appropriate proceedings for the enforcement of the rights conferred by this Part is guaranteed.

(2) The Supreme Court shall have power to issue directions or orders or writs, including writs in the nature of *habeas corpus, mandamus*, prohibition, *quo warranto* and *certiorari,* whichever may be appropriate, for the enforcement of any of the rights conferred by this Part.

(3) Without prejudice to the powers conferred on the Supreme Court by clauses (1) and (2), Parliament may by law empower any other court to exercise within the local limits of its jurisdiction all or any of the powers exercisable by the Supreme Court under clause (2).

(4) The right guaranteed by this article shall not be suspended except as otherwise provided for by this Constitution.

[40]**32A.** [*Constitutional validity of State laws not to be considered in proceedings under article* 32.] *Rep. by the Constitution (Forty-third Amendment) Act,* 1977, *s.* 3 (*w.e.f.* 13-4-1978).

33. *Power to Parliament to modify the rights conferred by this Part in their application to Forces.*—Parliament may by law determine to what extent any of the rights conferred by this Part shall, in their application to the members of the Armed Forces or the Forces charged with the maintenance of public order, be restricted or abrogated so as to ensure the proper discharge of their duties and the maintenance of discipline among them.

34. *Restriction on rights conferred by this Part while martial law is in force in any area.*—Notwithstanding anything in the foregoing provisions of this Part, Parliament may by law indemnify any person in the service of the Union or of a State or any other person in respect of any act done by him in connection with the maintenance or restoration of order in any area within the territory of India where

---

tory of India or the secession of part of the territory of India or which incites any individual or association to bring about such cession or secession;

(*ii*) which disclaims, questions, threatens, disrupts or is intended to threaten or disrupt the sovereignty and integrity of India or the security of the State or the unity of the nation;

(*iii*) which is intended, or which is part of a scheme which is intended, to overthrow by force the government as by law established;

(*iv*) which is intended, or which is part of a scheme which is intended, to create internal disturbance or the disruption of public services;

(*v*) which is intended, or which is part of a scheme which is intended, to threaten or disrupt harmony between different religious, racial, language or regional groups or castes or communities;

(c) "anti-national association" means an association—

(*i*) which has for its object any anti-national activity;

(*ii*) which encourages or aids persons to undertake or engage in any anti-national activity;

(*iii*) the members whereof undertake or engage in any anti-national activity'."

[40] Ins. by the Const. (42nd Am.) Act, 1976, s. 6, w.e.f. 1.2.1977. The repealed clause ran as follows:

"6. *Insertion of new article 32A.*—After article 32 of the Constitution, the following article shall be *inserted*, namely:—

'32A. *Constitutional validity of State laws not to be considered in proceedings under article 32.*—Notwithstanding anything in article 32, the Supreme Court shall not consider the constitutional validity of any State law in any proceedings under that article unless the constitutional validity of any Central law is also in issue in such proceedings'."

martial law was in force or validate any sentence passed, punishment inflicted, forfeiture ordered or other act done under martial law in such area.

35. *Legislation to give effect to the provisions of this Part.*—Notwithstanding anything in this Constitution,—

(*a*) Parliament shall have, and the Legislature of a State shall not have, power to make laws—

(*i*) with respect to any of the matters which under clause (3) of article 16, clause (3) of article 32, article 33 and article 34 may be provided for by law made by Parliament; and

(*ii*) for prescribing punishment for those acts which are declared to be offences under this Part;

and Parliament shall, as soon as may be after the commencement of this Constitution, make laws for prescribing punishment for the acts referred to in sub-clause (*ii*);

(*b*) any law in force immediately before the commencement of this Constitution in the territory of India with respect to any of the matters referred to in sub-clause (*i*) of clause (*a*) or providing for punishment for any act referred to in sub-clause (*ii*) of that clause shall, subject to the terms thereof and to any adaptations and modifications that may be made therein under article 372, continue in force until altered or repealed or amended by Parliament.

Explanation.—In this article, the expression "law in force" has the same meaning as in article 372.

PART IV

DIRECTIVE PRINCIPLES OF STATE POLICY

36. *Definition.*—In this Part, unless the context otherwise requires, "the State" has the same meaning as in Part III.

37. *Application of the principles contained in this Part.*—The provisions contained in this Part shall not be enforceable by any court, but the principles therein laid down are nevertheless fundamental in the governance of the country and it shall be the duty of the State to apply these principles in making laws.

38. *State to secure a social order for the promotion of welfare of the people.*—[41][(1)] The State shall strive to promote the welfare of the people by securing and protecting as effectively as it may a social order in which justice, social, economic and political, shall inform all the institutions of the national life.

[42][(2) The State shall, in particular, strive to minimise the inequalities in income, and endeavour to eliminate inequalities in status, facilities and opportunities, not only amongst individuals but also amongst groups of people residing in different areas or engaged in different vocations.]

39. *Certain principles of policy to be followed by the State.*—The State shall, in particular, direct its policy towards securing—

(*a*) that the citizens, men and women equally, have the right to an adequate means of livelihood;

(*b*) that the ownership and control of the material resources of the community are so distributed as best to subserve the common good;

(*c*) that the operation of the economic system does not result in the concentration of wealth and means of production to the common detriment;

(*d*) that there is equal pay for equal work for both men and women;

(*e*) that the health and strength of workers, men and women, and the tender age of children are not abused and that citizens are not forced by economic necessity to enter avocations unsuited to their age or strength;

---

[41] Art. 38 renumbered as cl. (1) thereof by the Const. (44th Am.) Act, 1978, s. 9 (w.e.f. 20.6.1979).

[42] Ins. by s. 9, *ibid.* (w.e.f. 20.6.1979).

[43][(*f*) that children are given opportunities and facilities to develop in a healthy manner and in conditions of freedom and dignity and that childhood and youth are protected against exploitation and against moral and material abandonment.]

[44][**39A.** *Equal justice and free legal aid.*—The State shall secure that the operation of the legal system promotes justice, on a basis of equal opportunity, and shall, in particular, provide free legal aid, by suitable legislation or schemes or in any other way, to ensure that opportunities for securing justice are not denied to any citizen by reason of economic or other disabilities.]

40. *Organisation of village panchayats.*—The State shall take steps to organise village panchayats and endow them with such powers and authority as may be necessary to enable them to function as units of self-government.

41. *Right to work, to education and to public assistance in certain cases.*—The State shall, within the limits of its economic capacity and development, make effective provision for securing the right to work, to education and to public assistance in cases of unemployment, old age, sickness and disablement, and in other cases of undeserved want.

42. *Provision for just and humane conditions of work and maternity relief.*—The State shall make provision for securing just and humane conditions of work and for maternity relief.

43. *Living wage, etc., for workers.*—The State shall endeavour to secure, by suitable legislation or economic organisation or in any other way, to all workers, agricultural, industrial or otherwise, work, a living wage, conditions of work ensuring a decent standard of life and full enjoyment of leisure and social and cultural opportunities and, in particular, the State shall endeavour to promote cottage industries on an individual or co-operative basis in rural areas.

[45][**43A.** *Participation of workers in management of industries.*—The State shall take steps, by suitable legislation or in any other way, to secure the participation of workers in the management of undertakings, establishments or other organisations engaged in any industry.]

44. *Uniform civil code for the citizens.*—The State shall endeavour to secure for the citizens a uniform civil code throughout the territory of India.

45. *Provision for free and compulsory education for children.*—The State shall endeavour to provide, within a period of ten years from the commencement of this Constitution, for free and compulsory education for all children until they complete the age of fourteen years.

46. *Promotion of educational and economic interests of Scheduled Castes, Scheduled Tribes and other weaker sections.*—The State shall promote with special care the educational and economic interests of the weaker sections of the people, and, in particular, of the Scheduled Castes and the Scheduled Tribes, and shall protect them from social injustice and all forms of exploitation.

47. *Duty of the State to raise the level of nutrition and the standard of living and to improve public health.*—The State shall regard the raising of the level of nutrition and the standard of living of its people and the improvement of public health as among its primary duties and, in particular, the State shall endeavour to bring about prohibition of the consumption except for medicinal purposes of intoxicating drinks and of drugs which are injurious to health.

---

[43] Subs. by the Const. (42nd Am.) Act, 1976, s. 7 for cl. (*f*), w.e.f. 3.1.1977. The original clause ran as follows:

"(*f*) that childhood and youth are protected against exploitation and against moral and material abandonment."

[44] Ins. by the Const. (42nd Am.) Act, 1976, s. 8 (w.e.f. 3.1.1977).

[45] Ins. by the Const. (42nd Am.) Act, 1976, s. 9 (w.e.f. 3.1.1977).

48. *Organisation of agriculture and animal husbandry.*—The State shall endeavour to organise agriculture and animal husbandry on modern and scientific lines and shall, in particular, take steps for preserving and improving the breeds, and prohibiting the slaughter, of cows and calves and other milch and draught cattle.

[46][**48A.** *Protection and improvement of environment and safeguarding of forests and wild life.*—The State shall endeavour to protect and improve the environment and to safeguard the forests and wild life of the country.]

49. *Protection of monuments and places and objects of national importance.*—It shall be the obligation of the State to protect every monument or place or object of artistic or historic interest, [47][declared by or under law made by Parliament] to be of national importance, from spoliation, disfigurement, destruction, removal, disposal or export, as the case may be.

50. *Separation of judiciary from executive.*—The State shall take steps to separate the judiciary from the executive in the public services of the State.

51. *Promotion of international peace and security.*—The State shall endeavour to—

(*a*) promote international peace and security;

(*b*) maintain just and honourable relations between nations;

(*c*) foster respect for international law and treaty obligations in the dealings of organised peoples with one another; and

(*d*) encourage settlement of international disputes by arbitration.

[48][PART IVA

FUNDAMENTAL DUTIES

51A. *Fundamental duties.* It shall be the duty of every citizen of India—

(*a*) to abide by the Constitution and respect its ideals and institutions, the National Flag and the National Anthem;

(*b*) to cherish and follow the noble ideals which inspired our national struggle for freedom;

(*c*) to uphold and protect the sovereignty, unity and integrity of India;

(*d*) to defend the country and render national service when called upon to do so;

(*e*) to promote harmony and the spirit of common brotherhood amongst all the people of India transcending religious, linguistic and regional or sectional diversities; to renounce practices derogatory to the dignity of women;

(*f*) to value and preserve the rich heritage of our composite culture;

(*g*) to protect and improve the natural environment including forests, lakes, rivers and wild life, and to have compassion for living creatures;

(*h*) to develop the scientific temper, humanism and the spirit of inquiry and reform;

(*i*) to safeguard public property and to abjure violence;

(*j*) to strive towards excellence in all spheres of individual and collective activity so that the nation constantly rises to higher levels of endeavour and achievement.]

---

[46] Ins. by the Const. (42nd Am.) Act, 1976, s. 10 (w.e.f. 3.1.1977).
[47] Subs. by the Const. (7th Am.) Act, 1956, s. 27, for "declared by Parliament by law".
[48] Ins. by the Const. (42nd Am.) Act, 1976, s. 11 (w.e.f. 3.1.1977).

PART V

THE UNION

CHAPTER I.—THE EXECUTIVE

The President and Vice-President

52. *The President of India.*—There shall be a President of India.

53. *Executive power of the Union.*—(1) The executive power of the Union shall be vested in the President and shall be exercised by him either directly or through officers subordinate to him in accordance with this Constitution.

(2) Without prejudice to the generality of the foregoing provision, the supreme command of the Defence Forces of the Union shall be vested in the President and the exercise thereof shall be regulated by law.

(3) Nothing in this article shall—

(*a*) be deemed to transfer to the President any functions conferred by any existing law on the Government of any State or other authority; or

(*b*) prevent Parliament from conferring by law functions on authorities other than the President. [s. 7, G.I. Act]

54. *Election of President.*—The President shall be elected by the members of an electoral college consisting of—

(*a*) the elected members of both Houses of Parliament; and

(*b*) the elected members of the Legislative Assemblies of the States.[49]

55. *Manner of election of President.*—(1) As far as practicable, there shall be uniformity in the scale of representation of the different States at the election of the President.

(2) For the purpose of securing such uniformity among the States *inter se* as well as parity between the States as a whole and the Union, the number of votes which each elected member of Parliament and of the Legislative Assembly of each State is entitled to cast at such election shall be determined in the following manner:—

(*a*) every elected member of the Legislative Assembly of a State shall have as many votes as there are multiples of one thousand in the quotient obtained by dividing the population of the State by the total number of the elected members of the Assembly;

(*b*) if, after taking the said multiples of one thousand, the remainder is not less than five hundred, then the vote of each member referred to in sub-clause (*a*) shall be further increased by one;

(*c*) each elected member of either House of Parliament shall have such number of votes as may be obtained by dividing the total number of votes assigned to the members of the Legislative Assemblies of the States under sub-clauses (*a*) and (*b*) by the total number of the elected members of both Houses of Parliament, fractions exceeding one-half being counted as one and other fractions being disregarded.

(3) The election of the President shall be held in accordance with the system of proportional representation by means of the single transferable vote and the voting at such election shall be by secret ballot.

[50][*Explanation.*—In this article, the expression "population" means the population as ascertained at the last preceding census of which the relevant figures have been published:

---

[49] See the Presidential and Vice-Presidential Elections Act, 1952.

[50] Subs. by the Const. (42nd Am.) Act, 1976, s. 12, for *Explanation* (w.e.f. 3.1.1977). The *Explanation*, as originally enacted, ran as follows:

"*Explanation.*—In this article, the expression "population" means the population as ascertained at the last preceding census of which the relevant figures have been published."

Provided that the reference in this *Explanation* to the last preceding census of which the relevant figures have been published shall, until the relevant figures for the first census taken after the year 2000 have been published, be construed as a reference to the 1971 census.]

56. *Term of office of President.*—(1) The President shall hold office for a term of five years from the date on which he enters upon his office:

Provided that—

(*a*) the President may, by writing under his hand addressed to the Vice-President, resign his office;

(*b*) the President may, for violation of the Constitution, be removed from office by impeachment in the manner provided in article 61;

(*c*) the President shall, notwithstanding the expiration of his term, continue to hold office until his successor enters upon his office.

(2) Any resignation addressed to the Vice-President under clause (*a*) of the proviso to clause (1) shall forthwith be communicated by him to the Speaker of the House of the People.

57. *Eligibility for re-election.*—A person who holds, or who has held office as President shall, subject to the other provisions of this Constitution be eligible for re-election to that office.

58. *Qualifications for election as President.*—(1) No person shall be eligible for election as President unless he—

(*a*) is a citizen of India,

(*b*) has completed the age of thirty-five years, and

(*c*) is qualified for election as a member of the House of the People.

(2) A person shall not be eligible for election as President if he holds any office of profit under the Government of India or the Government of any State or under any local or other authority subject to the control of any of the said Governments.

Explanation.—For the purposes of this article, a person shall not be deemed to hold any office of profit by reason only that he is the President or Vice-President of the Union or the Governor [51]* * of any State or is a Minister either for the Union or for any State.

59. *Conditions of President's office.*—(1) The President shall not be a member of either House of Parliament or of a House of the Legislature of any State, and if a member of either House of Parliament or of a House of the Legislature of any State be elected President, he shall be deemed to have vacated his seat in that House on the date on which he enters upon his office as President.

(2) The President shall not hold any other office of profit.

(3) The President shall be entitled without payment of rent to the use of his official residences and shall be also entitled to such emoluments, allowances and privileges as may be determined by Parliament by law and, until provision in that behalf is so made, such emoluments, allowances and privileges as are specified in the Second Schedule.

(4) The emoluments and allowances of the President shall not be diminished during his term of office.

60. *Oath or affirmation by the President.*—Every President and every person acting as President or discharging the functions of the President shall, before entering upon his office, make and subscribe in the presence of the Chief Justice of India or, in his absence, the seniormost Judge of the Supreme Court available, an oath or affirmation in the following form, that is to say—

"I, A. B., do $\frac{\text{swear in the name of God}}{\text{solemnly affirm}}$ that I will faithfully execute the

---

[51] The words "or Rajpramukh or Uparajpramukh" omitted by the Const. (7th Am.) Act, 1956, s. 29 and Sch.

office of President (or discharge the functions of the President) of India and will to the best of my ability preserve, protect and defend the Constitution and the law and that I will devote myself to the service and well-being of the people of India."

61. *Procedure for impeachment of the President.*—(1) When a President is to be impeached for violation of the Constitution, the charge shall be preferred by either House of Parliament.

(2) No such charge shall be preferred unless—

(*a*) the proposal to prefer such charge is contained in a resolution which has been moved after at least fourteen days' notice in writing signed by not less than one-fourth of the total number of members of the House has been given of their intention to move the resolution, and

(*b*) such resolution has been passed by a majority of not less than two-thirds of the total membership of the House.

(3) When a charge has been so preferred by either House of Parliament, the other House shall investigate the charge or cause the charge to be investigated and the President shall have the right to appear and to be represented at such investigation.

(4) If as a result of the investigation a resolution is passed by a majority of not less than two-thirds of the total membership of the House by which the charge was investigated or caused to be investigated, declaring that the charge preferred against the President has been sustained, such resolution shall have the effect of removing the President from his office as from the date on which the resolution is so passed.

62. *Time of holding election to fill vacancy in the office of President and the term of office of person elected to fill casual vacancy.*—(1) An election to fill a vacancy caused by the expiration of the term of office of President shall be completed before the expiration of the term.

(2) An election to fill a vacancy in the office of President occurring by reason of his death, resignation or removal, or otherwise shall be held as soon as possible after, and in no case later than six months from, the date of occurrence of the vacancy; and the person elected to fill the vacancy shall, subject to the provisions of article 56, be entitled to hold office for the full term of five years from the date on which he enters upon his office.

63. *The Vice-President of India.*—There shall be a Vice-President of India.

64. *The Vice-President to be ex-officio Chairman of the Council of States.*—The Vice-President shall be *ex-officio* Chairman of the Council of States and shall not hold any other office of profit:

Provided that during any period when the Vice-President acts as President or discharges the functions of the President under article 65, he shall not perform the duties of the office of Chairman of the Council of States and shall not be entitled to any salary or allowance payable to the Chairman of the Council of States under article 97.

65. *The Vice-President to act as President or to discharge his functions during casual vacancies in the office, or during the absence of President.*—(1) In the event of the occurrence of any vacancy in the office of the President by reason of his death, resignation or removal, or otherwise, the Vice-President shall act as President until the date on which a new President elected in accordance with the provisions of this Chapter to fill such vacancy enters upon his office.

(2) When the President is unable to discharge his functions owing to absence, illness or any other cause, the Vice-President shall discharge his functions until the date on which the President resumes his duties.

(3) The Vice-President shall, during, and in respect of, the period while he is so acting as, or discharging the functions of, President, have all the powers and immunities of the President and be entitled to such emoluments, allowances and

privileges as may be determined by Parliament by law and, until provision in that behalf is so made, such emoluments, allowances and privileges as are specified in the Second Schedule.

66. *Election of Vice-President.*—(1) The Vice-President shall be elected by the [52][members of an electoral college consisting of the members of both Houses of Parliament] in accordance with the system of proportional representation by means of the single transferable vote and the voting at such election shall be by secret ballot.

(2) The Vice-President shall not be a member of either House of Parliament or of a House of the Legislature of any State, and if a member of either House of Parliament or of a House of the Legislature of any State be elected Vice-President, he shall be deemed to have vacated his seat in that House on the date on which he enters upon his office as Vice-President.

(3) No person shall be eligible for election as Vice-President unless he—

(*a*) is a citizen of India;

(*b*) has completed the age of thirty-five years; and

(*c*) is qualified for election as a member of the Council of States.

(4) A person shall not be eligible for election as Vice-President if he holds any office of profit under the Government of India or the Government of any State or under any local or other authority subject to the control of any of the said Governments.

Explanation.—For the purposes of this article, a person shall not be deemed to hold any office of profit by reason only that he is the President or Vice-President of the Union or the Governor [53]* * * of any State or is a Minister either for the Union or for any State.

67. *Term of office of Vice-President.*—The Vice-President shall hold office for a term of five years from the date on which he enters upon his office:

Provided that—

(*a*) a Vice-President may, by writing under his hand addressed to the President, resign his office;

(*b*) a Vice-President may be removed from his office by a resolution of the Council of States passed by a majority of all the then members of the Council and agreed to by the House of the People; but no resolution for the purpose of this clause shall be moved unless at least fourteen days' notice has been given of the intention to move the resolution;

(*c*) a Vice-President shall, notwithstanding the expiration of his term, continue to hold office until his successor enters upon his office.

68. *Time of holding election to fill vacancy in the office of Vice-President and the term of office of person elected to fill casual vacancy.*—(1) An election to fill a vacancy caused by the expiration of the term of office of Vice-President shall be completed before the expiration of the term.

(2) An election to fill a vacancy in the office of Vice-President occurring by reason of his death, resignation or removal, or otherwise shall be held as soon as possible after the occurrence of the vacancy, and the person elected to fill the vacancy shall, subject to the provisions of article 67, be entitled to hold office for the full term of five years from the date on which he enters upon his office.

69. *Oath or affirmation by the Vice-President.*—Every Vice-President shall, before entering upon his office, make and subscribe before the President, or some

---

[52] Subs. by the Const. (11th Am.) Act, 1961, s. 2, for "members of both Houses of Parliament assembled at a joint meeting".

[53] The words "or Rajpramukh or Uparajpramukh" omitted by the Const. (7th Am.) Act, 1956, s. 29 and Sch.

person appointed in that behalf by him, an oath or affirmation in the following form, that is to say—

"I, A. B., do $\frac{\text{swear in the name of God}}{\text{solemnly affirm}}$ that I will bear true faith and allegiance to the Constitution of India as by law established and that I will faithfully discharge the duty upon which I am about to enter."

70. *Discharge of President's functions in other contingencies.*—Parliament may make such provision as it thinks fit for the discharge of the functions of the President in any contingency not provided for in this Chapter.[54]

[55][**71.** *Matters relating to, or connected with, the election of a President or Vice-President.*—(1) All doubts and disputes arising out of or in connection with the election of a President or Vice-President shall be inquired into and decided by the Supreme Court whose decision shall be final.

(2) If the election of a person as President or Vice-President is declared void by the Supreme Court, acts done by him in the exercise and performance of the powers and duties of the office of President or Vice-President, as the case may be, on or before the date of the decision of the Supreme Court shall not be invalidated by reason of that declaration.

(3) Subject to the provisions of this Constitution, Parliament may by law regulate any matter relating to or connected with the election of a President or Vice-President.

---

[54] See the President (Discharge of Functions) Act, 1969.

[55] Art. 71 has been successively subs. by the Const. (39th Am.) Act, 1975, s. 2 (w.e.f. 10.8.1975) and the Const. (44th Am.) Act, 1978, s. 10, to read as above, w.e.f. 20.6.1979. The Article, as originally enacted read as follows:

"71. *Matters relating to or connected with the election of a President or Vice-President.*—(1) All doubts and disputes arising out of or in connection with the election of a President or Vice-President shall be inquired into and decided by the Supreme Court whose decision shall be final. (2) If the election of a person as President or Vice-President is declared void by the Supreme Court, acts done by him in the exercise and performance of the powers and duties of the office of President or Vice-President, as the case may be, on or before the date of the decision of the Supreme Court shall not be invalidated by reason of that declaration. (3) Subject to the provisions of this Constitution, Parliament may by law regulate any matter relating to or connected with the election of a President or Vice-President."

The following clause was inserted by the Const. (11th Am.) Act, 1961, w.e.f. 19.12.1961:—

"(4) The election of a person as President or Vice-President shall not be called in question on the ground of the existence of any vacancy for whatever reason among the members of the electoral college electing him."

Art. 71 was substituted by the Const. (39th Am.) Act, 1975, by s. 2, w.e.f. 10.8.1975, with the following:

"71. *Matters relating to or connected with the election of a President or Vice-President.*—(1) Subject to the provisions of this Constitution, Parliament may by law regulate any matter relating to or connected with the election of a President or Vice-President, including the grounds on which such election may be questioned:

Provided that the election of a person as President or Vice-President shall not be called in question on the ground of the existence of any vacancy for whatever reason among the members of the electoral college electing him.

(2) All doubts and disputes arising out of or in connection with the election of a President or Vice-President shall be inquired into and decided by such authority or body and in such manner as may be provided for by or under any law referred to in clause (1).

(3) The validity of any such law as is referred to in clause (1) and the decision of any authority or body under such law shall not be called in question in any Court.

(4) If the election of a person as President or Vice-President is declared void under any such law as is referred to in clause (1), acts done by him in the exercise and performance of the powers and duties of the office of President or Vice-President, as the case may be, on or before the date of such declaration shall not be invalidated by reason of that declaration."

(4) The election of a person as President or Vice-President shall not be called in question on the ground of the existence of any vacancy for whatever reason among the members of the electoral college electing him.]

72. *Power of President to grant pardons, etc., and to suspend, remit or commute sentences in certain cases.*—(1) The President shall have the power to grant pardons, reprieves, respites or remissions of punishment or to suspend, remit or commute the sentence of any person convicted of any offence—

(*a*) in all cases where the punishment or sentence is by a Court Martial;

(*b*) in all cases where the punishment or sentence is for an offence against any law relating to a matter to which the executive power of the Union extends;

(*c*) in all cases where the sentence is a sentence of death.

(2) Nothing in sub-clause (*a*) of clause (1) shall affect the power conferred by law on any officer of the Armed Forces of the Union to suspend, remit or commute a sentence passed by a Court Martial.

(3) Nothing in sub-clause (*c*) of clause (1) shall affect the power to suspend, remit or commute a sentence of death exercisable by the Governor [56]* * * of a State under any law for the time being in force. [s. 295, G.I. Act]

73. *Extent of executive power of the Union.*—(1) Subject to the provisions of this Constitution, the executive power of the Union shall extend—

(*a*) to the matters with respect to which Parliament has power to make laws; and

(*b*) to the exercise of such rights, authority and jurisdiction as are exercisable by the Government of India by virtue of any treaty or agreement:

Provided that the executive power referred to in sub-clause (*a*) shall not, save as expressly provided in this Constitution or in any law made by Parliament, extend in any State [57]* * * to matters with respect to which the Legislature of the State has also power to make laws.

(2) Until otherwise provided by Parliament, a State and any officer or authority of a State may, notwithstanding anything in this article, continue to exercise in matters with respect to which Parliament has power to make laws for that State such executive power or functions as the State or officer or authority thereof could exercise immediately before the commencement of this Constitution.

[s. 8, G.I. Act]

Council of Ministers

74. *Council of Ministers to aid and advise President.*—[58][(1) There shall be a Council of Ministers with the Prime Minister at the head to aid and advise the President who shall, in the exercise of his functions, act in accordance with such advice:]

[59][Provided that the President may require the Council of Ministers to reconsider such advice, either generally or otherwise, and the President shall act in accordance with the advice tendered after such reconsideration.]

(2) The question whether any, and if so what, advice was tendered by Ministers to the President shall not be inquired into in any court. [s. 9, G.I. Act]

---

[56] The words "or Rajpramukh" omitted by the Const. (7th Am.) Act, 1956, s. 29 and Sch.

[57] The words and letters "specified in Part A or Part B of the First Schedule" omitted by s. 29 and Sch., *ibid.*

[58] Subs. by the Const. (42nd Am.) Act, 1976, s. 13, for cl. (1) w.e.f. 3.1.1977. The Clause, as originally enacted, ran as follows:

"74. (1) There shall be a Council of Ministers with the Prime Minister at the head to aid and advise the President in the exercise of his functions."

[59] Ins. by the Const. (44th Am.) Act, 1978, s. 11, w.e.f. 20.6.1979.

75. *Other provisions as to Ministers.*—(1) The Prime Minister shall be appointed by the President and the other Ministers shall be appointed by the President on the advice of the Prime Minister.

(2) The Ministers shall hold office during the pleasure of the President.

(3) The Council of Ministers shall be collectively responsible to the House of the People.

(4) Before a Minister enters upon his office, the President shall administer to him the oaths of office and of secrecy according to the forms set out for the purpose in the Third Schedule.

(5) A Minister who for any period of six consecutive months is not a member of either House of Parliament shall at the expiration of that period cease to be a Minister.

(6) The salaries and allowances of Ministers shall be such as Parliament may from time to time by law determine and, until Parliament so determines, shall be as specified in the Second Schedule. [s. 10, G.I. Act]

The Attorney-General for India

76. *Attorney-General for India.*—(1) The President shall appoint a person who is qualified to be appointed a Judge of the Supreme Court to be Attorney-General for India.

(2) It shall be the duty of the Attorney-General to give advice to the Government of India upon such legal matters, and to perform such other duties of a legal character, as may from time to time be referred or assigned to him by the President, and to discharge the functions conferred on him by or under this Constitution or any other law for the time being in force.

(3) In the performance of his duties the Attorney-General shall have right of audience in all courts in the territory of India.

(4) The Attorney-General shall hold office during the pleasure of the President, and shall receive such remuneration as the President may determine.

[s. 16, G.I. Act]

Conduct of Government Business

77. *Conduct of business of the Government of India.*—(1) All executive action of the Government of India shall be expressed to be taken in the name of the President.

(2) Orders and other instruments made and executed in the name of the President shall be authenticated in such manner as may be specified in rules[60] to be made by the President, and the validity of an order or instrument which is so authenticated shall not be called in question on the ground that it is not an order or instrument made or executed by the President.

(3) The President shall make rules for the more convenient transaction of the business of the Government of India, and for the allocation among Ministers of the said business. [s. 17, G.I. Act]

[61]* * * *

---

[60] See Notification No. S.O. 2297, dated the 3rd November, 1958, Gazette of India, Extraordinary, 1958, Pt. II, Sec. 3(*ii*), p. 1315, as amended from time to time.

[61] Cl. (4) was ins. by the Const. (42nd Am.) Act, 1976, s. 14, w.e.f. 3.1.1977 and omitted by the Const. (44th Am.) Act, 1978, s. 12 w.e.f. 20.6.1979. The omitted clause ran as follows:

"14. *Amendment of article* 77.—In article 77 of the Constitution, after clause (3), the following clause shall be *inserted*, namely:—

'(4) No court or other authority shall be entitled to require the production of any rules made under clause (3) for the more convenient transaction of the business of the Government of India.'"

78. *Duties of Prime Minister as respects the furnishing of information to the President, etc.*—It shall be the duty of the Prime Minister—

(*a*) to communicate to the President all decisions of the Council of Ministers relating to the administration of the affairs of the Union and proposals for legislation;

(*b*) to furnish such information relating to the administration of the affairs of the Union and proposals for legislation as the President may call for; and

(*c*) if the President so requires, to submit for the consideration of the Council of Ministers any matter on which a decision has been taken by a Minister but which has not been considered by the Council. [s. 17, G.I. Act]

CHAPTER II.—PARLIAMENT

General

79. *Constitution of Parliament.*—There shall be a Parliament for the Union which shall consist of the President and two Houses to be known respectively as the Council of States and the House of the People. [s. 18, G.I. Act]

80. *Composition of the Council of States.*—(1) [62][[63]* * * The Council of States] shall consist of—

(*a*) twelve members to be nominated by the President in accordance with the provisions of clause (3); and

(*b*) not more than two hundred and thirty-eight representatives of the States [64][and of the Union territories].

(2) The allocation of seats in the Council of States to be filled by representatives of the States [64][and of the Union territories] shall be in accordance with the provisions in that behalf contained in the Fourth Schedule.

(3) The members to be nominated by the President under sub-clause (*a*) of clause (1) shall consist of persons having special knowledge or practical experience in respect of such matters as the following, namely:—

Literature, science, art and social service.

(4) The representatives of each State [65]* * * in the Council of States shall be elected by the elected members of the Legislative Assembly of the State in accordance with the system of proportional representation by means of the single transferable vote.

(5) The representatives of the [66][Union territories] in the Council of States shall be chosen in such manner as Parliament may by law prescribe. [s. 18, G.I. Act]

[67][**81.** *Composition of the House of the people.*—(1) [68][Subject to the provi-

---

[62] Subs. by the Const. (35th Am.) Act, 1974, s. 3. for "The Council of States", w.e.f. 1.3.1975.

[63] The words "Subject to the provisions of paragraph 4 of the Tenth Schedule," omitted by the Const. (36th Am.) Act, 1975, w.e.f. 26.4.1975.

[64] Added by the Const. (7th Am.) Act, 1956, s. 3.

[65] The words and letters "specified in Part A or Part B of the First Schedule" omitted by s. 3, *ibid.*

[66] Subs. by the Const. (7th Am.) Act, 1956, s. 3, for "States specified in Part C of the First Schedule".

[67] Subs. for the original Art. 81, which had itself been amended by the Const. (2nd Am.) Act, 1952, w.e.f. 1.5.1953: s. 4, *ibid.* As originally enacted, the Article read:

"(1) (*a*) Subject to the provisions of clause (2) and of articles 82 and 331, the House of the People shall consist of not more than five hundred members directly elected by the voters in the States.

(*b*) For the purpose of sub-clause (*a*), the States shall be divided, grouped or formed into territorial constituencies and the number of members

sions of article 331 [69]* * *], the House of the People shall consist of—

(*a*) not more than [70][five hundred and twenty-five members] chosen by direct election from territorial constituencies in the States, and

(*b*) not more than [71][twenty members] to represent the Union territories, chosen in such manner as Parliament may by law provide.

(2) For the purposes of sub-clause (*a*) of clause (1),—

(*a*) there shall be allotted to each State a number of seats in the House of the People in such manner that the ratio between that number and the population of the State is, so far as practicable, the same for all States; and

(*b*) each State shall be divided into territorial constituencies in such manner that the ratio between the population of each constituency and the number of seats allotted to it is, so far as practicable, the same throughout the State:

[72][Provided that the provisions of sub-clause (*a*) of this clause shall not be applicable for the purpose of allotment of seats in the House of the People to any State so long as the population of that State does not exceed six millions.]

---

to be allotted to each such constituency shall be so determined as to ensure that there shall be [not less than one member for every 750,000 of the population and] not more than one member for every 500,000 of the population.

(*c*) The ratio between the number of members allotted to each territorial constituency and the population of that constituency as ascertained at the last preceding census of which the relevant figures have been published, shall, so far as practicable, be the same throughout the territory of India.

(2) The representation in the House of the People of the territories comprised within the territory of India but not included within any State shall be such as Parliament may by law provide.

(3) Upon the completion of each census, the representation of the several territorial constituencies in the House of the People shall be readjusted by such authority, in such manner and with effect from such date as Parliament may by law determine:

Provided that such readjustment shall not affect representation in the House of the People until the dissolution of the then existing House.

The portion in square brackets in cl. 1(*b*) was deleted by the Const. (2nd Am.) Act, 1952.

Note: Paragraph (2) of the Constitution (Removal of Difficulties) Order No. VIII as amended by the Const. (7th Am.) Act, 1956, provides as follows:

For the period during which the tribal areas specified in Part B of the Table appended to paragraph 20 of the Sixth Schedule to the Constitution or any parts thereof are administered by the President by virtue of sub-paragraph (2) of paragraph 18 of the said Schedule, the Constitution of India shall have effect subject to the following adaptations:—

In article 81,—

(*a*) in sub-clause (*b*) of cl. (1), after the words "Union territories", the words, letter and figures "and the tribal areas specified in Part B of the Table appended to paragraph 20 of the Sixth Schedule" shall be inserted; and

(*b*) to cl. (2), the following proviso shall be added, namely:—

"Provided that the constituencies into which the State of Assam is divided shall not comprise the tribal areas specified in Part B of the Table appended to paragraph 20 of the Sixth Schedule."

[68] Subs. by the Const. (35th Am.) Act, 1974, s. 4, for "Subject to the provisions of article 331" w.e.f. 1.3.1975.

[69] The words and figure "and paragraph 4 of the Tenth Schedule" omitted by the Const. (36th Am.) Act, 1975, w.e.f. 26.4.1975.

[70] Subs. by the Const. (31st Am.) Act, 1973, s. 2, for "five hundred members" w.e.f. 17.10.1973.

[71] Subs. by s. 2, *ibid.*, for "twenty-five members".

[72] Ins. by s. 2, *ibid.*

(3) In this article, the expression "population" means the population as ascertained at the last preceding census of which the relevant figures have been published:

[73][Provided that the reference in this clause to the last preceding census of which the relevant figures have been published shall, until the relevant figures for the first census taken after the year 2000 have been published, be construed as a reference to the 1971 census.] [s. 18, G.I. Act]

[74][82. *Readjustment after each census.*—Upon the completion of each census, the allocation of seats in the House of the People to the States and the division of each State into territorial constituencies shall be readjusted by such authority and in such manner as Parliament may by law[75] determine:

Provided that such readjustment shall not affect representation in the House of the People until the dissolution of the then existing House:]

[76][Provided further that such readjustment shall take effect from such date as the President may, by order, specify and until such readjustment takes effect, any election to the House may be held on the basis of the territorial constituencies existing before such readjustment:

Provided also that until the relevant figures for the first census taken after the year 2000 have been published, it shall not be necessary to readjust the allocation of seats in the House of the People to the States and the division of each State into territorial constituencies under this article.]

83. *Duration of Houses of Parliament.*—(1) The Council of States shall not be subject to dissolution, but as nearly as possible one-third of the members thereof shall retire as soon as may be on the expiration of every second year in accordance with the provisions made in that behalf by Parliament by law.

(2) The House of the People, unless sooner dissolved, shall continue for [77][five years] from the date appointed for its first meeting and no longer and the expiration of the said period of [77][five years] shall operate as a dissolution of the House:

Provided that the said period may, while a Proclamation of Emergency is in operation, be extended by Parliament by law for a period not exceeding one year at a time and not extending in any case beyond a period of six months after the Proclamation has ceased to operate. [s. 18, G.I. Act]

84. *Qualification for membership of Parliament.* A person shall not be qualified to be chosen to fill a seat in Parliament unless he—

[78][(*a*) is a citizen of India, and makes and subscribes before some person authorized in that behalf by the Election Commission an oath or affirmation according to the form set out for the purpose in the Third Schedule;]

(*b*) is, in the case of a seat in the Council of States, not less than thirty years of age and, in the case of a seat in the House of the People, not less than twenty-five years of age; and

---

[73] Ins. by the Const. (42nd Am.) Act, 1976, s. 15 (w.e.f. 3.1.1977).

[74] Subs. by the Const. (7th Am.) Act, 1956, w.e.f. 1.11.1956, for the original Article which read as follows:

"Notwithstanding anything in clause (1) of article 81, Parliament may by law provide for the representation in the House of the People of any State specified in Part C of the First Schedule or of any territories comprised within the territory of India but not included within any State on a basis or in a manner other than that provided in that clause."

[75] See the Delimitation Commission Act, 1962.

[76] Ins. by the Const. (42nd Am.) Act, 1976, s. 16, w.e.f. 3.1.1977.

[77] Subs. by the Const. (44th Am.) Act, 1978, s. 13 for "six years", w.e.f. 20.6.1979. The words "six years" were subs. for the original words "five years" by the Const. (42nd Am.) Act, 1976, w.e.f. 3.1.1977.

[78] Subs. by the Const. (16th Am.) Act, 1963, s. 3, for cl. (*a*), w.e.f. 5.10.1963. The original clause (*a*) read as follows:

"(*a*) is a citizen of India;"

(c) possesses such other qualifications as may be prescribed in that behalf by or under any law made by Parliament.[79]

[80][85. *Sessions of Parliament, prorogation and dissolution.*—(1) The President shall from time to time summon each House of Parliament to meet at such time and place as he thinks fit, but six months shall not intervene between its last sitting in one session and the date appointed for its first sitting in the next session.

(2) The President may from time to time—

(a) prorogue the Houses or either House;

(b) dissolve the House of the People.] [s. 19, G.I. Act]

86. *Right of President to address and send messages to Houses.*—(1) The President may address either House of Parliament or both Houses assembled together, and for that purpose require the attendance of members.

(2) The President may send messages to either House of Parliament, whether with respect to a Bill then pending in Parliament or otherwise, and a House to which any message is so sent shall with all convenient despatch consider any matter required by the message to be taken into consideration. [s. 20, G.I. Act]

87. *Special address by the President.*—(1) At the commencement of [81][the first session after each general election to the House of the People and at the commencement of the first session of each year] the President shall address both Houses of Parliament assembled together and inform Parliament of the causes of its summons.

(2) Provision shall be made by the rules regulating the procedure of either House for the allotment of time for discussion of the matters referred to in such address[82] * * *.

88. *Rights of Ministers and Attorney-General as respects Houses.*—Every Minister and the Attorney-General of India shall have the right to speak in, and otherwise to take part in the proceedings of, either House, any joint sitting of the Houses, and any committee of Parliament of which he may be named a member, but shall not by virtue of this article be entitled to vote. [s. 21, G.I. Act]

Officers of Parliament

89. *The Chairman and Deputy Chairman of the Council of States.*—(1) The Vice-President of India shall be *ex-officio* Chairman of the Council of States.

(2) The Council of States shall, as soon as may be, choose a member of the Council to be Deputy Chairman thereof and, so often as the office of Deputy Chairman becomes vacant, the Council shall choose another member to be Deputy Chairman thereof. [s. 22, G.I. Act]

90. *Vacation and resignation of, and removal from, the office of Deputy Chairman.*—A member holding office as Deputy Chairman of the Council of States—

(a) shall vacate his office if he ceases to be a member of the Council;

(b) may at any time, by writing under his hand addressed to the Chairman, resign his office; and

---

[79] See the Representation of the People Act, 1951.

[80] Subs. by the Const. (1st Am.) Act, 1951, s. 6 w.e.f. 18.6.1951, for the original article which read as follows:

"85. (1) The Houses of Parliament shall be summoned to meet twice at least in every year, and six months shall not intervene between their last sitting in one session and the date appointed for their first sitting in the next session.

(2) Subject to the provisions of clause (1), the President may from time to time—

(a) summon the Houses or either House to meet at such time and place as he thinks fit;

(b) prorogue the Houses;

(c) dissolve the House of the People."

[81] Subs. by s. 7, *ibid.*, for "every session".

[82] The words "and for the precedence of such discussion over other business of the House" omitted by the Const. (1st Am.) Act, 1951, s. 7, w.e.f. 18.6.1951.

(c) may be removed from his office by a resolution of the Council passed by a majority of all the then members of the Council:

Provided that no resolution for the purpose of clause (c) shall be moved unless at least fourteen days' notice has been given of the intention to move the resolution. [s. 22, G.I. Act]

91. *Power of the Deputy Chairman or other person to perform the duties of the office of, or to act as, Chairman.*—(1) While the office of Chairman is vacant, or during any period when the Vice-President is acting as, or discharging the functions of, President, the duties of the office shall be performed by the Deputy Chairman, or, if the office of Deputy Chairman is also vacant, by such member of the Council of States as the President may appoint for the purpose.

(2) During the absence of the Chairman from any sitting of the Council of States the Deputy Chairman, or, if he is also absent, such person as may be determined by the rules of procedure of the Council, or, if no such person is present, such other person as may be determined by the Council, shall act as Chairman. [s. 22, G.I. Act]

92. *The Chairman or the Deputy Chairman not to preside while a resolution for his removal from office is under consideration.*—(1) At any sitting of the Council of States, while any resolution for the removal of the Vice-President from his office is under consideration, the Chairman, or while any resolution for the removal of the Deputy Chairman from his office is under consideration, the Deputy Chairman, shall not, though he is present, preside, and the provisions of clause (2) of article 91 shall apply in relation to every such sitting as they apply in relation to a sitting from which the Chairman, or, as the case may be, the Deputy Chairman, is absent.

(2) The Chairman shall have the right to speak in, and otherwise to take part in the proceedings of, the Council of States while any resolution for the removal of the Vice-President from his office is under consideration in the Council, but, notwithstanding anything in article 100, shall not be entitled to vote at all on such resolution or on any other matter during such proceedings.

93. *The Speaker and Deputy Speaker of the House of the People.*—The House of the People shall, as soon as may be, choose two members of the House to be respectively Speaker and Deputy Speaker thereof and, so often as the office of Speaker or Deputy Speaker becomes vacant, the House shall choose another member to be Speaker or Deputy Speaker, as the case may be. [s. 22, G.I. Act]

94. *Vacation and resignation of, and removal from, the offices of Speaker and Deputy Speaker.*—A member holding office as Speaker or Deputy Speaker of the House of the People—

(a) shall vacate his office if he ceases to be a member of the House of the People;

(b) may at any time, by writing under his hand addressed, if such member is the Speaker, to the Deputy Speaker, and if such member is the Deputy Speaker, to the Speaker, resign his office; and

(c) may be removed from his office by a resolution of the House of the People passed by a majority of all the then members of the House:

Provided that no resolution for the purpose of clause (c) shall be moved unless at least fourteen days' notice has been given of the intention to move the resolution:

Provided further that, whenever the House of the People is dissolved, the Speaker shall not vacate his office until immediately before the first meeting of the House of the People after the dissolution. [s. 22, G.I. Act]

95. *Power of the Deputy Speaker or other person to perform the duties of the office of, or to act as, Speaker.*—(1) While the office of Speaker is vacant, the duties of the office shall be performed by the Deputy Speaker or, if the office of Deputy Speaker is also vacant, by such member of the House of the People as the President may appoint for the purpose.

(2) During the absence of the Speaker from any sitting of the House of the People the Deputy Speaker or, if he is also absent, such person as may be determined by the rules of procedure of the House, or, if no such person is present, such other person as may be determined by the House, shall act as Speaker.
[s. 22, G.I. Act]

96. *The Speaker or the Deputy Speaker not to preside while a resolution for his removal from office is under consideration.*—(1) At any sitting of the House of the People, while any resolution for the removal of the Speaker from his office is under consideration, the Speaker, or while any resolution for the removal of the Deputy Speaker from his office is under consideration, the Deputy Speaker, shall not, though he is present, preside, and the provisions of clause (2) of article 95 shall apply in relation to every such sitting as they apply in relation to a sitting from which the Speaker, or, as the case may be, the Deputy Speaker, is absent.

(2) The Speaker shall have the right to speak in, and otherwise to take part in the proceedings of, the House of the People while any resolution for his removal from office is under consideration in the House and shall, notwithstanding anything in article 100, be entitled to vote only in the first instance on such resolution or on any other matter during such proceedings but not in the case of an equality of votes.

97. *Salaries and allowances of the Chairman and Deputy Chairman and the Speaker and Deputy Speaker.*—There shall be paid to the Chairman and the Deputy Chairman of the Council of States, and to the Speaker and the Deputy Speaker of the House of the People, such salaries and allowances as may be respectively fixed by Parliament by law and, until provision in that behalf is so made, such salaries and allowances as are specified in the Second Schedule.[83] [s. 22, G.I. Act]

98. *Secretariat of Parliament.*—(1) Each House of Parliament shall have a separate secretarial staff:

Provided that nothing in this clause shall be construed as preventing the creation of posts common to both Houses of Parliament.

(2) Parliament may by law regulate the recruitment, and the conditions of service of persons appointed, to the secretarial staff of either House of Parliament.

(3) Until provision is made by Parliament under clause (2), the President may, after consultation with the Speaker of the House of the People or the Chairman of the Council of States, as the case may be, make rules regulating the recruitment, and the conditions of service of persons appointed, to the secretarial staff of the House of the People or the Council of States, and any rules so made shall have effect subject to the provisions of any law made under the said clause.

Conduct of Business

99. *Oath or affirmation by members.*—Every member of either House of Parliament shall, before taking his seat, make and subscribe before the President, or some person appointed in that behalf by him, an oath or affirmation according to the form set out for the purpose in the Third Schedule. [s. 24, G.I. Act]

100. *Voting in Houses, power of Houses to act notwithstanding vacancies and quorum.*—(1) Save as otherwise provided in this Constitution, all questions at any sitting of either House or joint sitting of the Houses shall be determined by a majority of votes of the members present and voting, other than the Speaker or person acting as Chairman or Speaker.

The Chairman or Speaker, or person acting as such, shall not vote in the first instance, but shall have and exercise a casting vote in the case of an equality of votes.

(2) Either House of Parliament shall have power to act notwithstanding any vacancy in the membership thereof, and any proceedings in Parliament shall be

---

[83] See the Salaries and Allowances of Officers of Parliament Act, 1953.

valid notwithstanding that it is discovered subsequently that some person who was not entitled so to do sat or voted or otherwise took part in the proceedings.

(3) Until Parliament by law otherwise provides, the quorum to constitute a meeting of either House of Parliament shall be one-tenth of the total number of members of the House.

(4) If at any time during a meeting of a House there is no quorum, it shall be the duty of the Chairman or Speaker, or person acting as such, either to adjourn the House or to suspend the meeting until there is a quorum. [s. 23, G.I. Act]

Disqualifications of Members

101. *Vacation of seats.*—(1) No person shall be a member of both Houses of Parliament and provision shall be made by Parliament by law for the vacation by a person who is chosen a member of both Houses of his seat in one House or the other.

(2) No person shall be a member both of Parliament and of a House of the Legislature of a State [84]* * *, and if a person is chosen a member both of Parliament and of a House of the Legislature of [85][a State], then, at the expiration of such period as may be specified in rules[86] made by the President, that person's seat in Parliament shall become vacant, unless he has previously resigned his seat in the Legislature of the State.

(3) If a member of either House of Parliament—

(*a*) becomes subject to any of the disqualifications mentioned in clause (1) of article 102, or

[87][(*b*) resigns his seat by writing under his hand addressed to the Chairman or the Speaker, as the case may be, and his resignation is accepted by the Chairman or the Speaker, as the case may be,]

his seat shall thereupon become vacant:

[88][Provided that in the case of any resignation referred to in sub-clause (*b*), if from information received or otherwise and after making such inquiry as he thinks fit, the Chairman or the Speaker, as the case may be, is satisfied that such resignation is not voluntary or genuine, he shall not accept such resignation.]

(4) If for a period of sixty days a member of either House of Parliament is without permission of the House absent from all meetings thereof, the House may declare his seat vacant:

Provided that in computing the said period of sixty days no account shall be taken of any period during which the House is prorogued or is adjourned for more than four consecutive days. [s. 25, G.I. Act]

102. *Disqualifications for membership.*—(1) A person shall be disqualified for being chosen as, and for being, a member of either House of Parliament—

(*a*) if he holds any office of profit under the Government of India or the Government of any State, other than an office declared by Parliament by law not to disqualify its holder;[89]

(*b*) if he is of unsound mind and stands so declared by a competent court;

---

[84] The words and letters "specified in Part A or Part B of the First Schedule" omitted by the Const. (7th Am.) Act, 1956, s. 29 and Sch., w.e.f. 1.11.1956.

[85] Subs. by s. 29 and Sch., *ibid.*, for "such a State".

[86] *See* the prohibition of Simultaneous Membership Rules, 1950, published with the Ministry of Law Notification No. F.46/50-C, dated the 26th January, 1950, Gazette of India, Extraordinary, p. 678.

[87] Subs. by the Const. (33rd Am.) Act, 1974, s. 2, for Sub-clause (*b*), w.e.f. 19.5.1974. The original sub-cl. (*b*) read as follows:

"(*b*) resigns his seat by writing under his hand addressed to the Chairman or the Speaker, as the case may be,"

[88] Ins. by s. 2, *ibid.*, w.e.f. 19.5.1954.

[89] See the Parliament (Prevention of Disqualification) Act, 1959.

(*c*) if he is an undischarged insolvent;

(*d*) if he is not a citizen of India, or has voluntarily acquired the citizenship of a foreign State, or is under any acknowledgment of allegiance or adherence to a foreign State;

(*e*) if he is so disqualified by or under any law made by Parliament.

(2) For the purposes of this article a person shall not be deemed to hold an office of profit under the Government of India or the Government of any State by reason only that he is a Minister either for the Union or for such State.

[s. 26, G.I. Act]

[90][**103.** *Decision on questions as to disqualifications of members.*—(1) If any question arises as to whether a member of either House of Parliament has become subject to any of the disqualifications mentioned in clause (1) of article 102, the question shall be referred for the decision of the President and his decision shall be final.

(2) Before giving any decision on any such question, the President shall obtain the opinion of the Election Commission and shall act according to such opinion.]

104. *Penalty for sitting and voting before making oath or affirmation under article 99 or when not qualified or when disqualified.*—If a person sits or votes as a member of either House of Parliament before he has complied with the requirements of article 99, or when he knows that he is not qualified or that he is disqualified for membership thereof, or that he is prohibited from so doing by the provisions of any law made by Parliament, he shall be liable in respect of each day on which he so sits or votes to a penalty of five hundred rupees to be recovered as a debt due to the Union. [s. 27, G.I. Act]

Powers, Privileges and Immunities of Parliament and its Members

105. *Powers, privileges, etc., of the Houses of Parliament and of the members and committees thereof.*—(1) Subject to the provisions of this Constitution and to the rules and standing orders regulating the procedure of Parliament, there shall be freedom of speech in Parliament.

(2) No member of Parliament shall be liable to any proceedings in any court in respect of anything said or any vote given by him in Parliament or any committee thereof, and no person shall be so liable in respect of the publication by or under the authority of either House of Parliament of any report, paper, votes or proceedings.

(3) In other respects, the powers, privileges and immunities of each House of Parliament, and of the members and the committees of each House, shall be such as may from time to time be defined by Parliament by law, and, until so defined,

---

[90] Art. 103 has been successively subs. by the Const. (42nd Am.) Act, 1976, s. 20 w.e.f. 3.1.1977 and the Const. (44th Am.) Act, 1978, s. 14 to read as above, w.e.f. 20.6.1979. The Article as substituted by the 42nd Amendment ran as follows:

"103. *Decision on questions as to disqualification.*—(1) If any question arises—

(*a*) as to whether a member of either House of Parliament has become subject to any of the disqualifications mentioned in clause (1) or article 102, or

(*b*) as to whether a person, found guilty of a corrupt practice at an election to a House of Parliament under any law made by Parliament, shall be disqualified for being chosen as, and for being, a member of either House of Parliament, or of a House of the Legislature of a State, or as to the period for which he shall be so disqualified, or as to the removal of, or the reduction of the period of, such disqualification,

the question shall be referred for the decision of the President and his decision shall be final.

(2) Before giving any decision on any such question, the President shall consult the Election Commission and the Election Commission may, for this purpose, make such inquiry as it thinks fit."

[91][shall be those of that House and of its members and committees immediately before the coming into force of section 15 of the Constitution (Forty-fourth Amendment) Act, 1978].

(4) The provisions of clauses (1), (2) and (3) shall apply in relation to persons who by virtue of this Constitution have the right to speak in, and otherwise to take part in the proceedings of, a House of Parliament or any committee thereof as they apply in relation to members of Parliament. [s. 28, G.I. Act]

106. *Salaries and allowances of Members.*—Members of either House of Parliament shall be entitled to receive such salaries and allowances as may from time to time be determined by Parliament by law and, until provision in that respect is so made, allowances at such rates and upon such conditions as were immediately before the commencement of this Constitution applicable in the case of members of the Constituent Assembly of the Dominion of India.[92] [s. 29, G.I. Act]

Legislative Procedure

107. *Provisions as to introduction and passing of Bills.*—(1) Subject to the provisions of articles 109 and 117 with respect to Money Bills and other financial Bills, a Bill may originate in either House of Parliament.

(2) Subject to the provisions of articles 108 and 109, a Bill shall not be deemed to have been passed by the Houses of Parliament unless it has been agreed to by both Houses, either without amendment or with such amendments only as are agreed to by both Houses.

(3) A Bill pending in Parliament shall not lapse by reason of the prorogation of the Houses.

(4) A Bill pending in the Council of States which has not been passed by the House of the People shall not lapse on a dissolution of the House of the People.

(5) A Bill which is pending in the House of the People, or which having been passed by the House of the People is pending in the Council of States, shall, subject to the provisions of article 108, lapse on a dissolution of the House of the People.
[s. 30, G.I. Act]

108. *Joint sitting of both Houses in certain cases.*—(1) If after a Bill has been passed by one House and transmitted to the other House—

(*a*) the Bill is rejected by the other House; or

(*b*) the Houses have finally disagreed as to the amendments to be made in the Bill; or

(*c*) more than six months elapse from the date of the reception of the Bill by the other House without the Bill being passed by it,

the President may, unless the Bill has lapsed by reason of a dissolution of the House of the People, notify to the Houses by message if they are sitting or by public notification if they are not sitting, his intention to summon them to meet in a joint sitting for the purpose of deliberating and voting on the Bill:

Provided that nothing in this clause shall apply to a Money Bill.

(2) In reckoning any such period of six months as is referred to in clause (1) no account shall be taken of any period during which the House referred to in

---

[91] Subs. by the Const. (44th Am.) Act, 1978, for certain words, w.e.f. 20.6.1979. Clause (3) of the Article, inserted by the Const. (42nd Am.) Act w.e.f. 18.12.1976 ran as follows:

"(3) In other respects, the powers, privileges and immunities of each House of Parliament, and of the members and the committees of each House, shall be those of that House, and of its members and committees, at the commencement of section 21 of the Constitution (42nd Amendment) Act, 1976, and as may be evolved by such House of Parliament from time to time."

[92] See the Salaries and Allowances of Members of Parliament Act, 1954. See also the Salaries and Allowances of Ministers Act, 1952.

sub-clause (c) of that clause is prorogued or adjourned for more than four consecutive days.

(3) Where the President has under clause (1) notified his intention of summoning the Houses to meet in a joint sitting, neither House shall proceed further with the Bill, but the President may at any time after the date of his notification summon the Houses to meet in a joint sitting for the purpose specified in the notification and, if he does so, the Houses shall meet accordingly.

(4) If at the joint sitting of the two Houses the Bill, with such amendments, if any, as are agreed to in joint sitting, is passed by a majority of the total number of members of both Houses present and voting, it shall be deemed for the purposes of this Constitution to have been passed by both Houses:

Provided that at a joint sitting—

(*a*) if the Bill, having been passed by one House, has not been passed by the other House with amendments and returned to the House in which it originated, no amendment shall be proposed to the Bill other than such amendments (if any) as are made necessary by the delay in the passage of the Bill;

(*b*) if the Bill has been so passed and returned, only such amendments as aforesaid shall be proposed to the Bill and such other amendments as are relevant to the matters with respect to which the Houses have not agreed;

and the decision of the person presiding as to the amendments which are admissible under this clause shall be final.

(5) A joint sitting may be held under this article and a Bill passed thereat, notwithstanding that a dissolution of the House of the People has intervened since the President notified his intention to summon the Houses to meet therein.

[s. 31, G.I. Act]

109. *Special procedure in respect of Money Bills.*—(1) A Money Bill shall not be introduced in the Council of States.

(2) After a Money Bill has been passed by the House of the People it shall be transmitted to the Council of States for its recommendations and the Council of States shall within a period of fourteen days from the date of its receipt of the Bill return the Bill to the House of the People with its recommendations and the House of the People may thereupon either accept or reject all or any of the recommendations of the Council of States.

(3) If the House of the People accepts any of the recommendations of the Council of States, the Money Bill shall be deemed to have been passed by both Houses with the amendments recommended by the Council of States and accepted by the House of the People.

(4) If the House of the People does not accept any of the recommendations of the Council of States, the Money Bill shall be deemed to have been passed by both Houses in the form in which it was passed by the House of the People without any of the amendments recommended by the Council of States.

(5) If a Money Bill passed by the House of the People and transmitted to the Council of States for its recommendations is not returned to the House of the People within the said period of fourteen days, it shall be deemed to have been passed by both Houses at the expiration of the said period in the form in which it was passed by the House of the People. [s. 37, G.I. Act]

110. *Definition of "Money Bills".*—(1) For the purposes of this Chapter, a Bill shall be deemed to be a Money Bill if it contains only provisions dealing with all or any of the following matters, namely—

(*a*) the imposition, abolition, remission, alteration or regulation of any tax;

(*b*) the regulation of the borrowing of money or the giving of any guarantee by the Government of India, or the amendment of the law with respect to any financial obligations undertaken or to be undertaken by the Government of India;

(c) the custody of the Consolidated Fund or the Contingency Fund of India, the payment of moneys into or the withdrawal of moneys from any such Fund;

(d) the appropriation of moneys out of the Consolidated Fund of India;

(e) the declaring of any expenditure to be expenditure charged on the Consolidated Fund of India or the increasing of the amount of any such expenditure;

(f) the receipt of money on account of the Consolidated Fund of India or the public account of India or the custody or issue of such money or the audit of the accounts of the Union or of a State; or

(g) any matter incidental to any of the matters specified in sub-clauses (a) to (f).

(2) A Bill shall not be deemed to be a Money Bill by reason only that it provides for the imposition of fines or other pecuniary penalties, or for the demand or payment of fees for licences or fees for services rendered, or by reason that it provides for the imposition, abolition, remission, alteration or regulation of any tax by any local authority or body for local purposes.

(3) If any question arises whether a Bill is a Money Bill or not, the decision of the Speaker of the House of the People thereon shall be final.

(4) There shall be endorsed on every Money Bill when it is transmitted to the Council of States under article 109, and when it is presented to the President for assent under article 111, the certificate of the Speaker of the House of the People signed by him that it is a Money Bill. [s. 37, G.I. Act]

111. *Assent to Bills.*—When a Bill has been passed by the Houses of Parliament, it shall be presented to the President, and the President shall declare either that he assents to the Bill, or that he withholds assent therefrom:

Provided that the President may, as soon as possible after the presentation to him of a Bill for assent, return the Bill if it is not a Money Bill to the Houses with a message requesting that they will reconsider the Bill or any specified provisions thereof and, in particular, will consider the desirability of introducing any such amendments as he may recommend in his message, and when a Bill is so returned, the Houses shall reconsider the Bill accordingly, and if the Bill is passed again by the Houses with or without amendment and presented to the President for assent, the President shall not withhold assent therefrom. [s. 32, G.I. Act]

Procedure in Financial Matters

112. *Annual financial statement.*—(1) The President shall in respect of every financial year cause to be laid before both the Houses of Parliament a statement of the estimated receipts and expenditure of the Government of India for that year, in this Part referred to as the "annual financial statement".

(2) The estimates of expenditure embodied in the annual financial statement shall show separately—

(a) the sums required to meet expenditure described by this Constitution as expenditure charged upon the Consolidated Fund of India; and

(b) the sums required to meet other expenditure proposed to be made from the Consolidated Fund of India,

and shall distinguish expenditure on revenue account from other expenditure.

(3) The following expenditure shall be expenditure charged on the Consolidated Fund of India:—

(a) the emoluments and allowances of the President and other expenditure relating to his office;

(b) the salaries and allowances of the Chairman and the Deputy Chairman of the Council of States and the Speaker and the Deputy Speaker of the House of the People;

(*c*) debt charges for which the Government of India is liable including interest, sinking fund charges and redemption charges, and other expenditure relating to the raising of loans and the service and redemption of debt;

(*d*) (*i*) the salaries, allowances and pensions payable to or in respect of Judges of the Supreme Court;

(*ii*) the pensions payable to or in respect of Judges of the Federal Court;

(*iii*) the pensions payable to or in respect of Judges of any High Court which exercises jurisdiction in relation to any area included in the territory of India or which at any time before the commencement of this Constitution exercised jurisdiction in relation to any area included in [93][a Governor's Province of the Dominion of India];

(*e*) the salary, allowances and pension payable to or in respect of the Comptroller and Auditor-General of India;

(*f*) any sums required to satisfy any judgment, decree or award of any court or arbitral tribunal;

(*g*) any other expenditure declared by this Constitution or by Parliament by law to be so charged. [s. 33, G.I. Act]

113. *Procedure in Parliament with respect to estimates.*—(1) So much of the estimates as relates to expenditure charged upon the Consolidated Fund of India shall not be submitted to the vote of Parliament, but nothing in this clause shall be construed as preventing the discussion in either House of Parliament of any of those estimates.

(2) So much of the said estimates as relates to other expenditure shall be submitted in the form of demands for grants to the House of the People, and the House of the People shall have power to assent, or to refuse to assent, to any demand, or to assent to any demand subject to a reduction of the amount specified therein.

(3) No demand for a grant shall be made except on the recommendation of the President. [s. 34, G.I. Act]

114. *Appropriation Bills.*—(1) As soon as may be after the grants under article 113 have been made by the House of the People, there shall be introduced a Bill to provide for the appropriation out of the Consolidated Fund of India of all moneys required to meet—

(*a*) the grants so made by the House of the People; and

(*b*) the expenditure charged on the Consolidated Fund of India but not exceeding in any case the amount shown in the statement previously laid before Parliament.

(2) No amendment shall be proposed to any such Bill in either House of Parliament which will have the effect of varying the amount or altering the destination of any grant so made or of varying the amount of any expenditure charged on the Consolidated Fund of India, and the decision of the person presiding as to whether an amendment is inadmissible under this clause shall be final.

(3) Subject to the provisions of articles 115 and 116, no money shall be withdrawn from the Consolidated Fund of India except under appropriation made by law passed in accordance with the provisions of this article.

115. *Supplementary, additional or excess grants.*—(1) The President shall—

(*a*) if the amount authorised by any law made in accordance with the provisions of article 114 to be expended for a particular service for the current financial year is found to be insufficient for the purposes of that year or when a need has arisen during the current financial year for supplementary or additional expenditure upon some new service not contemplated in the annual financial statement for that year, or

---

[93] Subs. by the Const. (7th Am.) Act, 1956, s. 29 and Sch., for "a Province corresponding to a State specified in Part A of the First Schedule", w.e.f. 1.11.1956.

(b) if any money has been spent on any service during a financial year in excess of the amount granted for that service and for that year,

cause to be laid before both the Houses of Parliament another statement showing the estimated amount of that expenditure or cause to be presented to the House of the People a demand for such excess, as the case may be.

(2) The provisions of articles 112, 113, and 114 shall have effect in relation to any such statement and expenditure or demand and also to any law to be made authorising the appropriation of moneys out of the Consolidated Fund of India to meet such expenditure or the grant in respect of such demand as they have effect in relation to the annual financial statement and the expenditure mentioned therein or to a demand for a grant and the law to be made for the authorisation of appropriation of moneys out of the Consolidated Fund of India to meet such expenditure or grant. [s. 36, G.I. Act]

116. *Votes on account, votes of credit and exceptional grants.*—(1) Notwithstanding anything in the foregoing provisions of this Chapter, the House of the People shall have power—

(a) to make any grant in advance in respect of the estimated expenditure for a part of any financial year pending the completion of the procedure prescribed in article 113 for the voting of such grant and the passing of the law in accordance with the provisions of article 114 in relation to that expenditure;

(b) to make a grant for meeting an unexpected demand upon the resources of India when on account of the magnitude or the indefinite character of the service the demand cannot be stated with the details ordinarily given in an annual financial statement;

(c) to make an exceptional grant which forms no part of the current service of any financial year;

and Parliament shall have power to authorise by law the withdrawal of moneys from the Consolidated Fund of India for the purposes for which the said grants are made.

(2) The provisions of articles 113 and 114 shall have effect in relation to the making of any grant under clause (1) and to any law to be made under that clause as they have effect in relation to the making of a grant with regard to any expenditure mentioned in the annual financial statement and the law to be made for the authorisation of appropriation of moneys out of the Consolidated Fund of India to meet such expenditure.

117. *Special provisions as to financial Bills.*—(1) A Bill or amendment making provision for any of the matters specified in sub-clauses (a) to (f) of clause (1) of article 110 shall not be introduced or moved except on the recommendation of the President and a Bill making such provision shall not be introduced in the Council of States:

Provided that no recommendation shall be required under this clause for the moving of an amendment making provision for the reduction or abolition of any tax.

(2) A Bill or amendment shall not be deemed to make provision for any of the matters aforesaid by reason only that it provides for the imposition of fines or other pecuniary penalties, or for the demand or payment of fees for licences or fees for services rendered, or by reason that it provides for the imposition, abolition, remission, alteration or regulation of any tax by any local authority or body for local purposes.

(3) A Bill which, if enacted and brought into operation, would involve expenditure from the Consolidated Fund of India shall not be passed by either House of Parliament unless the President has recommended to that House the consideration of the Bill. [s. 37, G.I. Act]

Procedure Generally

118. *Rules of procedure.*—(1) Each House of Parliament may make rules for regulating, subject to the provisions of this Constitution, its procedure and the conduct of its business.[94]

(2) Until rules are made under clause (1), the rules of procedure and standing orders in force immediately before the commencement of this Constitution with respect to the Legislature of the Dominion of India shall have effect in relation to Parliament subject to such modifications and adaptations as may be made therein by the Chairman of the Council of States or the Speaker of the House of the People, as the case may be.

(3) The President, after consultation with the Chairman of the Council of States and the Speaker of the House of the People, may make rules as to the procedure with respect to joint sittings of, and communications between, the two Houses.

(4) At a joint sitting of the two Houses the Speaker of the House of the People, or in his absence such person as may be determined by rules of procedure made under clause (3), shall preside. [s. 38, G.I. Act]

119. *Regulation by law of procedure in Parliament in relation to financial business.*—Parliament may, for the purpose of the timely completion of financial business, regulate by law the procedure of, and the conduct of business in, each House of Parliament in relation to any financial matter or to any Bill for the appropriation of moneys out of the Consolidated Fund of India, and, if and so far as any provision of any law so made is inconsistent with any rule made by a House of Parliament under clause (1) of article 118 or with any rule or standing order having effect in relation to Parliament under clause (2) of that article, such provision shall prevail.

120. *Language to be used in Parliament.*—(1) Notwithstanding anything in Part XVII, but subject to the provisions of article 348, business in Parliament shall be transacted in Hindi or in English:

Provided that the Chairman of the Council of States or Speaker of the House of the People, or person acting as such, as the case may be, may permit any member who cannot adequately express himself in Hindi or in English to address the House in his mother tongue.

(2) Unless Parliament by law otherwise provides, this article shall, after the expiration of a period of fifteen years from the commencement of this Constitution, have effect as if the words "or in English" were omitted therefrom. [s. 39, G.I. Act]

121. *Restriction on discussion in Parliament.*—No discussion shall take place in Parliament with respect to the conduct of any Judge of the Supreme Court or of a High Court in the discharge of his duties except upon a motion for presenting an address to the President praying for the removal of the Judge as hereinafter provided. [s. 40, G.I. Act]

122. *Courts not to inquire into proceedings of Parliament.*—(1) The validity of any proceedings in Parliament shall not be called in question on the ground of any alleged irregularity of procedure.

(2) No officer or member of Parliament in whom powers are vested by or under this Constitution for regulating procedure or the conduct of business, or for maintaining order, in Parliament shall be subject to the jurisdiction of any court in respect of the exercise by him of those powers. [s. 41, G.I. Act]

CHAPTER III.—LEGISLATIVE POWERS OF THE PRESIDENT

123. *Power of President to promulgate Ordinances during recess of Parliament.* —(1) If at any time, except when both Houses of Parliament are in session, the

---

[94] Both Houses have made such Rules. See for the Lok Sabha Rules, the Gaz. of India, dt. 7.4.1952, Pt. 1, s. 1, Ext. p. 834; and for the Rajya Sabha Rules, the Gaz. of India, dt. 1.7.1964, Pt. 1, s. 1, p. 1171.

President is satisfied that circumstances exist which render it necessary for him to take immediate action, he may promulgate such Ordinances as the circumstances appear to him to require.

(2) An Ordinance promulgated under this article shall have the same force and effect as an Act of Parliament, but every such Ordinance—

(a) shall be laid before both Houses of Parliament and shall cease to operate at the expiration of six weeks from the reassembly of Parliament, or, if before the expiration of that period resolutions disapproving it are passed by both Houses, upon the passing of the second of those resolutions; and

(b) may be withdrawn at any time by the President.

Explanation.—Where the Houses of Parliament are summoned to reassemble on different dates, the period of six weeks shall be reckoned from the later of those dates for the purposes of this clause.

(3) If and so far as an Ordinance under this article makes any provision which Parliament would not under this Constitution be competent to enact, it shall be void.

[s. 42, G.I. Act]

[95]* * * *

CHAPTER IV.—THE UNION JUDICIARY

124. *Establishment and constitution of Supreme Court.*—(1) There shall be a Supreme Court of India consisting of a Chief Justice of India and, until Parliament by law prescribes a larger number, of not more than seven[96] other Judges.

(2) Every Judge of the Supreme Court shall be appointed by the President by warrant under his hand and seal after consultation with such of the Judges of the Supreme Court and of the High Courts in the States as the President may deem necessary for the purpose and shall hold office until he attains the age of sixty-five years:

Provided that in the case of appointment of a Judge other than the Chief Justice, the Chief Justice of India shall always be consulted:

Provided further that—

(a) a Judge may, by writing under his hand addressed to the President, resign his office;

(b) a Judge may be removed from his office in the manner provided in clause (4).

[97][(2A) The age of a Judge of the Supreme Court shall be determined by such authority and in such manner as Parliament may by law provide.]

(3) A person shall not be qualified for appointment as a Judge of the Supreme Court unless he is a citizen of India and—

(a) has been for at least five years a Judge of a High Court or of two or more such Courts in succession; or

(b) has been for at least ten years an advocate of a High Court or of two or more such Courts in succession; or

(c) is, in the opinion of the President, a distinguished jurist.

Explanation I.—In this clause "High Court" means a High Court which exercises, or which at any time before the commencement of this Constitution exercised, jurisdiction in any part of the territory of India.

---

[95] Cl. (4) ins. by the Const. (38th Am.) Act, 1975, s. 2 w.e.f. 1.8.1975 and omitted by the Const. (44th Am.) Act, 1978, s. 16 w.e.f. 20.6.1979. The omitted clause was as follows:

"(4) Notwithstanding anything in this Constitution, the satisfaction of the President mentioned in clause (1) shall be final and conclusive and shall not be questioned in any court on any ground."

[96] Now "seventeen", *vide* Act 48 of 1977.

[97] Ins. by the Const. (15th Am.) Act, 1963, s. 2, w.e.f. 5.10.1963.

Explanation II.—In computing for the purpose of this clause the period during which a person has been an advocate, any period during which a person has held judicial office not inferior to that of a district judge after he became an advocate shall be included.

(4) A Judge of the Supreme Court shall not be removed from his office except by an order of the President passed after an address by each House of Parliament supported by a majority of the total membership of that House and by a majority of not less than two-thirds of the members of that House present and voting has been presented to the President in the same session for such removal on the ground of proved misbehaviour or incapacity.

(5) Parliament may by law regulate the procedure for the presentation of an address and for the investigation and proof of the misbehaviour or incapacity of a Judge under clause (4).[98]

(6) Every person appointed to be a Judge of the Supreme Court shall, before he enters upon his office, make and subscribe before the President, or some person appointed in that behalf by him, an oath or affirmation according to the form set out for the purpose in the Third Schedule.

(7) No person who has held office as a Judge of the Supreme Court shall plead or act in any court or before any authority within the territory of India.

[s. 200, G.I. Act]

125. *Salaries, etc., of Judges.*—(1) There shall be paid to the Judges of the Supreme Court such salaries as are specified in the Second Schedule.

(2) Every Judge shall be entitled to such privileges and allowances and to such rights in respect of leave of absence and pension as may from time to time be determined by or under law made by Parliament and, until so determined, to such privileges, allowances and rights as are specified in the Second Schedule:[99]

Provided that neither the privileges nor the allowances of a Judge nor his rights in respect of leave of absence or pension shall be varied to his disadvantage after his appointment.

[s. 201, G.I. Act]

126. *Appointment of acting Chief Justice.*—When the office of Chief Justice of India is vacant or when the Chief Justice is, by reason of absence or otherwise, unable to perform the duties of his office, the duties of the office shall be performed by such one of the other Judges of the Court as the President may appoint for the purpose.

[s. 202, G.I. Act]

127. *Appointment of ad hoc Judges.*—(1) If at any time there should not be a quorum of the Judges of the Supreme Court available to hold or continue any session of the Court, the Chief Justice of India may, with the previous consent of the President and after consultation with the Chief Justice of the High Court concerned, request in writing the attendance at the sittings of the Court, as an *ad hoc* Judge, for such period as may be necessary, of a Judge of a High Court duly qualified for appointment as a Judge of the Supreme Court to be designated by the Chief Justice of India.

(2) It shall be the duty of the Judge who has been so designated, in priority to other duties of his office to attend the sittings of the Supreme Court at the time and for the period for which his attendance is required, and while so attending he shall have all the jurisdiction, powers and privileges, and shall discharge the duties, of a Judge of the Supreme Court.

[s. 202, G.I. Act]

128. *Attendance of retired Judges at sittings of the Supreme Court.*—Notwithstanding anything in this Chapter, the Chief Justice of India may at any time, with the previous consent of the President, request any person who has held the office of a Judge of the Supreme Court or of the Federal Court [1][or who has held

---

[98] See the Judges (Inquiry) Act, 1968.

[99] See the Supreme Court Judges (Condition of Service) Act, 1958.

[1] Ins. by the Const. (15th Am.) Act, 1963, s. 3, w.e.f. 5.10.1963.

the office of a Judge of a High Court and is duly qualified for appointment as a Judge of the Supreme Court] to sit and act as a Judge of the Supreme Court, and every such person so requested shall, while so sitting and acting, be entitled to such allowances as the President may by order determine and have all the jurisdiction, powers and privileges of, but shall not otherwise be deemed to be, a Judge of that Court:

Provided that nothing in this article shall be deemed to require any such person as aforesaid to sit and act as a Judge of that Court unless he consents so to do.

129. *Supreme Court to be a court of record.*—The Supreme Court shall be a court of record and shall have all the powers of such a court including the power to punish for contempt of itself. [s. 203, G.I. Act]

130. *Seat of Supreme Court.*—The Supreme Court shall sit in Delhi or in such other place or places, as the Chief Justice of India may, with the approval of the President, from time to time, appoint. [s. 203, G.I. Act]

131. *Original jurisdiction of the Supreme Court.*—Subject to the provisions of this Constitution, the Supreme Court shall, to the exclusion of any other court, have original jurisdiction in any dispute—

(*a*) between the Government of India and one or more States; or

(*b*) between the Government of India and any State or States on one side and one or more other States on the other; or

(*c*) between two or more States,

if and in so far as the dispute involves any question (whether of law or fact) on which the existence or extent of a legal right depends:

[2][Provided that the said jurisdiction shall not extend to a dispute arising out of any treaty, agreement, covenant, engagement, *sanad* or other similar instrument which, having been entered into or executed before the commencement of this Constitution, continues in operation after such commencement, or which provides that the said jurisdiction shall not extend to such a dispute.]

[s. 204, G.I. Act]

[3]**131A.** [*Exclusive jurisdiction of the Supreme Court in regard to questions as to constitutional validity of Central laws.*] *Rep. by the Constitution (Forty-third Amendment) Act, 1977, s. 4 (w.e.f. 13-4-1978).*

---

[2] Subs. by the Const. (7th Am.) Act, 1956, s. 5, w.e.f. 1.11.1956, for the original proviso which read as follows:

"Provided that the said jurisdiction shall not extend to—(*i*) a dispute to which a State specified in Part B of the First Schedule is a party, if the dispute arises out of any provision of a treaty, agreement, covenant, engagement, *sanad* or other similar instrument which was entered into or executed before the commencement of this Constitution and has, or has been, continued in operation after such commencement; (*ii*) a dispute to which any State is a party, if the dispute arises out of any provision of a treaty, agreement, covenant, engagement, *sanad* or other similar instrument which provides that the said jurisdiction shall not extend to such a dispute."

[3] Ins. by the Const. (42nd Am.) Act, 1976, s. 23, w.e.f. 1.2.1977. The repealed article ran as follows:

"131A. *Exclusive jurisdiction of the Supreme Court in regard to questions as to Constitutional validity of Central laws.*—(1) Notwithstanding anything contained in any other provision of this Constitution, the Supreme Court shall, to the exclusion of any other court, have jurisdiction to determine all questions relating to the constitutional validity of any Central law.

(2) Where a High Court is satisfied—(*a*) that a case pending before it or before a court subordinate to it involves questions as to the constitutional validity of any Central law or, as the case may be, of both Central and State laws; and (*b*) that the determination of such questions is necessary for the disposal of the case,

the High Court shall refer the question for the decision of the Supreme Court.

(3) Without prejudice to the provisions of clause (2), where on an application made by the Attorney-General of India, the Supreme Court is satisfied,—(*a*) that a case pending before a High Court or before a court subordinate to a

132. *Appellate jurisdiction of Supreme Court in appeals from High Courts in certain cases.*—(1) An appeal shall lie to the Supreme Court from any judgment, decree or final order of a High Court in the territory of India, whether in a civil, criminal or other proceeding, [4][if the High Court certifies under article 134A] that the case involves a substantial question of law as to the interpretation of this Constitution.[5]

[6]* * * *

(3) Where such a certificate is given, [7]* * * any party in the case may appeal to the Supreme Court on the ground that any such question as aforesaid has been wrongly decided [7]* * *.

Explanation.—For the purposes of this article, the expression "final order" includes an order deciding an issue which, if decided in favour of the appellant, would be sufficient for the final disposal of the case.

133. *Appellate jurisdiction of Supreme Court in appeals from High Courts in regard to civil matters.*—[8][(1) An appeal shall lie to the Supreme Court from any

---

High Court involves questions as to the constitutional validity of any Central law, or, as the case may be, of both Central and State laws; and (*b*) that the determination of such questions is necessary for the disposal of the case, the Supreme Court may require the High Court to refer the questions to it for its decision.

(4) When a reference is made under clause (2) or clause (3), the High Court shall stay all proceedings in respect of the case until the Supreme Court decides the questions so referred.

(5) The Supreme Court shall, after giving the parties an opportunity of being heard, decide the questions so referred, and may—(*a*) either dispose of the case itself; or (*b*) return the case to the High Court together with a copy of its judgment on such questions for disposal of the case in conformity with such judgment by the High Court or, as the case may be, the court subordinate to it."

[4] Subs. by the Const. (44th Am.) Act, 1978, s. 17, w.e.f. 1.8.1979 for "if the High Court certifies".

[5] For the purpose of this article and articles 133 and 134 certain Judicial Commissioners' Courts have been declared by Parliament to be High Courts. See the Judicial Commissioners' Courts (Declaration as High Courts) Act, 1950; and the Goa, Daman & Diu Judicial Commissioner's Court (Declaration as High Court) Act, 1964.

[6] Cl. (2) omitted by the Const. (44th Am.) Act, 1978, w.e.f. 1.8.1979. The omitted clause was as follows:

"(2) Where the High Court has refused to give such a certificate, the Supreme Court may, if it is satisfied that the case involves a substantial question of law as to the interpretation of this Constitution, grant special leave to appeal from such judgment, decree or final order."

[7] Certain words omitted by s. 17, *ibid.*, w.e.f. 1.8.1979. The original cl. (3) was as follows:—

"(3) Where such a certificate is given, or such leave is granted, any party in the case may appeal to the Supreme Court on the ground that any such question as aforesaid has been wrongly decided and, with the leave of the Supreme Court, on any other ground."

[8] Subs. by the Const. (30th Am.) Act, 1972, s. 2, for cl. (1) w.e.f. 27.2.1973. The original cl. (1) was as follows:

"(1) An appeal shall lie to the Supreme Court from any judgment, decree or final order in a civil proceeding of a High Court in the territory of India if the High Court certifies—

(*a*) that the amount or value of the subject-matter in dispute in the court of first instance and still in dispute on appeal was and is not less than twenty-thousand rupees or such other sum as may be specified in that behalf by Parliament by law; or

(*b*) that the judgment, decree or final order involves directly or indirectly some claim or question respecting property of the like amount or value; or

(*c*) that the case is a fit one for appeal to the Supreme Court;

and, where the judgment or final order appealed from affirms the decision of the court immediately below in any case other than a case referred to in sub-clause (*c*) if the High Court certifies that the appeal involves some substantial question of law."

judgment, decree or final order in a civil proceeding of a High Court in the territory of India [9][if the High Court certifies under article 134A—]

(*a*) that the case involves a substantial question of law of general importance; and

(*b*) that in the opinion of the High Court the said question needs to be decided by the Supreme Court.]

(2) Notwithstanding anything in article 132, any party appealing to the Supreme Court under clause (1) may urge as one of the grounds in such appeal that a substantial question of law as to the interpretation of this Constitution has been wrongly decided.

(3) Notwithstanding anything in this article, no appeal shall, unless Parliament by law otherwise provides, lie to the Supreme Court from the judgment, decree or final order of one Judge of a High Court.

134. *Appellate jurisdiction of Supreme Court in regard to criminal matters.*—(1) An appeal shall lie to the Supreme Court from any judgment, final order or sentence in a criminal proceeding of a High Court in the territory of India if the High Court—

(*a*) has on appeal reversed an order of acquittal of an accused person and sentenced him to death; or

(*b*) has withdrawn for trial before itself any case from any court subordinate to its authority and has in such trial convicted the accused person and sentenced him to death; or

(*c*) [10][certifies under article 134A] that the case is a fit one for appeal to the Supreme Court:

Provided that an appeal under sub-clause (*c*) shall lie subject to such provisions as may be made in that behalf under clause (1) of article 145 and to such conditions as the High Court may establish or require.

(2) Parliament may by law confer on the Supreme Court any further powers to entertain and hear appeals from any judgment, final order or sentence in a criminal proceeding of a High Court in the territory of India subject to such conditions and limitations as may be specified in such law.[11]

[12][**134A.** *Certificate for appeal to the Supreme Court.*—Every High Court, passing or making a judgment, decree, final order, or sentence, referred to in clause (1) of article 132 or clause (1) of article 133, or clause (1) of article 134,—

(*a*) may, if it deems fit so to do, on its own motion; and

(*b*) shall, if an oral application is made, by or on behalf of the party aggrieved, immediately after the passing or making of such judgment, decree, final order or sentence,

determine, as soon as may be after such passing or making, the question whether a certificate of the nature referred to in clause (1) of article 132, or clause (1) of article 133 or, as the case may be, sub-clause (*c*) of clause (1) of article 134, may be given in respect of that case.]

135. *Jurisdiction and powers of the Federal Court under existing law to be exercisable by the Supreme Court.*—Until Parliament by law otherwise provides, the Supreme Court shall also have jurisdiction and powers with respect to any matter to which the provisions of article 133 or article 134 do not apply if juris-

---

This amendment governs all appeals from the date the amendment came into force except appeals pending on that date in the Supreme Court, and appeals in respect of which certificates had been given before that date.

[9] Subs. by the Const. (44th Am.) Act, 1978, s. 18, for "if the High Court certifies—" w.e.f. 1.8.1979.

[10] Subs. by the Const. (44th Am.) Act, 1978, s. 19, for "certifies" w.e.f. 1.8.1979.

[11] See the Supreme Court (Enlargement of Criminal Appellate Jurisdiction) Act, 1970.

[12] Ins. by the Const. (44th Am.) Act, 1978, s. 20, w.e.f. 1.8.1979.

diction and powers in relation to that matter were exercisable by the Federal Court immediately before the commencement of this Constitution under any existing law.

136. *Special leave to appeal by the Supreme Court.*—(1) Notwithstanding anything in this Chapter, the Supreme Court may, in its discretion, grant special leave to appeal from any judgment, decree, determination, sentence or order in any cause or matter passed or made by any court or tribunal in the territory of India.

(2) Nothing in clause (1) shall apply to any judgment, determination, sentence or order passed or made by any court or tribunal constituted by or under any law relating to the Armed Forces.

137. *Review of judgments or orders by the Supreme Court.*—Subject to the provisions of any law made by Parliament or any rules made under article 145, the Supreme Court shall have power to review any judgment pronounced or order made by it.

138. *Enlargement of the jurisdiction of the Supreme Court.*—(1) The Supreme Court shall have such further jurisdiction and powers with respect to any of the matters in the Union List as Parliament may by law confer.

(2) The Supreme Court shall have such further jurisdiction and powers with respect to any matter as the Government of India and the Government of any State may by special agreement confer, if Parliament by law provides for the exercise of such jurisdiction and powers by the Supreme Court.

139. *Conferment on the Supreme Court of powers to issue certain writs.*—Parliament may by law confer on the Supreme Court power to issue directions, orders or writs, including writs in the nature of *habeas corpus, mandamus,* prohibition, *quo warranto* and *certiorari,* or any of them, for any purposes other than those mentioned in clause (2) of article 32.

[13][**139A.** *Transfer of certain cases.*—[14][(1) Where cases involving the same or substantially the same questions of law are pending before the Supreme Court and one or more High Courts or before two or more High Courts and the Supreme Court is satisfied on its own motion or on an application made by the Attorney-General of India or by a party to any such case that such questions are substantial questions of general importance, the Supreme Court may withdraw the case or cases pending before the High Court or the High Courts and dispose of all the cases itself:

Provided that the Supreme Court may after determining the said questions of law return any case so withdrawn together with a copy of its judgment on such questions to the High Court from which the case has been withdrawn, and the High Court shall on receipt thereof, proceed to dispose of the case in conformity with such judgment.]

(2) The Supreme Court may, if it deems it expedient so to do for the ends of justice, transfer any case, appeal or other proceedings pending before any High Court to any other High Court.]

140. *Ancillary powers of Supreme Court.*—Parliament may by law make provision for conferring upon the Supreme Court such supplemental powers not inconsistent with any of the provisions of this Constitution as may appear to be necessary or desirable for the purpose of enabling the Court more effectively to exercise the jurisdiction conferred upon it by or under this Constitution.

[s. 215, G.I. Act]

---

[13] Ins. by the Const. (42nd Am.) Act, 1976, s. 24 (w.e.f. 1.2.1977).

[14] Subs. by the Const. (44th Am.) Act, 1978, s. 21, for cl. (1) (w.e.f. 1.8.1979). The original clause as enacted was as follows:

"(1) If, on an application made by the Attorney-General of India, the Supreme Court is satisfied that cases involving the same or substantially the same questions of law are pending before it and one or more High Courts or before two or more High Courts and that such questions are substantial questions of general importance, the Supreme Court may withdraw the case or cases pending before the High Court or the High Courts and dispose of all the cases itself."

141. *Law declared by Supreme Court to be binding on all courts.*—The law declared by the Supreme Court shall be binding on all courts within the territory of India. [s. 212, G.I. Act]

142. *Enforcement of decrees and orders of Supreme Court and orders as to discovery, etc.*—(1) The Supreme Court in the exercise of its jurisdiction may pass such decree or make such order as is necessary for doing complete justice in any cause or matter pending before it, and any decree so passed or order so made shall be enforceable throughout the territory of India in such manner as may be prescribed by or under any law made by Parliament and, until provision in that behalf is so made, in such manner as the President may by order[15] prescribe.

(2) Subject to the provisions of any law made in this behalf by Parliament, the Supreme Court shall, as respects the whole of the territory of India, have all and every power to make any order for the purpose of securing the attendance of any person, the discovery or production of any documents, or the investigation or punishment of any contempt of itself. [s. 210, G.I. Act]

143. *Power of President to consult Supreme Court.*—(1) If at any time it appears to the President that a question of law or fact has arisen, or is likely to arise, which is of such a nature and of such public importance that it is expedient to obtain the opinion of the Supreme Court upon it, he may refer the question to that Court for consideration and the Court may, after such hearing as it thinks fit, report to the President its opinion thereon.

(2) The President may, notwithstanding anything in [16]* * * the proviso to article 131, refer a dispute of the kind mentioned in the [17][said proviso] to the Supreme Court for opinion and the Supreme Court shall, after such hearing as it thinks fit, report to the President its opinion thereon. [s. 213, G.I. Act]

144. *Civil and judicial authorities to act in aid of the Supreme Court.*—All authorities, civil and judicial, in the territory of India shall act in aid of the Supreme Court. [s. 210, G.I. Act]

[18]**144A.** [*Special provisions as to disposal of questions relating to constitutional validity of laws.*] *Rep. by the Constitution (Forty-third Amendment) Act,* 1977, s. 5 (*w.e.f.* 13-4-1978).

145. *Rules of Court, etc.*—(1) Subject to the provisions of any law made by Parliament, the Supreme Court may from time to time, with the approval of the President, make rules for regulating generally the practice and procedure of the Court including—

(*a*) rules as to the persons practising before the Court;

(*b*) rules as to the procedure for hearing appeals and other matters pertaining to appeals including the time within which appeals to the Court are to be entered;

(*c*) rules as to the proceedings in the Court for the enforcement of any of the rights conferred by Part III;

---

[15] *See* the Supreme Court (Decrees and Orders) Enforcement Order, 1954, published with the Ministry of Law Notification No. C.O. 47, dated the 14th January, 1954.

[16] The words, brackets and figure "clause (*i*) of" omitted by the Const. (7th Am.) Act, 1956, s. 29 and Sch. w.e.f. 1.11.1956.

[17] Subs. by s. 29 and Sch., *ibid.*, for "said clause".

[18] Ins. by the Const. (42nd Am.) Act, 1976, s. 25 (w.e.f. 1.2.1977). The repealed article ran as follows:

"144A. *Special provisions as to disposal of questions relating to constitutional validity of laws.*—(1) The minimum number of Judges of the Supreme Court who shall sit for the purpose of determining any question as to the constitutional validity of any Central law or State law shall be seven. (2) A Central law or a State law shall not be declared to be constitutionally invalid by the Supreme Court unless a majority of not less than two-thirds of the Judges sitting for the purpose of determining the question as to the constitutional validity of such law hold it to be constitutionally invalid".

[19][(cc) rules as to the proceedings in the Court under [20][article 139A];]

(d) rules as to the entertainment of appeals under sub-clause (c) of clause (1) of article 134;

(e) rules as to the conditions subject to which any judgment pronounced or order made by the Court may be reviewed and the procedure for such review including the time within which applications to the Court for such review are to be entered;

(f) rules as to the costs of and incidental to any proceedings in the Court and as to the fees to be charged in respect of proceedings therein;

(g) rules as to the granting of bail;

(h) rules as to stay of proceedings;

(i) rules providing for the summary determination of any appeal which appears to the Court to be frivolous or vexatious or brought for the purpose of delay;

(j) rules as to the procedure for inquiries referred to in clause (1) of article 317.

(2) Subject to the [21][provisions of [22]* * * clause (3)], rules made under this article may fix the minimum number of Judges who are to sit for any purpose, and may provide for the powers of single Judges and Division Courts.

(3) [23][[22]* * * The minimum number] of Judges who are to sit for the purpose of deciding any case involving a substantial question of law as to the interpretation of this Constitution or for the purpose of hearing any reference under article 143 shall be five:

Provided that, where the Court hearing an appeal under any of the provisions of this Chapter other than article 132 consists of less than five Judges and in the course of the hearing of the appeal the Court is satisfied that the appeal involves a substantial question of law as to the interpretation of this Constitution the determination of which is necessary for the disposal of the appeal, such Court shall refer the question for opinion to a Court constituted as required by this clause for the purpose of deciding any case involving such a question and shall on receipt of the opinion dispose of the appeal in conformity with such opinion.

(4) No judgment shall be delivered by the Supreme Court save in open Court, and no report shall be made under article 143 save in accordance with an opinion also delivered in open Court.

(5) No judgment and no such opinion shall be delivered by the Supreme Court save with the concurrence of a majority of the Judges present at the hearing of the case, but nothing in this clause shall be deemed to prevent a Judge who does not concur from delivering a dissenting judgment or opinion. [s. 214, G.I. Act]

146. *Officers and servants and the expenses of the Supreme Court.*—(1) Appointments of officers and servants of the Supreme Court shall be made by the Chief Justice of India or such other Judge or officer of the Court as he may direct:

Provided that the President may by rule require that in such cases as may be specified in the rule, no person not already attached to the Court shall be appointed to any office connected with the Court, save after consultation with the Union Public Service Commission.

---

[19] Ins. by the Const. (42nd Am.) Act, 1976, s. 26 (w.e.f. 1.2.1977).

[20] Subs. by the Const. (43rd Am.) Act, 1977, s. 6, for "articles 131A and 139A" (w.e.f. 13.4.1978).

[21] Subs. by the Const. (42nd Am.) Act, 1976, s. 26, for "provisions of clause (3)" w.e.f. 1.2.1977.

[22] Certain words, figures and letters, omitted by the Const. (43rd Am.) Act, 1977, s. 6, w.e.f. 13.4.1978. The omitted words in cl. (2) are "Article 144A and of"; and in cl. (3) "Subject to the provisions of Article 144A".

[23] Subs. by the Const. (42nd Am.) Act, 1976, s. 26, for "The Minimum number" w.e.f. 1.2.1977.

(2) Subject to the provisions of any law made by Parliament, the conditions of service of officers and servants of the Supreme Court shall be such as may be prescribed by rules made by the Chief Justice of India or by some other Judge or officer of the Court authorised by the Chief Justice of India to make rules for the purpose:

Provided that the rules made under this clause shall, so far as they relate to salaries, allowances, leave or pensions, require the approval of the President.

(3) The administrative expenses of the Supreme Court, including all salaries, allowances and pensions payable to or in respect of the officers and servants of the Court, shall be charged upon the Consolidated Fund of India, and any fees or other moneys taken by the Court shall form part of that Fund. [s. 216, G.I. Act]

147. *Interpretation.*—In this Chapter and in Chapter V of Part VI, references to any substantial question of law as to the interpretation of this Constitution shall be construed as including references to any substantial question of law as to the interpretation of the Government of India Act, 1935 (including any enactment amending or supplementing that Act), or of any Order in Council or order made thereunder, or of the Indian Independence Act, 1947, or of any order made thereunder.

CHAPTER V.—COMPTROLLER AND AUDITOR-GENERAL OF INDIA

148. *Comptroller and Auditor-General of India.*—(1) There shall be a Comptroller and Auditor-General of India who shall be appointed by the President by warrant under his hand and seal and shall only be removed from office in like manner and on the like grounds as a Judge of the Supreme Court.

(2) Every person appointed to be the Comptroller and Auditor-General of India shall, before he enters upon his office, make and subscribe before the President, or some person appointed in that behalf by him, an oath or affirmation according to the form set out for the purpose in the Third Schedule.

(3) The salary and other conditions of service of the Comptroller and Auditor-General shall be such as may be determined by Parliament by law and, until they are so determined, shall be as specified in the Second Schedule:[24]

Provided that neither the salary of a Comptroller and Auditor-General nor his rights in respect of leave of absence, pension or age of retirement shall be varied to his disadvantage after his appointment.

(4) The Comptroller and Auditor-General shall not be eligible for further office either under the Government of India or under the Government of any State after he has ceased to hold his office.

(5) Subject to the provisions of this Constitution and of any law made by Parliament, the conditions of service of persons serving in the Indian Audit and Accounts Department and the administrative powers of the Comptroller and Auditor-General shall be such as may be prescribed by rules made by the President after consultation with the Comptroller and Auditor-General.

(6) The administrative expenses of the office of the Comptroller and Auditor-General, including all salaries, allowances and pensions payable to or in respect of persons serving in that office, shall be charged upon the Consolidated Fund of India. [s. 166, G.I. Act]

149. *Duties and powers of the Comptroller and Auditor-General.*—The Comptroller and Auditor-General shall perform such duties and exercise such powers in relation to the accounts of the Union and of the States and of any other authority or body as may be prescribed by or under any law made by Parliament and, until provision in that behalf is so made, shall perform such duties and exercise such powers in relation to the accounts of the Union and of the States as were conferred on or exercisable by the Auditor-General of India immediately before the com-

[24] See the Comptroller & Auditor-General (Conditions of Service) Act, 1953.

mencement of this Constitution in relation to the accounts of the Dominion of India and of the Provinces respectively. [s. 166, G.I. Act]

[25][**150.** *Form of accounts of the Union and of the States.*—The accounts of the Union and of the States shall be kept in such form as the President may, [26][on the advice of] the Comptroller and Auditor-General of India, prescribe.] [s. 168, G.I. Act]

151. *Audit reports.*—(1) The reports of the Comptroller and Auditor-General of India relating to the accounts of the Union shall be submitted to the President, who shall cause them to be laid before each House of Parliament.

(2) The reports of the Comptroller and Auditor-General of India relating to the accounts of a State shall be submitted to the Governor [27]* * * of the State, who shall cause them to be laid before the Legislature of the State. [s. 169, G.I. Act]

PART VI

THE STATES [28]***

CHAPTER I.—GENERAL

152. *Definition.*—In this Part, unless the context otherwise requires, the expression "State" [29][does not include the State of Jammu and Kashmir]. [s. 46, G.I. Act]

CHAPTER II.—THE EXECUTIVE

The Governor

153. *Governors of States.*—There shall be a Governor for each State:

[30][Provided that nothing in this article shall prevent the appointment of the same person as Governor for two or more States.]

154. *Executive power of State.*—(1) The executive power of the State shall be vested in the Governor and shall be exercised by him either directly or through officers subordinate to him in accordance with this Constitution.

(2) Nothing in this article shall—

(*a*) be deemed to transfer to the Governor any functions conferred by any existing law on any other authority; or

(*b*) prevent Parliament or the Legislature of the State from conferring by law functions on any authority subordinate to the Governor. [s. 49, G.I. Act]

155. *Appointment of Governor.*—The Governor of a State shall be appointed by the President by warrant under his hand and seal. [s. 48, G.I. Act]

156. *Term of office of Governor.*—(1) The Governor shall hold office during the pleasure of the President.

(2) The Governor may, by writing under his hand addressed to the President, resign his office.

---

[25] Subs. by the Const. (42nd Am.) Act, 1976, s. 27, for Art. 150 w.e.f. 1.4.1977. The article, as originally enacted, ran as follows:

"150. *Power of Comptroller and Auditor-General to give directions as to accounts.*—The accounts of the Union and of the States shall be kept in such form as the Comptroller and Auditor-General of India may, with the approval of the President, prescribe."

[26] Subs. by the Const. (44th Am.) Act, 1978, s. 22 for "after consultation with", w.e.f. 20.6.1979.

[27] The words "or Rajapramukh" omitted by the Const. (7th Am.) Act, 1956, s. 29 and Sch. w.e.f. 1.11.1956.

[28] The words "IN PART A OF THE FIRST SCHEDULE" omitted by the Const. (7th Am.) Act, 1956, s. 29 and Sch. w.e.f. 1.11.1956.

[29] Subs. by s. 29 and Sch., *ibid.*, for "means a State specified in Part A of the First Schedule", w.e.f. 1.11.1956.

[30] Added by s. 6, *ibid.*, w.e.f. 1.11.1956.

(3) Subject to the foregoing provisions of this article, a Governor shall hold office for a term of five years from the date on which he enters upon his office:

Provided that a Governor shall, notwithstanding the expiration of his term, continue to hold office until his successor enters upon his office.

157. *Qualifications for appointment as Governor.*—No person shall be eligible for appointment as Governor unless he is a citizen of India and has completed the age of thirty-five years.

158. *Conditions of Governor's office.*—(1) The Governor shall not be a member of either House of Parliament or of a House of the Legislature of any State specified in the First Schedule, and if a member of either House of Parliament or of a House of the Legislature of any such State be appointed Governor, he shall be deemed to have vacated his seat in that House on the date on which he enters upon his office as Governor.

(2) The Governor shall not hold any other office of profit.

(3) The Governor shall be entitled without payment of rent to the use of his official residences and shall be also entitled to such emoluments, allowances and privileges as may be determined by Parliament by law and, until provision in that behalf is so made, such emoluments, allowances and privileges as are specified in the Second Schedule.

[31][(3A) Where the same person is appointed as Governor of two or more States, the emoluments and allowances payable to the Governor shall be allocated among the States in such proportion as the President may by order determine.]

(4) The emoluments and allowances of the Governor shall not be diminished during his term of office.

159. *Oath or affirmation by the Governor.*—Every Governor and every person discharging the functions of the Governor shall, before entering upon his office, make and subscribe in the presence of the Chief Justice of the High Court exercising jurisdiction in relation to the State, or, in his absence, the seniormost Judge of that Court available, an oath or affirmation in the following form, that is to say—

"I, A. B., do $\frac{\text{swear in the name of God}}{\text{solemnly affirm}}$ that I will faithfully execute the office of Governor (or discharge the functions of the Governor) of .... (*name of the State*) and will to the best of my ability preserve, protect and defend the Constitution and the law and that I will devote myself to the service and well-being of the people of .... (*name of the State*)."

160. *Discharge of the functions of the Governor in certain contingencies.*—The President may make such provision as he thinks fit for the discharge of the functions of the Governor of a State in any contingency not provided for in this Chapter.

161. *Power of Governor to grant pardons, etc., and to suspend, remit or commute sentences in certain cases.*—The Governor of a State shall have the power to grant pardons, reprieves, respites or remissions of punishment or to suspend, remit or commute the sentence of any person convicted of any offence against any law relating to a matter to which the executive power of the State extends.

162. *Extent of executive power of State.*—Subject to the provisions of this Constitution, the executive power of a State shall extend to the matters with respect to which the Legislautre of the State has power to make laws:

Provided that in any matter with respect to which the Legislature of a State and Parliament have power to make laws, the executive power of the State shall be subject to, and limited by, the executive power expressly conferred by this Constitution or by any law made by Parliament upon the Union or authorities thereof.

[s. 49, G.I. Act]

---

[31] Ins. by the Const. (7th Am.) Act, 1956, s. 7, w.e.f. 1.11.1956.

Council of Ministers

163. *Council of Ministers to aid and advise Governor.*—(1) There shall be a Council of Ministers with the Chief Minister at the head to aid and advise the Governor in the exercise of his functions, except in so far as he is by or under this Constitution required to exercise his functions or any of them in his discretion.

(2) If any question arises whether any matter is or is not a matter as respects which the Governor is by or under this Constitution required to act in his discretion, the decision of the Governor in his discretion shall be final, and the validity of anything done by the Governor shall not be called in question on the ground that he ought or ought not to have acted in his discretion.

(3) The question whether any, and if so what, advice was tendered by Ministers to the Governor shall not be inquired into in any court. [ss. 50, 51, G.I. Act]

164. *Other provisions as to Ministers.*—(1) The Chief Minister shall be appointed by the Governor and the other Ministers shall be appointed by the Governor on the advice of the Chief Minister, and the Ministers shall hold office during the pleasure of the Governor:

Provided that in the States of Bihar, Madhya Pradesh and Orissa, there shall be a Minister in charge of tribal welfare who may in addition be in charge of the welfare of the Scheduled Castes and backward classes or any other work.

(2) The Council of Ministers shall be collectively responsible to the Legislative Assembly of the State.

(3) Before a Minister enters upon his office, the Governor shall administer to him the oaths of office and of secrecy according to the forms set out for the purpose in the Third Schedule.

(4) A Minister who for any period of six consecutive months is not a member of the Legislature of the State shall at the expiration of that period cease to be a Minister.

(5) The salaries and allowances of Ministers shall be such as the Legislature of the State may from time to time by law determine and, until the Legislature of the State so determines, shall be as specified in the Second Schedule.

[s. 51, G.I. Act]

The Advocate-General for the State

165. *Advocate-General for the State.*—(1) The Governor of each State shall appoint a person who is qualified to be appointed a Judge of a High Court to be Advocate-General for the State.

(2) It shall be the duty of the Advocate-General to give advice to the Government of the State upon such legal matters, and to perform such other duties of a legal character, as may from time to time be referred or assigned to him by the Governor, and to discharge the functions conferred on him by or under this Constitution or any other law for the time being in force.

(3) The Advocate-General shall hold office during the pleasure of the Governor, and shall receive such remuneration as the Governor may determine.

Conduct of Government Business

166. *Conduct of business of the Government of a State.*—(1) All executive action of the Government of a State shall be expressed to be taken in the name of the Governor.

(2) Orders and other instruments made and executed in the name of the Governor shall be authenticated in such manner as may be specified in rules to be made by the Governor, and the validity of an order or instrument which is so authenticated shall not be called in question on the ground that it is not an order or instrument made or executed by the Governor.

(3) The Governor shall make rules for the more convenient transaction of the business of the Government of the State, and for the allocation among Ministers

of the said business in so far as it is not business with respect to which the Governor is by or under this Constitution required to act in his discretion.

[s. 59, G.I. Act]

[32]* * * *

167. *Duties of Chief Minister as respects the furnishing of information to Governor, etc.*—It shall be the duty of the Chief Minister of each State—

(*a*) to communicate to the Governor of the State all decisions of the Council of Ministers relating to the administration of the affairs of the State and proposals for legislation;

(*b*) to furnish such information relating to the administration of the affairs of the State and proposals for legislation as the Governor may call for; and

(*c*) if the Governor so requires, to submit for the consideration of the Council of Ministers any matter on which a decision has been taken by a Minister but which has not been considered by the Council. [s. 59, G.I. Act]

CHAPTER III.—THE STATE LEGISLATURE

General

168. *Constitution of Legislatures in States.*—(1) For every State there shall be a Legislature which shall consist of the Governor, and

(*a*) in the States of [33][Andhra Pradesh], Bihar[34] * * *[35] [36][Tamil Nadu], [37][Maharashtra], [38][Karnataka], [39]* * * [40][and Uttar Pradesh], two Houses;

(*b*) in other States, one House.

(2) Where there are two Houses of the Legislature of a State, one shall be known as the Legislative Council and the other as the Legislative Assembly, and where there is only one House, it shall be known as the Legislative Assembly.

[s. 60, G.I. Act]

169. *Abolition or creation of Legislative Councils in States.*—(1) Notwithstanding anything in article 168, Parliament may by law provide for the abolition of the Legislative Council of a State having such a Council or for the creation of such a Council in a State having no such Council, if the Legislative Assembly of the State passes a resolution to that effect by a majority of the total membership of the Assembly and by a majority of not less than two-thirds of the members of the Assembly present and voting.

---

[32] Cl. (4) was ins. by the Const. (42nd Am.) Act, 1976, s. 28 w.e.f. 3.1.1977 and *omitted* by the Const. (44th Am.) Act, 1978, s. 23 w.e.f. 20.6.1979. The omitted clause (4) ran as follows:

"(4) No court or other authority shall be entitled to require the production of any rules made under clause (3) for the more convenient transaction of the business of the Government of the State."

[33] Ins. by the Legislative Councils Act, 1957 (37 of 1957), s. 3 (w.e.f. 1.7.1958).

[34] The word "Bombay" omitted by the Bombay Reorganisation Act, 1960 (11 of 1960), s. 20 (w.e.f. 1.5.1960).

[35] No date has been appointed under s. 8(2) of the Const. (7th Am.) Act, 1956 for the insertion of the words "Madhya Pradesh" in this sub-clause.

[36] Subs. by the Madras State (Alteration of Name) Act, 1968 (53 of 1968), s. 4, for "Madras" (w.e.f. 14.1.1969).

[37] Ins. by the Bombay Reorganisation Act, 1960 (11 of 1960), s. 20 (w.e.f. 1.5.1960).

[38] Subs. by the Mysore State (Alteration of Name) Act, 1973 (31 of 1973), s. 4, for "Mysore" (w.e.f. 1.11.1973), which was inserted by the Const. (7th Am.) Act, 1956, s. 8(1).

[39] The word "Punjab" omitted by the Punjab Legislative Council (Abolition) Act, 1969 (46 of 1969), s. 4 (w.e.f. 7.1.1970).

[40] Subs. by the West Bengal Legislative Council (Abolition) Act, 1969 (20 of 1969), s. 4, for "Uttar Pradesh and West Bengal" (w.e.f. 1.8.1969).

Earlier, by the Const. (Am. of 1st and 4th Sch.) Order, 1950, "Uttar Pradesh" had been substituted for "United Provinces".

(2) Any law referred to in clause (1) shall contain such provisions for the amendment of this Constitution as may be necessary to give effect to the provisions of the law and may also contain such supplemental, incidental and consequential provisions as Parliament may deem necessary.

(3) No such law as aforesaid shall be deemed to be an amendment of this Constitution for the purposes of article 368.

[41][**170.** *Composition of the Legislative Assemblies.*—(1) Subject to the provisions of article 333, the Legislative Assembly of each State shall consist of not more than five hundred, and not less than sixty, members chosen by direct election from territorial constituencies in the State.

(2) For the purposes of clause (1), each State shall be divided into territorial constituencies in such manner that the ratio between the population of each constituency and the number of seats allotted to it shall, so far as practicable, be the same throughout the State.

[42][*Explanation.*—In this clause, the expression "population" means the population as ascertained at the last preceding census of which the relevant figures have been published:

Provided that the reference in this *Explanation* to the last preceding census of which the relevant figures have been published shall, until the relevant figures for the first census taken after the year 2000 have been published, be construed as a reference to the 1971 census.]

(3) Upon the completion of each census, the total number of seats in the Legislative Assembly of each State and the division of each State into territorial consti-

---

[41] Subs. by the Const. (7th Am.) Act, 1956, w.e.f. 1.11.1956, for the original Article which read as follows:

"170. (1) Subject to the provisions of article 333, the Legislative Assembly of each State shall be composed of members chosen by direct election.

(2) The representation of each territorial constituency in the Legislative Assembly of a State shall be on the basis of the population of that constituency as ascertained at the last preceding census of which the relevant figures have been published and shall, save in the case of the autonomous districts of Assam and the constituency comprising the cantonment and municipality of Shillong, be on a scale of not more than one member for every seventy-five thousand of the population:

Provided that the total number of members in the Legislative Assembly of a State shall in no case be more than five hundred or less than sixty.

(3) The ratio between the number of members to be allotted to each territorial constituency in a State and the population of that constituency as ascertained at the last preceding census of which the relevant figures have been published shall, so far as practicable, be the same throughout the State.

(4) Upon the completion of each census, the representation of the several territorial constituencies in the Legislative Assembly of each State shall be readjusted by such authority, in such manner and with effect from such date as Parliament may by law determine:

Provided that such readjustment shall not affect representation in the Legislative Assembly until the dissolution of the then existing Assembly."

Note: Paragraph 2 of the Const. (Removal of Difficulties) Order No. VIII as amended by the Const. (7th Am.) Act, 1956, s. 29 and Sch. I provides as follows:

"For the period during which the tribal areas specified in Part B of the Table appended to paragraph 20 of the Sixth Schedule to the Constitution or any parts thereof are administered by the President by virtue of sub-paragraph (2) of paragraph 18 of the said Schedule, the Constitution of India shall have effect subject to the following adaptation:—

In clause (2) of article 170, after the words 'throughout the State', the following proviso shall be inserted, namely:—

'Provided that the constituencies into which the State of Assam is divided shall not comprise the tribal areas specified in Part B of the Table appended to paragraph 20 of the Sixth Schedule'."

[42] Subs. by the Const. (42nd Am.) Act, 1976, s. 29, for the *Explanation* w.e.f. 3.1.1977.

tuencies shall be readjusted by such authority and in such manner as Parliament may by law determine:

Provided that such readjustment shall not affect representation in the Legislative Assembly until the dissolution of the then existing Assembly:]

[43][Provided further that such readjustment shall take effect from such date as the President may, by order, specify and until such readjustment takes effect, any election to the Legislative Assembly may be held on the basis of the territorial constituencies existing before such readjustment:

Provided also that until the relevant figures for the first census taken after the year 2000 have been published, it shall not be necessary to readjust the total number of seats in the Legislative Assembly of each State and the division of such State into territorial constituencies under this clause.] [s. 61, Sch. V, G.I. Act]

171. *Composition of the Legislative Councils.*—(1) The total number of members in the Legislative Council of a State having such a Council shall not exceed [44][one-third] of the total number of members in the Legislative Assembly of that State:

Provided that the total number of members in the Legislative Council of a State shall in no case be less than forty.

(2) Until Parliament by law otherwise provides, the composition of the Legislative Council of a State shall be as provided in clause (3).

(3) Of the total number of members of the Legislative Council of a State—

(*a*) as nearly as may be, one-third shall be elected by electorates consisting of members of municipalities, district boards and such other local authorities in the State as Parliament may by law specify;

(*b*) as nearly as may be, one-twelfth shall be elected by electorates consisting of persons residing in the State who have been for at least three years graduates of any university in the territory of India or have been for at least three years in possession of qualifications prescribed by or under any law made by Parliament as equivalent to that of a graduate of any such university;

(*c*) as nearly as may be, one-twelfth shall be elected by electorates consisting of persons who have been for at least three years engaged in teaching in such educational institutions within the State, not lower in standard than that of a secondary school, as may be prescribed by or under any law made by Parliament;

(*d*) as nearly as may be, one-third shall be elected by the members of the Legislative Assembly of the State from amongst persons who are not members of the Assembly;

(*e*) the remainder shall be nominated by the Governor in accordance with the provisions of clause (5).

(4) The members to be elected under sub-clauses (*a*), (*b*) and (*c*) of clause (3) shall be chosen in such territorial constituencies as may be prescribed by or under any law made by Parliament, and the elections under the said sub-clauses and under sub-clause (*d*) of the said clause shall be held in accordance with the system of proportional representation by means of the single transferable vote.

(5) The members to be nominated by the Governor under sub-clause (*e*) of clause (3) shall consist of persons having special knowledge or practical experience in respect of such matters as the following, namely:—

Literature, science, art, co-operative movement and social service.

[s. 61, Sch. V, G.I. Act]

172. *Duration of State Legislatures.*—(1) Every Legislative Assembly of every State, unless sooner dissolved, shall continue for [45][five years] from the date ap-

---

[43] Ins. by the Const. (42nd Am.) Act, 1976, s. 29 (w.e.f. 3.1.1977).
[44] Subs. by the Const. (7th Am.) Act, 1956, s. 10, for "one-fourth".

pointed for its first meeting and no longer and the expiration of the said period of [45][five years] shall operate as a dissolution of the Assembly:

Provided that the said period may, while a Proclamation of Emergency is in operation, be extended by Parliament by law for a period not exceeding one year at a time and not extending in any case beyond a period of six months after the Proclamation has ceased to operate.

(2) The Legislative Council of a State shall not be subject to dissolution, but as nearly as possible one-third of the members thereof shall retire as soon as may be on the expiration of every second year in accordance with the provisions made in that behalf by Parliament by law. [s. 61, G.I. Act]

173. *Qualification for membership of the State Legislature.*—A person shall not be qualified to be chosen to fill a seat in the Legislature of a State unless he—

[46][(*a*) is a citizen of India, and makes and subscribes before some person authorised in that behalf by the Election Commission an oath or affirmation according to the form set out for the purpose in the Third Schedule;]

(*b*) is, in the case of a seat in the Legislative Assembly, not less than twenty-five years of age and, in the case of a seat in the Legislative Council, not less than thirty years of age; and

(*c*) possesses such other qualifications as may be prescribed in that behalf by or under any law made by Parliament.[47] [Sch. 5, G.I. Act]

[48][**174.** *Sessions of the State Legislature, prorogation and dissolution.*—(1) The Governor shall from time to time summon the House or each House of the Legislature of the State to meet at such time and place as he thinks fit, but six months shall not intervene between its last sitting in one session and the date appointed for its first sitting in the next session.

(2) The Governor may from time to time:—

(*a*) prorogue the House or either House;

(*b*) dissolve the Legislative Assembly.] [s. 62, G.I. Act]

175. *Right of Governor to address and send messages to the House or Houses.*—(1) The Governor may address the Legislative Assembly or, in the case of a State having a Legislative Council, either House of the Legislature of the State, or both Houses assembled together, and may for that purpose require the attendance of members.

(2) The Governor may send messages to the House or Houses of the Legislature of the State, whether with respect to a Bill then pending in the Legislature or otherwise, and a House to which any message is so sent shall with all convenient despatch consider any matter required by the message to be taken into consideration. [s. 63, G.I. Act]

---

[45] Subs. by the Const. (44th Am.) Act, 1978, s. 24, for "six years" (w.e.f. 6-9-1979). The words "six years" were subs. for the original words "five years" by the Const. (42nd Am.) Act, 1976, s. 30 (w.e.f. 3.1.1977).

[46] Subs. by the Const. (16th Am.) Act, 1963, w.e.f. 5.10.1963, for the original clause which read as follows:

"(*a*) is a citizen of India";

[47] See the Representation of the People Act, 1951.

[48] Subs. by the Const. (1st Am.) Act, 1951, w.e.f. 18.6.1951, for the original article which read as follows:

"174. (1) The House or Houses of the legislature of the State shall be summoned to meet twice at least in every year, and six months shall not intervene between their last sitting in one session and the date appointed for their first sitting in the next session.

(2) Subject to the provisions of clause (1), the Governor may from time to time—

(*a*) summon the House or either House to meet at such time and place as he thinks fit;

(*b*) prorogue the House or Houses;

(*c*) dissolve the Legislative Assembly."

176. *Special address by the Governor.*—(1) At the commencement of [49][the first session after each general election to the Legislative Assembly and at the commencement of the first session of each year], the Governor shall address the Legislative Assembly or, in the case of a State having a Legislative Council, both Houses assembled together and inform the Legislature of the causes of its summons.

(2) Provision shall be made by the rules regulating the procedure of the House or either House for the allotment of time for discussion of the matters referred to in such address [50]* * *.

177. *Rights of Ministers and Advocate-General as respects the Houses.*—Every Minister and the Advocate-General for a State shall have the right to speak in, and otherwise to take part in the proceedings of, the Legislative Assembly of the State or, in the case of a State having a Legislative Council, both Houses, and to speak in, and otherwise to take part in the proceedings of, any committee of the Legislature of which he may be named a member, but shall not, by virtue of this article, be entitled to vote. [s. 64, G.I. Act]

Officers of the State Legislature

178. *The Speaker and Deputy Speaker of the Legislative Assembly.*—Every Legislative Assembly of a State shall, as soon as may be, choose two members of the Assembly to be respectively Speaker and Deputy Speaker thereof and, so often as the office of Speaker or Deputy Speaker becomes vacant, the Assembly shall choose another member to be Speaker or Deputy Speaker, as the case may be. [s. 65, G.I. Act]

179. *Vacation and resignation of, and removal from, the offices of Speaker and Deputy Speaker.*—A member holding office as Speaker or Deputy Speaker of an Assembly—

(*a*) shall vacate his office if he ceases to be a member of the Assembly;
(*b*) may at any time by writing under his hand addressed, if such member is the Speaker, to the Deputy Speaker, and if such member is the Deputy Speaker, to the Speaker, resign his office; and
(*c*) may be removed from his office by a resolution of the Assembly passed by a majority of all the then members of the Assembly:

Provided that no resolution for the purpose of clause (*c*) shall be moved unless at least fourteen days' notice has been given of the intention to move the resolution:

Provided further that, whenever the Assembly is dissolved, the Speaker shall not vacate his office until immediately before the first meeting of the Assembly after the dissolution. [s. 65, G.I. Act]

180. *Power of the Deputy Speaker or other person to perform the duties of the office of, or to act as, Speaker.*—(1) While the office of Speaker is vacant, the duties of the office shall be performed by the Deputy Speaker or, if the office of Deputy Speaker is also vacant, by such member of the Assembly as the Governor may appoint for the purpose.

(2) During the absence of the Speaker from any sitting of the Assembly the Deputy Speaker or, if he is also absent, such person as may be determined by the rules of procedure of the Assembly, or, if no such person is present, such other person as may be determined by the Assembly, shall act as Speaker [s. 65, G.I. Act]

181. *The Speaker or the Deputy Speaker not to preside while a resolution for his removal from office is under consideration.*—(1) At any sitting of the Legislative Assembly, while any resolution for the removal of the Speaker from his office is under consideration, the Speaker, or while any resolution for the removal of the Deputy Speaker from his office is under consideration, the Deputy Speaker, shall not,

---

[49] Subs. by the Const. (1st Am.) Act, 1951, s. 9, for "every session," w.e.f. 18.6.1951.

[50] The words "and for the precedence of such discussion over other business of the House" omitted by s. 9, *ibid*.

though he is present, preside, and the provisions of clause (2) of article 180 shall apply in relation to every such sitting as they apply in relation to a sitting from which the Speaker or, as the case may be, the Deputy Speaker, is absent.

(2) The Speaker shall have the right to speak in, and otherwise to take part in the proceedings of, the Legislative Assembly while any resolution for his removal from office is under consideration in the Assembly and shall, notwithstanding anything in article 189, be entitled to vote only in the first instance on such resolution or on any other matter during such proceedings but not in the case of an equality of votes.

182. *The Chairman and Deputy Chairman of the Legislative Council.*—The Legislative Council of every State having such Council shall, as soon as may be, choose two members of the Council to be respectively Chairman and Deputy Chairman thereof and, so often as the office of Chairman or Deputy Chairman becomes vacant, the Council shall choose another member to be Chairman or Deputy Chairman, as the case may be. [s. 65, G.I. Act]

183. *Vacation and resignation of, and removal from, the offices of Chairman and Deputy Chairman.*—A member holding office as Chairman or Deputy Chairman of a Legislative Council—

(*a*) shall vacate his office if he ceases to be a member of the Council;

(*b*) may at any time by writing under his hand addressed, if such member is the Chairman, to the Deputy Chairman, and if such member is the Deputy Chairman, to the Chairman, resign his office; and

(*c*) may be removed from his office by a resolution of the Council passed by a majority of all the then members of the Council:

Provided that no resolution for the purpose of clause (*c*) shall be moved unless at least fourteen days' notice has been given of the intention to move the resolution. [s. 65, G.I. Act]

184. *Power of the Deputy Chairman or other person to perform the duties of the office of, or to act as, Chairman.*—(1) While the office of Chairman is vacant, the duties of the office shall be performed by the Deputy Chairman or, if the office of Deputy Chairman is also vacant, by such member of the Council as the Governor may appoint for the purpose.

(2) During the absence of the Chairman from any sitting of the Council the Deputy Chairman or, if he is also absent, such person as may be determined by the rules of procedure of the Council, or, if no such person is present, such other person as may be determined by the Council, shall act as Chairman. [s. 65, G.I. Act]

185. *The Chairman or the Deputy Chairman not to preside while a resolution for his removal from office is under consideration.*—(1) At any sitting of the Legislative Council, while any resolution for the removal of the Chairman from his office is under consideration, the Chairman, or while any resolution for the removal of the Deputy Chairman from his office is under consideration, the Deputy Chairman, shall not, though he is present, preside, and the provisions of clause (2) of article 184 shall apply in relation to every such sitting as they apply in relation to a sitting from which the Chairman or, as the case may be, the Deputy Chairman is absent.

(2) The Chairman shall have the right to speak in, and otherwise to take part in the proceedings of, the Legislative Council while any resolution for his removal from office is under consideration in the Council and shall, notwithstanding anything in article 189, be entitled to vote only in the first instance on such resolution or on any other matter during such proceedings but not in the case of an equality of votes.

186. *Salaries and allowances of the Speaker and Deputy Speaker and the Chairman and Deputy Chairman.*—There shall be paid to the Speaker and the Deputy Speaker of the Legislative Assembly, and to the Chairman and the Deputy Chairman of the Legislative Council, such salaries and allowances as may be respectively

fixed by the Legislature of the State by law and, until provision in that behalf is so made, such salaries and allowances as are specified in the Second Schedule.
[s. 65, G.I. Act]

187. *Secretariat of State Legislature.*—(1) The House or each House of the Legislature of a State shall have a separate secretarial staff:

Provided that nothing in this clause shall, in the case of the Legislature of a State having a Legislative Council, be construed as preventing the creation of posts common to both Houses of such Legislature.

(2) The Legislature of a State may by law regulate the recruitment, and the conditions of service of persons appointed, to the secretarial staff of the House or Houses of the Legislature of the State.

(3) Until provision is made by the Legislature of the State under clause (2), the Governor may, after consultation with the Speaker of the Legislative Assembly or the Chairman of the Legislative Council, as the case may be, make rules regulating the recruitment, and the conditions of service of persons appointed, to the secretarial staff of the Assembly or the Council, and any rules so made shall have effect subject to the provisions of any law made under the said clause.

Conduct of Business

188. *Oath or affirmation by members.*—Every member of the Legislative Assembly or the Legislative Council of a State shall, before taking his seat, make and subscribe before the Governor, or some person appointed in that behalf by him, an oath or affirmation according to the form set out for the purpose in the Third Schedule.
[s. 67, G.I. Act]

189. *Voting in Houses, power of Houses to act notwithstanding vacancies and quorum.*—(1) Save as otherwise provided in this Constitution, all questions at any sitting of a House of the Legislature of a State shall be determined by a majority of votes of the members present and voting, other than the Speaker or Chairman, or person acting as such.

The Speaker or Chairman, or person acting as such, shall not vote in the first instance, but shall have and exercise a casting vote in the case of an equality of votes.

(2) A House of the Legislature of a State shall have power to act notwithstanding any vacancy in the membership thereof, and any proceedings in the Legislature of a State shall be valid notwithstanding that it is discovered subsequently that some person who was not entitled so to do sat or voted or otherwise took part in the proceedings.

(3) Until the Legislature of the State by law otherwise provides, the quorum to constitute a meeting of a House of the Legislature of a State shall be ten members or one-tenth of the total number of members of the House, whichever is greater.

(4) If at any time during a meeting of the Legislative Assembly or the Legislative Council of a State there is no quorum, it shall be the duty of the Speaker or Chairman, or person acting as such, either to adjourn the House or to suspend the meeting until there is a quorum.
[s. 66, G.I. Act]

Disqualifications of Members

190. *Vacation of seats.*—(1) No person shall be a member of both Houses of the Legislature of a State and provision shall be made by the Legislature of the State by law for the vacation by a person who is chosen a member of both Houses of his seat in one House or the other.

(2) No person shall be a member of the Legislatures of two or more States specified in the First Schedule and if a person is chosen a member of the Legislatures of two or more such States, then, at the expiration of such period as may be

specified in rules[51] made by the President, that person's seat in the Legislatures of all such States shall become vacant, unless he has previously resigned his seat in the Legislatures of all but one of the States.

(3) If a member of a House of the Legislature of a State—

(*a*) becomes subject to any of the disqualifications mentioned in clause (1) of article 191; or

[52][(*b*) resigns his seat by writing under his hand addressed to the Speaker or the Chairman, as the case may be, and his resignation is accepted by the Speaker or the Chairman, as the case may be,]

his seat shall thereupon become vacant:

[53][Provided that in the case of any resignation referred to in sub-clause (*b*), if from information received or otherwise and after making such inquiry as he thinks fit, the Speaker or the Chairman, as the case may be, is satisfied that such resignation is not voluntary or genuine, he shall not accept such resignation.]

(4) If for a period of sixty days a member of a House of the Legislature of a State is without permission of the House absent from all meetings thereof, the House may declare his seat vacant:

Provided that in computing the said period of sixty days no account shall be taken of any period during which the House is prorogued or is adjourned for more than four consecutive days.

[s. 68, G.I. Act]

191. *Disqualifications for membership.*—(1) A person shall be disqualified for being chosen as, and for being, a member of the Legislative Assembly or Legislative Council of a State—

(*a*) if he holds any office of profit under the Government of India or the Government of any State specified in the First Schedule, other than an office declared by the Legislature of the State by law not to disqualify its holder;

(*b*) if he is of unsound mind and stands so declared by a competent court;

(*c*) if he is an undischarged insolvent;

(*d*) if he is not a citizen of India, or has voluntarily acquired the citizenship of a foreign State, or is under any acknowledgment of allegiance or adherence to a foreign State;

(*e*) if he is so disqualified by or under any law made by Parliament.[54]

(2) For the purposes of this article, a person shall not be deemed to hold an office of profit under the Government of India or the Government of any State specified in the First Schedule by reason only that he is a Minister either for the Union or for such State.

[s. 69, G.I. Act]

[55][**192.** *Decision on questions as to disqualifications of members.*—(1) If any question arises as to whether a member of a House of the Legislature of a

---

[51] *See* the Prohibition of Simultaneous Membership Rules, 1950 published with the Ministry of Law Notification No. F.46/50-C, dated the 26th January, 1950, Gazette of India, Extraordinary, p. 678.

[52] Subs. by the Const. (33rd Am.) Act, 1974, s. 3, for sub-clause (*b*) w.e.f. 19.5.1974. The original clause ran as follows:

"(*b*) resigns his seat by writing under his hand addressed to the Speaker or the Chairman, as the case may be."

[53] Ins. by s. 3, *ibid.* w.e.f. 19.5.1964.

[54] See the Representation of the People Act, 1951.

[55] Article 192 has been successively subs. by the Const. (42nd Am.) Act, 1976, s. 33 w.e.f. 3.1.1977 and the Const. (44th Am.) Act, 1978 s. 25 to read as above w.e.f. 20.6.1979. The original article as enacted was as follows:

"192. (1) If any question arises as to whether a member of a House of the Legislature of a State has become subject to any of the disqualifications mentioned in clause (1) of article 191, the question shall be referred for the decision of the Governor and his decision shall be final.

(2) Before giving any decision on any such question, the Governor shall obtain the opinion of the Election Commission and shall act according to such opinion."

State has become subject to any of the disqualifications mentioned in clause (1) of article 191, the question shall be referred for the decision of the Governor and his decision shall be final.

(2) Before giving any decision on any such question, the Governor shall obtain the opinion of the Election Commission and shall act according to such opinion.]

193. *Penalty for sitting and voting before making oath or affirmation under article 188 or when not qualified or when disqualified.*—If a person sits or votes as a member of the Legislative Assembly or the Legislative Council of a State before he has complied with the requirements of article 188, or when he knows that he is not qualified or that he is disqualified for membership thereof, or that he is prohibited from so doing by the provisions of any law made by Parliament or the Legislature of the State, he shall be liable in respect of each day on which he so sits or votes to a penalty of five hundred rupees to be recovered as a debt due to the State.

[s. 70, G.I. Act]

Powers, Privileges and Immunities of State Legislatures and their Members

194. *Powers, privileges, etc., of the Houses of Legislatures and of the members and committees thereof.*—(1) Subject to the provisions of this Constitution and to the rules and standing orders regulating the procedure of the Legislature, there shall be freedom of speech in the Legislature of every State.

(2) No member of the Legislature of a State shall be liable to any proceedings in any court in respect of anything said or any vote given by him in the Legislature or any committee thereof, and no person shall be so liable in respect of the publication by or under the authority of a House of such a Legislature of any report, paper, votes or proceedings.

(3) In other respects, the powers, privileges and immunities of a House of the Legislature of a State, and of the members and the committees of a House of such Legislature, shall be such as may from time to time be defined by the Legislature by law, and, until so defined, [56][shall be those of that House and of its members

---

The substituted article by the 42nd Const. Amendment read as follows:

"192. (1) If any question arises—

(a) as to whether a member of a House of the Legislature of a State has become subject to any of the disqualifications mentioned in clause (1) of article 191, or

(b) as to whether a person, found guilty of a corrupt practice at an election to a House of the Legislature of a State under any law made by Parliament, shall be disqualified for being chosen as, and for being, a member of either House of Parliament or of a House of the Legislature of a State, or as to the period for which he shall be so disqualified, or as to the removal of, or the reduction of the period of, such disqualification,

the question shall be referred for the decision of the President and his decision shall be final.

(2) Before giving any decision on any such question, the President shall consult the Election Commission and the Election Commission may, for this purpose, make such inquiry as it thinks fit."

[56] Subs. by the Const. (44th Am.) Act, 1978, s. 26, for certain words w.e.f. 20.6.1979. The Const. (42nd Am.) Act, 1976, by s. 34, had amended cl. (3) to read as follows:

"(3) In other respects, the powers, privileges and immunities of a House of the Legislature of a State, and of the members and the committees of a House of such Legislature, shall be those of that House, and of its members and Committees, at the commencement of s. 34 of the Const. (42nd Am.) Act, 1976, and as may be evolved by such House of the Legislature of a State, so far as may be, in accordance with those of the House of the People, and of its members and committees where such House is the Legislative Assembly and in accordance with those of the Council of States, and of its members and committees where such House is the Legislative Council."

Clause (3), as originally enacted ran as follows:

"(3) In other respects, the powers, privileges and immunities of a House of the Legislature of a State, and of the members and the committees of a House of such Legislature, shall be such as may from time to time be defined by the

and committees immediately before the coming into force of section 26 of the Constitution (Forty-fourth Amendment) Act, 1978].

(4) The provisions of clauses (1), (2) and (3) shall apply in relation to persons who by virtue of this Constitution have the right to speak in, and otherwise to take part in the proceedings of, a House of the Legislature of a State or any committee thereof as they apply in relation to members of that Legislature.

[s. 71, G.I. Act]

195. *Salaries and allowances of members.*—Members of the Legislative Assembly and the Legislative Council of a State shall be entitled to receive such salaries and allowances as may from time to time be determined by the Legislature of the State by law and, until provision in that respect is so made, salaries and allowances at such rates and upon such conditions as were immediately before the commencement of this Constitution applicable in the case of members of the Legislative Assembly of the corresponding Province.

[s. 72, G.I. Act]

Legislative Procedure

196. *Provisions as to introduction and passing of Bills.*—(1) Subject to the provisions of articles 198 and 207 with respect to Money Bills and other financial Bills, a Bill may originate in either House of the Legislature of a State which has a Legislative Council.

(2) Subject to the provisions of articles 197 and 198, a Bill shall not be deemed to have been passed by the Houses of the Legislature of a State having a Legislative Council unless it has been agreed to by both Houses, either without amendment or with such amendments only as are agreed to by both Houses.

(3) A Bill pending in the Legislature of a State shall not lapse by reason of the prorogation of the House or Houses thereof.

(4) A Bill pending in the Legislative Council of a State which has not been passed by the Legislative Assembly shall not lapse on a dissolution of the Assembly.

(5) A Bill which is pending in the Legislative Assembly of a State, or which having been passed by the Legislative Assembly is pending in the Legislative Council, shall lapse on a dissolution of the Assembly. [ss. 73, 74, G.I. Act]

197. *Restriction on powers of Legislative Council as to Bills other than Money Bills.*—(1) If after a Bill has been passed by the Legislative Assembly of a State having a Legislative Council and transmitted to the Legislative Council—

(*a*) the Bill is rejected by the Council; or

(*b*) more than three months elapse from the date on which the Bill is laid before the Council without the Bill being passed by it; or

(*c*) the Bill is passed by the Council with amendments to which the Legislative Assembly does not agree,

the Legislative Assembly may, subject to the rules regulating its procedure, pass the Bill again in the same or in any subsequent session with or without such amendments, if any, as have been made, suggested or agreed to by the Legislative Council and then transmit the Bill as so passed to the Legislative Council.

(2) If after a Bill has been so passed for the second time by the Legislative Assembly and transmitted to the Legislative Council—

(*a*) the Bill is rejected by the Council; or

(*b*) more than one month elapses from the date on which the Bill is laid before the Council without the Bill being passed by it; or

(*c*) the Bill is passed by the Council with amendments to which the Legislative Assembly does not agree,

---

Legislature by law, and, until so defined, shall be those of the House of Commons of the Parliament of the United Kingdom, and of its members and committees, at the commencement of this Constitution."

the Bill shall be deemed to have been passed by the Houses of the Legislature of the State in the form in which it was passed by the Legislative Assembly for the second time with such amendments, if any, as have been made or suggested by the Legislative Council and agreed to by the Legislative Assembly.

(3) Nothing in this article shall apply to a Money Bill.

198. *Special procedure in respect of Money Bills.*—(1) A Money Bill shall not be introduced in a Legislative Council.

(2) After a Money Bill has been passed by the Legislative Assembly of a State having a Legislative Council, it shall be transmitted to the Legislative Council for its recommendations, and the Legislative Council shall within a period of fourteen days from the date of its receipt of the Bill return the Bill to the Legislative Assembly with its recommendations, and the Legislative Assembly may thereupon either accept or reject all or any of the recommendations of the Legislative Council.

(3) If the Legislative Assembly accepts any of the recommendations of the Legislative Council, the Money Bill shall be deemed to have been passed by both Houses with the amendments recommended by the Legislative Council and accepted by the Legislative Assembly.

(4) If the Legislative Assembly does not accept any of the recommendations of the Legislative Council, the Money Bill shall be deemed to have been passed by both Houses in the form in which it was passed by the Legislative Assembly without any of the amendments recommended by the Legislative Council.

(5) If a Money Bill passed by the Legislative Assembly and transmitted to the Legislative Council for its recommendations is not returned to the Legislative Assembly within the said period of fourteen days, it shall be deemed to have been passed by both Houses at the expiration of the said period in the form in which it was passed by the Legislative Assembly. [s. 82, G.I. Act]

199. *Definition of "Money Bills."*—(1) For the purposes of this Chapter, a Bill shall be deemed to be a Money Bill if it contains only provisions dealing with all or any of the following matters, namely—

(*a*) the imposition, abolition, remission, alteration or regulation of any tax;

(*b*) the regulation of the borrowing of money or the giving of any guarantee by the State, or the amendment of the law with respect to any financial obligations undertaken or to be undertaken by the State;

(*c*) the custody of the Consolidated Fund or the Contingency Fund of the State, the payment of moneys into or the withdrawal of moneys from any such Fund;

(*d*) the appropriation of moneys out of the Consolidated Fund of the State;

(*e*) the declaring of any expenditure to be expenditure charged on the Consolidated Fund of the State, or the increasing of the amount of any such expenditure;

(*f*) the receipt of money on account of the Consolidated Fund of the State or the public account of the State or the custody or issue of such money; or

(*g*) any matter incidental to any of the matters specified in sub-clauses (*a*) to (*f*).

(2) A Bill shall not be deemed to be a Money Bill by reason only that it provides for the imposition of fines or other pecuniary penalties, or for the demand or payment of fees for licences or fees for services rendered, or by reason that it provides for the imposition, abolition, remission, alteration or regulation of any tax by any local authority or body for local purposes.

(3) If any question arises whether a Bill introduced in the Legislature of a State which has a Legislative Council is a Money Bill or not, the decision of the Speaker of the Legislative Assembly of such State thereon shall be final.

(4) There shall be endorsed on every Money Bill when it is transmitted to the Legislative Council under article 198, and when it is presented to the Governor for assent under article 200, the certificate of the Speaker of the Legislative Assembly signed by him that it is a Money Bill. [s. 82, G.I. Act]

200. *Assent to Bills.*—When a Bill has been passed by the Legislative Assembly of a State or, in the case of a State having a Legislative Council, has been passed by both Houses of the Legislature of the State, it shall be presented to the Governor and the Governor shall declare either that he assents to the Bill or that he withholds assent therefrom or that he reserves the Bill for the consideration of the President:

Provided that the Governor may, as soon as possible after the presentation to him of the Bill for assent, return the Bill if it is not a Money Bill together with a message requesting that the House or Houses will reconsider the Bill or any specified provisions thereof and, in particular, will consider the desirability or introducing any such amendments as he may recommend in his message and, when a Bill is so returned, the House or Houses shall reconsider the Bill accordingly, and if the Bill is passed again by the House or Houses with or without amendment and presented to the Governor for assent, the Governor shall not withhold assent therefrom:

Provided further that the Governor shall not assent to, but shall reserve for the consideration of the President, any Bill which in the opinion of the Governor would, if it became law, so derogate from the powers of the High Court as to endanger the position which that Court is by this Constitution designed to fill.

[s. 75, G.I. Act]

201. *Bills reserved for consideration.*—When a Bill is reserved by a Governor for the consideration of the President, the President shall declare either that he assents to the Bill or that he withholds assent therefrom:

Provided that, where the Bill is not a Money Bill, the President may direct the Governor to return the Bill to the House or, as the case may be, the Houses of the Legislature of the State together with such a message as is mentioned in the first proviso to article 200 and, when a Bill is so returned, the House or Houses shall reconsider it accordingly within a period of six months from the date of receipt of such message and, if it is again passed by the House or Houses with or without amendment, it shall be presented again to the President for his consideration.

[s. 76, G.I. Act]

Procedure in Financial Matters

202. *Annual financial statement.*—(1) The Governor shall in respect of every financial year cause to be laid before the House or Houses of the Legislature of the State a statement of the estimated receipts and expenditure of the State for that year, in this Part referred to as the "annual financial statement".

(2) The estimates of expenditure embodied in the annual financial statement shall show separately—

(*a*) the sums required to meet expenditure described by this Constitution as expenditure charged upon the Consolidated Fund of the State; and

(*b*) the sums required to meet other expenditure proposed to be made from the Consolidated Fund of the State;

and shall distinguish expenditure or revenue account from other expenditure.

(3) The following expenditure shall be expenditure charged on the Consolidated Fund of each State—

(*a*) the emoluments and allowances of the Governor and other expenditure relating to his office;

(*b*) the salaries and allowances of the Speaker and the Deputy Speaker of the Legislative Assembly and, in the case of a State having a Legislative Council, also of the Chairman and the Deputy Chairman of the Legislative Council;

(*c*) debt charges for which the State is liable including interest, sinking fund charges and redemption charges, and other expenditure relating to the raising of loans and the service and redemption of debt;

(*d*) expenditure in respect of the salaries and allowances of Judges of any High Court;

(e) any sums required to satisfy any judgment, decree or award of any court or arbitral tribunal;

(f) any other expenditure declared by this Constitution, or by the Legislature of the State by law, to be so charged. [s. 78, G.I. Act]

203. *Procedure in Legislature with respect to estimates.*—(1) So much of the estimates as relates to expenditure charged upon the Consolidated Fund of a State shall not be submitted to the vote of the Legislative Assembly, but nothing in this clause shall be construed as preventing the discussion in the Legislature of any of those estimates.

(2) So much of the said estimates as relates to other expenditure shall be submitted in the form of demands for grants to the Legislative Assembly, and the Legislative Assembly shall have power to assent, or to refuse to assent, to any demand, or to assent to any demand subject to a reduction of the amount specified therein.

(3) No demand for a grant shall be made except on the recommendation of the Governor. [s. 79, G.I. Act]

204. *Appropriation Bills.*—(1) As soon as may be after the grants under article 203 have been made by the Assembly, there shall be introduced a Bill to provide for the appropriation out of the Consolidated Fund of the State of all moneys required to meet—

(a) the grants so made by the Assembly; and

(b) the expenditure charged on the Consolidated Fund of the State but not exceeding in any case the amount shown in the statement previously laid before the House or Houses.

(2) No amendment shall be proposed to any such Bill in the House or either House of the Legislature of the State which will have the effect of varying the amount or altering the destination of any grant so made or of varying the amount of any expenditure charged on the Consolidated Fund of the State, and the decision of the person presiding as to whether an amendment is inadmissible under this clause shall be final.

(3) Subject to the provisions of articles 205 and 206, no money shall be withdrawn from the Consolidated Fund of the State except under appropriation made by law passed in accordance with the provisions of this article.

205. *Supplementary, additional or excess grants.*—(1) The Governor shall—

(a) if the amount authorised by any law made in accordance with the provisions of article 204 to be expended for a particular service for the current financial year is found to be insufficient for the purposes of that year or when a need has arisen during the current financial year for supplementary or additional expenditure upon some new service not contemplated in the annual financial statement for that year, or

(b) if any money has been spent on any service during a financial year in excess of the amount granted for that service and for that year,

cause to be laid before the House or the Houses of the Legislature of the State another statement showing the estimated amount of that expenditure or cause to be presented to the Legislative Assembly of the State a demand for such excess, as the case may be.

(2) The provisions of articles 202, 203 and 204 shall have effect in relation to any such statement and expenditure or demand and also to any law to be made authorising the appropriation of moneys out of the Consolidated Fund of the State to meet such expenditure or the grant in respect of such demand as they have effect in relation to the annual financial statement and the expenditure mentioned therein or to a demand for a grant and the law to be made for the authorisation of appropriation of moneys out of the Consolidated Fund of the State to meet such expenditure or grant. [s. 81, G.I. Act]

206. *Votes on account, votes of credit and exceptional grants.*—(1) Notwithstanding anything in the foregoing provisions of this Chapter, the Legislative Assembly of a State shall have power—

(*a*) to make any grant in advance in respect of the estimated expenditure for a part of any financial year pending the completion of the procedure prescribed in article 203 for the voting of such grant and the passing of the law in accordance with the provisions of article 204 in relation to that expenditure;

(*b*) to make a grant for meeting an unexpected demand upon the resources of the State when on account of the magnitude or the indefinite character of the service the demand cannot be stated with the details ordinarily given in an annual financial statement;

(*c*) to make an exceptional grant which forms no part of the current service of any financial year;

and the Legislature of the State shall have power to authorise by law the withdrawal of moneys from the Consolidated Fund of the State for the purposes for which the said grants are made.

(2) The provisions of articles 203 and 204 shall have effect in relation to the making of any grant under clause (1) and to any law to be made under that clause as they have effect in relation to the making of a grant with regard to any expenditure mentioned in the annual financial statement and the law to be made for the authorisation of appropriation of moneys out of the Consolidated Fund of the State to meet such expenditure.

207. *Special provisions as to financial Bills.*—(1) A Bill or amendment making provision for any of the matters specified in sub-clauses (*a*) to (*f*) of clause (1) of article 199 shall not be introduced or moved except on the recommendation of the Governor, and a Bill making such provision shall not be introduced in a Legislative Council:

Provided that no recommendation shall be required under this clause for the moving of an amendment making provision for the reduction or abolition of any tax.

(2) A Bill or amendment shall not be deemed to make provision for any of the matters aforesaid by reason only that it provides for the imposition of fines or other pecuniary penalties, or for the demand or payment of fees for licences or fees for services rendered, or by reason that it provides for the imposition, abolition, remission, alteration or regulation of any tax by any local authority or body for local purposes.

(3) A Bill which, if enacted and brought into operation, would involve expenditure from the Consolidated Fund of a State shall not be passed by a House of the Legislature of the State unless the Governor has recommended to that House the consideration of the Bill. [s. 82, G.I. Act]

Procedure Generally

208. *Rules of procedure.*—(1) A House of the Legislature of a State may make rules for regulating, subject to the provisions of this Constitution, its procedure and the conduct of its business.

(2) Until rules are made under clause (1), the rules of procedure and standing orders in force immediately before the commencement of this Constitution with respect to the Legislature for the corresponding Province shall have effect in relation to the Legislature of the State subject to such modifications and adaptations as may be made therein by the Speaker of the Legislative Assembly, or the Chairman of the Legislative Council, as the case may be.

(3) In a State having a Legislative Council the Governor, after consultation with the Speaker of the Legislative Assembly and the Chairman of the Legislative Council, may make rules as to the procedure with respect to communications between the two Houses.

209. *Regulation by law of procedure in the Legislature of the State in relation to financial business.*—The Legislature of a State may, for the purpose of the timely completion of financial business, regulate by law the procedure of, and the conduct of business in, the House or Houses of the Legislature of the State in relation to any financial matter or to any Bill for the appropriation of moneys out of the Consolidated Fund of the State, and, if and so far as any provision of any law so made is inconsistent with any rule made by the House or either House of the Legislature of the State under clause (1) of article 208 or with any rule or standing order having effect in relation to the Legislature of the State under clause (2) of that article, such provision shall prevail.

210. *Language to be used in the Legislature.*—(1) Notwithstanding anything in Part XVII, but subject to the provisions of article 348, business in the Legislature of a State shall be transacted in the official language or languages of the State or in Hindi or in English:

Provided that the Speaker of the Legislative Assembly or Chairman of the Legislative Council, or person acting as such, as the case may be, may permit any member who cannot adequately express himself in any of the languages aforesaid to address the House in his mother-tongue.

(2) Unless the Legislature of the State by law otherwise provides, this article shall, after the expiration of a period of fifteen years from the commencement of this Constitution, have effect as if the words "or in English" were omitted therefrom:

[57][Provided that in relation to the [58][Legislatures of the States of Himachal Pradesh, Manipur, Meghalaya and Tripura] this clause shall have effect as if for the words "fifteen years" occurring therein, the words "twenty-five years" were substituted.]

[s. 85, G.I. Act]

211. *Restriction on discussion in the Legislature.*—No discussion shall take place in the Legislature of a State with respect to the conduct of any Judge of the Supreme Court or of a High Court in the discharge of his duties.

212. *Courts not to inquire into proceedings of the Legislature.*—(1) The validity of any proceedings in the Legislature of a State shall not be called in question on the ground of any alleged irregularity of procedure.

(2) No officer or member of the Legislature of a State in whom powers are vested by or under this Constitution for regulating procedure or the conduct of business, or for maintaining order, in the Legislature shall be subject to the jurisdiction of any court in respect of the exercise by him of those powers.

[s. 87, G.I. Act]

CHAPTER IV.—LEGISLATIVE POWER OF THE GOVERNOR

213. *Power of Governor to promulgate Ordinances during recess of Legislature.*—(1) If at any time, except when the Legislative Assembly of a State is in session, or where there is a Legislative Council in a State, except when both Houses of the Legislature are in session, the Governor is satisfied that circumstances exist which render it necessary for him to take immediate action, he may promulgate such Ordinances as the circumstances appear to him to require:

Provided that the Governor shall not, without instructions from the President, promulgate any such Ordinance if—

(*a*) a Bill containing the same provisions would under this Constitution have required the previous sanction of the President for the introduction thereof into the Legislature; or

---

[57] Ins. by the State of Himachal Pradesh Act, 1970 (53 of 1970), s. 46 (w.e.f. 25.1.1971).

[58] Subs. by the North-Eastern Areas (Reorganisation) Act, 1971 (81 of 1971), s. 71, for "Legislature of the State of Himachal Pradesh" (w.e.f. 21.1.1972).

(*b*) he would have deemed it necessary to reserve a Bill containing the same provisions for the consideration of the President; or

(*c*) an Act of the Legislature of the State containing the same provisions would under this Constitution have been invalid unless, having been reserved for the consideration of the President, it had received the assent of the President.

(2) An Ordinance promulgated under this article shall have the same force and effect as an Act of the Legislature of the State assented to by the Governor, but every such Ordinance—

(*a*) shall be laid before the Legislative Assembly of the State, or where there is a Legislative Council in the State, before both the Houses, and shall cease to operate at the expiration of six weeks from the reassembly of the Legislature, or if before the expiration of that period a resolution disapproving it is passed by the Legislative Assembly and agreed to by the Legislative Council, if any, upon the passing of the resolution or, as the case may be, on the resolution being agreed to by the Council; and

(*b*) may be withdrawn at any time by the Governor.

Explanation.—Where the Houses of the Legislature of a State having a Legislative Council are summoned to reassemble on different dates, the period of six weeks shall be reckoned from the later of those dates for the purposes of this clause.

(3) If and so far as an Ordinance under this article makes any provision which would not be valid if enacted in an Act of the Legislature of the State assented to by the Governor, it shall be void:

Provided that, for the purposes of the provisions of this Constitution relating to the effect of an Act of the Legislature of a State which is repugnant to an Act of Parliament or an existing law with respect to a matter enumerated in the Concurrent List, an Ordinance promulgated under this article in pursuance of instructions from the President shall be deemed to be an Act of the Legislature of the State which has been reserved for the consideration of the President and assented to by him. [s. 88, G.I. Act]

[59] * * * * *

CHAPTER V.—THE HIGH COURTS IN THE STATES

214. *High Courts for States.*—[60]* * There shall be a High Court for each State. [s. 219, G.I. Act]

[61] * * * * *

215. *High Courts to be courts of record.*—Every High Court shall be a court of record and shall have all the powers of such a court including the power to punish for contempt of itself. [s. 220, G.I. Act]

---

[59] Cl. (4) was ins. by the Const. (38th Am.) Act, 1975, s. 3 (retrospectively) and omitted by the Const. (44th Am.) Act, 1978, s. 27 (w.e.f. 20.6.1979).

The omitted clause (4) ran as follows:

"(4) Notwithstanding anything in this Constitution, the satisfaction of the Governor mentioned in clause (1) shall be final and conclusive and shall not be questioned in any court on any ground."

[60] The brackets and figure "(1)" omitted by the Const. (7th Am.) Act, 1956, s. 29 and Sch. w.e.f. 1.11.1956.

[61] Cls. (2) and (3) omitted by s. 29 and Sch., *ibid.* The original clauses (2) and (3) read as follows:

"(2) For the purposes of this Constitution the High Court exercising jurisdiction in relation to any Province immediately before the commencement of this Constitution shall be deemed to be the High Court for the corresponding State.

(3) The provisions of this Chapter shall apply to every High Court referred to in this article.

216. *Constitution of High Courts.*—Every High Court shall consist of a Chief Justice and such other Judges as the President may from time to time deem it necessary to appoint. [s. 220, G.I. Act]

[62] * * * * *

217. *Appointment and conditions of the office of a Judge of a High Court.*—(1) Every Judge of a High Court shall be appointed by the President by warrant under his hand and seal after consultation with the Chief Justice of India, the Governor of the State, and, in the case of appointment of a Judge other than the Chief Justice, the Chief Justice of the High Court, and [63][shall hold office, in the case of an additional or acting Judge, as provided in article 224, and in any other case, until he attains the age of [64][sixty-two years]]:

Provided that—

(*a*) a Judge may, by writing under his hand addressed to the President, resign his office;

(*b*) a Judge may be removed from his office by the President in the manner provided in clause (4) of article 124 for the removal of a Judge of the Supreme Court;

(*c*) the office of a Judge shall be vacated by his being appointed by the President to be a Judge of the Supreme Court or by his being transferred by the President to any other High Court within the territory of India.

(2) A person shall not be qualified for appointment as a Judge of a High Court unless he is a citizen of India and—

(*a*) has for at least ten years held a judicial office in the territory of India; or

(*b*) has for at least ten years been an advocate of a High Court [65] * * * or of two or more such Courts in succession; [66] * * *

[66] * * * * *

Explanation.—For the purposes of this clause—

[67][(*a*) in computing the period during which a person has held judicial office in the territory of India, there shall be included any period, after he has held any judicial office, during which the person has been an advocate of a High Court or has held the office of a member of a tribunal or any post, under the Union or a State, requiring special knowledge of law;]

---

[62] Proviso omitted by s. 11, *ibid.* The original proviso read as follows:

"Provided that the Judges so appointed shall at no time exceed in number such maximum number as the President may, from time to time, by order fix in relation to that Court.

[63] Subs. by *ibid.* s. 12 for "shall hold office until he attains the age of sixty years".

[64] Subs. by the Const. (15th Am.) Act, 1963, s. 4, for "sixty years", w.e.f. 5.10.1963.

[65] The words "in any State specified in the First Schedule" omitted by the Const. (7th Am.) Act, 1956, s. 29 and Sch. w.e.f. 1.11.1956.

[66] The word "or" and cl. (c) were ins. by the Const. (42nd Am.) Act, 1976, s. 36 w.e.f. 3.1.1977 and omitted by the Const. (44th Am.) Act, 1978, s. 28 w.e.f. 20.6.1979. The omitted cl. (c) ran as follows:

"(c) is, in the opinion of the President, a distinguished jurist";

[67] Ins. by the Const. (44th Am.) Act, 1978, s. 28, w.e.f. 20.6.1979. Clause (*a*) as originally enacted, was as follows:

"(*a*) in computing the period during which a person has been an advocate of a High Court, there shall be included any period during which the person has held judicial office after he became an advocate";

The above clause (*a*) was amended by the Const. (42nd Am.) Act, 1976, s. 36(c) to read as follows:

"(c) In the *Explanation*, in clause (*a*), for the words 'has held judicial office' the words 'has held judicial office or the office of a member of a tribunal or any post, under the Union or a State, requiring special knowledge of law" shall be substituted."

[68][(*aa*)] in computing the period during which a person has been an advocate of a High Court, there shall be included any period during which the person [69][has held judicial office or the office of a member of a tribunal or any post, under the Union or a State, requiring special knowledge of law] after he became an advocate;

(*b*) in computing the period during which a person has held judicial office in the territory of India or been an advocate of a High Court, there shall be included any period before the commencement of this Constitution during which he has held judicial office in any area which was comprised before the fifteenth day of August, 1947, within India as defined by the Government of India Act, 1935, or has been an advocate of any High Court in any such area, as the case may be.

[70][(3) If any question arises as to the age of a Judge of a High Court, the question shall be decided by the President after consultation with the Chief Justice of India and the decision of the President shall be final.] [s. 220, G.I. Act]

218. *Application of certain provisions relating to Supreme Court to High Courts.*—The provisions of clauses (4) and (5) of article 124 shall apply in relation to a High Court as they apply in relation to the Supreme Court with the substitution of references to the High Court for references to the Supreme Court. [s. 220, G.I. Act]

219. *Oath or affirmation by Judges of High Courts.*—Every person appointed to be a Judge of a High Court [71] * * * shall, before he enters upon his office, make and subscribe before the Governor of the State, or some person appointed in that behalf by him, an oath or affirmation according to the form set out for the purpose in the Third Schedule. [s. 220, G.I. Act]

[72][**220.** *Restriction on practice after being a permanent Judge.*—No person who, after the commencement of this Constitution, has held office as a permanent Judge of a High Court shall plead or act in any court or before any authority in India except the Supreme Court and the other High Courts.

Explanation.—In this article, the expression "High Court" does not include a High Court for a State specified in Part B of the First Schedule as it existed before the commencement[73] of the Constitution (Seventh Amendment) Act, 1956.]

221. *Salaries, etc., of Judges.*—(1) There shall be paid to the Judges of each High Court such salaries as are specified in the Second Schedule

(2) Every Judge shall be entitled to such allowances and to such rights in respect of leave of absence and pension as may from time to time be determined by or under law made by Parliament[74] and, until so determined, to such allowances and rights as are specified in the Second Schedule:

Provided that neither the allowances of a Judge nor his rights in respect of leave of absence or pension shall be varied to his disadvantage after his appointment. [s. 221, G.I. Act]

---

[68] Cl. (*a*) re-lettered as cl. (*aa*) by the Const. (44th Am.) Act, 1978, s. 28 w.e.f. 20.6.1979.

[69] Subs. by the Const. (42nd Am.) Act, 1976, for "has held judicial office" w.e.f. 3.1.1977.

[70] Ins. by the Const. (15th Am.) Act, 1963, s. 4 on 5.10.1963 w.e.f. 26.1.1950.

[71] The words "in a State" omitted by the Const. (7th Am.) Act, 1956, s. 29 and Sch. w.e.f. 1.11.1956.

[72] Subs. by the Const. (7th Am.) Act, 1956, w.e.f. 1.11.1956 for the original article 220, which read as follows:

"220. No person who has held office as a Judge of a High Court after the commencement of this Constitution shall plead or act in any Court or before any authority within the territory of India."

[73] i.e. 1st November, 1956.

[74] See the High Court Judges (Conditions of Service) Act, 1954.

222. *Transfer of a Judge from one High Court to another.*—(1) The President may, after consultation with the Chief Justice of India, transfer a Judge from one High Court to any other High Court [75] * * *.

[76][(2) When a Judge has been or is so transferred, he shall, during the period he serves, after the commencement of the Constitution (Fifteenth Amendment) Act, 1963, as a Judge of the other High Court, be entitled to receive in addition to his salary such compensatory allowance as may be determined by Parliament by law and, until so determined, such compensatory allowance as the President may by order fix.]

223. *Appointment of acting Chief Justice.*—When the office of Chief Justice of a High Court is vacant or when any such Chief Justice is, by reason of absence or otherwise, unable to perform the duties of his office, the duties of the office shall be performed by such one of the other Judges of the Court as the President may appoint for the purpose. [s. 222, G.I. Act]

[77][**224.** *Appointment of additional and acting Judges.*—(1) If by reason of any temporary increase in the business of a High Court or by reason of arrears of work therein, it appears to the President that the number of the Judges of that Court should be for the time being increased, the President may appoint duly qualified persons to be additional Judges of the Court for such period not exceeding two years as he may specify.

(2) When any Judge of a High Court other than the Chief Justice is by reason of absence or for any other reason unable to perform the duties of his office or is appointed to act temporarily as Chief Justice, the President may appoint a duly qualified person to act as a Judge of that Court until the permanent Judge has resumed his duties.

(3) No person appointed as an additional or acting Judge of a High Court shall hold office after attaining the age of [78][sixty-two years].

[79][**224A.** *Appointment of retired Judges at sittings of High Courts.*—Notwithstanding anything in this Chapter, the Chief Justice of a High Court for any State may at any time, with the previous consent of the President, request any person who has held the office of a Judge of that Court or of any other High Court to sit and act as a Judge of the High Court for that State, and every such person so requested shall, while so sitting and acting, be entitled to such allowances as the President may by order determine and have all the jurisdiction, powers and privileges of, but shall not otherwise be deemed to be, a Judge of that High Court:

---

[75] The words "within the territory of India" omitted by the Const. (7th Am.) Act, 1956, s. 14 w.e.f. 1.11.1956.

[76] Ins. by the Const. (15th Am.) Act, 1963, w.e.f. 5.10.1963. The original clause (2) as in force in 1950, which had been deleted by the Const. (7th Am.) Act, 1956, w.e.f. 1.11.1956, read as follows:

> "(2) When a Judge is so transferred, he shall, during the period he serves as a Judge of the other Court, be entitled to receive in addition to his salary such compensatory allowance as may be determined by Parliament by law, and, until so determined, such compensatory allowance as the President may by order fix."

[77] Subs. by the Const. (7th Am.) Act, 1956, w.e.f. 1.11.1956, for the original Article which read as follows:

> "Notwithstanding anything in this Chapter, the Chief Justice of a High Court for any State may at any time, with the previous consent of the President, request any person who has held the office of a Judge of that Court or of any other High Court to sit and act as a Judge of the High Court for that State, and every such person so requested shall, while so sitting and acting, be entitled to such allowances as the President may by order determine and have all the jurisdiction, powers and privileges of, but shall not otherwise be deemed to be, a Judge of that High Court. Provided that nothing in this article shall be deemed to require any person as aforesaid to sit and act as a Judge of that High Court unless he consents so to do."

[78] Subs. by the Const. (15th Am.) Act, 1963, w.e.f. 5.10.1963 for "sixty years".

[79] Ins. by the Const. (15th Am.) Act, 1963, s. 7, w.e.f. 5.10.1963.

Provided that nothing in this article shall be deemed to require any such person as aforesaid to sit and act as a Judge of that High Court unless he consents so to do.]

225. *Jurisdiction of existing High Courts.*—Subject to the provisions of this Constitution and to the provisions of any law of the appropriate Legislature made by virtue of powers conferred on that Legislature by this Constitution, the jurisdiction of, and the law administered in, any existing High Court, and the respective powers of the Judges thereof in relation to the administration of justice in the Court, including any power to make rules of Court and to regulate the sittings of the Court and of members thereof sitting alone or in Division Courts, shall be the same as immediately before the commencement of this Constitution:

[80][Provided that any restriction to which the exercise of original jurisdiction by any of the High Courts with respect to any matter concerning the revenue or concerning any act ordered or done in the collection thereof was subject immediately before the commencement of this Constitution shall no longer apply to the exercise of such jurisdiction.] [ss. 223, 226, G.I. Act]

[81][226. *Power of High Courts to issue certain writs.*—(1) Notwithstanding anything in article 32 [82] * * *, every High Court shall have power, throughout the territories in relation to which it exercises jurisdiction, to issue to any person or authority, including in appropriate cases, any Government, within those territories directions, orders or writs, including [83][writs in the nature of *habeas corpus, mandamus,* prohibition, *quo warranto* and *certiorari,* or any of them, for the enforcement of any of the rights conferred by Part III and for any other purpose.]

(2) The power conferred by clause (1) to issue directions, orders or writs to any Government, authority or person may also be exercised by any High Court exercising jurisdiction in relation to the territories within which the cause of action, wholly or in part, arises for the exercise of such power, notwithstanding that the seat of such Government or authority or the residence of such person is not within those territories.

[84][(3) Where any party against whom an interim order, whether by way of injunction or stay or in any other manner, is made on, or in any proceedings relating to, a petition under clause (1), without—

---

[80] Ins. by the Const. (44th Am.) Act, 1978, s. 29 w.e.f. 20.6.1979. The original proviso was omitted by the Const. (42nd Am.) Act, 1976, s. 37 w.e.f. 1.2.1977.

[81] Subs. by the Const. (42nd Am.) Act, 1976, s. 38, for Art. 226 w.e.f. 1.2.1977.

[82] The words, figures and letters "but subject to the provisions of article 131A and article 226A" omitted by the Const. (43rd Am.) Act, 1977, s. 7 w.e.f. 13.4.1978.

[83] Subs. by the Const. (44th Am.) Act, 1978, s. 30, for the portion beginning with the words "writs in the nature of *habeas corpus, mandamus,* prohibition, *quo warranto* and *certiorari,* or any of them, — (*a*) for the enforcement of any of the rights conferred by the provisions of Part III; or (*b*) for the redress of any injury of a substantial nature by reason of the contravention of any other provision of this Constitution or any provision of any enactment or Ordinance or any order, rule, regulation, bye-law or other instrument made thereunder; or (*c*) for the redress of any injury by reason of any illegality in any proceedings by or before any authority under any provision referred to in sub-clause (*b*) where such illegality has resulted in substantial failure of justice." w.e.f. 1.8.1979.

[84] Subs. by s. 30, *ibid.*, for cls. (3), (4), (5) and (6) w.e.f. 1.8.1979. The clauses substituted read as follows:

"(3) No petition for the redress of any injury referred to in sub-clause (*b*) or sub-clause (*c*) of clause (1) shall be entertained if any other remedy for such redress is provided for by or under any other law for the time being in force.

(4) No interim order (whether by way of injunction or stay or in any other manner) shall be made on, or in any proceedings relating to, a petition under clause (1) unless—

(*a*) copies of such petition and of all documents for such interim order are furnished to the party against whom such petition is filed or proposed to be filed; and

(*b*) opportunity is given to such party to be heard in the matter.

(*a*) furnishing to such party copies of such petition and all documents in support of the plea for such interim order; and

(*b*) giving such party an opportunity of being heard,

makes an application to the High Court for the vacation of such order and furnishes a copy of such application to the party in whose favour such order has been made or the counsel of such party, the High Court shall dispose of the application within a period of two weeks from the date on which it is received or from the date on which the copy of such application is so furnished, whichever is later, or where the High Court is closed on the last day of that period, before the expiry of the next day afterwards on which the High Court is open; and if the application is not so disposed of, the interim order shall, on the expiry of that period, or, as the case may be, the expiry of the said next day, stand vacated.]

[85][(4) The power conferred on a High Court by this article shall not be in derogation of the power conferred on the Supreme Court by clause (2) of article 32.][85a]

[86]**226A.** [*Constitutional validity of Central laws not to be considered in proceedings under article* 226.] *Rep. by the Constitution (Forty-third Amendment) Act,* 1977, *s.* 8 (*w.e.f.* 13-4-1978).

---

(5) The High Court may dispense with the requirements of sub-clauses (*a*) and (*b*) of clause (4) and make an interim order as an exceptional measure if it is satisfied for reasons to be recorded in writing that it is necessary so to do for preventing any loss being caused to the petitioner which cannot be adequately compensated in money but any such interim order shall, if it is not vacated earlier, cease to have effect on the expiry of a period of fourteen days from the date on which it is made unless the said requirements have been complied with before the expiry of that period and the High Court has continued the operation of the interim order.

(6) Notwithstanding anything in clause (4) or clause (5), no interim order (whether by way of injunction or stay or in any other manner) shall be made on, or in any proceedings relating to, a petition under clause (1) where such order will have the effect of delaying any inquiry into a matter of public importance or any investigation or inquiry into an offence punishable with imprisonment or any action for the execution of any work or project of public utility, or the acquisition of any property for such execution, by the Government or any corporation owned or controlled by the Government."

[85] Cl. (7) renumbered as cl. (4) by the Const. (44th Am.) Act, 1978, s. 30, w.e.f. 1.8.1979.

[85a] Article 226 as originally enacted, and prior to the Const. (42nd Am.) Act, 1976, ran as follows:

"226. (1) Notwithstanding anything in article 32, every High Court shall have power, throughout the territories in relation to which it exercises jurisdiction, to issue to any person or authority, including in appropriate cases any Government, within those territories directions, orders or writs, including writs in the nature of *habeas corpus, mandamus,* prohibition, *quo warranto* and *certiorari,* or any of them, for the enforcement of any of the rights conferred by Part III and for any other purpose.

[(1A) The power conferred by clause (1) to issue directions, orders or writs to any Government, authority or person may also be exercised by any High Court exercising jurisdiction in relation to the territories within which the cause of action wholly or in part, arises for the exercise of such power, notwithstanding that the seat of such Government or authority or the residence of such person is not within those terrritories.]

(2) The power conferred on a High Court by [clause (1) or clause (1A)] shall not be in derogation of the power conferred on the Supreme Court by clause (2) of article 32."

Note: Article (1A) was inserted by the Const. (15th Am.) Act, 1963 w.e.f. 5.10.1963. The words and figures in square brackets in clause (2) were substituted by *ibid.*, for "clause (1)".

[86] The repealed article 226A ran as follows:

"226A. Notwithstanding anything in article 226, the High Court shall not consider the constitutional validity of any Central law in any proceedings under that article."

227. *Power of superintendence over all courts by the High Court.*—[87][(1) Every High Court shall have superintendence over all courts and tribunals throughout the territories in relation to which it exercises jurisdiction.]

(2) Without prejudice to the generality of the foregoing provision, the High Court may—

(*a*) call for returns from such courts;

(*b*) make and issue general rules and prescribe forms for regulating the practice and proceedings of such courts; and

(*c*) prescribe forms in which books, entries and accounts shall be kept by the officers of any such courts.

(3) The High Court may also settle tables of fees to be allowed to the sheriff and all clerks and officers of such courts and to attorneys, advocates and pleaders practising therein:

Provided that any rules made, forms prescribed or tables settled under clause (2) or clause (3) shall not be inconsistent with the provision of any law for the time being in force, and shall require the previous approval of the Governor.

(4) Nothing in this article shall be deemed to confer on a High Court powers of superintendence over any court or tribunal constituted by or under any law relating to the Armed Forces. [s. 224, G.I. Act]

[88] * * * * *

228. *Transfer of certain cases to High Court.*—If the High Court is satisfied that a case pending in a court subordinate to it involves a substantial question of law as to the interpretation of this Constitution the determination of which is necessary for the disposal of the case, [89][it shall withdraw the case and [90]* * * may—]

(*a*) either dispose of the case itself, or

(*b*) determine the said question of law and return the case to the court from which the case has been so withdrawn together with a copy of its judgment on such question, and the said court shall on receipt thereof proceed to dispose of the case in conformity with such judgment. [s. 225, G.I. Act]

[91] **228A** [*Special provisions as to disposal of questions relating to constitutional validity of State laws.*] *Rep. by the Constitution (Forty-third Amendment) Act,* 1977, *s.* 10 (*w.e.f.* 13-4-1978).

---

[87] Cl. (1) has been successively subs. by the Const. (42nd Am.) Act, 1976, s. 40 w.e.f. 1.2.1977 and the Const. (44th Am.) Act, 1978, s. 31 to read as above, w.e.f. 20.6.1979. The 42nd Am. Act had substituted cl. (1) to read as follows:

"(1) Every High Court shall have superintendence over all courts subject to its appellate jurisdiction."

[88] Cl. (5) was ins. by the Const. (42nd Am.) Act, 1976, s. 40 w.e.f. 1.2.1977 and omitted by the Const. (44th Am.) Act, 1978, s. 31 w.e.f. 20.6.1979. The omittted clause ran as follows:

"(5) Nothing in this article shall be construed as giving to a High Court any jurisdiction to question any judgment of any inferior court which is not otherwise subject to appeal or revision."

[89] Subs. by the Const. (42nd Am.) Act, 1976, s. 41 for "it shall withdraw the case and may—" w.e.f. 1.2.1977.

[90] The words, figures and letter, "subject to the provisions of article 131A" omitted by the Const. (43rd Am.) Act, 1977, s. 9 w.e.f. 13.4.1978.

[91] Ins. by the Const. (42nd Am.) Act, 1976, s. 42, w.e.f. 1.2.1977. The repealed article ran as follows:

"228A. (1) No High Court shall have jurisdiction to declare any Central law to be constitutionally invalid.

(2) Subject to the provisions of article 131A, the High Court may determine all questions relating to the constitutional validity of any State law.

(3) The minimum number of Judges who shall sit for the purpose of determining any question as to the constitutional validity of any State law shall be five:

Provided that where the High Court consists of less than five Judges, all the Judges of the High Court may sit and determine such question.

229. *Officers and servants and the expenses of High Courts.*—(1) Appointments of officers and servants of a High Court shall be made by the Chief Justice of the Court or such other Judge or officer of the Court as he may direct:

Provided that the Governor of the State [92] * * * may by rule require that in such cases as may be specified in the rule no person not already attached to the Court shall be appointed to any office connected with the Court save after consultation with the State Public Service Commission.

(2) Subject to the provisions of any law made by the Legislature of the State, the conditions of service of officers and servants of a High Court shall be such as may be prescribed by rules made by the Chief Justice of the Court or by some other Judge or officer of the Court authorised by the Chief Justice to make rules for the purpose:

Provided that the rules made under this clause shall, so far as they relate to salaries, allowances, leave or pensions, require the approval of the Governor of the State [93] * * *.

(3) The administrative expenses of a High Court, including all salaries, allowances and pensions payable to or in respect of the officers and servants of the Court, shall be charged upon the Consolidated Fund of the State, and any fees or other moneys taken by the Court shall form part of that Fund. [ss. 228, 242, G.I. Act]

[94][**230.** *Extension of jurisdiction of High Courts to Union territories.*—(1) Parliament may by law extend the jurisdiction of a High Court to, or exclude the jurisdiction of a High Court from, any Union territory.

(2) Where the High Court of a State exercises jurisdiction in relation to a Union territory,—

(*a*) nothing in this Constitution shall be construed as empowering the Legislature of the State to increase, restrict or abolish that jurisdiction; and

(*b*) the reference in article 227 to the Governor shall, in relation to any rules, forms or tables for subordinate courts in that territory, be construed as a reference to the President. [s. 230, G.I. Act]

[95]**231.** *Establishment of a common High Court for two or more States.*—(1) Notwithstanding anything contained in the preceding provisions of this Chapter,

---

(4) A State law shall not be declared to be constitutionally invalid by the High Court unless—

(*a*) where the High Court consists of five Judges or more, not less than two-thirds of the Judges sitting for the purpose of determining the validity of such law, hold it to be constitutionally invalid; and

(*b*) where the High Court consists of less than five Judges, all the Judges of the High Court sitting for the purpose hold it to be constitutionally invalid.

(5) The provisions of this article shall have effect notwithstanding anything contained in this Part.

Explanation.—In computing the number of Judges of a High Court for the purposes of this article, a Judge who is disqualified by reason of personal or pecuniary bias shall be excluded."

[92] The words "in which the High Court has its principal seat" omitted by the Const. (7th Am.) Act, 1956, s. 29 and Sch. w.e.f. 1.11.1956.

[93] The words "in which the High Court has its principal seat" omitted by the Const. (7th Am.) Act, 1956, s. 29 and Sch. w.e.f. 1.11.1956.

[94] Subs. by s. 16, *ibid.* for the original article 230 which read as follows:

"230. (1) Parliament may by law—

(*a*) extend the jurisdiction of a High Court to, or

(*b*) exclude the jurisdiction of a High Court from,

any State specified in the First Schedule other than, or any area not within, the State in which the High Court has its principal seat."

[95] Subs. by s. 16, *ibid.* for the original article 231 which read as follows:

"231. Where a High Court exercises jurisdiction in relation to any area outside the State in which it has its principal seat, nothing in this Constitution shall be construed—

Parliament may by law establish a common High Court for two or more States or for two or more States and a Union territory.

(2) In relation to any such High Court,—

(*a*) the reference in article 217 to the Governor of the State shall be construed as a reference to the Governors of all the States in relation to which the High Court exercises jurisdiction;

(*b*) the reference in article 227 to the Governor shall, in relation to any rules, forms or tables for subordinate courts be construed as a reference to the Governor of the State in which the subordinate courts are situate; and

(*c*) the references in articles 219 and 229 to the State shall be construed as a reference to the State in which the High Court has its principal seat:

Provided that if such principal seat is in a Union territory, the references in articles 219 and 229 to the Governor, Public Service Commission, Legislature and Consolidated Fund of the State shall be construed respectively as references to the President, Union Public Service Commission, Parliament and Consolidated Fund of India.] [s. 230, G.I. Act]

[96] **232.** * * * * *

CHAPTER VI.—SUBORDINATE COURTS

233. *Appointment of district judges.*—(1) Appointments of persons to be, and the posting and promotion of, district judges in any State shall be made by the Governor of the State in consultation with the High Court exercising jurisdiction in relation to such State.

(2) A person not already in the service of the Union or of the State shall only be eligible to be appointed a district judge if he has been for not less than seven years an advocate or a pleader and is recommended by the High Court for appointment. [s. 254, G.I. Act]

[97][**233A.** *Validation of appointments of, and judgments, etc., delivered by, certain district judges.*—Notwithstanding any judgment, decree or order of any court,—

(*a*) (*i*) no appointment of any person already in the judicial service of a State or of any person who has been for not less than seven years an advocate or a pleader, to be a district judge in that State, and

---

(*a*) as empowering the Legislature of a State in which the Court has its principal seat to increase, restrict or abolish that jurisdiction;

(*b*) as empowering the Legislature of a State specified in Part A or Part B of the First Schedule in which any such area is situate, to abolish that jurisdiction; or

(*c*) as preventing the Legislature having power to make laws in that behalf for any such area, from passing, subject to the provisions of clause (*b*), such laws with respect to the jurisdiction of the Court in relation to that area as it would be competent to pass if the principal seat of the Court were in that area."

[96] Deleted by the Const. (7th Am.) Act, 1956 w.e.f. 1.11.1956. The original article 232 read as follows:

"232. Where a High Court exercises jurisdiction in relation to more than one State specified in the First Schedule or in relation to a State and an area not forming part of the State—

(*a*) references in this Chapter to the Governor of the State in which the Court shall be construed as references to the Governor of the State in which the Court has its principal seat;

(*b*) the reference to the approval by the Governor of rules, forms and tables for subordinate Courts shall be construed as a reference to the approval thereof by the Governor or the Rajapramukh of the State in which the subordinate Court is situate, or if it is situate in an area not forming part of any State specified in Part A or Part B of the First Schedule, by the President; and

(*c*) references to the Consolidated Fund of the State shall be construed as references to the Consolidated Fund of the State in which the Court has its principal seat."

[97] Ins. by the Const. (20th Am.) Act, 1966, s. 2, w.e.f. 22.12.1966.

(*ii*) no posting, promotion or transfer of any such person as a district judge, made at any time before the commencement of the Constitution (Twentieth Amendment) Act, 1966, otherwise than in accordance with the provisions of article 233 or article 235 shall be deemed to be illegal or void or ever to have become illegal or void by reason only of the fact that such appointment, posting, promotion or transfer was not made in accordance with the said provisions;

(*b*) no jurisdiction exercised, no judgment, decree, sentence or order passed or made, and no other act or proceeding done or taken, before the commencement of the Constitution (Twentieth Amendment) Act, 1966 [98]by, or before, any person appointed, posted, promoted or transferred as a district judge in any State otherwise than in accordance with the provisions of article 233 or article 235 shall be deemed to be illegal or invalid or ever to have become illegal or invalid by reason only of the fact that such appointment, posting, promotion or transfer was not made in accordance with the said provisions.]

234. *Recruitment of persons other than district judges to the judicial service.*—Appointments of persons other than district judges to the judicial service of a State shall be made by the Governor of the State in accordance with rules made by him in that behalf after consultation with the State Public Service Commission and with the High Court exercising jurisdiction in relation to such State.

235. *Control over subordinate courts.*—The control over district courts and courts subordinate thereto including the posting and promotion of, and the grant of leave to, persons belonging to the judicial service of a State and holding any post inferior to the post of district judge shall be vested in the High Court, but nothing in this article shall be construed as taking away from any such person any right of appeal which he may have under the law regulating the conditions of his service or as authorising the High Court to deal with him otherwise than in accordance with the conditions of his service prescribed under such law.

[s. 255, G.I. Act]

236. *Interpretation.*—In this Chapter—

(*a*) the expression "district judge" includes judge of a city civil court, additional district judge, joint district judge, assistant district judge, chief judge of a small cause court, chief presidency magistrate, additional chief presidency magistrate, sessions judge, additional sessions judge and assistant sessions judge;

(*b*) the expression "judicial service" means a service consisting exclusively of persons intended to fill the post of district judge and other civil judicial posts inferior to the post of district judge. [Ss. 254, 255 G.I. Act]

237. *Application of the provisions of this Chapter to certain class or classes of magistrates.*—The Governor may by public notification direct that the foregoing provisions of this Chapter and any rules made thereunder shall with effect from such date as may be fixed by him in that behalf apply in relation to any class or classes of magistrates in the State as they apply in relation to persons appointed to the judicial service of the State subject to such exceptions and modifications as may be specified in the notification.

[99]*PART VII.*—[*The States in Part B of the First Schedule.*] *Rep. by the Constitution (Seventh Amendment) Act,* 1956, *s.* 29 *and Sch.*

---

[98] i.e., 22.12.1966.

[99] The whole of Part VII was repealed by s. 29 and Sch. of the Const. (7th Am.) Act, 1956, w.e.f. 1.11.1956. Before its appeal Part VII read as follows:

"238. *Application of provisions of Part VI to States in Part B of the First Schedule.*—The provisions of Part VI shall apply in relation to the States specified in Part A of that Schedule subject to the following modifications and omissions, namely:—

(1) For the word 'Governor' wherever it occurs in the said Part VI, except where it occurs for the second time in clause (*b*) of article 232, the word 'Rajapramukh' shall be substituted.

(2) In article 152, for the word and letter 'Part A' the word and letter 'Part B' shall be substituted.

(3) Articles 155, 156 and 157 shall be omitted.

(4) In article 158,—

(*i*) in clause (1), for the words 'be appointed' the word 'becomes' shall be substituted;

(*ii*) for clause (3), the following clause shall be substituted, namely:—

'(3) The Rajapramukh shall, unless he has his own residence in the principal seat of Government of the State, be entitled without payment of rent to the use of an official residence and shall be also entitled to such allowances and privileges as the President may, by general or special order, determine';

(*iii*) in clause (4), the words 'emoluments and' shall be omitted.

(5) In article 159, after the words 'seniormost Judge of that Court available' the words 'or in such other manner as may be prescribed in that behalf by the President' shall be inserted.

(6) In article 164, for the proviso to clause (1) the following proviso shall be substituted, namely:—

'Provided that in the State of Madhya Bharat there shall be a Minister in charge of tribal welfare who may in addition be in charge of the welfare of the Scheduled Castes and backward classes or any other work.'

(7) In article 168, for clause (1) the following clause shall be substituted, namely:—

'(1) For every State there shall be a Legislature which shall consist of the Rajpramukh and—

(*a*) in the State of Mysore, two Houses,

(*b*) in other States, one House.'

(8) In article 186, for the words 'as were immediately before the commencement of this Constitution applicable in the case of members of the Legislative Assembly of the corresponding Province' the words 'as the Rajpramukh may determine' shall be substituted.

(9) In article 195, for the words 'as were immediately before the commencement of this Constitution applicable in the case of members of the Legislative Assembly of the corresponding Province' the words 'as the Rajpramukh may determine' shall be substituted.

(10) in clause (3) of article 202—

(*i*) for sub-clause (*a*), the following sub-clause shall be substituted, namely:—

'(*a*) the allowances of the Rajpramukh and other expenditure relating to his office as determined by the President by general or special order';

(*ii*) for sub-clause (*f*) the following sub-clause shall be substituted, namely:—

'(*f*) in the case of the State of Travancore-Cochin, a sum of fifty-one lakhs of rupees required to be paid annually to the Devaswom fund under the covenant entered into before the commencement of this Constitution by the Rulers of the Indian States of Travancore and Cochin for the formation of the United State of Travancore and Cochin;

(*g*) any other expenditure declared by this Constitution, or by the Legislature of the State by law, to be so charged.'

(11) In article 208, for clause (2), the following clause shall be substituted, namely:—

'(2) Until rules are made under clause (1), the rules of procedure and standing orders in force immediately before the commencement of this Constitution with respect to the Legislature for the State, or, where no House of the Legislature for the State existed, the rules of procedure and standing orders in force immediately before such commencement with respect to the Legislative Assembly of such Province as may be specified in that behalf by the Rajpramukh of the State, shall have effect in relation to the Legislature of the State subject to such modifications and adaptations as may be made therein by the Speaker of the Legislative Assembly or the Chairman of the Legislative Council, as the case may be.'

(12) In clause (2) of article 214, for the word 'Province' the words 'Indian State' shall be substituted.

(13) For article 221, the following article shall be substituted, namely:—

PART VIII

[1][THE UNION TERRITORIES]

[2][**239.** *Administration of Union territories.*—(1) Save as otherwise provided by Parliament by law, every Union territory shall be administered by the President acting, to such extent as he thinks fit, through an administrator to be appointed by him with such designation as he may specify.

(2) Notwithstanding anything contained in Part VI, the President may appoint the Governor of a State as the administrator of an adjoining Union territory, and where a Governor is so appointed, he shall exercise his functions as such administrator independently of his Council of Ministers. [s. 94, G.I. Act]

[3][**239A.** *Creation of local Legislatures or Council of Ministers or both for certain Union territories.*—(1) Parliament may by law create for any of the Union territories of [4]* * * * [5]* * * * [6][Goa, Daman and Diu], [7][Pondicherry, Mizoram and Arunachal Pradesh]]—

(*a*) a body, whether elected or partly nominated and partly elected, to function as a Legislature for the Union territory, or

(*b*) a Council of Ministers,

or both with such constitution, powers and functions, in each case, as may be specified in the law.

(2) Any such law as is referred to in clause (1) shall not be deemed to be an amendment of this Constitution for the purposes of article 368 notwithstanding that it contains any provision which amends or has the effect of amending this Constitution.]

[8][**239B.** *Power of administrator to promulgate Ordinances during recess of Legislature.*—(1) If at any time, except when the Legislature of a Union territory referred to in clause (1) of article 239A is in session, the administrator thereof is

---

'221. *Salaries, etc. of Judges.*—(1) There shall be paid to the Judges of each High Court such salaries as may be determined by the President after consultation with the Rajpramukh. (2) Every Judge shall be entitled to such allowances and to such rights in respect of leave of absence and pension as may from time to time be determined by or under law made by Parliament and, until so determined, to such allowances and rights as may be determined by the President after consultation with the Rajpramukh:

Provided that neither the allowances of a Judge nor his rights in respect of leave of absence or pension shall be varied to his disadvantage after his appointment.' "

[1] Subs. by the Const. (7th Am.) Act, 1956, s. 17 for the heading "THE STATES IN PART C OF THE FIRST SCHEDULE" w.e.f. 1.11.1956.

[2] Subs. by *ibid.*, for the original article 239 which read as follows:

"(1) Subject to the other provisions of this Part, a State specified in Part C of the First Schedule shall be administered by the President acting, to such extent as he thinks fit, through a Chief Commissioner or a Lieutenant-Governor to be appointed by him or through the Government of a neighbouring State:

Provided that the President shall not act through the Government of a neighbouring State save after—

(*a*) consulting the Government concerned; and

(*b*) ascertaining in such manner as the President considers most appropriate the views of the people of the State to be so administered.

(2) In this article, references to a State shall include references to a part of a State."

[3] Ins. by the Const. (14th Am.) Act, 1962, s. 4, w.e.f. 28.12.1962.

[4] The words "Himachal Pradesh" omitted by the State of Himachal Pradesh Act, 1970 (53 of 1970), s. 46, w.e.f. 25.1.1971.

[5] The words "Manipur, Tripura," omitted by the North-Eastern Areas (Reorganisation) Act, 1971 (81 of 1971), s. 71 w.e.f. 21.1.1972.

[6] Subs. by the Const. (27th Am.) Act, 1971, s. 2 for "Goa, Daman and Diu, and Pondicherry" w.e.f. 15.2.1972.

[7] Subs. by the Const. (37th Am.) Act, 1975, s. 2, for "Pondicherry and Mizoram".

[8] Ins. by the Const. (27th Am.) Act, 1971, s. 3 (w.e.f. 30.12.1971).

satisfied that circumstances exist which render it necessary for him to take immediate action, he may promulgate such Ordinances as the circumstances appear to him to require:

Provided that no such Ordinance shall be promulgated by the administrator except after obtaining instructions from the President in that behalf:

Provided further that whenever the said Legislature is dissolved, or its functioning remains suspended on account of any action taken under any such law as is referred to in clause (1) of article 239A, the administrator shall not promulgate any Ordinance during the period of such dissolution or suspension.

(2) An Ordinance promulgated under this article in pursuance of instructions from the President shall be deemed to be an Act of the Legislature of the Union territory which has been duly enacted after complying with the provisions in that behalf contained in any such law as is referred to in clause (1) of article 239A, but every such Ordinance—

(a) shall be laid before the Legislature of the Union territory and shall cease to operate at the expiration of six weeks from the reassembly of the Legislature or if, before the expiration of that period, a resolution disapproving it is passed by the Legislature, upon the passing of the resolution; and

(b) may be withdrawn at any time by the administrator after obtaining instructions from the President in that behalf.

(3) If and so far as an Ordinance under this article makes any provision which would not be valid if enacted in an Act of the Legislature of the Union territory made after complying with the provisions in that behalf contained in any such law as is referred to in clause (1) of article 239A, it shall be void.]

[9] * * * * *

[10]**240.** *Power of President to make regulations for certain Union territories.*—(1) The President may make regulations for the peace, progress and good government of the Union territory of—

(a) the Andaman and Nicobar Islands;

[11][(b) Lakshadweep;]

[12][(c) Dadra and Nagar Haveli;]

[13][(d) Goa, Daman and Diu;]

[14][(e) Pondicherry;]

---

[9] Cl. (4) was ins. by the Const. (38th Am.) Act, 1975, s. 4 (retrospectively) and omitted by the Const. (44th Am.) Act, 1978, s. 32, w.e.f. 20.6.1979. The omitted clause read as follows:

"(4) Notwithstanding anything in this Constitution, the satisfaction of the administrator mentioned in clause (1) shall be final and conclusive and shall not be questioned in any court on any ground."

[10] Subs. by the Const. (7th Am.) Act, 1956, w.e.f. 1.11.1956, for the original article 240 which read as follows:

"240. (1) Parliament may by law create or continue for any State specified in Part C of the First Schedule and administered through a Chief Commissioner or Lieutenant-Governor—

(a) a body, whether nominated, elected or partly nominated and partly elected, to function as a Legislature for the State; or

(b) a Council of Advisers or Ministers, or both with such constitution, powers and functions, in each case, as may be specified in the law.

(2) Any such law as is referred to in clause (1) shall not be deemed to be an amendment of this Constitution for the purposes of article 368 notwithstanding that it contains any provision which amends or has the effect of amending the Constitution."

[11] Subs. for "the Laccadive, Minicoy and Amindivi Islands" by the Laccadive, Minicoy and Amindivi Islands (Alteration of Name) Act, 1973 (34 of 1973), s. 4, w.e.f. 1.11.1973.

[12] Ins. by the Const. (10th Am.) Act, 1961, s. 3, w.e.f. 16.8.1961.

[13] Ins. by the Const. (12th Am.) Act, 1962, s. 3, w.e.f. 20.12.1961.

[14] Ins. by the Const. (14th Am.) Act, 1962, ss. 5 and 7 w.e.f. 16.8.1962.

[15][(*f*) Mizoram;

(*g*) Arunachal Pradesh:]

[16][Provided that when any body is created under article 239A to function as a Legislature for the [17][Union territory of Goa, Daman and Diu, [18][Pondicherry, Mizoram or Arunachal Pradesh]], the President shall not make any regulation for the peace, progress and good government of that Union territory with effect from the date appointed for the first meeting of the Legislature:]

[19][Provided further that whenever the body functioning as a Legislature for the Union territory of Goa, Daman and Diu, [18][Pondicherry, Mizoram or Arunachal Pradesh] is dissolved, or the functioning of that body as such Legislature remains suspended on account of any action taken under any such law as is referred to in clause (1) of article 239A, the President may, during the period of such dissolution or suspension, make regulations for the peace, progress and good government of that Union territory.]

(2) Any regulation so made may repeal or amend any Act made by Parliament or [20][any other law] which is for the time being applicable to the Union territory and, when promulgated by the President shall have the same force and effect as an Act of Parliament which applies to that territory.]

241. *High Courts for Union territories.*—(1) Parliament may by law constitute a High Court for a [21][Union territory] or declare any court in any [22][such territory] to be a High Court for all or any of the purposes of this Constitution.

(2) The provisions of Chapter V of Part VI shall apply in relation to every High Court referred to in clause (1) as they apply in relation to a High Court referred to in article 214 subject to such modifications or exceptions as Parliament may by law provide.

[23][(3) Subject to the provisions of this Constitution and to the provisions of any law of the appropriate Legislature made by virtue of powers conferred on that Legislature by or under this Constitution, every High Court exercising jurisdiction immediately before the commencement of the Constitution (Seventh Amendment) Act, 1956, in relation to any Union territory shall continue to exercise such jurisdiction in relation to that territory after such commencement.

(4) Nothing in this article derogates from the power of Parliament to extend or exclude the jurisdiction of a High Court for a State to, or from, any Union territory or part thereof.]

---

[15] Ins. by the Const. (27th Am.) Act, 1971, s. 4 w.e.f. 15.2.1973.

[16] Ins. by the Const. (14th Am.) Act, 1962, s. 2, w.e.f. 16.8.1962.

[17] Subs. by the Const. (27th Am.) Act, 1971, s. 4, for "Union territory of Goa, Daman and Diu or Pondicherry" w.e.f. 15.2.1972.

[18] Subs. by the Const. (37th Am.) Act, 1975, s. 3, for "Pondicherry or Mizoram" w.e.f. 3.5.1975.

[19] Subs. by the Const. (27th Am.) Act, 1971, s. 4, w.e.f. 15.2.1972.

[20] Subs. by s. 4, *ibid.*, for "any existing law" w.e.f. 15.2.1972.

[21] Subs. by the Const. (7th Am.) Act, 1956, s. 29 and Sch. for "State specified in Part C of the First Schedule", w.e.f. 1.11.1956.

[22] Subs. by s. 29 and Sch. *ibid.*, for "such State" w.e.f. 1.11.1956.

[23] Subs. by the Const. (7th Am.) Act, 1956, s. 29 and Sch. for cls. (3) and (4), w.e.f. 1.11.1956.. Those clauses read as follows:

"(3) Subject to the provisions of this Constitution and to the provisions of any law of the appropriate Legislature made by virtue of powers conferred on that Legislature by or under this Constitution, every High Court exercising jurisdiction immediately before the commencement of this Constitution in relation to any State specified in Part C of the First Schedule or any area included therein shall continue to exercise such jurisdiction in relation to that State or area after such commencement.

(4) Nothing in this article derogates from the power of Parliament to extend or exclude the jurisdiction of a High Court in any State specified in Part A or Part B of the First Schedule to, or from, any State specified in Part C of that schedule or any area included within that State."

[24]242. *[Coorg.] Rep. by the Constitution (Seventh Amendment) Act,* 1956, *s.* 29 *and Sch.*

[25]*PART IX.—[The territories in Part D of the First Schedule and other territories not specified in that Schedule.] Rep. by the Constitution (Seventh Amendment) Act,* 1956, *s.* 29 *and Sch.*

PART X

THE SCHEDULED AND TRIBAL AREAS

244. *Administration of Scheduled Areas and Tribal Areas.*—(1) The provisions of the Fifth Schedule shall apply to the administration and control of the Scheduled Areas and Scheduled Tribes in any State [26] * * * other than [27][the States of Assam and Meghalaya].

(2) The provisions of the Sixth Schedule shall apply to the administration of the tribal areas in [28][the States of Assam and Meghalaya and the Union territory of Mizoram].

[29][**244A.** *Formation of an autonomous State comprising certain tribal areas in Assam and creation of local Legislature or Council of Ministers or both therefor.*—(1) Notwithstanding anything in this Constitution, Parliament may, by law, form within the State of Assam an autonomous State comprising (whether wholly or in part) all or any of the tribal areas specified in [30][Part I] of the table appended to paragraph 20 of the Sixth Schedule and create therefor—

(*a*) a body, whether elected or partly nominated and partly elected, to function as a Legislature for the autonomous State, or

(*b*) a Council of Ministers,

or both with such constitution, powers and functions, in each case, as may be specified in the law.

---

[24] The repealed article 242 read as follows:

"(1) Until Parliament by law otherwise provides, the Constitution, powers and functions of the Coorg Legislative Council shall be the same as they were immediately before the commencement of this Constitution.

(2) The arrangements with respect to the revenues collected in Coorg and expenses in respect of Coorg shall, until other provision is made in that behalf by the President by order, continue unchanged." [s. 97, G.I. Act]

[25] The whole of Part IX was repealed by s. 29 and Sch. of the Const. (7th Am.) Act, 1956, w.e.f. 1.11.1956. Before its repeal Part IX read as follows:

"PART IX — THE TERRITORIES IN PART D OF THE FIRST SCHEDULE AND OTHER TERRITORIES NOT SPECIFIED IN THAT SCHEDULE.

243. *Administration of territories specified in Part D of the First Schedule and other territories not specified in that Schedule.*—(1) Any territory specified in Part D of the First Schedule and any other territory comprised within the territory of India but not specified in that Schedule shall be administered by the President acting, to such extent as he thinks fit, through a Chief Commissioner or other authority to be appointed by him.

(2) The President may make regulations for the peace and good government of any such territory and any regulation so made may repeal or amend any law made by Parliament or any existing law which is for the time being applicable to such territory and, when promulgated by the President, shall have the same force and effect as an Act of Parliament which applies to such territory." [s. 96, G.I. Act]

[26] The words and letters "specified in Part A or Part B of the First Schedule" omitted by the Const. (7th Am.) Act, 1956, s. 29 and Sch. w.e.f. 1.11.1956.

[27] Subs. by the North-Eastern Areas (Reorganisation) Act, 1971, s. 71, w.e.f. 21.1.1972, for "the State of Assam".

[28] Subs. by the North-Eastern Areas (Reorganisation) Act, 1971, s. 71, w.e.f. 21.1.1972, "the State of Assam".

[29] Ins. by the Const. (22nd Am.) Act, 1969, s. 2, w.e.f. 25.9.1969.

[30] Subs. by the North-Eastern Areas (Reorganisation) Act, 1971 (81 of 1971), s. 71, for "Part A" w.e.f. 21.1.1972.

(2) Any such law as is referred to in clause (1) may, in particular,—

(a) specify the matters enumerated in the State List or the Concurrent List with respect to which the Legislature of the autonomous State shall have power to make laws for the whole or any part thereof, whether to the exclusion of the Legislature of the State of Assam or otherwise;

(b) define the matters with respect to which the executive power of the autonomous State shall extend;

(c) provide that any tax levied by the State of Assam shall be assigned to the autonomous State in so far as the proceeds thereof are attributable to the autonomous State;

(d) provide that any reference to a State in any article of this Constitution shall be construed as including a reference to the autonomous State; and

(e) make such supplemental, incidental and consequential provisions as may be deemed necessary.

(3) An amendment of any such law as aforesaid in so far as such amendment relates to any of the matters specified in sub-clause (a) or sub-clause (b) of clause (2) shall have no effect unless the amendment is passed in each House of Parliament by not less than two-thirds of the members present and voting.

(4) Any such law as is referred to in this article shall not be deemed to be an amendment of this Constitution for the purposes of article 368 notwithstanding that it contains any provision which amends or has the effect of amending this Constitution.]

PART XI

RELATIONS BETWEEN THE UNION AND THE STATES

CHAPTER I.—LEGISLATIVE RELATIONS

Distribution of Legislative Powers

245. *Extent of laws made by Parliament and by the Legislatures of States.* (1) Subject to the provisions of this Constitution, Parliament may make laws for the whole or any part of the territory of India, and the Legislature of a State may make laws for the whole or any part of the State.

(2) No law made by Parliament shall be deemed to be invalid on the ground that it would have extra-territorial operation. [s. 99, G.I. Act]

246. *Subject-matter of laws made by Parliament and by the Legislatures of States.*—(1) Notwithstanding anything in clauses (2) and (3), Parliament has exclusive power to make laws with respect to any of the matters enumerated in List I in the Seventh Schedule (in this Constitution referred to as the "Union List").

(2) Notwithstanding anything in clause (3), Parliament, and, subject to clause (1), the Legislature of any State [30] * * * also, have power to make laws with respect to any of the matters enumerated in List III in the Seventh Schedule (in this Constitution referred to as the "Concurrent List").

(3) Subject to clauses (1) and (2), the Legislature of any State [30] * * * has exclusive power to make laws for such State or any part thereof with respect to any of the matters enumerated in List II in the Seventh Schedule (in this Constitution referred to as the "State List").

(4) Parliament has power to make laws with respect to any matter for any part of the territory of India not included [31][in a State] notwithstanding that such matter is a matter enumerated in the State List. [s. 100, G.I. Act]

247. *Power of Parliament to provide for the establishment of certain additional courts.*—Notwithstanding anything in this Chapter, Parliament may by law provide

[30] The words and letters "specified in Part A or Part B of the First Schedule" omitted by the Const. (7th Am.) Act, 1956, s. 29 and Sch. w.e.f. 1.11.1956.

[31] Subs. by the Const. (7th Am.) Act, 1956, s. 29 and Sch., for "in Part A or Part B of the First Schedule", w.e.f. 1.11.1956.

for the establishment of any additional courts for the better administration of laws made by Parliament or of any existing law with respect to a matter enumerated in the Union List. [s. 104, G.I. Act]

248. *Residuary powers of legislation.*—(1) Parliament has exclusive power to make any law with respect to any matter not enumerated in the Concurrent List or State List.

(2) Such power shall include the power of making any law imposing a tax not mentioned in either of those Lists.

249. *Power of Parliament to legislate with respect to a matter in the State List in the national interest.*—(1) Notwithstanding anything in the foregoing provisions of this Chapter, if the Council of States has declared by resolution supported by not less than two-thirds of the members present and voting that it is necessary or expedient in the national interest that Parliament should make laws with respect to any matter enumerated in the State List specified in the resolution, it shall be lawful for Parliament to make laws for the whole or any part of the territory of India with respect to that matter while the resolution remains in force.

(2) A resolution passed under clause (1) shall remain in force for such period not exceeding one year as may be specified therein:

Provided that, if and so often as a resolution approving the continuance in force of any such resolution is passed in the manner provided in clause (1), such resolution shall continue in force for a further period of one year from the date on which under this clause it would otherwise have ceased to be in force.

(3) A law made by Parliament which Parliament would not but for the passing of a resolution under clause (1) have been competent to make shall, to the extent of the incompetency, cease to have effect on the expiration of a period of six months after the resolution has ceased to be in force, except as respects things done or omitted to be done before the expiration of the said period.

250. *Power of Parliament to legislate with respect to any matter in the State List if a Proclamation of Emergency is in operation.*—(1) Notwithstanding anything in this Chapter, Parliament shall, while a Proclamation of Emergency is in operation, have power to make laws for the whole or any part of the territory of India with respect to any of the matters enumerated in the State List.

(2) A law made by Parliament which Parliament would not but for the issue of a Proclamation of Emergency have been competent to make shall, to the extent of the incompetency, cease to have effect on the expiration of a period of six months after the Proclamation has ceased to operate, except as respects things done or omitted to be done before the expiration of the said period. [s. 102, G.I. Act]

251. *Inconsistency between laws made by Parliament under articles 249 and 250 and laws made by the Legislatures of States.*—Nothing in articles 249 and 250 shall restrict the power of the Legislature of a State to make any law which under this Constitution it has power to make, but if any provision of a law made by the Legislature of a State is repugnant to any provision of a law made by Parliament which Parliament has under either of the said articles power to make, the law made by Parliament, whether passed before or after the law made by the Legislature of the State, shall prevail, and the law made by the Legislature of the State shall to the extent of the repugnancy, but so long only as the law made by Parliament continues to have effect, be inoperative. [s. 102, G.I. Act]

252. *Power of Parliament to legislate for two or more States by consent and adoption of such legislation by any other State.*—(1) If it appears to the Legislatures of two or more States to be desirable that any of the matters with respect to which Parliament has no power to make laws for the States except as provided in articles 249 and 250 should be regulated in such States by Parliament by law, and if resolutions to that effect are passed by all the Houses of the Legislatures of those States, it shall be lawful for Parliament to pass an Act for regulating that matter accordingly, and any Act so passed shall apply to such States and to any other State by which it is adopted afterwards by resolution passed in that behalf by the House or, where there are two Houses, by each of the Houses of the Legislature of that State.

(2) Any Act so passed by Parliament may be amended or repealed by an Act of Parliament passed or adopted in like manner but shall not, as respects any State to which it applies, be amended or repealed by an Act of the Legislature of that State. [s. 103, G.I. Act]

253. *Legislation for giving effect to international agreements.*—Notwithstanding anything in the foregoing provisions of this Chapter, Parliament has power to make any law for the whole or any part of the territory of India for implementing any treaty, agreement or convention with any other country or countries or any decision made at any international conference, association or other body. [s. 106, G.I. Act]

254. *Inconsistency between laws made by Parliament and laws made by the Legislatures of States.*—(1) If any provision of a law made by the Legislature of a State is repugnant to any provision of a law made by Parliament which Parliament is competent to enact, or to any provision of an existing law with respect to one of the matters enumerated in the Concurrent List, then, subject to the provisions of clause (2), the law made by Parliament, whether passed before or after the law made by the Legislature of such State, or, as the case may be, the existing law, shall prevail and the law made by the Legislature of the State shall, to the extent of the repugnancy, be void.

(2) Where a law made by the Legislature of a State [32] * * * with respect to one of the matters enumerated in the Concurrent List contains any provision repugnant to the provisions of an earlier law made by Parliament or an existing law with respect to that matter, then, the law so made by the Legislature of such State shall, if it has been reserved for the consideration of the President and has received his assent, prevail in that State:

Provided that nothing in this clause shall prevent Parliament from enacting at any time any law with respect to the same matter including a law adding to, amending, varying or repealing the law so made by the Legislature of the State. [s. 107, G.I. Act]

255. *Requirements as to recommendations and previous sanctions to be regarded as matters of procedure only.*—No Act of Parliament or of the Legislature of a State [33] * * *, and no provision in any such Act, shall be invalid by reason only that some recommendation or previous sanction required by this Constitution was not given, if assent to that Act was given—

(a) where the recommendation required was that of the Governor, either by the Governor or by the President;

(b) where the recommendation required was that of the Rajpramukh, either by the Rajpramukh or by the President;

(c) where the recommendation or previous sanction required was that of the President, by the President. [s. 109, G.I. Act]

CHAPTER II.—ADMINISTRATIVE RELATIONS

General

256. *Obligation of States and the Union.*—The executive power of every State shall be so exercised as to ensure compliance with the laws made by Parliament and any existing laws which apply in that State, and the executive power of the Union shall extend to the giving of such directions to a State as may appear to the Government of India to be necessary for that purpose. [s. 122, G.I. Act]

257. *Control of the Union over States in certain cases.*—(1) The executive power of every State shall be so exercised as not to impede or prejudice the exercise of the executive power of the Union, and the executive power of the Union shall

---

[32] The words and letters "specified in Part A or Part B of the First Schedule" omitted by the Const. (7th Am.) Act, 1956, s. 29 and Sch., w.e.f. 1.11.1956.

[33] The words and letters "specified in Part A or Part B of the First Schedule" omitted by the Const. (7th Am.) Act, 1956, s. 29 and Sch., w.e.f. 1.11.1956.

extend to the giving of such directions to a State as may appear to the Government of India to be necessary for that purpose.

(2) The executive power of the Union shall also extend to the giving of directions to a State as to the construction and maintenance of means of communication declared in the direction to be of national or military importance:

Provided that nothing in this clause shall be taken as restricting the power of Parliament to declare highways or waterways to be national highways or national waterways or the power of the Union with respect to the highways or waterways so declared or the power of the Union to construct and maintain means of communication as part of its functions with respect to naval, military and air force works.

(3) The executive power of the Union shall also extend to the giving of directions to a State as to the measures to be taken for the protection of the railways within the State.

(4) Where in carrying out any direction given to a State under clause (2) as to the construction or maintenance of any means of communication or under clause (3) as to the measures to be taken for the protection of any railway, costs have been incurred in excess of those which would have been incurred in the discharge of the normal duties of the State if such direction had not been given, there shall be paid by the Government of India to the State such sum as may be agreed, or, in default of agreement, as may be determined by an arbitrator appointed by the Chief Justice of India, in respect of the extra costs so incurred by the State. [s. 126, G.I. Act]

[34]**257A.** [*Assistance to States by deployment of armed forces or other forces of the Union.*] *Rep. by the Constitution (Forty-fourth Amendment) Act*, 1978, *s.* 33 (*w.e.f.* 20-6-1979).

258. *Power of the Union to confer powers, etc., on States in certain cases.*—(1) Notwithstanding anything in this Constitution, the President may, with the consent of the Government of a State, entrust either conditionally or unconditionally to that Government or to its officers functions in relation to any matter to which the executive power of the Union extends.

(2) A law made by Parliament which applies in any State may, notwithstanding that it relates to a matter with respect to which the Legislature of the State has no power to make laws, confer powers and impose duties, or authorise the conferring of powers and the imposition of duties, upon the State or officers and authorities thereof.

(3) Where by virtue of this article powers and duties have been conferred or imposed upon a State or officers or authorities thereof, there shall be paid by the Government of India to the State such sum as may be agreed, or, in default of agreement, as may be determined by an arbitrator appointed by the Chief Justice of India, in respect of any extra costs of administration incurred by the State in connection with the exercise of those powers and duties. [s. 124, G.I. Act]

[35][**258A.** *Power of the States to entrust functions to the Union.*—Notwith-

---

[34] Ins. by the Const. (42nd Am.) Act. 1976, s. 43 w.e.f. 3.1.1977. The repealed Act read as follows:

"257A. (1) The Government of India may deploy any armed force of the Union or any other force subject to the control of the Union for dealing with any grave situation of law and order in any State.

(2) Any armed force or other force or any contingent or unit thereof deployed under clause (1) in any State shall act in accordance with such directions as the Government of India may issue and shall not, save as otherwise provided in such directions, be subject to the superintendence or control of the State Government or any officer or authority subordinate to the State Government.

(3) Parliament may, by law, specify the powers, functions, privileges and liabilities of the members of any force or any contingent or unit thereof deployed under clause (1) during the period of such deployment."

[35] Ins. by the Const. (7th Am.) Act, 1956, s. 18, w.e.f. 1.11.1956.

standing anything in this Constitution, the Governor of a State may, with the consent of the Government of India, entrust either conditionally or unconditionally to that Government or to its officers functions in relation to any matter to which the executive power of the State extends.]

[36]**259.** [*Armed Forces in States in Part B of the First Schedule.*] *Rep. by the Constitution (Seventh Amendment) Act*, 1956, *s.* 29 *and Sch.*

260. *Jurisdiction of the Union in relation to territories outside India.*—The Government of India may by agreement with the Government of any territory not being part of the territory of India undertake any executive, legislative or judicial functions vested in the Government of such territory, but every such agreement shall be subject to, and governed by, any law relating to the exercise of foreign jurisdiction for the time being in force.

261. *Public acts, records and judicial proceedings.*—(1) Full faith and credit shall be given throughout the territory of India to public acts, records and judicial proceedings of the Union and of every State.

(2) The manner in which and the conditions under which the acts, records and proceedings referred to in clause (1) shall be proved and the effect thereof determined shall be as provided by law made by Parliament.

(3) Final judgments or orders delivered or passed by civil courts in any part of the territory of India shall be capable of execution anywhere within that territory according to law.

Disputes relating to Waters

262. *Adjudication of disputes relating to waters of inter-State rivers or river valleys.*—(1) Parliament may by law provide for the adjudication of any dispute or complaint with respect to the use, distribution or control of the waters of, or in, any inter-State river or river valley.

(2) Notwithstanding anything in this Constitution, Parliament may by law provide that neither the Supreme Court nor any other court shall exercise jurisdiction in respect of any such dispute or complaint as is referred to in clause (1).

[Ss. 131, 132, 133, G.I. Act]

Co-ordination between States

263. *Provisions with respect to an inter-State Council.*—If at any time it appears to the President that the public interests would be served by the establishment of a Council charged with the duty of—

(*a*) inquiring into and advising upon disputes which may have arisen between States;

(*b*) investigating and discussing subjects in which some or all of the States, or the Union and one or more of the States, have a common interest; or

(*c*) making recommendations upon any such subject and, in particular, recommendations for the better co-ordination of policy and action with respect to that subject,

it shall be lawful for the President by order to establish such a Council, and to define the nature of the duties to be performed by it and its organisation and procedure.

[s. 135, G.I. Act]

---

[36] The deleted article read as follows:

"259. (1) Notwithstanding anything in this Constitution, a State specified in Part B of the First Schedule having any Armed Forces immediately before the commencement of this Constitution may, until Parliament by law otherwise provides, continue to maintain the said Forces after such commencement subject to such general or special orders as the President may from time to time issue in that behalf.

(2) Any such Armed Forces as are referred to in clause (1) shall form part of the Armed Forces of the Union."

PART XII

FINANCE, PROPERTY, CONTRACTS AND SUITS

CHAPTER I.—FINANCE

General

[37][**264.** *Interpretation.*—In this Part, "Finance Commission" means a Finance Commission constituted under article 280.]

265. *Taxes not to be imposed save by authority of law.*—No tax shall be levied or collected except by authority of law.

266. *Consolidated Funds and public accounts of India and of the States.*—(1) Subject to the provisions of article 267 and to the provisions of this Chapter with respect to the assignment of the whole or part of the net proceeds of certain taxes and duties to States, all revenues received by the Government of India, all loans raised by that Government by the issue of treasury bills, loans or ways and means advances and all moneys received by that Government in repayment of loans shall form one consolidated fund to be entitled "the Consolidated Fund of India", and all revenues received by the Government of a State, all loans raised by that Government by the issue of treasury bills, loans or ways and means advances and all moneys received by that Government in repayment of loans shall form one consolidated fund to be entitled "the Consolidated Fund of the State".

(2) All other public moneys received by or on behalf of the Government of India or the Government of a State shall be credited to the public account of India or the public account of the State, as the case may be.

(3) No moneys out of the Consolidated Fund of India or the Consolidated Fund of a State shall be appropriated except in accordance with law and for the purposes and in the manner provided in this Constitution. [s. 136, G.I. Act]

267. *Contingency Fund.*—(1) Parliament may by law establish a Contingency Fund in the nature of an imprest to be entitled "the Contingency Fund of India" into which shall be paid from time to time such sums as may be determined by such law, and the said Fund shall be placed at the disposal of the President to enable advances to be made by him out of such Fund for the purposes of meeting unforeseen expenditure pending authorisation of such expenditure by Parliament by law under article 115 or article 116.[38]

(2) The Legislature of a State may by law establish a Contingency Fund in the nature of an imprest to be entitled "the Contingency Fund of the State" into which shall be paid from time to time such sums as may be determined by such law, and the said Fund shall be placed at the disposal of the Governor [39] * * * of the State to enable advances to be made by him out of such Fund for the purposes of meeting unforeseen expenditure pending authorisation of such expenditure by the Legislature of the State by law under article 205 or article 206.

Distribution of Revenues between the Union and the States

268. *Duties levied by the Union but collected and appropriated by the States.*—(1) Such stamp duties and such duties of excise on medicinal and toilet prepara-

---

[37] Subs. by the Const. (7th Am.) Act, 1956, s. 29 and Sch. w.e.f. 1.11.1956, for the original article 264 which read as follows:
"In this Part, unless the context otherwise requires,—
(*a*) 'Finance Commission' means a Finance Commission constituted under article 280;
(*b*) 'State' does not include a State specified in Part C of the First Schedule;
(*c*) references to States specified in Part C of the First Schedule and any other territory comprised within the territory of India but not specified in that Schedule."

[38] See the Contingency Fund of India Act, 1950.

[39] The words "or Rajpramukh" deleted by the Const. (7th Am.) Act, 1956, w.e.f. 1.11.1956.

tions as are mentioned in the Union List shall be levied by the Government of India but shall be collected—

(*a*) in the case where such duties are leviable within any [40][Union territory], by the Government of India, and

(*b*) in other cases, by the States within which such duties are respectively leviable.

(2) The proceeds in any financial year of any such duty leviable within any State shall not form part of the Consolidated Fund of India, but shall be assigned to that State. [s. 137, G.I. Act]

269. *Taxes levied and collected by the Union but assigned to the States.*—(1) The following duties and taxes shall be levied and collected by the Government of India but shall be assigned to the States in the manner provided in clause (2), namely:—

(*a*) duties in respect of succession to property other than agricultural land;

(*b*) estate duty in respect of property other than agricultural land;

(*c*) terminal taxes on goods or passengers carried by railway, sea or air;

(*d*) taxes on railway fares and freights;

(*e*) taxes other than stamp duties on transactions in stock-exchanges and futures markets;

(*f*) taxes on the sale or purchase of newspapers and on advertisements published therein;

[41][(*g*) taxes on the sale or purchase of goods other than newspapers, where such sale or purchase takes place in the course of inter-State trade or commerce.]

(2) The net proceeds in any financial year of any such duty or tax, except in so far as those proceeds represent proceeds attributable to [42][Union territories], shall not form part of the Consolidated Fund of India, but shall be assigned to the States within which that duty or tax is leviable in that year, and shall be distributed among those States in accordance with such principles of distribution as may be formulated by Parliament by law.

[41][(3) Parliament may by law formulate principles for determining when a sale or purchase of goods takes place in the course of inter-State trade or commerce.] [s. 137, G.I. Act]

270. *Taxes levied and collected by the Union and distributed between the Union and the States.*—(1) Taxes on income other than agricultural income shall be levied and collected by the Government of India and distributed between the Union and the States in the manner provided in clause (2).

(2) Such percentage, as may be prescribed[43], of the net proceeds in any financial year of any such tax, except in so far as those proceeds represent proceeds attributable to [42][Union territories] or to taxes payable in respect of Union emoluments, shall not form part of the Consolidated Fund of India, but shall be assigned to the States within which that tax is leviable in that year, and shall be distributed among those States in such manner and from such time as may be prescribed.

(3) For the purposes of clause (2), in each financial year such percentage as may be prescribed of so much of the net proceeds of taxes on income as does not represent the net proceeds of taxes payable in respect of Union emoluments shall be deemed to represent proceeds attributable to [44][Union territories].

---

[40] Subs. by the Const. (7th Am.) Act, 1956, s. 29 and Sch., for "States specified in Part C of the First Schelule", w.e.f. 1.11.1956.

[41] Ins. by the Const. (6th Am.) Act, 1956, s. 3, w.e.f. 11.9.1956.

[42] Subs. by the Const. (7th Am.) Act, 1956, s. 29 and Sch., for "States specified in Part C of the First Schedule", w.e.f. 1.11.1956.

[43] *See* the Constitution (Distribution of Revenues) Order, 1979 (C.O. 112).

[44] Subs. by the Const. (7th Am.) Act, 1956, s. 29 and Sch., for "States specified in Part C of the First Schedule", w.e.f. 1.11.1956.

(4) In this article—

(*a*) "taxes on income" does not include a corporation tax;

(*b*) "prescribed" means—

(*i*) until a Finance Commission has been constituted, prescribed by the President by order, and

(*ii*) after a Finance Commission has been constituted, prescribed by the President by order after considering the recommendations of the Finance Commission;

(*c*) "Union emoluments" includes all emoluments and pensions payable out of the Consolidated Fund of India in respect of which income-tax is chargeable. [s. 138, G.I. Act]

271. *Surcharge on certain duties and taxes for purposes of the Union.*—Notwithstanding anything in articles 269 and 270, Parliament may at any time increase any of the duties or taxes referred to in those articles by a surcharge for purposes of the Union and the whole proceeds of any such surcharge shall form part of the Consolidated Fund of India. [Ss. 137, 138 G.I. Act]

272. *Taxes which are levied and collected by the Union and may be distributed between the Union and the States.*—Union duties of excise other than such duties of excise on medicinal and toilet preparations as are mentioned in the Union List shall be levied and collected by the Government of India, but, if Parliament by law so provides, there shall be paid out of the Consolidated Fund of India to the States to which the law imposing the duty extends sums equivalent to the whole or any part of the net proceeds of that duty, and those sums shall be distributed among those States in accordance with such principles of distribution as may be formulated by such law. [s. 140, G.I. Act]

273. *Grants in lieu of export duty on jute and jute products.*—(1) There shall be charged on the Consolidated Fund of India in each year as grants-in-aid of the revenues of the States of Assam, Bihar, Orissa and West Bengal, in lieu of assignment of any share of the net proceeds in each year of export duty on jute and jute products to those States, such sums as may be prescribed.

(2) The sums so prescribed shall continue to be charged on the Consolidated Fund of India so long as any export duty on jute or jute products continues to be levied by the Government of India or until the expiration of ten years from the commencement of this Constitution, whichever is earlier.

(3) In this article, the expression "prescribed" has the same meaning as in article 270. [s. 140, G.I. Act]

274. *Prior recommendation of President required to Bills affecting taxation in which States are interested.*—(1) No Bill or amendment which imposes or varies any tax or duty in which States are interested, or which varies the meaning of the expression "agricultural income" as defined for the purposes of the enactments relating to Indian income-tax, or which affects the principles on which under any of the foregoing provisions of this Chapter moneys are or may be distributable to States, or which imposes any such surcharge for the purposes of the Union as is mentioned in the foregoing provisions of this Chapter, shall be introduced or moved in either House of Parliament except on the recommendation of the President.

(2) In this article, the expression "tax or duty in which States are interested" means—

(*a*) a tax or duty the whole or part of the net proceeds whereof are assigned to any State; or

(*b*) a tax or duty by reference to the net proceeds whereof sums are for the time being payable out of the Consolidated Fund of India to any State. [s. 141, G.I. Act]

275. *Grants from the Union to certain States.*—(1) Such sums as Parliament may by law provide shall be charged on the Consolidated Fund of India in each year as grants-in-aid of the revenues of such States as Parliament may determine to be in need of assistance, and different sums may be fixed for different States:

Provided that there shall be paid out of the Consolidated Fund of India as grants-in-aid of the revenues of a State such capital and recurring sums as may be necessary to enable that State to meet the costs of such schemes of development as may be undertaken by the State with the approval of the Government of India for the purpose of promoting the welfare of the Scheduled Tribes in that State or raising the level of administration of the Scheduled Areas therein to that of the administration of the rest of the areas of that State:

Provided further that there shall be paid out of the Consolidated Fund of India as grants-in-aid of the revenues of the State of Assam sums, capital and recurring, equivalent to—

(*a*) the average excess of expenditure over the revenues during the two years immediately preceding the commencement of this Constitution in respect of the administration of the tribal areas specified in [45][Part I] of the table appended to paragraph 20 of the Sixth Schedule; and

(*b*) the costs of such schemes of development as may be undertaken by that State with the approval of the Government of India for the purpose of raising the level of administration of the said areas to that of the administration of the rest of the areas of that State.

[46][(1A) On and from the formation of the autonomous State under article 244A,—

(*i*) any sums payable under clause (*a*) of the second proviso to clause (1) shall, if the autonomous State comprises all the tribal areas referred to therein, be paid to the autonomous State, and, if the autonomous State comprises only some of those tribal areas, be apportioned between the State of Assam and the autonomous State as the President may, by order, specify;

(*ii*) there shall be paid out of the Consolidated Fund of India as grants-in-aid of the revenues of the autonomous State sums, capital and recurring, equivalent to the costs of such schemes of development as may be undertaken by the autonomous State with the approval of the Government of India for the purpose of raising the level of administration of that State to that of the administration of the rest of the State of Assam.]

(2) Until provision is made by Parliament under clause (1), the powers conferred on Parliament under that clause shall be exercisable by the President by order and any order made by the President under this clause shall have effect subject to any provision so made by Parliament:

Provided that after a Finance Commission has been constituted no order shall be made under this clause by the President except after considering the recommendations of the Finance Commission. [s. 142, G.I. Act]

276. *Taxes on professions, trades, callings and employments.*—(1) Notwithstanding anything in article 246, no law of the Legislature of a State relating to taxes for the benefit of the State or of a municipality, district board, local board or other local authority therein in respect of professions, trades, callings or employments shall be invalid on the ground that it relates to a tax on income.

(2) The total amount payable in respect of any one person to the State or to any one municipality, district board, local board or other local authority in the State by way of taxes on professions, trades, callings and employments shall not exceed two hundred and fifty rupees per annum:

Provided that if in the financial year immediately preceding the commencement of this Constitution there was in force in the case of any State or any such municipality, board or authority a tax on professions, trades, callings or employments the rate, or the maximum rate, of which exceeded two hundred and fifty

---

[45] Subs. by the North-Eastern Areas (Reorganisation) Act, 1971 (81 of 1971), s. 71, for "Part A" (w.e.f. 21.1.1972).

[46] Ins. by the Const. (22nd Am.) Act, 1969, s. 3, w.e.f. 25.9.1969.

rupees per annum, such tax may continue to be levied until provision to the contrary is made by Parliament by law, and any law so made by Parliament may be made either generally or in relation to any specified States, municipalities, boards or authorities.

(3) The power of the Legislature of a State to make laws as aforesaid with respect to taxes on professions, trades, callings and employments shall not be construed as limiting in any way the power of Parliament to make laws with respect to taxes on income accruing from or arising out of professions, trades, callings and employments. [s. 142A, G.I. Act]

277. *Savings.*—Any taxes, duties, cesses or fees which, immediately before the commencement of this Constitution, were being lawfully levied by the Government of any State or by any municipality or other local authority or body for the purposes of the State, municipality, district or other local area may, notwithstanding that those taxes, duties, cesses or fees are mentioned in the Union List, continue to be levied and to be applied to the same purposes until provision to the contrary is made by Parliament by law. [s. 143, G.I. Act]

[47]**278.** [*Agreement with States in Part B of the First Schedule with regard to certain financial matters.*] *Rep. by the Constitution (Seventh Amendment) Act,* **1956**, *s.* 29 *and Sch.*

279. *Calculation of "net proceeds", etc.*—(1) In the foregoing provisions of this Chapter, "net proceeds" means in relation to any tax or duty the proceeds thereof reduced by the cost of collection, and for the purposes of those provisions the net proceeds of any tax or duty, or of any part of any tax or duty, in or attributable to any area shall be ascertained and certified by the Comptroller and Auditor-General of India, whose certificate shall be final.

(2) Subject as aforesaid, and to any other express provision of this Chapter, a law made by Parliament or an order of the President may, in any case where under this Part the proceeds of any duty or tax are, or may be, assigned to any State, provide for the manner in which the proceeds are to be calculated, for the time from or at which and the manner in which any payments are to be made, for the making of adjustments between one financial year and another, and for any other incidental or ancillary matters. [s. 144, G.I. Act]

280. *Finance Commission.*—(1) The President shall, within two years from the commencement of this Constitution and thereafter at the expiration of every fifth year or at such earlier time as the President considers necessary, by order constitute

---

[47] The original article repealed by the Const. (7th Am.) Act, 1956, w.e.f. 1.11.1956 read as follows:

"(1) Notwithstanding anything in this Constitution, the Government of India may, subject to the provisions of clause (2), enter into an agreement with the Government of a State specified in Part B of the First Schedule with respect to—

(*a*) the levy and collection of any tax or duty leviable by the Government of India in such State and for distribution of the proceeds thereof otherwise than in accordance with the provisions of this Chapter;

(*b*) the grant of any financial assistance by the Government of India to such State in consequence of the loss of any revenue which that State used to derive from any tax or duty leviable under this Constitution by the Government of India or from any other sources;

(*c*) the contribution by such State in respect of any payment made by the Government of India under clause (1) of article 291,

and, when an agreement is so entered into the provisions of this Chapter shall in relation to such State have effect subject to the terms of such agreement.

(2) An agreement entered into under clause (1) shall continue in force for a period not exceeding ten years from the commencement of this Constitution;

Provided that the President may at any time after the expiration of five years from such commencement terminate or modify any such agreement if after consideration of the report of the Finance Commission he thinks it necessary to do so."

a Finance Commission which shall consist of a Chairman and four other members to be appointed by the President.

(2) Parliament may by law determine the qualifications which shall be requisite for appointment as members of the Commission and the manner in which they shall be selected.[48]

(3) It shall be the duty of the Commission to make recommendations to the President as to—

(*a*) the distribution between the Union and the States of the net proceeds of taxes which are to be, or may be, divided between them under this Chapter and the allocation between the States of the respective shares of such proceeds;

(*b*) the principles which should govern the grants-in-aid of the revenues of the States out of the Consolidated Fund of India;

[49] * * * * *

[50][(*c*)] any other matter referred to the Commission by the President in the interests of sound finance.

(4) The Commission shall determine their procedure and shall have such powers in the performance of their functions as Parliament may by law confer on them.

281. *Recommendations of the Finance Commission.*—The President shall cause every recommendation made by the Finance Commission under the provisions of this Constitution together with an explanatory memorandum as to the action taken thereon to be laid before each House of Parliament.

Miscellaneous Financial Provisions

282. *Expenditure defrayable by the Union or a State out of its revenues.*—The Union or a State may make any grants for any public purpose, notwithstanding that the purpose is not one with respect to which Parliament or the Legislature of the State, as the case may be, may make laws. [s. 150, G.I. Act]

283. *Custody, etc., of Consolidated Funds, Contingency Funds and moneys credited to the public accounts.*—(1) The custody of the Consolidated Fund of India and the Contingency Fund of India, the payment of moneys into such Funds, the withdrawal of moneys therefrom, the custody of public moneys other than those credited to such Funds received by or on behalf of the Government of India, their payment into the public account of India and the withdrawal of moneys from such account and all other matters connected with or ancillary to matters aforesaid shall be regulated by law made by Parliament, and, until provision in that behalf is so made, shall be regulated by rules made by the President.[51]

(2) The custody of the Consolidated Fund of a State and the Contingency Fund of a State, the payment of moneys into such Funds, the withdrawal of moneys therefrom, the custody of public moneys other than those credited to such Funds received by or on behalf of the Government of the State, their payment into the public account of the State and the withdrawal of moneys from such account and all other matters connected with or ancillary to matters aforesaid shall be regulated by law made by the Legislature of the State, and, until provision in that behalf is so made, shall be regulated by rules made by the Governor [52] * * * of the State. [s. 151, G.I. Act]

---

[48] See the Finance Commission (Miscellaneous Provisions) Act, 1951.

[49] Sub-clause (c) which was omitted by the Const. (7th Am.) Act, 1956, s. 29 and Sch. w.e.f. 1.11.1976 read as follows:

"(c) The continuance or modification of the terms of any agreement entered into by the Government of India with the Government of any State specified in Part B of the First Schedule under clause (1) of article 278 or under article 306; and"

[50] Sub-clause (*d*) was re-lettered as sub-clause (*c*) by s. 29 and Sch., *ibid.*, w.e.f. 1.11.1956.

[51] See the Contingency Fund of India Act, 1950.

[52] The words "or Rajpramukh" omitted by the Const. (7th Am.) Act, 1956, s. 29 and Sch. w.e.f. 1.11.1956.

284. *Custody of suitors' deposits and other moneys received by public servants and courts.*—All moneys received by or deposited with—

(*a*) any officer employed in connection with the affairs of the Union or of a State in his capacity as such, other than revenues or public moneys raised or received by the Government of India or the Government of the State, as the case may be, or

(*b*) any court within the territory of India to the credit of any cause, matter, account or persons,

shall be paid into the public account of India or the public account of the State, as the case may be.

285. *Exemption of property of the Union from State taxation.*—(1) The property of the Union shall, save in so far as Parliament may by law otherwise provide, be exempt from all taxes imposed by a State or by any authority within a State.

(2) Nothing in clause (1) shall, until Parliament by law otherwise provides, prevent any authority within a State from levying any tax on any property of the Union to which such property was immediately before the commencement of this Constitution liable or treated as liable, so long as that tax continues to be levied in that State. [s. 154, G.I. Act]

286. *Restrictions as to imposition of tax on the sale or purchase of goods.*—(1) No law of a State shall impose, or authorise the imposition of, a tax on the sale or purchase of goods where such sale or purchase takes place—

(*a*) outside the State; or

(*b*) in the course of the import of the goods into, or export of the goods out of, the territory of India.

[53] * * * * *

[54][(2) Parliament may by law formulate principles for determining when a sale or purchase of goods takes place in any of the ways mentioned in clause (1).[55]

(3) Any law of a State shall, in so far as it imposes, or authorises the imposition of, a tax on the sale or purchase of goods declared by Parliament by law to be of special importance in inter-State trade or commerce, be subject to such restrictions and conditions in regard to the system of levy, rates and other incidents of the tax as Parliament may by law specify.]

---

[53] The *Explanation* to clause (1) was deleted by the Const. (6th Am.) Act, 1956, s. 4, w.e.f. 11.9.1956. As originally enacted, the *Explanation* read as follows:

"*Explanation.*—For the purposes of sub-clause (*a*), a sale or purchase shall be deemed to have taken place in the State in which the goods have actually been delivered as a direct result of such sale or purchase for the purpose of consumption in that State, notwithstanding the fact that under the general law relating to sale of goods the property in the goods has by reason of such sale or purchase passed in another State".

[54] Subs. by s. 4, *ibid.*, for cls. (2) and (3). As originally enacted, the clauses read as follows:

"(2) Except in so far as Parliament may by law otherwise provide, no law of a State shall impose, or authorise the imposition of, a tax on the sale or purchase of any goods where such sale or purchase takes place in the course of inter-State trade or commerce:

Provided that the President may by order direct that any tax on the sale or purchase of goods which was being lawfully levied by the Government of any State immediately before the commencement of this Constitution shall, notwithstanding that the imposition of such tax is contrary to the provisions of this clause, continue to be levied until the thirty-first day of March, 1951.

(3) No law made by the Legislature of a State imposing or authorising the imposition of, a tax on the sale or purchase of any such goods as have been declared by Parliament by law to be essential for the life of the community shall have effect unless it has been reserved for the consideration of the President and has received his assent."

[55] See the Central Sales Tax Act, 1956.

287. *Exemption from taxes on electricity.*—Save in so far as Parliament may by law otherwise provide, no law of a State shall impose, or authorise the imposition of, a tax on the consumption or sale of electricity (whether produced by a Government or other persons) which is—

(*a*) consumed by the Government of India, or sold to the Government of India for consumption by that Government; or

(*b*) consumed in the construction, maintenance or operation of any railway by the Government of India or a railway company operating that railway, or sold to that Government or any such railway company for consumption in the construction, maintenance or operation of any railway.

and any such law imposing, or authorising the imposition of, a tax on the sale of electricity shall secure that the price of electricity sold to the Government of India for consumption by that Government, or to any such railway company as aforesaid for consumption in the construction, maintenance or operation of any railway shall be less by the amount of the tax than the price charged to other consumers of a substantial quantity of electricity. [s. 154A, G.I. Act]

288. *Exemption from taxation by States in respect of water or electricity in certain cases.*—(1) Save in so far as the President may by order otherwise provide, no law of a State in force immediately before the commencement of this Constitution shall impose, or authorise the imposition of, a tax in respect of any water or electricity stored, generated, consumed, distributed or sold by any authority established by any existing law or any law made by Parliament for regulating or developing any inter-State river or river-valley.

Explanation.—The expression "law of a State in force" in this clause shall include a law of a State passed or made before the commencement of this Constitution and not previously repealed, notwithstanding that it or parts of it may not be then in operation either at all or in particular areas.

(2) The Legislature of a State may by law impose, or authorise the imposition of, any such tax as is mentioned in clause (1), but no such law shall have any effect unless it has, after having been reserved for the consideration of the President, received his assent; and if any such law provides for the fixation of the rates and other incidents of such tax by means of rules or orders to be made under the law by any authority, the law shall provide for the previous consent of the President being obtained to the making of any such rule or order.

289. *Exemption of property and income of a State from Union taxation.*—(1) The property and income of a State shall be exempt from Union taxation.

(2) Nothing in clause (1) shall prevent the Union from imposing, or authorising the imposition of, any tax to such extent, if any, as Parliament may by law provide in respect of a trade or business of any kind carried on by, or on behalf of, the Government of a State, or any operations connected therewith, or any property used or occupied for the purposes of such trade or business, or any income accruing or arising in connection therewith.

(3) Nothing in clause (2) shall apply to any trade or business, or to any class of trade or business, which Parliament may by law declare to be incidental to the ordinary functions of Government. [s. 155, G.I. Act]

290. *Adjustment in respect of certain expenses and pensions.*—Where under the provisions of this Constitution the expenses of any court or Commission, or the pension payable to or in respect of a person who has served before the commencement of this Constitution under the Crown in India or after such commencement in connection with the affairs of the Union or of a State, are charged on the Consolidated Fund of India or the Consolidated Fund of a State, then, if—

(*a*) in the case of a charge on the Consolidated Fund of India, the court or Commission serves any of the separate needs of a State, or the person has served wholly or in part in connection with the affairs of a State; or

(*b*) in the case of a charge on the Consolidated Fund of a State, the court or Commission serves any of the separate needs of the Union or another State, or the person has served wholly or in part in connection with the affairs of the Union or another State,

there shall be charged on and paid out of the Consolidated Fund of the State or, as the case may be, the Consolidated Fund of India or the Consolidated Fund of the other State, such contribution in respect of the expenses or pension as may be agreed, or as may in default of agreement be determined by an arbitrator to be appointed by the Chief Justice of India. [s. 156, G.I. Act]

[56][**290A.** *Annual payment to certain Devaswom Funds.*—A sum of forty-six lakhs and fifty thousand rupees shall be charged on, and paid out of, the Consolidated Fund of the State of Kerala every year to the Travancore Devaswom Fund; and a sum of thirteen lakhs and fifty thousand rupees shall be charged on, and paid out of the Consolidated Fund of the State of [57][Tamil Nadu] every year to the Devaswom Fund established in that State for the maintenance of Hindu temples and shrines in the territories transferred to that State on the 1st day of November, 1956, from the State of Travancore-Cochin.]

[58]**291.** [*Privy purse sums of Rulers.*] *Rep. by the Constitution (Twenty-sixth Amendment) Act,* 1971, s. 2.

CHAPTER II.—BORROWING

292. *Borrowing by the Government of India.*—The executive power of the Union extends to borrowing upon the security of the Consolidated Fund of India within such limits, if any, as may from time to time be fixed by Parliament by law and to the giving of guarantees within such limits, if any, as may be so fixed. [s. 162, G.I. Act]

293. *Borrowing by States.*—(1) Subject to the provisions of this article, the executive power of a State extends to borrowing within the territory of India upon the security of the Consolidated Fund of the State within such limits, if any, as may from time to time be fixed by the Legislature of such State by law and to the giving of guarantees within such limits, if any, as may be so fixed.

(2) The Government of India may, subject to such conditions as may be laid down by or under any law made by Parliament, make loans to any State or, so long as any limits fixed under article 292 are not exceeded, give guarantees in respect of loans raised by any State, and any sums required for the purpose of making such loans shall be charged on the Consolidated Fund of India.

(3) A State may not without the consent of the Government of India raise any loan if there is still outstanding any part of a loan which has been made to the State by the Government of India or by its predecessor Government, or in respect

---

[56] Ins. by the Const. (7th Am.) Act, 1956, s. 19, w.e.f. 1.11.1956.

[57] Subs. by the Madras State (Alteration of Name) Act, 1968, s. 4 for "Madras" w.e.f. 14.1.1969.

[58] The repealed article read as follows:

"291. (1) Where under any covenant or agreement entered into by the Ruler of any Indian State before the commencement of this Constitution, the payment of any sums, free of tax, has been guaranteed or assured by the Government of the Dominion of India to any Ruler of such State as privy purse—

(*a*) such sums shall be charged on, and paid out of, the Consolidated Fund of India; and

(*b*) the sums so paid to any Ruler shall be exempt from all taxes on income.

(2) Where the territories of any such Indian State as aforesaid are comprised within a State specified in Part A or Part B of the First Schedule, there shall be charged on, and paid out of, the Consolidated Fund of that State such contribution, if any, in respect of the payments made by the Government of India under clause (1) and for such period as may, subject to any agreement entered into in that behalf under clause (1) of article 278, be determined by order of the President."

By the Const. (7th Am.) Act, 1956, clause (2) was omitted, and clause (1) became the only clause w.e.f. 1.11.1956.

of which a guarantee has been given by the Government of India or by its predecessor Government.

(4) A consent under clause (3) may be granted subject to such conditions, if any, as the Government of India may think fit to impose. [s. 163, G.I. Act]

CHAPTER III.—PROPERTY, CONTRACTS, RIGHTS, LIABILITIES, OBLIGATIONS AND SUITS

294. *Succession to property, assets, rights, liabilities and obligations in certain cases.*—As from the commencement of this Constitution—

(*a*) all property and assets which immediately before such commencement were vested in His Majesty for the purposes of the Government of the Dominion of India and all property and assets which immediately before such commencement were vested in His Majesty for the purposes of the Government of each Governor's Province shall vest respectively in the Union and the corresponding State, and

(*b*) all rights, liabilities and obligations of the Government of the Dominion of India and of the Government of each Governor's Province, whether arising out of any contract or otherwise, shall be the rights, liabilities and obligations respectively of the Government of India and the Government of each corresponding State,

subject to any adjustment made or to be made by reason of the creation before the commencement of this Constitution of the Dominion of Pakistan or of the Provinces of West Bengal, East Bengal, West Punjab and East Punjab.

[Ss. 172, 173, G.I. Act]

295. *Succession to property, assets, rights, liabilities and obligations in other cases.*—(1) As from the commencement of this Constitution—

(*a*) all property and assets which immediately before such commencement were vested in any Indian State corresponding to a State specified in Part B of the First Schedule shall vest in the Union, if the purposes for which such property and assets were held immediately before such commencement will thereafter be purposes of the Union relating to any of the matters enumerated in the Union List, and

(*b*) all rights, liabilities and obligations of the Government of any Indian State corresponding to a State specified in Part B of the First Schedule, whether arising out of any contract or otherwise, shall be the rights, liabilities and obligations of the Government of India, if the purposes for which such rights were acquired or liabilities or obligations were incurred before such commencement will thereafter be purposes of the Government of India relating to any of the matters enumerated in the Union List,

subject to any agreement entered into in that behalf by the Government of India with the Government of that State.

(2) Subject as aforesaid, the Government of each State specified in Part B of the First Schedule shall, as from the commencement of this Constitution, be the successor of the Government of the corresponding Indian State as regards all property and assets and all rights, liabilities and obligations, whether arising out of any contract or otherwise, other than those referred to in clause (1).

[Ss. 172, 173, G.I. Act]

296. *Property accruing by escheat or lapse or as bona vacantia.*—Subject as hereinafter provided, any property in the territory of India which, if this Constitution had not come into operation, would have accrued to His Majesty or, as the case may be, to the Ruler of an Indian State by escheat or lapse, or as *bona vacantia* for want of a rightful owner, shall, if it is property situate in a State, vest in such State, and shall, in any other case vest in the Union:

Provided that any property which at the date when it would have so accrued to His Majesty or to the Ruler of an Indian State was in the possession or under the control of the Government of India or the Government of a State shall, according as the purposes for which it was then used or held were purposes of the Union or of a State, vest in the Union or in that State.

Explanation.—In this article, the expressions "Ruler" and "Indian State" have the same meanings as in article 363. [s. 174, G.I. Act]

[59] [**297.** *Things of value within territorial waters or continental shelf and resources of the exclusive economic zone to vest in the Union.*—(1) All lands, minerals and other things of value underlying the ocean within the territorial waters, or the continental shelf, or the exclusive economic zone, of India shall vest in the Union and be held for the purposes of the Union.

(2) All other resources of the exclusive economic zone of India shall also vest in the Union and be held for the purposes of the Union.

(3) The limits of the territorial waters, the continental shelf, the exclusive economic zone, and other maritime zones, of India shall be such as may be specified, from time to time, by or under any law made by Parliament.]

[60] [**298.** *Power to carry on trade, etc.*—The executive power of the Union and of each State shall extend to the carrying on of any trade or business and to the acquisition, holding and disposal of property and the making of contracts for any purpose:

Provided that—

(*a*) the said executive power of the Union shall, in so far as such trade or business or such purpose is not one with respect to which Parliament may make laws, be subject in each State to legislation by the State; and

(*b*) the said executive power of each State shall, in so far as such trade or business or such purpose is not one with respect to which the State Legislature may make laws, be subject to legislation by Parliament.]

[s. 175, G.I. Act]

299. *Contracts.*—(1) All contracts made in the exercise of the executive power of the Union or of a State shall be expressed to be made by the President, or by the Governor[61] * * * of the State, as the case may be, and all such contracts and all assurances of property made in the exercise of that power shall be executed on behalf of the President or the Governor[61] * * * by such persons and in such manner as he may direct or authorise.

(2) Neither the President nor the Governor[62] * * * shall be personally liable in respect of any contract or assurance made or executed for the purposes of this Constitution, or for the purposes of any enactment relating to the Government of India heretofore in force, nor shall any person making or executing any such contract or assurance on behalf of any of them be personally liable in respect thereof.

---

[59] Subs. by the Const. (40th Am.) Act, 1976, s. 2 w.e.f. 27.5.1976. Article 297, as originally enacted, ran as follows:

"297. *Things of value lying within territorial waters [or continental shelf] to vest in the Union.*—All lands, minerals and other things of value underlying the ocean within the territorial waters [or the continental shelf] of India shall vest in the Union and be held for the purposes of the Union."

The words in square brackets were inserted by the Const. (15th Am.) Act, 1963, w.e.f. 5.10.1963.

[60] Subs. by the Const. (7th Am.) Act, 1956, w.e.f. 1.11.1956, for the original article 298 which read as follows:

"298. (1) The executive power of the Union and of each State shall extend, subject to any law made by the appropriate Legislature, to the grant, sale, disposition or mortgage of any property held for the purposes of the Union or of such State, as the case may be, and to the purchase or acquisition of property for those purposes respectively, and to the making of contracts.

(2) All property acquired for the purposes of the Union or of a State shall vest in the Union or in such State, as the case may be."

[61] The words "or the Rajpramukh" omitted by the Const. (7th Am.) Act, 1956, s. 29 and Sch., w.e.f. 1.11.1956.

[62] The words "nor the Rajpramukh" omitted by s. 29 and Sch., *ibid.*

300. *Suits and proceedings.*—(1) The Government of India may sue or be sued by the name of the Union of India and the Government of a State may sue or be sued by the name of the State and may, subject to any provisions which may be made by Act of Parliament or of the Legislature of such State enacted by virtue of powers conferred by this Constitution, sue or be sued in relation to their respective affairs in the like cases as the Dominion of India and the corresponding Provinces or the corresponding Indian States might have sued or been sued if this Constitution had not been enacted.

(2) If at the commencement of this Constitution—

(*a*) any legal proceedings are pending to which the Dominion of India is a party, the Union of India shall be deemed to be substituted for the Dominion in those proceedings; and

(*b*) any legal proceedings are pending to which a Province or an Indian State is a party, the corresponding State shall be deemed to be substituted for the Province or the Indian State in those proceedings.

[s. 176, G.I. Act]

[63][CHAPTER IV.—RIGHT TO PROPERTY

300A. *Persons not to be deprived of property save by authority of law.*—No person shall be deprived of his property save by authority of law.]

PART XIII

TRADE, COMMERCE AND INTERCOURSE WITHIN THE TERRITORY OF INDIA

301. *Freedom of trade, commerce and intercourse.*—Subject to the other provisions of this Part, trade, commerce and intercourse throughout the territory of India shall be free.

302. *Power of Parliament to impose restrictions on trade, commerce and intercourse.*—Parliament may by law impose such restrictions on the freedom of trade, commerce or intercourse between one State and another or within any part of the territory of India as may be required in the public interest.

303. *Restrictions on the legislative powers of the Union and of the States with regard to trade and commerce.*—(1) Notwithstanding anything in article 302, neither Parliament nor the Legislature of a State shall have power to make any law giving, or authorising the giving of, any preference to one State over another, or making, or authorising the making of, any discrimination between one State and another, by virtue of any entry relating to trade and commerce in any of the Lists in the Seventh Schedule.

(2) Nothing in clause (1) shall prevent Parliament from making any law giving, or authorising the giving of, any preference or making, or authorising the making of, any discrimination if it is declared by such law that it is necessary to do so for the purpose of dealing with a situation arising from scarcity of goods in any part of the territory of India. [s. 297, G.I. Act]

304. *Restrictions on trade, commerce and intercourse among States.*—Notwithstanding anything in article 301 or article 303, the Legislature of a State may by law—

(*a*) impose on goods imported from other States [64][or the Union territories] any tax to which similar goods manufactured or produced in that State are subject, so, however, as not to discriminate between goods so imported and goods so manufactured or produced; and

(*b*) impose such reasonable restrictions on the freedom of trade, commerce or intercourse with or within that State as may be required in the public interest:

---

[63] Ins. by the Const. (44th Am.) Act, 1978, s. 34 (w.e.f. 20.6.1979).
[64] Ins. by the Const. (7th Am.) Act, 1956, s. 29 and Sch. w.e.f. 1.11.1956.

Provided that no Bill or amendment for the purposes of clause (*b*) shall be introduced or moved in the Legislature of a State without the previous sanction of the President. [s. 297. G.I. Act]

[65] [**305.** *Saving of existing laws and laws providing for State monopolies.*—Nothing in articles 301 and 303 shall affect the provisions of any existing law except in so far as the President may by order otherwise direct; and nothing in article 301 shall affect the operation of any law made before the commencement of the Constitution (Fourth Amendment) Act, 1955, in so far as it relates to, or prevent Parliament or the Legislature of a State from making any law relating to, any such matter as is referred to in sub-clause (*ii*) of clause (6) of article 19.]

[66]**306.** [*Power of certain States in Part B of the First Schedule to impose restrictions on trade and commerce.*] *Rep. by the Constitution (Seventh Amendment) Act,* 1956, *s.* 29 *and Sch.*

307. *Appointment of authority for carrying out the purposes of articles 301 to 304.*—Parliament may by law appoint such authority as it considers appropriate for carrying out the purposes of articles 301, 302, 303 and 304, and confer on the authority so appointed such powers and such duties as it thinks necessary.

PART XIV

SERVICES UNDER THE UNION AND THE STATES

CHAPTER I.—SERVICES

308. *Interpretation.*—In this Part, unless the context otherwise requires, the expression "State" [67][does not include the State of Jammu and Kashmir].

309. *Recruitment and conditions of service of persons serving the Union or a State.*—Subject to the provisions of this Constitution, Acts of the appropriate Legislature may regulate the recruitment, and conditions of service of persons appointed, to public services and posts in connection with the affairs of the Union or of any State:

Provided that it shall be competent for the President or such person as he may direct in the case of services and posts in connection with the affairs of the Union, and for the Governor [68] * * * of a State or such person as he may direct in the case of services and posts in connection with the affairs of the State, to make rules regulating the recruitment, and the conditions of service of persons appointed, to such services and posts until provision in that behalf is made by or under an Act of the appropriate Legislature under this article, and any rules so made shall have effect subject to the provisions of any such Act. [s. 241, G.I. Act]

---

[65] Subs. by the Const. (4th Am.) Act, 1955, s. 4, w.e.f. 27.4.1955, for the original article which read as follows:

"305. Nothing in articles 301 and 303 shall affect the provisions of any existing law except in so far as the President may by order otherwise provide."

[66] The repealed article read as follows:

"306. Notwithstanding anything in the foregoing provisions of this Part or in any other provisions of this Constitution, any State specified in Part B of the First Schedule which before the commencement of this Constitution was levying any tax or duty on the import of goods into the State from other States or on the export of goods from the State to other States may, if an agreement in that behalf has been entered into between the Government of India and the Government of that State, continue to levy and collect such tax or duty subject to the terms of such agreement and for such period not exceeding ten years from the commencement of this Constitution as may be specified in the agreement:

Provided that the President may at any time after the expiration of five years from such commencement terminate or modify any such agreement if, after consideration of the report of the Finance Commission constituted under article 280, he thinks it necessary to do so."

[67] Subs. by the Const. (7th Am.) Act, 1956, s. 29 and Sch., for "means a State specified in Part A or Part B of the First Schedule", w.e.f. 1.11.1956.

[68] The words "or Rajpramukh" omitted by s. 29 and Sch., *ibid.*

310. *Tenure of office of persons serving the Union or a State.*—(1) Except as expressly provided by this Constitution, every person who is a member of a defence service or of a civil service of the Union or of an all-India service or holds any post connected with defence or any civil post under the Union holds office during the pleasure of the President, and every person who is a member of a civil service of a State or holds any civil post under a State holds office during the pleasure of the Governor [69] * * * of the State.

(2) Notwithstanding that a person holding a civil post under the Union or a State holds office during the pleasure of the President or, as the case may be, of the Governor [70] * * * of the State, any contract under which a person, not being a member of a defence service or of an all-India service or of a civil service of the Union or a State, is appointed under this Constitution to hold such a post may, if the President or the Governor [71] * * *, as the case may be, deems it necessary in order to secure the services of a person having special qualifications, provide for the payment to him of compensation, if before the expiration of an agreed period that post is abolished or he is, for reasons not connected with any misconduct on his part, required to vacate that post. [s. 240, G.I. Act]

311. *Dismissal, removal or reduction in rank of persons employed in civil capacities under the Union or a State.*—(1) No person who is a member of a civil service of the Union or an all-India service or a civil service of a State or holds a civil post under the Union or a State shall be dismissed or removed by an authority subordinate to that by which he was appointed.

[72][(2) No such person as aforesaid shall be dismissed or removed or reduced in rank except after an inquiry in which he has been informed of the charges against him and given a reasonable opportunity of being heard in respect of those charges [73] * * *:

[74][Provided that where it is proposed after such inquiry, to impose upon him any such penalty, such penalty may be imposed on the basis of the evidence adduced during such inquiry and it shall not be necessary to give such person any opportunity of making representation on the penalty proposed:

---

[69] The words "or, as the case may be, the Rajpramukh" omitted by the Const. (7th Am.) Act, 1956, s. 29 and Sch. w.e.f. 1.11.1956.

[70] The words "or Rajpramukh" omitted by s. 29 and Sch., *ibid.*

[71] The words "or the Rajpramukh" omitted by s. 29 and Sch., *ibid*

[72] Subs. by the Const. (15th Am.) Act, 1963, s. 10, w.e.f. 5.10.1963 for the original clauses (2) and (3) which read as follows:

"(2) No person as aforesaid shall be dismissed or removed or reduced in rank until he has been given a reasonable opportunity or showing cause against the action proposed to be taken in regard to him:

Provided that this clause shall not apply—

(*a*) where a person is dismissed or removed or reduced in rank on the ground of conduct which has led to his conviction on a criminal charge;

(*b*) where an authority empowered to dismiss or remove a person or to reduce him in rank is satisfied that for some reason, to be recorded by that authority in writing, it is not reasonably practicable to give to that person an opportunity or showing cause; or

(*c*) where the President or Governor, as the case may be, is satisfied that in the interest of the security of the State it is not expedient to give to that person such an opportunity.

(3) If any question arises whether it is reasonably practicable to give to any person an opportunity of showing cause under clause (2), the decision thereon of the authority empowered to dismiss or remove such person or to reduce him in rank, as the case may be, shall be final."

[73] Certain words omitted by the Const. (42nd Am.) Act, 1976, s. 44 w.e.f. 3.1.1977. The omitted words are as follows:

"and where it is proposed, after such inquiry, to impose on him any such penalty, until he has been given a reasonable opportunity of making representation on the penalty proposed, but only on the basis of the evidence adduced during such inquiry".

[74] Subs. by s. 44, *ibid.*, w.e.f. 3.1.1977 for "Provided that this clause shall not apply—".

Provided further that this clause shall not apply—]

(*a*) where a person is dismissed or removed or reduced in rank on the ground of conduct which has led to his conviction on a criminal charge; or

(*b*) where the authority empowered to dismiss or remove a person or to reduce him in rank is satisfied that for some reason, to be recorded by that authority in writing, it is not reasonably practicable to hold such inquiry; or

(*c*) where the President or the Governor, as the case may be, is satisfied that in the interest of the security of the State it is not expedient to hold such inquiry.

(3) If, in respect of any such person as aforesaid, a question arises whether it is reasonably practicable to hold such inquiry as is referred to in clause (2), the decision thereon of the authority empowered to dismiss or remove such person or to reduce him in rank shall be final.] [s. 240, G.I. Act]

312. *All-India services.*—(1) Notwithstanding anything in [75][Chapter VI of Part VI or Part XI], if the Council of States has declared by resolution supported by not less than two-thirds of the members present and voting that it is necessary or expedient in the national interest so to do, Parliament may by law provide for the creation of one or more all India service [76][(including an all-India judicial service)] common to the Union and the States, and, subject to the other provisions of this Chapter, regulate the recruitment, and the conditions of service of persons appointed, to any such service.[77]

(2) The services known at the commencement of this Constitution as the Indian Administrative Service and the Indian Police Service shall be deemed to be services created by Parliament under this article.

[76][(3) The all-India judicial service referred to in clause (1) shall not include any post inferior to that of a district judge as defined in article 236.

(4) The law providing for the creation of the all-India judicial service aforesaid may contain such provisions for the amendment of Chapter VI of Part VI as may be necessary for giving effect to the provisions of that law and no such law shall be deemed to be an amendment of this Constitution for the purposes of article 368.]

[78][**312A.** *Power of Parliament to vary or revoke conditions of service of officers of certain services.*—(1) Parliament may by law—

(*a*) vary or revoke, whether prospectively or retrospectively, the conditions of service as respects remuneration, leave and pension and the rights as respects disciplinary matters of persons who, having been appointed by the Secretary of State or Secretary of State in Council to a civil service of the Crown in India before the commencement of this Constitution, continue on and after the commencement of the Constitution (Twenty-eighth Amendment) Act, 1972, to serve under the Government of India or of a State in any service or post;

(*b*) vary or revoke, whether prospectively or retrospectively, the conditions of service as respects pension of persons who, having been appointed by the Secretary of State or Secretary of State in Council to a civil service of the Crown in India before the commencement of this Constitution, retired or otherwise ceased to be in service at any time before the commencement of the Constitution (Twenty-eighth Amendment) Act 1972:

Provided that in the case of any such person who is holding or has held the office of the Chief Justice or other Judge of the Supreme Court or a High Court, the Comptroller and Auditor-General of India, the Chairman or other member of

---

[75] Subs. by the Const. (42nd Am.) Act, 1976, s. 45, for "Part XV" w.e.f. 3.1.1977.
[76] Ins. by s. 45, *ibid.* w.e.f. 3.1.1977.
[77] See the All India Services Act, 1951.
[78] Ins. by the Const. (28th Am.) Act, 1972, w.e.f. 29.8.1972.

the Union or a State Public Service Commission or the Chief Election Commissioner, nothing in sub-clause (*a*) or sub-clause (*b*) shall be construed as empowering Parliament to vary or revoke, after his appointment to such post, the conditions of his service to his disadvantage except in so far as such conditions of service are applicable to him by reason of his being a person appointed by the Secretary of State or Secretary of State in Council to a civil service of the Crown in India.

(2) Except to the extent provided for by Parliament by law under this article, nothing in this article shall affect the power of any legislature or other authority under any other provision of this Constitution to regulate the conditions of service of persons referred to in clause (1).

(3) Neither the Supreme Court nor any other court shall have jurisdiction in—

(*a*) any dispute arising out of any provision of, or any endorsement on, any covenant, agreement or other similar instrument which was entered into or executed by any person referred to in clause (1), or arising out of any letter issued to such person, in relation to his appointment to any civil service of the Crown in India or his continuance in service under the Government of the Dominion of India or a Province thereof;

(*b*) any dispute in respect of any right, liability or obligation under article 314 as originally enacted.

(4) The provisions of this article shall have effect notwithstanding anything in article 314 as originally enacted or in any other provision of this Constitution.]

313. *Transitional provisions.*—Until other provision is made in this behalf under this Constitution, all the laws in force immediately before the commencement of this Constitution and applicable to any public service or any post which continues to exist after the commencement of this Constitution, as an all-India service or as service or post under the Union or a State shall continue in force so far as consistent with the provisions of this Constitution. [s. 276, G.I. Act]

[79]**314.** [*Provision for protection of existing officers of certain services.*] *Rep. by the Constitution (Twenty-eighth Amendment) Act,* 1972, *s.* 3 (*w.e.f.* 29-8-1972).

CHAPTER II.—PUBLIC SERVICE COMMISSIONS

315. *Public Service Commissions for the Union and for the States.*—(1) Subject to the provisions of this article, there shall be a Public Service Commission for the Union and a Public Service Commission for each State.

(2) Two or more States may agree that there shall be one Public Service Commission for that group of States, and if a resolution to that effect is passed by the House or, where there are two Houses, by each House of the Legislature of each of those States, Parliament may by law provide for the appointment of a Joint State Public Service Commission (referred to in this Chapter as Joint Commission) to serve the needs of those States.

(3) Any such law as aforesaid may contain such incidental and consequential provisions as may be necessary or desirable for giving effect to the purposes of the law.

---

[79] The repealed article, as originally enacted, read as follows:

"314. Except as otherwise expressly provided by this Constitution, every person who having been appointed by the Secretary of State or Secretary of State in Council to a civil service of the Crown in India continues on and after the commencement of this Constitution to serve under the Government of India or of a State shall be entitled to receive from the Government of India and the Government of the State, which he is from time to time serving, the same conditions of service as respects remuneration, leave and pension, and the same rights as respects disciplinary matters or rights as similar thereto as changed circumstances may permit as that person was entitled to immediately before such commencement." *Cf.* Secs. 247-9, G.I. Act.

(4) The Public Service Commission for the Union, if requested so to do by the Governor [80] * * * of a State, may, with the approval of the President, agree to serve all or any of the needs of the State.

(5) References in this Constitution to the Union Public Service Commission or a State Public Service Commission shall, unless the context otherwise requires, be construed as references to the Commission serving the needs of the Union or, as the case may be, the State as respects the particular matter in question.

[s. 264, G.I. Act]

316. *Appointment and term of office of members.*—(1) The Chairman and other members of a Public Service Commission shall be appointed, in the case of the Union Commission or a Joint Commission, by the President, and in the case of a State Commission, by the Governor [81] * * * of the State:

Provided that as nearly as may be one-half of the members of every Public Service Commission shall be persons who at the dates of their respective appointments have held office for at least ten years either under the Government of India or under the Government of a State, and in computing the said period of ten years any period before the commencement of this Constitution during which a person has held office under the Crown in India or under the Government of an Indian State shall be included.

[82][(1A) If the office of the Chairman of the Commission becomes vacant or if any such Chairman is by reason of absence or for any other reason unable to perform the duties of his office, those duties shall, until some person appointed under clause (1) to the vacant office has entered on the duties thereof or, as the case may be, until the Chairman has resumed his duties, be performed by such one of the other members of the Commission as the President, in the case of the Union Commission or a Joint Commission, and the Governor of the State in the case of a State Commission, may appoint for the purpose.]

(2) A member of a Public Service Commission shall hold office for a term of six years from the date on which he enters upon his office or until he attains, in the case of the Union Commission, the age of sixty-five years, and in the case of a State Commission or a Joint Commission, the age of [83][sixty-two years], whichever is earlier:

Provided that—

(*a*) a member of a Public Service Commission may, by writing under his hand addressed, in the case of the Union Commission or a Joint Commission, to the President, and in the case of a State Commission, to the Governor [84] * * * of the State, resign his office;

(*b*) a member of a Public Service Commission may be removed from his office in the manner provided in clause (1) or clause (3) of article 317.

(3) A person who holds office as a member of a Public Service Commission shall, on the expiration of his term of office, be ineligible for re-appointment to that office.

[s. 265, G.I. Act]

317. *Removal and suspension of a member of a Public Service Commission.*—(1) Subject to the provisions of clause (3), the Chairman or any other member of a Public Service Commission shall only be removed from his office by order of the President on the ground of misbehaviour after the Supreme Court, on reference being made to it by the President, has, on inquiry held in accordance with the

---

[80] The words "or Rajpramukh" omitted by the Const. (7th Am.) Act, 1956, s. 29 and Sch. w.e.f. 1.11.1956.

[81] The words "or Rajpramukh" omitted by the Const. (7th Am.) Act, 1956, s. 29 and Sch., w.e.f. 1.11.1956.

[82] Ins. by the Const. (15th Am.) Act, 1963, s. 11, w.e.f. 5.10.1963.

[83] Subs. by the Const. (41st Am.) Act, 1976, s. 2, for "sixty years", w.e.f. 7.11.1976.

[84] The words "or Rajpramukh" omitted by the Const. (7th Am.) Act, 1956, s. 29, and Sch., w.e.f. 1.11.1956.

procedure prescribed in that behalf under article 145, reported that the Chairman or such other member, as the case may be, ought on any such ground to be removed.

(2) The President, in the case of the Union Commission or a Joint Commission, and the Governor [85] * * *, in the case of a State Commission, may suspend from office the Chairman or any other member of the Commission in respect of whom a reference has been made to the Supreme Court under clause (1) until the President has passed orders on receipt of the report of the Supreme Court on such reference.

(3) Notwithstanding anything in clause (1), the President may by order remove from office the Chairman or any other member of a Public Service Commission if the Chairman or such other member, as the case may be—

(*a*) is adjudged an insolvent; or

(*b*) engages during his term of office in any paid employment outside the duties of his office; or

(*c*) is, in the opinion of the President, unfit to continue in office by reason of infirmity of mind or body.

(4) If the Chairman or any other member of a Public Service Commission is or becomes in any way concerned or interested in any contract or agreement made by or on behalf of the Government of India or the Government of a State or participates in any way in the profit thereof or in any benefit or emolument arising therefrom otherwise than as a member and in common with the other members of an incorporated company, he shall, for the purposes of clause (1), be deemed to be guilty of misbehaviour.

318. *Power to make regulations as to conditions of service of members and staff of the Commission.*—In the case of the Union Commission or a Joint Commission, the President and, in the case of a State Commission, the Governor [86] * * * of the State may by regulations—

(*a*) determine the number of members of the Commission and their conditions of service; and

(*b*) make provision with respect to the number of members of the staff of the Commission and their conditions of service:

Provided that the conditions of service of a member of a Public Service Commission shall not be varied to his disadvantage after his appointment.

[s. 265, G.I. Act]

319. *Prohibition as to the holding of offices by members of Commission on ceasing to be such members.*—On ceasing to hold office—

(*a*) the Chairman of the Union Public Service Commission shall be ineligible for further employment either under the Government of India or under the Government of a State;

(*b*) the Chairman of a State Public Service Commission shall be eligible for appointment as the Chairman or any other member of the Union Public Service Commission or as the Chairman of any other State Public Service Commission, but not for any other employment either under the Government of India or under the Government of a State;

(*c*) a member other than the Chairman of the Union Public Service Commission shall be eligible for appointment as the Chairman of the Union Public Service Commission or as the Chairman of a State Public Service Commission, but not for any other employment either under the Government of India or under the Government of a State;

(*d*) a member other than the Chairman of a State Public Service Commission shall be eligible for appointment as the Chairman or any other member of

---

[85] The words "or Rajpramukh" omitted by the Const. (7th Am.) Act, 1956, s. 29 and Sch., w.e.f. 1.11.1956.

[86] The words "or Rajpramukh" omitted by the Const. (7th Am.) Act, 1956, s. 29 and Sch., w.e.f. 1.11.1956.

the Union Public Service Commission or as the Chairman of that or any other State Public Service Commission, but not for any other employment either under the Government of India or under the Government of a State.

[s. 265, G.I. Act]

320. *Functions of Public Service Commissions.*—(1) It shall be the duty of the Union and the State Public Service Commissions to conduct examinations for appointments to the services of the Union and the services of the State respectively.

(2) It shall also be the duty of the Union Public Service Commission, if requested by any two or more States so to do, to assist those States in framing and operating schemes of joint recruitment for any services for which candidates possessing special qualifications are required.

(3) The Union Public Service Commission or the State Public Service Commission, as the case may be, shall be consulted—

(*a*) on all matters relating to methods of recruitment to civil services and for civil posts;

(*b*) on the principles to be followed in making appointments to civil services and posts and in making promotions and transfers from one service to another and on the suitability of candidates for such appointments, promotions or transfers;

(*c*) on all disciplinary matters affecting a person serving under the Government of India or the Government of a State in a civil capacity, including memorials or petitions relating to such matters;

(*d*) on any claim by or in respect of a person who is serving or has served under the Government of India or the Government of a State or under the Crown in India or under the Government of an Indian State, in a civil capacity, that any costs incurred by him in defending legal proceedings instituted against him in respect of acts done or purporting to be done in the execution of his duty should be paid out of the Consolidated Fund of India, or, as the case may be, out of the Consolidated Fund of the State;

(*e*) on any claim for the award of a pension in respect of injuries sustained by a person while serving under the Government of India or the Government of a State or under the Crown in India or under the Government of an Indian State, in a civil capacity, and any question as to the amount of any such award,

and it shall be the duty of a Public Service Commission to advice on any matter so referred to them and on any other matter which the President, or, as the case may be, the Governor [87]* * * of the State, may refer to them:

Provided that the President as respects the all-India services and also as respects other services and posts in connection with the affairs of the Union, and the Governor [88]* * *, as respects other services and posts in connection with the affairs of a State, may make regulations specifying the matters in which either generally, or in any particular class of case or in any particular circumstances, it shall not be necessary for a Public Service Commission to be consulted.

(4) Nothing in clause (3) shall require a Public Service Commission to be consulted as respects the manner in which any provision referred to in clause (4) of article 16 may be made or as respects the manner in which effect may be given to the provisions of article 335.

(5) All regulations made under the proviso to clause (3) by the President or the Governor [89]* * * of a State shall be laid for not less than fourteen days before each House of Parliament or the House or each House of the Legislature of the

---

[87] The words "or Rajpramukh" omitted by the Const. (7th Am.) Act, 1956, s. 29 and Sch., w.e.f. 1.11.1956.

[88] The words "or Rajpramukh, as the case may be" omitted by the Const. (7th Am.) Act, 1956, s. 29 and Sch., w.e.f. 1.11.1956.

[89] The words "or Rajpramukh" omitted by s. 29 and Sch., *ibid.*

State, as the case may be, as soon as possible after they are made, and shall be subject to such modifications, whether by way of repeal or amendment, as both Houses of Parliament or the House or both Houses of the Legislature of the State may make during the session in which they are so laid. [s. 266, G.I. Act]

321. *Power to extend functions of Public Service Commissions.*—An Act made by Parliament or, as the case may be, the Legislature of a State may provide for the exercise of additional functions by the Union Public Service Commission or the State Public Service Commission as respects the services of the Union or the State and also as respects the services of any local authority or other body corporate constituted by law or of any public institution. [s. 267, G.I. Act]

322. *Expenses of Public Service Commissions.*—The expenses of the Union or a State Public Service Commission, including any salaries, allowances and pensions payable to or in respect of the members or staff of the Commission, shall be charged on the Consolidated Fund of India or, as the case may be, the Consolidated Fund of the State.

323. *Reports of Public Service Commissions.*—(1) It shall be the duty of the Union Commission to present annually to the President a report as to the work done by the Commission and on receipt of such report the President shall cause a copy thereof together with a memorandum explaining, as respects the cases, if any, where the advice of the Commission was not accepted, the reasons for such non-acceptance to be laid before each House of Parliament.

(2) It shall be the duty of a State Commission to present annually to the Governor [90]* * * of the State a report as to the work done by the Commission, and it shall be the duty of a Joint Commission to present annually to the Governor [90]* * * of each of the States the needs of which are served by the Joint Commission a report as to the work done by the Commission in relation to that State, and in either case the Governor [91]* * *, shall, on receipt of such report, cause a copy thereof together with a memorandum explaining, as respects the cases, if any, where the advice of the Commission was not accepted, the reasons for such non-acceptance to be laid before the Legislature of the State.

[92][PART XIVA

TRIBUNALS

323A. *Administrative tribunals.*—(1) Parliament may, by law, provide for the adjudication or trial by administrative tribunals of disputes and complaints with respect to recruitment and conditions of service of persons appointed to public services and posts in connection with the affairs of the Union or of any State or of any local or other authority within the territory of India or under the control of the Government of India or of any corporation owned or controlled by the Government.

(2) A law made under clause (1) may—

(*a*) provide for the establishment of an administrative tribunal for the Union and a separate administrative tribunal for each State or for two or more States;

(*b*) specify the jurisdiction, powers (including the power to punish for contempt) and authority which may be exercised by each of the said tribunals;

(*c*) provide for the procedure (including provisions as to limitation and rules of evidence) to be followed by the said tribunals;

(*d*) exclude the jurisdiction of all courts, except the jurisdiction of the Supreme Court under article 136, with respect to the disputes or complaints referred to in clause (1);

---

[90] The words "or Rajpramukh" omitted by the Const. (7th Am.) Act, 1956, s. 29 and Sch., w.e.f. 1.11.1956.

[91] The words "or Rajpramukh, as the case may be" omitted by s. 29 and Sch., *ibid.*

[92] Ins. by the Const. (42nd Am.) Act, 1976, s. 46 (w.e.f. 3.1.1977).

(e) provide for the transfer to each such administrative tribunal of any cases pending before any court or other authority immediately before the establishment of such tribunal as would have been within the jurisdiction of such tribunal if the causes of action on which such suits or proceedings are based had arisen after such establishment;

(f) repeal or amend any order made by the President under clause (3) of article 371D;

(g) contain such supplemental, incidental and consequential provisions (including provisions as to fees) as Parliament may deem necessary for the effective functioning of, and for the speedy disposal of cases by, and the enforcement of the orders of, such tribunals.

(3) The provisions of this article shall have effect notwithstanding anything in any other provision of this Constitution or in any other law for the time being in force.

323B. *Tribunals for other matters.*—(1) The appropriate Legislature may, by law, provide for the adjudication or trial by tribunals of any disputes, complaints, or offences with respect to all or any of the matters specified in clause (2) with respect to which such Legislature has power to make laws.

(2) The matters referred to in clause (1) are the following, namely:—

(a) levy, assessment, collection and enforcement of any tax;

(b) foreign exchange, import and export across customs frontiers;

(c) industrial and labour disputes;

(d) land reforms by way of acquisition by the State of any estate as defined in article 31A or of any rights therein or the extinguishment or modification of any such rights or by way of ceiling on agricultural land or in any other way;

(e) ceiling on urban property;

(f) elections to either House of Parliament or the House or either House of the Legislature of a State, but excluding the matters referred to in article 329 and article 329A;

(g) production, procurement, supply and distribution of food-stuffs (including edible oilseeds and oils) and such other goods as the President may, by public notification, declare to be essential goods for the purpose of this article and control of prices of such goods;

(h) offences against laws with respect to any of the matters specified in sub-clauses (a) to (g) and fees in respect of any of those matters;

(i) any matter incidental to any of the matters specified in sub-clauses (a) to (h).

(3) A law made under clause (1) may—

(a) provide for the establishment of a hierarchy of tribunals;

(b) specify the jurisdiction, powers (including the power to punish for contempt) and authority which may be exercised by each of the said tribunals;

(c) provide for the procedure (including provisions as to limitation and rules of evidence) to be followed by the said tribunals;

(d) exclude the jurisdiction of all courts, except the jurisdiction of the Supreme Court under article 136, with respect to all or any of the matters falling within the jurisdiction of the said tribunals;

(e) provide for the transfer to each such tribunal of any cases pending before any court or any other authority immediately before the establishment of such tribunal as would have been within the jurisdiction of such tribunal if the causes of action on which such suits or proceedings are based had arisen after such establishment;

(f) contain such supplemental, incidental and consequential provisions (including provisions as to fees) as the appropriate Legislature may deem necessary for the effective functioning of, and for the speedy disposal of cases by, and the enforcement of the orders of, such tribunals.

(4) The provisions of this article shall have effect notwithstanding anything in any other provision of this Constitution or in any other law for the time being in force.

Explanation.—In this article, "appropriate Legislature", in relation to any matter, means Parliament or, as the case may be, a State Legislature competent to make laws with respect to such matter in accordance with the provisions of Part XI.]

PART XV

ELECTIONS

324. *Superintendence, direction and control of elections to be vested in an Election Commission.*—(1) The superintendence, direction and control of the preparation of the electoral rolls for, and the conduct of, all elections to Parliament and to the Legislature of every State and of elections to the offices of President and Vice-President held under this Constitution [93]* * * shall be vested in a Commission (referred to in this Constitution as the Election Commission).

(2) The Election Commission shall consist of the Chief Election Commissioner and such number of other Election Commissioners, if any, as the President may from time to time fix and the appointment of the Chief Election Commissioner and other Election Commissioners shall, subject to the provisions of any law made in that behalf by Parliament, be made by the President.

(3) When any other Election Commissioner is so appointed the Chief Election Commissioner shall act as the Chairman of the Election Commission.

(4) Before each general election to the House of the People and to the Legislative Assembly of each State, and before the first general election and thereafter before each biennial election to the Legislative Council of each State having such Council, the President may also appoint after consultation with the Election Commission such Regional Commissioners as he may consider necessary to assist the Election Commission in the performance of the functions conferred on the Commission by clause (1).

(5) Subject to the provisions of any law made by Parliament, the conditions of service and tenure of office of the Election Commissioners and the Regional Commissioners shall be such as the President may by rule determine:

Provided that the Chief Election Commissioner shall not be removed from his office except in like manner and on the like grounds as a Judge of the Supreme Court and the conditions of service of the Chief Election Commissioner shall not be varied to his disadvantage after his appointment:

Provided further that any other Election Commissioner or a Regional Commissioner shall not be removed from office except on the recommendation of the Chief Election Commissioner.

(6) The President, or the Governor [94]* * * of a State, shall, when so requested by the Election Commission, make available to the Election Commission or to a Regional Commissioner such staff as may be necessary for the discharge of the functions conferred on the Election Commission by clause (1).

325. *No person to be ineligible for inclusion in, or to claim to be included in a special electoral roll on grounds of religion, race, caste or sex.*—There shall be one general electoral roll for every territorial constituency for election to either House of Parliament or to the House or either House of the Legislature of a State and no person shall be ineligible for inclusion in any such roll or claim to be in-

---

[93] The words "including the appointment of election tribunals for the decision of doubts and disputes arising out of or in connection with elections to Parliament and to the Legislatures of States" omitted by the Const. (19th Am.) Act, 1966, s. 2, w.e.f. 11.12.1966.

[94] The words "or Rajpramukh" omitted by the Const. (7th Am.) Act, 1956, s. 29 and Sch., w.e.f. 1.11.1956.

cluded in any special electoral roll for any such constituency on grounds only of religion, race, caste, sex or any of them.

326. *Elections to the House of the People and to the Legislative Assemblies of States to be on the basis of adult suffrage.*—The elections to the House of the People and to the Legislative Assembly of every State shall be on the basis of adult suffrage; that is to say, every person who is a citizen of India and who is not less than twenty-one years of age on such date as may be fixed in that behalf by or under any law made by the appropriate Legislature and is not otherwise disqualified under this Constitution or any law made by the appropriate Legislature on the ground of non-residence, unsoundness of mind, crime or corrupt or illegal practice, shall be entitled to be registered as a voter at any such election.

327. *Power of Parliament to make provision with respect to elections to Legislatures.*—Subject to the provisions of this Constitution, Parliament may from time to time by law make provision with respect to all matters relating to, or in connection with, elections to either House of Parliament or to the House or either House of the Legislature of a State including the preparation of electoral rolls, the delimitation of constituencies and all other matters necessary for securing the due constitution of such House or Houses.

328. *Power of Legislature of a State to make provision with respect to elections to such Legislature.*—Subject to the provisions of this Constitution and in so far as provision in that behalf is not made by Parliament, the Legislature of a State may from time to time by law make provision with respect to all matters relating to, or in connection with, the elections to the House or either House of the Legislature of the State including the preparation of electoral rolls and all other matters necessary for securing the due constitution of such House or Houses.

329. *Bar to interference by courts in electoral matters.*—[95][Notwithstanding anything in this Constitution [96]* * *—]

(*a*) the validity of any law relating to the delimitation of constituencies or the allotment of seats to such constituencies, made or purporting to be made under article 327 or article 328, shall not be called in question in any court;

(*b*) no election to either House of Parliament or to the House or either House of the Legislature of a State shall be called in question except by an election petition presented to such authority and in such manner as may be provided for by or under any law made by the appropriate Legislature.

[97]**329A.** [*Special provision as to elections to Parliament in the case of Prime Minister and Speaker.*] *Rep. by the Constitution (Forty-fourth Amendment) Act*, 1978, *s.* 36 (*w.e.f.* 20-6-1979).

---

[95] Subs. by the Const. (39th Am.) Act, 1975, s. 3 for certain words, w.e.f. 10.8.1975. (The words "Notwithstanding anything in this Constitution" was substituted by the words, figures and letter "Notwithstanding anything in this Constitution but subject to the provisions of Article 329A.")

[96] The words, figures and letter "but subject to the provisions of Article 329A" omitted by the Const. (44th Am.) Act, 1978, w.e.f. 20.6.1979.

[97] Ins. by the Const. (39th Am.) Act, 1975, s. 4, w.e.f. 10.8.1975. The repealed article ran as follows:

"329A. (1) Subject to the provisions of Chapter II of Part V [except sub-clause (*e*) of clause (1) of Article 102], no election—

(*a*) to either House of Parliament of a person who holds the office of Prime Minister at the time of such election or is appointed as Prime Minister after such election;

(*b*) to the House of the People of a person who holds the office of Speaker of that House at the time of such election or who is chosen as the Speaker for that House after such election;

shall be called in question, except before such authority [not being any such authority as is referred to in clause (*b*) of article 329] or body and in such manner as may be provided for by or under any law made by Parliament and any such law may provide for all other matters relating to doubts and disputes in relation to such election including the grounds on which such election may be questioned.

PART XVI

SPECIAL PROVISIONS RELATING TO CERTAIN CLASSES

330. *Reservation of seats for Scheduled Castes and Scheduled Tribes in the House of the People.*—(1) Seats shall be reserved in the House of the People for—

(*a*) the Scheduled Castes;

(*b*) the Scheduled Tribes [98][except the Scheduled Tribes—

(*i*) in the tribal areas of Assam;

(*ii*) in Nagaland;

(*iii*) in Meghalaya;

(*iv*) in Arunachal Pradesh; and

(*v*) in Mizoram; and]

(*c*) the Scheduled Tribes in the autonomous districts of Assam.

(2) The number of seats reserved in any State [99][or Union territory] for the Scheduled Castes or the Scheduled Tribes under clause (1) shall bear, as nearly as may be, the same proportion to the total number of seats allotted to that State [99][or Union territory] in the House of the People as the population of the Scheduled Castes in the State [99][or Union territory] or of the Scheduled Tribes in the State [99][or Union territory] or part of the State [99][or Union territory], as the case may be, in respect of which seats are so reserved, bears to the total population of the State [99][or Union territory.]

[1][(3) Notwithstanding anything contained in clause (2), the number of seats reserved in the House of the People for the Scheduled Tribes in the autonomous districts of Assam shall bear to the total number of seats allotted to that State a

---

(2) The validity of any such law as is referred to in clause (1) and the decision of any authority or body under such law shall not be called in question in any court.

(3) Where any person is appointed as Prime Minister or, as the case may be, chosen to the office of the Speaker of the House of the People, while an election petition referred to in clause (*b*) of Article 329 in respect of his election to either House of Parliament or, as the case may be, to the House of the People is pending, such election petition shall abate upon such person being appointed as Prime Minister or, as the case may be, being chosen to the office of the Speaker of the House of the People, but such election may be called in question under any such law as is referred to in clause (1).

(4) No law made by Parliament before the commencement of the Constitution (Thirty-ninth Amendment) Act, 1975, in so far as it relates to election petitions and matters connected therewith, shall apply or shall be deemed ever to have applied to or in relation to the election of any such person as is referred to in clause (1) to either House of Parliament and such election shall not be deemed to be void or ever to have become void on any ground on which such election could be declared to be void, or has before such commencement, been declared to be void under any such law and notwithstanding any order made by any court, before such commencement, declaring such election to be void, such election shall continue to be valid in all respects and any such order and any finding on which such order is based shall be and shall be deemed always to have been void and of no effect.

(5) Any appeal or cross appeal against any such order of any court as is referred to in clause (4) pending immediately before the commencement of the Constitution (Thirty-ninth Amendment) Act, 1975, before the Supreme Court shall be disposed of in conformity with the provisions of clause (4).

(6) The provisions of this article shall have effect notwithstanding anything contained in this Constitution".

In *Indira Nehru Gandhi* v. *Raj Narain* ('75) A.SC. 2299, the Supreme Court struck down cl. (4) of Article 329 as violating the basic structure of the Constitution, and also on the ground that the Amendment was not a law but a legislative judgment in favour of Mrs. Gandhi.

[98] Subs. by the Const. (31st Am.) Act, 1973, s. 3, for certain words w.e.f. 17.10.1973. The words substituted read "except the Scheduled Tribes in the tribal areas of Assam and in Nagaland, and".

[99] Ins. by the Const. (7th Am.) Act, 1956, s. 29 and Sch. w.e.f. 1.11.1956.

[1] Ins. by the Const. (31st Am.) Act, 1973, s. 3, w.e.f. 17.10.1973.

proportion not less than the population of the Scheduled Tribes in the said autonomous districts bears to the total population of the State.]

[2][*Explanation.*—In this article and in article 332, the expression "population" means the population as ascertained at the last preceding census of which the relevant figures have been published:

Provided that the reference in this *Explanation* to the last preceding census of which the relevant figures have been published shall, until the relevant figures for the first census taken after the year 2000 have been published, be construed as a reference to the 1971 census.]

331. *Representation of the Anglo-Indian community in the House of the People.*—Notwithstanding anything in article 81, the President may, if he is of opinion that the Anglo-Indian community is not adequately represented in the House of the People, nominate not more than two members of that community to the House of the People.

332. *Reservation of seats for Scheduled Castes and Scheduled Tribes in the Legislative Assemblies of the States.*—(1) Seats shall be reserved for the Scheduled Castes and the Scheduled Tribes, [3][except the Scheduled Tribes in the tribal areas of Assam, in Nagaland and in Meghalaya], in the Legislative Assembly of every State [4]* * *.

(2) Seats shall be reserved also for the autonomous districts in the Legislative Assembly of the State of Assam.

(3) The number of seats reserved for the Scheduled Castes or the Scheduled Tribes in the Legislative Assembly of any State under clause (1) shall bear, as nearly as may be, the same proportion to the total number of seats in the Assembly as the population of the Scheduled Castes in the State or of the Scheduled Tribes in the State or part of the State, as the case may be, in respect of which seats are so reserved, bears to the total population of the State.

(4) The number of seats reserved for an autonomous district in the Legislative Assembly of the State of Assam shall bear to the total number of seats in that Assembly a proportion not less than the population of the district bears to the total population of the State.

(5) The constituencies for the seats reserved for any autonomous district of Assam shall not comprise any area outside that district [5]* * *.

(6) No person who is not a member of a Scheduled Tribe of any autonomous District of the State of Assam shall be eligible for election to the Legislative Assembly of the State from any constituency of that district [5]* * *.

333. *Representation of the Anglo-Indian community in the Legislative Assemblies of the States.*—Notwithstanding anything in article 170, the Governor [6]* * * of a State may, if he is of opinion that the Anglo-Indian community needs representation in the Legislative Assembly of the State and is not adequately represented therein, [7][nominate one member of that community to the Assembly].

334. *Reservation of seats and special representation to cease after thirty years.*—Notwithstanding anything in the foregoing provisions of this Part, the provisions of this Constitution relating to—

---

[2] Ins. by the Const. (42nd Am.) Act, 1976, s. 47, w.e.f. 3.1.1977.

[3] Subs. by the Const. (31st Am.) Act, 1973, s. 4, for certain words w.e.f. 17.10.1973. The words substituted read "except the Scheduled Tribes in the tribal areas of Assam and in Nagaland".

[4] The words and letters "specified in Part A or Part B of the First Schedule" omitted by the Const. (7th Am.) Act, 1956, s. 29 and Sch. w.e.f. 1.11.1956.

[5] The words "except in the case of the constituency comprising the cantonment and municipality of Shillong" omitted by the North-Eastern Areas Reorganisation Act, 1971, w.e.f. 21.1.1972.

[6] The words "or Rajpramukh" omitted by the Const. (7th Am.) Act, 1956, s. 29 and Sch. w.e.f. 1.11.1956.

[7] Subs. by the Const. (23rd Am.) Act, 1969, s. 4, for "nominate such number of members of the community to the Assembly as he considers appropriate" w.e.f. 23-1-1970.

(a) the reservation of seats for the Scheduled Castes and the Scheduled Tribes in the House of the People and in the Legislative Assemblies of the States; and

(b) the representation of the Anglo-Indian community in the House of the People and in the Legislative Assemblies of the States by nomination,

shall cease to have effect on the expiration of a period of [8][thirty years] from the commencement of this Constitution:

Provided that nothing in this article shall affect any representation in the House of the People or in the Legislative Assembly of a State until the dissolution of the then existing House or Assembly, as the case may be.

335. *Claims of Scheduled Castes and Scheduled Tribes to services and posts.*—The claims of the members of the Scheduled Castes and the Scheduled Tribes shall be taken into consideration, consistently with the maintenance of efficiency of administration, in the making of appointments to services and posts in connection with the affairs of the Union or of a State.

336. *Special provision for Anglo-Indian community in certain services.*—(1) During the first two years after the commencement of this Constitution, appointments of members of the Anglo-Indian community to posts in the railway, customs, postal and telegraph services of the Union shall be made on the same basis as immediately before the fifteenth day of August, 1947.

During every succeeding period of two years, the number of posts reserved for the members of the said community in the said services shall, as nearly as possible, be less by ten per cent. than the numbers so reserved during the immediately preceding period of two years:

Provided that at the end of ten years from the commencement of this Constitution all such reservations shall cease.

(2) Nothing in clause (1) shall bar the appointment of members of the Anglo-Indian community to posts other than, or in addition to, those reserved for the community under that clause if such members are found qualified for appointment on merit as compared with the members of other communities.

337. *Special provision with respect to educational grants for the benefit of Anglo-Indian community.*—During the first three financial years after the commencement of this Constitution, the same grants, if any, shall be made by the Union and by each State [9]* * * for the benefit of the Anglo-Indian community in respect of education as were made in the financial year ending on the thirty-first day of March, 1948.

During every succeeding period of three years the grants may be less by ten per cent. than those for the immediately preceding period of three years:

Provided that at the end of ten years from the commencement of this Constitution such grants, to the extent to which they are a special concession to the Anglo-Indian community, shall cease:

Provided further that no educational institution shall be entitled to receive any grant under this article unless at least forty per cent of the annual admissions therein are made available to members of communities other than the Anglo-Indian community.

338. *Special Officer for Scheduled Castes, Scheduled Tribes, etc.*—(1) There shall be a Special Officer for the Scheduled Castes and Scheduled Tribes to be appointed by the President.

(2) It shall be the duty of the Special Officer to investigate all matters relating to the safeguards provided for the Scheduled Castes and Scheduled Tribes under this Constitution and report to the President upon the working of those

[8] Subs. by s. 5, *ibid.*, for "twenty years".

[9] The words and letters "specified in Part A or Part B of the First Schedule" omitted by the Const. (7th Am.) Act, 1956, s. 29 and Sch., w.e.f. 1.11.1956.

safeguards at such intervals as the President may direct, and the President shall cause all such reports to be laid before each House of Parliament.

(3) In this article, references to the Scheduled Castes and Scheduled Tribes shall be construed as including references to such other backward classes as the President may, on receipt of the report of a Commission appointed under clause (1) of article 340, by order specify and also to the Anglo-Indian community.

339. *Control of the Union over the administration of Scheduled Areas and the welfare of Scheduled Tribes.*—(1) The President may at any time and shall, at the expiration of ten years from the commencement of this Constitution by order appoint a Commission to report on the administration of the Scheduled Areas and the welfare of the Scheduled Tribes in the States [10]* * *.

The order may define the composition, powers and procedure of the Commission and may contain such incidental or ancillary provisions as the President may consider necessary or desirable.

(2) The executive power of the Union shall extend to the giving of directions to [11][a State] as to the drawing up and execution of schemes specified in the direction to be essential for the welfare of the Scheduled Tribes in the State.

340. *Appointment of a Commission to investigate the conditions of backward classes.*—(1) The President may by order appoint a Commission consisting of such persons as he thinks fit to investigate the conditions of socially and educationally backward classes within the territory of India and the difficulties under which they labour and to make recommendations as to the steps that should be taken by the Union or any State to remove such difficulties and to improve their condition and as to the grants that should be made for the purpose by the Union or any State and the conditions subject to which such grants should be made, and the order appointing such Commission shall define the procedure to be followed by the Commission.

(2) A Commission so appointed shall investigate the matters referred to them and present to the President a report setting out the facts as found by them and making such recommendations as they think proper.

(3) The President shall cause a copy of the report so presented together with a memorandum explaining the action taken thereon to be laid before each House of Parliament.

341. *Scheduled Castes.*—(1) The President [12][may with respect to any State [13][or Union territory], and where it is a State [14]* * * after consultation with the Governor [15]* * * thereof,] by public notification[16], specify the castes, races or tribes or parts of or groups within castes, races or tribes which shall for the purposes of this Constitution be deemed to be Scheduled Castes in relation to that State [13][or Union territory, as the case may be].

(2) Parliament may by law include in or exclude from the list of Scheduled Castes specified in a notification issued under clause (1) any caste, race or tribe or part of or group within any caste, race or tribe, but save as aforesaid a notification issued under the said clause shall not be varied by any subsequent notification.

---

[10] The words and letters "specified in Part A and Part B of the First Schedule" omitted by the Const. (7th Am.) Act, 1956, s. 29 and Sch., w.e.f. 1.11.1956.

[11] Subs. by s. 29 and Sch., *ibid.*, for "any such State".

[12] Subs. by the Const. (1st Am.) Act, 1951, s. 10, for "may, after consultation with the Governor or Rajpramukh of a State," w.e.f. 18.6.1951.

[13] Ins. by the Const. (7th Am.) Act, 1956, s. 29 and Sch. w.e.f. 1.11.1956.

[14] The words and letters "specified in Part A or Part B of the First Schedule" omitted by s. 29 and Sch., *ibid.*

[15] The words "or Rajpramukh" omitted by s. 29 and Sch., *ibid.*

[16] See the Const. (Scheduled Castes) Order, 1950; the Const. (Scheduled Castes), (Union Territories) Order, 1951; the Const. (Jammu and Kashmir) Scheduled Castes Order, 1956; the Const. (Dadra and Nagar Haveli) Scheduled Castes Order, 1962; the Const. (Pondicherry) Scheduled Castes Order, 1964; the Const. (Goa, Daman and Diu) Scheduled Castes Order, 1968 and the Const. (Sikkim) Scheduled Castes Order, 1978.

342. *Scheduled Tribes.*—(1) The President [17][may with respect to any State [13][or Union territory], and where it is a State [18]* * * after consultation with the Governor [19]* * * thereof,] by public notification,[20] specify the tribes or tribal communities or parts of or groups within tribes or tribal communities which shall for the purposes of this Constitution be deemed to be Scheduled Tribes in relation to that State [21][or Union territory, as the case may be.]

(2) Parliament may by law include in or exclude from the list of Scheduled Tribes specified in a notification issued under clause (1) any tribe or tribal community or part of or group within any tribe or tribal community, but save as aforesaid a notification issued under the said clause shall not be varied by any subsequent notification.

PART XVII

OFFICIAL LANGUAGE

CHAPTER I.—LANGUAGE OF THE UNION

343. *Official language of the Union.*—(1) The official language of the Union shall be Hindi in Devanagari script.

The form of numerals to be used for the official purposes of the Union shall be the international form of Indian numerals.

(2) Notwithstanding anything in clause (1), for a period of fifteen years from the commencement of this Constitution, the English language shall continue to be used for all the official purposes of the Union for which it was being used immediately before such commencement:

Provided that the President may, during the said period, by order[22] authorise the use of the Hindi language in addition to the English language and of the Devanagari form of numerals in addition to the international form of Indian numerals for any of the official purposes of the Union.

(3) Notwithstanding anything in this article, Parliament may by law provide for the use, after the said period of fifteen years, of—

(*a*) the English language, or

(*b*) the Devanagari form of numerals,

for such purposes as may be specified in the law.[23]

344. *Commission and Committee of Parliament on official language.*—(1) The President shall, at the expiration of five years from the commencement of this Constitution and thereafter at the expiration of ten years from such commencement, by order constitute a Commission which shall consist of a Chairman and such other members representing the different languages specified in the Eighth Schedule as the President may appoint, and the order shall define the procedure to be followed by the Commission.

---

[17] Subs. by the Const. (1st Am.) Act, 1951, s. 11, for "may, after consultation with the Governor or Rajpramukh of a State," w.e.f. 18.6.1951.

[18] The words and letters "specified in Part A or Part B of the First Schedule" omitted by the Const. (7th Am.) Act, 1956, s. 29 and Sch. w.e.f. 1.11.1956.

[19] The words "or Rajpramukh" omitted by s. 29 and Sch., *ibid.*

[20] See the Const. (Scheduled Tribes) Order, 1950; the Const. (Scheduled Tribes) (Union Territories) Order, 1951; the Const. (Andaman and Nicobar Islands) Scheduled Tribes Order, 1959; the Const. (Dadra and Nagar Haveli) Scheduled Tribes Order, 1962; the Const. (Scheduled Tribes) (Uttar Pradesh) Order, 1967; the Const. (Goa, Daman and Diu) Scheduled Tribes Order, 1968; the Const. (Nagaland) Scheduled Tribes Order, 1970; and the Const. (Sikkim) Scheduled Tribes Order, 1978.

[21] Ins. by the Const. (7th Am.) Act, 1956, s. 29 and Sch. w.e.f. 1.11.1956.

[22] See C.O. 41.

[23] See the Official Languages Act, 1963.

(2) It shall be the duty of the Commission to make recommendations to the President as to—

(a) the progressive use of the Hindi language for the official purposes of the Union;

(b) restrictions on the use of the English language for all or any of the official purposes of the Union;

(c) the language to be used for all or any of the purposes mentioned in article 348;

(d) the form of numerals to be used for any one or more specified purposes of the Union;

(e) any other matter referred to the Commission by the President as regards the official language of the Union and the language for communication between the Union and a State or between one State and another and their use.

(3) In making their recommendations under clause (2), the Commission shall have due regard to the industrial, cultural and scientific advancement of India, and the just claims and the interests of persons belonging to the non-Hindi speaking areas in regard to the public services.

(4) There shall be constituted a Committee consisting of thirty members, of whom twenty shall be members of the House of the People and ten shall be members of the Council of States to be elected respectively by the members of the House of the People and the members of the Council of States in accordance with the system of proportional representation by means of the single transferable vote.

(5) It shall be the duty of the Committee to examine the recommendations of the Commission constituted under clause (1) and to report to the President their opinion thereon.

(6) Notwithstanding anything in article 343, the President may, after consideration of the report referred to in clause (5), issue directions in accordance with the whole or any part of that report.

CHAPTER II.—REGIONAL LANGUAGES

345. *Official language or languages of a State.*—Subject to the provisions of articles 346 and 347, the Legislature of a State may by law adopt any one or more of the languages in use in the State or Hindi as the language or languages to be used for all or any of the official purposes of that State:

Provided that, until the Legislature of the State otherwise provides by law, the English language shall continue to be used for those official purposes within the State for which it was being used immediately before the commencement of this Constitution.[24]

346. *Official language for communication between one State and another or between a State and the Union.*—The language for the time being authorised for use in the Union for official purposes shall be the official language for communication between one State and another State and between a State and the Union:

Provided that if two or more States agree that the Hindi language should be the official language for communication between such States, that language may be used for such communication.

347. *Special provision relating to language spoken by a section of the population of a State.*—On a demand being made in that behalf the President may, if he is satisfied that a substantial proportion of the population of a State desire the use of any language spoken by them to be recognised by that State, direct that such language shall also be officially recognised throughout that State or any part thereof for such purpose as he may specify.

---

[24] See the Acts passed by the various State Legislatures.

CHAPTER III.—LANGUAGE OF THE SUPREME COURT, HIGH COURTS, ETC.

348. *Language to be used in the Supreme Court and in the High Courts and for Acts, Bills, etc.*—(1) Notwithstanding anything in the foregoing provisions of this Part, until Parliament by law otherwise provides—

(*a*) all proceedings in the Supreme Court and in every High Court,

(*b*) the authoritative texts—

(*i*) of all Bills to be introduced or amendments thereto to be moved in either House of Parliament or in the House or either House of the Legislature of a State,

(*ii*) of all Acts passed by Parliament or the Legislature of a State and of all Ordinances promulgated by the President or the Governor [25]* * * of a State, and

(*iii*) of all orders, rules, regulations and bye-laws issued under this Constitution or under any law made by Parliament or the Legislature of a State,

shall be in the English language.

(2) Notwithstanding anything in sub-clause (*a*) of clause (1), the Governor [26]* * * of a State may, with the previous consent of the President, authorise the use of the Hindi language, or any other language used for any official purposes of the State, in proceedings in the High Court having its principal seat in that State:

Provided that nothing in this clause shall apply to any judgment, decree or order passed or made by such High Court.

(3) Notwithstanding anything in sub-clause (*b*) of clause (1), where the Legislature of a State has prescribed any language other than the English language for use in Bills introduced in, or Acts passed by, the Legislature of the State or in Ordinances promulgated by the Governor [26]* * * of the State or in any order, rule, regulation or bye-law referred to in paragraph (*iii*) of that sub-clause, a translation of the same in the English language published under the authority of the Governor [26]* * * of the State in the Official Gazette of that State shall be deemed to be the authoritative text thereof in the English language under this article.

[ss. 214, 227, G.I. Act]

349. *Special procedure for enactment of certain laws relating to language.*—During the period of fifteen years from the commencement of this Constitution, no Bill or amendment making provision for the language to be used for any of the purposes mentioned in clause (1) of article 348 shall be introduced or moved in either House of Parliament without the previous sanction of the President, and the President shall not give his sanction to the introduction of any such Bill or the moving of any such amendment except after he has taken into consideration the recommendations of the Commission constituted under clause (1) of article 344 and the report of the Committee constituted under clause (4) of that article.

CHAPTER IV.—SPECIAL DIRECTIVES

350. *Language to be used in representations for redress of grievances.*—Every person shall be entitled to submit a representation for the redress of any grievance to any officer or authority of the Union or a State in any of the languages used in the Union or in the State, as the case may be.

[27][**350A.** *Facilities for instruction in mother-tongue at primary stage.*—It shall be the endeavour of every State and of every local authority within the State to provide adequate facilities for instruction in the mother-tongue at the primary stage of education to children belonging to linguistic minority groups; and the President

---

[25] The words "or Rajpramukh" omitted by the Const. (7th Am.) Act, 1956, s. 29 and Sch., w.e.f. 1.11.1956.

[26] The words "or Rajpramukh" omitted by s. 29 and Sch., *ibid.*

[27] Ins. by s. 21, *ibid.*

may issue such directions to any State as he considers necessary or proper for securing the provision of such facilities.

350B. *Special Officer for linguistic minorities.*—(1) There shall be a Special Officer for linguistic minorities to be appointed by the President.

(2) It shall be the duty of the Special Officer to investigate all matters relating to the safeguards provided for linguistic minorities under this Constitution and report to the President upon those matters at such intervals as the President may direct, and the President shall cause all such reports to be laid before each House of Parliament, and sent to the Governments of the States concerned.]

351. *Directive for development of the Hindi language.*—It shall be the duty of the Union to promote the spread of the Hindi language, to develop it so that it may serve as a medium of expression for all the elements of the composite culture of India and to secure its enrichment by assimilating without interfering with its genius, the forms, style and expressions used in Hindustani and in the other languages of India specified in the Eighth Schedule, and by drawing, wherever necessary or desirable, for its vocabulary primarily on Sanskrit and secondarily on other languages.

PART XVIII

EMERGENCY PROVISIONS

352. *Proclamation of Emergency.*—(1) If the President is satisfied that a grave emergency exists whereby the security of India or of any part of the territory thereof is threatened, whether by war or external aggression or [28][armed rebellion], he may, by Proclamation, make a declaration to that effect [29][in respect of the whole of India or of such part of the territory thereof as may be specified in the Proclamation.]

[30][*Explanation.*—A Proclamation of Emergency declaring that the security of India or any part of the territory thereof is threatened by war or by external aggression or by armed rebellion may be made before the actual occurrence of war or of any such aggression or rebellion, if the President is satisfied that there is imminent danger thereof.]

[31][(2) A Proclamation issued under clause (1) may be varied or revoked by a subsequent Proclamation.

---

[28] Subs. by the Const. (44th Am.) Act, 1978, s. 37 for "internal disturbance" w.e.f. 20.6.1979.

[29] Ins. by the Const. (42nd Am.) Act, 1976, s. 48, w.e.f. 3.1.1977.

[30] Ins. by the Const. (44th Am.) Act, 1978, s. 37, w.e.f. 20.6.1979.

[31] Subs. by s. 37, *ibid.*, for cls. (2), (2A) and (3) w.e.f. 20.6.1979. The clauses as originally enacted read as follows:

"(2) A Proclamation issued under clause (1)—

(*a*) may be revoked by a subsequent proclamation;

(*b*) shall be laid before each House of Parliament;

(*c*) shall cease to operate at the expiration of two months unless before the expiration of that period it has been approved by resolutions of both Houses of Parliament;

Provided that if any such Proclamation is issued at a time when the House of the People has been dissolved or the dissolution of the House of the People takes place during the period of two months referred to in sub-clause (*c*), and if a resolution approving the Proclamation has been passed by the Council of States, but no resolution with respect to such Proclamation has been passed by the House of the People before the expiration of that period, the Proclamation shall cease to operate at the expiration of thirty days from the date on which the House of the People first sits after its reconstitution unless before the expiration of the said period of thirty days a resolution approving the Proclamation has been also passed by the House of the People.

[(2A) Where a Proclamation issued under clause (1) is varied by a subsequent Proclamation, the provisions of clause (2) shall, so far as may be, apply in relation to such subsequent Proclamation as they apply in relation to a

(3) The President shall not issue a Proclamation under clause (1) or a Proclamation varying such Proclamation unless the decision of the Union Cabinet (that is to say, the Council consisting of the Prime Minister and other Ministers of Cabinet rank appointed under article 75) that such a Proclamation may be issued has been communicated to him in writing.

(4) Every Proclamation issued under this article shall be laid before each House of Parliament and shall, except where it is a Proclamation revoking a previous Proclamation, cease to operate at the expiration of one month unless before the expiration of that period it has been approved by resolutions of both Houses of Parliament:

Provided that if any such Proclamation (not being a Proclamation revoking a previous Proclamation) is issued at a time when the House of the People has been dissolved, or the dissolution of the House of the People takes place during the period of one month referred to in this clause, and if a resolution approving the Proclamation has been passed by the Council of States, but no resolution with respect to such Proclamation has been passed by the House of the People before the expiration of that period, the Proclamation shall cease to operate at the expiration of thirty days from the date on which the House of the People first sits after its reconstitution, unless before the expiration of the said period of thirty days a resolution approving the Proclamation has been also passed by the House of the People.

(5) A Proclamation so approved shall, unless revoked, cease to operate on the expiration of a period of six months from the date of the passing of the second of the resolutions approving the Proclamation under clause (4):

Provided that if and so often as a resolution approving the continuance in force of such a Proclamation is passed by both Houses of Parliament the Proclamation shall, unless revoked, continue in force for a further period of six months from the date on which it would otherwise have ceased to operate under this clause:

Provided further that if the dissolution of the House of the People takes place during any such period of six months and a resolution approving the continuance in force of such Proclamation has been passed by the Council of States but no resolution with respect to the continuance in force of such Proclamation has been passed by the House of the People during the said period, the Proclamation shall cease to operate at the expiration of thirty days from the date on which the House of the People first sits after its reconstitution unless before the expiration of the said period of thirty days, a resolution approving the continuance in force of the Proclamation has been also passed by the House of the People.

(6) For the purposes of clauses (4) and (5), a resolution may be passed by either House of Parliament only by a majority of the total membership of that House and by a majority of not less than two-thirds of the members of that House present and voting.

(7) Notwithstanding anything contained in the foregoing clauses, the President shall revoke a Proclamation issued under clause (1) or a Proclamation varying such Proclamation if the House of the People passes a resolution disapproving, or, as the case may be, disapproving the continuance in force of, such Proclamation.

(8) Where a notice in writing signed by not less than one-tenth of the total number of members of the House of the People has been given, of their intention to move a resolution for disapproving, or, as the case may be, for disapproving the continuance in force of, a Proclamation issued under clause (1) or a Proclamation varying such Proclamation,—

Proclamation issued under clause (1).]

(3) A Proclamation of Emergency declaring that the security of India or of any part of the territory thereof is threatened by war or by external aggression or by internal disturbance may be made before the actual occurrence of war or of any such aggression or disturbance if the President is satisfied that there is imminent danger thereof."

Clause (2A) was inserted by the Const. (42nd Am.) Act, 1976, s. 48, w.e.f. 3.1.1977.

(*a*) to the Speaker, if the House is in session; or

(*b*) to the President, if the House is not in session,

a special sitting of the House shall be held within fourteen days from the date on which such notice is received by the Speaker, or, as the case may be, by the President, for the purpose of considering such resolution.]

[32][[33][(9) The power conferred on the President by this article shall include the power to issue different Proclamations on different grounds, being war or external aggression or [34][armed rebellion] or imminent danger of war or external aggression or [34][armed rebellion], whether or not there is a Proclamation already issued by the President under clause (1) and such Proclamation is in operation.

[35] * * * * *]

[ss. 12, 102, G.I. Act]

353. *Effect of Proclamation of Emergency.*—While a Proclamation of Emergency is in operation, then—

(*a*) notwithstanding anything in this Constitution, the executive power of the Union shall extend to the giving of directions to any State as to the manner in which the executive power thereof is to be exercised;

(*b*) the power of Parliament to make laws with respect to any matter shall include power to make laws conferring powers and imposing duties, or authorising the conferring of powers and the imposition of duties, upon the Union or officers and authorities of the Union as respects that matter, notwithstanding that it is one which is not enumerated in the Union List:

[36][Provided that where a Proclamation of Emergency is in operation only in any part of the territory of India,—

(*i*) the executive power of the Union to give directions under clause (*a*), and

(*ii*) the power of Parliament to make laws under clause (*b*),

shall also extend to any State other than a State in which or in any part of which the Proclamation of Emergency is in operation if and in so far as the security of India or any part of the territory thereof is threatened by activities in or in relation to the part of the territory of India in which the Proclamation of Emergency is in operation.]

[s. 102, G.I. Act]

354. *Application of provisions relating to distribution of revenues while a Proclamation of Emergency is in operation.*—(1) The President may, while a Proclamation of Emergency is in operation, by order direct that all or any of the provisions of articles 268 to 279 shall for such period, not extending in any case beyond the expiration of the financial year in which such Proclamation ceases to operate, as may be specified in the order, have effect subject to such exceptions or modifications as he thinks fit.

(2) Every order made under clause (1) shall, as soon as may be after it is made, be laid before each House of Parliament.

---

[32] Ins. by the Const. (38th Am.) Act, 1975, s. 5 (retrospectively) on 1.8.1975 w.e.f. 26.1.1950.

[33] Cl. (4) re-numbered as cl. (9) by the Const. (44th Am.) Act, 1978, s. 37, w.e.f. 20.6.1979.

[34] Subs. by s. 37, *ibid.*, for "internal disturbance" w.e.f. 20.6.1979.

[35] Cl. (5) omitted by s. 37, *ibid.*, w.e.f. 20.6.1979. The omitted clause inserted by the Const. (38th Am.) Act, 1975 (retrospectively) ran as follows:

"(5) Notwithstanding anything in this Constitution,— (*a*) the satisfaction of the President mentioned in clause (1) and clause (3) shall be final and conclusive and shall not be questioned in any court on any ground; (*b*) subject to the provisions of clause (2), neither the Supreme Court nor any other court shall have jurisdiction to entertain any question, on any ground, regarding the validity of—

(*i*) a declaration made by Proclamation by the President to the effect stated in clause (1); or

(*ii*) the continued operation of such Proclamation."

[36] Ins. by the Const. (42nd Am.) Act, 1976, s. 49 (w.e..f 3.1.1977).

355. *Duty of the Union to protect States against external aggression and internal disturbance.*—It shall be the duty of the Union to protect every State against external aggression and internal disturbance and to ensure that the government of every State is carried on in accordance with the provisions of this Constitution.

356. *Provisions in case of failure of constitutional machinery in States.*—(1) If the President, on receipt of a report from the Governor [37]* * * of a State or otherwise, is satisfied that a situation has arisen in which the government of the State cannot be carried on in accordance with the provisions of this Constitution, the President may by Proclamation—

(*a*) assume to himself all or any of the functions of the Government of the State and all or any of the powers vested in or exercisable by the Governor [38]* * * or any body or authority in the State other than the Legislature of the State;

(*b*) declare that the powers of the Legislature of the State shall be exercisable by or under the authority of Parliament;

(*c*) make such incidental and consequential provisions as appear to the President to be necessary or desirable for giving effect to the objects of the Proclamation, including provisions for suspending in whole or in part the operation of any provisions of this Constitution relating to any body or authority in the State:

Provided that nothing in this clause shall authorise the President to assume to himself any of the powers vested in or exercisable by a High Court, or to suspend in whole or in part the operation of any provision of this Constitution relating to High Courts.

(2) Any such Proclamation may be revoked or varied by a subsequent Proclamation.

(3) Every Proclamation under this article shall be laid before each House of Parliament and shall, except where it is a Proclamation revoking a previous Proclamation, cease to operate at the expiration of two months unless before the expiration of that period it has been approved by resolutions of both Houses of Parliament:

Provided that if any such Proclamation (not being a Proclamation revoking a previous Proclamation) is issued at a time when the House of the People is dissolved or the dissolution of the House of the People takes place during the period of two months referred to in this clause, and if a resolution approving the Proclamation has been passed by the Council of States, but no resolution with respect to such Proclamation has been passed by the House of the People before the expiration of that period, the Proclamation shall cease to operate at the expiration of thirty days from the date on which the House of the People first sits after its reconstitution unless before the expiration of the said period of thirty days a resolution approving the Proclamation has been also passed by the House of the People.

(4) A Proclamation so approved shall, unless revoked, cease to operate on the expiration of a period of [39][six months from the date of issue of the Proclamation]:

Provided that if and so often as a resolution approving the continuance in force of such a Proclamation is passed by both Houses of Parliament, the Proclamation shall, unless revoked, continue in force for a further period of [40][six months] from

---

[37] The words "or Rajpramukh" omitted by the Const. (7th Am.) Act, 1956, s. 29 and Sch., w.e.f. 1.11.1956.

[38] The words "or Rajpramukh, as the case may be" omitted by s. 29 and Sch., *ibid.*

[39] Subs. by the Const. (44th Am.) Act, 1978, s. 38, for "one year from the date of the passing of the second of the resolutions approving the Proclamation under clause (3)" (w.e.f. 20.6.1979). The words "one year" were subs. for the original words "six months" by the Const. (42nd Am.) Act, 1976, s. 50 (w.e.f. 3.1.1977).

[40] Subs. by the Const. (44th Am.) Act, 1978, s. 38, for "one year" w.e.f. 20.6.1979. The words "one year" were subs. for the original words "six months" by the Const. (42nd Am.) Act, 1976, s. 50, w.e.f. 3.1.1977.

the date on which under this clause it would otherwise have ceased to operate, but no such Proclamation shall in any case remain in force for more than three years:

Provided further that if the dissolution of the House of the People takes place during any such period of [40][six months] and a resolution approving the continuance in force of such Proclamation has been passed by the Council of States, but no resolution with respect to the continuance in force of such Proclamation has been passed by the House of the People during the said period, the Proclamation shall cease to operate at the expiration of thirty days from the date on which the House of the People first sits after its reconstitution unless before the expiration of the said period of thirty days a resolution approving the continuance in force of the Proclamation has been also passed by the House of the People.

[41][(5) Notwithstanding anything contained in clause (4), a resolution with respect to the continuance in force of a Proclamation approved under clause (3) for any period beyond the expiration of one year from the date of issue of such Proclamation shall not be passed by either House of Parliament unless—

(*a*) a Proclamation of Emergency is in operation, in the whole of India or, as the case may be, in the whole or any part of the State, at the time of the passing of such resolution, and

(*b*) the Election Commission certifies that the continuance in force of the Proclamation approved under clause (3) during the period specified in such resolution is necessary on account of difficulties in holding general elections to the Legislative Assembly of the State concerned.] [s. 93, G.I. Act]

357. *Exercise of legislative powers under Proclamation issued under article 356.*—(1) Where by a Proclamation issued under clause (1) of article 356, it has been declared that the powers of the Legislature of the State shall be exercisable by or under the authority of Parliament, it shall be competent—

(*a*) for Parliament to confer on the President the power of the Legislature of the State to make laws, and to authorise the President to delegate, subject to such conditions as he may think fit to impose, the power so conferred to any other authority to be specified by him in that behalf;

(*b*) for Parliament, or for the President or other authority in whom such power to make laws is vested under sub-clause (*a*), to make laws conferring powers and imposing duties, or authorising the conferring of powers and the imposition of duties, upon the Union or officers and authorities thereof;

(*c*) for the President to authorise when the House of the People is not in session expenditure from the Consolidated Fund of the State pending the sanction of such expenditure by Parliament.

[42][(2) Any law made in exercise of the power of the Legislature of the State by Parliament or the President or other authority referred to in sub-clause (*a*) of clause (1) which Parliament or the President or such other authority would not,

---

[41] Subs. by the Const. (44th Am.) Act, 1978, s. 38 for cl. (5) w.e.f. 20.6.1979. Clause (5) was ins. by the Const. (38th Am.) Act, 1975, s. 6, (retrospectively) which read as follows:

"(5) Notwithstanding anything in this Constitution, the satisfaction of the President mentioned in clause (1) shall be final and conclusive and shall not be questioned in any court on any ground."

[42] Subs. by the Const. (42nd Am.) Act, 1976, s. 51 for cl. (2) w.e.f. 3.1.1977. Cl. (2) as originally enacted was as follows:

"(2) Any law made in exercise of the power of the Legislature of the State by Parliament or the President or other authority referred to in sub-clause (*a*) of clause (1) which Parliament or the President or such other authority would not, but for the issue of a Proclamation under article 356, have been competent to make shall, to the extent of the incompetency, cease to have effect on the expiration of a period of one year after the Proclamation has ceased to operate except as respects things done or omitted to be done before the expiration of the said period, unless the provisions which shall so cease to have effect are sooner repealed or re-enacted with or without modification by Act of the appropriate Legislature."

but for the issue of a Proclamation under article 356, have been competent to make shall, after the Proclamation has ceased to operate, continue in force until altered or repealed or amended by a competent Legislature or other authority.]

[s. 93, G.I. Act]

358. *Suspension of provisions of article 19 during emergencies.*—[43][(1)] [44][While a Proclamation of Emergency declaring that the security of India or any part of the territory thereof is threatened by war or by external aggression is in operation], nothing in article 19 shall restrict the power of the State as defined in Part III to make any law or to take any executive action which the State would but for the provisions contained in that Part be competent to make or to take, but any law so made shall, to the extent of the incompetency, cease to have effect as soon as the Proclamation ceases to operate, except as respects things done or omitted to be done before the law so ceases to have effect:

[45][Provided that [46][where such Proclamation of Emergency] is in operation only in any part of the territory of India, any such law may be made, or any such executive action may be taken, under this article in relation to or in any State or Union territory in which or in any part of which the Proclamation of Emergency is not in operation, if and in so far as the security of India or any part of the territory thereof is threatened by activities in or in relation to the part of the territory of India in which the Proclamation of Emergency is in operation.]

[47][(2) Nothing in clause (1) shall apply—

(*a*) to any law which does not contain a recital to the effect that such law is in relation to the Proclamation of Emergency in operation when it is made; or

(*b*) to any executive action taken otherwise than under a law containing such a recital.]

359. *Suspension of the enforcement of the rights conferred by Part III during emergencies.*—(1) Where a Proclamation of Emergency is in operation, the President may by order declare that the right to move any court for the enforcement of such of [48][the rights conferred by Part III (except articles 20 and 21)] as may be mentioned in the order and all proceedings pending in any court for the enforcement of the rights so mentioned shall remain suspended for the period during which the Proclamation is in force or for such shorter period as may be specified in the order.

[49][(1A) While an order made under clause (1) mentioning any of [48][the rights conferred by Part III (except articles 20 and 21)] is in operation, nothing in that Part conferring those rights shall restrict the power of the State as defined in the said Part to make any law or to take any executive action which the State would but for the provisions contained in that Part be competent to make or to take, but any law so made shall, to the extent of the incompetency, cease to have effect as soon as the order aforesaid ceases to operate, except as respects things done or omitted to be done before the law so ceases to have effect.

[50][Provided that where a Proclamation of Emergency is in operation only in any part of the territory of India, any such law may be made, or any such executive action may be taken, under this article in relation to or in any State or Union territory in which or in any part of which the Proclamation of Emergency is not

---

[43] Art. 358 renumbered as cl. (1) thereof by the Const. (44th Am.) Act, 1978, s. 39, w.e.f. 20.6.1979.
[44] Subs. by s. 39, *ibid.*, for "While a Proclamation of Emergency is in operation" w.e.f. 20.6.1979.
[45] Ins. by the Const. (42nd Am.) Act, 1976, s. 52, w.e.f. 3.1.1977.
[46] Subs. by the Const. (44th Am.) Act, 1978, s. 39, for "where a Proclamation of Emergency" w.e.f. 20.6.1979.
[47] Ins. by the Const. (44th Am.) Act, 1978, s. 39 (w.e.f. 20.6.1979).
[48] Subs. by s. 40, *ibid.*, for "the rights conferred by Part III" (w.e.f. 20.6.1979).
[49] Ins. by the Const. (38th Am.) Act, 1975, s. 7 (retrospectively), on 1.8.1975 w.e.f. 26.1.1950.
[50] Ins. by the Const. (42nd Am.) Act, 1976, s. 53 (w.e.f. 3.1.1977).

in operation, if and in so far as the security of India or any part of the territory thereof is threatened by activities in or in relation to the part of the territory of India in which the Proclamation of Emergency is in operation.]

[51][(1B) Nothing in clause (1A) shall apply—

(*a*) to any law which does not contain a recital to the effect that such law is in relation to the Proclamation of Emergency in operation when it is made; or

(*b*) to any executive action taken otherwise than under a law containing such a recital.]

(2) As order made as aforesaid may extend to the whole or any part of the territory of India:

[50][Provided that where a Proclamation of Emergency is in operation only in a part of the territory of India, any such order shall not extend to any other part of the territory of India unless the President, being satisfied that the security of India or any part of the territory thereof is threatened by activities in or in relation to the part of the territory of India in which the Proclamation of Emergency is in operation, considers such extension to be necessary.]

(3) Every order made under clause (1) shall, as soon as may be after it is made, be laid before each House of Parliament.

360. *Provisions as to financial emergency.*—(1) If the President is satisfied that a situation has arisen whereby the financial stability or credit of India or of any part of the territory thereof is threatened, he may by a Proclamation make a declaration to that effect.

[52][(2) A Proclamation issued under clause (1)—

(*a*) may be revoked or varied by a subsequent Proclamation;

(*b*) shall be laid before each House of Parliament;

(*c*) shall cease to operate at the expiration of two months, unless before the expiration of that period it has been approved by resolutions of both Houses of Parliament:

Provided that if any such Proclamation is issued at a time when the House of the People has been dissolved or the dissolution of the House of the People takes place during the period of two months referred to in sub-clause (*c*), and if a resolution approving the Proclamation has been passed by the Council of States, but no resolution with respect to such Proclamation has been passed by the House of the People before the expiration of that period, the Proclamation shall cease to operate at the expiration of thirty days from the date on which the House of the People first sits after its reconstitution, unless before the expiration of the said period of thirty days a resolution approving the Proclamation has been also passed by the House of the People.]

(3) During the period any such Proclamation as is mentioned in clause (1) is in operation, the executive authority of the Union shall extend to the giving of directions to any State to observe such canons of financial propriety as may be specified in the directions, and to the giving of such other directions as the President may deem necessary and adequate for the purpose.

(4) Notwithstanding anything in this Constitution—

(*a*) any such direction may include—

(*i*) a provision requiring the reduction of salaries and allowances of all or any class of persons serving in connection with the affairs of a State;

(*ii*) a provision requiring all Money Bills or other Bills to which the provisions of article 207 apply to be reserved for the consideration of the President after they are passed by the Legislature of the State;

---

[51] Ins. by the Const. (44th Am.) Act, 1978, s. 40 (w.e.f. 20.6.1979).

[52] Subs. by the Const. (44th Am.) Act, 1978, s. 41, for cl. (2) w.e.f. 20.6.1979. Clause (2) as originally enacted read as follows:

"(2) The provisions of clause (2) of article 352 shall apply in relation to a Proclamation of Emergency issued under article 352."

(b) it shall be competent for the President during the period any Proclamation issued under this article is in operation to issue directions for the reduction of salaries and allowances of all or any class of persons serving in connection with the affairs of the Union including the Judges of the Supreme Court and the High Courts.

[53] * * * * *

PART XIX

MISCELLANEOUS

361. *Protection of President and Governors and Rajpramukhs.*—(1) The President, or the Governor or Rajpramukh of a State, shall not be answerable to any court for the exercise and performance of the powers and duties of his office or for any act done or purporting to be done by him in the exercise and performance of those powers and duties:

Provided that the conduct of the President may be brought under review by any court, tribunal or body appointed or designated by either House of Parliament for the investigation of a charge under article 61:

Provided further that nothing in this clause shall be construed as restricting the right of any person to bring appropriate proceedings against the Government of India or the Government of a State.

(2) No criminal proceedings whatsoever shall be instituted or continued against the President, or the Governor [54]* * * of a State, in any court during his term of office.

(3) No process for the arrest or imprisonment of the President, or the Governor [54]* * * of a State, shall issue from any court during his term of office.

(4) No civil proceedings in which relief is claimed against the President, or the Governor [54]* * * of a State, shall be instituted during his term of office in any court in respect of any act done or purporting to be done by him in his personal capacity, whether before or after he entered upon his office as President, or as Governor [55]* * * of such State, until the expiration of two months next after notice in writing has been delivered to the President or the Governor [56]* * *, as the case may be, or left at his office stating the nature of the proceedings, the cause of action therefor, the name, description and place of residence of the party by whom such proceedings are to be instituted and the relief which he claims. [s. 306, G.I. Act]

[57][**361A.** *Protection of publication of proceedings of Parliament and State Legislatures.*—(1) No person shall be liable to any proceedings, civil or criminal, in any court in respect of the publication in a newspaper of a substantially true report of any proceedings of either House of Parliament or the Legislative Assembly, or, as the case may be, either House of the Legislature, of a State, unless the publication is proved to have been made with malice:

---

[53] Cl. (5) was ins. by the Const. (38th Am.) Act, 1975, s. 8 (retrospectively) and omitted by the Const. (44th Am.) Act, 1978, s. 41, w.e.f. 20.6.1979. The omitted clause read as follows:

"(5) Notwithstanding anything in this Constitution,—

(a) the satisfaction of the President mentioned in clause (1) shall be final and conclusive and shall not be questioned in any court on any ground;

(b) subject to the provisions of clause (2), neither the Supreme Court nor any other court shall have jurisdiction to entertain any question, on any ground, regarding the validity of— (i) a declaration made by Proclamation by the President to the effect stated in clause (1); or (ii) the continued operation of such Proclamation."

[54] The words "or Rajpramukh" omitted by the Const. (7th Am.) Act, 1956, s. 29 and Sch., w.e.f. 1.11.1956.

[55] The words "or Rajpramukh" omitted by the Const. (7th Am.) Act, 1956, s. 29 and Sch., w.e.f. 1.11.1956.

[56] The words "or the Rajpramukh" omitted by s. 29 and Sch., *ibid.*

[57] Ins. by the Const. (44th Am.) Act, 1978, s. 42 (w.e.f. 20.6.1979).

Provided that nothing in this clause shall apply to the publication of any report of the Proceedings of a secret sitting of either House of Parliament or the Legislative Assembly, or, as the case may be, either House of the Legislature, of a State.

(2) Clause (1) shall apply in relation to reports or matters broadcast by means of wireless telegraphy as part of any programme or service provided by means of a broadcasting station as it applies in relation to reports or matters published in a newspaper.

Explanation.—In this article, "newspaper" includes a news agency report containing material for publication in a newspaper.]

362. [*Rights and privileges of Rules of Indian States.*] *Rep. by the Constitution (Twenty-sixth Amendment) Act,* 1971, *s.* 2.

363. *Bar to interference by courts in disputes arising out of certain treaties, agreements, etc.*—(1) Notwithstanding anything in this Constitution but subject to the provisions of article 143, neither the Supreme Court nor any other court shall have jurisdiction in any dispute arising out of any provision of a treaty, agreement, covenant, engagement, *sanad* or other similar instrument which was entered into or executed before the commencement of this Constitution by any Ruler of an Indian State and to which the Government of the Dominion of India or any of its predecessor Governments was a party and which has or has been continued in operation after such commencement, or in any dispute in respect of any right accruing under or any liability or obligation arising out of any of the provisions of this Constitution relating to any such treaty, agreement, covenant, engagement, *sanad* or other similar instrument.

(2) In this article—

(*a*) "Indian State" means any territory recognised before the commencement of this Constitution by His Majesty or the Government of the Dominion of India as being such a State; and

(*b*) "Ruler" includes the Prince, Chief or other person recognised before such commencement by His Majesty or the Government of the Dominion of India as the Ruler of any Indian State.

[58][**363A.** *Recognition granted to Rulers of Indian States to cease and privy purses to be abolished.*—Notwithstanding anything in this Constitution or in any law for the time being in force—

(*a*) the Prince, Chief or other person who, at any time before the commencement of the Constitution (Twenty-sixth Amendment) Act, 1971, was recognised by the President as the Ruler of an Indian State or any person who, at any time before such commencement, was recognised by the President as the successor of such Ruler shall, on and from such commencement, cease to be recognised as such Ruler or the successor of such Ruler;

(*b*) on and from the commencement of the Constitution (Twenty-sixth Amendment) Act, 1971, privy purse is abolished and all rights, liabilities and obligations in respect of privy purse are extinguished and accordingly the Ruler or, as the case may be, the successor of such Ruler, referred to in clause (*a*) or any other person shall not be paid any sum as privy purse.]

364. *Special provisions as to major ports and aerodromes.*—(1) Notwithstanding anything in this Constitution, the President may by public notification direct that as from such date as may be specified in the notification—

(*a*) any law made by Parliament or by the Legislature of a State shall not apply to any major port or aerodrome or shall apply thereto subject to such exceptions or modifications as may be specified in the notification, or

(*b*) any existing law shall cease to have effect in any major port or aerodrome except as respects things done or omitted to be done before the said date, or shall in its application to such port or aerodrome have effect subject to such exceptions or modifications as may be specified in the notification.

---

[58] Ins. by the Const. (26th Am.) Act, 1971, s. 3, w.e.f. 28.12.1971.

(2) In this article—

(*a*) "major port" means a port declared to be a major port by or under any law made by Parliament or any existing law and includes all areas for the time being included within the limits of such port;[59]

(*b*) "aerodrome" means aerodrome as defined for the purposes of the enactments relating to airways, aircraft and air navigation.[60]

365. *Effect of failure to comply with, or to give effect to, directions given by the Union.*—Where any State has failed to comply with, or to give effect to, any directions given in the exercise of the executive power of the Union under any of the provisions of this Constitution, it shall be lawful for the President to hold that a situation has arisen in which the government of the State cannot be carried on in accordance with the provisions of this Constitution.

366. *Definitions.*—In this Constitution, unless the context otherwise requires, the following expressions have the meanings hereby respectively assigned to them, that is to say—

(1) "agricultural income" means agricultural income as defined for the purposes of the enactments relating to Indian income-tax.[61]

[s. 311(2), G.I. Act]

(2) "an Anglo-Indian" means a person whose father or any of whose other male progenitors in the male line is or was of European descent but who is domiciled within the territory of India and is or was born within such territory of parents habitually resident therein and not established there for temporary purposes only;

(3) "article" means an article of this Constitution;

(4) "borrow" includes the raising of money by the grant of annuities, and "loan" shall be construed accordingly; [s. 311(2), G.I. Act]

[62] * * * * *

(5) "clause" means a clause of the article in which the expression occurs;

(6) "corporation tax" means any tax on income, so far as that tax is payable by companies and is a tax in the case of which the following conditions are fulfilled:—

(*a*) that it is not chargeable in respect of agricultural income;

(*b*) that no deduction in respect of the tax paid by companies is, by any enactments which may apply to the tax, authorised to be made from dividends payable by the companies to individuals;

(*c*) that no provision exists for taking the tax so paid into account in computing for the purposes of Indian income-tax the total income of individuals receiving such dividends, or in computing the Indian income-tax payable by, or refundable to, such individuals;

[s. 311(2), G.I. Act]

(7) "corresponding Province", "corresponding Indian State" or "corresponding State" means in cases of doubt such Province, Indian State or State as may be determined by the President to be the corresponding Province, the corresponding Indian State or the corresponding State, as the case may be, for the particular purpose in question;

[s. 311(2), G.I. Act]

(8) "debt" includes any liability in respect of any obligation to repay capital sums by way of annuities and any liability under any guarantee,

---

[59] See the Indian Ports Act, 1908 and the Major Port Trusts Act, 1963.

[60] See the Indian Aircraft Act, 1934.

[61] See the Income-tax Act, 1961.

[62] Cl. (4A) was ins. by the Const. (42nd Am.) Act, 1976, s. 54 w.e.f. 1.2.1977 and omitted by the Const. (43rd Am.) Act, 1977, s. 11 w.e.f. 3.4.1978. The omitted clause was as follows:

"(4A) 'Central law' means any law other than a State law but does not include any amendment of this Constitution made under article 368;".

and "debt charges" shall be construed accordingly;
[s. 311(2), G.I. Act]

(9) "estate duty" means a duty to be assessed on or by reference to the principal value, ascertained in accordance with such rules as may be prescribed by or under laws made by Parliament or the Legislature of a State relating to the duty, of all property passing upon death or deemed, under the provisions of the said laws, so to pass;[63]

(10) "existing law" means any law, Ordinance, order, bye-law, rule or regulation passed or made before the commencement of this Constitution by any Legislature, authority or person having power to make such a law, Ordinance, order, bye-law, rule or regulation; [s. 311(2), G.I. Act]

(11) "Federal Court" means the Federal Court constituted under the Government of India Act, 1935;

(12) "goods" includes all materials, commodities, and articles;
[s. 311(2), G.I. Act]

(13) "guarantee" includes any obligation undertaken before the commencement of this Constitution to make payments in the event of the profits of an undertaking falling short of a specified amount;
[s. 311(2), G.I. Act]

(14) "High Court" means any Court which is deemed for the purposes of this Constitution to be a High Court for any State and includes—

(*a*) any Court in the territory of India constituted or reconstituted under this Constitution as a High Court, and

(*b*) any other Court in the territory of India which may be declared by Parliament by law to be a High Court for all or any of the purposes of this Constitution; [s. 311(2), G.I. Act]

(15) "Indian State" means any territory which the Government of the Dominion of India recognised as such a State; [s. 311(2), G.I. Act]

(16) "Part" means a Part of this Constitution;

(17) "pension" means a pension, whether contributory or not, of any kind whatsoever payable to or in respect of any person, and includes retired pay so payable, a gratuity so payable and any sum or sums so payable by way of the return, with or without interest thereon or any other addition thereto, of subscriptions to a provident fund;
[s. 311(2), G.I. Act]

(18) "Proclamation of Emergency" means a Proclamation issued under clause (1) of article 352;

(19) "public notification" means a notification in the Gazette of India, or, as the case may be, the Official Gazette of a State; [s. 311(2), G.I. Act]

(20) "railway" does not include—

(*a*) a tramway wholly within a municipal area, or

(*b*) any other line of communication wholly situate in one State and declared by Parliament by law not to be a railway;
[s. 311(2), G.I. Act]

[64] * * * * *

---

[63] See the Estate Duty Act, 1953.

[64] Cl. (21) omitted by the Const. (7th Am.) Act, 1956, s. 29 and Sch. w.e.f. 1.11.1956. As originally enacted, the clause read:

"(21) 'Rajpramukh' means—

(*a*) in relation to the State of Hyderabad, the person who for the time being is recognised by the President as the Nizam of Hyderabad;

(*b*) in relation to the State of Jammu and Kashmir or the State of Mysore, the person who for the time being is recognised by the President as the Maharaja of that State; and

(*c*) in relation to any other State specified in Part B of the First Schedule, the person who for the time being is recognised by the President as the Rajpramukh of that State,

[65][(22) "Ruler" means the Prince, Chief or other person who, at any time before the commencement of the Constitution (Twenty-sixth Amendment) Act, 1971, was recognised by the President as the Ruler of an Indian State or any person who, at any time before such commencement, was recognised by the President as the successor of such Ruler;]

(23) "Schedule" means a Schedule to this Constitution;

(24) "Scheduled Castes" means such castes, races or tribes or parts of or groups within such castes, races or tribes as are deemed under article 341 to be Scheduled Castes for the purposes of this Constitution;

(25) "Scheduled Tribes" means such tribes or tribal communities or parts of or groups within such tribes or tribal communities as are deemed under article 342 to be Scheduled Tribes for the purposes of this Constitution;

(26) "securities" includes stock; [s. 311(2), G.I. Act]

[66] * * * * *

(27) "sub-clause" means a sub-clause of the clause in which the expression occurs;

(28) "taxation" includes the imposition of any tax or impost, whether general or local or special, and "tax" shall be construed accordingly; [s. 311(2), G.I. Act]

(29) "tax on income" includes a tax in the nature of an excess profits tax; [s. 311(2), G.I. Act]

[67][(30) "Union territory" means any Union territory specified in the First Schedule and includes any other territory comprised within the territory of India but not specified in that Schedule.]

---

and includes in relation to any of the said States any person for the time being recognised by the President as competent to exercise the powers of the Rajpramukh in relation to that State."

[65] Subs. by the Const. (26th Am.) Act, 1971, s. 4, for cl. (22) w.e.f. 28.12.1971. As originally enacted, the clause read as follows:

"(22) 'Ruler' in relation to an Indian State means the Prince, Chief or other person by whom any such covenant or agreement as is referred to in clause (1) of article 291 was entered into and who for the time being is recognised by the President as the successor of such Ruler." [*Cf.* s. 311(1), G.I. Act]

[66] Cl. (26A) was ins. by the Const. (42nd Am.) Act, 1976, s. 54 w.e.f. 1.2.1977 and omitted by the Const. (43rd Am.) Act, 1977, s. 11 w.e.f. 13.4.1978. The omitted clause ran as follows:

"(26A) 'State Law' means—

(*a*) a State Act or an Act of the Legislature of a Union territory;

(*b*) an Ordinance promulgated by the Governor of a State under article 213 or by the administrator of a Union territory under article 239B;

(*c*) any provision with respect to a matter in the State List in a Central Act made before the commencement of this Constitution;

(*d*) any provision with respect to a matter in the State List or the Concurrent List in a Provincial Act;

(*e*) any notification, order, scheme, rule, regulation or bye-law or any other instrument having the force of law made under any Act, Ordinance or provisions referred to in sub-clause (*a*), sub-clause (*b*), sub-clause (*c*) or sub-clause (*d*);

(*f*) any notification, order, scheme, rule, regulation or bye-law or any other instrument having the force of law, not falling under sub-clause (*e*), and made by a State Government or the administrator of a Union territory or an officer or authority subordinate to such Government or administrator; and

(*g*) any other law (including any usage or custom having the force of law) with respect to a matter in the State List."

[67] Subs. by the Const. (7th Am.) Act, 1956, s. 29 and Sch. w.e.f. 1.11.1956, for cl. (30), which read as follows:

"(30) 'Uparajpramukh' in relation to any State specified in Part B of the First Schedule means the person who for the time being is recognised by the President as the Uparajpramukh of that State."

367. *Interpretation.*—(1) Unless the context otherwise requires, the General Clauses Act, 1897, shall, subject to any adaptations and modifications that may be made therein under article 372, apply for the interpretation of this Constitution as it applies for the interpretation of an Act of the Legislature of the Dominion of India.

(2) Any reference in this Constitution to Acts or laws of, or made by, Parliament, or to Acts or laws of, or made by, the Legislature of a State [68]* * *, shall be construed as including a reference to an Ordinance made by the President or, to an Ordinance made by a Governor [69]* * *, as the case may be.

(3) For the purposes of this Constitution "foreign State" means any State other than India:

Provided that, subject to the provisions of any law made by Parliament, the President may by order[70] declare any State not to be a foreign State for such purposes as may be specified in the order.

PART XX

AMENDMENT OF THE CONSTITUTION

368. [71][*Power of Parliament to amend the Constitution and procedure therefor.*]—[72][(1) Notwithstanding anything in this Constitution, Parliament may in exercise of its constituent power amend by way of addition, variation or repeal any provision of this Constitution in accordance with the procedure laid down in this article.]

[73][(2)] An amendment of this Constitution may be initiated only by the introduction of a Bill for the purpose in either House of Parliament, and when the Bill is passed in each House by a majority of the total membership of that House and by a majority of not less than two-thirds of the members of that House present and voting, [74][it shall be presented to the President who shall give his assent to the Bill and thereupon] the Constitution shall stand amended in accordance with the terms of the Bill:

Provided that if such amendment seeks to make any change in—

(*a*) article 54, article 55, article 73, article 162 or article 241, or

(*b*) Chapter IV of Part V, Chapter V of Part VI, or Chapter I of Part XI, or

(*c*) any of the Lists in the Seventh Schedule, or

(*d*) the representation of States in Parliament, or

(*e*) the provisions of this article,

the amendment shall also require to be ratified by the Legislatures of not less than one-half of the States [75]* * * by resolutions to that effect passed by those Legislatures before the Bill making provision for such amendment is presented to the President for assent.

[76][(3) Nothing in article 13 shall apply to any amendment made under this article.]

[77][(4) No amendment of this Constitution (including the provisions of Part III) made or purporting to have been made under this article [whether before or after

---

[68] The words and letters "specified in Part A or Part B of the First Schedule" omitted by s. 29 and Sch., *ibid.*

[69] The words "or Rajpramukh" omitted by s. 29 and Sch., *ibid.*

[70] See the Constitution (Declaration as to Foreign States) Order, 1950 (C.O. 2), dated 23rd January, 1950.

[71] Subs. by the Const. (24th Am.) Act, 1971, s. 3, for "*Procedure for amendment of the Constitution*", w.e.f. 5.11.1971.

[72] Ins. by s. 3, *ibid.*

[73] Art. 368 renumbered as cl. (2) by s. 3, *ibid.*

[74] Subs. by s. 3, *ibid.*, for "it shall be presented to the President for his assent and upon such assent being given to the Bill".

[75] The words and letters "specified in Parts A and B of the First Schedule" omitted by the Const. (7th Am.) Act, 1956, s. 29 and Sch. w.e.f. 1.11.1956.

[76] Ins. by the Const. (24th Am.) Act, 1971, s. 3, w.e.f. 5.11.1971.

[77] Ins. by the Const. (42nd Am.) Act, 1976, s. 55, w.e.f. 3.1.1977.

the commencement of section 55 of the Constitution (Forty-second Amendment) Act, 1976] shall be called in question in any court on any ground.

(5) For the removal of doubts, it is hereby declared that there shall be no limitation whatever on the constituent power of Parliament to amend by way of addition, variation or repeal the provisions of this Constitution under this article.]

PART XXI

[78][TEMPORARY, TRANSITIONAL AND SPECIAL PROVISIONS]

369. *Temporary power to Parliament to make laws with respect to certain matters in the State List as if they were matters in the Concurrent List.*—Notwithstanding anything in this Constitution, Parliament shall, during a period of five years from the commencement of this Constitution, have power to make laws with respect to the following matters as if they were enumerated in the Concurrent List, namely—

(*a*) trade and commerce within a State in, and the production, supply and distribution of, cotton and woollen textiles, raw cotton (including ginned cotton and unginned cotton or *kapas*), cotton seed, paper (including newsprint), foodstuffs (including edible oilseeds and oil), cattle fodder (including oil-cakes and other concentrates), coal (including coke and derivatives of coal), iron, steel and mica;

(*b*) offences against laws with respect to any of the matters mentioned in clause (*a*), jurisdiction and powers of all courts except the Supreme Court with respect to any of those matters, and fees in respect of any of those matters but not including fees taken in any court;

but any law made by Parliament, which Parliament would not but for the provisions of this article have been competent to make, shall, to the extent of the incompetency, cease to have effect on the expiration of the said period, except as respects things done or omitted to be done before the expiration thereof.

[79]**370.** *Temporary provisions with respect to the State of Jammu and Kashmir.*—(1) Notwithstanding anything in this Constitution,—

(*a*) the provisions of article 238 shall not apply in relation to the State of Jammu and Kashmir;

(*b*) the power of Parliament to make laws for the said State shall be limited to—

(*i*) those matters in the Union List and the Concurrent List which, in consultation with the Government of the State, are declared by the President to correspond to matters specified in the Instrument of Accession governing the accession of the State to the Dominion of India as the matters with respect to which the Dominion Legislature may make laws for that State; and

(*ii*) such other matters in the said Lists as, with the concurrence of the Government of the State, the President may by order specify.

Explanation.—For the purposes of this article, the Government of the State means the person for the time being recognised by the President as the Maharaja

---

[78] Subs. by the Const. (13th Am.) Act, 1962, s. 2, for "TEMPORARY AND TRANSITIONAL PROVISIONS", w.e.f. 1.12.1963.

[79] In exercise of the powers conferred by this article the President, on the recommendation of the Constituent Assembly of the State of Jammu and Kashmir, declared that, as from the 17th day of November, 1952, the said art. 370 shall be operative with the modification that for the *Explanation* in cl. (1) thereof, the following *Explanation* is substituted, namely:—

"*Explanation.*—For the purposes of this article, the Government of the State means the person for the time being recognised by the President on the recommendation of the Legislative Assembly of the State as the *Sadar-i-Riyasat of Jammu and Kashmir, acting on the advice of the Council of Ministers of the State for the time being in office."

(Ministry of Law Order No. C.O. 44, dated the 15th November, 1952)

* Now "Governor".

of Jammu and Kashmir acting on the advice of the Council of Ministers for the time being in office under the Maharaja's Proclamation dated the fifth day of March, 1948;

(*c*) the provisions of article 1 and of this article shall apply in relation to that State;

(*d*) such of the other provisions of this Constitution shall apply in relation to that State subject to such exceptions and modifications as the President may by order[80] specify:

Provided that no such order which relates to the matters specified in the Instrument of Accession of the State referred to in paragraph (*i*) of sub-clause (*b*) shall be issued except in consultation with the Government of the State:

Provided further that no such order which relates to matters other than those referred to in the last preceding proviso shall be issued except with the concurrence of that Government.

(2) If the concurrence of the Government of the State referred to in paragraph (*ii*) of sub-clause (*b*) of clause (1) or in the second proviso to sub-clause (*d*) of that clause be given before the Constituent Assembly for the purpose of framing the Constitution of the State is convened, it shall be placed before such Assembly for such decision as it may take thereon.

(3) Notwithstanding anything in the foregoing provisions of this article, the President may, by public notification, declare that this article shall cease to be operative or shall be operative only with such exceptions and modifications and from such date as he may specify:

Provided that the recommendation of the Constituent Assembly of the State referred to in clause (2) shall be necessary before the President issues such a notification.

[81][**371.** *Special provision with respect to the States of* [83]* * * *Maharashtra and Gujarat.*—

[82]* * * * *

(2) Notwithstanding anything in this Constitution, the President may by order made with respect to [84][the State of Maharashtra or Gujarat], provide for any special responsibility of the Governor for—

---

[80] *See* the Const. (Application to Jammu and Kashmir) Order, 1954 (C.O. 48), as amended from time to time.

[81] Subs. by the Const. (7th Am.) Act, 1956, s. 22, for Art. 371, w.e.f. 1.11.1956, for the original article which read as follows:

"371. Notwithstanding anything in this Constitution, during a period of ten years from the commencement thereof, or during such longer or shorter period as Parliament may by law provide in respect of any State, the Government of every State specified in Part B of the First Schedule shall be under the general control of, and comply with such particular directions, if any, as may from time to time be given by, the President:

Provided that the President may by order direct that the provisions of this article shall not apply to any State specified in the order."

[82] Cl. (1) omitted by the Const. (32nd Am.) Act, 1973, s. 2, w.e.f. 1.7.1974. The omitted clause ran as follows:

"(1) Notwithstanding anything in this Constitution, the President may, by order made with respect to the State of Andhra Pradesh * * *, provide for the constitution and functions of regional committees of the Legislative Assembly of the State, for the modifications to be made in the rules of business of the Government and in the rules of procedure of the Legislative Assembly of the State and for any special responsibility of the Governor in order to secure the proper functioning of the regional committees."

(* * * The words "or Punjab" omitted by the Punjab Reorganisation Act, 1966, w.e.f. 1.11.1966.)

[83] The words "Andhra Pradesh" omitted by s. 2, *ibid.* w.e.f. 1.7.1974.

[84] Subs. by the Bombay Reorganisation Act, 1960, s. 85, for "the State of Bombay" w.e.f. 1.5.1960.

(a) the establishment of separate development boards for Vidarbha, Marathwada, [85][and the rest of Maharashtra or, as the case may be,] Saurashtra, Kutch and the rest of Gujarat with the provision that a report on the working of each of these boards will be placed each year before the State Legislative Assembly;

(b) the equitable allocation of funds for developmental expenditure over the said areas, subject to the requirements of the State as a whole; and

(c) an equitable arrangement providing adequate facilities for technical education and vocational training, and adequate opportunities for employment in services under the control of the State Government, in respect of all the said areas, subject to the requirements of the State as a whole.]

[86][**371A.** *Special provision with respect to the State of Nagaland.*—(1) Notwithstanding anything in this Constitution,—

(a) no Act of Parliament in respect of—

(i) religious or social practices of the Nagas,

(ii) Naga customary law and procedure,

(iii) administration of civil and criminal justice involving decisions according to Naga customary law,

(iv) ownership and transfer of land and its resources,

shall apply to the State of Nagaland unless the Legislative Assembly of Nagaland by a resolution so decides;

(b) the Governor of Nagaland shall have special responsibility with respect to law and order in the State of Nagaland for so long as in his opinion internal disturbances occurring in the Naga Hills-Tuensang Area immediately before the formation of that State continue therein or in any part thereof and in the discharge of his functions in relation thereto the Governor shall, after consulting the Council of Ministers, exercise his individual judgment as to the action to be taken:

Provided that if any question arises whether any matter is or is not a matter as respects which the Governor is under this sub-clause required to act in the exercise of his individual judgment the decision of the Governor in his discretion shall be final, and the validity of anything done by the Governor shall not be called in question on the ground that he ought or ought not to have acted in the exercise of his individual judgment:

Provided further that if the President on receipt of a report from the Governor or otherwise is satisfied that it is no longer necessary for the Governor to have special responsibility with respect to law and order in the State of Nagaland, he may by order direct that the Governor shall cease to have such responsibility with effect from such date as may be specified in the order;

(c) in making his recommendation with respect to any demand for a grant, the Governor of Nagaland shall ensure that any money provided by the Government of India out of the Consolidated Fund of India for any specific service or purpose is included in the demand for a grant relating to that service or purpose and not in any other demand;

(d) as from such date as the Governor of Nagaland may by public notification in this behalf specify, there shall be established a regional council for the Tuensang district consisting of thirty-five members and the Governor shall in his discretion make rules providing for—

(i) the composition of the regional council and the manner in which the members of the regional council shall be chosen:

Provided that the Deputy Commissioner of the Tuensang district shall be the Chairman *ex-officio* of the regional council and the Vice-Chairman of the regional council shall be elected by the members thereof from amongst themselves;

---

[85] Subs. by s. 85, *ibid.*, for "rest of Maharashtra", w.e.f. 1.5.1960.
[86] Ins. by the Const. (13th Am.) Act, 1962, s. 2, w.e.f. 1.12.1963.

(*ii*) the qualifications for being chosen as, and for being, members of the regional council;

(*iii*) the term of office of, and the salaries and allowances, if any, to be paid to members of, the regional council;

(*iv*) the procedure and conduct of business of the regional council;

(*v*) the appointment of officers and staff of the regional council and their conditions of services; and

(*vi*) any other matter in respect of which it is necessary to make rules for the constitution and proper functioning of the regional council.

(2) Notwithstanding anything in this Constitution, for a period of ten years from the date of the formation of the State of Nagaland or for such further period as the Governor may, on the recommendation of the regional council, by public notification specify in this behalf,—

(*a*) the administration of the Tuensang district shall be carried on by the Governor;

(*b*) where any money is provided by the Government of India to the Government of Nagaland to meet the requirements of the State of Nagaland as a whole, the Governor shall in his discretion arrange for an equitable allocation of that money between the Tuensang district and the rest of the State;

(*c*) no Act of the Legislature of Nagaland shall apply to the Tuensang district unless the Governor, on the recommendation of the regional council, by public notification so directs and the Governor in giving such direction with respect to any such Act may direct that the Act shall in its application to the Tuensang district or any part thereof have effect subject to such exceptions or modifications as the Governor may specify on the recommendation of the regional council:

Provided that any direction given under this sub-clause may be given so as to have retrospective effect;

(*d*) the Governor may make regulations for the peace, progress and good government of the Tuensang district and any regulations so made may repeal or amend with retrospective effect, if necessary, any Act of Parliament or any other law which is for the time being applicable to that district;

(*e*) (*i*) one of the members representing the Tuensang district in the Legislative Assembly of Nagaland shall be appointed Minister for Tuensang affairs by the Governor on the advice of the Chief Minister and the Chief Minister in tendering his advice shall act on the recommendation of the majority of the members as aforesaid[87];

(*ii*) the Minister for Tuensang affairs shall deal with, and have direct access to the Governor on, all matters relating to the Tuensang district but he shall keep the Chief Minister informed about the same;

(*f*) notwithstanding anything in the foregoing provisions of this clause, the final decision on all matters relating to the Tuensang district shall be made by the Governor in his discretion;

(*g*) in articles 54 and 55 and clause (4) of article 80, references to the elected members of the Legislative Assembly of a State or to each such member shall include references to the members or member of the Legislative Assembly of Nagaland elected by the regional council established under this article;

---

[87] Paragraph 2 of the Constitution (Removal of Difficulties) Order, No. X provides (w.e.f. 1.12.1963) that article 371A of the Constitution of India shall have effect as if the following proviso were added to paragraph (*i*) of sub-clause (*e*) of clause (2) thereof, namely:—

"Provided that the Governor may, on the advice of the Chief Minister, appoint any person as Minister for Tuensang affairs to act as such until such time as persons are chosen in accordance with law to fill the seats allocated to the Tuensang district in the Legislative Assembly of Nagaland."

(*h*) in article 170—

(*i*) clause (1) shall, in relation to the Legislative Assembly of Nagaland, have effect as if for the word "sixty", the words "forty-six" had been substituted;

(*ii*) in the said clause, the reference to direct election from territorial constituencies in the State shall include election by the members of the regional council established under this article;

(*iii*) in clauses (2) and (3), references to territorial constituencies shall mean references to territorial constituencies in the Kohima and Mokokchung districts.

(3) If any difficulty arises in giving effect to any of the foregoing provisions of this article, the President may by order do anything (including any adaptation or modification of any other article) which appears to him to be necessary for the purpose of removing that difficulty:

Provided that no such order shall be made after the expiration of three years from the date of the formation of the State of Nagaland.

Explanation.—In this article, the Kohima, Mokokchung and Tuensang districts shall have the same meanings as in the State of Nagaland Act, 1962.]

[88][**371B.** *Special provision with respect to the State of Assam.*—Notwithstanding anything in this Constitution, the President may, by order made with respect to the State of Assam, provide for the constitution and functions of a committee of the Legislative Assembly of the State consisting of members of that Assembly elected from the tribal areas specified in [89][Part I] of the table appended to paragraph 20 of the Sixth Schedule and such number of other members of that Assembly as may be specified in the order and for the modifications to be made in the rules of procedure of that Assembly for the constitution and proper functioning of such committee.]

[90][**371C.** *Special provision with respect to the State of Manipur.*—(1) Notwithstanding anything in this Constitution, the President may, by order made with respect to the State of Manipur, provide for the constitution and functions of a committee of the Legislative Assembly of the State consisting of members of that Assembly elected from the Hill Areas of that State, for the modifications to be made in the rules of business of the Government and in the rules of procedure of the Legislative Assembly of the State and for any special responsibility of the Governor in order to secure the proper functioning of such committee.

(2) The Governor shall annually, or whenever so required by the President, make a report to the President regarding the administration of the Hill Areas in the State of Manipur and the executive power of the Union shall extend to the giving of directions to the State as to the administration of the said areas.

Explanation.—In this article, the expression "Hill Areas" means such areas as the President may, by order, declare to be Hill Areas.]

[91][**371D.** *Special provisions with respect to the State of Andhra Pradesh.*—(1) The President may by order made with respect to the State of Andhra Pradesh provide, having regard to the requirements of the State as a whole, for equitable opportunities and facilities for the people belonging to different parts of the State, in the matter of public employment and in the matter of education, and different provisions may be made for various parts of the State.

(2) An order made under clause (1) may, in particular,—

(*a*) require the State Government to organise any class or classes of posts in a civil service of, or any class or classes or civil posts under, the State into different local cadres for different parts of the State and allot in

---

[88] Ins. by the Const. (22nd Am.) Act, 1969, s. 4, w.e.f. 25.9.1969.

[89] Subs. by the North-Eastern Areas (Reorganisation) Act, 1971, s. 71, for "Part A" w.e.f. 21.1.1972.

[90] Ins. by the Const. (27th Am.) Act, 1971, s. 5, w.e.f. 15.2.1972.

[91] Ins. by the Const. (32nd Am.) Act, 1973, s. 3 (w.e.f. 1.7.1974).

accordance with such principles and procedure as may be specified in the order the persons holding such posts to the local cadres so organised;

(*b*) specify any part or parts of the State which shall be regarded as the local area—

(*i*) for direct recruitment to posts in any local cadre (whether organised in pursuance of an order under this article or constituted otherwise) under the State Government;

(*ii*) for direct recruitment to posts in any cadre under any local authority within the State; and

(*iii*) for the purposes of admission to any University within the State or to any other educational institution which is subject to the control of the State Government;

(*c*) specify the extent to which, the manner in which and the conditions subject to which, preference or reservation shall be given or made—

(*i*) in the matter of direct recruitment to posts in any such cadre referred to in sub-clause (*b*) as may be specified in this behalf in the order;

(*ii*) in the matter of admission to any such University or other educational institution referred to in sub-clause (*b*) as may be specified in this behalf in the order,

to or in favour of candidates who have resided or studied for any period specified in the order in the local area in respect of such cadre, University or other educational institution, as the case may be.

(3) The President may, by order, provide for the constitution of an Administrative Tribunal for the State of Andhra Pradesh to exercise such jurisdiction, powers and authority [including and jurisdiction, power and authority which immediately before the commencement of the Constitution (Thirty-second Amendment) Act, 1973, was exercisable by any court (other than the Supreme Court) or by any tribunal or other authority] as may be specified in the order with respect to the following matters, namely:—

(*a*) appointment, allotment or promotion to such class or classes of posts in any civil service of the State, or to such class or classes of civil posts under the State, or to such class or classes of posts under the control of any local authority within the State, as may be specified in the order;

(*b*) seniority of persons appointed, allotted or promoted to such class or classes of posts in any civil service of the State, or to such class or classes of civil posts under the State, or to such class or classes of posts under the control of any local authority within the State, as may be specified in the order;

(*c*) such other conditions of service of persons appointed, allotted or promoted to such class or classes of posts in any civil service of the State or to such class or classes of civil posts under the State or to such class or classes of posts under the control of any local authority within the State, as may be specified in the order.

(4) An order made under clause (3) may—

(*a*) authorise the Administrative Tribunal to receive representations for the redress of grievances relating to any matter within its jurisdiction as the President may specify in the order and to make such orders thereon as the Administrative Tribunal deems fit;

(*b*) contain such provisions with respect to the powers and authorities and procedure of the Administrative Tribunal (including provisions with respect to the powers of the Administrative Tribunal to punish for contempt of itself) as the President may deem necessary;

(*c*) provide for the transfer to the Administrative Tribunal of such classes of proceedings, being proceedings relating to matters within its jurisdiction and pending before any court (other than the Supreme Court) or tribunal or other authority immediately before the commencement of such order, as may be specified in the order;

(*d*) contain such supplemental, incidental and consequential provisions (including provisions as to fees and as to limitation, evidence or for the application of any law for the time being in force subject to any exceptions or modifications) as the President may deem necessary.

(5) The order of the Administrative Tribunal finally disposing of any case shall become effective upon its confirmation by the State Government or on the expiry of three months from the date on which the order is made, whichever is earlier:

Provided that the State Government may, by special order made in writing and for reasons to be specified therein, modify or annual any order of the Administrative Tribunal before it becomes effective and in such a case, the order of the Administrative Tribunal shall have effect only in such modified form or be of no effect, as the case may be.

(6) Every special order made by the State Government under the proviso to clause (5) shall be laid, as soon as may be after it is made, before both Houses of the State Legislature.

(7) The High Court for the State shall not have any powers of superintendence over the Administrative Tribunal and no court (other than the Supreme Court) or tribunal shall exercise any jurisdiction, power or authority in respect of any matter subject to the jurisdiction, power or authority of, or in relation to, the Administrative Tribunal.

(8) If the President is satisfied that the continued existence of the Administrative Tribunal is not necessary, the President may by order abolish the Administrative Tribunal and make such provisions in such order as he may deem fit for the transfer and disposal of cases pending before the Tribunal immediately before such abolition.

(9) Notwithstanding any judgment, decree or order of any court, tribunal or other authority,—

(*a*) no appointment, posting, promotion or transfer of any person—

(*i*) made before the 1st day of November, 1956, to any post under the Government of, or any local authority within, the State of Hyderabad as it existed before that date; or

(*ii*) made before the commencement of the Constitution (Thirty-second Amendment) Act, 1973, to any post under the Government of, or any local or other authority within, the State of Andhra Pradesh; and

(*b*) no action taken or thing done by or before any person referred to in sub-clause (*a*),

shall be deemed to be illegal or void or ever to have become illegal or void merely on the ground that the appointment, posting, promotion or transfer of such person was not made in accordance with any law, then in force, providing for any requirement as to residence within the State of Hyderabad or, as the case may be, within any part of the State of Andhra Pradesh, in respect of such appointment, posting, promotion or transfer.

(10) The provisions of this article and of any order made by the President thereunder shall have effect notwithstanding anything in any other provision of this Constitution or in any other law for the time being in force.

371E. *Establishment of Central University in Andhra Pradesh.*—Parliament may by law provide for the establishment of a University in the State of Andhra Pradesh.]

[92][**371F.** *Special provisions with respect to the State of Sikkim.*—Notwithstanding anything in this Constitution,—

(a) the Legislative Assembly of the State of Sikkim shall consist of not less than thirty members;

---

[92] Ins. by the Const. (36th Am.) Act, 1975, s. 3 (w.e.f. 26.4.1975).

(*b*) as from the date of commencement of the Constitution (Thirty-sixth Amendment) Act, 1975 (hereafter in this article referred to as the appointed day)—

(*i*) the Assembly for Sikkim formed as a result of the elections held in Sikkim in April, 1974 with thirty-two members elected in the said elections (hereinafter referred to as the sitting members) shall be deemed to be the Legislative Assembly of the State of Sikkim duly constituted under this Constitution;

(*ii*) the sitting members shall be deemed to be the members of the Legislative Assembly of the State of Sikkim duly elected under this Constitution; and

(*iii*) the said Legislative Assembly of the State of Sikkim shall exercise the powers and perform the functions of the Legislative Assembly of a State under this Constitution;

(*c*) in the case of the Assembly deemed to be the Legislative Assembly of the State of Sikkim under clause (*b*), the references to the period of [93][five years] in clause (1) of article 172 shall be construed as references to a period of [94][four years] and the said period of [94][four years] shall be deemed to commence from the appointed day;

(*d*) until other provisions are made by Parliament by law, there shall be allotted to the State of Sikkim one seat in the House of the People and the State of Sikkim shall form one parliamentary constituency to be called the parliamentary constituency for Sikkim;

(*e*) the representative of the State of Sikkim in the House of the People in existence on the appointed day shall be elected by the members of the Legislative Assembly of the State of Sikkim;

(*f*) Parliament may, for the purpose of protecting the rights and interests of the different sections of the population of Sikkim make provision for the number of seats in the Legislative Assembly of the State of Sikkim which may be filled by candidates belonging to such sections and for the delimitation of the assembly constituencies from which candidates belonging to such sections alone may stand for election to the Legislative Assembly of the State of Sikkim;

(*g*) the Governor of Sikkim shall have special responsibility for peace and for an equitable arrangement for ensuring the social and economic advancement of different sections of the population of Sikkim and in the discharge of his special responsibility under this clause, the Governor of Sikkim shall, subject to such directions as the President may, from time to time, deem fit to issue, act in his discretion;

(*h*) all property and assets (whether within or outside the territories comprised in the State of Sikkim) which immediately before the appointed day were vested in the Government of Sikkim or in any other authority or in any person for the purposes of the Government of Sikkim shall, as from the appointed day, vest in the Government of the State of Sikkim;

(*i*) the High Court functioning as such immediately before the appointed day in the territories comprised in the State of Sikkim shall, on and from the appointed day, be deemed to be the High Court for the State of Sikkim;

(*j*) all courts of civil, criminal and revenue jurisdiction, all authorities and all officers, judicial, executive and ministerial, throughout the territory of the State of Sikkim shall continue on and from the appointed day to exercise their respective functions subject to the provisions of this Constitution;

---

[93] Subs. by the Const. (44th Am.) Act, 1978, s. 43 for "six years" w.e.f. 6.9.1979. The words "six years" were subs. for the original words "five years" by the Const. (42nd Am.) Act, 1976, s. 56, w.e.f. 3.1.1977.

[94] Subs. by the Const. (44th Am.) Act, 1978, s. 43, for "five years" w.e.f. 6.9.1979. The words "five years" were subs. for the original words "four years" by the Const. (42nd Am.) Act, 1976, s. 56, w.e.f. 3.1.1977.

(*k*) all laws in force immediately before the appointed day in the territories comprised in the State of Sikkim or any part thereof shall continue to be in force therein until amended or repealed by a competent Legislature or other competent authority;

(*l*) for the purpose of facilitating the application of any such law as is referred to in clause (*k*) in relation to the administration of the State of Sikkim and for the purpose of bringing the provisions of any such law into accord with the provisions of this Constitution, the President may, within two years from the appointed day, by order, make such adaptations and modifications of the law, whether by way of repeal or amendment, as may be necessary or expedient, and thereupon, every such law shall have effect subject to the adaptations and modifications so made, and any such adaptation or modification shall not be questioned in any court of law;

(*m*) neither the Supreme Court nor any other court shall have jurisdiction in respect of any dispute or other matter arising out of any treaty, agreement, engagement or other similar instrument relating to Sikkim which was entered into or executed before the appointed day and to which the Government of India or any of its predecessor Governments was a party, but nothing in this clause shall be construed to derogate from the provisions of article 143;

(*n*) the President may, by public notification, extend with such restrictions or modifications as he thinks fit to the State of Sikkim any enactment which is in force in a State in India at the date of the notification;

(*o*) if any difficulty arises in giving effect to any of the foregoing provisions of this article, the President may by order[95], do anything (including any adaptation or modification of any other article) which appears to him to be necessary for the purpose of removing that difficulty;

Provided that no such order shall be made after the expiry of two years from the appointed day;

(*p*) all things done and all actions taken in or in relation to the State of Sikkim or the territories comprised therein during the period commencing on the appointed day and ending immediately before the date on which the Constitution (Thirty-sixth Amendment) Act, 1975, receives the assent of the President shall, in so far as they are in conformity with the provisions of this Constitution as amended by the Constitution (Thirty-sixth Amendment) Act, 1975, be deemed for all purposes to have been validly done or taken under this Constitution as so amended.]

372. *Continuance in force of existing laws and their adaptation.*—(1) Notwithstanding the repeal by this Constitution of the enactments referred to in article 395 but subject to the other provisions of this Constitution, all the law in force in the territory of India immediately before the commencement of this Constitution shall continue in force therein until altered or repealed or amended by a competent Legislature or other competent authority.

(2) For the purpose of bringing the provisions of any law in force in the territory of India into accord with the provisions of this Constitution, the President may by order[96] make such adaptations and modifications of such law, whether by way of repeal or amendment, as may be necessary or expedient, and provide that

---

[95] *See* the Constitution (Removal of Difficulties) Order No. XI (C.O. 99).

[96] *See* the Adaptation of Laws Order, 1950, dated the 26th January, 1950, Gazette of India, Extraordinary, p. 449, as amended by Notification No. S.R.O. 115, dated the 5th June, 1950, Gazette of India, Extraordinary, Part II, Section 3, p. 51, Notification No. S.R.O. 870, dated the 4th November, 1950, Gazette of India, Extraordinary, Part II, Section 3, p. 903, Notification No. S.R.O. 508, dated the 4th April, 1951, Gazette of India, Extraordinary, Part II, Section 3, p. 287, Notification No. S.R.O. 1140B, dated the 2nd July, 1952, Gazette of India, Extraordinary, Part II, Section 3, p. 616/I and the Adaptation of the Travancore-Cochin Land Acquisition Laws Order, 1952, dated the 20th November, 1952, Gazette of India, Extraordinary, Part II, Section 3, p. 923.

the law shall, as from such date as may be specified in the order, have effect subject to the adaptations and modifications so made, and any such adaptation or modification shall not be questioned in any court of law.

(3) Nothing in clause (2) shall be deemed—

(*a*) to empower the President to make any adaptation or modification of any law after the expiration of [97][three years] from the commencement of this Constitution; or

(*b*) to prevent any competent Legislature or other competent authority from repealing or amending any law adapted or modified by the President under the said clause.

Explanation I.—The expression "law in force" in this article shall include a law passed or made by a Legislature or other competent authority in the territory of India before the commencement of this Constitution and not previously repealed, notwithstanding that it or parts of it may not be then in operation either at all or in particular areas.

Explanation II.—Any law passed or made by a Legislature or other competent authority in the territory of India which immediately before the commencement of this Constitution had extra-territorial effect as well as effect in the territory of India shall, subject to any such adaptations and modifications as aforesaid, continue to have such extra-territorial effect.

Explanation III.—Nothing in this article shall be construed as continuing any temporary law in force beyond the date fixed for its expiration or the date on which it would have expired if this Constitution had not come into force.

Explanation IV.—An Ordinance promulgated by the Governor of a Province under section 88 of the Government of India Act, 1935, and in force immediately before the commencement of this Constitution shall, unless withdrawn by the Governor of the corresponding State earlier, cease to operate at the expiration of six weeks from the first meeting after such commencement of the Legislative Assembly of that State functioning under clause (1) of article 382, and nothing in this article shall be construed as continuing any such Ordinance in force beyond the said period. [Ss. 292, 293, G.I. Act]

[98][**372A.** *Power of the President to adapt laws.*—(1) For the purposes of bringing the provisions of any law in force in India or any part thereof, immediately before the commencement of the Constitution (Seventh Amendment) Act, 1956, into accord with the provisions of this Constitution as amended by that Act, the President may by order[99] made before the first day of November, 1957, make such adaptations and modifications of the law, whether by way of repeal or amendment, as may be necessary or expedient, and provide that the law shall, as from such date as may be specified in the order, have effect subject to the adaptations and modifications so made, and any such adaptation or modification shall not be questioned in any court of law.

(2) Nothing in clause (1) shall be deemed to prevent a competent legislature or other competent authority from repealing or amending any law adapted or modified by the President under the said clause.]

373. *Power of President to make order in respect of persons under preventive detention in certain cases.*—Until provision is made by Parliament under clause (7) of article 22, or until the expiration of one year from the commencement of this Constitution, whichever is earlier, the said article shall have effect as if for any reference to Parliament in clauses (4) and (7) thereof there were substituted a reference to the President and for any reference to any law made by Parliament in those clauses there were substituted a reference to an order made by the President.

374. *Provisions as to Judges of the Federal Court and proceedings pending in the Federal Court or before His Majesty in Council*—(1) The Judges of the Federal Court holding office immediately before the commencement of this Constitution shall,

---

[97]Subs. by the Const. (1st Am.) Act, 1951, s. 12, for "two years", w.e.f. 18.6.1951.
[98] Ins. by the Const. (7th Am.) Act, 1956, s. 23, w.e.f. 1.11.1956.
[99] *See* the Adaptation of Laws Orders of 1956 and 1957.

unless they have elected otherwise, become on such commencement the Judges of the Supreme Court and shall thereupon be entitled to such salaries and allowances and to such rights in respect of leave of absence and pension as are provided for under article 125 in respect of the Judges of the Supreme Court.

(2) All suits, appeals and proceedings, civil or criminal, pending in the Federal Court at the commencement of this Constitution shall stand removed to the Supreme Court, and the Supreme Court shall have jurisdiction to hear and determine the same, and the judgments and orders of the Federal Court delivered or made before the commencement of this Constitution shall have the same force and effect as if they had been delivered or made by the Supreme Court.

(3) Nothing in this Constitution shall operate to invalidate the exercise of jurisdiction by His Majesty in Council to dispose of appeals and petitions from, or in respect of, any judgment, decree or order of any court within the territory of India in so far as the exercise of such jurisdiction is authorised by law, and any order of His Majesty in Council made on any such appeal or petition after the commencement of this Constitution shall for all purposes have effect as if it were an order or decree made by the Supreme Court in the exercise of the jurisdiction conferred on such Court by this Constitution.

(4) On and from the commencement of this Constitution the jurisdiction of the authority functioning as the Privy Council in a State specified in Part B of the First Schedule to entertain and dispose of appeals and petitions from or in respect of any judgment, decree or order of any court within that State shall cease, and all appeals and other proceedings pending before the said authority at such commencement shall be transferred to, and disposed of by, the Supreme Court.

(5) Further provision may be made by Parliament by law to give effect to the provisions of this article.

375. *Courts, authorities and officers to continue to function subject to the provisions of the Constitution.*—All courts of civil, criminal and revenue jurisdiction, all authorities and all officers, judicial, executive and ministerial, throughout the territory of India, shall continue to exercise their respective functions subject to the provisions of this Constitution.

376. *Provisions as to Judges of High Courts.*—(1) Notwithstanding anything in clause (2) of article 217, the Judges of a High Court in any Province holding office immediately before the commencement of this Constitution shall, unless they have elected otherwise, become on such commencement the Judges of the High Court in the corresponding State, and shall thereupon be entitled to such salaries and allowances and to such rights in respect of leave of absence and pension as are provided for under article 221 in respect of the Judges of such High Court.

[1][Any such Judge shall, notwithstanding that he is not a citizen of India, be eligible for appointment as Chief Justice of such High Court, or as Chief Justice or other Judge of any other High Court].

(2) The Judges of a High Court in any Indian State corresponding to any State specified in Part B of the First Schedule holding office immediately before the commencement of this Constitution shall, unless they have elected otherwise, become on such commencement the Judges of the High Court in the State so specified and shall, notwithstanding anything in clauses (1) and (2) of article 217 but subject to the proviso to clause (1) of that article, continue to hold office until the expiration of such period as the President may by order determine.

(3) In this article, the expression "Judge" does not include an acting Judge or an additional Judge.

377. *Provisions as to Comptroller and Auditor-General of India.*—The Auditor-General of India holding office immediately before the commencement of this Constitution shall, unless he has elected otherwise, become on such commencement the Comptroller and Auditor-General of India and shall thereupon be entitled to such salaries and to such rights in respect of leave of absence and pension as are provided for under clause (3) of article 148 in respect of the Comptroller and Auditor-

---

[1] Added by the Const. (1st Am.) Act, 1951, s. 13, w.e.f. 18.6.1951.

General of India and be entitled to continue to hold office until the expiration of his term of office as determined under the provisions which were applicable to him immediately before such commencement.

378. *Provisions as to Public Service Commissions.*—(1) The members of the Public Service Commission for the Dominion of India holding office immediately before the commencement of this Constitution shall, unless they have elected otherwise, become on such commencement the members of the Public Service Commission for the Union and shall, notwithstanding anything in clauses (1) and (2) of article 316 but subject to the proviso to clause (2) of that article, continue to hold office until the expiration of their term of office as determined under the rules which were applicable immediately before such commencement to such members.

(2) The members of a Public Service Commission of a Province or of a Public Service Commission serving the needs of a group of Provinces holding office immediately before the commencement of this Constitution shall, unless they have elected otherwise, become on such commencement the members of the Public Service Commission for the corresponding State or the members of the Joint State Public Service Commission serving the needs of the corresponding States, as the case may be, and shall, notwithstanding anything in clauses (1) and (2) of article 316 but subject to the proviso to clause (2) of that article, continue to hold office until the expiration of their term of office as determined under the rules which were applicable immediately before such commencement to such members.

[2][**378A.** *Special provision.*—Notwithstanding anything contained in article 172, the Legislative Assembly of the State of Andhra Pradesh as constituted under the provisions of sections 28 and 29 of the States Reorganisation Act, 1956, shall, unless sooner dissolved, continue for a period of five years from the date referred to in the said section 29 and no longer and the expiration of the said period shall operate as a dissolution of that Legislative Assembly.]

[3]**379-391.** *Rep. by the Constitution (Seventh Amendment) Act, 1956, s. 29 and Sch.*

---

[2] Ins. by the Const. (7th Am.) Act, 1956, s. 24, w.e.f. 1.11.1956.

[3] The repealed articles 379-391 read as follows:

"**379.** *Provisions as to provisional Parliament and Speaker and Deputy Speaker thereof.*—(1) Until both Houses of Parliament have been duly constituted and summoned to meet for the first session under the provisions of this Constitution, the body functioning as the Constituent Assembly of the Dominion of India immediately before the commencement of this Constitution shall be the provisional Parliament and shall exercise all the powers and perform all the duties conferred by the provisions of this Constitution on Parliament.

Explanation.—For the purposes of this clause, the Constituent Assembly of the Dominion of India includes—

(*i*) the members chosen to represent any State or other territory for which representation is provided under clause (2), and

(*ii*) the members chosen to fill casual vacancies in the said Assembly.

(2) The President may by rules provide for—

(*a*) the representation in the provisional Parliament functioning under clause (1) of any State or other territory which was not represented in the Constituent Assembly of the Dominion of India immediately before the commencement of this Constitution,

(*b*) the manner in which the representatives of such States or other territories in the provisional Parliament shall be chosen, and

(*c*) the qualifications to be possessed by such representatives.

(3) If a member of the Constituent Assembly of the Dominion of India was, on the sixth day of October, 1949, or thereafter at any time before the commencement of this Constitution, a member of a House of the Legislature of a Governor's Province or of an Indian State corresponding to any State specified in Part B of the First Schedule or a Minister for any such State, then, as from the commencement of this Constitution the seat of such member in the Constituent Assembly shall, unless he has ceased to be a member of that Assembly earlier, become vacant and every such vacancy shall be deemed to be a casual vacancy.

(4) Notwithstanding that any such vacancy in the Constituent Assembly of the Dominion of India as is mentioned in clause (3) has not occurred under that clause,

steps may be taken before the commencement of this Constitution for the filling of such vacancy, but any person chosen before such commencement to fill the vacancy shall not be entitled to take his seat in the said Assembly until after the vacancy has so occurred.

(5) Any person holding office immediately before the commencement of this Constitution as Speaker or Deputy Speaker of the Constituent Assembly when functioning as the Dominion Legislature under the Government of India Act, 1935, shall on such commencement be the Speaker or, as the case may be, the Deputy Speaker of the provisional Parliament functioning under clause (1).

380. *Provision as to President.*—(1) Such person as the Constituent Assembly of the Dominion of India shall have elected in that behalf shall be the President of India until a President has been elected in accordance with the provisions contained in Chapter I of Part V and has entered upon his office.

(2) In the event of the occurrence of any vacancy in the office of the President so elected by the Constituent Assembly of the Dominion of India by reason of his death, resignation, or removal, or otherwise, it shall be filled by a person elected in that behalf by the Provisional Parliament functioning under article 379, and until a person is so elected, the Chief Justice of India shall act as President.

381. *Council of Ministers of the President.*—Such persons as the President may appoint in that behalf shall become members of the Council of Ministers of the President under this Constitution, and, until appointments are so made, all persons holding office as Ministers for the Dominion of India immediately before the commencement of this Constitution shall on such commencement become, and shall continue to hold office as, members of the Council of Ministers of the President under this Constitution.

382. *Provisions as to provisional Legislatures for States in Part A of the First Schedule.*—(1) Until the House or Houses of the Legislature of each State specified in Part A of the First Schedule has or have been duly constituted and summoned to meet for the first session under the provisions of this Constitution, the House or Houses of the Legislature of the corresponding Province functioning immediately before the commencement of this Constitution shall exercise the powers and perform the duties conferred by the provisions of this Constitution on the House or Houses of the Legislature of such State.

(2) Notwithstanding anything in clause (1), where a general election to reconstitute the Legislative Assembly of a Province has been ordered before the commencement of this Constitution, the election may be completed after such commencement as if this Constitution had not come into operation, and the Assembly so reconstituted shall be deemed to be the Legislative Assembly of that Province for the purposes of that clause.

(3) Any person holding office immediately before the commencement of this Constitution as Speaker or Deputy Speaker of the Legislative Assembly or President or Deputy President of the Legislative Council of a Province shall on such commencement be the Speaker or Deputy Speaker of the Legislative Assembly or the Chairman or Deputy Chairman of the Legislative Council, as the case may be, of the corresponding State specified in Part A of the First Schedule while such Assembly or Council functions under clause (1):

Provided that where a general election has been ordered for the reconstitution of the Legislative Assembly of a Province before the commencement of this Constitution and the first meeting of the Assembly as so reconstituted is held after such commencement, the provisions of this clause shall not apply and the Assembly as reconstituted shall elect two members of the Assembly to be respectively the Speaker and Deputy Speaker thereof.

383. *Provision as to Governors of Provinces.*—Any person holding office as Governor in any Province immediately before the commencement of this Constitution shall on such commencement be the Governor of the corresponding State specified in Part A of the First Schedule until a new Governor has been appointed in accordance with the provisions of Chapter II of Part VI and has entered upon his office.

384. *Council of Ministers of Governors.*—Such persons as the Governor of a State may appoint in that behalf shall become members of the Council of Ministers of the Governor under this Constitution, and, until appointments are so made, all persons holding office as Ministers for the corresponding Province immediately before the commencement of this Constitution shall on such commencement become, and shall continue to hold office as, members of the Council of Ministers of the Governor of the State under this Constitution.

385. *Provision as to provisional Legislatures in States in Part B of the First Schedule.*—Until the House or Houses of the Legislature of a State specified in Part B of the First Schedule has or have been duly constituted and summoned to meet for the first session under the provisions of this Constitution, the body or authority functioning immediately before the commencement of this Constitution as the Legislature of the corresponding Indian State shall exercise the powers and perform the duties conferred by the provisions of this Constitution on the House or Houses of the Legislature of the State so specified.

386. *Council of Ministers for States in Part B of the First Schedule.*—Such persons as the Rajpramukh of a State specified in Part B of the First Schedule may appoint in that behalf shall become members of the Council of Ministers of such Rajpramukh under this Constitution, and, until appointments are so made, all persons holding office as Ministers for the corresponding Indian State immediately before the commencement of this Constitution shall on such commencement become, and shall continue to hold office as, members of the Council of Ministers of such Rajpramukh under this Constitution.

387. *Special provision as to determination of population for the purposes of certain elections.*—For the purposes of elections held under any of the provisions of this Constitution during a period of three years from the commencement of this Constitution, the population of India or of any part thereof may, notwithstanding anything in this Constitution, be determined in such manner as the President may by order direct, and different provisions may be made for different States and for different purposes by such order.

388. *Provisions as to the filling of casual vacancies in the provisional Parliament and provisional Legislatures of the States.*—(1) Casual vacancies in the seats of members of the provisional Parliament functioning under clause (1) of article 379, including vacancies referred to in clauses (3) and (4) of that article, shall be filled, and all matters in connection with the filling of such vacancies (including the decision of doubts and disputes arising out of, or in connection with, elections to filll such vacancies) shall be regulated—

(*a*) in accordance with such rules as may be made in that behalf by the President, and

(*b*) until rules are so made, in accordance with the rules relating to the filling of casual vacancies in the Constituent Assembly of the Dominion of India and matters connected therewith in force at the time of the filling of such vacancies or immediately before the commencement of this Constitution, as the case may be, subject to such exceptions and modifications as may be made therein before such commencement by the President of that Assembly and thereafter by the President of India:

Provided that where any such seat as is mentioned in this clause was, immediately before it became vacant, held by a person belonging to the Scheduled Castes or to the Muslim or the Sikh community and representing a Province or, as the case may be, a State specified in Part A of the First Schedule, the person to fill such seat shall, unless the President of the Constituent Assembly or the President of India, as the case may be, considers it necessary or expedient to provide otherwise, be of the same community:

Provided further that at an election to fill any such vacancy in the seat of a member representing a Province or a State specified in Part A of the First Schedule, every member of the Legislative Assembly of that Province or of the corresponding State or of that State, as the case may be, shall be entitled to participate and vote.

Explanation.—For the purposes of this clause—

(*a*) all such castes, races or tribes or parts of or groups within castes, races or tribes as are specified in the Government of India (Scheduled Castes) Order, 1936, to be Scheduled Castes in relation to any Province shall be deemed to be Scheduled Castes in relation to that Province or the corresponding State until a notification has been issued by the President under clause (1) of article 341 specifying the Scheduled Castes in relation to that corresponding State;

(*b*) all the Scheduled Castes in any Province or State shall be deemed to be a single community.

(2) Casual vacancies in the seats of members of a House of the Legislature of a State functioning under Article 382 or article 385 shall be filled, and all matters in connection with the filling of such vacancies (including the decision of doubts and disputes arising out of, or in connection with, elections to fill such vacancies) shall be regulated in accordance with such provisions governing the

392. *Power of the President to remove difficulties.*—(1) The President may, for the purpose of removing any difficulties, particularly in relation to the transition from the provisions of the Government of India Act, 1935, to the provisions of this Constitution, by order direct that this Constitution shall, during such period as may be specified in the order, have effect subject to such adaptations, whether by way of modification, addition or omission, as he may deem to be necessary or expedient:

Provided that no such order shall be made after the first meeting of Parliament duly constituted under Chapter II of Part V.

(2) Every order made under clause (1) shall be laid before Parliament.

(3) The powers conferred on the President by this article, by article 324, by clause (3) of article 367 and by article 391 shall, before the commencement of this Constitution, be excercisable by the Governor-General of the Dominion of India.

PART XXII

SHORT TITLE, COMMENCEMENT AND REPEALS

393. *Short title.*—This Constitution may be called the Constitution of India.

394. *Commencement.*—This article and articles 5, 6, 7, 8, 9, 60, 324, 366, 367, 379, 380, 388, 391, 392 and 393 shall come into force at once, and the remaining provisions of this Constitution shall come into force on the twenty-

---

filling of such vacancies and regulating such matters as were in force immediately before the commencement of this Constitution subject to such exceptions and modifications as the President may by order direct.

389. *Provision as to Bills pending in the Dominion Legislature and in the Legislatures of Provinces and Indian States.*—A bill which immediately before the commencement of this Constitution was pending in the Legislature of the Dominion of India or in the Legislature of any Province or Indian State may, subject to any provision to the contrary which may be included in rules made by Parliament or the Legislature of the corresponding State under this Constitution, be continued in Parliament or the Legislature of the corresponding State, as the case may be, as if the proceedings taken with reference to the Bill in the Legislature of the Dominion of India or in the Legislature of the Province or Indian State had been taken in Parliament or in the Legislature of the corresponding State.

390. *Moneys received or raised or expenditure incurred between the commencement of the Constitution and the 31st day of March, 1950.*—The provisions of this Constitution relating to the Consolidated Fund of India or the Consolidated Fund of any State and the appropriation of moneys out of either of such Funds shall not apply in relation to moneys received or raised or expenditure incurred by the Government of India or the Government of any State between the commencement of this Constitution and the thirty-first day of March, 1950, both days inclusive, and any expenditure incurred during that period shall be deemed to be duly authorised if the expenditure was specified in a schedule of authorised expenditure authenticated in accordance with the provisions of the Government of India Act, 1935, by the Governor-General of the Dominion of India or the Governor of the corresponding Province or is authorised by the Rajpramukh of the State in accordance with such rules as were applicable to the authorisation of expenditure from the revenues of the corresponding Indian State immediately before such commencement.

391. *Power of the President to amend the First and Fourth Schedules in certain contingencies.*—(1) If at any time between the passing of this Constitution and its commencement any action is taken under the provisions of the Government of India Act, 1935, which in the opinion of the President requires any amendment in the First Schedule and the Fourth Schedule, the President may, notwithstanding anything in this Constitution, by order, make such amendments in the said Schedules as may be necessary to give effect to the action so taken, and any such order may contain such supplemental, incidental and consequential provisions as the President may deem necessary.

(2) When the First Schedule or the Fourth Schedule is so amended, any reference to that Schedule in this Constitution shall be construed as a reference to such Schedule as so amended."

sixth day of January, 1950, which day is referred to in this Constitution as the commencement of this Constitution.

395. *Repeals.*—The Indian Independence Act, 1947, and the Government of India Act, 1935, together with all enactments amending or supplementing the latter. Act, but not including the Abolition of Privy Council Jurisdiction Act, 1949, are hereby repealed.

[4][FIRST SCHEDURE

[Articles 1 and 4]

I. THE STATES

	Name	*Territories*
1.	Andhra Pradesh ...	[5][The territories specified in sub-section (1) of section 3 of the Andhra State Act, 1953, sub-section

---

[4] The whole of the First Schedule was substituted by the Consti. (7th Am.) Act, 1956, w.e.f. 1.11.1956. The Schedule as originally enacted read as follows:

"FIRST SCHEDULE

(Articles 1, 4 and 391)

The States and the territories of India

PART A

	Names of States	*Names of corresponding Provinces*
1.	Assam	Assam
2.	Bihar	Bihar
3.	Bombay	Bombay
4.	Madhya Pradesh	The Central Provinces and Berar
5.	Madras	Madras
6.	Orissa	Orissa
7.	Punjab	East Punjab
8.	The United Provinces	The United Provinces
9.	West Bengal	West Bengal

Territories of States

The territory of the State of Assam shall comprise the territories which immediately before the commencement of this Constitution were comprised in the Province of Assam, the Khasi States and the Assam Tribal Areas.

The territory of the State of West Bengal shall comprise the territory which immediately before the commencement of this Constitution was comprised in the Province of West Bengal.

The territory of each of the other States in this Part shall comprise the territories which immediately before the commencement of this Constitution were comprised in the corresponding Province and the territories which, by virtue of an order made under section 290A of the Government of India Act, 1935, were immediately before such commencement being administered as if they formed part of that Province.

Part B

Names of States

1. Hyderabad.
2. Jammu and Kashmir.
3. Madhya Bharat.
4. Mysore.
5. Patiala and East Punjab States Union.
6. Rajasthan.
7. Saurashtra.
8. Travancore-Cochin.
9. Vindhya Pradesh.

Territories of States

The territory of each of the States in this Part shall comprise the territory which immediately before the commencement of this Constitution was comprised in the corresponding Indian State, and

(*a*) in the case of each of the States of Rajasthan and Saurashtra, shall also comprise the territories which immediately before such commencement were being administered by the Government of the corresponding Indian State, whether under the provisions of the Extra-Provincial Jurisdiction Act, 1947, or otherwise; and

(*b*) in the case of the State of Madhya Bharat, shall also comprise the territory which immediately before such commencement was comprised in the Chief Commissioner's Province of Panth Piploda.

Name		*Territories*
		(1) of section 3 of the States Reorganisation Act, 1956, the First Schedule to the Andhra Pradesh and Madras (Alteration of Boundaries) Act, 1959, and the Schedule to the Andhra Pradesh and Mysore (Transfer of Territory) Act, 1968, but excluding the territories specified in the Second Schedule to the Andhra Pradesh and Madras (Alteration of Boundaries) Act, 1959.]
2. Assam	...	The territories which immediately before the commencement of this Constitution were comprised in the Province of Assam, the Khasi States and the Assam Tribal Areas, but excluding the territories specified in the Schedule to the Assam (Alteration of Boundaries) Act, 1951, [6][and the territories specified in sub-section (1) of section 3 of the State of Nagaland Act, 1962] [7][and the territories specified in sections 5, 6 and 7 of the North-Eastern Areas (Reorganisation) Act, 1971].
3. Bihar	...	[8][The territories which immediately before the commencement of this Constitution were either comprised in the Province of Bihar or were being administered as if they formed part of that Province and the territories specified in clause (a) of sub-section (1) of section 3 of the Bihar and Uttar Pradesh (Alteration of Boundaries) Act, 1968, but excluding the territories specified in sub-section (1) of section 3 of the Bihar and West Bengal (Transfer of Territories) Act, 1956, and the territories specified in clause (b) of sub-section (1) of section 3 of the first mentioned Act.]
[9][4. Gujarat	...	The territories referred to in sub-section (1) of section 3 of the Bombay Reorganisation Act, 1960.]

Part C

Names of States

1. Ajmer.
2. Bhopal.
3. Bilaspur.
4. Cooch-Behar.
5. Coorg.
6. Delhi.
7. Himachal Pradesh.
8. Kutch.
9. Manipur.
10. Tripura.

Territories of States

The territory of each of the States of Ajmer, Coorg and Delhi shall comprise the territory which immediately before the commencement of this Constitution was comprised in the Chief Commissioners' Provinces of Ajmer-Merwara, Coorg and Delhi, respectively.

The territory of each of the other States in this Part shall comprise the territories which, by virtue of an order made under section 290A of the Government of India Act, 1935, were immediately before the commencement of this Constitution being administered as if they were a Chief Commissioner's Province of the same name.

Part D

The Andaman and Nicobar Islands."

[5] Subs. by the Andhra Pradesh and Mysore (Transfer of Territory) Act, 1968, s. 4, for the former entry w.e.f. 1.10.1968.

[6] Added by the State of Nagaland Act, 1962, s. 4 w.e.f. 1.12.1963.

[7] Added by the North-Eastern Areas (Reorganisation) Act, 1971 (81 of 1971), s. 9 (w.e.f. 21.1.1972).

[8] Subs. by the Bihar and Uttar Pradesh (Alteration of Boundaries) Act, 1968 (24 of 1968), s. 4, for the former entry (w.e.f. 10.6.1970).

[9] Subs. by the Bombay Reorganisation Act, 1960 (11 of 1960), s. 4, for entry 4 (w.e.f. 1.5.1960).

Name		*Territories*
5. Kerala	...	The territories specified in sub-section (1) of section 5 of the States Reorganisation Act, 1956.
6. Madhya Pradesh	...	The territories specified in sub-section (1) of section 9 of the States Reorganisation Act, 1956 [10][and the First Schedule to the Rajasthan and Madhya Pradesh (Transfer of Territories) Act, 1959].
[11][7. Tamil Nadu]	...	The territories which immediately before the commencement of this Constitution were either comprised in the Province of Madras or were being administered as if they formed part of that Province and the territories specified in section 4 of the States Reorganisation Act, 1956, [12][and the Second Schedule to the Andhra Pradesh and Madras (Alteration of Boundaries) Act, 1959,] but excluding the territories specified in sub-section (1) of section 3 and sub-section (1) of section 4 of the Andhra State Act, 1953 and [13][the territories specified in clause (b) of sub-section (1) of section 5, section 6 and clause (d) of sub-section (1) of section 7 of the States Reorganisation Act, 1956 and the territories specified in the First Schedule to the Andhra Pradesh and Madras (Alteration of Boundaries) Act, 1959].
[14][8. Maharashtra	...	The territories specified in sub-section (1) of section 8 of the States Reorganisation Act, 1956, but excluding the territories referred to in sub-section (1) of section 3 of the Bombay Reorganisation Act, 1960].
[15][9. Karnataka]	...	The territories specified in sub-section (1) of section 7 of the States Reorganisation Act, 1956 [16][but excluding the territory specified in the Schedule to the Andhra Pradesh and Mysore (Transfer of Territory) Act, 1968].
[17][10.] Orissa	...	The territories which immediately before the commencement of this Constitution were either comprised in the Province of Orissa or were being administered as if they formed part of that Province.

---

[10] Ins. by the Rajasthan and Madhya Pradesh (Transfer of Territories) Act, 1959 (47 of 1959), s. 4 (w.e.f. 1.10.1959).

[11] Subs. by the Madras State (Alteration of Name) Act, 1968 (53 of 1968), s. 5, for "7. Madras" (w.e.f. 14.1.1969).

[12] Ins. by the Andhra Pradesh and Madras (Alteration of Boundaries) Act, 1959 (56 of 1959), s. 6 (w.e.f. 1.4.1960).

[13] Subs. by s. 6, *ibid.*, for certain words (w.e.f. 1.4.1960). The words substituted read: "the territories specified in clause (*b*) of sub-section (1) of section 5, section 6 and clause (*d*) of sub-section (1) of section 7 of the States Reorganisation Act, 1956".

[14] Ins. by the Bombay Reorganisation Act, 1960 (11 of 1960), s. 4 (w.e.f. 1.5.1960).

[15] Subs. by the Mysore State (Alteration of Name) Act, 1973 (31 of 1973), s. 5, for "9. Mysore" (w.e.f. 1.11.1973).

[16] Ins. by the Andhra Pradesh and Mysore (Transfer of Territory) Act, 1968 (36 of 1968), s. 4 (w.e.f. 1.10.1968).

[17] Entries 8 to 14 renumbered as entries 9 to 15 by the Bombay Reorganisation Act, 1960 (11 of 1960), s. 4 (w.e.f. 1.5.1960).

Name		*Territories*
[17][11.] Punjab	...	The territories specified in section 11 of the States Reorganisation Act, 1956 [18][and the territories referred to in Part II of the First Schedule to the Acquired Territories (Merger) Act, 1960] [19][but excluding the territories referred to in Part II of the First Schedule to the Constitution (Ninth Amendment) Act, 1960] [20][and the territories specified in sub-section (1) of section 3, section 4 and sub-section (1) of section 5 of the Punjab Reorganisation Act, 1966].
[21][12.] Rajasthan	...	The territories specified in section 10 of the States Reorganisation Act, 1956 [22][but excluding the territories specified in the First Schedule to the Rajasthan and Madhya Pradesh (Transfer of Territories) Act, 1959].
[21][13.] Uttar pradesh	...	[23][[24]The territories which immediately before the commencement of this Constitution were either comprised in the Province known as the United Provinces or were being administered as if they formed part of that Province and the territories specified in clause (b) of sub-section (1) of section 3 of the Bihar and Uttar Pradeh (Alteration of Boundaries) Act, 1968, but excluding the territories specified in clause (a) of sub-section (1) of section 3 of that Act.]
[25][14.] West Bengal	...	The territories which immediately before the commencement of this Constitution were either comprised in the Province of West Bengal or were being administered as if they formed part of that Province and the territory of Chandernagore as defined in clause (c) of section 2 of the Chandernagore (Merger) Act, 1954 and also the territories specified in sub-section (1) of section 3 of the Bihar and West Bengal (Transfer of Territories) Act, 1956.
[25][15.] Jammu and Kashmir	...	The territory which immediately before the commencement of this Constitution was comprised in the Indian State of Jammu and Kashmir.

[18] Ins. by the Acquired Territories (Merger) Act, 1960 (64 of 1960), s. 4 (w.e.f. 17.1.1961).

[19] Added by the Constitution (Ninth Amendment) Act, 1960, s. 3 (w.e.f. 17.1.1961).

[20] Ins. by the Punjab Reorganisation Act, 1966 (31 of 1966) s. 7 (w.e.f. 1.11.1966).

[21] Entries 8 to 14 renumbered as entries 9 to 15 by the Bombay Reorganisation Act, 1960 (11 of 1960), s. 4 (w.e.f. 1.5.1960).

[22] Ins. by the Rajasthan and Madhya Pradesh (Transfer of Territories) Act, 1959 (47 of 1959), s. 4 (w.e.f. 1.10.1959).

[23] Subs. by the Bihar and Uttar Pradesh (Alteration of Boundaries) Act, 1968 (24 of 1968), s. 4, for the former entry (w.e.f. 10.6.1970).

[24] On the enforcement of s. 5 of the Haryana and Uttar Pradesh (Alteration of Boundaries) Act, 1979 (31 of 1979), the entry against "13. Uttar Pradesh" shall stand subs. as directed in s. 5 of that Act. For the text of s. 5 of that Act, *see* Appendix III.

[25] Entries 8 to 14 renumbered as entries 9 to 15 by the Bombay Reorganisation Act, 1960 (11 of 1960), s. 4 (w.e.f. 1.5.1960).

[26] Ins. by the State of Nagaland Act, 1962 (27 of 1962), s. 4 (w.e.f. 1.12.1963).

Name		Territories
[26][16. Nagaland	...	The territories specified in sub-section (1) of section 3 of the State of Nagaland Act, 1962.]
[27][17. Haryana	...	[28]The territories specified in sub-section (1) of section 3 of the Punjab Reorganisation Act, 1966.]
[29][18. Himachal Pradesh	...	The territories which immediately before the commencement of this Constitution were being administered as if they were Chief Commissioners' Provinces under the names of Himachal Pradesh and Bilaspur and the territories specified in sub-section (1) of section 5 of the Punjab Reorganisation Act, 1966.]
[30][19. Manipur	...	The territory which immediately before the commencement of this Constitution was being administered as if it were a Chief Commissioner's Province under the name of Manipur.
20. Tripura	...	The territory which immediately before the commencement of this Constitution was being administered as if it were a Chief Commissioner's Province under the name of Tripura.
21. Meghalaya	...	The territories specified in section 5 of the North-Eastern Areas (Reorganisation) Act, 1971.]
[31][22. Sikkim	...	The territories which immediately before the commencement of the Constitution (Thirty-Sixth Amendment) Act, 1975, were comprised in Sikkim.]

II. THE UNION TERRITORIES

Name		Extent
1. Delhi	...	The territory which immediately before the commencement of this Constitution was comprised in the Chief Commissioner's Province of Delhi.
[32] * *		* * *
[33] * *		* * *
[34][2.] The Andaman and Nicobar Islands	...	The territory which immediately before the commencement of this Constitution was comprised in the Chief Commissioner's Province of the Andaman and Nicobar Islands.
[34][3.] [35][Lakshadweep]	...	The territory specified in section 6 of the States Reorganisation Act, 1956.

[27] Ins. by the Punjab Reorganisation Act, 1966 (31 of 1966), s. 7 (w.e.f. 1.11.1966).

[28] On the enforcement of s. 5 of the Haryana and Uttar Pradesh (Alteration of Boundaries) Act, 1979 (31 of 1979), the entry against "17. Haryana" shall stand subs. as directed in s. 5 of that Act. For text of s. 5 of that Act, *see* Appendix III.

[29] Ins. by the State of Himachal Pradesh Act, 1970 (53 of 1970), s. 4 (w.e.f. 25.1.1971).

[30] Ins. by the North-Eastern Areas (Reorganisation) Act, 1971 (81 of 1971), s. 9 (w.e.f. 21.1.1972).

[31] Ins. by the Const. (36th Am.) Act, 1975, s. 2, w.e.f. 26.4.1975.

[32] Entry 2 relating to "Himachal Pradesh" omitted by the State of Himachal Pradesh Act, 1970 (53 of 1970), s. 4 (w.e.f. 25.1.1971).

[33] Entries relating to Manipur and Tripura omitted by the North-Eastern Areas (Reorganisation) Act, 1971 (81 of 1971), s. 9 (w.e.f. 21.1.1972.)

[34] Entries 4 to 9 renumbered as entries 2 to 7 by s. 9, *ibid.* (w.e.f. 21.1.1972).

[35] Subs. by the Laccadive, Minicoy and Amindivi Islands (Alteration of Name) Act, 1973 (34 of 1973), s. 5, for "The Laccadive, Minicoy and Amindivi Islands," (w.e.f. 1.11.1973).

Name		*Territories*
[36][34][4.] Dadra and Nagar Haveli	...	The territory which immediately before the eleventh day of August, 1961 was comprised in Free Dadra and Nagar Haveli.]
[37][38][5.] Goa, Daman and Diu	...	The territories which immediately before the twentieth day of December, 1961 were comprised in Goa, Daman and Diu.]
[39][38][6.] Pondicherry	...	The territories which immediately before the sixteenth day of August, 1962, were comprised in the French Establishments in India known as Pondicherry, Karikal, Mahe and Yanam.]
[40][38][7.] Chandigarh	...	The territories specified in section 4 of the Punjab Reorganisation Act, 1966.]
[41][8. Mizoram	...	The territories specified in section 6 of the North-Eastern Areas (Reorganisation) Act, 1971.
9. Arunachal Pradesh	...	The territories specified in section 7 of the North-Eastern Areas (Reorganisation) Act, 1971.]

SECOND SCHEDULE

[Articles 59(3), 65(3), 75(6), 97, 125, 148(3), 158(3), 164(5), 186 and 221]

PART A

PROVISIONS AS TO THE PRESIDENT AND THE GOVERNORS OF STATES[42]* * *

1. There shall be paid to the President and to Governors of the States [42]* * * the following emoluments per mensem, that is to say:—

The President	...	...	...	...	10,000 rupees.
The Governor of a State		...	...	...	5,500 rupees.

2. There shall also be paid to the President and to the Governors of the States [43]* * * such allowances as were payable respectively to the Governor-General of the Dominion of India and to the Governors of the corresponding Provinces immediately before the commencement of this Constitution.

3. The President and the Governors of [44][the States] throughout their respective terms of office shall be entitled to the same privileges to which the Governor-General and the Governors of the corresponding Provinces were respectively entitled immediately before the commencement of this Constitution.

4. While the Vice-President or any other person is discharging the functions of, or is acting as, President, or any person is discharging the functions of the Governor, he shall be entitled to the same emoluments, allowances and privileges as the President or the Governor whose functions he discharges or for whom he acts, as the case may be.

[45]* * * * *

---

[36] Ins. by the Const. (10th Am.) Act, 1961, s. 2, w.e.f. 11.8.1961.
[37] Ins. by the Const. (12th Am.) Act, 1962, s. 2, w.e.f. 20.12.1961.
[38] Entries 4 to 9 renumbered as entries 2 to 7 by the North-Eastern Areas (Reorganisation) Act, 1971 (81 of 1971), s. 9 (w.e.f. 21.1.1972).
[39] Ins. by the Const. (14th Am.) Act, 1962, ss. 3 and 7 w.e.f. 16.8.1962.
[40] Ins. by the Punjab Reorganisation Act, 1966 (31 of 1966), s. 7 (w.e.f. 1.11.1966).
[41] Ins. by the North-Eastern Areas (Reorganisation) Act, 1971 (81 of 1971), s. 9 (w.e.f. 21.1.1972).
[42] The words and letter "specified in Part A of the First Schedule" omitted by the Const. (7th Am.) Act, 1956, s. 29 and Sch., w.e.f. 1.11.1956.
[43] The words "so specified" omitted by s. 29 and Sch., *ibid.*
[44] Subs. by s. 29 and Sch., *ibid.*, for "such States".
[45] Part B omitted by the Const. (7th Am.) Act, 1956, s. 29 and Sch. w.e.f. 1.11.1956. The omitted Part read as follows:—

PART C

PROVISIONS AS TO THE SPEAKER AND THE DEPUTY SPEAKER OF THE HOUSE OF THE PEOPLE AND THE CHAIRMAN AND THE DEPUTY CHAIRMAN OF THE COUNCIL OF STATES AND THE SPEAKER AND THE DEPUTY SPEAKER OF THE LEGISLATIVE ASSEMBLY [46]* * * AND THE CHAIRMAN AND THE DEPUTY CHAIRMAN OF THE LEGISLATIVE COUNCIL OF [47][A STATE].

7. There shall be paid to the Speaker of the House of the People and the Chairman of the Council of States such salaries and allowances as were payable to the Speaker of the Constituent Assembly of the Dominion of India immediately before the commencement of this Constitution, and there shall be paid to the Deputy Speaker of the House of the People and to the Deputy Chairman of the Council of States such salaries and allowances as were payable to the Deputy Speaker of the Constituent Assembly of the Dominion of India immediately before such commencement.

8. There shall be paid to the Speaker and the Deputy Speaker of the Legislative Assembly [48]* * * and to the Chairman and the Deputy Chairman of the Legislative Council of [49][a State] such salaries and allowances as were payable respectively to the Speaker and the Deputy Speaker of the Legislative Assembly and the President and the Deputy President of the Legislative Council of the corresponding Province immediately before the commencement of this Constitution and, where the corresponding Province had no Legislative Council immediately before such commencement, there shall be paid to the Chairman and the Deputy Chairman of the Legislative Council of the State such salaries and allowances as the Governor of the State may determine.

PART D

PROVISIONS AS TO THE JUDGES OF THE SUPREME COURT AND OF THE HIGH COURTS [50]* * *

9. (1) There shall be paid to the Judges of the Supreme Court, in respect of time spent on actual service, salary at the following rates per mensem, that is to say:—

The Chief Justice	5,000 rupees.
Any other Judge	4,000 rupees:

Provided that if a Judge of the Supreme Court at the time of his appointment is in receipt of a pension (other than a disability or wound pension) in respect of any previous service under the Government of India or any of its predecessor Governments or under the Government of a State or any of its predecessor Governments, his salary in respect of service in the Supreme Court [51][shall be reduced—

"PART B

PROVISIONS AS TO THE MINISTERS FOR THE UNION AND FOR THE STATES IN PART A AND PART B OF THE FIRST SCHEDULE

5. There shall be paid to the Prime Minister and to each of the other Ministers for the Union such salaries and allowances as were payable respectively to the Prime Minister and to each of the other Ministers for the Dominion of India immediately before the commencement of this Constitution.

6. There shall be paid to the Ministers for any State specified in Part A or Part B of the First Schedule such salaries and allowances as were payable to such Ministers for the corresponding Province or the corresponding Indian State, as the case may be, immediately before the commencement of this Constitution."

[46] The words and letter "of a State in Part A of the First Schedule" omitted by s. 29 and Sch., *ibid.*

[47] Subs. for "any such State" by s. 29 and Sch., *ibid.*

[48] The words and letter "of a State specified in Part A of the First Schedule" omitted by s. 29 and Sch., *ibid.*

[49] Subs. by s. 29 and Sch., *ibid.*, for "such State".

[50] The words and letter "in States in Part A of the First Schedule" omitted by the Const. (7th Am.) Act, 1956, s. 25, w.e.f. 1.11.1956.

[51] Subs. by s. 25, *ibid*; for "shall be reduced by the amount of that pension".

(a) by the amount of that pension, and

(b) if he has, before such appointment, received in lieu of a portion of the pension due to him in respect of such previous service the commuted value thereof, by the amount of that portion of the pension, and

(c) if he has, before such appointment, received a retirement gratuity in respect of such previous service, by the pension equivalent of that gratuity].

(2) Every Judge of the Supreme Court shall be entitled without payment of rent to the use of an official residence.

(3) Nothing in sub-paragraph (2) of this paragraph shall apply to a Judge who, immediately before the commencement of this Constitution,—

(a) was holding office as the Chief Justice of the Federal Court and has become on such commencement the Chief Justice of the Supreme Court under clause (1) of article 374, or

(b) was holding office as any other Judge of the Federal Court and has on such commencement become a Judge (other than the Chief Justice) of the Supreme Court under the said clause,

during the period he holds office as such Chief Justice or other Judge, and every Judge who so becomes the Chief Justice or other Judge of the Supreme Court shall, in respect of time spent on actual service as such Chief Justice or other Judge, as the case may be, be entitled to receive in addition to the salary specified in sub-paragraph (1) of this paragraph as special pay an amount equivalent to the difference between the salary so specified and the salary which he was drawing immediately before such commencement.

(4) Every Judge of the Supreme Court shall receive such reasonable allowances to reimburse him for expenses incurred in travelling on duty within the territory of India and shall be afforded such reasonable facilities in connection with travelling as the President may from time to time prescribe.

(5) The rights in respect of leave of absence (including leave allowances) and pension of the Judges of the Supreme Court shall be governed by the provisions which, immediately before the commencement of this Constitution, were applicable to the Judges of the Federal Court.

10. [52][(1) There shall be paid to the Judges of High Courts, in respect of time spent on actual service, salary at the following rates per mensem, that is to say,—

The Chief Justice	4,000 rupees.
Any other Judge	3,500 rupees:

Provided that if a Judge of a High Court at the time of his appointment is in receipt of a pension (other than a disability or wound pension) in respect of any previous service under the Government of India or any of its predecessor Governments or under the Government of a State or any of its predecessor Governments, his salary in respect of service in the High Court shall be reduced—

(a) by the amount of that pension, and

(b) if he has, before such appointment, received in lieu of a portion of the pension due to him in respect of such previous service the commuted value thereof, by the amount of that portion of the pension, and

(c) if he has, before such appointment, received a retirement gratuity in respect of such previous service, by the pension equivalent of that gratuity.]

(2) Every person who immediately before the commencement of this Constitution—

[52] Subs. by the Const. (7th Am.) Act, 1956, s. 25, for sub-paragraph (1) w.e.f. 1.11.1956. The original sub-paragraph read as follows:

"(1) There shall be paid to the Judges of the High Court of each State specified in Part A of the First Schedule, in respect of time spent on actual service, salary at the following rates per mensem, that is to say:—

The Chief Justice	4,000 rupees
Any other Judge	3,500 rupees."

(*a*) was holding office as the Chief Justice of a High Court in any Province and has on such commencement become the Chief Justice of the High Court in the corresponding State under clause (1) of article 376, or

(*b*) was holding office as any other Judge of a High Court in any Province and has on such commencement become a Judge (other than the Chief Justice) of the High Court in the corresponding State under the said clause,

[53]shall, if he was immediately before such commencement drawing a salary at a rate higher than that specified in sub-paragraph (1) of this paragraph, be entitled to receive in respect of time spent on actual service as such Chief Justice or other Judge, as the case may be, in addition to the salary specified in the said sub-paragraph as special pay an amount equivalent to the difference between the salary so specified and the salary which he was drawing immediately before such commencement

[54][(3) Any person who, immediately before the commencement of the Constitution (Seventh Amendment) Act, 1956, was holding office as the Chief Justice of the High Court of a State specified in Part B of the First Schedule and has on such commencement become the Chief Justice of the High Court of a State specified in the said Schedule as amended by the said Act, shall, if he was immediately before such commencement drawing any amount as allowance in addition to his salary, be entitled to receive in respect of time spent on actual service as such Chief Justice, the same amount as allowance in addition to the salary specified in sub-paragraph (1) of this paragraph.]

11. In this Part, unless the context otherwise requires,—

(*a*) the expression "Chief Justice" includes an acting Chief Justice, and a "Judge" includes an *ad hoc* Judge;

(*b*) "actual service" includes—

(*i*) time spent by a Judge on duty as a Judge or in the performance of such other functions as he may at the request of the President undertake to discharge;

(*ii*) vacations, excluding any time during which the Judge is absent on leave; and

(*iii*) joining time on transfer from a High Court to the Supreme Court or from one High Court to another.

---

[53] Paragraph 2 of the Const. (Removal of Difficulties) Order No. IV provides that as from 26th January, 1950, the Second Schedule to the Constitution of India shall have effect subject to the following adaptation, namely,—

"* * * * *

(2) In sub-paragraph (2) of paragraph 10, for all words after cl. (*b*), the following shall be substituted:—

'shall, in respect of time spent of actual service as such Chief Justice or other Judge, as the case may be, be entitled to receive in addition to the salary specified in sub-paragraph (1) of this paragraph as special pay the amount, if any, by which that salary falls short of the salary payable to the Chief Justice, or, as the case may be, any other Judge, of the High Court in the Province immediately before such commencement'."

[54] Subs. by the Const. (7th Am.) Act, 1956, s. 25, for sub-paragraphs (3) and (4) w.e.f. 1.11.1956. The original sub-paragraphs read as follows:

"(3) Every Judge of a High Court shall receive such reasonable allowances to reimburse him for expenses incurred in travelling on duty within the territory of India and shall be afforded such reasonable facilities in connection with travelling as the President may from time to time prescribe.

(4) The rights in respect of leave of absence (including leave allowances) and pension of the Judges of the High Court of any State shall be governed by the provisions which, immediately before the commencement of this Constitution, were applicable to the Judges of the High Court in the corresponding Province."

PART E

PROVISIONS AS TO THE COMPTROLLER AND AUDITOR-GENERAL OF INDIA

12. (1) There shall be paid to the Comptroller and Auditor-General of India a salary at the rate of four thousand rupees per mensem.

(2) The person who was holding office immediately before the commencement of this Constitution as Auditor-General of India and has become on such commencement the Comptroller and Auditor-General of India under article 377 shall in addition to the salary specified in sub-paragraph (1) of this paragraph be entitled to receive as special pay an amount equivalent to the difference between the salary so specified and the salary which he was drawing as Auditor-General of India immediately before such commencement.

(3) The rights in respect of leave of absence and pension and the other conditions of service of the Comptroller and Auditor-General of India shall be governed or shall continue to be governed, as the case may be, by the provisions which were applicable to the Auditor-General of India immediately before the commencement of this Constitution and all references in those provisions to the Governor-General shall be construed as references to the President.

THIRD SCHEDULE

[Articles 75(4), 99, 124(6), 148(2), 164(3), 188 and 219]

FORMS OF OATHS OR AFFIRMATIONS

I

Form of oath of office for a Minister for the Union:—

"I, A.B., do swear in the name of God / solemnly affirm that I will bear true faith and allegiance to the Constitution of India as by law established, [55][that I will uphold the sovereignty and integrity of India,] that I will faithfully and conscientiously discharge my duties as a Minister for the Union and that I will do right to all manner of people in accordance with the Constitution and the law, without fear or favour, affection or illwill."

II

Form of oath of secrecy for a Minister for the Union:—

"I, A.B., do swear in the name of God / solemnly affirm that I will not directly or indirectly communicate or reveal to any person or persons any matter which shall be brought under my consideration or shall become known to me as a Minister for the Union except as may be required for the due discharge of my duties as such Minister."

[56][III

A

Form of oath or affirmation to be made by a candidate for election to Parliament:—

---

[55] Ins. by the Const. (16th Am.) Act, 1963, s. 5, w.e.f. 5.10.1963.

[56] Subs. by s. 5, *ibid.*, for Form III. The original Form III was as follows:
"Form of oath or affirmation to be made by a member of Parliament:—
'I, A.B., having been elected (or nominated) a member of the Council of States (or the House of the People) do swear in the name of God / solemnly affirm that I will bear true faith and allegiance to the Constitution of India as by law established and that I will faithfully discharge the duty upon which I am about to enter.'"

"I, A.B., having been nominated as a candidate to fill a seat in the Council of States (or the House of the People) do swear in the name of God / solemnly affirm that I will bear true faith and allegiance to the Constitution of India as by law established and that I will uphold the sovereignty and integrity of India."

B

Form of oath or affirmation to be made by a member of Parliament:—

"I, A.B., having been elected (or nominated) a member of the Council of States (or the House of the People) do swear in the name of God / solemnly affirm that I will bear true faith and allegiance to the Constitution of India as by law established, that I will uphold the sovereignty and integrity of India and that I will faithfully discharge the duty upon which I am about to enter."]

IV

Form of oath or affirmation to be made by the Judges of the Supreme Court and the Comptroller and Auditor-General of India:—

"I, A.B., having been appointed Chief Justice (or a Judge) of the Supreme Court of India (or Comptroller and Auditor-General of India) do swear in the name of God / solemnly affirm that I will bear true faith and allegiance to the Constitution of India as by law established, [57][that I will uphold the sovereignty and integrity of India,] that I will duly and faithfully and to the best of my ability, knowledge and judgment perform the duties of my office without fear or favour, affection or illwill and that I will uphold the Constitution and the laws."

V

Form of oath of office for a Minister for a State:—

"I, A.B., do swear in the name of God / solemnly affirm that I will bear true faith and allegiance to the Constitution of India as by law established, [58][that I will uphold the sovereignty and integrity of India,] that I will faithfully and conscientiously discharge my duties as a Minister for the State of .... and that I will do right to all manner of people in accordance with the Constitution and the law without fear or favour, affection or illwill."

VI

Form of oath of secrecy for a Minister for a State:—

"I, A.B., do swear in the name of God / solemnly affirm that I will not directly or indirectly communicate or reveal to any person or persons any matter which shall be brought under my consideration or shall become known to me as a Minister for the State of ...., ... except as may be required for the due discharge of my duties as such Minister."

---

[57] Ins. by the Const. (16th Am.) Act, 1963, s. 5, w.e.f. 5.10.1963.
[58] Ins. by s. 5, *ibid.*

[59][VII

A

Form of oath or affirmation to be made by a candidate for election to the Legislature of a State:—

"I, A.B., having been nominated as a candidate to fill a seat in the Legislative Assembly (or Legislative Council), do swear in the name of God / solemnly affirm that I will bear true faith and allegiance to the Constitution of India as by law established and that I will uphold the sovereignty and integrity of India."

B

Form of oath or affirmation to be made by a member of the Legislature of a State:—

"I, A.B., having been elected (or nominated) a member of the Legislative Assembly (or Legislative Council), do swear in the name of God / solemnly affirm that I will bear true faith and allegiance to the Constitution of India as by law established, that I will uphold the sovereignty and integrity of India and that I will faithfully discharge the duty upon which I am about to enter."]

VIII

Form of oath or affirmation to be made by the Judges of a High Court:—

"I, A.B., having been appointed Chief Justice (or a Judge) of the High Court at (or of) .... do swear in the name of God / solemnly affirm that I will bear true faith and allegiance to the Constitution of India as by law established, [60][that I will uphold the sovereignty and integrity of India,] that I will duly and faithfully and to the best of my ability, knowledge and judgment perform the duties of my office without fear or favour, affection or illwill and that I will uphold the Constitution and the laws."

[61][**FOURTH SCHEDULE**

[Articles 4(1) and 80(2)]

Allocation of seats in the Council of States

To each State or Union territory specified in the first column of the following table, there shall be allotted the number of seats specified in the second column thereof opposite to that State or that Union territory, as the case may be.

---

[59] Subs. by s. 5, *ibid.*, for Form VII. The original Form VII was as follows:

"Form of oath or affirmation to be made by a member of the Legislature of a State:—

"I, A.B., having been elected (or nominated) a member of the Legislative Assembly (or Legislative Council), do swear in the name of God / solemnly affirm that I will bear true faith and allegiance to the Constitution of India as by law established and that I will faithfully discharge the duty upon which I am about to enter.'"

[60] Ins. by s. 5, *ibid.*

[61] Subs. by the Const. (7th Am.) Act, 1956, s. 3, w.e.f. 1.11.1956, for the original Fourth Schedule which read as follows:

"FOURTH SCHEDULE

[Articles 4(1), 80(2) and 391]

Allocation of seats in the Council of States

To each State or group of States specified in the first column of the table of seats appended to this Schedule there shall be allotted the number of seats specified

TABLE

1.	Andhra Pradesh	18
2.	Assam	7
3.	Bihar	22
[62][4.	Gujarat	11]
[63][5.	Haryana	5]
[64][6.]	Kerala	9
[64][7.]	Madhya Pradesh	16
[65][8.	Tamil Nadu]	[66][18]
[67][[64] [9.]	Maharashtra	19]
[68][10.	Karnataka]	12
[64][11.]	Orissa	10
[64][12.]	Punjab	[69][7]
[70][13.]	Rajasthan	10
[70][14.]	Uttar Pradesh	34
[70][15.]	West Bengal	16
[70][16.]	Jammu and Kashmir	4
[71][[70] [17.]	Nagaland	1]
[72][18.	Himachal Pradesh	3]

in the second column of the said table opposite to that State or group of States, as the case may be.

TABLE OF SEATS

The Council of States

Representatives of States specified in Part A of the First Schedule

1 *States*	2 *Total Seats*
1. Assam	6
2. Bihar	21
3. Bombay	17
4. Madhya Pradesh	12
5. Madras	27
6. Orissa	9
7. Punjab	8
8. The United Provinces	31
9. West Bengal	14
Total ...	145"

[62] Subs. by the Bombay Reorganisation Act, 1960, s. 6, for "Bombay" w.e.f. 1.5.1960.

[63] Ins. by the Punjab Reorganisation Act, 1966, s. 9, w.e.f. 1.11.1966.

[64] Entries 5 to 21 renumbered as entries 6 to 22 by s. 9, *ibid.*, w.e.f. 1.11.1966.

[65] Subs. by the Madras State (Alteration of Name) Act, 1968, s. 5 for "8. Madras" w.e.f. 14.1.1969.

[66] Subs. by the Andhra Pradesh and Madras (Alteration of Boundaries) Act, 1969, s. 8, for "17", w.e.f. 1.4.1960.

[67] Ins. by the Bombay Reorganisation Act, 1960, s. 6, w.e.f. 1.5.1960.

[68] Subs. by the Mysore State (Alteration of Name) Act, 1973, s. 5, for "10. Mysore" w.e.f. 1.11.1973.

[69] Subs. by the Punjab Reorganisation Act, 1966, s. 9, for "11" w.e.f. 1.11.1966.

[70] Entries 5 to 21 renumbered as entries 6 to 22 by the Punjab Reorganisation Act, 1966, s. 9, w.e.f. 1.11.1966.

[71] Ins. by the State of Nagaland Act, 1962, s. 6, w.e.f. 1.12.1963.

[72] Ins. by the State of Himachal Pradesh Act, 1970, s. 5, w.e.f. 25.1.1971.

[73][19.	Manipur	1
20.	Tripura	1
21.	Meghalaya	1
[74][22.	Sikkim	1]
[75][23.]	Delhi	3
[75][24.]	Pondicherry	1
[75][25.]	Mizoram	1
[75][26.]	Arunachal Pradesh	1]
	Total	[76][232]]

FIFTH SCHEDULE

[Article 244(1)]

Provisions as to the Administration and Control of Scheduled Areas and Scheduled Tribes

PART A

GENERAL

1. *Interpretation.*—In this Schedule, unless the context otherwise requires, the expression "State" [77]* * * does not include the [78][States of Assam and Meghalaya].

2. *Executive power of a State in Scheduled Areas.*—Subject to the provisions of this Schedule, the executive power of a State extends to the Scheduled Areas therein.

3. *Report by the Governor [79]* * * to the President regarding the administration of Scheduled Areas.*— The Governor [79]* * * of each State having Scheduled Areas therein shall annually, or whenever so required by the President, make a report to the President regarding the administration of the Scheduled Areas in that State and the executive power of the Union shall extend to the giving of directions to the State as to the administration of the said areas.

PART B

ADMINISTRATION AND CONTROL OF SCHEDULED AREAS AND SCHEDULED TRIBES

4. *Tribes Advisory Council.*—(1) There shall be established in each State having Scheduled Areas therein and, if the President so directs, also in any State having Scheduled Tribes but not Scheduled Areas therein, a Tribes Advisory Council consisting of not more than twenty members of whom, as nearly as may be, three-fourths shall be the representatives of the Scheduled Tribes in the Legislative Assembly of the State:

Provided that if the number of representatives of the Scheduled Tribes in the Legislative Assembly of the State is less than the number of seats in the Tribes Advisory Council to be filled by such representatives, the remaining seats shall be filled by other members of those tribes.

---

[73] Subs. by the North-Eastern Areas (Reorganisation) Act, 1971, s. 10, for entries 19 to 22, w.e.f. 21.1.1972.

[74] Ins. by the Const. (36th Am.) Act, 1975, s. 4, w.e.f. 26.4.1975.

[75] Entries 22 to 25 renumbered as entries 23 to 26 by s. 4, *ibid.*, w.e.f. 26.4.1975.

[76] Subs. by s. 4, *ibid.*, for "231" w.e.f. 26.4.1975.

[77] The words and letters "means a State specified in Part A or Part B of the First Schedule but" omitted by the Const. (7th Am.) Act, 1956, s. 29 and Sch., w.e.f. 1.11.1956.

[78] Subs. by the North-Eastern Areas (Reorganisation) Act, 1971, s. 71, for "State of Assam" w.e.f. 21.1.1972.

[79] The words "or Rajpramukh" omitted by the Const. (7th Am.) Act, 1956, s. 29 and Sch. w.e.f. 1.11.1956.

(2) It shall be the duty of the Tribes Advisory Council to advise on such matters pertaining to the welfare and advancement of the Scheduled Tribes in the State as may be referred to them by the Governor [80]* * *.

(3) The Governor [81]* * * may make rules prescribing or regulating, as the case may be,—

(*a*) the number of members of the Council, the mode of their appointment and the appointment of the Chairman of the Council and of the officers and servants thereof;

(*b*) the conduct of its meetings and its procedure in general; and

(*c*) all other incidental matters.

5. *Law applicable to Scheduled Areas.*—(1) Notwithstanding anything in this Constitution, the Governor [80]* * *, may by public notification direct that any particular Act of Parliament or of the Legislature of the State shall not apply to a Scheduled Area or any part thereof in the State or shall apply to a Scheduled Area or any part thereof in the State subject to such exceptions and modifications as he may specify in the notification and any direction given under this sub-paragraph may be given so as to have retrospective effect.

(2) The Governor [82]* * * may make regulations for the peace and good government of any area in a State which is for the time being a Scheduled Area.

In particular and without prejudice to the generality of the foregoing power, such regulations may—

(*a*) prohibit or restrict the transfer of land by or among members of the Scheduled Tribes in such area;

(*b*) regulate the allotment of land to members of the Scheduled Tribes in such area;

(*c*) regulate the carrying on of business as moneylender by persons who lend money to members of the Scheduled Tribes in such area.

(3) In making any such regulation as is referred to in sub-paragraph (2) of this paragraph, the Governor [83]* * * may repeal or amend any Act of Parliament or of the Legislature of the State or any existing law which is for the time being applicable to the area in question.

(4) All regulations made under this paragraph shall be submitted forthwith to the President and, until assented to by him, shall have no effect.

(5) No regulation shall be made under this paragraph unless the Governor [84]* * * making the regulation has, in the case where there is a Tribes Advisory Council for the State, consulted such Council.

PART C

SCHEDULED AREAS

6. *Scheduled Areas.*—(1) In this Constitution, the expression "Scheduled Areas" means such areas as the President may by order[85] declare to be Scheduled Areas.

---

[80] The words "or Rajpramukh, as the case may be" omitted by s. 29 and Sch., *ibid.*

[81] The words "or Rajpramukh" omitted by s. 29 and Sch., *ibid.*

[82] The words "or Rajpramukh, as the case may be" omitted by s. 29 and Sch., *ibid.*

[83] The words "or Rajpramukh" omitted by s. 29 and Sch., *ibid.*

[84] The words "or the Rajpramukh" omitted by s. 29 and Sch., *ibid.*

[85] *See* the Scheduled Areas (Part A States) Order, 1950 (C.O. 9), the Scheduled Areas (Part B States) Order, 1950 (C.O. 26), the Scheduled Areas (Himachal Pradesh) Order, 1975 (C.O. 102) and the Scheduled Areas (States of Bihar, Gujarat, Madhya Pradesh and Orissa) Order, 1977 (C.O. 109).

(2) The President may at any time by order[86]—

(*a*) direct that the whole or any specified part of a Scheduled Area shall cease to be a Scheduled Area or a part of such an area;

[87][(*aa*) increase the area of any Scheduled Area in a State after consultation with the Governor of that State;]

(*b*) alter, but only by way of rectification of boundaries, any Scheduled Area;

(*c*) on any alteration of the boundaries of a State or on the admission into the Union or the establishment of a new State, declare any territory not previously included in any State to be, or to form part of, a Scheduled Area;

[87][(*d*) rescind, in relation to any State or States, any order or orders made under this paragraph, and in consultation with the Governor of the State concerned, make fresh orders redefining the areas which are to be Scheduled Areas;]

and any such order may contain such incidental and consequential provisions as appear to the President to be necessary and proper, but save as aforesaid, the order made under sub-paragraph (1) of this paragraph shall not be varied by any subsequent order.

PART D

AMENDMENT OF THE SCHEDULE

7. *Amendment of the Schedule.*—(1) Parliament may from time to time by law amend by way of addition, variation or repeal any of the provisions of this Schedule and, when the Schedule is so amended, any reference to this Schedule in this Constitution shall be construed as a reference to such Schedule as so amended.

(2) No such law as is mentioned in sub-paragraph (1) of this paragraph shall be deemed to be an amendment of this Constitution for the purposes of article 368.

SIXTH SCHEDULE

[Articles 244(2) and 275(1)]

Provisions as to the Administration of Tribal Areas in [88][*the States of Assam and Meghalaya and in the Union territory of Mizoram*]

1. *Autonomous districts and autonomous regions.*—(1) Subject to the provisions of this paragraph, the tribal areas in each item of [88][Parts I and II and in Part III] of the table appended to paragraph 20 of this Schedule shall be an autonomous district.

(2) If there are different Scheduled Tribes in an autonomous district, the Governor may, by public notification, divide the area or areas inhabited by them into autonomous regions.

(3) The Governor may, by public notification,—

(*a*) include any area in [89][any of the Parts] of the said table,

(*b*) exclude any area from [89][any of the Parts] of the said table,

(*c*) create a new autonomous district,

(*d*) increase the area of any autonomous district,

(*e*) diminish the area of any autonomous district,

---

[86] *See* the Madras Scheduled Areas (Cessor) Order, 1950 (C.O. 30) and the Andhra Scheduled Areas (Cessor) Order, 1955 (C.O. 50).

[87] Ins. by the Fifth Schedule to the Constitution (Amendment) Act, 1976 (101 of 1976), s. 2.

[88] Subs. by the North-Eastern Areas (Reorganisation) Act, 1971 (81 of 1971), s. 71(*i*) and Eighth Sch., "Assam" (w.e.f. 21.1.1972).

[89] Subs. by s. 71(*i*) and Eighth Schedule, *ibid.*, for "Part A" (w.e.f. 21.1.1972).

(*f*) unite two or more autonomous districts or parts thereof so as to form one autonomous district,

[90][(*ff*) alter the name of any autonomous district,]

(*g*) define the boundaries of any autonomous district:

Provided that no order shall be made by the Governor under clauses (*c*), (*d*), (*e*) and (*f*) of this sub-paragraph except after consideration of the report of a Commission appointed under sub-paragraph (1) of paragraph 14 of this Schedule:

[91][Provided further that any order made by the Governor under this sub-paragraph may contain such incidental and consequential provisions (including any amendment of paragraph 20 and of any item in any of the Parts of the said table) as appear to the Governor to be necessary for giving effect to the provisions of the order.]

2. *Constitution of District Councils and Regional Councils.*—[92][(1) There shall be a District Council for each autonomous district consisting of not more than thirty members, of whom not more than four persons shall be nominated by the Governor and the rest shall be elected on the basis of adult suffrage.]

(2) There shall be a separate Regional Council for each area constituted an autonomous region under sub-paragraph (2) of paragraph 1 of this Schedule.

(3) Each District Council and each Regional Council shall be a body corporate by the name respectively of "the District Council of (*name of district*)" and "the Regional Council of (*name of region*)", shall have perpetual succession and a common seal and shall by the said name sue and be sued.

(4) Subject to the provisions of this Schedule, the administration of an autonomous district shall, in so far as it is not vested under this Schedule in any Regional Council within such district, be vested in the District Council for such district and the administration of an autonomous region shall be vested in the Regional Council for such region.

(5) In an autonomous district with Regional Councils, the District Council shall have only such powers with respect to the areas under the authority of the Regional Council as may be delegated to it by the Regional Council in addition to the powers conferred on it by this Schedule with respect to such areas.

(6) The Governor shall make rules for the first constitution of District Councils and Regional Councils in consultation with the existing tribal Councils or other representative tribal organisations within the autonomous districts or regions concerned, and such rules shall provide for—

(*a*) the composition of the District Councils and Regional Councils and the allocation of seats therein;

(*b*) the delimitation of territorial constituencies for the purpose of elections to those Councils;

(*c*) the qualifications for voting at such elections and the preparation of electoral rolls therefor;

(*d*) the qualifications for being elected at such elections as members of such Councils;

(*e*) the term of office of members of [93][Regional Councils];

---

[90] Ins. by the Assam Reorganisation (Meghalaya) Act, 1969 (55 of 1969), s. 74 and Fourth Sch. (w.e.f. 2.4.1970).

[91] Ins. by the North-Eastern Areas (Reorganisation) Act, 1971 (81 of 1971), s. 71(*i*) and Eighth Sch. (w.e.f. 21.1.1972).

[92] Subs. by the Assam Reorganisation (Meghalaya) Act, 1969 (55 of 1969), s. 74 and Fourth Sch., for sub-paragraph (1), w.e.f. 2.4.1970, which read as follows:

"(1) There shall be a District Council for each autonomous district consisting of not more than twenty-four members, of whom not less than three-fourths shall be elected on the basis of adult suffrage."

[93] Subs. by the Assam Reorganisation (Meghalaya) Act, 1969 (55 of 1969), s. 74 and Fourth Sch., for "such Councils" (w.e.f. 2.4.1970).

(f) any other matter relating to or connected with elections or nominations to such Councils;

(g) the procedure and the conduct of business [94][(including the power to act notwithstanding any vacancy)] in the District and Regional Councils;

(h) the appointment of officers and staff of the District and Regional Councils.

[94][(6A) The elected members of the District Council shall hold office for a term of five years from the date appointed for the first meeting of the Council after the general elections to the Council, unless the District Council is sooner dissolved under paragraph 16 and a nominated member shall hold office at the pleasure of the Governor:

Provided that the said period of five years may, while a Proclamation of Emergency is in operation or if circumstances exist which, in the opinion of the Governor, render the holding of elections impracticable, be extended by the Governor for a period not exceeding one year at a time and in any case where a Proclamation of Emergency is in operation not extending beyond a period of six months after the Proclamation has ceased to operate:

Provided further that a member elected to fill a casual vacancy shall hold office only for the remainder of the term of office of the member whom he replaces.]

(7) The District or the Regional Council may after its first constitution make rules [95][with the approval of the Governor] with regard to the matters specified in sub-paragraph (6) of this paragraph and may also make rules [95][with like approval] regulating—

(a) the formation of subordinate local Councils or Boards and their procedure and the conduct of their business; and

(b) generally all matters relating to the transaction of business pertaining to the administration of the district or region, as the case may be:

Provided that until rules are made by the District or the Regional Council under this sub-paragraph the rules made by the Governor under sub-paragraph (6) of this paragraph shall have effect in respect of elections to, the officers and staff of, and the procedure and the conduct of business in, each such Council.

[96]* * * * *

3. *Powers of the District Councils and Regional Councils to make laws.*—(1) The Regional Council for an autonomous region in respect of all areas within such region and the District Council for an autonomous district in respect of all areas within the district except those which are under the authority of Regional Councils, if any, within the district shall have power to make laws with respect to—

(a) the allotment, occupation or use, or the setting apart, of land, other than any land which is a reserved forest, for the purposes of agriculture or grazing or for residential or other non-agricultural purposes or for any other purpose likely to promote the interests of the inhabitants of any village or town:

Provided that nothing in such laws shall prevent the compulsory acquisition of any land, whether occupied or unoccupied, for public purposes

---

[94] Ins. by s. 74 and Fourth Sch., *ibid.* (w.e.f. 2.4.1970).

[95] Ins. by the Assam Reorganisation (Meghalaya) Act, 1969 (55 of 1969), s. 74 and Fourth Sch. (w.e.f. 2.4.1970).

[96] Second proviso omitted by s. 74 and Fourth Sch., *ibid.* (w.e.f. 2.4.1970). The original second proviso read as follows:

"Provided further that the Deputy Commissioner or the Sub-Divisional Officer, as the case may be, of the North Cachar and Mikir Hills shall be the Chairman *ex officio* of the District Council in respect of the territories included in items 5 and 6 respectively of Part A of the table appended to paragraph 20 of this Schedule and shall have power for a period of six years after the first constitution of the District Council, subject to the control of the Governor, to annual or modify any resolution or decision of the District Council or to issue such instructions to the District Council, as he may consider appropriate, and the District Council shall comply with every such instruction issued."

[97][by the Government of the State concerned] in accordance with the law for the time being in force authorising such acquisition;

(b) the management of any forest not being a reserved forest;

(c) the use of any canal or water-course for the purpose of agriculture;

(d) the regulation of the practice of *jhum* or other forms of shifting cultivation;

(e) the establishment of village or town committees or councils and their powers;

(f) any other matter relating to village or town administration, including village or town police and public health and sanitation;

(g) the appointment or succession of Chiefs or Headmen;

(h) the inheritance of property;

[98][(i) marriage and divorce;]

(j) social customs.

(2) In this paragraph, a "reserved forest" means any area which is a reserved forest under the Assam Forest Regulation, 1891, or under any other law for the time being in force in the area in question.

(3) All laws made under this paragraph shall be submitted forthwith to the Governor and, until assented to by him, shall have no effect.

4. *Administration of justic in autonomous districts and autonomous regions.*—(1) The Regional Council for an autonomous region in respect of areas within such region and the District Council for an autonomous district in respect of areas within the district other than those which are under the authority of the Regional Councils, if any, within the district may constitute village councils or courts for the trial of suits and cases between the parties all of whom belong to Scheduled Tribes within such areas, other than suits and cases to which the provisions of sub-paragraph (1) of paragraph 5 of this Schedule apply, to the exclusion of any court in the State, and may appoint suitable persons to be members of such village councils or presiding officers of such courts, and may also appoint such officers as may be necessary for the administration of the laws made under paragraph 3 of this Schedule.

(2) Notwithstanding anything in this Constitution, the Regional Council for an autonomous region or any court constituted in that behalf by the Regional Council or, if in respect of any area within an autonomous district there is no Regional Council, the District Council for such district, or any court constituted in that behalf by the District Council, shall exercise the powers of a court of appeal in respect of all suits and cases triable by a village council or court constituted under sub-paragraph (1) of this paragraph within such region or area, as the case may be, other than those to which the provisions of sub-paragraph (1) of paragraph 5 of this Schedule apply, and no other court except the High Court and the Supreme Court shall have jurisdiction over such suits or cases.

(3) The High Court[99]* * * shall have and exercise such jurisdiction over the suits and cases to which the provisions of sub-paragraph (2) of this paragraph apply as the Governor may from time to time by order specify.

(4) A Regional Council or District Council, as the case may be, may with the previous approval of the Governor make rules regulating—

(a) the constitution of village councils and courts and the powers to be exercised by them under this paragraph;

(b) the procedure to be followed by village councils or courts in the trial of suits and cases under sub-paragraph (1) of this paragraph;

---

[97] Subs. by the North-Eastern Areas (Reorganisation) Act, 1971 (81 of 1971), s. 71(*i*) and Eighth Sch., for "by the Government of Assam" (w.e.f. 21.1.1972).

[98] Subs. by the Assam Reorganisation (Meghalaya) Act, 1969 (55 of 1969), s. 74 and Fourth Sch., for cl. (*i*) (w.e.f. 2.4.1970), for "marriage".

[99] The words "of Assam" omitted by the North-Eastern Areas (Reorganisation) Act, 1971 (81 of 1971), s. 71(*i*) and Eighth Sch. (w.e.f. 21.1.1972).

(c) the procedure to be followed by the Regional or District Council or any court constituted by such Council in appeals and other proceedings under sub-paragraph (2) of this paragraph;

(d) the enforcement of decisions and orders of such Councils and courts;

(e) all other ancillary matters for the carrying out of the provisions of sub-paragraphs (1) and (2) of this paragraph.

[1][(5) On and from such date as the President may, [2][after consulting the Government of the State concerned], by notification appoint in this behalf, this paragraph shall have effect in relation to such autonomous district or region as may be specified in the notification, as if—

(i) in sub-paragraph (1), for the words "between the parties all of whom belong to Scheduled Tribes within such areas, other than suits and cases to which the provisions of sub-paragraph (1) of paragraph 5 of this Schedule apply", the words "not being suits and cases of the nature referred to in sub-paragraph (1) of paragraph 5 of this Schedule, which the Governor may specify in this behalf," had been substituted;

(ii) sub-paragraphs (2) and (3) had been omitted;

(iii) in sub-paragraph (4)—

(a) for the words "A Regional Council or District Council, as the case may be, may with the previous approval of the Governor make rules regulating", the words "The Governor may make rules regulating" had been substituted; and

(b) for clause (a), the following clause had been substituted, namely:—

"(a) the constitution of village councils and courts, the powers to be exercised by them under this paragraph and the courts to which appeals from the decisions of village councils and courts shall lie;";

(c) for clause (c), the following clause had been substituted, namely:—

"(c) the transfer of appeals and other proceedings pending before the Regional or District Council or any court constituted by such Council immediately before the date appointed by the President under sub-paragraph (5);"; and

(d) in clause (e), for the words, brackets and figures "sub-paragraphs (1) and (2)", the word, brackets and figure "sub-paragraph (1)" had been substituted.]

5. *Conferment of powers under the Code of Civil Procedure, 1908, and the Code of Criminal Procedure, 1898*[3], *on the Regional and District Councils and on certain courts and officers for the trial of certain suits, cases and offences.*—(1) The Governor may, for the trial of suits or cases arising out of any law in force in any autonomous district or region being a law specified in that behalf by the Governor, or for the trial of offences punishable with death, transportation for life, or imprisonment for a term of not less than five years under the Indian Penal Code or under any other law for the time being applicable to such district or region confer on the District Council or the Regional Council having authority over such district or region or on courts constituted by such District Council or on any officer appointed in that behalf by the Governor, such powers under the Code of Civil Procedure, 1908, or, as the case may be, the Code of Criminal Procedure, 1898,[3] as he deems appropriate, and thereupon the said Council, court or officer shall try the suits, cases or offences in exercise of the powers so conferred.

---

[1] Ins. by the Assam Reorganisation (Meghalaya) Act, 1969 (55 of 1969), s. 74 and Fourth Sch. (w.e.f. 2.4.1970).

[2] Subs. by the North-Eastern Areas (Reorganisation) Act, 1971 (81 of 1971), s. 71(*i*) and Eighth Sch., for certain words (w.e.f. 21.1.1972). The words substituted read as follows: "after consulting the Government of Assam or, as the case may be, the Government of Meghalaya".

[3] *See* now the Code of Criminal Procedure, 1973 (Act 2 of 1974).

(2) The Governor may withdraw or modify any of the powers conferred on a District Council, Regional Council, court or officer under sub-paragraph (1) of this paragraph.

(3) Save as expressly provided in this paragraph, the Code of Civil Procedure, 1908, and the Code of Criminal Procedure, 1898[3] shall not apply to the trial of any suits, cases or offences in an autonomous district or in any autonomous region to which the provisions of this paragraph apply.

[4][(4) On and from the date appointed by the President under sub-paragraph (5) of paragraph 4 in relation to any autonomous district or autonomous region, nothing contained in this paragraph shall, in its application to that district or region, be deemed to authorise the Governor to confer on the District Council or Regional Council or on courts constituted by the District Council any of the powers referred to in sub-paragraph (1) of this paragraph.

[5][**6.** *Powers of the District Council to establish primary schools, etc.*—(1) The District Council for an autonomous district may establish, construct, or manage primary schools, dispensaries, markets, [6][cattle pounds], ferries, fisheries, roads, road transport and waterways in the district and may, with the previous approval of the Governor, make regulations for the regulation and control thereof and, in particular, may prescribe the language and the manner in which primary education shall be imparted in the primary schools in the district.

(2) The Governor may, with the consent of any District Council, entrust either conditionally or unconditionally to that Council or to its officers functions in relation of agriculture, animal husbandry, community projects, co-operative societies, social welfare, village planning or any other matter to which the executive power of the State [7]* * * extends.]

7. *District and Regional Funds.*—(1) There shall be constituted for each autonomous district, a District Fund and for each autonomous region, a Regional Fund to which shall be credited all moneys received respectively by the District Council for that district and the Regional Council for that region in the course of the administration of such district or region, as the case may be, in accordance with the provisions of this Constitution.

[8][(2) The Governor may make rules for the management of the District Fund, or, as the case may be, the Regional Fund and for the procedure to be followed in respect of payment of money into the said Fund, the withdrawal of moneys therefrom, the custody of moneys therein and any other matter connected with or ancillary to the matters aforesaid.

---

[4] Ins. by the Assam Reorganisation (Meghalaya) Act, 1969 (55 of 1969), s. 74 and Fourth Sch. (w.e.f. 2.4.1970).

[5] Subs. by *ibid.*, for paragraph 6. The original para 6 read as follows:

"(6) The District Council for an autonomous district may establish, construct, or manage primary schools, dispensaries, market, cattle pounds, ferries, fisheries, roads and waterways in the district and, in particular, may prescribe the language and the manner in which primary education shall be imparted in the primary schools in the district."

[6] Subs. by the Repealing and Amending Act, 1974 (56 of 1974), s. 4, for "cattle ponds".

[7] The words "of Assam or Meghalaya, as the case may be," omitted by the North-Eastern Areas (Reorganisation) Act, 1971 (81 of 1971), s. 71(*i*) and Eighth Sch., w.e.f. 21.1.1972.

[8] Subs. by the Assam Reorganisation (Meghalaya) Act, 1969 (55 of 1969), s. 74 and Fourth Sch., for sub-paragraph (2) w.e.f. 2.4.1970. The original sub-paragraph (2) read as follows:

"(2) Subject to the approval of the Governor, rules may be made by the District Council and by the Regional Council for the management of the District Fund or, as the case may be, the Regional Fund, and the rules so made may prescribe the procedure to be followed in respect of payment of money into the said Fund, the withdrawal of moneys therefrom, the custody of moneys therein and any other matter connected with or ancillary to the matters aforesaid."

(3) The accounts of the District Council or, as the case may be, the Regional Council shall be kept in such form as the Comptroller and Auditor-General of India may, with the approval of the President, prescribe.

(4) The Comptroller and Auditor-General shall cause the accounts of the District and Regional Councils to be audited in such manner as he may think fit, and the reports of the Comptroller and Auditor-General relating to such accounts shall be submitted to the Governor who shall cause them to be laid before the Council.]

8. *Powers to assess and collect land revenue and to impose taxes.*—(1) The Regional Council for an autonomous region in respect of all lands within such region and the District Council for an autonomous district in respect of all lands within the district except those which are in the areas under the authority of Regional Councils, if any, within the district, shall have the power to assess and collect revenue in respect of such lands in accordance with the principles for the time being followed [9][by the Government of the State in assessing lands for the purpose of land revenue in the State generally].

(2) The Regional Council for an autonomous region in respect of areas within such region and the District Council for an autonomous district in respect of all areas in the district except those which are under the authority of Regional Councils, if any, within the district, shall have power to levy and collect taxes on lands and buildings, and tolls on persons resident within such areas.

(3) The District Council for an autonomous district shall have the power to levy and collect all or any of the following taxes within such district, that is to say—

(*a*) taxes on professions, trades, callings and employments;
(*b*) taxes on animals, vehicles and boats;
(*c*) taxes on the entry of goods into a market for sale therein, and tolls on passengers and goods carried in ferries; and
(*d*) taxes for the maintenance of schools, dispensaries or roads.

(4) A Regional Council or District Council, as the case may be, may make regulations to provide for the levy and collection of any of the taxes specified in sub-paragraphs (2) and (3) of this paragraph [10][and every such regulation shall be submitted forthwith to the Governor and, until assented to by him, shall have no effect].

9. *Licences or leases for the purpose of prospecting for, or extraction of, minerals.*—(1) Such share of the royalties accruing each year from licences or leases for the purpose of prospecting for, or the extraction of, minerals granted by [11][the Government of the State] in respect of any area within an autonomous district as may be agreed upon between [11][the Government of the State] and the District Council of such district shall be made over to that District Council.

(2) If any dispute arises as to the share of such royalties to be made over to a District Council, it shall be referred to the Governor for determination and the amount determined by the Governor in his discretion shall be deemed to be the amount payable under sub-paragraph (1) of this paragraph to the District Council and the decision of the Governor shall be final.

10. *Power of District Council to make regulations for the control of money-lending and trading by non-tribals.*—(1) The District Council of an autonomous district may make regulations for the regulation and control of money-lending or trading within the district, by persons other than Scheduled Tribes resident in the district.

---

[9] Subs. by the North-Eastern Areas (Reorganisation) Act, 1971 (81 of 1971), s. 71(*i*) and Eighth Sch., for certain words (w.e.f. 21.1.1972). The substituted words read: "the Government of Assam in assessing lands for the purpose of land revenue in the State of Assam generally".

[10] Ins. by the Assam Reorganisation (Meghalaya) Act, 1969 (55 of 1969), s. 74 and Fourth Sch. (w.e.f. 2.4.1970).

[11] Subs. by the North-Eastern Areas (Reorganisation) Act, 1971 (81 of 1971), s. 71(*i*) and Eighth Sch., for "the Government of Assam" (w.e.f. 21.1.1972).

(2) In particular and without prejudice to the generality of the foregoing power, such regulations may—

(*a*) prescribe that no one except the holder of a licence issued in that behalf shall carry on the business of money-lending;

(*b*) prescribe the maximum rate of interest which may be charged or be recovered by a money-lender;

(*c*) provide for the maintenance of accounts by money-lenders and for the inspection of such accounts by officers appointed in that behalf by the District Council;

(*d*) prescribe that no person who is not a member of the Scheduled Tribes resident in the district shall carry on whole-sale or retail business in any commodity except under a licence issued in that behalf by the District Council:

Provided that no regulations may be made under this paragraph unless they are passed by a majority of not less than three-fourths of the total membership of the District Council:

Provided further that it shall not be competent under any such regulations to refuse the grant of a licence to a money-lender or a trader who has been carrying on business within the district since before the time of the making of such regulations.

(3) All regulations made under this paragraph shall be submitted forthwith to the Governor and, until assented to by him, shall have no effect.

11. *Publication of laws, rules and regulations made under the Schedule.*—All laws, rules and regulations made under this Schedule by a District Council or a Regional Council shall be published forthwith in the Official Gazette of the State and shall on such publication have the force of law.

12. [12][*Application of Acts of Parliament and of the Legislature of the State of Assam to autonomous districts and autonomous regions in the State of Assam.*]—(1) Notwithstanding anything in this Constitution—

(*a*) no Act of the [13][Legislature of the State of Assam] in respect of any of the matters specified in paragraph 3 of this Schedule as matters with respect to which a District Council or a Regional Council may make laws, and no Act of the [13][Legislature of the State of Assam] prohibiting or restricting the consumption of any non-distilled alcoholic liquor shall apply to any autonomous district or autonomous region [14][in that State] unless in either case the District Council for such district or having jurisdiction over such region by public notification so directs, and the District Council in giving such direction with respect to any Act may direct that the Act shall in its application to such district or region or any part thereof have effect subject to such exceptions or modifications as it thinks fit;

(*b*) the Governor may, by public notification, direct that any Act of Parliament or of the [13][Legislature of the State of Assam] to which the provisions of clause (*a*) of this sub-paragraph do not apply shall not apply to an autonomous district or an autonomous region [14][in that State], or shall apply to such district or region or any part thereof subject to such exceptions or modifications as he may specify in the notification.

(2) Any direction given under sub-paragraph (1) of this paragraph may be given so as to have retrospective effect.

---

[12] Subs. by the North-Eastern Areas (Reorganisation) Act, 1971 (81 of 1971), s. 71(*i*) and Eighth Sch., for the heading (w.e.f. 21.1.1972). The original heading was as follows: *"Application of Acts of Parliament and of the Legislature of the State to autonomous districts and autonomous regions."*

[13] Subs. by *ibid.*, for "Legislature of the State", w.e.f. 21.1.1972.

[14] Ins. by s. 71(1) and Eighth Sch., *ibid.*, w.e.f. 21.1.1972.

[15][12A. *Application of Acts of Parliament and of the Legislature of the State of Meghalaya to autonomous districts and autonomous regions in the State of Meghalaya.*—Notwithstanding anything in this Constitution,—

(*a*) if any provision of a law made by a District or Regional Council in the State of Meghalaya with respect to any matter specified in sub-paragraph (1) of paragraph 3 of this Schedule or if any provision of any regulation made by a District Council or a Regional Council in that State under paragraph 8 or paragraph 10 of this Schedule, is repugnant to any provision of a law made by the Legislature of the State of Meghalaya with respect to that matter, then, the law or regulation made by the District Council or, as the case may be, the Regional Council whether made before or after the law made by the Legislature of the State of Meghalaya, shall, to the extent of repugnancy, be void and the law made by the Legislature of the State of Meghalaya shall prevail;

(*b*) the President may, with respect to any Act of Parliament, by notification, direct that it shall not apply to an autonomous district or an autonomous region in the State of Meghalaya, or shall apply to such district or region

---

[15] Subs. by s. 71(*i*) and Eighth Sch., *ibid.*, for paragraph 12A w.e.f. 21.1.1972. The former paragraph 12A, which had been inserted by the Assam Reorganisation (Meghalaya) Act, 1969, w.e.f. 2.4.1970, read as follows:

"12A. *Special provisions as respects application of laws in Meghalaya.*—(1) Notwithstanding anything contained in paragraph 12: (*a*) if any provision of a law made by a District or Regional Council in Meghalaya with respect to any of the matters specified in clause (*b*) or clause (*c*) of sub-paragraph (1) of paragraph 3 of this Schedule is repugnant to any provision of a law made by the Legislature of the State of Assam with respect to any project declared by the Legislature of that State to be of State importance, then, the law made by the District Council or, as the case may be, the Regional Council, whether made before or after the law made by the Legislature of the State of Assam, shall, to the extent of the repugnancy, be void and the law made by the Legislature of the State of Assam shall prevail; (*b*) if any provision of a law made by a District or Regional Council in Meghalaya with respect to any of the matters specified in clause (*b*) or clause (*c*) or clause (*f*) of sub-paragraph (1) of paragraph 3 of this Schedule is repugnant to any provision of a law made by the Legislature of Meghalaya with respect to that matter, then, the law made by the District Council or, as the case may be, the Regional Council, whether made before or after the law made by the legislature of Meghalaya shall, to the extent of repugnancy, be void and the law made by the Legislature of Meghalaya shall prevail.

(2) If it appears to two or more District Councils or Regional Councils in Meghalaya to be desirable that any of the matters with respect to which they have power to make laws under paragraph 3 of this Schedule should be regulated by the Legislature of Meghalaya by law, and if resolutions to that effect are passed by the said District Councils or Regional Councils, it shall be lawful for the Legislature of Meghalaya to pass an Act regulating that matter accordingly, and any Act so passed shall apply to the autonomous districts or regions concerned, and to any other autonomous district or region the District or Regional Council whereof adopts it afterwards by resolution passed in this behalf.

(3) Any Act passed by the Legislature of Meghalaya under sub-paragraph (2) of this paragraph may be amended or repealed by an Act of the Legislature of Meghalaya passed in like manner, but shall not, as regards any autonomous district or region to which it applies, be amended or repealed by any law made by the District or Regional Council thereof.

(4) The Governor may, with respect to any Act of the Legislature of the State of Assam, and the President may, with respect to any Act of Parliament, by public notification direct, that it shall not apply to Meghalaya, or shall apply thereto, or to any part thereof subject to such exceptions or modifications as he may specify in the notification, and any such direction may be so given as to have retrospective effect.

(5) The provisions of clause (*b*) of sub-paragraph (1) of paragraph 12 shall not apply to Meghalaya."

or any part thereof subject to such exceptions or modifications as he may specify in the notification and any such direction may be given so as to have retrospective effect.

[16][**12B.** *Application of Acts of Parliament and of the Legislature of the Union territory of Mizoram to autonomous districts and autonomous regions in the Union territory of Mizoram.*—Notwithstanding anything in this Constitution,—

(*a*) if any provision of a law made by a District Council or a Regional Council in the Union territory of Mizoram with respect to any matter specified in sub-paragraph (1) of paragraph 3 of this Schedule or if any provision of any regulation made by a District Council or a Regional Council in that Union territory under paragraph 8 or paragraph 10 of this Schedule, is repugnant to any provision of a law made by the Legislature of the Union territory of Mizoram with respect to that matter, then, the law or regulation made by the District Council or, as the case may be, the Regional Council, whether made before or after the law made by the Legislature of the Union territory of Mizoram, shall, to the extent of repugnancy, be void and the law made by the Legislature of the Union territory of Mizoram shall prevail;

(*b*) the President may with respect to any Act of Parliament, by notification, direct that it shall not apply to an autonomous district or an autonomous region in the Union territory of Mizoram, or shall apply to such district or region or any part thereof subject to such exceptions or modifications as he may specify in the notification and any such direction may be given so as to have retrospective effect.]

13. *Estimated receipts and expenditure pertaining to autonomous districts to be shown separately in the annual financial statement.*—The estimated receipts and expenditure pertaining to an autonomous district which are to be credited to, or is to be made from, the Consolidated Fund of the State [17]* * * shall be first placed before the District Council for discussion and then after such discussion be shown separately in the annual financial statement of the State to be laid before the Legislature of the State under article 202.

14. *Appointment of Commission to inquire into and report on the administration of autonomous districts and autonomous regions.*—(1) The Governor may at any time appoint a Commission to examine and report on any matter specified by him relating to the administration of the autonomous districts and autonomous regions in the State, including matters specified in clauses (*c*), (*d*), (*e*) and (*f*) of sub-paragraph (3) of paragraph 1 of this Schedule, or may appoint a Commission to inquire into and report from time to time on the administration of autonomous districts and autonomous regions in the State generally and in particular on—

(*a*) the provision of educational and medical facilities and communications in such districts and regions;

(*b*) the need for any new or special legislation in respect of such districts and regions; and

---

[16] Subs. by the Government of Union Territories (Amendment) Act, 1971 (83 of 1971), s. 13, for paragraph 12B (w.e.f. 29.4.1972). The former paragraph 12B, which had been inserted by the North-Eastern Areas (Reorganisation) Act, 1971, w.e.f. 21.1.1972, read as follows:

"12B. *Application of Acts of Parliament and other Acts to autonomous districts and autonomous regions in the Union territory of Mizoram.*—Notwithstanding anything in this Constitution, the President may with respect to any Act of Parliament and the Administrator may with respect to any other Act, by notification, direct that it shall not apply to an autonomous district or an autonomous region in the Union territory of Mizoram or shall apply to such district or region or any part thereof subject to such exceptions or modifications as he may specify in the notification and any such direction may be given so as to have retrospective effect."

[17] The words "of Assam" omitted by the North-Eastern Areas (Reorganisation) Act, 1971 (81 of 1971), s. 71(*i*) and Eighth Sch. (w.e.f. 21.1.1972).

(c) the administration of the laws, rules and regulations made by the District and Regional Councils;

and define the procedure to be followed by such Commission.

(2) The report of every such Commission with the recommendations of the Governor with respect thereto shall be laid before the Legislature of the State by the Minister concerned together with an explanatory memorandum regarding the action proposed to be taken thereon by [18][the Government of the State].

(3) In allocating the business of the Government of the State among his Ministers the Governor may place one of his Ministers specially in charge of the welfare of the autonomous districts and autonomous regions in the State.

15. *Annulment or suspension of acts and resolutions of District and Regional Councils.*—(1) If at any time the Governor is satisfied that an act or resolution of a District or a Regional Council is likely to endanger the safety of India [19][or is likely to be prejudicial to public order], he may annual or suspend such act or resolution and take such steps as he may consider necessary (including the suspension of the Council and the assumption to himself of all or any of the powers vested in or exercisable by the Council) to prevent the commission or continuance of such act, or the giving of effect to such resolution.

(2) Any order made by the Governor under sub-paragraph (1) of this paragraph together with the reasons therefor shall be laid before the Legislature of the State as soon as possible and the order shall, unless revoked by the Legislature of the State, continue in force for a period of twelve months from the date on which it was so made:

Provided that if and so often as a resolution approving the continuance in force of such order is passed by the Legislature of the State, the order shall unless cancelled by the Governor continue in force for a further period of twelve months from the date on which under this paragraph it would otherwise have ceased to operate.

16. *Dissolution of a District or a Regional Council.*—[20][(1)] The Governor may on the recommendation of a Commission appointed under paragraph 14 of this Schedule by public notification order the dissolution of a District or a Regional Council, and—

(a) direct that a fresh general election shall be held immediately for the reconstitution of the Council, or

(b) subject to the previous approval of the Legislature of the State assume the administration of the area under the authority of such Council himself or place the administration of such area under the Commission appointed under the said paragraph or any other body considered suitable by him for a period not exceeding twelve months:

Provided that when an order under clause (a) of this paragraph has been made, the Governor may take the action referred to in clause (b) of this paragraph with regard to the administration of the area in question pending the reconstitution of the Council on fresh general election:

Provided further that no action shall be taken under clause (b) of this paragraph without giving the District or the Regional Council, as the case may be, an opportunity of placing its views before the Legislature of the State.

[21][(2) If at any time the Governor is satisfied that a situation has arisen in which the administration of an autonomous district or region cannot be carried on

---

[18] Subs. by the North-Eastern Areas (Reorganisation) Act, 1971 (81 of 1971), s. 71(*i*) and Eighth Sch., for "the Government of Assam" (w.e.f. 21.1.1972).

[19] Ins. by the Assam Reorganisation (Meghalaya) Act, 1969 (55 of 1969), s. 74 and Fourth Sch. (w.e.f. 2.4.1970).

[20] Paragraph 16 renumbered as sub-paragraph (1) thereof by the Assam Reorganisation (Meghalaya) Act, 1969 (55 of 1969), s. 74 and Fourth Sch. (w.e.f. 2.4.1970).

[21] Ins. by s. 74 and Fourth Sch., *ibid* (w.e.f. 2.4.1970).

in accordance with the provisions of this Schedule, he may, by public notification, assume to himself all or any of the functions or powers vested in or exercisable by the District Council or, as the case may be, the Regional Council and declare that such functions or powers shall be exercisable by such person or authority as he may specify in this behalf, for a period not exceeding six months:

Provided that the Governor may by a further order or orders extend the operation of the initial order by a period not exceeding six months on each occasion.

(3) Every order made under sub-paragraph (2) of this paragraph with the reasons therefor shall be laid before the Legislature of the State and shall cease to operate at the expiration of thirty days from the date on which the State Legislature first sits after the issue of the order, unless, before the expiry of that period it has been approved by the State Legislature.]

17. *Exclusion of areas from autonomous districts in forming constituencies in such districts.*—For the purposes of elections to [22][the Legislative Assembly of Assam or Meghalaya], the Governor may by order declare that any area within an autonomous district [23][in the State of Assam of Meghalaya, as the case may be,] shall not form part of any constituency to fill a seat or seats in the Assembly reserved for any such district but shall form part of a constituency to fill a seat or seats in the Assembly not so reserved to be specified in the order.

[24]* * * * *

19. *Transitional provisions.*—(1) As soon as possible after the commencement of this Constitution the Governor shall take steps for the constitution of a District Council for each autonomous district in the State under this Schedule and, until a District Council is so constituted for an autonomous district, the administration of such district shall be vested in the Governor and the following provisions shall apply to the administration of the areas within such district instead of the foregoing provisions of this Schedule, namely:—

(*a*) no Act of Parliament or of the Legislature of the State shall apply to any such area unless the Governor by public notification so directs; and the Governor in giving such a direction with respect to any Act may direct that the Act shall, in its application to the area or to any specified part thereof, have effect subject to such exceptions or modifications as he thinks fit;

(*b*) the Governor may make regulations for the peace and good government of any such area and any regulations so made may repeal or amend any

---

[22] Subs. by the North-Eastern Areas (Reorganisation) Act, 1971 (81 of 1971), s. 71(*i*) and Eighth Sch., for "the Legislative Assembly of Assam" (w.e.f. 21.1.1972).

[23] Ins. by s. 71(*i*) and Eighth Sch., *ibid.* (w.e.f. 21.1.1972).

[24] Paragraph 18 omitted by s. 71(*i*) and Eighth Sch., *ibid.* (w.e.f. 21.1.1972). Paragraph 18, as originally enacted, read as follows:

"18. *Application of the provisions of this Schedule to areas specified in Part B of the table appended to paragraph 20.*—(1) The Governor may—

(*a*) subject to the previous approval of the President, by public notification, apply all or any of the foregoing provisions of this Schedule to any tribal area specified in Part B of the table appended to paragraph 20 of this Schedule or any part of such area and thereupon such area or part shall be administered in accordance with such provisions, and

(*b*) with like approval, by public notification, exclude from the said table any tribal area specified in Part B of that table or any part of such area.

(2) Until a notification is issued under sub-paragraph (1) of this paragraph in respect of any tribal area specified in Part B of the said table or any part of such area, the administration of such area or part thereof, as the case may be, shall be carried on by the President through the Governor of Assam as his agent and the provisions of *article 240* shall apply thereto as if such area or part thereof were *a Union territory specified in that article*. [The italicised words were substituted, respectively, for "Part IX", and "territory specified in Part D of the First Schedule" by the Const. (7th Am.) Act, 1956, w.e.f. 1.11.1956.]

(3) In the discharge of his functions under sub-paragraph (2) of this paragraph as the agent of the President the Governor shall act in his discretion."

Act of Parliament or of the Legislature of the State or any existing law which is for the time being applicable to such area.

(2) Any direction given by the Governor under clause (*a*) of sub-paragraph (1) of this paragraph may be given so as to have retrospective effect.

(3) All regulations made under clause (*b*) of sub-paragraph (1) of this paragraph shall be submitted forthwith to the President and, until assented to by him, shall have no effect.

[25][**20.** *Tribal areas.*—(1) The areas specified in Parts I, II and III of the table below shall respectively be the tribal areas within the State of Assam, the State of Meghalaya and the Union territory of Mizoram.

(2) Any reference in the table below to any district shall be construed as a reference to the territories comprised within the autonomous district of that name

---

[25] Subs. by the North-Eastern Areas (Reorganisation) Act, 1971 (81 of 1971) s. 71(*i*) and Eighth Sch. for para 20 w.e.f. 21.1.1972. The original paragraph 20 read as follows:

"20. *Tribal areas.*—(1) The areas specified in Parts A and B of the table below shall be the tribal areas within the State of Assam.

(2) The United Khasi-Jaintia Hills District shall comprise the territories which before the commencement of this Constitution were known as the Khasi States and the Khasi and Jaintia Hills District, excluding any areas for the time being comprised, within the cantonment and municipality of Shillong, but including so much of the area comprised within the municipality of Shillong as formed part of the Khasi State of Mylliem:

Provided that for the purposes of clauses (*e*) and (*f*) of sub-paragraph (2), clauses (*a*), (*b*) and (*d*) of sub-paragraph (3) and sub-paragraph (4) of paragraph 8, and clause (*d*) of sub-paragraph (2) of paragraph 10 of this Schedule, no part of the area comprised within the municipality of Shillong shall be deemed to be within the District.

(2A) The Mizo District shall comprise the area which at the commencement of this Constitution was known as the Lushai Hills District. [This sub-paragraph was inserted by the Lushai Hills District (Change of Name) Act, 1954].

[Sub-paragraph 2-B which had been inserted by the Naga Hills-Tuensang Area Act, 1957, w.e.f. 1.12.1957 read as follows before it was deleted by the State of Nagaland Act, 1962, w.e.f. 1.12.1963: 2-B. The Naga Hills-Tuensang Area shall comprise the areas which at the commencement of this Constitution were known as the Naga Hills District and the Naga Tribal Area.]

(3) Any reference in the table below to any district (other than the United Khasi-Jaintia Hills District *and the Mizo District*) or administrative area [other than the Naga Hills-Tuensang Area] shall be construed as a reference to that district or area at the commencement of this Constitution:

Provided that the tribal areas specified in Part B of the table below shall not include any such areas in the plains as may, with the previous approval of the President, be notified by the Governor of Assam in that behalf. [The words in *italics* introduced by the Lushai Hills District (Change of Name) Act, 1954. The words in square brackets inserted by the Naga Hills-Tuensang Area Act, 1957, w.e.f. 1.12.1957, but deleted by the State of Nagaland Act, 1962, w.e.f. 1.12.1963.]

TABLE

PART A

1. The United Khasi-Jaintia Hills District.
2. The Garo Hills District.
3. The Mizo District [sub. for "Lushai Hills District" by the Lushai Hills District (Change of Name) Act, 1954.]
4. [The original item 4, "The Naga Hills District" was deleted by the Naga Hills-Tuensang Area Act, 1957, w.e.f. 1.12.1957.]
5. The North Cachar Hills.
6. The Mikir Hills.

PART B

1. North East Frontier Tract including Balipara Frontier Tract, Tirap Frontier Tract, Abor Hills District and Misimi Hills District.
2. . . . [The original item 2, "The Naga Tribal Area" was sub. by "The Naga Hills-Tuensang Area" by the Naga Hills-Tuensang Area Act, 1957, w.e.f. 1.12.1957, and the item was deleted by the State of Nagaland Act, 1962, w.e.f. 1.12.1963.]"

existing immediately before the day appointed under clause (*b*) of section 2 of the North-Eastern Areas (Reorganisation) Act, 1971:

Provided that for the purposes of clauses (*e*) and (*f*) of sub-paragraph (1) of paragraph 3, paragraph 4, paragraph 5, paragraph 6, sub-paragraph (2), clauses (*a*), (*b*) and (*d*) of sub-paragraph (3) and sub-paragraph (4) of paragraph 8 and clause (*d*) of sub-paragraph (2) of paragraph 10 of this Schedule, no part of the area comprised within the municipality of Shillong shall be deemed to be within the [26][Khasi Hills District].

TABLE

PART I

1. The North Cachar Hills District.
2. The Mikir Hills District.

PART II

[26][1. Khasi Hills District.
2. Jaintia Hills District.]
3. The Garo Hills District.

PART III

[27]* * * * *

[28][1. The Chakma District.
2. The Lakher District.
3. The Pawi District.]]

[29][**20A.** *Dissolution of the Mizo District Council.*—(1) Notwithstanding anything in this Schedule, the District Council of the Mizo District existing immediately before the prescribed date (hereinafter referred to as the Mizo District Council) shall stand dissolved and cease to exist.

(2) The Administrator of the Union territory of Mizoram may, by one or more orders, provide for all or any of the following matters, namely:—

(*a*) the transfer, in whole or in part, of the assets, rights and liabilities of the Mizo District Council (including the rights and liabilities under any contract made by it) to the Union or to any other authority;

---

[26] Subs. by the Government of Meghalaya Notification No. DCA 31/72/11, dated the 14th June, 1973, Gazette of Meghalaya, Pt. VA, dated 23-6-1973, p. 200.

[27] The words "The Mizo District" omitted by the Government of Union Territories (Amendment) Act, 1971 (83 of 1971), s. 13 (w.e.f. 29.4.1972).

[28] Ins. by the Mizoram District Councils (Miscellaneous Provisions) Order, 1972, published in the Mizoram Gazette, 1972, dated the 5th May 1972, Vol. I, Pt. II, p. 17 (w.e.f. 29.4.1972).

[29] Subs. by the Government of Union Territories (Amendment) Act, 1971 (83 of 1971), s. 13, for paragraph 20A (w.e.f. 29.4.1972). The original paragraph 20A which had been inserted by the Assam Re-organisation (Meghalaya) Act, 1969, w.e.f. 2.4.1970 read as follows:

"20A. *Interpretation.*—(1) In this Schedule,—

(*a*) 'Governor' in relation to Meghalaya, means the Governor of Assam acting in the aid and advice of the Council of Ministers for Meghalaya, except in so far as he is by or under this Schedule required to exercise his functions in his discretion or to exercise his powers under sub-paragraph (4) of paragraph 12A.

(2) Subject to any express provision made in this behalf, the provisions of this Schedule shall, in their application to Meghalaya, have effect—

(*i*) as if references to the Government of Assam, State of Assam, State and Legislature of the State were references respectively to the Government of Meghalaya, the autonomous State of Meghalaya, Meghalaya and the Legislature of Meghalaya;

(*ii*) as if in paragraph 13, the words and figures 'under article 202' had been omitted."

(*b*) the substitution of the Union or any other authority for the Mizo District Council, or the addition of the Union or any other authority, as a party to any legal proceedings to which the Mizo District Council is a party;

(*c*) the transfer or re-employment of any employees of the Mizo District Council to or by the Union or any other authority, the terms and conditions of service applicable to such employees after such transfer or re-employment;

(*d*) the continuance of any laws, made by the Mizo District Council and in force immediately before its dissolution, subject to such adaptations and modifications, whether by way of repeal or amendment, as the Administrator may make in this behalf, until such laws are altered, repealed or amended by a competent Legislature or other competent authority;

(*e*) such incidental, consequential and supplementary matters as the Administrator considers necessary.

Explanation.—In this paragraph and in paragraph 20B of this Schedule, the expression "prescribed date" means the date on which the Legislative Assembly of the Union territory of Mizoram is duly constituted under and in accordance with the provisions of the Government of Union Territories Act, 1963.

20B. *Autonomous regions in the Union territory of Mizoram to be autonomous districts and transitory provisions consequent thereto.*—(1) Notwithstanding anything in this Schedule,—

(*a*) every autonomous region existing immediately before the prescribed date in the Union territory of Mizoram shall, on and from that date, be an autonomous district in that Union territory (hereafter referred to as the corresponding new district) and the Administrator thereof may, by one or more orders, direct that such consequential amendments as are necessary to give effect to the provisions of this clause shall be made in paragraph 20 of this Schedule (including Part III of the table appended to that paragraph) and thereupon the said paragraph and the said Part III shall be deemed to have been amended accordingly;

(*b*) every Regional Council of an autonomous region in the Union territory of Mizoram existing immediately before the prescribed date (hereafter referred to as the existing Regional Council) shall, on and from that date and until a District Council is duly constituted for the corresponding new district, be deemed to be the District Council of that district (hereafter referred to as the corresponding new District Council).

(2) Every member whether elected or nominated of an existing Regional Council shall be deemed to have been elected or, as the case may be, nominated to the corresponding new District Council and shall hold office until a District Council is duly constituted for the corresponding new district under this Schedule.

(3) Until rules are made under sub-paragraph (7) of paragraph 2 and sub-paragraph (4) of paragraph 4 of this Schedule by the corresponding new District Council, the rules made under the said provisions by the existing Regional Council and in force immediately before the prescribed date shall have effect in relation to the corresponding new District Council subject to such adaptations and modifications as may be made therein by the Administrator of the Union territory of Mizoram.

(4) The Administrator of the Union territory of Mizoram may, by one or more orders, provide for all or any of the following matters, namely:—

(*a*) the transfer in whole or in part of the assets, rights and liabilities of the existing Regional Council (including the rights and liabilities under any contract made by it) to the corresponding new District Council;

(*b*) the substitution of the corresponding new District Council for the existing Regional Council as a party to the legal proceedings to which the existing Regional Council is a party;

(*c*) the transfer or re-employment of any employees of the existing Regional Council to or by the corresponding new District Council, the terms and conditions of service applicable to such employees after such transfer or re-employment;

(*d*) the continuance of any laws made by the existing Regional Council and in force immediately before the prescribed date, subject to such adaptations and modifications, whether by way of repeal or amendment, as the Administrator may make in this behalf until such laws are altered, repealed or amended by a competent Legislature or other competent authority;

(*e*) such incidental, consequential and supplementary matters as the Administrator considers necessary.

20C. *Interpretation.*—Subject to any provision made in this behalf, the provisions of this Schedule shall, in their application to the Union territory of Mizoram, have effect—

(1) as if references to the Governor and Government of the State were references to the Administrator of the Union territory appointed under article 239, references to State (except in the expression "Government of the State") where references to the Union territory of Mizoram and references to the State Legislature were references to the Legislative Assembly of the Union territory of Mizoram;

(2) as if—

(*a*) in sub-paragraph (5) of paragraph 4, the provision for consultation with the Government of the State concerned had been omitted;

(*b*) in sub-paragraph (2) of paragraph 6, for the words "to which the executive power of the State extends", the words "with respect to which the Legislative Assembly of the Union territory of Mizoram has power to make laws" had been substituted;

(*c*) in paragraph 13, the words and figures "under article 202" had been omitted.]

21. *Amendment of the Schedule.*—(1) Parliament may from time to time by law amend by way of addition, variation or repeal any of the provisions of this Schedule and, when the Schedule is so amended, any reference to this Schedule in this Constitution shall be construed as a reference to such Schedule as so amended.

(2) No such law as is mentioned in sub-paragraph (1) of this paragraph shall be deemed to be an amendment of this Constitution for the purposes of article 368.

SEVENTH SCHEDULE

[Article 246]

List I — Union List

1. Defence of India and every part thereof including preparation for defence and all such acts as may be conducive in times of war to its prosecution and after its termination to effective demobilisation.

2. Naval, military and air forces; any other armed forces of the Union. [I, 1, G.I. Act]

[30][2A. Deployment of any armed force of the Union or any other force subject to the control of the Union or any contingent or unit thereof in any State in aid of the civil power; powers, jurisdiction, privileges and liabilities of the members of such forces while on such deployment.]

3. Delimitation of cantonment areas, local self-government in such areas, the constitution and powers within such areas of cantonment authorities and the regulation of house accommodation (including the control of rents) in such areas. [I, 2, G.I. Act]

4. Naval, military and air force works. [I, 2, G.I. Act]

5. Arms, firearms, ammunition and explosives. [I, 29, 30, G.I. Act]

6. Atomic energy and mineral resources necessary for its production.

---

[30] Ins. by the Const. (42nd Am.) Act, 1976, s. 57 (w.e.f. 3.1.1977).

7. Industries declared by Parliament by law to be necessary for the purpose of defence or for the prosecution of war.

8. Central Bureau of Intelligence and Investigation. [I, 1, G.I. Act]

9. Preventive detention for reasons connected with Defence, Foreign Affairs, or the security of India; persons subjected to such detention. [I, 1, G.I. Act]

10. Foreign affairs; all matters which bring the Union into relation with any foreign country.

11. Diplomatic, consular and trade representation.

12. United Nations Organisation.

13. Participation in international conferences, associations and other bodies and implementing of decisions made thereat. [I, 3, G.I. Act]

14. Entering into treaties and agreements with foreign countries and implementing of treaties, agreements and conventions with foreign countries. [I, 3, G.I. Act]

15. War and peace.

16. Foreign jurisdiction.

17. Citizenship, naturalisation and aliens. [I, 49, G.I. Act]

18. Extradition. [I, 3, G.I. Act]

19. Admission into, and emigration and expulsion from, India; passports and visas. [I, 17, G.I. Act]

20. Pilgrimages to places outside India. [I, 17, G.I. Act]

21. Piracies and crimes committed on the high seas or in the air; offences against the law of nations committed on land or the high seas or in the air.

22. Railways. [I, 20, G.I. Act]

23. Highways declared by or under law made by Parliament to be national highways.

24. Shipping and navigation on inland waterways, declared by Parliament by law to be national waterways, as regards mechanically propelled vessels; the rule of the road on such waterways. [I, 21, G.I. Act]

25. Maritime shipping and navigation, including shipping and navigation on tidal waters; provision of education and training for the mercantile marine and regulation of such education and training provided by States and other agencies. [I, 21, G.I. Act]

26. Lighthouses, including lightships, beacons and other provision for the safety of shipping and aircraft. [I, 25, G.I. Act]

27. Ports declared by or under law made by Parliament or existing law to be major ports, including their delimitation, and the constitution and powers of port authorities therein. [I, 22, G.I. Act]

28. Port quarantine, including hospitals connected therewith; seamen's and marine hospitals. [I, 18, G.I. Act]

29. Airways; aircraft and air navigation; provision of aerodromes; regulation and organisation of air traffic and of aerodromes; provision for aeronautical education and training and regulation of such education and training provided by States and other agencies. [I, 24, G.I. Act]

30. Carriage of passengers and goods by railway, sea or air, or by national waterways in mechanically propelled vessels. [I, 26, G.I. Act]

31. Posts and telegraphs; telephones, wireless, broadcasting and other like forms of communication. [I, 7, G.I. Act]

32. Property of the Union and the revenue therefrom, but as regards property situated in a State [31]* * * subject to legislation by the State, save in so far as Parliament by law otherwise provides. [I, 10, G.I. Act]

[32]* * * * *

34. Courts of wards for the estates of Rulers of Indian States.

35. Public debt of the Union. [I, 6, G.I. Act]

36. Currency, coinage and legal tender; foreign exchange. [I, 5, G.I. Act]

37. Foreign loans.

38. Reserve Bank of India.

39. Post Office Savings Bank. [I, 7, G.I. Act]

40. Lotteries organised by the Government of India or the Government of a State. [I, 48, G.I. Act]

41. Trade and commerce with foreign countries; import and export across customs frontiers; definition of customs frontiers. [I, 19, G.I. Act]

42. Inter-State trade and commerce.

43. Incorporation, regulation and winding up of trading corporations, including banking, insurance and financial corporations but not including co-operative societies. [I, 33, G.I. Act]

44. Incorporation, regulation and winding up of corporations, whether trading or not, with objects not confined to one State, but not including universities.

45. Banking. [I, 38, G.I. Act]

46. Bills of exchange, cheques, promissory notes and other like instruments. [I, 28, G.I. Act]

47. Insurance. [I, 37, G.I. Act]

48. Stock exchanges and futures markets.

49. Patents, inventions and designs; copyright; trade-marks and merchandise marks. [I, 29, G.I. Act]

50. Establishment of standards of weight and measure. [I, 51, G.I. Act]

51. Establishment of standards of quality for goods to be exported out of India or transported from one State to another.

52. Industries, the control of which by the Union is declared by Parliament by law to be expedient in the public interest.[33] [I, 34, G.I. Act]

53. Regulation and development of oilfields and mineral oil resources; petroleum and petroleum products; other liquids and substances declared by Parliament by law to be dangerously inflammable.[34] [I, 36, G.I. Act]

54. Regulation of mines and mineral development to the extent to which such regulation and development under the control of the Union is declared by Parlia-

---

[31] The words and letters 'specified in Part A or Part B of the First Schedule' omitted by the Const. (7th Am.) Act, 1956, s. 29 and Sch. w.e.f. 1.11.1956.

[32] Entry 33 omitted by s. 26, *ibid*. The original entry 33 read as follows:
"33. Acquisition or requisitioning of property for the purposes of the Union". [II, 9, G.I. Act]

[33] In addition to the Industries specified in the Schedule to the Industries (Development and Regulation) Act, 1951, the following industries have been declared to be industries, the control of which by the Union is expedient in the public interest: Cardamom, by the Cardamom Act, 1965; Coffee, by the Coffee Act, 1942; Coir Industry, by the Coir Industry Act, 1953; Power Alcohol, by the Indian Power Alcohol Act, 1948; Rice Milling, by the Rice Milling Industry (Regulation) Act, 1958; Rubber, by the Rubber Act, 1947; Silk Industry, by the Central Silk Board Act, 1948; and Tea, by the Tea Act, 1953.

[34] Acetone, Calcium Phosphide and several other substances have been declared by Parliament to be dangerously inflammable by the Inflammable Substances Act, 1952.

ment by law to be expedient in the public interest.[35] [I, 36, G.I. Act]

55. Regulation of labour and safety in mines and oilfields. [I, 35, G.I. Act]

56. Regulation and development of inter-State rivers and river valleys to the extent to which such regulation and development under the control of the Union is declared by Parliament by law to be expedient in the public interest.[36] [I, 23, G.I. Act]

57. Fishing and fisheries beyond territorial waters. [I, 23, G.I. Act]

58. Manufacture, supply and distribution of salt by Union agencies; regulation and control of manufacture, supply and distribution of salt by other agencies. [I, 47, G.I. Act]

59. Cultivation, manufacture, and sale for export, of opium. [I, 31, G.I. Act]

60. Sanctioning of cinematograph films for exhibition. [III, 33, G.I. Act]

61. Industrial disputes concerning Union employees.

62. The institutions known at the commencement of this Constitution as the National Library, the Indian Museum, the Imperial War Museum, the Victoria Memorial and the Indian War Memorial, and any other like institution financed by the Government of India wholly or in part and declared by Parliament by law to be an institution of national importance. [I, 11, G.I. Act]

63. The institutions known at the commencement of this Constitution as the Benares Hindu University, the Aligarh Muslim University and the [37][Delhi University; the University established in pursuance of article 371E;] any other institution declared by Parliament by law to be an institution of national importance.[38] [I, 13, G.I. Act]

64. Institutions for scientific or technical education financed by the Government of India wholly or in part and declared by Parliament by law to be institutions of national importance.[38]

65. Union agencies and institutions for—

(a) professional, vocational or technical training, including the training of police officers; or

(b) the promotion of special studies or research; or

(c) scientific or technical assistance in the investigation or detection of crime. [I, 12, G.I. Act]

66. Co-ordination and determination of standards in institutions for higher education or research and scientific and technical institutions.

67. Ancient and historical monuments and records, and archaeological sites and remains, [39][declared by or under law made by Parliament] to be of national

---

[35] See Mines and Minerals (Regulation and Development) Act, 1957, which prescribes the extent to which such regulation and development has been declared to be expedient in the public interest.

[36] See the River Board Act, 1956, which prescribes the extent to which such regulation and development has been declared by Parliament to be expedient in the public interest

[37] Subs. by the Const. (32nd Am.) Act, 1973, s. 4, for "Delhi University, and" (w.e.f. 1.7.1974).

[38] The following are some of the institutions which have been declared to be institutions of national importance: All India Institute of Medical Sciences, by Act 25 of 1956; Dakshina Bharat Hindi Prachar Sabha, by Act 14 of 1964; Hindi Sahitya Sammelan, by Act 13 of 1962; Indian Institutes of Technology at Bombay, Delhi, Kanpur, Kharagpur and Madras, by Act 59 of 1961, as amended from time to time; Indian Statistical Institute, by Act 57 of 1959; Salar Jung Museum and Salar Jung Library, by Act 26 of 1961; Visva Bharati, by Act 29 of 1951; the Khuda Baksh Oriental Public Library, by Act 43 of 1969; and the Post-Graduate Institute of Medical Education and Research, Chandigarh, by Act 51 of 1966.

[39] Subs. by the Const. (7th Am.) Act, 1956, s. 27, w.e.f. 1.11.1956 for "declared by Parliament by law".

importance.[40] [I, 15, G.I. Act]

68. The Survey of India, the Geological, Botanical, Zoological and Anthropological Surveys of India; Meteorological organisations. [I, 14, G.I. Act]

69. Census. [I, 16, G.I. Act]

70. Union Public Services; All-India Services; Union Public Service Commission. [I, 8, G.I. Act]

71. Union pensions, that is to say, pensions payable by the Government of India or out of the Consolidated Fund of India. [I, 9, G.I. Act]

72. Elections to Parliament, to the Legislatures of States and to the offices of President and Vice-President; the Election Commission.

73. Salaries and allowances of members of Parliament, the Chairman and Deputy Chairman of the Council of States and the Speaker and Deputy Speaker of the House of the People. [I, 41, G.I. Act]

74. Powers, privileges and immunities of each House of Parliament and of the members and the Committees of each House; enforcement of attendance of persons for giving evidence or producing documents before committees of Parliament or commissions appointed by Parliament. [I, 41, G.I. Act]

75. Emoluments, allowances, privileges, and rights in respect of leave of absence, of the President and Governors; salaries and allowances of the Ministers for the Union; the salaries, allowances, and rights in respect of leave of absence and other conditions of service of the Comptroller and Auditor-General. [I, 41, G.I. Act]

76. Audit of the accounts of the Union and of the States.

77. Constitution, organisation, jurisdiction and powers of the Supreme Court (including contempt of such Court), and the fees taken therein; persons entitled to practise before the Supreme Court. [I, 53, G.I. Act]

78. Constitution and organisation [41][(including vacations) of the High Courts except provisions as to officers and servants of High Courts; persons entitled to practise before the High Courts.

[42][79. Extension of the jurisdiction of a High Court to, and exclusion of the jurisdiction of a High Court from, any Union territory.]

80. Extension of the powers and jurisdiction of members of a police force belonging to any State to any area outside that State, but not so as to enable the police of one State to exercise powers and jurisdiction in any area outside that State without the consent of the Government of the State in which such area is situated; extension of the powers and jurisdiction of members of a police force belonging to any State to railway areas outside that State. [I, 39, G.I. Act]

81. Inter-State migration; inter-State quarantine. [I, 50, G.I. Act]

82. Taxes on income other than agricultural income. [I, 54, G.I. Act]

83. Duties of customs including export duties. [I, 44, G.I. Act]

84. Duties of excise on tobacco and other goods manufactured or produced in India except— [I, 45, G.I. Act]

---

[40] The list of monuments and sites so declared was contained in the Schedule to the Ancient and Historical Monuments and Archaeological Sites and Remains (Declaration of National Importance) Act, 1951. That Act was repealed by the Ancient Monuments and Archaeological Sites and Remains Act, 1958 (Act 24 of 1958) which declared that those monuments and sites as well as those listed under s. 126 of the States Re-organization Act, 1956 (Act 37 of 1956), were of national importance and, further, authorised the Central Government to declare other monuments or sites to be of national importance.

[41] Ins. by the Const. (15th Am.) Act, 1963, w.e.f. 26.1.1950.

[42] Subs. by the Const. (7th Am.) Act, 1956, w.e.f. 1.11.1956, for the original entry which read as follows:

"79. Extension of the jurisdiction of a High Court having its principal seat in any State to and exclusion of the jurisdiction of any such High Court from, any area outside that State."

(a) alcoholic liquors for human consumption;

(b) opium, Indian hemp and other narcotic drugs and narcotics, but including medicinal and toilet preparations containing alcohol or any substance included in sub-paragraph (b) of this entry.

85. Corporation tax. [I, 46, G.I. Act]

86. Taxes on the capital value of the assets, exclusive of agricultural land, of individuals and companies; taxes on the capital of companies. [I, 55, G.I. Act]

87. Estate duty in respect of property other than agricultural land. [I, 56A, G.I. Act]

88. Duties in respect of succession to property other than agricultural land. [I, 56, G.I. Act]

89. Terminal taxes on goods or passengers, carried by railway, sea or air; taxes on railway fares and freights. [I, 58, G.I. Act]

90. Taxes other than stamp duties on transactions in stock exchanges and futures markets.

91. Rates of stamp duty in respect of bills of exchange, cheques, promissory notes, bills of lading, letters of credit, policies of insurance, transfer of shares, debentures, proxies and receipts. [I, 57, G.I. Act]

92. Taxes on the sale or purchase of newspapers and on advertisements published therein. [II, 48, G.I. Act]

[43][92A. Taxes on the sale or purchase of goods other than newspapers, where such sale or purchase takes place in the course of inter-State trade or commerce.] [II, 48, G.I. Act]

93. Offences against laws with respect to any of the matters in this List. [I, 42, G.I. Act]

94. Inquiries, surveys and statistics for the purpose of any of the matters in this List. [I, 43, G.I. Act]

95. Jurisdiction and powers of all courts, except the Supreme Court, with respect to any of the matters in this List; admiralty jurisdiction. [I, 53, G.I. Act]

96. Fees in respect of any of the matters in this List, but not including fees taken in any Court. [I, 59, G.I. Act]

97. Any other matter not enumerated in List II or List III including any tax not mentioned in either of those Lists.

List II—State List

1. Public order (but not including [44][the use of any naval, military or air force or any other armed force of the Union or of any other force subject to the control of the Union or of any contingent or unit thereof] in aid of the civil power). [II, 1, G.I. Act]

[45][2. Police (including railway and village police) subject to the provisions of entry 2A of List I.] [II, 3, G.I. Act]

3. [46]* * * Officers and servants of the High Court; procedure in rent and revenue courts; fees taken in all courts except the Supreme Court. [II, 2, G.I. Act]

---

[43] Ins. by the Const. (6th Am.) Act, 1956, s. 2, w.e.f. 11.9.1956.

[44] Subs. by the Const. (42nd Am.) Act, 1976, s. 57, for certain words w.e.f. 3.1.1977. The original entry was as follows:

"1. Public order (but not including the use of naval, military or air forces or any other armed forces of the Union in aid of the civil power)."

[45] Subs. by s. 57, *ibid.*, for entry 2 w.e.f. 3.1.1977. The original entry read: "Police, including railway and village police."

[46] The words "Administration of justice; constitution and organisation of all courts, except the Supreme Court and the High Court" omitted by s. 57, *ibid.*, w.e.f. 3.1.1977.

4. Prisons, reformatories, Borstal institutions and other institutions of a like nature, and persons detained therein; arrangements with other States for the use of prisons and other institutions. [II, 4, G.I. Act]

5. Local government, that is to say, the constitution and powers of municipal corporations, improvement trusts, district boards, mining settlement authorities and other local authorities for the purpose of local self-government or village administration. [II, 13, G.I. Act]

6. Public health and sanitation; hospitals and dispensaries. [II, 14, G.I. Act]

7. Pilgrimages, other than pilgrimages to places outside India. [II, 15, G.I. Act]

8. Intoxicating liquors, that is to say, the production, manufacture, possession, transport, purchase and sale of intoxicating liquors. [II, 31, G.I. Act]

9. Relief of the disabled and unemployable. [II, 32, G.I. Act]

10. Burials and burial grounds; cremations and cremation grounds. [II, 16, G.I. Act]

[47]* * * * *

12. Libraries, museums and other similar institutions controlled or financed by the State; ancient and historical monuments and records other than those [48][declared by or under law made by Parliament] to be of national importance. [II, 10, G.I. Act]

13. Communications, that is to say, roads, bridges, ferries, and other means of communication not specified in List I; municipal tramways; ropeways; inland waterways and traffic thereon subject to the provisions of List I and List III with regard to such waterways; vehicles other than mechanically propelled vehicles. [II, 18, G.I. Act]

14. Agriculture, including agricultural education and research, protection against pests and prevention of plant diseases. [II, 20, G.I. Act]

15. Preservation, protection and improvement of stock and prevention of animal diseases; veterinary training and practice. [II, 20, G.I. Act]

16. Pounds and the prevention of cattle trespass. [II, 20, G.I. Act]

17. Water, that is to say, water supplies, irrigation and canals, drainage and embankments, water storage and water power subject to the provisions of entry 56 df List I. [II, 19, G.I. Act]

18. Land, that is to say, rights in or over land, land tenures including the relation of landlord and tenant, and the collection of rents; transfer and alienation of agricultural land; land improvement and agricultural loans; colonization. [II, 21, G.I. Act]

[49]* * * * *

21. Fisheries. [II, 24, G.I. Act]

22. Courts of wards subject to the provisions of entry 34 of List I; encumbered and attached estates. [II, 21, G.I. Act]

23. Regulation of mines and mineral development subject to the provisions of List I with respect to regulation and development under the control of the Union. [II, 23, G.I. Act]

---

[47] Entry 11 omitted by the Const. (42nd Am.) Act, 1976, s. 57, w.e.f. 3.1.1977. The omitted entry 11 read as follows: "Education including universities, subject to the provisions of entries 63, 64, 65 and 66 of List I and entry 25 of List III." [II, 10, G.I. Act]

[48] Subs. by the Const. (7th Am.) Act, 1956, s. 27, for "declared by Parliament by law" w.e.f. 1.11.1956.

[49] Entries 19 and 20 omitted by the Const. (42nd Am.) Act, 1976, s. 57 w.e.f. 3.1.1977. The omitted entries were as follows:
"19. Forests; 20. Protection of wild animals and birds." [II, 22, 25, G.I. Act]

24. Industries subject to the provisions of [50][entries 7 and 52] of List I. [II, 29, G.I. Act]

25. Gas and gas-works. [II, 26, G.I. Act]

26. Trade and commerce within the State subject to the provisions of entry 33 of List III. [II, 27, G.I. Act]

27. Production, supply and distribution of goods subject to the provisions of entry 33 of List III. [II, 29, G.I. Act]

28. Markets and fairs. [II, 27, G.I. Act]

[51]* * * * *

30. Money-lending and money-lenders; relief of agricultural indebtedness. [II, 27, G.I. Act]

31. Inns and inn-keepers. [II, 28, G.I. Act]

32. Incorporation, regulation and winding up of corporations, other than those specified in List I, and universities; unincorporated trading, literary, scientific, religious and other societies and associations; co-operative societies. [II, 33, G.I. Act]

33. Theatres and dramatic performances; cinemas subject to the provisions of entry 60 of List I; sports, entertainments and amusements. [II, 35, G.I. Act]

34. Betting and gambling. [II, 36, G.I. Act]

35. Works, lands and buildings vested in or in the possession of the State. [II, 8, G.I. Act]

[52]* * * * *

37. Elections to the Legislature of the State subject to the provisions of any law made by Parliament. [II, 11, G.I. Act]

38. Salaries and allowances of members of the Legislature of the State, of the Speaker and Deputy Speaker of the Legislative Assembly and, if there is a Legislative Council, of the Chairman and Deputy Chairman thereof. [II, 12, G.I. Act]

39. Powers, privileges and immunities of the Legislative Assembly and of the members and the committees thereof, and, if there is a Legislative Council, of that Council and of the members and the committees thereof; enforcement of attendance of persons for giving evidence or producing documents before committees of the Legislature of the State. [II, 12, G.I. Act]

40. Salaries and allowances of Ministers for the State. [II, 10, G.I. Act]

41. State public services; State Public Service Commission. [II, 6, G.I. Act]

42. State pensions, that is to say, pensions payable by the State or out of the Consolidated Fund of the State. [II, 7, G.I. Act]

43. Public debt of the State. [II, 5, G.I. Act]

44. Treasure trove. [II, 21, G.I. Act]

45. Land revenue, including the assessment and collection of revenue, the maintenance of land records, survey for revenue purposes and records of rights, and alienation of revenues. [II, 39, G.I. Act]

46. Taxes on agricultural income. [II, 41, G.I. Act]

47. Duties in respect of succession to agricultural land. [II, 43, G.I. Act]

48. Estate duty in respect of agricultural land [II, 43A, G.I. Act]

49. Taxes on lands and buildings. [II, 42, G.I. Act]

---

[50] Subs. by the Const. (7th Am.) Act, 1956, s. 28, w.e.f. 1.11.1956 for "entry 52".

[51] Entry 29 omitted by the Const. (42nd Am.) Act, 1976, s. 57, w.e.f. 3.1.1977. Originally enacted, the entry read as follows:

"29. Weights and measures except establishment of standards." [II, 30, G.I. Act]

[52] Entry 36 omitted by s. 26, *ibid.* As originally enacted, the entry read as follows:

"Acquisition or requisitioning of property, except for the purposes of the Union, subject to the provisions of entry 42 of List III." [II, 9, G.I. Act]

50. Taxes on mineral rights subject to any limitations imposed by Parliament by law relating to mineral development. [II, 44, G.I. Act]

51. Duties of excise on the following goods manufactured or produced in the State and countervailing duties at the same or lower rates on similar goods manufactured or produced elsewhere in India:—

(a) alcoholic liquors for human consumption;

(b) opium, Indian hemp and other narcotic drugs and narcotics;

but not including medicinal and toilet preparations containing alcohol or any substance included in sub-paragraph (b) of this entry. [II, 40, G.I. Act]

52. Taxes on the entry of goods into a local area for consumption, use or sale therein. [II, 49, G.I. Act]

53. Taxes on the consumption or sale of electricity. [II, 48B, G.I. Act]

[53][54. Taxes on the sale or purchase of goods other than newspapers, subject to the provisions of entry 92A of List I.] [II, 48, G.I. Act]

55. Taxes on advertisements other than advertisements published in the newspapers [54][and advertisements broadcast by radio or television] [II, 48, G.I. Act]

56. Taxes on goods and passengers carried by road or on inland waterways. [II, 52, G.I. Act]

57. Taxes on vehicles, whether mechanically propelled or not, suitable for use on roads, including tramcars subject to the provisions of entry 35 of List III. [II, 48A, G.I. Act]

58. Taxes on animals and boats. [II, 47, G.I. Act]

59. Tolls. [II, 53, G.I. Act]

60. Taxes on professions, trades, callings and employments. [II, 46, G.I. Act]

61. Capitation taxes. [II, 45, G.I. Act]

62. Taxes on luxuries, including taxes on entertainments, amusements, betting and gambling. [II, 50, G.I. Act]

63. Rates of stamp duty in respect of documents other than those specified in the provisions of List I with regard to rates of stamp duty. [II, 51, G.I. Act]

64. Offences against laws with respect to any of the matters in this List. [II, 37, G.I. Act]

65. Jurisdiction and powers of all courts, except the Supreme Court, with respect to any of the matters in this List. [II, 2, G.I. Act]

66. Fees in respect of any of the matters in this List, but not including fees taken in any court. [II, 54, G.I. Act]

List III—Concurrent List

1. Criminal law, including all matters included in the Indian Penal Code at the commencement of this Constitution but excluding offences against laws with respect to any of the matters specified in List I or List II and excluding the use of naval, military or air forces or any other armed forces of the Union in aid of the civil power. [III, 1, G.I. Act]

2. Criminal procedure, including all matters included in the Code of Criminal Procedure at the commencement of this Constitution. [III, 11, G.I. Act]

3. Preventive detention for reasons connected with the security of a State, the maintenance of public order, or the maintenance of supplies and services essential to the community; persons subjected to such detention. [I, 1; II, 1, G.I. Act]

4. Removal from one State to another State of prisoners, accused persons and persons subjected to preventive detention for reasons specified in entry 3 of this List. [III, 3, G.I. Act]

[53] Subs. by the Const. (6th Am.) Act, 1956, w.e.f. 11.9.1956, for the original entry which read as follows:

"54. Taxes on the sale or purchase of goods other than newspapers."

[54] Ins. by the Const. (42nd Am.) Act, s. 57, w.e.f. 3.1.1977.

5. Marriage and divorce; infants and minors; adoption; wills, intestacy and succession; joint family and partition; all matters in respect of which parties in judicial proceedings were immediately before the commencement of this Constitution subject to their personal law. [III, 6, 7, G.I. Act]

6. Transfer of property other than agricultural land; registration of deeds and documents. [III, 8, G.I. Act]

7. Contracts, including partnership, agency, contracts of carriage, and other special forms of contracts, but not including contracts relating to agricultural land. [III, 10, G.I. Act]

8. Actionable wrongs. [III, 14, G.I. Act]

9. Bankruptcy and insolvency. [III, 12, G.I. Act]

10. Trust and Trustees. [III, 9, G.I. Act]

11. Administrators-general and official trustees. [III, 12, G.I. Act]

[55][11A. Administration of justice; constitution and organisation of all courts, except the Supreme Court and the High Courts.

12. Evidence and oaths; recognition of laws, public acts and records, and judicial proceedings. [III, 5, G.I. Act]

13. Civil procedure, including all matters included in the Code of Civil Procedure at the commencement of this Constitution, limitation and arbitration. [III, 4, G.I. Act]

14. Contempt of court, but not including contempt of the Supreme Court.

15. Vagrancy; nomadic and migratory tribes. [III, 23, G.I. Act]

16. Lunacy and mental deficiency, including places for the reception or treatment of lunatics and mental deficients. [III, 18, G.I. Act]

17. Prevention of cruelty to animals [III, 22, G.I. Act]

[56][17A. Forests.

17B. Protection of wild animals and birds.]

18. Adulteration of foodstuffs and other goods. [II, 30, G.I. Act]

19. Drugs and poisons, subject to the provisions of entry 59 of List I with respect to opium. [III, 19, G.I. Act]

20. Economic and social planning.

[56][20A. Population control and family planning.]

21. Commercial and industrial monopolies, combines and trusts.

22. Trade unions; industrial and labour disputes. [III, 29, G.I. Act]

23. Social security and social insurance; employment and unemployment. [III, 27, 28, G.I. Act]

24. Welfare of labour including conditions of work, provident funds, employers' liability, workmen's compensation, invalidity and old age pensions and maternity benefits. [III, 27, G.I. Act]

[57][25. Education, including technical education, medical education and universities, subject to the provisions of entries 63, 64, 65 and 66 of List I; vocational and technical training of labour.]

26. Legal, medical and other professions. [III, 26, G.I. Act]

27. Relief and rehabilitation of persons displaced from their original place of residence by reason of the setting up of the Dominions of India and Pakistan.

---

[55] Ins. by the Const. (42nd Am.) Act, 1976, s. 57, w.e.f. 3.1.1977.
[56] Ins. by the Const. (42nd Am.) Act, 1976, s. 57, w.e.f. 3.1.1977.
[57] Subs. by s. 57, *ibid.*, for entry 25, w.e.f. 3.1.1977. The original entry read as follows:

"25. Vocational and technical training of labour".

28. Charities and charitable institutions, charitable and religious endowments and religious institutions. [II, 34, G.I. Act]

29. Prevention of the extension from one State to another of infectious or contagious diseases or pests affecting men, animals or plants. [III, 30, G.I. Act]

30. Vital statistics including registration of births and deaths. [II, 14, G.I. Act]

31. Ports other than those declared by or under law made by Parliament or existing law to be major ports. [II, 18, G.I. Act]

32. Shipping and navigation on inland waterways as regards mechanically propelled vessels, and the rule of the road on such waterways, and the carriage of passengers and goods on inland waterways subject to the provisions of List I with respect to national waterways. [III, 32, G.I. Act]

[58][33. Trade and commerce in, and the production, supply and distribution of,—

(a) the products of any industry where the control of such industry by the Union is declared by Parliament by law to be expedient in the public interest, and imported goods of the same kind as such products;

(b) foodstuffs, including edible oilseeds and oils;

(c) cattle fodder, including oilcakes and other concentrates;

(d) raw cotton, whether ginned or unginned, and cotton seed; and

(e) raw jute.]

[59][33A. Weights and measures except establishment of standards.]

34. Price control.

35. Mechanically propelled vehicles including the principles on which taxes on such vehicles are to be levied. [III, 20, G.I. Act]

36. Factories. [III, 26, G.I. Act]

37. Boilers. [III, 21, G.I. Act]

38. Electricity. [III, 31, G.I. Act]

39. Newspapers, books and printing presses. [III, 17, G.I. Act]

40. Archaeological sites and remains other than those [60][declared by or under law made by Parliament] to be of national importance. [I, 15, G.I. Act]

41. Custody, management and disposal of property (including agricultural land) declared by law to be evacuee property.

[61][42. Acquisition and requisitioning of property.] [II, 9, G.I. Act]

43. Recovery in a State of claims in respect of taxes and other public demands, including arrears of land-revenue and sums recoverable as such arrears, arising outside that State. [III, 4, G.I. Act]

44. Stamp duties other than duties or fees collected by means of judicial stamps, but not including rates of stamp duty. [III, 13, G.I. Act]

45. Inquiries and statistics for the purposes of any of the matters specified in List II or List III. [III, 35, G.I. Act]

---

[58] Subs. by the Const. (3rd Am.) Act, 1954, s. 2, for entry 33, w.e.f. 22.2.1955, for the original entry which read as follows:

"Trade and commerce in, and the production, supply and distribution of, the products of industries where the control of such industries by the Union is declared by Parliament by law to be expedient in the public interest."

[59] Ins. by the Const. (42nd Am.) Act, 1976, s. 57, w.e.f. 3.1.1977.

[60] Subs. by the Const. (7th Am.) Act, 1956, s. 27, for "declared by Parliament by law" w.e.f. 1.11.1956.

[61] Subs. by s. 26, *ibid.*, for entry 42. The original entry read as follows:

"42. Principles on which compensation for property acquired or requisitioned for the purposes of the Union or of a State or for any other public purpose is to be determined, and the form and the manner in which such compensation is to be given."

46. Jurisdiction and powers of all courts, except the Supreme Court, with respect to any of the matters in this List. [III, 15, G.I. Act]

47. Fees in respect of any of the matters in this List, but not including fees taken in any court. [III, 25, 36, G.I. Act]

EIGHTH SCHEDULE

[Articles 344(1) and 351]

Languages

1. Assamese.
2. Bengali.
3. Gujarati.
4. Hindi.
5. Kannada.
6. Kashmiri.
7. Malayalam.
8. Marathi.
9. Oriya.
10. Punjabi.
11. Sanskrit.

[62][12. Sindhi]
[63][13.] Tamil.
[63][14.] Telugu.
[63][15.] Urdu.

[64][NINTH SCHEDULE

[Article 31B]

1. The Bihar Land Reforms Act, 1950 (Bihar Act XXX of 1950).
2. The Bombay Tenancy and Agricultural Lands Act, 1948 (Bombay Act LXVII of 1948).
3. The Bombay Muleki Tenure Abolition Act, 1949 (Bombay Act LXI of 1949).
4. The Bombay Taluqdari Tenure Abolition Act, 1949 (Bombay Act LXII of 1949).
5. The Panch Mahals Mehwassi Tenure Abolition Act, 1949 (Bombay Act LXIII of 1949).
6. The Bombay Khoti Abolition Act, 1950 (Bombay Act VI of 1950).
7. The Bombay Paragana and Kulkarni Watan Abolition Act, 1950 (Bombay Act LX of 1950).
8. The Madhya Pradesh Abolition of Proprietary Rights (Estates, Mahals, Alienated Lands) Act, 1950 (Madhya Pradesh Act I of 1951).
9. The Madras Estates (Abolition and Conversion into Ryotwari) Act, 1948 (Madras Act XXVI of 1948).
10. The Madras Estates (Abolition and Conversion into Ryotwari) Amendment Act, 1950 (Madras Act I of 1950).
11. The Uttar Pradesh Zamindari Abolition and Land Reforms Act, 1950 (Uttar Pradesh Act I of 1951).

---

[62] Added by the Const. (21st Am.) Act, 1967, s. 2, w.e.f. 10.4.1967.
[63] Entries 12 to 14 renumbered as entries 13 to 15 by s. 2, *ibid.*
[64] Added by the Const. (1st Am.) Act, 1951, s. 14, on 18.6.1951.

12. The Hyderabad (Abolition of Jagirs) Regulation. 1358F (No. LXIX of 1358, Fasli).

13. The Hyderabad Jagirs (Commutation) Regulation, 1359F (No. XXV of 1359, Fasli).]

[65][14. The Bihar Displaced Persons Rehabilitation (Acquisition of Land) Act, 1950 (Bihar Act XXXVIII of 1950).

15. The United Provinces Land Acquisition (Rehabilitation of Refugees) Act, 1948 (U.P. Act XXVI of 1948).

16. The Resettlement of Displaced Persons (Land Acquisition) Act, 1948 (Act LX of 1948).

17. Sections 52A to 52G of the Insurance Act, 1938 (Act IV of 1938), as inserted by section 42 of the Insurance (Amendment) Act, 1950 (Act XLVII of 1950).

18. The Railway Companies (Emergency Provisions) Act, 1951 (Act LI of 1951).

19. Chapter III-A of the Industries (Development and Regulation) Act, 1951 (Act LXV of 1951), as inserted by section 13 of the Industries (Development and Regulation) Amendment Act, 1953 (Act XXVI of 1953).

20. The West Bengal Land Development and Planning Act, 1948 (West Bengal Act XXI of 1948), as amended by West Bengal Act XXIX of 1951.]

[66][21. The Andhra Pradesh Ceiling on Agricultural Holdings Act, 1961 (Andhra Pradesh Act X of 1961).

22. The Andhra Pradesh (Telangana Area) Tenancy and Agricultural Lands (Validation) Act, 1961 (Andhra Pradesh Act XXI of 1961).

23. The Andhra Pradesh (Telangana Area) Ijara and Kowli Land Cancellation of Irregular Pattas and Abolition of Concessional Assessment Act, 1961 (Andhra Pradesh Act XXXVI of 1961).

24. The Assam State Acquisition of Lands belonging to Religious or Charitable Institution of Public Nature Act, 1959 (Assam Act IX of 1961).

25 The Bihar Land Reforms (Amendment) Act, 1953 (Bihar Act XX of 1954).

26. The Bihar Land Reforms (Fixation of Ceiling Area and Acquisition of Surplus Land) Act, 1961 (Bihar Act XII of 1962), (except section 28 of this Act).

27. The Bombay Taluqdari Tenure Abolition (Amendment) Act, 1954 (Bombay Act I of 1955).

28. The Bombay Taluqdari Tenure Abolition (Amendment) Act, 1957 (Bombay Act XVIII of 1958).

29. The Bombay Inams (Kutch Area) Abolition Act, 1958 (Bombay Act XCVIII of 1958).

30. The Bombay Tenancy and Agricultural Lands (Gujarat Amendment) Act, 1960 (Gujarat Act XVI of 1960).

31. The Gujarat Agricultural Lands Ceiling Act, 1960 (Gujarat Act XXVII of 1961).

32. The Sagbara and Mehwassi Estates (Proprietary Rights Abolition, etc.) Regulation, 1962 (Gujarat Regulation I of 1962).

33. The Gujarat Surviving Alienations Abolition Act, 1963 (Gujarat Act XXXIII of 1963), except in so far as this Act relates to an alienation referred to in sub-clause (*d*) of clause (3) of section 2 thereof.

---

[65] Added by the Const. (4th Am.) Act, 1955, s. 5, on 27.4.1955.
[66] Added by the Const. (17th Am.) Act, 1964, s. 3, on 20.6.1964.

34. The Maharashtra Agricultural Lands (Ceiling on Holdings) Act, 1961 (Maharashtra Act XXVII of 1961).
35. The Hyderabad Tenancy & Agricultural Lands (Re-enactment, Validation and Further Amendment) Act, 1961 (Maharashtra Act XLV of 1961).
36. The Hyderabad Tenancy and Agricultural Lands Act, 1950 (Hyderabad Act XXI of 1950).
37. The Jenmikaram Payment (Abolition) Act, 1960 (Kerala Act III of 1961).
38. The Kerala Land Tax Act, 1961 (Kerala Act XIII of 1961).
39. The Kerala Land Reforms Act, 1963 (Kerala Act I of 1964).
40. The Madhya Pradesh Land Revenue Code, 1959 (Madhya Pradesh Act XX of 1959).
41. The Madhya Pradesh Ceiling on Agricultural Holdings Act, 1960 (Madhya Pradesh Act XX of 1960).
42. The Madras Cultivating Tenants Protection Act, 1955 (Madras Act XXV of 1955).
43. The Madras Cultivating Tenants (Payment of Fair Rent) Act, 1956 (Madras Act XXIV of 1956).
44. The Madras Occupants of Kudiyiruppu (Protection from Eviction) Act, 1961 (Madras Act XXXVIII of 1961).
45. The Madras Public Trust (Regulation of Administration of Agricultural Lands) Act, 1961 (Madras Act LVII of 1961).
46. The Madras Land Reforms (Fixation of Ceiling on Land) Act, 1961 (Madras Act LVIII of 1961).
47. The Mysore Tenancy Act, 1952 (Mysore Act XIII of 1952).
48. The Coorg Tenants Act, 1957 (Mysore Act XIV of 1957).
49. The Mysore Village Offices Abolition Act, 1961 (Mysore Act XIV of 1961).
50. The Hyderabad Tenancy and Agricultural Lands (Validation) Act, 1961 (Mysore Act XXXVI of 1961).
51. The Mysore Land Reforms Act, 1961 (Mysore Act X of 1962).
52. The Orissa Land Reforms Act, 1960 (Orissa Act XVI of 1960).
53. The Orissa Merged Territories (Village Offices Abolition) Act, 1963 (Orissa Act X of 1963).
54. The Punjab Security of Land Tenures Act, 1953 (Punjab Act X of 1953).
55. The Rajasthan Tenancy Act, 1955 (Rajasthan Act III of 1955).
56. The Rajasthan Zamindari and Biswedari Abolition Act, 1959 (Rajasthan Act VIII of 1959).
57. The Kumaun and Uttarakhand Zamindari Abolition and Land Reforms Act, 1960 (Uttar Pradesh Act XVII of 1960).
58. The Uttar Pradesh Imposition of Ceiling on Land Holdings Act, 1960 (Uttar Pradesh Act I of 1961).
59. The West Bengal Estates Acquisition Act, 1953 (West Bengal Act I of 1954).
60. The West Bengal Land Reforms Act, 1955 (West Bengal Act X of 1956).
61. The Delhi Land Reforms Act, 1954 (Delhi Act VIII of 1954).
62. The Delhi Land Holdings (Ceiling) Act, 1960 (Central Act 24 of 1960).
63. The Manipur Land Revenue and Land Reforms Act, 1960 (Central Act 33 of 1960).
64. The Tripura Land Revenue and Land Reforms Act, 1960 (Central Act 43 of 1960).

[67][65. The Kerala Land Reforms (Amendment) Act, 1969 (Kerala Act 35 of 1969).

66. The Kerala Land Reforms (Amendment) Act, 1971 (Kerala Act 25 of 1971).]

[68][67. The Andhra Pradesh Land Reforms (Ceiling on Agricultural Holdings) Act, 1973 (Andhra Pradesh Act 1 of 1973).

68. The Bihar Land Reforms (Fixation of Ceiling Area and Acquisition of Surplus Land) (Amendment) Act, 1972 (Bihar Act I of 1973).

69. The Bihar Land Reforms (Fixation of Ceiling Area and Acquisition of Surplus Land) (Amendment) Act, 1973 (Bihar Act IX of 1973).

70. The Bihar Land Reforms (Amendment) Act, 1972 (Bihar Act V of 1972).

71. The Gujarat Agricultural Lands Ceiling (Amendment) Act, 1972 (Gujarat Act 2 of 1974).

72. The Haryana Ceiling on Land Holdings Act, 1972 (Haryana Act 26 of 1972).

73. The Himachal Pradesh Ceiling on Land Holdings Act, 1972 (Himachal Pradesh Act 19 of 1973).

74. The Kerala Land Reforms (Amendment) Act, 1972 (Kerala Act 17 of 1972).

75. The Madhya Pradesh Ceiling on Agricultural Holdings (Amendment) Act, 1972 (Madhya Pradesh Act 12 of 1974).

76. The Madhya Pradesh Ceiling on Agricultural Holdings (Second Amendment) Act, 1972 (Madhya Pradesh Act 13 of 1974).

77. The Mysore Land Reforms (Amendment) Act, 1973 (Karnataka Act 1 of 1974).

78. The Punjab Land Reforms Act, 1972 (Punjab Act 10 of 1973).

79. The Rajasthan Imposition of Ceiling on Agricultural Holdings Act, 1973 (Rajasthan Act 11 of 1973).

80. The Gudalur Janmam Estates (Abolition and Conversion into Ryotwari) Act, 1969 (Tamil Nadu Act 24 of 1969).

81. The West Bengal Land Reforms (Amendment) Act, 1972 (West Bengal Act XII of 1972).

82. The West Bengal Estates Acquisition (Amendment) Act, 1964 (West Bengal Act XXII of 1964).

83. The West Bengal Estates Acquisition (Second Amendment) Act, 1973 (West Bengal Act XXXIII of 1973).

84. The Bombay Tenancy and Agricultural Lands (Gujarat Amendment) Act, 1972 (Gujarat Act 5 of 1973).

85. The Orissa Land Reforms (Amendment) Act, 1974 (Orissa Act 9 of 1974).

86. The Tripura Land Revenue and Land Reforms (Second Amendment) Act, 1974 (Tripura Act 7 of 1974).]

[69][[70]* * * * *

88. The Industries (Development and Regulation) Act, 1951 (Central Act 65 of 1951).

---

[67] Ins. by the Const. (29th Am.) Act, 1972, s. 2, w.e.f. 9.6.1972.

[68] Ins. by the Const. (34th Am.) Act, 1974, s. 2, w.e.f. 7.9.1974.

[69] Ins. by the Const. (39th Am.) Act, 1975, s. 5, w.e.f. 10.8.1975.

[70] Entry 87 omitted by the Const. (44th Am.) Act, 1978, s. 44, w.e.f. 20.6.1979. Entry 87, which was ins. by the Const. (39th Am.) Act, 1975, s. 5, read as follows:

"The Representation of the People Act, 1951 (Central Act 43 of 1951), the Representation of the People (Amendment) Act, 1974 (Central Act 58 of 1974) and the Election Laws (Amendment) Act, 1975 (Central Act 40 of 1975)."

89. The Requisitioning and Acquisition of Immovable Property Act, 1952 (Central Act 30 of 1952).

90. The Mines and Minerals (Regulation and Development) Act, 1957 (Central Act 67 of 1957).

91. The Monopolies and Restrictive Trade Practices Act, 1969 (Central Act 54 of 1969).

[71]* * * * *

93. The Coking Coal Mines (Emergency Provisions) Act, 1971 (Central Act 64 of 1971).

94. The Coking Coal Mines (Nationalisation) Act, 1972 (Central Act 36 of 1972).

95. The General Insurance Business (Nationalisation) Act, 1972 (Central Act 57 of 1972).

96. The Indian Copper Corporation (Acquisition of Undertaking) Act, 1972 (Central Act 58 of 1972).

97. The Sick Textile Undertakings (Taking Over of Management) Act, 1972 (Central Act 72 of 1972).

98. The Coal Mines (Taking Over of Management) Act, 1973 (Central Act 15 of 1973).

99. The Coal Mines (Nationalisation) Act, 1973 (Central Act 26 of 1973).

100. The Foreign Exchange Regulation Act, 1973 (Central Act 46 of 1973).

101. The Alcock Ashdown Company Limited (Acquisition of Undertakings) Act, 1973 (Central Act 56 of 1973).

102. The Coal Mines (Conservation and Development) Act, 1974 (Central Act 28 of 1974).

103. The Additional Emoluments (Compulsory Deposit) Act, 1974 (Central Act 37 of 1974).

104. The Conservation of Foreign Exchange and Prevention of Smuggling Activities Act, 1974 (Central Act 52 of 1974).

105. The Sick Textile Undertakings (Nationalisation) Act, 1974 (Central Act 57 of 1974).

106. The Maharashtra Agricultural Lands (Ceiling on Holdings) (Amendment) Act, 1964 (Maharashtra Act XVI of 1965).

107. The Maharashtra Agricultural Lands (Ceiling on Holdings) (Amendment) Act, 1965 (Maharashtra Act XXXII of 1965).

108. The Maharashtra Agricultural Lands (Ceiling on Holdings) (Amendment) Act, 1968 (Maharashtra Act XVI of 1968).

109. The Maharashtra Agricultural Lands (Ceiling on Holdings) (Second Amendment) Act, 1968 (Maharashtra Act XXXIII of 1968).

110. The Maharashtra Agricultural Lands (Ceiling on Holdings) (Amendment) Act, 1969 (Maharashtra Act XXXVII of 1969).

111. The Maharashtra Agricultural Lands (Ceiling on Holdings) (Second Amendment) Act, 1969 (Maharashtra Act XXXVIII of 1969).

112. The Maharashtra Agricultural Lands (Ceiling on Holdings) (Amendment) Act, 1970 (Maharashtra Act XXVII of 1970).

113. The Maharashtra Agricultural Lands (Ceiling on Holdings) (Amendment) Act, 1972 (Maharashtra Act XIII of 1972).

114. The Maharashtra Agricultural Lands (Ceiling on Holdings) (Amendment) Act, 1973 (Maharashtra Act L of 1973).

---

[71] Entry 92 omitted by the Const. (44th Am.) Act, 1978, s. 44 (w.e.f. 20.6.1979).

115. The Orissa Land Reforms (Amendment) Act, 1965 (Orissa Act 13 of 1965).

116. The Orissa Land Reforms (Amendment) Act, 1966 (Orissa Act 8 of 1967).

117. The Orissa Land Reforms (Amendment) Act, 1967 (Orissa Act 13 of 1967).

118. The Orissa Land Reforms (Amendment) Act, 1969 (Orissa Act 13 of 1969).

119. The Orissa Land Reforms (Amendment) Act, 1970 (Orissa Act 18 of 1970).

120. The Uttar Pradesh Imposition of Ceiling on Land Holdings (Amendment) Act, 1972 (Uttar Pradesh Act 18 of 1973).

121. The Uttar Pradesh Imposition of Ceiling on Land Holdings (Amendment) Act, 1974 (Uttar Pradesh Act 2 of 1975).

122. The Tripura Land Revenue and Land Reforms (Third Amendment) Act, 1975 (Tripura Act 3 of 1975).

123. The Dadra and Nagar Haveli Land Reforms Regulation, 1971 (3 of 1971).

124. The Dadra and Nagar Haveli Land Reforms (Amendment) Regulation, 1973 (5 of 1973).]

[72][125. Section 66A and Chapter IVA of the Motor Vehicles Act, 1939 (Central Act 4 of 1939).

126. The Essential Commodities Act, 1955 (Central Act 10 of 1955).

127. The Smugglers and Foreign Exchange Manipulators (Forfeiture of Property) Act, 1976 (Central Act 13 of 1976).

128. The Bonded Labour System (Abolition) Act, 1976 (Central Act 19 of 1976).

129. The Conservation of Foreign Exchange and Prevention of Smuggling Activities (Amendment) Act, 1976 (Central Act 20 of 1976).

[73]* * * * * *

131. The Levy Sugar Price Equalisation Fund Act, 1976 (Central Act 31 of 1976).

132. The Urban Land (Ceiling and Regulation) Act, 1976 (Central Act 33 of 1976).

133. The Departmentalisation of Union Accounts (Transfer of Personnel) Act, 1976 (Central Act 59 of 1976).

134. The Assam Fixation of Ceiling on Land Holdings Act, 1956 (Assam Act I of 1957).

135. The Bombay Tenancy and Agricultural Lands (Vidarbha Region) Act, 1958 (Bombay Act XCIX of 1958).

136. The Gujarat Private Forests (Acquisition) Act, 1972 (Gujarat Act 14 of 1973).

137. The Haryana Ceiling on Land Holdings (Amendment) Act, 1976 (Haryana Act 17 of 1976).

138. The Himachal Pradesh Tenancy and Land Reforms Act, 1972 (Himachal Pradesh Act 8 of 1974).

139. The Himachal Pradesh Village Common Lands Vesting and Utilization Act, 1974 (Himachal Pradesh Act 18 of 1974).

---

[72] Ins. by the Const. (40th Am.) Act, 1976, s. 3. w.e.f. 27.5.1976.

[73] Entry 130 omitted by the Const. (44th Am.) Act, 1978, s. 44, w.e.f. 20.6.1979. The omitted entry read as follows:

"130. The Prevention of Publication of Objectionable Matter Act, 1976 (Central Act 27 of 1976)."

140. The Karnataka Land Reforms (Second Amendment and Miscellaneous Provisions) Act, 1974 (Karnataka Act 31 of 1974).

141. The Karnataka Land Reforms (Second Amendment) Act, 1976 (Karnataka Act 27 of 1976).

142. The Kerala Prevention of Eviction Act, 1966 (Kerala Act 12 of 1966).

143. The Thiruppuvaram Payment (Abolition) Act, 1969 (Kerala Act 19 of 1969).

144. The Sreepadam Lands Enfranchisement Act, 1969 (Kerala Act 20 of 1969).

145. The Sree Pandaravaka Lands (Vesting and Enfranchisement) Act, 1971 (Kerala Act 20 of 1971).

146. The Kerala Private Forests (Vesting and Assignment) Act, 1971 (Kerala Act 26 of 1971).

147. The Kerala Agricultural Workers Act, 1974 (Kerala Act 18 of 1974).

148. The Kerala Cashew Factories (Acquisition) Act, 1974 (Kerala Act 29 of 1974).

149. The Kerala Chitties Act, 1975 (Kerala Act 23 of 1975).

150. The Kerala Scheduled Tribes (Restriction on Transfer of Lands and Restoration of Alienated Lands) Act, 1975 (Kerala Act 31 of 1975).

151. The Kerala Land Reforms (Amendment) Act, 1976 (Kerala Act 15 of 1976).

152. The Kanam Tenancy Abolition Act, 1976 (Kerala Act 16 of 1976).

153. The Madhya Pradesh Ceiling on Agricultural Holdings (Amendment) Act, 1974 (Madhya Pradesh Act 20 of 1974).

154. The Madhya Pradesh Ceiling on Agricultural Holdings (Amendment) Act, 1975 (Madhya Pradesh Act 2 of 1976).

155. The West Khandesh Mehwassi Estates (Proprietary Rights Abolition, etc.) Regulation, 1961 (Maharashtra Regulation I of 1962).

156. The Maharashtra Restoration of Lands to Scheduled Tribes Act, 1974 (Maharashtra Act XIV of 1975).

157. The Maharashtra Agricultural Lands (Lowering of Ceiling on Holdings) and (Amendment) Act, 1972 (Maharashtra Act XXI of 1975).

158. The Maharashtra Private Forests (Acquisition) Act, 1975 (Maharashtra Act XXIX of 1975).

159. The Maharashtra Agricultural Lands (Lowering of Ceiling on Holdings) and (Amendment) Amendment Act, 1975 (Maharashtra Act XLVII of 1975).

160. The Maharashtra Agricultural Lands (Ceiling on Holdings) (Amendment) Act, 1975 (Maharashtra Act II of 1976).

161. The Orissa Estates Abolition Act, 1951 (Orissa Act 1 of 1952).

162. The Rajasthan Colonisation Act, 1954 (Rajasthan Act XXVII of 1954).

163. The Rajasthan Land Reforms and Acquisition of Landowners' Estates Act, 1963 (Rajasthan Act 11 of 1964).

164. The Rajasthan Imposition of Ceiling on Agricultural Holdings (Amendment) Act, 1976 (Rajasthan Act 8 of 1976).

165. The Rajasthan Tenancy (Amendment) Act, 1976 (Rajasthan Act 12 of 1976).

166. The Tamil Nadu Land Reforms (Reduction of Ceiling on Land) Act, 1970 (Tamil Nadu Act 17 of 1970).

167. The Tamil Nadu Land Reforms (Fixation of Ceiling on Land) Amendment Act, 1971 (Tamil Nadu Act 41 of 1971).

168. The Tamil Nadu Land Reforms (Fixation of Ceiling on Land) Amendment Act, 1972 (Tamil Nadu Act 10 of 1972).

169. The Tamil Nadu Land Reforms (Fixation of Ceiling on Land) Second Amendment Act, 1972 (Tamil Nadu Act 20 of 1972).

170. The Tamil Nadu Land Reforms (Fixation of Ceiling on Land) Third Amendment Act, 1972 (Tamil Nadu Act 37 of 1972).

171. The Tamil Nadu Land Reforms (Fixation of Ceiling on Land) Fourth Amendment Act, 1972 (Tamil Nadu Act 39 of 1972).

172. The Tamil Nadu Land Reforms (Fixation of Ceiling on Land) Sixth Amendment Act, 1972 (Tamil Nadu Act 7 of 1974).

173. The Tamil Nadu Land Reforms (Fixation of Ceiling on Land) Fifth Amendment Act, 1972 (Tamil Nadu Act 10 of 1974).

174. The Tamil Nadu Land Reforms (Fixation of Ceiling on Land) Amendment Act, 1974 (Tamil Nadu Act 15 of 1974).

175. The Tamil Nadu Land Reforms (Fixation of Ceiling on Land) Third Amendment Act, 1974 (Tamil Nadu Act 30 of 1974).

176. The Tamil Nadu Land Reforms (Fixation of Ceiling on Land) Second Amendment Act, 1974 (Tamil Nadu Act 32 of 1974).

177. The Tamil Nadu Land Reforms (Fixation of Ceiling on Land) Amendment Act, 1975 (Tamil Nadu Act 11 of 1975).

178. The Tamil Nadu Land Reforms (Fixation of Ceiling on Land) Second Amendment Act, 1975 (Tamil Nadu Act 21 of 1975).

179. Amendments made to the Uttar Pradesh Zamindari Abolition and Land Reforms Act, 1950 (Uttar Pradesh Act I of 1951) by the Uttar Pradesh Land Laws (Amendment) Act, 1971 (Uttar Pradesh Act 21 of 1971) and the Uttar Pradesh Land Laws (Amendment) Act, 1974 (Uttar Pradesh Act 34 of 1974).

180. The Uttar Pradesh Imposition of Ceiling on Land Holdings (Amendment) Act, 1976 (Uttar Pradesh Act 20 of 1976).

181. The West Bengal Land Reforms (Second Amendment) Act, 1972 (West Bengal Act XXVIII of 1972).

182. The West Bengal Restoration of Alienated Land Act, 1973 (West Bengal Act XXIII of 1973).

183. The West Bengal Land Reforms (Amendment) Act, 1974 (West Bengal Act XXXIII of 1974).

184. The West Bengal Land Reforms (Amendment) Act, 1975 (West Bengal Act XXIII of 1975).

185. The West Bengal Land Reforms (Amendment) Act, 1976 (West Bengal Act XII of 1976).

186. The Delhi Land Holdings (Ceiling) Amendment Act, 1976 (Central Act 15 of 1976).

187. The Goa, Daman and Diu Mundkars (Protection from Eviction) Act, 1975 (Goa, Daman and Diu Act 1 of 1976).

188. The Pondicherry Land Reforms (Fixation of Ceiling on Land) Act, 1973 (Pondicherry Act 9 of 1974).]

Explanation.—Any acquisition made under the Rajasthan Tenancy Act, 1955 (Rajasthan Act III of 1955) in contravention of the second proviso to clause (1) of article 31A shall, to the extent of the contravention, be void.]

[74]*TENTH SCHEDULE.—[PART A—Territories of Sikkim. PART B—Terms and conditions of association of Sikkim with the Union.] Rep. by the Constitution (Thirty-sixth Amendment) Act, 1975, s. 5 (w.e.f. 26th April, 1975).*

---

[74] Added by the Const. (35th Am.) Act, 1974, s. 5, w.e.f. 22.2.1975. The repealed Schedule ran as follows:

"TENTH SCHEDULE

[Articles 2A, 80(1) and 81(1)]

PART A

Territories of Sikkim

1. *Sikkim.*—Sikkim comprises the following territories, namely:— The territories which, immediately before the coming into force of the Government of Sikkim Act, 1974, were comprised in Sikkim.

PART B

Terms and conditions of Association of Sikkim with the Union

2. *Responsibilities of the Government of India.*—(1) The Government of India—

(*a*) shall be solely responsible for the defence and territorial integrity of Sikkim and for the conduct and regulation of the external relations of Sikkim, whether political, economic or financial;

(*b*) shall have the exclusive right of constructing, maintaining and regulating the use of railways, aerodromes, landing grounds and air navitation facilities, posts, telegraphs, telephones and wireless installations in Sikkim;

(*c*) shall be responsible for securing the economic and social development of Sikkim and for ensuring good administration and for the maintenance of communal harmony therein;

(*d*) shall be responsible for providing facilities for students from Sikkim in institutions for higher learning in India and for the employment of people from Sikkim in the public services of India (including the All-India Services), at par with those available to citizens of India;

(*e*) shall be responsible for providing facilities for the participation and representation of the people of Sikkim in the political institutions of India.

(2) The provisions contained in the paragraph shall not be enforceable by any Court.

3. *Exercise of certain powers by the President.*—The President may by general or special order, provide—

(*a*) for the inclusion of the planned development of Sikkim within the ambit of the planning authority of India while that authority is preparing plans for the economic and social development of India, and for appropriately associating officials from Sikkim in such work;

(*b*) for the exercise of all or any of the powers vested or sought to be vested in the Government of India in or in relation to Sikkim under the Government of Sikkim Act, 1974.

4. *Representation in Parliament.*—Notwithstanding anything in this Constitution—

(*a*) there shall be allotted to Sikkim one seat in the Council of States and one seat in the House of the People;

(*b*) the representative of Sikkim in the Council of States shall be elected by the members of the Sikkim Assembly;

(*c*) the representative of Sikkim in the House of the People shall be chosen by direct election, and for this purpose, the whole of Sikkim shall form one parliamentary constituency to be called the parliamentary constituency for Sikkim:

Provided that the representative of Sikkim in the House of the People in existence at the commencement of the Constitution (Thirty-fifth Amendment) Act, 1974, shall be elected by the members of the Sikkim Assembly;

(*d*) there shall be one general electoral roll for the parliamentary constituency for Sikkim and every person whose name is for the time being entered in the electoral roll of any constituency under the Government of Sikkim Act, 1974, shall be entitled to be registered in the general electoral roll for the parliamentary constituency for Sikkim;

(*e*) a person shall not be qualified to be the representative of Sikkim in the Council of States or the House of the People unless he is also qualified to be chosen to fill a seat in the Sikkim Assembly and in the case of any such representative—

(*i*) clause (*a*) of Article 84 shall apply as if the words 'is a citizen of India and' had been omitted therefrom;

(*ii*) clause (3) of article 101 shall apply as if sub-clause (*a*) had been omitted therefrom;

(*iii*) sub-clause (*d*) of clause (1) of Article 102 shall apply as if the words 'is not a citizen of India, or' had been omitted therefrom;

(*iv*) Article 103 shall not apply;

(*f*) every representative of Sikkim in the Council of States or in the House of the People shall be deemed to be a member of the Council of States or the House of the People, as the case may be, for all the purposes of this Constitution except as respects the election of the President or the Vice-President:

Provided that in the case of any such representative, clause (2) of Article 101 shall apply as if for the words 'a House of the Legislature of a State', in both the places where they occur, and for the words 'Legislature of the State', the words 'the Sikkim Assembly' had been substituted;

(*g*) if a representative of Sikkim, being a member of the Council of States or the House of the People, becomes subject to any of the disqualifications for being the representative of Sikkim in the Council of States or the House of the People, his seat as a member of the Council of States or the House of the People, as the case may be, shall thereupon become vacant;

(*h*) if any question arises as to whether a representative of Sikkim, being a member of the Council of States or the House of the People, has become subject to any of the disqualifications mentioned in clause (*g*) of this paragraph, the question shall be referred for the decision of the President and his decision shall be final:

Provided that before giving any decision on any such question, the President shall obtain the opinion of the Election Commission and shall act according to such opinion;

(*i*) the superintendence, direction and control of the preparation of the electoral rolls for and the conduct of elections to Parliament under this paragraph of the representatives of Sikkim shall be vested in the Election Commission and provisions of clauses (2), (3), (4) and (6) of Article 324 shall so far as may be, apply to and in relation to all such elections;

(*j*) Parliament may, subject to the provisions of this paragraph, from time to time by law make provision with respect to all matters relating to, or in connection with such elections to either House of Parliament;

(*k*) no such election to either House of Parliament shall be called in question except by an election petition presented to such authority and in such manner as may be provided for by or under any law made by Parliament.

Explanation.—In this paragraph, the expression 'the Sikkim Assembly' shall mean the Assembly for Sikkim constituted under the Government of Sikkim Act, 1974.

5. *Schedule not to derogate from agreements, etc.*—The provisions of this Schedule shall be in addition to, and not in derogation of, any other power, jurisdiction, rights and authority which the Government of India has or may have in or in relation to Sikkim under agreement, grant, usage, sufference or other lawful arrangement."

APPENDIX 1

[75]THE CONSTITUTION (APPLICATION TO JAMMU AND KASHMIR) ORDER, 1954

C.O. 48

In exercise of the powers conferred by clause (1) of article 370 of the Constitution, the President, with the concurrence of the Government of the State of Jammu and Kashmir, is pleased to make the following Order:—

1. (1) This Order may be called the Constitution (Application to Jammu and Kashmir) Order, 1954.

(2) It shall come into force on the fourteenth day of May, 1954, and shall thereupon supersede the Constitution (Application to Jammu and Kashmir) Order, 1950.

2. [76][The provisions of the Constitution as in force on the 20th day of June, 1964 and as amended by the Constitution (Nineteenth Amendment) Act, 1966, the Constitution (Twenty-first Amendment) Act, 1967, section 5 of the Constitution (Twenty-third Amendment) Act, 1969, the Constitution (Twenty-fourth Amendment) Act, 1971, section 2 of the Constitution (Twenty-fifth Amendment) Act, 1977, the Constitution (Twenty-sixth Amendment) Act, 1971, the Constitution (Thirtieth Amendment) Act, 1972, section 2 of the Constitution (Thirty-first Amendment) Act, 1973, section 2 of the Constitution (Thirty-third Amendment) Act, 1974, sections 2, 5, 6 and 7 of the Constitution (Thirty-eighth Amendment) Act, 1975, the Constitution (Thirty-ninth Amendment) Act, 1975 and the Constitution (Fortieth Amendment) Act, 1976 which, in addition to article 1 and article 370, shall apply in relation to the State of Jammu and Kashmir and the exceptions and modifications subject to which they shall so apply shall be as follows:—]

(1) THE PREAMBLE.

(2) PART I.

To article 3, there shall be added the following further proviso, namely:—

"Provided further that no Bill providing for increasing or diminishing the area of the State of Jammu and Kashmir or altering the name or boundary of that State shall be introduced in Parliament without the consent of the Legislature of that State."

(3) PART II.

(a) This Part shall be deemed to have been applicable in relation to the State of Jammu and Kashmir as from the 26th day of January, 1950.

(b) To article 7, there shall be added the following further proviso, namely:—

"Provided further that nothing in this article shall apply to a permanent resident of the State of Jammu and Kashmir who, after having so migrated to the territory now included in Pakistan, returns to the territory of that State under a permit for resettlement in that State or permanent return issued by or under the authority of any law made by the Legislature of that State, and every such person shall be deemed to be a citizen of India.".

(4) PART III.

(a) In article 13, references to the commencement of the Constitution shall be construed as references to the commencement of this Order.

---

[75] Published with the Ministry of Law Notification No. S.R.O. 1610, dated the 14th May, 1954, Gazette of India, Extraordinary, Part II, Section 3, page 821.

[76] The opening words have been successively amended by C.O. 74, C.O. 76, C.O. 89, C.O. 91, C.O. 94, C.O. 98, C.O. 103, C.O. 104, C.O. 105 and C.O. 108 to read as above.

(b) In clause (4) of article 15, the reference to Scheduled Tribes shall be omitted.

(c) In clause (3) of article 16, the reference to the State shall be construed as not including a reference to the State of Jammu and Kashmir.

(d) In article 19, for a period of [77][[78][twenty-five] years] from the commencement of this Order:—

(i) in clauses (3) and (4), after the words "in the interests of", the words "the security of the State or" shall be inserted;

(ii) in clause (5), for the words "or for the protection of the interests of any Scheduled Tribe", the words "or in the interests of the security of the State" shall be substituted; and

(iii) the following new clause shall be added, namely:—

'(7) The words "reasonable restrictions" occurring in clauses (2), (3), (4) and (5) shall be construed as meaning such restrictions as the appropriate Legislature deems reasonable.'.

(e) In clauses (4) and (7) of article 22, for the word "Parliament", the words "the Legislature of the State" shall be substituted.

(f) In article 31, clauses (3), (4) and (6) shall be omitted; and for clause (5), there shall be substituted the following clause, namely:—

"(5) Nothing in clause (2) shall affect—

(a) the provisions of any existing law; or

(b) the provisions of any law which the State may hereafter make—

(i) for the purpose of imposing or levying any tax or penalty; or

(ii) for the promotion of public health or the prevention of danger to life or property; or

(iii) with respect to property declared by law to be evacuee property.".

(g) In article 31A, the proviso to clause (1) shall be omitted; and for sub-clause (a) of clause (2), the following sub-clause shall be substituted, namely:—

'(a) "estate" shall mean land which is occupied or has been let for agricultural purposes or for purposes subservient to agriculture, or for pasture, and includes—

(i) sites of buildings and other structures on such land;

(ii) trees standing on such land;

(iii) forest land and wooded waste;

(iv) area covered by or fields floating over water;

(v) sites of *jandars* and *gharats;*

(vi) any *jagir, inam, muafi* or *mukarrari* or other similar grant, but

does not include—

(i) the site of any building in any town, or town area or village *abadi* or any land appurtenant to any such building or site;

(ii) any land which is occupied as the site of a town or village; or

(iii) any land reserved for building purposes in a municipality or notified area or cantonment or town area or any area for which a town planning scheme is sanctioned.'.

[79][(h) In article 32, clause (3) shall be omitted.]

(i) In article 35—

(i) references to the commencement of the Constitution shall be construed as references to the commencement of this Order;

---

[77] Subs. by C.O. 69, for "ten years".
[78] Subs. by C.O. 97, for "twenty".
[79] Subs. by C.O. 89, for cl. (*h*).

(ii) in clause (a)(i), the words, figures and brackets "clause (3) of article 16, clause (3) of article 32" shall be omitted; and

(iii) after clause (b), the following clause shall be added, namely:—

"(c) no law with respect to preventive detention made by the Legislature of the State of Jammu and Kashmir whether before or after the commencement of the Constitution (Application to Jammu and Kashmir) Order, 1954 shall be void on the ground that it is inconsistent with any of the provisions of this Part, but any such law shall, to the extent of such inconsistency, cease to have effect on the expiration of [80][[81][twenty-five] years] from the commencement of the said Order, except as respects things done or omitted to be done before the expiration thereof.".

(j) After article 35, the following new article shall be added, namely:—

"35A. *Saving of laws with respect to permanent residents and their rights.*—Notwithstanding anything contained in this Constitution, no existing law in force in the State of Jammu and Kashmir, and no law hereafter enacted by the Legislature of the State,—

(a) defining the classes of persons who are, or shall be, permanent residents of the State of Jammu and Kashmir; or

(b) conferring on such permanent residents any special rights and privileges or imposing upon other persons any restrictions as respects—

(i) employment under the State Government;

(ii) acquisition of immovable property in the State;

(iii) settlement in the State; or

(iv) right to scholarships and such other forms of aid as the State Government may provide,

shall be void on the ground that it is inconsistent with or takes away or abridges any rights conferred on the other citizens of India by any provision of this Part.".

(5) PART V.

[82][(a) For the purposes of article 55, the population of the State of Jammu and Kashmir shall be deemed to be sixty-three lakhs.

(b) In article 81, for clauses (2) and (3), the following clauses shall be substituted, namely:—

"(2) For the purposes of sub-clause (a) of clause (1),—

(a) there shall be allotted to the State six seats in the House of the People;

(b) the State shall be divided into single member territorial constituencies by the Delimitation Commission constituted under the Delimitation Act, 1972, in accordance with such procedure as the Commission may deem fit;

(c) the constituencies shall, as far as practicable, be geographically compact areas, and in delimiting them regard shall be had to physical features, existing boundaries of administrative units, facilities of communication and public convenience; and

(d) the constituencies into which the State is divided shall not comprise the area under the occupation of Pakistan.

(3) Nothing in clause (2) shall affect the representation of the State in the House of the People until the dissolution of the House existing on the date of publication in the Gazette of India of the final order or orders of the Delimitation Commission relating to the delimitation of parliamentary constituencies under the Delimitation Act, 1972.

---

[80] Subs. by C.O. 69, for "ten years".
[81] Subs. by C.O. 97, for "twenty".
[82] Subs. by C.O. 98, for cls. (*a*) and (*b*).

(4) (a) The Delimitation Commission shall associate with itself for the purpose of assisting it in its duties in respect of the State, five persons who shall be members of the House of the People representing the State.

(b) The persons to be so associated from the State shall be nominated by the Speaker of the House of the People having due regard to the composition of the House.

(c) The first nominations to be made under sub-clause (b) shall be made by the Speaker of the House of the People within two months from the commencement of the Constitution (Application to Jammu and Kashmir) Second Amendment Order, 1974.

(d) None of the associate members shall have a right to vote or to sign any decision of the Delimitation Commission.

(e) If owing to death or resignation, the office of an associate member falls vacant, it shall be filled as soon as may be practicable by the Speaker of the House of the People and in accordance with the provisions of sub-clauses (a) and (b)."].

[83][(c) In article 133, after clause (1), the following clause shall be inserted, namely:—

'(1A) The provisions of section 3 of the Constitution (Thirtieth Amendment) Act, 1972, shall apply in relation to the State of Jammu and Kashmir subject to the modification that references therein to "this Act", "the commencement of this Act", "this Act had not been passed" and "as amended by this Act" shall be construed respectively as references to "the Constitution (Application to Jammu and Kashmir) Second Amendment Order, 1974", "the commencement of the said Order", "the said Order had not been made" and "as it stands after the commencement of the said Order".'].

[84][(d)] In article 134, clause (2), after the words "Parliament may", the words "on the request of the Legislature of the State" shall be inserted.

[84][(e)] Articles 135, [85]* * * and 139 shall be omitted.

[86]* * * * *

[87][(5A) PART VI.

[88][(a) Articles 153 to 217, article 219, article 221, articles 223, 224, 224A and 225 and articles 227 to 237 shall be omitted.]

(b) In article 220, references to the commencement of the Constitution shall be construed as references to the commencement of the Constitution (Application to Jammu and Kashmir) Amendment Order, 1960.

[89][(c) In article 222, after clause (1), the following new clause shall be inserted, namely:—

"(1A) Every such transfer from the High Court of Jammu and Kashmir or to that High Court shall be made after consultation with the Governor.".]]

(6) PART XI.

[90][(a) In article 246, for the words, brackets and figures "clauses (2) and (3)" occurring in clause (1), the word, brackets and figure "clause (2)" shall be substituted, and the words, brackets and figure "Notwithstanding anything in clause (3)," occurring in clause (2) and the whole of clauses (3) and (4) shall be omitted.]

---

[83] Ins. by C.O. 98.
[84] Cls. (c) and (d) relettered as cls. (d) and (e) by C.O. 98.
[85] The figure "136" omitted by C.O. 60.
[86] Cls. (f) and (g) omitted by C.O. 56.
[87] Ins. by C.O. 60 (w.e.f. 26.1.1960).
[88] Subs. by C.O. 89, for cl. (a).
[89] Subs. by C.O. 74, for cl. (c) (w.e.f. 24.11.1965).
[90] Subs. by C.O. 66, for cl. (a).

[91][[92][(b) For article 248, the following article shall be substituted, namely—

"248. *Residuary powers of legislation.*—Parliament has exclusive power to make any law with respect to—

(a) prevention of activities directed towards disclaiming, questioning or disrupting the sovereignty and territorial integrity of India or bringing about cession of a part of the territory of India or secession of a part of the territory of India from the Union or causing insult to the Indian National Flag, the Indian National Anthem and this Constitution; and

(b) taxes on—

(i) foreign travel by sea or air;

(ii) inland air travel;

(iii) postal articles, including money orders, phonograms and telegrams.".]

(bb) Article 249 shall be omitted.]

(c) In article 250, for the words "to any of the matters enumerated in the State List", the words "also to matters not enumerated in the Union List" shall be substituted.

(d) In article 251, for the words and figures "articles 249 and 250", the word and figures "article 250" shall be substituted, and the words "under this Constitution" shall be omitted; and, for the words "under either of the said articles", the words "under the said article" shall be substituted.

(e) To article 253, the following proviso shall be added, namely:—

"Provided that after the commencement of the Constitution (Application to Jammu and Kashmir) Order, 1954, no decision affecting the disposition of the State of Jammu and Kashmir shall be made by the Government of India without the consent of the Government of that State.".

[93]* * * * *

[94][(f)] Article 255 shall be omitted.

[94][(g)] Article 256 shall be re-numbered as clause (1) of that article, and the following new clause shall be added thereto, namely:—

"(2) The State of Jammu and Kashmir shall so exercise its executive power as to facilitate the discharge by the Union of its duties and responsibilities under the Constitution in relation to that State; and in particular, the said State shall, if so required by the Union, acquire or requisition property on behalf and at the expense of the Union, or if the property belongs to the State, transfer it to the Union on such terms as may be agreed, or in default of agreement, as may be determined by an arbitrator appointed by the Chief Justice of India.".

[95]* * * * *

[96][(h)] In clause (2) of article 261, the words "made by Parliament" shall be omitted.

(7) PART XII.

[97]* * * * *

[98][(a)] Clause (2) of article 267, article 273, clause (2) of article 283 [99][and article 290] shall be omitted.

---

[91] Subs. by C.O. 85, for cl. (*b*).
[92] Subs. by C.O. 93, for cl. (*b*).
[93] Cl. (*f*) omitted by C.O. 66.
[94] Cls. (*g*) and (*h*) relettered as cls. (*f*) and (*g*), *ibid.*
[95] Cl. (*i*) omitted by C.O. 56.
[96] Cl. (*j*) relettered as cl. (*i*) by C.O. 56 and again relettered as cl. (*h*) by C.O. 66.
[97] Cls. (*a*) and (*b*) inserted by C.O. 55 have been omitted by C.O. 56.
[98] Cls. (*a*), (*b*) and (*c*) [relettered as (*c*), ((*d*) and (*e*) respectively by C.O. 55] have again been relettered as (*a*), (*b*) and (*c*) respectively by C.O. 56.
[99] Subs. by C.O. 94, for "articles 290 and 291".

[98][(b)] In articles 266, 282, 284, 298, 299 and 300, references to the State or States shall be construed as not including references to the State of Jammu and Kashmir.

[98][(c)] In atricles 277 and 295, references to the commencement of the Constitution shall be construed as references to the commencement of this Order.

(8) PART XIII.

[1]* * * In clause (1) of article 303, the words "by virtue of any entry relating to trade and commerce in any of the Lists in the Seventh Schedule" shall be omitted.

[1]* * * * *

(9) PART XIV.

[2][In 'article 312, after the words "the States", the brackets and words "(including the State of Jammu and Kashmir)" shall be inserted.]

[3][(10) PART XV.

(a) In clause (1) of article 324, the reference to the Constitution shall, in relation to elections to either House of the Legislature of Jammu and Kashmir, be construed as a reference to the Constitution of Jammu and Kashmir.

[4][(b) In articles 325, 326, 327 and 329, the reference to a State shall be construed as not including a reference to the State of Jammu and Kashmir.

(c) Article 328 shall be omitted.

(d) In article 329, the words and figures "or article 328" shall be omitted.]

[5][(e) In article 329A, clauses (4) and (5) shall be omitted.]]

(11) PART XVI.

(a) In article 330, references to the "Scheduled Tribes" shall be omitted.

(b) Articles 331, 332, 333, 336, 337, 339 and 342 shall be omitted.

(c) In articles 334 and 335, references to the State or the States shall be construed as not including references to the State of Jammu and Kashmir.

(12) PART XVII.

The provisions of the Part shall apply only in so far as they relate to—

(i) the official language of the Union;

(ii) the official language for communication between one State and another, or between a State and the Union; and

(iii) the language of the proceedings in the Supreme Court.

(13) PART XVIII.

(a) To article 352, the following new clause shall be added, namely:—

"[6][(6)] No Proclamation of Emergency made on grounds only of internal disturbance or imminent danger thereof shall have effect in relation to the State of Jammu and Kashmir (except as respects article 354) [7][unless—

(a) it is made at the request or with the concurrence of the Government of that State, or

(b) where it has not been so made, it is applied subsequently by the President to that State at the request or with the concurrence of the Government of that State.]".

---

[1] Brackets and letter '(*a*)' and cl. (b) omitted by C.O. 56.
[2] Subs., *ibid*., for the previous modification.
[3] Subs. by C.O. 60, for sub-paragraph (10) (w.e.f. 26.1.1960).
[4] Subs. by C.O. 75, for cls. (b) and (c).
[5] Ins. by C.O. 105.
[6] Subs. by C.O. 104, for "(4)".
[7] Subs. by C.O. 100, for certain words

[8][(b) In clause (1) of article 356, references to provisions or provision of this Constitution shall, in relation to the State of Jammu and Kashmir, be construed as including references to provisions or provision of the Constitution of Jammu and Kashmir.

(c) Article 360 shall be omitted.]

(14) PART XIX.

[9]* * * * *

[10][(a)] [11][Article 365] shall be omitted.

[12]* * * * *

[10][(b)]To article 367, there shall be added the following clause, namely:—

"(4) For the purposes of this Constitution as it applies in relation to the State of Jammu and Kashmir—

(a) references to this Constitution or to the provisions thereof shall be construed as references to the Constitution or the provisions thereof as applied in relation to the said State;

[13][(aa) references to the person for the time being recognised by the President on the recommendation of the Legislative Assembly of the State as the Sadar-i-Riyasat of Jammu and Kashmir, acting on the advice of the Council of Ministers of the State for the time being in office, shall be construed as references to the Governor of Jammu and Kashmir;

(b) references to the Government of the said State shall be construed as including references to the Governor of Jammu and Kashmir acting on the advice of his Council of Ministers:

Provided that in respect of any period prior to the 10th day of April, 1965, such references shall be construed as including references to the Sadar-i-Riyasat acting on the advice of his Council of Ministers;]

(c) references to a High Court shall include references to the High Court of Jammu and Kashmir;

[14]* * * * *

[15][(d)] references to the permanent residents of the said State shall be construed as meaning persons who, before the commencement of the Constitution (Application to Jammu and Kashmir) Order, 1954, were recognised as State subjects under the laws in force in the State or who are recognised by any law made by the Legislature of the State as permanent residents of the State; and

[16][(e) references to a Governor shall include references to the Governor of Jammu and Kashmir:

Provided that in respect of any period prior to the 10th day of April, 1965, such references shall be construed as references to the person recognised by the President as the Sadar-i-Riyasat of Jammu and Kashmir and as including references to any person recognised by the President as being competent to exercise the powers of the Sadar-i-Riyasat.]".

---

[8] Subs. by C.O. 71, for cl. (*b*).
[9] Cl. (*a*) omitted by C.O. 74.
[10] Cls. (*b*) and (*c*) relettered as cls. (*a*) and (*b*) by C.O. 74
[11] Subs. by C.O. 94, for "Articles 362 and 365".
[12] Original cl. (*c*) omitted by C.O. 56.
[13] Subs. by C.O. 74, for cl. (*b*).
[14] Cl. (*d*) omitted by C.O. 56.
[15] Cl. (*e*) relettered as cl (*d*), ibid.
[16] Subs. by C.O. 74, for cl. (*e*).

(15) PART XX.

[17][(a)] [18][To clause (2) of article 368], the following proviso shall be added, namely:—

"Provided further that no such amendment shall have effect in relation to the State of Jammu and Kashmir unless applied by order of the President under clause (1) of article 370.".

[19][(b) After clause (3) of article 368, the following clause shall be added, namely:—

"(4) No law made by the Legislature of the State of Jammu and Kashmir seeking to make any change in or in the effect of any provision of the Constitution of Jammu and Kashmir relating to—

(a) appointment, powers, functions, duties, emoluments, allowances, privileges or immunities of the Governor; or

(b) superintendence, direction and control of elections by the Election Commission of India, eligibility for inclusion in the electoral rolls without discrimination, adult suffrage and composition of the Legislative Council, being matters specified in sections 138, 139, 140 and 50 of the Constitution of Jammu and Kashmir,

shall have any effect unless such law has, after having been reserved for the consideration of the President, received his assent.".]

(16) PART XXI.

(a) Articles 369, 371, [20] [371A], [21] [372A], 373, clauses (1), (2), (3) and (5) of article 374 and [22] [articles 376 to 378A and 392] shall be omitted.

(b) In article 372—

(i) clauses (2) and (3) shall be omitted;

(ii) references to the laws in force in the territory of India shall include references to *hidayats, ailans, ishtihars*, circulars, *robkars, irshads, yadashts*, State Council Resolutions, Resolutions of the Constituent Assembly, and other instruments having the force of law in the territory of the State of Jammu and Kashmir; and

(iii) references to the commencement of the Constitution shall be construed as references to the commencement of this Order.

(c) In clause (4) of article 374, the reference to the authority functioning as the Privy Council of a State shall be construed as a reference to the Advisory Board constituted under the Jammu and Kashmir Constitution Act, 1996 and references to the commencement of the Constitution shall be construed as references to the commencement of this Order.

(17) PART XXII.

Articles 394 and 395 shall be omitted.

(18) FIRST SCHEDULE.

(19) SECOND SCHEDULE.

[23]* * * * *

(20) THIRD SCHEDULE.

Forms V, VI, VII and VIII shall be omitted.

(21) FOURTH SCHEDULE.

---

[17] Numbered as cl. (*a*) by C.O. 101.
[18] Subs. by C.O. 91, for "To article 368".
[19] Ins. by C.O. 101.
[20] Ins. by C.O. 74.
[21] Ins. by C.O. 56.
[22] Subs., *ibid*., for "articles 376 to 392".
[23] Modification relating to paragraph 6 omitted by C.O. 56.

[24][(22) SEVENTH SCHEDULE.

(a) In the Union List—

(i) for entry 3, the entry "3. Administration of cantonments," shall be substituted;

[25][(ii) entries 8, 9 [26][and 34], [27]* * * entry 79, and the words "Inter-State migration" in entry 81 shall be omitted;]

[28]* * * * *

[29][(iii) in entry 72, the reference to the States shall be construed,—

(a) in relation to appeals to the Supreme Court from any decision or order of the High Court of the State of Jammu and Kashmir made in an election petition whereby an election to either House of the Legislature of that State has been called in question, as including a reference to the State of Jammu and Kashmir;

(b) in relation to other matters, as not including a reference to that State]; [30][and]

[31][(iv) for entry 97, the following entry shall be substituted, namely:—

"97. Prevention of activities directed towards disclaiming, questioning or disrupting the sovereignty and territorial integrity of India or bringing about cession of a part of the territory of India or secession of a part of the territory of India from the Union or causing insult to the Indian National Flag, the Indian National Anthem and this Constitution; taxes on foreign travel by sea or air, on inland air travel and on postal articles, including money orders, phonograms and telegrams.".]

(b) The State List shall be omitted.

[32][(c) In the Concurrent List—

[33][(i) for entry 1, the following entry shall be substituted, namely:

"1. Criminal law (excluding offences against laws with respect to any of the matters specified in List I and excluding the use of naval, military or air forces or any other armed forces of the Union in aid of the civil power) in so far as such criminal law relates to offences against laws with respect to any of the matters specified in this List."];

[34][(ia) for entry 2, the entry "2. Criminal procedure in so far as it relates to administration of oaths and taking of affidavits by diplomatic and consular officers in any foreign country." shall be substituted;

(ib) for entry 12, the entry "12. Evidence and oaths in so far as they relate to administration of oaths and taking of affidavits by diplomatic and consular officers in any foreign country." shall be substituted;

(ic) for entry 13, the entry "13. Civil procedure in so far as its relates to administration of oaths and taking of affidavits by doplomatic and consular officers in any foreign country." shall be substituted;]

[35]* * * * *

[24] Subs. by C.O. 66, for sub-paragraph (22).
[25] Subs. by C.O. 85, for item (*ii*).
[26] Subs. by C.O. 92, for "34 and 60".
[27] The words 'the words "and records" in entry 67' omitted by C.O. 95.
[28] Original item (iii) omitted by C.O. 74.
[29] Subs. by C.O. 83, for item (iii).
[30] Ins. by C.O. 85.
[31] Subs. by C.O. 93, for item (iv).
[32] Subs. by C.O. 69, for cl. (c).
[33] Subs. by C.O. 70, for item (i).
[34] Ins. by C.O. 94.
[35] Items (ii) and (iii) omitted by C.O. 74.

[36][[37][(ii)]for entry 30, the entry "30. Vital statistics in so far as they relate to births and deaths including registration of births and deaths." shall be substituted;]

[38]* * * * *

[39][(iii) entry 3, entries 5 to 10 (both inclusive), entries 14, 15, 17, 20, 21, 27, 28, 29, 31, 32, 37, 38, 41 and 44 shall be omitted;

(iiia) for entry 42, the entry "42. Acquisition and requisitioning of property, so far as regards acquisition of any property covered by entry 67 of List I or entry 40 of List III or of any human work of art which has artistic or aesthetic value." shall be substituted; and]

[40][(iv)] in entry 45, for the words and figures "List II or List III", the words "this List" shall be substituted.]]

(23) EIGHTH SCHEDULE.

[41][(24) NINTH SCHEDULE.

[42][(a)] After entry 64, the following entries shall be added, namely:—

[43][64A.] The Jammu and Kashmir State Kuth Act (No. 1 of Svt. 1978).

[43][64B.] The Jammu and Kashmir Tenancy Act (No. II of Svt. 1980).

[43][64C.] The Jammu and Kashmir Alienation of Land Act (No. V of Svt. 1995).

[44]* * * * *

[45][64D.] The Jammu and Kashmir Big Landed Estates Abolition Act (No. XVII of Svt. 2007).

[45][64E.] Order No. 6-H of 1951, dated the 10th March, 1951, regarding Resumption of Jagirs and other assignments of land revenue, etc.

[46][64F. The Jammu and Kashmir Restitution of Mortgaged Properties Act, 1976 (Act XIV of 1976).

64G. The Jammu and Kashmir Debtors' Relief Act, 1976 (Act XV of 1976).]

[47][(b) Entries 87 to 124, inserted by the Constitution (Thirty-ninth Amendment) Act, 1975, shall be re-numbered as entries 65 to 102 respectively.]]

[48][(c) Entries 125 to 188 shall be re-numbered as entries 103 to 166 respectively.]

---

[36] Ins. by C.O. 70.
[37] Item (iv) renumbered as item (ii) by C.O. 74.
[38] Items (v) and (vi) omitted by C.O. 72.
[39] Subs. by C.O. 95, for item (iii).
[40] Item (vii) renumbered as item (iv) by C.O. 74.
[41] Subs., *ibid.*, for sub-paragraph (24).
[42] Relettered by C.O. 105.
[43] Renumbered by C.O. 98.
[44] Omitted by C.O. 106.
[45] Relettered, *ibid.*
[46] Ins., *ibid.*
[47] Ins. by C.O. 105.
[48] Ins. by C.O. 108 (w.e.f. 31.12.1977).

RE-STATEMENT, WITH REFERENCE TO THE PRESENT TEXT OF THE CONSTITUTION, OF THE EXCEPTIONS AND MODIFICATIONS SUBJECT TO WHICH THE CONSTITUTION APPLIES TO THE STATE OF JAMMU AND KASHMIR.

[*Note*:—The exceptions and modifications subject to which the Constitution applies to the State of Jammu and Kashmir are either those provided in the Constitution (Application to Jammu and Kashmir) Order, 1954 or those consequential to the non-application to the State of Jammu and Kashmir of certain amendments to the Constitution. All the exceptions and modifications which have a practical significance are included in this re-statement which is only for facility of quick reference. For ascertaining the exact position, reference will have to be made to the Constitution (Application to Jammu and Kashmir) Order, 1954 and to the text of the Constitution on the 20th June, 1964, as amended by the subsequent amendments to the Constitution mentioned in clause 2 of the said Order.]

(1) THE PREAMBLE.

(*a*) In the first paragraph, omit "SOCIALIST SECULAR";

(*b*) in the penultimate paragraph, omit "and integrity".

(2) PART I.

Article 3.—

(*a*) Add the following further proviso, namely:—

"Provided further that no Bill providing for increasing or diminishing the area of the State of Jammu and Kashmir or altering the name or boundary of that State shall be introduced in Parliament without the consent of the Legislature of that State.";

(*b*) omit *Explanation I* and *Explanation II*.

(3) PART II.

(*a*) This Part shall be deemed to have been applicable in relation to the State of Jammu and Kashmir as from the 26th day of January, 1950.

(*b*) *Article* 7.—Add the following further proviso, namely:—

"Provided further that nothing in this article shall apply to a permanent resident of the State of Jammu and Kashmir who, after having so migrated to the territory now included in Pakistan, returns to the territory of that State under a permit for resettlement in that State or permanent return issued by or under the authority of any law made by the Legislature of that State, and every such person shall be deemed to be a citizen of India.".

(4) PART III.

(*a*) *Article* 13.—References to the commencement of the Constitution shall be construed as references to the commencement of the Constitution (Application to Jammu and Kashmir) Order, 1954 (C.O. 48), *i.e.*, the 14th day of May, 1954.

(*b*) *Article* 15.—In clause (4), omit reference to Scheduled Tribes.

(*c*) *Article* 16.—In clause (3), reference to the State shall be construed as not including a reference to the State of Jammu and Kashmir.

(*d*) *Article* 19.—

(*A*) In clause (1),—

(*i*) in sub-clause (*e*), omit "and" at the end;

(*ii*) after sub-clause (*e*), insert the following clause, namely:—
"(*f*) to acquire, hold and dispose of property; and";

(*B*) in clause (5), for "sub-clauses (*d*) and (*e*)", substitute "sub-clauses (*d*), (*e*) and (*f*)".

(*e*) *Article* 22.—In clauses (4) and (7), for "Parliament" substitute "the Legislature of the State".

(*f*) *Article* 30.—Omit clause (1A).

(*g*) After article 30, insert the following, namely:—

"Right to Property

31. *Compulsory acquisition of property.*—(1) No person shall be deprived of his property save by authority of law.

(2) No property shall be compulsorily acquired or requisitioned save for a public purpose and save by authority of a law which provides for acquisition or requisitioning of the property for an amount which may be fixed by such law or which may be determined in accordance with such principles and given in such manner as may be specified in such law, and no such law shall be called in question in any court on the ground that the amount so fixed or determined is not adequate or that the whole or any part of such amount is to be given otherwise than in cash:

Provided that in making any law providing for the compulsory acquisition of any property of an educational institution established and administered by a minority, referred to in clause (1) of article 30, the State shall ensure that the amount fixed by or determined under such law for the acquisition of such property is such as would not restrict or abrogate the right guaranteed under that clause.

(2A) Where a law does not provide for the transfer of the ownership or right to possession of any property to the State or to a Corporation owned or controlled by the State, it shall not be deemed to provide for the compulsory acquisition or requisitioning of property, notwithstanding that it deprives any person of his property.

(2B) Nothing in sub-clause (*f*) of clause (1) of article 19 shall affect any such law as is referred to in clause (2).

* * * * *

(5) Nothing in clause 2 shall affect—

(*a*) the provisions of any existing law; or

(*b*) the provisions of any law which the State may hereafter make—

(*i*) for the purpose of imposing or levying any tax or penalty; or

(*ii*) for the promotion of public health or the prevention of danger to life or property; or

(*iii*) with respect to property declared by law to be evacuee property.";

(*h*) After article 31, omit the following sub-heading, namely:—

"Saving of Certain Laws"

(*i*) *Article* 31A.—

(*A*) In clause (1),—

(*i*) for "article 14 or article 19" substitute "article 14, article 19 or article 31";

(*ii*) omit the first proviso to clause (1);

(*iii*) in the second proviso omit "further";

(*B*) in clause (2), for sub-clause (*a*), substitute the following sub-clause, namely:—

'(*a*) "estate" shall mean land which is occupied or has been let for agricultural purposes or for purposes subservient to agriculture, or for pasture, and includes—

(*i*) sites of buildings and other structures on such land;

(*ii*) trees standing on such land;

(*iii*) forest land and wooded waste;

(*iv*) area covered by or fields floating over water;

(*v*) sites of *jandars* and *gharats;*

(*vi*) any *jagir, inam, muafi* or *mukarrari* or other similar grant,

but does not include—

(*i*) the site of any building in any town, or town area or village *abadi* or any land appurtenant to any such building or site;

(*ii*) any land which is occupied as the site of a town or village; or

(*iii*) any land reserved for building purposes in a municipality or notified area or cantonment or town area or any area for which a town planning scheme is sanctioned;'.

(*i*) *Article* 31C.—This article is not applicable to the State of Jammu and Kashmir.

(*k*) *Article* 32.—Omit clause (3).

(*l*) *Article* 35.—

(*A*) References to the commencement of the Constitution shall be construed as references to the commencement of the Constitution (Application to Jammu and Kashmir) Order, 1954 (C.O. 48), *i.e.*, the 14th day of May, 1954;

(*B*) in clause (*a*)(*i*), omit "clause (3) of article 16, clause (3) of article 32";

(*C*) after clause (*b*), add the following clause, namely:—

"(*c*) no law with respect to preventive detention made by the Legislature of the State of Jammu and Kashmir whether before or after the commencement of the Constitution (Application to Jammu and Kashmir) Order, 1954 shall be void on the ground that it is inconsistent with any of the provisions of this Part, but any such law shall, to the extent of such inconsistency, cease to have effect on the expiration of twenty-five years from the commencement of the said Order, except as respects things done or omitted to be done before the expiration thereof.".

(*m*) After article 35, add the following article, namely:—

"35A. *Saving of laws with respect to permanent residents and their rights.*—Notwithstanding anything contained in this Constitution, no existing law in force in the State of Jammu and Kashmir, and no law hereafter enacted by the Legislature of the State,—

(*a*) defining the classes of persons who are, or shall be permanent residents of the State of Jammu and Kashmir; or

(*b*) conferring on such permanent residents any special rights and privileges or imposing upon other persons any restrictions as respects—

(*i*) employment under the State Government;

(*ii*) acquisition of immovable property in the State;

(*iii*) settlement in the State; or

(*iv*) right to scholarships and such other forms of aid as the State Government may provide,

shall be void on the ground that it is inconsistent with or takes away or abridges any rights conferred on the other citizens of India by any provision of this Part.".

(5) PART IV.—This Part is not applicable to the State of Jammu and Kashmir.

(6) PART IVA.—This Part is not applicable to the State of Jammu and Kashmir.

(7) PART V.

(*a*) Article 55.—

(*A*) For the purposes of this article, the population of the State of Jammu and Kashmir shall be deemed to be sixty-three lakhs:

(*B*) in the *Explanation* omit the proviso.

(*b*) *Article* 81.—For clauses (2) and (3), substitute the following clauses, namely:—

"(2) For the purposes of sub-clause (*a*) of clause (1),—

(*a*) there shall be allotted to the State six seats in the House of the People;

(*b*) the State shall be divided into single-member territorial constituencies by the Delimitation Commission constituted under the Delimitation Act, 1972, in accordance with such procedure as the Commission may deem fit;

(*c*) the constituencies shall, as far as practicable, be geographically compact areas, and in delimiting them regard shall be had to physical features, existing boundaries of administrative units, facilities of communication and public convenience; and

(*d*) the constituencies into which the State is divided shall not comprise the area under the occupation of Pakistan.

(3) Nothing in clause (2) shall affect the representation of the State in the House of the People until the dissolution of the House existing on the date of publication in the Gazette of India of the final order or orders of the Delimitation Commission relating to the delimitation of parliamentary constituencies under the Delimitation Act, 1972.

(4) (*a*) The Delimitation Commission shall associate with itself for the purpose of assisting it in its duties in respect of the State, five persons who shall be members of the House of the People representing the State.

(*b*) The persons to be so associated from the State shall be nominated by the Speaker of the House of the People having due regard to the composition of the House.

(*c*) The first nominations to be made under sub-clause (*b*) shall be made by the Speaker of the House of the People within two months from the commencement of the Constitution (Application to Jammu and Kashmir) Second Amendment Order, 1974.

(*d*) None of the associate members shall have a right to vote or to sign any decision of the Delimitation Commission.

(*e*) If owing to death or resignation, the office of an associate member falls vacant, it shall be filled as soon as may be practicable by the Speaker of the House of the People and in accordance with the provisions of sub-clauses (*a*) and (*b*).".

(*c*) *Article* 82.—Omit the second and third provisos.

(d) *Article* 105.—In clause (3), for "shall be those of that House and of its members and committees immediately before the coming into force of section 15 of the Constitution (Forty-fourth Amendment) Act, 1978" substitute "shall be those of the House of Commons of the Parliament of the United Kingdom, and of its members and committees, at the commencement of this Constitution".

(*e*) For article 132, substitute the following article, namely:—

'132. *Appellate jurisdiction of Supreme Court in appeals from High Courts in certain cases.*—(1) An appeal shall lie to the Supreme Court from any judgment, decree or final order of a High Court in the territory of India, whether in a civil, criminal or other proceeding, if the High Court certifies that the case involves a substantial question of law as to the interpretation of this Constitution.

(2) Where the High Court has refused to give such a certificate, the Supreme Court may, if it is satisfied that the case involves a substantial question of law as to the interpretation of this Constitution, grant special leave to appeal from such judgment, decree or final order.

(3) Where such a certificate is given, or such leave is granted, any party in the case may appeal to the Supreme Court on the ground that any such question as aforesaid has been wrongly decided and, with the leave of the Supreme Court, on any other ground.

Explanation.—For the purposes of this article, the expression "final order" includes an order deciding an issue which, if decided in favour of the appellant, would be sufficient for the final disposal of the case.'.

(*f*) *Article* 133.—

(*A*) In clause (1), omit "under article 134A";

(*B*) after clause (1), insert the following clause, namely:—

'(1A) The provisions of section 3 of the Constitution (Thirtieth Amendment) Act, 1972, shall apply in relation to the State of Jammu and Kashmir subject to the modification that references therein to "this Act", "the commencement of this Act", "this Act had not been passed" and "as amended by this Act" shall be construed respectively as references to "the Constitution (Application to Jammu and Kashmir) Second Amendment Order, 1974", "the commencement of the said Order", "the said Order had not been made" and "as it stands after the commencement of the said Order".'.

(*g*) *Article* 134.—

(*A*) In clause (1), in sub-clause (*c*), omit "under article 134A";

(*B*) in clause (2), after "Parliament may" insert "on the request of the Legislature of the State".

(*h*) *Articles* 134A, 135, 139 and 139A.—These articles are not applicable to the State of Jammu and Kashmir.

(*i*) *Article* 145.—In clause (1), omit sub-clause (*cc*).

(*j*) *Article* 150.—For "as the President may, on the advice of the Comptroller and Auditor-General of India, prescribe" substitute "as the Comptroller and Auditor-General of India may, with the approval of the President prescribe".

(8) PART VI.

(*a*) Omit articles 153 to 217, article 219, article 221, articles 223, 224, 224A and 225, articles 227 to 233, article 233A and articles 234 to 237.

(*b*) *Article* 220.—References to the commencement of the Constitution shall be construed as references to the commencemnt of the Constitution (Application to Jammu and Kashmir) Amendment Order, 1960, i.e., the 26th January, 1960.

(*c*) *Article* 222.—After clause (1), insert the following clause, namely:—

"(1A) Every such transfer from the High Court of Jammu and Kashmir or to that High Court shall be made after consultation with the Governor.".

(*d*) *Article* 226.—

(*A*) Renumber clause (2) as clause (1A);

(*B*) omit clause (3);

(*C*) renumber clause (4) as clause (2); and in clause (2) as so renumbered, for "this article" substitute "clause (1) or clause (1A)".

(9) PART VIII.—This Part is not applicable to the State of Jammu and Kashmir.

(10) PART X.—This Part is not applicable to the State of Jammu and Kashmir.

(11) PART XI.

(a) *Article* 246.—

(A) In clause (1), for "clauses (2) and (3)" substitute "clause (2)";
(B) in clause (2), omit "Notwithstanding anything in clause (3),";
(C) omit clauses (3) and (4).

(b) For article 248, substitute the following article, namely:—

"248. *Residuary powers of legislation.*—Parliament has exclusive power to make any law with respect to—

(a) prevention of activities directed towards disclaiming, questioning or disrupting the sovereignty and territorial integrity of India or bringing about cession of a part of the territory of India or secession of a part of the territory of India from the Union or causing insult to the Indian National Flag, the Indian National Anthem and this Constitution; and

(b) taxes on—

(i) foreign travel by sea or air;
(ii) inland air travel;
(iii) postal articles, including money orders, phonograms and telegrams.",

(c) Omit article 249.

(d) *Article* 250.—For "to any of the matters enumerated in the State List" substitute "also to matters not enumerated in the Union List".

(e) *Article* 251.—

(i) For "Articles 249 and 250" substitute "article 250";
(ii) omit "under this Constitution";
(iii) for "under either of the said articles" substitute "under the said article".

(f) *Article* 253.—Add the following proviso, namely:—

"Provided that after the commencement of the Constitution (Application to Jammu and Kashmir), Order, 1954, no decision affecting the disposition of the State of Jammu and Kashmir shall be made by the Government of India without the consent of the Government of that State.".

(g) Omit article 255.

(h) *Article* 256.—Renumber this article as clause (1) thereof, and add the following new clause thereto, namely:—

"(2) The State of Jammu and Kashmir shall so exercise its executive power as to facilitate the discharge by the Union of its duties and responsibilities under the Constitution in relation to that State; and in particular, the said State shall, if so required by the Union, acquire or requisition property on behalf and at the expense of the Union, or if the property belongs to the State, transfer it to the Union on such terms as may be agreed, or in default of agreement, as may be determined by an arbitrator appointed by the Chief Justice of India.".

(i) *Article* 261.—In clause (2), omit "made by Parliament".

(12) PART XII.

(a) *Articles* 266, 282, 284, 298, 299 and 300.—In these articles references to the State or States shall be construed as not including references to the State to Jammu and Kashmir;

(*b*) omit clause (2) of article 267, article 273, clause (2) of article 283 and article 290.

(*c*) *Articles* 277 and 295.—In these articles references to the commencement of the Constitution shall be construed as references to the commencement of the Constitution (Application to Jammu and Kashmir) Order, 1954, *i.e.*, the 14th day of May, 1954.

(*d*) Omit the sub-heading "Chapter IV.—Right to Property" and article 300A.

(13) PART XIII.

In article 303, in clause (1), omit "by virtue of any entry relating to trade and commerce in any of the Lists in the Seventh Schedule".

(14) PART XIV.

Except in article 312, reference to "State" in this part does not include the State of Jammu and Kashmir.

(15) PART XIVA.

This Part is not applicable to the State of Jammu and Kashmir.

(16) PART XV.

(*a*) *Article* 324.—(*a*) In clause (1), the reference to the Constitution shall, in relation to elections to either House of the Legislature of Jammu and Kashmir, be construed as a reference to the Constitution of Jammu and Kashmir.

(*b*) *Articles* 325, 326 and 327.—In these articles the references to a State shall be construed as not including a reference to the State of Jammu and Kashmir.

(*c*) Omit article 328.

(*d*) *Article* 329.—

(*A*) Reference to a State shall be construed as not including a reference to the State of Jammu and Kashmir;

(*B*) omit "or article 328".

(17) PART XVI.

(*a*) *Article* 330.—

(*A*) Omit references to the Scheduled Tribes;

(*B*) Omit the *Explanation*.

(*b*) Omit articles 331, 332, 333, 336, 337, 339 and 342.

(*c*) *Articles* 334 *and* 335.—References to the State or the States shall be construed as not including references to the State of Jammu and Kashmir.

(18) PART XVII.—The provisions of this Part shall apply to the State of Jammu and Kashmir only in so far as they relate to—

(*i*) the official language of the Union;

(*ii*) the official language for communication between one State and another, or between a State and the Union; and

(*iii*) the language of the proceedings in the Supreme Court.

(19) PART XVIII.

(*a*) For article 352, substitute the following article, namely:—

"352. *Proclamation of Emergency.*—(1) If the President is satisfied that a grave emergency exists whereby the security of India or of any part of the territory thereof is threatened, whether by war or external aggression or internal disturbance, he may, by Proclamation, make a declaration to that effect.

(2) A Proclamation issued under clause (1)—

(*a*) may be revoked by a subsequent Proclamation;

(*b*) shall be laid before each House of Parliament;

(*c*) shall cease to operate at the expiration of two months unless before the expiration of that period it has been approved by resolutions of both Houses of Parliament:

Provided that if any such Proclamation is issued at a time when the House of the People has been dissolved or the dissolution of the House of the People takes place during the period of two months referred to in sub-clause (*c*), and if a resolution approving the Proclamation has been passed by the Council of States, but no resolution with respect to such Proclamation has been passed by the House of the People before the expiration of that period, the Proclamation shall cease to operate at the expiration of thirty days from the date on which the House of the People first sits after its reconstitution unless before the expiration of the said period of thirty days a resolution approving the Proclamation has been also passed by the House of the People.

(3) A Proclamation of Emergency declaring that the security of India or of any part of the territory thereof is threatened by war or by external aggression or by internal disturbance may be made before the actual occurrence of war or of any such aggression or disturbance if the President is satisfied that there is imminent danger thereof.

(4) The power conferred on the President by this article shall include the power to issue different Proclamations on different grounds, being war or external aggression or internal disturbance or imminent danger of war or external aggression or internal disturbance, whether or not there is a Proclamation already issued by the President under clause (1) and such Proclamation is in operation.

(5) Notwithstanding anything in this Constitution,—

(*a*) the satisfaction of the President mentioned in clause (1) and clause (3) shall be final and conclusive and shall not be questioned in any court on any ground;

(*b*) subject to the provisions of clause (2), neither the Supreme Court nor any other Court shall have jurisdiction to entertain any question, on any ground, regarding the validity of—

(*i*) a declaration made by Proclamation by the President to the effect stated in clause (1); or

(*ii*) the continued operation of such Proclamation.

(6) No Proclamation of Emergency made on grounds only of internal disturbance or imminent danger thereof shall have effect in relation to the State of Jammu and Kashmir (except as respects article 354) unless—

(*a*) it is made at the request or with the concurrence of the Government of that State; or

(*b*) where it has not been so made, it is applied subsequently by the President to that State at the request or with the concurrence of the Government of that State.".

(*b*) *Article* 353.—Omit the proviso.

(*c*) *Article* 356.—

(*A*) In clause (1), reference to provisions or provision of this Constitution shall, in relation to the State of Jammu and Kashmir, be construed as including references to provisions or provision of the Constitution of Jammu and Kashmir;

(*B*) in clause (4) for the opening portion, substitute the following, namely:—

"A Proclamation so approved shall, unless revoked, cease to operate on the expiration of a period of six months from the date of the passing of the second of the resolutions approving the Proclamation under clause (3)";

(C) for clause (5), substitute the following clause, namely:—

"(5) Notwithstanding anything in this Constitution, the satisfaction of the President mentioned in clause (1) shall be final and conclusive and shall not be questioned in any court on any ground.".

(d) *Article* 357.—For clause (2), substitute the following clause, namely:—

"(2) Any law made in exercise of the power of the Legislature of the State by Parliament or the President or other authority referred to in sub-clause (*a*) of clause (1) which Parliament or the President or such other authority would not, but for the issue of a Proclamation under article 356, have been competent to make shall, to the extent of the incompetency, cease to have effect on the expiration of a period of one year after the Proclamation has ceased to operate except as respects things done or omitted to be done before the expiration of the said period, unless the provisions which shall so cease to have effect are sooner repealed or re-enacted with or without modification by Act of the appropriate Legislature.".

(e) For article 358, substitute the following article, namely:—

"358.—*Suspension of provisions of article 19 during emergencies.*— While a Proclamation of Emergency is in operation, nothing in article 19 shall restrict the power of the State as defined in Part III to make any law or to take any executive action which the State would but for the provisions contained in that Part be competent to make or to take, but any law so made shall, to the extent of the incompetency, cease to have effect as soon as the Proclamation ceases to operate, except as respects things done or omitted to be done before the law so ceases to have effect.".

(*f*) *Article* 359.—

(*A*) In clause (1) omit "(except articles 20 and 21)";

(*B*) in clause (1A);

(*i*) omit "(except articles 20 and 21)";

(*ii*) omit the proviso;

(*C*) omit clause (1B);

(*D*) in clause (2), omit the proviso.

(*g*) Omit article 360.

(20) PART XIX.

(*a*) *Article* 361A.—This article is not applicable to the State of Jammu and Kashmir.

(*b*) Omit article 365.

(*c*) *Article* 367.—After clause (3), add the following clause, namely:—

"(4) For the purposes of this Constitution as it applies in relation to the State of Jammu and Kashmir.

(*a*) references to this Constitution or to the provisions thereof shall be construed as references to the Constitution or the provisions thereof as applied in relation to the said State;

(*aa*) references to the person for the time being recognised by the President on the recommendation of the Legislative Assembly of the State as the Sadar-i-Riyasat of Jammu and Kashmir, acting on the advice of the Council of Ministers of the State for the time being in office, shall be construed as references to the Governor of Jammu and Kashmir;

(*b*) references to the Government of the said State shall be construed as including references to the Governor of Jammu and Kashmir acting on the advice of his Council of Ministers:

Provided that in respect of any period prior to the 10th day of April, 1965, such references shall be construed as including references to the Sadar-i-Riyasat acting on the advice of his Council of Ministers;

(*c*) references to a High Court shall include references to the High Court of Jammu and Kashmir;

(*d*) references to the permanent residents of the said State shall be construed as meaning persons who, before the commencement of the Constitution (Application to Jammu and Kashmir) Order, 1954, were recognised as State subjects under the laws in force in the State or who are recognised by any law made by the Legislature of the State as permanent residents of the State; and

(*e*) references to a Governor shall include references to the Governor of Jammu and Kashmir:

Provided that in respect of any period prior to the 10th day of April, 1965, such references shall be construed as references to the person recognised by the President as the Sadar-i-Riyasat of Jammu and Kashmir and as including references to any person recognised by the President as being competent to exercise the powers of 'the Sadar-i-Riyasat.".

(21) PART XX.

Article 368.—

(*a*) In clause (2), add the following further proviso, namely:—

"Provided further that no such amendment shall have effect in relation to the State of Jammu and Kashmir unless applied by order of the President under clause (1) of article 370.";

(*b*) omit clauses (4) and (5) and after clause (3) add the following clause, namely:—

"(4) No law made by the Legislature of the State of Jammu and Kashmir seeking to make any change in or in the effect of any provision of the Constitution of Jammu and Kashmir relating to:—

(*a*) appointment, powers, functions, duties, emoluments, allowances, privileges or immunities of the Governor; or

(*b*) superintendence, direction and control of elections by the Election Commission of India, eligibility for inclusion in the electoral rolls without discrimination, adult suffrage and composition of the Legislative Council, being matters specified in sections 138, 139, 140 and 50 of the Constitution of Jammu and Kashmir,

shall have any effect unless such law has, after having been reserved for the consideration of the President, received his assent.".

(22) PART XXI.—

(*a*) Omit articles 369, 371, 371A, 372A, 373 and articles 376 to 378A and 392.

(*b*) *Article* 372.—

(*A*) Omit clauses (2) and (3);

(*B*) references to the laws in force in the territory of India shall include references to *hidayats, ailans, ishtihars,* circulars, *robkars, irshads, yadashts,* State Council Resolutions, Resolutions of the Constituent Assembly, and other instruments having the force of law in the territory of the State of Jammu and Kashmir;

(C) references to the commencement of the Constitution shall be construed as references to the commencement of the Constitution (Application to Jammu and Kashmir) Order, 1954 (C.O. 48), *i.e.*, the 14th day of May, 1954.

(c) *Article* 374.—

(A) Omit clauses (1), (2), (3) and (5);

(B) in clause (4), the reference to the authority functioning as the Privy Council of a State shall be construed as a reference to the Advisory Board constituted under the Jammu and Kashmir Constitution Act, Svt. 1996, and references to the commencement of the Constitution shall be construed as references to the commencement of the Constitution (Application to Jammu and Kashmir) Order, 1954, *i.e.*, the 14th day of May, 1954.

(23) PART XXII.—Omit articles 394 and 395.

(24) THIRD SCHEDULE.—Omit forms V, VI, VII and VIII.

(25) FIFTH SCHEDULE.—This Schedule is not applicable to the State of Jammu and Kashmir.

(26) SIXTH SCHEDULE.—This Schedule is not applicable to the State of Jammu and Kashmir.

(27) SEVENTH SCHEDULE.—

(a) List I—Union List.—

(A) Omit entry 2A

(B) for entry 3, substitute the following entry, namely:—

"3. Administration of cantonments.";

(C) omit entries 8, 9, 34 and 79;

(D) in entry 72, the reference to the States shall be construed,—

(i) in relation to appeals to the Supreme Court from any decision or order of the High Court of the State of Jammu and Kashmir made in an election petition whereby an election to either House of the Legislature of that State has been called in question, as including a reference to the State of Jammu and Kashmir;

(ii) in relation to other matters, as not including a reference to that State;

(E) in entry 81, omit "Inter-State migration";

(F) for entry 97, substitute the following entry, namely:—

"97. Prevention of activities directed towards disclaiming, questioning or disrupting the sovereignty and territorial integrity of India or bringing about cession of a part of the territory of India or secession of a part of the territory of India from the Union or causing insult to the Indian National Flag, the Indian National Anthem and this Constitution; taxes on foreign travel by sea or air, on inland air travel and on postal articles, including money orders, phonograms and telegrams.".

(b) Omit List II—State List.

(c) List III—Concurrent List.—

(A) For entry 1, substitute the following entry, namely:—

"1. Criminal law (excluding offences against laws with respect to any of the matters specified in List I and excluding the use of naval, military or air forces or any other armed forces of the Union in aid of the civil power) in so far as such criminal law relates to offences against laws with respect to any of the matters specified in this List.";

(B) for entry 2, substitute the following entry, namely:—

"2. Criminal procedure in so far as it relates to administration of oaths and taking of affidavits by diplomatic and consular officers in any foreign country.";

(*C*) omit entry 3, entries 5 to 10 (both inclusive), entries 14, 15, 17, 20, 21, 27, 28, 29, 31, 32, 37, 38, 41 and 44;

(*D*) entries 11A, 17A, 17B, 20A and 33A are not applicable to the State of Jammu and Kashmir;

(*E*) for entry 12, substitute the following entry, namely:—

"12. Evidence and oaths in so far as they relate to administration of oaths and taking of affidavits by diplomatic and consular officers in any foreign country.";

(*F*) for entry 13, substitute the following entry, namely:—

"13. Civil procedure in so far as it relates to administration of oaths and taking of affidavits by diplomatic and consular officers in any foreign country.";

(*G*) for entry 25, substitute the following entry, namely:—

"25. Vocational and technical training of labour.";

(*H*) for entry 30, substitute the following entry, namely:—

"30. Vital statistics in so far as they relate to births and deaths including registration of births and deaths.";

(*I*) for entry 42, substitute the following entry, namely:—

"42. Acquisition and requisitioning of property, so far as regards acquisition of any property covered by entry 67 of List I or entry 40 of List III or of any human work of art which has artistic or aesthetic value.";

(*J*) in entry 45, for "List II or List III" substitute "this List".

(28) NINTH SCHEDULE.—

(*a*) After entry 64, add the following entries, namely:—

"64A. The Jammu and Kashmir State Kuth Act (No. I of Svt. 1978).

64B. The Jammu and Kashmir Tenancy Act (No. II of Svt. 1980).

64C. The Jammu and Kashmir Alienation of Land Act (No. V of Svt. 1995).

64D. The Jammu and Kashmir Big Landed Estates Abolition Act (No. XVII of Svt. 2007).

64E. Order No. 6-H of 1951, dated the 10th March, 1951, regarding Resumption of Jagirs and other assignments of land revenue, etc.

64F. The Jammu and Kashmir Restitution of Mortgaged Properties Act, 1976 (Act XIV of 1976).

64G. The Jammu and Kashmir Debtors' Relief Act, 1976 (Act XV of 1976).";

(*b*) entries 65 to 86 are not applicable to the State of Jammu and Kashmir;

(*c*) after entry 86, insert the following entry, namely:—

'87. The Representation of the People Act, 1951 (Central Act 43 of 1951), the Representation of the People (Amendment) Act, 1974 (Central Act 58 of 1974) and the Election Laws (Amendment) Act, 1975 (Central Act 40 of 1975).";

(*d*) after entry 91, insert the following entry, namely:—

"92. The Maintenance of Internal Security Act, 1971 (Central Act 26 of 1971).";

(*e*) after entry 129, insert the following entry, namely:—

"130. The Prevention of Publication of Objectionable Matter Act, 1976 (Central Act 27 of 1976).";

(*f*) after insertion of the entries 87, 92 and 130 as indicated above, renumber entries 87 to 188 as entries 65 to 166 respectively.

APPENDIX 2

BILLS TO AMEND FUNDAMENTAL RIGHTS

The various Amendments to the Constitution have been incorporated in the text of the Constitution printed in this work. It is however desirable as far as certain amendments to the Chapter on Fundamental Rights and Art. 368 are concerned to note the actual Bills introduced by the Government in Parliament and the reasons for introducing them as reflected in the Statement of Objects and Reasons presented to the House.

The provisions of the Bills which subsequently became the Constitution (1st Amendment) Act, 1951, the Constitution (4th Amendment) Act, 1954, the Constitution (7th Amendment) Act, 1956, the Constitution (16th Amendment) Act, 1963, and the Constitution (17th Amendment) Act, 1964, are therefore set out in this Appendix along with the Statement of Objects and Reasons accompanying them. In order, however, to conserve space, the clauses of the Bills which have in fact been incorporated in the Constitution without any amendment at all have not been re-printed. Further, for the convenience of the reader the changes made between the provisions in the Bill and the provisions in the final Act are indicated in the foot notes.

The Constitution (1st Amendment) Act, 1951

Statement of Objects and Reasons

During the last fifteen months of the working of the Constitution, certain difficulties have been brought to light by judicial decisions and pronouncements specially in regard to the chapter on fundamental rights. The citizen's right to freedom of speech and expression guaranteed by article 19(1)(*a*) has been held by some courts to be so comprehensive as not to render a person culpable even if he advocates murder and other crimes of violence. In other countries with written constitutions, freedom of speech and of the press is not regarded as debarring the State from punishing or preventing abuse of this freedom. The citizen's right to practise any profession or to carry on any occupation, trade or business conferred by article 19(1)(*g*) is subject to reasonable restrictions which the laws of the State may impose "in the interests of the general public." While the words cited are comprehensive enough to cover any scheme of nationalisation which the State may undertake, it is desirable to place the matter beyond doubt by a clarificatory addition to article 19(6). Another article in regard to which unanticipated difficulties have arisen is article 31. The validity of agrarian reform measures passed by the State Legislatures in the last three years has, in spite of the provisions of clauses (4) and (6) of article 31, formed the subject-matter of dilatory litigation, as a result of which the implementation of these important measures, affecting large numbers of people has been held up.

The main objects of this Bill are, accordingly, to amend article 19 for the purposes indicated above and to insert provisions fully securing the constitutional validity of zamindari abolition laws in general and certain specified State Acts in particular. The opportunity has been taken to propose a few minor amendments to other articles in order to remove difficulties that may arise.

It is laid down in article 46 as a directive principle of State policy that the State should promote with special care the educational and economic interests of the weaker sections of the people and protect them from social injustice. In order that any special provision that the State may make for the educational, economic or social advancement of any backward class of citizens may not be challenged on the ground of being discriminatory, it is proposed that article 15(3) should be suitably amplified. Certain amendments in respect of articles dealing with the convening and proroguing of the sessions of Parliament have been found necessary and are also incorporated in this Bill. So also a few minor amendments in respect of articles 341, 342, 372 and 376.

The Constitution (1st Amendment) Bill, 1951

1. *Art. 15*: The original proposal to amend Art. 15 was:
words "or for the educational, economic or social advancement of any back-
words "or for the educational, economic or social advancement of any backward class of citizens" shall be added.

2. *Art. 19(2)*: The original proposal to amend Art. 19(2) was:
"(2) Nothing in sub-clause (*a*) of clause (1) shall affect the operation of any existing law in so far as it imposes, or prevent the State from making any law imposing, in the interests of the security of the State, friendly relations with foreign States, public order, decency or morality, restrictions on the exercise of the right conferred by the said sub-clause, and, in particular, nothing in the said sub-clause shall affect the operation of any existing law in so far as it relates to, or prevent the State from making any law relating to, contempt of court, defamation or incitement to an offence."[1]

3. *Art. 19(6)*: Art. 19(6) as proposed in the Bill was incorporated in the Constitution without any changes.

4. *Art. 31A(1)*: The whole of Cl. (1) was inserted in the Constitution with the addition of the Proviso thereto which was not contained in the Bill.

5. *Art. 31A(2)*: The original Cl. (*a*) as proposed in the Bill was:
"(*a*) the expression 'estate' shall, in relation to any local area have the same meaning as in the existing law relating to the land tenures in force in that area."

6. *Art. 31A(2)*: The original Cl. (*b*) was incorporated in the Constitution without any changes.

7. *Art. 31B*: The original Art. 31B as proposed in the Bill was:
"31B. *Validation of certain Acts.*—Without prejudice to the generality of the provisions contained in article 31A, none of the Acts specified in the Ninth Schedule nor any of the provisions thereof shall be deemed to be void, or ever to have become void, on the ground that such Act or provision is inconsistent with, or takes away or abridges any of the rights conferred by, any provisions of this Part, and notwithstanding any judgment, decree or order of any court or tribunal to the contrary, each of the said Acts shall continue in force until altered or repealed by a competent Legislature."[2]

8. *Ninth Schedule*: Items 1 to 11 in that Schedule were contained in the Bill. Items 12 and 13 as incorporated by the Act were not in the Bill as originally introduced.

The Constitution (4th Amendment) Act, 1954

Statement of Objects and Reasons

This Bill seeks to amend Articles 31, 31A and 305 of, and the Ninth Schedule to, the Constitution.

2. Recent decisions of the Supreme Court have given a very wide meaning to clauses (1) and (2) of article 31. Despite the difference in the wording of the two clauses, they are regarded as dealing with the same subject. The deprivation of property referred to in clause (1) is to be construed in the widest sense as including any curtailment of a right to property. Even where it is caused by a purely regulatory provision of law and is not accompanied by an acquisition or taking possession of that or any other property right by the State, the law, in order to be valid according to these decisions, has to provide for compensation under clause (2) of the article. It is considered necessary, therefore, to re-state more precisely the

---

[1] The clause as enacted is substantially the same as that proposed but has been re-drafted.

[2] The only change in the Article as enacted is to enable Regulations to be included in the 9th Schedule.

State's power of compulsory acquisition and requisitioning of private property and distinguish it from cases where the operation of regulatory or prohibitory laws of the State results in "deprivation of property". This is sought to be done in clause 2 of the Bill.

3. It will be recalled that the zamindari abolition laws which came first in our programme of social welfare legislation were attacked by the interests affected mainly with reference to articles 14, 19 and 31, and that in order to put and end to the dilatory and wasteful litigation and place these laws above challenge in the courts, articles 31A and 31B and the Ninth Schedule were enacted by the Constitution (First Amendment) Act. Subsequent judicial decisions interpreting articles 14, 19 and 31 have raised serious difficulties in the way of the Union and the States putting through other and equally important social welfare legislation on the desired lines, e.g., the following:—

(*i*) While the abolition of zamindaris and the numerous intermediaries between the State and the tiller of the soil has been achieved for the most part, our next objectives in land reform are the fixing of limits to the extent of agricultural land that may be owned or occupied by any person, the disposal of any land held in excess of the prescribed maximum and the further modification of the rights of land owners and tenants in agricultural holdings.

(*ii*) The proper planning of urban and rural areas require the beneficial utilisation of vacant and waste lands and the clearance of slum areas.

(*iii*) In the interests of national economy the State should have full control over the mineral and oil resources of the country, including in particular, the power to cancel or modify the terms and conditions of prospecting licences, mining leases and similar agreements. This is also necessary in relation to public utility undertakings which supply power, light or water to the public under licences granted by the State.

(*iv*) It is often necessary to take over under State management for a temporary period a commercial or industrial undertaking or other property in the public interest or in order to secure the better management of the undertaking or property. Laws providing for such temporary transference to State management should be permissible under the Constitution.

(*v*) The reforms in company law now under contemplation, like the progressive elimination of the managing agency system, provision for the compulsory amalgamation of two or more companies in the national interest, the transfer of an undertaking from one company to another, etc. require to be placed above challenge.

It is accordingly proposed in clause 3 of the Bill to extend the scope of article 31A so as to cover these categories of essential welfare legislation.

4. As a corollary to the proposed amendment of article 31A, it is proposed in clause 5 of the Bill to include in the Ninth Schedule to the Constitution two more State Acts and four Central Acts which fall within the scope of sub-clauses (*d*) and (*f*) of clause (1) of the revised article 31A. The effect will be their complete, retrospective validation under the provisions of article 31B.

5. A recent judgement of the Supreme Court in *Saghir Ahmed* v. *the State of U.P.* has raised the question whether an Act providing for a State monopoly in a particular trade or business conflicts with the freedom of trade and commerce guaranteed by article 301, but left the question undecided. Clause (6) of article 19 was amended by the Constitution (First Amendment) Act in order to take such State monopolies out of the purview of sub-clause (*g*) of clause (1) of that article, but no corresponding provision was made in Part XIII of the Constitution with reference to the opening words of article 301. It appears from the judgment of the Supreme Court that notwithstanding the clear authority of Parliament or of a State Legislature to introduce State monopoly in a particular sphere of trade or commerce, the law might have to be justified before the courts as being "in the public interest" under article 301 or as amounting to a "reasonable restriction"

under article 304(*b*). It is considered that any such question ought to be left to the final decision of the Legislature. Clause 4 of the Bill accordingly proposes an amendment of article 305 to make this clear.

The Constitution (4th Amendment) Bill, 1954

1. *Art. 31*: Cl. (2) of that Article as originally proposed in the bill was:

"No property shall be compulsorily acquired or requisitioned by the State save for a public purpose and save by authority of a law which provides for compensation for the property so acquired or requisitioned and either fixes the amount of the compensation or specifies the principles on which, and the manner in which, the compensation is to be determined and given."[3]

2. Cl. 2(A) of that Article was incorporated in the Constitution as proposed in the Bill.

3. *Art. 31A*: Clause (1) as proposed in the Bill was as follows:

"(1) Notwithstanding anything contained in article 13, no law providing for—

(*a*) the acquisition by the State of any estate or of any rights therein, or

(*b*) the extinguishment or modification of any rights in estates *or in agricultural holdings*,[4] or

(*c*) *the maximum extent of agricultural land that may be owned or occupied by any person and the disposal of any agricultural land held in excess of such maximum, whether by transfer to the State or otherwise*,[5] or

(*d*) *the acquisition or requisitioning of any immoveable property for the relief or rehabilitation of persons displaced from their original place of residence by reason of the setting up of the Dominions of India and Pakistan*,[5] or

(*e*) *the acquisition or requisitioning for a public purpose of any land, buildings or huts declared in pursuance of law to constitute a slum or of any vacant or waste land*,[6] or

(*f*) the taking over of the management of any property by the State for a limited period either in the public interest or in order to secure the proper management of the property, or

(*g*) *the transfer of any undertaking, wholly or in part, from one company to another or* the amalgamation of two or more companies either in the public interest or in order to secure the proper management of the undertaking or of any of the companies,[7] or

(*h*) the extinguishment or modification of any rights of managing agents, managing directors, directors, managers or shareholders of companies,[8] or

(*i*) the extinguishment or modification of any rights accruing by virtue of any agreement, lease or licence for the purpose of searching for, or winning, any mineral or mineral oil, *or for the purpose of supplying power, light or water to the public*, or the premature termination or cancellation of any such agreement, lease or licence,[9]

---

[3] The last clause in the clause as enacted: "and no such law shall be called into question in any court on the ground that the compensation provided by that is not adequate" was not in the clause as proposed.

[4] Sub-clauses (*a*) and (*b*) have been enacted as clause (*a*), and the italicised words in the original sub-clause (*b*) have not been enacted.

[5] Sub-clauses (*c*) and (*d*) have not been enacted in the Constitution.

[6] This sub-clause was not enacted in the Constitution.

[7] The italicised words have not been enacted.

[8] The sub-clause as enacted is different in two respects: (*a*) it refers to the extinguishment or modification of the rights of secretaries and treasurers; (*b*) *qua* share-holders, it only refers to the voting rights of share-holders.

[9] The italicised words have not been enacted.

shall be deemed to be void on the ground that it is inconsistent with, or takes away or abridges any of the rights conferred by, article 14, article 19 or article 31;

Provided that where such law is a law made by the Legislature of a State, the provisions of this article shall not apply thereto unless such law, having been reserved for the consideration of the President, has received his assent."

4. In cl. (2) the amendments proposed were as follows:
"(*i*) after the words 'an estate', the words 'or agricultural holding' shall be, and shall be deemed always to have been inserted;[10] and (*ii*) after the word 'tenure-holder', the words '*raiyat, under-raiyat*' shall be, and shall be deemed always to have been, inserted."[11]

5. *9th Schedule*: Items 14 to 19 in the 9th Schedule were proposed in the original Bill but item 20 which was inserted by the Amendment was not contained therein.

The Constitution (7th Amendment) Act, 1956

The Statement of Objects and Reasons and the clause are not printed as the only change made is a change in Art. 16(3) consequent upon the re-organisation of States, the abolition of Part B and Part C States, and the creation of Union Territories.

The Constitution (16th Amendment) Act, 1963

Statement of Objects and Reasons

The Committee on National Integration and Regionalism appointed by the National Integration Council recommended that article 19 of the Constitution be so amended that adequate powers become available for the preservation and maintenance of the integrity and sovereignty of the Union. The Committee were further of the view that every candidate for the membership of a State Legislature or Parliament, and every aspirant to, and incumbent of, public office should pledge himself to uphold the Constitution and to preserve the integrity and sovereignty of the Union and that forms of oath in the Third Schedule to the Constitution should be suitably amended for the purpose. It is proposed to give effect to these recommendations by amending clauses (2), (3) and (4) of article 19 for enabling the State to make any law imposing reasonable restrictions on the exercise of the rights conferred by sub-clauses (*a*), (*b*) and (*c*) of clause (1) of that article in the interests of the sovereignty and integrity of India. It is also proposed to amend articles 84 and 173 and forms of oath in the Third Schedule to the Constitution so as to provide that every candidate for the membership of Parliament or State Legislature, Union and State Ministers, Members of Parliament and State Legislatures, Judges of the Supreme Court and High Courts and the Comptroller and Auditor-General of India should take an oath to uphold the sovereignty and integrity of India.

2. The Bill seeks to achieve these objects.

The Constitution (16th Amendment) Bill, 1963

The changes proposed have been incorporated in Art. 19.

The Constitution (17th Amendment) Act, 1964

Statement of Objects and Reasons

The Kerala Agrarian Relations Act, 1961 was struck down by the Supreme Court in its application to ryotwari lands transferred from the State of Madras to Kerala. The Act was further struck down by the High Court of Kerala in its application to lands other than estates in Malabar and Travancore. It was held that the provisions

---

[10] This proposal was not enacted.
[11] The variations were enacted as proposed.

of the Act were violative of Articles 14, 19 and 31 of the Constitution and that the protection of Article 31A of the Constitution was not available to those lands, as they were not estates.

2. The protection of article 31A is available only in respect of such tenures as were estates on the 26th January, 1950, when the Constitution came into force. The expression "estate" has been defined differently in different States and, as a result of the transfer of land from one State to another on account of the reorganisation of States, the expression has come to be defined differently in different parts of the same State. Moreover, many of the land reform enactments relate to lands which are not included in an estate. It is, therefore, proposed to amend the definition of "estate" in Article 31A of the Constitution by including therein lands held under ryotwari settlement and also other lands in respect of which provisions are normally made in land reform enactments. It is also proposed to amend the Ninth Schedule by including therein the State enactments relating to land reform in order to remove any uncertainty or doubt that may arise in regard to their validity.

3. The Bill seeks to achieve these objects.

The Constitution (17th Amendment) Bill, 1964

1. *Art. 31A*: The 2nd Proviso to Cl. (1) as enacted by the amendment Act was not contained in the Bill as introduced in Parliament.
2. The new sub-cl. (*a*) of Cl. (2) as enacted by the amending Act was the same as that proposed in the Bill.
3. *9th Schedule*: The amending Act incorporates items 21 to 64 and enacts an exception to item 55.[12]

(*a*) The proposed items under the Bill, numbered items 21 to 144, contained, in addition to the items actually incorporated, the following:[13]

21. The Andhra Pradesh (Andhra Areas) Estates (Abolition and Conversion into Ryotwari) Act, 1948 (Madras Act XXVI of 1948).

23. The Andhra Pradesh (Telangana Area) Jagirs (Commutation) Regulations (Amendment) Act, 1961 (Andhra Pradesh Act XVIII of 1961).

24. The Assam State Acquisition of Zamindaris Act, 1951 (Assam Act XVIII of 1951).

26. The Assam Fixation of Ceiling on Land Holdings Act, 1956 (Assam Act 1 of 1957).

28. The Assam Consolidation of Holdings Act, 1960 (Assam Act XIX of 1961).

30. The Bihar Land Reforms (Amendment) Act, 1959 (Bihar Act XVI of 1959).

32. The Bombay Bhagdari and Narwadari Tenures Abolition Act, 1949 (Bombay Act XXXII of 1949).

33. The Bombay Watwa Vazifdari Rights Abolition Act, 1950 (Bombay Act LXII of 1950).

34. The Bombay Tenancy and Agricultural Lands (Amendment) Act, 1951 (Bombay Act XII of 1951).

35. The Bombay Tenancy and Agricultural Lands (Second Amendment) Act, 1951 (Bombay Act XXXIV of 1951).

36. The Bombay Tenancy and Agricultural Land (Third Amendment) Act, 1951 (Bombay Act XLV of 1951).

37. The Salsette Estates (Land Revenue Exemption Abolition) Act, 1951 (Bombay Act XLVII of 1951).

---

[12] The exception is enacted as an Explanation at the end of the 9th Schedule. This was not contained in the Bill.

[13] The Acts are numbered as in the Bill.

38. The Bombay Land Tenures Abolition (Compensation Application Extension of Date) (Amendment) Act, 1952 (Bombay Act III of 1952).

39. The Bombay Tenancy and Agricultural Land (Amendment) Act, 1952 (Bombay Act XXXIII of 1952).

40. The Bombay Saranjam Jahagirs and other Inams of Political Nature Resumption Rules, 1952.

41. The Bombay Land Tenures Abolition (Amendment) Act, 1953 (Bombay Act XXXVIII of 1953).

42. The Bombay Personal Inams Abolition Act, 1952 (Bombay Act XLII of 1953).

43. The Bombay Merged Territories (Ankadia Tenure Abolition) Act, 1953 (Bombay Act XLIII of 1953).

44. The Bombay Kauli and Katuban Tenures (Abolition) Act, 1953 (Bombay Act XLIV of 1953).

45. The Bombay Merged Territories (Baroda Mulgiras Tenure Abolition) Act, 1953 (Bombay Act XLV of 1953).

46. The Bombay Merged Territories (Baroda Watan Abolition) Act, 1953 (Bombay Act XLVI of 1953).

47. The Bombay Merged Territories Matadari Tenure Abolition Act, 1953 (Bombay Act XLVIII of 1953).

48. The Bombay Land Tenures Abolition (Recovery of Records) Act, 1953 (Bombay Act L of 1953).

49. The Bombay Tenancy and Agricultural Lands (Amendment) Act, 1953 (Bombay LX of 1953).

50. The Bombay Service Inams (Useful to Community) Abolition Act, 1953 (Bombay Act LXX of 1953).

51. The Bombay Merged Territories (Janjira and Bhor) Khoti Tenure Abolition Act, 1953 (Bombay Act LXXI of 1953).

52. The Bombay (Okhamandal Salami Tenure Abolition) Act, 1953 (Bombay Act I of 1954).

53. The Bombay Pargana and Kulkarni Watans (Abolition) Amendment Act, 1954 (Bombay Act XXIX of 1954).

54. The Bombay Merged Territories and Areas (Jagirs Abolition) Act, 1953 (Bombay Act XXXIX of 1954).

55. The Bombay Amending Act, 1954 (Bombay Act LVIII of 1954).

56. The Bombay Service Inams (Useful to Community) Gujarat and Konkan) Resumption Rules, 1954.

58. The Bombay Bhil Naik Inams Abolition Act, 1955 (Bombay Act XXI of 1955).

59. The Bombay Merged Territories Miscellaneous Alienation Abolition Act, 1955 (Bombay Act XXII of 1955).

60. The Bombay Shilotri Rights (Kolaba) Abolition Act, 1955 (Bombay Act XLVII of 1955).

61. The Bombay Pargana and Kulkarni Watans (Abolition) (Amendment) Act, 1955 (Bombay Act L of 1955).

62. The Bombay Land Tenures Abolition (Amendment) Act, 1955 (Bombay Act LI of 1955).

63. The Bombay Tenancy and Agricultural Lands (Amendment) Act, 1955 (Bombay Act XIII of 1956).

64. The Bombay Land Tenures Abolition (Amendment) Act, 1956 (Bombay Act XL of 1956).

65. The Bombay Tenancy and Agricultural Land (Amendment) Act, 1957 (Bombay Act XV of 1957).

66. The Bombay Tenancy and Agricultural Lands (Second Amendment) Act, 1957 (Bombay Act XXXVIII of 1957).

68. The Bombay Land Tenure Abolition Laws (Amendment) Act, 1958 (Bombay Act LVII of 1958).

69. The Bombay Tenancy and Agricultural Lands (Amendment) Act, 1958 (Bombay Act LXIII of 1958).

70. The Bombay Land Tenures Abolition (Amendment) Act, 1958 (Bombay Act XCIII of 1958).

72. The Bombay Tenancy and Agricultural Land (Vidarbha Region and Kutch Area) Act, 1958 (Bombay Act XCIX of 1958).

73. The Bombay Inferior Village Watans Abolition Act, 1958, (Bombay Act I of 1959).

74. The Bombay Ankadia Tenure (Saurashtra Area) Abolition Act, 1959 (Bombay Act XXXI of 1959).

75. The Bombay Bandhijama, Udhad and Ugadia Tenures Abolition Act, 1959 (Bombay Act XXXV of 1959).

76. The Bombay (Saurashtra Area) Aghat Tenure and Ijaras Abolition Act, 1959 (Bombay Act LXV of 1959).

77. The Bombay Taluqdari Tenure (Abolition) Amendment Act, 1960 (Bombay Act XVIII of 1960).

80. The Gujarat Patel Watans Abolition Act, 1961 (Gujarat Act XLVII of 1961).

81. The Bombay Taluqdari Tenure Abolition (Gujarat Amendment) Act, 1962 (Gujarat Act XV of 1962).

83. The Saurashtra Land Reforms Act, 1951 (Saurashtra Act XXV of 1951).

84. The Saurashtra Barkhali Abolition Act, 1951 (Saurashtra Act XXVI of 1951).

85. The Saurashtra Estates Acquisition Act, 1952 (Saurashtra Act III of 1952).

86. The Bombay Tenancy and Agricultural Land (Amendment) Act, 1960 (Maharashtra Act IX of 1961).

88. The Maharashtra Revenue Patels (Abolition of Office) Act, 1962 (Maharashtra Act XXXV of 1962).

89. The Bombay Tenancy and Agricultural Lands (Amendment) Act, 1962 (Maharashtra Act XXXVI of 1962).

90. The Bombay Tenancy and Agricultural Lands (Second Amendment) Act, 1962 (Maharashtra Act VIII of 1963).

91. The West Khandesh Mehwassi Estates (Proprietary Rights Abolition, etc.) Regulation, 1961 (Maharashtra Regulation I of 1962).

93. The Hyderabad Abolition of Inams Act, 1954 (Hyderabad Act VIII of 1955).

94. The Kerala Agrarian Relations Act, 1960 (Kerala Act IV of 1961).

95. The Madhya Bharat Zamindari Abolition Act, Samvat 2008 (Madhya Bharat Act XIII of 1951).

96. The Madhya Bharat Abolition of Jagirs Act, Samvat 2008 (Madhya Bharat Act XXVIII of 1951).

99. The Madras Estates (Abolition and Conversion into Ryotwari) Amendment Act, 1951 (Madras Act XVII of 1951).

100. The Madras Estates (Abolition and Conversion into Ryotwari) Second Amendment Act, 1951 (Madras Act XXXV of 1951).

101. The Madras Estates (Abolition and Conversion into Ryotwari) Amendment Act, 1953 (Madras Act IX of 1953).

102. The Madras Estates (Abolition and Conversion into Ryotwari) Amendment Act, 1954 (Madras Act XXXIV of 1954).

105. The Madras Estates (Supplementary) Act, 1956 (Madras Act XXX of 1956).

106. The Madras Estates (Abolition and Conversion into Ryotwari) Amendment Act, 1956 (Madras Act XLIV of 1956).

107. The Madras Estates (Abolition and Conversion into Ryotwari), Estates Land (Reduction of Rent) and Estates (Supplementary) (Amendment) Act, 1958 (Madras Act XXXIV of 1958).

108. The Madras Estates (Abolition and Conversion into Ryotwari) Amendment Act, 1961 (Madras Act XVIII of 1961).

109. The Madras Estates (Supplementary) Amendment Act, 1961 (Madras Act XXXV of 1961).

114. The Mysore (Personal and Miscellaneous) Inams Abolition Act, 1954 (Mysore Act I of 1955).

115. The Mysore (Religious and Charitable) Inams Abolition Act, 1955 (Mysore Act XVIII of 1955).

121. The PEPSU Tenancy and Agricultural Lands Act, 1955 (PEPSU Act XIII of 1955).

122. The Rajasthan Land Reforms and Resumption of Jagirs Act, 1952 (Rajasthan Act VI of 1952).

125. The Rajasthan Kasar Bhom Abolition Act, 1961 (Rajasthan Act XXXV of 1961).

126. The Ajmer Abolition of Intermediaries and Land Reforms Act, 1955 (Ajmer Act III of 1955).

127. The Uttar Pradesh Zamindari Abolition and Land Reforms (Amendment) Act, 1952 (U.P. Act XVI of 1953).

128. The Uttar Pradesh Land Reforms (Amendment) Act, 1954 (U.P. Act XX of 1954).

129. The Jaunsar Bawar Zamindari Abolition and Land Reforms Act, 1956 (U.P. Act XI of 1956).

130. The Uttar Pradesh Land Reforms (Amendment) Act, 1956 (U.P. Act XVIII of 1956).

131. The Uttar Pradesh Urban Areas Zamindari Abolition and Land Reforms Act, 1956 (U.P. Act IX of 1957).

132. The Uttar Pradesh Zamindari Abolition and Land Reforms (Amendment) Act, 1958 (U.P. Act XIV of 1958).

133. The Uttar Pradesh Land Reforms (Amendment) Act, 1958 (U.P. Act XXXVII of 1958).

134. The Uttar Pradesh Government Estates Thekedari Abolition Act, 1958 (U.P. Act I of 1959).

137. The Uttar Pradesh Land Laws (Amendment) Act, 1962 (U.P. Act XXI of 1962).

142. The Himachal Pradesh Abolition of Big Landed Estates and Land Reforms Act, 1953 (Himachal Pradesh Act XV of 1954).

(b) The following Acts were incorporated in the 9th Schedule by the Constitution (17th Amendment) Act, 1964, though they were not included in the Bill:[14]

[14] The Acts are numbered as in the 9th Schedule.

22. The Andhra Pradesh (Telangana Area) Tenancy and Agricultural Lands (Validation) Act, 1961 (Andhra Pradesh Act XXI of 1961).

33. The Gujarat Surviving Alienations Abolition Act, 1963 (Gujarat Act XXXIII of 1963), except in so far as this Act relates to an alienation referred to in sub-clause (*d*) of clause (3) of section 2 thereof.

35. The Hyderabad Tenancy and Agricultural Lands (Re-enactment, Validation and Further Amendment) Act, 1961 (Maharashtra Act XLV of 1961).

37. The Jenmikaram Payment (Abolition) Act, 1960 (Kerala Act III of 1961).

38. The Kerala Land Tax Act, 1961 (Kerala Act XIII of 1961).

39. The Kerala Land Reforms Act, 1963 (Kerala Act I of 1964).

50. The Hyderabad Tenancy and Agricultural Lands (Validation) Act, 1961 (Mysore Act XXXVI of 1961).

52. The Orissa Land Reforms Act, 1960 (Orissa Act XVI of 1960).

The Constitution (Twenty-fourth Amendment) Act, 1971

Statement of Objects and Reasons

The Supreme Court in the well-known *Golak Nath's Case* [(1967) 2 S.C.R. 762] reversed, by a narrow majority, its own earlier decisions upholding the power of Parliament to amend all parts of the Constitution including Part III relating to fundamental rights. The result of the judgment is that Parliament is considered to have no power to take away or curtail any of the fundamental rights guaranteed by Part III of the Constitution even if it becomes necessary to do so for giving effect to the Directive Principles of State Policy and for the attainment of the objectives set out in the Preamble to the Constitution. It is, therefore, considered necessary to provide expressly that Parliament has power to amend any provision of the Constitution so as to include the provisions of Part III within the scope of the amending power.

2. The Bill seeks to amend article 368 suitably for the purpose and makes it clear that article 368 provides for amendment of the Constitution as well as procedure therefor. The Bill further provides that when a Constitution Amendment Bill passed by both Houses of Parliament is presented to the President for his assent, he should give his assent thereto. The Bill also seeks to amend article 13 of the Constitution to make it inapplicable to any amendment of the Constitution under article 368.

The Constitution (Twenty-fifth Amendment) Act, 1971

Statement of Objects and Reasons

Article 31 of the Constitution as it stands specifically provides that no law providing for the compulsory acquisition or requisitioning of property which either fixes the amount of compensation or specifies the principles on which and the manner in which the compensation is to be determined and given shall be called in question in any court on the ground that the compensation provided by that law is not adequate. In the *Bank Nationalization Case* (1970, 3 S.C.R. 530) the Supreme Court has held that the Constitution guarantees right to compensation, that is, the equivalent in money of the property compulsorily acquired. Thus in effect the adequacy of compensation and the relevancy of the principles laid down by the Legislature for determining the amount of compensation have virtually become justiciable inasmuch as the Court can go into the question whether the amount paid to the owner of the property is what may be regarded reasonably as compensation for loss of property. In the same case, the Court has also held that a law which seeks to acquire or requisition property for a public purpose should also satisfy the requirements of article 19(1)(*f*).

2. The Bill seeks to surmount the difficulties placed in the way of giving effect to the Directive Principles of State policy by the aforesaid interpretation. The word "compensation" is sought to be omitted from article 31(2) and replaced by the word "amount". It is being clarified that the said amount may be given otherwise than in cash. It is also proposed to provide that article 19(1)(*f*) shall not apply to any law relating to the acquisition or requisitioning of property for a public purpose.

3. The Bill further seeks to introduce a new article 31C which provides that if any law is passed to give effect to the Directive Principles contained in clauses (*b*) and (*c*) of article 39 and contains a declaration to that effect, such law shall not be deemed to be void on the ground that it takes away or abridges any of the rights contained in article 14, 19 or 31 and shall not be questioned on the ground that it does not give effect to those principles. For this provision to apply in the case of laws made by State Legislatures, it is necessary that the relevant Bill should be reserved for the consideration of the President and receive his assent.

INDEX

 For the Constitution, see pages [I-3] to [I-7]

For the Constitution, see pages [I-3] to [I-7]

For the Constitution, see pages [I-3] to [I-7]

 For the Constitution, see pages [I-3] to [I-7]

 For the Constitution, see pages [I-3] to [I-7]

 For the Constitution, see pages [I-3] to [I-7]

 For the Constitution, see pages [I-3] to [I-7]

For the Constitution, see pages [I-3] to [I-7]

 For the Constitution, see pages [I-3] to [I-7]

 For the Constitution, see pages [I-3] to [I-7]

 For the Constitution, see pages [I-3] to [I-7]

 For the Constitution, see pages [I-3] to [I-7]

 For the Constitution, see pages [I-3] to [I-7]

For the Constitution, see pages [I-3] to [I-7]

 For the Constitution, see pages [I-3] to [I-7]

 For the Constitution, see pages [I-3] to [I-7]

 For the Constitution, see pages [I-3] to [I-7]

 For the Constitution, see pages [I-3] to [I-7]